THE COMMON LAW LIBRARY

PROFESSIONAL LIABILITY

AUSTRALIA
Law Book Co.
Sydney

CANADA and USA
Carswell
Toronto

HONG KONG
Sweet and Maxwell Asia

NEW ZEALAND
Brookers
Wellington

SINGAPORE and MALAYSIA
Sweet & Maxwell Asia
Singapore and Kuala Lumpur

THE COMMON LAW LIBRARY

JACKSON & POWELL

ON

PROFESSIONAL LIABILITY

SIXTH EDITION

LONDON
SWEET & MAXWELL
2007

First edition (1982)
Second edition (1987)
Second impression (1988)
Third edition (1992)
Second impression (1994)
Fourth edition (1997)
Fifth edition (2002)

Published in 2007 by
Sweet & Maxwell Limited
100 Avenue Road, London NW3 3PF
http://www.sweetandmaxwell.co.uk
Computerset by Interactive Sciences Ltd, Gloucester
Printed and bound in Great Britain by
William Clowes Ltd, Beccles, Suffolk

A catalogue record for this book is available from the British Library

ISBN–10 0–421–95510–4
ISBN–13 978–0–421–95510–3

GENERAL EDITORS

JOHN L. POWELL, Q.C., M.A., LL.B.
Of the Middle Temple

ROGER STEWART, Q.C., M.A., LL.M.
Of the Inner Temple

EDITORS

SCOTT ALLEN, B.A.
Of the Inner Temple, Barrister

MARK CANNON, B.A.
Of the Middle Temple, Barrister

GRAHAM CHAPMAN, B.A.
Of the Inner Temple, Barrister

ANNELIESE DAY, M.A.
Of the Inner Temple, Barrister

BEN ELKINGTON, M.A., LL.M.
Of Gray's Inn and of Lincoln's Inn, Barrister

HUGH L. EVANS, M.A., B.C.L.
Of the Middle Temple, Barrister

DAVID HALPERN, Q.C., M.A.
Of Gray's Inn

GRAEME MCPHERSON, M.A.
Of Gray's Inn, Barrister

SIAN MIRCHANDANI, M.A., Vet, MB.
Of the Inner Temple, Barrister

LEIGH-ANN MULCAHY, M.A., LL.M.; Dip. EC Law
Of the Inner Temple, Barrister

AMANDA SAVAGE, LL.B., BCL, B.A.
Of the Middle Temple, Barrister

FIONA SINCLAIR, M.A., LL.M.
Of the Inner Temple and of Lincoln's Inn, Barrister

PAUL SUTHERLAND, M.A.
Of the Middle Temple, Barrister

DAVID TURNER, M.A.
Of Gray's Inn, Barrister

CONSULTANT EDITOR

SIR RUPERT JACKSON, M.A., LL.B.
*One of Her Majesty's Judges of the
Queen's Bench Division, Of the Middle Temple*

PREFACE

This sixth edition is marked by a change of title for reasons explained in Chapter 1. It is also marked by the addition of two new chapters, the first on Professional Indemnity Insurance and the second on Actuaries. The first is the work of David Turner whom we welcome to the team of editors. The second is the work of David Halpern who was elevated to silk this year. A *vale* and thanks to Christopher Gibson Q.C. who was an editor of the fifth edition.

As in relation to the last three editions, this edition is very much a "chambers" endeavour. The proliferation of UK and European legislation and case law, as well as Commonwealth case law, necessarily demands a large team, especially given that all members are full-time practitioners. The roles of Mark Cannon and Hugh Evans have again been as significant as those of the general editors in bringing this edition to fruition. Mark's role of editing the main general chapters and Hugh's role of editing the chapters on Solicitors and Barristers are especially demanding. Fiona Sinclair has again singly met the huge challenge of editing the chapter on Construction Professionals. A major task was also undertaken by Anneliese Day and Sian Mirchandani in taking over the editorship of the chapter on Medical Practitioners and by Ben Elkington in again singly editing the chapter on Insurance Brokers and that on Members and Managing Agents at Lloyd's. The unrelenting flow of human rights cases imposes a considerable burden for the editors of the chapter on Human Rights and Professionals, Leigh-Ann Mulcahy and Anneliese Day. It is a much expanded chapter, as is that on Information Technology Professionals edited by Paul Sutherland and Scott Allen. The writing of new chapters by David Turner and David Halpern has required major endeavours by each.

With the revision demanded by each edition, the footprints of the original authors and previous editors become less distinct. Nevertheless, the stamp of Rupert Jackson (as the original author) on the general chapters, as well as on the chapters on Solicitors, Barristers, Medical Practitioners and Insurance Brokers, remains distinct. His perspicacity and prodigiousness on the High Court Bench portends an output of original material on professional liability as taxing for his successor editors as his example when a general editor. In his capacity as Consultant Editor, we are well aware that Big Brother is watching us.

The book consists of two categories of chapters. The first eight chapters deal with subjects of general application. The remaining chapters deal with specific professions. Chapter 1 (the Nature of Professions) has been edited by John Powell. Chapters 2 (Duties and Obligations), 3 (Remedies), 4 (Contribution between Defendants) and 5 (Defences) have been edited by Mark Cannon, assisted by Amanda Savage and Graham Chapman. Chapter 6 (Litigation) has been edited by Hugh Evans and Fiona Sinclair. Chapter 7 (Human Rights and Professionals) has been edited by Leigh-Ann Mulcahy, assisted by Anneliese

Day. Chapter 8 (Professional Indemnity Insurance) is a new chapter written by David Turner.

As to the chapters on specific professions, Chapter 9 (Construction Professionals) has been edited by Fiona Sinclair and Chapter 10 (Surveyors) has been edited by Roger Stewart, as in the last edition. Those chapters were written originally by John Powell. In the third and fourth editions, the chapter on Construction Professionals was edited by Roger Stewart and that on Surveyors by Iain Hughes (now His Honour Judge Iain Hughes Q.C.). Chapters 11 (Solicitors) and 12 (Barristers) have been edited by Hugh Evans, as in the last three editions. Chapter 13 (Medical Practitioners) has been edited by Anneliese Day and Sian Mirchandani. In the third edition it was edited by Fiona Sinclair and in the fourth edition by Christopher Gibson. Chapters 14 (Financial Services Regulation) and Chapter 15 (Financial Services Practitioners) are separate chapters on a subject which, in the last edition, was addressed in a new single chapter written by John Powell together with Graeme McPherson. They have edited those chapters in this edition. Chapter 17 (Accountants and Auditors) has again been edited by David Halpern. He also wrote the new Chapter 18 (Actuaries). The chapter on Accountants was originally written by John Powell and edited by him in previous editions. Chapters 16 (Insurance Brokers) and Chapter 19 (Members and Managing Agents at Lloyd's) have again been edited by Ben Elkington. Mark Cannon edited Chapter 16 in the third and fourth editions. He was the original author of Chapter 19 in the third edition and edited it in the fourth edition. Chapter 20 (Information Technology Professionals) was a new chapter in the last edition written by Paul Sutherland and Scott Allen. It has been edited by them in this edition. Chapter 21 (Patent Agents and Trade Mark Attorneys) was also a new chapter in the last edition, written by Hugh Evans. It has been edited in this edition by Roger Stewart.

We also thank Tim Chelmick, Emilie Jones, Richard O'Brien and George Spalton for their assistance in respect of various chapters and Professor Eva Lomnicka for her advice and many suggestions in relation to Chapters 14 and 15. We are indebted to our senior clerk, Lizzy Wiseman, for her encouragement and understanding.

We two retain overall editorial responsibility for the whole book.

The law is stated as of September 30, 2006.

We are grateful to Kate Auer, Renée Kerman, Susannah Shaw and Victoria Wilson of Sweet & Maxwell for their support and encouragement in relation to this edition. We also thank Fiona Mullen for preparing the Index.

John L. Powell
Roger Stewart

4 New Square,
Lincoln's Inn,
London WC2A 3RJ

November 6, 2006

CONTENTS

CONTENTS

[xv]

TABLE OF CASES

TABLE OF STATUTES

TABLE OF STATUTORY INSTRUMENTS

TABLE OF PRACTICE DIRECTIONS

TABLE OF ABBREVIATIONS

A.A.S. = Australian Accounting Standard
ABCA = Alberta Court of Appeal
ABI = Association of British Insurers
ABTA = Association of British Travel
    Agents
A.C. = Appeal Cases (Law Reports)
A.C.D. = Administrative Court Digest
A.C.E. = Association of Consulting
    Engineers
A.C.S.R. = Australian Corporations and
    Securities Reports
A.C.T.R. = Australian Capital Territory
    Reports
A.G. = Auditing Guideline
AIDS = Acquired Immune Deficiency
    Syndrome
A.L.J. = Australian Law Journal
A.L.J.R. = Australian Law Journal
A.L.R. = Australian Law Reports
An-Am = Anglo American Law Review
APB = Auditing Practices Board
A.P.R. = Atlantic Provinces Reports
ARP = Assigned Risks Pool
A.S.B. = Accounting Standards Board
A.S.C. = Accounting Standards
    Committee
ATE = after the event insurance
AUTH = Authorisation Manual
AVSC = Assets Valuation Standards
    Committee
Ad E = Adolphus and Ellis Reports
All E.R. = All England Law Reports
Alta.L.R. = Alberta Law Reports
App.Cas. = Law Reports Appeal Cases
    1875–1890
Atk. = Atkyn's Reports
Aust. = Australia

B.Ad = Barnewall and Adolphus King's
    Bench Reports
B. Ald = Barnewall and Alderson King's
    Bench Reports
BAS = Board of Actuarial Standards
B. & C. = Bamewall & Cresswell
B.C.C. = British Company Law Cases

B.C.C.A. = British Columbia Court of
    Appeal
BCD = Banking Consolidation Directive
B.C.L.C. = Butterworths Company Law
    Cases
B.C.L.R. = British Columbia Law
    Reports
B.L.R. = Business Law Review
B.M.J. = British Medical Journal
B.M.L.R. = Butterworths Medico–Legal
    Reports
B. P. or Bos. & Pul. (N.R.) = Bosanquet
    and Puller's New Reports
BTE = before the event insurance
Beav. = Beavan's Report
Bing = Bingham's Reports
Bos. & Pul. (N.R.). See B.P.
Brod. B. = Broderip and Bingham's
    Reports
Build.L.R. = Building Law Reports
Burr. = Burrow's Reports

c. = Chapter (of an Act of Parliament)
CA = Court of Appeal
CAA = Civil Aviation Authority
CASS = Client Assets sourcebook
C.B. (N.S.) = Common Bench Reports
    (New Series)
CCAB = Consultative Committee of
    Accounting Bodies
C.C.L.T. = Canadian Cases on the Law of
    Torts 1976–
CDM Reg's = Construction (Design and
    Management) Regulations 1994
C. & F. = Clerk & Finnelly
C.I.L.L. = Construction Industry Law
    Letter
C.J. = Lord Chief Justice
CJD = Cretzfelt-Jacob disease
C.J.Q. = Civil Justice Quarterly
C.L.J. = Cambridge Law Journal
C.L.R. = Commonwealth Law Reports
C.L.Y.B. = Current Law Year Book
C.O.D. = Crown Office Digest
COMP = Compensation Sourcebook

[cxci]

C.P. = Construction Practice

C. P. or Car. & P. = Carrington and Payne's Report

C.P.D. = Law Reports Common Pleas Division 1875–1880

C.P.L. = Current Property Law

C.P.R. = Civil Procedure Rules

C.P.S. = Crown Prosecution Service

CTF = Child Trust Fund

Cal. Rptr. = Californian Reporter

Camp = Campbell's Reports

Can. = Canada

Car. & P. *See* C. P.

Ch. = Chancery (Law Reports)

Ch D. = Chancery Division

Cl. Fin. = Clark and Finnelly's House of Lords Reports

Cmnd = Command Paper

Coll = Collyer's Report

Com.Cas = Commercial Cases

Con. L.R. = Construction Law Report

Const. L.J. = Construction Law Journal

Cr. J. = Crompton and Jervis's Reports

Cr.App.R. = Criminal Appeal Reports

DCI = decompression illness

DES = diethylstilboestrol

DISP = Dispute Resolution the Complaints Sourcebook

DPB = designated professional body

D.L.R. = Dominion Law Reports (Canada)

D.R. = Decisions and Reports

DSDM = Dynamic Systems Development Method

De G.F. & J. = De Gex, Fisher & Jones

De G.M. & G.= De Gex, Macnaghten and Gordon's Reports

Dow. Cl = Dow and Clark's Reports

E.C. = European Community

E. E. = Ellis and Ellis's Reports

E.E.C. European Economic Community

E.G. = Estates Gazette

E.G.C.S. = Estates Gazette Case Summaries

E.G.D. = Estates Gazette Digest of Cases

E.G.L.R. = Estates Gazette Law Reports

E.H.R.L.R. = European Human Rights Law Review

E.H.R.R. = European Human Rights Report

EMD = Emerging Debt Market

EMLR = Entertainment and Media Law Reports

E.N.T. = ear, nose & throat

Eq = Law Reports Equity

ERP = executive retirement plan

EWCA = England and Wales Court of Appeal

EWHC = England and Wales High Court

EZ PUT = Enterprise Zone Property Unit Trust

Env. L.R. = Environment Law Reports

Eur. Comm. H.R. = European Commission of Human Rights

Ex = Exchequer Law Reports

F. = Sessions Cases, 5th Series [Fraser] (Scotland)

F. F. = Foster and Finalson's Reports

FCA = Federal Court of Appeal

FCE = fibro-cartilaginous embolism

F.C.R. = Federal Court Reports

FIMBRA = Financial Intermediaries, Managers and Brokers Regulatory Organisation

FLR = Financial Law Report

F.L.R. = Federal Law Reports

F.L.R. or Fam L.R. = Family Law Report

FOS = Financial Ombudsman Service

FRC = Financial Reporting Council

F.R.I.C.S. = Fellow of the Royal Institute of Chartered Surveyors

FRS = Financial Reporting Standard

FSA = Financial Services Authority

FSA 1986 = Financial Services Act 1986

FSCS = Financial Services Compensation Scheme Limited

FSMA = Financial Services and Markets Act 2000

FSMA 2000 = Financial Services and Markets Act 2000

F.S.R. = Fleet Street Patent Law Report

FTLR = Financial Times Law Report

Fam. = Family Division (Law Reports)

Fed. Rep. = Federal Reports

GEN = General provisions

GISC = General Insurance Standards Council

GLO = Group Litigation Order

GMC = General Medical Council

GN = Guidance Note

GTT = glucose tolerance test

G.W.D. = Green's Weekly Digest
Giff = Giffard's Reports

H.C. = Health Circular
HCA = High Court of Australia
HBRV = House Buyer's Report and
 Valuation
H.I.V. = Human Immuno-Deficiency
 Virus
H.K.C.A. = Hong Kong Court of Appeal
H.K.L.R. = Hong Kong Law Reports
H.K.L.R.D. = Hong Kong Law Reports
 and Digest
HL = House of Lords
H.L.C. = House of Lords Cases
H.L.R. Housing Law Report
H. & M. = Hemming & Miller
H.M.S.O. = Her Majesty's Stationary
 Office
HRA = Human Rights Act

IAS's = International Accounting
 Standards
IATA = International Air Transport
 Association
IBNR = Incurred but not reported
IBRC = Insurance Brokers Registration
 Council
ICAEW = Institute of Chartered
 Accountants of England and Wales
I.C.E. = Institute of Civil Engineers
ICOB = Insurance Conduct of Business
 sourcebook
I.C.R. = Industrial Cases Reports
ICVC = Investment Company with
 Variable Capital
I.E.E. = Institute of Electrical Engineers
IEHC = Irish Eire High Court
I.E.S.C. = Irish Supreme Court
IFRS's = international financial reporting
 standards
I.L.Pr. = International Legal Practitioner
I.L.R.M. = Irish Law Reports Monthly
IMRO = Investment Managers
 Regulatory Organisation
IOB = Insurance Ombudsman
IPRU (INS) Interim Prudential
 Sourcebook: Insurers
IPRU (INV) = Interim Prudential
 sourcebook for Investment Business
I.R.C. = Inland Revenue Commissioners
I.R.C.L. = Irish Reports Common Law
I.R. or Ir.R = Irish Reports (Eire)

I.R.L.R. = Industrial Relations Law
 Reports
ISA = International Standards on
 Auditing
ISD = Investment Services Directive
ISQC = International Standard on Quality
 Control
I.S.V.A. = Incorporated Society of
 Valuers and Auctioneers
I.T.L. or Ir.L.T. = Irish Law Times
I.Mech.E = Institute of Mechanical
 Engineers
Imm. A.R. = Immigration Appeal Reports
Int.Con.L.Rev. = International
 Construction Law Review
Ir. Eq. Rep. = Irish Equity Reports
I.Struct.E = Institute of Structural
 Engineers

JCT = Joint Contracts Tribunal

K. J. = Kay and Johnson's Reports
K.B. = King's Bench (Law Reports)

L.G.E.R.A. = Local Government and
 Environmental Reports of Australia
L.J. = Law Journal Newspapers
L.J. = Lord Justice
L.J.K.B. = Law Journal Reports, Kings
 Bench
L.J.P.C. = Law Journal reports Privy
 Council
L.J.Q.B. = Law Journal Queen's Bench
 (N.S. 1831–1946)
L.M.C.L.Q. = Lloyd's Maritime and
 Commercial Quarterly
L.M.X. = London market excess of loss
L.Q.R. = Law Quarterly Review
L.R. = Land Report
L.R.L.R. = Lloyds Reinsurance Law
 Reports
L.T. = Law Times
L.T.J. = Law Times Journal
L.T.L. = Lawtel
Ll.L.Rep. = Lloyd's List Reports (pre-
 1951)
Lloyd's L.R.P.N. = Lloyd's Law Reports
 Professional Negligence
Lloyds P.N. and Lloyd's Rep. P.N. =
 Lloyd's Law Reports Professional
 Negligence
Lloyd's Rep I.R. = Lloyd's Law Reports
 Insurance and Reinsurance

Lloyd's Rep = Lloyd's List Reports (1951 onwards)

Lloyd's Rep. Med. = Lloyd's Law Reports Medical

MAD = Market Abuse Directive (03/6)

MiFID = Markets in Financial Instruments Directive (2004/39)

M.I.G.s = Mortgage Indemnity Guarantees

M.L.R. = Modern Law Journal

M.O.D. = Ministry of Defence

M.R. = Master of the Rolls

M.R.I.C.S = Member of the Royal Institute of Chartered Surveyors

M. & W. = Meeson & Welsby

MYCA = Malaysia Court of Appeal

Macq. = Macqueen's Scotch Appeals

Man.G = Manning and Granger's Common Pleas Reports

Med.L.R. = Medical Law Reports

Med. L. Rev. = Medical Law Review

N.B.R. = New Brunswick Reports

NBQB = New Brunswick QB

NCIS = National Criminal Intelligence Service

N.E. = North Eastern Reports

N.H.B.C. = National House Builder Registration Council

N.H.S. = National Health Service

N.I. = Northern Ireland; Northern Ireland Reports

NICO = National Insurance Contributions Office

N.I.L.R. = Northern Ireland Law Reports

N.I.Q.B. = Northern Ireland Queen's Bench

N.L.J. = New Law Journal

N.P.C. = New Property Cases

NSCA = Nova Scotia Court of Appeal

N.S.R. = Nova Scotia Reports

N.S.W.C.A. = New South Wales Court of Appeal

N.S.W.L.R. = New South Wales Law Reports

N.Y. = New York Court of Appeal Reports

NZCA = New Zealand Court of Appeal

N.Z.L.R. = New Zealand Law Reports

New L.J. = New Law Journal

Nfld. CA = Newfoundland Court of Appeal

Nfld. P.E.I.R. = Newfoundland & Prince Edward Island Reports

OBO = Office of the Banking Ombudsman

OBSO = Office of the Building Societies Ombudsman

OH = Outer House of the Court of Session

OIO = Office of the Investment Ombudsman

O.R. = Ontario Reports

Ord = Order

P. = Probate, Divorce and Admiralty (Law Reports)

PC = Privy Council

PCC = Professional Conduct Committee

PCCC = Professional Conduct and Complaints Committee

PEP = Personal Equity Plan

PERG = Perimeter Guidance Manual

PERLS = principal exchange rate linked security

PIAOB = Personal Insurance Arbitration Ombudsman Bureau

PIAS = Personal Insurance Arbitration Service

P.I.Q.R. = Personal Injury and Quantum Reports

P.L. = Public Law

PML = probable maximum loss

P.N. = Professional Negligence

P.N.L.R. = Professional Negligence and Liability Reports

POD = Prospectus Directive (2003/71)

PPH = Primary Pulmonary Hypertension

PRIN = Principles for Businesses

PRINCE = Projects in Controlled Environments

PRU = Integrated Prudential Sourcebook

PTSD = post traumatic stress disorder

para. = paragraph

Price = Price's Reports

Q.B. = Queen's Bench (Law Reports)

Q.B.D. = Queen's Bench Division

Q.C. = Queen's Counsel

QCA = Queensland Court of Appeal

QdR. = Queensland Papers

r. = rule

RAO = Financial Services and Markets Act 2000 (Regulated Activities) Order 2001

RCH = recognised clearing houses

R.I.B.A. = Royal Institute of British Architects

R.I.C.S. = Royal Institution of Chartered Surveyors

RIE = recognised investment exchanges

RLF = retrolental fibroplasias

R.L.R = Restitution Law Review

R.P.B. = recognised professional body

R.P.C. = Reports of Patent Design and Trade Mark Cases

R.P.R. = Real Property Reports (Canada)

RSB = recognised supervisory body

R.S.C. = Rules of the Supreme Court

RTA = Road Traffic Accident

reg. = regulation

Russ. M = Russell and Mylne's Reports, Chancery

s. or ss. = section, sections (of an Act of Parliament)

S.A. = South Africa

SAS = Statement of Auditing Standard

S.A.S.C. = Supreme Court of South Australia

SAH = sub-arachnid haemorrhage

S.A.L.R. = South Africa Law Reports

SAR's = Rules Governing Substantial Acquisition of Shares

S.A.S.R. = South Australian State Reports

SBC = JCT Standard Building Contract

S.C. = Session Cases

S.C. (H.L.) = Session Cases (House of Lords)

S.C.C. = Supreme Court of Canada

S.C.L.R. = Scottish Council of Law Reporting

S.C.R. = Canada Law Reports, Supreme Court

SERPS = State Earnings Related Pension Scheme

SFA = Securities and Futures Authority

SFA = Standard Form Agreement

SFACB = SFA Complaints Bureau and Arbitration Service

SGHC = Singapore High Court

SI = Statutory Instrument

SIF = Solicitors Indemnity Fund

S.J. = Solicitors Journal

SKCA = Saskatchewan Court of Appeal

S.L.R. = Scottish Law Review (Sheriff Court Reports 1885–1963)

S.L.T. = Scottish Law Times

S.R.O. = self regulatory organisation

SSADM = Structural Systems Analysis and Design Method

S.S.A.P.'s = Statements of Standard Accounting Practice

Sask.R. = Saskatchewan Reports

Sch. = Schedule (to and Act of Parliament)

Stark = Starkie's Reports

TCC = Technology and Construction Court

T.C.L.R. = Trade and Competition Law Reports

T.L.R. = Times Law Report

TOD = Transparency Obligations Directive (2004/109)

TR = Taxation Reports

TSA = Securities Association

Taunt. = Taunton's Reports

Tru. L.I. = Trust Law International

U.C.C.P. = Upper Canada Common Pleas

U.C.T.A. = Unfair Contract Terms Act

UK GAPP = United Kingdom generally accepted accounting practice

UKHL = United Kingdom House of Lords

U.K.H.R.R. = United Kingdom Human Rights Reports

UKLA = UK Listing Authority

UKPC = United Kingdom Privy Council

U.S. = United States Supreme Courts Reports

V.C. = Vice Chancellor

V.L.R. = Victorian Report

V.R. = Victoria Reports

VSCA = Victorian Court of Appeal

W.A.R. = Western Australian Law Reports

WASC = Supreme Court of Western Australia

W.L.R. = Weekly Law Reports

W.N. = Weekly Notes (Law Reports)

W.N. (N.S.W.) = Weekly Notes (New South Wales)

TABLE OF ABBREVIATIONS

W.T.L.R. = Wills and Trusts Law Reports
W.W.R. = Western Weekly Reports
Wils.K.B. = J. Wilson's Reports, Kings
    Bench

XL = excess of loss reinsurance

Y.C.Ex = Younge and Collier's
    Exchequer Reports

CHAPTER 1

THE NATURE OF PROFESSIONAL LIABILITY

1. THE CHANGE OF TITLE

In its first and subsequent editions, the title to this book has been *Professional* **1–001**
Negligence. The title has become all too anachronistic and constricting. It is time
to escape from the original straitjacket and to adopt the more fitting title of
Professional Liability. This is not a function of mission creep. It is to recognise
a long established reality in relation to the claims associated with the term
"professional negligence".

The term "professional negligence" invites association with the tort of negli- **1–002**
gence. Contract rather than tort, however, provides the framework for resolving
the vast majority of claims against members of professions. Analysis follows the
conventional course of first ascertaining the nature of the bargain as reflected in
express and implied terms. Tort needs to be considered only to the extent
necessary to overcome perceived obstacles arising from the contractual analysis.
Statutory liabilities may also be incurred under various statutes for defective
service. Fiduciary duties are conceptually distinct from duties of care which
underpin claims for professional liability based on contract and tort. Nevertheless, such duties not only are highly pertinent to a text on the liability of
lawyers, accountants and financial practitioners, but also provide important
context for claims based on contract, tort and statute.

"Professional liability" as a title defines a wider realm of causes of action than **1–003**
"professional negligence". The former additionally includes causes of action of
a more heinous nature. The discussion in this work excludes the latter. The
etymology of "professional" suggests a moral boundary within which to confine
discussion. Intentional wrongdoing is all the more unexpected in members of a
profession. This is far from suggesting that moral rectitude is actually inherent in
all such members. The conduct of all too many has prompted caricature in press
and literature from long before Dickens. Nevertheless, intentional wrongdoing
remains conduct which merits forfeiture of the "professional" epithet and hence
exclusion from consideration in a book with that epithet in its title. It follows that,
in terms of a moral keyboard, the causes of action considered do not range far
from middle C—Bach rather than Rachmaninov.

The title remains deficient in another respect. "Professional" is too narrow to **1–004**
describe the range of occupations which attract claims perceived as professional
negligence or liability claims. "Professional" is an acquisitive concept, acquisitive of aspirations as well as expectations and liabilities. Yet perceptions as to its

contours are indistinct, subjective and continually changing. The penumbra enlarges with language and context. A professional is not synonymous with a member of a profession and a professional service is professed by others also. The occupations which today are regarded as professions extend far beyond those regarded as such a century ago. They have increased as human knowledge, skill and consequent specialisation have increased. Judicial attempts to define a "profession" recognise that the meaning of the word long ago ceased to be confined to the three learned professions, the Church, Medicine and Law. For the purposes of discussion, the term "practitioner" is useful as a neutral and chameleon term which leaves at large the inevitably imprecise and changing boundary between those generally recognised as members of professions and others.

2. THE PROFESSIONS

1–005   In previous editions of this book it was suggested that a definition of "the professions" is pre-eminently a matter for social historians rather than lawyers.[1] That remains the case although the effect of the addition of the definite article and the plural is that the term "the professions" connotes a narrower meaning than that connoted today by "a profession". It was ventured in previous editions that the occupations which are regarded as professions have four characteristics.

(1) **The nature of the work:** The work done is skilled and specialised. A substantial part of the work is mental rather than manual. A period of theoretical and practical training is usually required before the work can be adequately performed.

(2) **The moral aspect:** Practitioners are usually committed, or expected to be committed, to certain moral principles, which go beyond the general duty of honesty.[2] They are expected to provide a high standard of service for its own sake. They are expected to be particularly concerned about the duty of confidentiality. They also, normally, owe a wider duty to the community, which may on occasions transcend the duty to a particular client or patient.[3]

(3) **Collective organisation:** Practitioners usually belong to a professional association which regulates admission and seeks to uphold standards of

---

[1] A helpful collection of definitions of "profession" is to be found in App.5 to the Monopolies Commission's Report on the Professions (October 1970). For a general introduction to the sociology of professions, see T. J. Johnson, *Professions and Power* (Macmillan, 1972).

[2] See, e.g. discussion of the professions in Tawney, *The Acquisitive Society* (Harvester Press, 1982) and Durkheim, *Professional Ethics and Civil Morals* (Greenwood Press, 1983).

[3] For example, a doctor's duty to prevent the spread of contagious diseases may outweigh his duty to a particular patient. An accountant, certifying the accounts of a firm of solicitors or auditing the accounts of a public company, may find himself obliged to act contrary to the immediate interests of his clients. Similarly, a barrister or solicitor is under a professional obligation to draw the court's attention to relevant authorities, even if they are adverse to his client's case. Architects have a responsibility for public safety and environmental considerations, which go beyond their immediate duty to the client. This public responsibility of professions is discussed by Sir Gordon Borrie in "The Professions—Expensive Monopolies or Guardians of the Public Interests?" (Fourth Hamptons Lecture given at the Society of Valuers and Auctioneers on November 14, 1983).

the profession. Such associations commonly set examinations to test competence and issue professional codes on matters of conduct and ethics.[4]

(4) **Status**: Most professions have a high status in the community. Some of their privileges are conferred by Parliament. Some are granted by common consent.

These characteristics still hold true,[5] with some qualifications.

As to the moral aspect, it is more accurate to describe practitioners as having   1–006
a strong sense of a wider duty to the community and public at large. Generally, however, that sense of a duty must not constrain practitioners from giving primacy to the interests of their clients and to act in their interests, unless it would be legally, morally or ethically repugnant to do so.

As to collective organisation, an important function of this is self-regulation in   1–007
relation to admission, standards and other matters. Over recent decades there has been increasing statutory imposition of regulatory requirements on the organisation of many occupations, including members of professions. The degree of statutory intervention has varied, but generally it has been to supplement rather than replace the self-regulatory model. The exception has been in relation to the financial sector. The statute based self-regulatory regime imposed by the Financial Services Act 1986 has been replaced by the fully statute-based regime imposed by the Financial Services and Markets Act 2000. The raising of standards was an important purpose of both statutes. Their effect, coupled with increasing sophistication and specialisation in the financial sector, has been to mould public perception of occupations in the financial sector as professions—as well as public expectation of a professional service. Enhancing this perception is the regular generation of associations and societies around new specialisations.

Assertion of high status in society as an attribute of the professions does not   1–008
synchronise well with the avowedly egalitarian culture of our age. A strong feature of that culture is tilting at privileges attaching to status, whether real or imagined, in the cause of equality. Another feature is the espousal of a dichotomy between the interests of the professions and the interests of consumers, spiced by

---

[4] Ralf Dahrendorf argues that the crucial distinction between professions in Britain and those on the European Continent is that in Britain the professions are self-governing and independent, whereas elsewhere in Europe they are regulated by the state. He points out that if any major profession is slack in the enforcement of its own standards, public confidence in all professions is undermined. On Dahrendorf's analysis, this would have far-reaching social consequences. Dahrendorf argues that the condition of the British professions is "an index of the state of liberty in this country". See Dahrendorf, "Defence of the English Professions", (1984) *Journal of the Royal Society of Medicine*, Vol.77, p.178.

[5] A leading article in *The Times*, January 5, 1980, discussing the recent expansion of the professions, summarised what the community expected of the professions in these terms: "For an occupation to become a profession in the commonly accepted sense of the word means more than for its practitioners to enjoy the privileges of controlling their own entry and regulating their own conduct. It means also that they must have specialised skills acquired by intellectual and practical training, that they have a high degree of detachment and integrity, and, above all, that they have a strong sense of responsibility and an exceptional commitment to the interests of their clients which transcends all other commitments." The authors are grateful to *The Times* for permission to use this quotation. However, some sociologists argue that the traditional view of the professions (described above) is no longer valid: see Dingwall and Lewis (edns), *The Sociology of the Professions* (Macmillan, 1983).

inclusion of the professions within "the establishment" for the purposes of popular pillory and political advantage. The defence that we are all professionals now, implies a comforting egalitarian evolution from the worker of an earlier age. But it is mere rhetorical refrain and lacks conviction. In the mouths of members of recognised professions it smacks of insincerity and condescension, which compound the original sin of perceived higher status. The reality is that high status in society is a distinguishing feature of the professions. It is status based on recognition of high education. The mantra "education, education and education" as the recipe to remove inequality serves to encourage recognition of degrees of achievement in education. It also reinforces the perception of the higher status of those who are highly educated and the recognition of the professions as higher echelons of occupations.

1–009   Fortunately, it is not necessary for the purpose of this book to attempt a comprehensive definition of the professions.[6] There is no serious dispute as to the professional status of many of the specific occupations discussed in the following chapters. The editors are conscious of other occupational groups which are equally regarded as professions, which are not dealt with in this book. The choice which has been made is largely governed by the amount of litigation which each profession has generated.[7] The main focus is not upon particular occupational groups but rather upon the principles applicable to professional liability generally, as illustrated in their application in respect of different occupational groups, some of which may be recognised as professions and others not (or not quite yet). What is apparent is the enduring nature of these principles and their ready adaptability to other occupations, including some which may be regarded as "new professions", as illustrated in the cases of financial practitioners[8] and information technology professionals.[9]

3. RISK TRANSFERRED AND RISK RETAINED

1–010   Regulation, especially in the financial sector, brings its own influences. Situations which attract the assertion of investment liability provide the cutting edge for developments in the law relating to professional liability. Regulatory influences have relevance not only in the investment field but right across the domain of professional liability. The confluence of regulatory rules and conventional common law principles is as fertile for ideas as is the confluence of the Amazon with the Atlantic for sea life. The task of the lawyer is to be acute to their interrelationship and the scope for development.

1–011   The fertility is generated by different starting points. The conventional professional liability lawyer starts from the concept of reasonable care and the

---

[6] Judicial discussion about the nature of professions occurs principally in tax cases, see *IRC v Maxse* [1919] 1 K.B. 647 at 657, *per* Scrutton L.J.; *Currie v IRC* [1921] 2 K.B. 332 at 343, *per* Scrutton L.J.; *Carr v IRC* [1944] 2 All E.R. 163 at 166–167, *per* Du Parcq L.J.

[7] The principles which are discussed in the following chapters are, of course, equally applicable to the other professions: see, e.g. the reasoning of the Court of Appeal in *Luxmoore-May v Messenger May Baverstock* [1990] 1 W.L.R. 1009 (concerning art auctioneers).

[8] See Ch.15, below.

[9] See Ch.20, below.

premise of what would have been done in the relevant circumstances by that paragon of virtue, the reasonably competent solicitor, accountant or whatever. The regulator, perhaps more familiar with economics than the ordinary lawyer, starts from the concept of risk. To seek to achieve a fair allocation of risk, and to prescribe rules accordingly, inevitably produces huge rules books. The greater the fine tuning, the longer the rules. Nor are judges more virtuous. What are law reports of cases other than illustrations of fine tuning to specifics? The difference between regulators and judges is that the former do it prospectively and the latter do it retrospectively.

A fair allocation of risk requires a realistic appreciation of the nature and   **1–012** degree of risk transferred *and* a realistic appreciation of the degree of risk retained by the person to whom the duty is owed. Starting from a concept of reasonable care and the competent professional too easily, if perhaps subconsciously, downplays scrutiny of the claimant's role. Worse, it encourages a priori reasoning. In contrast, the concept of risk and its evaluation in a particular case, that is the nature and extent of the risk transferred to the defendant and the risk retained by the claimant, encourages a more open-minded evaluation.

Different investors have different appetites for risk and different capacities to   **1–013** absorb risk. Different investment products have different risk profiles, as do different investment services. Our regime for regulation of financial services responds accordingly: hence the regulatory focus on the type of product, service, consumer and provider, with rules fine-tuned accordingly. This focus and the consequent evaluation of the risks transferred and risks retained are far better than the approach of focussing on the unrealistic ideal of the reasonably competent practitioner. It also avoids artificial problems created by the latter approach, such as the problem of whether there is a different standard of care for the specialist practitioner.[10] Also, regulatory concepts such as customers' understanding of risk, "know your client" and "suitable advice" have wider currency. The task of the lawyer is to be acute to the interrelationship between common law principles and regulatory concepts and to the scope for development by analogy.

4. CONTRACT

A final plea for the importance of contract. For too long the assertion of failure   **1–014** to exercise reasonable care has been a portmanteau term which has aided the less than rigorous practitioner or judge to avoid articulation of more precise reasons for his contention or conclusion. A proper evaluation of risks transferred and retained requires greater scrutiny of the particular task undertaken for the particular client and of the precise contractual obligations undertaken. The tortious focus on not causing harm linked to the Atkin concept of care is too blunt. It has dominated too long the analysis of professional liability cases. Also their description as professional negligence cases as opposed to professional liability cases encourages false parallax and sometimes blind spots as to other bases of liability.

---

[10] See, e.g. in the context of solicitors: *Duchess of Argyll v Beuselinck* [1972] 2 Lloyd's Rep. 172. See Ch.11, paras 11–096 to 11–097.

Other than in medical contexts, contract provides the basis for most professional relationships. Contract principles rather than tort principles should provide the prime basis for analysis in such cases, supplemented in regulatory contexts by regulatory principles and rules. A rigorous contractual analysis should also lead to better determination of the scope of the contract and the services agreed to be provided and to the articulation of more precise express and implied duties than the too general duty to exercise reasonable care and skill.

CHAPTER 2

DUTIES AND OBLIGATIONS

1. PROFESSIONAL LIABILITY

(a) *Positive Duties*

2–001 Traditionally, the professions operate in spheres where success cannot be achieved in every case. Very often success or failure depends upon factors beyond the professional person's control (such as the patient's stamina during a long operation or the credibility of a particular witness at trial). Even where the critical factors are within the professional person's control, he still cannot guarantee success. In matters of fine judgment or great complexity no human being can be right every time.

2–002 The problem which the courts have faced in devising the standard of perform-ance which the law will require of professional persons is to find a standard which provides proper protection for the consumer, whilst allowing for the factors mentioned in the previous paragraph.[1] Broadly speaking, the solution which has been found is to require that professional persons should possess a certain minimum degree of competence and that they should exercise reasonable care in the discharge of their duties. At this level of generality, the approach of the courts (and, on occasions, the formulation of this approach) has hardly changed over the last 170 years. In *Lanphier v Philpos*[2] (a clinical negligence case tried in 1838), Tindal C.J. directed the jury in these terms:

> "Every person who enters into a learned profession undertakes to bring to the exercise of it a reasonable degree of care and skill. He does not undertake, if he is an attorney, that at all events you shall gain your case, nor does a surgeon undertake that he will perform a cure; nor does he undertake to use the highest possible degree of skill."

In *Greaves & Co (Contractors) Ltd v Baynham Meikle & Partners*[3] (a claim against consulting engineers decided in 1975), Lord Denning M.R. stated:

> "Apply this to the employment of a professional man. The law does not usually imply a warranty that he will achieve the desired result, but only a term that he will use reasonable care and skill. The surgeon does not warrant that he will cure the patient. Nor does the solicitor warrant that he will win the case."[4]

A professional person may owe this duty to exercise reasonable skill and care

---

[1] See, e.g. the judgment of Scott L.J. in *Mahon v Osborne* [1939] 2 K.B. 14 at 16:
"The case is one of general importance because its facts illumine the principles which apply. It calls for close attention by reason of the double need, on the one hand, of enforcing a high standard of care in the surgeon against the grave danger of an overlooked swab, and, on the other, of protecting the surgeon from the risk of condemnation for actionable want of care where he has in reality been doing his best for his patient."

[2] (1838) 8 Car. & P. 475. See also the judgment of Willes J. in *Harmer v Cornelius* (1858) 5 C.B.(N.S.) 236:
"*Spondes peritiam artis*. Thus, if an apothecary, a watchmaker, or an attorney be employed for reward, they each impliedly undertake to possess and exercise reasonable skill in their several arts. The public profession of an art is a representation and undertaking to all the world that the professor possesses the requisite ability and skill."

[3] [1975] 1 W.L.R. 1095.

[4] *ibid*. at 1100D. However, on the particular facts of that case, it was held that the consulting engineers had given a warranty that they would achieve a certain result.

as a contractual obligation, in the tort of negligence or as a statutory duty, although in the case of statutory duty, a stricter duty may be prescribed so that there could be fault without want of skill and care.

The striking feature of the passages quoted in the previous paragraph (and of **2–003** many similar pronouncements about professional liability)[5] is that they focus upon professions which are bound to have an appreciable failure rate. In practice, however, different professions enjoy varying degrees of success. It is not surprising if a litigating solicitor says that some of his clients lose their cases or if a doctor says that some of his patients do not recover. It is most surprising if an engineer says that some of the bridges which he designs fall down; or if a conveyancing solicitor says that some of his clients do not acquire good title to their properties. The expectations created by different professions or by different branches within the same profession vary. The reasonable expectation of consumers is bound to have some impact on the application of the general principle stated in the previous paragraph. This may explain the divergence of judicial approach between medical negligence cases (such as *Maynard v West Midlands RHA*)[6] and cases concerning solicitors engaged in non-contentious work[7] (such as *GK Ladenbau v Crawley & De Reya*[8] and *Edward Wong Finance Co Ltd v Johnson Stokes & Master*[9]). The cases concerning individual professions have tended to develop along their own separate lines. It is therefore convenient to consider each profession separately, as is done in Section 2 of this book. The one common feature of all professions, however, is that they are not generally held to warrant that they will achieve the results which their clients desire.

Thus the professional person as defendant enjoys a privileged position. Unlike **2–004** the building contractor[10] or the shopkeeper,[11] he does not normally guarantee his product. However, his privileged position has been eroded in certain respects by developments in the law of contract and tort.[12] These are summarised in the following paragraphs and more specifically discussed in the chapters dealing with the individual professions in Section 2.

(b) *Restrictions and Inhibitions*

As well as coming under a positive duty to exercise reasonable skill and care in **2–005** the performance of his duties, a professional person may also find that, as a result

---

[5] See, e.g. the well-known direction to the jury given by McNair J. in *Bolam v Friern Hospital Management Committee* [1957] 1 W.L.R. 582. See Ch.13, para.13–022, below.

[6] [1984] 1 W.L.R. 634. See Ch.13, below.

[7] The policy considerations which underlie the apparently higher standard demanded of conveyancing solicitors were explored by Hoffmann L.J. in a lecture to the Professional Negligence Bar Association on October 14, 1992: "The reasonableness of lawyers' lapses" (1994) 10 P.N. 6. See also Evans, Ch.1, above.

[8] [1978] 1 W.L.R. 266. See Ch.11, para.11–093, below.

[9] [1984] A.C. 296. See Ch.11, paras 11–088 to 11–090, below.

[10] See, e.g. *Miller v Cannon Hill Estates Ltd* [1931] 2 K.B. 113; *Hancock v BW Brazier (Anerley) Ltd* [1966] 1 W.L.R. 1317; *Barclays Bank Plc v Fairclough Building Ltd* [1995] Q.B. 214.

[11] See the Sale of Goods Act 1979, ss.13–15, as amended by the Sale and Supply of Goods Act 1994.

[12] For example, as a result of decisions on concurrent liability (discussed later in this chapter), in relation to limitation architects and engineers are in a substantially worse position than contractors and sub-contractors.

of having undertaken those duties, he is prevented in law from acting in certain ways. While it is possible to describe these inhibitions in terms of positive duties, they are better considered as restrictions on a professional's conduct rather than as goals which he must attain. The obligations of a fiduciary are, in general, negative: for example a duty not to make a secret profit. In the same way a professional person will generally be under a duty not to reveal to third parties information given to him in confidence. Attempts are sometimes made to extend professional liability by pleading alternative claims based upon breach of a fiduciary duty to exercise reasonable skill and care. However, this approach was deprecated by Lord Browne-Wilkinson in *Henderson v Merrett Syndicates Ltd*[13] and rejected decisively by the Court of Appeal in *Bristol and West Building Society v Mothew.*[14]

2–006   These restrictions on the conduct of a professional person fall into three categories:

(1) *Fiduciary obligations*: These are the varying restrictions imposed in equity on professional persons acting in a fiduciary capacity, having at their heart a core duty of undivided loyalty. The extent to which a professional person will be subject to such obligations will depend upon the extent to which the client is entitled to expect such undivided loyalty.

(2) *Undue influence*: A professional person who acquires (or is deemed to have acquired) a degree of ascendancy over a client is not permitted to abuse that client's confidence by using it to obtain some material advantage whether by gift or a transaction which favours the professional person.

(3) *Confidentiality*: A professional person is generally not permitted to reveal confidential information acquired from or on behalf of a client.

The first two are discussed in detail in paras 2–128 to 2–154, below and the third in paras 2–155 to 2–179, below. Where appropriate they are also considered in the context of particular professions in Section 2.

2. CONTRACTUAL LIABILITY

2–007 Historically, the law of contract is the principal means by which the courts have exercised control over the standard of performance of professional persons.[15] In most instances there is a contract between the professional person and his client, whereby the former agrees to render certain services and the latter agrees to pay a specified, alternatively a reasonable, fee. In such a contract there is generally

---

[13] [1995] 2 A.C. 145 at 204–206. See further (1995) 111 L.Q.R. 1, *per* Heydon.
[14] [1998] Ch. 1 at 16C–18F. Discussed further in para.2–130, below.
[15] See Atiyah, *The Rise and Fall of Freedom of Contract* (Clarendon Press, 1979), p.416.

implied by law a term that the professional person will exercise reasonable skill and care.[16]

As Oliver J. pointed out in *Midland Bank Trust Co Ltd v Hett, Stubbs & Kemp*,[17] the obligation to exercise reasonable skill and care is not the only contractual term which ought to be considered in a professional negligence action:

2–008

"The classical formulation of the claim in this sort of case as 'damages for negligence and breach of professional duty' tends to be a mesmeric phrase. It concentrates attention on the implied obligation to devote to the client's business that reasonable care and skill to be expected from a normally competent and careful practitioner as if that obligation were not only a compendious, but also an exhaustive, definition of all the duties assumed under the contract created by the retainer and its acceptance. But, of course, it is not. A contract gives rise to a complex of rights and duties of which the duty to exercise reasonable care and skill is but one. If I employ a carpenter to supply and put up a good quality oak shelf for me, the acceptance by him of that employment involves the assumption of a number of contractual duties. He must supply wood of an adequate quality and it must be oak. He must fix the shelf. And he must carry out the fashioning and fixing with the reasonable care and skill which I am entitled to expect of a skilled craftsman. If he fixes the brackets but fails to supply the shelf or if he supplies and fixes a shelf of unseasoned pine, my complaint against him is not that he has failed to exercise reasonable care and skill in carrying out the work but that he has failed to supply what was contracted for."[18]

The particular illustration chosen by Oliver J. in the above passage must be used with caution, since the obligations of a carpenter to his employer are generally of a different nature to those owed by a professional person to his client.[19] Nevertheless, in every contract between a professional person and his client there will be express or implied terms defining the nature of the engagement. Thus if a surveyor is instructed to produce a report on certain property, there is an express or implied obligation to inspect it.[20] If a surgeon agrees with his patient to perform a particular operation, there may be an implied term that he will "give the necessary supervision thereafter until the discharge of the patient".[21] If a solicitor is instructed to effect the grant of an option, there are implied terms that he will draw up the option agreement and effect registration.[22] The importance of specific terms such as these is that: (i) a professional person will be liable if he breaks them, quite irrespective of the amount of skill and care which he has exercised; and (ii) the defence of contributory negligence is not available.[23]

2–009

---

[16] This common law principle is now embodied in s.13 of the Supply of Goods and Services Act 1982.

[17] [1979] Ch. 384.

[18] *ibid.* at 434E–H. See also Ch.11, para.11–007, below.

[19] See para.2–004, above.

[20] See Ch.10, para.10–020, below.

[21] See *Morris v Winsbury-White* [1937] 4 All E.R. 494 at 500C–D; and Ch.13, para.13–004, below.

[22] See *Midland Bank Trust Co Ltd v Hett, Stubbs & Kemp* [1979] 1 Ch. 384 at 435B; and Ch.11, para.11–007, below. See also Nicholls L.J.'s analysis of the solicitors' duties in *Bell v Peter Browne & Co* [1990] 2 Q.B. 495 at 500.

[23] See Ch.5, para.5–143, below.

2–010   Where a professional is retained on express terms the court may have to construe those terms to determine whether they create absolute obligations or whether the professional merely promises to exercise reasonable skill and care in undertaking a specified task or to achieve a specified result. The decision of the Court of Appeal in *Midland Bank Plc v Cox McQueen*[24] provides helpful guidance as to how to approach such questions of construction. In that case solicitors were retained by a bank to obtain the signatures of a Mr and Mrs Duke to various documents and to explain the implications of a mortgage to them. Mr Duke introduced to the solicitors an imposter, telling them she was Mrs Duke. In an action against the solicitor the bank contended that the solicitors had undertaken an absolute duty to obtain Mrs Duke's signature. The Court of Appeal rejected that argument. Lord Woolf M.R. (with whom the other members of the Court agreed) said:

> "If commercial institutions such as banks wish to impose an absolute liability on members of a profession they should do so in clear terms so that the solicitors can appreciate the extent of their obligation which they are accepting . . . Unless the language used in a retainer clearly has this consequence, the courts should not be ready to impose obligations on solicitors which even the most careful solicitor may not be able to meet."

This suggests that courts will be slow to construe professionals' retainers as giving rise to strict obligations, although it does not follow that in appropriate cases they will not do so.[25]

2–011   However, much of the professional person's work is not regulated by specific contractual terms such as these. Within the framework set by his instructions the professional person normally attempts to achieve a particular result (e.g. the solution of an engineering problem or the restoration of the patient to good health) or he renders a certain kind of service (e.g. financial advice or architectural design). In the absence of express terms[26] to the contrary effect, there is implied by law a term that the professional person will carry out these activities with reasonable skill and care.[27]

2–012   By way of exception to the general principles stated above, there are a small number of cases in which the professional person is simply required to achieve a specified result[28] and there is no need for a contractual term defining the skill and care which he must use. Engagements of this kind are the most onerous undertaken by professional persons. For example, where a dentist agrees to make a denture for his patient, his obligation is not to exercise reasonable skill and care (nor even exceptional skill and care) but to produce a denture which will be fit

---

[24] [1999] P.N.L.R. 593; [1999] Lloyd's Rep. P.N. 223.

[25] See also *Mercantile Credit Company Ltd v Fenwick* [1999] Lloyd's Rep. P.N. 408; and *Barclays Bank Plc v Weeks Legg & Dean (a firm)* [1999] Q.B. 309. A strict construction was placed on a solicitor's undertaking in *Zwebner v The Mortgage Corp Ltd* [1998] P.N.L.R. 769. See further Ch.11, paras 11–009 and 11–010, below.

[26] Or implied terms arising from the particular circumstances of the retainer: e.g. *Greaves & Co (Contractors) Ltd v Baynham Meikle & Partners* [1975] 1 W.L.R. 1095, discussed in Ch.9, paras 9–165 and 9–166, below.

[27] See ss.13 and 16 of the Supply of Goods and Services Act 1982.

[28] See, e.g. Ch.11, para.11–009 and Ch.16, para.16–012, below.

for its purpose.[29] An IT consultant may also owe the same standard in respect of computer software provided under a contract with a client.[30] In *IBA v EMI and BICC*,[31] it was argued that contracts by architects or engineers to do design work fell into the same category. The point did not arise directly for decision in the House of Lords. However, Lord Scarman, founding himself on *Samuels v Davis*[32] expressed the opinion obiter that "one who contracts to design an article for a purpose made known to him undertakes that the design is reasonably fit for the purpose".[33]

3. TORTIOUS LIABILITY

(a) *The Tort of Negligence*

The tort of negligence[34] is complete when three conditions are satisfied:　　**2–013**

  (1) the defendant owes a duty of care to the claimant;

  (2) the defendant has acted or spoken in such a way as to break that duty of care; and

  (3) the claimant has suffered relevant damage as a consequence of the breach.

The first condition. This is discussed below.[35] The essential questions to be　**2–014** considered in every case are whether a duty of care existed and, if so, what was its scope.

The second condition. Once the existence and scope of the duty of care have　**2–015** been established, the question of breach turns upon whether the defendant exercised the requisite degree of skill and care in the performance of his tortious duty.[36]

The third condition. The third condition is satisfied if the claimant suffers　**2–016** damage within the scope of the defendant's duty.[37] Thus if the defendant's duty

---

[29] *Samuels v Davis* [1943] K.B. 526.
   "It does not help to consider cases of an artist painting a picture or a sculptor making a bust, or to refer to cases of surgical operations in the ordinary sense. Clearly a dentist is in the same position as any other surgeon from the point of view of the law. If a dentist takes out a tooth or a surgeon removes an appendix, he is bound to take reasonable care and to show such skill as may be expected from a qualified practitioner. The case is entirely different, where a chattel is ultimately to be delivered."
[30] See Ch.9, paras 9–165 to 9–171 and Ch.20, paras 20–010 to 20–026, below.
[31] (1978) 11 Build.L.R. 29, CA; (1980) 14 Build.L.R. 1, HL.
[32] [1943] 1 K.B. 526.
[33] (1980) 14 Build.L.R. 48. See further at Ch.9, para.9–167, below.
[34] For a general discussion of the tort of negligence, which is beyond the scope of this book, see *Charlesworth & Percy*.
[35] See paras 2–017 to 2–080, below.
[36] See Section 4, below and the chapters in Section 2 on individual professions, especially on "Liability for Breach of Duty".
[37] See the discussion of minimum actionable damage in Stapleton, "The Gist of Negligence" (1988) 104 L.Q.R. 213.

is only to protect the claimant against personal injury or physical damage, then that kind of damage (rather than pure financial loss) must be inflicted, in order to complete the tort of negligence.[38] Accordingly, the questions of duty and damage (the first and third conditions) are interrelated. In determining whether the defendant owed any relevant duty to the claimant, it is necessary to characterise the damage flowing from the breach of such duty. Once damage of the requisite character has been established, the subsequent inquiry is directed to quantum.[39]

2–017   **Situations in which a duty of care exists.** A owes a duty to exercise reasonable care in relation to B in those situations where the courts have held (or Parliament has enacted) that a duty of care exists. Obvious examples are: where A is a car driver and B is anyone who might be injured by A's careless driving (e.g. another motorist, a cyclist, a pedestrian or a passenger); where A is the occupier of premises and B is a visitor; where A is B's employer; or where A is a medical practitioner and B is his patient. However, obvious situations, whether covered by earlier decisions or an Act of Parliament, do not necessarily answer the question whether a particular duty of care is owed in a novel situation. In order to decide whether a duty of care is owed in a novel situation, some analogy or guiding principle must be derived from earlier authorities.

2–018   Over the last 80 years or so, a series of new situations have been considered by the House of Lords and either accepted as giving rise to a duty of care, or alternatively held not to do so. Important examples are:

(1) The manufacturer of a product owes a duty to take reasonable care to protect the ultimate consumer against personal injury.[40]

(2) A bank giving a reference on behalf of its customer to a third party owes a duty (in the absence of any effective disclaimer) to take reasonable care to protect the third party against financial loss.[41]

(3) Borstal officers, when allowing borstal boys to work on an island, have been held to owe a duty to the owners of nearby yachts to take reasonable care to prevent the boys escaping and causing damage to property.[42]

(4) A local authority exercising its supervisory functions in relation to the construction of dwelling-houses has been held to owe a duty to future owners and occupiers to protect them against the cost of repairing defects which would be liable to affect health or safety.[43] This decision was

---

[38] *Nitrigin Eireann Teoranta v Inco Alloys Ltd* [1992] 1 W.L.R. 498, *per* May J. is a good illustration of this. Damage to the pipes supplied by the defendant was economic loss in respect of which the defendant owed the claimant no duty of care. Only when damage was caused to other property nearly a year later was the claimant's cause of action in tort complete. See further Ch.5, paras 5–031 to 5–074, below.

[39] See Ch.3, paras 3–001 to 3–007, below and the sections on "Liability for Breach of Duty" in the chapters on individual professions.

[40] *Donoghue v Stevenson* [1932] A.C. 562.

[41] *Hedley Byrne & Co Ltd v Heller & Partners Ltd* [1964] A.C. 465.

[42] *Dorset Yacht Co v Home Office* [1970] A.C. 1004.

[43] *Anns v Merton London BC* [1978] A.C. 728.

subsequently departed from by the House of Lords,[44] pursuant to the Practice Statement (Judicial Precedent) 1966.[45]

(5) A surveyor instructed by a building society to value a modest house for mortgage purposes, has been held to owe a duty to protect the prospective mortgagor against economic loss flowing from unreported defects.[46]

(6) Auditors of a public company have been held not to owe a duty of care to persons who might purchase shares (or to shareholders who might purchase more shares) in reliance upon the audited accounts.[47]

(7) Solicitors instructed to prepare a will have been held to owe a duty of care to the intended beneficiaries.[48]

Appellate decisions in the major "duty of care" cases have normally com- **2–019** prised two elements: first, there is a line of reasoning leading to the specific result; secondly, there is a more general discussion about the law of tort and duties of care, which is intended to justify (or to provide a theoretical basis for) the specific line of reasoning which has been adopted. The *ratio* of these decisions is always to be found in the first element, namely the line of reasoning leading to the specific result.[49] However, the other element (the general discussion) often attracts more attention from commentators and sometimes is treated almost as if it were the *ratio* of the case.[50] This is unfortunate, because the "theoretical discussion" element in these cases is not consistent and could hardly be expected to be so, in view of the broad jurisprudential problems with which it grapples. It is submitted that any attempt to rationalise the numerous appellate decisions on duty of care should begin by analysing those decisions into their two principal elements.

The line of reasoning leading to the specific result. This is dealt with in the **2–020** chapters on individual professions in the sections dealing with duty of care.[51]

---

[44] *Murphy v Brentwood DC* [1991] 1 A.C. 398.
[45] [1966] 1 W.L.R. 1234.
[46] *Smith v Eric S Bush* [1990] 1 A.C. 831.
[47] *Caparo Industries Plc v Dickman* [1990] 2 A.C. 605.
[48] *White v Jones* [1995] 2 A.C. 207.
[49] It is always essential to consider "the detailed circumstances of the particular case and the particular relationship between the parties in the context of their legal and factual situation as a whole": Lord Bingham in *Commissioners of Customs and Excise v Barclays Bank Plc* [2006] UKHL 28; [2006] 3 W.L.R. 1 at [8].
[50] See the warning in Lord Atkin in *Donoghue v Stevenson* [1932] A.C. 562 at 583–584: discussed at para.2–022, below.
" . . . in the branch of the law which deals with civil wrongs, dependent in England at any rate entirely upon the application by judges of general principles also formulated by judges, it is of particular importance to guard against the danger of stating propositions of law in wider terms than is necessary, lest essential factors be omitted in the wider survey and the inherent adaptability of English law be unduly restricted. For this reason it is very necessary in considering reported cases in the law of torts, that the actual decision alone should carry authority, proper weight, of course, being given to the dicta of the judges."
(See also *Heaven v Pender* (1883) 11 Q.B.D. 503, where Cotton and Bowen L.JJ. declined to agree with Brett M.R. "in laying down unnecessarily the larger principle which he entertains".)
[51] See the sections headed "Duties to Third Parties" in the chapters on individual professions.

2–021   **The theoretical discussion.** The theoretical discussion which occurs in the major "duty of care" cases is referred to below.[52] It is part of the continuing quest by the courts to find some rational explanation for the conclusions to which they are driven in individual cases. Although (as previously stated) these passages are not part of the *rationes* of the cases in which they occur and, inevitably, they are not consistent and are not of universal application,[53] nevertheless they have assumed great importance in the development of the law of negligence and so to any general consideration of professional negligence (which is the business of this part of this chapter).

(b) *Theoretical Basis for the Duty of Care*[54]

(i) *Lord Atkin's Approach*

2–022   In *Donoghue v Stevenson*,[55] the House of Lords by a majority of 3:2 held that the manufacturer of ginger beer owed a duty of care to the ultimate consumer. The majority (Lords Atkin, Thankerton and Macmillan) dealt principally with authorities concerning the liability of manufacturers and analogous cases. But also, in the general part of their speeches, they discussed whether there was some broad principle which underlay all cases where the law imposed a duty of care. The leading speech for the majority was given by Lord Atkin. He noted that the courts decide whether there is a duty of care in the specific cases, which come before them, and thus the law has been developed in respect of particular relationships: salesman and customer, landlord and tenant and so forth.[56] He continued:

> "And yet the duty which is common to all the cases where liability is established must logically be based upon some element common to the cases where it is found to exist. To seek a complete logical definition of the general principle is probably to go beyond the function of the judge, for the more general the definition the more likely it is to omit essentials or to introduce non-essentials.
> . . . At present I content myself with pointing out that in English law there must be, and is, some general conception of relations giving rise to a duty of care, of which the particular cases found in the books are but instances . . . . The rule that you are to love your neighbour becomes in law, you must not injure your neighbour; and the lawyer's question, Who is my neighbour? receives a restricted reply. You must take reasonable care to avoid acts or omissions which you can reasonably foresee would be likely to injure your neighbour. Who, then, in law is my neighbour? The answer seems to

---

[52] See paras 2–022 to 2–080, below.

[53] In his speech in *Dorset Yacht Co Ltd v Home Office* [1970] A.C. 1004 at 1060D (discussed in para.2–026, below), Lord Diplock said at 1060E of the well-known passage in Lord Atkin's speech in *Donoghue v Stevenson* [1932] A.C. 562 (set out in para.2–022, below):

"Used as a guide to characteristics which will be found to exist in conduct and relationships which give rise to a legal duty of care this aphorism marks a milestone in the modern development of the law of negligence. But misused as a universal, it is manifestly false."

(See also Lord Devlin in *Hedley Byrne & Co Ltd v Heller & Partners Ltd* [1964] A.C. 465 at 525.)

[54] This section focuses mainly on the principal House of Lords and Privy Council decisions on duty of care over the last 75 years. The varying approaches adopted in the major Commonwealth jurisdictions are also considered.

[55] [1932] A.C. 562.

[56] *ibid.* at 579.

be—persons who are so closely and directly affected by my act that I ought reasonably to have them in contemplation as being so affected when I am directing my mind to the acts or omissions which are called in question."[57]

In the context of Lord Atkin's speech the phrase "injure your neighbour" means to cause some kind of physical or psychological harm to the claimant. If the soft drink in *Donoghue v Stevenson* had been perfectly harmless but of lower nutritional value than advertised, Mrs Donoghue would have had no claim against the manufacturer for any financial loss which she might suffer.[58]   **2–023**

(ii) *Hedley Byrne*

Compared with the duty of care to prevent physical injury, the duty to prevent   **2–024**
economic loss has caused the courts great problems, outside the obvious areas of economic loss consequent upon personal injury or damage to property. In *Hedley Byrne & Co Ltd v Heller & Partners Ltd*,[59] the claimants suffered financial losses as a result of acting in reliance on favourable references given by the bankers of Easipower Ltd (which subsequently went into liquidation). The House of Lords held that the bankers owed no duty to the claimants only because the references had been given "without responsibility". Thus the House of Lords recognised, in principle, that a person making a statement could owe a duty to the recipient (with whom he has no contract) to take reasonable care and that, in the event of breach, he could be liable for economic losses suffered by the recipient.

In the general part of their speeches the Law Lords discussed two interrelated   **2–025**
problems, the extent of liability for words as opposed to deeds and the extent of liability for financial loss rather than (or not resulting from) physical injury. In general terms, all five Law Lords recognised that it would be unacceptable to impose liability on third parties for all financial losses foreseeably suffered as a result of negligent mis-statement. They saw as the principal mechanism for restricting such liability the nature of the relationship between the parties, rather than the nature of the loss.[60] Although different formulations were used, they emphasised the need for a special relationship. Lord Reid said that expressly or by implication from the circumstances, the defendant must have undertaken some responsibility to the claimant. Lord Devlin said that a duty to take care in respect of words arises when the relationship between the parties is contractual, fiduciary or "equivalent to contract", i.e. there would be a contract but for the lack of consideration.[61] Significantly, the House of Lords overruled *Candler v Crane, Christmas & Co*[62] and held that the law was correctly stated in the dissenting judgment of Denning L.J.

---

[57] [1932] A.C. 562 at 580.
[58] For example, paying an excessive price for the drink; alternatively, purchasing additional ingredients to bring the drink up to the advertised nutritional value.
[59] [1964] A.C. 465.
[60] Lord Devlin protested that the distinction between pure financial loss and financial loss consequent upon physical injury was irrational: see *ibid.* at 517. See also, *per* Lord Hodson at the bottom of 509, *ibid.*
[61] *ibid.* at 483, *per* Lord Reid and at 528–529, *per* Lord Devlin.
[62] [1951] 2 K.B. 164. See paras 2–113 to 2–116, below.

(iii) *The Inclusive Approach*

2–026   **The *Dorset Yacht* case.** In *Dorset Yacht Co Ltd v Home Office*,[63] the House of Lords held, on a preliminary issue, that borstal officers supervising borstal boys staying on Brownsea Island owed a duty to the owners of nearby yachts to take reasonable care to prevent the boys escaping and causing damage. In the general part[64] of his speech Lord Reid said:

> " . . . there has been a steady trend towards regarding the law of negligence as depending on principle so that, when a new point emerges, one should ask not whether it is covered by authority but whether recognised principles apply to it. *Donoghue v Stevenson* may be regarded as a milestone, and the well-known passage in Lord Atkin's speech[65] should I think be regarded as a statement of principle. It is not to be treated as if it were a statutory definition. It will require qualification in new circumstances. But I think that the time has come when we can and should say that it ought to apply unless there is some justification or valid explanation for its exclusion. For example, causing economic loss is a different matter . . . "

2–027   ***Anns v Merton*, the two-stage test.** In *Anns v Merton LBC*,[66] structural movement occurred causing cracking in a block of flats in Wimbledon. The lessees of seven flats claimed damages against the local authority for the negligence of its employees in approving foundations of inadequate depth. The House of Lords held on a preliminary issue that in performing its supervisory functions the local authority owed a duty of care to future owners and occupiers of the flats. The principal speech was given by Lord Wilberforce, with whom Lords Diplock, Simon and Russell agreed. In the general part of his speech Lord Wilberforce said[67]:

> "Through the trilogy of cases in this House—*Donoghue v Stevenson* [1932] A.C. 562, *Hedley Byrne & Co Ltd v Heller & Partners Ltd* [1964] A.C. 465 and *Dorset Yacht Co Ltd v Home Office* [1970] A.C. 1004—the position has now been reached that in order to establish that a duty of care arises in a particular situation, it is not necessary to bring the facts of that situation within those of previous situations in which a duty of care has been held to exist. Rather the question has to be approached in two stages. First, one has to ask whether, as between the alleged wrongdoers and the person who has suffered damage there is a sufficient relationship of proximity or neighbourhood such that, in the reasonable contemplation of the former, carelessness on his part may be likely to cause damage to the latter—in which case a prima facie duty of care arises. Secondly, if the first question is answered affirmatively, it is necessary to consider whether there are any considerations which ought to negative, or to reduce or limit the scope of the duty or the class of person to whom it is owed or the damages to which a breach of it may give rise: see *Dorset Yacht* case [1970] A.C. 1004 at 1027, *per* Lord Reid. Examples of this are *Hedley Byrne*'s case [1964] A.C. 465 where the class of potential plaintiffs was reduced to those shown to have relied upon the correctness of statements made, and *Weller & Co v Foot and Mouth Disease Research Institute* [1966] 1 Q.B. 569; and (I cite these merely as illustrations, without discussion) cases about 'economic loss' where, a duty having been held to exist, the nature of the recoverable damages was

---

[63] [1970] A.C. 1004.
[64] *ibid.* at 1026–1027.
[65] See para.2–022, above.
[66] [1978] A.C. 728.
[67] *ibid.* at 751G–752B.

limited: see *SCM (United Kingdom) Ltd v WJ Whittall & Son Ltd* [1971] 1 Q.B. 137 and *Spartan Steel & Alloys Ltd v Martin & Co (Contractors) Ltd* [1973] Q.B. 27."

Subsequent use of the two-stage test. This two-stage test gained wide 2–028 currency and was used as the rationale of the decision in numerous novel situations where a duty of care was alleged.[68] The problem with this test was the undue weight which it attributed to foreseeability of damage, and the substantial extension of tortious liability which it appeared to presage. Indeed the *Anns* decision itself, which was justified by reference to this test, was the subject of strong criticism[69] and the High Court of Australia declined to follow it.[70] In England, the retreat began in 1984, with the decision of the House of Lords in *Governors of the Peabody Donation Fund v Sir Lindsay Parkinson & Co Ltd*.[71] In that case developers claimed damages against a local authority for permitting the developers' own contractor to depart from the approved drainage design. Lord Keith, with whom the other four Law Lords agreed, held that the local authority owed no relevant duty to the developers. In the general part of his speech he said:

"There has been a tendency in some recent cases to treat these passages [i.e. the passages set out above[72]] as being themselves of a definitive character. This is a temptation which should be resisted. The true question in each case is whether the particular defendant owed to the particular plaintiff a duty of care having the scope which is contended for, and whether he was in breach of that duty with consequent loss to the plaintiff. A relationship of proximity in Lord Atkin's sense must exist before any duty of care can arise, but the scope of the duty must depend on all the circumstances of the case ... So in determining whether or not a duty of care of particular scope was incumbent upon a defendant it is material to take into consideration whether it is just and reasonable that it should be so."[73]

In *Candlewood Navigation Corp Ltd v Mitsui OSK Lines Ltd*,[74] the Privy 2–029 Council emphasised the importance of limiting liability for economic loss, although they considered that this could be achieved within the *Anns* two-stage test.[75] In *Leigh & Sillivan Ltd v Aliakmon Shipping Co Ltd*,[76] buyers of goods,

---

[68] See, e.g. the reasoning in *Yianni v Edwin Evans & Sons* [1982] Q.B. 438; and *Ross v Caunters* [1980] Ch. 297 in relation to the liability of surveyors and solicitors respectively to third parties. Interestingly, despite the subsequent demise of the *Anns* two-stage test, the House of Lords has held that the results in both cases were correct. This illustrates the point made in paras 2–051 to 2–052, below.

[69] See, e.g. *D&F Estates Ltd v Church Commissioners for England* [1989] A.C. 177; *Murphy v Brentwood DC* [1991] 1 A.C. 38; I. N. Duncan Wallace Q.C., "Negligence and Defective Buildings: Confusion Confounded?" (1989) 105 L.Q.R. 46.

[70] *Shire of Sutherland v Heyman* (1985) 60 A.L.R. 1. In a percipient article, I. N. Duncan Wallace Q.C. suggested that this case was a turning point in the law of tort and that the higher judiciary both in England and the Commonwealth were beginning to apply the traditional principles more rigorously: see "The Shire of Sutherland Case in the High Court of Australia" in (1986) 3 Int.Const.L. Rev., Pt 2.

[71] [1985] A.C. 210.

[72] See paras 2–026 to 2–027, above.

[73] [1985] A.C. 210 at 240–241.

[74] [1986] A.C. 1.

[75] *ibid.* at 24H–25D.

[76] [1986] A.C. 785.

to whom risk but not property had passed, unsuccessfully claimed against the ship owners in respect of damage caused to the goods in transit. The reasoning leading to the specific decision was that the claimants could not claim for loss of or damage to property unless they had either legal ownership or possessory title to the property at the time when the loss or damage occurred. The decision was given in a single speech by Lord Brandon, with whom the other four Law Lords agreed. In rejecting an argument based on the *Anns* two-stage test, Lord Brandon commented that it was not intended to provide a universally applicable test of the existence and scope of a duty of care in the law of negligence. In particular, it should not be adopted in situations where previously it has been repeatedly held that a duty of care does not exist.[77] This decision may have been the death knell of the *Anns* two-stage test. Once it is recognised that this is inconsistent with a substantial body of earlier duty of care cases, the test has little utility as a guide to the solution of future problems.

(iv) *The Threefold Test*

2–030   Once the shortcomings of the inclusive approach were recognised, the courts moved towards a more neutral framework within which to consider the existence of a duty of care.[78] In *Smith v Eric S Bush*,[79] a surveyor instructed by a building society failed to spot a serious defect in a house (inadequate support for upstairs chimneys) and the building society granted a mortgage to the claimant. Both the mortgage application form and the report contained a disclaimer of liability for the accuracy of the report, but that disclaimer was ineffective by reason of the Unfair Contract Terms Act 1977.[80] The House of Lords held that the surveyor, though instructed by the mortgagee, owed a duty to the prospective mortgagor to exercise reasonable care when inspecting and reporting. The line of reasoning leading to the specific result is set out in Ch.9, below.[81] In the more general part of his speech Lord Griffiths (with whom Lord Keith and Lord Brandon agreed) stated:

> "In what circumstances should a duty of care be owed by the adviser to those who act upon his advice? I would answer—only if it is foreseeable that if the advice is negligent

---

[77] [1986] A.C. 785 at 815.
[78] For example in *Yuen Kun Yeu v Att-Gen of Hong Kong* [1988] A.C. 175 proceedings by investors (who had suffered losses) against the Commissioner of Deposit-taking Companies in Hong Kong were dismissed as disclosing no reasonable cause of action. Lord Keith, delivering the judgment of the Privy Council, emphasised the importance of proximity as well as foreseeability in relation to the first stage of the *Anns* test (*ibid.* at 191–192). He also said that in future that test should not be regarded in all circumstances as a suitable guide to the existence of a duty of care. Factors which weighed heavily in the actual decision were the large number of potential claimants (anyone who might invest in Hong Kong), the nature of the Commissioner's functions and his limited powers. See also *Davis v Radcliffe* [1990] 1 W.L.R. 821, where the Privy Council reached a similar conclusion. See further para.2–088, below.
[79] [1990] 1 A.C. 831. *Smith v Eric S Bush* and *Harris v Wyre Forest DC* were heard together. The reasoning in relation to both cases is important and should be considered together. These cases are discussed more fully in Ch.10, paras 10–046 to 10–051, below.
[80] See Ch.5, para.5–012, below.
[81] See paras 10–046 to 10–051, below.

the recipient is likely to suffer damage, that there is a sufficiently proximate relationship between the parties and that it is just and reasonable to impose the liability."[82]

Shortly after the decisions discussed in the previous paragraph the House of **2–031** Lords returned to the same issues in *Caparo Industries Plc v Dickman*.[83] The claimants, having taken over a public limited company ("F"), alleged that the audited accounts on which they had relied were inaccurate and misleading. They brought proceedings against two directors of F for fraud and against the auditors for negligence in certifying that the accounts showed a true and fair view of F's position on the stated date. On a preliminary issue the House of Lords held that the auditors owed no duty to the claimants, either as potential investors or as existing shareholders considering the purchase of further shares. Three principal speeches were delivered by Lord Bridge, Lord Oliver and Lord Jauncey.

In the general part of his speech Lord Bridge said that the quest for a single **2–032** general principle to determine the existence and scope of the duty of care in any situation had failed. He continued:

"What emerges [from the recent decisions] is that, in addition to the foreseeability of damage, necessary ingredients in any situation giving rise to a duty of care are that there should exist between the party owing the duty and the party to whom it is owed a relationship characterised by the law as one of 'proximity' or 'neighbourhood' and that the situation should be one in which the court considers it fair, just and reasonable that the law should impose a duty of a given scope upon the one party for the benefit of the other. But it is implicit in the passages referred to that the concepts of proximity and fairness embodied in these additional ingredients are not susceptible of any such precise definition as would be necessary to give them utility as practical tests, but amount in effect to little more than convenient labels to attach to the features of different specific situations which, on a detailed examination of all the circumstances, the law recognises pragmatically as giving rise to a duty of care of a given scope."[84]

Lord Bridge went on to say that the law attached more significance to the traditional categorisations as guides to the existence and scope of the duty of care. He then focused on the authorities concerning negligent advice/economic loss ("this relatively narrow corner of the field"[85]) for the purpose of determining the instant case.

In the general part of his speech Lord Oliver expressed similar views. Having **2–033** referred to the extensive financial losses which could foreseeably result from negligent statements, he continued:

"Thus the postulate of a simple duty to avoid any harm that is, with hindsight, reasonably capable of being foreseen becomes untenable without the imposition of some intelligible limits to keep the law of negligence within the bounds of common sense and practicality. Those limits have been found by the requirement of what has been called a 'relationship of proximity' between plaintiff and defendant and by the imposition of a further requirement that the attachment of liability for harm which has occurred be 'just and reasonable'. But although the cases in which the courts have imposed or withheld liability are capable of an approximate categorisation, one looks

---

[82] [1990] 1 A.C. 831 at 864H–865A.
[83] [1990] 2 A.C. 605. Discussed in Ch.17, paras 17–051 to 17–060, below.
[84] *ibid.* at 617–618.
[85] *ibid.* at 619E.

in vain for some common denominator by which the existence of the essential relationship can be tested. Indeed it is difficult to resist a conclusion that what have been treated as three separate requirements are, at least in most cases, in fact merely facets of the same thing, for in some cases the degree of foreseeability is such that it is from that alone that the requisite proximity can be deduced, whilst in others the absence of that essential relationship can most rationally be attributed simply to the court's view that it would not be fair and reasonable to hold the defendant responsible. 'Proximity' is, no doubt, a convenient expression so long as it is realised that it is no more than a label which embraces not a definable concept but merely a description of circumstances from which, pragmatically, the courts conclude that a duty of care exists."[86]

2–034   The same threefold test was adopted by three members of the House of Lords in *Spring v Guardian Assurance Plc*.[87] In that case the claimant was frustrated in his efforts to set up in business selling insurance by an adverse reference from the defendants, his former employers. The trial judge held that the defendants had been negligent but not malicious in preparing the adverse reference. The Court of Appeal allowed an appeal by the defendants on the grounds that they owed no relevant duty of care to the claimant.[88] The House of Lords allowed the claimant's appeal by a majority of four to one. Out of that majority Lord Lowry,[89] Lord Slynn[90] and Lord Woolf[91] all approached the issues using the threefold test.

2–035   **Summary.** It appeared that following the demise of the *Anns* two-stage test ("the inclusive approach") a new framework emerged for considering, or at least for explaining, some of the major decisions on duty of care. This involved considering three questions:

(1) whether it was reasonably foreseeable that the claimant would suffer the kind of damage which occurred;

(2) whether there was sufficient proximity between the parties;

(3) whether it was just and reasonable that the defendant should owe a duty of care of the scope alleged.

(v) *The Exclusive Approach*

2–036   The perceived difficulty with the threefold approach set out in the previous paragraph is that questions (2) and (3) are so broad that it is frequently impossible to tell how they would be answered on the facts of any individual case. The questions are highly subjective. Furthermore, every new case must be approached from first principles.

---

[86] [1990] 2 A.C. 605 at 633A–D.
[87] [1995] 2 A.C. 296. For a discussion of this decision see "The Right of Spring" by Lord Cooke in Cane and Stapleton (eds), *The Law of Obligations, Essays in Celebration of John Fleming* (Clarendon Press, 1998). Lord Cooke considers the decision in the context of the law of defamation and the law of employment.
[88] The Court of Appeal's decision was strongly criticised by Weir, "The case of the careless referee" (1993) 52 C.L.J. 376.
[89] [1995] 2 A.C. 296 at 325–326.
[90] *ibid.* at 334–336.
[91] *ibid.* at 342.

Lord Oliver grappled with these problems in *Caparo Industries Plc v Dick-* **2–037**
man[92] in the passage quoted in para.2–033, above. He recognised that it was
impossible to state "some general principle which will determine liability in an
infinite variety of circumstances".[93] He went on to commend the incremental
approach stated by Brennan J. in *Sutherland Shire Council v Heyman*.[94]

The incremental approach. In *Sutherland Shire Council v Heyman*, the High **2–038**
Court of Australia declined to hold a local authority liable to a subsequent house
purchaser for negligent inspection of foundation works. In considering the proper
approach to the duty of care question, Brennan J. stated:

> "Of course, if foreseeability of injury to another were the exhaustive criterion of a
> prima facie duty to act to prevent the occurrence of that injury, it would be essential to
> introduce some kind of restrictive qualification—perhaps a qualification of the kind
> stated in the second stage of the general proposition in *Anns*. I am unable to accept that
> approach. It is preferable, in my view, that the law should develop novel categories of
> negligence incrementally and by analogy with established categories, rather than by a
> massive extension of a prima facie duty of care restrained only by indefinable con-
> siderations which ought to negative, or to reduce or limit the scope of the duty or the
> class of person to whom it is owed."[95]

Adoption of incremental approach by House of Lords. In *Murphy v Brent-* **2–039**
wood DC,[96] the claimant purchased a house which had been built with defective
foundations, and claimed damages against the local authority for negligence in
approval of the plans. The official referee awarded him £35,000, representing his
loss on resale of the house in its defective condition. The decision was upheld by
the Court of Appeal (on the basis of *Anns v Merton LBC*[97]) but reversed by the
House of Lords. An enlarged committee of seven Law Lords heard the appeal.
They rejected both the general statement of principle in *Anns* (the two-stage test)
and the specific decision in that case. Accordingly the House departed from its
own previous decision in *Anns* pursuant to the Practice Statement (Judicial
Precedent),[98] and overruled *Dutton v Bognor Regis UDC*[99] and "all cases
subsequent to *Anns* which were decided in reliance on it".[1] The House of Lords
held[2] that the correct manner to determine the existence and scope of the duty of

---

[92] [1990] 2 A.C. 605.
[93] *ibid.* at 633.
[94] (1984–1985) 157 C.L.R. 424.
[95] *ibid.* at 481. See also Lord Devlin in *Hedley Byrne & Co Ltd v Heller & Partners Ltd* [1964] A.C.
465 at 536: "Is the relationship between the parties in this case such that it can be brought within a
category giving rise to a special duty? As always in English law, the first step is such an inquiry is
to see how far the authorities have gone, for new categories in the law do not spring into existence
overnight." The second sentence in that passage was cited by Lord Diplock in *Dorset Yacht Co Ltd
v Home Office* [1970] A.C. 1004 at 1058F in the course of a rigorous analysis of the role of authority
in the law of negligence.
[96] [1991] 1 A.C. 398.
[97] [1978] A.C. 728.
[98] [1966] 1 W.L.R. 1234.
[99] [1972] 1 Q.B. 373.
[1] [1991] 1 A.C. 398 at 472G in the speech of Lord Keith. In total five substantive speeches were
delivered, but the speech of Lord Keith was the only one with which all members of the Committee
expressed their agreement.
[2] See *ibid.* at 461E–F, *per* Lord Keith.

care in novel situations was the incremental approach stated by Brennan J. in *Sutherland Shire Council v Heyman*.[3] They went on to hold that the damage in *Anns* should be characterised as pure economic loss.[4] Recognition of a duty of care owed by local authorities and builders in respect of such loss would, in effect, introduce a "transmissible warranty of quality".[5] That would be inconsistent with existing authority and principle as to the scope of a duty of care owed by the manufacturers of chattels. The three-stage test was not invoked, although it was not disapproved.[6] *Anns* was disapproved because, on the analysis in *Murphy v Brentwood DC* and the earlier related decision in *D&F Estates Ltd v Church Commissioners for England*,[7] it introduced a wide-ranging novel category of duty of care which conflicted with established principle.

2–040 **Relationship between the incremental approach and the threefold test.** The incremental approach did not supplant the threefold test discussed in paras 2–030 to 2–035, above. It can be seen as providing guidance to the application of the threefold test and a warning of the potential danger of deciding whether a particular duty of care is owed simply by reference to general statements of principle.[8] It can also be analysed as providing an alternative approach which should lead to the same answer in any given case.[9]

2–041 **Continued application of the threefold test.** However the relationship between it and the incremental approach is analysed, *Murphy* did not mark the demise of the threefold test. In *X (minors) v Bedfordshire CC*,[10] the House of Lords decided two groups of cases brought against local authorities, "the child care cases" and "the education cases". In the child care cases, the House of Lords struck out claims by children against local authorities for negligence in the exercise of their powers under the Children Act 1989 and preceding statutes. In

---

[3] (1984–1985) 157 C.L.R. 424 at 481.

[4] See, *per* Lord Keith at 466, *per* Lord Bridge at 475–479, *per* Lord Oliver at 484 and *per* Lord Jauncey at 496–497.

[5] *ibid., per* Lord Keith at 469B.

[6] Lord Oliver in particular continued to speak of the need to establish "proximity" in cases of economic loss, although recognising that it was "an expression which persistently denies definition": *ibid.* at 487G.

[7] [1989] A.C. 177 discussed in Ch.9, below.

[8] "The incremental approach also has been the subject of criticism but in the absence of some guiding principle of universal application this approach ensures that developments in the law will take place in measured steps": *Bank of Credit and Commerce International (Overseas) Ltd v Price Waterhouse (No.2)* [1998] P.N.L.R. 564 at 586, *per* Sir Brian Neill. In *Reeman v Department of Transport* [1997] P.N.L.R. 618, Phillips L.J., having said that the threefold test was the correct approach, said at 625A–C:

"When confronted with a novel situation the court does not, however, consider these matters in isolation. It does so by comparison with established categories of negligence to see whether the facts amount to no more than a small extension of a situation already covered by authority, or whether a finding of the existence of a duty of care would effect a significant extension of the law of negligence. Only in exceptional cases will the court accept that the interests of justice justify such an extension of the law."

[9] See para.2–049, below.

[10] [1995] 2 A.C. 633; see also (1996) 112 L.Q.R. 134, *per* Cane. The actual decision in *X (minors) v Bedfordshire CC* [1995] 2 A.C. 633 in relation to the claims by children is no longer good law: see *D v East Berkshire Community NHS Trust* [2003] EWCA Civ 1151; [2004] Q.B. 558 at [83]. This is a consequence of the enactment of the Human Rights Act 1998.

the first case, five children claimed damages for the local authority's wrongful failure to take them into care. In the second case, a child claimed damages for wrongly being taken into care. In the education cases the House of Lords declined to strike out claims by pupils with special needs against a number of education authorities for negligence in the exercise of their powers under the Education Acts.[11] Lord Browne-Wilkinson (with whom Lord Jauncey, Lord Lane and Lord Ackner agreed) set out the general approach in the first part of his speech, before dealing with the individual cases. When Lord Browne-Wilkinson came to determine the duty of care question applying "the usual principles", he asked himself:

"Was the damage to the plaintiff reasonably foreseeable? Was the relationship between the plaintiff and the defendant sufficiently proximate? Is it just and reasonable to impose a duty of care?"[12]

However, when considering whether it was fair, just and reasonable to impose a common law duty on the local authorities in the child care cases, Lord Browne-Wilkinson referred to the decision in *Caparo Industries Plc v Dickman*[13]:

"that, in deciding whether to develop novel categories of negligence the court should proceed incrementally and by analogy with decided categories."[14]

Thus the two approaches co-exist.[15] The incremental approach may assist the court in determining the question of proximity or the "just and reasonable" question. The incremental approach may determine the answer in such a way that the court need not even consider the threefold test.[16] If existing authority provides an answer by way of analogy, then there is no (or less) need to consider the question on the basis of more general principle.[17]

Criticisms of incremental approach. Whereas the *Anns* two-stage test had   2–042
been criticised as unduly expansive, the incremental approach adopted by the
House of Lords in *Murphy* was seen by some commentators as too restrictive.[18]

---

[11] This decision is considered further in paras 2–086 to 2–087, below.

[12] [1995] 2 A.C. 633 at 739A–B (see also 749D–E). Lord Jauncey (who re-affirmed the threefold test at 728E–F), Lord Lane and Lord Ackner agreed with Lord Browne-Wilkinson.

[13] [1990] 2 A.C. 605.

[14] [1995] 2 A.C. 633 at 751C (see also at 762C—the education cases).

[15] See also *Hill v Van Erp* (1995–1997) 188 C.L.R. 159 (discussed in para.2–065, below) at 178, *per* Dawson J. and at 190, *per* Toohey J. commenting on the lack of real difference between the approach based on proximity (discussed in paras 2–064 to 2–067, below) and the incremental approach.

[16] See, e.g. *Henderson v Merrett Syndicates Ltd* [1995] 2 A.C. 145 at 181C–D. The claimants succeeded on the incremental approach, viz. an extension of the *Hedley Byrne* principle, and Lord Goff did not consider it necessary to embark upon the threefold test. In *Goodwill v British Pregnancy Advisory Service* [1996] 1 W.L.R. 1397 the claimant failed on the incremental approach and her claim was struck out. There was no separate consideration of the threefold test.

[17] This can be characterised as a justification of intellectual sloth or as an application of the doctrine of judicial precedent.

[18] The "pockets of case law" approach favoured by the House of Lords in *Caparo* and *Murphy* was strongly criticised by J. Stapleton in her article "Duty of care and economic loss: a wider agenda" (1991) 107 L.Q.R. 249. She criticised the manner in which pockets were selected and the grouping of cases which resulted. She argued that "pocket analysis" should be abandoned and replaced by an agenda of policy concerns (at 284–286).

The view was expressed that the "new orthodoxy" was empty and would freeze the law of negligence at the stage it had then reached.[19] These criticisms were expressed in varying forms by the courts of Canada and New Zealand, who declined to adopt the incremental approach.[20] In giving the majority judgment in *Canadian National Railway Co v Norsk Pacific Steamship Co*,[21] McLachlin J. stated:

> "They [the Canadian courts] will refuse to accept injustice merely for the sake of the doctrinal tidiness which is the motivating spirit of *Murphy*. This is in the best tradition of the law of negligence, the history of which exhibits a sturdy refusal to be confined by arbitrary forms and rules where justice indicates otherwise ... "[22]
> 'I consider that, from a doctrinal point of view, this court should continue on the course charted in *Kamloops* rather than reverting to the narrow exclusionary rule as the House of Lords did in *Murphy*.' "[23]

2–043   These criticisms were not entirely fair. Whilst in general terms the approach of the courts to duty of care issues has been more conservative since the demise of *Anns*, the House of Lords is quite prepared to take substantial "incremental" steps in order to achieve a just result, even if not always adopting the incremental approach. This is most vividly demonstrated in the extensions of the *Hedley Byrne* principle made in the 1990s.

(vi) *Extensions of* Hedley Byrne

2–044   In *Spring v Guardian Assurance Plc*[24] (discussed in para.2–034, above), Lord Goff reached his conclusion on a different basis to the majority. He concluded that the defendants were liable on the basis of the *Hedley Byrne* principle. He considered that the concept of "special skill" which featured in the reasoning in *Hedley Byrne* included "special knowledge". Thus an employer giving a reference about a former employee had the requisite special skill. Lord Goff also extended the concept of reliance to include the situation where a person trusts his former employer to give an accurate reference. This latter extension was a substantial leap. Two apparently cardinal features of the *Hedley Byrne* principle were: (i) that the claimant had received the negligent statement; and (ii) that the claimant had acted in the belief that the negligent statement was true. In the instant case Mr Spring did not satisfy either of those two conditions.

2–045   **Application of *Hedley Byrne* to parties in contractual relationship.** Once the House of Lords in *Murphy* had characterised defects in buildings as pure economic loss, the question immediately arose whether previous claims against architects and engineers, brought in tort in order to defeat a limitation defence, were rightly decided. The pre-eminent case to which this question applied was

---

[19] D. Howarth, "Negligence after Murphy: time to rethink" (1991) 50 C.L.J. 58.
[20] See paras 2–054 to 2–063, below.
[21] (1992) 91 D.L.R. (4th) 289.
[22] *ibid.* at 365.
[23] *ibid.* at 371.
[24] [1995] 2 A.C. 296.

Pirelli General Cable Works Ltd v Oscar Faber & Partners.[25] In a passage of considerable importance to professional negligence Lord Keith said[26]:

> "It would seem that in a case such as *Pirelli*, where the tortious liability arose out of a contractual relationship with professional people, the duty extended to take reasonable care not to cause economic loss to the client by the advice given. The plaintiffs built the chimney as they did in reliance on that advice. The case would accordingly fall within the principle of *Hedley Byrne & Co Ltd v Heller & Partners Ltd.*"[27]

This question arose for decision in *Henderson v Merrett Syndicates Ltd.*[28] The names on a number of syndicates at Lloyd's brought actions against both their members' agents and managing agents in respect of massive losses which they had suffered. Saville J., the Court of Appeal and the House of Lords all held that, in addition to their various contractual duties, managing agents owed a duty of care in tort both to direct and indirect names to carry out their functions with reasonable skill and care. The principal speech was given by Lord Goff, with whom Lord Keith, Lord Mustill, Lord Nolan and Lord Browne-Wilkinson agreed. Lord Goff stated that the governing principle was that contained in *Hedley Byrne*. This established liability for words as well as deeds, and for pure economic loss as well as physical damage. The assumption of responsibility, although it had been criticised,[29] was "at least in cases such as the present" a crucial feature for establishing *Hedley Byrne* liability.[30] Towards the end of his discussion of general principle Lord Goff stated:

> "It follows that, once the case is identified as falling within the *Hedley Byrne* principle, there should be no need to embark upon any further enquiry whether it is 'fair, just and reasonable' to impose liability for economic loss—a point which is, I consider, of some importance in the present case."[31]

On that basis if a case can be brought within the *Hedley Byrne* principle by means of the incremental approach, it is not necessary to embark upon the threefold test discussed in paras 2–030 to 2–035, above.

The disappointed beneficiary. A further extension of the *Hedley Byrne* principle occurred in *White v Jones.*[32] In July 1986, the testator wrote to his

2–046

2–047

---

[25] [1983] 2 A.C. 1, discussed in Ch.5, paras 5–056 to 5–065, below.

[26] *Murphy v Brentwood DC* [1991] 1 A.C. 398 at 466F–G.

[27] [1964] A.C. 465.

[28] [1995] 2 A.C. 145. Discussed in Ch.19. Further discussed by Powell in "Professional and client: the duty of care", published in Birks (edn), *Wrongs and Remedies in the Twenty-First Century* (Clarendon Press, 1996), pp.58–61.

[29] *Smith v Eric S Bush* [1990] 1 A.C. 831 at 862B–F and 864H, *per* Lord Griffiths; *Caparo Industries Plc v Dickman* [1990] 2 A.C. 605 at 628G, *per* Lord Roskill. For more recent criticism, see *Phelps v Hillingdon BC* [2000] 3 W.L.R. 776 at 791F, *per* Lord Slynn: "The phrase means simply that the law recognises that there is a duty of care. It is not so much that responsibility is assumed as that it recognised or imposed by law." References to recent academic criticism are listed in the speech of Lord Steyn in *Williams v Natural Health Life Foods Ltd* [1998] 1 W.L.R. 830 at 837C–D.

[30] *Henderson v Merrett* [1995] 2 A.C. 145 at 180–181.

[31] *ibid.* at 181.

[32] [1995] 2 A.C. 207. Discussed in Ch.11, paras 11–048 to 11–050. Further discussed by Powell in "Professional and client: the duty of care", published in Birks (edn), *Wrongs and Remedies in the Twenty-First Century*, (Clarendon Press, 1996) pp.61–62; and by Murphy, "Expectation Losses, Negligent Omissions and the Tortious Duty of Care" (1996) C.L.J. 43.

solicitors stating that he wished to make a new will leaving most of his estate to his daughters, who had been cut out of the existing will. The solicitors failed to give effect to these instructions before the testator died. By a bare majority the House of Lords held that the solicitors owed a duty of care to the daughters, the intended beneficiaries. The majority comprised Lord Goff, Lord Browne-Wilkinson and Lord Nolan. Both Lord Goff and Lord Browne-Wilkinson based their decision on an extension of *Hedley Byrne*. They considered that on a number of grounds justice required the solicitors to have a liability to intended beneficiaries, and that the *Hedley Byrne* principle afforded the proper means of overcoming the conceptual difficulties which would otherwise arise. They concluded that solicitors who undertook the task of preparing a will "assumed responsibility" for that task and so towards the intended beneficiaries. This decision involves a further substantial extension of the *Hedley Byrne* principle. The intended beneficiary, unlike the representee in *Hedley Byrne* or the employee in *Spring*, need have had no prior connection with, or even knowledge of, the testator's solicitors. The relevant conduct is not a statement but the performance of a task (preparing a will) or, as in *White v Jones*, the omission to perform a task.

2–048   **Practical application of the extended *Hedley Byrne* principle.** In *Williams v Natural Life Health Foods Ltd*,[33] Lord Steyn (with whom Lord Goff, Lord Hoffmann, Lord Clyde and Lord Hutton agreed) described the extended *Hedley Byrne* principle as:

> "the rationalisation or technique adopted by English law to provide a remedy for the recovery of damages in respect of economic loss caused by the negligent performance of services."[34]

Once a case is identified as falling within that principle, then there is no need to consider whether it is "fair, just and reasonable" to impose liability.[35] In that case the director and principal shareholder of Natural Life Health Foods Ltd was sued for negligent advice which had been given by the company. The House of Lords, reversing the Court of Appeal, dismissed the claim, because the director (as opposed to the company) had not assumed responsibility to the claimants. Lord Steyn gave guidance as to the practical application of the extended *Hedley Byrne* principle.[36] The court must focus not on the state of mind of the defendant, but on communications between the claimant and the defendant. The claimant must show that he reasonably relied upon an assumption of responsibility by the defendant.[37]

---

[33] [1998] 1 W.L.R. 830. Discussed in Grantham and Rickett, "Directors' 'Tortious' Liability: Contract, Tort or Company Law?" (1999) 62 M.L.R. 133.

[34] *ibid.* at 834F.

[35] *ibid.* at 834G; see also *Brooks v Commissioner of Police of the Metropolis* [2005] UKHL 24; [2005] 1 W.L.R. 1495 at [29], *per* Lord Steyn; and *Lennon v Commissioner of the Police of the Metropolis* [2004] EWCA Civ 130; [2004] 1 W.L.R. 2594.

[36] *ibid.* at 835–837.

[37] It is clear that claimants face a substantial hurdle in any case where they seek to hold personally liable in negligence the employee of a company providing professional services: see, e.g. *Hale v Guildarch Ltd* [1999] P.N.L.R. 44 (claim in tort against employees of a limited company which gave financial advice dismissed). The position of directors and employees of limited liability companies is discussed in paras 2–089 to 2–095, below.

(vii) *The Co-existence of Different Approaches*

Relationship of the extended *Hedley Byrne* principle with the threefold   2–049
test and the incremental approach. It is not entirely clear whether the decisions
which involved the extended *Hedley Byrne* principle were putting that principle
forward in place of the threefold test[38] and the incremental approach or as an
alternative approach to be adopted in appropriate cases (and, if the latter, in
which cases one approach should be applied rather than another). Nor was the
relationship between the threefold test and the incremental approach spelt out in
Murphy v Brentwood DC.[39] So long as extensions of the *Hedley Byrne* principle
are legitimate and consistent with its underlying rationale, then there should be
no conflict between them and decisions made by applying the threefold test or the
incremental approach. The are simply different routes to the same conclusion and
are based upon the same decisions and principles, however expressed in terms of
general principle.

In *Marc Rich & Co AG v Bishop Rock Marine Co Ltd*,[40] the House of Lords   2–050
had to consider whether a classification society owed a duty of care to cargo
owners when surveying a vessel. Such a claim had not been recognised in the
English courts, nor in any foreign court. The damage suffered was physical
damage, but the majority[41] held that the threefold test applied.[42] However, it was
emphasised that the law developed incrementally in this area[43] and the possibility, on different facts, that direct contact between the classification society and
cargo owners might have given rise to an assumption of responsibility by the
former was recognised.[44] The majority concluded that on the facts pleaded no
duty of care was owed because, even if there were sufficient proximity (which
was not decided), it would not be fair, just and reasonable to impose such a duty.
They did not explain the relationship between the different approaches, but were
able to use all of them without practical difficulty.[45]

Three routes to the same destination. In *Stovin v Wise*,[46] a motorcyclist was   2–051
injured in a collision with a car at a dangerous road junction. The car driver was
held liable to the motorcyclist, but both at first instance and in the Court of
Appeal recovered a 30 per cent contribution from the county council for failing

---

[38] In his dissenting speech in *Marc Rich & Co AG v Bishop Rock Marine Co Ltd* [1996] A.C. 211 at
229H, Lord Lloyd described the decisions on the *Hedley Byrne* principles as "a parallel movement
in the opposite direction" to that in which the House of Lords had moved when developing the
threefold test. See also P. Cane "Contract, Tort and the Lloyd's Debacle" in F. D. Rose, (edn),
Consensus ad Idem (Sweet & Maxwell, 1996), pp.115–116.
[39] [1991] 1 A.C. 398. See para.2–039, above.
[40] [1996] A.C. 211.
[41] *ibid.*, Lord Lloyd dissented. Lords Keith, Jauncey and Browne-Wilkinson agreed with Lord Steyn
who gave the only reasoned speech of the majority.
[42] *ibid., per* Lord Steyn at 235D–236B. This was followed in *British Telecommunications Plc v James
Thomson & Sons (Engineers) Ltd* [1999] 1 W.L.R. 9.
[43] [1996] A.C. 211 at 236B–C.
[44] *ibid.* at 237H–238A.
[45] In *Aiken v Stewart Wrightson Members Agency Ltd* [1995] 1 W.L.R. 1281 (discussed in Ch.19,
para.19–028) Potter J. applied the threefold test, but in doing so referred to assumption of responsibility when considering whether there was proximity and concluded that the duty of care was a
"justifiable increment".
[46] [1996] A.C. 923; discussed by Harris, (1997) 113 L.Q.R. 398.

to take steps to make the junction safer. The House of Lords by a bare majority allowed the council's appeal. The opinion of the majority was set out in the speech of Lord Hoffmann. After discussing the distinction between acts and omissions, he considered the decision in *Anns*, the House of Lords in *Murphy v Brentwood DC* having left open the possibility that the council might have owed a duty of care in respect of physical injury. He said:

"Lord Wilberforce, who gave the leading speech, first stated the well-known two-stage test for the existence of a duty of care. This involves starting with the prima facie assumption that a duty of care exists if it is reasonably foreseeable that carelessness may cause damage and then asking whether there are any considerations which ought to 'negative, or to reduce or limit the scope of the duty or the class of person to whom it is owed or the damages to which a breach of it may give rise'. Subsequent decisions in this House and the Privy Council have preferred to approach the question the other way round, starting with situations in which a duty has been held to exist and then asking whether there are considerations of analogy, policy, fairness and justice for extending it to cover a new situation: see for example Lord Bridge of Harwich in *Caparo Industries Plc v Dickman* [1990] 2 A.C. 605 at 617–618. It can be said that, provided that the considerations of policy, etc., are properly analysed, it should not matter whether one starts from one end or the other."[47]

Lord Hoffmann then turned to the position of public authorities, which is discussed below.[48]

2–052 In *Bank of Credit and Commerce International (Overseas) Ltd v Price Waterhouse (No.2)*,[49] Sir Brian Neill, with whom Brooke and Nourse L.JJ. agreed, suggested that it might be useful to look at a new set of facts by using each of the three approaches used and approved by the House of Lords and that:

"if the facts are properly analysed and the policy considerations are correctly evaluated the several approaches will yield the same result."[50]

This approach has found favour with the editors of *Clerk & Lindsell on Torts*[51] and was restated by a slightly differently constituted Court of Appeal in *Parkinson v St James and Seacroft University Hospital NHS Trust*.[52]

---

[47] [1996] A.C. 923 at 410–411. There is a useful discussion of the relationship between the *Anns* two-stage test and the threefold test in the dissenting speech of Lord Nicholls at 931H–932H.
[48] See para.2–081, below.
[49] [1998] P.N.L.R. 564.
[50] *ibid.* at 586F.
[51] 19th edn, para.8–90.
[52] [2002] Q.B. 266; [2001] EWCA Civ 530 at [17], *per* Brooke L.J. with whom Hale L.J. and Sir Martin Nourse agreed.

See also *Welton v North Cornwall DC* [1997] 1 W.L.R. 570 at 580E–F where Rose L.J., having remarked on the varying use of assumption of responsibility, the fair just and reasonable test and reliance on policy considerations said:

"But I confess that I am unable to discern in the authorities any material difference attributable to that difference in language, either in the route charted or in the ultimate destination, when the existence of a duty of care is recognised or denied."

In *Kyrris v Oldham* [2003] EWCA Civ 1506; [2004] 1 B.C.L.C. 305 the same result was reached whether by adopting the three-stage test of *Caparo Industries Plc v Dickman* [1990] 2 A.C. 605 or the assumption of responsibility approach of *Henderson v Merrett Syndicates Ltd* [1995] 2 A.C. 145.

No single test. The difficulty in stating a single, practical test which can be **2–053**
applied to determine all novel claims in negligence was recognised by the House
of Lords in *Customs and Excise Commissioners v Barclays Bank Plc.*[53] In
holding that a bank which received notice of a freezing order made against one
of its customers did not owe a duty of care in tort to the person who had obtained
the freezing order, the House of Lords considered the advantages and limits of
the test of assumption of responsibility, the threefold test and the incremental
approach. The solution suggested by Lord Hoffmann[54] and Lord Mance[55] was
lower-level principles or factors which were of more practical use and guidance
than the more abstract concepts used in formulating the various tests. Nevertheless, even if those concepts are just "labels", they remain useful in giving a
structure to the task of deciding whether a duty of care exists[56] and any law of
tort must propound a test of liability in negligence if "it is not to become a
morass of single instances".[57] However, once it is appreciated that the correct
result is or should be reached whatever test is applied in a particular case, it
becomes clear that the focus should always be on the particular facts and
relationship between the parties.[58]

(viii) *Commonwealth Approaches to Duty of Care Issues*

New Zealand. In *South Pacific Manufacturing Co Ltd v New Zealand Security* **2–054**
Consultants and Investigations Ltd[59] two actions were brought against the agents
of insurers for alleged negligence in investigating fires. In the first case, the
claimant was the creditor and principal shareholder of the insured who had lost
property in the fire. In the second case, the claimant was the insured who had
suffered losses as a result of the fire. In each case, the insurers, relying upon the
investigations and report of their agents, had refused to pay out. The New
Zealand Court of Appeal held that both actions should be struck out. In neither
case did the investigators for the insurers owe a duty of care to the claimant. All
five judges favoured a modified version of the *Anns* two-stage test.

Cooke P. (with whom Hardie Boys J. agreed) formulated the correct approach **2–055**
in 15 propositions.[60] He began by stating (it is submitted quite correctly):

> "A broad two-stage approach or any other approach is only a framework, a more or less
> methodical way of tackling a problem. How it is formulated should not matter in the
> end. Ultimately the exercise can only be a balancing one and the important object is that
> all relevant factors be weighed. There is no escape from the truth that, whatever formula
> be used, the outcome in a grey area case has to be determined by judicial judgment.
> Formulae can help to organise thinking but they cannot provide answers."

---

[53] [2006] UKHL 28; [2006] 3 W.L.R. 1.
[54] [2006] UKHL 28; [2006] 3 W.L.R. 1 at [36].
[55] [2006] UKHL 28; [2006] 3 W.L.R. 1 at [83].
[56] [2006] UKHL 28; [2006] 3 W.L.R. 1 at [71], *per* Lord Rodger, approving an observation of Kirby
J. in *Perre v Apand Pty Ltd* [1999] H.C.A. 36; (1999) 198 C.L.R. 180 at [283]: "As against the
approach which I favour, it has been said that the three identified elements are mere 'labels'. So
indeed they are . . . . Labels are commonly used by lawyers. They help steer the mind through the task
in hand." (See also the judgment of Kirby J. at [258].)
[57] [2006] UKHL 28; [2006] 3 W.L.R. 1 at [8], *per* Lord Bingham.
[58] *ibid.*
[59] [1992] 2 N.Z.L.R. 282.
[60] *ibid.* at 294–299.

The considerations which Cooke P. set out in the propositions which followed were familiar common law principles of equal validity both in England and New Zealand, although their application may vary according to the differing social conditions of the two countries. It is also fairly clear that the actual decision reached would have been the same in England, whether reached by reference to the threefold test, the incremental approach or by applying the extended *Hedley Byrne* principle, or some combination of them.[61]

2–056   In *Invercargill CC v Hamlin*,[62] the New Zealand Court of Appeal faced substantially the same issue as had confronted the House of Lords in *Murphy v Brentwood DC*.[63] In 1972, the claimant purchased a newly constructed house. The foundations were defective and gave rise to minor problems for the first 17 years. Then in 1989, the back door stuck badly and the claimant commissioned a report, which revealed the defective foundations. In 1990, the claimant commenced proceedings against the council for negligence by their building inspector in having approved the foundations in 1972. The New Zealand Court of Appeal held that the council was liable in negligence to the claimant.[64] In coming to the opposite decision from the House of Lords in *Murphy*, the court drew attention to the respects in which social factors, economic factors and the legislative framework prevailing in New Zealand differed from that in England. Cooke P. also commented at a more general level on the divergences between the Commonwealth jurisdictions.[65]

2–057   The Privy Council upheld the decision of the New Zealand Court of Appeal.[66] In delivering the opinion of the Privy Council Lord Lloyd stated that this branch of the law of negligence was not suited to a single monolithic solution. He noted that in New Zealand community standards and expectations demanded the imposition of a duty of care on local authorities and builders alike to ensure compliance with local byelaws. He placed particular emphasis on the different

---

[61] The New Zealand Court of Appeal applied a broadly similar approach in *Fleming v Securities Commission* [1995] 2 N.Z.L.R. 514, in which the Commission was held to owe no duty of care to investors who suffered loss. See the reasoning of Richardson J. (with whom most members of the court agreed) at 527–533. See also *Wellington District Law Society v Price Waterhouse* [2002] 2 N.Z.L.R. 767 at [42] in the judgment of the Court of Appeal where the approach to novel claims in New Zealand was helpfully summarised. The Court quoted from the speech of Lord Pearson in *Dorset Yacht Co Ltd v Home Office* [1970] A.C. 1004 at 1052 and drew attention to the relevance of the kind of damage from which it was being alleged there was a duty to protect the claimant when considering whether a duty was owed. Another helpful overview of current position in New Zealand can be found in paras [22]–[32] of the judgment of Tipping J. in *Att-Gen v Carter* [2003] 2 N.Z.L.R. 160.

[62] [1994] 3 N.Z.L.R. 513. Discussed by I. N. Duncan Wallace, "No Somersault after Murphy: New Zealand follows Canada" (1995) 111 L.Q.R. 285.

[63] [1991] 1 A.C. 398.

[64] The limitation aspect is dealt with in Ch.5, below.

[65] [1994] 3 N.Z.L.R. 513 at 523:

"While the disharmony may be regrettable, it is inevitable now that the Commonwealth jurisdictions have gone on their own paths without taking English decisions as the invariable starting point. The ideal of a uniform common law has proved as unattainable as any ideal of a uniform civil law. It could not survive the independence of the United States; constitutional evolution in the Commonwealth has done the rest. What of course is both desirable and feasible, within the limits of judicial and professional time, is to take into account and learn from decisions in other jurisdictions."

[66] *Invercargill CC v Hamlin* [1996] A.C. 624. Discussed by I. N. Duncan Wallace, "No surprises in the Privy Council" (1996) 112 L.Q.R. 369.

statutory backgrounds in England and New Zealand. In particular, New Zealand had no legislation corresponding to our Defective Premises Act 1972. It can thus be seen that the application of broadly the same common law principles leads to opposing results in England and New Zealand.

Canada. In 1984, in *City of Kamloops v Nielson*,[67] the Supreme Court of **2–058** Canada by a majority of 3:2 followed both the general approach and the actual decision of the House of Lords in *Anns*. It held a local authority liable in tort for failing to ensure compliance with building byelaws. In giving the majority judgment Wilson J. assessed an array of relevant factors (the distinction between acts and omissions, the area of local authorities' discretion, the nature of the loss, the floodgates argument and so forth) before concluding that a duty of care should be imposed. The Supreme Court of Canada continues to apply the *Anns* test.[68]

Following the change of tack by the House of Lords in *Murphy*, the Canadian **2–059** Supreme Court again had to consider whether or not to follow England. In *Canadian National Railway Co v Norsk Pacific Steamship Co Ltd*,[69] the claimant railway company was the principal user, but not the owner of a bridge negligently damaged by the defendant. The claimant claimed its economic loss suffered through re-routing traffic while the bridge was being repaired. The Canadian Supreme Court by a majority of 4:3 held that the claimant was entitled to recover. The principal judgment for the majority was given by McLachlin J. with whom L'Heureux-Dube and Cory JJ. concurred. McLachlin J. defined the underlying problem as the search for a principled mechanism to limit liability for foreseeable economic loss flowing from negligence. She reviewed the different approaches adopted in the principal civil and common law jurisdictions. She rejected the House of Lords' approach in *Murphy* as unduly restrictive.[70]

McLachlin J. summarised the proper approach in these terms: **2–060**

"The matter may be put thus: before the law will impose liability there must be a connection between the defendant's conduct and plaintiff's loss which makes it just for the defendant to indemnify the plaintiff. In contract, the contractual relationship provides this link. In trust, it is the fiduciary obligation which establishes the necessary connection. In tort, the equivalent notion is proximity. Proximity may consist of various forms of closeness—physical, circumstantial, causal or assumed—which serve to identify the categories of case in which liability lies."[71]

After discussing the numerous disparate factors relevant to determining whether there is sufficient proximity, McLachlin J. continued:

---

[67] (1984) 10 D.L.R. (4th) 641.
[68] See, for example, *Martel Building Ltd v The Queen* (2000) 193 D.L.R. (4th) 1: no duty of care owed by tenant to landlord to conduct negotiations for renewal of lease with reasonable skill and care. Perhaps surprisingly, the Court found that there was proximity, but that the existence of a duty of care was negated by ancillary policy factors which precluded the extension of the law of tort into commercial negotiations. This decision is discussed at (2001) 117 L.Q.R. 351: see Duncan Wallace Q.C., "Tender Call Obligations in Canada" (Duncan Wallace Q.C.).
[69] (1992) 91 D.L.R. (4th) 289.
[70] See para.2–042, above.
[71] (1992) 91 D.L.R. (4th) 289 at 369.

"While proximity is critical to establishing the right to recover pure economic loss in tort, it does not always indicate liability. It is a necessary but not necessarily sufficient condition of liability. Recognising that proximity is itself concerned with policy, the approach adopted in *Kamloops* (parallelled by the second branch of *Anns*), requires the court to consider the purposes served by permitting recovery as well as whether there are any residual policy considerations which call for a limitation on liability. This permits courts to reject liability for pure economic loss where indicated by policy reasons not taken into account in the proximity analysis."[72]

2–061   In Canada, as in England, if a case falls within the *Hedley Byrne* principle, the court will impose a duty of care without any wider consideration of the policy factors. This is illustrated by *Edgeworth Construction Ltd v ND Lea and Associates Ltd.*[73] The claimant successfully tendered to build a section of highway in British Columbia. The claimant lost money on the project, allegedly due to errors in the specifications and construction drawings. The construction contract excluded any liability on the part of the employer (the province) in respect of representations in the tender documents. The Canadian Supreme Court declined to strike out the claimant's claim against the engineering firm which had prepared the tender documents, including the specifications and construction drawings. The Court held that the claim fell directly within the *Hedley Byrne* principle. The defendants had provided information in the tender package for use by a definable group of persons. The claimant reasonably relied upon that information in preparing its bid. The contract between the claimant and the province, which protected the province from liability, was not inconsistent with a duty of care on the part of the engineers towards the claimants. At a superficial level, it may be said that this decision is contrary to *Pacific Associates Inc v Baxter*,[74] decided by the English Court of Appeal. In reality, however, the appellate courts were applying the same legal principles in both cases, but the circumstances and contractual matrices were different.[75] The Court did, however, strike out the claim against individual engineers who had fixed their seals to the design documents.[76]

2–062   More recently, the Canadian Supreme Court has had to consider the question of tortious liability for defects in buildings. In *Winnipeg Condominium Corp v Bird Construction Co*,[77] the defendant constructed an apartment building, which the claimant subsequently acquired. Defects in the cladding emerged, and in order to avoid accidents the claimant carried out remedial works at substantial

---

[72] (1992) 91 D.L.R. (4th) 289 at 371. The Canadian Supreme Court adopted a similar approach in *Bow Valley Husky (Bermuda) Ltd v Saint John Shipbuilding Ltd* (1997) 153 D.L.R. (4th) 385. In that case the hirers of an oil rig suffered economic loss, as a result of a defective part which caused a fire on the rig. Their action in negligence against the manufacturers was dismissed. McLachlin J. (with whom La Forest J. agreed) held that a prima facie duty of care arose, but that this was negatived by policy considerations, in particular the problem of indeterminate liability: *ibid.* at 404–413. For discussion and analysis of this judgment see Feldthusen, "Dynamic change to maritime law— gracious retreat on relational economic loss" (1998) 6 Tort L.Rev. 164.

[73] (1993) 107 D.L.R. (4th) 169.

[74] [1990] 1 Q.B. 993; see further Ch.9, para.9–108.

[75] In the English case the claimant contractors had more extensive remedies available against the employers and on the facts there was no assumption of responsibility by the engineers towards the claimants.

[76] This aspect of the decision is discussed further at para.2–091, below.

[77] (1995) 121 D.L.R. (4th) 193.

cost. The Court declined to strike out the claim. In coming to this conclusion the Court declined to follow the specific decisions of the House of Lords in *D&F Estates Ltd v Church Commissioners for England*[78] and *Murphy v Brentwood DC*.[79] The Court held that policy considerations militated in favour of imposing a duty of care. The classification of the claim as economic loss carried less weight than it would in England, especially since the building defect before rectification was a source of danger. In *Ingles v City of Toronto*,[80] the Canadian Supreme Court held that a local authority which inspected a building's under-pinnings owed a duty of care to the owner of the building, applying the *Anns* test.

In *Cooper v Hobart*[81] the Supreme Court of Canada gave an authoritative   **2–063** re-statement of the *Anns* test as it is applied in Canada. The first stage involves two questions: (1) Was the harm that occurred the reasonably foreseeable con-sequence of the defendant's act? (2) Are there reasons, notwithstanding the proximity between the parties established in the first part of the test, that tort liability should not be recognised here? The first part focuses primarily on the specific relationship between the parties. At the second stage of the test wider policy considerations fall to be considered, such as "the effect of recognising a duty of care on other legal obligations, the legal system and society more generally". This is very similar in effect to the threefold test laid down by the House of Lords in *Smith v Eric S Bush*[82] and *Caparo Industries Plc v Dickman*.[83] The Supreme Court explained that proximity was generally used to characterise the type of relationship in which a duty of care may arise and that such relationships were usually identified by categories. The factors needed to satisfy the requirement of proximity are, however, "diverse and depend on the circum-stances of the case. One searches in vain for a single unifying characteristic". The present position in Canada is that a modified *Anns* test is applied, but with explicit recognition of the limited value of producing a clear definition of what will constitute proximity.

Australia. As set out earlier, the incremental approach adopted by the House   **2–064** of Lords in *Murphy* has its origins in Australia.[84] However, in the 1980s and 1990s, the Australian courts made more use of the concept of proximity as the vehicle for determining whether or not a duty of care exists.[85] Proximity might be established by precedent, namely if the parties stood in a relationship which was the subject of previous judicial decision. Absent any binding decision which is in point, a consideration of proximity enabled the court to assess and weigh all those factors which in England would be considered in applying the threefold

---

[78] [1989] A.C. 177.
[79] [1991] 1 A.C. 398.
[80] (2000) 183 D.L.R. (4th) 193.
[81] (2001) 206 D.L.R. (4th) 193, discussed by Neyers, "Distilling Duty: The Supreme Court of Canada Amends Anns" (2002) 118 L.Q.R. 221.
[82] [1990] 1 A.C. 831.
[83] [1990] 2 A.C. 605.
[84] *Sutherland Shire Council v Heyman* (1984–1985) 157 C.L.R. 424 at 481. See para.2–038, above.
[85] Indeed the High Court of Australia came to treat "proximity" as the governing test for the existence and scope of a duty of care. The authorities are helpfully set out and analysed by Vaggelas, "Proximity, economic loss and the High Court of Australia" (1997) 5 Tort L.Rev. 127.

test. This approach was exemplified in *Bryan v Maloney*.[86] The defendant built a house with inadequate foundations on clay soil. The High Court of Australia held that the defendant was liable in negligence to a subsequent purchaser for the cost of remedial works. After a full review and weighing of the policy factors, the court held that sufficient proximity was established between the builder and the subsequent purchaser. The fact that the claimant's loss was economic did not justify denying recovery. In particular, recognition of a duty of care to avoid economic loss suffered by reason of defects to the house did not impose liability "in an indeterminate amount for an indeterminate time to an indeterminate class".[87] Nor did the imposition of such a duty unduly limit the builder's legitimate pursuit of his own economic advantage.[88]

2–065   In *Hill v Van Erp*,[89] the High Court of Australia considered the vexed question of whether a testator's solicitor owes a duty of care to the intended beneficiary. By a majority of 5:1 the Court held that the testator's solicitor does owe such a duty. Despite the mass of jurisprudence devoted to this topic throughout the common law world, the Court did not find its task an easy one. Brennan C.J., Gaudron and Gummow JJ. rejected the English route of expanding the *Hedley Byrne* principle to embrace the relationship between solicitor and intended beneficiary. The other two members of the majority, Dawson and Toohey JJ., considered that there were both assumption of responsibility and reliance in the more general sense. This case (like *White v Jones* in England) also provided an opportunity for the highest appellate court to reappraise its approach to duty of care problems. The court recognised the limitations of "proximity" as an universal test for determining the existence and scope of a duty of care, but the majority (of the majority) were not prepared to abandon that approach. Dawson J. said:

> " . . . the requirement of proximity is at least a useful means of expressing the proposition that in the law of negligence reasonable foreseeability of harm may not be enough to establish a duty of care. Something more is required and it is described as proximity. Proximity in that sense expresses the result of a process of reasoning rather than the process itself, but it remains a useful term because it signifies that the process of reasoning must be undertaken. But to hope that proximity can describe a common element underlying all those categories of case in which a duty of care is recognised is to expect more of the term than it can provide."[90]

Toohey J. said that "the general conception [of proximity] must be taken as controlling the circumstances which might otherwise, by application of reasonable foreseeability alone, give rise to a duty of care".[91] Gaudron J. also found proximity a satisfactory analytical tool for resolving the duty of care problem. However, Brennan C.J. analysed all relevant factors without reference to proximity. Gummow J. found proximity to be of limited use; he noted Fleming's

---

[86] (1995) 182 C.L.R. 609, discussed by Duncan Wallace Q.C. (1997) 113 L.Q.R. 355. See also *Gala v Preston* (1991) 172 C.L.R. 243.
[87] *ibid.* at 618 and 623, *per* Mason C.J., Deane J. and Gaudron J. quoting Cardozo C.J. in *Ultramares Corp v Touche* (1931) 174 N.E. 441 at 444.
[88] *ibid.* at 623–624, *per* Mason C.J., Deane J. and Gaudron J.
[89] (1995–1997) 188 C.L.R. 159.
[90] *ibid.* at 177–178.
[91] *ibid.* at 188.

dismissal of proximity as "the currently fashionable touchstone of duty".[92] If "proximity" survived, it was not in good health.[93]

The marked decline in the fortunes of "proximity" as a useful test continued **2–066** in the decision of the High Court of Australia in *Perre v Apand Pty Ltd*.[94] The defendant sold potato seeds to a farmer in South Australia, who planted them. The resulting potato crop was infected with bacterial wilt. The claimants were neighbouring farmers who were unable to export their crops to Western Australia, which banned the entry of potatoes grown within 20 miles of an outbreak of bacterial wilt. They suffered financial loss as a result. The loss suffered was accepted by the defendant to have been reasonably foreseeable and the defendant in fact knew that persons such as the claimants would suffer such loss in the circumstances. It was held that the defendant owed a duty of care to the claimants in respect of their losses. In reaching that conclusion the seven members of the court addressed the question of the appropriate approach to novel cases. There was no unanimity of approach, however. McHugh J., who had long been sceptical as to the value of proximity as a guide,[95] said:

" . . . since the fall of proximity, the court has not made any authoritative statement as to what is to be the correct approach for determining the duty of care question. Perhaps none is possible. At all events, the differing views of the members of this court in the present case suggest that the search for a unifying element may be a long one."[96]

He went on to ask:

" . . . where does one find a conceptual framework that will promote predictability and continuity and at the same time facilitate change in the law when it is needed? I think that the existing legal materials already contain part of the answer. We have the established categories, a considerable body of case law and the useful concept of reasonably foreseeability. If a case falls outside an established category, but the defendant should reasonably have foreseen that its conduct would cause harm to the plaintiff, we have only to ask whether the reasons that called for or denied a duty in other (usually similar) cases require the imposition of a duty in the instant case. No doubt that may sometimes mean that, whether or not a duty is imposed at a particular time, will depend on the extent to which the case law has progressed to that time. But

---

[92] (1995–1997) 188 C.L.R. 159 at 237.
[93] *ibid*. at 238 of the judgment of Kirby J. in *Pyrenees Shire Council v Day* [1998] H.C.A. 3 (reported at (1998) 192 C.L.R. 330):
"Finally, in *Hill v Van Erp*, four members of this Court recognised the limitations in the usefulness of the notion of proximity in determining individual claims to the existence of a duty of care enforceable at law. When to these voices is added the consistent criticism of 'proximity' expressed for a decade by Brennan C.J., it is tolerably clear that proximity's reign in this Court, at least as a universal identifier of the existence of a duty of care at common law, has come to an end."
(The four members of the High Court of Australia in *Hill v Van Erp* to whom Kirby J. was referring were Dawson J. at (1997) 188 C.L.R. 159 at 177–178, Toohey J. at 188–189, McHugh J. at 210–211 and Gummow J. at 237–239. As an example of the views of Brennan C.J. Kirby J. cited *Bryan v Maloney* (1995) 182 C.L.R. 609 at 653. Kirby J. explained what he meant in the passage quoted in *Modbury Triangle Shopping Centre Pty Ltd v Anzil* [2000] H.C.A. 61 at para.60. The decision in *Pyrenees* is discussed at (1998) 114 L.Q.R. 377, *per* Lunney).
[94] [1999] H.C.A. 36, reported in (1999) 198 C.L.R. 180. See further Witting, "The Three-stage Test Abandoned in Australia—or Not" (2002) 118 L.Q.R. 214.
[95] See his dissenting judgment in *Hill v Van Erp* (1995–1997) 188 C.L.R. 159 at 210–211.
[96] [1999] H.C.A. 36 at 76; (1999) 198 C.L.R. 180 at 624. See also, *per* Gaudron J. at 614–615, *per* Kirby J. at 683–684 and, *per* Hayne J. at pp.697–698.

that is the way of the common law, the judges preferring to go 'from case to case, like the ancient Mediterranean mariners, hugging the coast from point to point, and avoiding the dangers of the open sea of system or science'.[97] It is not an approach that appeals to grand theorists who prefer to decide cases by general principles applicable to all cases. But in an area of law such as awarding damages for negligently inflicting economic loss, which is still developing and which has been recently cast aside from any unifying principle, there is no alternative to a cautious development of the law on a case by case basis."[98]

Gummow J. saw the absence of a "simple formula which can mask the necessity for examination of the particular facts" as a benefit, allowing the development of a coherent body of precedent against which the facts of particular cases can be judged, not by "the imposition of a fixed system of categories", but identifying relevant "salient features" and considering whether, allowing for the operation of appropriate "control mechanisms", the relationship gave rise to a duty of care.[99]

2–067　　In *Sullivan v Moody*[1] the High Court of Australia held that medical practitioners and others investigating allegations of child abuse did not owe a duty of care in tort to the relations of the children. They also held that the threefold test did not apply in Australia.[2] It is now clear that "proximity" has ceased to be the test in Australia.[3] More recently, in *Woolcock Street Investments Pty Ltd v CDG Pty Ltd*[4] the High Court of Australia has identified "vulnerability" as an important requirement, its significance having emerged from the decisions in *Caltex Oil (Australia) Pty Ltd v The Dredge Willemstad*[5] and *Perre v Apand Pty Ltd*.[6] "Vulnerability" refers to the injured party's inability to protect himself from the defendant's carelessness, either entirely or so that any resulting loss would fall on the defendant.[7] However, this is not put forward as a universal test. Australia appears to have abandoned any single, simple "test" and to be applying an incremental approach while still seeking to identify guiding principles.

(ix) *Analysis*

2–068　　**The problem.** If the only claims before the courts were in respect of personal injuries caused by swallowing snails lurking in opaque ginger beer bottles then

---

[97] Lord Wright, "The Study of Law" (1938) 54 L.Q.R. 185 at 196.
[98] (1999) 198 C.L.R. 180 at 629–630. See further McHugh J.'s judgment in *Crimmins v Stevedoring Industry Finance Committee* [1999] H.C.A. 59 para.78; reported in (1999) 167 A.L.R. 1 at 19–20.
[99] *ibid.* at 659–660. Gummow J.'s reference to "salient features" was taken from the judgment of Stephen J. in *Caltex Oil (Australia) Pty Ltd v The Dredge Willemstad* (1976) 136 C.L.R. 529 at 576–577.
[1] [2001] H.C.A. 59; (2001) 183 A.L.R. 404.
[2] Although Kirby J. supported it in *Graham Barclay Oysters Pty Ltd v Ryan* [2002] H.C.A. 54 at [229]–[244].
[3] See also *Woolcock Street Investments Pty Ltd v CDG Pty Ltd* [2004] H.C.A. 16 at [18] in the judgment of Gleeson C.J., Gummow, Hayne and Heydon JJ.
[4] [2004] H.C.A. 16; [2005] B.L.R. 92.
[5] (1976) 136 C.L.R. 529.
[6] [1999] H.C.A. 36; (1999) 198 C.L.R. 180.
[7] [2004] H.C.A. 16 at [23] in the judgment of Gleeson C.J., Gummow, Hayne and Heydon JJ., [80] in the judgment of McHugh J., [168] in the judgment of Kirby J. and [222] in the judgment of Callinan J.

the law would have been settled by *Donoghue v Stevenson*.[8] There would be no need for the courts to search for principles upon which to base their decisions in novel situations. That is not the case. Novel claims come before the courts and have to be decided. However, the search for guiding principles or a useful test has not resulted in an answer which commands widespread acceptance.[9] Members of the House of Lords and Privy Council appear to proceed on different bases[10] and there is no unanimity between (or to an extent within) the major Commonwealth jurisdictions. This is not to say that the same result would not be reached in a particular case by the application of any of the different tests and approaches propounded in recent years by the House of Lords, nor in different Commonwealth jurisdictions, although, as the differing status of *Anns v Merton LBC*[11] demonstrates, that would not always be the case.[12]

Limited role of statements of general principle. It is submitted that the starting point should be to establish the purpose for which statements of general principle or of the appropriate test to be applied are made. That purpose is to try to provide guidance as to the approach to novel claims, based upon analysis of existing authority. The purpose is not to provide a test against which the body of existing authority should be tested for consistency or orthodoxy. Moreover, the need to resort to general principle should be limited. It is now over 70 years since the decision in *Donoghue v Stevenson*[13] and 40 since *Hedley Byrne & Co Ltd*   **2–069**

---

[8] [1932] A.C. 562.

[9] "The fundamental problem is that a single unifying principle for liability in negligence, easy to apply and predictable in outcome, has proved elusive. Differing theories hold the legal stage for a time. But then their defects and inadequacies are exposed. None has won permanent acceptance. The best that observers of this branch of the common law have been able to offer is the cautionary advice to study the cases in the hope of deriving guidance from analogies. However, in order to do this it is necessary to have some concept of the principle by which the analogy is to be discovered." *per* Kirby J. in *Pyrenees Shire Council v Day* [1998] H.C.A. 3 at 189 (reported in (1998) 192 C.L.R. 330).

See also *Customs and Excise Commissioners v Barclays Bank Plc* [2006] UKHL 28; [2006] 3 W.L.R. 1 discussed in para.2–053, above.

[10] See, e.g. "The random element of their lordships' infallible judgments: an economic and comparative analysis of the tort of negligence from *Anns* to *Murphy*" by Markesinis and Deakin, (1992) 55 M.L.R. 619. It is pointed out that the House of Lords has considered "duty of care" issues on 12 occasions in the preceding 15 years. It is argued that the decisions show "an unsystematic and not fully thought-out series of shifts", and that inadequate consideration has been given to economic factors, foreign law and academic literature.

[11] [1978] A.C. 728.

[12] In *Woolcock Street Investments Pty Ltd v CDG Pty Ltd* [2004] H.C.A. 16 McHugh J. said at [48]:

"One can be sure that the Law Lords who decided *Hedley Byrne* did not foresee the consequences that their decision would have for the law of negligence. Although their Lordships' reasons differ, they appear to have believed that, in the case of negligent statements, a claim for economic loss would lie only where the defendant had or could be supposed to have assumed responsibility for the statement. But, once the Law Lords indicated that the so-called exclusionary rule concerning economic loss was no longer exclusionary, actions for 'pure' economic loss could not be confined to claims of negligent statement. As a result, appellate courts in the United Kingdom, Canada, New Zealand and Australia have spent much time deciding whether or not defendants owed a duty of care to prevent pure economic loss to plaintiffs. It is not unfair to say that the results have been less than successful. Not only have the courts of different jurisdictions formulated different principles and rules for determining the issue of duty but ultimate appellate courts have reached conflicting decisions in cases where the material facts were similar, if not identical."

[13] [1932] A.C. 562.

v Heller & Partners Ltd.[14] It should not be necessary and is not necessary to consider every claim in negligence from first principles. In many cases, indeed most, the existence of a duty of care is not in issue or falls to be decided by the application of what is a substantial body of existing authority.[15] The purpose of general tests or statements of principle should be to provide, or at least to assist in the provision of, answers in truly novel situations, where there is no direct or closely analogous decision.

2–070 **Role of authority.** This suggests that the judicial decision-making process should not usually consist of a series of headings taken from statements of general principle or tests with two, three or more stages, but should begin with careful analysis of the facts relied upon as giving rise to the particular duty of care coupled with investigation of the existing authorities to see whether there is any direct or close authority which determines the answer.[16] This not only accords with the doctrine of precedent, but enables judges to reach consistent and predictable decisions. It also recognises the limits of general statements or tests as useful guides to the decision-making process as opposed to statements of the results of that process.[17]

2–071 **Need for guiding principles.** However, there is still a need to establish guiding principles, not just because there should be some coherence and consistency between different decisions, but in order to afford guidance in truly novel situations.[18] This introduces an inevitable tension between the need to

---

[14] [1964] A.C. 465.

[15] See for example *Perrett v Collins* [1998] 2 Lloyd's Rep. 255, *per* Hobhouse L.J. at 263, col.2, explaining that the decision of the Houses of Lords in *Marc Rich & Co AG v Bishop Rock Marine Co Ltd* [1996] A.C. 211 (see para.2–050, above) did not throw into doubt decided cases as to liability in negligence for personal injury and death.

[16] "There is I suspect a danger here of the method of approach becoming more important than the objective. The objective is to ascertain whether it is appropriate that there be a duty of care in the particular case. So long as that objective is realised, I cannot think that it is of great moment whether it is attained by a two-stage test, an incremental approach, or some combination of the two. What matters is that there is an identification, an analysis and a weighing of all the competing considerations . . ."

(*South Pacific Manufacturing Co Ltd v New Zealand Security Consultants and Investigations Ltd* [1992] 2 N.Z.L.R. 282, *per* Hardie Boys J. at 316 lines 12–18).

[17] See, e.g. the observations of Hobhouse L.J. in *Perrett v Collins* [1998] 2 Lloyd's Rep. 255 at 258, col.1, where he spoke of "the dangers of substituting for clear criteria, criteria which are incapable of precise definition and involve what can only be described as an element of subjective assessment by the Court: such ultimately subjective assessments tend inevitably to lead to uncertainty and anomaly which can be avoided by a more principled approach".

[18] In *Customs and Excise Commissioners v Barclays Bank Plc* [2006] UKHL 28; [2006] 3 W.L.R. 1 at [8] Lord Bingham referred to "the value of and need for a test of liability in tortious negligence, which any law of tort must propound if it is not to become a morass of single instances".

See also (1) *Perrett v Collins* [1998] 2 Lloyd's Rep. 255 at 273, *per* Buxton L.J., col.1:

"For my part, if it were literally the case that considerations determining whether a duty exists in law do indeed collapse into a pragmatic decision whether there should be a duty in the particular circumstances, then I would see little role for an Appellate Court in elucidating that question. Deciding pragmatic issues, especially issues of fairness and reasonableness, would seem to be eminently a task for a first instance Judge, with which an Appellate Court will only interfere on very limited and special grounds, which do not include disagreement with the Judge's conclusion."

(2) para.240 of the judgment of Kirby J. in *Pyrenees Shire Council v Day* [1998] H.C.A. 3 (reported in (1998) 192 C.L.R. 330):

avoid formulations so short as to afford no practical guidance[19] and the recitation of numerous principles to which different weight will be given by different judges in different cases.[20] The difficulty with the threefold test and with the extended *Hedley Byrne* principle, as with the test of "proximity" in Australia, is that they can amount to little more than statements that in law a particular duty of care exists or does not exist. They do not explain why that result is reached.[21] It is therefore not surprising that the different tests should lead to the same result,[22] although it may be easier to be led astray by one test than another.[23]

"whatever the defects of the notions of 'foreseeability', 'proximity' and the imprecision of the policy evaluation inherent in measurement of 'fairness', 'justice' and 'reasonableness', some guidance must be given by the Court as to how the duty question is to be answered when it is contested in a particular case. Otherwise, confronted with a suggested new category, lawyers in their offices and courts in Australia would have no instruction for their task of reasoning by analogy from past categories. It would then be all too easy to declare that those categories are closed, leaving all future extensions to the unpredictable vagaries of specific legislation. This would amount to an abdication of the function of common law courts. Legislatures simply cannot anticipate the myriad of circumstances presenting with the assertion that a duty of care is, or is not, to be imposed by the common law. To perform the task of reasoning by analogy, accepting or rejecting new categories, the individual affected, the lawyer advising and the court deciding have a right to know at least the general approach which they should adopt in order to resolve the controversy." (footnotes omitted)

[19] In *Customs and Excise Commissioners v Barclays Bank Plc* [2006] UKHL 28; [2006] 3 W.L.R. 1 Lord Rodger said, succinctly, at [52]: "appellate judges should follow the philosopher's advice to 'Seek simplicity, and distrust it'."

[20] See, e.g. *Crimmins v Stevedoring Industry Finance Committee* [1999] H.C.A. 59 (reported in (1999) 167 A.L.R. 1, *per* McHugh J. at para.77 (page 20)):

"Since the demise of any unifying principle for the determination of the duty of care and the general acknowledgement of the importance of frank discussion of policy factors, the resolution of novel cases has increasingly been made by reference to a 'checklist' of policy factors (See Stapleton, 'Duty of Care Factors: a Selection from the Judicial Menus' in Cane and Stapleton (eds), *The Law of Obligations—Essays in Celebration of John Fleming* (1998), p.59.) The result has been the proliferation of 'factors' that may indicate or negative the existence of a duty, but without a chain of reasoning linking these factors with the ultimate conclusion. Left unchecked, this approach becomes nothing more than the exercise of a discretion—like the process of sentencing, where the final result is determined by the individual 'judge's synthesis of all the various aspects' (*R. v Williscroft* [1975] V.R. 292 at 300, *per* Adam and Crockett J.J.)."

[21] See, e.g. the passages from the speeches of Lord Bridge and Lord Oliver in *Caparo Industries Plc v Dickman* [1990] 2 A.C. 605 set out in paras 2–032 and 2–033, above as to the three-stage test. In *Phelps v Hillingdon LBC* [2001] 2 A.C. 619, Lord Slynn said at 654E that "assumption of responsibility" means simply that the law recognises that there is a duty of care. It is not so much that responsibility is assumed as that it is recognised or imposed by the law. As May L.J. said in *Merrett v Babb* [2001] EWCA Civ 214, para.41; [2001] Q.B. 1174 at [41]:

"I also think that it is reaching for the moon—and not required by authority—to expect to accommodate every circumstance which may arise within a single short abstract formulation. The question in each case is whether the law recognises that there is a duty of care."

For criticism of the value of the "proximity" test in Australia see paras 2–065 and 2–066, above and *Sullivan v Moody* [2001] H.C.A. 59; (2001) 183 A.L.R. 403 at [48].

For Canada see *Hercules Managements Ltd v Ernst & Young* (1997) 146 D.L.R. (4th) 577 at para.23, *per* La Forest J.: " . . . the term 'proximity' itself is nothing more than a label expressing a result, judgment or conclusion; it does not, in and of itself, provide a principled basis on which to make a legal determination." See also *Cooper v Hobart* (2001) 206 D.L.R. (4th) 193 at [35] (Supreme Court of Canada).

[22] See para.2–051, above.

[23] See, e.g. Lord Hoffmann in *Stovin v Wise* [1996] A.C. 923 at 949A–D (partly set out in para.2–051, above).

2–072   **The correct approach to existing authority.** The solution should lie in the correct analysis of existing authority. What needs to be deduced is not so much the result on the facts of the particular decision, but which were the important facts and why they were important. This has two results. First, an informed understanding of existing authority should allow most cases to be decided in accordance with that authority or by close analogy to it. Secondly, it should elicit more general principles to which recourse must be had in truly novel situations.[24] A good example of how this has been achieved in practice is to be found in decisions as to whether accountants owe duties of care to third parties for negligent misstatements (either in accounts or otherwise). Building on the dissenting judgment of Denning L.J. in *Candler v Crane Christmas & Co*,[25] in *James McNaughton Group Ltd v Hicks Anderson*,[26] the Court of Appeal identified a number of factors which were likely to be relevant when deciding whether a duty of care was owed.[27] It is submitted that this level of analysis is more valuable than attempts to state principles which apply in all circumstances.[28]

2–073   **The underlying principles.** That is not to say that there are not underlying principles to the law of negligence. There are. They include the following:

(1) A tortious duty of care is imposed by law on A in relation to B. A does not himself agree to the imposition of the duty, although it may result from his voluntary acts or agreement. A finding that A owes B a duty of care is therefore a legal conclusion drawn from the relevant facts.

(2) At the heart of liability for negligence is that A should reasonably have foreseen that carelessness on his part could result in damage to B or to a "relevant" class to which B belongs.[29] It does not follow that A owes a duty of care to B, but absent reasonable foreseeability of damage, he will not do so.[30]

---

[24] See, e.g. the judgment of Lord Philips M.R. in *Watson v British Boxing Board of Control Ltd* [2001] Q.B. 1134. Faced with a novel claim, Lord Philips M.R. first identified the material facts, then analysed the authorities to deduce their underlying principles, and then applied those principles to the facts.

[25] [1951] 2 K.B. 164: see paras 2–113 to 2–116, below.

[26] [1991] 2 Q.B. 113.

[27] See Ch.17, paras 17–061 to 17–072. See also *Precis (521) Plc v William M Mercer Ltd* [2004] EWCA Civ 114; [2005] P.N.L.R. 28 at [24].

[28] However, if such an approach is to be adopted, it is important to guard against over-restrictive categorisation: see Stapleton, "Duty of care and economic loss: a wider agenda" (1991) 107 L.Q.R. 249.

[29] If A is driving a car and the duty of care requires A to take care to avoid causing personal injury or death, then the "relevant" class would be other road users, passengers, pedestrians, etc. If A is making a statement, then the "relevant" class will not necessarily extend to all those whom A should reasonably foresee might act to their detriment in reliance on the statement. "Relevant" here is not definitive, but indicative of the need for further analysis.

[30] See *Hamilton v Papakura DC* [2002] UKPC 9; [2002] 3 N.Z.L.R. 308 at [37]–[39]. There is no single, fixed standard of reasonable foreseeability. The degree of foreseeability required is related to the consequences which might be foreseen. The more serious the damage, the lesser the degree of likelihood of its occurrence that is needed: see *Jolley v Sutton LBC* [2000] 1 W.L.R. 1082 at 1091, *per* Lord Hoffmann; and *Att-Gen of the British Virgin Islands v Hartwell* [2004] UKPC 4; [2004] 1 W.L.R. 1273 at [21], *per* Lord Nicholls.

(3) While the careless infliction of reasonably foreseeable physical injury or of reasonably foreseeable damage to goods or other property requires to be justified if A is not to be required to compensate B for having inflicted it, that is not the case where the damage suffered does not involve personal injury or damage to goods or other property.[31]

(4) In the latter case (which covers both "pure economic loss"[32] and the failure to confer a benefit), the law of tort recognises both the difficulties in imposing a potentially wide liability on A[33] and that it may be entirely legitimate and consistent with public policy for A to cause "pure economic loss"[34] or to fail to confer a benefit.

(5) Whatever the nature of the damage, a duty of care should be found where, and only where, it is reasonable for A to be liable to compensate B for having negligently caused the damage in question.[35]

It is not suggested that these underlying principles provide a mechanism for deciding whether a duty of care is owed in a novel situation. They do, however,

---

[31] See, e.g., *per* Lord Oliver in *Murphy v Brentwood DC* [1991] 1 A.C. 398 at 487B–C:
"The infliction of physical injury to the person or property of another universally requires to be justified. The causing of economic loss does not. If it is to be categorised as wrongful it is necessary to find some factor beyond the mere occurrence of the loss and the fact that this occurrence could be foreseen."
But see the comment of Cooke P. in *South Pacific Manufacturing Co Ltd v New Zealand Security Consultants and Investigations Ltd* [1992] 2 N.Z.L.R. 282 and 296:
"The first concern of the law is naturally personal safety. Injury to the person is a kind of damage in a class of its own. Or at least most people would, I think, say so. On the other hand, a plaintiff awarded damages for harm to property is being compensated essentially for economic loss. It would be a crude system of law that drew a vital distinction for this purpose between tangible and intangible property interests"
[32] "Pure economic loss" now includes damage to a building or chattel caused by an inherent defect if A has supplied that building or chattel to B.
[33] See Cardozo C.J. in *Ultramares Corp v Touche* (1931) 174 N.E. 441; and in *Wagner v International Railway Co* (1921) 232 N.Y. 176.
[34] See, e.g. Lord Reid in *Dorset Yacht Co Ltd v Home Office* [1970] A.C. 1004 at 1027B:
"For example, causing economic loss is a different matter; for one thing, it is often caused by deliberate action. Competition involves traders being entitled to damage their rivals' interests by promoting their own, and there is a long chapter of the law determining in what circumstances owners of land can and in what circumstances they may not use their proprietary rights so as to injure their neighbours."
See also *Martel Building Ltd v The Queen* (2000) 196 D.L.R. (4th) 1, paras 62–67 (discussed in para.2–058, fn.68, above).
[35] See, e.g. Lord Reid in *Hedley Byrne & Co Ltd v Heller & Partners Ltd* [1964] A.C. 465 at 482 ("The law ought so far as possible to reflect the standards of the reasonable man . . . ").
In *Frost v Chief Constable of South Yorkshire* [1999] 2 A.C. 455 at 495B, when considering whether to recognise a duty of care to protect from psychiatric harm in the absence of physical injury (an area of law in which the courts adopt a more restrictive approach akin to that adopted to cases of pure economic loss), Lord Steyn referred to "the man on the Underground". In *McFarlane v Tayside Health Board* [2000] 2 A.C. 59 at 82B–C, Lord Steyn conducted a notional poll of commuters on the Underground when considering whether the parents of an unwanted but healthy child should recover damages for the cost of the child's upbringing. (However, care is needed when adopting this approach: the High Court of Australia disagreed with the result of Lord Steyn's poll: see *Catanach v Melchior* [2003] H.C.A. 38.)
See also *Graham Barclay Oysters Pty Ltd v Ryan* [2002] H.C.A. 54, *per* Gleeson C.J. at [6]: "At the centre of the law of negligence is the concept of reasonableness."

provide some assistance in understanding decisions on particular facts and in identifying which facts were important.

2–074 The last of the underlying principles identified, namely that a duty of care should be imposed where it is reasonable for A to be liable to compensate B for having negligently caused the damage in question, can be criticised for being hopelessly vague and for inviting individual judges to decide particular cases according to their personal assessment of the reasonable outcome.[36] However, in this context reasonableness is not assessed by the judge solely on the basis of his own, personal criteria. Rather, existing authority is to be seen as representing "the cumulative experience of the judiciary of the actual consequences of lack of care in particular circumstances".[37] Reasonableness may underlie a decision that a manufacturer should owe a duty of care to a consumer who suffers personal injury as a result of a latent defect caused by the manufacturer's negligence,[38] and may be more explicitly stated as a factor in cases of negligent misstatement,

---

Similar views were expressed by Tipping J. giving the judgment of the New Zealand Court of Appeal in *Att-Gen v Carter* [2003] 2 N.Z.L.R. 160 at [30]:

"The outcome of a duty of care issue should not depend on what analytical method is employed. The ultimate enquiry is whether it is fair, just and reasonable to require the defendant to take reasonable care to avoid causing the plaintiff loss or damage of the kind for which compensation is being sought."

[36] See, e.g. *Perre v Apand Pty Ltd* [1999] H.C.A. 36; (1999) 198 C.L.R. 180 at para.80, *per* McHugh J.:

"almost everyone would agree that courts should not impose a duty of care on a person unless it is fair, just and reasonable to do so. But attractive as concepts of fairness and justice may be in appellate courts, in law reform commissions, in the academy and among legislators, in many cases they are of little use, if they are of any use at all, to the practitioners and trial judges who must apply the law to concrete facts arising from real life activities. While the training and background of judges may lead them to agree as to what is fair or just in many cases, there are just as many cases where using such concepts as the criteria for duty would mean that "each judge would have a distinct tribunal in his own breast, the decisions of which would be as irregular and uncertain and various as the minds and tempers of mankind." *Donaldson v Beckett* (1774) 2 Brown 129, *per* Lord Camden cited in "The Judge and Case Law" in Devlin, *The Judge* (1979) at 181. Lord Devlin was surely right when he said ("The Judge and Case Law" in Devlin, *The Judge* (1979) at 181):

"For a judge to decide fairly and convincingly every case that comes before him in the light only of his own sense of justice, he would have to be a superman. I doubt if there have ever been more than a handful of men on the bench who could do it, though doubtless there are slightly more who think that they could."

In *Sullivan v Moody* [2001] H.C.A. 59; (2001) 183 A.L.R. 403 the High Court of Australia expressed reservations about the "fair, just and reasonable" element of the three-stage test, saying at [49]:

"The question as to what is fair, and just and reasonable is capable of being misunderstood as an invitation to formulate policy rather than to search for principle. The concept of policy, in this context, is often ill-defined. There are policies at work in the law which can be identified and applied to novel problems, but the law of tort develops by reference to principles, which must be capable of general application, not discretionary decision-making in individual cases."

The Court went on to quote from the speech of Lord Diplock in *Dorset Yacht Co Ltd v Home Office* [1970] A.C. 1004.

[37] *per* Lord Diplock in *Dorset Yacht Co Ltd v Home Office* [1970] A.C. 1004 at 1058. Lord Diplock was discussing questions of public policy when deciding whether a duty of care was owed, but the principle is the same.

See also *D v East Berkshire Community NHS Trust* [2005] UKHL 23; [2005] 2 A.C. 373 at [100], *per* Lord Rodger.

[38] *Donoghue v Stevenson* [1932] A.C. 562; see also para.2–022, above.

where the reasonableness of the claimant's reliance will be relevant in determining whether he was owed a duty of care.[39]

Beyond such general statements, there is little to be gained in seeking to enunciate universal principles which could provide practical assistance, for example, both in deciding whether a local authority owes a duty of care when assessing a child's educational needs and in deciding the extent to which an accountant who audits accounts or who makes a statement as to accounts (whether audited or management) at a meeting in the course of the takeover of his client company owes a duty of care. The situations are far removed from each other and the factors which emerge from the authorities have little in common.[40] Those factors, rather than a test of assumption of responsibility or the threefold test, provide the most useful and principled guidance when deciding whether a particular duty of care was owed.[41]   **2-075**

Nevertheless, the threefold test, the extended *Hedley Byrne* principle, based on assumption of responsibility, and the incremental approach continue to be invoked and applied. It is therefore appropriate to say something about each.   **2-076**

The question of proximity. The concept of proximity is protean. In cases of personal injury or damage to property, it may arise as a direct consequence of foreseeability of the harm.[42] In cases of pure economic loss, the purpose underlying the defendant's statements or actions is highly material in determining whether there was sufficient proximity. Indeed, this consideration was decisive in *Caparo Industries Plc v Dickman*,[43] in which the claimants failed on proximity because the manner in which they used the accounts was not within the "purpose" for which those accounts had been prepared, having regard in particular to the statutory context. This consideration was also decisive in leading to the different results in *James McNaughton Paper Group Ltd v Hicks Anderson &*   **2-077**

---

[39] See, e.g. Ch.17, para.17–071, below. See also *Att-Gen v Carter* [2003] 2 N.Z.L.R. 160 at [26], *per* Tipping J., giving the judgment of the New Zealand Court of Appeal.

[40] In relation to local authorities see paras 2–081 to 2–087, below and in relation to accountants, see Ch.17, paras 17–077 to 17–080.

[41] See *Customs and Excise Commissioners v Barclays Bank Plc* [2006] UKHL 28; [2006] 3 W.L.R. 1 at [36], *per* Lord Hoffmann and at [83], *per* Lord Mance. (Lord Hoffmann referred to his judgment at first instance in *Morgan Crucible Co Plc v Hill Samuel & Co Ltd* [1991] Ch. 292 at 300–303. While the passage to which he refers remains helpful, his judgment was overturned on appeal.)

See, e.g. Sir Brian Neill in *Bank of Credit and Commerce International (Overseas) Ltd v Price Waterhouse (No.2)* [1998] P.N.L.R. 564 at 5876D:

"The threefold test and the assumption of responsibility test indicate the criteria which have to be satisfied if liability is to attach. But the authorities also provide some guidance as to the factors which are to be taken into account in deciding whether these criteria are met."

His lordship then went on to list various factors (see also his judgment in *James McNaughton Paper Group Ltd v Hicks Anderson* [1991] 2 Q.B. 113 at 125–127 discussed in Ch.17, paras 17–062 to 17–072).

[42] However, if the claimant is one of a vast number of persons who are foreseeably at risk of personal injury/death, the claimant could still fail for lack of proximity (*Hill v Chief Constable of West Yorkshire* [1989] A.C. 53) and special factors apply to claims for psychiatric injury or "nervous shock" (*Alcock v Chief Constable of South Yorkshire Police* [1992] 1 A.C. 310; and *Frost v Chief Constable of South Yorkshire Police* [1999] 2 A.C. 455). See also *Sutradhar v Natural Environment Research Council* [2004] EWCA Civ 175; [2004] P.N.L.R. 30 where a claim for personal injuries against the makers of a report to an authority responsible for providing drinking water failed for lack of proximity.

[43] [1990] 2 A.C. 605. See Ch.17, paras 17–051 to 17–060.

Co^{44} and *Morgan Crucible Plc v Hill Samuel & Co Ltd.*[45] The underlying purpose of the defendant's functions is also relevant to the "just and reasonable" question,[46] discussed in the next paragraph. In terms of the development of the law of negligence, proximity served a useful purpose in focusing attention on the need to show more than foreseeability of loss and an absence of policy considerations if a duty of care, particularly in relation to pure economic loss, were to be found. However, as the Australian experience demonstrates,[47] the concept can be overworked.

2–078 **The "just and reasonable" question.** This was an important feature of the House of Lords decision in *Governors of the Peabody Donation Fund v Sir Lindsay Parkinson & Co Ltd*[48] and of many subsequent duty of care decisions,[49] in particular *Marc Rich & Co AG v Bishop Rock Marine Co Ltd.*[50] When considering this question, it is submitted that judges are not bringing to bear purely personal or subjective opinions.[51] They are considering the application of established legal principles to the unique facts of individual cases (this is implicit in the word "just") as well as purely pragmatic considerations.

2–079 **Policy considerations in the context of "just and reasonable".** In this context, the role of the courts in policy matters falls to be considered. A cautious approach was advocated in decisions such as *D&F Estates Ltd v Church Commissioners for England*[52] and *Murphy v Brentwood DC.*[53] However, the courts do have to reach decisions which involve policy factors.[54] They should not and, on occasions, do not shy away from doing so. On one view the law of negligence itself is based upon judicial assessment of "the demands of society for protection from the carelessness of others"[55] so that to an extent every decision involves

---

[44] [1991] 2 Q.B. 113. Discussed in Ch.17, paras 17–062 to 17–072.

[45] [1991] Ch. 295. Discussed in Ch.17, para.17–077. Further authorities on this area are discussed in paras 17–077 to 17–080.

[46] *Peabody Donation Fund v Sir Lindsay Parkinson & Co Ltd* [1985] A.C. 210.

[47] See paras 2–064 to 2–067, above.

[48] [1985] A.C. 210.

[49] See, e.g. the cases discussed in paras 2–029 to 2–034, above.

[50] [1996] 1 A.C. 211, discussed in para.2–050, above.

[51] See para.2–074, above.

[52] [1989] A.C. 177. See the speech of Lord Bridge at 210E: " . . . it is again, in my opinion, a dangerous course for the common law to embark upon the adoption of novel policies which it sees as instruments of social justice but to which, unlike the legislature, it is unable to set carefully defined limitations."

[53] [1991] 1 A.C. 398. See the speech of Lord Oliver at 491F–492B:
"But, in any event, like my noble and learned friends, I think that the achievement of beneficial social purposes by the creation of entirely new liabilities is a matter which properly falls within the province of the legislature . . . I do not, for my part, think that it is right for the courts not simply to expand existing principles but to create at large new principles in order to fulfil a social need in an area of consumer protection which has already been perceived by the legislature but for which, presumably advisedly, it has not thought it necessary to provide."

[54] "The test for the existence of a duty of care which looks to what the court considers is fair, just and reasonable is of a different order from the test of proximity or neighbourhood with its further ingredient of foreseeability. The test of fairness is a test which may principally involve considerations of policy.": *per* Lord Clyde in *Phelps v Hillingdon LBC* [2001] 2 A.C. 619 at 671H.

[55] *per* Lord Pearce in *Hedley Byrne & Co Ltd v Heller & Partners Ltd* [1964] A.C. 465 at 536. See also, *per* Lord Denning M.R. in *Dorset Yacht Co Ltd v Home Office* [1969] 2 Q.B. 412 at 426B: "It is, I think, at bottom a matter of public policy, which we as judges must resolve. This talk of 'duty' or 'no duty' is simply a way of limiting the range of liability for negligence." In his speech in the

questions of policy. For example, it was the House of Lords and not Parliament which removed an advocate's immunity from suit.[56] In doing so, they were assisted by knowledge that the absence of such immunity in Canada had not led to the dire consequences predicted by those who sought to uphold the existing position.[57] The experience of other jurisdictions and systems of law can assist when broad questions of policy arise.[58] The courts are less well equipped to consider questions such as the cost of insurance[59] or the possible inhibiting consequences of finding a duty of care on those found to owe it, although, such arguments have not always found favour.[60] However, there is a danger that when considering such questions they will fall back on speculation and their own, subjective views.[61] An important safeguard, more usually mentioned when a duty

House of Lords in the *Dorset Yacht Co* case [1970] A.C. 1004 at 1058D, Lord Diplock agreed with this passage from the judgment of Lord Denning and then went on to explain how this policy decision was to be made by reference to existing authority.

[56] *Arthur J Hall & Co v Simons* [2002] 1 A.C. 615. "The judges created the immunity and the judges should say that the grounds for maintaining it no longer exist": *per* Lord Hoffmann at 704H–705A.

[57] *ibid.* at 681D–F, *per* Lord Steyn and 695B–G, *per* Lord Hoffmann.

[58] See, e.g. Markesinis, Auby, Coester-Waltjen and Deakin, *Tortious Liability of Statutory Bodies* (Hart Publishing, 1999).

[59] See, e.g. Lord Hoffmann in *Frost v Chief Constable of South Yorkshire* [1999] 2 A.C. 455 at 510D, where he admitted that he was "not in a position to form a view one way or the other" on the likely volume of claims and consequent burden on insurers and public funds if the claim for psychiatric damage were allowed. However, see, *per* Lord Steyn at 494E where he set out his fourth "objective policy consideration": "the imposition of liability for pure psychiatric harm in a wide range of situations *may* result in a burden of liability on defendants which *may* be disproportionate to tortious conduct involving perhaps momentary lapses of concentration, e.g. in a motor car accident" (emphasis added).

[60] See, e.g. Lord Reid in *Dorset Yacht Co Ltd v Home Office* [1970] A.C. 1004 at 1033B, where having cited the decision of the Court of Appeals of New York in *Williams v State of New York* (1955) 127 N.E. (2d) 545 (where it was held that finding a duty of care would impact on the rehabilitative work done with prisoners), he said:

"It may be that the public servants of the State of New York are so apprehensive, easily dissuaded from doing their duty and intent on preserving public funds from costly claims that they could be influenced in that way. By my experience leads me to believe that Her Majesty's servants are made of sterner stuff."

See also *Barrett v Enfield LBC* [1998] Q.B. 367 at 380A–C, *per* Evans L.J.:

"I would agree that what is said to be a 'policy' consideration, namely, that imposing a duty of care might lead to defensive conduct on the part of the person concerned and might require him to spend time or resources on keeping full records or otherwise providing for self-justification, if called upon to do so, should normally be a factor of little, if any, weight. If the conduct in question is of a kind which can be measured against the standards of the reasonable man, placed as the defendant was, then I do not see why the law in the public interest should not require those standards to be observed."

(Lord Slynn agreed with this when the case reached the House of Lords: [2001] 2 A.C. 550 at 568F.)

[61] For example, it is interesting to contrast the approach of Lord Hoffmann in *Arthur J Hall & Co v Simons* [2002] 1 A.C. 615 at 692D–693E (where he rejected an argument based upon the anticipated effect on advocates of abolition of their immunity from suit in negligence) with his speech in *Stovin v Wise* [1996] A.C. 923 at 958C:

"I think that it is important, before extending the duty of care owed by public authorities, to consider the cost to the community of the defensive measures which they are likely to take in order to avoid liability. It would not be surprising if one of the consequences of the *Anns* case and the spate of cases which followed was that local council inspectors tended to insist upon stronger foundations than were necessary."

In *Arthur J Hall & Co*, Lord Hoffmann had the benefit of Canadian experience and of the wasted

of care is found to be owed, is that liability will only be found if there is negligence and not just an error of judgment.[62] It is submitted that this is an important factor and that courts should, while avoiding leaps in the dark if at all possible, bear in mind that to sound in damages, the error has to be such that no reasonably careful or reasonably competent defendant would have made it. The courts should be slow to accept unsupported assertions as to the deleterious consequences that would follow from finding that a duty of care was owed.[63]

2–080   **Assumption of responsibility and the extended *Hedley Byrne* principle.** In *Hedley Byrne & Co Ltd v Heller & Partners Ltd*[64] Lord Reid identified as the additional requirement which needed to be satisfied to give rise to a duty of care for a misstatement "that expressly or by implication from the circumstances the speaker or writer has undertaken some responsibility".[65] Whether someone has undertaken or assumed responsibility towards another in relation to a task or a statement can be a useful test when deciding whether he owed that other person a duty of care.[66] However, there are two difficulties. First, assumption of responsibility is of little use if the person making the statement or carrying out the task has expressly disclaimed liability in circumstances where that disclaimer is itself

---

costs jurisdiction in the English courts to guide him. In *Stovin v Wise*, he and the other members of the House of Lords had no information as the likely consequences of a finding that a local authority owed a duty to exercise reasonable skill and care when deciding which dangerous junctions to render safer. Markesinis, Auby, Coester-Waltjen and Deakin, *Tortious Liability of Statutory Bodies* (Hart Publishing, 1999), p.79, postulate a "counter-hunch" to that made by Lord Hoffmann in *Stovin v Wise*, namely that "the post-*Murphy* situation may be encouraging sloppy verification of building calculations" (See also (1) *South Pacific Manufacturing Co Ltd v New Zealand Security Consultants and Investigations Ltd* [1992] 2 N.Z.L.R. 282 at 312, lines 25–29: "And since the imposition of liability on local authorities effected by decisions such as *Bowen v Paramount Builders (Hamilton) Ltd* [1977] 1 N.Z.L.R. 394, it is reasonable to assume there has been an improvement in their supervision of new house building. In my own trial experience I have heard statements by local body witnesses to that effect." (2) *Rowling v Takaro Properties Ltd* [1988] A.C. 473 at 502D–E, where Lord Keith expressed a similar apprehension as that evinced by Lord Hoffmann in *Stovin v Wise*.)
[62] See, e.g. *Dorset Yacht Co Ltd v Home Office, per* Lord Denning M.R. in the Court of Appeal [1969] 2 Q.B. 412 at 427B–H and, *per* Lord Reid in the House of Lords [1970] A.C. 1004 at 1032C–E ("I cannot believe that negligence or dereliction of duty is widespread among prison or Borstal officers"); *Arthur J Hall & Co v Simons* [2002] 1 A.C. 615 at 682B–C, *per* Lord Steyn; and *Phelps v Hillingdon LBC* [2001] 2 A.C. 619 at 654H–655D, *per* Lord Slynn and at 672B–G, *per* Lord Clyde.
[63] See, e.g. the discussion of policy arguments advanced against a duty of care in *Capital and Counties Plc v Hampshire CC* [1997] Q.B. 1004 at 1043D–1044F. The Court of Appeal had, however, found that there was no sufficient proximity, so that there was no duty of care.
[64] [1964] A.C. 465; see also paras 2–024 to 2–025, above.
[65] *ibid.* at 483. Lords Morris and Hodson considered that a duty would arise where a person with special skill or information "takes it upon himself" to give information or advice (*ibid.* at 502 and 514). Lord Devlin spoke of "a responsibility that is voluntarily accepted or undertaken" (*ibid.* at 529) and Lord Pearce of "persons holding themselves out in a calling or situation or profession [who] take on a task within that calling or situation or profession" (*ibid.* at 538).
See also *Customs and Excise Commissioners v Barclays Bank Plc* [2006] UKHL 28; [2006] 3 W.L.R. 1 at [38], *per* Lord Hoffmann:
"... the notion of assumption of responsibility serves a ... useful purpose in drawing attention to the fact that a duty of care is ordinarily generated by something which the defendant has decided to *do* ... " (Lord Hoffmanns's emphasis)
[66] See, in particular the discussion of this point by Lord Hoffmann in *Customs and Excise Commissioners v Barclays Bank Plc* [2006] UKHL 28; [2006] 3 W.L.R. 1 at [35] to the effect that assumption of responsibility is a useful test in cases where information is provided. However, Lord Hoffmann also explained that the concept was less illuminating, but still legitimate and useful in other situations

challenged as was the case in *Smith v Eric S Bush*.[67] References to *voluntary* assumption of responsibility tend "to import a degree of subjectivity".[68] Secondly, if the subjective, voluntary element is excised, so that the test is one of deemed assumption of responsibility, then as a test "assumption of responsibility" becomes little more than a statement that the law recognises a duty of care.[69] That is not to say that an objective assessment as to whether a defendant has undertaken responsibility to a claimant is not without value, for example, in the context of cases of negligent misstatement.[70] However, it is to recognise that in many cases in which a duty of care is found, the concept of assumption of responsibility affords little, if any, practical assistance in understanding why that conclusion is reached. As with proximity in the threefold test, assumption of responsibility can only be taken so far.

(c) *Particular Situations*

(i) *Public and Local Authorities: Duty of Care and Statute*[71]

The tort of negligence and statute. Although the law of negligence is   2–081
essentially judge-made, statute is increasingly important. Statute has clarified or changed existing common law duties,[72] provided the context in which common

---

(*ibid.* at [35]–[38]). In the same case the speeches of Lord Rodger at [73] and Lord Mance at [93] address the sort of case in which the notion of voluntary assumption of responsibility is useful.

See also, e.g. *Williams v Natural Health Life Foods Ltd* [1998] 1 W.L.R. 830 (discussed in para.2–049, above); *Al-Kandari v JR Brown & Co* [1988] Q.B. 665 (discussed in Ch.11, para.11–063); and *Pryke v Gibbs Hartley Cooper Ltd* [1991] 1 Lloyd's Rep. 602 (discussed in Ch.16, para.16–025).

[67] [1990] 1 A.C. 831 (discussed in para.2–030, above).

[68] *Merrett v Babb* [2001] EWCA Civ 214; [2001] Q.B. 1174 at [41], *per* May L.J.

[69] See para.2–071, fn.21, above. See also the comments of Tipping J. giving the judgment of New Zealand Court of Appeal in *Att-Gen v Carter* [2003] 2 N.Z.L.R. 160 at [23] for a defence of the expression "deemed assumption of responsibility". In *Precis (521) Plc v William M Mercer Ltd* [2004] EWCA Civ 114; [2005] P.N.L.R. 28 Arden L.J. (with whom the other members of the Court agreed) said, at [24]:

"It is, however, apparent from the foregoing that the precise limits of the concept of assumption of responsibility are still in a state of development. A difficulty which the court faces is that there is no comprehensive list of guiding principles to help the courts determine when an assumption of responsibility can be said to arise ... The courts have, therefore, to look at all the relevant circumstances, and (following their approach to the duty of care generally: see above) determine whether the circumstances fall within the situations in which an assumption of responsibility has previously been held to exist or whether the circumstances are closely analogous to and consistent with the situations in which liability has been imposed in previous cases."

Or, as Lord Bingham said *Customs and Excise Commissioners v Barclays Bank Plc* [2006] UKHL 28; [2006] 3 W.L.R. 1 at [5]:

"The problem here is, as I see it, that the further this test is removed from the actions and intentions of the actual defendant, an the more notional the assumption of responsibility becomes, the less difference there is between this test and the threefold test."

[70] See, e.g. *Peach Publishing Ltd v Slater & Co* [1998] B.C.C. 139 at 146C, *per* Morritt L.J.; and at 161E, *per* Nourse L.J.; and *Electra Private Equity Partners v KPMG Peat Marwick (a firm)* [1999] Lloyd's P.N. 670 at 682, *per* Auld L.J. These decisions are discussed in Ch.17, para.17–080.

[71] See *Statutory Torts* by Stanton, Skidmore, Harris and Wright (2003); and *The Negligence Liability of Public Authorities* by Booth and Squires (2006).

[72] See, e.g. the Occupiers' Liability Act 1957 and the Occupiers' Liability Act 1984.

law issues have to be decided,[73] created statutory duties actionable by those for whose protection the statutory duty was enacted[74] or those specified as being entitled to bring claims,[75] and has created powers and duties to be exercised by a variety of public bodies which may give rise to common law duties of care.[76] In recent years, the courts have had to grapple with a number of novel claims against public bodies or authorities in which it has been alleged that the body or authority was in breach of a tortious duty of care in relation to the exercise (or non-exercise) of its powers, duties or functions.

2–082   **Lord Browne-Wilkinson's classification.** In *X (minors) v Bedfordshire CC*[77] Lord Browne-Wilkinson identified four classes of claims[78]:

(1) Actions for breach of statutory duty *simpliciter* (i.e. irrespective of carelessness).

(2) Actions based solely on the careless performance of a statutory duty in the absence of any other common law right of action.

(3) Actions based on a common law duty of care arising either from the imposition of a statutory duty or from the performance of it.

(4) Misfeasance in public office, i.e. the failure to exercise, or the exercise of, statutory powers either with the intention to injure the claimant or in the knowledge that the conduct is unlawful.

In this section some brief consideration will be given to the first class and then the vexed question of the circumstances in which the existence or exercise of a statutory power or duty gives rise to a common law duty of care (the third class) will be addressed. The fourth class, misfeasance in public office, is beyond the scope of this book.[79] Before doing so, however, the second class needs to be explained.

2–083   **Careless exercise of a statutory duty.** Where Parliament has authorised an authority to carry out a particular act, the fact that carrying it out involves what would otherwise be a tortious act (e.g. nuisance) does not render the authority liable in damages: the authority has a complete defence to a claim—it is not wrongful to carry out an act which Parliament has authorised.[80] However, Parliament is not taken to have authorised the authority to carry out the act

---

[73] See, e.g. *Caparo Industries Plc v Dickman* [1990] 2 A.C. 605, discussed in Ch.17, para.17–059).
[74] *Clerk and Lindsell on Torts* (19th ed.), paras 9–10 to 9–48 and see para.2–084, below.
[75] See, e.g. s.150 of the Financial Services and Markets Act 2000.
[76] *Clerk & Lindsell on Torts* (19th edn), Ch.14 and see paras 2–085 to 2–086, below.
[77] [1995] 2 A.C. 633; see also para.2–042 above. The actual decision in *X (minors) v Bedfordshire CC* [1995] 2 A.C. 633 in relation to the claims by children is no longer good law as a result of the passing of the Human Rights Act 1998 (*D v East Berkshire Community NHS Trust* [2003] EWCA Civ 1151; [2004] Q.B. 558 at [83]). However, Lord Browne-Wilkinson's classification remains valuable.
[78] *ibid.* at 730H–731B.
[79] See *Clerk & Lindsell on Torts* (19th edn), (paras 14–56 to 14–68); and *Three Rivers DC v Governor and Company of the Bank of England (No.3)* [2003] 2 A.C. 1.
[80] See, e.g. *Allen v Gulf Oil Refining Ltd* [1981] A.C. 1001.

carelessly, so that if the authority has done the act carelessly, so as to cause damage, it has no defence based upon statutory authority. It follows that Lord Browne-Wilkinson's second class is concerned with the negation of a defence, rather than the recognition of a duty of care or other tortious claim.[81] The fact that a statutory power is exercised carelessly does not of itself give rise to a cause of action in tort. The claimant has to show that the circumstances were such that the person exercising the power owed him a duty of care when exercising it.[82]

Breach of statutory duty *simpliciter* **(Lord Browne-Wilkinson's first class).** 2–084
Breach of statutory duty only gives rise to a private law cause of action if, on the true construction of the statute, the duty was imposed in order to protect a limited class of the public and Parliament intended to confer on members of that class a private right of action for breach of the duty.[83] Where there is an express provision in the statute, this principle is easy to apply.[84] It is more difficult to apply where there is no express provision. The most important factors in determining whether Parliament intended there to be a private right of action are:

(1) Whether the provision was designed to protect a limited class of individuals.

(2) Whether the statute provides for any other sanction for breach of the duty.

(3) Whether the claimant has alternative remedies.

Of these, the first is the most important, with less weight being attached to the absence of other sanction or remedy. A broad analysis of the statute is required.[85] Analysis of the considerable body of authority as to the application of these factors is beyond the scope of this book.[86]

Common law duty of care arising either from the imposition of a statutory 2–085
duty or from the performance of it. The courts have not found an easy answer to the question when the imposition of a statutory duty or the performance of it should give rise to a common law duty of care. There is a reluctance to recognise the possibility of claims for negligent policy decisions, although there is also a recognition that the distinction between policy and operational questions is not always easy to make or useful in practice. The result has been a tendency to find that the natural persons through whom authorities discharge their statutory functions themselves owe common law duties of care, for breach of which their employees are vicariously liable. So, an education authority does not itself owe a common law duty to pupils to assess their educational needs, but the educational psychologist who makes the assessments is under a common law duty to

---

[81] See *X (minors) v Bedfordshire CC* [1995] 2 A.C. 633 at 732C–733F, explaining *Geddis v Proprietors of Bann Reservoir* (1878) 3 App.Cas. 430.
[82] *ibid*. at 734H–735A.
[83] *ibid*. at 731D–E.
[84] Examples are given in para.9–10 of *Clerk & Lindsell on Torts* (19th edn).
[85] *Phelps v Hillingdon LBC* [2001] 2 A.C. 619 at 652D–G, *per* Lord Slynn.
[86] See *Clerk & Lindsell on Torts* (19th edn), paras 9–10 to 9–41.

them to carry out the assessments with reasonable skill and care.[87] In the same way, a fire authority owes no duty of care to property owners in its area, but if its employees attend a fire, they owe a common law duty of care to exercise reasonable skill and care not to create some new danger.[88] This distinction may have arisen because different considerations apply to claims based on alleged common law duties said to arise solely from the existence of some broad public law duty and cases in which public authorities have chosen to enter into relationships or to accept responsibilities which give rise to a common law duty of care.[89] However, in each case, it is still necessary to show that the specific employee of the public authority has so conducted himself as to give a duty of care to the particular claimant.

2–086   **The narrow scope for a common law duty of care.** Recent decisions of the House of Lords, particularly in *X (minors) v Bedfordshire CC*[90] and *Stovin v Wise*,[91] have established a number of formidable obstacles to a finding that a common law duty of care arises.[92] In considering whether a public body owes a duty of care when acting under a statute, the following questions need to be addressed[93]:

(1) Did the statute impose a duty or confer a power or discretion?

(2) If the latter, then does the exercise of the power or discretion involve consideration of "policy" matters? If it does, then no duty of care will be

---

[87] *Phelps v Hillingdon LBC* [2001] 2 A.C. 619. This distinction appears clearly from the decision of the Court of Appeal in *Carty v Croydon LBC* [2005] EWCA Civ 19; [2005] 1 W.L.R. 2312. There it was held that the mere fact that an education authority officer failed to make an assessment in accordance with the applicable statutory requirements was not actionable in tort, but that, once the officer entered into a relationship with or assumed responsibility towards a child, then a duty of care could arise.

[88] *Capital and Counties Plc v Hampshire CC* [1997] Q.B. 1004.

[89] *Gorringe v Calderdale MBC* [2004] UKHL 15; [2004] 1 W.L.R. 1057, *per* Lord Hoffmann at [38].

[90] [1995] 2 A.C. 633.

[91] [1996] A.C. 923.

[92] Recent appellate decisions have been criticised and compared with the approaches adopted in French and German law in Markesinis, Auby, Coester-Waltjen and Deakin, *Tortious Liability of Statutory Bodies* (Hart Publishing, Oxford and Portland, Oregon, 1999). See also Craig, "Negligence in the Exercise of a Statutory Power" (1978) 94 L.Q.R. 428; Bowman and Bailey, "Negligence in the Realms of Public Law—Positive Obligation to Rescue?" [1984] P.L. 27; Bowman and Bailey, "The Policy/Operational Dichotomy—a Cuckoo in the Nest" [1986] C.L.J. 430; Howarth, "Negligence after Murphy: Time to Rethink" [1991] C.L.J. 58 at 94–95; Bailey and Bowman, "Public Authority Negligence Revisited" [2000] C.L.J. 85. This area of the law could be important in claims against health authorities if the defence of lack of resources is advanced: see Ch.13, below. It is also relevant in the regulated financial services industry: see Ch.14.

[93] See also the judgment of Hale L.J. in *A v Essex CC* [2003] EWCA Civ 1848; [2004] 1 W.L.R. 1881, at [33], where she set out 3 areas of inquiry which follow the scheme of this paragraph. In *Carty v Croydon LBC* [2005] EWCA Civ 19; [2005] 1 W.L.R. 2312 at [28]–[32] Dyson L.J. expressed the view that Hale L.J.'s second area of inquiry (whether the decision involved the exercise of a statutory discretion) would be better merged into the third, namely the three stage test in *Caparo Industries Plc v Dickman* [1990] 2 A.C. 605.

owed because the courts will not begin to assess whether a particular decision was negligent,[94] at least where the decision involved weighing of competing public interests.[95]

[94] In *Anns v Merton LBC* [1978] A.C. 728 (see paras 2–027 and 2–039, above) the House of Lords concluded that in the operational sphere a public authority could owe a duty of care to persons affected by its acts or omissions. In the sphere of policy, a public authority's tortious liability would be much more limited, but it did not enjoy total immunity.

However, in *Rowling v Takaro Properties Ltd* [1988] A.C. 473 at 501B–D, the Privy Council opined that it might be more helpful to identify a class of "policy or planning" decisions, such as "discretionary decisions on the allocation of scarce resources or the distribution of risks" which are simply not suitable for judicial resolution at all (strictly speaking this was obiter because it was held that the decision in issue was not negligent). The reason why such decisions are not suitable for judicial resolution may be because of a reluctance to become involved in political questions, or because it will be extremely difficult to show that such a decision was negligent: when that difficulty is considered together with the probable availability of public law remedy and the possible consequences on public administration, then policy factors dictate that no duty of care should be owed: *ibid.* at 502A–F.

This was taken further in *X (minors) v Bedfordshire CC* [1995] 2 A.C. 633, where, at 737F–G Lord Browne-Wilkinson said if the matters relevant to the exercise of discretion included "policy" matters, which might be difficult to identify, then the court could not begin to assess them. Having noted the difference of approach in *Anns v Merton LBC* [1978] A.C. 728; and *Rowling v Takaro Properties Ltd* [1988] A.C. 473, Lord Browne-Wilkinson concluded that "a common law duty of care in relation to the taking of decisions involving policy matters cannot exist": [1995] A.C. 633 at 738H.

On the policy/operational distinction, see also *Barratt v Enfield LBC* [2002] 1 A.C. 550 at 571F, *per* Lord Slynn; and *Phelps v Hillingdon LBC* [2001] 2 A.C. 619 at 673H–674C, *per* Lord Clyde.

However, in *Tomlinson v Congleton BC* [2003] UKHL 43; [2004] 1 A.C. 46 the House of Lords did address the question of liability under s.1(3) of the Occupiers' Liability Act 1984 by weighing up various policy considerations, including to a limited extent the cost of taking measures to reduce or eliminate a perceived risk (see paras [34]–[50] of the speech of Lord Hoffmann, with whom Lords Nicholls, Hobhouse and, to an extent, Scott agreed).

[95] See the analysis of Lord Hutton in *Barratt v Enfield LBC* [2001] 2 A.C. 559 at 578E–584C; and *Phelps v Hillingdon LBC* [2002] A.C. 619 at 653B, *per* Lord Slynn. See also *Sutherland Shire Council v Heyman* (1985) 157 C.L.R. 424 at 469, where Mason J. observed:

"[T]he dividing line between [policy and operational factors] will be observed if we recognize that a public authority is under no duty of care in relation to decisions which involve or are dictated by financial, economic, social or political factors or constraints. Thus budgetary allocations and the constraints which they entail in terms of allocation of resources cannot be made the subject of a duty of care. But it may be otherwise when the courts are called upon to apply a standard of care to action or inaction that is merely the product of administrative direction, expert or professional opinion, technical standards or general standards of reasonableness."

See also *Graham Barclay Oysters Pty Ltd v Ryan* [2002] H.C.A. 54, *per* Gleeson C.J. at [6]:

"Citizens blame governments for many kinds of misfortune. When they do so, the kind of responsibility they attribute, expressly or by implication, may be different in quality from the kind of responsibility attributed to a citizen who is said to be under a legal liability to pay damages in compensation for injury. Subject to any insurance arrangements that may apply, people who sue governments are seeking compensation from public funds. They are claiming against a body politic or other entity whose primary responsibilities are to the public. And, in the case of an action in negligence against a government of the Commonwealth or a State or Territory, they are inviting the judicial arm of government to pass judgment upon the reasonableness of the conduct of the legislative or executive arms of government; conduct that may involve action or inaction on political grounds. Decisions as to raising revenue, and setting priorities in the allocation of public funds between competing claims on scarce resources, are essentially political. So are decisions about the extent of government regulation of private and commercial behaviour that is proper. At the centre of the law of negligence is the concept of reasonableness. When courts are invited to pass judgment on the reasonableness of governmental action or inaction, they may be confronted by issues that are inappropriate for judicial resolution, and that, in a representative democracy, are ordinarily decided through the political process. Especially is this so when criticism is addressed to legislative action or inaction. Many citizens may believe that, in various matters, there should

(3) If the decision whether to exercise the power or discretion[96] did not involve "policy" matters, then only if the authority or body acted so unreasonably that its act or decision fell outside the scope of the power or discretion conferred by Parliament, could there be a breach of any duty of care.[97]

(4) In cases where there might be a duty of care (i.e. where the statute imposed a duty) or in which the exercise of a power or discretion did not involve "policy" matters and was so unreasonable as to fall outside the scope of the power or discretion, then, in deciding whether a duty of care is owed in a particular case the courts apply normal principles,[98] but with particular regard to the statute which is the source of the duty, power or discretion.[99] In cases concerning the exercise of statutory powers, a duty of care could only arise in exceptional circumstances.[1]

---

be more extensive government regulation. Others may be of a different view, for any one of a number of reasons, perhaps including cost. Courts have long recognised the inappropriateness of judicial resolution of complaints about the reasonableness of governmental conduct where such complaints are political in nature."

[96] In a sense every decision involves an element of discretion so this cannot be a decisive test: see *Barrett v Enfield LBC* [2001] 2 A.C. 550 at 571D–E, *per* Lord Slynn; *Phelps v Hillingdon LBC* [2001] 2 A.C. 619 at 652H–653D, *per* Lord Slynn; and *Carty v Croydon LBC* [2005] EWCA Civ 19; [2005] 1 W.L.R. 2312 at [25]–[32], *per* Dyson L.J.

[97] In *X (minors) v Bedfordshire CC* [1995] 2 A.C. 633 at 736A–737E, Lord Browne-Wilkinson considered the extent to which a decision involving the exercise of discretion might be justiciable in the law of negligence. If the decision was not so unreasonable as to fall outside the ambit provided by the statute (i.e. if it was not unreasonable in the *Associated Provincial Picture Houses Ltd v Wednesbury Corp* [1948] 1 K.B. 223 sense), then it was authorised by Parliament and so not actionable (this reflects Lord Browne-Wilkinson's second class: see para.2–082 above). In *Barratt v Enfield BC* [2001] 2 A.C. 550 at 570D–571C, Lord Slynn queried whether it was strictly necessary to show *Wednesbury* unreasonableness, but said that if the test were instead whether there had been "no real exercise of the discretion", then this was "very much the administrative law test". In the same case Lord Hutton observed at 586C–F that where the claim arose from the exercise of a power (as opposed to a decision whether to exercise it) then the common law concept of negligence was to be preferred to the public law concept of *Wednesbury* unreasonableness.

[98] In *X (minors) v Bedfordshire CC* [1995] 2 A.C. 633 at 739A–D, when considering whether a common law duty of care arose in the operational sphere, Lord Browne-Wilkinson said that the usual principles in the threefold test should be applied, albeit that particular regard had to be had to the statutory framework: *ibid.* at 739A–D. Lord Browne-Wilkinson also attached significance to the fact that in the nearest analogies, *Hill v Chief Constable of West Yorkshire* [1989] A.C. 53; and *Yuen Ken Yeu v Att-Gen of Hong Kong* [1988] A.C. 175, no duty of care had been found: *ibid.* at 751C–G. The threefold test was also applied in *Barratt v Enfield LBC* [2001] 2 A.C. 550 at 572D, *per* Lord Slynn.
Lord Nicholls provided a helpful summary of earlier authority as to proximity in his dissenting speech in *Stovin v Wise* [1996] A.C. 923 at 937B–F.

[99] *Stovin v Wise* [1996] A.C. 923 at 952F–953A. Lord Nicholls, who dissented as to the result, expressed the position in these terms at 935B–C:
"Public authorities operate within a statutory framework. Since the will of the legislature is paramount in this field, the common law should not impose a concurrent duty inconsistent with this framework. A common law duty must not be inconsistent with the performance by the authority of its statutory duties and powers in the manner intended by Parliament, or contrary in any other way to the presumed legislative intention."

[1] *Stovin v Wise* [1996] A.C. 923. Giving the speech with which the majority agreed, Lord Hoffmann stated that the policy/operation distinction (which had first been formulated in *Anns*: see fn.94, above) was an inadequate tool. He considered that the Canadian cases (*Just v British Columbia* (1989) 64 D.L.R. (4th) 689; and *Brown v British Columbia (Minister of Transportation and Highways)* (1994) 112 D.L.R. (4th) 1) which proceeded on that basis were unsatisfactory. After reviewing the public

(5) Finally, it should be borne in mind that once a decision has been taken to exercise a statutory power, then the exercise of it may give rise to circumstances in which the public body or authority owes a duty of care to the claimant.[2] In such cases, if a duty of care would be owed if the relevant acts were performed otherwise than in the exercise of a statutory power, a duty of care is not excluded because the acts were performed in the exercise of such a power.[3, 4] However, it will still be necessary to consider whether a duty of care was owed to the given claimant.[5]

Vicarious liability. The fact that a public authority or body does not itself owe   **2–087**
a duty of care does not mean that the employees through whom it performs its functions do not themselves owe duties of care for breach of which their employer may be vicariously liable.[6] So, if an employee gives advice in circumstances akin to those in *Hedley Byrne & Co Ltd v Heller & Partners Ltd*,[7] he will owe a duty of care and his employer will be vicariously liable for his negligence.[8] However, it will always be necessary to consider the employee's purpose in giving advice and whether it would tend to discourage the performance of the statutory duty being performed.[9] Thus in *X (minors) v Bedfordshire*

---

authority line of cases and observing that the fact that Parliament had conferred a discretion rather than imposed a statutory duty indicated that Parliament had not intended to create a common law right of compensation, Lord Hoffmann concluded:

> "In summary, therefore, I think that the minimum preconditions for basing a duty of care upon the existence of a statutory power, if it can be done at all, are, first, that it would in the circumstances have been irrational not to have exercised the power, so that there was in effect a public law duty to act, and secondly, that there are exceptional grounds for holding that the policy of the statute requires compensation to be paid to persons who suffer loss because the power was not exercised." [1996] A.C. 923 at 953D–E.

Lord Hoffmann went on to find that neither condition was satisfied in that case.

[2] *Barratt v Enfield LBC* [2001] 2 A.C. 550 at 577D–578E, *per* Lord Hutton; citing *Fisher v Ruislip-Northwood UDC* [1954] K.B. 584; *Dorset Yacht Co Ltd v Home Office* [1970] A.C. 1004; and *Sutherland Shire Council v Heyman* (195) 157 C.L.R. 424. See, e.g. *Kent v Griffiths* [2001] Q.B. 36, CA: ambulance service, having accepted an emergency call, owed a duty of care (no question arose as to the adequacy or allocation of resources). See also *A v Essex CC* [2003] EWCA Civ 1848; [2004] 1 W.L.R. 1881 where the Court of Appeal held that, although a local authority adoption agency owed no general duty of care when deciding what information to provide to prospective adopters, once a decision had been made to provide information, then there was a duty of care to ensure that the information was both given and received.

[3] *Phelps v Hillingdon LBC* [2001] 2 A.C. 619 at 653C–D, *per* Lord Slynn.

[4] For an alternative approach see the judgment of McHugh J. in *Crimmins v Stevedoring Industry Finance Committee* (1999) 200 C.L.R. 1 at [39]–[40].

[5] See, for example, *D v East Berkshire Community Health NHS Trust* [2005] UKHL 23; [2005] 2 A.C. 373, where it was held that healthcare professionals and social workers owed no duty of care to the parents of children who might have been abused by those parents. (See also *D v Bury MBC* [2006] EWCA Civ 1; [2006] 1 W.LR. 917; and *Sullivan v Moody* [2001] H.C.A. 59; (2001) 183 A.L.R. 404.)

[6] *Lister v Hesley Hall Ltd* [2001] UKHL 22; [2001] 2 A.C. 215.

[7] [1964] A.C. 465.

[8] *Welton v North Cornwall DC* [1997] 1 W.L.R. 570: environmental health officer taking it upon himself to advise guest house owners as to works needed to comply with statutory requirements.

[9] *Harris v Evans* [1998] 1 W.L.R. 1285: health and safety inspector reporting to local authorities did not owe a duty of care to the proprietors of the business about which he reported. His statements were made to the authorities to advise them and it would discourage proper reporting if the subjects of reports could bring claims for damages. The distinction between this case and *Welton* is narrow. It is for the defendant to establish that the imposition of a duty of care would have this effect and it will

CC[10] claims in the child care cases based on breach of duties of care owed by social workers and psychiatrists were struck out because the individuals concerned were working for and reporting to their employer.[11] There was also obvious potential for conflict between parents and social services in such cases.[12] However, in the education cases, there was an arguable case that educational psychologists owed duties of care: in contrast to the child care cases, there was no conflict between their duty to their employer and a duty of care owed to the children referred to them.[13] The willingness of the courts to recognise vicarious liability provides a means of redress which their reluctance to find direct duties of care would otherwise deny. Although it might be thought that this consequence would weigh against finding vicarious liability, in fact it is the availability of redress by way of vicarious liability which makes it easier to find against direct liability.[14]

2-088   **Supervisors and regulators.** The banking and financial services fields are and have been subject to regulation and supervision in a number of common law jurisdictions for some time.[15] When a financial institution or bank fails, customers who suffer losses will often complain that the regulator failed them. Given that at least one of the purposes of the regulatory/supervisory systems is to provide protection to investors, it might be thought that the regulator would owe investors a duty of care in relation to the exercise of its powers and functions. However, such claims have not met with success. In *Yuen Kun Yeu v Att-Gen of Hong Kong*[16] the claimants were depositors in a registered deposit-taking company, which had been run fraudulently. They brought a claim against the Commissioner of Deposit-Taking Companies, established under an Ordinance whose purposes included "to make provision for the protection of persons who deposit money". The Privy Council struck out the claim. Having criticised the *Anns* test,[17] the Privy Council turned to the question whether there were sufficiently

---

only be possible to do so in exceptional cases: *Phelps v Hillingdon LBC* [2001] 2 A.C. 619 at 653E–F, *per* Lord Slynn.

[10] [1995] 2 A.C. 633: see para.2–041, above.

[11] *ibid.* at 752D–753F, *per* Lord Browne-Wilkinson:

"In my judgment in the present cases, the social workers and the psychiatrist did not, by accepting the instructions of the local authority, assume any duty of care to the plaintiff children. The professionals were employed or retained to advise the local authority in relation to the well-being of the plaintiffs but not to advise or treat the plaintiffs."

(See also *Kapfunde v Abbey National Plc* [1999] I.C.R. 1, discussed in para.2–116, below.)

[12] *Phelps v Hillingdon LBC* [2001] 2 A.C. 619 at 674G–H, *per* Lord Clyde; and *D v East Berkshire Community Health NHS Trust* [2005] UKHL 23; [2005] 2 A.C. 373. There should be no potential for conflict between the interests of children and the interests of local authorities.

[13] *X (Minors) v Bedfordshire CC* [1995] 2 A.C. 633 at 764F–764B. Despite the misgivings expressed in *Barrett v Enfield LBC* [2001] 2 A.C. 550 at 557G–558B by Lord Browne-Wilkinson about this part of his speech, it was vindicated in *Phelps v Hillingdon LBC* [2001] 2 A.C. 619.

[14] *Phelps v Hillingdon LBC* [2001] 2 A.C. at 671A–D, *per* Lord Clyde. It is submitted, however, that the readiness to recognise vicarious liability undermines many of the "policy" considerations said to militate against direct liability. The recognition of duties of care owed by employees for advice given presents its own difficulties: see para.2–095, below.

[15] See Ch.14 for the position in the United Kingdom under the Financial Services and Markets Act 2000.

[16] [1988] A.C. 175.

[17] See para.2–030, fn.78, above.

close and direct relations between the Commissioner and would-be depositors to give rise to a duty of care. While loss by would-be depositors was foreseeable, the Commissioner had to balance their interests with those of existing depositors (who might be prejudiced were he to exercise his power to remove the company from the register and so, in effect, put it out of business).[18] This did not suggest an intention by the legislature that the Commissioner should owe would-be depositors a duty of care. The Commissioner had no wider powers to control the day-to-day management of the company[19] and the claimants were members of a very wide class of those inhabitants of Hong Kong who might deposit money with the company.[20] The failure of the claim in *Yuen Kun Yeu v Att-Gen of Hong Kong*[21] and the striking out of the similar claim in the later decision of the Privy Council in *Davis v Radcliffe*[22] provide a useful warning of the difficulties of establishing a duty of care where the statutory duty, power or function is for the general benefit of society or of a wide section of society.[23]

(ii) *Directors and Employees*

Many professions are allowed to provide their services by way of limited liability companies, e.g. architects, engineers, surveyors, valuers, insurance brokers and financial advisers. However, the actual work must be done by natural persons, either directors or other employees. Other professionals provide services through their employees, themselves often professionally qualified. In such cases there will be no contract between the client and the employee. In cases in which the limited company or other principal is solvent and insured the position of the directors or employees is rarely controversial. However, that is not always the case and it is not uncommon for a claimant to allege that a director or employee owed a duty of care in tort. **2–089**

Limited liability companies. In *Williams v Natural Life Health Foods Ltd*[24] advice as to taking a franchise of a health food shop was given by a limited company acting principally by its managing director, whose personal experience was trumpeted in the company's brochure and who played a prominent part in producing detailed financial projections provided to the claimant. The claimant claimed that the managing director owed him a duty of care. The House of Lords **2–090**

---

[18] *cf. Davis v Radcliffe* [1990] 1 W.L.R. 821 at 827A–D where the Privy Council held that the need to balance competing interests was also a factor weighing against the existence of a duty of care.
[19] *Dorset Yacht Co Ltd v Home Office* [1970] A.C. 1004 was distinguished on this ground. The degree of control exercised by a defendant over a third party usually has to be high for a defendant to owe a duty of care to prevent the third party causing loss and damage: see *Smith v Leurs* (1945) 70 C.L.R. 256; and *Modbury Triangle Shopping Centre Pty Ltd v Anzil* [2000] H.C.A. 61. See generally *Smith v Littlewoods Organisation Ltd* [1987] A.C. 241 (particularly at 270–274).
[20] *cf. Davis v Radcliffe* [1990] 1 W.L.R. 821, where the Finance Board of the Isle of Man was operating a licensing system "in the interests of the public as a whole" (at 827A).
[21] [1988] A.C. 175.
[22] [1990] 1 W.L.R. 821.
[23] See also (1) *Cooper v Hobart* (2001) D.L.R. (4th) 193, Supreme Court of Canada: claim against registrar appointed under Mortgage Brokers Act struck out; (2) *Att-Gen v Carter* [2003] 2 N.Z.L.R. 160, New Zealand Court of Appeal: claim against shipping regulators struck out following *Yuen Kun Yeu v Att Gen of Hong Kong* [1988] A.C. 175; *Fleming v Securities Commission* [1995] 2 N.Z.L.R. 514; and *Cooper v Hobart* (2001) 206 D.L.R. (4th) 193.
[24] [1998] 1 W.L.R. 890.

reversed the decision of the trial judge and Court of Appeal that he did.[25] Lord Steyn, who gave the only reasoned speech, agreed with Sir Patrick Russell, who dissented in the Court of Appeal, that it was an inevitable feature of a one-man company that the managing director would be the person who was possessed of the qualities essential for the functioning of the company, but that this did not mean that the managing director assumed personal responsibility to the company's customers. Nor did the fact that the company's brochure placed great emphasis on the managing director's experience and expertise. He held that the managing director had not "crossed the line" and assumed personal responsibility.[26] Lord Steyn placed particular reliance on two judgments of La Forest J. in the Supreme Court of Canada.

2–091   **The Canadian cases.**[27] In the first, *London Drugs Ltd v Kuehne & Nagel International Ltd*,[28] the claimant delivered a valuable transformer to the first defendant, a limited company, under a contract which limited the company's liability to $40. It was then damaged through the negligence of the company's employees. They were also sued. The majority held that the employees owed a duty of care, but that their liability was limited by the terms of the contract between their employer and the claimant. La Forest J. dissented on the question of duty. He said[29]:

> "In my view, where the plaintiff has suffered injury to his property pursuant to contractual relations with the company, he can be considered to have chosen to deal *with a company*.
>   A plaintiff who chooses to enter into a course of dealing with a limited liability company can, in most cases, be held to have voluntarily assumed the risk of the company being unable to satisfy a judgment in contract or for vicarious liability. That the customer takes this risk in matters of contract has been accepted since *Salomon v A. Salomon and Co* [1897] A.C. 22, HL. Now that many contractual claims are bought concurrently as tort claims, the customer should not be able to shift this risk to the employee by claiming in tort."

La Forest J. agreed with the other members of the Court in the second decision, *Edgeworth Construction Ltd v ND Lea & Associates Ltd*.[30] That was a claim by a contractor who had entered a road building contract, the specifications and drawings for which had been prepared by a limited company of engineers. The contractor sued both the limited company and the individual engineers who affixed their seals to the drawings. The claim against the individuals was struck

---

[25] [1998] 1 W.L.R. 890. See also the decision of the New Zealand Court of Appeal in *Trevor Ivory Ltd v Anderson* [1992] 2 N.Z.L.R. 517.

[26] See also *Hale v Guildarch Ltd* [1999] P.N.L.R. 44.

[27] See also *Sealand of the Pacific v Robert C McHaffie Ltd* (1974) 51 D.L.R. (3d) 702 (British Columbia Court of Appeal: an architect employed by a limited company did not owe a personal duty of care to a third party with whom the company entered a contract).

[28] (1992) 97 D.L.R. (4th) 261.

[29] *ibid.* at 289d and 290h–291a.

[30] [1993] 3 S.C.R. 206.

out. In *Williams v Natural Life Health Foods Ltd*,[31] Lord Steyn set out this passage from the judgment of La Forest J.[32]:

> "The situation of the individual engineers is quite different. While they may, in one sense, have expected that persons in the position of the appellant would rely on their work, they would expect that the appellant would place reliance on their firm's pocketbook and not theirs for indemnification; see *London Drugs*, at 386–387. Looked at the other way, the appellant could not reasonably rely for indemnification on the individual engineers. It would have to show that it was relying on the particular expertise of an individual engineer without regard to the corporate character of the engineering firm. It would seem quite unrealistic, as my colleague observes, to hold that the mere presence of an individual engineer's seal was sufficient indication of personal reliance (or for that matter voluntary assumption of risk)."

In *Williams v Natural Health Life Foods Ltd*,[33] Lord Steyn said that this reasoning was "instructive" and "consistent with English law".

Assumption of personal responsibility and reasonable reliance. The 2–092 approach of La Forrest J. is instructive in a number of respects. First, in the explicit recognition that, usually, a person who agrees to deal with a limited company takes the risk that the company will prove to be insolvent. Analysis in terms of which party assumed a particular risk is or should be an important feature of the law of negligence. Secondly, in recognising that the relevant reliance had to be not on the individual director or employee's skill or ability, but on his pocket. Thirdly, in approaching the question both from the perspective of the individual employees as well as from that of the claimants—what was it reasonable for the defendant employees to assume in terms of their personal responsibility towards the claimants?[34] It would be reasonable for them to assume that they would be personally liable if they had done something which, viewed objectively, indicated that they were assuming direct responsibility to the claimants. In general, directors and employees should not be taken to have assumed personal responsibility, at least in cases of economic loss,[35] although there will be occasions on which they have done so.[36]

Employees of firms and individuals. Where the employer is not a limited 2–093 liability company, then one element in the reasoning of La Forest J. is not present, at least in the same terms. There has been no assumption by the claimant of the risk of dealing with a limited liability company. However, it could be said

---

[31] [1998] 1 W.L.R. 803 at 836H–837A.
[32] [1993] 3 S.C.R. 206 at 212.
[33] [1998] 1 W.L.R. 830 at 837B.
[34] *cf.* the approach of Evans J. in *MacMillan v AW Knott Becker Scott Ltd* [1990 1 Lloyd's Rep. 98.
[35] In cases of personal injury, directors and employees have no special protection: see, e.g. *Alder v Dickson* [1955] 1 Q.B. 158, discussed by Hobhouse L.J. in *Perrett v Collins* [1998] 2 Lloyd's Rep. 255.
[36] As in *Fairline Shipping Corp v Adamson* [1975] Q.B. 180. In *Partco Group Ltd v Wragg* [2002] EWCA Civ 594; [2002] 2 B.C.L.C. 323, Leveson J. and Court of Appeal held that there was an arguable case that company directors had assumed personal responsibility for statements made during friendly takeover.

a client who contracts with a firm or principal is generally to be taken to be relying on that firm or principal, rather than on its employees. As Lord Hoffmann observed in *Standard Chartered Bank v Pakistan National Shipping Corp (Nos 2 and 4)*,[37] the decision in *Williams v Natural Health Life Foods Ltd*[38] was to the effect that, "just as an agent can contract on behalf of another without incurring personal liability, so an agent can assume responsibility on behalf of another for the purposes of the *Hedley Byrne* rule without assuming personal responsibility". It is not limited to company law.[39] Moreover, while the fact that a defendant has or does not have insurance is not, apparently, a relevant consideration when considering whether to impose a duty of care,[40] the fact that the client, employer and employee were proceeding (or objectively are to be taken to have been proceeding) on the basis that the employer and not the employee would have professional indemnity insurance would, on the approach of La Forest J., be a telling consideration against finding that the employee personally owed a duty of care, absent some further factor indicating personal responsibility.[41]

2-094   ***Merrett v Babb.*** The position of an employed valuer who personally signs a mortgage valuation which his employer has been retained to provide was considered by the Court of Appeal in *Merrett v Babb*.[42] The employer in that case was a firm, not a limited liability company. The mortgage valuation was signed by the defendant employee personally and contained the statement required by s.13 of the Building Societies Act 1986 that he was not disqualified from providing a valuation. It was not seen by the claimant, whose claim was based on *Smith v Eric S Bush*.[43] The majority[44] held that a duty of care was owed by the defendant employee, Mr Babb. His position was said to be indistinguishable from that of Mr Lee, the individual surveyor in *Harris v Wyre Forest DC*, the case heard at the same time as *Smith v Eric S Bush*. Since Mr Lee had been held to owe a duty of care (for breach of which his local authority employer was vicariously liable), so did Mr Babb.

2-095   This decision illustrates the potential danger of finding that individual employees personally owe duties of care when discharging duties on behalf of their employers in cases where individual employees are not separately represented

---

[37] [2002] UKHL 43; [2003] 1 A.C. 959 at [21]; see also [23].
[38] [1998] 1 W.L.R. 830.
[39] *BP Plc v Aon Ltd* [2006] EWHC 424, Comm; [2006] Lloyd's Rep. I.R. 577, (Colman J.) at [80].
[40] See, e.g. *Watson v British Boxing Board of Control Ltd* [2001] Q.B. 1134 at 1163, *per* Lord Philips M.R., agreeing with Buxton L.J. in *Perrett v Collins* [1998] 2 Lloyd's Rep. 255 at 276–277. But see *Customs and Excise Commissioners v Barclays Bank Plc* [2006] UKHL 28; [2006] 1 W.L.R. 1 at [35], *per* Lord Mance where he considered that the availability of insurance was a relevant factor when considering whether it was fair, just and reasonable to find that a duty of care in tort was owed.
[41] These considerations do not arise in claims in the tort of deceit: *Standard Chartered Bank v Pakistan Shipping Corp (Nos 2 and 4)* [2002] UKHL 43; [2003] 1 A.C. 959. See also the judgment of Toulson J. in *Noel v Poland* [2002] 2 B.C.L.C. 645.
[42] [2001] EWCA Civ 214; [2001] Q.B. 1174.
[43] [1990] 1 A.C. 831. See Ch.10, paras 10–046 to 10–051, below.
[44] May L.J. and Wilson J. Aldous L.J. dissented.

and the employer is solvent.[45] Those decisions are then found to have unintended consequences. *Merrett v Babb*[46] is best explained as a decision on the special facts involved in cases such as *Smith v Eric S Bush*.[47] However, it should not be applied more generally and the conflict between it and *Williams v Natural Health Life Foods Ltd*[48] should be resolved.[49]

(iii) *Sub-agents and Sub-contractors*

Sometimes a professional will not discharge his obligations to his client person-   **2–096** ally or by an employee, but by sub-contracting with another professional. In such cases the question can arise as to whether the sub-contractor/agent owes a duty of care in tort to the ultimate client. In considering the duties owed by sub-agents to the ultimate principal the editor of *Bowstead & Reynolds on Agency* says that the position in English law cannot be stated as clearly as it can for the United States, "because of the existence of old case law which has not been reconsidered".[50] Older authority suggests that no duty of care is owed,[51] but must be treated with caution in the light of subsequent developments and in particular of the decision of the House of Lords in *Henderson v Merrett Syndicates Ltd.*[52] The finding as to concurrent liability was merely part of the reasoning leading to the conclusion that a managing agent at Lloyd's owed a duty of care not only to direct names (with whom he had contracted), but also to indirect names, who had contracted with a members' agent who had in turn contracted with the managing agent.[53] The members' agents remained contractually liable to these indirect

---

[45] See, e.g. the decision of the Court of Appeal in *Punjab National Bank v de Boinville* [1992] 1 W.L.R. 1138 (discussed in Ch.16, para.16–028) that insurance brokers employed by two limited companies themselves owed a duty of care to the claimant. This is hard to reconcile with *Williams v Natural Health Life Foods Ltd* [1998] 1 W.L.R. 830. In *Punjab National Bank v de Boinville* the individuals were not separately represented. See also the cases on the vicarious liability of public bodies and authorities discussed in para.2–087, above and *Smith v Eric S Bush* [1990] 1 A.C. 831 itself.

[46] [2001] EWCA Civ 214; [2001] Q.B. 1174.

[47] [1990] 1 A.C. 831. See *Williams v Natural Health Life Foods Ltd* [1998] 1 W.L.R. 830 at 837D, *per* Lord Steyn; and *Merrett v Babb* [2001] EWCA Civ 214, paras 23 and 40, *per* May L.J. and para.58, *per* Wilson J.

[48] [1998] 1 W.L.R. 830.

[49] In *Yazhou Travel Investment Co Ltd v Bateson Starr (a firm)* [2005] P.N.L.R. 31 H.H. Judge GP Muttrie, sitting as a Deputy High Court Judge in the Court of First Instance, High Court of Hong Kong Special Administrative Region, held that employed solicitors personally owed a duty of care in tort to clients of their employer firm for whom they acted. The client had dealt exclusively with the employees and had had no dealings with any partner in the firm. In the circumstances it was held that the employees had assumed responsibility to the client. On the approach taken by the judge the individual professional who undertakes work for a client who has contracted with his employer will almost invariably owe a duty of care in tort to the client. It is suggested, however, that the analysis confuses the acceptance by an employee of a task which his employer has contracted to perform for a client and acceptance by the employee of personal responsibility to the client, a key factor referred to in the speech of Lord Steyn in *Williams v Natural Health Life Foods Ltd* [1998] 1 W.L.R. 830 at 837B and the speech of Lord Mance in *Custom and Excise Commissioners v Barclays Bank Plc* [2006] UKHL 28; [2006] 3 W.L.R. 1 at [93].

[50] *Bowstead & Reynolds on Agency* (17th edn), para.5–012.

[51] See, e.g. *Calico Printers Association v Barclays Bank Ltd* (1931) 145 L.T. 151.

[52] [1995] 2 A.C. 145. See para.2–046, above and, in relation to concurrent liability, para.2–108, below.

[53] See Ch.19, paras 19–014 and 19–015, below for an explanation of the relevant factual background.

names for loss suffered as a result of any want of care on the part of the managing agent. The House of Lords allowed the indirect names to sue the managing agents for the same loss. In rejecting the argument on behalf of the managing agents that the parties had agreed to structure their relationships by a chain of contracts so as to exclude any duty of care on the part of managing agents to indirect names, Lord Goff gave this guidance for future cases:

> "I wish however to add that I strongly suspect that the situation which arises in the present case is most unusual; and that in many cases in which a contractual chain comparable to that in the present case is constructed it may well prove to be inconsistent with an assumption of responsibility which has the effect of, so to speak, short circuiting the contractual structure so put in place by the parties. It cannot therefore be inferred from the present case that other sub-agents will be held directly liable to the agent's principal in tort."[54]

Lord Goff then went on to give the example of a subcontractor in a building contract who would not ordinarily be liable to the employer for economic loss.[55]

2–097　　　Lord Goff had approached the question by considering whether a duty of care was owed without considering the impact of the contractual context and then, having concluded that, subject to consideration of the contractual context, a duty was owed, he found nothing in the contractual context to displace that conclusion. This was because the contractual and tortious duties were not materially different.[56] There was no conflict between the contractual and tortious duties.[57] "The Names were not seeking to impose on the managing agents any obligation beyond that which the retainer itself required to be performed."[58] The managing agents were writing insurance contracts on behalf of direct and indirect names and it was they who would suffer loss in the first instance should the managing agents be careless. As for other situations, the position has been summarised in these terms by Lord Browne-Wilkinson in *White v Jones*[59]:

> " . . . the fact that the defendant assumed to act in the plaintiffs' affairs pursuant to a contract with a third party is not necessarily incompatible with the finding that, by so acting, the defendant also entered into a special relationship with the plaintiff . . . this factor should not lead to the conclusion that a duty of care will necessarily be found to exist even where there is a contractual chain of obligations designed by the parties to regulate their dealings."

2–098　　　**Competing considerations.** In deciding whether a duty of care is owed, the courts have to balance competing considerations. On the one hand, the sub-agent

---

[54] [1995] 2 A.C. 145 at 195G–H.
[55] Lord Goff approved the decision of the Court of Appeal in *Simaan General Contracting Co v Pilkington Glass Ltd (No.2)* [1988] Q.B. 758.
[56] [1995] 2 A.C. 145 at 195A.
[57] *X (minors) v Bedfordshire CC* [1995] 2 A.C. 633 at 739D, *per* Lord Browne-Wilkinson.
[58] *ibid.* at 753D.
[59] [1995] 2 A.C. 207 at 274D–E.

or contractor will be providing part of the service which the intermediate agent or contractor has promised to provide to the ultimate client. He will owe a contractual duty to exercise reasonable skill and care and a concurrent tortious duty. There should be little scope for conflict between those duties and a duty of care owed to the ultimate client. On the other hand, there is no direct contractual relationship and the parties have chosen to regulate their relations by a chain of contracts. The client has his remedy against the intermediate contractor or agent, who will in turn have recourse against the sub-contractor or agent should he fail to exercise reasonable skill and care.[60] Moreover the relations and dealings between two professional firms may not readily translate into a duty of care owed to the client of one firm.[61]

However, in each case it is necessary to analyse the facts to see whether there **2–099** has been an assumption of direct responsibility by the sub-agent to the principal. So, in cases in which there is direct communication and where the agent's role was (and was always intended to be) limited, a duty of care may be found. It would be wrong to approach claims in negligence by principals against sub-agents on the basis that the mere fact of a contractual chain excluded the possibility of a duty of care.[62]

(iv) *Immunity*

By tradition certain professions enjoyed immunity from suit on the grounds of **2–100** public interest. The development of the law of tort and a reappraisal of the public interest have led to the narrowing of such immunity. In England and Wales the immunity of advocates was first limited to work done in court and to a small category of pre-trial work and was then removed entirely.[63] The immunity of expert witnesses is now limited to work done in court and to related pre-trial work.[64] Architects are no longer immune from suit in respect or certificates

---

[60] See, e.g. *Pacific Associates Inc v Baxter* [1990] 1 Q.B. 993; and Stapleton, "Duty of care: peripheral parties and alternative opportunities for deterrence" (1995) 111 L.Q.R. 301.

[61] See, e.g. *Pangood Ltd v Barclay Brown & Co Ltd* [1999] Lloyd's Rep. I.R. 405, discussed in Ch.16, para.16–035.

[62] See *Riyad Bank v Ahli United Bank (UK) Plc* [2006] EWCA Civ 780; [2006] 2 Lloyd's Rep. 292; and *BP Plc v Aon Ltd* [2006] EWHC 424, Comm; [2006] Lloyd's Rep. I.R. 577 (Coleman J.) for cases in which, on the particular facts, it was held that the sub-contractor/sub-agent defendants owed a duty of care to the principal notwithstanding the interposition of a contractual chain.

[63] *Arthur J Hall & Co v Simons* [2002] 1 A.C. 615. See Chs 11 and 12, para.11–112 and para.12–009. Advocates should continue to enjoy the same immunity as others from any action brought against them on the ground that things said or done in proceedings were said or done maliciously or falsely: *Taylor v Director of Public Prosecutions* [1999] 2 A.C. 177; and *Darker v Chief Constable of West Midlands* [2001] 1 A.C. 435.

Advocates retain immunity in Scotland: *Wright v Paton Farrell* [2003] P.N.L.R. 20 (T.G. Coutts Q.C., sitting as a temporary judge in the Outer House). The same is true in Australia (*D'Orta-Ekenaike v Victoria Legal Aid* [2005] H.C.A. 12), but not in New Zealand (*Lai v Chamberlains* [2006] NZSC 70).

[64] *Palmer v Durnford Ford* [1992] 1 Q.B. 483 at 488. Other aspects of the decision in *Palmer* (but not this aspect) were doubted by the Court of Appeal in *Walpole v Partridge & Wilson* [1994] Q.B. 106 at 123–125. See further *Stanton v Callaghan* [1999] P.N.L.R. 116: expert immune both in respect of his evidence at trial and in respect of the contents of a report prepared for exchange, but not for advice given as to the merits of his client's claim.

negligently given.[65] Similarly, "mutual valuers" have lost their immunity.[66] There are suggestions in the authorities that the surviving immunities may be further cut down, or even abolished, in the future.[67]

2–101   Certainly when new situations arise in which there is a case for immunity on grounds of public interest, there is now a tendency to deal with the matter under the rubric of duty of care. Thus in *Yuen Kun Yeu v Att-Gen of Hong Kong*,[68] the Privy Council acknowledged that there was a case for giving the Commissioner of Deposit-Taking Companies immunity on the grounds of public policy, but they based their decision on the absence of any relevant duty of care. Likewise, in *Hill v Chief Constable of West Yorkshire*,[69] Lord Keith (with whom Lords Brandon, Oliver and Goff agreed) considered that the police should be immune from claims of the kind made by Mrs Hill, on grounds similar to those justifying advocates' immunity. But he based his decision on the absence of any duty of care owed by the police to the deceased.[70]

2–102   The concept of immunity as a device to protect the judicial process[71] serves a useful function. It is submitted that immunity should now be limited to the established categories. The question whether or not a new class of persons should be "immune" in respect of specified activities (e.g. the fire service in putting out fires) involves consideration of substantially the same factors as the "just and reasonable" question in the threefold test. It is unhelpful for the courts to consider (and indeed for advocates to argue) the same matters twice under different headings. The concept of immunity evolved before the courts had developed a satisfactory framework within which to assess all factors relevant to the existence and scope of a duty of care. Now that such a framework exists, the concept of immunity as a separate ground for denying liability in new situations which arise is otiose. Thus, the liability of fire brigades was extensively reviewed by the Court of Appeal in *Capital and Counties Plc v Hampshire CC*.[72] The ratio of the decision that the fire brigade owed no tortious duty in respect of any failure to fight fires adequately was that there was no assumption of responsibility towards the property owners. It is submitted that the court was right to base its decision on the established tests for duty of care, rather than on immunity (which the fire brigades were claiming). The principles governing duty of care are now sufficiently developed that it is unnecessary to create new categories of immunity.

---

[65] See Ch.9, para.9–255.

[66] See Ch.10, below; *Arenson v Arenson* [1977] A.C. 405; *Palacath Ltd v Flanagan* [1985] 2 All E.R. 161.

[67] In *Arenson v Arenson* [1977] A.C. 405 Lord Kilbrandon stated that even arbitrators are not immune from suit (at 430–431). Lords Salmon and Fraser suggested that this may be the case, but expressed no firm opinion on the point (at 440D–E and 442D). But see now s.29 of the Arbitration Act 1996. See also *Darker v Chief Constable of the West Midlands* [2001] 1 A.C. 435, where the House of Lords held that witness immunity in relation to evidence given or to be given in court proceedings did not extend to the earlier investigative process undertaken by the police.

[68] [1988] A.C. 175 at 198. See para.2–088, above.

[69] [1989] A.C. 53 at 63–64. See also *Brooks v Commissioner of Police of the Metropolis* [2005] UKHL 24; [2005] 1 W.L.R. 1495.

[70] In the light of the decision of the European Court of Human Rights in *Z v United Kingdom* (2001) 34 E.H.R.R. 97, para.110, this is the better formulation: see *Brooks v Commissioner of Police of the Metropolis* [2005] UKHL 24; [2005] 1 W.L.R. 1495 at [27], *per* Lord Steyn.

[71] By freeing those involved from undue pressure and by preventing relitigation.

[72] [1997] Q.B. 1004.

(d) *Concurrent Liability, Contracts and Tortious Duties of Care*

The question whether a professional person owes a duty of care in tort to his **2–103** client, in addition to his contractual obligations, is one which exercised the courts intermittently throughout the last century and gave rise to conflicting authority.[73] The authorities relevant to each profession will be discussed in the chapters which follow. At the present stage, the topic is dealt with only at the level of generality.

(i) *Competing Considerations*

The existence of a contract under which the client pays the professional person **2–104** for his services can be said to militate in favour of imposing a tortious duty co-extensive with the contractual obligations. The relationship between the parties is a close one, and its objective is to confer a benefit (often an economic benefit) on the client. The client relies upon the professional person and the latter can readily foresee the kind of loss or damage which will ensue if he is careless. The professional person has chosen to contract with the client and so has assumed responsibility. There can be little doubt, but that if the professional were acting without charging, he would owe a duty of care in tort. On the other hand, it can be said that the existence of the contract militates against imposing a duty of care: the only practical result of imposing a concurrent duty of care is to give the client the benefit of an alternative limitation period.[74]

(ii) *Authority*

Whilst there has been strong judicial support for both sides of this debate, the **2–105** weight of authority has supported concurrent liability. In *Donoghue v Stevenson*[75] Lord Macmillan stated:

> " . . . there is the equally well-established doctrine that negligence apart from contract gives a right of action to the party injured by that negligence—and here I use the term negligence, of course, in its technical legal sense, implying a duty owed and neglected. The fact that there is a contractual relationship between the parties which may give rise to an action for breach of contract, does not exclude the co-existence of a right of action founded on negligence as between the same parties, independently of the contract, though arising out of the relationship in fact brought about by the contract. Of this the best illustration is the right of the injured railway passenger to sue the railway company either for breach of the contract of safe carriage or for negligence in carrying him."[76]

---

[73] For cases in which it was held that a professional man's liability lay only in contract, see e.g. *Jarvis v Moy, Davies, Smith, Vandervell & Co* [1936] 1 K.B. 399 (stockbrokers); *Groom v Crocker* [1939] 1 K.B. 194 (solicitors); *Bagot v Stevens Scanlan & Co Ltd* [1966] 1 Q.B. 197 (architects). For cases in which a concurrent duty of care in tort was recognised, see e.g. *Boorman v Brown* (1842) 3 Q.B. 511; and (1844) 11 Cl. & Fin. 1; *Nocton v Lord Ashburton* [1914] A.C. 932 at 956, *per* Viscount Haldane L.C.; *Esso Petroleum Co Ltd v Mardon* [1976] Q.B. 801 at 819, *per* Lord Denning M.R.; *Midland Bank Trust Co Ltd v Hett, Stubbs & Kemp* [1979] Ch. 384.

[74] See Ch.5, paras 5–031 to 5–074, below.

[75] [1932] A.C. 562.

[76] *ibid.* at 609–610.

Lord Macmillan cited the 13th edition of *Pollock on Torts*, which suggested that two previous decisions[77] of the Court of Exchequer, said to support the contrary view, had been misunderstood.

2–106   A number of more recent decisions concerning solicitors,[78] insurance brokers[79] and engineers/architects[80] either held or proceeded on the basis that there was concurrent liability in contract and tort. Concurrent liability has been accepted in principle, although it seldom arises in practice, in medical negligence cases.[81] Furthermore, in several pre-1994 duty of care cases the House of Lords indicated obiter the view that professional persons owe concurrent duties to their clients in contract and tort. In *Smith v Eric S Bush*,[82] Lord Jauncey (with whom Lords Keith and Brandon agreed), discussing the relationship between the defendant surveyors and the building society, said that the surveyors "not only entered into contractual relations with the building society but also came under a duty in tort to it to exercise reasonable care in carrying out their survey and preparing their report".[83] In *Caparo Industries Plc v Dickman*,[84] Lord Bridge (with whom Lords Roskill and Ackner agreed) began his discussion of the professional man's liability to third parties from the premise that he owed a duty in tort to his own client.[85] Finally in *Murphy v Brentwood DC*[86] Lord Keith (with whom all other Law Lords agreed) explained that the engineers' tortious liability to their clients in *Pirelli* was based upon the *Hedley Byrne* principle.[87] Logically, this must be correct. If "a relationship equivalent to contract" gives rise to a tortious duty to protect against economic loss, as Lord Devlin maintained in *Hedley Byrne*,[88] a fortiori a contractual relationship between the parties should have the same result.

2–107   The principal authority upon which opponents of concurrent liability relied was the decision of the Privy Council in *Tai Hing Cotton Mill Ltd v Liu Chong Hing Bank Ltd*.[89] Lord Scarman, giving the opinion of the Judicial Committee of the Privy Council, stated:

---

[77] *Winterbottom v Wright* (1852) 10 M. & W. 109; *Longmeid v Holliday* (1851) 6 Ex. 761.

[78] See, e.g. *Midland Bank Trust Co Ltd v Hett, Stubbs & Kemp* [1979] 1 Ch. 384; *Forster v Outred & Co* [1982] 1 W.L.R. 86; *DW Moore & Co Ltd v Ferrier* [1988] 1 W.L.R. 267; *Bell v Peter Browne & Co* [1990] 2 Q.B. 495. But see the caveat expressed by Lloyd L.J. in *Lee v Thompson* (1990) 6 P.N. 91.

[79] Set out in Ch.16, para.16–014, below. See in particular the decision of the Court of Appeal in *Forsikringsaktieselskapet Vesta v Butcher* [1989] A.C. 852 at 860B, *per* O'Connor L.J. and at 879E–F, *per* Sir Roger Ormrod.

[80] *Pirelli General Cable Works Ltd v Oscar Faber & Partners* [1983] 2 A.C. 1; *London Congregational Union Inc v Harriss & Harriss* [1988] 1 All E.R. 15. See Ch.9, paras 9–049 to 9–050, below.

[81] See Ch.13, paras 13–006 and 13–007, below.

[82] [1990] 1 A.C. 831. Discussed in para.2–030, above.

[83] *ibid.* at 870E.

[84] [1990] 2 A.C. 605. Discussed in paras 2–031 to 2–033, above.

[85] *ibid.* at 619C: "In advising the client who employs him the professional man owes a duty to exercise that standard of skill and care appropriate to his professional status and will be liable both in contract and in tort for all losses which his client may suffer by reason of any breach of that duty."

[86] [1991] 1 A.C. 398. Discussed in para.2–039, above.

[87] See the passage from Lord Keith's speech quoted in para.2–045, above.

[88] [1964] A.C. 464 at 528–529.

[89] [1986] A.C. 80.

"Their Lordships do not believe that there is anything to the advantage of the law's development in searching for a liability in tort where the parties are in a contractual relationship. This is particularly so in a commercial relationship. Though it is possible as a matter of legal semantics to conduct an analysis of the rights and duties inherent in some contractual relationships including that of banker and customer either as a matter of contract law when the question will be what, if any, terms are to be implied or as a matter of tort law when the task will be to identify a duty arising from the proximity and character of the relationship between the parties, their Lordships believe it to be correct in principle and necessary for the avoidance of confusion in the law to adhere to the contractual analysis: on principle because it is a relationship in which the parties have, subject to a few exceptions, the right to determine their obligations to each other, and for the avoidance of confusion because different consequences do follow according to whether liability arises from contract or tort, e.g. in the limitation of action."[90]

The *Tai Hing* case was an appeal from Hong Kong and it concerned the relationship of banker and customer.[91] The professional negligence cases referred to earlier in this section were not expressly disapproved. Indeed in his careful choice of words in this passage, although Lord Scarman deprecated the introduction of tortious liability in a contractual situation, he stopped short of saying that there was no such liability. The other authority sometimes relied upon by opponents of concurrent liability was *Greater Nottingham Co-operative Society Ltd v Cementation Piling and Foundations Ltd*,[92] but it is submitted that properly understood this case is authority for the proposition that a contract limits the scope of any tortious duties arising, not that it excludes such duties.

(iii) Henderson v Merrett

The issue finally arose for decision by the House of Lords in *Henderson v Merrett Syndicates Ltd*.[93] The facts are set out in para.2–046, above. In the case of the direct names there was, of course, a contract between the claimants and the managing agents. Lord Goff, with whom the other law lords agreed, considered that all the elements of a *Hedley Byrne* relationship were present. He recognised that there were two possible views about the effect of the contractual relationship: first, the view taken in France that the contract excludes a remedy in tort; secondly, the view taken in Germany that contractual and tortious claims may be concurrent. After a full analysis of the authorities and the literature, Lord Goff **2–108**

---

[90] [1986] A.C. 80 at 107B–D. This passage was considered by the Court of Appeal in *Banque Keyser Ullmann SA v Skandia (UK) Insurance Co Ltd* [1990] 1 Q.B. 665 at 800: "Lord Scarman's opinion contains a valuable warning as to the consequences of an ever-expanding field of tort. It should not be part of the general function of the law of tort to fill in contractual gaps." The same passage was considered and applied by the House of Lords in *Scally v Southern Health and Social Services Board* [1992] 1 A.C. 294 in the context of a contract of employment.

[91] Lord Scarman's point is more apposite in the commercial context than other contexts, as he himself said. In this regard, see the decisions of the Court of Appeal (both of which subsequently went to the House of Lords) in *National Bank of Greece SA v Pinios Shipping Co (No.1)* [1990] 1 A.C. 637; and *Bank of Nova Scotia v Hellenic Mutual War Risks Association (Bermuda) Ltd, The "Good Luck"* [1990] 1 Q.B. 818.

[92] [1989] Q.B. 71.

[93] [1995] 2 A.C. 145.

rejected the view that the existence of a contractual duty excluded any parallel duty in tort between the same parties.[94]

(iv) *The Scope of the Concurrent Duty*

2–109   The tortious duty arises from the relationship between the parties and the function which the professional person/firm is performing. It is a duty to use reasonable care in identified respects. Thus the tortious and contractual duties have different origins. Although concurrent, these duties are not necessarily co-extensive. Since the contract of retainer may impose obligations to achieve specific results[95] or may impose liability for sub-agents,[96] the concurrent duty of care imposed by the law of tort may fall short of, or be less onerous than, the contractual obligations of the retainer.

(v) *Can the Concurrent Duty in Tort be More Extensive than the Contractual Obligations?*

2–110   As a matter of principle, if the contract of retainer governs the whole of the parties' relationship, the answer should be no. If, however, the contract governs only part of the parties' dealings, in other aspects of the parties' mutual activities there may be a tortious duty of care but no parallel contractual obligation.[97] Examples might be: an architect instructed to design a project, who later gratuitously assists in marketing the building; an accountant retained to audit a company's accounts, who gives general management advice upon which the directors reasonably rely (perhaps because of the accountant's experience in that field of business). In any particular case, it will be important to establish whether the professional in effect undertook some further task or gave some advice beyond that which he had contracted to give.

(vi) *Further Significance of the Contract*

2–111   Absent some act or advice beyond the scope of his contract, it is in the contract between the professional and his client that the extent of his tortious duty will be found. His tortious duty of care will be no greater in scope than the implied contractual promise to exercise reasonable skill and care. Moreover, the contract can have greater significance: by defining what the professional is to do, it may explain the scope of his responsibility and the extent to which responsibility or risk is to rest with his client or is to be borne by others.

(e) *Liability to Third Parties*

2–112   The extent to which a professional person owes duties of care to persons other than his client has been the source of considerable litigation, as well as academic

---

[94] The decision is supported by Burrows, "Solving the Problem of Concurrent Liability" in *Understanding the Law of Obligations* (Hart Publishing, 1998). The countervailing arguments are discussed by Powell: see "Professional and client: the duty of care", published in Birks (edn), *Wrongs and Remedies in the Twenty-First Century* (Clarendon Press, 1996).
[95] See paras 2–008 to 2–010, above.
[96] See, e.g. for example, the position of the members' agents in *Aiken v Stewart Wrightson Members Agency Ltd* [1995] 1 W.L.R. 1281 at 1293–1305.
[97] *Pryke v Gibbs Hartley Cooper Ltd* [1991] 1 Lloyd's Rep. 602, discussed in Ch.16, para.16–025, below; *Holt v Payne Skillington* (1995) 77 B.L.R. 51 at 71–74.

debate, over the last 40 years. A significant proportion of the major "duty of care" cases arises in the context of professional negligence. There appear to be three reasons for this. First, much of a professional man's work consists of supplying advice or information, errors in which can lead to (sometimes extensive) financial loss. The courts' reluctance to award damages for negligence causing economic loss is reduced (but not eliminated) when negligent advice was given in a professional context. Thus a number of borderline economic loss claims arise. Secondly, because of the standards which the professions are expected to uphold and the status which they still enjoy, it is commonplace for a third party to rely upon a professional man to perform his task skilfully and impartially, even when the interests of the third party and the client are opposed. Third, professional persons are usually insured. They are therefore attractive targets. The widespread reliance upon the professions by society lies at the root of a legal problem, which is expressed in the plethora of third-party liability cases. If professional persons were liable to all who relied upon them to act skilfully, their liability would be unduly wide and oppressive. If professional men were liable only to their clients, this would be hopelessly out of step with the reasonable expectations of society.

(i) *Denning L.J.'s Dissenting Judgment*

Any general discussion of professional liability to third parties must start from the dissenting judgment of Denning L.J. in *Candler v Crane Christmas & Co.*[98] This had the distinction of being approved by the House of Lords in *Hedley Byrne & Co Ltd v Heller & Partners Ltd*[99] and in some landmark cases it has been heavily relied upon by the House of Lords.[1] In *Candler v Crane Christmas & Co*,[2] the claimant invested £2,000 in a company in reliance on the company's accounts. The company's accountants had given the claimant a copy of those accounts and discussed them with him. The accounts had been prepared negligently and the claimant lost the whole of his investment. The majority of the Court of Appeal (in a decision now overruled) held that the accountants owed no relevant duty to the claimant. In his dissenting judgment Denning L.J. said:

2–113

> "Let me now be constructive and suggest the circumstances in which I say that a duty to use care in statement does exist apart from a contract in that behalf.
>
> First, what persons are under such a duty? My answer is those persons such as accountants, surveyors, valuers and analysts, whose profession and occupation it is to examine books, accounts and other things, and to make reports on which people—other than their clients—rely in the ordinary course of business . . .[3]
>
> Secondly, to whom do these professional people owe this duty? I will take accountants, but the same reasoning applies to the others. They owe the duty, of course, to their employer or client; and also I think to any third person to whom they themselves show the accounts, or to whom they know their employer is going to show the accounts, so

---

[98] [1951] 2 K.B. 164. Discussed in Ch.17, paras 17–051 and 17–052, below.
[99] [1964] A.C. 465.
[1] See *Smith v Eric S Bush* [1990] 1 A.C. 831 at 844–845, *per* Lord Templeman and at 867–868, *per* Lord Jauncey; and *Caparo Industries Plc v Dickman* [1990] 2 A.C. 605 at 621–623, *per* Lord Bridge and at 656–657, *per* Lord Jauncey.
[2] [1951] 2 K.B. 164.
[3] *ibid.* at 179.

as to induce him to invest money or take some other action on them. But I do not think the duty can be extended still further so as to include strangers of whom they have heard nothing and to whom their employer without their knowledge may choose to show their accounts . . . . The test of proximity in these cases is: did the accountants know that the accounts were required for submission to the plaintiff and use by him? . . . [4]

Thirdly, to what transactions does the duty of care extend? It extends, I think, only to those transactions for which the accountants knew their accounts were required. For instance, in the present case it extends to the original investment of £2,000 which the plaintiff made in reliance on the accounts, because the accountants knew that the accounts were required for his guidance in making that investment; but it does not extend to the subsequent £200 which he made after he had been two months with the company. This distinction, that the duty only extends to the very transaction in mind at the time, is implicit in the decided cases."[5]

(ii) Analysis of Denning L.J.'s Dissenting Judgment

2–114   **What persons are under the duty?** Denning L.J. explained that the reason why professional men owed the duty was because their callings required particular knowledge and skill. They can, therefore, reasonably be expected to apply that knowledge and exercise that skill. Thus the level of performance required by the duty is not unreasonable or unduly burdensome. The special knowledge and skill of professional persons also go to whether it is reasonable for a third party to rely on them.[6]

2–115   **To whom is the duty owed?** The duty is owed to the client and to those third parties with whom the professional person deals directly with a view to influencing their future conduct (e.g. by making an investment or loan). It also extends to third parties to whom the professional person knows his views will be conveyed by his client for the same purpose. This limits the class of those to whom the duty is owed. It recognises that there are limits to the extent to which it is reasonable to impose a duty of care on a professional person and so limits to the extent to which it is reasonable for a third party to rely on him. It is reasonable to impose liability (and for there to be reliance) where the advice or information is conveyed by the professional person himself or by his client in circumstances in which the former is to be taken as knowing that it will be conveyed and relied on.[7]

2–116   **To what transactions does the duty of care extend?** Denning L.J. limited the duty to the specific transaction for which the professional knew that the advice or information was required. He emphasised that the purpose for which a professional man produces a report or information is of crucial importance, giving a number of examples which remain sound today:

---

[4] [1951] 2 K.B. 164 at 180–181.

[5] *ibid.* at 182–183.

[6] Denning L.J. explained that professional persons "are not liable, of course, for casual remarks made in the course of conversation, nor for other statements made outside their work, or not made in their [professional] capacity" (*ibid.* at 180).

[7] See, e.g. the decision of the High Court of Australia in *Tepko Pty Ltd v Water Board* [2001] H.C.A. 19 (reported in (2001) 75 A.L.J.R. 775), at para.47 and the decision of the New Zealand Court of Appeal in *Brownie Wills v Shrimpton* [1998] 2 N.Z.L.R. 321.

(1) "... a doctor, who negligently certifies a man to be a lunatic when he is not, is liable to him, although there is no contract in the matter, because the doctor knows that his certificate is required for the very purpose of deciding whether the man should be detained or not; but an insurance company's doctor owes no duty to the insured person, because he makes his examination only for the purposes of the insurance company: see *Everett v Griffiths* [1920] 3 K.B. 163 at 211 and 217."[8]

Over 40 years later, the Court of Appeal held that a doctor who was retained to examine the claimant for his potential employer owed no duty of care in tort[9]:

(2) "So also, a Lloyd's surveyor who, in surveying for classification purposes, negligently passes a mast as sound when it is not, is not liable to the owner for damage caused by it breaking, because the surveyor makes his survey only for the purpose of classifying the ship for the Yacht Register and not otherwise: *Humphrey v Bowers* (1929) 45 T.L.R. 297."[10]

In *The "Morning Watch"*,[11] Phillips J. held that a classification society which prepared a special survey of a vessel owed no duty of care in tort to an intending purchaser: the survey was needed if the vessel was to be kept classed at Lloyd's and the purchaser was not intended to act on the result of the survey[12]:

(3) "Again, a scientist or expert (including a marine hydrographer) is not liable to his readers for careless statements in his published works. He publishes his work simply for the purpose of giving information, and not with any particular transaction in mind at all. But when a scientist or an expert makes an investigation and report for the very purpose of a particular transaction, then, in my opinion, he is under a duty of care in respect of that transaction."[13]

The decision of the House of Lords in *Caparo Industries Plc v Dickman*[14] reflected the courts' continuing concern to limit those who could bring claims against the maker of a widely published statement (in *Caparo* the auditors of company accounts). The purpose for which the relevant statement was made in *Caparo* was found in the statutory context and provided the answer as to who could bring a claim and for what loss.

(iii) *Intended Beneficiaries*

Denning L.J. did not have in mind cases such as *White v Jones*,[15] which has **2–117** already been applied by analogy to the intended beneficiaries of pension and life assurance cover in *Gorham v British Telecommunications Plc*.[16] There will be a

---

[8] [1998] 2 N.Z.L.R. 321 at 183.
[9] *Kapfunde v Abbey National Plc* [1999] I.C.R. 1. See further *X (minors) v Bedfordshire CC* [1995] 2 A.C. 633 at 752D–753F, *per* Lord Browne-Wilkinson.
[10] [1951] 2 K.B. 164 at 183.
[11] [1990] 1 Lloyd's Rep. 547.
[12] See also *Marc Rich & Co AG v Bishop Rock Marine Co Ltd* [1996] A.C. 211.
[13] [1951] 2 K.B. 164 at 183.
[14] [1990] 2 A.C. 605. Discussed in Ch.17, paras 17–054 to 17–060, below.
[15] [1995] 2 A.C. 207, discussed in para.2–050, above. See also *Sutradhar v Natural Environmental Research Council* [2006] UKHL 33; [2006] 4 All E.R. 490.
[16] [2000] 1 W.L.R. 2129, CA.

limited number of cases in which the client engages the professional person to effect a transaction designed to benefit third parties in circumstances in which, by the time the failure to effect the transaction by reason of the professional person's breach of duty is discovered, the client is no longer in a position (as opposed to no longer willing) to effect the transaction. In those circumstances, the intended beneficiaries may be owed a duty of care by the professional person. This approach to duty of care was applied by the Court of Appeal in *Dean v Allin & Watts (a firm).*[17] The defendant solicitors had been retained to give effect to a loan transaction, it being intended by their borrower clients and by the lender (who was not their client) that the loan would be secured. They negligently failed to arrange the intended security and, when the borrowers were unable to repay the loan, were held to have owed a duty of care to the lender on the basis of assumption of responsibility. As with the will cases, by the time the problem came to light, it was too late to make good the earlier failure.[18]

(iv) *Particular Professions*

2–118   The above general principles apply to all professional persons. Cases concerning particular professions are considered in Section 2, below.

4. The Standard of Skill and Care

(a) *The Meaning of Reasonable Skill and Care*

2–119   In order to discharge the implied contractual obligation stated above[19] as well as the duty of care in tort,[20] the professional person must exercise reasonable skill and care. The cases abound with paraphrases of this term and explanations of what it means, and some of these are quoted in the chapters concerning individual professions.[21] No single formulation commands universal assent. It is common ground that the standard of skill and care must be determined by reference to members of the profession concerned, rather than the man on the Clapham omnibus. Where the authorities differ, however, is on the question whether the requisite standard is (a) that which members of the particular profession do in

---

[17] [2001] EWCA Civ 758; [2001] P.N.L.R. 39.

[18] See also *Richards (t/a Colin Richards & Co) v Hughes* [2004] EWCA Civ 266; [2004] P.N.L.R. 35, where the Court of Appeal refused to strike out a claim by the intended beneficiaries of an offshore trust established by their parents on the advice of the defendant accountant, but which failed because of his allegedly negligent advice.

[19] See para.2–007, above.

[20] There is a suggestion by Megarry J. in *Argyll v Beuselinck* [1972] 2 Lloyd's Rep. 172 at 183 that the implied contractual duty to exercise reasonable skill and care may, on occasions, impose a higher standard than the duty of care in tort. The editors are unaware of any decision in which the claimant has succeeded in contract but failed in tort by reason of this distinction. For the opposite view, see *Esso Petroleum Co Ltd v Mardon* [1976] 1 Q.B. 801 at 820A–B.

[21] See in particular Ch.13, para.13–022, below. The definition of "negligent" and "non-negligent" mistakes is a matter which occurs with particular frequency in the medical cases.

fact achieve ordinarily,[22] or (b) that which, in the opinion of the court, members of the profession ought to achieve.[23] The distinction is frequently blurred, for example, in definitions which refer to the standard attained by "reasonably competent" members of the profession.[24] These definitions, however, properly fall into the second category, since it is for the court to decide what is meant by "reasonably competent" members of the profession. They may or may not be equated with practitioners of average competence.[25]

It is submitted that of the two approaches discussed in the preceding paragraph, the second is correct.[26] Suppose a profession collectively adopts extremely lax standards in some aspect of its work. The court does not regard itself as bound by those standards and will not acquit practitioners of negligence simply because they have complied with those standards.[27] Thus, evidence as to general and approved practice, although of very considerable importance, is not automatically conclusive in every case. It was pointed out above[28] that there is a

2-120

---

[22] See, e.g. *Hunter v Hanley* (1955) S.C. 200 at 204–205; *Bolam v Friern Hospital Management Committee* [1957] 1 W.L.R. 582 at 586; *Andrew Master Hones Ltd v Cruikshank & Fairweather* [1980] R.P.C. 16 at 18, *per* Graham J.; the finding of negligence was not challenged on appeal; *Whitehouse v Jordan* [1981] 1 W.L.R. 246 at 257–258, *per* Lord Wilberforce; *Smith v Eric S Bush* [1990] 1 A.C. 831 at 851C–D; *Luxmoore-May v Messenger May Baverstock* [1990] 1 W.L.R. 1009 at 1020. This is the view adopted in *Halsbury*:

"When a person has held himself out as being capable of attaining standards of skill either in relation to the public generally, for example by driving a car, or in relation to some person for whom he is performing a service, he is required to show the skill normally possessed by persons doing that work. Doctors and members of other professions and callings must, therefore, exercise the standard of skill which is usual in their profession or calling."

Halsbury's Laws of England (4th edn), Vol.34, para.12 (reproduced by kind permission of Butterworths Ltd).

[23] See, e.g. *Midland Bank Trust Co Ltd v Hett, Stubbs & Kemp* [1979] 1 Ch. 384: "The extent of the legal duty in any given situation must, I think, be a question of law for the court" (*per* Oliver J. at 402C); *Bown v Gould & Swayne* [1996] P.N.L.R. 130.

[24] See, e.g. *Saif Ali v Sydney Mitchell & Co* [1980] A.C. 198 at 218C–E and 220D–E, *per* Lord Diplock; *Whitehouse v Jordan* [1981] 1 W.L.R. 246 at 263E–F, *per* Lord Fraser; *Eckersley v Binnie & Partners* (1988) 18 Con.L.R. 1 at 79, *per* Bingham L.J.; and *McFarlane v Wilkinson* [1997] 2 Lloyd's Rep. 259 at 275, *per* Brooke L.J.

[25] The last part of this paragraph and the first part of the next paragraph were cited with approval by Phillips J. in *Deeny v Gooda Walker* [1996] L.R.L.R. 183 at 207; and by Cresswell J. in *Henderson v Merrett Syndicates Ltd (No.2)* [1996] 1 P.N.L.R. 32 at 36.

[26] The second approach was adopted by the House of Lords in *Bolitho v City and Hackney HA* [1998] A.C. 232. At 241–242, Lord Browne-Wilkinson (with whom Lords Slynn, Nolan, Hoffmann and Clyde agreed) said: "The use of these adjectives—responsible, reasonable and respectable—all show that the court has to be satisfied that the exponents of the body of opinion relied upon can demonstrate that such opinion has a logical basis." Lord Browne-Wilkinson went on to say that it would very seldom be right for a judge to reach the conclusion that views genuinely held by a competent medical expert were unreasonable; and that the case before the House was not one of those rare cases. See further Ch.13, paras 13–032 and 13–033, below.

This decision was applied to solicitors by the Court of Appeal in *Patel v Daybells (a firm)* [2001] EWCA Civ 1229; [2002] P.N.L.R. 6. (See further Ch.11, para.11–091). It was held:

"If a practice in the profession exposes clients or patients to a foreseeable and avoidable risk, the practice may not be capable of being defended on rational grounds, and in those circumstances the fact that it is commonly (or even universally) followed will not exclude liability for negligence."

[27] Conversely, if a profession adopts unduly high standards the practitioner is not necessarily negligent if he fails to comply with them: see, e.g. *United Mills Agencies Ltd v Harvey Bray & Co* [1951] 2 Lloyd's Rep. 631 at 643, col.2.

[28] See para.2–003, above.

divergence in the approach of the courts towards the different professions. This divergence of approach is illustrated in the extent to which the courts are willing to override or disregard evidence of established practice within individual professions. This will be analysed and discussed in the chapters which follow on the individual professions. At the level of generality, however, there is now a perceptible trend on the part of the courts to question more closely the practices of the professions. This has been seen in the Lloyd's litigation in the 1990s, where the practices of part of the Lloyd's market have been closely scrutinised following the catastrophic losses suffered by many names.[29] This trend has also been seen in medical negligence cases, where the courts have made their own assessment of the reasonableness of certain clinical practices.[30]

(b) *Relevance of Defendant's Qualifications and Experience*

2–121 Another problem[31] which arises in this context is whether the professional person should be judged by reference to (a) the standard of skill and care appropriate to a practitioner with his particular qualifications and experience or (b) the standard of skill and care appropriate to his profession generally. There is some support for the former approach to be found in the earlier medical negligence cases,[32] (obiter) in a decision of Megarry J. concerning a solicitor[33] and in one decision concerning insurance brokers.[34] However, the latter view is more generally adopted.[35] In *Andrew Master Hones Ltd v Cruikshank & Fairweather*,[36] a case concerning patent agents in which this point was argued, Graham J. stated:

> "The degree of knowledge and care to be expected is thus seen to be that degree possessed by a notional duly qualified person practising that profession. The test is, therefore, if I may put it that way, an objective test referable to the notional member of the profession and not a subjective test referable to the particular professional man employed."[37]

2–122 It is submitted that neither the subjective approach nor the objective approach is wholly satisfactory. As to the subjective approach, it is unrealistic and impracticable in each case (a) to formulate a standard by reference to the defendant's

---

[29] See Ch.19.

[30] See Ch.13, paras 13–032 and 13–033, below.

[31] This is part of a wider problem (which is outside the scope of this book), namely the extent to which the personal attributes of the defendant are relevant in determining whether he was negligent. Thus the learner driver is judged by the standard of a competent and experienced driver: see *Nettleship v Weston* [1971] 2 Q.B. 691. But certain qualifications or disabilities cannot sensibly be disregarded (for example, the fact that the defendant only has one arm). There is a general discussion of this problem in *The Common Law* by O. W. Holmes (Little, Brown & Co, 1881), Lecture 3.

[32] See the first edition of this book, Ch.6, para.6–11.

[33] *Argyll v Beuselinck* [1972] 2 Lloyd's Rep. 172 at 183, discussed in Ch.11, para.11–096, below. See also *Yates Property Corp v Boland* (1998) 157 A.L.R. 30; [1999] Lloyd's Rep. P.N. 459, Federal Court of Australia.

[34] *Sharp and Roarer Investments Ltd v Sphere Drake Insurance Plc, The Moonacre* [1992] 2 Lloyd's Rep. 501, discussed in Ch.16, para.16–037, below.

[35] See, e.g. Ch.9, para.9–163, below, concerning architects; *Wilsher v Essex AHA* [1987] Q.B. 730 concerning medical practitioners (discussed in Ch.13, para.13–027, below).

[36] [1980] R.P.C. 16. The case went to the Court of Appeal, but not on the issue of negligence.

[37] *ibid.* at 18.

assumed capabilities, and then (b) to determine if he has achieved that particular standard. As to the objective approach, it seems equally unrealistic to demand identical standards of competence from persons who come from different ranks of the same profession (for example, junior hospital doctors and consultants, or leading and junior counsel). It is suggested that the correct approach (and that which is in practice adopted) is to judge the defendant by reference to the standard of skill and care appropriate to members of his profession,[38] who have the same status or formal position as the defendant. Where the defendant holds himself out as a specialist in a particular field, he should be judged by the standards appropriate to a specialist in that field, even if there is no formal recognition of his specialisation.[39]

(c) *Formulation of the Standard*

It is therefore suggested that the standard of skill and care which a professional **2–123** person is required to exercise may be defined as follows: that degree of skill and care which is ordinarily exercised by reasonably competent members of the profession, who have the same rank[40] and profess the same specialisation (if any) as the defendant. If the standard is formulated in this way, it is fair to both parties. The professional person will not be held liable in the absence of personal fault on his part. The client is adequately protected, because it is normally actionable negligence if a professional person undertakes work beyond his competence.[41]

(d) *Organisation Offering Professional Services*

Where the defendant is an organisation offering professional services (e.g. a firm **2–124** or a hospital) rather than an individual, different considerations arise. Such an organisation possesses the skills of specialists and generalists and of senior and junior staff. It should deploy such skills as necessary. Thus if, in a hospital, a houseman is required to do the work of a consultant, the standard by which his services will be judged is the standard of the consultant.[42] In other words, an organisation is judged by the standard of skill and care appropriate to the professional staff who ought to have been undertaking the work in question.

(e) *Undertaking Work of Other Professions*

Where a person strays across the boundaries of his own profession and under- **2–125** takes work normally performed by some allied profession, it is submitted that he should be judged by the standard of skill and care applicable to members of the latter profession. Thus if a surveyor agrees to design and to supervise the

---

[38] But see para.2–124, below.
[39] See Ch.11, para.11–097 and Ch.13, para.13–028, below.
[40] The term "rank" is not entirely satisfactory. It is intended to describe the different levels within hierarchical professions such as medicine.
[41] See, e.g. Ch.11, para.11–101 and Ch.13, para.13–028, below.
[42] See *Wilsher v Essex AHA* [1987] Q.B. 730 at 750–751, *per* Mustill L.J., with whom Glidewell L.J. agreed. This issue did not arise on the appeal to the House of Lords.

construction of a building, he should be judged by the standard of a reasonably competent architect.[43]

(f) New Techniques

2–126 One problem which commonly occurs in the scientific professions, such as medicine and engineering, is that posed by new techniques. At the general level, innovation and the development of new techniques is plainly desirable. In individual cases, however, where the new technique has failed, the defendant usually faces the allegation that he was negligent to depart from general and approved practice. Such cases are discussed later.[44] It is doubted that any general principle[45] can be formulated in respect of such cases, beyond that stated above.[46] However, important matters in determining whether the defendant exercised reasonable skill and care are: (a) whether there was any necessity to attempt a new technique in the instant case[47]; (b) whether the client was adequately informed of the risks involved; and (c) the amount and quality of the preliminary research carried out.

(g) Changes in the Standard Required

2–127 It follows from what has been said above that the standard of skill and care required by law of any given profession is not fixed for all time. Advances in knowledge may render certain courses of conduct "negligent", which were formerly quite acceptable.[48] Furthermore, quite independently of any advances in knowledge, there may be a general improvement in the standards of a particular profession. If so, the standard of the reasonably competent practitioner changes and mistakes which were formerly tolerable come to be regarded as negligent. In addition, the publication of written standards by a profession's governing body may itself bring about a raising or a changing of the quality of work which is required to constitute "reasonable skill and care". There is now a growing trend amongst professional bodies to publish written standards which reflect the best practices of the profession.[49]

5. FIDUCIARY OBLIGATIONS

(a) The Nature of Fiduciary Obligations

2–128 The contractual obligations owed by a professional person are agreed by him in return for his clients' promise to pay for his services. In broad terms, the law

---

[43] See Ch.10, below.
[44] See Ch.9, para.9–133 and Ch.13, paras 13–035 and 13–036, below.
[45] The statement of the Court of Appeal in *Landau v Werner* (1961) 105 S.J. 1008 that "success was the best justification for unusual and unestablished treatment" is of little assistance.
[46] See para.2–122, above.
[47] There was such necessity in *IBA v EMI and BICC* (1980) 14 Build.L.R. 1.
[48] See, e.g. Ch.13, para.13–025, below.
[49] See, e.g. surveyors (see Ch.10, paras 10–022 to 10–025), solicitors (see Ch.11, para.11–094) and accountants (see Ch.17, paras 17–094 to 17–098).

imposes a tortious duty of care on him where a client or third party is reasonably relying upon his professional skill and knowledge or where his client has retained him to confer a benefit on others. Fiduciary obligations are of a different order. They are based upon the trust reposed by a client in his professional adviser, and in particular the trust that the professional will act solely in his client's interests and not in his own. This is sometimes described as a "duty of loyalty", but in effect it amounts to an inhibition: a professional should not put himself in a position in which his duty to act in his client's interests is in conflict with his own interests, let alone prefer his own interests to those of his client should there be a conflict.[50] The obligations which flow from this general prohibition are called fiduciary obligations.

"Fiduciary duty of care". Before considering fiduciary obligations, it is **2–129** necessary to identify those obligations which are not fiduciary. Fiduciary relationships played an important part in the development of the law of tort in the last century, particularly in the context of claims against professional and other advisers. In *Nocton v Lord Ashburton*,[51] damages (by way of equitable compensation) were awarded for breach of fiduciary duty by a solicitor who gave bad advice which led a client to act in the interests of the solicitor rather than himself. Viscount Haldane L.C. held that the trial judge had been wrong to treat the claim as based upon deceit. "It was really an action based on the exclusive jurisdiction of a Court of Equity over a defendant in a fiduciary position in respect of matters which at law would also have given a right to damages for negligence."[52] Thereafter, until the decision in *Hedley Byrne & Co Ltd v Heller & Partners Ltd*,[53] the existence of a fiduciary relationship was seen as a means of enabling damages to be recovered for negligent advice.[54] In *Hedley Byrne* itself the House of Lords relied upon its earlier decision in *Nocton v Lord Ashburton* and recognised that damages could be recovered if there were a "special relationship".

This led some to allege and, at least in Canada,[55] to hold that a professional **2–130** who gave negligent advice would be liable not only in contract and tort, but also for breach of fiduciary duty. It is hard to see what purpose was served by adding

---

[50] See, e.g. the formulation by Millett L.J. in *Bristol & West Building Society v Mothew* [1998] Ch. 1 at 18B–C:

"The distinguishing obligation of a fiduciary is the obligation of loyalty. The principal is entitled to the single-minded loyalty of his fiduciary. This core liability has several facets. A fiduciary must act in good faith; he must *not* make a profit out of his trust. he must *not* place himself in a position where his duty and his interest may conflict; he may *not* act for his own benefit or the benefit of a third person without the informed consent of his principal." (emphasis added)

See also *Att-Gen v Blake* [1998] Ch. 439 at 455, where Lord Woolf M.R. giving the judgment of the Court of Appeal (himself and Millett and Mummery L.JJ.) said at 455E:

" . . . equity is proscriptive, not prescriptive: see *Breen v Williams* (1996) 186 CLR 71. It tells the fiduciary what he must not do. It does not tell him what he ought to do."

[51] [1914] A.C. 932.
[52] *ibid.* at 957.
[53] [1964] A.C. 465, discussed in paras 2–024 to 2–025, above.
[54] See, e.g. the decision of Salmon J. in *Wood v Martins Bank Ltd* [1959] 1 Q.B. 55.
[55] See, e.g. the authorities concerning doctors discussed in Ch.13, para.13–012, below. For an example of similar confusion see *Wickstead v Browne* (1992) 30 N.S.W.L.R. 1. In *Breen v Williams* (1996) 186 C.L.R. 71 several members of the High Court of Australia remarked upon the different approach of the Canadian courts to that adopted in Australia.

a third cause of action, unless it was hoped to circumvent a limitation period which would defeat both the contractual and tortious claim.[56] It may be that this trend arose from a misconception that any breach of any duty by a fiduciary is a breach of fiduciary duty.[57] It is not.[58] It is now clear that there is no separate "fiduciary duty of care". Rather, the liability of a negligent fiduciary is "a paradigm of the general duty to act with care imposed by law on those who take it upon themselves to act for or advise others".[59] The duty to exercise skill and care may be owed by a fiduciary, but it is not a fiduciary duty: it is a tortious and, where appropriate, contractual duty.[60]

2–131   **Effect of fiduciary obligations on contractual and tortious duties.** The fact that a professional person is subject to fiduciary obligations and so may be called a fiduciary, does not mean that all his duties to his client are fiduciary duties. His contractual and tortious duties are still owed in contract and tort. They do not become fiduciary duties because he is a fiduciary.[61] Nor is the scope of the

---

[56] As to which see *Cia de Seguros Imperio v Heath (REBX) Ltd* [2001] 1 W.L.R. 112 discussed in Ch.5, paras 5–119 to 5–122, below.

[57] See the judgment of Southin J. in *Giradet v Crease & Co* (1987) 11 B.C.L.R. (2d) 361 at 362:
"Counsel for the plaintiff spoke of this case in his opening as one of breach of fiduciary duty and negligence. It became clear during his opening that no breach of fiduciary duty is in issue. What is in issue is whether the defendant was negligent in advising on the settlement of a claim for personal injuries suffered in an accident. The word 'fiduciary' is flung around now as if it applied to all breaches of duty by solicitors, directors of companies and so forth. But 'fiduciary' comes from the Latin 'fiducia' meaning 'trust'. Thus, the adjective, 'fiduciary' means of or pertaining to a trustee or trusteeship. That a lawyer can commit a breach of the special duty of a trustee, e.g. by stealing his client's money, by entering into a contract with the client without full disclosure, by sending the client a bill claiming disbursements never made and so forth is clear. But to say that simple carelessness is giving advice is such a breach is a perversion of words. The obligation of a solicitor of care and skill is the same obligation of any person who undertakes for reward to carry out a task. One would not assert of an engineer or physician who had given bad advice and from whom common law damages were sought that he was guilty of a breach of fiduciary duty. Why should it be said of a solicitor?"
(This passage has been approved by La Forest J. in *LAC Minerals Ltd v International Corona Resources Ltd* (1989) 61 D.L.R. (4th) 14, by Ipp J. in *Permanent Building Society v Wheeler* (1994) 14 ACSR 109 and by Millett L.J. in *Bristol & West Building Society v Mothew* [1998] Ch. 1.)

[58] See para.2–132, below.

[59] *Henderson v Merrett Syndicates Ltd* [1995] 2 A.C. 145 at 205F, *per* Lord Browne-Wilkinson. See (1995) 111 L.Q.R. 1, *per* Heydon.

[60] *Bristol & West Building Society v Mothew* [1998] Ch. 1 at 16C–18F, *per* Millett L.J., applying *Permanent Building Society (in liq) v Wheeler* (1994) 14 A.C.S.R. 109 and *Nocton v Lord Ashburton* [1914] A.C. 932 at 956, where Viscount Haldane L.C. said:
"My Lords, the solicitor contracts with his client to be skilful and careful. For failure to perform his obligation he may be made liable at law in contract or even in tort, for negligence in breach of a duty imposed on him. In the early history of the action of assumpsit this liability was indeed treated as one for tort. There was a time when in cases of liability for breach of a legal duty of this kind the Court of Chancery appears to have exercised a concurrent jurisdiction. That was not remarkable, having regard to the defective character of legal remedies in those days. But later on, after the action of assumpsit had become fully developed, I think it probable that a demurrer for want of equity would always have lain to a bill which did no more than seek to enforce a claim for damages for negligence against a solicitor."
There may also be an equitable duty on a mortgagee or receiver to exercise skill and care: *Downsview Nominees Ltd v First City Corp Ltd* [1993] A.C. 295; and *Medforth v Blake* [2000] Ch. 86. However, this is not a fiduciary duty.

[61] "The expression 'fiduciary duty' is properly confined to those duties which are peculiar to fiduciaries and the breach of which attracts legal consequences differing from those consequent upon

contractual or tortious duties enlarged because the professional person also owes fiduciary duties,[62] even if in certain circumstances they might he said to require him to advise his client.[63] The courts will not impose fiduciary obligations to make good a failure by a party to a contract to obtain adequate protection of his interests which could have been achieved by the inclusion of appropriate contractual provisions.[64] Nor should fiduciary duties by superimposed on common law duties "simply to improve the nature or extent of the remedy".[65]

The nature of fiduciary obligations. Fiduciary duties or obligations are a **2–132** difficult area of the law.[66] In essence they represent equity's attempt to regulate the conduct of those whom it regards as bound to act in the interest of others rather than for themselves.[67] Where one person (the principal) is to be taken as trusting another (the fiduciary) to act in the principal's interests, equity will not allow the fiduciary to act in his own interests or in those of a third party. The

---

the breach of other duties. Unless the expression is so limited it is lacking in practical utility. In this sense it is obvious that not every breach of duty by a fiduciary is a breach of fiduciary duty." *per* Millett L.J. in *Bristol & West Building Society v Mothew* [1998] Ch. 1 at 16C–D. See also, *per* La Forest J. in *LAC Minerals Ltd v International Corona Resources Ltd* (1989) 61 D.L.R. (4th) 14 at 28. In *Noranda Australia Ltd v Lachlan Resources NL* (1988) 13 N.S.W.L.R. 1, the parties to a joint venture provided in their contract that the "relationship of the parties shall be fiduciary in nature". It was held that this did not mean that every term of the contract was also a fiduciary obligation: the provision as to the fiduciary relationship only applied to terms relevant to the duty of each party to act in the mutual interest of both.

[62] See *Clark Boyce v Mouat* [1994] 1 A.C. 428, discussed in para.2–136, below.

[63] If a professional person chooses to deal with his client in relation to property within the scope of his fiduciary obligation of loyalty, then if he is to uphold the transaction he must show that he gave certain advice: see para.2–140, below. However, he owes no contractual or tortious duty to give that advice: the consequence of a failure to give it is to expose him to a claim to have the transaction set aside (or possibly for equitable compensation), not to a claim for damages in contract or tort.

[64] *Hospital Products Ltd v United States Surgical Corp* (1984) 156 C.L.R. 41 at 147, *per* Dawson J.

[65] *Nornberg v Wynrib* [1992] 2 S.C.R. 226, *per* Sopinka J. at 272; quoted with approval in *Pilmer v Duke Group Ltd* [2001] 2 B.C.L.C. 773 at 733c–d.

[66] Finn, *Fiduciary Obligations* (The Law Book Company Ltd, Australia, 1977) remains the classic text. See also McKendrick (edn), *Commercial Aspects of Trusts and Fiduciary Obligations* (Clarendon Press, Oxford, 1992); and Bean, *Fiduciary Obligations and Joint Ventures* (Clarendon Press, Oxford, 1995).

[67] "A fiduciary is someone who has undertaken to act for or on behalf of another in a particular matter in circumstances which give rise to a relationship of trust and confidence." *per* Millett L.J. in *Bristol & West Building Society v Mothew* [1998] Ch. 1 at 18A, cited with approval by the Privy Council in *Arklow Investments Ltd v Maclean* [2000] 1 W.L.R. 594.

In *Brandeis (Brokers) Ltd v Black* [2001] 2 All E.R. (Comm) 980 at 991e–g Toulson J. adopted the definition of fiduciary given by Professor Finn in *Commercial Aspects of Trust and Fiduciary Relations* (1992) at p.9: "A person will be a fiduciary in his relationships with another when and insofar as that other is entitled to expect that he will act in that other's interest or (as in a partnership) in their joint interests, to the exclusion of their several interests."

See also *Chirnside v Fay* [2004] N.Z.C.A. 111; [2004] 3 N.Z.L.R. 637 at [51] in the judgment of the New Zealand Court of Appeal (Anderson P. McGrath and Hammond JJ.):

"Fiduciary law is not concerned with private ordering. That is, it is not the function of fiduciary law to mediate between the various interests of parties who are dealing with each other. That is for contract law. Fiduciary law serves to support the integrity and utility of relationships in which the role of one party is perceived to be the service of the interests of the other. It does so by imposing a specific duty of loyalty. As La Forest J. said (for the majority) in *Hodgkinson v Simms* (1994) 117 D.L.R. (4th) 161 (SCC):

'... the question to ask is whether, given all the surrounding circumstances, one party could

obligation of the fiduciary is not to allow his own self interest to conflict with his duty to act in the principal's interests. The extent of that duty will depend upon the extent to which he is trusted[68] to act in the interests of the principal so that it is not possible to postulate a series of fiduciary duties which apply to all fiduciaries.[69] Fletcher Moulton L.J. explained this in his much quoted judgment in *Re Coomber*[70]:

"Fiduciary relations are of many different types; they extend from the relation of myself to an errand boy who is bound to bring back my change up to the most intimate and confidential relations which can possibly exist between one party and another where the one is wholly in the hands of the other because of his infinite trust in him. All these are cases of fiduciary relations, and the Courts have again and again, in cases where there has been a fiduciary relation, interfered and set aside acts which, between persons in a wholly independent position, would have been perfectly valid. Thereupon in some minds there arises the idea that if there is any fiduciary relation whatever any of these types of interference is warranted by it. They conclude that every kind of fiduciary relation justifies every kind of interference. Of course that is absurd. The nature of the fiduciary relation must be such that it justifies the interference."[71]

---

reasonably have expected that the other party would act in the former's best interests with respect to the subject matter at issue. Discretion, influence, vulnerability and trust were mentioned as non-exhaustive examples of evidential factors to be considered in making this determination.' (at 176)"

[68] The extent of the trust depends upon the application of principle to the particular facts: it is not just a matter of the subjective intent of the principal.

[69] Professor Finn proffered this definition of a fiduciary in his essay in McKendrick (edn), *Commercial Aspects of Trusts and Fiduciary Obligation*:

"A person will be a fiduciary in his relationship with another when and in so far as that other is entitled to expect that he will act in that other's interests or (as in a partnership) in their joint interests, to the exclusion of his own several interest".

In its Report "Fiduciary Duties and Regulatory Rules" (Law Com. No.236), the Law Commission gave the following definition:

"Broadly speaking, a fiduciary relationship is one in which a person undertakes to act on behalf of or for the benefit of another often as an intermediary with a discretion or power which affects the interests of the other who depends on a fiduciary for information and advice."

See also the judgment of Mummery L.J. in *Peskin v Anderson* [2001] 1 B.C.L.C. 372 at 379 (paras [32]–[34]) and *Sinclair Investment Holdings SA v Versailles Trade Finance Ltd* [2005] EWCA Civ 722; [2006] 1 B.C.L.C. 61 at [20] *per* Arden L.J.

[70] [1911] 1 Ch. 723 at 728–729.

[71] In *Re Goldcorp Exchange Ltd* [1995] 1 A.C. 74, Lord Mustill, giving the opinion of the Privy Council, said at 98A–B:

"To describe someone as a fiduciary, without more, is meaningless. As Frankfurter J. said in *S.E.C. Chenery Corp* (1943) 318 US 80 at 885–86, cited in *Goff & Jones, The Law of Restitution* (4th edn, 1993), p.644:

'To say that a man is a fiduciary only begins analysis; it gives direction to further inquiry. To whom is he a fiduciary? What obligations does he owe as a fiduciary? In what respect has he failed to discharge these obligations? And what are the consequences of his deviation from duty?' "

See also *Maguire v Makaronis* (1997) 188 C.L.R. 449 at 464, where Brennan C.J. and Gaudron, McHugh and Gummow JJ. said:

" . . . to say that the appellants stood as fiduciaries to the respondents calls for the ascertainment of the particular obligations owed to the respondents and consideration of what acts and omissions amounted to failure to discharge those obligations."

See also *Brandeis (Brokers) Ltd v Black* [2001] 2 All E.R. (Comm) 980 at [40], *per* Toulson J.:

"Fiduciaries are not all required, like the victims of Procrustes, to lie on a bed of the same length."

Toulson J. then referred to the speech of Lord Browne-Wilkinson in *Henderson v Merrett Syndicates Ltd* [1995] 2 A.C. 145, at 206.

So, in each case it is important to establish the extent of the trust, for that will   **2–133**
define the extent to which equity will intervene.[72–73] The trust and confidence
which gives rise to fiduciary obligations is not, or need not, be emotional. For
example, a director owes fiduciary obligations to his company. In this sense it is
to be contrasted with the confidence which is the basis for the equitable doctrine
of undue influence. It is based upon reliance, but not the same sort of reliance
which may underlie a tortious duty of care.[74] Nor is it simply reliance on another
party to a contract to perform his obligations under it.[75] Rather it is the fact that
the principal so relies on the fiduciary as to leave the principal vulnerable to any
disloyalty by the fiduciary and so reliant on his good faith.[76] It follows that a
commercial relationship at arm's length, with both parties on an equal footing is
unlikely to give rise to fiduciary obligations.[77]

The significance of the retainer. When considering the extent of a pro-   **2–134**
fessional person's fiduciary obligations the scope and terms of any retainer
(together with the scope of any tortious duty of care) need to be considered. In
particular, it is necessary to ascertain what a professional person has been
retained to do and the terms upon which he has agreed to do it in order to
establish whether and to what extent he is in a position of trust.[78] If, for example,
a professional person is retained to advise or act in relation to a particular piece
of property, there is no fiduciary obligation preventing him from purchasing other
property as to which he was not retained to advise.[79] So, a solicitor who was
retained to act on a libel action can purchase from his client property unrelated

---

[72–73] So, while usually a company director owes a fiduciary duty to the company to promote its
interests, each case must be looked at on its facts. In *Plus Group Ltd v Pyye* [2002] EWCA Civ 370;
[2002] 2 B.C.L.C. 201 the company had ceased to pay the director and had excluded him from its
management. The Court of Appeal held that he was not in breach of fiduciary duty when he set up
his own company in the same area of business. Brooke L.J., with whom Jonathan Parker J. agreed,
said at [75]: "the facts and circumstances of each case must be carefully examined to see whether a
fiduciary relationship exists in relation to the matter of which complaint is made".
[74] For example, an engineer asked to design foundations may be relied upon by the building owner,
but the engineer will not owe any fiduciary obligations as to the adequacy of his design.
[75] *Re Goldcorp Exchange Ltd* [1995] 1 A.C. 74 at 98C–G.
[76] *Hospital Products Ltd v United States Surgical Corp* (1984) 156 C.L.R. 41 at 142, *per* Dawson
J.:
  "There is, however, the notion underlying all the cases of fiduciary obligation that inherent in the
  nature of the relationship itself is a position of disadvantage or vulnerability on the part of one of
  the parties which causes him to place reliance upon the other and requires the protection of equity
  acting upon the conscience of that other . . . From that springs the requirement that a person under
  a fiduciary obligation shall not put himself in a position where his interest and duty conflict or, if
  conflict is unavoidable, shall resolve it in favour of duty and shall not, except by special
  arrangement, make a profit out of his position."
[77] *ibid.* at 170, *per* Gibbs C.J. See also *Halton International Inc (Holdings) SARL v Guernroy Ltd*
[2005] EWHC 1968, Ch (Patten J.).
[78] "Even in the case of a solicitor client relationship, long accepted as a status based fiduciary
relationship, the duty is not derived from the status. As in all such cases, the duty is derived from what
the solicitor undertakes, or is deemed to have undertaken, to do in the particular circumstances . . .
Whether the relationship derives from retainer, less formal arrangement or self-appointment, it must
be examined to see what duties are thereby imposed on the fiduciary and the scope and ambit of those
duties.": New South Wales Court of Appeal in *Beach Petroleum NL v Kennedy* [1999] N.S.W.C.A.
408 (reported (1999) 48 N.S.W.L.R. 1), paras 188 and 192 (pp.45–46 of the report).
[79] *Montesquieu v Sandys* (1811) 18 Ves.Jun. 302; *Cane v Allen* (1814) 2 Dow 289; and *Edwards v
Meyrick* (1842) 2 Hare 60.

to that action in the same way as a complete stranger could.[80] In every case, it is a question of determining what the subject-matter of the professional's retainer was.[81]

2–135   The terms of the retainer are also of importance. Equity will not impose a fiduciary obligation which is inconsistent with the terms agreed. So in *Kelly v Cooper*[82] the Privy Council had to decide whether an estate agent owed a client, who instructed him on the sale of his house, a fiduciary duty not to act simultaneously for the owner of a neighbouring house, which might interest prospective purchasers of the client's house. The client argued that an agent owed his principal an undivided duty of loyalty, so that if the agent acted for the neighbour without the client's informed consent he would be in breach of contract and in breach of fiduciary duty. Both claims failed. It is well known that estate agents act for many clients at the same time and that there may well be a conflict of interest between their various clients. Nevertheless, estate agents are regularly instructed on that basis. The Privy Council accordingly held that a term was to be implied into the estate agent's retainer that he would be entitled to act for other, competing clients. That left the claim for breach of fiduciary duty. The Privy Council approved a passage from the judgment of Mason J. in *Hospital Products Ltd v United States Surgical Corp*[83] and held that, since the contract

---

[80] *Alison v Clayhills* (1907) 97 L.T. 709 at 712. A solicitor would still have to show that he was not exercising undue influence.

     In *Longstaff v Birtles* [2001] Lloyd's Rep. P.N. 826 the Court of Appeal held that the fiduciary obligations of a solicitor retained by a client on a proposed purchase of a hotel business extended to a proposed investment by the client in a different hotel business owned by a partnership of which the solicitor was a partner. This decision is at best borderline. The solicitor's retainer was to act on the proposed purchase and not, it would seem, a more general retainer to advise as to how the client should invest in the hotel business.

[81] In the context of the fiduciary obligations between partners, Dixon J. said in *Birtchnell v Equity Trustees, Executors & Agency Co Ltd* (1929) 42 C.L.R. 384 at 408:

     "The subject matter over which the fiduciary obligations extend is determined by the character of the venture or undertaking for which the partnership exists; and this is to be ascertained, not merely from the express agreement of the parties, whether embodied in written instruments or not, but also from the course of dealing actually pursued by the firm."

     In all cases where a fiduciary obligation is alleged it is necessary to identify the "subject matter" in this way: see *Breen v Williams* (1996) 186 C.L.R. 71, para.14, *per* Brennan C.J.

[82] [1993] A.C. 205.

[83] (1984) 156 C.L.R. 41 at 97:

     "That contractual and fiduciary relationships may co-exist between the same parties has never been doubted. Indeed, the existence of a basic contractual relationship has in many situations provided a foundation for the erection of a fiduciary relationship. In these situations it is the contractual foundation which is all important because it is the contract that regulates the basic rights and liabilities of the parties. The fiduciary relationship, if it is to exist at all, must accommodate itself to the terms of the contract so that it is consistent with, and conforms to, them. The fiduciary relationship cannot be superimposed upon the contract in such a way as to alter the operation which the contract was intended to have according to its true construction."

     This passage from the judgment of Mason J. has been followed at first instance in the English courts: see *Global Container Lines Ltd v Bonyard Shipping Co* [1998] 1 Lloyd's Rep. 528 (Rix J.); and *Land Rover Group Ltd v UPF (UK) Ltd (in administrative receivership)* [2003] 2 B.C.L.C. 232 (H.H. Judge Norris Q.C., sitting as a judge of the High Court). In the same way a fiduciary duty cannot modify the terms of a contract, it cannot alter the operation of a statute. Parliament, not equity is sovereign: see *Tito v Waddell (No.2)* [1977] Ch. 106, at 139; followed in *Cubillo v Commonwealth of Australia* [2001] FCA 1213; (2001) 183 A.L.R. 249 at [465].

allowed the estate agent to act for other clients whose interests might conflict with those of the claimant, he would not be in breach of any fiduciary duty by so acting. This reflected the general rule that a principal who gives his informed consent to a fiduciary acting also for someone else with a conflicting interest (or potentially conflicting interest), cannot complain that the principal faces a potential conflict between his duty to him and to his other client.[84] However, contractual terms do not always have the effect of preventing one contracting party from being subject to a fiduciary obligation which is inconsistent with his contractual obligations. A fiduciary cannot rely upon the fact that he has entered a contract with a third party which creates a conflict between his obligations to his two clients. If he does so, he cannot rely upon the fact that proper discharge of his duty to one client would place him in breach of obligations owed to the other, absent the former's informed consent.[85]

The Privy Council came to a similar conclusion in *Clark Boyce v Mouat*.[86] In **2–136** that case solicitors acted both for a son, who was borrowing a sum of money, and for his mother, who was charging her house as security for the loan. They advised the mother to seek independent legal advice, but she declined to do so. In due course the son became bankrupt and the mother had to repay the loan. She sued the solicitors for breach of contract, negligence and breach of fiduciary duty. The Privy Council held that there was no reason why a solicitor should not act for two parties with competing interests so long as each had been advised of the conflict. Whether there was a conflict and, if there was, what its extent was depended upon what the solicitor was being retained to do for each party. Therefore, the crucial question was the extent of their retainer by the mother. The Privy Council upheld the trial judge's decision that the mother had not retained the solicitors to advise as to the wisdom of the proposed transaction. Their retainer required them to carry out the necessary conveyancing and to explain the legal consequences of the transaction. This had been done, so that the claims in contract and negligence failed. The Privy Council then rejected the claim, because, in the words of Lord Jauncey:

> "A fiduciary duty concerns disclosure of material facts in a situation where the fiduciary has either a personal interest in the matter to which the facts are material or acts for another party who has such an interest. It cannot be prayed in aid to enlarge the scope of contractual duties."[87]

---

[84] *Bristol & West Building Society v Mothew* [1998] Ch. 1 at 18H–19B, *per* Millett L.J. The fiduciary must, however, act in good faith in the interests of each of his clients and, if an actual conflict of interest arises, then he may have to cease acting for one or possibly both clients: *ibid*. at 19D–H. See further the decision of the New Zealand Court of Appeal in *Armitage v Paynter Construction Ltd* [1999] 2 N.Z.L.R. 534, where the solicitor's instructions to act for both parties to a joint venture did create a conflict when the solicitor became aware that one party was in financial difficulties. By paying joint venture money to that party he consciously preferred its interests to that of the other party. In *Bolkiah v KPMG (a firm)* [1999] 2 A.C. 222 at 235A–C, Lord Millett said that companies which competed with each other were to be inferred to have consented to the same firm of auditors acting for them and for their competitors.
[85] *Hilton v Barker Booth & Eastwood (a firm)* [2005] UKHL 8; [2005] 1 W.L.R. 567.
[86] [1994] 1 A.C. 428.
[87] *ibid*. at 437G. See also *Norberg v Wynrib* (1992) 92 D.L.R. (4th) 449 at 481, *per* Sopinka J.: "Fiduciary duties should not be superimposed on these common law duties simply to improve the nature or extent of the remedy." In *Att-Gen v Blake* [1998] Ch. 439 at 453D, Lord Woolf M.R., giving

(b) *Dealing with the Principal*

2–137　　**"Self-dealing" and "fair-dealing".** There is a well-established distinction in the authorities between cases in which the fiduciary is himself the seller or buyer on behalf of the principal ("self-dealing") and cases where the role of the fiduciary is limited to advising or assisting in the transaction or some earlier involvement in the subject-matter of the transaction ("fair dealing").[88] In cases of self-dealing, the transaction is usually said to be voidable without more at the instance of the principal. In cases of fair dealing, it is for the fiduciary to show that he took no advantage of his position in that he gave full value and made full disclosure to the principal. In fact, if a fiduciary who was "self-dealing" did give full value and make full disclosure to his principal, then the transaction would not be voidable—the principal would have given his full consent. In effect, it is open to a fiduciary to turn what would be a self-dealing case into a fair-dealing case,[89] although his close connection with the relevant property may make it more difficult for him to show that he has made full disclosure.[90] In all such cases, liability of the fiduciary does not depend upon whether the fiduciary was actually acting in bad faith or not,[91] but on whether full value and disclosure were given.

2–138　　**Self-dealing.** The prohibition on self-dealing is strict. The conflict between duty and interest is so great that a fiduciary is presumed not to have succeeded in ignoring his own interests[92] and the sale is voidable at the instance of the principal.[93] There is no need for the principal to show that the transaction was on

---

the judgment of the Court of Appeal (himself, Millett and Mummery L.JJ.) referred to this as a "salutary warning".

[88] The distinction was made in early cases such as *Ex p. Lacey* (1802) 6 Ves.Jun. 625; *Randall v Errington* (1805) 10 Ves.Jun. 423; *Morse v Royal* (1806) 12 Ves.Jun. 355; and *Cane v Allen* (1814) 2 Dow. 289. In *Tito v Waddell (No.2)* [1977] Ch. 106 at 241, Megarry V.C. rejected an argument that there was only one rule (see also *Re Thompson's Settlement* [1986] Ch. 99 at 110–116, *per* Vinelott J.).

[89] *Ex p. Lacey* (1802) 6 Ves. Jun. 625; *Randall v Errington* (1805) 10 Ves.Jun. 423, as explained by Megarry V.C. in *Tito v Waddell (No.2)* [1977] Ch. 106 at 242D; *Sanderson v Walker* (1807) 13 Ves.Jun. 60; *Andrews v Mowbray* (1805–07) Wils.Ex. 71 at 73; *Downes v Grazebrook* (1817) 3 Mer. 200; *Luff v Lord* (1864) 34 Beav. 220 at 227, *per* Romilly M.R.; *Lagunas Nitrate Company v Lagunas Syndicate* [1899] 2 Ch. 392; and *Movietex Ltd v Bulfield* [1988] B.C.L.C. 104 at 118e–g, *per* Vinelott J.

[90] *Ex p. Lacey* (1802) 6 Ves.Jun. 625 at 626.

[91] As required, for example, to establish a claim for breach of fiduciary duty against a solicitor who is acting for both borrower and lender: see *Bristol & West Building Society v Mothew* [1998] Ch. 1 at 18D–E *per* Millett L.J.; and *Johnson v (1) EBS Pensioner Trustees Ltd (2) O'Shea* [2002] Lloyd's Rep. P.N. 308 at paras 37–39 of the judgment of Mummery L.J., with whom the other members of the Court of Appeal agreed.

[92] *Cook v Collingridge* (1823) Jacob 607 at 621, *per* Lord Eldon L.C.

[93] *Campbell v Walker* (1800) 5 Ves.Jun. 678; *Ex p. Lacey* (1802) 6 Ves.Jun. 625; *Att-Gen v Clarendon* (1810) 17 Ves.Jun. 491 at 500; *Downes v Glazebrook* (1817) 3 Mer. 200; *Aberdeen Railway Co v Blaikie Brothers* (1854) 1 Macq. 461; *Phosgate Sewage Company v Hartmount* (1875) 5 Ch.D. 394; *Erlanger v New Sombrero Phosphate Company* (1878) 3 App.Cas. 1218; *Williams v Scott* [1900] A.C. 499; *Wright v Morgan* [1926] A.C. 788; *Glennon v Commissioner for Taxation of the Commonwealth of Australia* (1972) 127 C.L.R. 503; and *Re Thompson's Settlement* [1986] Ch. 99.

unfavourable terms or that the fiduciary has made a profit.[94] While the rule might seem harsh, the usual remedy is to set aside the transaction on terms which reflect the consideration given by the fiduciary and any work or improvement he has carried out on the property concerned. It does not usually involve the payment of compensation by the fiduciary to the principal.[95]

Fair dealing. The fair dealing rule is also based on a conflict between duty and interest. It will apply where the fiduciary has a sufficient duty to act in the interests of the principal in respect of a transaction that he will not be permitted to advance his own interest unless he obtains the informed consent of the principal and gives full value. In considering what role a person must have in order to be subject to this fiduciary obligation, the approach of Dixon J. in *McKenzie v McDonald*[96] is instructive:

2–139

> "Did the defendant occupy such a position of confidence towards the plaintiff as to bring him within the equitable requirements of full disclosure and open dealing? In my opinion he did. He assumed the function of advising and assisting a woman in a difficult situation in the acquisition of a residence by means of the disposal or pledging of her property. He was necessarily furnished with an intimate knowledge of her financial position, her obligations, and family needs. He proceeded to advise her upon the wisdom and practicability of raising money by mortgage, and acted for her in an effort to do so. He undertook the sale of her farm, and acquired such information as he could in relation to it, and offered his counsel as to its condition and the price she had asked and in effect should ask."

This emphasises the need for there to be confidence and trust in a person, so as to render the principal vulnerable to an abuse of that trust.[97] For example, 19th century authority suggests that it is enough to be a close friend of the principal consulted about a proposed sale,[98] but that a person whose role is confined to providing details of a proposed sale is not subject to the fair dealing rule.[99] In the same way, a person who occupies a fiduciary position is nevertheless permitted

---

[94] *Ex p*. Lacey (1802) 6 Ves.Jun. 625 at 627, *per* Lord Eldon L.C.; *Ex p. James* (1803) 8 Ves.Jun. 337 at 348, *per* Lord Eldon L.C.; *Randall v Errington* (1805) 10 Ves.Jun. 423; and *Att-Gen v Dudley* (1915) C.Coop. 146. It is no defence that the fiduciary purchased the property at auction (*Whichote v Lawrence* (1798) 3 Ves.Jun. 740; *Lister v Lister* (1802) 6 Ves.Jun. 631; *Beningfield v Baxter* (1886) 12 App.Cas. 167), nor that the price paid by the fiduciary was as good or better as could be obtained elsewhere (*Baker v Carter* (1935) 1 Y. & C.Ex. 259; *De Bussche v Alt* (1878) 8 Ch.D. 286). In short "it is no answer to a claim to set aside a transaction which infringes the self-dealing rule that the transaction was fair or even generous to the trust estate" (*Re Thompson's Settlement* [1986] Ch. 99 at 118B, *per* Vinelott J.).

[95] See Ch.3, paras 3–011 and 3–012, below.

[96] [1927] V.L.R. 134 at 145.

[97] *cf. Holder v Holder* [1968] Ch. 353, where a named executor performed some slight functions in that capacity and then purported to renounce his executorship and subsequently bought estate property at a fair price. The Court of Appeal declined to apply the self-dealing rule to him. He "had never acted as executor in a way which could be taken to amount to acceptance of a duty to act in the interests of the beneficiaries": *per* Vinelott J. in *Re Thompson's Settlement* [1986] Ch. 99 at 116C.

[98] *Taylor v Obee* (1816) 3 Price 83.

[99] *Andrews v Mowbray* (1805–07) Wils.Ex. 71; and *Guest v Smythe* (1870) L.R. 5 Ch.App. 551.

to exercise rights and options which were acquired before he did so: there is no abuse of trust or confidence in doing so.[1]

2–140   **Full advice and disclosure.** In *Gibson v Jeyes*,[2] Lord Eldon L.C. applied the fair-dealing rule is these terms to a claim against an attorney who had sold an annuity to a client he had been advising:

> "he might contract: but then he should have said, if he was to deal with her for this, she must get another attorney to advise her as to the value: or, if she would not, then out of that state of circumstances this clear duty results from the rule of this Court, and throws upon him the whole onus of the case; that, if he will mix with the character of attorney that of vendor, he shall, if the propriety of the contract comes in question, manifest, that he has given her all that reasonable advice against himself that he would have given her against a third person."[3]

The fiduciary must show not only that he disclosed all the relevant information which he had, but that he had obtained all the information which he should have done.[4] However, he is not obliged to give advice which he would not have given had he had no personal interest in the transaction.[5] It is not enough for the fiduciary simply to resign from his position: if he adopts that course, then he still has to show that he disclosed all relevant information.[6]

2–141   Particular difficulties arise when the known value of property increases after it is acquired by a fiduciary because of some subsequent discovery or event. The fiduciary would have to show that he disclosed all that he knew[7] and if there were suspicion that he might have known what was discovered later, then the transaction would probably be set aside on the application of the principal.[8] However, if the subsequent event was not anticipated, then the fact that it increased the value of the property sold to the fiduciary does not render the sale voidable.[9]

---

[1] *Vyse v Foster* (1874) L.R. 7 H.L. 318; *Hordern v Hordern* [1910] A.C. 465; and *Re Mullholland's Will Trusts* [1949] 1 All E.R. 460.

[2] (1801) 6 Ves.Jun. 266 at 278.

[3] See also *Harris v Treemenheere* (1808) 15 Ves.Jun. 34; *Dunbar v Tredenick* (1813) 2 Ball & Beatty 304; *Champion v Rigby* (1830) 1 Russ. & M. 539; *Gresley v Mousley* (1859) 4 De G. & J. 78; *Pisani v Att-Gen of Gibraltar* (1874) L.R. 5 P.C. 516; *Robinson v Abbott* (1894) 20 V.L.R. 346; *Moody v Cox & Hatt* [1917] 2 Ch. 71; and *Swindle v Harrison* [1997] 4 All E.R. 705.

[4] *Gresley v Mousley* (1858) 4 De G. & J. 78. The fiduciary is required to disclose all material information (which does not involve considering the actual causative effect of the non-disclosure): see *Johnson v (1) EBS Pensioner Trustees Ltd (2) O'Shea* [2002] Lloyd's Rep. P.N. 308: see para.55 of the judgment of Mummery L.J.

[5] *Pisani v Att-Gen of Gibraltar* (1974) L.R. 5 P.C. 516 at 537–538.

[6] *Ex p. Lacey* (1802) 6 Ves.Jun. 625 at 626; *Ex p. James* (1803) 8 Ves.Jun. 337 at 348; *Spring v Pride* (1864) 4 De G.J. & S. 395; and *Wright v Morgan* [1926] A.C. 788.

[7] *Haywood v Roadknight* [1927] V.L.R. 512.

[8] See *Ex p. Lacey* (1802) 6 Ves.Jun. 625 at 627; *Ex p. James* (1803) 8 Ves.Jun. 337 at 349; *Coles v Trescothick* (1804) 9 Ves.Jun. 234 at 248; and *Ex p. Bennett* (1805) 10 Ves.Jun. 391, where Lord Eldon L.C. discusses the approach to be adopted in a case where land was sold to a fiduciary and valuable mineral deposits were later found. See also *Lowther v Lowther* (1806) 13 Ves.Jun. 95, where Lord Erskine L.C. appears to have thought that if the defendant had acted as agent on the sale of a painting subsequently found to be a Titian, then the sale would be set aside.

[9] *Montesquieu v Sandys* (1811) 18 Ves.Jun. 302 (value of reversionary interest increased dramatically when the healthy incumbent died and the successor appointed was aged 60); and *Demerara Bauxite Co Ltd v Hubbard* [1924] A.C. 673. *Edwards v Meyrick* (1842) 2 Hare 60 is a borderline case.

Full value. Full value will mean the current market value[10] on the basis of the knowledge which the principal should have had. It may be at least as favourable as what could have been obtained from a third party[11] and, if the fiduciary had an advisory role, on terms which the fiduciary would have advised the principal to accept from a third party.[12]

2–142

The fiduciary's interest. The fiduciary will have an interest in any transaction to which he personally is a party. Equity looks at the substance rather than the form of a transaction, so that if a party to the transaction is a limited company which is no more than the fiduciary's *alter ego*, the transaction will be subject to the rule.[13] A share holding which is not so small that it can be disregarded is sufficient to bring the rule into effect.[14] If the other party is the fiduciary's partner or a firm in which he is a partner the rule applies.[15] The fact that a fiduciary was acting for a third party who was a party to the transaction is sufficient, for the fiduciary has divided loyalties.[16] It is always worth bearing in mind the dictum of Upjohn L.J. in *Boulting v Association of Cinematograph, Television and Allied Technicians*[17]:

2–143

> "A broad rule like this[18] must be applied with common sense and with an appreciation of the sort of circumstances in which over the last 200 years and more it has been applied and thrived. It must be applied realistically to a state of affairs which discloses a real conflict of duty and interest and not to some theoretical conflict."[19]

---

[10] *Demerara Bauxite Co Ltd v Hubbard* [1926] A.C. 673.
[11] *Denton v Donner* (1856) 23 Beav. 285; *Plowright v Lambert* (1885) 52 L.T. 646; and *Lunghi v Sinclair* [1966] W.A.R. 172.
[12] *Champion v Rigby* (1830) 1 Russ. & M. 539; *Holman v Loynes* (1852) 4 De G.M. & G. 270; and *Widgery v Tepper* (1878) 38 L.T. 434; *cf. Blackham v Heythorpe* (1917) 23 C.L.R. 156.
[13] *Silkstone and Haigh Moor Coal Co v Edey* [1900] 1 Ch. 167, where the company was "a mere trustee" for the fiduciary.
[14] *Transvaal Lands Co v New Belgium (Transvaal) Land & Development Co* [1914] 2 Ch. 488; *Re Clark; Clark v Moore, Moores (Chemists) Ltd* (1920) 150 L.T.J. 94; and *Movietex Ltd v Bulfield* [1988] B.C.L.C. 104 at 122e–g.
[15] *Re Moore* (1881) 51 L.J. (N.S.) Ch. 72; and *Re Thompson's Settlement* [1986] Ch. 99.
[16] *Ex p. Bennett* (1805) 10 Ves.Jun. 381; *Hesse v Briant* (1856) 4 De G.M. & G. 623; *Moody v Cox & Hatt* [1917] 2 Ch. 71; *Imeson v Lister* (1920) L.T.Jo. 446; and *Heywood v Roadknight* [1927] V.L.R. 512; *cf. North and South Trust Co v Berkeley* [1971] 1 W.L.R. 470 at 484H–485A, *per* Donaldson J.
[17] [1964] 2 Q.B. 606 at 637–638.
[18] Upjohn L.J. was considering the rule that a fiduciary should not allow his personal interest to conflict with his duty.As Lord Upjohn, the same judge expressed similar views in his speech in *Boardman v Phipps* [1967] 2 A.C. 721, at 756:
"The phrase 'possibly may conflict' requires consideration. In my view it means that the reasonable man looking at the relevant facts and circumstances of the particular case would think that there was a real sensible possibility of conflict; not that you could imagine some situation arising which might, in some conceivable possibility in events not contemplated as real sensible possibilities by any reasonable person, result in conflict."
  See also *Bhullar v Bhullar* [2003] EWCA Civ 241; [2003] 2 B.C.L.C. 241 at [30], *per* Jonathan Parker L.J.
[19] See also *Pilmer v Duke Group Ltd* [2001] 2 B.C.L.C. 773 at [78], where the statement by Mason J. in *Hospital Products Ltd v United States Surgical Corp* (1984) 156 C.L.R. 41 that the fiduciary is precluded from pursing a gain in circumstances in which there is "a conflict or a real or substantial possibility of a conflict" between the interests of the fiduciary and the person to whom the duty is owed was cited by McHugh, Gummow, Hayne and Callinan JJ. with approval. Mason J. (and

(c) *Unauthorised Profits and Diversion of Opportunities*

2-144   While acting in the interests of his principal a fiduciary may be able to further his own interests by profiting from his fiduciary position or by diverting to himself opportunities which properly belong to his principal. The classic case of the latter is *Keech v Sandford*,[20] where a trustee of a lease took the reversion personally, having failed to obtain a renewal for the trust, and was held to hold it on trust for the beneficiary. In the same way, a fiduciary whose role is to negotiate for a purchase on behalf of his principal cannot purchase for himself.[21] Nor can he exploit confidential information which he learns in his fiduciary capacity for his own benefit.[22] Again, it is important to establish the extent of the subject-matter of the fiduciary obligation. In relation to bribes and secret commissions the courts have been willing to stretch the definition of fiduciary to provide a remedy.[23]

(d) *Undue Influence*

(i) Royal Bank of Scotland Plc v Etridge (No.2) *and Undue Influence*

2-145   *Royal Bank of Scotland Plc v Etridge (No.2).* In 2001 the law in this area was clarified and explained by the House of Lords in *Royal Bank of Scotland Plc v*

McHugh, Gummow, Hayne and Callinan JJ.) went on to quote with approval a statement by Judge Learned Hand in *Phelan v Middle States Oil Corp* (1955) 220 F (2d) 593 at 602–603:

"[If] the doctrine be inexorably applied and without regard to the particular circumstances of the situation, every transaction will be condemned once it is shown that the fiduciary had such a hope or expectation, however unlikely to be realized it may be, and however trifling an inducement it will be, if it is realized ... We have found no decisions that have applied this rule inflexibly to every occasion in which the fiduciary has been shown to have had a personal interest that might in fact have conflicted with his loyalty. On the contrary in a number of situations courts have held that the rule does not apply, not only when the putative interest, though in itself strong enough to be an inducement, was too remote, but also when, though not too remote, it was too feeble an inducement in determining motive."

[20] (1726) Cas. t. K. 61; *cf. Aberdeen Town Council v Aberdeen University* (1877) 2 App.Cas. 544. The principle was recently summarised by the Court of Appeal in *Gwembe Valley Development Co Ltd v Koshy (No.3)* [2003] EWCA Civ 1048; [2004] 1 B.C.L.C. 131 at [44]–[45] by reference to the judgment of Rich, Dixon and Evatt JJ. in the High Court of Australia in *Furs Ltd v Tomkies* (1936) 54 C.L.R. 583 at 592 and to the decision of the House of Lords in *Regal (Hastings) Ltd v Gulliver* [1967] A.C. 134.

[21] *Lees v Nuttall* (1834) 2 My. & K. 891; and *Cook v Deeks* [1916] 1 A.C. 554.

[22] *Boardman v Phipps* [1967] 2 A.C. 46; and *Regal (Hastings) Ltd v Gulliver* [1967] 2 A.C. 134 (note). This may overlap with a claim for breach of confidence: see paras 2–155 to 2–175, below.

A fiduciary who resigns from the position which gave rise to his fiduciary obligations and then exploits for himself an opportunity of which he learnt from his fiduciary position will be liable to account for the profits he makes, as will a company which he forms in order to exploit the opportunity: *CMS Dolphin Ltd v Simonet* [2001] 2 B.C.L.C. 704 (Lawrence Collins J.). In any particular case, what matters is whether the opportunity was one which the fiduciary was under a duty to refer to the beneficiary. If he was so that there was a real conflict of interest, then he will be accountable: *Bhullar v Bhullar* [2003] EWCA Civ 241; [2003] 2 B.C.L.C. 241.

[23] *Reading v Att-Gen* [1951] A.C. 507; affirming [1949] 2 K.B. 232: ex-sergeant using uniform to assist smuggling operation.

Etridge (No.2).[24] While the decision was mainly concerned with the relationship between banks and other lenders and guarantor spouses, it is important for understanding undue influence more generally. Earlier authority needs to be read subject to this decision.

Undue influence. Gifts, deeds and other transactions may be set aside if **2–146** procured by undue influence of one person over another. Equity provides relief for undue influence where the common law principle of duress might not. It extends to more subtle, less overt pressure or improper persuasion. In every case the question is whether the intention to enter the transaction or to confer the benefit was produced by the improper exercise of another's influence. No more precise definition of the circumstances in which equity will intervene is possible, because of the varied circumstances in which influence may arise and be improperly exercised.[25]

(ii) *Undue Influence and the Burden of Proof*

Presumptions and classes. Before the decision in *Royal Bank of Scotland Plc* **2–147** *v Etridge (No.2)*[26] the first issue in any claim for undue influence was which class of relationship existed between the parties.[27] Depending upon which class a relationship fell into, presumptions arose as to whether undue influence had been exercised or not. However, once it is appreciated that undue influence must be proved in each case, the true significance of the "presumptions" and "classes" referred to in the earlier cases can be seen. So, where the person seeking relief establishes both that he was in a relationship of trust and confidence with another, such as to give the other influence over him, and that the transaction is not one readily explained—as would be, for example, a moderate Christmas present by a client to a solicitor—then the evidential burden falls on the other to show that the transaction was not produced by the improper or undue exercise of his influence. The person seeking relief has done all that is needed to establish his entitlement to relief. There is no need to prove any improper conduct by the other party.[28] If the other party does not adduce evidence to show that the transaction was entered otherwise than under his undue influence it will be set aside.[29]

Relationships which are presumed to give one person influence over **2–148** **another.** Certain relationships are expected to have given one person influence

---

[24] [2001] UKHL 44; [2002] 2 A.C. 773. Noted in (2002) 118 L.Q.R. 337; applied by the Privy Council in *R. v Her Majesty's Att-Gen for England and Wales* [2003] UKPC 22.
[25] *Royal Bank of Scotland Plc v Etridge (No.2)* [2001] UKHL 44; [2002] 2 A.C. 773, *per* Lord Nicholls at [7].
[26] [2001] UKHL 44; [2002] 2 A.C. 773.
[27] See *Barclays Bank Plc v O'Brien* [1994] 1 A.C. 180; *Royal Bank of Scotland Plc v Etridge (No.2)* [1998] 4 All E.R. 705 at 711f–j, *per* Stuart-Smith L.J. giving the judgment of the Court of Appeal (himself, Millett and Morritt L.JJ.) and paras 2–142 to 2–145 of the 5th edition of this book.
[28] *Hammond v Osborne* [2002] EWCA Civ 885; [2002] W.T.L.R. 125; *Jennings v Cairns* [2003] EWCA Civ 1935.
[29] *Royal Bank of Scotland Plc v Etridge (No.2)* [2001] UKHL 44; [2002] 2 A.C. 773, *per* Lord Nicholls at [13]–[20] and, *per* Lord Scott at [151]–[161].

over another. These include doctor and patient,[30] solicitor and client,[31] parent and child,[32] guardian and ward[33] and religious adviser and disciple.[34] They are all relationships in which one party is likely to trust and be influenced by the other. They are essentially personal relationships. The trust and confidence involved is different from that which characterises fiduciary relationships, for example the relationship between a commercial principal and his agent or between a limited company and its directors.[35]

2–149   If the party seeking to set aside a transaction or gift proves such a relationship then there is a further presumption that the other party was in a position to influence him. However, although this presumption is irrebuttable,[36] it remains open to the party alleged to have exercised his influence unduly to show that the transaction was in fact entered free from that presumed influence. So a solicitor who enters a transaction with a corporate client may find it relatively easy to show that the client was acting of its own free, informed will and so uphold the transaction.[37]

2–150   **Proving specific relationships.** Where the relationship is not one which is presumed to give one party influence over another, the specific relationship will have to be proved if the evidential presumption is to be established. It is important to bear in mind that it is not only the relationship but also a transaction which, as Lord Nicholls said in *Royal Bank of Scotland Plc v Etridge (No.2)*,[38] "cannot be accounted for by the ordinary motives of ordinary persons in that relationship" which must be proved.[39] In relation to the latter, the relevant

---

[30] See, e.g. *Mitchell v Homfray* (1881) 8 Q.B.D. 587; *Radcliffe v Price* (1902) 18 T.L.R. 466; *Williams v Johnson* [1937] 4 All E.R. 34; and *Brooks v Alker* (1975) 60 D.L.R. (3d) 577.

[31] See, e.g. *Liles v Terry* [1895] Q.B. 679; *Wills v Barron* [1902] A.C. 271; *Wright v Carter* [1903] 1 Ch. 27; *Allison v Clayhills* (1907) 97 L.T. 709; and *Lloyd v Coote & Ball* [1915] 1 K.B. 242.

[32] See, e.g. *Powell v Powell* [1900] 1 Ch. 243; *O'Connor v Foley* [1905] 1 I.R. 1; *M'Mackin v Hibernian Bank* [1905] 1 I.R. 296; *Lancashire Loans Ltd v Black* [1934] 1 K.B. 380; *Bullock v Lloyds Bank Ltd* [1955] 1 Ch. 817; and *Re Pauling's Settlement Trusts* [1964] Ch. 303. The presumption weakens and eventually disappears as the child is emancipated by age, marriage and living away from the parent.

[33] See, e.g. *Smith v Kay* (1859) 7 H.L.C. 750; and *Dettman v Metropolitan and Provincial Bank Ltd* (1863) 1 H. & M. 641.

[34] See, e.g. *Allcard v Skinner* (1887) 36 Ch.D. 145; *Morley v Loughnan* [1893] 1 Ch. 736; *Chennells v Bruce* (1939) 55 T.L.R. 422; and *Roche v Sherrington* [1982] 2 All E.R. 426.

[35] There is an overlap between fiduciary relationships and relationships giving rise to a presumption of undue influence (e.g. solicitor and client). However, they involve different types of unconscionable conduct.

[36] *Royal Bank of Scotland Plc v Etridge (No.2)* [2001] UKHL 44; [2002] 2 A.C. 773, *per* Lord Nicholls at [18].

[37] Ss in *Westlemetton (Vic) Pty Ltd v. Archer* [1982] V.R. 305.

[38] [2001] UKHL 44; [2002] 2 A.C. 773 at [13].

[39] It is preferable not to use the expression "manifest disadvantage" (which came from the speech of Lord Scarman in *National Westminster Bank Plc v Morgan* [1985] A.C. 686 at 703–707): see *Bank of Scotland Plc v Etridge (No.2)* [2001] UKHL 44; [2002] 2 A.C. 773, *per* Lord Nicholls at [26] and *per* Lord Scott at [220]. It is wrong to approach claims for undue influence by analysing the benefits and disadvantages of the transaction in issue, rather than to consider whether it can be readily explained otherwise than by the abuse of influence: see *Macklin v Dowsett* [2004] EWCA Civ 904; (2004) 34 E.G. 68 at [16]–[19], *per* Auld L.J. with whom Sedley and Jacob L.JJ. agreed.

circumstances were described in *Allcard v Skinner*[40] by Lindley L.J. in the context of gifts. He said[41]:

"But if the gift is so large as not to be reasonably accounted for on the ground of friendship, relationship, charity or some other ordinary motives on which ordinary men act, the burden is upon the donee to support the gift."[42]

There is a deliberate reluctance to define the circumstances in which one **2-151** person will be found on the facts to be in such a relationship to another as to be able to influence him, because the courts will not fetter their powers to prevent victimisation.[43] Nevertheless, it is possible to analyse the decided cases so as to discover what has led to a finding that, on the particular facts, one person was in a position to influence another. As with those relationships which are presumed to give one party influence over the other, such relationships will usually be intimate and personal. In *Yerkey v Jones*,[44] Dixon J. said that examination of the relations which were presumed to give influence showed that not only did they give one party "an opportunity of obtaining ascendancy or confidence and of abusing it" but also that "in none of those relations is it natural to expect the one party to give property to the other". In *Re Brocklehurst's Estate*,[45] Bridge L.J. found three characteristics of those relationships presumed to give one party influence over the other: a duty to advise, a position of actual or potential dominance and the existence of trust and confidence. He suggested that the first two were the most useful. In *Goldsworthy v Brickell*,[46] Nourse L.J. said:

"In all of these relationships ... the principle is the same. It is that the degree of trust and confidence is such that the party in whom it is reposed, either because he is or has become an adviser of the other or because he has been entrusted with the management of his affairs or everyday needs or for some other reason, is in a position to influence him into effecting the transaction of which complaint is later made."

So, undue influence is often found where an old person is looked after by **2-152** someone else,[47] but where a reasonable degree of independence is retained,

---

[40] (1887) 36 Ch.D. 145.

[41] *ibid.* at 185.

[42] For a case in which the transaction in issue was not such as to give rise to any presumption that influence had been abused in order to procure it see *Turkey v Awadh* [2005] EWCA Civ 382, where the transaction was not a normal commercial transaction, but was explained by the ordinary motives of people in the position of the parties.

[43] *Hunter v Atkins* (1832–4) 3 My. & Cr. 113 at 140–141, *per* Lord Brougham L.C.; *Allcard v Skinner* (1887) 36 Ch.D. 145 at 183, *per* Lindley L.J.; *National Westminster Bank Plc v Morgan* [1985] A.C. 686 at 709, *per* Lord Scarman; and *Bank of Scotland Plc v Etridge (No.2)* [2001] UKHL 44; [2002] 2 A.C. 773, *per* Lord Nicholls at [11].

[44] (1938–1939) 63 C.L.R. 649 at 675.

[45] [1978] Ch. 14 at 41.

[46] [1987] Ch. 378 at 401D.

[47] See, e.g. *Inche Noriah v Sheik Allie Bin Omar* [1929] A.C. 127; *Johnson v Buttress* (1936) 56 C.L.R. 113; *Stewart v Rundle* [1940] 2 D.L.R. 503; *Re Craig, Meneces v Middleton* [1971] Ch. 95; and *Goldsworthy v Brickell* [1987] Ch. 378. See also *Abbey National Bank Plc v Stringer* [2006] EWCA Civ 338 (vulnerable mother under influence of son).

influence will not be found.[48] In the same way, a woman in her fifties was found to be under the influence of her uncle because she relied on him completely in business matters and always followed his advice.[49] On the other hand, strong evidence will be needed to show that one businessman had influence over another.[50] Professional relationships which are commercial in character are unlikely to give rise to influence, whereas those which are more intimate and personal may well do so.

2–153   **Actual undue influence.** Finally, it is possible to set aside a transaction by proving the actual exercise of undue influence rather than a relationship which gave one person influence over another and a transaction which requires justification. Cases of actual undue influence are relatively infrequent and turn upon their own special facts. In the leading case of *Allcard v Skinner*[51] Lindley L.J. referred to four earlier decisions as instances of actual undue influence. One was a case where coercion was shown[52] and the others were cases involving charlatans.[53] What is needed is proof that something was done to "twist the mind of a donor".[54]

(iii) *Discharging the Burden of Proof*

2–154   Once it is appreciated that the presumption is evidential, it is clear that there is no defined way in which it can be rebutted. It is for the person seeking to uphold a transaction or gift to prove that it was not procured by the improper exercise of his influence. The evidence needed to rebut the presumption will depend on how strongly the presumption has been established. In *Powell v Powell*[55] the presumption extremely strong: it was proved that strong moral pressure had been applied on a girl only just of age by her stepmother. In such an extreme case, proof of independent advice might not be enough. However, in a more usual case, proof of independent advice will rebut the presumption. In the words of Fletcher Moulton L.J. in *Re Coomber; Coomber v Coomber*[56]:

> "All that is necessary is that some independent person, free from any taint of the relationship, or of the consideration of interest which would affect the act, should put clearly before the person what are the nature and the consequences of the act. It is for adult persons of competent mind to decide whether they will do an act, and I do not think that independent and competent advice means independent and competent approval. It simply means that the advice shall be removed entirely from the suspected

---

[48] *Jenkins v Public Curator* (1953) 90 C.L.R. 113; *Re Brockehurst's Estate* [1978] Ch. 14; and *R. v Hutton* [1978] N.I. 139.
[49] *Bank of New South Wales v Rogers* (1941) 65 C.L.R. 42.
[50] *Fowler v Wyatt* (1857) 24 Beav. 232 at 236–237, *per* Romilly M.R.
[51] (1887) 36 Ch.D. 145 at 181.
[52] *White v Mead* (1840) 2 Ir. Eq. Rep. 240.
[53] *Norton v Relly* (1764) 2 Eden 286; *Nottidge v Prince* (1860) 2 Giff. 246; and *Lyon v Home* (1868) L.R. 6 Eq. 655.
[54] *Daniel v Drew* [2005] EWCA Civ 507; *The Times*, May 18, 2005 at [31], *per* Ward L.J., with whom Buxton L.J. and Wilson J. agreed.
[55] [1900] 1 Ch. 243.
[56] [1911] 1 Ch. 723 at 730.

atmosphere; and that from the clear language of an independent mind, they should know what they are doing."[57]

6. CONFIDENTIALITY[58]

(a) *Introduction*

A duty of confidence arises when confidential information comes to the knowl-   2–155
edge of a person in circumstances where he has notice, or is held to have agreed, that the information is confidential, with the effect that it would be just in all the circumstances that he should be precluded from disclosing the information to others.[59] Although not intended to be a definitive statement when it was given, this proposition provides a useful starting point for the consideration of this area of predominantly judge-made law that reflects the willingness of judges to afford protection to people from being taken advantage of by those to whom they have entrusted confidential information.[60] It is a subject of particular importance to the professional and, indeed, the obligation to keep matters confidential is one of the defining features of a professional relationship.

The English Appellate courts have recently confirmed that that is no separate   2–156
cause of action for breach of the right to privacy.[61] However, with the advent of the Human Rights Act 1998 and the consequent need to give effect to Article 8 and protect, where appropriate, the wrongful disclosure or misuse of private information, the role and scope of actions for breach of confidence has been considerably adapted and developed.[62] A detailed analysis and discussion of the development and scope of the law of confidentiality, particularly so far as it concerns the protection of rights to privacy, is outside the scope of this book, which concentrates on the position of professionals. Issues concerning the protection of privacy tend to arise outside the sphere of professional relationships, although the impact on professionals may increase as the jurisprudence develops.

---

[57] This passage was quoted with approval by Lord Nicholls in *Royal Bank of Scotland Plc v Etridge (No.2)* [2001] UKHL 44; [2002] 2 A.C. 773 at [60].
[58] See generally Toulson and Phipps, *Confidentiality* (Sweet & Maxwell, 1996) ("Toulson and Phipps"). Gurry, *Breach of Confidence* (Clarendon Press, Oxford, 1984) ("Gurry") is also useful, if rather dated. Meagher, Gummow and Lehane, *Equity, Doctrines and Remedies* (4th edn, Butterworths, 2002) provide a helpful analysis in Ch.41
[59] *Att-Gen v Guardian Newspapers (No.2)* [1990] 1 A.C. 109 at 281B, *per* Lord Goff.
[60] *ibid.* at 267H, *per* Lord Griffiths.
[61] *Campbell v MGN Ltd* [2004] 2 A.C. 547; and *Douglas v Hello! Ltd (No.3)* [2005] EWCA Civ 595; [2006] Q.B. 125.
[62] See *Campbell v MGN Ltd* [2004] 2 A.C. 547, *per* Lord Nicholls at paras 17 and 18; and *Douglas v Hello! Ltd (No.3)* [2005] EWCA Civ 595; [2006] Q.B. 125, in particular paras 47–53. The Court of Appeal in *Douglas* (at para.53) noted that they could not "pretend that we find it satisfactory to shoehorn within the cause of action of breach of confidence claims for publication of unauthorised photographs of a private occasion" (the subject matter of that case). See further Mulheron "A Potential Framework for Privacy?" (2006) M.L.R. 679.

(b) *Origins of the Duty of Confidence*

2–157   ***Prince Albert v Strange.*** A duty of confidence and a remedy for its breach
have long been recognised by English law.[63] The jurisdiction is most often
thought to be equitable in nature but until the foundation stone of the modern law
was laid in *Prince Albert v Strange*[64] there was no general right of relief in
respect of the misuse (threatened or actual) of confidential information.[65] In
Prince Albert v Strange the claimant obtained an injunction restraining the
defendant from publishing a catalogue containing a collection of private etchings
made by Queen Victoria and Prince Albert. The collection was to be published
by the defendant in a catalogue that described the etchings, announced an
exhibition of them and included a false statement to the effect that the catalogue
had royal consent. The defendant had obtained copies of the etchings from an
employee of a printer who had received plates of the etchings in order to make
copies for the Queen. The claimant sought an injunction to prevent publication
of the catalogue on two grounds. The first was that publication would infringe the
claimant's proprietary rights in the etchings. The second was that the contents of
the catalogue had been derived from a breach of trust and thus that the claimant
was entitled to an injunction on the basis of knowing receipt. The claimant was
successful on both arguments both at first instance and on appeal. On appeal,
while asserting that its facts brought it squarely within the existing law,[66] Lord
Cottenham L.C. stated that "this case by no means depends solely upon the
question of property, for a breach of trust, confidence, or contract, would of itself
entitle the Plaintiff to an injunction".[67]

2–158   The defendant argued that there was no infringement of the claimant's proprietary rights in the etchings by mere descriptions of them appearing in the
catalogue. Further, he denied on affidavit having any reason to suspect that the
etchings had been obtained by unlawful means. It has been suggested that these
submissions, directed as they were to the two principle strands of the claimant's
case had some force.[68] It is for this reason that it might be thought that the case
went some way in establishing a more general (equitable) jurisdiction for obtaining a remedy of a threatened or actual breach of confidence.

2–159   **Theoretical bases for the jurisdiction after *Prince Albert v Strange*.**[69] Lord
Cottenham's list of grounds upon which the injunction in the Prince Albert case
may have been granted has been used to broaden the jurisdiction. Nevertheless,
a coherent theoretical justification for this extension was lacking with its existence being more assumed than explained:

---

[63] The jurisdiction was described as "ancient" by Megarry J. in *Coco v AN Clark (Engineers) Ltd*
[1969] R.P.C. at 46. See Ch.I of Toulson and Phipps, *op.cit.*, for an historical review of the jurisdiction.
[64] (1849) 1 De.G & Sm. 652; (1849) 1 Mac. & G. 25.
[65] A comprehensive summary of the older cases can be found in Toulson and Phipps, *op.cit.*, at paras
1–01 to 1–05 inclusive.
[66] The established categories of liability being infringement of proprietary rights, breach of contract,
breach of trust by the defendant and knowing receipt.
[67] (1849) 1 Mac. & G. 25 at 43.
[68] See Toulson and Phipps, *op.cit.*, at para.1–07.
[69] A detailed examination of this subject is beyond the scope of this work but reference should be
made to the helpful analysis in Toulson and Phipps, *op.cit.*, Ch.II.

"In some cases it has been referred to as property, in others contract, and in others again, it has been treated as founded upon trust or confidence, meaning, as I conceive, that the Court fastens the obligation on the conscience of the party . . . but whatever grounds the jurisdiction is founded, the authorities leave no doubt as to the exercise of it."[70]

Nevertheless, the basis upon which the courts act is not merely a matter of academic interest. It goes to the practical question of the remedies available, in particular to the questions whether the courts can award damages or equitable compensation and, if so, on what basis. Lord Cottenham mentioned three possibilities: property, contract or some trust-like obligation that binds the recipient's conscience. In the *Spycatcher* case,[71] Lord Goff noted that at least one member of the House of Lords deliberately avoided the "fundamental" question of whether or not, contract apart, the duty arose out of some obligation of conscience arising from the circumstances of the receipt of the information or whether confidential information was itself property.[72]

A proprietary right? This last question has led to a sharp division of opinion. **2–160** This is most obviously demonstrated by the decision of the House of Lords in *Boardman v Phipps*.[73] In that case purchasers of shares in a company made a profit by reason of their special position in relation to a trust which owned a substantial holding in the company. At the date they acquired their shares both purchasers were agents of the trustees and were able to obtain information about the company by reason of their position. One of the purchasers was the solicitor to the trustees. Neither purchaser reported these matters to the trustees. The House of Lords held by a majority of 3:2 that the purchasers were liable to account for the profits made, subject to an allowance for the value of their work. In the course of their speeches differing views were expressed as to whether information was or could be property. A majority (but not the same majority as that which concurred in the actual result) expressed doubts as to whether information could strictly be property.[74] Their views accord with much earlier authority that there was no property in a set of ideas.[75]

---

[70] *Morision v Moat* (1851) 9 Hare 241 at 255, *per* Turner V.C.

[71] *Att-Gen v Guardian Newspapers Ltd (No.2)* [1990] 1 A.C. 109.

[72] *ibid.* at 281, *per* Lord Goff, referred to in *Douglas v Hello! Ltd (No.3)* [2005] EWCA Civ 595; [2006] Q.B. 125 at [59].

[73] [1967] 2 A.C. 46.

[74] Viscount Dilhorne (dissenting) thought that "some information and knowledge can be properly regarded as property", but that the information in question was not "to be regarded as property of the trust in the same way as shares held by the trust" (*ibid.* at 89–90). Lord Cohen said that "Information is, of course, not property in the strict sense of that word" (*ibid.* at 102). Lord Upjohn (dissenting) was of the opinion that "information is not property at all" (*ibid.* at 127). Lord Hodson dissented "from the view that information is of its nature something which is not properly to be described as property" (*ibid.* at 107). Finally, Lord Guest thought that the information acquired "became trust property" (*ibid.* at 115). It is submitted that there is little to be gained from debating this point, which was not the point of difference between the majority and the minority.

[75] *Jeffreys v Boosey* (1854) 4 H.L.C. 814. See also *Bowstead and Reynolds on Agency* (17th edn), para.6–076. In *Att-Gen v Guardian Newspapers Ltd* [1987] 1 W.L.R. 1248 at 1264D–F, Browne-Wilkinson V.C. accepted that information "is not property in any sense", but still preferred an analysis based on "the traditional terms of equitable rights over property".

2–161   Although the notion that confidential information may have the character—or at least some of the characteristics—of property persisted,[76] the contrary view has been confirmed by recent authority. In particular, in *Douglas v Hello! Ltd (No.3)* the Court of Appeal rejected an argument that the claimants had a right to protection of information about their wedding because they had a proprietary interest in it. Rather, they had such a right because the information was private.[77] The Court of Appeal also held that an action for breach of confidence did not fall to be considered as a "tort" for the purposes of English law.[78] Nevertheless, aspects of such claims remain similar to claims in tort and it is important to bear tortious concepts in mind when considering this jurisdiction.

2–162   **Contract.** Here the position is more straight-forward. Particular contractual relationships, of which many professional relationships are good examples, give rise to express or implied terms imposing duties of confidence. In such circumstances, an award of damages for breach of the duty is not problematic. However, given that many claims for breach of confidence will not have a basis in contract, if the justification for the extra-contractual jurisdiction is not to be found in concepts of property (be it equitable or tort-based), a theoretical basis for the award of damages in equity must be found. This is amply demonstrated by recent claims concerned with the protection from publication of photographs or "private" information in circumstances where there was no pre-existing contractual or other relationship.

2–163   **A free-standing equitable duty.** The most coherent justification for the existence of an equitable duty of confidence and a jurisdiction to provide a remedy for its breach would seem to lie in the notion that the recipient of confidential information has his conscience bound in such a way that breach of his duty should properly be actionable. Here, the conceptual analysis is similar to

---

[76] See, for example, *Seager v Copydex Ltd (No.2)* [1969] 1 W.L.R. 809 in which the Court of Appeal ordered damages for the misuse of confidential information to be assessed by reference to the market value of the information and held that once the damages had been paid the right to use the information in question would belong to the defendants. This approach was adopted by analogy with the assessment of damages for conversion. As pointed out by Toulson and Phipps at para.2–16, the difficulty with this approach is that, ordinarily, liability for breach of confidence is founded upon conduct that binds the conscience, whereas the liability to pay damages for conversion may exist where the defendant is unaware of the true ownership of the property. In *Dowson & Mason Ltd v Potter* [1986] 1 W.L.R. 1419, damages were assessed on the basis that confidential information was property. However, this was because of the terms of a consent order.

[77] [2005] EWCA Civ 595; [2006] Q.B. 1265 at [119] and [126]–[127]. Lord Upjohn's statement *in Boardman v Phipps* [1967] 2 A.C. 46 at 127 was cited as an accurate summary of the law.

[78] See [2005] EWCA Civ 595; [2006] Q.B. 1265 at [96], citing *Kitechnology BV v Unicor GmbH* [1995] I.L. Pr. 568; [1995] F.S.R. 795 at para.40; and Clerk & Lindsell on Torts, (18th edn, 2000) at 2 and 3 to para.27–001. Their Lordships also found persuasive the suggestion in *Dicey & Morris on the Conflict of Laws* (13th edn, 2000, paras 34–029ff) that a claim for breach of confidence fell to be categorised as a restitutionary claim for unjust enrichment. Note, however, that Lord Nicholls, in *Campbell v MGN Ltd* [2004] 2 A.C. 547 (at, inter alia, [14]) referred to the cause of action for breach of confidence as a tort, at least in the context of a claim which concerned the misuse of private information. See also Goff and Jones, *The Law of Restitution* (6th edn) para.34–014, where it is suggested that there may be concurrent liability for a breach of confidence in contract and tort and the court may act on the assumption that the information was the property of the confider which the recipient had converted.

that employed in the case of fiduciary obligations.[79] The focus is on the relationship between the parties, the knowledge and conscience of one of them and the type of duty imposed is in the nature of an inhibition rather than a requirement (as in the case of a tortious duty of care) to meet a required standard of conduct. This approach is not without support from the authorities. Thus in *Fraser v Evans*,[80] Lord Denning M.R. commented:

> "The jurisdiction is based not so much on property or on contract as on the duty to be of good faith. No person is permitted to divulge to the world information which he had received in confidence, unless he had just cause or excuse for doing so."[81]

This approach has also been adopted in Australia where it has been said that **2–164** the rational basis for the general equitable jurisdiction "lies in the notion of an obligation of conscience arising from the circumstances in or through which the information was communicated or obtained".[82] Quite apart from its conceptual lucidity, such an approach has the advantage of providing a clear justification for an award of damages (or equitable compensation) for breach of confidence. Other attempts have been made to justify the availability of this remedy for breach of what would appear to be an exclusively equitable duty, but these have largely been unpersuasive.[83] However, the recognition of a free-standing equitable duty of confidence and a corresponding jurisdiction to provide a full range of remedies, including damages (or equitable compensation), for its breach appears consistent with developments in the analogous area of the law of fiduciary obligations.[84] The question remains as to whether this free-standing equitable jurisdiction simply augments the existing bases for the recognition of a duty of

---

[79] Indeed, it is sometimes described as a fiduciary obligation: see *Att-Gen v Blake* [1998] Ch. 439 at 454F. However, as Henry J. observed when giving the opinion of the Privy Council in *Arklow Investments Ltd v Maclean* [2000] 1 W.L.R. 594 at 600F–G, little is gained by attaching this label. What matters is whether in the particular circumstances equity requires that information be kept confidential. The better view is that, while a fiduciary may well find himself obliged to maintain the confidentiality of information, "Where ... the essence of the complaint is misuse of confidential information, the appropriate cause of action in favour of the party aggrieved is breach of confidence and not breach of fiduciary duty" (*per* Sopinka J. in *LAC Minerals Ltd v International Corona Resources Ltd* (1989) 61 D.L.R. (4th) 14 (cited by Otton L.J. in *Indata Equipment Supplies Ltd v ACL Ltd* [1998] 1 B.C.L.C. 412 at 419h–420a).

[80] [1969] 1 Q.B. 349 at 361.

[81] See also, e.g. *Morison v Moat* (1851) 9 Hare 241; and *Seager v Copydex Ltd* [1967] 1 W.L.R. 923 at 931F, *per* Lord Denning M.R.:

> "The law on this subject does not depend on any implied contact. It depends on the broad principle of equity that he who has received information in confidence shall not take unfair advantage of it. He must not make use of it to the prejudice of him who gave it without obtaining his consent."

See also *Att-Gen v Guardian Newspapers Ltd (No.2)* [1990] 1 A.C. 109 at 215G–H, *per* Bingham L.J.

[82] *Moorgate Tobacco Co Ltd v Philip Morris Ltd (No.2)* (1984) 156 C.L.R. 415 at 438, *per* Deane J., High Court of Australia; cited with approval in *Smith, Kline & French Laboratories (Australia) Ltd v Secretary to the Department of Community Services and Health* [1990] F.S.R 617 (affirmed [1991] F.C.R 291) at 673.

[83] See, e.g. the suggestion by Lord Goff that damages are available by reason of a "beneficent interpretation" of Lord Cairns' Act in *Att.-Gen. v Guardian Newspapers (No.2)* [1990] 1 A.C. 109 at 286D–E and the alternative justification for the award of damages in *Seager v Copydex Ltd* [1967] 1 W.L.R. 923 on the basis of a quantum meruit in Goff and Jones, *The Law of Restitution* (6th edn, 2002), para.34–013.

[84] See Ch.3, paras 3–017 and 3–018, below.

confidence, or whether it is of itself the single basis upon which the jurisdiction as a whole may be explained.

2–165   In New Zealand the jurisdiction is seen as deriving historically from equity, but it has been suggested that its origins are of less relevance than its existence: the New Zealand courts will now award damages for breach of a duty of confidence.[85] In *Hosking v Runting*[86] the New Zealand Court of Appeal reiterated the equitable, "conscience based" foundation of an action for breach of confidence. However, the majority declined to follow the English approach of developing the equitable remedy of breach of confidence to encompass protection from invasion of privacy, preferring to recognise breaches of confidence and privacy as separate causes of action.[87]

2–166   In Canada, there is support for the view that an action for breach of confidence is now to be regarded as *sui generis* with a wide variety of available remedies.[88] In Australia the existence of an independent equitable jurisdiction has been recognised for some time.[89] The latter is the preferable view.[90] There is a coherent justification for an independent equitable jurisdiction, namely that the recipient of information which he knows or should know is confidential, should maintain that confidentiality. To bring all cases of breach or threatened breach of confidence within other categories such as claims for abuse of property or breach of a fiduciary obligation would or might involve stretching those categories beyond their proper limits. To exclude claims which did not fall within the proper limits of such categories would be to deny a remedy where one should be given.[91] It is with this independent duty of confidence that the rest of this section is concerned.

---

[85] *Aquaculture Corp v New Zealand Green Mussel Co Ltd* [1990] 3 N.Z.L.R. 299 at 301, *per* Cooke P.

[86] [2004] N.Z.C.A. 34.

[87] *ibid.* at [45] and [48]. Tipping J. said that the English Courts had, in adopting this approach, found it necessary to strain the boundaries of the remedy to the point where the concept of confidence has become somewhat artificial.

[88] *LAC Minerals Ltd v International Corona Resources Ltd* (1989) 61 D.L.R. (4th) 14, *per* Sopinka J. The remedies available included an award of damages and the imposition of a constructive trust. This analysis was followed in *Cadbury Schweppes Inc v FBI Foods Ltd* (1999) 167 D.L.R. (4th) 577.

[89] *Moorgate Tobacco Co Ltd v Philip Morris Ltd (No.2)* (1984) 156 C.L.R. 415 at 437–438, *per* Deane J:

"It is unnecessary, for the purposes of the present appeal, to attempt to define the precise scope of the equitable jurisdiction to grant relief against an actual or threatened abuse of confidential information not involving any tort or any breach of some express or implied contractual provision, some wider fiduciary duty or some copyright or trade mark right. A general equitable jurisdiction to grant such relief has long been asserted and should, in my view, now be accepted: see *Commonwealth of Australia v John Fairfax & Sons Ltd* (1980) 147 C.L.R. 39 at 50–52. Like most heads of exclusive equitable jurisdiction, its rational basis does not lie in proprietary right. It lies in the notion of an obligation of conscience arising from the circumstances in or through which the information was communicated or obtained."

This was approved by Scott J. and Bingham L.J. in *Att-Gen v Guardian Newspapers (No.2)* [1990] 1 A.C. 109 at 147H and 216B. For subsequent development of the law in Australia see Toulson and Phipps, para.2–23.

[90] Lord Keith recognised "an independent equitable principle of confidence" in *Att-Gen v Guardian Newspapers Ltd (No.2)* [1990] 1 A.C. 109 at 255E. See also *Duchess of Argyll v Duke of Argyll* [1967] Ch. 302 at 318–322, *per* Ungoed-Thomas J.; and *Douglas v Hello! Ltd* [2001] Q.B. 967 at [121], *per* Sedley L.J.

[91] See also Toulson and Phipps, at para.2–24.

(c) *Elements of the Cause of Action*

A claim for breach of confidence may be established if three essential require- **2–167**
ments are met:

(1) the information that forms the subject-matter of the action must be of a
confidential nature;

(2) it must have been imparted by the confider to the recipient in circumstances which justify the imposition of a duty of confidence; and

(3) the recipient must have used or disclosed the information without the
authority or consent of the confider, possibly to the detriment of the
confider.[92]

Confidentiality of the information. The information which it is alleged is the **2–168**
subject of a duty of confidence must display a "necessary quality of confidence
about it" and must not be "something which is public property and public
knowledge".[93] It must not be something which is public property and public
knowledge.[94] Nevertheless, it is possible for confidential information to be
comprised of information that is in the public domain. What is essential, at least
in a commercial context, is that the confider has used his brain in compiling that

---

[92] See *Coco v AN Clark (Engineers) Ltd* [1969] R.P.C. 41 at 47, *per* Megarry J.; described by Simon
Brown L.J. in *R. v Department of Health Ex p. Source Informatics Ltd* [2001] Q.B. 424 at [14] as the
"conventional starting point for considering the nature and scope of the duty of confidentiality"; and
by Lord Nicholls in *Campbell v MGN Ltd* [2004] UKHL 24; [2004] 2 A.C. 457 at [13] as the "classic
exposition" of the cause of action. See also *Murray v Yorkshire Fund Managers Ltd* [1998] 1 W.L.R.
951 at 956G–H, *per* Nourse L.J. The Court of Appeal in *Douglas v Hello! Ltd (No.3)* noted that the
essential feature creating the duty of confidence was the circumstances in which the information was
communicated from the confider to the confidant: [2005] EWCA Civ 595; [2006] Q.B. 1265 at
[55].
[93] *Saltman Engineering Co Ltd v Campbell Engineering Co Ltd* (1948) 65 R.P.C. 203 at 215, *per* Lord
Greene M.R. In *Douglas v Hello! Ltd*, [2005] EWCA Civ 595; [2006] Q.B. 1265 the Court of Appeal
observed that this was "not the clearest of definitions", commenting that information will be
confidential if it is available to one person (or group of people) and not generally available to others,
provided that the person or group possessing the information does not intend that it should become
available to others (para.55). See also *Hilton v Barker Booth & Eastwood (a firm)* [2005] UKHL 8;
[2005] 1 W.L.R. 567 at [7], *per* Lord Scott and [33]–[34], *per* Lord Walker (the facts that a solicitor's
client had been adjusted bankrupt and found guilty of criminal offences were not confidential
information, being matters of public record). However, the solicitor still had a professional obligation
not to disclose them, but this was not because of a duty of confidence, but because of his duty to
further his client's interests which would be prejudiced by disclosure of the information.
[94] *Seager v Copydex Ltd* [1967] 1 W.L.R. 923 at 931G, *per* Lord Denning M.R. ("public knowledge"); and *Woodward v Hutchins* [1977] 1 W.L.R. 760 at 764D, *per* Lord Denning M.R. ("in the
public domain"). Information "in the public domain" has been described as meaning "no more than
that the information is so generally accessible that, in all the circumstances, it cannot be regarded as
confidential": *per* Lord Goff in *Att-Gen v Guardian Newspapers (No.2)* [1990] 1 A.C. 109 at
282C–D. See also *Christofi v Barclays Bank Plc* [2000] 1 W.L.R. 937, CA (no breach of confidentiality by claimant's bank in advising trustee in bankruptcy of claimant's husband that a caution the
trustee had registered had been warned off the register—the trustee should have been advised of this
anyway).

information or using it in a particular way and has produced a result that can only be achieved by another person if that same exercise is performed.[95] Alternatively (and more relevantly in a non commercial context) it must have "the basic attribute of inaccessibility".[96] So taking unauthorised photographs of a confidential event could amount to a breach of confidence (even where the claimants had contracted for the authorised publication of other photographs).[97] Information can lose its confidential quality with time.[98] However, although, in general, once information is in the public domain it will no longer be confidential or entitled to the protection of the law of confidence (so that once personal information about an individual's private life has been widely published it may serve no useful purpose to prohibit further publication) the same is not necessarily true of photographs which may do more than convey information but also intrude on privacy.[99] A duty of confidence will not apply to mere trivia or useless information.[1] It is important to identify what information is at issue: for example, it is one thing to disclose the identities of patients who are prescribed various drugs, but another just to disclose information as to which doctors prescribed which drugs, while not revealing the identities of their patients.[2]

2–169 The obligation of confidentiality "extends to matter which a reasonable person would understand to be intended to be secret, or to be available to a limited group to which that person does not belong".[3] In the context of information about a

---

[95] *Saltman Engineering Co Ltd v Campbell Engineering Co Ltd* (1948) 65 R.P.C. 203 at 215, *per* Lord Greene M.R.

[96] *Att-Gen v Guardian Newspapers Ltd (No.2)* [1990] 1 A.C. 109 at 215B, *per* Bingham L.J. referring to Gurry, at p.70. See also Toulson and Phipps, at para.3–09.

[97] *Douglas v Hello! Ltd* [2001] Q.B. 967 at [71], *per* Brooke L.J. and at [165], *per* Keene L.J, followed on this point in *Douglas v Hello! Ltd (No.3)* [2005] EWCA Civ 595; [2006] Q.B. 1265. See also *Shelley Films Ltd v Rex Features* Ltd [1994] E.M.L.R. 134; *Hellewell v Chief Constable of Derbyshire* [1995] 1 W.L.R. 804 at 807H; *Creation Records Ltd v News Group Newspapers Ltd* [1997] E.M.L.R. 444; and *Australian Broadcasting Corp v Lenah Game Meats Pty Ltd* [2001] H.C.A. 63; (2001) 185 A.L.R. 1 at [53].

[98] See, e.g. *Att-Gen v Guardian Newspapers Ltd (No.2)* [1990] 1 A.C. 109 at 215C–E, *per* Bingham L.J., giving the example of the planned date for D-Day, which was highly confidential before the landings, but became known to the world at large within a few days. See also *Arklow Investments Ltd v Maclean* [2000] 1 W.L.R. 594 at 600H. However, a person who has received the information while it was confidential will not be allowed to obtain advantage from his early receipt when it ceases to be confidential: *Coco v AN Clark (Engineers) Ltd* [1969] R.P.C. 41 at 47 referring to *Seager v Copydex Ltd* [1967] 1 W.L.R. 923.

[99] As to the nature of photographs and the special considerations that attach thereto, see *Theakston v MGN Ltd* [2002] E.M.L.R. 398 (para.78); *Von Hannover v Germany* (2005) 40 E.H.R.R.1, at [59]; and *Campbell v MGN Ltd* [2004] 2 A.C. 457 at [123] and [155].

[1] See, e.g. Lord Goff in *Att-Gen v Guardian Newspapers (No.2)* [1990] 1 A.C. 109 at 282D. The information has to be significant to the confider in that it is important to him to maintain its confidentiality (see *Moorgate Tobacco Co Ltd v Philip Morris Ltd (No.2)* (1984) 156 C.L.R. 414 at 438, *per* Deane J.). It follows that details of someone's private life are not "trivia": *Stephens v Avery* [1988] Ch. 499; and *Barrymore v News Group Newspapers Ltd* [1997] F.S.R. 600. For an example of confidential information which was also useless, see *McNicol v Sportsman's Book Stores* [1930] MaG. C.C. 116, where Maugham J. refused to restrain a threatened breach of confidence as to a "perfectly useless" betting system based on the age of the moon (see *Att-Gen v Guardian Newspapers (No.2)* [1990] 1 A.C. 109 at 149C–D, *per* Scott J.).

[2] *R. v Department of Health Ex p. Source Informatics Ltd* [2001] Q.B. 424, CA.

[3] *per* Gleeson C.J. in *Australian Broadcasting Corp v Lenah Game Meats Pty Ltd* [2001] H.C.A. 63; (2001) 185 A.L.R. 1 at [36].

person's private life, it has been recognised that the privacy of personal information is something worthy of protection in its own right[4] and, as such, the duty of confidence will arise where the party subject to the duty knows or ought to know that the other person can reasonably expect his privacy to be protected.[5]

Circumstances in which the information is imparted. The information must   2–170
be confided in the sense that the recipient knows or should know that he should keep it confidential. This will largely be a question of fact in any particular case. In the case of a professional person to whom information is imparted by a client, it will not usually be hard to show.

Misuse. The third requirement for liability for breach of a duty of confidence   2–171
is that the confidential information has been or is threatened to be misused by the recipient. Misuse will usually involve unauthorised disclosure of the information to a third party, but need not do so.[6] The recipient will have been given the information so that he can use it for some purpose or purposes. To be actionable the use must involve taking some improper use of the information.[7] So, while it may be possible to misuse only part of the information confided,[8] if that part of the information can be used so as to preserve the confidential interest in it which the recipient is bound to protect, then there will be no misuse.[9] So, in a case concerning use of confidential information which had been given to pharmacists Simon Browne L.J. said:

"To my mind the one clear and consistent theme emerging from all these authorities is this: the confidant is placed under a duty of good faith to the confider and the touchstone

---

[4] per Lord Hoffmann in *Campbell v MGN Ltd* [2004] 2 A.C. 457 at [46].
[5] See *A v B Plc* [2003] Q.B. 195 at 96; and *Douglas v Hello! Ltd* [2005] EWCA Civ 595; [2006] Q.B. 1265 at [78]–[82]. It was recognised in the latter case at [82] that the comments cited by the Court of Appeal underlined Lord Nicholls' observation in *Campbell v MGN Ltd* [2004] 2 A.C. 457 at [14] that the use of the phrase "duty of confidence" and the description of private information as "confidential" are "not altogether comfortable".
[6] For example, using confidential information to compete against the confider's commercial interests.
[7] *Smith Kline and French Laboratories (Australia) Ltd v Secretary to the Department of Community Services and Health* (1991) 99 A.L.R. 679 at 691–692, (Federal Court of Australia). In *Murray v Yorkshire Fund Managers Ltd* [1998] 1 W.L.R. 951, CA, the claimant was one of a group of six people who had come together to produce a confidential business plan for the takeover of a company. He provided a copy to a third party so the third party could consider whether to invest. The third party then approached the other members of the group and proceeded with them, but without the claimant. He had not been provided with the confidential plan to approach the others, but it involved no breach of confidence in discussing it with them—they knew its contents already. Nor, given the loose relationship between the claimant and the other members of the group, had there been any misuse of the information.
[8] See Gurry, p.258.
[9] *R. v Department of Health Ex p. Source Informatics Ltd* [2001] 2 Q.B. 424: pharmacists providing details of drugs prescribed by doctors not in breach of duty of confidentiality to the patients, because the information had been anonymised; *cf. W v Edgell* [1990] Ch. 359 at 417, where Bingham L.J. suggested that a psychiatrist could discuss an individual case in an article or in memoirs or in gossiping with friends if he took appropriate steps to conceal the identity of his patient.

by which to judge the scope of his duty and whether or not it has been fulfilled or breached is his own conscience, no more and no less. One asks, therefore, on the facts of this case: would a reasonable pharmacist's conscience be troubled by the proposed use to be made of patients' prescriptions? Would he think that by entering [the applicants'] scheme he was breaking his customers' confidence, making unconscientious use of the information they provide?"[10]

2–172   **Justified use.** The protection afforded by equity is against misuse of confidential information. The conscience of the pharmacist in Simon Brown L.J.'s test would not be troubled if disclosure, although unauthorised, were in the public interest or required by law. While these aspects of the law of confidentiality can be treated as defences, they are better seen as examples of unauthorised use, which is not a misuse.[11]

2–173   **Disclosure justified in the public interest.** Where it is said by a defendant that his unauthorised disclosure was required in the public interest, the court has to weigh two competing interests: the public interest in maintaining confidence against a countervailing public interest favouring disclosure.[12] The latter extends to all matters of which disclosure is required in the public interest, and not just to information relating to a crime or fraud.[13] However, publication to the world at large or to the media may not be justified, while more limited publication may be.[14] So, in *Francombe v Mirror Group Newspapers*,[15] publication in a national newspaper of information obtained in breach of confidence by illegal wire tapping was not justified, whereas in *Lion Laboratories Ltd v Evans*,[16] employees of a company which made intoximeters were justified in informing another

---

[10] [2001] 2 Q.B. 424 at 952E–F.

[11] See, e.g. *Att-Gen v Guardian Newspapers Ltd (No.2)* [1990] 1 A.C. 109 at 282E–F, where Lord Goff treated the possibility that public interest might favour disclosure as a limiting principle to the broad general principle. Other limiting principles were that the information must still be confidential and must not be useless or trivial.

[12] See, e.g. *Att-Gen v Guardian Newspapers Ltd (No.2)* [1990] 1 A.C. 109 at 282E–F, *per* Lord Goff.

[13] *ibid.* at 282G–H, *per* Lord Goff, citing *Beloff v Pressdram Ltd* [1973] 1 All E.R. 241 at 260F, *per* Ungoed-Thomas J.; and *Lion Laboratories Ltd v Evans* [1985] Q.B. 526 at 550C, *per* Griffiths L.J. (see also the judgment of Bingham L.J. in [1990] 1 A.C. 109 at 222A–E and that of Scott J. at 159H–161A which are to like effect); *cf.* the Public Interest Disclosure Act 1998, which applies to disclosure by employees.

[14] "The disclosure must, I should think, be to one who has a proper interest to receive the information. Thus it would be proper to disclose a crime to the police; or a breach of the Restrictive Trade Practices Act to the registrar. There may be cases where the misdeed is of such a character that the public interest may demand, or at least excuse, publication on a broader field, even to the press.": *Initial Services Ltd v Putterill* [1968] 1 Q.B. 396 at 405–406, *per* Lord Denning M.R. (see further *Att-Gen v Guardian Newspapers Ltd (No.2)* [1990] 1 A.C. 109 at 282E–F and 222E–H, *per* Bingham L.J.)

The earlier authorities on confidentiality and the press now need to be read subject to Art.10 of the Convention for the Protection of Human Rights and Fundamental Freedoms, which requires interference with the freedom of the press to be justified: see *A v B* [2002] EWCA Civ 337; [2003] Q.B. 195; and *Campbell v MGN Ltd* [2004] UKHL 22; [2004] 2 A.C. 467.

[15] [1984] 1 W.L.R. 893, CA.

[16] [1985] Q.B. 526, CA.

national newspaper that the intoximeters were unreliable.[17] A useful example of this balancing exercise in the context of auditors is *Price Waterhouse v BCCI Holdings (Luxembourg) SA*.[18] Price Waterhouse ("PW") acted as auditors to the BCCI group of companies. The firm also performed a variety of other functions including reporting to an internal committee of BCCI on problem loans made by that bank. PW were also required to report to BCCI's solicitors in order that they could advise BCCI. After the financial collapse of BCCI the Serious Fraud Office and the Bank of England served a number of notices on PW demanding the production of documents under s.2 of the Criminal Justice Act 1987 and s.39 of the Banking Act 1987. PW wished to co-operate with these demands and sought declarations that the information sought was not protected by either legal professional privilege or a duty of confidence. Having found that the information was not subject to legal professional privilege and that even if it was, s.39 of the Banking Act 1987 could nevertheless require its disclosure, Millett J. turned to consider the issue of confidence. He found that the public interest in the effective regulation and supervision of authorised banking institutions outweighed the public interest in maintaining the confidence in the information.[19]

Disclosure required by law. It is no misuse of confidential information to disclose it if that disclosure is required by law. So, for example, disclosure of confidential and even privileged documents may be required by statute.[20] Confidential documents may have to be disclosed in litigation.[21]   **2–174**

---

[17] Other examples include *Stephens v Avery* [1988] Ch. 499; *X v Y* [1988] 2 All E.R. 648; *Woolgar v Chief Constable of Sussex Police* [2000] 1 W.L.R. 25; and *Frankson v Home Office* [2003] EWCA Civ 655; [2003] 1 W.L.R. 1952.

   More recent examples are helpfully collected in the judgment of Gray J. in *Jockey Club v Buffham* [2002] EWHC 1866, QB; [2003] Q.B. 462 at paras [46]–[51]. Having set out the authorities, Gray J. held that the public interest in horse racing justified use by the BBC of otherwise confidential information.

[18] [1992] B.C.L.C. 583, *per* Millett J.

[19] See also *W v Edgell* [1990] Ch. 359, *per* Scott J., CA (disclosure of psychiatric report to mental health review tribunal justified and overrode the duty of confidence owed by a doctor to his patient); and *Re a Company's Application* [1989] Ch. 477, *per* Scott J. (disclosure to FIMBRA and the Inland Revenue by former employee of FIMBRA member of member's alleged breaches of FIMBRA rules and tax irregularities permitted). These cases are discussed in Toulson and Phipps, at paras 6–12 to 6–20.

   The decision of the Court of Appeal in *H (a healthcare worker) v Associated Newspapers Ltd* [2002] EWCA Civ 195; [2002] Lloyd's Rep. Med. 210 illustrates the fine balance that has to be struck between confidentiality (in particular the information imparted in confidence by a healthcare worker to his employer that he was HIV positive) and the public interest and freedom of the press. A solicitor who knows from confidential information obtained from his client that his client might lack mental capacity might be justified in making an application to the Court of Protection, but not in disclosing that information to another solicitor retained by the client on another matter: *Marsh v Sofaer* [2003] EWHC 3334, Ch; [2004] P.N.L.R. 24 (Morritt V.C.).

[20] See, e.g. *Price Waterhouse v BCCI Holdings (Luxembourg) SA* [1992] B.C.L.C. 583, where Millett J. held that s.37 of the Banking Act 1987 empowered the Bank of England to require production of privileged, confidential documents. See also *R. (Kent Pharmaceuticals Ltd) v Director of the Serious Fraud Office* [2004] EWCA Civ 1494; [2005] W.L.R. 1302.

[21] See, e.g. *Robertson v Canadian Imperial Bank of Commerce* [1994] 1 W.L.R. 1493, PC. See also *Barclays Bank Plc (trading as Barclaycard) v Taylor* [1989] 1 W.L.R. 1066, CA (banks not in breach of contractual duty of confidentiality in complying with and not challenging access orders under Police and Criminal Evidence Act 1984).

2–175   **Detriment.** It is sometimes suggested that a claimant must also establish that he has suffered or will suffer detriment as a result of a breach of confidence.[22] There are powerful arguments that he need not.[23] In any event, the answer will lie in the nature of the confidential interest which the recipient is bound to preserve and in the remedy being sought. For example, where the confidential information concerns the claimant's health or personal life, a claim for an injunction to restrain unauthorised disclosure could be allowed even though the claimant might not be able to show that he would suffer financial detriment were the information to be publicised. However, once the information had been made public then, unless there were a claim for an account of profits, he would have no obvious remedy unless he could show actual damage.[24] There is a danger in this area of descending into semantics.[25]

(d) *The Continuing Duty to Former Clients*[26]

2–176   **A continuing duty.** A distinctive feature of a duty of confidence is that it is a continuing duty that survives the termination of the professional client relationship so that the professional will be obliged to preserve the confidentiality of information imparted during the course of the retainer after that retainer has come to an end.[27] In many cases (e.g. medical records) this will not create any difficulty. However, there are circumstances in which the continuing duty of confidentiality owed to a former client might conflict with duties owed to a

---

[22] See, e.g. *Att-Gen v Guardian Newspapers Ltd (No.2)* [1990] 1 A.C. 109 at 270F, *per* Lord Griffiths. On this topic generally see Toulson and Phipps, paras 6–01 to 6–04.

[23] See, e.g. the judgment of Gummow J. in *Smith Kline and French Laboratories (Australia) Ltd v Department of Community Services* (1990) A.L.R. 87 at 126:
> "The basis of the equitable jurisdiction to protect obligations of confidence lies, as the present case illustrates, in an obligation of conscience arising from the circumstances in or through which the information, the subject of the obligation, was communicated or obtained: *Moorgate Tobacco Co Ltd v Philip Morris Ltd (No.2)* (1984) 156 C.L.R. 414 at 438. The obligation of conscience is to respect the confidence, not merely to refrain from causing detriment to the plaintiff. The plaintiff comes to equity to vindicate his right to observance of the obligation, not necessarily to recover loss or to restrain infliction of apprehended loss. To look into a related field, when has equity said that the only breaches of trust to be restrained are those that would prove detrimental to the beneficiaries?"

Once it is appreciated that to be confidential the information must be of significance to the claimant, the need to show detriment would appear to be superfluous or readily fulfilled.

[24] *Att-Gen v Guardian Newspapers Ltd (No.2)* [1990] 1 A.C. 109 at 255H–256A, *per* Lord Keith, who was not of the view that detriment should have to be shown.

[25] *ibid.* at 281H–282B, *per* Lord Goff:
> "I would also, like Megarry J. in *Coco v AN Clark (Engineers) Ltd* [1969] R.P.C. 41 at 48, wish to keep open the question whether detriment to the plaintiff is an essential ingredient of an action for breach of confidence. Obviously, detriment or potential detriment to the plaintiff will nearly always form part of his case: but this may not always be necessary . . . In the present case the point is immaterial, since it is established that in cases of Government secrets the Crown has to establish not only that the information is confidential, but also that publication would be to its 'detriment' in the sense that the public interest requires that it should not be published. That the word 'detriment' should be extended so far as to include such a case perhaps indicates that everything depends upon how wide a meaning can be given to the word 'detriment' in this context."

[26] See generally Hollander and Salzedo, *Conflicts of Interest and Chinese Walls* (2nd edn, Sweet & Maxwell, 2004).

[27] *Bolkiah v KPMG* [1999] 2 A.C. 222 at 235D, *per* Lord Millett.

different client. Absent the informed consent of the former client, the professional person or firm will be prevented from acting for the second client unless there is no risk of disclosure.[28] In this context "no risk" means that there is no real risk, as opposed to a merely fanciful risk. The risk need not be substantial, at least in cases where questions of legal professional privilege arise.[29]

The basis upon which the court acts is not to prevent a conflict between duty to one client and duty to another: there is no fiduciary duty to advance the interests of a former client.[30] Rather it is to protect and preserve the confidentiality in information which has been imparted during the course of the retainer or other professional relationship.[31]

Bolkiah v KPMG (a firm). The law in this area has been authoritatively stated   **2–177** by Lord Millett in *Bolkiah v KPMG (a firm).*[32] The defendant firm of chartered accountants were the auditors of an investment agency established to hold and manage various assets of the government of Brunei. The claimant was a member of the royal family of Brunei and chairman of the agency. In 1996, he instructed the firm to provide forensic accountancy and litigation support services in relation to litigation concerning his financial affairs. In the course of this work the firm was given access to highly confidential information concerning the claimant's assets. The litigation was settled in 1998 and the firm then undertook no further work for the claimant. In 1998, the claimant was removed from his position as chairman of the agency and the government of Brunei began an investigation into the activities of the agency during the period when the claimant had been its chairman. As part of this investigation the agency retained the firm to investigate the whereabouts of certain assets which it was suspected had been misappropriated by the claimant. The firm took steps to try to protect the claimant's confidentiality by erecting "Chinese walls" between those who had

---

[28] Particular problems arise where the professional firm owes a duty to a new client to divulge confidential information imparted by a former client. In such circumstances, unless the new client agrees to release the firm from that duty, it may well be impossible for the firm to act: *Re A Firm of Solicitors* [1992] Q.B. 959; and *Re A Firm of Solicitors* [1997] Ch. 1.

[29] *Bolkiah v KPMG (a firm)* [1999] 2 A.C. 222 at 237B, *per* Lord Millett. See also *Re A Firm of Solicitors* [1997] Ch. 1 at 9, *per* Lightman J.

[30] *ibid.* at 235C–D, *per* Lord Millett. See also *Att-Gen v Blake* [1998] Ch. 439 at 453H, CA:

"We do not recognise the concept of a fiduciary obligation which continues notwithstanding the determination of the particular relationship which gives rise to it. Equity does not demand a duty of undivided loyalty from a former employee to his former employer . . . "

In *Longstaff v Birtles* [2001] Lloyd's Rep. P.N. 826, Mummery L.J., with whom the other members of the Court of Appeal agreed, said that a solicitor's fiduciary duty to tell a client to obtain independent advice before dealing with him could extend beyond the termination of the retainer if the trust and confidence engendered by that retainer remained. While this may be the case in relation to the specific subject matter of the retainer and while questions of undue influence might arise in relation to a transaction entered after the termination of the retainer, as a wider statement of the law this must be doubted. In particular the authorities referred to above were not cited in *Longstaff.*

[31] It is no answer to a claim for breach of a duty owed to client A not to disclose information to client B, that the solicitor has contracted with client B on terms which require him to disclose the information to client B: *Hilton v Barker Booth & Eastwood (a firm)* [2005] UKHL 8; [2005] 1 W.L.R. 567, *per* Lord Scott at [6] and, *per* Lord Walker at [35].

[32] [1999] 2 A.C. 222.

worked on the claimant's litigation and those who were to undertake the investigative work for the agency. The claimant commenced an action for breach of confidence and sought an injunction restraining the firm from acting for the agency.

2–178   The information obtained by the firm during the course of its retainer by the claimant was clearly confidential, he had not consented to its disclosure and it was of obvious relevance to the investigation that the agency now wished the firm to carry out. The House of Lords was not convinced that the proposed Chinese walls would be sufficiently strong to avoid a risk of information passing through them. While there was no rule of law that such measures were ineffective, the assumption was that information would move within a firm. The firm had to show by clear and convincing evidence that effective measures had been taken to ensure that no disclosure would occur.[33] Lord Millett recognised the importance of Chinese walls, for example in the City of London and in the Core Conduct of Business Rules published by the Financial Services Authority. However, he was not satisfied that ad hoc measures such as those proposed by the defendant firm would be sufficiently effective, not least because the proposed Chinese wall would be within a single department and office, between colleagues who were accustomed to working with each other.[34]

2–179   **Factors to consider.** In order to justify the court's intervention there must be a non-fanciful risk that confidential information will leak to the new client. It will be important in any case to consider the nature of the information in question and its relevance to the new client's affairs. It may also be relevant to consider

---

[33] [1999] 2 A.C. 222 at 237H–238A. Lord Millett adapted a dictum of Sopinka J. in *MacDonald Estate v Martin* (1999) 77 D.L.R. (4th) 249 at 269 that the court should grant an injunction "unless satisfied on the basis of clear and convincing evidence that all reasonable measures have been taken to ensure that no disclosure will occur". However, Lord Millett's formulation replaced "all reasonable" with "effective".

[34] Lord Millett also referred to the Law Commission, Consultation Paper on Fiduciary Duties and Regulatory Rules (1992) (Law. Com. No.124) which described Chinese walls as normally involving some combination of (i) physical separation of the various departments so as to insulate them from each other (often extending to separate dining arrangements, etc.); (ii) an educational programme, normally recurring, to emphasise the importance of not improperly or inadvertently imparting confidential information; (iii) strict and detailed procedures for dealing with a breach of a Chinese wall and the maintenance of proper records when it occurred; (iv) monitoring by compliance officers of the effectiveness of the wall; (v) disciplinary sanctions for breach of it. He did not appear to doubt that such a wall would be effective. For a case where a Chinese wall was held to be sufficient between those members of firm A, who had acted for the claimant as experts in relation to a claim against firm B, when firm A and firm B merged, see *Young v Robson Rhodes (a firm)* [1999] 3 All E.R. 524, *per* Laddie J.

For a less favourable view of Chinese walls see the judgment of Bryson J. in *D & J Constructions Pty Ltd v Head* (1987) 9 N.S.W.L.R. 118, at 122–123; quoted by Clarke L.J. in *Koch Shipping Inc v Richards Butler (a firm)* [2002] EWCA Civ 1280; [2003] P.N.L.R. 11 at [31].

See also *Re a firm of Solicitors* [1999] P.N.L.R. 950; *In the matter of T & A (children)* [2000] Lloyd's Rep. P.N. 452; *Halewood International Ltd v Addleshaw Booth & Co* [2000] P.N.L.R. 788; *Re a firm of Solicitors* [2000] 1 Lloyd's Rep. 31; *Ball v Druce & Atlee* [2002] P.N.L.R. 23; *Bolde v Coutts & Co* [2003] EWHC 1865, Ch; *Marks & Spencer Group Plc v Freshfields Bruckhaus Deringer* [2004] EWHC 1337, Ch; [2004] 1 W.L.R. 2331; and *GUS Consulting GmbH v Leboeuf Lamb Greene & Macrae* [2006] EWCA Civ 683; [2006] P.N.L.R. 32.

whether the information is still remembered by those to whom it was imparted.[35] When considering these matters, it must be borne in mind that there has to be a real risk, but, at least in cases involving legal professional privilege, the risk need not be substantial. The number of those who are in possession of the confidential information may also be relevant. The risk of disclosure is very different if only one, experienced professional is involved, rather than members of a large team. In the former case, personal undertakings may suffice to render the risk of disclosure fanciful. The decision of the Court of Appeal in *Koch Shipping Inc v Richards Butler (a firm)*[36] illustrates this. Holding that there was no real risk of disclosure Tuckey L.J.:

> "In these days of professional and client mobility it is of course important that client confidentiality should be preserved. Each case must depend upon its own facts. But I think there is a danger inherent in the intensity of the adversarial process of courts being persuaded that a risk exists when, if one stands back a little, that risk is no more than fanciful or theoretical. I advocate a robust view with this in mind, so as to ensure that the line is sensibly drawn."[37]

---

[35] "Confidential information passing between solicitor and client and otherwise acquired by a solicitor on behalf of his client may, like any other confidential information communicated to anyone else, subsequently cease to be confidential. Confidential documents and information may become common knowledge or at least known to an opponent in the course of a trial. Some information may be memorable and some eminently forgettable. Common sense requires recognition that not all confidential information acquired by a solicitor will remain in the mind of the solicitor or be susceptible of being triggered as a recollection after the lapse of a period of time. For the purpose of the law imposing constraints upon solicitors acting against the interests of former clients, the law is concerned with the protection of information which (a) was originally communicated in confidence, (b) at the date of the later proposed retainer is still confidential and may reasonably be considered remembered or capable, on the memory being triggered, of being recalled and (c) relevant to the subject matter of the subsequent proposed retainer.": *Re A Firm of Solicitors* [1997] Ch. 1 at 9G–10A, *per* Lightman J.

See also *In the matter of T & A (children)* [2000] Lloyd's Rep. P.N. 452 (no reason to suppose that a solicitor remembered details of a client's personal circumstances imparted 13 years earlier and no reason to suppose that information imparted more recently to a firm of solicitors' criminal department, even if recollected, would filter through to another department during the relevant period of a few days).

[36] [2002] EWCA Civ 1280; [2003] P.N.L.R. 11. For a Canadian decision on similar facts see *Freyn v Bank of Montreal* (2002) 224 D.L.R. (4th) 337 (New Brunswick Court of Appeal).

[37] *ibid.* at [52]. See also *Ball v Druces & Attlee (a firm)* [2002] P.N.L.R. 23, where Burton J. granted an interim injunction restraining a firm of solicitors from acting for a defendant when they had earlier acted for the claimant and another individual in relation to the subject matter of the current action.

CHAPTER 3

REMEDIES

1. DAMAGES

The principal object of an award of damages is to put the claimant[1] in the position **3–001** he would have occupied if the breach of duty had not occurred, so far as money can do this and subject to the rules as to remoteness and mitigation of damage.[2] There are no general principles which apply to damages for professional negligence (as opposed to damages for negligence or breach of contract generally). The damage which professionals inflict, when things go wrong, covers the whole spectrum from personal injury through damage to property and economic loss. The most that can be said at the general level is that within individual professions or clusters of professions certain kinds of loss or damage commonly recur and

---

[1] The term "claimant" will be used in this chapter to describe the client or patient. The term "defendant" will be used for the professional man. Often the roles are the other way round in practice, as when the professional sues for fees owed and the client counterclaims for professional negligence.

[2] In *Att-Gen v Blake* [2001] 1 A.C. 268 the House of Lords, by a majority of 4:1, recognised that in exceptional cases a defendant in breach of contract could be ordered to account to the claimant for the profits made from his breach. Such cases will be extremely rare: see further *Experience Hendrix LLC v Enterprises Inc* [2003] EWCA Civ 323; [2003] 1 All E.R. (Comm) 830. For circumstances in which the court will make an award for non-pecuniary damage other than personal injury see *Farley v Skinner (No.2)* [2001] UKHL 49; [2002] 2 A.C. 732. In New Zealand exemplary damages may be awarded in exceptional cases of negligence: see *A v Bottrill* [2002] UKPC 44; [2003] 1 A.C. 449.

these have given rise to particular rules.[3] See, for example, the solicitors' negligence cases in which the claimant loses his opportunity to bring proceedings[4] or the surveyors' negligence cases where the claimant purchases a property with defects of which he was unaware.[5] A general discussion of the law of damages is beyond the scope of this book. In the chapters relating to individual professions, an attempt will be made to show how the general principles governing damages are commonly applied to claims against the individual professions.[6]

3–002 ***Banque Bruxelles Lambert SA v Eagle Star Insurance Co Ltd.*** In *Banque Bruxelles Lambert SA v Eagle Star Insurance Co Ltd*[7] the House of Lords introduced a new factor into the assessment of damages. The facts and the reasoning of the decision are set out and analysed in Ch.10.[8] Although the group of cases before the House of Lords concerned surveyors, the decision plainly affects recoverability of damage across the whole field of professional negligence. Before considering questions of remoteness or causation, it is necessary to determine the scope of the duty which was breached. Where the negligence lies in what the defendant said (as opposed to what he did), it is first necessary to characterise the negligent statement as "advice" or "information". In cases of advice, the defendant will be responsible for all the foreseeable loss which is a consequence of the claimant having acted on that advice.[9] In cases of negligent information (on which the claimant has acted) the defendant is only responsible "for all the foreseeable consequences of the information being wrong".

---

[3] Strictly speaking, these may not be "rules" at all. It may simply be that the courts, in applying the general principle of restitution to similar factual situations, inevitably adopt similar methods of assessment. See *Radford v De Froberville* [1977] 1 W.L.R. 1262 at 1268–1271; *Johnson v Agnew* [1980] A.C. 367; *Dodds Properties (Kent) v Canterbury CC* [1980] 1 W.L.R. 433; *County Personnel Ltd v Alan R Pulver & Co* [1987] 1 W.L.R. 916; *Ruxley Electronics & Construction Ltd v Forsyth* [1996] 1 A.C. 344. Jane Stapleton's article "The normal expectancies measure in tort damages" (1997) 113 L.Q.R. 257 provides an interesting review of the topic. On Stapleton's analysis the "normal expectancies" measure (rather than the "entitled result" measure) applies in most professional negligence actions. This is so whether the defendant has inflicted injury or merely failed to secure a benefit, and whether the claim is formulated in contract or in tort.

[4] Ch.11, paras 11–284 to 11–301.

[5] Ch.10, paras 10–131 to 10–150.

[6] See the sections of the chapters concerning individual professions titled "Damages".

[7] [1997] A.C. 191. See (1997) 113 L.Q.R. 1 and (1999) 115 L.Q.R. 527 (Stapleton) and (2001) 17 P.N. 146 (Evans). Lord Hoffmann has accepted the views of Professor Stapleton, but not in a speech given in his judicial capacity: see (2005) 121 L.Q.R. 592 at 596.

[8] See Ch.10, paras 10–113 to 10–116.

[9] See, e.g. *Aneco Reinsurance Underwriting Ltd v Johnson & Higgins* [2001] UKHL 51; [2002] 1 Lloyd's Rep. 157. The distinction between "information" and "advice" is better seen as a way of expressing two related questions, namely (i) what is the scope of the duty and (ii) what is the prospective harm, or kind of harm, from which the person to whom the duty is owed falls to be protected? (see *Equitable Life Assurance Co v Ernst & Young* [2003] EWCA Civ 1114; [2003] 2 B.C.L.C. 603 at [105]). The advice/information distinction is helpful in some cases, but in others the professional's duties will be more complex and a wider inquiry will be appropriate. In determining the scope of a professional's duty, the acts of his client and the professional acted with appropriate skill and care should be considered. For example, if the client would have sought further information with a view to adopting a particular course of action, then that decision and loss resulting from failure to take it, might fall within the scope of the original duty: *Equitable Life Assurance Co v Ernst & Young* [2003] EWCA Civ 1114; [2003] 2 B.C.L.C. 603 at [129].

In practice,[10] this generally means that one takes the damages which would be recoverable on a "restitution" basis and then excludes those losses which the claimant would have suffered even if the negligent information had been correct. This further narrows the scope of potential liability: in *Candler v Crane Christmas & Co*[11] Denning L.J. suggested that a professional person would only be liable to a third party in respect of losses incurred on the transaction for which he knew his views were required. The effect of *Banque Bruxelles Lambert SA v Eagle Star Insurance Co Ltd*,[12] at least in cases of "information", is to restrict the liability of the defendant to the specific consequences of the information which he provided being inaccurate. It matters not that the claimant can show that he would not have entered the transaction had he been given non-negligent information.

Allocation of risk. The same result could have been achieved by considering the allocation of risk between the lender and the valuer.[13] The valuer takes the risk that his valuation negligently misstates the current value of the property. The lender takes the risks that the borrower will be unable to meet his obligations and that the value of his security will fall (and/or the amount outstanding on the loan will rise) so that, on the assumption that the valuer has given a non-negligent valuation, he will be out of pocket. The lender will often have insured against that eventuality. On that analysis, a decision that a negligent valuer should pay all the losses suffered as a result of entering the loan transaction would transfer loss which was at the lender's risk (or at the risk of his insurers) to the valuer (and, in most cases, to his insurers).[14] **3–003**

Subsequent developments. Following its decision in *Banque Bruxelles Lambert SA v Eagle Star Insurance Co Ltd*,[15] the House of Lords has had to resolve related issues as to interest on damages[16] and contributory negligence.[17] **3–004**

---

[10] We say "in practice", because the House of Lords rejected the "cap" as the theoretical basis of their decision.

[11] [1951] 2 K.B. 164: see Ch.2, paras 2–113 to 2–116.

[12] [1997] A.C. 191. In *Kenny & Good Pty Ltd v MGICA (1992) Ltd* [2000] Lloyd's Rep. PN 25; (1999) 163 A.L.R. 611 the High Court of Australia declined to follow the House of Lords' decision. The New Zealand Court of Appeal referred to it with apparent approval in *Boyd Knight v Purdue* [1999] 2 N.Z.L.R. 278.

[13] See Powell, "Damages: The judiciary at sea?" (2001) 17 P.N. 206. See also Ch.2, para.2–092.

[14] *Aneco Reinsurance Underwriting (in liquidation) Ltd v Johnson and Higgins Ltd* [2001] UKHL 51 provides a useful illustration. The claimants were reinsurers whose claim against the retrocessionaires failed because of negligence by the defendant brokers. The total risk reinsured was US$30 million of which US$10 million was subject to retrocession cover. The claimants would not have reinsured the risk at all had the brokers not been in negligent (cover would not have been available in practice had full disclosure been made). The Court of Appeal increased damages to US$30 million (Aldous L.J. dissenting), even though the claimants had taken the risk of a claim of US$20 million without retrocession cover. The House of Lords dismissed the appeal (Lord Millett dissenting) because the defendants had been under a duty to advise, not just to provide information. The claimant had not taken the risk of proceeding on negligent advice.

[15] [1997] A.C. 191.

[16] *Nykredit Mortgage Bank Plc v Edward Edrman Group Ltd (No.2)* [1997] 1 W.L.R. 1627 (see Ch.9).

[17] *Platform Home Loans Ltd v Oyston Shipways Ltd* [2000] 2 A.C. 190 (see Ch.5, para.5–117). This decision was adopted by the New Zealand Court of Appeal in *Benton v Miller & Poulgrain (a firm)* [2005] 1 N.Z.L.R. 66.

3–005 **Causation.** In order to recover damages, the injured party must show that the damage was caused by the defendant's wrongful act or omission. This is discussed further in the chapters on particular professions. However, the House of Lords has recently made one clear and one arguable departure from the conventional approach, in both cases for reasons of policy. First, in *Fairchild v Glenhaven Funeral Services Ltd*[18] the conundrum arose of a claimant who had suffered personal injury (mesothelioma caused by exposure at work to asbestos dust) and who could show that more than one employer had wrongfully exposed him to absestos dust, but who could not prove the any one employer's wrongful acts or omissions had caused the disease. On the conventional basis, the ex-employee failed against each of his former employers. The House of Lords adopted the pragmatic and plainly just solution of holding all those whose wrongful acts had materially increased the risk of him contracting the disease liable. The implications of this decision are still being worked out.[19]

3–006 The second decision, *Chester v Asfar*,[20] is more controversial. In that case the House of Lords held by a majority[21] that a patient who was not advised of a risk entailed in a proposed operation in breach of duty by the surgeon, but who would have undergone the surgery had the risk been explained on a later date, could recover damages for the injury which resulted when the risk eventuated. The majority appear to have been motivated by the fact that the claimant had consented to invasive surgery without having given informed consent. They held that the scope of the surgeon's duty was such that he should be liable for the fact that the possible adverse consequence of which he had failed to advise had occurred. It is clear, however, that this decision is limited to cases of clinical negligence and is not to be applied to other cases of negligent failure to warn of possible risks, for example in relation to financial investments.[22]

3–007 **Assessing damages on a hypothetical basis.** A common feature of professional negligence litigation is that the court must determine what course events would have taken if the defendant had properly discharged his professional duty. If given competent treatment, would the patient have recovered? If given competent advice, would the client have taken the lease? If proceedings had been started within the limitation period (or had not been dismissed for want of prosecution), what damages would the claimant have recovered? If the broker had obtained suitable insurance cover, would the insurers have paid out in the events which subsequently occurred? Although these topics will be dealt with individually in the subsequent chapters, the general principle[23] is this:

(i) Where the question is what the claimant would have done, if the defendant had given competent advice or had otherwise acted competently, this is determined by the court on the balance of probabilities. Damages are

[18] [2002] UKHL 22; [2003] 1 A.C. 32.
[19] See, e.g., *Barker v Corus* [2006] UKHL 20; [2006] 2 W.L.R. 1027, reversed retrospectively by s.3 of the Compensation Act 2006.
[20] [2004] UKHL 41; [2005] 1 A.C. 134: see Ch.13, paras.13–137 and 13–138. The High Court of Australia reached the same decision in *Chappel v Hart* [1999] Lloyd's Rep. Med. 223.
[21] Lords Steyn, Hope and Walker. Lord Bingham and Lord Hoffmann dissented.
[22] *Beary v Pall Mall Investments (a firm)* [2005] EWCA Civ 415; [2005] P.N.L.R. 674.
[23] See *Allied Maples Group Ltd v Simmons & Simmons* [1995] 1 W.L.R. 1602.

then assessed on that hypothesis without any discount to reflect the possibility that the claimant might have acted differently.[24]

(ii) Where the question is what some third party would have done, if the defendant had performed competently, damages are assessed on a "loss of a chance" basis. The court must consider what are the chances that the insurers would have paid out; or that the "other side" would have yielded; or that the judge in the original action would have found for the claimant on liability; and so forth. The damages must then reflect the value of this chance which has been lost.

(iii) The medical cases[25] fall into a different category. It is generally a question of past fact whether the claimant's condition was amenable to treatment at the time of the negligent diagnosis or treatment. The court must determine this question on the balance of probabilities (like any other question of past fact) and then award damages on that basis.[26]

2. LOSS OF REMUNERATION

A further question which commonly arises is whether a finding of negligence disentitles the professional person to his fees. If the fees have been paid, the client will probably seek to recover them. If they have not been paid, there will often be a counterclaim for the amount owing. In spite of the frequency with which this question arises, the courts have not been entirely consistent in their approach to it: see, for example, the surveyors' cases mentioned below.[27]   **3–008**

The first matter to consider in every case is the nature of the contract between the parties. A solicitor's retainer to bring or defend an action is usually an entire contract.[28] An agreement with an architect to provide the normal services as   **3–009**

---

[24] In the context of claims for "lost litigation", where the issue is the assessment which would have been made of what the claimant would have done had the "lost litigation" proceeded, the issue is not decided on the balance of probabilities, but as part of the assessment of the value of the lost claim: see *Dixon v Clement Jones Solicitors (a firm)* [2004] EWCA Civ 1005; [2005] P.N.L.R. 6.

[25] Sub-para.(iii) refers to the negligent diagnosis and negligent treatment cases. The negligent advice cases (where the patient contends that properly advised, he would not have undergone the treatment) fall within sub-para.(i), above.

[26] *Hotson v East Berkshire AHA* [1987] A.C. 750. See also Ch.13, paras 13–139 to 13–141, which indicates a different approach to hypothetical questions in the medical context. However, see *Smith v National Health Service Litigation Authority* [2001] Lloyd's Rep. Med. 90 where Andrew Smith J. held that *Allied Maples Ltd v Simmons & Simmons (a firm)* [1995] 1 W.L.R. 1602 applied to a claim for damages for failure to undertake an examination which might, but might not, have revealed an existing condition, leading to earlier treatment. However, this aspect of the decision in *Smith v National Health Service Litigation Authority* [2001] Lloyd's Rep. Med. 90 has been held by Burnton J. to have been reached *per incuriam*: see *Hardaker v Newcastle HA and Chief Constable of Northumbria* [2001] Lloyd's Rep. Med. 512.

[27] See Ch.10, para.10–110.

[28] *Underwood, Son & Piper v Lewis* [1894] 2 Q.B. 306; *Heywood v Wellers* [1976] Q.B. 446 at 458.

defined in the RIBA conditions of engagement is not entire, but severable into stages.[29] In a contract of the latter kind there can be no dispute as to the defendant's entitlement to be paid for those stages of the work which have been properly carried out.[30] The crucial questions are:

(a) In the case of an entire contract, what remuneration can be recovered where the defendant was negligent? and

(b) In the case of a severable contract, what remuneration can be recovered for that part or stage of the work which was negligently performed?

3–010 This topic is discussed in the chapters on individual professions.[31] The approach which is adopted in most cases, and which, it is submitted, is correct, is that where the defendant's negligence renders his services valueless, he is not entitled to recover (or to retain) any remuneration for the work in question.[32] In any other case, where the defendant has substantially (albeit negligently) performed the work, he is entitled to be paid the normal remuneration and the client must rely upon his remedy in damages.[33] A more difficult question is whether there is an intermediate band of cases in which the defendant's entitlement to fees is neither wholly extinguished by his negligence nor wholly preserved. In *Mondel v Steel*[34] (which concerned a shipbuilder's claim for the balance of the price of a ship) it was held that there could be an abatement of the price to reflect "how much less the subject matter of the action was worth, by reason of the breach of contract". In *Hutchinson v Harris*[35] the Court of Appeal expressed doubt whether the principle of *Mondel v Steel* could ever be applied to contracts for professional services. It is submitted that this doubt is well founded. Once it is established that the professional person has substantially performed his task and that his services were of some value to the client, an award of damages (if properly computed) should afford sufficient compensation to the client.

---

[29] *Hutchinson v Harris* (1978) 10 Build.L.R. 19.

[30] The same principle applies to quantity surveyors: *Du Bosky & Partners v Shearwater Property Holdings Plc* (1992) 61 B.L.R. 64.

[31] See Ch.9, para.9–322 (architects), Ch.10, para.10–110 (surveyors), and Ch.11, para.11–318 (solicitors).

[32] e.g. *Heywood v Wellers* [1976] Q.B. 446. The same also applies in a case of non-performance as in *Adrian Alan Ltd v Fuglers* [2002] EWCA Civ 1655; [2003] P.N.L.R. 14.

[33] See, e.g. *Moneypenny v Hartland* (1824) 1 Car. & P. 352; (1826) 2 Car. & P. 378: " . . . unless that negligence or want of skill has been to an extent that has rendered the work useless to the defendants, they must pay him, and seek their remedy in a cross action. For if it were not so, a man, by a small error, might deprive himself of his whole remuneration", (*per* Best C.J.). Furthermore an award of damages coupled with a remission of liability for fees would often result in the client receiving double compensation; see *Hutchinson v Harris* (1978) 10 Build.L.R. 19 at 32, (*per* Stephenson L.J.) and at 46, (*per* Waller L.J.).

[34] (1841) 8 M. & W. 858.

[35] (1978) 10 Build.L.R. 19 at 31. In *Turner Page Music Ltd v Torres Design Associates Ltd* [1997] C.I.L.L. 1263 the official referee distinguished *Hutchinson v Harris* on the grounds that in the instant case the contract between the parties was not an entire contract. He ordered an abatement of the professional fees due to the defendants, to reflect the fact that they had failed to produce a bill of quantities.

3. EQUITABLE REMEDIES[36]

(a) *Rescission*

Rescission of the impugned transaction is the usual remedy for breach of   **3–011**
fiduciary duty in dealings between principal and fiduciary[37] or undue influence.[38]
Rescission involves setting aside the transaction so as to place each party in the
position in which he would have been had it not been entered.[39] Where a contract
is avoided at the instance of a claimant, he must himself do equity by restoring
the benefit he received under the contract and by giving an allowance for any
capital expenditure by the defendant which has enhanced the value of any
property or other asset which had been transferred to the defendant under the
impugned transaction.[40] If he has received money under the impugned transaction, it must be returned with interest.[41] So, where the transaction is a loan by a
fiduciary to his principal by way of mortgage, the principal must repay the
principal with interest.[42] The defendant must also account for any profits or other
benefits derived from the subject property.[43]

Rescission will not be ordered where, even by making all possible allowances,   **3–012**
it would not be possible to undo the transaction.[44] So, where third parties have
acquired the relevant property or interests in it for value and without notice,
rescission will not be possible.[45] However, if the property has been sold on by the

---

[36] A full discussion of equitable remedies is beyond the scope of this book. See Spry, *Equitable
Remedies* (6th edn, Sweet & Maxwell, 2001); *Snell's Equity* (31st edn, Sweet & Maxwell, 2005); and
Meagher, Gummow & Lehane, *Equity, Doctrines and Remedies* (4th edn, Butterworths, 2004).
Remedies such as specific performance and rectification are not considered at all, since they are rarely
sought in claims against professional persons.

[37] See Ch.2, paras 2–137 to 2–143.

[38] If a guarantee or other security has been given under undue influence, then the usual remedy is an
order that the document be delivered up and cancelled.

[39] It is therefore very different from a common law award of damages for breach of contract or
negligence, which seeks only to place the claimant in the position which he would have been had
there been no breach of contract or duty.

[40] *York Buildings Company v Mackenzie* (1795) 8 Bro.P.C. 42; *Ex p. Hughes* (1802) 6 Ves.Jun. 617;
Ex p. Bennett (1805) 10 Ves.Jun. 381; *Robinson v Ridley* (1821) 6 Madd. 2; *Luddy's Trustee v Peard*
(1886) 33 Ch.D. 500; and *Beningfield v Baxter* (1886) 12 App.Cas. 167. If the fiduciary has
diminished the value of the estate, then that is taken into account to: see, for example, *Sidny v Ranger*
(1841) 12 Sim. 118 (fiduciary had cut down timber on estate).

[41] *York Buildings Co v Mackenzie* (1795) 8 Bro.P.C. 42; *Luddy's Trustee v Peard* (1886) 33 Ch.D. 500;
and *Re Sherman* [1954] Ch. 658.

[42] *Maguire v Makaronis* (1996–97) 188 C.L.R. 449 (High Court of Australia). But see *Swindle v
Harrison* [1997] 4 All E.R. 707, CA, discussed in paras 3–012 to 3–013, below, for a possible
alternative remedy.

[43] *York Buildings Co v Mackenzie* (1795) 8 Bro.P.C. 42; *Randall v Errington* (1805) 10 Ves.Jun. 423;
Aberdeen Town Council v Aberdeen University (1877) 2 App.Cas. 544; *Erlanger v New Sombrero
Phosphate Co* (1878) 3 App.Cas. 1218; *Beningfield v Baxter* (1886) 12 App.Cas. 167; and *Re
Sherman* [1954] Ch. 658.

[44] *Erlanger v New Sombrero Phosphate Co* (1878) 3 App.Cas. 1218. See also *Dunbar Bank Plc v
Nadeem* [1998] 3 All E.R. 876 at 884H–J, *per* Millett L.J.; applied in *Johnson v (1) EBS Pensioner
Trustees Ltd (2) O'Shea* [2002] EWCA Civ 164; [2002] Lloyd's Rep. P.N. 308. In the latter case it
was held that rescission is a discretionary remedy. While this is true, it is the usual remedy unless it
is not possible to undo the transaction for both parties.

[45] *McKenzie v McDonald* [1927] V.L.R. 134.

defendant at a profit, then he will be liable to account for that profit.[46] Particular problems arise in cases in which the claimant has rendered rescission impossible by selling on the subject property. If he has done so with knowledge of his right to rescind, then he has no good reason to complain.[47] If he has done so in ignorance, then he may have no remedy, although he may be able to claim equitable compensation.[48] A claim to rescission is also lost if the claimant has affirmed the transaction with knowledge of the relevant facts and of his right to seek rescission.[49]

(b) *Equitable Compensation*

(i) *Compensation for Loss Caused by Breach of Fiduciary Obligation*

3–013 The usual remedies for breach of fiduciary duty are rescission of the transaction in which the fiduciary had an undisclosed interest or an account of the fiduciary's secret profits. In his speech in *Nocton v Lord Ashburton*[50] Viscount Haldane L.C. explained that in appropriate cases equitable compensation akin to damages had been awarded by equity against a fiduciary. This element of his speech was not immediately developed. Although an award of damages is not usually regarded as a remedy for breach of an equitable obligation,[51] there has been a recognition in the English authorities that damages may be awarded for breach of an equitable duty of confidence.[52] More recently, courts in Australia, New Zealand and Canada have taken the lead in awarding compensation for damage suffered as a result of breach of fiduciary duty.[53] Equitable compensation may also be awarded when rescission of a transaction entered after a fiduciary has failed to make proper disclosure is no longer possible.[54]

3–014 The remedy is now recognised in English law for breaches of fiduciary obligation. In *Swindle v Harrison*[55] the Court of Appeal had to consider to what extent proof of a causal link between a breach of fiduciary duty and loss should be established if compensation or damages were to be awarded. The existence of

---

[46] *Hall v Hallett* (1784) 1 Cox 134; *Fox v Mackreth* (1788) 2 Bro.C.C. 400, 2 Cox 320; affirmed (1791) 4 Bro.P.C. 258; *Ex p. Reynolds* (1800) 5 Ves.Jun. 707; and *De Bussche v Alt* (1878) 8 Ch.D. 286.

[47] See, e.g., *Great Luxembourg Railway Co v Magnay (No.2)* (1858) 23 Beav. 586; and *Re Cape Breton Ltd* (1885) 29 Ch.D. 795.

[48] *Re Cape Breton Ltd* (1885) 29 Ch.D. 795 at 805, *per* Cotton L.J. and 811, *per* Fry L.J.; *Jacobus Marler Estates Ltd v Marler* (1913) 85 L.J.P.C. 167n.

[49] *Peyman v Lanjani* [1985] Ch. 457, CA; applying *Leathley v John Fowler & Co Ltd* [1946] K.B. 579, CA.

[50] [1914] A.C. 932. See also *McKenzie v McDonald* [1927] V.R. 134 (Dixon AJ).

[51] See, e.g., *Ex p. Adamson* (1878) 8 Ch.D. 807 at 819, *per* James and Baggallay L.JJ.

[52] *Swinney v Chief Constable of Northumbria Police Force* [1997] Q.B. 464; applying a dictum of Lord Goff in *Att-Gen v Guardian Newspapers (No.2)* [1990] 1 A.C. 109; and *Seager v Copydex Ltd* [1967] 1 W.L.R. 923; and [1969] 1 W.L.R. 809.

[53] See, e.g., the authorities cited by Professor Finn at p.40 of *Commercial Aspects of Trusts and Fiduciary Obligations* (McKendrick, edn), which include *Hill v Rose* [1990] V.R. 129; *McKaskell v Benseman* [1989] 3 N.Z.L.R. 75; and *Canson Enterprises Ltd v Boughton & Co* (1991) 85 D.L.R. (4th) 129.

[54] *Meara v Fox* [2002] P.N.L.R. 93 at para.[49], *per* Pomfrey J.; citing *Moody v Cox & Hatt* [1917] 2 Ch. 71. Equitable compensation is discussed by Congalen in *"Equitable Compensation for Breach of Fiduciary Dealing Rules"* (2003) 119 L.Q.R. 246.

[55] [1997] 4 All E.R. 707.

the remedy of compensation or damages appears to have been accepted. Mr Swindle was a solicitor. Mrs Harrison wished to mortgage her house to acquire a restaurant business for her son to run. Part of the money was to be raised by a loan from a brewery. That loan had not been agreed when Mrs Harrison exchanged contracts for the restaurant and paid a deposit of £44,000, despite warnings from her solicitor as to the risk to which she was exposing herself. The date for completion approached, but the brewery declined to make the loan. Mrs Harrison and her son were unable to borrow the money needed from their bank. Mr Swindle offered to advance the money needed at five per cent over base and for an arrangement fee of £1,000. The terms offered were reasonable and Mrs Harrison accepted them. Mr Swindle did not reveal that his firm would receive half the arrangement fee itself, paying the balance to its bank, and that he was borrowing the money at two and a half per cent over base and so, if Mrs Harrison made the payments due, would make a modest profit. Mrs Harrison was able to complete, but the restaurant was not a success. She lost her home and any equity in the restaurant. Mr Swindle brought proceedings to enforce the charge. Mrs Harrison counterclaimed for damages for negligence and breach of fiduciary duty, alleging that Mr Swindle was in breach of duty in failing to reveal the profit he would be making. She claimed her entire loss on the venture.

The claim in negligence was bound to fail because Mrs Harrison was unable   **3–015** to show that, had Mr Swindle informed her of the profit he would be making, she would not have proceeded. That left her claim for breach of fiduciary duty. There had clearly been a breach of fiduciary duty, albeit not serious. The usual remedy would have been rescission of the loan, so that Mrs Harrison would have had to repay the principal sum borrowed together with interest either at a rate assessed by the Court or at the contractual rate.[56] That remedy was of little use to Mrs Harrison. She claimed her entire loss on the restaurant business, relying on a dictum of Lord Thankerton in *Brickenden v London Loan & Savings Co.*[57] The argument failed. Evans L.J. rejected it on the basis that considerations of causation applied to claims for compensation for non-fraudulent breaches of fiduciary

---

[56] *Maguire v Makaronis* (1996–97) 188 C.L.R. 449 (High Court of Australia).

[57] [1934] 3 D.L.R. 465 at 469: "When a party, holding a fiduciary relationship, commits a breach of his duty by non-disclosure of material facts, which his constituent is entitled to know in connection with the transaction, he cannot be heard to maintain that disclosure would not have altered the decision to proceed with the transaction, because the constituent's action would be solely determined by some other fact, such as the valuation by another party of the property proposed to be mortgaged. Once the court has determined that the non-disclosed facts were material, speculation as to what course the constituent, on disclosure, would have taken is not relevant." This is discussed as part of a wider analysis of causation in relation to equitable remedies in the judgments of Brennan C.J. and Gaudron, McHugh and Gummow JJ. in *Maguire v Makaronis* (1996–97) 188 C.L.R. 449 at 467–474. See also (1994) 110 L.Q.R. 238 (Heydon). In *Nationwide Building Society v Balmer Radmore (a firm)* [1999] Lloyd's Rep. P.N. 241, Blackburne J., having explained the factual background to the decision in *Brickenden*, said at 274: "It may be therefore that, although couched in entirely general terms, it is appropriate to approach Lord Thankerton's remarks with caution and avoid elevating what he said in the context of that case into a statement of inflexible principle."

See also (1) *Johnson v (1) EBS Pensioner Trustees Ltd (2) O'Shea* [2002] EWCA Civ 164; [2002] Lloyd's Rep. P.N. 308 at [55] of the judgment of Mummery L.J.; (2) *Gwembe Valley Development Co Ltd v Koshy (No.3)* [2003] EWCA Civ 1048; [2005] 1 B.C.L.C. 131 at [144]–[147] where the Court of Appeal considered the dictum of Lord Thankerton in *Brickenden v London Loan & Savings Co* [1934] 3 D.L.R. 465, at 469 and explained that it applied to claims to rescind transactions entered into in breach of fiduciary duty, but not to claims for equitable compensation, where causation had to be established.

duty, following *Bristol & West Building Society v Mothew.*[58] Hobhouse L.J.'s analysis was more subtle. He distinguished between the traditional remedies for a breach of fiduciary duty involving non-disclosure by the fiduciary of his interest in the transaction (which rendered it voidable at the election of the beneficiary, so that, as stated by Lord Thankerton in *Brickenden*, considerations as to the causative effect of non-disclosure did not arise) and a claim for damages for breach of fiduciary duty. As to the latter, Hobhouse L.J. held that it was necessary to satisfy the test of common law if damages were to be recovered. Mrs Harrison failed to satisfy that test, so her claim failed. Mummery L.J., the third member of the Court, expressly recognised the availability of equitable compensation as a remedy for breach of fiduciary duty. Having observed that common law considerations of remoteness and foreseeability were generally irrelevant to restitutionary remedies for breach of trust or fiduciary duty, he held that:

> "Although equitable compensation, whether awarded in lieu of rescission or specific restitution or whether simply awarded as monetary compensation, is not damages, it is still necessary for Mrs Harrison to show that the loss suffered has been caused by the relevant breach of fiduciary duty. Liability is not unlimited. There is no equitable by-pass of the need to establish causation."[59]

He went on to apply the decision of the House of Lords in *Banque Bruxelles Lambert SA v Eagle Star Insurance Co Ltd*[60] and to hold that Mrs Harrison's loss arose not from any want of information about the loan from her solicitors, but from her purchase of the restaurant.

3–016   Thus, in claims for compensation for loss caused by breach of a fiduciary obligation, the claimant will have to establish causation, i.e. that he would have acted differently had the fiduciary complied with his obligations.[61] In assessing compensation, the courts are trying to compensate for the consequences of the breach of the fiduciary obligation and in doing so they apply common sense views as to what loss resulted from the breach and so falls to be compensated.[62]

---

[58] [1998] Ch. 1, CA.
[59] [1997] 4 All E.R. 707 at 733h. See also *Halton International Inc (Holdings) SARL v Guernroy Ltd* [2005] EWHC 1968, Ch; [2006] 1 B.C.L.C. 78 (Patten J.) at [155].
[60] [1997] 1 A.C. 191.
[61] See also *Rama v Millar* [1996] 1 N.Z.L.R. 257, where, giving the opinion of the Privy Council, Lord Nicholls said at 260–261: "This is not a case of a claim that a fiduciary should account for an unauthorised profit. The claim is for the amount of loss Mr Millar is said to have sustained by Mr Rama's breach of fiduciary duty. This calls for consideration of what would have happened if Mr Rama had fulfilled his fiduciary duties and kept Mr Millar informed." In *Nationwide Building Society v Balmer Radmore (a firm)* [1999] Lloyd's Rep. P.N. 241, Blackburne J., having reviewed the authorities, including a passage from the speech of Lord Browne-Wilkinson in *Target Holdings Ltd v Redferns* [1996] A.C. 421 at 432E–H, said at 278: "That broad statement encourages me to think that where, as in the cases before me, what is at issue is the consequence of a misrepresentation or non-disclosure made by the fiduciary which has caused the beneficiary to authorise the application of his monies in a particular way, the only sensible approach to the question of compensation for the consequences of the misrepresentation or non-disclosure is to consider what would have happened if there had been no misrepresentation or the appropriate disclosure had been made."
[62] *Canson Enterprises Ltd v Boughton & Co* (1991) 85 D.L.R. (4th) 129 at 163, *per* McLachlin J.; approved by the House of Lords in *Target Holdings Ltd v Redferns (a firm)* [1996] A.C. 421 at 439A. See also *Youyang Pty Ltd v Minter Ellison Morris Fletcher* [2003] H.C.A. 15 where the trustee's liability to repay in full moneys paid away in breach of trust was not reduced by subsequent events.

The remedy is compensatory, not punitive, so that there is no power to make an exemplary award.[63]

(ii) *Equitable Compensation for Breach of Confidence*[64]

There is jurisdiction under Lord Cairns' Act 1858 to award damages in lieu of an **3–017** injunction. This has been used to justify awards of damages for breach of confidence. However, it could not justify an award of damages where a grant of an injunction would not be ordered—most obviously when the confidential information had already been disclosed.[65] The English courts have awarded damages for breach of confidence.[66]

Once it is appreciated that there is an equitable obligation of confidence,[67] then **3–018** the availability of equitable compensation in appropriate cases resolves this problem. Such compensation should be awarded for actual loss and damage, but there is no reason in principle why it should not compensate the claimant for distress and inconvenience.[68]

(c) *Account of Profits*

An account of profits is the appropriate remedy where a fiduciary has made an **3–019** unauthorised profit by breaching his fiduciary obligations[69] or where profit has been made from a breach of confidence.[70]

(d) *Injunction*

An injunction—both interim and final—can be used to restrain a breach or **3–020** threatened breach of confidence. In such cases it is essential that the injunction be unambiguous and that it extend only to information which is truly confidential.[71]

---

[63] *Harris v Digital Pulse Pty Ltd* [2003] N.S.W.C.A. 10.

[64] See Toulson and Phipps, *Confidentiality* (Sweet & Maxwell, 1996), paras 10–09 to 10–13.

[65] *Malone v Metropolitan Police Commissioner* [1979] Ch. 344 at 360A–C, *per* Megarry V.C.

[66] *Seager v Copydex Ltd (No.2)* [1969] 1 W.L.R. 809. Damages were awarded on the basis of the value of the information, after which the information would belong to the defendant. Meagher, Gummow & Lehane, *Equity, Doctrines and Remedies,* (4th edn, Butterworths, 2002) are scathing about this decision: see paras [41–090] and [41–135].

[67] See Ch.2, para.2–163.

[68] *cf. Farley v Skinner (No.2)* [2001] UKHL 49; [2002] 2 A.C. 732.

[69] See, for example, *Regal (Hastings) Ltd v Gulliver* [1967] 2 A.C. 134n, *per* Lord Russell of Killowen at 149F.

[70] *Peter Pan Manufacturing Corp v Corsets Silhouette Ltd* [1963] R.P.C. 45 (claim was made both in equity and in contract); *Att-Gen v Guardian Newspapers Ltd* [1990] 1 A.C. 109.

[71] See Toulson and Phipps, *Confidentiality* (Sweet & Maxwell, 1996), paras 10–01 to 10–02.

4. INTEREST

(a) *Interest under the Supreme Court Act 1981*

(i) *General*

3–021   The court has a discretion to award simple interest on any damages awarded to a claimant and will generally do so.[72] The discretion extends to both the rate of interest awarded and the period for which it should run, commencing with the date when the cause of action arose and ending with the date of the judgment.[73] In the purely commercial context (i.e. most claims against insurance brokers, auditors, underwriting agents, etc.) commercial rates of interest are awarded and no further discussion is called for here.

(ii) *Clinical Negligence: Claims for Personal Injuries*

3–022   In respect of damages for personal injuries the rules as to interest are clear and well settled. In brief, interest must be awarded unless the court is satisfied that there are special reasons to the contrary.[74] Interest is normally awarded on special damages at half the appropriate rate from the date of accident until trial. The appropriate rate is the Special Account Rate (formerly the Short Term Investment Rate). The details of this rate, together with much other useful information, are conveniently set out in "Facts and Figures", an annual publication by the Professional Negligence Bar Association. No interest is awarded on damages for future loss of earnings or earning capacity. Interest on general damages for pain, suffering and loss of amenities should be awarded at the rate of two per cent per annum from the date of service of the writ until the date of trial.[75]

(iii) *Damages for Inconvenience and Discomfort*

3–023   In respect of general damages for inconvenience and discomfort, interest at two per cent will generally[76] be awarded from the date of the inconvenience to trial, applying the principles applicable to the award of interest on general damages in personal injury actions.

---

[72] s.35A of the Supreme Court Act 1981 empowers the court to award interest on sums paid before judgment. However, this power does not extend to sums recovered by the claimant before the commencement of proceedings: see *IM Properties Plc v Cape & Dalgleish* [1999] Q.B. 297. In that case the claimants claimed against their auditors losses flowing from negligent audits. They had recovered part of the losses from their former chief executive before issuing the writ. The Court of Appeal held that no interest could be awarded in respect of that part of the loss.

[73] s.35A(1) of the Supreme Court Act 1981. In *Nykredit Mortgage Bank Plc v Edward Erdman Group Ltd* [1997] 1 W.L.R. 1627 the House of Lords rejected the (ingenious) argument that there was a distinction between the date when a cause of action accrued and the date when it "arose" within the meaning of s.35A of the Supreme Court Act 1981: see 1638B.

[74] s.35A(2) of the Supreme Court Act 1981.

[75] *Wright v British Railways Board* [1983] 2 A.C. 773; and see the analysis by Purchas L.J. in *Auty v National Coal Board* [1985] 1 W.L.R. 784 at 809.

[76] Such interest was awarded in *Heatley v William H Brown Ltd* [1992] 1 E.G.L.R. 289, 297. Occasionally such interest has not been awarded, but no reasons have been given: *Wilson v Baxter Payne & Lepper* [1985] 1 E.G.L.R. 141.

(iv) *Interest on Damages for Pecuniary Losses in Solicitors' and Surveyors' Negligence Actions*

Interest is awarded to compensate the claimant for being deprived of his damages for a period of time, not as compensation for the damage done to him[77] or as a punishment for the defendant. For this reason the nature of the transaction giving rise to the claim will be material to the choice of the rate of interest. A commercial transaction will more readily attract a commercial rate of interest than a domestic house purchase. The decisions of the Court of Appeal in *Pinnock v Wilkins & Sons*[78] and *Watts v Morrow*[79] establish that the court may take the rate applicable to judgments by s.17 of the Judgments Act 1838. However, that is only an option and should not be applied without considering whether some other, more flexible rate is more appropriate.[80]

3–024

(b) *Interest under the Civil Procedure Rules*

Part 36 of the Civil Procedure Rules concerns offers to settle and payments into court. Unlike the Rules of the Supreme Court and the County Court Rules which they replaced, the Civil Procedure Rules enable claimants to make offers to settle their claims. If the offer is made more than 21 days before the start of the trial, a defendant has 21 days to accept the claimant's offer without needing the court's permission, but may only accept it after that with the court's permission.[81] Rule 36.21 applies where a claimant obtains a judgment against a defendant which is more advantageous than the proposals contained in his offer. In such circumstances the court may award interest on the whole or part of any sum of money (excluding interest) awarded to the claimant at a rate of up to 10 per cent above the base rate for some or all of the period from the latest date on which the defendant could have accepted the offer without needing the permission of the court.

3–025

(c) *Interest in Equity*

Equity has its own independent jurisdiction to award interest.[82] It has the power to award compound interest if appropriate. Equity's purpose in cases against delinquent fiduciaries is not to punish them, but to ensure that they have made no

3–026

---

[77] *per* Lord Herschell L.C. in *London, Chatham and Dover Railway Co v South Eastern Railway Co* [1893] A.C. 429 at 437. And see the dicta of Lord Denning M.R. in *Jefford v Gee* [1970] 2 Q.B. 130 at 146.

[78] *The Times*, January 29, 1990.

[79] [1991] 1 W.L.R. 1421.

[80] For a detailed critique of these decisions see paras 1–182 to 1–188 of the fourth edition of this work. In *Harrison v Bloom Camillin (No.2)* [2000] Lloyd's Rep. P.N. 404 (Neuberger J); and *Griffiths v Last Cawthra Feather (a firm)* [2002] P.N.L.R. 27 (H.H. Judge Grenfell sitting in the TCC) interest was awarded on damages awarded against solicitors at the short term investment rate.

[81] CPR, r.36.12(1).

[82] *Wallersteiner v Moir (No.2)* [1975] Q.B. 373, CA; *Rama v Millar* [1996] 1 N.Z.L.R. 257, PC.

profit from abuse of their position.[83] Therefore, compound interest will only be awarded if either the defendant has himself received compound interest or should have done so. Otherwise, equity is likely to adopt a similar approach in deciding which is the appropriate rate as that adopted under s.35A of the Supreme Court Act 1981.

---

[83] *Wallersteiner v Moir (No.2)* [1975] Q.B. 373 at 388B–D, *per* Lord Denning M.R, at 397C–F and 406D–E, *per* Scarman L.J. The earlier authorities are set out in this decision.

CHAPTER 4

CONTRIBUTION BETWEEN DEFENDANTS

1. INTRODUCTION

Where the claimant's injury or loss was caused by the breach of duty of more than one person, contribution proceedings are often instituted between the parties alleged to be responsible. Earlier editions of this book have discussed the Law Reform (Married Women and Tortfeasors) Act 1935, the Civil Liability (Contribution) Act 1978 and the somewhat complicated interrelationship between the two Acts. The time has now passed, however, when any proceedings are likely to be brought under the 1935 Act.[1] For discussion of that Act and the transitional provisions, see the second and third editions of this book and the Court of Appeal's decision in *Lampitt v Poole BC (Taylor, Third Party)*.[2] This chapter is concerned with the Civil Liability (Contribution) Act 1978.[3]

4–001

2. ENTITLEMENT TO CONTRIBUTION

Section 1(1) of the Civil Liability (Contribution) Act 1978 provides that, subject to the qualifications thereafter set out, "any person liable in respect of any damage suffered by another person may recover contribution from any other person liable in respect of the same damage (whether jointly with him or otherwise)".

4–002

---

[1] Such proceedings might be brought if the limitation period had been suspended, because the claimant was under a disability or because of fraud or deliberate concealment by the defendant.

[2] [1991] 2 Q.B. 545.

[3] The Act was passed following the Law Commission's Report on Contribution (Law Com. No. 79) and replaces s.6(1)(c) of the Law Reform (Married Women and Tortfeasors) Act 1935. For a comprehensive review of the working of the Act, see C. Mitchell, "The Civil Liability (Contribution) Act 1978" [1997] R.L.R. 27.

3. LIABILITY OF THE PERSON CLAIMING CONTRIBUTION

4–003 Section 1(1) gives a right to claim contribution to "any person liable". In practice contribution claims are often made between co-defendants who are both denying liability and against whom no finding of liability has been made. There is no difficulty in those circumstances, because their respective liability to the claimant will be determined at the trial of the claimant's action against them. However, there are two respects in which the requirement of liability is qualified. First, the fact that by the time the claim for contribution is made the person making it has acquired a defence of limitation which bars the remedy, but not the right,[4] provides no defence.[5] This is sensible, because if a claim were made against a defendant at the end of the applicable limitation period, he might otherwise be unable to claim contribution.[6] Secondly, if the person claiming contribution has made or agreed to make any payment in bona fide settlement or compromise of a claim, then he is entitled to claim contribution "without regard to whether or not he himself is or ever was liable in respect of the damage, provided, however, that he would have been liable assuming the factual basis of the claim against him could be established".[7] Two issues arise in relation to this provision: (i) what is the "factual basis" of the claim; and (ii) for the purposes of assessing contribution, is the settling party to be deemed to have been liable on that basis, or is it for the party against whom contribution is sought to establish that he was.[8]

4–004 Most issues in most claims are issues of fact. However, there will also be issues of law or of mixed fact and law, or of pure law. Where, for example, there is an issue as to whether a duty of care in tort was owed in particular circumstances, that is a question of law, not of fact. The effect of s.1(4) is that the party claiming contribution must show that, had the factual basis of the claim against him been proved, then any issues of law as to his liability would have been resolved against him. For example, if a claim were brought against an accountant for allegedly making a representation to a third party as to his client company's accounts, then it would not matter that the accountant denied making the statement: that was an allegation of fact. However, it would be open to the party against whom contribution was claimed to argue that in the circumstances alleged, no duty of care was imposed as a matter of law.

4–005 The question of what a party who had settled a claim had to prove in order to claim a contribution arose in *Dubai Aluminium Co Ltd v Salaam*.[9] In that case the original claim had been brought against a number of defendants, including a firm of solicitors, one of whose partners was alleged to have knowingly participated

---

[4] Most limitation periods bar the remedy, but not the right. Of those relevant to claims against professional persons, s.14B of the Limitation Act 1980 is the only one which might be thought to bar the right. However, it appears that it too only bars the remedy: see *Financial Services Compensation Scheme Ltd v Larnell (Insurances) Ltd (in creditors' voluntary liquidation)* [2005] EWCA Civ 1408; [2006] P.N.L.R. 13 at [44], *per* Lloyd L.J. and at [71], *per* Moore-Bick L.J. Sir Peter Gibson agreed with both judgments. See further, Ch.5, para.5–077.

[5] Civil Liability (Contribution) Act 1978, s.1(2).

[6] See para.4–017, below, for the time for bringing a claim for contribution.

[7] Civil Liability (Contribution) Act 1978, s.1(4).

[8] The second issue is addressed in para.4–014, below.

[9] [2002] UKHL 48; [2002] 2 A.C. 366.

in a major fraud. The other partners reached a settlement with the claimant on terms that the allegations against them and against the allegedly fraudulent partner were withdrawn. They then claimed a contribution against other defendants (but not against their partner). One issue was whether that partner had been acting in the ordinary course of the business of the firm so as to render his partners vicariously liable for his wrongful acts.[10] Reversing the decision of the Court of Appeal[11] the House of Lords held that whether a partner was acting in the ordinary course of the business of his firm was "a question of law, based on primary facts, rather than a simple question of fact"[12] so that it was open to challenge by the party against whom contribution was claimed. On the limited material before them on the appeal they held that the partner had been acting in the ordinary course of his firm's business.

(a) Basis of Liability

Section 6(1) provides: 4–006

"A person is liable in respect of any damage for the purposes of this Act if the person who suffered it (or anyone representing his estate or dependents) is entitled to recover compensation from him in respect of that damage (whatever the legal basis of his liability, whether tort, breach of contract, breach of trust or otherwise)."

This is widely drafted and has been so interpreted. However, it has been stated authoritatively that is not so widely drafted as to enable a claim to be made between defendants where the claimant has a claim against one for professional negligence and against the other for restitution in respect of the same matter.[13] It does not appear to extend to a claim in debt.[14] Obviously the person against whom contribution is claimed must be liable to the person to whom the person

---

[10] Partnership Act 1890, s.10.

[11] [2001] Q.B. 113.

[12] [2002] UKHL 48; [2002] 2 A.C. 366 at [24], *per* Lord Nicholls with whom Lords Slynn, Hutton and Hobhouse agreed; Lord Millett considered that it was "a factual conclusion based on an assessment of the primary facts": see para.[112] of his speech; he then went on to conclude that the conclusion that the partner was so acting was "legally open to the trial judge had the case proceeded to trial": para.[131].

[13] *Royal Brompton Hospital National Health Service Trust v Hammond* [2002] UKHL 14; [2002] 1 W.L.R. 1397 at [33], *per* Lord Steyn, with whom the other members of the House of Lords agreed, disapproving this aspect of the decision of the Court of Appeal in *Friends' Provident Life Office v Hillier Parker May & Rowden* [1997] Q.B. 85. Lord Steyn accepted the criticisms made in *Goff & Jones, The Law of Restitution* (5th edn) p.396: a claim in restitution is not for "damage suffered" by the claimant, but in respect of the unjust enrichment of the defendant. It is not a claim for compensation and so does not fall within s.1(1). At [26] Lord Steyn also stated that the 1978 Act was intended to extend the reach of the contribution principle to a wider range of cases than before. However, it may be that *Friends' Provident* remains authoritative, notwithstanding the decision in *Royal Brompton*: see *Niru Battery Manufacturing Co v Milestone Trading Ltd* [2004] EWCA Civ 487; [2004] 2 Lloyd's Rep. 379, where what was said on this point was clearly obiter. Whether it is technically correct that this part of Lord Steyns's speech in *Royal Brompton* was not the ratio decidendi, the views expressed by him are highly persuasive.

[14] *Hampton v Minns* [2002] 1 W.L.R. 1, where Kevin Garnett Q.C., sitting as a deputy High Court judge, held that the Civil Liability (Contribution) Act 1978 did not apply to a claim in debt, including a claim against a guarantor of a debtor. See also *Howkins & Harrison v Taylor* [2001] Lloyd's Rep. P.N. 1, CA.

claiming contribution is or may be liable. So, where no claim would lie by an employer under a building contract against the building contractor because of the contractual provisions as to insurance, architects and engineers sued by the employer could not claim contribution from the building contractor.[15]

(b) *Meaning of "the same damage"*

4–007　While contribution may be claimed on the basis of the widest possible range of liabilities, both the person claiming and the person from whom contribution is claimed must be liable to the same person in respect of the same damage.[16] This problem was considered by the Court of Appeal in *Birse Construction Ltd v Haiste*.[17] Birse contracted with Anglian Water to design and construct a reservoir. Birse engaged Haiste, consulting engineers, to assist in preparing their tender and designing the reservoir. N, an employee of Anglian, administered the project as engineer. Following completion, defects emerged. Birse settled Anglian's claim against it by constructing a new reservoir at its own expense. Birse brought proceedings against Haiste for negligence. Haiste brought contribution proceedings against N under the Civil Liability (Contribution) Act 1978. The Court of Appeal held that the contribution proceedings should be struck out. The ground of the decision was that the damage allegedly caused by N to Anglian was not "the same damage" as the damage allegedly caused by Haiste to Birse. Sir John May stated:

> "The Act is in my opinion concerned with the relatively simple sharing of existing liability. I would be surprised if against this background the Act created potentially complicated and some might say tortuous legal relationships."[18]

Roch L.J. summarised his reasoning and conclusion:

> "The word 'damage' in the phrase 'the same damage' in section 1(1) does not mean 'damages' . . .
> The damage suffered by Anglian in this case was the physical defects in the reservoir. The damage suffered by Birse was the financial loss of having to construct a second reservoir for Anglian. Anglian and Birse did not suffer the same damage."[19]

4–008　　In the same way, where a claimant suffers personal injuries and his claim against the person who negligently caused them is not issued in time, he may have a claim against his former solicitor. His claim against the solicitor is clearly

---

[15] *Co-operative Retail Services Ltd v Taylor Young Partnership Ltd (Carillion Construction Ltd, Part 20 Defendants)* [2002] UKHL 17; [2002] 1 W.L.R. 1419
[16] In the light of the decision of the House of Lords in *Banque Bruxelles Lambert SA v Eagle Star Insurance Co Ltd* [1997] A.C. 191 (see Ch.3, para.3–002, above), it is now possible for one party to be liable only for some of the damage suffered. This does not prevent another party responsible for the whole damage from claiming contribution: *Ball v Banner* [2000] Lloyd's Rep. P.N. 569, *per* Hart J. See also *Rahman v Areanose Ltd* [2001] Q.B. 351, CA.
[17] [1996] 1 W.L.R. 675.
[18] *ibid.* at 680C.
[19] *ibid.* at 682C–F. See also *Mahony v J Kruschich (Demolitions) Pty Ltd* (1985) 156 C.L.R. 522 (High Court of Australia).

related to the original claim, but it is not for the same damage.[20] The damage in the original claim was the personal injuries themselves. The damage in the second claim is the loss of the chance to bring the original claim (or the reduced value of that claim if he has to rely on s.33 of the Limitation Act 1980).[21] In *Royal Brompton Hospital National Health Service Trust v Hammond*[22] the claimant sought damages against the architect for negligently granting the contractor extensions of time. The architect sought to claim a contribution from the contractor. The House of Lords held that the claim against the architect was for damage in the sense of impairment of the claimant's rights against the contractor. That was not the same damage as the claimant's claim against the contractor to have the extensions of time set aside. The position would be different if the claim against the architect were for negligent supervision or inspection of the contractor's work. In that case both would be liable for the defective work and so liable for the same damage.[23]

The same reasoning was applied by the Court of Appeal in *Howkins &* **4–009** *Harrison v Tyler*.[24] In that case the claimant was a firm of valuers which had compromised a claim against it by a building society. The claim had been for allegedly negligent overvaluation of a property taken as security for a loan to the defendants. Having settled the building society's claim, the firm brought an action for contribution. The claim failed on a preliminary issue as to whether the firm and the defendants had been liable for the same damage. Scott V.C., with whom Aldous and Sedley L.JJ. agreed, proposed this test:

"Suppose that A and B are the two parties who are said each to be liable to C in respect of 'the same damage' that has been suffered by C. So C must have a right of action of some sort against A and a right of action of some sort against B. There are two questions that should then be asked. If A pays C a sum of money in satisfaction, or on account, of A's liability to C, will that sum operate to reduce or extinguish, depending upon the amount, B's liability to C? Secondly, if B pays C a sum of money in satisfaction or on account of B's liability to C, would that operate to reduce or extinguish A's liability to C? It seems to me that unless both of those questions can be given an affirmative answer, the case is not one to which the 1978 Act can be applied. If the payment by A or B to C does not *pro tanto* relieve the other of his obligations to C, there cannot, it seems to me, possibly be a case for contending that the non-paying

---

[20] *Wallace v Litwiniuk* (2001) 92 Alta.L.R. (3d) 249 (Alberta Court of Appeal); approved in *Royal Brompton Hospital National Health Service Trust v Hammond* [2002] UKHL 14; [2002] 1 W.L.R. 1397.

[21] As to which see Ch.5, paras 5–093 to 5–098, below.

[22] [2002] UKHL 14; [2002] 1 W.L.R. 1397, dismissing an appeal from the decision of the Court of Appeal reported at [2000] Lloyd's Rep. P.N. 643.

[23] The decision of the House of Lords in *Royal Brompton Hospital National Health Service Trust v Hammond* [2002] UKHL 14; [2002] 1 W.L.R. 1397 was followed by the Court of Appeal in Northern Ireland in *Dingles Building (NI) Ltd v Brooks* [2003] P.N.L.R. 8. It *Dingles Building* it was held that the damage which formed the subject of a claim by the claimant company for breach of warranty of authority against a sole trustee who purported to contract on behalf of his fellow trustees was not the same as that suffered by reason of any negligent failure of the claimant company's solicitors to advise that the other trustees be asked to sign the contract. The damage for which the solicitors might be liable was the loss of the chance to obtain those signatures, whereas the sole trustee was liable for the damage suffered by reason of his lack of authority.

[24] [2001] Lloyd's Rep. P.N. 1.

party, whose liability to C remains un-reduced, will also have an obligation under section 1(1) to contribute to the payment made by the paying party."[25]

Applying that test to the facts, payment by the valuers to the building society did not reduce the debt secured on the property.[26]

4–010   The test suggested in *Howkins & Harrison v Tyler*[27] was considered by the House of Lords in *Royal Brompton Hospital National Health Service Trust v Hammond*.[28] Lord Steyn, with whom the other members of the House of Lords agreed, said that the *Howkins & Harrison* test might render questions of contribution unnecessarily complex if it were regarded as a threshold and that it was best regarded as "a practical test to be used in considering the very statutory question whether two claims under consideration are for 'the same damage'."[29] However, he said that the safest course was to apply the statutory test. Lord Bingham, with whom the other members of the House of Lords agreed, said:

> "When any claim for contribution falls to be decided the following questions in my opinion arise. (1) What damage has A suffered? (2) Is B liable to A in respect of that damage? (3) Is C also liable to A in respect of that damage or some of it? .... I do not think it matters greatly whether, in phrasing these questions, one speaks (as the 1978 Act does) of 'damage', or of 'loss' or 'harm', provided it is borne in mind that 'damage' does not mean 'damages' (as pointed out by Roch L.J. in *Birse Construction Ltd v Haiste Ltd* [1996] 1 W.L.R. 675, 682) and that B's right to contribution by C depends on the damage, loss or harm for which B is liable to A corresponding (even if in part only) with the damage, loss or harm for which C is liable to A."[30]

4. THE CLAIM

(a) *Matters which cannot be Raised in Defence to a Claim*

4–011   It is no defence to a claim for contribution that had the original claimant brought the claim he would have faced a good limitation defence, unless that defence barred the right and not the remedy.[31] It would also appear that it is no defence

---

[25] [2001] Lloyd's Rep. P.N. 1 at 4. See also *Eastgate Group Ltd v Lindsey Morden Group Inc* [2001] EWCA Civ 1446; [2002] 1 W.L.R. 642.

[26] Scott V.C. then considered to what extent the valuers might have a claim were the building society subsequently to recover the full debt or by joining the building society to a claim for the debt. Such claims, however, would be matters of subrogation and restitution and had nothing to do with the Civil Liability (Contribution) Act 1978: *ibid.* at 5.

[27] [2001] Lloyd's Rep. P.N. 1.

[28] [2002] UKHL 14; [2002] 1 W.L.R. 1397.

[29] *ibid.* at [28].

[30] *ibid.* at [6]. See also *Alexander v Perpetual Trustees WA Ltd* [2004] H.C.A. 7; (2004) 216 C.L.R. 109. Deciding whether B and C are both liable to A for the same damage can raise difficult questions of causation and, in particular, as to whether the subsequent negligence of C has broken the chain of causation in relation to B's earlier negligence. The decision of Davies J. in *Luke v Kingsley Smith & Co (a firm)* [2003] EWHC 1559, QB; [2004] P.N.L.R. 12 contains a helpful discussion.

[31] Civil Liability (Contribution) Act 1978, s.1(3). See para.4–003, fn.4, above.

that the person from whom contribution is sought has reached a settlement with the original claimant.[32]

(b) *Matters which can be Raised in Defence to a Claim*

Judgments given in any part of the United Kingdom between the original claimant and the person from whom contribution is claimed are conclusive as to any issue determined in the latter's favour.[33] So, if there has been a judgment on liability in his favour, there is no right to claim contribution, even if the party seeking contribution disagrees with that result.[34]

4–012

(c) *Basis of Assessment of Contribution*

The principles of apportionment are set out in s.2 of the Civil Liability (Contribution) Act 1978. Section 2(1) provides that "the amount of the contribution recoverable from any person shall be such as may be found by the court to be just and equitable having regard to the extent of that person's responsibility for the damage in question". It is for the person seeking contribution to prove that the person from whom contribution is sought would have been liable to the original claimant and the basis of his responsibility for the relevant damage.

4–013

The question arises whether, in a case in which the person claiming contribution settled the claim against him,[35] his liability is to be assumed or whether it has to be proved by the person against whom contribution is sought if he wishes contribution to be assessed on the basis that the other was also responsible. It might be said that s.1(4) envisages a claim by someone who denies that he was liable to the original claimant on the facts, but claims that he nevertheless made a bona fide settlement.[36] This provision would serve little purpose if the assessment of contribution proceeds on the basis that he is deemed to have been liable. However, the decision of the House of Lords in *Dubai Aluminium Co Ltd v Salaam*[37] proceeds on the basis that liability is to be assumed and does not have to be proved by the person against whom contribution is sought. Their Lordships also held that the assessment of contribution should take account of the receipt of the proceeds of the original fraud by those against whom contribution was sought.

4–014

---

[32] See *Kenburgh Investments (Northern) Ltd (in liquidation) v Minton* [2000] Lloyd's Rep. P.N. 736 at 743, CA; and *Logan v Uttlesford DC* (1986) 136 New L.J. 541 and the decision of the Court of Appeal in *Jameson v Central Electricity Generating Board* [1998] Q.B. 323. However, the settlement may have extinguished the original claimant's right to make any further claim, so that the person seeking contribution was not liable to him: see *Jameson v Central Electricity Generating Board* [2001] 1 A.C. 455, HL (reversing the decision of the Court of Appeal on this ground).

[33] Civil Liability (Contribution) Act 1978, s.1(5).

[34] In *James Hardie & Coy Pty Ltd v Seltsam Pty Ltd* (1998) 196 C.L.R. 53 the High Court of Australia held that a consent judgment entered between the original claimant and the person from whom contribution was claimed provided a complete defence to the claim for contribution. However, the person claiming contribution was entitled to be heard in opposition to the entry of judgment by consent.

[35] See paras 4–003 to 4–005, above.

[36] See para.4–003, above.

[37] [2002] UKHL 48; [2002] 2 A.C. 366.

4-015   The person against whom contribution is claimed can rely upon any defence of contributory negligence which he would have had against the original claimant[38] and on any limitation on his liability under statute or under any agreement made before the damage occurred.[39] Contribution can only be claimed to the extent that the party from whom it is claimed would in fact have been liable and not by reference to settlement of an overstated claim.[40] Where the party claiming contribution has settled the original claim on a costs-inclusive basis, then he is able to recover a contribution towards the whole sum paid in settlement. He is also able to recover sums paid in respect of the injured party's costs under s.51 (3) of the Supreme Court Act 1981.[41]

4-016   Where the client suffers loss or injury as a result of the negligence of two or more of his professional advisers, the apportionment of liability between them is governed by the same general principles as apply to any other wrongdoers. The court should have regard both to the culpability of the various parties and to the extent to which each party's conduct "caused" the damage in question.[42] This includes consideration of each party's "moral responsibility in the sense of culpability and organisational responsibility in the sense of where in the hierarchy of decision-making and in the organisational structure leading to the damage the contributing party was located".[43] The "just and equitable" criterion is wide enough to enable the apportionment take account of blameworthiness as well as causative potency,[44] and even, to an extent, of non-causative matters.[45] However, the main factor to consider is each party's responsibility for the damage.[46] Questions of apportionment arise most commonly in the building professions and these are discussed in Ch.9.[47] Apportionment of liability for medical accidents is discussed in Ch.13.[48] Apportionment of liability between successive solicitors or between solicitors and members of other professions is discussed in Ch.11.[49] The question of apportionment between defendants should be considered separately from the assessment of contributory negligence as between the claimant and all defendants.[50] It is not possible to proceed upon

---

[38] Civil Liability (Contribution) Act 1978, s.2(3)(b) and (c).

[39] *ibid.*, s.3(3)(a).

[40] *J Sainsbury Plc v Broadway Malyan* [1999] P.N.L.R. 286, *per* Judge Lloyd Q.C.

[41] *BICC Ltd v Cumbrian Industrial Ltd* [2001] EWCA Civ 1621; [2002] Lloyd's Rep. P.N. 526 at [114]–[123], *per* Henry L.J. giving the judgment of the Court of Appeal.

[42] Where one partner was culpable and his "innocent" partners seek a contribution, they are to be treated as culpable when seeking contribution: *Dubai Aluminium Co Ltd v Salaam* [2002] UKHL 48; [2002] 2 A.C. 366. But it seems inconceivable that "innocent" partners would be treated as culpable were they to claim contribution against the culpable partner.

[43] *BICC Ltd v Cumbrian Industrial Ltd* [2001] EWCA Civ 1621; [2002] Lloyd's Rep. P.N. 526 at [106]–[108], *per* Henry L.J. giving the judgment of the Court of Appeal.

[44] *Madden v Quirk* [1989] 1 W.L.R. 702 (Simon Brown J).

[45] *Re-Source America International Ltd v Platt Site Services Ltd* [2004] EWCA Civ 665; (2004) 95 Con.L.R. 1; followed in *Brian Warwick Partnership v HOK International Ltd* [2005] EWCA Civ 962; [2006] P.N.L.R. 5.

[46] *Brian Warwick Partnership v HOK International Ltd* [2005] EWCA Civ 962; [2006] P.N.L.R. 5 at [45], *per* Arden L.J., with whom Keene L.J. agreed on this point at [51].

[47] See Ch.9, paras 9–345 and 9–346, below.

[48] See Ch.13, paras 13–064 and 13–065, below.

[49] See Ch.11, paras 11–038 to 11–342, below.

[50] *Fitzgerald v Lane* [1989] A.C. 328.

assumptions as to the existence and breach of a duty for the purposes of making an apportionment. The actual duty and breach need to be found.[51]

(d) *Time for bringing a Claim for Contribution*

Section 10 of the Limitation Act 1980 provides that a claim for contribution   **4–017** within two years of a judgment or arbitration award against him in favour of the original claimant or of the date of any agreement to make a payment in settlement of a claim against him. Where an agreement is later embodied in a consent order, time will run from when the agreement was made and not from the date of the order.[52]

---

[51] *Amaca Pty Ltd v The State of New South Wales* [2003] H.C.A. 44.
[52] *Knight v Rochdale Healthcare NHS Trust* [2003] EWHC 1831, QB; [2004] 1 W.L.R. 371 (Crane J.).

CHAPTER 5

DEFENCES

1. EXCLUSION OR RESTRICTION OF LIABILITY

Previous editions of this work have stated that, traditionally, professional persons **5–001** have not normally sought to exclude or restrict their liability to clients or patients for breach of duty. Reference has been made to evidence to the Royal Commission on Legal Services, in which the Law Society argued that it was "one of the marks of a fully developed profession" that they should not do so.[1] However, times change and with them the attitude of professionals and professional bodies

---

[1] Quoted in para.23.39 of the Royal Commission's Report, Cmnd. 7648 (1979). The Royal Commission was not persuaded by this view and recommended that an enquiry should be set up to review the question of limiting liability for all professions: see para.23.30 of the Report. In 1987, the Law Society Council decided that there was "no objection as a matter of conduct" to solicitors seeking to limit liability to their level of insurance cover: see the Council statement published in the *Law Society's Gazette*, May 27, (1987), p.1545.

to exclusion or limitation of liability. It is now not at all uncommon to find provisions in professional retainers or reports which seek either to limit in one or more ways the damages which clients can recover in the event of breach of duty by the professionals whom they have engaged or to exclude or limit any duty to persons other than their clients. The very high potential liability to which some professionals are exposed, not least when compared with the fees properly charged for the work which gives rise to the exposure, and the availability and cost of professional indemnity insurance are the obvious explanations for this as for the rapid adoption of LLP status by many firms.

5–002   In 1988–1989, the Secretary of State for Trade and Industry appointed three study teams to look into the problems of auditors, surveyors and the construction industry professions. Their reports together with the report of the Steering Group, chaired by Professor Likierman, were published in April 1989.[2] These established that there had been a significant increase in the number and size of professional negligence claims in the 1980s, unrelated to any discernible increase in negligence; that professional indemnity premiums had increased proportionately (despite cyclical fluctuations due to changes in the insurance market); that increased costs were being passed on to the clients and that professionals were becoming more cautious to the detriment of their clients. Possible solutions, including contractual limitations of liability, were discussed. In a later consultation paper,[3] the Common Law Team of the Law Commission, whilst opposing the principle of proportionate liability, recognised "the very real problems faced by many professional defendants in obtaining affordable insurance".[4] They considered that professional persons ought to be able to limit their liability and that they were entitled to greater certainty in this regard.

> "It seems unsatisfactory to tell the professional who structures his liability and insurance position with great care that the reasonableness of carefully drafted clauses on which he will rely will be assessed on a 'case by case' basis."[5]

(a) The Position at Common Law

5–003   There are various methods by which liability can be excluded or limited by contractual provision. The first is to exclude a duty which would otherwise be accepted. An example would be a term that the professional will not have a duty to do something. For example, it is and has long been usual for architects to accept a duty to carry out periodic inspection of the building works, but to state expressly that they are under no duty to supervise the execution of the works.[6] In the same way, it is and has long been common for survey reports to include a standard clause to the effect that no responsibility can be accepted by the surveyor for defects in parts of the property which were inaccessible or had not been inspected.[7] It could be said that such clauses do not exclude or limit liability

---

[2] See "Professional Liability: Report of the Study Teams", Chairman: Professor Andrew Likierman (HMSO, 1989).
[3] "Feasibility Investigation of Joint and Several Liability" (HMSO, 1996).
[4] *ibid*. para.5.1.
[5] *ibid*. para.5.18.
[6] See Ch.9, para.9–236.
[7] See Ch.10, para.10–073.

in that all they do is to define what the professional undertakes to do. Such clauses do serve to limit the scope of the professionals' duties, but there is a practical limit to their effect. To develop the examples given, an architect who had been retained on the basis that he was not obliged to supervise the works, can still be liable for failure to notice poor workmanship if a competent architect would have done so during a periodic inspection,[8] and a surveyor may be in breach of duty in either failing to inspect particular areas or warn that he had not done so or in failing to uncover or open up areas if he should have appreciated that there were grounds for suspecting that there was a defect.[9] In other words, such clauses do not prevent liability arising for any want of skill and care in the execution of those duties which have been assumed.

Another type of clause is that which seeks to exclude or limit liability for a **5–004** breach of duty, rather than to restrict or limit the scope of the duty. Such clauses vary from clauses which provide for a complete exclusion of all liability[10] to clauses which limit liability to a particular sum or which exclude liability for one or more types of loss or which specify a time in which a claim may be brought. Those who draft such clauses usually do so with applicable statutory provisions in mind.[11] No doubt it is for this reason, as well as a remaining sense that it is inappropriate for professional persons to seek to exclude all liability, that it is far more usual to encounter clauses which seek to limit rather than to exclude liability.

In order to exclude or restrict liability for breach of contractual duty of care **5–005** and negligence, the professional must ensure the following:

(1) if a contractual term is relied upon, it is expressly incorporated into the contract of engagement[12];

(2) if a notice is relied upon, it was drawn to the client's attention; and

(3) in either case, the wording used is sufficiently clear to apply to negligence.[13]

In order to be effective an exemption clause must be expressed clearly and **5–006** must also clearly apply to the liability in respect of which the professional seeks protection.[14] In one recent case, a clause provided that accountants who were advising on a scheme intended to produce a significant saving for their client were retained on terms which included a clause under which they accepted liability in respect of loss and damage suffered by their client "as a direct result of [the accountants] providing the Services" but which went on to exclude "all other liability . . . in particular consequential loss, failure to realise anticipated

---

[8] See Ch.9, para.9–241.
[9] See Ch.10, para.10–084.
[10] Or require one party to indemnify the other against the consequences of the other's breach.
[11] See paras 5–012 to 5–020, below.
[12] As to which, see *Chitty*, Ch.12, paras 12–013 *et seq.* and Ch.14, para.14–002.
[13] As to which, see *Chitty*, Ch.14, particularly at paras 14–010 to 14–012. By far the safest way of excluding or restricting liability for negligence is to use the word "negligence" or some synonym for it. See, generally *Smith v South Wales Switchgear Co Ltd* [1978] 1 W.L.R. 165 and *Photo Production Ltd v Securicor Transport Ltd* [1980] A.C. 827.
[14] *Chitty*, Ch.14, paras 14–005 and 14–006.

savings and benefits ... ". The accountants were negligent and as a result the scheme failed. The client claimed for the lost opportunity of obtaining the benefits from a non-negligent scheme. The accountants sought unsuccessfully to rely on the express exclusion of liability for "failure to realise anticipated savings and benefits". It was held that the loss claimed fell within the first part of the clause, being the direct result of the provision of the "Services" as defined.[15]

5-007   If there is any doubt as to the meaning of an exemption clause or any ambiguity, the courts will apply the *contra proferentem* rule and construe the clause against the party seeking to rely on it so that the doubt or ambiguity will be resolved against him and in favour of the injured party.[16]

5-008   Where the exemption clause seeks to exclude liability in respect of negligence, then, if there is room for any real doubt as to the parties' intention,[17] the principles summarised in *Canada Steamship Lines Ltd v The King* fall to be applied.[18] Those principles are:

"(1) If the clause contains language which expressly exempts the person in whose favour it is made (hereafter called 'the proferens') from the consequence of the negligence of his own servants, effect must be given to that provision ...

(2) If there is no express reference to negligence, the court must consider whether the words used are wide enough, in their ordinary meaning, to cover negligence on the part of the servants of the proferens ...

(3) If the words used are wide enough for the above purpose, the court must then consider whether 'the head of damage may be based on some ground other than that of negligence' ... The 'other ground' must not be so fanciful or remote that the proferens cannot be supposed to have desired protection against it; but subject to this qualification ... the existence of a possible head of damage other than that of negligence is fatal to the proferens even if the words used are prima facie wide enough to cover negligence on the part of his servants."[19]

In applying this test, which is not a statute but merely a guide as to how to ascertain the intention of the parties to a contract,[20] the court must bear in mind that it is "inherently improbable that one party to the contract should intend to absolve the other party from the consequences of the latter's own negligence".[21] It might be thought to be unlikely that a client would intend to absolve a

---

[15] *University of Keele v Price Waterhouse* [2004] EWCA Civ 583; [2004] P.N.L.R. 43. See also, on very different facts, *Caledonia North Sea Ltd v British Telecommunications Plc* [2002] UKHL 4; [2002] B.L.R. 139 where an attempt to imply an exemption into an indemnity provision in a contract failed.

[16] See *Lewison, The Interpretation of Contracts*, (3rd edn, Sweet & Maxwell, 2004), para.12.05.

[17] *Scottish & Newcastle Plc v GD Construction (St Albans) Ltd* [2003] EWCA Civ 16; [2003] B.L.R. 131, at [57], *per* Longmore L.J., with whom Ward L.J. agreed.

[18] [1952] A.C. 192.

[19] *ibid.* at 208.

[20] See the authorities referred to in para.12-06 of *Lewison, The Interpretation of Contracts*, (3rd edn, Sweet & Maxwell, 2004) and *Chitty*, para.14-010, n.64.

[21] *Gillespie Bros & Co Ltd v Roy Bowles Transport Ltd* [1973] 1 Lloyd's Rep. 10, at p.19, col.2, *per* Buckley L.J., cited with approval by Stephenson L.J. in *The Raphael* [1982] 2 Lloyd's Rep. 42, at 50–51 and by Schiemann L.J. in *Casson v Osterly PJ Ltd* [2001] EWCA Civ 1013; [2003] B.L.R. 1476 at [12]. It is for this reason that the Courts adopt a less strict approach to clauses which limit rather than exclude liability: *Ailsa Craig Fishing Co Ltd v Malvern Fishing Co Ltd* [1983] 1 W.L.R. 964, HL, *per* Lord Wilberforce at 966H and, *per* Lord Fraser at 970D–E.

professional he retains from liability for his own negligence, but, as a matter of construction it may be difficult to find any other head of liability (other than dishonesty), although, as explained in the chapters on individual professions, professionals may owe strict contractual obligations and statutory duties, as well as fiduciary obligations and obligations of confidentiality. The courts have emphasised that strained constructions of exemption and limitation clauses should be avoided, not least because they are now subject to control by statute.[22]

(b) *The Statutory Framework*

Solicitors.[23] Section 60(5) of the Solicitors Act 1974 provides that any provision in a "contentious business agreement"[24] between a solicitor and his client "that that the solicitor shall not be liable in negligence, or that he shall be relieved from any responsibility to which he would otherwise be subject as a solicitor, shall be void".[25] It is clear that this provision prevents any exclusion of liability for negligence (or breach of a contractual duty to exercise reasonable skill and care) in a contentious business agreement. That raises the question, yet to be answered by the courts, whether it also renders void any provision in such an agreement which limits liability for negligence to a specified amount. Such a provision could be said to have the effect that the solicitor "shall not be liable for negligence", because it would exclude liability above the specified limit and so be void because of the first limb of the provision. It could also be said to relieve the solicitor of "responsibility to which he would otherwise be subject as a solicitor" and so fall foul of the second limb too. On the other hand, it could be said that the words "shall not be liable" in the first limb are directed at a total exclusion of liability, because a limitation clause would still leave the solicitor liable, albeit only to a limited extent, and that the second limb is concerned with responsibility other than liability in negligence. A difficulty with the latter interpretation is that it would permit a very low limit of liability for negligence, which would defeat the apparent purpose of the provision.[26] However, as has already been stated, the point remains undecided by the Courts. The Law Society has called for this provision be removed.[27]

5–009

---

[22] *Mitchell (George) (Chesterhall) Ltd v Finney Lock Seeds Ltd* [1983] 2 A.C. 803, at 813D–814D, *per* Lord Bridge, with whom the other members of the House of Lords agreed.

[23] See Ch.11, para.11–142 below.

[24] Defined in the Solicitors Act 1974, ss.59(1) and 87(1) (see also Sch.2, paras 1(4) and (5) and 22(1) of the Administration of Justice Act 1985). See also *Chamberlain v Boodle & King* [1982] 1 W.L.R. 1443.

[25] See also Sch.2, para.24 of the Administration of Justice Act 1985. There is no similar provision affecting agreements for non-contentious business, but see the Law Society Statement "Limitation of Liability by Contract", discussed in Ch.11, para.11–142, below.

[26] Nor can the Unfair Contract Terms Act 1977 be prayed in aid of the construction of s.60(5) which limits it to a complete exclusion of liability, because, self-evidently, Parliament did not pass the Solicitors Act 1974 (and its predecessors, which contained provisions to the same effect) on the basis that it was to be construed subject to an Act passed three years later.

[27] In a speech given by the President, Peter Williamson, on June 23, 2006.

5–010 **Auditors.** In the case of auditors engaged by a company to carry out a statutory audit, any provision in their contract of engagement[28] purporting to exempt them from liability for negligence or breach of duty is also void.[29]

5–011 **Financial Services and Markets Act 2000.** The Financial Services and Markets Act 2000 and rules made under it contain a number of restrictions on the exclusion of duties and liabilities. These are addressed in Ch.14 below.[30]

5–012 **Unfair Contract Terms Act 1977.** The statute of most general application, however, is the Unfair Contract Terms Act 1977. Section 2(1) provides that a person cannot "by reference to any contract term or to a notice given to persons generally or to particular persons exclude or restrict his liability for death or personal injury resulting from negligence". The term "negligence" embraces both the tort of negligence and breach of any contractual obligation to exercise reasonable skill or care.[31] The profession principally affected by s.2(1) is, of course, the medical profession. Since the damage resulting from clinical negligence is almost always some form of personal injury,[32] doctors are effectively prevented from excluding or restricting liability for negligence. Other professions affected to a lesser extent are architects and engineers, whose negligence could on occasion lead to personal injury.[33]

5–013 Negligence which results in damage other than personal injury or death is dealt with in s.2(2). A person cannot exclude or restrict liability for such negligence by reference to a contract term or notice, except in so far as that term or notice satisfies "the requirement of reasonableness". The test of "reasonableness" is explained in s.11.[34] In the case of a contract term, the court must consider whether it was a fair and reasonable one having regard to the circumstances in the actual or constructive knowledge of the parties at the time the contract was made.[35] In the case of a notice, the court must consider whether it would be fair and reasonable to allow reliance on it, having regard to all the circumstances

---

[28] Or in the articles of the company.

[29] Companies Act 1985, s.310. See further Ch.17, para.17–102, below. The Companies Bill currently before Parliament retains the prohibition on exclusion of liability, but does permit (i) the company to indemnify the auditors against the costs of successfully defending civil or criminal proceedings and (ii) the auditor to limit liability, if specified conditions are met and then only if the limitation is "fair and reasonable in all the circumstances". The Unfair Contract Terms Act 1977 will not apply to such limitation clauses. There is no equivalent provision for the auditors of limited liability partnerships.

[30] Ch.14, para.14–005.

[31] Unfair Contract Terms Act 1977, s.1(1).

[32] See Ch.13, para.13–155, below.

[33] See, e.g. *Clay v AJ Crump & Sons Ltd* [1964] 1 Q.B. 533 and *Eckersley v Binnie & Partners* (1988) 18 Con.L.R. 1.

[34] The operation of s.11 is briefly discussed by the House of Lords in *George Mitchell (Chesterhall) Ltd v Finney Lock Seeds Ltd* [1983] 2 A.C. 803 at 815–816. J. Adams and R. Brownsword review the earlier authorities in "The Unfair Contract Terms Act: A Decade of Discretion" in (1988) 104 L.Q.R. 94. They criticise the *George Mitchell* decision as having given rise to undue uncertainty. For a general discussion of the "reasonableness" test, see *Chitty*, paras 14–081 to 14–094.

[35] Unfair Contract Terms Act 1977, s.11(1).

when the alleged liability arose.[36] It is thought that it would generally be unreasonable for a professional person to exclude liability altogether for negligence vis-à-vis his client.[37] There can, of course, be no objection to a term limiting the task which a professional person undertakes.[38] However, once the task has been defined, it is unlikely that a complete exclusion of liability would be fair and reasonable. Notices or contractual terms which merely seek to limit a professional person's liability to a specified sum may fall into a different category, although they are subject to the requirement of reasonableness.[39]

The requirement of reasonableness. In considering the requirement of rea-   **5–014** sonableness, the courts will have regard the guidelines provided in Sch.2 to the Act, although these are not an exhaustive list.[40] The first four of the five guidelines provided in the Act are likely to be relevant in the context of professionals. In summary, they are: (a) the strength of the bargaining position of the parties; (b) whether the customer/client received an inducement to agree to the term or had an opportunity to engage another without having to accept the term in question; (c) whether the customer/client knew or ought reasonably to have known of the term and its extent and (d) where the clause attempts to exclude liability in respect of a particular condition, whether it was reasonable at the time of making the contract to expect that compliance with the condition would be practicable. Further, where the clause seeks to limit liability to a specified sum, s.11(4) of the Act provides that the court shall have regard in particular to (a) the resources which he could expect to be available to him for the purpose of meeting the liability; and (b) how far it was open to him to cover himself by insurance.[41]

Professional persons commonly practise individually or in small firms. The   **5–015** damages resulting from professional negligence (particularly in the realms of auditing, the provision of financial advice or the design of buildings) may be far beyond the means of the practitioner or firm which is liable. It may be impossible to obtain insurance cover for the full amount of such liabilities or the cost of the

---

[36] Unfair Contract Terms Act 1977, s.11(3). The distinction between subss. (1) and (3) is of considerable importance in the context of professional negligence. Where there is no contract between the parties the court can have regard to the nature and quality of the defendant's negligent conduct, when deciding whether the disclaimer satisfies the "reasonableness" test. Where there is a contract, the court can only take account of the actual negligence in the instant case as being an example of the kind of negligence for which the contract purports to exclude liability. Thus the relevance of the defendant's actual conduct is much diminished.

[37] See the reasoning of the House of Lords in *Smith v Eric S Bush* [1990] 1 A.C. 831, where a disclaimer of liability towards a party one stage removed from the client was held to be unreasonable.

[38] See para.5–003, above.

[39] See, e.g. *St Albans City and DC v International Computers Ltd* [1996] 4 All E.R. 481, CA and *South West Water Services Ltd v International Computers Ltd* [2001] Lloyd's Rep. P.N. 353, *per* (Judge Toulmin Q.C.) cases concerning the supply of computers.

[40] *Overseas Medical Supplies Ltd v Orient Transport Services Ltd* [1999] 2 Lloyd's Rep. 273, CA.

[41] The availability of insurance may also be a relevant factor in applying the test of reasonableness under s.11(1) (although it is not a relevant factor that the party seeking to limit or exclude liability has or has not in fact obtained insurance): see *Chitty*, para.14–087, n.432 for the relevant authorities.

maximum insurance cover available for a particular profession may be such as to require an increase in fees which clients would not willingly accept. It may be, therefore, that if a professional firm takes out the maximum insurance cover which is available (or which is reasonable in the circumstances), and then seeks to restrict its liability to that sum, such restriction would satisfy the requirement of reasonableness.[42]

5–016   A further consideration is the nature of the client. Limitation (or even exclusion) clauses in contracts between commercial organisations and their professional advisers are more likely to be upheld than in retainers entered between private individuals and professional firms.[43] In this context, what matters is not whether the client was "dealing as a consumer",[44] but whether the contract of retainer was between two commercial persons, or between a professional person or firm and a private individual.

5–017   Section 3 of the Act applies to contracts in which one party deals as a consumer[45] or on the other party's written standard terms of business. Any term which excludes or restricts any liability for breach of contract or which purports to entitle the party relying on the terms to render a contractual performance substantially different from that which was reasonably expected or to fail to render all or part of his contractual obligations is subject to the test of reasonableness. In the context of claims against professionals and the general application of s.2 of the Act, this is of practical relevance only to clauses which attempt to exclude, restrict or avoid liability for contractual obligations other than the implied obligation to exercise reasonable skill and care or which purported to permit the professional to provide some modified or alternative method of performance of his agreed duties.

5–018   **Unfair Terms in Consumer Contracts Regulations 1999.** In 1993, the EC Directive on Unfair Terms in Consumer Contracts was adopted[46] under Art.100a of the EC Treaty. This has now been implemented in England and Wales by the

---

[42] See *Smith v Eric S Bush* [1990] 1 A.C. 831 at 859, *per* Lord Griffiths. See also paras 5.18–5.19 of "Feasibility investigation of joint and several liability" by the Common Law Team of the Law Commission (HMSO, 1996).

[43] See *Photo Productions Ltd v Securicor Transport Ltd* [1980] A.C. 827, at 843D–E, *per* Lord Wilberforce; *Monarch Airlines Ltd v London Luton Airport Ltd* [1998] 1 Lloyd's Rep. 403 (Clarke J.); and *Watford Electronics Ltd v Sanderson CFL Ltd* [2001] EWCA Civ 317; [2001] 1 All E.R. (Com) 696. In *Watford Electronics* Chadwick L.J. (with whom Buckley J. agreed) said at [55]:

"Where experienced businessmen representing substantial companies of equal bargaining power negotiate an agreement, they may be taken to have had regard to the matters known to them. They should, in my view be taken to be the best judge of the commercial fairness of the agreement which they have made; including the fairness of each of the terms in that agreement. They should be taken to be the best judge on the question whether the terms of the agreement are reasonable. The court should not assume that either is likely to commit his company to an agreement which he thinks is unfair, or which he thinks includes unreasonable terms., Unless satisfied that one party has, in effect, taken unfair advantage of the other—or that a term is so unreasonable that it cannot properly have been understood or considered—the court should not interfere."

See also the judgment of Peter Gibson L.J. in the same case at [63].

[44] A necessary precondition to the application of s.3 of the Unfair Contract Terms Act 1977, which applies to liability in contract where either one party deals "as a consumer" or on the other party's written standard terms of business. As to the former see *R&B Customs Brokers Co Ltd v United Dominions Trust* [1988] 1 W.L.R. 321, CA and *Chitty*, para.14–066.

[45] See fn.44 to para.5–016 above.

[46] Directive 93/13. Discussed in *Chitty*, paras 15–004 to 15–007.

Unfair Terms in Consumer Contracts Regulations 1999.[47] The regulations apply to any contract between a seller or supplier and a consumer. A professional person or firm is, of course, a "supplier" of professional services. A "consumer" is "any natural person . . . acting for purposes which are outside his trade, business or profession".[48] The regulations require any written term in a contract to be in "plain, intelligible language"[49] and that any term which has not been individually negotiated to be "fair".[50] The regulations apply to all terms of the contract which have not been individually negotiated, and any terms which were negotiated if an overall assessment indicates that they are in fact a pre-formulated standard contract. The operative provision is in reg.8, which provides that any "unfair term" in a contract with a consumer shall not be binding on the consumer. The definition of "unfair term" is in reg.5(1), namely:

> "A contractual term which has not been individually negotiated shall be regarded as unfair, if, contrary to the requirement of good faith, it causes a significant imbalance in the parties' rights and obligations under the contract, to the detriment of the consumer."[51]

The 1999 Regulations apply to all kinds of contract terms, and are not limited to exemption clauses. Attempts have been made to use the 1999 Regulations to impugn the validity of dispute resolution clauses in contracts such as those requiring disputes to be referred to arbitration or adjudication (or permitting one party unilaterally to refer a dispute to adjudication). In one case, a clause which would have required the claimant to bring one claim against a building contractor in court and another by way of arbitration, the clause was held to be unfair.[52] In relation to adjudication under the Housing Grants, Construction and Regeneration Act 1996,[53] such attempts to date have been unsuccessful, but this is not to say that the 1999 Regulations could not be used successfully to impugn the validity of contractual clauses other than exemption clauses in the future.[54] It should be noted that any term of a contract (and not the contract overall) needs to have been "individually negotiated" if it is not to be subject to the test of fairness.[55] A term will not be "individually negotiated" if it was drafted in advance and the consumer was not able to influence its substance.[56]

5–019

---

[47] Replacing the Unfair Terms in Consumer Contracts Regulations 1994, which continue to apply to contracts made between July 1, 1995 and the coming into force of the 1999 Regulations on October 1, 1999.

[48] reg.3(1). This is not the same as "dealing as a consumer" for the purposes of the Unfair Contract Terms Act 1977 (as to which see n.44 to para.5–016 above): see *Chitty*, paras 15–023 and 15–0024.

[49] reg.7.

[50] reg.5.

[51] See further reg.6(1) which amplifies this provision.

[52] *Zealander v Laing Homes Ltd* [2000] T.C.L.R. 724 (H.H. Judge Havery Q.C.), a decision under the Unfair Terms in Consumer Contracts Regulations 1994: see Ch.9, para.9–025 below.

[53] As to which, see Ch.9, paras 9–024 to 9–025, below.

[54] *Picardi v Cuniberti* [2002] EWHC 2923, TCC; [2003] B.L.R. 487; *Westminster Building Co Ltd v Beckingham* [2004] EWHC 138, TCC; (2004) 94 Con. L.R. 107.

[55] This is emphasised by reg.5(3). It is for the person who claims that a term was individually negotiated to prove that it was: reg.5(4).

[56] reg.5(2).

5–020   The test of fairness has been held to be a composite test covering both the making and the substance of the contract.[57] A term is unfair if it causes a significant imbalance in the rights of the parties which is contrary to the requirements of good faith. A "significant imbalance" will occur when the term tilts the parties' contractual rights and obligations in favour of the supplier. The requirements of "good faith" have not, prior to the Regulations, been recognised in the law of contract save for in particular circumstances (such as contracts of insurance). The House of Lords has held that in the context of the Regulations the concept of "good faith" was not an artificial or technical concept but connoted fair and open dealing.[58] In assessing the fairness of the term it would appear that an objective test is to be applied by considering the position of typical parties when the contract in question is made.[59] In practice, it seems unlikely that any clause limiting the liability of a professional, which satisfies the requirement of reasonableness under the Unfair Contract Terms Act 1977, would be held to be "unfair" under the 1994 Regulations.[60]

(c) *Exclusion of Liability to Third Parties*

5–021   The exclusion of liability to third parties presents special problems. In the ordinary way, by reason of the doctrine of privity of contract, an exemption clause contained in the professional person's contract of engagement will not be binding upon third parties.[61] Thus an architect cannot avoid liability to future purchasers of a building which he designs, by reference to an exemption clause contained in his original contract of engagement.[62] However, the professional person may in some cases be able to avoid undertaking any duty to third parties in the first place, by means of a suitably worded disclaimer.[63] Thus in *Hedley Byrne & Co Ltd v Heller & Partners Ltd*,[64] it was held that, since the defendant bankers stipulated that their references were given "without responsibility", they did not undertake any duty to the claimants. "A man cannot be said voluntarily to be undertaking a responsibility if at the very moment when he is said to be accepting it he declares that in fact he is not" (*per* Lord Devlin).[65] This aspect of *Hedley Byrne* (which was in fact the ratio of the decision) has been less fully explored than the general part of the speeches concerning duty of care. However,

---

[57] *Director General of Fair Trading v First National Bank Plc* [2001] UKHL 52; [2002] 1 A.C. 481, at [17], *per* Lord Bingham.
[58] *ibid.*
[59] *ibid* at [20].
[60] See *Chitty*, para.15–068.
[61] *Haseldine v Daw & Son* [1941] 2 K.B. 343 illustrates the general principle. The position would be otherwise if the client contracted as agent for the third party: *New Zealand Shipping Co Ltd v AM Satterthwaite & Co Ltd* [1975] A.C. 154.
[62] However, the terms of the contract of engagement may still be relevant in determining whether the third parties have a claim in negligence: see Ch.9.
[63] *Henderson v Merrett Syndicates Ltd* [1995] 2 A.C. 145, at 181E, *per* Lord Goff. The question whether the Unfair Contract Terms Act 1977 applies to such a disclaimer is discussed by K. M. Stanton, "Disclaiming Tort Liability: The Unfair Contract Terms Act 1977" in (1985) 1 P.N. 132.
[64] [1964] A.C. 465, discussed in Ch.2, paras 2–024 to 2–025, above.
[65] *ibid.* at 533. See also at 493, *per* Lord Reid, at 504, *per* Lord Morris, at 511, *per* Lord Hodson and at 540, *per* Lord Pearce. On "assumption of responsibility" see Ch.2, para.2–080, above.

the principle was applied in *McCullagh v Lane Fox & Partners*.[66] In that case the purchaser of a house claimed damages against the vendor's agents for negligently mis-stating the size of the garden. The Court of Appeal held that the disclaimer in the agents' particulars (which satisfied the requirement of reasonableness under the Unfair Contract Terms Act 1977) negatived any assumption of responsibility by the agents to the purchaser.[67] Thus the first question to consider in every case is whether the defendant has incurred a duty of care to the third party,[68] and in relation to that the existence of a disclaimer or attempted disclaimer is relevant but not decisive.[69, 70]

Contracts (Rights of Third Parties) Act 1999. Under the Contracts (Rights 5–022 of Third Parties) Act 1999 a person who is not a party to a contract may acquire rights under that contract if, and to the extent that, the parties to that contract intend that he should do so. He can do so if either (i) the contract expressly provides that he can or (ii) if a term of the contract confers a benefit on him, unless it appears that the party to the contract other than the party against whom the term is to be enforced did not intend term to be enforceable by the third party.[71] Where the third party is entitled to enforce contractual rights under the Act, then the party against whom is seeking to enforce those rights will be able to rely on any relevant exemption clause in the contract which he would be entitled to rely on had the claim been brought by his contractual counter-party rather than the third party.[72] It has been suggested that even where the exemption clause is invalid between the contracting parties (because, for example, it fails to satisfy the test of reasonableness under the Unfair Contract Terms Act 1977) it may nevertheless apply to a claim brought by the third party under the Act.[73]

Exclusion clauses in mortgage applications. The effect of disclaimers on 5–023 third party liability has been considered extensively in the context of mortgage applications. This topic is dealt with in Ch.10, below.[74] The principal authority is the decision of the House of Lords in *Smith v Eric S Bush* and *Harris v Wyre Forest DC*.[75] It is clear from the facts of *Smith* and *Harris* that there were strong

---

[66] [1996] 1 E.G.L.R. 35.
[67] The same principle was applied in *Omega Trust Co Ltd v Wright Son & Pepper* [1997] 1 E.G.L.R. 120. The defendant surveyors prepared a report for lender clients which contained the following disclaimer:
    "This report shall be for private and confidential use of the clients for whom the report is undertaken and should not be reproduced in whole or in part or relied upon by third parties for any use whatsoever without the express written authority of the surveyors."
    The Court of Appeal held that this disclaimer satisfied the test of reasonableness under the Unfair Contract Terms Act 1977; and that it prevented any duty of care arising to lenders who were not the clients, but who relied upon the report.
[68] As to which see Ch.2, paras 2–112 to 2–118, above.
[69] See *Smith v Eric S Bush* [1990] 1 A.C. 831.
[70] The equivalent passage in the fourth edition of this work was approved by Lord Eassie in *The Governor and Company of the Bank of Scotland v Fuller Peiser* [2002] P.N.L.R. 13.
[71] Contracts (Rights of Third Parties) Act 1999, s.1.
[72] s.3(2).
[73] See *Chitty* at para.14–041.
[74] See further Ch.10, paras 10–064 to 10–070, below.
[75] [1990] 1 A.C. 831.

grounds in both cases for holding that the disclaimers were not fair and reasonable. The House of Lords' decision was closely tied to the facts of those cases, and may have been otherwise if the property were an expensive one, where the purchaser might be expected to commission his own survey report.[76]

5–024   **General comment.** There are powerful policy arguments for restricting professional liability within sensible bounds, as was shown by the Likierman Report.[77] It is submitted that in situations where the third party has not paid for the services, it may well be reasonable for a professional person to exclude liability altogether (especially in a commercial context, which the *Smith* and *Harris* cases were not).[78] Furthermore in any case where third party liability is likely to be substantial, it ought to be "fair and reasonable" to limit such liability to the amount of insurance cover sensibly available.

2. Limitation in Contract and Tort

(a) *The Limitation Period*

5–025   Under the Limitation Act 1980 claims founded on tort[79] or simple contract[80] are barred after the expiration of six years from the date on which the cause of action accrues. In the case of persons under a disability (defined as infants or persons of unsound mind)[81] "the action may be brought at any time before the expiration of six years from the date when he ceased to be under a disability or died (whichever first occurred)".[82] The limitation period is also extended in cases of fraud, concealment or mistake.[83]

5–026   **Latent damage.** In cases of latent damage other than personal injuries, an alternative limitation period for claims in negligence is available to the claimant, namely three years from the "starting date" as defined in s.14A of the Limitation Act 1980.[84]

---

[76] [1990] 1 A.C. 831 at 859G–H, *per* Lord Griffiths. A disclaimer of liability by a valuer was held to be reasonable in a commercial context in *The Governor and Company of the Bank of Scotland v Fuller Peiser* [2002] P.N.L.R. 13.

[77] See para.5–002, above.

[78] However, in *McCullagh v Lane Fox and Partners* [1996] 1 E.G.L.R. 35 at 46 it was held reasonable to exclude liability to third parties for misstatement in the context of a house sale.

[79] Limitation Act 1980, s.2. For a general discussion of limitation of actions in tort, see A. McGee, *Limitation Periods* (3rd edn, Sweet & Maxwell, 1998) and *Clerk & Lindsell*, Ch.33. For an overview of limitation of actions in general and proposals for reform, see the Law Commission Report on Limitation of Actions (Law Com. 270; 2001). This book is concerned only with limitation in the context of professional liability.

[80] *ibid.* s.5. For a general discussion of limitation of actions in contract, see A. McGee, *Limitation Periods, op. cit.*, *Chitty*, Ch.29 and the Law Commission Report on Limitation of Action (Law Com. 270; 2001). Claims based on a specialty (i.e. a contract under seal) have a limitation period of 12 years: Limitation Act 1980, s.8.

[81] *ibid.* s.38(2). An "infant" is a person under 18: see Family Law Reform Act 1969, s.1. For the definition of "unsound mind", see Limitation Act 1980, s.38(2) and (3).

[82] *ibid.* s.28(1).

[83] See paras 5–099 to 5–104, below.

[84] See paras 5–075 to 5–084, below.

Personal injuries and death. Claims in respect of personal injuries or death 5–027
are subject to a time limit of three years and are governed by special rules.[85]
These special rules determine the date upon which time begins to run[86] and
confer a discretion on the court to disapply the time limit.[87]

Characterising the claim. It is clearly important at the outset to determine 5–028
whether the damages claimed are "in respect of personal injuries",[88] in order to
establish what the limitation period is and whether there is discretion to extend
it. Obviously most, but not all, claims against medical practitioners fall into this
category. In *Walkin v South Manchester HA*,[89] the Court of Appeal held that a
mother's claim for a failed sterilisation operation was a claim for damages "in
respect of personal injuries". Although the losses for which she claimed were
economic, the unwanted pregnancy was an "impairment" and thus fell within the
definition of "personal injuries" in s.38(1) of the Limitation Act 1980. The court
left open whether a claim by a man for a failed vasectomy, leading to the
unwanted pregnancy of his partner, would also be classified as a claim for
personal injuries.[90] Somewhat different considerations may arise if a medical
practitioner fails to diagnose an incurable defect in an unborn child, so that the
child is born rather than aborted.[91] In this scenario (unlike the failed sterilisation
cases) the pregnancy is a desired state of affairs at the time and the claim should
only be for the costs of rearing a disabled child.[92] It may be appropriate to
distinguish *Walkin* on this basis. In the same way, if a medical practitioner
negligently fails to diagnose the true extent of the condition of a claimant who is
pursuing a claim for personal injuries, a claim for damages against him will not
be for personal injuries, but for financial loss.[93] Turning to other professions,
sometimes claims are made against architects and engineers in respect of personal injury (for example following the Abbeystead disaster).[94] But where a
solicitor errs in the prosecution of litigation, with the result that his client fails to
recover damages for personal injuries, it is submitted that the client's claim
against the solicitor should not be characterised as one "in respect of personal
injuries". His claim is one for pure financial loss, namely the value of the chose
in action which he has lost. Thus s.11 of the Limitation Act 1980 would not apply

---

[85] Limitation Act 1980, ss.11–14 and 33. Section 11 of the Limitation Act 1980 does not apply to
actions for trespass to the person, even where the consequence is personal injury. Accordingly, the
limitation period for such claims is six years, and the court has no discretion to extend that period:
Stubbings v Webb [1993] A.C. 498.

[86] See paras 5–085 to 5–092, below.

[87] See paras 5–093 to 5–098, below.

[88] Limitation Act 1980, s.11(1).

[89] [1995] 1 W.L.R. 1543. Followed by Leveson J. in *Godfrey v Gloucestershire Royal Infirmary NHS
Trust* [2003] Lloyd's Rep. Med. 398.

[90] As to which see *McFarlane v Tayside Health Board* [2000] 2 A.C. 59 and *Parkinson v St James
and Seacroft University Hospital NHS Trust* [2001] EWCA Civ 530; [2002] Q.B. 266, particularly at
[56]–[73], *per* Hale L.J.

[91] As to which see Ch.13, paras 13–144 and 13–161, below.

[92] See also *Arndt v Smith* (1996) 7 Med. L.R. 108: the British Columbia Supreme Court held that
claims by the parents of a disabled child (who would have been aborted in the event of competent
ante-natal advice) were claims for economic loss and thus subject to a six-year limitation period.

[93] See *Oakes v Hopcroft* [2000] Lloyd's Rep. P.N. 946, CA, where this was common ground.

[94] *Eckersley v Binnie & Partners* (1988) 18 Con.L.R. 1.

to such a professional negligence action and the limitation period would be six years.[95] In *Bennett v Greenland Houchen & Co*[96] the claimant sued his former solicitors for allegedly mishandling earlier litigation, with the result that he became clinically depressed. The Court of Appeal held that this was an action in respect of personal injuries:

> "In asking, 'what is this case all about?' the obvious conclusion here must be that it does include a claim for personal injury. Consequently the action should have been brought within the three year period."[97]

So a claim for failure to diagnose dyslexia is a claim for personal injuries.[98]

(b) *Date when Cause of Action in Contract Accrues*

5–029   In claims for breach of contract the cause of action accrues when the breach occurs, whether or not damage is suffered at that time.[99] Thus where the professional person does something contrary to the express or implied terms of his retainer, time begins to run (at least for the contractual claim) on the date of that act. Where the professional person omits to do something which is required by his retainer, it is less easy to identify when his breach of contract occurred.[1] In *Midland Bank Trust Co Ltd v Hett, Stubbs & Kemp*,[2] Oliver J. held that the solicitors' obligation to register the option continued until the date when effective registration became impossible, and that an action for breach of contract against the solicitors could be begun up to six years from the date when the obligation lapsed.[3] The question of a solicitor's continuing duty was considered by the

---

[95] This view is supported by *Ackbar v CF Green & Co Ltd* [1975] Q.B. 582, a claim against insurance brokers for failing to obtain passenger liability insurance as instructed. The claimant was subsequently injured when travelling as a passenger in his lorry. Croom-Johnson J. held that the proviso to s.2(1) of the Limitation Act 1939 (as amended) did not apply and that the limitation period was six years. He observed that the same principles would apply to claims against solicitors for failing to issue proceedings in time or for allowing proceedings to be dismissed for want of prosecution: *ibid.* at 586C. See also Ch.4, para.4–008 above. But *cf. Paterson v Chadwick* [1974] 1 W.L.R. 890: the words "a claim in respect of personal injuries" are construed differently in s.32(1) of the Administration of Justice Act 1970 (discovery against third parties).

[96] [1998] P.N.L.R. 458.

[97] *ibid.* at 465, *per* Otton L.J. It is possible that the claim for personal injuries was too remote to sound in damages.

[98] *Adams v Bracknell Forest BC* [2004] UKHL 29; [2005] 1 A.C. 76.

[99] Thus claims against solicitors were held to be statute-barred in *Short v McCarthy* (1820) 3 B. & Ald. 626; *Brown v Howard* (1820) 2 Brod. & B. 73; *Howell v Young* (1826) 5 B. & C. 259. In *Bagot v Stevens Scanlan & Co Ltd* [1966] 1 Q.B. 197 a claim against architects was held to be statute-barred. In so far as these cases decided that there is no concurrent liability in tort, they are no longer good law: see Ch.2, paras 2–103 to 2–111, above.

[1] This issue is discussed by Evans, "Negligent Omissions by Solicitors and Limitation" in (1991) 7 P.N. 50.

[2] [1979] Ch. 384. For the facts see Ch.11, para.11–007, below.

[3] *Bean v Wade* (1885) 2 T.L.R. 157, which appears to be to the contrary effect, was distinguished with some difficulty. For a detailed analysis of this decision, see *Midland Bank v Hett, Stubbs & Kemp* [1979] 1 Ch. 384 at 435–438.

Court of Appeal in *Bell v Peter Browne & Co.*[4] In that case the claimant transferred his former matrimonial home to his wife in 1978, on the understanding that whenever it was sold he would receive one-sixth of the proceeds. The solicitors who were acting for him failed to protect his interest by a declaration of trust or mortgage or by entering a caution on the land register. In 1986, the former wife sold the matrimonial home and spent the proceeds. The claimant started proceedings against the solicitors in 1987. The Court of Appeal held that the contractual claim accrued in 1978 and was therefore statute-barred. The fact that the solicitors could have remedied their breach at any time before the wife sold the house did not mean that there was a continuing breach of contract right up to 1986.[5] The Court of Appeal ostensibly distinguished *Midland Bank Trust Co Ltd v Hett, Stubbs & Kemp*,[6] but the distinctions drawn were so fine that the authority of *Midland Bank* on this particular issue has been substantially weakened.[7]

An architect, who is engaged to design and supervise the construction of a   **5–030**
building, is sometimes said to be under a continuing duty to keep his design under review during the construction period.[8] Such a duty generally would continue until practical completion. Indeed, in *University of Glasgow v William Whitfield*,[9] Judge Bowsher Q.C. (rejecting the architects' limitation defence) held that the duty continued beyond practical completion.[10] An engineer has been held to be under a similar continuing duty.[11] These decisions antedate the introduction of s.14A of the Limitation Act.[12] More recently, the nature of any continuing duty was considered by Dyson J. in *New Islington and Hackney Housing Association Ltd v Pollard Thomas & Edwards Ltd*.[13] He suggested that an architect would not be under a duty to review the design of foundations unless there was some particular reason for him to do so. He rejected the suggestion that absent some such reason any breach of duty in relation to design was a continuing breach. This decision accords with common sense and is to be welcomed.[14]

---

[4] [1990] 2 Q.B. 495.

[5] See, *per* Nicholls L.J. at 500–501 and, *per* Beldam L.J. at 509.

[6] [1979] Ch. 384.

[7] In *Morfoot v W F Smith & Co* [2001] Lloyd's Rep. P.N. 658, H.H. Judge Havelock-Allan Q.C., sitting as an additional judge of the High Court, applied the reasoning of the Court of Appeal in *Bell v Peter Browne & Co* [1990] 2 Q.B. 495 when considering whether a failure to obtain a deed of release was a continuing breach of contract. He held that it was not.

[8] *Brickfield Properties Ltd v Newton* [1971] 1 W.L.R. 862 at 873F, *per* Sachs L.J.; *Equitable Debenture Assets Corp Ltd v William Moss Group Ltd* (1984) 2 Con.L.R. 1 at 24, *per* Judge Newey Q.C.

[9] (1988) 42 B.L.R. 66. Distinguished in *Chesham Properties Ltd v Bucknall Austin Project Management Services Ltd* (1996) 82 B.L.R. 92 (H.H. Judge Hicks Q.C.).

[10] *ibid.* at 78. In *New Islington and Hackney Housing Association Ltd v Pollard Thomas & Edwards Ltd* [2001] P.N.L.R. 515, Dyson J. suggested at 522 that this decision was "heavily coloured by the special facts of the case" and that Judge Bowsher Q.C. was not "stating a general principle". See also the obiter discussion about duties continuing after practical completion in the dissenting judgment of Bingham L.J. in *Eckersley v Binnie & Partners* (1988) 18 Con.L.R. 1 at 146–147.

[11] *Chelmsford DC v TJ Evers* (1983) 25 Build.L.R. 99 at 106, *per* Judge Smout Q.C.

[12] See paras 5–075 to 5–084, below.

[13] [2001] P.N.L.R. 515.

[14] This decision was followed by H.H. Judge LLoyd Q.C. in *Payne v Satchell* [2002] P.N.L.R. 7 and by H.H. Judge Seymour Q.C. in *Tesco Stores Ltd v Costain Construction Ltd* [2003] EWHC 1487, TCC.

(c) *Date when Cause of Action in Tort Accrues*

5-031   In claims based on the tort of negligence the cause of action accrues when the claimant suffers actionable damage.[15] This may be when the breach of duty occurs or it may be at some later date (for example, when the client acts in reliance on negligent advice). Where the claimant is unaware that he has suffered damage until many years after the event, the basic limitation period would effectively prevent him from obtaining any remedy. Parliament has intervened on a number of occasions to relieve the injustice which this causes. The Limitation Acts 1963 and 1975 introduced special provisions for the protection of claimants in personal injury actions.[16] The Latent Damage Act 1986 provided an alternative limitation period in cases of latent damage not involving personal injuries.[17] But none of this legislation has dispensed with the need to consider when, on basic common law principles, the cause of action in negligence accrued. For example, in a case of latent damage a claimant who does not begin proceedings within three years of the "starting date" is still entitled to do so within six years of the accrual of his cause of action.[18]

5-032   **Two key questions.** It is submitted that in every case the correct approach is to answer the following questions:

(1) For what kind of damage is the defendant liable?

(2) At what time did the claimant first suffer non-negligible damage of that kind?

In answering these questions (at least in jurisdictions which have s.14A of the Limitation Act 1980 or an equivalent provision) no regard should be had as to the fact that the answer to these questions may mean that the primary period of limitation expired before the claimant knew or could reasonably have been expected to know sufficient facts to bring a claim.[19] Nor should the answer to either question be determined by how the claimant has sought to portray or characterise the loss.[20]

5-033   **The first question.** The answer to the first question is clear in relation to most professions: the duty of care owed in tort clearly extends to a duty to take

---

[15] The damage must be "beyond what can be regarded as negligible": *Cartledge v E Jopling & Sons Ltd* [1963] A.C. 758 at 772, *per* Lord Reid. It must be "real damage as distinct from purely minimal damage" (*per* Lord Evershed at 774). See further, *Bank of East Asia v Tsien Wui Marble Factory Ltd* [2000] H.K.L.R.D. 268, below. If the claimant suffers damage which is irrecoverable in law, that does not start the limitation period running: *Nitrigin Eireann Teoranta v Inco Alloys Ltd* [1992] 1 W.L.R. 498, (May J.).

[16] These are now consolidated in the Limitation Act 1980 and are dealt with in paras 5–085 to 5–092, below.

[17] Dealt with in paras 5–075 to 5–084, below.

[18] Limitation Act 1980, s.14(4)(a).

[19] By enacting ss.14A and 14B of the Limitation Act 1980 "Parliament thus re-affirmed that a cause of action for damages for negligence may accrue, without its beneficiary knowing or having reason to know of it.": *Law Society v Sephton* [2006] UKHL 22; [2002] 2 W.L.R. 1091, *per* Lord Mance, with whom Lords Scott, Rodger and Walker agreed, at [56].

[20] *Law Society v Sephton* [2006] UKHL 22; [2002] 2 W.L.R. 1091.

reasonable care to avoid causing economic loss. Claims for personal injury or damage to goods or property may arise, but the vast bulk of claims are for economic loss. In this regard the position of medical practitioners is, in effect, the mirror image of that of other professions in that liability for negligence is mainly, if not exclusively, for personal injury. So, in the following paragraphs, the authorities in respect of each profession are set out so as to show when, in fact, it has been held that non-negligible damage has been suffered. However, it should be borne in mind that the principles being applied to different professions and to different factual situations are, or should be, the same.

The liability of construction professionals is or has been, bedevilled by debate **5–034** as to whether damage to a building is physical damage or economic loss. In cases concerning the limitation period in tort against construction professionals this issue has not always been addressed or assumptions have been made as to the nature of the loss for which construction professional defendant is liable. The position has been complicated by different views as to the nature of damage in different jurisdictions. Given that the better view is that construction profession-als are liable in tort for economic loss (at least to their clients),[21] the question of when causes of action accrue against them in negligence should be answered in the same way as it is in relation to claims against other members of other professions. However, as is explained below, the authorities do not disclose a clear or consistent approach.[22]

The second question. While in many cases it will be clear on the facts when **5–035** actionable damage is first suffered, difficult issues can arise in practice. A covenient starting point remains the submission of counsel recorded and accepted by Stephenson L.J. in *Forster v Outred & Co*[23] and approved by Lord Nicholls, with whom the other members of the House of Lords agreed, in *Nykredit Mortgage Bank Plc v Edward Erdman Group Ltd (No.2)*[24]

"What is meant by actual damage? Mr. Stuart-Smith says that it is any detriment, liability or loss capable of assessment in money terms and it includes liabilities which may arise on a contingency, particularly a contingency over which the plaintiff has no control; things like loss of earning capacity, loss of a chance or bargain, loss of profit, losses incurred from onerous provisions or covenants in leases. They are all illustrations of a kind of loss which is meant by 'actual' damage. It was also suggested in argument ... that 'actual' is really used in contrast to 'presumed' or 'assumed'. Whereas damage is presumed in trespass and libel, it is not presumed in negligence and has to be proved. There has to be some actual damage."

However, there is an ambiguity in that submission, namely the reference to **5–036** "liabilities which may arise on a contingency". The courts have had to grapple with a number of cases, mainly concerning solicitors, where the immediate or

---

[21] Ch.9, para.9–058.
[22] See paras 5–056 to 5–074, below.
[23] [1982] 1 W.L.R. 86, at 94 and 98.
[24] [1997] 1 W.L.R. 1627, at 1630B–G.

short term consequence of negligence by a professional is to expose the claimant to a risk of some future loss.[25] The issue which then arises is whether the mere fact that the claimant is subject to that risk itself constitutes loss. The authorities now show that the key distinction is between cases where there is an immediate loss of value of some asset or interest in an asset as a result of the acceptance of the contingent liability (for example, if it is charged to secure that liability) and cases in which the claimant has merely become subject to a contingency which may or may not lead to loss in the future. In the former cases, actionable damage is suffered when the contingent liability is accepted.[26] In the latter cases, time does not run until the risk or contingency materialises causing actual loss.[27] This is a very fine distinction.

(i) *Claims against Solicitors*[28]

5–037   **Where client incurs an obligation.** In the leading case of *Forster v Outred & Co*[29] the claimant signed a mortgage deed charging her property to H, as security for a loan by H to her son. She claimed that she had done so as the result of the defendant solicitors' negligence. The Court of Appeal held, on an interlocutory appeal, that the claimant's loss accrued when she signed the mortgage deed and not at a later date when the demand for payment was made under the deed. Accordingly the claimant's claim[30] was statute-barred. Stephenson L.J., who gave the leading judgment, said:

> " . . . the plaintiff has suffered actual damage through the negligence of her solicitors by entering into the mortgage deed, the effect of which has been to encumber her interest in her freehold estate with this legal charge and subject her to a liability which may, according to matters completely outside her control, mature into financial loss—as indeed it did. It seems to me that the plaintiff did suffer actual damage in those ways; and subject to that liability and with that encumbrance on the mortgage property was then entitled to claim damages."[31]

Dunn L.J. gave a short concurring judgment, in which he said:

> "I would hold that in cases of financial or economic loss the damage crystallises and the cause of action is complete at the date when the plaintiff, in reliance on negligent advice, acts to his detriment."[32]

---

[25] See paras 5–037 to 5–041, below.

[26] *Forster Outred & Co* [1982] 1 W.L.R. 86. See paras 5–037 to 5–040, below.

[27] *Law Society v Sephton* [2006] UKHL 22; [2002] 2 W.L.R. 1091. See para.5–050, below.

[28] See also Evans, *op. cit.*, Ch.10.

[29] [1982] 1 W.L.R. 86. Approved by the House of Lords in *Nykredit Mortgage Bank Plc v Edward Erdman Group Ltd (No.2)* [1997] 1 W.L.R. 1627.

[30] Under the second writ. The first action was struck out for want of prosecution.

[31] *ibid.* at 98D–E.

[32] *ibid.* at 99F. It is better to say "financial detriment": *Law Society v Sephton* [2006] UKHL 22; [2002] 2 W.L.R. 1091, at [43], *per* Lord Walker, with whom Lords Scott, Rodger and Mance agreed.

The same approach was adopted by the Court of Appeal in *Baker v Ollard &*   **5–038**
Bentley[33] and *Costa v Georghiou*[34] and by Nourse J. in *Melton v Walker &*
Stanger.[35] This line of authority was reviewed in some detail by the High Court
of Australia in *Wardley Australia Ltd v Western Australia.*[36] The claimant in that
case gave an indemnity in 1987 in reliance on representations made by the
defendants. In 1989, the claimant was called upon to make payment pursuant to
the indemnity. In 1991, the claimant sought to amend its statement of claim by
adding a statutory claim (for which there was a three year limitation period) to
the effect that it had been induced to give the indemnity by the defendant's
misleading representations. The High Court held that the claimant suffered loss
when it was called upon to pay, not when it entered into the indemnity agreement.
Therefore, the amendment was made within the limitation period and should not
be struck out. Four of the seven members of the court gave a single judgment to
the following effect: where P enters into a contract which exposes him to a
contingent liability, he does not suffer damage until the contingency is fulfilled.
The High Court of Australia held that if *Forster v Outred & Co*[37] and the other
English cases contradict this principle, then they ought not to be followed in
Australia. It is unreasonable to expect P to commence proceedings before the
contingency is fulfilled. Moreover, if damages are assessed on a contingency
basis, they might not be adequate.

In *Gilbert v Shanahan*[38] the New Zealand Court of Appeal has considered   **5–039**
Wardley and stated the provisional view that "the Australian approach is in
general terms preferable to the English". In that case the claimant claimed
damages for negligent lack of advice, as a result of which the claimant guaranteed the performance of certain obligations under a lease. The court held that,
since the guarantee imposed present liabilities rather than contingent liabilities,
the claimant's cause of action accrued when he signed the guarantee and accordingly his claim in negligence was statute barred.

Contingent liability or actual loss? Whether the English decisions were   **5–040**
inconsistent with the decisions in Australia and New Zealand depends upon
whether they went as far as holding that exposure to a contingent liability
constituted actionable damage. Any doubt on this point has now been resolved:
the wider interpretation of *Forster v Outred & Co*[39] is incorrect.[40] In *Forster v*
Outred & Co[41] the claimant had charged her property as security for her son's

---

[33] (1982) 126 S.J. 593: alleged cause of action accrued on date when property conveyed to claimant,
not at later date when problems arose.
[34] (1984) 1 P.N. 201: cause of action accrued when claimant entered into sub-underlease with
defective rent review clause, not 9 years later when the rent review clause was intended to operate.
[35] (1981) 125 S.J. 861: alleged cause of action accrued when claimant executed agreement drafted by
defendant solicitors, not at later date when High Court held that agreement did not have effect
intended by claimant.
[36] (1992) 109 A.L.R. 247.
[37] [1982] 1 W.L.R. 86.
[38] [1998] 3 N.Z.L.R. 528 at 542. New Zealand has no equivalent of s.14A of the Limitation Act
1980.
[39] [1982] 1 W.L.R. 86.
[40] *Law Society v Sephton* [2006] UKHL 22; [2002] 2 W.L.R. 1091, in particular at [16]–[18], *per* Lord
Hoffmann, with whom the other members of the House of Lords agreed.
[41] [1982] 1 W.L.R. 86.

debt. The value of her interest in the property was reduced at once. She could and did suffer loss before her son's creditor enforced the security. If, for example, at the trial of the claimant's claim against her solicitors the debt was £100,000 and the son was not in a position to repay it, the court would not have held that she had suffered no loss merely because the creditor had yet to enforce the security. No doubt in assessing damages the court would have to take due account of the possibility that the son's fortunes might improve so that he could repay his debt, but that would not preclude the award of any damages at all.

5-041   However, the decision of the House of Lords in *Law Society v Sephton*,[42] a claim against accountants, makes it clear that in English law exposure to a mere contingency of a future claim does not constitute actionable damage. Holding that mere exposure to a contingent loss did not constitute actionable damage, the House of Lords questioned the decision of the Court of Appeal in *Gordon v JB Wheatley & Co*.[43] In that case the defendant solicitors had negligently advised their client that a collective investment scheme did not need authorisation under the Financial Services Act 1986. Some time later the Securities and Investment Board ordered the client to indemnify his clients. The Court of Appeal held that loss was suffered when the client continued to take investments without authorisation, thereby incurring a contingent liability. That part of their reasoning was disapproved.[44] This provides a useful example, apart from *Law Society v Sephton* itself, of circumstances which do not constitute actionable damage.

5-042   **Where client acquires less valuable rights than intended.** If a solicitor's negligence diminishes the value of rights acquired by the client, actionable damage normally occurs at the time of acquisition of those rights rather than at the moment when they are exercised. This is illustrated by the decision of the Court of Appeal in *DW Moore & Co Ltd v Ferrier*.[45] In 1971, the claimant insurance brokers engaged solicitors to draft a contract between themselves and F, who was to become an employee/director. The contract contained a restrictive covenant. In 1975, the parties entered into a further agreement drafted by the solicitors, containing a restrictive covenant in similar terms. In 1980, F ceased to be employed by the claimants and started to compete with them. It emerged that the restrictive covenant did not provide the protection which had been expected. The claimants started proceedings in May 1985, but it was held on a preliminary issue that their claim was statute-barred. The Court of Appeal held that *Forster v Outred & Co*[46] was not inconsistent with *Pirelli* and was still good law. They further held that a valid restrictive covenant was a thing of value, so that the claimants must have suffered some loss (capable of quantification) both in 1971 and in 1975. Therefore the claimants' causes of action against the solicitors

---

[42] [2006] UKHL 22; [2006] 2 W.L.R. 1091. See further para.5–055, below.
[43] [2000] Lloyd's Rep. P.N. 605.
[44] *Law Society v Sephton* [2006] UKHL 22; [2002] 2 W.L.R. 1091, at [23]–[25], *per* Lord Hoffmann who was "inclined to think that [the case] was wrongly decided; at [50]–[51], *per* Lord Rodger who thought that the reasoning based upon contingent liablity "cannot be sustained", but that there was another way of explaining the decision which was "more sustainable"; and at [80]–[81], *per* Lord Mance who considered the reasoning "open to objection".
[45] [1988] 1 W.L.R. 267.
[46] [1982] 1 W.L.R. 267.

had accrued in 1971 and 1975. The same principle was applied by the Court of Appeal in *Lee v Thompson*,[47] *Sullivan v Layton Lougher & Co*[48] and *McCarroll v Statham Gill Davis*.[49]

However, it may be unclear whether the claimant has actually suffered loss by **5–043** reason of having entered a transaction. The answer may depend upon the difference, from time to time, between the value of the rights acquired and the burden assumed.[50] In such cases proof is needed that actual loss was suffered at a particular time. This is the explanation of the decision of the Court of Appeal in *UBAF Ltd v European American Banking Corp*.[51] The claimants claimed that in December 1974 they had agreed to participate in two loans to shipping companies in reliance on incorrect information supplied by the defendants, and that in March 1976 the shipping companies had defaulted. The writ was issued in December 1981. The Court of Appeal declined to strike out the action on the grounds that it was statute-barred. Ackner L.J., giving the judgment of the court, said:

"The defendants successfully contended before Leggatt J. that the accrual of the cause of action occurred when the plaintiffs parted with their money and acquired instead claims for repayment of money lent against borrowers, whose ability to repay was, contrary to the alleged representations, a matter of considerable doubt. Again, there is a short answer to this question—it depends upon the facts as found at the trial. The plaintiffs do not assert that they are entitled to damages to be measured by the difference in the value of the chose in action which they acquired by making this loan as compared with the value it would have had if the representations had been accurate, as in a claim for a breach of warranty. Their case is that, if they had known the respects in which the representations were inaccurate, they would not have entered into the contract. Accordingly, it is argued by the defendants that, at the very moment of entering into that contract, the plaintiffs must have suffered damage. In our judgment, this bare proposition is not self-evident. The plaintiffs are suing in tort—the tort of negligence. To establish a cause of action they must establish not only a breach of duty, but that that breach of duty occasioned them damage. This is axiomatic. It is possible, although it may be improbable, that, at the date when the plaintiffs advanced their money, the value of the chose in action which they then acquired was, in fact, not less than the sum which the plaintiffs lent, or indeed even exceeded it."[52]

---

[47] (1990) 6 P.N. 91: claim against solicitor for failing to obtain good title to house; cause of action accrued at time of purchase (1975) not when the problem came to light (1984).

[48] [1995] 2 E.G.L.R. 111: defendant solicitors acted for claimant in the purchase of a 63-year lease of premises; it was alleged that the solicitors failed to explain circumstances which would make subsequent enfranchisement more expensive; held that the claimant suffered "damage" on the date of purchase (because the leasehold interest was less valuable than he was entitled to expect) and not when he became entitled to leasehold enfranchisement; claim statute barred.

[49] [2003] EWCA Civ 425; [2003] P.N.L.R. 509: claimant suffered actionable damage when he signed an agreement which (on his case) contained less favourable terms than it should have done.

[50] The obvious example is a case in which money is advanced by way of loan on the basis of security which is less valuable than the lender realised. It may be that, even so, the loan is fully secured, at least initially, so that no immediate loss is suffered. See para.5–050, below.

[51] [1984] Q.B. 713. This was not a case involving solicitors: but the same principles were involved. The court distinguished *Forster Outred & Co* [1982] 1 W.L.R. 86.

[52] *ibid.* at 725. This reasoning is criticised by K. M. Stanton, "Reforming Limitations of Actions" in (1986) 2 P.N. 75.

This was, in effect, a striking out application, rather than a trial of the limitation issue. It may have limited impact on the solicitor cases.[53]

5–044 The line of cases following *Forster v Outred & Co* was reviewed by the House of Lords in *Nykredit Mortgage Bank Plc v Edward Erdman Group Ltd (No.2)*.[54] It follows from *Nykredit* that a cause of action by a mortgage lender against a solicitor will only accrue in tort when the value of the security (i.e. the mortgaged property and the borrower's covenant) is less than the amount owed.[55]

5–045 **Previous action dismissed for want of prosecution.** In *Hopkins v Mac-Kenzie*,[56] as a result, allegedly, of negligence by the defendant solicitor, the claimant's claim against a hospital for clinical negligence had been dismissed for want of prosecution. The Court of Appeal held that the cause of action in tort against the solicitor accrued when the original claim was actually dismissed, and not at any earlier date. This decision was open to considerable doubt.[57] It is now clear that it is of, at most, very limited application.

5–046 This is the result of the later decisions of the Court of Appeal in *Khan v RM Falvey*[58] and *Hatton v Chafes (a firm)*.[59] The first decision, *Khan*, was another case against a solicitor following the striking out of earlier litigation for want of prosecution. The losses suffered included sums paid to the defendant more than six years before the action commenced, so the claims were statute barred in any event. However, the Court of Appeal took the opportunity to reconsider the decision in *Hopkins v MacKenzie* in the light of the decision of the House of Lords in *Nykredit Mortgage Bank Plc v Edward Erdman Group Ltd (No.2)*.[60] They held that where it was inevitable or there was a serious risk that an action would be struck out, actionable damage was suffered even if the action was not struck out until some time later. This decision is to be welcomed. It is wrong to consider when the claimant first suffered actionable damage solely by reference to the way that the claimant pleads his loss. *Hopkins v MacKenzie* was always hard to reconcile with other authorities and the effect of *Khan* is to bring limitation in this area back into line with other areas. This was confirmed by the decision in *Hatton* which followed *Khan* and held, on the facts, that the underlying action had been bound to be struck out more than six years before the proceedings against the solicitors were issued. The Court of Appeal left open the question whether it would have sufficed if it was either more probable than not that the earlier action would have been struck out or whether there was a real (as

---

[53] See Evans, *op. cit.*, pp.179–180. The decision appears to be consistent with *Nykredit Mortgage Bank Plc v Edward Erdman Group Ltd* [1997] 1 W.L.R. 1627, since it was possible that at trial the claimants would show that they were not under-secured until within six years of the issue of proceedings.

[54] [1997] 1 W.L.R. 1627. See para.5–050, below.

[55] *Lloyds Bank Plc v Burd Pearse* [2000] P.N.L.R. 71, *per* Evans-Lombe J. (failure to advise on restrictive covenants which reduced value of claimant bank's security. Held that it was for the defendant to prove that loss had been suffered more than six years before the issue of proceedings in accordance with *Nykredit Mortgage Bank Plc v Edward Erdman Group Ltd* and that the defendant had failed to do so).

[56] (1995) 6 Med.L.R. 26. Discussed in Evans, *op. cit.*, pp.186–188.

[57] See para.5–043 of the fifth edition of this work.

[58] [2002] EWCA Civ 400; [2002] P.N.L.R. 28.

[59] [2003] EWCA Civ 341; [2003] P.N.L.R. 24.

[60] [1997] 1 W.L.R. 1627 (see para.5–050).

opposed to a minimal or fanciful) risk that it would have been struck out more than six years before the issue of the later proceedings. The same result was reached on slightly different facts in *Polley v Warner Goodman & Street (a firm)*[61] and in *Cohen v Kingsley Napley (a firm)*.[62]

Where the client purchases a property. Usually, time will run from the date **5–047** of exchange of contracts in the same way that it does in cases involving surveyors.[63] However, solicitors may be in breach of duty in failing to advise that the property, although worth what the client is paying for it, is unsuitable for his intended purposes. In such a case, there are a number of ways in which loss could be said to have first been suffered. The first is the date of purchase: even if the property is worth what the claimant has paid for it, it is not suitable for his purpose and so he should not have bought it and incurred the costs of doing so. The second is when the claimant spends money on the property in order to carry out work which is rendered futile by its unsuitability. The third is when the unsuitability became manifest and caused disruption to the use of the property. All three were considered by the Court of Appeal in *Havenledge Ltd v Graeme John and Partners (a firm)*[64] and, rather unfortunately, each member of the court held that a different one was correct. The result was a majority view that the particular claim was statute-barred. It is submitted that it will rarely be the case that damage is not suffered when an unsuitable property is purchased.

Omissions capable of being remedied. The final problem to consider is **5–048** analogous to that referred to above.[65] When does the cause of action accrue in tort in respect of breaches which are capable of being remedied? So long as the matter can be put right, it may be thought that the client has suffered no loss. Indeed this was the view taken by Oliver J. in *Midland Bank Trust Co Ltd v Hett, Stubbs and Kemp*.[66] He held that the claimant did not suffer actual damage until August 1967, when the property was conveyed and the option was defeated. However, in *Bell v Peter Browne & Co*[67] the Court of Appeal held that the claimant suffered damage in 1978 and that his cause of action in tort accrued then.[68] In essence, if the claimant's legal or equitable rights were diminished in value, then he suffered damage, despite the fact that it would have been possible to restore their value in the unlikely event that anyone had turned his mind to the matter. Similar considerations apply in claims by disappointed beneficiaries under *White v Jones*.[69] On one view, loss is suffered when the will is not made (or not properly made) in their favour, so depriving them of a saleable expectancy. On the other, it is only on the death of the solicitor's client that the earlier failure becomes incapable of remedy. In *Bacon v Howard Kennedy (a firm)*,[70]

---

[61] [2003] EWCA Civ 1013; [2003] P.N.L.R. 40: order extending validity of writ bound to be set aside so that time did not start to run only when it was in fact set aside.
[62] [2005] EWHC 899, QBD; [2005] P.N.L.R. 37 (Tugenhadt J.).
[63] See para.5–049, below.
[64] [2001] P.N.L.R. 419, CA.
[65] See para.5–029, above.
[66] [1979] Ch. 384.
[67] [1990] 2 Q.B. 495. For the facts see para.5–029, above.
[68] See the reasoning of Nicholls L.J. at 502–503 and of Beldam L.J. at 509–510, *ibid.*
[69] [1995] 2 A.C. 207, discussed in Ch.11, paras 11–048 to 11–050.
[70] [1998] P.N.L.R. 1.

Judge Bromley Q.C., sitting as a judge of the High Court, held that the latter analysis was correct. In many such cases (but not in *Bacon*) the disappointed beneficiaries will be able to rely on s.14A of the Limitation Act 1980.[71]

(ii) *Claims against Surveyors*

5–049 **Claims by purchasers.** Where a person purchases property in reliance on a survey report which fails to disclose material defects, the courts have repeatedly held that the measure of damages is the difference between the price paid and the value of the property as it ought to have been described.[72] Quite consistently with this approach, Judge Hawser Q.C. held in *Secretary of State for the Environment v Essex Goodman & Suggitt*[73] that the cause of action accrued when the claimants acted in reliance upon the survey report (and became irrevocably committed to lease the property in question). In the case of a house purchaser, the cause of action would normally accrue when contracts are exchanged. This approach was adopted in *Horbury v Craig Hall & Rutley*.[74] In *Byrne v Hall Pain & Foster*,[75] the claimants exchanged contracts to purchase the lease of a flat on July 8, 1988. They completed the purchase on July 22, 1988. They issued their writ against the allegedly negligent surveyors on July 18, 1994. The Court of Appeal held that the cause of action accrued on exchange of contracts rather than completion, and accordingly that the claim was statute barred.

5–050 **Mortgagees.** Where a mortgagee lends money upon inadequate security as a consequence of a negligent valuation, he generally suffers loss when he makes or agrees to make the loan. The cause of action, therefore, should accrue on that date and not on the date when the borrower defaults. Different considerations arise, however, in marginal cases where the value of the mortgaged property, although lower than stated in the negligent valuation, equals or exceeds the sum lent. In that situation the Court of Appeal has held that the claimant does not suffer loss, and the cause of action in tort does not accrue, until such time as the indebtedness exceeds the value of the security.[76] The approach of the Court of Appeal in *First National Commercial Bank* was approved by the House of Lords in *Nykredit Mortgage Bank Plc v Edward Erdman Group Ltd (No.2)*[77] (which was the sequel to its decision in *Banque Bruxelles Lambert SA v Eagle Star Insurance Co Ltd*[78]). The House of Lords held that the lender's cause of action in tort against a negligent valuer accrues on the date when the value of the security plus the value of the borrower's covenant is less than the amount owed

---

[71] See paras 5–075 to 5–084, below.
[72] See Ch.10, paras 10–131 to 10–150, below.
[73] [1986] 1 W.L.R. 1432.
[74] [1991] C.I.L.L. 692: cause of action accrued when claimant exchanged contracts to purchase.
[75] [1999] 1 W.L.R. 1849, CA.
[76] *First National Commercial Bank Plc v Humberts* [1995] 2 All E.R. 673. It was, however, a material fact in this case that the commitment fee paid by the borrower covered the claimant's initial costs of making the advance: *ibid.* at 676–677.
[77] [1997] 1 W.L.R. 1627.
[78] [1997] A.C. 191.

by the borrower.[79] It is necessary to assess the balance between the detriment suffered and the benefit received to see when, on the facts, the claimant became financially worse off.[80] In *Kenny & Good Pty Ltd v MGICA (1992) Ltd*,[81] the High Court of Australia held that loss occurs when it is reasonably ascertainable that sale of the mortgaged property will result in a loss.

(iii) *Claims against Insurance Brokers*

Claims against insurance brokers in relation to the obtaining of insurance (or **5–051** failure to do so) fall into the category of claims in which the claimant acquires less valuable rights then he should have done and so suffers immediate loss.[82] Thus *Iron Trades Mutual Insurance Co Ltd v JK Buckenham Ltd*[83] involved a claim against brokers for obtaining reinsurance contracts which proved to be voidable. Kenneth Rokison Q.C. held that the cause of action in tort accrued when the reinsurance contracts were executed, not when the reinsurers sought to avoid them. In *Islander Trucking Ltd v Hogg Robinson & Gardner Mountain (Marine) Ltd*,[84] brokers arranged "goods in transit" insurance for the claimant in 1980. In 1985, the insurers avoided the policy for alleged non-disclosure and misrepresentation. Evans J. held that the cause of action in tort accrued when the insurance contract was made, not when the insurers avoided.

The Court of Appeal approved both *Iron Trades Mutual* and *Islander Trucking* **5–052** in *Knapp v Ecclesiastical Insurance Group Plc*.[85] The Court held that if an insurance broker negligently procured a voidable insurance policy, the cause of action against the broker accrued when the policy incepted, not on the date of avoidance by the insurers. Ten days later the House of Lords came to the same conclusion in *Nykredit Mortgage Bank Plc v Edward Erdman Group Ltd (No.2)*.[86] In *Compannia de Seguros Imperio v Heath (REBX) Ltd*,[87] Langley J. held that the cause of action against a broker for wrongly committing an insurer to fronting a risk under a binding authority arose when the insurer was committed the risk and so was exposed to a greater liability or potential liability.[88] The

---

[79] This decision was applied in *DNB Mortgages Ltd v Bullock & Lees (a firm)* [2000] P.N.L.R. 427, where the Court of Appeal grappled with the questions as to how the value of the mortgagor's covenant was to be valued and how to value the mortgaged property over a period of falling prices.

[80] See the analysis of the House of Lords of the lending cases in *Law Society v Sephton* [2006] UKHL 22; [2002] 2 W.L.R. 1091.

[81] [2000] Lloyd's Rep. P.N. 25 and (1999) 163 A.L.R. 611, *per* Gaudron J.; McHugh J. stated that this would be, at the earliest, when the mortgagor defaulted.

[82] For cases in this category concerning solicitors see para.5–042, above.

[83] [1990] 1 All E.R. 808. Discussed by K. M. Stanton, "Limitation of Actions: Latent Damage and the Insurance Broker" in (1989) 1 P.N. 158.

[84] [1990] 1 All E.R. 826.

[85] [1998] P.N.L.R. 172.

[86] [1997] 1 W.L.R. 1627 at 1634C.

[87] [1999] Lloyd's Rep. 571.

[88] However, insurers do not necessarily suffer loss when they insure a risk: their aim is to make a profit from the premiums received. The cases referred to in these two paragraphs were distinguished on the facts by Gloster J. in *Gaughan v Tony McDonagh & Co Ltd* [2005] EWHC 739, Comm; [2005] P.N.L.R. 689. In that case the alleged breach concerned not the initial obtaining of insurance (more than six years before the issue of proceedings) but the provision of allegedly false information by the brokers to the insurers some months later (less than six years before the issue of proceedings).

reasoning in these decisions was approved by the House of Lords in *Law Society v Sephton*.[89]

(iv) *Claims against Financial Advisers*

5–053 Consistently with the approach to claims against surveyors, solicitors and insurance brokers, a client of a financial adviser will suffer loss and damage when he makes an investment or otherwise acts to his detriment in reliance upon negligent advice.[90]

(v) *Claims against Accountants*

5–054 The principles to be found in the cases concerning solicitors, surveyors and financial advisers apply equally to claims against accountants. In particular, it is a decision in a claim against accountants that has established the important distinction between acceptance of a contingent liability by charging an asset or interest in an asset (so as to suffer immediate actionable damage) and mere exposure to a contingent claim (which is not actionable damage).[91]

5–055 **Law Society v Sephton.** This is the decision of the House of Lords in *Law Society v Sephton*.[92] The claim in that case was for alleged negligent certification by the defendant accountant of the books and accounts of a solicitor who was misappropriating his clients' money. The alleged negligence had occurred more than 10 years before the issue of proceedings and, indeed, some 10 years after the claimant, through its investigating accountant, had discovered the deficiency. The defendant argued that actionable damage had been suffered more than six years before the issue of the proceedings, as and when further misappropriations took place, so exposing the claimant to the contingent liability of claims by defrauded clients. In due course, but within six years of the issue of proceedings, those claims had been met. The total paid, including interest, was claimed as damages. The House of Lords rejected the limitation defence. Exposure to the contingency of future claims, which the claimant had a discretion whether to accept, was not itself actionable damage. Even if an accountant might have advised that some provision be made for such contingent liabilities, it did not follow that the Courts would consider that to be actionable damage.[93]

(vi) *Claims against Construction Professionals*

5–056 **Pirelli.** The leading case is *Pirelli General Cable Works Ltd v Oscar Faber & Partners*,[94] hereafter referred to as *Pirelli*. *Pirelli* was decided on December 9, 1982 and substantially changed what was previously thought to be the law.[95] All

---

[89] [2006] UKHL 22; [2006] 2 W.L.R. 1091.
[90] *Martin v Britannia Life Ltd* [2000] Lloyd's Rep. P.N. 412, *per* Jonathan Parker J. (damage suffered when inappropriate policies were issued to the claimant and the claimant made payments associated with them).
[91] See para.5–041, above.
[92] [2006] UKHL 22; [2006] 2 W.L.R. 1091.
[93] *ibid.* at [29], *per* Lord Hoffmann with whom the other members of the House of Lords agreed.
[94] [1983] 2 A.C. 1. Discussed by K. M. Stanton, "Limitation of Actions in Professional Negligence Cases" in (1983) 99 L.Q.R. 175.
[95] See the first edition of this book, para.1–048.

cases on this topic decided before December 9, 1982 must, therefore, be treated with caution. In *Pirelli*, the principal speech was given by Lord Fraser.[96] Lords Bridge, Brandon and Templeman expressed agreement with that speech and made no further comment. Lord Scarman also expressed agreement with that speech, but added a brief comment deploring the current state of the law and looking forward to future legislation on latent damage.

Facts of *Pirelli*. The brief facts of *Pirelli* were as follows: the claimants **5–057** engaged the defendants, a firm of consulting engineers, to advise on and design an addition to their factory premises, which included a chimney. The chimney was constructed in June and July 1969. An unsuitable material (Lytag) was used in its construction. By April 1970, cracks developed at the top of the chimney. The claimants could not have discovered the damage with reasonable diligence before October 1972. They did not in fact discover the damage until November 1977. The writ was issued in October 1978. The House of Lords rejected the argument that the cause of action accrued when the damage to the chimney became discoverable (October 1972). The House of Lords held that the cause of action accrued in the spring of 1970 when damage, in the form of cracks near the top of the chimney, must have come into existence.[97] Therefore, the claimant's claim was statute-barred.

House of Lords reasoning in *Pirelli*. Lord Fraser, who made the only **5–058** substantive speech,[98] reasoned as follows:

(1) In *Cartledge v E Jopling & Sons Ltd*,[99] the House of Lords held that a cause of action for personal injury accrues when the injury occurs, not when it is capable of being discovered by the claimant.[1]

(2) The principle of *Cartledge v E Jopling & Sons Ltd*[2] is applicable to cases of damage to property as well as to personal injury claims.[3]

(3) The fact that the owners of damaged property suffer no financial loss unless and until the damage is discovered is irrelevant. They "have a damaged article when, but for the defendant's negligence, they would have had a sound one".[4]

(4) There is a distinction between a defect in property and damage to that property.

"Unless the defect is very gross, it may never lead to any damage at all to the building. It would be analogous to a predisposition or natural weakness in the human body which may never develop into disease or injury. The plaintiff's cause of action will not accrue until damage occurs, which will commonly

---

[96] Summarised at para.5–058, below.
[97] [1983] 2 A.C. 1 at 19D.
[98] See para.5–056, above.
[99] [1963] A.C. 758.
[1] [1983] 2 A.C. 1 at 13.
[2] [1963] A.C. 758.
[3] [1983] 2 A.C. 1 at 14.
[4] *ibid.* at 16D.

consist of cracks coming into existence as a result of the defect even though the cracks or the defect may be undiscovered and undiscoverable. There may perhaps be cases where the defect is so gross that the building is doomed from the start, and where the owner's cause of action will accrue as soon as it is built, but it seems unlikely that such a defect would not be discovered within the limitation period. Such cases, if they exist, would be exceptional."[5]

(5) The reasoning of the Court of Appeal in *Sparham-Souter v Town & Country Developments (Essex) Ltd*[6] on the limitation issue was incorrect. The reference to that decision by the House of Lords in *Anns v Merton LBC*[7] did not amount to approval of the whole decision.[8]

(6) (Obiter) The duty of the builder and the local authority[9] is owed to owners of the property as a class; "if time runs against one owner, it also runs against all his successors in title".[10]

(7) (Obiter) There is probably no analogy between the negligent design of the chimney in the present case and cases of negligent advice by a solicitor.

"It seems to me that, except perhaps where the advice of an architect or consulting engineer leads to the erection of a building which is so defective as to be doomed from the start, the cause of action accrues only when physical damage occurs to the building."[11]

5–059   **"Doomed from the start".** The decision in *Pirelli* opened up a number of matters for debate. One frequently discussed question was when it could be said that a building was "doomed from the start", with the result that time began to run upon practical completion. A number of enterprising defendants contended that the defects alleged against them were so serious as to fall within this category. Such arguments usually failed. In a series of cases the courts held that Lord Fraser's comments on buildings which were "doomed from the start" were of very limited application. In *Dove v Banhams Patent Locks Ltd*,[12] Hodgson J. held that an inadequate security gate installed by burglary prevention specialists was not doomed from the start. The claimants' cause of action did not accrue until a burglar broke the gate down some 12 years later. In *London Congregational Union Inc v Harriss & Harriss*,[13] Judge Newey Q.C. rejected the argument that a church and hall were doomed from the start merely because design errors had created the likelihood of flooding. The cause of action accrued when the first flooding occurred. Judge Newey's decision on this issue was upheld by the Court of Appeal.[14] A similar approach was adopted in *Kensington and Chelsea and*

---

[5] [1983] 2 A.C. 1 at 16F–H.
[6] [1976] Q.B. 858.
[7] [1978] A.C. 728 at 760.
[8] [1983] 2 A.C. 1 at 15–18.
[9] And by implication the duty of the designer, although Lord Fraser did not expressly say this. But this obiter passage must now be read subject to *Murphy v Brentwood DC* [1991] 1 A.C. 398.
[10] *ibid.* at 18B–E.
[11] *ibid.* at 18G–H.
[12] [1983] 1 W.L.R. 1436.
[13] [1985] 1 All E.R. 335.
[14] [1988] 1 All E.R. 15.

Westminster AHA v Wettern Composites.[15] Stone mullions were inadequately fixed to the external walls of a hospital extension. Judge Smout Q.C. rejected the argument that the building or part of the building was doomed from the start. The cause of action accrued when the mullions moved. In *Ketteman v Hansel Properties Ltd,*[16] the Court of Appeal treated Lord Fraser's references in *Pirelli* to buildings "doomed from the start" as being of very limited application, and their decision was upheld by the House of Lords.[17] The House of Lords held that a building was not "doomed from the start" merely because it had a latent defect which would inevitably result in damage in due course.[18]

A case,[19] however, where the "doomed from the start" argument succeeded **5–060** was *Tozer Kemsley & Millburn (Holdings) Ltd v J Jarvis & Sons Ltd.*[20] The claim concerned an allegedly defective air conditioning plant. Judge Stabb Q.C. held, obiter, that on the basis of the claimant's allegations, the cause of action accrued when the plant was installed. The fact that the defects manifested themselves subsequently with increasing severity was irrelevant.[21] A similar result was reached in the more recent decision of Dyson J. in *New Islington and Hackney Housing Association v Pollard Thomas & Edwards Ltd.*[22] In cases in which the defect to the property is self-contained in that it does not cause damage to any other part, the latest date (if knowledge or discoverability of the defect is not the test) on which damage occurs is practical completion of the building.

Degree of damage required. A separate problem[23] arising from *Pirelli* is what **5–061** degree of damage to the building must occur in order for the cause of action to accrue (assuming that physical damage to the building is the relevant damage). This question has arisen since *Pirelli* a number of times. In *Bromley LBC v Rush & Tompkins Ltd,*[24] a case concerning alleged defects in reinforced concrete, Judge Stabb Q.C. held that depassivation and the commencement of corrosion of the steel reinforcement did not constitute "relevant and significant damage". However, the occurrence of hairline cracking of the concrete, caused by the

---

[15] [1985] 1 All E.R. 346.

[16] [1984] 1 W.L.R. 1274 at 1288–1289.

[17] [1987] A.C. 189.

[18] This issue was considered by Litton L.J. in *Bank of East Asia v Tsien Wui Marble Factory Ltd* [2000] H.K.L.R.D. 268. His comments are strictly obiter because the court below had found as a fact that the defective cladding, which formed the subject matter of the dispute, was not doomed from the start. Litton P.J. noted that it would be a rare case where a defect which was so profound as to render a building "bound to fail" did not give rise to physical damage within six years. He rejected the notion that a cause of action could accrue prior to the occurrence of quantifiable physical damage. Implicit in this is a rejection of the argument that a different accrual date applies where a building is "doomed from the start". See further paras 5–066 to 5–071, below.

The "doomed from the start" argument failed in *O'Donnell v Kilrasan Concrete Ltd* [2001] 4 I.R. 183 (Herbet J.).

[19] For two further examples (one of which is doubted), see A. McGee, *Limitation Periods, op. cit.,* pp.64–66.

[20] (1983) 4 Con.L.R. 24.

[21] *ibid.* at 30–32. See also *London Congregational Union Inc v Harriss & Harriss* [1988] 1 All E.R. 15 at 23G, *per* Ralph Gibson L.J.

[22] [2001] P.N.L.R. 515.

[23] For general guidance, see *Cartledge v E Jopling & Sons Ltd* [1963] A.C. 758.

[24] (1985) 4 Con.L.R. 44.

progress of corrosion of the steel reinforcement, did constitute relevant and significant damage. Therefore, the cause of action accrued when the hairline cracking occurred.[25] In *University of Glasgow v William Whitfield*,[26] Judge Bowsher Q.C. held that condensation alone was not damage; the cause of action in tort only accrued when the condensation caused structural damage to the building.

5–062   **Successive owners.** Separate problems arise from that part of Lord Fraser's speech which is summarised in sub-paragraph (6) above.[27] The notion that time may run against a future owner of damaged property before he has acquired any interest in the property is curious in theory and bizarre in practice.[28] As Judge Newey Q.C. pointed out in *Perry v Tendring DC*,[29] if the second owner is to sue, the first owner must assign his cause of action to him. On the hypothesis that all parties are unaware of the damage, this is an unlikely event, at least at the time of sale. Moreover, the first owner, having incurred no remedial costs and having sold at market price, has suffered no loss. It is therefore arguable that the assignee (the subsequent owner who actually suffers loss) can recover nothing. These problems have now been resolved by s.3 of the Latent Damage Act 1986.[30]

5–063   **Effect of *Murphy* on *Pirelli*.** The most important question to consider in relation to Pirelli is the impact of *Murphy v Brentwood DC*.[31] As stated earlier,[32] the House of Lords in that case held that defects in buildings should be characterised as economic loss. Lord Keith, with whom all other law lords agreed, explained *Pirelli* as a case of reliance on negligent advice falling within the *Hedley Byrne* principle. As to the accrual of the cause of action, Lord Keith said:

> "The defendants there had in relation to the design been in contractual relations with the plaintiffs, but it was common ground that a claim in contract was time-barred. If the plaintiffs had happened to discover the defect before any damage had occurred there would seem to be no good reason for holding that they would not have had a cause of action in tort at that stage, without having to wait until some damage had occurred. They would have suffered economic loss through having a defective chimney upon which they required to expend money for the purpose of removing the defect. It would seem that in a case such as *Pirelli*, where the tortious liability arose out of a contractual relationship with professional people, the duty extended to take reasonable care not to cause economic loss to the client by the advice given. The plaintiffs built the chimney

---

[25] (1985) 4 Con.L.R. 44 at 52–53.
[26] (1988) 42 Build. L.R. 66 at 76.
[27] See para.5–058, above.
[28] The problem is discussed by G. Robertson, "Defective Premises and Subsequent Purchasers" in (1983) 99 L.Q.R. 559 and J. Holyoak, "Limitation Periods in Economic Loss" in (1984) 128 S.J. 234.
[29] (1984) 30 Build. L.R. 118 at 142–143. See also *R L Polk & Co (Great Britain) Ltd v Edwin Hill and Partners* (1988) 41 Build.L.R. 84.
[30] See below.
[31] [1991] 1 A.C. 398.
[32] See Ch.2, para.2–039, above.

as they did in reliance on that advice. The case would accordingly fall within the principle of *Hedley Byrne v Heller & Partners Ltd.*"[33]

Thus *Pirelli* is a case in which economic loss was recoverable. It is arguable that the effect of this analysis is to push back the accrual of the cause of action in such a case, to an earlier date than has previously been assumed—namely the date when the claimant acted in reliance on the negligent design.[34] If this analysis is correct, then the decisions in *London Congregational Union v Harriss and Harriss*[35] and *Kensington and Chelsea and Westminster AHA v Wettern Composites*[36] have been impliedly overruled. Furthermore, this analysis would create some consistency between the architect/engineer cases discussed in this section and the solicitor/insurance broker cases discussed above.[37] This approach would not appear to work injustice, since Parliament has made adequate provision for cases where defects are concealed by the Latent Damage Act 1986.[38]   **5–064**

An alternative view which has been canvassed by some commentators is that the reconciliation of *Murphy* and *Pirelli* requires the substitution of the date of discoverability for the date of occurrence of physical damage, as the date when "damage" is suffered for the purposes of determining when the cause of action in negligence accrues. In other words, it is said that the start date has become later rather than earlier.[39] This view was rejected at first instance in *Western*   **5–065**

---

[33] [1991] 1 A.C. 398 at 466F. This view was accepted by Ching P.J. in *Bank of East Asia* [2000] 1 H.K.L.R.D. 268 at 339E. Litton P.J. was critical of this "re-classification" of *Pirelli* as a case of economic loss. See further paras 5–066 to 5–071, below and Mullany, "Limitation of actions—where are we now?" in [1993] L.M.C.L.Q. 34.

[34] See in this respect the judgment of Judge Smout in *Imperial College of Science and Technology v Norman & Dawbarn* (1986) 8 Con.L.R. 107 at 125 where, although the judge held following *Pirelli* that a cause of action in respect of design against a firm of architects did not arise until actual damage had occurred, he also held that any damage flowing from a failure to warn as to a limited design life must have accrued when the client acted on the architect's design recommendations. See also *New Islington and Hackney Housing Association Ltd v Pollard Thomas & Edwards Ltd* [2001] P.N.L.R. 515 at 529, *per* Dyson J.: "If as Lord Keith said, *Pirelli* falls within the principle of *Hedley Byrne & Heller & Partners* [1964] A.C. 465 and is an economic loss case, then it is difficult to see why the cause of action in *Pirelli* did not accrue when the plaintiffs relied on the advice of the engineers by instructing them to proceed with the construction of the chimney." However, Dyson J. held that he was bound to follow *Pirelli* and hold that knowledge or discoverability of the defect was not the relevant test.

In *Abbott v Will Gannon & Smith* [2005] EWCA Civ 198; [2005] P.N.L.R. 30 it was held that *Pirelli* had not been overruled by *Murphy* but that, if it had, and time ran when economic loss was suffered, economic loss was only suffered when the latent defect became manifest (see para.5–072, below).

[35] [1985] 1 All E.R. 335 and [1988] 1 All E.R. 15, discussed in para.5–059, above.

[36] [1985] 1 All E.R. 346, discussed in para.5–059, above.

[37] See paras 5–037 to 5–052, above.

[38] See paras 5–075 to 5–084, below. See *New Islington and Hackney Housing Association Ltd v Pollard Thomas & Edwards Ltd* [2001] P.N.L.R. 515 at 529, *per* Dyson J. But see *Bank of East Asia v Tsien Wui Marble Factory* [2000] 1 H.K.L.R.D. 268 and, in particular, *per* Ching P.J. at 341–343, *per* Bokhary P.J at 358A and, *per* Lord Nicholls at 363B (this decision is discussed further in paras 5–066 to 5–071, below).

[39] See Mullany, "Limitation of actions and latent damage" in (1991) 54 M.L.R. 216 at 227–228; McKendrick,"*Pirelli* re-examined" in (1991) 11 Journal of Legal Studies 326 at 335–336; Mullany, "Limitation of actions—where are we now?" in [1993] L.M.C.L.Q. 34 at 43. In *Pullen v Gutteridge Haskins & Davey Pty Ltd* [1993] 1 V.R. 27, the Appeal Division of the Supreme Court of Victoria declined to follow *Pirelli*, holding that damage occurred only when the latent defect became known or manifest.

Challenge Housing Association Ltd v Percy Thomas Partnership.[40] However, in the context of New Zealand law it was considered more favourably by the Privy Council in *Invercargill CC v Hamlin.*[41] The facts of *Invercargill* and the relevant dates are set out in Ch.2, para.2–056, above. The Privy Council upheld the decision of the New Zealand Court of Appeal that Mr Hamlin's cause of action accrued in 1989, when the defective foundations first became reasonably discoverable and were in fact discovered. The Privy Council referred to some of the criticisms which have been expressed of Pirelli and concluded:

> "Once it is appreciated that the loss in respect of which the plaintiff in the present case is suing is loss to his pocket, and not for physical damage to the house or foundations, then most, if not all the difficulties surrounding the limitation question fall away. The plaintiff's loss occurs when the market value of the house is depreciated by reason of the defective foundations, and not before. If he resells the house at full value before the defect is discovered, he has suffered no loss. Thus in the common case the occurrence of the loss and the discovery of the loss will coincide."[42]

The Privy Council left open the question whether *Pirelli* should still be regarded as good law in England, although it was not such in New Zealand.[43]

5–066   ***Bank of East Asia.*** The above contrasting approaches views have recently been considered by the Hong Kong Court of Final Appeal in *Bank of East Asia Ltd v Tsien Wui Marble Factory Ltd.*[44] The claim in *Bank of East Asia* concerned the granite cladding of a tower block being built for the claimant. Palmer and Turner were the architects and engineers. The cladding was completed in March 1982, the building as a whole in July 1983. The cladding failed. Proceedings were issued against Palmer and Turner in 1996. Palmer and Turner admitted negligence but argued that the claim was time barred; more than six years having elapsed since the occurrence of damage and the accrual of the cause of action.[45]

5–067   Latent damage provisions mirroring those in s.14A of the Limitation Act 1980[46] were introduced into the Limitation Ordinance in 1991 by s.31. However, the claimant could not avail itself of s.31 if the action had already become statute barred by the date on which they came into force, July 31, 1991. The central issue for the Court was therefore when the cause of action accrued. By a majority of 3:2 the Court of Final Appeal held that the limitation period had expired before

---

[40] (1995) C.I.L.L. 1018.

[41] [1996] A.C. 624.

[42] *ibid.* at 648C–D. Had they not been bound by *Pirelli*, the Court of Appeal would have reached a similar conclusion as was reached in *Abbott v Will Gannon & Smith* [2005] EWCA Civ 198; [2005] P.N.L.R. 30, discussed in para.5–072, below.

[43] *ibid.* at 649C. In *Havenledge Ltd v Graeme John & Partners (a firm)* [2001] P.N.L.R. 419, CA, Sir Antony Evans said at 424 that *Pirelli* remained binding as an authoritative statement of English law. In *New Islington and Hackney Housing Association Ltd v Pollard Thomas & Edwards Ltd* [2001] P.N.L.R. 515 at 529 Dyson J. held that he was bound to follow *Pirelli* and that "the knowledge test has not been applied in English law".

[44] [2000] 1 H.K.L.R.D. 268. See (2001) 117 L.Q.R. 20 (Limitation and Latent Damage in Hong Kong: Mullany).

[45] The contractual action against both parties was clearly time barred. The sub-contractor did not admit negligence and sought unsuccessfully to argue that it had relied on independent contractors.

[46] See paras 5–075 to 5–084, below.

the issue of proceedings. All five judges gave reasons for their decision. Substantive judgments were delivered by Litton P.J. and Ching P.J. in the majority and by Bokhary P.J. in the minority; Nazareth N.P.J. delivered a short judgment agreeing with the majority and Lord Nicholls N.P.J. delivered a short dissenting judgment agreeing with Bokhary P.J. The parties agreed that the loss to the claimant should properly be characterised as economic loss. All members of the court agreed, except for Litton P.J. who favoured a return to the "common sense" view that the loss suffered was both economic and physical. It was not right to "unhook" the physical element.

When was damage first suffered? The majority endorsed the approach of the 5–068
House of Lords in *Pirelli* and rejected the alternative approach of the Privy Council in *Invercargill CC v Hamlin*.[47] The majority were considerably influenced by the fact that the approach adopted in *Invercargill* was not reconcilable with the statutory scheme in Hong Kong. There was no equivalent of s.31 (or s.14A) in New Zealand, such provision was unnecessary because the law in New Zealand had developed along different lines from that in England. Of the discoverability test, Ching P.J. said "the discovery of damage is self-evidently not the occurrence of damage".[48]

Some variance of views is apparent between the judgments of Litton P.J. and 5–069
Ching P.J. Litton P.J. concluded that the cause of action accrued in 1985 when, on the evidence, physical damage in a "real and substantial sense" first occurred.[49] Ching P.J. accepted that the loss under consideration in this case was economic. In the absence of proof as to when such economic loss occurred, the court "may, if not must, take the date of the occurrence of the physical damage as being the date of the economic loss".[50]

The views of the minority. The minority fully endorsed the approach of the 5–070
Privy Council in *Invercargill CC v Hamlin*.[51] Bokhary P.J. expressed the view that the approach could not sensibly be confined to New Zealand: "Either it is convincing or it is not".[52] The approach of the Privy Council in *Invercargill* recognised that economic loss in building defects cases occurred when the market value of the building was diminished. This was the only manner in which the term "economic loss" had substance and real meaning.[53] So far as he statutory position was concerned, Bokhary P.J. rejected the notion that, merely because legislation had been passed to give relief against an unjust judicial decision, the legislature was to be taken to have set that judicial decision in stone.[54]

---

[47] [1996] A.C. 624.
[48] [2000] 1 H.K.L.R.D. 268 at 319C.
[49] *ibid.* at 301D–F, 303F–H and 310B. In following *Pirelli* and rejecting *Invercargill*, Litton P.J. placed great reliance on the judgment of Lord Reid in *Cartledge v Jopling (E) & Sons Ltd* [1963] A.C. 758 at 772. Litton L.J. said: "it cannot be the policy of the legislature to encourage speculative lawsuits".
[50] *ibid.* at 344C.
[51] [1996] A.C. 624.
[52] [2000] 1 H.K.L.R.D. 268 at 356D.
[53] *ibid.* at 356F–G.
[54] *ibid.* at 358H.

5–071   Lord Nicholls emphasised that physical damage to the building and financial loss to its owner were not necessarily linked. Financial loss might be suffered before any physical damage occurred. "To make the accrual of the cause of action dependent on the presence or absence of physical damage to a building is to ignore the realities of defectively designed or defectively constructed building works."[55] He also agreed with Bokhary P.J. that the statutory provisions should not be taken to freeze the common law in effect at the time of its enactment.[56] Lord Nicholls considered that there were two possibilities for the date of accrual of the action: the first was when the claimants accepted and paid for the building. At that date it acquired something which, because of the defect, was inherently less valuable. The second alternative was when the defect became patent. Until then, the market value of the building was undiminished. In Lord Nicholls' view, "despite powerful arguments to the contrary, the preponderance of high authority now supports the view that, as regards latent defects in buildings, the second possibility is to be preferred".[57]

5–072   **The position in English law.** If the *Invercargill* analysis is adopted as part of English law, then in respect of claims against architects and engineers the reforms introduced by the Latent Damage Act 1986[58] will be largely otiose. However, it appears that a decision of the House of Lords will be needed to establish the position in English law. In *New Islington and Hackney Housing Association Ltd v Pollard Thomas & Edwards Ltd*,[59] Dyson J. held that the claimant housing association suffered loss and damage in relation to inadequate sound-proofing at practical completion of the building at the latest. This decision was consistent with those relating to other professions, but required a reappraisal of the effect of *Pirelli*. It was not referred to by the Court of Appeal in the later decision of *Abbott v Will Gannon & Smith Ltd*.[60] The facts in that case were found to be indistinguishable from those in *Pirelli*. Having so concluded, the Court of Appeal held that they remained bound by that decision so that time ran from when physical damage was first suffered. It was for the House of Lords and not the Court of Appeal to consider whether *Pirelli* remained good law. Had they not been bound by *Pirelli* the Court of Appeal would have held that economic loss was not suffered when the building was first constructed with its defect, but when the defect became manifest and so reduced the value of the building.

5–073   **Uncertainty.** The present state of the law in this area cannot be regarded as satisfactory.[61] The difference of view between the appellate courts and their members who have had to grapple with this issue indicates its difficulty. The "discoverability" test is attractive in that it goes to the market value of the building. It is, however, an ignorant market and the claimant will not have sold

---

[55] [2000] 1 H.K.L.R.D. 268 at 362E–F.
[56] *ibid.* at 363J.
[57] *ibid.* at 363B.
[58] See paras 5–075 to 5–084, below.
[59] [2001] P.N.L.R. 515.
[60] [2005] EWCA Civ 198; [2005] P.N.L.R. 30.
[61] In *Abbott v Will Gannon & Smith Ltd* [2005] EWCA Civ 198; [2005] P.N.L.R. 30 Tuckey L.J., with whom Clarke and Mummery L.JJ. agreed, said at [17] that he could not state with any confidence what the present state of the law was in England.

the building before the defect is in fact discovered—otherwise he would not be a claimant. The alternative, that loss is suffered when an inherently less valuable building is constructed, threatens to revive "doomed from the start" arguments.[62]

Inadequate or incorrect specification. Where an architect or engineer negligently specifies inappropriate materials or equipment, damage is not suffered until the materials or equipment are delivered. Until then, the client has not suffered any quantifiable loss or damage.[63]　　　　　　　　　5–074

(d) Effect of the Latent Damage Act 1986

This Act is based upon the recommendations made by the Law Reform Committee in its 24th Report,[64] published in November 1984. The Act deals with latent damage not including personal injuries.[65] Its main objects are to protect claimants who, for good reason, are unaware that they have a cause of action for a number of years, and at the same time to protect defendants against unduly stale claims.[66]　　　　　　　　　5–075

The Act provides[67] for the insertion of s.14A into the Limitation Act 1980. Section 14A provides, in effect, two alternative periods of limitation in cases of latent damage.[68] The claimant may either bring his claim within six years from the date on which the cause of action accrued or within three years from the "starting date". The "starting date" is defined as follows:　　　5–076

"The earliest date on which the plaintiff or any person in whom the cause of action was vested before him first had both the knowledge required for bringing an action for damages in respect of the relevant damage and a right to bring such an action."[69]

The knowledge referred to in this passage means knowledge both:

"(a) of the material facts about the damage in respect of which damages are claimed; and

(b) of the other facts relevant to the current action mentioned in subsection (8) below."[70]

---

[62] See generally *New Islington and Hackney Housing Association Ltd v Pollard Thomas & Edwards Ltd* [2001] P.N.L.R. 515, *per* Dyson J.

[63] *Proctor & Gamble (Health and Beauty Care) Ltd v Carrier Holdings Ltd* [2003] EWHC 83, TCC; [2003] Build L.R. 255 (Forbes J.)

[64] Cmnd. 9390 (1984).

[65] The Act came into force on September 18, 1986. It does not affect any actions commenced before that date: s.4(1)(b). Nor does it enable actions to be brought which had become statute-barred before that date: s.4(1)(a).

[66] For a fuller account of the thinking which led up to the Act, see the Law Reform Committee's 24th Report.

[67] Latent Damage Act 1986, s.1.

[68] It should be noted, however, that s.14A of the Limitation Act 1980 does not apply in cases of deliberate concealment by the defendant. In such cases the claimant can still rely upon s.32(1)(b) of the Limitation Act 1980, which is more favourable to him. (See s.2(2) of the Latent Damage Act 1986.)

[69] Limitation Act 1980, s.14A(5).

[70] *ibid.* s.14A(6).

The phrase "material facts about the damage" means such facts as would lead a reasonable person to consider the damage sufficiently serious to justify instituting proceedings.[71] The "other facts" referred to in (b) above are:

"(a) that the damage was attributable in whole or in part to the act or omission which is alleged to constitute negligence; and

(b) the identity of the defendant; and

(c) if it is alleged that the act or omission was that of a person other than the defendant, the identity of that person and the additional facts supporting the bringing of an action against the defendant."[72]

However, knowledge that the particular acts or omissions did or did not, as a matter of law, involve negligence is irrelevant.[73] For the purposes of these provisions a person is deemed to know matters which he ought reasonably to have observed or ascertained or (in appropriate circumstances) learnt from experts.[74] Where different heads of damage occurred at different times, a claimant cannot circumvent these provisions by abandoning heads of damage which are inconvenient to his case on limitation.[75] It is for the claimant to prove that the "starting date" was within three years of the issue of proceedings.[76]

5–077 **The 15-year long stop.** The Act also provides for a long stop, as recommended by the Law Reform Committee.[77] This is contained in s.14B of the Limitation Act 1980,[78] which prevents an action for damages for negligence being brought:

" . . . after the expiration of fifteen years from the date (or, if more than one, from the last of the dates) on which there occurred any act or omission—

(a) which is alleged to constitute negligence; and

(b) to which the damage in respect of which damages are claimed is alleged to be attributable (in whole or in part)."

---

[71] Limitation Act 1980, s.14A(7).

[72] *ibid.* s.14A(8).

[73] *ibid.* s.14A(9). See further para.5–079, below.

[74] For the full provision as to constructive knowledge see *ibid.* s.14A(10). The claimant is also fixed with the knowledge of his solicitors: *Heathcote v David Marks & Co* [1996] 1 E.G.L.R. 123 (but see *Lloyds Bank Plc v Crosse & Crosse (a firm)* [2001] P.N.L.R. 830, CA for the significance of the scope of the solicitors' retainer).

[75] *Horbury v Craig Hall & Rutley* [1991] C.I.L.L. 692; approved by the Court of Appeal in *Hamlin v Edwin Evans* (1996) C.I.L.L. 1173. Dugdale discusses the decision in *Horbury* in "Latent damage: the application of the discoverability principle to survey reports" (1991) 7 P.N. 193. Dugdale argues that *Horbury* illustrates some of the flaws in the Latent Damage Act 1986 and that the Act is in urgent need of revision.

In *McKillen v Russell* [2002] P.N.L.R. 29 the Court of Appeal in Northern Ireland, considering the Northern Irish equivalent of s.14A, held that where the claimant had learnt of some damage (in this case that his surveyor had failed to detect one problem with his house), time began to run in respect of his claim, even though there was further damage of which he was not then aware. Similar views were expressed by Lord Woolf L.C.J. in *Babicki v Rowlands (a firm)* [2001] EWCA Civ 1720; [2002] Lloyd's Rep. P.N. 122.

[76] *Haward v Fawcetts (a firm)* [2006] UKHL 6; [2006] 1 W.L.R. 682.

[77] See paras 4–10 to 4–14 of their 24th report.

[78] By s.1 of the Latent Damage Act 1986.

This provision overrides s.14A. It bars the commencement of proceedings 15 years after the breach of duty, even if the claimant remains unaware of his cause of action throughout the 15-year period, and even if the cause of action does not accrue during that period.[79] It does not operate to bar the right itself, merely the remedy.[80] However, the long stop does not operate in cases to which s.32(1)(b) of the Limitation Act 1980 applies (postponement of limitation period in cases of deliberate concealment).[81]

Miscellaneous provisions. The Latent Damage Act 1986 makes consequential   **5–078**
provisions in respect of persons under a disability.[82] The Act also makes special provision for successive owners of property which is affected by latent damage.[83] Section 3 provides that a fresh cause of action shall accrue to the subsequent owner upon his acquisition of the property; but that for limitation purposes the cause of action shall be deemed to have accrued on the date when a cause of action accrued to his predecessor in title. This overcomes the problem discussed above.[84] Furthermore, even if the subsequent owner acquires the property more than six years after the cause of action accrued, he still has three years[85] from the "starting date"[86] in which to bring proceedings.[87] However, in view of the House of Lords' decision in *Murphy v Brentwood DC*,[88] these provisions may be more of academic interest than of practical importance.

Meaning of "negligence". One important question[89] of construction arises in   **5–079**
respect of the Act as a whole. Does the word "negligence" mean the tort of negligence? Or does it also include the breach of a contractual duty to exercise reasonable skill and care? In the Unfair Contract Terms Act 1977 the word "negligence" is used in the wider sense, and is so defined in s.1(1). There is no definition of the word "negligence" in the Latent Damage Act 1986. There is

---

[79] Limitation Act 1980, s.14B(2). See also *Pearson Education Ltd v Charter Partnership Ltd* [2005] EWHC 2021, TCC; [2006] P.N.L.R. 14 (H.H. Judge Thornton Q.C.).

[80] *Financial Services Compensation Scheme Ltd v Larnell (Insurances) Ltd (in creditors' voluntary liquidation)* [2005] EWCA Civ 1408; [2006] 2 W.L.R. 751.

[81] Latent Damage Act 1986, s.2(2).

[82] Latent Damage Act 1986, s.2, which inserts s.28A into the Limitation Act 1980.

[83] This provision only applies to damage which was latent when the property was transferred from one owner to his successor: see subss.3(1)(b), (5) and (6) of the Latent Damage Act 1986.

[84] See para.5–062, above.

[85] Subject to the long stop: see s.14B of the Limitation Act 1980.

[86] As defined in s.14A(5) of the Limitation Act 1980.

[87] Section 3 of the Latent Damage Act 1986 is subject to special transitional provisions: Latent Damage Act 1986, subss. 4(3) and (4). In brief, the section only applies where the claimant acquired his interest in the damaged property after September 18, 1986. The alternative limitation period (3 years from the "starting date") is not available where the original cause of action accrued before September 18, 1986. The object of these provisions appears to be that the defendant should not be deprived of any limitation defence which accrued before the Act came into force. (This is the objective of all transitional provisions in s.4. But the achievement of this object is rather more complex in the case of s.3. The transitional provisions affecting s.3 did not appear in the Latent Damage Bill, as originally published. They were added during the Bill's passage through Parliament.)

[88] [1991] 1 A.C. 398.

[89] This question is discussed by K. M. Stanton, "Reforming Limitations of Actions" in (1986) 2 P.N. 75. This article was written shortly after the Latent Damage Bill was first published.

little doubt that the draughtsman of the Act intended to use the word "negligence" in the narrow sense, meaning the tort of negligence.[90] It is so used in the Law Reform Committee's 24th Report on which the Act is based.[91] In *Société Commerciale de Réassurance v ERAS (International) Ltd*,[92] the Court of Appeal held, with regret, that s.14A of the Limitation Act 1980 applied only to actions for the tort of negligence. It did not apply to claims framed in contract. Nor does s.14A apply to claims under the Defective Premises Act 1972.[93]

5–080　　**Date of knowledge.** The language of s.14A echoes that of s.14.[94] Accordingly the authorities on the construction of s.14 are valuable by way of analogy.[95] However, more recent authority has accumulated on the application of s.14A itself. Section 14A does not require the claimant to know that he has a possible cause of action. What it does require is that he must know the material facts founding that cause of action.[96] If the time comes when the claimant expresses a clear view that the defendant is responsible for the mishap, it is difficult for him thereafter to deny that he had sufficient "knowledge" to trigger s.14A. The mere fact that the claimant would need expert evidence to confirm his view before launching proceedings does not alter the situation.[97] In *Hallam-Eames v Merrett Syndicates Ltd*,[98] the Court of Appeal considered what degree of knowledge the Lloyd's names on a long tail syndicate must have in order to trigger s.14A in respect of their claims against the managing agents and the auditors. The court gave a single judgment. It stated that the act or omission of which the claimant must have knowledge "must be that which is causally relevant for the purposes of an allegation of negligence". The court applied s.14A to the facts of the *Merrett* litigation as follows:

> "What, on these principles, are the facts which constitute the negligence of which the Names complain? It would in our view be incomplete to say that it was the writing of the run off reinsurance policies or the RITCs or the certification of the syndicate accounts. These facts in themselves do not amount to acts of which the Names would even prima facie be entitled to complain. It is necessary to add the allegation that the run off policies and the RITCs exposed the Names to potentially huge liabilities and that

---

[90] Since this view has now been judicially confirmed, no lengthy justification is offered. However, the editors' arguments in support of this view can be found in para.1–124 of the third edition of this book.

[91] See, e.g. 24th Report, para.2.1, third sentence and n.3.

[92] [1992] 2 All E.R. 82. See also the decision of Mr K. Rokison Q.C. in *Iron Trades Mutual Insurance Co Ltd v JK Buckenham Ltd* [1990] 1 All E.R. 808 at 821–823; discussed by N. J. Mullany, "Reform of the Law of Latent Damage" in (1991) 54 M.L.R. 349 at 359–360.

[93] *Payne v John Setchell Ltd* [2002] P.N.L.R. 7 (H.H. Judge Humphrey Lloyd Q.C.).

[94] See paras 5–085 to 5–091, below.

[95] See *Haward v Fawcetts (a firm)* [2006] UKHL 6; [2006] 1 W.L.R. 682, where the House of Lords, considering the application of s.14A, referred to numerous authorities concerning the equivalent provision in s.14. See also *Spencer-Ward v Humberts* [1995] 1 E.G.L.R. 123 at 125; *Hallam-Eames v Merrett Syndicates Ltd* [1995] 7 Med.L.R. 122 at 125.

[96] *Higgins v Hatch & Fielding* [1996] 1 E.G.L.R. 133. Knowledge of facts founding a different cause of action from that sued on will not cause time to run in respect of the latter claim: *Birmingham Midshires Building Society v Wretham* [1999] P.N.L.R. 685 at 692D–693A citing *Hamlin v Edwin Evans* [1996] P.N.L.R. 398, CA.

[97] *Spencer-Ward v Humberts* [1995] 1 E.G.L.R. 123; *Wilson v Le Fevre Wood & Royle* [1996] P.N.L.R. 107.

[98] [1995] 7 Med.L.R. 122.

the certified accounts attributed values to IBNRs, none of which were in fact capable of reasonable quantification."[99]

This decision was approved by the House of Lords in *Haward v Fawcetts (a*   **5–081** *firm).*[1] In the latter case the claim was against a firm of accountants for allegedly negligent advice as to a proposed investment in a company. The House of Lords took the opportunity to review existing authority as to the date of knowledge under both s.14 and s.14A of the Limitation Act 1980. What is needed is knowledge that the damage is attributable to the act or omission of the defendant which forms the essence of the claim in negligence. This first requires knowledge that damage has been suffered. So, it is insufficient for a claimant to know, for example, that he has made a payment. He needs to know that he has made a payment with adverse consequences.[2] In the same way, in a claim for the negligent removal of a healthy breast, it is not enough for the claimant to know that her breast has been removed. She needs to know that the breast was healthy.[3] In such cases the claimant needs to know that something has gone wrong, but not that the act or omission which caused something to go wrong was itself negligent.[4] More generally, what is required is that the claimant should know the essence of his case, apart from the fact that the defendant's relevant acts or omissions were negligent. So, in *Haward v Fawcetts (a firm)* itself, time began to run when the claimant knew that he had lost his investment and that he had done so because the advice given by the accountant was flawed (because he knew the true state of the finances of the company in which he had invested)[5] or when the claimant knew enough for it to be reasonable for him to embark on preliminary investigations into the possibility that it was flawed.[6]

In applying s.14A the courts have been ready to fix claimants with knowledge   **5–082** which they should have acquired. In *Finance for Mortgages Ltd v Farley and Co*[7] the claimant lenders claimed damages against surveyors for allegedly negligent valuation. Kay J. held that the claimants ought to have commenced possession proceedings against the borrowers at a much earlier date and ought to have procured a valuation of the property within about six weeks from obtaining

---

[99] [1995] 7 Med.L.R. 122 at 126. See also *Oakes v Hopcroft* [2000] Lloyd's Rep. P.N. 946, CA. Hoffmann L.J.'s approach in *Hallam-Eames* was followed in *Markes v Coodes* [1997] P.N.L.R. 252 (solicitor's negligence).

[1] [2006] UKHL 6; [2006] 1 W.L.R. 682.

[2] The House of Lords therefore disapproved of the decision in *HF Pensions Trustees Ltd v Ellison* [1999] P.N.L.R. 489 (Jonathan Parker J.) doubted at para.5–054, note 27, of the fifth edition of this work: see [2006] UKHL 6; [2006] 1 W.L.R. 682 at [60]–[61], *per* Lord Walker, at [88], *per* Lord Brown and at [117], *per* Lord Mance. (See also *3M United Kingdom Plc v Linklaters & Paines (a firm)* [2005] EWHC 1382, Ch; [2006] P.N.L.R. 903 (Hart J.) at [31].)

[3] *Dobbie v Medway HA* 1994] 1 W.L.R. 1234, CA, discussed in para.5–088 below) as explained by Hoffmann L.J. in *Hallam-Eames v Merrett Syndicates Ltd* [1995] 7 Med.L.R. 122. See *Haward v Fawcetts (a firm)* [2006] UKHL 6; [2006] 1 W.L.R. 682 at [14], *per* Lord Nicholls, [62], *per* Lord Walker, at [88], *per* Lord Brown and at [120], *per* Lord Mance.

[4] *Haward v Fawcetts (a firm)* [2006] UKHL 6; [2006] 1 W.L.R. 682 at [14], *per* Lord Nicholls.

[5] *ibid.* at [51], *per* Lord Scott. Lord Walker referred at [72] to the claimant's knowledge that his investment was "completely lost". Lord Brown held at [89]–[90] that the claimant knew that he had suffered the relevant damage and that the investment which had been lost had been recommended by the accountant. That was sufficient.

[6] *ibid.* at [20], *per* Lord Nicholls, who held that the claimant had not discharged the burden of proof. Lord Mance reached the same conclusion at [138].

[7] [1998] P.N.L.R. 145.

possession. The claimants were fixed with constructive knowledge of the value of the property as from that time, and accordingly their claim was statute barred.[8] In the same way, in *Webster v Cooper & Burnett*[9] the claimant had failed to read carefully a statement sent to her eight years before she issued proceedings. Had she done so, she would have realised that her house had been charged to secure her husband's business debts (her claim being that her solicitors had failed to advise her of the effect of the charge). She was fixed with the knowledge which she should have acquired and her claim was statute-barred.[10]

5–083　　However, the question will always be whether the claimant should reasonably have acquired the relevant knowledge. So, in *The Mortgage Corp v Lambert and Co (a firm)*[11] the claimant lender had received reports from a debt collection agency indicating a current value of the property well below that reported by the defendant surveyor a year or so earlier. While that might have led the lender to query the original valuation, a reasonable lender would not necessarily have obtained a retrospective valuation at that stage, or more than three years before the issue of proceedings. It followed that the lender could rely on s.14A.[12] In cases in which the claimant has had the benefit of expert or professional advice, it is important to bear in mind the scope of the instructions given.[13] However, a claimant who instructs an appropriate expert is not penalised for shortcomings in

---

[8] A similar approach was adopted in *Birmingham Midshires Building Society v Infields* [1999] Lloyd's Rep. P.N. 874, *per* Judge Bowsher Q.C. The defendant solicitor acted for the borrower and claimant lender. The defendant knew that the borrower planned to let the flat in contravention of the written mortgage terms, but did not notify the claimant of this fact. The claimant lender sued the defendant, who raised a limitation defence. The claimant argued that it was entitled to rely on s.14A. Although the claimant lender's arrears department had the requisite knowledge more than 3 years prior to issue of the writ, the claimant argued that such knowledge had not been passed on to the legal department. Judge Bowsher held that, if true, it was a matter for criticism of the claimants, who should have had a system in place to ensure important information was passed on. However, the judge found as a fact that the legal department must have had sight of the relevant correspondence which revealed the reasons for the borrower's default. See also *Halifax Plc v Ringrose & Co (a firm)* [2000] Lloyd's Rep. P.N. 309, *per* Bell J. (claim by lenders against solicitors) and *New Islington and Hackney Housing Association Ltd v Pollard Thomas & Edwards Ltd* [2001] P.N.L.R. 515, *per* Dyson J. (claim by housing association against architects).

[9] [2000] P.N.L.R. 240, CA.

[10] See also *Fennon v Anthony Hodari & Co (a firm)* [2001] Lloyd's Rep. P.N. 183, CA: client knew that her damage was attributable to a failure to tell her the nature and effect of the document she had signed and it did not matter that she was not aware that the failure was negligent.

This decision was followed by Nelson J. in *Bowie v Southorns* [2002] EWHC 1389, QB; [2003] P.N.L.R. 7. In the latter case the claimant did not know that the solicitor who had failed to explain to her the meaning and effect of a guarantee owed her a legal duty to do so, but did know that he had not done so. Time ran against her on the basis of actual knowledge. She did not have constructive knowledge by reason of having instructed lawyers to act for her in defence to a possession claim, having taken all reasonable steps to obtain legal advice (see s.14A(10)).

See also *Swansea Building Society v Bradford & Bingley (t/a BBG Surveyors)* [2003] P.N.L.R. 38 (H.H. Judge Tyzack Q.C. sitting as a deputy High Court judge) where the claimant was held to have acquired constructive knowledge once it received advice to obtain further specialist reports.

[11] [2000] P.N.L.R. 820.

[12] See also the approach of Evans-Lombe J. in *Lloyds Bank Plc v Burd Pearse* [2000] P.N.L.R. 71 (for the facts see para.5–054, fn.12, above), at 81D–F (claimant bank had no reason to check the documents of title when it had no reason to suppose that its security was inadequate; the bank was not to be fixed with constructive knowledge of facts which its solicitors might have learnt, but did not).

[13] *Lloyds Bank Plc v Crosse & Crosse (a firm)* [2001] EWCA Civ 366 (reported at [2001] P.N.L.R. 830, CA: solicitors retained at later date by claimant on relatively narrow basis).

that expert's work. If the expert fails to discover or advise of something which he should have discovered or advised of, the claimant is not fixed with constructive knowledge by reason of the expert's failing.[14]

If the claimant has a number of employees, it will be appropriate to combine **5–084** the knowledge of one or more of those employees if, on the facts, it would be reasonable to suppose that their knowledge would be aggregated within the claimant's organisation.[15] For the purposes of s.14A, where the claim is brought by insurers by way of subrogation, their knowledge is relevant as well as that of the nominal claimant.[16]

(e) *Special Rules re Personal Injury and Death*

(i) *Primary Limitation Periods*

Personal injuries. Where the claimant claims damages for negligence, nui- **5–085** sance or breach of duty in respect of personal injuries,[17] the limitation period (which is only three years) begins on the date when the cause of action accrued or on "the date of knowledge", if later.[18] If the injured person dies before the expiry of three years, the limitation period begins on the date of death or on "the date of the personal representative's knowledge" if later.[19] The "date of knowledge" is defined in s.14(1) of the Limitation Act 1980 as the date on which the claimant or his personal representative first knew:

"(a)   that the injury in question was significant[20]; and
 (b)   that the injury was attributable in whole or in part to the act or omission which is alleged to constitute negligence, nuisance or breach of duty; and
 (c)   the identity of the defendant; and
 (d)   if it is alleged that the act or omission was that of a person other than the defendant, the identity of that person and the additional facts supporting the bringing of an action against the defendant."

Knowledge that any acts or omissions did or did not, as a matter of law, involve negligence is irrelevant.[21] For the purpose of s.14(1) a person is deemed

---

[14] *Gravgaard v Aldridge & Brownlee (a firm)* [2004] EWCA Civ 1529; [2005] P.N.L.R. 319 at [9], *per* Arden L.J., with whom the other members of the Court agreed.
[15] *3M United Kingdom Plc v Linklaters & Paines (a firm)* [2005] EWHC 1382, Ch; [2006] P.N.L.R. 903 (Hart J.) at [29].
[16] *Graham v Entec Europe Ltd (trading as Exploration Associates)* [2003] EWCA Civ 1177; [2003] 4 All E.R. 1345.
[17] As to which, see para.5–028, above.
[18] Limitation Act 1980, s.11(4).
[19] *ibid.*, s.11(5).
[20] "Significant" is defined in s.14(2). From the decision of the Court of Appeal in *H v Northampton County Council* [2004] EWCA Civ 526; [2005] P.I.Q.R. P7 it would appear that the injury in question is that complained of in the action and the fact that the claimant had earlier knowledge of some other injury is not decisive (claim for post-traumatic stress disorder, rather than for immediate injuries sustained by reason of sexual abuse).
[21] See the last part of s.14(1).

to know matters which he ought reasonably to have observed or ascertained or (in appropriate circumstances) learnt from experts.[22]

5–086 *Nash v Eli Lilly & Co.* The Court of Appeal considered in detail the construction and application of s.14(1) in *Nash v Eli Lilly & Co.*[23] The court proceeded on the basis that "knowledge" in s.14(1):

> "is a condition of mind which imports a degree of certainty and that the degree of certainty which is appropriate for this purpose is that which, for the particular plaintiff, may reasonably be regarded as sufficient to justify embarking upon the preliminaries to the making of a claim for compensation such as the taking of legal or other advice."[24]

The court discussed the difference between knowledge and belief. If a claimant held a firm belief that his injury was attributable to[25] an act or omission by the defendant, but he thought it necessary to obtain reassurance or confirmation by experts, then he would not be regarded as having "knowledge" until his enquiries were (or ought to have been) completed.[26]

5–087 **Application to clinical negligence.**[27] In the context of clinical negligence actions, the most important part of the definition of "date of knowledge" is sub-paragraph (b). The claimant is often aware that his medical treatment has not been wholly successful. This in itself does not necessarily indicate that there has been any mishap. If the claimant is not alerted to the relevant act or omission until he consults another doctor or specialist, that may well be that date when

---

[22] For the full provision as to constructive knowledge, see s.14(3). Where the claimant instructs an expert who fails to ascertain the material facts, and erroneously advises that there is no claim, the claimant is not expected to be unduly sceptical; nor is he thereby fixed with constructive knowledge: *Hepworth v Kerr* (1995) 6 Med.L.R. 139.

[23] [1993] 1 W.L.R. 782. Applied in *Coban v Allen* [1997] 8 Med.L.R. 316.

[24] *ibid.* at 792C–D.

[25] The meaning of "attributable" was discussed in *Nash v Eli Lilly & Co* [1993] 1 W.L.R. 782 at 797–799 and in *Spargo v North Essex District HA* [1997] 8 Med.L.R. 125 at 130.

[26] *ibid.* at 795. Constructive knowledge is discussed below.

[27] For other cases illustrating the principles in this section see: *Skitt v Khan* [1997] 8 Med.L.R. 104; *Parry v Clwyd HA* [1997] 8 Med.L.R. 243; *Slevin v Southampton and SW Hampshire HA* [1997] 8 Med.L.R. 175; *Saxby v Morgan* [1997] 8 Med.L.R. 293; *Hind v York HA* [1997] 8 Med.L.R. 377; *Smith v Leicester HA* [1998] Lloyd's Rep. Med. 77; *Bates v Leicester HA* [1998] Lloyd's Rep. Med. 93; *O'Driscoll v Dudley HA* [1998] Lloyd's Rep. Med. 211; *Briggs v Pitt-Payne & Lias* [1999] Lloyd's Rep. Med. 1; *Pavey v Ministry of Defence* [1999] Lloyd's Rep. Med. 9; *Roberts v Winbow* [1999] Lloyd's Rep. Med. 31; *Davis v Jacobs & Camden Islington HA* [1999] Lloyd's Rep. Med. 72; *Appleby v Walshall HA* [1999] Lloyd's Rep. 154; *Briody v St Helen's and Knowsley AHA* [1999] Lloyd's Rep. 185; *Das v Ganju* [1999] Lloyd's Rep. Med. 198; *Ali v Courthaulds Textiles Ltd* [1999] Lloyd's Rep. Med. 301; *French v East London and City HA* [2000] Lloyd's Rep. Med. 35; *Corbin v Penfold Metallising Co Ltd* [2000] Lloyd's Rep. Med. 246; *Harrild v Ministry of Defence, Robert Jones, Agnes Hunt* [2001] Lloyd's Rep. Med. 117; *Rowe v Kingson-upon-Hull CC* [2003] EWCA Civ 1281; [2004] P.I.Q.R. P16. For a detailed and comprehensive review of this aspect of limitation, see R. James, "The Limitation Period in Medical Negligence Claims" in (1998) Med.L.R. 62. See also *Rowbottom v Royal Masonic Hospital* [2002] EWCA Civ 87; [2002] Lloyd's Rep. Med. 173, a borderline case.

time begins to run.[28] In *Broadley v Guy Clapham & Co*,[29] however, it must have been obvious to the claimant, even without the benefit of expert advice, that there was something significantly wrong and she was thereby fixed with knowledge. Hoffmann L.J. summarised the approach in this way:

"Section 14(1)(b) requires that one should look at the way the plaintiff puts his case, distill what he is complaining about and ask whether he had, in broad terms, knowledge of the facts on which that complaint is based."[30]

The crucial question is when the claimant became aware, or constructively   **5–088** aware, that the injury was attributable to the defendant's act or omission. The claimant need not be alerted to the question of negligence. In *Dobbie v Medway HA*,[31] the claimant's breast was removed unnecessarily during an operation in 1973. Shortly after the operation the claimant learnt that the removal was unnecessary, in that the lump in her breast (the original cause for concern) was benign. Even though the claimant was unaware of any possible negligence until many years later, the Court of Appeal held that the claimant had the requisite knowledge, and that time had begun to run, in 1973. All that the claimant needed to know was that she had suffered significant harm (namely the removal of a healthy breast) and that this was due to the act or omission of the health authority.[32]

Similar reasoning was adopted in *Spargo v North Essex District HA*.[33] The   **5–089** Court of Appeal held that a claimant would not have the requisite knowledge "if she thinks she knows that her condition is capable of being attributed to the act or omission alleged to constitute negligence, but she is not sure about this and would and would need to check with an expert before she could properly be said to know that it was".[34] However, where the claimant was "clear in her mind" that there was a connection between an alleged misdiagnosis and her injury, there was no need for the court to go further and inquire whether a rational person would be willing to say that the claimant knew there was a possible causal connection

---

[28] As in *Scuriaga v Powell* (1979) 123 S.J. 406; *Driscoll-Varley v Parkside HA* (1991) 2 Med.L.R. 346; *Davis v City & Hackney HA* (1989) 2 Med.L.R. 366 and *Harrild v Ministry of Defence, Robert Jones, Agnes Hunt* [2001] Lloyd's Rep. Med. 117.

[29] [1994] 4 All E.R. 439: claimant's foot dropped after operation on knee.

[30] *ibid*. at 448. This decision and other authorities on s.14 were reviewed by the House of Lords in *Haward v Fawcetts (a firm)* [2006] UKHL 6; [2006] 1 W.L.R. 682.

[31] [1994] 1 W.L.R. 1234.

[32] As explained by Hoffmann L.J. in *Hallam-Eames v Merrett Syndicates Ltd* [1995] 7 Med.L.R. 122 and in *Haward v Fawcetts (a firm)* [2006] UKHL 6; [2006] 1 W.L.R. 682 at [14], *per* Lord Nicholls; [62], *per* Lord Walker; at [88], *per* Lord Brown and at [120], *per* Lord Mance.

[33] [1997] 8 Med. L.R. 125.

[34] *ibid*. at 130, *per* Brooke L.J. Brooke L.J. laid down four principles concerning the application of s.14(1) at pp.129–130 of the judgment. The Court of Appeal in *Corbin v Penfold Metallising Co Ltd* [2000] Lloyd's Rep. Med 247 at 249(12) held that the principles laid down by Brooke L.J. were "not merely guidelines but authoritative statements of how section 14 should be interpreted".

However, in *Babicki v Rowlands (a firm)* [2001] EWCA Civ 1720; [2002] Lloyd's Rep. P.N. 121 Lord Woolf L.C.J., with whom Simon Brown and Buxton L.JJ. agreed, said that, while Brooke L.J.'s judgment in *Spargo v North Essex District HA* [1997] 8 Med.L.R. 125 provided "some very helpful guidance", on the facts of *Babicki* it was better to turn to the words of the statute (s.14A, rather than s.14) rather than to seek to place a gloss on them.

between her suffering and the omission she had identified without first going to a doctor to seek confirmation.[35]

5–090 Pursuant to s.14(3), a person is deemed to know matters which he ought reasonably to have observed or ascertained or (in appropriate circumstances) learnt from experts. The burden of proof of showing want of reasonable action is on the defendant.[36] Where the claimant instructs an expert who fails to ascertain the material facts, and erroneously advises that there is no claim, the claimant is not expected to be unduly sceptical; nor is he thereby fixed with constructive knowledge.[37] However, if prior to seeking such advice the claimant has a sufficiently firm belief that his or her injury is attributable to the defendant's negligence to amount to knowledge, time begins to run then.[38] While it has been suggested that for this purpose a solicitor is not treated as being an "expert",[39] in *Henderson v Temple Pier Co*[40] the Court of Appeal held that, for the purposes of s.14, the claimant was fixed with constructive knowledge of facts which her solicitors ought to have ascertained.[41]

5–091 These principles were applied in *Forbes v Wandsworth HA*.[42] The claimant had two operations on his leg, which was subsequently amputated. Nine years later he consulted a solicitor, who obtained an expert report. This indicated that the leg could have been saved but for a negligent delay in carrying out the second operation. On the basis of this expert evidence, the claimant began his action. The Court of Appeal held by a majority that the claimant was fixed with constructive knowledge from about 12 to 18 months following the operation. The court reasoned as follows: if medical treatment does not have the desired result, the patient is not to know whether "it is just one of those things" or whether there has been negligence. If he might want to claim, he should obtain expert advice reasonably promptly. He cannot sit back for years, then obtain an expert report and commence proceedings in reliance on s.14. In this case, a reasonable man would have taken advice within 12–18 months of the operation.[43] The test of what knowledge a person might reasonably have been expected to have acquired under s.14(3) is essentially objective: what would a reasonable person who had suffered the injury have done? Any

---

[35] [1997] 8 Med. L.R. 125 at 131.

[36] *Nash v Eli Lilly & Co* [1993] 1 W.L.R. 782 and *Forbes v Wandsworth HA* (1996) 7 Med. L.R. 175.

[37] *Hepworth v Kerr* (1995) 6 Med.L.R. 139.

[38] See *Spargo v North Essex District HA* [1997] 8 Med L.R.. 125, discussed at para.5–089, above.

[39] *Fowell v National Coal Board, The Times*, May 28, 1986.

[40] [1998] 1 W.L.R. 1540.

[41] *ibid.* at 1545D–E, *per* Bracewell J.:
"Even if the solicitor is to be regarded as a appropriate expert, the facts were ascertainable by him without the use of legal expertise. The proviso (section 14(1)(c)) is not intended to give an extended period of limitation to a person whose solicitor acts dilatorily in acquiring information which is obtainable without particular expertise."

[42] [1997] Q.B. 402.

[43] *ibid.* at 412, *per* Stuart-Smith L.J. Both Stuart-Smith and Evans L.JJ. held that the test was wholly objective, dicta in *Nash v Eli Lilly & Co* [1993] 1 W.L.R. 782 at 799H, to the effect that the objective test should be qualified by reference to the claimant's character and intelligence were doubted. Roch L.J., whilst expressing some difficulty with the qualification set out in *Nash v Eli Lilly & Co*, regarded himself as bound by that qualification.

special characteristics of a particular claimant can be taken into account under s.33 of the Limitation Act 1980.[44]

Death. The limitation period for claims under the Fatal Accidents Act 1976 **5–092** (which is three years) begins to run on the date of death or the "date of knowledge"[45] of the person for whose benefit the claim is brought.[46]

(ii) *Discretionary Exclusion of Time Limit*

The statutory discretion. In the case of actions in respect of personal injuries **5–093** or death,[47] the court has discretion under s.33(1) of the Limitation Act 1980 to disapply the time limits,

"having regard to the degree to which:

(a) the provisions of section 11 or 12 of this Act prejudice the plaintiff or any person whom he represents; and

(b) any decision of the court under this subsection would prejudice the defendant or any person whom he represents."

Section 33(3) provides that in acting under the section the court shall have regard to all the circumstances of the case, including a number of matters which are specifically set out.[48]

Manner in which the discretion is exercised. This provision first appeared in **5–094** the Limitation Act 1975. It has generated a great deal of case law, principally arising from road traffic accidents or accidents at work. Broadly speaking, it is a precondition for success that the claimant has suffered some prejudice by reason of the existence of the limitation period. This may be the case even if he has previously issued a claim form in time, if that action had not proceeded, because he will suffer prejudice if a fresh action would be time barred.[49] If the claimant would be prejudiced then the court does have an unfettered discretion[50] to be

---

[44] *Adams v Bracknell Forest BC* [2004] UKHL 4; [2005] 1 A.C. 76. On the facts of *Adams* the claimant should reasonably have sought professional advice more than three years before proceedings were commenced and so could not rely on s.14 of the Limitation Act 1980.

[45] As to which, see paras 5–085 and 5–086, above.

[46] Limitation Act 1980, s.12(2). It is a precondition that the deceased died before the expiry of the period when he could maintain an action in respect of the injury: see s.12(1). There may be different limitation periods for different dependants.

[47] As to which, see para.5–028, above.

[48] Limitation Act 1980, s.33(3)(a)–(e). For a discussion of the six matters set out therein see the speech of Lord Diplock in *Thompson v Brown* [1981] 1 W.L.R. 744 at 751–752. For the purposes of sub-para.(f) the claimant may, in appropriate cases, be required to provide further information as to the general nature of any medical, legal or other expert advice which he has received: *Jones v GD Searle & Co* [1979] 1 W.L.R. 101.

[49] *Horton v Sadler* [2006] UKHL 27; [2006] W.L.R. 1346 where the House of Lords departed from its earlier ruling in *Walkley v Precision Forgings Ltd* [1979] 1 W.L.R. 606. The latter decision had been applied by the House of Lords in *Deerness v John R Keeble & Son (Brantham) Ltd* [1983] 2 Lloyd's Rep. 260. On several occasions the Court of Appeal had distinguished the decision in *Walkley* on technical grounds and in *Horton* the House of Lords recognised this and decided to apply the Practice Statement (Judicial Precedent) [1996] 1 W.L.R. 1234.

[50] The Court of Appeal is generally reluctant to interfere with the judge's exercise of this discretion: see *Conry v Simpson* [1983] 3 All E.R. 369.

exercised generally (in accordance with the statutory criteria) so as to reach an equitable and fair decision.[51] If the claimant's substantive case is weak, that factor weighs against the exercise of the discretion in his favour.[52] Furthermore, the sheer length of the delay between the mishap and the issue of proceedings may be a powerful factor against disapplying the time limit.[53] The discretion should not be exercised in a different way in large group actions from the way in which it is exercised in ordinary cases.[54] In exercising its discretion the court may have regard to the insurance position of any other defendants against whom the claimant has begun proceedings in time.[55]

5-095   In the context of claims for clinical negligence the following points should be noted in considering prejudice to the defendant:

(1) It is not correct to say that the defendant is not prejudiced, simply because he is insured. The defendant and his insurer should be treated as a composite unit.[56]

(2) Where the factual evidence depends upon surviving medical records rather than the recollection of witnesses, it may be more difficult for the defendant to show sufficient prejudice flowing from delay for the purpose of s.33.[57]

(3) Even where medical records have been lost, the defendant may still be unable to show prejudice, as in *Hammond v West Lancashire HA*.[58]

5-096   **Relevance of fault on the part of the claimant's legal advisers.** The fact that the claimant would have a claim against his own solicitors, in the event that no direction is made under s.33, has been held to be a highly relevant consideration, at least in relation to the question whether he would suffer prejudice if the time limit were not disapplied.[59] However, even in cases where "if the action were not allowed to proceed the claimant would have a cast-iron case against his solicitor in which the measure of damages will be no less than those that he would be able

---

[51] *Horton v Sadler* [2006] UKHL 27; [2006] 2 W.L.R. 1346 at [32] *per* Lord Bingham, with whom the other members of the House of Lords agreed.
[52] *Nash v Eli Lilly & Co* [1993] 1 W.L.R. 782 at 807–808; *Forbes v Wandsworth HA* [1997] Q.B. 402.
[53] See, e.g. *Dobbie v Medway HA* [1994] 1 W.L.R. 1234. In considering the length of, and the reasons for, the delay "on the part of the claimant", the test is subjective rather than objective. The court must have regard to the claimant's actual state of mind, rather than to what a reasonable person would think or do in the claimant's position: *Coad v Cornwall HA* [1997] 1 W.L.R. 189. Delay after the claimant has consulted solicitors may be particularly relevant to the exercise of the court's discretion, particularly in the absence of any explanation of such delay: e.g. *Berry v Calderdale HA* [1998] Lloyd's Rep. Med. 179.
[54] *Nash v Eli Lilly & Co* [1993] 1 W.L.R. 782 at 810.
[55] *Liff v Peasley* [1980] 1 W.L.R. 781 at 788–789.
[56] *Kelly v Bastible* [1997] 8 Med.L.R. 15.
[57] See, e.g. *Farthing v NE Essex HA* [1998] Lloyd's Rep. Med. 37.
[58] [1998] Lloyd's Rep. Med. 146. In that case X-rays had been destroyed with the result that there was no evidence to refute the conclusions which the hospital had drawn from those X-rays.
[59] *Thompson v Brown* [1981] 1 W.L.R. 744 at 752–753; *Donovan v Gwentoys Ltd* [1990] 1 W.L.R. 472; *Ramsden v Lee* [1992] 2 All E.R. 204. For further discussion, see J. Steiner, "Solicitors' Liability and the Limitation Act 1980—Tipping the Scales" (1990) 6 P.N. 183, where it is argued that courts should refrain from prejudging the outcome of subsequent solicitors' negligence litigation.

to recover against the defendant if the action were allowed to proceed", this factor is not conclusive. The claimant may still, quite reasonably, prefer to sue the original tortfeasor rather than his own solicitors.[60]

Moreover, generally any failings by the claimant's solicitor will not be attrib-   **5–097**
uted to the claimant. This emerges from three decisions of the Court of Appeal. The first of these is *Das v Ganju*.[61] Sir Christopher Staughton, giving the leading judgment of the Court of Appeal, quoted from the earlier decision of *Whitfield v North Durham HA*[62] and said: "If that passage means that as a matter of law anything done by the lawyers must be visited on the client, it cannot in my view be reconciled with other authority ... that other authority is *Thompson v Brown*". Buxton L.J. held that the availability of a remedy against solicitors only arose as a factor where it was established that otherwise the claimant should be permitted to proceed. Buxton L.J. expressly reserved his view as to whether such alternative remedy might ever be relevant except where the claimant's case against his solicitors was unanswerable. *Das v Ganju* was followed in *Corbin v Penfolds Metallising Co Ltd*.[63] The trial judge has attributed delay on the part of the claimant's solicitors to the claimant. Buxton L.J. said that, unless, as a matter of law a claimant was bound by and bore responsibility for his solicitor's actions, such attribution was not right. On the evidence, the claimant had done what any man his position might have been expected to have done, namely gone to apparently efficient and responsible solicitors and left them to get on with it. He was not persuaded that each case should be considered on its own facts, holding that the court was speaking more generally and saying that there was certainly no rule of law to visit the faults of the lawyers on the claimant.[64] Finally, in *Steeds v Peverel Management Services*,[65] Sir Christopher Slade (giving the judgment of the Court of Appeal) concluded that the above authorities demonstrated that fault on the part of the claimant's solicitors was not to be attributed to the claimant personally. This was not to say, however, that the existence of a claim by the claimant against the solicitors was irrelevant—it was a factor in weighing the prejudice suffered by the claimant if the discretion under s.33 were not exercised.

The relevance of s.33 to professional negligence litigation. The principal   **5–098**
relevance of s.33 of the Limitation Act 1980 to professional negligence is therefore twofold. First, it will sometimes enable solicitors who have failed to issue a writ in time to escape the consequences of their own negligence. In such a situation it is not uncommon for the solicitors' insurers to finance the claimant's

---

[60] *Thompson v Brown* [1981] 1 W.L.R. 744 at 750. See also *Hartley v Birmingham DC* [1992] 1 W.L.R. 968. In the latter case the writ in a personal injuries action was issued one day late owing to the negligence of the claimant's solicitors. An important factor in the Court of Appeal's decision to disapply the time limit was the prejudice which the claimant would suffer, if suing her own solicitor rather than the original tortfeasor. The new defendant, i.e. the claimant's own solicitor, would know much more about the weak points of her case than the original defendant: see, *per* Parker L.J. at 980D–E and, *per* Leggatt L.J. at 983D–E.
[61] [1999] Lloyd's Rep. Med. 198.
[62] [1995] 6 Med. L.R. 32 at 35.
[63] [2000] Lloyd's Rep. Med. 247.
[64] *ibid.* at para.26.
[65] [2001] EWCA Civ 419, March 30, 2001.

application under s.33.[66] Secondly, it will sometimes enable patients (or their personal representatives) to begin clinical negligence actions after the expiry of the normal limitation period.[67] In such cases the court will apply the same general principles in exercising its discretion as were discussed in the previous paragraphs. However, the fact that the action is one for professional negligence may be an additional factor in the defendant's favour.

(f) *Fraud or Concealment*

5–099   Section 32(1) of the Limitation Act 1980 provides that where:

"(a) the action is based upon the fraud of the defendant; or
 (b) any fact relevant to the plaintiff's right of action has been deliberately concealed from him by the defendant[68] the period of limitation shall not begin to run until the plaintiff has discovered the fraud [or] concealment ... or could with reasonable diligence have discovered it."[69]

Section 32(2) provides:

"For the purposes of subsection (1) above, deliberate commission of a breach of duty in circumstances in which it is unlikely to be discovered for some time amounts to deliberate concealment of the facts involved in that breach of duty."

This form of wording appeared for the first time in s.7 of the 1980 Limitation (Amendment) Act, amending s.26 of the 1939 Act.[70] Section 7 was based on (although not identical to) the recommendations of the Law Reform Committee in its 21st Report.[71] The Law Reform Committee reviewed cases in which the then s.26 had been considered[72] and concluded that the provision should be reformulated so as to incorporate the feature of unconscionability but to "reproduce in a more intelligible form the construction placed on that section by the courts".[73]

---

[66] See Ch.11, para.11–331, below.
[67] See, e.g. *Hills v Potter* [1984] 1 W.L.R. 641 at 653–654.
[68] The claimant is entitled to rely on s.32(1)(b), even where he is making a claim for fraud: see *UBAF Ltd v European American Banking Corp* [1984] Q.B. 713 at 727.
[69] The parts relating to mistakes have been omitted from the quotation, as they are not specifically relevant to professional negligence actions.
[70] Consolidated by the Limitation Act 1980.
[71] Final Report on Limitation of Actions, Cmnd. 6923 (1977). Note that the Committee deliberately did not make any reference to the likelihood of the defendant's act remaining undiscoverable for a substantial period, or at all. See para.2.25 of the 21st Report.
[72] *Kitchen v Royal Air Force Association* [1958] 1 W.L.R. 563; *Clark v Woor* [1965] 1 W.L.R. 650; *Applegate v Moss* [1971] 1 Q.B. 406; *King v Victor Parsons & Co* [1973] 1 W.L.R. 29.
[73] See the Final Report, para.2.22. Given the nature of the 1980 Act, however, pre–1980 legislation and authorities should not be relied on in construing s.32, unless there is ambiguity in the wording: see the speeches of Lords Keith and Browne-Wilkinson and in *Sheldon v RHM Outhwaite (Underwriting Agencies) Ltd* [1996] A.C. 102 at 140E and 144E–G respectively, *cf., per* Lord Lloyd at 146D. See also *Cave v Robinson Jarvis & Rolfe (a firm)* [2002] UKHL 18; [2003] 1 A.C. 384 at [58], *per* Lord Scott (but see the approach of Lord Millett in the same case at [19]–[23]: three other members of the House of Lords, agreed with Lord Scott, only two with Lord Millett).

Effect of deliberate concealment some time after breach. In *Sheldon v RHM* **5–100**
Outhwaite (Underwriting Agencies) Ltd,[74] the House of Lords held by a bare
majority that s.32(1)(b) operates to postpone the start of the limitation period
even where the deliberate concealment occurs some time after accrual of the
cause of action. When time starts to run again, the claimant will have the full
limitation period, not just the balance that was left at the time of the deliberate
concealment.[75]

"Any fact relevant to the right of action." The claimant may only invoke **5–101**
s.32(1)(b) where the defendant has deliberately[76] concealed "any fact relevant to
the right of action". "Action" is defined broadly in s.38(1) of the Act. By virtue
of s.38(9) references in s.32 to a right of action include references to a cause of
action. The meaning of "any fact relevant to the right of action" was considered
by the Court of Appeal in *Johnstone v The Chief Constable of Surrey*.[77] The court
applied a "statement of claim" test; a fact is only relevant for the purposes of
s.32(1)(b) if it is one which has to be pleaded in order to constitute the cause of
action. "Any fact" means that if one relevant fact is deliberately concealed, then
the provision will apply and, if more than one relevant fact is concealed, then
time will only begin to run when all of them have been discovered (or could have
been discovered with reasonable diligence).[78]

When time runs again. Under s.32(1), time begins to run when the claimant **5–102**
discovers the fraud or concealment or could, with reasonable diligence, have
discovered it. The claimant bears the burden of proving that the fraud or
concealment could not have been discovered with reasonable diligence.[79] Guidance as to the test of reasonable diligence is to be found in the judgment of
Millett L.J. in *Paragon Finance Plc v DB Thackerar*[80]:

> "the question is not whether the claimant **should** have discovered the fraud sooner but
> whether they **could** with reasonable diligence have done so. The burden of proof is on
> them. They must establish that they **could not** have discovered the fraud without
> exceptional measures which they could not reasonably be expected to take ... in the
> course of argument May L.J. observed that the test was how a person carrying on a

---

[74] [1996] 1 A.C. 102.
[75] However, as held by the Court of Appeal in *Ezekiel v Lehrer* [2002] EWCA Civ 16; [2002] Lloyd's
Rep. P.N. 260. Once a claimant is aware of the relevant facts, a subsequent attempt to conceal them
from him did not allow the claimant to invoke s.32. The genie is not deemed to have been put back
in the bottle.
[76] The reason why a defendant deliberately concealed a fact relevant to the right of action is
irrelevant; what matters is whether he did so deliberately: see *Williams v Fanshaw Porter Hazelhurst
(a firm)* [2004] EWCA Civ 157; [2004] 1 W.L.R. 3185.
[77] *The Times*, November 23, 1992, CA (Civil Division) Transcript No.961 of 1992. See further *C v
Mirror Group Newspapers Ltd* [1997] 1 W.L.R. 131. The "statement of claim" test was also applied
by Gray J. in *McCarroll v Statham Gill Davis* [2002] EWHC 2558, QB; [2003] P.N.L.R. 19. His
decision was upheld on appeal: [2003] EWCA Civ 425; [2003] P.N.L.R. 25.
[78] *Halifax Plc v Ringrose & Co (a firm)* [2000] P.N.L.R. 483 at 494A–B, *per* Bell J. Cited in *Ezekiel
v Lehrer* [2001] P.N.L.R. 812, *per* Evans-Lombe J.
[79] *Paragon Finance Plc v DB Thakerar* [1999] 1 All E.R. 400. See also *Halifax Plc v Ringrose & Co
(a firm)* [2000] P.N.L.R. 492, *per* Bell J. at 493E. See also *Leeds & Holbeck Building Society v Arthur
& Cole (a firm)* [2002] P.N.L.R. 4.
[80] [1999] 1 All E.R. 400, at 418d.

business of the relevant kind would act if he had adequate but not unlimited staff and resources and were motivated by reasonable but not excessive sense of urgency. I respectfully agree."[81]

5–103   **Section 32(2): "Deliberate commission of a breach of duty".** The decision of the House of Lords in *Cave v Robison Jarvis & Rolf (a firm)*[82] confirmed the understanding of this provision which was generally held before the decision of the Court of Appeal in *Brocklesby v Armitage & Guest*,[83] which is now over-ruled. Lord Millett, with whom Lord Mackay and Lord Hobhouse agreed, said at [25]:

"In my opinion, section 32 deprives a defendant of a limitation defence in two situations: (i) where he takes active steps to conceal his own breach of duty after he has become aware of it; and (ii) where he is guilty of deliberate wrongdoing and conceals or fails to disclose it in circumstances where it is unlikely to be discovered for some time. But it does not deprive a defendant of a limitation defence where he is charged with negligence if, being unaware of his error or that he has failed to take proper care, there has been nothing for him to disclose."

Lord Scott, with whom Lord Slynn, Lord Mackay and Lord Hobhouse agreed, said at [58]:

"The relevant words in section 32 (2) are 'deliberate commission of a breach of duty . . . amounts to deliberate concealment of the facts involved in that breach of duty'. These are clear words of English. 'Deliberate commission of a breach of duty' is to be contrasted with a commission of a breach of duty which is not deliberate, a breach of duty which is inadvertent, accidental unintended—there are a number of adjectives that can be chosen for the purpose of the contrast, and it does not matter which is chosen. Each would exclude a breach of duty that the actor was not aware he was committing."

He went on to explain at [60] that under subsection (2):

"The claimant need not concentrate on the allegedly concealed facts but can instead concentrate on the commission of the breach of duty. If the claimant can show that the defendant knew he was committing a breach of duty, or intended to commit a breach of duty—I can discern no difference between the two formulations; each would constitute, in my opinion, a deliberate commission of the breach—then, if the circumstances are such that the claimant is unlikely to discover for some time that the breach

---

[81] In para.50 of her judgment in *Biggs v Sotnicks (a firm)* [2002] Lloyd's Rep. P.N. 331, Arden L.J., with whom Robert Walker and Aldous L.JJ. agreed, described this as "the classic statement of what section 32(1) requires". In the same case Robert Walker and Aldous L.J. declined to adopt a qualification of this passage of the judgment of Millett L.J. suggested by Crane J. in *UCB Home Loans v Carr* [2000] Lloyd's Rep. P.N. 754. On the facts of the case it was held that the claimant had sufficient knowledge more than six years before the issue of proceedings and so was out of time. The claimant's suggestion that time did not run until he received a copy of the defendant's solicitor's file was rejected: with reasonable diligence it would have been obtained more than six years before proceedings began.

[82] [2002] UKHL 18; [2003] 1 A.C. 384.

[83] [2001] 1 W.L.R. 599 (Note): discussed in para.5–075 of the fifth edition of this work.

of duty has been committed, the facts involved in the breach are taken to have been deliberately concealed for subsection (1)(b) purposes."

This decision is clear and requires no elaboration.

Section 32(2): "Circumstances in which it is unlikely to be discovered for   **5–104**
some time". The "it" referred to here must be the deliberate commission of a breach of duty. There is no case law concerning at what point in time the unlikelihood must exist, the degree of unlikelihood required or what period constitutes "some time". It is suggested that the unlikelihood must exist at the time of the breach, that it has to be significant (i.e. not fanciful), and that "some time" must mean a material time in the context of the period of limitation.

3. LIMITATION IN EQUITY

The application of the Limitation Act 1980 to claims for equitable relief is   **5–105**
somewhat complex. The applicable principles have been developed over a considerable period of time and many of the relevant cases on the subject were decided in the 19th century.[84] However, this area of law has been subjected to scrutiny in several recent cases in the Court of Appeal and the High Court. Those judgments contain discussion of the previous authorities and the relevant principles, and provide the focus of this section.[85]

For present purposes, the application of the Limitation Act 1980 to claims for equitable relief can be divided into two categories: (1) express application or (2) application by analogy. Each will be considered in turn.

Before considering those two above categories, a third category deserves brief   **5–106**
mention. This is where equity acts "in obedience" to the statute. Equity is said to act "in obedience" in cases where a legal right sought to be enforced in equity is time barred under the Act. The authorities do not consistently make the distinction between cases where equity acts in obedience, and cases where it acts by analogy. The distinction is also ignored in s.36 of the 1980 Act (below), which should be construed broadly so as to encompass both categories.[86]

(a) *Express Application of the Limitation Act 1980*

The 1980 Act contains express provisions in respect of the following equitable   **5–107**
claims:

---

[84] A matter about which two members of the Court of Appeal in *Cia de Seguros Imperio v Heath (REBX) Ltd* [2001] 1 W.L.R. 112 expressed dissatisfaction: see para.5–122, below.
[85] For a fuller discussion of limitation in the context of claims for equitable relief, see: Spry, *Equitable Remedies* (6th edn, Sweet & Maxwell, 2001), pp.244–245 and 416–427; Snell *Equity* (31st edn, Sweet & Maxwell, 2005), paras 5–16—5–18 and 13–20 and the Law Commission Report on Limitation of Actions (Law Com. 270), paras 2.39–2.47 and 2.52–2.66 (and proposals for reform at paras 4.94–4.137 and 4.158–4.196). The equitable doctrines of laches and acquiescence are discussed separately, at paras 5–126 to 5–140, below.
[86] See Spry *Equitable Remedies*, *op. cit.*, pp.417–418. The authorities discussed below concern the application of the Act by analogy.

(1) Actions in respect of trust property.[87]

(2) Actions claiming personal estate of a deceased person.[88]

(3) Actions to recover land.[89]

(4) Actions to redeem mortgaged land.[90]

5–108   The first of these is the most important in the context of claims against professionals. As will be seen, attempts by claimants to rely on s.21 against professional defendants have not met with success. Section 21 provides as follows:

"*Time limit for actions in respect of trust property*

(1) No period of limitation prescribed by this Act shall apply to an action by a beneficiary under a trust, being an action—

(a) in respect of any fraud or fraudulent breach of trust to which the trustee was a party or privy; or

(b) to recover from the trustee trust property or the proceeds of trust property in the possession of the trustee, or previously received by the trustee and converted to his use . . .

(3) Subject to the preceding provisions of this section, an action by a beneficiary to recover trust property or in respect of any breach of trust, not being an action for which a period of limitation is prescribed by any other provision of this Act, shall not be brought after the expiration of six years from the date on which the cause of action accrued."

This provision clearly applies to an action based upon a fraudulent breach of trust or to recover trust property or its proceeds from a trustee. In recent years, there have been attempts to extend its effect to other claims.[91]

5–109   Section 21 was considered by the Court of Appeal in *Paragon Finance Plc v DB Thakerar & Co (a firm).*[92] In two cases conjoined on appeal, the defendant solicitors acted for the claimant mortgage lender and for a number of borrowers in relation to the purchase and mortgage of several flats. The defendants were alleged to have known that the borrowers were sub-purchasers buying at prices significantly higher than the prices paid by the sub-vendor to the vendor, but to have failed to inform the claimant of this fact. The borrowers defaulted on the mortgages and the security proved to be of substantially less value than the sums advanced by the claimant. The claimant brought claims for breach of contract, negligence and breach of fiduciary duty, and, after expiry of six years from the

---

[87] Limitation Act 1980, s.21.

[88] *ibid.*, s.22.

[89] *ibid.*, ss.15, 20(2) and 20(4).

[90] *ibid.*, s.16.

[91] A claim against a company director who has acquired and disposed of the company's property is a claim against him as a trustee and falls within s.21(1)(b): *JJ Harrison (Properties Ltd) v Harrison* [2001] EWCA Civ 1467; [2002] 1 B.C.L.C. 162, CA. However, a claim against a company director for an account of secret or unauthorised profits does not, because there was no pre-existing fiduciary responsibility for the relevant property (i.e. the profits): see *Gwembe Valley Development Co Ltd v Koshy (No.3)* [2003] EWCA Civ 1048; [2004] 1 B.C.L.C. 131 at [119].

[92] [1999] 1 All E.R. 400.

last transaction, sought to amend their claim to allege fraud, conspiracy to defraud, fraudulent breach of trust and intentional breach of fiduciary duty.[93] The claimants submitted that no period of limitation applied to the claims for fraudulent breach of trust and intentional breach of fiduciary duty.

Millett L.J., delivering the judgment of the Court of Appeal, distinguished two **5–110** categories of constructive trusteeship. The first category covers cases where the defendant, although not expressly appointed as a trustee, assumes the duties of a trustee by a lawful transaction which is independent of, and precedes the breach of trust. The second category covers those cases where the trust obligation arises as a direct consequence of the unlawful transaction impeached by the claimant. The constructive trustee in the first category is a "real" trustee. His possession of the trust property is affected from the outset by the trust and confidence by means of which he obtained it. The "constructive trustee" in the second category is not in fact a trustee at all, although he may be liable to account as if he were. The constructive trust is a remedial mechanism by which equity gives relief for fraud.[94] Millett L.J. observed:

> " . . . any principled system of limitation should be based on the cause of action and not the remedy. There is a case for treating fraudulent breach of trust differently from other frauds, but only if what is involved really is a breach of trust. There is no case for distinguishing between an action for damages for fraud at common law and its counterpart in equity based on the same facts merely because equity employs the formula of constructive trust to justify the exercise of the equitable jurisdiction."[95]

Millett L.J. held that the defendants were fiduciaries and held the claimants' **5–111** money on a resulting trust for them pending completion. However, the claimants could not establish and did not rely on a breach of this trust. They alleged that the money which was obtained from them was obtained by fraud, and sought to raise a constructive trust in their favour in its place. The constructive trust was thus of the second type and s.21 of the Limitation Act 1980 did not apply. It followed that the defendants had an arguable limitation defence of which they should not be deprived by amendment.[96]

Millett L.J.'s twofold categorisation of constructive trusts was applied in *UCB* **5–112** *Home Loans v Carr*.[97] The claimant lender brought proceedings for damages and/ or equitable compensation for deceit, breach of trust, breach of contract and/or negligence against the defendant firm of solicitors in connection with two residential mortgage transactions in which the defendant had acted for the claimant. At trial of the preliminary issue on limitation Crane J. followed *Paragon Finance Plc v DB Thakerar & Co (a firm)*[98] and held that a constructive trust of the second kind did not fall within s.21 so that the claim in relation to it was time barred, because the claimants had failed to bring themselves with s.32 of the Limitation Act 1980.[99] However, he concluded that the claimants could, in

---

[93] The application of s.36 of the Limitation Act 1980 to the proposed amendment to allege intentional breach of fiduciary duty is discussed at paras 5–116 to 5–123, below.
[94] [1999] 1 All E.R. 400 at 408j–409f.
[95] *ibid*. at 414a–b.
[96] *ibid*. at 409g–h and 414e–g.
[97] [2000] Lloyd's Rep. P.N. 754.
[98] [1999] 1 All E.R. 400.
[99] See paras 5–099 to 5–104, above.

principle, rely on the first type of constructive trust given the terms of the solicitors' retainer. That claim for fraudulent breach of trust, if proved, would not subject to a limitation period by reason of s.21(1) of the Limitation Act 1980.[1]

5–113   The analysis in *Paragon Finance Plc v DB Thakerar & Co (a firm)*[2] was also applied in *Coulthard v Disco Mix Club Ltd*.[3] The claimant sued the defendants in respect of various agency and management agreements allegedly entered into for the commercial exploitation of dance mixes prepared and recorded by the claimant. The claimant's principal complaint involved allegations of under-accounting. That allegation formed the basis of claims for breach of duty to account, fraudulent breach of contract, breach of fiduciary duty and dishonest breach of fiduciary duty. The claimant also claimed that two of the defendants were liable to account as constructive trustees. Jules Sher Q.C., sitting as a Deputy High Court judge, cited passages of Millett L.J.'s judgment in *Paragon Finance Plc v DB Thakerar & Co (a firm)*[4] and continued:

> "What the *Paragon Finance* case makes clear is that the critical boundary in these cases lies between those cases where the defendant is a true trustee (be it of an express trust or a constructive trust) and those where he is not. In the *Nelson v Rye*[5] relationship, which is the same in this respect as Mr Coulthard's and Mr Prince [the third defendant]'s relationship, the relationship is not that of trustee and beneficiary. The touchstone of a true trusteeship is trust property . . . at no stage in Mr Coulthard's pleading or evidence is an asset or fund identified as an asset or fund which is or should have been held in a trustee capacity. This is why the dispute attracts the application of the six year limit under section 5 of the Act, directly or by analogy. Had there been a true trust of property alleged, the relevant section would have been section 21; and to the extent to which there was fraud, or a receipt by the trustee and conversion to his use, there would not have been any limitation defence."[6]

In the circumstances, the constructive trust which arose was merely remedial and s.21 did not apply.

5–114   The same disctinction was made in *Gwembe Valley Development Co Ltd v Koshy (No.3)*.[7] The managing director of a join venture company was found to have deliberately and dishonestly failed to disclose his personal interest in transactions with the company. The Court of Appeal took the opportunity to review recent Court of Appeal authority in this area.[8] The court concluded that claims against fiduciaries who were in a fiduciary relationship before the claim arose (rather than against those whose fiduciary obligation only arises by reason of their wrongful acts) fall within s.21 of the Limitation Act 1980 and will be

---

[1] *UCB Home Loans v Carr* [2000] Lloyd's Rep. P.N. 754. at 768–769. Crane J. stated that the evidence relating to the possible breach of trust of either kind had not been fully presented to him and as such, he could only express his views on the matter. Further, s.30(1) of the Trustee Act 1925 might prevent the claimants from establishing breach of trust against the defendants for the default of their employee in the absence of wilful default on their part, such default not being alleged.
[2] [1999] 1 All E.R. 400.
[3] [2000] 1 W.L.R. 707. See also *Clarke v Marlborough Fine Art (London) Ltd* (unreported, May 15, 2001, *per* Patten J.)
[4] [1999] 1 All E.R. 400.
[5] [1996] 1 W.L.R. 1378, *per* Laddie J.
[6] [2000] 1 W.L.R. 707 at 732A–D.
[7] [2003] EWCA Civ 1048; [2004] 1 B.C.L.C. 131 at [89].
[8] *ibid*. at [71]–[111].

subject to a six-year time limit unless they are either for a fraudulent breach (s.21(1)(a)) or for the recovery of property held on trust (s.21(1)(b)). Section 21 would not apply to claims against the second type of fiduciary, although some other limitation period might be applied by analogy. The Court of Appeal disapproved the decision of Sir Robert McGarry V.C. in *Tito v Waddell*[9] that the liability of a fiduciary to account for profits for breach of the self-dealing rule and the fair-dealing rule did not fall within s.21, and the decision of Harman J. in an earlier stage of the litigation before the Court of Appeal that the claim was simply one for an account and so not barred by the Limitation Act 1980.[10] The Court of Appeal summarised the application of the Limitation Act 1980 to claims against fiduciaries as follows[11]:

"The starting assumption should be that a six year limitation period will apply—under one or other provision of the Act, applied directly or by analogy—unless it is specifically excluded by the Act or established case-law. Personal claims against fiduciaries will normally be subject to limits by analogy with claims in tort or contract (1980 Act s.2, 5; see *Seguros*). By contrast, claims for breach of fiduciary duty, in the special sense explained in *Mothew*, will normally be covered by section 21. The six-year time-limit under section 21(3) will apply, directly or by analogy, unless excluded by subsection 21(1)(a) (fraud) or (b) (Class 1 trust)."[12]

(b) *Application of the Limitation Act 1980 by Analogy*

The relevant provision of the Limitation Act 1980 is s.36, which provides as follows: 5-115

"Equitable jurisdiction and remedies

    (1) The following time limits under this Act, that is to say—

        (a) the time limit under section 2 for actions founded on tort

        (b) the time limit under section 5 for actions founded on simple contract ... shall not apply to any claim for specific performance of a contract or for an injunction or for other equitable relief, except in so far as any such time limit may be applied by the court by analogy in like manner as the corresponding time limit under any enactment repealed by the Limitation Act 1939 was applied before 1 July 1940.

---

[9] [1977] Ch. 107 at 248–251.

[10] *Gwembe Valley Development Co Ltd v Koshy* [1998] 2 B.C.L.C. 613.

[11] [2003] EWCA Civ 1048; [2004] 1 B.C.L.C. 131 at [89].

[12] In the result, the claim for an account was excluded by 21(1)(a). In *Halton International Inc (Holdings) SARL v Guernoy Ltd* [2006] EWCA Civ 801; [2006] 1 B.C.L.C. 78 (para.22) Carnwath L.J. stated that, although the judgment in *Gwembe* (to which he was a party) proceeded on the premise that fraud was sufficient to bring the case within s.21(1)(a)) the ultimate decision may be better explained by reference to the alternative ground of fraudulent concealment (s.32 Limitation Act 1980). *Halton* concerned a shareholders' agreement that gave the defendant a power of attorney in respect of the claimant's shares in a company. It was held that even if the defendant had breached a fiduciary duty in exercising the power of attorney so as to cause the company to issue shares which he then acquired, those shares had not existed until the breach of duty complained of and therefore s.21(1)(b) could not apply.

(2) Nothing in this Act shall affect any equitable jurisdiction to refuse relief on the ground of acquiescence or otherwise."

5–116   The application of s.36 to claims for breach of fiduciary duty was considered in *Paragon Finance Plc v DB Thakerar & Co (a firm)*.[13] The claimants argued that a claim for account in respect of a breach of fiduciary duty was outside the scope of the 1980 Act, relying on *Nelson v Rye*.[14] Millett L.J. held that *Nelson v Rye* was wrongly decided, and, in any case irrelevant.[15] Millett L.J. stated:

> "the law on this subject has been settled for more than a hundred years. An action for an account brought by a principal against his agent is barred by the statutes of limitation unless the agent is a trustee of the money which he received: see *Burdick v Garrick* (1870) L.R. 5 Ch. App. 233, *Knox v Gye* (1872) L.R. 5 H.L. 656 and *Re Sharpe, Re Bennett, Mason and General Life Assurance Co v Sharpe* [1892] 1 Ch. 154. A claim for an account in equity, absent any trust, has no equitable element; it is based on legal, not equitable rights: see *How v Earl Winterton* [1896] 2 Ch. 626 at 693, *per* Lindley L.J. Where the agent's liability to account was contractual, equity acted in obedience to the statute: see *Hovenden v Lord Annesley* (1806) 2 Sch. & Lef. 607 at 631, *per* Lord Resedale. Where, as in *Knox v Gye*, there was no contractual relationship between the parties, so that the liability was exclusively equitable, the court acted by analogy with the statute. Its power to do so is implicitly preserved by section 36 of the 1980 Act ... Accordingly the defendant's liability to account for more than six years before the issue of the writ depended on whether he was, not merely a fiduciary (for every agent owes fiduciary duties to his principal), but a trustee, that is to say whether he owed fiduciary duties in relation to the money."[16]

5–117   Further explanation as to the application of s.36 was provided by Jules Sher Q.C., sitting as a Deputy High Court Judge in *Coulthard v Disco Mix Club Ltd*.[17] He held that most of the claims for breach of fiduciary duty were in reality claims for simple breach of the contractual duty to account, not breaches of fiduciary duty. As such, the claim was governed by s.5 of the Act:

---

[13] [1999] 1 All E.R. 400.

[14] [1996] 1 W.L.R. 1378, *per* Laddie J. The defendant, in his capacity as the claimant musician's business manager, collected the claimant's fees and royalties and accounted to him annually for his net income, after deduction of his own commission. After the relationship ended, the claimant claimed an account. Laddie J. recognised that the defendant's liability to account was contractual, but held that this was irrelevant because the claimant had chosen to sue for breach of fiduciary duty, rather than for breach of contract. The defendant's failure to account was either a breach of fiduciary duty, which fell outside the 1980 Act, or was a breach of constructive trust, which fell within s.21(1)(b) of the Act.

[15] In Millett L.J.'s judgment, *Nelson v Rye* was not on point because in that case the defendant's liability arose from his receipt of money in circumstances which made him an accounting party. In the *Paragon Finance* case, unless and until the underlying transactions were set aside, the defendants had duly accounted for the money advanced by the claimants. The claimants did not claim an account on the basis that the receipt of the money by the defendants made them accounting parties. Rather, they claimed equitable compensation for breach of fiduciary duty and sought all necessary accounts to enable that compensation to be quantified: see [1999] 1 All E.R. 400 at 416g–h.

[16] [1999] 1 All E.R. 400 at 415h–j. Millett L.J. doubted that the defendant in *Nelson v Rye* was a trustee of the money, since he was not obliged to keep the trust property separate from his own and apply it exclusively for the benefit of the claimant beneficiary. As such, he was not a (true) constructive trustee.

[17] [2000] 1 W.L.R. 707.

"The Act of 1980 cannot be side-stepped by describing [the claims for breach of contract] as claims in breach of fiduciary duty".[18]

In so far as the pleaded claims were in reality claims for breach of fiduciary duty—such as the claim that the "deliberately and dishonestly" withheld money due to the claimant—the question was whether the Act would be applied by analogy. The judge cited this passage from *Knox v Gye*[19]:

" . . . For where the remedy in equity is correspondent to the remedy at law, and the latter is subject to a limit in point of time by the Statute of Limitations, a court of equity acts by analogy to the statute and imposes on the remedy it affords the same limitation. This is the meaning of the common phrase, that a court of equity acts by analogy to the Statute of Limitations, the meaning being, that where the suit in equity corresponds with an action at law which is included in the words of the statute, a court of equity adopts the enactment of the statute as its own rule or procedure. But if any proceedings in equity be included in the words of the statute, there a court of equity, like a court of law, acts in obedience to the statute . . . where the court of equity frames its remedy on the basis of the common law and supplements the common law by extending the remedy to parties who cannot have an action at common law, there the court of equity acts in analogy to the statute, that is, it adopts the statute as the rule of procedure regulating the remedy it affords."[20]

He then said: **5–118**

"Two things emerge from these passages. First, where the court of equity was simply exercising a concurrent jurisdiction giving the same relief as was available in a court of law the statute of limitation would be applied. But secondly, even if the relief afforded by equity was wider than that available at law the court of equity would apply the statute by analogy where there was 'correspondence' between the remedies available at law or in equity.

Now, in my judgment, the true breaches of fiduciary duty—i.e. the allegations of deliberate and dishonest under-accounting, are based on the same factual allegations as the common law claims of fraud. The breaches of fiduciary duty are thus no more than the equitable counterparts of the claims at common law. The court of equity, in granting relief for such breaches would be exercising a concurrent jurisdiction with that of the common law . . .

[Counsel for the plaintiff] argues that the court of equity will apply the statute by analogy only where the equitable remedy is being sought in support of a legal right or the court of equity is being asked to apply a purely legal right, and he cites passages from *Hicks v Sallitt* (1853) 3 De G.M & G. 783 and *Hovenden v Lord Anersley* (1806) 2 Sch. & Lef. 697. I have no doubt that the principles of application by analogy to the statute (or, in obedience to the statute, as the Lord Chancellor preferred to describe it in its application to the facts of Hovenden's case) are quite apposite in the situations envisaged by [counsel for the plaintiff]. But, in my judgment, they have a much wider scope than that: one could scarcely imagine a more correspondent set of remedies as damages for fraudulent breach of contract and equitable compensation for breach of fiduciary duty in relation to the same factual situation, namely the deliberate withholding of money due by a manager to his artist. It would have been a blot on our

---

[18] [2000] 1 W.L.R. 707 at 728B–G, relying on the classification of fiduciary duties proposed by Millett L.J. in *Bristol & West Building Society v Mothew* [1998] Ch. 1 at 18.
[19] (1872) L.R. 5 H.L. 656.
[20] *ibid*. at 674–675.

jurisprudence if those self same facts gave rise to a time bar in the common law courts but none in the courts of equity."[21]

5–119   The application of s.36 of the Limitation Act 1980 arose in a very different context in *Cia de Seguros Imperio v Heath (REBX) Ltd.*[22] The claimant, an insurance and re-insurance company, brought proceedings against the defendant brokers, in respect of the latter's operation of various binding authorities. The claimant sought damages for breach of contract, negligence and breach of fiduciary duty in respect of various agreements, and for negligent misstatements, negligent misrepresentation and collateral warranty in respect of certain documents. At trial of the preliminary issue of limitation, Langley J. held that all the claims were time barred.[23] The defendant appealed in respect of the time limit in respect of fiduciary duty. The Court of Appeal upheld Langley J.'s judgment.[24]

5–120   Waller L.J., with whom Sir Christopher Staughton and Clarke L.J. agreed, accepted the claimant's submission that the claim included breaches of fiduciary duty independent from causes of action in contract or tort, so that ss.2 and 5 of the Limitation Act 1980 were not directly applicable. The question, then, was whether, by s.36, ss.2 and 5 were to be applied by analogy. In his judgment, in applying s.36, the court was not looking to see whether a limitation period had actually been applied to a dishonest breach of fiduciary duty by analogy before July 1, 1940, but rather asking whether it would have been applied had the issue arisen. The court must act "in a like manner" to a court sitting prior to July 1, 1940.[25] Waller L.J. held that the principles set out in relevant passages from *Knox v Gye*[26] and Spry's *Equitable Remedies*,[27] combined with authorities cited by the defendant,[28] supported the submission that equity would have taken the view that it should apply the statute by analogy to a claim for damages or compensation for dishonest breach of fiduciary duty:

"... what is alleged against the defendants as giving rise to a dishonest breach of duty are precisely those facts which are relied on for alleging breach of contract and tort. It

---

[21] [2000] 1 W.L.R. 707, at 730A–E. The judgment of Ebsworth J. in *Kershaw v Wheelan (No.2)*, *The Times*, February 10, 1997 might have assisted the claimant but was based on *Nelson v Rye* [1996] 2 All E.R. 186, which had been disapproved in *Paragon Finance Plc v DB Thakerar & Co (a firm)* [1999] 2 All E.R. 400. The approach in *Coulthard* was adopted by Morland J. in *Leeds & Holbeck Building Society v Arthur & Cole* [2001] Lloyd's Rep. P.N. 649 (claim for breach of fiduciary duty against a solicitor).

[22] [2001] 1 W.L.R. 112. Followed in *Leeds & Holbeck Building Society v Arthur & Cole* [2001] Lloyd's Rep. P.N. 649.

[23] [1999] Lloyd's Rep. I.R. 571. Langley J.'s judgment contains detailed consideration of the authorities and the arguments raised by counsel on both sides. For discussion of the first instance decision and, in particular, Langley J.'s implied acceptance of an exception to the principle that the statute of limitations applied by analogy to claims for breach of fiduciary duty, where the fiduciary validly received or held property for the person to whom he owes the duty, see McGee, "Fiduciary Duties and Limitation Periods" in [2001] 20 C.J.Q. 171.

[24] [2001] 1 W.L.R. 112.

[25] [2001] 1 W.L.R. 112 at 120A.

[26] (1872) L.R. 5 H.L. 656 at 674.

[27] 5th edn, Sweet & Maxwell, 1997, pp.419–420 (see now the same pages in the 6th edn).

[28] *Hovenden v Lord Annesley* (1806) 2 Sch. & Lef. 607; *Burdick v Garrick* (1870) L.R. 5 Ch. App. 233; *Friend v Young* [1897] 2 Ch. 421 and *North American Land & Timber Co Ltd v Watkins* [1904] 1 Ch. 242.

is true that there is an extra allegation of 'intention' but that does not detract from the fact that the essential factual allegations are the same. Furthermore the claim is one for 'damages'. The prayer for relief has now been amended with out leave to add a claim for 'equitable relief' but the reality of the claim is that it is one for damages, the assessment of which would be no different whether the claim was maintained as a breach of contract or continued simply as a dishonest breach of fiduciary duty claim."[29]

Counsel for the claimant had argued that the line to be drawn between those **5–121** cases where equity applied the statute of limitation by analogy and those where it did not was defined by the question whether equity was acting in its "exclusive" jurisdiction or its "concurrent" jurisdiction. He relied on the speech of Viscount Haldane L.C. in *Nocton v Lord Ashburton*[30] and the judgment of Millet L.J. in *Paragon Finance Plc v DB Thakerar & Co (a firm)*. Waller L.J. disagreed with both submissions. So far as *Nocton v Lord Asburburton* was concerned, the claimant was faced with the difficulty, as expressed by Langley J., that limitation was not in issue in that case, and, further, that *Knox v Gye*[31] was not cited. So far as *Paragon Finance* was concerned, Waller L.J. stated:

"In my view, it is fundamentally to misunderstand the judgment of Millett L.J. to suggest that he would have approved the view that a claim for *damages* brought against a fiduciary, even alleging a dishonest breach of that duty, would be free from limitation. In my view, his treatment of *Nelson v Rye* demonstrates that point and demonstrates beyond peradventure that the question whether equity was exercising its exclusive as opposed to its concurrent jurisdiction does *not* supply the definitive answer as to whether equity applied the statute by analogy."[32]

Waller L.J. cited a passage from Millett L.J.'s judgment in *Paragon Finance* **5–122** *Plc v DB Thakerar & Co (a firm)*[33] and concluded: "This made it clear that, even where equity was acting in its exclusive jurisdiction, the statute was applied by analogy".[34] Sir Christopher Staughton and Clarke L J., agreeing with Waller L.J., noted that it was not obvious why it was still necessary to have special rules for specific performance, or an injunction, or other equitable relief. If a distinction, for limitation purposes, still had to be drawn, it was to be hoped that a revised statute would enact with some precise where that distinction should be drawn, rather than leaving it to "research into cases decided long ago".[35]

---

[29] [2001] 1 W.L.R. 112 at 121D–E.
[30] [1914] A.C. 932 at 958.
[31] (1872) L.R. 5 H.L. 656.
[32] [2001] 1 W.L.R. 112 at 122B–D.
[33] [1999] 1 All E.R 400 at 415–416.
[34] [2001] 1 W.L.R. 112 at 122D–G.
[35] *ibid.* at 124. See also *Leeds & Holbeck Building Society v Arthur & Cole (a firm)* [2002] P.N.L.R. 4 where Morland J. held that s.5 of the Limitation Act 1980 applied by analogy to a claim for breach of fiduciary duty. In *Meara v Fox* [2002] P.N.L.R. 5, Pumfrey J. would have applied a six-year period of limitation to a claim for breach of fiduciary duty provided that to do so would not cause injustice which could not be avoided by application of other provisions of the Limitation Act, such as s.32. It is doubtful, however, whether all breaches of fiduciary duty can be said to be analogous to claims for breach of contract.

5–123   Where a period of limitation is now prescribed, but was not before July 1, 1940, then s.36 of the Limitation Act 1980 does not apply and that period will not be applied by analogy. An example is the two-year limitation for bringing a claim for contribution under the Civil Liability (Contribution) Act 1978.[36]

(c) Where there is no Analogy or Correspondence

5–124   It follows from the above that, whether equity is acting in its exclusive or auxiliary jurisdiction, statutory limitation periods will be applied by analogy where equity gives the same relief as was available at law, or where there is "correspondence" between the remedies available at law or in equity. Where there is no such equivalent or correspondent legal remedy, no analogy can be drawn so that, in the absence of an express statutory provision, the claim will not be subject to a limitation period.[37]

5–125   A claim to set aside a transaction on the grounds of undue influence would fall within this exception. The matter was considered, albeit indirectly, in *Clarke v Marlborough Fine Art (London) Ltd*.[38] The case concerned a claim by the executor of the estate of Francis Bacon in respect of various agreements between Francis Bacon and the defendants. The particulars of claim alleged breach of fiduciary duty, breach of duty to account under an agency agreement, and undue influence. The defendants argued that each of the claims based on breach of fiduciary duty and undue influence were time barred.[39] So far as the former was concerned, they relied on *Coulthard v Disco Mix Club Ltd*[40] and *Paragon Finance Plc v DB Thakerar & Co (a firm)*[41] and argued that the constructive trusts pleaded were remedial and the claims for breach of fiduciary duty underlying them were time barred. Patten J. was not satisfied that the claim was one which clearly fell into the remedial category, although the claims were difficult, and preferred to leave the question to trial. So far as the claim in undue influence was concerned, he said:

> "I am very far from satisfied that a Court of Equity would ever have barred a claim in undue influence by analogy with the statute. No case has been found in which this was done and in *Coulthard* Mr Sher Q.C. seems to have accepted (see p.725G) that the only available defences would be laches and acquiescence.[42] Further confirmation of this can

---

[36] *Hampton v Minns* [2002] 1 W.L.R. 1 Kevin Garnett Q.C. (sitting as a deputy High Court).
[37] The doctrines of laches and acquiescence may apply on the facts: see paras 5–126 to 5–140, below.
[38] May 15, 2001, *The Times*, July 5, 2001, *per* Patten J.
[39] The limitation point was one of several arguments raised by the defendants in support of their application to strike out the claim under CPR r.3.4(2)(a) and obtain summary judgment under Pt 24 of the CPR.
[40] [2000] 1 W.L.R. 707; see para.5–117, above.
[41] [1999] 1 All E.R. 400; see paras 5–109 to 5–111, above.
[42] Jules Sher Q.C. stated at follows: "Mr Coulthard claims in the alternative to set aside [the agreement] . . . on the grounds of undue influence and abuse of confidence. I see considerable problems ahead in terms of laches and acquiescence in this claim for equitable relief . . . " [2000] 1 W.L.R. 707 at 725G.

be found in *Allcard v Skinner* (1887) 36 Ch. D 145 at 174 and 186. I am not therefore prepared to strike out these claims on the basis that they are time barred."[43]

This reasoning would apply to other equitable claims which had no correspondence or analogy with those for which a period of limitation is specified in the Limitation Act 1980.

4. OTHER EQUITABLE DEFENCES: LACHES AND ACQUIESCENCE[44]

The equitable defences of laches and acquiescence are expressly preserved by **5–126** s.36(2) of the Limitation Act 1980.[45] The doctrine of laches concerns unreasonable delay on the part of the claimant in the commencement or prosecution of proceedings which, in all the circumstances, renders it inequitable to grant the equitable relief sought. The defence of acquiescence arises where the claimant assents or "lies by" in respect of the acts of another, and it is unjust in all the circumstances to grant the relief sought. This will be satisfied where, for example, the claimant has expressly or impliedly represented that he will not rely on his rights.[46] Both are doctrines of equity and apply to claims for equitable relief. Where a period of limitation is prescribed by statute, equity will not reduce the period which Parliament has stipulated.[47]

(a) *Laches*

The classic statement of the defence is to be found in *Lindsay Petroleum Co v* **5–127** *Hurd*[48]:

---

[43] In *Allcard v Skinner* (1887) 36 Ch. D 145, A sought to recover property transferred to S, on the grounds of undue influence. At 174, Cotton L.J. said:
"The defendant has not pleaded the Statute of Limitations, and I do not suggest that she could successfully have done so. In cases where the fact of undue influence depends on the result of conflicting evidence, delay must be important, but it cannot be disputed that the plaintiff was in a state which necessarily subjected here to a powerful influence . . . ."
Cotton L.J. then considered the application of the defence of laches. Lindley L.J. said, at 186:
"More than six years had elapsed between the time when the plaintiff left the sisterhood and the commencement of the present action. The action is not one of those to which the state of limitation in terms applied, nor is that statute pleaded. But this action very closely resembles an action for money had and received where laches and acquiescence are relied upon . . . "
[44] See, in general, Spry, *Equitable Remedies* (6th edn, Sweet & Maxwell, 2001), pp.224–244 and 431–444; Snell, *Equity* (31st edn, Sweet & Maxwell, 2005) para.5–19; Meagher, Gummow and Lehane, *Equity: Doctrines and Remedies* (4th edn, Butterworths, 2002) and Law Commission, *Limitation of Actions*, (Consultation Paper No.151), paras 9.12 to 9.20 and Law Commission Report on Limitation of Actions (Law Com. 270), paras 2.97–2.99.
[45] See para.5–115, above.
[46] The terms laches and acquiescence are used interchangeably and without consistency in the authorities and the textbooks. The interrelationship between laches, acquiescence and estoppel and the scope of each is a matter of academic debate, full exploration of which is beyond the scope of this work (see the comments of Nourse L.J. in the Court of Appeal in *Goldsworthy v Brickell* [1987] Ch. 378 at 410A–D.)
[47] But see para.5–136, below.
[48] (1874) L.R. 5 P.C. 221.

"Now the doctrine of laches in the courts of equity is not an arbitrary or technical doctrine. Where it would be practically unjust to give a remedy, either because the party has, by his conduct, done that which might fairly be regarded as a waiver of it, or where by his conduct or neglect he has, though perhaps not waiving that remedy, yet put the other party in a situation in which it would not be reasonable to place him if the remedy were afterwards to be asserted, in either of these cases lapse of time and delay are most material. But in every case, if an argument against relief, which otherwise would be just, is founded upon mere delay, that delay of course not amounting to bar by statute of limitations, the validity of that defence must be tried upon principles substantially equitable. Two circumstances, always important in such cases, are length of delay and the nature of the acts done during the interval, which might affect either party and cause a balance of justice or injustice in taking the one course or the other, so far as relates to the remedy."[49]

So, mere passage of time is not the only factor, as in limitation. Equity considers the claimant's acts as well to see whether it would now be equitable to allow him the relief sought.

5–128   The above passage was cited by Lord Blackburn in *Erlanger v New Sombrero Phosphate Co*,[50] who continued:

"I have looked in vain for any authority which gives a more distinct and definite rule that this; and, I think from the nature of the inquiry, it must always be a question of more or less, depending on the degree of diligence which might reasonably be required, and degree of change which has occurred, whether the balance of justice or injustice is in favour of granting the remedy or withholding it. The determination of such a question must largely depend on the turn of mind of those who have to decide, and must therefore be subject to uncertainty; but that, I think, is inherent in the nature of the inquiry."[51]

The flexibility of the defence was stressed more recently by Laddie J. in *Nelson v Rye*[52]:

"It can be misleading to approach the equitable defence of laches and acquiescence as if they consisted of a series of precisely defined hurdles which a litigant must struggle before the defence is made out ... these defences are not technical or arbitrary. The courts have indicated over the years some of the factors which must be taken into consideration in deciding whether the defence runs. Those factors include the period of delay, the extent to which the defendant's position has been prejudiced by the delay and the extent to which that prejudice was caused by the actions of the plaintiff. I accept that mere delay alone will almost never suffice, but the court has to look at all the circumstances, including in particular those factors set out above, and then decide whether the balance of justice or injustice is in favour of granting the remedy or

---

[49] (1874) L.R. 5 P.C. 221 at 239–40, *per* Lord Selbourne L.C.: applied by the Supreme Court of Canada in *Wewakym Indian Band v The Queen* (2002) 220 D.L.R. (4th) 1, by the Supreme Court of New Zealand in *Eastern Services Ltd v No.68 Ltd* [2006] NZSC 44 (in which an order for specific performance was upheld notwithstanding a delay of more than 20 years). Note, however, that courts are particularly reluctant to accept that an equitable interest in land can be lost or destroyed by mere inaction: *see* (inter alia) *Williams v Greatrex* [1957] 1 W.L.R. 31, CA, cited in *Eastern Services Ltd* (para.39).
[50] (1878) 3 App. Cas. 1218.
[51] *ibid.* at 1279. See also *Nwakobi v Nzekwu* [1964] 1 W.L.R. 1019, PC, where Viscount Radcliffe, giving the opinion of the Privy Council said: "Laches is an equitable defence, and to maintain it and obtain relief a defendant must have an equity which on balance outweighs the plaintiff's right."
[52] [1996] 1 W.L.R. 1378 (but see para.5–116, above).

withholding it. If substantial prejudice will be suffered by the defendant, it is not necessary for the defendant to prove that it was caused by the delay. On the other hand, the plaintiff's knowledge that the delay will cause such prejudice is a factor to be taken into account."[53]

In *Frawley v Neil*,[54] Aldous L.J., whilst recognising that previous authorities **5–129** might be relevant to the question whether it would be conscionable to unconscionable for the relief to be granted, emphasised that the modern approach does not require an inquiry into whether the circumstances of a particular case can be fitted within the confines of a preconceived formula derived from earlier cases. Rather, the court should adopt a broad approach, to ascertain whether it would in all the circumstances be unconscionable for a party to be permitted to assert his beneficial right.

It follows that it is neither possible nor desirable to formulate a precise test or **5–130** list of factors necessary for the defence to be satisfied. However, the authorities do provide some useful guidance as to what is meant by delay and the circumstances in which such delay might render the remedy unconscionable.[55] These will be discussed below.

(i) *Unreasonable Delay*

Length of delay. Whether the claimant's delay is unreasonable depends on all **5–131** the circumstances of the case. Delay which might otherwise be unreasonable might be reasonable depending upon the defendant's conduct or whether the parties are in negotiations.[56] However, mere protest by the claimant, where, following negotiations, the defendant continues to act in contravention of the claimant's rights will not justify delay.[57] It should be remembered that the crucial question is whether the delay is such as to render grant of the relief equitable. As such, even a short delay may trigger the defence, if the defendant has been prejudiced as a result.[58]

It has been suggested that where relief is sought in the exclusive jurisdiction **5–132** of the court, as opposed to its auxiliary or concurrent jurisdiction, a longer delay might be required before the defence of laches operates. This is because the claimant has no remedies at law, and denial of equitable relief is, in effect, a denial of his rights altogether.[59] However, there are contrary observations in *Habib Bank Ltd v Habib Bank AG Zurich*[60] in which counsel for the claimants

---

[53] [1996] 1 W.L.R. 1378 at 1392.
[54] *The Times*, April 5, 1999 (transcript CHANF 97/1573/3).
[55] The principles derived from the authorities are also relevant to the defence of acquiescence, discussed in paras 5–131 to 5–133, below.
[56] *Southcomb v Bishop of Exeter* (1847) 6 Ha. 213, followed in *McMurray v Spicer* (1868) L.R. 5 Eq. 527 at 537. See also *Re H. (Abduction: Acquiescence)* [1998] A.C. 72 at 88–89, HL(E).
[57] *Lehmann v McArthur* (1868) L.R. 3 Ch. 496.
[58] See, e.g. in an example rather removed from claims against professionals, where the claimant seeks specific performance of a contract the subject matter of which is of a fluctuating value, the claimant would be required to act more expeditiously than otherwise might be the case. See *Mills v Haywood* (1877) 6 Ch. D. 196; *Pollard v Clayton* (1855) 1 K. & J. 463 and *Wroth v Tyler* [1974] Ch. 30 at 53.
[59] See Spry, *op. cit.*, p.437, citing as an example *Knight v Bowyer* (1858) 2 De G.F & J. 421.
[60] [1981] 1 W.L.R. 1265, albeit in the context of acquiescence—the defences are so similar that the same must be said of laches.

sought to make such a distinction. Faced with arguments as to whether the claimant was asserting a legal or an equitable right, Oliver L.J., with whom Watkins and Stephenson L.JJ. agreed, stated:

> "I have to confess that I detect in myself, despite the erudition displayed by both counsel, a strong predilection for the view that such distinctions are both archaic and arcane and that in the year 1980 they have but little significance for anyone but a legal historian. For myself, I believe that the law as it has developed over the past 20 years has now evolved a far broader approach to the problem than that suggested by Mr Aldous and one which is in no way dependent upon the historical accident of whether any particular right was first recognised by the common law or was invented by the Court of Chancery."[61]

5–133   **Time from which delay judged.** Prima facie, the time from which the claimant's delay is judged is the time at which he became aware of the facts giving rise to a right to claim the equitable relief in question. In *Lindsay Petroleum Co v Hurd*,[62] it was said: "In order that the remedy should be lost by laches or delay, it is, if not universally, at all events ordinarily . . . necessary that there should be sufficient knowledge of the facts constituting the title to relief."[63] The extent of knowledge required depends on the circumstances of the case and the remedy claimed.[64] It is clear that time will not begin to "run" where the claimant is under undue influence.[65]

(ii) *Prejudice to the Defendant or a Third Party*

5–134   There are several bases on which it might be held that the claimant's delay has resulted in prejudice to the defendant or a third party, such that the remedy should not be granted.[66] Examples are:

(1) Where the defendant loses access to documentary evidence which affects his ability to defend himself, or the lapse of time renders it difficult for the defendant to recall material facts.[67]

(2) Where dispositions are made by the defendant or a third party and it would be unjust in all the circumstances to disturb them.[68]

---

[61] [1981] 1 W.L.R. 1265 at 1284–1285. The dicta was subsequently followed by the Court of Appeal in *Gafford v Graham* (1999) 77 P. & C.R. 73 and *Jones v Stones* [1999] 1 W.L.R. 1793 at 1744.

[62] (1874) L.R. 5 P.C. 221.

[63] *ibid.* at 241.

[64] See *Holder v Holder* [1968] Ch. 353 at 369 (approved on this point on appeal at 383), approving *Re Pauling's Settlement* [1962] 1 W.L.R. 86 at 108. Examples of cases in which it has been held that that knowledge of the relevant facts gives rise to a presumption of knowledge of the right to an equitable remedy are: *Stafford v Stafford* (1857) 1 De. G. & J. 193 at 202 and *Allcard v Skinner* (1887) 36 Ch. D. 145 at 188, *per* Lindley L.J. Authorities to the contrary are: *Cockerell v Cholmeley* (1830) 1 Russ. & M. 418 at 425; *Wilmott v Barber* (1880) 15 Ch. D. 96 at 105; *Re Howlett* [1949] Ch. 676 at 775.

[65] *Allcard v Skinner* (1887) 36 Ch. D 145; *Beale v Kyte* [1907] 1 Ch. 564.

[66] See, generally Spry, *op. cit.*, pp.230–235 and 434–438.

[67] *Bourne v Swan & Edgar* [1903] 1 Ch. 211 at 219 and *Watts v Assets Co Ltd* [1905] A.C. 317 at 333. See also *Tanna v Tanna* (unreported, May 25, 2001).

[68] Whether or not they were made for value.

(3) Where the defendant expends money or incurs and additional liability, or has let pass opportunities to mitigate his position.[69]

(4) Where, by delaying, the claimant has placed the defendant under unfair suspense or gained an unfair advantage.[70]

Where the defence is made out the claimant is not necessarily deprived of a **5–135** remedy altogether. For example, the claimant who seeks an injunction may be granted a limited injunction, or conditions may be imposed to ensure the defendant is not prejudiced. Alternatively, damages in lieu of the injunction may be obtained.[71]

(iii) *Relationship between Laches and The Limitation Act 1980*

It was held in *Re Pauling's Settlement*[72] that, there being an express statutory **5–136** provision providing a limitation period in respect of the claim, there was no room for the equitable doctrine of laches.[73] On the other hand, in *Kleinwort Benson Ltd v Sandwell BC*,[74] Hobhouse J. noted that it was common ground between the parties that (in so far as s.5 of the Limitation Act 1980 applied) a six-year limitation period should be applied by analogy under s.36 of the Act, and there remained jurisdiction to refuse relief on the grounds of laches.[75] It appears to be now settled that the equitable doctrine may apply even where there is an express limitation period: see the recent Court of Appeal decision in *Green v Gaul*.[76]

(b) *Acquiescence*

As mentioned above, there is considerable overlap between the defences of **5–137** laches and acquiescence. The principles underlying laches set out at paras 5–127 to 5–136, above apply equally to the defence of acquiescence, and will not be repeated. However, several authorities concerned specifically with the defence of acquiescence deserve mention. These are discussed below.

A leading case in this area is *Shaw v Applegate*.[77] The claimant sought to **5–138** enforce a covenant entered into in 1967 not to use his land as an "amusement arcade". Breaches of the covenant had occurred since 1971. The claimant brought injunction proceedings in 1973 but did not apply for an interlocutory

---

[69] See *Shaw v Applegate* [1977] 1 W.L.R. 970; *Fysh v Page* (1956) 96 C.L.R. 233.
[70] See *Allcard v Skinner* (1887) 36 Ch. D 145; *Lamshed v Lamshed* (1963) 109 C.L.R. 440 at 453 and *Pollard v Clayton* (1855) 1 K. & J. 462 (where the price of the subject matter of the contract was fluctuating). Delay will be particularly relevant where the claim is to a business; the claimant is not permitted to wait and see if the business prospers: *Re Jarvis* [1958] 1 W.L.R. 815.
[71] *Sayers v Collyer* (1884) 28 Ch. D 103 at 110; *Shaw v Applegate* [1977] 1 W.L.R. 970 at 978–979 and 981.
[72] [1961] 1 W.L.R. 86.
[73] *ibid.* at 115, *per* Wilberforce J. (approved by the Court of Appeal in [1964] Ch. 303 at 353).
[74] [1994] All E.R. 890.
[75] *ibid.* at 943d–e. See also *West Sussex Properties Ltd v Chichester DC* (ureported, June 28, 2000) at para.32. Presumably, the same remarks apply to the defence of acquiescence.
[76] [2006] EWCA Civ 1124. Chadwick L.J. (giving the judgment of the Court) found that, to the extent that Mummery L.J. had expressed the contrary view in *Gwembe v Koshy* [2003] EWCA Civ 1048; [2004] 1 B.C.L.C. 131, such view was "obviously wrong" (para.40).
[77] [1977] 1 W.L.R. 970.

injunction. The trial occurred in 1976. In the meantime, the defendant had continued to carry on his business. Buckley L.J. considered that it was unnecessary for the defendant to establish each of the five elements of the defence set out by Fry J. in *Willmott v Barber*.[78] In his judgment, the test to be applied was whether upon the facts of the case it would be dishonest or unconscionable for the claimant to rely on his rights.[79]

5–139   A similar approach was adopted in *Habib Bank Ltd v Habib Bank AG Zurich*[80]:

"[The defence] requires a very much broader approach which is directed rather than ascertaining whether, in particular individual circumstances, it would be unconscionable for a party to be permitted to deny that which, knowingly or unknowingly, he has allowed or encouraged another to assume to his detriment, than to inquiring whether the circumstances can be fitted within the confines of some preconceived formula . . . . ."[81]

This was said by the Court of Appeal in *Jones v Stones* to encapsulate the law.[82] So far as previous authorities were concerned, they assisted in showing was acts could be relevant in deciding whether it would be unconscionable to allow a party to proceed upon a particular basis, but did not lay down principles which had to be met and applied in every case. At the heart of estoppel or acquiescence lay an encouragement or allowance of a party to believe something to his detriment.

5–140   Finally, it should be noted that the fact that the claimant has acquiesced in a small and limited breach does not preclude him for all time from complaining about wider and more important breaches: see *Richards v Revitt*.[83]

---

[78] (1880) 15 Ch. D 105 at 106. The five elements were: (1) the defendant must have made a mistake as to his legal rights; (2) the defendant must have expended some money or must have done some act (not necessarily upon the claimant's land) on the faith of his mistaken belief; (3) the claimant must know of the existence of his own right which is inconsistent with the right claimed by the defendant; (4) the claimant must know of the defendant's mistaken belief of his rights; (5) the claimant must have encouraged the defendant in his expenditure of money or in the other acts which he has done, either directly or by abstaining from asserting his legal right.

[79] *ibid.* at 978. The judge held that it was not dishonest or unconscionable for the claimant to seek to enforce his rights, since he had been in doubt as to his legal rights. However, the defendant had been lulled into a false sense of security, so that the appropriate remedy was damages in lieu of an injunction.

[80] [1981] 1 W.L.R. 1265.

[81] *ibid.* at 128, *per* Oliver L.J., with whom Watkins and Stephenson L.JJ. agreed. See also *Taylors Fashions Ltd v Liverpool Trustees Co* [1982] Q.B. 133 at 155.

For a recent example of a successful defence of acquiescence see the decision of the British Columbia Court of Appeal in *Roeder v Blues* (2004) 248 D.L.R. (4th) 211. In that case lawyers acting for the beneficiary of a trust advised the trustee that the beneficiary had no objection to the early release of trust property, contrary to the express terms of the trust. The property was released and no complaint at all was made for about two months. It was only on the eve the expiration of the limitation period that proceedings were issued. In the circumstances it would have been "unfair and unjust" to permit the beneficiary to recover against the trustee.

[82] [1999] 1 W.L.R. 1739 at 1744H, *per* Aldous L.J. Aldous L.J. also approved dicta to the effect that the modern approach should not depend upon the historical accident of whether any particular right existed at common law or was invented by the Court of Chancery. See also *Gafford v Graham* (1999) 77 P. & C.R. 73 and para.5–132, above.

[83] (1877) 7 Ch.D 22 4 at 226.

5. CONTRIBUTORY NEGLIGENCE

Where a person suffers damage: **5–141**

> "as a result partly of his own fault and partly of the fault of any other person or persons . . . the damages recoverable in respect thereof shall be reduced to such extent as the court thinks just and equitable having regard to the claimant's share in the responsibility for the damage".[84]

In the context of professional negligence a successful plea of contributory negligence by the defendant is less common than in other areas of negligence. This is because the parties often do not stand on an equal footing (as they do in, say, claims arising from road traffic accidents). If the defendant makes a mistake, it may be difficult to say that the client was negligent not to spot it or correct its effect, unless the client is expected to be wiser than his own professional advisers.[85]

There are, of course, exceptions to the very general statements made in the **5–142** previous paragraph. First, the claimant may be particularly well placed to spot or correct the defendant's mistake.[86] Secondly, the claimant may do something quite separate which aggravates the consequences of the defendant's breach of duty. For example, a lender having received a negligently high valuation of the proposed security, may proceed to make a loan which would in any event be imprudent[87]; a patient may take larger doses than instructed of a drug which it was negligent of his doctor to prescribe.[88] In *De Meza v Apple*,[89] the claimants,

---

[84] Law Reform (Contributory Negligence) Act 1945, s.1(1). For a general discussion of contributory negligence, see G. Williams, *Joint Torts and Contributory Negligence* (Stevens & Sons, 1951), Pt Two. For an analysis of the three principal types of case in which contributory negligence arises, see N. Gravells, "Three Heads of Contributory Negligence" in (1977) 93 L.Q.R. 581.

[85] It is sometimes argued on behalf of a claimant that there can be no contributory negligence because it was the duty of the defendant to protect him from the very damage which he suffered. This argument was rejected by the High Court of Australia in *Astley v Austrust Ltd* (1999) 161 A.L.R. 155; [1999] Lloyd's Rep. P.N. 758. The Court stated that, while in some circumstances a claimant might be able to have relied upon the defendant to perform his duty and so not be held to have been contributorily negligent, there is no absolute rule. The question is always whether the claimant took reasonable care and while the role and duty of the defendant are relevant factors, they will not always be determinative.

[86] Thus in claims against auditors for failing to detect defalcations by company employees, it is quite often argued that the directors were similarly negligent. See, e.g. *Nelson Guarantee Corp Ltd v Hodgson* [1958] N.Z.L.R. 609 at 619–620; *Simonius Vischer & Co v Holt & Thompson* [1979] 2 N.S.W.L.R. 322; *Daniels v Anderson* (1995) 16 A.C.S.R. 607. *Morash v Lockhart & Ritchie Ltd* (1979) 95 D.L.R. (3rd) 647, the claimant was 75 per cent contributorily negligent for failing to keep himself informed about his insurance cover for a long period.

[87] See Ch.10, paras 10–168 to 10–174, below.

[88] See also *Grossman v Stewart* (1977) 5 C.C.L.T. 45, British Columbia Supreme Court: defendant prescribed drug for claimant's skin disorder, without warning her that there were risks involved in the prolonged use of the drug. The claimant continued to use the drug for a long period after defendant had stopped prescribing it. Damages were reduced by two-thirds for contributory negligence. See also *Fredette v Wiebe* (1986) 29 D.L.R. (4th) 534 and *Brushett v Cowan* (1990) 3 C.C.L.T. (2d) 195.

[89] [1974] 1 Lloyd's Rep. 508. The issue of contributory negligence did not arise on appeal: [1975] 1 Lloyd's Rep. 498.

a firm of solicitors, engaged the defendants, a firm of auditors, to complete some consequential loss insurance certificates. The defendants made certain mistakes which Brabin J. held amounted to breaches of duty, and as a result the claimants were under-insured when a fire occurred at one of their offices. However, Brabin J. considered that the claimants themselves had also been negligent in regard to their insurance. He apportioned responsibility 70 per cent to the defendants and 30 per cent to the claimants. Where a relevant fact is not communicated by the client to his professional advisers, the question commonly arises whether the client was negligent to withhold it or the defendant was negligent not to elicit it. If the client is an experienced businessman, the court is more likely to treat his omission as amounting at least to contributory negligence.[90]

(a) *Contributory Negligence and Contract*

5–143 One important question, until relatively recently the subject of conflicting English authority and still the subject of a divergence between the English and Australian courts, is whether the defence of contributory negligence is available when the claimant's claim is brought in contract alone.[91] If the defendant is in breach of an implied contractual duty to exercise reasonable care, does this amount to "fault" within s.1 of the Act?[92] Paull J. in *Quinn v Burch Bros (Builders) Ltd*[93] and Brabin J. in *De Meza v Apple*[94] held that it did, but in each case the Court of Appeal found it unnecessary to decide the point. The Supreme Court of Victoria, construing a statute which closely followed the English Act, came to the opposite conclusion.[95] In *Basildon DC v JE Lesser Properties Ltd*,[96] Judge Newey Q.C., after considering a number of English and Commonwealth authorities, concluded that in a claim for breach of contract apportionment of liability under the Law Reform (Contributory Negligence) Act 1945 was not permissible. This conclusion was based upon the fact that before the passing of the Act contributory negligence by the claimant was a complete defence to actions in tort, but not to actions in contract. Neill L.J. came to the same

---

[90] See, e.g. *Carradine Properties Ltd v DJ Freeman & Co* (1989) 5 Const. L.J. 267, discussed in Ch.11, below.

[91] The seminal academic discussion of this question is G. Williams, *Joint Torts and Contributory Negligence, op. cit.*, Ch.8. Williams argues forcefully that the Act ought to, and does, apply to actions for breach of contract: see pp.214–222.

[92] The word "fault" is defined in s.4 as meaning "negligence, breach of statutory duty or other act or omission which gives rise to a liability in tort or would, apart from this Act, give rise to the defence of contributory negligence".

[93] [1966] 2 Q.B. 370.

[94] [1974] 1 Lloyd's Rep. 508, QBD; [1975] 1 Lloyd's Rep. 498, CA.

[95] *Belous v Willetts* [1970] V.R. 45; *AS James Pty Ltd v CB Duncan* [1970] V.R. 705; *Read v Nerey Nominees Pty Ltd* [1979] V.R. 47. The point was considered, but not decided, by the New South Wales Court of Appeal in *Simonius Vischer & Co v Holt & Thompson* [1979] 2 N.S.W.L.R. 322. For a discussion of the earlier Australian cases, see J. Swanton, "Contributory Negligence as a Defence to Actions for Breach of Contract" in 55 A.L.J. 278. Swanton argues that the defence of contributory negligence ought to be available whether the action is framed in contract or tort. See now *Daniels v Anderson* (1995) 16 A.C.S.R. 607.

[96] [1985] 1 Q.B. 839.

conclusion in *AB Marintrans v Comet Shipping*[97] (an appeal from arbitrators to the Queen's Bench Division by way of a special case stated pursuant to s.21 of the Arbitration Act 1950). Neill L.J. commented that his conclusions as to the construction of the Act may well lead to unsatisfactory results in some cases. Claimants would be able to avoid the apportionment provisions by suing in contract, even when a claim in tort would be equally appropriate or more appropriate. The next decision on the point was that of Hobhouse J. in *Forsikringsaktieselskapet Vesta v Butcher*.[98] Hobhouse J. declined to follow the reasoning of Judge Newey in *Basildon DC v JE Lesser Properties Ltd*[99] and Neill L.J. in *AB Marintrans v Comet Shipping*.[1] Instead, he divided the cases where the problem arises into three categories:

"(1) Where the defendant's liability arises from some contractual provision which does not depend on negligence on the part of the defendant.
(2) Where the defendant's liability arises from a contractual obligation which is expressed in terms of taking care (or its equivalent) but does not correspond to a common law duty to take care which would exist in the given case independently of contract.
(3) Where the defendant's liability in contract is the same as his liability in the tort of negligence independently of the existence of any contract."

Hobhouse J. held that the case before him fell into category (3) and that in such a case liability could be apportioned under the Act, except where this was expressly prohibited by some term of the contract between the parties. The Court of Appeal (one of whose members, significantly, was Neill L.J.) upheld Hobhouse J.'s conclusion and the reasoning on which it was based.[2] This analysis was applied by Alliott J. in *Lipkin Gorman v Karpnale Ltd*[3] and upheld by the Court of Appeal.[4] In *Tennant Radiant Heat Ltd v Warrington Development Corp*,[5] the Court of Appeal held that contributory negligence had no application in the context of a claim for breach of a repairing covenant. This decision is consistent with *Forsikringsaktieselskapet Vesta*, since such a claim would fall into category (1).[6] The Court of Appeal applied the same analysis in *Barclays Bank Plc v Fairclough Building Ltd*.[7] The New Zealand Court of Appeal

5–144

---

[97] [1985] 1 W.L.R. 1270.
[98] [1986] 2 All E.R. 488.
[99] [1985] 1 Q.B. 839.
[1] [1985] 1 W.L.R. 1270.
[2] [1989] A.C. 852. See the judgment of O'Connor L.J. at 860–867 and Neill L.J. at 875 and Sir Roger Ormrod at 879. This issue did not arise on the subsequent appeal by the reinsurers to the House of Lords.
[3] [1987] 1 W.L.R. 987 at 997.
[4] [1989] 1 W.L.R. 1340 at 1360.
[5] [1988] 1 E.G.L.R. 41.
[6] This case was decided six weeks after the Court of Appeal's decision in *Forsikringsaktieselskapet Vesta* and it appears that only a brief report of the earlier decision was available.
[7] [1995] Q.B. 214. Since the defendant was in breach of a strict contractual duty, this was a category (1) case and the defence of contributory negligence was held not to be available. For an example of a category (2) case where a defence of contributory negligence was not available see *Raflatac v Eade* [1999] 1 Lloyd's Rep. 506, *per* Colman J. (defendant contractor owed contractual duty to exercise reasonable skill and care, but no duty of care in tort to avoid economic loss).

considered these questions obiter in *Mouat v Clarke Boyce*[8] in relation to the
New Zealand Contributory Negligence Act 1947. It favoured the approach
adopted by the English Court of Appeal.[9] However, the High Court of Australia
has declined to follow Hobhouse J. and the Court of Appeal, holding in *Astley v
Austrust Ltd*[10] that s.27A of the South Australian Wrongs Act 1937 (which is to
similar effect as s.1 of the Law Reform (Contributory Negligence) Act 1945) did
not allow the court to reduce damages for breach of a contractual duty which was
concurrent with the tortious duty of care owed by a solicitor. In view of the
importance of the issues involved and the division of judicial opinion to which
they have given rise, the matter cannot be regarded as finally resolved until it has
been considered by the House of Lords.[11]

(b) *Application to Professional Negligence*

5-145   The debate as to the applicability of the Law Reform (Contributory Negligence)
Act 1945 to actions for breach of contract is of considerable importance in the
context of professional negligence. In the great majority of such cases the client
has concurrent claims against his professional adviser both in contract and tort.[12]
It would seem both unjust and illogical if the client is able to escape the
consequences of his own negligence by suing in contract alone. In the ordinary
way professional negligence cases fall into category (3), as defined by Hobhouse
J. in *Forsikringsaktieselskapet Vesta v Butcher*.[13] As the law now stands, therefore, in most professional negligence actions, whether the claimant chooses to
sue in contract or tort or both, the defence of contributory negligence is available.

5-146   The decision of the House of Lords in *Banque Bruxelles Lambert SA v Eagle
Star Insurance Co Ltd*[14] identifies a two-stage inquiry which will be appropriate
in many professional negligence actions: (i) What is the overall damage which P
has suffered as a result of acting on D's report? (ii) Which part of that loss is
recoverable in damages against D? The interaction between this approach to

---

[8] [1992] 2 N.Z.L.R. 559.
[9] See the judgment of Cooke P. at 564, *ibid*. Although the underlying decision on liability has now
been reversed (see [1994] 1 A.C. 428), this separate judgment on contributory negligence was not
considered by the Privy Council. The New Zealand Court of Appeal had earlier held that contributory
negligence applied to a claim for breach of fiduciary duty: *Davy v Mead* [1987] 2 N.Z.L.R. 443.
[10] [1999] H.C.A. 6, reported at (1999) 161 A.L.R. 155 and [1999] Lloyd's Rep. 758 This decision is
discussed by Blom, "Contributory Negligence and Contract—A Canadian view of *Astley v Austrust
Ltd*" in [2000] Tort Law Rev. 70. As he explains, the Canadian statutory provisions are different,
antedating the Law Reform (Contributory Negligence) Act 1945, although different Provinces have
different provisions.
[11] In *Standard Chartered Bank v Pakistan National Shipping Corp (Nos 2 and 4)* [2002] UKHL 43;
[2003] 1 A.C. 959, the House of Lords held that a defence of contributory negligence only arose
under the Law Reform (Contributory Negligence) Act 1945 in cases in which it would have provided
a complete defence of contributory negligence before that Act came into force. The claim in that case
was in deceit, so that the position in contract was not decided.
[12] See Ch. 2, paras 2–103 to 2–111, above.
[13] [1986] 2 All E.R. 488 and [1989] A.C. 852.
[14] [1997] A.C. 191: see Ch. 3, para.3–002, above.

damages and s.1 of the Law Reform (Contributory Negligence) Act 1945 gave rise to disagreement between first instance judges. This was resolved by the decision of the House of Lords in *Platform Home Loans Ltd v Oyston Shipways Ltd*.[15] "Damage" for the purpose of s.1 means the overall loss, not merely that part for which the defendant is liable on *Banque Bruxelles Lambert* principles. In cases where the whole of the overall damage is recoverable in damages against the defendant (subject to contributory negligence), there is no difficulty. However, where only part of the overall loss is recoverable in damages, then it is not just and equitable to reduce the damages twice, once to take account of the *Banque Bruxelles Lambert* decision and then again for contributory negligence: the total amount of damage should be reduced and then damages awarded at whichever is the lower of that figure and the damages recoverable on *Banque Bruxelles Lambert* principles. The same principles apply in respect of any profession whose function it is to produce reports.

(c) *Methods by which Claimants might seek to Circumvent a Plea of Contributory Negligence*

The plea of contributory negligence is not available in answer to a claim for **5–147** deceit.[16] Thus where the facts warrant pleading deceit, as opposed to mere negligence, the defence of contributory negligence can be pre-empted by this means. However, before proceeding to plead and prove a claim for deceit, the claimant's advisers should consider the possible impact upon the defendant's insurance arrangements. An alternative possible method of forestalling the defence of contributory negligence would be to base the claim upon some specific term in the retainer which does not require the use of reasonable care.[17] The Court of Appeal stated in *Barclays Bank Plc v Fairclough Building Ltd*[18] that it was "at least arguable" that contributory negligence could be defeated by proving a failure to possess the requisite skill, as opposed to a failure to exercise that skill. This passage is obiter and, it may be thought, the reasoning is not attractive. The gravamen of the claim is that the defendant did not deploy reasonable skill and care in performing his task. Whether the defendant lacked the requisite abilities or simply did not bother to use them is at one remove from the real complaint. It is part of the background. Nor is the distinction easy to draw in practice. Suppose the defendant had part of the requisite skill and could have acquired the rest by consulting a reference book from his shelf? It may be thought undesirable that claimants should avoid the consequences of their own negligence by means of such rarified distinctions.

---

[15] [2000] 2 A.C. 190. Discussed by Dugdale, "Contributory Negligence applied to Economic Loss: *Platform Home Loans* and *Fancy & Jackson*" in (1999) 62 M.L.R. 281 and by Stapleton, "Risk Taking by Commercial Lenders" in (1999) 115 L.Q.R. 527.
[16] *Standard Chartered Bank v Pakistan National Shipping Corp (Nos 2 and 4)* [2002] UKHL 43; [2003] 1 A.C. 959; *Alliance & Leicester Building Society v Edgestop Ltd* [1993] 1 W.L.R. 1462.
[17] *Bristol & West Building Society v Kramer & Co, The Times*, February 6, 1995, but see Ch.2, para.2–010, above.
[18] [1995] Q.B. 214 at 222–223.

(d) *Attribution*[19]

5-148 Where two professionals have been negligent, the question may arise whether either can establish contributory negligence on the basis that the other's mistakes should be "imputed" to the client. Whilst for certain purposes the conduct of an agent is treated as that of the principal, such an argument is unattractive in this context. Proportionate liability is not part of English law and has been rejected by the Law Commission.[20] It should not be introduced by this circuitous means. The appropriate course for a defendant is to sue the agent for contribution. In *Henderson v Merrett Syndicates Ltd (No.2)*,[21] Cresswell J. rejected a contention by the defendant auditors that the negligence of the managing agents should be "attributed" to the claimant names and thus constitute contributory negligence. Whilst this decision was based upon the "unusual and complex structure of Lloyd's", it may perhaps be followed on a more general basis.[22]

---

[19] This question has arisen in the context of claims against auditors and is discussed in Ch.17, paras 17–149 to 17–152.

[20] See para.5–002, above.

[21] [1996] P.N.L.R. 32.

[22] The question of attribution in the context of contributory negligence is discussed in depth by A. Bartlett Q.C., "Attribution of contributory negligence: agents, company directors and fraudsters" in (1998) 114 L.Q.R. 460. Bartlett supports the "both ways" test, viz.:

> "The fault of the connected person should be attributed to the plaintiff as contributory negligence where—and only where—the relationship between them is such that the plaintiff would in principle be liable to a third party because of errors of the connected person."

Bartlett argues (a) that the actual results of most reported cases can be reconciled with this test and (b) that this approach can be justified on policy grounds. He is accordingly critical of the sparse reasoning which supports the decision in *Henderson v Merrett Syndicates Ltd (No.2)* [1996] P.N.L.R. 32.

CHAPTER 6

LITIGATION

1. GROUP ACTIONS

(a) *General*

Group actions, also known as multi-party actions, and as class actions in other **6–001** jurisdictions, concern the litigation of a number of claims having some similarity, usually the same claimant or defendants and similar legal and factual issues, which are administered together by the same judge. There has been an upsurge in group actions during the 1980s and 1990s. They may cover a large variety of types of claims, including actions against employers for personal injury,[1] litigation alleging cancer from industrial plants,[2] transport disaster claims,[3] claims for environmental nuisance,[4] perhaps most well known of all a number of pharmaceutical product liability claims,[5] other product liability actions,[6] claims against

---

[1] The British Coal Vibration White Finger Litigation and the Respiratory Disease Litigation, which mostly resulted in success for the claimants.

[2] The Sellafield childhood leukemia cases, which failed on causation in *Reay and Hope v British Nuclear Fuels Plc* (1994) 5 Med. L.R. 1; *B & D v X Co.*

[3] See, e.g. the *Herald of Free Enterprise* disaster of 1987 (where three arbitrators set landmark awards for post-traumatic stress disorder), and the Hillsborough football stadium disaster of 1989.

[4] The Docklands Nuisance actions (some of which settled, some of which were withdrawn).

[5] The Pertussis Vaccine Litigation (see *Loveday v Renton* [1990] 1 M.L.R. 117, where the case effectively ended with failure by the claimants on a preliminary issue on causation); the Opren Litigation (where proceedings were discontinued); the Myodil Litigation (where a core cohort achieved settlements), the large and expensively unsuccessful Benzodiazepene Litigation; the Norplant Litigation (where legal aid was withdrawn shortly before trial) and the Hepatitis C Litigation where the claimants succeeded at trial (reported as *A v National Blood Authority* [2001] 3 All E.R. 289). In many of these cases, causation has been the key issue on which the claimants failed.

[6] See, e.g. the Tobacco Litigation, which ended in failure for the claimants following a preliminary issue on limitation.

arms of the state for negligence causing personal injury,[7] and financial loss by investors from alleged negligent misstatements in prospectuses.[8] There have also been a number of professional negligence group actions, which will be briefly considered below. As a result of all this litigation, there has been a great deal of experience in how to manage and litigate group actions. Some of it is reflected in reported decisions and in the provisions for group actions in the Civil Procedure Rules ("CPR"), but many of the techniques are necessarily of a more informal kind which is best found in the leading books on the subject.[9]

(b) *Professional Negligence*

6–002 A number of group actions have arisen in the field of professional negligence. The most prominent are as follows. The massive losses suffered by names at Lloyd's in the late 1980s and early 1990s gave rise to a number of group actions against members' agents, managing agents and underwriters.[10] The fall in the property market at about the same time led to many actions by lenders against the solicitors and surveyors they had retained, and there were two multi-party actions against solicitors brought by two of the building societies.[11] Home Income Plans, a scheme to raise income on the strength of mortgages which caused clients loss, led to unsuccessful litigation by the assignee of the investors against many firms of solicitors.[12] Several of the pharmaceutical group actions involve subsidiary allegations of clinical negligence,[13] and there have been clinical negligence group actions.[14] Group litigation is currently underway involving claims against solicitors arising out of the collapse of the Accident Group concerning monitoring of a large number of personal injury claims.

(c) *Procedure*

6–003 CPR Pt 19 rr.10–15, and the accompanying Practice Direction, are concerned with group litigation. No similar body of rules existed before 2000. The rules can be summarised as follows. A court can make a Group Litigation Order, ("GLO"), where there are or are likely to be a number of claims giving rise to

---

[7] The HIV Haemophilac Litigation, which was settled following a preliminary hearing in the Court of Appeal (reported at [1996] P.N.L.R. 290); the Creutzfeldt Jakob Disease Litigation, where the claimants succeeded in establishing liability (reported at [1996] 7 Med. L.R. 309).

[8] The Lockton Litigation.

[9] See Hodges, *Multi-Party Actions* (Oxford, 2001) and Day, *Multi-Party Actions* (LAG, 1996). While the latter was written long before the new Civil Procedure Rules, it still provides valuable insights, and it includes helpful pleadings and orders in the appendices.

[10] See Ch.16, below.

[11] The Bristol and West Building Society and the Nationwide Building Society. See further Ch.10, paras 10–208 *et seq.*

[12] *Investors Compensation Scheme Ltd v West Bromwich Building Society* [1999] Lloyd's Rep. P.N. 496; see further Ch.10, para.10–164.

[13] See, e.g. the HIV Haemophiliac Litigation and the Hepatitis Litigation.

[14] See, e.g. the cervical screening cases brought against East Kent HA.

GLO issues.[15] A GLO must[16] contain directions about the establishment of a register,[17] specify the GLO issues to identify the claims, and identify a management court. Judgments or orders in one claim are generally binding on other claims.[18] Directions may be given[19] varying the GLO issues, providing for tests claims to proceed,[20] appointing lead solicitors,[21] specifying what is to be included in a statement of case,[22] and providing for a cut-off-date for joining the litigation and for publicising the GLO.[23] Co-ordinated litigation may be carried out outside the framework of GLOs in appropriate cases, for instance by the use of representative actions.

The new rules only lay down, and can only lay down, a very broad framework, **6–004** as the circumstances of potential group actions can be very diverse. A fundamental issue in many cases is likely to be whether the group action should progress by deciding generic issues without investigating any or many individual cases first, or whether individual cases should be properly pleaded and scrutinised before deciding on which generic issues should be tried.[24] In general, a high degree of co-operation is required between the lawyers for the opposing sides,[25] and judges have had to be active and interventionist in these type of actions long before the Woolf reforms.

(d) Costs

CPR r.48.6A provides special rules where a court has made a GLO.[26] The **6–005** fundamental rules are that any order for common costs against group litigants will generally impose on an individual claimant several liability for an equal proportion of those costs, and that the paying party will also generally be liable for the individual costs of his claim and an equal proportion of the common costs. These rules reflect the general practice which had already developed in a number

---

[15] CPR r.19.11(1). No guidance is given as to how the court should exercise the discretion. The Practice Direction at paras 2.1–3.9 sets out a number of preliminary steps which must be undertaken before applying for a GLO, the information required for making an application, and which judges must approve any order.

[16] CPR r.19.11(2).

[17] While para.6.5 of the Practice Direction envisages that this will normally be kept by the court, it may well be more convenient for a lead solicitor to do so.

[18] CPR r.19.12.

[19] CPR r.19.13.

[20] See also para.15 of the Practice Direction.

[21] This is a necessary provision of last resort. Selection of a lead solicitor in almost always voluntary, and para.2.2 of the Practice Direction assists in this process.

[22] There is often provision for "Master pleadings", and para.14.1 of the Practice Direction envisages that "Group Particulars of Claim" may be provided.

[23] See also para.13 of the Practice Direction.

[24] See Hodges, *op. cit.*, pp.15–18.

[25] For instance, in the selection of test cases. In general, it will be in the interests of all parties for the test cases to include as many contentious issues as reasonably possible, and to include both strong and weak cases, so that judgment in those test cases will provide the maximum assistance in settling the remaining cases.

[26] See further the notes to the White Book accompanying CPR r.48.6A.

of cases.[27] The costs of test cases are generally generic costs. It is common in practice for claimants joining a group action to become immediately responsible for an equal proportion of generic costs. When a claim is removed from the group register, the court may order that the litigation pays a proportion of the common costs to that date.[28]

2. EXPERT EVIDENCE

(a) The Functions of the Expert Witness

6–006   In the context of liability issues in professional negligence actions, the expert witness commonly performs two functions. First, he sets out and explains the relevant technical matters, e.g. the relevant principles of engineering and how they were applied to the building project in question, or the principles of valuation and how they were applied in the defendant surveyor's valuation or report. To this extent, the expert witness is performing a didactic role: he is explaining the technical aspects of the case in language comprehensible to laymen. Expert evidence of this sort may be largely or wholly uncontroversial. For example, the expert witnesses in a clinical negligence case may agree that the claimant's condition is the result of an adverse reaction to a new drug administered by the defendant. The court must understand and resolve any conflicts between expert evidence of this sort before it can consider the question of negligence. Where there is a dispute on questions of technical fact, the court may prefer the theory advanced by one expert witness over that advanced by another, but it will not assume technical expertise: it will not substitute a theory of its own where that theory is not supported by the evidence of any of the expert witnesses.[29]

6–007   The second function of the expert witness is to assist the court in deciding whether the acts or omissions of the defendant constituted negligence. He will recount the current state of knowledge at the material time and the standards

---

[27] See, e.g. *Davies (Joseph Owen) v Eli Lilly & Co* [1987] 1 W.L.R. 1136, CA; *Nationwide Building Society v Various Solicitors (No.4)* [2000] Lloyd's Rep. P.N. 70. Further guidance on costs can be found in the cases referred to in the White Book at paras 19.0.10 and 48.6A, and in particular *Sayers v Merck SmithKline Beecham Plc* [2001] EWCA Civ 2017; [2002] 1 W.L.R. 2274, CA, and *AB v Liverpool City Council (Costs)* [2003] EWHC 1539, QB.

[28] But this may well be unfair to the claimant, see *Sayers v Merck SmithKline Beecham Plc* [2001] EWCA Civ 2017; [2002] 1 W.L.R. 2274, CA.

[29] In the clinical negligence case *McLean v Weir* (1977) 3 C.C.L.T. 87 in the British Columbia Supreme Court, Gould J. summarised the position in a manner which, it is submitted, is equally applicable in England (at 101):

"It is true that the court may accept in whole or in part or reject in whole or in part the evidence of any witness on the respective grounds of credibility or plausibility, or a combination of both. But in technical matters, unlike in lay matters within the traditional intellectual competence of the court, it cannot substitute its own medical opinion for that of qualified experts. The court has no status whatsoever to come to a medical conclusion contrary to unanimous medical evidence before it even if it wanted to, which is not the situation in this case. If the medical evidence is equivocal, the court may elect which of the theories advanced it accepts. If only two medical theories are advanced, the court may elect between the two or reject them both; it cannot adopt a third theory of its own, no matter how plausible such might be to the court."

ordinarily observed in his profession, including any relevant general and approved practice or differing schools of thought. Expert evidence that a reasonably competent member of the defendant's profession would not have committed the act or omission in question is generally necessary before the court will find that he was negligent. Thus in *Sansom v Metcalfe Hambleton and Co*[30] Butler-Sloss L.J. said[31]:

> " . . . a court should be slow to find a professionally qualified man guilty of a breach of his duty of skill and care towards a client (or third party) without evidence from those within the same profession as to the standard expected on the facts of the case and the failure of the professionally qualified man to measure up to that standard."

The evidence of a professional accused of negligence as to why he believes that his conduct did not fall below the standard of reasonable care and skill is admissible, but the fact that his evidence lacks the objectivity of an independent expert may reduce the weight given to it.[32]

(b) *Cases where Expert Evidence is Not Required*

In two categories of cases, supportive expert evidence is not necessary for a **6–008** finding of negligence. The first category is solicitors' negligence cases. Expert evidence is rarely admitted upon the question whether a solicitor has discharged his duty of skill and care. The rationale appears to be that the courts themselves possess the necessary professional expertise to decide the question. In *Midland Bank v Hett, Stubbs & Kemp*,[33] Oliver J. criticised the practice of calling solicitors to give evidence as to what they would have done in a particular situation and doubted that such evidence was admissible.[34] This dictum was approved and applied by the Court of Appeal in *Bown v Gould & Swayne*,[35] in which the Court upheld an order disallowing the evidence of a conveyancing expert in a solicitors' negligence action. Millett L.J. commented that if a judge needed assistance with regard to conveyancing practice, the proper way was to cite the relevant textbooks.[36]

The second category of cases where a finding of negligence may be made **6–009** notwithstanding expert evidence in support of the defendant's conduct or the lack

---

[30] [1998] P.N.L.R. 542. The defendant surveyor's appeal from a finding that he had negligently conducted a survey was allowed on the basis that the only relevant expert evidence called by the claimant had been from a structural engineer.

[31] *ibid.* at 549.

[32] *DN v Greenwich LBC* [2004] EWCA Civ 1659.

[33] [1979] Ch. 384 at 402.

[34] *ibid.* This passage is quoted in full and discussed further in Ch.10, para.10–143, below.

[35] [1996] 1 P.N.L.R. 130.

[36] See *May v Woollcombe Beer & Watts* [1999] P.N.L.R. 283: expert evidence held admissible in relation to conveyancing matters where there was no answer provided by textbooks; *Archer v Hickmotts* [1997] P.N.L.R. 318: expert evidence concerning advice which should have been given in relation to a mortgage to secure a loan which the client was taking to assist her brother setting up his solicitor's practice was admitted, as the court had no familiarity with the matters in question and there were no text books which could assist (the judgment was reversed on appeal but without mention of expert evidence: see *sub nom. Northern Rock Building Society v Archer* (1998) 78 P.& C.R. 65).

of evidence critical of it are those cases in which the *Bolam* test does not apply. Three types of case make up this category[37]:

6–010 (1) Cases in which the court considers that there is no logical basis for the body of opinion in accordance with which the defendant acted. In *Bolitho v City and Hackney Health Authority*,[38] a clinical negligence case, Lord Browne-Wilkinson said[39]:

> " . . . the Court is not bound to hold that a defendant doctor escapes liability for negligent treatment or diagnosis just because he leads evidence from a number of medical experts who are genuinely of the opinion that the defendant's treatment or diagnosis accorded with sound medical practice. In the *Bolam* case itself, McNair J. [1957] 1 W.L.R. 583, 587 stated that the defendant had to have acted in accordance with the practice accepted as proper by a '*responsible* body of medical men'. Later, at 588, he referred to 'a standard of practice recognised a proper by a competent *reasonable* body of opinion'. Again, in the passage which I have cited from *Maynard*'s case, Lord Scarman refers to a 'respectable' body of professional opinion. The use of these adjectives—responsible, reasonable and respectable—all show that the court has to be satisfied that the exponents of the body of opinion relied upon can demonstrate that such opinion has a logical basis."

He concluded[40]:

> " . . . if, in a rare case, it can be demonstrated that the professional opinion is not capable of withstanding logical analysis, the judge is entitled to hold that the body of opinion is not reasonable or responsible."

(2) Cases in which the expert evidence called by the defendant is in reality no more than the personal opinion of an expert witness as to what he would have done in the position of the defendant. Such evidence does not establish that the defendant's conduct was in line with a responsible *body* of opinion or with a recognised *practice* within his profession. In *Midland Bank Trust Co Ltd v Hett Stubbs & Kemp*,[41] a solicitors' negligence case, Oliver J. said[42]:

> "Clearly, if there is some practice in a profession, some accepted standard of conduct which is laid down by a professional institute or sanctioned by common usage, evidence of that can and ought to be received. But evidence which really amounts to no more than an expression of opinion by a particular practitioner of what he thinks that he would have done had he been placed, hypothetically and without the benefit of hindsight, in the position of the defendants, is of little assistance to the court . . . "

It is thought that this does not prevent the court receiving assistance from expert witnesses in cases where there is no general and approved practice or

---

[37] See *Michael Hyde & Associates Ltd v JD Williams & Co Ltd* [2001] P.N.L.R. 233, CA.
[38] [1998] A.C. 232, HL.
[39] *ibid.* at 241.
[40] *ibid.* at 243.
[41] [1979] Ch. 384.
[42] *ibid.* at 402. This passage was approved by the Court of Appeal in *Bown v Gould & Swayne* [1996] P.N.L.R. 130 and in the architect's negligence case of *Michael Hyde & Associates Ltd v JD Williams & Co Ltd* [2001] P.N.L.R. 233 and was applied in the solicitors' negligence case of *X v Woollcombe Yonge* [2001] Lloyd's Rep. P.N. 274. See also *Linden Homes South East Ltd v LBH Wembley Ltd* [2002] EWHC 3115, TCC (finding of negligence by construction professionals in face of evidence of defendant's expert witness because there was not evidence of two respectable but differing bodies of opinion, merely of differing views as between the two individual experts).

specific school of thought by reference to which the defendant's conduct can either be justified or condemned as negligent. In such cases, the court may still be assisted by the evidence of an expert witness as to how, in his experience and opinion, an ordinarily competent member of his profession would have acted in the position of the defendant. This may be quite different to the manner in which he personally would have acted.

(3) Cases in which it is not necessary to apply any particular professional expertise in order to decide whether the defendant has failed to exercise the skill and care expected of an ordinary member of his profession. For example, in the architect's negligence case of *Worboys v Acme Investments Ltd*[43] Sachs L.J. recognised that there were cases where an omission on a plan was so glaring as to require no evidence of general practice and instanced a house without provision for a staircase. In the architect's negligence case of *Royal Brompton Hospital NHS Trust v Hammond (No.7)*,[44] Judge Seymour Q.C. put it this way[45]:

" . . . if I am satisfied on the evidence that an obvious mistake was made which would not have been made by any careful person of whatever profession, or, indeed, of none, then I can find that the person who made that mistake was negligent. What I cannot do, as it seems to me, is to substitute my own view for that of a professional person of the appropriate discipline on any matter in respect of which any special skill, training or expertise is required to make an informed assessment."

In *Michael Hyde & Associates Ltd v JD Williams & Co Ltd*,[46] also an **6–011** architect's negligence case, the Court of Appeal held that the trial judge had been entitled to conclude that, on the facts of that case, the exercise of judgment involved in deciding whether the defendant was negligent did not of itself require any special architectural skills. He did not have to "get under the skin of a different profession" in order to assess whether or not the defendants had failed to use reasonable skill and care and, accordingly, was entitled to make a finding of negligence in spite of expert evidence which supported the defendant's conduct.[47] For a detailed discussion of the role of expert evidence in professional negligence claims, particularly claims against construction professionals, see the judgment of Judge Lloyd Q.C. in *Royal Brompton Hospital NHS Trust v Hammond*.[48] The judge commented that expert evidence may be needed to assist the court to assess the evidence, for example, by indicating which factors or

---

[43] (1969) 210 E.G. 335, CA. See also the clinical negligence case of *Gold v Haringey HA* [1988] 1 Q.B. 481 at 490, *per* Lloyd L.J.:
"If the giving of contraceptive advice required no special skill, then I could see an argument that the *Bolam* test should not apply."
[44] (2001) 76 Con. L.R. 148.
[45] *ibid.* at 170.
[46] [2001] P.N.L.R 233, CA.
[47] *ibid.* at para.27. Ward L.J. also observed (at para.26) that the judge would also have been entitled to disapply the *Bolam* test on the basis that the case fell into the second category:
"He may well have been able to discount the evidence on that basis for I find little to suggest that there were two recognised but contrary views of an accepted practice governing the decision in question. As I read the evidence the experts were doing no more than putting themselves forward as reasonably competent architects and then saying what they would have done in the circumstances in which Mr Warrington found himself."
[48] [2002] EWHC 2037, TCC.

technical considerations would influence the judgment of a professional person, in cases where the negligence alleged is not a failure to follow an established professional practice. Otherwise, in such cases, expert evidence is not indispensable. The issue of breach of duty may be determined as a matter of common sense. Alternatively, the court may itself possess the necessary expertise to assess the evidence; the Technology and Construction Court has such expertise in disputes arising in the construction industry and in other areas of commerce. Even so, expert evidence may remain desirable in order to satisfy the court that its decision on the required standard of care is in line with the expectations and understanding of the profession. The judge also pointed out that, since the role of the expert witness under the Civil Procedure Rules is to assist the court rather than to make a case for the expert's instructing party, it is not necessary for a party which alleges negligence to adduce supporting expert evidence, provided that in a case where such evidence is necessary or desirable it is available from an expert called by another party.

(c) *The Civil Procedure Rules*

6–012 Lord Woolf's final report on the civil justice system, published in July 1996,[49] heralded a new and restrictive approach to expert evidence which has been embodied in England and Wales in Pt 35 of the Civil Procedure Rules. Under CPR r.35.4, no party may call an expert witness without the court's permission. The principle which guides the court in deciding whether or not to permit expert evidence is set out in CPR r.35.1: expert evidence is to be restricted to that which is reasonably required to resolve the proceedings. Thus the use of expert evidence is now wholly subject to the control of the court and the court is encouraged to exercise its powers to decide that no expert evidence shall be called upon a particular issue, that a single expert shall be jointly instructed by the parties[50] or that expert evidence shall be adduced in writing only.[51] For example, in the solicitors' negligence case of *Mann v Chetty & Patel*,[52] the Court of Appeal held that expert evidence would be permitted on only one of the quantum issues which arose in the case, whereas the claimant sought to adduce expert evidence on three such issues. The Court of Appeal stated that, in deciding whether to allow expert evidence, the court had to make a judgment on at least three matters:

  (i) how cogent the proposed expert evidence would be ("cogency");

  (ii) how helpful that evidence would be in resolving any of the issues in the case ("usefulness"); and

---

[49] *Access to Justice* (HMSO, 1996).
[50] See paras 6–021 to 6–024, below.
[51] CPR r.35.5(1) provides that expert evidence shall be given in a written report unless the court directs otherwise. In fast-track cases (those worth less than £15,000) experts will not be permitted to give oral evidence unless that is necessary in the interests of justice: CPR r.35.5(2).
[52] [2001] Lloyd's Rep. P.N. 38, CA. See also the accountants' negligence case of *Barings Plc (in liquidation) v Coopers & Lybrand* [2001] Lloyd's Rep. P.N. 379.

(iii) how much the evidence would cost and the relationship between that cost and the sums at stake ("proportionality"). Further guidance as to the use of expert evidence in civil proceedings is found in the Protocol for the Instruction of Experts to give Evidence in Civil Proceedings, which was published by the Civil Justice Council in June 2005 and referred to with approval by the Court of Appeal in *General Medical Council v Meadow.*[52a]

(d) *Relevance and Admissibility of Expert Evidence*

The modern approach to expert evidence encourages the court to be vigilant in its scrutiny of expert evidence, both before and at trial. If permission has been given to call expert evidence, objection may be made to its admissibility and this should be done as soon as possible. It is no longer necessary to make such objection to the trial judge only,[53] nor is it desirable to leave such a challenge until trial.   **6–013**

(i) *The Appropriate Discipline*

Particular care is required in the instructing of expert witnesses and the presentation of their evidence. The first question must be whether the task undertaken by the defendant was one within his own proper and usual professional sphere. If it was not, there may be a question whether he should be judged not according to the practice of his own profession but rather according to the professional practice of the specialism in which he purported to operate.[54] If so, an expert of that discipline should be instructed.   **6–014**

(ii) *The Appropriate Questions*

Secondly, it is important that the evidence of an expert witness is confined to matters which are relevant to the issues before the court. In *Pozzolanic Lytag Ltd v Bryan Hobson Associates,*[55] Dyson J. stated that the expert witnesses should have confined themselves to the question whether there was a common practice in the engineering profession as to what engineers who are engaged as project managers do in relation to the insurance obligations of building contractors.   **6–015**

[52a] [2006] EWCA Civ 1390 at [21].

[53] The position used to be more complicated. Where it was disputed whether expert evidence was admissible, the master or judge in chambers was not entitled to rule on the admissibility of such evidence, see *Sullivan v West Yorkshire Passenger Transport Executive* [1985] 2 All E.R. 134, CA. However, in *Woodford & Ackroyd v Burgess* [1999] Lloyd's Rep. P.N. 231, the Court of Appeal held that a judge who was not the trial judge could rule on admissibility under the inherent jurisdiction. See also *Liverpool Roman Catholic Archdiocese Trustees Incorporated v Goldberg (No.2)* [2001] Lloyd's Rep. P.N. 518, where Neuberger J. set out in six steps the proper approach to an application to exclude expert evidence on the grounds that it was inadmissible.

[54] See, e.g. *Investors in Industry Commercial Properties v South Bedfordshire DC* [1986] 1 All E.R. 787 and *Sansom v Metcalfe Hambleton & Co* [1998] P.N.L.R. 542, discussed further at Ch.9, para.9–147, below.

[55] [1999] B.L.R. 267.

Instead, they considered numerous other issues including contributory negligence, which was a matter for the court. He warned[56]:

"Prolix expert reports directed to issues with which they should not be concerned merely add to the expense of litigation. Everything possible should be done to discourage this. In appropriate cases, this will include making special orders for costs."

(iii) *Appropriate Qualifications and Experience*

6–016 Thirdly, the expert witness must be properly qualified to provide an opinion upon the issues to be determined. The court will consider "whether the witness has acquired by study or experience sufficient knowledge of the subject to render his opinion of value in resolving the issues before the court".[57] In *Royal Brompton Hospital NHS Trust v Hammond (No.7)*[58] Judge Seymour Q.C. rejected the evidence of the claimant's expert architect in its entirety. He warned that, if experts are to give useful evidence, they must be given sufficient time to master the relevant documents. Further, they should avoid making assumptions (or accepting instructions to make assumptions) the accuracy of which is central to the questions which they are to address.[59] Finally, they should make sure that they have contemporary knowledge of practice in their own profession. The evidence from the claimant's expert architect was found wanting in each of these respects. The latter point serves to remind that an expert who has a working knowledge of contemporary practice in the relevant profession may often be more credible than an expert, however highly qualified, who has not practised for many years.

(iv) *Impartiality*

6–017 Fourthly, the evidence of an expert witness must be independent and impartial. CPR, r.35.3 provides expressly that the duty of an expert to assist the court overrides any obligation to the party from whom he receives his instructions or by whom he is paid. The expert's report must be addressed to the court and not to his instructing party.[60] It is counter-productive to instruct a "hired gun", i.e. an expert whose evidence is biased towards the instructing party and who will seek

---

[56] [1999] B.L.R. 267 at 275. See also *Pride Valley Food Ltd v Hall and Partners (Contract Management) Ltd* (2000) 76 Con. L.R. 1, where Judge Toulmin C.M.G., Q.C. concluded that the claimant's expert evidence provided little or no assistance. Amongst other criticisms, he pointed out that the report was overlong, included opinions on matters of fact and law which were questions for decision by the court and included expressions of opinion as to what the expert himself would have done in the defendant's position. The Court of Appeal did not comment on this passage: [2001] EWCA Civ 1001. See also *Stephen Donald Architects Ltd v Christopher King* [2003] EWHC 1867, TCC (evidence of defendant's expert architect unhelpful because he did not address the question whether any reasonably competent architect would have prepared a different design in response to the client's brief).

[57] *The Queen v Bonython* (1984) 38 S.A.S.R. 45 at 46, *per* King C.J.

[58] (2001) 76 Con. L.R. 148.

[59] See also the *Commercial Court Guide*, para.H2.12: an expert should state the assumptions upon which his opinion is based, and if a stated assumption is, in the opinion of the expert, unreasonable or unlikely, he should state that clearly.

[60] CPR Pt 35, Practice Direction 1.1.

to advocate his instructing party's case.[61] In *Anglo Group Plc v Winther Brown & Co Ltd*,[62] Judge Toulmin C.M.G., Q.C. disregarded the evidence of two expert witnesses who had failed to act independently of their instructing parties. The judge also restated and extended the guidelines as to the duties and responsibilities of expert witnesses in civil cases which were set out by Cresswell J. in *National Justice Compania Naviera SA v Prudential Assurance Co Ltd (The Ikarian Reefer)*[63] so as to reflect the principles enshrined in the Civil Procedure Rules and emphasise the need for an expert witness to be impartial:

"1. An expert witness should at all stages in the procedure, on the basis of the evidence as he understands it, provide independent assistance to the court and the parties by way of objective unbiased opinion in relation to matters within his expertise. This applies as much to the initial meetings of experts as to evidence at trial. An expert witness should never assume the role of an advocate.

2. The expert's evidence should normally be confined to technical matters on which the court will be assisted by receiving an explanation, or to evidence of common professional practice. The expert witness should not give evidence or opinions as to what the expert himself would have done in similar circumstances or otherwise seek to usurp the role of the judge.

3. He should co-operate with the expert of the other party or parties in attempting to narrow the technical issues in dispute at the earliest possible stage of the procedure and to eliminate or place in context any peripheral issues. He should co-operate with the other expert(s) in attending without prejudice meetings as necessary and in seeking to find areas of agreement and to define precisely areas of disagreement to be set out in the joint statement of experts ordered by the court.

4. The expert evidence presented to the court should be, and be seen to be, the independent product of the expert uninfluenced as to form or content by the exigencies of the litigation.

5. An expert witness should state the facts or assumptions upon which his opinion is based. He should not omit to consider material facts which could detract from his concluded opinion.

6. An expert witness should make it clear when a particular question or issue falls outside his expertise.

7. Where an expert is of the opinion that his conclusions are based on inadequate factual information he should say so explicitly.

8. An expert should be ready to reconsider his opinion, and if appropriate, to change his mind when he has received new information or has considered the opinion of the other expert. He should do so at the earliest opportunity."

In *Stevens v Gullis*,[64] the defendant's expert building surveyor had failed in his   **6–018** duty to act impartially and had also failed to comply with the requirements of the

---

[61] In the valuer's negligence case of *Cemp Properties (UK) Ltd v Dentsply Research and Development Corp* [1991] 2 E.G.L.R. 197 at 200, the Court of Appeal commented that:

"It is a sad feature of modern litigation that expert witnesses, particularly in valuation cases, instead of giving evidence of their actual views as to the true position, enter into the arena and, as advocates, put forward the maximum or minimum figures as best suited to their side's interests. If experts do this, they must not be surprised if their views carry little weight with the judge. In this case, such evidence rightly led the judge to reject the expert evidence on both sides."

One of the main objectives of CPR Pt 35 is to eliminate partisan expert evidence.

[62] Unreported, March 1, 2000.

[63] [1993] 2 Lloyd's Rep. 68 at 81.

[64] [2000] 1 All E.R. 527.

Civil Procedure Rules in relation to his report[65] and to a joint memorandum of matters agreed with the claimant's expert. The value which the court places upon the impartiality of expert evidence is demonstrated by the Court of Appeal's decision to uphold an order debarring the defendant from calling his expert, notwithstanding that both claimant and defendant had invited the court to accept his evidence. In *Great Eastern Hotel Co Ltd v John Laing Construction Ltd*,[66] the evidence of the defendant's construction management expert was rejected because, in failing to carry out thorough research, in accepting uncritically the factual account given by the defendant and in failing to take account of material evidence, he demonstrated "no concept of his duty to the court as an independent expert".[67]

6–019   The Court of Appeal held in *Toth v Jarman*[68] that a conflict of interest does not necessarily disqualify an expert from giving evidence, as the expert is under a duty to give an independent opinion. However, where a material or significant conflict of interest is identified, the court is likely to decline to act on that evidence or, indeed, to give permission for that evidence to be adduced. Accordingly, all potential conflicts of interest should be disclosed at an early stage in proceedings.[69] Further, the court suggested[70] that an expert's report should contain a declaration that:

(i) that he has no conflict of interest of any kind, other than any which he has disclosed in his report;

(ii) that he does not consider that any interest which he has disclosed affects his suitability as an expert witness on any issue on which he has given evidence;

(iii) that he will advise the party by whom he is instructed if, between the date of his report and the trial, there is any change in circumstances which affects his position on (i) or (ii) above.

6–020   Where there is a close pre-existing professional or personal relationship between the defendant and an expert whom he wishes to give evidence on his behalf, the test for admissibility of the expert's evidence flows from the principle that justice must be seen to be done. In *Liverpool Roman Catholic Archdiocesan Trust v Goldberg (No.3)*,[71] Evans-Lombe J. held that the test is whether a reasonable observer might think that the relationship between the expert and the party calling him is capable of affecting the views of the expert so as to make them unduly favourable to that party. If so, the evidence will not be admitted. It is not necessary, for the evidence to be excluded, to show that the relationship *has* so affected the expert's views. (In that case, the defendant tax barrister was not permitted to adduce the expert evidence of a colleague in his chambers, with

---

[65] CPR r.35.10(1) imposes requirements as to the contents of an expert's report, which are set out in CPR Pt 35, Practice Direction, paras 1.2–1.6.
[66] [2005] EWHC 181, TCC.
[67] *ibid., per* H.H. Judge Wilcox at para.128.
[68] [2006] EWCA Civ 1028.
[69] *ibid.*, at para.102.
[70] *ibid.*, at para.120.
[71] [2001] 1 W.L.R. 2337.

whom the defendant had a close personal and professional relationship of long-standing.) Furthermore, in expressing his opinion of the defendant's performance, an expert must not be deterred by the fact that the defendant is held in high esteem by the members of their common profession. In *Hubbard v Lambeth, Southwark & Lewisham HA*,[72] the Court of Appeal held that the court should generally order experts of like disciplines to engage in "without prejudice" discussions in order to narrow the issues in a case once their reports have been exchanged. Good reason was required before such an order would not be made. The claimants' experts' reluctance to subject the competence of a colleague to critical discussion because he was a well-known and highly respected practitioner was not good reason.

(e) *The Single Joint Expert*

A notable innovation introduced by the Civil Procedure Rules is the court's   **6–021** power, at any stage in an action, to direct that expert evidence on a particular issue shall be given by a single joint expert.[73] Either party is entitled to give the joint expert instructions but such instructions must be copied to the other party.[74] The parties are jointly and severally liable for the joint expert's fees and expenses unless the court directs otherwise.[75] In professional negligence cases, the use of single joint experts will commonly be restricted to issues which allow little scope for disagreement, such as matters of scientific or technical fact or quantum, rather than to issues of breach of duty which require the court to consider the range of professional practice. *The Queen's Bench Guide*[76] supports this approach:

> "In very many cases it is possible for the question of expert evidence to be dealt with by a single expert. Single experts are, for example, often appropriate to deal with questions of quantum in cases where primary issues are as to liability. Likewise, where expert evidence is required in order to acquaint the court with matters of expert fact, as opposed to opinion, a single expert will usually be appropriate. There remain, however, a body of cases where liability will turn upon expert opinion evidence and where it will

---

[72] [2001] EWCA Civ 1455.

[73] CPR r.35.7. In practice, an order that evidence shall be given by a single joint expert may be refused until the issues in the case have been clarified by the service of a defence: see *Simms v Birmingham HA* [2001] Lloyd's Rep. Med. 382. In *Coopers Payen Ltd v Southampton Container Terminal Ltd* [2003] EWCA Civ 1223, the Court of Appeal provided guidance upon how the court should approach the evidence of a single joint expert. While it will be a rare case in which the court will disregard the evidence of a single joint expert, it was necessary for the judge to evaluate that evidence in the light of all the evidence in the case (see the judgment of Clarke L.J. at paras [41]–[43]); *cf. Tucker v Wyatt* [2005] EWCA Civ 1420.

[74] CPR r.35.8(1) and (2). Similarly, discussion between one party and a jointly instructed expert will not be permitted unless the other party is present or gives its consent to such discussion taking place in its absence. In *Peet v Mid-Kent Healthcare Trust (Practice Note)* [2001] EWCA Civ 1703, the Court of Appeal held that for a party to test the evidence of a jointly instructed expert by means of an unilateral discussion was inconsistent with the structure and overriding objective of the Civil Procedure Rules on joint experts and would never be permitted against the wishes of the other party. In an earlier decision to like effect, the judge pointed out that if a party wished to test the evidence of a joint expert, it should use the procedure for submission of written questions to the expert which is set out in CPR r.35.6: *Smith v Stephens* [2001] C.I.L.L. 1802.

[75] CPR r.35.8(5).

[76] Para.7.9.5.

be appropriate for the parties to instruct their own experts. For example, in cases where the issue for determination is as to whether a party acted in accordance with proper professional standards, it will often be of value to the court to hear opinions of more than one expert as to the proper standard in order that the court becomes acquainted with the range of views existing upon the question and in order that the evidence can be tested in cross-examination."

6–022 In *Oxley v Penwarden*,[77] the Court of Appeal confirmed that the Civil Procedure Rules do not create a presumption that a single joint expert will be instructed in every case. It permitted the parties in a complex clinical negligence case to instruct separate experts on the issue of causation, as to which there were two schools of thought in the medical profession.

6–023 It may happen that one party will be dissatisfied with the report of a single joint expert when it is produced and will wish to apply for permission to instruct another expert with a view to deciding whether there are aspects of the single joint expert's report which he should challenge. In *Daniels v Walker*,[78] the Court of Appeal held that such permission might be granted where the dissatisfied party's reasons were not fanciful, especially where (as was the case in *Daniels*) the parties had initially agreed to instruct a single joint expert and the sum at stake was substantial. The question whether the dissatisfied party might go further and call his own expert at trial was considered in *Cosgrove v Pattison*.[79] In that case, which involved a boundary dispute, a party was permitted to call evidence from a second expert when that party alleged that the single joint expert might be biased. Neuberger J. provided the following, non-exhaustive list of factors which would be relevant upon any application to call a second expert: the nature of the dispute, the number of issues to which the expert evidence was relevant, the reasons for requiring another expert's report, the amount of money at stake, the effect of allowing a further expert witness upon the conduct of the trial, the delay that calling a further expert would cause, any other special features and the overall justice to the parties in the context of the litigation. In certain circumstances, a party may secure the appointment of a second joint expert.[80]

6–024 In *Layland v Fairview New Homes Plc*,[81] it was held that a claimant could resist summary judgment if it showed a realistic prospect of successfully challenging a single joint expert's evidence by either submissions or cross-examination, but it is clear that the parties do not enjoy an unfettered right to challenge the evidence of a joint expert by cross-examining him at trial. In *Peet v Mid-Kent Healthcare Trust (Practice Note)*,[82] Lord Woolf C.J. explained that, normally, the evidence of a joint expert should be contained in his written report so that he would not be required to give oral evidence at trial and the parties would not be entitled to cross-examine him. Those remarks were obiter in *Peet* but Lord Woolf's approach was adopted and applied by the Court of Appeal *Popek v*

---

[77] [2001] Lloyd's Rep. Med. 347, CA. See, for a further example, *ES v Chesterfield and North Derbyshire Royal Hospital NHS Trust* [2003] EWCA Civ 1284.
[78] [2000] 1 W.L.R. 1382.
[79] [2001] T.L.R. 113.
[80] See *Smolen v Solon Co-operative Housing Services Ltd* [2003] EWCA Civ 1240.
[81] [2002] EWHC 1350, Ch.
[82] [2001] EWCA Civ 1703; [2002] 1 W.L.R. 210.

National Westminster Bank Plc.[83] There, the trial judge's decision to strike out the claimant's case as hopeless in the light of the joint expert's report was upheld, notwithstanding that the claimant had not had the opportunity to put his version of the facts to the expert by way of cross-examination. Cross-examination of a joint expert was not to be the norm. The claimant should have tested the expert's evidence in advance of trial by submitting written questions to him in accordance with the procedure set out in CPR r.35.6.

(f) *Experts' Immunity from Suit*

The scope of an expert witness's immunity from suit was considered by the Court of Appeal in *Stanton v Callaghan.*[84] Chadwick L.J.[85] derived the following conclusions from authority: 6–025

> "(i) an expert witness who gives evidence at a trial is immune from suit in respect of anything which he says in court, and that immunity will extend to the contents of the report which he adopts as, or incorporates in, his evidence (ii) where an expert witness gives evidence at trial the immunity which he would enjoy in respect of that evidence is not to be circumvented by a suit based on the report itself and (iii) the immunity does not extend to protect an expert who has been retained to advise as to the merits of a party's claim in litigation from a suit by the party by whom he has been retained in respect of that advice, notwithstanding that it was in contemplation at the time when the advice was given that the expert would be a witness at the trial if that litigation were to proceed."

The court held that the expert witness in that case was immune from suit, both in respect of a joint statement which he had signed after a meeting of experts and in respect of his report. The immunity was justified by public policy and, in particular, the need to avoid the tension between a desire to assist a court and fear of the consequences of a departure from previous advice.

Although immunity from suit will protect an expert even when he is dishonest,[86] the immunity does not protect an expert from every kind of sanction. First, the expert's professional body may conduct disciplinary proceedings against him. An argument that the immunity should be extended to include subsequent disciplinary proceedings was rejected by the Court of Appeal in *General Medical Council v Meadow.*[87–88] Second, a costs order may be made against an expert who, by his evidence, causes significant expense to be incurred, and does so in "flagrant reckless disregard of his duties to the court".[89] Mere negligence is not sufficient. The hurdle before such a costs order is made is set high in order to avoid discouraging experts from giving frank evidence. Accordingly, it is expected that costs orders against experts will be exceptional. 6–026

---

[83] [2002] EWCA Civ 42.
[84] [2000] Q.B. 75.
[85] *ibid.* at 100. Nourse and Otton L.JJ. delivered concurring judgments.
[86] *Darker v Chief Constable of the West Midlands* [2001] 1 A.C. 435, applied in *Paimano v Reiss* [2001] P.N.L.R. 21 and in *Gayle v Lord Chancellor* [2004] EWHC 3394, QB.
[87–88] [2006] EWCA Civ 1390.
[89] *Phillips v Symes (a bankrupt) (Expert Witnesses: Costs)* [2004] EWHC 2330, Ch; [2005] 1 W.L.R. 2043. See, *per* Peter Smith J. at para.95.

HUMAN RIGHTS AND PROFESSIONALS

1. INTRODUCTION

The Human Rights Act 1998 ("HRA") was passed to give "further effect" to the **7–001**
European Convention for the Protection of Human Rights and Fundamental
Freedoms 1950 ("the Convention") in domestic law. The Act does this by four
key methods:

> (1) by s.6 of the HRA, it creates a statutory tort, making it unlawful for a
> "public authority" to act incompatibly with the Convention. A "public
> authority" is defined to include courts and tribunals and any person or

body who exercises a "public function".[1] The court's duty arising from s.6 means that the Convention has effect on both the common law and equity;

(2) by s.7 of the HRA, it empowers a "victim"[2] of a violation of Convention rights to bring proceedings against a "public authority" guilty of such a violation or to raise the violation in any legal proceedings;

(3) by s.3 of the HRA, it has creates a strong interpretive obligation on judges and administrative decision-makers to construe all past and future legislation compatibly with the Convention, "so far as it is possible to do so"; and

(4) by s.2 of the HRA, it places a duty on courts to "take into account" Strasbourg jurisprudence whenever a Convention issue arises.

7–002　　The HRA came into force on October 2, 2000.[3] The primary effect of the HRA is in relation to issues of procedure and in relation to substantive legal areas such as tort, administrative law and equity. As a general rule, it has limited application to contract law. This chapter seeks to provide an introduction to the interaction between the HRA and professional liability. For a full analysis of the Convention and the operation of the HRA, the reader should consult the current editions of the leading human rights texts.[4]

2. Relevant Convention Rights

7–003　　The Articles of the Convention that are of principal relevance to professional liability are:

(a) Article 6: the right to a fair trial;

---

[1] For the definition of a "public authority" for the purpose of s.6 HRA, see *R. (on the application of Heather) v Leonard Cheshire Foundation* [2002] EWCA Civ 366; [2002] A.C. 271; *Poplar Housing and Regeneration Communication Association Ltd v Donaghue* [2001] EWCA Civ 595; [2001] A.C. 415; and *R. (on the application of Johnson, Thomas, Manning) v Havering London BC* [2006] EWHC 1714, Admin; *R. (on the application of Moreton) v Medical Defence Union* [2006] EWHC 1948, Admin (MDU not a "public body" and did not exercise a "public function"); *Cameron v Network Rail Infrastructure Ltd* [2006] EWHC 1133, *The Times*, June 14, 2006 (Railtrack was not a public authority for the purposes of the HRA and was not acting as such).

[2] HRA, s.7(7). The test is the same as under Art.34 of the Convention. An individual only has standing if he is actually and directly affected by the act or omission which is the subject of the complaint, although he may also be a victim if he could potentially be affected by the act or omission: *Dudgeon v United Kingdom* [1982] 4 E.H.R.R. 149.

[3] The Human Rights Act 1998 (Commencement No.2) Order 2000 (SI 2000/1851) (c.47)—apart from s.18 (appointment of judges), s.20 (powers of ministers to make orders under the HRA) and s.21(5) (substitution of other sentences for the death penalty) which came into force on the passing of the Act on November 9, 1998: s.22(2) of the HRA; and s.19 (statements of compatibility) which came into force on November 24, 1998; see the Human Rights Act 1998 (Commencement) Order 1998 (SI 1998/2882) (c.71).

[4] e.g. Simor & Emmerson Q.C., *Human Rights Practice* (Sweet & Maxwell); Lester & Pannick, *Human Rights Law & Practice* (Butterworths). For an accessible overview of the Convention and the HRA, see *European Human Rights Law* (Legal Action Group, 1999). The authors are grateful for the assistance of the above texts in relation to the summary of the Convention rights which follows.

(b) Article 8: the right to respect for private and family life, home and correspondence;

(c) Article 10: the right to freedom of expression;

(d) Article 11: the right to freedom of assembly; and

(e) Article 1 of Protocol No.1: the right to peaceful enjoyment of possessions.

(a) *Article 6*

Article 6 states: **7–004**

"(1) In the determination of his civil rights and obligations or of any criminal charge against him, everyone is entitled to a fair and public hearing within a reasonable time by an independent and impartial tribunal established by law. Judgment shall be pronounced publicly but the press and public may be excluded from all or part of the trial in the interests of morals, public order or national security in a democratic society, where the interests of juveniles or the protection of private life of the parties so require, or to the extent strictly necessary in the opinion of the court in special circumstances where publicity would prejudice the interests of justice.

(2) Everyone charged with a criminal offence shall be presumed innocent until proved guilty according to law.

(3) Everyone charged with a criminal offence has the following minimum rights:

(a) to be informed promptly, in a language which he understands and in detail, of the nature and cause of the accusation against him;

(b) to have adequate time and facilities for the preparation of his defence;

(c) to defend himself in person or through legal assistance of his own choosing or, if he has not sufficient means to pay for legal assistance, to be given it free when the interests of justice so require;

(d) to examine or have examined witnesses against him and to obtain the attendance and examination of witnesses on his behalf under the same conditions as witnesses against him; and

(e) to have the free assistance of an interpreter if he cannot understand or speak the language used in court."

Article 6 concerns the "determination" of "civil rights and obligations" or of   **7–005**
a "criminal charge". These expressions have autonomous meanings within
European human rights law. The classification of proceedings in domestic law as
civil will not necessarily be determinative. The European Court has adopted an
incremental approach to the definition of "civil rights and obligations". They
include issues arising in contract, tort,[5] commercial law, insurance law, real and
personal property, intellectual property,[6] restitution,[7] planning,[8] education, family

---

[5] A pending negligence claim is a possession within the meaning of Art.1 of Protocol No.1 (*Pressos Compania SA v Belgium* (1996) 21 E.H.R.R. 301) and will therefore attract Art.6. See also *Osman v United Kingdom* (2000) 29 E.H.R.R. 245.

[6] *British American Tobacco Co Ltd v Netherlands* (1996) 21 E.H.R.R. 409.

[7] *Krcmár v Czech Republic*, Application No.35376/97, March 3, 2000, European Court.

[8] *Allan Jacobbson v Sweden (No.2)*, Application No.16970/90, Judgment of February 19, 1998 at para.39.

law and succession. Preliminary investigative procedures, such as a DTI investigation, are not determinative of a civil right.[9] Pure "public" law rights are not generally regarded as "civil rights", e.g. the entry and removal of immigrants.[10] Matters concerning public employment may be regarded as "public rights".[11] Further, proceedings regarding political rights are not within Art.6(1).[12] The European Court has focused on identification of a pecuniary right or interest in determining whether a right was a "civil" right: *Editions Périscope v France*.[13]

7–006   The requirement for a "determination" means that there must be a dispute (in the French text, a *contestation*) concerning the civil right or obligation in question. Preliminary issues, issues of liability or quantum and issues solely as to costs all fall within the definition. Proceedings are not determinative of a civil right or obligation if they merely constitute a preliminary investigative stage[14] or form part of an administrative process.[15] The requirement that there be a dispute over a civil right in order to bring Art.6(1) into play has been construed to cover not only disputes concerning the scope of a right but also its very existence under domestic law.[16] In *Aït-Mouhoub v France*,[17] in determining the applicability of Art.6(1), the court asked itself whether there was a dispute over a "civil right" which could be "said, at least on arguable grounds to be recognised under domestic law" and whether the proceedings were "directly decisive" of that right. Article 6(1) "does not in itself guarantee any particular content for the "rights and obligations" in the substantive law of the Contracting States". A civil right or obligation only attracts Art.6(1) when it is "recognised" by national law: *Powell and Rayner v United Kingdom*,[18] though it is not always easy to distinguish between procedural and substantive limitations: *Fayed v United Kingdom*.[19]

7–007   Proceedings may be designated as a "criminal charge" irrespective of the domestic law designation by reference to three criteria formulated by the European Court in *Engel v Netherlands*[20]:

(1) the classification in domestic law;

(2) the nature of the offence or conduct in question; and

---

[9] *Fayed v United Kingdom* (1994) 18 E.H.R.R. 393.
[10] *Uppal v United Kingdom* (1981) 3 E.H.R.R. 391.
[11] *Koseck v Germany* (1987) 9 E.H.R.R. 328; *Neigel v France* [1997] E.H.R.L.R. 424; *Argento v Italy* (1999) 28 E.H.R.R. 719. See now *Pellegrin v France* (2001) 31 E.H.R.R. 651 in which the European Court has reviewed the law in this area and narrowed the employment disputes excluded from the scope of Art.6(1) to those which are raised by public servants whose duties typify the specific activities of the public service insofar as they are designed to safeguard the general interests of the State and of other public authorities (e.g. the armed forces or police).
[12] *Pierre-Bloch v France* (1998) 26 E.H.R.R. 202.
[13] (1992) 14 E.H.R.R. 597, para.40.
[14] *Fayed v United Kingdom* (1994) 18 E.H.R.R. 393.
[15] *R. v Lord Chancellor Ex p. Lightfoot* [2000] 2 W.L.R. 318, CA; [1999] 2 W.L.R. 1126, *per* Laws J.
[16] *Ashingdane v United Kingdom* (1985) 7 E.H.R.R. 528.
[17] (2000) 30 E.H.R.R. 382.
[18] (1990) 12 E.H.R.R. 355. See also *W v United Kingdom* (1988) 10 E.H.R.R. 29.
[19] (1994) 18 E.H.R.R. 393, para.67.
[20] *Engel v Netherlands* (1979) 1 E.H.R.R. 647.

(3) the severity of any possible penalty.

If a domestic court can impose imprisonment, this will generally be sufficient to define the proceedings as "criminal" unless the "nature, duration or manner of execution of the imprisonment" is not "appreciably detrimental".[21] So, for instance, prison disciplinary proceedings[22] and contempt proceedings[23] have been held to be criminal proceedings for the purpose of Art.6, notwithstanding their domestic designation.

The European Court reviewed the applicability of Art.6 to civil proceedings in **7-008** *Perez v France*.[24] It stated that a new approach was necessary in order to end the uncertainty surrounding Art.6(1)'s applicability. Whether or not a right is to regarded as "civil" must be determined by reference not only to its legal classification but also to its substantive content and effects under domestic law. Moreover the European Court, in the exercise of its supervisory function, must also take account of the object and purpose of the Convention. The right to a fair trial holds such a prominent place in a democratic society that there can be no justification for a restrictive interpretation of Art.6(1). Conformity with the spirit of the Convention requires that the word *"contestation"* should not be construed too technically. Article 6(1) may apply even in the absence of a claim for financial reparation. It is sufficient if the outcome of the proceedings is decisive for the "civil right" in question.

Article 6(1), which applies to both civil and criminal proceedings, encom- **7-009** passes various express and implied rights. The express rights are:

(1) the right to a fair hearing;

(2) the right to a public hearing except to the extent that it is strictly necessary where publicity would prejudice the interests of justice or in the interests of morals, public order, national security, juveniles or the protection of the private life of the parties;

(3) the right to a hearing within a reasonable time;

(4) the right to an independent and impartial tribunal established by law; and

(5) public judgment.

The right of access to a court, which has been implied into Art.6,[25] is of **7-010** general importance in relation to any restrictions on the liability of potential defendants. This right is not absolute but is qualified. However, any restriction must be justified in that:

---

[21] (1979) 1 E.H.R.R. 647, para.82.
[22] *Campbell & Fell v United Kingdom* (1985) 7 E.H.R.R. 165; *cf. McFeeley v United Kingdom* (1981) 3 E.H.R.R. 161. See also *Greenfield v Secretary of State for the Home Department, The Times*, March 6, 2001, Div. Ct.; *R. v Carroll Ex p. Secretary of State for the Home Department*, unreported, February 16, 2001, Admin. Ct. (adjudications relating to prisoners not legal proceedings but disciplinary proceedings).
[23] *Harman v United Kingdom* (1984) 38 D.R. 53; Application No.10038/82.
[24] (2005) 40 E.H.R.R. 39.
[25] See *Golder v United Kingdom* (1979) 1 E.H.R.R. 524.

(a) it must have a legitimate aim;

(b) it must not impair the very essence of the right; and

(c) the restriction must be proportionate to the aim to be achieved.[26]

7–011   Other implied rights are the right to equality of arms, which means that each party must be afforded a reasonable opportunity to present his case (including his evidence) under conditions which do not place him at a substantial disadvantage vis-à-vis his opponent,[27] and the right to effective participation in a hearing.

7–012   Article 6(1) is applicable to all proceedings including actions between private parties and is therefore of particular relevance to the professional liability context, which will often involve purely private parties. In addition to the rights set out above, a defendant to a criminal charge also enjoys the following additional rights:

(a) the right against self-incrimination implied into Art.6(1);

(b) the presumption of innocence set out in Art.6(2); and

(c) the specific procedural guarantees set out in Art.6(3) including the right to know the nature of the charge against him, the right to have sufficient time and facilities to adequately prepare a defence and the right to legal aid where the interests of justice so require.

(b) *Article 8*

7–013   Article 8 states:

"(1) Everyone has the right to respect for his private and family life, his home and his correspondence.

(2) There shall be no interference by a public authority with the exercise of this right except such as is in accordance with the law and is necessary in a democratic society in the interests of national security, public safety or the economic well-being of the country, for the prevention of disorder or crime, for the protection of health or morals, or for the protection of the rights and freedoms of others."

Article 8(1) provides a right to respect for private and family life, home and correspondence. The right to private life provided by this section is a qualified right and is subject to restrictions justified by reference to Art.8(2), e.g. national security, the economic well-being of the country and the protection of the rights and freedoms of others. Any derogation from the right must also be "in accordance with the law", which means that it must have a positive legal basis and must be "necessary in a democratic society" which means that the interference must (i) have a pressing social aim and (ii) be proportionate to the aim to be achieved. It is important to note that Art.8 has "vertical effect" in that it restrains infringements of privacy by a public authority. It does not, prima facie, apply

---

[26] *Stubbings v United Kingdom* (1997) 23 E.H.R.R. 213.
[27] *Dombo Beheer BV v Netherlands* (1994) 18 E.H.R.R. 213, para.33. See also *Neumeister v Austria* (1979) 1 E.H.R.R. 91.

between individuals (so-called "horizontal effect"). However, since the court is a public body, it can be argued that it should ensure that there are no unwarranted interferences with the interests protected by Art.8, even by private bodies.[28]

(c) *Article 10*

Article 10 states: **7–014**

"(1) Everyone has the right to freedom of expression. This right shall include freedom to hold opinions and to receive and impart information and ideas without interference by public authority and regardless of frontiers. This article shall not prevent States from requiring the licensing of broadcasting, television or cinema enterprises.

(2) The exercise of these freedoms, since it carries with it duties and responsibilities, may be subject to such formalities, conditions, restrictions and penalties as are pre-scribed by law and are necessary in a democratic society, in the interests of national security, territorial integrity or public safety, for the prevention of disorder or crime, for the protection of health or morals, for the protection of the reputation or rights of others, for preventing the disclosure of information received in confidence, or for maintaining the authority and impartiality of the judiciary."

Article 10 protects the "freedom to hold opinions and to receive and impart   **7–015** information and ideas without interference by public authority and regardless of frontiers". "Expression" is not defined in Art.10. It clearly covers words, pictures, cinema, video and conduct intended to convey an idea or information. It extends to a wide range of types of expression including political, journalistic, artistic and commercial expression (in particular advertising).

Article 10 protects the freedom to both receive and impart "information" and   **7–016** "ideas": *Open Door Counselling and Dublin Well Woman v Ireland* (1993) 15 E.H.R.R. 244. No limit is placed on the definition of "information and ideas". Article 10 does not impose any general duty on the State to provide information. Further, it does not protect individuals from being compelled to disclose informa-tion: *Goodwin v United Kingdom* (1996) 22 E.H.R.R. 123.

A restriction on the rights conferred by Art.10 (other than a licensing restric-   **7–017** tion) will be compatible with the Convention only if its aim is to protect one of the interests set out in Art.10(2), namely, national security, territorial integrity, public safety, the prevention of disorder or crime, the protection of health or morals, the protection of the rights of others, preventing the disclosure of information received in confidence or maintaining the authority and impartiality of the judiciary. This list is exhaustive and the interest is to be narrowly construed. The restriction must be "prescribed by law", "necessary in a demo-cratic society" and proportionate. Freedom of expression has a special position under the Convention and the European Court has required a strong justification for interference with the right: *Sunday Times (No.2) v United Kingdom* (1991) 14 E.H.R.R. 229, para.50.

---

[28] *R. v Lambert* [2001] 3 W.L.R. 206, para.114; *Venables v Newsgroup Newspapers Ltd* [2001] 2 W.L.R. 1038, QBD, para.27.

(d) *Article 11*

7–018   Article 11 states:

> "(1) Everyone has the right to freedom of peaceful assembly and to freedom of association with others, including the right to form and to join trade unions for the protection of his interests.
>
> (2) No restrictions shall be placed on the exercise of these rights other than such as are prescribed by law and are necessary in a democratic society in the interests of national security or public safety, for the prevention of disorder or crime, for the protection of health or morals or for the protection of the rights and freedoms of others. This article shall not prevent the imposition of lawful restrictions on the exercise of these rights by members of the armed forces, of the police or of the administration of the State."

7–019   Article 11 protects the right to freedom of peaceful assembly and to freedom of association with others. The rights are expressly qualified by Art.11(2). The limitation "for the protection of the rights and freedoms of others" set out in Art.11(2) means that it is necessary to balance Art.11 rights with rights under other Articles of the Convention. States may place limitations on the exercise of Art.11 rights by, e.g. members of the armed forces, police or members of the administration of the State: *Rekvényi v Hungary.*[29] Article 11 contains a positive obligation for authorities to protect the exercise of the rights contained in it: *Young, James & Webster v United Kingdom.*[30] The term "association" has an autonomous meaning under the Convention and the classification in national law is only a starting point: *Chassagnou v France.*[31]

7–020   The right to freedom of association protects the right to form or join trade unions and other associations. Professional regulatory bodies set up by statute to regulate a profession do not fall within the definition of an "association" and compulsory membership does not violate Art.11: *Le Compte v Belgium.*[32]

(e) *Article 1 of Protocol No.1*

7–021   Article 1 of Protocol No.1 to the Convention states:

> "Every natural or legal person is entitled to the peaceful enjoyment of his possessions. No one shall be deprived of his possessions except in the public interest and subject to the conditions provided for by law and by the general principles of international law.
>
> The preceding provisions shall not, however, in any way impair the right of a State to enforce such laws as it deems necessary to control the use of property in accordance with the general interest or to secure the payment of taxes or other contributions or penalties."

7–022   Article 1 of Protocol No.1 encompasses three principles:

(1) the right to peaceful enjoyment of possessions;

---

[29] (2000) 30 E.H.R.R. 519.
[30] (1982) 4 E.H.R.R. 38.
[31] (2000) 29 E.H.R.R. 615.
[32] (1982) 4 E.H.R.R. 1.

(2) the right not to be deprived of possessions except in the public interest and in accordance with the law; and

(3) the State's right to exercise control over possessions in accordance with the general interest or to secure the payment of taxes, etc.

Article 1 of Protocol No.1 protects economic rights. Possessions include all **7–023** movable and immovable property, contractual rights including leases, orders for possession of property,[33] judgment debts,[34] shares,[35] goodwill[36] and even a claim for compensation in tort.[37] Both natural and legal persons are expressly conferred with rights under this Article.

The European Court has shown a tendency to assimilate the assessment of all **7–024** interferences with the peaceful enjoyment of possessions under a single test of fair balance: any interference must not place a disproportionate burden on the individual owner or result in discriminatory treatment. It has in general seen the availability of an effective remedy and the provision of compensation[38] as a necessary element in preserving a fair balance, whether the interference involves the deprivation of property or the control of its use. In relation to compensation, Art.1 of Protocol No.1 requires payment of an amount reasonably related to the value of the property, but does not guarantee a right to full compensation in all circumstances.[39]

Other Articles of the Convention which are relevant to clinical negligence such **7–025** as Art.2 (the right to life) are discussed at para.7–051, below.

3. NEGLIGENCE AND DUTY OF CARE

In 1998, the European Court gave what was perceived to be a landmark judgment **7–026** in *Osman v United Kingdom*.[40] The case concerned a claim brought against the police arising out of the failure to protect a child, Ahmet Osman, from the threatening and obsessive attentions of a teacher culminating in serious injury to Ahmet and the death of his father. The Court of Appeal struck out the claim applying the rule formulated by the House of Lords in *Hill v Chief Constable of the West Yorkshire Police*[41] that it was not fair, just and reasonable for the police to owe a duty to an individual member of the public in relation to the investigation and suppression of crime. The European Court of Human Rights held that to strike out a claim based on the failure of a claimant to establish a duty of care where the court had held that it was not fair, just and reasonable to impose such

---

[33] *Immobiliare Saffi v Italy* (2000) 30 E.H.R.R. 756.
[34] *Agneessens v Belgium* (1988) 58 D.R. 63; Application No.12164/86.
[35] *Bramelid and Malmstrom v Sweden* (1982) 5 E.H.R.R. 249.
[36] *Van Marle v Netherlands* (1986) 8 E.H.R.R. 483.
[37] *Pressos Compania Naviera SA v Belgium* (1996) 21 E.H.R.R. 301.
[38] See, e.g. *Holy Monasteries v Greece* (1995) 20 E.H.R.R. 1.
[39] *Papachelas v Greece* (2000) 30 E.H.R.R. 923, para.48 (legitimate objectives of "public interest" may call for less than reimbursement of full market value).
[40] (2000) 29 E.H.R.R. 245.
[41] [1989] A.C. 53, HL.

a duty[42] in that class of case was a disproportionate restriction on the claimant's right of access to a court and violated Art.6 of the Convention. The Court held that the approach created a blanket "immunity" for the police in relation to their primary function.

7–027   The application of Art.6 as formulated in *Osman* undoubtedly hindered the use of striking out, a very important tactical weapon in professional negligence cases, for a few years. The European Court subsequently resiled from this position in *Z v United Kingdom*[43] and *TP & KM v United Kingdom*[44] (both complaints to Strasbourg arising out of the child abuse cases in *X (minors) v Bedfordshire County Council*[45]) conceding that the striking out of the cases where domestic courts held that it was not fair, just and reasonable to impose a duty of care was a matter of substantive law and did not violate Art.6(1). However, the Court found a violation of Art.13 of the Convention (the right to an effective remedy before a national authority for violation of a Convention right). This restored the ability to strike out on this ground and has some potential impact on substantive law.

(a) *Z v United Kingdom*

7–028   The applicants in *Z* were four siblings. Over a period of four-and-a-half years, serious concerns were raised about the health and well-being of the applicants, including reports that some of the children were stealing food from school bins, that they were kept in filthy rooms or had physical bruising. Ultimately, the children were placed in emergency foster care after their mother threatened to batter them if they were not taken into care. The Official Solicitor commenced proceedings on behalf of the applicants against the local authority, claiming damages for negligence on the basis that the authority, through its child protection staff including psychiatrists and social workers, failed to have proper regard for the children's welfare and to take effective steps to protect them. The applicants' claims were struck out in proceedings culminating in the House of Lords. Lord Browne-Wilkinson, who gave the leading judgment, stated that public policy considerations were such that local authorities should not be held liable in negligence in respect of the exercise of their statutory duties safeguarding the welfare of children under the Children Act 1989. The applicants made a complaint to the European Commission of Human Rights. The Commission applied the principles established in *Osman* to the facts of *Z* and held that there had been a breach of the right of access to court in Art.6 and a breach of Art.3 (the prohibition on inhuman or degrading treatment). The case was then referred to the European Court.[46] In its judgment,[47] the Court also found a violation of Art.3, agreeing with the Commission that the failure to provide the

---

[42] This is the third limb of the three-limb test for the existence of a duty of care established in *Caparo Industries Plc v Dickman* [1990] 2 A.C. 605, HL, the first two being reasonable foreseeability of loss or damage and proximity between the claimant and defendant.
[43] Application No.29392/95, May 10, 2001; *The Times*, May 31, 2001.
[44] Application No.28945/95, May 10, 2001; *The Times*, May 31, 2001.
[45] [1995] 2 A.C. 633, HL.
[46] (1999) 28 E.H.R.R. CD 65; [2000] 2 F.C.R. 245, Eur. Comm. H.R.
[47] Application No.29392/95, May 10, 2001; *The Times*, May 31, 2001.

applicants with appropriate protection against serious, long-term neglect and abuse breached the prohibition on inhuman and degrading treatment.[48] In relation to Art.6(1) and the claimed violation of the right of access to a court, the Court considered Art.6(1) to be applicable to the case on the grounds that there was a serious and genuine dispute about the existence of the right asserted by the applicants under the domestic law of negligence, as shown by the grant of legal aid to the applicants and permission to appeal to the House of Lords. However, it did not consider Art.6(1) to have been violated. The Court expressly resiled from *Osman*, stating that it considered its reasoning in that judgment to have been based on an understanding of the law of negligence which had to be reviewed. It accepted the Government's argument that the inability of the applicants to sue the local authority flowed not from an "immunity" but from the applicable principles governing the substantive right of action in domestic law.[49] Accordingly, the Court appeared to have effectively accepted that *Osman* was decided *per incuriam* although it did not expressly overrule the decision in relation to its application to Art.6. However, the Court having found that there was no violation of Art.6(1), went on to hold that there was a violation of Art.13 (the right to an effective remedy before a national authority for breach of a Convention right)[50] and awarded damages by way of just satisfaction for breach of the applicants' rights under Art.3. The European Court's decision in *TP & KM v United Kingdom*[51] was to the same effect as *Z* although it involved a primary breach of a different Article, namely Art.8.

(b) *Striking Out*

In light of *Z*, there is almost certainly now no restraint on domestic courts imposed by Art.6(1) in relation to striking out claims based on a failure to establish a duty of care because it is not fair, just and reasonable to impose one. The European Court has accepted that this constitutes a matter of substantive domestic law and that Art.6(1) is not violated in principle. However, there is still scope for an *Osman* argument if a decision concerns more than one aspect of the exercise of local authorities' powers and duties such that it can be said to amount to an arbitrary removal of the courts' jurisdiction to determine a whole range of civil claims.[52]

7–029

(c) *Switch from Article 6(1) to Article 13*

Article 13 guarantees an "effective remedy before a national authority" to everyone who claims that his rights and freedoms under the Convention have been violated,[53] so long as that claim is arguable in terms of the Convention.[54] Unlike Art.6(1) which applies to protect the right of access to a court in relation

7–030

---

[48] Application No.29392/95, May 10, 2001; *The Times*, May 31, 2001, para.75.
[49] Application No.29392/95, May 10, 2001; *The Times*, May 31, 2001, para.100.
[50] *ibid.*, para.111.
[51] Application No.28945/95, May 10, 2001; *The Times*, May 31, 2001.
[52] *Z v United Kingdom*, Application No.29392/95, May 10, 2001; *The Times*, May 31, 2001, para.98.
[53] *Klass v Germany* (1980) 2 E.H.R.R. 214, para.64.
[54] *Boyle and Rice v United Kingdom* (1988) 10 E.H.R.R. 425, para.52.

to *any* civil right or obligation which is arguable in domestic law, the right to an effective remedy under Art.13 is limited to providing an effective remedy for an "arguable" breach of another Convention right. Accordingly, Art.13 is parasitic upon establishing the arguability of another Convention right. It is therefore weaker in the protection given to a complainant than Art.6. Article 13 requires that where an individual considers himself to have been prejudiced by a measure allegedly in breach of the Convention, he should have a remedy before a national authority in order to have the claim decided and, if appropriate, to obtain redress.[55] The authority referred to in Art.13 does not need to be a judicial authority[56] and Art.13 does not require any particular remedy.[57] The aggregate of the possible channels of redress in the national legal system may be taken into account.[58]

7–031　　Article 6(1) is incorporated into domestic law through the HRA whilst Art.13 is not. Accordingly, on the face of it, the courts will not be in breach of their obligation under s.6 of the HRA to act compatibly with Convention rights if they fail to provide an effective remedy pursuant to Art.13. However, before the European Court, the State (in the "person" of the UK Government) can be liable for its collective failure (including by its courts) to provide an effective remedy before a national authority for an individual to argue that his Convention rights have been violated. Since courts do have a duty under s.2 of the HRA to take into account Strasbourg case law, including that relating to Art.13,[59] this may influence courts in favour of allowing a claim to proceed to a full hearing on the merits as a matter of existing domestic law in order to avoid the State subsequently being found by the European Court to be in breach of Art.13 for having struck out the claim. The Court recognised in *Z* that a claimant who wishes to complain of a breach of his Convention rights does post-HRA have an effective remedy for Art.13 purposes through the claim mechanism in s.7(1) of the HRA. However, the operation of the limitation provision in s.22(4) of the HRA means that a claim can only be brought under s.7(1)(a) if the act or omission occurs on or after the date of the HRA coming into force, i.e. October 2, 2000. This gives rise to a potential inconsistency in treatment between claims based on acts or omissions which occurred prior to October 2, 2000 where no HRA claim will lie, and those based on acts or omissions following that date, where a claimant can bring a claim under the HRA based on the same set of facts and circumstances. This inconsistency may also influence the willingness of the courts to countenance claims in tort in order to avoid divergence of treatment in similar cases solely related to the date the cause of action arose.

(d) *Tort or Convention?*

7–032　　One likely result of *Z* is that in circumstances where a cause of action in tort is not clearly established as a matter of domestic law, claims are now more likely

---

[55] *Klass v Germany* (1980) 2 E.H.R.R. 214, para.64; *Leander v Sweden* (1987) 9 E.H.R.R. 433, para.77(a).
[56] *Leander v Sweden* (1987) 9 E.H.R.R. 433, para.77(b).
[57] *Vilvarajah v United Kingdom* (1992) 14 E.H.R.R. 248, para.122.
[58] *Silver v United Kingdom* (1983) 5 E.H.R.R. 347, paras 113(c) and 118; *Leander v Sweden* (1987) 9 E.H.R.R. 433, para.77(c).
[59] See *Hansard*, HL col.476 (November 18, 1997).

to be framed as claims under s.7(1)(a) of the HRA either independently of or, more probably in addition to, a tortious claim. Examples include the following:

(1) actions against the police arising out of death or serious injury—Art.2 (right to life);

(2) clinical negligence—Art.2 (right to life);

(3) claims based on failures in child protection against psychiatrists, social workers and local authorities—Art.3 (prohibition on torture inhuman or degrading treatment), or if less serious, Art.8 (right to respect for private life); and

(4) claims against educational psychologists based on failure to diagnose dyslexia or other special needs—Art.8 (right to respect for private life) or possibly, Art.2 of Protocol No.1 (right to education).

Framing a claim under the HRA instead of or in addition to a claim in tort has **7–033** the following implications:

(1) a one-year limitation period applies rather than the usual limitation periods in tort[60];

(2) there may be a potential difference in level of damages awarded. Domestic courts are obligated by s.8 of the HRA to award damages on same principles as the European Court, whose awards have generally been low[61];

(3) under certain Convention Articles (e.g. Arts 8 and 10), once an interference is established by the claimant or admitted by the defendant, the burden of proof is then on the defendant to justify his conduct. This amounts to an effective reversal of the traditional burden of proof in civil claims; and

(4) the evidential requirements in a Convention claim may be different. Evidence of social statistics, government policy and the existence of other remedies may be required, in contrast to traditional common law claims.

(e) *Claims not Governed by the HRA*

In the case of claims arising out of acts and omissions which took place prior to **7–034** October 2, 2000, where no s.7(1)(a) of the HRA claim lies, there may be an indirect effect arising from the Court's finding in Z of a violation of Art.13. If a

---

[60] s.7(5) HRA.
[61] For the approach to damages under the HRA, see the guidance given by the House of Lords in *R. (on the application of Greenfield) v Secretary of State for the Home Department* [2005] UKHL 14; [2005] 2 All E.R. 240. Their Lordships summarised the approach taken by the European Court under Art.41 of the Convention and stated that domestic courts when exercising their power to award damages under s.8 of the HRA should not apply domestic scales of damages.

claim based on an act or omission which pre-dates the coming into force of the HRA can be:

(1) framed as an arguable breach of a substantive Convention right; and

(2) there is no adequate alternative extra-judicial remedy;
    this may lead to reluctance on the part of domestic courts to strike out a claim brought in tort because to do so will encourage the claimant who has been shut out to take his case to the European Court. Such a claimant is likely to succeed in Strasbourg in showing a violation of Art.13 if he can make out an arguable breach of a substantive Convention right and show that he has been denied the opportunity to argue that right and, if appropriate, to obtain redress before a national authority.

(f) *Further Developments since Z*

7–035   Since Z, there have been several European Court cases in the same vein. In the social care context, the decisions of *E v United Kingdom*,[62] *Venema v The Netherlands*[63] and *Yousef v The Netherlands*[64] have considered allegations of breach of Arts 3 and 8 and taken a similar approach to Z and *TP & KM*.

Lam v United Kingdom[65] concerned the failure by domestic courts to find that a duty of care existed in negligence in respect of the manner in which a local authority failed to exercise its enforcement functions to put an end to a statutory nuisance because it was not fair, just and reasonable to impose one. The courts had assumed for the purposes of a strike-out application that it might be possible on the facts to establish foreseeability of harm and proximity. The applicants complained that the domestic courts invoked public policy considerations in order to bestow an immunity on the local authority for its wrongful acts and omissions with the result that they were denied access to a court in breach of Art.6(1). The Court dismissed the complaint as manifestly ill-founded.[66]

In *Reid v United Kingdom*,[67] the European Court of Human Rights held that the applicant's inability to sue the Crown Prosecution Service for negligence in assessing whether there was sufficient evidence against him for a prosecution resulted from principles governing the substantive cause of action and not from an immunity. In *Patel v United Kingdom*,[68] the European Court of Human Rights declared inadmissible a complaint that the applicant had been denied access to a court under Art.6(1). The applicant had brought a claim for negligence against his former counsel in earlier criminal proceedings. Part of the claim was struck out on the ground of advocates' immunity and the rest of the claim was stayed. The action was discontinued in 2001 with no order as to costs. The European

---

[62] (2002) 36 E.H.R.R. 519.
[63] (2002) 36 E.H.R.R. 345.
[64] (2002) 36 E.H.R.R. 345.
[65] Application No.41671/98, July 5, 2001.
[66] In the social care context, see also *DP and JC v United Kingdom* (2003) 36 E.H.R.R. 14 following the Z and *TP & KM* approach to Arts 6(1) and 13; and *E v United Kingdom* (2003) 36 E.H.R.R. 31; [2003] 1 F.L.R. 348 on Art.13.
[67] Application No.33221/96, June 26, 2001.
[68] Application No.38199/97, February 19, 2002.

Court held that there was no restriction on the applicant's access to court under Art.6(1) since his stayed High Court action would have permitted him to apply to amend the statement of claim to cover the barrister's alleged negligent conduct in court which was no longer covered by immunity following the House of Lords decision in *Arthur JS Hall v Simons*.[69]

Turning to domestic cases, in *Walters v North Glamorgan National Health*   **7–036**
Service Trust,[70] Mr Justice Thomas held that the inability of the applicant to sue for damages for "nervous shock" as a result of a pathological grief reaction following the death of her son whilst in the Trust's care flowed from the applicable principles governing the substantive right of action, not from any immunity. In *Re A Debtor No.SD 38 of 2001 Miller v Law Society*,[71] Geoffrey Vos Q.C. held that a solicitor was confined to the statutory rights of appeal to the High Court under the Solicitors Act 1974 regarding the conduct of an investigation of his affairs under the Solicitors Accounting Rules 1991 before any intervention. It was not contrary to Art.6(1) that a solicitor could not bring a claim against the Law Society for breach of a private law duty of care arising from its conduct of the investigation. In *D v East Berkshire Community Health NHS Trust, Dewsbury Health Care NHS Trust & Kirklees Metropolitan Council; Oldham NHS Trust & Dr Blumenthal*,[72] the House of Lords dismissed appeals by parents from the dismissal of their damages claims against local and health authorities for psychiatric harm arising from false allegations made against them by child welfare professionals. An attempt by the claimants to resurrect *Osman* failed. There were strong public policy reasons for concluding that no common law duty of care was owed to parents in relation to childcare decisions.[73]

4. IMMUNITIES

European human rights law does not look favourably on immunities from suit. In   **7–037**
Fayed v United Kingdom,[74] the European Court held that it would not be consistent with the rule of law or the basic principle of access to a court underlying Art.6(1) if a state could:

> "without restraint or control by the Convention enforcement bodies, remove from the jurisdiction of the courts a whole range of civil claims or confer immunities from civil liability on large groups or categories of persons".[75]

---

[69] [2000] 3 W.L.R. 543, HL.
[70] [2002] Lloyd's Rep. Med. 227, QBD.
[71] [2002] 4 All E.R. 312; (2003) P.N.L.R. 4; *The Times*, June 3, 2002, Ch. D.
[72] [2005] UKHL 23; [2005] 2 A.C. 373.
[73] See also *AD v Bury Metropolitan BC* [2006] EWCA Civ 1. The approach was recently confirmed in *L v Pembrokeshire County Council* [2006] EWHC 1029. Field J. held that the policy consideration underlying the principle in *JD* was not rendered invalid or otherwise inapplicable by the fact that after the coming into force of the HRA, such a parent might have a claim under Art.8 of the Convention.
[74] (1994) 18 E.H.R.R. 393.
[75] *ibid.*, para.65.

7–038   Had it survived *Arthur JS Hall v Simons*,[76] advocates' immunity may potentially have infringed Art.6 although it is noted that in *Trevor Rush McCafferty
Wright v Paton Farrell*,[77] the Outer House of the Court of Session held that
advocates' immunity from suit in respect of their conduct in court of criminal
proceedings did not of itself give rise to a violation of Art.6(1).[78] There remains
scope for Art.6 arguments in relation to the *Hunter v Chief Constable of the West
Midlands Police*[79] principle that it is an abuse of process for a person to bring a
civil action by way of a collateral attack on a final decision of a court if that
principle is extended beyond narrow limits. Further, there are possible Convention arguments in relation to the outstanding issue of whether the abolition of
advocates' immunity has prospective or retrospective effect.[80]

7–039   Any extension to the current immunities of arbitrators, experts or witnesses
could arguably contravene Art.6.[81] However, the extent of existing immunities
would appear to be generally compatible with Art.6. In *Taylor v United Kingdom*[82] the applicant solicitor had been prevented from pursuing a libel action
against the Serious Fraud Office by reason of witness immunity attaching to
certain documents. Following his unsuccessful appeal to the House of Lords
against the High Court's decision to strike out his claim, the applicant alleged a
breach of Art.6 before the European Court of Human Rights. Referring to *Z v
United Kingdom*,[83] the Court stated that whilst Art.6 applied to the proceedings
brought by the applicant, it did not guarantee any particular content for his civil
rights. The Court held that the immunity from suit was necessary to encourage
freedom of speech and communication in the judicial process, such that the
limitation it imposed on the applicant's access to court was proportionate and
compatible with the spirit of Art.6(1). In *Benjamin Gray v Laurie Avadis*,[84]
Tugendhat J. found that letters sent to the Office for the Supervision of Solicitors
in connection with a complaint it was investigating attracted absolute privilege
and that the consequent immunity from suit was compatible with Art.6. In *Heath
v Commissioner of Police for the Metropolis*,[85] the appellant argued that the
application of the absolute immunity rule to her claim for unlawful sex discrimination in relation to alleged conduct by members of a disciplinary board in the
conduct of a quasi-judicial proceeding violated her right to a fair hearing under
Art.6(1) because it denied her access to the Employment Tribunal. The Court of

---

[76] [2000] 3 W.L.R. 543, HL.
[77] (2003) P.N.L.R. 410; L.T.L. August 29, 2002, Ct. Sess. (Scot).
[78] See also the cases of *Reid v United Kingdom* and *Patel v United Kingdom* in para.7–035 above.
[79] [1982] A.C. 539, HL.
[80] Whilst a claimant might argue in favour of retrospective effect using Art.6(1), a defendant might
argue that such a course would infringe his legitimate expectation contrary to Art.6(1) or Art.1 of
Protocol No.1 (though even where an individual has a legitimate expectation that a certain state of
affairs will prevail, Art.1 of Protocol No.1 does not necessarily protect such an expectation from the
retrospective effect of a judicial decision: *Antoniades v United Kingdom* (1990) 64 D.R. 232).
[81] Consistent with the theme of the courts being unwilling to create new immunities or extend existing
immunities, in *Id v Home Office* [2005] EWCA Civ 1554; *The Times*, February 10, 2005 the Court
of Appeal was unwilling to construe the Immigration Act 1971, Sch.2 so as to confer immunity from
suit on immigration officers from an action for damages for false imprisonment. In so ruling, the
Court chose not to follow *Ulla v The Home Office, Independent*, July 5, 1994.
[82] Application No.49589/99, June 10, 2003, ECtHR.
[83] *ibid.*
[84] [2003] EWHC 1830; *The Times*, August 19, 2003.
[85] [2004] EWCA Civ 943; *The Times*, July 22, 2004.

Appeal stated that the appellant's right of access to the Employment Tribunal under Art.6(1) was not absolute. It was confined to overcoming procedural bars and immunities, as distinguished from rules as to substantive rights or the lack of them. The Court held that the immunity operated as a substantive bar to the appellant's claim so as not to engage Art.6(1). However, if that conclusion was wrong and the immunity operated as a procedural bar so as to engage Art.6(1), the Court held that the immunity was for a legitimate purpose and was necessary and proportionate in the public interest for the protection of the integrity of the judicial system.[86]

5. Lawyers

The HRA itself may raise new lawyers' liability issues where lawyers have failed   **7–040**
to consider or raise HRA points or where wasted costs orders are made for the raising of what a judge regards as unnecessary arguments,[87] possibly including unnecessary human rights arguments.[88] Three areas of relevance to lawyers' liabilities—the wasted costs jurisdiction, legal professional privilege and freedom of expression/association—are now considered.

(a) *Wasted Costs Orders*

The applicability of Art.6(1) to the wasted costs jurisdiction is not wholly clear.   **7–041**
In *B v United Kingdom*,[89] the European Commission stated that the making of a wasted costs order in that case against a solicitor who had failed to arrange legal representation in a criminal case did not involve the determination of "civil rights and obligations" but concerned the administration of justice and that Art.6(1) was not applicable. However, the European Court has not yet considered the applicability of Art.6(1) to the wasted costs jurisdiction and its general approach to Art.6(1) would suggest that it might well consider it to be applicable. The formulation by the European Court of the "identification of a pecuniary right or interest" test for deciding whether a procedure is determinative of civil rights or obligations in *Editions Périscope v France*[90] (which post-dates *B v United Kingdom*) might now be argued to encompass a wasted costs application. Where considerations of impropriety are in issue, it is likely that Art.6(1) is engaged in light of the settled view of the European Court that professional disciplinary

---

[86] See also the Court of Appeal decision in *D v East Berkshire Community Health NHS Trust* [2003] EWCA Civ 1151; [2003] 4 All E.R. 796 where the Court held that the judge had erred in finding that witness immunity precluded liability in circumstances where it was not clear that the circumstances fell within the scope of the immunity.
[87] *Arthur JS Hall v Simons* [2000] 3 W.L.R. 543 at 589B–C, *per* L. Hope, HL (the power of the judge to make a wasted costs order in a criminal case in regard to advancing what the judge may regard as unnecessary arguments may breach the HRA).
[88] See, e.g. *Daniels v Walker, Practice Note* [2000] 1 W.L.R. 1382 at 1386H–1387C.
[89] (1984) 38 D.R. 213, Application No.10615/83.
[90] (1992) 14 E.H.R.R. 597.

proceedings regulating the right to practice a profession concern the determination of civil rights and must conform to Art.6(1).[91] In *Medcalf v Mardell*,[92] the House of Lords held that it was unfair to make wasted costs orders against leading and junior counsel who had put their signatures to allegations of fraud and other impropriety in a draft notice of appeal where legal professional privilege prevented them from adducing evidence as to whether they had reasonably credible material before them to justify making the allegations. Despite *B v United Kingdom* cited above, the House of Lords was prepared to assume that Art.6(1) was relevant to the wasted costs jurisdiction. If Art.6(1) applies on the ground that a wasted costs application does determine the respondent's civil rights and obligations, the procedure will attract the express and implied rights set out at paras 7–009 and 7–011, above.

(b) *Lawyer/Client Confidentiality and the Convention*

7–042 The European Court has recognised under Art.8 the principle of the right to respect for communications between a person and his lawyer (this being important for the furtherance of a person's rights under Art.6): *Silver v United Kingdom*.[93] The issue has principally arisen in the context of control over prisoners' correspondence by prison authorities. In *Campbell v United Kingdom*,[94] the Court stated:

> "It is clearly in the general interest that any person who wishes to consult a lawyer should be free to do so under conditions which favour full and uninhibited discussion. It is for this reason that the lawyer-client relationship is, in principle, privileged.
>   ... the Court sees no reason to distinguish between the different categories of correspondence with lawyers which, whatever their purpose, concern matters of a private and confidential character. In principle, such letters are privileged under Article 8. This means that the prison authorities may open a letter from a lawyer to a prisoner when they have reasonable cause to believe that it contains an illicit enclosure which the normal means of detection have failed to disclose. The letter should, however, only be opened and should not be read. Suitable guarantees preventing the reading of the letter should be provided, e.g. opening the letter in the presence of the prisoner. The reading of a prisoner's mail to and from a lawyer, on the other hand, should only be permitted in exceptional circumstances when the authorities have reasonable cause to believe that the privilege is being abused in that the contents of the letter endanger prison security or the safety of others or are otherwise of a criminal nature."

7–043 In *Niemietz v Germany*,[95] police searched a lawyer's offices looking for information to reveal the identity and possible whereabouts of a person who was the subject of a criminal investigation. The European Court held that the search violated Art.8, recognising that activities of a professional character could fall within the concept of private life and correspondence in Art.8. It recognised that where a lawyer was involved, an encroachment on professional secrecy might

---

[91] *Le Compte v Belgium* (1982) 4 E.H.R.R. 1; *Gautrin v France* (1999) 28 E.H.R.R. 196.
[92] [2002] 3 W.L.R. 172; [2002] 3 All E.R. 721, HL.
[93] (1983) 5 E.H.R.R. 347.
[94] (1993) 15 E.H.R.R. 137.
[95] (1993) 16 E.H.R.R. 97.

have repercussions on the proper administration of justice and the rights guaranteed by Art.6.[96] In *Foxley v United Kingdom*,[97] the European Court found a violation of Art.8 when the applicant's trustee in bankruptcy, to whom the applicant's post was being redirected by order under s.371 of the Insolvency Act 1986, had opened and made copies of correspondence addressed to the applicant from his legal advisers. Lawyer/client confidentiality is also protected by EC law, which is another legal source of fundamental rights protection.[98]

In the United Kingdom, the common law recognises the right to legal confi-　**7–044** dentiality which arises between a person and their legal adviser as a matter of substantive law, not just procedure (except that the recognition is not afforded where the client is trying to use the relationship to commit a crime or for some unlawful purpose). Legal confidentiality is regarded as a right of great constitutional importance because it is seen as necessary bulwark of a person's right of access to justice whether as a claimant or as a defendant: *R. v Derby Magistrates' Court Ex p. B*.[99] The general protection given to legal confidentiality in English law, through both the common law doctrine of legal professional privilege and the equitable doctrine of confidence, is likely to satisfy, and arguably go beyond, the requirements of Art.8.[1] The protection of legal professional privilege in domestic law is so strong that it will not be abrogated even where it may be relevant to the defence of a defendant charged with murder in a criminal trial.[2] However, the interrelationship between legal confidentiality and the right to a fair trial may need to be further scrutinised in light of the Convention, especially since Art.8(2) permits of an interference with Art.8(1) rights in the interests of the "the protection of the rights and freedoms of others" including the right to a fair trial under Art.6. The Rules Committee attempted to make a limited though unsuccessful inroad into privilege through the legislative route. However, in *General Mediterranean Holdings v Patel*,[3] Toulson J. held that CPR, r.48.7(3) (subsequently revoked), which permitted the court to order disclosure of privileged documents to the court and/or to the other party in the context of a wasted costs application against solicitors, was *ultra vires* to the extent that it cut down the substantive right to legal confidentiality. He had regard to the "high value which the [Strasbourg] court accorded to legal confidentiality" in coming to his decision. In *Medcalf v Mardell*, Lord Hobhouse at para.60 of the judgment appeared to suggest that legal professional privilege may not be absolute by reference to the Convention. He stated:

"The need of a lawyer to be able to ask a court to look at privileged material when a lawyer's conduct is in question may not be so intractable . . . It may be that, as in the context of Article 6 and 8 of the European Convention on Human Rights, the privilege may not always be absolute and a balancing exercise may sometimes be necessary."

---

[96] See also *Panteleyenko v Ukraine*, Application No.00011901/02, June 29, 2006 (illegal search of private notary's office was breach of Art.8).

[97] Application No.33274/96, June 20, 2000; *The Times*, July 4, 2000.

[98] Case 155/79 *AM & S Europe Ltd v Commission of the European Communities* [1983] Q.B. 878.

[99] [1996] A.C. 487, HL.

[1] See, e.g. *R. v Special Commissioners Ex p. Morgan Grenfell & Co*, November 8, 2000, Admin. Ct.

[2] *R. v Derby Magistrates' Court Ex p. B* [1996] A.C. 487, HL.

[3] [1999] 3 All E.R. 673.

This approach of balancing competing rights, inherent in the Convention, is potentially inconsistent with *R. v Derby Magistrates Ex p. B*[4] in which the House of Lords held that legal professional privilege was absolute and trumped all other competing interests. It may be that Lord Hobhouse's dictum will provide some encouragement for a future attack on the absolutist approach to privilege in *Ex p. B*.

7–045   The HRA may come into play in the context of disclosure applications. In *Three Rivers DC & Bank of Credit & Commerce International SA (in liquidation) v Governor & Company of the Bank of England*,[5] the Court of Appeal held that material prepared by Bank of England employees for the Bingham inquiry into the collapse of BCCI was not covered by legal advice privilege since the dominant purpose of such material was to put relevant factual material before the inquiry, not to obtain legal advice. At first instance, Tomlinson J. held that Art.8 was not relevant as any incursion into privacy that might be involved was necessary for the protection of the rights and freedoms of the parties to the litigation, except in specific instances where, for example, the parties agreed to preserve the anonymity of an informant.[6] In *R. (on the application of Millar Gardner Solicitors) v Minshull Street Crown Court*,[7] the Divisional Court held that a warrant to obtain telephone contact details held at a solicitors' office in documents including the office diary was lawful since these details were not subject to legal professional privilege. Whilst Art.8 was engaged, it was justified as necessary in a democratic society for the prevention of crime and protection of others. In *Bodle v Coutts & Co*,[8] the claimant was seeking an order that Coutts & Co's solicitors be restrained from acting for the bank in proceedings brought by the claimant to set aside a statutory demand. The basis for the application was that the solicitors had previously represented the claimant in matrimonial proceedings and during the early stages of her negotiation with the bank. The solicitors refused to release the files to the claimant's new solicitors as the claimant had failed to pay their legal fees. The judge directed that the files be produced to the court in order to ascertain whether or not they contained confidential information that was germane to the unresolved issues. The judge decided that there was no such material. The claimant objected to the solicitors' files being inspected by the judge without her own solicitors having access to the same files on the basis that it would be procedurally unfair to her and in breach of Art.6. Peter Smith J. accepted that it would have been procedurally unfair for the court to have had regard to documents deployed by one side without the other side having access to them and such would have been an arguable breach of Art.6. However, this was not an absolute rule and in the present case to disclose the files to the claimant's solicitors would have entirely circumvented the solicitors' lien. He found that there was no Art.6 infringement of the claimant's rights as the court had to balance her rights against those of the solicitors. It was relevant that the solicitors did not have any relevant confidential information

---

[4] [1996] 1 A.C. 487, HL.
[5] [2003] QB 1556; [2003] 3 W.L.R. 667, CA; *The Times*, April 19, 2003.
[6] [2002] EWHC 2039, Comm.
[7] [2002] EWHC 2079, Admin.
[8] [2003] EWHC 1865, Ch.

concerning the issues between the claimant and the bank and there was no risk of disclosure of any confidential information to the bank.

(c) *Freedom of Expression/Association*

Article 10 may occasionally arise in the context of lawyers' liabilities. The 7–046 European Court held that the conviction of a defence lawyer in criminal proceedings for "negligent defamation" as a result of a memorandum denouncing the tactics of a public prosecutor as "manipulation and unlawful presentation of evidence" was a violation of Art.10 since it was only in exception cases that restriction of defence counsel's freedom of expression could be "necessary in a democratic society": *Nikula v Finland*.[9]

In *Amihalachioaie v Moldova*,[10] the European Court found a violation of 7–047 Art.10 where the chairman of the Moldovan Bar Council strongly criticised a decision of the Constitutional Court holding that the provisions of an Act which required all lawyers practicing in Moldova to be members of the Moldovan Bar Council were unconstitutional. He was subsequently fined for showing a lack of regard for the Constitutional Court and there was no right of appeal. The Court held that the applicant's conviction interfered with his right to freedom of expression. Lawyers are entitled to freedom of expression and to comment in public on the administration of justice, provided that their criticism does not overstep certain bounds. In performing its supervisory role the Court has to look at the interference complained of in the light of the case as a whole, including the tenor of the applicant's remarks and the context in which they were made, and determine whether it "corresponds to a pressing social need", was "proportionate to the legitimate aim pursued" and whether the reasons adduced by the national authorities to justify it are "relevant and sufficient".

In *Steur v Netherlands*,[11] the European Court held that a decision of the 7–048 Disciplinary Appeals Tribunal upholding a complaint against the applicant lawyer and censuring him where in the conduct of a case he had made uncorroborated allegations on behalf of his client against a social security investigating officer (to the effect that he could only have obtained statements from the applicant's client by the application of pressure in an unacceptable manner) was a violation of Art.10. It was stated that the finding might have had a discouraging effect on the applicant, making him feel restricted in the way in which he defended future clients. The Court noted that censuring and placing excessive and unnecessary restrictions on the freedom of expression of a lawyer may have a "chilling effect" on the manner in which he defends future cases. Further, the interference with a lawyer's freedom of expression during the proceedings of a trial may also lead to the violation of the right of a fair trial in some circumstances. In light of the principles in *Nikula*, the "special status" of lawyers had to be considered: not only were they subject to restrictions but they also benefited from exclusive rights and privileges. Their conduct must be discreet, honest and dignified. The applicant's criticism had been aimed at the manner in which the evidence was obtained. It was restricted to the actions of the complainant as an

---

[9] Application No.31611/96, March 21, 2002; (2004) 38 E.H.R.R. 45.
[10] Application No.60115/00; (2005) 40 E.H.R.R. 35.
[11] Application No.39657/98; (2004) 39 E.H.R.R. 33.

investigating officer and focused on his "general professional or other qualities". Further, the statement was confined to the courtroom and did not amount to a personal insult. It was noted that the disciplinary authorities did not attempt to establish whether the impugned statement was true or whether it was made in good faith and at no point did they call into question the honesty of the applicant.

6. MEDICAL PRACTITIONERS

(a) *Introduction*

7–049   Patients have become increasingly aware of their "rights" in relation to those who treat them and expectations of medical care and treatment have increased. As advances in science have brought benefits, there are also increasing legal and moral difficulties as to how such technology should be applied. It is in this area of professional liability that the HRA has proved to have the most immediate impact.

7–050   National Health Service ("NHS") patients being treated by general practitioners, health authorities and trusts can expect them as public authorities to act compatibly with Convention rights in relation to the provision of health care services. Individual rights of action under the HRA will also lie against the Department of Health in appropriate circumstances. However, the position of private patients is less clear. Whilst it would appear that Parliamentary intention was that those who treated patients privately would not be "public authorities" for the purpose of the HRA,[12] the position is less clear where, for example, NHS Trusts contract the treatment of patients out to private clinics. In *R. (on the application of A) v Partnerships in Care*,[13] the managers of a private psychiatric hospital which was acting under statutory powers were held to be a public authority.

(b) *Relevant Articles in relation to Medical Practitioners*

7–051   Medical issues encompass a fairly wide range of Convention articles, namely:

- Article 2:   the right to life;
- Article 3:   the right not to be subject to inhuman and degrading treatment;
- Article 6:   the right to a fair trial, including proceedings before the General Medical Council and the General Dental Council[14];
- Article 8:   the right to respect for private and family life;

---

[12] Hansard, HL col.811 (November 24, 1997) (Lord Chancellor stated that doctors would be public authorities within the meaning of s.6 of the HRA in relation to their NHS practice but not their private practice).
[13] [2002] 1 W.L.R. 2610.
[14] See at paras 7–087 *et seq.*, below.

- Article 9: the right to respect to freedom of thought, conscience and religion;
- Article 12: the right to marry and found a family; and
- Article 14: the prohibition of discrimination in relation to Convention rights.

(i) *Article 2*

Article 2 concerns the protection by law of human life. The right is absolute and, with one limited exception,[15] cannot be subject to derogation. The Article imposes two duties on the State (and through s.6 of the HRA, on health authorities, NHS Trusts and the Department of Health): 7–052

(1) not to take a person's life save in the limited circumstances set out in Art.2(2)[16]; and

(2) to take reasonable measures to protect life.

The Article imposes both a negative obligation to refrain from depriving someone of their life and a positive duty to take reasonable measures to protect life: *X v United Kingdom*.[17] It also includes a duty on the State to take preventative operational measures to protect an individual whose life is at risk from the criminal acts of another individual: *Osman v United Kingdom*.[18] Recognised as one of the most fundamental of all human rights, this Article is likely to play a significant role in medical law issues. Despite the reference to "life", Art.2 is not restricted to cases where actual loss of life occurs. It is sufficient if loss of life is one possible consequence of the conduct complained of.[19] 7–053

Examples of the application of Article 2. Article 2 can be invoked in the following situations: 7–054

(a) *Abortion*: Prior to the HRA, the position in English law was that an unborn child had no existence separate from its mother and could be aborted under the terms of the Abortion Act 1967.[20] In *Paton v United Kingdom*,[21]

---

[15] The only derogation permitted by Art.15 is in respect of deaths resulting from lawful acts of war.

[16] Art.2 expressly provides that deprivation of life shall not be regarded as inflicted in contravention of the Article when it results from the use of force which is no more than absolutely necessary: (a) in defence of any person from unlawful violence; (b) in order to effect a lawful arrest or to prevent the escape of a person lawfully detained; or (c) in action lawfully taken for the purpose of quelling a riot or insurrection.

[17] (1978) 14 D.R. 31.

[18] (2000) 29 E.H.R.R. 245. See also *R. v Amit Misra: R. v Rajeev Srivastava* (2005) 1 Cr. App. R. 21; *The Times*, October 13, 2004. The appellant doctor sought to appeal against his conviction for manslaughter by gross negligence as a result of his post-operative care of a patient who subsequently died of toxic shock syndrome. The Court of Appeal held that the offence of manslaughter by gross negligence was based on well established principles and was not incompatible with the Convention.

[19] Reaffirmed by the European Court of Human Rights in *William and Anita Powell v United Kingdom* [2000] E.H.R.L.R. 650 at 654; Application No.45305/99, May 4, 2000.

[20] *Re F (in utero)* [1988] Fam. 122, CA; *St George's Healthcare NHS Trust v S* [1998] 3 W.L.R. 936 at 957A.

[21] (1980) 3 E.H.R.R. 408.

the Commission held that a foetus had no absolute right to life as the term "everyone" in Art.2 generally only applied post-natally but it left open the question whether the foetus did have some right to life (for example, if it was able to live independently of its mother). In *H v Norway*,[22] the Commission held that the abortion of a foetus for social reasons was not contrary to Art.2 where there was "a difficult situation of life" in relation to the mother. These decisions, which allow a wide margin of appreciation in relation to the right to life, were relied on by one member of the Court of Appeal in the case of the conjoined twins in *Re A (Minors) (Conjoined Twins: Separation)*.[23] Ward L.J. stated that Art.2 was subject to an implied limitation that justified the balancing approach taken by the Court in allowing the twins to be separated despite the fact that this would cause certain death to one of the twins.[24] In *Vo v France*[25] the European Court stated that it was unnecessary to answer in the abstract the question of whether the unborn child was a "person" for the purposes of Art.2, thereby reinforcing the margin of appreciation of the Member States in this area and highlighting the view of the European Group of Ethics that "it would be inappropriate to impose one exclusive moral code". The Court chose to focus instead on the legal protection to which the applicant was entitled in respect of the loss of the unborn child and on the procedural requirements of Art.2. The Court concluded that recourse should have been made to the administrative courts, thereby allowing the applicant to prove medical negligence on the part of the doctor whose failure to examine the applicant prior to the medical procedure caused her to lose her child. See also in *R. v Secretary of State for Health Ex p. John Smeaton (on behalf of the Society for the Protection of Unborn Children)*,[26] in which the legality of the sale and use of the morning after pill was unsuccessfully challenged.

(b) *Euthanasia*: Article 2 confers a right to life but not a right to die. The national court's duty to respect the sanctity of human life and the refusal to sanction a course of conduct aimed at terminating life or accelerating death was affirmed at first instance in *A National Health Service Trust v D*.[27] The issue of euthanasia has now been extensively considered by the House of Lords and the European Court: see *Pretty v Director of Public Prosecutions and Home Secretary*[28] and *Pretty v United Kingdom*.[29] The House of Lords held that:

---

[22] (1992) 73 D.R. 155.

[23] [2001] 2 W.L.R. 480; [2000] Lloyd's Rep. Med. 425, CA.

[24] Walker L.J. and Brooke L.J. preferred to base their decision on the fact that the doctor's purpose in performing the operation was to save life, even if the extinction of another life was a virtual certainty and therefore this was not intentional killing. The word "intentionally" in Art.2 was said to apply only where the purpose of the prohibited action was death (consistent with existing domestic law on this subject). The Court's consideration of the human rights aspects of the appeal is extremely brief.

[25] Application No.53924/00.

[26] [2002] 2 F.L.R. 146, Admin.

[27] [2000] 2 F.L.R. 677; [2000] Lloyd's Rep. Med. 411; *The Times*, July 19, 2000, *per* Cazalet J.

[28] [2001] 3 W.L.R. 1598; [2002] 1 All E.R. 1, HL.

[29] [2002] 35 E.H.R.R. 1.

(i) the right to life set out in Art.2 could not be interpreted as conferring a right to die or to enlist the aid of another in bringing about one's death;

(ii) the Art.3 right not to be subjected to inhuman or degrading treatment did not bear on an individual's right to live or die; it could not plausibly be suggested that the respondent was inflicting such treatment on Mrs Pretty whose suffering derived from her disease[30];

(iii) the Art.8 right to respect for private life covered protection of personal autonomy in living; it did not extend to the choice not to live any longer. Further, even if Art.8 applied, the present legislative regime was justifiable under Art.8(2) and it was notable that the United Kingdom's response to this problem was in accordance with a broad international consensus;

(iv) a belief in the virtue of assisted suicide could not found a requirement pursuant to Art.9(1) for Mrs Pretty's husband to be absolved from the consequences of criminal conduct and the same arguments on justification applied in any event;

(v) even if one of the ECHR Articles was engaged and Mrs Pretty could therefore rely in principle on Art.14, s.2 of the Suicide Act 1961 did not discriminate against the disabled whilst allowing the able-bodied to commit suicide; the law conferred no right on anyone to commit suicide.

The European Court largely agreed with the English court's interpretation of the Convention, holding that:

(i) Article 2 did not impose on States a positive obligation to protect a "right to die";

(ii) A State's obligation to prevent ill treatment pursuant to Art.3 could not be considered to include permitting actions designed to cause death. Nor was the State required to provide a means of lawfully committing assisted suicide;

(iii) Whilst the right to refuse medical treatment was within Art.8, the interference with Mrs Pretty's ability to end her life was legitimate and "necessary in a democratic society";

(iv) Article 9 did not protect all convictions or beliefs: a strongly held belief about assisted suicide did not fall within its meaning;

(v) The State had an objective and reasonable justification for not distinguishing in law between individuals who were and were not capable of committing suicide and therefore there had been no violation of Arts 8 and 14.

However, in contrast to the *Pretty* case, in *Ms B v An NHS Hospital Trust*[31] a patient's right to refuse treatment and have the ventilator which kept her alive switched off even if this would result in her death was upheld on the ground that this amounted to refusal of treatment as opposed to active ending of life. Many commentators have called for reform of the law in

---

[30] In *R. (on the application of Q) v Secretary of State for the Home Department* [2004] Q.B. 36 the Court of Appeal approved the approach taken to Art.3 in *Pretty*.
[31] [2002] 2 All E.R. 449.

light of the anomalies which arguably arise as a result of the two cases.[32]

(c) *Withdrawal of treatment*: This is dealt with at paras 7–069 *et seq.*, below;

(d) *Right to information on life-threatening risks*: Art.2 has been applied in the health and environmental contexts to life-threatening hazards in so far as these hazards may be attributed to the State.[33] Applying analogous principles, the HRA ought to be considered by medical authorities when deciding how to deal with potential life-threatening health risks and particularly in relation to the provision of advice or information relating to those risks. However in *Patricia Howard v Secretary of State for Health*[34] Mr Justice Scott Baker held that the Secretary of State for Health had been entitled to refuse public access to two inquiries that he had instigated into serious malpractice by doctors, although it was relevant that the Secretary of State had conceded access by interested parties and their representatives throughout the oral hearings and there was no prohibition on witnesses communicating with the media. The judge noted that Art.10(1) did not confer a right on individuals to receive information that others were not willing to impart and the Secretary of State's decision had not interfered with the applicants' ability to impart information by any means available to them. He also held that Art.3 was not engaged because clinical negligence was not a sufficient foundation for such a claim.

(e) *Inquests*: There has been a great deal of case law in this area since the HRA came into force and the House of Lords has re-emphasised the scope of Art.2 protection in the case of deaths post the Human Rights Act coming into force: see *R. (on the application of Khan) v Secretary of State for Health*.[35] Their Lordships held that the State's investigatory obligations included a duty to require a public inquiry with the participation of the deceased's family and that the holding of an inquest would not satisfy that obligation as the claimant was in no fit state to take part in it himself unless he had legal representation. It was emphasised that a public investigation had to be held which was both judicial and effective. See also *R. v Secretary of State for the Home Department Ex p. Amin*[36] in which the House of Lords again re-emphasised the importance of a proper (namely an independent public) investigation under Art.2 where a death occurs in

---

[32] For further analysis of the case law in this area see *"Assisted Suicide under the European Convention on Human Rights: a Critique"* [2003] E.H.R.L.R. 65. See also *A Local Authority (Claimant) v MR Z (Defendant) & The Official Solicitor (Advocate to the Court)* (2005) 1 W.L.R. 959 in which Hedley J. held that a local authority had a duty to investigate the position of a disabled person who wished her husband to arrange assisted suicide for her in Switzerland and to consider whether she was legally competent. However, where she was competent, the local authority had no duty to seek the continuation of an injunction restraining the husband from removing his wife from England. In the context of a person of full capacity, the right to life under Art.2 of the European Convention on Human Rights 1950 did not assume primacy over the rights of autonomy and self-determination.

[33] *LCB v United Kingdom* (1999) 27 E.H.R.R. 212.

[34] [2002] 3 W.L.R. 738; *The Times*, March 28, 2002, Admin. Ct.

[35] [2003] 4 All E.R. 1239.

[36] [2001] A.C.D. 11.

custody. However, there is no absolute need for a full public inquiry. See *Yvonne Scholes v Secretary of State for the Home Department*[36a] for an example of where the United Kingdom's duty under Art.2 of the Convention to investigate a suicide at a young offender institution had been discharged without a full public inquiry having been held. It is also important to note that in *Re McKerr*[37] the House of Lords made clear that the duty to investigate an unlawful killing under Art.2 did not arise in domestic law in respect of deaths before October 2, 2000, when the Human Rights Act came into force.[38] However, in *Commissioner of Police for the Metropolis v Christine Hurst*[39] it was held that where there were very strong reasons of public policy why an inquiry of the kind mandated in Art.2 should take place and no unfairness would be caused to an individual by the holding of such an inquiry, s.3 of the HRA 1998 could be given a limited retrospective application in order to bring about the resumption of the inquest.

The leading authority on inquests and what Art.2 requires is now *R. (on the application of Middleton) v West Somerset Coroner*.[40] The House of Lords made clear that where an inquest is the means by which the State discharges its procedural obligation to initiate an effective public investigation into a death involving or possibly involving a breach of the Convention, it has ordinarily to culminate in an expression of the jury's conclusion on the disputed factual issues at the heart of the case in order to be compliant with the Convention. This could be achieved by interpreting the word "how" in the Coroners Act 1988, s.11(5)(b)(ii) in a broad sense, meaning "by what means and in what circumstances", rather than simply "by what means" the deceased came by his death. The Convention would not be complied with where there was no exploration of the facts surrounding the death or where short verdicts in the traditional form were given. It was for the coroner to decide how best to elicit the jury's conclusion on the central issues and this might be done by inviting an expanded or narrative form of verdict or by inviting the jury's answers to factual questions put by the coroner.[41]

[36a] [2006] EWCA Civ 1343.

[37] [2004] 1 W.L.R. 807.

[38] *Re McKerr* appears to be inconsistent with the approach of the European Court in *Cyprus v Turkey* (2002) 35 E.H.R.R. 487 (which was not cited in *McKerr*) and this has led to suggestions that *McKerr* was wrongly decided. However, *Re McKerr* was applied in *Jean Pearson v HM Coroner for Inner London North* [2005] EWHC 833; and *Louie Clayton v HM Coroner for South Yorkshire (East District) & Chief Constable of South Yorkshire & PC Cross* [2005] EWHC 1196.

[39] *The Times*, August 11, 2005.

[40] [2004] 2 A.C. 182.

[41] *Middleton* was applied by the House of Lords in a decision made on the same day: see *R. (on the application of Sacker) v HM Coroner for the County of West Yorkshire* (2004) 1 W.L.R. 796. See also *Rita Goodson v HM Coroner for Bedfordshire and Luton & Luton and Dunstable Hospital NHS Trust* (2005) 2 All E.R. 791 in which Richards J. held that there was no separate procedural obligation to investigate under Art.2 of the Convention where a death in hospital raised no more than a potential liability in negligence. Accordingly, it could not be argued that a coroner was required to seek the assistance of an independent medical expert witness at the inquest into the death of a patient in an NHS hospital. In *Plymouth CC v HM Coroner for Devon & Secretary of State for Education and Skills* [2005] EWHC 1014, Wilson J. held that it was not appropriate to extend an inquest into the death of a child to the role played by the statutory child protection agencies in relation to the child's

(ii) *Article 3*

7–055   The right not to be subjected to inhuman or degrading treatment may be invoked in relation to issues of forced treatment or the maintenance of life by artificial support. It will often conflict with the right to life, but may nonetheless be relied upon as a basis for complaint. Article 3 will also apply to issues arising in relation to the refusal of treatment and experimental treatment.[42] In *R. (on the application of PS) v (1) Responsible Medical Officer (Dr G) (2) Second Opinion Appointed Doctor (Dr W)*[43] forcible administration of anti-psychotic drugs was held to be permissible under the Mental Health Act even where the patient had capacity and had elected not to give consent. The claimant's rights were held not to be engaged under Art.3 because (i) the treatment did not achieve the minimum level of severity to amount to inhuman or degrading treatment; and/or (ii) medical or therapeutic necessity had been convincingly shown to exist. The treatment was also said to be proportionate and justified under Art.8. The limits of Art.3 rights in this context were recently re-emphasised by the House of Lords in *R. (B) v Ashworth Hospital Authority.*[44] Their Lordships held that no breach of Arts 3 or 8 arose in respect of a claimant who was treated compulsorily under s.63 of the Mental Health Act 1983 for his psychopathic disorder in a personality disorder ward without the need for reclassification as such treatment was justified by therapeutic necessity.

(iii) *Article 6*[45]

7–056   Article 6 is perhaps the most important article as far as clinical negligence generally and tribunal procedure is concerned. It is also possible for medical practitioners (and other healthcare professionals) to invoke Art.6 to protect their rights in disciplinary proceedings before their regulatory bodies. Even prior to the coming into force of the HRA, regulatory bodies were changing certain procedures in order to ensure compatibility with the Convention. Article 6 in the disciplinary context is dealt with at paras 7–087 *et seq.*, below.

7–057   In *Hubbard v Lambeth Southwark & Lewisham HA*[46] a decision by the master to order a private pre-trial meeting of both parties' expert witnesses was upheld on the grounds that it would usefully identify and narrow the issues, notwithstanding the genuine sensitivity of the claimants' experts in criticising the professional competence of a distinguished colleague at such a meeting. The Court of Appeal held that the order did not raise any issues under Art.6.

---

life since the trigger for the investigative duty under Art.2 of the Convention had not been activated as there was no evidence to justify a conclusion that the statutory child protection agencies knew or ought to have known of a real and immediate risk to the child's life.

[42] The European Commission has held that experimental medical treatment may amount to inhuman treatment, if not torture, in the absence of consent: *X v Denmark* (1983) D.R. 282; Application No.9974/82.

[43] [2003] EWHC 2335.

[44] [2005] UKHL 20; [2005] 2 A.C. 278. See also *R. (on the application of B) v (1) SS (Responsible Medical Officer) (2) Second Opinion Appointed Doctor* [2006] EWCA Civ 28; (2006) 1 W.L.R. 810 (Art.3 not engaged in respect of patient detained under Mental Health Act 1983 as proposed compulsory administration of medication unlikely to reach a level of severity sufficient to engage the Convention and the treatment was a medical or therapeutic necessity).

[45] For an introduction to Art.6 please see paras 7–004 *et seq.*, above.

[46] [2002] Lloyd's Rep. Med. 8.

However, in *William Cassie Powell and Anita Diane Powell v Paul Boladz*[47] Art.6 was used to defeat the defendant's application to strike out a libel action on the basis that the interference with the claimant's rights under Art.6 would be more serious if the application was granted than the interference with the defendant's rights under the same Article if the application was refused.

See also *R. (on the application of Alliss) v Legal Service Commission*[48] in **7–058** which the claimant succeeded in establishing that the withdrawal of funding by the Legal Services Commission five months before a three-week personal injury and wrongful death claim was in breach of Art.6(1). The Court held that the grant of legal aid might be required pursuant to Art.6 where it was indispensable to ensure effective and fair access to the court which might be by reason of the complexity or type of case. On the facts of that case the claimant was a young man with psychiatric problems and limited education and the trial would be lengthy and complex with the opposing party being represented by leading and junior counsel. In these circumstances, having supported the case for five years it had become too late for funding to be withdrawn (although the Court did say that had public funding been discharged at an early stage of the case, that would have been acceptable).

(iv) *Article 8*

The right to respect for private and family life affects a wider range of issues than **7–059** might at first be thought including, for example, consent to treatment,[49] the right to information on life-threatening risks,[50] the confidentiality of medical records,[51] a patient's right of access to medical records[52] or disclosure of the fact that a person has HIV or AIDS. It might also be arguable that the right to respect for private life in Art.8 supports an entitlement to abortion. However, in *Greenfield v Irwin*,[53] Buxton L.J. indicated (albeit obiter[54]) that the claimant was highly unlikely to be able to rely on Art.8 in order to allow her to claim for loss of employment caused by reason of a negligent failure to diagnose a pregnancy. The court drew attention to the fact that states were permitted a wide margin of appreciation in relation to Art.8.

Examples of the application (or attempted application) of Art.8 since the Act **7–060** came into force include the following:

(a) *Joanna Rose v Secretary of State for Health*,[55] in which Scott Baker J. held that the desire by a person born as a result of artificial insemination by donor to know details of their origin did engage Art.8 and placed the State under a positive obligation. The information the claimants were trying to obtain was about their biological fathers and was something which went to the heart of their identity and to their make-up as people. Respect for

---

[47] [2003] EWHC 2160.
[48] [2002] EWHC 2079, Admin.
[49] See para.7–073, below.
[50] *Guerra v Italy* (1998) 26 E.H.R.R.357; *López Ostra v Spain* (1995) 20 E.H.R.R. 277.
[51] See paras 7–082 to 7–085, below.
[52] See para.7–076, below.
[53] [2001] 1 W.L.R. 1279.
[54] By reason of the fact that the HRA was not in force at the time of the original judgment.
[55] [2002] 2 F.L.R. 962; [2002] EWHC 1593, Admin; L.T.L. July 26, 2002.

private and family life incorporated the concept of personal identity. However, it should be noted that the issue as to whether Art.8 had in fact been breached was left open.

(b) *Re R (A Child) sub nom. Re R (A Child) (IVF: Paternity of Child)*[56] in which it was held that a husband whose sperm had mistakenly not been used in fertility treatment was, as a result of ss.28 and 29 of the Human Fertilisation and Embryology Act 1990, not the legal father of the resultant children. This was held to amount to an interference with his Art.8 rights but it was not necessary to consider the question of incompatibility because within domestic legislation there were remedies which could protect his position in relation to the twins (even if he was not entitled to a declaration of paternity), thereby making any breach of his Art.8 rights proportionate.

(c) In *Natallie Evans v Amicus Healthcare*[57] the Court of Appeal held that the female claimants were not entitled to use frozen embryos created by IVF treatment after the claimants had separated from their male partners who had withdrawn their consent to treatment. Article 2 was said not to be engaged as an embryo was not a human life. However, the wishes of the claimants to continue with the IVF treatment and to have the embryos released from storage and transferred to them was held to engage their right to respect for their private lives under Art.8 which was also engaged by their former partners' opposition to that course of action. The provisions of Sch.3 to the Human Fertilisation and Embryology Act 1990 which permitted the former partners to refuse to allow the claimants access to the embryos was an interference with their Convention rights but that interference was both necessary for the protection of the rights of all four parties and proportionate.

(d) In *Deep Vein Thrombosis & Air Travel Group Litigation*[58] Nelson J. (whose decision was upheld by the Court of Appeal) held that neither Arts 6 nor 8 of the ECHR gave the claimants a remedy outside of the Warsaw Convention, nor was Art.17 of the latter Convention incompatible with ECHR rights.

(e) In *Collins v United Kingdom*[59] a severely disabled claimant had been moved to a purpose built complex within a hospital where she was promised a "home for life". However in 2000 the Health Authority decided to close down that complex and transfer future care to the Social Services Directorate. The claimant unsuccessfully brought judicial review proceedings to challenge that decision. It was held that the decision to move her into alternative care was not disproportionate, gave proper consideration to her interests and was based on relevant and sufficient reasons;

---

[56] (2003) 2 All E.R. 131; [2003] EWCA Civ 182.
[57] [2004] 2 W.L.R. 713.
[58] [2004] Q.B. 234; *The Times*, July 14, 2003.
[59] Application No.11909/02, October 15, 2002.

(f) In *R. (on the application of Sue Axon) v Secretary of State for Health & Family Planning Association*[60] there was held to be no infringement of Art.8(1) rights of a young person's parents if a health professional was permitted to withhold information relating to advice or treatment of the young person on sexual matters.

(g) In *R. (on the application of TB) v Stafford Combined Court & Crown Prosecution Service*[61] there was held to be a breach of Art.8 where a Crown Court Judge had ordered disclosure of the psychiatric records of a minor who was a witness in a trial relating to sexual offences against her without serving her with notice of the witness summons directed to her NHS trust requiring the records.

(h) In *Evans v United Kingdom*[61a] a woman was prevented from using previously created embryos when her ex-partner refused to provide consent to the same being used. Before the European Court she sought to rely on Arts 8 and 14, complaining that the Human Fertilisation and Embryology Act 1990 violated her right to private life and discriminated against women dependent on IVF. She further complained that it violated the embryo's right to life contrary to Art.2. The European Court dismissed her application holding that:

   (i) the question of when a right to life begins was within the margin of appreciation and under English law embryos had no right to life and hence no violation of Art.2.

  (ii) the rules in the 1990 Act were within the margin of appreciation and there was no breach of Art.8.

 (iii) there was an objective and reasonable justification for any difference between a woman able to conceive without assistance compared to a woman dependent on IVF and therefore no breach of Art.14.

(v) *Article 9*

The right to freedom of thought, conscience and belief may be invoked in relation to issues of refusal of treatment. It may also be relevant where a medical practitioner holds a conscientious objection to abortion and the extent to which they may lawfully object to having any association whatsoever with an abortion procedure.[62] **7–061**

(vi) *Article 12*

The right to marry and found a family may be relevant to issues of who is entitled to receive fertility treatment on the NHS.[63] Article 12 was unsuccessfully sought **7–062**

---

[60] [2006] EWHC 372; (2006) Q.B. 539.
[61] [2006] EWHC 1645; *Independent*, July 6, 2006.
[61a] (2006) 43 E.H.R.R. 21.
[62] See further Leonard Hammer, "Abortion Objection in the United Kingdom Within the Framework of the European Convention on Human Rights and Fundamental Freedoms" [1999] E.H.R.L.R. 564 at 575, who argues that s.4 of the Abortion Act 1967 does not provide sufficient protection for abortion objectors.
[63] See, e.g. *R. v Human Fertilisation and Embryology Authority Ex p. Blood* [1999] Fam. 151; [1997] 2 All E.R. 687; and para.7–053, below.

to be invoked in *Briody v St Helen's & Knowsley AHA*[64] in which the Court of Appeal held that damages were not recoverable for surrogacy treatment which, although lawful, had a vanishingly small chance of success (assessed at 1 per cent). The right to a family founded by marriage set out in Art.12 was held to be quite different from having a right to be supplied with a child.

7. Particular Issues Arising under the HRA in Relation to Medical Practitioners

(a) *Clinical Negligence and the Bolam Test*

7–063   Prior to the coming into force of the Act, it had been suggested by some practitioners that Art.2 may provide a means for challenging the long established *Bolam* test and the court's adherence to the "respectable body of medical opinion" approach.[65] The argument put forward was that the *Bolam* test is inconsistent with the right to life unless the domestic courts construe the requirement to take reasonable care as equivalent to the requirement to make adequate provision for medical care. If the care provided is negligent then, by definition, it will not have been adequate. However, the converse may not apply and care that is inadequate is not necessarily negligent. Despite such anticipation, such a challenge is yet to be successfully mounted.

(b) *Right to Treatment*

7–064   There is scope for arguing under the HRA that health authorities and NHS Trusts are obliged to make adequate provision for medical care in all cases where the right to life of the patient in question would otherwise be endangered. The question was raised in *X v Ireland*,[66] but the Commission held that it was unnecessary to determine this issue because the applicant had in fact received treatment and her life had not been endangered. In *Association X v United Kingdom*,[67] it was held that the State must take adequate and appropriate steps to protect life and that this might raise issues with respect to the adequacy of medical care. The case concerned the steps taken by the state to reduce the risks to life by introducing a vaccination programme for children. On the facts before it, the Commission found no evidence to suggest that the vaccinations had been administered poorly or that proper steps had not been taken to minimise any risks.

7–065   The European Court has allowed Contracting States an almost unfettered discretion in relation to the allocation of resources pursuant to the doctrine of the margin of appreciation. Prior to the implementation of the HRA, domestic courts also showed a marked reluctance to become involved in decisions in this area. For example, in *R. v Cambridge HA Ex p. B*,[68] the Health Authority decided not

---

[64] [2002] 2 W.L.R. 394, CA.
[65] See further Philip Havers Q.C. in Powers and Harris (eds), *Medical Law* (Butterworths, 1999).
[66] (1974) 7 D.R. 78.
[67] (1978) 14 D.R. 31.
[68] [1995] 1 W.L.R. 898.

to give a particular treatment to a young female patient suffering from leukaemia on the basis that it might only have a 20 per cent chance of success. It was therefore held not to be in her best interests and scarce resources should not be allocated to it. The Court of Appeal upheld the Health Authority's decision stating that this was an area in which the Court could not make a judgment as to how a limited budget was best allocated to the maximum advantage of the maximum number of patients.[69]

It might at first appear that such an approach would no longer be consistent   **7-066**
with the Convention. The right to life is an absolute right to which, in theory, lack of financial resources to provide the care in question provides no defence. However, the European Court stated in *Osman v United Kingdom*,[70] albeit in the context of the obligations on the police to take positive steps to protect life, that the Art.2 obligation must be interpreted in a way which "does not impose an impossible or disproportionate burden on the authorities".[71] Further, in *Powell v United Kingdom*,[72] the Court stated that whilst Art.2 required the State to take appropriate steps to safeguard the lives of those within its jurisdiction, where the State made adequate provision for securing high professional standards among health professionals and the protection of patients' lives, matters such as errors of judgment or negligent co-ordination among health professionals were insufficient to call a Contracting State to account from the standpoint of its obligations under Art.2. The HRA, however, allows courts to look at both the decision-making process and the merits of the decision. Thus, resource allocation decisions should become more transparent.[73]

Blanket bans on treatment may be challenged as being incompatible with the   **7-067**
Convention. For example, a blanket ban on the basis of age may arguably contravene Arts 3, 8 and 14. If the ban related to resuscitation, it might also breach Art.2. A decision not to fund fertility treatment could potentially violate Arts 8 and 12.

Hospital waiting lists may also be challenged if the facts merit it. In *Passan-*   **7-068**
nante v Italy,[74] the Commission held that excessive delay by a public authority in providing a medical service to which a patient is entitled, and the fact that such delay has (or is likely to have) a serious impact on the patient's health could amount to an interference with the right to respect for private life under Art.8(1). In *R. v North and East Devon HA Ex p. Coughlan*,[75] the Court of Appeal held that the decision of the health authority to close an NHS home in which the applicant was a resident constituted a breach of Art.8. Although Art.8(2) permits justification for an interference with the right to respect for private life on the ground of

[69] [1995] 1 W.L.R. 898 at 906, *per* Sir Thomas Bingham M.R. See also James and Longley, "Judicial Review and Tragic Choices" [1995] P.L. 367; and O'Sullivan, "The Allocation of Scarce Resources and the right to life under the ECHR" [1998] P.L. 389.
[70] (2000) 29 E.H.R.R. 245.
[71] (2000) 29 E.H.R.R. 245, para.116.
[72] [2000] E.H.R.L.R. 650.
[73] Lord Irvine of Lairg, "The Development of Human Rights in Britain under an Incorporated Convention on Human Rights" [1998] P.L. 221 at 224.
[74] (1998) 26 E.H.R.R. C.D. 153.
[75] [2000] 2 W.L.R. 622; [1999] C.O.D. 340, CA. *cf. Frank Cowl v Plymouth CC* [2001] EWHC Admin. 734 (September 14, 2001) in which Scott Baker J. held that the consultation process carried out by a local authority prior to closing a residential care home for the elderly was adequate and not in breach of the Convention.

resources, such derogation would have to be applied without discrimination "on any ground" pursuant to Art.14.

(c) Withdrawal of Treatment

7–069 As stated above, Art.2 provides for a right to live. It does not state that there is a duty to live. Equally, there is no right to die. This area is further complicated by the potential incapacity of patients to make clear their own wishes by reason of their medical condition. In *D v United Kingdom*,[76] the European Court emphasised the importance of dying with dignity, although it declined to rule on the Art.2 contentions.

7–070 In *A National Health Service Trust v D*,[77] a 19-month-old child suffered from a severe, chronic and worsening lung disease which meant that his life expectancy was very short. The paediatricians involved in his care were firmly of the opinion that it would not be in the child's best interest to be readmitted to intensive care to undergo further resuscitation involving artificial ventilation. His parents were totally opposed to any such inaction but the paediatrician they instructed for the purpose of the hearing expressed the same opinion as the doctors in charge of their child's care. Cazalet J. agreed with the expressed medical opinion as to what was in the child's best interests in granting a declaration that treatment to prolong the child's life would not be required. Such a declaration was held not to infringe Art.2 because the decision was in the child's best interests. Article 3 was also relied upon to support the argument that a person had a right to die with dignity. The judge set out four general principles to be used as a framework in such cases:

(1) the court's paramount consideration is the best interests of the child and this involves a careful consideration of the views of the parents. However, those views cannot override the court's views of the child's best interests;

(2) the court's respect for the sanctity of human life imposes a strong obligation to take all steps capable of preserving life, save in exceptional circumstances;

(3) there is no question of approving a course of action aimed at terminating life or accelerating death; and

(4) it is well established that a court will not direct a doctor to provide treatment which he or she is unwilling to give and which is against clinical judgment.

7–071 In *NHS Trust A v M; NHS Trust B v H*,[78] Dame Butler-Sloss held that a decision to cease treatment in a patient's best interests was not an intentional deprivation of life contrary to Art.2, which imported a deliberate act, not an

---

[76] (1997) 24 E.H.R.R. 423.
[77] [2000] 2 F.L.R. 677; [2000] Lloyd's Rep. Med. 411; *The Times*, July 19, 2000, *per* Cazalet J.
[78] [2001] 2 W.L.R. 942; [2001] 1 All E.R. 801; [2001] Lloyd's Rep. Med. 28; *The Times*, November 29, 2000, Dame Elizabeth Butler-Sloss P.

omission. In relation to the State's positive obligation under Art.2 to take adequate and appropriate steps to safeguard life, where a responsible clinical decision was made to withhold treatment that was not in the patient's best interests, and that accorded with a respectable body of medical opinion, the State's positive obligation was discharged.

In *R. (on the application of Oliver Leslie Burke) v General Medical Council*   **7–072** *& (1) The Disability Rights Commission (Interested Party) and (2) The Official Solicitor to the Supreme Court (Intervener)*[79] it was held that under both the Convention and at common law, if a patient was competent, or although incompetent had made an advance directive which was valid and relevant to the treatment in question, his decision to require the provision of artificial nutrition and hydration (ANH) during his dying days was determinative of the issue. If neither such circumstances applied, the duty would be to treat the patient in his or her best interests (with there being a strong presumption in favour of preservation of life). It was stated that a failure to provide life-prolonging treatment in circumstances exposing the patient to "inhuman or degrading treatment" would in principle involve a breach of Art.3. Alternatively even if the patient's suffering had not reached the severity required to breach Art.3, a withdrawal of treatment in the same circumstances might still breach Art.8 if there were sufficiently adverse effects on his physical or moral integrity or mental stability. Thus, at the final stage when the patient had lapsed into a coma and lacked awareness of what was happening, there would not be a breach if ANH was withdrawn in circumstances where its continuation was futile and of no benefit to the patient. However, the prior authorisation of the court was required as a matter of law where it was proposed to withdraw or withhold ANH. In *R. (on the application of Oliver Leslie Burke) v General Medical Council & the Disability Rights Commission*[80] the Court of Appeal held that there was nothing in the General Medical Council's guidance paper on the withholding and withdrawing of artificial nutrition and hydration that was unlawful or that constituted a breach of the Convention. Where a competent patient indicated his or her wish to be kept alive by the provision of ANH, any doctor who deliberately brought that patient's life to an end by discontinuing the supply of ANH would not merely be in breach of duty but would be guilty of murder and in violation of Art.2.

(d) *Consent to Treatment*

When the courts are asked to consider the issue of the extent of a doctor's duty   **7–073** to warn the patient of the risks and complications of a procedure, this Article could be sought to be relied upon in support of a doctrine of "informed consent" based on a patient's right to know, in place of the doctor-based duty which is currently favoured by the English courts. Consent can, however, be overridden in certain circumstances. For example, in *Acmanne v Belgium*,[81] the applicant's challenge to compulsory tuberculosis screening failed. It was held that although

---

[79] [2004] EWHC 1879.
[80] [2005] EWCA Civ 1003; (2005) 3 W.L.R. 1132.
[81] (1983) 40 D.R. 251.

there was interference with private life, it was justified in order to protect health.[82]

7–074   In *Glass v United Kingdom*[83] there was held to be a violation of Art.8 where a hospital imposed treatment on a severely mentally and physically handicapped child contrary to the wishes of his mother. The decision to impose treatment was held to give rise to interference with the right to respect for the child's private life and in particular his right to physical integrity. It was further stated that, save in emergency situations, the requirement of parental consent required doctors to seek the intervention of the court. Thus the decision to override the mother's objection to the proposed treatment in the absence of authorisation by the court violated Art.8.

7–075   Further, in *R. (on application of B) v Dr SS (Responsible Medical Officer Broadmoor Hospital) & Dr G (Second Opinion Appointed Doctor) & Secretary of State for the Department of Health*[84] the court was dealing with a patient who did not have capacity to consent to treatment as he did not believe he was or might be mentally ill as a result of which he was not able to use and weigh in the balance the relevant information concerning the treatment in reaching a decision as to whether or not to accept it. Charles J. held that Art.3 of the Convention was not engaged (as it was unlikely that compulsory administration of an anti-psychotic drug would result in intense physical or mental suffering) and it was only when the treatment proposed reached the appropriate level of severity to engage Art.3 that the question of medical or therapeutic necessity arose.

(e) *Right of Access to Confidential Information*

7–076   Article 8 may confer a right of access by a person to personal or confidential information. For example, in *Gaskin v United Kingdom*,[85] the Strasbourg Court upheld Mr Gaskin's argument that his rights under Art.8 had been breached by the refusal of the local authority to disclose documents relating to his upbringing in care.[86]

7–077   In *MG v United Kingdom*[87] the European Court upheld a claim similar to *Gaskin* concluding that there had been a failure to fulfil the State's positive obligation to protect the applicant's rights under Art.8 in respect of his access to his records from April 1995. The applicant had been in local authority voluntary care for five periods during his childhood and he requested access to his social services records relating to his time spent in the local authority care. He specifically requested information as to whether he had ever been on the "at risk

---

[82] See also *Grare v France* (1993) 15 E.H.R.R. C.D. 100 (even if the treatment regime of a voluntary patient in a psychiatric hospital which had unpleasant side effects could be said to be an invasion of the applicant's private life, it was justified by need); and *X v Germany* (1985) 7 E.H.R.R. 152 (force feeding detainees on hunger strike).

[83] Application No.61827/00, March 9, 2004

[84] [2005] EWHC 1936.

[85] (1990) 12 E.H.R.R. 36.

[86] See also *Gunn-Russo v Nugent Care Society and Secretary of State for Health* [2001] EWHC Admin., July 20, 2001: the disclosure of adoption records by a voluntary adoption agency required a balancing exercise to be conducted between disclosure and confidentiality. Domestic law in this field was held to be compatible with the Convention.

[87] Application No.39393/98, September 24, 2002.

register", whether his father had been investigated or convicted of crimes against children and about the responsibility of the local authority for abuse he suffered as a child. A year later he was provided with summary information and certain documents from his file. The Court held that this refusal breached his Art.8 rights. However, from March 1, 2000 he could have but had not appealed to an independent authority against the disclosure of certain records on the grounds of a duty of confidentiality to third parties under the Data Protection Act 1998. Therefore, the Court held that his rights under Art.8 had been breached between April 1995 and March 1, 2000 only.

This has implications for the English common law position that a former   **7–078** patient had no right of access to records at common law in *R. v Mid-Glamorgan Family Health Services Ex p. Martin*.[88] In *Rose v Secretary of State for Health*[89] claimants born as a result of artificial insemination by donor complained that the defendant's refusal to provide them with non-identifying information relating to the donor's medical history, ethnic and cultural identity and with identifying information where possible breached their Art.8 rights. The Court held that the provision of information about the claimants' biological fathers went to the very heart of their identity and to their make-up as people and so the right to respect for private and family life pursuant to Art.8 was engaged.

(f) Disclosure of Confidential Information

Equally, the disclosure of confidential information may breach Art.8. In *Z v*   **7–079** *Finland*,[90] a reference in a published judgment to an applicant's full name which led to the disclosure of her HIV status breached her right to a private life. See also *H (A Healthcare Worker) v Associated Newspapers Ltd and H (A Healthcare Worker) v N (A Health Authority)*[91] in which a health worker with HIV ("H") was held to have a right to confidentiality which could properly be protected by an injunction against the soliciting or publication of information which might lead to deductive disclosure of H's identity. H was also entitled to bring proceedings under a cloak of anonymity because to hold otherwise would have been to frustrate the decision of the court on the issues before it.

In *A Local Authority v (1) W (2) L (3) W (4) T & R (By the children's*   **7–080** *guardian)*[92] a local authority was held to be entitled to an injunction restraining the publication of the identity of a defendant and her victim in a criminal trial, and that they were suffering from the HIV virus, in order to protect the privacy of her children who had not been involved in the trial but who were the subject of care proceedings. It was held that the naming of the parents was bound to have an adverse effect upon the children in a manner which engaged and was likely to inflict substantial damage on their Art.8 rights. See also *A London BC v (1) Mr and Mrs N (Foster Carers of the Child) (2) P (A Child by her Guardian Pauline Bennett)*[93] in which Sumner J. held that a local authority was not under a duty to

---

[88] [1995] 1 W.L.R. 110; [1995] 1 All E.R. 356, CA.
[89] [2002] EWHC 1593.
[90] (1998) 25 E.H.R.R. 371.
[91] [2002] Lloyd's Med. Rep. 210, CA.
[92] *The Times*, July 21, 2005.
[93] [2005] EWHC 1676, Fam.

inform the father of a child in care that a foster parent with whom the child was staying was HIV positive as the risk of infection was negligible and disclosure would breach the foster parent's right to confidentiality about his condition pursuant to Art.8.

7–081   In *R. (on the application of Szuluk) v HM Prison Sutton*[94] it was held (on the specific facts of that case) to be a breach of Art.8 to require the content of correspondence between a prisoner with a life-threatening medical condition and his medical advisors outside prison to be examined by a prison medical officer.

(g) *Disclosure of Medical Records and Confidentiality*

7–082   The European Court of Human Rights has confirmed that a patient's medical records are included in Art.8. In *MS v Sweden*,[95] the applicant claimed she had suffered a back injury as a result of a fall at work with the consequence that she was unable to return to work. She therefore made a claim against the Social Insurance Office. However, she was a long-term sufferer from spondylolisthesis, which can cause chronic back pain. Without her consent, the Social Insurance Office obtained her medical records from the clinic that had treated her back injury and rejected her claim for compensation on the basis that they showed her injuries had not been caused at work. The records revealed that the applicant had had an abortion after the alleged injury at work but the abortion records related the abortion to serious back problems suffered during an earlier pregnancy and not a work-related injury. Importantly, the Court held that the applicant had not waived her rights by commencing the action and that:

> "The protection of personal data not least medical data is of fundamental importance to a person's enjoyment of his or her right to respect for private and family life . . . "

However, on the facts, it was held that whilst there was an interference with the applicant's rights, Art.8(2) was satisfied because there was a proportionate and legitimate aim in the information being sought, namely the protection of the economic well-being of the country by reason of the allocation of public funds. It may be harder to impose a duty of confidentiality on a large Health Trust where files are passed from one department to another and viewed by doctors, nurses, secretaries and administrators alike.[96]

7–083   In *A Health Authority v X*,[97] Munby J. applied the principles set out in *Z v Finland*[98] and *MS v Sweden*[99] in holding that there was a compelling public interest requiring the disclosure of medical records by a health authority investigating allegations that medical practitioners had breached their terms of service. However, he also emphasised that such disclosure was an interference with a

---

[94] [2004] A.C.D. 45; [2004] EWCA 514, Admin.
[95] (1999) 28 E.H.R.R. 313. See also *Z v Finland* (1998) 25 E.H.R.R. 371.
[96] In relation to disclosure of medical reports, see also *R. v Secretary of State for the Home Department Ex p. Amnesty International*, unreported, February 15, 2000, DC: fairness required that medical reports on Senator Pinochet should be disclosed to the four States which had requested sight of them.
[97] *Independent*, June 25, 2001, *per* Munby J.
[98] (1997) 25 E.H.R.R. 371.
[99] (1997) 28 E.H.R.R. 313.

patient's rights under Art.8 and could only be justified where there were effective and adequate safeguards against abuse. The following safeguards were said to be typically required:

(1) the maintenance of the confidentiality of the documents themselves;

(2) the minimum public disclosure of any information derived from the documents; and

(3) the protection of the patient's anonymity.

It was also emphasised that it was the duty of every public body, including the court, to ensure that that confidentiality was preserved and that there were effective and adequate safeguards against abuse before authorising the transfer of medical records from one doctor to a public body or from one public body to another. In *Cornelius v De Taranto*,[1] Morland J. found a breach of the duty of confidentiality when a consultant forensic psychiatrist disclosed a medico-legal report to a third party without the client's express consent and awarded damages of £3,750 for the breach.[2] The judge rejected an argument that the only remedy should be nominal damages, stating that it would be a hollow protection of the right to respect for private and family life in Art.8 of the Convention if nominal damages were the only remedy for disclosure of details in breach of that right.[3]

Munby J.'s decision was upheld by the Court of Appeal: *A Health Authority*   **7–084** *v X*.[4] The judge was found to have correctly balanced the public interest in effective disciplinary procedures for the investigation and eradication of medical malpractice against the confidentiality of the documents, and to have correctly used his power to attach conditions to disclosure.[5]

In *A v X & B (Non Party)*[6] an application was made for disclosure of medical   **7–085** records by a non party. The application arose in circumstances where the main cause of the claimant's injuries in a road traffic accident was a bipolar mood disorder or hypomania. As the disorder could have a genetic origin and the claimant's brother also appeared to suffer from it, the defendant sought disclosure of the brother's medical records in order to seek to prove that the claimant's disorder would have occurred in any event. However, the court refused to make such an order stating that only in a very exceptional factual situation would such disclosure be justified in civil proceedings and this was not such a case. In particular, it was noted that there was already clear evidence that the claimant was mentally disturbed whilst at university and disclosure was therefore not necessary for a fair disposal of the claim.

---

[1] (2001) E.M.L.R. 329.
[2] *ibid.*, para.66.
[3] The Court of Appeal did not disturb the judge's decision on this point on appeal [2001] EWCA Civ 1511 (October 10, 2001).
[4] [2002] 1 F.L.R. 1045; [2002] 2 All E.R. 780, CA
[5] The Court of Appeal has also upheld the decision on liability of Morland J. in *Cornelius v De Taranto* [2002] E.M.L.R. 6 (although an appeal against a costs order was allowed). The Court of Appeal reiterated that a client's express consent was required before a medicolegal report was transmitted to a third party.
[6] [2004] EWHC 447.

(h) *Patient's Complaints Procedures*

7–086 On applications for disclosure of documents created pursuant to patients' complaints procedures, Art.8 may have to be considered, both in relation to the rights of the patient and the rights of those being investigated.

8. Professional Disciplinary Proceedings

(a) *Introduction*

7–087 Professional disciplinary proceedings will amount to the determination of civil rights and obligations for the purpose of Art.6(1) if the private right of the professional to practice his profession is actually or potentially interfered with.[7] In *Gautrin v France*,[8] the European Court confirmed that Art.6(1) applies to hearings before medical and dental disciplinary bodies where these affect the professional's right to continue to practise his profession. This confirmed the position set out in several earlier cases including *Diennet v France*,[9] in which it was held that the French Medical Disciplinary Council fell within the Article.[10] The European Court has left open the question whether professional disciplinary proceedings amount to the determination of a criminal charge, an issue which became superfluous following the finding that there was a determination of civil rights and obligations.[11] If they were to constitute determination of a criminal charge, they would additionally attract the application of Art.6(2) which enshrines the presumption of innocence, and Art.6(3) which gives a number of specific additional guarantees to those subjected to criminal charges.[12] The domestic courts appear unlikely to find that professional disciplinary proceedings will amount to determination of a "criminal charge" for the purposes of Art.6(1). However, the distinction is of diminished importance because it has been accepted that there is a hierarchy of civil proceedings in relation to the penal element or stigma involved and at the upper end of the hierarchy, due process guarantees similar to those conferred by Arts 6(2) and 6(3) are implied in Art.6(1): *Albert and Le Compte v Belgium*[13]; *Official Receiver v Stern*[14]; *R. v*

---

[7] *Le Compte, Van Leuven and De Meyere v Belgium* (1982) 4 E.H.R.R. 1, paras 47–49.

[8] (1999) 23 E.H.R.R. 196.

[9] (1996) 21 E.H.R.R. 554.

[10] See also *König v Germany* (1980) 2 E.H.R.R. 170; and *Albert and Le Compte v Belgium* (1983) 5 E.H.R.R. 533.

[11] *Le Compte, Van Leuven and De Meyere v Belgium* (1982) 4 E.H.R.R. 1, para.53. The Divisional Court in *Pine v Solicitors Disciplinary Tribunal; sub. nom. In the Matter of a Solicitor*, unreported, January 11, 2001, held that proceedings before the Solicitors Tribunal relating to failure to maintain proper accounts and permitting misleading information to be delivered to the Law Society were not the determination of a criminal charge. This finding was not challenged on a subsequent appeal to the Court of Appeal [2001] EWCA Civ 1574; [2002] 1 W.L.R. 2189; [2002] 2 All E.R. 658; (2002) U.K.H.R.R. 81, CA.

[12] See para.7–012, above.

[13] (1983) 5 E.H.R.R. 533, paras 30, 39.

[14] [2001] 1 W.L.R. 2230, CA at 2254h and 2257c.

Security & Futures Authority Ex p. Fleurose[15]; and *Pine v Law Society*.[16] Proceedings on the admission to a profession also involve the determination of a civil right: *Bakker v Austria*.[17]

It follows that any disciplinary tribunal which can interfere with a practitio-   **7–088** ner's ability to practice will in general have to itself comply with the requirements of Art.6. However, any defect in procedure may be saved if there is a full appeal to, or review by, an Art.6 compliant court or tribunal with jurisdiction to rectify factual errors or to examine whether the sanction is proportionate to the fault or which can remedy any incompatibility below.[18] In practice, appeals from professional disciplinary tribunals tend only to examine whether the body made an error of law, whether by breaching the duty of fairness or otherwise. There is not usually a full review on the merits. A limited power of appeal may be sufficient for the purposes of meeting the Art.6 requirement to provide a fair hearing in some cases though not in others. Accordingly, there is increasing pressure for the disciplinary proceedings to themselves embody the procedural protections required by Art.6 (and other procedural safeguards). Professional bodies with power to suspend or debar professionals from practice are therefore being subjected to greater procedural scrutiny in light of the HRA. These include:

(1) the respective disciplinary tribunals of the Law Society and the Bar Council;

(2) the disciplinary tribunal of the Institute of Chartered Accountants; and

(3) the Professional Conduct Committee and Health Committee of the General Medical Council and the General Dental Council and the equivalent bodies for other medical practitioners such nurses, midwives, health visitors and physiotherapists.[19]

Articles 10 and 11 may have some relevance to disciplinary proceedings. The   **7–089** application of Art.10 to disciplinary proceedings involving lawyers and the interrelationship between Art.10 and the Art.6 right to a fair trial is discussed above at para.7–046 particularly in relation to the case of *Steur v Netherlands*. In *Maestri v Italy*[20] the European Court considered the application of Art.11 to disciplinary proceedings involving a judge. It held that there had been a violation of Art.11 where following disciplinary proceedings the applicant who was acting

---

[15] [2002] I.R.L.R. 297, *The Times*, January 15, 2002, CA, para.14.
[16] [2001] EWCA Civ 1574; (2002) U.K.H.R.R. 81 [2002] 1 W.L.R. 2189; [2002] 2 All E.R. 658, CA. See also *Macpherson v Law Society* [2005] EWHC 2837, Admin.
[17] (2004) 39 E.H.R.R. 26.
[18] *Le Compte, Van Leuven and De Meyere v Belgium* (1982) 4 E.H.R.R. 1, para.51; *Gautrin v France* (1999) 28 E.H.R.R. 196, para.57; *R. v United Kingdom Central Council for Nursing, Midwifery and Health Visiting Ex p. Tehrani* [2001] I.R.L.R. 208. See also *R. (on the application of Malik) v Waltham Forest Primary Care Trust* [2006] EWHC 487, Admin; [2006] 3 All E.R. 71; [2006] Lloyd's Rep. Med. 298; *The Times*, May 26, 2006 (procedure as a whole, including right to claim judicial review, Art.6 compliant).
[19] On the European Court's analysis, it seems unlikely that proceedings which do not have direct power to interfere with a practitioner's right to practise will be subject to Art.6: see *Fayed v United Kingdom* (1994) 18 E.H.R.R. 393.
[20] Application No.39748/98; (2004) 39 E.H.R.R. 38.

president of the La Spezia District Court was convicted of having been a Freemason from 1981 until March 1993. The disciplinary section of the National Council of the Judiciary reprimanded him as a result. It relied on directives issued by the National Council in March 1990 and July 1993 which highlighted the conflict between membership of the Freemasons and membership of the judiciary. The European Court held that in relation to the period before March 1990, domestic law did not contain sufficient information to satisfy the condition of foreseeability. In relation to the period after March 1990, it was clear from an overall examination of a debate held in March 1990 that the National Council of the Judiciary was questioning whether it was advisable for a judge to be a Freemason but there was no indication that membership of the Freemasons could constitute a disciplinary offence in every case. The wording of the 1990 Directive was not sufficiently clear to enable the applicant to realise that membership of a Masonic lodge could lead to sanctions being imposed on him. The condition of foreseeability was not satisfied and the accordingly the interference was not "prescribed by law" and violated Art.11.

7–090   Decisions interfering with the right to practice as a professional may also engage Art.1 of Protocol No.1. In *R. (on the application of Malik) v Waltham Forest Primary Care Trust*,[21] Collins J. held that the unlawful suspension of the claimant by his primary care trust from its list of performers pursuant to the National Health Service (Performers) List Regulations 2004 interfered with the claimant's right to peaceful enjoyment of his possession (namely the possession of a licence by virtue of inclusion on the list) and entitled him to damages in the event that he could establish loss.

(b) *Procedural Guarantees*

7–091   In general, a professional disciplinary tribunal will be required to satisfy at least the following requirements to comply with Art.6(1) in conjunction with domestic law principles of natural justice:

    (i) independence and impartiality;

    (ii) equality of arms;

    (iii) right to a public/oral hearing;

    (iv) the giving of reasons;

    (v) legal representation;

    (vi) procedure for challenging interim suspensions.

A right of appeal to an Art.6(1) compliant tribunal may cure any defects in the procedure at first instance.

---

[21] [2006] EWHC 487, Admin; [2006] 3 All E.R. 71; [2006] Lloyd's Rep. Med. 298; *The Times*, May 26, 2006.

Independence and impartiality. The tribunal must be independent and 7–092
impartial: *Gautrin v France.*[22] The European Court has upheld complaints based
not just on actual independence or bias but on its mere appearance.[23] In *Thaler
v Austria*,[24] the Court held that situations falling short of the direct involvement
of a member of a tribunal in the subject-matter to be decided could give rise to
legitimate doubts about its independence and impartiality.[25]

Since the HRA came into force, there have been a number of challenges to
domestic professional disciplinary bodies on the ground that they were not
sufficiently independent and impartial. In *Sadler v General Medical Council*,[26]
the Privy Council found that the GMC's Committee on Professional Performance
satisfied the requirements of independence, impartiality and fairness under Art.6
and stated:

> "There is no general principle of Convention jurisprudence which prevents professional
> self-regulation: see *Albert and Le Compte v Belgium* (1983) 5 E.H.R.R. 533 especially
> at pages 541–542, paragraph 29. Whether a tribunal satisfies the requirements of Article
> 6 depends on all the relevant circumstances, including how the members of the tribunal
> are appointed, their tenure of office, their protection from outside pressure and their
> apparent independence (as evidenced by their standing and procedure)".

In *R. v United Kingdom Central Council for Nursing, Midwifery and Health
Visiting & Nursing and Midwifery Council Ex p. Celia Mary Hamilton*,[27] a
challenge was made to the impartiality of the United Kingdom Central Council
("UKCC") on the grounds that there was insufficient insulation between the
prosecutorial and adjudicative functions of the UKCC, the names of professional
screeners had not been supplied to the claimant and the requirement that a
medical examiner should attend the hearing and could ask questions with the
leave of the chairman created an appearance of bias. Crane J. held that the
UKCC's procedures did not breach Art.6 because neither the professional screeners nor anyone else had a prosecutorial or even a presentational role in the
context of an application for termination of suspension, the screeners' role was
limited and the medical examiners were independent experts who acted only as
witnesses and advisers. The tenure of the members of the Council did not raise
concerns and the committee sat with an independent legal assessor. Although the
issue of fitness to practise could involve consideration of the practitioner's ability
to comply with professional standards in the context of the code of conduct, this

---

[22] (1999) 28 E.H.R.R. 196.
[23] *ibid.* In *R. v General Medical Council Ex p. Kyros Nicolaides* [2001] EWHC 625; [2001] Lloyd's
Rep. Med. 525, Sir Richard Tucker held that the Professional Conduct Committee of the GMC was
not biased or in breach of Art.6 when it gave a decision concerning the conduct of a professional
during a previous disciplinary hearing before the GMC.
[24] Application No.58141/00, February 3, 2005; (2005) 41 E.H.R.R. 33.
[25] See further *Cosson v France* Application No.00038498/03, July 18, 2006; *Syndicat National des
Professionnels des Procedures Collectives v France* Application No.00070387/01 (participation by
state commissioner in court deliberations contrary to Art.6(1)); *cf. Gubler v France* Application
No.00069742/01, July 27, 2006 (where the disciplinary section members of a medical council had
withdrawn from the sitting at which the medical council had decided to bring a complaint against the
applicant and had had no involvement in the decision, there was no violation of Art.6(1)).
[26] [2003] UKPC 59; [2004] Lloyd's Rep. Med. 44; (2004) H.R.L.R. 8.
[27] [2002] EWHC 2770, Admin.

was not sufficient to deprive the committee of independence and impartiality. The case was the subject of an unsuccessful appeal.[28]

In *Aaron v Law Society*[29] the Court stated that, in relation to claims of objective bias the test was whether in the circumstances a fair minded observer would have considered that there had been a real possibility of bias. In *Holder v Law Society*,[30] the Divisional Court held that the Solicitors Disciplinary Tribunal was an independent and impartial tribunal that complied with Art.6. It noted that appointments to the tribunal were made by the Master of the Rolls through an open selection process and the Law Society was not involved in those appointments.[31]

7–093   By contrast, in *P (A Barrister) v General Council of the Bar* [2005] P.N.L.R. 32, the Visitors (Inns of Court) held that where a lay representative who was a member of the Professional Conduct and Complaints Committee ("PCCC") of the Bar Council sat as a panel member at a Visitors Tribunal hearing, that person was acting as a judge in his/her own cause and was therefore automatically disqualified from sitting on the panel. Further, the presence of such a person on the panel meant that it could not be said to be independent within the meaning of Art.6. In *Shrimpton v General Council of the Bar*,[32] the inclusion of two lay members of the PCCC on the disciplinary tribunal again meant the tribunal was not independent and impartial. The Visitors (Inns of Court) held that where there was any suggestion of bias affecting a tribunal, anything less than a full, careful and independent review of the evidence by an appellate tribunal, leading to its own findings of fact, would suggest a continuance of the breach of natural justice.

In *R. (on the application of Mahfouz) v Professional Conduct Committee of the General Medical Council & The General Medical Council (Third Party)*[33] allowed the appellant's appeal in part from a decision of Davis J[34] who had held that the Professional Conduct Committee ("PCC") of the GMC did not breach Art.6 in rejecting an application to discharge themselves based on an allegation of unconscious bias following the publication of newspaper articles concerning the claimant during his hearing for professional misconduct. The Court stated that knowledge of prejudicial publicity need not be fatal to the fairness of a hearing by the PCC but its effect had to be considered in the context of the proceedings as a whole including the impact of the legal advice available. Where there was a possible breach of the rules of natural justice as well as a potential procedural irregularity, the legal assessor to the committee was under a duty to provide advice, looking at it in the same way as a judge directing a jury.

7–094   **Equality of arms.** The right to a fair hearing means that all parties must have a reasonable opportunity of presenting their respective cases under conditions

---

[28] [2003] EWCA Civ 1600; *The Times*, November 12, 2003.
[29] [2003] EWHC 2271, Admin.
[30] [2005] EWHC 2023, Admin; [2006] P.N.L.R. 10.
[31] See also *Simms v Law Society* [2005] EWHC 408, Admin; *Pine v Law Society* [2001] EWCA Civ 1574; (2002) U.K.H.R.R. 81; [2002] 1 W.L.R. 2189; [2002] 2 All E.R. 658, CA.
[32] Reported on *Lawtel*, May 16, 2005.
[33] *The Times*, March 19, 2004, CA.
[34] [2003] EWHC 1695, Admin.

that do not place them at a substantial disadvantage vis-à-vis their opponents.[35] There should be sufficient disclosure of documents to meet the requirement of fairness: the right to a fair hearing may require that documents which form the basis of a complaint or defence should be provided to the complainant or the professional. It might be necessary to impose conditions on disclosure (e.g. confidentiality) in order to maintain fairness to another party's rights: *R. v General Medical Council Ex p. Toth*.[36] Where a disciplinary tribunal is assisted by a legal adviser or assessor fairness requires that the parties are afforded an opportunity to comment on that advice and the committee should have an opportunity to consider their comments before making their determination: *Nwabuaze v General Medical Council*.[37] In *Boodoo v General Medical Council*,[38] Silber J. held that there had been an obligation on the Health Committee of the GMC to inform the parties of the advice given to it by the medical assessors so that they could respond but that the failure to do so had not undermined the committee's finding which was neither wrong nor unjust. The Court was influenced by the fact that the essential ingredients give rise to the conclusion that the doctor concerned was suffering from alcohol dependency were present in the uncontradicted medical evidence. In *R. (on the application of S) v Knowsley NHS Primary Care Trust; R. (on the application of Ghosh v Northumberland NHS Care Trust*,[39] Toulson J. held that a general practitioner who was the subject of a proposed removal from the trust's list of medical performers should in fairness be entitled to have the opportunity to cross-examine the relevant witnesses.

Right to a public/oral hearing. Article 6(1) generally requires that proceed- 7–095 ings are held in public, unless the limited exceptions set out in the Article apply.[40] This particular Art.6(1) right includes the right to an oral hearing. In *Bakker v Austria*,[41] the applicant complained about the lack of a public hearing before a tribunal in proceedings relating to his request for authorisation to practise as a self-employed physiotherapist. The European Court held that there was a violation of Art.6(1) when the applicant had not had an oral hearing before the Administrative and Constitutional Courts (who were the only courts who could qualify as "tribunals" within the meaning of Art.6). Where matters of professional secrecy or protection of the private life of a professional or his patient or client are concerned, this may justify sitting in private.[42] Where the professional waives his right to a public hearing expressly or tacitly, the conduct of disciplinary proceedings in private does not contravene the Convention.[43]

It may nevertheless be permissible for a professional disciplinary body to proceed without an oral or public hearing in certain circumstances. In *Das v*

---

[35] See *Dombo Beheer v Netherlands* (1994) 18 E.H.R.R. 213; *De Haes & Gijsels v Belgium* (1997) 25 E.H.R.R. 1.
[36] [2000] 1 W.L.R. 2129.
[37] [2000] 1 W.L.R. 1760.
[38] [2004] EWHC 2712, Admin.
[39] [2006] EWHC 26, Admin; [2006] Lloyd's Rep. Med. 123; *The Times*, February 2, 2006.
[40] *Gautrin v France* (1999) 28 E.H.R.R. 196, para.42.
[41] (2004) 39 E.H.R.R. 26.
[42] *Le Compte, Van Leuven and De Meyere v Belgium* (1982) 4 E.H.R.R. 1, para.59. See also *Hurter v Switzerland* Application No.00053146/99, December 15, 2005.
[43] *ibid.*

General Medical Council,[44] the appellant appealed against a determination by the GMC's Committee on Professional Performance. The Committee had made several findings against him in his absence, and had withdrawn his registration for 12 months. The appellant claimed that, by proceeding in his absence, the Committee had breached Art.6(1) of the Convention. Evidence was adduced to show that notice of the hearing was sent to the appellant's address and signed for by him. The Privy Council held that the Committee's determination was a model of its kind and was unassailable. Its findings had been fully particularised, supported by clear evidence that the appellant's performance was seriously defective, and the hearing was eminently fair. The Committee had been entitled to conclude that proper notice of the hearing had been received by the appellant, and its decision to proceed in his absence was a proper exercise of its discretion. In *R. (on the application of Thompson) v Law Society,*[45] the Office for the Supervision of Solicitors ("OSS") had considered complaints of inadequate professional services against the appellant solicitor. The appellant sought judicial review on the ground that his rights at common law or under Art.6 of the Convention had been infringed by the failure of the OSS to afford him an oral hearing. The Court of Appeal stated that, at common law, the duty of the OSS adjudicator and appellate adjudication panel was to act fairly and what was fair depended on the circumstances of the particular case. Similarly, under Art.6, there might be cases in which an oral hearing was required at first instance and others where it was not. The Court held that no breach of the Convention arose if the tribunal was subject to control by a court which had full jurisdiction and itself complied with the requirements of Art.6. It noted that while some disciplinary proceedings could give rise to disputes over civil rights within Art.6(1) if what was at stake was the right to continue to exercise a profession, a decision to reprimand, as in this case, did not amount to a determination of civil rights.

7-096   **The giving of reasons.** An Art.6 compliant disciplinary tribunal also has to give reasons for its decision.[46] In *Perez v France,*[47] the European Court stated that while Art.6(1) obliges the courts to give reasons for their decisions, it cannot be understood as requiring a detailed answer to every argument.[48]

7-097   In *Selvanathan v General Medical Council,*[49] the Privy Council referred to the then new obligation on the General Medical Council to give reasons and Lord Hope indicated that a general explanation would be required identifying the reasons for the finding made; and the reasons for the imposition, or non-imposition of a penalty. In *Gupta v General Medical Council*[50] the Privy Council held that the Professional Conduct Committee of the General Medical Council

---

[44] [2003] UKPC 75.

[45] [2004] EWCA Civ 167; [2004] 1 W.L.R. 2522; [2004] 2 All E.R. 113; *The Times*, April 1, 2004, CA.

[46] See *Ruiz Torija v Spain* (1995) 19 E.H.R.R. 553; *Georgiadis v Greece* (1997) 24 E.H.R.R. 606; *Helle v Finland* (1998) 26 E.H.R.R. 159.

[47] (2005) 40 E.H.R.R. 39.

[48] At para.81.

[49] [2001] Lloyd's Rep. Med. 1; (2001) 59 B.M.L.R. 95; *The Times*, October 26, 2000.

[50] [2001] UKPC 61; [2002] 1 W.L.R. 1691; [2002] Lloyd's Rep. Med. 82; (2002) 64 B.M.L.R. 56.

was not obliged to give reasons for its factual findings. More recently, in *Watson v General Medical Council*,[51] Collins J. held that good practice required that reasons should normally be given for decisions. They need not be at all lengthy and where credibility was in issue it would usually not be necessary to do more than indicate that the evidence of particular witnesses was accepted. It might be unnecessary for the panel to do more than indicate its conclusions if it is apparent from the transcript of evidence why the particular decision had been reached. In *R. (on the application of Luthra) v General Dental Council*,[52] the Professional Conduct Committee of the General Dental Council had found the appellant guilty of serious professional misconduct involving dishonesty, and had suspended his registration. The appellant complained that the Committee had violated Art.6 by failing to give any or any sufficient reasons for its finding. Elias J. held that the basis of the Committee's decision was clear from its conclusions when considered in light of the transcript of evidence and that this was sufficient to amount to adequate reasons. He stated there was usually no need for the committee to identify why, in reaching its findings of fact, it accepted some evidence and rejected other evidence. In *Threlfall v General Optical Council*,[53] Stanley Burnton J. held that the disciplinary committee of the General Optical Council was under a duty both at common law and under Art.6 ECHR to give adequate reasons for a finding of serious professional misconduct and to do so in good time for the optician to be able to exercise a right of appeal.

Hearing within a reasonable time. The hearing should take place within a **7–098** reasonable time: *Doran v Ireland*.[54] In assessing the reasonableness of the length of the proceedings, the Court will take into account all the circumstances of the case including the complexity of the dispute, the conduct of the applicant and the relevant authorities and what was at stake for the applicant in the dispute.[55] The right to a hearing within a reasonable time may affect whether extensions of interim orders should be given. In *General Medical Council v Pembrey*,[56] it was held that the GMC was entitled to an extension of an interim conditional registration order against a consultant pending a hearing of complaints by the Professional Conduct Committee where the delay in progressing the matter did not breach Art.6. It may also affect whether there should be a re-hearing of any complaint: *R. (on the application of Aziz) v General Medical Council*.[57] A stay of proceedings is only necessary if, due to the misconduct of the prosecution, it is unfair for the defendant to be tried or a fair trial is no longer possible: *General Dental Council v Price*.[58] In *Langford v Law Society*,[59] the Divisional Court held that there was a relatively high threshold to be crossed before it could be said in

[51] [2006] EWHC 18, Admin.
[52] [2004] EWHC 458, Admin.
[53] [2004] EWHC 2683, Admin; [2005] Lloyd's Rep. Med. 250; *The Times*, December 2, 2004.
[54] Application No.50389/99, July 31, 2003; (2006) 42 E.H.R.R. 13.
[55] *Stelios Lerios v Cyprus* Application No.00068448/01, March 23, 2006.
[56] [2002] EWHC 1602 Admin; [2002] Lloyd's Rep. Med. 434; L.T.L. August 8, 2002.
[57] [2005] EWHC 2695.
[58] L.T.L. July 19, 2001, DC.
[59] [2002] EWHC 2802, Admin.

any particular case that a period of delay was unreasonable so as to give grounds for real concern that a Convention right had been violated.[60]

7–099   **Legal representation.** Article 6(1) does not necessarily require the provision of legal representation in disciplinary proceedings: *Pine v Law Society*.[61] On a challenge arising out of the refusal of a request to be legally represented in *R. (on the application of S) v Knowsley NHS Primary Care Trust; R. (on the application of Ghosh v Northumberland NHS Care Trust*,[62] Toulson J. held that the question in each case had to be whether the doctor could reasonably be expected to undertaken his own representation, having regard to the complexity of the allegations and the evidence.

7–100   **Procedure to challenge interim suspension.** A professional should be warned about the possibility of interim suspensions pending the substantive disciplinary hearing and should have an opportunity to make representations and if necessary, call witnesses: *Gupta v The General Medical Council*.[63]

7–101   **Appeals.** As stated above, an appeal may cure unfairness in the disciplinary tribunal procedure. In *Ghosh v General Medical Council*,[64] an appeal to the Privy Council was sufficient to cure any alleged unfairness in the composition of the Professional Conduct Committee of the General Medical Council because it was by way of full rehearing. In *Chaudhary v Specialist Training Authority Appeal Panel*,[65] the claimant wished to complain against a decision not to appoint the claimant to the register of specialists eligible to be appointed as consultants in the NHS. The Court of Appeal held that a right of appeal to the Specialist Training Authority Appeal Panel under the European Specialist Medical Qualifications Order 1995 together with the possibility of judicial review of its decision was a lawful alternative to a procedure by way of complaint to an employment tribunal and did not breach the right to a fair trial under Art.6.

The HRA has influenced the approach taken to appeals from disciplinary proceedings in the direction of rehearing rather than mere review. In *R. v Royal*

---

[60] In *Aaron v Law Society* [2003] EWHC 2271, Admin the appellant appealed against the Solicitors' Disciplinary Tribunal's finding of "conduct unbecoming a solicitor". The appellant complained, inter alia, of unreasonable delay by the Tribunal with reference to Art.6 of the Convention, submitting that the only effective remedy for the delay of up to 14 or 15 years between the first instance of alleged improper conduct and the institution of disciplinary proceedings was to quash the whole of the Tribunal's findings. The Court held that the delays involved in the proceedings did not reach the Art.6(1) threshold, and that none of the delays caused the appellant any prejudice. However, the Court did note that those responsible for regulation of solicitors should now have the "reasonable time" requirement of Art.6 in the forefront of their minds in any disciplinary process.

[61] [2001] EWCA Civ 1574; [2002] 1 W.L.R. 2189; [2002] 2 All E.R. 658; (2002) U.K.H.R.R. 81, CA.

[62] [2006] EWHC 26, Admin; [2006] Lloyd's Rep. Med. 123; *The Times*, February 2, 2006.

[63] [2001] EWHC 631, Admin; *The Times*, October 16, 2001. See also *Sudesh Madan v The General Medical Council* [2001] EWHC Admin 577; [2001] Lloyd's Rep. Med. 539, DC.

[64] [2001] UKPC 29; [2001] 1 W.L.R. 1915; [2001] Lloyd's Rep. Med. 443; (2001) U.K.H.R.R. 987; *The Times*, June 25, 2001, PC. Lord Millett said: "The Board's jurisdiction is appellate, not supervisory. The appeal is by way of a rehearing in which the Board is fully entitled to substitute its own decision for that of the committee".

[65] [2005] EWCA Civ 282.

Pharmaceutical Society of Great Britain Ex p. Panjawani,[66] the Divisional Court held that an appeal had to be conducted by way of rehearing in order to comply with Art.6 because the statutory procedure for cases before the Statutory Committee of the Royal Pharmaceutical Society allowed for the same body to initiate, prosecute and determine complaints.[67] In *Preiss v General Dental Council*,[68] the Privy Council said:

> "Since the coming into operation of the Human Rights Act 1998, with its adjuration in section 3 to read and give effect to legislation, so far as it is possible to do so, in a way compatible with the Convention rights, any tendency to read down rights of appeal in disciplinary cases is to be resisted.".[69]

In cases such as *Chohan v Law Society*[70] and *Hayes v Law Society*[71] the Court has applied this approach to appeals from solicitors' disciplinary proceedings, treating the case as a rehearing, albeit one within which the decision-making body is accorded appropriate respect. A similar approach was taken to appeals from osteopaths' disciplinary proceedings in *Moody v General Osteopathic Council*.[72]

(c) Law Society Interventions and Investigations

There have been a number of recent cases challenging interventions and investigations by the Law Society on human rights grounds. In relation to interventions, in *Holder v Law Society*,[73] the Court of Appeal held that although intervention by the Law Society in a solicitor's practice involved an interference with the claimant's peaceful enjoyment of his possessions in Art.1 of Protocol No.1, it was justified in the public interest and the statutory scheme complied with the Convention. The Law Society has a "margin of discretion" and the Court in discharging its separate duty to consider the merits of the case must pay due regard to the views of the Law Society as the relevant professional body. The Court of Appeal held that the Law Society's intervention in the case in question as a matter of the exercise of its discretion was entirely justified.[74] The Court of Appeal in *Murugesu Kanapathipillai Sritharan v Law Society* followed its

7–102

---

[66] [2002] EWHC 1127 Admin; L.T.L., July 10, 2002.

[67] See also *Preiss v General Dental Council* [2001] 1 W.L.R. 1926; [2001] Lloyd's Rep. Med. 491; *The Times*, August 14, 2001, PC; and *R. v United Kingdom Central Council for Nursing Midwifery & Health Visiting Ex p. Tehrani* [2001] I.R.L.R. 208, Ct. Sess. (Scot.).

[68] [2001] UKPC 36; [2001] 1 W.L.R. 1926; [2001] Lloyd's Rep. Med. 491; [2001] I.R.L.R. 696; (2001) H.R.L.R. 56.

[69] Rose L.J. made similar comments in *Langford v Law Society* [2002] EWHC 2802, Admin.

[70] [2004] EWHC 1145, Admin.

[71] [2004] EWHC 1165, Admin.

[72] [2004] EWHC 967, Admin.

[73] [2003] EWCA Civ 39; [2003] 1 W.L.R. 1059; [2003] 3 All E.R. 62, CA.

[74] See also *Michael John Harvey v The Law Society* [2003] EWHC 535, Ch in which it was accepted by the claimant that the intervention procedure was in principle compatible with the HRA, both at the stage at which the Law Society comes to decide on intervention and at the stage at which the Court considers whether the intervention should continue and *Gauntlett v Law Society* [2006] EWHC 1954, Ch in which Evans-Lombe J. upheld the intervention procedure as Convention compliant.

decision in *Holder v Law Society* in relation to the compatibility of interventions with Art.1 of Protocol 1.[75]

7–103　　In *R. (on the application of Pamplin) v Law Society*,[76] Mr Justice Newman declined to find that the reasonable disclosure of confidential information by the police to the Law Society in connection with an investigation by the Office for the Supervision of Solicitors in the public interest violated Art.8.

[75] [2005] EWCA Civ 476; [2005] 4 All E.R. 1105; *The Times*, May 11, 2005.
[76] [2001] EWHC Admin 300; *Independent*, July 9, 2001.

PROFESSIONAL INDEMNITY INSURANCE

1. INTRODUCTION

Professional indemnity insurance can be summarised as insurance against the risk of civil liability arising in the course of a professional's business. The precise scope of cover will, inevitably, depend upon the wording of the relevant contract of insurance.

8–001

2. REGULATORY REQUIREMENTS

Many professions require their members to take out and maintain professional indemnity insurance. Some professions require cover to be taken out with an

8–002

approved carrier and/or on approved terms, and specify minimum levels of cover. Examples are set out below.[1]

(a) *Insurance Brokers*

8–003 Insurance brokers are now regulated by the FSA and are therefore subject to the requirements set out in Ch.9 of the Integrated Prudential Sourcebook (PRU). PRU 9.2.7 requires any firm to take out and maintain professional indemnity insurance which satisfies the requirements of PRU 9.2.10. PRU 9.2.10 in turn stipulates that the professional indemnity insurance must:

(a) provide cover in respect of claims for which the firm may be liable as a result of the conduct of itself, its employees or agents;

(b) contain "appropriate cover" for defence costs;

(c) provide a minimum limit of indemnity of €1,000,000 for a single claim and, in the aggregate, the higher of €1,500,000 or 10 per cent of annual income up to a maximum of £30,000,000[2];

(d) not have an excess greater than the higher of £2,500 or 1.5 per cent of annual income.[3]

(b) *Surveyors*

8–004 Every member of the RICS must ensure that any firm of which he or she is sole principal, a partner or director to be insured[4] on terms no less comprehensive than the RICS Professional Indemnity Insurance Policy in force from time to time.[5] The minimum levels of cover are graded according to gross fee income as follows[6]:

GFI	Minimum Level of Cover
£100,000	£250,000
£200,000	£500,000
>£200,000	£1,000,000

8–005 The maximum uninsured excess for policies with a limit of indemnity of up to and including £500,000 is 2.5 per cent of sum insured or £10,000, whichever is

---

[1] See also the FSA Handbook, the Interim Prudential Sourcebook for Investment Business (IPRU (INV)) at section 1 ("Purpose") and in particular IPRU(INV) 2.3.1R which imposes a requirement for "authorised professional firms" to effect and maintain adequate professional indemnity insurance. As to the regulatory regime under the Financial Services and Markets Act 2000, see generally Ch.15.

[2] PRU 9.2.13.

[3] PRU 9.2.17. If the broker holds client money or other clients assets then the maximum deductible can be doubled.

[4] r.4 of Sch.1 to RICS Conduct Regulation 27.1.

[5] *ibid.* r.6.2.

[6] *ibid.* r.6.1.

the greater; for policies with a limit of indemnity greater than £500,000 the maximum excess is 2.5 per cent of the sum insured.[7]

The RICS maintains an Assigned Risks Pool for members who are unable to obtain open market cover. **8–006**

(c) *Architects*

Architects are prohibited from undertaking professional work without "*adequate and appropriate professional indemnity insurance cover*".[8] The Architects' Professional Indemnity Insurance Guidelines indicate that cover should be written on terms wider than a policy which responds to liability only for neglect, error or omission. Minimum limits of indemnity are specified[9] in accordance with gross fee income for the preceding year as follows: **8–007**

GFI	Minimum Level of Cover
£100,000	£250,000
£200,000	£500,000
>£200,000	£1,000,000

(d) *Accountants*

Any firm of accountants registered with the Institute of Chartered Accountants of England and Wales, Institute of Chartered Accountants of Scotland or Institute of Chartered Accountants in Ireland must arrange minimum professional indemnity insurance cover.[10] Firms with a gross fee income of less than £400,000 must maintain insurance with a minimum limit of indemnity of £50,000 for a sole practitioner or £100,000 in every other case.[11] Firms with a gross fee income of more than £400,000 must maintain professional indemnity insurance with a minimum limit of indemnity of £1,000,000.[12] The limits of indemnity can include an excess of not more than £30,000 per principal.[13] The policy wording must be in accordance with the ICAEW's Minimum Approved Policy Wording[14] and must include retroactive cover for claims arising up to six years prior to the commencement of cover. **8–008**

---

[7] r.6.1 of Sch.1 to RICS Conduct Regulation 27.1.
[8] Standard 8 of the Architects Code: Standards of Conduct and Practice, issued by the Architects Registration Board.
[9] RIBA Professional Indemnity Insurance Minimum Requirements, cl.2.
[10] See, for example, ICAEW's Professional Indemnity Insurance Regulations, reg.3.1.
[11] *ibid.*, reg.3.3.
[12] *ibid.*, reg.3.2.
[13] *ibid.*, reg.3.5.
[14] *ibid.*, regs 3.1, 1.7. The requirement for compliance with the minimum terms does not prevent insured and insurer agreeing terms which are more advantageous to the insured.

8–009 The ICAEW Minimum Approved Policy Wording provides for payment of defence costs incurred with Insurers' written consent (such consent not unreasonably to be withheld or delayed) in the investigation, defence or settlement of any claim or circumstance in addition to the sums payable under the primary insuring clauses.[15] Any self-insured excess is subject to an annual aggregate limit.[16] Insurers are entitled to stipulate an aggregate limit on their liabilities under the insurance.[17]

8–010 The various Institutes maintain an Assigned Risks Pool ("ARP") for practices which are unable to obtain cover through the open market. Firms entering the ARP are required to pay a premium determined by a Joint Advisory Panel, comprised of members of the relevant Institutes and representatives of the participating insurers.

(e) Solicitors

8–011 Solicitors are under a statutory obligation to obtain professional indemnity cover in accordance with the relevant Minimum Terms and Conditions for the year in which cover is sought.[18] Until September 1, 2000, solicitors' compulsory cover was effected through the Solicitors Indemnity Fund. Since that date, solicitors' practices have been required to take out professional indemnity insurance on the open market from one of an approved list of insurers (known as Qualifying Insurers). SIF continues to exist, but only to run off claims which had been notified prior to September 1, 2000.

8–012 Rule 4.1 of the Solicitors Indemnity Insurance Rules 2006[19] requires insurance to be effected in accordance with the Law Society's Minimum Terms and Conditions. Until October 1, 2005, the minimum levels of cover were £1,000,000 for ordinary firms and £1,500,000 for bodies corporate (such as LLPs). Since that date, the minimum levels of cover have increased to £2,000,000 and £3,000,000 respectively.[20] Although insurance may be subject to an excess, such an excess cannot operate to reduce the limit of indemnity payable.[21] Defence costs are payable in addition to the limit of indemnity[22] and must not be the subject of any monetary limit[23] or excess.[24]

8–013 For the renewal period commencing on October 1, 2006, there are 23 Qualifying Insurers of whom seven are Lloyd's underwriters and the balance operate in the Companies Market.[25] The overwhelming majority of Qualifying Insurers require placement of risks via brokers.

---

[15] cl.B.3 of the ICAEW's Minimum Approved Policy Wording 2005.
[16] *ibid.*, cl.B.5.
[17] *ibid.*, cl.B.1.
[18] s.37 of the Solicitors Act 1974; s.9 of the Administration of Justice Act 1985.
[19] r.4 of the Solicitors Indemnity Insurance Rules 2005.
[20] cl.2.1 of the Law Society's Minimum Terms and Conditions.
[21] *ibid.*, cl.3.2.
[22] *ibid.*, cl.1.2.
[23] *ibid.*, cl.2.2.
[24] *ibid.*, cl.3.3.
[25] The figures for 2005 were nine and sixteen respectively.

In order to provide temporary cover[26] for firms which cannot afford or obtain **8–014** open market cover, the Law Society has established an Assigned Risks Pool. The ARP is underwritten by the Qualifying Insurers in proportion to their premium income from open market business. Firms covered by the ARP must pay premiums calculated as a percentage of turnover which are markedly higher than would *normally* apply in the open market.

Qualifying Insurers are required to enter into a Qualifying Insurer's Agree- **8–015** ment with the Law Society, by which they agree inter alia to underwrite the ARP.

(f) *Barristers*

Paragraph 402.1 of the Bar Code of Conduct requires all self-employed practis- **8–016** ing barristers to be members of the Bar Mutual Indemnity Fund. Premiums are calculated by reference to turnover which is weighted according to practice area. Limits of indemnity depend upon the premium payable, and vary between £500,000 and £2,500,000. Excess of loss cover up to £2,500,000 in excess of £2,500,000 can be purchased through BMIF although it is underwritten by open market insurers. Greater excess of loss cover must be purchased through the open market.

3. THE NATURE/SCOPE OF PROFESSIONAL INDEMNITY INSURANCE

Professional indemnity insurance normally operates to indemnify the Insured **8–017** against legal liability established against the Insured (whether directly or vic- ariously) and arising out of the Insured's business and caused by any negligent error, act or omission on the part of the Insured. Many policies, however, go further and provide (subject to any relevant exclusions[27]) an indemnity in respect of any civil liability "howsoever arising". It is also common for extensions to the policy to provide additional cover, for example in respect of first party legal costs, fidelity and "sue and labour" costs.

As with any other form of insurance, it will be necessary for the Insured to **8–018** establish that its loss (in the form of legal liability) has been proximately caused[28] by a peril insured against. The English law of insurance now recognises that there may be more than one proximate cause[29]—if so, then (and subject to the application of any exclusion) the policy *will* respond provided that at least one of

---

[26] For up to 24 months in any five-year period.

[27] For example, some policies exclude liability for fraud; others only exclude any right of indemnity on the part of a fraudulent insured.

[28] Proximate means "proximate" in efficiency and not the latest causally relevant factor to the exclusion of all others: *Leyland Shipping v Norwich Union* [1918] A.C. 350 at pp.363, 369.

[29] *Wayne Tank & Pump Co v Employers Liability Assurance* [1973] 2 Lloyd's Rep. 237; *The Miss Jay Jay* [1987] 1 Lloyd's Rep. 32; *Midland Mainline v Eagle Star* [2004] 2 Lloyd's Rep. 604. *cf. West Wake Price v Ching* [1956] 2 Lloyd's Rep. 618 at p.624 col.2 where Devlin J. appears to have viewed the possibility that an insured loss might have more than one proximate cause as an heresy.

the causes falls within the scope of cover.[30] If, however, any proximate cause of the liability is excluded from cover then the policy will not respond at all.[31]

8–019   Under the primary insuring clause of a professional indemnity policy, an Insured will not, without more, be entitled to be indemnified against any *claim* made against it but only in respect of legal liability arising in consequence of a claim. Since the decisions of the Court of Appeal in *Post Office v Norwich Union Fire Insurance Society Ltd*[32] and the House of Lords in *Bradley v Eagle Star*[33] it has been beyond argument[34] that this means a liability whose existence *and* amount have been respectively ascertained and defined by judgment, award or binding compromise. Expense incurred by an Insured to avoid such liability will, accordingly, not normally fall within the scope of the insuring clause of a professional indemnity insurance policy[35] unless covered by an appropriate extension to the policy.[36]

8–020   In *Lumbermens Mutual Casualty Co v Bovis Lend Lease*,[37] Colman J. held that, because the Insured's liability must ordinarily be both established and quantified before any claim can be brought on any liability policy,[38] a settlement which made no allocation as between insured and uninsured losses was insufficient to "ascertain" liability in order to crystallise a right of action under the policy. While *Lumbermens* was settled before the point could be tested on appeal, in *Enterprise Oil Ltd v Strand Insurance Company Ltd*[39] Aikens J. held, obiter, that *Lumbermens* was wrong since the requirement for the liability to be ascertained referred to the Insured's liability to the third party and not to the amount of Insurers' liability to the Insured—thus it would be permissible to establish the extent of the insured liability by evidence extrinsic to the terms of the settlement with the third party. While the point remains open, the views expressed in *Enterprise Oil* are probably the less controversial.

8–021   In order to ascertain whether the Insured's liability to the third party has been caused proximately by a peril insured against, the Court will look at the true nature of the circumstances giving rise to the Insured's liability. The basis upon which any claim was advanced against the Insured is unlikely to be determinative,[40] so it would (for example) remain open to an Insured to allege that its liability was proximately caused by a peril covered by the insuring clause even if the third party's claim had been brought on some different basis.[41]

---

[30] *Capel Cure Myers Capital Management v McCarthy* [1995] 1 L.R.L.R. 498.
[31] *Wayne Tank & Pump Co v Employers Liability Assurance* [1973] 2 Lloyd's Rep. 237; *Midland Mainline v Eagle Star* [2004] 2 Lloyd's Rep. 604.
[32] [1967] 2 Q.B. 363.
[33] [1989] A.C. 957.
[34] See also *The Mercandian Continent* [2001] Lloyd's Rep. I.R. 802.
[35] See, e.g. *Walton v National Employers' Mutual General Insurance Association Ltd* [1974] 2 Lloyd's Rep. 385 where the NSW Supreme Court held that such costs were no more than costs incurred in rendering the contractual performance which the insured had contracted to provide.
[36] As in *Mabey & Johnson Ltd v Ecclesiastical Insurance Office* [2004] Lloyd's Rep. I.R. 10.
[37] [2005] Lloyd's Rep. I.R. 47 at para.42.
[38] Which would include any professional indemnity policy.
[39] [2006] 1 Lloyd's Rep. 500 at paras 164–72 (obiter).
[40] *West Wake Price v Ching* [1956] 2 Lloyd's Rep. 618 where Devlin J. acknowledged that any underlying proceedings might not be determinative of the issue of causation as between insurers and insured; *Enterprise Oil v Strand Insurance* [2006] 1 Lloyd's Rep. 500. *cf. Charterhouse Development v Sharp* [1998] Lloyd's Rep. I.R. 266 at p.277.
[41] *Johns v Kelly* [1986] 1 Lloyd's Rep. 468 at p.474 col.1.

In *London Borough of Redbridge v Municipal Mutual Insurance Ltd*,[42] how-   **8–022**
ever, it was held that Insurers were not entitled to raise an issue of illegality
which had not been addressed in the underlying proceedings. The decision in the
Redbridge case is difficult to reconcile with *West Wake Price*[43] as well other
recent authorities such as *Commercial Union v NRG Victory Re*[44] and *Enterprise
Oil*[45]: if *Redbridge* were correct then an insurer who has rightly but pre-
emptively repudiated liability for any third party claim could nevertheless find
itself being obliged to provide an indemnity unless it has had the foresight to
issue non-liability declaratory relief proceedings against its Insured and obtained
any necessary declaration before the Insured's liability to the third party has been
ascertained. The alternative would be for the insurer who wished to challenge the
proximate cause of the Insured's liability to the third party to apply to be joined
under CPR Pt 19.2 as a necessary party to any action between the third party and
Insured.[46] In any event, it is not certain that the decision in *Redbridge* would be
followed

Even where the policy wording purports to indemnify the Insured "in respect   **8–023**
of any claim *alleging* neglect", it is likely that the Insured will still have to
establish that negligence/neglect was the proximate cause of the liability and will
not be able to rely upon the way in which the third party's claim has been
formulated.[47]

Insurers will not, without more, be bound by every settlement entered into by   **8–024**
the Insured. Prima facie, it will be for the Insured to establish, on a proper
analysis of the applicable law and the relevant facts, that it was under an actual
liability to the third party in an amount at least as great as the settlement sum.[48]
In the majority of cases this requirement is likely to be of no consequence since
either Insurers will have approved or (if exercising claims control) made the
settlement and so be bound by it, or the policy will contain a provision requiring
Insurers' consent as a condition precedent to Insurers' liability.

Professional indemnity insurance will often exclude cover in respect of any   **8–025**
liability which arises purely by reason of a contractual term and which would not
attach in the absence of that term. In practice, therefore, such insurance would
not provide cover against a liability to a third party which could not be established in negligence.[49]

---

[42] [2001] Lloyd's Rep. I.R. 545.
[43] [1956] 2 Lloyd's Rep. 618. Caution is needed when applying *West Wake Price*: the decision
proceeds from the premises that (1) there could only be one proximate cause of a loss and (2) a
"mixed" claim in negligence and fraud would be not fall within cover since fraud was not insured.
Neither premise would now be regarded as sound—see para.8–017, above.
[44] [1998] 2 Lloyd's Rep. 600.
[45] [2006] 1 Lloyd's Rep. 500.
[46] See *Chubb Insurance Co of Europe SA v Davies* [2005] Lloyd's Rep. I.R. 1; *Wood v Perfection
Travel* [1996] L.R.L.R. 233.
[47] *MDIS v Swinbank* [1999] Lloyd's Rep. I.R. 516. Although there was force in Peter Gibson L.J.'s
dissent on this issue, it is likely that the principle set out in *West Wake Price* will now be seen as being
of general application rather than confined to its own wording.
[48] *Commercial Union v NRG Victory Re* [1998] 2 Lloyd's Rep. 600 (this was a reinsurance case, and
there is some uncertainty as to the extent to which contracts of reinsurance are to be equated to
liability policies); *MDIS v Swinbank* [1999] Lloyd's Rep. I.R. 516; *Enterprise Oil v Strand Insurance*
[2006] 1 Lloyd's Rep. 500 at paras 74–82.
[49] See, e.g. *Ham v Somak Travel*, unreported, (1998) CA; *cf. Wimpey Construction UK Ltd v DV
Poole* [1984] 2 Lloyd's Rep. 499.

4. Policy Trigger: Claims Made/Circumstances Notified

8–026   It is standard market practice for PI policies to be written on a "claims made" basis.[50] Thus the policy will normally operate in respect of any claim first made against an Insured during the period of insurance. A claim is normally to be construed by reference to the relief claimed not the grounds advanced for such relief.[51]

8–027   Policies will ordinarily exclude liability for any claim or circumstance which might give rise to a claim of which an Insured is aware prior to inception of the policy in question. There is accordingly a requirement for insureds to be protected against the possibility of claims falling through the gaps between succeeding policies[52] by a provision by which any claim arising from a circumstance which might give rise to a claim of which the Insured becomes aware during the period of insurance and which is notified to Insurers as such shall be deemed to have been made for the first time during that period of insurance. This protection is almost universally to be found in an express deeming provision.[53]

8–028   Occasionally an express deeming provision is omitted during the preparation of bespoke policies.[54] In the absence of an express deeming provision there would be strong grounds for contending that such a provision should nevertheless be implied: if not as a consequence of universal market custom[55] then in order to give business efficacy to the terms of the contract.[56]

8–029   In *Robert Irving & Burns v Stone*[57] the Court of Appeal[58] held that a claim is normally made when an expression of discontent (1) is communicated to the Insured and (2) which might result in a remedy expected from the Insured. The Court also held that the issue of a claim form which is neither served nor brought to the Insured's attention does not amount to a claim.[59] Conversely, where a claim form is served or brought to the attention of an Insured, it does constitute notification of a claim encompassing all matters subsequently particularised in

---

[50] This has the practical benefit for the insurance market of allowing professional indemnity risks to be written on a short tail basis; the disadvantage for the insured is the need to maintain run-off cover after a cessation of business.

[51] *West Wake Price v Ching* [1956] 2 Lloyd's Rep. 618 at p.629 col.1; *Haydon v Lo & Lo* [1997] 1 W.L.R. 198.

[52] It is extremely likely if not certain that the succeeding year's cover will exclude liability in respect of any claim or circumstance previously notified to insurers.

[53] See, for example, cl.1.1(b) of the Law Society's Minimum Terms and Conditions; cl.B.9 of the ICAEW's Minimum Approved Policy Wording.

[54] In a recent Canadian case, *Jesuit Fathers of Upper Canada v Guardian Insurance Co* [2006] S.C.C. 21, a deeming provision was omitted from a standard form of liability policy.

[55] *cf. Baker v Black Sea & Baltic General Insurance* [1996] L.R.L.R. 353 at p.362. It would be surprising if an insurer would not accept (and expert evidence would not establish), that it is the universal practice of the London market to treat circumstances notified as being "locked in" to the year against which they are first notified.

[56] See *J Rothschild Assurance v Collyear* [1999] Lloyd's Rep. I.R. 6 at p.22 col.2; *Friends Provident v Sirius* [2005] Lloyd's Rep. I.R. 135 at para.13. The possible implication of a deeming provision was not considered by the Supreme Court of Canada in *Jesuit Fathers of Upper Canada v Guardian Insurance Co* [2006] S.C.C. 21.

[57] [2003] 1 Lloyd's Rep. P.N. 46 at p.48 col.1.

[58] Applying *St Paul Fire & Marine v Guardian Insurance Company of Canada* [1983] 1 D.L.R. 342. See also *Jesuit Fathers of Upper Canada v Guardian Insurance Co* [2006] S.C.C. 21 at para.53.

[59] *Robert Irving & Burns v Stone* [2003] 1 Lloyd's Rep. P.N. 46 at p.50 col.2.

the Particulars of Claim.[60] A claim is "made" even where the Insured volunteers the need for both investigation and recompense.[61]

5. COMPOSITE AND JOINT POLICIES

Many professional indemnity policies will provide cover for more than one   **8–030**
Insured. This gives rise to considerations as to the true nature of the contracts of insurance which have been created. If the interests of each Insured were identical in each and every respect, then it would be arguable that the policies were joint in nature, with consequent implications as to underwriters' entitlement to avoid the whole policy for pre-inception non-disclosure of any material fact or to repudiate a claim in the event of a breach of policy conditions. It is unlikely that multiple insureds under a professional indemnity policy would ever have a truly identical interest in the policy—and most if not all policies provide that each Insured is insured for his or her interest. Accordingly a professional indemnity policy is conventionally to be viewed as composite in nature—i.e. a bundle of separate contracts between Insurers on the one hand and each Insured on the other—to the clear potential benefit of innocent Insureds where there has been a non-disclosure by another Insured.[62]

6. CONTRACT FORMATION IN THE LLOYD'S AND COMPANIES' MARKETS

(a) *Generally*

In both the Lloyd's and Companies' markets, contracts of insurance are com-   **8–031**
monly formed using a broker's slip. The slip is a piece of paper recording, normally in shorthand, the essential details of the contract including, typically, information as to:

- the risk insured
- the parties assured/insured
- period of cover (including any retroactive date)
- limit of indemnity
- deductible
- aggregation
- premium
- terms of cover

---

[60] *Thorman v New Hampshire Insurance Company (UK) Ltd* [1988] 1 Lloyd's Rep. 7 at p.18; *cf. Steamship Mutual Underwriting Association Ltd v Trollope and Colls Ltd* (1986) 33 B.L.R. 77.
[61] *J Rothschild Assurance v Collyear* [1999] Lloyd's Rep. I.R. 6 at p.28.
[62] *Arab Bank Plc v Zurich Insurance Co* [1999] 1 Lloyd's Rep. 262.

- essential information relevant to the risk.

8–032   The broker (who places the risk as the Insured's agent) will typically first approach an underwriter with an acknowledged reputation for the type of risk in question. This underwriter will then normally become the lead underwriter on the slip.

8–033   Each underwriter will stamp and then "scratch" the slip, the scratch normally consisting of an illegible monogram accompanied by the date. Mere stamping of the slip without a scratch will not normally suffice to bind the underwriter's syndicate or company to the insurance.[63] Against the syndicate or company's stamp and his scratch the underwriter will indicate the percentage of the risk which he is prepared to write.

8–034   Each Insurer is severally but not jointly liable for its proportionate share of the risk. Where the slip is not fully subscribed (i.e. the broker cannot place 100 per cent of the risk) then the Insured will stand as co-insurer for the uninsured portion of the risk. Where, as is common, the slip is oversubscribed then market practice dictates that the each Insurer's scratched percentage is "written down" (i.e. reduced *pro rata*) to achieve a 100 per cent subscription.[64] The process of writing down can become complicated where some underwriters annotate the slip with "to stand" against the specified percentage: thus preventing any reduction of share for the particular syndicate/company in the writing down process.

8–035   Once the slip is fully subscribed, the broker is normally responsible for preparing appropriate policy wording unless standard wording applies. The wording to apply is typically identified in the body of the slip.

8–036   One the policy has been issued, its terms will normally be treated as constituting the entire agreement between Insured and Insurers, and reference to the slip thereafter as a contractual document, or as an aid to construction, may not be permissible.[65] Where the policy does not reflect the terms of the slip, the appropriate remedy for the disappointed party is to seek rectification of the policy.[66] In some instances, however, the slip may be a self-contained contractual document to which the policy is purely supplementary. In such cases, it may be permissible to construe both the slip and the policy side by side.[67]

(b) *Leading Underwriter Clauses*

8–037   To avoid the need for the broker to notify all subscribing underwriters of matters such as changes to details of the cover; claims etc, the slip may contain a leading underwriter clause. Such a clause will empower the leading underwriter to negotiate changes to cover, receive information, agree claims etc without the express consent of the following market. The extent of the leading underwriter's powers is obviously dependent upon the precise terms of any leading underwriter clause.[68]

---

[63] *Denby v English and Scottish Maritime Insurance* [1998] Lloyd's Rep. I.R. 343.
[64] *The Zephyr* [1985] 2 Lloyd's Rep. 529.
[65] *Youell v Bland Welch & Co (No.1)* [1992] 2 Lloyd's Rep. 127; *Great North Eastern Railway v Avon Insurance Plc* [2001] Lloyd's Rep. I.R. 793.
[66] See, e.g. *Wilson Holgate v Lancashire & Cheshire Insurance* (1922) 13 Ll. L.R. 486.
[67] *HIH Casualty and General Insurance Ltd v New Hampshire* [2001] Lloyd's Rep. I.R. 596.
[68] See, e.g. *Denby v Marchant* [1996] L.R.L.R. 301.

It should, however, be noted that many underwriters' stamps provide expressly **8–038** that all changes to cover are to be agreed individually; alternatively following underwriters may place an appropriate qualification next to their stamp and scratch. In such circumstances the requirement to obtain consent from each such underwriter becomes a term of the contract with that underwriter.

7. THE PRE-CONTRACTUAL DUTY OF UTMOST GOOD FAITH

(a) *The Duty*

In his seminal speech in *Carter v Boehm*,[69] Lord Mansfield recognised that an **8–039** Insured is peculiarly in a privileged position to know those matters which would affect any assessment of the risk proposed. A contract of insurance was accordingly, by its nature, a contract of utmost good faith. This meant, in turn, that an insured was obliged to disclose prior to inception[70] of the contract of insurance all facts material to the risk. On the facts of *Carter v Boehm*, this meant that Insurers were entitled to be told that the fort which was the subject matter of the insurance had been captured by the French prior to placement of the risk. The codification of that law within the Marine Insurance Act 1906 means that Lord Mansfield's analysis remains as pertinent today as it did when the Duke of Wellington was born.[71]

The test for materiality is straightforward: a fact is material if it would have **8–040** acted upon the mind of a reasonably prudent underwriter in his assessment of the risk (i.e. if he would have wanted to have known about it).[72] It is not necessary, however, that the hypothetically prudent underwriter would have been decisively influenced[73] in his assessment of the risk by the non-disclosure.[74]

The remedy for non-disclosure is avoidance. To mitigate the potentially **8–041** disproportionate effect of any non-disclosure, the House of Lords held in *Pan Atlantic Insurance v Pine Top Insurance*[75] that Insurers' entitlement to avoid any particular policy is implicitly subject to a requirement to establish that the particular non-disclosure relied upon induced Insurers to write the risk.

Until relatively recently it was unclear whether Insurers had to prove that they **8–042** were decisively influenced in their acceptance of the risk by the non-disclosure or misrepresentation in question.[76] In *Assicurazioni Generali v Arab Insurance Group*,[77] however, the Court of Appeal confirmed that in order to prove inducement Insurers must establish that, but for the non-disclosure, they would not have

---

[69] (1766) 3 Burr. 1905.
[70] Inception equates to "execution" of the contract (i.e. when the contract is concluded). It should not be confused with the date on which cover commences.
[71] In 1769.
[72] [1995] 1 A.C. 501.
[73] i.e. would have changed the terms of cover or have declined to write the risk.
[74] *Container Transport International Ltd v Oceanus Mutual Underwriting* [1984] 1 Lloyd's Rep. 476; *St Paul Fire & Marine v McConnell Dowell Constructors* [1995] 2 Lloyd's Rep. 116.
[75] [1995] 1 A.C. 501.
[76] See, e.g. *St Paul Fire & Marine v McConnell Dowell Constructors* [1995] 2 Lloyd's Rep. 116; *Avon v Swire Fraser* [2000] Lloyd's Rep. I.R. 535.
[77] [2003] 1 W.L.R. 577.

written the risk or would have done so on different terms (the difference being adverse to the insured). Inducement can be established by hearsay evidence[78] and there is no reason in principle why, like other facts, it should not be inferred in an obvious case; but it should probably be established by direct evidence if possible, to guard against the risk that a Court might draw an adverse inference from the absence of such direct evidence.[79] When considering evidence of inducement, the Court is likely to be sensitive to the possibility that the evidence may be self-serving in nature.[80]

8–043   Both materiality and inducement are to be assessed at the time of inception.[81]

(b) *The Scope of the Duty*

8–044   The obligation to disclose material facts is not, however, limitless. It extends only to those facts within the actual knowledge of the Insured. For these purposes, "the Insured" means a directing mind thereof (someone with a predominant position within the company) or someone sufficiently concerned with insurance transactions,[82] and knowledge is not to be imputed on a quasi-vicarious basis.[83] Moreover, in matters of opinion at least, the obligation will not be breached on account of an honest albeit mistaken belief on the part of the Insured.[84] Where each director is a separate Insured under the policy, then a director cannot without more be treated as the directing mind or alter ego of the company.[85]

8–045   For the purposes of the obligation of disclosure, the Insured is deemed to know facts of which it should be aware in the ordinary course of its business.[86] The Insured is also (effectively) obliged to disclose matters known to its agent to insure (normally its broker).[87] Where a director is authorised to act on behalf of the principal Insured and other directors in effecting cover, the normal rules of agency may be displaced if, on a true construction of the policy, the parties intended to protect innocent directors from the dishonesty of the former.[88] In assessing the knowledge of an agent to insure, knowledge acquired otherwise than in the ordinary course of the agent's business or held in the agent's capacity as agent to insure will be disregarded.[89]

---

[78] *Manolakaki v Constantinides* [2004] EWHC 749, Ch.
[79] *Wisniewski v Central Manchester HA* [1998] P.I.Q.R. P324; *Walker International v Republique Populaire du Congo* [2005] EWHC 2813, Comm at para.18.
[80] *North Star Shipping Limited v Sphere Drake Insurance Plc* [2005] 2 Lloyd's Rep. 76 at para.254.
[81] *Brotherton v Asegurdora Colseguros SA* [2003] Lloyd's Rep. I.R. 746.
[82] *Regina Fur Company Ltd v Bossom* [1957] 2 Lloyd's Rep. 466 at p.484 col.2.
[83] *The Eurysthenes* [1976] 2 Lloyd's Rep. 171 at p.179 col.2.
[84] *Economides v Commercial Union Assurance Co Plc* [1998] Q.B. 587.
[85] *Arab Bank v Zurich Insurance* [1999] 1 Lloyd's Rep. 262 at p.279. The answer would possibly be different if the director held the majority of the shares or if the actions in question were condoned by the Board.
[86] s.18(1) of the Marine Insurance Act 1906.
[87] s.19 of the Marine Insurance Act 1906.
[88] *Arab Bank v Zurich Insurance* [1999] 1 Lloyd's Rep. 262 at p.278.
[89] *Group Josi Re v Walbrook Insurance Co Ltd* [1996] 1 Lloyd's Rep. 345 at pp.366–7; *PCW Syndicates v PCW Reinsurers* [1996] 1 Lloyd's Rep. 241 at pp.255–6.

Conversely, the Insured is not obliged to disclose[90] facts: 8–046

(a) known to Insurers; or

(b) of which Insurers are deemed to be aware in the ordinary course of their business; or

(c) in respect of which Insurers have waived any requirement for disclosure. Waiver may be by non-enquiry where the Insurer is on notice of particular facts, but only if there has been a fair presentation of the risk[91]; such waiver is not to be inferred lightly.[92] Alternatively, waiver may arise as a matter of inference due to the nature of questions asked in a proposal form—it is likely that the Courts will be more willing to find waiver in such circumstances[93];

(d) which are immaterial as their subject matter is covered by an express warranty.

(c) *Avoidance*

Provided that Insurers can establish that they were induced to write the risk by   8–047
non-disclosure of a material fact, such a state of affairs does not automatically vitiate the cover. It gives rise only to a right of election on the part of Insurers as to whether to treat the policy as subsisting (affirmation) or cancelled from inception (avoided *ab initio*). Upon avoidance of a policy, an insurer is under an obligation to return any premium received, unless the policy was procured by fraud.[94]

Any unequivocal act consistent only with the policy continuing in force will   8–048
affirm the policy, *provided that* Insurers had *actual* knowledge of the fact not disclosed at the time of the act relied upon as constituting the affirmation.[95] Insurers are entitled to a reasonable period in which to make their election, and the facts must be such that a reasonable Insured would appreciate that an informed choice has been made.[96]

Insurers' common law right of avoidance may be modified or extinguished by   8–049
the terms of the policy.[97] Restrictions on Insurers' rights of avoidance are often

---

[90] Generally, s.18(3) of the Marine Insurance Act 1906.
[91] *Container Transport International Ltd v Oceanus Mutual Underwriting* [1984] 1 Lloyd's Rep. 476 at p.511; *Newbury International Ltd v Reliance National Insurance Co (UK) Ltd* [1994] Lloyd's Rep. 83; *Marc Rich v Portman* [1997] 1 Lloyd's Rep. 225 at pp.233–4.
[92] *Container Transport International Ltd v Oceanus Mutual Underwriting* [1984] 1 Lloyd's Rep. 476; *Wise v Grupo Nacional* [2004] Lloyd's Rep. I.R. 764.
[93] *Roselodge v Castle* [1966] 2 Lloyd's Rep. 113; *Roberts v Plaisted* [1989] 2 Lloyd's Rep. 341 (arguably a case where insurers knew the facts which they alleged had not been disclosed); *Schoolman v Hall* [1951] 1 Lloyd's Rep. 139. In *Doheny v New India Assurance* [2005] Lloyd's Rep. I.R. 251 at para.16, the inclination of the Court of Appeal (obiter), was to treat this as a species of waiver outside the scope of s.18(3)(c) of the Marine Insurance Act 1906—although it is questionable whether this view could be correct given the terms of s.18(1) of the Marine Insurance Act 1906.
[94] s.84(3) of the Marine Insurance Act 1906.
[95] *Insurance Corp of the Channel Island v The Royal Hotel* [1998] Lloyd's Rep. I.R. 151.
[96] *Spriggs v Wessington Court School* [2005] Lloyd's Rep. I.R. 474; *cf. Callaghan v Thompson* [2000] Lloyds Rep. I.R. 125.
[97] *HIH Casualty and General Insurance Ltd v Chase Manhattan* [2001] Lloyd's Rep. I.R. 191.

found in professional indemnity policies, including both solicitors' and account-ants' insurance,[98] recognising a public policy requirement to protect the interests of the clients of the firms concerned above the interests of the insurance market. The scope of such provisions differ and are to be construed accordingly. It is now clear[99] that a clause providing, without more, that the policy was neither cancel-lable nor voidable *would* exclude a right of avoidance in respect of innocent and negligent, material misrepresentation or non-disclosure.[1]

8–050   The ICAEW's Minimum Approved Policy Wording prohibits Insurers from exercising their right of avoidance on the grounds of "any" alleged non-disclosure or misrepresentation.[2] The clause is, however, subject to a proviso by which the burden lies on the Insured to satisfy Insurers that the non-disclosure or misrepresentation was free from fraudulent conduct or intent to deceive. It is therefore clear from the terms of the proviso that the clause would not operate to prevent avoidance where there had been fraudulent non-disclosure or mis-representation.

8–051   Under the Law Society's Minimum Terms and Conditions of Professional Indemnity Insurance 2006, Insurers are prohibited[3] from avoiding the insurance "on any grounds whatsoever including, without limitation, non-disclosure or misrepresentation, whether fraudulent or not". Prima facie the breadth of the restriction is self-evident, although it is open to question whether the clause would truly be effective to exclude the right of avoidance where the making of the contract *had* been induced by fraud[4]: as a matter of practice, the conundrum may be unlikely to arise since each participating insurer has to make a formal commitment to the Law Society to provide insurance in accordance with the Minimum Terms—and no doubt the Law Society would, if necessary, intervene to secure observance of the restriction. It is open to argument, however, that Insurers' right to claim damages (amounting to a set-off against any liability under the policy) would not be affected by the clause given the general rule of law that a party cannot exclude liability for its own fraud.[5]

8–052   The Courts have recently grappled with the possibility that Insurers rights to avoid a contract of insurance for breach of the pre-contractual duty of utmost good faith might be restricted by an application of the doctrine of post-con-tractual good faith. This concept stems from recognition that the duty of utmost good faith:

---

[98] cl.4.1 of the Law Society's Minimum Terms and Conditions of Professional Indemnity Insurance 2006 (in force from October 1, 2006); cl.C.1 of ICAEW's Minimum Approved Policy Wording 2005.
[99] *cf. Toomey v Eagle Star (No.2)* [1995] 2 Lloyd's Rep. 88 in which the Court distinguished between innocent and "negligent" non-disclosure/misrepresentation.
[1] See *HIH Casualty and General Insurance Ltd v Chase Manhattan Bank* [2001] 2 Lloyd's Rep. 483, CA, at p.512, [2003] 2 Lloyd's Rep. 61, HL, at p.76.
[2] cl.C.1.
[3] cl.4.1.
[4] See, e.g. *S Pearson & Son Ltd v Dublin Corp* [1907] A.C. 351, (*per* Lord Loreburn L.C. at pp.353–4, Lord Halsbury at p.356 and Lord James at p.362), *HIH Casualty and General Insurance Ltd v Chase Manhattan* [2001] 2 Lloyd's Rep. 483 at para.75, *HIH Casualty and General Insurance Ltd v Chase Manhattan* [2003] 2 Lloyd's Rep. 61 at para.16.
[5] *HIH Casualty and General Insurance Ltd v Chase Manhattan* [2003] 2 Lloyd's Rep. 61 at para.76.

- endures after inception of the policy
- is mutual in nature.

Although the Court of Appeal recognised in *North Star Shipping Limited v*   **8–053**
Sphere Drake Insurance Plc[6] that the present state of the law[7] is unsatisfactory,
the basic principle remains that provided an insurer can establish both materiality
and inducement, then it will be entitled to avoid the policy.[8] In *Drake Insurance
v Provident Insurance*,[9] however, the same Court left open the possibility that
Insurers would not be entitled to avoid where, at the time of any election to avoid,
they were aware of matters which would have made their decision unreasonable.[10]

8. RULES OF CONSTRUCTION

(a) *Generally*

Under English law, there is no magic to the construction of an insurance contract.   **8–054**
The relevant principles are of application to all commercial contractual provisions and are generally well established[11]:

(1) The words used must be given their ordinary meaning albeit that they
    should reflect the commercial setting of the contract—thus the contract
    must be construed in context[12] and the meaning of the document is the
    meaning which would be attributed to the words in context as distinct
    from their dictionary definition[13];

(2) A literal construction that leads to an absurd result or one otherwise
    manifestly contrary to the real intention of the parties should be rejected,
    if an alternative more reasonable construction can be adopted without
    doing violence to the language used.[14] Where one of two possible

---

[6] [2006] 2 Lloyd's Rep. 183 at para.53.

[7] Which is ossified by the statutory codification of the law of insurance as it stood at the turn of the
twentieth century by the Marine Insurance Act 1906.

[8] *Brotherton v Aseguradora Colseguros SA* [2003] Lloyd's Rep. I.R. 746.

[9] [2004] Lloyd's Rep. I.R. 277.

[10] The views expressed are obiter and tentative. In *North Star Shipping Ltd v Sphere Drake Insurance
Plc* [2006] 2 Lloyd's Rep. 183 the Court of Appeal (again obiter) expressed the view that the
approach contemplated in *Drake* might arise in very few cases and was in any event difficult to
reconcile with the recognition under existing law that insurers would be entitled to avoid upon having
established materiality and inducement.

[11] See generally *Investors Compensation Scheme Ltd v West Bromwich BS* [1998] 1 W.L.R. 896 at
pp.912H–913C; *Yorkshire Water v Sun Alliance & London Insurance Plc* [1997] 2 Lloyd's Rep. 21
at p.28, cited with approval in *Pilkington United Kingdom Ltd v CGU Insurance Plc* [2004] Lloyd's
Rep. I.R. 891 at p.46 and *Blackburn Rovers Football & Athletic Club Plc v Avon Insurance Plc*
[2005] Lloyd's Rep. I.R. 447 at para.9.

[12] *Charter Reinsurance Co Ltd v Fagan* [1996] 2 Lloyd's Rep. 113 at p.117, col.1; [1996] 3 All E.R.
46 at p.51e.

[13] *Gan v Tai Ping (No.2)* [2001] Lloyd's Rep. I.R. 667 at pp.684–5.

[14] *Antaios Naviera SA v Salen Rederierna AB* [1985] A.C. 191 at p.201; *cf. Gan v Tai Ping (No.2)*
[2001] Lloyd's Rep. I.R. 667 at para.85.

constructions would be repugnant to the commercial purpose of the contract, it will be disregarded.[15]

(3) In the case of a genuine ambiguity,[16] the construction which is more favourable to the Insured should be adopted.

(4) The Court must recognise that commercial contracts are often imperfect instruments—it is therefore permissible to overlook obvious grammatical errors or even disregard redundant words or phrases as surplusage.[17] At the same time, the Court must also be astute not to "make" for the parties a contract which they did not make for themselves.[18]

(5) The Court will not be deflected from finding the obvious meaning of any contractual provision by any errors of language or grammar.[19]

(6) It is not the function of the Court to punish Insurers guilty of unclear and inaccurate wording.[20]

8–055   Some US jurisdictions tend to adopt an approach to policy construction which is weighted towards the Insured and may be based on a combination of public policy considerations as well as a principle of giving effect to the objectively reasonable expectations of the *Insured*.[21] Such an approach is not recognised by the English Courts.[22]

8–056   As noted above,[23] once the policy has been issued, its terms will normally be treated as constituting the entire agreement between Insured and Insurers, and reference to the slip thereafter as a contractual document, or as an aid to construction, may not be permissible. Where the policy does not reflect the terms

---

[15] *Fraser v BN Furman (Productions) Ltd* [1967] 2 Lloyd's Rep. 1 at p.12 where the Court of Appeal held that a clause requiring the insured under a liability policy to take reasonable precautions to prevent accidents would be breached only by reckless conduct on the part of the insured itself since to construe the clause as being breached by mere negligence would be repugnant to the commercial purpose of the contract.

[16] i.e. where following steps 1 and 2 there remain clearly two commercially realistic meanings which could be attributed to the words—see *Gan v Tai Ping (No.2)* Lloyd's Rep. I.R. 667 at p.686 col.2.

[17] See, e.g. *Blackburn Rovers Football & Athletic Club Plc v Avon Insurance Plc* [2005] Lloyd's Rep. I.R. 239 at para.13.

[18] *Charter Reinsurance Co Ltd v Fagan* [1997] A.C. 313 at p.388C; *Gan v Tai Ping (No.2)* [2001] Lloyd's Rep. I.R. 667 at para.85; *Great North Eastern Railway Ltd v Avon Insurance Plc* [2001] 2 Lloyd's Rep. 649 at para.34; *Royal & Sun Alliance Plc v Dornoch* [2005] Lloyd's Rep. I.R. 544 at para.16.

[19] *Gan v Tai Ping (No.2)* [2001] Lloyd's Rep. I.R. 667 at para.83; *Doheny v New India Assurance* [2005] Lloyd's Rep. I.R. 251 at paras 7–8 and 12.

[20] *Doheny v New India Assurance* [2005] Lloyd's Rep. I.R. 251 at para.12.

[21] See, e.g. *Broadwell Realty Services Inc v Fidelity and Casualty Co of New York* 528 Atlantic Reporter 2d series 76 Superior Court of New Jersey; *Slay Warehousing Co Inc v Reliance Insurance Co* (1973) 471 Fed. Rep. (2nd) series 1364; *cf.* the Canadian approach which lies somewhere in between—see *Consolidated-Bathurst Export Ltd v Mutual Boiler and Machinery Insurance Co* [1980] 1 S.C.R. 888 at pp. 901–902; *Non-Marine Underwriters, Lloyd's of London v Scalera* [2000] 1 S.C.R. 551 at para.71; *Jesuit Fathers of Upper Canada v Guardian Insurance Co* [2006] S.C.C. 21 at paras 27–9.

[22] *Yorkshire Water v Sun Alliance & London Insurance Plc* [1997] 2 Lloyd's Rep. 21 at p.28 col.1.

[23] para.8–036.

of the slip, the appropriate remedy for the disappointed party is to seek rectification of the policy.

Beyond terms relating to the time for payment of premium and/or of any **8–057** indemnity falling due under the policy, there is limited scope for the implication of terms into a contract of insurance as a matter of law. The requirement to establish a universal market custom[24] makes difficult (although it does not preclude) the implication of a term through usage. Difficulties in defining terms for implication or in establishing their necessity are manifest in the authorities.[25] A possible exception would be if a "claims made" policy omitted an express deeming provision.[26]

(b) *Exclusion Clauses and Insuring Clauses*

Exclusion clauses are to be construed in accordance with the principles set out **8–058** above. The Courts will not strike down an exclusion clause on the grounds of repugnancy unless its effect is to empty the contract of insurance of meaningful content.[27]

The causative relationship required for the operation of any relevant clause **8–059** must be considered and understood. Wording requiring that the liability or loss result "directly, independently and exclusively of all other causes" from the insured peril will exclude liability in the event that there is any other *proximate* cause; but a concurrent but non-proximate cause would not entitle Insurers to refuse indemnity.[28] An exclusion in the event that loss is "caused by" or "arises from" an excluded peril requires that the excluded peril be a proximate cause, if not the sole proximate cause.[29] Conversely, an exclusion in respect of liability or loss caused "directly or indirectly" from some excluded cause will bite in the event that the excluded cause is operative even if not proximate.[30]

9. CLASSIFICATION OF TERMS/CONSEQUENCES OF BREACH

It is a matter of notoriety that insurance contracts contain a variety of different **8–060** terms; and that breach of different types of term by an Insured will result in significantly different consequences. The principal types of term and the consequences of breach are explored below. It must be remembered that the label given in the contract to a term is not necessarily conclusive.

---

[24] *Baker v Black Sea & Baltic General Insurance Co Ltd* [1998] 1 W.L.R. 974 at p.984, approving [1996] L.R.L.R. 353 at p.362.
[25] *Gan v Tai Ping (No.2)* [2001] Lloyd's Rep. I.R. 667 at paras 93–7; *Insurance Company of Africa v Scor (UK) Reinsurance Co Ltd* [1985] 1 Lloyd's Rep. 312 at p.324 col.1; *Bonner v Cox* [2005] EWCA Civ 1512 at paras 96, 105–110; *cf. Phoenix v Halvanon* [1985] 2 Lloyd's Rep. 599 (doubted in *Bonner v Cox*).
[26] See para.8–028, above.
[27] *Great North Eastern Railway v Avon Insurance Plc* [2001] Lloyd's Rep. I.R. 793 at para.31.
[28] *Fidelity and Casualty Co of New York v Mitchell* [1917] A.C. 529.
[29] *Wayne Tank & Pump Co v Employers Liability Assurance* [1973] 2 Lloyd's Rep. 237; *Midland Mainline v Eagle Star* [2004] 2 Lloyd's Rep. 604. "*Resulting from*" is also likely to be construed as having the same effect.
[30] *Jason v British Traders' Insurance Co* [1969] 1 Lloyd's Rep. 281 at p.290.

(a) *"Warranties"*

8–061 In ordinary contracts a warranty is a term that is collateral to the main purpose of the contract, breach of which gives rise to a right in damages only. In insurance law a "warranty" has the effect of a "condition" in any ordinary contract.

8–062 A warranty arises when the Insured undertakes that some particular thing shall or shall not be done; or that a condition will be fulfilled; or that a particular state of facts does or does not exist. Normally the condition in question must go to the root of the contract of insurance. A warranty can be express or implied. It must be exactly complied with, irrespective of its materiality to the risk: see s.33(3) of the Marine Insurance Act 1906. Thus where the truth of statements in a proposal form is warranted, any misdescription would constitute a breach regardless of materiality to the risk.[31]

8–063 Mere use of the label "warranty" does not mean that the term is a warranty. Conversely, a term may be a warranty without being expressed as such.[32] Terms described as warranties are often no more that terms delimiting the risk or suspensive conditions: cover is suspended by breach until such time as the breach is remedied.[33]

8–064 In *The Good Luck*,[34] the House of Lords confirmed that a breach of warranty does not have the effect of avoiding the contract *ab initio*, or bringing the contract to an end. Instead, it has the immediate effect of discharging the insurer from any *further* liability under the policy. Breach does not affect any liability arising before the date of breach, and the obligations on the Insured (such as to pay premium) continue.

8–065 A breach of warranty may, however, be waived.[35] Following the decisions of the House of Lords in *The Kanchenjunga*,[36] and at first instance and in the Court of Appeal in *HIH Casualty and General Insurance Ltd v Axa Corporate Solutions*,[37] the principles relevant to waiver of a breach of warranty can be summarised as follows:

   (a) Waiver by election can have no application to a case of breach of an insurance warranty: the breach of warranty automatically discharges the cover so that there is no election to be made.

---

[31] See, e.g. *Yorkshire Insurance v Campbell* [1917] A.C. 218 the words: *"I, the undersigned, do hereby warrant and declare the truth of all the above statements . . . "* meant a description of the insured animal in the proposal form was held to be a warranty that had not been exactly complied with. The claim for loss failed, and the immateriality to the risk was irrelevant.

[32] See, e.g. *HIH Casualty and General Insurance Ltd v New Hampshire* [2001] Lloyd's Rep. I.R. 596.

[33] *CTN Cash & Carry v General Accident Fire and Life Assurance Corp* [1989] 1 Lloyd's Rep. 299; *Kler Knitwear Ltd v Lombard General Insurance Co Ltd* [2000] Lloyd's Rep. I.R. 47.

[34] [1992] 2 A.C. 233.

[35] s.34(3) of the Marine Insurance Act 1906.

[36] [1990] 2 Lloyd's Rep. 391.

[37] [2002] Lloyd's Rep. I.R. 325 (first instance) and [2003] Lloyd's Rep. I.R. 1, CA—the clearer analysis is to be found in the decision of Jules Sher Q.C. at first instance which was adopted and approved by the Court of Appeal.

(b) If waiver is to operate in respect of a breach of an insurance warranty, it must be waiver by estoppel.

(c) Waiver by estoppel involves a clear and unequivocal representation that the insurer will not stand on its right to treat the cover as having been discharged in circumstances where the insured has relied to its detriment on the representation, and it would be inequitable to allow the insurer to resile from it.

(d) The essence of the representation must go to the willingness of the insurer to forego his rights. Thus it is of the essence of the doctrine of promissory estoppel that one side is reasonably seen by the other to be foregoing its rights.

(e) Mere inaction founds a representation, if at all, only in circumstances required for an estoppel by silence, and silence can only amount to a representation where there is a duty to speak.

At first sight, the above principles restrict the circumstances in which post-   **8–066** inception waiver of a breach of warranty might be said to arise. There has, however, been little (if any) express consideration of the potential for estoppel by silence to arise in the context of an insurance policy. As to that:

(a) it is beyond question that the obligation of utmost good faith is mutual[38];

(b) it is therefore difficult to see why there should not, in appropriate circumstances, be an obligation on Insurers to speak out where they are deemed to know of a legal right (even if they are subjectively ignorant of it).

The policy terms themselves may suffice to waive at least *some* breaches of   **8–067** warranty. While a basis clause[39] will have the effect that full disclosure is warranted, a non-avoidance clause may be couched in terms wide enough to encompass repudiation of the insurance or of any claim and so preclude reliance upon the basis clause. A term that Insurers would "not seek to avoid, repudiate or rescind this Insurance on any ground whatsoever" would preclude reliance on a basis clause[40] as would cover written on the Law Society's Minimum Terms and Conditions[41] and the ICAEW's Minimum Approved Policy Wording.[42]

---

[38] *Drake Insurance v Provident Insurance* [2004] Lloyd's Rep. I.R. 277 at para.83.
[39] A clause typically along the following lines "It is agreed that the proposal form and any information given therein is incorporated herein and shall form the basis of the contract". Since such forms almost invariably require the insured to declare the accuracy and completeness of the answers given, issues of materiality and inducement can often be bypassed by insurers—as in *Doheny v New India Assurance* [2005] Lloyd's Rep. I.R. 251 at para.13.
[40] *Kumar v AGF Insurance Ltd* [1999] Lloyd's Rep. I.R. 147.
[41] See cl.4.1 of the 2006 wording, preventing insurers from repudiating the insurance on any grounds whatsoever.
[42] See cl.C.1 by which insurers agree not to exercise any right to claim to be discharged from liability (language encapsulating the consequence of a breach of warranty—see *The Good Luck* [1992] A.C. 233) on the grounds of any non-disclosure or misrepresentation of fact.

(b) *Conditions Precedent to Cover*

8–068   A "condition precedent" to cover is a requirement that must be satisfied before a contract comes into existence. In *The "Zeus V"* [43] the Court of Appeal held a provision that cover was "subject to" a marine survey of the insured ship was to be construed as a condition precedent to cover. The decision was clearly influenced by expert evidence as to market usage and understanding and therefore cannot be relied upon as establishing a universal principle.

(c) *Condition Precedent to Liability*

8–069   Some obligations upon an Insured are expressed as being conditions precedent to liability. For example, notification of a claim within a certain time is sometimes (but not always) so expressed.[44] If such a condition is not complied with, then no liability arises regardless of whether the breach is causative of any loss.[45]

8–070   Even if the relevant obligation is not itself expressed to be a condition precedent, many policies contain a "due observance" clause, by which the due observance of the terms and conditions of the policy, in so far as they relate to anything to be done by the Insured, shall be a condition precedent to Insurers' liability. In *Pilkington United Kingdom Ltd v CGU Insurance Plc*[46] the Court of Appeal held that a standard "due observance" clause would have the effect of elevating the Insured's obligations under the policy to the status of conditions precedent to liability.[47] Conversely, the Courts will not strain to find that successive provisions form part of a condition precedent unless that is a necessary and grammatical consequence of the language used,[48] although effect will be given to language or formatting which indicates that subordinate provisions form part of a condition precedent.[49]

(d) *Collateral Promise and Innominate Terms*

8–071   A condition precedent requires clear wording, and if the wording is not clear, the term is likely to be construed as a collateral promise. Where a term is merely a collateral promise, and the Insured's right to recover is not dependent on the fulfilment of the promise, the term is "innominate" and breach would not discharge the insurer from its obligations; it merely gives a right to counterclaim for damages. Following the Court of Appeal's decision in *Alfred McAlpine Plc v BAI (Run-Off) Ltd*[50] it was thought that in extreme cases a breach of an

---

[43] [2000] 2 Lloyd's Rep. 587.

[44] *George Hunt Cranes Ltd v Scottish Boiler & General Insurance Co Ltd* [2002] Lloyd's Rep. I.R. 178.

[45] *Pioneer Concrete (UK) Ltd v National Employers Mutual General Insurance Association Ltd* [1985] 1 Lloyd's Rep. 274 at 281.

[46] [2004] Lloyd's Rep. I.R. 891.

[47] *cf. Re Bradley and Essex and Suffolk Accident Indemnity Society* [1912] 1 K.B. 415, which the Court of Appeal distinguished in *Pilkington.*

[48] *Insurance Company of Africa v Scor (UK) Reinsurance Co Ltd* [1985] 1 Lloyd's Rep. 312 at p.330 col.2.

[49] *Gan v Tai Ping (No.2)* [2001] Lloyd's Rep. I.R. 667.

[50] [2000] 1 Lloyd's Rep. 437 (obiter).

innominate term might entitle Insurers to treat the claim as repudiated by the Insured. This "heresy" was corrected by the same Court in *Friends Provident Life & Pensions v Sirius International*,[51] which applied a conventional contractual analysis (that Insurers' remedy for breach of such a term should be limited to damages), although in many cases a contractual right to damages will be of little if any value to the Insurer.[52]

10. THE CONTINUING DUTY OF UTMOST GOOD FAITH AND THE RULE AGAINST FRAUDULENT CLAIMS

It was clear even before the passing of the Marine Insurance Act 1906 that an   **8–072** Insured has a duty of good faith prior to inception of any contract of insurance.[53] The duty of good faith was codified (and so preserved in aspic) by s.17 of that Act.[54] Unlike the immediately following provisions of the Act, which are expressly limited to the pre-contractual context, there is no explicit temporal limitation on the duty of good faith. It is therefore now universally accepted (even if contemporary judicial acceptance is generally qualified with regret) that the duty of good faith endures beyond inception of the contract.[55] However the House of Lords' decision in *The Star Sea* [2003] 1 A.C. 469 made clear that the obligation has a different application and content after inception[56] and does not amount to a continuing obligation to disclose facts material to the risk.[57]

The practical effect of the House of Lords decision in *The Star Sea* has been   **8–073** to encourage the Courts to make clear that the post-inception duty of good faith is an historical oddity and a practical irrelevance. It is now clear beyond serious argument that, following inception, the rights of the parties are governed primarily by the terms of their contract[58]; but there is a rule of law against the making of fraudulent claims,[59] a sub-species of which is the use of a fraudulent means or device to support an otherwise bona fide claim provided that the lie:

(1) relates directly to the claim;

(2) was told in order to improve the Insured's prospects of obtaining a settlement or winning the case; and

(3) would, if believed, tend objectively (but prior to a final determination of the parties' rights) materially to improve the Insured's prospects of obtaining a settlement (including as to timing) or winning at trial.[60]

---

[51] [2006] Lloyd's Rep. I.R. 45 at paras 31–2.
[52] *ibid.*, at para.33.
[53] *Carter v Boehm* (1766) 3 Burr 1905; *Rozanes v Bowen* (1828) L.R.L.R. 98 at p.102.
[54] "A contract of . . . insurance is a contract based upon the utmost good faith and, if the utmost good faith be not observed by either party, the contract may be avoided by the other party".
[55] *The Star Sea* [2003] 1 A.C. 469 at paras 7, 48, 81 and 96.
[56] *ibid.*, para.48.
[57] *ibid.*, paras 97–101.
[58] *The Mercandian Continent* [2001] Lloyd's Rep. I.R. 802; *The Aegon* [2002] Lloyd's Rep. I.R. 573.
[59] *The Star Sea* [2003] 1 A.C. 469 at para.62; *The Aegon* [2002] Lloyd's Rep. I.R. 573 at para.45; *Axa General Insurance Ltd v Gottlieb* [2005] Lloyd's Rep. I.R. 369.
[60] *The Aegon* [2002] Lloyd's Rep. I.R. 573 at para.45 (obiter).

Once litigation is joined, the parties' obligations *inter se* are governed by the rules and orders of Court so that the rule against fraudulent claims no longer applies in relation to the subject matter of the litigation.[61]

8–074   The consequences of a fraudulent claim are not entirely settled, although any claim tainted by the fraud will be wholly forfeited even if the majority of the claim is bona fide.[62] The weight of judicial opinion is consistent with the fraud discharging the insurer from all future liability under the policy, with effect from the time of the fraud.[63] Such language treats the making of a fraudulent claim as if it were a breach of warranty on the part of the Insured, with the effect that any prospective bona fide claims are forfeited, but the Insured's accrued rights are not affected. More recently, however, the Court of Appeal suggested (obiter) in *Axa General Insurance v Gottlieb*[64] that only the claim tainted by the fraud should be treated as forfeited, and that any bona fide claim arising after the fraud should be payable[65]: at first sight, such an approach would be difficult to reconcile with the earlier authorities, which it is highly arguable are determinative of the issue.

8–075   The rule against fraudulent claims is, however, likely to be of limited effect in the context of professional indemnity insurance. First, the Court of Appeal determined in *The Mercandian Continent*[66] that the rule only operates once the Insured has a crystallised cause of action against Insurers. Secondly, in the absence of collusion between an Insured and the third party to whom liability has been incurred, the potential for fraudulent claims arising out of liability insurance is smaller than in the context of insurance against first party loss[67] rather than against liability to a third party.

11. POLICY RESPONSE TO THE INSURED'S LIABILITY FOR FRAUD OR ILLEGALITY

8–076   Section 55(2)(a) of the Marine Insurance Act 1906 codified a general exclusion in respect of any loss attributable to the wilful misconduct of an assured. In *Beresford v Royal Insurance Co Ltd*,[68] Lord Atkin held that:

> "On ordinary principles of insurance law an assured cannot by his own deliberate act cause the event upon which the insurance money is payable. The insurers have not agreed to pay on that happening. The fire assured cannot recover if he intentionally burns down his house, nor a marine assured if he scuttles his ship, nor the life assured

---

[61] [2002] Lloyd's Rep. I.R. 573, at para.52.

[62] See, e.g. *Axa General Insurance v Gottlieb* [2005] Lloyd's Rep. I.R. 369 at para.27.

[63] *The Star Sea* [2003] 1 A.C. 469 at paras 66 and 110–1; *Orakpo v Barclays Insurance Services* [1995] L.R.L.R. 443 at p.451 col.2; *Galloway v Guardian Royal Exchange (UK) Ltd* [1999] Lloyd's Rep. I.R. 209 at p.212 col.2.

[64] [2005] Lloyd's Rep. I.R. 369 at para.22.

[65] The views expressed in *Gottlieb* are tentative as well as obiter.

[66] [2001] Lloyd's Rep. I.R. 802 at para.11, following *Post Office v Norwich Union Fire Insurance Society Ltd* [1967] 2 Q.B. 363 and *Bradley v Eagle Star* [1989] A.C. 957. This finding was obviously based on a strict view as to the meaning of "claim" in the relevant context and ignored the insured's accrued rights, under a policy extension, to defence costs.

[67] Although it might arise, for example, in order to persuade an insurer that a claim was caused by negligence rather than deceit on the part of the insured.

[68] [1938] A.C. 586.

if he deliberately ends his own life. This is not the result of public policy, but of the correct construction of the contract".

Although Lord Atkin's speech was addressed to policies insuring against first party loss, similar principles have been applied to liability policies, so that an Insured will not normally be entitled to an indemnity in respect of the consequences of his own deliberate or wilful act.[69]   8–077

In the absence of any relevant exclusion in the policy (or any relevant limitation to the scope of the insuring clause), there is no reason why a liability policy should not provide an indemnity in respect of legal liability arising out of deliberate and criminal acts of those for whom the Insured is, in law, responsible.[70] This may involve issues of attribution where the Insured is a limited company and the criminal acts are perpetrated by the Insured's directing mind or alter ego—in such cases it would appear that the policy will respond if the criminal acts were performed for the perpetrator's own ends rather than for the benefit of the company.[71]   8–078

Whether a particular policy will in fact respond to liability arising out of fraud or illegality perpetrated by someone other than the Insured but for whom the Insured is in law responsible will naturally turn on the wording of the policy in question. Both the Law Society's Minimum Terms and Conditions and the ICAEW's Minimum Approved Policy Wording would provide cover which is sufficiently wide. Conversely, insurance in respect of liability caused by "neglect, error or omission" would not be construed as extending to liability caused by fraud.[72]   8–079

12. CLAIMS NOTIFICATION & CO-OPERATION CLAUSES

(a) *Generally*

The general conditions of an insurance policy typically include provisions as to when a claim or potential claim must be notified to Insurers, and as to the obligation upon an Insured thereafter to provide Insurers with information and/or assistance in relation to that claim.   8–080

The obligation to notify is normally expressed as arising when the Insured becomes aware of any circumstance which *may* give rise to a claim; such a requirement is logical since the Insured is likely to be unable to obtain cover in any succeeding year in respect of any such circumstance.[73] Some policies, however, provide that the obligation to notify arises only when the Insured is aware of circumstances which are *likely* to give rise to a claim. Such wording is more generous to an Insured in terms of when the obligation to notify arises,[74] although it is better suited to other forms of liability insurance written on a   8–081

---

[69] *Gray v Barr* [1971] 2 Q.B. 554; *Charlton v Fisher* [2001] Lloyd's Rep. I.R. 387.
[70] See, e.g. *Hawley v Luminar Lesiure Ltd* [2006] Lloyd's Rep. I.R. 307 at para.107.
[71] *KR v Royal & Sun Alliance Plc* [2006] Lloyd's Rep. I.R. 327 at paras 51–2. This case is under appeal.
[72] See para.8–018, above.
[73] *J Rothschild Assurance v Collyear* [1999] Lloyd's Rep. I.R. 6 at p.22 col.2.
[74] *Layher v Lowe* [2000] Lloyd's Rep. I.R. 510; *Jacobs v Coster* [2000] Lloyd's Rep. I.R. 506.

"claims arising" or "liability incurred" basis rather than professional indemnity policy written on a "claims made" basis.

8–082   It is likely (but not decided) that the obligation to notify should be construed objectively, but taking into account the actual knowledge of the Insured.[75]

8–083   Notification provisions may be composite. Where there is an issue as to whether effective notification has been made, it is accordingly necessary first to establish the precise nature and scope of any (and all) obligation(s) to notify, and then to ask whether the Insured has satisfied any such obligation.[76]

8–084   A claims notification will be valid even where it is general in nature.[77] Conversely, a notification which is precisely defined may be limited in its effect.[78]

8–085   Not only is there no justification in demanding too much of the requirement to notify circumstances, but the requirement for materiality imposed by an obligation to notify circumstances which *may* give rise to a claim is weak; a Court is likely to take a broad approach when determining whether a circumstance has been notified, recognising that the imposition of too formulaic an approach might leave an Insured in the position where no "valid" notification had been given to one year's Insurers and the relevant circumstance was excluded from the succeeding year's cover.[79] Accordingly, unless the contractual requirement as to notification is expressly prescriptive as to the content of the notification required, the provision of less than complete detail as to any relevant claim or circumstance will not invalidate any notification—Insurers' rights in relation to the provision of detail by the Insured will, in such cases, be found in any claims information/co-operation clause.

8–086   The nature and scope of the information to which an insurer is entitled under any claims information/co-operation clause will be expressly defined on the face of the clause. Insurers' entitlement to information is, however, circumscribed by the context in which the obligations under the clause arise: any information sought must have some bearing on the claim (and Insurers' liability to meet it) and it would probably be an impermissible use of the clause for Insurers to seek information relevant only to a general review of the pre-inception underwriting decision. Thus, in *Gan v Tai Ping (No.3)*,[80] the Court of Appeal held that while information may be sought which bears on a possible ground for avoidance for non-disclosure, or repudiation for breach of warranty, the potential ground of avoidance or repudiation must have some connection with the claim in question.

(b) Solicitors

8–087   The Law Society's Minimum Terms and Conditions contain no proforma wording for either a claims notification or claims co-operation/information clause.

---

[75] *Jacobs v Coster* [2000] Lloyd's Rep. I.R. 506 at para.10(2).
[76] *Hamptons Residential v Field* [1998] 2 Lloyd's Rep. 248.
[77] *Alexander Forbes Europe Ltd v SBJ Ltd* [2003] Lloyd's Rep. P.N. 137 at para.19.
[78] *Hamptons Residential v Field* [1997] 1 Lloyd's Rep. 302 (overturned on different grounds on appeal, [1998] 2 Lloyd's Rep. 248).
[79] *J Rothschild Assurance v Collyear* [1999] Lloyd's Rep. I.R. 6 at p.22 col.2.
[80] [2002] Lloyd's Rep. I.R. 612 at paras 36–8.

While Insurers are entitled to include such clauses within any policy wording, they must not conflict with the other provisions of the Minimum Terms.[81] In practice, this precludes any such provision from being a condition precedent to liability.[82]

(c) *Accountants*

The ICAEW's Minimum Approved Policy Wording requires an Insured, as a **8–088** condition precedent to liability, to give notice "as soon as practicable" of any claim made or notified, or of any loss or of the discovery of reasonable cause for suspicion of dishonesty or fraud on the part of any past or present partner, director, employee etc.[83] A similar obligation, also expressed as a condition precedent to liability, arises upon the Insured becoming aware during the period of insurance of any circumstance which may give rise to a loss or claim.[84] Although notification must be in writing, no other formalities are prescribed.

The ICAEW's Minimum Approved Policy Wording entitles Insurers to con- **8–089** duct an investigation into any circumstances notified and to receive at all times the Insured's full co-operation for such purpose.[85] There is also a claims control clause[86] by which Insurers would be entitled at any time to take over and conduct (at their own expense) the defence, investigation or settlement of any claim. This latter provision is subject to a Q.C. clause.

13. Q.C. CLAUSES

In liability insurance there often may be a divergence of interest between insurer **8–090** and Insured as to whether to defend a claim brought by a third party. It may be that the Insured recklessly wishes to fight on using the unwilling Insurers' funds.[87] This situation is usually dealt with by a control clause within the policy. The converse situation, where the insurer wishes to fight on, but the Insured does not, is often regulated by a Q.C. Clause.

A typical clause[88] provides that the insurer will pay: **8–091**

> "any such claim(s) which may arise without requiring the Insured to dispute any claim, unless a Queen's Counsel (to be mutually agreed upon by the Underwriters and Insured) advise that the same could be successfully contested by the Insured and the Insured consents to such a claim being contested, but such consent not to be unreasonably withheld".

---

[81] [2002] Lloyd's Rep. I.R. 612 at paras 36–8, cl.7.1.
[82] See cl.4.2 which prohibits insurers from reducing or denying liability under the insurance by reason of any breach of term, save in certain defined circumstances.
[83] cl.B.8, ICAEW Minimum Approved Policy Wording.
[84] *ibid.*, cl.B.9.
[85] *ibid.*, cl.B.7. The provision is innominate.
[86] *ibid.*, cl.B.7.
[87] Very often the case where the insured has a small deductible.
[88] A comparable provision appears in the ICAEW Minimum Approved policy Wording as part of cl.B.7.

8–092   Indeed, a Q.C. Clause may be framed so as to apply to any dispute between the insurer and the Insured. Conversely, it may be limited to matters relating to the amount payable under the insurance, the liability of Insurers having otherwise been established or admitted.

8–093   In *David Wilson Homes v Surrey Services Ltd*,[89] the Court of Appeal held that a Q.C. Clause in terms:

> " . . . any dispute or difference arising hereunder between the Assured and the Insurers shall be referred to a Queen's Counsel of the English Bar to be mutually agreed between the Insurers and the Assured or in the event of disagreement by the Chairman of the Bar Council"

was an arbitration clause falling within s.6 of the Arbitration Act 1996. Court proceedings were therefore stayed.

14. DEDUCTIBLES AND LIMITS OF INDEMNITY; AGGREGATION OF CLAIMS

(a) *Generally*

8–094   The contract of insurance will define the maximum sum payable by Insurers in respect of each claim and/or in the aggregate. In addition, the Insured will normally bear a self-insured excess or deductible which must be paid in respect of each claim.

8–095   Insurance policies often seek to group claims together, for the purpose of determining both the deductible (or excess) payable by the Insured and also the sums payable by Insurers, and/or to impose an absolute limit on the aggregate deductible payable by the Insured or the sums payable by Insurers. It might be expected that a policy will aggregate both the deductible and the limit of indemnity on the same basis so as to avoid one or other party to the contract bearing what would at first sight appear to be a disproportionate share of the risk. There is, however, no presumption that deductibles and limits of indemnity will be aggregated on the same basis, and the correct treatment of both will accordingly depend on the policy wording in question.[90]

8–096   Provision for aggregation is often, if not exclusively, made by means of defining "claim" or "loss" or "liability" within the policy wording. Beyond that common approach, different aggregation clauses employ different language. It is important not to try and impose upon any particular aggregation clause a preconception that the particular claims should or should not be aggregated—but instead to give effect to the language used. Any attempt to identify and then impose a single, coherent philosophy of aggregation would inevitably be insensitive to differences in policy wording and accordingly doomed to failure.

8–097   Typical phrases found in aggregation clauses include "any one event", "each and every claim", "any one occurrence", "any one occurrence, any one location", "each series of occurrences arising out of one event", "series of claims resulting from any related series of acts or omissions" and "arising from or

---

[89] [2001] EWCA Civ 34, CA.
[90] *Countrywide Assured Group Plc v D J Marshall* [2003] Lloyd's Rep. P.N. 1 at para.13.

attributable to one originating cause or source". It can thus be seen that it may be necessary to consider issues both of causation and also relationship, although it would be artificial to consider, or define, such issues in isolation from each other.

An "event" or "occurrence" is generally to be regarded as "something which happens at a particular time, at a particular place, in a particular way"[91] or which (1) can properly be described as an event (in the relevant contractual or factual context), (2) satisfies any necessary test of causation imposed by the clause and (3) is not too remote. Accordingly, repeated but separate acts of negligence, albeit of a similar nature, could not properly be described as a single "event".[92] A similar approach can be anticipated to the construction of the word "occurrence"[93] although that word does not exclude the possibility that what may be viewed as multiple acts might nevertheless form part of the same event[94]; although related acts which are causally and temporally distinct may not.[95] Perhaps counter-intuitively, "cause", "original cause" and "originating cause" connote a wider relationship than "event".[96]   **8–098**

"Claim" is not to be construed narrowly as relating to a discrete cause of action but in a broader and more robust sense, by reference to the relief claimed rather than the basis upon which it is so claimed.[97]   **8–099**

A requirement in an aggregation clause that claims should "result from a related series of acts or omissions" is not satisfied simply by the identification of some common characteristic between the different claims—both because similarity does not create a relationship and also because there needs to be a sufficient causal relationship.[98]   **8–100**

Wording such as "originating from one cause" requires the establishment of a causative link between the relevant cause and the relevant liability or loss.[99] The phrase "arising out of a single event" indicates a requirement for a significant causal relationship.[1]   **8–101**

(b) *Solicitors*

The Law Society's Minimum Terms and Conditions provide for aggregation by a permissive definition of "One Claim"—it is implicit that a qualifying insurer can chose from the list of acceptable definitions. Thus claims *may*   **8–102**

---

[91] *Axa Reinsurance (UK) Plc v Field* [1996] 1 W.L.R. 1026 at p.1035.

[92] *B F Caudle v Alec Sharp* [1995] L.R.L.R. 433 at p.438 col.2.

[93] *Mann v Lexington Insurance Co* [2001] 1 Lloyd's Rep. 1; in *Scott v Copenhagen Reinsurance* [2002] Lloyd's Rep. I.R. 775 at para.62, Langley J held that the terms "event" and "occurrence" were usually synonymous.

[94] *Kuwait Airways Corp v Kuwait Insurance Co* [1996] 1 Lloyd's Rep. 664.

[95] *Scott v Copenhagen Reinsurance* [2003] Lloyd's Rep. I.R. 696.

[96] *Axa Reinsurance (UK) Plc v Field* [1996] 1 W.L.R. 1026 at p.1035—use of the word "originating" was intended to "open up the widest possible search for a unifying factor"; *Countrywide Assured Group Plc v D J Marshall* [2003] Lloyd's Rep. P.N. 1.

[97] *Haydon v Lo & Lo* [1997] 1 W.L.R. 198.

[98] *Lloyd's TSB General Insurance v Lloyds Bank Group Insurance* [2003] Lloyd's Rep. I.R. 623 at paras 24–5, 52.

[99] *American Centennial Insurance Co v INSCO Ltd* [1996] 1 L.R.L.R. 407; *RE Brown v GIO Insurance* [1998] Lloyd's Rep. I.R. 201.

[1] *Scott v Copenhagen Reinsurance* [2003] Lloyd's Rep. I.R. 696.

(subject to the actual policy wording) be aggregated[2] against any one or more Insured[3] which arise from:

    (i) one act or omission;

    (ii) one series of related acts or omissions[4];

    (iii) the same act or omission in a series of related matters or transactions;

    (iv) similar acts or omissions in a series of related matters or transactions;

    (v) one matter or transaction.

15. Limitation

8–103   As noted above,[5] the Insured's right of action under a liability policy will normally arise only when the Insured's liability to the third party is ascertained by judgment, award or settlement.[6] Since any claim will be contractual in nature, it must be brought within six years from the date of ascertainment.[7] It should be noted that claims under other sections of a professional indemnity policy may arise at different times: for example, depending on the precise wording of the policy in question, a claim under a fidelity extension might arise at the time of loss *or* at the time at which it should with reasonable diligence have been discovered; a claim in respect of defence costs might arise as and when such costs were incurred.

8–104   In *Seechurn v ACE Insurance SA*,[8] the Court of Appeal held that the continuation of negotiations between Insurers and Insured after the expiry of a contractual or statutory limitation period will not give rise to any waiver or estoppel in respect of Insurers' rights to rely upon limitation.[9]

16. Third Party Rights

8–105   Contracts of liability insurance confer a benefit (the right to indemnity) upon the Insured but do not purport to confer any benefit upon the third party who might establish a liability against the Insured. Accordingly, such a third party

---

[2] cl.2.5 of the Law Society's Minimum Terms and Conditions.

[3] It is implicit that "one or more insured" is referring to one or more insured under the same policy.

[4] Similar to the wording considered *Lloyds TSB General Insurance v Lloyds Bank Group Insurance* [2003] Lloyd's Rep. I.R. 623.

[5] See para.8–017, above.

[6] *Post Office v Norwich Union Fire Insurance Society Ltd* [1967] 2 Q.B. 363; *Bradley v Eagle Star* [1989] A.C. 957; *The Mercandian Continent* [2001] Lloyd's Rep. I.R. 802.

[7] s.5 of the Limitation Act 1980; *Lefevre v White* [1990] 1 Lloyd's Rep. 569.

[8] [2002] 2 Lloyd's Rep. 390.

[9] See also *Super Chem Products Ltd v American Life and General Insurance Co Ltd* [2004] Lloyd's Rep. I.R. 446 and *Fortis Bank SA v Trenwick International Insurance* [2005] Lloyd's Rep. I.R. 464.

would not be entitled to bring any action under the Contracts (Rights of Third Parties) Act 1999 to enforce the terms of the policy.

A third party claimant may, however, obtain rights under the Third Parties **8–106** (Rights Against Insurers) Act 1930. Section 1 of the Act prescribes a scheme for the statutory transfer to any third party to whom the Insured has incurred liability of the Insured's right of action in relation to that liability against Insurers. The transfer takes place upon any one of the insolvency events listed in s.1(1) of the Act occurring, even though the liability itself may not have been ascertained.[10] In order to exercise any rights against Insurers it will therefore be necessary for the statutory assignee to establish an ascertained liability against the Insured.[11] The Insurers' liability under the Act to the third party will be materially the same as any liability to the Insured would have been[12]—thus Insurers are entitled to maintain, as against the third party, any defence which could have been maintained as against the Insured.

It has long been recognised that the 1930 Act is an imperfect instrument—not **8–107** least on account of the requirement formally to establish an ascertained liability against the Insured before proceeding against Insurers. There are also uncertainties within the legislation (for example as to whether obligations imposed on the Insured as conditions precedent to liability must be performed (and if so, by whom) if the third party is to be entitled to any indemnity). The Law Commission has made detailed proposals for the replacement of the 1930 Act.[13] Although its recommendations were accepted in principle by the Department of Constitutional Affairs in July 2002, no substantive steps have yet been taken to translate the principal recommendations into legislation.

---

[10] *Post Office v Norwich Union Fire Insurance Society Ltd* [1967] 2 Q.B. 363.
[11] *Post Office v Norwich Union Fire Insurance Society Ltd*, above; *Bradley v Eagle Star* [1989] A.C. 957.
[12] s.1(4) of the Act.
[13] Law Commission Report No.272, July 2001.

CHAPTER 9

CONSTRUCTION PROFESSIONALS

1. INTRODUCTION

(a) *The Construction Professionals*

9–001　The professions which are the subject of this chapter are those concerned with building and engineering works: principally architects, engineers and quantity surveyors. Given the variety of modern contractual arrangements, building methods and titles, it is sometimes difficult both to identify the professional man and to distinguish him from a building contractor. For further discussion and fuller treatment of the required qualifications, professional bodies and terms and conditions of engagement of construction professionals, reference should be made to the relevant sections in the standard textbooks on building law generally.[1] This chapter includes consideration of tasks traditionally undertaken by professional men under an obligation to exercise reasonable skill and care even although such tasks (for example, design) may in fact be undertaken by a building contractor. Moreover, in considering the liability of construction professionals, it will be necessary briefly to consider other types of case and in particular the liability in tort of builders and local authorities.[2]

9–002　**Architects.** An "architect" is: "one who possesses, with due regard to aesthetic as well as practical considerations, adequate skill and knowledge to enable him (i) to originate, (ii) to design and plan, (iii) to arrange for and supervise the erection of such buildings or other works calling for skill in design and planning as he might, in the course of his business, reasonably be asked to carry out or in respect of which he offers his services as a specialist."[3] For convenience, in this chapter, the term "architect" is used to denote the person carrying out the functions referred to above, whatever his particular professional qualifications might be. In practice, however, the use of the description "architect" is controlled by legislation. Subject to certain qualifications, statute restricts practising or carrying on business under any name, style or title containing the word "architect" to persons registered by the Architects' Registration Board.[4] Architects are currently the only construction professionals who are subject to a

---

[1] See Hudson's *Building and Engineering Contracts* (11th edn), Ch.2; *Keating on Construction Contracts* (8th edn), Ch.13; and Emden's *Construction Law* (8th edn, revised 1990 with later updates), Part IV, Ch.6.

[2] See further paras 9–060 to 9–125, below.

[3] This is the definition adopted and acted upon by the Tribunal of Appeal from the Architects' Registration Council and cited by the Divisional Court in *R. v Architects' Registration Tribunal Ex p. Jaggar* [1945] 2 All E.R. 131 at 134. The use of the word "supervise" may now be open to question. In the then current edition of the RIBA Conditions, clause B provided "The Architect shall give such periodical supervision and inspection as may be necessary to ensure that the works are being executed in general accordance with the contract." In all editions of the Conditions from 1971 onwards, the obligation to supervise has been replaced with an obligation to carry out periodic inspections. See further, paras 9–236 and 9–237, below.

[4] See the Architects Act 1997, s.20. The 1997 Act consolidated earlier legislation including orders made under the European Communities Act 1972. In *Munkenbeck and Marshall v Kensington Hotel* (1999) 15 Const. L.J. 231, the defendant argued that he was not obliged to pay fees as he had contracted for the services of registered architects. The court rejected this as, on a true analysis of the contract, the defendant had contracted only for the services of architecturally qualified personnel.

statutory requirement of registration. The Board, through the Registrar of Architects, admits applicants to registration who fulfil the requisite qualifications. The usual qualification is that the applicant has passed an examination in architecture recognised by the Board. Architects also belong to one of the professional bodies, chief among which is the Royal Institute of British Architects (RIBA). Both the Architects' Registration Board and the RIBA prescribe codes of conduct.[5]

Engineers. "Engineer" is a term descriptive of a much wider range of occupations and professions than those the subject of this chapter.[6] No precise definition of the term is available. The term is applied here to a person who in a contract for engineering works performs functions analogous to those of an architect under a "traditional" building contract[7] or a person who is employed in connection with a building or engineering project for more specialist skills than those usually possessed by an architect, for example a civil, structural, mechanical or electrical engineer. There is an increasingly wide range of specialist engineers and consequently a wide range of qualifications and professional bodies. The most important professional body for civil engineers is the Institution of Civil Engineers (ICE).[8] Membership of the Institution entitles a person to describe himself as a Chartered Civil Engineer.[9] Other important professional bodies include the Institution of Structural Engineers (I.Struct.E),[10] the Institution of Mechanical Engineers (I.Mech.E)[11] and the Institution of Engineering and Technology.[12]

9–003

Quantity surveyors. The duties of a quantity surveyor were judicially described in the 19th century as "taking out in detail the measurements and quantities from plans prepared by an architect, for the purpose of enabling builders to calculate the amounts for which they would execute the plans."[13] This description is rather anachronistic, as a quantity surveyor's duties today commonly extend to the preparation of estimates, bills of quantities and schedules for

9–004

---

[5] Copies of the current codes of conduct and further information are available on the website of the Architects' Registration Board at *www.arb.org.uk* and on the RIBA websites at *www.riba.org* and *www.architecture.com*.

[6] In his 1994 Presidential Address to the Institution of Civil Engineers, Dr Edmund Hambly described the range of activities undertaken by civil engineers as follows: "Civil engineers manage the conception, innovation, promotion, design, construction, operation, maintenance and eventual removal of the amenities of modern civilisation. These amenities range from water supply to offshore energy, transport systems to buildings, land reclamation to municipal services and industrial production to environmental improvement."

[7] As provided for in the ICE Conditions of Contract.

[8] Further information is available on the ICE's website at *www.ice.org.uk*.

[9] See Hudson, *op. cit.* pp.248–249.

[10] Further information is available on the Institution of Structural Engineers' website at *www. istructe.org.uk*. Historically, structural engineers had a particular expertise in the use and properties of reinforced concrete.

[11] Further information is available at the Institution of Mechanical Engineers' website at *www. imeche.org.uk*.

[12] A professional association formed in early 2006 by the amalgamation of the Institution of Electrical Engineers (IEE) and the Institute of Incorporated Engineers (IIE). The IET's website is at *www.theiet.org*.

[13] *Taylor v Hall* (1870) 4 I.R.C.L. 467, *per* Morris J. at 476.

pricing by contractors together with negotiation with contractors and the valuation of work done for the purpose of interim and final certificates issued by the architect. Although often perceived as the professional man most closely concerned with controlling cost on the part of the client, it has been pointed out that a quantity surveyor's powers in this regard are strictly limited. As a quantity surveyor neither designs the works, nor issues variation instructions nor assesses extensions of time:

> "all that a quantity surveyor can do is (a) to check that tenders of contractors or subcontractors are reasonably priced before he recommends acceptance; (b) to measure work executed accurately; (c) exercise vigilance in the valuation of variations or the checking of the valuation of variations submitted to him by the contractor; (d) make a fair assessment of any additional sums which may be due to a contractor as a result of extension of time, acceleration instructions and so forth."[14]

In the wider context of the construction industry, however, quantity surveyors are commonly recognised as possessing an expertise in construction economics beyond that of other construction professionals. They are used extensively as claims consultants in connection with contractual disputes between building owners and building contractors. Qualifications or registration are not prescribed by law for practice, but quantity surveyors commonly belong to the Royal Institution of Chartered Surveyors (RICS).[15] Practical training and examination are today the usual prerequisites to admission to membership of the RICS, which prescribes a code of conduct for its members.

9–005 **Building surveyors.** Surveyors who qualify within the building surveying division of the RICS are known as building surveyors. They commonly undertake work traditionally performed by architects, such as the design and inspection of construction works, but have a particular expertise in the interpretation and application of the Building Regulations, which are designed to preserve the safety of people using new or refurbished buildings.

9–006 **Project managers.** When a construction project is particularly large or complex, the owner may appoint a project manager to act as his representative. There is, as yet, no recognised professional body for project managers in the United Kingdom, although the RICS has a Project Management Forum and both the RIBA and the Association of Consulting Engineers (ACE) publish standard forms of contract for the appointment of a project manager.[16] The obligations of

---

[14] *per* Mr Recorder Jackson Q.C. in *Burrell Hayward & Budd v Chris Carnell and David Green*, unreported, February 20, 1992 (dismissal of counterclaim by a firm of architects against a firm of quantity surveyors for alleged negligence in failing to control costs and failing to keep the architects properly informed of the likely costs of the project).

[15] Further information is available on the RICS website at *www.rics.org.uk*, on the RIBA website at *www.riba.org* and on the ACE website at *www.acenet.co.uk*.

[16] The RIBA Form of Appointment as a Project Manager (PM/99); the ACE Conditions of Engagement, 1995—Agreement E for use where a Consulting Engineer is engaged as a Project Manager.

a project manager will commonly include many of the functions traditionally performed by an architect or engineer who is acting for the employer.[17] In *Royal Brompton Hospital NHS Trust v Hammond (No.9)*,[18] Judge Lloyd Q.C. observed that project management is still an emergent professional discipline, in which professional practices as such have not yet developed or become clearly discernible. The standard of care required of a project manager is likely to depend upon his particular terms of engagement and the demands of the particular project. Nevertheless, it was clear that a central part of the role of the project manager was to be "co-ordinator and guardian of the client's interests". Moreover, the terms of engagement of other consultants will be material in defining the scope of the project manager's duties, since duplication of function is not expected. Thus, in that case, although the architect was the contract administrator formally appointed under the building contract, that function had been transferred de facto to the project manager. The judge also considered the effect of the appointment of a project manager on the obligations of other professional consultants appointed by the client. The project manager is the client's primary representative and should be regarded by other consultants as, in effect, a client (albeit a highly informed client) and kept fully advised by them. The expertise and knowledge of the project manager will affect only the extent to which such advice needs to be spelled out; the essential elements of such advice must always be clearly given even although it may be thought to be pointing out the obvious.

(b) *Claims against Construction Professionals*

The Pre-Action Protocol. Anyone who is contemplating making or defending a claim against a construction professional must bear in mind the Pre-Action Protocol for Construction and Engineering Disputes. The protocol was published

9–007

---

[17] It follows that care must be taken to see that an expert witness in a claim against a project manager has the appropriate qualification(s). See *Pride Valley Foods Ltd v Hall & Partners (Contract Management) Ltd* (2001) 76 Con. L.R. 1 at 24, *per* Judge Toulmin C.M.G., Q.C, "There is an initial difficulty in accepting expert opinion evidence in relation to the duties of project managers. There is no chartered or professional institution of project managers nor a recognisable profession of project managers. In so far as it may be appropriate to accept expert evidence, the nature of the evidence that might be acceptable will depend on what the project manager has agreed to do. In some cases the project manager will be the architect who will design the project and then, acting as project manager, supervise the contractor and the sub-contractors in carrying out the work. . . . At the other end of the scale the project manager will supervise the work of the contractor and sub-contractors and ensure that the work is carried out in conformity with the design drawings. In these circumstances the project manager will have no design function even to the extent of providing an outline specification.". The Court of Appeal did not comment on this part of the judgment: [2001] EWCA Civ 1001. For further detailed discussion of project managers' responsibilities, see C. Leong, "The duty of care in project management" (2001) 17 P.N. 250. For a case where project managers were held liable for failing to prevent works which created a risk of fire, see *Six Continents Retail Ltd v Carford Catering Ltd* [2003] EWCA Civ 1790. See also *Great Eastern Hotel Co Ltd v John Laing Construction Ltd* [2005] EWHC 181, TCC, where the duties of a building contractor operating under a construction management contract were regarded as akin to those of a professional project manager.

[18] [2002] EWHC 2037, TCC.

in September 2000 and came into force on October 2, 2000. It was originally drafted for use in cases destined for the Technology and Construction Court, but has been approved for use in all courts.[19] It applies to "all construction and engineering disputes (including professional negligence claims against architects, engineers and quantity surveyors)".[20] It is thought that the reference to architects, engineers and quantity surveyors is not exclusive, so that claims for professional negligence against other construction professionals, such as building surveyors or project managers, should be treated as subject to the protocol. If proceedings are then commenced, the court will be able to treat the standards set in the protocol as the normal reasonable approach to pre-action conduct.[21] This is significant, because the court will take into account compliance or non-compliance with the protocol when giving directions for the management of subsequent proceedings and when making costs orders.[22] In particular, a party which fails to comply may be ordered to pay all or part of the other party's costs of later proceedings, which may be on the indemnity basis.[23] A successful claimant who has failed to comply with the protocol may recover interest for a shorter period or at a lower rate than he otherwise would; conversely, an unsuccessful defendant who did not comply may be ordered to pay interest at a higher rate.[24] The pre-action protocol applies equally to claims made under Pt 20 of the Civil Procedure Rules.[25]

9–008   **The Technology and Construction Court.** Many cases which include claims of professional negligence against construction professionals are brought in the Technology and Construction Court (TCC),[26] which is a division of the High Court of Justice. Proceedings in the TCC are specialist proceedings governed by Pt 49 of the Civil Procedure Rules. Accordingly, the Civil Procedure Rules apply to proceedings in the TCC only subject to the provisions of Practice Direction— Technology and Construction Court. The Practice Direction also includes Forms to be used in drafting orders made at case management conferences and pre-trial reviews in the TCC and are designed to take into account the special nature of the

---

[19] Pursuant to para.1.1 of the Civil Procedure Rules Practice Direction—Protocols.
[20] Protocol, para.1.1.The protocol does not apply to certain types of claim, which are described in para.1.2. Those exceptions include a claim in which an application for summary judgment under Pt 24 of the Civil Procedure Rules will be made and a claim to enforce the decision of an adjudicator to whom a dispute has been referred under s.108 of the Housing Grants, Construction and Regeneration Act 1996.
[21] Protocol, para.1.4.
[22] CPR Practice Direction—Protocols, para.2.1.
[23] CPR Practice Direction—Protocols, para.2.3(1) and (2).
[24] CPR Practice Direction—Protocols, para.2.3(3) and (4).
[25] In *Daejan Investments Ltd v The Park West Club Ltd* [2003] EWHC 2872, TCC, the claimant on a claim made under CPR Pt 20 was penalised by an adverse costs order for its failure to follow the protocol before issuing the claim. See also *Alfred McAlpine Ltd v SIAC Construction Ltd* [2005] EWHC 3139, TCC, where the Court refused to grant a stay of existing proceedings to allow the protocol procedure to be followed in relation to a new Pt 20 defendant but made clear that any consequent financial loss suffered by the new party would be compensated by an adverse costs order against the Pt 20 claimant at the end of the case.
[26] Formerly known as the Official Referees' Court.

issues in TCC cases, which are typically both complex and technical.[27] Users of the TCC should also consult *The Technology and Construction Court Guide*.[28]

Adjudication. Part II of the Housing Grants, Construction and Regeneration Act 1996 introduced a form of mandatory dispute resolution known as "adjudication". A claim for damages for professional negligence against a construction professional may be referred to adjudication in certain circumstances. The decision of an adjudicator is binding upon the parties, and will be enforced by the court, pending any formal legal or arbitral proceedings which may be taken in order to obtain a final decision on the same dispute. The important subject of adjudication is considered more fully in a later section of this chapter.[29] **9–009**

(c) *Forms of Building Contract*

Before embarking on a discussion of professional liability in the context of the construction professions, it is important to outline the usual position of each in relation to other persons involved in a construction project. This position will depend upon the type of contractual arrangement used. Most building projects will use one of three types of contractual arrangement: (a) a "traditional" building contract; (b) a "design and build" or "turnkey" contract; or (c) a "management" contract. **9–010**

(i) *The "Traditional" Building Contract*

In the traditional form of building contract,[30] there will be a contract between the employer and the building contractor and a separate contract between the employer and the architect (and/or other professional consultant). The price payable for the building works may be fixed either by reference to works identified on drawings or specifications (in which event the contractor will generally be obliged to carry out all such works for a fixed sum) or for works quantified in a bill of quantities (in which event the contractor will generally be entitled to be paid additional moneys in the event that the actual quantities exceed those identified in the contractual documents).[31] The basic principle is that the **9–011**

---

[27] And as such, may give rise to special problems on appeal on questions of fact: see *Yorkshire Water Services Ltd v Taylor Woodrow Construction Northern Ltd* [2005] EWCA Civ 894, and *Ove Arup & Partners International Ltd v Mirant Asia-Pacific Construction (Hong Kong) Ltd (No.2)* [2005] EWCA Civ 1585.

[28] The 2nd edition of the TCC Guide was published on October 3, 2005. The organisation of the TCC is currently under review; a Practice Direction setting out interim arrangements for the allocation of cases to the judges of the TCC was published on June 7, 2005: [2005] 3 All E.R. 289. See also the Annual Report for the Technology and Construction Court 2004/5 at (2006) 22(3) Const.L.J. 149–159. For comment on the effects of implementation of the Civil Procedure Rules upon procedure in the Technology and Construction Court, see A. Burr and R. Honey, "The Post-Woolf TCC: Any Changes?" (2001) 17 Const.L.J. 378.

[29] See paras 9–351 to 9–359, below.

[30] For a good example, see the JCT Standard Building Contract 2005 edition (known as SBC 2005) (which is published in With Quantities and Without Quantities versions). Further information about the various standard form building contracts published by the Joint Contracts Tribunal Limited is available on its website at *www.jctltd.co.uk* and the principal JCT contracts are conveniently reprinted in Emden, *op. cit.*.

[31] Hudson, *op. cit.*, pp.415–416.

employer, through his professional consultants, provides the design and the contractor builds to that design. Thus, subject to variations or other events leading to a change in the contract price, the employer under a traditional building contract should know at the outset of a project both its likely final costs and the precise nature and scope of the building project.

9–012 At the initial stages, where the architect's services will mainly be of an advisory nature, he is unlikely to be the employer's agent.[32] But on being instructed to act as architect in relation to a building project and to proceed with the works, for many purposes he becomes the employer's agent.[33] His general function will be to act on behalf of the employer and to protect his interests.[34] It was formerly held that in relation to the issue of certificates, or at least the final certificate, the architect ceased to be the employer's agent and became an arbitrator or quasi-arbitrator,[35] but this is no longer the law.[36] A specialist engineer or quantity surveyor may be employed pursuant to a contract with the employer only, with the main contractor or sub-contractor only, or with the architect only. As a result of the growth in multi-disciplinary practices, a single firm may be able to provide to an employer the skills of architects, specialist engineers and quantity surveyors. Except in quite unusual circumstances, however, an architect in private practice remains an independent contractor.[37] He is not generally the agent of the contractor.[38] In general, a contractor will be responsible both for his own method of working and for the design of necessary temporary works.[39]

---

[32] Hudson, *op. cit.*, p.269.

[33] See, e.g. *Chambers v Goldthorpe* [1901] 1 K.B. 624, CA at 634; *R B Burden Ltd v Swansea Corp* [1957] 1 W.L.R. 1167, CA at 1172; *Clayton v Woodman & Son (Builders) Ltd* [1962] 2 Q.B. 533 at 539; *AMF International Ltd v Magnet Bowling Ltd* [1968] 1 W.L.R. 1028 at 1046; *Hosier & Dickinson Ltd v P & M Kaye Ltd* [1970] 1 W.L.R. 1611, CA at 1615. For an example of a case where an architect was held not to be the employer's agent see *District of Surrey v Carroll-Hatch and Associates Ltd* (1979) 101 D.L.R. (3d) 218 at 222.

[34] See, e.g. *R B Burden Ltd v Swansea Corp* [1957] 1 W.L.R. 1167, CA at 1172. When he issues certificates for payment, however, "he stands apart from the owner (i.e. employer) and enjoys to some extent an independent authority of his own", *per* Lord Radcliffe, *ibid.* at 1172. See para.9–255, below for the status of architect when issuing certificates.

[35] e.g. *Chambers v Goldthorpe* [1901] 1 Q.B. 624.

[36] See *Sutcliffe v Thackrah* [1974] A.C. 727 and generally on this issue para.9–255, below.

[37] *AMF International Ltd v Magnet Bowling Ltd* [1968] 1 W.L.R. 1028 at 1045; also *Clayton v Woodman & Son (Builders) Ltd* [1962] 2 Q.B. 533 at 539. In the latter case (reversed, although not on the instant point, on appeal) Salmon J. stated unequivocally: " . . . an architect is clearly an independent contractor. The building owner has no control over the manner in which the architect does his work." This statement requires qualification. As observed by Lord Reid in *Sutcliffe v Thackrah* [1974] A.C. 727 at 737 the architect in many matters is bound to act on the employer's instructions, whether he agrees with them or not. In this regard see the Australian case of *Perini Corp v Commonwealth of Australia* (1969) 12 B.L.R. 82: held that there was an implied term in the contract between the claimant contractor and defendant employer that the latter would ensure that the Director of Works (an employee of the defendants but discharging the functions of an architect) did his duty as certifier; *cf.* the South African case of *Alfred McAlpine & Son (Pty) Ltd v Transvaal Provincial Administration* [1974] (3) S.A.L.R. 506 (no implied term in contract between contractor and employer that engineer would introduce variations "at reasonable times").

[38] *Hosier & Dickinson Ltd v P & M Kaye Ltd* [1970] 1 W.L.R. 1611, CA at 1615.

[39] See *Plant Construction Ltd v Clive Adams Associates and JMH Construction Services Ltd* [2000] B.L.R. 137, CA; *Aurum Investments Ltd v Avonforce Ltd* [2001] Lloyd's Rep. P.N. 285.

In larger traditional building projects the employer may appoint a clerk of **9–013** works. Although employed pursuant to a contract with the employer his status and function in relation to other parties in a building project may be difficult to analyse legally. His powers and duties are frequently set out in the contract between the employer and the contractor,[40] but only to a limited extent is he likely to be the employer's agent. As between the architect and the clerk of works the general division of function is that the latter is to attend to matters of detail.[41] The clerk of works is not the representative of the architect unless he is the architect's employee.[42]

(ii) The "Design and Build" or "Turnkey" Contract

In the "traditional" form of building contract, the architect plays a central role **9–014** not just in design but also in contract administration as the leader of the professional team.[43] In large modern building projects this role can be criticised as outdated.[44] The increasingly specialised nature of such matters as structural and services design means that the architect may have little to contribute to the most important aspects of buildings. Moreover it is likely to be the contractor rather than the architect to whom the employer will have to look to ensure that the project is effectively co-ordinated and controlled so as to be produced on time and at the right price.

---

[40] See the various forms of the JCT Standard Building Contract 2005, cl.3.4. The RIBA and the Institute of Clerks of Works have co-operated to produce the *Clerk of Works Manual* (1994, 3rd edn) and the *Clerk of Works and Site Inspector Handbook* (2006), which describe the position and duties of the clerk of works when the JCT Standard Form is used. The Manual and Handbook are obtainable from RIBA Publications Ltd, 56–64 Leonard St., London EC2A 4LT and at *www.ribabookshops.com*.

[41] See *Leicester Guardians v Trollope* (1911) 75 J.P. 197; and *Gray v T P Bennett & Son* (1987) 43 B.L.R. 63 where, at 78, the clerk of works was described as "the eyes and ears of the architect" (architects and engineers not liable for defective construction of brickwork to nurses' home which the contractor had deliberately concealed—see further para.9–246, below).

[42] *East Ham Corp v Bernard Sunley & Sons Ltd* [1966] A.C. 406 at 443. Note *Kensington and Chelsea and Westminster AHA v Wettern Composites Ltd* (1984) 1 Con. L.R. 114 at 139: employer held vicariously liable for the negligence of the clerk of works. In *Gray v T P Bennett & Son* (1987) 43 B.L.R. 63 the architects refused to employ the clerk of works unless given an indemnity by the claimant, which the claimant was not prepared to provide. The clerk of works thus remained the employee of the claimant but was held not negligent on the facts in failing to spot deliberatively destructive workmanship by the contractor. See further paras 9–246 and 9–247, below. Note that the "engineer's representative" under the ICE Conditions of Contract 1999 (7th edn), cl.2(3), although performing similar tasks to a clerk of works, is in a different contractual position and is responsible to the engineer.

[43] In an article "*Anns* beyond repair" (1991) 107 L.Q.R. 228, I. N. Duncan Wallace Q.C. criticises some professional institutions for asserting a "captain of the ship status" and failing to correct "the serious judicial and public misunderstanding and exaggeration of the effectiveness and degree of supervision, or of day-to-day control over methods of working, which can be afforded either in practice or contractually by a supervising architect or engineer."

[44] In a paper "Supervision: an architect's view" for the Society of Construction Law on April 5, 1988 (see the Society's website at *www.scl.org.uk*), Francis Goodall suggests that an architect is a designer, who may have little skill or talent for the supervision and inspection role assigned to him: "Supervision, inspection, are things for a manager, the man who can sieve sand and organize the wrought iron gate or the fountain, once someone with other, dare I say more creative, talents than his has designed it in the first place."

9–015   There are many forms of contract[45] in which the employer employs a contractor both to design and construct a building. Such contracts may have both advantages and disadvantages for the employer. In the absence of express provision, the contractor will be required to produce works fit for their intended purpose.[46] It will generally not be possible, as often occurs in a traditional contract, for a designer to blame the contractor for defective workmanship and for the contractor to respond with allegations of defective design. However, in providing the design, a contractor is likely to seek to minimise the cost of a design in a way which may be unnecessary for an independent professional man. If the employer's right to a building which is reasonably fit for its purpose is replaced by an obligation merely to exercise reasonable care and skill in design,[47] an employer is likely to have substantially less protection in respect of the quality of the design than he would have under a traditional contract. Although consultants may be retained by the employer directly (particularly to provide a check on the design carried out by the contractor), the main designers are likely to be retained by the contractor with the result that disputes concerning alleged professional negligence are likely to be between the contractor and one or more professional men.[48]

(iii) *Management Contracts*

9–016   Many large building projects now involve a "management" contractor. Although The Joint Contracts Tribunal Limited in the United Kingdom has, since 1987, published a standard form of management contract together with associated works contracts,[49] many different forms of management contract are found. Typically, the management contractor is paid the actual cost of the works, plus a fee. The construction works are carried out by separate "works" or "trade"

---

[45] Such contracts are given a variety of different names such as "turnkey", "design and build" or "package deal". Many are major contractors' own standard forms but others, such as JCT Standard Form of Contract With Contractor's Design (1998), the JCT Design and Build Contract (2005) and the ICE Design and Construct Conditions of Contract (1992, revised 1998), are provided by industry bodies. The names are not always helpful in ascertaining the precise obligations undertaken: see the article by I. N. Duncan Wallace Q.C., "Contracts for industrial plant projects" (1984) 1 I.C.L.R. 322; and Hudson, *op. cit.*, at pp.426 to 431.

[46] See e.g. *Viking Grain Storage Ltd v T H White Installations Ltd* (1986) 33 B.L.R. 103 (held to be an implied term that completed works would be reasonably fit for their purpose as a grain drying and storage installation where the defendant contractor had offered to carry out a package deal of design, execution and management). See further the cases of *Greaves & Co (Contractors) Ltd v Baynham Meikle & Partners* [1974] 1 W.L.R. 1261; and *Consultants Group International v John Worman Ltd* (1985) 9 Con. L.R. 46, discussed further at paras 9–165 to 9–171, below, which both concerned the extent of liability of design sub-contractors in situations where their immediate employers had undertaken an obligation to provide works reasonably fit for their purpose to the ultimate employer.

[47] As, for example, in the JCT Standard Form With Contractor's Design (1998) which, by cl.2.5, restricts the contractor's liability in respect of design to that of an independent designer under a separate contract with the employer. The JCT Design and Build Contract (2005), cl.2.17.1, is in similar terms.

[48] For an example see *Consultants Group International v John Worman Ltd* (1987) 9 Con. L.R. 46 (specialist architects found to owe design obligations to contractor which were co-extensive with those owed by contractor to client with the result that architects owed an obligation to design building so that it was fit for its purpose) discussed at para.9–169, below.

[49] Now the JCT Management Building Contract 2005, with standard Management Works Contract Conditions.

contractors. Typically, the management contractor enters into the works or trade contracts with the works or trade contractors. Sometimes, the works contracts are made directly with the employer (in which case, the management contractor is often known as the "construction manager"[50]). Although each works contract may be for a fixed price, it is very unlikely that there will be an overall fixed price at the commencement of the works as all of the packages will not then have been let. In the absence of some form of bonus agreement whereby the management contractor is rewarded for achieving reductions in price, there is no direct financial incentive for the management contractor to achieve economies. Further there may be considerable scope for claims by one works contractor that he has been disrupted by the activities of another. Whereas in a traditional contract it is the main contractor who has the financial incentive to sort such disputes out, in a management contract, such disputes may well fall for the account of the employer.[51] In most management contracts, professional consultants will still be employed by the employer but their precise role, particularly in the supervision of works, is likely to be substantially affected by the presence and powers of the management contractor. Conversely, depending upon the particular terms of its contract, a construction manager may be regarded as owing obligations more akin to those traditionally owed by a construction professional than to those traditionally owed by a building contractor.[52]

2. DUTIES

(a) *Duties to Client*

(i) *Contractual Duties*

Express terms. As in the case of other professions the primary basis for the   **9–017** duties of a construction professional in a particular case is the contract pursuant to which he is engaged. More commonly than with other professions, construction professionals are engaged pursuant to written contracts in standard form.[53]

---

[50] See, for example, the JCT Construction Management Appointment and Construction Management Trade Contract.

[51] For powerful criticism of most management contracts see Hudson, *op. cit.* pp.431–435.

[52] See, for example, *Great Eastern Hotel Co Ltd v John Laing Construction Ltd* [2005] EWHC 181, TCC (construction management contract imposed upon the construction manager duties to exercise reasonable professional skill and care in the performance of its services, rather than the absolute obligations normally undertaken by a contractor under a building contract).

[53] By para.2.1 of its Code of Professional Conduct (1997) the RIBA requires that a member undertake "when making an engagement, whether by an agreement for professional services, by a contract of employment or by a contract for the supply of services and goods, to state whether or not professional indemnity insurance is held and to have defined beyond reasonable doubt and recorded the terms of the engagement including the scope of the service, the allocation of responsibilities and any limitation of liability, the method of calculation or [*sic*] remuneration and the provision for termination and adjudication." Para.2.3 of the RIBA Code of Conduct (2005) states, "Members should ensure that their terms of appointment, the scope of their work and the essential project requirements are clear and recorded in writing . . . ." The failure of construction professionals to comply with good practice in this respect contributed to their later breaches of duty in regard to procurement advice, project planning and the production of timely design information in *Plymouth & South West Co-operative Society v Architecture, Structure & Management Ltd* [2006] EWHC 5, TCC.

In the case of architects, those most frequently used are published in standard form by the RIBA[54] whilst the most common forms for engineers are the ACE Conditions of Engagement Agreements.[55] Standard forms are also produced by the RICS for building surveying services and for quantity surveying services.[56] Whether oral or written the contract will need to be carefully scrutinised in a professional negligence claim in order to determine the nature and extent of the engagement undertaken. For example, an architect engaged by an employer may have been engaged for only some or all of the following duties: advising, examining the site, preparing designs, drawings and plans, supervising the works and certifying their value for the purpose of the payment provisions of the building contract.[57]

9–018   Although a construction professional's duties are defined by the terms of his contract (and any concurrent duty of care or fiduciary duty), it will often be necessary to look beyond the terms of that contract in order to ascertain what precisely is required by way of discharge of those duties. This necessity arises from the fact that a building project involves a whole matrix of relationships where each party's individual responsibilities can only be evaluated in the light of the responsibilities assumed by others. Thus in ascertaining the scope of an architect's express contractual duties under a retainer made in connection with a "traditional" building contract it may be necessary to examine closely the terms of the contract between the employer and the main contractor[58] or whether

---

[54] Until 1982, the RIBA issued various editions of their Conditions of Engagement. In 1982, the Conditions were superseded by a document entitled "Architect's Appointment" (and known as the "Blue Book") which was intended to be used for ordinary building works and another entitled "Architect's Appointment Small Works" for use with smaller works. In 1990 the RIBA issued the RIBA Architect's Appointment Historic Buildings: Repairs and Conservation Works for use with such works. In 1992, the "Architects Appointment" document was superseded by the RIBA Standard Form of Agreement for the Appointment of an Architect, which is now in its 1999 edition and is known as SFA/99. In 1992 the RIBA also issued the Standard Form of Agreement for the Appointment of an Architect for Design and Build in two different forms according to whether the Architect was to work for the employer or the contractor. The current editions are obtainable from RIBA Publications Ltd.

[55] A total of nine agreements are published by the ACE according to the role being undertaken by the Engineer. All were originally published in 1995, superseding eight forms which had been published in 1981, and were most recently revised in 2002. The current editions with amendments are obtainable from the ACE at 12 Caxton St, London SW1H 0QL or at *www.acenet.co.uk*.

[56] The RICS standard forms of engagements are obtainable from RICS Bookshop, 12 Great George St, London SW1P 3AD.

[57] For example, see *Tesco v Norman Hitchcox Partnership* (1997) 56 Con. L.R 42 (upon the terms of the defendant architects' engagement, they had undertaken an obligation to design the works, but no obligation to supervise their construction). For the list of architect's duties drawn up by Hudson (an architect as well as a lawyer) for architects in the United Kingdom when retained by the employer, see Hudson, *op.cit.* pp.266–267.

[58] For examples, see : *T A Bickerton & Son Ltd v NW Metropolitan Hospital Board* [1969] 1 All E.R. 977, CA (having regard to the terms of the main building contract which required the architect to issue instructions in regard to the expenditure of prime cost, it was the duty of the architects to issue such instructions whenever necessary); *West Faulkner Associates v London Borough of Newham* (1994) 71 B.L.R. 1, CA (architects in breach of duty to clients in failing to issue notice under the main building contract to contractor as a prelude to determination); *Royal Brompton Hospital NHS Trust v Hammond (No.4)* [2000] B.L.R. 75 (mechanical and electrical engineers' obligation to use reasonable skill and care to see that co-ordination drawings were provided in time to allow the building contractor to meet the contract programme was not diluted or altered by provisions in the building contract which required the contractor to co-ordinate drawings); *South Lakeland DC v Curtins Consulting Engineers Plc*, unreported, May 23, 2000 (argument by engineers who designed

special responsibility for design or materials has been undertaken direct to the employer by specialist engineers or sub-contractors.[59]

It is common for design and build contractors to take over the appointment of design and other consultants originally engaged by the employer by novation of the consultants' contracts with the employer. In this way, the contractor typically hopes to secure both continuity in the design and other professional services required to complete the project and redress against the relevant consultant if defective services provided to the employer before the novation result in the contractor suffering loss under the building contract. Careful examination of the terms of any novation agreement will be required to determine whether the latter objective is actually achieved. It was not achieved in *Blyth & Blyth Ltd v Carillion Construction Ltd*.[60] In that case, the Scottish Court of Session held that a novation agreement made between the employer, the design and build contractor and the consulting engineers originally engaged by the employer required the engineers to regard the contractor as their client only in respect of services provided *after* the date of the novation. Accordingly, the contractor was not entitled to recover damages for loss which it suffered as a result of defective services provided by the engineers to the employer *before* the novation. **9–019**

Limitation of liability. The standard conditions of engagement published by the professional bodies for use in retaining construction professionals include terms which are designed to allow the professional to limit his liability for breach of those conditions in various ways. For example, the RIBA Standard Form of Agreement for the Appointment of an Architect (SFA/99) includes: **9–020**

(a) a clause which imposes a contractual limitation period for the bringing of a claim against the architect (by action or arbitration) which may be shorter than the statutory limitation period[61];

(b) a clause which limits the architect's liability for loss and damage to a specified sum[62]; and

(c) a clause which limits the architect's liability to that sum which he would be liable to pay assuming that there had been an apportionment of liability similar to that permitted by the Civil Liability (Contribution) Act 1978 between the architect and other parties liable in respect of the same

---

multi-storey car park that they owed no duty in respect of structural elements supplied by a specialist supplier was rejected; the engineers owed a duty to specify performance standards for those elements and to check the specialist supplier's design calculations; *Try Build Ltd v Invicta Leisure Tennis Ltd* (2000) 71 Con. L.R. 141 (argument by engineers that they were entitled to leave elements of the design to the specialist supplier was rejected; the engineers ought to have specified those elements or at least made clear in their specification that design of those elements was left to the specialist supplier).

[59] See *IBA v EMI and BICC* (1980) 14 B.L.R. 1 (for the facts, see para.9–095, below).

[60] (2001) 79 Con. L.R. 142. The effects of novation of an architect's appointment from employer to design and build contractor were also explored in *J Jarvis & Sons Ltd v Castle Wharf Developments Ltd* [2001] EWCA Civ 19; discussed at para.9–110, below.

[61] Condition 7.2.

[62] Condition 7.3.1.

damage (such as contractors and other consultants) and that such other parties had already satisfied their liability to the claimant.[63]

It can readily be seen that such provisions claim significant benefits for the architect if sued by his employer; the latter clause, in particular, places upon the employer the risk that other parties who might be liable to the employer will become insolvent and so unable to contribute to the employer's loss. Such terms may be open to challenge under the Unfair Contract Terms Act 1977 and/or the Unfair Terms in Consumer Contracts Regulations 1999.

9–021   In broad terms, s.3 of the Unfair Contract Terms Act 1977 provides that a contract term which seeks to exclude or restrict liability for negligence is unenforceable unless the term satisfies the statutory test of reasonableness.[64] The prohibition applies only where one party deals as a consumer or on the other's written standard terms of business. Unless the client is a home-owner or otherwise retains the construction professional outside the course of any business, so that he is a consumer, the question will become whether the incorporation of standard conditions of engagement into the construction professional's retainer means that the contract is made on the professional's written standard terms of business. For the Act to apply to standard forms drafted by a professional body, there must be proof that either by practice or by express statement a party has adopted a standard form as his standard terms of business.[65]

9–022   Assuming that the Act can be shown to apply, the question whether the term challenged will survive the statutory test of reasonableness will depend upon the facts in each case. In *Moores v Yakeley*,[66] the defendant architect contracted to provide his services in connection with the construction of a new bungalow for the claimant. The contract was made on the 1992 edition of the RIBA Standard Form of Agreement for the Appointment of an Architect (SFA/92), which provided that the defendant's liability for loss and damage caused by breach of the Agreement would be limited to £250,000. Since the claimant was a consumer, it was common ground that the statutory test of reasonableness under the Unfair Contract Terms Act 1977 applied. Dyson J. held that the term satisfied that test. Relevant factors were that the sum referred to was based on the defendant's reasonable assessment of the likely total construction cost of the bungalow, that the sum was over ten times the defendant's anticipated fee for the project and that the claimant was in a stronger bargaining position than the defendant (there was a severe recession in the building industry at the time, the claimant's financial resources were far in excess of the defendant's and the claimant had solicitors to protect his interest in negotiations with the defendant). The Court of Appeal upheld the judge's decision[67] for the reasons which he gave.

[63] Condition 7.3.2.
[64] See generally Ch.5, paras 5–012 to 5–017. By s.2(1), any term or non-contractual notice which seeks to exclude or restrict liability for death or personal injury is void, but the standard forms under discussion contain no such terms.
[65] *British Fermentation Products Ltd v Compair Reavell Ltd* [1999] B.L.R. 352.
[66] (1998) 62 Con. L.R. 76.
[67] Unreported, March 23, 2000.

The protection afforded to consumers by the Unfair Contract Terms Act 1977 **9-023**
is supplemented by the Unfair Terms in Consumer Contracts Regulations 1999,[68]
which implement in English law the E.C. Council's Directive on Unfair Terms in
Consumer Contracts.[69] The Regulations apply only to terms in contracts made by
consumers who are natural persons: a company cannot rely upon them. For the
purposes of a challenge to the standard terms of engagement published by the
construction-related professional bodies, two potential areas of dispute are clear.
First, the Regulations apply only where a term has not been "individually
negotiated".[70] Terms in standard form conditions of engagement, such as the
financial limitation clause which was considered in *Moores v Yakeley*,[71] are
typically published in a form which allows the parties to choose and insert the
figure or period of time which is to form the limitation in question. It will be a
question of fact in each case whether such a term was individually negotiated, but
the extent to which the consumer has been able to influence the figure or period
of time inserted, and thereby, the substance of the term, will always be a relevant
consideration.[72]

The second likely area of challenge arises because the standard conditions **9-024**
used for the engagement of construction professionals commonly include a
clause requiring that disputes arising under the engagement be referred to
arbitration. This may be to the detriment of the consumer, particularly where he
has claims against both professional and contractor in respect of the same loss.
Unless all parties consent, he would be required to bring separate proceedings
against each defendant (i.e. by separate arbitrations with the professional and the
contractor or by arbitration with the professional and legal proceedings against
the contractor) which will inevitably increase his costs of securing compensation.
The Arbitration Act 1996 provides, by ss.89–91, that a term which constitutes an
arbitration agreement with a consumer[73] is unfair for the purposes of the Unfair
Terms in Consumer Contracts Regulations so far as it relates to a claim for a
pecuniary remedy which does not exceed £5,000.[74] A clause requiring a claim in
excess of that sum to be referred to arbitration, unless individually negotiated,
will be open to challenge under the Regulations in the normal way. The Regulations contain a "grey list" of terms which, subject to the facts of any particular

---

[68] Revoking and replacing the Unfair Terms in Consumer Contracts Regulations 1994, which came
into force on July 1, 1995. Detailed consideration of the Regulations is outside the scope of this work
and the reader is referred to *Chitty on Contracts* (29th edn), paras 15–004 to 15–099.
[69] Directive 93/13. For consideration of the test of unfairness under the 1994 Regulations, which is
substantially the same under the 1999 Regulations, see *Director General of Fair Trading v First
National Bank Plc* [2000] 2 W.L.R. 1353, CA; and commentaries at (2000) 116 L.Q.R. 557 and
[2000] C.L.J. 242. For general discussion of the Regulations, see E. Macdonald, "The Emperor's old
clauses: misleading terms and the unfair terms in consumer contracts regulations" [1999] C.L.J.
413.
[70] Reg.5(1).
[71] (1998) 62 Con. L.R (Dyson J.); unreported, March 23, 2000, CA.
[72] Reg.5(2) provides that "a term shall always be regarded as not having been individually negotiated
where it has been drafted in advance and the consumer has therefore not been able to influence the
substance of the term."
[73] Which, for these purposes, includes a legal person such as a company as well as a natural person:
Arbitration Act 1996, s.90.
[74] The sum in question is prescribed by order, currently the Unfair Arbitration Agreements (Specified
Amount) Order 1999 (SI 1999/2167) (effective January 1, 2000).

case, may be regarded as unfair.[75] A challenge to an arbitration agreement in standard conditions of engagement is likely to be assisted by the fact that the "grey list" includes any term which has the object or effect of "excluding or hindering the consumer's right to take legal action or exercise any other legal remedy, particularly by requiring the consumer to take disputes exclusively to arbitration not covered by legal provisions".[76]

9–025   The authorities demonstrate the operation of both kinds of challenge. In *Zealander & Zealander v Laing Homes Ltd*,[77] a case decided under the 1994 Regulations, it was held that an arbitration agreement contained in the National House Builders Council's (NHBC) "Buildmark" guarantee was unfair and unenforceable. Similarly, in *Picardi v Cuniberti*,[78] Judge Toulmin C.M.G., Q.C, obiter, considered that the adjudication clause in the RIBA Standard Form of Agreement for the Appointment of an Architect (SFA/99) was deprived of effect by the operation of the 1999 Regulations in a case where it had not been individually negotiated. The decision in *Picardi* was distinguished on its facts in *Lovell Projects Ltd v Legg and Carver*[79] and in *Westminster Building Company Ltd v Beckingham*.[80] In each of those cases, it was the party which sought to invoke the Regulations which had insisted upon the particular standard form contracts used and had done so in circumstances where it had taken (or had had the opportunity to take) appropriate professional advice. In *Bryen & Langley Ltd v Boston*,[81] the Court of Appeal explained that, in those circumstances, the other party could not be said to have fallen short of the requirements of fair dealing stipulated by the Regulations. The *Lovell*, *Westminster* and *Bryen* cases involved standard forms of building contract rather than standard forms of professional appointment. The application of the Regulations to SFA/99 was considered further in *Munkenbeck & Marshall v Michael Harold*.[82] It was held that, on the facts of that case, cl.9.6 (requiring the client to pay the architect's legal and other costs of a claim on which the architect succeeded) and 5.13 (requiring the client to pay interest at a high rate on sums due to the architect) were unfair and unenforceable.

9–026   **Implied terms.** As the employer's agent the construction professional will owe to his principal all the usual duties of an agent. In particular he will owe his principal contractual duties to serve him with reasonable care, skill and diligence and also to serve him faithfully. He will also as agent have authority to bind his principal. As a corollary of that authority, he must not exceed it and if he does he may incur personal liability to third parties for breach of warranty of authority. Treatment of a construction professional's authority as agent is, however, outside

---

[75] reg.5(5), Sch.2, para.1.
[76] *ibid.*, para.1(q).
[77] [2000] T.C.L.R. 724.
[78] [2002] EWHC 2923, QB.
[79] [2003] B.L.R. 452.
[80] [2004] EWHC 138, TCC. For discussion of these cases, see P. Britton, "The architect, the banker, his wife and the adjudicator: construction and the changing law of unfair contract terms" (2006) 22(1) Const. L.J. 23–51.
[81] [2005] EWCA Civ 973; the decision at first instance is at [2004] EWHC 2450, TCC and was followed in *Allen Wilson Shopfitters and Builders Ltd v Buckingham* [2005] EWHC 1165, TCC.
[82] [2005] EWHC 356, TCC.

the scope of this book and reference should be made to the standard building law textbooks.[83]

The contractual duty to serve his client with reasonable care and skill will, however, arise irrespective of whether the nature of the engagement is such as to make the construction professional the client's agent and irrespective of whether standard form conditions of engagement are used. The Supply of Goods and Services Act 1982 provides that such a duty is implied in a contract for the supply of a service where the supplier is acting in the course of a business.[84] This duty is further discussed below, together with the circumstances in which a construction professional may be under the more onerous contractual duty to ensure that his design is reasonably fit for its required purpose.[85] **9–027**

The duty to exercise reasonable care and skill is frequently pleaded as if it were a comprehensive or exhaustive definition of all the duties of a construction professional to his client. It is not.[86] Other duties may properly be implied as terms of the relevant contract. In the circumstances stated in s.14(1) of the Supply of Goods and Services Act 1982[87] there will be an implied term that the supplier will carry out the required service within a reasonable time. What is a reasonable time is a question of fact.[88] Whether other terms should be implied will be decided through application of the usual common law rules for implication of terms.[89] The following paragraphs consider two examples of implied terms which are of particular importance in the construction context: a term giving a **9–028**

---

[83] See Hudson, *op. cit.*, pp.269–281; Keating, *op. cit.*, pp.415–424.

[84] Supply of Goods and Services Act 1982, s.13.

[85] See paras 9–165 to 9–171.

[86] Note the passage quoted in Ch.11, para.11–007 from Oliver J.'s judgment in the solicitor's negligence case, *Midland Bank & Trust Co Ltd v Hett, Stubbs & Kemp* [1979] Ch. 384 at 435.

[87] The circumstances are where "the time for the service to be carried out is not fixed by the contract, left to be fixed in a manner agreed by the contract or determined by the course of dealing between the parties". Even where the circumstances referred to in s.14(1) of the Supply of Goods and Services Act 1982 exist, the facts may render impossible the implication of any meaningful term requiring the performance of services within a reasonable time. For example, in *Munckenbeck & Marshall v The Kensington Hotel Ltd* (2001) 78 Con. L.R. 171, it was held that a firm of architects' contract of engagement contained no implied term that they would provide tender drawings within a reasonable time. Since it was not possible to identify the date upon which the architects first came under an obligation to produce such drawings, an implied term that they were to produce them within a reasonable time could not arise.

[88] Supply of Goods and Services Act 1982, s.14(2).

[89] e.g. in *Adams Holden & Pearson v Trent R.H.A.* (1989) 47 B.L.R. 34, the Court of Appeal rejected an attempt by architects to imply a term as to extra payment for extra services into a contract under seal so as to take advantage of the resulting 12-year limitation period on the grounds that the term sought to be implied was not necessary to fill an obvious omission in the express terms of the contract. In *Chesham Properties Ltd v Bucknall Austin Project Management Services* (1996) 82 B.L.R. 92, Judge Hicks Q.C. gave detailed consideration to the question whether there were to be implied into the contracts of engagements of architects, engineers, quantity surveyors and project managers terms that they should report on the actual or possible deficiencies of themselves or their fellow professionals. Having considered the detailed terms of each engagement, he found: (a) that the project managers were obliged to report on the deficiencies of others (but not themselves); (b) that the architects were obliged to report on the deficiencies of the engineer and quantity surveyor but not the project manager (who was employed long after the architect and could not, accordingly, have been in the contemplation of the parties at the time of the contract); and (c) that the engineers and quantity surveyors had no duty to report on their own deficiencies or on those of fellow professionals. For further consideration of the decision in *Chesham Properties Ltd v Bucknall Austin Project Management Services*, see C. Leong, "The duty of care in project management" (2001) 17 P.N. 250.

professional appointment retrospective effect and a term imposing a duty upon a designer to review his design.

9–029 **Retrospectivity.** Since professional engagements are sometimes formalised only some time after the construction professional has begun providing his services, the implication of a term which provides that the written appointment has retrospective effect may be important. One or other party may wish to allege that conduct which took place before the written appointment was made amounted to a breach of that appointment. In the absence of an express term providing that the appointment has retrospective effect, an implication of retrospectivity will arise where parties have been conducting themselves as if there is an agreement in place and on the mutual assumption that such agreement will be formalised in due course. But no such implication arises where parties have been proceeding without any certainty as to whether an agreement will ultimately be concluded.[90]

9–030 **The duty to review a design.** An unusual feature of contracts for the services of construction professionals, when compared to those of other professionals, is that the building projects in connection with which they are retained may continue for many months or, often, years. The question may then arise, particularly in the context of limitation, whether the construction professional has a duty to revisit or review the services which he has provided at an earlier stage of the project. A prominent example of this is the question whether a designer is under a continuing obligation to review his design. Although it will be necessary to look at the circumstances of each engagement, a designer who also supervises or inspects work will generally be obliged to review his design up until that design has been included in the work. In *Brickfield Properties Ltd v Newton*[91] Sachs L.J. said:

> "The architect is under a continuing duty to check that his design will work in practice and to correct any errors which may emerge. It savours of the ridiculous for the architect to be able to say ' . . . true my design was faulty, but of course, I saw to it that the contractors followed it faithfully. . . .' ".[92]

9–031 After *Brickfield*, there were several decisions holding that a designer owes a continuing duty to review his design. It remained unclear, however, whether the duty requires proactive conduct by the designer (whereby he takes positive steps to see that his design was and remains appropriate), or merely reactive conduct (whereby he is under an obligation to reconsider the appropriateness of his design only if and when some potential defect in the design comes to his notice). The duration of the duty also remained unclear: in particular, whether it extended beyond the date of practical completion of the works designed.[93]

---

[90] *Consarc Design Ltd v Hutch Investments Ltd* [2002] P.N.L.R. 712 (no implied term that an architect's appointment had retrospective effect and hence the architects owed no prior obligation to warn that the building contract completion date was unlikely to be achieved).
[91] [1971] 1 W.L.R. 862.
[92] *ibid.* at 873.
[93] It is not always clear when, as a matter of law or as a matter of fact, practical completion takes place. For discussion, see T. Thompson, "Practical Completion in Building Contracts: A Legal Definition?" (2004) 20 Const. L.J. 301.

Common sense suggests that a duty to take proactive steps to review a design **9–032** after it has been built will be rare. In his dissenting judgment in *Eckersley v Binnie & Partners*[94] Bingham L.J. said obiter[95]:

"It has never, to my knowledge, been held that a professional man who advises on a tax scheme or on draft trading conditions, is thereafter bound to advise his client if, within a period of years, the statutory provisions or the relevant authorities change. Nor has it ever to my knowledge been suggested that a retired practitioner is bound, during his retirement, to keep in touch with developments in his profession in this way. These would be novel and burdensome obligations. On the other hand, counsel for the claimants was able to advance persuasive examples, involving dangers to life and health, where some response by a professional man might well be called for. What is plain is that if any such duty at all is to be imposed, the nature, scope and limits of such a duty require to be very carefully and cautiously defined. The development of the law on this point, if it ever occurs, will be gradual and analogical."

In *London Borough of Merton v Lowe*,[96] the defendant architects were retained **9–033** to design and supervise the construction of an indoor swimming pool. Part of their design called for suspended ceilings rendered with a coat of Pyrok, a proprietary material. After practical completion but before the final certificate had been issued, cracks were discovered in the ceilings. The architects required the contractor to remedy those defects, but did not consider whether the use of Pyrok was an inappropriate design. Judge Stabb Q.C. held that the architects were in breach of duty in failing to do so. He said[97]:

"I am now satisfied that the architect's duty of design is a continuing one, and it seems to me that the subsequent discovery of a defect in the design, initially and justifiably thought to have been suitable, reactivated or revived the architect's duty in relation to design and imposed upon them the duty to take such steps as were necessary to correct the results of that initially defective design."

The Court of Appeal upheld Judge Stabb's decision on this point. This case appears to support a purely reactive duty to review design; the duty arises only if the designer is asked to conduct a review or some event occurs which would cause a reasonably competent designer to look again at his design.[98]

Two authorities appear to suggest a proactive duty to review design which also **9–034** continues beyond practical completion. In *University of Glasgow v William Whitfield*,[99] where continuing problems with water ingress were experienced at the date of practical completion, Judge Bowsher Q.C. said obiter that an architect's duty to design extended beyond practical completion until the building was in fact "complete". In *Department of National Heritage v Steensen Varming*

---

[94] (1988) 18 Con. L.R. 1. For outline facts of the case see para.9–074, below.
[95] *ibid.* at 146. Neither of the other Lords Justices considered this point in view of their findings.
[96] (1981) 18 B.L.R.130, CA.
[97] This passage from the unreported judgment of Judge Stabb Q.C. is quoted at (1981) 18 B.L.R. 130 at 133.
[98] See to like effect the subsequent first instance decisions in *Tesco v Norman Hitchcox Partnership* (1997) 56 Con. L.R. 42; and *J Sainsbury Plc v Broadway Malyan* [1999] P.N.L.R. 286.
[99] (1988) 42 B.L.R. 66 at 78.

Mulcahy,[1] the same judge held that mechanical engineers were under a continuing duty to keep their design under review to see whether in fact it was and remained appropriate as construction progressed; it was not open to a designer, he said, to defend an allegation of negligent design by claiming that the design was executed with reasonable care and skill at the outset but became inappropriate by reason of external factors over which the designer had no control.

9–035   It is difficult to reconcile these suggestions of a proactive continuing duty to review design with authority to the effect that, in the absence of an express term or express instructions to investigate and report upon the causes of defects, there will be no implied obligation upon a professional man to report to a client upon his own deficiencies. In *Chesham Properties Ltd v Bucknall Austin Project Management Services Ltd*,[2] Judge Hicks Q.C. in finding that no such duty was owed stated:

> "The duty sought to be pleaded here—to advise, warn or inform of their own actual or potential deficiencies in performance—is more specific, more directly contrary to the architects' own interests, and therefore less likely to arise by construction or implication than the duty postulated by Judge Bowsher in *Glasgow University v Whitfield* to reveal 'what he knows of the design defects as possible causes of the problem'."

9–036   The position is plainly different if the professional man accepts express instructions to investigate and report upon defects, thereby accepting a new obligation to review his original design. This occurred in the Australian case of *Pullen v Gutteridge*.[3] The Victoria Court of Appeal found that the defendant engineers were liable for the negligent design of a swimming pool complex and found that the claim in respect of that design was not statute barred. However the court also found that the engineers were at fault in not reporting properly on the cause of the defects which were subsequently discovered when instructed to do so:

> "Had the respondent acted with reasonable care when asked to investigate and report to the appellant, its investigations would have had two consequences. In the first place, it would have come to realise, or at the very least to entertain a strong suspicion, that its own design of the sub-structure was seriously deficient and that the deficiency was

---

[1] (1998) 60 Con. L.R. 33 at 89.

[2] (1996) 82 B.L.R. 92. See also *Midland Bank & Trust Co Ltd v Hett, Stubbs & Kemp* [1979] 1 Ch. 384, *per* Oliver J. at 403B: "It is not seriously arguable that a solicitor who or whose firm has acted negligently comes under a continuing duty to take care to remind himself of the negligence of which, ex hypothesi, he is unaware"; *Rees Hough Ltd v Redland Reinforced Plastics Ltd* (1984) 27 B.L.R. 136 at 149 (manufacturers and sellers of pipes not obliged to warn that they had been unable to design to the contractual specification); *Southern Water Authority v Carey* [1985] 2 All E.R. 1077 (sub-contractors on sewage project not obliged to warn main contractor or engineer of defects in sub-contract works); *cf. Stag Line v Tyne Shiprepair Group Ltd* [1984] 2 Lloyd's Rep. 211 (implied duty on ship-repairer to inform ship-owner of the use of potentially hazardous lining material contrary to specification when ship-repairer became aware of the same).

[3] [1993] 1 V.R. 27, Victoria CA. For further consideration of the decision in *Chesham Properties Ltd v Bucknall Austin Project Management Services*, see C. Leong, "The duty of care in project management" (2001) 17 P.N. 250.

responsible for many of the defects that had emerged and were emerging. In the second place, it would have communicated this realisation or suspicion to its client."[4]

The English authorities referred to above (with the apparent exception of **9-037** *Chesham Properties Ltd v Bucknall Austin Project Management Services Ltd*[5]) were considered by Dyson J. in *New Islington Health Authority v Pollard Thomas & Edwards*.[6] The defendant architects were engaged to design and supervise the construction of flats for the claimant, under two building contracts. After practical completion but before issue of the final certificates under the building contracts, the claimant received complaints from its tenants that sound-proofing in the properties was poor. It asked the architects for details of their design for sound insulation of the flats and whether that design complied with the Building Regulations. The architects provided the information requested but took no steps to review their design for the sound insulation. The claimant argued that the architects owed a continuing duty to check and review their design until the end of their retainer, which was marked by the issue of the final certificates. Dyson J. rejected that submission. He held, first, that a designer who also supervised or inspected work would generally be obliged to review that design up until the design had been included in the work. If his design was for part of the works only, his duty would extend only until that part had been built. Secondly, the duty to review design will arise only if the designer has good reason to reconsider his original design. Giving as an example an architect who designs and supervises the construction of the foundations of a building only, Dyson J. said[7]:

> "In my view, in the absence of an express term or express instructions, he is not under a duty specifically to review the design of the foundations, unless something occurs to make it reasonably necessary, or at least prudent, for a reasonably competent architect to do so. For example, a specific duty might arise if, before completion, the inadequacy of the foundations causes the building to show signs of distress; or if the architect reads an article which shows that the materials that he has specified for the foundations are not fit for their purpose; or if he learns from some other source that the design is dangerous. In such circumstances, I am in no doubt that the architect would be under a duty to review the design, and, if necessary, issue variation instructions to the contractor to remedy the problem. But in the absence of some reason such as this, I do not think that an architect who has designed and supervised the construction of foundations is thereafter under an obligation to review his design."

Thirdly, Dyson J held that an architect who, as in *New Islington HA*, had been engaged on the RIBA Standard Conditions of Engagement to design and super-vise the construction of the entire works would owe a duty to review his design up until practical completion. Thereafter, the architect was not entitled to issue variation instructions to the building contractor and the terms of his own engage-ment imposed no express or implied duty to review his design. If the employer

---

[4] *Pullen v Gutteridge* [1993] 1 V.R. 27 at 86.
[5] (1996) 82 B.L.R. 92.
[6] [2001] P.N.L.R. 515. The reasoning deployed in this case was foreshadowed in A. Nissen, "The duty to review a design—is it real or artificial?" (1997) 13 Con. L.J. 221.
[7] *ibid.* para.16.

asks the architect to investigate a potential design defect after practical completion, the architect is entitled to refuse or to say that he will do so only if paid an
additional fee, since the work of investigating the effectiveness of his original
design is not part of his original contract of engagement.[8] Finally, Dyson J. held
that whenever the duty to review arises, it is limited in scope to a reactive
duty[9]:

> "In my judgment, the duty does not require the architect to review any particular aspect
> of the design that he has already completed unless he has good reason for so doing.
> What is a good reason must be determined objectively, and the standard is set by
> reference to what a reasonably competent architect would do in the circumstances."

It was held that the claimant's request for information about the defendants'
design for sound insulation was not sufficient to activate the defendants' duty to
review their design: it was merely a request for information and not a request that
the defendant investigate the noise insulation problem at the flats.

9–038   Dyson J.'s approach has subsequently been adopted and applied at first
instance.[10] The weight of authority, therefore, is to the effect that an architect
owes no duty to review his design unless something occurs which would bring
the need to review to the attention of a reasonably competent architect. Accordingly, an architect does not owe a continuing duty to his client to review his
design such that his failure to prepare a competent design is a breach of duty
which continues until completion of the structure he has designed.

(ii) *Duties Independent of Contract*

9–039   Duties may be imposed by law on a construction professional towards his client
as well as towards the rest of the world. The statutory duties which are imposed
are reasonably clear. The nature and extent of duties imposed by common law are
less clear. The principal practical importance of tortious claims is that contractual
claims in respect of latent defects against construction professionals are often
statute-barred before the defects in respect of which complaint is made are
discovered. The Latent Damage Act 1986 provides considerable relief to a

---

[8] On that basis, Dyson J. distinguished the decision of Judge Bowsher Q.C. in *University of Glasgow
v William Whitfield* (see para.9–033, above): on the facts of that case, the architect's failure to review
his design had been in breach of a duty imposed by a fresh retainer created by the employer's request
that the architect investigate problems of water ingress at the building after practical completion. It
remains difficult, however, to reconcile Dyson J.'s view of the scope of the duty with that of Judge
Bowsher Q.C., who clearly had in mind a proactive duty which existed before the defects arose and
before the employer's request was made. At (1988) 42 B.L.R. 66 at 78, he said, "Equally, I take the
view that where, as here, an architect has had drawn to his attention that damage has resulted from
a design which he knew or ought to have known was bad from the start, he has a particular duty to
his client to disclose what he had been under a continuing duty to reveal, namely what he knows of
the design defects as possible causes of the problem."
[9] *ibid.* para.20.
[10] *Payne v John Setchell Ltd* [2002] P.N.L.R. 7 (where Judge Lloyd Q.C. said, at para.21: "It is now
in my view well established that a designer's duty of care only requires a reconsideration of the
design if the designer becomes aware or should have been aware of the need to reconsider the
design." For the facts of that case, see para.9–057, below); *Tesco Stores Ltd v Costain Construction
Ltd* [2003] EWHC 1487, TCC.

claimant making such claims if he is able to bring his claim in negligence. The Act has no application to contractual claims.[11]

Duties imposed by statute. Two pieces of legislation significantly affect the duties which construction professionals owe to their clients: the Defective Premises Act 1972 and the Construction (Design and Management) Regulations 1994.
9-040

The Defective Premises Act 1972. Section 1(1) of the Defective Premises Act 1972[12] provides:
9-041

"(1) A person taking on work for or in connection with the provision of a dwelling (whether the dwelling is provided by the erection or by the conversion or enlargement of a building) owes a duty—

(a) if the dwelling is provided to the order of any person, to that person; and
(b) without prejudice to paragraph (a) above, to every person who acquires an interest (whether legal or equitable) in the dwelling; to see that the work which he takes on is done in a workmanlike or, as the case may be, professional manner, with proper materials and so that as regards that work the dwelling will be fit for habitation when completed."

Section 2 of the Act states that provided certain requirements are fulfilled no action shall be brought under s.1 where rights in respect of defects are conferred by an "approved scheme". At present there are no such approved schemes.[13] Until March 31, 1979, the main approved scheme was the 10-year protection scheme of the National House-Builders Registration Council which covered the vast majority of new houses constructed in this country and thus provided an enormous restriction on the practical operation of s.1.[14]
9-042

The duty set out in s.1 applies only to work taken on after the commencement date of the Act, which was January 1, 1974. Furthermore, the Act applies only to "dwellings". The term is not defined in the Act. The term has been interpreted, for the purposes of other legislation, as meaning a person's home (or one of his
9-043

---

[11] See Ch.5, paras 5-075 to 5-084. The existence of tortious liability will also affect a claim for contribution under the Law Reform (Married Women and Tortfeasors) Act 1935 although any such claims are now likely to be very rare as the Act applies only to cases where the relevant damage occurred or the relevant obligations were assumed before January 1, 1979. In practice the 1935 Act is now only likely to be of importance where the operation of the limitation period is suspended by reason of the fact that a claimant is an infant or patient. For discussion of the 1935 Act, see Ch.1 of the 3rd edn, paras 1-77 to 1-79.

[12] The Act does not apply in Scotland or Northern Ireland.

[13] The House Building Standards (Approved Scheme etc.) Orders 1973, 1975 and 1977 (SI 1973/7 1843, SI 1975/1402 and SI 1977/642) were replaced by the House Building Standards (Approved Scheme etc.) Order 1979 (SI 1979/381) which did not apply to the NHBC scheme due to changes in the NHBC scheme. This was resolved following a little known agreement between the Secretary of State and the NHBC. Through most of the 1980s it was widely thought that the NHBC scheme was an excluded scheme. Thus in *Warner v Basildon Corp* (1991) 7 Const. L.J. 146, CA, Ralph Gibson L.J. said: "About 97 per cent of houses constructed in any year are built under the NHBC Scheme approved under s.2 of the Defective Premises Act 1972 and, in consequence, the section 1 remedy is excluded." For further discussion of this matter see I. N. Duncan Wallace Q.C., "*Anns* beyond repair" (1991) 107 L.Q.R. 228, 242.

[14] For criticism of this restriction and other comments on the operation of the Act see J. R. Spencer, "The Defective Premises Act 1972—defective law and defective law reform" [1974] C.L.J. 307.

homes).[15] It has been held that, for the purposes of the Act, a dwelling house is a building used or capable of being used as a dwelling house, not being a building which is used predominantly for commercial or industrial purposes.[16]

9–044   Section 1 of the Act applies to the failure to carry out necessary remedial work as well as to the carrying out of work badly. In *Andrews v Schooling*,[17] the purchasers of a leasehold flat claimed damages against the freehold owners and developers from whom the flat was purchased on the basis that the cellar was unfit for habitation through damp. The defendants had carried out no work to the cellar, but were held liable under s.1 of the Act for failing to do so.

9–045   There is a question of construction as to whether s.1(1) of the Act imposes three separate duties to carry out work (a) in a workmanlike or professional manner; (b) with proper materials; and (c) so that the dwelling will be fit for habitation when completed or whether there is a single duty and the requirement of fitness for habitation is a measure of the standard required in the performance of that duty. In *Thompson v Clive Alexander & Partners*[18] Judge Lewis Q.C. considered this matter and held the latter construction to be correct. He based his reasoning first on statements by members of the Court of Appeal in *Alexander v Mercouris*[19] and secondly on his view that the plain intention of the Act was only to see that dwellings were built in such a way as to ensure that they were fit for habitation on completion. The decision is somewhat difficult to reconcile both with the words of the statute and with observations by Buckley and Goff L.JJ. in *Alexander v Mercouris* that a cause of action would arise during the course of construction once bad workmanship had taken place (although it appears to have been implicit that the bad workmanship would be such as to render the dwelling unfit for habitation if and when the dwelling was completed). If correct, the decision imposes a significant limit on the scope of the Act, since failure to carry out work in a workmanlike or professional manner or with proper materials will not amount to a breach of the duty imposed by s.1(1) if the dwelling is nevertheless fit for habitation.

9–046   Subsection 1(5) provides that any cause of action under the section shall be deemed for limitation purposes to have accrued at the time when the dwelling was completed. This has been interpreted as a "longstop" provision.[20] However, in *Payne v John Setchell Ltd*,[21] Judge Lloyd Q.C. held that a claim under the Defective Premises Act does not amount to an "action for damages for negligence" within the meaning of s.14A of the Limitation Act 1980 (introduced by the Latent Damage Act 1986). Accordingly, a claimant under the Act does not

---

[15] *Uratemp Ventures v Collins* [2001] UKHL 43; [2002] 1 A.C. 301, for the purposes of the Housing Act 1988.

[16] *Catlin Estates Ltd v Carter Jonas* [2005] EWHC 2315.

[17] [1991] 1 W.L.R. 783, CA.

[18] (1992) 28 Con. L.R. 49. In *Mirza v Bhandal*, unreported, April 27, 1999, Latham J. proceeded as if the former construction were correct, so that there would be no breach of the duty imposed by s.1(1) if the dwelling was in fact fit for habitation. It is not clear, however, whether Latham J. had heard argument on the point.

[19] [1979] 1 W.L.R. 1270.

[20] See the observations made in the Court of Appeal in *Alexander v Mercouris*, referred to in para.45 above, which were applied in *Catlin Estates Ltd v Carter Jonas* [2005] EWHC 2315.

[21] [2002] P.N.L.R. 7, approving the view adopted in the 4th edition of this work. For the facts, see para.9–057, below.

have the benefit of an extension of time of three years from the date of knowledge subject to the long-stop of 15 years. This result would in any event follow from the construction of s.1(1) adopted in *Thompson v Clive Alexander & Partners*[22]: a duty to ensure that a dwelling is fit for habitation goes beyond a duty to exercise reasonable skill and care. Subsection 1(5) contains an important proviso: if, after completion of the dwelling, further work is done to rectify defects in the original work, any cause of action in relation to such further work accrues only when it is finished. Thus in *Alderson v Beetham Organisation Ltd*[23] it was held that the leaseholders of flats acquired a fresh cause of action upon completion of the developer's ineffective works to remedy the originally installed but defective damp proof system in the building.

A dwelling will be unfit for habitation when completed notwithstanding that a **9–047** defect is latent rather than patent. In *Andrews v Schooling*,[24] Balcombe L.J. said:

> "If, when the work is completed, the dwelling is without some essential attribute—e.g. a roof or a damp course—it may well be unfit for human habitation even though the problems resulting from the lack of that attribute have not then become patent. A house without a roof is unfit for habitation even though it does not rain until some months after the house has been completed."

The Construction (Design and Management) Regulations 1994. In addition **9–048** to statutory duties which provide a directly enforceable civil remedy, there are also statutory obligations which impose extensive obligations upon professional men which do not give rise to direct civil rights but are nonetheless likely to be of importance in civil proceedings. Thus reg.13 of the Construction (Design and Management) Regulations 1994[25] imposes obligations upon a designer:

(a) not to prepare a design for any project unless he has taken reasonable steps to ensure that a client is aware of the (extensive) duties to which the client is subject by reason of the regulations;

---

[22] (1992) 28 Con. L.R. 49. In *Mirza v Bhandal*, unreported, April 27, 1999, Latham J. proceeded as if the former construction were correct, so that there would be no breach of the duty imposed by s.1(1) if the dwelling was in fact fit for habitation. It is not clear, however, whether Latham J. had heard argument on the point.

[23] [2003] EWCA Civ 408.

[24] [1991] 1 W.L.R. 783, CA at 790. This approach was followed in *Mirza v Bhandal*, unreported, April 27, 1999: rejecting the argument that a dwelling was fit for habitation at the time of its completion since its inadequate foundations had not by then brought about its collapse, although they were expected to do so within fifteen years thereafter unless underpinned, Latham J. said, "The dwelling, when completed, carried with it the seeds of its destruction. It seems to me that such a dwelling cannot properly be described as fit for habitation. . . . Although the effects of defective foundations are not as immediately dramatic as the lack of a roof, it seems to me that the principle remains the same. The inadequacy of the foundations was inevitably going to produce a situation in which the house would collapse. I do not consider that a house with foundations as inadequate as that can be described as fit for habitation when completed."

[25] SI 1994/3140, made under s.15 of the Health and Safety at Work etc. Act 1974 which came into force on March 31, 1995. See also The Construction (Design and Management) (Amendment) Regulations 2000, SI 2000/2380.

(b) (subject to a requirement of reasonable practicality) to ensure that any design that he prepares[26] and which he is aware will be used for the purposes of construction work includes among the design consideration adequate regard to the need:

   (i) to avoid foreseeable risks to the health and safety of any person at work carrying out construction work or cleaning work in or on the structure at any time, or of any person who may be affected by the work of such a person at work;

   (ii) to combat at source risks to the health and safety of any person at work carrying out construction work or cleaning work in or on the structure at any time or of any person who may be affected by the work of such a person at work; and

   (iii) to give priority to measures which will protect all persons at work who may carry out construction work or cleaning work at any time and all persons who may be affected by the work of such persons at work over measures which only protect each person carrying out such work;

(c) (subject to a requirement of reasonable practicality) to ensure that the design includes adequate information about any aspect of the project or structure or materials which might affect the health or safety of any person at work carrying out construction work or cleaning work in or on the structure at any time or of any person who may be affected by the work of such a person at work; and

(d) to co-operate with the planning supervisor (who is responsible for the preparation of a health and safety plan) and with any other designer to enable each of them to comply with the requirements and prohibitions placed upon them in relation to the project.

Although reg.21 expressly states that a breach of the majority of the Regulations shall not confer a right of action in civil proceedings, which would otherwise be given by s.47(2) of the Health and Safety at Work etc. Act 1974, it is likely that a court would find that a breach of the regulations amounted to a breach of a common law duty of care.[27]

9–049   **Duties imposed at common law.** Claims made against construction professionals in tort by their clients will generally be for economic loss. Until recently there was a very real debate as to whether the existence of a contract precluded the existence of a concurrent duty of care.[28] In England and Canada it

---

[26] For discussion of the meaning of "prepares a design" in the context of a criminal prosecution under the CDM Regulations, see *R. v Paul Wirth SA* [2000] I.C.R. 860, CA (a design and build contractor which approved a latch design prepared by its specialist sub-contractor did not prepare the design of the latch for the purposes of reg.13(2)(a)).

[27] See *Hewett v Alf Brown's Transport Ltd* [1991] I.C.R. 471 where the court accepted a submission that requirements of the Control of Lead at Work Regulations 1980 (SI 1980/1248) were equivalent to the common law requirements in dismissing a claim against an employer in respect of an employee's exposure to lead. See also J. Barber, "Potential side-effects of the CDM Regulations" (1997) 13 Const. L.J. 95.

[28] See Ch.2, paras 2–103 to 2–108.

has now been decided that the mere existence of a contract will not exclude a concurrent duty of care although the parties will be able (subject to statutory limitations) to restrict such a duty if they wish to do so. Although the position is less well established, it appears likely that courts in Australia and New Zealand would take the same view.

In *Henderson v Merrett Syndicates Ltd*,[29] the House of Lords conducted an extensive analysis of previous English and Commonwealth authorities before concluding that under the *Hedley Byrne* principle, the claimants who were direct Names at Lloyds of London were owed a duty of care in tort as well as in contract by the managing agents. Lord Goff gave the leading speech. He praised and substantially adopted the analysis of Oliver J. in *Midland Bank Trust Co v Hett, Stubbs & Kemp*[30] and expressly considered[31] *Bagot v Stevens Scanlan & Co Ltd*,[32] in which Diplock L.J., sitting at first instance on the trial of a preliminary issue as to whether the action was barred by limitation, held that an architect employed under a contract with the employer to supervise the laying of a drainage system owed him a duty in contract only and not in tort. In reaching this decision, Diplock L.J. had felt compelled to recognise that a different conclusion might be reached "where the law in the old days recognised either something in the nature of a status like a public calling (such as common carrier, common innkeeper, or a bailor and bailee) or the status of master and servant".[33] Having pointed out that it was also necessary to add claims against doctors and dentists to the list, Lord Goff stated that he found it startling "that, in the second half of the 20th century, a problem of considerable practical importance should fall to be solved by reference to such an outmoded form of categorisation as this". Later, Lord Goff stated[34]:

> "Attempts have been made to explain how doctors and dentists may be concurrently liable in tort while other professional men may not be so liable, on the basis that the former cause physical damage whereas the latter cause pure economic loss . . . . But this explanation is not acceptable, if only because some professional men, such as architects, may also be responsible for physical damage. As a matter of principle, it is difficult to see why concurrent remedies in tort and contract, if available against the medical profession, should not also be available against members of other professions, whatever form the relevant damage may take."

The rationale for the concurrent duty of care in tort was provided by the *Hedley Byrne* principle[35]:

> "However, at least in cases such as the present . . . there seems to be no reason why recourse should not be had to the concept, which appears after all to have been adopted, in one form or another, by all of their Lordships in *Hedley Byrne* . . . . In addition, the concept provides its own explanation why there is no problem in cases of this kind about liability for pure economic loss; for if a person assumes responsibility to another

---

[29] [1995] 2 A.C. 145.
[30] [1979] Ch. 384.
[31] *ibid.* at 185.
[32] [1966] 1 Q.B. 197.
[33] *ibid.* at 204–205.
[34] *ibid.* at 190.
[35] *ibid.* at 181. See Ch.2, paras 2–103 to 2–110.

in respect of certain services, there is no reason why he should not be liable in damages for that other in respect of economic loss which flows from the negligent performance of those services. It follows that, once the case is identified as falling within the *Hedley Byrne* principle, there should be no need to embark upon any further enquiry whether it is 'fair, just and reasonable' to impose liability for economic loss . . . The concept indicates too that in some circumstances, for example where the undertaking to furnish the relevant service is given on an informal occasion, there may be no assumption of responsibility; and likewise that an assumption of responsibility may be negatived by an appropriate disclaimer."

His conclusion[36] was that:

" . . . the common law is not antipathetic to concurrent liability, and that there is no sound basis for a rule which automatically restricts the claimant to either a tortious or a contractual remedy. The result may be untidy; but, given that the tortious duty is imposed by the general law, and the contractual duty is attributable to the will of the parties, I do not find it objectionable that the claimant may be entitled to take advantage of the remedy which is most advantageous to him, subject only to ascertaining whether the tortious duty is so inconsistent with the applicable contract that, in accordance with ordinary principle, the parties must be taken to have agreed that the tortious remedy is to be limited or excluded."

Even before *Henderson*, there were many architects' negligence cases pleaded in contract and in tort where the availability of the concurrent remedy was not questioned.[37] An example of a leading case where it was assumed that a duty lay in tort as well as contract was *Pirelli General Cable Works Ltd v Oscar Faber & Partners*.[38] The claimant building owners sued the defendant consulting engineers for the negligent design of a chimney extension. The claim was initially in contract and in tort for the costs of rectification of a chimney which had cracked but the claimants conceded that the contractual claim was time-barred. In *Murphy v Brentwood DC*,[39] Lord Keith, with whom all the other law lords agreed, explained *Pirelli* as a case in which tortious liability arose out of a contractual relationship as a consequence of the *Hedley Byrne* principle,[40] thus presaging the result in *Henderson*.[41]

9–051   **The importance of concurrent liability.** The main practical reason for the debate as to the existence of concurrent liability arises from the different treatment accorded to contractual and tortious claims. Since a tortious claim requires damage, it may accrue later and the Latent Damage Act 1986, which extends the limitation period to three years from the "date of knowledge" as defined (up to

---

[36] *Bagot v Stevens Scanlon & Co Ltd* [1966] 1 Q.B. 197 at 194–195.
[37] See fn.70 to para.2–21 of the 3rd edition of this work for examples of such cases.
[38] [1983] 2 A.C. 1.
[39] [1991] 1 A.C. 398.
[40] *ibid.* at 466F.
[41] Courts in Canada, New Zealand and Australia have also reached the conclusion that a person who has performed professional services may be held liable concurrently in contract and in negligence unless the terms of the contract preclude the tortious liability: see, for examples, *Central Trust & Co v Rafuse* (1986) 31 D.L.R. (4th) 481 (a solicitors' case); *Frost & Sutcliffe v Tuara* [2004] 1 N.Z.L.R. 782 and *Pullen v Gutteridge* [1993] 1 V.R. 27.

a maximum "long-stop" period of 15 years), applies only to claims in negligence. Some commentators have criticised the apparent influence of procedure on substantive law. Thus I.N. Duncan Wallace Q.C., in an article prior to *Henderson*,[42] stated:

"These rather complicated concepts of concurrent liability, relatively recently developed throughout the Commonwealth countries over the past 20 years, appear to have been principally dictated by the need of defendants to secure the benefit of statutory limitation, contribution or apportionment remedies not then currently available in contract, rather than on any substantive principle. By contrast the current climate in the House of Lords seems disposed, many may think wisely, to restore and affirm the important distinctions between tort and contract. This would be facilitated, it is suggested, by eliminating the artificial pressures arising from purely procedural differences of remedy. The extension of the Act of 1986 to liability in contract (or, to the exact contrary, repealing the 1986 Act altogether), therefore would reduce the artificial arguments and litigation arising from questions of concurrent liability, as well as provide a means of doing justice to contractual plaintiffs."[43]

Such calls were decisively rejected. In *Henderson*, Lord Goff stated[44]:

"I think it is desirable to stress at this stage that the question of concurrent liability is by no means only of academic significance. Practical issues, which can be of great importance to the parties, are at stake. Foremost among these is perhaps the question of limitation of actions. If concurrent liability in tort is not recognised, a plaintiff may find his claim barred at a time when he is unaware of its existence. This must moreover be a real possibility in the case of claims against professional men, such as solicitors or architects, since the consequences of their negligence may well not come to light until long after the lapse of six years from the date when the relevant breach of contract occurred. Moreover the benefits of the Latent Damage Act 1986, under which the time of the accrual of the cause of action may be postponed until after the plaintiff has the relevant knowledge, are limited to actions in tortious negligence. This leads to the startling possibility that a client who has had the benefit of gratuitous advice from his solicitor may in this respect be better off than a client who has paid a fee. Other practical problems arise, for example, from the absence of a right to contribution between negligent contract-breakers; from the rules as to remoteness of damage, which are less restricted in tort than they are in contract; and from the availability of the opportunity to obtain leave to serve proceedings out of the jurisdiction. It can of course be argued that the principle established in respect of concurrent liability in contract and tort should not be tailored to mitigate the adventitious effects of rules of law such as these, and that one way of solving such problems would no doubt be to rephrase such incidental rules as have to remain in terms of the nature of the harm suffered rather than the nature of the liability asserted (see Tony Weir, XI Int.Encycl.Comp.L. ch.12, para.72). But this is perhaps crying for the moon; and with the law in its present form, practical considerations of this kind cannot sensibly be ignored."

---

[42] "Anns beyond repair" (1991) 107 L.Q.R. 228 at 247.

[43] For consideration of how best to protect sufferers from latent damage see "Limitation of actions and latent damage—an Australian perspective" (1991) 54 M.L.R. 216; and N. J. Mullany, "Reform of the law of latent damage" (1991) 54 M.L.R. 349.

[44] *ibid.* at 185.

9–052   If a claimant pleads his claim in tort as well as in contract, the defendant may raise a defence of contributory negligence.[45] Although it is probable that the defence will also be available in an action brought in contract alone, the matter has yet to reach the House of Lords.[46]

9–053   **The scope of the concurrent duty in tort.** The question, "what does the concurrent duty of care in tort require?" begs the response, "duty of care in doing what?" That response focuses the inquiry on what was agreed to be done, i.e. on the terms of the contract. Moreover the touchstone of implication is necessity not reasonableness. Recognition of this principle prompts caution against patching over perceived holes in the matrix of contractual duties as between parties to a building project with duties of care in tort and against construing the duty to exercise reasonable care and skill as a duty to do that which is reasonable. Normally, however, the contractual relationship between a construction professional and his client will establish sufficient proximity, assumption of responsibility and reliance to found a coterminous duty of care in tort. The construction professional will owe a duty to his client in tort to exercise reasonable skill and care in providing the services which he contracted to provide.

9–054   It will be rare that a concurrent duty of care in tort will require the taking of steps extending beyond those required to discharge the duties expressed or implied in the contract, including in particular the duty to exercise reasonable care and skill. However, should the professional contracting party provide advice or services which are outside the ambit of his retainer, he may be held to have owed a duty of care in tort in respect of such advice or services which is necessarily wider in scope than his contractual duties.[47]

9–055   The contract may go further than defining the duties undertaken. It may contain terms qualifying, limiting or even excluding any concurrent duty of care in tort. Such express terms are rare in contracts with professional men (as distinct from contracts with building contractors, sub-contractors or suppliers).[48] It may often be the case, however, that a professional man has a defence to an action in tort which is not available to him in contract. If a professional engages a sub-consultant to perform part of his tasks, he will owe no duty of care in tort to his

---

[45] Conversely, to the extent that a concurrent duty of care in tort is narrower than contractual duties, there will be no defence of contributory negligence. See, for example, *Raflatac Ltd v Eade* [1999] B.L.R. 261, discussed at para.9–057, below. Contributory negligence is discussed in relation to the construction professions at paras 9–347 to 9–348, below.

[46] See the discussion at Ch.5, paras 5–141 to 5–147.

[47] See, for an example, *Kensington and Chelsea and Westminster AHA v Wettern Composites Ltd* (1984) 1 Con. L.R. 114 (defendant structural engineers' contractual duties included checking the drawings for the adequacy of fixings to cladding but not supervision of the installation of the fixings; defects in the installation of the fixings were observed by the engineers; held that although there was no contractual duty requiring the engineers to follow up their observations, their duty of care to the claimant client in tort did require them to do so). For an example involving surveyors, see *Holt v Payne Skillington* (1995) 77 B.L.R. 51.

[48] e.g. *Rumbelows Ltd v AMK* (1980) 19 B.L.R. 25; *William Hill Organisation Ltd v Bernard Sunley and Sons Ltd* (1982) 22 B.L.R. 1, CA; *Twins Transport Ltd v Patrick and Brocklehurst* (1983) 25 B.L.R. 65; *Southern Water Authority v Lewis and Duvivier (No.1)* (1984) 1 Con. L.R. 40 and *(No.2)* (1984) 1 Con. L.R. 50; *Greater Nottingham Co-operative Society Ltd v Cementation Piling and Foundations Ltd* [1989] Q.B. 71.

client in relation to that work unless he owed a duty to carry out that work which was a non-delegable duty for the purposes of the law of tort.[49]

There is a conflict of authority at first instance as to whether the concurrent **9–056** duty of care in tort owed by a construction professional to his client is limited to a duty to avoid causing personal injury or damage to other property of his client, or extends to taking care to avoid economic loss. In *Storey v Charles Church Developments Ltd*,[50] the defendant designed and built a house for the claimant. Structural faults appeared as a result of defective design of the foundations. The claimant claimed damages for breach of the defendant's concurrent duty of care in tort. It was common ground that the claimant's loss was economic loss. Judge Hicks Q.C. held that the defendant did owe a duty of care in respect of such loss. In accordance with the reasoning of the House of Lords in *Henderson*, the judge applied the *Hedley Byrne* principle to the question of the defendant's concurrent duty. He held that, by reason of its contract with the claimant, the defendant had assumed a responsibility to him to exercise reasonable skill and care in designing the house and the claimant had relied upon him to do so. That assumption of responsibility and concomitant reliance occurred because of the relationship created by the contract between the parties and the resulting duty of care in tort was not limited by the terms of the contract. It followed that the defendant's duty in tort was a duty to avoid causing economic loss to his client.[51] It was argued that a builder can never be liable in tort for economic loss, in reliance upon the decision of the House of Lords in *Murphy v Brentwood DC*.[52] Judge Hicks dismissed that argument. *Murphy* was distinguishable on the facts, particularly since there was no contract between the parties in *Murphy*. Furthermore, Lord Keith in *Murphy*[53] had referred with approval to the decision in *Pirelli General Cable Works Ltd v Oscar Faber and Partners*[54] in which it was assumed that a designer owed a concurrent duty in tort to avoid causing economic loss to his client.[55]

In *Payne v John Setchell Ltd*,[56] Judge Lloyd Q.C. declined to follow the **9–057** decision in *Storey*. In that case, the claimants were the purchasers of cottages which had been built for a Mrs Wright. Mrs Wright had engaged the defendant civil and structural engineer to assist in the construction of the cottages. The

---

[49] *D & F Estates Ltd v Church Commissioners for England* [1989] A.C. 177 at 208, *per* Lord Bridge; *Aiken v Stewart Wrightson Members Agency Ltd* [1995] 1 W.L.R. 1281 (member's agents at Lloyd's did not owe a duty of care in tort to the Names with whom they had contracts in respect of work delegated to managing agents, who had no contracts with the Names); *Raflatac Ltd v Eade* [1999] B.L.R. 261 (main contractor did not owe a duty of care in tort to the employer in respect of work which had been sub-contracted, with the employer's consent, to a specialist contractor). For a general iscussion of non-delegable duties in tort, see *Clerk & Lindsell on Tort* (19th edn), paras 6–52 to 6–69.
[50] (1995) 73 Con. L.R. 1. For discussion of this and other decisions, see I. Ndekugri, "Concurrent liability in contract and tort in the construction industry" (2000) 16 Const. L.J. 13.
[51] See, to similar effect *Barclays Bank Plc v Fairclough Building Ltd (No.2)* (1995) 76 B.L.R. 1 (a sub-sub-contractor owed a duty of care in tort to the sub-contractor in performing the sub-sub-contract works; duty not limited to physical damage).
[52] [1991] 1 A.C. 398; discussed further at para.9–070, below.
[53] *ibid.* at 466.
[54] [1983] 2 A.C. 1.
[55] See para.9–050, above.
[56] [2002] P.N.L.R. 7. For discussion of the case, see A. Pigott, "Economic loss, transmissible warranties and extensions to the boundaries of *Murphy v Brentwood*" (2005) 21 Const. L.J. 95.

defendant had designed raft foundations for the cottages, inspected the construction of those foundations and certified that they were satisfactorily constructed and suitable for support of the cottages. The claimants alleged that raft foundations were an inappropriate design and had caused structural problems which required remedial work. The claimants argued that, until Mrs Wright sold the cottages to them, she had had a cause of action against the defendant for breach of his concurrent duty of care in tort in designing the foundations and certifying their suitability. It was common ground that if Mrs Wright had had such a cause of action, the claimants would have acquired an identical cause of action upon their acquisition of the cottages, under s.3 of the Latent Damage Act 1986.[57] The judge regarded the decisions of the House of Lords in *Murphy* and, to the like effect, in *Department of the Environment v Thomas Bates & Son*[58] as establishing that[59]:

> "as a matter of policy, any person undertaking work or services in the course of a construction process is ordinarily liable only for physical injury or for property damage other than to the building itself but is not liable for other losses—ie economic loss. If any liability for such economic loss is to arise it must be for other reasons, e.g. as a result of advice or statements made upon which reliance is placed in circumstances which create a relationship where there is in law to be an assumption of the responsibility for loss—i.e. within the principle of *Hedley Byrne v Heller* . . . . In my judgment a designer is not liable in negligence to the client or to a subsequent purchaser for the cost of putting right a flaw in a design that the designer has produced that has not caused physical injury or damage, just as a contractor is not liable."

Accordingly, the judge held that the defendant did not owe to his client, Mrs Wright, any duty of care in tort to avoid causing economic loss. Since the claimants had suffered economic loss only (the cost of remedial works to cure the defects in the cottages' foundations), they acquired no useful cause of action upon acquisition of the cottages under s.3 of the Latent Damages Act 1986.

9–058   Judge Lloyd's analysis of the decisions in *Murphy* and *DOE v Bates* is entirely apposite in relation to the scope of the duty of care owed by the builder or designer of a property to a person with whom he has no contract, but questionable in relation to the scope of the duty in tort owed by such a person *to his client*. That duty was not the subject of discussion in those cases. Furthermore, it is difficult to reconcile the judge's approach with the words of Lord

---

[57] s.3(1) states:
"Subject to the following provisions of this section, where—
    (a) a cause of action ('the original cause of action') has accrued to any person in respect of any negligence to which damage to any property in which he has an interest is attributable (in whole or in part); and
    (b) another person acquires an interest in that property after the date on which the original cause of action accrued but before the material facts about the damage have become known to any person who, at the time when he first has knowledge of those facts, has any interest in the property;
a fresh cause of action in respect of that negligence shall accrue to that other person on the date on which he acquires his interest in the property."

[58] [1991] 1 A.C. 499; discussed further at para.9–071, below.

[59] [2002] P.N.L.R. 7 at [30].

Goff in *Henderson*, explaining that the concurrent duty of care in tort is a *Hedley Byrne* duty, which encompasses economic loss[60]:

"However, at least in cases such as the present . . . there seems to be no reason why recourse should not be had to the concept, which appears after all to have been adopted, in one form or another, by all of their Lordships in *Hedley Byrne* . . . . In addition, the concept provides its own explanation why there is no problem in cases of this kind about liability for pure economic loss; for if a person assumes responsibility to another in respect of certain services, there is no reason why he should not be liable in damages for that other in respect of economic loss which flows from the negligent performance of those services. It follows that, once the case is identified as falling within the *Hedley Byrne* principle, there should be no need to embark upon any further enquiry whether it is 'fair, just and reasonable' to impose liability for economic loss . . . ."

In *Ove Arup & Partners International Ltd v Mirant Asia-Pacific Construction (Hong Kong) (No.2)*,[61] the defendant engineers were alleged to have prepared a defective foundations design for a power station. When sued by their client in negligence, they argued (relying upon the decision in *Payne v John Setchell*) that their concurrent duty of care at common law did not extend to a duty to protect their client against economic loss. Judge Toulmin C.M.G. Q.C. rejected the argument, holding that the principles enunciated by Lord Goff in *Henderson* applied to a professional designer as they did to other professionals. Pending appellate consideration of the scope of the concurrent duty of care in tort owed by a construction professional to his client, it is thought that this is the better view.[62]

Fiduciary duties. Although the vast majority of claims against construction   **9–059** professionals are brought either in contract or in the tort of negligence, other claims are sometimes made which overlap with those discussed in this book. As set out above,[63] a construction professional may act as agent for his client and have the power to alter the client's legal relationships. As a consequence, when acting in such capacity, he is likely to owe fiduciary duties to his client. However such fiduciary duties will not enlarge the scope of contractual duties. In *Chesham Properties Ltd v Bucknall Austin Project Management Services Ltd*[64] the claimant sought to make out a case that the defendant project managers, architects, engineers and quantity surveyors owed fiduciary duties to warn their employer client of their own actual or potential deficiencies in performance and/or those of their fellow professionals. In finding that no such fiduciary duty was owed, Judge

---

[60] [1995] 2 A.C. 146 at 181. See also *Bellefield Computer Services Ltd v E. Turner & Sons Ltd* [2000] B.L.R. 97, where Schiemann L.J. (at 102) clearly regarded a designer's concurrent duty of care in tort as a duty to avoid causing economic loss; see also *Gable House Estates Ltd v The Halpern Partnership* (1995) 48 Con. L.R. 1 at 106 *per* Judge Lewis Q.C.; and *Gloucestershire HA v Torpy* (1997) 55 Con. L.R. 124 at 135, *per* Judge Bowsher Q.C.
[61] [2004] EWHC 1750, TCC. This part of the decision was not challenged on appeal: [2005] EWCA Civ 1585. See also *Tesco v Costain Construction Ltd* [2003] EQHC 1487, TCC, where Judge Seymour Q.C. reached the same conclusion on this issue as did Judge Toulmin CMG QC.
[62] For further discussion, see A. Pigott, "Economic loss, transmissible warranties and extensions to the boundaries of *Murphy v Brentwood*" (2005) 21(2) Const. L.J., 95–101.
[63] See para.9–026. For a general discussion of fiduciary obligations owed by professionals, see Ch.2, paras 2–128 to 2–154.
[64] (1996) 82 Build. L.R. 92.

Hicks Q.C. adopted the statement of the Privy Council in the solicitors' case of *Clarke Boyce v Mouat*[65]:

> "A fiduciary duty concerns disclosure of material facts in a situation where the fiduciary has either a personal interest in the matter to which the facts are material or acts for another party who has such an interest. It cannot be prayed in aid to enlarge the scope of contractual duties."

(b) *Duties to Third Parties*

9–060   **Contractual warranties.** A construction professional may undertake express contractual duties to a person other than his immediate client. For example, a building owner who contracts with a design and build contractor may wish to make sure that he will have a remedy for defective design in the event that the contractor becomes insolvent. If the contractor has sub-contracted the design work to an architect, the employer may require the architect to sign a collateral warranty. In consideration for the employer awarding the main contract to the contractor, who is the architect's client, or for nominal consideration, the architect undertakes an obligation to the employer to use reasonable skill and care in performing the work sub-contracted to him.[66] Sometimes, such a document is executed under seal, when it may be known as a "duty of care deed". In that case, not only will the employer be entitled to bring an action for any breach of duty in respect of design against a party which is likely to have the benefit of professional indemnity insurance, but he will also have 12 years within which to bring such an action.[67] The liability of the construction professional to such a third party will then be governed by ordinary contractual rules.[68]

9–061   **Non-contractual duties.** Just as an architect, engineer or quantity surveyor may have duties imposed upon him towards his client by the operation either of

---

[65] [1994] 1 A.C. 428 at 437G. Any claim for breach of fiduciary duty brought now would need to take into account the decision of the Court of Appeal in *Bristol & West Building Society v Mothew* [1998] Ch. 1 that a breach of fiduciary duty requires intentional misconduct and is not made out where the conduct complained of is consistent with mere oversight; the latter gives rise to a claim for breach of contract or negligence only.

[66] The British Property Federation has published two Forms of Agreement for Collateral Warranties after consultation with RIBA, ACE, RICS and the insurance industry. One form (referred to as "CoWa/F"), is for use where the warranty is given to a funding institution; the other ("CoWa/P") is for use with a purchaser or tenant. Each form contains an undertaking by the professional in these terms: "The Firm warrants that it has exercised and will continue to exercise reasonable skill [and care] [care and diligence] in the performance of its duties to the Client under the Agreement . . .".

[67] The limitation period for an action brought on a contract under seal is 12 years: Limitation Act 1980, s.8.

[68] An issue which commonly arises in connection with a collateral warranty given by a construction professional to a non-client is whether that warranty has been effectively assigned by the non-client to a third party. Whether a collateral warranty is capable of being assigned will depend upon its terms, and in particular, upon the correct construction of any covenant against assignment which it contains. In *Allied Carpets Group Plc v Macfarlane* [2002] EWHC 1155, TCC a collateral warranty was given by a firm of architects and structural engineers which was engaged in the development of a warehouse by its owner to the intended tenant of the warehouse. The tenant assigned its lease to the claimant and purported to assign the collateral warranty. Judge Bowsher Q.C. held that there had not been any effective assignment of the warranty.

statute or of common law so he may have duties imposed towards third parties.

Duties imposed by statute. In England and Wales,[69] the major relevant **9–062** statutory duty in relation to dwellings is the Defective Premises Act 1972. Section 1(1) of that Act is set out and discussed above.[70] As is apparent from the words of the section, any duty is owed to "every person who acquires an interest (whether legal or equitable) in the dwelling".

The Contracts (Rights of Third Parties) Act 1999. Strictly speaking, this **9–063** Act[71] does not impose duties on construction professionals. Rather, it creates an exception to the doctrine of privity of contract so as to enable a third party to acquire rights under a contract if that is what the parties to the contract intended. However, because construction professionals operate in circumstances in which their services may well be regarded as conferring a benefit on parties other than their immediate client, the Act is of potential importance in any consideration of the liability of construction professionals. Detailed consideration of the Act is outside the scope of this work and only the principal provisions are outlined below.[72] Section 1 of the Act gives a third party a right to enforce a term of a contract if the contract expressly provides that he may[73] or if the relevant term purports to confer a benefit on him.[74] The third party will have such a right unless, on a true construction of the contract, the parties to it did not intend the term to be enforceable by the third party.[75] The third party must be expressly identified in the contract by name, class or description, but he does not need to have existed at the date when the contract was made.[76] He is entitled to the same remedies for breach of contract as would be available if he were a party to the contract, i.e. he can recover his own loss.[77] Defences available to the promisor[78] include defences and set-off which the promisor would have had against the other contracting party if that party had sought to enforce the term,[79] and also any defence or counterclaim which the promisor would have had against the third party if the third party had been a party to the contract.[80] Thus, if the promisor

---

[69] By s.7(3) the Act does not apply to Scotland or Northern Ireland.

[70] See paras 9–041 to 9–047, above.

[71] The Act substantially implements "Privity of Contract: Contracts for the Benefit of Third Parties", Law Commission Report No. 242 (Cm. 3329, 1996).

[72] For detailed consideration, see *Chitty on Contracts* (29th edn), paras 18–084 to 18–112; C. MacMillan, "A birthday present for Lord Denning: The Contracts (Rights of Third Parties) Act 1999" (2000) 63 M.L.R. 721; T. Roe, "Contractual intention under section 1(1)(b) and 1(2) of the Contracts (Rights of Third Parties) Act 1999" (2000) 63 M.L.R. 887; N. Andrews, "Strangers to justice no longer: the reversal of the privity rule under the Contracts (Rights of Third Parties) Act 1999" [2001] C.L.J. 353; A. Burrows, "The Contracts (Rights of Third Parties) Act 1999 and its implications for commercial contracts", a lecture given to the Society of Construction Law on May 23, 2000.

[73] s.1(1)(a).

[74] s.1(1)(b).

[75] s.1(2).

[76] s.1(3).

[77] s.1(5).

[78] i.e. the contracting party which bears the burden of performing the relevant term.

[79] s.3(2) and (3).

[80] s.3(4).

was induced to enter the contract by the third party's misrepresentation, he could set up this defence in the third party's claim even although it would not have been available had the promisee brought the claim.

9–064   The Act came into force on November 11, 1999. It applies only to contracts entered into on or after May 11, 2000, unless expressly incorporated into a contract made before that date.[81] Its effect upon claims against construction professionals is not yet widely apparent. It is likely that employers and other third parties who are in a position to do so will continue to require collateral warranties from construction professionals engaged by others, so as to avoid the potentially difficult questions of contractual construction which may arise upon a claim under the Act. Moreover, it is to be anticipated that construction professionals will take care to see that the operation of the Act is expressly excluded from their professional appointments.[82]

9–065   **Duties imposed at common law.** The general principles upon which the courts act in seeking to decide whether a duty of care should be imposed at common law are discussed in Ch.2 above.[83] Although it is submitted that courts throughout the Commonwealth have regard to the same principles, there has been a considerable divergence in the results in similar factual situations. This divergence has been most marked when considering whether a subsequent purchaser can recover damages for economic loss (generally the cost of repair of a defective building) from a person involved in the original building operation. In England and Wales, the House of Lords has expressed considerable reluctance to allow such claims[84] and it is likely that a subsequent purchaser will only be able to claim damages for economic loss if he can rely upon the *Hedley Byrne*[85] principle. Although the courts of Canada, Australia and New Zealand (including the Privy Council on a New Zealand appeal[86]) have discussed (and differed upon) the precise importance and significance of economic loss, none have limited claims for economic loss to the same extent as the House of Lords has done. The differing approaches taken throughout the Commonwealth render a unified discussion of this area both unsatisfactory and, potentially, misleading. Accordingly, this part of the chapter is organised in the following way:

(i) The definition of the type of loss. In view of the differing approaches taken in respect of different types of loss and different categorisations of such loss, it is important to define the type of loss which is sought to be recovered.

(ii) Recovery by third parties in respect of personal injury and damage to "other property". This area presents little difference of approach between the various Commonwealth jurisdictions.

---

[81] s.10(2) and (3).
[82] The RIBA Standard Form of Agreement for the Appointment of an Architect (SFA/99) expressly excludes the operation of the Act: cl.7.6.
[83] See Ch.2, paras 2–013 to 2–080.
[84] See paras 9–082 to 9–085, below.
[85] See paras 9–094 to 9–102, below.
[86] *Invercargill CC v Hamlin* [1996] A.C. 624. See further paras 9–072 and 9–116, below.

(iii) The general exclusionary rule adopted in England with regard to the recovery of economic loss. This section considers the basic English rule as set out in *Murphy v Brentwood DC*.[87]

(iv) The English exceptions to the general exclusionary rule. This section discusses the possibility of escaping the general exclusionary rule by one of the three exceptions contemplated in *Murphy*: the complex structure theory; the prevention of damage to third party property; and the application of the *Hedley Byrne* principle.

(v) The positions in other Commonwealth jurisdictions.

(vi) Problems of scope of duty. This section discusses the problem of defining the scope of duty in the absence of a contract.

(i) *The Definition of the Type of Loss*

In *Sutherland Shire Council v Heyman*[88] Brennan J., in a passage which has been   **9–066**
substantially approved in the House of Lords[89] and which it is submitted accurately summarises the common law as applied in England, stated:

> "Liability in tort is for damage done, not for damage merely foreseeable or threatened or imminent. . . . The corollary is that a postulated duty of care must be stated in reference to the kind of damage that a plaintiff has suffered and in reference to the claimant or a class of which the plaintiff is a member. I venture to repeat what I said in *John Pfeiffer Pty Ltd v Canny*[90]: 'His duty of care is a thing written on the wind unless damage is caused by the breach of that duty; there is no actionable negligence unless duty, breach and consequential damage coincide. . . . For the purposes of determining liability in a given case, each element can be defined only in terms of the others.' It is impermissible to postulate a duty of care to avoid one kind of damage— say, personal injury—and, finding the defendant guilty of failing to discharge that duty, to hold him liable for the damage actually suffered that is of another and independent kind—say, economic loss. Not only may the respective duties differ in what is required to discharge them: the duties may be owed to different persons or classes of person. That is not to say that a plaintiff who suffers damages of some kind will succeed or fail in an action to recover damages according to his classification of the damage he suffered. The question is always whether the defendant was under a duty to avoid or prevent that damage, but the actual nature of the damage suffered is relevant to the existence and extent of any duty to avoid or prevent it."

The above passage is a clear reaffirmation of the importance of classifying the   **9–067**
type of damage which had been blurred in *Dutton v Bognor Regis UDC*[91] and *Anns v Merton LBC*.[92] In *Dutton* the Court of Appeal held that a local authority which negligently inspected the foundations of a house built on an old rubbish tip

---

[87] [1991] 1 A.C. 398, HL.
[88] (1984–1985) 157 C.L.R. 425: local authority held not liable to the subsequent purchasers of a house for structural defects caused by inadequate footings. Although all members of the High Court of Australia were agreed as to the result, only a bare majority held that there was no duty of care.
[89] See *Caparo Industries Plc v Dickman* [1990] 2 A.C. 605, *per* Lord Oliver at 651, *per* Lord Bridge at 627; *Murphy v Brentwood DC* [1991] A.C. 398, *per* Lord Keith at 464B.
[90] (1981) 148 C.L.R. 218 at 241–242.
[91] [1972] 1 Q.B. 373.
[92] [1978] A.C. 728.

was liable to a subsequent purchaser of the house for the costs of strengthening the foundations so that there was no danger to health and safety and for a (presumably continuing) diminution in value. In a famous dictum,[93] Lord Denning said:

> "The damage done here was not solely economic loss. It was physical damage to the house. If [counsel for the defendant's] submission were right, it would mean that if the inspector negligently passes the house as properly built and it collapses and injures a person, the council are liable: but if the owner discovers the defect in time to repair it—and he does repair it—the council are not liable. That is an impossible distinction. They are liable in either case."

9–068   In *Anns v Merton LBC*[94] a local council was sued for the costs of remedying defects in a block of flats caused by movement of the foundations and consequential losses by seven lessees of the flats by reason of having negligently approved or inspected the foundations. At first instance and in the Court of Appeal, the only issue was whether the claims were statute-barred. In the House of Lords, the council was granted leave to challenge the existence of a duty of care. The House of Lords held that the council would be liable for the negligence of its inspector in inspecting the foundations and that such a duty was not statute-barred as it arose only when there was a present or imminent danger to the health of the persons occupying it. Lord Wilberforce (with whom three other Law Lords agreed) accepted that the position of a local authority should be no worse than that of a builder.[95] Later in his judgment he said[96]:

> "In my opinion [the damages recoverable] may also include damage to the dwelling house itself. . . . To allow recovery for such damage to the house follows, in my opinion, from normal principle. If classification is required, the relevant damage is in my opinion material, physical damage, and what is recoverable is the amount of expenditure necessary to restore the dwelling to a condition in which it is no longer a danger to the health or safety of persons occupying and possibly (depending on the circumstances) expenses arising from necessary displacement."

9–069   The decisions in *Dutton* and *Anns* have now been respectively overruled and departed from. In *D & F Estates Ltd v Church Commissioners for England*,[97] the claimant lessees of a flat sued the main contractors who had built the claimants' flat for the cost of remedying defective plasterwork originally installed by subcontractors together with associated consequential costs. The House of Lords held inter alia that the loss sustained in renewing the plasterwork amounted to irrecoverable pure economic loss, i.e. either the cost of repairing the defects or the diminution in the value of the property as a result of the defects. Both Lord Bridge[98] and Lord Oliver[99] were clear that the plasterwork had caused no significant damage to any other relevant property. Both, however, left open the question whether individual items of a "complex structure" such as a house

---

[93] [1972] 1 Q.B. 373 at 396.
[94] [1978] A.C. 728.
[95] *ibid.* at 758.
[96] *ibid.* at 759G.
[97] [1989] 1 A.C. 177.
[98] *ibid.* at 207.
[99] *ibid.* at 214E.

could be treated separately with the result that the defective construction of one part of the house, such as the foundations, which gave rise to damage to another part, such as the walls, could be said to give rise to damage which was not pure economic loss.[1]

In *Murphy v Brentwood DC*[2] Mr Murphy, a subsequent purchaser of a house, **9–070** sued a local authority for having negligently passed plans with the result that the foundations cracked and extensive damage was caused to the walls and pipes of the house. The judge held that the damage was such as to cause an imminent danger to Mr Murphy's health and safety. Mr Murphy's claim was for £35,000, being the reduction in the price which he obtained on a sale of the house in its defective condition. £35,000 was less than the cost of repair would have been. The House of Lords unanimously departed from *Anns*, holding that where a defect in a house was discovered before any injury to person or health or damage to property other than the defective house itself had occurred, no action lay against a local authority. The question whether a local authority owed a duty in respect of injury to persons[3] or "other" property[4] was expressly left open, as was the question whether the builder of defective premises could be held responsible for the cost necessarily incurred by a building owner in protecting himself from potential liability to third parties in respect of personal injury.[5] Lord Keith (with whom all the other law lords agreed) stated[6]:

"In my opinion it must now be recognised that, although the damage in *Anns* was characterised as physical damage by Lord Wilberforce, it was purely economic loss."[7]

In *Department of the Environment v Thomas Bates and Son Ltd*,[8] the defendant **9–071** builders who built an office complex were sued by underlessees of part of the complex in respect of the cost of strengthening the pillars of a building so as to allow it to carry its design load. The House of Lords applied their decision in *Murphy* in finding that the loss suffered by the claimants was purely economic and thus irrecoverable against the builders.[9]

---

[1] See, *per* Lord Bridge at 207 and, *per* Lord Oliver at 212. See further paras 9–087 to 9–092, below.
[2] [1991] 1 A.C. 398.
[3] *per* Lord MacKay at 457H.
[4] *per* Lord Keith at 463H.
[5] *per* Lord Bridge at 475H and, *per* Lord Oliver at 489C; discussed further at para.9–093, below.
[6] *ibid.* at 466H.
[7] See also, *per* Lord Oliver at 484A.
[8] [1991] 1 A.C. 499.
[9] The precise characterisation of the economic loss may be important for limitation purposes. In *Abbott v Will Gannon & Smith Ltd* [2005] EWCA Civ 198, structural engineers who had designed allegedly ineffective remedial works argued that the claimant owner had suffered economic loss upon completion of the remedial works, since the owner had then been in possession of a defective building which was worth less than it would have been had the remedial works been effective. The Court of Appeal rejected the argument, deciding that it was bound by the pre-*Murphy* decision of the House of Lords in *Pirelli General Cable Works Ltd v Oscar Faber & Partners* [1983] 2 A.C. 1 to hold that damage occurred only when cracks subsequently appeared in the building and that such damage was physical damage. The Court also stated that if, contrary to its holding, the loss was properly characterised as economic loss, it was not suffered until the defect was discovered because only then would there be any depreciation in market value or cost of repairs.

9–072   Although they have been unwilling to accept that the categorisation is as important as the House of Lords has found it to be, the Supreme Court of Canada,[10] the High Court of Australia[11] and the Privy Council (on a New Zealand appeal)[12] have all made it clear that they accept that the House of Lords was correct to categorise loss claimed by a subsequent purchaser in respect of defects in a structure as economic loss.

(ii) *Recovery by Third Parties in respect of Personal Injury and Damage to "Other Property"*

9–073   **Personal injury.** It has long been held that architects and other construction professionals owe a duty of care not to cause personal injury to those whom they could reasonably foresee might be injured as a result of their negligence.[13] Thus in *Clay v AJ Crump & Sons Ltd*[14] the employer requested demolition contractors to leave a wall standing as protection against intruders. The architect promised the employer to look into the matter and inquired of the demolition contractors whether it was safe to leave the wall standing. They replied that it was, relying on the advice of a foreman. Subsequently the architect visited the site but never inspected the wall, which was left standing in a *dangerous* condition. When the building contractors came on site their managing director cursorily examined the wall but failed to appreciate its condition. The wall collapsed, injuring the claimant, a labourer employed by the building contractors. The Court of Appeal held that the architect, demolition contractors and building contractors owed a duty of care and were liable to the claimant. Responsibility was apportioned 42 per cent to the architect, 38 per cent to the demolition contractors and 20 per cent to the building contractors. The case was argued and resolved upon a general level, the main issues being whether the claimant was within the contemplation of the architect and whether the examination by building contractors absolved the architect from his duty to the claimant. The court reached its result as a result of the application of the principles in *Donoghue v Stevenson*[15] Ormerod L.J. stated[16]:

---

[10] See *Winnipeg Condominium Corp v Bird Construction Co* (1995) 74 B.L.R. 1; (1995) 121 D.L.R. (4th) 193 (Supreme Court of Canada); *Ingles v Tutkaluk Construction Ltd* [2000] 1 S.C.R. 298; (2001) 17 Const. L.J. 540 *sub nom. Ingles v City of Toronto*.

[11] See *Bryan v Maloney* (1995) 74 B.L.R. 35 (High Court of Australia) but note that the finding in *Bryan* that the purchaser was entitled to recover her economic loss from the careless builder may be confined to claims by residential purchasers: see *Woolcock Street Investments v DG Pty Ltd* [2005] B.L.R. 92 (High Court of Australia), considered further at para.9–115, below.

[12] See *Invercargill CC v Hamlin* [1996] A.C. 624 (Lord Lloyd for the Privy Council said, "Once it is appreciated that the loss in respect of which the claimant in the present case is suing is loss to his pocket, and not for physical damage to the house or foundations, then most, if not all the difficulties surrounding the limitation question fall away. The claimant's loss occurs when the market value of the house is depreciated by reason of the defective foundations and not before. If he resells the house at full value before the defect is discovered, he has suffered no loss. Thus in the common case the occurrence of the loss and the discovery of the loss will coincide.").

[13] See, for example, *Murphy v Brentwood DC* [1991] 1 A.C. 398 at 487, *per* Lord Oliver; and *Mobil Oil Hong Kong Ltd v Hong Kong United Dockyards Ltd (The Hu Lien)* [1991] 1 Lloyd's Rep. 309 at 329, *per* Lord Brandon.

[14] [1964] 1 Q.B. 533, CA.

[15] [1932] A.C. 562, HL.

[16] *ibid.* at 557.

"The architect, by reason of his contractual arrangement with the building owner, was charged with the duty of preparing the necessary plans and making arrangements for the manner in which the work should be done. This involved taking precautions or giving instructions for them to be taken so that the work could be done with safety. It must have been in the contemplation of the architect that builders would go on the site as the whole object of the work was to erect buildings there. It would seem impossible to contend that the plaintiff would not be affected by the decisions and plans drawn up by the architect."[17]

The decision in *Clay* was considered by the Court of Appeal in *Perrett v Collins*,[18] where the defendants had certified as airworthy an aircraft which later crashed and injured the claimant, a passenger. The submission that the defendants owed no duty of care to the claimant was rejected. Hobhouse L.J. said[19]:

" . . . it has never been a requirement of the law of the tort of negligence that there be a particular antecedent relationship between the defendant and the plaintiff other than one that the plaintiff belongs to a class which the defendant contemplates or should contemplate would be affected by his conduct. Nor has it been a requirement that the defendant should inflict the injury upon the claimant. . . . In cases of personal injury, it suffices that the activity of the defendant has given rise to the situation which has caused the injury to the plaintiff. Where the defendant is involved in an activity which, if he is not careful, will create a foreseeable risk of personal injury to others, the defendant owes a duty of care to those others to act reasonably having regard to the existence of that risk. . . .

and, later[20]:

"Where the plaintiff belongs to a class which either is or ought to be within the contemplation of the defendant and the defendant by reason of his involvement in an activity which gives him a measure of control over and responsibility for a situation which, if dangerous, will be liable to injure the plaintiff, the defendant is liable if as a result of his unreasonable lack of care he causes a situation to exist which does in fact cause the plaintiff injury."

There are relatively few cases concerning design defects which have caused **9–074** physical injuries to persons after completion of the works. Provided that injury is foreseeable, personal injuries caused by such defects will give rise to an actionable duty of care. In *Eckersley v Binnie Partners*,[21] the defendants were consulting engineers who had been employed by a water authority to design and supervise the construction of a water tunnel and associated valve house. They were found liable in negligence to 31 claimants who were, or were representatives of, members of a visiting party who were injured or killed in an explosion at the valve house caused by the ignition of methane gas. Neither at first instance nor on appeal was there any dispute that the consulting engineers owed a duty of

---

[17] See also *Florida Hotels Pty Ltd v Mayo* (1965) 113 C.L.R. 588. The majority in the High Court of Australia held that an architect owed a duty of care in supervising building works to an injured labourer employed by the employer who engaged no main contractor but employed his own tradesmen and labourers. This case is discussed further at paras 9–242 and 9–250, below.
[18] [1998] 2 Lloyd's Rep. 255.
[19] *ibid.* at 261.
[20] *ibid.* at 262.
[21] (1988) 18 Con. L.R. 1.

care, although there was considerable dispute as to whether the presence of methane gas was reasonably foreseeable.[22] In *Targett v Torfaen BC*[23] the Court of Appeal held that a local authority that had designed and built a council house was liable to a tenant who had been injured as a result of the negligent failure to provide a handrail or adequate lighting, notwithstanding the claimant's knowledge of the defects that had caused his injuries. The Court refused to accede to the defendant's argument that the effect of *Murphy v Brentwood DC*[24] was that the local authority was not liable for injuries caused by patent defects. Both Leggatt L.J.[25] and Sir Donald Nicholls V.C.[26] emphasised that the essential question was whether it was reasonable for a claimant to avoid a danger once he was aware of the same. On the facts of the case a weekly tenant was in no position to remedy the dangerous situation and the council was therefore liable, although a deduction of 25 per cent was appropriate for the claimant's contributory negligence in failing to look where he was going.[27] In *Berwick v Wickens Holdings Ltd*,[28] injury was caused many years after completion of the defective building. The claimant's husband was an employee of a building contractor (John Lay) which was engaged to refurbish a 25-year-old building. He was killed when the building collapsed. The building was originally constructed by another contractor (Wickens), which had added two floors to an existing single-storey building. The claimant sued Wickens, John Lay and the structural engineer retained by John Lay to assess the structural stability of the building. The expert witnesses who gave evidence at trial agreed that the method of construction adopted by Wickens was "so remote from acceptable building practice as to be beyond reasonable expectation". The judge held that Wickens was in breach of its duty of care to the claimant's husband, but that neither John Lay nor the structural engineers were liable. Wickens had created a building which was at risk of collapse in the event of any interference with its structure, but with no outward signs that this was so: the building was a trap and the collapse was caused by the trap being sprung in a way which was foreseeable by Wickens. John Lay and its structural engineers also owed a duty of care to avoid causing personal injury to the claimant's husband, but neither was in breach of that

---

[22] As to which see para.9–285, below.

[23] [1992] 3 All E.R. 27.

[24] [1991] 1 A.C. 398.

[25] [1992] 3 All E.R. 27, 36.

[26] *ibid.* at 37.

[27] For further examples of cases where a duty of care to avoid personal injury has been held to exist in respect of building professionals see: *Driver v William Willett (Contractors) Ltd* [1969] 1 All E.R. 665 (engineers employed by building contractors as consulting safety and inspecting engineers held to owe a duty of care to the claimant, a labourer employed by the contractors, who was injured by the collapse of a scaffold board from a hoist. The contractors were also held liable and responsibility was apportioned in the ratio of 40 per cent to the contractors and 60 per cent to the engineers); *Canberra Formwork Pty Ltd v Civil & Civic Ltd* (1982) 41 A.C.T.R. 1 (site engineer employed by a building contractor liable for the death of a workman for failing to take reasonable steps to prevent the use of a dangerous formwork box on site); *Voli v Inglewood Shire Council* [1963] A.L.R. 657 (defendant architect liable to claimant injured by collapse of a stage in a public hall designed by the architect)—see further para.9–123, below; *cf. Introvigne v Commonwealth of Australia* (1980) 32 A.L.R. 251 (defendant architect not liable to claimant schoolboy who had swung on a flagpole designed by the architect, as there was no duty to guard against schoolboy abuses).

[28] Unreported, October 1, 2000, Bell J.

duty.[29] John Lay was entitled to rely upon the structural engineers' advice as to the safety of the building and the engineers had carried out proper investigations before giving that advice. The collapse of the building was not foreseeable upon the information reasonably available to them.

Damage to other property. Although it might be possible for the law to impose a duty of care only in respect of personal injuries, it is generally accepted that a construction professional will owe a duty not to cause physical damage to property other than that in respect of which he is engaged. Thus in *North West Water Authority v Binnie Partners*,[30] there was no argument that the defendant engineers who had been found liable for the personal injury caused to the claimants in *Eckersley v Binnie Partners*[31] owed a different duty to the water authority in respect of damage suffered to its property. Drake J. found that there was no practical difference between the issues that the defendant wished to raise in the second case from those that it had raised in the first case. In *Nitrigin Eireann Teoranta v Inco Alloys Ltd*,[32] May J., on the hearing of preliminary issues, found that no cause of action had arisen when a pipe supplied by specialist pipe-makers to a building owner cracked and was repaired as the cost of repair amounted to irrecoverable economic loss. However he found the pipe-makers liable for the losses caused by a subsequent explosion when the pipe cracked again a year later causing damage to the surrounding plant, on the basis that such damage amounted to damage to other property and was recoverable. His finding was based on the assumption that it was reasonable for the claimant not to discover (and thus repair) the cause of cracking when it first occurred. In the light of *Targett*,[33] this finding appears correct. However the judge's further statement, obiter,[34] that even if the claimant ought reasonably to have diagnosed the cause of the cracking on the first occasion, this would not have affected the accrual of a cause of action on the second, appears inconsistent with the reasoning in *Targett*.

Where the defective construction causes damage to other parts of the same property, the damage is unlikely to be characterised as damage to "other property".[35] In *Bellefield Computer Services Ltd v E Turner & Sons Ltd*,[36] the subsequent purchaser of a diary processing plant claimed damages in tort against the builder of the plant for damage caused when fire spread from the storage area to the rest of the plant. The storage area was designed to be separated from the rest of the plant by an internal fire-stop compartment wall. The builder had failed

9–075

9–076

---

[29] Bell J. further held that there was no material difference between John Lay's duty at common law and its statutory duty under reg.50(2) of the Construction (General Provisions) Regulations 1961, which was also subject to the requirement that harm be foreseeable.

[30] (1989) 30 Con. L.R. 136. For a further example, see *Offer-Hoar v Larkstore Ltd* [2005] EWHC 2742, where the developer and a geo-technical engineer involved in the development of a site were held to owe a duty of care to the owners of neighbouring properties damaged as a result of excavations at the site. There was no appeal on this point: [2006] EWCA Civ 1079.

[31] (1988) 18 Con. L.R. 1. See para.9–074, above.

[32] [1992] 1 W.L.R. 498. See also A. McGee, "Back to Pirelli" (1992) 108 L.Q.R. 364, where this decision is discussed.

[33] See para.9–074, above.

[34] *ibid.* at 506.

[35] See also the discussion of the "complex structure theory" at paras 9–087 to 9–092, below.

[36] [2000] B.L.R. 97, CA.

to construct the wall to full height, with the result that fire was able to pass over the top of the wall. On a trial of preliminary issues, Bell J. held that the builder owed a duty of care to the claimant in respect of damage to his plant, equipment, stock and other chattels in the areas of the building outside the storage area. The principle discussed in this section applied: damage to those items was a foreseeable result of the builder's failure properly to construct the wall and they were property distinct from the building itself. By contrast, the judge held that no duty of care was owed in relation to damage to the fabric of the building outside the storage area, and losses consequential upon such damage. The Court of Appeal upheld the judge's decision on all points. The claimant argued that the damage caused to the fabric of the building outside the storage area was physical damage rather than economic loss, because the defective wall itself did not cause any damage in the way that defective foundations cause cracking in the structures which they support. The wall merely created a situation in which the fire was able to cause more damage than it otherwise would. The Court of Appeal rejected this argument, approving this statement from the judgment of Bell J.[37]:

> " . . . there is no conceptual or qualitative difference (and certainly none which I feel able to formulate) between the case of defective foundations which fail to cope with shrinkage or heave in the subsoil and to support the building, resulting in cracked walls and pipes, and the case of a defective roof which fails to cope with and to keep out water, and the case of the defective fire stop wall which fails to cope with and to contain fire which goes on to injure other parts of the building. If the resulting injury to the fabric of the building itself is to be seen as purely economic loss in the first two of those cases, it must, in my view, be seen as economic loss in the third."

The Court also rejected as artificial the claimant's argument that the parts of the dairy which were separated from the storage area by the defective wall should be regarded as "other property" because those parts were put to different uses.

9–077   The House of Lords confirmed in *Murphy v Brentwood DC*[38] that a builder owes to a subsequent occupier of a property which he has built a duty of care in tort to avoid causing personal injury or damage to other property of the occupier. The question whether a construction professional owes the same duty to a subsequent occupier arose for decision in *Baxall Securities Ltd v Sheard Walshaw Partnership*.[39] The defendants were architects who had been engaged by a developer for the design and construction of a warehouse. The claimant was a lessee of the warehouse and used it to store electrical goods. Due to the inability of the siphonic roof drainage system to cope with rainfall, rainwater flooded through the roof of the warehouse on two occasions, damaging the claimant's goods. The claimant sued in tort, alleging that the defendants had negligently failed to see that adequate overflows were installed and to design a roof drainage system which was able to cope with the rainfall levels which ought to have been anticipated. The defendants argued that they owed no duty of care in tort to the claimant because it was a subsequent occupier. Alternatively, they argued that no

---

[37] [2000] B.L.R. 97 at 108.
[38] [1991] 1 A.C. 398.
[39] [2001] P.N.L.R. 256. Such a duty had been held to exist by Judge Lewis Q.C. in *Tesco v Norman Hitchcox Partnership* (1998) 56 Con. L.R. 42, but the judge preferred to consider the matter afresh and from first principles.

such duty arose in relation to the lack of overflows because the claimant ought reasonably to have discovered that defect before taking the lease.

Judge Bowsher Q.C. held that since, following *Murphy*, a builder owes a duty **9–078** of care to avoid physical damage to a subsequent occupier in appropriate circumstances, there was no reason why an architect should not owe the same duty in appropriate circumstances. However, the reasoning deployed in *Donoghue v Stevenson* and in *Murphy* meant that there would be no duty where there was a reasonable possibility of inspection by the subsequent occupier.[40] The possibility of inspection meant that there would not be a sufficiently proximate relationship between the parties to justify the imposition of a duty; alternatively, it would not be just, fair and reasonable to impose a duty since the defendant's liability would then depend upon the assiduity of the claimant's advisers. The claimant did have a reasonable opportunity to inspect the building before entering the lease; it would be normal for a prospective tenant to have the building inspected by a surveyor and that is what the claimant had done. It was irrelevant that the claimant's surveyor did not discover the defects. Accordingly, the judge held, the defendants owed no duty to the claimant in respect of the lack of overflows. However, the defendants did owe a duty in respect of damage attributable to the use of an inadequate design rainfall rate since neither the claimant nor its surveyor could reasonably have been expected to discover that the drainage system was under-designed in that way. The judge's reasoning and decision on the issues of duty were upheld by the Court of Appeal.[41] This decision is an important reminder that the *Donoghue v Stevenson* duty to avoid causing physical harm is subject to the "intermediate examination" exception which is commonly discussed in relation to the liability of a manufacturer to a consumer for a dangerously defective product, but less commonly considered in building cases. Since it will be reasonable to expect that most subsequent occupiers of buildings will carry out some form of inspection before taking up occupation, the exception is likely to prove important in the defence of claims against construction professionals for negligently causing physical harm.[42] Necessarily, the duty of care exists only in respect of latent defects: a defect is not latent if it is reasonably discoverable by a subsequent occupier with the benefit of such skilled third party advice as he might be expected to obtain before going into occupation.

Forbes J. gave judgment in the contribution proceedings in *Bellefield Com-* **9–079** *puter Services Ltd v E Turner and Sons Ltd*[43] shortly before the Court of Appeal delivered its decision in *Baxall*. Forbes J. followed the reasoning of Judge Bowsher Q.C. in *Baxall*. He held that architects engaged by a design and build contractor owed a duty of care in tort to a subsequent occupier of the building in respect of latent defects because there had been no reasonable possibility that the claimant would carry out an inspection which was likely to discover those defects

---

[40] [2001] P.N.L.R. 256 at 275–276, quoting the speech of Lord Atkin in *Donoghue v Stevenson* at 580–582, and at 280–281, quoting the speech of Lord Keith in *Murphy* at 464.

[41] [2002] EWCA Civ 9. This decision is the subject of an article by I. N. Duncan Wallace, "Lucky Architects: Snail in an Opaque Bottle?" (2003) 119 L.Q.R. 17.

[42] But, as was recognised in *Baxall*, there are cases in which an occupier who discovers a defect is unable to rectify the defect or move from the property; in such cases, that person is not deprived of a remedy: *Targett v Torfaen BC* [1992] 3 All E.R. 27, discussed at para.9–074, above.

[43] Unreported, November 9, 2001. For the facts, see para.9–119, below.

before it went into occupation. Again, the judge's findings and reasoning were upheld on appeal.[44] Potter L.J. (with whom May L.J. and Sir Anthony Evans agreed) identified the following four principles concerning the existence and scope of an architect's duty to a subsequent owner or occupier in respect of defects in a structure which cause physical damage to other property:

(1) An architect may, in appropriate circumstances, owe a duty of care in tort and be liable to a subsequent occupier of the building which the architect has designed and/or the construction of which he has supervised in respect of latent defects in the building of which there is no reasonable possibility of inspection.

(2) The question whether a particular defect in a building comes within the scope of an architect's duty of care to a subsequent occupier will depend upon the original design and/or supervisory obligations of the architect in question. The architect will not owe a duty of care in respect of defects for which he never had any design or supervisory responsibility in the first place.

(3) If a dangerous defect arises as the result of a negligent omission on the part of the architect, he cannot excuse himself from liability on the grounds that he delegated the duty of design of the relevant part of the building works, unless he obtains the permission of his employer to do so.

(4) The detailed duties of an architect in relation to his design function depend upon the application of the general principles above stated to the particular facts of the case, including any special terms agreed. The precise ambit of such duties will usually depend upon expert evidence from members of the profession as to what a competent, experienced architect would do in the circumstances.

9–080   The question whether a construction professional owed a duty of care to a subsequent owner came before the court again in *Sahib Foods Ltd v Paskin Kyriades Sands*.[45] A fire in a food production factory spread beyond the room in which it ignited because combustible panels had been used to line that room. The subsequent purchaser of the factory claimed damages from the architects who designed the refurbishment of the factory. Applying the principles identified in *Baxall* and *Bellefield*, Judge Bowsher Q.C. held that the architects owed a duty of care to the purchaser in respect of latent defects in the factory of which there had been no reasonable possibility of an inspection. The purchaser's claim failed, however, because there was no evidence to suggest that the use of the combustible panels was a defect which would not have been revealed by a pre-purchase survey.[46]

9–081   It should be noted that the loss claimed in *Baxall*, *Bellefield* and *Sahib* was physical damage to property. In *Bellefield*, May L.J. expressly reserved for future consideration the question whether or to what extent the scope of an architect's

---

[44] [2002] EWCA Civ 1823.
[45] [2003] EWHC 142, TCC.
[46] This point was not the subject of the appeal: [2003] EWCA Civ 1832.

duty of care to a subsequent owner or occupier extended to loss which was not associated with physical damage.[47]

(iii) *The General Exclusionary Rule adopted in England with regard to the Recovery of Economic Loss*

The core of the modern English exclusionary rule concerning the recovery of economic loss is to be found in three decisions of the House of Lords: *D & F Estates Ltd v Church Commissioners for England*[48]; *Murphy v Brentwood DC*[49]; and *Department of the Environment v Thomas Bates and Son.*[50] The three decisions rely on three main arguments: (a) that the recovery of "pure" economic loss goes beyond existing decisions based upon the *Donoghue v Stevenson*[51] principle; (b) that there are policy reasons for not allowing such an extension; and (c) that the courts should not intervene in an area where Parliament has legislated (by the Defective Premises Act 1972). **9–082**

The first two arguments were foreshadowed in the dissenting speech of Lord Brandon in *Junior Books Ltd v Veitchi Co Ltd*[52]: **9–083**

"My Lords, it appears to me clear beyond doubt that, there being no contractual relationship between the respondents and the appellants in the present case, the foundation, and the only foundation, for the existence of a duty of care owed by the defenders to the pursuers, is the principle laid down in the decision of your Lordships' House in *Donoghue v Stevenson* [1932] A.C. 562. The actual decision in that case related only to the duty owed by a manufacturer of goods to their ultimate user or consumer, and can be summarised in this way: a person who manufactures goods which he intends to be used or consumed by others, is under a duty to exercise such reasonable care in their manufacture as to ensure that they can be used or consumed in the manner intended without causing physical damage to persons or their property. While that was the actual decision in *Donoghue v Stevenson*, it was based on a much wider principle embodied in passages in the speech of Lord Atkin, which have been quoted so often that I do not find it necessary to quote them again here. Put shortly, that wider principle is that, when a person can or ought to appreciate that a careless act or omission on his part may result in physical injury to other persons or their property, he owes a duty to all such persons to exercise reasonable care to avoid such careless act or omission. It is, however, of fundamental importance to observe that the duty of care laid down in *Donoghue v Stevenson* was based on the existence of a danger of physical injury to persons or their property. That this is so, is clear from the observations made by Lord Atkin at pp.581–582 with regard to the statements of law of Brett M.R. in *Heaven v Pender* (1883) 11 Q.B.D. 503, 509. It has further, until the present case, never been doubted, so far as I know, that the relevant property for the purpose of the wider principle on which the decision in *Donoghue v Stevenson* was based, was property other than the very property which gave rise to the danger of physical damage concerned . . . .

. . . There are two important considerations which ought to limit the scope of the duty of care which it is common ground was owed by the appellants to the respondents on the assumed facts of the present case. The first consideration is that, in *Donoghue v Stevenson* itself and in all the numerous cases in which the principle of that decision has

---

[47] The existing authorities on this question are discussed at paras 9–100 to 9–102, below.
[48] [1989] A.C. 177.
[49] [1991] 1 A.C. 398.
[50] [1991] 1 A.C. 490. The facts of each of the cases are set out in paras 9–069 to 9–071, above.
[51] [1932] A.C.562, HL.
[52] [1983] 1 A.C. 520 at 549 and 550–551.

been applied to different but analogous factual situations, it has always been either stated expressly, or taken for granted, that an essential ingredient in the cause of action relied on was the existence of danger, or the threat of danger of physical damage to persons or their property, excluding for this purpose the very piece of property from the defective condition of which such danger, or threat of danger, arises. To dispense with that essential ingredient in a cause of action of the kind concerned in the present case would, in my view, involve a radical departure from long-established authority. The second consideration is that there is no sound policy reason for substituting the wider scope of the duty of care put forward for the respondents for the more restricted scope of such duty put forward by the appellants. The effect of accepting the respondents' contention with regard to the scope of the duty of care involved would be, in substance, to create, as between two persons who are not in any contractual relationship with each other, obligations of one of those two persons to the other which are only really appropriate as between persons who do have such a relationship between them. In the case of a manufacturer or distributor of goods, the position would be that he warranted to the ultimate user or consumer of such goods that they were as well designed, as merchantable and as fit for their contemplated purpose as the exercise of reasonable care could make them. In the case of sub-contractors such as those concerned in the present case, the position would be that they warranted to the building owner that the flooring, when laid, would be as well designed, as free from defects of any kind and as fit for its contemplated purpose as the exercise of reasonable care could make it. In my view, the imposition of warranties of this kind on one person in favour of another, when there is no contractual relationship between them, is contrary to any sound policy requirement. It is, I think, just worthwhile to consider the difficulties which would arise if the wider scope of the duty of care put forward by the respondents were accepted. In any case where complaint was made by an ultimate consumer that a product made by some persons with whom he himself had no contract was defective, by what standard or standards of quality would the question of defectiveness fall to be decided? In the case of goods bought from a retailer, it could hardly be the standard prescribed by the contract between the retailer and the wholesaler, or between the wholesaler and the distributor, or between the distributor and the manufacturer, for the terms of such contracts would not even be known to the ultimate buyer. In the case of sub-contractors such as the appellants in the present case, it could hardly be the standard prescribed by the contract between the sub-contractors and the main contractors, for, although the building owner probably be aware of those terms, he could not, since he was not a party to such contract, rely on any standard or standards prescribed in it. It follows that the question by what standard or standards alleged defects in a product complained of by its ultimate user or consumer are to be judged remains entirely at large and cannot be given any just or satisfactory answer."

Lord Brandon's speech received express approval in *D & F Estates* from Lord Bridge,[53] with whom all of the other law lords agreed, and from Lord Oliver[54] who gave the only other substantive speech. The general rule, therefore, is that a local authority, a contractor and a construction professional do not owe a duty of care in tort to avoid causing pure economic loss to persons with whom they have no contract.

9–084   The importance of the Defective Premises Act 1972 and the preceding Law Commission Report in setting out and limiting the scope of duties owed to

---

[53] [1989] A.C. 177 at 202.
[54] *ibid.* at 215.

subsequent purchasers was emphasised by Lord Bridge in *D & F Estates*,[55] and by all five law lords who gave substantive speeches in *Murphy*.[56] Lord Mackay[57] considered that there were two options open to the House of Lords: either the overruling of *Anns* or a removal of the qualifications in *Anns* (i.e. that a cause of action should arise only when a defect became dangerous). In deciding which of the options should be taken, he made express reference to the Defective Premises Act before deciding that it would not be a proper exercise of the judicial function to create a large new area of common law liability.[58] In the light of: (a) the fact that the Defective Premises Act does not apply in Scotland or Northern Ireland[59]; and (b) the subsequent decision of the Privy Council in *Invercargill v Hamlin*[60] to the effect that the New Zealand courts were justified in finding that, in the absence of an equivalent statute to the Defective Premises Act, social conditions required the imposition of extensive common law duties of the sort contemplated by Lord Mackay, there was created the intriguing possibility of the House of Lords deciding on a Scottish or Northern Irish appeal, that the law of Scotland or Northern Ireland should be the same as that of New Zealand rather than England.[61]

In Scotland, at least, that possibility has not materialised. In *Strathford East* **9–085** *Kilbride Ltd v HLM Design Ltd*,[62] Lord MacLean in the Outer House of the Court of Session held that architects employed by a landlord owed no duty to the tenants to avoid causing them economic loss in the absence of any assumption of responsibility by the architect to the tenants. He thus followed *Murphy* in preference to numerous Commonwealth decisions which had continued to follow *Anns* and had declined to adopt *Murphy*.[63]

(iv) *The English Exceptions to the General Exclusionary Rule*

The House of Lords has contemplated three situations in which claimants may **9–086** seek to recover "pure" economic loss against construction professionals with whom they have no contract: (i) the application of the "complex structure theory"; (ii) expenditure necessary to avoid liability to third parties; and (iii) the application of the *Hedley Byrne* or reliance principle. However, as explained below, the first of these "exceptions" to the general exclusionary rule has not matured.

---

[55] [1989] A.C. 177 at 208.
[56] [1991] 1 A.C. 398, *per* Lord Mackay at 457, Lord Keith at 472, Lord Bridge at 480, Lord Oliver at 491 and Lord Jauncey at 498.
[57] *ibid.* at 457.
[58] It is arguable, however, that the limitations on the availability of a remedy under the Defective Premises Act 1972 (see paras 9–041 to 9–047, above) are such that reliance upon this statute as providing a remedy for third parties in all cases where a remedy might be thought appropriate is unjustified.
[59] See s.7(3) of the Act.
[60] [1996] A.C. 624. See further para.9–116, below.
[61] See also the note "A prophet not rejected in his own land" by J. M. Thompson in (1994) 110 L.Q.R. 361 and the cases there cited. Thompson points out that *Junior Books* is followed in Scotland and is not treated as lacking authority in the way that it is in England.
[62] 1997 S.C.L.R. 877.
[63] The Commonwealth decisions are discussed further at paras 9–112 to 9–117, below.

9–087   **The complex structure theory.** The complex structure theory was first raised in *D & F Estates* by Lords Bridge[64] and Oliver.[65] Lord Bridge stated:

> "However, I can see that it may well be arguable that in the case of complex structures, as indeed possibly in the case of complex chattels, one element of the structure should be regarded for the purpose of the application of the principles under discussion as distinct from another element, so that damage to one part of the structure caused by a hidden defect in another part may qualify to be treated as damage to 'other property', and whether the argument should prevail may depend on the circumstances of the case."

The theory was discussed again in *Murphy*. Lord Oliver[66] contented himself with making it clear that he had not put forward the theory with any enthusiasm. Each of the other law lords plainly thought that the theory might apply in the future although they gave differing examples of its possible application.[67]

9–088   It is difficult to find a policy justification for the existence of the complex structure theory. The theory entails that the cost of repairing damage to a building caused by the explosion of a boiler would be treated as recoverable physical damage against a heating engineer engaged solely in relation to the installation of a boiler one month after the construction of a house but as irrecoverable economic loss against an engineer engaged in relation to the construction of the whole of the house. Such a distinction surely cannot be justified, as it would mean that the greater the responsibility undertaken, the smaller the subsequent liability and vice versa.

9–089   Although the complex structure theory was applied at first instance in *Jacobs v Morton & Partners*,[68] there is now a considerable body of English case law which suggests that the complex structure theory is not a viable route to recovery in respect of pure economic loss. In *Ernst & Whinney v Willard Engineering (Dagenham) Ltd*,[69] a case decided prior to *Murphy*, the claimant assignees of the lease of an office building discovered defective air conditioning ductwork. They sued in negligence two sub-contractors who had originally installed the ductwork together with the consulting mechanical and electrical engineers. On the hearing of a preliminary issue, the judge held that no duty of care was owed by the engineers or the sub-contractors. His judgment paid deference to the then exist-ing authority of *Anns* and the primary basis for it was that it would be neither just nor reasonable to impose liability on the defendants. However, he was also asked to find whether the defects alleged amounted to physical damage. He said[70]:

> "In my view, the answer is 'No.' I cannot think that a defect in a constituent part of a building can be regarded as constituting physical damage to the building of which it forms part. I find it even more difficult to accede to the notion that the purchaser of a building comprising such a defect can make such an assertion in respect of the building he bought."

---

[64] [1989] A.C. 177 at 207.
[65] *ibid.* at 213.
[66] [1991] 1 A.C. 398 at 484D.
[67] *ibid., per* Lord Keith at 470H, *per* Lord Bridge at 478E and *per* Lord Jauncey at 497C.
[68] (1994) 72 B.L.R. 92.
[69] (1987) 40 B.L.R. 67.
[70] *ibid.* at 81.

In *Warner v Basildon Development Corp*,[71] a decision given the day before the   **9–090**
decision in *Murphy*, the purchaser of a house sought to rely on the complex
structure theory in his claim in tort against the contractor responsible for building
the foundations of the house. The Court of Appeal held that it was not open to
it to adopt the theory of complex structures (or complex chattels) as an adjunct
to the principle of *Donoghue v Stevenson* as applied to building operations, since
the theory formed no part of the principles set out in *DF Estates*.[72] In *Tesco v
Norman Hitchcox Partnership*,[73] Judge Esyr Lewis Q.C. rejected an attempt to
apply the complex structure theory in respect of a supermarket so as to allow
recovery for damage to the supermarket as a result of the defective design of the
fire inhibition structures within the building. In *Tunnel Refineries v Bryan
Donkin*,[74] Mr Recorder Susman Q.C. accepted a submission that he was bound
by the decision of the Court of Appeal in *Warner* to find that there was no room
for the complex structure theory in English law.

The Court of Appeal again considered a submission based upon the complex   **9–091**
structure theory in *Bellefield Computer Services Ltd v E Turner & Sons Ltd*.[75]
The claimant argued that it was entitled to recover for damage caused to parts of
the dairy other than the storage area which was bounded by the inadequately
constructed fire-stop wall because those parts of the building were put to different
uses from the storage area. The argument was rejected and the decision of Bell
J. at first instance was upheld, albeit without comment upon the status of the
complex structure theory as such. Schiemann L.J. pointed out that it was unrealistic to regard parts of the diary as separate properties just because different parts
were put to different uses: the dairy was constructed as one unit, marketed as a
unit, bought for use as a unit and used by the claimant as a unit.[76]

In *Payne v John Setchell Ltd*,[77] having considered the speeches of the various   **9–092**
members of the House of Lords in *DF Estates* and *Murphy*, HHJ Lloyd Q.C. held
that the complex structure theory was no longer tenable. That case concerned two
cottages which were built off the same foundation slab. The defendant was
responsible for the design of the foundations. Each of the claimants was a
subsequent purchaser of one of the cottages. They argued that, because the
foundations were inadequate, each of the cottages constituted a danger to the
adjacent cottage. They claimed an indemnity against their liabilities to each other
to make their respective properties safe. They sought to rely upon the complex
structure theory, arguing that the foundation slab and each of the cottages were
"other property" so far as the other cottage was concerned. The judge rejected
the complex structure theory and the argument. He held that in applying the
concept of "other property", it was necessary to be realistic. It would be

---

[71] (1991) 7 Const. L.J. 146.
[72] [1989] 1 A.C. 177 and see para.9–069, above.
[73] (1997) 56 Con. L.R. 42.
[74] (1998) C.I.L.L. 1392.
[75] [2000] B.L.R 97, CA. For the facts, see para.9–076, above. For discussion, see the commentary by
I. N. Duncan Wallace Q.C., "*Donoghue v Stevenson* and "complex structure": *Anns* revisted?"
[2000] 116 L.Q.R. 530.
[76] *ibid.* at 100.
[77] [2002] P.N.L.R. 7. For the facts, see para.9–057, above.

completely unrealistic to treat the part of the foundation slab under one cottage as if it were separate from the part under the other cottage.[78]

9–093   **Expenditure necessary to avoid liability to third parties.** In *Murphy*, Lord Bridge suggested the following as a possible exceptional case wherein economic loss might be recoverable[79]:

> " . . . if a building stands so close to the boundary of the building owner's land that after discovery of the dangerous defect it remains a potential source of injury to person or property on the neighbouring land or on the highway, the building owner ought, in principle, to be entitled to recover in tort from the negligent builder the cost of obviating the danger, whether by repair or demolition, so far as that cost is necessarily incurred in order to protect himself from potential liability to third parties."

Lord Oliver[80] (with whom Lord Ackner agreed, whilst also agreeing with Lord Bridge) expressly deferred consideration of whether such a qualification existed whilst expressing his doubt as to its basis. If Lord Bridge is correct it would seem that the owner of a house in the centre of a city may be able to claim the cost of repairing the house so as to prevent it collapsing into a busy highway whilst the owner of an identical property set in its own land will not be able to recover. The exception was applied in *Morse v Barrett (Leeds) Ltd*.[81] The claimants, who were largely subsequent purchasers of houses, joined together to re-build an old wall which had been rendered dangerous by the action of the defendant, the original builder of the houses. The judge found that the claim fell squarely within Lord Bridge's suggested qualification.[82] However in *George Fischer Holding Ltd v Multi Design Consultants Ltd*,[83] Judge Hicks Q.C. refused to follow *Morse*. Having found that a design sub-contractor owed a collateral contractual duty to the claimant, the judge went on to consider what would have been the position had he been wrong. In that case, he considered the costs of averting a danger to the public would not have been recoverable since the statements of Lords Bridge and Oliver amounted only to minority dicta and were contrary to the decision of the majority in *Murphy*.

9–094   **The *Hedley Byrne* or reliance principle.** Both Lord Oliver in *D & F Estates*[84] and Lords Bridge and Keith in *Murphy*[85] drew attention to the possibility that economic loss would be recoverable by the application of the decision of the

---

[78] [2002] P.N.L.R. 7 at para.39.
[79] [1991] 1 A.C. at 475F.
[80] *ibid.* at 489C.
[81] (1993) 9 Const. L.J. 158, Ch.D.
[82] In an article, "Has construction law been taken to the wreckers?" (1991) 65 A.L.J. 270, 274, P. Gerber and R. Jackson point out that although a person may be obliged, if he is not to be liable in nuisance, to remedy a mischief on his own land once he is aware of the same, it does not follow that he is entitled to recover the cost of remedy from the author of the mischief. *cf. Privest Properties Ltd v Foundation Co of Canada Ltd* (1995) 128 D.L.R. (4th) 577 where Drost J. in the British Columbia Supreme Court found that the defendant architects would have been liable to the claimant owners of a building for the cost of removing negligently installed asbestos products but for his finding that the products did not constitute a danger to the health and safety of the occupants of the building. The British Columbia Court of Appeal dismissed the claimant's appeal: (1997) 143 D.L.R. (4th) 635.
[83] (1998) 61 Con. L.R. 85 at 109–111.
[84] [1989] A.C. 177 at 213.
[85] [1991] 1 A.C. 398 at 465 and 481.

House of Lords in *Hedley Byrne v Heller & Partners*.[86] Although that decision is typically associated with the giving of information or advice, Lord Goff in *Henderson* made clear that it extends to a broad range of circumstances in which "special skill" is exercised[87]:

"[T]he facts of *Hedley Byrne* itself . . . show that the concept of a 'special skill' must be understood broadly . . . . [T]hough *Hedley Byrne* was concerned with the provision of information and advice, the example given by Lord Devlin of the relationship between solicitor and client . . . show[s] that the principle extends beyond the provision of advice and information to include the performance of other services."

The last decade of the 20th century saw a considerable extension to the ambit of the *Hedley Byrne* principle in other areas of the law,[88] and recent decisions suggest that it is by this route that liability of construction professionals to persons other than their clients will be found to the greatest extent in the future in England.

There is, of course, no reason in principle why a construction professional **9–095** should not incur liability by a straight application of the decision in *Hedley Byrne*, namely where he makes a statement to a person who is entitled to and does rely on such statement. In *Townsend (Builders) Ltd v Cinema News and Property Management*[89] an architect wrote to the building contractors that he would be responsible for serving all notices required by building byelaws. The Court of Appeal held that he was under a duty to the contractors to serve such notices and liable in tort for damages caused by late service. Although the case was decided before *Hedley Byrne*, it is submitted that it was decided in accordance with the principles later set out by the House of Lords. Similarly the concession made in the House of Lords in *IBA v EMI and BICC*[90] is explicable on the basis of a direct application of *Hedley Byrne*. The claimant employers (IBA) engaged the first defendants (EMI) as main contractors for the design, construction and erection of a television mast and EMI in turn engaged the second defendants (BICC) as sub-contractors for design, construction and erection of the mast. There was no contract between IBA and BICC but it was conceded by the latter that they owed a duty of care to IBA, possibly because BICC gave IBA a direct assurance, in response to a specific request, that the mast would not oscillate dangerously. The assurance proved false and the mast collapsed. The House of Lords held that BICC were negligent in the design of the mast and consequently in giving the assurance and were accordingly directly liable to IBA O'Connor J. and the Court of Appeal both held that the assurance by BICC amounted to a contractual warranty but this finding was unanimously rejected by the House of Lords.[91]

---

[86] [1964] A.C. 465.

[87] [1995] 2 A.C. 145 at 178–181.

[88] See Ch.2, paras 2–044 to 2–048 and particularly the cases of *Spring v Guardian Assurance Plc* [1995] 2 A.C. 296; *Henderson v Merrett Syndicates Ltd* [1995] 2 A.C. 145; *White v Jones* [1995] 2 A.C. 207; and *Williams v Natural Life Health Foods Ltd* [1998] 1 W.L.R. 830.

[89] (1958) 20 B.L.R. 118. Donald Keating Q.C. questioned whether this case was still good law at (1992) 8 Const. L.R. 405 at 406.

[90] (1980) 14 B.L.R. 1, HL; (1979) 11 B.L.R. 29, CA.

[91] *ibid.* at 22–24 at 32, 41.

9–096   In *Machin v Adams*,[92] an architect was asked by his clients, who were in the process of selling their house to the claimant for use as a care home, to write a letter setting out the then state of alteration and refurbishment works at the house together with the amount of time necessary to complete the same. The defendant knew that the letter was to be shown to persons other than his clients, probably including the purchaser of the house. The Court of Appeal held that the defendant owed no duty of care to the claimant in respect of the letter. Simon Brown L.J. considered that the defendant would have owed a duty of care to the claimant in respect of the letter but for the fact that he understood that he would be required to return on completion of the works in order to certify the same before the completion of the sale. Because of this understanding, the defendant could not have anticipated that the claimant would take some irrevocable step based upon the letter. Morritt L.J. agreed with this reasoning but added that no duty of care would have been owed even had the defendant not intended to return for final certification. There was no identifiable harm from which the defendant assumed responsibility to guard the claimant in writing the letter: it was not a signal to her to proceed with the purchase without further enquiry. On this basis, Sir Brian Neill agreed with Morritt L.J.

9–097   No *Hedley Byrne* duty will be imposed in respect of reports or advice provided for persons other than the claimant unless the defendant was, at least, aware that his report or advice might be so used.[93] Similarly an express disclaimer will be effective to prevent a duty of care arising.[94]

---

[92] (1997) 84 B.L.R. 79. See also *Howes v Crombie* [2002] P.N.L.R. 60 (Sc. Ct. Sess.) (defendant engineer provided letter to house owner the structural integrity of the house; defendant unaware that the letter was required by the mortgage lender to a prospective purchaser; the letter was forwarded to the lender, but not to the purchaser; Lord Eassie held that the engineer owed no duty of care to the purchaser in providing the letter to the vendor).

[93] See *Rolls-Royce Power Engineering v Ricardo Consulting Engineers* [2003] EWHC 2871, TCC (defendant engineers engaged to provide design services to a wholly-owned subsidiary of the claimant; the claimant acquired the subsidiary's business to the claimant and suffered loss due to defendants' allegedly negligent design; held that the defendant owed no duty of care in tort to avoid causing economic loss to the claimant, since the defendant was unaware of the claimant's interest and the claimant had not relied upon the defendant's design); *British Columbia Ltd v HBT Agra Ltd* (1994) 120 D.L.R. (4th) 726 (British Columbia Court of Appeal) (defendant engineer, who had prepared a report for an owner of land which stated that the land was "essentially free of risk of subsidence associated with abandoned mines", did not owe a duty to a subsequent owner of part of the land who relied on the report because the defendant was not aware that his report would be supplied to the claimant or to persons in the position of the claimant); *Offer-Hoar v Larkstore Ltd* [2006] EWHC 2742 (geo-technical engineer which provided a site investigation report owed no duty of care to avoid causing economic loss to a subsequent developer of the site whose use of the report was not reasonably foreseeable. This finding was not challenged on the subsequent appeal: [2006] EWCA Civ).

[94] See, for examples: *Wolverine Tube (Canada) Inc v Noranda Metal Industries Ltd* (1995) 26 O.R. 577 (Ontario Court of Appeal) (defendant prepared environmental reports for an industrial client under a contract which provided that the reports were not be used outside the client's organisation without the defendant's permission; the reports each contained a clear disclaimer of liability to third parties; a purchaser from the defendant's client relied upon the reports; held that the disclaimers and the terms of the contract with the client were such as to prevent a duty of care from arising); *McKinlay Hendry Ltd v Tonkin Taylor Ltd* [2005] N.Z.L.R. 318 (New Zealand Court of Appeal) (an express disclaimer in the defendants' report, as well as the contractual arrangements put in place by the parties, precluded a finding that the defendants were liable for negligent misstatement in a ground investigation report which was relied upon by a party which was not their client).

The scope of a *Hedley Byrne* duty of care will be limited by the extent of the   **9–098**
claimant's foreseeable reliance upon the advice or information which the defendant provides. The case of *Lidl Properties v Clarke Bond Partnership*[95] illustrates this principle. The claimant claimed that it had purchased a site for the
development of a supermarket in reliance upon advice given to it by the defendant engineers as to the level of ground contamination at the site and the likely
cost of decontamination. At the time, the defendants were retained by developers
who intended to purchase the site, decontaminate it and sell it on to the claimant.
Even although the defendants' advice was given gratuitously, at a hastily
arranged ad hoc meeting, it was held that the defendants owed a duty of care in
respect of that advice. They were giving advice within the scope of their
expertise and experience to a party who would foreseeably rely upon it for the
purposes of making an offer to purchase the site. Accordingly, the defendants had
assumed responsibility to the claimant to advise with reasonable care and skill.
The extent of their duty was limited, however, by the purpose of the meeting,
which had been called in order that the claimant might form a view as to the
likely cost of the defendants' proposed decontamination scheme. The defendants
did not owe a duty to give a comprehensive presentation of the history and
investigation of the site. In the event, the claim was dismissed because the
defendants were not in breach of their duty and the claimant had not in fact relied
upon the defendants' advice.

The *Hedley Byrne* duty found in *Payne v John Setchell Ltd*[96] was also limited,   **9–099**
but in time. The claimants were the subsequent purchasers of cottages. The
defendant civil and structural engineer had been engaged by the vendor of the
cottages to assist in their construction. The defendant had designed raft foundations for the cottages, inspected the construction of those foundations and
certified that they were satisfactorily constructed and suitable for support of the
cottages. The claimants alleged that they had purchased the cottages in reliance
upon the defendant's certificates. On a trial of preliminary issues, Judge Lloyd
Q.C. observed that the purpose of providing the certificates was to furnish the
vendor with a document which could be used to satisfy a prospective purchaser
that the foundations had been soundly built to a satisfactory design, even
although NHBC cover was not available. The defendant intended that his certificates would be seen and relied upon by subsequent purchasers and it followed
that he owed such purchasers a duty to take care that the statements made in or
to be inferred from the certificates were reliable. The certificates were to be
regarded as statements that the design of the foundations had been prepared with
reasonable care.[97] The judge added, obiter, that the defendant's duty was not
unlimited in time. Since, for all practical purposes, the certificates were to be
treated as tantamount to NHBC cover, it was foreseeable only that they would be
regarded as valid for a period of 10 years from completion of the building
works.

---

[95] [1998] Env. L.R. 622. The opposite conclusion was reached in *McKinlay Hendry Ltd v Tonkin
Taylor Ltd* [2005] N.Z.L.R. 318 (New Zealand Court of Appeal) (engineers not liable for negligent
misstatement in a ground investigation report which was relied upon by a party other than their
client).
[96] [2002] P.N.L.R. 7.
[97] *ibid.* at para.46.

9–100   Greater difficulties can be expected to occur in deciding when construction professionals owe duties to persons other than their clients to prevent economic loss on the grounds that such persons are entitled to rely upon the professionals or are in a sufficiently close relationship that a duty of care should be imposed, even although no misleading communication is made by a professional to the claimant. In *Junior Books Ltd v Veitchi Co Ltd*,[98] nominated flooring sub-contractors were found liable to a building owner for the costs of remedying a defective floor which they had laid. In *Murphy*, Lord Bridge stated[99]:

> "There may, of course, be situations where, even in the absence of contract, there is a special relationship of proximity between builder and building owner which is sufficiently akin to contract to introduce the element of reliance so that the scope of the duty of care owed by the building to the owner is wide enough to embrace purely economic loss. The decision in *Junior Books Ltd v Veitchi Co Ltd* can, I believe, only be understood on this basis."[1]

As has been pointed out on many occasions,[2] such an explanation for the decision in *Junior Books* is difficult to justify. The building owner in *Junior Books* chose to enter into a single contract with a main contractor, presumably relying on the competence and financial solvency of that contractor. The use of nominated sub-contractors is (or was) generally thought to give the owner some of the benefits of choice of sub-contractor without the burdens of a direct contract. It is difficult to see why the law should decide to provide further benefits to the owner.[3]

---

[98] [1983] 2 A.C. 520.

[99] [1991] 1 A.C. at 481D.

[1] See also *per* Lord Keith at 466G.

[2] See, e.g. per Robert Goff L.J. in *Muirhead v Industrial Tank Specialities Ltd* [1986] Q.B. 507 at 528. In *Nitrigin Eireann Teoranta v Inco Alloys Ltd* [1992] 1 W.L.R. 498 at 505, May J. stated that it would be intellectually dishonest to distinguish that case from *Junior Books* and did not do so. The judge simply declined to apply *Junior Books* on the basis that it was unique and depended in some (unspecified) way on *Hedley Byrne*. The British Columbia Court of Appeal declined to follow *Junior Books* in *Hasegawa v Pepsi* [2002] B.C.C.A. 324.

[3] See also the pre-*Murphy* decision of *Equitable Debenture Assets Corp Ltd v William Moss Group Ltd* (1984) 2 Con. L.R. 1, where the question arose whether curtain walling consultants, Winmart, engaged not by the claimant employer but by the employer's architects, Morgan, owed a duty of care to the employer. Judge Newey Q.C. answered the question affirmatively but emphasised the circumscribed nature of the duty: "The duties which Winmart owed had to be performed within the scope of their employment by Morgan. They would and I think did on occasions draw attention to the need for further work to be done to avoid risks, but they could not officiously advise or inspect when not asked to do so. They would therefore only be blamed if they failed to perform correctly what their instructions allowed them to do." On the facts Winmart were held not liable. See also *Midland Bank v Bardgrove Property Services Ltd* (1990) 24 Con. L.R. 98: a claim by a landowner against engineers engaged by a neighbouring landowner's developer failed because inter alia the claim was for irrecoverable economic loss and irrecoverable in the absence of a "special relationship" between the parties. The claimant's appeal (which concerned the action against the landowner alone) was dismissed and is reported at 60 B.L.R. 1. An attempt to rely upon *Junior Books Ltd v Veitchi Co. Ltd* also failed in *Architype Projects Ltd v Dewhurst Macfarlane & Partners* [2003] EWHC 3341, TCC. The claim was brought by a building owner against an engineer which had been a sub-consultant to the owner's architect. Judge Toulmin C.M.G. Q.C. regarded himself as bound by *Junior Books* only if the facts if the case were identical to the facts in *Junior Books*. They were not (for example, the engineer was not a nominated sub-contractor) and there was no other factor to negative the general rule that, in the context of construction contracts, a sub-contractor owes no duty of care to the building owner.

The increasing popularity of design and build contracts in the procurement of **9–101**
construction projects prompts the question whether a construction professional
appointed by the design and build contractor owes a duty of care to avoid causing
economic loss to the employer. Such a claim will rarely succeed. In *Henderson
v Merrett Syndicates*,[4] Lord Goff emphasised that the existence of a contractual
chain which has been structured so as not to include a contract between claimant
and defendant will commonly prove inconsistent with such a duty of care[5]:

> "Let me take the analogy of the common case of an ordinary building contract, under
> which main contractors contract with the building owner for the construction of the
> relevant building, and the main contractor sub-contracts with sub-contractors or suppli-
> ers (often nominated by the building owner) for the performance of work or the supply
> of materials in accordance with standards and subject to terms established in the sub-
> contract. I put on one side cases in which the sub-contractor causes physical damage to
> property of the building owner, where the claim does not depend on an assumption of
> responsibility by the sub-contractor to the building owner; though the sub-contractor
> may be protected from liability by a contractual exemption clause authorised by the
> building owner. But if the sub-contracted work or materials do not in the result conform
> to the required standard, it will not ordinarily be open to the building owner to sue the
> sub-contractor or supplier direct under the *Hedley Byrne* principle, claiming damages
> from him on the basis that he has been negligent in relation to the performance of his
> functions. For there is generally no assumption of responsibility by the sub-contractor
> or supplier direct to the building owner, the parties having so structured their relation-
> ship that it is inconsistent with any such assumption of responsibility. This was the
> conclusion of the Court of Appeal in *Simaan General Contracting Co v Pilkington
> Glass Ltd. (No. 2)* [1988] Q.B. 758."

The effect of contractual arrangements in preventing a duty of care arising is **9–102**
well illustrated by the decision in *Ove Arup & Partners International Ltd v
Mirant Asia-Pacific Construction (Hong Kong) Ltd (No.2)*.[6] The defendant
engineers were alleged to have prepared a defective foundations design for a
power station. In addition to the claim by the person with whom they had a
contract for design services, they were sued by another company on the
employer-side of the project. The claimant argued that it had foreseeably relied
upon the engineers to exercise skill and care in performing their contract for
design services and had suffered loss when the engineers failed to do so. The
claim was dismissed. The many companies on the employer-side of the project
had deliberately created an intricate contractual chain which excluded a direct
contract between the claimant and the engineers. That the chain had been so
structured purely for tax reasons was irrelevant: the contractual structure chosen
by the parties remained inconsistent with an assumption of responsibility by the
engineers to the claimant for the proper performance of their services.[7] As this

---

[4] [1995] 2 A.C. 145.
[5] *ibid.* at 195–196.
[6] [2004] EWHC 1750, TCC.
[7] This part of the decision was not challenged on appeal: [2005] EWCA 1585. See also *Tesco v
Norman Hitchcox Partnership* (1997) 56 Con. L.R. 42 (defendant architects engaged under separate
contracts by the developer and the tenant of a supermarket did not owe a duty of care in tort to the
tenant to carry out inspections which were required only under their contract with the developer;
detailed contractual relationships entered into by the parties showed that the tenant did not rely on the
architects carrying out any such wider inspections). The position is the same in New Zealand: see
Rolls-Royce New Zealand Ltd v Carter Holt Harvey Ltd [2004] N.Z.L.R. 97 (New Zealand Court of

case demonstrates,[8] the mere existence of an established contractual chain of rights is not sufficient to exclude a duty of care in tort; the question is, rather, whether that contractual chain indicates that the parties' intentions as to the assumption or allocation of risk and responsibility were inconsistent with the alleged duty.

9–103   **Duties of care to subsequent purchasers.** An attempt to apply the wider *Hedley Byrne* principle was denied by the Court of Appeal in *Preston v Torfaen BC*.[9] The claimants were the first purchasers from a local authority of a house which had been built on an in-filled quarry. The defendants were the engineers who had carried out the site investigation for the local authority. It was accepted, for the purposes of a preliminary issue: (1) that the defendants had held themselves out as experts to give specific advice for a specific purpose; (2) that they must have known that the local authority would rely on that advice as it in fact did; (3) that the local authority had power to sell the house; and (4) that the defendants must have known that whoever occupied the house at the time that the defects became manifest would inevitably suffer economic loss as a result of any negligent advice. In the absence of any form of negligent misstatement by the defendants to the claimants, the Court of Appeal found that the above facts were not sufficient to ground liability in negligence. Sir Michael Fox pointed out that a builder would not have been liable to the claimant and did not consider that there was any reason for the defendants to be placed in any different position.

9–104   The existence of a *Hedley Byrne* duty of care owed by a construction professional to a purchaser from the professional's client was also considered in *Machin v Adams*[10] and in *Lidl Properties v Clarke Bond Partnership*,[11] which are discussed above.[12]

Appeal) (specialist sub-contractor owed no duty of care in tort to the employer). See also *Sealand of the Pacific v Robert C. McHaffie Ltd* (1974) 51 D.L.R. (3d) 702, where the claimant employer sued the defendant naval architects and their employee, Mr McHaffie. The British Columbia Court of Appeal rejected the claim against both the employer and the employee for negligent misrepresentation. At 706, *per* Seaton J.A.:

"Here Mr McHaffie did not undertake to apply his skill for the assistance of Sealand. He did exercise, or fail to exercise, his skill as an employee of McHaffie Ltd in the carrying out of its contractual duty to Sealand. Further, while Sealand may have chosen to consult McHaffie Ltd because it had the benefit of Mr McHaffie's services as an employee, it was with McHaffie Ltd that Sealand made a contract and it was upon the skill of McHaffie Ltd that it relied."

The claim against McHaffie Ltd failed on the basis that "the duty and liability ought to be discovered in the contract" but the company was held liable for breach of contract in failing to consider and make inquiries about the suitability of a product which proved unsuitable for the required construction, on an underwater aquarium.

[8] And as the New Zealand Court of Appeal pointed out in *RM Turton & Co Limited (In Liquidation) v Kerslake* [2000] 3 N.Z.L.R. 407 at [9]. In *McKinlay Hendry Ltd v Tonkin Taylor Ltd* [2005] N.Z.L.R. 318 (New Zealand Court of Appeal) the contractual chain, as well as an express disclaimer in the defendants' report, precluded a finding that the defendants were liable for negligent misstatement in a ground investigation report which was relied upon by a party which was not their client.

[9] [1993] C.I.L.L. 864.

[10] (1997) 84 B.L.R. 79.

[11] [1998] Env. L.R. 622.

[12] See paras 9–096 and 9–098, above.

Duties of care to contractors. It may be that the English courts will, in the   9-105
future, be prepared to use the *Hedley Byrne* principle to permit claims to be made
by contractors against construction professionals engaged by the employer in
respect of either negligent certificates or tender information.[13] Although there is
a decision of the Court of Appeal[14] which suggests that it will be rare for such
a duty to be owed, a more recent decision in the same court[15] confirms that there
is no reason in principle why such a duty may not be found in appropriate circumstances.

In the 19th century case of *Stevenson v Watson*[16] a building contractor claimed   9-106
that an architect owed him a duty to exercise due care and skill in ascertaining
sums due to him for building work and that the architect was in breach of that
duty in certifying as payable by the employer a sum much lower than that
properly due. The court expressed much sympathy for the claim[17] but felt
constrained by previous authorities to hold that in carrying out his certifying
functions the architect was in the position of an arbitrator and was immune from
action in the absence of fraud or collusion with the employer. In *Sutcliffe v
Thackrah*[18] however, the House of Lords held that an architect did not, in the
absence of specific agreement, act as arbitrator between the employer and the
contractor and was not immune from an action in negligence at the suit of the
employer for over-certification. The question whether in the same circumstances
the architect might owe a duty to the contractor was expressly left undecided.[19]
In *Arenson v Arenson*[20] Lord Salmon expressed the view that the architect in
Sutcliffe v Thackrah owed the contractor a duty to use reasonable care in issuing
his certificates "arising out of their proximity" and referred to *Hedley Byrne* in
support.[21]

The only reported English case[22] of a successful claim in tort by a contractor   9-107
against an architect, engineer or quantity surveyor for late or under-certification

---

[13] See the Canadian cases discussed at para.9-111, below.
[14] *Pacific Associates Inc v Baxter* [1990] 1 Q.B. 993 discussed at para.9-108, below.
[15] *J Jarvis & Sons Ltd v Castle Wharf Developments Ltd* [2001] EWCA Civ 19; [2001] Lloyd's Rep.
P.N. 308, discussed at para.9-110, below.
[16] (1879) 4 C.P.D. 148.
[17] *ibid.* at 156.
[18] [1974] A.C. 727.
[19] *ibid.* at 736, *per* Lord Reid.
[20] [1977] A.C. 405 at 438.
[21] Similarly in *F G Minter Ltd v Welsh Health Technical Services Organisation* (1979) 11 B.L.R. 1,
the contractor and sub-contractor were respectively entitled to be reimbursed for certain direct loss
and expense caused by variations and delay in issuing instructions. There were a number of variations
and the progress of works was affected by lack of necessary instructions. Claims for consequent direct
loss and expense were made and ultimately paid with the exception of claims for finance charges and
for being kept out of moneys for the periods between the occurrence and certification of the direct loss
and expense. Parker J. rejected the latter claims in an action by the contractor against the employer
but expressed the view, obiter, at 13 that the charges "might give rise to a claim against the architect".
[22] But note *Lubenham Fidelities and Investment Co Ltd v South Pembrokeshire DC* (1986) 6 Con.
L.R. 85, CA in which the Court of Appeal heard an appeal from Judge Newey who had decided at
first instance that such a duty existed. There was no argument upon the point in the Court of Appeal
and the court was not therefore required to consider whether a duty in fact existed. Also note the
Hong Kong case of *Shui On Construction Co Ltd v Shui Kay Co Ltd* (1984-85) 1 Con. L.J. 305 in
which Hunter J. refused to strike out allegations in a statement of claim that the defendant architects

is *Michael Salliss & Co Ltd v Calil and William F Newman & Associates*.[23] The claimant contractor was employed by the first defendants in *respect* of refurbishment works under the JCT 1963 Private Form of Contract. The second defendants were the architects and quantity surveyors under the contract. At the hearing of preliminary issues, Judge Fox-Andrews Q.C. held[24]:

> "If the architect unfairly promotes the building employer's interest by low certification or merely fails properly to exercise reasonable care and skill in his certification it is reasonable that the contractor should not only have the right as against the owner to have the certificate reviewed in arbitration but also should have the right to recover damages against the unfair architect."

9–108   The leading case on the existence of a duty of care owed by construction professionals to a contractor after building works have begun is *Pacific Associates Inc v Baxter*.[25] The claimant contractors had been engaged in extensive dredging and reclamation work in the Persian Gulf for the ruler of Dubai. Conditions of the contract provided that in the event of encountering unforeseeable obstructions, the claimant was, after certification by the defendant engineers, entitled to payment for costs. Another condition provided for arbitration of disputes between the Ruler and the claimants whilst General Condition 86 provided:

> "Neither . . . the engineer nor any of his staff, nor the engineer's representative shall be in any way personally liable for the acts or obligations under the contract, or answerable for any default or omission on the part of the employer in the observance or performance of any of the acts, matters or things which are herein contained."

Following a certification dispute, the claimant commenced arbitration proceedings against the Ruler which were settled on payment of £10 million. The claimants then issued proceedings against the defendants seeking a further £45 million claiming that the losses had been caused by the defendants' negligent certification. The judge decided on the hearing of a preliminary issue that the loss claimed could not be recoverable and struck the claim out. This decision was upheld by the Court of Appeal. Purchas, Gibson and Russell L.JJ.[26] all made it clear that they regarded both the presence of the arbitration clause, whereby the contractor was entitled to challenge the engineer's decision in proceedings against the employer, and the disclaimer as fatal to the imposition of a duty of care.

9–109   Although not expressly overruled, it is now doubtful whether *Salliss* is good law. Purchas L.J. stated specifically[27] that a question mark must reside over the decision. More importantly there would appear to be no reason to attribute less importance to an arbitration clause in the JCT 1963 Standard Form than to that

---

owed to the claimant main contractors a duty of care in the performance of mainly administration functions and also a duty to act fairly and impartially.
[23] (1987) 13 Con. L.R. 68.
[24] *ibid.* at 78.
[25] [1990] 1 Q.B. 993. For discussion, see T. Trottman, *"Pacific Associates v Baxter*: time for re-consideration?" (1999) 15 Const. L.J. 449.
[26] At 1022–1024, 1031–1034 and 1037–1039, respectively.
[27] *ibid.* at 1020C.

in the *Pacific Associates* case. *Pacific Associates* was followed in the Hong Kong case of *Leon Engineering & Construction Co Ltd v Ka Duk Investment Co Ltd*[28] where Bokhary J. refused leave to the claimant building contractors to join architects as defendants to an action on the ground that they owed a duty to give proper, timely and impartial consideration to the claimants' claims under the building contract. The basis of the decision was that there was adequate machinery under the contract between the employer and the contractor to enforce the contractor's rights. There may, however, be exceptional cases where a case can be brought in the absence both of a disclaimer and a valid and effective arbitration clause or other method of challenging a decision by an architect or engineer. It may be possible to circumvent the restrictions imposed by the Court of Appeal's decision by alleging alternative causes of action providing, of course, that the appropriate factual basis exists.[29]

The cases discussed above involved unsuccessful attempts to argue that a **9–110** construction professional acting for the employer owes a duty to the contractor in the administration of the building contract.[30] The situation is different before the contractor has committed himself to build the works by entering the building contract. In *J Jarvis & Sons Ltd v Castle Wharf Developments Ltd*,[31] the defendant was the developer of a office and leisure complex on flagship site in Nottingham. It engaged project managers (GMS) to act on its behalf in seeking tenders for the design and construction of the works. The claimant contractor was invited to tender. It proposed a scheme which differed from the developer's scheme. Following discussions between the contractor and GMS, at which certain modifications to the contractor's proposed scheme were agreed, the developer sent to the claimant a letter stating its intention to enter a design and build contract with the claimant. The claimant then commenced work on site. Some months later, the local planning authority informed the claimant that the scheme which it was building was not in accordance with the planning permission which had been issued to the developer and threatened enforcement proceedings. The claimant alleged that it had begun work in reliance upon negligent misstatements made to it by GMS to the effect that the claimant's proposed scheme, modified as discussed, would be in line with the existing planning permission. GMS argued that it owed no duty of care to the claimant, relying upon *Pacific Associates v Baxter*. The Court of Appeal held that, although generally a professional acting for a principal which had entered or was about to enter a contract would not owe a duty of care in tort to the other party to the contract, there was no reason in principle why a construction professional retained by an employer could not owe a *Hedley Byrne* duty of care in relation to statements made to a contractor and upon which the contractor relied in tendering for the building contract.[32] At that stage, there was no contract between

---

[28] (1990) 47 B.L.R. 139. See further the Canadian cases discussed at para.9–111, below.
[29] See para.9–125, below.
[30] A similar claim failed for similar reasons in *John Holland Construction Engineering Ltd v Majorca Products* (2000) 16 Const. L.J. 114, Supreme Court of Victoria. In that case, Byrne J. went further and held that the employer's architects did not owe a duty in tort to the contractor to act fairly and impartially in the administration of the building contract. It is submitted that this does not represent the position in English law: see *Sutcliffe v Thakrah* [1974] A.C. 727, HL.
[31] [2001] EWCA Civ 19.
[32] *ibid.* at [53] in the judgment of the court, which was given by Peter Gibson L.J.

the contractor and the employer which might negate such a duty by providing the contractor with alternative remedies; indeed, on the facts of this case, a building contract was never concluded. In the event, although the court was not persuaded that the claimant had proved the statements which it attributed to GMS, it was not necessary to decide whether GMS owed a duty of care to the claimant. It was clear that the claimant had not relied upon the statements which it alleged and, therefore, the claim failed on causation.[33]

9–111   The decision of the Supreme Court of Canada in *Edgeworth Construction v ND Lea & Associates Ltd*[34] was not cited in *Jarvis v Castle Wharf*. The judgment of McLachlin J. (with whom five of the other six judges concurred) in that case provides powerful reasoning in support of the existence of a *Hedley Byrne* duty of care owed by a construction professional to a tendering contractor. The Supreme Court held that a contractor which relied on tender documents prepared by engineers for the employer in order to put forward a price could sue the engineers for economic losses sustained as a result of negligent errors in such documents. This was so even though there was an express term in the contract between the employer and the contractor that any representations in the tender documents were furnished merely for information and did not amount to warranties. McLachlin J. took the view that the errors amounted to negligent misrepresentations which the engineers knew would be likely to be relied on by the contractor and were in fact relied upon. The claim fell within the principle set out in *Hedley Byrne* and the subsequent decision of the Supreme Court of Canada in *Haig v Bamford*.[35] She considered the only real question to be whether the terms of the contract between the contractor and the employer negated the duty of care which would otherwise have been held to have arisen. It was held that the contract did not provide the engineers with protection (a) because it did not purport to do so; and (b) because the engineers could have taken alternative measures to protect themselves by, for example, putting a disclaimer on their design documents. McLachlin J. did not consider that there were any policy considerations militating against the imposition of a duty of care: she pointed out that it made greater practical sense for the pre-tender engineering work to be done by one firm rather than have all tenderers checking such work.[36] By contrast

---

[33] See para.9–282, below.

[34] (1993) 107 D.L.R. (4th) 169 overturning the decision of the British Columbia Court of Appeal reported at (1991) 54 B.L.R. 16.

[35] [1977] 1 S.C.R. 466.

[36] Similar reasoning is found in the dissenting judgment of Thomas J. in *RM Turton & Co Ltd v Kerslake & Partners* [2000] Lloyd's Rep. P.N. 967, New Zealand Court of Appeal (the majority regarded the contractual chain as inconsistent with a duty of care). See also *District of Surrey v Carroll-Hatch and Associates Ltd* (1979) 101 D.L.R. (3d) 218, British Columbia CA (structural engineers engaged by an architect were held to owe a duty of care to the employer despite the absence of a contract with the employer. The engineers were held guilty of negligent misrepresentation first by implying in a letter to the employer that an adequate soils investigation had been done and secondly by certifying to the employer that the design work performed by them complied with the Canadian National Building Code. Both representations were incorrect. It is unclear whether the representations formed the basis of the finding that the engineers were negligent in failing to warn the employer of the need for a deep soils report and of the risk in proceeding with the construction without such report. Although the engineers had warned the architect of the need for the report, the architect was not the agent of the employer for this purpose. The engineers should have warned the employer directly. The architect was similarly held liable in negligence, including negligent misrepresentation, and in contract.)

in *Auto Concrete Curb Ltd v South Nation River Conservation Authority*[37] the Supreme Court overruled the Ontario Court of Appeal which had held that an engineer was liable to a contractor for negligence in the pre-engineering stage of a tender process for a contract for dredging a river.[38] The trial judge had made findings of fact: (a) that two alternative methods of performing the contract would have been within the contemplation of a reasonably competent engineer who was preparing tender documents; (b) that a reasonably competent engineer would have made inquiries of statutory authorities having jurisdiction in relation to the project and included relevant information in the tender documents (such inquiries would have revealed the need for additional permits for one of the methods); (c) that the engineer knew or ought to have known that the contractor and other bidders would rely on the information contained in the tender documents and the failure to include relevant information constituted a negligent misrepresentation; (d) that the need to obtain permits was not one that was made known or was reasonably foreseeable from the bid documents; and (e) that it was not reasonable to expect the contractor within a two-week period for tender to canvass and make enquiries when the engineer had had some four months to make appropriate enquiries. The Supreme Court held that it was no part of the function of the engineer to advise the contractor as to his method of work. Accordingly the engineer was under no duty to proffer such advice.[39] The decision would, presumably, have been different if the engineer had taken it upon himself to give misleading advice.

(v) *The Position in Other Jurisdictions*

Canada. The Supreme Court of Canada has declined to follow the decision in **9–112** *Murphy.* In *Winnipeg Condominium Corporation v Bird Construction Co,*[40] La Forest J. (with whom all the other judges agreed) stated that he was in favour of allowing the possibility of tortious recovery by a building owner in respect of the cost of repairing dangerous defects from the original builder of the apartment

---

[37] [1993] 3 S.C.R. 201.

[38] (1992) 89 D.L.R. (4th) 393.

[39] See also *Vermont Construction Inc v Beatson* (1976) 67 D.L.R. (3rd) 95 where the Supreme Court of Canada, by a majority, rejected a claim in tort by a contractor against an architect for loss caused by delay occasioned by defective plans. Although arising from the civil law jurisdiction of Quebec, the common law position was extensively analysed.

[40] (1995) 1221 D.L.R. (4th) 193. In *Cook v Bowen* (1997) 39 B.C.L.R. (3d) 12, Owen-Flood J. followed *Bird* in finding that an engineer who negligently designed a sewage system for a developer so as to create a health risk owed a duty of care to a subsequent purchaser. In *Blair v Alderney Consultants* (1998) 168 N.S.R.(2d) 287, Hamilton J. in the Supreme Court of Nova Scotia found an engineer, who had negligently designed a storm water drainage system for a developer, liable to a builder who bought a plot of land with the intention of selling it on. The builder, who himself built the property in breach of the building code, claimed that flooding at the property led to a delay in selling the property and a diminution in its value. The judge does not appear to have considered the relevant Canadian authorities (particularly *Bird*) but simply decided that the loss was, in principle, recoverable on the basis of *Anns*. Although he found the builder liable for 50 per cent of his losses (as a result of his own breaches of the building code), it is submitted that this decision is difficult to reconcile with either principle or authority. No danger to health was alleged (the only flooding was to the basement of the property) and the case was not put upon the basis of recovering works necessary to avert such a danger. Moreover the builder was able to inspect the sewer system and should have taken it into account when deciding how much he should pay for purchasing the land.

building. La Forest J. made it clear that he drew no distinction between a builder and anyone else who was negligent in the planning or construction of a building[41] and expressly left open the question whether a claim should be allowed against negligent builders or professionals in respect of non-dangerous defects in a building.[42] In *Ingles v Tutkaluk Construction Ltd*,[43] the Supreme Court of Canada considered the question which arose in *Murphy* upon similar facts. The claim was brought by a homeowner against the contractor which had agreed to lower the basement of his house and against the Corporation of the City of Toronto. The City's building inspectors had carried out a partial inspection of the works, but had accepted the contractor's assurance that underpinning which it had installed had been carried out in accordance with the City's requirements. That was not the case. Applying the two-stage test developed in *Anns*,[44] and declining to follow *Murphy*, the Supreme Court held that the City owed to the claimant a duty of care at common law to avoid the economic loss represented by the contractor's inherently defective building works.

9–113   The Canadian courts have also applied an approach similar to Lord Wilberforce's two-stage test for a duty of care in *Anns*[45] to claims which are capable of justification in England under the *Hedley Byrne* principle.[46] One example is provided by the decision of the Supreme Court of Canada *Edgeworth Construction v ND Lea & Associates Ltd*,[47] discussed above. By contrast, in *Auto Concrete Curb Ltd v South Nation River Conservation Authority*[48] and *Martel Building Ltd v Canada*,[49] the Supreme Court declined to find that an employer's engineer and an employer, respectively, owed a duty of care to a tendering contractor during the tender process.

9–114   **Australia.** In *Bryan v Maloney*,[50] the High Court of Australia held, by a majority of four to one, that a professional builder owed a duty of care to a subsequent purchaser in respect of financial loss caused by a failure to construct the house with proper footings. It is notable that it was not alleged that the

---

[41] (1995) 1221 D.L.R. (4th) 193 at 14C.
[42] *ibid.* at 26I.
[43] [2000] 1 S.C.R. 298; (2001) 17 Const. L.J. 540 *sub nom. Ingles v City of Toronto.*
[44] Originally adopted in Canada in *City of Kamloops v Nielsen* [1984] 2 S.C.R. 2.
[45] [1978] A.C. 728; see para.9–068, above. In *Henderson v Merrett Syndicates Ltd* [1995] 2 A.C. 145, Lord Goff stated that the *Hedley Byrne* principle comprehended policy considerations, so that it would not be necessary to consider matters of policy in a case which fell within the principle: see para.9–058, above.
[46] See also the Canadian cases discussed at para.9–111, above. Scrutiny of the facts may reveal a contractual relationship between the employer and "third party" who is sought to be made liable under the Hedley Byrne principle: see *City of Brantford v Kemp and Wallace-Carruthers & Associates Ltd* (1960) 23 D.L.R. (2d) 640, Ontario CA, the facts of which are described at para.9–184, below; *cf. IBA v EMI and BICC* (1978) 11 B.L.R. 29, CA; (1980) 14 B.L.R. 1, HL, the facts of which are set out at para.9–095, above. The Court of Appeal's finding that BICC's assurance amounted to a contractual warranty to IBA was reversed by the House of Lords.
[47] (1993) 107 D.L.R. (4th) 169 overturning the decision of the British Columbia Court of Appeal reported at (1991) 54 B.L.R. 16. See para.9–111, above.
[48] [1993] 3 S.C.R. 201, discussed at para.9–111, above.
[49] [2000] 2 S.C.R. 860.
[50] (1995) 74 B.L.R. 35. See I. N. Duncan Wallace Q.C., "*Murphy* rejected: the *Bryan v Maloney* landmark" (1995) 3 Tort L.R. 231; and "The *Murphy* saga in Australia: *Bryan* in difficulties?" (1997) 113 L.Q.R. 355.

foundations caused a danger to the subsequent purchaser with the result that the decision goes significantly further than that of the Supreme Court of Canada in *Winnipeg*. Four factors were held to give rise to a sufficient degree of proximity to found a duty of care: (a) the house was a permanent structure which was intended to be used indefinitely; (b) it was obviously foreseeable that the negligent construction of the footings was likely to cause economic loss to a subsequent purchaser; (c) a subsequent purchaser would have less opportunity to inspect the footings than the first purchaser to whom the builder plainly owed a duty of care; and (d) in the absence of competing or intervening negligence or some other causative event, the causal proximity between negligence on the part of the builder and subsequent economic loss was the same regardless of whether the loss was suffered by the first or a subsequent purchaser. Brennan J. (who dissented) expressly approved the decision in *Winnipeg* to the effect that economic loss to remedy dangerous defects in a property should be recoverable.[51] Thus all of the members of the High Court would have been prepared to allow a greater degree of recovery than contemplated by the House of Lords in *Murphy*.

Bryan v Maloney emphasised "proximity" as the pre-eminent tool for seeking   **9–115**
to establish when the law will impose a duty of care. The High Court of Australia has since rejected the notion of proximity as the primary test for the existence of a duty of care to avoid causing pure economic loss to a party with whom the defendant has no contract.[52] One consequence has been a retrenchment from the permissive approach to recovery for pure economic loss which was seen in *Bryan v Maloney*. In *Woolcock Street Investments v CDG Pty Ltd*,[53] a majority in the High Court of Australia held that engineers who designed a commercial building owed no duty of care to avoid economic loss suffered by a purchaser from the engineers' client. *Bryan v Maloney* was distinguished on the grounds that the decision in that case depended upon a finding that there was no reason to differentiate between the obligations owed by the defendant builder to the original owner and those which it owed to the subsequent purchaser. No such finding was available in *Woolcock* since the purchaser was not similarly vulnerable to the economic consequences of negligence by the designer: there were numerous steps which the purchaser could reasonably have been expected to take to protect itself. There was therefore no assumption of responsibility by the defendant to the subsequent purchaser.

New Zealand. The courts in New Zealand have consistently refused to follow   **9–116**
either the principles set out in *Murphy* or the actual result in the case. In *South Pacific Manufacturing Co Ltd v New Zealand Security Consultants & Investigations Ltd*,[54] the New Zealand Court of Appeal stated that negligence law in New Zealand had not changed as a result of the decision. In *Invercargill CC v*

---

[51] (1994) 74 B.L.R. 35 at 71–72.
[52] See *Sullivan v Moody* (2001) 207 C.L.R. 562.
[53] [2005] B.L.R. 92.
[54] [1992] 2 N.Z.L.R. 282 (claims by assured for negligence against professional fire investigators employed by insurer struck out for disclosing no reasonable cause of action).

Hamlin,[55] the Privy Council held that it was settled law in New Zealand that councils were liable to house owners and subsequent owners for defects caused or contributed to by building inspectors' negligence. The Court of Appeal of New Zealand had identified differences between New Zealand and English law which might justify a difference in approach, including: (a) most people owned homes built for them by small-scale builders; (b) there had been extensive government support for low cost housing; (c) it had not been the practice for reports by engineers and surveyors to be commissioned on house purchases; and (d) standard byelaws considered comfort and standards of workmanship. The Privy Council recognised that New Zealand judges were better able to interpret conditions in New Zealand than they were. Given the upheavals in England as compared with the comparative uniformity of approach in New Zealand, the Privy Council had no difficulty in adopting the reasoning of the New Zealand Court of Appeal.

9–117   **Other jurisdictions.** A similar position to that in England and Wales was adopted by the Hong Kong Court of Final Appeal in *Bank of East Asia v Tsien Wui Marble Factory Ltd*.[56] By contrast, the courts in Singapore[57] and Malaysia[58] have indicated their preference for the decisions of other Commonwealth countries over that of the House of Lords in *Murphy*.

(vi) *Problems of Scope of Duty*

9–118   Given the absence of a contract, there may be difficulties in assessing the scope of a construction professional's duty of care to third persons and in particular the extent to which such a duty may be limited by the terms of the professional's contract with his own client. This is an area where there is likely to be a difference in attitude according to whether the loss sought to be recovered is physical injury (where the contract is likely to be relevant only to the ambit of the task that the professional was undertaking) or economic loss (where the terms of the contract may be relevant in assessing whether a duty of care will arise, at all, to a third party).[59]

---

[55] [1996] A.C. 624, PC; upholding [1994] 3 N.Z.L.R. 513, New Zealand CA. The regulation of building works in New Zealand has since been reorganised under the Building Act 1991 so that compliance with the building code is monitored by approved certifiers rather than by local authorities. In *Attorney General v Body Corporate No. 2002000* [2005] NZCA 296, the New Zealand Court of Appeal held that the statutory body responsible for approving certifiers did not owe duties of care in tort to building owners, but accepted that the individual approved certifiers did owe such duties.

[56] [1998] 2 HKLRD 373. For further discussion, see R. Glofcheski, "The law of limitations as applied to latent building defects" (2000) 16 Const. L.J. 379; and N. J. Mullaney, "Limitation and Latent Damage in Hong Kong" (2001) 117 L.Q.R. 21.

[57] See the decisions of the Singapore Court of Appeal in *MC Strata Title Plan No.1272 v Ocean Front Pte Ltd* [1996] 1 S.L.R. 113; and *MC Strata Title Plan No.1075 v RSP Architects & Planners & Engineers* [1999] 2 S.L.R. 449 (the management corporation of a residential condominium could recover damages from the developers and the developer's architects for pure economic loss arising from the faulty construction of the common parts of the building).

[58] See *Lim Teck King v Dr. Rashid* [2005] M.Y.C.A. 13 (Court of Appeal of Malaysia).

[59] See paras 9–065 to 9–111, above. See also *Rumbelows Ltd v AMK* (1980) 19 B.L.R. 25 (specialist pipework sub-contractors' duty in tort to building owner was not limited by a clause in the sub-contract limiting their liability to the replacement of defective materials); *Twins Transport Ltd v Patrick and Brocklehurst* (1983) 25 B.L.R. 65 (main contractor's duty in tort to the building owner was not limited by the terms of the contractor's contract with the developer). Note that these cases,

The decision of the Court of Appeal in *Bellefield Computer Services Ltd v E*   **9–119**
Turner and Sons Ltd[60] illustrates the way in which contract terms agreed between
a construction professional and his client may limit the scope of the professional's duty of care to a third party. The purchaser of a dairy processing plant which
was damaged by fire due to defects in the design of its fire-resisting features
brought an action against the contractor which had carried out the design and
construction of the plant. The contractor settled the claim and sought contribution
under the Civil Liability (Contribution) Act 1978 from the architects whom it had
engaged to carry out some of its design duties under the main contract. It was
held that the architects were not liable for any contribution because they owed no
relevant duty of care to the original claimant (and so were not persons liable in
respect of the same damage as the contractor, as required by the Act). The
architects owed no relevant duty of care because of the way in which the scope
of their design obligations was limited by their contract with the contractor. In
particular, they had undertaken no responsibility to provide a detailed design for
the critical fire-resisting features and they had not agreed to carry out any
supervision or inspection of the works during construction.

In *Pacific Associates Inc v Baxter*,[61] the terms of a contract to which the   **9–120**
defendant engineers were not a party were nevertheless effective to prevent a
duty of care being imposed upon the engineers. Engineers engaged by the
building owner did not owe a duty in tort to the main contractor in respect of
payment certificates issued by them because the building contract provided (a)
that the main contractor was entitled to challenge the engineers' certificates in
arbitral proceedings against the employer; and (b) that the engineers were not to
be held personally liable for their conduct in administering the contract. Purchas
L.J. said[62]:

> " . . . where the parties have come together against a contractual structure which
> provides for compensation in the event of failure of one of the parties involved, the
> court will be slow to superimpose an added duty of care beyond that which was in the
> contemplation of the parties at the time that they came together."

Insurance clauses in building contracts have proved particularly important in   **9–121**
determining the existence and scope of duties of care owed in tort to third parties,
at least where the duty is alleged to have been owed by a sub-contractor
responsible for causing physical damage to property. In *Norwich CC v Harvey*,[63]
the Court of Appeal dismissed a claim by a building owner against a roofing sub-

---

as well as *Southern Water Authority v Lewis & Duvivier*, were decided before the decision in *Murphy
v Brentwood DC*: it is doubtful whether the sub-contractors would be held to owe a duty in tort on
the same facts today.
[60] [2002] EWCA Civ 1823. For an earlier example, see *Southern Water Authority v Lewis & Duvivier*
(1984) 27 B.L.R. 111, where it was held that sub-contractors owed no duty of care to the employer
in respect of events after the issue of taking-over certificates under the main contract. Judge Smout
Q.C. said, "The contractual setting may not necessarily be overriding, but is relevant in the
consideration of the scope of the duty in tort for it indicates the extent of the liability which the
claimants' predecessors wished to impose. To put it more crudely . . . the contractual setting defines
the area of risk which the claimants' predecessors chose to accept and for which they may or may not
have sought insurance."
[61] [1990] 1 Q.B. 993. For the facts, see para.9–108, above.
[62] *ibid.* at 1010.
[63] [1989] 1 W.L.R. 828.

contractor for damages for negligently-caused fire damage. Both the owner and the sub-contractor had contracted with the main contractor on the basis that the owner had assumed, and would insure against, the risk of damage by fire. In those circumstances, it was not fair, just or reasonable to impose a duty of care in tort to avoid such damage upon the sub-contractor. On similar facts, but different contract terms, the sub-contractor was held to owe a duty in tort to avoid causing damage to the property of the building owner in *British Telecommunications Plc v Thomson Ltd.*[64] The House of Lords on a Scottish appeal held that the provisions of the main building contract reinforced rather than undermined the existence of a duty of care owed by a domestic sub-contractor to the owner. The insuring obligations set out in the main building contract provided that the owner, the main contractor and nominated sub-contractors were to be joint insureds under a policy of insurance to be maintained by the owner in respect of fire damage. One assured cannot sue a co-assured for a loss in respect of which the co-assured is entitled to the benefit of the same insurance.[65] As a domestic sub-contractor, the defendant was outside the class of persons vis-à-vis whom the owner had assumed the risk of fire. Accordingly, he could not rely upon the contract terms so as to avoid liability to the building owner for negligently caused fire damage. The defendant engineers in *Hopewell Project Management Ltd v Ewbank Preece Ltd*[66] argued that they were joint insureds with the employer under two policies of insurance taken out in accordance with the provisions of the building contract and that, therefore, they could not be held liable on a sub-rogated claim brought by insurers in the name of the employer. The argument failed. The parties insured under the policies included "contractors and sub-contractors". Mr Recorder Jackson Q.C. held that the engineers were not insured under the policies. He observed that it is not normal practice to describe a professional firm as a contractor or sub-contractor, even although that firm enters into contracts with its clients.[67] Similarly, it is unusual for contracts made by

---

[64] [1999] 1 W.L.R. 9, HL.

[65] *Petrofina (UK) Ltd v Magnaload Ltd* [1984] QB 127; *National Oil Wells (UK) Ltd v Davy Off-Shore Ltd* [1993] 2 Lloyd's Rep. 582. The significance of this principle in the context of contribution claims was considered by the House of Lords in *Co-operative Retail Services Ltd v Taylor Young Partnership* [2002] UKHL 17; [2002] 1 W.L.R. 1419, discussed further at paras 9–332 to 9–335, below. In every case where the existence of a policy of insurance in joint names is said to be relevant to liability for breach of contract, it will be important to identify correctly the particular loss(es) covered by the policy. In *Scottish & Newcastle Plc v GD Construction (St Albans) Ltd* (2001) 80 Con. L.R. 75, the claimant engaged the defendant building contractor to refurbish a public house. The defendant's roofing sub-contractor used a blow-torch on the thatched roof of the public house, causing a fire, extensive damage and delay to the opening of the public house for business. The building contract provided that the claimant would take out a policy of insurance in the joint names of the claimant, the defendant and the roofing sub-contractor in respect of loss and damage caused by fire to the existing structure and contents of the public house. Judge Seymour Q.C. held that this provision was not effective to exclude liability on the part of the defendant to the claimant for damage caused by the fire to the existing structure and contents of the public house, because loss due to negligently caused fire was outside the scope of the policy. Nor was it effective to exclude liability for the claimant's business interruption loss because that was not a type of loss which was covered by the policy. The defendant remained liable to the claimant for the cost of the delay to the opening of the public house for business. On appeal, the judge's decision in relation to damage to the structure of the public house was reversed (there was no appeal against the balance of his decision): [2003] EWCA Civ 16.

[66] [1998] 2 Lloyd's Rep. 448.

[67] *ibid.* at 455.

construction professionals to contain insurance provisions such as those considered in the *Norwich CC* and *British Telecommunications* cases.[68] In the light of those decisions, it would certainly be prudent for an architect or engineer engaged by a design and build contractor to make sure that, if the building contract provides that the employer shall insure against (and thereby assume the risk of) physical damage to the property, such provision is replicated or incorporated in his own contract.

Clayton v Woodman & Son (Builders) Ltd[69] is a personal injuries case where the architect's contract was relevant to the scope of his duties in tort. In that case a building project entailed incorporation of an old gable and the cutting of a groove along its base in order to take the concrete floor of a new lift motor house. During a site inspection by the architect the claimant, an experienced bricklayer and an employee of the building contractors, suggested to him that owing to the difficulty of incorporating the gable it would be better to pull it down. The architect rejected the suggestion, having satisfied himself that the gable could be safely incorporated. The specification required the retention of the gable and the provision of necessary shoring by the contractors. The groove was cut but the gable collapsed, injuring the claimant. At first instance Salmon J. held the contractors negligent and in breach of statutory duty in failing to shore and strut the gable. He further held that given their "exceptionally close relationship" the architect owed a duty to the claimant to take reasonable care for his safety and that he was in breach of that duty since he had in effect instructed the claimant to cut the groove. The Court of Appeal took a different view and held that the architect did not owe a duty in the circumstances. The architect had not given any direct instructions to the claimant but, given his decision that the gable could be safely incorporated, had taken the right decision in the interests of the employer to adhere to the specification. The manner of executing the groove was within the province of the contractors and it was the manner of execution adopted, namely without shores or struts, which had caused the injury. If, in contrast, the architect had directed the claimant as to how the groove was to be cut he would have been stepping outside his own province. Moreover, if he had so directed when he knew or ought to have known that it would have been done in a dangerous manner, a duty might have been imposed upon him.[70]

9–122

Windeyer J. summarised the position in relation to personal injury actions in the Australian case of *Voli v Inglewood Shire Council*[71]:

9–123

" . . . neither the terms of the architect's engagement, nor the terms of the building contract, can operate to discharge the architect from a duty of care to persons who are strangers to those contracts. Nor can they directly determine what he must do to satisfy his duty to such persons. That duty is cast upon him by law, not because he made a contract, but because he entered upon the work. Nevertheless his contract with the building owner is not an irrelevant circumstance. It determines what was the task upon

---

[68] Although such contracts do commonly impose upon the professional an obligation to maintain professional indemnity insurance.
[69] [1962] 1 W.L.R. 585, CA, reversing Salmon J. at first instance, [1962] 2 Q.B. 533.
[70] *ibid.* at 592, *per* Donovan L.J. and at 595, *per* Pearson L.J.
[71] [1963] A.L.R. 657.

which he entered. If, for example, it was a design for a stage to bear only some specified weight, he would not be liable for the consequence of someone thereafter negligently permitting a greater weight to be put upon it."[72]

The facts of *Voli* were that the claimant was injured by the collapse of a stage in a public hall designed by the defendant architect. The claimant was held to owe a duty of care so to design the platform as to make it safe for any burden reasonably to be expected. The specified joists supporting the stage were not strong enough to bear such a burden and the architect was consequently liable in negligence to the claimant. In *Introvigne v Commonwealth of Australia*[73] the issue of injury to a third party through misuse of an article designed by an architect was considered. The claimant schoolboy was swinging from the halyard of a flagpole in the school quadrangle when the truck fastened to the top of the pole collapsed and injured him. In an action against the architects, inter alios, the court recognised that an abuse of a particular article in a particular way might be so notorious as to make such abuse reasonably foreseeable.[74] On the facts, however, it was held that the architects when designing the flagpole were not under a duty of care to guard against schoolboy abuses.

9–124   The extent of a duty of care to a contractor in respect of design and supervision causing loss to adjoining property was considered obiter by Judge Stabb Q.C., in *Oldschool v Gleeson (Construction) Ltd.*[75] While abjuring the view that the relationship of consulting engineer and contractor did not admit a duty of care owed by the former to the latter, he continued:

" . . . it seems abundantly plain that the duty of care of an architect or of a consulting engineer in no way extends into the area of how the work is carried out. Not only has he no duty to instruct the builder how to do the work or what safety precautions to take but he has no right to do so, nor is he under any duty to the builder to detect faults during the progress of the work. The architect, in that respect, may be in breach of his duty to his client, the building owner, but this does not excuse the builder for faulty work. I take the view that the duty of care which an architect or a consulting engineer owes to a third party is limited by the assumption that the contractor who creates the work acts at all material times as a competent contractor. The contractor cannot seek to pass blame for incompetent work on to the consulting engineer on the grounds that he failed to prevent it. . . . But if . . . the design was so faulty that the competent contractor in the course of executing the works could not have avoided the resulting damage, then on principle it seems to me that the consulting engineer responsible for that design should bear the loss."[76]

---

[72] [1963] A.L.R. 657 at 662.
[73] (1980) 32 A.L.R. 251, Federal Court of Australia.
[74] *ibid.* at 273.
[75] (1976) 4 B.L.R. 103: consulting engineers held not negligent on the facts.
[76] *ibid.* at 131. See also *AMF International Ltd v Magnet Bowling Ltd* [1968] 1 W.L.R. 1028 at 1053, *per* Mocatta J.; *East Ham Corp v Bernard Sunley & Sons Ltd* [1966] A.C. 406 at 444, 449. In *Victoria University of Manchester v Hugh Wilson* (1984) 2 Con. L.R. 43 Judge Newey Q.C. expressed the view, obiter, that the words of Judge Stabb Q.C. in *Oldschool* must now be regarded as too widely expressed. However, it is suggested that Judge Newey's criticism is itself now out of line with modern authority.

(c) *Other Torts*

Although there is scarce authority in this area, there is no reason why, on **9–125** appropriate facts, a construction professional who undertakes an appointment as contract administrator should not be held liable to the building contractor or the employer for the torts of inducing breach of contract or wrongful interference with contract. Claims are most likely to be made by a contractor which is disappointed with the way in which a contract administrator has exercised his certification function. An illustration is provided by *Lubenham Fidelities Investment Co Ltd v South Pembrokeshire DC*.[77] The claimant contractor claimed damages against the defendant architect and contract administrator for financial loss alleged to have been caused by the architect's interim payment certificates. There was an issue as to the correct interpretation of terms of the building contract which provided for the deduction of liquidated damages payable by the contractor from sums certified by the architect as payable to the contractor. The Court of Appeal held that, although the architect's interpretation of those provisions was incorrect, so that excessive sums had been deducted as against the contractor, the architect was not liable for wrongful interference with the building contract (or for procuring a breach of contract by the employer). The architect had applied his erroneous interpretation in good faith, albeit negligently, and had not intended deliberately to misapply the provisions of the contract so as to deprive the claimant of its entitlements. It was recognised that the architect would have been exposed to such liability had he deliberately misapplied the provisions of the building contract in issuing his certificates with the intention of depriving the contractor of the larger sums to which it would otherwise be entitled.[78]

(d) *The Standard of Care and Skill*

(i) *The Ordinary Competent and Skilled Practitioner*

As in the case of other professions the standard generally required of an architect **9–126** in discharging his duties is the reasonable skill, care and diligence of an ordinary competent and skilled architect. The standard was more fully described by Windeyer J. in the Australian case of *Voli v Inglewood Shire Council*[79] as follows:

> "An architect undertaking any work in the way of his profession accepts the ordinary liabilities of any man who follows a skilled calling. He is bound to exercise due care, skill and diligence. He is not required to have an extraordinary degree of skill or the highest professional attainments. But he must bring to the task he undertakes the competence and skill that is usual among architects practising their profession. And he must use due care. If he fails in these matters and the person who employed him thereby

---

[77] (1986) 6 Con. L.R. 85.
[78] *ibid.* at 114. See, to similar effect: *John Mowlem v Eagle Star* (1992) 62 B.L.R. 126; *John Holland Construction and Engineering Ltd v Majorca Products* (2000) Const. L.J. 114, Supreme Court of Victoria.
[79] [1963] A.L.R. 657.

suffers damage, he is liable to that person. This liability can be said to arise either from a breach of his contract or in tort."[80]

The standard may be similarly expressed for engineers,[81] quantity surveyors and other construction professionals. In *Eckersley v Binnie Partners*,[82] Bingham L.J. who dissented on the result but not, it is submitted, on the standard to be applied said:

> " . . . a professional man should command the corpus of knowledge which forms part of the professional equipment of the ordinary member of his profession. He should not lag behind other ordinarily assiduous and intelligent members of his profession in knowledge of new advances, discoveries and developments in his field. He should be alert to the hazards and risks inherent in any professional task he undertakes to the extent that other ordinarily competent members of the profession would be alert. He must bring to any professional task he undertakes no less expertise, skill and care than other ordinarily competent members would bring but need bring no more. The standard is that of the reasonable average. The law does not require of a professional man that he be a paragon combining the qualities of polymath and prophet."[83]

9–127   What is required to fulfil the standard will vary according to the facts and circumstances of each case. Thus in *Larche v Ontario*,[84–85] the Ontario Court of Appeal upheld the trial judge's rejection of a claim that architects were liable to a patient at a psychiatric hospital who was injured when he fell from the roof as a result of alleged negligence in the design of a railing. The Court upheld the judge's finding that "what was designed was reasonable and represented the discharge of the architects' duty to design a barrier which met an acceptable security standard in the particular location it was constructed at this type of psychiatric facility".[86] An English illustration is provided by the decision at first instance in *Ministry of Defence v Scott Wilson Kirkpatrick*.[87] The third defendants were structural engineers. They were engaged by the Ministry of Defence to design a scheme of works for the repair and refurbishment of a wooden shipbuilding slip at its Plymouth dockyard. The original slip was a large wooden structure which had been built in the early 17th century using the same methods

---

[80] [1963] A.L.R. 657 at 661. See also, e.g. *Armstrong v Jones* (1869) cited in *Hudson's Building Contracts* (4th edn, 1914), Vol.2, at pp.6, 7, *per* Baron Fitzgerald; *BL Holdings Ltd v Robert J Wood & Partners* (1978) 10 B.L.R. 48 at 80; *Kensington and Chelsea and Westminster AHA v Wettern Composites* (1984) 1 Con. L.R. 114 at 131.

[81] e.g. *Greaves & Co (Contractors) Ltd v Baynham Meikle & Partners* [1975] 1 W.L.R. 1095, CA at 1101, *per* Lord Denning M.R.; *Wimpey Construction UK Ltd v Poole* [1984] 2 Lloyd's Rep. 499 at 505 *et seq.*, *per* Webster J. (this case is discussed further at para.9–163, below in relation to the specialist practitioner).

[82] (1988) 18 Con. L.R. 1. For the facts see para.9–074, above and for further discussion on the question of foreseeability see para.9–285, below.

[83] *ibid.* at 80. This passage was quoted with approval by the Court of Appeal in *Michael Hyde & Associates Ltd v JD Williams & Co Ltd* [2001] P.N.L.R. 233, at para.24, *per* Ward L.J. (with whom Sedley and Nourse L.JJ. agreed). For further discussion of this case, see para.9–141, below.

[84–85] (1990) 75 D.L.R. (4th) 377.

[86] *ibid.* at 380.

[87] Unreported, July 1997, Mr Recorder Coles Q.C. The dismissal of the claim against the third defendants was not the subject of the appeal at [2000] B.L.R. 20. The decision is discussed further at para.9–243, below.

as were then used to build ships. The roof timbers had been attached to the main structure using cast iron nails which varied in length from 8 inches to 12 inches. The engineers' design for repair of the roof included the replacement of rotten timbers with sound wood and the instruction that such new timbers be "well fixed as existing", i.e. that nails of similar length and strength as the original nails should be used. The repair works were not carried out for some years, by which time the engineers' involvement had ceased. Later, during bad weather, the roof of the slip was lifted off the main structure by wind and came to rest in a nearby playing field. The Ministry of Defence alleged that the third defendants had been negligent in designing the repairs on a "like-for-like" basis and that they ought to have followed modern codes of practice which would have required the use of steel angles, straps and bolts to fix the roof timbers to the main structure. The claim failed. The judge held that the engineers' design was appropriate since the original building had remained intact for nearly 200 years, proving the adequacy of nails of the type originally used. Furthermore, the principles of design which were appropriate in new buildings were not necessarily appropriate in the repair of older buildings; in particular, the slip was of considerable historic and architectural significance and the engineers were right to seek to replicate the original method of construction in the repairs which they designed.

The qualifications and experience of his client may also influence what is **9–128** required of the professional man in discharge of his duties. The claim against the architects in *J Jarvis & Sons Ltd v Castle Wharf Developments Ltd*[88] provides an example. The first defendant was the developer of an office and leisure complex on a flagship site in Nottingham. The third defendants were architects who, initially, were engaged by the developer to obtain planning permission for the development. The claimant contractor was invited to tender for the detailed design and construction of the development. It proposed a scheme which differed from the developer's scheme. Following discussions between the contractor and the developer's project manager at which certain modifications to the contractor's proposed scheme were agreed, the developer sent to the contractor a letter stating its intention to enter a design and build contract with the contractor. The architects were not involved in the tender process or in the discussions with the contractor. The architects' contract with the developer was then novated to the contractor and the contractor began work on site. Some months later, the local planning authority informed the claimant that the scheme which it was building was not in accordance with the planning permission which had been issued to the developer and threatened enforcement proceedings. The contractor alleged that, until then, it had believed that its proposed scheme, modified as discussed with the developer's project manager, would be in line with the existing planning permission. It claimed that the architects should have advised it of the true planning position at the outset of their novated engagement and, in failing to do so, were in breach of their duty of care in contract and in tort. The claim succeeded at first instance but the architects' appeal was upheld.

The Court of Appeal accepted the architects' submission that, in the absence **9–129** of any express or implied request for advice, a professional has a duty to offer

---

[88] [2001] EWCA Civ 19; [2001] Lloyd's Rep. P.N. 308. For discussion of the claim against the project managers, see para.9–110, above; for discussion of the findings on causation, see para.9–282, below.

unsolicited advice only when his reasonable perception of his client's skill and experience suggests that his client needs such advice. The following words of Donaldson L.J. in the solicitors' case of *Carradine Properties Ltd v DJ Freeman*[89] applied equally to architects:

> "A solicitor's duty to his client is to exercise all reasonable skill and care in and about his client's business. In deciding what he should do and what advice he should tender the scope of his retainer is undoubtedly important, but it is not decisive. If a solicitor is instructed to prepare all the documentation needed for the sale or purchase of a house, it is no part of his duty to pursue a claim by the client for unfair dismissal. But if he finds unusual covenants or planning restrictions, it may indeed be his duty to warn of the risks and dangers of buying the house at all, notwithstanding that the client has made up his mind and is not seeking advice about that. I say only that this *may* be his duty because the precise scope of that duty will depend inter alia upon the extent to which the client appears to need advice. An inexperienced client will need and will be entitled to expect the solicitor to take a much broader view of the scope of his retainer and of his duties than will be the case with an experienced client."

The claimant in *Jarvis*, the Court held, was a design and build contractor which had taken on a major development. The architects were entitled to suppose that the claimant had informed itself of and understood the planning position. Furthermore, the architects did not know that the claimant in fact had a limited and erroneous understanding of the position and the claimant failed to establish that the architects were put on inquiry as to the accuracy of the claimant's understanding. In those circumstances, the architects' duty to exercise reasonable care and skill did not require them to volunteer advice to the claimant as to the planning position.

9–130   However, once it is established that a professional man owes a duty to provide advice or services to his client, the fact that his client has special skills in the same area does not reduce the standard of care which is required in order to discharge that duty. In *Gloucestershire HA v Torpy*,[90] the defendant mechanical services engineers argued that the fact that their client was experienced and knowledgeable in the area of incinerator technology meant that their obligations to him were reduced. Judge Bowsher Q.C. rejected that argument, saying[91]: "I cannot see how it can possibly be right to suggest that, for example, conveyancing counsel should accept from a solicitor engaged to convey his house a lower than usual standard of care."

9–131   The starting point for any consideration of what must be done to discharge his duty to exercise reasonable care and skill is the professional man's contract.[92] In

---

[89] [1999] Lloyd's Rep. P.N. 483 at 487. This passage was also approved by the Court of Appeal in the solicitors' case *Virgin Management Ltd v Defendant Morgan Group Plc*, unreported, January 24, 1996.

[90] (1997) 55 Con. L.R. 124.

[91] *ibid.* at 146.

[92] See *Investors in Industry Commercial Properties v South Bedfordshire DC; Ellison & Partners and Hamilton Associates (Third Parties)* [1986] 1 All E.R. 787, CA at 806F; *Nordic Holdings Ltd v Mott MacDonald Ltd* (2001) 77 Con. L.R. 88, *per* Judge Seymour Q.C. at para.82. See also *Neisner-Kratt Enterprises v Building Design 2* (1988) 39 B.L.R. 98 where the Saskatchewan Court of Queen's Bench examined closely the inspection provisions in the Royal Architectural Institute of Canada's standard form agreement (similar to the RIBA agreement), before concluding no breach had occurred.

a claim against a construction professional it may also be relevant to look not only at the terms of the contracts between the professional and the employer but also at the terms of other contracts to which the professional is not party, such as a building contract in which he is named as contract administrator.

The relevant standard is that of competent practitioners prevailing at the time **9–132** when the particular professional services are performed,[93] as distinct from the (perhaps higher) standard of competent practitioners prevailing at the time of the trial.

On the other hand, what is required to fulfil the standard is not static and will **9–133** vary as circumstances change. In particular the standard will reflect the need for the construction professions to keep pace with new skills and technology.[94] It will apply even if the architect embarks on a novel design as illustrated by *IBA v EMI and BICC*.[95] In that case the design of the cylindrical television mast by the sub-contractors BICC was at and beyond the frontiers of professional knowledge. The House of Lords nevertheless held that they were in breach of their duty to exercise reasonable skill and care in the design of the mast. The relation of the required standard to the novel design was considered by Lord Edmund-Davies:

> "Judgment on hindsight has to be avoided. . . . Justice requires that we seek to put ourselves in the position of BICC when first confronted by their daunting task, lacking all empirical knowledge and adequate expert advice in dealing with the many problems awaiting solution. But those very handicaps created a clear duty to identify and to think through such problems, including those of static and dynamic stresses, so that dimensions of the venture into the unknown could be adequately assessed and the ultimate decision as to its practicability arrived at."[96]

The exercise of reasonable skill and care may even require the abandonment of a project:

> "The project may be alluring. But the risks of injury to those engaged in it, or others, or to both, may be so manifest and substantial, and their elimination may be so difficult to ensure with reasonable certainty that the only proper course is to abandon the project altogether. Learned Counsel for BICC appeared to regard such a defeatist outcome as unthinkable. Yet circumstances can and have at times arisen in which it is plain commonsense, and any other decision foolhardy. The law requires even pioneers to be prudent."[97]

---

[93] e.g. *Newham LBC v Taylor Woodrow* (1982) 19 B.L.R. 99, CA at 128; *Kensington and Chelsea and Westminster AHA v Wettern Composites* (1984) 1 Con. L.R. 114 at 131; *Perry v Tendring DC* (1984) 3 Con. L.R. 75 at 97 ("On the totality of the evidence I must . . . conclude that at the material time [1965] the competent engineer would not have known of long-term heave"); *Eckersley v Binnie & Partners* (1988) 18 Con. L.R. 1, *per* Bingham L.J. at 80; *Privest Properties Ltd v Foundation Co of Canada Ltd* (1995) 128 D.L.R. (4th) 577 upheld at (1997) 143 D.L.R. (4th) 635 (architects should have known in early 1970s that a specified product contained asbestos).
[94] See *Moresk Cleaners Ltd v Hicks* [1966] 2 Lloyd's Rep. 338 at 343.
[95] (1980) 14 B.L.R. 1, HL. For facts see para.9–095, above.
[96] *ibid.* at 31.
[97] *ibid.* at 28.

Similarly, in *Victoria University of Manchester v Wilson*,[98] Judge Newey Q.C. said[99]:

> "For architects to use untried, or relatively untried, materials or techniques cannot in itself be wrong, as otherwise the construction industry can never make any progress. I think, however, that architects who are venturing into the untried or little tried would be wise to warn their clients specifically of what they are doing and to obtain their express approval."

9–134   Where a design involves an element of risk as compared to an available alternative, the exercise of reasonable care and skill may require an architect or engineer to inform the employer of the element of risk and the superior safety of the alternative design. For example, in *Pullen v Gutteridge*,[1] the Court of Appeal of Victoria held that engineers were liable for failing to warn their employer of the risks attaching to their foundation design for a swimming pool complex and for failing to advise upon possible alternative designs. On the other hand, judged by the standard of reasonable care, an architect will generally not be liable for misuse of a structure designed by him. Thus the architect who designed the flagpole in *Introvigne v Commonwealth of Australia*[2] was not liable to the claimant schoolboy who sustained injury as a result of swinging from its halyard. The court considered that to ask the architect at the design stage to assume that ordinary precautions would not be taken, such as padlocking the halyard to the pole and reasonable supervision of the pupils by the teachers, would have imposed too heavy a duty upon the architects. Again, in *Voli v Inglewood Shire Council*[3] the architect who designed the stage would not have been liable for a collapse caused by someone permitting a greater weight to be placed upon it than it was designed to bear. Nevertheless, as recognised by the court in *Introvigne*,[4] the duty to take reasonable care might impose liability upon an architect in the case of abuse of an article designed by him if the abuse were so notorious as to be reasonably foreseeable.

9–135   It will be no answer to a claim for professional negligence that the practitioner had insufficient time to undertake a competent job unless the professional has pointed out the inevitable risks caused by a lack of time and the client has consented to taking such a risk. However if a professional is asked to undertake a task quickly, the time available (which is known to both parties) may affect the court's assessment of the scope of the defendant's retainer.[5]

9–136   A practitioner may not have the particular knowledge or expertise required by his client. In that event the exercise of reasonable care and skill may require the

---

[98] (1984) 2 Con. L.R. 43.

[99] *ibid.* at 74. See also *Try Build Ltd v Invicta Leisure Tennis Ltd* (2000) 71 Con. L.R. 141 (engineers held in breach of duty for failing to advise their client, a design and build contractor, upon the need for tests to establish that the novel features of a sports hall roof construction had been developed successfully by the specialist supplier).

[1] [1993] 1 V.R. 27.

[2] (1980) 32 A.L.R. 251. For facts see para.9–123, above.

[3] [1963] A.L.R. 657 at 662, *per* Windeyer J. For the facts, see para.9–123, above.

[4] (1980) 32 A.L.R. 251 at 273.

[5] See, for example: *Hilton Canada v SNC Lavalin* (1999) 176 N.S.R. (2d) 155 (engineers asked to undertake a survey of a hotel within one and a half days of the proposed purchase; held that lack of sufficient time to perform the task provided no defence since, in that case, the engineers should either have refused the retainer or pointed out the risks clearly to their client).

practitioner to inform the client accordingly and either to decline acceptance of instructions or to seek himself, or advise the client to seek, specialist advice and assistance.[6] The importance of an architect expressly informing his client as to the limits of his own knowledge or as to the need for further specialist advice appears from the decision of Judge Newey Q.C. in *Richard Roberts Holdings Ltd v Douglas Smith Stimson Partnership*[7] where architects were retained in relation to alterations to a dyeworks. The architects had enjoyed a long-standing relationship with the claimants as a result of friendship between the managing director of the claimants and a partner in the architects. No consulting engineer specialising in dyeworks was engaged on the project although one had been engaged on a previous similar project. In initially preparing their drawings, the architects assumed that an effluent tank would be lined with stainless steel. The employer was concerned by the anticipated cost of £35,000 for the lining and requested that cheaper alternatives be sought. Eventually an alternative lining was designed and installed for £3,240 by a specialist contractor with whom the employer contracted direct. Upon the failure of the lining, the claimant sued both the subcontractor for defective design and the architect, alleging breach of contract in recommending or permitting the alternative method of lining the tank. The subcontractor took no part in the trial. The architects were found liable notwithstanding that they neither charged nor recovered fees in respect of the lining of the effluent tank. The judge found[8]:

> "In my view the architects were employed by [the plaintiffs] to act as architects for the creation of the Hinckley Dyeworks. They were not responsible for equipment . . . which [the plaintiffs'] staff would design and fix for themselves, but their position was not as it had been at Loughborough, in that they were to design the effluent cooling tanks and also the mixing room floor. The lining was I think an integral part of the tank. The architects did not know about linings, but part of their expertise as architects was to be able to collect information about materials of which they lacked knowledge and/or experience and to form a view about them. If the architects felt that they could not form a reliable judgment about a lining for the tank, they should have informed [the plaintiffs] of that fact and advised them to take other advice, possibly from a chemist."

(ii) *General Practice and Knowledge as Evidence of the Standard*

The knowledge required of an architect, engineer or quantity surveyor will generally be judged by the standard of the ordinary competent practitioner in the profession concerned.[9] If a man is unqualified but holds himself out as possessing a skill, he will be judged by the standards of a reasonably competent qualified person. Thus in *Cardy v Taylor*,[10] an unqualified person practising as an architect was judged by the standards of a reasonably competent architect. If a practitioner   **9–137**

---

[6] See *Moresk Cleaners Ltd v Hicks* [1966] 2 Lloyd's Rep. 338 at 343; see also *Young v Tomlinson* [1979] 2 N.Z.L.R. 441 at 458.
[7] (1988) 46 B.L.R. 50.
[8] *ibid.* at 66.
[9] See Ch.2, paras 2–119 to 2–127.
[10] (1994) 38 Con. L.R. 79.

carries out tasks usually carried out by the members of another profession, he will be judged by the standards of that other profession.[11]

9–138   The standard of reasonable care and skill is usually established by reference to the general practice of the construction profession concerned. In *Nye Saunders and Partners v Alan E Bristow*[12] Stephen Brown L.J. expressly applied the test in *Bolam v Friern Hospital Management Committee*[13] to decide whether an architect had fulfilled the required standard:

> "Where there is a conflict as to whether he has discharged that duty, the courts approach the matter upon the basis of considering whether there was evidence that at the time a responsible body of architects would have taken the view that the way in which the subject of enquiry had carried out his duties was an appropriate way of carrying out the duty, and would not hold him guilty of negligence merely because there was a body of competent professional opinion which held that he was at fault."

9–139   Although evidence of general practice may materially assist a court, it is not decisive of what is required to discharge the standard of reasonable care. That is for the court to decide having regard to the circumstances of the particular case.[14]

9–140   Furthermore, the *Bolam* test will not be applied to determine whether a professional is in breach of a duty to exercise reasonable skill and care in every case in which such an allegation is made. There are three categories of case in which the court is entitled not to apply the *Bolam* test and, therefore, to make a finding of negligence notwithstanding expert evidence that a body of professional opinion supports the course which the defendant took:

> (i) Cases in which the court considers that there is no logical basis for the body of opinion in accordance with which the defendant acted. In *Bolitho v City & Hackney HA*,[15] a medical negligence case, Lord Browne-Wilkinson said[16]:
>
> > "the Court is not bound to hold that a defendant doctor escapes liability for negligent treatment or diagnosis just because he leads evidence from a number of medical experts who are genuinely of the opinion that the defendant's treatment or diagnosis accorded with sound medical practice. In the *Bolam* case itself,

---

[11] The finding in the Irish case of *Sunderland v McGreavey* [1987] I.R. 372 that the duty of an architect engaged to carry out a pre-purchase property survey was to "inspect the building with the eye of a competent architect and to draw the inferences which such an architect would draw from what he sees" is questionable. In so far as the architect was carrying out a task normally undertaken by a surveyor, the other view is that the architect should have been judged by the standard of a reasonably competent surveyor.

[12] (1987) 37 B.L.R. 92 at 103 (for the facts see para.9–194, below). This dictum was cited by Judge Bowsher Q.C. in *Department of National Heritage v Steensen Varming Mulcahy* (1998) 60 Con. L.R. 33 at 84.

[13] [1957] 1 W.L.R. 582. This is in fact the second part of the *Bolam* test. The first part states merely that the performance of a skilled professional will be judged by reference to the care and skill practised by the ordinary member of his profession.

[14] See *Florida Hotels Pty Ltd v Mayo* (1965) 113 C.L.R. 588 at 593, *per* Barwick C.J. and 601, *per* Windeyer J.; *Jameson v Simon* (1899) 1 F. 1211, Ct of Sess. at 1222, *per* Lord Trayner; *Greaves & Co (Contractors) Ltd v Baynham Meikle & Partners* [1975] 1 W.L.R. 1095, CA, discussed at para.9–165, below.

[15] [1998] A.C. 232, HL.

[16] *ibid.* at 241.

McNair J. [1957] 1 W.L.R. 583, 587 stated that the defendant had to have acted in accordance with the practice accepted as proper by a '*responsible* body of medical men'. Later, at p.588, he referred to 'a standard of practice recognised a proper by a competent *reasonable* body of opinion.' Again, in the passage which I have cited from *Maynard's case*, Lord Scarman refers to a 'respectable' body of professional opinion. The use of these adjectives—responsible, reasonable and respectable—all show that the court has to be satisfied that the exponents of the body of opinion relied upon can demonstrate that such opinion has a logical basis."

He concluded[17]:

"if, in a rare case, it can be demonstrated that the professional opinion is not capable of withstanding logical analysis, the judge is entitled to hold that the body of opinion is not reasonable or responsible."

(ii) Cases in which the expert evidence called by the defendant is in reality no more than the personal opinion of an expert witness as to what he would have done in the position of the defendant. Such evidence does not establish that the defendant's conduct was in line with a responsible *body* of opinion or with a recognised *practice* within his profession. In *Midland Bank Trust Co Ltd v Hett Stubbs & Kemp*,[18] a solicitors' negligence case, Oliver J. said[19]:

"Clearly, if there is some practice in a profession, some accepted standard of conduct which is laid down by a professional institute or sanctioned by common usage, evidence of that can and ought to be received. But evidence which really amounts to no more than an expression of opinion by a particular practitioner of what he thinks that he would have done had he been placed, hypothetically and without the benefit of hindsight, in the position of the defendants, is of little assistance to the court . . . ."

(iii) Cases in which it is not necessary to apply any particular expertise in, for example, the field of architectural practice, in order to decide whether the defendant has failed to exercise the skill and care expected of an ordinary member of his profession. For example, in *Worboys v Acme Investments Ltd*[20] Sachs L.J. recognised that there were cases where an omission on a plan was so glaring as to require no evidence of general practice and instanced a house without provision for a staircase.

Those three categories of case in which the *Bolam* test will not be applied were **9–141** recognised by the Court of Appeal in *Michael Hyde & Associated Ltd v JD*

---

[17] [1998] A.C. 232, HL at 243.
[18] [1979] Ch. 384. See also *Linden Homes South East Ltd v LBH Wembley Ltd* [2002] EWHC 3115, TCC; (2003) 87 Con. L.R. 180 (finding of negligence in face of evidence of defendant's expert witness because there was not evidence of two respectable but differing bodies of opinion, merely of differing views as between the two individual experts).
[19] *ibid.* at 402. This passage was quoted with approval in the architects' case *Michael Hyde & Associates Ltd v JD Williams & Co Ltd* [2001] P.N.L.R 233, para.26, *per* Ward L.J. (with whom Sedley and Nourse L.JJ. agreed): see para.9–141, below. In this category of case, it would perhaps be more accurate to say that the initial criteria for application of the *Bolam* test are not met rather than that the test is disapplied.
[20] (1969) 210 E.G. 335, CA. See also the medical negligence case of *Gold v Haringey HA* [1988] 1 Q.B. 481 at 490, *per* Lloyd L.J. : "If the giving of contraceptive advice required no special skill, then I could see an argument that the *Bolam* test should not apply."

Williams & Co Ltd,[21] holding that the instant case fell into the third category. The trial judge found that the defendant architects were negligent in failing to investigate the seriousness of a risk of discoloration of stored textiles caused by a gas heating system. This finding was made despite evidence from experts who confirmed that they would have done no more than the defendants did. The judge held that the defendants failed to apply reasonable care when they failed to realise that the system supplier's refusal to remove a disclaimer of liability for discoloration of materials suggested that the risk might be more serious than the supplier's salesman would admit. The judge declined to apply the *Bolam* test, saying: "These factors in my judgment are not peculiar to architectural or engineering practice. It was a matter of weighing risks against benefits . . .". The Court of Appeal dismissed the claimant's appeal. Ward L.J. (with whom Sedley and Nourse L.JJ. agreed) held that the judge was entitled to come to the conclusion that the exercise of judgment involved in deciding whether further investigation of the risk of discoloration was required did not of itself require any special architectural skills. He did not have to "get under the skin of a different profession" in order to assess whether or not the defendants had failed to use reasonable skill and care.[22]

9–142   In *Royal Brompton Hospital NHS Trust v Hammond (No.7)*,[23] Judge Seymour Q.C. considered the analysis in *Michael Hyde v Williams* and summarised the principles applying in the third category of cases thus:

> "if I am satisfied on the evidence that an obvious mistake was made which would not have been made by any careful person of whatever profession, or, indeed, of none, then I can find that the person who made that mistake was negligent. What I cannot do, as it seems to me, is to substitute my own view for that of a professional person of the appropriate discipline on any matter in respect of which any special skill, training or expertise is required to make an informed assessment."[24]

In that case, the claimant alleged that its architects had been negligent in granting unwarranted extensions of time to the contractor which was engaged in building a new hospital for the claimant. Having rejected as unhelpful the evidence of the claimant's expert architect, the judge held that he could find the architects negligent only if he was satisfied that they had made an error which no one applying reasonable common sense would have made. On the facts, and without the assistance of supportive expert evidence, the majority of the claimant's allegations of breach failed. The case illustrates the importance of the correct

---

[21] [2001] P.N.L.R 233, CA.
[22] *ibid.* at para.27. Ward L.J. also observed (at para.26) that the judge would also have been entitled to disapply the *Bolam* test on the basis that the case fell into the second category: "He may well have been able to discount the evidence on that basis for I find little to suggest that there were two recognised but contrary views of an accepted practice governing the decision in question. As I read the evidence the experts were doing no more than putting themselves forward as reasonably competent architects and then saying what they would have done in the circumstances in which Mr Warrington found himself."
[23] (2001) 76 Con. L.R. 148.
[24] *ibid.* at 170.

application and presentation of expert evidence in professional negligence cases.[25]

It might be thought that the issue of breach of duty in *Adams v Rhymney Valley DC*[26] could have been decided without the application of any particular professional skill, but the Court of Appeal reached a different view. The defendant local authority installed window locks with removable keys in housing occupied by the claimants. The keys to the windows were kept out of reach of the claimants' three children. In a house fire, the family were unable to reach the keys in order to use the bedroom windows as a means of escape, and the three children perished as a result. The claimants alleged that the defendant was negligent and in breach of statutory duty in failing to install push-button locks, which could have been readily opened in an emergency. The locks had been chosen by the defendant's housing department, which had not consulted the local fire or police services and had not considered the relative merits of different types of lock design. Sir Christopher Staughton identified[27] the key issue as:

> "whether the *Bolam* test still applies, although the particular defendant did not in fact have the qualifications of a professional in the relevant field of activity, and although he did not go through the process of reasoning which a qualified professional could consider before making a choice."

The majority in the Court of Appeal held that the test did apply and that, in the light of expert evidence to the effect that a reasonably competent window designer could have chosen a lock with removable keys in preference to the push-button type, the defendant was not in breach of its duty of care to the claimants. In his dissenting judgment Sedley L.J. held that the *Bolam* test was not appropriate to determine whether a defendant has failed to exercise reasonable skill and care in a case where the defendant has not exercised, and has not purported to exercise, any special skill. In other words, to have one's performance measured by reference to the *Bolam* test is a privilege reserved to those who have considered and reflected upon the alternative courses available and made a conscious choice between them.[28] It is submitted that this is an impracticably stringent requirement for the application of the test, since many reasonably careful and competent professionals properly practice in accordance with the manner which they have been taught rather than from first principles. It was expressly rejected by Sir Christopher Staughton[29]:

> "Seeing that, upon the hypothesis which is inherent in the problem, a respectable body of professionals have been and are in favour of each course, I do not see that the defendant is required to go through the same thought process in order to deserve the support of those who favour the course which he chooses. The consultant who naturally chooses one method out of long experience is as much entitled to rely on the *Bolam*

---

[25] See further paras 9–144 to 9–149, below.
[26] [2001] P.N.L.R 68.
[27] *ibid.* at para.42.
[28] See, to similar effect, the judgment of the same judge in *Michael Hyde & Associates Ltd v JD Williams & Co Ltd* [2001] P.N.L.R 233 at para.46.
[29] [2001] P.N.L.R 68 at para.43.

doctrine as one who sits down in his chair and goes through the whole process of choice again."

However, it remains difficult to see why the defendants in *Adams* should have enjoyed the benefit of the *Bolam* test. As demonstrated by the reasoning set out in the judgment of Sedley L.J., the relative merits of locks with removable keys and push-button locks for use in local authority housing for families were capable of being assessed without the exercise of any particular professional expertise, as a matter of reasonable common sense. As such, the case arguably fell into the third category of cases identified in *Michael Hyde v Williams* as not requiring the application of the *Bolam* test.[30]

(iii) *Expert Evidence*

9–144 The decision as to the standard of skill and care required of a defendant professional is ultimately a matter for the court, and not for the profession in the form of expert witnesses. In *F v R*,[31] King C.J. put it this way:

> "The ultimate question, however, is not whether the defendant's conduct accords with the practices of his profession or some part of it, but whether it confirms to the standard of reasonable care demanded by the law. That is a question for the court and the duty of deciding it cannot be delegated to any profession or group in the community."

9–145 However, in most cases in which construction professionals are alleged to have fallen below the required standard of skill and care, the court will be assisted by expert evidence as to either or both:

(i) matters of scientific or technical fact. To this extent, the expert's function is merely didactic, in that he explains the technical aspects of the case in terms comprehensible to the layperson. Expert evidence of this sort may be largely or wholly uncontroversial;

(ii) the standards ordinarily observed in his profession, including the existence of schools of thought, bodies of opinion or of recognised practices within the profession.

Indeed, save in those (relatively rare) cases in which the issue of breach of duty can properly be decided as a matter of ordinary common sense,[32] expert evidence that the reasonably competent professional would not have committed the act or omission complained of will be essential for a finding of breach of duty.

9–146 The judgment of Judge Lloyd Q.C. in *Royal Brompton Hospital NHS Trust v Hammond (No.9)* includes a detailed discussion of the role of expert evidence in

---

[30] See paras 9–140 to 9–141, above. In her article "Something 'old', something 'new', something 'borrowed' . . . The continued evolution of *Bolam*" (2001) 17 P.N. 75, Paula de Prez criticises the application of the *Bolam* test in *Adams* and comments that it is distasteful for negligence litigation to be successfully defended on the basis of coincidence rather than competence.

[31] (1983) S.A.S.R. 189 at 194, Supreme Court of South Australia. See further C. Leong, and P. Chan, "Architects' design duties: a shift from *Bolam's* to the objective test" (1999) 15 P.N. 3.

[32] See paras 9–140 to 9–141, above.

claims against construction professionals.[33] The judge commented that expert evidence may be needed to assist the court to assess the evidence, for example, by indicating which factors or technical considerations would influence the judgment of a professional person, in cases where the negligence alleged is not a failure to follow an established professional practice. Otherwise, in such cases, expert evidence is not indispensable. The issue of breach of duty may be determined as a matter of common sense. Alternatively, the court may itself possess the necessary expertise to assess the evidence; the Technology and Construction Court has such expertise in disputes arising in the construction industry and in other areas of commerce. Even so, expert evidence may remain desirable in order to satisfy the court that its decision on the required standard of care is in line with the expectations and understanding of the profession. The judge also pointed out that, since the role of the expert witness under the Civil Procedure Rules is to assist the court rather than to make a case for the expert's instructing party, it is not necessary for a party which alleges negligence to adduce supporting expert evidence, provided that in a case where such evidence is necessary or desirable it is available from an expert called by another party.

Care is required in the selection and presentation of expert evidence. In the first place, evidence will be admitted only from a member of the profession to which the defendant belongs.[34] In *Investors in Industry Commercial Properties v South Bedfordshire DC*[35] the Court of Appeal held that there was no sustainable claim against architects, primarily because there was no relevant evidence from other architects as to standards in the profession. Slade L.J. said[36]: **9–147**

> "Expert evidence from suitably qualified professional persons is, in our judgment, admissible to show what competent architects in the position of Hamiltons could reasonably have been expected to know and do in their position at the relevant time. Indeed, in our judgment, there could be no question of the Court condemning them for professional negligence . . . unless there were appropriate expert evidence to support the allegation that their conduct fell below the standard which might reasonably be expected of an ordinarily competent architect . . . . The expert evidence before the judge consisted of evidence from three engineers and one architect, Mr Foster. The questions put to the engineers and answered by them included questions relating to the nature and extent of the professional duties owed by Hamiltons to Anglia. However, we think that little reliance can be placed on their answers to these particular questions, which related to a profession other than their own."

The only expert architect, Mr Foster, was called by the defendants. In the face of his evidence, the Court held that the claimant had not established that the architects were in breach of duty. The claim in *Sansom v Metcalfe Hambleton & Co*[37] arose out of a building surveyor's failure to draw his client's attention to a crack in the wall of the property. The trial judge found the defendant to have been

---

[33] [2002] EWHC 2037, TCC, at paras 16–25.
[34] Or, where the defendant was providing services normally provided by members of another profession, from a member of that profession: see para.9–137, above.
[35] [1986] 1 All E.R. 787. For the facts, see para.9–185, below.
[36] *ibid.* at 808–809.
[37] [1998] P.N.L.R. 542.

negligent and in so doing accepted the evidence of the claimant's expert structural engineer in preference to that of the defendant's expert building surveyor. The Court of Appeal held that this finding was not supported by relevant and admissible evidence. Butler-Sloss L.J. said[38]:

> "a court should be slow to find a professionally qualified man guilty of a breach of his duty of skill and care towards a client (or third party) without evidence from those within the same profession as to the standard expected on the facts of the case and the failure of the professionally qualified man to measure up to that standard."

9–148   Secondly, it is important that the evidence of an expert witness is confined to matters which are relevant to the issues before the court and upon which the witness is properly qualified to comment. In *Pozzolanic Lytag Ltd v Bryan Hobson Associates*[39] the defendant engineers were engaged in connection with the construction of a storage dome for pulverised fuel ash. The services which they agreed to provide included project management in relation to the contract for construction of the dome, which was awarded to a design and build contractor. The dome collapsed due to design defects. It transpired that the contractor was insolvent and uninsured. The claimant alleged that the defendants were in breach of duty as project managers in that they had failed to see that the contractor had taken out indemnity insurance against claims for design defects, as required by the building contract. Dyson J. stated that the expert witnesses should have confined themselves to the question whether there was a common practice in the engineering profession as to what engineers, who are engaged as project managers, do in relation to the insurance obligations of contractors. Instead, they considered numerous other issues including contributory negligence, which was a matter for the court. He warned[40]:

> "Prolix expert reports directed to issue with which they should not be concerned merely add to the expense of litigation. Everything possible should be done to discourage this. In appropriate cases, this will include making special orders for costs."

9–149   In *Pride Valley Food Ltd v Hall and Partners (Contract Management) Ltd*,[41] the claimant sought to adduce the expert evidence of an architect in support of its

---

[38] [1998] P.N.L.R. 542 at 549. Note also the Scottish case of *J. Dykes Ltd v Littlewoods Mail Order Stores Ltd*, 1982 S.L.T. 50 (action against firm of consulting engineers dismissed after allegations of breach of duty against the firm were held to be irrelevant in that the pursuers did not link the alleged duties to the standard of ordinary professional competence of consultant engineers); and *Pride Valley Foods Ltd v Hall & Partners (Contract Management) Ltd* (2000) 76 Con. L.R. 1 at 24 (there being no established profession of project manager, care was needed to select expert witnesses who were able to give useful evidence as to the standard of care to be applied in the discharge of a project manager's duty of care: see the passage from the judgment of Judge Toulmin C.M.G. Q.C. which is quoted at n.17 to para.9–006, above) (the Court of Appeal did not comment on this passage: [2001] EWCA Civ 1001; [2001] 76 Con. L.R. 1 at 36).
[39] [1999] B.L.R. 267.
[40] *ibid.* at 275.
[41] (2001) 76 Con. L.R. 1; the claimant's appeal on causation succeeded ([2001] EWCA 1001; (2001) 76 Con. L.R. 1 at 36).

claim against the defendant project manager. Judge Toulmin C.M.G. Q.C. concluded that the evidence provided little or no assistance. Amongst other criticisms,[42] he pointed out that the report was overlong, included opinions on matters of fact and law which were questions for decision by the court and included expressions of opinion as to what the expert himself would have done in the defendant's position. In *Royal Brompton Hospital NHS Trust v Hammond (No.7)*,[43] the evidence of the claimant's expert architect was rejected in its entirety by the trial judge. Judge Seymour Q.C. warned that, if experts are to give useful evidence, they must be given sufficient time to master the relevant documents. In a typical construction case, the volume of documentation which an expert will need to digest may be very large. Further, experts should avoid making assumptions (or accepting instructions to make assumptions) the accuracy of which is central to the questions which they are to address.[44] Finally, experts should make sure that they have contemporary knowledge of practice in their own profession. The claimant's expert architect's evidence was found wanting in each of these respects. The more restrictive attitude of modern courts towards expert evidence was confirmed when the Court of Appeal upheld an order debarring the defendant from calling his expert building surveyor in *Stevens v Gullis*.[45] The expert had failed in his duty to act impartially and had also to comply with the requirements of the Civil Procedure Rules in relation to his report and a joint memorandum of matters agreed with the claimant's expert.

(iv) *Res Ipsa Loquitur*

It follows from the considerations set out above that it will be very rarely that **9–150** there is room for the application of the maxim *res ipsa loquitur*[46] in a professional negligence action against a construction professional. The failure of a building or the issue of a certificate for the wrong amount will very rarely be

---

[42] See the passage quoted at fn.17 to para.9–006, above on the need for care in selecting an expert to give evidence on a claim against a project manager.

[43] (2001) 76 Con. L.R. 148. For the facts, see para.9–142, above. See also *Anglo Group Plc v Winther Brown & Co Ltd*, unreported, March 1, 2000, and *Catlin Estates Ltd v Carter Jonas* [2005] EWHC 2315, TCC (evidence of defendant's experts disregarded for failure to comply with duty of impartiality). See also *Stephen Donald Architects Ltd v Christopher King* [2003] EWHC 1867, TCC (evidence of defendant's expert architect unhelpful because he did not address the question whether any reasonably competent architect would have prepared a different design in response to the client's brief). In *Great Eastern Hotel Co Ltd v John Laing Construction Ltd* [2005] EWHC 181, TCC, the evidence of the defendant's construction management expert was rejected because, in failing to carry out thorough research, in accepting uncritically the factual account given by the defendant and in failing to take account of material evidence, he demonstrated "no concept of his duty to the court as an independent expert" (*per* Judge Wilcox at [128]).

[44] Compare the Commercial Court Guide, para.H2.6: an expert should state the assumptions upon which his opinion is based, and if a stated assumption is, in the opinion of the expert, unreasonable or unlikely, he should state that clearly.

[45] [2000] 1 All E.R. 527.

[46] The doctrine has been abandoned in Canada: *Fontaine v Loewen Estate* (1997) 156 D.L.R. (4th) 181, Supreme Court of Canada. See also *Pearson v Fryer*, The Times, April 4, 2000, in which Roch L.J. said of the maxim: "It troubles me that we still tend to fall into the habit of talking about maxims or doctrines which go under labels in Latin whose meaning does not express a defined principle, and which those for whose benefit [they exist] will probably not understand." For further discussion, see C. Witting, "*Res Ipsa Loquitur*: Some Last Words?" (2001) 117 L.Q.R. 392.

sufficient, of itself, to demonstrate that there has been a failure to take reasonable care on the part of a construction professional. In *Copthorne Hotel (Newcastle) Ltd v Arup Associates*,[47] Judge Hicks Q.C. found that the claimant had failed to make out a case of negligent estimation in respect of piling costs where the defendants had estimated a figure of £425,000 against an out-turn cost of £975,000. No evidence had been led as to what figure the defendants should have used for pile diameter, which was an essential element in arriving at a price. The judge said:

> "I hope and believe that I am not over-simplifying if I record the impression that the plaintiff's main hope was that I would be persuaded to find in their favour simply by the size of the gap, absolutely and proportionately, between the cost estimate and the successful tender.
> The gap was indeed enormous. It astonished and appalled the parties at the time, and it astonishes me. I do not see, however, how that alone can carry the plaintiff home. There is no plea or argument that the maxim 'res ipsa loquitur' applies. Culpable under-estimation is of course one obvious explanation of such a discrepancy, but far from the only one . . . ."

9–151   It will be particularly important to adduce cogent evidence of a failure to exercise reasonable care where the task performed by the construction pro-fessional requires the application of skill and judgment to complex facts. In *Royal Brompton Hospital NHS Trust v Hammond (No.7)*[48] the complaint was that architects had granted extensions of time to the building contractor which were too lengthy. The project, the construction of a new hospital, was large and complex. In considering claims for extensions of time, the architects were required to calculate the effect of various delaying factors upon the programme for the works so as to arrive at a revised contractual completion date. Expert evidence adduced on the question of contract programming was to the effect that the accuracy with which works can be reprogrammed depends upon the quality of the information available. Judge Seymour Q.C. said[49]:

> "All of this does, of course, emphasise the vital point that the duty of a professional man, generally stated, is not to be right, but to be careful. While, unless in a particular case the professional man is actually wrong, the fact that he has not been careful will probably not cause his client any loss, the fact that he is in the event proved to be wrong is not, in itself, any evidence that he has been negligent. His conduct has to be judged having regard to the information available to him, or which ought to have been available to him, at the time that he gave his advice or made his decision or did whatever else it is that he did."

(v) *Codes of Practice and Legislation*

9–152   A feature of the construction professions is the large number of codes of practice and published standards relating to the manner of construction. Moreover, the

---

[47] (1996) 58 Con. L.R. 105.
[48] (2001) 76 Con. L.R. 148. For the facts, see para.9–142, above.
[49] *ibid.* at 1717.

manner of construction is extensively regulated by statutory regulations both in the United Kingdom[50] and in the Commonwealth. The purpose of such codes, standards and regulations is to provide for standards of safety and good building practice. Since they broadly reflect good practice, the question frequently arises as to whether non-compliance with relevant codes or regulations is indicative of negligence. Claims against construction professionals are frequently based on alleged breach of a duty to take reasonable care to ensure that the design was in accordance with the requirements of building regulations or byelaws. The premise behind such formulations of the duty is that non-compliance is indicative of negligence. In the case of specific requirements such formulations need qualification to provide for forms of construction which, although they do not comply with the regulations, may be wholly consistent with their broad purpose, in particular safety. Many regulations, however, are sufficiently broad to allow wide flexibility of form of construction.

The effect of non-compliance with codes of practice was extensively considered in relation to a claim against an engineer for negligent design by Beattie J. in *Bevan Investments Ltd v Blackhall and Struthers (No.2)*.[51] He took the view that: **9–153**

"Bearing in mind the function of codes, a design which departs substantially from them is prima facie a faulty design, unless it can be demonstrated that it conforms to accepted engineering practice by rational analysis. If I am correct in this appreciation, and if on the evidence it is established that the design in several material respects fails to comply with the relevant codes, then [the defendant engineer] and his experts must show that the design is capable of rational analysis and is adequate and safe. I do not go so far as to say however that the mere circumstance that a client is unaware that the designer is working outside a code can of itself categorise a designer's actions as negligent."[52]

Expert evidence was given in the same case that rigid application of codes would stifle a number of progressive advances. Beattie J. nevertheless commended the view that experimental proposals should have the encouragement or actual approval of the client and would need to embody sound engineering design and practice. This view was followed in *Kaliszewska v John Clague & Partners*[53] where the defendant architect was found to have been negligent in his design of foundations for a bungalow, having failed:

". . . to call evidence or to show by rational analysis that although the defendant's design did not comply with the current Codes of Practice and did not appear to be

---

[50] See the Building Regulations 2000 which came into force on January 1, 2001 (as now amended by the Building Regulations (Amendment) (No.3) Regulations 2004) and the Construction (Design and Management) Regulations 1994 discussed in para.9–046, above.

[51] [1973] 2 N.Z.L.R. 45.

[52] *ibid.* at 65–66. Also note *Victoria University of Manchester v Hugh Wilson* (1984) 2 Con. L.R. 43, 74 *per* Judge Newey Q.C.: "CP 212 and other literature were not binding on the architects in the sense that they were obliged to follow their recommendations precisely, but they should certainly have taken them into account and disregarded them only if they had good scientific reasons for so doing."

[53] (1984) 5 Con. L.R. 62.

within the mainstream of knowledge, it was nevertheless as a result of local conditions adequate."[54]

9–154   A professional is not, however, entitled slavishly to follow the provisions of a code of practice without considering its precise relevance to the project in hand. In *IBA v EMI and BICC*,[55] Lord Fraser said[56]:

"I have reached the firm conclusion that BICC failed in their duty of care when they applied the code of practice that had been found appropriate for lattice masts to the new cylindrical mast at Emley Moor without noticing that the reason for disregarding ice on the stays was not applicable to a cylindrical mast. They were therefore negligent in their design."

9–155   Similarly in *Holland Hannen and Cubitts (Northern) Ltd v Welsh Health Technical Services Organisation*,[57] Robert Goff L.J. said[58]:

"The structural engineer will therefore simply consider the profile of the floor as such; and ask himself the question whether there is a significant risk that the floor, with that profile, in the building in question, may be unacceptable. In considering that question he cannot simply rely on the codes of practice. It is plain from the evidence that the code of practice is no more than a guide for use by professional men, who have to exercise their own expertise; this must moreover be especially true in a case such as the present, where the design was a novel one, omitting as it did a finishing screed. Practice alone can, I consider, provide of itself no reliable guide where, as here, a novel design concept is being used."

(vi) *Knowledge of the Law*

9–156   The knowledge of law required of an architect was considered by Gibson J. at first instance in *B L Holdings Ltd v Robert J Wood and Partners*.[59] It was

---

[54] (1984) 5 Con. L.R. 62 at 77. In *Turner Page Music Ltd v Torres Design Associates* (1997) C.I.L.L. 1263, Judge Hicks Q.C. found that the defendant architects were negligent in failing to provide adequate means of escape for a refurbished theatre, with the result that Building Regulations approval was refused. He rejected the defendants' submission that refusal of Building Regulations approval was a routine experience which did not reflect upon the designer. In *Munkenbeck & Marshall v Regent Health and Fitness Club Ltd (No.2)* (1997) 59 Con. L.R. 145, Judge Rich Q.C., accepted a submission that where plans were submitted to a local authority which were not in accordance with "an approved document" relating to the provision of adequate fire escapes and recognised by s.7 of the Building Act 1984, it was for the architects who had submitted the plans to demonstrate that the plans would nonetheless be acceptable under the Building Regulations. See also *Storey v Charles Church Developments Plc* (1995) 73 Con. L.R. 1, where designers of a house were held negligent for failing to take proper account of the Building Regulations, British Standards and other published guidance in designing for a site upon which there were various mature trees.
[55] (1980) 14 B.L.R. 1, HL. For facts see para.9–095, above.
[56] *ibid.* at 36–37.
[57] (1985) 35 B.L.R. 1. For facts see para.9–213, below. A Canadian decision to the same effect is *Homes by Jayman v Kellam Berg* (1997) 54 Alta. L.R. (3d) 272 (Alberta Court of Appeal) (although septic tanks designed by an engineer complied with the relevant codes they were nonetheless too small).
[58] *ibid.* at 25; Goff L.J. dissented as to whether the engineers were obliged to consider the aesthetic importance of the floor and consequently the other members of the court did not regard the engineer as bound to ask himself the question which Goff L.J. poses. Nonetheless it is submitted that his words are relevant and apposite to questions which a professional man is obliged to ask.
[59] (1978) 10 B.L.R. 48.

conceded in that case that when an architect agrees to act in some field of activity commonly carried on by architects, in which a knowledge and understanding of certain principles of law are required, and if the work is to be done properly and the client's interest protected, the architect must have a sufficient knowledge of those principles of law in order reasonably to protect his client from danger and loss. The judge added that in many particular cases a professional man engaging in such work would have, and display, a sufficient knowledge of the relevant principles of law by knowing, and by advising his client, that he knows little or nothing of them, and by refusing to incur expense on behalf of his client or to expose him to risk of financial loss, until his client had obtained legal advice or decided to act upon his own judgment.[60] This passage was approved by the Court of Appeal in *West Faulkner Associates v London Borough of Newham*[61] where the Court was considering whether the mistaken construction of a standard form clause in a building contract was one which a reasonably competent architect could have held. The Court held that it was not and Brown L.J. (with whom the other members of the Court agreed) went on: "At the very least [the architect] should have realised that the clause might fall to be construed differently . . . and in those circumstances should either himself have sought, or asked his client to seek, legal advice specifically upon the point."[62]

In the *B L Holdings* case the defendant architects agreed to act for the claimant **9–157** clients in the obtaining of planning permission for an office building. They thereby, in the judge's view, took upon themselves the obligation of knowing enough of the principles of law relating to office development control to be able to advise their clients adequately and reasonably to protect them from damage and loss. The defendants were wrongly advised by an officer of the local planning authority that certain areas were to be excluded in calculating the area of a building for the purpose of determining whether the limit was exceeded beyond which an office development permit was required. Acting on that advice the architects designed a building which exceeded those limits. Planning permission was granted and the building was erected. On subsequent discovery of the need for a permit and that the planning permission was accordingly void, the claimants were unable to let the building for some three years until the permit limits were raised. Notwithstanding the misleading advice of the local planning officer, Gibson J. held that the architects were in breach of their relevant obligation and accordingly liable in failing to warn their clients of the danger of the planning application being of no effect in law. The Court of Appeal,[63] although not disapproving Gibson J.'s statements of principle, reversed the decision and absolved the architects of liability on the facts. One passage in Gibson J.'s judgment was particularly referred to in reversing his decision: "I think that not a few architects engaged in this work would have been misled exactly as [the particular architect concerned] was and I think that he might well have been followed in error by some lawyers."[64] The decision of the Court of Appeal can thus be viewed as a rare example of the errors of other members of

---

[60] (1978) 10 B.L.R. 48 at 70.
[61] (1994) 71 B.L.R. 1 at 15.
[62] *ibid.* at 18H.
[63] (1979) 12 B.L.R. 1.
[64] (1978) 10 B.L.R. 48, 77; and see (1979) 12 B.L.R. 1, CA at 16, *per* Browne L.J., and at 18, *per* Lawton L.J.

the profession being invoked to absolve the defendant architects of negligence.

9–158 In *Royal Brompton Hospital NHS Trust v Hammond*[65] Judge Lloyd Q.C. took the view that construction professionals acting as contract administrators or project managers must have both a knowledge of the fundamental principles of construction law and an ability to apply those principles in the administration of building contracts and the management of construction projects. He observed that, in many cases, what is required is not so much knowledge of the general law but rather a good understanding of the operation of the standard forms of building contracts. In that case, both architects and project managers were held to have been in breach of duty to their client in advising on the (incorrect) basis that the building contractor would be entitled to determine its employment under the building contract if it were not given a particular instruction for additional work.

9–159 Building regulations and byelaws provide the context in which designers are most commonly required to consider matters of law. Here, also, the construction professional will discharge his duty of care unless no reasonably competent and careful member of his profession would have interpreted the relevant provisions in the way that he has. In *J Sainsbury Plc v Broadway Malyan*,[66] consulting engineers were retained by architects acting in connection with the design and construction of a superstore. The design included a compartment wall separating the sales area of the store from the service area. The architects' design provided for one side only of the wall above roof girder level to be fire-resistant. When a fire spread from the service area to the sales area, the store owner claimed damages against the architects for defective design of the compartment wall. The architects compromised the store owner's action and claimed contribution from the engineers, alleging that they ought to have appreciated and warned that the roof girder was part of the compartment wall and therefore subject to the fire-resistance requirements of the Building Regulations. Judge Lloyd Q.C. held that, on the correct construction of the relevant Building Regulations, the girder was not an "element of structure" which required fire protection but that, if he was wrong about that, the engineers would not have been negligent had they failed to appreciate that the girder was an "element of structure" within the meaning of the Regulations. He said[67]:

> "The interpretation of the Building Regulations is ultimately a question of law, but it is relevant to consider how they strike the non-lawyers, such as engineers, for whom they are intended and who have to understand and apply them. It does not of course follow that if the correct meaning is not recognised by such a reasonably competent person then that person is negligent. The degree to which such a person is expected to be familiar with the meaning and operation of [the] Regulations is a separate issue."

---

[65] [2002] EWHC 2037, TCC.
[66] [1999] P.N.L.R. 286.
[67] *ibid.* at 302–303.

(vii) *Not Every Error is Negligence*

The standard of reasonable care and skill is not a standard of perfection. It does **9–160** not make an architect, for example, the insurer[68] or guarantor[69] that work has been properly done. It is not sufficient to prove an error in order to show that there has been a failure to exercise reasonable care and skill. Actual negligence must be proven.[70] Similarly an error of judgment or wrong opinion is not necessarily negligent.[71]

Moreover trivial or few errors may not necessarily be negligent. Thus in **9–161** *London School Board v Northcroft, Son and Neighbour*[72] as a result of two errors by a clerk employed by the defendant quantity surveyors, builders were overpaid two sums of £118 and £15 15s. on buildings to the value of £12,000. The judge rejected the claimant employer's claim that the clerk was negligent in making the two errors. A stricter view was taken in another quantity surveyor's case, *Tyrer v District Auditor of Monmouthshire*.[73] In that case in one particular contract the quantity surveyor had made a simple mathematical error in issuing an interim certificate. Lord Widgery C.J. conceded that this was an error which could happen at any time, "but the obligation was on the appellant to ensure that adequate checks were made".[74] The quantity surveyor was, however, held on the facts to have been "negligent over and over again". It may well be that if there had only been the one error in the interim certificate and if it had involved a small sum, a different view might have been taken. Clearly the more and the greater in consequence the errors, the more difficult it will be to resist a finding of negligence, if only because there will be a strong suggestion of a fault in the system adopted by the quantity surveyor to produce his valuations.

In the case of errors in supervision (or inspection) the question frequently **9–162** arises whether the error pertains to a matter of detail or not. Thus where what is

---

[68] See *Moresk Cleaners Ltd v Hicks* [1966] 2 Lloyd's Rep 338 at 342, *per* Judge Sir Walker Carter O.R.

[69] See *East Ham Corp v Bernard Sunley & Sons Ltd* [1966] A.C. 406 at 427, *per* Viscount Dilhorne. See also the Canadian case of *Meredith v Macfarlane* (1915) 9 O.W.N. 160: microscopic perfection of an architect's work is not required.

[70] See *Sutcliffe v Thackrah* [1974] A.C. 727 at 760, *per* Lord Salmon: "It by no means follows that a professional valuation was negligently given because it turns out to have been wholly wrong. Nor does the fact that an architect's certificate was given for the wrong amount of itself prove negligence against the architect." See also Robert Goff L.J.'s judgment in *Holland Hannen and Cubitts (Northern) Ltd v Welsh Health Technical Services Organisation* (1985) 35 B.L.R. 1 at 22 where he states: "The true answer must be to recognise that his obligation is only to exercise due care and skill, though, where he is held to have been negligent, to identify precisely the negligence to which he is held guilty." Goff L.J.'s dissent on one aspect of the case is not thought to affect this. See further para.9–216, below. See also *Copthorne Hotel (Newcastle) Ltd v Arup Associates* (1996) 12 Const. L.J. 402 where Judge Hicks Q.C. found that an enormous difference between a predicted piling price and the tender price was insufficient, of itself, to establish that the prediction had been negligent; and the extract from the judgment of Judge Seymour Q.C. in *Royal Brompton Hospital NHS Trust v Hammond (No.7)* (2001) Con. L.R. 148 which is quoted at para.9–151, above.

[71] See *Armitage v Palmer* (1960) 175 E.G. 315, CA, *per* Harman L.J.; *East Ham Corp v Bernard Sunley & Sons Ltd* [1966] A.C. 406 at 443 *per* Lord Upjohn; *J. Sainsbury Plc v Broadway Malyan* [1999] P.N.L.R. 286 at 300, *per* Judge Lloyd Q.C. The qualification "not necessarily negligent" is important: see the medical negligence case of *Whitehouse v Jordan* [1981] 1 W.L.R. 246 at 257–258, 263 and 268.

[72] (1889) cited in *Hudson's Building Contracts* (4th edn), Vol.2, p.147.

[73] (1973) 230 E.G. 973.

[74] *ibid.* at 974.

required of an architect is reasonable examination of the building works, it is recognised that some defects and insufficiencies might escape his notice.[75] Where an employer directly employs a clerk of works and also engages an architect, examining matters of detail are for the former leaving the latter to attend to more important matters.[76] Moreover, a certain degree of tolerance must be allowed for in determining the quality of work supervised, although this does not entail giving an architect a general dispensing power.[77] In a mid-19th century case Erle J. expressed the view: "if you employ [an architect] about a novel thing, about which he has had little experience, if it has not had the test of experience, failure may be consistent with skill. The history of all great improvements show failure of those who embark in them."[78] While it is correct in principle to state that failure may be consistent with skill, Erle J.'s view seems generally reflective of a less safety-conscious age than the present. A reflection of modern standards in relation to a novel design, particularly where there are safety implications, is found in Lord Edmund-Davies's speech in *IBA v EMI and BICC*.[79] It must be recognised, however, that it is unrealistic to expect standards of perfection in construction works. The case of *Christopher Moran Holdings Ltd v Carden & Godfrey*[80] concerned the reconstruction of a historic building on the site of Thomas More's garden in Chelsea, London, at a total cost of "many millions of pounds".[81] In response to its architect's claim for unpaid fees, the building owner counterclaimed damages for negligence in four respects. One of the complaints was that there was inadequate headroom on the stairs leading to a tower room looking over the River Thames. Judge Wilcox found, on the facts, that the problem was not the result of breach of duty on the part of the architects, but he also noted that the defect could be repaired at a cost of £450.75 and remarked[82]:

> "Looked at in its proper context, this is a minor complaint. It is easy of resolution and is typical of the minor matters that crop up in complex schemes such as this and does not necessarily connote negligence on anyone's part."

(viii) *The Specialist Practitioner*

9–163   When the client deliberately obtains and pays for an architect, engineer or quantity surveyor of especially high skills, is the required standard not the conventional standard of the ordinary competent and skilled practitioner but some higher standard? This question was answered negatively in the case of engineers by Webster J. in *Wimpey Construction UK Ltd v Poole*.[83] In that case

---

[75] See *East Ham Corp v Bernard Sunley & Sons Ltd* [1966] A.C. 406 especially at 427. Also see *Cedar Transport Group Ltd v First Wyvern Property Trustees Co Ltd* (1981) 258 E.G. 1077.
[76] See para.9–246, below. Somewhat anomalously in *London Hospital Trustees v TP Bennett & Son* (1987) 13 Con. L.R. 22 Judge Stabb Q.C. said (at 28) that, although a clerk of works was the employee of the building owner, "in fact he was also the eyes and ears of the architect".
[77] See *Cotton v Wallis* [1955] 1 W.L.R. 1168, CA at 1176 and 1177.
[78] *Turner v Garland and Christopher* (1853) cited in *Hudson's Building Contracts* (4th edn, 1914) Vol.2, p.1.
[79] (1980) 14 B.L.R. 1 at 18: see para.9–095, above.
[80] (1999) 73 Con. L.R. 28.
[81] *ibid.* at 30.
[82] *ibid.* at 40.
[83] [1984] 2 Lloyd's Rep. 499 at 506.

the claimant company was alleged to have been negligent in the design of a new quay wall at Southampton. The design had been carried out by the company's engineering department which employed some most experienced designers and at least one designer of exceptionally high qualifications. Applying the conventional test the judge held that the company had not been negligent in that design. The judge nevertheless accepted that it was the duty of a professional man to exercise reasonable care in light of his actual knowledge and that the question whether he had exercised reasonable care could not be answered by reference to a lesser degree of knowledge than in fact he had, on the grounds that the ordinarily competent practitioner would only have that lesser degree of knowledge.[84]

Moreover, where a practitioner holds himself out as a specialist in a well **9–164** recognised speciality practised by some but not all within a wider profession, such as geotechnical engineers within the engineering profession, the relevant standard is that of the ordinary competent and skilled practitioner in that speciality.[85] In *Gloucestershire HA v Torpy*,[86] the defendant engineers were engaged in connection with the design and specification of new incinerators for a hospital. The incinerators installed failed to meet performance requirements and were unsuitable. Judge Bowsher Q.C. drew a distinction between specialist engineers (who were to be judged by the standards appropriate to such specialists) and general practice engineers with experience of a particular specialism (who were to be judged by the standard of such general practitioners). The defendants were mechanical and engineering building services engineers who claimed to have extensive experience in incinerator technology. The judge rejected the argument that, on that account, the defendants were to be judged by the standard of specialists. They were general practitioners with experience in a particular field, rather than specialists in that field, and were to be judged by reference to the care and skill exercised by ordinary mechanical and engineering building services engineers.

(ix) *Special Steps and Warranty of Reasonable Fitness*

While generally in the course of his ordinary employment a construction pro- **9–165** fessional is under no higher duty than the duty to use reasonable care and skill, the circumstances of a particular case may require special steps to be taken in order to fulfil that duty. In *Greaves & Co (Contractors) Ltd v Baynham Meikle & Partners*[87] the claimant contractors were required to design and build a warehouse for the storage of heavy oil drums. They sub-contracted the structural design of the warehouse to the defendant engineers. It was made known to the engineers that the first floor had to take the weight of loaded fork-lift trucks. After the warehouse was built the first floor began to crack owing to vibration

---

[84] [1984] 2 Lloyd's Rep. 499 at 506–507.
[85] See further Ch.11, para.11–006 to 11–007.
[86] (1997) 55 Con. L.R. 124. On very similar facts, Judge Toulmin C.M.G., Q.C., in *Hammersmith Hospitals NHS Trust v Troup Bywaters & Anders* [2000] Env. L.R. 343 held that the defendants were to be judged by the standard of ordinarily competent building services engineers and not as if they were experts in combustion, incineration or waste handling technology. On the facts in that case, the engineers were not in breach of duty: affirmed on appeal: [2001] EWCA Civ 793.
[87] [1974] 1 W.L.R. 1261.

caused by the movement of the trucks. It was held that the engineers had not designed the floor with sufficient strength to withstand the vibration. Further, the engineers had misconstrued a warning of vibration in the type of construction used in the relevant code of practice. Kilner-Brown J. at first instance, confronted with evidence indicating a divergence of view as to what a competent engineer would have done and a strong body of opinion that the defendant engineers had not failed, held that the engineers were not in breach of their duty to exercise reasonable care and skill. But on the facts he held that the engineers owed a higher duty and that they were in breach of that duty. The Court of Appeal,[88] although upholding the judge's decision, reversed him on this point. It held that there was no such higher duty on professional men and that what the judge meant was that in the circumstances of the case, special steps were required to discharge the duty to exercise reasonable care and skill and that those steps had not been taken.

9–166   It was held in *Greaves* that the defendant engineers were in breach of an implied term in their contract with the contractors that their design would be reasonably fit for the purpose, namely for use of loaded fork-lift trucks. The judges in the Court of Appeal were at pains to emphasise that the term was implied in the particular circumstances of the case and that they were not deciding the question whether an architect or an engineer employed to design a house or a bridge impliedly warranted that his design would be fit for the purpose.[89] Lord Denning M.R. mooted that that question might have to be answered some day as a matter of law.

9–167   This question was subsequently considered in *IBA v EMI and BICC*.[90] It was argued for the sub-contractors, BICC, who had designed the television mast, that since design was normally a function for a professional man they should be under no higher duty than that generally applicable to such a man namely a duty to exercise reasonable care and skill according to the accepted standards of his profession. The argument was rejected by the Court of Appeal on two grounds.[91] First, the issue of the extent of the contractors' and sub-contractors' obligations in relation to design had to be determined in the ultimate analysis by reference to the interpretation of the contract concerned. There was no good reason for not importing into the contract between IBA, the employer, and EMI, the main contractor, and between EMI and BICC, an obligation as to reasonable fitness for the purpose or for importing a different obligation in relation to design from the obligation which plainly existed in relation to materials. Secondly, there was a good commercial reason in favour of such an obligation. Contracts such as the one concerned should be interpreted so that ultimate liability, if something went wrong, should rest where it properly belonged. The Court of Appeal's decision on the point is the more striking in view of its decision that BICC were not liable in negligence. On appeal the House of Lords[92] held that BICC were negligent and most of their lordships, therefore, did not consider it necessary to decide the issue of the extent of the contractual obligation as to design. The issue was, however,

---

[88] [1975] 1 W.L.R. 1095.
[89] *ibid.* at 1100, 1102 and 1103.
[90] (1980) 14 B.L.R. 1, HL. For the facts see para.9–095, above.
[91] (1978) 11 B.L.R. 29 at 49–52.
[92] (1980) 14 B.L.R. 1.

considered obiter by Lord Scarman.[93] He saw no reason why one who in the course of his business contracted to design, supply and erect a television aerial mast was not under an obligation to ensure that it was reasonably fit for the purpose for which he knew it was intended to be used. He did not accept that the design obligation of the supplier of an article was to be equated with the obligation of a professional man in the practice of his profession. In support of his view he relied upon the Court of Appeal's decision in *Samuels v Davis*.[94] In that case it was held that, where a dentist undertook for reward to make a denture for a patient, it was an implied term of the contract that the denture would be reasonably fit for its intended purpose. The fact of the article being supplied, as well as being designed, was invoked both by the Court of Appeal in the latter case and by Lord Scarman in *IBA* as the crucial distinction justifying the higher duty to ensure that the design was reasonably fit for the purpose, as opposed to the duty to take reasonable care and skill in the design.[95]

Both *Greaves* and Lord Scarman's dictum were considered in *George Hawkins* **9–168** *v Chrysler (UK)*[96] where engineers were engaged to design showers to be installed at a foundry. An employee slipped and sued the foundry owners, who in turn brought third-party proceedings against the engineers. The judge at first instance found that the engineers were not in breach of their duty to exercise reasonable care but were in breach of an implied warranty to provide "as safe a floor as was practicable in the expertise of the profession to provide a safe floor for these men in these conditions".[97] The Court of Appeal dismissed the foundry owners' appeal on the negligence issue but upheld the engineer's appeal on the warranty. On the evidence there were no grounds upon which a warranty going beyond an engineer's normal obligation to exercise reasonable skill and care should be founded and there was no basis for the implication of such a warranty in law.[98]

In *Consultants Group International v John Worman Ltd*[99] the claimants (CGI) **9–169** provided specialist architectural and consultancy services under an agreement

---

[93] (1980) 14 B.L.R. 1 at 47. Viscount Dilhorne added (*ibid.* at 26) however that he "would have been surprised" had not E.M.I. and B.I.C.C. undertaken an obligation to supply a mast "reasonably fit for its intended purpose".

[94] [1943] K.B. 526.

[95] Lord Scarman's final formulation of the circumstances giving rise to the higher duty seems, in isolation, not to reflect this distinction: "In the absence of any term (express or to be implied) negativing the obligation, one who contracts to design an article for a purpose made known to him undertakes that the design is reasonably fit for the purpose" (1980) 14 B.L.R. 1 at 48. From the context, however, it is clear that he contemplates both design and supply of the article by its designer.

[96] (1986) 38 B.L.R. 36.

[97] Which was not, in fact, the warranty pleaded. The pleaded warranty was that the material used for the floor would be fit for use in a wet shower room.

[98] See *per* Fox L.J. at 49–51, *per* Dillon L.J. at 53–54 and, *per* Neill L.J. at 54–56. See also *Balcomb v Wards Construction (Medway) Ltd* (1980) 259 E.G. 765, where Sir Douglas Frank Q.C., sitting as a High Court judge, rejected an argument that a warranty, apparently as to the reasonable fitness of foundation specifications provided by engineers, was to be implied in a contract between developers and the engineers. In *B.C. Rail Ltd v Canadian Pacific Consulting Services Ltd* (1990) 47 B.C.L.R. 49 the British Columbia Court of Appeal found there to be an implied warranty of fitness for purpose in a contract where the defendant engineers had agreed to design and install an overhead contact system for a railway line. The warranty was found to be both reasonable and necessary on a proper construction of the contract.

[99] (1985) 9 Con. L.R. 46.

with the defendant contractors ("the CGI agreement") in connection with the refurbishment of an abattoir by the defendant under a contract with the abattoir owner, Turner ("the Turner agreement"). Provided that the design and construction of the abattoir fulfilled certain criteria, Turner was entitled automatically to a domestic United Kingdom grant and was entitled to be considered for a further EC grant. When CGI sued the defendant for fees, the defendant counterclaimed for alleged breaches of the CGI agreement. Preliminary issues were ordered to decide inter alia whether: (a) it was a term of the Turner agreement that the works and/or designs would be fit for their purpose; (b) whether it was a term of the CGI agreement that CGI would carry out their works so that the completed project would be fit for its purpose; and (c) whether CGI would be liable to the defendants if the designs and specifications of CGI were not such as to comply with the design requirements entitling Turner to be considered for an EC grant. Judge Davies Q.C. held that, in the context of the case, "fitness for purpose" really meant that works should be designed and executed to the standards demanded by United Kingdom and EC requirements for grant aid[1] with the result that issues (b) and (c) fell to be considered together. He then held that on a true construction of the contract documents it was an express term of the Turner contract that the works should be fit for this purpose and further held that if he was wrong, such a term would have been implied.[2] The judge found that the defendants had made it clear to CGI that they had no experience of abattoir work and would be dependent on CGI's experience and expertise[3] and that CGI were the "prime movers in the project from start to finish".[4] As a result he found that it was also an express, alternatively an implied, term of the CGI agreement that the works would be so designed by CGI that the completed project would be fit for its purpose.[5]

9–170　　It is submitted that the Court of Appeal in *Hawkins* and Judge Davies Q.C. in *Consultants Group International* adopted the correct approach to analysis of the relationship between the designer and his client. There will be no absolute answer as to whether one who designs but does not supply an article or build a structure is under a duty to ensure that it is reasonably fit for its intended purpose, but such a duty will not be implied by law. It will therefore arise either on a true construction of the parties' agreement[6] or as an implication from the common intention of the parties.

---

[1] (1985) 9 Con. L.R. 46 at 49.

[2] The judge had little difficulty with this, having already decided in *Viking Grain Storage Ltd v T.H. White Installations Ltd* (1985) 3 Con. L.R. 53 that a term of fitness for purpose was to be implied into a contract for the design and construction of a grain drying and storage installation.

[3] *ibid.* at 34.

[4] *ibid.* at 59.

[5] *ibid.* at 60.

[6] For a further example, see *Associated British Ports v Hydro Soil Services NV* [2006] EWHC 1187 (the main design and build contract included an express term that the design of works to strengthen a quay wall would be fit for purpose; the contract by which the design and build contractor appointed architects to carry out the design expressly incorporated the terms of the main contract; held that the architects' obligation was to provide a design for the strengthening works which was fit for the employer's purpose). Similarly, it was held that, on the true construction of the architects' appointment in *CFW Architects v Cowlin Construction Ltd* [2006] EWHC 6, TCC, they had warranted that their design drawings would be provided by a particular time, and not merely that they would exercise reasonable skill and care to meet the target date.

Similarly, in the absence of special circumstances, a construction professional **9–171**
who designs a structure, inspects its construction and issues a certificate to that
effect will not normally be taken thereby to have warranted or represented by his
certificate that the structure is fit for its purpose. In *Payne v John Setchell Ltd*,[7]
the defendant engineer was responsible for the design of foundations for cottages
which were later purchased by the claimants. The claimants alleged that they
relied in making their purchases upon certificates issued by the defendant which
stated that he was satisfied that the foundations had been constructed in accordance with his design and were suitable for support of dwellings. Judge Lloyd
Q.C. rejected the claimant's contention that the defendant had thereby certified
that the foundations were fit for their purpose. The judge pointed out that a
certificate has to be construed in the light of the obligations pursuant to which it
has been issued. He said[8]:

> "A certificate expresses the judgment, opinion or skill of the person issuing it, usually,
> but not always, in relation to a matter called for by a construction contract (where the
> certifier is sometimes also acting in a quasi-arbitral capacity). . . . It is not normally a
> warranty nor is it to be read as tantamount to a warranty, particularly if issued by a
> professional person, although it may amount to a warranty. If issued by a contractor
> who has undertaken full and complete performance of the contract it may be taken as
> its formal confirmation that it has duly fulfilled all the obligations undertaken under the
> contract which will probably include obligations of an absolute nature. To that extent
> it might be or be equivalent to a warranty especially if given to or intended for a third
> party. The other contracting party will not normally need such a document as it will
> have its rights under the contract. A professional person however does not normally
> undertake obligations of an absolute nature but only undertakes to exercise reasonable
> professional skill and care in performance of the relevant service or in the production
> of the product. Thus the certificate of 20 October 1988, particularly since it refers to the
> two visits to the site, can only be read as an expression of the opinion of the defendant
> that as the result of such inspections the defendant had reasonable grounds for believing
> that the construction of the foundation had been satisfactorily carried out to its design
> and, by implication, that there were no circumstances known to the defendant as a result
> of those inspections which cast doubt on the defendant's original judgment in the
> production of that design."

(x) *Reliance Upon Specialists and Delegation to them*

Modern developments in materials and technologies in the construction indus- **9–172**
try have been so numerous and so rapid as to exceed the ability of even the most
talented and assiduous professional men to master them all. Architects and others
must of necessity seek the assistance of specialists when they reach the limits of
their knowledge.[9] This consideration raises the question whether it is a defence
to a construction professional alleged to have been negligent in the performance

---

[7] [2002] P.N.L.R. 7. For the facts, see para.9–057, above.
[8] *ibid.* at para.20.
[9] *Equitable Debenture Assets Corp Ltd v William Moss Group Ltd* (1984) 2 Con. L.R. 1 at 25, *per*
Judge Newey Q.C. The same judge in *Richard Roberts & Holdings Ltd v Douglas Smith Stimson
Partnership* (1988) 46 B.L.R. 50 at 66 said: "If the architects felt that they could not form a reliable
judgment about a lining for the tank, they should have informed Holdings of that fact and advised
them to take other advice, possibly from a chemist." For the facts and further discussion of this case
see para.9–136, above.

of a task which he agreed to perform to show (a) that he relied upon the advice or work of specialists or even delegated the performance of the task to them; and (b) that such reliance or delegation was reasonable. The question is the more acute given that a construction professional in some circumstances may be negligent in not seeking specialist assistance. Much as sympathy for his dilemma may favour an affirmative answer to the question, at least upon initial impression, there is the countervailing consideration that such an answer may leave the client without remedy either against the construction professional or the specialist in the absence of a direct agreement between the client and the specialist.

9–173   The question admits of no general answer. In principle, it is submitted that the question should be approached as follows. First, the concept of reliance in this context needs to be defined. At one extreme, a construction professional may wholly rely upon specialists effectively to the extent of complete delegation. At the other extreme the professional may only rely on specialists to the extent that in the formulation of his design he takes account of articles by them in professional journals or detailed product specifications reflecting specialist research. The key distinction is between: (a) the case where a professional relies upon specialist assistance to a point that on any objective assessment it must be recognised that the relevant task is performed by the specialists and not the professional; and (b) the case where, despite reliance upon specialists, an objective assessment results in the conclusion that the task is still essentially performed by the professional. In making the distinction a crucial criterion, albeit not the only one, is the extent to which the professional exercises an independent judgment. But the distinction is ultimately one of degree. It is only reliance of the kind in case (a) which is the subject of the question. Where the reliance is of the kind in case (b), the question does not arise since the performance was that of the professional and not specialists.

9–174   In answering the question, the starting point is the construction professional's contract. If he agreed to perform the relevant task personally, reasonable reliance upon specialists would not be a defence; in such a case the relevant breach of duty would, logically, not be failure to choose competent specialists but incompetence by the construction professional himself. On the other hand, the contract may expressly or by implication permit reliance upon specialists or the client may otherwise permit it. In that case, reasonable reliance upon specialists will provide a defence in appropriate circumstances. In the same case, however, the construction professional may be shown to have been in breach of his duty in not initially choosing specialists of appropriate competence or in not properly reviewing the specialists' advice or other work, and thus not discovering errors which a member of his profession of ordinary competence ought to have discovered upon such review. Nevertheless, it is submitted that the client's permission and the professional's consequent power to rely upon or to delegate to specialists cannot be derived, without more specific provision in the professional's contract, from his duty to exercise reasonable care and skill nor from the standard applicable to that duty, being that of the ordinary competent member of his profession.

9–175   The authorities are not entirely consistent as to the answer to the question. In *Moresk Cleaners Ltd v Hicks*[10] it was held that it was not the ordinary practice

---

[10] [1966] 2 Lloyd's Rep. 338.

of the profession for an architect to delegate his work on design and then to seek to disown responsibility for it.[11] The defendant architect was held negligent in the design of the reinforced concrete frame to a building; the architect had delegated that part of the building's design to a structural engineer.[12] *Moresk* is to be contrasted with *Merton LBC v Lowe*[13] where the defendant architect was appointed in 1964 under then existing RIBA Conditions of Engagement to design and supervise the construction of a swimming pool. His design included suspended ceilings surfaced with a proprietary product called Pyrok supplied by Pyrok Ltd. That company was nominated as the sub-contractor for the purpose of plastering the ceilings. In the event the ceiling surfacing failed and had to be replaced. The cause was an imbalance of the mix of the undercoats and the Pyrok finishing coat. Pyrok Ltd alone knew the constituents of that coat. Two facts are important. First, it was accepted that mix was part of the design of the specialist sub-contractor's product. Secondly, the judge found that that element of the design formed part of the detailed design for which the architect was responsible. Nevertheless he was held not negligent in originally accepting and approving Pyrok Ltd's specification for the ceiling.[14] At first instance Judge Stabb Q.C. held that the architect was entitled (a) to assume that the specification which did not specify the mix, provided for the same proper mix as specified in an earlier quotation by Pyrok Ltd; and (b) to rely on Pyrok Ltd to apply a proper mix. On appeal this finding was upheld, but apparently on the basis, as expressed by Waller L.J., that the original decision to employ Pyrok Ltd was reasonable in view of its successful work done elsewhere. *Moresk* was distinguished on the ground that in that case the architect "had virtually handed over to another the whole task of design" and "could not escape responsibility for the work which he was supposed to do by handing it over to another".[15] *Merton LBC v Lowe* thus

---

[11] See also in this respect the decision of the Court of Appeal in *Nye Saunders and Partners v Alan E Bristow* (1987) 37 B.L.R. 92. The facts are set out at para.9–191, below. The court rejected the contention that an architect was entitled too rely wholly on the fact that he had referred a request for a cost estimate to a quantity surveyor. At 107 Stephen Brown L.J. said:

"Of course it was a very sensible and prudent step for Mr Nye to take to consult a quantity surveyor who is an expert in computing costs. But in my judgment he cannot avoid responsibility for the fact that he did not draw the attention of his client to the fact that inflation was not taken into account. The duty rested fairly and squarely upon Mr Nye and it cannot be avoided by, as it were, seeking to move the responsibility onto Mr Parker."

[12] Note also the judgment of Judge Sir Walker Carter O.R. at 343:

"If the [architect] was not able, because this form of reinforced concrete was a comparatively new form of construction to design it himself, he had three courses open to him. One was to say, 'This is not my field.' The second was to go to his client, the building owner, and say, 'This reinforced concrete is out of my line. I would like you to employ a structural engineer to deal with this aspect of the matter.' Or he can, while retaining responsibility for the design, himself seek the advice and assistance of a structural engineer, paying for his service out of his own pocket but having at any rate the satisfaction of knowing that if he acts upon that advice and it turns out to be wrong, the person whom he employed to give the advice will owe the same duty to him as he, the architect, owes to the building owners."

On the subject of delegation of design functions by architects to engineers or other specialists, see Hudson (*op. cit.*), pp.302–307.

[13] Unreported at first instance, but reported on appeal at (1981) 18 B.L.R. 130.

[14] The architect was nevertheless held negligent on another ground: in failing to carry out a proper investigation after cracking in the ceilings had developed. See para.9–033, above.

[15] (1981) 18 B.L.R. 130 at 148, CA. Note also Pigeon J.'s majority judgment in the Canadian case of *Vermont Construction Inc v Beatson* (1976) 67 D.L.R. (3d) 95. In holding that a party charged with

appears to provide an affirmative answer to the question posed above,[16] at least where the relevant reliance by the architect relates to a limited aspect of his design responsiblity. It is inconsistent, however, with the approach adumbrated above[17] and also with that of the judge in *Moresk*.

9–176   The particular RIBA Conditions incorporated in the architect's contract in *Merton London BC v Lowe* did not contain the specific provisions relating to specialist sub-contractors and suppliers contained in more recent editions. They provide that the architect may recommend that the specialist sub-contractors and suppliers should design and execute any part of the work and that while he will be responsible for the direction and integration of their design and for general inspection of their work, he will not be responsible for the detailed design or performance of the work entrusted to them.[18] There is a similar specific provision relating to consultants. This provides that the architect will advise on the need for independent consultants, and will be responsible for the direction and integration of their work but not for the detailed design, inspection and performance of the work entrusted to them.[19] The effect of this and related provisions were considered by the Court of Appeal in *Investors in Industry Commercial Properties v South Bedfordshire DC; Ellison & Partners and Hamilton Associates (Third Parties)*[20]:

> "Whether or not in any given instance these conditions apply, it must generally be the duty of an architect to exercise reasonable care in the work he is engaged to perform. However, clauses 1.20, 1.22 and 1.23 of the RIBA conditions, in our judgment, clearly contemplate that, where a particular part of the work involved in a building contract involves specialist knowledge or skill beyond that which an architect of ordinary competence may reasonably be expected to possess, the architect is at liberty to recommend to his client that a reputable independent consultant, who appears to have the relevant specialist knowledge or skill, shall be appointed by the client to perform this task. If following such a recommendation a consultant with these qualifications is appointed, the architect will normally carry no legal responsibility for the work to be done by the expert which is beyond the capability of an architect of ordinary competence; in relation to the work allotted to the expert, the architect's legal responsibility

---

negligence could "clear his feet" if he shows that he acted in accordance with general and approved practice, he found (at 103) that the defendant architects had acted in accordance with the practice of architects generally in relying on engineers to make stress calculations for the structures for which they prepared plans. Accordingly he absolved the architects of negligence in not checking the engineers' calculations even though they could have done so.

[16] See para.9–172, above.

[17] See paras 9–173 to 9–174, above.

[18] RIBA 1971 Conditions of Engagement with 1975, 1976 and 1979 amendments, cl.1.40; RIBA Architect's Appointment 1982 with 1982, 1987 and 1988 amendments, cl.3.8; RIBA Standard Form of Agreement for the Appointment of an Architect (1992), cl.4.2.5 and, to similar effect, RIBA Standard Form of Agreement for the Appointment of an Architect (1999), cl.3.12. See also n.52 to para.9–017, above. Similar provisions are found in the various forms of the ACE Conditions of Engagement for engineer and in the RICS Conditions of Engagement for Building Surveying Services.

[19] *ibid.*, cl.1.22, cl.3.6, cl.4.1.7 and cl.3.11. Similar provisions are found in the various forms of the ACE Conditions of Engagement for engineers and in the RICS Conditions of Engagement for Building Surveying Services (for consideration of the letter, see *Catlin Estates Ltd v Carter Jonas* [2005] EWHC 2315).

[20] [1986] 1 All E.R. 787, CA. This case is reported at first instance *sub nom. Anglia Commercial Properties Ltd v South Bedfordshire DC* (1984) 2 Con. L.R. 99. The relevant facts so far as they related to the architects are stated at para.9–185, below.

will normally be confined to directing and co-ordinating the expert's work in the whole. However, this is subject to one important qualification. If any danger or problem arises in connection with the work allotted to the expert, of which an architect of ordinary competence reasonably ought to be aware and reasonably could be expected to warn the client, despite the employment of the expert, and despite what the expert says or does about it, it is in our judgment the duty of the architect to warn the client. In such a contingency he is not entitled to rely blindly on the expert, with no mind of his own, on matters which must or should have been apparent to him."[21]

Two points should be noted. Under the relevant RIBA Conditions the architect's responsibility is excluded only where the client follows his recommendation or advice as to the use of specialist sub-contractors and suppliers or consultants. Secondly, the propositions of law in the quoted passage deal only with the position where the architect's advice as to the use of consultants is followed by the client.

3. LIABILITY FOR BREACH OF DUTY

This part of the chapter considers breach of duty by an architect, engineer or quantity surveyor which consists of: **9–177**

(i) breach of the implied contractual duty to exercise reasonable care and skill[22];

(ii) breach of any duty of care owed to the client independently of his contractual duties[23]; and

(iii) breach of any duty of care owed to a third party.[24]

These breaches will be jointly described as negligence. Instances in which the relevant professions have been or may be liable for breach of duty are discussed

---

[21] [1986] 1 All E.R. 787 at 807–808. Construction professionals were found negligent in failing to check and warn of deficiencies in the designs prepared by specialist sub-contractors in *Try Build Ltd v Invicta Leisure Tennis Ltd* (2000) 71 Con. L.R. 141 (engineers failed to appreciate that novel features of a design for a sports hall roof developed by a specialist supplier had not been successfully developed and were inadequate); and *Baxall Securities Ltd v Sheard Walshaw Partnership* [2001] P.N.L.R 256 (architects failed to specify and check the design rainfall rate to be used in the design by a specialist sub-contractor of a roof drainage system. Judge Bowsher Q.C. pointed out that the sub-contractor would naturally adopt a low rate in order to reduce his tender price and increase his chance of securing the sub-contract; that was a matter against which the architects should have protected their client by specifying the appropriate rate in the tender documentation). The judge's finding of breach of duty by the architects was not challenged on the appeal in *Baxall Securities Ltd v Sheard Walshaw Partnership* [2002] EWCA Civ 9. See also *Catlin Estates Ltd v Carter Jonas* [2005] EWHC 2315 (on the terms of their engagement, building surveyors had not divested themselves of responsibility for design work carried out by specialists retained by them; but in any event they would have retained a responsibility to identify defects in the work which would have been identified by a reasonably competent building surveyor); and *Atwal Enterprises Ltd v Toner* 2006 S.L.T. 537 (inspecting architect failed to require specialist sub-contractors who had designed part of the works to explain apparent defects in them and consequently failed to take appropriate corrective action).
[22] See paras 9–026 to 9–038, above
[23] See paras 9–039 to 9–059, above.
[24] See paras 9–060 to 9–124, above.

below under 12 heads generally descriptive of the tasks commonly undertaken by them. Those tasks are considered broadly in the order in which they are likely to be performed over the course of a building project. Finally, the question of breach of duty by a construction professional acting as an expert witness for the purpose of litigation is discussed.

(a) *Examination of Site*

9–178   A construction professional, typically an architect or engineer, who is charged with the design of a building or other structure will owe a duty to satisfy himself that the chosen site is suitable for the proposed works. This may involve him in one or more of the following activities:

  (i) measuring the site;

  (ii) ascertaining the nature and properties of the ground below the site;

  (iii) considering the likely effects of the proposed works on the ground conditions;

  (iv) considering the effects of non-physical constraints on building, such as planning requirements.

The work of other consultants or contractors may overlap with the architect or engineer's work in respect of each activity: in those cases, it will be necessary to consider the extent to which the architect or engineer is entitled to rely upon information provided by such persons.

9–179   **Measuring the site.** The site must be neither too small nor too large for the building to be erected upon it. Liability for failure to appreciate that the site and the proposed works are not compatible in this way has arisen in cases where the architect or engineer has attempted a "short-cut", relying upon inaccurate information provided by others rather than carrying out or organising his own measured survey.[25]

9–180   Construction professionals who make preliminary investigations into the nature of a site should give clear and appropriate warnings as to any risks or inaccuracies in their results. This is illustrated by *Gable House Estates v The Halpern Partnership*.[26] The defendant architects advised that the redevelopment of a building would result in useable office space of between 35,056 and 34,163 square feet, depending upon which of four schemes was adopted. It was found that the actual area was only 31,769 square feet. The judge found that it would not have been possible for the architects to have forecasted the useable office

---

[25] For examples, see *Columbus Co v Clowes* [1903] 1 K.B. 244; and *Cardy v Taylor* (1994) 38 Con. L.R. 79.
[26] (1995) 48 Con. L.R. 1.

space to an accuracy of 500 square feet. In those circumstances, the architects did not discharge their duty simply by qualifying their estimates with the words "All areas approximate". That was an insufficient warning of errors of up to 500 square feet.[27]

Ground investigations. An architect or engineer who designs a building 9–181 should take reasonable care to see that there is adequate information, from his own investigations or from those of a specialist consultant or contractor, as to the sub-soil conditions. It is particularly important to bear in mind that conditions below ground may vary between different areas of the site. In *Moneypenny v Hartland*[28] an engineer relied upon the results of a site investigation which revealed that the proposed site for the foundations of a planned bridge was founded on rock. The engineer then changed the location of the foundations to an area which was not covered by the site investigation. In consequence he grossly underestimated the cost of construction because the underlying ground there turned out to be clay, which was unable to support the foundations. The engineer was held negligent in failing to carry out his own investigation into ground conditions at the location which he chose for the foundations.

The nature of a site may require extensive tests and examinations, both during 9–182 and after excavations. This will be particularly important where the nature of the ground is poor or presents special difficulties for the proposed building, for example, if there is made ground (i.e. non-natural, man-made ground). In *Eames London Estates Ltd v North Hertfordshire DC*[29] an industrial building was constructed on made ground. The foundations proved inadequate with the result that extensive repairs and possible rebuilding was required. The architect entrusted with the design of the building including the foundations had made no examination of the soil. Although knowing that it was made ground, he thought that it was an old railway embankment. Judge Edgar Fay Q.C. held that the architect should have satisfied himself about the land's bearing capacity,[30] and that he could not shed his responsibility for foundations by ascertaining what would "get by the local authority", as he appeared to have done. He was held negligent in two respects: first, in specifying the loading for piers without any attempt to ascertain for himself whether the ground was suitable for the loading, and secondly in putting aside a query as to the adequacy of the depth of excavations for foundations properly raised by a practical man on the spot.[31]

Often ascertainment of the ground conditions at a site will be beyond the 9–183 expertise of an architect or engineer. In such a case the exercise of due care may require the architect to advise the employer accordingly and either to engage himself or to advise the employer to engage specialists to carry out the requested

---

[27] For further discussion of this case see para.9–190, below.
[28] (1824) 1 Car. & P. 351 (first instance); (1826) 2 Car. & P. 378.
[29] (1980) 259 E.G. 491.
[30] The judge observed that "the 25 in. Ordnance Survey maps are part of the furnishings of local architects' offices" and that a glance at the relevant map would have shown that the railway had crossed only part of the site: *ibid.* at 495.
[31] *ibid.* at 495.

ground investigation.[32] As the cases discussed in the following paragraphs demonstrate, he may nevertheless retain a responsibility to consider carefully the value of the information provided by specialists and to advise as to its limitations.

9–184   In the Canadian case of *District of Surrey v Carroll-Hatch and Associates Ltd*,[33] an engineer engaged by architects to inspect trial pits was held negligent for failing to warn that the information available from the pits was inadequate to establish the load-bearing capacity of the ground. In *City of Brantford v Kemp and Wallace-Carruthers & Associates Ltd*,[34] the site for a new fire hall and police station consisted of an old rubbish tip. The safer design entailed supporting the whole building on piles. The riskier but cheaper design, which the defendant engineers adopted, was a "floor on earth" method which entailed supporting the main walls on piles but placing partition walls on floors laid on granular fill and suspended from the main walls. Proper examination of the site would have demonstrated the need for the safer design but the engineers had not carried out such examination either before or during excavations. They were held liable in negligence for the subsequent failure of the internal walls and floors. The Ontario Court of Appeal also held that in the circumstances of the case it was not enough for the defendant engineers to rely on the result of percussion tests made by a soil testing firm, knowing the limitations of sampling tests of any kind on ground of this sort.

9–185   Similarly in *Investors in Industry Commercial Properties v South Bedfordshire DC; Ellison & Partners and Hamilton Associates (Third Parties)*[35] the claimant developer engaged a firm of architects to design and act as architects in relation to the construction of four warehouses on a site known to be infilled land, formerly the site of a large swimming pool. The architect's contract incorporated the then RIBA Conditions of Engagement including the particular clause, cl.1.22, discussed above.[36] Upon the architect's recommendation a firm of structural engineers was engaged by the claimant to design and superintend the construction of the foundations. At first instance, the engineers were held to have been at fault in failing to see that a proper site investigation had been carried out. Only "quite useless" trial holes had been dug, when the only possible way of investigating the particular ground was by means of bore holes and subsequent laboratory analysis of the undisturbed samples.[37] The claim against the architects in respect of the foundations, however, failed. Judge Stabb Q.C. held that the architects were entitled to rely upon the engineers' judgment as to what foundations were suitable and that the architects had properly met the risk presented by the nature of the ground by seeing that consulting engineers were appointed to deal with it.[38] The Court of Appeal affirmed the judge's finding on the point, also

---

[32] See, for example, *District of Surrey v Carroll-Hatch and Associates Ltd* (1979) 10 D.L.R. (3d) 218, considered at para.9–184, below. Also see the passage from *Moresk Cleaners Ltd v Hicks* [1966] 2 Lloyd's Rep. 338 at 343 set out in fn.11 under para.9–175, above.

[33] (1979) 10 D.L.R. (3d) 218, British Columbia CA.

[34] (1960) 23 D.L.R. (2d) 641, Ontario CA.

[35] [1986] 1 All E.R. 787, CA. This case is reported at first instance *sub nom. Anglia Commercial Properties Ltd v South Bedfordshire DC* (1984) 2 Con. L.R. 99.

[36] See para.9–176, above.

[37] (1984) 2 Con. L.R. 99 at 100–101.

[38] *ibid.* at 103.

holding that, in the circumstances, cl.1.22 read together with other relevant RIBA Conditions defined and limited the scope of the architects' contractual duty to the claimant employer in respect of the foundations.[39]

Design assumptions. As the cases discussed above illustrate, available infor-   **9–186** mation about the ground conditions may be limited at the time when the construction professional is required to provide a design. The designer is then obliged to prepare his design on the basis of assumptions as to the existing ground conditions. If he does so, then he has an obligation to see to it that the requisite additional information to verify those assumptions is acquired (by him or by someone else) and that the client knows that the information is required. If the designer does not gather the requisite information himself, he must normally see to it that the information is conveyed back to him so that the may judge whether it is sufficient for the purposes of his design. So much was made clear in *Ove Arup & Partners International Ltd v Mirant Asia-Pacific Construction (Hong Kong) Ltd (No.2)*,[40] where the Court of Appeal upheld a finding that foundations designers had failed to take adequate steps to see that the assumptions as to ground conditions upon which their design was based were verified.[41]

The effect of the proposed works. In some cases, it will be necessary for the   **9–187** designer to take into account the likely effect on ground conditions of the proposed works themselves. For example, the drought of 1976 gave rise to a number of cases which explored the effect of the removal of trees from sites founded on London clay. In *Acrecrest Ltd v WS Hattrell & Partners*,[42] architects were held negligent in giving insufficient regard to the removal of trees from a site for development. Water which would have been absorbed by the trees was absorbed by the ground, giving rise to swelling or "heave" of the clay, and damage to the new building.[43] In another case,[44] an architect designing foundations for a new bungalow who failed to appreciate the significance of removal of trees from a site based on London clay was found negligent. He had failed to

---

[39] [1986] 1 All E.R. 787, CA at 807. Note also the passage from the judgment quoted at para.9–176, above. For further examples of failure to examine site properly, see *Blair v Alderney Consultants* (1998) 168 N.S.R. (2d) 287 (engineer employed by developer to design storm drainage for a development was negligent in not having gone onto adjoining Crown land a short distance from the development itself. Had he done so, he would have seen a drain outlet which was not shown either on aerial plans or plans from the Department of Transportation. The engineer's argument that it was unreasonable to expect him to walk between adjoining developments and that he was entitled to rely on the plans was rejected on the basis that access was, in this case, possible and experience showed that the plans often contained errors); *Dalgliesh v Bromley Corp* (1953) 162 E.G. 623 (architects negligently failed to warn that the slope of the site was such that the development would be uneconomical as a result of the need for expensive levelling works).
[40] [2005] EWCA Civ 1585.
[41] *ibid.*; see, in particular, *per* May L.J. at [91].
[42] (1979) 252 E.G. 1107 (first instance); [1983] Q.B. 260, CA.
[43] Engineers were held liable on similar facts in *Balcomb v Wards Construction (Medway) Ltd* (1980) 259 E.G. 765.
[44] *Kaliszewska v John Clague & Partners* (1984) 5 Con. L.R. 62.

address the problem in any methodical way or to use the current knowledge in his profession which was available to him.[45]

9–188   **Non-physical constraints.** Even in the absence of instructions so to do, the exercise of reasonable care may require an architect to make reasonable enquiries concerning the rights of neighbours, for example, about easements[46] and restrictive covenants, or planning restrictions,[47] lest they be infringed by subsequent building. The circumstances of each case will usually require detailed examination in order to establish whether the duty to make such enquiries was undertaken by the architect or by other agents of the employer, for example, his solicitors,[48] or even by the employer himself. Where he has not carried out such enquiries, the prudent course for an architect is to warn his client that he has not done so.

(b) *Cost Estimates and Budgets*

9–189   Before embarking on a building project a client will commonly ask an architect, engineer or quantity surveyor for an estimate of the cost. Although in giving the estimate precision is not required, reasonable care and skill must be exercised.[49]

9–190   One of the principal reasons for instructing a construction professional to provide an estimate of likely construction costs is that the client wishes to know and plan for the total expenditure which he faces if he proceeds with the project in question. Accordingly, it is important that the professional should advise his client in clear terms as to any matters which he has not taken into account in his estimate but which might affect the actual final cost and any factors which he has included but which may change during over the life of the project. It may also be appropriate to indicate the level of accuracy to which his estimate has been prepared. A good example of the last consideration is provided by the decision of Judge Lewis Q.C. in *Gable House Estates v The Halpern Partnership*.[50] The defendant architects provided a preliminary cost plan and elemental specification showing a cost for the works of £5.8 million and useable office space of 33,928

---

[45] *Kaliszewska v John Clague & Partners* (1984) 5 Con. L.R. 62 at 77.

[46] See *Armitage v Palmer* (1959) 173 E.G. 91, *per* Lloyd Jacob J.: "If by reason of the manner in which an architect sited a building it infringed an easement enjoyed by a neighbouring owner of which the architect had actual or constructive notice, he had not exercised reasonable skill and care." On the facts, which concerned a neighbour's allegation that his right of light had been infringed, the architect was held not negligent.

[47] The primary restriction imposed by planning legislation is that the owner of the land must consent to the proposed development. In *John Harris & Partnership v Groveworld Ltd* [1999] P.N.L.R. 697, architects failed to notice that part of the proposed site was owned not by their client but by the local authority. They were liable for increased costs incurred in obtaining a revised planning permission. See also *Hancock v Tucker* [1999] Lloyd's Rep. P.N. 814, where it was alleged that architects' conduct of a planning application had caused unnecessary delays on obtaining permission. On the facts, they were not negligent: see further para.9–320, below.

[48] See Ch.11, para.11–201, below.

[49] See, for examples, *Moneypenny v Hartland* (1826) 2 Car. & P. 378 (see also para.9–181, above); and *Gordon Shaw Concrete Products Ltd v Design Collaborative Ltd* (1985) 35 C.C.L.T. 100 (although it is doubted whether the findings of total failure of consideration in those cases can be justified).

[50] (1995) 48 Con. L.R. 1.

square feet. It was found that the actual area was only 31,769 square feet. The judge found that the architects could not have estimated the area to an accuracy of more than 500 square feet. However, they knew that the amount of the lettable square feet, rather than its quality, was of great importance to the claimant. In those circumstances, the formula "All areas approximate" was an insufficient warning of the possibility that the stated square footage could not be achieved.

The decision of the Court of Appeal in *Nye Saunders and Partners v Alan E* **9-191** *Bristow*[51] illustrates the importance of clear warnings as to matters which may cause the final cost to differ from the estimated cost. The facts were that the claimant architects were retained by the defendant, a well-known businessman, in 1973 to prepare and submit a planning application for the renovation of his mansion. The defendant informed the claimants that he had about £250,000 to spend and asked the claimants to provide a written estimate of the likely cost of the works. The claimants consulted a quantity surveyor and wrote to the defendant enclosing a schedule of costs amounting to some £238,000. Neither the schedule nor the architects' covering letter mentioned the effect of likely increases in inflation: in fact, it was wholly based on then current prices. Mr Bristow assumed that inflation had been taken into account. Following the grant of planning permission the claimants were engaged in March 1974 to proceed with the scheme. At a meeting in September of the same year, an up-to-date statement showed likely costs to completion of £440,000, including a figure for inflation during the 18 months' contract period. Mr Bristow thereupon cancelled the project and refused to pay the claimants' fees on the grounds that their services had been valueless. The claimants sued for their fees. The claim was defended upon the basis that had a proper estimate been provided Mr Bristow would not have commenced the project. The defence succeeded and the claimant's appeal was rejected. It was held that the claimants did not avoid liability to Mr Bristow for the costs advice given by passing the preparation of that advice to a quantity surveyor, since the claimants retained a responsibility to warn Mr Bristow that inflation had not been taken into account.[52] The claimants were also found negligent at first instance for failing to warn that the estimate included no sum for contingencies.

Saunders is consistent with the Canadian case of *Savage v Board of School* **9-192** *Trustees*[53] where it was held that an architect had failed to exercise reasonable care and skill in providing an estimate of $110,000 for building a school. The lowest tender received was $157,000. The court asserted that if an architect furnished an estimate as part of his contract, it must at his peril be reasonably near the ultimate cost, and that where any deficiency appeared on its face to be unreasonable, the burden rested upon the architect to show how it arose and that he was not at fault. Much of the discrepancy was explained by inadequate checking and rechecking of the estimate. The main defence that the events happened in a period of rising prices was rejected on the facts, including on the ground that the trend in prices was known to the architect and should have been allowed for in his estimates.

---

[51] (1987) 37 Build. L.R. 92.
[52] See the passage from the judgment of Slade L.J. quoted at para.9–147, above.
[53] [1951] 3 D.L.R. 39.

9–193   It is submitted that *Savage* was incorrect to the extent that the court found that the burden was upon the defendant to explain a discrepancy in his estimate. Subsequent events should not, as a matter of principle, cause the burden of proof to shift. Thus a finding of negligence should not follow merely from the fact that the final cost is very significantly higher than a construction professional's estimate. In *Copthorne Hotel (Newcastle) Ltd v Arup Associates,*[54] Judge Hicks Q.C. found that the claimant had failed to make out a case of negligent estimation in respect of piling costs where the defendants had estimated a figure of £425,000 against an out-turn cost of £975,000. No evidence had been led as to what figure the defendants should have used for pile diameter which was an essential element in arriving at a price. The judge said:

> "I hope and believe that I am not over-simplifying if I record the impression that the claimant's main hope was that I would be persuaded to find in their favour simply by the size of the gap, absolutely and proportionately, between the cost estimate and the successful tender.
> The gap was indeed enormous. It astonished and appalled the parties at the time, and it astonishes me. I do not see, however, how that alone can carry the claimant home. There is no plea or argument that the maxim 'res ipsa loquitur' applies. Culpable under-estimation is of course one obvious explanation of such a discrepancy, but far from the only one . . . ."

9–194   Subject to the question of burden of proof, however, it is submitted that both *Saunders* and *Savage* were correctly decided. Although the construction professional is in no better position than anybody else to foretell the rate of future general inflation, he should know more about the effect of inflation on the building industry in the short term so that, for example, he should know when the next wage increase is expected and what is the current trend in costs of materials. Moreover he and he alone knows to what extent, if at all, he has taken inflation into account. However, if he bases his estimate on current building costs and makes it plain that he has done so,[55] that ought to be sufficient. Ultimately, the issue whether an estimate is so wrong as to be negligent and the issue whether the estimated figure should take account of future inflation are questions of fact dependent on the particular circumstances of each case. Much will turn upon the terms of the quantity surveyor's or architect's contract of engagement. If he agrees to estimate the ultimate cost of the project then the estimate which he provides will be judged on this basis.

9–195   If an architect, engineer or quantity surveyor knows that his client has a financial limit for a building project, the duty to exercise reasonable care requires that he consider whether the limit is likely to be exceeded and warn the client accordingly. Even if a costs limit is not specified an architect should plan works capable of being carried out at a reasonable cost having regard to their scope and

---

[54] (1996) 58 Con. L.R. 105.
[55] The estimate should indicate whether (i) it is based on building costs as at that date; or (ii) it represents the anticipated tender figure (which will presumably be received some months or even years in the future); or (iii) it represents the total anticipated costs of construction (which will presumably be very much more than the tender figure unless a fixed price contract is proposed). If (i), the estimator should indicate those matters which may affect the tender and/or final price.

function.[56] In *Stephen Donald Architects Ltd v Christopher King*,[57] Judge Seymour Q.C. declined to find that an architect had been in breach of duty in the steps which he took when he realised that the construction costs of his design would exceed his client's budget. In those circumstances, any reasonably competent architect would embark on the process of "value engineering", that is, the consideration with the preferred building contractor and any other members of the professional team whether there were ways in which the cost of construction could be reduced to an affordable level. If that failed, the next step was to inquire of other contractors whether they could build the design within the client's budget.

(iii) *Compliance with Legislation, Planning and Building Control Requirements and Codes of Practice*

This subject, including the important case of *BL Holdings Ltd v Robert J Wood & Partners*[58] is more fully considered above.[59] Generally a member of the construction professions is not expected to have a detailed knowledge of the law but rather such knowledge as is expected of the reasonably competent practitioner. If he lacks sufficient knowledge, or considers that there is a specific point upon which his client should be advised but upon which he is not qualified to advise, he should warn his client to consult a specialist.   **9–196**

An architect or engineer engaged to design a building is expected to be familiar with planning and building control requirements and, usually, will be responsible for ensuring compliance with them. In *Townsends (*Builders*) Ltd v Cinema News Property Management*[60] an architect was held liable in negligence to building contractors for late service of notices required by building byelaws because he had undertaken to be responsible for serving such notices. Whether an architect is responsible for ensuring compliance with such requirements, however, ultimately depends on the facts of each case and in particular the scope of his instructions.[61]   **9–197**

It will normally be prudent for an architect or engineer who is instructed to make an application for planning permission or building regulations approval to liaise informally with the relevant officers of the local authority before submitting any application. In this way, he is able to tailor his design to the authority's requirements, conserving time and cost. The claimant in *Hancock v Tucker*[62] engaged the defendant architects to seek planning permission for his intended   **9–198**

---

[56] See Hudson, *op. cit.* at 325.
[57] [2003] EWHC 1867, TCC.
[58] (1978) 10 B.L.R. 48 (first instance); (1979) 12 B.L.R. 1, CA.
[59] See paras 9–152 to 9–155, above.
[60] (1958) 20 B.L.R. 118
[61] See para.9–188, above in relation to inquiries concerning rights of neighbours and planning restrictions. In *Strongman v Sincock* [1955] 2 Q.B. 525, CA, it was conceded that it was "the universal practice" for the architect and not the builder to obtain licences then required for certain building work. Such a concession is unlikely to reflect current practice. Also note the briefly reported cases of *Stern and Sirotkin v Oakfield Estates Ltd* [1937] E.G.D. 70 (term of contract with architects that plans should be such as to comply with and satisfy the local authority. Plans held defective and architects held liable in several respects); and *Leach v Crossley* (1984) 8 Con. L.R. 7, CA (engineer failed to use a revised Code of Practice when asked the maximum weight of a particular material allowable on a roof: see para.9–215, below, where this case is more fully discussed).
[62] [1999] P.N.L.R. 814.

conversion of a hotel to residential flats. Over the following year, in the course of their informal discussions with the local planning authority, the architects proposed four different schemes, as they sought to take into account the planners' comments. By the time that planning permission was achieved, the value of the property had fallen significantly. The claimant alleged that the architects had wasted time, and should have either persisted with their initial scheme or sought permission at an early stage for the scheme which was ultimately passed by the planners. Toulson J. dismissed the claim. He approved the architects' decision to seek, through informal liaison with the planners, the scheme which was most likely to be permitted before submitting any formal application, as a rational and understandable approach.

(d) *Design and Specification*

9–199　　One of the primary functions of an architect or engineer is design, including the preparation of plans, drawings, specifications, the selection of materials and proprietary products and advice as to suitable specialist contractors. Whilst the standard commonly applicable in designing is that of reasonable care, particular circumstances may require special steps to be taken in order to fulfil that standard and there may even be a duty to ensure that the design is reasonably fit for its intended purpose.[63] An architect or engineer who has agreed to design a structure may not escape liability for a negligent design on the ground that he delegated the design to another person unless by the terms of his contract delegation is permitted and his liability for the delegated design is excluded or limited.[64] If a design is outside his expertise the proper course is for him to inform his client accordingly and either himself to engage, or to advise the employer to engage, a person with the required expertise.[65] In the New Zealand case of *Young v Tomlinson*[66] architects were held negligent in the design of a wall which was defective "owing to the architects having moved a little out of their specialised field." They were also held negligent in not having sought the advice of structural engineers for the design.[67]

9–200　　**Approvals.** The approval of defective plans or drawings by the employer will not absolve the architect from liability in circumstances in which the employer is relying on him to avoid defects, unless the employer has given his approval with full knowledge of the defects.[68] Where the client is a layperson, even a layperson who has experience of building matters, merely copying plans to him will not be

---

[63] See paras 9–165 to 9–171, above. Note also *Sealand of the Pacific v Robert C McHaffie Ltd* (1974) 51 D.L.R. (3d) 702: naval architects held on the facts to have agreed to make enquiries as to the suitability of certain concrete for an aquarium beyond talking to the suppliers and looking at a pamphlet concerning the use of the concrete in a different manner from that intended.

[64] See paras 9–172 to 9–176, above.

[65] *ibid.*

[66] [1979] 2 N.Z.L.R. 441.

[67] Compare *Christopher Moran Holdings Ltd v Carden & Godfrey* (1999) 73 Con. L.R. 28, where architects who advised their client that the provision of mechanical and electrical services for a swimming pool was outside their expertise and that he should retain specialist consultants were held to have discharged their duty.

[68] Note in this regard *Voli v Inglewood Shire Council* [1963] A.L.R. 657 at 663–664.

sufficient to apprise him of a defect or material change in design.[69] It is submitted that the position will be different where the client is a developer or design and build contractor which maintains its own in-house design expertise and is sent the plans for the purpose of checking and approving them.

Architects and engineers commonly seek to defend their designs against **9–201** criticism by relying on approvals granted by building control and other authorities. This defence typically fails. In *Eames London Estates Ltd v North Hertfordshire DC*[70] an industrial building was constructed on made ground. The foundations proved inadequate because the architect entrusted with the design of the building including the foundations had made no investigation of ground conditions. It was held that the architect should have satisfied himself about the land's bearing capacity and that he could not shed his responsibility for foundations by ascertaining what would "get by the local authority", as he appeared to have done. The Commonwealth authorities are to the same effect. In *Voli v Inglewood Shire Council*,[71] the defendant architects designed a stage which collapsed because the joists supporting it were insufficiently strong. The High Court of Australia held that it was no defence for the architects to point to the fact that their design had been passed by the Public Works Department. Windeyer J. conceded that the fact that plans were approved by a public authority might in some cases, although not on the facts of that particular case, be relevant in considering whether or not an architect was in fact negligent. In the common situation of an architect's or engineer's negligent design having been approved by a local authority building inspector, it is submitted that such approval will be treated by the courts as irrelevant to the issue of the architect's or engineer's liability. *Murphy v Brentwood DC*[72] makes it clear that, in England, in the usual exercise of its statutory powers a local authority owes no duty to anyone to protect them against economic loss. Such responsibility will rest solely with the architect or engineer who is employed to draw up the plans.[73] Accordingly, the fact that the defendants' design complied with the Building Regulations was held to be no defence to the claim that the design was negligently deficient in *Sahib Foods Ltd v Paskin Kyriades Sands*.[74]

Compliance with the client's brief. The designer should take reasonable care **9–202** to provide a design which meets his client's requirements. If the client expresses his instructions in terms which leave the designer in doubt as to what the client's purpose is, the designer has a duty to seek clarification so as to ascertain what is the purpose he is instructed to achieve. Judge Bowsher Q.C. made this point in *Stormont Main Working Men's Club v J Roscoe Milne Partnership*.[75] In that

---

[69] See *Christopher Moran Holdings Ltd v Carden & Godfrey* (1999) 73 Con. L.R. 28, where Judge Wilcox held that architects were in breach of duty in failing to explain to their client the nature of a revision to their design, the reasons for it and the options open to him in respect of it.

[70] (1980) 259 E.G. 491. See para.9–182, above.

[71] [1963] A.L.R. 657.

[72] [1991] 1 A.C. 398. For discussion of this case see paras 9–070 and 9–077, above.

[73] In *Targett v Torfaen BC* [1992] 3 All E.R. 27, the Court of Appeal emphasised that the essential question, in deciding whether a tortfeasor was liable for personal injuries caused by a defect of which the claimant had knowledge, was whether it was reasonable for the claimant to avoid the danger given the knowledge. See further para.9–074, above.

[74] [2003] EWHC 142, TCC. This point was not taken upon the appeal: [2003] EWCA Civ 1832.

[75] (1988) 13 Con. L.R. 126 at 133.

case, the claimant complained that an extension to the club which had been designed by the defendant architects was defective because the position of pillars meant that the space around the snooker tables was less than that required for national competitions. The judge found, on the facts, that the claimant had not intended to create facilities for playing competition snooker and had given no instructions to that effect. The architects reasonably understood that their client's purpose in instructing them was to get planning permission for an extension allowing whatever improvement to the games facilities was practicable and were not negligent in designing the same.

9–203   **Novel designs.** Where a design is experimental or in need of amplification as the construction progresses, an architect should be astute to consider whether his design will work in practice and to correct any errors which may emerge.[76] In the case of a novel design, the failure of the design may be consistent with the exercise of reasonable care and skill by the designer. In *Turner v Garland and Christopher*,[77] Erle J. directed the jury:

> "You should bear in mind that if the building is of an ordinary description, in which he [the architect] has an abundance of experience, and it proved a failure, this is evidence of a want of skill and attention. But if out of ordinary course, and you employ him about a novel thing, about which he has little experience, if it has not had the test of experience, failure may be consistent with skill. The history of all great improvements shows failure of those who embark in them; this may account for the defect of the roof."

But, particularly where the failure of a novel design may present danger and a threat to safety, it will be incumbent on the designer to show that his design, albeit novel, is capable of rational analysis and to anticipate, and to provide for, all possible causes of failure.[78] Prudence may even justify the abandonment of a design.[79]

9–204   Where specialist suppliers or sub-contractors are involved in the development of a novel design, the construction professional must avoid the temptation to assume that any failure of the design will not result in a finding of liability against him. It will be in the short-term interests of suppliers or sub-contractors to under-specify so as to keep their prices low and increase their prospects of obtaining the work. The construction professional should take care to protect his client against loss resulting from inadequate design or specification by others. In *Try Build Ltd v Invicta Leisure Tennis Ltd*,[80] structural and civil engineers were engaged by a building owner in connection with the design and construction of two tennis halls. The claimant was the design and build contractor, to whom the engineers' contract was novated. The claimant contracted with a specialist sub-contractor

---

[76] For discussion of the nature and scope of the designer's duty to review his design, see paras 9–030 to 9–038, above.

[77] (1853) cited in *Hudson's Building Contracts* (4th edn), Vol.2, p.1 (architect employed to plan and superintend buildings incorporating new patent concrete roofs absolved of want of competent skill despite failure of roofs).

[78] See *Eckersley v Binnie* (1988) 18 Con. L.R. 1, discussed further at para.9–206, below.

[79] See *IBA v EMI and BICC* (1980) 14 B.L.R. 1, 14 discussed in para.9–095, above; and *Bevan Investments Ltd v Blackhall and Struthers (No. 2)* [1973] 2 N.Z.L.R. 45 at 65–66.

[80] (2000) 1 Con. L.R. 141.

for the design, supply and construction of the roofs of the halls. The design was novel: each roof comprised four inflated foil cushions held in place by a rope edge detail. The roofs leaked. Having carried out remedial works pursuant to its obligations under the building contract, the claimant sought damages from the engineers in respect of its losses. It was common ground that the causes of the leakage were (a) tearing of the foil at the edge details because the foil was too thin; and (b) faulty design of the waterproofing details. Judge Bowsher Q.C. held that both matters were the result of breach of duty on the part of the engineers. They should have specified the conditions in which the roofs were required to be watertight and the required thickness of the edge foils. The judge rejected the engineers' arguments that those were matters which they were entitled to leave to the specialist contractor, and held that even if they were, the engineers should have advised their clients that this was what they were doing. Furthermore, the engineers should have advised on the need for tests to establish that the novel features of the design had been successfully developed by the sub-contractor. Had they done so, such tests would have revealed that the edge foils were too thin. The engineers' evidence that they had trusted in the expertise of the specialist sub-contractor was no answer:

"Engineers who are engaged to supervise and check the work of others are not paid to trust those others blindly, though the degree of trust or lack of it may affect the depth of enquiries made."[81]

Judge Bowsher Q.C. applied the same principles in *Baxall Securities Ltd v* **9–205** *Sheard Walshaw Partnership*.[82] The defendant architects were held to have been negligent in failing to specify which of the rainfall rates identified in the relevant British Standard was to be assumed by a specialist sub-contractor in its design of a roof drainage system. They ought to have appreciated that, left to its own devices, the sub-contractor would be tempted to design on the basis of the lowest (and therefore the cheapest) rainfall rate. The foreseeable use of the property was such that this was not the appropriate rate.

Assessment of risk. A designer must take reasonable care to assess and cater **9–206** in his design for all those risks which he can reasonably foresee. In *Eckersley v Binnie*,[83] the defendant engineers were found negligent and thus responsible for the Abbeystead disaster in which 16 people died and others were injured. As the judge at first instance held,[84] the central issue in the case was whether the accumulation of methane in the tunnel and valve house in sufficient quantities to

---

[81] (2000) 1 Con. L.R. 141 at 169.
[82] [2001] P.N.L.R. 256. For the facts, see para.9–077, above. See also *South Lakeland DC v Curtins Consulting Engineers Plc*, unreported, May 23, 2000, Judge Thornton Q.C. (engineers were negligent in failing to specify performance standards for car park slabs to be supplied by a specialist sub-contractor and to check the sub-contractor's design calculations). The judge's finding of breach of duty by the architects was not challenged on the appeal in *Baxall Securities Ltd v Sheard Walshaw Partnership* [2002] EWCA Civ 9.
[83] (1988) 18 Con. L.R. 1. For the facts, see para.9–074, above. See also *Adams v Rhymney Valley DC* [2001] P.N.L.R. 68, CA (design of window locking systems for local authority housing held not negligent although the choice of design led to fatalities when the windows could not be used as means of escape during a house fire).
[84] *ibid.* at 4.

cause the explosion ought reasonably to have been foreseen at the design stage. A majority in the Court of Appeal held that it ought.[85] Russell L.J. identified[86] the risks which a careful designer would not ignore by reference to the speech of Lord Reid in *The Wagon Mound*,[87] where, dealing with remote risks, Lord Reid said:

> "It does not follow that, no matter what the circumstances may be, it is justifiable to neglect a risk of such a small magnitude. A reasonable man would only neglect such a risk if he had a valid reason for doing so: eg. that it would involve considerable expense to eliminate the risk. He would weigh the risk against the difficulty of eliminating it . . . a person must be regarded as negligent if he does not take steps to eliminate a risk which he knows or ought to know is a real risk and not a mere possibility which would never influence the mind of a reasonable man."

9–207   Similarly, in *Pride Valley Foods Ltd v Hall & Partners (Contract Management) Ltd*,[88] it was held that project managers engaged for the design and construction of a bread-making factory had negligently failed to warn the client that the expanded polystyrene panels which he wished to use in order to keep costs down were highly combustible and, if ignited, would lead to a rapid spread of fire through the factory. The defendants' case was that they had indeed given such advice in the course of several conversations with their client, but it was found on the facts that they had not. The case illustrates the value of written confirmation of important advice to the client as to the risks of a design; had the defendants in *Pride Valley Foods* adopted that course, the issues in the case would have been considerably narrower.

9–208   The use of combustible panels was also the basis of a successful claim in *Sahib Foods Ltd v Paskin Kyriades Sands*.[89] It was held that a fire in a food production factory was started as a result of lack of care by the leasehold owner and occupier, but that its spread beyond the room where it started was caused by the use of combustible panels to line that room. The panels had been specified by the defendant architects as part of their design for the refurbishment of the factory. Although the expert witnesses called by the parties agreed that not all reasonably competent architects would have been aware of the risk of fire spreading as a result of use of the panels in question, it was found that the defendants were in breach of duty for specifying the use of such panels because they in fact had knowledge of the risk. The decision is of particular interest because of Judge Bowsher Q.C.'s analysis of the significance of the client's knowledge of the risk.

---

[85] Although Bingham L.J.'s dissenting judgment (especially at 84–114) appears to provide a coherent and convincing argument to the effect that it was not foreseeable at the time of the design to a reasonably competent engineer.

[86] *ibid.* at 52.

[87] [1967] A.C. 617 at 642.

[88] (2001) 76 Con. L.R. 1 (first instance). The Court of Appeal upheld the judge's finding on breach of duty, but remitted the case for retrial on the issue of causation: [2001] EWCA Civ 1001. For further consideration of the decision in *Pride Valley Foods Ltd v Hall & Partners (Contract Management) Ltd*, see C. Leong, "The duty of care in project management" (2001) 17 P.N. 250. For a discussion of this case, see T. Dugdale, "Out of the frying pan, into the fire: how much was the cook to blame?" (2004) P.N. 113.

[89] [2003] EWHC 142, TCC.

Holding that the client's knowledge provided the architects with no defence, the judge said[90]:

> "A competent architect does not present a design that he knows to be deficient in an important respect and then discuss with the client whether the deficiency should be removed. Still less does he present such a design and say, I did not need to tell the client about the deficiency because the client already knew that such a feature was required. Take a simple example. An architect designs a house as a residence for a client who happens to be a surveyor and forgets to require a damp-proof course under a parapet wall. If after construction the client complains, it is no answer for the architect to say, 'Well you knew about the need for the damp proof course as well as I did'. The architect is employed to use his own skill and judgment. There is no duty on the client who happens to have a particular skill to examine the architect's designs and tell the architect where he has gone wrong. If I, as a lawyer, go to a solicitor for advice and pay him for it, I do not see why I should be criticised if I fail to do that solicitor's work all over again and check whether he has got it right."

The cause of the start of the fire was particularly careless use of equipment by the claimant's employees. The judge found that, in the light of the gravity of the consequences should a fire start in the room in question, the architects had not been entitled to assume that equipment would be correctly used or only slightly misused. This part of the decision was upheld by the Court of Appeal.[91] Thus if a designer is aware of a serious danger against which his design must guard, he should consider all the ways in which the danger might be brought about, including unusually careless behaviour by the client. In order to avoid liability, he should give clear advice to his client as to the risks of cost-cutting in design and ensure that the client accepts those risks.[92]

Published standards. In preparing a design the provisions of relevant build-   **9–209**
ing regulations and byelaws will need to be observed. Codes of practice should
be considered and departed from only with the most careful consideration of the
consequences. This topic is more fully considered above.[93]

Level of detail. A difficult question is the degree of detail required to be   **9–210**
included in plans, drawings and specifications. Some omissions may be clearly
negligent.[94] Generally, however, the degree of detail required will depend upon
the facts of each case, in particular the nature of the architect's instructions and
the documents concerned. There will be wide differences of detail and even
accuracy required as between a preliminary design plan, a plan submitted for
planning permission and a working drawing. The expertise and resources of the

---

[90] [2003] EWHC 142, TCC at [40].

[91] [2003] EWCA Civ 1832.

[92] Engineers were also held liable for failing to advise on risks inherent in their designs where alternative designs were available in *City of Brantford v Kemp and Wallace-Carruthers & Associates Ltd* (1960) 23 D.L.R. (2d) and *Pullen v Gutteridge* [1993] 1 V.R. 27.

[93] See paras 9–152 to 9–155 and 9–196 to 9–198, above.

[94] Note Sachs L.J.'s example of a design of a house without a staircase in *Worboys v Acme Investments Ltd* (1969) 210 E.G. 335, CA. Also see paras 9–137 to 9–143, above concerning the importance of evidence of general practice.

contractor, insofar as known to the designer, will also be relevant.[95] Owing to these varying circumstances many reported cases concerning negligence in design provide scant indication as to a court's approach on other albeit superficially similar facts.

9–211   **Choice of materials.** Choice of materials is an essential part of design. Usually materials will be so familiar as to require no inquiry as to their suitability. In the case of untried or novel materials, whether used alone or in conjunction with established materials, the exercise of reasonable care may require an architect or engineer to make proper enquiries as to their suitability.[96] The same applies to the choice of proprietary products or systems: a construction professional may be required to make extensive enquiries as to the design assumptions adopted by the specialist supplier in developing such product or system. Thus, in *Michael Hyde & Associated Ltd v JD Williams & Co Ltd*,[97] the defendant architects were found negligent in accepting the assurances of a gas heating system salesman that the risk of discoloration of stored textiles by the system was minimal. When discoloration to materials stored by their client did occur, it was held that the defendants should have appreciated that the supplier's refusal to withdraw its disclaimer of liability for discoloration suggested that the risk was a serious one, notwithstanding the salesman's denials, and made enquiries of the supplier's technical department. The cases of *Gloucestershire HA v Torpy*[98] and *Hammersmith Hospitals NHS Trust v Troup Bywaters & Anders*[99] both concerned complaints that building services engineers had negligently failed to make adequate investigations into the suitability and capacity of proprietary incinerator systems before advising that they be installed in hospitals. In the *Gloucestershire HA* case, the engineers were found negligently to have failed to appreciate that the incinerators did not have the required output, because they had failed to investigate their capacity before advising the employer to accept the supplier's tender. In the *Hammersmith Hospitals* case, it was held that the engineers were not negligent, primarily because there was expert evidence that a reasonably competent building services engineer in 1991 would have accepted the manufacturer's data without independent verification and because the engineers were aware that the client would be required to accept the incinerators only if they passed post-installation performance tests.

---

[95] In *Catlin Estates Ltd v Carter Jonas* [2005] EWHC 2315 at [340], it was held that the designer's duty was "to communicate the design to the contractor in a manner which was clear and unambiguous" and suggested that the inclusion of references to British Standards in the specification was inadequate in the circumstances of that case.
[96] See *Sealand of the Pacific v Robert C McHaffie* (1974) 51 D.L.R. (3d) 702. Note also the facts of *Merton LBC v Lowe* (1981) 18 B.L.R. 130, CA discussed at para.9–176, above; *Richard Roberts & Holdings Ltd v Douglas Smith Stimson Partnership* (1988) 46 B.L.R. 50 (architects negligent in failing adequately to investigate linings of effluent tanks: see para.9–136, above and *Privest Properties v Foundation Co of Canada* (1995) 128 D.L.R. (4th) 577 upheld at (1997) 143 D.L.R. (4th) 635 (architects who specified product should have been aware that it contained asbestos before specification); *George Hawkins v Chrysler (UK)* (1986) 38 B.L.R. 36 (engineers who selected shower room tiles after careful consideration of product data sheets and trade brochures and consultation with specialist flooring firm was held not negligent even although tiles turned out to be slippery).
[97] [2001] P.N.L.R 233, CA.
[98] (1997) 55 Con. L.R. 124.
[99] [2000] Env. L.R. 343, affirmed on appeal ([2001] EWCA Civ 793; unreported, May 25, 2001).

Buildability. Two aspects of design which a designer should bear in mind are **9–212** "buildability" and "supervisability". The Construction (Design and Management) Regulations 1994 require a designer to ensure that his design is safely buildable.[1] Further, as Judge Newey Q.C said in *Equitable Debenture Assets Corp Ltd v William Moss Group Ltd*[2]:

> "I think that if implementation of part of a design requires work to be carried out on site, the designer should ensure that the work can be performed by those likely to be employed to do it, in the conditions which can be foreseen, by the exercise of the care and skill ordinarily to be expected by them. If the work would demand exceptional skill, and particularly if it would have to be performed partly from scaffolding and often in windy conditions, then the design will lack what the experts in evidence described as 'buildability'. Similarly, I think that if a design requires work to be carried out on-site in such a way that those whose duty it is to supervise it and/or check that it has been done will encounter great difficulty in doing so, then the design will again be defective. It may perhaps be described as lacking 'supervisability'."

In *Department of National Heritage v Steenson Varming Mulcahy*,[3] Judge Bowsher Q.C. cited Judge Newey's dictum with approval, pointing out[4]:

> " . . . the words 'those likely to be employed to do [the work]' used by Judge Newey are important and are to be related to the differing facts of each case. It is not to be assumed in every case that the work is to be done by the 'ordinary' tradesman, in this case 'the ordinary electrician' . . . The designer is entitled to look at the facts of the project on which he is engaged and consider what is the standard of workmanship required by the employer and agreed by the contractor to be provided to do the particular work."

On the facts of that case, the judge rejected a contention that there was such widespread installation of defective cabling on the British Library project as to give rise to an inference that the design was at fault. Further, he held that the defendant engineers were entitled to expect that their design, which specified a high standard of finish, would be executed by a contractor which was able to meet that high standard. The roof design chosen by the defendants in *George Fischer Holding Ltd v Multi Design Consultants Ltd*[5] for a warehouse was found to have been negligent because of, apparently, its lack of buildability. The design required the roof slopes to be clad using panels which were not continuous from eaves to ridge, but comprised a series of panels laid end to end and joined by "end laps". The design required perfect construction of the end lap joints if the roof was to be watertight. That was an unrealistic expectation. The use of end lap joints could and should have been avoided altogether.

Integration of design. It will often be the case that a designer instructed to **9–213** design only a part of a building will need to take account of the design of other

---

[1] The regulations are discussed at para.9–048, above.
[2] (1984) 2 Con. L.R. 1 at 21 (architects held negligent in various respects in relation to the design of curtain walling which was subject to extensive leaking).
[3] (1998) 60 Con. L.R. 33.
[4] *ibid.* at 85.
[5] (1998) 61 Con. L.R. 85.

parts.[6] However it appears from the decision of the majority in the Court of Appeal in *Holland Hannen & Cubitts (Northern) Ltd v Welsh Health Technical Services Organisation*[7] that designers will not generally be required to consider their design from a point of view which goes beyond the extent of their own discipline. In that case CED were nominated sub-contractors to the claimant main contractors in respect of the design and supply of concrete floors for a hospital. AMP were engineers employed by CED who advised on the structural aspects of the floors. The original design was such that the profile of the floors would comply with CP116 but there was a subsequent change, made without reference to AMP, so that the floors were required to comply with CP204. The main contractors experienced difficulties in erecting partitions and a survey discovered that the floors complied with CP116 but not CP204. It was apparent upon a visual inspection that the floors were not completely level, although there would have been no difficulty in pushing trolleys over the floors. The architects sought to condemn the floors and a delay resulted. The main contractors then sued both the employer and CED for loss and expense occasioned by the delay, whereupon CED brought in AMP. The Court of Appeal was agreed that AMP's obligation was to exercise the reasonable skill and care of ordinarily competent engineers but were divided as to the result of the application of this test. Lawton L.J. said[8]:

> "It would not be part of their function to visualise what the floors would look like when the final finishes had been applied. The appearance of the floors would be for the architect to visualize."

Dillon L.J. agreed[9]:

> "As I see it, however, matters of visual appearance or aesthetic effect are matters for the architect and are not within the province of the structural engineer. It is for the structural engineer to work out what the deflections of a floor will be; it is for the architect to decide whether a floor with those deflections will be visually or aesthetically satisfactory when the finishes chosen by the architect have been applied."

Robert Goff L.J. disagreed, taking the view[10] that the engineer was under a duty to ask himself the question "whether there is a significant risk that the floor, with that profile, in the building in question, may be unacceptable." He would have held that, as CED were effectively lay clients of AMP, they were under:

> "a duty to draw to the attention of their clients any matter within their expertise which might result in a significant risk of the structure being unacceptable to the building

---

[6] See, for example, the South Australian case of *Carosella v Ginos and Gilbert* (1981) 27 S.A.S.R. 515 (engineers held negligent in recommending foundations designed without regard to the nature of the superstructure).

[7] (1985) 35 B.L.R. 1.

[8] *ibid.* at 11. In their article "Are architects and engineers responsible for buildability in design?" (2000) 16 Const. L.J. 3, Philip Harris and Jonathan Leach argue that buildability is the sole province of the building contractor. It is submitted that the better view is that both the construction professional charged with design and the building contractor have a responsibility in relation to buildability; the extent of their respective responsibilities will depend on the facts in each case.

[9] *ibid.* at 31.

[10] *ibid.* at 25.

owner or his architect, and I can see no reason why this should exclude a risk that an aspect of the configuration of the structure might render it visually unacceptable."[11]

It is submitted that, whilst a designer may have no duty to consider his design from the point of view of a discipline which is not his own, he ought to take care to see that his design is compatible with the design of the remainder.

Co-ordination of design. As modern buildings have become more sophisti-   **9–214**
cated, there has been an increasing use of specialist suppliers, sub-contractors and consultants. As the parties involved in a building project proliferate, the employer's desire for a single point of professional contact increases. The result is that a construction professional in general practice may find himself appointed "lead consultant", with responsibility for co-ordinating the work of numerous specialists who have greater expertise in their respective areas than he does. The duty to co-ordinate elements of the overall design which have been prepared by others can be an onerous duty. In *Equitable Debenture Assets Corp Ltd v William Moss Group Ltd*,[12] the defendant architects properly sought the assistance of specialist walling consultants, but failed properly to co-ordinate their work. They failed, amongst other things, to ask the consultants to make inquiries about the curtain walling sub-contractor, to enlist the consultants' help in checking and approving the sub-contractor's tender, to take steps to bring about co-operation between the contractor and the consultants in the preparation of working draw-ings and to involve the consultants fully in the supervision and inspection of the curtain walling installation.[13] In *Royal Brompton Hospital NHS Trust v Ham-mond*,[14] project managers were held liable for failing to monitor and co-ordinate the production of drawings by mechanical and engineering services consultants. As a result, they failed to advise the client that it was premature to award the building contract on the basis of the information available and, after award of the contract, they failed to see that the necessary information was provided to the contractor so as to allow it to build to programme.

Client-instructed change to design. A designer will often be found to have   **9–215**
particularly onerous obligations if he is asked to review his design in order to overcome a specific obstacle. Thus in *Leach v Crossley*,[15] the defendant engi-neers were engaged to produce engineering plans for the construction of a warehouse with a car park on its roof. A perfectly satisfactory initial design was prepared for the structural support of the car park assuming the use of a lightweight waterproofing material supplied by a particular company. Through no fault of the defendants, it was discovered that the material would not be satisfactory and an alternative would have to be used. The defendants were asked

---

[11] (1985) 35 B.L.R. 1 at 26.
[12] (1984) 2 Con. L.R. 1 at 21 (architects held negligent in various respects in relation to the design of curtain walling which was subject to extensive leaking).
[13] Where specialists are used to supply and install proprietary systems, there is a particular temptation for the generalist construction professional to neglect his duty by placing too much reliance upon the assumed expertise of those specialists: see the cases discussed at paras 9–204 and 9–211, above.
[14] [2002] EWHC 2037, TCC.
[15] (1984) 8 Con. L.R. 7. See, further, paras 9–118 to 9–124, above.

for the maximum weight that the car deck could carry so that possible alternatives could be investigated. Instead of re-doing the calculations, the defendants simply gave the figure for the weight of material allowed for in the design. They were held to have been negligent and liable to the claimants when another light material which was within this weight failed on the basis that the roof could, in fact, have carried a heavier material.[16]

9–216 **Over-design.** Occasionally, the complaint will be that a designer has taken excessive precautions in his design. One such case was *London Underground v Kenchington Ford Plc*.[17] The defendant engineers were engaged to design the station concourse slab for one of the new stations on the Jubilee Line extension. London Underground alleged that reasonably competent engineers would have designed a thinner, and therefore cheaper, slab than that which the defendants designed. Judge Wilcox dismissed the claim. There was expert evidence of a respectable school of thought in the structural engineering profession which would have adopted the defendants' approach.

9–217 **Review of design.** Cases in which a designer has been held to have breached a duty to review his design are considered in the section above which discusses the circumstances in which a duty to review will arise.[18]

(e) *Preparation of Bills of Quantities*

9–218 It is usually the function of a quantity surveyor to prepare bills of quantities. But when the task is undertaken by an architect or engineer he will be under the same duty as that required of a quantity surveyor, namely to take reasonable care and skill. Quantities are commonly prepared by reference to standard methods of measurements, with which a quantity surveyor is expected to be familiar. As demonstrated by *London School Board v Northcroft, Son and Neighbour*,[19] minor errors may be insufficient to establish negligence in the preparation of quantities. Conversely, the greater the errors, whether in number or consequence, the more difficult it will be to resist a finding of negligence.[20] A quantity surveyor should

---

[16] See also *Richard Roberts Holdings Ltd v Douglas Smith Stimson Partnership* (1988) 46 B.L.R. 50 (architects held to have been negligent in design of effluent tank lining where original satisfactory lining rejected by client on grounds of cost); *Governors of Board of Hospitals for Sick Children v McLaughlin & Harvey* (1987) 19 Con. L.R. 25 (engineers found negligent in respect of pile design which had been revised in order to save money where original design would have been satisfactory); *Pride Valley Foods Ltd v Hall & Partners (Contract Management) Ltd* (2001) 76 Con. L.R. 1 (first instance); [2001] EWCA Civ 1001; (2001) 76 Con. L.R. 1 at 36, CA (project managers held negligent in failing to warn the client that his chosen materials were highly combustible and if ignited would allow rapid spread of fire throughout the factory).
[17] (1998) 63 Con. L.R. 1.
[18] See paras 9–030 to 9–038, above.
[19] (1889) *Hudson's Building Contracts* (4th edn, 1914), Vol.2, p.149.
[20] See generally para.9–164, above including reference to the quantity surveyor case of *Tyrer v District Auditor of Monmouthshire* (1973) 230 E.G. 973.

take care to ensure that the quantities are reasonably sufficient and not exces-sive.[21] In practice a quantity surveyor often operates through the architect to whom he reports matters for onward transmission to the client if necessary. The quantity surveyor should take reasonable care to procure that the information is transmitted to the client, since he is under a direct obligation to him, although normally the quantity surveyor can assume that the architect will pass it on.[22] In addition to his duties to the client employer, a quantity surveyor may owe a *Hedley Byrne* duty to a contractor in respect of the preparation of bills of quantities included in tender documentation.[23]

(f) *Selection of Contractor and the Tender Process*

A construction professional engaged by a building owner may be required to   **9–219**
advise as to the means by which a contractor for the works should be selected. Unless the works require the unique skills of a particular contractor, or there is some particular urgency which makes a tender process impracticable, a construc-tion professional should normally advise his client to select a contractor through a process of competitive tender rather than enter negotiations for a contract with a single contractor. In *Hutchinson v Harris*,[24] an architect was held negligent in failing to put the work of converting a house out to competitive tender.

A construction professional acting for a building owner or developer will   **9–220**
commonly be required by his terms of engagement to advise as to the list of contractors who are to be invited to tender and to appraise the tenders received. In each case, the exercise of reasonable care and skill may require him to make reasonable inquiries as to the solvency and capabilities of contractors, including nominated sub-contractors. An example is *Equitable Debenture Assets Corp Ltd v William Moss Group Ltd*,[25] where Judge Newey Q.C. held that architects were negligent in failing to make inquiries into the experience and capabilities of the nominated subcontractor which designed, supplied and installed what turned out to be defective curtain walling. Inquiries should have been made both before the subcontractor was invited to tender and after its tender had been submitted, in order properly to appraise that tender. In *Valerie Pratt v George J. Hill Asso-ciates*,[26] architects were held to be in breach of their duty to recommend suitable reliable builders and guilty of negligent misrepresentation in describing as "very

---

[21] Note *Keete v King* [1938] E.G.D. 65; *Saunders and Collard v Broadstairs Local Board* (1890) reported in *Hudson's Building Contracts* (4th edn), Vol.2, p.164; *Tyrer v District Auditor of Mon-mouthshire* (1973) 230 E.G. 973 (quantity surveyor approved excessive quantities and prices in some contracts with builders when it was his duty not to accept rates he must have known to be ridiculously high: held negligent).

[22] *Aubrey Jacobus and Partners v Gerrard*, unreported, June 1981, *per* Judge Stabb Q.C.

[23] See generally paras 9–060 to 9–124, above on the subject of duty of care to third parties and in particular paras 9–105 to 9–111 concerning duties owed to contractors.

[24] 1977 (unreported), a decision of Judge Edgar Fay Q.C. at first instance. The appeal in the case is reported in (1978) 10 B.L.R. 19, from which the decision at first instance is apparent. An application by the architect for leave to cross-appeal out of time was refused.

[25] (1984) 2 Con. L.R. 1 (architects held negligent in various respects in relation to the design of curtain walling which was subject to extensive leaking) at 26.

[26] Unreported; a decision of Recorder Barry Green Q.C. at first instance. The appeal is at (1987) 38 B.L.R. 25 where the only issue is as to damages but the issues at first instance are reasonably apparent.

reliable" a builder who was, in fact, wholly unreliable. In *Partridge v Morris*,[27] Judge Hicks Q.C. held that an architect who advised a lay client as to the acceptability of building tenderers should have checked their financial position. This they could and should have done by making enquiries of building merchants, obtaining bank references, obtaining trade credit references, making inquiries of other architects, arranging a company search or asking the contractor to provide its audited accounts for examination.

9–221   Further, the construction professional should take care, when examining the amounts of quotations or tenders, not to advise the acceptance of rates which are unreasonable in the circumstances. In *Tyrer v District Auditor of Monmouthshire*,[28] the quantity surveyor was found to have been in breach of duty when he approved quantities and prices in contracts with a contractor when he must have known that they were based on rates which were "ridiculously high".

(g) *Advice on Choice and Terms of a Building Contract*

9–222   A construction professional's engagement to advise upon choice of contractors will commonly carry with it the obligation, whether express or implied, to consider the choice and terms of the contract between the employer and the contractor. There are many standard forms of building and engineering contract[29] and different forms will be appropriate for different types and sizes of project. In some cases, a contract drafted specifically for the project in hand will be appropriate. The exercise of reasonable care and skill may require the construction professional to advise the employer to reject a particular form of contract or a particular term if disadvantageous to the employer's interests.[30] Given the large number of different standard forms which now exist and the multitude of decisions as to what particular provisions of the contract mean, it may be prudent for the architect either to seek himself or to advise his client to seek legal advice as to the meaning or effect of a particular term in a contract.[31] He should certainly do so if he is in real doubt as to the correct construction of an important term. It has been suggested that a construction professional may incur liability in negligence for recommending without modification (or proper explanation) one of the standard forms in general use in the United Kingdom,[32] but a professional should be cautious about recommending amendments to standard terms and, if in doubt as to the legal consequences of any proposed amendment, should take legal advice or recommend that the client does so.

9–223   If nominated sub-contractors or suppliers are to be used, the construction professional should normally advise the employer to refuse to nominate a particular sub-contractor unless that sub-contractor is prepared to guarantee or

---

[27] [1995] C.I.L.L. 1095.
[28] (1973) 230 E.G. 973
[29] See paras 9–010 to 9–016, above.
[30] See the unreported decision in *Burrell Hayward & Budd v Chris Carnell and David Green*, February 20, 1992, where a deputy official referee found that both the claimant quantity surveyors and the defendant architects were partially responsible for the use of an inappropriate building contract by the architect's clients; this had no causal effect, however, as the terms of the building contract were, in practice, ignored.
[31] See para.9–156, above.
[32] Hudson, *op. cit.*, pp.331–341.

warrant directly to the employer the quality or fitness of his work and materials.

A building contract will normally comprise conditions of contract, contract **9–224** drawings, a specification and a bill of quantities. Where professionals of different disciplines are involved in the preparation of the various constituent parts of the contract, care must be taken to see that they are consistent with each other. The drawings, specification and bill of quantities should together provide the contractor with a full and clear description of the work to be done. An architect may incur liability in negligence as well as for excess of authority if through failure to scrutinise contract documents he allows his client to enter into a contract for building works different from those which the client required him to provide for in specifications.[33]

From a wider perspective, there is now available a wide range of methods by **9–225** which to procure the construction of a building (of which the traditional building contract, the design and build contract and the construction management contract are merely the principal forms). A construction professional may well be required to advise as to the appropriate method(s) of procurement for a particular development and should take care to see that he does not overestimate his client's expertise and experience in this respect.[34]

(h) Administration of the Building Contract

Particularly when engaged in respect of a larger building project, a construction **9–226** professional will commonly be responsible for performing a number of tasks which may collectively be described as administration of the main building contract. All the standard forms of building and engineering contracts provide for a named architect[35] or engineer.[36] The building contract gives certain powers and duties to that person to regulate the mutual rights and obligations of the employer and the building contractor. His tasks will include inspecting the works, issuing payment certificates, issuing orders for variation of the contract works, making decisions on the contractor's claims for extensions of time or for payment for delay and disruption, instructing the removal of defective work, determining the date of practical completion and loss and expense, and approving work to make good defects. The important functions of inspection and certification are considered in detail in the following sections of this chapter.[37]

---

[33] See *Kenny & Reynolds Ltd v Pyper* [1964] E.G.D. 419 (error by architect in not deleting from specifications a percentage sum for a central heating system after decision to exclude the item, held to be inexcusable and negligent. On the facts the claim against the architect failed since the client was taken to have signed the building contract in the knowledge of the architect's error).

[34] For a case where the architect failed to give detailed and cogent advice in this respect, see *Plymouth & South West Co-operative Society v Architecture, Structure & Management Ltd* [2006] EWHC 5, TCC.

[35] See, for example, the JCT Standard Building Contract (2005), Art.3, where the title is "Architect/Contract Administrator" to cater for the appointment of a person who is not a registered architect.

[36] See, for example, the ICE Conditions of Contract (2002 edn).

[37] See paras 9–236 to 9–253 and 9–254 to 9–260, below.

9–227   **Issuing instructions and information.** Generally an architect should issue instructions and information required for the execution of works within a reasonable time. In *Neodox Ltd v Borough of Swindon Pendlebury*,[38] Diplock J. held that there was no implied term in a civil engineering contract which required the employer, by his engineer, to provide information and instructions necessary for the execution of the works in sufficient time to enable the contractor to complete the works on time. He drew attention to the fact that the contract (like most building contracts) did not contemplate that the contractor would have all the required information before works commenced. Rather, it was anticipated that further information would be provided by the engineers during the course of the contract. There was therefore an implied term that necessary information and instructions would be given within a reasonable time. What amounts to a reasonable time will depend on the facts of each case, in particular the terms of the main building contract, but Diplock J. pointed out that reasonableness is not to be determined solely by reference to the interests of the contractor, but also by reference to the position of the engineer, his staff and the employer. Relevant factors would include the order in which the works are to be carried out, whether requests for particular information or instructions have been made by the contractor, whether the instructions relate to a variation to the works or to the original works and the time by which the contractor was required to complete the works.[39] Similarly, in *London Borough of Merton v Stanley Hugh Leach Ltd*,[40] it was held that there was an implied term of the building contract (the JCT Standard Form of Building Contract, 1963 edition, July 1971 revision) that the architect would supply the contractor with accurate drawings and information during the course of the works. But for the fact that there were express terms in the building contract which required the architect to supply such instructions, drawings and information as were necessary for the contractor to complete its works in a regular and orderly manner and on time, it appears that such a term would have been implied.[41] Vinelott J. explained the position of the architect in the contractual relationship between employer and contractor[42]:

> "under the standard conditions the architect acts as the servant or agent of the building owner in supplying the contractor with the necessary drawings, instructions, levels and the like and in supervising the progress of the work and in ensuring that it is properly carried out. He will of course normally though not invariably have been responsible for

---

[38] (1958) 5 B.L.R. 34.

[39] *ibid.* at 41–42. See also *Royal Brompton Hospital NHS Trust v Hammond (No.4)* [2000] B.L.R. 75, where Judge Hicks Q.C. held that consulting mechanical and electrical engineers had an obligation to use reasonable care and skill to see that their co-ordination drawings were provided in time to enable contractor to prepare his installation drawings and thus to carry out and complete the works in accordance with the contract programme. Provisions in the building contract which required the contractor to co-ordinate drawings did not dilute or alter the engineers' responsibility.

[40] (1985) 32 B.L.R. 51.

[41] *ibid.* at 81–83.

[42] *ibid.* at 79–79. In *Costain Ltd v Bechtel Ltd* [2005] EWHC 1018, TCC, the defendant project managers argued that, on the particular terms of the building contract in that case, their position was not analogous to that of an architect or other contract administrator under conventional building contracts and that they were employed to protect the interests of the employer rather than to act impartially as between employer and contractor. Jackson J. rejected that argument so far as the project manager's functions (e.g. the issuing of certificates under the building contract) corresponded with those of a contract administrator under a traditional contract.

the design of the work. To the extent that the architect performs these duties the building owner contracts with the contractor that the architect will perform them with reasonable diligence and with reasonable skill and care. The contract also confers on the architect discretionary powers which he must exercise with due regard to the interests of the contractor and the building owner. The building owner does not undertake that the architect will exercise his discretionary powers reasonably; he undertakes that although the architect may be engaged or employed by him he will leave him free to exercise his discretion fairly and without improper interference by him . . . . [T]o the extent that the architect exercises these discretions his duty is to act fairly; 'the building owner and the contractor make their contract on the understanding that in all such matters the architect will act in a fair and unbiased manner and it must therefore be implicit in the owner's contract with the architect that he shall not only exercise due care and skill but also reach such decisions fairly, holding the balance between his client and the contractor' (see *Sutcliffe v Thackrah* [1974] A.C. 727 *per* Lord Reid at p.737)."

Implied terms such as those found in *Neodox* and in *Merton v Leach* describe   **9–228**
what the contract administrator has to do, as the employer's agent, to meet the employer's obligations to the contractor. Normally, the contractor's preferred remedy for late issue of information or instructions will be a claim against the employer under the building contract for an extension of time for completion or for payment in respect of delay and disruption, rather than a claim against the contract administrator in tort.[43] However, the contract administrator may be liable to indemnify the employer as his principal if his breach of duty puts the employer in breach of the building contract, renders him liable to the contractor for additional payments or causes him to incur costs by entitling the contractor to extensions of time.

On a complex or large project, the duties of a contract administrator may be   **9–229**
onerous and require the exercise of good organisational and management skills. In *Corfield v Grant*[44] an architect was held to be in breach of duty by reason of his failure properly to control a building project. The judge was particularly critical of the architect's failure to appoint and direct a suitably skilled and experienced assistant in a situation where the architect knew that speed was of the essence and it was necessary to organise a large number of matters at the same time. The judge found the architect to be responsible for the resultant "inadequately controlled muddle". In *The Royal Brompton Hospital NHS Trust v Hammond (No.1)*,[45] the Trust's predecessor had engaged Taylor Woodrow as main building contractor to carry out extensive building work at a hospital. The Trust settled Taylor Woodrow's claim for extra payments under the building contract and then claimed the costs of the settlement as damages against the various defendants, who had been the Trust's architects, engineers and project managers for the works. One of the Trust's allegations was that Taylor Woodrow had suffered loss and expense, which the Trust had been obliged under the building contract to pay, as a result of the "sheer number" of variation orders and instructions issued by the professional team during the course of the works. Judge Hicks Q.C. refused to strike out the allegation as bad in law, but made clear that it would require careful particularisation and proof.

---

[43] See paras 9–105 to 9–111 for discussion of the difficulties facing a claim in tort.
[44] (1992) 29 Con. L.R. 58.
[45] [1999] B.L.R. 162.

9–230   Before ordering work additional to that agreed in the building contract, it will be both prudent and necessary in most cases to seek the express authority of the employer to do so. In *Wilks v Thingoe (Suffolk) Regional DC*[46] an architect was held negligent in having embarked on a course of extravagant expenditure without his employers' authority.

9–231   **Applications for extensions of time and for extra payment.** A construction professional acting as contract administrator should take care in acceding to contractor's claims for extra payment and extensions of time. Any extensions granted and payments awarded should be reasonable and justified according to the terms of the main building contract. The contract administrator's duty in relation to applications for extensions of time was considered by the Supreme Court of New South Wales in *Perini Corporation v Commonwealth of Australia*.[47] In that case, the building contract provided that the power to grant extensions of time lay with an official of the defendant, called the director of works. It was held that the director of works had a discretion whether to grant an extension of time, but was bound to give his decision on any application for an extension within a reasonable time; in the circumstances, that meant that he should give a decision as soon as his investigation into the facts was completed and he had to make available sufficient time to carry out that investigation.

9–232   The building contract in *London Borough of Merton v Stanley Hugh Leach Ltd*[48] provided that, if it became apparent that the progress of the works was delayed, the contractor should give written notice of the delay to the architect and the architect, if of the opinion that the works had been or were likely to be delayed, should grant an extension of time for completion.[49] The question arose whether the architect should grant an extension of time in the absence of written notice from the contractor. Vinelott J. held that the contract required the architect to estimate delay and, if appropriate, grant an extension of time, if he became aware of any event which was likely to cause delay and would entitle the contractor to an extension of time, regardless of whether he had received notice of delay from the contractor. The architect was not entitled to ignore events which were likely to cause delay to the works beyond the contractual completion date just because the contractor was not aware of the likely delay. However, if delay was reasonably apparent to the contractor but he failed to give written notice of it to the architect, that was a breach of contract by the contractor and could be taken into account by the architect in considering an extension of time.[50] It may be, for example, that the delay could have been reduced had the architect

---

[46] (1954) 164 E.G. 86.
[47] (1969) 12 B.L.R. 82.
[48] (1985) 32 B.L.R. 51.
[49] The JCT Standard Form of Building Contract, 1963 edn, July 1971 revision, cl.23. Care should be taken in applying the decision in cases concerning different contracts. Some contracts stipulate that the provision of notice by the contractor is a condition precedent to the contractor's entitlement to an extension of time.
[50] (1985) 32 B.L.R. 51 at 89–90. The decision in *London Borough of Merton v Stanley Hugh Leach Ltd* (1985) 32 B.L.R. 51 was followed in *Sindall Ltd v Solland* (2001) 80 Con. L.R. 152: Judge Lloyd Q.C. held that both as a matter of law and as a matter of established good practice, a contract administrator should always consider whether there are any factors known to him which might justify the grant of an extension of time. This is so even where the contractor has not given written notice of such factors as required by the particular building contract.

been given earlier notice of it; in that case, it may be appropriate to grant a shorter extension of time so that the contractor does not benefit from his breach of contract.

An architect is obliged to act fairly, lawfully, rationally and logically in **9–233** considering an extension of time. In *John Barker Construction Ltd v London Portman Hotel Ltd*,[51] it was held that the architect had failed to meet that standard. He had not carried out a logical analysis in a methodical manner of the impact which the delaying events had or were likely to have on the contractor's planned programme. He had made an impressionistic, rather than a calculated, assessment of the delay. He misapplied the provisions of the building contract and, where he allowed an extension of time, the allowances which he made bore no logical or reasonable relation to the delay in fact caused. The analysis required in order to assess the impact of delaying events upon the contractual completion date can be complex and the accuracy of the assessment will depend upon the quality of the information which is available to the architect, as the court recognised in *The Royal Brompton Hospital NHS Trust v Hammond (No.7)*.[52] Judge Seymour Q.C. heard evidence from an expert in construction programming, a Mr Gibson, and observed[53]:

"Because the construction of a modern building, other than one of the most basic type, involves the carrying out of a series of operations, some of which, possibly, can be undertaken at the same time as some of the others, but many of which can only be carried out in a sequence, it may well not be immediately obvious which operations impact upon which other operations. In order to make an assessment of whether a particular occurrence has affected the ultimate completion of the work, rather than just a particular operation it is desirable to consider what operations, at the time the event with which one is concerned happens, are critical to the forward progress of the work as a whole. . . . the establishment of the critical path of a particular construction project can itself be a difficult task if one does not know how the contractor planned the job. Not only that, but the critical path may well change during the course of the works, and almost certainly will do if the progress of the works is affected by some unforeseen event. Mr Gibson frankly accepted that the various different methods of making an assessment of the impact of unforeseen occurrences upon the progress of construction works are likely to produce different results, perhaps dramatically different results. He also accepted that the accuracy of any of the methods in common use critically depends upon the quality of the information upon which the assessment exercise was based. All of this does, of course, emphasise the vital point that the duty of a professional man, generally stated, is not to be right, but to be careful. While, unless in a particular case the professional man is actually wrong, the fact that he has not been careful will probably not cause his client any loss, the fact that he is in the event proved to be wrong

---

[51] (1996) 83 B.L.R. 31.

[52] (2001) 76 Con. L.R. 148. The Society for Construction Law has published a Protocol for Determining Extensions of Time and Compensation for Delay and Disruption which may be adopted by contracting parties as an aid to interpretation of their building contract and may be used by contract administrators as guidance in dealing with contractors' claims for extensions of time. The Protocol was published in October 2002 and is available at *www.eotprotocol.com*. For discussion, see A. Burr and N. Lane, "The SCL Delay and Disruption Protocol: Hunting Snarks" (2003) 19 Const. L.J. 135.

[53] *ibid.* at para.[32]. On the facts, only one of the employer's allegations of negligent grant of an unwarranted extension of time by the architect succeeded.

is not, in itself, any evidence that he has been negligent. His conduct has to be judged having regard to the information available to him, or which ought to have been available to him, at the time he gave his advice or made his decision or did whatever else it is that he did."

9–234   **Insurance and performance bonds.** Building contracts commonly contain provisions designed to preserve the employer's prospect of recovering losses if a defaulting contractor goes into liquidation. For example, the contractor may be required to provide a performance bond. Or he may be obliged to put in place insurance cover against his liabilities to the employer. Where such provisions are found, a construction professional acting for the employer should take care to see that his client's position is protected in the manner contemplated by the contract. The main action in *Convent Hospital v Eberlin & Partners*[54] came about because the contractor had become insolvent without providing the performance bond required under the building contract. The employers alleged that their architect had been negligent in failing to see that a suitable bond was in force when the building contract was executed. Summary judgment was given for the employers. In *Pozzolanic Lytag Ltd v Bryan Hobson Associates*,[55] the defendant engineers were appointed project managers in relation to the design and construction of storage facilities for pulverised fuel ash. Part of the works designed by the contractor collapsed due to design deficiencies. Although, under the building contract, the contractors should have been insured in respect of liability for such a collapse, they were not. Dyson J. held that the engineers, as project managers, were responsible for ensuring that insurance was in place and were liable to the claimant accordingly. He held that the fact that the project managers lacked the expertise necessary to assess the adequacy of the insurance arrangements which the contractor did have in place did not relieve them of their responsibility. He said[56]:

> "If a project manager does not have the expertise to advise his client as to the adequacy of the insurance arrangements proposed by the contractor, he has a choice. He may obtain expert advice from an insurance broker or lawyer. Questions may arise as to who has to pay for this. Alternatively, he may inform the client that expert advice is required, and seek to persuade the client to obtain it. What he cannot do is simply act as a 'postbox' and send the evidence of the proposed arrangements to the client without comment."

9–235   **Notices of non-performance.** Some standard form contracts contain provisions allowing the contract administrator, on behalf of the employer, to issue

---

[54] Unreported, May 1, 1984. The facts of the main action are apparent from the first instance ((1989) 14 Con. L.R. 1) and Court of Appeal ((1989) 23 Con. L.R. 112) reports of the architects' third party proceedings against the contractors' managing director for fraudulently and/or negligently misrepresenting the position. For discussion of performance bonds in connection with certification, see para.9–234, below.

[55] [1999] B.L.R. 267. For further consideration of the decision in *Pozzolanic Lytag Ltd v Bryan Hobson Associates*, see C. Leong, "The duty of care in project management" (2001) 17 P.N. 250.

[56] *ibid.* at 272.

notices warning a recalcitrant contractor of the consequences of poor perform-ance.[57] The decision to issue such a notice should be the result of careful consideration. If a notice is negligently issued, the contractor may well incur loss and expense which he is entitled to recover from the employer and which the employer, in turn, will be able to recover from the contract administrator. On the other hand, a failure to act decisively to deal with a contractor's incompetence can also result in liability on the part of the contract administrator, as happened in *West Faulkner Associates v London Borough of Newham*.[58] The defendant architects were engaged by a local authority to act as architect in respect of the refurbishment of a large number of flats which was being carried out by the contractor pursuant to JCT Standard Form of Building Contract, 1963 edition, 1977 revision. As a result of the contractor's inability properly to programme and supervise the works, the contractual completion date was substantially exceeded. The architects were negligent in failing to serve a notice under cl.25(1)(b) of the contract stating that the contractor was failing to proceed regularly and diligently with the works (which notice would have led to the local authority being able to terminate the contractor's employment if its performance did not improve). The judge said[59]:

> "The architects were without authoritative guidance as to the meaning of 'regularly and diligently'. They thought that provided [the contractor] had men and materials on site and were doing some work within the contractual period they were proceeding regularly and diligently. They did not seek to confirm this belief by consulting more experienced architects than themselves, taking legal advice or urging the council to take legal advice and communicate it to them . . .
>
> I think that if [the contractor's] failures had been less glaringly obvious the architects might have been justified in not serving a notice upon them—at least until they had obtained reliable guidance. Since however, [the contractor's] failures were so very extreme, I think that the architects should have realised that [the contractor] could not possibly be proceeding regularly and diligently and have given a notice to them. I feel sure that the ordinary competent architect would have taken that course . . . This was not a marginal case."

The Court of Appeal upheld the judge's decision. Brown L.J., with whom the other members of the Court agreed, held that a reasonably competent architect, who was required to have "a general knowledge of the law as applied to the most important clauses . . . of standard forms of building contract", could not have misconstrued the clause in the way that the defendant did. At the very least, he should have realised that it could be construed differently and either himself have taken legal advice or advised his client so to do.

---

[57] See, for examples, the JCT Standard Form of Building Contract (1998 edn), cl.27 (continuation of the specified default for 14 days after receipt of the notice entitles the employer to give notice to terminate the contractor's employment) and the ICE Conditions of Contract (7th edn, 1999), cl.46(1) (if the rate of progress of the works is too slow to ensure completion by the contractual completion date, for any reason which does not entitle the contractor to an extension of time, the engineer may issue a notice to effect and the contractor must take steps to accelerate his progress).

[58] (1994) 71 B.L.R. 1, CA; and (1992) 31 Con. L.R. 105, first instance.

[59] *ibid.* at 140.

(i) *Supervision or Inspection of the Works*

9–236 **Supervision or inspection?** Early forms of the RIBA Conditions of Engagement for the Appointment of an Architect provided that the architect was required to perform "periodical supervision" of the works.[60] Successive versions of the RIBA Conditions have sought progressively to restrict the nature and scope of the architect's function in this respect. Thus the 1992 edition of the Standard Form of Agreement for the Appointment of an Architect referred, instead, to an obligation to carry out periodic inspections,[61] whereas the 1999 edition provides merely that the architect shall "make visits to the works in connection with [his] design"[62] and shall advise the client, where appropriate, that site inspectors should be appointed.[63] Such attempts by express terms to reduce the burden of the architect's obligation to consider the quality of the works as they progress are a reflection of the fact that claims against construction professionals in respect of defective works are very common.[64]

9–237 The difference between "supervision" and "inspection" is not merely academic. In *Rowlands v Collow*[65] Thomas J. drew a distinction between an engineer's obligation to "supervise" a building contract which involved "detailed and continuous direction" and an obligation to provide observation by way of oversight which required an engineer to carry out such inspections as were necessary to confirm that a design was being interpreted correctly and to ascertain that the works were being carried out in accordance with the contract documents.[66] A client who believes that his architect is supervising the building contractor will naturally consider that the architect has a greater responsibility if the works are defective than the client who understands that his architect is not on site for all or most of the time, but is carrying out inspections which are limited in number, duration and frequency. Accordingly, although the reported cases seldom reflect an understanding that a construction professional was obliged to maintain a full-time presence on site, caution is required when considering the older authorities which address an obligation to "supervise" rather than to inspect. For convenience, however, the term "supervision'" is used below to refer generally to the obligation of a construction professional to monitor the quality of construction works.

9–238 **The scope of the duty to supervise.** The employer is entitled to expect his architect or engineer so to administer and supervise the work so as to ensure, as far as is reasonably possible, that the quality of the work matches up to the standard contemplated by the building contract.[67] In practice, the professional

---

[60] See, for example, Condition B of the 1962 Revision of the Conditions of Engagement, which was the clause under consideration in *Sutcliffe v Chippendale and Edmondson* (1982) 18 B.L.R. 149: see para.9–236, below.

[61] cl.3.1.

[62] Work Stage K1 and cl.2.8.

[63] cl.2.5.

[64] It may not be coincidence that inspection of the works is typically not a well-remunerated part of a construction professional's engagement; but the level of fee will not dictate the standard of care required: see *Brown v Gilbert-Scott* (1992) 35 Con. L.R. 120 at 123, *per* Mr Recorder Coles Q.C.

[65] [1992] 1 N.Z.L.R. 178 at 197.

[66] It was held that the engineer in an informal contract concerning the provision of a driveway was under an obligation to inspect only, but was nonetheless in breach of the same.

[67] *Sutcliffe v Chippendale and Edmondson* (1982) 18 B.L.R. 149 at 162, *per* Judge Stabb Q.C.

charged with supervising the works is likely also to be the professional whose responsibility it is to carry out administration of the building contract, including the task of certifying that the interim and final payments are due to the contractor. The certification function may require the architect or engineer to carry out detailed and frequent inspections.[68] This is not to say that a construction professional who certifies payment for work which is fact defective because, despite reasonable skill and care, he is unaware of the defects, is in breach of his duty to supervise. His duty is to exercise reasonable skill and care in seeking to achieve a particular result; he does not (normally) guarantee that a particular result will be achieved.

Equally, however, a construction professional charged with managing construction must take reasonable care to see that the intended result is achieved. In *Six Continents Retail Ltd v Carford Catering Ltd*,[69] the defendant project manager was retained for the design and installation of kitchen equipment in a restaurant, which was later damaged by fire arising from the fixing of a rotisserie to a combustible wall. It had warned the owner that the installation might create a fire risk but the owner had taken no steps in response. The Court of Appeal held that the project manager had not discharged its duty to the owner by giving the warning. Its duty was to take care to bring about a safe installation and it should have done more to avoid the risk arising.

9–239

Reasonable examination of the works does not require the architect to go into every matter in detail.[70] It is recognised that some defects and insufficiencies may escape his notice.[71] Further, it by no means follows that in failing to discover a defect which a reasonable examination would have disclosed the architect is necessarily negligent. The omission may be explicable as no more than an error of judgment or a deliberately calculated risk which in all the circumstances of the case was reasonable and proper.[72] Similarly in assessing the standard of materials and workmanship especially of a house "built down to a price" a certain degree of tolerance must be allowed for, although this does not give an architect a general dispensing power.[73]

9–240

Inspections by reference to stages of the works. As Judge Bowsher Q.C. pointed out in *Corfield v Grant*,[74] the frequency and duration of inspections should be tailored to the nature of the works going on at site from time to time.

9–241

---

[68] The inter-relationship between the supervision and certification functions was recognised by Judge Stabb Q.C. in *Sutcliffe v Chippendale and Edmondson* (1982) 18 B.L.R. 149: "Plainly it is part of an architect's duty of supervision, as agent for his employer, to see that the work is properly executed, and therefore to my mind supervision and the issuing of interim certificates cannot be regarded as wholly separate and distinct functions. . . . in a well supervised contract an architect would not certify for work not properly executed." Similarly, in the Scottish case of *Jameson v Simon* (1899) 1 F. (Ct of Sess.) 1211 at 1222. "reasonable supervision" was defined by Lord Trayner as such supervision as would enable the architect to certify that the work had been executed according to the contract.
[69] [2003] EWCA Civ 1790.
[70] *Clemence v Clarke* (1880) cited in *Hudson's Building Contracts* (4th edn), Vol.2, p.54 at 59, *per* Grove J.
[71] *East Ham Corp v Bernard Sunley & Sons Ltd* [1966] A.C. 406 at 428, *per* Viscount Dilhorne. See also *Victoria University of Manchester v Hugh Wilson* (1984) 2 Con. L.R. 43 at 76: on the facts the architects were held negligent in their supervision of the fixing of tiles.
[72] *ibid.* at 443, *per* Lord Upjohn.
[73] *Cotton v Wallis* [1955] 1 W.L.R. 1168, CA at 1175–1177.
[74] (1992) 29 Con. L.R. 58 at 58–59.

The inspecting professional will not avoid a finding of negligence if he fails to see defects in the works because he has not arranged to examine critical stages of the works. This is illustrated by the decision in *Jameson v Simon*.[75] In that case the architect was held negligent in failing to inspect the bottoming of the cement floor of a house either before or at the time the floor was laid. The bottoming was subsequently found to consist of waste material and to be the cause of dry rot. Evidence was adduced that the architect had visited the site on average once a week and had given as much supervision and inspection as it was customary to give according to the practice of architects. But that practice was insufficient to absolve the architect for failure to inspect so important a part of the work. Lord Trayner said[76]:

> "It is contended that the architect cannot be constantly at the work, and this is obviously true. But he or someone representing him should undoubtedly see to the principal parts of the work before they are hid from view, and if need be I think he should require a contractor to give notice before an operation is to be done which will prevent his so inspecting an important part of the work as to be able to give his certificates upon knowledge, and not an assumption, as to how work hidden from view had been done."

The defender architect had directed the plasterer who was to put down the cement to proceed with his work without knowing whether the work to be covered up by it had been properly done or not. Similarly, in *Brown v Gilbert-Scott*[77] it was held that the architect was only obliged to inspect the works but was nevertheless in breach of duty because he had failed to carry out an inspection at a critical time, namely, the laying of the damp proof membrane.[78]

9–242   The responsibility for notifying the contractor that certain parts of the works should not be covered up before they have been inspected lies with the inspecting professional. In the Australian case of *Florida Hotels Pty Ltd v Mayo*[79] the building works included the construction of a hotel swimming pool. The employer did not engage a main contractor but employed his own tradesmen, labourers and foremen. He also engaged an architect pursuant to a contract whereby the latter agreed to: "give such periodical supervision and inspection as may be necessary to ensure that the works are being executed in general accordance with the contract; constant supervision does not form part of the duties undertaken by him." A labourer was injured by the collapse of concrete around the pool, following the removal of framework. The collapse was due to reinforcing mesh being laid longitudinally, not transversely, thereby reducing its

---

[75] (1899) 1 F. (Ct of Sess.) 1211 at 1222.
[76] *ibid.* at 1219 (also note Lord Moncrieff at 1224). See also *Kensington and Westminster and Chelsea AHA v Wettern Composites* (1984) 1 Con. L.R. 114 at 123, *per* Judge Smout Q.C. (architects negligent in failing to appreciate that much of the work of fixing mullions would be speedily covered up in the course of the works and as such called for closer supervision than would otherwise be the case).
[77] (1992) 35 Con. L.R. 120 (Note).
[78] See also the Alberta case *Homes by Jayman Ltd v Kellam Berg* (1995) 29 Alta. L.R. (3d) 1, where engineers were held to be liable for breach of a duty to provide some level of inspection and supervision in respect of the provision of a new septic tank system for a condominium. On appeal ((1998) 54 Alta. L.R. (3d) 272), the Alberta Court of Appeal found that the engineers were also liable for negligently designing the septic tanks so that they were too small.
[79] (1965) 113 C.L.R. 588.

strength. The mesh had been laid and the concrete had been poured between two visits of the architect. The labourer sued the employer, who sought contribution from the architect on the basis that he was in breach of his duty of care to the employer and also in breach of his contractual duty to the employer, in failing to supervise the works properly. Expert witnesses maintained that an architect should be present when concrete was poured and before this should satisfy himself that the formwork and reinforcing mesh were properly prepared. The architect was held in breach of his contractual duty to the employer in failing to make arrangements of a reliable nature to be informed before the concrete was poured and to give instructions that there was to be no covering up of the formwork and mesh before he inspected them. He was not entitled to rely on the contractor to give him notice of when the concrete was to be poured, even in circumstances where the contractor had given such notices in the past.[80] Similarly, in *George Fischer Holding Ltd v Multi Design Consultants Ltd*,[81] Judge Hicks Q.C. found that employer's representatives (DLE) who failed to make any visits at all to the roof of a warehouse during its construction were "in gross breach of duty". He rejected their excuse that access was unsafe, on the basis that the representatives were entitled to require the contractor to provide safe access. He also rejected the defence that defective work would not have been detected even if inspections had taken place, because the work of making the joints would not necessarily or probably have been going on during visits, and if it were the workman would have taken untypical care while under the eye of the employer's representative:

"That defence fails at every level. As to missing the relevant phase of the operation, first, it is clear on the evidence that on visits of the frequency and length which Mr Gardiner says he carried out elsewhere on site, and even without any special attention to this point, the likelihood is that he would on many occasions have had the opportunity of seeing lap joints formed and sealed. Secondly, the formation of the joints was so obviously crucial that even if the overall frequency of visits was not increased special attention should have been paid to ensuring that they fully covered this aspect. But, thirdly, since this whole discussion predicates the acceptance by DLE of the very risky and inadvisable inclusion of lap joints in such shallow slopes, it was incumbent upon them to exercise the closest and most rigorous inspection and supervision of the process. The last point also disposes of the suggestion that workmen will 'put on a show'—either they cannot do that all the time, or if they do, that achieves the object anyway. Moreover it is any event part of the necessary skill of a competent inspecting officer to detect and make allowances for such behaviour."[82]

A part of the works which involves the repetition of the same small operation many times will not always be so critical as it was in the *George Fischer* case.[83]

9–243

---

[80] This decision may be justified in light of the expert evidence given and also of the employer having used his own labourers. Accordingly, he depended more on the architect than would have been reasonable if a main contractor had been engaged. Nevertheless, particularly on larger building projects, it seems unduly burdensome to expect an architect to carry out checks before, and be present during, the pouring of the concrete. Ultimately, however, the question is one for expert evidence of general practice relevant to a particular case.

[81] (1998) 61 Con. L.R. 85.

[82] *ibid.* at 126.

[83] The judge also held that a design which required perfect seals to be made between roof panels was a bad design: see para.9–212, above.

In other cases, it may be sufficient for the inspecting professional to satisfy himself, by inspecting random examples, that the contractor's method of performing the operation is satisfactory. That was the situation in *Ministry of Defence v Scott Wilson Kirkpatrick*,[84] where the second defendants were engineers engaged to act as superintending officers in relation to repair works at a dockyard slip. The roof of the slip was blown off during a storm because the contractor had not followed the method of fixing the roof timbers which was required by the building contract. The engineers were held to have been negligent in failing to satisfy themselves that the contractor was using a compliant method of fixing, although they were not required to check every one of the 350-odd joints (having inspected and improved the contractor's method, it would have been sufficient for the engineers to instruct the clerk of works that all of the connections should be formed in the same way). The connections in question were "at the heart of the contractual work".[85]

9–244   **Confidence in the contractor.** In *Sutcliffe v Chippendale and Edmondson*, Judge Stabb Q.C. linked the level of supervision required to the supervisor's understanding of the contractor's level of competence:

> "In think that the degree of supervision required of an architect must be governed to some extent by his confidence in the contractor. If and when something occurs which should indicate to him a lack of competence in the contractor, then, in the interests of his employer, the standard of his supervision should be higher."[86]

The discovery of defective works might not be necessary to put the superintending professional on notice that a particular contractor requires closer supervision. It has been held that a "lack of frankness" on the part of subcontractors when defects were discovered was relevant to the level of supervision required, because it ought to have put the defendant architects "on their guard".[87] In another case, the court accepted that the architect should have taken into account the lack of relevant experience of the builder in deciding how often, and in how much detail, he would inspect the works.[88]

9–245   **Defects intended by the contractor.** Whether a contractor's wrongdoing was accidental or deliberate may also affect the liability of the architect. In *London Hospital (Trustees) v T P Bennett*[89] the defendant architects and engineers were held not to be in breach of duty to the claimant building owners where a building contractor's employees had deliberately planned to carry out hacking to concrete nibs. They knew that this was wrong in the absence of the professional team and the clerk of works. The contractual claim against the architects and engineers

---

[84] Unreported, July 1997, Mr Recorder Coles Q.C. This point was not the subject of the appeal at [2000] B.L.R. 20.
[85] See also *Sandown Hotels Ltd v Phelps* (1953) 167 E.G. 595 (architect engaged to take out specifications and superintend the repainting of a seaside hotel negligently failed to give sufficient attention to the preparation of woodwork, with the result that the paintwork flaked).
[86] *ibid.* at 162.
[87] *Kensington and Westminster and Chelsea AHA v Wettern Composites* (1984) 1 Con. L.R. 114 at 132.
[88] *Brown v Gilbert-Scott* (1992) 35 Con. L.R. 120 (Note).
[89] (1987) 13 Con. L.R. 22.

being statute-barred, the judge also held that if he was wrong, he would have found that there was no duty of care in tort to prevent third parties from causing damage and that the deliberate wrongdoing amounted to a *novus actus interveniens*.[90]

The clerk of works. In larger building projects where the employer employs   **9–246**
a clerk of works as well as engaging an architect,[91] the usual division of functions is for the former to attend to matters of detail and for the latter to attend to more important matters. The issue then becomes what amounts to a matter of detail and what does not. In *Leicester Guardians v Trollope*[92] an architect was held negligent in failing to supervise the laying of concrete. He had contended that it was for the clerk of works to supervise. Channel J. rejected the contention, considering that the laying of the concrete was a very important matter since a large area had to be covered. He continued:

> "if the architect had taken steps to see that the first block was all right, and had then told the clerk of works that the work in the others was to be carried out in the same way, I would have been inclined to hold that the architect had done his duty; but in fact he did nothing to see that the design was complied with. In my view this was not a matter of detail which could be left with the clerk of works."[93]

Save where a clerk of works is employed by the architect, the architect will   **9–247**
usually not be liable for negligence on the part of the clerk of works in carrying out work within the clerk's sphere of function.[94] But the appointment of a clerk of works, whilst a factor to be taken into account, does not reduce the architect's liability to use reasonable skill and care to ensure compliance with design, as opposed to mere detail.[95] That view was noted by Mr Recorder Coles Q.C. in *Ministry of Defence v Scott Wilson Kirkpatrick*.[96] There, the clerk of works was employed by the client but was substantially exercising powers delegated to him by the engineers retained to superintend the works. It was held that, insofar as the clerk of works was performing functions delegated to him by the engineers, the engineers remained liable for his acts and omissions. In *Saunders and Collard v*

---

[90] (1987) 13 Con. L.R. 22 at 35, basing himself on the reasoning of Lord Goff in *Smith v Littlewoods Organisation Ltd* [1987] A.C. 241.
[91] For the status of the clerk of works see para.9–013, above.
[92] (1911) 75 J.P. 197.
[93] *ibid.* at 200; the architect was held negligent even assuming, as was alleged, the deviation from the design was attributed to the fraud of the clerk of works. The latter finding would not be correct if a case were brought in tort alone: see *London Hospital (Trustees of) v T P Bennett* (1987) 13 Con. L.R. 22, discussed in para.9–245, above. Similarly, in *Lee v Bateman, The Times*, October 31, 1893, Cave J. directed the jury that the issue of whether certain beams in a fire-damaged building needed to be replaced was a matter for the architect and not the clerk of works.
[94] Note *Victoria University of Manchester v Hugh Wilson* (1984) 2 Con. L.R. 43 at 60, *per* Judge Newey Q.C.: "The architects should also have inspected the sub-contractors' work as it proceeded, but not as frequently as would the [clerk of works] since they were not permanently on the site and they were entitled to rely on [him] doing his work properly." On the facts, the architects were held negligent in their supervision of the fixing of tiles.
[95] *Kensington and Westminster and Chelsea AHA v Wettern Composites* (1984) 1 Con. L.R. 114 at 133, *per* Judge Smout Q.C. See, further, para.9–242, above.
[96] Unreported, July 1997, Mr Recorder Coles Q.C. The Court of Appeal held that it was unnecessary for it to express a view on this point: [2000] B.L.R. 20 at 32.

Broadstairs Local Board,[97] it was held that superintending engineers were negligent if they relied on the clerk of works since they knew him to be unreliable.

9–248   **The contractor's method of working.** That it is no part of an architect's usual function to instruct the contractor as to the manner of performance of his work and the safety precautions to be taken has already been discussed.[98] This proposition is best illustrated by the case of *Clayton v Woodman & Son (Builders) Ltd.*[99] Pearson L.J. considered the respective roles of builder and architect[1]:

> "It is quite plain, in my view, both as a general proposition and under the particular contract in this case, that the builder, as employer, has the responsibility at common law to provide a safe system of work . . . . It is important that that responsibility of the builder should not be overlaid or confused by any doubt as to where his province begins or some other person's province ends in that respect. The architect, on the other hand, is engaged as the agent of the owner for whom the building is being erected, and his function is to make sure that in the end, when the work has been completed, the owner will have a building properly constructed in accordance with the contract, plans, specification and drawings and any supplementary instructions which the architect may have given. The architect does not undertake (as I understand the position) to advise the builder as to what safety precautions should be taken or, in particular, as to how he should carry out his building operations. It is the function and the right of the builder to carry out his own building operations as he thinks fit, and, of course, in doing so, to comply with his obligations to the workman."

9–249   Moreover, in general, an architect owes no duty to a contractor to tell him promptly during the course of construction, even as regards permanent work, where he is going wrong; he may, if he wishes, leave that to the final stages notwithstanding that the correction of a fault then may be much more costly to the builder than had his error been pointed out earlier[2] and notwithstanding that the architect in that respect may be in breach of his duty to the employer.[3] If, however, an architect is informed that the contractors are embarking on an "incredible act of folly" then as a matter of common sense he should intervene. Moreover, if he sees them not taking special precautions without which a risk of damage to property is likely to arise, he may be under a duty to his employer to warn them to take the precautions necessary.[4]

9–250   In the Australian case of *Florida Hotels Pty Ltd v Mayo*[5] the employer did not engage a main contractor but employed his own workmen for the construction of a swimming pool. He also engaged an architect to: "give such periodical

---

[97] (1890) cited in *Hudson's Building Contracts* (4th edn, 1914), vol.2, p.164.
[98] See paras 9–122 to 9–123, above.
[99] [1962] 1 W.L.R. 585, CA reversing Salmon J. at first instance, [1962] 2 Q.B. 533. The case is discussed at para.9–122, above.
[1] *ibid.* at 593.
[2] *per* Mocatta J. *in AMF International Ltd v Magnet Bowling Ltd* [1968] 1 W.L.R. 1028 at 1052.
[3] See *Oldschool v Gleeson (Construction) Ltd* (1976) 4 B.L.R. 103 at 131 quoted at para.9–124, above. But *cf.* the differing views expressed by Judge Newey Q.C. in *Victoria University of Manchester v Hugh Wilson* (1984) 2 Con. L.R. 43 at 92.
[4] *Oldschool v Gleeson (Construction) Ltd* (1976) 4 B.L.R. 103 at 124–126.
[5] (1965) 113 C.L.R. 588, discussed at para.9–242, above.

supervision and inspection as may be necessary to ensure that the works are being executed in general accordance with the contract; constant supervision does not form part of the duties undertaken by him." A labourer was injured by the collapse of concrete, due to inadequate reinforcement. The architect was held in breach of his contractual duty to the employer in failing to make arrangements of a reliable nature to be informed before the concrete was poured and to give instructions that there was to be no covering up of the reinforcement before he inspected it. The majority of the court also held that the architect owed a duty of care to the injured labourer and was in breach of it. This decision may be justified in light of the expert evidence given and also of the employer having used his own labourers. Accordingly he depended more on the architect than would have been reasonable if a main contractor had been engaged.

A more difficult decision is *AMF International Ltd v Magnet Bowling Ltd.*[6] In **9–251** that case the defendant employers, Magnet, engaged contractors, T, to build a bowling centre and also engaged the claimants, AMF, to supply and install equipment for the bowling centre. Owing to lack of temporary precautions by T, the partially constructed building was flooded after heavy rain and AMF's equipment was damaged. In an action by AMF against Magnet and T, Mocatta J. held them both to be in breach of the common duty of care imposed on them as occupiers of the building by s.2 of the Occupiers' Liability Act 1957 and liable to AMF in the proportions of 40 and 60 per cent respectively. Magnet's breach consisted of the failure of the architect, their employee, either to check himself or to request the private architect engaged by Magnet to check that the building had been ready and safe to receive the valuable and sensitive property which Magnet were inviting AMF to bring into the building. It is submitted that crucial to the decision were the facts that the equipment was valuable, that AMF had a contract with Magnet as opposed to being a mere sub-contractor and, in particular, that by that contract Magnet were themselves responsible for ensuring that the building was ready to accept delivery of the equipment.[7]

An architect may always undertake a duty to consider and advise upon the **9–252** need for precautions to be taken by a contractor as, for example, in the case of *Clay v A J Crump & Sons Ltd.*[8] In that case, the architect was expressly requested by the employer to consider whether it was safe to leave standing a wall which subsequently collapsed. Similarly, interference by a professional in the contractor's method of working may result in liability if that interference results in injury or loss. In *Plant Construction Ltd v Clive Adams Associates*

---

[6] [1968] 1 W.L.R. 1028.

[7] The following passage at 1046 of Mocatta J.'s judgment is significant: "Accordingly, if [B, an employee of the private architects] was not consulted by [T] about flood precautions and never gave them his advice on the subject, there is considerable difficulty on the facts as I have so far stated them, and on the statements as to the functions of an architect in *Clayton v Woodman & Sons (Builders) Ltd*, which I have cited, in blaming [B] for what occurred. Unless he was asked by Magnet for his advice as to the fitness of the building to receive AMF's timber, or to ensure its safety, I do not think, on the authority of *Clayton v Woodman*, that I could hold him in law to blame for not warning Magnet to prevent AMF coming in until the position had been secured and in not seeking to persuade [T] to do more than he did."

[8] [1964] 1 Q.B. 533, CA, discussed in para.9–078, above.

(No.1),[9] the claimant contracted with the Ford Motor Company to construct pits to take engine mount rigs at its research engineering centre. It sub-contracted the excavation of the pits to JMH. The excavation of one pit required the removal of part of the base of a stanchion which supported the roof of the centre. JMH was responsible under the sub-contract for the design of the necessary works of temporary support for the stanchion and roof. Ford's in-house engineer, Mr Furley, vetoed JMH's design and issued instructions dictating the manner of support. The engineer's design was inadequate and the roof collapsed. Judge Hicks Q.C. held that JMH owed a contractual duty of care to warn the claimant that the design was unsafe and had failed to discharge that duty.[10] However, he made a deduction of 80 per cent for contributory negligence on the part of the claimant which, through Mr Furley, was principally to blame for the adoption of an unsafe method of building temporary supports. The claimant's action against its independent consulting engineers had been settled, but the judge found that any reasonably competent engineer would have appreciated that Mr Furley's design was unsafe. Clearly, independent engineers who had interfered with the design of the temporary works as Mr Furley did would have been held liable to the claimant.

9–253   In *Consarc Design Ltd v Hutch Investments Ltd*,[11] Judge Bowsher Q.C. approved and incorporated within his judgment the entirety of paras 9–236 to 9–252, above, as they appeared in the fifth edition of this work.[12] In that case, the judge held that architects engaged to inspect construction works, including the laying of a new floor, were not in breach of duty when they failed to notice defects in the floor. The particular defects were such that a reasonably competent and careful architect could not have been expected to notice them.

(j) *Certification*

9–254   **The certification procedure.** The standard forms of building and engineering contracts provide that, on a monthly or other regular basis throughout the course of construction, the named architect or engineer must certify sums for payment to the contractor. The contractor is entitled to be paid for work properly carried out. The architect or engineer therefore has an obligation to see that work has been executed in compliance with the contract before issuing a payment certificate. In addition, a quantity surveyor may be engaged to value the works for the purposes of the architect's or engineer's certificate. In that case, the role of the quantity surveyor is simply to assess the quantities of work carried out; the

---

[9] Unreported, September 3, 1998, Judge Hicks Q.C. See also the appeal, which concerned the scope of the contractor's implied contractual duty to warn of an unsafe design ([2000] B.L.R. 137) and the subsequent decision of Judge Hicks Q.C. on causation ([2000] B.L.R. 205). This important decision of the Court of Appeal was applied by Dyson J. in *Aurum Investments Ltd v Avonforce Ltd* [2001] Lloyd's Rep. P.N. 285.

[10] This finding was upheld on appeal ([2000] B.L.R. 205) but the Court of Appeal differed from the judge as to the scope of the duty and accordingly, remitted the issue of causation to him for retrial.

[11] [2002] P.N.L.R. 712.

[12] See the 5th edition, paras 8–236 to 8–249.

architect or engineer remains responsible for seeing that the work valued by the quantity surveyor has been properly carried out.[13] Payment certificates issued up to practical completion are referred to as "interim certificates"; at the end of the contract, a "final certificate" may be issued.

Duty to client. In issuing interim and final certificates the architect or engineer 9–255 will generally not be immune from liability in negligence to the employer. In *Chambers v Goldthorpe*[14] it was held by a majority of the Court of Appeal that in issuing a final certificate stating the amount due to the contractor, an architect occupied the position of an arbitrator or quasi-arbitrator and was immune from action by the employer for alleged negligence in over-certification. This position was said to follow from the fact that in issuing the certificate he had to act impartially towards the employer and the contractor and was no longer the former's agent. The immunity appears never to have been extended to an architect in issuing an interim certificate.[15] Moreover, the correctness of the decision was doubted.[16] Finally, the case was overruled by the House of Lords in *Sutcliffe v Thackrah*.[17] In that case it was held at first instance[18] that architects were negligent in having over-certified sums in interim certificates as due to contractors who were turned off site and subsequently went into liquidation. The Court of Appeal[19] reversed the judge's decision on the grounds that the architects were acting in an arbitral capacity but the House of Lords restored his decision. It was held that an architect did not enjoy an arbitrator's immunity unless certain indicia were met. These indicia were summarised by Lord Wheatley in a subsequent decision of the House of Lords, *Arenson v Arenson*,[20] in which *Sutcliffe v Thackrah* was applied to a case of auditors engaged to value shares:

"The indicia are as follows: (a) there is a dispute or a difference between the parties which has been formulated in some way or another; (b) the dispute or difference has been remitted by the parties to the person to resolve in such a manner that he is called upon to exercise a judicial function; (c) where appropriate, the parties must have been provided with an opportunity to present evidence and/or submissions in support of their respective claims in the dispute; and (d) the parties have agreed to accept his decision."[21]

---

[13] *Sutcliffe v Chippendale and Edmondson* (1982) 18 B.L.R. 149.

[14] [1901] 1 K.B. 624, CA.

[15] See *Wisbech RDC v Ward* [1927] 2 K.B. 556 at 565, *per* Sankey J.; [1928] 2 K.B. 1 at 23, *per* Atkin L.J.; and *R B Burden Ltd v Swansea Corp* [1957] 1 W.L.R. 1167 at 1172, *per* Lord Radcliffe.

[16] *Hosier & Dickinson Ltd v P & M Kaye Ltd* [1970] 1 W.L.R. 1611 at 1616, *per* Lord Denning M.R.

[17] [1974] A.C. 727.

[18] Reported *sub nom. Sutcliffe v Chippendale and Edmondson* (1982) 18 B.L.R. 149.

[19] [1973] 1 W.L.R. 888.

[20] [1977] A.C. 405.

[21] *ibid.* at 428. In *Cedar Transport Group Ltd v First Wyvern Property Trustees Co Ltd* (1981) 258 E.G. 1077 at 1080 a claim to immunity by architects in issuing a final certificate pursuant to the then current JCT Standard Form of Building Contract was rejected as the required indicia were not fulfilled. On the facts, however, the architects were absolved of negligence.

9–256   **Interim certificates.** The question of the degree of error likely to amount to negligence is more fully discussed above.[22] In *Sutcliffe v Thackrah*,[23] Lord Salmon stated that the fact that an architect's certificate was given for the wrong amount did not of itself prove negligence against the architect.[24] Clearly, however, in assessing amounts to be certified, an architect and any quantity surveyor engaged for the purpose must take care to ensure that claims for payment are reasonable and justified by the work done at the time, in quality and amount respectively.[25] The *locus classicus* in relation to the proper approach by an architect in issuing interim certificates remains the judgment of Judge Stabb Q.C. at first instance in *Sutcliffe v Chippendale and Edmondson*.[26] Among the points made by the judge were the following. First, while any prolonged or detailed inspection or measurement at an interim stage is impracticable and not to be expected, more than a glance round is expected. Secondly, so long as the contractual basis of an interim certificate is the valuation of work properly executed, the architect should first satisfy himself as to the quality of the work, before requiring his employer by way of certificate to make payment for it. Thirdly, where a quantity surveyor is also engaged by the employer, the architect should keep him continually informed of any defective or improperly executed work observed so as to give him the opportunity of excluding it from interim valuations. Not to adopt this approach would entail the risk of the employer making excessive payments to the contractor which might prove irrecoverable, particularly in the event of the contractor's insolvency.[27]

9–257   **Final certificates.** Although the obligations of an architect or engineer in issuing a final certificate do not differ materially from those which he owes in respect of interim certificates, the consequences of negligently issuing a final certificate are likely to be much more serious. This is because the final certificate may be held to be binding and conclusive as between the parties to the building contract. After issue of such a final certificate, an employer will have no remedy against the building contractor should defects become apparent in the building. Whether or not a final certificate is conclusive will depend upon the terms of the

---

[22] See paras 9–160 to 9–162, above.

[23] [1974] A.C. 727 at 760.

[24] In *Cedar Transport Group Ltd v First Wyvern Property Trustees Co Ltd* (1981) 258 E.G. 1077, £30 was claimed against the architects in respect of the contractor's failure to plaster a doorway. The judge rejected the claim, holding that it was *de minimis* and that in any event it amount to a failure to exercise such proper skill and judgment so as to constitute a breach of duty by the architects.

[25] This may require careful liaison between the architect and the quantity surveyor. Thus in *Sutcliffe v Thackrah* [1974] A.C. 727 the negligent overpayment on interim certificates was the result of one of the architects failing to pass on his knowledge of defects to quantity surveyors who assumed all the work was satisfactory. In *RB Burden v Swansea Corp* [1957] 1 W.L.R. 1167, it was held that the quantity surveyor had carried out his valuation improperly: he had been in too great a hurry and had omitted to make a visual valuation at site.

[26] (1982) 18 B.L.R. 149.

[27] *ibid.* at 165–166. See also *Victoria University of Manchester v Hugh Wilson* (1984) 2 Con. L.R. 43 at 78. In *Rowlands v Collow* [1992] 1 N.Z.L.R. 178 at 200 Thomas J. held that an engineer who certified the value of work done in an informal contract for the provision of a driveway accepted an obligation to inspect and assess the value of the work which had, in fact, been completed.

particular building contract, so that no general rule can be stated.[28] In *Crown Estates Commissioners v John Mowlem & Co Ltd,*[29] the Court of Appeal held that a final certificate issued under cl.30.9 of the 1980 JCT Standard Form of Building Contract was conclusive evidence not merely in relation to those materials and workmanship which were expressly required by the contract to be to the reasonable satisfaction of the architect, but also in relation to any materials or workmanship where approval was inherently for the opinion of the architect. The decision has been criticised[30] and it led to an amendment (No.15) to the 1980 edition of the JCT Standard Form of Contract. The implications of the decision continue to be felt, however. Judge Lloyd Q.C. held in *Oxford University Fixed Assets Ltd v Architects Design Partnership*[31] that an architect sued by his client in respect of defects in a building was not entitled to claim contribution from the building contractor pursuant to the Civil Liability (Contribution) Act 1978. A final certificate had been issued under cl.30.9 of the J.C.T. 1980 Standard Form of Building Contract. This was because the effect of the final certificate would have been to defeat any claim brought by the client directly with the result that no liability could be established against the contractor (by reason of s.1(6) of the 1978 Act). In *London Borough of Barking & Dagenham v Terrapin Construction Ltd,*[32] the Court of Appeal followed the decision in *Crown Estates* in holding that the agreement of the contractor's final account issued under cl.30.8.1 of the JCT Standard Form of Building Contract with Contractor's Design (1981 edition) was conclusive evidence as to the quality and standard of all materials and workmanship which were inherently for approval by the architect, including compliance of the works with statutory requirements such as the Building Regulations. However, the Court rejected the defendant design and build contractor's argument that the certificate was also conclusive evidence that its design complied with the requirements of the contract. Thus an architect who negligently issues a final certificate which is conclusive evidence as to the quality and standards of materials and workmanship may find that he is unable to claim contribution from the contractor when defects appear; and an architect engaged by a design and

---

[28] In addition to the cases mentioned in the text, see for further examples: *East Ham Corp v Bernard Sunley* [1966] A.C. 406, HL (RIBA Standard Form of Building Contract, 1950 revision); *P & M Kaye v Hosier & Dickinson* [1972] 1 W.L.R. 146, HL (1963 JCT Standard Form of Building Contract); *Fairweather v Asden Securities* (1979) 13 B.L.R. 40; *cf. HW Nevill (Sunblest) v Wm Press & Son* (1981) 20 B.L.R. 78 (both cases concerning a pre-1976 version of 1963 JCT Standard Form of Building Contract); *Crestar v Carr* (1987) 37 B.L.R. 113, CA (pre-1980 JCT Minor Works Contract); *Matthew Hall Ortech v Tarmac Roadstone* (1997) 87 B.L.R. 96 (ICE Model Form of Conditions of Contract for Process Plants).

[29] (1994) 70 B.L.R. 1.

[30] See the commentary by I.N. Duncan Wallace Q.C. at (1995) 11 Const. L.J. 184; see also the Scottish case *Belcher Food Products Ltd v Miller & Black* 1999 S.L.T. 142, a case concerning the 1963 JCT Standard Form of Building Contract, where Lord Gill distinguished *Crown Estates* and held that the final certificate was not conclusive evidence for all purposes of the standard and quality of the works.

[31] (1999) 64 Con. L.R. 13. For further discussion, see para.9–331, below.

[32] [2000] B.L.R. 479, CA. For commentary on the decision in *London Borough of Barking & Dagenham v Terrapin Construction Ltd* [2002] B.L.R. 479, see I.N.D. Wallace Q.C., "RIBA/JCT Final Certificates Again (*London Borough of Barking and Dagenham v Terrapin Construction Limited*)" (2002) 18 Const. L.J. 4.

build contractor will be vulnerable to a claim for contribution by the contractor if his design proves defective and the contractor is held liable to the employer.

9–258   **Other certificates.** The building contract may provide for the architect or engineer to issue certificates which are not connected with valuation of the works. For example, the JCT Standard Forms provide for the issue of a certificate of practical completion. Normally, all but a small percentage of the contract price will become payable to the contractor upon issue of the certificate of practical completion. If the contractor then becomes insolvent and the certificate turns out to have been negligently issued, the employer is likely to seek redress from the architect or engineer. Furthermore, if a certificate of practical completion is issued before the works are in fact complete, when a certificate of non-completion should be issued instead, the employer will be unable to deduct liquidated damages from the sum payable to the contractor. An example is *George Fischer Holding Ltd v Multi Design Consultants Ltd*,[33] where the issue of a certificate of practical completion by the employer's representatives was held to be premature in the light of "the host of items of incomplete or defective work" which remained.

9–259   Another kind of certificate was considered in *Try Build Ltd v Invicta Leisure Tennis Ltd*.[34] Structural and civil engineers were engaged by a building owner in connection with the design and construction of two tennis halls. The claimant was the design and build contractor, to whom the engineers' contract was novated. The claimant contracted with a specialist sub-contractor for the design, supply and construction of the roofs of the halls. The design was novel: each roof comprised four inflated foil cushions held in place by a rope edge detail. The roofs leaked. Having settled the employer's claim, the claimant sought damages from the engineers in respect of its losses. Judge Bowsher Q.C. found that the engineers had agreed with the claimant to issue a certificate in an agreed form which required them to have reviewed the sub-contractor's shop drawings and materials and inspected the components of the roof system at the sub-contractor's factory in Germany and on site. It was held that the engineers had signed the certificate when they knew that in doing so they were giving a certificate which was in part false and in part not supported by relevant investigations on their part. As such, the certificate was signed in breach of their duty to the claimant.

9–260   **Duty to the contractor.** Following the decision of the Court of Appeal in *Pacific Associates Inc v Baxter*,[35] the circumstances in which it is now possible that a claim by a contractor against an architect for negligent certification could still succeed are discussed above.[36] A construction professional may certainly be held liable to his own client if default in carrying out his certification function puts the client in breach of the building contract. The employer warrants to the contractor that the certifier, as his agent, will perform his function fairly and

---

[33] (1998) 61 Con. L.R. 85 at 132, 134–139; see also *Catlin Estates Ltd v Carter Jonas* [2005] EWHC 2315. It is not always clear when, as a matter of law or as a matter of fact, practical completion takes place. For discussion, see T. Thompson, "Practical Completion in Building Contracts: A Legal Definition?" (2004) 20 Const. L.J. 301.
[34] (2000) 71 Con. L.R. 141.
[35] [1990] 1 Q.B. 993.
[36] See paras 9–105 to 9–111, above.

impartially. If the certifier allows himself to be unduly influenced by the interests of the employer, he will place the employer in breach of the building contract and render himself liable to the employer.[37]

(k) *Specialist Survey*

Specialist engineers may be asked to inspect and report upon buildings with regard to their particular speciality. Thus, following widespread claims for subsidence, potential mortgagees and insurance companies often insist upon a property being inspected before purchase by a structural engineer if there is any indication of pre-existing movement. When carrying out such an inspection, the specialist will be judged by the standards of a reasonably competent specialist.   **9–261**

The reported cases reveal a number of examples. In *Pfeiffer v E & E Installations*,[38] a surveyor had advised the claimants who were considering buying a house to obtain specialist advice as the state of the gas-fired heating system, which was believed to be about 15-years-old. As a result the claimants approached the defendant heating engineers who inspected the system and pronounced it satisfactory. In fact, there were potentially dangerous cracks in the heat exchanger. The Court of Appeal, having established that it was common ground between the expert witnesses that an inspection for cracks should have been carried out by a heating engineer where a system was 15-years-old, found that the defendants had been negligent.[39] In another case,[40] it was held that a specialist site investigation company was in breach of duty in not making sufficiently specific or urgent recommendations for further investigations at a land-slip site.   **9–262**

The authorities illustrate that a survey will not, necessarily, reveal all defects even if competently carried out. In *Trizec Equities v Ellis-Don Management Services Ltd*,[41] a claim against geotechnical engineers failed on the basis that the ground conditions encountered were unforeseen and unforeseeable with the result that the engineers had not acted negligently when designing the foundations of a substantial office complex. In *Hilton Canada v SNC Lavalin*,[42] the defendant engineers were engaged to carry out a "due diligence" survey of a hotel in which the claimant was contemplating taking an equity stake. The judge found that the extent of the engineers' obligations was to "determine if major defects were to be found and to assess the general condition of the building". He found that the engineers were not negligent in discovering that the steel structure   **9–263**

---

[37] For a discussion of the circumstances in which the employer will be held to have interfered with or obstructed the due performance of the certifer's function, see *RB Burden Ltd v Swansea Corp* [1957] 1 W.L.R. 1167. See also *John Holland Construction and Engineering Ltd v Majorca Products* (2000) Const. L.J. 114, Supreme Court of Victoria, where it was held on the facts that the certifying architects had not made their decisions with regard exclusively or predominantly to the interests of the employer.

[38] [1991] 1 E.G.L.R. 162.

[39] For further and much fuller discussion of negligent surveys and their consequences, see Ch.10.

[40] *Holbeck Hall & Hotel Ltd v Scarborough BC* (1997) 57 Con. L.R. 113, where the claim failed on the issue of reliance. For the appeal on a different point, see [2000] B.L.R. 109, CA. See further para.9–274, below.

[41] (1998) 66 Alta. L.R. (3d) 1.

[42] (1999) 176 N.S.R. (2d) 155.

of the hotel suffered from significant corrosion on the basis that there were no signs which should have alerted the engineers, undertaking a visual inspection, to the existence of the problem. In *Berwick v Wickens Holdings Ltd*,[43] the claimant was the widow of a workman who was killed when the building upon which he was working collapsed. She brought a claim against the structural engineers who had been engaged by the building contractor to survey the building before refurbishment works commenced. It was held that the building was originally constructed in a manner "so remote from acceptable building practice as to be beyond reasonable expectation." Bell J. held that the engineers had carried out proper investigations before advising the contractor that the building was safe; the collapse of the building was not foreseeable upon the information reasonably available to them and accordingly they had not been negligent.

(l) *Investigation of Defects*

9–264   It may sometimes be the case that a primary cause of action will be statute-barred against designers but a claimant will allege that he should nonetheless be entitled to recover on the basis that the designers did not point out the deficiencies in their original design when instructed to consider defects which had arisen. This interesting question arose in *Pullen v Gutteridge*[44] where the Court of Appeal of Victoria considered two actions against a firm of engineers. In the first action, the claimant alleged that the engineers had negligently designed a swimming pool complex. The engineers claimed that this action was statute-barred both in contract and in tort. The claimant accordingly commenced a second action alleging (1) that the engineers had failed to investigate defects properly during the limitation period; (2) that as a result of their negligence, the claimant had lost the opportunity of obtaining competent advice from other sources; and (3) that if they had obtained such advice, proceedings would have been commenced during the limitation period. The Court of Appeal found that the engineers were liable in the first action and that the defence of limitation failed, but nonetheless went on to consider the second action in case they were wrong in respect of their treatment of the first action. The Court's conclusion was expressed as follows[45]:

> "Had the respondent acted with reasonable care when asked to investigate and report to the appellant, its investigations would have had two consequences. In the first place, it would have come to realise, or at the very least to entertain a strong suspicion, that its own design of the sub-structure was seriously deficient and that the deficiency was responsible for many of the defects that had emerged and were emerging. In the second place, it would have communicated this realisation or suspicion to its client."

4. DAMAGES

9–265   As in the case of other professions the usual remedy for breach of duty by an architect, engineer or quantity surveyor is an award of damages. This may be a

---

[43] Unreported, October 1, 2000, Bell J. See further para.9–074, above.
[44] [1993] 1 V.R. 27.
[45] *ibid.* at 86.

provisional award, following from the decision of an adjudicator appointed under the Housing Grants, Construction and Regeneration Act 1996,[46] or it may be a final award made in legal or arbitral proceedings. The principles upon which damages are awarded in each case are identical.

(a) *The Scope of the Duty*

Following the decision of the House of Lords in *Banque Bruxelles Lambert SA*   **9–266**
v Eagle Star Insurance Co Ltd (BBL),[47] it may be necessary in any case where damages are claimed for breach of contract or negligence to decide what for what kind of loss the claimant is entitled to compensation; in other words, to decide whether the loss claimed is within the scope of the duty breached.[48] This enquiry will go beyond that which is already necessary as to whether a duty of care will be imposed, at common law, in respect of economic loss as distinct from physical injury or damage to "other" property.[49] It follows, as Judge Bowsher Q.C. pointed out in *Department of National Heritage v Steensen Varming Mulcahy*,[50] that the damages claimed will affect the scope of the duty which it is necessary for a claimant to establish:

"The duty defines the relevant consequences. But the reverse is also true. If the Plaintiff by his pleading limits the relevant consequences, the limit on the consequences necessarily limits the number of relevant duties. In considering SVM's duties, it is important to remember what has been sometimes overlooked in this case, that because the damage claim is limited to loss arising out of damage to cables, the only relevant duties are duties to avoid the consequences of cable damage and loss of DNH arising from cable damage."

In *Hancock v Tucker*,[51] Toulson J. put it this way:

" . . . in relation to the proper approach in law in respect of damages, the concepts of duty, causation and remoteness are connected, for if A's duty to B is defined in such a way as to exclude the relevant loss, B cannot claim that such loss has been caused by any breach of duty on the part of A. However, in some cases there may be no dispute about the scope of the duty and the real question is whether the loss should fairly and sensibly be regarded as a consequence of the breach or is too remote. Given that most events could be traced back to an almost infinite number of preceding events, it is a matter of judgment whether the connection between the wrongdoer's conduct and the plaintiff's loss is sufficiently close to make it fair to hold the wrongdoer responsible for the loss. In other cases the real argument may be as to the scope of the duty and, once that is established, there may be no room for serious argument over the causal connection between the breach of duty and the loss."

The decision in *BBL* also means that, in cases involving the giving of negligent   **9–267**
advice, it will be necessary to distinguish between a duty to provide information

---

[46] Adjudication is discussed below at paras 9–351 to 9–367.
[47] [1997] A.C. 191.
[48] For full discussion of this case see Ch.10.
[49] See paras 9–075 to 9–081, above.
[50] (1998) 60 Con. L.R. 33 at 82.
[51] [1999] Lloyd's Rep. P.N. 814 at 822. For the facts, see para.9–195, above.

for the purpose of enabling another to decide upon a course of action and a duty to advise another as to what course of action to adopt.[52] In respect of the former duty, the House of Lords stated[53]:

> "The measure of damages in an action for breach of duty to provide accurate information . . . is the loss attributable to the inaccuracy of the information which the plaintiff has suffered by reason of having entered into the transaction on the assumption that the information was correct. One therefore compares the loss he has actually suffered with what his position would have been if he had not entered into the transaction and asks what element of this loss is attributable to the inaccuracy of the information."

9–268   There are plainly some cases involving construction professionals providing information where the decision in *BBL* is likely to be directly relevant: most obviously providing a misleading cost estimate or providing misleading information to a client which forms part of the basis for his decision to proceed with a project.[54] In such cases the loss recoverable will be restricted to the amount by which the cost estimate was wrong or the information misleading. In *Gable House v The Halpern Partnership*[55] the judge found (a) that the defendant architects had been negligent in their assessment of the nett lettable area of a development; and (b) that, given competent advice, it was unlikely that the claimant developers would have proceeded with the development. It appears that the claimant's recoverable loss would now be restricted to the difference between the value of the development with the advised lettable area and that with its actual lettable area. Such a measure would be likely to be very much less than the loss recoverable before the decision in *BBL*, which would have been likely to have been taken to include all losses incurred in the development.

9–269   In *HOK Sport Ltd v Aintree Racecourse Co Ltd*,[56] Judge Thornton Q.C. held that the *BBL* principle applied generally to claims against construction professionals and would be particularly important where (i) a professional is engaged to provide information for a specific project; (ii) the client is to decide whether to proceed with the project; (iii) the information to be provided by the professional is to be relied on by the client as part of its decision-making process; and (iv) the decision is neither participated in by nor dependent upon the advice of that professional. In that case, in breach of their appointment, the claimant

---

[52] [1997] A.C. 191 at 216. See further Ch.9. *cf. Kvaerner Construction (Regions) Ltd v Kirkpatrick & Partners Consulting Engineers Ltd* 1999 S.C. 291, where a majority in the Scottish Court of Session held that a design and build contractor which had tendered on the basis of the defendant engineers' initial design work was entitled to recover from the engineers the extra cost to it of performing the building contract when the defendants' detailed design turned out to be more expensive than the initial design had suggested. Lord Marnoch, dissenting, preferred the defendant's argument (based on the passage quoted from *BBL*) that the claimant could recover its additional cost only if it could show that, if the defendants had provided the correct design information pre-tender, their tender price would have been increased by an amount equivalent to the additional costs and would have been accepted by the employer.

[53] *ibid.* at 97.

[54] See paras 9–189 to 9–195, above.

[55] (1995) 48 Con. L.R. 1. In *Copthorne Hotel (Newcastle) Ltd v Arup Associates* (1996) 58 Con. L.R. 105, Judge Hicks Q.C. rejected an argument that the effect of the decision in *BBL* was to increase a defendant's liability for a misstatement so that damages equivalent to the difference between the amount of an estimate actually given and the amount of a competent estimate could be recovered even if (as was the case) the claimant would have proceeded with the project in any event.

[56] [2002] EWHC 3094, TCC.

architect failed to warn the client racecourse owner that various design changes
during the development of a new stand would mean that fewer standing places
would be available than had been expected. As a result, the racecourse owner was
deprived of the opportunity to postpone development of the new stand and
redesign the project so as to remedy the loss of places. The arbitrator awarded the
racecourse owner damages based on the financial loss which it suffered as a
result of the lack of those places. The judge held that, in the light of *BBL*, this was
the wrong approach. The architect's duty was to provide information as to the
number of places which its design would provide. It was not to advise the
racecourse owner on whether it should postpone the project to allow a redesign.
The loss which fell within the scope of the architect's duty was limited to the loss
attributable to the racecourse owner's decision to proceed with the project on the
incorrect assumption that a larger number of places would be provided.

It is likely that some advice from building professionals can properly be   **9–270**
categorised as advice as to which course of action to adopt, rather than information. In *Hancock v Tucker*,[57] the defendant architect was engaged to design and
seek planning permission for a scheme to convert his hotel into sheltered
accommodation for the elderly. He alleged that, as a result of the defendant's
negligence, he would have obtained planning permission for a suitable scheme
two years earlier than in fact he did. By that time, the value of the property had
fallen. The claimant sought to recover the difference between the values of the
hotel with planning permission at the date when planning permission was granted
and the date when it should have been granted. The defendant argued that this
loss was caused by a fall in the property market and was outside the scope of his
duty. Toulson J. held that there had been no breach of duty by the defendant, but
said that if there had, he would have found that loss caused by a fall in the market
was within the scope of his duty. The defendant had advised the claimant as to
which course he should take in the matter of seeking planning permission for the
development of the property, knowing that the purpose for which he was retained
was to enable the claimant to realise the maximum value of the property by
selling it with the best planning permission which he could obtain in the shortest
time. It was reasonably foreseeable that if the defendant was negligent, the
claimant might lose a marketing opportunity which it was his purpose to obtain.
Accordingly, the claimant would have recovered the loss claimed.[58] Further
examples of advice as to which course a client should adopt might include an
architect advising that a house should be situated in a particular position or an
engineer advising that the way in which to cross a river was to use a tunnel. In
such cases, as in *Hancock*, the decision in *BBL* is likely to be of limited assistance
to the construction professional.

---

[57] [1999] Lloyd's Rep. P.N. 814. For the facts, see para.9–198, above. For another example of the
failure of an argument that the loss claimed was outside the scope of the defendant's duty, see *Try
Build Ltd v Invicta Leisure Tennis Ltd* (2000) 71 Con. L.R. 141 (engineers' duty to certify the
adequacy of sub-contractor's roof design and materials was not limited to protecting the main
contractor against overpayment to the sub-contractor; the duty arose before the engineers' contract
was novated from the employer to the main contractor; had the engineers discharged their duty while
still engaged by the employer, the sub-contractor's design would not have been adopted and the loss
claimed would have been avoided); see further para.9–258, above.
[58] *ibid.* at 824.

9-271   Unusually, the concept of scope of duty operated to increase the claimant's recovery in *Earl Terrace Properties Ltd v Nilsson Design Ltd*.[59] It was alleged that breach of duty by the architect had caused a delay in completion of a development and that, as a result, the claimant developer had suffered losses. The consequence of the delay in completion of the development was a delay in sale of the developed properties. The architect argued that the developer was obliged to give credit against its recoverable losses for the profit it would make upon the eventual sales of the developed properties, the property market having moved upwards during the period of delay. The judge held that market movements were outside the scope of the architect's duty and too remote. Accordingly, since the developer could not have recovered additional damages if the market had moved downwards during the delay, neither could the architect enjoy the benefit of a rising market.

(b) *Remoteness*

9-272   It is trite law that although a breach of duty is established no loss and damage will be recoverable if too remote. The claimant must establish that, broadly, the loss and damage were (a) caused by the relevant breach of duty[60] and (b) foreseeable.[61]

(i) *Causation*

9-273   A breach of duty may be so clearly the cause of loss, for example negligence in design consisting of inadequate foundations, that causation is scarcely an issue. Nevertheless causation is essentially an issue of fact to be determined according to the particular circumstances of each case, and by the common sense of ordinary men rather than the logic of philosophers.[62] A finding as to causation in one case is, therefore, of limited guidance as to the appropriate finding as to causation in a different case even though the facts of each case may be similar.[63] Some general principles may be discerned, however.

---

[59] [2004] EWHC 136, TCC.
[60] As to which see paras 9–273 to 9–283, below.
[61] As to which see paras 9–284 to 9–288, below.
[62] *Knightley v Johns* [1982] 1 W.L.R. 349 at 367, *per* Stephenson L.J.; *Galoo v Bright Grahame Murray* [1994] 1 W.L.R. 1360, *per* Glidewell L.J. at 1375A (discussed further in Ch.17, para.17–125, below). In *Department of National Heritage v Steensen Varming Mulcahy* (1998) 60 Con. L.R. 33 at 102, Judge Bowsher Q.C. provided a helpful review of the authorities bearing upon questions of causation and stated: "The test is what an informed person in the building industry (not the man in the street) would take to be the cause without too much microscopic analysis but on a broad view. Where a loss has been occasioned by more than one cause, a claimant must show on the balance of probabilities that the breach complained of caused or materially contributed to the loss complained of."
[63] See, for example, the finding on the facts in *Lubenham Fidelities & Investment Co Ltd v South Pembrokeshire DC* (1986) 6 Con. L.R. 85, CA. Following upon the issue by architects of interim certificates containing erroneous deductions, contractors suspended the execution of works and the employer eventually terminated the building contract. But both employer's and contractors' claims against the architects in respect of their losses failed. The necessary causal link between the architects' erroneous certificates and the losses consequent upon suspension of the works and termination of the building contract was not established.

Advice to the claimant. In cases where the breach of duty is a failure to advise **9–274** the claimant, he must establish on the balance of probabilities that, had the correct advice been given, he would have acted upon it.[64] The reported cases reveal many examples of the application of this rule. In *Gable House v The Halpern Partnership*,[65] the judge found that the claimants would not have commenced a development given proper advice from the defendants as to its nett lettable area even although the correct advice would still have given a development which fell within the claimant's investment criteria. An example going the other way is the case of *Copthorne Hotel (Newcastle) Ltd v Arup Associates*,[66] where Judge Hicks Q.C. rejected a claim based upon an allegedly negligent cost estimate on the basis that, by the time of the estimate, the claimant was already committed to the project and would have proceeded with it in any event.[67] Causation must be proved as a matter of fact. In *Holbeck Hall & Hotel Ltd v Scarborough BC*,[68] the defendant local authority faced a claim by hotel owners for failing to take steps to stabilise the cliff upon which the hotel was sited, leading to its collapse. The local authority, in turn, sued the site investigation company which had investigated and reported upon earlier land-slips in the area. The authority's claim failed because there was no evidence that, had the company given definite and urgent warnings about the need for further investigation, such warnings would have been heeded. Judge Hicks Q.C. rejected the submission that it was possible to infer as a matter of law that the authority would have heeded such warnings; the issue was entirely one of fact.

Advice to a third party. A breach of duty may consist, however, in failure to **9–275** order or advise another person to do a particular act and as a result of that other person's omission damage may be suffered. In order to establish that the damage was caused by the original breach of duty it is necessary to prove, on a balance of probabilities, that the other person would have complied with the order or advice given. Many breaches of duty in the context of supervision by an architect fall into this category. The point was expressly dealt with in *Driver v William Willett (Contractors) Ltd*.[69] Having concluded that consultant safety engineers were in breach of their duty in failing to advise the contractors to have enclosed

[64] *Sykes v Midland Bank* [1971] 1 Q.B. 113.
[65] (1995) 48 Con. L.R. For the facts, see para.9–190, above.
[66] (1996) 58 Con. L.R. 105.
[67] For further examples, see *Hill & Samuel Bank Ltd v Frederick Brand Partnership* (1993) 45 Con. L.R. 141 (claim against architects and engineers for recommending defective panels failed because the employer would have chosen to use those panels in any event); *Nordic Holdings Ltd v Mott MacDonald Ltd* (2001) 77 Con. L.R. 88, Judge Seymour Q.C. (claim failed on causation because even if advised that a suspended warehouse floor would not crack whereas a fibre reinforced concrete slab floor would crack to a limited extent, the claimant would have "run the risk" of the latter because it was by far the less expensive option and minor cracking would not affect the claimant's use of the warehouse); *Pride Valley Foods Ltd v Hall & Partners (Contract Management) Ltd* (2001) 76 Con. L.R. 1 (first instance); [2001] EWCA Civ 1001, CA (appeal against finding that employer would have insisted upon the use of cheaper panels in the construction of a factory even if warned by the defendant project managers that the panels were highly combustible succeeded; on the evidence, there was a low-cost method of complying with the defendants' advice; issue of causation remitted to the trial judge).
[68] (1997) 57 Con. L.R. 113 at 149. The appeal at [2000] 2 All E.R. 705 does not deal with this issue.
[69] [1969] 1 All E.R. 665.

with wire mesh the hoist from which the claimant had fallen, Rees J. still had to go on to consider whether the claimant had established that, if the requisite advice had been given, the advice would have been accepted, the precautions taken and the accident prevented. He concluded that, on a balance of probabilities, the contractors would have implemented the advice and the accident would have been prevented.[70] The engineers were accordingly liable for the claimant's injuries.

9–276   **Concurrent causes.** In tort, if there are competing causes of the claimant's loss and he is responsible for none of them, he will recover in full if he establishes that the cause for which the construction professional is responsible materially contributed to his loss.[71] The decision in *IBA v EMI and BICC*[72] provides an illustration of this principle. The claimant employers (IBA) engaged the first defendants (EMI) as main contractors for the design, construction and erection of a television mast and EMI in turn engaged the second defendants (BICC) as sub-contractors for design, construction and erection of the mast. There was no contract between IBA and BICC but it was conceded by the latter that they owed a duty of care to IBA. The mast collapsed as a result of the combined operation of two causes: aerodynamic stress and asymmetric ice loading. BICC's design for the mast had provided for the former stress but, negligently, had made no provision for the latter. Although aerodynamic stress was by far the more important cause of the collapse, asymmetric ice loading had materially contributed to the collapse. BICC was therefore liable in full for IBA's loss.

9–277   In contract, the position is less clear but there is authority for the following propositions:

> (i) if a breach of contract is one of two causes of a loss, both causes co-operating and of approximately equal efficacy, the claimant can recover his loss in full on the basis that the breach materially contributed to the loss[73];
>
> (ii) if one cause of a loss is the defendant's breach of contract and another cause is the contractual responsibility of the claimant, the claimant will recover if he can establish that the cause for which the defendant is responsible is the effective, dominant cause.[74]

9–278   The first situation is illustrated by those cases in which defective works may be attributed both to the contractor's poor workmanship and the architect's failure properly to inspect the works. In *Hutchinson v Harris*,[75] the architect argued that she was not liable for damages for negligent supervision of works,

---

[70] [1969] 1 All E.R. 665 at 673. A case where the occurrence of loss depends upon the hypothetical actions of a third party may also be treated as a claim for a lost chance: see further para.9–291, below.

[71] *Bonington Castings v Wardlaw* [1956] A.C. 613, HL; *McGhee v National Coal Board* [1972] 3 All E.R. 1008.

[72] (1980) 14 B.L.R. 1 at 37, HL.

[73] *Heskell v Continental Express Ltd* [1950] 1 All E.R. 1033 at 1048, *per* Devlin J.

[74] *Leyland Shipping v Norwich Union* [1918] A.C. 350 at 370, HL.

[75] (1978) 10 B.L.R. 19, CA. The extract of the judgment at first instance, which was unaffected by the appeal, appears from the commentary at 22.

because the primary fault was that of the builder and the employer had not demonstrated that she was unable to recover damages from the builder. Judge Fay Q.C. rejected that argument:

" . . . where the duty of a contracting party is to supervise the work of another contracting party, it seems to me that there is a direct causal connection between the supervisor's negligent failure to prevent negligent work, and the damage represented by that negligent work. No doubt the builder is also liable. It is a case of concurrent breaches of contract producing the same damage. In my judgment the claimant has an action against both, although she cannot obtain damages twice over."[76]

Similarly, in *Wessex Regional HA v HLM Design Ltd*, it was held that the employer had independent, concurrent and unlimited causes of action arising out of over-certification against the building contractor and the supervising architect. Accordingly, the settlement of the employer's claims against the contractor in an arbitration did not give the architect a defence to the employer's claim against him.

An example of the second situation would be a claim against a designer for **9–279** delay in production of his design, where part of the reason for the delay was the employer's late issue of instructions or necessary information. If, as a matter of fact, the designer's own delay was the dominant cause, the employer should recover in full; in certain circumstances, the employer's default may be recognised by a deduction for contributory negligence.[77]

Intervening act of a third party. The chain of causation may be broken by **9–280** the act or omission of some third person. Thus in *London Hospital (Trustees) v TP Bennett & Son*,[78] Judge Stabb held that if he had found the engineers or the architects to have been negligent in the performance of their supervisory functions, he would nonetheless have found that the contractor's employees' wrongdoing in hacking off concrete nibs amounted to a break in the chain of causation.[79] The familiar problem of whether the possibility of intermediate examination by a third person precluded the originally negligent person being liable for the claimant's damage or injury was considered in the following two architect's negligence cases. In *Clay v AJ Crump Sons Ltd*[80] both the defendant architect and demolition contractors argued that the building contractors had the last opportunity of examination of the safety of the site, that this broke the chain of causation and that accordingly they did not cause or contribute to the cause of the accident. The Court of Appeal rejected this argument, referring to a number of authorities on the subject of intermediate examination in the process. Upjohn L.J. posed the relevant question as: "Judged as a matter of fact: were the acts or omissions of the architect or the demolition contractors so remote that in the field

---

[76] (1995) 71 B.L.R. 32.
[77] For an example, see *Raflatac v Eade* [1999] B.L.R. 261. Contributory negligence is discussed at paras 9–347 to 9–350, below.
[78] (1987) 43 B.L.R. 63.
[79] *ibid.* at 87. For further discussion of this case see para.9–245, above
[80] [1964] 1 Q.B. 533, CA. For full facts see para.9–073, above.

of causation it can properly be said that they did not contribute to the accident?"[81] The answer was "No". Similarly in *Voli v Inglewood Shire Council*[82] it was argued that the architect was exonerated from liability because before construction of the stage to his negligent design the plans and specifications had been submitted for approval to the state public works department and no objection had been made to the design and details of the stage. The examination by the department was said to be an intermediate examination breaking the chain of causation between the negligent design and the collapse of the stage causing injury to the claimant. The argument succeeded at first instance but failed on appeal when the architect was held liable. The approval of the public works department was required in order to obtain a state subsidy for the building and did not mean that the officers who examined the plans undertook to correct the architect's plans. Windeyer J. conceded that the fact that plans were approved by a public authority might in some cases, although not on the facts of the particular case, be relevant in considering whether or not an architect was in fact negligent. In the common situation of an architect's or engineer's negligent design having been approved by a local authority building inspector, it is submitted that such approval will be treated by the courts as irrelevant to the issue of the architect's or engineer's liability. *Murphy v Brentwood DC*[83] makes it clear that, in England, in the usual exercise of its statutory powers a local authority owes no duty to anyone to protect them against economic loss. Such responsibility will rest solely with the architect or engineer who is employed to draw up the plans.[84]

9–281   It is thought that a negligent survey or the lack of a survey before purchase should be irrelevant to the issue of causation in a claim by a subsequent purchaser of a building against those concerned in its original construction, including the architect or an engineer.[85] Such claims are now likely to be rare, in England, given the limited circumstances in which a tortious duty not to cause economic loss is owed[86] but may arise either under the Defective Premises Act 1972[87] or as a result of the assignment of a contractual warranty. In the case of a claim under the Defective Premises Act, it is submitted that the courts would be unwilling to allow causation or contributory negligence to amount to a defence

---

[81] [1964] 1 Q.B. 533 at 569.

[82] [1963] A.L.R. 657. For facts see para.9–123, above.

[83] [1991] 1 A.C. 398. For discussion of this case see para.9–070, above.

[84] In *Targett v Torfaen BC* [1992] 3 All E.R. 27, the Court of Appeal emphasised that the essential question, in deciding whether a tortfeasor was liable for personal injuries caused by a defect of which the claimant had knowledge, was whether it was reasonable for the claimant to avoid the danger given the knowledge. See further para.9–074, above.

[85] But *cf. Baxall Securities Ltd v Sheard Walshaw Partnership* [2002] EWCA Civ 9, the facts of which appear at para.9–078 in the main text. The Court of Appeal decided that the sole effective cause of both floods was the lack of adequate overflows in the roof drainage system. That was a patent defect which ought to have been detected by the surveyors instructed to report to the claimant prior to the claimant's purchase of the property. Had the architects owed a duty of care to the claimant in respect of the lack of overflows, the architects would have been in breach of such duty but the surveyors' failure to detect the lack of overflows would have broken the chain of causation between the architects' breach and the claimant's loss. However, since the Court of Appeal had confirmed that the prospect that the claimant would commission a pre-purchase survey which ought reasonably to have discovered the lack of overflows prevented the architects owing any relevant duty of care, the court's remarks on the issue of causation were obiter.

[86] See para.9–103, above.

[87] As to which see paras 9–041 to 9–047, above.

given Parliament's expressed desire to allow subsequent purchasers to claim in specific, limited, situations. Where other specialists are retained by the client, the relative roles of the construction professional and such specialists will require careful consideration in order to decide whose conduct was the effective cause of the client's loss. It may be open to the construction professional to argue that the conduct of another specialist was sufficient to break the chain of causation between his own breach of duty and the client's loss. Such an argument failed, however, in *Linden Homes South East Ltd v LBH Wembley Ltd.*[88] Geotechnical and engineering consultants were engaged to carry out an investigation of the site which the claimant wished to develop, for the purpose of identifying an appropriate foundations design. When the chosen design was found to be unsuitable after work had begun, the consultants argued that although they had recommended that design, the final say on foundations design lay with the specialist contractor engaged by the client and it was that contractor's choice of design which was the effective cause of the loss. The argument failed because the specialist contractor had relied, and had been entitled to rely, upon the consultants' site investigation report in choosing the foundations' design. The report had negligently failed to disclose that there were reasons why the design ultimately chosen would not be effective.

Intervening act of the claimant. In some cases, it will be the claimant's own conduct which breaks the chain of causation.[89] In *AMF International Ltd v Magnet Bowling Ltd,*[90] Mocatta J., having apportioned liability to AMF as between Magnet and T in the proportions of 40 and 60 per cent respectively, allowed Magnet to recover, to the extent of their liability to AMF, damages for breach of contract by T. Magnet's negligence vis-à-vis AMF was irrelevant as an answer to their claim in contract against T on the authority of *Mowbray v Merryweather.*[91] He was satisfied that on the facts it would not be proper to hold that Magnet's acts or omissions broke the chain of causation between the breaches of contract by T and the loss suffered by Magnet in the shape of their liability to AMF. In *J Jarvis & Sons Ltd v Castle Wharf Developments Ltd,*[92] the claimant design and build contractor suffered loss when it had to redesign a development which was halted by the local planning authority. The claimant alleged that it had believed that there was planning permission for the development in the form in which it had begun to build, and that this mistaken belief was the result of negligent misstatements made to it by the employer's project managers and by breaches of duty on the part of its own architects. On the facts, however, the claimant had not entered into any contract for the works and been provided with all of the relevant information regarding the planning position by

9–282

---

[88] [2002] EWHC 3115, TCC.

[89] *Quinn v Burch Bros. (Builders)* [1966] 2 Q.B. 370, CA.

[90] [1968] 1 W.L.R. 1028, especially at 1060 (for facts see para.9–250, above). In *Cardy v Taylor* (1994) 38 Con. L.R. 79, Judge Bowsher Q.C. rejected an argument that a builder who failed to check that his architect had carried out a site survey was thereby negligent. The consequence was that the architect was obliged to indemnify the builder for the damages that the builder was obliged to pay to his client.

[91] [1895] 2 Q.B. 640.

[92] [2001] EWCA Civ 19; [2001] Lloyd's Rep. P.N. 308. The project managers and architects were held not to have been in breach of any relevant duty: see paras 9–110 and 9–128, above.

the time that it commenced works on site. By its decision in those circumstances to proceed with construction in advance of planning approval for its intended development, it had broken the chain of causation between any breach of duty by the construction professionals and its own loss.[93]

9–283   The Court of Appeal considered what was required before a client could be said to have broken the chain of causation between its own loss and the breach of contract or negligence of a construction professional in *Six Continents Retail Ltd v Carford Catering Ltd.*[94] The defendant project manager was retained for the design and installation of kitchen equipment in a restaurant, which was later damaged by fire arising from the fixing of a rotisserie to a combustible wall. It had warned the owner that the installation might create a fire risk but the owner had taken no steps in response. The Court of Appeal held that the project manager had not discharged its duty to the owner by giving the warning. Its duty was to take care to bring about a safe installation. Further, the owner's failure to heed the warning had not broken the chain of causation between the project manager's breach of duty and the owner's loss, since the risk of such a fire was within the range of outcomes which the project manager's contractual obligations were designed to avoid. Laws L.J. said[95]:

"... it was a warning of an outcome which the respondents themselves should have prevented from happening. I find it very difficult to see how the giving of such a warning ought to transpose the burden of avoiding that very outcome from the respondents, who owed a duty in effect to prevent it, to the appellants who were the beneficiaries of that duty."

(ii) *Foreseeability*

9–284 In order to succeed, the claimant must establish not only that the damage was caused by the breach of duty of the architect, engineer or quantity surveyor, but also that it was foreseeable. If the claim is brought in contract, this means that the loss must either (a) arise naturally in the usual course of things from such a breach, or (b) have been in the contemplation of the parties at the time the contract was made as the probable result of the breach.[96] If the claim is brought in tort, it means that, at the time the breach of duty was committed, the damage (or at least the type of damage) was reasonably foreseeable as a consequence of the breach.[97]

---

[93] [2001] EWCA Civ 19; [2001] Lloyd's Rep. P.N. 308 at 321–323 and 325–327. See also *Ford Motor Co Ltd v HLM Design Ltd* 1997 S.L.T. 837, Court of Session, OH (application to strike out claim by employer against architects for negligent design of building on basis that, after discovering the defects, the employer had let the building to tenants but had voluntarily waived the tenant's repairing obligations so far as the defects were concerned. The application was dismissed; the employer could not be said to have suffered no loss merely because he could have avoided that loss by suing others).

[94] [2003] EWCA Civ 1790.

[95] *ibid.* at para.22.

[96] *Hadley v Baxendale* (1854) 9 Exch. 341. In *Czarnikow Ltd v Koufos* [1969] 1 A.C. 350 at 388; and in *Balfour Beatty Construction (Scotland) Ltd v Scottish Power Plc* (1994) 71 B.L.R. 20 at 26, the House of Lords has said that the test in relation to the second limb was whether the loss was likely to occur "with a very substantial degree of probability." For a full discussion of the requirement of foreseeability in contract, see *McGregor on Damages*, paras 6–144—6–184.

[97] For a full discussion of the requirement of foreseeability in tort, see *McGregor*, paras 6–004—6–143.

The issue of foreseeability is frequently considered in the context of liability **9–285** as opposed to damages, although relevant to both issues. For example, in *Eckersley v Binnie & Partners*[98] the main issue both at first instance and on appeal was whether it was reasonably foreseeable to the defendant engineers that methane might gather in the valve house in quantities potentially dangerous to life and limb. Both the trial judge and the majority of the Court of Appeal considered that, on the facts, the engineers ought to have foreseen and guarded against the risk of methane. Similarly in *IBA v EMI and BICC*[99] in considering whether BICC had been negligent the Court of Appeal regarded the crucial issue as whether BICC should have foreseen the combination of causes which resulted in the collapse of the mast; namely, asymmetric ice loading on the stays and oscillation to the mast structure induced by an aerodynamic stress known as vortex shedding. O'Connor J. at first instance[1] held that the combination of causes was foreseeable and that BICC was negligent. His finding was reversed by the Court of Appeal but restored by the House of Lords.[2]

The type of loss. If it is foreseeable that breach of duty will cause the type of **9–286** loss which is in fact suffered, it is irrelevant that neither the extent nor the precise nature of the loss could have been foreseen.[3] Whether the foreseeable loss was of the same type as the loss suffered will be a question of fact in each case. Thus, in *Balfour Beatty Construction (Scotland) Ltd v Scottish Power Plc*,[4] it was held that the demolition and reconstruction of an aqueduct was not a foreseeable consequence of the interruption of the electricity supply to the claimant's concrete batching plant. The electricity supplier did not know that the claimant had contracted to build the aqueduct using continuous pouring of concrete and so could not reasonably have foreseen the result of failure of the power supply. Demolition of the aqueduct was a different type of loss from wastage of concrete or site resources, which were foreseeable results of loss of power. A further illustration is provided by the unusual facts of *Sea Harvest Corporation (Pty) Ltd v Duncan Dock Cold Storage (Pty) Ltd*.[5] The claimants stored frozen fish in a cold store in the Table Bay harbour. The store and its contents were destroyed when a distress flare, which had been fired in the harbour as part of New Year celebrations, landed on the roof of the store and set it alight. The roof of the store was non-combustible, but the fibreglass gutters were not. The claimants alleged that the defendant had negligently failed to install a sprinkler system at the store.

---

[98] (1988) 18 Con. L.R. 1.
[99] (1978) 11 B.L.R. 29 at 99, CA.
[1] Unreported.
[2] (1980) 14 B.L.R. 1. For facts see para.9–276, above. See also *Acrecrest Ltd v W S Hattrell & Partners* (1979) 252 E.G. 1107 (at first instance) where one issue was whether the defendant architects should have foreseen, as they had not, the possibility of Dutch Elm Disease and that there would be "heave" damage in consequence. The unchallenged evidence was that such was the state of knowledge of architects at the relevant time that these matters were not reasonably foreseeable. If they had been the original and only cause of damage, the architects would not have been negligent nor liable for the damage which occurred by reason of those matters.
[3] *H Parsons (Livestock) Ltd v Uttley Ingham & Co Ltd* [1978] 3 Q.B. 791, CA; *Brown v KMR Services Ltd* [1995] 2 Lloyd's Rep. 513, CA.
[4] (1994) 71 B.L.R. 20, HL.
[5] (2000) 1 S.A. 827.

It was common ground that such a system would have extinguished or at least controlled the fire. A sprinkler system had not been installed, upon the advice of consulting engineers who had designed the store for the defendants. The Supreme Court of Appeal of South Africa held that while the precise manner in which harm occurs need not be foreseeable, the general manner of its occurrence must be foreseeable. The question was whether the engineers ought reasonably to have foreseen the danger of fire emanating from an external source on the roof of the building with sufficient intensity to ignite the fibreglass gutters. The only conceivable such source was a flare. The engineers were not aware of the practice of firing flares in the harbour to celebrate New Year and a flare had never been known to cause a fire such as this, since they were designed and required by regulation to burn out at 150 feet above ground. It was held that the fire which occurred was not reasonably foreseeable. It is thought that the same decision would have been reached by an English court on the facts of that case.

9–287   **Date for assessment of loss.** In the New Zealand case of *Bevan Investments Ltd v Blackhall and Struthers (No.2)*[6] the issue of foreseeability arose in the context of consideration of the appropriate date for assessment of loss. There, attempts to build a leisure centre to the original negligent design of the defendant engineer were effectively abandoned in September 1969. It would have been possible to have commenced completion of the building to a modified design in October 1970. But owing to financial difficulties, disputes as to liability and uncertainty as to the enforceability of any judgment obtained, the claimant employer resolved that he could do nothing until his claims against the architect engaged by him and the engineer engaged by the architect were settled or adjudicated. Beattie J. at first instance held that the primary measure of damages was essentially the costs of completing the building to the modified design and that such costs should be assessed as at the date of trial in May 1972. On appeal it was argued for the engineer that the appropriate date for assessment was October 1970 and that the delay between then and the date of trial, which had the effect of increasing the costs of completion, was not within the contemplation of the parties at the time when the engineer entered his contract of engagement with the architect. The argument was rejected. Richmond P. said:

> "If then [the engineer] had actually considered the likely effects of breaches of contract of the kind which occurred in the present case ought he reasonably to have had in contemplation, as 'a serious possibility' or 'a real danger' the possibility that a situation might develop which would make it commercially impossible for Bevan Investments to proceed with the completion of the building for reasons of the kind which were explained in evidence and which were accepted by Beattie J.? In my opinion [the engineer] ought to have done so. The particular design failure was of a kind unlikely to be discovered until an attempt was made to lift the first floor slab into place. At that stage Bevan Investments would be heavily involved financially with the contractors and very likely to be faced with difficult problems as between itself and the contractors. There would be a real danger of differences arising in matters of a technical nature and as to liability. In such circumstances there would be a real risk of difficulties also arising in relation to the availability of mortgage finance. Putting the matter more generally, there would be a real risk of a situation developing in which, even if Bevan Investments

---

[6] [1973] 2 N.Z.L.R. 45 (first instance); [1978] 2 N.Z.L.R. 97 (on appeal).

could by some means or other find the money to do so, it would simply not make sense, from a commercial point of view, to proceed with the work of completion until the complex difficulties facing Bevan Investments were resolved, if need be by litigation. I am therefore satisfied that in the circumstances of the present case [the engineer] should be regarded as having had in contemplation a real risk of serious delays over and beyond those likely to be caused merely by the need of Bevan Investments to secure the technical advice and modified plans necessary for it to let a contract for the completion of the building to a safe design."[7]

Richmond P. further saw no reason in principle why the engineer should not have had the contingency of the employers being unable to complete the work for the material reasons in contemplation as a sufficiently real danger to bring the case within the first rule in *Hadley v Baxendale*.[8]

In *Alcoa Minerals of Jamaica Inc v Herbert Broderick*,[9] the Privy Council had **9–288** to consider similar questions arising from a claim in tort. Mr Broderick owned a house which was damaged by pollutants emanating from Alcoa's alumina smelting plant. He could not afford the necessary repairs. At first instance, he recovered damages for nuisance which were measured as the cost of repairs at the time of trial. By that time, inflation and a fall in the value of the Jamaican dollar meant that the repair cost was significantly higher than at the date when the house was damaged. On appeal, Alcoa argued (a) that the recoverable cost of repair was that at the date of the breach, because that is the date in tort when damages should be assessed; and (b) alternatively, that the recoverable cost of repair was that at the date when Mr Broderick ought reasonably to have carried out repairs. In deciding that date, his lack of funds should be ignored. The appeal was dismissed. It was held that the general rule that damages should be assessed at the date of the breach was subject to exceptions and should not be applied where it would cause injustice. Further, there was no absolute rule (in contract or in tort) that where a claimant does not have funds to repair damage at the date of the breach, his lack of funds was to be ignored in all cases when choosing a date for the assessment of damages. Here, it was "obviously foreseeable" by Alcoa that if a house of a person such as Mr Broderick were to be seriously damaged, he might not have the means to repair it and his ability to do so would depend on recovery of damages.[10]

(c) *The Measure of Damages*

Following the decision of the House of Lords in *Banque Bruxelles Lambert SA* **9–289** *v Eagle Star Insurance Co Ltd*[11] it is necessary to consider the type of loss which is recoverable before considering the measure of such loss. When the measure is

---

[7] [1978] 2 N.Z.L.R. 97 at 118. See also as to the appropriate dates for assessment of damages *London Congregational Union Inc v Harriss and Harriss* [1985] 1 All E.R. 335 (at first instance). The appeal, at [1988] 1 All E.R. 15, did not deal with this point.

[8] (1854) 9 Ex. 341. See para.9–284, above. For the relevant passage in Richmond P.'s judgment see [1978] 2 N.Z.L.R. 97 at 117.

[9] [2000] B.L.R. 279. *Alcoa Minerals of Jamaica Inc v Herbert Broderick* is now reported at [2002] 1 A.C. 371

[10] *ibid.* at 286. This case is discussed further in relation to mitigation of loss at para.9–321, below.

[11] [1997] A.C. 191. See further paras 9–266 to 9–271, above and Ch.10, below.

considered, whether the claim is brought in contract or tort, the fundamental principle governing the measure of damages is that the claimant must be put so far as money can do it in the position he would have occupied if the construction professional had properly discharged his duty.[12] Broadly speaking, this can be achieved in one of two ways, depending upon the particular facts of the case: (i) by paying to the claimant the monetary equivalent of any benefits of which he has been deprived[13]; or (ii) by indemnifying the claimant against any expenses or liability which he has incurred.[14]

9–290   Where as a result of the relevant breach of duty the claimant suffers non-pecuniary loss, such as physical injury or inconvenience, then (subject to the rules as to remoteness) the claimant is entitled to general damages.[15] However, recovery will not extend to general damages for temporary loss of use of a property (for example, while repairs are carried out) which are calculated by reference to notional interest on the value of the property.[16] The position is different where pecuniary loss has been suffered as a result of the unavailability of the property for use: such loss will be recoverable (unless too remote) as special damage. Thus a building owner cannot recover general damages for loss of use of capital which is tied up in a building lying idle, but it will recover special damages if it can demonstrate that it would profitably have used that capital in some other way. Recovery is available in the latter situation even where the building owner cannot prove the precise nature and extent of its loss: in that case, damages will be calculated by reference to a notional reasonable rate of interest.[17]

9–291   **Loss of a chance.** In assessing damages, it will be necessary to consider what would have happened if the architect, engineer or quantity surveyor had properly discharged his duty. There are two possible approaches to dealing with the issue. The first is to assess on a balance of probabilities what would have happened. The second is to assess damages by reference to the value of the chance of a particular hypothesis being fulfilled. In the light of the decision of the Court of Appeal in the solicitors' case of *Allied Maples Group Ltd v Simmons & Simmons*,[18] it appears that, unless it is clear what would have happened, in a case where avoidance of the claimant's loss depends upon the hypothetical actions of a third party, damages should be assessed on the latter basis. For example, if an architect negligently failed to provide the correct information to the planning authority for the purposes of an application for planning permission which was in fact dismissed, the question will be: what was the chance that the authority would have granted permission had it been provided with the correct information? The claimant must prove on the balance of probabilities that it was a real

---

[12] See *Livingstone v Rawyards Coal Co* (1880) 5 App.Cas. 25 at 39; and *Dodds Properties (Kent) v Canterbury CC* [1980] 1 W.L.R. 433 at 451, 454, 456 (as to general principles); *Bevan Investments Ltd v Blackhall & Struthers (No.2)* [1978] 2 N.Z.L.R. 97.

[13] See the heads of damage discussed at paras 9–294 to 9–313, below.

[14] See the head of damage discussed at para.9–314, below.

[15] See the head of damage discussed at paras 9–315 to 9–318, below.

[16] *Bella Casa Ltd v Vinestone Ltd* [2005] EWHC 2807, TCC.

[17] *Earl's Terrace Properties v Nilsson Design* [2004] EWHC 136, TCC, considered further at para.9–271, above.

[18] [1995] 1 W.L.R. 1602 followed in *Stovold v Barlows* [1996] 1 P.N.L.R. 91. See further the discussion in Ch.3, para.3–007 and in Ch.11, paras 11–261 to 11–268.

and not a merely speculative chance; if he does that, the evaluation of the chance will be a matter for the quantification of damages. Normally, damages will be assessed as a percentage of the claimant's maximum possible recovery. By contrast, where the hypothetical outcome depends upon the action of the claimant, the claimant must prove, on the balance of probabilities, that he would have acted in such a way as to avoid the loss which he in fact suffered.[19] If he does that, then he will recover in full and no discount is made for the chance that he would not have acted in the relevant way.

The principles explained in *Allied Maples* were applied in *J Sainsbury Plc v* **9–292** *Broadway Malyan*.[20] The claimant was the owner of a superstore in Chichester which was destroyed by a fire. The defendants were the architects who had designed the store. The claimant claimed the cost of reinstatement of the building on the basis that, had the defendants properly designed a compartment wall, the wall would have contained the fire for sufficient time to allow the fire brigade to prevent its spread. The architects settled the case against them on this basis, and then sought contribution from consulting engineers, EGP, who had been involved in the design. EGP argued that the settlement was not reasonable because the claimant's claim was, correctly analysed, a claim for the value of the lost chance that the fire brigade (a third party) would have contained the fire. Judge Lloyd Q.C. accepted this submission. He found on the facts that there was only a 35 per cent chance that the fire brigade would have contained the fire had the wall not been defective. The architects had unreasonably settled the main action at too high a figure because no discount had been given by the claimant for the 65 per cent chance that the fire would have spread out of control in any event.[21]

(d) *Heads of Damage*

The losses which may result from breach of duty by architects and engineers and, **9–293** to a much lesser extent, quantity surveyors cover a wide variety. Certain types of losses, however, are of common occurrence and are considered below. The discussion is not definitive of the type of loss for which liability may be incurred and ultimately the appropriate measure of loss and the types of loss depend upon the facts of each case. In particular much will depend upon the nature of any contractual term broken, the relationship of the claimant to the defendant and how far a building project has proceeded at the time the breach of duty is discovered.

(i) *Costs of Rectification*

The costs of rectification will usually be the prime head of recoverable damage **9–294** when a building suffers from defects which are consequent upon negligence by

---

[19] See, for example, para.9–274, above.
[20] [1999] P.N.L.R. 286.
[21] *ibid.* at 325–326. The judge contrasted the case with a case where a storeowner wished to sell the store but found that its market value was reduced because of the defective wall: a claim for the diminution in value did not involve the hypothetical actions of a third party and so would not be a claim for loss of a chance.

an architect or engineer in examination of the site,[22] design[23] or superintendence.[24] In a case[25] of negligent supervision by an architect resulting in a house
not being built by the contractor in accordance with the building contract it was
said:

> " . . . the measure of damages could not by any possibility be what would be necessary
> to put the work in the condition required by the contract—that would be against the
> party who was paid for the performance of the work; but now the damages should be
> measured as to what loss the plaintiff has suffered by reason of the negligent perform-
> ance of his duty of superintendence."[26]

Construed as a statement that the architect's duty of care is not to be equated with
the builder's duty to carry out the work in the condition required by his contract,
this is clearly correct. Further, the recoverable loss consequent upon negligent
superintendence may not be the costs of rectification. If, for example, it were
shown that even given competent superintendence the work would not have been
carried out by the contractor in accordance with his contract then the recoverable
loss would rather be the amount which the architect should have withheld, but
did not withhold, on account of defective work in his interim or final certificates.
For example, in *Turner Page Music Limited v Torres Design Associates*,[27] Judge
Hicks Q.C. found that the employer would not have wished defective work,
which was negligently certified by the defendant architects, to have been remedied by the contractor due to pressure of time. As a result he found that the
amount of the negligent over-certification was the proper measure of loss. If, on
the other hand, it were shown that competent supervision would have resulted in
the contractor's work being carried out in accordance with his contract (and it
was reasonable for the employer to incur the costs necessary to rectify the
defect), the costs of rectification would be the appropriate loss recoverable.

---

[22] e.g. *City of Brantford v Kemp and Wallace-Carruthers & Associates Ltd* (1959) 21 D.L.R. (2d) 670
at 683–684, Ontario High Court. The issue of damage was not subject of the appeal to the Ontario
Court of Appeal reported at (1960) 23 D.L.R. (2d) 640. The facts of the case are given at para.9–184,
above.

[23] e.g. *Gilbride v Sincock* (1955) 166 E.G. 129; *Moresk Cleaners Ltd v Hicks* [1966] 2 Lloyd's Rep.
338 (damages agreed by reference to rectification cost). See also *Bevan Investments Ltd v Blackhall
and Struthers (No.2)* [1978] 2 N.Z.L.R. 97; *London Congregational Union Inc v Harriss and Harriss*
[1985] 1 All E.R. 335 at 343–345 (first instance. Damages assessed by reference to rectification costs,
but reduced on account of delay in bringing action to trial and of only one quotation for rectification
works having been obtained. The appeal at [1988] 1 All E.R. 15 did not deal with this issue); *George
Fischer Holding Ltd v Multi Design Consultants Ltd* (1998) 61 Con. L.R. 85 (professional fees
incurred by a claimant in working up a remedial scheme which was rejected by the court were also
not recoverable as damages on the basis that, although incurred, they were part and parcel of the
scheme which the court had found to be unnecessary; however, it was held that the fees were
nonetheless recoverable as part of the costs of the litigation); *Catlin Estates Ltd v Carter Jonas* [2005]
EWHC 2315 (reasonably necessary rectification costs assessed by reference to the quality of the
building which the employer was entitled to expect).

[24] See *Sandown Hotels Ltd v Phelps* (1953) 167 E.G. 595. Costs of rectification as such were not
awarded but rather the increased work of scheduled repainting because unsatisfactorily supervised
paintwork had to be burnt off as a whole.

[25] *Armstrong v Jones* (1869), cited in *Hudson's Building Contracts* (4th edn, 1914), Vol.2, p.6 (Court
of Exchequer (Ireland)).

[26] *ibid.* at 7, *per* Baron Fitzgerald.

[27] (1997) C.I.L.L. 1263.

An unusual claim for damages representing the costs of rectification was made   **9–295**
in *Consarc Design Ltd v Hutch Investments Ltd.*[28] The employer discovered that
a newly laid floor was defective during the defects liability period provided for
by the building contract. Under the contract, the employer was entitled to require
the building contractor to rectify the defects before issuing the final certificate or,
alternatively, to instruct another contractor to carry out the repair works and
deduct the cost from the payment due to the original contractor. The employer
took neither course. Instead, it paid the original contractor in full and then put the
floor repair works out to tender. The original contractor submitted the lowest
tender and was awarded the contract to repair its own defective floor. The
employer sought to recover the cost of the repair works as damages from its
architects on the grounds that they had failed to prevent the floor being completed
with defects during the original construction period. Judge Bowsher Q.C. dismissed the claim on the basis that the architects were not in breach of their duty
to inspect, but he remarked obiter that, in effect, the employer had made a
voluntary payment of the repair cost to the original contractor by failing to
invoke its rights under the original building contract. It could not be right, the
judge commented, that there should be a recovery from one wrongdoer of a
voluntary payment made to another wrongdoer.

A different problem arose in *McLaren Murdoch & Hamilton Ltd v Abercromby*   **9–296**
Motor Group Ltd.[29] The defender architects were responsible for the defective
design of a heating installation at four car showrooms under their contract with
the pursuer. Before remedial costs were incurred, the showrooms were sold to
another company in the group of which the pursuer was a member and it was the
purchaser which incurred the remedial costs. It was held that, as owner of the
building at the time that the defective installation was completed, the claimant
had suffered a loss for which it was entitled to compensation. The court went on
to state that, in any event, the court would permit the pursuer to recover those
costs so as to avoid the loss falling into a legal "black hole" (although it would
hold the damages on trust for the company which incurred the costs). That was
in accordance with the approach favoured obiter by the majority of the House of
Lords in *Alfred McAlpine Construction Ltd v Panatown Ltd.*[30]

The need for care in identifying the loss suffered as a result of the breach of   **9–297**
duty in question is also demonstrated by the New Zealand case of *Bevan*
Investments Ltd v Blackhall and Struthers (No.2).[31] In that case, construction of
a leisure centre to the original negligent design of the defendant engineer was
abandoned, but completion to a modified design was possible and intended.
Beattie J. held that the primary measure of damages was essentially the cost of
completing the building to the modified design. On appeal[32] it was argued for the
engineer that the appropriate measure of damages was the amount of wasted
expenditure incurred by the claimant employer, namely the amount of his legal
liability to the contractor less the salvage value of the partly completed structure
(after duly taking into account incidental expenses). Particular reliance was

---

[28] [2002] P.N.L.R. 712.
[29] (2002) 100 Con. L.R. 63, Sc. Ct. Sess. (OH).
[30] [2001] 1 A.C. 518.
[31] [1973] 2 N.Z.L.R. 45 (first instance).
[32] [1978] 2 N.Z.L.R. 97.

placed on the obiter dicta of Hutley J.A. in the Australian case of *Auburn Municipal Council v ARC Engineering Pty Ltd*,[33] the essence of the argument being (1) that the engineer's duty was not to construct the building but to exercise reasonable care and skill in design and supervision; and (2) that consequent upon breach of the latter duty "the loss which the [claimant employer] experienced *qua* the [engineer] was not the loss of the building which it contracted to get, but the loss of its money in a futile enterprise."[34] There was no contractual nexus between the employer and the engineer but only between the employer and the architect (who was also a defendant) and between the architect and the engineer. For purposes of the argument, however, both architect and engineer were treated as one. The argument was rejected. Richmond P. said:

> "I can see no reason why the general rule that a plaintiff is entitled to be placed in the same position as he would have been in had the contract been performed should not provide the starting point in the case of an action for damages brought against an engineer for failing to carry out his implied contractual undertaking to use proper care and skill in the design and supervision of a building."[35]

He conceded that if it had appeared that proper care and skill by the engineer would have led to a situation where the owner would have completely abandoned all idea of building, then he would have agreed with Hutley J.A. that wasted expenditure was the appropriate measure of damages.

9–298   In considering whether to award the costs of rectification, it will always be relevant for the court to consider whether the costs of rectification are in proportion to the benefit to be obtained by such rectification. This is clear from the decision of the House of Lords in *Ruxley Electronics and Construction Ltd v Forsyth*[36] where a contractor had, in breach of contract, constructed a private swimming pool to a depth of 6 feet rather than the required depth of 7 feet 6 inches. The trial judge had found as facts: (a) that the pool as constructed was perfectly safe to dive into; (b) that there was no evidence that the shortfall in depth decreased the value of the pool; and (c) the only practical method of achieving the required depth would be to demolish the pool and reconstruct it at a cost of £21,560. The judge further found that the cost of rectification was wholly disproportionate to the benefit to be gained by rectification and awarded damages for loss of amenity of £2,500. The Court of Appeal, by a majority, upheld the claimant's appeal against this award and awarded the costs of rectification but the House of Lords unanimously restored the decision of the trial judge. Before the House, the claimant sought to argue that damages for loss of amenity could not be awarded[37] and, as the claimant had undoubtedly suffered a real loss, he was entitled to the costs of rectification. The House of Lords declined to accept this proposition. As the defendant did not complain about the

---

[33] [1973] 1 N.S.W.L.R. 513, New South Wales CA especially at 529 *et seq.* (on the facts, the measure of damages for negligent design of footings was held to be costs of rectification, namely, the cost of demolition plus costs of reconstruction estimated at the date the employers reasonably ought to have commenced reconstruction).

[34] *ibid.* at 535.

[35] [1978] 2 N.Z.L.R. 97 at 108.

[36] [1996] 1 A.C. 344.

[37] By reason of the application of the decision in *Addis v Gramophone Co Ltd* [1909] A.C. 488.

award of £2,500, there was no issue before it which required it to consider whether damages for loss of amenity were properly awarded.[38] Nevertheless even if damages for loss of amenity were not properly awarded, it did not follow that the claimant was entitled to the cost of reinstatement since it would be wholly unreasonable of him to incur those costs.[39] Similarly the House of Lords considered it irrelevant that (before the House) the claimant had offered an undertaking to use any damages for the purpose of rectifying the swimming pool. The claimant could not manufacture a loss where one did not exist.[40]

The House of Lords in *Ruxley* thus also confirmed the relevance of a claim-   **9–299** ant's intention or lack of intention to carry out repair works, when those works have not already been carried out by the time of trial. The use to which the claimant intends to put his damages is relevant to the question whether rectification would be reasonable, and therefore to the question of whether he has suffered a loss to that extent.[41] Thus in *Department of National Heritage v Steensen Varming Mulcahy*,[42] project insurers brought a subrogated claim in the name of the Department of National Heritage against a firm of mechanical and electrical engineers who had provided the design and supervision for a part of the new National Library but were not themselves insured under the project insurance policy. The claim failed on liability but the judge found that even had liability been established he would have refused to permit recovery of the costs allegedly incurred in respect of remedying defective cables. The Department of National Heritage had publicly denied paying for any such remedial costs and the evidence suggested that the project insurers had paid for such works without reference to any obligation of the Department to reimburse the contractor. Similarly, in *Nordic Holdings Ltd v Mott MacDonald Ltd*,[43] the claimant warehouse owner complained that its engineers had negligently failed to advise that a suspended floor rather than a fibre reinforced concrete slab floor should be built in two extensions to the warehouse. Judge Seymour Q.C. held that the engineers were not in breach of duty and that the claim would anyway have failed on causation, but he also considered the measure of damages in case he was wrong on those points. The claim was for the wasted cost of laying fibre reinforced concrete floors in the extensions and the costs of demolishing those floors and constructing suspended floors in their place, as well as the costs of temporary works which had been carried out to repair cracks in the floors which were built. Judge Seymour Q.C. found that the claimant had no intention of demolishing the existing floors and building suspended floors. Accordingly, he held, the claimant

---

[38] Although Lord Bridge (at 354), Lord Mustill (at 360–361) and Lord Lloyd (at 374) opined that such a loss was recoverable. Lord Keith agreed with Lords Mustill and Lloyd and the latter thought that the claimant was lucky to have received such a large award. Damages for loss of amenity on comparable facts had been awarded in *Atkins (GW) Ltd v Scott* (1991) 7 Const. L.J. 215, CA.

[39] See, *per* Lord Lloyd at 374. See, for an unsuccessful attempt to apply *Ruxley* so as to reduce a claimant's damages, *McLaren Murdoch & Hamilton Ltd v The Abercromby Motor Group Ltd* (2003) 100 Con. L.R. 63, Sc. Ct. Sess. (OH) (replacement of the underfloor heating system in four car dealership showrooms was not an unreasonable and disproportionate response to the results of the architects' negligent failure properly to design the original system).

[40] See, *per* Lord Lloyd at 373.

[41] For criticism of this approach, see B. Coote, "Contract damages, *Ruxley*, and the performance interest" [1997] C.L.J. 537.

[42] (1998) 60 Con. L.R. 33.

[43] (2001) 77 Con. L.R. 88.

had suffered no loss which was represented by the costs of that exercise and the costs of laying the original floors had not been wasted. The claimant was entitled to recover only the cost of the temporary repairs which it had carried out.

9–300   **Credit for cost of proper design.** Where rectification costs are claimed as damages for negligent design, it may be that the cost of the building built to a hypothetically proper design would have been higher than the actual cost of the building which was negligently designed. In such a case, the claimant must give credit for the amount by which the cost of construction of a proper design would have exceeded the actual cost, provided that he would have incurred that extra cost had the designer discharged his duty.[44] In *Ministry of Defence v Scott Wilson Kirkpatrick*,[45] a contractor which had failed to secure the roof of a historic building in accordance with the building contract faced a claim from the Ministry for remedial works which were far more expensive than the original works would have been, even if performed in accordance with the contract. The contractors should have made critical connections between roof timbers using certain nails, but used much smaller nails instead. After the roof was blown off in a storm, the Ministry remade the connections using steel straps, saddles and bolts in accordance with a code of practice for the design of new buildings, rather than the large nails specified by the original contract. The Court of Appeal held that the cost of the steel components used by the Ministry was not recoverable as damages for the contractor's breach of contract. The relevant code of practice had not been incorporated into the original contract, so that the Ministry would have had to make additional payment for compliance with the code in any event.

9–301   **Date of assessment of repair costs.** The general rule for assessment of damages is the date when the cause of action arose, which in the case of breach of contract is the date of breach and in the case of the tort of negligence is the date when the damage was sustained. It is not, however, a universal rule, and a different date may be appropriate on the facts of a particular case.[46] In *Alcoa Minerals of Jamaica Inc v Herbert Broderick*,[47] the Privy Council confirmed that

---

[44] See *Bevan Investments Ltd v Blackhall and Struthers (No. 2)* [1973] N.Z.L.R. 45 (first instance); [1978] 2 N.Z.L.R. 97, New Zealand Court of Appeal. See also *City of Brantford v Kemp and Wallace-Carruthers & Associates Ltd* (1959) 21 D.L.R. (2d) 670 (first instance; credit given for extra costs of piling systems which should have been used over actual cost of "floor on earth" type of flooring used); and *Auburn Municipal Council v ARC Engineering Pty Ltd* [1973] 1 N.S.W.L.R. 513 (similar credit). *cf. Purdie v Dryburgh* 2000 S.C. 497 (Sc.Ct. Sess.), where the pursuers would not have proceeded with the project had they been advised as to the appropriate foundations design; the award to them of the cost of installing such foundations in this case might properly be regarded as loss caused by their reasonable effort to mitigate their loss.

[45] [2000] B.L.R. 20. For the facts, see para.9–127, above.

[46] See *East Ham Corp v Bernard Sunley & Sons Ltd* [1966] A.C. 406 (held that damages for breaches of contract by a building contractor were to be assessed by reference to cost of remedial works not at or shortly after the date of the breaches in 1954 but at the date of necessary investigations and remedial works were carried out in 1960 and 1961). Also see *Dodds Properties (Kent) v Canterbury CC* [1980] 1 W.L.R. 433, CA; and *London Congregational Union Inc v Harriss and Harriss* [1985] 1 All E.R. 335.

[47] [2002] 1 A.C. 371. For the facts, see para.9–288, above.

the rule should not be applied where it would result in injustice. Lord Slynn, who delivered the advice to Her Majesty, said[48]:

> "In a case where repairs have to be done at what is a heavy cost in relation to the plaintiff's financial position there may be stronger grounds for delaying the date of assessment that in a case where the claimant has undertaken a contractual obligation to buy and pay for goods where he could go out into the market and buy the goods at or near the same price."

The Court also saw force in the statement that "failure by a wrongdoer to accept liability will in many cases be a crucial factor in justifying a claimant in postponing work of repair until final judgment."[49] The claimant in that case did not have the means to carry out the necessary works without an award of damages, and the defendant had maintained strongly that it was liable to pay none. He recovered his costs of repair as at the date of trial.

Damages for failure to review a design. None of the cases has dealt specifi-   **9–302**
cally with the question whether the measure of damages for failing to correct a defective design will be the same as that for carrying out the defective design in the first place. The question would arise either where a professional was employed specifically to review another's design or where a claim in respect of the initial design was statute-barred but a claim in respect of reviewing it, was not. In the absence of concealment or an estoppel[50] such as to prevent a limitation defence from accruing, it is submitted that the contractual measure of damages for failing to review a design where a claim in respect of the original design obligations is statute-barred should be such as to put a claimant into the position that he would have been in if the design had been properly reviewed. Thus if the failure to review occurred immediately before practical completion, a claimant should be obliged to give credit for the (possibly substantial) costs which would have been incurred at that stage in correcting the design.

Betterment. In *Richard Roberts Holdings Ltd v Douglas Smith Stimson*   **9–303**
Partnership,[51] the question arose as to the circumstances in which a defendant professional may claim credit for "betterment", that is, when the claimant has re-built his building to a higher standard than that envisaged by the defendant's original design. Judge Newey Q.C. summarised the law as follows:

---

[48] [2002] 1 A.C. 371 at 283.
[49] *per* I. N. Duncan Wallace Q.C., "Costs of repairs: date for assessment"; (1980) 96 L.Q.R. 341 at 342–343.
[50] As to which see *Kaliszewska v John Clague & Partners* (1986) 5 Con. L.R. 62 (architect who negligently designed bungalow outside limitation period not guilty of deliberate concealment within the meaning of s.32(2) of the Limitation Act 1980 but was estopped from alleging that cause of action did not accrue within six years of commencement of action because of post-completion representation that claimant had nothing to worry about). In *Blaenau Gwent BC v Robinson Jones Design Partnership* (1997) 53 Con. L.R. 31 at 49–50, Judge Hicks Q.C. declined to follow the decision in *Kaliszewska* on the estoppel point on materially identical facts. He pointed out that where a defendant denies negligence but maintains a conditional plea that if, contrary to his primary case, he was negligent, the action is statute barred, it will be very difficult to assert that an earlier statement to the effect that he was not negligent can found an estoppel. The conditional case which is sought to be run at trial will be consistent with the original representation.
[51] (1988) 46 B.L.R. 50. For the facts, see para.9–136, above.

> "If the only practicable method of overcoming the consequences of a defendant's breach of contract is to build to a higher standard than the contract had required, the plaintiff may recover the cost of building to that higher standard. If, however, a plaintiff needing to carry out works because of a defendant's breach of contract, chooses to build to a higher standard than is strictly necessary, the courts will, unless the new works are so different as to break the chain of causation, award him the cost of the works less a credit to the defendant in respect of betterment."[52]

Whilst this summary of the law is unexceptionable, it does not mention any credit for the cost which would have been incurred by the claimant in building to a proper design in the first place. On the facts of *Richard Roberts*, where the original tank lining had cost only £3,240.52, it seems likely that a proper lining would, inevitably, have been more expensive at the time of installation and so a credit would have been appropriate.[53]

9–304   When a claimant has carried out remedial works before trial and seeks to recover the cost of those works, defendants very often produce expert evidence to support an assertion that the works were needlessly expensive and the claimant should, instead, have carried out an alternative cheaper scheme. It is submitted that the approach adopted by Judge Newey Q.C. in *Board of Governors of the Hospitals for Sick Children v McLaughlin and Harvey Plc*[54] in considering this question is correct. In that case there had been a fierce debate before trial between the defendants' experts and the claimants' expert as to the necessity for remedial works as a result of a defective pile design but the claimant had relied on its own expert's recommendations in carrying out remedial works before trial. In considering the law the judge stated:

> "The plaintiff who carries out either repair or reinstatement of his property must act reasonably. He can only recover as damages the costs which the defendant ought reasonably to have foreseen that he would incur and the defendant would not have foreseen unreasonable expenditure. Reasonable costs do not, however, mean the minimum amount which, with hindsight, it could be held would have sufficed. When the nature of the repairs is such that the claimant can only make them with the assistance of expert advice the defendant should have foreseen that he would take such advice and be influenced by it . . . [55]
>
> However reasonably the plaintiff acts, he can only recover in respect of loss actually caused by the defendant. If, therefore, part of a plaintiff's claim does not arise out of the defendant's wrong doing, but is due to some independent cause, the plaintiff cannot recover in respect of that part: *Owners of Liesbosch Dredger v Owners of Steamship Edison*,[56] and *Compania Financiera 'Soleada' SA v Hamoor Tanker Corp Inc, The*

---

[52] (1988) 46 B.L.R. 50 at 69. See also the same judge's judgment in *Board of Governors of the Hospitals for Sick Children v McLaughlin & Harvey Plc* (1987) 19 Con. L.R. 25 at 97–98. For consideration of some of the evidential difficulties which arise in connection with arguments on betterment in construction cases, see C. Ennis, "Credit for 'betterment' in quantum arguments" (2000) 16 Const. L.J. 31.

[53] See para.9–300, above. In *Turner Page Music Ltd v Torres Design Associates* (1997) C.I.L.L. 1263, it was held that a competent designer would have provided additional and improved fire exits in his original design. As a result of a Building Regulations refusal, the additional and improved fire exits had to be provided by way of variation. The judge found that it was likely that the late addition of the fire exits had increased their cost by one third and awarded this sum as damages.

[54] (1987) 19 Con. L.R. 25.

[55] *ibid.* at 94.

[56] [1933] A.C. 449.

Borag.[57] The independent cause may take the form of an event which breaks, that is to say, brings to an end, a chain of causation from the defendant's breach of duty, so that the plaintiff cannot recover damages for any loss which he sustains after the event. The event may take the form of negligent advice upon which the plaintiff has acted. Another way of expressing the matter might be that the defendant could not reasonably have foreseen that the plaintiff would act on negligent advice. Advice which is not negligent will not by itself break the chain . . . If at the date of the trial no remedial works have been carried out by the plaintiff, then the court has in order to assess damages to decide what works should be done. The parties are entitled to put forward rival schemes and the court has to choose between them or variants of them . . . The assessment has to be made on the basis of what the plaintiff can reasonably do. Contrary to Mr Potter Q.C.'s submissions, in my view where works have been carried out, it is not for the court to consider *de novo* what should have been done and what costs should have been incurred either as a check upon the reasonableness of the plaintiff's actions or otherwise."[58]

The judge went on to find that the claimant's expert had not been negligent and that the claimant was entitled to recover the costs of remedial works carried out on his advice.[59]

It is, of course, possible that matters other than reliance on a negligent expert **9–305** could break the chain of causation. Thus if a claimant sought a guarantee from its professional advisers in relation to remedial works instead of the normal obligation to exercise reasonable skill and care, it is submitted that remedial works will have been caused not by a defendant's breach of duty but rather by a claimant's desire to have a greater degree of security in respect of the repaired building than that to which he had been entitled in respect of the original works. This was the case in *Ministry of Defence v Scott Wilson Kirkpatrick*.[60] Between the date of the defective works carried out by the defendant contractor to the roof of the Ministry's building and the date when the roof was blown off in a storm, cladding to one side of the building was removed. The Ministry carried out remedial works after the storm and argued that it had reasonably relied upon professional advice as to the design of those works. The works were considerably more extensive and more expensive than the works required under the defendant's original contract. The Court of Appeal held that the relevant question was not whether the Ministry acted reasonably in following professional advice as to the appropriate remedial works. The removal of the cladding meant that circumstances had changed since the defendant's contract; at the time of the remedial works, the Ministry did not know whether, without the cladding, the original works would suffice even if properly performed. In those circumstances, it had

---

[57] [1981] 1 All E.R. 856, CA.

[58] (1987) 19 Con. L.R. 25 at 97.

[59] For a case where the same judge found that the claimant's expert engineer had been negligent and that the chain of causation was accordingly broken see *Frost v Moody Homes Limited* (1989) 6 Const. L.J. 43. See also *Skandia Property (UK) v Thames Water Utilities Ltd* [1999] B.L.R. 338, CA (claimant's expert's assumption that basement had been fully watertight before flooding was not reasonable; accordingly works to restore that level of waterproofing were not caused by the flood damage).

[60] [2000] B.L.R. 20. For the facts, see para.9–128, above. See also *Skandia Property (UK) v Thames Water Utilities Ltd* [1999] B.L.R. 338, CA (flooding to basement was not reasonably repaired by works to make the basement fully watertight. The basement had not been designed to be waterproof and the works were caused not by the damage caused by the defendant's neglect but by the claimant's desire to secure the basement against water ingress for the future).

acted reasonably, but the costs of so doing were not attributable to the defendant's breach of contract. Its damages were limited to the cost of carrying out remedial works to the standard specified in the defendant's contract.

(ii) *Diminution in Value*

9–306   In certain cases it may be appropriate to award the diminution in value of land or property rather than the cost of repairing the same.[61] In *Pantalone v Alaouie*[62] an engineer was found to be liable for the collapse of a building as a result of his negligence in failing to make clear to the owner of the adjoining property the precautions that would be required before undertaking excavations. Giles J. considered[63] that the essential question was whether it was reasonable to rebuild the building "judged in part by the advantages [to the claimants] of rebuilding in relation to the additional cost to the defendants over the diminution in value."[64] Having decided, on the facts, that it would not be reasonable he therefore awarded diminution in value plus conveyancing costs (to reflect the fact that it was likely that the site would be sold and a replacement property purchased). Similarly, in *Saigol v Cranley Mansion Ltd*,[65] negligent design and supervision by a building surveyor of works to the claimant's apartment led to the apartment being repossessed by her mortgagee. Although the costs of rectification were less than the diminution in the value of the apartment, the claimant was awarded the latter measure. The Court of Appeal held that the claimant, being out of possession, could not reasonably be expected to carry out remedial works. The appropriate measure of her loss was the diminution in the value of the apartment as a result of the need for rectification works. The costs of rectification were relevant only inasmuch as they might be taken into account by a valuer in deciding the market value of the apartment in its unrepaired state. It rejected the submission that the costs of rectification represented a ceiling on the amount which could be awarded for diminution in value.

9–307   In a few cases, it may be appropriate to award damages representing diminution in value as well as damages representing the costs of rectification. The effect of remedial works may not be to restore a property to the value which it would have had, all other things being equal, had the need for remedial works never existed. This is the result of purchasers being unwilling to purchase a property which has been associated with such remedial works and is known as "blight" or "stigma". It is commonly encountered in connection with works to repair subsidence damage.[66] The principle was approved by Judge Hicks Q.C. in *George Fischer Holding Ltd v Multi Design Consultants Ltd*[67] in awarding damages for negligent over-certification:

---

[61] See the approval by Lord Cohen in *East Ham Corp v Bernard Sunley Ltd* [1966] A.C. 406 at 434–435 of a statement in the then edition of *Hudson* to the effect that diminution of value of work done represented a possible measure of damages in an action against a building contractor.
[62] (1989) 18 N.S.W.L.R. 119.
[63] *ibid.* at 138.
[64] Thus anticipating the approach of the House of Lords in *Ruxley Electronics and Construction Ltd v Forsyth*—see para.9–298, above.
[65] (2000) 72 Con. L.R. 54, CA.
[66] See, for an example, *Hoadley v Edwards* [2001] P.N.L.R. 41.
[67] (1998) 61 Con. L.R. 85 at 145.

"In point of principle a plaintiff who carries out the best and most economical repair which can be devised to defective property but is left at the end with an asset for which purchasers in the market are not prepared to pay as much as for one which never had the defects has plainly lost both the money expended on the repair work and the residual difference in value."

(iii) *Wasted Expenditure*

Wasted expenditure will be the appropriate measure of damages where, for **9–308** example, in reliance upon an architect's negligent design or underestimate of construction cost, an employer embarks upon construction of a building, incurring expenditure on contractors, but, on appreciating that the building cannot be completed except to a substantially modified design or at a price greatly in excess of the estimated cost, he decides to abort the whole project.[68] Clearly, recovery of wasted expenditure is subject to the employer's duty to mitigate his loss and credit should be given for the salvage value of the partly constructed building. In contrast if an architect gives a negligent underestimate of construction cost but the building is completed, it is arguable that the damages recoverable by the employer against the architect should be nominal only, since he will have received a building to the value corresponding to the estimated construction cost plus the element of excess cost.

(iv) *Excess Expenditure*

Excess expenditure will be the appropriate measure of damages where the **9–309** employer has overpaid the contractor in consequence of the architect or quantity surveyor having negligently issued certificates for amounts greater than those properly due to the contractor. The certified amounts may be excessive owing to overcertification of the quantity of work done by the contractor[69] or, as is more often the case, owing to insufficient deductions being made for defective work.[70] If the overpayment were made in consequence of overcertification in interim certificates, it may be difficult for the employer to demonstrate more than nominal loss, since, if the errors are discovered in time, appropriate adjustments may be made in subsequent interim certificates or the final certificate. There may be no such difficulty, however, if in the interim the contractor has become insolvent.[71] An example of the recovery of such expenditure is *West Faulkner Associates v London Borough of Newham.*[72] Judge Newey Q.C. held that as a result of the architect's negligent failure to serve a notice under the building

---

[68] Damages for wasted expenditure would seem to have been awarded in *Dalgleish v Bromley Corp* (1953) 162 E.G. 623 but the matter is not clear from the brief report of the case. The fact that the refurbishment of the defendant's mansion would not have gone ahead was certainly the basis upon which the claimant's claim in *Nye Saunders v Alan Bristow* (1987) 37 B.L.R. 92, CA failed; see para.9–191, above. Note also the discussion of the *Bevan Investments Ltd* case at para.9–287, above.

[69] e.g. *Irving v Morrison* (1877) 27 U.C.C.P. 242; and *Saunders and Collard v Broadstairs Local Board* (1890) cited in *Hudson's Building Contracts* (4th edn, 1914), Vol.2, p.164.

[70] *Sutcliffe v Thackrah* [1974] A.C. 727.

[71] As in *Sutcliffe v Thackrah, ibid.*

[72] (1992) 31 Con. L.R. 105. The appeal at (1994) 71 B.L.R. 1 dealt only with liability. A further example of a case where the court found that the proper measure of damages for negligent over-certification of defective work was the amount negligently over-certified is *Turner Page Music Limited v Torres Design Associates* [1997] C.I.L.L. 1263.

contract stating that the contractor was not proceeding regularly and diligently with the works, the employer lost the opportunity to be placed in a favourable contractual situation with regard to the contractor. As a result the employer was entitled to recover the additional costs charged by new, replacement, contractors, professional fees and certain other consequential losses which should not have been incurred.

(v) *Underpayment*

9–310 Where a construction professional is employed to advise a contractor as to the level of recovery to which he is entitled from an employer, any claim by the contractor against the professional would be for the amount underpaid by the employer as a result of negligent advice. Similarly in the event that a claim in tort by a contractor against an architect, engineer or quantity surveyor appointed by the employer for undercertification were successful,[73] the measure of damages would also be the element of underpayment. It might well be open to the architect, however, to contend on the facts that the contractor's claim should be reduced or extinguished on account of his contributory negligence in not challenging the amount of the certificate within any time limited for doing so.

(vi) *Consequential Losses*

9–311 In addition to the primary measure of loss recoverable against an architect or engineer, certain consequential losses may be recoverable. Consequential loss has been defined as "loss and damage not directly and naturally resulting from the defendant's breach of contract".[74] In other words, it is loss which falls under the second limb of the test in *Hadley v Baxendale*[75] and must have been in the reasonable contemplation of the parties at the time of making the contract as likely to result from the breach of contract with a very substantial degree of probability. For example, in addition to the cost of rectifying a house built to a negligent design, the cost to the occupiers of alternative accommodation during the period of rectification works may be recovered. In the New Zealand case of *Bevan Investments Ltd v Blackhall & Struthers (No.2)*[76] a claim for loss of profits, consequent upon completion of the building of a leisure centre being delayed as a result of the defendant engineer's negligent design, was allowed.

9–312 Claims for consequential losses are more subject to successful resistance on grounds of remoteness or failure to mitigate than claims for other heads of loss.[77] A claim for extensive consequential losses succeeded, however, in *Earl Terrace*

---

[73] See paras 9–105 to 9–111, above.

[74] *British Sugar Plc v N.E.I. Power Projects Ltd* (1997) 87 B.L.R. 42, CA.

[75] (1854) 9 Ex. 341. See para.9–284, above.

[76] [1973] 2 N.Z.L.R. 45 (first instance); [1978] 2 N.Z.L.R. 97, CA. For facts and discussion of the case in the context of foreseeability, rectification costs and mitigation see paras 9–287 and 9–297, above and para.9–321, below.

[77] e.g. in *Hutchinson v Harris* (1978) 10 B.L.R. 19, a case of negligent supervision by an architect, the employer's claim for loss of rental income was disallowed on the grounds that she had failed to take reasonable steps to mitigate her loss. On the evidence in the same case a claim for interest charges on a bank loan was also rejected.

Properties Ltd v Nilsson Design Ltd.[78] It was alleged that breach of duty by the architect had caused a delay in completion of a development and that, as a result, the claimant developer had suffered losses. The consequence of the delay in completion of the development was a delay in sale of the developed properties, and that meant that the development capital was "locked into" the development for longer than it otherwise would have been. Judge Thornton Q.C. held that if a developer can show that it has lost the opportunity to use funds invested for a commercial purpose, it can recover damages (in the form of a reasonable rate of return) for the loss of its opportunity to use those funds elsewhere. It may do so even if it cannot reasonably or readily identify the nature or extent of its loss. Further, the developer was entitled to recover damages for loss of use of funds locked into the development even although its complex funding arrangements meant that some of the holding costs were incurred not by it but by its ultimate parent company. The judge held that since the architect knew that this was a speculative commercial development by a special purpose vehicle company, losses suffered by the parent company were within the scope of the architect's duty and recoverable by the claimant.

A head of consequential loss which is often claimed in cases concerning   **9–313**
construction professionals is the cost of managerial time spent dealing with the consequences of the professional's breach of duty. In principle, such costs are recoverable in contract and in tort as expenditure which has been wasted as a result of the defendant's breach of duty.[79] In *Try Build Ltd v Invicta Leisure Tennis Ltd*[80] Judge Bowsher Q.C. noted the typical evidential difficulties which attend claims for lost management time. The judge also pointed out the importance of distinguishing time spent by a claimant's employees in preparing claims for litigation and time spent preparing practical solutions to the defects complained of; only the latter may be compensated in damages. Finally, the judge rejected the defendant engineers' argument that the claimant would have incurred the cost of its senior management in any event, so that no damages were recoverable, and awarded damages based upon the cost to the claimant of the relevant employees' time:

> "Where the time of a senior manager has been taken up by extra duties made necessary by the wrongdoing of a defendant, the employer . . . has lost the benefit of that individual's time which ought to have been devoted to his ordinary duties even (or perhaps especially) if the time lost was time which might have been spent looking out of the window thinking. The value of that time lost to the company may be enormous or small, but it can only be assessed by reason of the cost of the employee to the company."[81]

---

[78] [2004] EWHC 136, TCC. Compare *Bella Casa Ltd v Vinestone Ltd* [2005] EWHC 2807, TCC, where the building owner's claim for *general* damages for loss of use of capital tied up in a building failed.

[79] See *Tate and Lyle Food and Distribution Ltd v Greater London Council* [1982] 1 W.L.R. 149 and 971; *Babcock Energy Ltd v Lodge Sturtervant Ltd* (1994) 41 Con. L.R. 45; *Lomond Assured Properties Ltd v McGrigor Donald* 1999 S.L.T. 797 (Note).

[80] (2000) 71 Con. L.R. 141, 180–182. For the facts, see paras 9–204 and 9–259, above.

[81] *ibid.* at 181–182. The same argument advanced by a defendant also failed in *Raflatac v Eade* [1999] B.L.R. 261 at 266.

A more restrictive approach to the award of damages for the cost of managerial time was taken in *Phee Farrar Jones Ltd v Connaught Mason Ltd.*[82] The claimant failed to recover damages for the cost of managerial time spent organising a relocation of its business following a flood caused by the defendant's breach of contract because it could not show that it had incurred a discrete expense, such as overtime, or any specific loss of revenue which it would have enjoyed had its manager not been occupied with the relocation.

(vii) *Liability to Third Parties*

9–314   One consequence of an architect's negligence may be to expose the employer to liability to some third party.[83] For example, owing to his failure to make a proper site examination or to make proper enquiries, an architect draws plans showing inaccurate site dimensions with the consequence that a building erected to the plans encroaches upon a third party's land. If the third party recovers damages against the employer for trespass, the architect will be liable to indemnify the employer. Similarly if owing to an architect's negligent design or supervision[84] a third party is injured and recovers damages from the employer, the architect will be liable to indemnify the employer, irrespective of any claim in tort which the injured third party may have had against the architect. If the damage or injury to the third party is caused partly by the employer's default and partly by the architect's default, liability may be apportioned between the employer and the architect.[85]

(viii) *Personal Injuries*

9–315   If in consequence of an architect's negligent design or supervision a person is injured[86] the measure of damages in a claim against the architect will be the usual measure for personal injuries. Quantum of damages for personal injuries is too vast a topic for this book and is more than adequately dealt with elsewhere.[87] In "disaster" situations where an architect or engineer's negligence caused or contributed to an explosion[88] or the collapse of a public building, such damages could, of course, be substantial. For discussion of procedural problems which arise in such matters with large numbers of claimants see above.[89]

---

[82] [2003] C.I.L.L. 2005.

[83] Thus in *Cardy v Taylor* (1994) 38 Con. L.R. 79, the architect was found liable to indemnify the building contractor who employed him against losses which the contractor was obliged to pay to his client by reason of the architect's failure to carry out a site survey.

[84] e.g. *Florida Hotels Pty Ltd v Mayo* (1965) 113 C.L.R. 588 (for facts see para.9–242, above). *Royal Brompton Hospital NHS Trust v Hammond (No.3)* [2002] UKHL 14; [2002] 1 W.L.R. 1397, is an example of a case where a client sued its professional advisers for impairing its prospects of achieving a favourable settlement with the building contractor: the case is discussed further at paras 9–327 to 9–330, below.

[85] See paras 9–324 to 9–350, below on shared responsibility.

[86] e.g. *Voli v Inglewood Shire Council* (1963) 110 C.L.R. 74; *Clay v A J Crump and Sons Ltd* [1964] 1 Q.B. 533, CA; *Driver v William Willett (Contractors) Ltd* [1969] 1 All E.R. 665 (safety engineer). Note also *Storey v Charles Church Developments Plc* (1995) 73 Con. L.R. 1 (claimants failed to recover damages for psychiatric illness caused by the consequences of the defendant's negligent foundation design).

[87] See Kemp and Kemp, *The Quantum of Damages* (Looseleaf, Sweet & Maxwell).

[88] As at Abbeystead: see *Eckersley v Binnie & Partners* (1988) 18 Con. L.R. 1.

[89] See Ch.6.

(ix) *Inconvenience, Distress and Loss of Amenity*

General damages for inconvenience and distress caused by the negligence of a   **9–316**
construction professional may be recovered provided that either (i) a major or
important part of the professional's engagement was to provide peace of mind,
pleasure of freedom from discomfort[90]; or (ii) the inconvenience is physical
inconvenience caused by the defendant's breach and the distress is the direct
result of that inconvenience.[91]

In *Hutchinson v Harris*[92] the claimant employer claimed damages for frustra-   **9–317**
tion, vexation and distress against an architect "friend" who was held to have
been negligent in failing to obtain competitive tenders, in supervising the conversion of a house into two maisonettes and a flat and in overcertifying payments to
the builder. The claim was under three heads: first, the distress consequent upon
continued litigation with the builder; secondly, the inconvenience of having to
organise remedial work; and thirdly, the aggravation suffered or to be suffered by
tenants, aggravation which would rebound on the employer. The official referee
refused to make any award in respect of those heads and the Court of Appeal,
after an extensive review of cases in other contexts in which damages for distress
and suchlike had been recovered, upheld his refusal. Stephenson L.J. said:

> "I am . . . clearly of the opinion that, in these days, we have reached a point where
> damages would have been properly awarded, as the judge thought, for any distress
> which had been caused to the plaintiff by her being kept out of her own house and home
> through having to do extensive repairs to it . . . . Here was a lady, no doubt wanting to
> do up these premises and convert them in order to obtain an income to support herself
> and her family but nevertheless embarking upon a commercial enterprise, converting
> these premises as a property owner, premises in which she had no intention of living
> herself but into which she intended to put tenants in order to draw rents from them. In
> those circumstances . . . the learned judge was quite right to hold that damages for
> distress and annoyance, under whichever of the heads now put by the claimant in this
> court, were not recoverable."[93]

In *Knott v Bolton*,[94] the Court of Appeal held that an architect was not liable   **9–318**
for damages for disappointment and distress to the claimants who had employed
him to build their house. It was alleged that the claimants were distressed as a
result of the failure to achieve a specified width for the staircase in their "dream
home". *Knott v Bolton* was overruled by the House of Lords in *Farley v
Skinner*.[95] In a case concerning a surveyor's negligent failure to report that a
property was unlikely to be affected by aircraft noise, it was held that damages
may be awarded for disappointment or distress caused by a breach of contract

---

[90] See, for example, the "holiday cases" of *Jarvis v Swans Tours Ltd* [1973] Q.B. 233; and *Jackson v Horizon Holidays Ltd* [1975] 1 W.L.R. 1468; and the solicitor's negligence case of *Heywood v Wellers* [1976] Q.B. 446.
[91] See the surveyors' cases of *Watts v Morrow* [1991] 1 W.L.R. 1421; and *Farley v Skinner* [2001] UKHL 49; [2001] 3 W.L.R. 899, discussed at Ch.10, paras 10–184 to 10–188.
[92] (1978) 10 B.L.R. 19, CA.
[93] (1978) 10 B.L.R. 19 at 37, see also Waller L.J. at 46 "[the plaintiff] had decided . . . to invest money in property, and in doing so, in my view, she has to concern herself with this sort of problem as an inevitable incident of being a landlord".
[94] (1995) 1 Con. L.J. 375.
[95] [2001] UKHL 49; [2001] 3 W.L.R. 899, discussed further at Ch.10, para.10–184 to 10–188, below.

even although the sole object of the contract was not to provide peace of mind, freedom from distress or discomfort, comfort or pleasure. It is sufficient that the provision of an amenity is a major or important part of the contract. The House of Lords also considered, but did not overrule, other decisions of the Court of Appeal concerning solicitors[96] and surveyors[97] which were consistent with that in *Knott v Bolton*. However, it remains likely that awards of such damages will be modest.[98]

(e) *Mitigation of Loss*

9–319   As in other classes of action, the claimant cannot recover damages in respect of any loss which he ought reasonably to have avoided. The nature of the steps which he ought to have taken will depend on the facts of each case. In *Board of Governors of Hospitals for Sick Children*[99] Judge Newey Q.C. stated:

> "The plaintiff has, whether as part of the requirement that he act reasonably or otherwise, a duty to mitigate his loss. This may require him if presented with two or more choices to choose the one which will keep his losses to the minimum. If he is incurring loss because he cannot use his property, his duty to mitigate may require him to repair it as quickly as possible, even if early repairs would cost more than later repairs would. The duty to mitigate may require the plaintiff to have regard to advice from third parties, or even from the defendant, or from the defendant's advisers."

9–320   It will often be the case that negligence by an architect or engineer leads to a client incurring additional professional fees in order to rectify or ameliorate an error. Such fees are, in principle, recoverable. Sometimes the original professional will be willing to rectify his own error for free but a client will wish to go elsewhere because he has lost confidence in his original adviser. The question then arises as to whether the client will be entitled to recover the additional fees paid to the replacement. It is submitted that unless the professional's breach has been such that, viewed objectively, the client is acting reasonably in taking the view that the professional may be incompetent, the failure to ask the original adviser to carry out the work will amount to a failure to mitigate. For example in *Columbus Co Ltd v Clowes*[1] Wright J. considered, obiter, that if the claimant employer were not to allow the defendant architect to make good at no extra charge the plans negligently prepared by him, but were to call in another architect who would probably insist on commencing the plans *de novo*, he would not be acting reasonably and would be incurring an unnecessary expense against the

---

[96] *Hayes v Dodd* [1990] 2 All E.R. 815. See further Ch.11, para.11–324.
[97] *Watts v Morrow* [1991] 1 W.L.R. 1421.
[98] *Watts v Morrow* [1991] 1 W.L.R. 1421; *Farley v Skinner* [2001] UKHL 49; [2001] 3 W.L.R. 899. See also the doubts expressed by Lord Lloyd in *Ruxley v Forsyth* [1996] A.C. 344 at 374 as to the award of £2,500 in that case. For summaries of other cases concerning damages for distress and inconvenience see K. Franklin, "Damages for Heartache" (1988) 4 Const. L.J. 264; and (1992) 8 Const. L.J. 318.
[99] (1987) 19 Con. L.R. 25 at 96. Compare *Sherson & Associates Pty Ltd v Bailey* [2000] N.S.W.C.A. 275, New South Wales CA (claimant did not fail to mitigate his loss in taking no action to stabilise a defectively constructed wall on professional advice which did not suggest a risk of collapse).
[1] [1903] 1 K.B. 244.

defendant. In *John Harris Partnership (a Firm) v Groveworld Ltd*,[2] the defendant architects argued that fees paid to replacement professionals should be disallowed as they themselves would have been obliged to carry out the work for free. Although the judge held that they would have been so obliged, he also found that the architects would not, at the time, have accepted this. As a result, the claim for fees was allowed.

The issue of mitigation of loss often arises where a claimant has not carried out   **9–321**
necessary remedial works before trial but has waited to see whether he will recover the cost of the works as damages. If the cost of the works has increased between the date of breach and the date of trial, the defendant is likely to argue that the claimant has failed to mitigate his loss by carrying out the works earlier and therefore at lower cost. It appears that if a claimant can justify his delay on reasonable commercial grounds, the argument will fail. In the New Zealand case of *Bevan Investments Ltd v Blackhall and Struthers (No.2)*,[3] considered previously in the discussion of the issue of foreseeability,[4] it was held that the claimant employer had not failed to mitigate his loss by choosing to postpone commencement of completion of the leisure centre to a modified design, owing to financial constraints on the company.[5] In *Alcoa Minerals of Jamaica Inc v Herbert Broderick*,[6] where the claimant householder lacked the means to carry out remedial work before trial, the Privy Council identified the real question as whether his delay was an unreasonable failure to mitigate his loss. It held that it was not; given his circumstances, it was entirely reasonable for the claimant to wait until funds were made available to him by way of an award of damages in the action.

(f) Abatement of Fees

A construction professional may be denied recovery of his fees if his breach of   **9–322**
duty is so serious as to be tantamount to non-performance.[7] In the more usual case, the normal course is to make an award of damages for the total of the loss sustained but to allow the recovery of fees.[8] In *Hutchinson v Harris*,[9] however, in addition to recovering damages for negligent supervision the claimants sought to resist the architect's claim for fees by invoking the defence adumbrated in *Mondel v Steel*.[10] In that case, which concerned a claim by a shipbuilder for the

---

[2] [1999] P.N.L.R. 697.
[3] [1973] 2 N.Z.L.R. 45 (first instance); and [1978] 2 N.Z.L.R. 97, especially at 115–116.
[4] See also *London Congregational Union Inc v Harriss and Harriss* [1985] 1 All E.R. 335 at 343–345.
[5] See the passage quoted at para.9–287, above and, to similar effect, *Dodd Properties (Kent) Ltd v Canterbury CC* [1980] 1 W.L.R. 433, CA; and *Perry v Sidney Phillips* [1982] 1 W.L.R. 1927, CA.
[6] [2002] 1 A.C. 371; [2000] B.L.R. 279. For the facts, see para.9–288, above.
[7] *Moneypenny v Hartland* (1826) 2 Car. & P. 378 at 380–381, *per* Best C.J.: "Supposing negligence or want of skill to be sufficiently made out, unless that negligence or want of skill has been to an extent that has rendered the work useless to the defendants, they must pay him, and seek their remedy in a cross action. For if it were not so, a man by a small error might deprive himself of his whole remuneration . . . ".
[8] e.g. *Columbus Co v Clowes* [1903] 1 K.B. 244
[9] (1978) 10 B.L.R. 19.
[10] (1841) 8 M. & W. 858.

price of a ship, Parke B. said that instead of claiming damages by way of set-off or counterclaim the defendant could:

> "defend himself by showing how much less the subject matter of the action was worth, by reason of the breach of contract; and to the extent that he obtains, or is capable of obtaining, an abatement of the price on that account, he must be considered as having received satisfaction for the breach of contract, and is precluded from recovering in another action to that extent; but no more."[11]

The defence failed in *Hutchinson v Harris* on several grounds. First, the defence had not been pleaded or argued at first instance and no evidence had been adduced on the matter, as there should have been. Since the architect's contract, being on the basis of the RIBA Conditions of Engagement, was not an entire contract but a severable contract divided into several distinct stages, the architect's right to payment had to be considered and evidence had to be adduced in respect of each stage. Secondly, allowing the defence would have had the effect of permitting double recovery by the claimant since any element of abatement was included in the damages awarded. Thirdly, Stephenson L.J. considered that there was the greatest difficulty in applying the defence of abatement to a claim for professional services, certainly to such a claim made by the particular claimant. The subject matter of the builder's contract, i.e. conversion works, was quite distinct from that of the architect's contract, i.e. services including supervision. The fact that the work certified by the architect had not been done by the builder did not mean that the architect had not done the equivalent amount of her own work. He also observed that no case had been drawn to his attention, with one possible exception,[12] in which a claim for professional services had been reduced or abated by the application of *Mondel v Steel*. He also noted that Parke B. in the latter case stated that the defence of abatement "had not . . . extended to all cases of work and labour, as for instance, that of an attorney, *Templer v M'Lachlen*,[13] unless no benefit whatever has been derived from it".

9–323   In *Turner Page Music Limited v Torres Design Associates Ltd*,[14] the defendant architects failed to produce a bill of quantities for the works although they had expressly agreed to do so. The contract was based upon the defendants' fee proposal, which divided their services into three phases. The provision of a bill of quantities was one item in Phase II. Judge Hicks Q.C. found that the price payable for the architects' services could be abated on the grounds of this failure. He distinguished *Hutchinson v Harris*, apparently on the grounds that, on its true construction, the contract imposed a series of severable obligations upon the defendants. As such he found that the defendants were entitled to be paid their fee less an allowance for the work not done.

---

[11] (1841) 8 M. & W. 858 at 872.
[12] *Sincock v Bangs (Reading)* (1952) 160 E.G. 134.
[13] (1806) 2 Bos. & Pul. (N.R.) 936.
[14] (1997) C.I.L.L. 1263. See also *Nye Saunders and Partners v Alan E Bristow* (1987) 37 B.L.R. 92: in response to the architects' claim for fees, the defendant sought entire abatement of those fees by way of counterclaim. The claim was dismissed at first instance and on appeal, without suggesting any difficulty with abatement of professional fees but without reference to *Hutchinson v Harris*.

5. SHARED RESPONSIBILITY

(a) *Apportionment of Liability*

A building project usually involves many participants with different functions **9–324**
and skills. Injury or damage to a claimant may be the result of breaches of duty
by more than one participant. The courts are often unwilling to accept arguments
from one negligent defendant that the negligence of another absolves them
entirely. Thus in *East Ham Corp v Bernard Sunley & Sons Ltd*,[15] Lord Pearson,
while conceding that the employers should be bound by the architect's examination or failure to examine the works in or after the defects liability period,
continued:

> "On the other hand, it seems to me unreasonable, too favourable to the contractors, to
> let them shelter behind the architect's failure to detect faults in the course of his visits
> during the progress of the work. The architect's duty is to the employers and not to the
> contractors, and the extent of his obligation to make inspections and tests depends upon
> the contract with the employers and the arrangements made and the circumstances of
> the case. Prima facie the contractors should be and remain liable for their own breaches
> of contract, and should not have a general release from liability in respect of all
> breaches which the architect should have detected but failed to detect during the
> currency of that contract."[16]

While one participant (D1) may be liable to the claimant (C) for the whole of **9–325**
C's damage, D1 may seek indemnity or contribution from any other person (D2)
who is liable in respect of the same damage.[17] The right to indemnity or
contribution may arise under a contract between D1 or D2. The Civil Liability
(Contribution) Act 1978 provides a statutory right to contribution. Section 1(1)
of the Act restricts recovery to where recovery can be made from another person
"liable in respect of the same damage".

"The same damage". The decision of the Court of Appeal in *Birse Construc-* **9–326**
tion v Haiste[18] established that "the same damage" means damage suffered by
the same person. In that case the claimant contractor (Birse) was awarded a
contract by an employer (Anglia Water Authority) to design and construct a
reservoir. The defendant (Haiste) was engaged by Birse to act as its consulting
engineers in relation to the project. Anglia engaged one Newton to act as the
"Engineer" under the building contract with Birse. The reservoir proved to be
defective. Birse settled Anglia's claim against it and sought an indemnity in
respect of the settlement from Haiste. Haiste, in turn, claimed contribution from
Newton on the grounds that Newton was liable in respect of the "same damage"
as Haiste were. The Court of Appeal found that the damage alleged against

---

[15] [1966] A.C. 406.
[16] *ibid.* at 449.
[17] The question of indemnity or contribution may arise not only as between defendants but also as
between defendants and persons joined to the action as CPR Pt 20 defendants.
[18] [1996] 1 W.L.R. 675. There is an exception to the rule that the "same damage" must be suffered
by the same person. If the person who originally suffered the damage assigns his cause of action to
another, the person who has suffered the damage will include the assignee: *Bovis Lend Lease Ltd v
Saillard Fuller & Partners* (2001) 77 Con. L.R. 134.

Haiste (i.e. Birse's loss in meeting Anglia's claim) was not the same damage as that in respect of which Newton could be held liable (i.e. Anglia's loss). The practical effect of the decision is significantly to restrict the ambit of the Act.

9–327   The need for care in identifying whether damage is "the same" for the purposes of a claim under the Act was emphasised by the House of Lords in *Royal Brompton Hospital NHS Trust v Hammond (No.3).*[19] The claimant (the Hospital) engaged a building contractor (the Contractor) to carry out major building works and the defendants (the Architects) as its project architects. On the Contractor's applications, the Architects granted extensions of time for completion of the works amounting to 43 weeks. As a result, the Contractor was entitled under the building contract to loss and expense payments in respect of the delay and the Hospital was not entitled to deduct liquidated damages for delayed completion from the contract price. In an arbitration against the Hospital, the Contractor claimed payment for loss and expense of £15 million, in addition to loss and expense payments which the Hospital had already made. The Hospital counterclaimed on the basis that the Contractor had not been entitled to any of the extensions of time certified by the Architects and that, accordingly, the Contractor was liable to pay liquidated damages under the contract and to repay the loss and expense payments already made. The arbitration was settled upon the Hospital agreeing to pay £6.2 million to the Contractor. The Hospital then brought proceedings against the Architects, claiming damages for negligent certification of the extensions of time. The Architect claimed contribution from the Contractor, on the basis that the Contractor was liable to the Hospital in respect of the same damage as the Architects. The Hospital's claim against the Architects was quantified by reference to the liquidated damages and the loss and expense payments which the Hospital had not been able to recover from the Contractor because of the Architects' extensions of time. The Architects argued, therefore, that they were liable to the Hospital in respect of the same damage as the Hospital had claimed from the Contractor in the arbitration. That damage was the Hospital's loss of capital in the form of liquidated damages foregone and loss and expense payments made.

9–328   At first instance, the Architects' claim was struck out on the grounds that the Architects and the Contractor were not liable to the Hospital in respect of the same damage. The Court of Appeal and the House of Lords dismissed the Architects' appeals. The following important observations were made in the House of Lords[20]:

(1) the purpose of the Civil Liability (Contribution) Act 1978 was to enlarge the category of persons from whom contribution could be claimed, by removing earlier restrictions on qualifying causes of action, but the root of the contribution principle remained "common liability to pay compensation for having caused the same harm";

(2) the words "the same damage" in the Act should be given their ordinary

---

[19] [2002] UKHL 14; [2002] 1 W.L.R. 1397.
[20] See the speeches of Lords Bingham and Steyn, who agreed with each other and with whom Lords Mackay, Hope and Rodger agreed.

meaning, without gloss. In particular, the words did *not* mean "substantially similar or materially similar damage";

(3) it was important to keep clearly in mind the distinction between "damage" and "damages". The fact that the *damages* payable by each of two parties to another are quantified in the same or similar ways does not necessarily mean that those parties are liable in respect of the same *damage*.

In order to decide whether the Architects and the Contractor were liable in respect of the same damage, it was necessary to analyse the nature of the damage in respect of which the Hospital claimed compensation from each of them. It was "the essence" of the claim in each case which had to be identified. The damage alleged to have been caused by the *Contractor's* breach of duty was the late delivery of the completed building, and the consequent disruption suffered by the Hospital. The compensation claimed in respect of that damage was liquidated damages and repayment of loss and expense payments. By contrast, the damage alleged to have been caused by the *Architects'* breach of duty was not delay in completion of the building—nor could negligent certification of extensions of time ever cause such delay. Rather, the damage caused by the negligent certification was the impairment of the Hospital's ability to obtain compensation for the delay from the Contractor. The issue of the certificates meant that the Hospital faced much greater difficulty in its claim against the Contractor than it would otherwise have done. The Hospital had to claim compensation from the Contractor in an arbitration in which its own architects' certificates were against it. Had the negligent certificates not been issued, the Hospital would not have had to go to arbitration, or at least would have gone to arbitration with the support of its architects. In summary, it was held that the damage suffered by the Hospital as a result of the Contractor's default was delay in completion of the building, whereas the damage suffered by the Hospital as a result of the Architects' alleged breaches was the weakening of its position in negotiating a financial settlement with the Contractor in relation to that delay. Thus the Architects and the Contractor were not persons who were liable to the Hospital in respect of the same damage.

The House of Lords took the opportunity in *Royal Brompton (No.3)* to identify **9–329** some decisions of the lower courts which had given too wide an interpretation to the phrase "the same damage". A notable example was *Hurstwood Developments Ltd v Motor & General and Andersley & Co Insurance Services Ltd*.[21] In that case, both parties were alleged to be liable to a building contractor for the costs of certain remedial works which the contractor was obliged under the building contract to carry out. The claimant was the contractor's insurance broker: its breach of duty was a failure to arrange insurance for the contractor against such costs. The defendant was the contractor's site investigation subcontractor: its breach of duty had brought about the need for the remedial works.

---

[21] [2001] EWCA Civ 1758.

The insurance broker's claim for contribution against the sub-contractor was, pound for pound, the same as the building contractor's claim against the insurance broker. Judge Gilliland Q.C. held that the parties were not liable to the building contractor in respect of the same damage. The damage caused by the sub-contractor was the need for remedial works. The damage caused by the insurance brokers was the financial loss caused by the absence of insurance cover. The Court of Appeal allowed the insurance brokers' appeal, holding that the parties were liable in respect of the same damage, but the House of Lords in *Royal Brompton (No.3)* held that the Court of Appeal had erred. Judge Gilliland Q.C.'s distinction between the different types of damage was correct and the parties were not liable in respect of the same damage.[22]

9–330 The House of Lords in *Royal Brompton (No.3)* also commented on the proper role of the "mutual discharge" test in determining whether parties are liable in respect of the same damage. This test was first formulated by Sir Richard Scott V.C. in *Howkins & Harrison v Tyler*,[23] as a threshold test. In order to decide whether the Civil Liability (Contribution) Act 1978 applied at all to a contribution claim made by A against B in respect of damage suffered by C, it was said, it was necessary to answer both of the following questions in the affirmative:

(1) If A pays C a sum of money in satisfaction, or on account of A's liability to C, will that sum operate to reduce or extinguish B's liability to C?

(2) If B pays C a sum of money in satisfaction, or on account of B's liability to C, will that sum operate to reduce or extinguish A's liability to C?

Thus, unless a payment made by one party to a contribution claim to the party who suffered the damage operated *pro tanto* to reduce the liability to the victim of the other party to the contribution claim, there could be no liability to make contribution under the Act. In *Royal Brompton (No.3)*, the House of Lords confirmed the proper role of the mutual discharge test. It is not a threshold test which determines whether the Act applies. Rather, as Lord Steyn put it[24]:

> "It is best regarded as a practical test to be used in considering the very statutory question whether two claims under consideration are for 'the same damage'. Its usefulness, however, may vary depending on the circumstances of individual cases. Ultimately, the safest course is to apply the statutory test."

It is difficult, however, to imagine circumstances in which the mutual discharge test will not be met but in which the parties will be liable in respect of the same damage, or *vice versa*. For example, on the facts in *Royal Brompton (No.3)*, the Hospital's claim against the Architects would be reduced *pro tanto* by

---

[22] Similarly, the House of Lords preferred the decision in *Bovis Construction v Commercial Union* [2001] 1 Lloyd's Rep. 416 to that in the related case of *Bovis Lend Lease Ltd v Saillard Fuller & Partners* (2001) 77 Con. L.R. 134. In those cases also, the House of Lords held, damage comprising pure financial loss could not be equated to damage representing the cost of repairing defective construction works, so that the parties were not liable in respect of the same damage.
[23] [2001] P.N.L.R. 27.
[24] [2002] UKHL 14 at [28].

any recovery which the Hospital made against the Contractor, but the converse would not be true.

The effect of a final certificate. An architect's claim for contribution against a building contractor failed for a different reason in *Oxford University Fixed Assets Ltd v Architects Design Partnership*.[25] The defendant architect had been engaged to design and supervise the construction of a pharmacology unit at the University. Following completion of the works, they had issued a final certificate under cl.30.9 of the JCT 1980 Standard Form of Building Contract. Defects in the works then emerged and the employer brought a claim against the architects. It was held that the architects were not entitled to claim contribution from the building contractor: as between the employer and the contractor, the final certificate was conclusive evidence that the standards and quality of workmanship and materials used by the contractor were in compliance with the building contract. According, the contractor would have been able to defeat any claim brought against him by the employer. It followed that the contractor was not a person liable in respect of the same damage as the architects. **9–331**

The effect of joint insurance. A construction professional will face a similar difficulty in claiming contribution from a building contractor to an employer's claim where the employer and the building contractor are jointly insured under a policy of insurance which covers the damage of which the employer complains. In *Co-operative Retail Services v Taylor Young Partnership*,[26] the defendants were architects and engineers who had been engaged by the claimant (CRS) for the construction of its new headquarters in Rochdale. The main building contract provided that the main contractor (Wimpey) should take out a policy of insurance of the works in the joint names of CRS, Wimpey and Wimpey's electrical sub-contractor (Hall). When the works were damaged by a fire, CRS sued the architects and engineers. They, in turn, sought to claim contribution from Wimpey and Hall. For the purposes of a trial of preliminary issues, it was assumed that the fire was caused by breach of duty on the part of each of the architects, the engineers, Wimpey and Hall. Nevertheless, the difficulty which the professionals faced was in showing that Wimpey and Hall were persons liable to the claimant in respect of the fire damage. All three were joint insureds under the policy of insurance which paid out in respect of the fire damage. One co-insured cannot sue another for a loss in respect of which both are entitled to the benefit of the same insurance.[27] **9–332**

The professionals sought in two ways to avoid the difficulty created by the fact that CRS, Wimpey and Hall were joint insureds in respect of the fire damage. First, they argued that the main building contract did not exclude the liability of Wimpey or Hall for loss caused by the fire if the fire was caused by their breach of duty to CRS. Rather, Wimpey remained liable to pay compensation to CRS for the loss caused by the fire save to the extent that such loss was recoverable from insurers under the joint names policy. This was important because the policy did **9–333**

---

[25] (1999) 64 Con. L.R. 13. For further discussion, see para.9–257, above.
[26] [2002] UKHL 17; [2002] 1 W.L.R. 1419.
[27] *Petrofina (UK) Ltd v Magnaload Ltd* [1984] QB 127; *National Oil Wells (UK) Ltd v Davy Off-Shore Ltd* [1993] 2 Lloyd's Rep. 582. See para.9–121, above.

not entirely cover CRS's losses: it excluded consequential loss and it was also subject to an excess. Secondly, the professionals argued that the question whether persons are liable in respect of the same damage for the purposes of the 1978 Act is to be determined at the date when the damage occurs. At the date of the fire, no claim had yet been made under the insurance policy, so that CRS could then have recovered damages from Wimpey and Hall. Accordingly, they were persons liable to CRS in respect of loss caused by the fire.

9–334   Both arguments failed, at first instance and on appeals to the Court of Appeal and to the House of Lords. In addressing the first argument, the House of Lords subjected to close analysis the manner in which the main building contract (JCT 80) allocated loss in the event of fire damage to the contract works.[28] They held that, on the true construction of the main contract, neither CRS nor Wimpey were entitled to sue each other for loss caused by fire damage to the contract works. Such liability was wholly excluded; it was not merely the case (as the professionals had argued) that Wimpey's liability was reduced by the amount of any insurance payment. In other words, the main contract provided a complete scheme for dealing with loss caused by fire damage which could not co-exist with a right in either party to the contract to recover damages for such loss from the other. If Wimpey could not be held liable under the contract for CRS's fire-related loss, it followed that Wimpey was not a person who could be held liable to CRS in respect of the same damage as the professionals and their claim for contribution failed. Since the sub-contract between Wimpey and Hall incorporated the provisions of the main contract, the claim against Hall failed in the same way.

9–335   Although not necessary for their decision, the House of Lords also considered, and rejected, the professionals' second argument. As had the Court of Appeal, they held that the relevant time for deciding whether persons are liable in respect of the same damage is the time when contribution is sought and *not* the time when the damage is suffered. However, the court did not distinguish between the date when contribution proceedings are brought and the date when judgment is given on the claim for contribution: that question remains for decision.

9–336   **Distinct types of damage.** It frequently happens in building cases that the claimant sustains numerous types of damage, for each of which, only some defendants are liable. If C sustains two types of damage and D1, D2 and D3 are liable for the first type of damage but only D1 and D3 are liable for the second type of damage, then in contribution proceedings between D1, D2 and D3 separate apportionment must be made between (a) D1, D2 and D3 and (b) D1 and D3. For example, in *Equitable Debenture Assets Corp Ltd v William Moss Group Ltd*,[29] liability in negligence for the defective design of curtain walling and so for

---

[28] The analysis deployed by the House of Lords in this case (viz., examination of the main contract to see whether there is an implied exclusion of liability between the joint insureds) is obviously sensitive to the particular terms of the main contract. Different contract terms can be expected to produce different results. Thus no exclusion of liability was found so that a contribution claim could proceed in *Surrey Heath BC v Lovell Construction Ltd* (1990) 48 B.L.R. 108 (where the contract was the JCT Standard Form of Building Contract With Contractor's Design: JCT WCD 81); and in *Bovis Lend Lease Ltd v Saillard Fuller & Partners* (2001) 77 Con. L.R. 134 (where the contract was a tailor-made construction management contract).
[29] (1984) 2 Con. L.R. 1 at 40.

the cost of its replacement was apportioned 75 per cent to the specialist design sub-contractors and 25 per cent to the architects; whereas liability for negligence resulting in bad workmanship to the parapet walling and causing loss due to additional leaks was apportioned 80 per cent to the specialist sub-contractors, 5 per cent to the architects and 15 per cent to the main contractors.

Distinct causes of damage. Similarly, if there are two distinct causes of damage it may be appropriate to come to an independent assessment as to responsibility for each head of damage even if the defendants are the same. In *Oxford University Press v John Stedman Design Group*,[30] the claimant bought an action against its architects and main contractors for defects in the floor of a warehouse. The defects consisted of (i) cracks, (ii) surface crazing, and (iii) breakdown in the edges. The architects settled with the claimant and sought a contribution from the main contractors under the 1978 Act. Judge Lewis Q.C. apportioned responsibility in respect of the cracking 60 per cent to the architects and 40 per cent to the contractors; in respect of the crazing, he apportioned responsibility equally between the architects and the contractor; and in respect of the damage to the edges, he apportioned responsibility wholly to the contractor.   **9–337**

Amount of contribution. Section 2(1) of the Act provides that the amount of contribution recoverable by D1 from D2 is such as may be found by the court to be just and equitable having regard to the extent of D2's responsibility for the damage. Section 2(2) goes on to provide that the court has power to exempt D2 from liability to make contribution or to direct that the contribution to be recovered from D2 should amount to a complete indemnity. In assessing contribution, the court takes a broad approach, taking into account both the extent to which D1 and D2 caused damage to C and their relative culpability. Indeed, the court is entitled to take into account conduct which was not causative of the damage in respect of which contribution is awarded, although causative responsibility is likely to be the most important factor in the assessment of the appropriate level of contribution.[31]   **9–338**

It is thought that listing factors which might generally point to greater apportionment of responsibility to one type of person in a building operation as opposed to another is a process best avoided, since so much depends on the facts of each case. Obviously, in the case of a design error, the design team are likely to have the heavier apportionment than the building contractor (if he has any at all). On the other hand, in the case of a workmanship error the heavier apportionment is likely to be to the builder and not to persons supervising him.[32] As between construction professionals, the apportionment of responsibility for an   **9–339**

---

[30] (1990) 34 Con. L.R. 1.

[31] *Brian Warwicker Partnership Plc v HOK International Ltd* [2005] EWCA Civ 962, following *Madden v Quirk* [1989] 1 W.L.R. 702, CA and *Re Source America International Ltd v Platt Site Services Ltd* [2004] EWCA Civ 665.

[32] As for the position where an architect relies upon specialists, (e.g. an engineer) or delegates work to them, see paras 9–172 to 9–176, above. As to the responsibility of a professional when the contractor has a duty to warn of unsafe works, see *Plant Construction Ltd v Clive Adams Associates and JMH Construction Services Ltd* [2000] B.L.R. 137, CA; and *Aurum Investments Ltd v Avonforce Ltd* [2001] Lloyd's Rep. P.N. 285.

error will depend upon the relative extent of their respective involvements and opportunities to avoid the error.[33]

9–340   **Settlement as damage.** Claims for contribution are often made by joining third parties in an action.[34] If satisfied that the defendant (D) is liable in respect of the damage suffered by the claimant (C), and that the third party (T) could also have been held liable for C's damage, the court will apportion liability under the Act as between D and T at the same time as it gives judgment for C against D. In those circumstances, it is obviously not open to T to argue that he and D are not persons liable in respect of the same damage under s.1 of the Act. The position is different if D has settled C's claim before seeking contribution from T. Section 1(4) of the Act provides that D is entitled to contribution in that case if D "would have been liable [to C] assuming that the factual basis of the claim against him could be established." This allows T to argue that D never had a liability to C and so should not have settled C's claim, or that D's liability to C was worth less than D supposed so that D should have paid less in settlement than he did. T will then argue that he is liable to make no contribution, or that he is liable to make contribution to a lower sum than the sum which D paid in settlement of C's claim.

9–341   An argument of this sort was made in *J. Sainsbury Plc v Broadway Malyan.*[35] The defendant architects, who had settled a claim for fire-damage caused by the negligent design of a wall at a superstore, claimed contribution from the employer's engineers for failing to point out a defect in the architects' design for a particular girder. The claim was rejected on its facts, but the judge considered the ambit of s.1 of the Act. He held that, where a settlement has been made, the party who seeks contribution must prove that the settlement was reasonable although he does not need to prove every ingredient of liability to do this. He went on to hold that the settlement concluded by the architects was unreasonable in two respects. First, the settlement was made on the basis that the architects were liable for the storeowner's entire loss. The loss alleged was the cost of reinstatement of all of the fire-damage, on the grounds that had the wall been properly designed, it would have contained the fire for sufficient time to allow the fire brigade to prevent its spread. On its true analysis, however, this was a claim for the loss of the chance that the fire brigade would have been able to control the fire, and that chance was no higher than 35 per cent. Secondly, the settlement failed to include any discount for the storeowner's contributory negligence, which the judge assessed at 20 per cent. For both reasons, the sum paid by the architects in settlement was too high, and the engineers, if liable, would have been ordered to pay a contribution based on the lower sum which should have been paid.

---

[33] See, for an example, *J Sainsbury v Broadway Malyan* (1988) 61 Con. L.R. 31 (discussed at para.9–341, below), where Judge Lloyd Q.C. rejected a claim by negligent architects for a contribution from engineers who had failed to point out defective fire-protection on a particular girder. He held, however, that had the failure been made out, he would have found the engineers to be 12.5% to blame on the basis that the architects' failures were far more basic and widespread than the single failure by the engineers would have been.

[34] Following the procedure set out in Pt 20 of the Civil Procedure Rules.

[35] (1998) 61 Con. L.R. 31.

The settlement upon which the claim for contribution is based may not, or not   **9-342**
exclusively, have involved the claimant in making a money payment to a third
party. It has been held that a right to contribution under the 1978 Act also arises
where the party claiming contribution has agreed, as part of his settlement with
a third party, to carry out works at his own expense rather than to pay a sum of
money. In that event, the contribution ordered will be assessed by reference to the
value of those works.[36]

There is a slight divergence of view at first instance as to whether the fact that   **9-343**
a settlement was entered into on legal advice is relevant to the question of
whether that settlement is reasonable. Judge Hicks Q.C. (in *DSL Group v Unisys
International Services Ltd*)[37] and Judge Lloyd Q.C. (in *J Sainsbury Plc v
Broadway Malyan*)[38] have taken the view that it is irrelevant whilst Judge
Bowsher Q.C. (in *P & O Developments Ltd v Guy's and St Thomas' NHS Trust*)[39]
has taken the view that the existence of such advice might go to the question of
whether the settlement was reasonable one. It is clear that a claimant for
contribution to a settlement must prove that the settlement was a reasonable one
(rather than merely that it was reasonable of him to settle the claim).[40] In most
cases, this follows from the fact that an unreasonable settlement will not be a
foreseeable loss.

Costs as damage. The settlement of a claim will typically involve the payment   **9-344**
of some sum (which may or may not be separately identified) on account of the
claimant's legal costs. The question whether the paying party may recover
contribution from a third party under the Civil Liability (Contribution) Act 1978
to sums paid on account of costs was decided in *Parkman Consulting Engineers
v Cumbrian Industrials Ltd*.[41] In that case, BICC Plc engaged both Parkman
(engineers) and Cumbrian (a building contractor) to decontaminate and develop
some land, which involved making the sub-soil layers watertight. The scheme
which was designed by Parkman and built by Cumbrian for this purpose failed.
Parkman settled BICC Plc's claim for £1.95 million including unspecified sums
for statutory interest and BICC Plc's costs, and then claimed contribution under
the 1978 Act from Cumbrian. Cumbrian argued that £1.95 million should not be
the starting point for the claim against it because that sum included an element
on account of BICC Plc's legal costs which should first be deducted. Judge
Thornton Q.C. rejected this argument and the Court of Appeal upheld his
decision. It held that the judge had been entitled to regard the whole of the
settlement sum, which was admitted to be a reasonable settlement, as the basis
and starting point for the claim for contribution. It was a global settlement and,
accordingly, the entire sum paid should be regarded as paid in settlement of
Parkman's liability to BICC Plc. The Court also suggested a way to recover a
contribution to costs without invoking the 1978 Act: it held that the power of the

---

[36] *Baker & Davies Plc v Leslie Wilks Associates* [2005] EWHC 1179, TCC.
[37] (1994) 41 Con. L.R. 33 at 39–43.
[38] (1998) 61 Con. L.R. 31 at 64.
[39] (1998) 62 Con. L.R. 38 at 55.
[40] *Biggin v Permanite* [1951] 2 K.B. 314 at 326, *per* Singleton L.J.; *P & O Developments Ltd v Guy's
and St. Thomas' NHS Trust* (1998) 62 Con. L.R. 38; *Royal Brompton Hospital NHS Trust v Hammond
(No.1)* [1999] B.L.R. 162.
[41] (2001) 79 Con. L.R. 112.

court under s.51(3) of the Supreme Court Act 1981 to order the payment of costs was wide enough to allow an order that the defendant in contribution proceedings make a payment in respect of the original claimant's costs. It was irrelevant that the original claimant (BICC Plc, in this case) was not a party to the proceedings in which the court would make such an order.

9–345   **The discretion on apportionment.** The Court of Appeal recognises that the trial judge has a discretion as to apportionment with which it will not interfere unless he has misdirected himself.[42] Unless the trial judge has failed to apply the relevant tests under the Act or has exercised his discretion in an unreasonable manner, the prospects of a successful appeal against his apportionment are slender. This was emphasised in *McKenzie v Potts*.[43] Both a builder and an architect were found to be liable to a claimant under s.1 of the Defective Premises Act 1972, by reason of the use of defective backfill behind foundation walls. The builder was liable for the actual use of the materials and had misinformed the architects as to the nature of the materials. The architects were held liable for negligent supervision in that they had wrongly relied on the builder's assurance. The trial judge considered the relevant tests of causation (where he found each defendant to have been equally responsible) and relative culpability (where he found the builder to have been more responsible than the architect) in apportioning damages as to 60 per cent to the builder and 40 per cent to the architect. Although the Court of Appeal expressed sympathy for the architect, they refused to interfere with the exercise of the judge's discretion. Russell L.J. said[44]:

> "I have to say that in my view other judges may have taken a more sympathetic view of the degree of culpability on the part of the architects, but, having acknowledged that to be the position, I cannot interfere with the apportionment as made by the judge. In my view he was entitled to make it; it was within the spectrum of his discretion . . . ."

9–346   One case in which the Court of Appeal did feel able to exercise the discretion afresh is *Holland Hannen and Cubitts (Northern) Ltd v Welsh Health Technical Services Organisation*.[45] The claimant building contractor sued both the employer and a nominated sub-contractor (CED) for losses occasioned by delay. Part of the delay was the responsibility of a design fault for which CED admitted liability and part of the delay was caused by a wrongful instruction which condemned the floors. The employer brought into the action both its architects (who had issued the wrongful instruction) and its engineers (WEP). CED brought in its own engineers (AMP). Judge Newey Q.C. held that responsibility for the delay should be apportioned two-thirds to the employer's architects and engineers (WEP) and one-third to CED. As between the design team, the judge took into account that the architects should have grappled with the problem at an

---

[42] *Holland Hannen and Cubitts (Northern) Ltd v Welsh Health Technical Services Organisation* (1985) 35 B.L.R. 1, *per* Lawton L.J. at 18.
[43] (1997) 50 Con. L.R. 40, CA.
[44] *ibid.* at 42.
[45] (1985) 35 B.L.R. 1.

earlier stage than they did and apportioned blame on an equal basis. He also found that AMP were liable to CED and should bear three-quarters of the sums for which CED were liable. The Court of Appeal by a majority reversed the finding that AMP were liable at all[46] and also found unanimously that the judge had erred in the exercise of his discretion in apportioning blame as between CED and the design team as he had not taken into account in that apportionment the architect's failure to grapple with the problem at an early stage.[47] The Court of Appeal therefore exercised its own discretion and re-apportioned blame two-thirds to the design team and one-third to CED.

(b) *Contributory Negligence*

The question of apportionment of responsibility will also arise as between a   **9–347** claimant and a defendant, if the latter successfully raises a defence of contributory negligence by the claimant.[48] Following the decision of the Court of Appeal in *Forsikringsaktieselskapet Vesta v Butcher*[49] contributory negligence may be raised as a defence to certain contractual claims.[50]

It is important to distinguish the principles governing contributory negligence   **9–348** and those which apply in the apportionment of liability between several wrongdoers.[51] In *Pride Valley Foods Ltd v Hall & Partners (Contract Management) Ltd*,[52] project managers engaged by the claimant to design a bread-making factory were held liable for negligently failing to advise him that the panels which he wished to use to line the factory were highly combustible and would allow rapid spread of fire throughout the factory if ignited. It was held that any damages recoverable by the claimant for damage caused by a subsequent fire at the factory should be reduced by 50 per cent for his contributory negligence in failing to take reasonable steps to prevent a fire starting in the factory.[53] Sedley L.J. considered[54] whether the issue of contributory negligence should be

---

[46] This is discussed at para.9–213, above.
[47] *ibid.*, *per* Lawton L.J. at 18, *per* Robert Goff L.J. at 28 and, *per* Dillon L.J. at 33.
[48] Note *Kensington and Chelsea and Westminster AHA v Wettern Composites Ltd* (1984) 1 Con. L.R. 114 at 135, *per* Judge Smout Q.C.: "I have reached the conclusion that the clerk of works' negligence whilst more than minimal is very much less than that of the architects. If I may adapt the military terminology, it was the negligence of the Chief Petty Officer as compared with that of the captain of the ship. I assess responsibility as to the clerk of works 20%, as to the architects 80%. By reason of the vicarious responsibility of the claimants (for the clerk of works) I make a finding of contributory negligence of 20%".
[49] [1989] A.C. 852.
[50] See Ch.4. See also Bartlett, A. "Attribution of contributory negligence: agents, company directors and fraudsters" (1998) 114 L.Q.R. 460.
[51] See paras 9–324 to 9–350, above.
[52] (2001) 76 Con. L.R. 1 (first instance); [2001] EWCA Civ 1001; (2001) 76 Con. L.R. 1 at 36, CA.
[53] The judge at first instance held that the claimant's case failed on causation, since he failed to prove that he would have accepted the advice which he should have been given by the defendants; the Court of Appeal remitted the case to the judge for a further trial on causation, but dismissed an appeal against his finding of 50% contributory negligence.
[54] (2001) 76 Con. L.R. 1 at 59–60.

approached in the same way as the issue of apportionment of liability between defendants, and concluded that it should not. He suggested that no deduction for contributory negligence will be made where the harm caused by the claimant's own negligence is wholly within the very risk which it was the defendants' duty to guard him against. In that case it was arguable that the claimant's neglect had such catastrophic consequences only because of the defendants' breach of their duty to guard against precisely those consequences. For that reason, Sedley L.J. would have deducted no more than one-third of the claimant's damages for contributory negligence but he, along with Brooke and Dyson L.JJ., declined to interfere with the exercise of the trial judge's discretion on this point.

9–349   The approach suggested by Sedley L.J. in *Pride Valley Foods Ltd v Hall & Partners (Contract Management) Ltd* was applied at first instance in *Sahib Foods Ltd v Paskin Kyriades Sands*.[55] A fire in a food production factory started because of negligence on the part of the claimant leaseholder's employees. It spread beyond the room in which it started because combustible panels had been used to line that room. The use of those panels was the result of negligent design by the defendant architects. Judge Bowsher Q.C. held that there was no contributory negligence by the leaseholder so far as its loss attributable to spread of the fire beyond the combustible panels was concerned, since the risk that fire would not be contained by the panels was the very risk against which the architects had a duty to guard in formulating their design. The correct analysis, the judge held, was that the parties were respectively responsible for two distinct elements of the claimants' loss: the leaseholder for loss caused by the fire inside the panels and the architects for loss caused by spread of the fire beyond the panels. The leaseholder's damages would be assessed as its entire loss as a result of the fire less the loss which it would have suffered had the fire been contained in the room in which it started (as would have been the case but for the architects' negligent choice of combustible panels).

9–350   The Court of Appeal reversed this part of the judge's decision.[56] It was held that the leaseholder was partly responsible for spread of the fire beyond the room where it started, because it had misinformed the architects as to the use to which the room would be put and that misinformation had contributed to the architects' decision to use combustible panels. Further, it was held that the judge ought to have adopted the conventional approach to contributory negligence and made a percentage deduction from the leaseholder's entire loss to reflect its contributory negligence in relation to both start and spread of the fire. Considering the analysis suggested by Sedley L.J. in *Pride Valley Foods Ltd v Hall & Partners (Contract Management) Ltd*, the Court of Appeal commented that a claimant may be guilty of contributory negligence even if the defendant in breach of duty has failed to protect the claimant against the very damage which it was employed to guard against. Only in a case where the whole of the responsibility for the damage was the defendant's failure to protect the claimant against his own negligence would it be appropriate not to hold the claimant guilty of contributory negligence. It is

---

[55] [2003] EWHC 142, TCC.
[56] [2003] EWCA Civ 1832. For a discussion of this case, see T. Dudgale, "Out of the frying pan, into the fire: how much was the cook to blame?" (2004) P.N. 113.

a matter of fact in each case: it may or may not be reasonable of the claimant to rely entirely upon the defendant rather than in part upon his own efforts to protect his person or property.[57]

6. ADJUDICATION

Part II of the Housing Grants, Construction and Regeneration Act 1996, which came into force on May 1, 1998,[58] introduced of new form of dispute resolution which applies only to the construction industry. Under s.108(1) of the Act, a party to a construction contract has the right to refer any dispute arising under the contract to adjudication. When that right is exercised, the other party to the contract must submit to adjudication. The decision of the adjudicator is final and binding if the contract so provides, but otherwise is binding only until the dispute is finally determined by legal proceedings, by arbitration (if the contract contains an arbitration agreement or the parties otherwise agree to arbitration) or by settlement of the dispute.[59]   **9–351**

Section 108(1)–(4) of the Act sets out a procedure for adjudication and requires that construction contracts include express terms which incorporate that procedure. In the absence of such express terms, a statutory scheme (the Scheme for Construction Contracts)[60] is implied into the contract.   **9–352**

Construction contracts. The Act applies to all "construction contracts" made after May 1, 1998.[61] This term is very widely defined. Section 104(1) provides that a construction contract is an agreement with a person for carrying out "construction operations" or arranging for them to be carried out by others by way of sub-contract or otherwise, providing his own or other labour to carry them out. Most importantly for present purposes, s.104(2) includes within the definition any agreement for the provision of advisory services whether architectural, design, surveying, building, engineering, interior or exterior decoration and landscaping. It follows that most engagements of construction professionals made after May 1, 1998 will be construction contracts under the Act, provided only that the project in connection with which the professional is retained is   **9–353**

---

[57] The position is the same in Australia: see *Astley v Austrust Ltd* [1999] H.C.A. 6 (High Court of Australia).

[58] Housing Grants, Construction and Regeneration Act (England and Wales) (Commencement No.4) Order 1998 (SI 1998/650).

[59] s.108(3). The parties by agreement can extend the scope of adjudication, but they cannot contract out of it: *RG Carter Ltd v Edmund Nuttall Ltd*, unreported, June 21, 2000, Judge Thornton Q.C.

[60] SI 1998/649.

[61] s.104(6)(a). Where novation of a contract takes place after May 1, 1998, the novation agreement may itself be a construction contract within the meaning of s.104. If the novated contract was made before May 1, 1998, the curious result will be that the parties have a right to refer to adjudication disputes which arose before the Act came into effect. In *Yarm Road Ltd v Costain Ltd*, unreported, July 30, 2001, Judge Havery Q.C. recognised that this construction of the Act created anomalies but regarded it as inescapable.

within the definition of "construction operations." Thus a professional engagement to administer a building contract was held to be a construction contract in *Gillies Ramsay Diamond v PJW Enterprises Ltd.*[62]

9–354   The Act applies only to agreements in writing, but the definition of writing in s.107 includes agreements which are merely evidenced in writing,[63] where the agreement refers to a document[64] or where there is merely an audio or visual record of the agreement.[65]

9–355   **Construction operations.** This term is also widely defined,[66] so that it will apply to most construction and engineering contracts and to most related contracts for professional services. There are exceptions,[67] notable amongst which are pure supply contracts, extraction and drilling for minerals, oil or natural gas, activities concerned with sites occupied primarily with the nuclear, power, water, sewage, chemical, pharmaceutical, oil, gas, steel and food industries, the making, installation and repair of artistic works, concession agreements for private finance initiative projects and the off site construction of building components, materials, plant and machinery unless the contract is also for their installation. A further important exception is made by s.106 of the Act, which excludes from the scope of the statutory adjudication scheme a construction contract with a residential occupier which principally relates to operations on a private dwelling-house or flat.

9–356   **The timetable.** The purpose of adjudication is to achieve early and swift resolution of disputes, albeit provisional resolution, so as to avoid construction projects being interrupted for long periods while disputing parties arbitrate or

---

[62] [2003] B.L.R. 58 (Sc. Ct. Sess. OH). Lady Paton rejected the argument that issues of professional negligence were not within the scope of adjudication under the Act but recognised that, " . . . it may on one view seem startling that a professional person acting as an Adjudicator should be invited to rule within 28 days on the important and often difficult and delicate question as to whether a fellow-professional has failed in his or her duty to such an extent that there has been professional negligence . . . ". A reclaiming motion was refused by the Inner House: [2004] B.L.R. 131.

[63] See s.107(2). In *RJT Consulting Engineers Ltd v DM Engineering Ltd* [2002] EWCA Civ 270; [2002] 1 W.L.R. 2344, a majority in the Court of Appeal held that the whole agreement had to be evidenced in writing. Written evidence of the existence (as opposed to the terms) of the agreement would not suffice. Nor would written evidence of only some of the terms, even if those terms (e.g. as to the identity of the parties, the scope of the works or the price) formed the substance of the agreement. This decision was followed in *Carillion Construction Ltd v Devonport Royal Dockyard* [2003] B.L.R. 79 (an oral agreement to vary the payment terms of a written contract was not a construction contract).

[64] See s.107(3). In *Total M and E Services Ltd v ABB Building Technologies Ltd* [2002] EWHC 248, TCC, it was held that orally agreed variations to the scope of works under a building contract referred to the written terms of the building contract for this purpose.

[65] See s.107(4) (an agreement is evidenced in writing if it is recorded by one of the parties, or by a third party, with the authority of the parties to the agreement) and s.107(5) (a purely oral agreement may be treated as in writing if reference is made to it in written submissions in adjudication, arbitral or judicial proceedings). In *Connex South Eastern Ltd v M J Building Services Group Plc* [2004] EWHC 1518, TCC, a contractor's tender was accepted by an oral instruction to proceed with the works which was given at a meeting. That instruction was recorded in the minutes of the meeting, which were written with the parties' authority. It was held that this was sufficient to evidence the contract in writing within the meaning of s.107. This part of the decision was not challenged on appeal: [2005] EWCA Civ 193.

[66] See s.105.

[67] See s.105(2). For examples, see the cases cited at para.9–362, fn.83, below.

---

litigate their differences. To this end, the Act permits a notice of referral to be served at any time[68] and requires[69] a timetable which enables the adjudicator to be appointed and the dispute referred to him within seven days of such notice. Thereafter, the adjudicator must reach his decision within 28 days, although the parties can agree a longer period and the adjudicator can extend the time by 14 days with the agreement of the referring party. The adjudicator is entitled to take the initiative in ascertaining the facts and law which are relevant in deciding the dispute. It will be immediately apparent that while adjudication is likely to serve a useful purpose in dealing with relatively straightforward disputes which might otherwise cause severe disruption to a project, such as some disputes as to payment between the parties to a building contract, its suitability as a means of resolving complex building contract disputes and professional negligence claims is questionable. In practice, the client is able to spend many months preparing his claim, possibly with the assistance of independent experts, before serving a notice of referral upon the construction professional. The professional will then have something in the order of a fortnight to prepare and present his defence before the adjudicator makes his decision.

Enforcement of adjudicator's decisions. The court has power to enforce an   **9–357** adjudicator's decision under s.42 of the Arbitration Act 1996.[70] The usual method of enforcement is by way of an order for summary judgment upon the application of the party in whose favour the decision was made, although where the decision requires a party to perform some obligation other than making a payment, a mandatory injunction will be available.

---

[68] This provision cannot be avoided by agreement: see *Midland Expressway Ltd v Carillion Construction Ltd (No.2)* [2005] EWHC 2963, TCC. Note that adjudication provisions, like arbitration agreements, survive the determination of the contract: *A Maintenance and Construction Ltd v Pagehurst Construction Services Ltd* (2000) 16 Const. L.J. 199. A reference to adjudication will be valid even after court proceedings have begun: *Herschel Engineering Ltd v Breen Property Ltd* [2000] B.L.R. 272. In *Connex South Eastern Ltd v M J Building Services Group Plc* [2004] EWHC 1518, TCC, it was held that an adjudication provision survived even the discharge of a contract by acceptance of a repudiatory breach. This part of the decision was not challenged on the appeal which, however, confirmed that there is no time limit for referring a dispute to adjudication: [2005] EWCA Civ 193; [2005] 1 W.L.R. 3323.

[69] s.104(2). In an article, "Adjudicators' Time Defaults" (2001) 17 Const. L.J. 371, David Blunt Q.C. notes that neither the Act nor the Scheme for Construction Contracts provides for the consequences in law when an adjudicator fails either to reach or to deliver his decision within the statutory time limits and considers what those consequences might be. See also para.9–362, below.

[70] *Macob Civil Engineering Ltd v Morrison Construction Ltd* [1999] B.L.R. 93; *Outwing Construction Ltd v H Randall & Son Ltd* [1999] B.L.R. 156. It will also create a debt which can be the subject of a statutory demand: *George Parke v The Fenton Gretton Partnership* [2001] C.I.L.L. 1712. The juridical basis for the enforcement of adjudicators' decisions was considered further in *David McLean Housing Contractors Ltd v Swansea Housing Association Ltd* [2002] B.L.R. 125, where Judge Lloyd Q.C. preferred to say that the cause of action enforced is not a debt created by the parties' agreement in their construction contract to be bound by the adjudicator's decision but, rather, the cause of action which underlay the dispute decided by the adjudicator. This remains the minority view at first instance, however. The more common view is that there is an express contractual agreement to be bound by the adjudicator's decision: see *VHE Construction Plc v RBSTB Trust Ltd* [2000] B.L.R. 187 (Judge Hicks Q.C.); *Bovis Lend Lease Ltd v Triangle Development Ltd* [2002] EWHC 3123, TCC (Judge Thornton Q.C.) and, in Scotland, *Construction Group Centre Ltd v The Highland Council* [2002] B.L.R. 476 (Lord MacFadyen).

9–358   **Challenging the adjudicator's decision.** During the relatively short time in which the Act has been in force, there has accumulated a large body of case law dealing with the extent to which it is possible to resist the enforcement of an adjudicator's decision. It is clear that the courts will enforce the decisions of adjudicators save where such decisions are made without jurisdiction. In *Bouygues UK Ltd v Dahl-Jensen UK Ltd*,[71] the adjudicator had made an obvious error in his calculations which meant that his decision was in favour of the claimant. It was common ground that, but for the error, the decision would have been in favour of the defendant. Nevertheless, the claimant obtained an order for summary judgment based on the decision. Dyson J., whose decision and reasoning were upheld by the Court of Appeal,[72] explained[73]:

> "the purpose of the scheme is to provide a speedy mechanism for settling disputes in construction contracts on a provisional interim basis, and requiring the decisions of adjudicators to be enforced pending final determination of disputes by arbitration, litigation or agreement, whether those decisions are wrong in point of law or fact. Sometimes those mistakes will be glaringly obvious and disastrous in their consequences for the losing party. The victims of mistakes will usually be able to recoup their losses by subsequent arbitration or litigation, and possibly even by a subsequent adjudication. Sometimes, they will not be able to do so, where, for example, there is intervening insolvency, either of the victim or of the fortunate beneficiary of the mistake. . . . But in deciding whether the adjudicator has decided the wrong question rather than given a wrong answer to the right question, the court should bear in mind that the speedy nature of the adjudication process means that mistakes will inevitably occur, and, in my view, it should guard against characterising a mistaken answer to an issue that lies within the scope of the reference as an excess of jurisdiction."

9–359   In *Sherwood and Casson Ltd v Mackenzie*,[74] Judge Thornton Q.C. summarised in five guidelines the approach which the court will take to enforcement of an adjudicator's decision:

---

[71] [2000] B.L.R. 49 (first instance).
[72] [2000] B.L.R. 522, CA.
[73] [2000] B.L.R. 49 at 55.
[74] Unreported, November 30, 1999, applied by Judge Bowsher Q.C. in *Northern Developments (Cumbria) Ltd v J & J Nichol* [2000] B.L.R. 158 at 162–163. Note also that, in an appropriate case, the court will sever and enforce those parts of his decision which the adjudicator did have jurisdiction to make: *Workplace Technologies Ltd v E Squared Ltd* [2000] C.I.L.L. 1607. For a further case where the court granted only partial enforcement of an adjudicator's decision, see *Griffin v Midas Homes Ltd* (2000) 78 Con. L.R. 152 (some of the disputes decided by the adjudicator were not properly identified in the notice of adjudication and others had not arisen at the date of his decision). However, partial enforcement will be possible only where it is possible to distinguish between several disputes decided by the same adjudicator. It is not open to a party to accept only part of an adjudicator's decision on a *single dispute*: see *K.N.S. Industrial Services (Birmingham) Ltd v Sindall Ltd* (2000) 75 Con. L.R. 71; and *Shimizu Europe Ltd v Automajor Ltd* [2002] EWHC 103, TCC. The particular terms of the construction contract may allow the unsuccessful party in the adjudication to set off against the sum due from him under the adjudicator's decision some other claim which was not determined by the adjudicator: see, for example, the Court of Appeal's decision in *Parsons Plastics (Research and Development) Ltd v Purac Ltd* [2002] EWCA Civ 459. But where such other claim is regulated by the payment provisions of the Act and the defendant has failed to comply with those provisions, set off will not be permitted: see, for example, *Solland International Ltd v Daraydan Holdings Ltd* [2002] EWHC 220, TCC; *cf. Shimizu Europe Ltd v LBJ Fabrications Ltd* [2003] EWHC 1229, TCC; and *Conor Engineering Ltd v Les Constructions Industrielles de la Mediterranee* [2004] EWHC 899. Similarly, set off between sums awarded in different adjudications was not permitted in *Interserve Industrial Services Ltd v Cleveland Bridge UK Ltd* [2006] EWHC 741, TCC. In *Ferson*

(1) A decision of an adjudicator whose validity is challenged as to its factual or legal conclusions or as to procedural error remains a decision that is both enforceable and should be enforced.

(2) A decision that is erroneous, even if the error is disclosed by the reasons, will still not ordinarily be capable of being challenged and should, ordinarily, still be enforced.

(3) A decision may be challenged on the ground that the adjudicator was not empowered by the 1996 Act to make that decision, because there was no underlying construction contract between the parties or because he had gone outside his terms of reference.

(4) The adjudication is intended to be a speedy process in which mistakes will inevitably occur. Thus, the court should guard against characterising a mistaken answer to an issue, which is within an adjudicator's jurisdiction, as being an excess of jurisdiction. Furthermore, the court should give a fair, natural and sensible interpretation to the decision in the light of the disputes that are the subject of the reference.

(5) An issue as to whether a construction contract ever came into existence, which is one challenging the jurisdiction of the adjudicator, so long as it is reasonably and clearly raised, must be determine by the Court on the balance of probabilities with, if necessary, oral evidence.

Those principles were approved by the Court of Appeal in *C& B Scene Concept Design Ltd v Isobars Ltd.*[75] The adjudicator decided in favour of the claimant's

---

Contractors Ltd v Levolux A T Ltd [2003] EWCA Civ 11, the Court of Appeal held that the particular terms of the contract did not permit an unsuccessful party in an adjudication to set off other contractual claims against the adjudicator's award and said, further, that where contractual provisions cannot be construed so as to give effect to the adjudication scheme required by the Act, such provisions will be struck out of the contract. In *Pegram Shopfitters Ltd v Tally Wiejl (UK) Ltd* [2003] EWCA Civ 1750; [2004] 1 W.L.R. 2082, May L.J.'s judgment contains a reminder that the Court's approach will normally be to enforce adjudicators' decisions in recognition of the policy of the legislation, although there will be cases "when legal principle has to prevail over broad brush policy" (at para.[9]).

[75] [2002] B.L.R. 93. Thus in *Gillies Ramsay Diamond v PJW Enterprises Ltd* [2003] B.L.R. 48 (Sc. Ct. Sess. OH), Lady Paton held that an adjudicator's decision awarding damages for professional negligence by a contract administrator was not justified on the material before him, but that his errors were within his jurisdiction and so his decision was enforceable. A reclaiming motion was refused by the Inner House: [2004] B.L.R. 131. In *Joinery Plus Ltd (in Administration) v Laing Ltd* [2003] EWHC 213, TCC, Judge Thornton Q.C. distinguished the decision in *C & B Scene Concept Design Ltd v Isobars Ltd* to find that an adjudicator who decided the dispute by reference to the wrong contract terms (as opposed to the wrong construction of the right terms) lacked jurisdiction. Similarly, in *Galliford Try Construction Ltd v Michael Heal Associates Ltd* [2003] EWHC 2886, TCC, an adjudicator's decision which was based on an erroneous conclusion that there was a contract between the parties was not enforced. Since the statutory regime of adjudication does not apply unless there is a (written) contract between the parties, the adjudicator had lacked jurisdiction. For the same reasons, an adjudicator's erroneous decision that there was a written contract between the parties led to refusal to enforce his decision in *Thomas-Fredric's (Construction) Ltd v Keith Wilson* [2003] EWCA Civ 1494 and in *Redworth Construction Ltd v Brookdale Healthcare Ltd* [2006] EWHC 1994, TCC.

claims to interim payments on the grounds that, under the contract, the defendant's failure to give notice of non-payment meant that it had no defence to the claims. The defendant sought to resist enforcement of this decision on the basis that the adjudicator had failed to appreciate that the Act operated to replace the relevant contract terms with the terms of the Scheme for Construction Contracts. It followed, argued the defendant, that the adjudicator had addressed himself to the wrong question and so exceeded his jurisdiction. The challenge succeeded at first instance but failed on appeal. It was held that the adjudicator had indeed mistaken the effect of the Act, but that this was an error of law which did not go to his jurisdiction. The Court of Appeal emphasised that an error of law, unless it be as to the scope of the dispute referred, does not take the adjudicator outside his jurisdiction. Stuart-Smith L.J., with whom Rix and Potter L.JJ. agreed, said[76]:

> "It is important that the enforcement of an adjudicator's decision by summary judgment should not be prevented by arguments that the adjudicator has made errors of law in reaching his decision, unless the adjudicator has purported to decide matters that are not referred to him. He must decide as a matter of construction of the referral, and therefore as a matter of law, what the dispute is that he has to decide. If he erroneously decides that the dispute referred to him is wider than it is, then, in so far as he has exceeded his jurisdiction, his decision cannot be enforced. But in the present case there was entire agreement as to the scope of the dispute, and the Adjudicator's decision, albeit he may have made errors of law as to the relevant contractual provisions, is still binding and enforceable until the matter is corrected in the final determination."

9–360   It is plain that the court will only rarely refuse to enforce an adjudicator's decision. In *Carillion Construction Ltd v Devonport Royal Dockyard Ltd*,[77] Chadwick L.J. (giving the judgment of the Court of Appeal) said[78]:

> " The objective which underlies the Act and the statutory scheme requires the courts to respect and enforce the adjudicator's decision unless it is plain that the question which he has decided was not the question referred to him or the manner in which he has gone about his task is obviously unfair. It should be only in rare circumstances that the courts will interfere with the decision of an adjudicator. . . .   In short, in the overwhelming majority of cases, the proper course for the party who is unsuccessful in an adjudication under the scheme must be to pay the amount that he has been ordered to pay by the adjudicator. If he does not accept the adjudicator's decision as correct (whether on the facts or in law), he can take legal or arbitration proceedings in order to establish the true position. To seek to challenge the adjudicator's decision on the ground that he has exceeded his jurisdiction or breached the rules of natural justice (save in the plainest cases) is likely to lead to a substantial waste of time and expense . . . ."

9–361   **The adjudicator's jurisdiction.** An adjudicator does not have jurisdiction to decide his own jurisdiction, unless the parties confer that jurisdiction upon him.[79]

---

[76] At para.[30].
[77] [2005] EWCA Civ 1358; followed in *Kier Regional Limited v City & General (Holborn) Ltd* [2006] EWHC 848, TCC.
[78] *ibid.* at paras [85] and [87].
[79] *Palmers Ltd v ABB Power Construction Ltd* [1999] B.L.R. 426; *Christiani and Nielsen Ltd v Lowry Centre Development Co Ltd*, unreported, June 29, 2000, Judge Thornton Q.C.; *Whiteways Contractors (Sussex) Ltd v Impresa Castelli Construction UK Ltd* (2000) 75 Con. L.R. 92; *Maymac Environmental Services Ltd v Faraday Building Services Ltd* (2000) 75 Con. L.R. 101. The parties

In *Fastrack Contractors Ltd v Morrison Construction Ltd*,[80] Judge Thornton Q.C. explained that there are four options available to a party who wishes to challenge the jurisdiction of an adjudicator:

"If a party challenges the entire jurisdiction of the adjudicator . . . it has four options. Firstly, it can agree to widen the jurisdiction of the adjudicator so as to refer the dispute as to the adjudicator's jurisdiction to the same adjudicator. If the referring party agrees to that course, and the appointed adjudicator accepts the reference to him of this second dispute, the jurisdiction of the adjudicator could then be resolved as part of the reference. The challenging party could, secondly, refer the dispute as to jurisdiction to second adjudicator. This would not put a halt to the first adjudication, if that had already led to an appointment, since the adjudicator has a statutory duty, unless both parties agree otherwise, to decide the reference in a very short timescale. The challenging party could, thirdly, seek a declaration from the court that the proposed adjudication lacked jurisdiction. This option is of little utility unless the adjudicator has yet to be appointed or the parties agree to put the adjudication into abeyance pending the relatively speedy determination of the jurisdiction question by the court. The Technology and Construction Court can, for example, resolve questions of that kind within days of them being referred to it. Fourthly, the challenging party could reserve its position, participate in the

---

may confer jurisdiction upon an adjudicator in various ways. At the time when they make their construction contract, they may adopt procedural rules for adjudication which expressly confer upon the adjudicator the power to decide his own jurisdiction: see, for example, *Farebrother Building Services Ltd v Frogmore Investments Ltd* [2001] C.I.L.L. 1762. Alternatively, at the time of the adjudication they may reach an express or implied ad hoc agreement that the adjudicator shall have such power: see, for example, *Nordot Engineering Services Ltd v Siemens Plc* [2001] C.I.L.L. 1778. An estoppel by convention may arise to prevent one or other party from denying that the adjudicator had jurisdiction: see *Oakley v Airclear Environmental Ltd* [2002] C.I.L.L. 1824 (where, however, no estoppel was found on the facts). A party which participates in an adjudication without expressing its objection to the jurisdiction of the adjudicator is likely to be held to have submitted to that jurisdiction: see, for example, *Cowlin Construction Ltd v CFW Architects* [2003] B.L.R. 241. In *Thomas-Fredric's (Construction) Ltd v Keith Wilson* [2003] EWCA Civ 1494, the Court of Appeal enunciated the following principles: (1) if the defendant has submitted to the adjudicator's jurisdiction in the full sense of having agreed not only that the adjudicator should rule on the issue of his own jurisdiction but also that he would then be bound by that ruling, then he is liable to enforcement even if the adjudicator's decision on jurisdiction is plainly wrong; (2) even if the defendant has not submitted to the adjudicator's jurisdiction in that sense, he still liable to enforcement if the adjudicator's decision on jurisdiction was plainly right. On appeal in *Pegram Shopfitters Ltd v Tally Wiejl (UK) Ltd* [2003] EWCA Civ 1750, it was held that the defendant had advanced its argument that the adjudicator lacked jurisdiction in the adjudication and so was not estopped from taking the same point in subsequent enforcement proceedings. By contrast, in *Shimizu Europe Ltd v Automajor Ltd* [2002] EWHC 103, TCC, Judge Seymour Q.C. remarked obiter that by paying part of the sum which the adjudicator had decided was due from it to the claimant and by asking the adjudicator to make a correction to his decision under the slip rule, the defendant had elected to treat the entire decision as made within the adjudicator's jurisdiction. Remarks to similar effect had been made in *K.N.S. Industrial Services (Birmingham) Ltd v Sindall Ltd* (2000) 75 Con. L.R. 71; and in *Farebrother Building Services Ltd v Frogmore Investments Ltd* (above). No such election occurred in *Joinery Plus Ltd (In Administration) v Laing Ltd* [2003] EWHC 213, TCC; where a party which was partly successful in an adjudication was not estopped from challenging the adjudicator's jurisdiction as to the balance of the decision by its conduct in banking a cheque sent in compliance with the decision: it made clear before doing so that the adjudicator's jurisdiction was disputed. Moreover, as Judge Seymour Q.C. emphasised in *R. Durtnell & Sons Ltd v Kaduna Ltd* [2003] EWHC 517, TCC, a party will not be held to have submitted to the adjudicator's jurisdiction unless he knew of the matters which meant that the adjudicator lacked jurisdiction.

[80] [2000] B.L.R. 168 at 178.

adjudication and then challenge any attempt to enforce the adjudicator's decision on jurisdictional grounds."

The court will not grant an interim injunction restraining an adjudication[81]; if a party wishes to challenge the adjudicator's jurisdiction before he reaches his decision, it must take the third option described by Judge Thornton Q.C. and claim a declaration or a final injunction using the procedure in Pt 7 of the Civil Procedure Rules.

9–362　　Successful challenges to the jurisdiction of an adjudicator have been made on the grounds that there was no dispute between the parties at the time of the notice of referral to adjudication[82]; that, in a case where the Scheme applied, the notice purported to refer more than one dispute for adjudication[83]; that the contract under which the dispute arose was not a construction contract within the meaning

---

[81] *Workplace Technologies Ltd v E Squared Ltd* [2000] C.I.L.L. 1607.

[82] *Fastrack Contractors Ltd v Morrison Construction Ltd* [2000] B.L.R. 168; *Shepherd Construction Ltd v Mecright Ltd* [2000] B.L.R. 489. The question whether and when a dispute can be said to exist for the purposes of adjudication has been considered in several cases. In *Sindall Ltd v Solland* (2001) 80 Con. L.R. 152, Judge Lloyd Q.C. said that for a dispute to exist, it must be clear that a point has emerged in the process of discussion or negotiation between the parties which needs to be decided. In *Watkin Jones & Son Ltd v Lidl UK GmbH* [2002] EWHC 183, TCC, Judge Moseley Q.C. regarded himself as bound by the decision of the Court of Appeal in *Halki Shipping Corp v Sopex Oils Ltd* [1998] 1 W.L.R. 726, a decision on when a dispute can be said to exist for the purposes of arbitration, to hold that a dispute may arise in the absence of a positive rejection of the claim or a refusal to meet it. A passive failure to admit a claim will suffice in certain circumstances. Forbes J. took the same approach in *Beck Peppiatt Ltd v Norwest Holst Construction Ltd* [2003] EWHC 822, TCC, as did Judge. Bowsher Q.C. in *Carillion Construction Ltd v Devonport Royal Dockyard* [2003] B.L.R. 79; and Judge Kirkham in *Cowlin Construction Ltd v CFW Architects* [2003] B.L.R. 241 and in *Orange EBS Ltd v ABB Ltd* [2003] B.L.R. 326; and the Court of Appeal in *Amec Capital Projects Ltd v Whitefriars City Estates Ltd* [2004] EWCA Civ 1418; and in *Collins (Contractors) Ltd v Baltic Quay Management (1994) Ltd* [2004] EWCA Civ 1757. In *CIB Properties Ltd v Birse Construction Ltd* [2004] EWHC 2365, TCC, Judge Toulmin C.M.G. Q.C. observed that tactical prolongation of discussions will not prevent a dispute arising: the question is whether the dispute has crystallised. The grounds for the claim must be adequately communicated to the defendant before a dispute can be said to have arisen, however, and any fundamental alteration to those grounds may result in a finding that the dispute ultimately decided by the adjudicator did not exist at the time of the referral to adjudication: *Edmund Nuttall Ltd v RG Carter Ltd* [2002] EWHC 400, TCC. In that case, Judge Seymour Q.C. refused to enforce the adjudicator's decision on the grounds that the claimant, after starting the adjudication, had abandoned wholesale the facts and arguments upon which it had previously relied in support of its claim to an extension of time and submitted new facts and arguments to the adjudicator, albeit in support of a claim to the same extension of time. The result was that the adjudicator decided a dispute which was different to that which existed at the time of the referral and which, therefore, he had no jurisdiction to decide. If correct, this decision means that a party wishing to refer a claim to adjudication must first make sure that the other party has been given full information and an adequate opportunity to answer the claim. As such, it should reduce the ability of a claiming party to use adjudication to "ambush" the other party to the contract. On the other hand, the decision significantly widens the scope for jurisdictional challenge to adjudicators' decisions. In many cases, the difference between (a) the refinement of a party's arguments and the abandonment by it of unmeritorious points after the referral to adjudication (both processes which are to be encouraged) and (b) the abandonment of facts and arguments originally relied upon to such a degree that the nature of the dispute is altered, may not be at all obvious. No dispute capable of reference to adjudication will exist, of course, if the same claim has been determined in a previous adjudication: *Watkin Jones & Son Ltd v Lidl UK GmbH (No.2)* [2002] EWHC 183, TCC.

[83] *Fastrack Contractors Ltd v Morrison Construction Ltd* [2000] B.L.R. 168; *Grovedeck Ltd v Capital Demolition Ltd* [2000] B.L.R. 181.

of the Act because it was not a contract for "construction operations"[84] or because it was concluded before May 1, 1998[85]; that the adjudicator's decision went beyond the bounds of the dispute referred to him.[86] An adjudicator who fails to decide the dispute referred to him commits an error of jurisdiction and any award which he makes will be a nullity.[87]

Finally, the failure by an adjudicator or by a party to the adjudication to comply with the procedural rules governing the adjudication process may deprive **9–363**

---

[84] *ABB Power Construction Ltd v Norwest Holst Engineering Ltd* (2001) 17 Const. L.J. 246; *Gibson & Lea Retail Interiors Ltd v Makro Self Service Wholesalers Ltd* [2001] B.L.R. 407; *cf. ABB Zantingh v Zedal Building Services* [2001] B.L.R. 66; *Palmers Ltd v ABB Power Construction* [1999] B.L.R. 426; and *Nottingham Community Housing Association Ltd v Powerminster Ltd* [2000] B.L.R. 309. For further examples of contracts held not to be for "construction operations", see *Mitsui Babcock Energy Services Ltd v Foster Wheeler Energia OY* 2001 S.L.T. 1158 (installation of boilers held to be an activity concerned with a site occupied primarily with oil and chemicals processing, exempted by s.105(2)(c)(ii) of the Act); and *Fence Gate Ltd v James R Knowles Ltd* (2001) 82 Con. L.R. 41 (a dispute over fees for litigation support services provided by architects and surveyors was not a dispute "in relation to construction operations", even although the litigation in question concerned such a dispute).

[85] *The Project Consultancy Group v The Trustees of the Gray Trust* [1999] B.L.R. 377; *cf. Atlas Ceiling and Partition Co Ltd v Crowngate Estates (Cheltenham) Ltd* (2002) 18 Const. L.J. 49; and *Christiani and Nielsen Ltd v Lowry Centre Development Co Ltd* [2005] T.C.L.R. 2.

[86] *FW Cook Ltd v Shimizu (UK) Ltd* [2000] B.L.R. 199. For further cases where decisions were not enforced because they were made outside the scope of the dispute referred to the adjudicator, see *Dean & Dyball Construction Ltd v Kenneth Grubb Associates Ltd* [2003] EWHC 2465, TCC; and *McAlpine PPS Pipeline Systems Ltd v Transco Plc* [2004] EWHC 2030, TCC.

[87] See, for examples, *Ballast Plc v The Burrell Company (Construction Management) Ltd* [2001] B.L.R. 529, Sc. Ct. Sess.; *Dean & Dyball Construction Ltd v Kenneth Grubb Associates Ltd* [2003] EWHC 2465, TCC and *McAlpine PPS Pipeline Systems Ltd v Transco Plc* [2004] EWHC 2030, TCC. There must be a failure to decide the entire dispute; the mere failure to consider a submission made by one or other party will not normally amount to an error of jurisdiction (although a serious failure of this sort may amount to a breach of the rules of natural justice so as to take the adjudicator outside his jurisdiction: see para.9–364). In *SL Timber Systems Ltd v Carillion Construction Ltd* [2001] B.L.R. 516, the adjudicator awarded payments to the pursuer purely on the grounds that the defender had failed, contrary to section 110 of the Act, to serve withholding notices in respect of those payments. The adjudicator decided that this was sufficient to entitle the pursuer to payment and that it did not have to establish any entitlement under the contract. The Court of Session accepted the defender's argument that the adjudicator's approach was wrong in law, but rejected its contention that this error had led the adjudicator to exceed his jurisdiction by declining to decide a dispute which was properly before him. It was simply an error of law as to the terms of the contract. In accordance with the decision of the Court of Appeal in *Bouygues UK Ltd v Dahl-Jensen UK Ltd* (for which, see para.9–358, above); it was an error within his jurisdiction. (For further discussion of *SL Timber Systems Ltd v Carillion Construction Ltd*, see the article by I.N.D. Wallace Q.C., "The HGCRA: A Critical Lacuna?" (2002) 18 Const. L.J. 117). Similarly, an adjudicator's error as to whether the Act operated to imply an entitlement to stage payments into a construction contract was merely an error of law as to the terms of the contract and did not go to the adjudicator's jurisdiction: see *C & B Scene Concept Design Ltd v Isobars Ltd* [2002] B.L.R. 93 (discussed at para.9–359, above) and *Tim Butler Contractors Ltd v Merewood Homes Ltd* (2002) 18 Const. L.J. 74; *cf. Barr Ltd v Law Mining Ltd* (2001) 80 Con. L.R. 134, Sc. Ct. Sess. Errors of law by the adjudicator did not prevent the enforcement of his decisions in *William Verry Ltd v North West London Communal Mikvah* [2004] EWHC 1300, TCC; and in *London & Amsterdam Properties Ltd v Waterman Partnership Ltd* (2003) EWHC 3059, TCC. The latter was a dispute arising out of allegations of professional negligence against structural engineers. Judge Wilcox held that it was strongly arguable that the adjudicator had failed properly to address the issue of professional negligence, but that this was an error of law which was within his jurisdiction.

the adjudicator of jurisdiction so that his decision will not be enforced.[88] In two cases, however, it has been held that an adjudicator's failure to issue his decision within the time period stipulated by the statutory scheme did not render his decision unenforceable.[89]

9–364 **Natural justice.** Where the statutory timetable for adjudication means that a construction professional is unable properly to prepare and present his defence to a client's claim, he may be able to resist enforcement of the adjudicator's decision if he can show that this amounted to a serious breach of the rules of natural justice. In *Amec Capital Projects Ltd v Whitefriars City Estates Ltd*,[90] the Court of Appeal confirmed that the rules of natural justice apply fully to the adjudicator's handling of the matters which he is empowered to determine. The decision also confirms that the relevant test for bias in this context is whether a fair-minded and informed observer, having considered all the circumstances which have a bearing on the suggestion that the decision-maker was biased, would conclude that there was a real possibility that he was biased. In that case, a challenge on grounds that there was a real possibility of bias on the part of the adjudicator succeeded at first instance, but failed on appeal.

9–365 Although mere procedural errors will not invalidate a decision,[91] conduct which seriously endangers the fair resolution of the dispute may well do so. The court has refused to enforce the decision of an adjudicator where: the decision was been reached after the adjudicator had discussed the substantive issues in the dispute during private telephone conversations with one of the parties, without recording the conversations or communicating their substance to the other party[92]; the adjudicator held discussions with third parties without informing the parties to the adjudication or allowing them an opportunity to comment on the information obtained[93]; the adjudicator became involved in without prejudice

---

[88] See, for example, *IDE Contracting Ltd v RG Carter Cambridge Ltd* [2004] B.L.R. 172. On the need for the referral notice to be served in time, see *William Verry Ltd v North West London Communal Mikvah* [2004] EWHC 1300, TCC. On the need to follow the contractual procedure for nomination of an adjudicator, see *Palmac Contracting Ltd v Park Lane Estates Ltd* [2005] EWHC 919, TCC. On the effect of para.9(2) of the Scheme, which prohibits an adjudicator from deciding a dispute which is the same or substantially the same as one which has previously been referred to adjudication, see *Michael John Construction Ltd v Golledge* [2006] EWHC 71, TCC; and *Quietfield v Vascroft Contractors Ltd* [2006] EWHC 174, TCC.

[89] See *Barnes & Elliott Ltd v Taylor Woodrow Holdings Ltd* [2004] B.L.R. 111; and *Simons Construction Ltd v Aardvark Developments Ltd* [2003] EWHC 2474, TCC. However, in *Ritchie Brothers (PWC) Ltd v David Philp (Commercials) Ltd* [2005] B.L.R. 384, the Scottish Court of Session came to the opposite conclusion.

[90] [2004] EWCA Civ 1418. For a post-*Amec* decision on compliance by adjudicators with the rules of natural justice, see *Carillion Construction Ltd v Devonport Royal Dockyard* [2005] EWHC 778, TCC.

[91] *Macob Civil Engineering Ltd v Morrison Construction Ltd* [1999] B.L.R. 93. Note that the adjudicator has a limited power to correct accidental omissions and errors in his decision, and doing so will not invalidate the decision: *Bloor Construction (UK) Ltd v Bowmer & Kirkland (London) Ltd* [2000] B.L.R. 315.

[92] *Discain Project Services Ltd v Opecprime Development Ltd* [2000] B.L.R. 402 (*ex tempore* reasons for granting permission to defend) and [2001] B.L.R. 285 (trial and full reasons).

[93] *Woods Hardwick Ltd v Chiltern Air-Conditioning Ltd* [2001] B.L.R. 23. The adjudicator was in breach of s.104(2)(e) of the 1996 Act, which requires him to act impartially, and para.19 of the Scheme, which requires him to communicate information which he has obtained to both parties. For a further example, see *Costain Ltd v Strathclyde Builders Ltd* [2004] S.L.T. 102 (Sc. Ct. Sess.).

negotiations between the parties[94]; in a case where a contractor claiming to be entitled to an extension of time advanced no delay analysis of its own, the adjudicator relied upon his own analysis of the causes and nature of the relevant delay.[95] However, a challenge to an adjudicator's appointment on the grounds that he had been appointed in an earlier adjudication between the same parties and so could not be relied upon to be impartial is unlikely to succeed.[96]

The Human Rights Act 1998. Section 6 of the Human Rights Act 1998[97] **9–366** provides that it is unlawful for a public authority to act in a manner which is incompatible with the European Convention on Human Rights. Article 6(1) of the Convention established the right to fair administration of justice:

> "In the determination of his civil rights and obligations . . . everyone is entitled to a fair and public hearing within a reasonable time by an independent and impartial tribunal established by law. Judgment shall be pronounced publicly . . . ."

Both the short timetable prescribed by statute for the adjudication process and the fact that adjudication is not a public process have been relied upon in attempts to challenge the adjudication process as incompatible with Art.6 of the Convention. Two such attempts have failed at first instance. In *Elanay Contracts Ltd v The Vestry*,[98] a decision made before the Human Rights Act 1998 came into force on October 1, 2000, Judge Havery Q.C. held that Art.6 of the Convention does not apply to an adjudicator's award or to proceedings before an adjudicator. The basis for his decision was that although adjudication is a determination of civil rights or obligations, it is not a final determination. By the time of the decision in *Austin Hall Building Ltd v Buckland Securities Ltd*,[99] the 1998 Act had come into force. The defendant to an application for summary judgment to enforce an adjudicator's decision argued that the whole system of adjudication established

---

[94] *Glencot Development and Design Company Ltd v Ben Barrett & Son (Contractors) Ltd* [2001] B.L.R. 202. See also *Specialist Ceiling Services Northern Ltd v ZVI Construction (UK) Ltd* [2004] B.L.R. 403.

[95] *Balfour Beatty Construction Ltd v Borough of Lambeth* [2002] B.L.R. 288. The failure of the adjudicator to allow the parties a fair hearing within the necessary constraints of the adjudication procedure also led to refusals to enforce decisions in *Shimizu Europe Ltd v LBJ Fabrications Ltd* [2003] EWHC 1229, TCC; *RSL (South West) Ltd v Stansell Ltd* [2003] EWHC 1390, TCC; *Buxton Building Contractors Ltd v The Governors of Durand Primary School* [2004] EWHC 7233, TCC (doubted in *Carillion Construction Ltd v Devonport Royal Dockyard Ltd* [2005] EWCA Civ 1358); *AWG Construction Ltd v Rockingham Motor Speedway Ltd* [2004] EWHC 888, TCC and *McAlpine PPS Pipeline Systems Ltd v Transco Plc* [2004] EWHC 2030, QB. However, a similar challenge failed in the Scottish case of *Karl Construction (Scotland) Ltd v Sweeney Civil Engineering (Scotland) Ltd* (2003) 85 Con. L.R. 59. *Balfour Beatty v Lambeth* was also distinguished on the facts in *Try Construction Ltd v Eton Town House Group Ltd* [2003] EWHC 60, TCC.

[96] *R.G. Carter Ltd v Edmund Nuttall Ltd* [2002] B.L.R. 359, where Judge Bowsher Q.C. held that the court had no power to revoke the appointment of an adjudicator and, in any event, there was no appearance of bias. The adjudicator was a surveyor. The judge observed that professionals such as surveyors and architects commonly act as certifiers under construction contracts and so are used to making decisions which they may later revise in the light of different evidence. See also *Amec Capital Projects Ltd v Whitefriars City Estates Ltd* [2004] EWCA Civ 1418.

[97] For further discussion as to the impact of the Human Rights Act 1998 upon claims for professional negligence, see Ch.7.

[98] [2001] B.L.R. 33.

[99] [2001] B.L.R. 272.

by the Housing Grants, Construction and Regeneration Act 1996 was incompatible with Art.6(1) of the Convention. Judge Bowsher Q.C. held that neither the 1998 Act nor the Convention applied to adjudication, although he described the question as "finely balanced".[1] The principal reason for the judge's decision was that an adjudicator is not a public authority.[2] He further held that, even if the Act and Convention applied, there was no breach of the requirement for a public hearing. In the first place, it was open to either party to ask the adjudicator to sit in public. A failure to make such a request amounted to waiver of the right to do so. Furthermore, it was necessary to look at the entire adjudication process, including enforcement of the adjudicator's decision by way of court proceedings, to see whether Art.6 was breached. Since the court dealing with enforcement of the decision would normally sit in public, there was no breach of Art.6.

9–367   **Impecuniosity.** The enforcement of an adjudicator's decision might work substantial injustice if, between enforcement and a subsequent reversal of the decision in arbitral or legal proceedings, the enforcing party falls into financial difficulty and is unable to repay the sum awarded by the adjudicator. The defendant in *Herschel Engineering Ltd v Breen Property Limited (No.2)*,[3] applied for a stay of execution on the basis of evidence which suggested that the claimant was or might be unable to repay the adjudicator's award if that award was reversed in subsequent arbitration or litigation. The application failed, in part because the claimant's financial position was the same as it had been, to the knowledge of the defendant, when the defendant contracted with it. The defendant had thus accepted the risks which attached to contracting with a party in that financial position.[4] In other cases, a stay of execution was refused because there was not compelling and uncontradicted evidence that the successful party in the adjudication would be unable to repay the award in the event that the adjudicator's decision was reversed in subsequent arbitration or litigation.[5] However, the Court of Appeal granted a stay of execution in *Bouygues UK Ltd v Dahl-Jensen UK Ltd*.[6] The defendant in that case was already in liquidation by the time of the claimant's application to enforce the adjudicator's award. That was a special circumstance which justified a stay pending the outcome of arbitration or litigation to achieve a final determination of the parties' dispute. Similarly, where the claimant was in administrative receivership, a stay on enforcement of an award was granted on terms that the defendant paid the sum at stake into court[7] and issued legal proceedings on the dispute within one month.[8]

---

[1] [2001] B.L.R. 272 at 280.

[2] See s.6(1) of the 1998 Act.

[3] Unreported, July 28, 2000.

[4] Similarly, a stay of execution will not be granted where the claimant's impecuniosity is attributable to the defendant's failure to pay the sum awarded by the adjudicator: *Absolute Rentals v Glencor Enterprises*, unreported, January 16, 2000.

[5] *Total M and E Services Ltd v ABB Building Technologies Ltd* [2002] EWHC 248, TCC; *Wimbledon Construction Co 2000 Ltd v Vago* [2005] EWHC 1086, TCC.

[6] [2000] B.L.R. 522.

[7] *Rainford House Ltd (in Administrative Receivership) v Cadogan Ltd* [2001] B.L.R. 416.

[8] *Baldwins Industrial Services Plc v Barr Ltd* [2003] B.L.R. 176.

CHAPTER 10

SURVEYORS

1. GENERAL

The general function of surveyors is to advise and act on behalf of clients in matters concerned with land, buildings and chattels. This description is so broad as to be virtually meaningless. It is, consequently, usually more useful to define a surveyor's job by reference to the particular task that he is carrying out than by reference to his own description. Although some surveyors are still general practitioners, sub-specialisms have been recognised by appropriate designation

10–001

and continue to develop. Given the professional knowledge required to carry out specialised tasks, a surveyor will very often be recognised by his specialism in much the same way that a heart surgeon is recognised as such rather than being simply a doctor. Many of the activities carried out by such specialists are close to, and sometimes overlap with, activities which are carried out by other professions, so that a building surveyor may carry out tasks which might otherwise be undertaken by an architect or structural engineer, whilst a minerals surveyor will require a substantial body of geotechnical knowledge of the sort familiar to a geotechnical engineer. For the purposes of this work, quantity and construction surveying is dealt with under the heading of construction professionals. The core activity of most (although not all) surveyors, and that which has generated the most considerable body of litigation, is the valuation of land and interests in land.

10–002   There is no statutory regulation of qualification and practice as a surveyor.[1] The profession is subject to self-regulation in respect of these matters by the main professional organisation, the Royal Institution of Chartered Surveyors (RICS), which amalgamated with the Incorporated Society of Valuers and Auctioneers (ISVA) in July 2000. The RICS is incorporated under a Royal Charter[2] which provides for the making of Bye-laws[3] with the approval of the membership and the Privy Council and also for the making of Regulations by the council of the RICS.[4] The RICS reorganised itself on January 1, 2001 into 16 faculties representing the different specialisations within the profession. A candidate for membership of the RICS must choose a specialisation, and therefore faculty of the profession, at an early stage. The professional and practical requirements of the various faculties of the RICS are extremely diverse. All prospective members must pass the Assessment of Professional Competence, which will involve mandatory parts (common to all faculties) together with core and optional parts which will reflect the particular area of specialisation.

10–003   **Chartered surveyors.** There is a variety of routes to becoming a chartered surveyor, but all involve graduating from an approved degree or diploma course or having equivalent senior professional experience. In addition, all candidates must complete the Assessment of Professional Competence. This test takes the form of a minimum period of two years' experience[5] with an approved firm of chartered surveyors, the submission by the candidate of a written summary of

---

[1] Estate agency work, defined as:
  "the introduction, in the course of business, of prospective vendors and purchasers of an interest in land and activities designed to ensure the disposal or acquisition of that interest",
is regulated by the Estate Agents' Act 1979. The Act does not apply to
  "things done . . . in the course of carrying out any survey or valuation pursuant to a contract which is distinct from that under which [estate agency work] is done" (see subss.1(1) and 1(2)(d)).
[2] The original charter was granted on August 26, 1881 and has been the subject of various supplementary charters, the most recent of which was in 1973.
[3] The present byelaws were promulgated in 1973, but have been the subject of substantial series of amendments up to January 2006. The byelaws are obtainable online at *www.rics.org*.
[4] The Regulations are, again, available online. The present set is as at February 2006.
[5] This period may be reduced if the candidate has relevant professional experience.

that experience and the solution to a practical task, relevant to their chosen specialisation, to be given at a formal interview.[6] Upon qualification a chartered surveyor becomes a member of the RICS and may describe himself as a chartered surveyor, and use the initials MRICS.[7] A chartered surveyor elected to the class of Fellow[8] may use the initials FRICS.[9] A firm or company where 50 per cent of its partners or directors consist of Fellows and Members may use, in conjunction with its title, the designation "Chartered Surveyors".[10]

Functions of surveyors. Their specific activities may be categorised under the   **10–004**
16 faculties and corresponding designations of the RICS. These are:

(a) Arts and antiques—Chartered arts and antiques surveyor

(b) Building control—Chartered building control surveyor

(c) Building surveying—Chartered building surveyor

(d) Commercial property—Chartered commercial property surveyor

(e) Dispute resolution

(f) Environment—Chartered environmental surveyor

(g) Facilities management—Chartered facilities management surveyor

(h) Geomatics—Chartered land surveyor or chartered hydrographic surveyor

(i) Machinery and business assets

(j) Management consultancy—Chartered management consultancy surveyor

(k) Minerals and waste management—Chartered minerals surveyor

(l) Planning and development—Chartered planning and development surveyor

(m) Quantity Surveying and Construction—Chartered construction surveyor or chartered quantity surveyor

(n) Residential property—Chartered valuation surveyor

(o) Rural

---

[6] Full details are provided in the appropriate Guide and Rules, published by RICS, and available from the Education and Membership Department, RICS, Surveyor Court, Westwood Way, Coventry CV4 8JE or see *www.rics.org*.
[7] RICS byelaw 13(1)(b).
[8] The requirements for election are set out in RICS byelaw 6 and the Regulations. The election to the status of Fellow is a recognition of achievement and status within the profession.
[9] RICS byelaw 13(1)(a).
[10] RICS byelaw 13(2).

(p) Valuation—chartered valuation surveyor

The descriptions of the divisions illustrate the extent to which surveyors operate in fields often more associated with other professions. In addition to the examples set out above,[11] a planning and development surveyor will often be instructed to appear as an advocate at a planning enquiry, rather than a solicitor or counsel. Similarly, surveyors are frequently retained to act in rent review arbitrations, rather than solicitors.[12] Most reported professional negligence cases against surveyors concern their activities of inspection and valuation and this chapter principally deals with those activities. Where surveyors act in planning enquiries and other contentious proceedings their conduct will be governed by principles similar to those that apply to solicitors acting in similar proceedings.[13] Surveyors frequently act as arbitrators (or "mutual valuers") in the context of rent reviews or agreements for the sale of property at market value.[14]

10–005 Four faculties of the RICS contain the overwhelming majority of the membership, those being commercial property, residential property, quantity surveying and construction and valuation. The building surveying division is relatively small. It is important to note that whilst inspection and valuation may be carried out by the same person in respect of relatively modest residential properties, they are really separate tasks involving the use of different skills. The assessment of defects, their importance and proper method of repair is a task for which a building surveyor should be suitably qualified and experienced. It is only because of the possible effect on value of significant defects and the requirement by lenders for accurate valuations that the public have become accustomed to an "ordinary" surveyor inspecting their house for defects rather than merely valuing it on the assumption that is free from significant defects. This tendency may have been reinforced by the search by lending institutions for cheap "surveys" on behalf of their clients and the willingness of valuers to undertake onerous tasks for very modest fees[15] whilst seeking to rely on exemption clauses in order to limit their liability.

The division of tasks is relevant to the competence of expert witnesses in actions involving the professional competence of surveyors. A chartered building surveyor is likely to have spent a considerable part of his professional life performing detailed examinations of different kinds buildings and their defects. A chartered surveyor qualified in, for example, the commercial/residential division of the RICS, is unlikely to have anything like the same degree of experience of defects, although he may have inspected many houses. Conversely a building

---

[11] See para.10–001.
[12] See, e.g. *Thomas Miller & Co v Richard Saunders and Partners* [1989] 1 E.G.L.R. 267 (where an analogy was drawn in argument between the position of counsel advising on evidence and a surveyor considering what evidence to submit to an arbitrator); and *Rajdev v Becketts* [1989] 2 E.G.L.R. 144, para.10–181 below.
[13] See Ch.11.
[14] A surveyor acting as an arbitrator (as distinct from an expert) will be immune from suit on the basis of judicial immunity. However, he will not be immune on any other basis: see *Hall v Simons* [2002] 1 A.C. 615; *Sutcliffe v Thackrah* [1974] A.C. 727; and *Arenson v Arenson* [1977] A.C. 405.
[15] Note the obligation imposed on building societies by s.62 of the Building Societies Act 1986.

surveyor is unlikely to be experienced in the valuation of property. For sub-stantial properties a valuation is likely to be subject to a detailed survey carried out by a specialist building surveyor.

Surveyors as expert witnesses. An expert's evidence is founded on his **10-006** training and experience. The court will consider "whether the witness has acquired by study or experience sufficient knowledge of the subject to render his opinion of value in resolving the issues before the court."[16] In England the court rules now expressly provide that the duty of an expert to assist the court overrides any obligation to the party from whom he receives instructions[17] and that an expert report must contain a statement that the expert understands his duty to the court.[18] Guidance as to the duties and responsibilities of expert witnesses in civil cases was given by Cresswell J. in *National Justice Compania Naviera SA v Prudential Assurance Co Ltd*.[19] This was generally approved by the Court of Appeal subject to the qualification that an experienced expert, when assessing the significance of certain evidence, is entitled to weigh the probabilities and this may involve making use of the skills of other experts or drawing on his more general knowledge.[20] Surveyors acting as expert witnesses must take care to try to put themselves in the position in which the defendant surveyor found him-self.[21] The use of hindsight when making criticisms is likely to devalue an expert's evidence.[22] The court has power under CPR 35.8 to appoint a court valuation expert, and will do so in an appropriate case whether the parties agree or not.[23] The separation of the RICS into 16 faculties, each representing a distinct area of practice, each with its own training and assessment syllabus, means that

---

[16] *per* King C.J. in *R. v Bonython* (1984) 38 S.A.S.R. 45 at 46. In *European Partners in Capital (EPIC) Holdings BV v Goddard & Smith* [1992] 2 E.G.L.R. 155, the Court of Appeal held:

"Issues of professional opinion, which must be chosen between if liability in negligence is to be established, will not as a general rule be issues suitable to be resolved on a summary judgment application."

(Scott L.J. at 157E.)

[17] CPR 35.3.

[18] CPR 35.10(2).

[19] [1993] 2 Lloyd's Rep. 68 at 81.

[20] [1995] 1 Lloyd's Rep. 455 at 496. In *Cemp Properties (UK) Ltd v Dentsply Research & Development Corp* [1991] 2 E.G.L.R. 197, 200 the Court of Appeal commented:

"It is a sad feature of modern litigation that expert witnesses, particularly in valuation cases, instead of giving evidence of their actual views as to the true position, enter into the arena and, as advocates, put forward the maximum or minimum figures as best suited to their side's interests. If experts do this, they must not be surprised if their views carry little weight with the judge. In this case, such evidence rightly led the judge to reject the expert evidence on both sides."

[21] See *per* Lord Hoffmann in *Banque Bruxelles Lambert SA v Eagle Star Insurance Co* [1997] A.C. 191 at 221, where he stated that:

" ... the court must form a view as to what a correct valuation would have been. This means the figure which it considers most likely that a reasonable valuer, *using the information available at the relevant date*, would have put forward as the amount which the property was most likely to fetch if sold upon the open market." [Emphasis added]

[22] For a recent example see *Preferred Mortgages Ltd v Countrywide Surveyors Ltd* [2006] P.N.L.R. 154; [2005] EWHC 2820, where the judge, at 168, rejected the evidence of the claimant's expert on the basis that he had been influenced by the subsequent sale price of the repossessed subject property stating that his "whole approach to valuation was, effectively, from the wrong end of the telescope." (For facts see para.10-125 below).

[23] *Abbey National v Key Surveyors Nationwide Ltd* [1996] 1 W.L.R. 1534.

care needs to be taken before describing or accepting without enquiry a chartered surveyor as an expert for the purpose of a surveying or valuation case. Given the multiplicity of tasks which a surveyor can undertake, it is suggested that two questions need to be considered: (a) Was the task one which the defendant undertook within his own proper and usual professional sphere? If not, there may be a question as to whether he should be judged not according to the practice of his own usual profession, but rather according to the professional practice of the specialism in which he purported to operate.[24] (b) If so, did the defendant act in accordance with practices which are regarded as acceptable by a respectable body of opinion in his profession?[25] Where a task is carried out by a professional man who is properly qualified to undertake the task, it will usually be necessary for there to be evidence from an expert of the same discipline to the effect that the defendant fell below the reasonable standard of his profession, before the court will be prepared to find him negligent.[26] Thus in *Sansom v Metcalfe Hambleton & Co*,[27] the Court of Appeal allowed an appeal by the defendant surveyor against a finding that he had negligently conducted a survey on the basis that the only relevant evidence called by the claimant had been from a structural engineer.[28] Butler-Sloss L.J., giving the judgment of the court, stated:

> "In my judgment, it is clear ... that a court should be slow to find a professionally qualified man guilty of a breach of his duty of skill and care towards a client (or third party), without evidence from those within the same profession as to the standard expected on the facts of the case and the failure of the professionally qualified man to measure up to that standard. It is not an absolute rule ... but, less it is an obvious case, in the absence of the relevant expert evidence the claim will not be proved."[29]

---

[24] See further para.9–137 above and para.11–097 below.

[25] See *Zubaida v Hargreaves* [1995] 1 E.G.L.R. 127 *per* Hoffmann L.J. at 128A–B applying the well-known passage in *Bolam v Friern Hospital Management Committee* [1957] 1 W.L.R. 582 at 587; and *Merivale Moore Plc v Strutt & Parker* [2000] P.N.L.R. 498 *per* Buxton L.J. at 515C–E.

[26] In *Routestone Ltd v Minories Finance Ltd* [1997] 1 E.G.L.R. 123 at 127B, Jacob J. held that the effect of the Civil Evidence Act 1972, s.3 was to make admissible the opinion of an expert on the question of whether or not a party had been negligent. He continued:
> "What really matters in most cases is the reasons given for the opinion. As a practical matter a well constructed expert's report containing opinion evidence sets out the opinion and the reasons for it. If the reasons stand up the opinion does, if not, not."

[27] [1998] P.N.L.R. 542.

[28] Similarly in *Whalley v Roberts & Roberts* [1990] 1 E.G.L.R. 164, Auld J., when considering whether or not there had been a breach by the defendant surveyors of their duty of care heard evidence from two surveyors as well as an architect and a civil engineer. On the question of liability, he held that it was only the evidence of the surveyors to which he should pay attention. See also the architect's case of *Investors in Industry v South Bedfordshire DC* [1986] 1 All E.R. 787 *per* Slade L.J. at 808 to 809, where the judge stated that little reliance was to be placed on the answers of three engineers as to the duties of an architect.

[29] At 549B. In *Merivale Moore Plc v Strutt & Parker* [2000] P.N.L.R. 498 at 517A, Buxton L.J. stated that he was not prepared to hold that the adduction of expert evidence as to the "bracket" within which a competent valuation might be provided was necessary in every case:
> "As at present advised, I think that it is still open to the judge in a suitable case to hold that the valuation is so far removed from what was the true value of the property that it must be regarded as a valuation that was outside the limits open to a competent valuer, without specific professional evidence as to what those limits were."

(a) *Bases of Liability*[30]

In England it is now settled law that surveyors may incur liability to their clients   **10–007**
for negligent valuations or reports both in contract and in tort.[31] If the appropriate
conditions are met, they may also incur liability to third parties in tort.[32] A
surveyor who dishonestly puts forward a mortgage valuation or any other
statement which causes loss will render himself liable to an action in deceit.
Given the prevalence of mortgage frauds in the late 1980s and early 1990s
together with the advantages of an action in deceit so far as foreseeability,[33]
contributory negligence[34] and (possibly) the effect of the decision in *BBL*,[35] there
has, recently, been a substantial increase in the number of fraud claims brought
against surveyors in England. It is also conceivable that the act or omission
complained of will give rise to liability under other torts,[36] but the claim so far
as based on tort will usually be for common law negligence including negligent
misrepresentation.

There is still discussion as to the full implications of the decision of the House   **10–008**
of Lords in *BBL v Eagle Star*.[37] Lord Hoffmann stated the *scope* of a valuer's
duty (and therefore the kind of damages arising) was to be deduced, in tort, from
the purpose of the rule imposing the duty. In the case of an implied contractual
duty, the nature and extent of the liability was to be defined by the term which
the law implied. This appears to go beyond a traditional analysis of contracts
where the court first deduces the extent of a party's obligations (whether by
reference to express or implied terms) and then considers the damages which
flow (by reference to considerations of causation, remoteness and foreseeability).
A new area of consideration is thus introduced.[38]

Limitation. Although a cause of action in negligence will have a different   **10–009**
measure of loss from a cause of action in contract, in surveyors' negligence
actions it is unlikely that there will be any practical difference in the result.[39]
There may, however, be significant differences in the limitation period where it
may well be beneficial to be able to sue in negligence as well as for breach of
contract as (a) the primary limitation period will often start to run later and (b)
the relief provided by s.14A of the Limitation Act 1980 whereby an action may

---

[30] Where compensation is sought the RICS has established an arbitration scheme as an alternative to
litigation between its members and their clients. It is intended to be inexpensive, swift and independent of the profession. The arbitration is conducted in writing and is administered independently from
the RICS by the Chartered Institute of Arbitrators, 12 Bloomsbury Square, London WC1A 2LP.
[31] See para.10–032 below. Following the decision of the House of Lords in *Henderson v Merrett*
[1995] 2 A.C. 145, cases such as *Hiron v Pynford South Ltd* [1992] 2 E.G.L.R. 138, where Judge
Newey Q.C. held that the fourth Defendant building surveyors did not owe a concurrent duty of care
in tort to that owed in contract are not good law.
[32] See para.10–032 below.
[33] See para.10–126 below.
[34] See para.10–011 below.
[35] [1997] A.C. 191; see para.10–157 below.
[36] Such as breach of confidence, trespass etc.
[37] [1997] A.C. 191.
[38] See generally paras 10–113 and 10–156 below.
[39] The decision of the House of Lords in *BBL v Eagle Star* [1997] A.C. 191 at 212D proceeds upon
this basis.

be commenced within three years of the "date of knowledge"[40] is available only for actions in negligence.[41] The first of these differences is illustrated by the decision of the Court of Appeal in *Byrne v Hall Pain & Foster*,[42] where the writ had been issued more than six years after the exchange of contracts, but less than six years after completion of the purchase. It followed that any contractual claim was statute barred as having occurred more than six years after any breach of contract. The question was thus as to whether the claimant had suffered loss so as to complete the cause of action in negligence. The court unanimously held that on exchange the purchaser acquired an interest in the property, there arose an immediate obligation to insure the same, and the seller acquired rights of action against the purchaser. On exchange the purchaser accordingly suffered loss and the cause of action was complete. The appeal was dismissed and the action was struck out as statute barred.[43] The second difference has been the subject of several reported cases, of which an example is *Mortgage Corp v Lambert*[44] where, on the assumed facts, an advance had been made following a negligent valuation on June 25, 1990. The borrowers defaulted almost immediately and an order for possession was obtained in May 1991. The borrowers made repeated partial payments and promises to repay arrears with the result that the order was postponed and the lender was unable to sell the property until August 1996. The writ was issued on October 15, 1996. The primary question for the court was, accordingly, whether the "date of knowledge" had occurred prior to October 15, 1993.[45] Prior to that date there had been several reports from debt-collectors which had put the estimated value of the property at substantially below the amount of the original valuation, but there had been no retrospective valuation. Although Chadwick L.J. (with whom the other members of the court agreed) considered that a prudent lender might well have been put on enquiry as to the

---

[40] Provided that it is within 15 years of the act of negligence.

[41] The Law Commission has recommended a uniform limitation period for actions not involving personal injuries with a single 10-year long-stop. Section 32 of the Limitation Act, dealing with deliberate concealment, applies to actions both in contract and in tort.

[42] [1999] P.N.L.R. 565.

[43] The only point which caused the court any difficulty was a passage in the speech of Lord Nicholls in *Nykredit v Edward Erdman* [1997] 1 W.L.R. 1627 at 1630, which it appeared to be suggested that the cause of action accrued in tort at the time of completion of the purchase. Simon Brown L.J. held, however, that Lord Nicholls had not, in that case, intended to draw a distinction between exchange and completion. In *Secretary of State for the Environment v Essex Goodman & Suggitt* [1986] 1 W.L.R. 1432, (Judge Hawser Q.C.); and *Horbury v Craig Hall & Rutley* [1991] C.I.L.L. 692, (Judge Bowsher Q.C.), Official Referees had previously determined that causes of action by house purchasers against surveyors in tort accrued on exchange of contracts (albeit, as was pointed out in *Byrne* at 568, the cases were of limited authorative value as the main issues were different: in *Essex Goodman* whether a cause of action accrued when damage occurred and in *Horbury* whether s.14A of the Limitation Act 1980 applied). See also *Kitney v Jones Lang Wootton* [1988] 1 E.G.L.R. 145 (cause of action in respect of organising repair works necessary in order to fulfil a covenant for repair accrued when the stipulated period for the works to be done expired rather than when the court subsequently held that the works had not been carried out) and *Westlake v Bracknell DC* [1987] 1 E.G.L.R. 161 (primary limitation period had expired at time of purchase, but deliberate concealment and estoppel found on basis of verbal reassurances by the surveyor on a later visit). The question of whether, on the facts, the cause of action in tort accrued after the cause of action in contract was also debated in *FG Whitley & Sons Ltd v Thomas Bickerton* [1993] 1 E.G.L.R. 139.

[44] [2000] P.N.L.R. 820.

[45] The court found it unnecessary to consider an alternative argument that no loss had been sustained prior to October 15, 1990.

validity of the original valuation, he considered the real question to be whether it was reasonable for a lender to obtain a retrospective valuation prior to October 15, 1993. On that issue there was no evidence. The court considered that a lender would be behaving reasonably if (with almost three years to go until the expiry of the primary period and with the benefit of an order for possession) it had decided to wait until it had obtained possession before obtaining a retrospective valuation.[46]

Liability may also be concurrent with that of other professional persons. The **10–010** depth of the recession in the early 1990s caused a very considerable volume of claims by lenders against both valuers and solicitors who had been retained prior to the making of the relevant loans where it was necessary to consider the respective liabilities of each. In such cases, the allegations of negligence will usually be distinct although, subject to the application of the decision in *BBL*,[47] the damage claimed will be the same. In other cases, the allegations of negligence will, themselves, overlap.[48]

Contributory negligence. A negligent surveyor has the same right as any **10–011** other defendant to defend an action against him by alleging that the claimant was

---

[46] In *Horbury v Craig Hall & Rutley* (1991) 7 P.N. 206; (1991) E.G.C.S. 81, the claimant purchased a property in November 1980 relying on the defendant's survey report. In March 1984 the claimant was told by a builder that certain chimney breasts were unsupported and dangerous and she paid £132 for repair work. In July 1985 the claimant discovered dry rot in the floors. In February 1988 the claimant issued a writ claiming damages in tort for the consequences of a negligent survey. The judge held that the defendants had been negligent in failing to observe the unsupported flues, and in failing to warn the claimant of the risk of rot affecting the floors. However the claimant's claim was statute barred. The three-year discoverability period under the Limitation Act 1980, s.14A ran from the date when the claimant first had knowledge of the material facts concerning the damage in respect of which damages were claimed. The damage was the purchase of the property in November 1980 in reliance on a negligent survey report. The claimant acquired the relevant knowledge in March 1984 when she was told of the unsupported flues. This was more than three years before the writ was issued. The judge held that the facts known in March 1984 were such as to meet the requirements of s.14A(7). In *Heathcote v David Marks & Co* [1996] 1 E.G.L.R. 123, Buckley J. held that the claimants' claim was statute barred, as their knowledge for the purpose of the Limitation Act 1980, s.14A included that of their solicitor, who had received a copy of the survey report in question more than three years prior to the expiry of the limitation period. See also *Spencer-Ward v Humberts* [1995] 1 E.G.L.R. 123, CA; *Sullivan v Layton Lougher & Co* [1995] 2 E.G.L.R. 111, CA; *Higgins v Hatch & Fielding* [1996] 1 E.G.L.R. 133, CA; *Etam v Baker Almond* [2001] E.G.C.S. 21, where in each case the claimants' claim was held by the court to be statute barred. For a discussion on the effect of the Latent Damage Act 1986 on surveyors reports and valuations, see T. Dugdale, "Latent damage: the application of the discoverability principle to survey reports" (1991) 7 P.N. 193.
[47] [1997] A.C.191, as to which see para.10–175 below.
[48] Thus in *Theodore Goddard v Fletcher King Services Ltd* [1997] 2 E.G.L.R. 131, a managing surveyor who failed to notice the deletion and omission of an upwards-only rent review provision in two leases was held to be 20% liable for the damages paid by the solicitor who was instructed to prepare the leases, and who was held to have a continuing obligation to consider and check the content of both leases. Although the surveyor was not under a duty to read the entire lease, he should have noticed these deletions and omissions, because he was aware that the provisions were vital to his client. Examples of other cases include: *Anglia Hastings & Thanet BS v House & Son* [1981] 2 E.G.L.R. 17; *Computastaff Ltd v Ingledew Brown & Bennison and Garrett* [1983] 2 E.G.L.R. 150; *Secretary of State for the Environment v Essex Goodman and Suggitt* [1986] 1 W.L.R. 1432; *GP & P Ltd v Bulcraig & Davis* [1988] 1 E.G.L.R. 138; *Green v Ipswich BC* [1988] 1 E.G.L.R. 239; *Banque Bruxelles Lambert SA v Eagle Star Insurance Co Ltd* [1994] 2 E.G.L.R. 108, Phillips J.; *McCullagh v Lane Fox & Partners Ltd* [1996] 1 E.G.L.R. 35; *Ball v Banner* [2000] Lloyd's L.R. P.N. 569 (although the liability of the property advisers was overturned on appeal).

negligent, and that such negligence caused, or contributed to, any loss proved. Contributory negligence does not involve breach of duty owed by a claimant to a defendant, but the failure by the claimant to use reasonable care to protect his own interests.[49] This topic is generally discussed in Ch.5 and below at para.10–167 in relation to claims by lenders where contributory negligence is most often alleged. A valuer personally or vicariously liable to the claimant for deceit is not entitled, either at common law or by reason of ss.1(1) and 4 of the Law Reform (Contributory Negligence) Act 1945, to plead by way of defence that the claimant was guilty of contributory negligence.[50] In relation to valuers who are personally liable, this would appear plainly correct. As a matter of policy, the position might not be thought to be so plain in relation to vicarious liability. Consider a situation where a careful firm of valuers employs a rogue who fraudulently prepares a valuation which is relied on, honestly but carelessly by a lender. Had a lender been careful, it would have appreciated that the valuer was fraudulent and alerted the firm. In such circumstances it is not immediately obvious why the law imposes the entire risk of the individual valuer's dishonesty on his employers. It might be said that experience shows that lenders need all the encouragement possible to be careful in their lending. However, in *Standard Chartered Bank v Pakistan National Shipping Corp (No.2)*,[51] the House of Lords held that contributory negligence was not available as a defence to employers who were vicariously liable to a careless claimant. At para.12, Lord Hoffmann pointed out that the purpose of the 1945 act was to enable a claimant to recover where previously he had been unable so to do rather than reduce the damages payable by a defendant. It follows that, absent re-consideration by the House of Lords or statutory change, an action in deceit offers considerable advantage to a careless claimant.

10–012   **Defective Premises Act 1972.** Since January 1, 1974, s.1 of the Defective Premises Act 1972 has imposed on a person taking on work for or in connection with the provision of a dwelling a duty to see that the work which he takes on is

---

[49] For example, the effect of a purchaser's failure to obtain a structural survey was considered by Cobb J. in *Sutherland v CR Maton & Son* [1979] 2 E.G.L.R. 81, who held that the failure neither broke the chain of causation nor constituted negligence on the part of the claimant. In *Yianni v Edwin Evans & Sons* [1982] Q.B. 438, Park J. had no doubt that such a failure could constitute contributory negligence. In *Perry v Tendring DC* [1995] 1 E.G.L.R. 260, Judge Newey Q.C. noted that whether or not such a failure was negligent would depend on the facts.

[50] See *Alliance & Leicester Building Society v Edgestop Ltd* [1993] 1 W.L.R. 1462. The claimants were the victims of a mortgage fraud, one of the actors being a valuer, at the time an employee of Hamptons Residential, and subsequently convicted of offences of dishonesty involving the material valuations. Hamptons applied to amend their defence to allege that the claimants were guilty of contributory negligence in failing to discover that the valuer was acting outside the scope of his employment, in failing to detect the dishonest nature of the applications for a mortgage, and in failing to act as a prudent lender in respect of the processing of the mortgage applications. Mummery J. held that prior to the 1945 Act, the contributory negligence of a claimant suing in deceit could not be pleaded as a defence (1474F) and that the position had not been changed by the 1945 Act (1477D). In a further decision in the same action, [1994] 2 E.G.L.R. 229, Mummery J. concluded that whilst the valuer had not been acting within the scope of his actual authority in valuing the properties, he had been acting within his ostensible authority, that the claimants had not had notice of his want of authority when they relied upon the valuations and that Hamptons were, therefore, vicariously liable for the valuer's deceit.

[51] [2003] 1 A.C. 959; [2002] UKHL 43.

done in a workmanlike, or as the case may be, professional manner, with proper materials and so that as regards that work the dwelling will be fit for habitation when completed. The duty is owed to the person to whose order the dwelling is provided and to every person who acquires an interest in the dwelling.[52] A surveyor carrying out a survey or valuation of a dwelling would not ordinarily be regarded as "taking on work in connection with the provision of a dwelling", and so it is submitted has no liability in respect of such work under this Act.[53]

Liability in respect of statements about property matters. The Property **10–013** Misdescriptions Act 1991[54] provides that where a statement that is false or misleading to a material degree is made about property matters in the course of estate agency business, the person by whom the business is carried on shall be guilty of an offence.[55] The commission of an offence under this Act does not of itself render any associated contract void or unenforceable.[56] Limitation periods for the commencement of a prosecution under the Act are three years from the date of the commission of the offence, or one year from the date of discovery of the offence by the prosecutor.[57] Civil liability for misdescriptions may also be founded in common law on the basis of *Hedley Byrne*.[58] In *Duncan Investments Ltd v Underwoods*,[59] the Court of Appeal upheld the finding of liability against the defendant estate agents who gave an oral estimate of the possible re-sale values of certain properties to an officer of the claimant property company during an inspection. The defendants' disclaimers were not effective, as they were limited to statements made on behalf of the vendors and the defendant had not been advising on behalf of the vendors. The defendants had advised the claimant knowing that the advice would be relied upon and that it was unlikely that the claimant would seek other independent advice. By contrast, in *McCullagh v Lane Fox & Partners Ltd*,[60] the Court of Appeal held that a written disclaimer was effective to prevent liability from arising for both written and oral misstatements. But for the disclaimer ("all statements contained in these particulars as to this property are made without responsibility . . . ") the defendant estate agents would have been liable to the claimant purchaser for an overpayment of £75,000.[61]

---

[52] Defective Premises Act 1972, s.1(1). See further para.9–041 above.

[53] For further analysis, see Holyoak and Allen, *Civil Liability for Defective Premises* (1982), Ch.4, and M. F. James, "The Defective Premises Act and 'fitness for habitation' " (1993) 9 P.N. 144.

[54] The Act received the Royal Assent on June 27, 1991 and came into force on that date. The Property Misdescriptions (Specified Matters) Order was made on November 11, 1992, and came into force on April 4, 1993. The Schedule to the Order sets out the specified matters for the purposes of s.1(1). For commentary on this Act, see D. W. Oughton, "The Property Misdescriptions Act 1991" (1992) 8 P.N. 59; G. Stephenson, "The regulation of estate agency" (1992) 8 P.N. 2; A. Reed, "Professional negligence and property sales" (1995) 2 P.N. 42; and S. Nield "Whose agent anyway?—estate agents' relationship with the buyer" (1995) 2 P.N. 49.

[55] Property Misdescriptions Act 1991, s.1(1) and (5).

[56] *ibid.*, s.1(4).

[57] *ibid.*, s.5(1).

[58] [1964] A.C. 465.

[59] [1998] P.N.L.R. 754.

[60] [1996] 1 E.G.L.R. 35.

[61] At first instance, [1994] 1 E.G.L.R. 35, Colman J. had held that a vendor's estate agent owed a duty of care at common law to a purchaser of a property in respect of the oral misstatement, but that the claimant had failed to prove that he had paid in excess of the market value for the property, with the result that his claim was dismissed. For a commentary on the first instance case see Mullan, "An 'undes res' " (1994) 3 P.N. 92.

There was no basis for saying that it would be unfair to the claimant to allow the agents to rely upon the disclaimer, nor that it would be unreasonable. When considering whether in general an estate agent, like a solicitor, does not himself owe a duty of care to the purchaser, Nourse L.J. commented:

> "the very function of an estate agent . . . is prone to take him out of the general and bring him under a particular duty to a prospective purchaser . . . an estate agent is well advised not to act for a vendor in a house sale without appropriate disclaimers, to which the attention of prospective purchasers is drawn".

10–014   **Liability of individuals.** In common with other professions, surveyors used to practice mainly as partners. However, many chartered surveyors now practise in companies or limited liability partnerships rather than in partnerships. The question therefore arises as to when an individual, who is not a partner, will incur personal liability—either as an employee or as a director of a company. As any relevant contract will not be with the individual, any liability will be tortious. In *Merrett v Babb*,[62] the Court of Appeal held, by a majority, that Mr Babb, an individual surveyor employed by a partnership, had a personal liability to a residential mortgagor as a result of having signed a mortgage valuation pursuant to s.13 of the Building Societies Act 1986. In reliance principally on the decisions of the House of Lords in *Smith v Bush* and *Harris v Wyre Forest DC*,[63] May L.J. held that it was unnecessary for there to be any personal dealings between an employee and a claimant in order for a duty of care to be imposed. He stated that it was irrelevant that Mr Babb was not insured and pointed out that in *Harris*, the House of Lords had imposed a duty of care on the employee of the local authority (although no distinction was drawn between the employee and his employer, the local authority in that case). In his dissenting judgment, Aldous L.J. relied on the decision in *Williams v Natural Life*,[64] where the House of Lords had considered the circumstances in which a duty of care would be imposed on a director of a limited company in addition to that imposed on the company. He pointed out that there was required not only to be a relationship between the claimant and the principal, but also between the claimant and the employee. Notwithstanding the personal signature of Mr Babb, he considered that no such relationship could be made out on the facts. It is submitted that the reasoning of Aldous L.J. is to be preferred to that of the majority. It is the economic entities which carry out (and benefit from) the provision of professional services which should bear responsibility for negligence acts or omissions. In the absence of fraud there appears no reason to impose a personal liability upon employees simply because they are the individuals through whom the services have been provided. If such duties are imposed, employees will be well advised to procure separate professional indemnity cover (so as to avoid the risk that their employers fail to take out or maintain appropriate insurance). Such insurance represents an extra and (largely) unnecessary cost. Aldous L.J.'s dissenting judgment is, moreover, consistent with the decision in *Edgeworth Construction v Lea and*

---

[62] [2001] Lloyd's L.Rep. P.N. 468; [2001] EWCA Civ 214.
[63] [1990] 1 A.C. 831.
[64] [1998] 1 W.L.R. 830.

Associates Ltd,[65] where the Canadian Supreme Court refused to impose a personal duty of care on engineers who had signed certificates. The decision in *Merrett v Babb* was distinguished by McKinnon J. in *Bradford & Bingley Plc v Hayes*.[66] A lender relied on a mortgage report signed by an individual valuer employed by a limited company. The instructions had been addressed by the limited company. The judge found no basis to impose a duty of care on the individual valuer. He pointed out that *Merrett* had been based on the decision of the House of Lords in *Smith v Bush* and that both cases had been concerned with individuals relying on mortgage reports in order to consider the purchase of domestic property. It therefore appears likely that the decision in *Merrett* will be confined to situations where the claimant is an individual contemplating the purchase of modest domestic property.

Whether valuers act as directors, partners or employees, there will be certain direct professional obligations imposed on them by the RICS.[67]

Liability in connection with company particulars. Part VI of The Financial   **10–015**
Services and Markets Act 2000 contains provisions governing the issue of prospectuses and have potential application so that a valuer may be held liable in respect of any false or misleading statement for which he is responsible in any listing particulars. In *Ball v Banner*,[68] the Court of Appeal had to consider the liability of the defendant surveyors (described as property advisors) for a statement which was attributed to them in the prospectus of an Enterprise Zone Property Unit Trust (which was an unregulated investment under the then Financial Services Act). Hart J. had found at first instance[69] that the statement in question, which related to the letting prospects of the property, had two possible meanings, one of which amounted to a statement which no competent surveyor could have made. He construed the statement to have the negligent meaning, but the Court of Appeal held that the statement bore the other, reasonable, meaning. The liability of a valuer in respect of statements in prospectus bears similarities to that of an accountant, and the matter is discussed in detail below.[70]

Liability in connection with a contravention of s.19 of the Financial   **10–016**
Services and Markets Act 2000. Valuers have a potential liability under this part of the Financial Services and Markets Act.[71]

Liability under the Financial Ombudsman scheme. Section 83(1) of the   **10–017**
Building Societies Act 1986 conferred on an individual the right as against a building society to have any complaint concerning action taken by the society in relation to certain matters investigated under a scheme recognised by the Building Societies Commission. On June 5, 1987, a building societies ombudsman

---

[65] [1993] 3 S.C.R. 206—see further para.9–111 above.
[66] Unreported, July 25, 2001.
[67] See RICS Bye-law 19, which requires every member, amongst other things, to comply with the Regulations and to comply with all relevant Practice Statements.
[68] Unreported, July 2000, Court of Appeal.
[69] The first instance judgment is reported at [2000] Lloyd's L.Rep. P.N. 569.
[70] See Ch.17, para.17–040. See *The Encyclopaedia of Financial Services*, edited by Professor E. Lomnicka and J. L. Powell Q.C. (Sweet & Maxwell).
[71] For further discussion see Ch.14, para.14–006.

scheme was recognised by the Commission. The ombudsman's duties included the obligation to investigate any complaint received by him from an individual if:

(a) the complaint related to action taken in the United Kingdom by a building society, and

(b) in relation to the grant or refusal to grant a borrowing member other or further advances secured on the same or different land, provided that the grounds of complaint was that

(c) the action complained of constituted in relation to the complainant, in the case of a participating society, a breach of its obligations under the Building Societies Act 1986, its rules or any other contract, or unfair treatment or maladministration.[72]

10–018 Schedule 12 of the Act omitted any reference to surveys and valuations of land, therefore the only relevant matter of complaint is that part of para.3 of Pt II of Sch.12 to the Act which refers to the grant or refusal to grant further advances to a borrowing member. The complainant had therefore to have been an existing borrower at the time of the grant or refusal. Further, because the complaint had to be about the acts or omissions of the society, the ombudsman had no jurisdiction to investigate complaints relating to valuations made by a non-employee surveyor. In *Halifax Building Society v Edell*,[73] Morritt J. held that the preparation, by surveyors directly employed by the claimant societies, of basic valuations, house buyers' reports and valuations, and structural surveys in connection with applications for further advances were all part of the society's process of administration. If negligently prepared, such work could amount to maladministration within Sch.12 to the 1986 Act, and that accordingly, the ombudsman had jurisdiction to investigate and determine the borrower's complaints. With effect from the coming into force of the relevant sections of the Financial Services and Markets Act, on December 1, 2001, the Buildings Societies Ombudsman came to an end when the Financial Ombudsman Service came into existence.[74] It seems that the Financial Ombudsman Service would take the same attitude towards surveys undertaken by financial institutions themselves as the old Building Societies Ombudsman.

(b) *Duties to Client*

(i) *Contractual Duties*

10–019 The primary basis of a surveyor's duties to his client is the contract of engagement between himself and his client. The contract may be written or oral or inferred from the conduct of the parties. By Practice Statement 2,[75] the RICS now requires a valuer to agree or confirm in writing the terms on which any valuation will be undertaken *before* issuing his report. The instructions must deal, at a

---

[72] See cll.14, 17 and 18 of the scheme, and Sch.12, Pt II of the Building Societies Act 1986. Details of the scheme were amended with effect from July 1, 1994.
[73] [1992] Ch. 436.
[74] The scope of this scheme is dealt with at para.14–103 below.
[75] For the application of RICS Practice Statements, see para.10–023, below.

minimum with a total of 17 matters, including the identity of the client, purpose of the valuation; the subject of the valuation; the basis or bases of valuation; any Assumptions or Special Assumptions[76] and reservations to be made; the date of the valuation; limits of liability to parties other than the client; the nature of information provided and the fee or basis thereof.[77] If he fails to do so and there is any subsequent dispute as to the terms of his instructions, he may be at a serious disadvantage.[78]

A surveyor's duties will vary according to the circumstances of each case and **10–020** in particular the purpose for which he is asked to report upon a particular property.[79] The RICS Practice Statements require a surveyor to use a Basis of Valuation recognised as being appropriate for the purpose of the valuation.[80] A surveyor's express duties will primarily depend upon the instructions given,[81] for example, to carry out a structural survey or valuation of a named property,[82] but the Practice Statements also define what may be required in order to carry out such instructions.[83] A surveyor will invariably be under an implied, if not an express, duty to exercise reasonable care and skill,[84] in both the work which results in the report, and the report itself.[85] In addition, certain specific duties may be implied. Thus a surveyor engaged to carry out a structural survey has been held to be under an implied duty to inspect the property so far as is reasonably

---

[76] Such Assumptions and Special Assumptions are dealt with separately. Special Assumptions must be agreed and confirmed in writing with the client before a report is issued and can only be made if they can "reasonably be regarded as realistic, relevant and valid, in connection with the particular circumstances of the valuation"—see PS2.3.

[77] Practice Statement 2, RICS Appraisal and Valuation Standards 5th Edition. The professional obligations imposed as to the confirmation of instructions have become steadily more extensive during the last 20 years both as to extent and as to timing.

[78] See *Fisher v Knowles* [1982] 1 E.G.L.R. 154 and para.10–077, below. Note that *Fisher v Knowles* was decided at a time when the very extensive Practice Statement 2 as to the content of instructions was not available from the RICS.

[79] See *Ker v John H Allan & Sons*, 1949 S.L.T. (Notes) 20 *per* Lord Birnam; and note the caution expressed in *Singer and Friedlander Ltd v John D. Wood & Co* [1977] 2 E.G.L.R. 84, 85 by Watkins J.:

"Whatever conclusion is reached, it must be without consideration for the purpose for which it is required. By this I mean that a valuation must reflect the honest opinion of the valuer of the true market value of the land at the relevant time, no matter why or by whom it is required, be it by merchant bank, land developer or prospective builder. So the expression, for example, 'for loan purposes' used in a letter setting out a valuation should be descriptive only of the reason why the valuation is required and not as an indication that were the valuation required for some other purpose a different value would be provided by the valuer to he who seeks the valuation. It might however be an indication that the valuer, knowing the borrowing of money was behind the valuation, acted with even more care than usual to try to be as accurate as possible."

RICS Practice Statement 3 now deals specifically with the Purposes of Valuations and seeks to provide that valuations for particular purposes have to be provided on specified bases.

[80] See Practice Statement 3.

[81] See para.10–031, below for the problems of construction of instructions.

[82] See *Predeth v Castle Phillips Finance Co Ltd* [1986] 2 E.G.L.R. 144 and para.10–078, below.

[83] See, e.g. Practice Statement 4, which expressly requires that "Investigations and investigations must always be carried out to the extent necessary to produce a valuation which is professionally adequate for its purpose" and goes on to provide a substantial commentary on this requirement.

[84] e.g. *Kenney v Hall, Pain and Foster* [1976] 2 E.G.L.R. 29 at 33. Surveyors' negligence cases are commonly determined only by reference to whether the surveyor failed to exercise reasonable care and skill. The word "negligence" is frequently used to indicate not only the specific tort, but also breach of the implied contractual duty to exercise reasonable care and skill. Such a term is implied by the Supply of Goods and Services Act 1982, s.13.

[85] *per* Denning L.J. in *Candler v Crane Christmas & Co* [1951] 2 K.B. 164 at 179.

practicable, whereas a surveyor carrying out a mortgage inspection and valuation may confine himself to a careful visual examination of the property.[86]

10–021 **The ambit of the decision in BBL.** As set out below,[87] in *BBL v Eagle Star*,[88] the House of Lords limited the damages recoverable by a lender who had made a loan in reliance on a negligent valuation so that no greater loss of principal could be recovered than the difference between the negligent valuation and a correct valuation at the time of the loan. It did so by restricting the kind of loss for which a lender could recover for breach of an implied term to exercise reasonable skill and care by reference to the reasonable expectations of lender and borrower. It thus appears possible that lenders (or other claimants) may seek to circumvent the effects of *BBL* by carefully worded express terms which, for example, expressly imposed liability for all damages incurred by a lender, including responsibility for subsequent fall in the property market, on a negligent valuer.[89] In the absence of such express terms, the scope of a valuer's duty, and thus the damages recoverable, will be the same whether a claim is made for breach of a common law duty of care or for breach of the ordinary implied term to exercise reasonable care and skill.[90]

10–022 **RICS Practice Statements.** Until December 31, 1995, chartered surveyors were under a professional duty to comply with all Practice Statements published by the RICS.[91] These were published from time to time by the Assets Valuation Standards Committee of the RICS. This committee sought to ensure uniform methods of valuing fixed assets by chartered surveyors on behalf of client

---

[86] Commenting about the level of expertise required of this class of service, Lord Griffiths in *Smith v Bush* [1990] 1 A.C. 831 at 858 said:

"It is only defects which are observable by a careful visual examination that have to be taken into account and I cannot see that it places any unreasonable burden on the valuer to require him to accept responsibility for the fairly elementary degree of skill and care involved in observing, following-up and reporting on such defects. Surely it is work at the lower end of the surveyor's field of professional expertise."

In *Whalley v Roberts & Roberts* [1990] 1 E.G.L.R. 164, Auld J. stated:

"The defendants were not instructed to undertake a structural survey or a survey of the detail called for in the standard form of the Royal Institution of Chartered Surveyors House Buyers' Report and Valuation inspection. They were instructed to inspect and to provide a mortgage valuation report. It is common ground that this involved them in making a brief and reasonably careful visual inspection to enable them, in the terms of the bank report form, to provide a valuation and general guide as to the condition of the property. I am satisfied on the evidence before me that this would not normally involve the use of a spirit-level unless the lack of level in the property became evident on a visual inspection so as to call for further investigation."

[87] See para.10–113 and 157, below.

[88] [1997] A.C. 191.

[89] In one of the cases considered in the *BBL* appeals, *Nykredit Mortgage Services Ltd v Edward Erdman*, the House of Lords rejected an argument by the lender that it was misled not merely by the final valuation figure, but by errors in the detailed valuation report which had been produced pursuant to a detailed letter of engagement. Lord Hoffmann did not consider, as a matter of construction, that the lender was entitled to place separate reliance on the information provided. See further para.10–115 below.

[90] Thus if the valuer in *Western Trust Savings Ltd v Strutt & Parker* [1999] P.N.L.R. 154 had been retained by the bank rather than merely owing it a duty of care at common law, the decision as to the scope of his duty is likely to have been the same—see further para.10–042 below.

[91] RICS byelaw 24(11), in force February 11, 1991, byelaw 19(7) and associated Conduct Regulation.

companies. As such valuations are often reproduced in the form of company accounts and prospectuses, consistency of method was important, to avoid the public being misled. These Practice Statements and guidance notes did not apply to valuations of domestic houses, or valuations for mortgages or loans secured on commercial property.[92] The position after December 31, 1995 is set out below.

RICS Appraisal and Valuation Manual. With effect from December 31,   **10–023**
1995, the RICS's Statement of Asset Valuation Practice and Guidance notes ("the Red Book") and its manual of Valuation Guidance notes ("the White Book") were withdrawn in respect of valuations undertaken after that date. The replacement of these works with the Appraisal and Valuation Standards[93] was intended to avoid confusion and to provide the profession, clients and the courts with authoritative guidance as to the assembly, interpretation and reporting of information relevant to the practice of valuation. A conscious decision was made by the RICS to prescribe minimum standards in respect of valuations over a much wider range of services than those to which the Red Book had applied. The manual contains Practice Statements in section one, and compliance with these remains mandatory.[94] Section two contains Guidance Notes[95] providing assistance on good valuation practice. Although compliance with the latter is not mandatory, the RICS warns that a departure should be made only for good reason.[96] The RICS also provides separate guidance in respect of valuations intended for inclusion in Financial Statements in accordance with UK Generally Accepted Accounting Principles. The principal aims of the Appraisal and Valuation Manual were expressed to be as follows:

(a) to encourage valuers carefully to establish and understand at the outset their clients' needs and requirements, and to satisfy themselves that they are equipped to meet them to a satisfactory standard;

(b) to promote the consistent use of bases and assumptions upon which valuations are provided and the selection on each occasion of the basis which will meet the clients' proper needs;

---

[92] See AVSC reg.25, agreed by RICS General Council July 9, 1990 and the notes thereto. The application of Guidance Notes was considered in *Allied Trust Bank Ltd v Edward Symmons & Partners* [1994] 1 E.G.L.R. 165.

[93] The manual is now published by RICS Business Services Ltd and is available both in a looseleaf format and on disk from RICS Books, Surveyor Court, Westwood Way, Coventry CV4 8JE. In the 11 years since publication of the Manual in October 1995, it has been subject to substantial amendments. It is now in its 5th Edition (although smaller amendments are made on a more regular basis). As a result, it is important, when considering the professional obligations of a surveyor at a particular moment, to ascertain the precise state of the Manual at the time he carried out his work.

[94] The scope of the Practice Statements is set out in Practice Statement 1.

[95] There are currently 5.

[96] In the introduction to the Appraisal and Valuation Manual, the RICS warns that:

"when an allegation of professional negligence is made against a surveyor, the court is likely to take account of any relevant Practice Statement published by the RICS in deciding whether or not the surveyor has acted with reasonable competence. Failure to comply with Practice Statements is likely to be adjudged negligent".

Surveyors are not required to follow the advice and recommendations contained in the Guidance Notes, but many firms assert in their reports that they have done so, see for example *Craneheath Securities Ltd v York Montague Ltd* [1994] 1 E.G.L.R. 159, Jacob J.; [1996] 1 E.G.L.R. 130, CA.

(c) to help valuers to achieve high standards of professional competence in the preparation of valuations and appraisals;

(d) to promote the provision of unambiguous and readily comprehensible valuation and appraisal reports which provide the advice and information their readers need and should have;

(e) to ensure that published references to valuations include clear, accurate and sufficient information which is not misleading.

Practice Statement 3 sets out the purposes of valuations and their bases which is now designed to comply with internationally accepted valuation standards. Valuers are required, in relation to valuations, based on market value to use the definition and conceptual framework settled by the International Valuation Standards Committee. Separate guidance is available in relation to building surveyors' inspections.

10-024   These documents, and other professional information published by the RICS, have a threefold importance. First, by their authorship and the type of surveyor to whom each publication is directed, the RICS implies that a chartered building surveyor is more competent to undertake building surveys than a "general purpose" surveyor. This has implications for those without such a qualification who nevertheless carry out such surveys. They should be judged according to the standard of the reasonably competent chartered building surveyor, whatever their training and experience. Secondly, any surveyor who materially departs from the good practice set out in the notes appropriate to the type of inspection undertaken, will be at risk in a professional negligence action, a point made in the introduction to the Guidance Notes by the RICS. Unless such a departure can be justified,[97] expert evidence that the notes represent general and approved practice within the profession[98] is likely to lead to a finding of negligence.[99] Thirdly, the

---

[97] As it was in *Hacker v Thomas Deal & Co* [1991] 2 E.G.L.R. 161, where the surveyor did not carry a mirror when carrying out a building survey:

"He is criticised for that by [counsel for the plaintiff], because that is one of the pieces of equipment that it is suggested in the literature put out by the Institute that every surveyor should consider carrying. But the passage that was read out says that this will depend upon the preferences of the individual surveyor."

The judge held that it would not be right to hold the surveyor negligent in failing to carry a mirror simply because there was an opportunity to use it, unless he had been put upon inquiry. The facts of the case are set out at para.10-086, below.

[98] See *Bolam v Friern Hospital Management Committee* [1957] 1 W.L.R. 582. An example of a failure to follow professional guidance is provided by the facts of *Montlake v Lambert Smith Hampton* [2004] EWHC 938. The claimants were the owners of the Wasps rugby ground and wished to raise money for expansion. They decided to form a company and float on the AIM market. The defendant valuers were asked to prepare a valuation. Given the length of time which the club had occupied the ground, there was concern as to possible CGT liability on a sale and the defendant valuers sought to maintain that establishing whether such liability existed was the only purpose of the valuation. The judge held, however, that the defendants appreciated that they were being asked to confirm the current value of the ground for fund raising purposes. The defendants had previously provided a valuation some two years previously for "accounting purposes" on a depreciated replacement cost basis. The new valuation was provided on the same basis and ignored the possibility of gaining planning consent. It was accepted at trial, that, even had the valuation only been for the purposes of calculating any CGT liability, it should have been on an Open Market basis.

[99] RICS guidance notes on the meaning of "open market value" and "forced sale value" were considered by the Court of Appeal in *Predeth v Castle Phillips Finance Co Ltd* [1986] 2 E.G.L.R.

various services offered by surveyors have been classified and standard conditions of engagement have been prepared. The public is now offered an ascending
level of service on defined terms. The existence of such a structure means that a
surveyor who neglects to make plain to his client the precise nature of the service
to be undertaken is doubly at risk. The surveyor will forfeit any protection the
standard conditions of engagement may offer, and he may be held by the court
to have in fact contracted to carry out a greater level of service than either he
intended or his fee warrants.

The existence of the professional obligation of compliance with the Practice   **10–025**
Statements, together with the publication by the RICS of the various Guidance
Notes and manuals discussed show that a body of guidance has been developed
for surveyors the breach of which is intended to have the same force and effect
in a professional negligence action as breach of the Auditing Standards issued by
the Auditing Practices Board would have in actions against accountants.[1]

Surveyors' standard conditions of engagement. To be incorporated into the   **10–026**
surveyor's contract of retainer, any standard conditions of engagement[2] must be
made known to the client and agreed upon at the time when instructions are
received. If they are not there is a real risk that they will be of no contractual
effect.[3] These rules of construction of a contract pose special difficulties for a
profession where time is frequently short, instructions are often received by
telephone and a course of dealing between the parties is unlikely in the domestic
context. This should be less of a problem where the surveyor is retained in
respect of a survey or valuation of commercial property. It is commonplace for
the fee to be agreed in advance and in such circumstances the surveyor has
sufficient opportunity to make known and secure the incorporation into his
contract of retainer suitable conditions of engagement.

Unfair Contract Terms Act 1977. Even if such standard conditions of   **10–027**
engagement are incorporated into the contract, the surveyor's contract of engagement will be subject to the Unfair Contract Terms Act 1977 and the Unfair Terms
in Consumer Contracts Regulations 1994.[4] By virtue of the provisions contained

---

144. In *Watts v Morrow* [1991] 1 E.G.L.R. 150, it was held at first instance that the surveyor's
departures from the RICS Practice Note on Structural Surveys of Residential Property made it more
difficult for him to come to the right answer and contributed to his failure to come to the right answer.
An appeal on the issue of liability was not pursued. In *Strover v Harrington* [1988] Ch. 390, the
absence of evidence that the defendant surveyors had acted contrary to accepted good professional
practice was fatal to the claimant's claim. In *PK Finians International (UK) Ltd v Andrew Downs &
Co Ltd* [1992] 1 E.G.L.R. 172, an allegation that the defendant valuer should not have made oral
enquiries of the planning authorities was held unsustainable in view of the terms of guidance note 6
of the RICS Guidance Notes on the Valuation of Assets. The deputy judge also commented, *ibid.* at
174K, that "these guidance notes are not to be regarded as a statute . . . mere failure to comply with
the guidance notes does not constitute negligence".
[1] For accountants, see Ch.17, para.17–051.
[2] Or such other conditions as the surveyor may wish to adopt.
[3] Save possibly as a warning notice.
[4] For discussions of this Act and the case of *Stewart Gill Ltd v Horatio Myer & Co Ltd* [1992] Q.B.
600, see Peel, "Making more use of the Unfair Contract Terms Act 1977" (1993) 56 M.L.R. 98; and
Brown and Chandler, "Unreasonableness and the Unfair Contract Terms Act" (1993) 109 L.Q.R.
41.

in Pt I of the Act which extends to England and Wales and to Northern Ireland,[5] a surveyor cannot by reference to any contract term or to any notice given to persons generally or to particular persons exclude or restrict his liability for death or personal injury resulting from negligence.[6] In the case of other loss or damage, a surveyor cannot by reference to any contract term or to any notice exclude or restrict his liability for negligence[7] except in so far as the term or notice satisfies the requirement of reasonableness. The Regulations provide that any "unfair term" shall not be binding on the consumer. It is submitted that any clause which satisfies the requirement of reasonableness under the Act, will not at the same time be held to be an "unfair term" within the meaning of the Regulations. The House of Lords considered the Act, its application to work undertaken by surveyors and valuers of domestic property, and the issue of reasonableness in *Smith v Eric S Bush*.[8]

10–028   The Court of Appeal considered an attempt by a claimant to avoid a written disclaimer in particulars issued by estate agents in *McCullagh v Lane Fox & Partners Ltd*.[9] The defendants, both orally and in their particulars, described a property to a prospective purchaser as having grounds of "nearly one acre" and "0.92 acre". The claimant told them he was going to demolish the property and rebuild on the site, and would not be obtaining his own survey. The claimant exchanged contracts to buy the property for £875,000, after which he discovered the true area of the grounds to be 0.48 acre. He sued, claiming he had overpaid for the property.[10] The Court of Appeal rejected the claimant's attempts to strike down the disclaimer by reliance on the Unfair Contract Terms Act 1977. Observing that it was for the defendants to establish that it was fair and reasonable that they should be allowed to rely upon the disclaimer, Hobhouse L.J.[11] noted that by his own observations at the time, the claimant put himself forward as a sophisticated and experienced member of the public, that he had had ample opportunity to read the particulars and was aware that it would contain a disclaimer, that he had ample opportunity to regulate his conduct in the light of the disclaimer and could have obtained an independent check on the area of the grounds. The claimant further had legal advice and representation, and enjoyed complete freedom of contract to negotiate as he chose. Hobhouse L.J. concluded that there was no basis for saying that it would be unfair to the claimant to allow

---

[5] Similar but not identical provisions are contained in Pt II of the Act, which extends to Scotland only. See para.10–072, below.

[6] s.2(1).

[7] A clause or notice that seeks to exclude a duty of care is subject to the provisions of the Unfair Contract Terms Act 1977 just as much as a clause or notice that attempts to exclude liability. See *Smith v Eric S Bush*; *Harris v Wyre Forest DC* [1990] 1 A.C. 831 *per* Lord Templeman at 848, Lord Griffiths at 856, and Lord Jauncey at 873, reversing the Court of Appeal on this point (*Harris v Wyre Forest DC* [1988] Q.B. 835).

[8] s.2(2). *Smith v Eric S Bush* [1990] 1 A.C. 831, see para.10–065, below.

[9] [1996] 1 E.G.L.R. 35. This case is also discussed at paras 10–013 above and 10–067 below.

[10] [1994] 1 E.G.L.R. 48, Colman J. The claimant failed; the judge held that although a duty of care was owed, the claimant had in fact bought the property for its true worth and had suffered no loss.

[11] [1996] 1 E.G.L.R. 35 at 46. The other members of the court agreed with this part of the judgment of Hobhouse L.J.

the defendants to rely upon the disclaimer, nor that it would be unreasonable.[12] That reasoning may be contrasted with the case of *St Marylebone Property Co Ltd v Payne*,[13] where a property for sale by auction was illustrated by a misleading photograph, which indicated the property to be of greater extent than in fact was owned by the vendor. Despite the claimant company being directed by a very experienced valuer and property dealer, who well knew the auctioneer's standard conditions, it was held not to be reasonable in the circumstances of an auction sale for the defendant vendor to rely upon them, as the particulars were dominated by the misleading photograph, upon which it was to be expected an investment purchaser would rely.

Building societies. Most purchases of private dwellings are now made with **10–029** the aid of an advance from a building society, bank, or centralised lender, secured by way of mortgage on the purchased property. In the case of a building society every director of the society is under a statutory duty to satisfy himself that arrangements are made for assessing the adequacy of the security to be taken in respect of advances to be made by the society.[14] The required arrangements as stated in the statute[15] include the provision of a written report as to the value of any freehold or leasehold estate comprised in the security and as to any factors likely to affect its value. The report must be provided by a:

"person who is competent to value, and is not disqualified under this section from making a report on, the land in question".[16]

A report from an employee of a building society may in certain circumstances render the society liable to an investigation by the building societies ombudsman.[17] Although banks (and other commercial lenders) are not subject to the same direct statutory duties as building societies, they are subject to supervision and adopt similar standards as a matter of practice. Lenders may also be required to obtain valuations in order to satisfy their own insurers. In the case of loans above a certain percentage of equity (usually in the region of 75 per cent), lenders often obtain Mortgage Indemnity Guarantees (referred to as "MIGs") to insure themselves against the risk of default by borrowers. There will be conditions attached to the MIGs which will almost invariably require the obtaining of valuations.[18]

Surveys for lenders. To the above ends building societies and other lenders **10–030** engage surveyors to inspect and report upon properties the subject of applications for mortgage advances. Some lenders employ their "in-house" surveyors for the

---

[12] The court went further. Even though the claimant had not read the disclaimer, since the claimant expected the particulars to contain a disclaimer it would "be unreasonable and unfair to the defendants to allow him to claim against the defendants as if there had been no such disclaimer". *ibid.*, at 46.

[13] [1994] 2 E.G.L.R. 25.

[14] The Building Societies Act 1986, s.13(1), with effect from January 1, 1987. Before that date a broadly similar obligation was imposed by the Building Societies Act 1962, s.25(1).

[15] Building Societies Act 1986, s.13(1)(c).

[16] *ibid.* The valuer need no longer be "prudent" or "experienced".

[17] See para.10–017, above.

[18] For further discussion of MIGs in the context of reliance, see para.10–123 below.

purpose. Formerly building societies generally did not show the surveyor's report to the applicant for an advance.[19] Now they invariably do show it[20] and the surveyor is generally instructed on the basis that the applicant will see his report. Lenders usually offer to their prospective borrowers a structured range of survey services. The range usually consists of:

(a) a mortgage inspection and valuation;

(b) a house or flat buyer's report and valuation;

(c) a building survey, formerly known as a full structural survey, with valuation.[21]

The depth of the inspection and the detail of the report vary proportionally with the fee charged. Attempts are invariably made to draw to the attention of the prospective borrowers the nature and scope of the service being offered, and in particular to make clear the limited nature of the basic service, the mortgage inspection and valuation. Such explanations and conditions of engagement are usually set out not only in leaflets describing the survey services offered, but also in mortgage application forms[22] and the surveyor's report itself.

10–031 The effect of these limitations will depend upon the wording of the particular documents and the facts in each case. Frequently, however, the effect of the documents is that two separate agreements are made. The first is an agreement between the building society and the prospective borrower whereby in consideration of the appropriate fee, the building society agrees:

(a) to instruct a surveyor to inspect the relevant property and to provide the required report on it;

(b) to provide a copy of the report to the applicant; and

(c) on the basis of the information contained in the mortgage application form, the surveyor's report and such further information as may be sought, to consider whether or not to offer the requested advance secured by mortgage on the property.

The second agreement is between the building society and the surveyor whereby in consideration for payment of the appropriate fee, the latter agrees to inspect the property and to provide a report to be shown to both the society and the applicant. In such a situation there may be no contractual nexus between the applicant and the surveyor. Accordingly, the applicant will be limited to making any claim against the surveyor in tort.[23] Where an independent surveyor has been instructed by the lender, the prospective borrower will generally have no remedy

---

[19] Note the criticism of this practice as long ago as 1956 by Devlin J. in *Eagle Star Insurance Co Ltd v Gale and Power* (1955) 166 E.G. 37.

[20] As in, for example, *Stevenson v Nationwide Buiding Society* [1984] 2 E.G.L.R. 165. See para.10–064, below.

[21] Although it will be rare for such a survey to be carried out by a building surveyor as a building surveyor will not usually hold himself out as competent to provide a valuation.

[22] As was the case in *Smith v Eric S Bush* [1990] 1 A.C. 831.

[23] See para.10–037, below.

against the society in respect of a negligent report, unless the original choice of surveyor can in some way be challenged.[24]

(ii) *Duties Independent of Contract*

The fact that there exists a contract between a surveyor and his client does not **10–032** preclude the surveyor being under a concurrent duty of care to his client[25] apart from contract.[26] Indeed, following the decision of the House of Lords in *Henderson v Merrett*,[27] there will usually be imposed a tortious duty where a contractual duty of care exists, although the tortious duty will not necessarily be co-extensive with all of the obligations assumed by contract. The existence of such a concurrent duty was expressly recognised by Lord Jauncey in *Smith v Eric S Bush*[28]:

> "the building society instructed the [surveyors] who, by accepting these instructions, not only entered into contractual relations with the building society but also came under a duty in tort to it to exercise reasonable care in carrying out their survey and preparing their report. To that extent they were in no different position to that of any other professional person who has accepted instructions to act on behalf of a client".

In *Holt v Payne Skillington and De Groot Collis*,[29] certain advice was given to the claimants by an employee of the second defendant surveyors as to the application of planning laws. This advice was outside the terms of the surveyor's contract of retainer. The Court of Appeal referred to *Midland Bank Trust Co Ltd v Hett Stubbs & Kemp*[30] and held that it was well-settled law that where there is a contract under which a party assumes contractual duties, a concurrent duty of care can also exist in tort. Furthermore, in the absence of a contractual term

---

[24] See the dicta by Lord Griffiths in *Smith v Bush* [1990] 1 A.C. 831, 865:
"I do not accept the view of the Court of Appeal in *Curran v Northern Ireland Co-ownership Housing Association Ltd* [1986] 8 N.I.J.B. 1, that a mortgagee who accepts a fee to obtain a valuation of a small house owes no duty of care to the mortgagor in the selection of the valuer to whom he entrusts the work. In my opinion, the mortagee in such a case, knowing that the mortgagor will rely upon the valuation, owes a duty to the mortgagor to take reasonable care to employ a reasonably competent valuer. Provided he does this the mortgagee will not be held liable for the negligence of the independent valuer who acts as an independent contractor."
In *Beresforde v Chesterfield BC* [1989] 2 E.G.L.R. 149, the defendant building society delivered under their own name an independent valuer's report to the claimants. The claimants claimed that the building society had therefore adopted the report as their own but the claim against the building society was struck out by the judge. Whilst expressing considerable doubt as to whether the claim could succeed ("very formidable difficulties indeed in any such claim achieving success" *per* Parker L.J. at 151) the Court of Appeal allowed the claimants' appeal on the ground that the claimants' claims were not so plainly unarguable that they ought to be stopped forthwith.
[25] See the discussion on concurrent liability in contract and tort in Ch.2, paras 2–103 *et seq.*
[26] See *Leigh v Unsworth* (1972) 230 E.G. 501, and the dicta of Judge Everett at 501, set out under fn.89, para.10–024 of the third edition of this work, and the Scottish case of *Drinnan v CW Ingram & Sons*, 1967 S.L.T. 205 and the dicta of Lord Milligan at 207, set out under fn.22, para.10–009 of the second edition of this work.
[27] [1995] 2 A.C. 145.
[28] [1990] 1 A.C. 831 at 870.
[29] [1996] P.N.L.R. 179.
[30] [1979] Ch. 384.

which precluded or restricted the duty of care in tort, it was open to the court to find that the duty of care in tort was wider than the concurrent duties in contract. The trial judge was therefore entitled to hold that a duty of care in tort was owed by the surveyors in respect of the advice as to the planning position. However, on the facts the claimants had failed to prove an unequivocal representation upon which they had relied.[31]

(c) Duties to Third Parties

(i) General Principles

10–033   **The traditional view.** It was formerly the prevailing view that a surveyor could only incur liability for professional negligence in contract and hence only to his client unless he were guilty of fraud.[32] Exceptionally for the period, in *Cann v Willson*[33] the defendant valuers were held liable to a third party. Instructed by the mortgagor, they had sent their valuation to the claimant mortgagee's solicitors. On later being informed by the solicitors that the valuation was required for mortgage purposes, the valuers confirmed their figure. Acting on the valuation, the claimant lent on mortgage and suffered loss upon the mortgagor's default, the amount realised on sale of the property being less than the valuation figure. Chitty J. held the valuers liable on two grounds. First, that they owed a duty of care to the mortgagees and had negligently failed to discharge it.[34] Secondly, that their statement as to the value was made recklessly and without reasonable ground for believing it to be true,[35] *Cann v Willson* was overruled, however, in *Le Lievre v Gould*,[36] in which the Court of Appeal reasserted the formerly prevailing view.[37]

---

[31] See also para.2–110 above.

[32] See *Scholes v Brook* (1891) 63 L.T. 837; (1892) 64 L.T. 674; *Le Lievre v Gould* [1893] 1 Q.B. 491, CA; *Love v Mack* (1905) 92 L.T. 345; *Davis v Sprott & Sons* (1960) 177 E.G. 9 (claim in negligence by mortgagors against estate agents in respect of a report and valuation of a bungalow as a security for a mortgage prepared by the latter upon the instructions of prospective mortgagees. Action dismissed upon estate agents' summons to strike out, on the ground that the statement of claim disclosed no reasonable cause of action against them. *Per* Pennycuick J.: " . . . it seemed that the statement of claim contained no allegation of a contractual relation between the plaintiffs and the second defendants. If there was no such relation there could be no liability in damages for breach of duty". Leave to appeal was granted, but apparently not pursued). An attempt to extend the doctrine in *Donoghue v Stevenson* [1932] A.C. 562 to valuers was made *in Old Gate Estates Ltd v Toplis and Harding and Russell* [1939] 3 All E.R. 209 (claim in negligence by company against valuers instructed by its promoters in respect of their excessive valuation of property known by the valuers to be used for the purpose of the company. Wrottesley J. dismissed the claim on the ground that the doctrine in *Donoghue v Stevenson* was confined to negligence resulting in danger to life, limb or health and accordingly did not extend to the facts of the case).

[33] (1888) 39 Ch.D. 39.

[34] *ibid.* at 43, following *Heaven v Pender* (1883) 11 Q.B.D. 503.

[35] *ibid.* at 44, following the Court of Appeal's decision in *Peek v Derry* (1887) 37 Ch.D. 541. The latter case had not at the time proceeded to the House of Lords.

[36] [1893] 1 Q.B. 491, CA.

[37] Following the House of Lords' decision in *Derry v Peek* (1889) 14 App.Cas. 337 overruling the Court of Appeal's decision in *Peek v Derry*, above.

Effect of *Hedley Byrne*. In *Hedley Byrne & Co Ltd v Heller and Partners*   **10–034**
Ltd,[38] the House of Lords took the view that *Cann v Willson* was rightly
decided.[39] Since *Hedley Byrne*[40] it is well established that in certain circumstances a surveyor owes a duty of care and may incur liability in negligence to
a third party.[41] It is rare that a surveyor's negligence leads to direct physical
injury and claims against surveyors are, accordingly, usually for economic loss.
Given the restrictive attitude adopted by English law to the recovery of pure
economic loss as exemplified by the decision in *Murphy v Brentwood DC*,[42] the
courts have had to consider the circumstances in which recovery of such loss will
be permitted.

The range of third persons who may be affected by a surveyor's default is   **10–035**
wide. For example, in the context of a property transaction the range may include
the vendor and purchaser, mortgagor and mortgagee, and possibly subsequent
purchasers.[43] However, the surveyor will not be under a duty of care to any
person unless the circumstances are such as to give rise to a duty of care. The
theoretical basis of valuers liability for economic loss was considered by May
L.J. in *Merrett v Babb*,[44] when he pointed out the dangers and difficulties in
seeking a single, universally applicable, test:

> "During the last twenty years or more, intense and repeated attempts have been made
> to refine a comprehensive test, shortly expressed, to define circumstances in which a
> person owes a duty of care to another, breach of which causing loss will give rise to a
> claim for damages. If the damage is physical damage directly inflicted, there is rarely
> a problem. If the damage is what has been characterised as foreseeable economic loss,
> there may be a problem—the more so if what causes the loss is the giving of advice or
> the providing of information. In such cases especially—but, I think, in every case—
> reliance is an intrinsically necessary ingredient which appears in every formulation of
> a test. Beyond that, two strands of consideration emerged. These may for convenience
> be called the *Caparo* strand and the *Henderson* strand. The *Caparo* strand asks whether,
> in addition to foreseeability, there is a sufficient relationship of proximity and whether
> the imposition of a duty of care is fair, just and reasonable. The *Henderson* strand asks
> whether the defendant is to be taken to have assumed responsibility to the claimant to
> guard against the loss for which damages are claimed. The difficulty with the *Caparo*

---

[38] [1964] A.C. 465.
[39] *ibid.* at 489, 502, 535. The case was also approved by the House of Lords in *Smith v Bush* [1990]
1 A.C. 831.
[40] Even prior to 1964 it was common for professional negligence claims by a client against a surveyor
instructed by him to proceed in both negligence and contract, e.g. *Gurd v A Cobden Soar & Son*
(1951) 157 E.G. 415; *Rayment v Needham* (1953) 163 E.G. 4.
[41] e.g. *Hingorani v Blower* [1976] 1 E.G.L.R. 104, especially at 106 (surveyor); *Singer and Friedlander Ltd v John D Wood & Co* [1977] 2 E.G.L.R. 84, especially at 85; *Corisand Investments Ltd
v Druce & Co* [1978] 2 E.G.L.R. 86; *Yianni v Edwin Evans & Sons* [1982] Q.B. 438; *Roberts v J
Hampson & Co* [1988] 2 E.G.L.R. 181; *Smith v Bush* [1990] 1 A.C. 831.
[42] [1991] 1 A.C. 398. For a full analysis and discussion see Ch.9, paras 9–070 *et seq.*
[43] Note that the possibility of a surveyor being under a duty to such a person was expressly excluded
by Lord Griffiths in *Smith v Bush* [1990] 1 A.C. 831 at 865.
[44] [2001] Lloyd's L.Rep. P.N. 468; [2001] EWCA Civ 214 [41]. For the facts and criticism of the
actual decision where by an individual employed surveyor who signed a valuation for a building
society was found to owe a duty of care to the purchaser, see para.10–014 above.

strand is that it sometimes seen as being unhelpfully vague. The difficulty with the *Henderson* strand is that it was originally expressed in terms of '*voluntary* assumption of responsibility' which tended to import a degree of subjectivity. *Henderson* itself put paid to that and, as Lord Slynn said in *Phelps*, '[assumption of responsibility] means simply that the law recognises that there is a duty of care. It is not so much that responsibility is assumed but that it is recognised or imposed by the law'. Thus the *Caparo* strand and the *Henderson* strand in reality merge. In my view, it is very often a helpful guide in particular cases to ask whether the defendant is to be taken to have assumed responsibility to the claimant to guard against the loss for which damages are claimed. But I also think that it is reaching for the moon—and not required by authority—to expect to accommodate every circumstance which may arise within a single short abstract formulation. The question in each case is whether the law recognises that there is a duty of care."

10–036   Given that no single factor leads to the imposition of a duty of care in a novel situation, the most helpful guidance is to be obtained by considering those circumstances in which duties of care have been imposed. The courts have had no difficulty in accepting the existence of a duty where a valuer expressly and voluntarily assumes a duty to a particular group of people.[45] Greater difficulties occur when no such responsibility is voluntarily assumed. The leading English decision extending the liability of valuers is *Smith v Bush*,[46] where the House of Lords held that valuers employed by lenders to value modest residential properties owed a duty to individual borrowers. Lord Templeman (who together with Lords Griffiths and Jauncey gave a speech with which the other members of the House agreed) upheld the submission that it was unnecessary, in order for liability to be founded, for there to be a *voluntary* assumption of responsibility by the valuer to the claimant—in fact a valuer would be likely to do everything that he could to avoid to avoid such responsibility. The real question was as to whether the law would impose such liability.[47] He stated:

> "I agree that by obtaining and disclosing a valuation, a mortgagee does not assume responsibility to the purchaser for that valuation. But in my opinion the valuer assumes responsibility to both mortgagee and purchaser by agreeing to carry out a valuation for mortgage purposes knowing that the valuation fee has been paid by the purchaser and knowing that the valuation will probably be relied on by the purchaser in order to decide whether or not to enter into a contract to purchaser the house."[48]

10–037   Aside from cases of concurrent contractual and tortious liability, cases where liability has been voluntarily assumed and the situation (exemplified by *Smith v Bush*) where a valuation is provided to a lender and relied on by a purchaser of a modest dwelling, the courts have been cautious in imposing duties of care to

---

[45] The existence of a duty of care to investors on behalf of a firm of surveyors was conceded in respect of statements in a prospectus which were expressly attributed to the surveyors in *Ball v Banner* [2000] Lloyd's L.Rep. P.N. 568, but the judge refused to impose liability for other, non-attributed, statements.

[46] [1990] 1 A.C. 831.

[47] See further para.10–047 below.

[48] *ibid.* at 847C.

third parties to prevent economic loss.[49] An attempt to impose a duty was made in *Preston v Torfaen BC*.[50] The claimant purchased a house on an estate built by the defendant council over, allegedly, an infilled quarry. The defendant engineers had provided the council with a report on soil conditions and, it was alleged, negligently failed to identify the nature of the site. The action against the council was abandoned after the decision in *Murphy*, but that against the engineers was pursued to the Court of Appeal on a preliminary issue as to whether the engineers owed a duty of care to the claimant. The Court of Appeal held that no duty was owed. The engineers were no more proximate to the claimant than the builders, who could not be sued by reason of *Murphy*. The duty owed by the engineers to the council could not be extended to the claimant; as a potential purchaser he was an unidentified member of a class, and further, a class that would not ask to see the report before purchase. These principles will apply to reports prepared in similar circumstances by surveyors.[51]

The High Court of Australia has considered whether liability should be **10–038** imposed upon a statutory water authority for negligently providing a "ball-park" figure to a developer for incurring the cost of bringing water to the developer's land.[52] By a majority of four to three, the court decided that liability should not be imposed. Both the majority and the minority relied upon Barwick C.J.'s formulation in *Mutual life and Citizens Assurance Co Ltd v Evatt*[53]:

"the speaker must realise or the circumstances be such that he ought to have realised that the recipient intends to act upon the information or advice in respect of his property or of himself in connection with some matter of business or serious consequence . . . The circumstances must be such that it is reasonable in all the circumstances for the recipient to seek, or to accept, and to rely upon the utterance of the speaker. The nature of the subject matter, the occasion of the interchange, and the identity and relative position of the parties as regards knowledge actual or potential and relevant capacity to form or exercise judgment will all be included in the factors which will determine the reasonableness of the acceptance of, and of the reliance by the recipient upon, the words of the speaker".

The fact that, despite reliance on the same test, the majority differed from the minority in deciding whether reliance was reasonable in the circumstances of the case shows how difficult it can be to predict whether a duty of care will be

---

[49] In *Thomson v Christie Manson & Woods* [2005] EWCA Civ 555; [2005] P.N.L.R. 713, the Court of Appeal accepted that the defendant auctioneers had voluntarily assumed a duty of care towards a purchaser with whom they had a special relationship: this relationship was such that they had assigned a member of staff to advise the purchaser. May L.J. emphasised that the existence of other duties did not cut down the scope of the duty owed:

"if the auctioneer in his relationship with potential purchasers goes beyond facilitation, he does so at his peril. His role is to sell the object for the best price. His duty to his client (the seller) and his own interest preclude true impartiality. The existence of such a conflict of interest predicates a duty of care owed by Christie's to Ms Thomson, as to which there is now little dispute. The characteristics of the duty of care are not diluted because Christie's had other interests and owed other duties. The potential for breach of duty to Ms Thomson is, if anything, enhanced" (at para.34)—see further para.10–117 below.

[50] 65 Build. L.R. 1.

[51] For further commentary on this case, see Ch.9, para.9–103.

[52] *Tepko Pty Ltd v Water Board* (2001) 75 A.L.J.R. 775 commented on by Dr Katter, "'Ball park' figures and the ambit of duty of care for negligent misstatement" at 75 A.L.J. 427.

[53] (1968) 122 C.L.R. 556 at 569–572.

imposed in a particular novel factual situation. The same difficulty was displayed in the Scottish case of *Smith v Carter*,[54] where Lord McCluskey held on a procedure roll debate that the pursuer, who was the co-purchaser of a property, was entitled to argue at trial that the defender valuer, who was unaware of her existence, nevertheless owed her a duty of care. Lord McCluskey held:

> "I am not prepared to affirm as a matter of general law that, in all circumstances, a surveyor who is instructed by an individual to carry out an inspection of property which that individual is considering buying owes no duty in the preparation and submission of his report of the inspection to any person who may join with the prospective purchaser in effecting the purchase. It cannot be uncommon for one person such as a relative or a friend who has some relevant experience in the property market to be acting as the undisclosed agent for another or as the spokesperson for a group interested in a possible property transaction."[55]

10–039   One important consideration in deciding whether or not a duty of care should be imposed in a particular factual situation is whether or not a claimant has alternative remedies available. In *Raja v Austin Gray*,[56] the claimant was the administrator of the owner of a property portfolio. Sixteen of the properties had been charged to a property development company which had itself borrowed money from a bank secured by a debenture. The bank appointed administrative receivers who, in turn, appointed the defendant valuers to carry out valuations and to act and advise and assist in relation to the sale of the properties. The question as to whether the defendants owed a duty of care to the deceased was tried as a preliminary issue. It was accepted for the purposes of the issue that the defendants knew that the deceased owned the properties and that the price obtained on sale would directly affect his equity in the properties. At first instance, Buckley J. held that a duty of care was owed. In doing so he relied on the facts: a) that the interests of the receiver and the deceased were essentially co-terminous in that they both wished to obtain the best price; b) that the deceased had no valuable remedies against anyone else as the receivers would be entitled to maintain that they had acted on the expert advice of the defendants; and c) that there was no substance in drawing a distinction between the property company's rights and those of the deceased. The judge did, however, consider that the valuers were bound to put their duty to the bank above any tortious duty to the deceased. It followed that the defendants could not be in breach of duty in the event of any conflict between the interests of the bank and those of the deceased.

The Court of Appeal reversed the decision and followed the earlier decision of H.H. Judge Jack Q.C. in *Huish v Ellis*.[57] It found that the claimant was within the group of persons to whom the receiver owed a duty in equity when exercising a power of sale. The court considered the question as to whether the receiver was entitled to rely on the advice of apparently competent valuers in effecting the sale and found, notwithstanding the absence of binding authority, that the answer was

---

[54] 1995 S.L.T. 295.
[55] *ibid.* at 297.
[56] [2003] Lloyd's Rep. P.N. 126; [2002] EWCA Civ 1965.
[57] [1995] B.C.C. 462.

"no".[58] It followed that the claimant was not without a remedy. Clarke L.J. stated:

> "Given that [the claimant] has an adequate remedy against [the receivers] and (on my view of the case) the receivers, I can see no reason why he should also have a remedy against the appellant valuers. I do not subscribe to the principle: 'the more the merrier'. Valuers in their position perform their services under a contract with the receivers which may contain limitations and restrictions of different kinds which may not be at all easy to fit into the concept of a duty of care in tort. I recognise Mr Douthwaite's point that the scope of any duty owed by the valuers would be limited by the scope of their instructions from their principals, the receivers, and that it would be likely to be a defence to valuers that they acted in accordance with the scope of their instructions. For that reason, I would not, for my part, regard problems of conflict as a conclusive consideration; but they do seem to me to be relevant factors."

Given the limitation on the duties sought to be imposed, it arguable that the court was wrong, as a matter of principle, to regard the existence of an alternative remedy as being decisive on the facts of the case. The practical effect of the court's decision may well be to impose the risk of insolvency of the receiver (who may be an individual) on the claimant. In many cases it may well be that the primary responsibility for selling at an undervalue will lie with the advisers to the receiver. Nevertheless both the question as to whether the receiver is liable even if he has taken apparently competent advice and whether the valuer owes a direct duty of care must be regarded as settled in England below the House of Lords. (The valuers sought and were refused leave to appeal by the House.) There are, however, analogous situations where similar questions are still open. Thus in *Cohen v TSB Bank Plc*,[59] the claimant was the guarantor of certain secured borrowings. Upon default, two partners in a surveying firm were appointed receivers and a separate firm of valuers appointed as selling agents. The claimant sued both the receivers and the agents for failing to obtain a proper price. The receivers accepted that they owed a duty of care subject to an exclusion clause. The agents denied the existence of any duty to the claimant. Having rejected the claim on its facts, the judge left open the questions as to whether any duties were, in fact, owed.

(ii) *Knowledge of Reliance*

A duty of care will be more difficult to establish where it is claimed that the **10–040** surveyor ought to have known, although he did not actually know, that reliance

---

[58] In *Francis v Barclays Bank Plc* [2005] P.N.L.R. 297; [2005] EWHC 2787, Sir Donald Rattee stated that it is now "clearly established" that in carrying out its duty to those interested in the equity of redemption, a mortgagee is responsible for the negligence of its agents—see further para.10–100 below. In *Mistry v Thakor* [2005] EWCA 953, the Court of Appeal left open what might be seen as the analogous question as to whether an owner should have imputed to him, for the purposes of an action in nuisance, the knowledge which his professional agent ought to have had (it being common ground that he had imputed his actual knowledge).

[59] [2002] B.C.L.C. 32.

would be placed on his advice by a third party.[60] As a matter of practice, surveyors and valuers will often include express disclaimers seeking to prevent third parties from relying on their report. Although these disclaimers will not be effective in a *Smith v Bush* context, they have been held to be effective in a commercial context.[61] An example of a duty being held to exist where the surveyor did not know that his report would be relied upon is *Bourne v McEvoy Timber Preservation Ltd*.[62] The defendant timber rot specialists were instructed by the vendors of a house to report on fungal infestation and to estimate for its eradication upon the basis that if their estimate was accepted they had the job and were paid for it, but if not, they had nothing. The defendants inspected the house and provided a report and an estimate. There was no evidence that the claimant purchaser was ever shown the defendants' report, but he, with the vendors' agreement, instructed and paid the defendants to carry out the work in the estimate. After completing the work the defendants provided a guarantee in which the claimant was named as client. Prior to the claimant instructing them to do the work, however, the defendants did not know of his existence or that he would see and rely upon their report. They did know that their report was connected with the proposed sale of the house. There was a later outbreak of dry rot in an area in which no dry rot had been reported. The defendants contended that in carrying out their inspection and report they did not owe a duty of care to the claimant since there was no "duty situation". Bristow J. rejected the defendants' contention:

> "I have to test whether there was sufficient proximity between the plaintiff and the defendants to give rise to a duty situation by asking myself the question: at the time the defendants made their inspection and reported to [the sellers] their principals, did they know, or ought they to have known, that the purchaser of the house might well be affected in the decisions which he took by the contents of their report? In my judgment the answer to that question on the evidence in this case must be 'yes'. The defendants knew the house was being 'tarted up' for sale. The defendants knew their report might go to the mortgagees. The fact that it might go to mortgagees meant that their findings must affect the value people would put on the house. What was the right value to put on the house must affect the . . . sellers, the mortgagees (if any), and most probably the third person concerned in the sale transaction, the buyer. The defendants regarded the buyer as the beneficiary of their work if they got the job. [The sellers] would fill in the buyer's name on the 20 year guarantee of their work, and the defendants would honour the guarantee in the hands of the occupiers from time to time of the house".[63]

On the facts, however, the defendants were held not negligent.

---

[60] See *Hingorani v Blower* [1976] 1 E.G.L.R. 104. The surveyor instructed to carry out structural survey by National House Owners' Association in turn so instructed by purchaser. Held: the surveyor owed a duty of care to the purchaser. It is unclear from the report whether the surveyor knew that the particular purchaser would place reliance upon his advice. He did know, however, that his advice was for the purpose of house purchase. The decision is explicable on the ground that the surveyor ought to have known that the purchaser would rely upon his advice.

[61] See *Omega Trust & Co Ltd v Wright Son & Pepper* [1997] P.N.L.R. 425 and further at para.10–071 below.

[62] [1976] 1 E.G.L.R. 100.

[63] *ibid.* at 101.

Similarly in *Shankie-Williams v Heavey*,[64] the defendant dry rot specialist was   **10–041**
instructed to inspect a ground floor flat by its vendor. He provided a report stating
that he had found no evidence of dry rot at the time of his inspection. He
nevertheless gave certain timbers a precautionary spray of fungicide and guaranteed these timbers against recurrence of dry rot infestation for 30 years. Soon
after the vendor sold not only the ground floor flat, but also the first floor flat
above. Dry rot appeared two years later in both flats and the defendant was sued
in negligence by each purchaser. The Court of Appeal held that the defendant
owed a duty of care to the purchasers of the ground floor flat because the
defendant knew that the vendor wanted a report or guarantee from him which he
could show to prospective purchasers of the ground floor flat. However, it was
held that he did not owe a duty of care to the purchaser of the first floor flat, since
his instructions, report and guarantee related to the ground floor flat only.[65]
Although in breach of his duty of care to the purchasers of the ground floor flat,
the Court of Appeal held that the defendant was not liable to them. There was no
evidence that those purchasers had seen the defendant's report and accordingly
there was no causal connection shown between the defendant's breach of duty
and the damage sustained by them.[66]

Where the surveyor neither knows nor ought to know that reliance is to be   **10–042**
placed upon his advice by a third party, no duty of care will arise. In *Le Lievre
v Gould*,[67] the claimant mortgagee agreed to advance to a builder sums secured
by the mortgage of land the subject of building works. The instalments were
quantified by reference to progress certificates provided by the mortgagee's
surveyor. The defendant, a surveyor employed by the builder, was unaware of the
agreement between the builder and the claimant mortgagee and his certificates
were addressed to the builder. His certificates were communicated, apparently
without his authority, by the builder to the mortgagee, who relied on them in
advancing the mortgage instalments. It was held that the surveyor owed no duty
of care to the mortgagee. The actual *ratio decidendi* was that there could be no
duty in the absence of a contract between the mortgagee and the surveyor. While
that *ratio* cannot survive *Hedley Byrne & Co Ltd v Heller and Partners Ltd*,[68]
four of their Lordships in that case were inclined to support the actual decision

---

[64] [1986] 2 E.G.L.R. 139, CA.
[65] *ibid.* at 141. May L.J. said:
  "In my judgment, on the facts as I have outlined them, there was an insufficient nexus between the
  appellant and the intending purchaser of a lease of the first-floor flat (the third plaintiff). I ask
  myself, in the circumstances of this case, where is one to stop in this inquiry? If the appellant owed
  to the third plaintiff a duty of care when reporting on the ground-floor flat, to be occupied by the
  first and second plaintiffs, did he owe a similar duty to any intending purchaser of the second-floor
  flat? . . . I think not. If, contrary, to that view, the answer has to be in the affirmative then I pose
  the question: 'What about an adjoining occupier?' Supposing that this was a company converting
  not one house but a row of five houses in the street. Did [the defendant] in those circumstances,
  asked to inspect and report only upon the ground-floor flat [of one house], owe any duty to
  intending lessees of flats in the yet to be converted adjoining premises . . . ? Again, I think
  not."
[66] See also *Duncan Investments v Underwoods* [1997] P.N.L.R. 521, where the defendant estate
agents gave an oral estimate of possible re-sale values to the claimant knowing that the advice was
likely to be relied upon and that it was unlikely that independent advice would be sought. The
imposition of a duty of care was upheld on appeal.
[67] [1893] 1 Q.B. 491.
[68] [1964] A.C. 465.

in *Le Lievre v Gould*.[69] Lord Reid in particular took the view that it would be difficult to establish the prerequisite degree of proximity to give rise to a duty of care on the facts of the case.[70]

10–043   A question which sometimes arises is as to whether a lender's reliance on a valuation is unreasonable so as to preclude him from recovering any loss. A range of possible results are possible in such a case: a court may decide that the particular transaction was outside the contemplation of the valuer so that no duty arises (or that the kind of damage suffered was beyond the scope of his duty); or that there was no causal link between the negligence and the loss suffered; or that the lender was guilty of contributory negligence or that the full loss should be recovered. In *Western Trust v Strutt & Parker*,[71] the question as to whether the lender was entitled to rely on a valuation arose in three different ways. A lender had agreed to provide a total loan of £1m in three tranches in order to enable farm buildings to be converted into a holiday cottages complex—the first of £500,000 and the next two of £250,000. The security taken was over 14 of the 15 properties and excluded the largest property. In addition, three of the charged properties were built slightly beyond the charged land. The valuer was instructed by the developer to provide a valuation on all of the properties after the first two tranches had been made. He negligently provided a valuation of the entire holiday complex on the basis that it would provide permanent accommodation (for which there was no planning permission). The lender then not only provided the third tranche of the loan, but also advanced two further loans of £500,000 and £150,000 ("the swimming pool loans") in order to build a swimming pool, sauna and café without, however, making any provision for the moneys to be advanced as the same were built. The questions arose (a) as to whether the lender was entitled to recover the first two tranches on the basis that had a competent valuation been provided, the lender would have sought to recover the same; (b) whether the lender could recover the third tranche given that the property valued (the whole complex) was different from that charged; and (c) whether the lender could recover the swimming pool loans. The Court of Appeal upheld the judge's decision that only the third tranche loan could be recovered, albeit with a reduction of 20 per cent for contributory negligence.[72] Both the first two tranches and the swimming pool loans were beyond the scope of the duty owed by the valuer. On the evidence, there was no reason for the valuer to suppose that his valuation was required in relation to the first two tranches.[73] So far as the swimming pool loans were concerned, the interval (some seven months) between the valuation and the further loans, together with the fact that there was no reason for the valuer to suppose that loans would be required other than immediately to

---

[69] [1964] A.C. 465 at 488 (Lord Reid), at 507 (Lord Hodson) at 519 (Lord Devlin) and at 535 (Lord Pearce). Lord Morris at 499 thought it unnecessary to consider the point.

[70] *ibid.* at 488. Lord Hodson at 507 and Lord Pearce at 535 preferred the justification of the decision given by Denning L.J. in *Candler v Crane Christmas & Co* [1951] 2 K.B. 164, namely that the claimant mortgagees not only had the opportunity, but had stipulated for inspection by their own surveyor.

[71] [1999] P.N.L.R. 154.

[72] Lord Woolf M.R. stated at 168 that he regarded the lender as being fortunate in only being held 20% to blame for the third tranche—see further para.10–174 below.

[73] See at 168—although Lord Woolf made it clear that even if his conclusion as to duty was different, he would have rejected the suggestion that the lender could have improved its position as to the first two tranches.

complete the development, were sufficient to take them beyond the valuer's duty. In relation to the third tranche, Lord Woolf accepted[74] that if the difference between the property which a valuer valued and the property relied on by the lender was of sufficient significance, it would mean that the lender had ventured beyond the scope of duty owed by the valuer. In deciding whether this was the case, he stated:

> "A useful working test would be to ask what would be a reasonable response of a valuer to the question can the valuation still be relied on notwithstanding the difference between the property he valued and the property which was actually the subject matter of the valuation. If, for example, the valuation was of a number of identical properties but the loan was made in relation to only some of the properties, you would expect the reasonable valuer to respond that the difference did not matter because the value of the lesser number of properties could be deduced by dividing the value given so as to reflect the reduction in the number of properties. If, however, no such calculation would be possible because the property being valued and the property which was the subject of the loan were significantly different, you would expect the response of the reasonable valuer to be otherwise."[75]

(iii) *Duty of Mortgagee's Valuer to Purchaser*

The prime example of the imposition of a duty of care by the English courts in **10–044** favour of third parties in this field has occurred in relation to valuation reports commissioned by lenders. In normal circumstances, a claim by a mortgagor against a lender's valuer will arise from the terms of the written report provided by the valuer. It is, of course, possible for the scope of the duty to be widened as a result of direct contact between the valuer and the mortgagor.[76] The existence of such a duty arising without such direct contact was first recognised in the case of *Yianni v Edwin Evans*,[77] confirmed in *Smith v Bush*.[78]

In *Yianni*, the defendants accepted that their valuation was negligent, but denied liability to the claimants, on the ground that they did not owe them a duty of care. Park J. held that the defendants did owe them a duty of care. He rejected arguments by the defendants that the claimants' reliance on the valuation was unforeseeable and that the claimants had been contributory negligent in not obtaining an independent surveyor's report:

> "It was plainly a house at the lower end of the property market. The applicant for a loan would therefore almost certainly be a person of modest means who, for one reason or another, would not be expected to obtain an independent valuation, and who would be certain to rely, as the plaintiffs in fact did, on the defendants' valuation as communicated to him in the building society's offer. I am sure that the defendants knew that their valuation would be passed on to the plaintiffs and that the defendants knew that the plaintiffs would rely upon it when they decided to accept the society's offer."[79]

---

[74] At 165.
[75] *ibid.* at 165–166.
[76] Thus in *Frost v James & Finlay Bank* [2001] Lloyd's L.R.P.N. 629, it was alleged that a valuer had provided express assurance to the mortgagor following an inspection at the property. Hart J. rejected the claim on its facts.
[77] [1982] Q.B. 438.
[78] [1990] 1 A.C. 831. See para.10–046, below.
[79] [1982] 1 Q.B. 438 at 456.

Park J. would appear to have been influenced in his conclusion by evidence adduced to the effect that only between 10 and 15 per cent of mortgage applicants to building societies had their own independent survey carried out. Although in accord with the expectations of consumer organisations, this decision represented a landmark in the extension of a surveyor's duty of care to third parties. Such a duty was held to exist despite the disclaimer of any implied warranty as to the reasonableness of the purchase price and the fact that the claimants did not see (and were not intended to see) the report.[80]

10–045   **The impact of *Yianni*.** This decision had a considerable impact on those concerned with the domestic housing market.[81] One lender[82] considered the implications of *Yianni* and introduced a scheme whereby prospective borrowers were offered a choice between a valuation without liability on the valuer and a report which accepted that the valuer was under a duty to exercise reasonable skill and care. Such a report cost at least £100 more than a valuation for a house worth £20,000. Noting that the report did not involve any more work for the valuer, Lord Templeman in *Smith v Bush*[83] was scathing about the scheme, its cost and the attempt to exclude liability for negligence:

> "On a million houses, this would represent increases of income to be divided between valuers, insurers and building societies of about £150m. It is hardly surprising that few purchasers have chosen the report instead of the valuation. Any increase in fees, alleged to be justified by the decision of this House in these appeals, will no doubt be monitored by the appropriate authorities. It is open to Parliament to provide that members of all professions or members of one profession providing services in the normal course of the exercise of their profession for reward shall be entitled to exclude or limit their liability for failure to exercise reasonable skill and care. In the absence of any such provision valuers are not, in my opinion, entitled to rely on a general exclusion of the common law duty of care owed to purchasers of houses by valuers to exercise reasonable skill and care in valuing houses for mortgage purposes."[84]

It is notable that such criticism was made shortly before the decline in property values at the end of the 1980s and beginning of the 1990s had become manifest. Given the modest fees charged for mortgage valuations and the extent of liability attaching to the same, it must be doubted that the criticism was fair. The standard conditions of engagement prepared by RICS now accept a duty of care to the prospective purchaser, whatever the level of service offered.

---

[80] In the reverse situation of a surveyor instructed by a mortgagor but told that reliance would be placed upon his advice by a mortgagee, a duty of care to the latter has been recognised: see *Singer & Friedlander Ltd v John D Wood & Co* [1977] 2 E.G.L.R. 84.

[81] Concern about the consequences of this case for the surveying profession in part led to the establishment of a fact finding study team, under the chairmanship of Professor Andrew Likierman, which considered the practice of surveying. The report, *Professional Liability*, was published in 1989 by HMSO. For a commentary on the report see M. F. James, "Surveyors and the Likierman Report" (1990) 3 P.N. 119.

[82] The Abbey National Building Society.

[83] [1990] 1 A.C. 831.

[84] *ibid.* at 853.

Smith v Bush. The House of Lords *in Smith v Bush*; and *Harris v Wyre Forest*   **10–046**
DC[85] considered both the question of the duty of care to third parties and the
application of the reasonableness test under the Unfair Contract Terms Act
1977.[86] The latter issue is considered below.[87] The facts of these cases are as
follows. In *Smith v Bush*, the claimant was sent a copy of the defendant
surveyor's valuation report by the building society. The report stated that no
essential repairs were necessary. The mortgage application form and report
contained a disclaimer of liability for the accuracy of the report and a recommendation to the effect that the claimant should obtain independent advice. The
claimant nevertheless relied on the report and bought the modest property. The
chimneys were in fact defective. The claimant claimed damages from the surveyor who, inter alia, relied upon the disclaimer. In *Harris v Wyre Forest DC* the
claimants purchased a small terraced house with a 95 per cent mortgage from the
defendant council. They paid the valuation fee and signed the standard mortgage
application which stated that the valuation was confidential, intended solely for
the council and that no responsibility was accepted for the value or condition of
the property. The claimants did not see the report, but accepted the mortgage
offered. Three years later they attempted to sell the house, but a survey revealed
structural defects in the property to the extent that it was uninhabitable and
unsaleable.

In deciding that the valuer[88] owed a duty of care to the purchasers in each case,   **10–047**
the House of Lords expressly approved the decision of Park J. in *Yianni v Edwin
Evans & Sons*.[89] Lord Templeman concluded that "the duty of care which the
valuer owes to the building society is exactly the same as the duty of care which
he owes to the purchaser"[90] and based his decision on his analysis of the
relationship between the valuer and the purchaser as "akin to contract". Lord
Templeman stated[91]:

> "The valuer knows that the consideration which he receives derives from the purchaser
> and is passed on by the mortgagee, and the valuer also knows that the valuation will
> determine whether or not the purchaser buys the house."

Lord Griffiths did not think that voluntary assumption of responsibility was a
helpful or realistic test for liability.[92] He answered the question, "in what
circumstances should a duty of care be owed by the adviser to those who act upon
his advice?" as follows:

---

[85] [1990] 1 A.C. 831. Save where the different facts of the two cases require, the case is referred to
as *Smith v Bush*.
[86] For further commentary on the case, see M. F. James, "Negligence in mortgage valuations" (1989)
3 P.N. 73; and *ibid.*, "Surveyor's liability after *Smith v Bush*" (1991) 3 P.N. 142.
[87] See para.10–065.
[88] In *Smith v Bush*, the valuer, in *Harris v Wyre Forest DC*, the council, who, it was accepted, were
vicariously liable for the acts and omissions of their employed valuer. In *Merrett v Babb* [2001]
Lloyd's L.Rep. P.N. 468, the question arose as to whether an employed valuer (as distinct from his
employer) owed a duty of care to a prospective purchaser. In deciding that such a duty was owed,
May L.J. placed heavy reliance on the fact that the House of Lords had considered the professional
status of the employed valuer in *Harris* to be important. See further para.10–014 above.
[89] [1982] Q.B. 438, and see para.10–044 above.
[90] [1990] 1 A.C. 831, at 851.
[91] *ibid.* at 846.
[92] *ibid.* at 862 and with less force, at 864.

"only if it is foreseeable that if the advice is negligent the recipient is likely to suffer damage, that there is a sufficiently proximate relationship between the parties and that it is just and reasonable to impose the liability. In the case of a surveyor valuing a small house for a building society or local authority, the application of these three criteria leads to the conclusion that he owes a duty of care to the purchaser. If the valuation is negligent and is relied upon damage in the form of economic loss to the purchaser is obviously foreseeable. The necessary proximity arises from the surveyor's knowledge that the overwhelming probability is that the purchaser will rely upon his valuation, the evidence was that surveyors knew that approximately 90 per cent of purchasers did so and the fact that the surveyor only obtains the work because the purchaser is willing to pay his fee. It is just and reasonable that the duty should be imposed for the advice is given in a professional as opposed to a social context and liability for breach of the duty will be limited both as to its extent and amount. The extent of the liability is limited to the purchaser of the house—I would not extend it to subsequent purchasers. The amount of the liability cannot be very great because it relates to a modest house. There is no question here of creating a liability of indeterminate amount to an indeterminate class.[93] I would certainly wish to stress that in cases where the advice has not been given for the specific purpose of the recipient acting upon it, it should only be in cases where the adviser knows that there is a high degree of probability that some other identifiable person will act upon the advice that a duty of care should be imposed. It would impose an intolerable burden upon those who give advice in a professional or commercial context if they were to owe a duty not only to those to whom they give the advice but to any other person who might choose to act upon it".[94]

10–048   Lord Jauncey considered that in three of the cases discussed, the existence of direct contact between the negligent provider of information, and the claimant or his agent was important.[95] The fact that such contact was absent in the case of *Smith v Bush* was noted by Lord Jauncey when he formulated his test, but on the facts, did not lead to a different result:

"I prefer to approach the matter by asking whether the facts disclose that the appellants in inspecting and reporting must, but for the disclaimers, by reason of the proximate relationship between them, be deemed to have assumed responsibility towards Mrs Smith as well as to the building society who instructed them.

There can only be an affirmative answer to this question. The four critical facts are that the appellants knew from the outset: (1) that the report would be shown to Mrs Smith; (2) that Mrs Smith would probably rely on the valuation contained therein in deciding whether to buy the house without obtaining an independent valuation; (3) that if, in those circumstances, the valuation was, having regard to the actual condition of the house, excessive, Mrs Smith would be likely to suffer loss; and (4) that she had paid to the building society a sum to defray the appellants' fee."[96]

---

[93] See the well-known dicta of Cardozo C.J. in *Ultramares Corp v Touche* (1931) 174 N.E. 441, quoted by Denning L.J. in *Candler v Crane Christmas & Co* [1951] 2 K.B. 164 at 183. The risk of creating such a liability led Phillips J. to reject the submission that Lloyd's Register of Shipping owed a duty of care to those foreseeably liable to suffer economic loss in consequence of reliance on an alleged negligent Classification Society survey of a ship. See *The Morning Watch* [1990] 1 Lloyd's Rep. 547 at 560.

[94] [1990] 1 A.C. 831 at 865.

[95] *ibid.* at 870, 871. The cases Lord Jauncey referred to were *Cann v Willson* (1888) 39 Ch.D. 39; *Candler v Crane Christmas & Co* [1951] 2 K.B. 164; and *Hedley Byrne & Co Ltd v Heller & Partners Ltd* [1964] A.C. 465.

[96] *ibid.* at 871E.

The Limitations on *Smith v Bush*. The Courts have, since the decision, been   **10–049**
careful to emphasise the limits of *Smith v Bush*. In *Caparo Industries Plc v
Dickman*,[97] Lord Oliver stressed the importance of the fact that the valuer knew
that his valuation was likely to be relied on by the purchaser:

> "[*Smith* and *Harris*] do not, I think, justify any broader proposition than that already set
> out, save that they make it clear that the absence of a positive intention that the advice
> shall be acted upon by anyone other than the immediate recipient—indeed an expressed
> intention that it shall not be acted upon by anyone else—cannot prevail against actual
> or presumed knowledge that it is likely to be relied upon in a particular transac-
> tion."[98]

In deciding that the knowledge of likely reliance should prevail against the
valuer's desire that the valuation should not be relied upon, the reasoning
resolves to a simple question of policy.[99] Such considerations were expressly
recognised by Lord Griffiths:

> "It must, however, be remembered that this is a decision in respect of a dwelling house
> of modest value in which it is widely recognised by surveyors that purchasers are in fact
> relying on their care and skill. It will obviously be of general application in broadly
> similar circumstances. But I expressly reserve my position in respect of valuations of
> quite different types of property for mortgage purposes, such as industrial property,
> large blocks of flats or very expensive houses."[1]

The above passage has been emphasised more than once. Moreover the courts   **10–050**
have warned against reliance on *Smith v Bush* in order to establish novel claims.
In *Saddington v Colley Professional Services*,[2] which concerned a claim for
consequential losses following an advance on an allegedly negligent mortgage,
Balcombe L.J. stated:

> "In my judgment [*Smith v Bush*] represents the high water mark in this field . . . Lord
> Griffiths took the view that *Smith v Bush* was at the outer limit".

Similarly in the Scottish case, *Wilson v DM Hall & Sons*,[3] Lady Paton rejected
a claim by a modest property developer against a valuer employed by the
developer's lender who had over-valued some flats. The developer claimed that
the sale had been delayed as a result. The judge emphasised that pricing and
marketing strategy was expected to be the preserve of the developer in conjunction with his own professionals and that a bank's valuer would not expect his

---

[97] [1990] 2 A.C. 605. See Ch.17, para.17–018. No duty of care was owed by the auditors of a public
company to potential investors.
[98] *ibid.* at 638–639. See also the statement by Brennan C.J. in *Esanda Finance Corp Ltd v Peat
Marwick Hungerfords* (1997) 188 C.L.R. 241 at 251–253, where he stressed the importance of the
knowledge that the claimant was likely to rely on the negligent mis-statement and para.15–083
below.
[99] For, it is submitted, the reasons adopted by the House of Lords when considering whether it was
reasonable for the valuer to exclude his duty. See para.10–065, below.
[1] *ibid.* at 859G. Such considerations were also relevant as to the application of the Unfair Contract
Terms Act—as to which see paras 10–065 and 10–073 below.
[2] [1999] Lloyd's Rep. P.N. 140 at 143.
[3] [2005] P.N.L.R. 375.

own report to be relied on, or, necessarily, passed to a developer. She drew attention to Lord Griffiths's own words when finding that different policy considerations applied to the question as to whether a duty of care should be imposed in favour of even a small scale developer.

Smith v Bush did not decide the extent to which a duty of care would be found to exist in unusual or expensive properties. *Beaumont v Humberts*[4] arose out of a valuation for reinstatement purposes of an unusual Grade II listed property in Dorset. The defendant valuers were instructed by the mortgagees and the claimant was the mortgagor. By a majority[5] the Court of Appeal held that the necessary degree of proximity between the valuer and the mortgagor had been established and a duty of care existed. The principal facts relied upon by the Court of Appeal in coming to that conclusion were that the valuer had earlier carried out a full structural survey of the property (but not a valuation) for the claimant, and the claimant had suggested to the mortgagees that they employ the valuer to obtain the reinstatement value that he would in any event have to pay for.

10–051   A consequence of the decision in *Smith v Bush* is that a valuer may be exposed to double jeopardy in respect of the same negligent valuation. In factual circumstances similar to those which obtained in *Smith v Bush*, the valuer will owe a contractual duty to the lender, and a duty of care at common law to the borrower. An overvaluation caused by a negligent failure to observe defects may result in the borrower suing the valuer. Having recovered damages the borrower may not carry out repairs, but instead may dissipate the fruits of the action. If there is a subsequent default by the borrower, the lender has a right to claim its loss from the valuer. The valuer cannot defeat such a claim on the basis that it has already met the claim by the borrower. The parties, the cause of action and the measure of damage would all be different.[6]

(d) *The Standard of Care and Skill*

(i) *Reasonable Standard*

10–052   In common with other professional persons and in the absence of an express term to the contrary, the standard required of a surveyor is that of the ordinary skilled man exercising the same skill as himself. He is variously described in the cases as the "reasonably skilled", "competent", "prudent" or "average" surveyor.[7] It

---

[4] [1990] 2 E.G.L.R. 166. Note that the purchaser was far removed from the archetypal purchaser of *Smith v Bush*, *per* Staughton L.J.: "Mr Beaumont is an intelligent and sophisticated businessman and not a humble purchaser of a house of modest value . . . "

[5] Taylor and Dillon L.JJ., Staughton L.J. dissenting. In fact Staughton and Dillon L.J. disagreed on every main issue, and Taylor L.J. did not agree on all issues with either.

[6] To reduce the risk of such a situation arising a potentially negligent valuer might wish to involve the lender at an appropriate stage in any action brought by the borrower.

[7] This passage in the third edition (1992) was cited with approval by the court in *Muldoon v Mays of Lilliput Ltd* [1993] 1 E.G.L.R. 43 at 45. This paragraph in the fourth edition (1997) was also approved by the Court of Appeal in *Sansom v Metcalfe Hambleton & Co* [1998] 2 E.G.L.R. 103 and by the court in *Lewisham Investment Partnership Ltd v Morgan* [1997] 2 E.G.L.R. 150. See generally on this topic *Tomlinson*, p.37.

will not be lower for a surveyor with no professional qualifications[8] or with limited experience whether generally[9] or of property in a particular area.[10] Nor will it make any difference that no fee[11] or a lower fee is charged or intended to be charged for the services rendered. Thus in *Roberts v J Hampson & Co*,[12] Ian Kennedy J. stated:

"In my judgment, it must be accepted that where a surveyor undertakes a Scheme 1 valuation it is understood that he is making a limited appraisal only. It is however, an appraisal by a skilled professional man. It is inherent in any standard fee work that some cases will colloquially be 'winners' and others 'losers' from the professional man's point of view. The fact that in an individual case he may need to spend two or three times as long as he would have expected, or as the fee structure would have contemplated, is something that he must accept. His duty to take reasonable care in providing a valuation remains the root of his obligation."[13]

The *standard* therefore remains constant irrespective both of the nature of the engagement and whether a claim is made in contract or tort. It is sometimes contended that when a limited task is required, for example, a "quick survey", the standard is lower. It is submitted that the contention is misconceived, as the dicta by Ian Kennedy J. in *Roberts v J Hampson & Co* illustrates. The point was also succinctly made by Lord Cameron in the Scottish case, *Stewart v HA Brechin & Co*[14]:

"The first question is what was the contract; because until that is decided, the extent of the defenders' obligation to the pursuer cannot be determined. Whatever the extent of that obligation, the measure of the defenders' duty in its discharge is the same, namely,

---

[8] See *Freeman v Marshall & Co* (1966) 200 E.G. 777 *per* Lawton J., 777:
"[The defendant surveyor] had . . . had no organised course of training as a surveyor and had never passed any professional examination in surveying. He was a member of the Valuers Institution through election, not examination . . . In fairness to him, he claimed only to have a working knowledge of structures from the point of view of buying and selling, but if he held himself out in practice as a surveyor he must be deemed to have the skills of a surveyor and be adjudged upon them."

[9] See *Kenney v Hall, Pain and Foster* [1976] 2 E.G.L.R. 29.

[10] See (on this point) *Baxter v FW Gapp & Co Ltd* [1938] 4 All E.R. 457 (first instance); [1939] 2 K.B. 752, CA, especially the passage from Goddard L.J.'s judgment at [1938] 4 All E.R. 459 quoted at para.10–081, below. This case has been overruled on the issue of the calculation of interest by *Swingcastle Ltd v Gibson* [1991] 2 A.C. 223.

[11] See *Kenney v Hall, Pain and Foster* [1976] 2 E.G.L.R. 29, a negligent valuation case, *per* Goff J. at 33:
"the defendants are right to concede that they owe such a duty of care to the plaintiff. It makes no difference whether or not they intended to charge a fee for their services. In point of law they could have done so, because whenever a professional man renders services to another at his request he is, in the absence of a contrary intention, entitled to charge for those services".

[12] [1990] 1 W.L.R. 94.

[13] *ibid.* at 101. In *Routestone Ltd v Minories Finance Ltd* [1997] 1 E.G.L.R. 123 at 126K, Jacob J. described the standard of care of an estate agent as follows:
"The relevant legal standard was not in dispute. [The claimant] had to show that the advice given by [the defendants] was more than erroneous—it had to amount to an error of the sort that would not have been made by a reasonably competent estate agent professing himself to have the standard and type of skill that [the defendants] held themselves out as having, and acting with ordinary care . . . "

[14] [1959] S.C. 306.

to display and apply reasonable care and a reasonable standard of professional competence in doing the work they were employed to do, provided that the work fell within the proper scope of their professional activities."[15]

As is apparent from Lord Cameron's dictum, it does not follow from the fact that the standard of care remains the same, that the scope and extent of the surveyor's instructions will be irrelevant to the result achieved.[16]

10–053   The *standard* is not relaxed if the required task is carried out in unusual circumstances, for example a valuation in a market showing signs of deep depression or of unusual buoyancy or volatility.[17] Whether the standard was complied with in a particular case, however, must be determined having regard to the circumstances and knowledge current at the time when the surveyor was required to carry out his instructions. The court must be careful "not to be wise after the event".[18] Genuinely unforeseeable events occurring after the valuation date must be disregarded whether they are adverse or beneficial to the surveyor's opinion of value. Thus in *Arab Bank v John D Wood Commercial*,[19] the Court of Appeal criticised the trial judge for "the use of inadmissible hindsight" in relying on an unusual renegotiation of rent which had occurred after the date of the first opinion of value in order to justify the overall valuation produced. Yet guarding against hindsight may be difficult where a long time has elapsed[20] between the allegedly negligent act and trial or where the state of knowledge at a particular time[21] is in issue.[22]

---

[15] [1959] S.C. 306 at 307.

[16] See further para.10–057 below.

[17] See *Nykredit Mortgage Bank Plc v Edward Erdman Group Ltd* [1996] 1 E.G.L.R. 119 at 122 *per* Peter Gibson L.J.:

"it is plain on the evidence that it is wrong to take speculations about the future movement of interest rates into account on a valuation, both in relation to demand and in relation to developer's costs",

and Singer & Friedlander Ltd v John D Wood & Co [1977] 2 E.G.L.R. 84 at 86 *per* Watkins J.:

"The unusual circumstances of his task impose upon [a valuer] a greater test of his skill and bid him to exercise stricter discipline in the making of assumptions without which he is unable to perform his task, and I think he must beware of lapsing into carelessness or over-confidence when the market is riding high. The more unusual be the nature of the problem, for no matter what reason, the greater the need for circumspection."

[18] *Hill v Debenham, Tewson and Chinnocks* (1958) 171 E.G. 835 *per* Judge Carter Q.C. For a recent example of a case where a judge considered that an expert had taken into account matters of which a valuer could not have known, see *Preferred Mortgages Ltd v Countrywide Surveyors Ltd* [2006] P.N.L.R. 154; [2005] EWHC 2820—see para.10–006 above.

[19] [2000] Lloyd's L.Rep. P.N. 173 at 186.

[20] Note *Leigh v Unsworth* (1972) 230 E.G. 501, where some seven-and-a-half years had elapsed. The delay may sometimes favour the defendant surveyor: *see MacKenzie v Hall & Co* (1951) 157 E.G. 492, a Scottish Court of Session case, the pursuers' claim against the defendant surveyors failed, effectively on this ground. *Per* Lord Mackintosh:

"the onus of proof which lay upon the pursuer of an action for professional negligence was a heavy one, and in this case that onus was made still heavier by the pursuers' long delay in bringing the action".

[21] Note the unsuccessful attempt in *Corisand Investments Ltd v Druce & Co* [1978] 2 E.G.L.R. 86, especially at 90, to establish that the defendant valuers were negligent in not anticipating or suspecting the impending collapse of the property market when carrying out a valuation in September 1973.

[22] This passage in the third edition (1992) was cited with approval by the court in *Muldoon v Mays of Lilliput Ltd* [1993] 1 E.G.L.R. 43, 46.

(ii) *General Practice and Knowledge as Evidence of the Standard*

What is required to fulfil the standard of care and skill in a particular case is **10–054**
usually determined by reference to the general practice of surveyors carrying out
similar work. Thus what ought to be done is usually determined by asking what
the "average"[23] or "ordinary competent"[24] surveyor would have done. While it
remains open to a court to reject a general practice as not achieving the required
standard, there has yet to be a precedent where a court has done so in the context
of surveyors. Gibson J.'s decision in *Corisand Investments Ltd v Druce & Co*[25]
that the defendants were negligent in not allowing for the speculative element in
the property market in making their valuation, was criticised by some in the
profession as going beyond general practice. The judge was nevertheless careful
to reach his decision by reference to what an "ordinary competent valuer"[26]
would have done. In his view, it would have included allowing for the speculative
element.

The knowledge required of a surveyor is likewise described by reference to a **10–055**
norm such as the "ordinary competent surveyor"[27] or "averaged skilled professional" as in *Daisley v BS Hall & Co*[28] In the latter case Bristow J. accepted
expert evidence that the risk to buildings on shrinkable clay subsoil adjacent to
poplar trees was notorious and was one of the subjects which was included in a
surveyor's education. The defendant surveyor who did not recognise the trees as
poplars was held negligent in failing, inter alia, to warn of the risk. In contrast in
Last v Post,[29] Lloyd Jacob J. held that the defendant surveyor was not negligent
in not recognising disintegration of roof tiles through efflorescence: "As the
character of the phenomenon was so rare it would not be right to apply as the
standard of a competent surveyor the detection of a phenomenon."[30]

Duty to keep up to date. The average skilled surveyor is, however, required **10–056**
to take reasonable steps to acquaint himself with changes and new developments
affecting his skill. From 1991 the RICS required its members to demonstrate a
commitment to their professional development, and now members of the Institution have an obligation to attend training and other events that are approved as
part of the Continuing Professional Development scheme. In *Hooberman v Salter*

---

[23] e.g. *Daisley v BS Hall & Co* (1972) 225 E.G. 1553 *per* Bristow J. at 1555:
"The duty of a practitioner of any professional skill which he undertakes to perform . . . is to see
the things that the average skilled professional in the field would see, draw from what he sees the
conclusions that the average skilled professional would draw, and take the action that the average
skilled professional would take."
[24] *Corisand Investments Ltd v Druce & Co* [1978] 2 E.G.L.R. 86 at 89. Note the Canadian case of
Seeward Mortgage Investment Corp v First Citizens Financial Corp (1983) 45 B.C.L.R. 87 at 100 *per*
Hamilton L.J.S.C.: "He could not expect from an appraiser the standard of inspection that would have
been required of a professional engineer."
[25] [1978] 2 E.G.L.R. 86.
[26] *ibid.* at 92, 97.
[27] See *Investors in Industry Commercial Properties v South Bedfordshire DC; Ellison & Partners and
Hamilton Associates (Third Parties)* [1986] 1 All E.R. 787 *per* Slade L.J. at 808 to 809.
[28] (1972) 225 E.G. 1553.
[29] (1952) 159 E.G. 240. The defendant was nevertheless held negligent in failing to observe the
deposit from the roof on the flooring and in failing consequently to warn the claimant of the condition
of the roof.
[30] *ibid.* at 240.

Rex,[31] a surveyor failed to take proper account of warnings in professional journals as to the lack of ventilation in flat roofs.[32] Judge Smout Q.C. stated:

"I am satisfied that in the light of knowledge in the construction industry and amongst surveyors in 1977 it was generally appreciated that flat roofs were vulnerable, that their construction had to be viewed with caution . . . and that a competent surveyor should have appreciated at that time that they reflected a serious potential danger."[33]

For the same reasons, a valuer must not only be familiar with the value of land throughout the country in a general way, but must inform himself adequately of market trends and be sensitive to them with particular regard for the locality in which the land he values lies.[34] Moreover, a surveyor must keep himself reasonably acquainted with the law and changes in the law so far as his skill is affected. Two cases illustrate this. In *Jenkins v Betham*,[35] the defendant surveyors and valuers were alleged to have negligently valued ecclesiastical property. Parke B. left to the jury the question whether the defendants supplied that ordinary degree of skill and care which could reasonably be expected from country surveyors and valuers. The jury found they did. The Court of Common Pleas ordered a new trial. Jervis C.J. stated:

"the defendants could not be expected to supply minute and accurate knowledge of the law; but we think that under the circumstances, they might properly be required to know the general rules applicable to the valuation of ecclesiastical property, and the broad distinction which exists between the cases of an incoming and outgoing tenant and incoming and outgoing incumbent".[36]

Similarly in *Weedon v Hindwood Clarke and Esplin*,[37] a valuer instructed in 1968 to negotiate with the district valuer the amount of compensation for land compulsorily acquired was held negligent either in not being aware of the change in the basis of valuation of such land brought about by the case of *West Midland Baptist (Trust) Association (Inc) v Birmingham Corp*[38] or because, being aware of it, he did not apply it as he should have. The Court of Appeal's decision in the *West Midland* case preceded the instructions and the House of Lords decision was pronounced in August 1979 preceding agreement on a figure between the defendant valuer and the district valuer in December 1969. Where, however, a surveyor is asked to advise on a matter of law it is submitted that the required standard of skill and care expected of him should be approached in the same way as by Hallet J. in *Sarginson Bros v Keith Moulton & Co*,[39] where he referred to "the steps which a reasonably prudent person would clearly have deemed necessary before that answer could be given with reasonable safety".

---

[31] [1985] 1 E.G.L.R. 144.
[32] *ibid.* at 146.
[33] *ibid.*
[34] *per* Watkins J. in *Singer & Friedlander Ltd v John D Wood & Co* [1977] 2 E.G.L.R. 84 at 85.
[35] (1855) 15 C.B. 167.
[36] *ibid.* at 393.
[37] (1974) 234 E.G. 121.
[38] [1968] 2 Q.B. 188, CA; [1970] A.C. 874, HL.
[39] (1942) 73 Ll. Rep. 104.

Extent of duty determined by type of service offered. As the different types **10–057** of service offered by surveyors become more defined, so there is a growing body of case law on whether particular steps are or are not required for a particular service. Although the *standard* of care will not vary according to the instructions received, the extent of the surveyor's duty may well do so. This was expressly recognised by the Court of Appeal in *Arab Bank v John D Wood Commercial*,[40] where a lender had lent £17.1m to a single purpose company to purchase an industrial estate in Darlington. It had received a valuation of £22m from one valuer (JDW) and had asked a second valuer (WGS) not to carry out its own valuation but only to review that of JDW. Having done so, WGS initially advised that a figure of £19m was appropriate and then revised the figure to £20.6m. The judge found that WGS were not obliged to conduct a full investigation and appraisal of the property as they would have had to do if instructed to carry out a free-standing open market valuation. The Court of Appeal approved a passage in the judge's judgment[41] in which he indicated that the consequence of the limited nature of WGS's instructions was that they would benefit from a greater margin of error than would have been appropriate to JDW.

Similarly, commenting on mortgage inspections and valuations, Lord Griffiths in *Smith v Bush*[42] said:

> "It is only defects which are observable by a careful visual examination that have to be taken into account and I cannot see that it places any unreasonable burden on the valuer to require him to accept responsibility for the fairly elementary degree of skill and care involved in observing, following-up and reporting on such defects. Surely it is work at the lower end of the surveyor's field of professional expertise."

Lord Templeman, in the same case[43] also commented on the standard of expertise required for such work: "The valuer is and, in my opinion, must be a professional person, typically a chartered surveyor in general practice, who, by training and experience and exercising reasonable skill and care, will recognise defects and be able to assess value." In *Whalley v Roberts & Roberts*,[44] Auld J. stated:

> "The defendants were not instructed to undertake a structural survey or a survey of the detail called for in the standard form of the Royal Institution of Chartered Surveyors House Buyers' Report and Valuation inspection. They were instructed to inspect and to provide a mortgage valuation report. It is common ground that this involved them in making a brief and reasonably careful visual inspection to enable them, in the terms of the bank report form, to provide a valuation and general guide as to the condition of the property. I am satisfied on the evidence before me that this would not normally involve the use of a spirit-level unless the lack of level in the property became evident on a visual inspection so as to call for further inspection."

In *Roberts v J Hampson Co*,[45] Ian Kennedy J. described a building society valuation as follows:

---

[40] [2000] Ll. Rep. P.N. 173.
[41] *ibid.* at 180 *per* Mance L.J.
[42] [1990] 1 A.C. 831 at 858.
[43] *ibid.* at 850.
[44] [1990] 1 E.G.L.R. 164 at 168.
[45] [1990] 1 W.L.R. 94 at 101.

"It is a valuation and not a survey, but any valuation is necessarily governed by condition. The inspection is, of necessity, a limited one. Both the expert surveyors . . . agreed that with a house of this size they would allow about half an hour for their inspection on site. That time does not admit of moving furniture, or of lifting carpets, especially where they are nailed down."

The Court of Appeal in *Sutcliffe v Sayer*[46] considered a valuation prepared by an estate agent, and Butler-Sloss L.J. commented:

"I do not consider that there is any duty upon a valuer to warn a purchaser as to the difficulty of resale . . . I can find no breach of the general duty of care to take proper steps to do the best that he can as a valuer and not as a qualified surveyor."[47]

(iii) *Not Every Error is Negligence*

10–058 The standard of reasonable care and skill allows for a margin of differing opinion and even a degree of error. As Buxton L.J. stated:

"It has frequently been observed that the process of valuation does not admit of precise conclusions, and thus that the conclusions of competent and careful valuers may differ, perhaps by a substantial margin, without one of them being negligent . . . "[48]

It is not enough to prove that the surveyor gave the wrong advice or that where there is room for two views he took the wrong view.[49] In *Luxmoore-May v Messenger May Baverstock*[50] Slade L.J. considered that problem in the context of the standard of care owed by a firm of provincial fine art auctioneers and valuers:

"The valuation of pictures of which the artist is unknown, pre-eminently involves an exercise of opinion and judgment, most particularly in deciding whether an attribution to any particular artist should be made. Since it is not an exact science, the judgment in the very nature of things may be fallible, and may turn out to be wrong. Accordingly, provided that the valuer has done his job honestly and with due diligence, I think that the court should be cautious before convicting him of professional negligence merely because he has failed to be the first to spot a 'sleeper' or the potentiality of a 'sleeper': see and compare the observations of Lord Wilberforce in relation to barristers in *Saif Ali v Sydney Mitchell & Co* [1980] A.C. 198, 214F–245G."[51]

The point was also well made by Judge Everett Q.C. in *Leigh v Unsworth*,[52] in which it was claimed that the surveyor was negligent in failing to observe signs of serious settlement in carrying out a structural survey:

---

[46] [1987] 1 E.G.L.R. 155.
[47] *ibid.* at 156. Contrast this case with the Scottish decision *of Martin v Bell-Ingram*, 1986 S.L.T. 575 (Second Division) where, on appeal, it was held (at 583) that a surveyor carrying out a mortgage valuation for a building society owes a duty to the mortgagor not only to identify those defects which affect the value of the property, but also those which materially would affect the decision whether or not to purchase.
[48] In *Merivale Moore v Strutt & Parker* [2000] P.N.L.R. 498 at 515.
[49] *per* Judge Carter Q.C., in *Hill v Debenham, Tewson and Chinnocks* (1958) 171 E.G. 835 at 835.
[50] [1990] 1 W.L.R. 1009.
[51] *ibid.* at 1020. See Ch.12, para.12–008, for a discussion of the duty of care owed by barristers.
[52] (1972) 230 E.G. 501.

"The carrying out of a survey and the reporting to a client involves observation, deduction and the exercise of professional skill and judgment. The mere fact that one professional man might suffer from an excessive caution does not mean that another man, exercising his judgment to the best of his skill and ability and taking perhaps a somewhat more optimistic view, is guilty of a departure from the appropriate standard of professional care and skill."[53]

The same point was made by Watkins J. in *Singer & Friedlander Ltd v John D Wood Co*[54] in respect of a valuation:

"The valuation of land by trained, competent and careful professional men is a task which rarely, if ever, admits of precise conclusion. Often beyond certain well-founded facts so many imponderables confront the valuer that he is obliged to proceed on the basis of assumptions. Therefore, he cannot be faulted for achieving a result which does not admit of some degree of error. Thus two able and experienced men, each confronted with the same task might come to different conclusions without any one being justified in saying that either of them lacked competence and reasonable care, still less integrity in doing his work."[55]

In *Craneheath Securities v York Montague Ltd*,[56] the Court of Appeal rejected the claimant's argument that if a sufficient number of errors in the defendants' valuation could be identified, the court should infer without direct evidence that the valuation figure itself was negligently wrong. Balcombe L.J. said:

"I reject [counsel's] submission, that if we were satisfied that there were a sufficient number of errors in the way [the valuer] has carried out his valuation we should in the circumstances of this case infer that his final result was wrong. Valuation is not a science, it is an art, and the instinctive 'feel' for the market of an experienced valuer is not something which can be ignored."[57]

In *Matto v Rodney Broom Associates*[58] the Court of Appeal commented that:

---

[53] (1972) 230 E.G. 501 at 649.
[54] [1977] 2 E.G.L.R. 84.
[55] *ibid.* at 86. See also to the same effect *Craneheath Securities Ltd v York Montague Ltd* [1994] 1 E.G.L.R. 159, Jacob J.; [1996] 1 E.G.L.R. 130, CA; *Allied Trust Bank Ltd v Edward Symmons & Partners* [1994] 1 E.G.L.R. 165; *Axa Equity & Law Home Loans Ltd v Goldsack Freeman* [1994] 1 E.G.L.R. 175; *Mortgage Express Ltd v Dunsmore, Reid and Smith* [1996] G.W.D. 10–590 (the lenders sued in two actions heard together in respect of valuations of two properties, succeeding in one case, but failing to prove that the other valuation was outside an acceptable degree of variation and had been negligently carried out).
[56] [1996] 1 E.G.L.R. 130.
[57] *ibid.* at 132. See also *Hardy v Wamsley-Lewis* (1967) 203 E.G. 1039, where the defendant surveyed a house and overlooked a piece of skirting with waviness characteristic of dry rot. Paull J. stated at 1041 that if the matter had remained there and there had been nothing else at all, he would have required argument as to whether one failure actually constituted negligence on the part of a professional man; *Lawrence v Hampton & Sons* (1964) 190 E.G. 107 *per* Mocatta J. at 111: "I have not overlooked [counsel's] argument that a competent surveyor may, without negligence, fail to notice a crack in a building"; *Fryer v Bunney* [1982] 2 E.G.L.R. 130 *per* Judge Newey Q.C. at 134: "The mere fact that a surveyor misses something in the course of a survey does not necessarily make him negligent." In *Frost v James & Finlay Bank* [2001] Lloyd's L.R.P.N. 629, Hart J. rejected a claim brought by a mortgagee against a valuer who had noticed and reported on cracking but considered it to be insignificant. He found that there was no basis upon which it could be shown that the valuer's conclusion was one to which no reasonably competent valuer could have come.
[58] [1994] 2 E.G.L.R. 163 at 168.

"if a surveyor fails to appreciate the extent of past damage, or to carry out the investigations which proper care and skill required, he will, in the absence of very special circumstances, commit no breach of duty in giving advice which is right and consistent with his having exercised proper care and skill. A professional man is entitled to be lucky".[59]

(iv) *The Relevance of "the bracket"*

10–059 Because competent valuers may legitimately differ from each other in providing competent valuations, a question which commonly arises is whether a valuer may be liable if he carelessly makes a material error in coming to his valuation, but nonetheless produces a final figure which can be justified by a competent assessment. Thus it may be possible to show that a valuer failed to take account of a specific characteristic of the property which every competent valuer should have taken into account and that, had the characteristic been considered, the valuer's own final figure would have been altered, although other valuers could nevertheless have justifiably arrived at the original figure. It is suggested that the answer to this question depends upon the nature of the instructions which the valuer has received. If his only material obligation is to produce a competent final valuation figure then it does not matter how he arrives at it. If, however, the valuer's obligations extend beyond the production of a final figure, the answer may be different. This analysis is supported by a dictum of Mance L.J. in *Arab Bank v John D Wood*,[60] in which he referred to the Privy Council decision in *Lion Nathan Ltd v C-C Bottlers Ltd*,[61] a case concerning the measure of damages in respect of a profit forecast which sellers of shares warranted to have been calculated on a proper basis and Lord Hoffmann gave an example which suggested that a small but discrete error in double-counting might lead through directly to an award of damages:

"Where, as in the present case, criticism is addressed to factors such as rental value and yield which bear proportionately on the ultimately assigned value, the issues of the permissible range and of negligence are on any view inseparably linked. The value estimated results from the estimated rental values and yields. Where there is some discrete error, like that postulated in *Lion Nathan*, it may be appropriate to examine more closely the nature of the valuer's engagement. Is it simply to produce an end result and to do so within the range of 'reasonable foreseeable deviation'? Or may be to exercise reasonable skill and care in the circumstances (including whatever instructions may have been given) both in forming and in expressing an opinion on value? In the *SAAMCO* case . . . the judgment given by Sir Thomas Bingham M.R. (as he then was) at pages 403H–404G lends some support to the latter analysis. On that basis, if as a result of clearly identifiable negligence, a valuer arrives at a figure lower than he would otherwise have put forward, the line of reasoning indicated in *Lion Nathan* might still be applicable, although the end figure could not itself be said to fall outside the margin of legitimate valuation by valuers generally."

---

[59] In *Routestone Ltd v Minories Finance Ltd* [1997] 1 E.G.L.R. 123, Jacob J. held that the fact that another estate agent would have marketed a property subject to a power of sale differently did not indicate negligence on the part of the defendant agents.
[60] [2000] P.N.L.R. 173 at 181.
[61] [1996] 1 W.L.R. 1438.

Despite the logic of the above approach, the English courts have held that it is a **10–060** necessary condition for liability, at least in the case of errors in the assessment of rentals or yields, that the final result should be outside "the bracket". The extent of authority is now such that it appears unlikely that a first instance judge will find a valuation negligent unless it is outside the bracket. The first relevant judicial statement is that of Watkins J. in *Singer & Friedlander Ltd v John D Wood & Co*[62]:

> "Pinpoint accuracy in the result is not, therefore, to be expected by he who requests the valuation. There is, as I have said, a permissible margin of error, the 'bracket' as I have called it. What can properly be expected from a competent valuer using reasonable care and skill is that his valuation falls within this bracket."

In *Craneheath Securities v York Montague*,[63] the Court of Appeal dismissed an appeal where the claimant sought to infer a negligent final valuation figure from a number of alleged discrete errors. It was made clear that it was a necessary pre-condition to liability that it could be shown that the final valuation figure was wrong. The matter was considered by Buxton L.J. in *Merivale Moore v Strutt & Parker*,[64] where he stated that it was a necessary condition for liability that a valuation should fall outside the permissible bracket. He adopted as helpful an observation of Judge Langan Q.C. in *Legal & General Mortgage Services v HPC Professional Services*[65] that once it is shown that the valuation falls outside the bracket:

> "the plaintiff will by that stage have discharged an evidential burden. It will be for the defendant to show that, notwithstanding that the valuation is outside the range within which careful and competent valuers may reasonably differ, he nonetheless exercised the degree of care and skill which was appropriate in the circumstances".

He went on to make the points (a) that if a valuer did adopt an unprofessional practice or approach, then that might be taken into account in considering whether his valuation contained an unacceptable degree of error; and (b) that where a valuation was shown to be outside the acceptable limit, that might be a strong indication that negligence had, in fact, occurred.[66]

In *David Goldstein v Levy Gee*,[67] which was a case concerning the valuation of shares by an accountant, Lewison J. considered the relevant authorities and stated that he found them difficult to reconcile. He found that he was bound by the decision in *Merivale Moore* so that the valuation had to be outside an

---

[62] [1977] 2 E.G.L.R. 84 at 86.
[63] [2001] Lloyd's L.Rep. P.N. 348 *per* Balcombe L.J. at 350.
[64] [2000] P.N.L.R. 498 at 515–517.
[65] [1997] P.N.L.R. 567 at 574F.
[66] In *Preferred Mortgages Ltd v Countrywide Surveyors Ltd* [2006] P.N.L.R. 154; [2005] EWHC 2820, the judge found that the valuation was just within the permissible bracket of 15% but also held, obiter, that even if it had not been, he would not have been prepared to find the valuation negligent given the competence with which the valuation had been prepared.
[67] [2003] EWHC 1574.

acceptable bracket before it was found to be negligent.[68] In this respect he followed the earlier decision of Mr Harvey Q.C. in *Currys Group v Martin*.[69]

10–061   **The extent of the bracket.** The margin of error approach is not a principle of law. It is an evidential approach to assist in the resolution of questions of primary liability. By itself, evidence as to the conclusion reached by a valuer does not prove that the valuer failed to exercise reasonable care and skill in coming to that conclusion, unless the doctrine of *res ipsa loquitur* applies.[70] The duty on the valuer is to exercise reasonable skill and care. If the valuer did so then the fact that the result of the exercise of reasonable skill and care fell outside the "bracket" may be rebuttable evidence of negligence, but does not of itself determine the issue of primary liability. Many properties do not have a single "true" value, and whilst the margin of error approach may be a convenient shorthand in many cases, it should not be applied without adequate consideration of the basic principles of negligence liability. The extent of permissible error will be determined by the judge having regard to the evidence. Plainly it will be much easier to value a property if it has itself been recently sold in the open market or if a number of closely comparable properties have recently been sold than will be the case if the property is unique or has very unusual characteristics.[71] In *Merivale Moore v Strutt & Parker*,[72] Buxton L.J. stated:

---

[68] This case was followed by H.H. Judge Richard Seymour Q.C. in *Lloyds TSB Bank v Edwards Symmons* [2003] EWHC 346, where it was alleged that the defendant valuers had negligently undervalued a shopping centre for a bank with the result that it was sold by the bank at too low a price. The judge considered a large number of alleged errors in methodology by the valuers, but found that, as the result of the valuation being within the appropriate bracket, no case had been made out. He did not consider whether the terms of the valuers' retainer were such that they were required to do more than simply produce an end figure.

[69] [1999] 3 E.G.L.R. 165.

[70] An example of the evidential nature of the bracket is provided by *Michael v Miller* [2004] EWCA Civ 282, where a mortgagor alleged that a mortgagee has disposed of a property at an undervalue. The mortagee had disposed of the property for £1.625m on the advice of an experienced agent. The judge found that the "true" value of the property was £1.75m, but that the figure of £1.625m nonetheless fell within an acceptable bracket which he considered was £1.6 to £1.9m. The Court of Appeal rejected the submission that the "bracket" had no relevance in such situations. Jonathan Parker L.J. stated (at paragraph 138):

> "In so far as the exercise of the mortgagee's power of sale calls for the exercise of informed judgment by the mortgagee, whether as to market conditions, or as to market value, or as to some other matter affecting the sale, the use of a bracket—or a margin of error—must in my judgment be available to the court as a means of assessing whether the mortgagee has failed to exercise that judgment reasonably".

He went on to doubt whether the judge had, in fact, been correct to find that the "true" value of the property was £1.75m in circumstances where no offer in that amount had been received despite sustained exposure to the market.

[71] The above passage was cited with approval by H.H. Judge Heppel Q.C. in *John D Wood & Co v Knatchbull* [2003] P.N.L.R. 351, [2002] EWHC 2822; in the context of advice by an estate agent to a vendor as to the appropriate asking price for a house. The agent had advised an asking price of £1.5m. The judge concluded that the true value of the property was £1.7m at the material time. He nonetheless held that the initial advice was not negligent both because of the limited information available to the agent and because the agent was entitled to a margin of error. He went on to hold that the agent was in breach of duty in that he should have informed the vendor when he became aware that a nearby similar property was on the market at £1.95m. See further para.10–107 below.

[72] [2000] P.N.L.R. 499 at 517.

"the 'bracket' is not to be determined in a mechanistic way, divorced from the facts of the instance case. We were shown a list of figures giving either the bracket determined, or the percentage divergence from the true figure found nonetheless not to have been negligent, in a series of recent cases. I did not find that of assistance, save as a graphic reminder that it is not enough simply to show that the valuation was different from the true value".

As a matter of practice, "the bracket" has usually been determined to lie in the range 10 to 20 per cent either side of a mean figure.[73] Judges have sometimes commented that expert evidence has suggested a closer correlation between competent valuations than they would suppose. In *Beaumont v Humberts*,[74] a case involving an alleged negligent valuation for reinstatement purposes, Staughton L.J. commented when dealing with the issue of breach of duty:

"It is accepted that a surveyor or valuer may be wrong by a margin of 10 per cent either way without being negligent. (That in itself seems, in my uninstructed opinion, a high standard to impose; but it is, as I have said, accepted.)"[75]

Similarly, in *Nykredit Mortgage Bank Plc v Edward Erdman Group Ltd*[76] the same Lord Justice commented:

---

[73] According to expert evidence in *Singer & Friedlander v John D Wood* [1977] 2 E.G.L.R. 84, the permissible margin was 10% either side of "the right figure", but in exceptional circumstances it could be extended to about 15% either way. In *Private Bank Trust & Co Ltd v S (UK) Ltd* [1993] 1 E.G.L.R. 144, the court concluded that on the evidence the defendant's valuations lay within a permissible margin of error of 15% either side of his valuation bracket. In *Banque Bruxelles Lambert SA v Lewis & Tucker Ltd* [1994] 2 E.G.L.R. 108, the evidence before Phillips J. was that when valuations are based on comparables, one competent valuation may differ from another by as much as 20%. See at 118C. In *BNP Mortgages Ltd v Barton Cook & Sams* [1996] 1 E.G.L.R. 239, the evidence proved an acceptable range for the property in question to be 15%. In *Assured Advances Ltd v Ashbee & Co* [1994] E.G.C.S. 169, the valuers were approached by brokers and not the lender, and asked for a "quick £50 valuation". The court considered the proper approach was
  "to find a central accurate valuation and to establish a percentage above and below it which was the non-negligent zone. Anything outside that zone would be prima facie a negligent valuation".
There was, however, no adequate evidence of the proper valuation, so the action failed. In *Arab Bank v John D Wood Commercial* [2000] Ll. Rep. P.N. 173 at 195, Mance L.J. plainly considered that a "bracket" of 20% above a correct figure was at the outer limits of a permissible range even for a "franking valuation"—see further para.10–057 above. In *Preferred Mortgages Ltd v Countrywide Surveyors Ltd* [2006] P.N.L.R. 154 [2005] EWHC 2820 the judge found that the bracket for an unusual converted chapel was 15%.
[74] [1990] 2 E.G.L.R. 166. See para.10–050 above.
[75] *ibid.* at 169. See *McIntyre v Herring Son & Daw* [1988] 1 E.G.L.R. 231, where Mr E.A. Machin Q.C., sitting as a deputy High Court judge, accepted at 233 that:
  "The widths of such brackets reflected only the evidence in that particular case and that there is no proposition of law that in valuation cases a valuer is not negligent if his valuation falls within such a bracket. The permissible width of the bracket must be a matter to be decided upon the evidence of any particular case."
In *Mount Banking Corp Ltd v Brian Cooper & Co* [1992] 2 E.G.L.R. 142 at 144, dicta to the same effect appear. The deputy judge at 145K considered the proper approach to be:
  "assess here whether [the valuer's] approach was proper and what a competent approach could properly have resulted in. If [the valuer's] end result was within a modest margin of that figure, then he is not to be adjudged negligent".
[76] [1996] 1 E.G.L.R. 119 at 120. The defendants carried out a residual land valuation, acknowledged to be sensitive to the variables used in its calculation. The method was not criticised, but certain of the variables were.

"There was evidence, which the judge accepted, that careful and skilled valuers did not inevitably arrive at precisely the same answer. If a given figure is taken as the true value, the range within which a valuer could arrive at some different amount without negligence was plus or minus 15 per cent. In the light of the sensitivity of the calculation I do not find that at all surprising."

If the property being valued is unique or unusual, then the use of a bracket may become inappropriate. Jacob J. commented in *Craneheath Securities Ltd v York Montague Ltd*[77]:

"The margin of error approach may well make sense when the property being valued has a number of good comparables (*e.g.* houses on an estate, forestry or farmland). Then one can in effect take an 'average' as the 'right' figure and look at the deviation from it . . . But, as I say, the approach depends on evidence. I had no evidence before me which would begin to support a permissible 'margin of error' for a property such as Kingsdown."

It will, nevertheless be open to a judge to find that a valuation fell outside the permissible bracket even without express expert evidence as to the extent of the bracket in a particular case.[78]

(v) *Onus of Proof*

10–062 The onus of proof rests "fairly and squarely" upon the claimant in an action for professional negligence against a surveyor.[79] It is not enough to prove that he was wrong. Negligence must be distinctly proved.[80] It may even be difficult to prove he was wrong by showing that the defendant's valuation was significantly higher or lower than another surveyor's valuation[81] or the price actually achieved[82] or that his estimate of individual items making up the calculation was on the high side.[83] It must be shown that his valuation and calculations were such that they

---

[77] [1994] 1 E.G.L.R. 159 at 162. His decision was upheld on appeal: [2001] Lloyd's L.Rep. P.N. 348.

[78] See *per* Buxton L.J. in *Merivale Moore v Strutt & Parker* [2000] P.N.L.R. 498 at 517.

[79] *Hill v Debenham, Tewson and Chinnocks* (1958) 171 E.G. 835 at 835.

[80] See *Singer & Friedlander Ltd v John D Wood & Co* [1977] 2 E.G.L.R. 84 at 93.

[81] *per* Geoffrey Lane L.J. in *Campbell v Edwards* [1976] 1 W.L.R. 403 at 408:
"There is nothing to suggest that the valuer here did not take into consideration all the matters which he should have taken into consideration; and where the only basis of criticism is that another valuer has subsequently produced a valuation a third of the original one it does not afford, in my view, any ground for saying that Chesterton's valuation must have been or may have been wrong".

[82] Note that Gibson J. in *Corisand Investments Ltd v Druce & Co* [1978] 2 E.G.L.R. 86 considered on the facts of that case that:
"the usefulness of comparing the valuation figure with the eventually realised sale price for the purpose of critical consideration of those valuation figures, is either non existent or extremely limited."

[83] See *Shacklock v Chas. Osenton, Lockwood & Co* (1964) 192 E.G. 819. The claimant sought to show that, defendant valuer was negligent, particularly his approach of estimating a maximum figure and making deductions for various items. *Per* Mocatta J. at 821:
"I do not think that [the defendant's] valuation can be faulted legally so as to show that he was professionally negligent . . . merely by going through these items and criticising them meticulously and suggesting that they are on the high side."

could not have been arrived at by the exercise of reasonable care and skill.[84] Although it is sometimes stated that the onus of proof in a professional negligence action is a heavy one,[85] the standard is no more than that applicable to civil actions generally, namely proof on a balance of probabilities.[86]

(e) *Limitation of Liability*

Surveyors' reports and valuations may seek to limit liability in two ways—either **10–063** by way of general limitations on the extent of liability owed to particular persons or groups or by clauses seeking to set out and limit the scope of particular services. The latter type of clause is discussed below.[87]

After *Yianni v Edwin Evans and Sons*[88] it became common to find terms seeking to limit a surveyor's liability generally and, in particular, when a report was sought through a building society upon an application for a mortgage advance. The decision of the House of Lords in *Smith v Eric S Bush*[89] to the effect that such terms will be regarded as unreasonable within the meaning of the Unfair Contract Terms Act 1977 has neutered the practical effect of such clauses so far as modestly priced domestic properties are concerned. The courts have, however, upheld such clauses in the case of expensive or unusual properties and are generally willing to uphold appropriate clauses in a commercial context, as is shown by the decision in *Omega Trust Co v Wright Son & Pepper.*[90]

Residential property. *Stevenson v Nationwide Building Society*[91] was the first **10–064** reported English case illustrating the effect of disclaimer clauses contained in a mortgage application form in respect of a valuation carried out upon the society's instructions but intended to be shown to the mortgage advance applicant. The claimant, who was an estate agent, sought an advance of £42,750 from the defendant building society. The defendant instructed a valuer employed by it to report upon the property. A copy of his report was provided to the claimant. The claimant was granted the requested advance and purchased the property. A month later part of the floor collapsed. The property had a number of structural defects which the valuer had not observed. The judge[92] held that the valuer had failed to exercise reasonable care and skill and that the society would have been vicariously liable for the valuer if liable. Nevertheless in view of two clauses contained in the mortgage application form completed by the claimant, the claim failed. The first of these clauses stated that the inspection carried out by the society's valuer was not a structural survey and there might be defects which

---

[84] The paragraph to this point in the fourth edition was stated to accurately state the law by Stuart-Smith L.J., with whom Mummery L.J. agreed in *Watts v Savills*, CA, June 16, 1998, para.38.
[85] *MacKenzie v Hall & Co* (1951) 157 E.G. 492.
[86] This paragraph in the third edition (1992) was cited with approval *in Macey v Debenham, Tewson & Chinnocks* [1993] 1 E.G.L.R. 149 at 151M, and cited by the court in *Muldoon v Mays of Lilliput Ltd* [1993] 1 E.G.L.R. 43 at 45M.
[87] See para.10–073, below.
[88] [1982] Q.B. 438. See para.10–041, above.
[89] [1990] 1 A.C. 831.
[90] [1997] P.N.L.R. 425—see further para.10–071, below.
[91] [1984] 2 E.G.L.R. 165.
[92] Mr J. Wilmers Q.C. sitting as a deputy High Court judge.

such a survey would reveal. The second clause contained the words that the report "was intended solely for the consideration of the society in determining what advance (if any) may be made on the security". The judge considered these words significant as indicating the limited purpose of the report. This was also made clear by the first clause. Nevertheless if those words had stood alone he would not have absolved the defendant from liability given the unusual nature of the building which demanded a careful inspection of its underside. The remaining words of the clause, however, were crucial:

"no responsibility is implied or accepted by the society or its valuer for either the value or condition of the property by reason of such inspection and report".

The judge stated that the words were unambiguous and free from doubt and it was accepted that, subject to the Unfair Contract Terms Act 1977, they constituted a valid disclaimer. It was further accepted as between the parties that the disclaimer was not a contract term, but was rather a "notice (not being a notice having contractual effect)".[93]

The relevant question was whether the notice satisfied the criterion of reasonableness under the Act, being that:

"it should be fair and reasonable to allow reliance on it, having regard to all the circumstances obtaining when the liability arose or (but for the notice) would have arisen".[94]

The judge, having noted that the onus of showing that the disclaimer is fair and reasonable was on the defendants and that the test was subjective, considered s.11(5) of the Act:

"When I bear in mind that the person affected by the disclaimer is someone well familiar with such disclaimers and with the possibility of obtaining a survey, and also familiar with the difference between a building society valuation and a survey and their different costs, it seems to me perfectly reasonable to allow the building society, in effect, to say to him that if he chooses the cheaper alternative he must accept that the society will not be responsible for the content to him."[95]

It is suggested that two facts were important to the resolution of the case. First, the claimant was an estate agent, a professional working in the precise area where his complaint lay. Secondly, the property was not a modest house at the lower end of the market. The claimant was buying a relatively expensive property, comprising two shops, a maisonette and a flat. There was to some extent an element of commercial dealing about the transaction. This case was cited to the House of Lords in *Smith v Bush*,[96] but not referred to in any of the speeches. On its facts *Stevenson v Nationwide Building Society* can stand with *Smith v Bush*, particularly given the decision of the Court of Appeal in *McCullagh v Lane Fox & Partners*.[97]

---

[93] Unfair Contract Terms Act 1977, s.11(3).
[94] *ibid.*
[95] [1984] 2 E.G.L.R. 165 at 170.
[96] [1990] 1 A.C. 831.
[97] [1996] 1 E.G.L.R. 35. For the facts and discussion see para.10–013 and 10–028 above.

The House of Lords considered in *Smith v Bush*[98] the application of the Unfair   **10–065**
Contract Terms Act 1977 to mortgage valuations.[99] Their Lordships concluded
that the Unfair Contract Terms Act 1977 applied to clauses or notices that sought
to exclude a duty, as well as to clauses or notices that sought to exclude liability.
Counsel for the valuers sought to argue that it was fair and reasonable for a valuer
to rely on an exclusion clause. Lord Templeman summarised the argument as
follows[1]:

"(a) the exclusion clause is clear and understandable and reiterated and is forcefully
       drawn to the attention of the purchaser;
 (b) the purchaser's solicitors should reinforce the warning and urge the purchaser to
       appreciate that he cannot rely on a mortgage valuation and should obtain and pay
       for his own survey;
 (c) if valuers cannot disclaim liability they will be faced by more claims from
       purchasers some of which will be unmeritorious but difficult and expensive to
       resist;
 (d) a valuer will become more cautious, take more time and produce more gloomy
       reports[2] which will make house transactions more difficult;
 (e) if a duty of care cannot be disclaimed the cost of negligence insurance for valuers
       and therefore the cost of valuation fees to the public will be increased."

It was also argued that there was no contract between a valuer and a purchaser,
that so far as the purchaser was concerned, the valuation was gratuitous,[3] and the
valuer should not be forced to accept a liability he was unwilling to undertake.

None of these arguments was accepted by the House of Lords. Lord Temple-   **10–066**
man stated[4]:

"All these submissions are inconsistent with the ambit and thrust of the Act of 1977.
The valuer is a professional man who offers his services for reward. He is paid for those
services. The valuer knows that 90 per cent of purchasers in fact rely on a mortgage
valuation and do not commission their own survey. There is great pressure on a
purchaser to rely on the mortgage valuation. Many purchasers cannot afford a second
valuation. If a purchaser obtains a second valuation the sale may go off and then both
valuation fees will be wasted. Moreover, he knows that mortgagees, such as building
societies and the council . . . are trustworthy and that they appoint careful and competent valuers and he trusts the professional man so appointed. Finally the valuer knows
full well that failure on his part to exercise reasonable skill and care may be disastrous
to the purchaser."

---

[98] [1990] 1 A.C. 831.
[99] For the facts of this case see para.10–046, above.
[1] *ibid.* at 851.
[2] This may allude to an area of tension within the practice of many surveyors carrying out surveys
and valuations of domestic property. Referrals from estate agents who have no such professional
capability can be important to a practice. If a surveyor, through fear of litigation produces (non-
negligent) reports that err on the side of gloom, a prospective sale may be lost, with it the estate
agent's commission, and as a consequence a source of work for the surveyor may disappear.
[3] Although the purchaser had of course paid for the valuation, through the building society or local
authority.
[4] [1990] 1 A.C. 831 at 852.

Lord Griffiths agreed that it would not be fair and reasonable for the surveyor to be permitted to exclude liability in the circumstances of the case.[5] He commented that it was impossible to draw up a complete list of the factors to be taken into account when a court has to decide whether an exclusion clause is fair and reasonable.[6] Lord Griffiths considered that the following matters should, in his view, always be considered:

(a) Were the parties of equal bargaining power?[7]

(b) Would it have been reasonably practicable to obtain the advice from an alternative source, taking into account considerations such as cost and time?[8]

(c) How difficult is the task being undertaken for which liability is being excluded?[9]

(d) What are the practical consequences of the decision on the question of reasonableness?[10]

(e) And, in the particular circumstances of the case, the question who employed the surveyor and paid his fees was material.[11]

10–067 It is important to emphasise that both *Smith v Bush* and *Harris v Wyre Forest DC* dealt with domestic property purchases at the least expensive end of the market.[12] The decision of the Court of Appeal to permit the defendants to rely upon their exclusion clause in *McCullagh v Lane Fox & Partners*[13] where the property was worth £800,000, illustrates the point made by the House of Lords.

10–068 Following *Smith v Bush*, the courts have sought to establish the circumstances in which liability can be disclaimed. *Beaton v Nationwide Building Society*[14] was another case involving the valuation of a modest property. A disclaimer notice within the meaning of s.11(3) of the 1977 Act was set out on the mortgage application form, the offer of advance and the copy of the valuation report

---

[5] [1990] 1 A.C. 831 at 852; at 859.

[6] *ibid.* at 858.

[7] Lord Griffiths contrasted the case with the position resulting from a one-off retainer between parties of equal bargaining power.

[8] Lord Griffiths noted the financial pressure many first-time buyers are under, and the strain that making them buy the same advice twice would cause.

[9] Lord Griffiths applied this to the sums of money potentially at stake and the ability of the parties to bear the loss involved, which in turn raised the question of insurance. He noted that all surveyors are obliged to carry indemnity insurance, and that had to be compared to the financial catastrophe for the purchaser.

[10] Lord Griffiths applied this to the sums of money potentially at stake and the ability of the parties to bear the loss involved, which in turn raised the question of insurance. He noted that all surveyors are obliged to carry indemnity insurance, and that had to be compared to the financial catastrophe for the purchaser.

[11] Lord Griffiths noted, at 859, that it had not been argued that had the purchaser employed and paid the surveyor directly, it would still have been reasonable for the surveyor to exclude his liability. He considered "the present situation is not far removed from that of a direct contract between the surveyor and the purchaser".

[12] See the comments by Lord Templeman at 854, Lord Griffiths at 859, and Lord Jauncey at 874. See further para.10–049 above.

[13] [1996] 1 E.G.L.R. 35. For the facts and discussion see paras 10–013 and 10–028, above.

[14] [1991] 2 E.G.L.R. 145.

provided to the claimants. The notices that the claimants accepted they had read included:

> "No responsibility is implied or accepted by the Society or its valuer for either the value or condition of the property by reason of the inspection and report. The Society does not undertake to give advice as to the value or condition of the property and accepts no liability for any such advice that may be given. The inspection carried out by the Society's valuer was not a structural survey and there may be defects which such a survey would reveal."

It was submitted that there were two specific matters which made it fair and reasonable for the defendant to rely upon the disclaimers. First, the claimants were advised by their own solicitors to have a structural survey carried out and made a positive decision not to have such a survey. The judge[15] noted that the statistics showed that only 10 to 15 per cent of all purchasers of modest dwelling houses trouble to obtain their own valuation and survey. The conduct of the claimants in not having a structural survey was thus to be anticipated. Further, the report of the surveyor went much further than simply approving the application for a mortgage at a stated valuation. The terms of the report stressed that certain matters should be brought to the attention of the applicants, some of those matters adversely affected the property and required remedial work, others, including the critical question of structural movement, were positively reassuring. The judge held that the very terms of the report made it unfair and unreasonable to permit the defendant to rely on disclaimers on this ground. The second ground relied on by the defendant was that the claimant had been told by the estate agent that the property had been partially underpinned. The judge considered that if he had concluded as a fact that the agent had made it plain to the claimant that there was cause for anxiety about the underpinning work, there would be force in the defendant's submission, but he did not so find. The judge therefore concluded that it would not be fair and reasonable to allow the defendant to rely on the disclaimers.

In *Davies v Idris Parry*,[16] the valuer sought to rely upon a blanket exclusion **10–069** of all liability for negligence in respect of a mortgage inspection and valuation. The surveyor was unable to escape liability for his negligence in failing to draw attention to major defects in the foundations of the property, defects that should have been reasonably apparent during his visual inspection. The property was at the lower end of the housing market and the surveyor knew that the claimant was likely to rely upon the valuation. McNeill J. held that such an exclusion notice was unreasonable.[17]

---

[15] Mr Neil Butterfield Q.C. (as he then was) sitting as a deputy High Court judge.

[16] [1988] 1 E.G.L.R. 147.

[17] See also *Henley v Cloke & Sons* [1991] 2 E.G.L.R. 141, Judge Thayne-Forbes Q.C.:
"The property is a detached house with four bedrooms, which had been built in the 1930s . . . It is, and was then, an attractive house, with central heating, garaging for two cars and a decent sized garden. It is situated in a pleasant residential area of Maidstone. It was being offered for sale at a price of £78,000."
This was in 1984. However, after considering *Smith v Bush*, counsel for the valuers (who prepared a mortgage inspection and valuation), did not attempt to rely upon the disclaimers, or to argue that the same were reasonable within the meaning of the 1977 Act.

10–070   The burden of proof is on the defendant to establish that in all the circumstances it is fair and reasonable that he should be allowed to rely upon his disclaimer of liability,[18] and the surveyor or lender will have to prove that any notices relied upon were brought to the attention of the claimant in time.[19]

10–071   **Commercial property.** In *Omega Trust Co Ltd v Wright Son & Pepper*,[20] the defendant valuer provided a borrower with valuations of three commercial retail properties in central London. The valuation contained a disclaimer:

> "This report shall be for private and confidential use of the clients for whom the report is undertaken and should not be reproduced in whole or in part or relied upon by third parties for any use whatsoever without the express written authority of [the surveyors]."

The borrower applied to Omega for a loan of £350,000, and the valuer retyped a copy of its valuation to Omega. Unknown to the valuer, Omega could not lend all that the borrower had requested, and so applied to its associate company, Banque Finindus, for £200,000 of the total and supported this request with a copy of the valuation addressed to Omega. After completion of the loan the borrower went into liquidation and the properties proved worthless. The valuers applied under RSC Order 14A for a ruling as to whether they owed a duty of care to Banque Finindus. The Court of Appeal held that as Banque Finindus was a separate legal entity of which the valuers were ignorant, that bank could not be regarded as a "client" within the meaning of the disclaimer. The only client was Omega. The Court of Appeal considered that the disclaimer satisfied the requirement of reasonableness under the Unfair Contract Terms Act 1977, relying on the commercial setting of the transaction, rather than the domestic situation in *Smith v Bush*. Henry L.J. said[21]:

> "The point that Lord Griffiths was making was that in a transaction involving a lot of money in a commercial context, both parties are well able to look after themselves, and it is not necessary to have any statutory protection for them. It is this point which, in my judgment, distinguishes this commercial case from those purchases of domestic houses with which other cases have dealt."

The Court of Appeal discussed the matters that would need to be considered: that the burden of proof to sustain the exemption clause was on the valuer, that the parties were of equal bargaining power, that it was reasonably practical for Banque Finindus to have obtained its own valuation from the valuer and within a reasonable timescale. Henry L.J. concluded[22]:

---

[18] See s.11(3) of the 1977 Act, and see *Smith v Bush, per* Lord Griffiths at 858.

[19] See *Goodall v Simpson* (1991) Outer House Cases, March 6, 1991, Court of Session (unreported); and *Martin v Bell-Ingram*, 1986 S.L.T. 575, where it was held that the surveyors could not rely upon a disclaimer of liability, as no disclaimer had been communicated to the prospective purchasers when the surveyors had communicated the terms of their report to the building society by telephone, and the same had been transmit onwards to the prospective purchasers or their solicitors. The terms of the disclaimer were not communicated to the prospective purchasers until after they had concluded their bargain to purchase the property.

[20] [1997] P.N.L.R. 425, CA.

[21] *ibid.* at 429D.

[22] *ibid.* at 430G.

"It seems to me that this professional valuer, valuing expensive properties in a commercial context, was entitled to know who his client was and to whom his duty was owed. He was entitled, it seems to me, to refuse to assume liability to any unknown lender, indeed I would go further and say that he is entitled to refuse to assume liability to any known lender to whom he had not agreed. He was entitled to increase the fee (or would have been) as a term of permitting the second lender to rely on the valuation because, as I have said, potentially it can be more expensive to be sued by two lenders rather than one. And if the second lender was not prepared to pay what is asked, it seems to me that the valuer would have been entitled to refuse to assume that liability to the bank, and the 1977 Act would not have required the contract to be rewritten."

Having found a valid and subsisting disclaimer, the Court of Appeal declined to rule on the question of whether a duty of care was owed by the valuers to Banque Finindus. The claim by Banque Finindus against the valuer was accordingly struck out.[23]

Scotland. The application of *Smith v Bush* to Scotland was restricted prior to April 1, 1991. The Unfair Contract Terms Act 1977, as it applied to Scotland, differed from the provisions that applied to England and Wales in that by s.15(1) the provisions in the Act preventing a party relying on an exclusion or restriction of liability clause applied only to contracts,[24] and by s.25(3)(d) any reference to excluding or restricting liability included only notices "having contractual effect". Where, therefore, a notice excluding liability had no contractual effect,[25]

10–072

---

[23] The extent to which a valuer may rely on a disclaimer in a commercial context was also considered in the Scottish case of *Commercial Financial Services Ltd v McBeth & Co* [1988] S.C.L.R. 248. The valuation report was not addressed to the pursuer lender, but to the borrower, which passed it on to the lender. The report contained the following disclaimer:

"In accordance with our standard practice, we must state that this valuation is for the use only of the parties to whom it is addressed and no responsibility is accepted to any third party for the whole or any part of its contents."

Lord Mayfield held that the lender's claim in negligence was irrelevant in that the terms of the "clear" disclaimer were such as to negative any claim in negligence. Further, the claim based on breach of contract was also irrelevant in that the document upon which the lenders relied when making the loan and which was claimed to be the contract with the valuers, was clearly addressed to the borrower, and that even if the lender had instructed the valuers to produce a report, the actual report they relied on was that addressed to the borrowers. The action was dismissed. A similar conclusion was reached by Lord Eassie in *Bank of Scotland v Fuller Peiser* [2002] P.N.L.R. 289. It appears that although the relevant English authorities were cited to him, he was not informed of the decision in *Commercial Funding Services v McBeth*. A borrower had commissioned a valuation of a hotel which she sent to her bank who were considering making a loan in connection with the purchase. The valuation contained an exclusion clause. Lord Eassie held that the effect of the exclusion clause was to prevent any duty of care from arising. He distinguished the decision in *Smith v Bush* on the ground that was a case concerned with domestic conveyancing where different considerations applied.

He pointed out that this case was set in a commercial context (albeit of modest value). Amongst the factors pointing to the reasonableness of the disclaimer were: the size of the claimant; its ability to obtain legal advice; the fact that the claimant could easily have obtained its own report (or paid a fee to the defendant to enable it to rely on his report); the lack of any time constraint upon obtaining alternative advice; and the fact that the bank was of at least equal bargaining power with the defendant.

[24] And not therefore to notices.

[25] As for example, a notice on a mortgage inspection and valuation report, prepared by a surveyor for a mortgagee pursuant to a contract of retainer, and subsequently provided by the mortgagee to the borrower. There is no contract between the surveyor and the borrower. See *Robbie v Graham & Sibbald* [1989] 2 E.G.L.R. 148.

and where the same was clear and unambiguous, a court was obliged to give effect to it.[26] Section 68 of the Law Reform (Miscellaneous Provisions) (Scotland) Act 1990, amended Pt II of the Unfair Contract Terms Act 1977 to bring non-contractual notices within the statutory restrictions. Scots law was thereby made equivalent to English law after *Smith v Bush*, as discussed in para.10–065, above. The amendments were not retrospective and will only apply to liability for loss and damage suffered after April 1, 1991 when the section came into force.[27]

10–073   **Clauses defining extent of service performed.** A distinction must be drawn, however, between those clauses that attempt to exclude or restrict liability in negligence to the client and/or third parties, and those clauses which attempt to define more clearly the nature and extent of the service performed. It is usual, for example, even for structural survey reports to include a standard clause to the effect that no responsibility can be accepted in respect of defects in inaccessible or uninspected parts of the property.[28] Unless agreed to before or at the time of the relevant contract, such a clause would not be incorporated as a contractual term.[29] Nevertheless such a clause operates as a warning[30] and may prevent the claimant from establishing breach of the duty to exercise reasonable care and skill or reliance on the report in relation to inaccessible or uninspected parts. Much will depend upon the proper construction of the clause. A simple disclaimer of responsibility in relation to uninspected parts will not absolve the surveyor from liability for defects therein if a careful surveyor would have suspected their existence from signs in inspected parts and would have given a

---

[26] *Robbie v Graham & Sibbald* [1989] 2 E.G.L.R. 148, where Lord Weir was unable to apply the reasoning in *Smith v Bush* [1990] 1 A.C. 831 as the disclaimer in the survey report obtained by a building society, and disclosed to the pursuers, was of no contractual effect. The action was dismissed. Lord Weir commented, at 149:

> "In reaching this conclusion I recognise that the pursuers may well feel a sense of injustice in that they are unable to take advantage of the Unfair Contract Terms Act 1977 as they would have been able to in England, with the possibility of succeeding in their action against the defenders. I am compelled, however, to apply the statutory law applicable to Scotland although I obtain no satisfaction in doing so in this particular case."

Contrast with *Melrose v Davidson & Robertson* [1993] S.C. 288, where Lord Morton of Shuna construed an exclusion clause as a term of the contract between the purchasers and the building society, thereby allowing s.16 of the Unfair Contract Terms Act 1977 to exclude the effect of the clause. Section 68 of the Law Reform (Miscellaneous Provisions) (Scotland) Act 1990 did not apply to the case. On a reclaiming motion, the First Division of the Inner House declined to interfere with the findings of Lord Morton; *ibid.*, 292. In *Wilson v D M Hall* [2005] P.N.L.R. 375, Lady Paton found that no duty of care was owed by a lender's valuer to a commercial property developer—see further para.10–050 above. Nonetheless she held, obiter, that had there been a duty, she would not have found a disclaimer to be effective as no notice had been given to the claimant of the same. She did not consider whether the existence of the disclaimer itself tended to show that there was no assumed duty.

[27] See s.68(6) and Law Reform (Miscellaneous Provisions) (Scotland) Act 1990 (Commencement No.3) Order 1991 (SI 1991/330).

[28] It is often a condition of a surveyor's professional indemnity insurance policy that his reports should contain such a clause. The Standard Conditions of Engagement prepared by the RICS for Home Buyers' Survey and Valuation contain such a clause, as do Model Conditions of Engagement for Building Surveys of Residential Property.

[29] See, e.g. *Olley v Marlborough Court Ltd* [1949] 1 K.B. 532; and *Thornton v Shoe Lane Parking Ltd* [1971] 2 Q.B. 163.

[30] See para.10–098, below.

warning or advised further investigations.[31] Moreover, a clause seeking to exclude or limit liability, whether amounting to a contractual term or only to a notice not having contractual effect, will be subject to the Unfair Contract Terms Act 1977.[32]

(f) *Mutual Valuer*

Frequently an agreement provides that in the event of a dispute between the parties as to valuation or assessment of rent of a property, they should be bound by the decision of a valuer jointly instructed by them or appointed on their behalf by a mutually selected third person.[33] The appointment must be made in accordance with the terms of the agreement. If it is not, any award will not be binding.[34] If the decision is honestly made the parties will be bound thereby even though the valuation or assessment is so high or so low as to be negligent.[35] In the latter events, however, the aggrieved party may pursue a professional negligence action for his loss against the valuer,[36] unless the valuer is entitled to immunity as an arbitrator or possibly a quasi-arbitrator.[37]

10–074

---

[31] See *Roberts v J Hampson & Co* [1988] 2 E.G.L.R. 181, also at [1990] 1 W.L.R. 94 (abbreviated), discussed at para.10–084, below.

[32] As discussed above, para.10–065. For a commentary on the Act see K.M. Stanton, "Disclaiming tort liability: the Unfair Contract Terms Act 1977" (1985) 4 P.N. 132.

[33] For example, the President of RICS. Where a rent review clause provides for such an appointment, the President of RICS owes no duty to the parties to such a clause to refrain from making an appointment where proceedings are contemplated. The President "should not be a pawn in tactical moves between the parties". See *United Co-operatives Ltd v Sun Alliance London Assurance Co Ltd* [1987] 1 E.G.L.R. 126. For a case where the Court of Appeal discussed the formalities of applying to the President of RICS for an appointment, see *Staines Warehousing Co Ltd v Montagu Executor & Trustee Co Ltd* [1987] 2 E.G.L.R. 130.

[34] In *Darlington BC v Waring & Gillow (Holdings) Ltd* [1988] 2 E.G.L.R. 159, the appointment of an independent valuer was held not to have been carried out in accordance with the terms of the lease, the award was therefore not binding and the current rent continued.

[35] *Campbell v Edwards* [1976] 1 W.L.R. 403, CA. For an extreme example, see *Rajdev v Becketts* [1989] 2 E.G.L.R. 144, where the independent valuer fixed the rent substantially above the proper open market rent. The increased rent had to be paid and the tenant sued his surveyors for failing to apply and operate the rent review provisions. See para.10–182, below. Where valuers appointed by each party are unable to agree a valuation because of differences as to the proper approach, the court may be prepared to make declarations as to the factors to be taken into account. See *Little Hayes Nursing Home Ltd v Marshall* [1993] E.G.C.S. 32 (valuation of property on the exercise of an option); and *Mid Kent Water Plc v Batchelor* [1994] 1 E.G.L.R. 185.

[36] *Campbell v Edwards* [1976] 1 W.L.R. 403 at 408 *per* Lord Denning M.R. Note *Belvedere Motors Ltd v King* [1981] 2 E.G.L.R. 131 (claim by landlords against the valuer appointed as an expert, not an arbitrator, to determine the rent under a rent review clause; the valuer was held not negligent). In *Wallshire Ltd v Aarons* [1989] 1 E.G.L.R. 147, a claim against an independent surveyor, appointed by the President of RICS, and acting as an expert; held, on the facts, the valuer was not negligent.

[37] *Palacath Ltd v Flanagan* [1985] 2 All E.R. 161: preliminary issue as to whether the surveyor appointed under a rent review clause was by the terms of the lease appointed as an arbitrator or quasi-arbitrator; it was held that he was not so appointed; he was appointed as an expert and was therefore not immune in respect of the landlord's claim against him for alleged negligence. See also *North Eastern Co-operative Society Ltd v Newcastle upon Tyne CC* [1987] 1 E.G.L.R. 142, where Scott J. held that on the facts it was intended that the independent surveyor should act as expert if appointed (as he was) by agreement between the parties, but that he should act as arbitrator if appointed, in default of agreement, by the President of RICS.

2. Liability for Breach of Duty

10–075   A surveyor's breaches of duty may take one of four forms:

(i) breach of a specific contractual duty;

(ii) breach of the implied contractual duty to exercise reasonable skill and care;

(iii) breach of the duty of skill and care owed by the surveyor to his client independently of the contract of engagement;

(iv) breach of the same duty as in (iii) but owed to a third party.

The word "negligence" is frequently used in surveyors' negligence cases as in other contexts to denote a default involving failure to exercise reasonable skill and care irrespective of whether the cause of action is contract or tort, and will be so used below. In a particular case, however, the negligent default will properly be analysed as one or more of the breaches of duty described in (i), (ii), (iii) and (iv). The default constituting the breach of duty in (i) need not necessarily involve negligence, but almost invariably it will and then it may also be characterised as such. Instances of default are categorised below under five heads, as follows:

(i) failing to carry out instructions;

(ii) insufficient knowledge or experience;

(iii) failing to inspect properly:

    (a) failing to inspect particular parts,

    (b) failing to uncover and open up,

    (c) failing to observe,

    (d) limited survey,

    (e) failing to recognise;

(iv) failing to make sufficient inquiries;

(v) inadequate report.

They are formulated primarily in the light of the broad steps required of a surveyor in carrying out a structural survey and/or a valuation. Nevertheless it must be emphasised that whether and, if so, to what extent each step has to be taken will vary according to the nature of the engagement and the circumstances of each case. For example, more will be required of a surveyor by way of inspection and examination of the property when instructed to carry out a building or structural survey as opposed to a domestic valuation. A commercial valuation, however, will usually require more beyond inspection of the subject property, as described by Watkins J. in *Singer and Friedlander Ltd v John D Wood and Co*,[38] a case of negligent valuation of development land:

---

[38] [1977] 2 E.G.L.R. 84.

"there is no diversion of opinion, save as to some details, about what in valuation is a general and approved practice between the valuers who have given evidence . . . . It consists of four fairly distinct stages of activity, namely, firstly, the sometimes tedious and laborious but vital approach work; secondly, analysing the information thereby gained, and so be enabled by the exercise of experience and judgment to accept facts and make assumptions; thirdly, applying the detailed discount method with comparables or some other justified by the circumstances as an alternative, or as a check, to the findings, and thereby produce the valuation; and fourthly informing the client of it".[39]

Owing to varying circumstances, it is dangerous to regard specific decisions as providing precedents. The facts of each case must be closely scrutinised and reported decisions regarded as providing indications at most as to the court's likely approach in similar situations. Individual cases are considered below under the appropriate heading for the primary default or one of the primary defaults. Several cases could be considered under a number of different headings. Moreover one default may lead to another, for example, a failure to observe may lead to a failure to report and to warn. Finally, the categories themselves do not cover the whole range of defaults for which a surveyor may incur liability, but they include the majority of acts and omissions likely to arise in the course of a surveyor's work within the scope of this chapter. **10–076**

(a) *Failing to Carry out Instructions*

Whilst many breaches considered under other heads may be characterised as a failure to carry out instructions, under this head are included cases where the surveyor has either failed completely to carry out his instructions or done something different. Extreme cases would be those of a surveyor instructed to survey a particular house either not inspecting it or inspecting the wrong property. More usual are cases where the surveyor carries out a more limited service than that for which he was engaged. Very often the crucial issue in such cases is one of fact, namely, what were the surveyors' instructions? In *Fisher v Knowles*,[40] the parties were in dispute both as to the nature of the terms of the surveyor's employment and how he was instructed. The judge, concluding that what the defendant was being instructed to do was something more than a bare valuation and less than a structural survey, held the defendant negligent. In *Moss v Heckingbottom*,[41] the defendant architect contended that his only instructions were to prepare plans. Barry J., however, preferred the evidence of the claimant that the defendant was instructed to make a structural survey of the house and outbuildings and to test and survey all services and equipment. He held the defendant in breach of contract in failing to do so and consequently in not **10–077**

---

[39] [1977] 2 E.G.L.R. 84 at 217. Note also the "matters of principle and of fact" listed by Gibson J. in *Corisand Investments Ltd v Druce & Co* [1978] 2 E.G.L.R. 86 at 89, to which an "ordinary competent valuer" in valuing property such as the hotel in that case should have regard. *cf.* Lord Cameron's caution in the final sentence of the passage quoted at para.10–082, below.
[40] [1982] 1 E.G.L.R. 154.
[41] (1958) 172 E.G. 207.

discovering defects.[42] An example of a case where a surveyor would not have been found liable but for the specific terms of his instructions is *Farley v Skinner*,[43] where the surveyor was specifically instructed to check that that there was no problem with aircraft noise at a house situated some 15 miles from Gatwick airport. Having accepted the claimant's account of the disputed instructions, the judge found that although there was no problem apparent at the time of his visit to the property, the surveyor should have made specific enquiries of the Civil Aviation Authority, in which event he would have ascertained that the house was close to a "stack" of aircraft used between 06.00 and 08.00 and between 17.30 and 19.00.

10–078 Failure to carry out instructions may result from misinterpretation or inadequate enquiry of the client. This error may arise where the instructions are unspecific or ambiguous. In *Buckland v Watts*,[44] the evidence was that the claimant instructed the defendant, a chartered surveyor, to survey a house and prepare some plans. The defendant took his instructions to mean a measured survey only. Although the county court judge held the instructions to imply a measured survey, the Court of Appeal reversed his decision and held the defendant negligent in failing to carry out his instructions, and consequently in not discovering a variety of defects. *Per* Salmon L.J.:

> "If a prospective buyer of a house goes to a chartered surveyor and says, 'I want a survey and plans' that ought to convey to any sensible surveyor that what the client wants to know is what is the structural condition of the house, and he also wants some plans of the house."[45]

Similarly in *Hellings v Parker Breslin Estate*,[46] the claimants instructed the defendant letting agents to let a flat, making it plain that it was very important that they be able to recover possession at the end of the term granted. The claimants intended to sell the flat for redevelopment purposes. The defendants failed to enquire as to their clients' intentions and to warn the claimants in plain terms that they could not recover possession under a Case 11 letting unless they required the flat as their residence. This failure to determine their clients' precise requirements and intentions was held to be in breach of duty. In *Predeth v Castle Phillips Finance Co Ltd*,[47] the instructions were specific, but the client, a finance

---

[42] (1958) 172 E.G. 207, *per* Barry J.:
"a structural survey entailed something more than the casual inspection of the building which had taken place when he and his assistant were preparing the plans. He might not have thought it necessary to draw attention to such defects as furniture beetle, loose frames and the like, which one would expect to find in any 200-year-old house. The truth was, however, that these were the type of defects to which attention should be drawn after a reasonably careful survey".

[43] [2001] UKHL 49. The reference is to the House of Lords report, which concerned the question of damages but from which the judge's findings, against, which there was no appeal, are apparent. See also para.10–184 below in relation to the recovery of damages.

[44] (1968) 208 E.G. 969.

[45] *ibid.* at 973. Although the basis of liability seems to have been negligence (whether the tort or breach of the implied term to use reasonable care and skill), the defendant could equally have been held in breach of the specific express term to carry out a structural survey. The latter creates an absolute duty and there can be no question of whether the defendant exercised reasonable care and skill in interpreting his instructions.

[46] [1995] 2 E.G.L.R. 99.

[47] [1986] 2 E.G.L.R. 144.

company, argued that there was an overriding duty on the valuer to provide a true market value. The Court of Appeal rejected this argument. The defendant valuers, having been instructed by the claimant finance company by letter to provide a "crash sale valuation", owed no duty to advise the company on the true market value of the property. Fox L.J. stated: "He was given a particular task to do. It seems to me that he did it."

(b) *Insufficient Knowledge or Experience*

A person engaging a surveyor is entitled to expect that he is sufficiently knowl-   **10–079**
edgeable and experienced to undertake the task required. If the surveyor lacks those qualifications and cannot make up for them, for example by making enquiries, he should refuse the engagement.[48] What constitutes insufficient knowledge has already been considered.[49] Insufficient experience is illustrated by two further cases.

In *Kenney v Hall, Pain and Foster*,[50] the claimant was advised as to the value   **10–080**
and reasonable asking price of a house by a property negotiator employed by the defendants. Both valuation and price were grossly excessive. Prior to giving his advice the negotiator had very limited experience. He had no formal qualifications and had only six months' experience working with estate agents in New Zealand and three months' experience working with the defendant. Goff J. held the defendant liable:

> "In my judgment, at the material time [the negotiator] lacked the skill which could reasonably have been expected of a person in his position, to give the valuation. Furthermore, in failing to refer the matter properly back to the office for their opinion, he failed to exercise reasonable care in making the valuation. Lastly, having regard to the nature of the plaintiff's request for a written opinion, he was entitled to assume that the valuation . . . had been the subject of full and informal consideration by a partner or responsible employee of the defendant, and I am satisfied that it was not."[51]

In *Baxter v FW Gapp & Co Ltd*,[52] the defendant valuer was experienced   **10–081**
generally but not in the value of properties in the locality of the bungalow, the subject of his advice. Goddard L.J. sitting at first instance stated:

> "His duty was, first of all, to use reasonable care in coming to the valuation which he was employed to make and he must be taken to have held himself out as possessing the experience and skill required to value the particular property. If he did not know enough

---

[48] Professional indemnity policies of insurance will very often restrict the category of persons who are entitled to sign off reports or valuations.

[49] See para.10–052, above. It is, of course, in the interests of a particular specialist to suggest that only a person with particular specialist expertise will be able to carry out a particular form of valuation. Thus in *Wilson v DM Hall & Sons* [2005] P.N.L.R. 375, the judge recorded that she had received expert evidence about the degree of specialist knowledge and experience necessary to carry out a residential valuation in Edinburgh. She indicated that had she considered it necessary, she would have ordered further evidence on this point. Although it will always depend on the evidence, it may well be that a specialist valuer will be able to provide a competent valuation "out of area", but will have to spend considerably more time than he would have done "in area".

[50] [1976] 2 E.G.L.R. 29; for further facts see para.10–124, below.

[51] *ibid.* at 34.

[52] [1938] 4 All E.R. 457.

about the property market, or the value of the property at the place where the property was situate, he ought to have taken steps to inform himself of the values of the properties there, or of any circumstances which might affect the property. It would be no defence, for instance, to say: I made this valuation, but the reason why my valuation has proved incorrect, if it has proved incorrect, is that I was not a person, as you know, who practised in that locality."[53]

The Court of Appeal affirmed the decision.[54]

(c) *Failing to Inspect Properly*

10–082 This is a very common cause of complaint against surveyors. The complaints may be sub-divided into more specific criticisms such as failure to inspect particular areas, failure to uncover or open up parts and failure to observe or to recognise. The latter are adopted as sub-headings below, together with a specific sub-category for the problem of the limited survey. The caution[55] concerning the varying nature of each case and not regarding any as establishing a precedent is particularly appropriate in the case of failure to inspect. That caution together with what generally is required by way of inspection on a visual survey is perhaps best expressed in a Scottish case, *Stewart v HA Brechin & Co*,[56] by Lord Cameron:

" . . . all that the defenders were under contract to do was to make such valuation of the property and to carry out such visual inspection as was reasonably practicable in the circumstances, reporting anything of significance to their client if such should be found. 'Anything of significance' in this context, in my opinion, means anything so material as would or might influence a reasonable man in fixing a price to be offered by him for the subjects, or anything which to the skilled eye of a surveyor would be an indication of possible and material defect structural or otherwise in the property, such as would, or might reasonably, be expected to affect its value to a prospective purchaser or cause him to reconsider an intention to make an offer for it. As was put by Lord President Cooper in the briefly reported case of *Ker v Allan*[57] ' . . . in conducting such an inspection a professional man should have a keen eye for anything showing or even raising a suspicion of, any material defect (including dry rot), but he need not, and usually cannot, conduct an exhaustive search—least of all in a furnished and occupied dwelling house for possible latent defects of which there is no overt symptom, and the existence of which he has no reason to suspect. . . . ' In such circumstances it is obviously difficult and probably impracticable as well as undesirable to attempt to lay down in specific terms and categories what must be looked at or looked for when a surveyor proceeds to value a house, or the extent to which failure to examine any

---

[53] [1938] 4 All E.R. 457 at 459; see also du Parcq L.J. on appeal, [1939] 2 K.B. 752.
[54] [1939] 2 K.B. 271. The House of Lords in *Swingcastle Ltd v Gibson* [1991] 2 A.C. 223 overruled the case on the issue of calculation of interest. The House of Lords in *Banque Bruxelles Lambert SA v Eagle Star Insurance Co Ltd* [1997] A.C. 191 concluded that on its facts, the decision to award the claimant the entire loss was correct.
[55] See para.10–076, above.
[56] (1959) S.C. 306.
[57] 1949 S.L.T. 20.

particular part or parts should be regarded as at least presumptive evidence of failure to exercise the due measure of professional care".[58]

(i) *Failing to Inspect Particular Parts*

A building or structural survey entails more than a casual inspection of a **10–083** property.[59] In carrying out such a survey a surveyor is expected to inspect all visible parts. In *Hill v Debenham, Tewson and Chinnocks*,[60] the defendant surveyor was instructed to survey and report on an old cottage which the claimant intended to buy and renovate. He was held negligent, inter alia, in giving no warning in respect of the rafters which had gone and the battens which needed renewing. The official referee concluded that the defendants' surveyor should in the circumstances have climbed up a ladder to a valley between two roofs and looked through gaps in missing tiles or, failing that, to warn that he did not know what the state of the rafters and battens would be. In *Stewart v HA Brechin & Co*,[61] the defendant surveyor failed to inspect the roof-spaces of an eighteenth-century mansion house and outbuildings and thus failed to discover extensive woodworm infestation. In *Conn v Munday*,[62] the surveyor was held negligent apparently[63] in failing, inter alia, to discover in the course of his survey woodworm in the cellar of a house. He gave evidence that he did not know there was a cellar. A surveyor may also be expected to inspect other areas in so far as they may affect the structure of the property.[64] Thus in the Scottish case of *Drinnan v CW Ingram & Sons*,[65] Lord Milligan stated that he could not see how a surveyor required to supply an estimate of the value of a top flat could do so

---

[58] [1959] S.C. 306 at 308. Note also *Fisher v Knowles* [1982] 1 E.G.L.R. 154 *per* Sir Douglas Frank Q.C., sitting as a deputy High Court judge, at 154:

"The word 'defect' is a word having a number of connotations. Defects may be something which is inherent in the type and age of a building. For example, an Elizabethan cottage is likely to have the defect of having low ceilings, a defect both in the ordinary sense and in the statutory sense. To some people, though, that would be considered to be an enhancement. There are defects of some kind in every home. There are creaking floorboards, gaps between the wainscot and the floor. There are cracks in the ceilings. One would be very lucky indeed to buy even a new house, let alone a 25-year-old house as this one was without finding some cracks in the ceiling. It seems that in approaching this matter in the instant case I should have regard to those defects which were of such a nature as a prudent person would have put right and which would have been apparent to the defendant exercising the ordinary skill of an ordinary competent chartered surveyor, and taking into account the type and age of the property."

[59] *per* Barry J. in *Moss v Heckingbottom* (1958) 172 E.G. 207. See the detailed guidance now provided by the RICS in "Building Surveys of Residential Property: A Guidance Note" (RICS, 1996, and earlier editions).

[60] (1958) 171 E.G. 835.

[61] (1959) S.C. 306.

[62] (1955) 166 E.G. 465. See also the Canadian case *Cantwell v Petersen* (1983) 139 D.L.R. (3d) 466 (failing to inspect crawlspace beneath the house and thus to discover dry rot and insect infestation).

[63] The case is only briefly reported.

[64] In *Mistry v Thakor* [2005] EWCA 953, the Court of Appeal expressed some surprise at the attitude of a surveyor employed by a building owner who refused to go up scaffolding to inspect a possible defect. Furthermore, this unwillingness was given as one of the reasons for the court's refusal to upset an apportionment as between the building owner and the surveyor in relation to liability to a third party in nuisance.

[65] [1967] S.L.T. 205.

without having at least some regard to the structure of the building as a whole.[66]

(ii) *Failing to Uncover and Open Up*

10–084 This is usually the substantive complaint where the surveyor has failed to discover defects which at the time of his inspection were concealed, for example, under carpets, floorboards or in a wall. In determining liability, much will depend upon the nature of the instructions, the presence of suspicious signs in visible parts and the practicality of uncovering and opening up. Liability on this ground was established in *Roberts v J Hampson & Co.*[67] The claimants purchased a property relying on a mortgage valuation provided by the defendant surveyor. The report drew attention to some dampness in the external walls and a certain amount of dry rot in the skirting board of a bedroom, the valuer recommended that a timber specialist be engaged to eradicate the rot. No retention was recommended. In fact the property was subject to a serious infestation of dry rot that manifested itself a few months after the claimants moved in. In a passage subsequently quoted by Lord Templeman with approval,[68] Ian Kennedy J. discussed the question of moving furniture and lifting carpets when the surveyor is instructed to carry out a mortgage valuation:

> "the position that the law adopts is simple. If a surveyor misses a defect because its signs are hidden, that is a risk that his client must accept. But if there is specific ground for suspicion and the trail of suspicion leads behind furniture or under carpets, the surveyor must take reasonable steps to follow the trail until he has all the information which it is reasonable for him to have before making his valuation".[69]

10–085 The principle underlying the striking phrase, "follow the trail of suspicion", although not new, having been endorsed by the House of Lords in *Smith v Bush*, has been applied in terms in a number of other cases. This obligation on the surveyor has also been described[70] as being "a diagnostic interpretation of a visual inspection". It is "judging what you cannot see by what you can see".[71] Other cases in which this principle has been applied include *Bere v Slades*,[72] where certain walls of a property were of unconventional and defective construction. The claimants conceded that this defect was not directly discoverable during a mortgage valuation. They complained however, that the valuer, when carrying

---

[66] [1967] S.L.T. 205 at 208. He continued:
> "It may be that in the absence of precise instructions to do so a surveyor is not bound to make a meticulous examination of the fabric of a whole tenement but I should be surprised if it is not the normal practice to have regard to anything clearly visible in the structure of the building."

The facts were that shortly after the defenders' report and in reliance upon it the pursuer purchased a tenement flat. Six months later the pursuer was informed by the city engineer that the whole tenement was in a dangerous condition and had to be demolished. The issue of liability was not decided, only preliminary issues being before the court.

[67] [1988] 2 E.G.L.R. 181. The case was described as one of "general application" by Lord Templeman in *Smith v Bush* [1990] 1 A.C. 831 at 850.

[68] In *Smith v Bush, op. cit.* at 851.

[69] [1988] 2 E.G.L.R. 181 at 185.

[70] By a Mr Anderson, a surveyor, whilst giving evidence in *Hacker v Thomas Deal & Co* [1991] 2 E.G.L.R. 161.

[71] *Hacker v Thomas Deal & Co*, see previous note.

[72] [1989] 2 E.G.L.R. 160.

out his inspection, had failed to follow up a number of other defects, either by declining to value or to refer for greater inspection. The judge agreed that the duty to follow a trail of suspicion existed, but held on the facts that the nature of the defects was not such as to give rise to such an obligation. He held that the valuer had prepared "a thoroughly competent report, carefully done and, I would add, masterly succinct".[73] In *Hipkins v Jack Cotton Partnership*[74] a surveyor failed to observe cracking and patching in the rendering of a wall. The cracks were the manifestation of a structural defect in the foundations of the property that made underpinning necessary. It was held that a reasonably competent surveyor would have seen the cracks and asked himself why they were there. Scott Baker J. said:

> "These were clues that he should not have missed. These clues led at least to the query that the building was unsound, yet he missed them."[75]

In *Whalley v Roberts & Roberts*,[76] the failure by a surveyor carrying out a mortgage valuation to detect that the house had been built out of level was, on the facts, and applying the test in *Roberts v J Hampson & Co*, held to be not negligent.

Hacker v Thomas Deal & Co[77] involved a building survey of a substantial and **10–086** expensive[78] property in Belgravia for an American investment banker. A virulent attack of dry rot was discovered by the defendant surveyors. The claimant alleged that there were a number of matters that indicated a particular risk of dry rot and the consequential need for careful inspection. These were the age and character of the building, the existence of a sauna compartment underneath the area where the outbreak was found, and the surveyors' failure to observe and inspect inside a small trap in the roof of the sauna, and the traces of damp noted in the report. Added by amendment were the significance of the existence of the sauna, the plunge pool and jacuzzi area, inherent dampness of the basement, and the likelihood of condensation in the area around the sauna, plunge pool and jacuzzi area. Judge Fawcus held that the age and character of the building were readily apparent to the surveyor and that he knew precisely what sort of building he was dealing with. The judge criticised the amendments as afterthoughts:

> " . . . an example of *ex post facto* rationalisation of a conclusion that he [the claimant's expert witness] has already come to. If he did not think that the plunge pool and jacuzzi area and the likelihood of condensation were significant, one asks oneself why he did not mention it in the first place".

The crucial question was whether the surveyor should have seen the small trap in the roof of the sauna and looked through, where he might have been able to see fruiting bodies of dry rot. Noting that the sauna was a prefabricated, self-

---

[73] [1989] 2 E.G.L.R. 160 at 163.
[74] [1989] 2 E.G.L.R. 157. This case was overruled on the issue of measure of loss by the Court of Appeal's decision in *Watts v Morrow* [1991] 1 W.L.R. 1421. See para.10–143, below.
[75] [1989] 2 E.G.L.R. 157 at 159.
[76] [1990] 1 E.G.L.R. 164.
[77] [1991] 2 E.G.L.R. 161.
[78] Purchased by the claimant for £1,625,000.

contained unit, the judge came to "the firm conclusion that he is not to be criticised for not seeing it", accepting the evidence of an expert surveyor that:

> "... although one is acting as a detective one does not start going into all the little crevices in the hopes of finding something unless there is some telltale sign which indicates that it would be advisable to do so".

The judge held that the claimant's claim failed.

10–087   Liability on the ground of failing to inspect particular parts was established in *Hill v Debenham, Tewson and Chinnocks*,[79] where the defendant surveyor reported: "Flooring on first floor appears to be in fair condition although we could only judge from superficial examination." In fact there was a second layer of floorboards underneath, riddled with woodworm. The official referee took the view that having found beetle in the woodwork and wet rot on the ground floor, any competent surveyor would have lifted one or two floorboards on the first floor. "I find that the general and proved practice of the profession is to take up floorboards when you are put on inquiry, if such course is practicable." In fact it was "eminently practicable" to take up the boards, since the cottage was unoccupied and little more than a shell at the time of the inspection. He continued:

> "Even if I am wrong as to this, it is plainly the duty to warn if he does not look, and no warning was given as to what might be found when the floorboards were lifted."[80]

10–088   Liability on this ground may be more difficult to establish where uncovering and opening up are not feasible, as may be the case where the premises are occupied and the floors have fitted carpets.[81] A more limited view of a surveyor's duty in such circumstances was taken in the briefly reported Scottish case of *Ker v John H Allan & Son.*[82] The defender surveyors were instructed by a prospective purchaser, the pursuer, to inspect a property and report verbally upon it the same day. This they did although the house was furnished and occupied and the time available before making the verbal report was very short. The pursuer failed to establish that the defenders were negligent in not looking under the floorboards. Lord Birnam accepted the evidence that the presence of dry rot ought always to be present in the mind of a surveyor and that he should always be on the lookout for any evidence that might to his skilled mind be suggestive of dry rot. He was nevertheless:

> "unable to accept the view that in such circumstances his duty requires him in the absence of any suspicious circumstances to cause carpets and linoleum to be lifted and to go underneath floors and make a detailed examination of every hidden corner of a building".[83]

---

[79] (1958) 171 E.G. 835.
[80] *ibid.* at 837.
[81] As indeed recognised by the Official Referee in *Hill v Debenham, Tewson and Chinnocks, ibid.* at 837.
[82] [1949] S.L.T. (Notes) 20, OH.
[83] *ibid.* In any event it was not proved that dry rot would have been visible if the defenders had looked beneath the floor.

On appeal to the Court of Session[84] the decision was affirmed. The Lord President, while expressly confining his attention to the facts of the case, added that the surveyors were not under a specific duty to inform the purchaser that they had not explored beneath the floors and in the hidden corners and concealed places. Similarly in *Thorne v Harris & Co*,[85] the surveyor was unable to make a complete survey at the time the bungalow was furnished. He probed and looked around for rot, but he could not examine under the floorboards. He was held not negligent in not discovering dry rot caused apparently by dampness spreading to the joists along sleeper plates attached to the outside wall and affecting the floorboards. By contrast in *Grove v Jackman and Masters*,[86] the defendant surveyors were held negligent. The presence of dry rot, caused by the sleeper walls not being honeycombed, could not have been discovered without taking up floorboards, which was not possible at the time of survey since the vendors were still in occupation. Lord Goddard C.J. concluded that there were indications which should have warned a competent and careful surveyor of the presence of dry rot. That being so, the defendants should have either arranged or advised the claimant to arrange for floorboards to be taken up and more thorough investigation made.[87]

Whether occupied or unoccupied, there are limits on the necessity to uncover or open up. Thus in *Bishop v Watson, Watson and Scoles*,[88] McKenna J. said: **10–089**

> "An architect like Mr Scoles who has agreed to make a visual survey is under no obligation to uncover those parts of the building where the flashings or damp proof courses should be found to see if they are there and, if they are, whether they are adequate. If he sees anything which would give a reasonably skilled person grounds to suspect that they are missing or inadequate he must draw his client's attention to the matter, but evidence that the building is of cavity construction is not itself ground for suspecting that the safeguards essential to that mode of construction have been omitted or botched."[89]

In that case the defendant was instructed to carry out a visual inspection and report upon a newly-built flat. Certain windows were covered on the inside with moisture, but he concluded that the likely cause was condensation, not dampness. It later transpired, however, that the flat was subject to penetrating dampness through the cavity walls caused apparently by the absence of flashings and of a damp proof course to a horizontal concrete ring beam and vertical concrete

---

[84] Briefly summarised in (1949) 154 E.G. 473.

[85] (1953) 163 E.G. 324.

[86] (1950) 155 E.G. 182.

[87] The surveyor reported that the bungalow was "soundly constructed on good modern principles of building", but Lord Goddard concluded that it was "as bad a piece of 'jerry building' as could be found in that district". In *Wooldridge v Stanley Hicks & Son* (1953) 162 E.G. 513, the defendant surveyors were held negligent although detailed examination of a guest house was not possible since all the rooms were occupied and furnished. Expert evidence established that there were probably signs of dry rot which the defendants should have discovered. In *Denny v Budgen* (1955) 166 E.G. 433, the surveyor was held negligent in not discovering woodworm in the floor. The defendant argued that he was protected by the fact that he said in his report that the floors were for the most part covered by linoleum, thus precluding examination. Pearce J., however, concluded that that indicated that some examination was possible.

[88] (1972) 224 E.G. 1881.

[89] *ibid.* at 1886.

columns respectively bridging the cavity walls. The defendant was held not negligent in failing to ascertain those facts and to observe what the claimant claimed were signs of defective construction or design.

(iii) *Failing to Observe*

10–090 Even though a surveyor may inspect all parts of a property and even uncover some, he may be insufficiently observant. This may be due to a failure to carry out a sufficiently detailed examination, or over-familiarity with the property, or type of property, bringing with it a sense of false security. Consequently he may fail to notice matters of significance.[90] In *Cross v David Martin and Mortimer*,[91] a surveyor whom Phillips J. described as having taken "a lot of care" over an HBRV[92] survey, failed to notice and consider the significance of a hump in the hall floor. Together with certain other indicators, the hump should have alerted the surveyor to the possibility of subsidence. The fact that the defendant firm had inspected the property on the occasion of its previous sale may have lulled the surveyor into a false sense of security.[93] The surveyor was held negligent.

10–091 **Dry rot and woodworm.** Failure to discover dry rot, woodworm, or similar infestation is the source of many claims against surveyors. In carrying out a survey particular regard should be paid to areas of suspicion.[94] In *Oswald v Countrywide Surveyors Ltd*,[95] a surveyor was held negligent in failing expressly to warn of an infestation of death watch beetle, a warning of "woodworm" being held insufficient. In *Lowry v Woodruffe, Buchanan and Coulter*,[96] a surveyor was held negligent in failing to discover dry rot in an area of suspicion, a wooden framework above the front door. Further, he should look out for signs characteristic of certain defects such as dry rot waviness or ribbiness in the skirtings. One or two errors of observation might, however, be insufficient to establish negligence.[97] Thus in *Tew v WM Whitburn & Son*,[98] Parker J. considered failure to observe "ribbiness" of skirting boards "very slender evidence" on which to hold a professional man guilty of negligence and in *Hacker v Thomas Deal & Co*[99] a failure to observe a small trap door in the roof of a sauna, through which the fruiting bodies of dry rot might have been observed, was held not to be negligent. Similarly in *Hardy v Wamsley-Lewis*,[1] if the defendant surveyor had only failed to observe dry rot waviness in the skirting board between the front door and the staircase, Paull J. would have required argument as to whether one failure constituted negligence. But the defendant also discovered on a door post an

---

[90] Note the definition of "anything of significance" in this context by Lord Cameron in *Stewart v H.A. Brechin & Co* [1959] S.C. 306 at 308: see para.10–082, above.
[91] [1989] 1 E.G.L.R. 154.
[92] House Buyer's Report and Valuation. Phillips J.'s abbreviation.
[93] [1989] 1 E.G.L.R. 154 at 158.
[94] This was a criticism made of the chartered surveyor in *Hacker v Thomas Deal & Co* [1991] 2 E.G.L.R. 161. See para.10–086, above.
[95] [1996] 2 E.G.L.R. 104.
[96] (1950) 156 E.G. 375.
[97] See para.10–058, above.
[98] (1952) 159 E.G. 56.
[99] [1991] 2 E.G.L.R. 161. See para.10–086, above.
[1] (1967) 203 E.G. 1039.

indication that there had been dry rot, although he concluded it was dormant. That being the case Paull J. was of the view that he ought to have "meticulously examined every bit of wood he could see, to see if there were signs of it spreading at all".[2] The evidence established that there were signs of active dry rot which the defendant ought to have seen despite the house being furnished and he was held negligent in failing to discover it.[3]

Defects in roof. Errors of observation are often alleged in respect of less   **10–092** accessible and visible areas of a property, particularly the roof and roofspace. Thus in *Parsons v Way and Waller Ltd*,[4] the defendant surveyors' employee was held negligent in not properly examining the roof. Rafters were not properly tied at their feet, with the result that the roof was spreading towards the rear and thrusting against the back wall. Moreover, the wall plate which held the rafters had receded and projected over the brickwork, as was plainly visible inside and outside the house. Similarly in *Last v Post*,[5] although the defendant surveyor genuinely and honestly thought he was paying adequate attention to everything visible and examined the roof from inside and then outside with binoculars, he failed to observe a considerable amount of deposit from tiles disintegrating through efflorescence. Although acquitted of not recognising that "rare phenomenon", he was held negligent in describing the roof as "soundly constructed" in his report, which no doubt he would not have done if he had observed the deposit. In *Eley v King & Chasemore*,[6] it was alleged that the chartered surveyor who carried out a structural survey of a property was negligent in failing to report on defects to the roof structure, including an absence of ventilation. The fact that the surveyor had failed to climb on to the roof was criticised by the claimant, but

---

[2] (1967) 203 E.G. 1039 at 1041.

[3] Surveyors were also held liable for not discovering dry rot and similar infestation in the following cases: *Legge v Young* [1949] E.G.D. 186 (dry rot in woodwork); *Grove v Jackman and Masters* (1950) 155 E.G. 182 (dry rot in floors and joists); *Sincock v Bangs (Reading)* [1952] C.P.L. 562 (dry rot and woodworm); *Wooldridge v Stanley Hicks & Son* (1953) 162 E.G. 513 (dry rot in bedroom); *Tremayne v T. Mortimer Burrows and Partners* (1954) 165 E.G. 232 (dry rot in shutters and window frames); *Denny v Budgen* (1955) 166 E.G. 433 (woodworm in floors); *Conn v Munday* (1955) 166 E.G. 465 (woodworm in cellar and dampness); *Leigh v William Hill & Son* (1956) 168 E.G. 396 (woodworm); *Fidgeon v Carroll* (1956) 168 E.G. 557 (woodworm in rafters, floors, shed and lavatory); *Philips v Ward* [1956] 1 W.L.R. 471 (death watch beetle); *Hill v Debenham, Tewson and Chinnocks* (1958) 171 E.G. 835 (woodworm in floorboards); *Stewart v HA Brechin & Co* [1959] S.C. 306 (woodworm in roof space); *Freeman v Marshall & Co* (1966) 200 E.G. 777 (rising damp, wet and dry rot); *Collard v Saunders* (1972) 221 E.G. 797 (death watch beetle); *Cantwell v Petersen* (1983) 139 D.L.R. (3d) 466 (dry rot and insect infestation); *Hooberman v Salter Rex* [1985] 1 E.G.L.R. 144 (dry rot); *Roberts v J Hampson & Co* [1988] 2 E.G.L.R. 181 (dry rot); *Steward v Rapley* [1989] 1 E.G.L.R. 159 (dry rot); *Syrett v Carr & Neave* [1990] 2 E.G.L.R. 161 (death watch beetle, note Court of Appeal considered case wrongly decided on measure of loss, see *Watts v Morrow* [1991] 1 W.L.R. 1421); *Oswald v Countrywide Surveyors Ltd* [1996] 2 E.G.L.R. 104 (death watch beetle); *Republic International Ltd v Fletcher Ramos*, unreported, August 30, 2000, H.H.J. Havery Q.C. (dry rot). Surveyors were held not liable in the following cases: *Ker v John H Allan & Sons*, 1949 S.L.T. (Notes) 20 (dry rot in floors); *MacKenzie v R & W Hall* (1951) 157 E.G. 492 (dry rot); *Tew v H.A. Whitburn & Son* (1952) 159 E.G. 56 (wet rot in woodwork); *Rona v Pearce* (1953) 162 E.G. 380 (woodworm); *Thorne v Harris & Co* (1953) 163 E.G. 324; *Hacker v Thomas Deal & Co* [1991] 2 E.G.L.R. 161, see para.10–086, above; *Kerridge v James Abbott & Partners* [1992] 2 E.G.L.R. 162 (dry rot and timber decay).

[4] (1952) 159 E.G. 524.

[5] (1952) 159 E.G. 240.

[6] [1989] 1 E.G.L.R. 181.

neither the trial judge nor the Court of Appeal agreed. The surveyor had inspected the roof space from inside the house, and the exterior of the roof from ground level. In the absence of any sign of defect, that degree of inspection and observation was held sufficient to discharge the surveyor's duty. That finding may be contrasted with the decision in *Heatley v William H Brown Ltd*,[7] where the surveyor retained to provide a structural survey was unable to gain access to the roof voids and discussed with the claimants the absence of such access. The report warned that parts of the property had fallen into disrepair. Despite the conversation, and the incorporation into the retainer of the defendants' written conditions of engagement which included reference to the limitations in a report where parts of the property were unexposed or inaccessible, the defendants were held to have provided a negligent report, in that further examinations and investigations ought to have been advised. A subsequent inspection, after the claimants had purchased the property and provided access to the roof voids, was also held to have been negligent.[8]

10–093   **Subsidence and cracking.** In carrying out a survey a surveyor must be particularly sensitive to signs of structural defects such as subsidence. This will require not only careful observation but also skilled inference, for example in evaluating a bulge or crack.[9] An example is *Matto v Rodney Broom Associates*.[10] The Court of Appeal, reversing the trial judge, held the defendant surveyor liable for failing to warn the claimant in sufficient terms of a risk in the future of further subsidence, even though the property had been stable for many years. Liability was found despite "the basic skill and experience of the defendant" not having been proved to be lacking. Ralph Gibson L.J. commented[11]:

> "A buyer, unless he says otherwise, is not concerned only with structural damage likely to occur while he is, in the immediate future, living in the house but also with structural damage which is likely to occur at a more remote date of which the impact upon him will result . . . from the effect of that apparent likelihood of structural damage upon his ability to sell the house."

Moreover, this is an area where the distinction between a reasonable (although in retrospect mistaken) opinion on the one hand and negligence on the other is critical. Where a claim is made, in the absence of satisfactory contemporaneous evidence of facts other than the defendant surveyor's, much will depend upon

---

[7] [1992] 1 E.G.L.R. 289 (official referee).

[8] Other cases illustrating negligent observation of the roof space include *Lowry v Woodroffe, Buchanan and Coulter* (1950) 156 E.G. 375 (defective roofing and guttering); *Chong v Scott Collins & Co* (1954) 164 E.G. 662 (reporting that the roof had been repaired in a good and workmanlike manner when this was not the case); *Hill v Debenham, Tewson and Chinnocks* (1958) 171 E.G. 835 (rafters gone and battens needing renewal); *Leigh v Unsworth* (1972) 230 E.G. 501 (no vertical hangers and stating that there was fibreglass insulation when there was none); *Perry v Sidney Phillips & Son* [1982] 1 All E.R. 1005 (first instance, leaky roof); *Hooberman v Salter Rex* [1985] 1 E.G.L.R. 144 (defects in flat roof and lack of ventilation in void); *Cross v David Martin & Mortimer* [1989] 1 E.G.L.R. 154 (loft conversion inadequate); *Watts v Morrow* [1991] 1 E.G.L.R. 150 (first instance, defective roof covering).

[9] See *Hipkins v Jack Cotton Partnership* [1989] 2 E.G.L.R. 157, where the surveyor negligently failed to observe cracks that were evidence of settlement.

[10] [1994] 2 E.G.L.R. 163.

[11] *ibid.* at 168.

expert evidence as to what should have been observed. Inevitably the problem of distinguishing accurate reconstruction from the revelation of hindsight is acute.[12] Accurate reconstruction will be more difficult the longer the period between the allegedly negligent inspection and trial as demonstrated by *Leigh v Unsworth*[13] where it amounted to over seven-and-a-half years. In that case it was claimed that the defendant surveyor was negligent in failing to detect indications of serious settlement subsequent to the usual initial settlement common in newly built houses. It was held there were only indications of the latter and the defendant was held not liable in respect of the settlement.[14] In *Lawrence v Hampton & Sons*,[15] in contrast the defendants were held negligent in failing to observe cracks and in failing to advise that underpinning was required and that there was a risk of even more underpinning being necessary.

The latter case also illustrates that a careful survey may require examination of   **10–094** matters extrinsic to the buildings themselves, such as the carrying out of further inquiries and advising the instruction of specialists. Thus also in *Daisley v B. S. Hall & Co*,[16] Bristow J. stated that:

> "a surveyor who finds a house under 10 years old built as close to a row of poplars as High Trees was, where two of those trees had been felled for no apparent reason other than to reduce the risk of root damage, is under a duty to ascertain by effective means the nature of the subsoil whether or not he finds evidence of settlement of the house which may be due to subsoil shrinkage".[17]

Camouflaged defects. A careful surveyor should be suspicious of recent   **10–095** redecoration or repairs as they may have been deliberately carried out to conceal defects, particularly structural defects. O'Connor J. expressed this warning in *Hingorani v Blower*,[18] where the vendor had "faked up" the house and redecorated it from "top to tail" internally and filled in a large external crack. The defendant surveyor was held negligent in failing to observe tell-tale signs of structural defects, in particular the filled-in external crack which was apparent. The same point was made in *Morgan v Perry*,[19] where what had been done by the vendor by way of repointing, in-filling and over-papering had the same effect as "a deliberate cover-up job". The defendant surveyor gave "a completely clean bill of health" to a house which two years later structural engineers advised should be demolished owing to subsidence. The house was built upon a steep slope and was slipping. The defendant was held negligent in failing to observe

---

[12] This was a criticism made of the claimants' experts in *Hacker v Thomas Deal & Co* [1991] 2 E.G.L.R. 161 (see para.10–086, above), and again in *Alliance & Leicester Building Society v J & E Shepherd* [1995] G.W.D. 11–608.

[13] (1972) 230 E.G. 501.

[14] In *Hipkins v Jack Cotton Partnership*, *ibid.*, the period between the date of the report and the trial was also some seven-and-a-half years. This did not prevent the learned judge making findings that at the time of the inspection, a crack in the rendering had probably been patched up but was still visible and that a vine growing up the wall was not then of such a height as to obscure the crack.

[15] (1964) 190 E.G. 107. See also *Gurd v A Cobden Soar and Son* (1951) 157 E.G. 415 (defective drains and subsidence).

[16] (1972) 225 E.G. 1553. Note also *Bolton v Puley* (1983) 267 E.G. 1161 (defective boundary wall).

[17] *ibid.* at 1555.

[18] [1976] 1 E.G.L.R. 104.

[19] (1973) 229 E.G. 1737.

clear signs of subsidence. These included the "known potential dangers of a steeply sloping site" and repairs to the adjacent highway due to causes other than traffic. Examination of the latter would have led the surveyor to enquire of the local highway authority. Not all camouflaged defects can reasonably be exposed during an inspection. Much will depend on the existence or otherwise of other pointers to there being a hidden defect. In *Whalley v Roberts & Roberts*,[20] a construction defect that caused the property to have been built out of level had been deliberately camouflaged, both inside and outside the house. That fact with others[21] contributed to the judge's finding that the defendant surveyor, who had carried out a mortgage valuation, was not negligent in having failed to observe the defect.[22]

10-096   **Total of unnoticed defects.** While failure to observe some defects may not amount to negligence,[23] the more numerous the material defects overlooked, the more difficult it will be to resist a finding of negligence. In *Hill v Debenham, Tewson and Chinnocks*,[24] the defendants were instructed to carry out a structural survey of a dilapidated cottage which the claimant wished to purchase and reinstate[25] into a habitable condition. The defendants were further required to prepare plans and estimate the cost of reinstatement and structural alterations based on the plans. They were held negligent in five respects. First, they failed to notice the absence of a damp-proof course and advise the claimant to install one since the cottage was subject to extensive damp. Secondly, they failed to observe that the rafters and battens were defective and needed replacement. Thirdly, they failed to lift floorboards and observe that a second layer of floorboards underneath was riddled with worm. Fourthly, although the estimate only purported to be rough and provisional, it was even by that standard "fantastically optimistic and most misleading". Fifthly, they failed to warn the claimant that decoration should be postponed until damp had been effectively

---

[20] [1990] 1 E.G.L.R. 164.

[21] These were: (a) it was unusual for a building to be constructed out of level in that way; (b) such lack of level was usually associated with movement cracks; there were no such signs; (c) detection of the slope by sight or feel in such a property was not easy; (d) the effort to camouflage the lack of true level; (e) the claimant, an experienced joiner, had failed to notice the defect when he first moved in; and (f) the previous owner had lived in the property for some eight years without becoming aware of the slope.

[22] To similar effect would appear to be the decision in *Preferred Mortgages v Countrywide Surveyors Ltd* [2006] P.N.L.R. 154; [2005] EWHC 2920, where the judge found that the defendant valuer was not liable for having failed to discover the absence of proper electricity, mains water and drainage. At the time of the relevant inspection, the property had been made to look attractive for the purposes of a mortgage fraud and at trial the claimant appears to have conceded that the valuer could not have been inspected to discover the relevant faults. The report does not make clear why this was so.

[23] See para.10-058, above.

[24] (1958) 171 E.G. 835.

[25] *ibid.* at 837 *per* Judge Carter Q.C.:

"I should like to pause and consider the nature of the advice which should be given to a client who is contemplating buying a house and converting it into living accommodation. What does he want to know? The first thing in my view he wants to know is: 'Is the fabric of this house good enough to justify the expense of conversion?' Any competent surveyor should realise that is the crucial question about which he is called upon to advise. Houses have a life and the cheaper the conversion the shorter the life. Before a surveyor advises spending money on conversion he should satisfy himself that the fabric of the house is good enough to justify the spending of money on conversion."

dealt with. Similarly in *Hood v Shaw*,[26] the defendant surveyor was held negligent in providing a report "very, very short of what one had the right to expect from a qualified surveyor".[27] It contained errors of commission and omission. He stated that he had not seen any sign of bulging or fractures and that the brickwork and pointing, window frames and surrounds were in good order. In fact the opposite was proved to be the case. Further, he failed to observe the installation of a solid floor underneath the suspended floor, indicative of previous damp or other defect.[28]

(iv) *Limited Survey*

The particular nature of an engagement may require a less extensive inspection **10–097** of a property than would ordinarily be the case. For example, a surveyor may be engaged to ascertain a reasonable asking price for a property by a vendor, or its value as security by a prospective mortgagee. In such circumstances the more limited nature of the inspection is an important factor to take into account in determining whether a surveyor has been negligent in overlooking a particular defect.[29] The court may also permit a valuer a wider margin of error in relation to a valuation than would other wise have been the case. Thus in *Arab Bank v John D Wood Commercial Ltd*,[30] a valuer was instructed to comment upon another valuation produced of a substantial industrial estate. The judge held that the valuer was not only entitled to rely on the factual matters contained in that report (for example as to floor areas which had been over-stated), but indicated that he considered that the appropriate margin of error was higher than that applicable for the original valuer.[31] Whether the limited instructions will be sufficient to preclude a finding of negligence will depend upon the circumstances of each case, in particular the precise nature of the instructions and of the mistake made by the valuer.[32]

The problem has arisen in cases where a surveyor has agreed to carry out a **10–098** limited, but ill-defined, survey, frequently for a reduced fee. In *Matto v Rodney Broom Associates*,[33] the Court of Appeal expressed sympathy for the defendant surveyor when finding him negligent, after delivering "a short report intended to serve his client swiftly and effectively and without a screen of qualification for

---

[26] (1960) 176 E.G. 1291.

[27] *ibid.* at 1291 *per* Paull J.

[28] See also *Hoadley v Edwards* [2001] P.N.L.R. 965, where the surveyor was held liable for failing to bring five significant defects relating to the condition of the plumbing, the windows and the wall ties to the attention of the claimants.

[29] See *Nash v Evens & Matta* [1988] 1 E.G.L.R. 130 (mortgage valuation, surveyor did not report wall tie failure. Held, by Ewbank J., that surveyors fulfilled their duty on the basis of the limited inspection he was asked to make).

[30] [2000] Lloyd's L.Rep. P.N. 173.

[31] The Court of Appeal did not criticise this approach of the judge, but did find that, even on the judge's findings and following his approach, the second valuer had been negligent.

[32] See also the discussion of *Roberts v J Hampson & Co* [1988] 2 E.G.L.R. 181; and *Smith v Bush* [1990] 1 A.C. 831, at para.10–057, above. In *Etam v Baker Almond* [2001] E.G.C.S. 21, the valuers were required to provide a letter of comfort to a shopping chain which had decided to buy a store in Truro. The judge found that the claimants were looking for reassurance that they were not paying a "daft price". In that context the advice given was not unreasonable.

[33] [1994] 2 E.G.L.R. 163.

his own protection", which nevertheless failed adequately to warn of the risk and possible expense of further subsidence.

As the majority of prospective purchasers choose one of the standard services now offered by surveyors, where the ambit of the inspection is known in advance, such survey cases are becoming unusual. The need for such standardised and defined services is illustrated by *Sincock v Bangs (Reading)*,[34] where a surveyor gave a prospective purchaser client the choice of a "detailed survey" or a "general opinion" of a farm. The client elected the latter. Following the inspection and later purchase, the client discovered settlement in one corner of the house, dry rot and woodworm necessitating costly repairs. The client sued the surveyor and recovered damages. Barry J. concluded that it was the surveyor's duty to "warn the [client] of any defects which might have a material effect on the value of the property". He conceded that at the initial survey the surveyor had neither the time nor opportunity for carrying out a detailed examination of the structure. He nevertheless concluded that "making all allowances for the circumstances" the surveyor was negligent. Similarly in *Sinclair v Bowden Son and Partners*,[35] the surveyor was asked to do a survey quickly, but not a full structural survey. He spent an hour-and-a-half at the property on a Saturday and at the prospective purchaser's request sent him his report over the weekend. He charged seven guineas, rather than his 38 guinea fee for a full structural survey. Although he was doing "a rush job he did not want to do", Stephenson J. held him negligent in failing to observe the significance of new air bricks and thus discover wet rot and weevil. In *Franses v Barnett*,[36] a purchaser required and was charged less for a limited report for the primary purpose of discovering dry rot. The claimant failed, in view of the limited instructions, to establish negligence on the part of surveyors who had not discovered serious defects to the property exterior.

(v) *Failing to Recognise*

10–099　Although a surveyor may carry out a comprehensive inspection and be sufficiently observant, he may incur liability through failing to recognise a particular defect. The failure may be due to lack of knowledge on his part or mistaken attribution of the symptoms of the defect to another cause. In *Bryan Peach v Iain G Chalmers & Co*,[37] a surveyor preparing a valuation and report misunderstood and misdescribed the construction of the house, which was of the Dorran-type construction. The property was valued as if it were of traditional construction. There was a risk, never explained to the purchasers, that the bolts holding together the pre-cast concrete panels could corrode, requiring expensive repairs. As a consequence the property could prove difficult to sell, as lending institutions

---

[34] (1952) C.P.L. 562.

[35] (1962) 183 E.G. 95. See also *Leigh v William Hill and Son* (1956) 168 E.G. 396 (surveyor engaged by prospective purchaser to inspect and advise on the value of a house held negligent in failing to discover woodworm. The decision was affirmed on appeal when Singleton L.J. commented: "I have great sympathy with him. It was a valuation which had to be done fairly quickly and it may be that the inspection was not as complete as it might otherwise have been").

[36] (1956) 168 E.G. 425. See also the Scottish case of *Ker v John Allan & Son*, 1949 S.L.T. (Notes) 20, and para.10–088, above. The short notice and time for the inspection may have been important factors contributing to the successful defence.

[37] (1992) S.C.L.R. 423; [1992] 2 E.G.L.R. 135, OH, Lord Caplan.

would be reluctant to lend on the security of the same. The pursuers overpaid by £9,000 and this sum was awarded. Lack of knowledge explains the failure to recognise in *Daisley v BS Hall & Co*[38] and *Last v Post*.[39] In *Freeman v Marshall*,[40] the surveyor wrongly attributed to condensation what in fact was rising damp. He was held negligent in doing so. Alternatively, the surveyor may correctly diagnose the defects and their causes, but err in his assessment of their significance. In *Watts v Morrow*,[41] where the chartered building surveyor's reassuring and detailed description of the roof was held to be negligent even though he correctly identified the principal defects, it was held by the official referee that the surveyor failed to recognise that the roof needed a comprehensive and expensive overhaul. As the first two cases demonstrate, the importance of expert evidence to establish the standard of a reasonably skilled surveyor is usually greater in cases of alleged failure to recognise than in cases of other inspection failure. Cases of failure to recognise, particularly when due to an error in attribution,[42] may involve differing views between experts as to the reasonable interpretation of particular symptoms at a certain time. Consequently, negligence may be more difficult to establish than in cases of other inspection failures.

(d) *Failing to Make Sufficient Inquiries*

Apart from inspecting a property, a surveyor may need to make a number of   **10–100**
enquiries in order to carry out his instructions. An example is provided by the facts of *Western Trust v Strutt & Parker*,[43] where a valuer was found liable for negligently valuing a holiday complex on the basis that it formed permanent accommodation. Had he made enquiries of the local authority, he could and should have discovered the true position. Two further recent examples of the negligent failure to make proper inquiries is provided by the facts of *Montlake v Lambert Smith Hampton*,[44] and *Francis v Barclays Bank Plc*.[45] In *Montlake*, the defendant surveyors did not make proper enquiries of the local planning authority before updating a valuation made two years previously. In the course of the two years, the local authority had changed the designation of a rugby ground from "Public and Private Open Space/Playing fields" to undesignated land. The consequence was that no allowance was made for the possibility of profitable residential development. In *Francis*, the third-party surveyors acted for the mortgagee in relation to a sale by the mortgagee of land to a developer. The initial sale agreement provided for additional payments in the event of the sale of the land within 10 years for development. The developer then proposed to limit the additional payment to a maximum of £80,000 in return for an immediate sum of £35,000. At the time the site lay outside the area designated by the local

---

[38] (1972) 225 E.G. 1553; see para.10–055, above.

[39] (1952) 159 E.G. 240; see para.10–055, above.

[40] (1966) 200 E.G. 777. *cf. Bishop v Watson, Watson and Scoles* (1972) 224 E.G. 1881 (see para.10–089 above).

[41] [1991] 1 E.G.L.R. 150 at first instance, reversed on appeal on the issue of measure of loss, [1991] 1 W.L.R. 1421, CA.

[42] e.g. disputes over interpretation of cracks in subsidence claims.

[43] [1999] P.N.L.R. 154—see further para.10–042, above.

[44] [2004] EWHC 938.

[45] [2005] P.N.L.R. 297, [2005] EWHC 2787.

planning authority for development, but subsequently a draft local plan was published showing the site within a development, area. The developer then sold the site and paid the maximum sum of £80,000. But for the variation, the sum payable would have been approximately £1m. The judge found that the mortgagee was in breach of its duty to the mortgagor in failing to make proper inquiries of the planning authority prior to agreeing to the variation. Similarly he found the surveyors liable to the mortgagee on the same grounds and held that had such inquiries been made, the mortgagee could not have been advised to agree to the variation.

As *Baxter v FW Gapp & Co Ltd*[46] and *Kenney v Hall, Pain and Foster*[47] illustrate, if a surveyor is insufficiently aware of local market values, he should take steps to ascertain them. It may be necessary to carry out research and to make enquiries of local agents or a specific class of prospective vendors or purchasers. Thus in *Bell Hotels (1935) Ltd v Motion*,[48] the defendants, instructed to make an approximate valuation of the last free house in Melton Mowbray, were held negligent in failing to advise the claimants that a brewery would be interested in buying. On the basis of the defendants' advice, the claimants sold the house to a buyer who almost immediately resold it at a considerable profit to a brewery. Although in the judgment the relevant default is described as failure to advise, clearly the effective default was failure to make sufficient enquiries of breweries themselves.

10–101 The more complex the task, the more detailed and painstaking the enquiries required of the surveyor. Authoritative guidance as to the appropriate methodology may be found in the appropriate Standards and Guidance Notes published by the RICS[49] and reference to the edition in force at the material time should always be made. A catalogue of factors and activities to be considered and undertaken at the stage of enquiry in carrying out a valuation is also set out in Watkins J.'s judgment in *Singer & Friedlander Ltd v John D Wood & Co.*[50] In

---

[46] [1938] 4 All E.R. 457 (first instance); [1939] 2 K.B. 752, CA; see para.10–081, above.

[47] [1976] 2 E.G.L.R. 29; for facts, see para.10–080, above. See also the Canadian case, *Avco Financial Services v Holstein* (1980) 109 D.L.R. (3d) 128.

[48] (1952) 159 E.G. 496.

[49] See paras 10–022 *et seq.*, above.

[50] [1977] 2 E.G.L.R. 84 at 86:

"The factors and activities which a competent valuer will consider and undertake in valuing land cannot be composed in such a way as to indicate an unvarying approach to every problem which confronts him. But a collection of them from which he will choose at will in a given circumstance must include the following:

(a) The kind of development of the land to be undertaken.

(b) The existence, if any, of planning permission in outline or in detail as to a part or the whole of the land. And if permission be for the building of houses, the situation and acreage of part of the land excluded from planning permission because, for example, of a tree preservation order, the need for schools and the layout of roads and other things. Furthermore, the number of houses permitted or likely to be permitted to be built by the planning authority is a relevant, indeed a vital factor.

(c) The history of the land, including its use, changes in ownership and the most recent buying prices, planning applications and permissions, the implementation or otherwise of existing planning permissions, the reason for the failure, if it be the fact that a planning permission had not been implemented.

(d) The position of the land in relation to surrounding countryside, villages and towns and places of employment; the quality of access to it, the attractiveness or otherwise of its situation.

that case the defendants were requested to value a site intended for development for the purpose of enabling the claimant finance houses to estimate the amount which they could advance to developers on a first mortgage of the site. The defendants were held negligent in valuing the site at £2,200,000. Three years later it was only worth £600,000. The primary ground for the finding of negligence was that the defendants had merely carried out "a hurried paper exercise" founded upon very little of the information that proper observance of the first of the four stages into which Watkins J. analysed the task of valuing land[51] would have provided. That stage consisted of "the sometimes tedious and laborious but vital approach work" consisting of inspecting the site, several enquiries and much research. The site had no comparable and a "dismal development record". Nevertheless the defendants were found to have only cursorily inspected it and ignored its imperfect characteristics and to have failed to make proper enquiries of the county planning authority.[52] It may also be necessary to carry out additional enquiries if unusual instructions are given.[53]

The professional use of hearsay information. To what extent may a surveyor, in carrying out a valuation, rely upon information gathered and provided by others without checking it? The answer will depend upon the nature of the information, the reputation of the person or body supplying it, and the ordinary practice of the profession. Of necessity, much useful information to a surveyor will be hearsay, for example comparable values provided by local estate agents, and specimen rental values published in the specialist press. Quite apart from the relaxations provided by the Civil Evidence Act 1995, it is not necessary for **10–102**

(e) The situation obtaining about the provision of services for example, electricity, sewage and other drainage and water.

(f) The presence, if it be so, of any unusual difficulties confronting development which will tend to increase the cost of it to an extent which affects the value of the land. A visit to the site must surely find a prominent place among physical activities to be undertaken.

(g) The demand in the immediate localities for houses of the kind likely to be built, with special regard to the situation of places of employment and increases to be expected in demand for labour. This will involve, inevitably, acquiring knowledge of other building developments recently finished or still in progress, especially having regard to rate of disposal, density and sale price of the houses disposed of. In this way the existence, if any, of local comparables, a valuable factor, can be discovered.

(h) Consultation with senior officers of the local planning authority is almost always regarded as an indispensable aid, likewise a knowledge of the approval planning policy for the local area; a study of the approved town or county map may prove rewarding.

(i) Whether ascertaining from the client if there have been other previous valuations of the land, and to what effect, should be undertaken is probably questionable because a valuer's mind should not be exposed to the possibilities of affectation by the opinion of a valuer.

(j) If he is a man whose usual professional activities do not bring him regularly into the locality, or what is more important has never done so, he will obviously need to be especially careful in collecting as much relevant local knowledge as he can, possibly by consulting valuers who work regularly in the area.

(k) The availability of a labour force which can carry out the prospective development."

[51] *ibid.* at 217 and set out at para.10–076, above.

[52] Guidance as to the proper approach of surveyors instructed in respect of rating valuations was given in *McIntyre v Herring Son and Daw* [1988] 1 E.G.L.R. 231.

[53] An example is provided by the facts of *Farley v Skinner* [2000] P.N.L.R. 441, where specific instructions were given to check that a house did not suffer from aircraft noise and the judge held that this required a check with the Civil Aviation Authority at Gatwick (the relevant local airport)—this decision was appealed on the measure of damages—see further para.10–184, below.

evidence of the value of comparable properties to be strictly proved by first-hand evidence where the evidence establishes that competent valuers make valuations on the basis of market intelligence which is hearsay. In a ruling in *Banque Bruxelles Lambert SA v Lewis & Tucker Ltd*,[54] Phillips J. distinguished *English Exporters (London) Ltd v Eldonwall Ltd*,[55] which itself had been approved by the Court of Appeal in *Rogers v Rosedimond Investments (Blakes Market) Ltd*.[56] These cases concerned the use of comparable evidence for the purposes of rent reviews. Phillips J. concluded:

> "One would of course normally expect the actual value of a property, *i.e.* the value that it would actually realise on the market, to tally with the opinion of competent valuers as to its value. But the questions what is the actual value and what opinion would a competent valuer form of the actual value are two different questions and it is the latter with which I am concerned. *English Exporters* and *Rogers v Rosedimond* were concerned with the former question and I do not consider that the principles pronounced in those cases are applicable in this."[57]

In *Abbey National Mortgages Plc v Key Surveyors Nationwide Ltd*,[58] the Court of Appeal, approving the approach and reasoning of Phillips J., held that an expert valuer was not confined to giving evidence based on comparables of which he had direct first-hand knowledge; having made careful and appropriate inquiries, the valuer was fully entitled to rely on what appeared to him to be reliable information. Direct first-hand knowledge was not required.[59]

10–103   A surveyor should be wary of relying on information from a person whose interests conflict with those of his client. Unless specifically instructed to rely on it, such information should be independently checked if possible. *In Old Gate Estates Ltd v Toplis and Harding and Russell*,[60] it was alleged that the surveyor instructed to value a property to be conveyed to the claimant company was negligent in not inquiring into figures as to its rents and outgoings provided by two directors of the company who were also sellers of the property. Since in calculating the figures the rates had been grossly understated, the valuation was

---

[54] *(No.1)*, unreported, February 26, 1993.
[55] [1973] 1 Ch. 415.
[56] [1978] 2 E.G.L.R. 48.
[57] The principle discussed by Phillips J. was considered and applied *in Zubaida v Hargreaves* [1993] 2 E.G.L.R. 170. The defendant valuer, appointed as an independent expert to determine the rent of a restaurant on a rent review, acted in accordance with a practice accepted as proper by competent, respected, and professional opinion, in using as comparables rents of similar shop units. An appeal was dismissed; see [1995] 1 E.G.L.R. 127. The Court of Appeal noted that the defendant's use of certain comparables was supported by a respectable body of professional opinion (see 128B), applied the test in *Bolam v Friern Hospital Management Committee* [1957] 1 W.L.R. 582 and dismissed the appeal.
[58] [1996] 3 All E.R. 183 at 189.
[59] In *Nyckeln Finance v Edward Symmons & Partners* [1999] Lloyd's L.Rep. P.N. 953, a case before the introduction of the Civil Procedure Rules and the Civil Evidence Act 1998, the Court of Appeal considered a case where the defendant wished to adduce evidence of a number of contemporaneous valuations of the subject property itself. The claimant was not prepared to concede that the valuations were themselves competent and objected to the valuers being called, on the basis that the defendant would benefit from a greater number of experts than it was permitted to call. The court considered that the defendant should have leave to call the original valuers, as their evidence was too potentially important to be excluded.
[60] [1939] 3 All E.R. 209.

excessive. The defendants conceded that in an ordinary valuation it would be negligent for a valuer to value a property without himself collecting the material such as rent and outgoings upon which the valuation was made. In the circumstances and particularly in view of the suppliers of the information being an accountant and surveyor respectively and hence competent to ascertain it, the defendants denied that they were negligent. In the event the issue was not resolved, the defendants escaping liability on other grounds. In *Love v Mack*,[61] a valuer instructed to value a mineral water factory was apparently "taken in and defrauded" by the mortgagor, who exaggerated the takings of the licensed houses. It was alleged that he was negligent in not checking the takings book and brewers' and distillers' invoices. Kekewich J., however, concluded that such checks were more than what was required by the necessities of the case and that "a man is not liable to an action because he is defrauded".[62] In *Craneheath Securities v York Montague*,[63] one of the respects in which it was alleged that the defendant surveyors were negligent was in relying on an estimate of turnover for a restaurant provided by directors of a vendor for the purposes of a valuation for the funders of a purchaser. The valuer made clear that he had not seen any audited accounts and the allegation was rejected on the basis that the claimant could not show that the estimate was, in fact, incorrect.

(e) *Failing to Make a Proper Appraisal*

A survey will usually entail no more than inspection and observation and   **10–104** reporting the results to the client. A valuation or a development brief,[64] however, will require detailed appraisal of the results of inspection and other enquiries before the client can be advised properly. Appraisal may, depending upon the property and the complexity of the assignment, be an extensive task. Apart from a detailed analysis of information obtained it may involve construction of terms in documents of title, consideration of statutory and planning requirements, calculation of periodic incomes and outgoings and investment returns. Any recent market history of the property will also have to be researched and considered. Where a property has recently been sold, a valuer who gives an open-market valuation without considering the implications of that recent sale is likely to be, in the absence of express instructions from the lender, negligent.[65] In arriving at a valuation figure a surveyor will be expected to apply a proper

---

[61] (1905) 92 L.T. 345.

[62] *ibid.* at 350. In *Tenenbaum v Garrod* [1988] 2 E.G.L.R. 178, a case described as "strange" by Mustill L.J. in the Court of Appeal, an estate agent who provided a "valuation" of certain factory buildings was held not liable to the claimant as the "valuation" had never been intended as a genuine independent valuation of the property, rather that it was a mere negotiating weapon for the claimant to use, who had not relied on it and who only sought to blame the defendant when his plan to purchase the property at undervalue failed.

[63] [2001] Lloyd's L.Rep. P.N. 348.

[64] i.e. instructions to assess the development potential of a site. It may also include instructions to plan and supervise the development. See article by J. Ratcliffe (1979) 251 E.G. 1260.

[65] See *Banque Bruxelles Lambert SA v Eagle Star Insurance Co Ltd* [1994] 2 E.G.L.R. 108 at 118 *per* Phillips J.

method of valuation and often check it by another method.[66] Moreover, it is a task that requires not only knowledge, skill and care, but also careful judgment.

10–105   The fact that a valuer makes a material and negligent error in reaching his figure will not usually establish liability where the total valuation figure was itself not negligently high, as defined by the principle expressed in *Bolam v Friern Hospital Management Committee*.[67] In *Mount Banking Corp Ltd v Brian Cooper & Co*,[68] the court rejected a submission by the claimant that provided it proved negligent errors in a valuer's calculation, it was entitled to recover even though the final valuation was within acceptable limits. The deputy judge rejected the argument that *Corisand Investments Ltd v Druce & Co*[69] was authority for such a proposition, and held[70]:

> "If the valuation that has been reached cannot be impeached as a total, then, however erroneous the method or its application by which the valuation has been reached, no loss has been sustained because, within the Bolam principle, it was a proper valuation."

The Court of Appeal reviewed the authorities and considered the proper approach to adopt for "margin of error" cases in *Merivale Moore Plc v Strutt & Parker*.[71] Buxton L.J. made four points. First, the "bracket" is not to be determined in a mechanistic way, divorced from the facts of the particular case. Secondly, if it is proved that in reaching the valuation, the valuer adopted an unprofessional practice or approach then that fact may be taken into account in considering whether the valuation contained an unacceptable degree of error. Thirdly, where it is shown that the valuation is outside the acceptable limit, that may be a strong indication that the valuer has been negligent. However, the question still remains whether the valuer has been negligent in accordance with the principle expressed in *Bolam*:

> "To find that his valuation fell outside the 'bracket' is, as held by this court in *Craneheath* and also, I consider, by the House of Lords in *Banque Lambert*, a necessary condition of liability, but it cannot in itself be sufficient."

---

[66] See *Singer & Friedlander Ltd v John D. Wood & Co* [1977] 2 E.G.L.R. 84 *per* Watkins J. The relevant passage is set out in para.10–101, fn.35, above. For examples of negligence in applying a wrong method of valuation, see *Jenkins v Betham* (1855) 15 C.B. 167; *Whitty v Lord Dillon* (1860) 2 F. & F. 67; *Weedon v Hindwood, Clarke and Esplin* (1974) 234 E.G. 121; *McIntyre v Herring Son & Daw* [1988] 1 E.G.L.R. 231; *Beaumont v Humberts* [1990] 2 E.G.L.R. 166. Cases in which the claimant's claim failed include: *Muldoon v Mays of Lilliput Ltd* [1993] 1 E.G.L.R. 43; and *Macey v Debenham, Tewson & Chinnocks* [1993] 1 E.G.L.R. 149; where the claimant, a solicitor, retained the defendant valuers to advise in respect of the proposed purchase for investment of certain freehold property. The advice given was to purchase the property; such advice included an analysis of yields. The claimant's claim failed, he having failed to prove that the valuer's report, and the calculations and deductions on which it was based, were such as could not have been arrived at if he had shown reasonable skill and care.

[67] [1957] 1 W.L.R. 582.

[68] [1992] 2 E.G.L.R. 142. See also *Legal & General Mortgage Services Ltd v HPC Professional Services* [1997] P.N.L.R. 567, where *Mount Banking* was followed. For a discussion on "the bracket" approach to valuation, see J. Murdoch, "The margin of error approach to negligence in valuations" (1997) 3 P.N. 31.

[69] [1978] 2 E.G.L.R. 86.

[70] [1992] 2 E.G.L.R. 142 at 145D.

[71] [1999] Lloyd's Rep. P.N. 734 at 744. See further para.10–061 above.

Fourthly, the adduction of expert valuation evidence is not a necessary pre-condition to a finding of negligence on the part of a valuer.

"I think that it is still open to the judge in a suitable case to hold that the valuation is so far removed from what was the true value of the property that it must be regarded as a valuation that was outside the limits open to a competent valuer, without specific professional evidence being given of what those limits were."

Buxton L.J. commented, however, that such evidence "plainly made the task of the trial judge much easier". As discussed above,[72] it has been suggested by Mance L.J. in *Arab Bank v John D Wood Commercial Ltd*,[73] that the above approach is only appropriate if the only relevant obligation is to produce a figure which a competent valuer could have produced. However, first instance judges have been unwilling to find such additional obligations.

Proper appraisal may be particularly difficult in a property "boom", but as **10–106** Phillips J. stated in *Banque Bruxelles Lambert SA v Eagle Star Insurance Co Ltd*,[74] when a property market is booming it is inevitable that the current market price will be affected by the entry into the market of property speculators hoping to make capital gains. No discount falls to be made from the open market valuation for that reason. The consequences of an earlier property market "boom" are illustrated by *Corisand Investments Ltd v Druce & Co*.[75] The defendant valuers were instructed to value a portfolio of properties including a hotel for the purpose of raising further finance secured upon a second mortgage. The claimants were willing to lend up to 70 per cent of the valuation and they advanced a total of £60,000. Shortly after, there was a collapse in the property market, the borrower defaulted, the first mortgagees appointed a receiver and the properties were sold, including the hotel, for a total of £125,250. There remained nothing on sale to satisfy the second mortgage debt of £60,000. The claimants sued the defendants, alleging that their valuation of the hotel was so excessive as to have been negligent. Gibson J. held that the defendants were negligent in three respects. First, the valuation reflected an estimate of the hotel's expenses which was excessively low. Secondly, while the defendants were not negligent in not anticipating or suspecting the impending collapse of the property market, they were negligent in not excluding from their valuation or identifying for the claimants' guidance the speculative content (put at 20 per cent) in the estimated open market price, characteristic of a price "boom".[76] This finding followed from the judge's view that it was the duty of the defendants in preparing a valuation for mortgage purposes to exclude from their valuation any apparent content which might well not be available for sale by the mortgagee when he

---

[72] See para.10–059 above.
[73] [2000] Lloyd's L.Rep. P.N. 173.
[74] [1994] 2 E.G.L.R. 108 at 117.
[75] [1978] 2 E.G.L.R. 86.
[76] Phillips J. pointed out in *Banque Bruxelles Lambert SA v Eagle Star Insurance Co Ltd* [1994] 2 E.G.L.R. 108 at 117, that the basis of valuation being described by Gibson J. is a forced sale valuation, and that his comments should not be applied to an open market valuation. It does not, however, necessarily follow that a "forced sale" value (i.e. one within a limited period of time) will be lower than an open market value. For an example of a case where it was found that it was reasonable for there to be no discount in respect of a sale within 90 days to a mortgagee in possession, see *UCB Corporate Services Ltd v Halifax (SW) Ltd* [2000] 1 E.G.L.R. 87.

attempted to realise his security.[77] Thirdly, the defendants failed to allow in their valuation for expenditure necessary to put the hotel into the condition required by the Fire Precautions Act 1971:

> "it was in my judgment the duty of a valuer preparing a valuation for mortgage purposes to make appropriate allowances for any significant defect or problem[78] in respect of which the purchasers in the market would calculate that they would have to spend money before being able to operate the hotel to make the estimated net income".[79]

Allowing reductions of 20 per cent for the speculative content and £8,000 for fire precaution works, the judge concluded that the hotel valuation was excessive by £63,000.[80]

In *Watts v Savills*,[81] the valuer was held negligent at first instance for his failure to value on the basis that the land had significant development potential. This decision was reversed on appeal, it being held that whether land had development potential (and therefore a greatly enhanced value) was a question of opinion, and not fact. A valuer could therefore be mistaken without being negligent. It was only if no reasonably competent valuer, acting with reasonable skill and care, could have formed the view that the land had no development potential, that the defendant valuer could be held liable.

(f) *Inadequate Report*

10–107 The nature of the report required will vary according to a surveyor's instructions and his role. There will, of course, be situations when there is an obligation to report information by reason of the law of agency. Thus where estate agents are employed for the sale of properties, they will be subject to the usual obligations of such agents to report matters affecting their principal to him.[82] Where, not acting as agent, a client may request only an oral report, although a written report is usually required and is always desirable. A written report is a vital document in surveyors' negligence cases not merely for its contents, but also because it

---

[77] *cf.* Watkins J. in *Singer & Friedlander Ltd v John D Wood & Co* [1977] 2 E.G.L.R. 84 at 85.

[78] e.g. the "dismal development record" of the site in *Singer & Friedlander Ltd v John D Wood & Co* [1977] 2 E.G.L.R. 84 (see para.10–101, above).

[79] [1978] 2 E.G.L.R. 86 at 99.

[80] Further cases arising out of valuations prepared during a booming property market are discussed at para.10–152 below.

[81] Unreported, June 26, 1998, CA.

[82] Thus in *John D Wood & Co v Knatchbull* [2003] P.N.L.R. 351; [2002] EWHC 351, agents had given an initial valuation of a property at £1.5m which the judge found to have been competent. The property was then marketed. During the course of the marketing campaign the agents became aware that a nearby similar property was on the market at £1.95m. H.H. Judge Heppel Q.C. found that the agents were in breach of duty in not bringing this knowledge to the attention of their principal. He stated:

> " . . . the agent has a duty to exercise reasonable care when marketing a property for sale and if in the course of so doing he becomes aware of a significant event in the market which might influence his principal's instructions to inform the principal thereof and to advise him accordingly".

is indicative of what was done or not done by the surveyor.[83] For example, errors of omission or commission in a report are commonly the consequences of earlier errors in inspecting. The detail required will vary according to the instructions and circumstances in each case. A building or structural survey report will usually be much more detailed than a valuation report. Where pro-forma or approved report forms are used there is less opportunity for omission or misunderstanding as to the extent of the inspection. Even in the case of a valuation, much more may be required than simple quotation of a figure. For example, Watkins J. in *Singer & Friedlander Ltd v John D Wood & Co*[84] stated that:

> "a bank, although interested mainly in a figure or valuation is entitled to be made aware by the valuer of the whole of the circumstances of the planning history of the site, including his firm's previous acquaintance with it".[85]

In the case of a building or structural survey the report should set out the facts and in particular state matters of significance and warn of material defects so as to enable a proper decision to be made.[86] In order to avoid a misleading impression, certain general words may need to be avoided.[87] Moreover, if a surveyor cannot ascertain any fact he should say that he was unable to do so and, therefore, unable to express any opinion on it.[88]

Failure to warn.[89] Failure to warn is the subject of numerous surveyors' **10–108** negligence cases and is frequently expressed to be the relevant default although

---

[83] Note *Barton v Stuart Hepburn & Co* [1926] E.G.D. 206. Rowlatt J. expressed the view that surveyors instructed to carry out a valuation should state in their report that they had not conducted a detailed inspection or thorough survey if that be the case.

[84] [1977] 2 E.G.L.R. 84.

[85] *ibid.* at 93.

[86] In *Summers v Congreve Horner & Co* [1991] 2 E.G.L.R. 139, Judge Fox-Andrews Q.C. held that there were four elements to a structural survey: the preparation for a visual inspection, the visual inspection, an evaluation of what had been seen at the inspection and the written report. The case went to the Court of Appeal on the issue of insurance cover, [1992] 2 E.G.L.R. 152. Note Lord Cameron's definition of "anything of significance" in *Stewart v HA Brechin & Co* 1959 S.C. 306 at 308. The relevant passage is set out in para.10–082, above. A surveyor abiding by the relevant Guidance Notes issued by the RICS should be able to demonstrate compliance with approved and general practice.

[87] e.g. in *Hood v Shaw* (1960) 176 E.G. 1291, the defendant surveyor's description of the structure of a house as "sound and substantial" was criticised by Paull J. See also *BFG Bank AG v Brown & Mumford Ltd* [1997] P.N.L.R. 202, where the Court of Appeal held that negligent valuers could only escape liability on their arguments that a letter was not a valuation and that the claimant should not have relied upon it if the claimant's interpretation of the same was unreasonable:

> "the question is whether an ordinary person to whom the letter was addressed could reasonably have thought that the extent of the risk being referred to was that there was no more than a 5 per cent risk of planning permission being refused" *per* Scott V.C. at 208F.

[88] See *Rona v Pearce* (1953) 162 E.G. 380 *per* Hilbery J.; also see *Hill v Debenham, Tewson and Chinnocks* (1958) 171 E.G. 835 at 837 *per* Judge Carter Q.C. "But applying the standard of the profession I entertain no doubt that the practice of the profession is 'If you do not look, you must warn.' "

[89] Despite the superficial attraction, there is no analogy between the cases discussed in this paragraph and the extensive jurisprudence on "failure to warn" in the context of medical negligence. See Ch.13, paras 13–089 *et seq.* None of the justifications for failing to warn of known risks of medical treatment applies in the context of advice about real property.

the effective default may be an antecedent failure to inspect or to observe.[90] Certain defects call for a specific warning, for example, dry rot[91] and death watch beetle.[92] Further, the warning given must be sufficient. Thus, for example, Bristow J. in *Daisley v BS Hall & Co*[93] in considering the risk of settlement owing to shrinkable clay stated:

> "If circumstances are such that the risk is high, clearly [the surveyor] should warn his client not to go on with the purchase. If circumstances are such that the risk is very small it must, in my judgment, be his duty to say so."[94]

In *Cross v David Martin and Mortimer*,[95] a surveyor carrying out an inspection for a RICS House Buyer's Report and Valuation correctly observed and briefly reported on the method of construction of a loft conversion. He was, however, held negligent[96] in failing to comment in his report more fully on the possible consequences of the conversion, namely that the original design concept of the roof had been violated, that the effect of what had been done could only be calculated with difficulty and that the roof space might not be capable of bearing the live loading imposed by a habitable room. The report should have expressly warned the claimants that unless the conversion had received building regulation approval, it would not be safe to use the loft for anything other than light storage. Similarly in *Izzard v Field Palmer*,[97] a mortgage valuer who (correctly) observed that a former Ministry of Defence property was built using the Jesperson system, was found liable for failing to point out the defects in such a system or the effect that such a construction had on mortgage value. Frequently, survey reports contain standard clauses to the effect that no responsibility can be accepted in respect of defects in inaccessible or uninspected parts of the property.[98] This may be construed as a general warning and is often pleaded to rebut liability for undiscovered defects. In deciding such a clause's efficacy, much will depend upon its particular terms and the particular defects overlooked.[99] Such a clause is unlikely to help the surveyor if he both should and could have examined in an

---

[90] See *Hill v Debenham, Tewson and Chinnocks* (*ibid.*) for several instances of failure to warn; also *Lees v English and Partners* [1977] E.G.D. 566 (failure to warn of bad "tie" between old and new brickwork); *Allen v Ellis & Co* [1990] 1 E.G.L.R. 170 (failure to warn of defective garage roof); *Alliance & Leicester Building Society v J. & E. Shepherd* [1995] G.W.D. 11–608, OH, Lord MacLean (complaint of failure to warn of risk of flooding on the property from the nearby River Tay and Inchewan Burn, held, the claimant had not established that at the date of the survey no reasonably competent surveyor would have failed to appreciate that the property was at risk of flooding).

[91] See, e.g. *Hardy v Wamsley-Lewis* (1967) 203 E.G. 1039. Paull J. there stated (at 1043) that it was clearly the surveyor's duty to report that what he found there had been dry rot, irrespective of its being dormant or not; also *Tremayne v T Mortimer Burrows and Partners* (1954) 165 E.G. 232.

[92] See *Oswald v Countrywide Surveyors Ltd* [1994] E.G.C.S. 150, an infestation of woodworm had been reported, but the failure to specify an active infestation by death watch beetle, which caused considerably more damage than woodworm, was held to be negligent.

[93] (1972) 225 E.G. 1553.

[94] *ibid.* at 1555.

[95] [1989] 1 E.G.L.R. 154.

[96] *ibid.* at 158.

[97] [2000] 1 E.G.L.R. 76.

[98] See para.10–073, above.

[99] See the discussion of exclusion clauses at paras 10–063 *et seq.*, above. The cases of *Stevenson v Nationwide Building Society* [1990] 1 A.C. 831 and *McCullagh v Lane Fox & Partners* [1996] 1 E.G.L.R. 35 are particularly relevant.

uninspected part where an existing material defect is subsequently discovered, as happened in *Heatley v William H Brown Ltd*.[1]

A valuer will not generally be liable to warn his client against the risk that others might reach a different, incorrect, valuation. This proposition is illustrated by the facts of the Australian case, *Flemington Properties Pty Ltd v Raine & Horne Commercial Pty Ltd*.[2] The valuer had been retained to provide an opinion as to the "unimproved" value of some land in accordance with a New South Wales statute. The claimant had then purchased the land in reliance on the valuation whereupon the Valuer General wrongly valued the land at lower than the "worse case" scenario provided by the valuer. The Full Court of the Federal Court of Australia held that the valuer was not under a duty to guard against the risk of a misapplication of the statute. Tamberlin J. stated[3]:

> "The suggestion that [the valuer] ought to have warned the applicant that an incorrect, one lot basis of valuation might be used, cannot be accepted. The retainer should not be construed to require a determination of a figure on a basis contrary to the provisions of the Act or to warn that such an approach might be followed. A 'worst case' assessment calls for an assessment based on the application of proper valuation principles, having due regard to the correct interpretation of the Act. The possibility that a valuation might be arrived at, which is based on principles or provisions outside or foreign to the requirements of the Act, is contrary to the role of the valuer. If it were otherwise it would be extremely difficult, if not impossible, to give any satisfactory valuation advice. The task of the valuer, in this case was to apply the correct principles as required by the Act.
>
> In other words, a valuer cannot reasonably be under a duty to provide to a client a valuation by way of warning, which presupposes that the land will be valued on an erroneous basis. In the present case, of course, the position is that the valuation was made on what has been found to be a correct basis. The possibility that it might have been made on another basis which is erroneous is irrelevant. There is no breach of the retainer or negligence in carrying out a valuation on correct principles and warning a client as to the lower range valuations arrived at by the application of correct principles in accordance with the Act."

10–109

3. DAMAGES

An award of damages will usually be the only remedy for breach of duty by a surveyor. In certain circumstances a surveyor may be deprived of his fees. Reported cases, however, do not reveal a consistent approach to the issue of whether a negligent surveyor should be so deprived. In some cases recovery of fees has been allowed,[4] presumably on the basis that such fees would have been incurred even if proper advice had been given. In other cases, despite a damages

10–110

---

[1] [1992] 1 E.G.L.R. 289. See para.10–092, above.
[2] (1998) 155 A.L.R. 345.
[3] At 346.
[4] *Last v Post* (1952) 1 9 E.G. 240; the claim for fees was admitted in *Bell Hotels (1935) Ltd v Motion* (1952) 159 E.G. 496; *Conn v Munday* (1955) 166 E.G. 465; *Corisand Investments Ltd v Druce & Co* [1978] 2 E.G.L.R. 86.

award for the extent of the loss sustained, fees have not been recovered[5] and even been ordered to be repaid.[6] The preferable approach is to allow recovery of fees where damages for the loss are awarded unless the surveyor's advice was so wrong as properly to be described as worthless.[7]

10–111   Once a breach of contract or act of negligence has been established, the following questions may arise as to the recoverability of damage:

     (a) Has the claimant sustained the loss claimed?[8]

     (b) Is the loss claimed within the scope of the defendant's duty?[9]

     (c) Are the damages claimed too remote?[10]

     (d) What is the correct measure of damages?[11]

(a) *Has the Claimant Sustained the Loss Claimed?*

10–112   A primary requirement for the recovery of damages is that the claimant should be able to establish that it has suffered the loss claimed or is to be taken as having suffered such loss. A court will, in appropriate circumstances, be prepared to disregard an artificial loss. Thus in *HIT Finance Ltd v Lewis & Tucker Ltd*,[12] the claimant was unable to recover contractual interest which it had had to pay to its two parents in order to make a loan following a negligent valuation from the defendants. The claimant had only one executive officer, whose salary was paid by a parent company. It had no other staff, no separate offices, no capital and any residual profits were passed to its parents. The claimant was unable to borrow funds to support its lending activities on the open market, but was constrained to borrow from its parent companies. Wright J. held that the claimant had no independence of operation, it was simply a financial arm of its two parents. Examining the underlying realities, the judge concluded that it was the parents who, in truth, provided the money for the loan, through the instrument of the claimant and that it was these two companies, rather than the claimant, which had suffered the loss that flowed from the negligence of the defendant. There was no evidence before the judge as to how the parent companies had financed the money that they passed to the claimant for onward loan. Nor was there any evidence showing how such money, if not lent to the claimant, would have been

---

[5] *Sincock v Bangs (Reading)* [1952] C.P.L. 562; *Hill v Debenham, Tewson and Chinnocks* (1958) 171 E.G. 835; *Buckland v Watts* (1968) 208 E.G. 969. In the first and third cases fees for other work were recovered. In *Whitty v Lord Dillon* (1860) 2 F. & F. 67, the defence of *non indebitatus* succeeded against a claim for fees in respect of advice held to have been negligent.

[6] *Chong v Scott Collins & Co* (1954) 164 E.G. 662; *Hoadley v Edwards* [2001] P.N.L.R. 965.

[7] See *Hill v Debenham, Tewson and Chinnocks* (1958) 171 E.G. 835 at 839, and the passages there quoted from Cockburn C.J.'s judgment in *Whitty v Lord Dillon* (1860) 2 F. & F. 67 and from Best C.J.'s judgment in *Moneypenny v Hartland* (1826) 2 C. & P. 378. In *Bigg v Howard Son & Gooch* [1990] 1 E.G.L.R. 173, the claimant conceded that the defendant surveyors were entitled to set off against the claimant's damages the sum counterclaimed for fees.

[8] See para.10–112 below.

[9] See para.10–113 below.

[10] See para.10–120 below.

[11] See para.10–129 below.

[12] [1993] 2 E.G.L.R. 231.

profitably employed. The judge felt able to take notice of the fact that both parent companies were, or were owned by major public limited companies and that surplus funds would be put to the best available use. The judge awarded 1 per cent over clearing bank base rate simple interest on the fluctuating balance due for the period since the loan was made.[13]

(b) *Is the Loss Claimed within the Scope of the Defendant's Duty?*

In England, this question may arise as a result of the decision of the House of **10–113** Lords in *BBL v Eagle Star*.[14] The cases arose in the context of losses claimed by lenders who had made secured loans on the basis of negligent valuations of real property which had subsequently fallen in value. Although the actual decision applies directly only to such cases, the potential application of the principle is much greater. The Court of Appeal had described as "the necessary point of departure" the well-known and well-established principle that where an injury was to be compensated by damages, the damages should be as nearly as possible the sum which would put the claimant in the position in which he would have been if he had not been injured. The House of Lords disagreed, holding that it was first necessary to decide for what kind of loss the claimant was entitled to compensation. Lord Hoffmann noted the following points:

1. The valuer was required by contract to provide an estimate of the price which the property might reasonably be expected to fetch if sold on the open market at the date of the valuation.

2. The estimate of the price was information that was to form part of the material on which the lender was to decide whether, and if so how much, to lend to the borrower. The valuation informs the lender of what the security is likely to be worth (at current values) if it has to be sold, and enables the lender to decide upon the appropriate loan to valuation cushion. This cushion is intended to cover contingencies such as a fall in the property market and non-negligent differences between the valuation and the actual market value.

---

[13] See also *GUS Property Management Ltd v Littlewoods Mail Order Stores Ltd*, 1982 S.L.T. 533 on the question of arm's-length transactions. In *Nykredit Mortgage Bank Plc v Edward Erdman Group Ltd*, October 1, 1993 (unreported), Judge Byrt Q.C. awarded the claimant interest at its borrowing rate on the money market, it being agreed that such a rate precisely reflected the loss suffered by the claimant. The rate varied between 0.25 to 0.4 over LIBOR from time to time and was calculated as simple interest on the capital sum lent, £2.45m, from the date of the advance, giving credit for receipts of capital by way of reduction in the capital sum. Subsequent appeals did not touch on this point: Court of Appeal, damages: [1995] Q.B. 375, Court of Appeal, liability: [1996] 1 E.G.L.R. 119, and House of Lords, damages: [1997] A.C. 191.

[14] [1997] A.C. 191, Lord Goff, Lord Jauncey, Lord Slynn, Lord Nicholls, Lord Hoffmann. Only one reasoned speech was delivered, by Lord Hoffmann. The cases heard together for this appeal were *South Australia Asset Management Corp v York Montague Ltd*, (unreported) April 6, 1995, May J.; *United Bank of Kuwait Plc v Prudential Property Services Ltd* [1994] 2 E.G.L.R. 100; Gage J., [1995] Q.B. 375, CA; *Nykredit Mortgage Services Ltd v Edward Erdman Group Ltd*, Judge Byrt Q.C. sitting as a judge of the Queen's Bench Division, unreported, October 1, 1993. An appeal on liability in the latter case was heard subsequent to the appeal on damages: [1996] 1 E.G.L.R. 119, CA. See also para.10–115 below.

3. Although the valuer knows that if he overvalues the property, the cushion will be reduced, he is not privy to the other considerations that the lender will take into account, such as the strength of the borrower's covenant, the value of other security to be offered, and the profitability of the proposed loan.

4. Because the valuer knows that the valuation is likely to be a very important element in the decisions to be made by the lender, the law implies a term into the contract of reasonable care and skill. The relationship between the parties also gives rise to a concurrent duty in tort,[15] the scope of the duty of care being the same as in contract.

5. A lender who sues a valuer, whether in contract or tort, must prove not only that the duty was owed, but that it was a duty in respect of the kind of loss which the lender has suffered.[16]

6. The scope of a valuer's duty is to be deduced in tort from the purpose of the rule imposing the duty. In the case of an implied contractual duty, the nature and extent of the liability is defined by the term which the law implies. The scope of the duty is that which the law regards as best giving effect to the express obligations assumed by the valuer, neither cutting them down so that the lender obtains less than he was reasonably entitled to expect, nor extending them so as to impose on the valuer a liability greater than he could reasonably have thought he was undertaking.

10–114 Lord Hoffmann enunciated an apparently general principle, that a person under a duty to take reasonable care to provide information on which someone else will decide upon a course of action is, if negligent, not generally regarded as responsible for all the consequences which flow from the course of action. He is responsible only for the consequences of the information being wrong. He made an apparently important distinction between a duty to provide information for the purpose of enabling another to decide upon a course of action, and a duty to advise another as to what course of action to adopt. In the former case, the informant must use reasonable skill and care to ensure that the information provided is correct. If it is not, and the informant is negligent, he will be responsible for all the reasonably foreseeable consequences of the information being wrong. In the latter case, the advisor must take reasonable care to consider all the potential consequences of that course of action, and if the advice is negligent, the advisor will be responsible for all the reasonably foreseeable loss which is a consequence of that course of action being taken. The work ordinarily carried out by surveyors and valuers will, in the absence of express agreement, almost always fall into the category of providers of information.

---

[15] *Henderson v Merrett Syndicates Ltd* [1995] 2 A.C. 145, HL.
[16] For this proposition, Lord Hoffmann relied upon *Caparo Industries Plc v Dickman* [1990] 2 A.C. 605, HL. See Ch.17, para.17–028 for discussion on this case. In *Caparo Industries Plc*, the House of Lords considered the duty in tort owed by auditors to shareholders. There was no contract between the parties, hence the need to consider the purposes of the audit. In the *Banque Bruxelles Lambert SA* cases, all the lenders, whether those who appeared in the Court of Appeal, or in the House of Lords, sued in contract as well as tort. It is not easy to transplant an analysis formulated for a tort only action to a case where the parties have regulated their position by contract.

In *Nykredit v Edward Erdman (No.2)*,[17] Lord Hoffmann emphasised that the   **10–115**
limitation on the damages recoverable by the lender arose not from any principle
relating to causation or the measure of damages but rather from a limitation on
the extent of the duty itself. He stated:

> "The principle approved by the House was that the valuer owes no duty of care to the
> lender in respect of his entering into the transaction as such and the it is therefore
> insufficient, for the purpose of establishing liability on the part of the valuer, to prove
> that the lender is worse off than he would have been if he had not lent the money at all.
> What he must show is that he is worse off as a lender than he would have been if the
> security had been worth what the valuer said . . .
>
> It is important to emphasise that this is a consequence of the limited way in which
> the House defined the valuer's duty of care and has nothing to do with questions of
> causation or any limit or 'cap' imposed upon damages which would otherwise be
> recoverable. It was accepted that the whole loss suffered by reason of the fall in the
> property market was, as a matter of causation, properly attributable to the lender having
> entered into the transaction and that, but for the negligent valuation, he would not have
> done so. It was not suggested that the possibility of a fall in the market was unforesee-
> able or that there was any other factor which negatived the causal connection between
> lending and losing the money."[18]

Since *BBL*, the general tendency in England has generally been to limit its   **10–116**
application so as to apply it as a form of special rule applicable so as to limit
damages in the case of valuations or other information provided for lenders.[19]
There has not been a case where it has been found that a valuer has advised as
to the course of action which a lender should adopt rather than merely providing
information. Similarly there has been no case where it has been found that the
foreseeable consequences of information being wrong extended beyond the
amount of damage which would have been sustained had the information been
correct.[20] Courts have, however, been prepared to consider the case beyond its
immediate factual context in claims against valuers. An example is provided by
Europe Mortgage Co Ltd v GA Property Services Ltd[21] where a valuer provided
a negligent valuation of a large country house. But for the valuation, the lender
would not have entered into the transaction at all. Some six years later the
claimant disposed of its interest in the loan at a discount to a subsidiary whilst
retaining its interest in any claim against the valuer. At that time, had there been
a default, the claimant would have been able to repossess the property and satisfy
its security. Moore-Bick J. upheld the defendant's contention that the scope of its

---

[17] [1997] 1 W.L.R. 1627.
[18] *ibid.* at 1638.
[19] For the application of the principle to solicitors, see paras 11–248 to 11–253 below. In *Aneco v Johnson*, HL, October 18, 2001, the majority of the House of Lords held that the important question was to determine the extent of a professional's instructions. That matter was simply a question of fact.
[20] For an example of a case where such a submission was rejected, see *Ball v Banner* [2000] Lloyd's L.Rep. P.N. 569 at 582–583 *per* Hart J., where it was found that damages recoverable by investors on the basis of statements attributed to a property advisor in an Enterprise Zone prospectus were limited to the difference between the value of the investment if the statements had been correct and the value on the basis of the incorrect statement. The decision that the property advisor was liable was overturned on a different basis on appeal.
[21] (1999) E.G.L.R. 77.

duty extended only to a loss represented by a shortfall in the value of the property and consequently dismissed the claim.[22]

10–117   There remains a debate about the precise legal nature of the "BBL principle". In *Platform Home Loans Ltd v Oyston Shipways*,[23] Lord Cooke, in his dissenting judgment, hinted that he would have been prepared to consider an argument that the decision in *BBL* should be overturned.[24] Lord Hobhouse, giving one of the two speeches of the majority stated:

> "The [BBL] principle is essentially a legal rule which is applied in a robust way without the need for fine tuning or a detailed investigation of causation."[25]

He went on to point out that the novelty in Lord Hoffmann's approach lay in applying principles which had previously been thought to apply to kinds of damage to its quantification.[26] Whatever the precise nature of the principle, the appellate courts have been cautious as to its application. Thus in *Western Trust v Strutt & Parker*,[27] the Court of Appeal rejected an argument that because a valuer had not valued precisely the same property as that on which a lender had lent, it was clear that the loan was outside the scope of his duty. Although Lord Woolf M.R. accepted that if the difference between the property which the valuer had valued and that relied upon by the lender for the purposes of making the loan was of sufficient significance, the proposition would be correct, that was not the case on the facts. In *Thomson v Christie Manson & Woods*,[28] the Court of Appeal considered the proper measure of damages arising from an allegedly negligent description of valuable vases at auction. The Court of Appeal upheld an appeal on the question of liability, finding that it had been reasonable not to qualify the catalogue description. May L.J. rejected[29] the submission that the defendants had acted as advisors, but found that it would, in any event, have made no difference, stating:

> "Ms Thomson does not contend that Christie's warranted their information. Lord Grabiner does however say that they were advisors and not mere providers of information. In so far as this matters, I do not think that Lord Grabiner is right here. Christie's duty was to provide advice in the nature of information to enable Ms Thomson to decide whether to bid or not. There were numerous elements of that decision which did not come within the scope of Christie's duty at all, such as her ability to afford the likely purchase price and the relative merits of spending the money on these vases rather than on something quite different.

---

[22] In *Housing Loan Corp v William H Brown* [1999] Lloyd's L.Rep. P.N. 185, the Court of Appeal held that a judge would have been entitled to find that a lender's loss occasioned as a result of making a loan based upon what it believed to be forced sale valuations of a property would have been beyond the scope of the valuer's duty given that the valuations were, in fact, given on an open-market basis. The Court of Appeal upheld the judge's conclusion that the claimant had failed to establish reliance. See further para.10–122 below.

[23] [2000] 2 A.C. 190—see further para.10–168 below.

[24] *ibid.* at 198D–E.

[25] *ibid.* at 207G.

[26] *ibid.* at 209G.

[27] [1999] P.N.L.R. 154 at 165.

[28] [2005] EWCA Civ 555; [2005] P.N.L.R. 713—see further in relation to the timing of information available to quantify damage at para.10–133 below.

[29] At paras 128–129.

I do not, however, think that a distinction between an advisor and a provider of advice in the nature of information is critical in determining the proper measure of damage. As I have said, the measure of damage has to relate to the scope of the responsibility assumed and to the breach of the resulting duty of care. Christie's duty did not extend to carrying out metallurgical analyses and the measure of damage should not embrace the result of such analyses. The breach of duty which the judge found related only to the provision of information."

Even when applied to lending cases, the reasoning in *BBL* has received far from **10–118** universal approval.[30] In *Kenny & Good v MGICA*,[31] the High Court of Australia had to consider a case where a valuer was required to provide an assessment of a development. The report expressly acknowledged that MGICA, the provider of a mortgage indemnity guarantee, might use and rely on the report. In addition to providing a valuation, the report stated that the property was "suitable security for investment of trust funds to the extent of 65% of our valuation for a term of 3–5 years". The property was valued at $5.35m as it stood and at $5.5m on completion, whereas the true value was between $3.9m and $4m. On sale under two years after valuation, the property fetched only $2.65m. The five members of the High Court unanimously decided that MGICA was entitled to recover the entirety of its loss, although the reasoning of the four different judgments differed. Guadron J. rejected the approach taken by Lord Hoffmann altogether. He regarded the critical question as being whether any part of the loss would have been avoided if the original valuation had been correct.[32] As he regarded the valuation as being the decisive consideration in MGICA's decision to insure the loan[33] and there was no suggestion that any loss would have been recoverable had the valuation been correct, the whole loss was recoverable. McHugh J. regarded the question as turning upon the proper construction of the contract between the valuer and the claimant or, in the case of a claim for negligent mis-statement, on the proper interpretation and ambit of the statement. In the ordinary case he regarded the valuer as being liable:

"only for such losses as a reasonable person would regard as flowing naturally from the negligent valuation or which are of a kind that should have been within the valuer's contemplation".[34]

Later he stated:

"In the case of money lent on a valuation, the damages are confined to the difference between what was lent and what would have been lent on the true value of the property together with such expenses and other losses that were sufficiently likely to result from the breach of duty or that they were within the reasonable contemplation of the parties

---

[30] See, e.g. Jane Stapleton, "Negligent valuers and falls in the property market" (1997) 113 L.Q.R. 1; Hugh Evans, "The scope of the duty revisited" (2001) 17 P.N. 146. It has been followed in New Zealand—see *Bank of New Zealand v New Zealand Guardian Trust & Co Ltd* [1999] 1 N.Z.L.R. 664 at 682–683.
[31] (1999) 163 A.L.R. 611.
[32] *ibid.* at 620.
[33] *ibid.* at 619.
[34] *ibid.* at 623.

to the contract or arrangement. In either case, losses do not include the consequences of subsequent market declines."[35]

The reason why losses would not ordinarily include subsequent market declines was in McHugh J.'s view that in so far as a possible decline in market values was reasonably foreseeable, such a decline would already be factored into the true value of the property at the date of valuation, whilst in so far as the decline was not reasonably foreseeable it was to be regarded as being outside the contemplation of the parties to the valuation arrangements.[36] In *Kenny* itself, however, McHugh J. took the view that the extent of the valuer's liability did extend to the whole of the loss—essentially because the statements made by the valuer related not merely to the value of the property, but to the safety of the investment proposed.[37] Gummow J. agreed with the essence of McHugh J.'s reasoning whilst drawing a further distinction arising from the fact that MGICA's loss could not have occurred any earlier than when the mortgagor defaulted.[38] Kirby and Callinan JJ. had no difficulty in finding that, on the particular facts in *Kenny*, the whole loss would be recoverable as having been "foreshadowed in plain terms by the language of the instructions to the appellant which made clear the purpose for which the valuation was being procured",[39] but did not consider it necessary to formulate "general principles for the determination of the quantification of damages generally in cases of negligent valuations of property".[40]

10–119   The position in Australia therefore appears to be as follows:

(a) there is no question of there being any special rule whether of contract or tort applicable to the negligent valuation of property;

(b) where a valuer makes statements not merely as to the value of property, but as to the wisdom of making a loan or otherwise extends the scope of his duty, he will be liable for losses occasioned by subsequent falls in the property market;

(c) it may be important to decide whether the lender would have sustained part of the loss even if the valuation had been correct (for example because he would have made a smaller loan)[41];

(d) where a valuer merely gives advice as to the value of a property, but a lender would not have made any loan but for such advice, the position is unclear.[42]

---

[35] (1999) 163 A.L.R. 611.
[36] *ibid.* at 627–629.
[37] *ibid.* at 630.
[38] *ibid.* at 636.
[39] *ibid.* at 645.
[40] *ibid.* at 644.
[41] Following Guadron J.'s reasoning.
[42] McHugh and Gummow JJ. considered that losses occasioned by subsequent falls in the value of the property would not be recoverable, whilst Guadron J. suggests that they would be. Kirby and Callinan JJ. reserved their position. The reasoning of McHugh and Gummow JJ. would tend to suggest that losses occasioned by the fall in the property market will not.

(c) *Remoteness*

Recovery of damages is subject to the overriding requirement that the loss or **10–120**
damage for which compensation is sought is not too remote. Broadly this
requirement demands that the loss or damage must have been (i) caused[43] by the
breach of duty; and (ii) be reasonably foreseeable[44]; and (iii) that recovery is not
precluded by considerations of public or social policy.[45]

(i) *Causation*

It is for the claimant to plead and prove causation of loss, and the mere fact that **10–121**
negligence has been established does not debar the negligent defendant from
contesting this issue.[46] The claimant must prove that a breach of duty[47] on the
part of the surveyor was the cause of the loss complained of. If the breach was
not the cause of any injury, a claim in contract would succeed to the extent of an
award of nominal damages only. A claim in tort would in those circumstances fail
completely, as damage is a necessary component of the cause of action.

Reliance. The essence of a surveyor's tasks discussed in this chapter being the **10–122**
giving of advice, the question of causation in such cases often resolves itself
primarily into a question of reliance. Was the particular loss or damage sustained
in consequence of reliance upon the surveyor's advice? However, although,
establishing that the damage was sustained in consequence of the negligent
advice is a necessary part of establishing reliance, it is not sufficient.[48] In *BBL* at
first instance[49] Phillips J. held that in order to establish reliance on a valuation,
a lender had to do more than establish that, but for the valuation, it would not
have made the loan. It had to establish that it believed the valuation to be correct.

---

[43] As to which see para.10–121, below.

[44] As to which see para.10–126, below.

[45] For a statement of the general principles, see *McGregor*, paras 6–004 (in relation to tort) and
para.6–125 (in relation to contract).

[46] See *Thomas Miller & Co v Richard Saunders & Partners* [1989] 1 E.G.L.R. 267, where it was
argued that negligence by surveyors having been found, causation had to be assumed. Reliance was
placed on certain dicta of Lord Denning M.R. in *Heywood v Wellers* [1976] Q.B. 446 at 459, and
Coldman v Hill [1919] 1 K.B. 443. The judge held that such cases were an exception to the general
rule and that the instant case did not fall within such an exception. He then held that there was no
causal link between the negligence and the loss and gave judgment for the defendants. The dicta in
Heywood v Wellers had in fact been disapproved by the House of Lords in *Wilsher v Essex AHA*
[1988] A.C. 1074, HL. See Ch.11, para.11–268 and Ch.13, para.13–118.

[47] In contract or tort.

[48] For examples of cases where it was not established that the loss or damage was sustained
consequential upon the advice, see *Rona v Pearce* (1953) 162 E.G. 380, where Hilbery J., although
satisfied that the defendant surveyor had failed to exercise proper diligence and care in making his
survey, "could not believe . . . that the report was a factor which influenced [the plaintiff] in buying
the bungalow". The surveyor therefore succeeded in defending the claimant's claim and he was
further given judgment on his counterclaim for survey fees. Similarly, in *Shankie-Williams v Heavey*
[1986] 2 E.G.L.R. 139, CA, the claimant purchasers' claim against the defendant dry rot specialist
failed because there was no evidence that they had seen his report.

[49] [1994] 2 E.G.L.R. 108 at 125.

It is submitted that this approach is correct.[50] Therefore, where a person does not consider a valuation correct, but would not have made a loan without it (because, for example, he needs the valuation to protect his own position), there will be no reliance. Thus, in *Tenenbaum v Garrod*,[51] the Court of Appeal upheld the finding of the trial judge that the claimant had not relied upon a "spoof" valuation, procured by the claimant from the defendant solely for use by him as part of a scheme to acquire property at undervalue.[52] Similarly if the claimant fundamentally misinterprets the valuation advice it has received such that, but for the misinterpretation, the claimant would not have acted as he did, there will be no reliance. This was the position in *Housing Loan Corp v William H Brown*,[53] where a tertiary lender was required by its own backers to make loans up to a maximum of 75 per cent of the lower of two forced sale values. In fact a loan was made on the basis of the defendants' negligent open market valuations. The judge fully accepted the claimant's evidence that it had, in fact, relied on the advice received, but found that such reliance hinged on its misinterpretation of the valuation as being made on a forced sale basis. Hirst L.J. held that the question as to whether a mistake was sufficiently fundamental to destroy reliance was one of fact and degree,[54] but that, on the facts, the judge had been fully entitled to come to his conclusion.[55] In *Speshal Investments Ltd v CorbyKane Howard Partnership*,[56] Hart J. emphasised the differences between believing in the veracity of a valuation and the reasonableness of such belief. Having found that it was necessary for a claimant to establish that he believed a valuation before reliance could be found, he summarised the relationship between duty, reliance and contributory negligence as follows:

> "So far as concerns the proposition that, even if the claimant did rely on the valuations believing them to be reliable, they were unreasonable in doing so, there is in my judgment some danger of confusion. The claim is based on the premise that the defendants owed the claimant a duty of care in tort. If the defendants did owe the claimants a duty of care in providing the valuations, and the claimant in fact relied on those valuations believing them to be reliable, the question whether it was 'reasonable' for the claimant to have relied appears to me to arise only in the context of considering whether it was contributorily negligent. If the proposition is that the caveats in the valuation report had the effect of negativing the existence of a duty of care, or of excepting the defendants from liability for a breach of it, then the issues relate to the nature of the relationship said to give rise to the duty of care and the true construction

---

[50] In *Cavendish Funding v Henry Spencer* [1998] P.N.L.R. 122, the Court of Appeal accepted the proposition, for the purposes of the appeal and did not find it necessary to consider an argument, based on the judgment of Millett L.J. in *Bristol and West Building Society v Mothew* [1996] 4 All E.R. 698, that it was unnecessary for a lender to establish that it would not have made the loan if the valuation had been different provided that the lender had, in fact, relied on the valuation and that it had been causative of the loan.

[51] [1988] 2 E.G.L.R. 178.

[52] See para.10–103, above.

[53] [1999] Lloyd's L.Rep. P.N. 185.

[54] *ibid*. at 193.

[55] For an example of a case where a similar submission was rejected, see *Arab Bank v John D Wood* [2000] Lloyd's L.Rep. P.N. 173 at 195. The claimant's evidence had been that it had instructed the defendant valuers to carry out a full open-market valuation. In fact only a check on another valuation had been requested. The claimant's evidence was, however, rejected with the result that there was no basis for the suggestion that it had misinterpreted the advice that it had received.

[56] [2003] EWHC 390.

of the provision alleged to exempt from liability. The question of the reasonableness of the reliance which was in fact placed on the valuations does not, it seems to me, arise at this stage. As I understand it, the defendants conceded the existence of a duty of care, and did not seek to argue that liability had effectively been excluded by the terms of the caveats. My approach is therefore to consider, first, whether there was actual reliance in the relevant sense and secondly to consider whether a case of contributory negligence has been made out."

In an appropriate case, a court will, however, be prepared to infer reliance (including therefore belief in the veracity of a valuation) even where there is no direct evidence of the same.[57]

Mortgage indemnity guarantees. Very often lenders will obtain "mortgage   **10–123** indemnity guarantees" from insurers or other financial institutions to protect themselves (at least in part) against the risk of default by a borrower. The question has therefore arisen as to the extent to which a lender has relied upon a valuation in making a loan with the benefit of such a guarantee. The question first arose at first instance in *BBL* where Phillips J. considered whether the lender relied upon the impugned valuation or a mortgage indemnity guarantee when lending the "top slice" of the loan.[58] Phillips J. considered the argument that the lender was not relying on the value of the security to justify lending the top slice fallacious, as it confused the question of whether the lender was relying on the valuation when deciding to lend the top slice of the loan and their motivation for so relying. The amount of the valuation was the factor which determined the amount that was lent, including the top slice of that amount. The reason why the lenders were prepared to run the risk of advancing more than 70 per cent of the valuation was the belief that this risk had been transferred to the insurers, but that did not mean that the lender was not relying on the valuation when deciding how much to lend. There was no break in the chain of causation that linked the valuations and the totality of the sums advanced by the lender. This reasoning was adopted by Mance L.J. when considering a similar submission in *Arab Bank v John D Wood*.[59] Mance L.J. pointed out that the valuation had permitted the negotiation of the mortgage indemnity policy which had, in turn, permitted the bank to lend the top slice of the loan which reinforced, rather than undermined, the alleged reliance. The courts have also consistently refused to require a lender to give credit for a mortgage indemnity guarantee on the basis that it represents a policy of insurance for which the law does not require the claimant to give

---

[57] For an extreme example of such a case, see *Cavendish Funding v Henry Spencer* [1998] P.N.L.R. 122, where the Court of Appeal refused to interfere with the judge's inference that a grossly negligent valuation had been a substantial cause of the making of a loan. This was so although there were two valuations in the case; the claimant appeared to have ignored the lower valuation; the loan was made in breach of the provisions of the claimant's lending manual and there appeared reasons to doubt (at the least) the competence of the relevant lending officer who was not called to give evidence. Aldous L.J. nonetheless viewed the history of the loan as being consistent only with reliance and causation.

[58] [1994] 2 E.G.L.R. 108 at 127. The "top slice" of the loan was the difference between an advance of 70% of valuation, and the 90% actually lent.

[59] [2000] Lloyd's L.Rep. P.N. 173 at 197.

credit.[60] Similarly a claimant does not have to give credit for its own building insurance policy or NHBC guarantee.[61]

10–124   *Novus actus interveniens.* The issue of causation may not be determined solely by reference to reliance. While recovery may be refused on the basis that the damage was not caused by reliance upon the negligent advice, the refusal may conversely be rationalised on the basis that the damage was attributable to another cause. The interplay of both bases is best illustrated in *Kenney v Hall, Pain and Foster.*[62] The claimant was advised by the defendant estate agents and surveyors that his house was worth not less than £90,000 and that adjoining flats leased to a third party were worth £50,000. He was also advised that a reasonable asking price for the whole property, called Culverlands House, was £150,000. Acting on the advice the claimant offered the property for sale for £150,000 in July 1973 through the defendants. Despite informal advice from another estate agent that the asking price was a "big handicap" and advice "off the record" from his bank manager that the bank had valued the whole of Culverlands House at £100,000, in September 1973 the claimant committed himself to buy another property, Wickham Lodge, for £47,500. That sum was some £10,000 above the price he originally thought he could afford. In October 1973 he committed himself to buy a cottage and a plot of land adjacent to Wickham Lodge, for a further £16,000. From November 1973 to April 1974 the claimant accepted estimates for extensive improvements to Wickham Lodge and the cottage, that expenditure totalling over £30,000. Expenditure on both purchases and improvements was financed by a bank bridging loan since Culverlands House remained unsold. A general decline in property prices intervened and it was ultimately sold in July 1974 for £60,000, of which £24,000 went to the leaseholder of the flats. The cottage was later sold for £14,000. At the date of the trial in 1976 Wickham Lodge was worth £57,000 but the claimant owed to the bank over £85,000 in respect of capital and interest, and to builders over £9,000.

10–125   Having held the defendants negligent, Goff J. dealt with four arguments on causation. First it was argued that the claimant's action in committing himself to buy Wickham Lodge before he had found a purchaser for Culverlands House was unreasonable. It amounted to a *novus actus interveniens* and the claimant could not hold the defendants liable for the consequences of his action. Goff J. rejected the argument, concluding that in the circumstances of a buoyant property market in September 1973 it was not unreasonable for the claimant to commit himself as he did in the light of the advice received from the defendants. Secondly, at the time he committed himself to buy Wickham Lodge the claimant was no longer acting in reliance on the defendants' advice, but on his own assessment of the situation. He had been warned by another estate agent that the asking price was a big handicap and he suspected that the defendants' valuation was too high. Goff J., however, considered the claimant was still relying substantially on the defendants' advice in the sense that, even allowing for his suspecting their figure to be rather high, the valuation still made him feel that he could safely commit himself to buy Wickham Lodge, and spend some money upon improvements, and cover

---

[60] *Arab Bank v John D Wood* [1999] Lloyd's Rep. P.N. 173.
[61] *Hanley Smith v Darlington* [2001] E.G. 160.
[62] [1976] 2 E.G.L.R. 29.

his commitments by a quick sale of Culverlands House by a dramatic reduction of 25 per cent in the asking price. Thirdly, it was argued that following the bank manager's informal advice as to the property's value, the causative effect of the defendants' valuation ceased and thereafter the claimant must have been relying exclusively on the bank's valuation. That argument was also rejected on the basis that the claimant was still acting in substantial reliance on the defendants' valuation. Fourthly, it was argued that while it was reasonable to take into account some expenditure on Wickham Lodge, nevertheless the actual expenditure on Wickham Lodge went beyond what was reasonable in the circumstances and was profligate. This argument partly succeeded, as £5,000 was disallowed in damages for economies which should reasonably have been made. This was justified by Goff J. on grounds of causation:

> "I conclude that a part of his expenditure was incurred not by reason of his reliance on the defendants' valuation, but by reason of his own under-estimate of the cost of repair and renovation."[63]

A lender will commonly allege that both a solicitor and a valuer are responsible for damage which has been suffered as a result of lending on inadequate security or where there has been a mortgage fraud. Although the facts of each case need to be examined with care, the general tendency of the courts is to deny one professional the opportunity to assert that all damage was caused by the fault of the other. Thus in *Preferred Mortgages v Countrywide Surveyors Ltd*,[64] Mr Bartley-Jones Q.C. found that the defendant valuers were not liable where an apparent mortgage fraud had been perpetrated on a lender,[65] but made clear that, had he found liability, he would have rejected the submission that the lender's solicitors were wholly to blame, stating:

> "[The valuer's] submission was that, had the Report been negligent, the sole cause of the claimant's loss was the failure of [the solicitors] in not drawing to the claimant's attention knowledge in its possession (in particular the direct deposit and the varying purchase price) which indicated that this transaction had all the hallmarks of a mortgage fraud. I fundamentally disagree . . . if [the solicitors] were in breach of contract or duty owed in tort to the claimant, it seems to me that the claimant's loss would have been caused by the activities of each, and both of [the valuers] and [the solicitors]."

(ii) *Foreseeability*

A claimant must establish not only that the loss was caused by the surveyor's breach of duty, but also that the loss was foreseeable. For a claim in contract, this **10–126**

---

[63] [1976] 2 E.G.L.R. 29 at 36. See also: *Thomas Miller & Co v Richard Saunders & Partners* [1989] 1 E.G.L.R. 267, where Rougier J., having found the defendant surveyors negligent in their handling of a rent review arbitration, concluded that such failure was not causative of the claimant's loss as the particular decision of the arbitrator constituted an intervening act; and *McGonigle v Hutton* [1995] 6 B.N.I.L. 68, where Girvan J. considered it "strongly arguable" that the failure by the puchaser's solicitor properly to investigate a warning given by the defendant surveyor as to whether certain roof space works were in breach of building control regulations, was a *novus actus interveniens* upon which the claimant had relied.

[64] [2006] P.N.L.R. 154; [2005] EWHC 2820.

[65] See further para.10–095 above.

means that, at the time the contract was made, the loss was "reasonably foresee-able as likely to result from the breach".[66] For a claim in tort, it means that at the time the breach of duty was committed, the loss was reasonably foreseeable as a consequence of the breach.[67]

10–127   Foreseeability of damage is often in issue in surveyors' negligence cases, although rarely in the context of compensation for loss. The apparent paradox is explained by the fact that the issue of foreseeability will often be relevant to liability and will be resolved by the determination on liability, hence making unnecessary further consideration of the issue in relation to damage. For exam-ple, the issue whether a surveyor should have anticipated a sudden outbreak of dry rot (because, for example, the conditions were ripe for such an outbreak) may be relevant to whether he was in breach of his duty to exercise reasonable care and skill. Foreseeability of damage was considered at length in the Scottish case of *Drinnan v CW Ingram & Sons*.[68] The pursuer contended that as a result of the defenders' negligent survey she was forced to leave her condemned flat and consequently suffered injury to her health, namely hypertension. The defenders contended that such injury was unforeseeable and they sought to have the relevant averments by the pursuer dismissed as irrelevant. After reviewing a number of authorities, including *Cook v Swinfen*,[69] Lord Milligan refused to accede to the defenders' application. The case established, however, no more than that the forseeability of such injury was arguable on the facts, since no final decision on the issue was made. In another Scottish case, *Hunter v J & E Shepherd*,[70] Lord Osborne refused to strike out a claim for the costs of alternative accommodation for the children of the family. Whilst repairs were being carried out, they stayed with relatives, the claimant paying for their board and lodging. The judge held that for the costs of the children's accommodation to be recover-able, it was not necessary for the claimant to have been legally obliged to support them; instead it was a question of foreseeability, and in the circumstances it was reasonably foreseeable that the claimant would regard himself as responsible for their accommodation during the period of remedial work.[71]

10–128   An issue which has arisen is whether a valuer should have foreseen a large rise in property prices. The general approach of the courts has been to refuse to permit claimants to recover additional losses because of such alleged foresee-ability. In one sense it is, of course, foreseeable that prices may rise or fall. However, a valuation of property should take into account the market expectation of such rises (or falls). Thus McHugh J. pointed out in *Kenny & Good v MGICA*[72]:

"in so far as a decline in the market was reasonably foreseeable, it will already be factored into the assessment of the true value of the property as at the date of valuation. In so far as the market decline was not reasonably foreseeable, any loss arising from the

---

[66] *per* Asquith L.J. in *Victoria Laundry (Windsor) Ltd v Newman Industries Ltd* [1949] 2 K.B. 528.
[67] See *McGregor*, paras 198–201.
[68] 1967 S.L.T. 205.
[69] [1967] 1 W.L.R. 457.
[70] 1992 S.L.T. 1095.
[71] See further at para.10–195, below.
[72] 163 A.L.R. 611 at 627.

decline must be regarded as outside the contemplation of the parties . . . and not recoverable in an action for negligence or breach of contract".

The question of the foreseeability of a large rise in property prices arose directly in *Morgan v Perry*.[73] In that case as a result of the defendant's survey in 1968 the claimant bought a house held to be valueless owing to settlement. The defendant argued that *Philips v Ward*[74] established only a prima facie rule for measuring damages, which should be displaced if its application to a particular case involved a departure from the fundamental principle in *Hadley v Baxendale*[75] and other cases. The motive for the argument was that in late 1971 and throughout 1972 house prices rose at an unprecedented rate. Therefore, damages assessed by reference to 1968 house values in accordance with the *Philips v Ward* principle would have been much less than damages assessed by reference to house values in 1971, when the extent of the damage had been properly investigated and ascertained. The defendant's argument was rejected, Judge Kenneth Jones Q.C. considering himself bound by *Philips v Ward*. The judge went on to say that, even accepting the argument, he did not consider that:

"the parties could be held reasonably to have contemplated that the plaintiff's loss would continue beyond the point where he first fully discovered the damage he had suffered; inflated 1973 values were far beyond the parties' horizon of contemplation."[76]

(d) *Measure of Damages*

Whether the claim is brought in contract or tort the fundamental principle **10–129** governing the measure of damages is that the claimant must be put, so far as money can, in the position he would have occupied if the surveyor had properly discharged his duty.[77] Evaluating that hypothetical position can present great practical difficulties.[78] There are two theoretical approaches to the evaluation of hypothetical events. The first is to assess on a balance of probabilities what would have happened.[79] The second is to assess damages by reference to the value of the chance of a particular hypothesis being fulfilled. Following the decision of the Court of Appeal in the solicitor's case *Allied Maples v Simmons*

---

[73] (1973) 229 E.G. 1737.

[74] [1956] 1 W.L.R. 471, CA. See further para.10–135 below.

[75] (1854) 9 Ex. 341.

[76] (1973) 229 E.G. 1737 at 1740. See also *Corisand Investments Ltd v Druce and Co* [1978] 2 E.G.L.R. 86, especially at 97: defendant valuers held not negligent in not anticipating or suspecting impending collapse of property market.

[77] See *Livingstone v Rawyards Coal Co* (1880) 5 App.Cas. 25 at 39; and *Dodd Properties (Kent) Ltd v Canterbury CC* [1980] 1 W.L.R. 433 at 451, 454, 456 (as to general principles). As to surveyors, see, e.g. *Swingcastle v Gibson* [1991] 2 A.C. 223 at 232 *per* Lord Lowry; *Watts v Morrow* [1991] 1 W.L.R. 1421; and *Banque Bruxelles Lambert SA v Eagle Star Insurance Co Ltd* [1997] A.C. 191.

[78] See, for example, the comments of Purchas L.J. in *Steward v Rapley* [1989] 1 E.G.L.R. 159 at 162.

[79] See, for example, the medical case of *Hotson v East Berkshire AHA* [1987] A.C. 750, and the other medical cases discussed in Ch.13, paras 13–117, *et seq.*

& Simmons,[80] the English courts now[81] take a hybrid approach: where a claimant must prove what he would have done, he must do so on the balance of probabilities, but the actions of third parties are assessed on the basis of determining the probability that they would have acted in a particular way. The logic for the differentiation is far from clear: if a claimant states honestly that it is extremely difficult for him to say what he would have done, it seems strange that he gets a full measure of damages if a court decides, on the balance of probabilities that he was more likely than not to take action to avoid damage, but nothing if its decision is just the other way. In either case, it is possible to assert that a claimant has lost a real "chance" which appears no different, in principle, from the "chance" of a third party acting differently in a hypothetical situation. An example of the current approach is provided by *Francis v Barclays Bank Plc*.[82] The claimant bank was a mortgagee in possession of land which it sold to a third party with a "clawback" provision which operated in the event that the land was on-sold within 10 years with the benefit of residential planning permission. The third party then approached the bank with an offer to modify the claw-back provision so as to restrict its total entitlement in return for an immediate payment. The bank sought the defendant surveyors' advice as to this offer who negligently failed to make proper enquiries of the local authority which would have ascertained that there was a real likelihood of the designation of the land being changed.[83] Had proper advice been given, the bank would not have agreed to the proposed variation. In fact the land was on-sold at a price which would have entitled the bank to some £1m rather than the total of £115,000 which it actually received. The surveyors sought to argue that, had the bank not agreed to the variation, the third party would not have acted so as to sell the land within the 10-year period and thus operate the original clawback provision. The judge considered the evidence of the financial position of the third party, the inherent probabilities and what the third party said that it would have done before reaching the conclusion that there was a two-thirds chance that the sale would have proceeded. On that basis he awarded that proportion of the sum that the bank would have received but for the variation of the clawback.

10–130   The damages recoverable for breach of duty by surveyors and associated topics are discussed below under the following headings:

(i) Negligent survey or valuation for a purchaser who completes a purchase:

    (a) The usual measure.
    (b) Relevance of cost of repairs.
    (c) Costs of extrication.
    (d) Collateral benefit.

---

[80] [1995] 1 W.L.R. 1390—see further Ch.11, para.11–261 below.
[81] This approach was not universally taken before *Allied* Maples. In Eagle *Star v Gale and Power* (1955) 166 E.G. 37, Devlin J. awarded a mortgagee damages of £100 against the defendant surveyor to indemnify it against the possibility of not being able to recover a loan money from the mortgagor.
[82] [2005] P.N.L.R. 297; [2005] EWHC 297.
[83] See further para.10–100 above with regard to liability.

   (ii) Negligent survey or valuation for a purchaser who withdraws from purchase before completion.

  (iii) Negligent survey or valuation for lender:

     (a) Assessment of the total loss.
     (b) Assessment of the scope of duty.
     (c) Interest on damages.
     (d) Contributory negligence by lender.

  (iv) Overvaluation for vendor.

   (v) Undervaluation for vendor.

  (vi) Other work.

 (vii) Inconvenience and discomfort.

(viii) Incidental expenses.

(i) *Negligent Survey or Valuation for a Purchaser who Completes a Purchase*

    The usual measure. Where a person has completed the purchase[84] of a   **10–131** property in reliance upon a negligent survey or overvaluation of the property by a surveyor,[85] the proper measure of damages has generally been expressed as the difference between (i) the value of the property without the defect and (ii) its value with the defect as at the date of purchase.[86] In calculating this difference in recent years, the value without the defect has generally been described as the price paid. The negligent surveyor's figure for the value of the property may, however, be the appropriate figure when it is lower than the price in fact paid for the property. The value with the defect is usually the market value of the property as at the date of purchase in its true condition.[87] Although the phrase "difference in value" is now in common use as a description of the proper measure, difference in value can usually be more accurately described as the overpayment or the excess paid for the property purchased. The premise underlying the assertion of difference in value as the proper measure is that the purchaser's loss

---

[84] Where the purchaser has not completed a purchase, he may maintain a claim for wasted expenditure. See para.10–151, below. Where a purchaser would not have bought a property and takes steps to extricate himself from the purchase, he may, on appropriate facts, maintain a claim for the costs of extrication. See para.10–148, below.

[85] Where the surveyor has not warranted the absence of any need for major or further repairs. No such warranty is expressed or, it is submitted, implied, in any of the conditions of engagement connected with standard services offered by surveyors to their clients. For the measure of damage where such a warranty has been given, see para.10–178, below.

[86] See *Watts v Morrow* [1991] 1 W.L.R. 1421, and para.10–145, below, and for further examples the succinct statement of the principle by the Lord Justice-Clerk in *Duncan v Gumleys* [1987] 2 E.G.L.R. 263 at 265, and by Hoffmann L.J. in *Sneesby v Goldings* [1995] 2 E.G.L.R. 102 at 105:
   "The formulation is the difference between its market value in good condition and its market value on the basis that the surveyor had made a proper report to the client."

[87] See *Philips v Ward* [1956] 1 W.L.R. 471, CA, as explained in *Ford v White & Co* [1964] 1 W.L.R. 885 and *Simple Simon Catering Ltd v Binstock Miller & Co* (1973) 228 E.G. 527 at 529, CA; also *Perry v Sidney Phillips & Son* [1982] 1 W.L.R. 1297, CA; *Watts v Morrow* [1991] 1 W.L.R. 1421. See also the Scottish cases of *Stewart v HA Brechin & Co* [1959] S.C. 306; and *Upstone v GDW Carnegie & Co*, 1978 S.L.T. (Sh Ct) 4 at 5. See also the discussion of *HTW Valuers v Astonland Pty Ltd* [2004] H.C.A. 54 at para.10–134 below.

is properly to be characterised as overpayment and not unacquired value, i.e. a money loss, not a value loss. The purchased property never had a value corresponding to the element of overpayment. The two expressions may therefore be properly defined as follows. "Diminution in value" means the amount by which the value of the property has been diminished by the unreported defects. "Excess purchase price paid" means the difference between the purchase price actually paid and the purchase price which would reasonably have been paid, if the claimant had persisted in his purchase after receipt of a competent survey report. In different cases and even in different judgments in the same cases, including *Philips v Ward*[88] and *Perry v Sidney Phillips & Son*,[89] difference in value and its two components have been expressed differently. This is mainly the consequence of there being on the particular facts of most cases no need for a more exact description, as the two components may readily be recognised.

10–132   Descriptions given for both components of the measure have obviously been based on the particular facts of each case.[90] In respect of the first component,[91] the price paid has usually been accepted to be the correct sum,[92] but the value of the property expressly stated in the negligent surveyor's report may on the facts be more appropriate,[93] or the value of the property to be deduced from the description in the negligent surveyor's report but in which the value is not stated,[94] or the value of the property in its assumed good condition,[95] or the value of the house without the defect.[96] For the second component,[97] descriptions given

---

[88] See para.10–137, below.

[89] See para.10–139, below.

[90] The problem of accurately describing both components of the measure was raised in acute form in *Shaw v Halifax (SW) Ltd* [1994] E.G.L.R. 95. In a rapidly rising market, the defendant valuers valued the property at £37,000, when due to unreported defects its value was in fact only £32,000, and the claimants purchased the property for £42,000 when its actual value due to the defects was £37,000. The claimants argued that they had suffered a loss of £5,000, being the difference between the price paid for the property and its actual value at the date of purchase. The defendants argued that the claimant had in fact suffered no loss, because the measure was the difference between the value of the property without the defect at the date of purchase (£37,000, as reported in June 1988) and the value with the defect at the date of purchase (also £37,000). The defendants relied upon *Hardy v Wamsley-Lewis* (1967) 203 E.G. 1039 and *Hingorani v Blower* [1976] 1 E.G.L.R 104 in support of their submissions. The judge held that the claimants were entitled to the difference between "the market value of the property without the defects and its market value in the defective condition" and noted that if the actual value of the property on August 11, 1988 was £37,000, then its value in an assumed condition without the defects was obviously higher. In the event the claimants recovered £5,000, on the basis that the price paid of £42,000 did represent the market value as at the date of purchase.

[91] See para.10–131, above.

[92] *Philips v Ward* [1956] 1 W.L.R. 471, CA, Romer L.J.; *Perry v Sidney Phillips & Son* [1982] 1 W.L.R. 1297, CA (all three judges); *Ford v White & Co* [1964] 1 W.L.R. 885; *Lees v English and Partners* [1977] 1 E.G.L.R. 65; *Bolton v Puley* [1983] 2 E.G.L.R. 138; *Treml v Ernest W Gibson and Partners* [1984] 2 E.G.L.R. 162; *Hooberman v Salter Rex* [1985] 1 E.G.L.R. 144; *Roberts v J Hampson & Co* [1988] 2 E.G.L.R. 181; *Steward v Rapley* [1989] 1 E.G.L.R. 159; *Watts v Morrow* [1991] 1 W.L.R. 1421.

[93] *Philips v Ward* [1956] 1 W.L.R. 471, CA 476, Morris L.J.; *Wilson v Baxter, Payne and Lepper* [1985] 1 E.G.L.R. 141.

[94] *Freeman v Marshall* (1966) 200 E.G. 777 at 779; *Hardy v Wamsley-Lewis* (1967) 203 E.G. 1039 at 1043; *Hingorani v Blower* [1976] 1 E.G.L.R. 104.

[95] *Philips v Ward* [1956] 1 W.L.R. 471, CA at 473, Denning L.J.; *Hoadley v Edwards* [2001] P.N.L.R. 965.

[96] *Duncan v Gumleys* [1987] 2 E.G.L.R. 263 at 265.

[97] See para.10–131 above.

have included the value of the property as it should have been described in a competent surveyor's report,[98] the market value of the property,[99] the value of the property in its actual condition,[1] the "real" or "fair" value,[2] the price which the particular purchaser would have been prepared to give,[3] its value with the defect,[4] and the price which the particular purchaser would have succeeded in negotiating with the particular vendor.[5]

The courts have also recognised the true measure of the loss in the context of limitation. In *Hamlin v Evans*,[6] the defendant valuers settled a claim based upon the presence of dry rot and were then presented with a claim based upon a fracture in one of the walls. The Court of Appeal considered that the only relevant damage was the diminution in value caused by purchasing the property in reliance on the negligent report. It followed that the second claim was statute barred. Waite L.J. distinguished cases brought against building contractors out of separate defects. *Hamlin* was followed by the Northern Irish Court of Appeal in *McKillen v Russell*,[7] where a claimant first discovered that a garage had been built without Building Regulations approval and made a claim against his surveyor which was settled. He later discovered that there had also been extensive works done to the house without the relevant approval. Kerr J. held that the claim was statute barred as the claimant knew of the relevant damage when he

---

[98] *Philips v Ward* [1956] 1 W.L.R. 471, CA, 473, Denning L.J. and 476, Morris L.J.; *Lees v English and Partner* [1977] 1 E.G.L.R. 65.

[99] *Perry v Sidney Phillips & Son* [1982] 1 W.L.R. 1297, CA at 1304, Oliver L.J. and 1306, Kerr L.J.; *Ford v White & Co* [1964] 1 W.L.R. 885 at 888; *Treml v Ernest W Gibson and Partners* [1984] 2 E.G.L.R. 162; *Hooberman v Salter Rex* [1985] 1 E.G.L.R. 144.

[1] *Perry v Sidney Phillips & Son* [1982] 1 W.L.R. 1297, CA, 1303, "the property which he actually got" (Oliver L.J.); *Hill v Debenham, Tewson and Chinnocks* (1958) 171 E.G. 835 at 839, "its value as it actually existed, namely as a bad shell"; *Hardy v Wamsley-Lewis* (1967) 203 E.G. 1039, 1043 "the value of it in the condition in which it truly was"; *Collard v Saunders* (1972) 221 E.G. 797, "its value in its actual bad condition"; *Morgan v Perry* (1973) 229 E.G. 1737 at 1740, "its value as [the property] in fact was"; *Hingorani v Blower* [1976] 1 E.G.L.R. 104 at 105, "the value of the house . . . as it really was"; *Bolton v Puley* [1983] 2 E.G.L.R. 138 at 143, "its value in its actual condition"; *Watts v Morrow* [1991] 1 W.L.R. 1421, "the value of the house in its true condition".

[2] See *HTW Valuers v Astonland Ptd Ltd* [2004] HCA 54 at [36].

[3] *Perry v Sidney Phillips and Son* [1982] 1 W.L.R. 1297, CA, 1302, Lord Denning M.R.; and *Bolton v Puley* [1983] 2 E.G.L.R. 138 at 142.

[4] *Duncan v Gumleys* [1987] 2 E.G.L.R. 263 at 265.

[5] See *Howard v Horne & Sons* [1990] 1 E.G.L.R. 272, where the claimants purchased the property for what was agreed by the independent surveyors to be its true market value of £200,250. A competent report, however, would have enabled them to negotiate a further reduction with the vendors. The official referee therefore awarded the claimants £1,500, being the further reduction in the purchase price that they could have, but were unable to secure (little more than one-half per cent). Although the judgment does not deal with the evidence of the surveyors on this point, the case is explicable on the basis of imprecise terminology and a difference in value that would generally be regarded as immaterial. If the property could have been purchased for £198,750 with the aid of a proper survey report, then that was the true market value. The claimants therefore recovered the difference between the price they paid and the price they would have paid with a proper report. The position may, of course, be different in a situation where a survey is carried out after exchange or where special contractual provisions apply. Thus in *Hanley Smith v Darlington* [2001] E.G. 160, a purchaser was entitled to have defects remedied by the vendor under a contract of sale. The survey was instituted after exchange and the measure of damages was held to be the costs of repair on the basis that but for the surveyor's negligence the claimant would have been entitled to have the defects remedied free of charge.

[6] [1996] 2 E.G.L.R. 106.

[7] [2002] P.N.L.R. 29.

first discovered that he had purchased the house at an over-value as a result of his surveyor's negligence.

10–133   **The use of hindsight in assessing damages.** The question as to whether it is ever permissible to take into account information which was not available at the time of purchase when assessing damages and, if so, in what circumstances, has arisen in two recent appellate cases which display a substantial difference of approach between England and Australia. In *Thomson v Christie Manson & Woods*,[8] the English Court of Appeal considered the proper measure of damages arising from an allegedly negligent description of valuable vases at auction. The auctioneer had described them in the catalogue, without qualification, as being "Louis XV". This description and the quality of the vases had been emphasised to the purchaser by the defendants who, it was held, had assumed a duty of care towards her. Following the purchase doubts had arisen as to the provenance of the vases and intensive investigations were carried out which went far beyond those which would have occurred prior to the preparation of a catalogue. These included metallurgical investigations. As a result of these investigations, the trial judge came to the conclusion that there was a 70 per cent probability that the vases had been manufactured during the reign of Louis XV, but that the description should have been qualified by words such as "possibly Italian". He awarded damages based on the difference between the price paid and the actual value of the vases taking into account all information available at the date of trial. The Court of Appeal upheld an appeal on the question of liability, finding that it had been reasonable not to qualify the catalogue description. However, the court also found that the measure of damages was wrong in principle—damages were to be assessed at the date of trial as being the difference between the price paid and the true value if correctly described. May L.J. considered that this followed both from the decision of the House of Lords in *BBL* and by analogy with the valuer's cases such as *Perry v Sidney Phillips* and *Phillips v Ward*.

10–134   In *HTW Valuers v Astonland Pty Ltd*,[9] the High Court of Australia displayed an approach which was markedly different. The claimant relied on valuation advice from the defendant valuers when purchasing a shopping mall in a small Queensland town for $485,000. Of considerable importance when considering the likely value of the mall was the view taken of possible competition from a new development which was due to be completed relatively shortly after the purchase completed. The judge found that although the defendant's view was that value would not be adversely affected, he should have given a warning to the effect that the effect the new development was uncertain. In fact the effect was disastrous. The evidence at trial was that the value of the mall at the time of purchase was $400,000, but had fallen within three years to $130,000. There was also evidence that the claimant had attempted, unsuccessfully, to sell the shopping mall from shortly after the new development opened. The court took the view that it was possible to assess the "real" value of the shopping centre at the time of the acquisition by reference to what subsequently occurred and thus, in effect, find that the market was mistaken. It is submitted that the decision can

---

[8] [2005] EWCA Civ 555; [2005] P.N.L.R. 713.
[9] [2004] H.C.A. 54.

only be justified on the basis that the claimant had been induced to take a risk which, given proper advice, he would not have been prepared to take and sought to extricate himself from the position when he discovered that he had been wrongly advised. It is otherwise difficult to see any principled reason for departing from the market's valuation at the date of purchase. Moreover, taking into account subsequent movements inevitably means that the defendant valuers are obliged to take the risk of such market movements when the claimant is in a position to decide whether or not to sell. It can, however, be the case that taking into account information obtained after purchase will work to the advantage of a defendant. Thus In *McKinnon v E Surv Ltd*,[10] the court was asked to consider the appropriate damages where a surveyor negligently failed to report on the true extent of structural movement and recommend monitoring, but where it was possible to show that the movement had, in fact, finished. The question arose as to whether the property should be valued as at the date of purchase, in which event, there would necessarily be uncertainty as to the position with a consequential effect on value or in the knowledge of the true facts, namely that movement had stopped. Mr Jonathan Gaunt Q.C. held, that in order to give effect to the overall compensatory rule in the assessment of damage, it was necessary to take account of information available at trial.

In earlier editions of this work it was stated: **10–135**

"In *Philips v Ward*,[11] *Perry v Sidney Phillips & Son*,[12] and *Watts v Morrow*,[13] the Court of Appeal has stated and re-stated that diminution in value is the proper measure of damage in respect of a negligent survey of a house for a private purchaser. This rule applies whether or not the purchaser has carried out repairs, whether or not the purchaser has retained or sold the property, and whether or not, if properly advised, the purchaser would not have bought the property. Unless and until the matter is considered by the House of Lords, that measure of damage will apply to virtually all cases arising out of domestic house surveys and/or valuations for prospective purchasers."[14]

In *Patel v Hooper & Jackson*,[15] Nourse L.J. endorsed the above statement from the fourth edition as being a correct statement of the prima facie rule applicable to the purchase of residential property. The only exception appears to be where it can be said that the purchaser is entitled to the costs of extrication from a purchase.[16]

Prior to *Philips v Ward*,[17] the measure of damages awarded in cases where a   **10–136** person had completed his purchase of a property in reliance upon a negligent survey or overvaluation was the cost of rectifying the defects unreported or

---

[10] [2003] P.N.L.R. 174.
[11] [1956] 1 W.L.R. 471.
[12] [1982] 1 W.L.R. 1297.
[13] [1991] 1 W.L.R. 1421.
[14] An exception would be where the surveyor has given a warranty. The decision of the Court of Appeal in *Watts v Morrow* [1991] 1 W.L.R. 1421 is discussed and criticised by T. Dugdale in "*Watts v Morrow*: penalising the house purchaser" (1992) 8 P.N. 152.
[15] [1999] Lloyd's L.Rep. P.N. 1 at 7–8.
[16] This was the measure of damages allowed in the actual case—see further para.10–149 below.
[17] [1956] 1 W.L.R. 471, CA.

misreported.[18] The official referee's decision[19] rejecting that measure was upheld by the Court of Appeal in *Philips v Ward*. In 1952 the claimant purchased a manor house for £25,000, in reliance upon the defendant surveyor's negligent report. It was later found to be affected by death watch beetle and woodworm. In his report the surveyor estimated the value of the property as somewhere between £25,000 and £27,000. It was found that in 1952 the necessary repair work would cost £7,000 at prices then prevailing, but that even if a purchaser knew of the defects, a fair price would have been £21,000. The claimant was awarded not £7,000 but £4,000 in damages, the difference between £25,000 and £21,000. The case was generally accepted as establishing two principles in respect of the measure of damages for a surveyor's breach of contract in such circumstances:

(i) the measure was the difference in value; and

(ii) the damages should be assessed as at the date when the damage occurred, that is 1952, not as at the date of trial in 1956.

10–137 **Formulation of measure of damage.** The difference in value was expressed by the three judges in *Philips v Ward* as follows. Denning L.J. described it as the difference between the value of the property in its assumed good condition and the value in the bad condition which should have been reported to the client.[20] Morris L.J. described it as the difference between the value of the property as it was described in the surveyor's report; and its value as it should have been described.[21] Romer L.J. did not precisely formulate the relevant difference, but he would appear to have taken it as the difference between the price paid and the market price of the property taking into account the defects which the surveyor failed to disclose.[22] As observed by Pennycuick J. in *Ford v White & Co*,[23] a solicitor's negligence case, each judge in *Philips v Ward* assumed or held the price paid to be equivalent to the value in assumed good condition (or as described in the defendant's report) and treated the two expressions as interchangeable. He further observed that the mind of each judge was not directed to the type of case where the purchaser had paid a price less than the value of the property in assumed good condition.[24] In Pennycuick J.'s view:

---

[18] See *Grove v Jackman and Masters* (1950) 155 E.G. 182; *Lowy v Woodroffe, Buchanan and Coulter* (1950) 156 E.G. 375; *Last v Post* (1952) 159 E.G. 240; *Wooldridge v Stanley Hicks and Son* (1953) 162 E.G. 513. The cost of rectifying defects would appear also to have been adopted in the following cases, although it is not clear from the brief reports: *Barton v Stuart Hepburn & Co* [1926] E.G.D. 206; *Legge v Young* [1949] E.G.D. 186; *Gurd v A Cobden Soar and Son* (1951) 157 E.G. 415; *Sincock v Bangs (Reading)* (1952) C.P.L. 562; *Thorne v Harris and Co* (1953) 163 E.G. 324; *Denny v Budgen* (1955) 166 E.G. 433. In *Tremayne v T Mortimer Burrows and Partners* (1954) 165 E.G. 232, McNair J. awarded £800 damages "as the cost of remedying the state of affairs that was found, or as the difference in value of the premises". The alternative basis of the award is no doubt indicative of the debate as to the proper measure, which was shortly thereafter resolved in *Philips v Ward* (above).
[19] Unreported.
[20] [1956] 1 W.L.R. 471 at 473.
[21] *ibid.* at 476.
[22] *ibid.* at 477–478.
[23] [1964] 1 W.L.R. 885.
[24] *ibid.* at 891.

"In the simple case of the purchase of property at a price in excess of the market value as a result of the wrong advice, the measure of damage must be the difference between (1) the market value of the property at the date of purchase, and (2) the price actually paid."[25]

He justified adopting the price paid as opposed to the higher value of the property in assumed good condition by taking a striking example:

"A sees a picture on sale at £100. He consults an art expert who negligently advises him that the picture is an old master worth £50,000. A buys the picture, but cannot in fact find a purchaser willing to pay more than £5 for it. Is his measure of damage £95 or £49,995? I should have thought obviously the former."[26]

Pennycuick J.'s observations were endorsed by Lord Denning M.R. in *Simple Simon Catering Ltd v Binstock Miller & Co*,[27] another solicitor's negligence case. Quoting Pennycuick J.'s painting example Lord Denning continued:

"An earlier case *Philips v Ward* [1956] 1 W.L.R. 471, when properly understood, proceeded on a similar basis . . . In those cases it was the difference between the price actually paid for the property on the basis that the advice was good, and the price at which it would be bought as it was in fact."[28]

In *Perry v Sidney Phillips and Son*,[29] the Court of Appeal confirmed the **10–138** explanation of *Philips v Ward* given in *Ford v White & Co* and the *Simple Simon Catering Ltd* cases. The claimant purchased a house in 1976 for £27,000 in reliance upon the defendant surveyors' report. In the report the value of the property was stated at £28,500. Subsequently the property was found to have a number of serious defects, including a leaking roof and a septic tank with an offensive odour. The defendants were held negligent in not properly inspecting and reporting upon the property. The correct method of assessing damages was tried as a preliminary issue. At first instance[30] the judge[31] held that difference in value was not the universal test in surveyors' negligence cases and that the proper measure of damages on the facts[32] was "the cost of repair of the defects which a proper inspection by a reasonably competent surveyor would have brought to light" assessed as at the date of his judgment.[33] The judge based his conclusion upon various passages from the Court of Appeal judgments in *Dodd Properties (Kent) Ltd v Canterbury CC*[34] relating to the primary compensatory principle of a damages award.[35] The deputy judge was also satisfied that if he had taken difference in value as the appropriate measure, he would have been entitled to

---

[25] [1964] 1 W.L.R. 885 at 888.
[26] *ibid.* at 888–889.
[27] (1973) 228 E.G. 527, CA.
[28] *ibid.* at 529.
[29] [1982] 1 W.L.R. 1297, CA.
[30] Reported at [1982] 1 All E.R. 1005.
[31] Mr Patrick Bennett Q.C. sitting as a deputy judge of the High Court.
[32] Including a finding of fact that the claimant did not intend to sell the property.
[33] [1982] 1 All E.R. 1005 at 1012, 1015.
[34] [1980] 1 W.L.R. 433, CA. Not a surveyor's negligence case, but a case where physical damage had been caused to the property. The measure of loss was therefore different.
[35] [1980] 1 W.L.R. 433 at 456 *per* Donaldson L.J., at 454–455 *per* Browne L.J.

consider the matter of assessment at the date of judgment,[36] again on the basis of the *Dodd Properties* case. By the time of the Court of Appeal hearing[37] and owing to financial difficulty, the claimant had sold the property for £43,000. Accordingly, before that court, the cost of repair was not defended as the appropriate measure of damages. Rather it was submitted on the claimant's behalf that the correct measure was the difference between (a) the value of the property at the date of trial if it had been in the condition in which it should have been, on the basis of the defendant surveyors' report, and (b) its value at the same date in its defective condition. This was tantamount to saying that the surveyors warranted their description and valuation of the property when their duty was the more limited one to exercise reasonable skill and care. The submission was rejected. The Court of Appeal reasserted the previously prevailing view that the appropriate measure of damages was the difference in value established in *Philips v Ward* as explained in *Ford v White & Co*. The claimant was entitled to interest on the difference. It was also held that the claimant was entitled to general damages for vexation and inconvenience.[38]

10–139   Each of the judges described the same calculation of loss somewhat differently. All agreed that the price paid by the claimant for the property was one element in the calculation. The other element was variously described. The *Dodd Properties* case[39] was distinguished as inapplicable essentially on the basis that it was concerned with physical damage being caused to the claimant's property. That being the case, the appropriate measure of damages justified by the primary compensatory principle was the cost of repairs. Moreover, in that case the question did arise as to the time for assessment of the cost of repair. In the case of a surveyor who does not cause defects but instead inadequately reports them, the measure of loss being the diminution in value, no question of a time for assessment other than the time of purchase arises.

10–140   **Nature of the loss.** It is submitted that this last point becomes more clear if the relevant measure is described not as the diminution in value, but as the overpayment or the excess price paid. The relevant measure is a money loss, not a value loss. The purchaser paid too much rather than obtained too little value. The property negligently reported upon never had an element of value corresponding to the overpayment. As a money loss, no question arises of assessing that loss other than when the money was lost on purchase. So long as English law, like virtually all jurisdictions, adheres to the principle of compensation by way of the actual sum as distinct from revaluation,[40] a claimant's entitlement in 1997 to £50,000 lost in 1990 is to £50,000 plus interest thereon for the interim period and not to the monetary equivalent (adjusted according to whatever inflation index as may appear appropriate) in 1997 of £50,000 in 1990.

10–141   Where the price paid exceeds the value of the property given in the negligent surveyor's report and valuation, that value and not the price paid may (although not invariably) be the appropriate figure, on the basis that the element of the

---

[36] [1980] 1 W.L.R. 433 at 1011.
[37] [1982] 1 W.L.R. 1297.
[38] See para.10–184, below.
[39] See para.10–138, above.
[40] See generally Professor F.A. Mann, *The Legal Aspect of Money* (4th edn).

overpayment comprising the difference between the price paid and the value described would not be attributable to the surveyor's default.[41] In *Hardy v Wamsley-Lewis*[42] for example, the value of the house as described in the defendant's report and its actual value were respectively assessed at £4,300 and £3,500. The claimant had nevertheless purchased it for £4,600. He was awarded the difference between £4,300 and £3,500 in damages.[43]

Other decisions. Despite attempts[44] to distinguish the difference in value   **10–142**
measure established in *Philips v Ward*,[45] it has since generally been followed and applied in all English and Scottish reported cases of a claim against a surveyor by a purchaser who completed the purchase in reliance upon a negligent survey or over-valuation.[46] The failure of attempts to distinguish *Philips v Ward* demonstrates the wide application of the measure of damages established by it. In *Lawrence v Hampton & Sons*,[47] it was argued that *Philips v Ward* was distinguishable where there was evidence that if there had been a proper report on the house, the purchaser would not have bought it. Mocatta J., although satisfied that there was positive evidence to that effect, held that that was no ground for

---

[41] For a similar approach, see Goff J.'s ground for not awarding the full expenditure on repairs in *Kenney v Hall, Pain and Foster* [1976] 2 E.G.L.R. 29 at 36, dealt with at paras 10–080, 10–100, 10–123, above.

[42] (1967) 203 E.G. 1039.

[43] The difference between £4,600 and £3,500 was not claimed. But it is submitted that that would not have been the appropriate measure because the element of the overpayment between £4,300 and £4,600 was attributable to the claimant's own action in overpaying. See also *Hingorani v Blower* [1976] 1 E.G.L.R. 104; difference in value apparently calculated by reference to the value of the property in the condition described by the defendant surveyor, assessed at £6,750, not the price paid of £7,000; and *Morgan v Perry* (1973) 229 E.G. 1737.

[44] Principally *Hipkins v Jack Cotton Partnership* [1989] 2 E.G.L.R. 157; *Syrett v Carr & Neave* [1990] 2 E.G.L.R. 161; and dicta by Staughton L.J. in *Steward v Rapley* [1989] 1 E.G.L.R. 159 at 164 to the effect that cost of repairs may be the appropriate measure on the hypothesis that the claimant may never have entered into the contract at all. This argument was finally rejected by the Court of Appeal in *Watts v Morrow* [1991] 1 W.L.R. 1421.

[45] [1956] 1 W.L.R. 471, CA.

[46] See *Fidgeon v Carroll* (1956) 168 E.G. 557, CA; *Hill v Debenham, Tewson and Chinnocks* (1958) 171 E.G. 835; *Moss v Heckingbottom* (1958) 172 E.G. 207; *Hood v Shaw* (1960) 176 E.G. 1291; *Lawrence v Hampton & Sons* (1964) 190 E.G. 107; *Freeman v Marshall* (1966) 200 E.G. 777; *Hardy v Wamsley-Lewis* (1967) 203 E.G. 1039; *Collard v Saunders* (1972) 221 E.G. 797 (a solicitor's negligence case); *Morgan v Perry* (1973) 229 E.G. 1737; *Bourne v McEvoy Timber Preservation Ltd* [1976] 1 E.G.L.R. 100; *Hingorani v Blower* [1976] 1 E.G.L.R. 104; *Lees v English and Partners* [1977] 1 E.G.L.R. 65; *Fisher v Knowles* [1982] 1 E.G.L.R. 154; *Perry v Sidney Phillips & Son* [1982] 1 W.L.R. 1297, CA; *Bolton v Puley* [1983] 2 E.G.L.R. 138; *Treml v Ernest W. Gibson and Partners* [1984] 2 E.G.L.R. 162; *Wilson v Baxter, Payne and Lepper* [1985] 1 E.G.L.R. 141; *Hooberman v Salter Rex* [1985] 1 E.G.L.R. 144; *Martin v Bell-Ingram*, 1986 S.L.T. 575 at 583 (Second Division); *County Personnel v Alan R. Pulver & Co* [1987] 1 W.L.R. 916 at 925F *per* Bingham L.J.; *Roberts v J. Hampson & Co* [1988] 2 E.G.L.R. 181, Ian Kennedy J.; *Miro Properties Ltd v J. Trevor & Sons* [1989] 1 E.G.L.R. 151, Mr Recorder Bernstein Q.C.; *Cross v David Martin & Mortimer* [1989] 1 E.G.L.R. 154, Phillips J.; *Steward v Rapley* [1989] 1 E.G.L.R. 159, CA; *Broadoak Properties Ltd v Young & White* [1989] 1 E.G.L.R. 263 (Judge Fox-Andrews Q.C.: "I find that in the absence of special circumstances the rule ought to be invariable. There should be certainty in this branch of the law"); *Bigg v Howard Son & Gooch* [1990] 1 E.G.L.R. 173, Judge Hicks Q.C.; *Rentokil Pty Ltd v Channon* [1990] 19 N.S.W.L.R. 417 (where the New South Wales Court of Appeal held that damages should be assessed on the basis of diminution in the value of the property, but, on the special facts of the case, by a majority, assessed at the date of hearing).

[47] (1964) 190 E.G. 107.

distinguishing the decision: "in that case[48] the possibility that the purchaser would not have bought the property was dealt with in each of the judgments".[49] It was also argued that the Court of Appeal was influenced by the fact that had the claimant in *Philips v Ward* recovered £7,000 he would have made a profit. The judge firmly rejected the argument[50]:

> "I do not think the existence of that possibility in *Philips v Ward* and its absence here, enables me to disregard the principle as to the measure of damages there laid down, which appears to me to be a general application in this kind of case, and was so regarded by Paull J. in *Hood v Shaw*." [51]

10–143   **(b) Relevance of cost of repairs.** Where an attempt has been made to displace the difference in value measure, it has usually been in favour of the cost of repairs. Except as a consequential loss item,[52] and the cases of *Hipkins v Jack Cotton Partnership*[53] and *Syrett v Carr and Neave*,[54] both first instance decisions overruled by the Court of Appeal in *Watts v Morrow*,[55] such cost has not been allowed as such and the difference in value measure has prevailed. Application of that measure is particularly noteworthy in cases where the cost of repairs was significantly less than the difference in value. *Daisley v BS Hall & Co*[56] provides a rare reported example of such a case.[57] Owing to the surveyor's negligent non-observance of soil shrinkage damage, the claimant paid in 1968 £1,750 more than the true value of a house. Three years later and before trial it was established that no more than £250 was required to rectify the damage and

---

[48] i.e. *Philips v Ward*.
[49] *ibid.* at 113. See *Philips v Ward* [1956] 1 W.L.R. 471, Denning L.J. at 473, Morris L.J. at 476, Romer L.J. at 477–478. Romer L.J. said:
> "On this hypothesis his ignorance of the defects may be said to have worsened his position to the extent of £4,000 for he parted with £25,000 and became the possessor of property worth only £21,000."

See also *Hardy v Wamsley-Lewis* (1967) 203 E.G. 1039 at 1043 *per* Paull J.:
> "[the parties] seem fairly clearly agreed, that if dry rot had been seen and reported the house would not have been bought. In those circumstances it seems to me that the proper measure of damage is the difference in value between the place as it was on the basis of the report and the value of it in the condition in which it truly was".

In *Lees v English and Partners* (1977) E.G.D. 566, the measure of the difference between the price paid and the value of the house in its actual condition was applied despite the vendor's contention that had his surveyor properly reported he would "not have touched the house with a barge pole". May J. commented: "the vendor might have been able to get the money from another purchaser when the remedial work had been done".
[50] (1964) 190 E.G. 107 at 113.
[51] (1960) 176 E.G. 1291 at 1293.
[52] See para.10–192, below.
[53] [1989] 2 E.G.L.R. 157.
[54] [1990] 2 E.G.L.R. 161.
[55] See para.10–145, below.
[56] (1972) 225 E.G. 1553. See next note for the argument advanced to distinguish *Philips v Ward*.
[57] See also *Hoadley v Edwards* [2001] P.N.L.R. 965, where it appears that unplanned expenditure of £12,500 was incurred by the claimants and that further expenditure of £6,800 was required to bring the house into the expected structural condition. The judge nonetheless awarded damages of £40,000 as representing the overpayment made by the claimants together with damages for physical inconvenience and discomfort.

eliminate the risk of further damage. Nevertheless, £1,750 was awarded in damages upon the express basis of *Philips v Ward*.[58]

A more usual situation is for the cost of repairs to be significantly higher than the difference in value assessed at the date of purchase owing to inflation, the state of the property market, or deterioration of the defect (e.g. subsidence or dry rot) between that date and the date of discovery of the defects. In such cases, the courts have equally awarded damages based upon difference in value at the time of purchase.[59] In *Watts v Morrow*,[60] a determined attempt was made in the Court of Appeal to displace difference in value as the proper measure of loss for this type of case. The claimants had purchased a farmhouse for £177,500 relying on the defendant's negligent structural survey report. By the time that serious defects had been discovered, the claimants had moved into the property and carried out repairs at a cost of £33,961. The unchallenged evidence of the claimant's expert valuer was that in October 1986, the date of the contract to purchase, the value of the house in its true condition was £162,500. The claimants therefore paid for the property £15,000 more than it was worth in its true condition. At first instance, the claimant's claim for the cost of repairs as the proper measure of damage was upheld. The official referee directed himself by

---

[58] See *ibid.* at 1557 *per* Bristow J.:

"[Counsel for the plaintiff] submits that since *Philips v Ward* clearly establishes that Mr Daisley would not in any circumstances have been entitled to more than £1,750 however much it might have cost him to do the necessary repairs if the hazard did bite so he cannot be said to have suffered less than that damage merely because the hazard never bites at all, and that the proper time to look at the assessment of loss is at the time of breach. I am satisfied that [counsel's] contention is right. What is sauce for the goose is sauce for the gander and if Mr Daisley would never be entitled to recover more than £1,750 as *Philips v Ward* appears to me clearly to establish, it must follow that he will never be entitled to recover less; therefore there must be judgment for the plaintiff for £1,750."

Contrast with the views to the contrary, obiter, of Staughton L.J. in *Steward v Rapley* [1989] 1 E.G.L.R. 159 at 164. See also on this point *Gardner v Marsh & Parsons* [1997] 1 W.L.R. 489, CA, para.10–144, fn.44 below.

[59] See, e.g. *Morgan v Perry* (1973) 229 E.G. 1737, where the claimant purchased a house in 1968 for £10,200, which later transpired to be valueless owing to soil subsidence. Investigations were only completed in 1971 and the case was tried in 1973. The recommended solution was demolition of the house, draining of the site and rebuilding. Estimates of the cost were £16,600 in 1969, £18,675 in 1971 and £24,000 in 1973. Due to the rise in house prices, the value of the house in the condition reported by the defendant would have been £24,000 or £25,000 at the date of trial. The claimant did not contend for the cost of repair, but the difference in value assessed at the completion of investigations in 1971. Kenneth Jones J. considered himself bound by *Philips v Ward* and held the proper measure was the "differential value" of the house in 1968, which was assessed as equal to its then whole value, £10,200. In *Collard v Saunders* (1972) 221 E.G. 797, the claimant sought the cost of repairs on the ground that repairs had been delayed owing to lack of means and accordingly cost more. Mocatta J. considered the case indistinguishable from that in *Philips v Ward* and assessed damages by reference to the difference in value. Similarly in *Hooberman v Salter Rex* [1985] 1 E.G.L.R. 144, the claimant purchased a maisonette in 1977 for £28,300. Dry rot so built up as to necessitate remedial work in 1980–81 at a cost of £6,391. If the remedial work required in 1977 had been carried out it was estimated that its cost would only have been £1,748 and the development of dry rot would have been prevented. Judge Smout Q.C. awarded the claimant damages of £875 in respect of his first head of claim, the difference between £28,300 and the market value of the maisonette in 1977 in its true condition. The judge considered that the principles expressed in those two cases precluded him from awarding the claimant anything in respect of the second head of claim, the increase in the cost of remedial work caused by the development of dry rot, £6,391, less the estimated cost of preventative repairs which could have been effected in 1977.

[60] [1991] 1 W.L.R. 1421.

reference to the principles stated by Bingham L.J. in *County Personnel Ltd v Alan R Pulver*,[61] to the effect that the diminution in value rule is almost always appropriate where property is acquired following negligent advice by surveyors, but that it is not an invariable approach and should not be mechanistically applied in inappropriate cases. The official referee noted that the facts of *Watts v Morrow* were broadly similar to those of *Syrett v Carr and Neave*,[62] a case also decided by him. The official referee held that the claimants had acted reasonably in deciding to repair the property rather than reselling the same, and concluded that the claimants were entitled to recover damages assessed as the cost of repairs, £33,961.

10–145   In the Court of Appeal the claimants argued that the principle in *Philips v Ward*, in so far as it could be regarded as a prima facie rule for the measure of damages in a claim against a negligent surveyor, was applicable only in cases where it is clear that the claimants would have bought the property in any event, even if it had been accurately described by the surveyor. Given that the judge had found that the claimants had acted reasonably in carrying out the repairs it was suggested that the full cost of such repairs should be awarded. Ralph Gibson L.J.[63] rejected the claimants' argument, stating:

> "It was rightly acknowledged for the plaintiffs that proof that the plaintiff, properly advised, would not have bought the property does not by itself cause the diminution in value rule to be inapplicable. It was contended, however, that it becomes inapplicable if it is also proved that it is reasonable for the plaintiff to retain the property and to do the repairs. I cannot accept that submission because:
>   (i) the fact that it is reasonable for the plaintiff to retain the property and to do the repairs seems to me to be irrelevant to determination of the question whether recovery of the cost of repairs is justified in order to put the plaintiff in the position in which he would have been if the contract, i.e. the promise to make a careful report, had been performed. The position is no different from that in *Philips*: the plaintiff would either have refused to buy or he would have negotiated a reduced price. Recovery of the cost of repairs after having gone into possession: that is to say in effect the acquisition of the house at the price paid less the cost of repairs at the later date of doing those repairs, is not a position into which the plaintiff could have been put as a result of proper performance of the contract. Nor is that cost recoverable as damages for breach of any promise by the defendant because, as stated above, there was no promise that the plaintiff would not incur any such cost.
>   (ii) In the context of the contract proved in this case, I have difficulty in seeing when or by reference to what principle it would not be reasonable for the purchaser of a house to retain it and to do the repairs. He is free to do as he pleases. He can owe no duty to the surveyor to take any cheaper course. The measure of damages should depend, and in my view does depend, upon proof of the sum needed to put the plaintiff in the position in which he would have been if the contract was properly performed, and a

---

[61] [1987] 1 W.L.R. 916 at 925. A solicitor's negligence action.
[62] [1990] 2 E.G.L.R. 161.
[63] With whom both the President and Bingham L.J. agreed, Bingham L.J. noted that there should be "sound, prima facie rules to be applied in the ordinary run of cases" and stated:
    "In the present field . . . the purchase of houses by private buyers in reliance on a negligent survey of structure or condition, *Philips v Ward* [1956] 1 W.L.R. 471 has been generally thought to lay down and in my view did lay down a prima facie rule for measuring damages."
There was nothing in the facts of the present case to take it outside the prima facie rule in *Philips v Ward*.

reasonable decision by him to remain in the house and to repair it, upon discovery of the defects, cannot alter that primary sum which remains the amount by which he was caused to pay more than the value of the house in its true condition.

(iii) If the rule were as contended for by the plaintiffs, what limit, if any, could be put on the nature and extent of the repairs of which the plaintiff could recover the cost? [Counsel for the plaintiffs] asserted that the cost of repairs awarded in this case was no more than putting the house in the condition in which, on reading the report, they believed the house to be. That, however, contains no relevant standard of reasonableness because, again, the defendant did not warrant that description to be true. To argue that to award damages on that basis is not to enforce a warranty never given but merely to 'reflect the losses which the claimants have incurred' seems to me to be a circular statement.

(iv) I have considered whether the reasonableness of the amount which a plaintiff might recover towards the cost of repairing unreported defects in excess of the diminution in value might be determined by reference to the amount which the plaintiff could recover if he sold the property: i.e. the diminution in value plus any other recoverable losses and expenses. Such a limit was not contended for by [counsel for the plaintiffs]. It has the apparent attraction of enabling a plaintiff who chooses to retain the property to recover as much as he would recover if he chose to sell it. It seems to me, however, to be impossible to hold that such is the law in the case of such a contract as was made in this case. The plaintiff must, I think, prove that the loss which he claims to have suffered was caused by the breach of duty proved and he cannot do that by proving what his loss would have been in circumstances which have not happened."[64]

Ralph Gibson L.J. also rejected an argument that the claimants could recover the cost of repairs as damages caused by entering into a transaction in reliance on the bad advice of the surveyor. The surveyor did not warrant that no repairs beyond those described in the survey report would be required within some period of time. In the absence of such a warranty, there was no basis for awarding the cost of repairs. The Court of Appeal held that *Hipkins v Jack Cotton Partnership*[65] and *Syrett v Carr and Neave*[66] were both wrongly decided on the issue of measure of damage.[67] In *Smith v Peter North*,[68] the Court of Appeal again rejected an attempt to distinguish previous authorities so as to claim the costs of repair. The claimants, who ran an equestrian business, instructed the defendants to advise as to the costs of repairing a property to bring it up to their required standard as well as on its value. The defendant surveyor advised that the property was in substantially good repair whereupon the claimants purchased it for £330,000. They then claimed that £130,000 was required to bring the property up to the required standard although the court-appointed valuer stated that the property was worth £340,000 (i.e. £10,000 more than the claimants paid for it) at the time of purchase. The judge struck out the claim for the cost of repairs, although allowed to remain a claim for the costs of seeking alternative accommodation together with the costs of moving and storing furniture during the

---

[64] [1991] 1 W.L.R. 1421 at 1435H.

[65] [1989] 2 E.G.L.R. 157.

[66] [1990] 2 E.G.L.R. 161.

[67] In *Hipkins*, the award should have been £8,900 plus interest. Given the delay between the purchase of the property and the trial, the total award would in any event have approached the cost of repairs.

[68] [2001] P.N.L.R. 274.

repair works. The Court of Appeal upheld the judge's conclusion. Jonathan Parker L.J. considered the case to be straightforward and emphasised (at para.50) that the effect of permitting the cost of repairs to be claimed would be to place them in a better position than had the valuer given a competent report.

10–146   The reaffirmation by the Court of Appeal that the diminution in value principle, as distinct from the cost of repairs, was the proper measure of damage in cases where a person completed the purchase of a domestic property in reliance upon a negligent survey or overvaluation by a surveyor has been followed in all subsequent cases.[69] It should, however, be noted that the cases discussed in this section have concerned the sale of domestic property. Even cases involving commercial property such as *Broadoak Properties Ltd v Young & White*[70] concerned the sale of a freehold. There is nothing in any of the reported cases to suggest that the diminution in value principle must apply to all land transactions, however far removed factually from those under consideration in the leading cases. Commercial transactions can often involve three parties: the developer of a new (and therefore apparently defect-free) building which is selling the freehold; an investor, typically a pension fund or similar institution, that is purchasing the freehold; and the purchaser of a leasehold interest from the developer, where the developer, with the benefit of the leasehold purchaser's covenants, is able to sell the "package" to the freehold purchaser. Should a negligent survey fail to reveal defects in such a building, it is by no means certain that the only measure of the leasehold purchaser's damage must be the diminution in value.

10–147   The cost of repairs can moreover assume considerable importance as part of the relevant material for an independent valuer attempting to establish the proper market value of a house at the time of the purchase. This was the situation in *Steward v Rapley*,[71] where the claimants' independent surveyor took the cost of repairs to a house badly affected by dry rot to be the measure of the fall in the market value. Purchas L.J. summarised the position:

"What in fact [the independent surveyor] has done is to take the costs of remedy as a measure and indication of the drop in the market value. He has not, and indeed it would be no part of his function, to say in law that it is open to the plaintiffs to recover the cost of repair and redecoration because, as the law stands at the moment, that is specifically not the position. But as I understand the state of the law, there is no objection to a person who wishes to present a professional assessment of a market value from arriving at that market value by taking a value based on a good state of condition in the house and then

---

[69] Examples include: *Heatley v William H Brown Ltd* [1992] 1 E.G.L.R. 289; *Ezekiel v McDade* [1995] 2 E.G.L.R. 107, CA; *Matto v Rodney Broom Associates* [1994] 2 E.G.L.R. 163, CA; and *Sneesby v Goldings* [1995] 2 E.G.L.R. 102 at 105, CA. In *Gardner v Marsh & Parsons* [1997] 1 W.L.R. 489, CA, surveyors negligently overlooked a serious structural defect. This was only discovered when the property was about to be sold, and the defect was later rectified at the landlord's expense. The claimants recovered damages on the diminution in value basis at the date of their original purchase. The surveyors appealed, arguing that had the defect been discovered on the original purchase the landlord would have rectified the same and the purchasers therefore suffered no loss. By a majority the Court of Appeal dismissed the surveyors' appeal, holding the actions of the landlord *res inter alios acta* and therefore collateral to the surveyors' negligence.
[70] [1989] 1 E.G.L.R. 263.
[71] [1989] 1 E.G.L.R. 159, CA.

deducting from it, either fully or appropriately discounted, the cost of putting it into an acceptable marketable condition."[72]

This approach, and the necessary limitation to it, was confirmed by Ralph Gibson L.J. in *Watts v Morrow*[73]:

> "The cost of doing repairs to put right defects negligently not reported may be relevant to the proof of the market price of the house in its true condition: *see Steward v Rapley*[74]; and the cost of doing repairs and the diminution in value may be shown to be the same. If, however, the cost of repairs would exceed the diminution in value, then the ruling in *Philips*, where it is applicable, prohibits recovery of the excess because it would give to the plaintiff more than his loss. It would put the plaintiff in the position of recovering damages for breach of a warranty that the condition of the house was correctly described by the surveyor and, in the ordinary case as here, no such warranty has been given."

(c) Costs of extrication. One possible factual situation which was expressly **10–148** left open by the Court of Appeal in *Watts v Morrow* was a case where a claimant purchased a property, discovered defects, and then took steps to extricate himself from the property. Ralph Gibson L.J. stated:

> "It is clear, and it was not argued to the contrary, that the ruling in *Philips* may be applicable to the case where the buyer has, after purchase, extricated himself from the transaction by selling the property. In the absence of any point on mitigation, the buyer will recover the diminution in value together with costs and expenses thrown away in moving in and out and of resale: see Romer L.J. in *Philips*. I will not here try to state the nature or extent of any additional recoverable items of damage. The damages recoverable where the plaintiff extricates himself from the transaction by resale are not necessarily limited to the diminution in value plus expenses. The consequences of the negligent advice and of the plaintiff entering into the transaction into which he would not have entered if properly advised, may be such that the diminution in value rule is not applicable. An example is the case of *County Personnel v Pulver* [1987] 1 W.L.R. 916, CA, a case of solicitors' negligence, where the plaintiff recovered the capital losses caused by entering into the transaction."[75]

Thus it would appear that a claimant who buys a property which he would not have bought had he been properly advised and discovers very serious defects which lead him to sell the property may be entitled to recover all the losses sustained by reason of entering into the transaction. It is possible to contemplate a situation where such losses would include the cost of repairs. Thus if very serious dry rot was discovered, a claimant might be advised that it would be impossible to sell the property unless at least some works of rectification were carried out in which event the costs of such repairs could be properly recoverable as mitigating the costs incurred in extricating the claimant from the transaction.

---

[72] [1989] 1 E.G.L.R. 159, CA at 161. The cost of repairs was used as a cross-check against the diminution in value in the Scottish case of *Wood v McVicar* [1990] G.W.D. 37–2143, Lord Morton of Shuna.
[73] [1991] 4 All E.R. 937 at 950F.
[74] [1989] 1 E.G.L.R. 159, CA.
[75] [1991] 1 W.L.R. 1421 at 1435D.

10–149   In *Patel v Hooper & Jackson*,[76] the Court of Appeal awarded damages based on the costs of extrication from the transaction. The claimants had purchased a house for £95,000 in reliance on a House Buyer's Report and Valuation. Having completed the purchase they discovered serious structural defects and damp which required to be corrected at substantial cost before the house was habitable. The claimants were unable to afford to carry out the repairs and attempted to sell the house whilst living in alternative rented accommodation. The Court of Appeal permitted an award of damages consisting of £25,250 being the difference in value; the costs of living in alternative accommodation for the five-year period until it was found that they ought reasonably to have put the house up for auction including the costs of moving from one set of rented accommodation to another and an award of £2,000 to each of the claimants by way of general damages. The Court of Appeal refused to allow an award of the actual mortgage payments made in respect of the house as the judge had found that, but for the defendant's negligence, the claimants would have bought a sound house for an equivalent price to that which they paid. The courts have also expressly contemplated awarding limited sums representing emergenccy work. In *Sneesby v Goldings*,[77] the trial judge had awarded the claimants not only damages representing the diminution in value, but also £2,434.76 which they paid to a builder to construct permanent support work. Hoffmann L.J. reviewed the submissions of counsel for the appellant:

> "The principle laid down in *Philips v Ward*, and followed by this court in *Watts v Morrow* [1991] 1 W.L.R. 1421, is that a plaintiff is not entitled to be paid the costs of repairs. There are cases in which plaintiffs have, in addition to the diminution in value, been awarded the cost of emergency work not affecting the value of the property, such as the cost of hiring the acrow props in this case . . . [the builders'] bill was for permanent work and that should not have been included. In my view that must be right. The work which they did was simply repair work, which is excluded by the principle in *Philips v Ward*."[78]

10–150   **(d) Collateral benefit.** As the difference in value represents the correct measure of damages in almost all cases, the courts have had to consider when it will be appropriate to oblige a claimant to give credit for collateral benefits received as a result of a purchase based upon negligent advice. The test applied by the courts has been whether the benefit received flowed directly from the transaction into which the claimant entered. The courts have had some difficulty in applying this test. The position may be complicated by the fact that to the extent that such benefits are foreseeable, they are likely to be reflected in the purchase price whilst to the extent that they are not, they could be regarded as irrelevant windfalls. The general tendency has been to restrict the taking into account of such benefits. An example of the approach adopted is to be found in *Gardner v Marsh & Parsons*.[79] The claimants purchased a long lease of a maisonette in a newly converted building in reliance on a full structural survey report. Under the terms of the lease the landlords were responsible for carrying

---

[76] [1999] Lloyd's L.Rep. P.N. 1.
[77] [1995] 2 E.G.L.R. 102 at 105, CA.
[78] *ibid.* at 105.
[79] [1997] 3 All E.R. 871.

out structural repairs. The defendant surveyors negligently failed to point out a serious structural defect which was discovered three years after purchase when the claimants attempted, unsuccessfully, to sell the property. After two years of negotiations, the necessary remedial works were carried out by the landlord. The Court of Appeal, by a majority, upheld the judge's award of £29,000, being the difference in value between the value of the maisonette in its assumed good condition and the actual value of the lease. The court unanimously rejected, on the facts, the contention that had the report not been negligent, the defect would have been remedied by the landlord prior to purchase. The majority (Hirst and Pill L.JJ.) also found that, particularly given the long delay, the remedying of the defect could not be said to have formed part of the same transaction as the purchase. It followed that although the defect had been remedied at no cost to the claimants, the benefit was collateral and not to be taken into account.[80] Similarly in *Treml v Ernest W Gibson and Partners*,[81] the claimant in reliance on the defendant surveyors' report purchased a house subsequently found to have serious defects. An issue arose as to whether credit should be given for a grant towards the cost of repair received by the claimant from the local authority. Popplewell J. held:

> "I am clearly of the view that the sum does not fall to be deducted. Firstly, because it is irrelevant to a claim where the difference in value is the measure of damage and, secondly, because, to use legal shorthand, it is a collateral benefit which does not have to be taken into account."[82]

In *Marder v Sautelle and Hicks*,[83] the defendant surveyors negligently failed to warn the claimants that the house had been constructed with defective materials. They purchased for £33,000 and then spent £26,000 on improvements and extensions. No repair was possible. The only solution was to demolish the defective part of the house and rebuild. The value of the house was taken to be £33,000, the site value, less demolition costs, was £13,500 with the difference between those two values being £19,500. That was the sum awarded by the judge. After the trial, the claimants sold the property for £70,000.[84] The defendants appealed out of time and argued in the Court of Appeal that the £70,000 ought to be taken into account. This argument failed. Staughton L.J. considered that there were four reasons why the price obtained for the property might be of no benefit to the defendants. First, changes in the planning climate may have persuaded purchasers to pay more in the hope of building two houses rather than one house when the existing property had been demolished. Secondly, the £70,000 was at least partly explained by the extensions built and financed by the claimants. Thirdly, the increase was accounted for to some extent by inflation in the property market, at rates that would have exceeded the 12 per cent simple

---

[80] Peter Gibson L.J. would have found that the claimants' actions in obliging the landlords to comply with their obligations under the lease represented reasonable acts of mitigation of the claimants' damage. As the acts were successful, the benefits were to be taken into account in the assessment of damages. Similarly a claimant does not have to give credit for an NHBC guarantee—see *Hanley Smith v Darlington* [2001] E.G. 160.

[81] [1984] 2 E.G.L.R. 162.

[82] *ibid.* at 72.

[83] [1988] 2 E.G.L.R. 187, CA.

[84] This was done openly, due notice of the intention having been given to the defendants.

interest awarded by the judge. Fourthly, the new purchasers may simply have paid too much: "in other words, the claimants obtained a windfall. That would be a collateral matter for which the defendants could claim no credit".[85] The appeal was dismissed.[86]

(ii) *Negligent Survey or Valuation for a Purchaser who Withdraws from Purchase before Completion*

10–151   Where after a negligent survey or valuation a purchaser enters a contract for the purchase of a property, but before completion discovers the defects overlooked and consequently does not proceed to completion, the purchaser will, prima facie, be entitled to damages for all the loss and expense incurred in entering and withdrawing from the contract to purchase so far as is attributable to the surveyors' default. Thus in *Buckland v Watts*,[87] the purchaser recovered in damages from the surveyor the amount of the deposit forfeited to the vendor, solicitors' fees incurred after the date of the surveyor's report and surveyor's fees attributable to the negligent survey.[88] Likewise in *Parsons v Way & Waller Ltd*,[89] the purchaser recovered the amount of his lost deposit.

(iii) *Negligent Survey or Valuation for Lender*

10–152   A money lender, for example a bank, building society,[90] or finance company, will usually require a valuation of a property for the purpose of deciding the sum, if any, it is prepared to advance secured by a mortgage thereon. Following the decision in *BBL v Eagle Star*,[91] it will almost invariably be necessary to carry out two tasks in order properly to assess the damages payable following a negligent valuation for a lender:

(a)   assess the total loss suffered by the lender in accordance with the principles understood to be applicable prior to the decision in *BBL*; and

(b)   assess whether the damages payable fall, in their entirety, within the scope of the duty undertaken by the valuer.

---

[85] [1988] 2 E.G.L.R. 187, CA at 189. The Lord Justice referred to the analysis of collateral benefits in the then edition of *McGregor*, para.16, and to *Slater v Hoyle & Smith Ltd* [1920] 2 K.B. 11, and concluded:

"I appreciate that this doctrine of collateral credit may not always seem very just to defendants who have to pay damages, but it is both logic and law."

[86] For an example of a case where it appears that the judge did find that claimants had suffered no loss, see *Devine v Jefferys* [2001] P.N.L.R. 407, where it appears that H.H.J. Jack Q.C. held that borrowers who had had their debt extinguished by their lender more than six years after purchase had not suffered any relevant loss. The reasoning in the decision is not entirely clear and appears to support a contrary result to that achieved.

[87] (1968) 208 E.G. 969.

[88] Recovery of such fees in damages is surprising since such fees would have been incurred even if the surveyor had not been negligent.

[89] (1952) 159 E.G. 524. He failed on grounds of remoteness to recover fees paid to a building society for a valuation for mortgage purposes: see para.10–092 above.

[90] In the case of a building society, a valuation is required by statute—s.62 of the Building Societies Act 1986.

[91] [1997] A.C. 191. For discussion as to the effects of the decision in relation to a valuer's scope of duty generally, see para.10–113 above.

(a) Assessment of the total loss. Prior to the decision in *BBL*, the courts had   **10–153**
simply sought to place a lender in the position which it would have been in had
a competent valuation been provided to it. This involved ascertaining the losses
sustained by entering into a loan and comparing them with the losses (if any)
which would have been incurred had a competent valuation been provided. After
BBL it is still necessary to carry out this task as a lender's recoverable losses
cannot, in any circumstances, exceed the losses incurred. In *Swingcastle Ltd v
Gibson*,[92] the House of Lords had made it clear that a valuer did not warrant the
accuracy of his valuation with the result that any profits which the lender had
hoped to make as a result of entering into the loan would, ordinarily, be
irrelevant. In 1985 the claimant, a finance company, agreed to lend £10,000 to
borrowers on the basis of a valuation of their house at £18,000 by a surveyor. The
valuation was negligent. The annual rate of interest under the mortgage was
36.51 per cent with a default rate of 45.619 per cent if the borrowers fell into
arrears. In 1986 the borrowers fell into arrears and surrendered possession to the
lenders. The house was sold in February 1987 for £12,000, leaving a shortfall if
accrued contractual interest were taken into account. The lenders brought an
action in negligence against the valuer seeking to recover a total of £9,297.56,
including accrued interest under the mortgage at the default rate. The county
court judge gave judgment for £7,136.41, having disallowed a claimed early
redemption penalty that could not properly have been awarded on the facts. The
Court of Appeal[93] considered itself bound by *Baxter v FW Gapp & Co Ltd*,[94] and
dismissed the appeal on the ground that the valuer was liable for the total amount
of the lender's loss, including any unpaid interest at a default rate stipulated in
the mortgage, as well as the principal sum advanced.

On the appeal to the House of Lords, the finance company decided neither to   **10–154**
appear nor to make representations.[95] The valuer's case throughout the proceedings was that the lenders' calculation of their loss was made on the wrong basis.
The damages should have been assessed on the basis that the lenders were
entitled to be placed in the position that they would have been in if they had
received a competent report from the valuer and had consequently made no loan
to the borrowers. On the facts, it was argued that the lenders' damages were to
be calculated on the basis that they should:

(a) take credit for the payment of £10,000 to the borrowers, £401.35 to their
     estate agents and £983.25 to their solicitors, and

(b) give credit for £1,734 paid by the borrowers between February 1985 and
     April 1986, and for £12,000 received on the sale of the property.

In addition, the finance company had for two years (or for such shorter period as
might be thought proper) been deprived of the use of the £10,000 which they

---

[92] [1991] 2 A.C. 223, HL.
[93] [1990] 1 W.L.R. 1223.
[94] [1939] 2 All E.R. 752, CA.
[95] A decision that did not find favour with their Lordships, [1991] 2 A.C. 223 at 239. The conduct of
the lenders may have contributed to the final order that the case be remitted with a direction that
judgment be entered for the valuers, despite the fact that liability had been admitted in the county
court and, on the appeal to the Court of Appeal, the valuers had asked for the substitution of a small
amount of damages which had been admitted to be due.

would not have lent but for the negligent valuation. The only speech was given by Lord Lowry, who began[96] by citing Lord Blackburn's dictum in *Livingstone v Rawyards Coal Co.*[97] He then cited (a) *Clerk and Lindsell on Torts*,[98] which supported the contention that a mortgagee who can establish that no advance would have been made is entitled to recover the difference between the sum advanced and the sum recovered on sale of the property, plus any consequential losses and expenses; and (b) *McGregor on Damages*,[99] which argued that (i) claims against valuers by the purchasers of property are to be assessed on a different basis from claims by the mortgagees of property; (ii) the relevant sum to be deducted from the amount of the unrecovered loan is not the true value of the property, but the amount that would have been lent if the valuer had not been negligent; (iii) the loss of the money advanced may be increased by expenses and reduced by receipts. Lord Lowry concluded: "The approach of the valuer in this case and the analysis of Neill L.J., which I have reproduced above, seem to me to be correct."[1] That statement then appeared to be of general application to circumstances where a lender proved it would not have lent with the benefit of non-negligent advice from a valuer. The case of *Baxter v F. W. Gapp & Co Ltd*[2] was then overruled by the House of Lords on the issue of calculation of damages:

"My Lords, *Baxter v F. W. Gapp & Co Ltd* [1939] 2 K.B. 271, is not an attractive precedent. For one thing, it does not clearly exemplify the proposition contended for by the lenders, even if that proposition can be teased out of it; secondly, the dispute was about all the plaintiff's consequential damage and the pecuniary effect of the difference in interest rates . . . was relatively insignificant; and, thirdly and most important, the approach, if carefully scrutinised, seems contrary to principle: the aggrieved party was entitled to be placed in the same position as if the wrong had not occurred, and not to receive from the wrongdoer compensation for lost interest at the rate which the borrower had contracted to observe."[3]

Lord Lowry then considered the case as advanced by the lenders:

"My Lords, it is clear that the lenders ought to have presented their claim on the basis that, if the valuer had advised properly, they would not have lent the money. Where they went wrong was to claim, not only correctly that they had to spend all the money which they did, but incorrectly that the valuer by his negligence deprived them of the interest which they would have received from the borrowers if the borrowers had paid up. The security for the loan was the property but the lenders did not have a further security consisting of a guarantee by the valuer that the borrowers would pay everything, or indeed anything, that was due from them to the lenders at the date, whenever it occurred, on which the loan transaction terminated. The fallacy of the lenders' case is that they have been trying to obtain from the valuer compensation for the borrowers' failure and not the proper damages for the valuer's negligence."[4]

---

[96] [1991] 2 A.C. 223 at 232D.
[97] (1880) 5 App. Cas. 25 at 39.
[98] (16th edn, 1989), para.11–45, pp.670–671.
[99] (15th edn, 1988), paras 1212–1218, pp.749–753.
[1] [1991] 2 A.C. 223 at 237A.
[2] [1939] 2 K.B. 271.
[3] [1991] 2 A.C. 223 at 236.
[4] *ibid.* at 238.

This passage, and in particular the first sentence, strongly suggests that the House of Lords accepted that a distinction was to be made between a "no transaction" and a "successful transaction" case when assessing damages in a lender/valuer case.[5] Lord Lowry then applied the reasoning to the facts of the case:

"Taking the figures I have mentioned of £10,000,[6] £401.35[7] and £983.25[8] on one side and £12,000[9] and £1,734[10] on the other, the lenders are £2,349.40 in credit. Clause 9 of the mortgage agreement provided that the lenders could debit the mortgage account with 'all costs expenses and disbursements incurred directly or indirectly in relation thereto'. This no doubt explains the claim for £344.99, though not the claim for interest thereon of £129.31. But I find it impossible to say whether the whole or part of the £344.99 should be taken into account against the valuer or simply be treated as administrative expenses of the mortgage chargeable by agreement against the borrowers. In the absence of any evidence as to how the lenders financed the loan or evidence showing how the money, if not lent to the borrowers, could have been profitably employed, I consider that 12 per cent interest, which would correspond to the 9 per cent allowed by Gibson J. in *Corisand Investments Ltd v Druce & Co* (1978) 248 E.G. 315, is the proper rate at which to recompense the lenders for being deprived of their £10,000. The actual time was two years, which would yield a result of £2,400, but one may ask whether it was reasonable for the tortfeasor to bear the liability up to the date of sale in February 1987, possession of the property having been surrendered on 30 June 1986. Moreover, it is not clear how a calculation of damages would be affected by the incidence of tax or whether this is a case in which it would have been reasonable for the court to contemplate partial recovery by the lenders against the borrowers: see

---

[5] A point made by the Court of Appeal in *Banque Bruxelles Lambert SA v Eagle Star Insurance Co Ltd* [1995] Q.B. 375 at 412. The measure of loss in a "no-transaction" case is:
   (a) the difference between the advance and any capital recovered, whether by way of repayment by the borrower, or from the sale of the mortgaged property; plus
   (b) consequential expenses, for example incurred in repossession proceedings against the borrower; plus
   (c) interest at an appropriate rate to reflect the loss of use of the capital sum advanced, credit being given for any interest payments made by the borrower.
Note the comment by Lord Lowry in *Swingcastle Ltd v Alastair Gibson* [1991] 2 A.C. 223 at 237:
   "There is, as Neill L.J. perceived, no cut and dried solution to calculating the amount of damages in cases of this kind. It depends on the evidence."
In a "transaction" case, that is where there has been a negligent survey or valuation for a lender who would have lent a lesser sum with a proper survey or valuation, an appropriate measure of loss in such cases is:
   (a) the difference between (i) the advance actually made less any capital recovered, whether by way of repayment by the borrower, or from the sale of the mortgaged property, and (ii) the lesser advance that would have been made, less any capital that would have been recovered in such circumstances; plus
   (b) any consequential expenses that would not have been incurred in any event; plus
   (c) interest at an appropriate rate to reflect the loss of use of the additional capital sum advanced, credit being given for any interest payments received by the lender on the additional capital.
[6] The original advance.
[7] The estate agent's charges.
[8] Solicitor's fees.
[9] The sum received on the sale of the property.
[10] Sums paid to the lenders by the borrowers in respect of capital and interest between February 1985 and April 1986. Note that no distinction was made between the two elements. Where larger sums are involved, substantial repayments of capital by the borrower may well have an effect on the interest calculation.

London and South of England Building Society v Stone [1983] 1 W.L.R. 1242. It was for the lenders to furnish the evidence by which to prove their case on the correct basis."[11]

10–155   Lord Lowry calculated interest to reflect the loss of use of capital at 12 per cent.[12] In doing so the House of Lords followed the 9 per cent awarded by Gibson J. in *Corisand Investments*. In neither case, however, did the lender adduce evidence of what it cost to finance the advance, and in the absence of such evidence a rate approximating to the Special Account rate[13] was selected. Some lenders will have no difficulty in proving what they paid for their funds, for example, from the money market, and higher rates are likely to be awarded where such evidence is presented and accepted. Even when the rates have been determined, the calculation of interest to reflect the loss of use of capital is likely to prove troublesome where the borrower has made payments of both capital and contractual interest. In some cases, the computerised records of the lender will permit an accurate calculation of interest to be made. In others, a broad brush approach will be necessary.[14]

10–156   There may be rare cases where the lender is able to prove that funds available to it for lending were limited, and that had it received a proper valuation it would not have lent to the borrower, but to a different and identified borrower who would have paid full contractual interest, but whose demand for finance from the lender could not be satisfied. In such circumstances, there would be the evidential basis for an argument by the lender that contractual interest should be awarded to reflect the loss of use of such capital. Recovery would be subject to such loss being reasonably foreseeable. This possibility was alluded to by Lord Lowry in *Swingcastle*:

> "In the absence of any evidence as to how the lenders financed the loan or evidence showing how the money, if not lent to the borrowers, could have been profitably employed . . . ",[15]

a reference to the analysis of Neill L.J. in the Court of Appeal[16] that he had cited with approval:

> "The lender could be awarded a sum equivalent to the amount he would have earned by way of interest on another loan if he had had the money available for this purpose. In my view, however, such an award should not be made in the absence of evidence that the money lent would have been used for another transaction. This evidence would have to be directed to proving an unsatisfied demand for loans and I anticipate that such evidence might seldom be forthcoming. Moreover, even if evidence of a lost transaction were available, I see no reason why the interest should be at the default rate rather than at the ordinary rate provided for in a standard contract for this type of business . . . "[17]

---

[11] *ibid.* at 239. For criticism of this decision, see Dugdale, "Causation and the professional's responsibility" (1991) 7 P.N. 78.

[12] *ibid.* at 239.

[13] Or its predecessor, the Short Term Investment Account rate.

[14] But note *Brandeis Goldschmidt & Co Ltd v Western Transport Ltd* [1981] Q.B. 864.

[15] [1991] 2 A.C. 223 at 239.

[16] [1990] 1 W.L.R. 1223, CA.

[17] Cited by Lord Lowry, [1991] 2 A.C. 223 at 230, approved at 237.

(b) Assessment of the scope of the duty. An apparent consequence of the way   **10–157**
in which damages were assessed in *Swingcastle* was that valuers bore the risk of
a fall in the property market, but conversely acquired an advantage when the
property market was rising. In a falling market, the price achieved for a property
disposed of by a mortgagee in possession will generally be lower, and consequently the difference between the sum advanced in reliance of the negligent
valuation, and the recovery by way of disposal of the property will be greater
than in a static market. In addition, it may take longer to sell property in such a
market, and so the period over which interest is awarded to reflect the loss of use
of capital may be longer. In a rising market, the consequences of a negligent
valuation will be mitigated, and even extinguished, as the rise in the market
brings the value of the property up towards the negligent valuation. In such a
market, the value of a claim can diminish to the point where there is little
commercial benefit in commencing proceedings.

The UK property market experienced a prolonged period of sustained growth   **10–158**
in the latter part of the 1980s, with a variety of established and new lending
institutions competing to lend funds to support dealing in property. This period
of rapid increase in values was followed by a severe market depression in the
early 1990s. Although property market fluctuations had been experienced
before,[18] the degree to which the property market collapsed was exceptional and
on this occasion (unlike the 1970s) the effect was not masked or mitigated by
high inflation. A consequence of the nature and extent of the collapse was that
lenders sought to recover some of their very substantial property lending losses
from allegedly negligent valuers and solicitors. They sought to avoid this consequence, and the case which finally determined the issue of who should bear
such losses was *BBL v Eagle Star*.[19] The practical effect of the decision was that
valuers were not held to be responsible for losses occasioned by the fall in the
property market. As set out above,[20] the House did this by finding that, in the
ordinary case, the scope of the duty undertaken by a valuer, whether in contract
or in tort, did not extend to losses occasioned by a subsequent fall in the property
market. Lord Hoffmann, giving the sole speech, stated:

> "The calculation of loss must . . . involve comparing what the plaintiff has lost as a
> result of making the loan with what his position would have been if he had not made
> it. If for example the lender would have lost the same amount of money on some other
> transaction, then the valuer's negligence has caused him no loss. Likewise if he had
> substantially overvalued the property so that the lender stands to make a loss if he has
> to sell the security at current values, but a rise in the property market enables him to
> realise enough to pay off the whole loan, the lender has suffered no loss."[21]

---

[18] "In 1972 the plaintiffs, in common with other finance houses, were obliged to raise their limits.
This was because much land development and speculation was then going on and inflation was
running high. There was a great deal of money in hand; interest rates were low in the first part of the
year. Finance houses, or some of them, so it was said, were almost falling over one another in their
eagerness to lend it."
per Watkins J., in *Singer & Friedlander Ltd v John D. Wood & Co* [1977] 2 E.G.L.R. 84.
[19] [1997] A.C. 191.
[20] See paras 10–113 *et seq.* above.
[21] [1997] A.C. 191 at 217G.

In this passage it is made clear that whilst it is the lender that in the ordinary course must bear the burden of a fall in the property market, the valuer also takes the benefit of any rise in the property market. Such a rise will reduce or extinguish any recoverable damages. Lord Hoffmann justified this by confirming that if the market rises, it reduces or eliminates the loss which the lender would otherwise have suffered. However, if it falls, "it may result in more loss than is attributable to the valuer's error. There is no contradiction in the asymmetry".[22] That loss did not fall within the scope of the valuer's duty of care.

10–159   The distinction between the "no-transaction" and "successful transaction" cases was declared to be "quite irrelevant to the scope of the duty of care" and "not based on any principle and should . . . be abandoned."[23] In either case, the negligent valuer is responsible for the loss suffered by the lender in consequence of having lent upon an inaccurate valuation. However, the House of Lords did not go so far as to say that the distinction was of no practical use. On the contrary, Lord Hoffmann conceded that the distinction had "a certain pragmatic truth" when it came to calculating the lender's loss. He conceded that, faced with a "no transaction" claim, the most likely alternative to be advanced by a negligent valuer was a "successful transaction" simply because of the difficulty in proving what else the lender would have done with the money. Despite Lord Hoffmann's injunction to abandon the distinction, it is a distinction that will naturally and necessarily arise from the evidence in most cases and will require a specific finding of fact to enable the calculation of damages to take place. In *South Australia Asset Management Corp v York Montague Ltd*, the House of Lords dismissed the appeal, yet May J. had carried out a conventional "no transaction/ successful transaction" analysis. The practicality of the distinction was adverted to by Lord Lowry in *Swingcastle Ltd v Gibson*[24] and Lord Hoffmann did not criticise the earlier decision; on the contrary, he invoked it as an example of the distinction he was making between the measure of damages for a breach of duty and the measure for a breach of warranty.[25]

10–160   The House of Lords dealt briefly with a number of other cases and submissions. Apart from the question of interest, the decision in *Baxter v FW Gapp & Co Ltd*[26] to award the whole of the loss suffered by the lender did not on its facts offend against the above principle.[27] The principle of causation that a claimant's reasonable attempt to cope with the consequences of the defendant's breach of duty does not break the causal connection between the breach of duty and the ultimate loss was reaffirmed.[28] The "cushion" theory was rejected. This theory involved calculating what the lender would have lost if a loan, of the same proportion of the true value of the property as the actual loan bore to the reported value, had been made. This permitted the lender to claim some of the losses

---

[22] [1997] A.C. 191 at 218B.
[23] *ibid.* at 218C.
[24] [1991] 2 A.C. 223 at 238F, and see para.10–154 above.
[25] [1997] A.C. 191 at 216G.
[26] [1938] 4 All E.R. 457, Goddard L.J.; [1939] 2 K.B. 752, CA.
[27] [1997] A.C. 191 at 217C.
[28] *ibid.* at 219A. Examples cited in support by Lord Hoffmann included *County Personnel (Employment Agency) Ltd v Alan R Pulver & Co* [1987] 1 W.L.R. 916; and *Hayes v James Charles Dodd* [1990] 2 All E.R. 815. It was in the latter case that Staughton L.J. first described and named the distinction between "no transaction" and "successful transaction" cases.

caused by a fall in the market but limited to the proportion represented by the "cushion". Lord Hoffmann commented that:

> "there seems no justification for deeming him, in the teeth of the evidence, to have been willing to lend the same proportion on a lower valuation".[29]

In so saying, Lord Hoffmann once again indicated that evidence as to whether the case was "no transaction" or "successful transaction" would be necessary. Only such evidence could provide the answer to whether the lender would indeed have lent nothing with a competent valuation, that being "the teeth of the evidence" which would make a cushion calculation involving the assumption that a lesser but proportionate loan would have been made, absurd. An argument that the rights acquired by the lender should be valued at the date of the loan, and compared with the amount of the loan, was rejected. Although such a procedure would ignore subsequent market movements, it would also ignore all subsequent events. Except in cases where all the loss caused by the breach could properly be quantified at once, the calculation of damages was bound to be affected by the extent to which loss in the future had to be estimated at the date of trial.[30] The House of Lords also rejected the argument that the damage falling within the scope of the duty should be limited to the excess over the highest non-negligent valuation, rather than the excess over the correct valuation. Lord Hoffmann said:

> "In deciding whether or not [the valuer] has been negligent, the court must bear in mind that valuation is seldom an exact science and that within a band of figures valuers may differ without one of them being negligent. But once the valuer has been found to have been negligent, the loss for which he is responsible is that which has been caused by the valuation being wrong. For this purpose the court must form a view as to what a correct valuation would have been. This means the figure which it considers most likely that a reasonable valuer, using the information available at the relevant date, would have put forward as the amount which the property was most likely to fetch if sold upon the open market. While it is true that there would have been a range of figures which the reasonable valuer might have put forward, the figure most likely to have been put forward would have been the mean figure of that range. There is no basis for calculating damages upon the basis that it would have been a figure at one or other extreme of the range."[31]

The "cap" theory whereby the lender's damages were limited to the amount of the overvaluation, was also rejected, but in so doing, Lord Hoffmann noted that in practice the application of the "cap" was generally likely to produce the same result as the requirement that loss should be a consequence of the valuation being

10-161

---

[29] [1997] A.C. 191 at 219G.

[30] *ibid*. at 220G.

[31] *ibid*. at 221G. The argument rejected by the House of Lords had never received judicial support. For example, in *United Bank of Kuwait v Prudential Property Services Ltd* [1994] 2 E.G.L.R. 100, the negligent valuer argued that the starting point for any assessment of damages was the difference between the highest non-negligent valuation and the defendant valuer's negligent valuation. Gage J. preferred the submission of the claimant that the starting point was the correct valuation, as found by the judge. The claimant had contracted to obtain from the defendant the correct valuation, not the highest non-negligent valuation.

wrong.[32] This was because the usual consequence would be that the lender had made an advance which was thought to be secured to a correspondingly greater extent. This is illustrated by the actual result in each of the three appeals before the House of Lords, where in each case the "cap" theory provides the same answer as that given by Lord Hoffmann.[33]

(i) *South Australia Asset Management Corp v York Montague Ltd.* The negligent valuation of a development site in 1990 was £15m, and a loan of £11m was made to a joint venture partnership. The actual value of the property in 1990 was £5m. In 1994 the property was sold for £2.477m. May J. quantified the loss at £9,753,000 and deducted 25 per cent for contributory negligence. The consequence of valuation being negligently wrong was that the lenders had £10m less security than they thought. If the lenders had had this margin, they would have suffered no loss. So the whole loss of £9,753,000 (less 25 per cent) was within the scope of the valuer's duty. The appeal was accordingly dismissed.

(ii) *United Bank of Kuwait Plc v Prudential Property Services Ltd.* The negligent valuation of the property in 1990 was £2.5m, a loan of £1.75m was made. In fact, in 1990 the actual value of the property was between £1.8m and £1.85m. In 1992 the property was sold for £950,000. Gage J. calculated the loss (including unpaid interest) at £1,309,000. Applying the principle that damages were to be limited to the consequences of the valuation being wrong, the lender had £700,000 or £650,000 less security than was thought. As this sum was less than the amount ordered by Gage J., the appeal was allowed, and the damages were reduced to the difference between the valuation and the correct value. In default of agreement as to what the correct value was, the case was remitted to Gage J. for decision on the basis of the facts called at trial. The important question of interest was not dealt with, and adjourned *sine die*.

(iii) *Nykredit Mortgage Services Ltd v Edward Erdman Group Ltd.* The negligent valuation in 1990 was £3.5m, and a loan of £2.45m was made. The actual value of the property in 1990 was £2m. In 1993 the property was sold for £345,000. Judge Byrt Q.C. calculated the loss at £3,058,000. Submissions by the lender based on what would have happened if the valuer had provided accurate information was held not to be the basis of the valuer's liability.[34] The appeal was allowed. The damages were the difference between £3.5m and the true value at the date of the valuation of £2m: £1.5m.

---

[32] [1997] A.C. 191 at 219H.
[33] *ibid.* at 222B. The three cases were *South Australia Asset Management Corp v York Montague Ltd*, May J., unreported April 6, 1995; *United Bank of Kuwait Plc v Prudential Property Services Ltd* [1994] 2 E.G.L.R. 100, Gage J.; [1995] Q.B. 375, CA; *Nykredit Mortgage Services Ltd v Edward Erdman Group Ltd*, Judge Byrt Q.C. sitting as a judge of the Queen's Bench Division, unreported, October 1, 1993. An appeal on liability in the latter case was heard subsequent to the appeal on damages: [1996] 1 E.G.L.R. 119, CA.
[34] *ibid.* at 222H.

Although the House of Lords rejected the "cap" argument, in practice the **10–162**
following steps appear to be required when calculating damages in a case where
a lender sues a valuer in respect of an admitted or proved negligent over-
valuation:

1. Distinguish between a duty on a valuer to provide information for the
   purpose of enabling a lender to decide upon a course of action, and a duty
   to advise a lender as to what course of action should be taken. In the
   absence of express contractual terms most, if not all, negligent valuation
   cases will be classified as negligent information cases.[35] If the case is one
   of the provision of negligent information, the procedure below is appropriate, which will limit damages to the foreseeable consequences of the
   information being wrong. If the case is one of negligent advice, the
   procedure adopted by the Court of Appeal in *BBL*[36] is appropriate, and the
   defendant will be liable for all the foreseeable loss which is a consequence
   of the claimant having acted on such advice.

2. Calculate the lender's actual loss. This is a conventional *Swingcastle*-type
   calculation of capital outlay less capital receipts, and loss of use of capital
   less income receipts. It will include losses caused by any fall in the
   property market. This will produce a number of heads of damage, for
   example irrecoverable losses on the capital sum lent, loss of use of the
   capital, and costs and expenses of repossession.[37]

3. Calculate the lender's hypothetical loss. This is an assessment on the basis
   that the lender's claim is for breach of warranty, that is damages assessed
   on the basis that the information provided by the valuer was accurate. This
   determines the position the lender would have been in if the valuation had
   been accurate, rather than a negligent over-valuation, and the lender had
   acted upon the same by lending the sum in fact lent. This will also produce
   a number of heads of damage, which may or may not be the same as those
   resulting from the actual loss calculation.

4. Damages are then calculated by deducting from the actual losses those
   hypothetical losses which would have been incurred in the event that the
   negligent valuation had been correct. The remaining losses fall within the
   scope of the duty that was breached. They may fairly be described as
   consequences of the valuation being wrong.

In almost every case, the same result will be obtained simply by comparing the
amount of the negligent overvaluation with the actual loss, calculated in the
conventional manner. Where the overvaluation exceeds the actual loss, the actual

---

[35] See the discussion at para.10–118 above in relation to the approach of the High Court of Australia
in *Kenny & Good v MGICA* [1999] H.C.A. 25.
[36] [1995] Q.B. 375, and see the guidance in *Swingcastle Ltd v Alastair Gibson* [1991] 2 A.C. 223.
These conventional ("transaction" and "no transaction") calculations have been set out in
para.10–154 at fn.5.
[37] It is important to note that it will be the actual outlay made by the lender which will be important
in this calculation. Monies retained by a lender (for example in "blocked" deposit accounts) will be
left out of a calculation of loss—see *Arab Bank v John D Wood* [2000] Lloyd's L.Rep. P.N. 173 at
198.

loss is awarded. Where the actual loss exceeds the overvaluation, the award is, for practical purposes, "capped" at the amount of the overvaluation. This is illustrated by comparing the result in *South Australia Asset Management Corp v York Montague Ltd* with that in *United Bank of Kuwait Plc v Prudential Property Services Ltd.*[38] It is, however, important to bear in mind that the House of Lords has rejected the concept of a "cap", and that the calculation described above is a measure of damages. This has consequences for example, for interest, which is applied to measures of damages, but would not be applied subsequent to an arbitrary "cap" on the claimant's damages.[39]

10–163   The above approach to the assessment of damages was confirmed by the House of Lords in the subsequent case *Nykredit Mortgage Bank Plc v Edward Erdman Group Ltd (No.2).*[40] In that case the question was as to the date upon which interest should run,[41] but the House of Lords also took the opportunity further to explain the substantive judgment delivered in the speech of Lord Hoffmann. Lord Nicholls went through the steps necessary to identify whether a lender had sustained "measurable, relevant loss":

> "The first step . . . is to identify the relevant measure of loss. It is axiomatic that in assessing loss caused by the defendant's negligence the basic measure is the comparison between (a) what the plaintiff's position would have been if the defendant had fulfilled his duty of care and (b) the plaintiff's actual position. Frequently, but not always, the claimant would not have entered into the relevant transaction had the defendant fulfilled his duty of care and advised the plaintiff, for instance, of the true value of the property. When this is so, a professional negligence claim calls for a comparison between the plaintiff's position had he not entered into the transaction in question and his position under the transaction. That is the basic comparison."[42]

Lord Nicholls illustrated the workings of this "basic comparison" in the context of a lender's action in respect of a negligent valuation:

> "The basic comparison is between (a) the amount of money lent by the plaintiff, which he would still have had in the absence of the loan transaction, plus interest at a proper rate, and (b) the value of the rights acquired, namely the borrower's covenant and the true value of the overvalued property."

The reference to interest in this context is to interest representing the cost to the lender of the money advanced, which would be claimed as special damages. Lord Nicholls then emphasised that in accordance with the opinion of Lord Hoffmann in the substantive judgments in the case the valuer was liable for the adverse consequences, flowing from entering into the transaction, which were attributable to the deficiency in the valuation. If the "basic comparison" demonstrated a loss, then it was necessary to enquire further and see whether all or part of that loss

---

[38] See para.10–161, above.
[39] Judges have, on occasions, referred to "the cap" as a convenient short-hand—see, e.g. *Preferred Mortgages Ltd v Countrywide Surveyors Ltd* [2006] P.N.L.R. 154 at 171, where the deputy judge calculated the damages that would have been awarded had he not found against the lender on liability.
[40] [1997] 1 W.L.R. 1627.
[41] As to which see para.10–164 below.
[42] [1997] 1 W.L.R. 1627 at 1631D.

was the consequence of the deficiency in the security. He answered this inquiry by showing that, in the ordinary case, the damages will be "capped" to the extent of the over-valuation:

> "Typically, the answer to this further inquiry will correspond with the amount of the loss as shown by the basic comparison, for the lender would not have entered into the transaction had he been properly advised, but limited to the extent of the over-valuation."[43]

(c) Interest on damages. The issue in *Nykredit* was as to the date from which interest should be payable to a lender making a claim against a negligent valuer following *BBL*. Lord Nicholls noted that the Supreme Court Act 1981, s.35A(1) (as amended) provided for statutory interest on damages for all or part of the period between the date when the cause of action arose and the date of judgment. This raised the question of when the lender's cause of action. Following his analysis of the decision in *BBL*,[44] Lord Nicholls concluded that this was the point when "relevant, measurable loss" occurred. This would be when the cause of action accrued and would provide the date from when statutory interest should run. Given that the "basic comparison" required an evaluation of the difference between the money lent plus interest and the value of the rights acquired by the lender, Lord Nicholls acknowledged that the borrower's covenant had to be evaluated. Lord Nicholls realised that this enquiry might produce "evidential and practical difficulties" and that the quantification of the lender's loss would be less certain and less satisfactory for being carried out prior to the disposal of the security property. However, valuing the worth of the borrower's covenant was not expected to be "unduly troublesome" and some guidance was provided.[45] On the facts of the case the borrower's covenant was worthless, there was immediate default and the amount lent at all times exceeded the true value of the property. The cause of action therefore arose at the date of completion of the loan in March 1990 and by December 1990 the lender had suffered its full allowable loss of £1.4m. Interest was awarded at the agreed rate of 0.4 per cent above LIBOR from December 1990. Lord Hoffmann pointed out[46] that the loss reached £1.4m by December 1990 because of the cost to the lender of the funds it had advanced to the borrower. The lender could not claim statutory interest from the date of the loan in March 1990 because such an award would be double recovery.

10–164

Mortgagor's covenants to repay. *Nykredit* emphasised the potential importance of a proper assessment of a borrower's covenant both to the date from which interest should run and to the date from which the primary limitation period should run in tort.[47] This issue had received only limited judicial attention prior to the decision in *Nykredit*. In *Swingcastle v Gibson*, the mortgagors'

10–165

---

[43] [1997] 1 W.L.R. 1627 at 1632A–B.
[44] See para.10–163 above.
[45] *ibid.* at 1632C.
[46] *ibid.* at 1637H.
[47] See para.10–009 above.

covenants to repay the money borrowed had been worthless and therefore irrelevant to the final calculation.[48] In *Eagle Star Insurance Co Ltd v Gale and Power*,[49] the covenants had, however, proved significant. Relying on the defendant surveyors' negligent survey and valuation the claimants advanced £3,015 to a purchaser on the security of a house and the personal covenants of himself and his wife. The purchaser further covenanted to reduce the mortgage by £1,500 to be received in the near future. Owing to subsidence the house was worth only £1,600. The claimants claimed damages measured by the difference between the valuation given and the actual value and contended that the covenants were irrelevant as *res inter alios acta*. Devlin J. rejected the argument, holding that the transaction had to be looked at as a whole and that the security could not be separated from the personal covenants. He considered that the only method of assessing damages was to calculate what the claimants would have obtained had they realised their security. Since the two main items of security, the value of the house, £1,600, and the covenant to repay the £1,500 together amounted to £3,100, quite apart from the personal covenants, the claimants would not have lost their money. He nevertheless concluded that it was not a case for nominal damages since something like illness might intervene, and the claimants were awarded £100 in damages to indemnify them against the possibility of not being able to recover their money from the mortgagor.

10–166   Devlin J.'s decision in the *Eagle Star* case may be contrasted with the Court of Appeal's decision in *London and South of England Building Society v Stone*.[50] In that case the claimant building society in reliance upon the defendant valuer's report advanced to borrowers £11,880 secured by way of mortgage on a house purchased by the latter for £14,880. The advance was repayable over 25 years and the legal charge contained covenants by the borrowers to repay the advance and to keep the property in repair. Subsequently the house was found to be in danger of collapse through subsidence. The borrowers could not afford to finance the necessary repairs themselves and looked to the claimant for assistance. The cost of repairs was originally estimated at £14,000. The claimant decided to proceed with repairs which eventually cost £29,000. The borrowers maintained payments under the legal charge throughout and after completion of the repairs sold the house for £26,500 and repaid the outstanding advance. Russell J. at first instance[51] held that the defendant had been negligent and awarded the claimant damages of £8,880 assessed by: (a) taking the difference between £11,880, the sum advanced, and what would have been advanced given a competent valuation, namely nil, and (b) crediting against that difference the sum of £3,000 being his assessment of the value to the building society of the borrowers' personal covenants. The judge refused to award the full cost of repairs in damages on the basis that the society had acted unreasonably in spending so much on repairs. The claimant successfully appealed against the deduction of £3,000. But the Court of Appeal was divided on the issue. Both O'Connor and Stephenson L.JJ. held that

---

[48] See, for another example, *Corisand Investments Ltd v Druce & Co* [1978] 2 E.G.L.R. 86.
[49] (1955) 166 E.G. 37.
[50] [1983] 1 W.L.R. 1242, CA.
[51] Reported in [1982] 1 E.G.L.R. 139.

the claimant was under no duty to mitigate its loss by seeking to enforce the borrowers' covenants. Stephenson L.J. said:

> "the valuer is not merely asking the court to take account of what has actually been paid to the lenders; he is requiring the lenders to have taken action in claiming payment from the borrowers; and it is one thing for a wrongdoer to claim the benefit of a benefit obtained by the wronged party under a contract with another; it is quite another thing—and, in my judgment, a far stronger thing—to claim the valuation of the chance of such a benefit which the wronged party has deliberately chosen not to take. In that case it seems to me the wrongdoer must show that the wronged party's reasoned choice to waive his contractual rights against the third party is unreasonable in the ordinary course of events in the particular field of commercial business and in all the circumstances (it may be something special) of the particular case."[52]

Sir Denys Buckley, dissenting, considered that the £3,000 was correctly deducted and endorsed the approach of Devlin J. in *Eagle Star Insurance Co Ltd v Gale and Power*[53] in taking into account the borrowers' personal covenants. O'Connor L.J. considered that the latter case was wrongly decided, but Stephenson L.J. expressed no view on the matter.

After *Nykredit*, the correct approach to the proper valuation of a borrower's **10–167** covenant was considered in the context of a dispute as to limitation, by the Court of Appeal in *DnB Mortgages v Bullock & Lees*.[54] In February 1990 the claimant had loaned £136,000 on the security of a house valued at £170,000 by the defendants. The borrowers continued to make mortgage payments until January 1991, when they defaulted. The writ was issued in May 1996. The judge found that the value of the house in May 1990 (i.e. six years before the writ) was £130,000 whilst the mortgage debt had, by then, reached £140,080, with the result that the value of the borrowers' covenant was critical in deciding whether or not the lender had suffered loss within the limitation period. The judge had found (largely taking into account the subsequent default) that the value of the covenant was not, by May 1990, worth as much as £10,000 with the result that the claim was statute barred. This conclusion would not, however, have been apparent at May 1990. Robert Walker L.J., giving the sole substantive judgment, commented that it was not entirely clear from the speeches in the House of Lords, how the borrowers' covenant was to be valued.[55] He stated that there was some degree of tension in *Nykredit*:

> "between the approach of valuing the mortgagor's covenant as part of a bundle of rights comprised in a marketable security (and to be valued as the market would have valued it at the time, without hindsight) and the approach of valuing it on fundamentals (that is, on the objective evidence, available when the case is heard, of the true state of affairs at the valuation date) . . . In this case the two approaches might lead to different results. So far as they would lead to different results, I consider that the mortgagor's covenant

---

[52] [1983] 1 W.L.R. 1242 at 1262, Stephenson L.J. rejected the argument that the borrowers' obligation to repay was so collateral or remote as to be disregarded altogether in measuring the lender's loss, *ibid.* at 1261.
[53] (1955) 166 E.G. 37.
[54] [2000] Lloyd's L.Rep. P.N. 290.
[55] *ibid.* at 295, col.1.

had to be valued on the evidence available to the deputy judge, restricted though it was, as to the true facts".[56]

It is now clear that the value of a borrower's covenant will be taken into account in deciding whether a lender has suffered loss following a negligent valuation. It will sometimes be necessary for a court to consider carefully the true financial circumstances of a borrower (rather than how they appeared at the time). This may widen the scope of the relevant enquiry.[57]

10–168   **(d) Contributory negligence by lender.** Because the lender's recovery is confined to the consequences of the incorrect valuation, two questions arose as to the proper relationship between the damages recoverable from a valuer and contributory negligence by a lender. The first was whether, given that the lender could not recover more than the consequences of the information as to value being wrong, it was possible to argue that matters unrelated to such a loss, for example, imprudent lending practices, should not be considered negligence that has contributed to the loss at all. The second was as to whether any deduction should be applied to the entire loss suffered by the lender or only to such damages for which the valuer was found liable. Following the decision of the House of Lords in *Platform Home Loans Ltd v Oyston Shipways Ltd*,[58] the law appears to be that any negligence which contributes to the decision to lend can be considered to be contributory negligence but that any reduction will be applied to the lender's total loss. In that case, the defendants negligently valued a property for £1.5m in 1990, when its true value was £1m. The overvaluation was therefore £500,000. The claimant lent the borrower £1.05m. The property was sold in 1993 for £435,000. The claimant sought to recover their overall loss of £680,174 in damages from the valuers. Jacob J. held that the claimants were responsible for £40,000 of their loss because of a failure to mitigate the same, and had been a total of 20 per cent contributorily negligent in two respects. First, in lending 70 per cent of a loan to value ratio on a loan over £1m, and secondly for failing to require the borrower properly to complete the mortgage application form. After further argument, Jacob J. rejected the argument that the two forms of contributory negligence should be treated differently, because one impinged on the duty of the valuer to provide the correct valuation, whereas the other did not. The contributory negligence of 20 per cent was applied across the board and judgment for £489,398 plus interest was given. On appeal,[59] Morritt L.J. concluded that the lender's overall loss was suffered partly as a result of its own fault and partly as a result of the fault of the valuers. The claim against the valuers, although limited in accordance with *BBL* was nonetheless a claim "in respect of" the overall loss suffered by the lender for it was an element in or ingredient of

---

[56] [2000] Lloyd's L.Rep. P.N. 290 at 295, col.1–2.
[57] For a post-*Nykredit* example of a case where a judge found that a borrower's covenant was worthless at the time of making a loan, see *Mortgage Corp v Lambert* [1999] Lloyd's L.Rep. P.N. 947. This conclusion was not challenged on the appeal, reported at [2000] P.N.L.R. 820, which considered s.14A of the Limitation Act 1980—see further para.10–009, above.
[58] [2000] 2 A.C. 190.
[59] [1998] Ch. 466.

that loss. On that basis, the court entitled to apportion the damages in respect of the claim by reference to the lender's share of responsibility for the overall loss. However, the Court of Appeal allowed the defendants' appeal and applied the 20 per cent deduction to the overvaluation of £500,000, rather than to the overall loss with the result that damages of £400,000 were awarded.

The House of Lords, by a majority of four to one, allowed the lender's appeal. **10–169** Lord Hobhouse concluded[60] that the totality of the claimants' loss was partly caused by the defendant's fault and therefore the case came within the scope of s.1(1) of the 1945 Act. The court then had to form a view as to what was just and reasonable having regard to the claimant's share in the responsibility for the damage and to reduce the claimants' recoverable damages accordingly. Lord Hobhouse concluded that the reduction of 20 per cent should be applied to the total loss (by then adjusted to £611,748) to give a figure of £489,398. That sum was below the overvaluation of £500,000 and therefore in accordance with *BBL* it was not just and equitable to make any further reduction. The House of Lords concluded that to apply the percentage reduction to the amount of the over-valuation would give rise to "unacceptable results".[61] The House of Lords criticised the methodology adopted by the trial judge and the reasoning adopted by the Court of Appeal, stating that the latter had "in effect" applied the same deduction twice over.

Evaluating a lender's negligence. A potentially negligent valuer will usually **10–170** wish to consider whether the lender can properly be criticised as imprudent. To succeed in a plea of contributory negligence,[62] the negligent valuer will have to prove that some lack of care on the part of the lender (in respect of the lender's business interests) caused or contributed to the loss, despite the negligent valua-tion. It is often a matter of importance in lending cases to appreciate that it is the conduct of the lender which has to be attacked. Thus a Defendant cannot impute the knowledge of, for example, a lender's solicitor to the Claimant for the

---

[60] [2000] 2 A.C. 190 at 211A.
[61] See *per* Lord Hobhouse at 211G and Lord Millett at 214H.
[62] The Law Reform (Contributory Negligence) Act 1945, s.1(1) provides:
"Where any person suffers damage partly of his own fault and partly of the fault of any other person or persons, a claim in respect of that damage shall not be defeated by reason of the fault of the person suffering the damage, but the damages recoverable in respect thereof shall be reduced to such extent as the court thinks just and equitable having regard to the claimant's share in the responsibility for the damage . . . "
In *UCB Bank Plc v David Pinder Plc* [1998] 2 E..G.L.R. 203; [1998] P.N.L.R. 398, the defendant valuer was in voluntary liquidation and took no part in the trial. A defence alleging contributory negligence by the claimant lender had, however, been served. The claimant attended to prove its case and contended that no effect could be given to the defence of contributory negligence, in the absence of attendance by the valuer, irrespective of the state of the evidence. It was held that since the defence had been pleaded it must be resolved on the evidence, however, all the evidence was tendered by the claimant, and the court was not under a duty to look at documents in the trial bundle which were not so tendered and were therefore not evidence of their contents. In the circumstances contributory negligence had not been established. Given the width of the discretion now afforded to the English courts as to the receipt of documentary evidence, this decision is unlikely to dissuade a court which wishes to do so from investigating the same. For further discussion of the topic of contributory negligence, see H. Evans, "Contributory negligence by lenders" (1998) 1 P.N. 42.

purpose of establishing contributory negligence.[63] Such a plea, if successful, can result in a finding of contributory negligence, a lack of causation of loss or a concurrent cause of loss. In order to constitute contributory negligence, the lender's fault must be causative of the damage in respect of which the lender claims. Fault which is not causative of damage is irrelevant for this purpose.[64] In general it is probably fair to say that the English courts became more receptive to allegations of contributory negligence in the spate of litigation that followed the property collapse in the early 1990s. This may have had something to do with the large amount of evidence which the courts received of what appeared to be a generally lax attitude towards the making of loans. The question of what conduct constitutes imprudent lending will usually be a matter for expert evidence and must be related to the nature of the business carried on by the lender. Different considerations may apply to the lending practices of a building society to those of a secondary bank. For example the Building Societies Act 1986, unlike the Banking Acts, restricts the primary security of a building society to that of freehold or leasehold estate and imposes an obligation of prudence on building societies. A building society, unlike a bank, is regulated by the Building Societies Commission, which from time to time issues DCE letters[65] and Prudential Notes that it expects to be observed, and the auditor of a building society has a statutory obligation to report to the Commission in respect of compliance.[66]

10–171   In *Housing Loan Corp v William H Brown*,[67] the Court of Appeal re-stated, albeit obiter, the correct approach to be adopted when considering contributory negligence by a lender, in that case in respect of a non-status loan. The court upheld the judge's conclusion that the lender had fundamentally misunderstood the nature of the valuations being provided to it with the result that there was no reliance.[68] However, it expressly considered the correct approach to contributory negligence in case the matter went further. Having found on the evidence instances of fault on the part of claimant which partly caused the damage suffered, the trial judge had to determine the causative potency of each particular factor, as well as its blameworthiness. On the facts, the Court of Appeal agreed with the trial judge that a 75 per cent reduction for contributory negligence would have been appropriate.

10–172   An issue which often arises is as to the relevance of internal controls to the assessment of fault on the part of a lender. It is suggested that their relevance may

---

[63] See *Preferred Mortgages Ltd v Countrywide Surveyors Ltd* [2006] P.N.L.R. 154 at 172; [2005] EWHC 2820 for an express statement to this effect. For the facts of the case see fn.22 to para.10–095 above.

[64] See, for example, the Scottish case of *Leeds Permanent Building Society v Walker, Fraser & Steele*, 1995 S.L.T. (Sh Ct) 72 at 77. The pursuers sued valuers in respect of an allegedly negligent overvaluation of a domestic property. The pursuers confined their claim to losses resulting from negligence on the part of the valuers, and excluded all losses resulting from a forced sale on repossession. The defenders pleaded contributory negligence in that the pursuer had failed to give adequate consideration to the financial circumstances of the borrowers. These were struck out by the sheriff on the ground that "the averments of fault attributed to the pursuers are not causative of the loss which the pursuers seek in this action".

[65] "Dear Chief Executive" letters, a method whereby matters of concern to the Building Societies Commission may be communicated to a building society relatively informally.

[66] See Wurtzburg and Mills, *Building Society Law* (looseleaf, Stevens & Sons), Ch.18.01.

[67] [1999] Lloyd's Rep. P.N. 185 at 198.

[68] See para.10–122 above.

be twofold: (a) in identifying precautions which will usually be sensible; and (b) as an evidential tool to help a court assess whether a lender has approached the making of a loan with care and common sense. Thus in *Housing Loan Corp v William H Brown*,[69] Hirst L.J. approved a passage from Mantell J.'s judgment where he had found that the lender should have complied with its own manual so as to act on the lower of two valuations, as being correct:

> "I fully accept that it is not necessarily negligent for an autonomous body to step outside self imposed controls. What matters is whether or not the controls were in place for a sensible purpose. I judge it to be a sensible precaution to act upon the lower of two valuations. It is a precaution which acknowledges the difficulty in making an accurate valuation of certain properties and it is intended to safeguard the interests of the lender. In my judgment, it was foolish in the extreme to ignore Mr Wagstaff's valuation."

The argument that once there is reliance on a negligent valuation there can be **10–173** no contributory negligence has been expressly rejected in a number of reported cases. This is inconsistent with the decision in *Platform Home Loans v Oyston*[70] and has received no significant judicial support.[71] A related question that has arisen is whether the lavishness of the security extinguishes the obligation to act as a prudent lender. The tendency of the courts has been to permit a lender a degree of latitude where there appears to be ample security whilst still reserving the right to find that a lender has acted imprudently. Thus in *Housing Loan Corp v William H Brown*,[72] Hirst L.J. was not prepared to go so far as to characterise the very act of non-status lending as being imprudent whilst nonetheless finding that, in the circumstances of the instant case, caution was called for. In *Preferred Mortgages Ltd v Countrywide Surveyors Ltd*,[73] the Judge would have held that the Claimant was contributorily negligent in lending over 80 per cent of valuation given the unusual nature of the property.[74] Similarly in *Kendall Wilson Securities v Barraclough*,[75] it was held that reasonable prudence in a solicitor lender advancing trust funds dictated an investigation into the affairs of the prospective borrower, rather than total reliance on the security. Contributory negligence in respect of this failure was assessed at one-third. In *HIT Finance v Lewis & Tucker Ltd*,[76] the negligent valuation was £2,200,000. The advance secured on the property was £1,540,000. Wright J. commented[77]:

---

[69] [1999] Lloyd's L.Rep. P.N. 185 at 199.
[70] [2000] 2 A.C. 190.
[71] The argument was rejected in the following reported cases: *Kendall Wilson Securities v Barraclough* [1986] 1 N.Z.L.R. 576; *PK Finans International (UK) Ltd v Andrew Downs & Co Ltd* [1992] 1 E.G.L.R. 172; *United Bank of Kuwait v Prudential Property Services Ltd* [1994] 2 E.G.L.R. 100; and *Housing Loan Corp v William H Brown* [1999] Lloyd's L.Rep. P.N. 185 at 198.
[72] [1999] Lloyd's L.Rep. P.N. 185 at 199.
[73] [2006] P.N.L.R. 154.
[74] The claim was rejected on liability—see further fn.22 to para.10–095, above. The judge would not have allowed any of the other allegations of contributory negligence which were made which had the effect of saying that the claimant should have realised that it was the victim of a mortgage fraud.
[75] [1986] 1 N.Z.L.R. 576, NZCA.
[76] [1993] 2 E.G.L.R. 231, Wright J.
[77] *ibid.* at 235E.

"The cushion apparently provided by the property, on the basis of the defendant's valuation was accordingly £660,000. In such circumstances, even if the borrowers turned out to be complete men of straw, the lenders were entitled to regard themselves as being more than adequately covered not merely in respect of the capital sum lent, but also any likely loss of interest, and indeed all the costs and expenses likely to be incurred in foreclosing upon and realising the security . . . it is very difficult to see how such a lender could properly be characterised as being imprudent."

However, the judge continued:

"I am not suggesting that the prudent lender, merely because he has the comfort of more than adequate security, is entitled to shut his eyes to any obviously unsatisfactory characteristics of the proposed borrower",

and gave as an example of a lender not acting prudently the making of a loan in circumstances where he had substantial reason for suspecting the honesty of the borrower.[78] In *Cavendish Funding v Henry Spencer*,[79] the Court of Appeal allowed a deduction of 25 per cent where a lender had decided to lend on the basis of a higher rather than a lower valuation of a property. The court made it plain that the reduction was limited because of the gross nature of the original over-valuation and that, even if the valuer had been given the opportunity to reconsider, the over-valuation would still have been gross.[80]

10–174　　The appropriate reduction for proved contributory negligence is, inevitably, a matter which will vary from case to case. It is possible only to give examples of reductions which have been made by reference to the facts of particular cases. In general criticisms tend to fall under the following general heads: (a) lending too much as a proportion of valuation; (b) failing properly to consider a valuation; (c) failing to make sufficient enquiries as to the status of a borrower; (d) failing to ascertain the purposes for which the loan was required; (e) failing to pick up on warning signs apparent from the transaction. In *Arab Bank v John D Wood*,[81] the Court of Appeal considered that the trial judge should reassess the issue of contributory negligence in the light of the lender's successful appeal on primary liability. It considered that the judge should consider issues arising from the facts: (1) that proper consideration had not been given as to how the loan was to be serviced and repaid at the end of its relatively short term; and (2) that the lender had not looked below the "bottom line" at the note of caution being sounded as to the valuation. On the facts, the court rejected a suggestion that the lender had been substantially at fault in failing to enquire as to the reasons for an apparent discrepancy between the purchase price and the valuation. Phillips J. in *BBL* at

---

[78] This general approach was followed by Gage J. in *United Bank of Kuwait v Prudential Property Services Ltd* [1994] 2 E.G.L.R. 100 at 106.

"It seems to me that it is important to bear in mind Mr Justice Wright's observation that the nature and extent of enquiries required may vary widely, and that an important factor will be the margin of safety provided by the security offered."

[79] [1998] P.N.L.R. 122.

[80] *ibid.* at 134.

[81] [2000] Lloyd's L.Rep. P.N. 173 at 204–206.

first instance[82] assessed contributory negligence by the bank at 30 per cent, on the grounds that the bank should have sought and obtained explanations for the substantial differences between the purchase prices of the properties and the reported values:

> "a prudent bank would have required a specific and convincing explanation for the disparity in each case before relying on the property as the sole source of repayment of a loan of 90 per cent of the valuation".

In *Nyckeln Finance Co Ltd v Stumpbrook Continuation Ltd*,[83] a commercial property was sold for £23.5m but after exchange of contracts was valued by Jackson-Stops & Staff at £30.5m. The claimant finance company then lent £21m to the purchaser. The loan, although only 70 per cent of the valuation, was 90 per cent of the sale price. Judge Fawcus, sitting as a judge of the High Court, held the claimants to be 20 per cent to blame for proceeding without satisfying

---

[82] [1994] 2 E.G.L.R. 108 at 137. In *Cavendish Funding Ltd v Henry Spenser & Sons Ltd* [1996] P.N.L.R. 554, the Court of Appeal held that the claimants' failure to review two valuations of the proposed security property received from different valuers at the same time in the light of their differences was negligent, and reduced the damages by 25%. In *UCB Bank Plc v David Pinder Plc* [1998] P.N.L.R. 398, the claimant lender was held one-third to blame, principally for failing properly to investigate the value of the borrower's covenants. In *The Mortgage Corp v Halifax (SW) Ltd* [1999] Lloyd's Rep. P.N. 159 at 178, the claimant lender was held 20% to blame, for failing to make proper enquiries as to the borrower's ability to service a very large loan and as to whether there were arrears on any existing or previous mortgages. In *Omega Trust & Co Ltd and Banque Finindus v Wright Son & Pepper (No.2)* [1998] P.N.L.R. 337, Douglas Brown J. held that the failings of Omega were
> "extensive and take this case well outside the range of percentage contributory negligence arrived at in a number of recent cases . . . on the remarkable facts of this case I assess the responsibility of Omega for failing to protect its own interests at 70 per cent".

The instances of Omega's failure included ignoring the obvious inadequacies of the valuation reports; failing to act on their knowledge of the borrowers' adverse financial history; failing to appreciate that a clearing bank had declined the loan proposal; failing to give even ordinary scrutiny to the borrower's accounts; disregarding the contents of an Infolink search which revealed county court judgments against the director of the borrower and 46 recent credit searches against the borrower; most seriously in failing to challenge the director of the borrower who had certified to Omega that there was no litigation outstanding or threatened against himself or the borrower when in fact as Omega knew from the Infolink search there were already three judgments in existence with two more pending; failing to verify the freehold property allegedly owned by the director of the borrower; and failing to obtain banking references. In *First National Commercial Bank Plc v Andrew S. Taylor Commercial Ltd* [1997] P.N.L.R. 37, the surveyor was held not negligent, but if negligence had been found, then the trial judge would have found contributory negligence by the claimant lender of 75% in failing to make adequate enquiries of the borrower and the guarantor. In *Speshal Investments Ltd v CorbyKane Howard Partnership* [2003] EWHC 390, the defendant valuers made grossly negligent valuations which, as the lender knew although the valuer did not, exceeded the amount of the purchase price of the properties concerned and were also called into question by other valuations (of which both the valuer and the lender were aware). Hart J. found that the lenders should have either withdrawn from the transaction or made further inquiries. He assessed the appropriate reduction for contributory negligence as 20 per cent stating:
> "A higher reduction would in my view be unjust. A valuer who gives negligent valuations as egregiously wrong as these cannot lightly be excused any part of his prima facie liability to pay for the full consequences of his negligence. A lesser reduction would risk appearing to be a recognition of an almost token nature only of some minor carelessness on the claimant's part."

[83] [1994] 2 E.G.L.R. 143. Jackson-Stops & Staff ceased trading on October 31, 1992 and changed its name to Stumpbrook Continuation Ltd. The name "Jackson-Stops & Staff" was then assigned to others.

themselves as to the reliability of the valuation. In *South Australian Asset Management Corp v York Montague Ltd*,[84] May J. held the bank negligent in failing to reassess the risk classification of the proposed loan as rigorously as the bank's own procedures required, negligent in failing to insist upon direct instructions from the bank to the valuer, as the bank's lending policy required, and causing or permitting a muddle to develop as to the extent to which certain joint venture proposals did or might contribute to an open market valuation. Making a "broad common-sense judgment" of the bank's share in the responsibility for this damage, May J. deducted 25 per cent from the loss.

10–175　　(e) **Joint responsibility.** Two practical questions which commonly arise in relation to claims against valuers by lenders are: (a) whether such a valuer is entitled to seek contribution from defaulting borrowers pursuant to the Civil Liability (Contribution) Act 1978; and (b) how damages should be apportioned as between a valuer and another defendant who has caused the making of the loan. The first issue was addressed by the Court of Appeal in *Howkins v Tyler and Powell*,[85] where the court decided that the lender's claims against the valuer and the borrower were not in respect of the same damage.

> "'The damage' for which the respondents are liable is that the [lender] has not been paid the sum of money contractually due. The damage for which the appellants were liable was the damage to the [lender] in lending money that the lender would not otherwise have lent. The respective formulations of the 'damage', it seems to me, carry the case outside the scope of section 1(1) of the 1978 Act."[86]

He went on to explain his reasoning as follows:

> " . . . it seems to me that a simple test should be applied to identify a claim capable of being one to which the 1978 act can apply. That test is this: Suppose that A and B are the two parties who are said to be liable to C in respect of 'the same damage' that has been suffered by C. So C must have a right of action of some sort against A and a right of action of some sort against B. There are two questions that should then be asked. If A pays C a sum of money in satisfaction, or on account, of A's liability to C, will that sum operate to reduce or extinguish, depending upon the amount, B's liability to C? Secondly, if B pays C a sum of money in satisfaction or on account of B's liability to C, would that operate to reduce or extinguish A's liability to C? It seems to me that unless both of those questions can be given an affirmative answer, the case is not one to which the 1978 Act can be applied".[87]

As the quantification of the claim for damages against the valuer should take into account the proper value of the borrower's covenant to repay, it could not be said that the above questions could be answered in the affirmative.

10–176　　The second question was considered by Hart J. in *Ball v Banner*,[88] where contribution was sought by the sponsors of an Enterprise Zone Property Trust from the property advisors to the issue in respect of allegedly negligent mis-

---

[84] [1995] 2 E.G.L.R. 219.
[85] [2001] P.N.L.R. 634. The Court of Appeal expressly left open an issue which had been inadequately pleaded as to whether the valuers were entitled to be subrogated to the lenders rights against the borrowers.
[86] *per* Sir Richard Scott V.C. at 639.
[87] *ibid.* at 639–640.
[88] [2000] Lloyd's L.Rep. P.N. 569.

statements attributed to the property advisors.[89] The sponsors accepted that they were liable in respect of all losses suffered by the investors whilst, following the reasoning in *BBL*, the losses recoverable against the property advisors were limited to those which were attributable to the specific statements attributed to them. Hart J., following the approach of the House of Lords in *Platform Home Loans v Oyston*,[90] found that the property advisors were, nonetheless, liable in respect of the same damage as that in respect of which the sponsors were liable. He drew attention to some apparently surprising consequences of his reasoning,[91] but nonetheless concluded that he was obliged to consider apportionment first before considering the application of the *BBL* "cap". The practical effect is that if a valuer and another defendant each cause a lender to make a loan of £1m and are held to be equally responsible for the same, the result of contribution proceedings will be determined by the relationship between the extent of the valuer's over-valuation and his degree of responsibility. Thus if the over-valuation is only of £250,000, that will be the limit of damages recoverable from him. If, on the other hand, the over-valuation is of £750,000, the recoverable damages will be £500,000.

(iv) *Overvaluation for Vendor*

Damages where there has been a negligent overvaluation for a vendor were **10–177** considered in *Kenney v Hall, Pain and Foster*,[92] the relevant facts of which are set out above.[93] Relying upon the defendants' overvaluation of his own house and expecting the proceeds of sale to cover him, the claimant vendor incurred expenditure on buying and improving two other properties greatly in excess of what he would have incurred if he had been properly advised. The proceeds proved insufficient and were considerably exceeded by the expenditure. The parties accepted that the measure of damages should be assessed on the principle stated by Lord Denning M.R. in *Esso Petroleum Co Ltd v Mardon*[94]:

> "You should look into the future so as to forecast what would have been likely to happen if he had never entered into this contract; and contrast it with his position as it is now as a result of entering into it."

The practical problems inherent in deciding what would have happened were avoided by the parties agreeing that if properly advised the claimant would have purchased another house at a cheaper price than the two actually purchased. Damages were thus arrived at by comparing the hypothetical with the actual situation.[95]

(v) *Undervaluation for Vendor*

Where as a result of a negligent undervaluation property is sold at a price less **10–178** than that which should have been achieved if proper advice had been given, the

---

[89] An appeal on the issue of liability was allowed.
[90] [2000] 2 A.C. 190.
[91] [2000] Lloyd's L.Rep. P.N. 569 at 585.
[92] [1976] 2 E.G.L.R. 29.
[93] See para.10–080.
[94] [1976] Q.B. 801.
[95] [1976] 2 E.G.L.R. 29 at 35.

normal measure of damages is the difference between the price at which the property was sold and the price that should have been achieved.[96] The usual difficulty is in assessing what the property would have sold at if there had been competent advice. This is usually done on the basis of "loss of a chance".[97] This is illustrated by *John D Wood & Co v Knatchbull*.[98] The property had been marketed and sold, in accordance with advice from estate agents, at a price of £1.5m. Although this advice was competent, the judge found that the agents were in breach of duty in failing to inform the vendor, prior to exchange of contracts, that they had learned that a nearby property was on the market at £1.95m. The judge further found that had this knowledge been imparted, the property would not have been sold for £1.5m but that there was a 66 per cent chance that it would have sold at £1.7m and awarded damages accordingly.

10–179   Surveyors may also be liable in respect of a negligent failure to sell development property for its true worth, because advice to maximise the development potential, for example to obtain appropriate planning permission, had not been given. In such circumstances the claimant may recover damages in respect of a loss of profit which he might, but for the negligence of the surveyor, have made. The claimant does not need to prove that on balance the profit would have been made, but the lost chance of such profit has to be substantial, and more than a mere speculative possibility. In *Montlake v Lambert Smith Hampton*,[99] the judge concluded that, if properly advised, Wasps Rugby Club would have received the difference between the value placed upon its ground and that which should have been put given a competent valuation. Much of the difference in value was explained by the fact that the negligent valuation did not take into account the possibility (although not the certainty) of obtaining planning permission, but the judge regarded the "chance" of obtaining planning permission as being only a check on his assessment of quantum. The judge also rejected, on the facts, suggestions that the claimants had been contributorily negligent in failing to minimise the loss that they had suffered. He emphasised that the club had been entitled to proceed on the basis that they had a proper valuation.

In *Obagi v Stanborough (Developments) Ltd*,[1] by contrast, the claimant failed to prove that even if the defendants had used their best endeavours, their chances of obtaining the necessary planning permission were more than a speculative possibility. The judge therefore awarded the claimants £5 in nominal damages in respect of the defendant's breach of contract. In *Weedon v Hindwood, Clarke and Esplin*,[2] the defendant valuers failed to take into account a change in the law.[3] In consequence they recommended to the claimant trustees for acceptance an amount lower than the actual amount due as compensation on compulsory

---

[96] Note *Garland v Ralph Pay and Ransom* [1984] 2 E.G.L.R. 147 (an estate agent's case).
[97] See further para.11–261, below.
[98] [2003] P.N.L.R. 351; [2002] EWHC 2822.
[99] [2004] EWHC 938.
[1] *The Times*, December 15, 1993; (1993) E.G.C.S. 205. For a discussion of *Allied Maples Group Ltd v Simmons Simmons* [1995] 1 W.L.R. 1602, CA, see para.11–263, below.
[2] (1974) 234 E.G. 121.
[3] See *West Midland Baptist (Trust) Association (Inc) v Birmingham Corp* [1968] 2 Q.B. 188, CA; [1970] A.C. 874, HL: relevant date for assessment under s.2, r.5, of the Acquisition of Land (Assessment of Compensation) Act 1919 held to be the date on which the work of reinstatement might reasonably have been commenced and not, as previously thought, the date of the service of the notice to treat.

purchase of the property concerned. Damages were awarded representing the difference between the value of the land, which under the statute would have been the price due from the acquiring authority, and the amount recommended for acceptance. In the last case the amount recommended for acceptance was the same as the price paid by the purchaser.

The measure of damages resulting from an alleged undervaluation of property **10–180** in the context of divorce proceedings was discussed in the Scottish case *of Shenkin v DM Hall Son.*[4] The pursuer obtained a valuation from the defenders of certain property he owned, advising the valuers that their report was needed for the purposes of his divorce settlement, and CGT. The property was valued by them at £115,000 and subsequently, as part of an overall divorce settlement, the pursuer transferred the property outright to his wife. When the pursuer's liability to CGT was finally determined, he discovered that the property was in fact worth £174,000 at the date of the defenders' valuation. The pursuer claimed that if he had been aware of the true value of the property, he would not have transferred the same to his wife and would have incurred no liability to CGT, or as part of the overall divorce settlement, he would have retained £60,000 of assets elsewhere. The pursuer claimed the £60,000 from the defenders, who sought to defeat the claim prior to trial by arguing that the underlying assumption was that the same divorce settlement would have been reached had the property been valued at £174,000, and that such an assumption was prima facie erroneous, in any event under Scots law.[5] Lord Osborne rejected the argument, deciding that it was open to the pursuer to try and quantify his loss at trial on the basis that the same settlement would have been achieved, as a question of fact.

(vi) *Other Work*

Breach of warranty. If the unlikely event that a surveyor expressly warrants **10–181** the accuracy of his valuation of property,[6] the measure of damage is the difference between the situation the lender is in, having relied upon the valuation, and the situation the lender would have been in, had the warranted valuation been true. In other words, the lender is to be put in as good a position against the valuer as he would have been in against the borrower had the property had the value warranted by the valuer at the time of the valuation. Thus property market movements subsequent to the warranted valuation may be taken into account in determining what position the lender would have been in at any particular time, for example when the mortgaged property was in fact sold. If a valuation is warranted, it may well have a profound effect on the quantum of damages recoverable from the surveyor.

Rent reviews. Surveyors are frequently instructed to act for their clients in **10–182** negotiations and arbitrations arising out of periodic rent reviews. There is no simple measure of damage, the factual circumstances being capable of considerable variation. In *County Personnel (Employment Agency) Ltd v Alan R Pulver*

---

[4] Unreported, January 23, 1996, Lord Osborne.
[5] See Family Law (Scotland) Act 1985, ss.8–10.
[6] Such a situation is only likely to occur where a surveyor provides his valuation on a standard form of report provided by, for example, a finance company and the form contains an express warranty.

& *Co*,[7] a solicitors' negligence action arising out of advice given in respect of an underlease with an unusual rent review clause, the Court of Appeal rejected the argument that the court was bound to apply the diminution in value rule, and instead held that on the facts, the costs of extrication from the situation in which the claimant company found itself as a consequence of the negligent advice were recoverable. In *Rajdev v Becketts*,[8] the defendant surveyors negligently failed to make representations on behalf of the claimant shopkeeper to an independent surveyor appointed by the president of the RICS to determine the rent of the shop. During negotiations the landlord had proposed an annual rental of £7,000, the claimant £4,600. The independent surveyor fixed a rent of £9,250. At trial the judge held that the proper open market rent at the review date was £7,000, and that the difference in value between a lease with a rent of £9,250, and one with a rent of £7,000, was £8,100. This was the sum awarded to the claimant in damages, a claim for additional sums in respect of a reduction in the value of the business carried on at the shop being rejected as containing elements of double recovery.[9]

10–183   The complications that can arise from applying the *restitutio* principle to rent review cases is well illustrated by *Knight v Lawrence*.[10] This involved a negligent failure by a receiver to serve trigger notices in respect of the rent reviews for a number of tenanted properties. When the properties came to be sold by the mortgagees the prices realised were less than they would have been had the rents been increased in accordance with the rent review provisions. The Vice-Chancellor said:

> "The starting point is to try to ascertain what would have been the sale price of the properties if on December 11, 1984, the rent reviews had properly taken place. That involves two stages. First, to find out at what the reviewed rents would properly have been agreed. Second, to find out, taking into account the higher rent payable as a result of such review, what increased price would have been obtainable for each of the properties."[11]

Having considered the expert evidence, and concluding that the properties would have achieved £35,000 more than they did, the Vice-Chancellor said:

> "But that is not the measure of loss recoverable by the claimants. The damages have to be assessed on the basis that they are to be put back into the position they would have been in had the sale taken place on that basis, that is to say if there had been a total realisation of £275,300. It is at that stage that the real complications are capable of arising."[12]

The Vice-Chancellor then sought to identify precisely how the additional sum would have been utilised, in order to put the claimants into the position they

---

[7] [1987] 1 W.L.R. 916. For further analysis, see Ch.11, para.11–276.
[8] [1989] 2 E.G.L.R. 144.
[9] The calculation of damages resulting from the negligent conduct of rent reviews was also considered in *Corfield v DS Bosher & Co* [1992] 1 E.G.L.R. 163; and *CIL Securities Ltd v Briant Champion Long* [1993] 2 E.G.L.R. 164.
[10] [1991] 1 E.G.L.R. 143.
[11] *ibid.* at 147.
[12] *ibid.* at 148.

would have been in, but for the negligence of the defendant.[13] This analysis could not be completed without the making of further enquiries.

(vii) *Inconvenience and Discomfort*

A contract breaker is not in general liable for any distress, frustration, anxiety, **10–184** displeasure, vexation, tension or aggravation which his breach of contract may cause to the innocent party. In *Watts v Morrow*,[14] Ralph Gibson L.J. stated:

> "As to the law, it is, in my judgment, clear that the claimants were not entitled to recover general damages for mental distress not caused by physical discomfort or inconvenience resulting from the breach of contract."

This follows what has become known as the rule in *Addis v Gramophone Co Ltd*,[15] to the effect that damages for mental distress are not recoverable in contract. In *Farley v Skinner (No.2)*,[16] the House of Lords[17] relaxed the rule so as to permit a claimant, who had specifically requested a surveyor to check on possible aircraft noise at a house that he was considering purchasing, to recover damages for inconvenience and discomfort when he discovered that the house was underneath one of the holding stacks for Gatwick Airport. Stuart-Smith L.J. had summarised the general reasons for refusing to permit damages to be recoverable as follows:

> "it is a policy decision that the law does not give compensation for distress, frustration, anxiety, displeasure, vexation or aggravation. But the reasons are understandable. In an action for damages for personal injury, the claimant must prove either physical injury or a recognised psychiatric injury. Distress and annoyance will not do. In an action against a professional man for negligent advice or information the damage that is normally within the contemplation of the parties is financial loss. But if the unreported defects have to be made good while the purchaser is living in the house, it is readily foreseeable that for a relatively short time whilst that work is being done, great physical discomfort and inconvenience of living on a building site, without facilities and in cramped conditions will be experienced. The court can appreciate the physical conditions and award an appropriate sum. But annoyance, vexation, etc., is entirely subjective; moreover as this case illustrates, I find it difficult to see how it can be assessed. The claimant decided, for his own personal reasons, not to move house. So if he is to be awarded damages for annoyance, over what period is it to be assessed: It is not just for a relatively short period while physical defects to the property are made good . . . "[18]

---

[13] The position of the claimants would have been radically different, because with the extra sum, a variety of debts could and would have been met, the discharge of which would have left the claimants free of liability.

[14] [1991] 1 W.L.R. 1421 at 1440.

[15] [1909] A.C. 488.

[16] House of Lords, October 11, 2001 overturning the decision of the Court of Appeal at [2000] P.N.L.R. 441.

[17] A two-judge court had, initially, been convened which disagreed. Mummery and Stuart-Smith L.J.J. formed the majority when the court re-convened, whilst Clarke L.J. dissented.

[18] *ibid.* at 449.

The majority had also rejected the suggestion that the contract was one which fell within the exceptional category of contracts to provide pleasure, relaxation or peace of mind. Following the decision in the architects case of *Knott v Bolton*,[19] Stuart-Smith L.J. pointed out that the contract as a whole, as distinct from one relatively minor part of the overall instructions, could not be said to fall within such a category.[20]

10–185 This reasoning was rejected by the House of Lords. Lord Steyn held[21] that the case has to be approached on the basis that the instruction to investigate aircraft noise formed a major part of the contract. It was thus permissible to award modest damages to effect the express term of the contract. He also rejected an argument that by failing to move out of the property, the claimant had lost the right to claim the damages.[22]

10–186 Where the interest of the claimant in the property is commercial, rather than domestic, no award of general damages will be made.[23] Moreover, where the inconvenience and discomfort consequent upon the necessary repairs has been taken into account in the valuation evidence presented to the court, it is likely that no further sum by way of general damages will be awarded,[24] to avoid double recovery.

10–187 The argument that damages for inconvenience should not be awarded was earlier expressly rejected by the Court of Appeal in *Perry v Sidney Phillips & Son*.[25] That case might be thought to be authority for a wider ambit of claim, encompassing distress and anxiety even where there were no specific instructions to the surveyor.[26] In that case Lord Denning M.R. stated:

> "It seems to me that Mr Perry is entitled to damages for all the vexation, distress and worry which he has been caused by reason of the negligence of the surveyor. If a man buys a house—for his own occupation—on the surveyor's advice that it is sound—and then finds out that it is in a deplorable condition, it is reasonably foreseeable that he will be most upset. He may, as here, not have the money to repair it and this will upset him all the more. That too is reasonably foreseeable. All this anxiety, worry and distress may nowadays be the subject of compensation."[27]

---

[19] (1995) 11 Const. L.J. 315—see para.9–318 above.
[20] [2000] P.N.L.R. 441 at 451 and see also *per* Mummery L.J. at 456.
[21] At para.18.
[22] At para.26.
[23] See the dicta of Staughton L.J. in *Hayes v Dodd* [1990] 2 All E.R. 815. In *Michael v Ensoncraft Ltd* [1990] E.G.C.S. 156, a claim against a negligent contractor by a landlord for damages for inconvenience in respect of damage to a house acquired for investment purposes, was rejected by the trial judge on the ground that the interest of the claimant in the premises was a commercial one.
[24] *Bigg v Howard Son & Gooch* [1990] 1 E.G.L.R. 173 at 1474.
[25] [1982] 1 W.L.R. 1297.
[26] The case has, indeed, been taken to be authority for such a proposition. For example, in *Bolton v Puley* [1982] 2 E.G.L.R. 138, an action in respect of a negligent survey that omitted reference to an unstable boundary wall, Talbot J. expressly relied on *Perry v Sidney Phillips* when awarding general damages of £500:
> "Finally there is the plaintiff's claim for damages for distress, vexation and worry resulting from the alarming cost he was advised was necessary to put the wall into a stable and safe condition. There had been the worry, for instance, of possible consequences to the public from a possible collapse of the wall. As pointed out in *Perry v Sidney Phillips & Son*, the damages under this heading may not be very substantial . . . "
[27] [1982] 1 W.L.R. 1297 at 1302.

It is, however, clear from the facts of the case,[28] and from the judgments of Oliver and Kerr L.JJ., that the general damages awarded in *Perry v Sidney Phillips & Son* were in respect of the physical discomfort suffered by the claimant, and that the case is therefore in accordance with the general proposition set out above.[29] Oliver L.J. summarised this part of the claimant's claim as being for:

" . . . vexation, that is the discomfort and so on suffered by the plaintiff as a result of having to live for a lengthy period in a defective house which for one reason or another was not repaired over the period between the acquisition by the plaintiff and the date of trial".[30]

Kerr L.J. commented:

"So far as the question of damages for vexation and inconvenience is concerned, it should be noted that the judge has awarded these not for the tension or frustration of a person who is involved in a legal dispute in which the other party refuses to meet its liabilities. If he had done so, it would have been wrong, because such aggravation is experienced by almost all litigants. He has awarded these damages because of the physical consequences of the breach which were all foreseeable at the time."[31]

Where properly made, a claim for general damages will not be reduced solely **10–188** because a less impecunious claimant could have mitigated or extinguished such physical discomfort by carrying out repairs. The defendant firm in *Perry v Sidney Phillips & Son* argued, on the basis of *The Liesbosch*,[32] that the claim for general damages by the claimant was an attempt to recover additional damages as a result of his poverty, that ought not to succeed. Oliver L.J. held that a proper formulation of the test to be applied was: "Was it reasonable in all the circumstances for the claimant not to mitigate his damage by carrying out the repairs which were required?"[33] and concluded on the facts[34] that the claimant's decision was reasonable. Kerr L.J. agreed and went further, drawing attention to the waning force of the decision in *The Liesbosch*.[35] Where, however, it would have been reasonable to carry out repairs earlier, then such damages will be either reduced or extinguished. In *Cross v David Martin and Mortimer*,[36] Phillips J. refused the

---

[28] The claimant was obliged to live in the property which he could not afford to repair, with serious defects in the roof, which leaked, and offensive smells from the defective septic tank.

[29] See para.10–181, above. This was the conclusion reached by Ralph Gibson L.J. in his analysis of *Perry v Sidney Phillips & Son* in *Watts v Morrow* [1991] 1 W.L.R. 1421 at 1440.

[30] [1982] 1 W.L.R. 1297 at 1304.

[31] *ibid.* at 1307.

[32] [1933] A.C. 449.

[33] [1982] 1 W.L.R. 1297 at 1305.

[34] Oliver L.J. noted at 1305 that the defendants "were strenuously resisting any liability at all for the repairs, and denying that they were responsible", and also that the finding of fact by the trial judge, that the claimant's conduct had been reasonable, could not be challenged in the Court of Appeal.

[35] *ibid.* at 1307:

"it seems to me that the authority of what Lord Wright said in *The Liesbosch* . . . is consistently being attenuated in more recent decisions of this court, in particular in *Dodd Properties (Kent) Ltd v Canterbury CC* [1980] 1 W.L.R. 433 and what was said there, at pp.458–459 by Donaldson L.J. If it is reasonably foreseeable that the claimant may be unable to mitigate or remedy the consequences of the other party's breach as soon as he would have done if he had been provided with the necessary means to do so from the other party, then it seems to me that the principle of *The Liesbosch* . . . no longer applies in its full rigour".

[36] [1989] 1 E.G.L.R. 154.

claimants general damages in respect of the distress and inconvenience caused by the existence for four years of a hole in their hall floor, on the ground that steps to mitigate such inconvenience could have been taken earlier. The judge did, however, award damages to reflect the considerable inconvenience that would be caused when repairs were carried out.

10–189   **Injury to health.** General damages for injury to health were awarded in *Allen v Ellis & Co*,[37] a professional negligence claim against a surveyor. The claimant obtained a structural survey that negligently described the garage as being in a satisfactory condition. In fact the roof of the garage was old, brittle, fragile and in need of replacement. About a year after moving into the property, the claimant climbed onto the garage roof to investigate the source of a leak. When he stepped onto the roof he fell through[38] and was injured. The claimant's case was that had the report properly described the roof he would either have had it replaced, or would not have attempted to climb on to it to investigate its condition. Garland J. considered the question of reliance and causation:

> "The negligence must operate to an extent which is beyond *de minimis*, but it need not be the only operative cause; it can be one among others, provided it is substantial. Remoteness is a matter of the requisite degree of foreseeability."[39]

On the facts of the case, the judge found the defendants negligent:

> "'The garage . . . is in satisfactory condition' is more than a failure to inform; it is positive misinformation. If the roof had been accurately described . . . he would never have been in peril of suffering the injuries which he did, in fact, suffer. I take the view that there is a sufficient causal connection, and also a sufficient degree of deemed foresight in the defendants at the time when they were negligent, connecting their negligence with what in fact occurred. In the circumstances, I take the view that the damages for personal injuries are not too remote from that negligence."[40]

An allegation of contributory negligence was dismissed, the judge pointing out that the claimant was a layman when it came to buildings. Accordingly, agreed general damages of £8,000 were awarded to the claimant.

10–190   In the Scottish case of *Drinnan v CW Ingram & Sons*,[41] the defender surveyors failed in their attempt to dismiss as too remote the pursuer's claim for injury to health. The point was only considered as a preliminary issue and the pursuer's right to damages for such injury was not finally determined. Damages for personal injury were included in the award in *Collard v Saunders*.[42] As a result of the defendant solicitor's advice, the claimant employed an unqualified surveyor. The defendant admitted liability. From the judgment it is clear that damages were considered as if the case were a surveyor's negligence case.

---

[37] [1990] 1 E.G.L.R. 170 at 73; *ibid.* at 172.
[38] Despite attempting to spread his weight with a piece of wood.
[39] *ibid.* at 172.
[40] 1967 S.L.T. 205.
[41] (1972) 221 E.G. 797.
[42] *per* Barry J. in *Bailey v Bullock* [1950] 2 All E.R. 1167 at 1172.

Quantum of damages. The quantum of awards of general damages for   **10–191**
inconvenience and discomfort has been variously described as "not extravagant", "not excessive but modest",[43] "may not be very substantial",[44] "modest",[45] and "restrained".[46] Each case must be decided on its own facts, and there
is no conventional award for such damages. The Court of Appeal has stated that
the proper approach is to fix a modest sum for the amount of physical discomfort
endured having regard to the period of time over which it was endured.[47] An
examination of reported cases suggests a broad tariff within which most negligent domestic survey cases will fall. Awards that fall well outside the ordinary
range will have to be capable of justification by reference to the facts of the case,
or be liable to be set aside on appeal.[48]

Examples of such awards include: *Roberts v J Hampson & Co*,[49] where a   **10–192**
young engaged couple of modest means were awarded a total of £1,500 in
respect of "extreme" and "particularly upsetting" disruption caused to them in
having to move out of their home during repairs; *Cross v David Martin and
Mortimer*,[50] where the claimants were each awarded £500 in respect of the
"considerable inconvenience and dislocation" that would be caused to them by
repairs to the defective ground floor; *Steward v Rapley*,[51] where at first instance,
each claimant was awarded £1,000 in respect of the inconvenience and disturbance caused by remedial works made necessary by an extensive outbreak of
dry rot. The award was not challenged on appeal; *Bigg v Howard Son and
Gooch*,[52] where the claimants were awarded a total of £1,600 in respect of the
discomfort and inconvenience caused by the extensive works necessary to make
their home structurally sound; *Hipkins v Jack Cotton Partnership*,[53] where the
claimants were obliged to move out of their home during underpinning works,
and were awarded damages for the "worry and inconvenience on the lines of
Perry v Sidney Phillips & Sons. The claimants seek £1,000. I think that is on the
high side and award £750"[54]; *Watts v Morrow*[55] where the claimants' weekend
home required substantial works over a period of eight months to the roof,
windows and walls. The trial judge awarded each claimant £4,000. Bingham L.J.
stated that such an award "far exceeded a reasonable award for the injury shown

---

[43] *per* Lord Denning M.R. in *Perry v Sidney Phillips & Son* [1982] 1 W.L.R. 1297 at 1303.
[44] *per* Oliver L.J., *ibid.* at 1305.
[45] *per* Ralph Gibson L.J. in *Watts v Morrow* [1991] 1 W.L.R. 1421, 1443 and *per* Nourse L.J.
approving the description of the judge at first instance in *Patel v Hooper & Jackson* [1999] Lloyd's
L.Rep. P.N. 1 at 10.
[46] *per* Bingham L.J., *ibid.* at 1445.
[47] *per* Ralph Gibson L.J. in *Watts v Morrow, ibid.* at 1443. In *Farley v Skinner*, Lord Steyn expressly
accepted that awards should be modest and that the award of £10,000 in that case was "certainly
high" (at para.28).
[48] The Court of Appeal will apply the principles reiterated by the House of Lords in *Pickett v British
Rail Engineering Ltd* [1980] A.C. 136. See also the commentary in Kemp & Kemp, *The Quantum of
Damages* (Sweet & Maxwell), Vol.1, Ch.19.
[49] [1989] 2 All E.R. 504. A full report is at [1988] 2 E.G.L.R. 181.
[50] [1989] 1 E.G.L.R. 154.
[51] [1989] 1 E.G.L.R. 159.
[52] [1990] 1 E.G.L.R. 173.
[53] [1989] 2 E.G.L.R. 157.
[54] *per* Scott Baker J. at 160.
[55] [1991] 1 W.L.R. 1421.

to have been suffered". The Court of Appeal substituted £750 for each claimant.[56] In *George Buchanan v Newington Property Centre*,[57] the pursuers were obliged to move into rented accommodation for some eight months whilst extensive dry rot was eradicated. The rented accommodation was in a tall block of council-owned flats where the general level of social amenity was considerably less than that to which the pursuers were accustomed. The second pursuer was frightened to remain in the rented accommodation whilst the first pursuer was at work, and so she travelled into central Edinburgh most days. She consulted her doctor. Both pursuers became irritable with one another. Sheriff Scott was satisfied that:

> "the pursuers had a miserable time of it, over a period, as a result of Mr Quinn's breach of duty. Happily, they have recovered. I consider that proper awards of solatium are £800 for the first pursuer and £1,200 for the second pursuer".

In *Heatley v William H Brown Ltd*,[58] the claimants, a couple with three young children, were compensated for two years of having to live in premises that became wholly unsuitable for family living because of warnings of danger. Financial pressures prevented the family from moving out. Safe access to the only bathroom facilities available involved leaving the house. This inconveience was made much worse when the children were unwell and could not be taken outside. Eventually a portaloo was purchased and placed in the inner hall. The health of the second claimant was adversely affected and family relationships generally became strained. The judge awarded the first claimant £1,500, the second claimant £3,000. In *Ezekiel v McDade*,[59] the claimant purchased a property built using the "Bison" system. The defendant surveyor negligently failed to identify a serious defect involving a concrete purlin. This and other defects were not discovered until after the claimant had been made redundant, and had been forced to offer the property for sale as he could not maintain the payments due on his mortgage. The property remained unsold, the claimant and his family endured lengthy eviction proceedings, and after eviction were housed in unsatisfactory temporary accommodation for some 12 months, before being rehoused to a proper standard. The official referee awarded £6,000 general damages for inconvenience and distress.[60] The Court of Appeal reduced this sum to £4,000, Nourse L.J. commenting that:

> "the judge proceeded in part on a wrong basis, in that he overlooked the fact that the first claimant's financial difficulties and falling into arrears with his payments under the mortgage started before the house was put on the market and not after it failed to sell".

---

[56] Ralph Gibson L.J. commented at 1442:
  "the award was excessive even if the judge had directed himself correctly. It was very substantially more than the awards made in similar cases apart from the award by the same judge in *Syrett*".
The latter is a reference to *Syrett v Carr & Neave* [1990] 2 E.G.L.R. 161, where an appeal was settled before hearing.
[57] 1992 S.C.L.R. 583.
[58] [1992] 1 E.G.L.R. 289.
[59] [1995] 2 E.G.L.R. 107.
[60] [1994] 1 E.G.L.R. 255.

In *Patel v Hooper & Jackson*,[61] the Court of Appeal upheld an award of £2,000 to each of the claimants who had been obliged not to move into their new home and to endure a succession of moves to different sets of rented accommodation over a five-year period.[62] In *Holder v Countrywide Surveyors*,[63] an award of £2,000 was made to a claimant against a negligent surveyor where the claimant had to move out of accommodation and clean dirty man-hole covers.

(viii) *Incidental Expenses*

It has been the usual,[64] but not invariable,[65] practice of the courts to reimburse **10–193** claimants for the incidental expenses of taking reasonable action to deal with defects to the property, despite the fact that the measure of damage has not been the reasonable cost of carrying out such repairs. This has been described as "not perhaps entirely logical, but it is well established and seems [to me] not unreasonable".[66] The objection is that such expenses are an adjunct of the remedial works. If the latter are not recoverable, why the former? In *Patel v Hooper & Jackson*,[67] the Court of Appeal permitted the recovery of the costs of alternative accommodation when allowing the claimants to recover on the basis of the "costs of extrication".[68] The Court of Appeal has yet to rule on whether such damages

---

[61] [2000] Lloyd's L.Rep. P.N. 1.

[62] See also *Hoadley v Edwards* [2001] P.N.L.R. 965, where Evans-Lombe J. made an award of £5,000 to the claimants who had had to endure works of structural improvement which they had not anticipated. From the reported facts, this award appears to have been high.

[63] [2003] P.N.L.R. 29.

[64] In *Morgan v Perry* (1973) 229 E.G. 1737, the cost of investigating the defects was held recoverable. In *Fryer v Bunney* [1982] 2 E.G.L.R. 130, the claimants were awarded £500 compensation in respect of the shrinkage to carpets moved to permit works to eradicate damp to take place. In *Treml v Ernest W Gibson & Partners* [1984] 2 E.G.L.R. 162, it was agreed between the parties that the claimant was entitled to recover the cost of reasonable accommodation during the period whilst the repairs were carried out, together with the cost of the removal and storage of her furniture. The judge also allowed the claimant to recover the cost of shoring up the property pending repair, and additional interest paid as a result of the claimant having to increase his mortgage to pay for the repairs. These cases were followed in *Shaw v Halifax (SW) Ltd* [1994] 2 E.G.L.R. 95 at 99, where as part of a preliminary issue, the cost of items including storage of furniture, consulting engineers' report, and building surveyors' report were held to be recoverable, subject to proof that they did not form part of the repair costs. In *Republic International Trust & Co Ltd v Fletcher Ramos*, unreported, August 30, 2000, H.H.J. Havery Q.C. awarded £4,000 by way of damages for loss of use whilst repairs were carried out to a property which would not have been purchased but for a negligent survey report.

[65] For example, Judge Hicks Q.C. in *Bigg v Howard Son & Gooch* [1990] 1 E.G.L.R. 173 at 175 refused to award the claimants the cost of alternative accommodation during repairs, stating that such an award was consistent only with a claim where the cost of repair was recoverable as the primary head of damages, which was not the case. The learned judge concluded:

"... no separate award of damages for the cost of accommodation during repair is appropriate in cases of this kind, alternatively that if such an award is ever appropriate it is not so when the likely need for and probable cost of vacating the premises during repair, as foreseeable by a purchaser buying at the relevant date with knowledge of the defects, has been taken into account in assessing what price he would have been prepared to pay".

[66] *per* Phillips J. in *Cross v David Martin & Mortimer* [1989] 1 E.G.L.R. 154 at 159. The judge awarded £2,500 in respect of incidental expenses such as the cost of alternative accommodation for the period of the repairs, the cost of removing furniture to storage and bringing it back.

[67] [1999] Lloyd's L.Rep. P.N.

[68] See further para.10–149 above.

are recoverable when damages are limited to the diminution in value,[69] but an indication that such claims would be permitted was provided in *Sneesby v Goldings*.[70]

10–194   In *Broadoak Properties Ltd v Young and White*,[71] Judge Fox-Andrews Q.C. decided as a preliminary issue, subject to liability, the basis upon which damages should be assessed:

> "if expenses were reasonably incurred in investigating the true state of the premises this will be a recoverable head of damage. If and in so far as moneys were spent, e.g. on the front wall in respect of temporary works (whether building or professional costs) to prevent a nuisance or danger, these will be recoverable. Reasonable management time expended in respect of such investigation and temporary works will likewise be recoverable."[72]

In the Scottish case of *Hunter v J&E Shepherd*,[73] Lord Osborne refused to strike out a claim for the costs of alternative accommodation against a firm of surveyors on the ground that:

> "The courts were not bound by rigid rules in assessing what amounted to fair compensation (*Duke of Portland v Wood's Trustees*, 1962 S.L.T. 321), and where damages were sought for the difference between the price paid and the true value of defective property, costs associated with remedying the defects might also be recoverable, notwithstanding that the costs of the remedial works themselves were not recoverable (*Martin v Bell-Ingram*, 1986 S.L.T. 575 followed)."[74]

In the common situation of a negligent survey for a purchase of a property the purchaser has been held entitled to recover the following costs and losses incurred during the period of necessary repairs: the costs of alternative accommodation[75] and of furniture removal and storage[76]; loss of use of part of the

---

[69] The point was expressly left open by the Court of Appeal in *Watts v Morrow* [1991] 1 W.L.R. 1421, Ralph Gibson L.J. commenting at 1441 that:
    "We do not have to decide whether, if the claimant has to rent other accommodation during the carrying out of repairs, such costs will be recoverable in the absence of any contractual warranty as to the existence of defects requiring repairs, and I would reserve my decision upon it."

[70] [1995] 2 E.G.L.R. 102 at 105K. See para.10–147.

[71] [1989] 1 E.G.L.R. 263.

[72] *ibid.* at 267. In *Holder v Countrywide Surveyors* [2003] P.N.L.R. 29, the judge stated that although the logic of the statement by H.H. Judge Hicks in *Bigg v Howard Son and Gooch* [1990] 1 E.G.L.R. 173 was unassailable, nevertheless the courts had awarded damages for the costs of accommodation during repair and proceeded to make an award under this head.

[73] March 28, 1991, OH, G.W.D. 17–1043.

[74] For an echo of this reasoning in a solicitor's negligence action, see the judgment of Bingham L.J. in *County Personnel Ltd v Alan R. Pulver & Co* [1987] 1 W.L.R. 916 at 925.

[75] *Hood v Shaw* (1960) 176 E.G. 1291 (the argument that such costs were irrecoverable since the difference in value was the only damage was rejected); *Collard v Saunders* (1972) 221 E.G. 797. In *Grove v Jackman and Masters* (1950) 155 E.G. 182, the costs of alternative accommodation were awarded additionally to the cost of repairs. *Treml v Ernest W Gibson and Partners* [1984] 2 E.G.L.R. 162; *Cross v David Martin and Mortimer* [1989] 1 E.G.L.R. 154; *Hunter v J&E Shepherd*, March 28, 1991, OH, G.W.D. 17–1043; *Shaw v Halifax (SW) Ltd* [1994] 2 E.G.L.R. 95 at 99; *Republic International Trust & Co Ltd v Fletcher Ramos*, unreported, August 30, 2000. See also *Patel v Hooper & Jackson* [2000] Lloyd's L.Rep. P.N. 1 and para.10–147 above.

[76] *Grove v Jackman and Masters* (1950) 155 E.G. 182; *Hill v Debenham, Tewson and Chinnocks* (1958) 171 E.G. 835; *Treml v Ernest W. Gibson and Partners* [1984] 2 E.G.L.R. 162; *Cross v David Martin and Mortimer* [1989] 1 E.G.L.R. 154.

property[77] and loss of rent.[78] In the same situation the purchaser has also been held entitled to recover the costs of emergency supports,[79] investigating the defects,[80] expenditure upon wasted decorations and plastering,[81] management time[82] and even the cost of a minor item of repair.[83] In *Philips v Ward*,[84] Romer L.J. added, obiter, that if on learning of the real condition of the house the claimant had decided to leave and resell, he would have been entitled to recover from the defendant, in addition to the £4,000 diminution in value, his costs and expenses of moving in and moving out and of the resale.[85] In *Hardy v Wamsley-Lewis*[86] where the claimant did decide to leave and resell, solicitors' costs on re-sale were allowed, but not, surprisingly, solicitors' costs on purchase.[87]

In the Scottish case of *Cochrane v Sibbald & Graham*,[88] a number of less **10–195** common incidental expenses were claimed. The pursuer was moving from Scone to Dundee, with contractual entry set for July 1982, and actual entry planned for September 1982. Dry rot was discovered in September 1982 and so actual entry had to be postponed until repairs had been completed, which was not until May 1983. The previous house had been retained as the family home and commuting costs between Scone and Dundee were claimed, and allowed. The pursuer had mitigated his loss (the costs of alternative accommodation, including removal costs) by commuting. In addition, the pursuer recovered bridging loan interest incurred because the previous house had to be withdrawn from the market.

In attempting to apply the principle of *restitutio* in surveyors' negligence **10–196** actions, the courts have been less than scrupulous in differentiating between the different measures of damage in contract and tort claims. In most of the cases there is a mix of compensation for the loss of the bargain with the surveyor,[89] which results in an award of the overpayment in the purchase price, and an

---

[77] *Tremayne v T Mortimer Burrows and Partners* (1954) 165 E.G. 232; *Rawlings v Rentokil Laboratories Ltd* (1972) 223 E.G. 1947 (not strictly a surveyor's negligence case).
[78] *Freeman v Marshall & Co* (1966) 200 E.G. 777.
[79] *Treml v Ernest W Gibson and Partners* [1984] 2 E.G.L.R. 162; *Broadoak Properties Ltd v Young & White* [1989] 1 E.G.L.R. 263.
[80] *Morgan v Perry* (1973) 229 E.G. 1737; *Broadoak Properties Ltd v Young & White* [1989] 1 E.G.L.R. 263; *Shaw v Halifax (SW) Ltd* [1994] 2 E.G.L.R. 95 at 99.
[81] *Hill v Debenham, Tewson and Chinnocks* (1958) 171 E.G. 835 (this expenditure was a result of the defendants' negligence in not warning the claimant to postpone decorations pending cure of damp).
[82] *Broadoak Properties Ltd v Young & White* [1989] 1 E.G.L.R. 263.
[83] *Hardy v Wamsley-Lewis* (1967) 203 E.G. 1039 (cost of sweeping up dry rot on floor and making it level again. The basis of recovery of this is not stated in the judgment. It may be justified as a reasonable measure to make the house habitable pending the resale, the claimant choosing the reasonable alternative of living in the property to seeking accommodation elsewhere during the same period).
[84] [1956] 1 W.L.R. 471 at 478.
[85] In *Rawlings v Rentokil Laboratories Ltd* (1972) 223 E.G. 1947, legal fees on abortive sales were allowed.
[86] (1967) 203 E.G. 1039.
[87] See *McGregor*, para.1285:
   " . . . it is however difficult to see the basis for this . . . denial of recovery, for on the assumption that the plaintiff would not have bought the property had the defendant submitted a true report, then the cost of neither purchase nor resale would have been incurred by him. True, he had contemplated incurring costs in purchasing a house, but such costs will still have to be incurred by him in acquiring a substitute for the defective house now disposed of".
[88] 1987 S.L.T. 622.
[89] The breach of the implied term to exercise reasonable skill and care.

attempt to put the claimant into the position he would have been in had the negligence never occurred, which permits consequential expenses to be awarded. In surveyors' negligence cases the practical difference between the different measures of damage is usually insignificant and with concurrent liability being assumed in most cases, there has been no incentive to determine the point on appeal.

10–197   Unless and until the point is otherwise determined by an appellate court, it is likely that courts of first instance will continue to permit claimants to recover damages in respect of reasonable and foreseeable expenses incurred in order to ascertain the true condition of the property, and reasonable and foreseeable incidental expenses incurred whilst repairing the same, on the ground that such expenses have been caused by the surveyor's breach of contract. This has the merit of achieving consistency with the situation that would be adopted where a claimant, on discovering the true condition of the property, immediately re-sells in order to purchase an alternative property. In addition to recovering any overpayment in price, such a claimant should recover the reasonable costs of the purchase and re-sale, on the basis that the former represented the recovery of expenses rendered futile by the breach, the latter expenses caused by the breach.

CHAPTER 11

SOLICITORS

1. GENERAL

11–001   **Function of solicitors.** It is the function of a solicitor to give advice on legal matters and to act on behalf of clients in transactions of a legal nature. In order to practise, the solicitor must (a) have been admitted as a solicitor, (b) have his name on the roll and (c) have a current practising certificate.[1] Solicitors have the right to practise as such in the Supreme Court, the county courts and certain other courts,[2] to undertake advocacy in the courts,[3] to convey real property,[4] and to prepare papers for the grant of probate or of letters of administration.[5] The skills which they are expected to possess include, e.g. expertise in negotiation, some business sense[6] and, sometimes, skill in the investment of moneys.[7] In practice, solicitors frequently advise clients or act for them upon matters which are not strictly "legal".[8]

11–002   **Other providers of legal services.** Solicitors no longer enjoy the monopoly on acting as a solicitor in the courts, conveyancing and probate, which existed before the Courts and Legal Services Act 1990. Authorised bodies may undertake such work, although no such body yet exists, save that in conveyancing the Act set up the Authorised Conveyancing Practitioners Board,[9] and Licensed Conveyancers have been allowed to practise since the Administration of Justice Act 1985. Lawyers from the European Union have a right to practise anywhere in the Union, subject to certain conditions[10] and thus continental lawyers have a right to practise in England and Wales. Such cross-border practice is regulated by the Lawyers' Service Directive,[11] and the Establishment of Lawyers Directive,[12] and such practitioners should follow the CCBE Code of Conduct for Lawyers in the European Community.

11–003   **Regulation.** Solicitors are subject to the discipline of the Law Society, whose powers are derived from the Solicitors Act 1974.[13] The core regulations are the Solicitors' Practice Rules.[14] The Council of the Law Society through the Consumer Complaints Service (formerly the Office for the Supervision of Solicitors)

---

[1] Solicitors Act 1974, s.1.
[2] *ibid.*, ss.19 and 20.
[3] See now the Access to Justice Act 1999, s.36.
[4] Solicitors Act 1974, s.22.
[5] *ibid.*, s.23.
[6] e.g. *Neushul v Mellish & Harkavy* (1967) 111 S.J. 399.
[7] e.g. *Dooby v Watson* (1888) 39 Ch. D 178 at 182–183.
[8] See Taylor L.J. in *Balabel v Air-India* [1988] Ch. 317 at 331H–332A.
[9] Courts and Legal Services Act 1990, ss.34 and 35.
[10] See *Gebhard v Consiglio dell'Ordine degli Avvocati e Procuratori di Milano* [1996] All E.R. (EC) 189.
[11] 77/249/EEC.
[12] 98/5/EC.
[13] s.31. The Law Society has powers to intervene in a solicitor's practice, which the Court of Appeal in *Holder v Law Society* [2003] EWCA Civ 39; [2003] 3 All E.R. 62 held raised no issue under the Human Rights Act 1998.
[14] Reprinted in the Law Society's *Guide to the Professional Conduct of Solicitors* (8th edn, 1999); the up-to-date version is to be found on the Law Society website.

is concerned with professional discipline. However, under the draft Legal Services Bill a new and independent Office for Legal Complaints will be established. Solicitors who carry on investment business were subject to the regime of the Financial Services Act 1986,[15] and since October 2001 have been subject to the Financial Services and Markets Act 2000.[16] All solicitors used to have to be insured with the Solicitors' Indemnity Fund, which indemnified members for civil liability. Since September 1, 2000, insurance has been provided commercially by insurers who comply with certain minimum terms.[17] For a general discussion of the solicitors' profession and its regulation, reference should be made to *Cordery*, or *The Law Society Guide to the Professional Conduct of Solicitors*.[18]

(a) Duties to Client

(i) Contractual Duties

Formation of the retainer. The *fons et origo* of a solicitor's duties is the retainer (or contract of engagement) between himself and the client.[19] The retainer may be written, oral, or inferred from conduct. In the case of formal instructions by lenders, the retainer is generally accepted either expressly in a letter, or impliedly by sending back the report on title.[20] A solicitor instructed by a lender to give independent advice to a potential mortgagor will generally be the

11–004

---

[15] See further the Solicitors' Investment Business Rules 1990 and the Financial Services (Conduct of Business) Rules 1990, both of which are reprinted in the Law Society's *Guide to the Professional Conduct of Solicitors* (8th edn, 1999); the up-to-date version is to be found on the Law Society website. Liabilities under the Act include the liability to pay compensation if knowingly concerned in contraventions under s.6 of the Act, on which see *Securities and Investment Board v Pantell* [1993] Ch. 256, CA. See also commentary by S. Fennell in (1992) 8 P.N. 157.

[16] See further the Solicitors' Financial Services (Scope) Rules 2001, the Solicitors' Financial Services (Conduct of Business) Rules 2001, and the Solicitors' Financial Services (Amendment) Rules 2001. The Law Society is a designated professional body under the new Act, and firms may carry out certain regulated actitivities without being regulated by the Financial Services Authority.

[17] The powers of the Law Society to regulate solicitors' insurance, with the concurrence of the Master of the Rolls, are provided by s.37 of the Solicitors Act 1974.

[18] The updated *Guide* can be found on the Law Society website. The last printed edition was the 8th in 1999.

[19] "The retainer when given puts into operation the normal terms of the contractual relationship, including in particular the duty of the solicitor to protect the client's interest and carry out his instructions in the matters to which the retainer relates, by all proper means. It is an incident of that duty that the solicitor shall consult with his client on all questions of doubt which do not fall within the express or implied discretion left him, and shall keep the client informed to such an extent as may be reasonably necessary according to the same criteria."

per Scott L.J. in *Groom v Crocker* [1939] 1 K.B. 194 at 222. See also *Midland Bank v Hett, Stubbs & Kemp* [1979] Ch. 384 at 402H: "The extent of his duties depends upon the terms and limits of that retainer and any duty of care to be implied must be related to what he is instructed to do." *per* Oliver J. In *Papparis v Charles Fulton & Co Ltd* [1981] I.R.L.R. 104 the Employment Appeal Tribunal considered that a general retainer to advise and conduct proceedings did not come to an end at the first stage of advice and resume when instructions were given to commence proceedings. For a detailed treatment of the retainer, including retainer by different types of persons and the determination of the retainer, see Roger Billins, *Solicitors' Duties and Liabilities* (Sweet & Maxwell, 1999), Ch.1.

[20] See *Bristol & West Building Society v Fancy & Jackson (a firm)* [1997] 4 All E.R. 582 at 604j–605b, (*per* Chadwick J.)

agent of that borrower, and not the lender: see *Royal Bank of Scotland v Etridge (No.2)*.[21] In some cases it may not be clear precisely who instructed the solicitor. In *Jewo Ferrous BV v Lewis Moore (a firm)*[22] the solicitor was instructed on behalf of a client who was to provide a charge, and who in fact also acted for the party in whose favour the charge was to be made. The solicitor reasonably understood his instructions to come from the provider of the charge only, and he was retained by that party alone.[23]

11–005   **Implied retainer.** In a situation where the parties act as if the relationship of solicitor and client existed, although there is no express agreement to that effect, the court will readily hold that there is an implied retainer to be inferred from the parties' conduct.[24] However, the facts of each case must be closely examined, and two cases illustrate circumstances where no retainer was implied. In *Dean v Allin & Watts (a firm)*[25] the solicitor acting for the borrower gave an undertaking to hold the deeds of a flat which belonged to an associate of the borrower to the order of the claimant, who was the proposed lender. The solicitor gave no advice about the security, but did not suggest that the claimant should seek independent legal advice. The Court of Appeal held that there was no implied retainer. The objective consideration of all the circumstances had to be considered, and included matters such as whether the party was liable for the solicitors' fees, instructed the solicitors directly, and whether there had been a contractual relationship in the past and if so whether there had been advice to obtain independent legal advice.[26] In *BDG Roof-Bond Ltd v Douglas*[27] the defendant solicitors acted for a client who sold his 50 per cent shareholding in the claimant

---

[21] [2002] 2 A.C. 773 at paras 75–78 (Lord Nicholls), 122 (Lord Hobhouse) and 178 (Lord Scott).

[22] [20001] P.N.L.R. 12, CA.

[23] The solicitor explained that the bill provided to the chargee in a form only appropriate to a client was an oversight.

[24] See *Bean v Wade* [1885] 2 T.L.R. 157, CA; *Blyth v Fladgate* [1891] 1 Ch. 337 esp. at 355, Ch. D; *Groom v Crocker* [1939] 1 K.B. 194, CA. A retainer was readily implied from the borrower's solicitor acting for the lender in *Pegrum v Fatharly* (1996) 14 W.A.R. 92, Western Australia CA. A retainer was also implied where the solicitor, who had acted for the company in past transactions and was also the company's legally qualified director, reviewed the documentation prior to exchange, see *Hanave Pt Ltd v Lfot Pt Ltd* (2000) 168 A.L.R. 318, Federal Court of Australia. *cf. Meerkin & Apel v Rossett Pty Ltd* [1998] 4 V.R. 54, where the Supreme Court of Victoria, reversing the trial judge, held that no retainer should be implied when solicitors prepared leases for a developer who passed them on to the owner of the property who had his own solicitors.

[25] [2001] Lloyd's Rep. P.N. 605; *cf. Madley v Cousins Coombe & Mustoe* [1997] E.G.C.S. 63, QBD, where the defendant solicitors acted for B in the purchase of property where a charge was to be taken over other property owned by the claimant and B. By delivering the charge to B for execution, the defendant had offered to act for both of them, and by sending the charge back the claimant had accepted that offer and thus retained the defendants. In any event, a retainer could be implied from the parties' conduct and relationship because the defendant had not suggested that the claimant should have independent legal advice. In contrast, in *HG & R Nominees Pty Ltd v Fava* [1997] 2 V.R. 366, Supreme Court Victoria, no retainer was to be implied from the fact that the defendant solicitors purportedly witnessed the claimants' signatures on a mortgage. In *International Trading Co Ltd v Lai Kam Man* [2004] 2 HKLRD 937 the Hong Kong High Court held that the vendor's solicitors were also retained by the purchaser in circumstances where they sent a bill to the purchaser describing him as their client, although it had been agreed that the purchaser was to pay the vendor's legal bill.

[26] To similar effect, the Ontario Court of Appeal considered that the usual indicia of a solicitor-client relationship were meetings between the parties, retainer agreements, correspondence, and bills for services, see *Filipovic v Upshall* (2000) 33 R.P.R. (3d) 178.

[27] [2000] P.N.L.R. 397. For the facts, see para.11–060, below.

company to that company. It was held that the solicitors were not retained by the company, despite the facts that they had acted for it in the past and their bill had been addressed to the company. No one from the company had instructed the solicitors, who acted for one of its directors on the opposite side of the transaction.

The need for writing.[28] Where the retainer is oral, the solicitor ought, for the **11–006** benefit of both parties, to record the terms in a letter to his client at the outset. At the very least, the nature of the retainer should be recorded in an attendance note. If the solicitor neglects this precaution and later there is a dispute as to what he was instructed to do, the solicitor will begin at a disadvantage.[29] If a solicitor considers that the services he is performing for a client are only limited, this should be put in writing to avoid misunderstanding.[30] Similarly, it is prudent for a solicitor to record in writing the advice that he gives during the retainer.[31] Thus, as an example, a solicitor should record in an attendance note and write to the client if he was not going to to give tax advice in a commercial transaction, see *Hurlingham Estates Ltd v Wilde & Partners.*[32] In that case, Lightman J. rejected the solicitor's evidence that he had agreed with the clients that he would not give tax advice, and he also stated that any such limitation would require the client's fully informed consent.[33]

The nature of the duties. The nature of a solicitor's contractual duties was **11–007** discussed in some detail by Oliver J. in *Midland Bank v Hett, Stubbs & Kemp.*[34] The claimants, as executors of Mr Green, claimed damages against the defendant solicitors for failing to register an option granted to Mr Green by his father on March 24, 1961. On August 17, 1967 the father conveyed the farm to his wife for £500 in order to defeat the option. Subsequently, the defendants sought to remedy their omission by registering the option, and Mr Green then purported to exercise it, but to no effect as the option was unregistered at the time the farm was conveyed by the father to the mother. Oliver J. analysed the contractual duties of the defendants in this way:

---

[28] A solicitor is obliged to give information about costs and other matters pursuant to the Solicitors' Practice Rules 1990, r.15, and the relevant code states that it is good practice to record all such information in writing.

[29] See *Crossley v Crowther* (1851) 9 Hare 384 and *Re Paine* (1912) 28 T.L.R. 201, Ch. D. "If the solicitor does not take the precaution of getting a written retainer, he . . . must take the consequences:" *per* Denning L.J. in *Griffiths v Evans* [1953] 1 W.L.R. 1424 at 1428. In *Gray v Buss Murton (a firm)* [1999] P.N.L.R. 882 Rougier J. explained that the underlying basis of this rule was that it was the client who knows what he wants done, and the solicitor should ascertain the client's wishes accurately. In *Mackie v Wilde* [1998] 2 I.R. 570, Irish High Court, Morris J. commented on this principle and made clear that any practice requiring one party's evidence to be preferred to another was unconstitutional, and the solicitor's evidence was in fact preferred.

[30] *Begusic v Clark, Wilson & Co* (1992) 92 D.L.R. (4th) 273, British Columbia Supreme Court. However, in *Silver v Morris* (1995) 139 N.S.R. (2d) 18, Nova Scotia CA, the defendant solicitor was retained by an experienced businesswoman in the sale of a business, in which he would be expected to give advice on tax implications. As he had orally made it clear to the claimant that he knew nothing about tax, it was held that the solicitor was not retained to give tax advice.

[31] See para.11–175, below.

[32] [1997] 1 Lloyd's Rep. 525.

[33] *Quaere* whether this is correct.

[34] [1979] Ch. 384.

"The classical formulation of the claim in this sort of case as 'damages for negligence and breach of professional duty' tends to be a mesmeric phrase. It concentrates attention on the implied obligation to devote to the client's business that reasonable care and skill to be expected from a normally competent and careful practitioner as if that obligation were not only a compendious, but also exhaustive, definition of all the duties assumed under the contract created by the retainer and its acceptance. But, of course, it is not. A contract gives rise to a complex of rights and duties of which the duty to exercise reasonable care and skill is but one.

. . . If one were to seek to write out in longhand the obligations which Mr Stubbs senior assumed when he engaged to act in the matter of the grant of the option, they were (1) to draw and have completed a proper and enforceable option agreement which would bind the parties; (2) to take such steps as were necessary and practicable to ensure that it was binding on the land into whosoever hands it might come before any third party acquired a legal estate; and (3) to carry out his work with the skill and care which a normally competent practitioner would bring to it."[35]

Oliver J.'s analysis of the solicitor's contractual duties is not easy to apply in cases where the solicitor is retained to do something more complex than effect an option, for example to conduct a personal injuries action. Presumably the solicitor's specific duties include (1) issuing the claim form within the limitation period, (2) obtaining a medical report and (3) instructing counsel. Suppose, however, the solicitor fails to send a letter before action, or to take a proof from a material witness before he dies, or to carry out the steps suggested in counsel's advice on evidence: is this a breach of the solicitor's specific duties or simply a breach of the general duty to exercise skill and care? If one attempts to "write out in longhand" all the duties assumed by a solicitor upon his retainer, the list in most cases is liable to run to considerable length, unless it is confined to the most basic steps involved in the particular business which the solicitor is undertaking. In practice, the solicitor's failure to carry out some necessary step is normally treated as a breach of the general duty to exercise skill and care rather than a breach of some specific duty implied in the retainer.[36] In most cases it is submitted that this is the correct approach, although the duty of skill and care implies a number of general obligations.[37]

11–008   **Express instructions.** In some cases there may be express instructions which the court will treat as express terms of the contract.[38] For example, in *Pilbrow v Pearless De Rougemont & Co*[39] there was an express term that the legal services were to be provided by a solicitor, and thus there was non-performance by the defendant firm when the work was handled competently by an employee who was not a solicitor, so that the solicitors were not able to obtain payment of their fees. Detailed express terms are common in retainers by lenders. An early

---

[35] [1979] Ch. 384 at 434E–F and 435A–B.
[36] See, e.g. *Sykes v Midland Bank Executor & Trustee Co Ltd* [1971] 1 Q.B. 113, CA, at 125H: failure to advise on lease; *County Personnel (Employment Agency) Ltd v Alan R Pulver & Co* [1987] 1 W.L.R. 916, CA: failure to advise on unusual term in lease.
[37] See para.11–082.
[38] This has particular importance in the context of contributory negligence, see para.11–337.
[39] [1999] 3 All E.R. 355, CA. *Pilbrow* was applied by the Court of Appeal in *Adrian Alan Ltd v Fuglers* [2002] EWCA Civ 1855; [2003] P.N.L.R. 14, where a former solicitor had fraudulently deceived the client into believing that he was qualified, and the client was able to recover fees paid.

example is *Bristol & West Building Society v Kramer*[40] where the defendant solicitors accepted standard form instructions to act for the claimant mortgage lenders, which included a requirement to notify the proposed mortgagee of certain matters. They were in breach of that instruction, which was held to be an express term of their retainer.

Construction of express duties.[41] An insertion by solicitors into their contract   **11–009**
with their client of a one-sided provision will be construed *contra proferentem*.[42]
Express instructions by lending institutions and the undertakings they require have been examined by the courts.[43] In particular, in a number of cases the Court of Appeal has addressed the issue of whether such duties should be construed as absolute obligations, or as qualified by the implied duty to use reasonable care and skill. Most have concluded that the duties are qualified, and it is likely to be a rare case where a court will impose an absolute obligation.[44] Exceptionally, a claim for breach of an undertaking succeeded regardless of whether the solicitors were at fault in *Zwebner v The Mortgage Corp Ltd*.[45] There, the solicitors' report on title undertook that all appropriate documents would be properly executed before completion of the mortgage transaction. This was construed as an absolute obligation to ensure (inter alia) that one of the borrower's signatures was genuine, when in fact it was a forgery. The Court of Appeal held that the defendant solicitors were strictly liable, although they also found them negligent.

However, in the other decisions, the obligations were not construed to be   **11–010**
absolute. In *Barclays Bank Plc v Weeks Legg & Dean (a firm)*,[46] the Court of Appeal determined appeals in three cases involving solicitors acting for purchasers of land who gave undertakings to the claimant bank on the bank's

---

[40] *The Times*, February 6, 1995. See Flenley and Leech, *Solicitors' Negligence* (Butterworths, 1999) at para.6.4 for a suggestion that *Kramer* would not be followed in any case which is not on all fours with it, given subsequent authority, on which see the next two paragraphs. More unusually, in *Polishuk v Hagarty* (1983) 149 D.L.R. (3d) 65, upheld on this point on appeal at (1985) 14 D.L.R. (4th) 446, solicitors accepted an undertaking in lieu of the discharge of a mortgage. It was no defence that they had fulfilled the standard of the ordinarily competent solicitor, as they had a contractual duty to complete the transaction according to the terms of the contract of purchase, which they were not able to vary without consent.
[41] For a different example of the construction of the retainer letter see *Twenty Two A Property Investments Ltd v Simpson Curtis (a firm)* [2000] E.G.C.S. 140, CA. The client had an interest in property where the sale by the owner had to be completed by a certain date. He instructed the defendant solicitors to make sure his interests were protected and to "keep actively pursuing to see that matters are progressing . . . .". As a result, the solicitor had a duty to keep himself informed at all times what the owner's solicitor was doing and proposed to do, and to exert pressure on him.
[42] *Re a Debtor (No.1594 of 1992), The Times*, December 18, 1992, Ch. D.
[43] For examples of a purposive constructions of such instructions see *Birmingham Midshires Mortgage Services Ltd v David Parry & Co* [1996] P.N.L.R. 494, upheld by CA [1997] N.P.C. 153 and [1997] E.G.C.S. 150 ("no other mortgages" construed as meaning on the security property only); *Bristol & West Building Society v Fancy & Jackson (a firm)* [1997] 4 All E.R. 582 (see the *Colin Bishop* case where a "back to back" sale was sufficiently close to a sub-sale to require reporting).
[44] But strict liability is also imposed for breach of a warranty of authority, see para.11–075, below.
[45] [1998] P.N.L.R. 769. See also *The Mortgage Corp v Mitchells Robertson* [1997] S.L.T. 1305, OH: mortgage instructions using the words "must", "should" and "will" were held to be capable of creating an absolute obligation.
[46] [1999] Q.B. 309.

standard form. In each case, the solicitor had undertaken that any sums received would be "applied solely for acquiring a good marketable title". The Court held that the undertaking was not absolute, but imposed a qualified obligation to obtain what a reasonably competent solicitor acting with skill and care would accept as a good marketable title. The undertaking was construed so that the solicitors' obligations pursuant to it were in conformity with the qualified obligations to their own clients and their trust obligations to the bank. In *Midland Bank Plc v Cox McQueen*[47] the Court of Appeal followed the *Barclays Bank* case, and distinguished *Zwebner*. In that case the retainer was to obtain the signature of a customer's wife to a legal charge, rather than properly to execute the documents, with no undertaking being given, and it was interpreted by the Court of Appeal as merely an obligation to use reasonable care and skill. The previous two cases were followed in *UCB Corporate Services Ltd v Clyde & Co (a firm)*[48] where the Court of Appeal held that an obligation to obtain an enforceable guarantee required the solicitors to do all that could be reasonably expected to achieve the desired result. Any absolute obligation would have to be in clear and unequivocal terms. Finally, in *Mercantile Credit Company Ltd v Fenwick*[49] the Court of Appeal similarly held, without referring to any previous authority, that if a lender wished to impose an absolute obligation on its solicitors it must do so in clear terms.[50] There, the solicitors' obligation to the lender with regard to guarantors for whom they did not act was to make enquiries to satisfy themselves that there would be no challenge to the security being taken, but they gave no warranty to that effect.

11–011   **Termination of the retainer.** A client can determine the retainer at will. If there is an entire contract, the solicitor can only terminate the retainer upon reasonable notice and for good cause.[51] However, at least some non-contentious[52] and contentious[53] retainers will not be entire contracts, so that the solicitor

---

[47] [1999] P.N.L.R. 593. This case, and not *Zwebner*, was followed by the Hong Kong Court of Appeal in *Ying Ho Co Ltd v Man Kwok Leung* [2000] 3 HKLRD 191, where an undertaking to send duly executed documents in a property transaction was held to be an obligation to use reasonable care to ensure that the documents were executed by the owner of the property. It was also followed by the Hong Kong High Court in *National Commercial Bank Ltd v Albert Hwang, David Chung & Co* [2002] 2 HKLRD 409.

[48] [2000] P.N.L.R. 841.

[49] [1999] Lloyd's Rep. P.N. 408.

[50] A point also made by Lord Woolf M.R. in *Midland Bank Plc v Cox McQueen* [1999] P.N.L.R. 593 at 603.

[51] *Summit Property Ltd v Pitmans (a firm)* [2001] Lloyd's Rep. P.N. 164, Park J. See the Law Society's *Guide to the Professional Conduct of Solicitors* (8th edn, 1999), para.12–12, which gives examples of what may amount to a good reason. (For the up-to-date version of the Guide see the Law Society website). An example of a good reason is non-payment of fees, see Solicitors Act 1974, s.65(2); see further para.11–193.

[52] There would be no entire contract where a solicitor agrees to act generally for a person or in a variety of matters, see *Warmingtons v McMurray* [1937] 1 All E.R. 562, CA. *Summit Property Ltd v Pitmans (a firm)* [2001] Lloyd's Rep. P.N. 164 is an example of an entire contract, which concerned one transaction.

[53] In *Perotti v Collyer-Bristow* [2003] EWHC 25, Ch; [2003] W.T.L.R. 1473, Lindsay J. doubted whether a retainer to conduct litigation was an entire contract, and concluded that old authority established that there was no such entire retainer in a complicated matter such as the administration of an estate. In any event, in that case the defendant solicitors had reason to determine their retainer

can determine the retainer at a natural break. A retainer will determine when it becomes impossible for the solicitors to carry it out.[54]

Continuing obligations. The question of whether an obligation is a continuing **11–012** one may be of particular importance in determining whether a cause of action is statute-barred. In *Midland Bank v Hett, Stubbs & Kemp*[55] the defendant solicitors contended that any claim against them for failing to register an option was statute-barred. Oliver J. rejected this contention, and held that the obligation, which was to take such steps as were necessary and practicable to ensure that the option agreement was binding on the land, was a continuing one until August 17, 1967, when it became incapable of effective performance. Therefore the claim for breach of contract was not statute-barred, since proceedings had been begun within six years of that date.[56] The concept of a continuing obligation has been subject to criticism in two subsequent Court of Appeal cases.[57] However, in *Carlton v Fulchers*[58] Waller L.J. considered that there could be a continuing obligation on the defendant solicitor to preserve the claimant's cause of action during the currency of the retainer.

(ii) *Tortious Duties*[59]

History. It used to be thought that a negligent solicitor was liable to his client **11–013** both in contract and in tort.[60] However, there were authorities to the effect that the solicitor's liability lay in contract alone[61] and the issue was far from clear. The point was ostensibly resolved by the Court of Appeal in *Groom v Crocker*,[62] in which it was held that the solicitor owed no duty to the client beyond the contractual duties arising from his retainer. For the next 37 years *Groom v Crocker* was followed without question.[63] However, the debate was reopened by

---

because there was a conflict of interest and a serious breakdown in confidence between client and solicitor, and a natural break had been reached.

[54] See *Morfoot v W F Smith & Co* [2001] Lloyd's Rep. P.N. 658, Ch. D. See further para.11–076 on the related question of a solicitor acting in breach of authority after the client ceases to have capacity.

[55] [1979] Ch. 384. For the facts see para.11–007, above.

[56] The defence of limitation also failed on other grounds. See para.11–013.

[57] *Lee v Thompson* (1990) 6 P.N. 91 at 93; *Bell v Peter Browne & Co* [1990] 2 Q.B. 495, especially at 514F–G, 521G and 525E–H; see also *Costiga v Rzicka* (1984) 33 Alta. L.R. (2d) 21. There will be some continuing fiduciary duties. For instance, a solicitor's duty of confidentiality continues, and thus he will have an obligation to decline to accept instructions from a new client because he has acquired knowledge from a former client, on which see paras 11–026 *et seq*. There was no continuing duty in *Morfoot v W F Smith & Co* [2001] Lloyd's Rep. P.N. 658, Ch. D, where it was held that the duty to obtain a deed of release was broken as soon as it was possible to obtain such a deed.

[58] [1997] P.N.L.R. 337, relying on passages in *Bell v Peter Browne & Co* [1990] 2 Q.B. 495 at 501 and 512. For the facts see para.11–187, below. See also *Hines v Willans* [2002] W.T.L.R. 299, summarised at para.11–023, below.

[59] See further Ch.2 para.2–013 *et seq*.

[60] See, e.g. *Boorman v Brown* (1844) 11 Cl. & Fin. 1 at 44; *Davies v Lock* (1844) 3 L.T. (O.S.) 125; *Davies v Hood* (1903) 88 L.T. 19, K.B.D. at 20; *Nocton v Ashburton* [1914] A.C. 932 at 956.

[61] *Howell v Young* (1826) 5B. & C. 259; *Bean v Wade* (1885) 2 T.L.R. 157, CA.

[62] [1939] 1 K.B. 194.

[63] See, for example, *Clarke v Kirby-Smith* [1964] 1 Ch. 506, Ch. D; *Cooke v Swinfen* [1967] 1 W.L.R. 457, CA; *Heywood v Wellers* [1976] Q.B. 446, CA.

the statement of Lord Denning M.R. in *Esso Petroleum Co Ltd v Mardon*[64] that *Groom v Crocker*[65] was wrongly decided. In *Midland Bank v Hett Stubbs & Kemp*[66] Oliver J. reviewed the authorities in considerable detail and came to the conclusion that *Groom v Crocker* was no longer good law and the defendant solicitors were liable in negligence (as well as contract) for failing to register an option.[67] In *Forster v Outred & Co*[68] the Court of Appeal (without hearing argument on the point) approved *Midland Bank v Hett Stubbs & Kemp*.[69] The Privy Council in *Tai Hing Cotton Mill Ltd v Liu Chong Hing Bank Ltd*[70] at least impliedly cast doubt upon the basis of the decision, and in *Lee v Thompson*[71] Lloyd L.J. considered the matter ripe for review.

11–014   **The current law.** In *Henderson v Merrett Syndicates Ltd*[72] the House of Lords decided that a duty of care in tort was owed by Lloyd's managing agents to Names, and that the existence of the duty of care was not excluded by the relevant contractual regime. The Names were free to pursue their remedy in contract or in tort. Lord Goff agreed with the reasoning of Oliver J. in *Midland Bank Trust Co Ltd v Hett, Stubbs & Kemp*.[73] The decision resolves this issue, at least for cases of professional negligence.

11–015   **The position in the Commonwealth.** Elsewhere in the Commonwealth the courts have now held that solicitors are liable to their clients both in contract and tort. In Canada the Supreme Court of Canada decided in *Central Trust Co v Rafuse*[74] that the law should allow concurrent liability, and this applied to solicitors as well as other professionals. In Australia, the High Court of Australia have also held that there is concurrent liability, see *Astley v Austrust Limited*.[75] The New Zealand Court of Appeal recognised concurrent liability in *Mouat v*

---

[64] [1976] Q.B. 801 at 819. He pointed out that cases of high authority, such as *Nocton v Ashburton* [1914] A.C. 932, had not been cited in *Groom v Crocker*.

[65] [1939] 1 K.B. 194.

[66] [1979] Ch. 384. For the facts see para.11–007.

[67] He held that the cause of action accrued when the option was incapable of being exercised. This decision on the date of the accrual of the cause of action is probably wrong given later decisions such as *DW Moore & Co Ltd v Ferrier* [1988] 1 W.L.R. 267, CA; and *Bell v Peter Browne & Co* [1990] 2 Q.B. 495, CA; see further Ch.5 para.5–029. The law in Australia is probably different: see *Wardley Australia Ltd v Western Australia* (1992) 66 A.L.J.R. 839 and (1992) 109 A.L.R. 247, discussed in Ch.5 para.5–038. The decision in *Hett Stubbs* on concurrent liability was criticised by J.M. Kaye: "The liability of solicitors in tort" (1984) 100 L.Q.R. 680.

[68] [1982] 1 W.L.R. 86. This decision was followed by the Court of Appeal in *Costa v Georghiou* (1985) 1 P.N. 201; *DW Moore & Co Ltd v Ferrier* [1988] 1 W.L.R. 267 and *Bell v Peter Browne & Co* [1990] 2 Q.B. 495.

[69] [1979] Ch. 384.

[70] [1986] A.C. 80 at 117.

[71] (1990) 6 P.N. 91, at 93 col. 2.

[72] [1995] 2 A.C. 145. See Ch.2. para.2–108.

[73] [1979] Ch. 384; see [1995] 2 A.C. 145 at 181H–182A.

[74] (1987) 31 D.L.R. (4th) 481. For the facts of this case see para.11–084. The same result had been reached in *Baldwin v Chalker* (1984) 48 Nfld. & P.E.I.R and 142 A.P.R. 86, Nfld. CA, and *Consumers Glass Co Ltd v Foundation Co of Canada* (1985) 20 D.L.R. (4th) 126, Ontario CA.

[75] [1999] Lloyd's Rep. P.N. 758: while there was concurrent liability, the defendant's plea of contributory negligence succeeded only in tort and not contract; see further para.11–334. See also the earlier case of *Hawkins v Clayton* (1988) 164 C.L.R. 539, High Court of Australia.

Clark Boyce.[76] In Ireland the Supreme Court has held that a solicitor is liable to his client both in contract and tort: see *Finlay v Murtagh*.[77]

(iii) *Fiduciary Duties*[78]

General. In addition to the contractual duties arising from his retainer and the   **11–016** general duty to exercise skill and care, the solicitor owes fiduciary duties to his client. Such duties are not necessarily to be found in or confined to the terms of the contractual retainer.[79] The relationship between a solicitor and his client has been described as "one of the most important fiduciary relations known to our law".[80] However, the limits of those duties must be recognised. In *Clark Boyce v Mouat*[81] the Privy Council concluded:

> "A fiduciary duty concerns disclosure of material facts in a situation where the fiduciary either has a personal interest in the matter to which the facts are material, or acts for another party who has such an interest. It cannot be prayed in aid to enlarge the scope of contractual duties."

The seven fiduciary duties listed below are of particular relevance to solicitors.[82] An allegation of breach of fiduciary duty or breach of trust may in some circumstances greatly assist a claimant, due to the different principles of compensation in many cases,[83] and the potentially different rules as to contributory negligence.[84] Indeed, the Court of Appeal in *Bristol & West Building Society v Mothew*[85] considered that the term "fiduciary duty" should be limited to those

---

[76] [1992] 2 N.Z.L.R. 559. The point was not considered by the Privy Council on appeal at [1994] 1 A.C. 428. The New Zealand Court of Appeal emphasised in *Frost & Sutcliffe v Tuiara* [2004] 1 N.Z.L.R. 782 that the duties in contract and tort would usually be concurrent and coextensive.

[77] [1979] I.R. 249 (claim against a solicitor for failing to issue proceedings within the limitation period).

[78] See also Ch.2 paras 2–128 *et seq*. For a more extensive treatment of this topic see H. Evans, *Lawyer's Liabilities* (2nd edn, 2002), Ch.3. All the cases in this section concern solicitors unless otherwise stated.

[79] See in particular the discussion in *Conway v Ratiu* [2005] EWCA Civ 1302; [2006] 1 All E.R. 571, CA. Some fiduciary duties may extend beyond the termination of the retainer. It was suggested by the Court that there may be powerful arguments to lift the corporate veil in appropriate cases to include those behind a client company who rely on the fiduciary.

[80] *per* Cozens-Hardy M.R. in *Re Van Laun* [1907] 2 K.B. 23, at 29. However, the fiduciary relationship does not generally extend beyond the retainer, see *Cox v Pemberton Holmes* [1993] 6 W.W.R. 603 British Columbia CA. The relationship of fiduciary and contractual duties was discussed by Lord Browne-Wilkinson in *Henderson v Merrett Syndicates Ltd* [1995] 2 A.C. 145 at 206A–D, a case which did not concern solicitors. Note that the seven fiduciary duties set out are not exhaustive. Thus, for instance, in *MacDonell v M & M Developments Ltd* (1998) 157 D.L.R. (4th) 240, Nova Scotia CA, a solicitor was in breach of his fiduciary duty in continuing to act generally for the claimant for two months after he had decided to assert his own title to lands ostensibly held by the claimant. Fiduciary duties may be owed by a solicitor to his partner or employer, which he must be careful not to breach when leaving a firm to set up business elsewhere, see for example *Kao Lee & Yip v. Koo Hoi Yan* [2003] HKEC 411; [2003] W.T.L.R. 1283, Hong Kong High Court.

[81] [1994] 1 A.C. 428 at 437F–G.

[82] This classification is to an extent one of convenience only. Categories (2) to (5) are all aspects of the same general principle.

[83] See further paras 11–228 *et seq.*, below.

[84] See further para.11–337, below.

[85] [1998] Ch. 1 at 16. For the facts see paras 11–023 and 11–304.

duties peculiar to fiduciaries where breach attracts different legal consequences from the breach of other duties.

11–017   **(1) Undue influence.**[86] A client may be induced by the undue influence of a solicitor to make a gift to him. It is well established that the solicitor-client relationship gives rise to a presumption of undue influence.[87] It applies to other transactions as well as gifts.[88] The presumption applies to gifts to the solicitor's relations. Thus a gift to the solicitor's son was set aside by the House of Lords in *Willis v Barron*,[89] where the defendant was the claimant's husband's solicitor rather than her own. In *Liles v Terry*[90] the Court of Appeal set aside a gift to the solicitor's wife on the basis of the presumption of undue influence. The presumption will apply after the relationship of client and solicitor has ended.[91] The presumption of undue influence does not strictly apply in the case of gifts by will,[92] although a similar but less rigorous doctrine does exist in such cases.[93] It is possible to rebut the presumption of undue influence by showing that the client exercised free will.[94] Legal advice is helpful in dispelling the presumption but it is probably not essential,[95] although some cases involving solicitors suggest the contrary.[96]

11–018   **(2) Personal dealings with clients.** In the well-known case of *Nocton v Ashburton*[97] a solicitor was found liable for breach of fiduciary duty when he had a personal interest in the transaction his client was entering, and he also acted for borrowers who were the other party to the transaction. In *Swindle v Harrison*[98] Mummery L.J explained that *Nocton v Ashburton* decided that a solicitor stands in a fiduciary relationship with his client, and when entering into a financial transaction with his client he was under a fiduciary duty to disclose all relevant facts known to him; such liability did not depend on proof of deceit or negligence. A solicitor is not permitted to enter transactions with his client, in circumstances where he has a duty to act in the interests of his client, without proof that he has given a fair price and that he has disclosed all the information

---

[86] Properly speaking, this is not a breach of fiduciary duty, but it is convenient and common to treat the issue under this head.
[87] See, e.g. *Liles v Terry* [1895] Q.B. 679, CA (voluntary conveyance of property by client to solicitor declared void); *Wright v Carter* [1903] 1 Ch. 27, CA (property donated in trust to solicitor by client declared void).
[88] *Wright v Carter* [1903] 1 Ch. 27 at 50, *per* Vaughan Williams L.J. *cf. Moody v Cox and Hatt* [1917] 2 Ch. 71 at 79–80, *per* Lord Cozens-Hardy M.R.
[89] [1902] A.C. 271.
[90] [1895] Q.B. 679.
[91] *Allison v Clayhills* (1907) 97 L.T. 709 at 712, *per* Parker J.
[92] *Hindson v Weatherill* (1854) 5 De G.M. & G. 301.
[93] See *Wintle v Nye* [1959] 1 W.L.R. 284, HL.
[94] As an illustration, see *Westmelton v Archer* [1982] V.R. 305 where a well-informed corporate client was not relying on any confidence or expectation of legal advice, and the presumption was easily dispelled.
[95] *Inche Noriah v Omar* [1929] A.C. 127; *Lancashire Loan Ltd v Black* [1934] 1 K.B. 380 at 412–413. These cases do not concern solicitors.
[96] e.g. *Rhodes v Bate* (1865) L.R. 1. Ch. 252 at 257.
[97] [1914] A.C. 932. For the facts of the case, see para.11–228, below.
[98] [1997] 4 All E.R. 705 at 732.

he has concerning the transaction.[99] This is sometimes relevant when a solicitor enters a joint venture with his client, which was permitted in *Hanson v Lorenz & Jones*.[1] In *Day v Cook*[2] the defendant solicitor presented a number of transactions to the claimant in which the solicitor had an interest. Although the claimant was fully informed, the solicitor was in breach of fiduciary duty as the transactions were not fair, because the solicitor obtained an unjustified advantage by them. In *Johnson v EBS Pensioner Trustees Ltd*[3] a solicitor acting for undisclosed lenders arranged a loan to his clients, but did not disclose that his firm would benefit from a 1.5 per cent service charge paid by the lenders. The Court of Appeal held:

(i) that the law of personal dealings with the client, described as the doctrine of abuse of confidence, applied in cases where property did not pass; by a majority that

(ii) the solicitor had failed to prove the transaction was a fair one as a result of the non-disclosure of the service charge; but that

(iii) the remedy was an account of the service charge, and rescission of the transaction was disproportionate.

In *Longstaff v Birtles*[4] the Court of Appeal held that a solicitor seeking to buy or sell property from a present or (as in that case) former client must insist that the client obtains independent legal advice.

The rule cannot be circumvented, for instance by purchasing property from the client in the name of the solicitor's brother when the solicitor is the real purchaser.[5] The rule may apply after the termination of the solicitor-client relationship, as in *McMaster v Byrne*.[6] The client had consistently resorted to the solicitor for advice about the formation and promotion of several companies and in relation to his will. The Privy Council held that a continuing relationship of confidence had arisen, and thus the solicitor was bound to disclose all material facts when the client granted him an option in relation to one of his companies after the termination of the solicitor-client relationship. A strict view was taken

11–019

[99] *Demerera Bauxite v Hubbard* [1923] A.C. 673, PC (solicitor failed to disclose a rival bid, and the transaction was unenforceable). Thus obtaining independent legal advice will not be sufficient if the solicitors fails to make a full disclosure to the new solicitor, see *Gibbs v Daniel* (1862) 4 Giff 1. The information must be sufficient for the client to give informed consent, see *Sims v Craig Bell & Bond* [1991] 3 N.Z.L.R. 535, CA. See also *Gibson v Jeyes* (1801) 6 Ves. Jun. 266.
[1] [1987] 1 F.T.L.R. 23. It would appear that the Court of Appeal considered it sufficient if the transaction was fair, and the client fully aware of its nature and effect. The question of the solicitor disclosing material facts does not seem to have been relevant. For illustrations of the dangers of joint ventures, see *Korz v St Pierre* (1988) 43 D.L.R. (4th) 528, Ontario CA, and *MacDonald Estate* (1994) 95 Man. R. (2d) 123, Manitoba CA. See also *Peterco Holdings v Calverton Holdings* 2003 BCCA 145; (2003) 11 B.C.L.R. (4th) 280, British Columbia CA, where it was held that, on the facts, the other partners trusted and relied on the solicitor as a partner but not as a solicitor, and there was no relationship sufficient to establish a fiduciary duty as a solicitor.
[2] [2000] P.N.L.R. 178, Bristol Mercantile Court. These findings were not appealed to the Court of Appeal, see [2001] EWCA Civ 592; [2001] P.N.L.R. 32.
[3] [2002] Lloyd's Rep. P.N. 309.
[4] [2001] EWCA Civ 1219; [2002] 1 W.L.R. 470.
[5] As in *McPherson v Watt* (1877) 3 A.C. 254.
[6] [1952] 1 All E.R. 1362.

in *Spector v Ageda*,[7] where the solicitor made a loan to the client. Megarry J. considered that as a general rule a solicitor ought never to act for a person in a transaction to which he himself is a party with an adverse interest, even after the fullest disclosure to the client, although he conceded that there may possibly be exceptions to this rule. If the solicitor has a significant interest in a company which is entering a transaction with his client, he may have to show at least that the sale was fair and honest.[8]

11–020   **(3) Obtaining a personal benefit.** A solicitor may not use his client's property to obtain a personal benefit. In *Brown v Inland Revenue Commissioners*[9] the solicitor possessed clients' money which was not worth investing individually, as it was in small sums or was required soon. He kept some of these moneys on deposit in the firm's name and retained the interest. It was not disputed that the solicitor should not make a profit out of the clients' money. However it was argued that he could keep the money by custom or by agreement, and the defendant relied on the approval by the Law Society of Scotland of the practice and on the difficulty of allocating to particular clients the interest earned. The House of Lords found against the solicitor. The custom, while common, was not universal or notorious, and there was insufficient evidence to found an implied term, despite the difficulty of accurately determining sums due.[10] However, in *Bogg v Raper*[11] a solicitor who inserted a standard clause in a will, exonerating the executors and trustees, of which he was to be one, from potential liabilities, was entitled to rely on it as a trustee. The clause did not confer a benefit, but defined the extent of the potential liabilities, and there was no conflict of interest.

11–021   **(4) Using a fiduciary position to make a personal profit.** A solicitor may not make use of his fiduciary position to gain a benefit for himself. In *Boardman v Phipps*[12] the defendant, Mr Boardman, acted as the solicitor to a trust that had a minority shareholding in a private company. The company was not performing satisfactorily, and he was asked to investigate. In his capacity as representative of the trust, Mr Boardman attended meetings and obtained information. As a result, it was decided by the trustees that the best solution was to obtain a majority of

---

[7] [1973] Ch. 30, at 47G–H. The transaction was set aside.

[8] *Farrar v Farrars Ltd* (1888) 40 Ch. D. 395 at 410 and 415; for an explanation of the case see *Movitex Ltd v Bulfield* [1988] B.C.L.C. 104 at 122–123, and see also *Day v Mead* [1987] 2 N.Z.L.R. 443, NZCA. Similarly, in *Recha and Klein v Yeamans and Gere* (1993) 135 N.B.R. (2d) 360, New Brunswick CA, the defendant solicitor was in breach of fiduciary duty in failing to disclose to his clients who were purchasing a restaurant that he had given a personal guarantee in relation to it for the vendor.

[9] [1965] A.C. 244, HL Scot. See also *Burdick v Garrick* (1870) L.R. 5 Ch. 233.

[10] Moneys held on account are now governed by s.33 of the Solicitors Act 1974 and the Solicitors' Accounts Rules 1991.

[11] *The Times*, April 22 1998, CA.

[12] [1967] 2 A.C. 46. See also *Official Assignee of Collier v Creighton* [1993] 2 N.Z.L.R. 534, NZCA, where the solicitor failed to inform his client who was considering purchasing a house that he was also still interested in purchasing it. A solicitor advising a client on a mortgage who had no knowledge that a likely object of the borrowed money was a company in which he had an interest was held not to be in breach of fiduciary duty in *Blythe v Northwood* (2005) 63 N.S.W.L.R. 531, NSWCA. For an unusual application of this principle, see *Stewart v Canadian Broadcasting Association* (1997) 150 D.L.R. (4th) 24, Ontario High Court, summarised at Ch.12, para.12–005.

the shareholdings, but they did not wish to seek the court's authority to do this. Mr Boardman therefore obtained shares in the company, with the approval of only some of the trustees. As a result of obtaining control of the company, he made a substantial profit, as did the trust from their shareholdings. A bare majority of the House of Lords held that Mr Boardman should disgorge the profits he had made to the beneficiaries. Exceptionally, Mr Boardman was remunerated on a liberal scale for the work he had undertaken. The primary reason for liability was that a fiduciary is not permitted to make a profit by reason of the opportunity or knowledge gained in that position, save with consent. A subsidiary reason was that there was a conflict between Mr Boardman's interest and his duties to the trust.[13]

(5) Bribes and secret commissions. A fiduciary is not allowed to accept   **11-022**
bribes or secret commissions. In *Islamic Republic of Iran v Denby*[14] the solicitor's client was the defendant in a shipping dispute. The other side paid the solicitor a commission to obtain a prompt and satisfactory settlement, which was described by the judge as a bribe, and the client was entitled to recover the sums from him. The rule applies to secret commissions that are not bribes, such as an introducing fee.[15] If the client expressly or impliedly accepts the payment's existence, he cannot later recover it from the solicitor, which is what happened in *Re Haslam v Hier-Evans*.[16] Solicitors were retained to act for a client in the purchase of a patent. They had a note from vendors offering them commission if they found a purchaser, and the solicitors showed it to the client before the patent was purchased by him. The Court of Appeal held that the client's executors were not allowed to deduct the commission from the solicitors' bill.

(6) Accepting inconsistent engagements. The issue of acting for both parties   **11-023**
in a transaction arises in the common law context of breach of the duty of reasonable care and skill,[17] but it also arises as a breach of fiduciary duty.[18] Common examples where there may be potential conflicts of duty are acting for

---

[13] *cf. Re Century Homes Pty Ltd (in liquidation)* (1984) 73 F.L.R. 462, Federal Court of Australia: the solicitor purchased company property with the consent and at the invitation of the company, and was thus not in breach of fiduciary duty.

[14] [1987] 1 Lloyd's Rep. 367. Leggatt J. was constrained by authority to hold that the recovery of the secret profit was a claim for money had and received, and no proprietary remedy was available. However, in *Att-Gen for Hong Kong v Reid* [1994] 1 A.C. 324, a public prosecutor accepted bribes as an inducement to exploit his position to obstruct the prosecution of some criminals. The Privy Council decided that the bribes were held on constructive trust, and thus could be traced into New Zealand houses.

[15] As in *Re Four Solicitors* [1901] 1 Q.B. 187.

[16] [1902] 1 Ch. 765.

[17] See paras 11–103 to 11–105.

[18] See *Moody v Cox and Hatt* [1917] 2 Ch. 71, especially at 79 and 81. A breach of duty was found in that case, and it was no defence to say that he owed a duty to his other client not to disclose relevant information. In *Hines v Willans* [2002] W.T.L.R. 299 the defendant solicitors acted for W and her husband on the making of identical reciprocal wills in 1985, and for W in various transactions thereafter, including in July 1990. In that month, the husband instructed the solicitors to change his will, leaving nothing to W, which they did. The Court of Appeal held that the defendants were in breach of fiduciary duty to W. As the evidence suggested that the husband would have changed his mind very soon afterwards, the court rejected the appeal against an award of substantial damages.

vendor and purchaser in a conveyancing transaction, and acting for lender and purchaser.[19] In the seminal case of *Bristol & West Building Society v Mothew*[20] the defendant solicitor acted for the claimant lender and the borrower in a mortgage transaction, an extremely common occurrence. The borrower arranged for a second charge on his existing property to be transferred to the new one. Despite knowing about this, the solicitor failed to report it to the claimants and misrepresented to them the fact that the borrowers had no other indebtedness. The Court of Appeal held that the subsequent receipt and misapplication of the lender's moneys was not a breach of trust, absent deliberate concealment or an intention to mislead, and the earlier misrepresentation did not change the position. Furthermore, the Court considered that the term "fiduciary duty" should be limited to those duties peculiar to fiduciaries where breach attracts different legal consequences from the breach of other duties, and used the concept of loyalty as an organising principle. Millett L.J. analysed the fiduciary obligations owed to two clients into four categories. First, the "double employment" rule prevented a solicitor acting for two clients whose interests may conflict, without obtaining informed consent.[21] Consent was implied in that case where the solicitor acted for lender and borrower. Secondly, there was a duty of good faith. There had to be an intention to further the interests of one client to the prejudice of the other for there to be a breach of this obligation, although the conduct would not have to be dishonest. Thirdly and relatedly, under the "no inhibition principle", a fiduciary must not be inhibited by his duties to one client from carrying out his duties to the other. Breach of this obligation also required intentional conduct. Finally, the "actual conflict" rule requires a solicitor not to be in a position where he cannot fulfil his obligations to one client without failing the other.

---

[19] Although there will generally be informed consent, see *Bristol & West Building Society v Mothew* [1996] 4 All E.R. 698. However, if there is a breach of r.6 of the Solicitors' Practice Rules 1990, for instance if a conflict of interest existed or arose, or if the seller was a builder or developer, the prohibition cannot be waived even by informed consent, see *Hilton v Parker Booth & Eastwood (a firm)* [2005] UKHL 8; [2005] 1 W.L.R. 567, at para.19.

[20] [1998] Ch. 1. For a critical commentary see S. Elliott, "Fiduciary liability for client mortgage frauds" (1999) 13 Tru. L.I. 74, where it is argued that previous cases show that a solicitor's negligence is also a breach of fiduciary duty where it is aggravated by conflicting interest or an adverse fiduciary engagement. In *Re Moage Ltd* (1998) 153 A.L.R. 711 the Federal Court of Australia, following *Mothew*, held that it had to be pleaded that the solicitor had intentionally preferred the interests of one client over another.

[21] There may be some cases where even express consent may not be sufficient, see the Canadian cases referred to below. For an example of breach of this duty see *Ball v Druces & Attlee (a firm)* [2004] EWHC 1402; [2004] P.N.L.R. 39, especially at para.339, where the defendant solicitors acted for The Eden Trust and their former client, the claimant, when there was a conflict of interest between them and the solicitors were in possession of confidential information. In *R. v Neil* (2003) 218 D.L.R. (4th) 671 the Supreme Court of Canada made it clear that the duty of loyalty went beyond the issue of confidentiality, and included a duty to avoid conflicting interests, a duty of commitment to the client's cause, and a duty of candour. There may be a breach of fiduciary duty even if the two retainers are unrelated if one client's interests are directly adverse to the immediate interests of another client. The rule applies not only to acting for clients with conflicts in the same transaction, but also where the conflict arises from different transactions, providing that there is a reasonable relationship between them; as a result, in *Marks & Spencer Plc v Freshfields Bruckhaus Deringer* [2004] 1 W.L.R. 2331 Lawrence Collins J. injuncted the defendants from acting for a third party. Permission to appeal was refused by the Court of Appeal, see [2004] EWCA Civ 741; [2005] P.N.L.R. 4.

Application of *Mothew*. There have been a number of reported cases in which **11–024**
Mothew has been applied.[22] In *Bristol & West Building Society v Fancy &
Jackson (a firm)*,[23] Chadwick J. held that one of the defendant firms in that
litigation, Steggles Palmer, were in breach of fiduciary duty by failing to inform
the claimant building society that they acted for the vendor, but that breach did
not assist the claimant in obtaining compensation. The solicitors had also failed
to inform the claimant of various important facts about the vendor and purchaser,
but Chadwick J. held that it had not been pleaded or proved that there had been
a deliberate suppression of that information, and there was no breach of fiduciary
duty. Thus the defendants were in breach of the "double employment" rule, but
not the "actual conflict" rule.[24] In the other "managed" action that tried a
number of individual test cases, *Nationwide Building Society v Balmer Radmore
(a firm)*[25] the judge also had to apply *Mothew*. In *Nationwide Building Society v
Balmer Radmore*[26] itself, Blackburne J. held that the defendant solicitors did not
know that the borrowers were living at a different address, that information
which might suggest such a fact which was on the purchase file was unavailable,
in any event they would not have to disclose it, and there was no deliberate
withholding of information. There were, however, findings of breach of fiduciary
duty in two of the Nationwide "managed cases". In *Nationwide Building Society
v Goodwin Harte*[27] the solicitor knew of other transactions concerning the
security property, and in particular that there had been four 125-year leases
granted, and he should not have returned an unqualified report on title or
confirmed that the borrower would reside there personally. Knowledge of these
other transactions pointed to fraud, and thus overrode the duty of confidentiality
to the borrower. Blackburne J. was prepared to hold that the solicitor acted
consciously, deliberately and in bad faith. In *Nationwide Building Society v
Richard Grosse & Co*[28] the solicitor submitted a clear report on title without
investigating title at all, which particularly influenced the judge in finding a
breach of fiduciary duty, and there was also a direct payment of deposit moneys.

---

[22] See also *Armitage v Paynter Construction Ltd* [1999] 2 N.Z.L.R 535. A solicitor acted for two
clients who were undertaking a joint venture. When he knew that one of the joint venturers was in
financial difficulties, he paid to it moneys which were due to both clients. Following *Mothew*, the New
Zealand Court of Appeal found that an actual conflict had arisen. In *Leeds & Holbeck Building
Society v Arthur & Cole (a firm)* [2002] P.N.L.R. 23, the claimant building society failed to prove that
the solicitor had known that he ought to disclose the lack of any deposit passing through his hands
or that his failure had been intentional and conscious. Morland J., having heard the solicitor's
evidence, found him to be frank, fair and honest.
[23] [1997] 4 All E.R. 582. In another case in that litigation, *Read & Rogers*, the judge was unwilling
to infer that the solicitor had been dishonest, rather than being guilty of honest oversight.
[24] For an example of an actual conflict, see *Barrett v Reynolds* (1998) 20 R.P.R. (3d) 14, Nova Scotia
CA, where the lawyer had agreed with the purchaser and vendor clients that he would withdraw if
there was a conflict, but on learning that the bank's approval of financing was conditional on the
purchasers' ability to sell their house, he did not withdraw and he was in breach of fiduciary duty in
failing to inform the vendor of the facts.
[25] [1999] P.N.L.R. 606. This report provides the introductory and general findings. The court's
conclusions on the facts of the individual cases are to be found in the Lloyd's Rep. P.N.
[26] [1999] Lloyd's Rep. P.N. 559. Nor was there breach of fiduciary duty in *Nationwide Building
Society v Vanderpump & Sykes* [1999] Lloyd's Rep. P.N. 422.
[27] [1999] Lloyd's Rep. P.N. 338.
[28] [1999] Lloyd's Rep. P.N. 348.

In *Birmingham Midshires Building Society v Infields*[29] the defendant solicitor admitted negligence for failing to inform the claimant that the proposed borrower lived abroad and intended to let the security property. The solicitor elected to give evidence (as in *Richard Grosse & Co*, and unlike in *Goodwin Harte*). The judge was influenced by his explanations and demeanour, and held that he was a good and honest man who did not deliberately prefer the interests of the borrower above those of the lender and was not in breach of fiduciary duty.

11–025   **Canadian cases.** Relatively few cases of this nature are framed as breach of fiduciary duty in this country, unlike Canada. If Canadian jurisprudence were followed in this country, it would provide some qualification to the rule in *Clark Boyce v Mouat*[30] that a solicitor might continue to act despite a potential conflict, if both clients give informed consent to his acting. Thus it has been held in Canada that a solicitor should not act where the transaction is very complicated, and particularly where a partner of the solicitor has a personal interest in that transaction,[31] or where the client is unsophisticated and clearly needs protection and independent advice.[32] It has been held in Australia that the solicitor should not act where the possibility of conflict is acute.[33] The breach of fiduciary duty in such cases will normally be a failure to disclose information to the client that the solicitor discovers in the course of the retainer. For example, in *Lapierre v Young*[34] the solicitor acted for both sides in a mortgage transaction, and was in breach of fiduciary duty by failing to disclose to the unsophisticated lender that a recent sale was for a smaller sum than he was lending, that the mortgage was in arrears, and that the borrower would pay a higher rate of interest. It has been held that the mere failure to advise about the existence of material retainers before and after the retainer with the claimant may be a breach of fiduciary duty,[35] as will be a failure to inform the purchaser client about the vendor's secret profit when the solicitor acted in the previous sale,[36] and the failure to inform the purchaser client of the vendor's secret profit which he did not know about but

---

[29] [1999] Lloyd's Rep. P.N. 874, H.H. Judge Bowsher Q.C., sitting as a judge of the Technology and Construction Court.

[30] [1994] 1 A.C. 428 at 435F–H. For the facts see para.11–104, below. Generally, disclosure of the conflict will be sufficient: in *422246 BC Ltd v 0909 Management Inc* (2000) 80 B.C.L.R. (3d) 299, British Columbia CA, the solicitor had made full disclosure of a conflict of interest and was not in breach of fiduciary duty.

[31] *Davey v Woolley, Hames, Dale & Dingwall* (1982) 133 D.L.R. (3d) 647, Ontario CA.

[32] *Ferris v Rusnak* (1984) 9 D.L.R. (4th) 183, Alberta QB.

[33] *Trade Practices Commission v CC (New South Wales) Pty Ltd* (1994) 125 A.L.R. 94.

[34] (1981) 117 D.L.R. (3d) 643, Ontario High Court. See also *MacCullough v Corbett* (1982) 133 D.L.R. (3d) 43, Nova Scotia CA; *Clarence Construction Ltd v Lavallee* (1980) 111 D.L.R. (3d) 582 British Columbia Supreme Court; *Skimming v Goldberg* (1993) 6 W.W.R. 59, Manitoba QB; *Stewart v Layton* (1992) 111 A.L.R. 687, Foster J.; *Hong Kong Bank of Canada v Phillips* [1998] 2 W.W.R. 606, Manitoba QB; *Barrett v Reynolds* (1998) 170 N.S.R. (2d) 201, Nova Scotia CA.

[35] *Confederation Life v Shepherd, McKenzie* (1992) 29 R.P.R. (2d) 271, Ontario High Court. In *3464920 Canada Inc v Strother* (2005) 256 D.L.R. (4th) 319 the defendant solicitors advised the claimant that tax sheltered financing which the claimant carried on was at an end by reason of statutory changes. While continuing to carry out other business for the claimant, the defendants acted for other clients, in which one of its solicitors had an interest, in successfully reopening the tax sheltered financing. The British Columbia Court of Appeal held that the defendants were in breach of fiduciary duty, as they had an ongoing duty to disclose any conflict of interest.

[36] See *Jacks v Davis* (1983) 141 D.L.R. (3d) 355, British Columbia CA. *Quaere* whether acting in the previous sale was material to the decision.

should have.[37] In Canada, unlike in England, there may be a breach of fiduciary duty in failing to disclose information to his client although the solicitor has no other client and no personal interest in the transaction.[38]

(7) Confidence.[39] Solicitors owe a duty to their clients[40] to preserve confidences, both as a matter of an implied contractual term,[41] and as a fiduciary duty.[42] In *Marsh v Sofaer*[43] the Vice-Chancellor held that the duty to keep communications confidential extend to the conclusions a solicitor draws from the material communicated, and thus a solicitor cannot communicate his conclusion that the client did or might lack capacity even to another solicitor acting for the client in a different matter, and lack of capacity did not provide implied consent for such disclosure. Thus the Court struck out the claimant's allegation that the solicitors should have informed other solicitors acting for her in criminal proceedings of her lack of capacity. However, in the earlier case of *Howell-Smith v Official Solicitor*,[44] the Court of Appeal held that a solicitor had a duty to protect the interests of a client who was under a disability, and in some circumstances that would require breaching his client's confidence In that case, the solicitor had acted properly in requiring the client's psychiatrist to return monies she had invested with him and reporting his professional conduct, although they had no instructions from the client to do so. **11–026**

Restraint of breach of confidence. The courts will restrain solicitors from potentially breaching confidences, as was established in *Rakusen v Ellis, Munday & Clark*.[45] The risk of breach of confidence is particularly acute when firms amalgamate, and the Law Society has issued guidance on conflict arising on this.[46] The law has been reviewed by the House of Lords in *Bolkiah v KPMG*.[47] **11–027**

---

[37] *Canson Enterprises Ltd v Boughton* [1996] 1 W.W.R. 412, British Columbia CA.

[38] See, e.g. *Cassey v Morrison* (1993) 15 O.R. (3d) 223, Ontario CA, aff'm'g (1989) 67 O.R. (2d) 65.

[39] See also Ch.2 paras 2–155 to 2–179 and Ch.17 paras 17–023 and 17–024. See generally Toulson and Phipps, *Confidentiality*, (Sweet & Maxwell, 1996, 2nd edn, 2007), and Hollander and Salzedo, *Conflicts of Interest and Chinese Walls* (Sweet & Maxwell, 2nd edn, 2004).

[40] There may be a duty to preserve a confidence for a person "as good as" a client, such as a director of a client company, but the relevant relationship must be proved, and it was not in *MacQuarie Bank Ltd v Myer* [1994] 1 V.R. 350, App. Div. Duties of confidentiality will be owed to a solicitors' partners, which were breached by the defendants misusing confidential information to their own benefit in *Deacons v White & Case Ltd LLP* [2003] HKLRD 670, Hong Kong High Court.

[41] See *Parry-Jones v Law Society* [1969] 1 Ch.1 at 7A–B, *per* Lord Denning.

[42] e.g. *Schering Chemicals Ltd v Falkman Ltd* [1982] Q.B. 1 at 27–28, a case which did not concern solicitors.

[43] [2003] EWHC 3334; [2004] P.N.L.R. 24.

[44] [2006] P.N.L.R. 21 (1996).

[45] [1912] 1 Ch. 831. Other significant cases before *Bolkiah* (below) include the following: *Re a firm of Solicitors* [1992] 1 Q.B. 959, CA; *Re a firm of Solicitors* [1997] Ch. 1, Lighman J.; *Re Schuppan (a bankrupt)* [1996] 2 All E.R. 664, Robert Walker J.

[46] See the Law Society's *Guide to the Professional Conduct of Solicitors* (8th edn, 1999), annex 15A; for the up-to-date version see the Law Society's website.

[47] [1999] 2 A.C. 222. Note that the requirements of Ch.15 of the Law Society's *Guide to the Professional Conduct of Solicitors* (8th edn, 1999) (and see the Law Society's website for the up-to-date version), are more onerous. For commentary see J. O'Sullivan: "Lawyers, conflicts of interest and Chinese walls" (2000) 16 P.N. 88, and Ter Kah Leng, "Protecting confidential client information" (2000) 16 P.N. 103. See also Stafford, Andrew: "Chinese walls and confidential information" (2003) 19 P.N. 306. For an early illustration of an injunction being granted applying *Bolkiah* see *Re*

While the case concerned accountants, they were undertaking litigation services, and the position of a solicitor would be at least as onerous, as the information would be privileged as well as confidential. The claimant must prove (i) that the solicitor is in possession of information which is confidential (and which he has not consented to disclose) and (ii) that the information may be relevant to the new matter in which the interest of the other client may be adverse to his own. The burden of proof is not a heavy one, and there is no presumption in favour of either side. The knowledge of one partner is not to be imputed to his fellow partners. If the two criteria mentioned above are satisfied, then the court will intervene unless satisfied that there is no risk of disclosure, in relation to which the defendant has the evidential burden. The risk has to be a real one, and not merely fanciful or theoretical. The court may be satisfied by clear and convincing evidence that effective measures have been taken to ensure that no disclosure will occur, such as the imposition of "Chinese walls" as an established part of the organisational structure. In *Bolkiah* itself, the House of Lords considered that the "Chinese walls" which were erected by KPMG were inadequate, as they were ad hoc and they were erected in a single department where personnel were accustomed to work together.

11–028   **No confidential information.** In some cases there is no confidential information to be imparted. In *T & A (children)*[48] a local authority applied for care orders in respect of children, which were opposed by the father. He sought to prevent solicitors acting for the guardian *ad litem*, as the solicitor concerned had acted for him in 1986 on burglary and theft charges, and the firm had acted for him in a number of minor criminal matters in 1997. The Court of Appeal upheld the judge's finding that the solicitor was not in possession of any confidential information, and there was no risk of a perception of injustice. The solicitor had no recollection of the 1986 matter, and she had no involvement in the criminal department of the firm, where the partner who had acted for the father had no

---

a firm of Solicitors [1999] P.N.L.R. 950. The applicant architects were involved in litigation brought by a claimant. That claimant retained B of firm X in that litigation. The architects had been involved in other litigation with some common features to the present one, in which they had instructed A of firm Y. A left firm Y and joined firm X. The Technology and Construction Court granted an injunction restraining firm X from continuing to act for the claimant. A had possession of relevant confidential information, some of which had already been passed to B, and there was a real risk of further inadvertent disclosure.

[48] [2000] Lloyd's Rep. P.N. 452. *cf. Davies v Davies* [1999] 3 F.C.R. 745, CA, where a solicitor was disqualified from acting for the husband in divorce proceedings where the solicitor had been consulted by the wife six years earlier about problems in the marriage. For another illustration see *Ball v Druces & Attlee (a firm)* [2002] P.N.L.R. 23. The defendant solicitors acted for the Eden Trust in litigation brought by the claimant. He alleged that the solicitors had acted for him in setting up the Eden project, and that there was a risk that they would give their clients confidential information to his prejudice. Burton J. held that there was an arguable case that the claimant's retainer of the solicitors had existed and that confidential information imparted to the solicitors might remain in their hands. He therefore granted an interlocutory injunction, as he was not satisfied that there was no risk of disclosure, on the basis of a cross-undertaking and guarantee in relation to the solicitors' potential lost profits and the Eden Trust's potential expense of instructing new solicitors. *cf. Re Recover Ltd (in liquidation)* [2003] EWHC 536, Ch; [2003] 2 B.C.L.C. 186, where Pumfrey J. required the alleged confidential information to be properly particularised, which it was not, and thus no injunction was granted.

recollection of him. The Court held that the unique nature of child care proceedings and the role of the guardian did not justify a departure from the principles of *Bolkiah*.

Adequate barriers. In several cases the Courts have found that there were sufficient barriers to prevent a risk of disclosure of confidential information. In *Re a firm of Solicitors*[49] a P&I Club sought to restrain solicitors from acting for defendants in litigation for unpaid release calls, where the defence alleged (inter alia) that supplementary calls were likely to be more than 25 per cent of advance calls. The club was also suing its insurance brokers for recommending certain reinsurers who had turned out to be worthless, where the brokers alleged that the club's managers were negligent in failing to check out the insurers. This was referred to the club's E underwriters, for whom the solicitors also acted. The failure of the reinsurers was one of the reasons for the difference between estimated and actual calls. The link between the two matters was held to be tenuous, but the Court did draw the inference that some of the existing information imparted by the club to its E underwriter's solicitors might be relevant to the proceedings. However, there was compelling evidence that the solicitor's information barrier, which was in place already, would work. The two matters had always been handled in two different departments, which were physically separated, there was no mixing of work, there was limited social contact and separate documentary storage. The solicitors had established the heavy burden of showing that the risk of inadvertent disclosure of confidential information was no more than theoretical, and Timothy Walker J. did not grant any injunction. More recently, in *GUS Consulting GMBH v Leboeuf, Lamb, Greene & Macrae*[50] the defendants were acting for a party to an arbitration which had made allegations of fraud against the other party, the claimant. Some of the partners in the defendants had acted for the claimant while in another firm. The Judge dismissed an application to restrain the defendants from acting for the claimant as there was an effective Chinese wall in relation to access to files, and an undertaking had been offered to instruct all staff who had acted for the claimant not to discuss the work they had done with the arbitration team, and to change its working arrangements so that the two teams would not work on the same floor. The Court of Appeal upheld the decision. Contrast *Halewood International Ltd v Addleshaw Booth & Co*[51] where the claimant owned the trade mark "Lambrini", and had been involved in injunctive proceedings in relation to the use of the name "Lamfresco". The solicitor who acted for the claimant moved to the defendant firm, which commenced acting for Italian wine growers who sold Lambrusco wine and who contended that the claimant was guilty of passing off. Applying

11-029

---

[49] [2000] 1 Lloyd's Rep. 31, Timothy Walker J. See also *Koch Shipping Inc v Richards Butler (a firm)* [2003] EWCA Civ 1280; [2003] P.N.L.R. 11, where the partner handling the applicant's shipping arbitration left her firm and joined Richards Butler, who acted for the opposing party. There were detailed undertakings from all the solicitors involved, and the Court of Appeal held that this made the risk of inadvertent disclosure of confidential information fanciful, and discharged the injunction which had been granted at first instance. cf. *Marks & Spencer Plc v Freshfields Bruckhaus Deringer* [2004] 1 W.L.R. 2331, where Lawrence Collins J. held that no effective barriers could be put in place because of the very large numbers of people concerned.
[50] [2006] EWCA Civ 683; [2006] P.N.L.R. 32.
[51] [2000] P.N.L.R. 788.

Bolkiah, Neuberger J. held that the solicitor had probably obtained confidential information in the Lamfresco litigation that might be relevant to the Lambrusco litigation, although most of the evidence was in the public domain. The judge held that the defendant solicitors then had a heavy evidential burden to show that there was no real risk of disclosure. They had set up an information barrier, and as the size of their intellectual property department in Leeds was relatively small and only one solicitor had confidential information, such a system would be easier to police than in the *Bolkiah* case. However, the judge thought that there was still a small risk of disclosure of confidential information as the solicitor worked in the same building as the Lambrusco litigation team. The defendant solicitors were prepared to undertake that the solicitor would work in a different building, and on that basis the judge did not grant the injunction.

11–030   **Commonwealth cases.** The position in the Commonwealth varies. In *MacDonald v Martin*[52] the Supreme Court of Canada adopted a two-fold approach. First, could the solicitor rebut the inference that he had received confidential information, without revealing any such information?[53] Secondly, was there a risk of using that information to prejudice the client? The court left open the possibility of professional bodies adopting effective screening rules, which subsequently happened, and the presumption that confidential information would be imparted was first rebutted in *Choukalos v Smith Lyons*[54] by undertakings and following the Law Society's guidelines for screening devices. In Australia the test is whether there is a real and sensible possibility of a breach of confidence,[55] and *Bolkiah* has recently been followed and applied.[56] In New Zealand the test used for granting injunctions to restrain breaches of confidence is similar to that found

---

[52] [1990] 3 S.C.R. 1235, which was applied in e.g. the following appellate decisions: *Baumgartner v Baumgartner* (1995) 122 D.L.R. (4th) 543, British Columbia CA; *Canada Southern Petroleum v Amoco Canada Petroleum Co* (1997) 144 D.L.R. (4th) 30, Alberta CA; *Canadian Pacific Railway Co v Aikins, MacAulay & Thorvaldson* (1998) 157 D.L.R. (4th) 473, Manitoba CA; *Davies, Ward & Beck v Baker and McKenzie* (1998) 164 D.L.R. (4th) 423, Ontario CA; *Everingham v Ontario* (1992) 88 D.L.R. (4th) 755, Ontario DC; *G v International Christian Mission Inc* (1995) 125 D.L.R. (4th) 712, Nova Scotia CA; *Gainers Inc v Pocklington* (1995) 125 D.L.R. (4th) 50, Alberta CA; *Grabber Industrial Products Central Ltd v Stewart & Co* (2000) 185 D.L.R. (4th) 303, British Columbia CA (refusing to restrain a solicitor married to a partner in the claimant's solicitors); *Oliver, Derksen Arkin v Fulmyk* (1995) 126 D.L.R. (4th) 123, Manitoba CA; *Rosin v MacPhail* (1997) 142 D.L.R. (4th) 304, British Columbia CA; *Trizec Properties Ltd v Husky Oil Operations Ltd* (1997) 148 D.L.R. (4th) 300, Alberta CA; *Bank of Montreal v Dresler* (2003) 224 D.L.R. (4th) 337, New Brunswick CA; *Ehsan v Begin* (2005) 247 D.L.R. (4th) 83, British Columbia CA. There are a large number of further cases, for which see the Canadian Abridgement.
[53] *cf.* the approach in Australia where the complainant has to identify the confidential information, see *Carindale Country Club Estate Pty Ltd v Astill* (1993) 115 A.L.R. 112, Drummond J. But *Unioil International Pty Ltd v Deloitte Touche Tohmatsu* [1997] 17 W.A.R. 98, High Court, followed the *McDonald v Martin* approach. For a helpful explanation of some aspects of the law, see C. Edmonds, "Trusing lawyers with confidences" (1997–98) 17 *Australian Bar Review* 222. However, in *Spincode Pty Ltd v Look Software Pty Ltd* [2001] VSCA 248; (2001) 4 V.R. 501, the Victoria Court of Appeal rejected the English law that an injunction could only be granted where there was a risk of disclosure of confidential information, and considered that an order could also be made on the basis of breach of a duty of loyalty or a solicitor's conduct being offensive to fairness and justice.
[54] (1994) 97 B.C.L.R. (2d) 122.
[55] *National Mutual v Sentry* (1989) A.L.R. 539 and *Murray v MacQuarie Bank Ltd* (1992) 105 A.L.R. 612, both Federal Court of Australia.
[56] *Newman v Phillips Fox* (1999) 21 W.A.R. 309, Supreme Court.

in *Bolkiah*, but in addition a balancing exercise is undertaken.[57] An injunction
was granted by the New Zealand Court of Appeal in favour of a party which had
not been a client of the solicitors in *Carter Holt Harvey Forests Ltd v Sunnex
Logging Ltd*.[58] The solicitors acted for Sunnex in proceedings against Carter
Holt. An injunction was granted as they had acted in a very similar claim by Rua
against Carter Holt. The earlier litigation had ended in a mediation in which the
lawyers had participated, and where they had signed a comprehensive confidentiality agreement on which Carter Holt were entitled to rely.

Overriding confidence. The duty of confidence may be overridden in some   **11–031**
circumstances.[59] For example, confidential matters may have to be disclosed to
the Law Society, which can insist on the inspection of books and documents to
check that there is compliance with its accounting rules.[60] The duty may be
negated if the lawyer has strong evidence of suspected fraud on the part of the
client, and if so he can apply to the court for directions.[61]

Restraint in other circumstances. Applications have been made to restrain   **11–032**
lawyers from acting in rather different circumstances, where there is no confidential information.[62] In *Re L (Minors) (Care proceedings: Solicitors)*[63] two
solicitors acting in care proceedings for the claimant mother and the local
authority were cohabiting. This could give rise to an apprehension of bias, and it
was crucial in this regard that the solicitor acted for the local authority, which was
an arm of the state, in care proceedings. The court declared that the local
authority's solicitor would no longer act unless the conduct of the case was
transferred to another solicitor. In *Christie v Wilson*[64] a solicitor-advocate was not
prevented from acting in a libel action for a claimant when he had previously
advised that the offending article was not defamatory. The case was decided on
the construction of the Law Society's Code for Advocacy 1993. In *Locabail
(UK) Ltd v Bayfield Properties Ltd*[65] the Court of Appeal gave guidance on when

---

[57] *Russell McVeagh McKenzie Bartleet & Co v Tower Corp* [1998] 3 N.Z.L.R. 641, NZCA.
[58] [2001] 3 N.Z.L.R. 343.
[59] See generally the Law Society's *Guide to the Professional Conduct of Solicitors* (8th edn, 1999),
Ch.16 (and for the up-to-date version see the Law Society website); Toulson and Phipps, *Confidentiality* (Sweet & Maxwell, 1996, 2nd edn, 2007).
[60] See *Parry-Jones v Law Society* [1969] 1 Ch. 1, CA.
[61] *Finers v Miro* [1991] 1 W.L.R. 35, CA. See also *R. v Cox and Railton* (1884) L.R. 14 Q.B.D. 153,
CA. The issue has arisen in a number of cases brought by lenders, on which see para.11–219,
below.
[62] See also *Geveran Trading Co Ltd v Skjevesland* [2002] EWCA Civ 1567; [2003] 1 W.L.R. 912,
CA, noted at Ch.12, para.12–005), and *Re Recover Ltd (in liquidation)* [2003] EWHC 536, Ch;
[2003] 2 B.C.L.C. 186, Pumfrey J. See also the guidance of the House of Lords in *Porter v Magill*
[2002] 2 A.C. 357. For an illustration of another potential area of dispute where the insurer appoints
solicitors to act for the insured but also denies liability, see *Nishimatsu-Costain-China Harbour Joint
Venture v Ip Kwan & Co* [2001] HKLRD 84, Hong Kong, CA.
[63] [2001] 1 W.L.R. 100, Wilson J.
[64] [1998] 1 W.L.R 1694.
[65] [2000] Q.B. 451. See also the earlier case of *Laker Airways Inc v FLS Aerospace Ltd and Burton*
[1999] Lloyd's Rep. 45, Rix J.: a barrister can generally act as arbitrator in a case where counsel
comes from his chambers.

a judge should disqualify himself from hearing a case in circumstances where his former firm had acted for one of the parties.

(iv) *Trust Duties*

11–033   **Express and implied trusts.** The subject of traditional express trusts is not considered in this work. A solicitor's liabilities, powers and duties will be governed by the trust deed. As a professional trustee acting for remuneration, a solicitor may have a higher standard of care than an unpaid trustee.[66] In conveyancing transactions, money received by the solicitor will normally be held under an implied trust, and will be subject to the Solicitors' Accounts Rules 1991.

11–034   **Trusts and lender claims.** Trust concepts have been deployed in litigation by mortgage lenders against their former solicitors in the hope that there might be more advantageous rules on causation and loss, and the cases are considered in more detail below under the heading of damages.[67] Such cases start from the uncontroversial principle that client moneys are held by solicitors on trust. The more difficult issue is to identify which breaches of instruction will result in a breach of trust. It would appear from *Target Holdings Ltd v Redferns*[68] that although a solicitor is a trustee with no authority to part with the mortgage moneys before completion, if he negligently completes before he has obtained good title, that is a breach of retainer and not a breach of trust. In *Bristol & West Building Society v Mothew*[69] it was argued that the lender's instructions to the solicitor made the solicitor's authority to complete the transaction conditional on complying with all his obligations to the lender, so that any breach of obligation would cause the payment of monies to be without authority and thus in breach of trust. Millett L.J. rejected this argument, and held that the instructions would have to be very clearly worded to lead to such an inconvenient result. The position is likely to be different and the solicitor's authority to release funds will be vitiated if he knows that the borrower has made fraudulent misrepresentations, but conceals this, see *Alliance & Leicester Building Society v Edgestop*.[70] In the unusual case of *Glantz v Polikoff & Co*,[71] the claimant loaned moneys to a purchaser involved in a fraud. The money was paid to the purchaser's solicitor, who was unaware of the fraud, and who held the money on trust. While the solicitor owed no duty of care to the claimant, he was in breach of trust in paying the money away, given the suspicious circumstances of which he was aware. In *Twinsectra v Yardley*[72] the House of Lords held that when solicitors receive monies from a lender on an undertaking that they will be retained until they are applied in the acquisition of property on behalf of the client, and will only be

---

[66] *Bartlett v Barclays Bank Trust Co Ltd (No.1)* [1980] Ch. 515 at 534.
[67] See further paras 11–228 *et seq.*, below.
[68] [1996] A.C. 421 at 428, *per* Lord Browne-Wilkinson, with whom all their Lordships agreed.
[69] [1998] Ch. 1, applied in *Nationwide Building Society v Balmer Radmore* [1999] P.N.L.R. 606.
[70] [1999] Lloyd's Rep. P.N. 868, Hoffman J. This 1991 case was approved but distinguished in *Target* [1996] A.C. 421 at 439.
[71] [1993] N.P.C. 145, QBD.
[72] [2002] UKHL 12; [2002] 2 A.C. 164.

used for that purpose, a trust was created. The power to apply the money "in the acquisition of property" was sufficiently certain to create a trust, and the fact that the lender had not intended to create a trust was irrelevant.

Constructive trusts. A solicitor's liability as a constructive trustee was **11-035** analysed by Millett L.J. in *Paragon Finance Plc v Thakerar & Co.*[73] He distinguished two classes of case. In the first the defendant was not expressly appointed a trustee, but he assumed the duties of a trustee in a lawful transaction. In the second, the trust obligation arose out of the unlawful transaction which was impeached by the claimant, and the constructive trust is nothing more than a formula for equitable relief. There are examples of the first class of case, where the solicitor takes it upon himself to act as a trustee where he is not one,[74] but the second class of case has received more attention. The traditional classification of this class distinguishes between knowing receipt of trust property and knowing assistance in a breach of trust.

Knowing receipt. Solicitors may be liable for knowing receipt of trust prop-   **11-036** erty transferred in breach of trust only when they have sufficient knowledge of the breach of trust, the relevant test for knowledge being unconscionability.[75] In *Re Blundell*,[76] solicitors were paid out of a trust estate for work they had done in administering it. It was held that an agent had no obligation to enquire how the trustee had administered the estate, and they were not liable as constructive trustees, as they had no actual knowledge of the breach.[77] While they knew that one trustee had purchased part of the trust property for himself in breach of trust, they did not have notice that the transaction was such as to preclude the trustee from resorting to the trust fund for payment of legal costs. A similar view was taken in *Carl Zeiss Stiftung v Herbert Smith & Co.*[78] The claimant, East German Carl Zeiss Stiftung, alleged that its West German counterpart held all its assets on trust. The defendants acted for the West German foundation, and the claimants claimed that fees and disbursements paid to them were held on constructive trust. The Court of Appeal considered that mere knowledge of a claim was insufficient and did not amount to notice of the trust, absent bad faith.

---

[73] [1999] 1 All E.R. 400 at 408–409.
[74] See *Mara v Browne* [1896] 1 Ch. 199 (now to be read subject to *Dubai Aluminium Co Ltd v Salaam* [2003] 2 A.C. 366), and *Blyth v Fladgate* [1891] 1 Ch. 337, where solicitors were held liable when they sold exchequer bills and reinvested the money badly on the direction of a sole trustee who had then died, but before the appointment of any new trustee.
[75] See *Bank of Credit and Commerce International (Overseas) Ltd v Akinidele* [2001] Ch. 437, CA (a case which did not involve solicitors). Dishonesty is not required here, see *Houghton v Fayers* [2000]1 B.C.L.C. 511 at 516h, *per* Nourse L.J. The cases discussed in this paragraph, while before the development of the test of unconscionability, are likely to be correct on their facts.
[76] (1888) 40 Ch. D. 370. For another example see *Williams v Williams* (1881) 17 Ch. D 437, where a solicitor acting on the instructions of the trustee misapplied moneys which were subject to a marriage settlement in the honest but mistaken belief there was in fact no settlement, and he was not liable. See also *Lee v Sankey* (1873) L.R. 15 Eq. 204 and *Williams-Ashman v Price & Williams* [1942] 1 Ch. 219.
[77] (1888) 40 Ch. D 370 at 383.
[78] [1969] 2 Ch. 276.

11–037   **Dishonest assistance.**[79] A solicitor may be liable as a constructive trustee in what used to be categorised as knowing assistance in a dishonest and fraudulent design.[80] The jurisdiction has been reformulated by the Privy Council in *Royal Brunei Airlines v Tan*,[81] who made it clear that there is no requirement of a dishonest and fraudulent design, and that the touchstone of liability is dishonesty by the party assisting the trustee. In *Twinsectra v Yardley*[82] the House of Lords applied *Royal Brunei Airlines v Tan* in a case against a solicitor. Monies were paid by the claimant lender to a Mr Sims pursuant to his undertaking that they would be applied in the acquisition of property, which created an express purpose trust. Most of those monies were paid to the defendant solicitor without the imposition of any restriction, although the solicitor knew of the undertakiing. The solicitor acquiesced in a short term advance of £34,000 for another venture, and used other parts of the money for the payment of his fees and other uses which were not the anticipated acquisition of property. A majority of the House of Lords (Lord Millett dissenting) held that the test for dishonesty[83] was that the defendant's knowledge of the transaction had to be such as to render his participation contrary to ordinary standards of honest behaviour, but he did not have to reflect about what those normal standards would be. The trial judge had held that the solicitor was mistaken rather than dishonest, as he believed that the undertaking was not his concern, and the House of Lords held that in the light of the judge's findings, the Court of Appeal should not have substituted its own findings of dishonesty.

11–038   **Further cases.** A number of relatively recent cases before *Twinsectra v Yardley* have considered allegations of dishonest assistance.[84] In *Walker v*

---

[79] Note that it may be sufficient if there is dishonest assistance in a breach of fiduciary duty, see *Brown v Bennett* [1999] 1 B.C.L.C. 649, CA.
[80] For two examples before the development of the modern law where solicitors did not have sufficient knowledge see: *Barnes v Addy* (1874) L.R. 9 Ch.App. 244 (solicitors had advised against the appointment as trustee of the husband of the tenant for life, but prepared the necessary deeds and introduced him to a broker to sell stock; they were not liable, as they had no knowledge of the dishonest intention to misappropriate trust funds); and *Equiticorp v Hawkins* [1991] 3 N.Z.L.R. 700 (Hong Kong solicitors assisted by supplying 50 shelf companies in what were alleged to be transactions which were illegal under New Zealand company law; the solicitors inquired about the transactions from other solicitors who had instructed them and were assured about the probity of the transactions, and they were entitled to rely on those assurances).
[81] [1995] 2 A.C. 378, a case which did not involve a claim against solicitors. *cf.* the position in New Zealand where in *Gathergood v Blundell* [1992] 3 N.Z.L.R. 643 the Court of Appeal held that the crucial question in knowing receipt or knowing assistance, where the knowledge in question was the breach of a fiduciary duty by a third party was knowledge of material facts giving rise to the existence of the duty and breach.
[82] [2002] UKHL 12; [2002] 2 A.C. 164. For a helpful commentary on the case see T.M. and Tjio H.: "Knowing what is dishonesty" (2002) 118 L.Q.R. 502.
[83] What precisely the House of Lords held has been interpreted by the Privy Council in *Barlow Clowes International Ltd v Eurotrust Ltd* [2006] 1 W.L.R. 1476, and the text reflects this. For helpful commentaries see Sir A. Clarke M.R., "Claims against professionals: negligence, dishonesty and fraud" (2006) 22 P.N. 70; M. Conaglen & A. Goymour, "Dishonesty in the context of assistance—again" [2006] C.L.J. 18, and T. Yeo: "Dishonest assistance: a restatement from the Privy Council" (2006) 122 L.Q.R. 171.
[84] *Quaere* the extent to which they are all reconcilable with *Twinsectra* (above); the reinterpretation of that case in *Barlow Clowes* (above) makes it more likely that they are.

Stones[85] the Court of Appeal held that a solicitor trustee who committed a breach of trust in the genuine belief that what he was doing was for the benefit of the beneficiaries, was nevertheless dishonest if his belief, by objective standards, was so unreasonable that no reasonable trustee could have thought that the breach was for the benefit of the beneficiaries. In *Gruppo Torras v Al-Sabah*[86] the Court of Appeal upheld a judge's finding of dishonest assistance against a Spanish lawyer. The Court considered that judicial restatements or refinements of the principles set out in *Royal Brunei* should be seen in the context of the factual circumstances before the Court, and emphasised that the test was whether the defendant was acting as an honest person would in the circumstances, which was an objective test. If there was "blind eye" dishonesty, which was refraining from asking questions which an honest man would, the Court should make this clear.

(b) *Duties to Third Parties*

(i) *General*

The general law.[87] It was formerly the law that solicitors owed no duty of care   **11–039** to persons who were not their clients for negligent misstatements relied upon by them.[88] The law changed after the case of *Hedley Byrne & Co Ltd v Heller & Partners Ltd*, which established liability for negligent misstatement relied upon by the claimant.[89] There has been considerable uncertainty about what principles *Hedley Byrne* established, and the test to be applied for determining whether a duty of care is owed. One approach has been the tripartite test developed in *Smith v Bush*,[90] *Caparo v Dickman*,[91] *Spring v Guardian Assurance Plc*[92] and *Marc Rich & Co v Bishop Rock Marine Co Ltd*[93] of foreseeability, proximity and whether it is just and reasonable to impose a duty of care. Side by side with this

---

[85] [2001] Q.B. 902, essentially repeating what was said in *Royal Brunei*. Other cases against solicitors dealing with dishonesty include *Abbey National v Solicitors' Indemnity Fund* [1997] P.N.L.R. 307 (where Steel J. held that a person acted dishonestly if his action was dishonest by the standards of ordinary decent people and he personally should have realised that this was the case; the case concerned the construction of the SIF rules; the decision was approved by Lord Hutton in *Twinsectra v Yardley* [2002] UKHL 12; [2002] 2 A.C. 164. at para.37), and *Mortgage Express v Newman* [2000] P.N.L.R. 298 (where the Court of Appeal held that in cases of alleged dishonesty the judge should consider the mind of the solicitor, the understanding and practice of solicitors at the time, and the events which took place, and then decide whether according to the standards of right-thinking members of society the act or omission was incompetent or dishonest. In *Mortgage Express Ltd v S Newman & Co (a firm)* [2001] Lloyd's Rep. P.N. 605 Etherton J. found, on the retrial, that the solicitor was not dishonest).
[86] [2001] Lloyd's Rep. P.N. 117.
[87] See generally Ch.2 paras 2–112 to 2–118.
[88] For instance, in *Fish v Kelly* (1864) 17 C.B. (N.S.) 194 the claimant consulted his employer's attorney, the defendant, about his rights if he gave notice terminating his employment. The defendant gave incorrect advice. The claimant's subsequent claim for damages was dismissed on the grounds that (i) the claimant was not the defendant's client and (ii) the advice was given during a casual conversation. This decision has subsequently been explained on the basis of the second ground only, see *Hedley Byrne & Co Ltd v Heller & Partners Ltd* [1964] A.C. 456 at 510 and 539.
[89] [1964] A.C. 465.
[90] [1990] 1 A.C. 837 at 865A, *per* Lord Griffiths.
[91] [1990] 2 A.C. 605 at 617H–618B (Lord Bridge) and 633B–C (Lord Oliver).
[92] [1995] 2 A.C. 296, *per* Lords Keith, Slynn and Woolf.
[93] [1996] A.C. 211.

general test, the courts have adopted an incremental approach from decided cases in *Murphy v Brentwood DC*.[94] Following this approach, *Hedley Byrne* has been interpreted as imposing liability when there has been a voluntary assumption of responsibility, and this has been applied by all of the House of Lords in *Henderson v Merrett Syndicates Ltd*,[95] a minority in *Spring v Guardian Assurance Plc*,[96] a majority in the solicitor's negligence case of *White v Jones*,[97] and and all their Lordships in *Williams v Natural Life Ltd*.[98] In *Customs and Excise Commissioners v Barclays Bank Plc*[99] the House of Lords have held that the various tests disclose no single common denominator, and the court should focus on the detailed circumstances of the case and the relationship between the parties.

11–040   **Reliance without retainer.** In *Crossan v Ward Bracewell & Co*[1] the claimant was charged with reckless driving, and consulted the defendant solicitors. They advised him that he should defend himself, or instruct the defendants, in which he case he would have to pay £50 on account of costs. They did not mention the possibilities of legal aid or of the claimant's insurers paying his costs. The claimant did not retain the defendants, but represented himself and pleaded guilty. He failed to notify his insurers of the accident, and they repudiated liability. Kennedy J. found the defendants liable, and decided that once they had elected to hold themselves out as qualified to assist the claimant as to how he could obtain funds to pay legal costs, they owed him a duty of care. Similarly, in *Throwley Homes v Sharratts*[2] the defendant solicitors acted for the claimant in a conveyancing transaction without fee. While there was no contractual retainer, Gage J. held that the defendants owed the claimant a duty of care in tort. It has been suggested in Australia[3] and Hong Kong[4] that a person employed by a firm who undertakes work for a client will generally owe the client a duty of care in tort. The position remains to be determined in England, and may depend on the precise circumstances.

11–041   **Reliance by non-client establishing duty.**[5] There are some cases where it has been held that a duty of care was owed to an associate of the client who relied

---

[94] [1991] 1 A.C. 398.

[95] [1995] 2 A.C. 145.

[96] [1995] 2 A.C. 296 (Lords Goff and Lowry).

[97] [1995] 2 A.C. 207. This case is discussed below at para.11–048.

[98] [1998] 1 W.L.R. 830.

[99] [2006] UKHL 28; [2006] 3 W.L.R. 1.

[1] (1989) 5 P.N. 103. Similarly for *Mathew v Maughold Life Assurance Co Ltd* [1955–1995] P.N.L.R. 51, CA. It is submitted that *Crossnan* is still good law on any of the modern test.

[2] [1998] N.P.C. 57.

[3] *Shigeva v Schafer* (1984) 5 N.S.W.L.R. 502, High Court.

[4] See *Yazhou Travel Investment Co Ltd* [2005] P.N.L.R. 31, High Court, relying on the personal nature of the solicitor-client relationship, and discussed in *Williams v Natural Life Health Foods Ltd* [1988] 1 W.L.R. 830, HL, and *Merrett v Babb* [2001] EWCA Civ 214; [2001] Q.B. 1174, two English cases which did not concern solicitors. See also J. Cooke and A. Harvey: "Babb and solicitor's negligence: can LLP status provide complete protection from personal liability?" (2006) 22 P.N. 106.

[5] The special case of whether a duty of care is owed to parties on the other side of litigation or a transaction from the solicitor's client is discussed below.

on the solicitor. In *Blackwell v Barroile Pty Ltd*[6] the Australian Federal Court of Appeal decided that a solicitor owed a duty of care to the client's trustee in bankruptcy as a result of the reliance by the trustee on the solicitor, which gave rise to a relationship of proximity. The solicitor had to inform the trustee properly in response to the trustee's request for information about the client's affairs. In *Re Foster*[7] it was held that the solicitors acting for a company also owed a duty of care to the two directors and secretary who had guaranteed the company's debts, where the solicitors were alleged to have negligently failed to register a legal charge which secured the debts.[8] In *Rothschild v Berenson*[9] solicitors acting for a lender which was obtaining funds from a consortium of banks were held by the Court of Appeal to have assumed responsibility to those banks.

Reliance by non-client without duty. However, recent cases have found no **11–042** duty of care in analogous circumstances.[10] In *A & J Fabrication (Batley) Ltd v Grant Thornton*[11] a creditor of a company wished to sue the solicitors who acted for its liquidators for failing to issue proceedings against the directors of the company within the limitation period. Astill J. refused leave to add the solicitors as additional defendants to an action the creditor had brought against the liquidator because no duty of care was owed. There had been no direct dealings or correspondence between the creditor and the solicitors, and it had primarily relied on the liquidator. The mere knowledge that advice might be passed on to and relied by the creditor, who was the principal funder of the liquidator's proceedings, did not create a duty of care. In *Brownie Wills v Shrimpton*[12] solicitors acted for a company which was obtaining an overdraft from a bank.

---

[6] (1994) 123 A.L.R. 81. To similar effect, see *Estill v Cowling* [2000] Lloyd's Rep. P.N. 378, discussed at Ch.12, para.12–006. See also *Wakim v HIH Casualty & General Insurance Ltd* [2001] FCA 103; [2001] 182 A.L.R. 353, discussed at Ch.12, para.12–006, where a duty of care was owed by a solicitor to the principal creditor of his client, the trustee in bankruptcy; the issue of reliance was not discussed.

[7] (1986) 2 P.N. 193. Also reported *sub nom. Foster v Crusts* [1986] B.C.L.C. 307.

[8] *Re Foster* was based on the two-part test for liability found in the speech of Lord Wilberforce in *Anns v Merton LBC* [1978] A.C. 728 which was decisively rejected by the House of Lords in *Murphy v Brentwood DC* [1991] 1 A.C. 398. On the facts of *Re Foster* it would not appear that there was a voluntary assumption of responsibility, and it must be questionable whether the case is correctly decided. See also *RP Howard Ltd v Woodman Matthews & Co* [1983] B.C.L.C. 117. The solicitor was acting for the company, and it was held to the principal shareholder too. Staughton J. stated, obiter, that the solicitor owed a duty of care to the company's principal shareholder, basing his conclusion in the two-stage test found in *Anns*. For possible limits to this case see *Verderame v Commercial Assurance Co Ltd* [1992] B.C.L.C. 793 (an insurance broker's case, see Ch.16, para.16–030), and *Huxford v Stoy Hayward & Co* (1989) 5 B.C.C. 421 (an accountant's case see Ch.17, para.17–083). *Howard* was followed with apparent approval by the New Zealand Court of Appeal in *Christensen v Scott* [1996] 1 N.Z.L.R. 273, who refused to strike out a claim by guarantors and shareholders of a company which retained solicitors in a particular transaction, although it was also alleged that the plaintiffs had been and remained personal clients of the solicitors.

[9] [1995] N.P.C. 107; E.G.C.S. 17.

[10] In *Budrewicz v Stojanowski* (1998) 41 O.R. (3d) 78 the Ontario High Court held that there was no duty of care by a solicitor who acted for a client lending money on mortgage towards the claimant who supplied the money, as there was no direct contact between the parties, no reliance, and any reliance would not have been reasonable. In *Midland Mortgage Corp v Jawl & Bundon* (1999) 64 B.C.L.R. (3d) 1. the British Columbia Court of Appeal held that there was no duty to another lender where such a duty might conflict with the duty owed to the lender client.

[11] [1999] P.N.L.R. 811.

[12] [1999] P.N.L.R. 553.

The claimant was a director of the company who guaranteed the overdraft, and signed it in the defendants' offices. He sued the defendant solicitors for failing to explain the nature of the guarantee to him. The New Zealand Court of Appeal held that the solicitors owed no duty of care to the director. To found a duty of care there needed to be reliance, and the reliance had to be reasonable, which depended on the reliance being induced by the conduct of the defendants. In fact the solicitors were instructed by the bank to obtain the guarantee, but the claimant knew nothing of that. The claimant assumed that the defendants, as the company's solicitors, would look after the interests of the directors, but that assumption was not reasonable.

11–043   **Liability without reliance.** A number of cases have found duties of care in circumstances where there was no reliance by the claimant. They may be justified on the tripartite test, or by extending the voluntary assumption of responsibility despite the absence of reliance, as was done in *White v Jones*.[13] In *Whelton Sinclair (a firm) v Hyland*[14] the claimant solicitors had acted for the defendant tenant in the assignment of a lease of a shop to him. The solicitors received a letter from the landlord informing them that he had served on the tenant a notice, under s.25 of the Landlord and Tenant Act 1954, to determine the lease of the shop. The Court of Appeal decided that there had subsequently been a contract between the solicitors and the tenant. They concluded, obiter, that in the context of the previous instructions and the landlord's letter, and knowing that there was a strict time-limit on the matter, the solicitors owed the tenants a duty of care either to indicate that they were not going to act or to take immediate steps to ensure that the defendant's interests were safeguarded. In *Penn v Bristol & West Building Society*[15] a husband instructed a solicitor to carry out the sale of a house that was owned by him and his wife, but the wife was ignorant of the transaction and did not instruct the defendant solicitor. The conveyance was achieved by the forgery of the husband. However, as the solicitors should have been aware that

---

[13] [1995] 2 A.C. 296. Disappointed beneficiary cases are discussed in paras 11–047 *et seq.* See also the following two cases. In *Harris v Nantes & Wilde* [1997] N.P.C. 7, the defendant solicitors acted for stepmother and stepson in the acquisition of property. She later instructed the firm to convey the estate into her sole name, which they did without informing the stepson. In fact she was involved in a fraudulent enterprise and forged his signature. The Court of Appeal declined to strike out an action by the stepson against the stepmother's solicitors in part because it was arguable that they owed him a duty of care, it being arguable that the instructions from the stepmother purported to be joint instructions from both of them. In *Woodward v Wolferstans (a firm)*, *The Times*, April 8, 1997; [1997] N.P.C. 51, the defendant solicitors were retained by the claimant's father in relation to the purchase of property where he was acting as guarantor. Despite the fact that she did not rely on them, it was held that they owed her a duty of care as they had assumed responsibility to her, although there was no breach.
[14] [1992] 2 E.G.L.R. 158.
[15] [1996] 2 F.C.R. 729. In *Esser v Brown* (2003) 223 D.L.R. (4th) 560, the British Columbia Supreme Court came to the same result on very similar facts in an action brought against a notary public who completed a transfer of property on the basis of a forged transfer document, but the decision was reversed on appeal, see (2004) 242 D.L.R. (4th) 112: the fact that there were suspicious circumstances in the transaction was not relevant to whether a duty of care was owed, and the court concluded that the notary had not purported to act for the claimant, unlike in *Penn*. In *Lee Siew Chun v Sourgrapes Packaging Products Trading Pte Ltd* [1993] 2 S.L.R. 297 a son obtained his mother's signature to a mortgage by deception and forged his father's signature after he had died. A solicitor purported to witness the signatures, and issued an attestation certificate. The Singapore High Court held that the solicitor owed the mother a duty of care.

the house was owned by the husband and the wife, and failed to check that she had given instructions too, a duty of care in tort arose. The judge referred to the proximity of the relationship, but by relying on *White v Jones*[16] he must have considered that there was a voluntary assumption of responsibility.

Commonwealth cases on liability without reliance. A number of Commonwealth cases have imposed a duty of care despite the absence of reliance.[17] In the first two cases the analogy with *White v Jones* is a strong one. In *Linsley v Kirstiuk*[18] solicitors retained by an estate to advise on its administration were held to owe a duty of care to the beneficiaries. In *Hawkins v Clayton*[19] the respondent solicitors prepared and kept the testator's will, which appointed the appellant sole executor and residual beneficiary, unknown to him. After the testator's death, the solicitors failed to locate the appellant for six years, as a result of which the estate suffered various losses. A majority of the High Court of Australia held that no term could be implied into the contract between the solicitors and testator that the solicitors would locate the executor or anyone else interested in the will when the testator died. However, a majority found that the solicitors owed a duty of care in tort to the executor, who stood in the place of the testator.[20] In *Seymour v Seymour*[21] a solicitor was retained by his aunt to act in relation to property. He mistakenly acted on the basis that she owned the fee simple. The New South Wales Court of Appeal held that he owed a duty to the aunt's children who were the remaindermen, as they would be damaged by the negligence, they were related to him, and they had entrusted him with the conduct of various matters for them. **11–044**

No duty. In *Yiu Chown Leung v Chow Wai Lam*[22] a solicitor acting for the borrower met the lenders twice, and at their request advised that there was no need to have a moneylender's licence, and explained the terms of the agreement. The Hong Kong Court of Final Appeal held that there had been no voluntary assumption of responsibility by the solicitor to look after the lenders' interest, they should have known that the solicitor was not acting for them, and in any event the lenders had not relied on him. In *Hants County Business Development* **11–045**

---

[16] See para.11–048.
[17] See also *Krambousanos v Jedda* (1996) 142 A.L.R. 604. Solicitors were retained by the applicants' son to advise them in respect of a mortgage to be taken over their property to provide him with a loan. The Federal Court of Australia found that there was a sufficient degree of proximity to establish a duty of care as there was an assumption of responsibility by the solicitors, although there had been no reliance by the applicants. On the facts, there was no breach of duty.
[18] (1986) 28 D.L.R. (4th) 495, British Columbia Supreme Court. Contrast *Rojack v Taylor & Buchalter* [2005] IEHC 28; [2005] 1 I.R. 416, where the Irish High Court held that a solicitor acting for an estate owed no duty to a beneficiary who might be able to make an application to court to increase his provision, even if that beneficiary were acting for the estate.
[19] (1988) 78 A.L.R. 69. This difficult case is explained by K. Nicholson, "The duty of care owed by a solicitor: recent developments—an Australian perspective" (1989) 5 P.N. 1, and J. Fleming, "Must a solicitor tell?" (1989) 105 L.Q.R. 15. It is not clear whether a similar conclusion would be reached in England.
[20] Similarly, in *Cancer Research Campaign v Ernest Brown & Co* [1998] P.N.L.R. 592. Harman J. held that the solicitors advising the executors owed a duty of care to the executor only, and not the beneficiary. For the facts, see para.11–223, below.
[21] (1996) 40 N.S.W.L.R. 358.
[22] [2005] 4 HKLRD 246.

Centre Ltd v Poole[23] a guarantor attended the lender's solicitor's offices to sign a guarantee. The Nova Scotia Court of Appeal held that the solicitors owed the guarantor no duty even to inform him that he should seek independent legal advice, although he was a former client, as there was no reliance and no reasonable perception by the solicitors of any reliance.

11–046   **Acting as an officer of the court.** It has been established for over a century that a solicitor acting as an officer of the court may be liable to persons who are not his clients.[24] For example, in *Batten v Wedgwood Coal & Iron Co*[25] the claimant's solicitor, M, had the conduct of a sale that took place pursuant to the order of the court. M failed to invest the proceeds in accordance with the court's order, with the result that no interest was earned. The defendants in the action, who would have been entitled to the interest, recovered the amount of their loss from M.[26] Presumably also, where the sale of the disputed property takes place by agreement between the parties, rather than by order of the court, the solicitor who has conduct of that sale will be liable both to his own client and to the other party.

(ii) *Liability to Beneficiaries without Reliance*

11–047   **History.**[27] It used to be the law that no duty of care was owed by a solicitor to persons who were not his client, and this included cases where there had been no reliance by the third party, as exemplified in the Scottish House of Lords case of *Robertson v Fleming*.[28] In *Ross v Caunters*[29] a disappointed beneficiary sued the testator's solicitors for negligently failing to notice that one of the attesting witnesses was the claimant's husband, as a result of which she forfeited her benefit under the will. After a detailed review of the authorities, Sir Robert Megarry V.C. found for the claimant. It was unclear for some time whether *Ross v Caunters* was good law,[30] on the basis that it was wholly inconsistent with the House of Lords' decision in *Robertson v Fleming*,[31] that its consequences may subvert the principle of privity of contract, and that Sir Robert Megarry V.C. based the decision in part on the test in *Anns v Merton LBC*,[32] which was overturned by the House of Lords in *Murphy v Brentwood DC*.[33]

---

[23] (1999) 172 N.S.R. (2d) 393.
[24] See *Stanford v Roberts* (1884) 26 Ch. D. 155 at 160; *Re Dangar's Trusts* (1889) 41 Ch. D. 178.
[25] (1886) 31 Ch. D. 346.
[26] Pearson J.:"I do not agree with the contention that [the solicitor] is not liable except to his own client . . . He was acting as an officer of the Court, and in that character was liable to the Court for the due discharge of his duty."
[27] For a more detailed treatment see the 3rd edn of this work at paras 4–16 to 4–24.
[28] (1861) 4 Macq. 167.
[29] [1980] 1 Ch. 297.
[30] The arguments are explored in H. Evans, "Is *Ross v Caunters* good law?" (1991) 7 P.N. 137. See also J. Dwyer, "Solicitors' duties in tort to person other than their clients" (1994) Tort L.R. 29.
[31] (1861) 4 Macq. 167. See in particular J. Kaye, "The liability of solicitors in tort" 100 L.Q.R. 680.
[32] [1978] A.C. 728, see *Ross v Caunters* [1980] 1 Ch. 297 at 309D–310E.
[33] [1991] 1 A.C. 398.

White v Jones.[34] In *White v Jones*[35] the House of Lords upheld the result   **11–048**
achieved in *Ross v Caunters* by a bare majority. Following a family row, a Mr
Barratt made a will that left nothing to his two children. He was soon reconciled
with them, and wanted to change it. He therefore sent a letter to the defendant
solicitors with instructions to draft a new will leaving £9,000 to each of the
claimants. The solicitors failed to have the will completed in the two months
before the testator died. They made two appointments to see Mr Barratt, but did
not keep them, and he died three days before a third one. Thus the relationship
on the facts was less close than in *Ross v Caunters*, as there had been no will,
rather than a defective one. The principal issue, however, was whether a duty of
care was owed in either case. In the leading judgment, Lord Goff considered the
reasons of justice that supported the imposition of a duty of care, and in particular
the fact that without such a duty the only person who has a valid claim has
suffered no loss, and the only person who has suffered a loss has no valid claim.[36]
He held that a remedy should be extended under the principle in *Hedley Byrne
v Heller*,[37] enlarging the solicitor's assumption of responsibility to include the
beneficiaries. Lord Browne-Wilkinson considered that a remedy should be
extended to them as there was a close analogy with existing categories of special
relationship such as fiduciary relationships or those within the principle of
Hedley Byrne v Heller.[38] Lord Nolan considered that the claim satisfied the
criteria laid down in *Caparo Industries Plc v Dickman*[39] and *Murphy v Brentwood DC*,[40] but he also seemed to consider that there was an implicit assumption
of responsibility.[41] It would appear, however, that only the reasoning in Lord
Goff's speech received the support of the majority in the House of Lords, and the
Court of Appeal has subsequently relied on it as expressing the *ratio* of the case
rather than the other majority speeches.[42]

The scope of the principle.[43] The extension in *White v Jones* of the principle   **11–049**
of the voluntary assumption of responsibility to include liability to disappointed
beneficiaries makes its further application unclear. In relation to the specific
liability to beneficiaries, Lord Goff considered that its scope should be worked

---

[34] For commentaries on this important decision, see J. Brady "Solicitors' duty of care in the drafting
of will" (1995) 46 N.I.L.Q. 434; J. Dwyer "A comedy of errors" [1996] Tort L.R. 77; H. Evans,
Lawyers' Liabilities (2nd edn, 2002), Ch.1; T. Weir, "A Damnosa Hereditas" (1995) 111 L.Q.R.
357.
[35] [1995] A.C. 207.
[36] See [1995] A.C. 207 at 259G–260G. Similarly, the Court of Appeal decided in *Daniels v Thomson*
[2004] EWCA Civ 307; [2004] P.N.L.R. 33 that, where the solicitor's negligence caused the payment
of inheritance tax, the testator could not suffer loss. The Court of Appeal also refused permission to
amend the particulars of claim to allege a breach of duty owed to the personal representative, in part
for the questionable reason that they had suffered no loss. For criticism of the decision see J.
O'Sullivan, "Loss, limitation and lawyers—digging a black hole" [2005] C.L.J. 29.
[37] [1964] A.C. 465.
[38] See [1995] A.C. 207 at 275D–F.
[39] [1990] 2 A.C. 605.
[40] [1991] 1 A.C. 398; see [1995] A.C. 207 at 292F–G.
[41] *ibid.* at 294A.
[42] See *Carr-Glynn v Frearsons (a firm)* [1999] Ch. 326 at 335D; *Worby v Rosser* [2000] P.N.L.R. 140
at 149B; *Corbett v Bond Pearce (a firm)* [2001] 3 All E.R. 769 at 775, para.18.
[43] See also paras 11–043 and 11–044. See further H. Evans, *Lawyers' Liabilities* (2nd edn, 2002),
Ch.1.

out in future cases.[44] There is guidance now from earlier cases, from decisions since *White v Jones*, and there are also a number of indications in *White v Jones* itself about the likely scope of the principle. It is clear from the facts of *White v Jones* that there does not have to be any prepared will for there to be a duty of care,[45] and thus on the facts there was a less close relationship than existed in *Ross v Caunters*. It should be noted that the scope of the duty owed to the beneficiary will not be wider than that owed to the testator, see *Cancer Research Campaign v Ernest Brown & Co.*[46] There is no requirement to prove that the testamentary intention continued until death, see *Humblestone v Martin Tolhurst Partnership (a firm).*[47]

11–050 **Identity of the beneficiary.** In *White v Jones* Lord Goff considered that the ordinary case was one where the intended beneficiaries are a small class of identified people, although he did not rule out liability in more remote circumstances.[48] Lord Nolan considered that there was no difficulty imposing liability where the disappointed beneficiaries were members of the testator's family, but that more remote beneficiaries would not necessarily be deprived of a remedy.[49] In *Gibbons v Nelsons*[50] Blackburne J. held that a duty of care was only owed to an unidentified intended beneficiary where the solicitor knew of the benefit that the testator wished to confer, and the class of persons he wished to benefit. In *Trusted v Clifford Chance*[51] Jonathan Parker J. held that no duty of care was owed to a disappointed beneficiary until the testator had decided to confer the particular testamentary benefit which it is complained was lost on that person.

11–051 **Conflict of interest.** A conflict between the duty owed by the solicitor to the testator and that to the potential beneficiary will prevent any duty of care being owed to the latter.[52] In *Clarke v Bruce Lance*[53] the claimant was a beneficiary

---

[44] [1995] A.C. 207 at 269G.

[45] See to similar effect *Gartside v Sheffield, Young & Ellis* [1983] N.Z.L.R. 37, NZCA: a solicitor who is instructed to prepare a will for a client, owes a duty of care to a beneficiary under the proposed will to carry out his instructions with due diligence and within a reasonable time.

[46] [1998] P.N.L.R. 592, discussed at para.11–223, below. The point is obvious from the formulation in *White v Jones* itself. The *Cancer Research* case also held that the solicitor owed no duty as solicitors of the executor to the beneficiaries following the testator's death, it being alleged that a deed of variation of the will would then have been executed.

[47] [2004] EWHC 151; [2004] P.N.L.R. 26. In fact Mann J. held that there was nothing to suggest that the testator's intentions had changed.

[48] *ibid.* at 269G–H.

[49] *ibid.* at 294H–295B.

[50] [2000] P.N.L.R. 734. There was also insufficiently unequivocal evidence of the testator's intentions. For a commentary see A. Sprince, "Disappointed beneficiaries and disappearing principles" (2001) 17 P.N. 104.

[51] [2000] W.T.L.R. 1219. It is submitted that the formulation of the decision was too restrictive, although the same result would have been reached on the wider basis that the testator had not yet decided what to do.

[52] See also the New Zealand case of *Sutherland v Public Trustees* [1980] 2 N.Z.L.R. 536. The testator had deliberately chosen not to name the claimants in his will as beneficiaries. The basis of the claimants' claim was that the Public Trustees (who in the preparation of wills owed the same duty as a solicitor in private practice) ought to have given certain advice which would have caused the testator to name the claimants as residuary beneficiaries. Jeffries J. held that the defendant owed no duty of care to the claimants.

[53] [1988] 1 W.L.R. 881.

under the testator's will of part of the income from a service station, and on the death of the testator's wife of the capital as well. The defendants were retained by the testator to act for him to vary the lease, granting the lessor an option to purchase the service station within six months of the death of the last survivor of the testator and his wife. Plainly, the claimant stood to lose out from the transaction. The Court of Appeal distinguished *Ross v Caunters* principally on the basis that none of the factors considered by Megarry V.C. to be material were present. There were four distinguishing features: there was no reason for the solicitors to contemplate that the claimant was likely to be affected by the deed of variation of the lease; the transaction did not have the benefit of the claimant as its object; if there were liability in such a case it would extend to an indeterminate class of potential beneficiaries; and if there were a breach to the client, he could sue for it, so that there might be double recovery.[54] This issue of a conflict of duties has recurred in recent cases.[55] In *Bacon v Howard Kennedy*[56] it was held that a duty of care was owed to the potential beneficiary, who did not in fact exert undue influence over the testator, as there was no conflict of interest. In *Knox v Till*[57] residuary beneficiaries under a will had to fight a probate action to establish that two later wills were made when the testator lacked testamentary capacity. The New Zealand Court of Appeal struck out a case brought by them against the solicitor who acted for the testator in relation to the later wills, as there would be a conflict between any duty owed to the testator, which was to carry out his instructions, and any duty owed to the original beneficiaries.

Double recovery. If the estate can recover damages, then it is unlikely that a **11–052** duty of care will be owed to the disappointed beneficiary, and if the disappointed beneficiary can recover then it is unlikely that the estate will be able to do so too. Three Court of Appeal decisions illustrate this principle. In the leading case of *Carr-Glynn v Frearsons (a firm)*[58] it was alleged that the defendant solicitors had failed to advise the testatrix about severing a joint tenancy in property that she jointly owned. Following *Clarke v Bruce Lance*, Lloyd J. held that a solicitor owed no duty of care to an intended beneficiary under a will whose gift was rendered ineffective where the solicitor caused loss to the estate, as the solicitor would otherwise be liable to the personal representatives and the beneficiary for an identical loss. The Court of Appeal reversed that decision, and held that a duty

---

[54] In "Solicitor's duty to intended legatees: *Clarke v Bruce Lance & Co*" (1988) 4 P.N. 129, David Goddard argues that the reasons given are compelling, with the exception of the third which is exaggerated.

[55] See also *Smolinski v Mitchell* (1995) 10 B.C.L.R. (3d) 366, British Columbia Supreme Court. Sigurdson J. held that no duty of care was owed to a potential beneficiary in somewhat unusual circumstances. The testator informed the defendant solicitor that she wished to leave everything to him and to her cousin. The defendant advised that she should obtain independent advice first, and a delay occurred during which she died. The solicitor owed no duty of care to the cousin because it would conflict with his duty to the client.

[56] [1999] P.N.L.R. 1.

[57] [2000] P.N.L.R. 67. Similarly in *Graham v Bonnycastle* (2004) 243 D.L.R. (4th) 617 the Alberta Court of Appeal struck out claims by beneficiaries under an earlier will against a solicitor who acted in relation to a new will, as such a duty would create inevitable conflicts of interest.

[58] [1999] Ch. 326. For an argument that the disappointed beneficiary has an action in restitution against the unintended recipient, see O'Dell, Eoin: "Restitution, Rectification, and Mitigation: Negligent Solicitors and Wills, Again" (2002) 65 M.L.R. 360.

of care was owed. The disappointed beneficiary would have received no benefit from a successful claim by the estate, as she had no interest in the residuary estate, and thus she should be permitted a remedy. The Court doubted whether the estate could in fact recover any substantial damages if it brought an action although it had suffered a loss, as the damages would fall into residue. The Court also held that the duty to the beneficiary extended beyond the preparation of the will to the service of a notice of severance, without which the relevant provision in the will could not take effect, as on a proper analysis it was part of the will-making process.[59] In contrast, in *Worby v Rosser*[60] the Court of Appeal held that no duty of care was owed to beneficiaries under an earlier will, as the loss claimed, which was the costs of a successful challenge to the subsequent will that were irrecoverable, could be claimed from the solicitors by the estate. Finally, in *Corbett v Bond Pearce (a firm)*[61] the defendant firm admitted negligence with regard to an invalid will. The validity of that will had been successfully challenged, and the defendants compensated the disappointed beneficiaries with the net value of the estate before deduction of the costs of the probate action. The estate then sued the defendants, but the Court of Appeal held that it had suffered no recoverable loss. The loss within the scope of the duty was that of those who would suffer as a result of the will being invalid, not the loss of the beneficiaries under an earlier valid will. Furthermore, there would effectively have been double recovery, which the Court was determined to avoid.

11–053   **Application beyond wills and solicitors.** It is noteworthy that in *Clarke v Bruce Lance*[62] the fact that the transaction that was under attack was the variation of a lease rather than the making of a will was not one of the features that the Court of Appeal considered distinguished the case from *Ross v Caunters*. In *White v Jones* in the Court of Appeal,[63] Sir Donald Nicholls V.C. considered that the principle would apply to a case where the solicitor is instructed to carry through a transaction of gift to a third party during the client's lifetime. In *Hemmens v Wilson Browne*[64] the settlor instructed the defendant solicitor to draft a document giving the claimant the right to call on the settlor to pay her a sum of money. The document gave the claimant no enforceable rights, but the solicitors owed no duty of care to the claimant, because the settlor was still alive and able to rectify the situation if he wanted to, which he did not. However, the judge considered[65] that if a settlor acts on the advice of his solicitor and executes an irrevocable deed of settlement benefiting X instead of the intended Y, the solicitor may owe a duty of care to Y. In contrast, in *White v Jones*, Lord Goff seemed to consider[66] that liability was confined to cases where a solicitor

---

[59] Thus duties to the testator outside the will-making process could not be translated into duties to a disappointed beneficiary.
[60] [2000] P.N.L.R. 140.
[61] [2001] 3 All E.R. 769. However, some heads of loss were later held to be recoverable by the estate, see *Corbett v Bond Pearce (a firm)* [2006] EWHC 909, Ch; [2006] W.T.L.R. 967, Rimer J.
[62] [1988] 1 W.L.R. 881.
[63] [1995] 2 A.C. 207 at 227A–B.
[64] [1995] Ch. 223, Ch. D.
[65] *ibid.* at 333H.
[66] [1995] 2 A.C. 207 at 262D–F and 268D. For further consideration of whether duties are owed to beneficiaries in relation to inter vivos transaction see the accountant's negligence case of *Richards (t/a Colin Richards & Co) v Hughes* [2004] EWCA Civ 266; [2004] P.N.L.R. 35, CA.

negligently drafted or failed to draft a will, and the testator had died, and Lord Browne-Wilkinson[67] also seemed to reject the extension of the principle to *inter vivos* transactions. In *Esterhuizen v Allied Dunbar Assurance Plc*[68] Longmore J. held that the defendant company which provided a will-making service to the testator owed a duty of care to the disappointed claimant beneficiaries, although it was not a firm of solicitors. *Chappell v Somers & Blake (a firm)*[69] shows an interesting and ingenious application of *White v Jones*. An executrix instructed the defendant solicitor to act in the administration of the estate. She alleged that they did nothing for five years, and thus the residuary beneficiary lost five years of income on two properties. The solicitor's application to strike out the claim on the grounds that the loss had been suffered by the beneficiaries was refused by Neuberger J. Relying on Lord Goff's speech in *White v Jones,* the beneficiary might have no claim, but it would be wrong for there to be a black hole with the duty owed to the executrix and the loss suffered by the beneficiaries. The judge therefore considered that the executrix could be treated as representing the interests of the owners of the property and thus would be entitled to recover damages for which she would account to the legatee. The beneficiaries were willing to be joined to the action, so there was no risk of double recovery.

Other jurisdictions. In Scotland, *Ross v Caunters* was not followed by the   **11–054**
Inner House of the Court of Session in *Weir v JM Hodge & Son*.[70] However, *White v Jones* was followed in the Scottish case of *Davidson v Bank of Scotland*.[71] In the Commonwealth, *Ross v Caunters* and *White v Jones* have generally been followed. Claims by disappointed beneficiaries have twice been considered by the New Zealand courts. In the first case, *Sutherland v Public Trustees, Ross v Caunters* was distinguished on the facts.[72] However, in *Gartside v Sheffield, Young & Ellis*, on facts quite close to those in *Ross v Caunters*, the Court of Appeal refused to strike out the case, and approved of the decision in *Ross v Caunters*.[73] In Australia the position was more fluid. In *Watts v Public Trustee*[74] the Supreme Court of Western Australia followed *Ross v Caunters*, but in *Seale v Perry*[75] the Supreme Court of Victoria declined to do so. In *Hill v Van Erp*[76] a majority of the High Court of Australia held that a solicitor who had a will

---

[67] [1995] 2 A.C. 207 at 276D.
[68] [1998] 2 F.L.R. 6. See also *Gorham v British Telecommunications* [2000] 4 All E.R. 867 where the Court of Appeal held that an insurance company advising a customer on pension and life cover owed the customer's dependants a duty of care, applying *White v Jones*. Other cases in which there was a successful reliance on *White v Jones* include: *Penn v Bristol & West Building Society* [1996] 2 F.C.R. 729, discussed at para.11–044; *Searles v Cann and Hallett (a firm)* [1999] P.N.L.R. 494, discussed at para.11–060; *Killick v PricewaterhouseCoopers (a firm)* [2001] P.N.L.R. 1, discussed at Ch.17 para.17–076.
[69] [2003] EWHC 1644; [2004] Ch. 19. For a commentary see J. O'Sullivan, "Solicitors, executors and beneficiaries: Who can sue and who can be sued?" (2003) 19 P.N. 507.
[70] [1990] S.L.T. 266. The Court decided that it was bound by *Robertson v Fleming* (1861) 4 Macq. 167. The case was followed in *MacDougall v MacDougall's Executors* [1994] S.L.T. 1178, OH.
[71] [2002] P.N.L.R. 740, OH. Also reported *sub nom. Holmes v Bank of Scotland* at [2002] S.L.T. 544.
[72] [1980] 2 N.Z.L.R. 536, High Court, see para.11–051, above.
[73] [1983] N.Z.L.R. 37. See para.11–049, above for the facts of the case.
[74] [1980] W.A.R. 97.
[75] [1982] V.R. 193, Full Court.
[76] (1997) 71 A.L.J.R. 487, 188 C.L.R. 159.

witnessed by a person she knew to be the husband of an intended beneficiary owed a duty of care to that beneficiary. The majority was influenced by the fact that the interests of the client and of the intended beneficiary were coincident. Although they considered that the notion of proximity was of limited use in the determination of particular disputes, they held that recovery could not be based upon any assumption of responsibility by the solicitor, which was the foundation of the decision of the House of Lords in *White v Jones*.[77] *Ross v Caunters* was followed in Ireland.[78] The decision in *White v Jones* has been followed in Canada.[79]

(iii) Duty of Care to the Other Side[80]

11–055   **General considerations.** Even if there would otherwise be a duty of care, additional problems arise where the claimant is the solicitor or client on the other side of a transaction or, to an even greater extent, on the other side in litigation. Any duty of care owed to the claimant would be likely to conflict with the solicitor's duty to his own client, and this implies that no duty will be owed to the other side. Much of a solicitor's work, both in contentious and non-contentious business, is adversarial in nature. It is the solicitor's duty to protect his own client's interests, where there is an actual or potential conflict with the interests of other parties.[81] There are two facts which may point in the opposite direction. First, solicitors are officers of the court and owe duties to the court, which may conflict with instructions from the client.[82] Second, they are expected to exercise professional restraint, when the advancement of their clients' interests would involve saying or doing something that is dishonest or disreputable.[83]

11–056   **Non-contentious business.** In the ordinary way (and consistent with the *caveat emptor* principle) a vendor's solicitor does not owe a duty of care to the purchaser, who can reasonably be expected to rely upon his own solicitor to investigate title and similar matters. The same result will apply for most non-contentious business. No duty will be owed even if the solicitors make misreprentations to the other side. The leading case is *Gran Gelato Ltd v Richcliff Ltd*.[84] Gran Gelato purchased an underlease from Richcliff. Gran Gelato's solicitors sent enquiries before contract to the second defendants, who were Richcliff's

---

[77] [1995] 2 A.C. 207. For further discussion of this case, see Ch.2 para.2–065.

[78] *Wall v Hegarty* [1980] I.L.R.M. 124, Barrington J.

[79] *Earl v Wilhelm* [2001] W.T.L.R. 1275; (2000) 183 D.L.R. (4th) 45, Saskatchewan, CA.

[80] For an attempt at a theoretical justification of the law, see H. Evans *Lawyers' Liabilities* (2nd edn, 2002), Ch.2.

[81] The solicitor's duty to protect his client's interests against those of a third party may exist even where the client wishes to benefit that third party: see, e.g. *Neushul v Mellish & Harkavy* (1967) 111 S.J. 399, CA.

[82] e.g. *Grosvenor (Mayfair) Estates Ltd v Raja, The Times*, November 2, 1990, CA: where a client instruct his solicitors to take no action in respect of his appeal, the solicitors should come off the record or inform the court of that situation.

[83] See the Law Society's *Guide to the Professional Conduct of Solicitors* (8th edn, 1999), p.346, para.17.01; for the up-to-date version see the Law Society website.

[84] [1992] Ch. 560, Nicholls V.C. For commentary, see P. Cane, "Negligent solicitor escapes liability" (1992) 109 L.Q.R. 539; S. Fennell, "Representations and statements by solicitors to third parties" (1992) 7 P.N. 25. In the earlier case of *Wilson v Bloomfield* (1979) 123 S.J. 860 the Court of Appeal refused to strike out a claim by purchasers of property alleging that the vendor's solicitors owed a duty of care to them in answering the enquiries before contract. The rule is the same in Singapore, see *Active Timber Agencies Pte Ltd v Allen & Gledhill* [1996] 1 S.L.R. 478, High Court.

solicitors, which included an enquiry as to whether there were any rights affecting the superior lease which might inhibit the enjoyment of the underlease. The second defendants mistakenly replied "Not to the lessor's knowledge." Richcliff was found liable for this misrepresentation, which Gran Gelato had relied upon to their loss, but not the second defendants. The Vice-Chancellor considered that:

> "in normal conveyancing transactions solicitors who are acting for a seller do not in general owe to the would-be buyer a duty of care when answering inquiries before contract or the like."[85]

The judge did not consider that it was a fair and reasonable reaction that there ought to be a remedy against the solicitor in such circumstances, and he was influenced by the fact that the buyer had a remedy against the seller. However, he was not impressed by the argument that to impose a duty of care on solicitors would expose them to conflicting duties to the client and to the other side.

Judicial comments on Gran Gelato. The decision in *Gran Gelato* was **11–057** referred to with approval by Lord Goff in *White v Jones*.[86] However, the Court of Appeal in *McCullagh v Lane Fox & Partners Ltd*[87] considered that the reasoning in *Gran Gelato* was inconsistent with *Punjab National Bank v DeBoinville*[88] unless it was confined to a special rule applicable to solicitors in conveyancing transactions, and the court was not wholly confident in identifying why such cases should differ. In *First National Bank Plc v Loxleys*[89] the Court of Appeal refused to strike out a similar action against solicitors who negligently replied to standard enquires before contract, and despite the existence of a disclaimer. However, in *Dean v Allin & Watts (a firm)*[90] the Court of Appeal appeared to approve *Gran Gelato*.

Exceptions to the general rule: reliance on solicitor's representations. A **11–058** duty may arise in some special circumstances where (a) the purchaser or his solicitor are intended to (and do) rely on information given by the vendor's solicitor and (b) such reliance is reasonable. Thus if a solicitor gives a formal report or certificate, which he intends some other person (whether or not his client) to rely upon, then he should owe a duty of care to that other person. This is illustrated by the New Zealand case of *Allied Finance & Investment Ltd v*

---

[85] [1992] Ch. 560, 570C–D. See also the dictum of Morritt J. in *CEMP Properties (UK) Ltd v Dentsply Research & Development Corp* [1989] 2 E.G.L.R. 205, 207.

[86] [1995] 1 A.C. 207 at 256D. See also *Memery Crystal v O'Higgins* [1997] 7 C.L. 457, QBD, where it was held that a solicitor acting for one party in a commercial transaction owed no duty to the other party; the fact that he was represented by his own lawyer meant that the court should be slow to impose a duty of care. In *Trend Publishing (HK) Ltd v Vivien Chan & Co (a firm)* [1996] 2 HKLRD 227, the High Court of Hong Kong followed *Gran Gelato* in deciding that the landlord's solicitor owed no duty of care to the tenant in drafting the tenancy agreement. In *Primosso Holdings Ltd v Alpers* [2006] 2 N.Z.L.R. 455 the New Zealand Court of Appeal held that a solicitor owed no duty to the other party to a transaction to check that his client is not using the solicitor to deceive the other party.

[87] [1996] 1 P.N.L.R. 205 at 226–234.

[88] [1992] 1 Lloyd's Rep. 7, CA.

[89] [1997] P.N.L.R. 21.

[90] [2001] Lloyd's Rep. P.N. 605.

Haddow & Co.[91] The claimants lent $25,000 to one Hill on the security of a yacht, which they understood that he was buying. In fact the yacht was bought by E. Ltd, a company owned and controlled by Hill. Before the transaction was entered into, Hill's solicitors (the defendants) sent a letter to the claimants' solicitors stating: "we . . . certify that the Instrument by way of Security is fully binding on Roger Kenneth Hill . . . We certify, on behalf of our client, that there are no other charges whatsoever on the yacht . . . ". This letter failed to disclose that Hill was not buying the yacht himself. The Court of Appeal, reversing the decision of Pritchard J., held that the defendant solicitors owed a duty of care to the claimants in respect of the letter and that the letter was misleading and negligent. Cooke J. stated:

> "I agree with Pritchard J. that the relationship between two solicitors acting for their respective clients does not normally of itself impose a duty of care on one solicitor to the client of the other . . . But surely the result of established principles is different when on request a solicitor gives a certificate on which the other party must naturally be expected to act. That is a classic duty of care situation . . . "[92]

11-059 Similarly, in the Scottish case of *Midland Bank Plc v Cameron, Thom, Peterkin & Duncans*[93] the defendant solicitors acted for an individual who wished to borrow money from the claimant bank. The solicitors wrote to the Bank setting out a statement of their client's affairs, which was inaccurate. They were held to owe no duty of care to the Bank on the pleaded facts. Lord Jauncey considered that four factors were relevant in determining whether a solicitor owed a duty of care:

> "(1) the solicitor must assume responsibility for the advice or information furnished to the third party; (2) the solicitor must let it be known to the third party expressly or impliedly that he claims, by reason of his calling, to have the requisite skill or knowledge to give the advice or furnish the information; (3) the third party must have relied upon that advice or information as matter for which the solicitor has assumed personal responsibility; and (4) the solicitor must have been aware that the third party was likely so to rely."[94]

---

[91] [1983] N.Z.L.R. 22.
[92] *ibid.* at 24. Richardson J. (at 30–31) and McMullin J. (at 35–36) came to the same conclusion by applying the two-stage test formulated by Lord Wilberforce in *Anns v Merton LBC* [1978] A.C. 729. See also *Connell v Odlum* [1993] 2 N.Z.L.R. 257. Under s.21 of the New Zealand Matrimonial Property Act 1978, people who had married or intended to marry could contract out of the provisions of the Act. This required a certificate signed by a solicitor, stating that he had explained the implications of the deed and given her independent legal advice. The defendant solicitor had signed such a certificate for Mrs Odlum. Six years later, Mrs Odlum succeeded in setting the deed aside on the basis that it had not been properly explained to her. The New Zealand Court of Appeal concluded that there was no conflict of interest between the duties owed by the solicitor to Mr and Mrs Odlum, and that Mr Connell owed a duty of care to Mr Odlum by signing such a certificate. The Court therefore refused to strike out Mr Odlum's action against the solicitor.
[93] [1988] S.L.T. 611, OH. While none of the cases referred to in this and the preceding paragraphs were cited to the Court, the result in *347671 BC Ltd v Heenan Blaikie* 2002 BCCA 126; (2002) 10 C.C.L.T. (3d) 306, British Columbia CA, is consistent with them. There, the lawyers acting for the borrower made specific misrepresentations to lenders in a telephone conversation, and were found liable to them as they reasonably relied on the misrepresentations.
[94] *ibid.* at 616.

Midland Bank Plc v Cameron, Thom, Peterkin & Duncans was relied upon by the Irish Supreme Court in *Doran v Delaney*.[95] The solicitors responded to requisitions on title asking the standard questions about whether there were any boundary disputes or threatened litigation with the answer "vendor says no". It was held that a duty of care was owed. The solicitors knew that there had been a dispute, but they were told by their client that it had been resolved, when in fact it had not been. The solicitors were held to owe a duty of care because they knew of the dispute and that the claimants would rely on the reply, and they assumed responsibility for the information given in reply being correct. The Court accepted that on many occasions there would be no assumption of responsibility because the answer would be a statement of professional opinion on which the purchaser's solicitors would form their own view, or because they would simply be transmitting information without any assumption of responsibility. It would appear that *Doran v Delaney* is difficult to reconcile with *Gran Gelato v Richcliffe*.

Other exceptions to the general rule. In *Searles v Cann and Hallett (a firm)*[96] **11–060** a duty of care was owed applying a different test. The solicitor acted for a businessman who borrowed money from the claimants on the security of their property, and he prepared a deed of assignment of insurance policies in favour of the claimants, which referred to a non-existent legal charge. Applying *White v Jones*,[97] the borrower would not suffer any loss from the solicitor's negligence, but the unrepresented claimants would do so. The duty of care was only to carry out the terms of the agreement between the parties, and there was thus no conflict between the duties owed by the solicitor to the claimants and to his client. While there was negligence in preparing a composite charge over the property, there was no loss as it was effectively worthless. Similarly a duty of care was held to be owed in *Dean v Allin & Watts (a firm)*.[98] The solicitor acting for the borrower gave an undertaking to hold the deeds of a flat which belonged to an associate of the borrower to the claimant's order. The form of security, which was ineffective, had not been agreed before the solicitor had been instructed. There was therefore a potential conflict between the duties of the solicitor to his client and to the claimant. The Court of Appeal held[99] that where there was such a conflict the court should be slow to find that the solicitor had assumed a duty of care, which would ordinarily be an improbable assumption. However a duty was owed in that case where the retainer was to take the necessary steps to provide effective security which was a necessary part of the transaction, the unsophisticated lender was known not to be instructing solicitors and would rely on the solicitors, there was no disclaimer of a duty, there was in fact an identity of interest in providing

---

[95] [1998] 2 I.L.R.M. 1, on appeal from the High Court. For a commentary, see U. de Vries, "Clients' instructions and solicitors' responsibilities" (1998) 14 P.N. 210.
[96] [1999] P.N.L.R. 494, QBD.
[97] [1995] 2 A.C. 207.
[98] [2001] Lloyd's Rep. P.N. 605.
[99] Applying the tripartite test, but also in the case of Lightman J. on the basis of an assumption of responsibility following *White v Jones*, which was approved by Lord Bingham in *Customs and Excise Commissioners v Barclays Bank Plc* [2006] UKHL 28; [2006] 3 W.L.R. 1 at para.22.

effective security, and in default only the lender would suffer loss. Contrast *BDG Roof-Bond Ltd v Douglas*[1] where no duty of care was held to be owed. The defendants were solicitors for a client who sold his 50 per cent shareholding in the claimant company to that company. The transaction was invalid, and after the company went into liquidation the liquidator sought to recover the £135,000 paid to the client from his solicitors. It was held that the solicitors were not retained by the company, and that they owed it no duty of care. Park J. observed that the general trend was a reluctance to find that a professional adviser owed a common law duty to someone who was not his own client. There was not a sufficiently proximate relationship between the parties, and it was not just and fair to impose a duty of care, as the company was on the opposite side of the transaction. Nor did the solicitors voluntarily assume responsibility to the company.

11–061   **Commonwealth cases.** Two Australian cases have come to the conclusion that a duty of care will generally not be owed to the other side in non-contentious business.[2] The decisions have been more mixed in Canada, some holding that there is no duty of care,[3] and others holding that there is,[4] and the fact that the other party is not legally represented is a crucial although not determinative

---

[1] [2000] P.N.L.R. 397.

[2] *Hardware Services Pty Ltd v Primac Association Ltd* (1988) 1 Qd.R. 393, Queensland Supreme Court: the mere reliance of the lessee on the lessor's solicitor to register a lease did not create a duty of care, for the solicitors never wrote to the lessee or conducted themselves in a way to raise the expectation of any such duty; *Thors v Weekes* (1990) 92 A.L.R. 131, Federal Court of Australia.

[3] *Re Abacus Cities Ltd* [1987] 1 W.W.R. 755, Alberta QB: solicitor acting for bank owes no duty of care to bank's debtor when advising bank; *Dorsch v City of Weyburn* (1986) 23 D.L.R. (4th) 379, Saskatchewan CA: solicitor acting for city held to owe no duty of care to landowner in negotiations for purchase of land; *Elms v Laurentian Bank of Canada* 2004 BCSC 1013; (2004) 27 C.C.L.T. (3d) 145, British Columbia Supreme Court: solicitors for investment company owed no duty to unrepresented investors; *Gerling Global General Insurance Co v Siskind, Cromarty, Ivey & Dowler* (2002) 59 O.R. (3d) 555, Ontario Supreme Court: solicitor assisting client in filling out proof of loss for insurance claim which was then sworn in front of him did not represent to the insurer that the document was true, but only the identity of the deponent, the place and time of swearing, and that the deponent had sworn that the contents were true; *Kamahap Enterprises Ltd v Chu's Central Market* (1990) 64 D.L.R. (4th) 167, British Columbia CA: solicitor acting for vendor held to owe no duty of care to purchaser; *Kwak v Odishaw* [1985] 2 W.W.R. 222, British Columbia CA: solicitor acting for other side in contract did not owe duty of care to claimant who signed promissory note drawn up by solicitor; *McPhail's Equipment Co v "Roxanne III"* (1994) 93 B.C.L.R. (2d) 73, British Columbia Supreme Court; affirmed on appeal at (1995) 2 B.C.L.R.(3d) 393; solicitor for the vendor owed no duty of care to the purchaser; *Patriquin v Laurentian Trust of Canada Inc* 2002 BCCA 6; (2002) 96 B.C.L.R. (3d) 318, British Columbia CA: broker's solicitor owed no duty to investor where he told investor that he did not represent his interests and the investor had own lawyer; *Seaway Trust Co v Markle* (1991) 7 C.C.L.T. (2d) 83, Ontario Court of Justice: even if a solicitor knows that the transaction in which his client participates is fraudulent, he owed no duty of disclosure to the other side; *Wynston v MacDonald* (1980) 105 D.L.R. (3d) 527, affirmed on appeal (1981) 119 D.L.R. (3d) 256, Ontario CA: mortgagor's solicitor held to owe no duty of care to mortgagee for negligent misstatement.

[4] *347671 BC Ltd v Blaikie* (2001) 2 C.C.L.T. (3d) 290, British Columbia Supreme Court: duty owed where law firm provided information that production company had ability to give claimants priority to recoup their investment from concert revenues, where claimants informed law firm that they would not be hiring their own lawyers and would be relying on information from defendant; *Bowles v Johnston* [1988] 4 W.W.R. 242, Manitoba QB: solicitor acting for vendor owed duty of care to unrepresented purchaser; *Clarence Construction Ltd v Lavallee* (1981) 132 D.L.R. (3d) 153, British Columbia CA: solicitor for purchaser owed duty to tell unrepresented vendor of change in mortgage,

factor in whether a duty of care is owed. In Hong Kong it has been held that a solicitor acting for a bank when witnessing the signature of an illiterate old lady on an assignment owed her no duty to advise her even to seek independent legal advice.[5]

Litigation. The existence of a conflict between a duty to the other side and to the solicitor's own client is all too apparent in litigation, and the court will not generally impose a duty of care, see *Al-Kandari v JR Brown & Co*.[6] This result has been reached in Scotland,[7] New Zealand,[8] and Canada.[9] Similarly, a solicitor acting for a judgment creditor will not owe a duty of care to the judgment debtor.[10]   **11–062**

---

where solicitor had undertaken work for vendor; *Klingspon v Ramsay* [1985] 5 W.W.R. 411 British Columbia Supreme Court: solicitor acting for company owed a duty of care to unrepresented claimant investing in company when he created misleading impression about solvency of company; *Peake v Vernon & Thompson* (1990) 49 B.C.L.R. (2d) 245, British Columbia Supreme Court: solicitor for mortgagee owed duty to mortgagee as it undertook to register the mortgage documents which it failed to do; *Tracy v Atkins* (1979) 105 D.L.R. (3d) 632, British Columbia CA: purchaser's solicitor held to owe a duty of care to the unrepresented vendor, who was relying on the defendant in certain respects, and the solicitor undertook work which would normally be carried out by the vendor's solicitor. But in *Granville Savings & Mortgage Corp v Slevin* (1992) 93 D.L.R. (4th) 268, a majority of the Manitoba Court of Appeal held that a solicitor representing a mortgagor owes no duty of care to the claimant mortgagee, where such a party is either represented or has declined to be represented as was the case there. The Supreme Court of Canada ((1994) 108 D.L.R. (4th) 383) reversed the decision of the Court of Appeal on the grounds that the evidence showed that the mortgagee had retained the solicitor.

[5] *Law Wan-lan v Well-Built Development Co Ltd* [1988] 2 H.K.L.R. 435, Hong Kong CA.

[6] [1988] 1 Q.B. 665, discussed in the next paragraph. For an example of where a duty of care was not owed see *Abrams v Abrams and Woodford & Ackroyd* [1997] C.L.Y. 3840, Gage J., where solicitors acting for the husband in the settlement of matrimonial proceedings had done nothing to step outside their role as solicitors for the husband, and owed no duty to the wife. *Al-Kandari* was relied upon in *Jensen v MacGregor* (1992) 93 D.L.R. (4th) 68, British Columbia Supreme Court, where the court struck out a claim by a husband that the advice of his wife's lawyers to her upon their separation had caused him damage. A similar result was reached by the Ontario Superior Court in *Baypark Investments Inc v Royal Bank of Canada* (2002) 57 O.R. (3d) 528.

[7] In *Bolton v Jameson & Mackay* [1989] S.L.T. 222, the Inner House of the Court of Session decided that a husband's solicitors owed no duty of care to the wife in divorce proceedings.

[8] In *New Zealand Social Credit Political League Inc v O'Brien* [1984] 1 N.Z.L.R. 84 the New Zealand Court of Appeal held that when drafting a pleading a solicitor did not owe a duty of care to the litigant on the other side.

[9] In *German v Major* (1985) 20 D.L.R. (4th) 703 the Alberta Court of Appeal held that prosecuting counsel did not owe a duty of care to the accused. In *Garrant v Moskal* [1985] 6 W.W.R. 31, the Saskatchewan Court of Appeal held that in divorce proceedings the husband's lawyer owed no duty of care to the wife. In *Lucky Venture Holdings v Hogue* (1988) 56 Man.R. (2d) 172 the Manitoba Court of Appeal held that a solicitor acting for a defendant owed no duty of care to his co-defendant. A solicitor was held to owe no duty of care to the opposite party in *Dube v Dionne* (1998) 201 N.B.R. (2d) 387, New Brunswick CA. Similarly, the Alberta Court of Appeal in *Martel v Spitz* 2005 ABCA 63; (2005) 40 Alta. L.R. (4th) 199 held that no duty of care was owed to the other side to verify the information in their client's affidavit. In *D'Amore Construction v Lawyers' Professional Indemnity* (2005) 249 D.L.R. (4th) 467, the Ontario Superior Court, Divisional Court, held that there was no duty owed by the defendant's lawyer to the represented claimant when he offered advice about sorting out priorities between the claimant's creditors, despite there being no conflict of interest.

[10] *Horner v WD Irwin & Sons Ltd* [1972] N.I.L.R. 202, Gibson J.: no duty owed with respect to action taken pursuant to a writ of *fieri facias*.

11-063   **Exceptions to the general rule.** In *Al-Kandari v JR Brown & Co*[11] a duty of care was held to be owed to the opposite party in litigation in very unusual circumstances. The case concerned a custody battle between the claimant mother and her Kuwaiti husband over their children, where the solicitors acted for the husband. There was a real risk that the husband would attempt to take the children to Kuwait, although custody had been granted to the claimant. It was agreed by the parties that the husband's passport, on which the children were registered, would be retained by the defendants to the order of the court. To enable the children's name to be removed from the passport, it was released to the Kuwaiti embassy, which assured the solicitors' agents that it would not be given to the husband. The husband managed to obtain his passport from the embassy, and kidnapped the children. The defendant solicitors were held to owe a duty of care to the claimant, which they breached by not informing her that the passport had been released to the embassy. The Court of Appeal made it clear that a solicitor does not normally owe a duty to the client's opponent.[12] However, the defendants had voluntarily agreed to hold the passport to the order of the court, although it would not seem that it was material whether that agreement amounted to an undertaking or not,[13] and had therefore "stepped outside their role as solicitors for their client and accepted responsibilities towards both their client and the claimant."[14]

11-064   **Criminal cases.** A further exception was established in *Welsh v Chief Constable of Merseyside*.[15] The claimant was on bail from a magistrate's court for two offences of theft. He was then sentenced in the Crown Court for other matters, and asked for the offences of the theft to be taken into consideration. It was alleged that the Crown Prosecution Service had failed to inform the magistrates' court that the offences had been taken into consideration, with the result that the unsuspecting claimant was arrested for failing to answer his bail. Tudor Evans J. refused the application to strike out the action against the Crown Prosecution Service and held that a duty of care was owed by the prosecutor to the defendant. He considered that the position of a prosecutor in criminal cases is very different from a solicitor in civil litigation; thus, for instance, there was a duty to make available to the defence witnesses who can give material evidence but who the prosecution do not intend to call. However, in *Elguzouli-Daf v Crown Prosecution Service*[16] the Court of Appeal considered that in general prosecutors owed no duty of care to defendants in criminal cases, because such a duty would have an inhibiting effect on the discharge of the prosecutor's central function of prosecuting crime. The Court of Appeal was careful to distinguish *Welsh*,

---

[11] [1988] 1 Q.B. 665. The case was referred to with apparent approval in *Customs and Excise Commissioners v Barclays Bank Plc* [2003] 3 W.L.R. 1 at paras 21 (Lord Bingham), 47 (Lord Rogers) and 109 (Lord Mance).
[12] See [1988] 1 Q.B. 665 at 672C (Lord Donaldson) and 7675F–H (Bingham L.J.).
[13] See at 576G, (*per* Bingham L.J.). It would seem that Lord Donaldson M.R. held the same view, because he does not use the concept "undertaking" in his discussion of whether a duty was owed at 672 A–F.
[14] *ibid.* at 672D, *per* Lord Donaldson M.R. See also Bingham L.J. at 675H–676A.
[15] [1993] 1 All E.R. 692 (see particularly 702A–703F).
[16] [1995] Q.B. 335.

because in that case there was assumed to be an assumption of responsibility by
the CPS to the defendant.

(iv) *Solicitors' Liability on Undertakings*

General.[17] Courts have the power to enforce summarily undertakings given by   **11–065**
solicitors. It is part of the general jurisdiction of the courts to control solicitors'
obligations, which is not confined to any fixed classification.[18] The jurisdiction is
not for the purpose of enforcing legal rights, but is to ensure honourable conduct
on the part of the court's officers.[19] While it has been suggested that dishonour-
able conduct is required before the court will enforce an undertaking,[20] the better
view is that this is not so and only misconduct is needed.[21] A failure to implement
an undertaking is prima facie to be regarded as misconduct, unless a solicitor can
give an explanation for it.[22] The general nature of the jurisdiction to enforce
solicitors' undertakings was summarised by Balcombe L.J. in the leading modern
authority of *Udall v Capri Lighting Ltd*.[23] The summary jurisdiction to enforce
solicitors' undertakings also exists in Canada,[24] Australia,[25] and New Zealand.[26]

Undertaking as solicitor. It has been long established[27] that an undertaking   **11–066**
must be given in the capacity of a solicitor if it is to be enforced.[28] In *Silver &
Drake v Baines*[29] a solicitor obtained advances of money for a client, and
undertook to repay the principal sums with interest. The Court of Appeal held
that such an undertaking was not given in his capacity of a solicitor. Lord

---

[17] See further *Halsbury's Laws* Vol.44, paras 255–257 (especially on pre-Judicature Act cases which
are not generally included here); *Cordery* section F4; the Law Society's *Guide to the Professional
Conduct of Solicitors* (8th edn, 1999), Ch.18 (for an up-to-date version see the Law Society website);
J. Adam, "Solicitors' undertakings—an analysis of legal and professional conduct aspects" (1990) 6
P.N. 58; H. Evans, "The unpredictability of undertakings" (1996) 12 P.N. 90; *ibid.*, *Lawyers'
Liabilities*, (2nd edn, 2002), Ch.6.
[18] See *Hastingwood Property Ltd v Saunders Bearman Anselm* [1991] 1 Ch. 114 at 125E–126B, *per*
Edward Nugee Q.C., sitting as a deputy High Court judge.
[19] *John Fox v Bannister King & Rigbeys* [1988] Q.B. 925 p.928B, *per* Nicholls L.J. Thus a
subsequent action on the same issues will not be an abuse of process, as the earlier application for
compensation for breach of an undertaking is disciplinary in nature, see *Ulster Bank Ltd v Fisher &
Fisher* [1999] P.N.L.R. 794, Girvan J.
[20] *Re a Solicitor, Ex p. Hales* [1907] 2 K.B. 539 at 545, DC.
[21] *United Mining & Finance Corp v Becher* [1910] 2 K.B. 296, K.B.D.; *Udall v Capri Lighting Ltd*
[1988] Q.B. 907 at 917E–F, *per* Balcombe L.J.
[22] *Udall v Capri Lighting Ltd* [1988] Q.B. 907 at 917E–F, *per* Balcombe L.J. (*cf.* Kerr L.J. at
924A–B); and *John Fox v Bannister King & Rigbeys* [1988] Q.B. 925 at 930E–G, *per* Nicholls L.J.,
with whom Sir John Donaldson M.R. agreed. But see *Bentley v Gaisford, The Times*, November 4,
1996.
[23] [1988] Q.B. 907 at 916C–918D.
[24] e.g. *115 Place Co-operative Housing Association v Burke, Tomchenko, Duprat* (1994) 116 D.L.R.
(4th) 657.
[25] e.g. *Wade v Licardy* (1993) 33 N.S.W.L.R. 1, Bryson J.
[26] e.g. *Countrywide Banking Corp Ltd v Kingston* [1990] 1 N.Z.L.R. 629.
[27] See e.g. *Re Gee* (1845) 10 Jur. 694; *Re Fairthorne* (1846) 3 Dow. & L. 548.
[28] An undertaking given in proceedings by solicitors who were a party to the proceedings will of
course be enforced in the normal way, although the undertaking was not given quae solicitor, see for
example *D v A & Co* [1900] 1 Ch. 484, Cozens-Hardy J.
[29] [1971] 1 Q.B. 396.

Denning M.R. considered that undertakings in relation to money were normally given by a solicitor to pay money that he has in his hands on trust, or that he will apply money in a particular way when he receives it.[30] In *United Bank of Kuwait v Hammoud*[31] an employed solicitor gave undertakings that moneys which were to come under his control which belonged or were owed to his clients would be transferred to the claimant, on the strength of which the claimant made a loan to the clients. The Court of Appeal held that the undertakings were given in the capacity of a solicitor, and that they bound the firm. The case is significant for three reasons. First, the tests for whether the undertaking was given in the capacity of a solicitor, whether it was made in the usual way of business of the firm so that the partners would be bound by an undertaking of another partner, and whether it was made with ostensible authority so that a firm would be bound by an undertaking of its employee, were all in effect the same.[32] Secondly, that question was to be answered, as it was in the case, with the assistance of expert evidence.[33] Thirdly and consequently, elderly decisions showing what is within the ordinary authority of a solicitor should be treated with caution.

11–067   **Examples of undertakings.** Some assistance may still be gained from decided cases, depending on their antiquity. Solicitors have been liable for giving undertakings in their capacity as solicitors in litigation in the following circumstances[34]: to enter an appearance in a proposed action and to give bail not exceeding the value of their client's ship and cargo in order to avoid its arrest[35]; to acknowledge service for a defendant[36]; to pay over funds given to the solicitor for a particular purpose[37]; to pay stamp duties and penalties in relation to documents used in evidence which were not stamped[38]; and as the solicitor of successful defendants to repay costs if the claimant's appeal succeeds.[39] In non-contentious matters solicitors have been liable for undertakings to the other party to repay moneys handed to them on behalf of their clients if no new agreement could be reached[40]; to pay over moneys recovered in litigation[41]; and to a bank to hold leases to the order of the bank and to account for the proceeds when

---

[30] [1971] 1 Q.B. 396 at 402F–G. Similar observations were made by Staughton L.J. in *United Bank of Kuwait Ltd v Hammoud* [1988] 1 W.L.R. 1051. Applying these observations, solicitors who gave an undertaking to pay sums of money, where there was no element of actual contemplated work or services in the capacity of a solicitor, did not give the undertaking as solicitors, see *Ruparel v Awan* [2001] Lloyd's Rep. P.N. 258, Ch. D.

[31] [1988] 1 W.L.R. 1051.

[32] See particularly Staughton L.J. at 1063B–D. *Hammoud* was followed by the Court of Appeal in *Hirst v Etherington* [1999] Lloyd's Rep P.N. 938. The promise to pay money to a third party in that case was not part of a solicitor's business, and the mistaken assurance by the solicitor giving such an undertaking that it was given in the normal course of business did not give him authority to bind his partners.

[33] *ibid.* at 1063F. See also Glidewell L.J. at 1059B–F.

[34] See also the facts of cases which are set out in this section, and the further cases cited in Halsbury, above.

[35] *The Crimdon* [1900] P. 171.

[36] *Re Kerly, Son & Verden* [1901] 1 Ch. 467.

[37] *Re a Solicitor, Ex p. Hales* [1907] 2 K.B. 539, DC.

[38] *Re Coolgardie Goldfields Ltd* [1900] 1 Ch. 475, Ch. D.

[39] *Swyny v Harland* [1894] 1 Q.B. 707, CA; *Att-Gen v Emerson* (1889) 24 Q.B.D. 56, CA.

[40] *United Mining & Finance Corp v Becher* [1910] 2 K.B. 296, KBD.

[41] *Re Pass* (1887) 35 W.R. 410, CA.

sold.[42] The Law Society has issued guidance on the form of undertakings for discharge of building society mortgages and for bridging finance.[43]

Construction of the undertaking. Where the existence or construction of an   **11–068** undertaking is in doubt, it will generally be construed in favour of its recipient. The critical question is how it would reasonably have been understood by the recipient in the circumstances he received it. Thus a letter reciting the solicitor's instructions "to confim to you that on completion of the sale . . . I am to remit £26,000 to you" was held to be an undertaking given a previous letter from the client to the solicitor and the recipient which instructed the solicitor to issue an undertaking to pay the moneys to the recipient.[44] An undertaking must be given by the solicitor personally and not merely on behalf of his client. This may not be obvious. In *Re C*[45] a solicitor undertook as follows:

> "in consideration of you, on behalf of your clients agreeing to the proceedings . . . being adjourned for one week . . . we on behalf of our clients undertake to apply [for various cross-summonses] and to pay to you on behalf of your clients whatever balance may be adjudged by the magistrate to be due to your clients."

The Divisional Court held that this was a personal undertaking, otherwise it would mean nothing as the client would be liable by the order of the magistrate in any event. However, even an undertaking by a client may impose an enforceable duty on his solicitors to act when their client is relying on them to implement it.[46] An undertaking need not use the word "undertaking", as is illustrated by *John Fox v Bannister King & Rigbeys*.[47] The claimant had acted as solicitors for Mr Watts, and was owed moneys by him. The defendants acted for Mr Watts in selling two properties, and in relation to some of the proceeds they informed the claimant: " . . . no doubt you and [Mr Watts] will sort out as to the £18,000 which is still in my account and which of course I shall retain until you have sorted everything out." The Court of Appeal held that this was an undertaking not to part with the £18,000. Furthermore an undertaking may be oral rather than in writing,[48] although it is good practice for the recipient to confirm it in writing.[49]

---

[42] *Re A Solicitor* [1966] 1 W.L.R. 1604.

[43] The Law Society's *Guide to the Professional Conduct of Solicitors* (8th edn, 1999), annex 25C; for an up-to-date version see the Law Society website.

[44] See *Reddy v Lachlan* [2000] Lloyd's Rep. P.N. 858, CA, which is authority for the propositions in the first two sentences of this paragraph.

[45] (1908) 53 S.J. 119. For another example see *Re Solicitors* (1916) 11 W.W.R. 529, British Columbia CA, where an undertaking "on behalf of our client" to execute an agreement and make payment was held to be an undertaking by the solicitor; *cf. Digby Brown & Co v Lyall* [1995] S.L.T. 932, OH, where such words were not so construed.

[46] As in *Refson & Co v Saggers* [1984] 1 W.L.R. 1025, Nourse J., although no action was taken against the solicitors in that case.

[47] [1988] Q.B. 925. Note that the undertaking there was to the solicitors. It is often a matter of construction whether the undertaking was given to the solicitor on the other side or his client. For an illustration of the latter see *Kutilin v Auerbach* (1989) 34 B.C.L.R. (2d) 23; for the facts, see below.

[48] Nor need it be embodied in an order of the court even though it be given in the context of litigation, see *Williams v Williams & Partridge* (1910) 54 Sol. Jo. 506, CA.

[49] *Udall v Capri Lighting Ltd* [1988] Q.B. 907 at 919H–920A, *per* Kerr L.J.

Solicitors' undertakings to lenders are generally not construed to impose absolute obligations.[50]

11–069   **Absolute nature of enforcement.** The courts are strict in their enforcement of undertakings, subject to the discretion referred to in the next paragraph. This may in part reflect the nature of the jurisdiction,[51] and also the fact that a solicitor is not obliged to give an undertaking.[52] Thus a court will enforce an undertaking even if it is made by mistake,[53] or the solicitor's authority is withdrawn or the client instructs the client not to perform it,[54] or the solicitor no longer acts for the client.[55] The solicitor will not be released from the undertaking save with the consent of its recipient.[56] It is irrelevant that the undertaking is given without the authority of the client, although if the recipient knows this then the Court's attitude to enforcing it may be affected.[57] A solicitor will not be able to rely on a defence of limitation,[58] or lack of consideration,[59] or the absence of writing

---

[50] See paras 11–009 and 11–010, above, and in particular *Barclays Bank Plc v Weeks Legg & Dean (a firm)* [1999] Q.B. 309. In that case, Millett L.J. observed that money, supplied pursuant to an undertaking to apply any sums received solely to acquire a good and marketable title, was held on trust to be applied only in accordance with the terms of the undertaking. In *Twinsectra v Yardley* [2000] Lloyd's Rep. P.N. 239 at 254 col.1. the Court of Appeal suggested that the observation should be applied more widely to money received by a solicitor from a third party to be held by him on express terms. An undertaking to apply the monies received in a particular way is likely to create a trust, see *Twinsectra v Yardley* [2002] UKHL; [2002] 2 A.C. 164 and para.11–034, above. For the meaning of an undertaking "to effect completion" see *1st Property Finance Ltd v Martin & Haigh (a firm)* [2006] P.N.L.R. 534, Ch. D.

[51] See para.11–065, above.

[52] See *Re Hilliard Ex p. Smith* (1845) 2 Dowl. & L. 919 and (less clearly) *Chilton v Blair* (1914) 8 B.W.C.C. 1, CA; *cf.* the unusual case of *Sturla v Freccia* (1880) 28 W.R. 360, where it would appear that the Court of Appeal ordered that an undertaking be given.

[53] Thus in *Dotesio v Biss (No.2)* (1912) 56 Sol. Jo. 736 the Court of Appeal enforced an undertaking that a solicitor should repay moneys paid if an appeal should succeed, as it did, although by an unfortunate error the original order required that the moneys should be paid to the solicitor's client rather than to him. *cf. Mullins v Howell* (1879) 11 Ch. D 673, where the court considered that it had a discretion whether to enforce an undertaking given by mistake; the undertaking was not made by a solicitor.

[54] As in *The Gertrude* [1927] W.N. 265, Hill J.: solicitors gave an undertaking to appear and put in bail in a collision action in rem. Their clients then said that they had never given any such instructions, and the solicitors immediately informed the other side. However, they were liable on their undertaking.

[55] As in *Williams v Williams & Partridge* (1910) 54 Sol. Jo. 506, where the Court of Appeal held that the undertaking to notify the other side to custody proceedings of any change of address by their client continued although the latter shortly changed her solicitors.

[56] See *Re Coolgardie Goldfields Ltd* [1900] 1 Ch. 475. Even a virtual waiver may be sufficient, see *Miller v James* (1823) 8 Moore C.P. 208.

[57] *John Fox v Bannister King & Rigbeys* [1988] Q.B. 925 at 929A–B, *per* Nicholls L.J.; *cf. The Gertrude* [1927] W.N. 265.

[58] *Bray v Stuart A West & Co* [1989] N.L.J.R. 753; see para.11–071 for the facts. The judge disapproved of the obiter dictum of Farwell J. in *Re Kerly, Son & Verden* [1901] 1 Ch. 467 (also apparently disapproved by Rigby L.J. at 477), it is submitted correctly, on the basis of *Re Grey* [1892] 2 Q.B. 440, a case concerning the summary jurisdiction over solicitors which was not concerned with undertakings. However, the court has a discretionary power to strike out the claim for delay, see *Taylor v Ribby Hall Leisure Ltd* [1998] 1 W.L.R. 400 summarised in para.11–071, below.

[59] This is implicit in *Goldman v Abbott* [1989] 48 E.G. 51 at 80 col.1. at F; see para.11–074 for the facts. The rule is long established, see *Re Hilliard Ex p. Smith* (1845) 2 Dowl. & L. 919.

with respect to a contract for land.[60] In contrast, the position with respect to illegality would appear to be exactly the same as in a common law action.[61] In *Rooks Rider v Steel*[62] the defendant solicitors gave an undertaking to the claimant solicitors to pay their proper fees and disbursements in connection with a loan agreement. Unknown to either solicitors, the claimant's client intended to use the loan agreement to obtain money fraudulently, although the loan was in fact not made. Knox J. applied the normal principle that in relation to an agreement tainted by illegality a third party is only affected if he has notice of the illegality, and the Judge held that the undertaking should be enforced.

Discretion. In tension with the absolute nature of the enforcement of under-   **11–070**
takings described above, the courts do retain a discretion whether or not to enforce them. This provides a good reason for the old rule that the full facts must be before the court.[63] In *Udall v Capri Lighting Ltd*[64] Balcombe L.J. considered that while the fact that the undertaking was for a third party to act, or that there was a defence to an action at law, would not preclude the summary enforcement of an undertaking, they would be factors which the court may take into account when exercising its discretion.[65] Similarly, Kerr L.J. stated that an undertaking that a third party will do or refrain from doing something may affect the manner in which the court exercises its power,[66] as may any difficulties with legal professional privilege.[67] However, he considered that an order for enforcement would normally be made as a matter of course.[68] The exercise of the court's discretion is illustrated by three cases, two of which are summarised in the next paragraph. In *Damodaran v Choe Kuan Him*[69] a solicitor acting for a purchaser gave the vendor an undertaking to pay over the purchase moneys on registration of transfer. There was (ultimately successful) litigation by a claimant against the vendor claiming an interest in the land, so that a *lis pendens* was entered on the register, as the solicitor knew when giving the undertaking. The Privy Council held that neither the existence of the suit, nor the protection of the interests of the claimant, nor the possibility of the purchaser suing the vendor for breach of contract were valid grounds to exercise a discretion to order payment of the sums into court rather than to the vendor.

Effect of delay. Two cases concerned with the exercise of the discretion   **11–071**
consider the issue of delay. In *Bray v Stuart A West & Co*[70] the vendor's solicitors

---

[60] *Udall v Capri Lighting Ltd* [1988] Q.B. 907 at 912C–E, *per* Balcombe L.J. The rule is of some antiquity, see e.g. *Evans v Duncombe* (1831) 1 Cr. & J. 372.
[61] Thus for instance, an illegal undertaking to give a bail bond to a sheriff was held to be void in *Lewis v Knight* (1832) 1 Dowl. 261.
[62] [1994] 1 W.L.R. 818.
[63] *Gilbert v Cooper* (1848) 17 L.J. Ch. 265.
[64] [1988] Q.B. 907.
[65] *ibid*. at 917G.
[66] *ibid*. at 919D–E.
[67] *ibid*. at 924D–E.
[68] *ibid*. at 923F, *per* Kerr L.J. The contrasting dicta by Megaw L.J. in *Silver & Drake v Baines* [1971] 1 Q.B. 396 at 405B–E suggesting a general discretion whether to enforce summarily are probably only applicable in the context of difficulties of proof.
[69] [1980] A.C. 497.
[70] [1989] N.L.J.R. 753.

undertook to the purchasers of land to discharge all subsisting charges. On completion in 1979 they did not discharge a local land charge that related to expenditure under the Public Health Act 1936. The local authority demanded payment only in 1987. Warner J. held that there was no limitation defence to a summary motion to enforce an undertaking. However, the judge considered that lapse of time was a factor that the court should have regard to in the exercise of its discretion. In that case, the purchaser was blameless and the solicitors careless, and the judge made an order in favour of the purchaser.[71] Contrast *Taylor v Ribby Hall Leisure Ltd*,[72] where the undertaking was given in June 1989 and the claimants suspected a breach in March 1990 but did not apply to the court until May 1995. The judge struck out the claim because there was inordinate and inexcusable delay that had seriously prejudiced the solicitor, and because no damage flowed from the breach of undertaking. The Court of Appeal considered that there was a discretionary power to strike out proceedings for contempt or which involved the court's supervisory power, and while it was generally preferable to make submissions on the effect of delay at the substantive hearing rather than by applying to strike out the claim, the court did not interfere with the judge's exercise of his discretion.

11–072   **Impossibility and compensation.** If the solicitor's undertaking is no longer capable of being carried out, then the court has a discretion whether to compensate the recipient. In *Udall v Capri Lighting Ltd*[73] the defendant's solicitors gave an undertaking during the course of litigation to the claimant's solicitors that the defendant's directors would provide security for its liabilities by creating second charges on their personal properties. It was established that the undertaking could not be performed. The Court of Appeal held that they would not make an order requiring performance of the undertaking, as no court will make an order in vain and disobedience would amount to contempt. However the court may exercise its discretion to order the solicitor to pay compensation, and the Court of Appeal in *Udall* remitted the case to the court below for it to investigate whether compensation should be ordered.[74] Where it is impossible to perform the undertaking, it would appear that the recipient will have to show that he has

---

[71] *cf. The Ring* [1931] P. 58, Bateson J., where solicitors undertook to accept service of a writ. The delay in issuing the writ was irrelevant, although the delay was only nine months. In the similar case of *Re Kerly, Son & Verden* [1901] 1 Ch. 467 at 477, Stirling L.J. considered that a delay of 18 months should be taken into account, but was not sufficient to prevent enforcement.

[72] [1998] 1 W.L.R. 400.

[73] [1988] Q.B. 907. In *Bentley v Gaisford, The Times*, November 4, 1996, a solicitor had unwittingly broken an undertaking preserving the previous solicitor's lien by photocopying documents. The Court of Appeal refused to order compensation as the conduct was not inexecusable and was insufficient to merit reproof.

[74] For a slightly different approach see *115 Place Co-operation Housing Association v Burke* (1994) 116 D.L.R. (4th) 657, British Columbia CA, where the claimant paid the defendant solicitors moneys owing to their client on an undertaking to deposit those moneys in their own name in a trust company. The trust company mistakenly paid out the moneys to the client. The claimant obtained judgment against the client, which later ceased to exist. The solicitors and the trust company were ordered to recreate the fund. They were not entitled to become involved in the assessment of damages against the client, but they could contest whether there were deficiencies in the contract covered by the undertaking.

suffered loss.[75] Contrast *Citadel Management Inc v Thompson*[76] where the solicitor alleged that an undertaking to make certain payments became impossible because his clients were unable to put him in funds. The Court of Appeal held that the undertaking could be performed. As the solicitor had not informed the claimant of the fact that his performance was dependent on others, he could not rely on that dependence to excuse his non-compliance. The Court also held that if circumstances changed so that it was no longer possible to fulfil an undertaking, the solicitor had to notify the recipient immediately, or be bound to honour it. In *Hole & Pugsley (a firm) v Sumption*[77] Hart J. made it clear that disclosure of a material change in circumstance would not relieve solicitors from liability in every case. There, the undertaking was to send proceeds of sale to the respondents or their bank. Disclosure of the change in circumstance, which was that the solicitors' client's bank now required the full net proceeds of sale to be paid to it, did not relieve the solicitors of their obligation.

Practice and procedure. Sir John Donaldson M.R. in *John Fox v Bannister* **11–073**
King & Rigbeys reaffirmed that the summary character of the jurisdiction lay not in the burden or standard of proof, but in the procedure, which was by originating summons[78] or simple application in existing proceedings.[79] While it was not usual, the court held that in an appropriate case the court can resolve issues of fact with the assistance of oral evidence and cross-examination, and can order pleadings and discovery.[80] As a consequence of its summary nature, the court will only exercise its jurisdiction in a clear case, see *Silver & Drake v Baines*.[81] The application should be entitled in the matter of the solicitor, rather than with the title of the action.[82] If the undertaking was made to the Court of Appeal, the application should be to that court.[83] An undertaking to a county court can be enforced in that court by committal.[84] An application for committal will normally result in an order for enforcement rather than for committal.[85] If the undertaking

---

[75] (1994) 116 D.L.R. (4th) 657 at 918F–G. See also *John Fox v Bannister King & Rigbeys* [1988] Q.B. 925 at 930C–D. Thus in *Kutilin v Auerbach* (1989) 34 B.C.L.R. (2d) 23 the defendant solicitor who acted for the wife in divorce proceedings gave an undertaking to the claimant to pay him or his wife moneys on determination of the entitlement to them. The claimant became so entitled, but the defendant mistakenly paid most of the moneys to the claimant's former lawyer, who deducted his fee before remitting the balance to the claimant. The British Columbia Court of Appeal did not award compensation for the moneys his lawyer had deducted, as the payment had reduced a legitimate obligation of the claimant. In *Commissioner of Inland Revenue v Bhanabhai* [2006] 1 N.Z.L.R. 797, it was no longer possible to pay the Inland Revenue tax from the consideration for property sales, which the solicitor had undertaken to do, as the monies had been dissipated. Laurenson J. ordered the solicitor to pay $300,000 compensation, less than the tax, as he took into account a global settlement reached between the solicitor and the liquidator of the client company, although all the liquidator's recoveries had been used to pay costs.
[76] [1999] 1 F.L.R. 21.
[77] [2002] P.N.L.R. 502.
[78] See *Re a Solicitor* (1969) 113 Sol. Jo. 549. In the Chancery Division it was by motion, see *Re FC* [1888] W.N. 77. Such procedures have been abolished by the Civil Procedure Rules 1999.
[79] [1988] 1 Q.B. 925 at 931H.
[80] *ibid.* at 930E–F (Nicholls L.J.) and 931H (Donaldson M.R.).
[81] [1971] 1 Q.B. 396 at 403B–C, *per* Lord Denning M.R. and at 403A–E, *per* Megaw L.J.
[82] According to the headnote of in *Re Kerly, Son & Verden* [1901] 1 Ch. 467.
[83] As in *Jonesco v Evening Standard Co Ltd* [1932] 2 K.B. 340.
[84] County Courts Act 1984, s.142.
[85] *Re a Solicitor* [1966] 1 W.L.R. 1604.

does not provide a period within which the act is to be done, it may be necessary to apply to the court first for an order fixing a period to do so.[86] It is not necessary to prove service of the undertaking on the respondent before an application for committal.[87]

11–074   **Methods of enforcement.** There are three ways in which undertakings can be enforced.[88] First, the recipient may apply to the court to exercise its inherent supervisory jurisdiction, which has been considered above. Secondly, there can be an application to the Law Society for professional misconduct. The Law Society can require implementation of the undertaking, but it does not have the power to order compensation or specific performance.[89] Thirdly, the recipient may have an action at law, most obviously in contract. Of the cases which have been cited above, only *United Bank of Kuwait v Hammoud*[90] and *Goldman v Abbott*[91] concerned the enforcement of an undertaking by an ordinary action, and both addressed the question of consideration. It was apparent that there was little difficulty in finding consideration in *Hammoud*,[92] which is surely typical. In *Goldman v Abbott*[93] the tenant's solicitors undertook to pay the landlord's costs in relation to a licence to assign. The licence to assign was not given, but on the construction of the correspondence the Court of Appeal held that the undertaking applied whether or not it was given. The Court found that there was consideration for the undertaking by the landlord processing the application, but significantly it seemed to consider that no consideration was required in any event.[94] Even if consideration is needed but is absent, there may be a duty of care in tort.[95]

(v) *Other Liabilities*

11–075   **Breach of warranty of authority.** In *Penn v Bristol & West Building Society*[96] a husband instructed a solicitor to carry out the sale of a house that was owned

---

[86] See *Cotton v Heyl* [1930] 1 Ch. 510 (where the undertaking was not by a solicitor).

[87] *Re Launder* (1908) 98 L.T. 554 (where the undertaking was not by a solicitor).

[88] *Udall v Capri Lighting Ltd* [1988] Q.B. 907 at 916C–E, *per* Balcombe L.J.

[89] See the Law Society's *Guide to the Professional Conduct of Solicitors* (8th edn, 1999), para.18.02.2; for the current version see the Law Society website.

[90] [1988] 1 W.L.R. 1051. In *Russo v Dupree* (2004) 217 A.L.R. 54, Bryson J. in the Supreme Court of New South Wales held that an undertaking by solicitors to protect the costs and disbursements of the previous solicitors on the handing over a file created a binding contractual arrangement.

[91] [1989] 2 E.G.L.R. 78.

[92] *ibid.* at 1057G–H.

[93] [1989] 2 E.G.L.R. 78.

[94] *ibid.* at 80 col.1 at F. In *Barclays Bank Plc v Lougher* (1996) 1 Con.L.R. 75 H.H. Judge Hicks Q.C., sitting as an Official Referee, held that consideration was required in an action to enforce an undertaking. It was given in that case by the claimant bank providing facilities to the defendant solicitor's client for the purchase of land, in return for the solicitor's undertaking to deal with the purchase moneys in a particular way. This issue was not considered on appeal, see [1999] Q.B. 309.

[95] As in *Al-Kandari v Brown* [1988] Q.B. 665; see para.11–063 for the facts. The court did not have to address the question of whether the solicitor's holding of the husband's passport amounted to an undertaking.

[96] [1997] 1 W.L.R. 1356. In a similar case in Singapore, a solicitor purportedly acted for a company pursuant to a forged resolution in a sale of property, and was found liable to the prospective purchaser for breach of warranty of authority, see *Fong Maun Yee v Yoong Weng Ho Robert* [1997] 2 S.L.R. 297, CA.

by him and his wife. She was ignorant of the transaction and did not instruct the defendant solicitor, although the solicitor mistakenly thought that he was acting for both husband and wife. The conveyance was in fact achieved by the forgery of the husband. As a result, the purchaser obtained no title to the property, and the building society which had loaned him money suffered loss. The Court of Appeal held that the solicitors were liable to the building society for breach of warranty of authority. In *Penn*, the solicitors did not act for the building society, which had its own lawyers. It was suggested by Chadwick J. in *Bristol & West Building Society v Fancy & Jackson (a firm)*[97] that solicitors would also be liable for breach of warranty of authority if they acted for borrowers and lenders, but the Court of Appeal held in *Zwebner v The Mortgage Corporation Ltd*[98] that the true position is that there is a duty to take any steps necessary to make up for the absence of such a warranty.

A solicitor negotiating the sale of property on a "subject to contract" basis **11–076** does not have ostensible authority to conclude a binding contract for the purchase of land,[99] nor does he have implied authority to accept notices for a client.[1] However, a solicitor has ostensible authority to settle litigation.[2] Any actual authority will end if the client ceases to have capacity, and as a result a solicitor may well be in breach of his warranty of authority.[3] Such a claim failed in *Donsland Ltd v Van Hoogstraten*[4] where it was alleged that proceedings were continued in breach of warranty of authority after the sole director of the claimant company had died. The Court of Appeal held that the retainer continued, as the company continued in existence, although there was no one to give instructions. The solicitors had authority to take all necessary steps to preserve the claim.[5] In litigation, a solicitor acting for a client warrants that he has a client who has authorised the proceedings, but not that the client had the name by which he appeared in the proceedings, nor that the client was solvent or had a good cause of action.[6] There is a summary jurisdiction to award damages against a solicitor who commenced proceedings without authority, which requires that the solicitor has a reasonable opportunity to make representations. However, Colman J. refused such an application in *Skylight Maritime SA v Ascot Underwriting Ltd*[7] because it was a complex case which was unsuitable for summary determination, but required a separate action instead. The judge also held that, as the damages were compensatory, the applicants could not be in a better position than if they

---

[97] [1997] 4 All E.R. 582 at 612F–613E.
[98] [1998] P.N.L.R. 769.
[99] *James v Evans* [2000] 3 E.G.L.R. 1, CA.
[1] *In Re Munro* [1981] 1 W.L.R. 1358 at 1361D.
[2] See para.11–191, below.
[3] *Younge v Toynbee* [1910] 1 K.B. 215; *James v Evans* [2000] 3 E.G.L.R. 1, CA.
[4] [2002] EWCA Civ 253; [2002] P.N.L.R. 26. The Court of Appeal stated at para.14 that it remained to be decided whether the representee had to prove that he had relied on the warranty or been induced to incur costs as a result of it.
[5] The case was applied by Cooke J. in *Euroafrica Shipping Lines Co Ltd v Zeguila Polska SA* [2004] EWHC 385, Comm; [2004] 2 B.C.L.C. 97, where there were difficulties in obtaining instructions as there was a dispute about the constitution of the client company.
[6] See *Nelson v Nelson* [1997] 1 W.L.R. 233, CA, and *SEB Trygg Liv AB v Manches* [2005] EWCA Civ 1237; [2006] 1 W.L.R. 276, CA. *SEB* decides that the obiter conclusion of McCowan L.J. in *Nelson,* that the solicitor warrants that the client did bear the name of the party to the proceedings, was wrong.
[7] [2005] EWHC 15; [2005] P.N.L.R. 25.

had been successful against the apparent party, and there was an issue as to whether the latter had any assets against which an order for costs could have been enforced.

11–077   **Fraud and other liabilities.** A solicitor may be liable in fraud to nonclients as much as to clients, as for example in *Henry Ansbacher & Co Ltd v Bins*.[8] A solicitor may be liable for other torts. In *Yellow Submarine Deli Inc v AGF Hospitality Associates Inc*.[9] it was alleged that the defendant solicitors had interfered in their clients' contractual relations with the claimant. Twaddle J.A., giving the judgment of the Manitoba Court of Appeal, rejected the claim as the claimant had not proved that the defendants had the intent necessary to establish the tort. In *Stevenson Estate v Siewert*[10] solicitors were held liable for conversion of a cheque, a strict liability tort, as the recipient to whom it was sent did not have capacity and it should have been sent to her trustee.

11–078   **Investment liabilities.** A solicitor may be liable to pay compensation under the financial regulations governing investment business, if knowingly concerned in contraventions under what was s.6 of the Financial Services Act 1987, on which see *Securities and Investment Board. v Pantell*.[11] The relevant provisions are now ss.380 and 382 of the Financial Services and Markets Act 2000,[12] and s.380 was successfully relied on by the Financial Services Authority acting on behalf of 84 investors who obtained a remedial order against a solicitor in *Financial Services Authority v Martin*.[13]

11–079   **Proceeds of Crime Act.** Lawyers have some limited duties to report matters to the authorities. In particular, under the Proceeds of Crime Act 2002 Pts 7 and 8, and particularly s.328, lawyers may commit a criminal offence if they are concerned in an arrangement which facilitates the use or control of criminal property by another person. There is protection if disclosure is made to the National Criminal Intelligence Service. There is also an offence of "tipping off" a person about a potential investigation by the NCIS. In *Bowman v Fels*[14] the Court of Appeal held that s.328 was not intended to affect the ordinary conduct of litigation by legal professionals, such as securing injunctive relief or settling

---

[8] [1998] P.N.L.R. 221, CA.

[9] [1998] 2 W.W.R. 701. In *Folland v Ontario* (2003) 225 D.L.R. (4th) 50, the Ontario Court of Appeal declined to strike out an action for malicious prosecution brought by a victim of a miscarriage of justice against a crown prosecutor, and see similarly *Lawrence v Peel Regional Police Force* (2005) 250 D.L.R. (4th) 287, Ontario CA.

[10] (2000) 86 Alta. L.R. (3d) 159, Alta. CA.

[11] [1993] Ch. 256, CA.

[12] There are a number of remedies apart from compensation. See further Ch.14 paras 14–081 to 14–102.

[13] [2005] EWCA Civ 1422; [2006] P.N.L.R. 11.

[14] [2005] EWCA Civ 226; [2005] 1 W.L.R. 3083. The Court of Appeal disapproved the earlier case of *P v P (Ancillary Relief: Proceeds of Crime)* [2004] Fam. 1. There, the wife's lawyers were concerned that the husband's assets were derived from untaxed income, and they sought the guidance of the Court. The President held that negotiating an ancillary relief settlement would amount to being concerned in a prohibited arrangement which facilitated the use or control of criminal property, which required reporting to the NCIS. See also the Law Society's Money Laundering Warning Card, which can be found on the Law Society's website.

any litigation. In any event s.328 would not override legal professional privilege.

(c) *The Standard of Skill and Care*

(i) *The Standard of Reasonableness*

Reasonable care and skill. The solicitor, in common with other professional men, is required to exercise reasonable care and skill.[15] At this level of generality, the law is unchanged since the nineteenth century.[16] However, lack of reasonable skill and care was then identified with "gross negligence" or *crassa negligentia*, and the courts tended to be more indulgent to practitioners in the degree of error which they allowed.[17] It is submitted that the nineteenth century authorities on the standard of skill and care to be expected of attorneys should now be treated with caution, save to the extent that the decisions or the statements of principle which they lay down have been approved more recently.[18]   **11–080**

The reasonably competent solicitor. The question whether the defendant solicitor made a mistake in any given case is usually capable of a definite answer. The question whether a particular mistake was negligent is a matter upon which (in borderline cases) the mere citation of authority is unlikely to be decisive. The judge applies what he perceives to be the standard of "the reasonably competent solicitor", a creature as mythical as the man on the Clapham omnibus. In *Midland Bank v Hett, Stubbs & Kemp*[19] Oliver J. emphasised that a solicitor should not be judged by the standard of a "particularly meticulous and conscientious practitioner . . . The test is what the reasonably competent practitioner would do having regard to the standards normally adopted in his profession . . . "[20]   **11–081**

Content of the duty. The duty of care and skill can be expressed as a number of general obligations: **11–082**

---

[15] Supply of Goods and Services Act 1982, s.13. This provision simply restates the common law.
[16] See, e.g. *Shilcock v Passman* (1836) 7 Car. & P. 289: "the question for us to consider is, whether the defendant has used reasonable skill and reasonable care", *per* Alderson B.; *Beale v South Devon Ry Co Ltd* (1864) 3 H. & C. 337: Crompton J. defined gross negligence as "the failure to exercise reasonable care, skill and diligence." In *Parker v Rolls* (1854) 14 C.B. 691 the judge's direction to the jury that an attorney was "bound to bring a fair and reasonable amount of care and skill to the performance of his professional duty" was approved.
[17] See, e.g. *Pitt v Yalden* (1767) 4 Burr. 2060; *Baikie v Chandless* (1811) 3 Camp. 17; *Godefroy v Dalton* (1830) 6 Bing. 460; *Purves v Landell* (1845) 12 C. & F. 91; *Lewis v Collard* (1853) 14 C.B. 208. The latest use of the test is *Faithfull v Kesteven* (1910) 103 L.T. 56, CA. In "The reasonableness of lawyers' lapses" (1994) 10 P.N. 6, Lord Hoffmann argues that the main reason for the change has been the availability of liability insurance.
[18] Recent years have seen the appearance of increasingly strict standards of liability (Report of the Royal Commission on Legal Services, Cmnd. 7648 (1979), para.23.27).
[19] [1979] Ch. 384. For the facts, see para.11–007.
[20] *ibid.* at 402–403. This dictum was approved by the Court of Appeal in *Martin Boston & Co v Roberts* [1996] 1 P.N.L.R. 45 at 50.

"The obligations of a lawyer are, I think, the following: (1) To be skilful and careful; (2) To advise his client on all matters relevant to his retainer, so far as may be reasonably necessary; (3) To protect the interest of his client; (4) To carry out his instructions by all proper means; (5) To consult with his client on all questions of doubt which do not fall within the express or implied discretion left to him; (6) To keep his client informed to such an extent as may be reasonably necessary, according to the same criteria." [21]

The precise content of the duty of reasonable skill and care will depend on the circumstances of each case. In particular, the standard of care must be judged by the nature and scope of the retainer.[22] Thus many cases will turn on an examination of the retainer.[23] When the solicitor is dealing with an enquiry from a third party, rather than with a client, the content of the standard of care is likely to be very much more limited in scope.[24]

11–083   **Judgment.** A solicitor is not expected to be faultless in his judgment.[25] The following statement of principle by Tindal C.J. in *Godefroy v Dalton*[26] was approved by Scrutton L.J. in *Fletcher & Son v Jubb, Booth & Helliwell*[27]:

"It would be extremely difficult to define the exact limit by which the skill and diligence which an attorney undertakes to furnish in the conduct of a cause is bounded; or to trace precisely the dividing line between that reasonable skill and diligence which appears to satisfy his undertaking, and that *crassa negligentia* or *lata culpa* mentioned in some of the cases, for which he is undoubtedly responsible. The cases, however, which have been cited and commented on at the bar, appear to establish, in general, that he is liable for the consequences of ignorance or non-observance of the rules of practice of this Court; for the want of care in the preparation of the cause for trial; or of the attendance thereon with his witnesses, and for the mismanagement of so much of the conduct of a cause as is usually and ordinarily allotted to his department of the profession. Whilst on the other hand, he is not answerable for error in judgment upon points of new occurrence, or of nice or doubtful construction, or of such as are usually entrusted to men in the higher branch of the profession of the law." [28]

11–084   **Knowledge of the law.**[29] The solicitor is not, and never has been, expected to possess encyclopedic knowledge:

---

[21] *Tiffin Hldg Ltd v Millican* 49 D.L.R. (2d) 216, *per* Riley J., approved by the Supreme Court of Canada (1967) 60 D.L.R. (2d) 469.

[22] See paras 11–004 to 11–010.

[23] e.g. *Spence v Bell* [1982] 6 W.W.R. 385, Alberta CA: defendant solicitor's retainer was limited to preparing a lease according to specific instructions, and did not extend to preparing a lease which financial institutions would accept for the purposes of financing.

[24] Thus in *Ouwens v Ace Builders Pty Ltd* (1989) 52 S.A.S.R. 344, Supreme Court of South Australia *in banco*, a solicitor told the respondent company that W, to whom the company was selling a house, would benefit from her father's estate. The solicitor owed no duty to the company to warn it of the limited enquiries made and of the possibility that W might divert her inheritance to her children. The warning would have been necessary if the solicitor was the company's adviser.

[25] For example, in *R Thew Ltd v Reeves (No.2)* (Note) [1982] Q.B. 1283, an error made by an articled clerk in the wording of an application for legal aid was held by Lord Denning M.R. not to amount to negligence: see 1287D.

[26] (1830) 6 Bing. 460.

[27] [1920] 1 K.B. 275 at 280; see also Bankes L.J. at 279.

[28] (1830) 6 Bing. 460 at 467–468.

[29] See further paras 11–153 and 11–154.

"No attorney is bound to know all the law; God forbid that it should be imagined that an attorney, or a counsel, or even a Judge is bound to know all the law; or that an attorney is to lose his fair recompense on account of an error, being such an error as a cautious man might fall into."[30]

Although a solicitor is not "bound to know all the law", he ought generally to know where and how to find out the law in so far as it affects matters within his field of practice. However, before the solicitor is held liable for failing to look a point up, circumstances must be shown which would have alerted the reasonably prudent solicitor to the point which ought to be researched. The last two sentences were cited with approval by the Supreme Court of Canada in *Central Trust Co v Rafuse*,[31] where it was stated that a solicitor "must have sufficient knowledge of the fundamental issues or principles of law applicable to the particular work he has undertaken to enable him to perceive the need to ascertain the law on the relevant points".[32]

Examples. In most cases, the solicitor's ignorance has been found to be negligent. In *Central Trust Co v Rafuse*[33] the defendant solicitors knew that a mortgage was being given to obtain a loan to assist in the purchase of the company's own shares. A solicitor should have known that the capacity of a company to borrow and give security may be limited by the Companies Acts, and he should have examined the relevant legislation to ascertain those limits.[34] In **11–085**

---

[30] *Montriou v Jefferys* (1825) 2C. & P. 113 at 116. See also *Fletcher & Son v Jubb, Booth & Helliwell* [1920] 1 K.B. 275: "Now it is not the duty of a solicitor to know the contents of every statute of the realm. But there are some statutes which it is his duty to know; and in these days when the defendants in so many actions are public authorities the Public Authorities Protection Act, 1893, is one of those statutes." (*per* Scrutton L.J. at 281.)

[31] (1987) 31 D.L.R. (4th) 481.

[32] *ibid.* at 524. Thus in *Melbourne Mortgages Ltd v Turtle* [2004] N.I.Q.B. 82; [2005] N.I.J.B. 297, QBD, solicitors acting for lenders in enforcing a large number of credit agreements should have kept up with significant developments in consumer credit law, and thus should have known of a recent English case reported in the Weekly Law Reports which decided that the form of agreement used was unenforceable. When there is a risk of a proposition of law being modified in the future, there is generally no duty to investigate whether any litigation is in the pipeline, or investigate whether an appeal was being followed up from a recent decision, see *Heydon v NRMA Ltd* [2000] N.S.W.C.A. 374; (2001) 51 N.S.W.L.R. 1.

[33] (1987) 31 D.L.R. (4th) 481, Supreme Court Canada.

[34] See also: *Elcano Acceptance Ltd v Richmond, Richmond, Stambler & Mills* (1989) 68 O.R. (2d) 165, Ontario High Court: solicitor failed to include an interest provision in promissory notes sufficient to satisfy the Interest Act; held negligent as any reasonably competent solicitor practising in commercial law in Canada should be aware of the relevant provisions. However, the Ontario Court of Appeal ((1991) 79 D.L.R. (4th) 154) found that the solicitor had been negligent because he had failed to follow his normal practice of inserting an interest provision, which was an isolated error. *MacCulloch v McInnes, Cooper & Robertson* 2001 NSCA 8; (2001) 178 N.S.R. (2d) 324, Nova Scotia CA: the lawyer was found to be negligent in failing to advise the client executor that before she could purchase estate assets she had to disclose a previous agreement to sell the assets on to a third party for more than three times the price. The law was clear that this was a breach of fiduciary duty, and the solicitor was aware of the potential problem but failed to research the issue. *Park Hall School v Overend* [1987] 2 I.R. 1, Irish High Court: a solicitor was expected to know that a "subject to contract" document might be a sufficient memorandum of writing to make enforceable an agreement for the sale of land.

Dean v Allin & Watts (a firm)[35] the Court of Appeal found solicitors liable for failing to know that there was a significant question mark whether s.2 of the Law of Property (Miscellaneous Provisions) Act 1989, whereby a disposition of an interest in land can only be made in writing, incorporating all the agreed terms in one document, applied to an equitable charge by way of deposit of title deeds.[36] An opposite result was reached in the New Zealand case of *Bannerman Brydone Folster & Co v Murray*.[37] Solicitors failed to appreciate that an option was a clog on the equity of redemption. The Court of Appeal in Wellington held that this failure was not negligent. Although the topic was dealt with in the textbooks on real property, the facts were not such as would have alerted "the average solicitor in New Zealand" to the need to refer to a text book on the point. Similarly, in the wasted costs case of *Ridehalgh v Horsefield*[38] the first of the six appeals concerned solicitors who misunderstood some landlord and tenant law. The Court of Appeal found they were not negligent, as the legislation was complex, the textbooks they consulted did not give a clear answer, they could not afford to consult specialist counsel, the county court judge saw nothing wrong with their analysis, and their argument was not discarded by counsel on appeal.

11–086   **Hindsight.** In determining whether the solicitor has exercised reasonable skill and care, he should be judged in the light of the circumstances at the time.[39] His actions or advice may, with the benefit of hindsight, be shown to have been utterly wrong, "but hindsight is no touchstone of negligence."[40]

(ii) *General Practice as Evidence of Reasonable Skill and Care*[41]

11–087   **The general rule.** Where the solicitor makes a mistake as a result of acting in accordance with the general practice of the profession, this will not normally be regarded as negligence. In *Simmons v Pennington*,[42] for example, solicitors acting for a vendor answered a requisition as to breaches of restrictive covenant in standard form, but "by ill luck", (*per* Denning L.J.) the court subsequently held that the answer entitled the purchaser to rescind. The defendants were acquitted

---

[35] [2001] Lloyd's Rep. P.N. 605. The textbooks were equivocal on the issue, and the issue was not decided until *United Bank of Kuwait v Sahib* [1997] Ch. 107 which occurred after the first three of the loan transactions. For the facts, see para.11–005, above. A similar finding of negligence where the lawyers did not know about s.2 was made in *Green v Collyer-Bristow* [1999] Lloyd's Rep. P.N. 798, in the context of matrimonial litigation, where two of the three main texts did not refer to the change. See further Ch.12, para.12–024.

[36] For another illustration, see *Bond v Livingstone* [2001] P.N.L.R. 30, QBD, where solicitors considered that the limitation period for personal injuries under a contract was six years rather than three. They were negligent as they overlooked s.11 of the Limitation Act 1980, "a mistake of the most basic kind".

[37] [1972] N.Z.L.R. 411.

[38] [1994] Ch. 205 at 240–245.

[39] *Bell v Strathairn & Blair* (1954) 104 L.J. 618.

[40] *per* Megarry J. in *Duchess of Argyll v Beuselinck* [1972] 2 Lloyd's Rep. 172 at 185 col.1.

[41] See further H. Evans, *Lawyers' Liabilities* (2nd edn, 2002), Ch.4.

[42] [1955] 1 W.L.R. 183.

of negligence. Conversely, where a solicitor falls into error as a result of departing from the general practice, this will generally be negligent.[43]

An exception. The relevance of the general practice of the profession to a charge of negligence was considered in detail in the Hong Kong case of *Edward Wong Finance Co Ltd v Johnson Stokes & Master.*[44] The claimants agreed to lend $1,355,000 to the purchasers of part of a factory, to be secured by a mortgage. The fifth defendants (the claimant's solicitors) handed over the money to Y, the vendor's solicitor, in return for an undertaking that Y would arrange for repayment of the existing mortgage on the property and that he would within 10 days forward an assignment of the property from the vendors to the purchasers. Y then left Hong Kong with the money. The existing mortgage on the property was not discharged and the claimant's intended charge over the property was worthless. It was established in evidence that, in the vast majority of conveyancing transactions in Hong Kong, the solicitor for the purchaser or mortgagee handed over the purchase price in return for an undertaking from the vendor's solicitor to forward the necessary documents of title within a stated time. This "Hong Kong style" completion enabled conveyancing transactions to be carried out far more quickly than elsewhere (where the money and the documents of title were handed over simultaneously). This was the first occasion on which such a transaction had fallen through because the vendor's solicitor had defaulted on his undertaking. The trial judge held that the solicitors were negligent in participating in a Hong Kong style completion, in view of the special circumstances of that case: Y was a recently established one-man firm and large sums of money were involved. The Hong Kong Court of Appeal by a majority reversed this decision. The Privy Council allowed an appeal by the claimants and held that the solicitors were negligent.

11–088

The Privy Council's reasoning was as follows: They did not condemn the practice of Hong Kong style completions. These were well suited to conditions in Hong Kong.[45] But it was foreseeable that the practice might result in loss, namely the embezzlement of the purchase moneys by the recipient. The foreseeability of this risk was proved by the fact that it was foreseen by a sub-committee of the Law Society of Hong Kong which had reported on conveyancing matters in 1965. Precautions could be taken to guard against the risk of embezzlement, without undermining the basic features of the Hong Kong style completion.[46]

11–089

"The risk inherent in the Hong Kong style of completion as operated in the instant case being foreseeable, and readily avoidable, there can only be an affirmative answer to the third question, whether the respondents were negligent in not foreseeing and avoiding that risk."[47]

---

[43] e.g. in *Stevenson v Rowand* (1830) 2 Dow. & Co. 104 the defendant, who was instructed to prepare a heritable bond, failed to give the necessary notice. Whether this rendered the bond invalid was a difficult question, which gave rise to a difference of judicial opinion but was ultimately decided against the client. The House of Lords held that the defendant had been negligent because he had "thought proper to depart from the ordinary mode of preparing heritable securities" (see at 119).

[44] [1984] A.C. 296. For an illuminating discussion of the policy reasons behind this decision see Lord Justice Hoffmann, "The reasonableness of lawyers' lapses" (1994) 10 P.N. 6.

[45] [1984] A.C. 296 at 306E.

[46] *ibid.* at 307H–308B.

[47] *ibid.* at 308G. See also the policy reasons mentioned at 307F–G.

The Privy Council only differed from the trial judge in that the solicitors' liability did not depend upon the special circumstances, which the judge had described as "warning bells".[48]

11–090   It appears that the "precautions" which the solicitors failed to take in this case were not normally taken by solicitors who participated in a Hong Kong style completion. Thus the defendant solicitors were held liable, despite the fact that they had complied in all material respects with the general practice of the profession in Hong Kong. Such a conclusion is not easily reconciled with the fact that the Privy Council did not condemn the general practice. This is an unusual case, in that the general practice of the profession (a) involved obvious risks and (b) did not take account of a report by the local Law Society that had drawn attention to such risks. It is submitted that it is only in relatively rare and extreme cases such as this that a solicitor, who complies with the general practice of the profession, will be held to have been negligent.

11–091   **Judicial treatment of *Wong*.**[49] *Wong* was referred to with approval by Lord Browne-Wilkinson in the clinical negligence case of *Bolitho v City & Hackney Health Authority.*[50] In *Patel v Daybells (a firm)*[51] solicitors completed a sale on the basis of undertakings given by the vendor's solicitors. The Court of Appeal held that this practice was not negligent, and distinguished *Wong* on the basis that the undertaking in *Wong* was wider, there was no official indemnity scheme in place in Hong Kong, and the Law Society of Hong Kong had already warned its members of the risk. They held that the principle in *Wong* was correct, which was that if a practice exposes clients to a foreseeable and avoidable risk, it may not be capable of being defended on rational grounds, and in those circumstances the fact that the practice is commonly or universally followed will not exclude liability.

11–092   **Unsafe common practice.** The courts are likely to be more ready to condemn an common practice which is unsafe. In *Roche v Peilow*[52] a house purchase was to be effected by a building contract. The building company had charged the property to their bank, but the defendant solicitors had not made a search in the Companies' Offices. The company went into liquidation after a number of stage payments had been made. The Irish Supreme Court held that the solicitors were negligent. Although they had followed a general practice of failing to make any

---

[48] [1984] A.C. 296 at 308G–H.
[49] The principle in *Wong* was applied in *National Commercial Bank Ltd v Albert Hwang, David Chung & Co* [2002] 2 HKLRD 409. The lender's solicitor released monies without verifying the authority of the person who purported to sign the agreement for the sale of property on behalf of the vendor company. This exposed the lender to a foreseeable risk that the mortgage would not be effective, which could have been avoided by making inquiries about the signer. The Hong Kong High Court held that the solicitors had been negligent. It was followed by the Court of Appeal of Singapore in *Yeo Yoke Mui v Ng Lian Poh* [1999] 3 S.L.R. 529. *Wong* was distinguished by the Court of Appeal, who did not criticise it, in the very different case of *Arbiter Group Plc v Gill Jennings & Every (a firm* [2000] P.N.L.R. 680, which concered delegability; for the facts, see para.11–150, below.
[50] [1998] A.C. 232 at 242–243.
[51] [2001] EWCA Civ 1229; [2002] P.N.L.R. 6.
[52] [1986] I.L.R.M. 189, Irish Supreme Court, on appeal from the High Court.

search before the granting of a lease, the inherent risks were well known to the solicitors. The court followed a dictum in *Donovan v Cork County Council*[53]:

> "If there is a common practice which has inherent defects, which ought to be obvious to any person giving the matter due consideration, the fact that it is shown to have been widely and generally adopted over a period of time does not make the practice any less negligent. Neglect of duty does not cease by repetition to be neglect of duty."[54]

Differing practices. The situation which more commonly arises is that there **11–093** are several different "practices of the profession" each of which is followed by a substantial number of respected and conscientious solicitors.[55] Applying the "*Bolam* principle",[56] a solicitor who complies with any one of the accepted practices ought to escape a finding of negligence. However, the court may be rather less reluctant to come to a different conclusion in this situation than in a case where the solicitor has complied with a practice of the profession which is universally adopted. This is illustrated by *G&K Ladenbau (UK) Ltd v Crawley & De Reya*,[57] where the issue was whether the defendants were negligent in failing to make a search of the commons register whilst acting for the claimants on the purchase of a plot of vacant land. Two conveyancing solicitors gave evidence on each side as to their practice in making commons searches. Both the solicitors called on behalf of the defendants stated that, in the particular circumstances of this case, it would not have been their practice to make a commons search. Mocatta J. acknowledged the conveyancing experience of both these witnesses, but nevertheless proceeded to hold that the defendants had been negligent. The Judge decided that it could not be said that "two equally well-established schools of practice had emerged" which it is submitted is not the correct test.[58]

The tendency to uniformity. In June 1985, in response to a recommendation **11–094** made by the Royal Commission on Legal Services,[59] the Law Society's Working Party on Professional Standards issued three written standards. Some of the material has been replaced by a new Practice Rule 15 dealing with client care and a Client Care Code, and they are now incorporated with modifications into the Law Society's *Guide to the Professional Conduct of Solicitors*.[60] The Law Society has issued a number of publications to assist solicitors in practice, the

---

[53] [1967] I.R. 173 at 193. That case concerned medical negligence.
[54] Similarly in the civil law case of *Roberge v Bolduc* [1991] 1 S.C.R. 374 the Supreme Court of Canada held that a common professional practice must be reasonable, and the defendant notary was found negligent as the practice he followed was not.
[55] See, e.g. P. Kenny, "The conveyancing retainer—1" (1982) 126 S.J. 387.
[56] *Bolam v Friern Hospital Management Committee* [1957] 1 W.L.R. 582 at 587. See Ch.13, para.13–022.
[57] [1978] 1 W.L.R. 266. See also para.11–246 for the facts.
[58] In *Ron Miller Realty Ltd v Honeywell, Wotherspoon & Beedell* (1992) 4 O.R. (3d) 492, Ontario High Court, affirmed (1993) 16 O.R. (3d) 255, summary judgment was granted despite the fact that the defendants had filed an affidavit from an expert suggesting that the mistake made by the defendants would have been made by most lawyers.
[59] Cmnd. 7648 (1979), Vol.I, para.22.57.
[60] The last printed edition was the 8th edn, 1999. For the current version see the Law Society's website.

most important of which is probably the Law Society's *Conveyancing Handbook*, which is reissued annually. These various guides are likely to carry great weight with the courts (a) as evidence of the general practice of the profession and (b), in certain situations, as an indication of what specific steps a reasonably careful and competent solicitor would take. Although these various sources are generally intended to reflect the existing practices of the profession, they are also likely to lead to a greater uniformity of practice. Thus with the passage of time it may become increasingly difficult for a solicitor to justify conduct which falls short of that described in the guides. In conveyancing, the "National Protocol" is likely to have the same effect.[61]

11–095 **An illustration: taking instructions.**[62] In *Johnson v Bingley Dyson & Furey*[63] the Court held that the principles laid down in the Law Society's *Guide to the Professional Conduct of Solicitors* were not the law, and a court must consider whether failure to observe the *Guide* was negligent in the particular case. However, the court condemned a common practice established by expert testimony that, in cut-price conveyancing, the lawyer does not see his client, because it preferred the more authoritative principle in the *Guide* that solicitors should see their clients. Similarly, in *Penn v Bristol & West Building Society*[64] the defendant solicitors were in breach of their duty to the claimant in the sale of the house she owned with her husband, as they failed to obtain instructions from her. The judge relied on the duty set out in the *Guide*[65] that when instructions were received from a third party, in that case her husband, the solicitor should obtain written instructions.

(iii) *The Specialist Solicitor and the Inexperienced Solicitor*

11–096 **An early statement of the law.** The position of the specialist solicitor was discussed, obiter, by Megarry J. in *Duchess of Argyll v Beuselinck*[66]:

"No doubt the inexperienced solicitor is liable if he fails to attain the standard of a reasonably competent solicitor. But if the client employs a solicitor of high standing and great experience, will an action for negligence fail if it appears that the solicitor did not exercise the care and skill to be expected of him, though he did not fall below the standard of a reasonably competent solicitor? If the client engages an expert, and doubtless expects to pay commensurate fees, is he not entitled to expect something more than the standard of the reasonably competent? I am speaking not merely of those expert in a particular branch of the law, as contrasted with a general practitioner, but also of those of long experience and great skill as contrasted with those practising in the same field of the law but being of a more ordinary calibre and having less experience.

---

[61] See further para.11–206.
[62] Note that the requirements of the Solicitors' Practice Rules 1990 are made under statute, and thus have the force of statute, see *Hughes v Kingston upon Hull CC* [1999] 2 All E.R. 49.
[63] *The Times*, February 28, 1995, [1995] N.P.C. 27, QBD.
[64] [1997] P.N.L.R. 393, Ch. D. Similarly, in *Al-Sabah v Ali* [1999] E.G.C.S. 11, Ferris J. relied on the *Guide* and held that a solicitor should see the client personally or obtain written confirmation from him, particularly in that case where the transaction was the sale of the purported client's flats to the agent from whom the solicitor obtained instructions.
[65] This has become para.12.05 in the 8th edn, 1999 and the current guide on the Law Society website.
[66] [1972] 2 Lloyd's Rep. 172.

The essence of the contract of retainer, it may be said, is that the client is retaining the particular solicitor or firm in question, and he is therefore entitled to expect from that solicitor or firm a standard of care and skill commensurate with the skill and experience which that solicitor or firm has. The uniform standard of care postulated for the world at large in tort hardly seems appropriate when the duty is not one imposed by the law of tort but arises from a contractual obligation existing between the client and the particular solicitor or firm in question."[67]

Insofar as it deals with the position of a solicitor specialising in a particular area of law, the passage quoted above has Canadian support.[68] It would be absurd if a large city firm with a substantial commercial practice were expected to know no more about the rules of international trade than the "average" solicitor in practice. However, it is respectfully submitted that, amongst solicitors practising in the same field of law, the proposed distinction between those "of long experience and great skill" and those "of a more ordinary calibre and having less experience" would be difficult to apply in practice. It would also be somewhat invidious. The judge would need to begin by assessing the "calibre" of the defendant solicitor, before deciding whether he was negligent. Where a profession is stratified (such as the medical profession)[69] it is easier for the court to exact different standards of skill and care from its members, according to their status and qualifications. In the case of solicitors, however, there is no formal distinction between those who possess great ability and experience and those who do not. Futhermore, if a complex matter comes before a solicitor with insufficient specialist experience, in appropriate cases he should surely refer it to a competent specialist, and if he does not he should be liable as if he did possess sufficient specialist knowledge.

Correct approach. It is suggested, therefore, that the correct approach is to judge the defendant solicitor by the standard of "the reasonably competent practitioner"[70] specialising in whatever areas of law the defendant holds himself out as a specialist.[71] This approach is consistent with principle and with authority in other areas of professional negligence.[72] In *Matrix Securities Ltd v Theodore*

11–097

---

[67] [1972] 2 Lloyd's Rep. 172 at 183.
[68] *Elcano Acceptance Ltd v Richmond, Richmond, Stambler & Mills* (1985) 31 C.C.L.T. 201 at 213, Ontario High Court, and *Confederation Life v Shepherd, McKenzie* (1992) 29 R.P.R. (2d) 271 at 297.
[69] See Ch.13, para.13–027.
[70] See *Midland Bank v Hett Stubbs & Kemp* [1979] Ch. 384 at 402–403.
[71] The sentence in the text was specifically adopted and applied by Douglas Brown J. in *Green v Collyer-Bristow* [1999] Lloyd's Rep. P.N. 798. A very similar test was adopted in *Hurlingham Estates Ltd v Wilde & Partners* [1997] 1 Lloyd's Rep. 525 by Lightman J. of a "reasonably competent conveyancer and commercial lawyer". The case concerned a commercial conveyance. It is consistent with the approach adopted in the earlier wasted costs case of *Locke v Camberwell HA* (1990) 140 N.L.J. 205 at 205 col.3. Moreland J., in considering the position of a solicitor inexperienced in medical negligence litigation, stated: "He is not expected to have the specialised expertise of a partner in a firm specialising in medical negligence work . . . He is expected to have the competence and the skill to be expected of a solicitor engaged in litigation in general practice." (The case was reversed on appeal on further facts coming to light, but nothing was said about the law: [2002] Lloyd's Rep. P.N. 23.)
[72] See Ch.2 paras 2–119 to 2–127. *cf. Marbel Developments Ltd v Pirani* (1994) 18 C.C.L.T. (2d) 229, where the British Columbia Supreme Court rejected the argument that there should be different standards applied to geographical areas or practising environments.

Goddard[73] Lloyd J. had to consider the conduct of a city firm giving tax advice. He held that they should be judged by the standard to be expected of a reasonably competent firm of solicitors with a specialist tax department. The fact that the defendants were established city solicitors who professed very high levels of skill and care did not increase this duty. He rejected a suggestion that in the context of obtaining clearance from the Inland Revenue of a tax avoidance scheme, the letter which they sent should have obtained a 100 per cent reliable result. Contrast *Balamoan v Holden & Co*,[74] where the defendant was a solicitor in a small country town instructed by a legally aided client in a comparatively small claim for nuisance. The Court of Appeal held that the courts should not apply too rigorous a standard of care in such circumstances, as the solicitor had to be anxious not to incur costs which could not be recovered from the other side. Great weight would therefore be placed on the judgment of a local circuit judge as to the standards reasonably to be required of local litigation solicitors.

11–098   **Non-solicitors.** The position of a legal executive, unqualified clerk or trainee might be different, because his qualifications are different. It has been held in an Australian case that a managing clerk who was sued for negligence had a duty to exercise the care expected of a managing clerk, not the higher standard of care expected of a solicitor.[75] In contrast, in *Balamoan v Holden & Co*[76] it was held that a one-man firm could not expect a lower standard of care to be applied to it merely because it delegated the case to an unqualified member of staff, if the conduct of that person fell below the standard appropriate for a solicitor.[77]

(iv) *Mitigating Factors*

11–099   **Non-negligent types of mistake.** Although every case turns on its own facts, certain types of mistake are less likely to be branded as negligent than others. The construction of documents, for example, is one of the most prolific sources of disagreement amongst lawyers. The fact that a solicitor erred in construing, or in advising on the construction of, a statute or document is unlikely to constitute negligence, so long as the construction which he favoured was a tenable one.[78] Again, where the solicitor is in a dilemma (which is not of his making) and is

---

[73] [1998] P.N.L.R. 290.
[74] [1999] N.L.J. Prac. 898.
[75] *Shigeva v Schafer* (1984) 5 N.S.W.L.R. 502, High Court.
[76] [1999] N.L.J. Prac. 898.
[77] Even if a lower standard of care is applied to unqualified staff, the same result may be reached in most cases. The less qualified person may be negligent in not seeking more expert advice, and the firm which employs him may be negligent in giving a less qualified person work which is too difficult for him, or in supervising him insufficiently.
[78] See, e.g., *Laidler v Elliott* (1825) 3 B. & C. 738 (incorrectly construing a rule of court, the meaning of which was obscure); *Elkington v Holland* (1842) 9 M. & W. 659 (incorrectly construing "a doubtful Act of Parliament"); *Bulmer v Gilman* (1842) 4 Man. & G. 108 (incorrectly construing an order of the House of Lords which was "doubtful in its terms"); *Dunlop v Woollahra Municipal Council* [1982] A.C. 158, PC (construction of two clauses in a planning scheme); *Ormindale Holdings Ltd v Ray, Wolfe, Connel, Lightbody & Reynolds* (1981) 116 D.L.R. (3d) 346 and (1982) 135 D.L.R. (3d) 557, British Columbia CA (construction of statute).

forced to choose between two or more evils, the court will be slow to castigate his actual decision as negligent.[79]

Lack of time. It is sometimes suggested that lack of time is a mitigating factor. **11–100** Where the lack of time arises because of pressure of other work, this is plainly not the case. No professional man ought to undertake more work than he is able to do properly. Where the lack of time arises because the client requires work to be done at great speed or because the solicitor is dealing with an emergency, then it is submitted that these are factors which should be taken into account in the solicitor's favour when determining whether or not a particular error was negligent. However, this is not an argument which can be pressed too far.[80] If the solicitor is required to perform a difficult task in inadequate time, he should clearly warn the client of the risks which are involved. The mere requirement to carry out work promptly is not a licence to be negligent.[81] On the other hand, solicitors are not justified in providing a second-rate service to clients who were slow in paying their fees.[82]

(v) Aggravating Factors

Creation of unnecessary risks. Where the solicitor creates, or incurs, unnec- **11–101** essary risks,[83] he is likely to be held liable for any consequential loss, however carefully he may have handled those risks and however skilfully he may have calculated the prospects of success at the outset. "It is negligence where there are two ways of doing a thing, and one is clearly right, and the other is doubtful, to

---

[79] He may, though, be able to apply to the court for directions or seek counsel's advice. This is illustrated by *Dunn v Fairs, Blissard, Barnes & Stowe* (1961) 105 S.J. 932: the deceased, who was dying of cancer, instructed a member of the defendant solicitors to purchase an annuity on her behalf. The solicitor carried out her instructions, even though her limited life expectancy made the transaction unwise. Barry J. dismissed a subsequent claim for negligence by the administrator of her estate.

"He had been placed in a dilemma, for he owed a duty to his client and was faced with having to proceed with the purchase or take action which would have led her to suspect that she was suffering from an incurable disease. The solicitor had considered the situation with great care and his Lordship was not satisfied that his decision to allow her to invest as she did could in any sense be regarded as negligent."

[80] Thus in *Whale View Investments Ltd v Kensland Realty Ltd* [2000] 2 HKLRD 261, High Court, a solicitor was negligent in failing to prepare mortgage documents properly when instructions were faxed on Saturday August 30, and the documents returned at 9.36 am on Tuesday September 2. The solicitors were negligent, as there was sufficient time to prepare the documents carefully and rather earlier than they did. On appeal, the finding of negligence was upheld, but the Court of Appeal held that the negligence caused no loss, see [2001] 2 HKLRD 342. In *Carew Counsel Pty Ltd v French* [2002] VSCA 1; (2002) 190 A.L.R. 690, the Victoria Court of Appeal took account of the fact that the solicitors had only two days in which to decide how to protect their client in relation to complex bankruptcy provisions, and the solicitors were held not to be negligent.

[81] In *Elcano Acceptance Ltd v Richmond, Richmond, Stambler & Mills* (1985) 31 C.C.L.T. 201, Ontario High Court, Smith J. put the matter in this way at 213:

"As a matter of policy, it seems to me that a Court should not lightly lower the requisite standard of care because the solicitor was rushed by his client. The solicitor's duty is, at a minimum, to tell the client very explicitly that certain dangers arise if, under the pressures of deadline, certain matters are not attended to, and, at a maximum, to withdraw from the relationship."

[82] See *F & G Reynolds (Whitchurch) Ltd v Joseph, The Times*, November 6, 1992.

[83] As by departing from the normal practice: see *Stevenson v Rowland* (1830) 2 Dow. & Cl. 104 at 119 and para.11–087, above.

do it in the doubtful way."[84] In *CW Dixey & Sons Ltd v Parsons*[85] the defendant solicitors acted for the claimants in granting a sub-lease of premises. Clause 2(10) of the head lease provided that the premises should not be used as a medical or quasi-medical establishment. The sub-lease as drafted by the defendants allowed the sub-lessee to use the premises for the purposes of a psychologist's consulting room. The head landlords took the view that this use infringed cl.2(10) of the head-lease and brought forfeiture proceedings, which were compromised. Salmon L.J. (sitting as an additional judge of the Queen's Bench Division) held that the defendants were negligent, and would have been negligent even if the use in question did not infringe cl.2(10):

> "In the present circumstances the solicitor owed a duty to his client to take reasonable care, not only to protect his client against committing a breach of the law but to protect him against a risk of being involved in litigation . . . In preparing a lease, as in the present case, a solicitor was presented with what was an obvious danger. It would not do for him to say that in his view it was all right. There was an obvious danger that a different view might be taken. In the present circumstances the ordinary careful solicitor would have gone to see his clients and advised them not to sign."[86]

11–102   **Acting beyond competence.** A solicitor creates unnecessary risks where he takes it upon himself to act in matters beyond his competence, or to advise on points which ought to be referred to counsel. In such circumstances he acts "at his peril".[87] If he errs, he may be held liable in negligence notwithstanding that he has exercised his utmost skill and care. In *Richards v Cox*,[88] for example, the claimant consulted the defendant solicitor about a road traffic accident in which she was injured. The defendant's clerk took the view that it was not worth suing her driver since he was uninsured. The Court of Appeal held that on a proper construction of the relevant insurance policy (which was extremely difficult to construe) the driver was insured. On the issue of negligence, which was not specifically argued on the appeal, Goddard L.J. stated:

> " . . . . it seems to me that the only negligence which can be alleged against [the solicitor's clerk] is that he took on himself to decide a somewhat difficult question."[89]

---

[84] *Levy v Spyers* (1856) 1 F. & F. 3, at 5 note (a): the defendant attorney was engaged to recover a sum due upon a judgment debt from one P. P. had agreed to give bills of exchange in discharge of the judgment debt. The defendant sent notes to P. rather than bills. It was held that the defendant acted negligently, even though the notes might have been sufficient.

[85] (1964) 192 E.G. 197.

[86] See also *Boros v Bodnar, Wanhella & Courtney* [1988] 6 W.W.R. 645, Saskatchewan QB: a solicitor delayed issuing proceedings against a hospital for wrongful dismissal until beyond the relevant limitation period of only one-year. He believed, as did most lawyers, that the one-year period only applied to negligence actions against hospitals, which view subsequently proved to be wrong. He was found to be negligent in not adopting a more cautious approach.

[87] *Ireson v Pearman* (1825) 3 B. & C. 799:

> "Now although it may not be part of the duty of an attorney to know the legal operation of conveyances, yet it is his duty to take care not to draw wrong conclusions from the deeds laid before him, but to state the deeds to counsel whom he consults, or he must draw conclusions at his peril."

[88] [1943] 1 K.B. 139.

[89] *ibid.* at 143.

If a situation is fraught with danger, particular care may be required. Thus in *Tonitto v Bassal*[90] a solicitor was found to be negligent in failing to comply strictly with the requirements of an option agreement, because it is common for grantees to seek to avoid the exercise of an option on the ground that its terms had not been complied with.

Acting for parties with opposed interests. Solicitors are not infrequently asked to act for two parties to a transaction with conflicting, or potentially conflicting, interests.[91] This practice, especially the practice of acting for both parties to a sale of land,[92] has frequently been condemned by the courts.[93] A solicitor who puts himself in this position may suddenly find that his duties to the respective clients require him to take two different, and mutually inconsistent, courses of action. In this situation, despite the exercise of the utmost skill and care, the solicitor must incur liability in negligence to one or other of the clients.[94] Such a situation arose in *Nash v Phillips*.[95] Even where so extreme a situation does not arise, the solicitor may encounter considerable difficulties as a result of acting in a dual capacity. If he makes a mistake or omission to the detriment of either party, the court will more readily castigate the error as

11–103

---

[90] (1992) 28 N.S.W.L.R. 564, NSWCA.

[91] For the rules of professional conduct as to when it is proper or improper to act for both parties see the Law Society's *Guide to the Professional Conduct of Solicitors*, (8th edn, 1999; current version on the Law Society website), Chs 15 and 25. There may also be a breach of fiduciary duty in such circumstances, see paras 11–023 to 11–025, above. If there is a breach of r.6 of the Solicitors' Practice Rules 1990, for instance if a conflict of interest existing or arose, or if the seller was a builder or developer, the prohibition cannot be waived even by informed consent, and the solicitors' duty in that case was to inform the client that they could not act for him, that he should seek legal advice from other solicitors, starting afresh, see *Hilton v Barker Booth & Eastwood (a firm)* [2005] UKHL 8; [2005] 1 W.L.R. 567 at paras 19 and 32, HL.

[92] The circumstances in which it is permissible for a solicitor to act for both parties to a conveyancing transaction are now specified in r.6 of the Solicitors Practice Rules 1990.

[93] e.g. *Goody v Baring* [1956] 1 W.L.R. 448, Ch.D; *Smith v Mansi* [1963] 1 W.L.R. 26, described by Danckwerts L.J. at 30 as "a shocking example of the trouble and expense which can arise from the employment (under a mistaken idea of saving time and expense) by the two parties to a sale of a solicitor who is already the solicitor of one of the parties." The Hong Kong Court of Appeal condemned this practice in *Yau Chin Kwan v Tin Shui Wai Development Ltd* [2003] 2 HKLRD 1.

[94] "The case has been put of a solicitor acting for vendor and purchaser who knows of a flaw in the title by reason of his acting for the vendor, and who, if he discloses that flaw in the title, which he knows as acting for the vendor, may be liable to an action by his vendor, and who, if he does not disclose the flaw in the title, may be liable to an action by the purchaser for not doing his duty as solicitor for him. It will be his fault for mixing himself up with a transaction in which he has two entirely inconsistent interests, and solicitors who try to act for both vendors and purchasers must appreciate that they run a very serious risk of liability to one or the other owing to the duties and obligations which such curious relation puts upon them."

per Scrutton L.J. in *Moody v Cox* [1917] 2 Ch. 71 at 91 (a fiduciary case, see at 79); cited and adopted by Danckwerts J. in *Goody v Baring* [1956] 1 W.L.R. at 450, and the Singapore High Court in *United Overseas Finance Ltd v Victor Sakayamary* [1997] 3 S.L.R. 211. The Federal Court of Australia expressed similar views in *Fox v Everingham* (1983) 50 A.L.R. 3371, basing them on *Moody v Cox* and *Goody v Baring*, and also in *Commonwealth Bank of Australia v Smith* (1992) 102 A.L.R. 453. See further *Wan v McDonald* (1992) 105 A.L.R. 473, Burchett J.; *Stewart v Layton* (1992) 111 A.L.R. 687, Foster J.; *Trade Practices Commission v CC (New South Wales) Pty Ltd* (1994) 125 A.L.R. 94, Hill J. In *Lizotte v Lizotte* 2002 NBCA 29; (2002) 249 N.B.R. (2d) 70, New Brunswick CA, a solicitor was held to be liable in the assignment of property between two brothers where he did not mention to his clients that there was a possible conflict of interest.

[95] (1974) 232 E.G. 1219, Ch. D.

"negligent," since he ought not to have put himself in such a position in the first place.[96] The same considerations apply a fortiori where the conflict is between the client and the solicitor himself.[97]

11–104   **Informed consent.** The Privy Council qualified this general principle in *Clark Boyce v Mouat*.[98] A solicitor may act for two parties whose interests may conflict providing that he had obtained the informed consent of both of them to his acting, which must be given in the knowledge that there is a conflict and that as a result the solicitor may be disabled from disclosing to each party the full knowledge he possesses or from giving some advice.[99] In that case, the claimant wished to assist her son by granting a mortgage over her home as security for loans to be made to him. The defendant solicitors acted for her and her son. They advised the claimant to obtain independent advice. She required no more than conveyancing and an explanation of the legal implications of the transaction. As she was in full command of her faculties and was aware of what she was doing, the defendant had no duty to give unsought advice. The requirement of informed consent may be onerous, depending on the circumstances, as is illustrated by *Mahoney v Purnell*.[1] The defendant solicitors acted for the claimant and his son-in-law on the sale of their jointly owned hotel from the claimant to the son-in-law. The solicitor had realised that the proposed transaction was potentially disadvantageous to the claimant, and knew that he trusted his son-in-law and was likely to be influenced by him. May J. held that the solicitor had advised the claimant that he ought to think about getting independent advice, but did not tell him he should, and did not advise the claimant about the conflict of interest in sufficiently clear and emphatic terms so that the claimant was enabled to give his informed consent.

11–105   **Borrower and lender.** Similar problems can arise when a solicitor acts for both borrower and lender.[2] This matter was briefly considered by the Court of

---

[96] e.g. *Lake v Bushby* [1949] 1 All E.R. 964, KBD; *Attard v Samson* (1966) 110 S.J. 249, QBD. See also *Powell v Powell* [1900] 1 Ch. 243 at 246–247, Ch. D. But *cf. Brinsden v Williams* [1894] 3 Ch. D 185. Canadian cases in which a solicitor acting for both parties has been held liable to one of them include *Clarence Construction Ltd v Lavallee* (1980) 111 D.L.R. (3d) 582, British Columbia CA; *Lapierre v Young* (1981) 117 D.L.R. (3d) 643, Ontario High Court; *Ferris v Rusnak* (1984) 9 D.L.R. (4th) 183, Alberta QB.
[97] *Apatu v Peach Prescott & Jamieson* [1985] 1 N.Z.L.R. 50 at 64, Eichelbaum J. There would be a breach of fiduciary duty, see para.11–018.
[98] [1994] 1 A.C. 428 at 435–436 (following Upjohn L.J. in *Boulting v Association of Cinematograph Television and Allied Technicians* [1963] 2 Q.B. 606 at 636). The Supreme Court of Ireland reached a similar conclusion in *O'Carroll v Diamond* [2005] I.E.S.C. 21; [2005] P.N.L.R. 34. A husband and wife approached their solicitors for advice in relation to surrendering their property to meet a debt of the husband. The defendant solicitors advised the wife to take independent legal advice, which they knew she did not do, and they refused to advise her on whether to give up her share of the property. They acted for both husband and wife in the drawing up of the documents, and were found not to be negligent.
[99] For possible qualifications to this rule see para.11–023, above. Further, the position is different when advising a client who is about to enter a transaction and who may be subject to undue influence, see para.11–207, below.
[1] [1996] 3 All E.R. 61.
[2] See, e.g. *Neushul v Mellish and Harkavy* (1967) 111 S.J. 399, CA, in which a solicitor acted for a lender in respect of a loan to one of his former clients. By reason of his knowledge of the borrower's financial affairs he "had put himself in hopeless difficulties."

Appeal in *Wills v Wood*,[3] a case where solicitors acted in connection with a loan between two of their private clients. Sir John Donaldson M.R. said that if the terms of the loans were already agreed, there might well be no problem.[4]

"But if either party were seeking advice or the solicitors were involved in the negotiation of the terms or either party might thereafter seek to say that sufficient was known to the solicitors to create a duty to advise, the solicitors were exposing themselves to the risk of criticism."

The commonest situation in which solicitors act for both lender and borrower is, of course, the domestic conveyance. Both the purchaser and the mortgagees who are lending part of the purchase price very often employ the same solicitor. In recent years this has given rise to difficulties in the voluminous litigation brought by lenders against solicitors, which is explored later.[5] The arrangement does on occasions infringe the guidelines proposed by the Master of the Rolls in *Wills v Wood*.[6] The fact that the solicitor in this situation acts for both the building society and the purchaser does not constitute an "aggravating factor" when considering whether a particular act or omission amounts to negligence, because there will normally be informed consent to the arrangement, as has been made clear by Millett L.J. in the leading judgment in *Bristol & West Building Society v Mothew*.[7] Furthermore, the lender will not be imputed with the knowledge of the solicitor who failed to inform it of the real intention of the borrower if such information was imparted to the solicitor before the retainer.[8]

Other circumstances of conflict. Potential conflict may arise in very different **11–106** circumstances. Thus in multi-party litigation, the requirement of confidentiality to existing clients in finalising a settlement may prevent a solicitor from acting for a new client to whom there would be a duty to give all available information.[9] There may be a conflict between an insured and his insurer.[10] Where a solicitor acts for a motorcyclist and his passenger in relation to injuries sustained in a road traffic accident, if the driver of the other vehicle alleges that the motorcyclist was at fault, the solicitor is in breach of fiduciary duty unless he advises the client of the conflict and ceases to act.[11] In criminal law, a solicitor who has acted for a defendant after his retainer is terminated cannot then act for a co-defendant where there has been a cut-throat defence.[12]

---

[3] *The Times*, March 24, 1984.
[4] For an even stricter view see *Ferris v Rusnak* (1984) 9 D.L.R. (4th) 183 at 191, Alberta QB.
[5] See paras 11–207 *et seq.*
[6] *The Times*, March 24, 1984.
[7] [1998] 1 Ch. 1.
[8] *Halifax Mortgage Services Ltd v Stepsky* [1996] Ch. D 207, CA. Applied by the New Zealand Court of Appeal in *Niak v Macdonald* [2001] 3 N.Z.L.R. 334, and see also *Kendall Wilson Securities Ltd v Barraclough* [1986] N.Z.L.R. 576, N.Z.CA, and *Waller v Davies* [2005] 3 N.Z.L.R. 814, High Court.
[9] See *Davies v Eli Lilly, The Times*, January 16, 1988.
[10] e.g. *Groom v Crocker* [1939] 1 K.B. 194, CA; see further para.11–192; *Nishimatsu-Costain-China Harbour Joint Venture v Ip Kwan & Co* [2001] HKLRD 84, Hong Kong CA.
[11] *Nadeau v Rice* (1990) 109 N.B.R. (2d) 243, New Brunswick CA.
[12] *Saminadhen v Khan* [1992] 1 All E.R. 963, CA.

(vi) *General Observations*[13]

11–107   **A serious matter.** Elderly cases suggest that allegations of negligence against a solicitor are a grave matter. A charge of negligence against a solicitor must be distinctly proved.[14] The issue of negligence should be approached "with the greatest care," even though the sum at stake may not be large.[15] Thus it is normally advisable to call the claimant, and not merely to rely on the correspondence.[16] In *Stewart Wrightson Group Ltd v Crocker*[17] Lord Denning M.R. observed that an error of judgment by solicitors did not amount to negligence. He added that, where there is delay in prosecuting a claim, negligence must be "most clearly established". Solicitors "should not be harassed by claims for negligence years after the event". In the analogous case of barrister's negligence, Lord Reid in *Rondel v Worsley* considered that "the onus of proving professional negligence over and above errors of judgment is a heavy one."[18]

11–108   **No requirement of moral censure.** On the other hand, as the courts are often at pains to emphasise, not every mistake amounting to professional negligence is deserving of moral censure. In *Creech v Mayorcas*[19] Pennycuick J. held the defendant liable "with some regret" for what he described as "an understandable slip" by the defendant's clerk. In *Sykes v Midland Bank Executor & Trustee Co Ltd*[20] a solicitor was held to have been negligent in failing to explain the effect of a particular provision in a sub-lease. In affirming this decision, Salmon L.J. observed.

> "The common law, of course, recognises no degrees of negligence, but I should like to say that, in my view, the degree of blame in the present case was slight. It was the sort of negligence many a competent professional man may have committed on some isolated occasion in the course of his career."[21]

The solicitor's state of mind is irrelevant, and it is his course of conduct which must be judged.[22]

---

[13] The observations in this paragraph presumably apply with equal force to all professions. They are included in this chapter since each of the cases cited concerns solicitors. Given the now common occurrence of professional negligence litigation, it may be doubted whether such observations carry the same force as they once did.

[14] *Farmer v Turner & Son* (1899) 15 T.L.R. 522, QBD.

[15] *per* Acton J. in *Ellis v Sampson* (1927) 71 S.J. 621.

[16] *Yager v Fishman & Co* [1944] 1 All E.R. 552 at 554D–E (Scott L.J.) and 556F (Goddard L.J.).

[17] (1979) 124 S.J. 83; *The Times*, December 19, 1979. Lord Denning based his comments, in part, on his own judgment in *Whitehouse v Jordan* given a few days previously. This must now be read subject to the House of Lords' decision in *Whitehouse v Jordan* [1981] 1 W.L.R. 246.

[18] [1969] 1 A.C. 191 at 230F. This was approved in the case of solicitors by Simon Brown L.J. in *Martin Boston & Co v Roberts* [1996] 1 P.N.L.R. 45 at 50D.

[19] (1966) 198 E.G. 1091.

[20] [1971] 1 Q.B. 113.

[21] *ibid.* at 126. These observations contrast markedly with the dicta in the 19th century cases referred to in para.11–080 (in particular, *Purves v Landell*).

[22] *Westway Homes Ltd v Gore Wood & Co, The Times*, July 9, 1991.

Illegality. It is no defence to a claim in negligence that the solicitor and client **11–109** were both engaged on a fraud, if the action could be pleaded and proved without reliance on the alleged fraud, see *Sweetman v Nathan*.[23]

(d) *Specific Defences to a Claim for Breach of Duty*

(i) *Immunity*

The abolition of immunity.[24] When a solicitor acted as an advocate, it used **11–110** to be the case that he enjoyed the same immunity against a claim for negligence as a barrister. The immunity of advocates has been abolished by the House of Lords in *Hall v Simons*[25] While that case concerned an attempt to strike out three cases brought against solicitors for negligence, the House of Lords primarily considered the position of barristers, and solicitor advocates were held to be in no different position.

(b) *Abuse of Process*[26]

Early cases. If a solicitor's negligence leads to the conviction of his client, **11–111** then the client may not be able to sue him because the action would be an abuse of process. There were three significant decision before the leading case of *Hall v Simons*[27] which need to be mentioned briefly.[28] The doctrine was first established in relation to solicitor's negligence in *Somasundaram v M Julius Melchior & Co*.[29] The claimant pleaded guilty to a charge of unlawfully wounding his wife. On release from prison, he sued his former solicitors, alleging that he had been overpersuaded to change his story and plead guilty. The Court of Appeal struck out the claim on the ground that it was frivolous and vexatious on its facts, but it also considered that the claim was an abuse of process because it was a collateral attack on the final decision of another court which the claimant had had

---

[23] [2003] EWCA Civ 1115; [2004] P.N.L.R. 7, CA.

[24] The topic is treated more extensively in the 5th edn of this work at paras 11–107 and 11–017 and Ch.11, paras 11–15 to 11–23. Earlier law may be relevant for acts and omissions before the date of the decision of the House of Lords if it is not of retrospective effect.

[25] [2002] 1 A.C. 615.

[26] For a more detailed treatment of the cases before the House of Lords decision in *Hall v Simons* [2002] 1 A.C. 615, see the 5th edn of this work at paras 10–108 to 10–111. See also H. Evans, *Lawyers' Liabilities*, (2nd edn, 2002), Ch.5; and *ibid.* "*Hall v Simons*" and abuse of process (2001) 17 P.N. 219.

[27] [2002] 1 A.C. 615. For the position in Canada see *Wernikowski v Kirkland, Murphy & Ain* (2000) 181 D.L.R. (4th) 625.

[28] And see also: *Oliver v McKenna & Co, The Times,* December 20 1995, Laddie J. (not struck out as sufficient new evidence which entirely changed the nature of the case); *Nestle v Best* [1996] P.N.L.R 444, CA (struck out, no fresh evidence available); *Acton v Graham Pearce & Co (a firm)* [1997] 3 All E.R. 909, Chadwick J. (conviction overturned on appeal, action allowed); *R.(L) v Witherspoon* [1999] P.N.L.R. 776, CA, (no collateral attack as significant differences from previous decision); *Channon v Lindley Johnstone* [2000] 2 F.L.R. 734, QBD, (no strike out where solicitor allegedly failed to adduce essential evidence in relation to ancillary relief proceedings).

[29] [1988] 1 W.L.R. 1394. The Court of Appeal relied on *Hunter v Chief Constable of the West Midlands Police* [1982] A.C. 529, HL.

a full opportunity of contesting. In *Walpole v Partridge & Wilson*[30] the claimant was convicted for obstructing a veterinary officer in the execution of his duty, and he appealed unsuccessfully. He brought proceedings alleging that the defendant solicitors had failed to lodge a further appeal on a point of law. The Court of Appeal declined to strike out the claim, considering that the initiation of proceedings which challenged the final decision of a court would not necessarily be an abuse of process. Ralph Gibson L.J. recognised four exceptions to the principle: where the challenged decision was obtained by fraud, collusion or perjury and there is sufficient fresh evidence to support the allegation; where there was sufficient fresh evidence which "entirely changes the character of the case"; where it was alleged that the solicitors failed to prosecute an appeal on an issue of law, as in *Walpole*; and in some circumstances, where there had been no decision on the merits such as where the claimant had submitted to judgment.[31] In *Smith v Linskills (a firm)*[32] the Court of Appeal held that the defendant had had a full opportunity of contesting his criminal trial where he was present throughout and could give instructions, even if criticism could be made of the defence. In considering the fresh evidence exception, the possibility of further alibi witnesses whose evidence was still not before the court did not entirely change the character of the case. The fact that he had now been released from prison did not prevent the action being a collateral attack, and his own motive was irrelevant.

11–112   *Hall v Simons.* In *Hall v Simons*[33] the House of Lords had to consider three cases where solicitors sought to strike out actions on the grounds of immunity and abuse of process. In the first, the client counterclaimed against his solicitors for failing to advise properly about the liability of other parties and as to timeous settlement in a building case that was settled on the eve of trial by a consent order. In the second action, the claimant sued his solicitors for negligent advice on the valuation of the matrimonial home in ancillary relief proceedings that were settled by a consent order approved by the court. In the third case, solicitors advised by counsel advised the claimant to settle matrimonial ancillary relief proceedings in a compromise approved by the court on an incorrect basis. The House of Lords refused to strike out the cases. Before considering the views of their Lordships, the relationship of the speeches should be noted. The leading speeches were given by Lords Steyn and Hoffmann, with whom Lords Browne-Wilkinson and Millett agreed, adding brief reasons of their own. Lords Hope, Hutton and Hobhouse agreed with the majority that immunity should be abolished for civil litigation, but disagreed in relation to criminal proceedings. In relation to abuse of process, the position of criminal and civil cases were treated

---

[30] [1994] Q.B. 106. Lord Hoffmann's suggested in *Hall v Simons* that Ralph Gibson L.J.'s judgment was "admirable" and the result correct, see [2002] 1 A.C. 615 at 703G at 706E, but it may be doubtful whether the reasoning in the case is in fact consistent with *Hall v Simons*.
[31] As a result of which the Court doubted the correctness of *Palmer v Durnford Ford* [1992] 1 Q.B. 483.
[32] [1996] 1 W.L.R. 763.
[33] [2002] 1 A.C. 615.

very differently. Most members of the House of Lords who considered the matter expressed their conclusions in substantially the same terms.

Criminal cases. In relation to criminal cases, the doctrine of abusive collateral attack was upheld, although it was recast in rather different form. The principle in *Hunter v Chief Constable of the West Midlands*[34] will generally prevent a claimant bringing proceedings unless and until his conviction has been set aside. However, it is clear that this is the general rule, and the principle was in fact expressed in slightly wider terms: **11–113**

> " . . . the court can strike out as an abuse of process the second action in which the plaintiff seeks to relitigate issues decided against him in earlier proceedings if such relitigation would be manifestly unfair to the defendant or would bring the administration of justice into disrepute."[35]

When the conviction has not been set aside, it would according to Lord Steyn be prima facie an abuse to bring civil proceedings,[36] and according to Lord Browne-Wilkinson it would only be in truly exceptional circumstances that such an action should be allowed.[37] Lord Hoffmann, with whom Lord Hutton agreed on this issue,[38] held[39] that such an action would ordinarily be an abuse but "there may be exceptional cases in which the issue can be tried without a risk that the conflict of judgments would bring the administration of justice into disrepute". Lord Hope did not consider the issue directly, although he agreed that the *Hunter* principle provided that a collateral challenge to a subsisting conviction would be struck out.[40] Lord Millett similarly held that such an action would ordinarily be struck out.[41] Finally, Lord Hobhouse's views were significantly different from the rest of the Court. He considered that the *Hunter* principle would rarely apply to a client suing his lawyer, as he could argue that his purpose was to recover compensation.[42] None of their Lordships indicated that there would ever be any impediment from the doctrine of abusive collateral attack to a defendant whose conviction had been quashed from suing his former lawyers.

Although the following is not necessarily a complete list, it would appear that the abuse of process principle will not prevent relitigation in the following circumstances: **11–114**

(1) Where the criminal conviction has been quashed. Lord Hoffmann made this clear, and he mentioned and approved *Acton v Graham Pearce & Co*

---

[34] [1982] A.C. 529. *Hunter* and *Hall v Simons* were relied on by the Saskatchewan Court of Appeal in *Fischer v Halyk* (2003) 239 D.L.R. (4th) 67. The claimant was convicted of theft and her appeal failed. Her action against her defence lawyer was an improper collateral attack on a criminal conviction, and was struck out as an abuse of process.
[35] [2002] 1 A.C. 615, 685B, *per* Lord Browne-Wilkinson; 702G, *per* Lord Hoffmann.
[36] *ibid.* at 679G.
[37] *ibid.* at 685C.
[38] *ibid.* at 727B–C.
[39] *ibid.* at 706E.
[40] *ibid* at 722G–H.
[41] *ibid.* at 753A.
[42] *ibid.* at 751C–D.

(a firm).[43] The point is also expressly mentioned by Lords Steyn,[44] Browne-Wilkinson,[45] and Millett.[46]

(2) According to Lord Hoffmann, where there has been a failure to appeal on a point of law. His Lordship cited *Walpole v Partridge & Wilson*[47] in this regard as such an exceptional case. Lord Hoffmann also seemed to suggest that the failure to take an obvious point of law in the Crown Court would equally be a case where there was no collateral challenge.[48]

(3) Following a suggestion made by Lord Hope[49] negligence causing delay or continued detention in custody, which may operate to the client's disadvantage irrespective of whether he is eventually acquitted or convicted.

11–115   **Civil cases.** In relation to civil proceedings, the position is a little less clear. The doctrine of abuse of process will play little part. According to Lord Steyn, the doctrines of *res judicata,* issue estoppel and abuse of process "as understood in private law" will generally be sufficient.[50] These doctrines will rarely be an impediment on a client suing his lawyer. Lord Steyn held that the *Hunter* principle would rarely be needed, but "it should still guard against unforeseen gaps."[51] Lord Hoffmann seemed to hold that the *Hunter* principle had no application at all in civil cases,[52] and consistent with his reasoning *res judicata* and issue estoppel would apply, if they were relevant.[53] However, he did consider that the interests of the successful claimant in a libel action might prevent the unsuccessful defendant from suing his former lawyers, as such an action would be unfair to him and thus would be an abuse of the process of the court.[54] The views of the other five of their Lordships on this issue are likely to carry very much less weight. It was not clear to Lord Browne-Wilkinson how far the *Hunter* principle would apply. Lords Hope, Hutton and Millett did not expressly address the issue. Lord Hobhouse took a very narrow view of the applicability of the *Hunter* principle in any context.[55]

---

[43] [1997] 3 All E.R. 909. See [2002] 1 A.C. 615 at 706E. The Ontario Court of Appeal reached the same conclusion in *Folland v Reardon* (2005) 249 D.L.R. (4th) 167 where they refused to strike out a claim by a claimant who had been wrongly convicted and imprisoned allegedly as a result of his lawyers negligence.

[44] [2002] 1 A.C. 615 at 679H.

[45] *ibid.* at 685D.

[46] *ibid.* at 753A.

[47] [1994] Q.B. 106.

[48] [2001] 1 A.C. 615 at 703H.

[49] *ibid.* at 722H. The suggestion was made in the context of a discussion of why he considered that the abuse of process principle would not provide sufficient protection because it would allow such exceptions.

[50] *ibid.* at 680A–B (Lord Steyn).

[51] *ibid.* at 680B.

[52] *ibid.* at 706G–H. His comments were relied on by *Feakins v Burstow* [2005] EWHC 1931, QB; [2006] P.N.L.R. 6, Jack J., in holding that an allegation that a solicitor had failed to produce documentary evidence in a trial which was lost was not an abuse of process.

[53] *ibid.* at 701A–G.

[54] *ibid.* at 706H–707B.

[55] See para.11–113, above.

Other types of abuse of process. In some cases brought against solicitors, the **11–116** issue of abuse of process is relevant, but raises no special issues peculiar to solicitors, as the solicitors did not represent the claimant in the unsuccessful proceedings which it is alleged give rise to the abuse. The governing principles in such cases are generally to be derived from *Henderson v Henderson*.[56] In *Gribbon v Lutton*[57] solicitors acted as stakeholder in relation to a deposit paid to their clients on the proposed sale of land. No contract was entered into, and a dispute arose between vendor and purchaser. The solicitors issued interpleader proceedings, in which it was held that the deposit was returnable to the proposed purchaser as no consideration had been paid. When later sued by the clients, the solicitors sought to argue that the deposit was not refundable. The Court of Appeal held that this was an abuse of process. While the solicitors could not plead or argue a case in the interpleader proceedings, by taking out such proceedings they sought a binding ruling and the benefits which flowed to them from such a ruling, and they were parties to such proceedings. In *Conlon v Simms*[58] the defendant was struck off for dishonest by the Solicitors Disciplinary Tribunal. His partners successfully sued him claiming that he should have disclosed his dishonesty to them. Lawrence Collins J. held that the claimants did not have to prove dishonesty and could rely on the Tribunal's findings, and it would be an abuse of process to relitigate the issue of dishonesty absent substantial fresh evidence.

There are a number of cases where such claims for abuse of process have **11–117** failed. It was not an abuse of process to run inconsistent cases where in one action against a guarantor who was sued to judgment, and in a subsequent case against a solicitor it was alleged that the guarantee was invalid.[59] It was held not to be an abuse of process to raise issues in ordinary proceedings against a solicitor which had been litigated in an application for compensation for breach of an undertaking, as the earlier proceedings were disciplinary in nature.[60] In *Johnson v Gore Wood & Co (a firm)*[61] the claimant's company sued the defendant solicitors, which action was settled, and then he sued the solicitors arising out of the same matters which were the subject of the original action. The House of Lords held that this was not an abuse of process. While there was a public interest in the finality of litigation and the defendant not being vexed twice for the same matter, the issue should be judged broadly on the merits taking account of all the public and private interests involved and the facts of the case. It was not necessary to identify an additional element such as a collateral attack on a previous decision or some dishonesty to found an abuse of process. In the case in question, the fact that the claimant had not undertaken the first action was not important, as he was identified with his company, nor did it matter that the first

---

[56] (1843) 3 Hare 100.

[57] [2001] EWCA Civ 1956; [2002] Q.B. 902.

[58] [2006] EWHC 401, Ch; [2006] 2 All E.R. 1024.

[59] *Finley v Connell Associates (a firm)* [1999] Lloyd's Rep. P.N. 895, Richards J. Similarly, in *Minton v Kenburgh Investments (Northern) Ltd (in liquidation), The Times*, July 11, 2000, liquidators who sued directors under the summary remedy under s.212 of the Insolvency Act 1986 could then sue solicitors in relation to the same transaction.

[60] *Ulster Bank Ltd v Fisher & Fisher* [1999] P.N.L.R. 794, Girvan J.

[61] [2002] 2 A.C. 1. For the analogous Canadian position, see *Martin v Goldfarb* (1999) 41 O.R. (3d) 161.

action culminated in a compromise rather than a judgment. However, the claimant had reasons which he regarded as compelling for deferring prosecuting his personal claim, and the defendants had not attempted to strike out the action which he brought over a long period of time.

(iii) *Acting on Counsel's Advice*

11–118   **History.**[62] It has been long established that if a solicitor acts in accordance with the advice of counsel, whom he has properly instructed, then usually he will not be held liable in negligence, even if counsel's advice proves to be mistaken or misconceived.[63] However, the law has changed to a marked degree in the last twenty years. The modern law was set in train by the decision of the Court of Appeal in *Davy-Chiesman v Davy-Chiesman*.[64] In that case a solicitor pressed on with proceedings when it was obvious that they would fail, acting in reliance on counsel's advice. Nevertheless the solicitor was ordered to pay all the wasted costs of both parties after the date when it was obvious that the proposed application would fail. May L.J., who delivered the leading judgment, said that it was the ordinary rule "that save in exceptional circumstances a solicitor cannot be criticised where he acts on the advice of properly instructed counsel."[65] He then qualified the proposition in this way:

> "However, this does not operate so as to give a solicitor an immunity in every such case. A solicitor is highly trained and rightly expected to be experienced in his particular legal fields. He is under a duty at all times to exercise that degree of care, to both client and the court, that can be expected of a reasonably prudent solicitor. He is not entitled to rely blindly and with no mind of his own on counsel's views."[66]

11–119   **Summaries of the modern law.** The law has been helpfully summarised in two Court of Appeal decisions. In *Locke v Camberwell Health Authority*[67] it was stated in these terms:

> "(1) In general, a solicitor is entitled to rely upon the advice of counsel properly instructed.
> (2) For a solicitor without specialist experience in a particular field to rely on counsel's advice is to make normal and proper use of the Bar.
> (3) However, he must not do so blindly, but must exercise his own independent judgment. If he reasonably thinks counsel's advice is obviously or glaringly wrong, it is his duty to reject it."

---

[62] For a helpful explanation of the law see P. Bartle, "The defence of reasonable reliance on counsel" (2002) 18 P.N. 111.

[63] For early cases see: *Kemp v Burt* (1833) 4 B. & Ad. 424; *Manning v Wilkin* (1848) 12 L.T. (O.S.) 249; *Re Clark* (1851) 1 De G.M. & G. 43; *Cates v Indermaur* (1858) 1 F. & F. 259; *Francis v Francis & Dickerson* [1956] P. 87.

[64] [1984] Fam. 48.

[65] [1984] Fam. 48 at 63E.

[66] *ibid.*, at 64A.

[67] [2002] Lloyd's Rep. P.N. 23 at 29. In *Harley v McDonald* [1999] 3 N.Z.L.R. 545 at 573 the New Zealand Court of Appeal helpfully stated: "ordinarily the advice of counsel will be a powerful factor upon which solicitors can rely, but only if the advice comes in properly reasoned form and the solicitor is satisfied, after appropriate consideration, that the advice is tenable." (The case was reversed by the Privy Council on appeal [2001] UKPC 18; [2001] 2 A.C. 678.)

In *Ridehalgh v Horsefield*[68] the court amplified the last point:

"A solicitor does not abdicate his professional responsibility when he seek the advice of counsel. He must apply his mind to the advice received. But the more specialist the nature of the advice, the more reasonable is it likely to be for a solicitor to accept it and act on it."

Illustrations: no defence. In a number of cases, reliance on counsel has been **11–120** held to be no defence.[69] In *Clark v Clark (No.2)*[70] solicitors acting for a wife, who was legally aided, sequestered the husband's assets. The costs were ordered to be paid from them first, leaving little for the wife. On counsel's advice, they subsequently attempted to vary the order, so that the assets should be applied first to the arrears of maintenance owed to the wife. The solicitors were found to be in breach of their duty to the Legal Aid Board in so doing. The breach of duty was clear and thus their defence of relying on counsel failed. In *Green v Collyer-Bristow*[71] matrimonial counsel negligently advised the claimant that she should seek specific enforcement of an agreement with her former husband to transfer real property to her. Both counsel and the solicitors failed to notice s.2 of the Law of Property (Miscellaneous Provisions) Act 1989, which imposed more onerous requirements with respect to the need for such an agreement to be in writing than the repealed s.40 of the Law of Property Act 1925. Although two of the three standard textbooks did not refer to the change in the law, both the barrister and

---

[68] [1994] Ch. 205 at 237G. In *Matrix Securities Ltd v Theodore Goddard* [1998] P.N.L.R. 290 Lloyd J. considered that when leading counsel had given considered advice to the client, a solicitor's duty was only to give separate advice if there was an important point on which he regarded counsel's advice as being seriously wrong. Neither solicitor nor counsel were negligent on the facts of that case, on which see Ch.12, para.12–029.

[69] The defence was also rejected in the following cases: *Bond v Livingstone* [2001] P.N.L.R. 30 (solicitors considered that the limitation period for personal injuries under a contract was six years, when it was plainly three years pursuant to s.11 of the Limitation Act 1980; the defence of relying on counsel failed as the defendants were personal injury solicitors and s.11 is a basic provision); *Dace v Redland Aggregates Ltd* [1997] E.G.C.S. 123 (see further Ch.12, para.12–019); *Darvall McCutcheon v HK Frost Holdings Pty Ltd* [2002] VSCA 85; (2002) 4 V.R. 570 (the underlying litigation concerned a breach of contract claim, considered by the judge, and a breach of confidence claim, which was not; the Victoria Court of Appeal held that the solicitors on the appeal were negligent in failing to take steps to have the breach of confidence claim remitted to the judge; the defence of reliance on counsel failed because counsel was not in fact asked to advise about the breach of confidence claim, but in any event the solicitors should have turned their mind to any advice which was given and examine it to ensure that it was sound, and should have sought and considered the reasons for such advice); *Estill v Cowling* [2000] Lloyd's Rep P.N. 378 (the solicitor should have given himself some general knowledge of inheritance tax, and thus been able to instruct counsel properly and spot that he had not advised on that issue; for the facts see Ch.12, para.12–033; *Green v Hancocks (a firm)* [2001] Lloyd's Rep. P.N. 212, CA (on an application for summary judgment, where the high street solicitors were entitled to rely on counsel for specialist advice, but arguably not on the question of whether the claimant had *locus standi* to sue, on which doubts had been raised in correspondence by other solicitors so that the firm should have informed the client that there were doubts about counsel's advice); *Locke v Camberwell HA* (1990) 140 N.L.J. 205 (the decision was reversed by the Court of Appeal on further facts coming to light: [2002] Lloyd's Rep. P.N. 23); *Miloslavsky v Aldington* [1996] 1 W.L.R. 736, CA (discussed at para.11–136).

[70] [1991] 1 F.L.R. 179 at 192, Booth J.

[71] [1999] Lloyd's Rep. P.N. 798.

the solicitor were held to be liable, and the solicitor could not absolve his responsibility by claiming to have relied on counsel.

11–121   **Illustrations: successful defence.** In contrast, in several cases the defence of relying on counsel was successful.[72] In *Watson v Watson*, one of the appeals in *Ridehalgh v Horsefield*[73] solicitors acting for a wife in divorce proceedings rejected an eminently sensible suggestion to amend a consent order dealing with the devolution of property, but they were not negligent in so doing in part because they relied on matrimonial and trust counsel. In *Reaveley v Safeway Stores Plc*[74] solicitors failed to advise a claimant in personal injury litigation that he was highly likely to lose the £2,500 offered by the defendants as he would not obtain in damages more than the benefits recoverable by the Compensation Recovery Unit of £16,000. The solicitors relied on counsel properly instructed who credibly advised that the action should proceed, and the defendants' doubts about the claimant's special damages claim did not alter that conclusion.

11–122   **Further limits to the defence.** In any event, a solicitor may still be liable for breach of contract if he acts contrary to the client's instructions, since counsel's advice, however prudent, cannot override the client's express instructions.[75] The defence will not avail a solicitor who has failed properly to instruct counsel,[76] or who has instructed counsel where it should have been obvious that counsel was

---

[72] The defence also succeeded in the following cases: *Afzal v Chubb Guarding Services Ltd (Wasted Costs Order)* [2002] EWHC 822; [2003] P.N.L.R. 33 (H.H. Judge Bowsher Q.C. held that solicitors were entitled to rely on counsel's opinion on whether the client was likely to establish that he was suffering genuine psychiatric injuries rather than making his symptoms up); *Firstcity Insurance Group Ltd v Orchard* [2003] P.N.L.R. 9 (summarised at Ch.12, para.12–040; neither counsel nor solicitors were held to be negligent in making an error of judgment, and the solicitors additionally succeeded on the basis that they were entitled to rely on counsel, applying the law as set out in para.11–119, above); *Heydon v NRMA Ltd* [2000] NSWCA 374; (2001) 51 N.S.W.L.R. 1 (summarised at Ch.12, para.12–036); *Luke v Wansboroughs (a firm)* [2003] EWHC 3151, QB; [2005] P.N.L.R. 1 (Davies J. held that solicitors who were not experienced in malicious falsehood claims were entitled to rely on counsel's advice that the claim was very likely to be struck out for want of prosecution; the barrister's advice was in any event not negligent); *R. v A (Wasted Costs Order)* [2000] P.N.L.R. 628 (solicitors were entitled to rely on counsel in making a bail application alleging that custody time limits had expired, where an unreported case not referred to in any standard textbook made it clear that there were no such limits in the circumstances of the case); *R. v Horsham DC* [1995] 1 W.L.R. 680 (Brooke J. held that solicitors could rely on counsel experienced in judicial review proceedings); *Sherman v Fitzhugh Gates (a firm)* [2003] EWCA Civ 886; [2003] P.N.L.R. 39 (solicitors issued proceedings on behalf of the executrix concerning what the defendant was entitled to in the testator's estate; the Court of Appeal held that they were not negligent and no wasted costs order was made against them as there was no easy solution to their client's dilemma to be found in the textbooks, and the solicitors relied on specialist counsel).

[73] [1994] Ch. 205 at 255–264. The decisions in *R. v Oxfordshire County Council Ex p. Wallace* (1987) 137 N.L.J. 542 and *Manor Electronics v Dickson, The Times,* February 8, 1990 are of limited assistance, as they were decided under the old Ord. 62 r. 11 wasted costs provisions, which required serious misconduct.

[74] [1998] P.N.L.R. 526, CA.

[75] *Fray v Voules* (1859) 1 E. & E. 839. But the client cannot insist upon matters which are not within his province, such as the contents of pleadings; see para.11–179.

[76] *Ireson v Pearman* (1825) 3 B. & C. 799: failure to place all relevant documents before counsel; *Andrews v Hawley* (1857) 26 L.J. Ex. 323; *Locke v Camberwell HA* (1990) 140 N.L.J. 205, Moreland J.; reversed on new facts coming to light by the Court of Appeal [2002] Lloyd's Rep. P.N. 23, CA.

not competent,[77] nor will it avail a solicitor who goes to counsel on matters which are within the solicitor's own province.[78]

The position of the client. In the kind of case under discussion the position   **11–123**
of the client was once unenviable: the solicitor was not liable because he had acted on counsel's advice and counsel had complete immunity on grounds of public interest. The client's position has now improved in both respects. The defence of "reliance on counsel's advice" is now rather more limited. Furthermore, counsel no longer enjoys immunity from suit.[79]

(iv) *Acting on Client's Instructions*

Duty to obey client. The solicitor will be in breach of duty if he does not   **11–124**
follow his client's instructions.[80] Indeed, it is in general[81] the client's privilege, if he so wishes, to mismanage his affairs. He is entitled to pursue litigation with little prospect of success,[82] to lend on insufficient security, or to enter an unwise bargain, if he so chooses. The solicitor has a duty to advise on the legal hazards of the transaction,[83] but no more:

> "It was the duty of the solicitor to inform and advise, ensuring that the information and advice was understood by the client. It was not part of his duty of care to force his advice on the client."[84]

---

[77] *Re A (a Minor)* (1988) 10 Fam.L. 339; *The Times*, February 25, 1988, CA.

[78] *Godefroy v Dalton* (1830) 6 Bing. 460 at 649:
  "We lay no stress upon the fact, that the attorney had consulted his counsel as to the sufficiency of the evidence; because, we think, his liability must depend upon the nature and description of the mistake or want of skill which has been shown; and he cannot shift from himself such responsibility by consulting another where the law would presume him to have the knowledge himself."
  (*per* Tindal C.J.). See also *Cook v S* [1966] 1 W.L.R. 635, QBD, (discussed in Ch.12, para.12–028) where counsel's erroneous advice exacerbated the consequences of solicitor's previous negligence. The solicitor was held liable for all the resulting loss.

[79] See Ch.12, para.12–009.

[80] For examples of solicitor being found to be negligent in failing to follow their client's instructions, resulting in bankruptcy, see see *Re Graham & Oldham (a firm)* [2000] B.P.I.R. 354, McKinnon J., and *Fraser v Gaskell* [2004] EWHC 894; [2004] P.N.L.R. 32, H.H. Judge Rich Q.C.

[81] The position may be more complicated if there is an insurer is funding litigation; see e.g. *Groom v Crocker* [1939] 2 All E.R. 397, CA. If there is a risk of undue influence from a third party who may benefit from a transaction, the solicitor may have to decline to act if his advice is not accepted: *Powell v Powell* [1900] 1 Ch. 243, Ch. D.

[82] The client, and not the attorney, is the *dominus litis*": *per* Erle J. in *Fray v Voules* (1859) 1 E. & E. 839, at 848. See further para.11–181.

[83] As to which see para.11–166. Thus in *Sutton v Mishcon de Reya* [2003] EWHC 3166, Ch; (2004) 1 F.L.R. 837, the claimant and another man agreed that they would enter a master-slave relationship, with the slave handing over his property and money to the claimant master. The claimant instructed the first defendant solicitors to draw up a deed to put into effect the agreement. They correctly advised that the agreement might not be enforceable. Hart J. struck out a claim (inter alia) that the deed should have been sanitised by not incorporating references to a "statement of trust." The instructions were to incorporate that reference, and as the "statement of trust" was part of the matrix of the cohabitation deed, it would have made no difference to the enforceability of the agreement to exclude reference to it.

[84] *Dutfield v Gilbert H Stephens & Sons* [1988] 18 Fam. Law 473, *per* Anthony Lincoln J.

Relying on this dictum, in *Middleton v Steeds Hudson*[85] Johnson J. held that the defendant solicitors were not negligent in their advice to the claimant with respect to the financial arrangements he proposed to make with his former wife. The defendants had advised that the arrangements were over-generous to the wife, and had discussed alternatives. The defendants had no duty to repeat the advice or ensure that the husband followed it. If the advice the solicitor gives is disregarded he must carry out the client's instructions or else determine the retainer if the circumstances justify him in doing so.[86]

11–125   **Exceptions to rule.** It is, therefore, a good defence to an action for negligence that the solicitor was acting on express instructions from the client.[87] The defence will fail, however, where the client's instructions were the result of inadequate advice by the solicitor.[88] Thus in *Morris v Duke-Cohan & Co*[89] solicitors were held liable for exchanging contracts on a purchase, despite express instructions from the clients, since the solicitors had failed to warn them of the risks. "A solicitor did not do his duty merely by reporting facts to clients and then seeking instructions", (*per* Caulfield J.). In the Irish case of *McMullen v Farrell*[90] Barron J. stated:

> "A solicitor cannot in my view fulfil his obligations to his client merely by carrying out what he is instructed to do. This is to ignore the essential element of any contract involving professional care or advice . . . In my view a solicitor when consulted has an obligation to consider not only what the client wishes him to do but also the legal implication of the facts which the client brings to his attention. If necessary, he must follow up these facts to ensure that he appreciates the real problem with which he is being asked to deal."

(e) *Solicitor's Liability for Costs*[91]

11–126   The courts have the power in certain circumstances to order a solicitor to pay to his client or to the litigant on the other side any costs which have been incurred by reason of the solicitor's misconduct. The exercise of this power may circum-

---

[85] [1998] 1 F.L.R. 738.
[86] See, e.g. *Sutherland v Public Trustee* [1980] 2 N.Z.L.R. 536 at 548, Supreme Court.
[87] *Waine v Kempster* (1859) 1 F. & F. 695: a solicitor, acting for the purchaser of a quantity of hay, omitted to make the usual enquiries, since the client stated that he had made the enquiries and the result was satisfactory; *Okafor v Malcolm Slowe & Co* (1968) 207 E.G. 345, QBD: the client insisted on completing the purchase before the result of searches was received; *Duncan v Cuelenaere* [1987] 2 W.W.R. 379, Saskatchewan QB: when a solicitor is given instructions about what has happened, he is entitled to rely on them.
[88] e.g. *Lee v Dixon* (1863) 3 F. & F. 744: an attorney brought proceedings in the wrong court. The express instructions of the client was no defence, unless he had been properly advised of the consequences.
[89] (1975) 119 S.J. 826; *The Times*, November 22, 1975.
[90] [1993] 1 I.R. 123 at 142–3.
[91] For a critical view of the jurisdiction, see H. Evans, "The wasted costs jurisdiction" (2001) 65 M.L.R. 51 and *ibid.*, *Lawyers' Liabilities* (2nd edn, 2002), Ch.7.

vent the need to bring a professional negligence action. The appropriate test, by reason of statutory amendment, is one of simple negligence.

History. Since at least the eighteenth century, the superior courts of record **11–127** have exercised jurisdiction over the attorneys on the roll of that court. The nature of the jurisdiction was reviewed by the House of Lords in *Myers v Elman*.[92] It is clear from all the speeches that something more serious was required than mere negligence. Lord Maugham required "a serious dereliction of duty",[93] Lord Atkin "gross negligence",[94] and Lord Wright considered that a "mere mistake or error of judgment is not generally sufficient, but a gross neglect or inaccuracy in a matter which it is a solicitor's duty to ascertain with accuracy may suffice."[95] While the inherent jurisdiction continues to exist after the statutory amendments discussed below, it is difficult to foresee many circumstances in which it will be used given the easier requirements of the new provisions.[96] An exception is the special rule that where a solicitor institutes proceedings on behalf of a company without authority, he will be ordered to pay the other side's costs even though he acted bona fide and without negligence.[97] Since 1960 there have existed parallel Rules of the Supreme Court which have regulated and modified the inherent jurisdiction, and which have been changed a number of times.[98]

The present rule. Section 4 of the Courts and Legal Services Act 1990, which **11–128** came into force on October 1, 1991, substituted for s.51 of the Supreme Court Act new provisions relating to costs which include the following:

"(6) In any proceedings mentioned in subsection (1),[99] the court may disallow or (as the case may be) order the legal or other representative concerned to meet, the whole of any wasted costs or such part of them as may be determined in accordance with rules of court.

(7) In subsection (6) 'wasted costs' means any costs incurred by a party—

---

[92] [1940] A.C. 282. The inherent jurisdiction remains the basis for the wasted costs jurisdiction in much of the commonwealth, see: *Harley v McDonald* [2001] UKPC 18; [2001] 2 A.C. 678, PC, a New Zealand appeal; *White Industries (QLD) Pty Ltd v Flower & Hart (a firm)* (1999) 163 A.L.R. 744, Federal Court of Australia., Full Court, and *Knaggs v JA Westaway & Sons* (1996) 40 N.S.W.L.R. 476, CA; *Steindl Nominees Pty Ltd v Laghaifar* [2003] QCA 157; [2003] 2 Qd.R. 683, CA; *Young v Young* [1993] 4 S.C.R. 3, Supreme Court of Canada; *Hunter v Hunter* [2001] 4 W.W.R. 28, Manitoba CA.
[93] [1940] A.C. 282 at 292.
[94] *ibid.* at 304.
[95] *ibid.* at 319.
[96] See para.11–129, below for an example.
[97] *Babury Ltd v London Industrial Plc* (1989) 139 N.L.J. 1596, QBD. However, the court may reduce the amount of costs payable where the defendants were in a position to know the status of the company, see *Padhiar v Patel* [2001] Lloyd's Rep. P.N. 328, QBD. There is a further exception in relation to wasted costs orders against non-parties, see para.11–129, below.
[98] For discussion of the old rules, see the third edition of this work at para.4–81 and the supplements thereto, and for a detailed review of the law up to 1986, see the second edition of this book, paras 4–59 to 4–63.
[99] That is, all proceedings in the civil division of the Court of Appeal, the High Court and any county court.

as a result of any improper, unreasonable, or negligent act or omission on the part of any legal or other representative or any employee of such a representative; or

which, in the light of any such act or omission occurring after they were incurred, the court considers it is unreasonable to expect that party to pay."

Order 62 r.11 of the Rules of the Supreme Court, which reflected this statutory provision, has now been replaced under the Civil Procedure Rules by CPR Pt 48.7 and paras 2.1–2.7 of the accompanying Practice Direction. There are similar provisions relating to the criminal courts.[1]

11–129 **Parties and the limits of the jurisdiction.** The Court of Appeal neither had under the old law nor has under the new law any jurisdiction to order that the costs of solicitors' successful appeals against wasted costs order should be paid out of central funds, see *Steele Ford & Newton v CPS*.[2] A wasted costs order cannot be made in favour of the Court, but only in favour of a party.[3] Furthermore, in *R. v Camden LBC Ex p. Martin*[4] Sedley J. held that a wasted costs order can only be made in favour of a party to the action, and thus cannot be made for the benefit of a local authority which chooses to appear at an ex parte application for leave to apply for judicial review. However, in *R. v Immigration Appeal Tribunal Ex p. Gulbamer Gulsen*[5] Buxton J. concluded that, although *Ex p. Martin* was correct in relation to the statutory wasted costs jurisdiction, at common law a wasted costs order could be made in favour of a non-party, although he declined to do so in that instance. In *Byrne v Sefton Health Authority*,[6] it was alleged that solicitors had negligently failed to issue proceedings within the limitation period, where subsequent solicitors had done so, and the action was then dismissed on limitation grounds. The Court of Appeal held that there was no jurisdiction to make a wasted costs order under s.51(6) as the solicitors had not conducted litigation. A similar result was reached on similar facts but slightly different grounds in *Radford & Co v Charles*.[7] The solicitors negligently failed to issue an appeal against the local authority decision on the claimant's housing needs within the permitted time. Neuberger J. held that the solicitors were not in breach of a duty owed to the court, but only to their client, so no wasted costs order could be made, and further the case was indistinguishable from *Byrne*. There are potential difficulties preventing contribution proceed-

---

[1] The Courts and Legal Services Act 1990, ss.111 and 112. As to attempts to limit the scope of the jurisdiction, see Ch.12, para.12–013. As to the last clause of subs.51(7), this may be relevant, for instance, where costs were reasonably incurred on behalf of a litigant but the action was later struck out as a result of the litigant's solicitors' defaults, see *Snowden v Ministry of Defence* [2001] EWCA Civ 1524; [2002] Costs L.R. 249, para.26, CA.
[2] *The Times*, May 28, 1993, HL. The same applies to any costs incurred by the solicitors in successfully resisting a wasted costs application
[3] See *Lawrence & Co* [1998] C.L.Y. 1016, CA.
[4] [1997] 1 W.L.R. 359.
[5] [1997] C.O.D. 430.
[6] [2001] EWCA Civ 1904; [2002] 1 W.L.R. 775.
[7] [2003] EWHC 3180; [2004] P.N.L.R. 25.

ings in relation to wasted costs between solicitors and barristers.[8] If only some of the potentially defaulting lawyers are respondents to a wasted costs application, the fact that others may be to blame does not prevent the Court from making the respondents liable for all the wasted costs.[9]

Court of Appeal guidelines. In *Re a Barrister (Wasted Costs Order) (No.1 of   **11–130** 1991)*[10] the Court of Appeal laid down six guidelines for use in criminal cases. While the decision was made in the context of a wasted costs order against a barrister in relation to his actions in court, the guidelines apply to all legal representatives.[11] In the leading case of *Ridehalgh v Horsefield*[12] the Court of Appeal gave detailed guidelines on wasted costs orders in civil litigation, which are summarised in the following paragraphs,[13] with illustrations of how the guidelines have been applied in subsequent cases. It is noteworthy that all the five appeals against wasted costs orders in *Ridehalgh* were successful, and the Court of Appeal did not make an order on the sixth case where the solicitors had been ordered to show cause why an order should not be made. The facts of five of the individual cases are summarised elsewhere.[14]

The meaning of the tests. The Court of Appeal in *Ridehalgh v Horsefield*[15]   **11–131** considered the meaning of "improper", "unreasonable" and "negligent". "Improper" includes conduct that would be a serious breach of a substantial duty of professional conduct. "Unreasonable" describes conduct which is vexatious or designed to harass the other side; the acid test is whether the conduct permits of a reasonable explanation. "Negligence" should be understood in an untechnical way as failure to act with the competence reasonably to be expected of ordinary members of the profession.

The position of the respondent lawyer. The Court of Appeal in *Ridehalgh v*   **11–132** *Horsefield*[16] stated that courts should bear in mind the peculiar vulnerability of legal representatives acting for the recipients of legal aid. Furthermore, the jurisdiction was not subject to the immunity of an advocate, which still existed at that time, although a court must make full allowance for the fact that an advocate in court has to make decisions quickly and under pressure. Where an applicant seeks a wasted costs order against the other side, full allowance has to be made for the respondent lawyers' inability to tell the whole story due to

---

[8] See the obiter remarks of the Court of Appeal in *Fletamentos Maritimos SA v Effjohn International SA* [2003] Lloyd's Rep. P.N. 26 at pp.34–35 and 43, and H. Evans *Lawyers' Liabilities* (2nd edn, 2002), para.7–06.
[9] See *Gandesh v Nandra* [2002] Lloyd's Rep. P.N. 558, Jacob J.
[10] [1993] Q.B. 293.
[11] See further Ch.12, para.12–012.
[12] [1994] Ch. 205. *Ridehalgh* was endorsed by the House of Lords *Medcalf v Mardell* [2002] UKHL 27; [2003] 1 A.C. 120, subject to *Hall v Simons* [2002] 1 A.C. 615, and subject to further amplification in relation to privilege, discussed at Ch.12, para.12–015.
[13] For the summary of where a solicitor can rely on counsel, see paras 11–118 *et seq.*, above.
[14] See paras 11–085, 11–121, 11–139, 11–184, and Ch.12, para.12–020.
[15] [1994] Ch. 205 at 232–233.
[16] [1994] Ch. 205 at 234G–237D.

professional privilege.[17] The threat of proposed applications should not be used as a means of intimidation, although it may not be objectionable to alert the other side to the possibility.[18]

11–133   **Procedure.** The Court of Appeal in *Ridehalgh v Horsefield*[19] gave guidance on the practice and procedure to be adopted in wasted costs application. First, in the ordinary way, applications for wasted costs orders are best left until after the end of the trial.[20] Secondly, save in obvious cases, the court should be slow to initiate an enquiry as to whether a wasted costs order should be made, and should leave it to the aggrieved party.[21] Thirdly, any procedure should be fair, simple, and summary. The court must be astute to control what could become a new and costly form of satellite litigation.[22] Fourthly, legal representatives should be

---

[17] CPR Pt 48.7(3) purportedly permitted the court to direct that privileged documents may be disclosed, which was struck out by Toulson J. in *General Mediterranean Holdings v Patel* [1999] 3 All E.R. 673, and subsequently revoked. For an illustration of the problems caused by privilege, see *Walter v Neville Eckley* [1997] B.C.C. 331. The registrar made a wasted costs order despite the solicitors swearing that they had relied on Counsel's opinion, which was privileged. Sir Richard Scott V.C. held that the registrar was wrong to make a costs order based on speculation that counsel's opinion would not have helped the solicitors. However, by the time of the appeal, privilege had been waived. The Judge held that the solicitors were entitled to rely on counsel's wrong opinions, but that further evidence had thereafter come to light which should have caused the solicitors to reconsider the decision to make a misconceived discovery application, and the wasted costs order was therefore affirmed on different grounds. In some cases the Court is able to come to a clear decision despite the absence of waiver of privilege by making assumptions in the lawyers' favour, see e.g. *B v B (Wasted Costs: Abuse of Process)* [2001] 1 F.L.R. 843, discussed at Ch.12, para.12–019. The protection of the lawyer who is unable to give his full account due to privilege has been developed further in *Medcalf v Mardell* [2002] UKHL 27; [2003] 1 A.C. 120, discussed at Ch.12, para.12–015. In *Dempsey v Johnstone (Wasted Costs Order)* [2003] EWCA Civ 1134; [2004] P.N.L.R 25 the Court of Appeal were unwilling to infer from the fact that legal aid had been extended to trial that the lawyers were asserting that there were good prospects of success.

[18] The court agreed at 237–238 with the disapproval of threats expressed in *Orchard v South Eastern Electricity Board* [1987] Q.B. 565, CA. In *Sushma Lal v Secretary of State for the Home Department* [1992] Imm. A.R. 303, the Court of Appeal distinguished *Orchard*. In an immigration case, the solicitor had failed to make full disclosure on an Ex p. application for leave to move for judicial review. It was held that in the circumstances it was not improper for the Treasury Solicitor to indicate that an application would be made for the solicitor to pay the costs personally if the proceedings were pursued.

[19] [1994] Ch. 205 at 238–239.

[20] The court approved of the views of Aldous J. in *Flimlab Systems International Ltd v Pennington* [1995] 1 W.L.R. 673. For an exceptional case where it was justified hearing the wasted costs application before the conclusion of the main action, see *B v B (Wasted Costs: Abuse of Process)* [20001] 1 F.L.R. 843, summarised at Ch.12, para.12–019. An application should be made timeously, or it may be refused: *Clark v Clark (No.2)* [1991] 1 F.L.R. 179 at 194, Booth J.

[21] In such a case the guidance of *R. v Knutsford Crown Ct Ex p. Middleweek, The Times*, March 23, 1992 is helpful. The Divisional Court stated that judges should seek the assistance of counsel upon their powers, and it was advisable to consider such matters and whether it was necessary to make an order at all. For an example of a judge-initiated wasted costs order see *Re G (Minors) (Care Proceedings: Wasted Costs)* [2000] Fam. 104, summarised at Ch.12, para.12–022.

[22] The effect of the summary nature of the wasted costs jurisdiction and the costs of an application have been considered in a number of cases. In *Re Freudiana Holdings Ltd, The Times*, December 4, 1995 the Court of Appeal held that allegations involving full scale relitigation of the issues in the original trial and which involved dishonesty should not proceed. In *Manzanilla Ltd v Corton Property & Investments Ltd* [1997] 3 F.C.R. 389 the Court of Appeal held that the jurisdiction was inappropriate where there needed to be a detailed investigation of the facts or dishonesty was alleged, as such matters were not capable of summary determination. In *Turner Page Music v Torres Design Associates Ltd, The Times*, August 7, 1998, the Court of Appeal held that a wasted costs application

given an opportunity to show why an order should not be made, but only when an apparently strong prima facie case had been made against them.[23] Fifthly, the court had a discretion as to whether the legal representative should show cause, which should not be automatic, and the costs of the enquiry compared with the costs claimed will be relevant. The court also has a discretion at the final stage of the enquiry whether to make an order.[24]

Cases since *Ridehalgh* have given further guidance on the procedure to be adopted. An application does not have to be made during the currency of the proceedings.[25] An application should normally be determined by the trial

11–134

---

was inappropriate if it would result in complex proceedings involving detailed investigations of fact. In *Wall v Lefever* [1998] 1 F.C.R. 605 the Court of Appeal held that the wasted costs jurisdiction should not be used to generate substantial additional costs in satellite litigation which was as expensive and complex as the original litigation. In *Royal Institution of Chartered Surveyors v Wiseman Marshall* [2000] P.N.L.R. 649 the Court of Appeal stated that it would rarely be appropriate to grant an adjournment to investigate whether the client was willing to waive privilege, as that would create complexity and delay. In the context of the inherent jurisdiction which exists in New Zealand, the Privy Council opined that allegations should be confined strictly to questions which are apt for summary disposal by the Court, see *Harley v McDonald* [2001] UKPC 18; [2001] 2 A.C. 678; see further Ch.12, para.12–016. Turner J. refused to allow a wasted costs application to proceed even to the first stage in *B v Pendelbury* [2002] EWHC 1797; [2003] P.N.L.R. 1, because there was substantial dispute on the facts, and the allegations which were based on impropriety and fraud were unsuitable to be determined in a summary jurisdiction. However, the fact that complex issues might arise in the wasted costs application did not preclude use of the procedure; account had to be taken of the prospects of success and how far time could be saved by appropriate case management, see *Wagstaff v Colls (Wasted Costs Order)* [2003] EWCA Civ 469; [2003] P.N.L.R. 29, CA. For a further example of a case where more time was spent on the wasted costs hearing than the substantive proceedings, see *Re Merc Property Ltd, The Times,* May 19, 1999, Ch. D; and for a case where the likely costs of the wasted costs hearing was disproportionate and was therefore not pursued see *Chief Constable of North Yorkshire v Audsley* [2000] Lloyd's Rep. P.N. 675.

[23] In *Livingstone v Frasso* [1997] C.L.Y. 604 a wasted costs order was quashed by the Court of Appeal when the solicitors were not given an opportunity to show why the order should not be made. In *Re Wiseman Lee (Solicitors) (Wasted Costs Order) (No.5 of 2000), The Times,* April 5, 2001, the Court of Appeal quashed a wasted costs order where the solicitors were given an opportunity to make representations by a certain date but failed to do so, as the procedure did not comply with natural justice or the Costs in Criminal Cases (General) Regulations 1986 (SI 1986/1335). In a straightforward case with limited costs involved, there may not need to be a full investigation: see *Woolwich Building Society v Fineberg* [1998] P.N.L.R. 216. It may not be necessary to have two separate hearings to establish a prima facie case and to show cause where the former can be determined at the hearing of the application about which complaint is made, see *B v B (Wasted Costs: Abuse of Process)* [2001] 1 F.L.R. 843, Wall J. *Quaere* whether the party seeking the costs should open at the hearing, as was suggested under the previous rules in *Bahai v Rashidian (No.2), The Times,* June 11, 1986, Drake J.

[24] For an example see *R. v Secretary of State for the Home Office Ex p. Wong* [1995] C.O.D. 331. The solicitor for an applicant for judicial review did not come off the record when legal aid was withdrawn and let the application go to sleep. That had caused wasted costs, as the Treasury Solicitor would otherwise have conceded the application much earlier. However, the solicitor was not made to pay the wasted costs, because if the solicitor had gone off the record, the point on which the case turned may never have come to light, and an injustice would have been done.

[25] subs.51(6) of the Supreme Court Act 1981 states that wasted costs applications can be made "in the proceedings mentioned in s.1", but this is a reference to the Court of Appeal Civil Division, High Court and County Court, and does not mean an application has to be made during the currency of the proceedings, see *Wagstaff v Colls (Wasted Costs Order)* [2003] EWCA Civ 469; [2003] P.N.L.R. 29, CA. In that case in any event proceedings were extant as they had merely been stayed, and the Court would have lifted the stay if necessary, which it was not. An application for wasted costs can be made after the order in relation to the proceedings have been drawn up, see *Gray v Going Places Leisure Travel Ltd* [2005] EWCA Civ 189; [2005] P.N.L.R. 26, CA.

judge.[26] The amount of wasted costs must be specified in the order, and the order cannot later be amended by adding a figure at a later date, see *Re Harry Jagdev & Co*.[27] In cases concerning children where an order for costs is sought against the Legal Aid Board or under the wasted costs jurisdiction, the procedure to be adopted is set out in *Re O (Costs: Liability of Legal Aid Board)*[28]: in general the applications should be drawn to the Legal Aid Board's attention. Where the Legal Aid Board or Community Legal Services Commission will be the beneficiary of the wasted costs order, it is also desirable to refer to them before making an application.[29] An appeal lies without leave.[30] It should be noted that it is permissible to compromise a wasted costs application. In *Manzanilla Ltd v Corton Property & Investments Ltd*[31] the Court of Appeal approved the practice of placing a succinct written statement before the court following settlement. This would deal with matters relevant to the reputations of the lawyers involved, which, as a result of the settlement, would not otherwise have been brought to the court's attention.

11–135   **Causation.**[32] The Court of Appeal in *Ridehalgh v Horsefield*[33] stated that it was essential to demonstrate a causal link between the improper, unreasonable or negligent conduct and the wasted costs.[34] The importance of demonstrating a causal link is shown by *Kilroy v Kilroy*,[35] where the Court of Appeal allowed an

---

[26] See *Bahai v Rashidian* [1985] 1 W.L.R. 1337, CA; *Re Freudiana Holdings Ltd, The Times*, December 4, 1995, CA; and *Gray v Going Places Leisure Travel Ltd* [2005] EWCA Civ 189; [2005] P.N.L.R. 26, CA.

[27] *The Times*, August 12, 1999, CA. In *R. v Johnson Partnership Solicitors* [2004] EWCA Crim 2343; [2005] P.N.L.R. 12 the Court of Appeal repeated the guidance in *Re Mintz (Wasted Costs Order), The Times*, July 16, 1999: the complaint and grounds need to be carefully and concisely formulated; where necessary a transcript of the relevant part of the proceedings should be available; and the sum ordered must be specified.

[28] [1997] 1 F.L.R. 465, CA.

[29] See *Tate v Hart* [1999] P.N.L.R. 787.

[30] *Thompson v Fraser, The Times,* October 4, 1985, CA. While there is a right of appeal against an order made in a wasted costs application, it should be exercised with great care where the judge at first instance had heard the evidence and seen the witnesses, see *Wall v Lefever* [1998] 1 F.C.R. 605, CA. Appeals against decisions as to whether there was a prima facie case will be even rarer, see *Royal Institution of Chartered Surveyors v Wiseman Marshall* [2000] P.N.L.R. 649, CA. Appeals from a District Judge will go to the Circuit Judge, see *Gray v Going Places Leisure Travel Ltd* [2005] EWCA Civ 189; [2005] P.N.L.R. 26, CA.

[31] [1997] 3 F.C.R. 389.

[32] There may be a tension between the relevant statute and the practice direction as to costs incurred before the misconduct, such as a case of inordinate delay, on which see Simpson, *Professional Negligence and Liability,* para.9.428. *Quaere* whether causation could be established in such cases. Costs for a period of delay of four years were awarded under the wasted costs jurisdiction in *Padhiar v Patel* [2001] Lloyd's Rep. P.N. 328, QBD.

[33] [1994] Ch. 205 at 237E–F.

[34] See also *R. v M (Wasted Costs Order)* [2000] P.N.L.R. 2, where solicitors issued a witness summons in unfortunately wide terms. The Court of Appeal held that no costs had been wasted, as a hearing would have been necessary at some stage, and the judge in fact dealt with the substance of the matter at the hearing of the defective summons in any event. The amount of wasted costs must be specified in the order, and the order cannot later be amended by adding a figure at a later date, see *Re Harry Jagdev & Co, The Times*, August 12, 1999, CA.

[35] [1997] P.N.L.R. 67. An example of a wasted costs application failing on causation is *Afzal v Chubb Guarding Services Ltd (Wasted Costs Order)* [2002] EWHC 822; [2003] P.N.L.R. 33. It was alleged that solicitors failed to put contrary views contained in other experts' reports to the key psychiatric expert in good time. However, when they were put to the expert, she did not waiver in her views, and

appeal against a wasted costs order as the judge had not identified the conduct of the solicitors which was improper, unreasonable or negligent, and he had failed to identify the costs wasted by the conduct, although a detailed enquiry was not required. In that case, there had been great delay in the litigation, but it was clear that much of the costs would have been incurred in any event. The court must ask whether the costs in question would have been incurred on the balance of probabilities but for the lawyers' conduct, not whether there was a substantial possibility that they would not have been incurred, see *Brown v Bennett (No.2)*.[36]

Hopeless litigation.[37] The Court of Appeal in *Ridehalgh v Horsefield*[38] stated that a legal representative has not acted improperly, unreasonably or negligently merely because he acted for a party who pursued a claim or defence which was plainly doomed to fail. However, he should not lend his assistance to proceedings which are an abuse of process.[39] A number of cases have concerned the bringing of hopeless proceedings or applications. In *Re a Company (No.006798 of 1995)*[40] Chadwick J. held that a solicitor who swore an affidavit in support of a winding-up petition asserting a belief that the company was insolvent acted improperly if he did not hold that belief, and unreasonably if there were no grounds upon which a competent solicitor could have reached that view. On the facts, the solicitor acted unreasonably as the amount owed was based on adjustments to an account made by the petitioner unilaterally and of which the company had no

11–136

---

causation was not established. In assessing the amount of wasted costs it is necessary to consider whether the costs claimed were reasonable, and in *R. (on the application of DPP) v Cheshire Justices* [2002] EWHC 466; [2002] P.N.L.R. 36, the Administrative Court reduced the wasted costs order made in relation to an adjournment of a speeding offence from £2,084.45 to £400.

[36] [2002] 1 W.L.R. 713, Neuberger J.

[37] See also the cases discussed at Ch.12, paras 12–016 to 12–019. For another example see *Da Sousa v Minister of State for Immigration, Local Government and Ethnic Affairs* (1993) 114 A.L.R. 708, Federal Court of Australia, where a wasted costs order was made against solicitors who pursued a misconceived application for judicial review of a decision refusing entry permits for which the applicant could not possibly have qualified; the solicitors failed to give reasonable attention to the relevant law and facts, and exposed their clients to possible prejudice by being excluded from applying for an entry permit in some other category.

[38] [1994] Ch. 205 at 233F–234F.

[39] See the similar comments by Sir John Donaldson M.R. in the context of the previous wasted costs jurisdiction in *Orchard v South Eastern Electricity Board* [1987] Q.B. 565 at 572 that it is not for lawyers to impose a pre-trial screen through which a litigant must pass before he can put his case to the court. As to the relationship between acting negligently or unreasonably in bringing a hopeless case and the question of abuse of process, see further *Dempsey v Johnstone (Wasted Costs Order)* [2003] EWCA Civ 1134; [2004] P.N.L.R 25 and Ch.12, para.12–017.

[40] [1996] 1 W.L.R. 491. Similarly, in *Re a Company (No.0022 of 1993)* [1993] B.C.C. 726, Knox J. held solicitors liable for wasted costs after they should have realised that an attempt to wind up a company was inappropriate because it was clear that the debt was disputed. In *Isaacs Partnership (a firm) v Umm Al-Jawaby Oil Service Co Ltd (Wasted Costs)* [2003] EWHC 2539, QB; [2004] P.N.L.R. 9 a wasted costs order was upheld by Gross J. against solicitors who had pursued hopeless litigation against the wrong defendant for breach of an employment contract, when they had both documentary evidence and a letter from the defendants pointing out that the claimant had been employed by another company. Wasted cost orders were made by Henrique J. in *Secretary of State for the Home Department v Zinovjev (Wasted Costs Order)* [2003] EWHC 100, Admin; [2004] P.N.L.R. 4 in four immigration appeals, all abandoned on the day of the appeal, where the appeal was made out of time without any explanation and on formulaic and unfocused grounds.

knowledge, and he was ordered to pay the wasted costs incurred by the company. In *Tolstoy-Miloslavsky v Aldington*[41] the claimant, a bankrupt, sought to set aside a libel judgment obtained by the defendant, on the grounds of fraud. The original libel was that the defendant was a major war criminal who had arranged the massacre of 70,000 people. The claimant relied on new evidence which purported to show that the defendant had lied at trial about the date he left Austria in May 1945. The new action was struck out as an abuse of process, as the new evidence could not show that the defendant had committed perjury, the date of departure had never been a crucial issue, the new evidence was not decisive even on that issue, and it had been available at the date of trial. The Court of Appeal made a wasted costs order against the solicitors as they held that it was unreasonable to commence an "utterly hopeless" case on the facts, which was also an abuse of process as being a collateral attack on the previous decision, when they were acting without fee,[42] given the other aggravating circumstances of that case which included the fact that the claimant had never paid any of the damages or costs in the original action. Solicitors have also been ordered to pay costs as a result of their unreasonableness in rejecting a *Calderbank* offer.[43]

11–137   However, solicitors were not liable for pursuing an action which proved wrong but was not manifestly inappropriate in *Re O (a minor) (Wasted Costs Application)*.[44] Nor were solicitors held liable in *R. v Westminster LBC Ex p. Geehan & Butler*,[45] where on careful analysis the application was probably not even arguable, but the solicitors had been forced to act very quickly as their clients had spent the night before the application sleeping rough. Solicitors were held not to

---

[41] [1996] 1 W.L.R. 736. Similarly, in *DCT v Levick* (2000) 168 A.L.R. 383 the Federal Court of Australia made a wasted costs order against laywers who advanced a case which was so hopeless that it had no real chance of success.

[42] In the pre-*Ridehalgh* case of *Mainwaring v Goldtech Investments Ltd, The Times*, February 19, 1991, it was accepted by the Court of Appeal that a wasted costs order could be made if solicitors conducted litigation in the knowledge that there was no real likelihood of their ever having their costs and expenses reimbursed by their client, although on the facts of the case no order was made. For further details of the case see the comment by S. Fennell at [1991] 7 P.N. 199. However, in *Hodgson v Imperial Tobacco Ltd* [1998] 1 W.L.R. 1056 the Court of Appeal held that a legal adviser acting under a conditional fee agreement permitted under s.58 of the Courts and Legal Services Act 1990 was no more at risk of being made personally liable for costs than if he did not act under such an agreement.

[43] *C v C (Wasted Costs Order)* [1994] 2 F.L.R. 34, Ewbank J. Some of the blame, and thus some of the costs, were shared by their former clients.

[44] [1994] 2 F.L.R. 842 Connell J. In *Gandesh v Nandra* [2002] Lloyd's Rep. P.N. 558 Jacob J. held that it may not be unreasonable to bring proceedings on behalf of a legally aided claimant who was later found to be a liar, in a case which depended on her credibility; for a similar factual case where the same conclusion was drawn, see *Persaud v Persaud* [2003] EWCA Civ 394; [2003] P.N.L.R. 26, CA. In *Marsh v Sofaer* [2006] EWHC 1217, Ch; [2006] P.N.L.R. 35 David Richards J. held that it was not unreasonable to allege that the claimant lacked capacity in answer to a plea of limitation, when there were two psychiatrists who supported that allegation. In *Terence Daly v Martin Bernard Hubner* [2002] Lloyd's Law Rep. P.N. 461, some of the allegations made by the successful defendant against the claimant's legal advisers were that the pleaded claim was manifestly unsustainable in law. Etherton J. held that the defendant could have applied to have the action struck out. Other allegations were dismissed for other reasons, and in refusing to permit the wasted application to continue to the second stage the judge also relied on the fact that the costs spent so far on the application were larger than the alleged wasted costs.

[45] [1995] C.O.D. 204, Dyson J.

be negligent in *Reaveley v Safeway Stores Plc*[46] for pursuing an action when they failed to advise a claimant that he was highly likely to lose the £2,500 offered by the defendants, as he would not obtain in damages more than the benefits recoverable by the Compensation Recovery Unit of £16,000. The solicitors relied on counsel properly instructed who credibly advised that the action should proceed.

Abuse of process. Solicitors have also been ordered to pay wasted costs where   **11-138**
the proceedings or application were for an improper purpose, an issue which is often closely allied to whether proceedings were hopeless. In *Flower & Hart (a firm) v White Industries (Qld) Pty Ltd*[47] a solicitor was ordered to pay wasted costs when his purpose in instituting proceedings was to gain a temporary bargaining position for his client and not to vindicate his client's rights, regardless of whether the cause of action was arguable or not. Similarly, in *Woolwich Building Society v Fineberg*[48] the improper use of a hopeless appeal to play for time in resisting the execution of a warrant for possession justified a wasted costs order. In *R. v Basra (Wasted Costs Order)*[49] the Court of Appeal upheld a wasted costs order made against solicitors in a criminal case who had issued a witness summons for the improper purpose of obtaining discovery or to obtain material for cross-examination.

Difficulties with public funding.[50] In *Roberts v Coverite*[51] no wasted costs   **11-139**
order was made against solicitors acting for claimants in litigation who sent notices of issue of legal aid to the court to pass on to the defendants. The defendants did not receive the notices, and as a result the case was not settled timeously and cheaply. It was not negligent to fail to notice that a sealed copy had not been returned as requested, or to rely on the court to pass on the notice. Compare *Re Stathams (Wasted Costs Order)*[52] where the Court of Appeal upheld a wasted costs order against solicitors who failed to inform the other side that their client's legal aid had been withdrawn. They had acted negligently and

---

[46] [1998] P.N.L.R. 526, CA. Similarly, in *R. v A (Wasted Costs Order)* [2000] P.N.L.R. 628, CA, no order was made against solicitors who pursued an application for release from custody in ignorance of an unreported case which showed that the application was hopeless, and in reliance on the advice of counsel.

[47] (1999) 163 A.L.R. 744, Federal Court Australia, Full Court. See also *Fletamentos Maritimos SA v Effjohn International SA* [2003] Lloyd's Rep. P.N. 26 (a case decided in 1997). The Court of Appeal made a wasted costs order against a solicitor for making a misconceived appeal against an arbitrator's decision refusing disclosure, which made allegations of actual or a risk of bias by the arbitrator, as it was an abuse of process.

[48] [1998] P.N.L.R. 216, Peter Gibson L.J. refusing leave to appeal. Similarly in *Morris v Roberts (Inspector of Taxes) (Wasted Costs)* [2005] EWHC 1040; [2005] P.N.L.R. 41, Lightman J. made a wasted costs order against solicitors who prosecuted hopeless appeals against tax decisions in order to evade or delay payment.

[49] [1998] P.N.L.R. 535. See also *Re a Solicitor (Wasted Costs Order)* [1996] 1 F.L.R. 40, CA, where a solicitor had to pay the wasted costs for issuing a witness summons for disclosure of documents in a criminal matter which was wholly speculative.

[50] In *Trill v Sacher, The Times*, November 14, 1992, the Court of Appeal made no wasted costs order where the delay which wasted costs was caused by the slow action of the legal aid authorities and delay in obtaining counsel's opinion.

[51] The third of the appeals in *Ridehalgh v Horsefield* [1994] Ch. 205 at 247–250.

[52] [1997] P.I.Q.R. 494.

unreasonably, and caused the defendants to waste costs by attending a hearing of an application for an adjournment of the claimant's appeal. But in *Tate v Hart*[53] the Court of Appeal held that there was no obligation to inform the other side of the discharge of the client's legal aid when the withdrawal was the subject of an appeal. The statutory code did not require notification in such circumstances, and the Court would be slow to add to a detailed statutory code of conduct.

11–140   **Misuse of procedure.** Procedural errors may often lead to wasted costs. In *Kleinwort Benson v Montenegro*[54] solicitors had to pay the wasted costs personally when they failed to disclose to the Court in an application for a Mareva injunction that their client was in fact bankrupt. In *Veasey v Millfeed Co Ltd*[55] the solicitor knew that the claimant was no longer in partnership, but served proceedings in the name of the partnership and failed to correct the error. He was found to be guilty of incompetence, and ordered to pay the costs of unnecessary striking out proceedings which were brought on account of the misnomer. In *R. v Liverpool City Council Ex p. May*[56] Laws J. made a wasted costs order against solicitors who issued proceedings to commit for breach of an undertaking without warning, where the breach was at most technical and did not justify the draconian steps proposed. In contrast, in three cases of procedural errors, no wasted costs order was made. In *R. v M (Wasted Costs Order)*[57] no order was made against solicitors who applied for unjustifiably wide disclosure of documents in a rape case, because the practice of seeking only more restricted classes of documents was recent. Similarly, in *Warren v Warren*[58] solicitors issued a summons to compel a district judge to give evidence about the terms of a disputed undertaking. The Court of Appeal determined that although the law had been undecided as to whether the district judge was compellable, in fact he was not. However, the solicitors could not be criticised for not appreciating that the judge was not compellable, it was not unreasonable to seek his attendance as he was in a position to give the best evidence about the terms of the undertaking, and in view also of the disproportionate conduct of both sides no wasted costs order was made. In *Neill v Crown Prosecution Service*[59] the Divisional Court considered that it was not improper for a solicitor to proceed with an old-style committal in an indecent assault case where the client had told him that the complainant had said that the prosecution may not go ahead, and where the

---

[53] [1999] P.N.L.R. 787.
[54] [1994] N.P.C. 46.
[55] [1997] P.N.L.R. 100. The court assumed without deciding that causation should be judged on the balance of probabilities, see para.11–266.
[56] [1994] C.O.D. 144.
[57] [1996] 1 F.L.R. 751, Scott Baker J. *cf. Wasted Costs Order (No.5 of 1997)*, *The Times*, September 7, 1999, discussed at Ch.12, para.12–019.
[58] [1997] Q.B. 488. In *Sherman v Fitzhugh Gates (a firm)* [2003] EWCA Civ 886; [2003] P.N.L.R. 39 the solicitors issued proceedings on behalf of the executrix as to what the defendant was entitled to in the testator's estate. This was not the correct procedure, but it was caused by the defendant unreasonably threatening proceedings but not commencing them, there was no easy solution found in the textbooks, and the solicitors relied on counsel. While the solicitors did not pass on the Master's views about the procedural difficulties, this was not improper, unreasonable or negligent within the meaning of s.51(7) of the Supreme Court Act 1981. The Court of Appeal held that no wasted costs order should be made.
[59] [1997] C.O.D. 171.

solicitor had agreed that oral evidence was not necessary in the committal when the complainant appeared to give evidence.

Other errors. The Court of Appeal considered the defendant solicitors to have **11–141** acted negligently and unreasonably in *Shah v Singh*.[60] The solicitors successfully applied immediately before trial of an action to come off the record as their bills had not been paid, but the claimants were not granted an adjournment of the trial. The solicitor concerned failed to impress upon the clerk who attended at court that the claimants had just received legal aid, which would have led to an adjournment.[61] In *R. v Secretary of State for the Home Department Ex p. Mahmood*[62] Richards J. made a wasted costs order against a solicitor who instructed a barrister for a hearing who had a known court commitment in the afternoon, when there was an obvious risk that their case might not be heard in the morning. In *R. v Qadi*[63] the Court of Appeal upheld a wasted costs order made against a solicitor's clerk who took instructions from his client in a corridor where he knew the jury were likely to pass, as a result of which the jury overheard the conversation and a re-trial was ordered. In *R. v Liverpool City Council Ex p. Horn*[64] Buxton J. made a wasted costs order when the solicitor had concealed the fraudulent conduct of his client.

(f) *Exclusion or Restriction of Liability by Contract*[65]

In a contentious business agreement, any provision exempting the solicitor from **11–142** liability for negligence or breach of duty is void.[66] In the Law Society Council Statement *Limitation of liability by contract*[67] it was considered acceptable to restrict liability to not below the minimum level of insurance cover (which is now £2,000,000). The Council recognised that this is subject to the general law, in particular the Unfair Contract Terms Act 1977. Any such restriction must be brought to the attention of the client and accepted by him, preferably in writing.

---

[60] [1996] 1 P.N.L.R. 83.

[61] *cf. Re A Solicitor (Wasted Costs Order)* [1993] 2 F.L.R. 959. No order was made by the Court of Appeal for a solicitor's error of judgment in failing to warn the court or his opponent that he might have to seek at a late stage an adjournment of a hearing because of difficulties with the Legal Aid Board.

[62] [1999] C.O.D. 119.

[63] [2000] P.N.L.R. 137.

[64] [1997] P.N.L.R. 95.

[65] The general principles of whether liability can be excluded or restricted are discussed in Ch.5, paras 5–001 to 5–024, which includes further discussion of the scope of the Solicitors Act 1974, s.60(5).

[66] Solicitors Act 1974, s.60(5). *Quaere* whether this permits the limitation of liability. "Contentious business agreement" is defined in s.59(1). See also *Chamberlain v Boodle & King* [1982] 1 W.L.R. 1443.

[67] Published in the *Law Society Gazette* on May 27, 1987. The revised version is substantially reproduced in the Law Society's *Guide to the Professional Conduct of Solicitors* (8th edn, 1999), para.12.11; the updated *Guide* is to be found on the Law Society's website.

(g) *Practice and Procedure*[68]

(i) *Expert Evidence*

11–143   In ascertaining the general practice or practices of the profession, the court will, of course, have regard to the evidence of solicitors who are called as witnesses by one or other party. However, in *Midland Bank v Hett, Stubbs & Kemp*,[69] Oliver J. criticised the practice of calling solicitors to give evidence as to what they would have done in a particular situation:

> "I must say that I doubt the value, or even the admissibility, of this sort of evidence, which seems to be becoming customary in cases of this type. The extent of the legal duty in any given situation must, I think, be a question of law for the court. Clearly, if there is some practice in a particular profession, some accepted standard of conduct which is laid down by a professional institute or sanctioned by common usage, evidence of that can and ought to be received. But evidence which really amounts to no more than an expression of opinion by a particular practitioner of what he thinks that he would have done had he been placed, hypothetically and without the benefit of hindsight, in the position of the defendants, is of little assistance to the court; whilst evidence of the witnesses' view of what, as a matter of law, the solicitor's duty was in the particular circumstances of the case is, I should have thought, inadmissible, for that is the very question which it is the court's function to decide."[70]

This dictum was approved by the Court of Appeal in *Bown v Gould & Swayne*,[71] where the Court rejected an application to allow a conveyancing expert. Millett L.J. commented that if a judge needed assistance with regard to conveyancing practice, the proper way was to cite the relevant textbooks. In *May v Woollcombe Beer & Watts*,[72] H.H. Judge Raymond Jack Q.C., sitting in the Bristol Mercantile Court, held that expert evidence was admissible in relation to conveyancing

---

[68] This section is not a complete or comprehensive account of practice and procedure relating to solicitor's negligence cases, but merely highlights two important issues that sometimes arise.

[69] [1979] Ch.384.

[70] *ibid.* at 402B–D. See also the very similar view of Lord Denning M.R. in *Carradine Properties Ltd v DJ Freeman & Co* [1999] Lloyd's Rep. P.N. 483 at 486 col.2; [1955–1995] P.N.L.R. 12. It is submitted that a wider view might be taken of the function of a solicitor as expert witness. Whilst, of course, the extent of the solicitor's duty is ultimately a question for the court, surely this is a mixed question of fact and law. Even if there is no directly relevant "practice of the profession", the evidence of other practitioners as to what they do in similar cases (and why) is likely to be of benefit to the court. A knowledge of the working of a solicitor's office, particularly of those departments handling non-contentious business, cannot be automatically imputed to the judge (or to counsel). In any event, experts are often called to give their view of what should have been done, e.g. the views of two Queen's Counsel were considered as to whether a fellow barrister had emphasised an important point with sufficient urgency in *Mathew v Maughold Life Assurance Co Ltd* [1955–1995] P.N.L.R. 15, CA. Furthermore, in medical negligence cases it is not uncommon for an expert witness to give evidence of what he would have done in the particular situation under consideration: see Ch.13, paras 13–037 to 13–038.

[71] [1996] 1 P.N.L.R. 130.

[72] [1999] P.N.L.R. 283. Similarly, in *Archer v Hickmotts* [1997] P.N.L.R. 318, H.H. Judge Brunning in the Nottingham County Court admitted expert evidence concerning the advice which should have been given in relation to a mortgage to secure a loan which the client was taking to assist her brother setting up his solicitor's practice, as the court had no familiarity with the matters in question and there were no textbooks which could assist. His judgment at the end of the trial was reversed by the Court of Appeal who made no mention of expert evidence, see *Northern Rock Building Society v Archer* (1998) 78 P.C.R. 65.

matters where there was no answer provided by textbooks. Under the Civil Procedure Rules no party may call an expert without the court's permission, see CPR r.35.4.[73] If permission has been given to call an expert, objection may be made to its admissibility, but this should be done so as soon as possible, and if there is real doubt as to whether the evidence should be admitted it should be allowed.[74]

Practice abroad. In Ireland the practice is similar to England.[75] In the Australian case of *Permanent Trustee Australia Ltd v Boulton*[76] Young J. considered that expert evidence was permitted as to "industry-wide" good practice and what was common amongst solicitor of good repute, and how long it would take ordinary competent solicitors to complete transactions, but not as to the expert's view of negligence, or what that witness would have done, or the time for reasonable notice. However, in Canada, expert evidence is frequently called in circumstances where it would not be permitted in England,[77] although some courts have restricted its use.[78]   **11–144**

(ii) *Privilege*[79]

Waiver of privilege. Privilege and its waiver can raise some difficult issues in solicitor's negligence cases, which have been explored in three decisions of the Court of Appeal. In *Lillicrap v Nalder*[80] the defendant solicitors acted for the claimant property developers, and admitted negligence for failing to advise their clients on rights of way in a transaction. The solicitors denied causation, and attempted to amend their defence to plead previous retainers in which their advice had been ignored by the claimant. The claimant claimed that such matters were privileged, although it was accepted that there was an implied waiver of privilege in relation to the transaction in question by the claimant suing the   **11–145**

---

[73] The position used to be more complicated. Where it was disputed whether expert evidence was admissible, the master or judge in chambers was not entitled to rule on the admissibility of such evidence, see *Sullivan v West Yorkshire Passenger Transport Executive* [1985] 2 All E.R. 134, CA. However, in *Woodford & Ackroyd v Burgess* [1999] Lloyd's Rep. P.N. 231 the Court of Appeal held that a judge who was not the trial judge could rule on admissibility under the inherent jurisdiction. Further, the Court of Appeal in *Bown* held that a judge on a pre-trial review was entitled to make such a ruling.
[74] See *Liverpool Roman Catholic Archdiocese Trustees Inc v Goldberg (No.2)* [2001] Lloyd's Rep. P.N. 518, Neuberger J. Subsequently, at trial, the expert's evidence was ruled inadmissible because of the close relationship between him and the defendant, see *Liverpool Roman Catholic Archdiocese Trustees Inc v Goldberg (No.3)* [2001] Lloyd's Rep. P.N. 823, Evans Lombe J.
[75] *McMullen v Caren Farrell* [1993] I.R.L.R. 123 at 141, Barron J.
[76] [1994] 33 N.S.W.L.R. 735.
[77] See, e.g. *Central Trust Co v Rafuse* (1987) 31 D.L.R. (4th) 481 and *Roberge v Bolduc* [1991] 1 S.C.R. 374, both Supreme Court of Canada.
[78] See, e.g. *Clarke v Poje & Kenney* (1989) 38 B.C.L.R. (2d) 110, at 117, British Columbia CA: in the absence of a standard practice within the profession, expert evidence is not admissible; *Deyong v Weeks* (1984) 33 Alta. L.R. (2d) 338, Alberta CA: expert evidence allowed on the standard of competence to be expected, but not as to what he would have done, and such evidence was of little value in an unusual transaction.
[79] Iniquity by a mortgagor will justify setting aside legal professional privilege so that a lender can obtain disclosure of the solicitor's file, although the solicitor had not participated in the iniquity, see *Abbey National Plc v David Prosser & Co (a firm)* [2001] P.N.L.R. Ch. D.
[80] [1993] 1 W.L.R. 94.

solicitors. The Court of Appeal appeared to hold that the waiver extended to matters which were relevant to an issue in the proceedings.[81] In *Muller v Linsley*[82] the claimant sued the defendant solicitors for negligence in the transfer of his shares which had resulted in litigation with other shareholders which was settled. The reasonableness of the settlement was in issue, and the Court of Appeal held that there should be discovery of without prejudice negotiations leading up to the settlement. The court held that the correspondence was not privileged as the public policy rule only applied to admissions. A majority also appeared to hold that any privilege was waived in relation to all matters relevant to the issues raised by the claimants in the action.[83] In *Paragon Finance Plc v Freshfields*[84] the Court of Appeal held that the implied waiver extended to the solicitor-client relationship, and not to communications to which the solicitor was not privy. Thus the claimant was not obliged to disclose communications with different solicitors whom they later instructed to pursue and settle a claim against a third party arising from the transactions over which the defendant solicitors were being sued.

11–146   **Two clients.** Where a solicitor has acted for two clients, such as a borrower and lender on a mortgage transaction, the lender will not be entitled to see privileged communications between the solicitor and the borrower, unless the solicitor's advice and assistance is employed in the furtherance of an iniquity.[85] The solicitors should consult their client with regard to an application for disclosure of privileged documents.[86] On the obligations of lenders to provide discovery in relation to contributory negligence, see *Portman Building Society v Royal Insurance Plc*.[87] As to the extent of waiver of privilege between insured and insured, see *TSB Bank Plc v Robert Irving & Burns*,[88] where it was held by the Court of Appeal that privilege was waived up until the emergence of an actual rather than possible conflict of interest, and the notification by the solicitors to the

---

[81] In *Paragon Finance Plc v Freshfields* [1999] Lloyd's Rep. P.N. 446 the Court of Appeal made clear that the decision did not go further than holding that the implied waiver extended to earlier tranactions of the client handled by the solicitors.

[82] [1996] 1 P.N.L.R. 74.

[83] In *Paragon Finance Plc v Freshfields* [1999] Lloyd's Rep. P.N. 446 at 447 col.2 the Court of Appeal stated that the case concerned "without prejudice" privilege, and the Court derived no statement of principle relevant to the case from the views which were expressed on waiver.

[84] [1999] Lloyd's Rep. P.N. 446. The Court overruled *Kershaw v Whelan* [1996] 1 W.L.R. 358, where it had been held that the implied waiver of privilege extended to advice received from other solicitors, and not just the defendants, which was material to the issues in the proceedings. The Court also overrulled *Hayes v Dowding* [1996] 1 W.L.R. 578.

[85] *Abbey National Plc v Clive Travers & Co* [1999] P.N.L.R. 819, CA, following *Nationwide Building Society v Various Solicitors* [1999] P.N.L.R. 52, Blackburne J., and to similar effect *Birmingham Midshires Mortgage Services Ltd v Ansell* [1998] P.N.L.R. 237, Ch. D; *Abbey National Plc v David Prosser & Co (a firm)* [2001] P.N.L.R. 15, Ch. D (where it was held that the fraud did not need to be pleaded), and *Darlington Building Society v O'Rourke James Scourfield & McCarthy* [1999] P.N.L.R 365, CA, discussed further at para.11–219, below. As to what is confidential, see para.11–219, and *Nationwide Building Society v Various Solicitors* [1999] P.N.L.R. 52.

[86] *Abbey National Plc v Clive Travers & Co* [1999] P.N.L.R. 819.

[87] [1998] P.N.L.R. 672, CA.

[88] [2000] P.N.L.R. 384. See also *Brown v Guardian Royal Exchange Assurance Plc* [1994] 2 Lloyd's Rep. 325.

insured of the conflict, with sufficient time for the insured to decide whether to instruct separate solicitors.[89]

(h) *Attribution and Vicarious Liability*[90]

Partners. A solicitor's partners are vicariously liable for his wrongful acts or **11-147** omissions acting in the ordinary course of business of the firm[91] or with the authority of his co-partners, see s.10 of the Partnership Act 1890.[92] In *Dubai Aluminium Co Ltd v Salaam*[93] the House of Lords held that "wrongful acts" in s.10 included equitable wrongs such as dishonest assistance in a breach of trust, as well as tortious liability. They also held that such acts would be done in the ordinary course of the business of the firm if it could fairly and properly be so regarded, which was a question of law. Thus the drafting of an agreement by a partner to assist in a fraudulent scheme was so closely connected with acts which he was authorised to do that he could be regarded as having acted in the ordinary course of the firm's business, and his innocent partners were liable for his assumed dishonest assistance. The case was applied by the Court of Appeal in *JJ Coughlan Ltd v Ruparelia*[94] where it was held that the motive or purpose of the solicitor was irrelevant, but one should not shut one's eyes to the true nature of the solicitor's acts when determining whether they fell within the ordinary business of a solicitor. It was necessary to look at the substance and detail of the transaction. In that case, the rogue solicitor attended meetings and acted as stakeholder, but the transactions promised absurd rates of return, and it was not part of a solicitor's business to be involved in such a scheme.

Under s.11 of the Partnership Act 1890 the firm is liable where a partner **11-148** receives money or property of another within the scope of his apparent authority and misapplies it, or the firm receives money or property in the course of business and a partner misapplies it. Merely accepting a draft to hold money to the client's order without any instructions is not acting within the course of

---

[89] For a detailed treatment of disclosure and privilege, see Ch.12 of Flenley and Leech's *Solicitor's Negligence* (Butterworths, 1999).

[90] See generally H. Evans, "Attribution and professional negligence" (2003) 19 P.N. 470.

[91] The test will be the same as for ostensible authority and acting in the ordinary course of business, see *United Bank of Kuwait Ltd v Hammoud* [1988] 1 W.L.R. 1051, CA, see para.11–066.

[92] See also ss.5, 9 and 11. It may be possible for the firm to obtain their excess from the defaulting partner who is in breach of a term to take reasonable care, see *Ross Harper & Murphy v Scott Banks* [2000] P.N.L.R. 631, OH. The same probably applies in England and Wales, although nineteenth century cases suggest the need to establish gross negligence.

[93] [2002] UKHL 48; [2003] 2 A.C. 366. In *Re Bell's Indenture* [1980] 1 W.L.R. 1217 Vinelott J. held that a solicitor had implied authority in the ordinary course of business to accept trust moneys, but not to accept office as a trustee. In *Scarborough Building Society v Howes Percival* (1998) 78 P.&C.R. D4 partners were liable for a fraudulent solicitor acting in the ordinary course of the firm's business. In *Walker v Stones* [2001] Q.B. 902 the Court of Appeal held that breaches of trust committed by a solicitor trustee fell outside the ordinary business of a partnership and could not give rise to vicarious liability under s.10. Cases decided before *Dubai* need to be treated with some caution.

[94] [2003] EWCA Civ 1057; [2004] P.N.L.R. 4. The claimant failed in any event because it had not believed that the defendant was engaged in a transaction in the ordinary course of a solicitor's business.

business of a solicitor nor is it within the scope of a partner's apparent authority.[95] Where two firms merge, regardless of the terms of the merger, partners in one firm could not be liable for the earlier acts of a partner in the other firm.[96] A defendant who is a "salaried partner", that is who is held held out as a partner but is in fact merely an employee of the firm, will only be liable for the firm's defaults if the claimant can prove he relied on the defendant holding himself out as a partner.[97]

11–149 **Staff.** A firm of solicitors is vicariously liable for breaches of duty committed by its own staff.[98] This will generally include liability for the fraud of the employee.[99] A firm will normally be liable for breaches committed by other solicitors acting as their agents within the scope of their authority.[1] Similarly if a solicitor entrusts his practice to a locum while he is away from the office for any reason, he will be liable for any breaches which the locum may commit. A solicitor will not, however, normally be liable for the defaults of a foreign lawyer he has instructed, who was an independent expert in the same way as an expert witness or counsel would be.[2]

11–150 **Delegation and organisation.** In *Arbiter Group Plc v Gill Jennings and Every (a firm)*[3] the claimants sought advice from the defendant patent agents as to whether their new kind of jukebox might infringe an existing US patent. The patent agents instructed US patent searchers to carry out a search to check this, who reported erroneously that the patent was not in force, which the defendants passed on to the claimant. Swinton Thomas L.J. held:

---

[95] *Antonelli v Allen* [2001] Lloyd's Rep. P.N. 487, Neuberger J.

[96] *HF Pension Trustees Ltd v Ellison* [1999] P.N.L.R. 894, Jonathan Parker J. In *Re Burton Marsden Douglas (a firm)* [2004] 3 All E.R. 222 a solicitor made representations to the client that a new firm had taken over the obligations of the his sold practice, but not that his liabilities had been too. Lloyd J. held that there was no special circumstances amounting to a novation, and the new firm was not liable to repay any monies which had been overpaid by the client to the solicitor.

[97] *Nationwide Building Society v Lewis* [1998] Ch. 482, CA. This principle was applied in *Sangster v Biddulph* [2005] EWHC 568; [2005] P.N.L.R. 33 where Etherton J. held that the claimant had successfully proved that she relied on the holding out of the defendant as a partner, as did the claimant in *All Link International Ltd v Ha Kai Cheong* [2005] HKLRD 65, Chiu J.

[98] e.g. *Floyd v Nangle* (1747) 3 Atk. 568; *Creech v Mayorcas* (1966) 198 E.G. 1091, Ch. D; *Heywood v Wellers* [1976] Q.B. 446, CA. The ostensible authority of both a partner and an employed solicitor was considered in a number of cases and in particular *United Bank of Kuwait Ltd v Hammoud* [1988] 1 W.L.R. 1051, CA, see further para.11–066. Subject to the question of co-insurance, the firm may be entitled to an indemnity from the employee; for an example see *Lee Siew Chun v Sourgrapes Packaging Products Trading Pte Ltd* [1993] 2 S.L.R. 297 Singapore High Court.

[99] e.g. see: *Lloyd v Grace Smith & Co* [1912] A.C. 716 (managing agent undertaking conveyancing work procured title deeds and stole the property); *Uxbridge Permanent Benefit Building Society v Pickard* [1939] 2 K.B. 248; and *Balfron Trustees Ltd v Karsten Peterson* [2002] Lloyd's Rep. P.N. 1, Laddie J., who emphasised that the relevant principles of vicarious liability are now to be found in *Lister v Hesley Hall Ltd* [2002] 1 A.C. 215.

[1] *Re Ward, Simmons v Rose; Weeks v Ward* (1862) 31 Beav. 1: solicitor held liable for negligent representations made by London agent.

[2] *Gregory v Shepherds* [2000] P.N.L.R. 769, CA. The solicitors were found liable on other grounds, see para.11–202 for the facts.

[3] [2000] P.N.L.R. 680. *Quaere* how this case should be reconciled with principles of agency and *Gregory v Shepherds* [2000] P.N.L.R. 769, CA; see further H. Evans, "Attribution and professional negligence" (2003) 19 P.N. 470 at 471–477.

"A professional man in appropriate circumstances is entitled to delegate tasks. Whether he is entitled to delegate a particular task will depend on the nature of the task. He is entitled to delegate some tasks to others but is not entitled to delegate others. It all depends on the nature of the task involved. If he does delegate he must delegate to a suitably qualified and experienced person."[4]

The court recognised that there was a risk that the person to whom the task is delegated may make a mistake, and the question to be considered was the degree of risk and whether it was appropriate that the delegator should take it. In that case, the defendants were entitled to delegate the search to US patent searchers, and they were entitled to rely on the results and not carry out further inquiries themselves.[5] If the drafting of documents is split between different departments of a firm, there is a potential for mismatch, and it is essential for someone with sufficiently general legal experience to have overall responsibility for reviewing the whole document, see *Summit Financial Group Ltd v Slaughter & May (a firm)*.[6]

2. LIABILITY FOR BREACH OF DUTY

(a) *General*

Classification of breaches. Broadly speaking, breach of duty by a solicitor **11–151** may take one of five forms:

(i) Breach of a specific contractual duty.[7]

(ii) Breach of the implied contractual duty to exercise reasonable skill and care.[8]

(iii) Breach of the duty of care owed by the solicitor to the client independently of his contractual duties.[9]

(iv) Breach of the duty of care owed by the solicitor to some third party who is not his client.[10]

(v) Breach of fiduciary or trust duties.[11]

Negligence is not an essential element of liability under the first head, although it is unusual for such a breach to occur without negligence.[12] The second, third

---

[4] [2000] P.N.L.R. 680 at 686.
[5] The claimant further relied on *Edward Wong Finance Co Ltd v Johnson Stokes & Master* [1984] A.C. 296, which was distinguished, see para.11–090, above.
[6] *The Times*, April 5, 1999.
[7] See paras 11–004 to 11–012.
[8] See paras 11–007 and 11–080.
[9] See paras 11–013 to 11–015.
[10] See paras 11–039 to 11–064.
[11] See paras 11–016 to 11–038.
[12] *Ferguson v Lewis* (1879) 14 L.J. 700 is an example of such a case. The defendant solicitor agreed to represent the claimant at the magistrate's court, but failed to attend. The defendant was acquitted of (gross) negligence, but held liable for breach of contract. For more modern examples, see paras 11–008 to 11–010, above.

and fourth heads involve breaches of the same standard of skill and care[13] and hereafter will jointly be described as "negligence",[14] a use of the term commonly adopted by professional negligence litigators which is apt to mislead other lawyers who confine the term to the third and fourth heads. Breach of trust and fiduciary duties used to play a comparatively small part in actions against solicitors, but have recently become more important. Breach of fiduciary duty may entail negligence,[15] but this is not necessary in order to establish liability.

11–152 Instances in which it has been held that solicitors are, or may be, liable for breach of duty are discussed below under four heads. It is not suggested that this catalogue is exhaustive. The cases serve to illustrate how the principles stated above operate in practice and, in particular, what the courts consider to be the standard of skill and care which may reasonably be expected of solicitors.[16]

(b) *Giving Wrong Advice*

11–153 **On the law.**[17] Giving advice is one of the principal functions of solicitors. If the solicitor gives incorrect advice on a point of common occurrence, where the law is clear, then he will be liable in negligence.[18] For example, in *Otter v Church Adams Tatham & Co*[19] the defendant solicitors advised that when M attained 21 his interest in certain settled property would become absolute. Subsequently (when M attained 21) they advised that there was no urgency about effecting the transfer of the property to him. In fact, M only had an equitable interest in tail in the property. In order to perfect his title, he should have executed a disentailing assurance. He died on active service before this was done. The point of law was a straightforward one, and Upjohn J. held that the defendants were negligent in not making a proper enquiry. In *Winston Cooper v Smith Llewellyn Partnership*[20] the defendant solicitors failed to advise their clients that the relevant limitation period was six years from the date of exchange of contracts, not completion. They had failed to distinguish the cause of actions in contract and tort, and had failed to look up the relevant case law. Curtis J. held that the solicitors were negligent.

11–154 If a solicitor errs in his advice on a matter where the law is difficult, then he is not liable in negligence so long as the opinion that he expresses is a reasonable

---

[13] In certain circumstances the contractual duty of skill and care may be higher than that imposed by the law of tort: see *Duchess of Argyll v Beuselinck* [1972] 2 Lloyd's Rep. 172 at 183 (discussed in para.11–096). It is theoretically possible, therefore, that a solicitor may be held liable to his client under head (ii) but escape liability under head (iii).

[14] The distinction between the second and third heads becomes important where a defence is raised under the Limitation Acts. The distinction may also be important when quantifying damages, in particular in relation to the test for foreseeability, as to which see s.3 of this chapter.

[15] As in *Nocton v Ashburton* [1914] A.C. 932: if negligence had been pleaded, it would not have been necessary to pursue the claim for breach of fiduciary duty. See also *Lapierre v Young* (1981) 117 D.L.R. (3d) 643, Ontario High Court.

[16] For a general discussion of the standard of skill and care, see paras 11–080 *et seq.*.

[17] See further paras 11–084 and 11–085.

[18] *Hill v Finney* (1865) 4F F. 616: erroneous advice in divorce proceedings; *Rumsey v Owen, White & Catlin* (1978) 245 E.G. 225, CA: advice based on a misunderstanding of the Landlord and Tenant Act 1954.

[19] [1953] Ch. 280.

[20] [1999] P.N.L.R. 576.

one.[21] In such a situation, however, the solicitor would be prudent to qualify his advice, by stating that the matter is in doubt. However, the contrary view was expressed by Lord Shand in *Blair v Assets Co*[22]:

> "It was (the solicitors') duty to form their own opinion, and to advise the liquidators accordingly. But it was not their duty, nor according to their instructions, to reason out the matter with the liquidators, to say whether their opinion was given with confidence or hesitation or to quote their authorities."

Where it is obvious that the solicitor's advice is no more than an expression of opinion on a moot point, then, according to Canadian authority,[23] a solicitor is not liable for failing to state this expressly: "The lawyer's advice in matters of statutory interpretation can never be more than an opinion . . . He is not, I think, normally required to warn experienced business clients of the possibility that the opinion, although firmly held, may not in fact prevail."[24] Contrast *Port of Sheerness Ltd v Brachers*[25] where the defendant solicitors advised their clients that dismissing dockers who refused to accept new terms would cause claims limited to redundancy payments. There were two competing schools of thought at the time as to whether such circumstances would have given rise to claims for redundancy or more costly claims for unfair dismissal. Buckley J. nevertheless found the defendant solicitors negligent for failing to mention the risk that the dismissals would be found to be unfair.

Practical advice. A solicitor is often called upon to give practical advice, in which legal considerations are only one factor. In such a situation, a mere error of judgment by the solicitor is less likely to amount to negligence.[26] Where, however, the solicitor advises a course of action that is plainly wrong, then he will be liable.[27] The more the advice is based on legal considerations, the more likely it is that an error will be found to be negligent. In *Worboys v Cartwright*[28] the vendor of a farm which the solicitor's client had purchased was resisting giving a date for vacant possession. The solicitors nevertheless advised the client

11–155

---

[21] *Bell v Strathairn & Blair* (1954) 104 L.J. 618 (Scottish case). In *Fordgate Wandsworth Ltd v Bernard Neville & Co* [1999] E.G.C.S. 98 the defendant solicitors were held by Lloyd J. not to be negligent in advising their client landlord that there had probably been a surrender of the lease by operation of law, and the client should accept it although it was not definite that there had been a surrender.

[22] [1896] A.C. 409 at 431; see also Lord Herschell at p.426.

[23] *Ormindale Holdings Ltd v Ray, Wolfe, Connel, Lightbody & Reynolds* (1981) 116 D.L.R. (3d) 346 and (1982) 135 D.L.R. (3d) 577, British Columbia CA

[24] *ibid.*, *per* Taylor J. at first instance. Taylor J.'s decision was upheld in all respects on appeal and this passage was specifically approved: see (1982) 135 D.L.R. (3d) 577 at 579.

[25] (1997) I.R.L.R. 214, and see also *Queen Elizabeth's Grammar School Blackburn Ltd v Banks Wilson (a firm)* [2001] EWCA Civ 1360; [2002] P.N.L.R. 14 noted at para.11–116, below. For a similar example see *Hall v Foong* (1995) 65 S.A.S.R. 281, where the Full Court of South Australia held that the defendant solicitor was negligent in giving the client definite advice that a contract to purchase property was void, when he knew his advice was contrary to a recent appellate decision, and he was in receipt of a preliminary advice from counsel that the contract was probably not void but that the client may be entitled to rescind it

[26] *Faithfull v Kesteven* (1910) 103 L.T. 56, CA.

[27] e.g. *Bryant v Goodrich* (1966) 110 S.J. 108: wrongly advising a wife to leave the matrimonial home after the breakdown of her marriage.

[28] [1992] E.G.C.S. 110.

to proceed to sell his farm at auction. Morritt J. held that the solicitors were negligent in their advice, as they had failed to assess the time an action for specific performance would take to be heard and the difficulty of making a decree effective.

(c) *Failing to Give Advice*

11–156   **Incomplete advice.** If a solicitor fails to give advice which is specifically requested, that is a clear breach of contract and a clear breach of duty.[29] However, claims of this nature seldom arise because (unless the retainer is terminated), the client usually presses the solicitor until he receives the advice which he is seeking. Claims for failure to give advice more commonly arise where the solicitor fails to give advice, which it was his duty to proffer, whether or not specifically requested[30]; or where (unknown to the client) the advice given is incomplete. An example of a solicitor giving incomplete advice is *Crossnan v Ward Bracewell & Co.*[31] The claimant was accused of reckless driving, and consulted a solicitor, who advised him that he could plead guilty unrepresented, or he could instruct the solicitor to act for him and pay £50 as a deposit against costs. The solicitor failed to inform the claimant that his insurance company would arrange and pay for his legal representation, and was held to be negligent. An allegation of failing to give advice that a particular course of action should be taken is often very closely related to an allegation of failing to take that action.[32]

11–157   **Who to advise.**[33] Where a solicitor is acting for a firm, it is generally sufficient if he conveys his advice to, and seeks instructions from, the particular partner who is handling the matter.[34] Where a solicitor is acting for husband and wife,

---

[29] If the matter is outside the solicitor's sphere of competence, he may, of course, quite properly refer the client to another solicitor or take counsel's opinion.

[30] e.g. *Stronghold Investments Ltd v Renkema* (1984) 7 D.L.R. (4th) 427, British Columbia CA: solicitor for purchaser of business failed to advise his client of the formalities necessary to transfer the fire insurance policy. A fire occurred and the claimant was uninsured.

[31] (1989) 4 P.N. 103, Kennedy J. See also *Cade v Cade* (1998) 71 S.A.S.R. 571, Full Court of South Australia, where solicitors gave advice in relation to the purchase of shares in a company by one of its directors and shareholders, who was their client, to the other. They negligently failed to read the articles of association of the company, which gave their client special rights which would probably have caused him to be able to purchase the shares at a lower value. For another example see *Campbell v Imray* [2004] P.N.L.R. 1, where the solicitors correctly advised the client that her action for damages for personal injury was statute-barred, but negligently failed to point out that there was a possibility of an application under the equivalent of s.33 of the Limitation Act 1980.

[32] e.g. *County Personnel Ltd v Alan R Pulver & Co* [1987] 1 W.L.R. 916, CA, considered at para.11–279, below.

[33] Advice to an agent with full authority is sufficient. In *Mean v Thomas* [1998] E.G.C.S. 2, QBD, the defendant solicitors were not liable to the claimant, an experienced builder, for failing to inform him of the existence of restrictive covenants over the land he intended to purchase at auction and develop. The defendants had informed the claimant's agent that it was his responsibility to satisfy himself that there was no obstruction to the proposed development.

[34] *Tomlinson v Broadsmith* [1896] 1 Q.B. 386, CA; *Sykes v Midland Bank Executor & Trustee Co Ltd* [1971] 1 Q.B. 113, CA; *Berlevy v Blyth Dutton (a firm)* [1997] E.G.C.S. 133, CA.

instructions are likely to be necessary from both.[35] Similarly, when instructed by two married couples in the purchase of property, a solicitor should not take instructions from the husband of one of the couples only, unless the three remaining parties have given him actual or ostensible authority to do so.[36] Where a solicitor engaged to act on behalf of three joint clients acts on instructions from one to the detriment of the first, he will be in serious breach of duty.[37]

As to the progress of the cause or matter. The solicitor owes a duty to inform **11–158** the client of the progress of the transaction which he is handling on the client's behalf. If he fails in this duty, the client may suffer unnecessary loss[38] or even be exposed to criminal liability.[39] In such circumstances there is unlikely to be any defence to an action for negligence. Apart from satisfying his legitimate curiosity, the client needs to know of material developments, in order to decide whether he should give further instructions to the solicitor or modify his existing instructions. Where appropriate, the solicitor should invite further instructions at the same time as informing the client of developments:

> "It is an incident of that duty[40] that the solicitor shall consult with his client in all questions of doubt which do not fall within the express or implied discretion left him, and shall keep the client informed to such an extent as may be reasonably necessary according to the same criteria."[41]

Thus in litigation a solicitor ought to inform his client of any offers of settlement made by the other party.[42] There may be some matters of pure procedure which do not need to be discussed with the client.[43]

Professional duty to inform. The duty to keep the client informed is now **11–159** reflected in the Solicitors Practice Rules 1990, r.15,[44] which requires solicitors to

---

[35] *Penn v Bristol & West Building Society* [1996] 2 F.C.R. 729, see para.11–043, above; *cf.* the outdated views expressed in *Morris v Duke-Cohan & Co* (1975) 119 S.J. 826; *The Times*, November 22, 1975: a solicitor should "not take instructions from a wife when a husband was also available". *per* Caulfield J.

[36] *Farrer v Messrs Copley-Singleton* [1998] P.N.L.R. 22, where the Court of Appeal held the defendant solicitors liable for failing to obtain instructions.

[37] *Perry v Edwin Coe, Independent,* April 1, 1994, Harman J.

[38] As in *Stinchcombe & Cooper Ltd v Addison, Cooper, Jesson & Co* (1971) 115 S.J. 368. Solicitors acted for the purchasers of land from the local authority. The contract provided that the vendors could rescind if the purchasers did not start building on the land within 12 months. The solicitors failed to inform the clients of this when contracts were exchanged (and the 12 months started to run). This failure was held to be negligent.

[39] As in *Ashton v Wainwright* [1936] 1 All E.R. 805. A solicitor acted for the officers of a club which was about to move premises. He applied to have the registration of the club transferred to the new premises, but the application was refused. He failed to communicate this to his clients, who proceeded with the move and were subsequently convicted for supplying drink at an unregistered club. The solicitor was held liable: " . . . in failing to inform the clients of the position so as to give them the chance, at any rate, of deciding whether they would risk a move, as I am satisfied they would not have done, he was clearly guilty of a breach of duty towards them", *per* Goddard J. at 809.

[40] i.e. the duty arising upon the solicitor's retainer.

[41] *per* Scott L.J. in *Groom v Crocker* [1939] 1 K.B. 194 at 222.

[42] See para.11–191.

[43] See *Beckmat Holdings Ltd v Tassou* (1982) 18 Alta. L.R. (2d) 300, Alberta CA.

[44] See The Law Society's *Guide to the Professional Conduct of Solicitors* (8th edn, 1999), p.27; the current version is on the Law Society's website.

give information about costs and other matters in accordance with the Client Care Code. The Code[45] which mostly concerns information about costs, also requires:

> "Every solicitor in private practice must ensure that the client . . . is given a clear explanation of the issues raised in a matter and is properly informed about its progress (including the likely timescale)."

This is amplified in the Law Society's *Guide to the Professional Conduct of Solicitors*[46]:

> "The solicitor should keep clients informed of the progress of matters. This may often be assisted by sending to clients copies of letters. In particular, it is important to tell clients of the reason for any serious delay. Requests for information should be answered promptly."

11–160   **In respect of matters which come to the solicitor's notice.** In the ordinary course of business a solicitor is likely to accumulate a substantial amount of information, much of which is of no interest to the client. It is the solicitor's duty, however, to identify any matters which are or may be important to the client and to bring them to his notice. In acting for a purchaser, for example, a solicitor would be negligent if he failed to advise his client of the existence of a right of way over the property[47] or of a defect in title.[48] In *Lake v Bushby*[49] the second defendant was instructed to act as solicitor for the claimant, after the claimant had contracted to purchase certain property. The solicitor discovered from a local search that there was no planning permission for a bungalow which stood upon the property, but he did not communicate this fact to the claimant. Pritchard J. held that the solicitor was in breach of duty. If a solicitor discovers that his clients are involved in a "contracts race", he ought to notify them promptly.[50]

11–161   The solicitor may reasonably decide not to burden his client with what appear to be pure legal technicalities. Provided that he takes care to explain the gist of any relevant information he has acquired or the results of his searches, that should be sufficient. In *Central Land Investments Ltd v Winn*[51] a solicitor was acting for the purchasers of a shop. He explained to them the nature of the redevelopment which was being undertaken in the vicinity of the shop and he pointed out that pedestrian traffic would be impeded. However, he did not tell his clients about the terms of a closure order affecting a nearby road, because he did not think it relevant. Melford Stevenson J. was "not prepared to differ from this view" and accordingly dismissed the claim.

11–162   **In respect of matters which he is not asked to investigate or advise upon.** In the ordinary way a solicitor is not obliged to travel outside his instructions and

---

[45] *ibid.*, p.270, para.7(a).
[46] *ibid.*, p.274, para.13.06.3.
[47] *Piper v Daybell Court-Cooper & Co* (1969) 210 E.G. 1047.
[48] *Pilkington v Wood* [1953] Ch. 770 (negligence admitted), Ch. D.
[49] [1949] 2 All E.R. 964.
[50] *Nash v Phillips* (1974) 232, E.G. 1219, Ch. D. For the professional obligations of a seller's solicitors in such circumstances, see r.6A of the Solicitors' Practice Rules 1990, discussed *in Jenmain v Steed* [2000] P.N.L.R. 616, CA.
[51] (1972) 223 E.G. 2334.

make investigations which are not expressly or impliedly requested by the client.[52] In *Clark Boyce v Mouat*[53] the Privy Council considered that where the client who was in full command of her faculties, and apparently aware of what she was doing, sought the assistance of a solicitor in the carrying out of a particular transaction, the solicitor is under no duty to go beyond those instructions by proffering unsought advice on the wisdom of the transaction.[54] While there are a number of cases which illustrate this principle,[55] it is not possible to lay down any hard and fast rule.[56]

---

[52] In *Pickersgill v Riley* [2004] UKPC 14 [2004] P.N.L.R. 31 the Privy Council held that this sentence correctly states the position. In that case, the defendant solicitors owed no duty to an experienced businessman who was entering a personal guarantee to advise him on the financial prudence of the project. They advised him in general terms about the risk of taking a guarantee from a limited company. See also Bingham L.J.'s views in *Mortgage Express Ltd v Bowerman & Partners* [1996] 2 All E.R. 836 at 842, quoted at para.11–210, below.

[53] [1994] 1 A.C. 428, at 437D.

[54] This is consistent with the House of Lords decision in *Royal Bank of Scotland Plc v Etridge (No.2)*, [2002] 2 A.C. 773, on which see para.11–207. The Privy Council's decision was applied by Harrison J. in *Bindon v Bishop* [2003] N.Z.L.R. 136. The defendant solicitor's retainer in that case was to provide advice on the legal risks and liabilities of the proposed guarantor, and he had no obligation to proffer advice on the wisdom of the transaction. See further para.11–170, below on the question of advice on the wisdom of a transaction.

[55] See the following further examples: *2475813 Nova Scotia Ltd v Lundrigan* (2003) 213 N.S.R. (2d) 53, Nova Scotia Supreme Court (a lawyer was presented with an agreement that his client had negotiated to sell her flat, and did not ask for any advice on it; he had no duty to draw the client's attention to a particular clause requiring her to release a prior mortgage and advise her on it); *Amersfort Ltd v Kelly Nichols & Blayney* [1996] E.G.C.S. 156, Ch. D (defendant solicitors answered the three questions asked of them, but had not been asked to review the claimants' lease generally; they had no duty to bring to the clients' attention any unusual features of the lease beyond answering the three questions); *Bartter v Gambrill* (1932) 76 S.J. 868 (claimant agreed with S, an adjoining landowner, to exchange part of her garden for a portion of S's land; after the agreement was made, the defendant solicitor was instructed to carry out the conveyancing, but the claimant subsequently regretted the transaction; Luxmoore J. held that "a solicitor was not obliged to point out to the person instructing him that he was not legally bound to carry out his bargain."); *Griffiths v Evans* [1953] 1 W.L.R. 1424 (claimant sustained an accident at work and thereafter received weekly payments from his employers under the Workmen's Compensation Acts, and consulted the defendant solicitor, because he feared a reduction of the weekly payments; they advised the claimant in respect of his claim under the Workmen's Compensation Acts, but not whether he had a claim for damages at common law in respect of the accident; the Court of Appeal (Denning L.J. dissenting) held that the defendant was not negligent); *Woodward v Wolferstans (a firm)*, *The Times*, April 8, 1997; [1997] N.P.C. 51 (defendant solicitors were retained by the claimant's father in relation to the purchase of property, where he was acting as guarantor; while they owed her a duty of care, there was no breach in failing to explain the details of the transaction to her, as the retainer from the father was simply to secure a good and marketable title).

[56] For a contrary case where the solicitor was held liable, see *Goody v Baring* [1956] 1 W.L.R. 448. The defendant was acting for the purchaser of a residential property, two floors of which were let to tenants. He ascertained from the vendor what rents were being paid by the tenants, but did not go on to check what were the standard rents fixed under the Rent Restriction Acts. In fact these were lower than the actual rents, with the result that the tenants subsequently recovered from the purchaser the amount of their overpayments. Danckwerts J. held that the defendant was in breach of duty in failing to make proper enquiries about the standard rent and to give the claimant "plain and clear advice" in that regard. *cf. Cady v Hanson* (1989) 51 D.L.R. (4th) 139, British Columbia CA: a solicitor acted for purchaser of property which turned out to have zoning problems; held that he had no reason to scrutinise the interim agreement for defects which might make it void, and thus he was not negligent in not advising the claimant that it might be void. See also the obiter discussion of the Court of Appeal in *Hall v Meyrick* [1957] 2 Q.B. 455 as to whether advice should be given to a couple that marriage would revoke the will the solicitor was retained to prepare.

11–163   **Statements of principle in this regard.** In *Carradine Properties Ltd v D J Freeman & Co*,[57] the claimants engaged contractors to demolish a building in Clacton. The contractors damaged an adjoining property, thereby exposing the claimants to liability. The claimants instructed the defendant solicitors to make a claim against the contractors and, subsequently, to consider making a claim against the estate agents who had selected those contractors. The claimants did not inform the defendants that they themselves had an insurance policy covering the incident and they did not ask the defendants to consider the claimants' insurance position. The Court of Appeal held that the defendants were not negligent in failing to think of the point themselves and to proffer advice upon it. Lord Denning M.R. attached importance to the fact that the claimants' managing director was very experienced in insurance matters. Donaldson L.J. said that the precise scope of the duty to advise would depend, inter alia, upon the extent to which the client appeared to need advice:

> "An inexperienced client will need and will be entitled to expect the solicitor to take a much broader view of the scope of his retainer and of his duties than will be the case with an experienced client."[58]

Oliver J. considered these questions in *Midland Bank v Hett, Stubbs & Kemp*[59] and formulated the general principle in these terms:

> " . . . the court must beware of imposing upon solicitors—or upon professional men in other spheres—duties which go beyond the scope of what they are requested and undertake to do. It may be that a particularly meticulous and conscientious practitioner would, in his client's general interest, take it upon himself to pursue a line of enquiry beyond the strict limits comprehended by his instructions. But that is not the test. The test is what the reasonably competent practitioner would do having regard to the standards normally adopted in his profession, and cases such as *Duchess of Argyll v Beuselinck* [1972] 2 Lloyd's Rep. 172; *Griffiths v Evans* [1953] 1 W.L.R. 1424 and *Hall v Meyrick* [1957] 2 Q.B. 455 demonstrate that the duty is directly related to the confines of the retainer."[60]

This should be contrasted with the dictum of the Court of Appeal of New Zealand in *Gilbert v Shanahan*, which it is submitted is consistent with the views of Oliver J.[61]:

---

[57] [1999] Lloyd's Rep. P.N. 48; [1955–1995] P.N.L.R. 12. In *John Mowlem Construction Plc v Neil F Jones & Co (a firm)* [2004] EWCA Civ 768; [2004] P.N.L.R. 925 the Court of Appeal similarly found that the defendants had no duty to inquire into and advise the clients about insurance issues. Judge L.J. emphasised that the professional obligations in this regard were fact specific. In *Cote v Rancourt* (2004) 244 D.L.R. (4th) 25 the defendant acted for the claimant in her criminal trial connected with a fire at her place of business. She sued him for failing to advise her to bring an action against her insurer within the limitation period. The defendant was ignorant of the civil law, and advised the claimant to consult another lawyer who specialised in it. The Supreme Court of Canada held that the lawyer was not negligent.

[58] [1999] Lloyd's Rep. P.N. 483 at 487 col.2, and see Lord Denning's similar remarks at 486. The view was adopted in *RP Howard Ltd v Woodman Matthews* [1983] B.C.L.C. 117 at 121–122, Staughton J.

[59] [1979] Ch. 384.

[60] *ibid.* at 402–403.

[61] [1988] 3 N.Z.L.R. 528. The solicitor, who was instructed in respect of a lease and guarantee, should have advised his client that he did not have any obligation to sign the guarantee, although the client had not expressly sought advice on the matter.

"Solicitors' duties are govered by the scope of their retainer, but it would be unreasonable and artificial to define that scope by reference only to the client's express instructions. Matters which fairly and reasonably arise in the course of carrying out those instructions must be regarded as coming within the scope of the retainer."

An illustration. In *Investors Compensation Scheme Ltd v West Bromwich Building Society*[62] a number of individuals had entered Home Income Plans, whereby they remortgaged their houses and the proceeds were invested, supplying an income. The interest on the mortgage was generally not paid, but was added to the amount secured. Rising property prices were supposed to keep the amount owed within 40 or 50 per cent of the value of the property. The scheme did not succeed, and the individuals suffered heavy losses. In complex proceedings brought by investors and their assignees, Evans-Lombe J. considered the scope of the duties owed by the solicitors in such transactions. They were instructed by the lenders to complete the mortgage transactions, and also by the investors. Most of the investors had taken out mortgages before, and therefore were not to be treated as ignorant or inexperienced. The solicitors were often justified in taking the view that the investors would be familiar with the usual provisions of a mortgage securing a loan on property. The solicitors plainly owed a duty to explain the unusual provisions whereby the interest was rolled-up, and the factors which might affect the performance of the scheme such as fluctuations in property prices and interest rates. They had no duty to advise on the merits of the transaction, or speculate as to how property prices and interests rates may vary in the future, as that was not part of their expertise, and the investors were advised by FIMBRA-registered financial advisers. 11–164

As to the solicitor's own negligence. In *Gold v Mincoff Science & Gold (a firm)*[63] Neuberger J. held that it would be a relatively exceptional case where a solicitor would have a duty to advise that he had been negligent on an earlier occasion, otherwise an onerous implied general retainer would be imposed on the solicitor. However, on the facts of that case the solicitors should have investigated the draft mortgages the client was going to enter, and they would have been led back to consider earlier mortgages he had entered and as a result they would have been obliged to advise the client that they had been negligent and he should seek separate legal advice. The judge relied on the solicitor's professional duty, where he discovers an action or omission which would justify a claim, to inform 11–165

---

[62] [1999] Lloyd's Rep. P.N. 496. For another example see *Accident Assistance Ltd v Hammonds Suddards Edge (a firm)* [2005] EWHC 202; [2005] P.N.L.R. 29. The claimants operated a credit hire business, hiring vehicles to motorists whose vehicles had been disabled in accidents, the costs being claimed in litigation against the motorist responsible for the accident. The defendant solicitors relayed leading counsel's advice that the repair agreements were regulated under the Consumer Credit Act and were not compliant. Hart J. held that the defendants had no duty to the experienced claimants to explain the ramifications of that advice, which were that the agreements would be totally unenforceable and that third party insurers could prevent recovery against them of the hire charges.

[63] [2001] Lloyd's Rep. P.N. 423. For a similar case see *Tucker v Allen Co (a firm)* [2001] P.N.L.R. 884, QBD, where solicitors failed to notice that there was no practicable access to the property the claimants were purchasing in 1988, and when a dispute arose about a right of way four years later they negligently failed to mention their own earlier default.

the client that he should seek independent legal advice.[64] In *Ezekiel v Lehrer*[65] the Court of Appeal appeared to accept that there was a duty upon a solicitor to advise his client that he had been negligent or ought to seek alternative advice to establish whether he had been negligent, but only where the solicitor knew or ought to have known that he was guilty of an earlier breach of duty.

11-166   **The duty to warn against particular risks.** There is generally a duty to point out any hazards of the kind which should be obvious to the solicitor but which the client, as a layman, may not appreciate.[66] In *Boyce v Rendells*[67] the Court of Appeal accepted the following as a general proposition:

> "If, in the course of taking instructions, a professional man like a land agent or a solicitor learns of facts which reveal to him as a professional man the existence of obvious risks, then he should do more than merely advise within the strict limits of his retainer. He should call attention to and advise upon the risks."[68]

By way of example, solicitors have been held negligent for: failing to warn a purchaser of property of the risks which he ran by moving in and carrying out works of repair before contracts were exchanged[69]; failing to advise clients of the dangers which they ran by exchanging contracts for the purchase of new property, before the prospective purchaser of their existing property had paid a deposit[70]; failing to warn the client of numerous risks involved in a conveyancing

---

[64] This is now para.29.09 in the Law Society's *Guide to the Professional Conduct of Solicitors* (8th edn, 1999). If there is a conflict of interest, then the solicitor is plainly bound not to continue to act. However the proposed legal duty to inform the client that the solicitor has been negligent may contradict *Bell v Lever Bros* [1932] A.C. 161, although in practice this is bound to emerge when the advice that they can no longer act or that the client should seek independent legal advice is given. In Canada there is such a duty, see *Vienneau v Arsenault* (1982) 41 N.B.R. (2d) 82, New Brunswick CA.

[65] [2002] Lloyd's Rep. P.N. 260 at para.24.

[66] *cf. Gosfield School Ltd v Birkett Long (a firm)* [2005] EWHC 2905; [2006] P.N.L.R. 19, noted at Ch.12, para.12–033, where the risk was not sufficiently significant to require warning. Contrast also *Foshan Hua Da Industrial Co v Johnson, Stokes & Master (a firm)* [1999] HKLRD 418. The claimant retained the defendant solicitors to prepare the documentation in respect of a loan it intended to make for the development of land on the security of shares in a company. The defendants advised the claimant not to proceed with the loan until the share certificate was produced, and advised that a legal mortgage over the shares was preferable to an equitable one. The High Court of Hong Kong held that the defendants were not negligent in failing to alert their clients to the possibility that the shares had been pledged elsewhere, nor for failing to detail the additional powers of a legal mortgage.

[67] (1983) 268 E.G. 268.

[68] *ibid.* at 272, col.2. In *Credit Lyonnais SA v Russell Jones & Walker (a firm)* [2002] EWHC 1310; [2003] P.N.L.R. 2, Laddie J. relied on this dictum, and held that it was not in conflict with the principle set out in *Clarke Boyce v Mouat* (see para.11–162, above) or the dictum of Bingham M.R. in *Mortgage Express Ltd v Bowerman & Partners* (see para.11–210, below). In any event, the terms of the particular solicitor's retainer when instructed in relation to the exercise of a break option in the lease included reading the break clause, and he should have advised that the payment required under it was a condition precedent. The dictum was also applied in *Keith v Davidson Chalmers* [2003] P.N.L.R. 10, OH, where a solicitor acting for the pursuer, who was setting up a property venture, failed to warn him that he may be in breach of his duties as director of an established property company.

[69] *Attard v Samson* (1966) 110 S.J. 249, QBD. For another example, see *Yazhou Travel Investment Co Ltd* [2005] P.N.L.R. 31, Hong Kong High Court, where the solicitors realised that the right to name a building would not run with the land, and devised a scheme to make the right enforceable. They should have advised that the validity of the scheme was open to question.

[70] *Morris v Duke-Cohan & Co* (1975) 119 S.J. 826; *The Times*, November 22, 1975, QBD.

transaction[71]; failing to warn a mortgagee of the risk of lending money when the mortgage could not be registered[72]; failing to warn the assignee of an insolvent debtor of the risk which he ran in costs from the continued prosecution of an action[73]; failing to warn trustees of circumstances which may render them personally liable for the loss of trust moneys[74]; failing to advise lessees of premises that the user permitted in the proposed sub-lease would (or at least might) infringe the head-lease[75]; failing to warn a businessman whose business he had just incorporated of the need to use the full corporate name[76]; and failing to warn the owner of a business of the risks of transferring the shares to an investor most of which were to be held on trust for the owner, with the owner being employed as manager. A solicitor instructed in a contentious matter ought always to consider the merits of his client's case. If he considers the proposed claim or defence to be hopeless, he should say so, whether or not he is asked to advise on the merits.[77] In *Queen Elizabeth's Grammar School Blackburn Ltd v Banks Wilson (a firm)*,[78] a solicitor advised a school that the meaning of a restrictive covenant, which limited the construction of any building to no greater in height than the buildings already existing on the property, should be construed as including the chimney pots and not just the roofline. The solicitor knew that a dispute was potentially to emerge with a neighbour about the effect of the clause. The Court of Appeal held that he was negligent in failing to advise that there was a risk as to what was the true construction of the clause, as the arguments against his construction were of sufficient significance.

---

[71] *Major v Buchanan* (1975) 9 O.R. (2d) 491, Ontario High Court; *Graybriar Industries Ltd v Davis & Co* (1992) 46 B.C.L.R. (2d) 164, British Columbia Supreme Court.

[72] *Income Trust Co v Watson* (1984) 26 B.L.R. 228, Ontario Hight Court.

[73] *Allison v Rayner* (1827) 7 B.C. 441.

[74] *Re A Solicitor Ex p. Incorporated Law Society* (1895) S.J. 219. See also *Stokes v Prance* [1898] 1 Ch. 212 at 223–225, Stirling J., as to the solicitor's duty when advising trustees who are lending trust funds, and *Austrust Pty Ltd v Astley* (1993) 60 S.A.S.R. 354, South Australia Supreme Court.

[75] *CW Dixey & Sons Ltd v Parsons* (1964) 192 E.G. 197, QBD. See also the restaurant cases referred to in the next paragraph. *Park Hall School v Overend* [1987] 2 I.R. 1, Irish High Court, is a surprising contrast to the cases cited above. A solicitor acted for a school in the proposed sale of land. The land had previously been sold at auction, although the sale had not gone ahead. Given the uncertain state of the law, it was not clear whether there existed a binding contract with the original proposed purchaser. The solicitor was found not to be negligent when he failed to warn his client that it might be already liable to convey the property, given that the original proposed purchaser had given no suggestion that he would assert his possible rights.

[76] *Turi v Swanik* (2002) 61 O.R. (3d), Ontario Superior Court.

[77] The last two sentences were cited with approval by the High Court of Hong Kong in *Delhaise v Ng & Co* [2004] 1 HKLRD 573, para.50. In *May v Mijatovic* [2002] WASC 151; (2002) 26 W.A.R. 95, Hasluck J. held that a solicitor who was instructed to apply for an injunction at short notice with insufficient time to read the documents presented to him should have warned the claimant of the risks associated with the application and the signing of an undertaking as to damages, and should have reviewed the documents in the time available and given a view as to the merits. See also *Jacks v Bell* (1828) 3 C. & P. 316; *Holmes v National Benzole Co* (1968) 109 S.J. 971:

> "A solicitor who, without any investigation of his client's claim, allowed or encouraged a client
> to pursue a claim which proper investigation would at an early stage have shown to be a hopeless
> one was in breach of duty to his client . . . ", (*per* Lyell J.).

[78] [2001] EWCA Civ 1360; [2002] P.N.L.R. 14. For criticism of the decision, see S. Gee, "The Solicitor's duty to warn that a court might take a different view" (2003) 19 P.N. 363.

11–167   **Explanation of legal documents.** One of the principal areas in which the client looks to his solicitor for guidance is in the explanation of legal documents. Normally, the client either signs such documents or permits them to be sent on his behalf in reliance upon the solicitor's advice. The solicitor owes a general duty to explain such documents to the client, or at least to ensure that he understands the material parts.[79] The solicitor's duty to explain legal documents is reflected in the Law Society's guidance[80]:

> "Solicitors should normally explain to clients the effect of important and relevant documents."

In the case of a will, a solicitor should take particular care to ensure that the client understands and agrees to its provisions.[81] With an experienced business client it may not be necessary to do this.[82] In particular, a solicitor should explain any unusual provisions[83] or any provisions of particular relevance to the client's proposed activities.[84] In *Sykes v Midland Bank Executor & Trustee Co Ltd*[85] the claimants took an underlease of office premises. The effect of one provision in

---

[79] e.g. *Watts v Hyde* (1846) 2 Coll. 368 at 380–381; *Meadows v Meadows* (1853) 16 Beav. 401; *Anderson v Elsworth* (1861) 3 Giff. 154 at 169: an attorney had to explain all the difference between a will and a deed when the client wanted to leave property by deed. *Clarence Construction Ltd v Lavallee* (1980) 111 D.L.R. (3d) 582 and (1982) 132 D.L.R. (3d) 153, British Columbia CA; *Booth v Davey* (1988) 138 N.L.J. 104, CA; *Donmez v Barnes* [1996] E.G.C.S. 129; *Titanic Investments v McFarlanes* [1997] N.P.C. 105, Ch. D.: there is a duty to give a proper explanation of any documents requiring signature, and where document were not to be signed by the client to ensure there were instructions to accept them based on an adequate explanation of their contents; risks which would not be obvious to a layman should be draw to the client's attention.

[80] The Law Society's *Guide to the Professional Conduct of Solicitors* (8th edn, 1999), p.274, para.13.04 n.5; the current *Guide* can be found on the Law Society website.

[81] See further para.11–222.

[82] *Aslan v Clintons* (1984) 134 N.L.J. 584, Leonard J.

[83] *Stannard v Ullithorne* (1834) 10 Bing. 491:

> "An attorney . . . is bound to take care, that his client does not enter into any covenant or stipulation that may expose him to a greater degree of responsibility than is ordinarily attached to the business in hand, or, at all events, that he does not do so till the consequences have been explained to him",

per Tindal C.J.; *Phillips v Millings* (1871) 7 Ch.App. 244; see also *Flandro v Mitha* (1992) 93 D.L.R. (4th) 222, British Columbia Supreme Court, (conveyancing notary failed to draw unusual rent revision clause to the attention of the purchaser). Thus solicitors were liable for failing to explain to their client that a proposed lease had been changed so that tenant's improvements were to be taken into account at rent reviews, see *Sonardyne Ltd v Firth & Co* [1997] E.G.C.S. 84, QBD.

[84] *Transportation Agency Ltd v Jenkins* (1972) 223 E.G. 1101, Kerr J.: clients proposed to use premises as a restaurant. Solicitor's clerk failed to point out that there was a covenant prohibiting cooking; *Simple Simon Catering Ltd v Binstock Miller & Co* (1973) 228 E.G. 527, CA: clients proposed to use premises as a restaurant. Solicitors failed to point out or explain a covenant whereby the landlords, or persons licensed by them, were permitted to share the use of the kitchen. However, there are obviously limits as to how far an explanation should go. In *Masons (a firm) v WD King Ltd* [2003] EWHC 3124, TCC; (2004) 92 Con.L.R. 144 the claimant solicitors adapted a clause in a standard building project to provide further mechanisms to enable the project manager to ensure that the contractor constructed the building in time, as it was vitally important that there was no significant delay in completion. They explained how the new clause worked in some detail, but did not say whether breach of the clause would give rise to unliquidated damages, or only the agreed liquidated damages. H.H. Judge Humphrey Lloyd Q.C. held that they had no such duty, particularly as the extent of the actual losses were only known after the condition had been drafted, and it was quite unclear what the answer would be.

[85] [1971] 1 Q.B. 113, CA.

the underlease was that whereas the sub-lessor could not unreasonably withhold his consent to a change of user, the head-lessor could do so. The solicitors failed to explain this to the claimants and it was held that they were thereby in breach of duty:

> "When a solicitor is asked to advise on a leasehold title it is, in my judgment, his duty to call his client's attention to clauses in an unusual form which may affect the interests of his client as he knows them."[86]

The Federal Court of Australia has formulated a solicitor's duty to explain legal documents in similar terms,[87] expressly relying upon *Sykes v Midland Bank Executor & Trustee Co Ltd*.[88]

There must of course be a sensible limit upon the solicitor's duty to explain **11–168** legal documents. When any such document (even a familiar document in common use) is put under the microscope, it will be found to abound with ambiguities, generalities or potential problems. In *Walker v Boyle*[89] Dillon J. rejected the contention that a solicitor acting for the purchaser of a house ought to advise his client of the implications of condition 17 of the National Conditions of Sale (19th edn). He put the matter in this way:

> "It is, of course, the duty of a solicitor to advise his client about any abnormal or unusual term in a contract, but I think it is perfectly normal and proper for a solicitor to use standard forms of conditions of sale such as the National Conditions of Sale. I do not think he is called on to go through the small print of those somewhat lengthy conditions with a toothcomb every time he is advising a purchaser to draw the purchaser's attention to every problem which on a careful reading of the conditions might in some circumstance or other conceivably arise. I cannot believe that purchasers of house property throughout the land would be overjoyed at having such lengthy explanations of the National Conditions of Sale ritually foisted upon them."[90]

Reminders. As a general rule, there is no duty on a solicitor to remind a client **11–169** of advice once it has been given. In *Yager v Fishman & Co*[91] the claimant's

---

[86] [1971] 1 Q.B. 113, CA at 124B, *per* Harman L.J. This dictum was cited in *County Personnel Ltd v Alan R Pulver & Co* [1987] 1 W.L.R. 916, CA, where the claimants took an underlease which had an unusual rent review lease whereby the rent was increased at the same percentage as the headlease. The defendant solicitors were held negligent in failing to advise the claimants of the risks they faced. See para.11–279 for further facts. In contrast, in *Commercial Bridging Plc v Nelsons* [1998] C.L.Y. 4018, Ch. D., the defendant solicitor was held to have no obligation to a sophisticated commercial client to explain a short and straightforward deed of priority of which it was aware.

[87] *Fox v Everingham* (1983) 50 A.L.R. 337 at 341.

[88] [1971] 1 Q.B. 113.

[89] [1982] 1 W.L.R. 495.

[90] *ibid.* at 507H–508A. In *Citibank Savings Ltd v Nicholson* (1997) 70 S.A.S.R. 206 Perry J. suggested that going through a guarantee clause by clause would be very misleading to a lay person, and a solicitor should give a clear account in summary of the salient features of the transaction.

[91] [1944] 1 All E.R. 552. See also *West London Observer v Parsons* (1955) 166 E.G. 749, QBD. The defendant solicitors acted for lessees. The lease could be renewed if the lessees gave notice on March 25, 1953 and were not, on that date, in breach of covenant. The defendants explained the provisions for renewal both in a letter dated October 1950 and during an interview in April 1951. It was held that the defendants were not negligent in failing to repeat that advice in or shortly before March 1953. For another illustration see *Atkins v Dunn & Baker (a firm)* [2004] EWCA Civ 263; [2004] W.T.L.R. 477, where the Court of Appeal held that a solicitor who had sent a draft will to the testator had no duty to chase the client up, although there may be such a duty in some circumstances.

company held a 21-year lease of premises, under which the claimant guaranteed the payment of rent. The lease could be terminated early if the company gave notice on or before December 24, 1940. In October 1940 the claimant asked his solicitors whether he could get his liability under the guarantee postponed. They replied that there was no way he could get out of his liabilities "at present". They did not go on to remind him that by giving notice before December 24 he could determine the underlease, nor did they advise him that he should take this course. The question of termination had been specifically referred to in earlier correspondence, and the Court of Appeal held that the solicitors were not negligent in failing to remind the claimant of the date by which notice should be given:

" . . . the respondent's solicitors were not bound to supply deficiencies in their client's memory unless they were clearly requested to do so. I am by no means sure that Yager would have welcomed a bill of costs which included charges for reminding him unasked of dates which he might be assumed to have in mind."[92]

Similarly, in *Elland Developments Ltd v Smith*[93] the defendant solicitors had advised a property development company before exchange of contracts about the risks involved in purchasing property with possessory title only, and the need to seek better evidence of title. Rattee J. held that they had no duty to repeat such advice after exchange of contracts. The rule is not an invariable one. In *RP Howard Ltd v Woodman Matthews*[94] the defendant solicitors were instructed by the claimants in relation to a business tenancy which was expiring. When first instructed in October 1975, the solicitors told their clients of the need to initiate an application to the county court to obtain a new tenancy under the provisions of the 1954 Landlord and Tenant Act Pt II. Negotiations then took place between the solicitors and their client's landlord. Staughton J. found that the solicitors were negligent in not reminding their client of the need to make the application to the court.

11–170   **Advice on matters of business.**[95] A solicitor is not a general adviser on matters of business (unless he specifically agrees to act in that capacity). Thus he is not generally under a duty to advise whether, legal considerations apart, the transaction which he is instructed to carry out is a prudent one,[96] or whether the

---

[92] *per* Du Parcq L.J. [1944] 1 All E.R. 552 at 558.

[93] [1995] E.G.C.S. 141.

[94] [1983] B.C.L.C. 117.

[95] One common problem which, strictly, falls under this heading is whether the solicitor for a lender should advise on the adequacy of the security. This is discussed in paras 11–210 to 11–212. For a criticism of this analysis of the law, see N. Patten, "The solicitor's liability for failing to spot mortgage fraud" (1995) 11 P.N. 2.

[96] See *Clarke v Boyce Mouat* [1994] 1 A.C. 428 and *Pickersgill v Riley* [2004] UKPC 14; [2004] P.N.L.R. 31 noted at para.11–162, above. For a further example, see *Rendel v Edgelow* (1909) 53 S.J. 237, Neville J.: solicitor acted for the purchaser of property intended as an investment. The purchaser subsequently alleged that the bargain was a bad one and the claimant was negligent in failing to advise against it, but the claim was dismissed. In *Bowdage v Harold Michelmore & Co* (1962) 106 S.J. 512 the claimant granted a six-month option to P to purchase a piece of land for £400, which was twice extended. Before the final expiry of the option the claimant received a much higher offer from a third party, which she was unable to accept since P then exercised the option. Melford Stevenson J. held that the solicitor had no duty to advise whether the transaction was a prudent or to recommend that she should consult an independent valuer. See also *Dunn v Fairs, Blissard, Barnes & Stowe* (1961) 105 S.J. 932: a solicitor accepted instructions from a woman aged 77 and dying of cancer to

other party is solvent and whether guarantees should be sought.[97] In *Yager v Fishman & Co*[98] one of the allegations against the solicitors was that they were negligent in failing to advise the claimant that he ought to determine the lease rather than keep it in existence and try to find a suitable tenant. The Court of Appeal rejected this contention. Scott L.J. pointed out that the solicitors were not specifically asked to advise on this question, and continued:

> "To impose on a solicitor the legal responsibility of answering such a business question would require both unequivocal instructions and unqualified acceptance; for it is no part of a solicitor's normal duty to profess the skill and experience for giving such advice."[99]

Goddard L.J. expressed the same view,[1] although he attached more weight to the fact that the claimant was an experienced business man:

> "The nature and amount of advice which, in a matter of this sort, a solicitor would be expected to give to a person wholly unacquainted with business may differ very materially from what he would offer to an experienced business man, who would naturally decide for himself the course he thought it in his interest to take."[2]

A similar approach was adopted by the Court of Appeal in *Carradine Proper-* **11–171** *ties Ltd v DJ Freeman & Co.*[3] Eveleigh L.J. rejected the contention that the defendant solicitors should have advised the claimants to consider whether they were insured in respect of the damage which had occurred. He stated:

> "The management of the company was well known to the defendants and they cannot be expected to tell the management to do that which commonsense would have told them to do as a simple matter of business."[4]

Similarly, in *Virgin Management v De Morgan*[5] solicitors were instructed by Virgin to carry a sale and development agreement into effect. The Court of Appeal held that the solicitors had no duty to advise their clients to try to negotiate a better deal by getting the purchaser to agree to pay VAT or to warn the clients that they may have to pay VAT.

---

purchase an annuity. She died before the first payment was due. Barry J. held that the solicitor was not negligent. But there were special circumstances, in that the client was unaware of her condition, and the solicitor had no wish to alarm her, see para.11–099. For a useful summary of the law, see *Law v Cunningham & Co (a firm)* [1993] E.G.C.S. 126.

[97] See *Football League Ltd v Edge Ellison (a firm)* [2006] EWHC 1462, Ch; [2006] All E.R. (D) 263, relying on *Pickersgill* above.

[98] [1944] 1 All E.R. 552. The facts are set out in para.11–169.

[99] *ibid.* at 555.

[1] *ibid.* at 557–558.

[2] *ibid.* at 556.

[3] [1999] Lloyd's Rep. P.N. 483; [1955–1995] P.N.L.R. 12. The facts are set out in para.11–163, above.

[4] *ibid.* at 487.

[5] [1996] N.P.C. 8. For another example see *Hallmark Financel Insurance Brokers Ltd v Fraser & Beatty* (1991) 1 O.R. (3d) 641, Ontario High Court.: a solicitor interpreted a letter of intent in a particular way when drafting an agreement. He could assume that his experienced business clients would check that their instructions were being discharged when reading the agreement.

11–172   **An exception.** *Neushul v Mellish & Harkavy*[6] is an example of a case in which solicitors were held to be negligent for failing to give "business" advice. The claimant, a widow, proposed to lend a substantial sum of money to F, a confidence trickster. F told her that he was contemplating marrying her, but gave no firm commitment. The claimant consulted the defendant solicitors for assistance in raising the money which she proposed to lend to F. The solicitors had previously acted for F and had some knowledge of his financial affairs. The Court of Appeal, by a majority, held that the solicitors were negligent in failing adequately to warn her against making the loan:

" . . . a solicitor who was carrying out a transaction for a client was not justified in expressing no opinion when it was plain that the client was rushing into an unwise, not to say disastrous, adventure"

(*per* Danckwerts L.J.). The facts of this case are unusual. The decision is consistent with dicta in the subsequent Court of Appeal case of *Carradine Properties v DJ Freeman & Co*[7] to the effect that the duty to advise is wider where the client is obviously inexperienced or in need of advice.

11–173   **Difficulty of drawing a distinction.** The distinction between legal and business matters is a question of degree. Thus in *County Personnel Ltd v Alan R Pulver & Co*[8] the claimants took an underlease which had an unusual rent review lease whereby the rent was increased at the same percentage as the headlease. The defendant solicitors were found to be negligent in failing to advise the claimants of the risks they faced unless the initial rents were known, because the mesne lessor might, as happened, have no reason to hold out for as low a rent as possible, for his lease was cheaper than the underlease which was at a considerably inflated value. They should have advised that both rents should be ascertained, and that the market level of rents should be investigated. Bingham L.J. said:

"I cannot accept the distinction drawn between legal consequences and financial implications, because in this case the significance of the legal consequences lay in the financial implications."[9]

The case should be contrasted with *Reeves v Thrings & Long*.[10] The claimant, who was a businessman, wished to purchase a hotel. His solicitors, the defendants, advised him that access to the hotel car park was by licence only, with no guarantee of renewal if and when the licence was brought to an end. A majority

---

[6] (1967) 111 S.J. 399. Similarly, in *O'Brien v Hooker Homes* (1993) A.S.C. 56–217, Supreme Court NSW a solicitor who arranged finance for the purchase of property by simple clients owed a duty to spell out the workings of their interest obligations.

[7] [1999] Lloyd's Rep. P.N. 483; [1955–1995] P.N.L.R. 12. For the facts of this case see paras 11–163 and 11–171, above. For a further example of the difference in the advice which should be given to experienced and inexperienced clients, see *Haigh v Wright Hassall & Co* [1994] E.G.C.S. 54. For the facts see para.11–201.

[8] [1987] 1 W.L.R. 916. See also comment by D. Clarke, (1987) 3 P.N. 40.

[9] *ibid.* at 924A. Similarly, Laskin J.A. held that legal and business advice was intermingled on some transactions, such as advice on negotiating security for a warranty on the purchase of property, see *Wong v 407527 Ontario Ltd* (1999) 26 R.P.R. (3d) 262, Ontario CA.

[10] [1996] 1 P.N.L.R. 265.

of the Court of Appeal considered that there was no duty on the solicitor to advise his client upon the commercial implications or risks of the access provisions. Unlike the clause in *County Personnel Ltd v Alan R Pulver & Co*, the implications of this clause were obvious. Similarly, in *Forbouys v Gadhavi*[11] the purchasers of property had considerable business experience. Their solicitors advised them about the date of the rent review. They were not negligent in preventing them taking the commercial risk to proceed with the purchase without knowledge of the figure under the rent review.

Unequal transactions. A solicitor may act for one party in circumstances **11-174** where the other is unrepresented and the transaction is potentially to the disadvantage of the latter. Common examples are guarantees, purchases of council houses under the right to buy scheme which are assisted by relations, and gifts. If there are indications that the donor might lack capacity to understand the document she was signing, the solicitor may owe a duty to his client, and potentially to the donor, to ensure that there is a medical examination to ascertain whether there is sufficient capacity.[12]

The importance of attendance notes and written communication. However **11-175** admirable and comprehensive the advice which a solicitor gives, it is of no benefit to his defence unless it can be proved what advice was given. The solicitor is unlikely to recall after a period of several years what advice he gave to his client on a routine matter. The best he can do is to describe his usual advice in the particular circumstances or to speculate as to what he "must" have said, which is unlikely to carry as much weight as the recollection of the claimant.[13] There is no substitute for a proper attendance note, recording the gist of the advice that was given. The lack of attendance notes has materially increased the number of successful claims that are brought against solicitors.[14] It is prudent to confirm advice and instructions in writing. The Law Society recommends that "Solicitors should consider whether it is appropriate to confirm in writing the

---

[11] [1993] N.P.C. 122.

[12] See *Dark v Boock* [1991] 1 N.Z.L.R. 496 at 500, *per* Heron J. See also para.11-221, below.

[13] See, e.g. *Goody v Baring* [1956] 1 W.L.R. 448 at 452, Danckwerts J. *cf.* the position with doctors: Ch.13, para.13-101. For an illustration see *Alliance & Leicester Building Society v Chopra* [1994] N.P.C. 52. The defendant solicitor claimed to have informed the claimant lender that the cash price being paid for shares in a hotel company was £2.6m. and not the £6m. that the proposed purchaser had told them, although there was no confirmatory letter or attendance note. It was argued that the evidence should be rejected as incredible, as the claimant would have immediately re-examined the proposed loan. A majority of the Court of Appeal granted unconditional leave to defend, as there were lurking doubts about whether the building society would have immediately reexamined the loan if so advised.

[14] The last two sentences were cited with approval by the Hong Kong High Court in *Delhaise v Ng & Co* [2004] 1 HKLRD 573, para.51. The defendant solicitors claimed that they had given advice on the poor merits of the claimant's case, but they had no attendance note to support that. However, two barristers had later given the same advice, and the defendants' evidence was accepted, as it was in *Lie Hendri Rusli v Wong Tan & Molly Lim (a firm)* [2004] 4 S.L.R. 594, Singapore High Court. On the issue of attendance notes see also N. von Benzon, "Avoiding solicitor's negligence" *Law Society Gazette*, May 29, 1985, p.1559. See also para.11-006 on the advisability of a written retainer.

advice given and the instructions received."[15] In *Robins v Meadows & Moran*[16] solicitors acted for lessors who wished to determine a lease. The documents were contradictory, so that it was not possible to ascertain with confidence the information necessary for a valid notice of determination. There was a dispute as to whether or not the solicitors were instructed not to contact the lessor's former solicitors to see whether there were any further documents that may clarify the position. The attendance note, which was very brief, did not record the instructions, and the judge found against the solicitors. The judge further considered, citing the Law Society recommendation quoted above, that it was appropriate to confirm the position in writing.[17]

(d) *Misconduct of Litigation*

11–176   **Funding of litigation.** The Client Care Code 1999, reproduced in Ch.13 of the *Guide,* suggests at para.4(j) that the solicitor should discuss with the client how and when costs are to be met, and consider whether the client may be eligible for legal aid, covered by insurance, should take out after the event insurance ("ATE"), or whether the costs may be paid by another person such as an employer. In the context of a claim by a passenger injured in a vehicle driven by someone in the same household, the Court of Appeal gave guidance as to what a solicitor should do in *Sarwar v Alam*,[18] relying on para.4(j). He should normally advise the client to bring to the first interview any relevant motor insurance policy, household insurance policy, or before the event ("BTE") policy belonging to him or any spouse or partner living in the same household. It is desirable for solicitors to send a standard form letter requesting sight of such documents. The solicitor should inquire whether a third person such as a trade union or employer might pay the costs, and should generally ask a passenger to obtain a copy of the driver's insurance if reasonably practicable. The solicitor's inquiries should be proportionate to the amount at stake. In most cases worth less than £5,000, the solicitor should refer the client to any BTE insurer, rather than seek ATE insurance.

11–177   **Procedure.** The conduct of litigation is in part a matter of routine and in part it is an art. By exceptional ingenuity or foresight the solicitor may secure advantages (sometimes decisive) for his client over the other party. The skilful use of a request for further information, or a timely application for specific

---

[15] The Law Society's *Guide to the Professional Conduct of Solicitors* (8th edn, 1999), para.13.06 n.6; see the Law Society website for the current *Guide.* Although there are many circumstances in which it is desirable to give advice in writing, it is not necessary to do so as a matter of law, see *Harwood v Taylor Vinters (a firm), The Times,* April 1, 2003, Ch. D.

[16] [1991] 29 E.G. 145, Judge Bates sitting as a judge of the High Court. See also *Middleton v Steeds Hudson* [1998] 1 F.L.R. 738, where Johnson J. expected that advice which was disregarded would be recorded in an attendance note, and the absence of any written records was "cogent" evidence in support of the claimant. On the facts, the judge did in fact accept the defendants' account.

[17] See also *Morton v Harper Grey Easton* (1995) 8 B.C.L.R. (2d) 53, British Columbia Supreme Court: if there is a conflict between the evidence of a lawyer and his client about the terms of retainer, the client's version is to be preferred unless the lawyer can shows that the agreement was in writing.

[18] [2001] EWCA Civ 1401; [2002] 1 W.L.R. 125.

disclosure, may bring the other party to its knees in civil litigation. Ingenious pre-trial research and preparation may lead to an acquittal (sometimes an unmeritorious acquittal) in criminal proceedings. However, the solicitor is not negligent if he fails to display exceptional ingenuity in matters of tactics or procedure.[19] What is required of a solicitor is reasonable competence and reasonable familiarity with the procedures of the courts in which he practises.[20] This requirement will include following local practice directions.[21] Thus in *Cox v Leech*[22] an attorney was held negligent for commencing proceedings in the Lord Mayor's Court, which did not have power to issue a commission for the examination of witnesses abroad, and it was obvious that such a commission would be necessary during the course of the action. A solicitor may well be negligent if he sues in the High Court in respect of a matter which clearly should have been litigated in the county court.[23] This is likely to involve the client in unnecessary delay and expense and, if successful, the client may be penalised in costs.[24] Given the flexibility introduced under the Civil Procedure Rules, and the powers of transfer between courts, this should rarely be an issue now.[25]

Issuing proceedings. Before issuing proceedings, the solicitor should obtain written instructions to commence them.[26] He should take care to identify the proper parties. In *Long v Orsi*[27] an attorney was held negligent when he issued proceedings on five bills of exchange, without first examining them. When he subsequently obtained the bills, it emerged that he had issued proceedings in the wrong name. In *Losner v Michael Cohen & Co*[28] solicitors were held negligent for issuing proceedings under the Dogs Act 1871, without first checking who owned the dogs in question or correctly naming all the owners in the summonses. **11–178**

---

[19] e.g. *Chapman v Van Toll, Van Toll v Chapman* (1857) 8 E. & B. 396: an attorney did not consider the procedural advantages of making an application under s.3 of the Common Law Procedure Act 1854. It was held that this would not necessarily have occurred to a reasonably competent attorney, and he was not negligent.

[20] e.g. *Frankland v Cole* (1832) 2 Cr. & J. 590; *Heywood v Wellers* [1976] Q.B. 446, CA.

[21] See *Langley v North West Water Authority* [1991] 3 All E.R. 610, CA. A solicitor was ordered to pay costs wasted through his failure to obey a local practice direction that required that, in personal injury litigation, authority to inspect hospital records should be sent with the particulars of claim.

[22] (1857) 1 C.B. (N.S.) 617. See also *Williams v Gibbs* (1836) 5 Ad. & E. 208; *Plant v Pearman* (1872) 41 L.J.Q.B. 169 (failing to register *lis pendens*).

[23] e.g. *Gill v Lougher* (1830) 1 Cr. & J. 170; *Lee v Dixon* (1863) 3 F. & F. 744. It is submitted that the principle is unaltered by the changes introduced by the Courts and Legal Services Act 1990 which provide for a greater parallel jurisdiction between the county court and the High Court, and a larger measure of flexibility between them. Similarly, it will be negligent to issue proceedings in Austria when greater damages could be recovered in the United Kingdom without taking proper advice from Austrian lawyers and counsel first: see *Waller v AB (a firm)* [2001] 2 C.L. 465, QBD.

[24] See s.51(9) of the Supreme Court Act 1981: where litigation should have been commenced in the county court, the recoverable costs can be reduced by up to 25%.

[25] But note that the amount at stake must be more than £15,000 if an action is to be commenced in the High Court, and a personal injury action must be commenced in the County Court unless worth more than £50,000. See the High Court and County Court Jurisdiction Order 1991, as amended.

[26] *Allen v Bone* (1841) 4 Beav. 493. It is submitted that proper attendance notes may be sufficient. See further para.11–175, above.

[27] (1836) 18 C.B. 610.

[28] (1975) 119 S.J. 340, CA.

However, in *Grima v MacMillan*[29] it was held not to be negligent to sue a defendant without checking first whether he was still alive. A solicitor has no general duty to verify the creditworthiness of a proposed defendant before commencing proceedings unless there are specific indications that something is wrong.[30]

11–179   **Statements of case.** A solicitor may be liable for errors in the statements of case, where he drafts them himself.[31] However, he is not obliged to put into his pleading everything which the client requests and, on occasions, it would be "very negligent" to do so.[32] A solicitor might also be liable if he failed to give the other party reasonable notice of any intended amendment to a statement of case.[33]

11–180   **Pursuing obvious remedy.** A solicitor may be liable if he fails to pursue an obvious remedy available to his client. Thus in *Martin Boston & Co v Roberts*[34] the defendant solicitors compromised a security for costs application by accepting a guarantee from a director of the company which was the claimant in the original litigation. At the successful conclusion to the litigation, the company was insolvent, and the director's house was subject to new charges which reduced the value of the equity to nil. A majority of the Court of Appeal held that the defendant solicitors were negligent because they did not insist on a caution on the director's property and they failed to demand further security for the company's appeal. Three cases involving family law further illustrate this principle. In *Dickinson v James Alexander & Co*[35] the defendant solicitors were instructed to deal with the break-up of the claimant's marriage. The defendants negligently failed to use ouster proceedings to remove the claimant's husband from the matrimonial home, when the children were suffering and the application would have succeeded. In *Griffiths v Dawson*[36] it was held that a solicitor, consulted by a wife in late middle age married for many years to a man in pensionable employment being divorced against her will on the grounds of separation, was negligent if he failed to file an application under s.10 of the Matrimonial Causes Act 1973, which would have the effect of delaying the hearing of a decree absolute while the financial circumstances were investigated. In *Beswarick v*

---

[29] (1972) 27 D.L.R. (3d) 666, Ontario High Court.
[30] *Thomson Snell & Passmore v Rose* [2000] P.N.L.R. 378, CA, where the defendant's counterclaim for negligence on such a ground was rejected. Similarly, Gray J. held in *Brinn v Russell Jones & Walker* [2002] EWHC 2727; [2003] P.N.L.R. 16 that the defendant solicitors were not negligent in failing to join the editor and journalist as defendants in libel proceedings, as there was nothing to put them on notice that the publisher may be in financial difficulties and the claim was not a large one.
[31] e.g. *Re Spencer* (1870) 39 L.J. Ch. 841 (erroneous statement in a petition).
[32] *per* Field J. in *Ibbotson v Shippey* (1879) 23 S.J. 388.
[33] See, e.g. Potter v London Transport Board (1965) 109 S.J. 233: leave was granted to amend and the hearing was adjourned. The solicitors were ordered to pay the costs thrown away.
[34] [1996] 1 P.N.L.R. 45.
[35] (1990) 6 P.N. 205 at 206 col.2, Douglas Brown J.
[36] *The Times*, April 5, 1993, Ewbank J.

Ripman[37] the defendant solicitors acted for the claimant in divorce proceedings against her husband, where there was a "clean break" settlement. The defendant solicitors were aware of the prospects of the claimant's children returning to live with her, and should have advised her to obtain a nominal periodical payment to ensure that she could apply to vary the order if this happened. Damages of £30,000 were awarded under this head.

Pursuing unmeritorious claims or defences. If a solicitor takes up or pursues   **11–181**
a hopeless case (at least without advising his client that it is hopeless) he is in breach of duty.[38] However, the mere fact that a claim or a defence proves unsuccessful does not imply that it was hopeless.[39] Furthermore:

> "it must never be forgotten that it is not for solicitors or counsel to impose a pre-trial screen through which a litigant must pass before he can put his complaint or defence before the court."[40]

The question whether a solicitor was negligent in allowing his client to bring or defend proceedings must be determined by reference to the circumstances at the material time: these include the instructions given by the client, the facts known to the solicitor, the expert reports available and so forth. If counsel, properly instructed, had advised that the proceedings should be brought or defended, this is very strong evidence (but not conclusive in every case) that the solicitor was not negligent.[41]

Evidence. Decisions on matters of evidence frequently involve a high degree   **11–182**
of judgment. Witnesses on the fringe of events or corroborative witnesses often turn out to do more harm than good (if, for example, they are shaken in cross-examination or their evidence conflicts with that given by the primary witnesses). Errors of judgment made by solicitors in this regard are unlikely to be held

---

[37] [2001] Lloyd's Rep. P.N. 698, H.H. Judge Griffith Williams Q.C., sitting as a High Court judge. The defendant solicitors were also found to be negligent in concluding that the claimant's half interest in a boat should be taken into account in calculating her assets for the purposes of eligibility for legal aid. However, if legally aided she would have had to repay the cost of her legal aid at some time, and no loss was suffered. They were not negligent with regard to an application for interim maintenance, which was not a sustainable claim, nor for settling the lump sum provision for £35,000 when an appropriate sum may have been as much as £40,000.

[38] *Davy-Chiesman v Davy-Chiesman* [1984] Fam. 48, CA. Where the client is legally aided, the Law Society too should be advised that the case is hopeless. In *Delhaise v Ng & Co* [2004] 1 HKLRD 573 the defendant solicitors acted for the claimant in litigation with a very poor prospect of success. The Hong Kong High Court held that the defendants had a duty to consider the merits of the case, and should say if it was hopeless even if not specifically asked to form a view. In that case, the defendants had given appropriate advice.

[39] e.g. *Pelky v Hudson Bay Insurance Co* (1981) 35 O.R. (2d) 97, Ontario High Court: solicitors' decision to run a defence of *volenti non fit injuria* (which failed) was an error of judgment, but not negligent.

[40] *Orchard v South Eastern Electricity Board* [1987] 1 Q.B. 565 at 572E, (*per* Sir John Donaldson M.R.). *cf. Ottley v Gilbey* (1845) 8 Beav. 602, where it was said that the solicitor has a duty to prevent useless litigation.

[41] See paras 11–118 *et seq.*

negligent.[42] For example, in *Roe v Robert McGregor & Sons Ltd*[43] the solicitors acted for contractors who erected a fence and were sued for negligence by claimants who crashed into it. The Court of Appeal held that the solicitors were not at fault in failing to interview a passenger in the car who it was reasonable to suppose would be extremely unlikely to give evidence against his friend the driver and might himself bring an action. If the solicitor is acting on the advice of counsel, he usually has a good defence,[44] and it will normally be negligent if he fails to follow the advice of counsel.[45]

11–183   It is negligent if a solicitor fails to take reasonable steps to trace potential witnesses,[46] or delays seeking evidence before the trail goes cold.[47] Thus in *Holden & Co v CPS*, a defendant was charged with possessing a shotgun without a licence, but claimed that it belonged to his brother.[48] The solicitors were told that the brother had gone to ground, and made no attempt to contact him despite knowing his address. The brother did attend court after the jury had retired, and the trial judge ordered a new trial. The Court of Appeal upheld the trial judge's order that the solicitors pay the cost of the aborted trial. Solicitors were found to be negligent in *Acton v Graham Pearce & Co (a firm)*.[49] They failed to obtain full statements from an employee's former employer, when told by their client that documents from the employee which were highly relevant to criminal charges brought against him were not genuine and that the employee had been dismissed. The defendant solicitors also failed to submit documents to a document analyser.

11–184   It may not be negligent if a solicitor fails to scrutinise all the evidence closely. For example, in *Allen v Unigate Dairies Ltd*[50] one of the complaints was that the solicitors failed to inquire as to the significance of a line on a plan, which in fact represented a wall between their client and the noise which he claimed induced his hearing loss, as a result of which the case collapsed at trial. In an application that the solicitors pay the costs personally, the Court of Appeal held that the solicitors were not negligent. Although it is generally a matter for counsel whether expert evidence should be called, the choice of expert is usually made

---

[42] e.g. *Godefroy v Dalton* (1830) 6 Bing. 460 (applying the old test of *crassa negligentia*; see para.11–080. In *Noble v Lourensse* (2003) 253 N.B.R. (2d) 293, the New Brunswick Court of Appeal upheld a decision that solicitors were not negligent in failing to obtain expensive evidence to contest one part of a relatively small claim, whether or not it was an error of judgment. *cf. Henderson v Hagblom* 2003 SKCA 40; [2003] 7 W.W.R. 590, where the Saskachewan Court of Appeal held a lawyer negligent for failing to obtain expert evidence which was needed to prove that a fire was caused by the negligent construction of a chimney.

[43] (1968) 1 W.L.R. 925 at 930G–H and 934G–H, CA.

[44] *Cates v Indermaur* (1858) 1 F. & F. 259. See also paras 11–118 *et seq.*

[45] See Johnson J. in *Gregg & Co v Gardner* [1897] 2 I.R. 122 at 126.

[46] e.g. *Scudder v Prothero Prothero* (1966) 110 S.J. 248, QBD. In *Rondel v Worsley* [1969] A.C. 191 Lords Reid at 231A and Upjohn at 285A expressed the view that this case may have been decided wrongly on its facts.

[47] *Balamoan v Holden & Co* [1999] N.L.J. Prac 898.

[48] [1990] 2 Q.B. 261, at 273–4. The case involved the (old) liability for wasted costs jurisdiction, and thus the test applied by the Court of Appeal was a more stringent one than mere negligence (see para.11–127).

[49] [1997] 3 All E.R. 909.

[50] The second appeal in *Ridehalgh v Horsefield* [1994] Ch. 205 at 245–247.

by the solicitor.[51] He may be held negligent, if he instructs an expert whose qualifications or experience render him unsuited to the task: " . . . Undoubtedly an attorney employed to conduct an action is bound to use due and proper care in the employment of persons whose evidence is material to the cause, to prepare themselves to give such evidences."[52]

At the hearing.[53] If the solicitor is acting as advocate, he is no longer immune   **11–185** from suit for negligence in respect of the manner in which he conducts the case.[54] He is liable for any failure to make proper arrangements for the hearing. Thus it is negligent if the solicitor fails to organise the attendance of witnesses.[55] In one old case[56] the attorney arranged for the attendance of a material witness, but did not physically check whether he had arrived. The attorney was held liable in that he "neglected to make any enquiries at the adjacent coffee houses."[57] Whether or not a witness should be *subpoenaed* is a matter of judgment. The solicitor might err in this regard, without being negligent.[58] In *Allen v Allen*[59] a material witness attended the hearing but "disappeared before giving evidence". Sir Jocelyn Simon P. expressed the view that there was no lack of reasonable diligence by solicitors in failing to ask for an adjournment. If a solicitor fails to instruct counsel[60] (where it was intended to do so) or to attend the hearing, he is plainly in breach of duty.[61]

---

[51] For an example of whether expert evidence had to be sought, see *Henderson v Hagblom* 2003 SKCA 40; [2003] 7 W.W.R. 590, Saskatchewan CA, where lawyers were found to be negligent when they failed to obtain expert evidence when they represented unsuccessful defendants in a claim for damages for fire caused by the negligent construction of a chimney.

[52] *per* Martin B. in *Mercer v King* (1859) 1 F. & F. 490. The attorney instructed a surveyor as expert witness, who became drunk and did not carry out the necessary measurements. There was some evidence that the attorney knew that the surveyor was addicted to drinking. Held that there was a sufficient case to go to the jury. It is usually negligent if the solicitor fails to take proofs of evidence from witnesses who are likely to be called (*Hatch v Lewis* (1861) 2F. & F. 467; *cf. Manley v Palache* (1895) 73 L.T. 98), although a client's full manuscript notes may be a sufficient proof from her (see *Waters v Maguire* [1999] Lloyd's Rep. P.N. 855, where Garland J. struck out a case against a barrister, who had no solicitor and was working for the Free Representation Unit, and held she was not negligent in failing to take a more detailed proof as she had a full note from the claimant); these principles are of limited application now witness statements have to be served.

[53] For an example where a solicitor acted as advocate at a criminal trial, and various allegations of negligence before and at trial were examined and dismissed, see *Paquet v Getty* 2002 NBBR 272; (2002) 253 N.B.R. (2d) 256, New Brunswick QB.

[54] See para.11–110.

[55] *Dunn v Hallen* (1861) 2 F. & F. 642.

[56] *Reece v Rigby* (1821) 4 B. & Ald. 202.

[57] *ibid., per* Abbot C.J.

[58] *Price v Bullen* (1825) 3 L.J. (O.S.) K.B. 39. The position would be different if the witness was plainly reluctant to attend. See also *Dax v Ward* (1816) 1 Stark. 409: the attorney wrote to a witness and reasonably expected that he would attend.

[59] (1968) 112 S.J. 965.

[60] *De Roufigny v Peale* (1811) 3 Taunt. 484; *Hawkins v Harwood* (1849) 4 Ex. 503. ("Instructing counsel" means instructing counsel properly, so as to enable him to discharge his duty. In that case "the brief . . . became mere waste paper.")

[61] *R. v Tew* (1752) Say. 50: the attorney failed to instruct counsel or attend trial; as a result client was non-suited "and afterwards thrown into gaol"; *Townley v Jones* (1860) 8 C.B. (N.S.) 289: the attorney failed to instruct counsel or attend trial, and was ordered to pay the costs; *Burgoine v Taylor* (1878) 9 Ch. D 1, CA: a solicitor was ignorant that the case had been transferred to another judge, and so watched the wrong list; he was ordered to pay costs; *Holden v Holden & Pearson* (1910) 102 L.T. 398; *Ridley v Tiplady* (1855) 20 Beav. 44 (failure to attend summons); *Swannell v Ellis* (1823) 1 Bing.

11–186   **After the hearing.** If there is a distinct possibility of an appeal, solicitors who represent clients who have lost litigation should advise them about their rights of appeal, and about the time-limits for implementing any appeal. Thus in *Corfield v DS Bosher & Co*[62] solicitors negligently failed to advise their client about an appeal from a rent review arbitration, when the client had requested a reasoned award which showed that he was unhappy with the way the proceedings were going. Similarly in *Hood v National Farmers Union*[63] the defendants were negligent in failing to advise on judicial review in relation to a decision of a Dairy Produce Quota Tribunal.

11–187   **Delay in commencing proceedings.** If solicitors delay issuing proceedings for so long that the claim becomes statute-barred, it is hard to see how there can ever[64] be a defence to a claim in negligence.[65] For instance, in *Fletcher & Son v Jubb, Booth & Helliwell*[66] the Court of Appeal held that the defendant solicitors were negligent in failing to appreciate that the limitation period for actions against local authorities was six months.[67] Contrast *Carlton v Fulchers*,[68] where the claimant instructed the defendant solicitors more than three years after she was injured in a road traffic accident. The Court of Appeal held that the defendants were not negligent in failing to issue proceedings immediately, as the insurers with whom they were dealing corresponded on the basis that there would be a trial or settlement. Thus an application under s.33 of the Limitation Act 1980 to disapply the limitation period would not have assisted the client, as those delays would not be held against the client. However, when the insurers took the limitation point, the defendants were negligent in failing to advise the claimant of the possibility of an application under s.33.

11–188   **Delay in defending proceedings.** Similarly, if solicitors acting for a defendant delay so long before entering an appearance or serving a defence, so that judgment is entered in default, it is hard to see how they could ever escape

---

347 (failure to attend arbitration). But compare *Lowry v Guildford* (1832) 5 C. & P. 234, in which there was a reasonable excuse for the attorney's absence. As to the solicitor's duty to remain in court see *Dauntly v Hyde* (1841) 6 Jur. 133.

[62] [1992] 1 E.G.L.R. 163, Judge Peter Crawford Q.C. sitting as a deputy High Court judge. For another illustration see *Darvall McCutcheon v HK Frost Holdings Pty Ltd* [2002] VSCA 85; (2002) 4 V.R. 570, summarised at para.11–120, above.

[63] [1994] 1 E.G.L.R. 109, CA.

[64] Unless the client refuses to give instructions or to put the solicitor in funds.

[65] e.g. *Clayton v Kearsey* (1935) 79 S.J. 180, K.B.D.; *Yardley v Coombes* (1963) 107 S.J. 575, Edmund Davies J.; *Gregory v Tarlo* (1964) S.J. 219, McNair J.; *Quevillon v Lamoureux* (1975) 52 D.L.R. (3d) 476, Quebec CA (error caused by solicitor's misapprehension of date of accident); *Cyr v Pelletier* (1991) 116 N.B.R. (2d) 137, New Brunswick CA; *Smith v Wells* (1993) 105 Nfld P.E.I.R. 351, Newfoundland CA. As to the delay in issuing proceedings to enforce a judgment, see *Russell v Palmer* (1767) 2 Wils. 325; *Harrington v Binns* (1863) 3 F. & F. 942.

[66] [1920] 1 K.B. 275.

[67] "Now it is not the duty of a solicitor to know the contents of every statute of the realm. But there are some statutes which it is his duty to know; and in these days when the defendants in so many actions are public authorities the Public Authorities Protection Act, 1893, is one of those statutes." (*Per* Scrutton L.J. at 281.) A Canadian decision to the same effect is *Prior v McNab* (1977) 78 D.L.R. (3d) 319. The Ontario High Court relied on, inter alia, Scrutton L.J.'s judgment in *Fletcher & Son v Jubb, Booth & Helliwell*.

[68] [1997] P.N.L.R. 337.

liability.[69] A defence which is sometimes put forward is that the client was applying for legal aid (now Community Legal Services funding) and the solicitor was awaiting the outcome of that application before taking any steps. It is hard to see how this defence could succeed. The solicitor in such circumstances is likely to have a number of choices: he can apply for a certificate; he could ensure that a sufficient extension of time is granted by the claimant's solicitors or the court; or he could make it plain to the client that he will not act unless and until public funding is granted, and that in the meantime the client must act in person.[70]

Delay after the action has commenced. Once proceedings are under way, the claimant's solicitor has a duty to prosecute the action with reasonable diligence.[71] If, therefore, the action is struck out for failing to comply with time limits or want of prosecution, he will have no defence to an action for breach of duty,[72] unless the client has caused or consented to the delay.[73] It appears that delay by counsel does not afford the solicitor a defence. If counsel is dilatory, the solicitor should regularly chase him up,[74] and if no response is forthcoming withdraw his instructions and pass them to another barrister "for a more ready response".[75]   **11–189**

Even where the solicitor's delay does not result in the loss of an action, he may still be liable for breach of duty.[76] Thus if an adjournment is sought at a late stage because of lack of preparation, the court may exercise its powers to disallow the solicitor's costs.[77] Even before the introduction of the Civil Procedure Rules, the attitude of the courts had become less tolerant towards delay; thus Lord Griffiths stated in a case concerning late amendment: **11–190**

> "We can no longer afford to show the same indulgence towards the negligent conduct of litigation as was perhaps possible in a more leisured age. There will be cases in

---

[69] e.g. *Godefroy v Jay* (1831) 7 Bing. 413.

[70] See the obiter remarks of the judge approved by Lord Griffiths in *Donovan v Gwentoys Ltd* [1990] 1 W.L.R. 472 at 476A–D, HL

[71] *The Flower Bowl (a firm) v Hodges Menswear Ltd, The Times*, June 14, 1988, CA.

[72] e.g. *Fitzpatrick v Batger & Co Ltd* [1967] 1 W.L.R. 706, CA; *Reggentin v Beecholme Bakeries Ltd* [1968] 2 Q.B. 276: "It follows, almost inevitably, that the solicitors for the claimant were at fault: and are liable . . . for negligence.", *per* Lord Denning M.R. at 278C; *Welburn v Mayberry* (1971) 115 S.J. 468, CA.

[73] See *Allen v Sir Alfred McAlpine & Sons Ltd* [1968] 2 Q.B. 229 at 256, *per* Diplock L.J. See also *Gouzenko v Harris* (1977) 72 D.L.R. (3d) 293, Ontario High Court: delay by the solicitors who first acted for claimant held not to be negligent.

[74] Thus in *Mansouri v Bloomsbury HA, The Times,* July 20, 1987 a writ was issued towards the end of the limitation period and the papers were sent to counsel for his advice. Dillon L.J. stated that "it was not satisfactory for the solicitors simply to send chasers to counsel once a month."

[75] *Mainz v James and Charles Dodd, The Times*, July 21, 1978, Watkins J.

[76] *Shilcock v Passman* (1836) 7 C. & P. 289: an attorney was engaged to secure the discharge of a client who was imprisoned for debt. As a result of delays caused by the attorney the client's discharge was delayed by about two months. The attorney was held liable. *cf. Lavanchy v Leverson* (1859) 1 F. & F. 615: an attorney was not liable for the delay in securing the discharge of debtor, because he believed negotiations were in progress. See also *Jones v Jones* [1970] 2 Q.B. 576 at 585, Salmon L.J., and *Thompson v Brown* [1981] 1 W.L.R. 744 at 750G–751A, *per* Cumming Bruce L.J.: a solicitor who delays issuing a writ for personal injuries, with the result that the client's right to interest is prejudiced, may be guilty of negligence.

[77] *Fowke v Duthie* [1991] 1 All E.R. 337, Macpherson J. See also *Sinclair-Jones v Kay* [1989] 1 W.L.R. 114, CA.

which justice will be better served by allowing the consequences of the negligence of the lawyers to fall upon their own heads rather than by allowing an amendment at a very late stage of the proceedings."[78]

11–191   **Settlement: consulting the client.** The solicitor has ostensible authority to compromise litigation on the client's behalf and any compromise which he makes (provided it does not involve a matter "collateral to the action") will bind the client.[79] Some nineteenth century authorities suggest that if a solicitor enters a reasonable compromise, without any reference to the client, there is no breach of duty,[80] unless the client has specifically forbidden that compromise.[81] The question presumably depends upon the terms of the particular retainer. Nowadays the courts would probably be reluctant to imply a term that the solicitor could settle without reference to his client, if no such term had been expressly agreed. The solicitor would be unwise if he took such a course in reliance on the authorities referred to above: they appear to be in conflict with *Sill v Thomas*[82]; and they are not in accord with the general duty to inform the client of the progress of his legal affairs.[83] There was some discussion of this subject (albeit obiter) in *Waugh v HB Clifford & Sons Ltd.*[84] Brightman L.J. considered that the solicitor's implied authority to compromise an action (as between himself and his client) was narrower than the ostensible authority. He took the example of a defamation action in which the defendant's solicitor may agree to settle at a large figure, which would be within his ostensible authority but not within his implied authority. "In the light of the solicitor's knowledge of his client's cash position it might be quite unreasonable and indeed grossly negligent for the solicitor to commit his client to such a burden without first inquiring if it were acceptable."[85] In the New Zealand case of *Thompson v Howley*[86] Somers J. decided that a solicitor is negligent unless he obtains the express instructions of his client to settle an action.

11–192   **Settlement: the merits.** A solicitor is bound to exercise reasonable care in the conduct of settlement negotiations and in advising on the merits of any settlement proposed. Such advice often entails weighing up imponderable factors, and a

---

[78] *Ketteman v Hansel Properties* [1987] 1 A.C. 189 at 220F–G.
[79] See *Waugh v HB Clifford & Sons Ltd* [1982] Ch. 374, CA. The court will not regard a matter as "collateral" unless it really is extraneous to the action: *ibid.* at 388D.
[80] *Wraight v Johnston* (1858) 1 F. & F. 128; *Chown v Parrott* (1863) 14 C.B. (N.S.) 74; *Re Newen* [1903] 1 Ch.812.
[81] *Fray v Voules* (1859) 1 E. & E. 839; *Butler v Knight* (1867) L.R. 2 Ex. 109.
[82] (1839) 8 C. & P. 762; see also *Pelky v Hudson Bay Insurance Co* (1981) 35 O.R. (2d) 97, Ontario High Court: solicitors for defendants and defendants' insurers failed to communicate an offer to settle at the policy limit.
[83] See para.11–158.
[84] [1982] Ch. 374. For discussion of this decision, see P. Kenny, "Authority to compromise" 126 S.J. 663.
[85] *ibid.* at 387 (the other members of the Court of Appeal agreed, at 383A and 390C). This passage marks a shift from the earlier cases referred to above. Communication between solicitor and client is much easier and quicker now than it was when those cases were decided. Even if the proposed settlement is comfortably within the client's means, it is surely reasonable to consult the client first.
[86] [1977] 1 N.Z.L.R. 16.

mere error of judgment is unlikely in practice to constitute negligence.[87] Solicitors have been held liable, however, for advising their client to settle at too low a figure, where they fail to assess the claim properly,[88] or as a result of their failure to make proper enquiries.[89] Particular problems arise where the defendant is insured, but with inadequate cover, and the same solicitor represents both the defendant and his insurers. Conflicts of interest can easily arise (e.g. if the claimant offers to accept the full amount for which the defendant is insured). The solicitor must keep both clients informed of offers which are made.[90] It may be necessary for separate solicitors to advise the insured defendant in respect of the settlement negotiations.

Ceasing to act. As a matter of law,[91] and of professional conduct,[92] the **11–193** solicitor can only determine the retainer for good reason and upon reasonable notice, although there may be exceptions in some cases where there is a natural break.[93] The solicitor is entitled to insist upon being put in funds by his client, in order to meet disbursements. If, after proceedings have begun, the client refuses to put him in funds, the solicitor is entitled to refuse to continue acting.[94] He must

---

[87] See the law in relation to barristers on this point, set out at Ch.12, paras 12–030 to 12–032. For an example see *Maillet and Pothier v Haliburton & Comeau* (1983) 55 N.S.R. (2d) and 114 A.P.R. 311, Nova Scotia Supreme Court: the claimant in a personal injuries action was awarded $75,000 by the jury at trial. The defendants appealed and on her solicitor's advice she accepted $40,000 in settlement. Her subsequent action against the solicitor was dismissed. Burchell J. said that the issue was not "what the Court of Appeal would have done." It was "whether a reasonably competent solicitor could have been sufficiently uncertain about the outcome of the appeal to conclude that the settlement at $40,000 was advisable" (*ibid.* at 315). It is submitted that this approach is correct. It is not desirable that a claimant should be able, too readily, to accept what is on offer from the original defendant (thus escaping the hazards of the original litigation) and then "top it up" by making a claim against his solicitors.

[88] In *Griffin v Kingsmill* [2001] EWCA Civ 93; [2001] Lloyd's Rep. P.N. 716 the solicitors were held to be liable for undersettling the action as well as counsel, and they did not seek to defend themselves on the basis that they relied on counsel. For the facts see Ch.12, para.12–032. For another example see *Hickman v Blake Lapthorn* [2005] EWHC 2714; [2006] P.N.L.R. 20, where no account was taken of the risk of the claimant not being able to work as a result of his injuries. For the facts see Ch.12, para.12–032. See also *Phippen v Palmers* [2002] 2 F.L.R. 415, Fam. Div., where solicitors were negligent in recommending acceptance of the husband's offer of a clean break in ancillary relief proceedings. This left the wife, who had no earning capacity, with inadequate income.

[89] In *McNamara v Martin Mears & Co* (1983) 126 S.J. 69 the solicitor for a wife in matrimonial proceedings proposed a figure of £15,000 in settlement of her financial claims and advised her to accept £12,000. The solicitor ought to have ascertained the total assets of the family, and should have proposed a figure of £24,000 and advised rejection of the £12,000.

[90] *Pelky v Hudson Bay Insurance Co* (1981) 35 O.R. (2d) 97, Ontario Hight Court. Solicitors failed to communicate an offer of settlement to insurers. Judgment was ultimately given for more than the insurance limit.

[91] *Summit Property Ltd v Pitmans (a firm)* [2001] Lloyd's Rep. P.N. 164, Park J. There, the solicitor withdrew because he was told to do so by a related party who was not his client, but was held to have no good reason to do so and he also gave the client inadequate notice. However, no loss was caused. For another example of a wrongful summary termination see *Young v Purdy* [1997] P.N.L.R. 130, where again no loss was caused.

[92] See further the Law Society's *Guide to the Professional Conduct of Solicitors* (8th edn, 1999), principle 12.12 (and for the current version see the Law Society website).

[93] See *Perotti v Collyer-Bristow* [2003] EWHC 25, Ch; [2003] W.T.L.R. 1473, discussed at para.11–011.

[94] Solicitors Act 1974, s.65(2). The section imposes a number of conditions, including the need for reasonable notice of the requirement of funds and of the withdrawal from the retainer.

give reasonable notice of his requirement for funds.[95] A solicitor is also entitled to withdraw from proceedings if, having reasonable and probable grounds for commencing the action, he later finds that it cannot be maintained.[96] A solicitor will be negligent if, after public funding has been withdrawn, he fails to advise the client of the consequences of withdrawal and what steps he could take, and he is also under a duty to consider making representations to restore the funding.[97]

(e) *Misconduct of Non-contentious Business*

11–194   The variety of non-contentious work undertaken by solicitors is so wide, that few generalisations about the solicitor's duty in such cases can usefully be offered, beyond that set out in the first part of this chapter.[98] If, however, the solicitor errs in carrying out a straightforward task of the kind customarily undertaken by the profession, he is unlikely to escape a finding of negligence.[99] He is also unlikely to escape liability if he causes the client loss through failing to maintain adequate office procedures.[1]

(i) *Conveyancing*[2]

11–195   **Protecting the client: customary searches.** A large part of a solicitor's activities are directed towards protecting the client against possible future hazards. This is particularly true in the realm of conveyancing. If a solicitor fails to protect his client by making the customary enquiries and searches then he is negligent[3]:

---

[95] In *Hoby v Built* (1832) B. & D. 350 the attorney told his client, five days before the commencement of the assizes in which the client's case was to be heard, that he needed funds in order to instruct counsel. The client failed to make any payment and the attorney did not instruct counsel. It was held that the attorney was in breach of duty in not giving reasonable notice. In *Noel v Lewis Holdings Ltd* (1990) 44 B.C.L.R. (2d) 37 the British Columbia Court of Appeal held that there was an implied term of the retainer that the solicitor may withdraw upon reasonable notice on non-payment of the accounts due.

[96] *Lawrence v Potts* (1834) 6 Car. & P. 428.

[97] *Casey v Hugh James Jones & Jenkins* [1999] Lloyd's Rep. P.N. 115, Thomas J.

[98] See paras 11–080 to 11–109.

[99] e.g. *Parker v Rolls* (1854) 14 C.B. 691: drawing up an agreement which was unenforceable, since it was not under seal; *Brown v Tolley* (1874) 31 L.T. 485: failure to give proper notices of creditors' meetings; *Carruthers v Hodgson* (1896) 100 L.T.J. 395: appointing an incompetent stockbroker to sell the claimant's stock; *Roberts v JW Ward & Son* (1982) 126 S.J. 120, CA: error in exercising option; *Harris v Carruthers* (1902) 2 N.S.W.S.R. 100, CA: failure to notice or properly understand material words in a deed. *cf. Elkington v Holland* (1842) 1 Dowl. (N.S.) 643.

[1] e.g. *Reeve v Palmer* (1859) 5 C.B. (N.S.) 84: attorney liable for loss of deeds, unless he proves that he exercised reasonable care; *North Western Rail Co v Sharp* (1854) 10 Exch. 451: attorney's duty to deliver up documents "in a reasonable state or order"; *D v D* (1962) 106 S.J. 959, DC: solicitor's duty to make quite sure that he has the client's correct address. The fact that he receives no answer to letters should put him on enquiry; *Frank v Seifert Sedley & Co* (1964) 108 S.J. 523, Melford Stevenson J.: solicitors accidentally sent draft contract to the wrong party; *Blood v Cotton* [1943] N.I.L.R. 68, Northern Ireland CA: duty to render true accurate and intelligible accounts.

[2] For an alternative analysis of the cases see H. Evans, *Lawyers' Liabilities*, (2nd edn, 2002), Ch.4.

[3] Thus, for instance, solicitors acting for the purchasers of a sub-lease should inspect the head lease, *Hill v Harris* [1965] 2 Q.B. 601, CA.

"It is clear negligence if an attorney suffers himself to be misled by the apparent respectability of the vendor, and thereby neglects his obvious duty of making reasonable inquiries into his title."[4]

A purchaser's solicitor should ensure that the vendor can show a good legal title free from adverse interests.[5] Thus in *Faragher v Gerber*[6] a solicitor was held liable for failing to make enquiries which would have elicited plans for a major new highway, despite a reply to a local search which advised checking with the London Docklands Development Corporation.

Proper confirmation. Some care needs to be taken with the searches and enquiries, and the replies received should be properly considered. Thus the plans should be closely scrutinised to ensure that the limits of the property accord with what is supposed to be conveyed.[7] Similarly, if the pre-contract enquiries stated that all consents had been obtained for major renovations, the solicitors should obtain copies of the consents either from the vendor or from another source such as the local authority.[8] If the purchaser's solicitors receive formal answers to enquiries from the vendor's solicitors which contradict information from the estate agent, further enquiry should be made.[9] In *Holmes v Kennard & Son*[10] the defendant solicitors, who acted for the purchasers, discovered that the vendor's wife had registered a notice protecting her rights under the Matrimonial Homes Act 1967. The wife's solicitors sent to the defendants a form for withdrawing a caution and not one for cancelling a notice. After completion, the wife succeeded in her objection to the cancellation of the charge. The defendants were found to be negligent in accepting a document which dealt with a caution and not a notice, and which had been signed by a person disclosing no authority to cancel the notice. In *Fashion Brokers Ltd v Clarke Hayes (a firm)*[11] the defendant solicitors relied on confirmation by telephone from a planning officer of the local authority

11–196

---

[4] *per* Mellor J. in *Allen v Clark* (1863) 7 L.T. 781. Thus the solicitors will be negligent if they hand over the purchase money before such searches are conducted, see para.11–202, below.

[5] See *Dogma Properties Ltd v Gale* (1984) 136 N.L.J. 453, Kilner Brown J.; *Holmes v Kennard & Son* (1984) 128 S.J. 854, CA: solicitors for purchasers were held liable for failing to take reasonable steps to protect their clients in respect of rights which had been registered by the vendor's wife.

[6] [1994] E.G.C.S. 122, QBD. In *Feerni Development Ltd v Daniel Wong & Partners* [2001] 2 HKLRD 13, Hong Kong High Court, the solicitors who acted for the purchaser failed to inspect an earlier assignment of the property; if they had done so they should have noticed that the person who had there signed as the vendor-administrator and the purchaser was the same, and thus that the transaction was voidable under a Hong Kong ordinance.

[7] *Nielsen v Watson* (1982) 125 D.L.R. 326, Ontario High Court: the plan showed the garage and the driveway outside the limits of property to be conveyed; solicitors held negligent. *Hondon Development Ltd Powerise Investments Ltd* [2005] HKCA 29; [2005] 3 HKLR 605; [2006] P.N.L.R. 1; HKCA: solicitor held negligent for failing to notice a significant discrepancy between the plan attached to the formal agreement and the plan attached to the provisional agreement. There is, however, no duty to inspect the property in the absence of special instructions, see *Bown v Gould & Swayne* [1996] P.N.L.R. 130, *per* Millett L.J.

[8] *Cottingham v Attey Bower & Jones (a firm)* [2000] P.N.L.R. 557, Rimer J. If they had known of the absence of consent, the solicitors should also have advised that although there could be no notice under s.36(1) or (2) of the Building Act 1984, as the works were carried out eight years before, there was a risk of injunction proceedings under s.36(6), which had no 12-month time limit.

[9] *Computastaff Ltd v Ingledew Brown Bennison & Garrett* (1983) 268 E.G. 906, at 911 col.1, McNeill J.

[10] (1984) 128 S.J. 854, CA.

[11] [2000] P.N.L.R. 473.

that the intended use of the property which their client was purchasing conformed with its planning consent. The Court of Appeal held that it was not reasonable to rely on such oral confirmation, and the solicitors should have obtained proper authentication before completion.[12]

11–197   **Suspicious circumstances.** There may be suspicious circumstances which should prompt further action. Thus in *McManus Developments Ltd v Barbridge Properties Ltd*[13] the claimant developers purchased some property. Between contract and completion a fence at the edge of the property was moved by the adjoining tenants to what they claimed was its true position. The defendants, who were the developers' solicitors and were told what had happened, only asked for the fence to be put back. The disputed strip did not belong to the property, and the developers had to buy it in order to proceed with their plans. The Court of Appeal decided that the intrusion should have set alarm bells ringing about whether there was an underlying problem, and the defendant solicitors should have taken further action. Similarly, in *Mercantile Building Society v JW Mitchell Dodds & Co*[14] the defendant solicitors acting on a remortgage obtained a land certificate, in which there were indications that should have put a conveyancer on enquiry that something might be amiss. They showed it to the borrower to check what he thought he owned, but they failed to confirm the plan with the client lender who could have compared it with their valuers' plan which would have shown a discrepancy, and were held to be negligent.

11–198   **Standard of care not absolute.** While the standard of care in conveyancing cases is high, it is not absolute, as is illustrated by *Neighbour v Barker*.[15] The defendant solicitors had advised the claimant clients to have a survey before purchase, but the advice was not followed. The claimants employed a surveyor

---

[12] The decision was in the context of third party proceedings brought by the defendant solicitor against the local authority.

[13] [1996] P.N.L.R. 431. However, the solicitors were not negligent in failing to supply a copy of the Land Registry plan to their clients, as that would not have added anything to the sale particulars which they had already. Similarly, in *Doran v Delaney* [1996] 1 I.L.R.M. 490 there was some doubt about the boundaries of the property, but the claimant's own solicitors negligently failed to have the boundaries staked out or to insist on the provision of an ordnance survey map in the contract which would show the boundaries. This part of the decision was not appealed to the Supreme Court (reported at [1998] 2 I.L.R.M. 1).

[14] [1993] N.P.C. 99, CA. *cf. UCB Bank Plc v David J Pinder Plc* [1998] P.N.L.R. 398, QBD, where solicitors could not have deduced from the plan that a small but significant part of the security property was outside the principal title. In accordance with normal practice, they sought the confirmation of the valuers that the area on the plan corresponded exactly with the area valued, and were informed " . . . we can confirm that the area shaded would appear to correspond with the premises". The solicitors were found not to be negligent.

[15] (1992) 40 E.G. 140. See also *Gorrie v Nielsen* [1989] 2 W.W.R. 437, Alberta CA. P owned W Ltd and M Ltd. W Ltd sold the lease of an aircraft hangar to M Ltd, but the assignment was not registered. P then sold his shares in W Ltd, which by then owned M Ltd, and secured the deferred part of the purchase price on the lease, with the mortgage executed by W Ltd. The purchaser defaulted, and an action under the mortgage was met with the defence that W Ltd did not have an interest in leasehold property. The failure to file a *caveat* against the title was held to be an error of judgment, and the defendant solicitor was found not to be negligent. Contrast *Peyman v Lanjani* [1985] 1 Ch. 457, where the Court of Appeal upheld a finding of negligence that a solicitor failed to advise his client that he could rescind the contract as the title was voidable, when the solicitor had sufficient grounds to enquire whether there were facts justifying such advice.

after purchase, who informed the defendants that the property their clients had just purchased had structural defects. The solicitors advised the claimants to complete the sale, because the consequences of not doing so could be financially disastrous, which advice was followed. In fact the vendors had made fraudulent misrepresentations, which would have enabled the claimants to escape from the transaction. They alleged that the defendants should have advised delay to investigate whether the claimants had any remedy. However, the Court of Appeal decided that the defendants were not liable, because there was no reason why they should have thought that there was any possible escape from the transaction.[16]

Remote contingencies. A solicitor is not liable for failing to protect his client **11–199** against a remote contingency.[17] The remoteness of the contingency is an important question. Thus in *G & K Ladenbau v Crawley & De Reya*[18] solicitors acting for a purchaser of vacant land failed to discover that rights of common had been registered against it. Mocatta J. held that the solicitors were negligent in failing to search the commons register even though, at the material time, it had seemed most unlikely that there would be any entry. The judge conceded that there was room for discretion in whether or not to make such a search "for example to densely built up land".[19] In contrast, in *Kotowich v Petursson*[20] a solicitor was held not liable for failing to check zoning, (i.e. planning permission) where his client already had a binding contract. The claimant was bound to complete, although she alleged she might have been able to exercise damage control.

Other errors. A solicitor is negligent if he fails to register any registrable **11–200** interest in, or rights over, land which his client may have.[21] In *Creech v*

---

[16] Similarly, there was no duty to advise a client to obtain security for a warranty from a shell company when the lawyer was instructed after the agreement had been signed, and the scope of the retainer was thus implicitly limited, see *Wong v 407527 Ontario Ltd* (1999) 26 R.P.R. (3d) 262, followed in *Vaz-Oxlade v Volkenstein* (2000) 35 R.P.R. (3d) 165 and *Baker v Turville* (2001) 38 R.P.R. (3d) 155, all Ontario CA.

[17] e.g. *Bryant v Busk* (1827) 4 Russ. 1: the title deeds of property were destroyed by fire between exchange and completion. Sir John Leach M.R. observed that the purchaser's solicitor (who had looked at the deeds before the fire) was not culpably negligent for failing to notice who the attesting witnesses were. At the time of inspecting the deeds the solicitor did not have a fire in contemplation. His purpose was to ascertain if the contents of the deeds corresponded with the statement of the abstract.

[18] [1978] 1 W.L.R. 266. See also para.11–093.

[19] *ibid.* at 289A. See also *Kolan v Solicitor* (1969) 7 D.L.R. (3d) 481 aff'd (1970) 11 D.L.R. (3d) 672, Ontario CA: solicitor negligent in not searching to see if the property was subject to a demolition order in the special circumstances of knowing that the property was old, having directed his mind to the possibility of the property being substandard.

[20] [1994] 4 W.W.R. 669, Manitoba QB. Similarly in *Wong v 407527 Ontario Ltd* (2000) 179 D.L.R. (4th) 38 the claimant purchased a block of flats with a warranty from a shell company as to the rental income. The Ontario Court of Appeal held that the defendant lawyer was not negligent in failing to advise an attempt to obtain security for the warranty, because by the time he was instructed the agreement was already executed. In contrast, in *Redmond v Densmore* (1997) 153 Nfld P.E.I.R. 181, Newfoundland CA, the defendant solicitor was negligent and caused the claimant loss in failing to report to him on zoning, as the contract for the purchase of the property could be rescinded on the grounds of misrepresentation.

[21] e.g. *Midland Bank v Hett Stubbs & Kemp* [1979] Ch. 384, Oliver J.: failure to register option; *Stratton Ltd v Weston, Financial Times*, April 11, 1990, Ch. D.: failure to register an equitable lease when a receiver was appointed over the landlord.

Mayorcas[22] a solicitor completed the purchase of the lease of a shop without obtaining the landlord's licence to assign and licence for change of user, or any undertaking from the vendor's solicitors to obtain such licences. Pennycuick J. described the omission (which was made by a legal executive) as an "understandable slip", but held that the solicitor was liable. In *Rickards v Jones (No.2)*[23] the defendant solicitors acted for the purchaser in the conveyance of a newly built house. The National House Building Council has a guarantee scheme for such properties. The defendants sent off the paperwork to the NHBC after completion, but they replied that the builder had ceased to be a member of the scheme. The house was defective and worthless. The Court of Appeal held that the defendants were negligent in failing to consider the NHBC paperwork properly. They should have confirmed with the NHBC that the builder was a member of the NHBC scheme and that cover would be granted once the paperwork was completed, and indeed as the house was already completed they should have obtained an NHBC certificate before completion of the purchase.

11–201   **Communicating with the client.** A solicitor should advise his client about important matters that come to his notice, such as the existence of a right of way, or a defect in title, or the absence of planning permission, or the existence of a "contracts race".[24] He should warn his client about risks that the client may not appreciate,[25] such as the nature and effect of a restrictive covenant and the risks attached to it,[26] or of the advisability of making inquiries about the financial standing of the tenants when the purchase agreement expressly provided that the vendor gave no warranty about the issue.[27] In *Lloyds Bank Plc v Parker Bullen (a firm)*[28] a solicitor was found liable for failing to inform the lender that the lease

---

[22] (1966) 198 E.G. 1091.

[23] [2002] EWCA Civ 1344; [2003] P.N.L.R. 13.

[24] See para.11–160. The client will be fixed with knowledge communicated by the other side to the solicitor: *Strover v Harrington* [1988] 1 Ch. 390, Ch. D., but *cf. Halifax Mortgage Services Ltd v Stepsky* [1996] Ch. D. 207, CA, see para.11–160.

[25] See para.11–166. Thus in *O'Brien v Hooker Homes* (1993) A.S.C. 56–217, Supreme Court N.S.W., a solicitor who arranged finance for the purchase of property by simple clients owed a duty to spell out the workings of their interest obligations. In *Keep Point Development Ltd v Chan Chi Yim* [2000] 3 HKLRD 166 the solicitors were found liable for failing to explain to unsophisticated clients the unusual danger of selling their property for option agreements on land which was not registered. In *Boateng v Hughmans (a firm)* [2002] EWCA Civ 593; [2002] P.N.L.R. 40, the claimant entered a property transaction where he sold a house to builders who were to convert it into flats, eventually conveying one of the flats back to the claimant. The builders required a mortgage to carry out the work. The Court of Appeal held that the claimant's solicitors were negligent in failing to explain to him that he was exposed to the inherent risk of being left without any interest in the property or remedy if the builders became insolvent, as happened. *cf. Carvin v Dunham Brindley & Linn* [1997] E.G.C.S. 90: part of the garden of a house was used as a storm drain which had not been adopted, and the purchaser was initially granted only a licence over it. It was intended that the remaining land would be conveyed to the purchaser in due course when the position had been finalised. The Court of Appeal upheld the judge's decision that the solicitor was not in breach of his duty to the prospective purchaser, a successful man of business, as he had explained the nature of the licence and the fact that the claimant would not immediately be acquiring the title to the whole property.

[26] *Bittlestone v Keegan Williams* [1997] E.G.C.S. 8; [1997] N.P.C. 3, Ch. D., unless the solicitor could satisfy himself that it was plainly unenforceable.

[27] *Hanave Pt Ltd v Lfot Pt Ltd* (2000) 168 A.L.R. 318, Federal Court of Australia.

[28] [2000] Lloyd's Rep. P.N. 51, Longmore J.

of the property prevented alienation. The solicitor should explain the effect of the conveyance, in particular any unusual or important provisions[29]:

> "A person who goes to a lawyer with respect to a land transaction is entitled to expect that lawyer to investigate the state of any title that is germane to the matter and to explain to the client exactly what it is that is portrayed by the state of the title."[30]

Thus in *Atkins v Atkins*[31] the solicitors failed explain the real purpose of the transaction to the claimant, which was to raise money on her house for her son, and was held to be negligent. In contrast, in *Haigh v Wright Hassall & Co*[32] a solicitor exchanged contracts on being assured by his client that a deposit cheque would be available that afternoon. The solicitor was held not to be liable; he had no duty to question how secure was the availability of the deposit cheque. However, the answer might have been different if the client was wholly inexperienced.

Handing over the purchase money. In *Gregory v Shepherds*[33] the claimant **11–202** instructed the defendant solicitors in connection with the purchase of Spanish property. They were not liable for the defaults of Spanish lawyers whom they instructed. However, the Court of Appeal held that the solicitors were negligent for paying over the client's money to the foreign purchaser without first obtaining specific confirmation that the searches which the Spanish lawyers had been instructed to carry out had been satisfactorily completed and that it was in order to make the payment. In *Edward Wong Finance Co Ltd v Johnson Stokes & Master*[34] it was held that solicitors for a prospective mortgagee were negligent to hand over funds to the vendor's solicitor in return for an undertaking. However, in *Patel v Daybells (a firm)*[35] the Court of Appeal distinguished *Wong*, and held that given the conditions in this jurisdiction it was not negligent to complete a sale on the basis of undertakings given by the vendor's solicitors. Where the purchaser wishes a deposit to be held until completion, his solicitor must inform the vendor's solicitor that the deposit is to be held as stakeholder.[36]

---

[29] See paras 11–167 to 11–168.

[30] *per* Thackray J. in *Graybriar Industries Ltd v Davis & Co* (1992) 46 B.C.L.R. (2d) 164, 181. British Columbia Supreme Court. Similarly, in *Behrooz Siasati v Bottoms & Webb (a firm)* [1997] N.P.C. 20; [1997] E.G.C.S. 22, QBD, the solicitor had a duty to a foreign client with limited English to take all reasonable steps to explain, if necessary through an interpreter, the nature and scope of the obligations of the lease of old commercial property which he intended to take on, of the risks involved, and to take reasonable steps to ensure that the client understood the advice, which should generally be reduced to writing so the client could obtain a translation.

[31] [1993] E.G.C.S. 54, Ch. D.

[32] [1994] E.G.C.S. 54, CA.

[33] [2000] P.N.L.R. 769, CA. In *Chua Ming Yuen v Hentron Investments Ltd* [2005] 1 HKLRD 611, Hong Kong High Court, a solicitor was held to be negligent in sending a cheque drawn on his client account for payment of the purchase of property by his client, which was dishonoured, when he knew that there had been technical problems in clearing his client's banker's draft into his own account.

[34] [1984] A.C. 296. See paras 11–088 to 11–091, above. The implications of *Wong* for conveyancing practice in England are discussed in B. George, "Can solicitors safely trust each other?" 128 S.J. 231.

[35] [2001] EWCA Civ 1229; [2002] P.N.L.R. 6, see further para.11–091, above.

[36] *Desmond v Boyles* [1985] I.R. 449, High Court.

11–203   **Acting for the vendor.**[37] Where the solicitor is acting for a vendor, his answers to enquiries before contract or requisitions on title are of the utmost importance. If the answers are erroneous, the client may be exposed to liability to the purchaser. In the ordinary way, any mistake by the solicitor in this respect is likely to be regarded as negligent, unless there is some justification such as incorrect instructions from the client. In *Simmons v Pennington*,[38] however, solicitors who gave the incorrect answer to a requisition escaped liability, since they had acted in accordance with the general practice of conveyancers and could not reasonably have foreseen the consequences of their answer. Clerical errors may be negligent. In *Stovold v Barlows*[39] the defendant solicitors were found to be negligent for failing to check whether the purchaser's solicitors were on the DX before sending the deeds in an urgent transaction. They sent them to a retailer with a similar name. In *Gribbon v Lutton*[40] solicitors acting for a prospective vendor received a deposit as stakeholder. No contract was entered, and the purchaser successfully argued that the deposit was returnable, despite being expressed to be non-refundable, as there was no consideration in the form of a lock-out agreement. The Court of Appeal held that the solicitors were negligent in failing to secure an enforceable agreement under which the deposit was forfeit if the vendor failed to purchase.

11–204   **Time limits.** Many conveyancing transactions are carried out within strict time limits. The most obvious example is the requirement under the Landlord and Tenant Act 1954, Pt II with respect to business tenancies, where there are the strict time limits for serving notices to renew leases and for applying to the court to renew the lease.[41] Time limits may be imposed by some third party (for example, the party "on the other side" of the transaction or the client's bank). They may be imposed by the circumstances of the client. Thus in many domestic conveyances it is essential that the exchange of contracts on the sale and the purchase should be synchronised and also that the completion of those two transactions should be synchronised. A failure by the solicitor to carry out his client's instructions in this regard will usually be both a breach of contract and negligent. The solicitor's task in synchronising exchanges of contracts has been

---

[37] See also the following two commonwealth examples. In *Slater Wilmshurst v Crown Group* [1991] 1 N.Z.L.R. 344, High Court, the vendor of commercial property asked its solicitor to check the legal description of land. The solicitor made no check on the register, and so missed a right of pre-emption to buy the property. Solicitors were found negligent as undisclosed encumbrances could have caused argument later. In *Savoie v Mailhot* [2004] N.B.C.A. 17; (2004) 268 N.B.R. (2d) 348, New Brunswick CA, a solicitor was found to be negligent for mistakenly putting in the wrong description of the property in the deed of sale.
[38] [1955] 1 W.L.R. 183, CA. See also para.11–087.
[39] [1996] P.N.L.R. 91, CA. *cf. Infantino v MacLean* [2001] 3 All E.R. 802, where in the context of the court's power under CPR r.6.9(1) to dispense with service of a claim form, Douglas Brown J. considered it arguable that solicitors were negligent for using the wrong DX address by reason of a computer error.
[40] [2001] EWCA Civ 1956; [2002] Q.B. 902.
[41] In general the duty of a solicitor, when his client as tenant is served with a notice under Pt II of the Landlord and Tenant Act 1954 is clear. He must tell his client of the two time limits. He must also take such steps as are sufficient, in all the circumstances of the case, to ensure that if either time limit is allowed to expire without the appropriate step being taken, that is the fault of the client." *Per* Staughton J. in *RP Howard Ltd v Woodman Matthews & Co* [1983] B.C.L.C. 117, at 121E.

made easier by the decision of the Court of Appeal in *Domb v Isoz*,[42] in which it was held that (subject to instructions to the contrary) a solicitor could achieve an exchange of contracts by means of a telephone conversation. Buckley L.J. stated that in view of the integrity and standing of solicitors, this procedure did not involve an undesirable degree of risk.[43] Where a conveyancing transaction is carried out as part of a legitimate scheme to reduce tax liability, this may impose special time constraints. In the New Zealand case of *Stirling v Poulgrain*[44] the first claimant instructed the defendant solicitors to transfer two farms to a trust, in order to reduce the estate duty payable on her death. The Inland Revenue agreed a valuation for both farms, provided that the transfers were effected by a specified date. The transaction was not completed in time, with the result that the valuation was increased by $90,000. Mahon J. held that the solicitors were in breach of contract,[45] and this decision was upheld by the Court of Appeal.[46]

Wider duties. A solicitor's duties in conveyancing may extend more widely **11–205** than to strictly conveyancing matters. Some duties will be obvious from the nature of the purchase. Thus if the client is purchasing a public house, then the solicitor will need to enquire as to the nature of the liquor license,[47] and if a solicitor acting for a vendor has to remit monies to a lender pursuant to an undertaking he may be in breach of duty if he does not first deduct the tax payable.[48] In *Raintree Ltd v Holmes*[49] the defendant solicitors acted for the claimant company in the purchase of land, which carried planning permission. The business of the company was to buy development land to build houses, as the solicitors knew. They failed to ascertain the expiry date of the planning permission, which was between the date of the conveyance and the date of the intended start of building works, and were held to be in breach of duty. When acting for a purchaser of property, the solicitor should, if he has any reason to doubt the matter, enquire whether the client has made proper financial arrangements.[50] If the client needs a mortgage in order to complete, the solicitor ought at least to

---

[42] [1980] Ch. 548.

[43] *ibid.* at 558.

[44] [1980] 2 N.Z.L.R. 402.

[45] *ibid.* at 407.

[46] *ibid.* at 413.

[47] *Kelly v Finbarr J Crowley* [1985] I.R. 212, Murphy J.

[48] *AMP General Insurance Ltd v Macalister Todd Phillips Bodkins* [2006] W.T.L.R. 189, New Zealand CA.

[49] (1984) 134 N.L.J. 522, Hobhouse J. *cf. Woodglen v Owens* (1999) 27 R.P.R. (3d) 237, Ontario CA, where the lawyer had no obligation to inform his developer client that the easement he obtained for him might not be sufficient if the "part lot" control provisions were imposed. The developer had other lawyers acting for him generally, and the defendant's retainer was limited. In *Finley v Connell Associates (a firm)* [2002] Lloyd's Rep. P.N. 62, the claimant acquired a building licence from the local council to build a hotel in 18 months. When he was running out of time and money, the council demanded a large premium for a change to a residential development. Ousley J. held that the defendant solicitor negligently failed to advise that on its true construction the building licence permitted such change, not to be unreasonably withheld, with recourse to arbitration in the event of a dispute.

[50] See further para.11–201. However, in *Citicorp Australia Ltd v O'Brien* (1996) 40 N.S.W.L.R. 398, the New South Wales Court of Appeal held that a solicitor acting for unsophisticated clients in the purchase of property owed no duty to inform them of their views of the financial prospects of the mortgage they were taking out. The solicitors had given a short explanation of terms of the loan and mortgage.

warn him of the risks involved if contracts are exchanged before the mortgage has been arranged.[51] A more difficult question is whether the solicitor is obliged to advise a house purchaser of the advantages of a structural survey. Certainly it is good practice to do so. It appears from *Buckland v Mackesy*[52] that where the client is inexperienced and the property is not new, the failure to give such advice could amount to negligence. The position with respect to an ordinary survey remains to be determined.[53] In *Johnson v Bingley Dyson & Furey*[54] Mr Ben Hytner Q.C. sitting as a deputy High Court judge held that although there was no general duty to advise a seller to obtain an independent valuation, there was one in the circumstances of that case, where the client was suffering from mental illness and her son was not in a position to give her sound advice on such matters. If a house is purchased in joint names, it may be negligent not to take steps to find out and declare the extent of the beneficial interests.[55]

11–206   **The National Protocol.** On March 21, 1990 the Law Society launched a "National Protocol" for domestic conveyancing and an accompanying Council Statement. The Council states that the protocol is to be "preferred practice", and there should be full disclosure to the other side of the extent to which the protocol will be followed.[56] The Law Society has also published formulae for exchanging contracts, and a code for completion by post.[57] These steps have led to a greater degree of standardisation of conveyancing transactions, and to be relevant to the question of negligence. The Law Society has also issued guidance on a solicitor's duties with regard to potential mortgage frauds, and with regard to property fraud generally (the "Green Card").[58]

11–207   **Mortgages and undue influence.** Solicitors are often instructed to advise in cases where there may be undue influence. The most typical example is a wife who is entering a mortgage of property to raise money from a bank for her

---

[51] *Buckland v Mackesy* (1968) E.G. 969, CA. See also H. Wilkinson, "The solicitor's duty on exchange of contracts" *New Law Journal*, February 23, 1978.

[52] (1968) 208 E.G. 969. The claim against the solicitor failed in this case, since it was held that he had given sufficient advice to his client. See Salmon L.J. at 971.

[53] In *Brenner v Gregory* (1972) 30 D.L.R. (3d) 672, Ontario High Court, a solicitor was not liable in not advising clients of the danger of purchasing property without any survey; expert evidence showed that it was not the local practice to do so. *cf. O'Connor v First National* [1991] I.L.R.M. 208 where Lynch J. held the solicitor liable in such circumstances, having regard to established conveyancing practice.

[54] [1997] P.N.L.R. 393.

[55] "The Courts might soon have to consider whether a solicitor who failed to do so was not guilty of negligence." *Per* Dillon L.J. in *Walker v Hall* (1983) 127 S.J. 550. The solicitor will probably have to advise his clients properly on the merits of a joint tenancy and tenancy in common: *Taylor v Warners*, (unreported, July 21, 1987), Warner J., commented upon by Crail, *Law Society Gazette*, June 29, 1988, 26.

[56] The protocol is reproduced in many books on conveyancing, including all editions of F. Silverman, *The Law Society's Conveyancing Handbook*. That book, published annually, is a good indication of standard conveyancing practice.

[57] Both are reproduced in the Law Society's *Guide to the Professional Conduct of Solicitors* (8th edn, 1999), Annexes 25D and 25E; for the current version see the Law Society website.

[58] Reproduced in *ibid.*, Annexes 25F and 25G.

husband's business affairs.[59] In *Royal Bank of Scotland Plc v Etridge (No.2)*[60] the House of Lords gave important guidance as to what should happen in such circumstances after that case had been decided. The leading speech of Lord Nicholls must be read with care to see precisely what is required of banks and solicitors, and the following is only a summary. The bank is put on inquiry whenever a wife offers to stand surety for her husband's debts, even if the wife held shares or was a director, and the same would apply whenever any person in a non-commercial relationship offers to guarantee the debts of another. Banks are unwilling to assume the responsibility of advising the wife, and their practice is to refer the wife to an independent legal adviser. For previous cases, it would be sufficient if the bank obtained confirmation that the solicitor had brought home to the wife the risks she was running by standing surety. After *Etridge* the bank has to write to the wife asking her to nominate solicitors, explaining a number of matters. If an appropriate response is received directly from the wife, the bank must provide the solicitor with the financial information needed to advise the wife, including such matters as the purpose of the new facility, the current amount of the indebtedness and the previous and proposed overdraft facility. In general, it is acceptable for the solicitor to also act for the husband and bank.[61] The solicitor should ensure that he has the financial information which the bank should have disclosed, and he should see the wife alone at a face to face meeting without the husband being present. The solicitor will typically have to advise[62] as a minimum: (1) on the nature of the documents and the practical implications, such as losing her home and bankruptcy; (2) on the seriousness of the risks involved, including the terms of the facility, the fact that it may increase, and whether there are other assets to cover the business if it were to fail; (3) that the wife has a choice whether to enter the transaction; and (4) the solicitor should obtain instructions that she wishes to proceed, or whether she would prefer the solicitor, for instance, to negotiate with the bank on the terms of the transaction. While such advice is onerous, unlike the Court of Appeal the House of Lords did not consider that the solicitor's duty was generally to ensure that the wife was

---

[59] For an earlier example see *Northern Rock Building Society v Archer* (1998) 78 P.R. 65, CA: Mrs Archer provided funds for her brother to set up a solicitor's practice on the security of her house, with the repayments to be made by her. She was to be principal borrower, and her brother the surety. Her solicitors explained to her the consequences of a mortgage, but negligently failed to advise her that she was being treated as the borrower, and that in the absence of a collateral arrangement with her brother which did not appear from the documents she did not even have the limited protection as surety. See also *Krambousanos v Jedda* (1996) 142 A.L.R. 604: solicitors were retained by the applicants' son to advise them in respect of a mortgage to be taken over their property. The Federal Court of Australia found that there was no breach of duty in failing to advise on the propriety of the transaction, as the retainer was only to explain the nature and effect of the mortgage.

[60] [2002] 2 A.C. 773.

[61] Note also the restrictions on acting for lenders and borrowers from October 1, 1999 in para.6(3) of the Solicitor's Practice Rules 1990 as amended (and published in the Law Society's *Guide to the Professional Conduct of Solicitors*, 8th edn, 1999; for the current version see the Law Society's website).

[62] See para.65 of Lord Nicholls' speech. Lord Scott concluded that in general the nature and effect of the documents had to be explained, although the facts of a particular case may add to or reduce the duty. Following that, it was held in *Colton v Graysons* [2003] Lloyd's Rep. P.N. 80, Ch. D., that there was nothing reckless or obviously imprudent in the transaction in question which required the solicitor to urge the clients to think hard against entering the transaction and to hunt around for alternatives. Lord Nicholls' observations were followed in *Oversea-Chinese Banking Corp Ltd v Tan Teck Khong* [2005] SGHC 61; [2005] 2 S.L.R. 694, Singapore High Court.

free from undue influence. The new scheme is only prospective as regards the bank, it is not wholly clear as to whether the solicitor's duties in the past would be the same as those imposed on them for the future, but it would seem that the duty is the same but without the need to have obtained the financial information.[63]

(ii) The Investment of Money and Claims by Lenders[64]

11–208   **Introduction.**[65] The property crash of the early 1990s caused serious losses to many mortgage lenders. As a result, there has been a large volume of litigation against the surveyors and solicitors that the lenders instructed, which have generated a substantial body of law. There are seven leading cases which should be particularly considered. There are two lengthy first instance decisions in "managed litigation" by two lenders against a number of solicitors, see *Bristol & West Building Society v Fancy & Jackson (a firm)*[66] and *Nationwide Building Society v Balmer Radmore (a firm)*.[67] These largely apply six appellate decisions: *Mortgage Express Ltd v Bowerman*[68] and *National Home Loans Corp Plc v Giffen Couch & Archer (a firm)*,[69] both concerned with the extent of the solicitors' common law duties to lenders; *Bristol & West Building Society v Mothew*,[70] where Millett L.J. analysed in particular the fiduciary obligations owed by the solicitors; *Target Holdings Ltd v Redferns*,[71] where the House of Lords considered the question of breach of trust; and *Banque Bruxelles Lambert v Eagle Star Insurance Co Ltd*,[72] a surveyor's case concerned with the scope of a professional's duty. Reference should also be made to the sections in this chapter dealing with express terms and their construction,[73] fiduciary duties and claims for breach of trust,[74] damages for breach of fiduciary duty,[75] damages for losses on loans secured by mortgage,[76] and contributory negligence.[77] A crucial feature which should be mentioned at the outset is that, unlike the vast majority of areas of a solicitor's work, the terms of the solicitor's retainer is normally governed by

---

[63] One of the cases in the *Etridge* appeals, *Kenyon-Brown v Desmond Banks & Co*, was an appeal by solicitors in relation to a claim brought by their former client. The House of Lords reversed the decision of the Court of Appeal and held that the solicitor had given proper advice, see the speech of Lord Scott at paras 373–375.

[64] This subject is affected by the Financial Services Act 1986 and the Financial Services and Markets Act 2000, see para.11–003, above.

[65] This topic is extensively treated in Ch.7 of Flenley and Leech's *Solicitor's Negligence* (Butterworths, 1999), and see in particular the helpful explanation of the roles of the lender and solicitor in mortgage transactions discussed at paras 7.7–7.13.

[66] [1997] 4 All E.R. 582; see paras 11–024, 11–075, 11–211, 11–215, 11–217, 11–305 and 11–336. For an interesting discussion of this case, see A. Sprince, "The liability of solicitors to lenders on borrower default" (1998) 14 P.N. 3.

[67] [1999] P.N.L.R. 606, see paras 11–024, 11–211, 11–216, 11–218, 11–219, 11–305 and 11–337.

[68] [1996] 2 All E.R. 836, see para.11–210.

[69] [1998] 1 W.L.R. 207, see para.11–213.

[70] [1998] Ch. 1, see paras 11–023, 11–034 and 11–304.

[71] [1996] 1 A.C. 421, see para.11–231.

[72] [1997] 1 A.C.191, see paras 11–248 and 11–304.

[73] Paras 11–008—11–010.

[74] Paras 11–023—11–025 and 11–034—11–038.

[75] Paras 11–228—11–234.

[76] Paras 11–303—11–307.

[77] Paras 11–333—11–337.

detailed instructions from the lender, which differ from one lender to another. While there is some room for the implication of implied duties in addition to the written duties, the scope for such implication is quite limited.

History. Before considering the modern law, some old and commonwealth **11–209** cases will be briefly summarised in this paragraph. They are now of limited importance given the wealth of modern English authority on this subject, and may not be wholly reconcilable with it. A solicitor acting for a lender of money is negligent if he does not take reasonable steps to protect his client's position.[78] Most obviously, if the solicitor missed or ignored a mortgage on the security property he will be liable.[79] In *Wilson v Tucker*,[80] for example, the client proposed to lend money on the security of a legacy given under a will. The attorney failed to read the whole of the will (which contained a clause rendering the legacy void in these circumstances) and was held to be negligent.[81] In *Anglia Hastings & Thanet Building Society v House & Son*,[82] solicitors, acting both for the purchaser of property and for the building society, were held liable for failing to report to the building society certain matters which cast doubt on the reliability of the purchaser. The solicitor is not, in the ordinary way, expected to advise on the value of the proposed security.[83] This is a matter on which the client must

---

[78] *Cooper v Stephenson* (1852) 21 L.J. Q.B. 292: if the attorney of a proposed mortgagee has reason to suspect that the proposed mortgagor has been bankrupt or insolvent, he ought to make proper searches to ascertain if this is so; *British Mutual Investment Co v Cobbold* (1875) L.R. 19 Eq. 627: a solicitor failed to spot a defect in the borrower's title to the property to be mortgaged. The defendant conceded that he would have been liable but for procedural error by claimant; *Pretty v Fowke* (1887) 3 T.L.R. 845: a solicitor was found to be liable for failing to make proper enquiries concerning the tenancy of a piece of land proposed as security for a loan; *Roe v Cullinane Turnbull Steele & Partners (No.2)* [1985] 1 N.Z.L.R. 37, Quillam J.: on a sale of land to a company without capital for payment which was mostly deferred, the vendor's solicitor was negligent in not obtaining personal guarantees when he knew that the security over the land was worth less than the debt; *County Natwest Ltd v Pinsent & Co* [1994] 4 Bank L.R. 4, Hobhouse J.: solicitors failed to point out mismatch between duration of insurance cover and loan facility. *Pegrum v Fatharly;* (1996) 14 W.A.R. 92, Western Australia CA: if the solicitor has reason to suspect that the borrower may be insolvent or the securities are inadequate in value, he should advise his client; *Yamada v Mock* (1996) 136 D.L.R. (4th) 124, Ontario High Court: solicitor found liable for failing to ask imposter for mortgagor to verify his identity (a claim which may be brought in England for breach of warranty of authority, see para.11–075, above); *Midland Mortgage Corp v Jawl & Bundon* (1999) 8 W.W.R. 535, British Columbia CA: solicitors were not negligent in failing to advise a lender of the riskiness of a mortgage over a short term lease, as their only duty was to implement lender's agreement with developer. But *cf. Bailey v Abraham* (1849) 14 L.T. (O.S.) 219: a material deed affecting the proposed security was not shown to the attorney.

[79] *Financeamerica Realty Ltd v Gillies* (1983) 40 Nfld. & P.E.I.R. 169, Newfoundland CA.

[80] (1822) 3 Stark. 154.

[81] "I am of the opinion, that by law it is the duty of an attorney not to content himself with a partial extract from a will, unless something pass between himself and his client which shows that it is unnecessary to consult the original." (*Per* Abbot C.J.)

[82] (1981) 260 E.G. 1128, [1955–1995] P.N.L.R. 11, Bingham J.

[83] *Hayne v Rhodes* (1846) 8 Q.B. 342; the issue in this case was whether the attorney had been specifically instructed to advise on the value of the security. *Rae v Meek* (1889) 14 App. Cas. 558: trustees consulted a law agent on the question whether they could lend on unfinished buildings. He replied, correctly, that they could. Held that the law agent was not negligent in failing to advise that the security was insufficient (see at 569); *Midland Bank Plc v Cameron, Thom, Peterkin & Duncans* [1988] S.L.T. 611, OH: instructions to solicitors to prepare a standard security does not import a duty to verify its value.

make up his own mind or take other professional advice. In *Brinsden v Williams*[84] a loan was made by one client to another. The solicitors acted for both parties. The security proved insufficient. North J. held that the solicitors were not liable. They "did not recommend the security at all, but merely acted as solicitors in respect of a security between two clients of theirs, the sufficiency of which the persons proposing to lend the money considered for themselves".[85] The solicitor's responsibility may be enlarged if he is specifically instructed to consider the adequacy of the security and he accepts such instructions.[86] If in the course of investigating the borrower's title to a proposed security, the solicitor happens to discover facts that suggest that the value is insufficient, then he ought to point this out, whatever the terms of his retainer. In *Scholes v Brook*[87] the valuers acting for a mortgagee substantially over-valued the property to be mortgaged. The solicitors had cause to doubt the accuracy of the valuation when, on investigating, they noticed the prices which had previously been paid for the property. They did not draw this to the attention of the client, but pointed it out to the valuers, who adhered to their original valuation. Romer J. held that the solicitors were not negligent. They "did what they ought to have done in calling [the valuers'] attention to the discrepancies."[88] It was not their duty to notify the client as well. Where a solicitor is trustee, it is his duty to check the sufficiency of any security before lending trust funds.[89] Where the security is insufficient and the beneficiaries claim against the trustees, the solicitor trustee is primarily liable.[90] The solicitor may constitute himself a trustee of money received from the client.[91] The solicitor may owe different duties as trustee and as solicitor.[92]

11–210   **The *Bowerman* duty.** In *Mortgage Express Ltd v Bowerman & Partners*[93] the defendant solicitor acted for a purchaser and a mortgagee. He became aware that the vendor was purchasing the property for £150,000 when he was selling it on

---

[84] [1894] 3 Ch. D. 185.

[85] *ibid.* at 191.

[86] e.g. *Green v Dixon* (1837) 1 Jur. 137. See also, *Donaldson v Haldane* (1840) 7 C. & F. 762; *Langdon v Godfrey* (1865) 4 F. & F. 445. See the analysis of Kekewich J. in *Dooby v Watson* (1888) 39 Ch. D. 178, followed in Canada by the Ontario Supreme Court in *Enola Apts Ltd v Young* (1979) 30 R.P.R. 94.

[87] (1891) 63 L.T. 837.

[88] However, the judge found that the valuers were negligent. This decision was affirmed on appeal: 64 L.T. 674.

[89] It is different if he is merely solicitor to the trust, rather than a trustee: *Johnstone v Thorburn* (1901) 3 F. 497, a Scottish case.

[90] *Re Partington, Partington v Allen* (1887) 57 L.T. 654, Stirling J.; *Blyth v Fladgate, Morgan v Blyth, Smith v Blyth* [1891] 1 Ch. 337, Stirling J. As to the position of the partners of a solicitor trustee, see *Re Bell's Indenture* [1980] 1 W.L.R. 1217, Vinelott J.

[91] As in *Craig v Watson* (1845) 8 Beav. 427. The facts were somewhat unusual, in that the solicitor "solicited his employment", suggested a loan of £3,000 and produced to the client a valuation of the proposed security in support of his advice.

[92] See, for example, *Bayer v Balkin* (1995) 31 A.T.R. 295, Cohen J.: a trust faced taxation difficulties. As a solicitor to the trust, the claimant had a duty to consider the law for the avoidance of tax. As trustee he had to consider what was the best interests of the trust as a whole. While the claimant negligently failed to advise on the transfer of a flat acting as solicitor, the failure to transfer the flat was the result of a decision as a trustee, and it was not beneficial to the trust as a whole to do so. The defendants' counterclaim therefore failed.

[93] [1996] 2 All E.R. 836. See commentary by M.P. Thompson, "Conflicts of interest" (1996) 60 Conv. 204.

for £220,000, and the valuation figure was £199,000. This should have caused the solicitor to consider that such information might cause the claimant lenders to doubt the correctness of the valuation they had obtained. The defendants were found to be negligent in failing to report these matters to the claimant lender and the Court of Appeal upheld the decision. Sir Thomas Bingham M.R. held[94]:

> "A client cannot expect a solicitor to undertake work he has not asked him to do and will not wish to pay him for such work. But if in the course of doing the work he is instructed to do the solicitor comes into possession of information which is not confidential and which is clearly of potential significance to the client, I think that the client would reasonably expect the solicitor to pass it on and feel understandably aggrieved if he did not . . . if in the course of investigating title a solicitor discovers facts which a reasonably competent solicitor would realise might have a material bearing on the valuation of the lender's security or some other ingredient of the lending decision, then it is his duty to point this out."

It should be noted that the information must not be confidential.[95] The judge suggested that the duty may be wider than matters relevant to the valuation of the security, although subsequent cases have placed limits on this duty.[96]

Application of this duty. The *Bowerman* duty has been considered in the two **11–211** "managed" lenders' cases. In *Bristol & West Building Society v Fancy & Jackson (a firm)*[97] Chadwick J. determined eight cases brought by the claimant lender against various solicitors which had acted for it on the mortgage of various properties owned by different purchasers. In most of the cases, the allegations of breach depended on the terms of the lender's instructions. However, in one of the four categories of breach that the judge considered, it was alleged that some of the defendants failed to inform the claimant that there was a subsale, although the instructions imposed no obligation on them to do so. The judge held that if the price differential between the two sales were sufficient to call into question the valuation, then it should be reported. He did not think that a discrepancy of 10 per cent between September 1988 and October 1989 required reporting in *Steggles Palmer*, although the solicitors were found liable for other reasons. In *Colin Bishop* there was an express obligation to report subsales, and the judge held that there was no relevant distinction between a subsale and a "back-to-back" sale, and the solicitors were liable for failing to report the latter. In *Nationwide Building Society v Balmer Radmore (a firm)*[98] Blackburne J. tried 12 representative claims brought by the Nationwide against various firms of solicitors. He concluded that the *Bowerman* duty to report to the lender would be confined to matters that were within the scope of the lender's interest which the solicitor was engaged to serve, and that this depended on the terms of the retainer. It would ordinarily be an implied obligation of the solicitors to pass on information obtained in the course of investigating title or preparing for completion

---

[94] [1996] 2 All E.R. 836 at 842D–F.
[95] See para.11–219, below, on confidential information and information obtained before the retainer.
[96] Compare the narrower formulation of the duty by Millett L.J. [1996] 2 All E.R. 836 at 845F, and see paras 11–213 and 11–214, below.
[97] [1997] 4 All E.R. 582.
[98] [1999] P.N.L.R. 606 at 637C–D.

which might cause the lender to doubt the correctness of the valuation or the bona fides of the borrower, but he expressed no view on whether the duty extended to information affecting some other ingredient of the lending decision. The *Bowerman* duty would be implied unless inconsistent with the express terms of the engagement, and it would only apply to information obtaining during the retainer which was not confidential. Thus in relation to subsales and back to back sales, the solicitor is generally under a duty to report them to the lender where the prices were significantly different.[99] These principles were applied in a number of individual cases. For instance, in *Nationwide Building Society v ATM Abdullah*[1] the solicitor was negligent in failing to report the fact that the transaction was a subsale at £63,000 when the principal sale was for £56,000 in a falling market and despite the fact that the head sale was from a mortgagee in possession who might be thought to be giving a discount.

11–212   **Further illustrations of the *Bowerman* duty.** A number of further cases illustrate the *Bowerman* duty. In *Mortgage Funding Corp v Tisdall Nelson Nari & Co*[2] the defendant solicitors were found to be negligent in failing to report the purchase price of £59,750 at which property had been purchased shortly before the remortgage funded by the claimant, which suggested that the claimant lender had an erroneous view of the valuation of the property of £98,500. Solicitors negligently failed to inform the lender of the substantial discrepancy in price on a subsale of £275,000 and £110,000, and the existence of shorthold tenancies, in *Mortgage Express Ltd v Newman & Co.*[3] Contrast *Paragon Finance Plc v Crangle & Co*[4] where the solicitor was not negligent in failing to report a subsale where there was no inflated purchase price. In *Halifax Plc v Ringrose & Co (a firm)*[5] Bell J. held that solicitors were negligent in failing to report back to back sales where the prices were £108,500 and £155,000, and in failing to report the possible non-payment of a deposit, but not the fact that the borrower had given different addresses, nor that there was a charging order and a possibility of a second mortgage on another property as the claimant had given no instructions in relation to the borrower's creditworthiness, a matter which will now be considered.

11–213   **The borrower's financial status.** A solicitor will generally not owe an implied duty to report to a lender client information casting doubt on the borrower's ability to repay the loan. The leading case suggesting a restrictive interpretation of the solicitor's retainer in this regard is *National Home Loans*

---

[99] [1999] P.N.L.R. 606 at 652G.
[1] [1999] Lloyd's Rep. P.N. 616. In *Nationwide Building Society v Archdeacons* [1999] Lloyd's Rep. P.N. 549 it was held to be negligent to fail to report that the transaction had been purchased a few weeks before for £45,000 when the sale on was for £59,000 in a stagnant market. The solicitor was liable in *Nationwide Building Society v JR Jones* [1999] Lloyd's Rep. P.N. 414 for failing to inform the lender of back to back transactions with a 53% price uplift. See also, the *Littlestone & Cowan* case summarised at para.11–218, below. *cf.* the *Vanderpump* case summarised at para.11–214, below.
[2] [1998] P.N.L.R. 81.
[3] [1996] P.N.L.R. 603, Ch. D.
[4] [1999] E.G.C.S. 25, Ch. D.
[5] [2000] P.N.L.R. 483.

Corp Plc v Giffen Couch & Archer (a firm).[6] The defendant solicitors knew that there were significant arrears on the proposed borrowers' existing mortgage, and that they had been threatened with proceedings. The claimant's instructions were detailed but did not require any reporting on the state of account of any existing mortgage. The Court of Appeal held that the defendant solicitors were not negligent in failing to advise the claimant of the matters in question, which did not relate to title or the adequacy of the security over the property. Peter Gibson L.J. set out five relevant factors[7]: (1) the solicitor's primary function in accordance with his instructions was to acquire a valid and effective first mortgage and a good and marketable title; (2) the lender provided detailed printed instructions, so that there was limited room for implying further duties[8]; (3) the only instructions concerning the borrower's financial circumstances were to undertake a bankruptcy search and report on what that revealed; (4) the lender did not send the solicitor a copy of the borrower's application, where the borrowers lied about the arrears; and (5) the report on title required the solicitors to certify that they were not aware of any material changes in the circumstances of the borrowers, implying that the lender was satisfied about such circumstances up to the offer. *Mortgage Express Ltd v Bowerman & Partners*[9] was distinguished.

　　Giffen Couch & Archer was followed in *Birmingham Midshire Mortgage* **11–214** *Services Ltd v David Parry & Co.*[10] The solicitor acting for the mortgagee had no obligation to investigate the borrower's position in relation to mortgages of other property he might hold unless he had express instructions to do so, as it was no part of his duty to supply information about the borrower's financial position. There are a number of cases that might suggest a more extensive duty, most importantly *Mortgage Express v Bowerman.*[11] In *Halifax Mortgage Services Ltd v S. S.*[12] Judge Humphrey Lloyd Q.C. found it difficult to reconcile *Giffen Couch & Archer* with *Mortgage Express v Bowerman.* He held that the scope of the duty was a matter of fact and degree, but that if a solicitor was obliged to discharge any general duty of care above the specific instructions of the claimant lender, then that would include reporting matters of potential significance to the lender. As a result, the Judge refused to strike out an allegation that the defendant

---

[6] [1998] 1 W.L.R. 207. In an earlier case, *Omega Trust Co Ltd v Wright Son & Pepper (No.2)* [1998] P.N.L.R. 337, Douglas Brown J. held that solicitors were negligent in representing that the borrower was up to date with his rent, and in failing to carry out a bankruptcy search, which would not normally be required, when they knew that the borrower's principal had been in dubious financial circumstances, albeit as a result of confidential information which they were not obliged to disclose.

[7] *ibid.* at 214A–G.

[8] See the similar comments of Chadwick J. in *Bristol & West Building Society v Fancy & Jackson* [1997] 4 All E.R. 582 at 603G.

[9] [1996] 2 All E.R. 836.

[10] [1997] N.P.C. 153 and [1997] E.G.C.S. 150, CA. The case also concerned a general condition that the borrower intended to reside in the property. The solicitor had to bring the clause to the borrower's attention, and report if he knew that the borrower did not so intend, but he had no duty to check that the borrower had such an intention. It was followed in *Nationwide Building Society v Balmer Radmore* [1999] Lloyd's Rep P.N. 558, where the solicitor did not know and did not in the circumstances have to infer that that the borrower was not resident at the property in a remortgage.

[11] [1996] 2 All E.R. 836, CA, see para.11–210.

[12] [1998] P.N.L.R. 616.

solicitors should have reported the knowledge they acquired of the borrower's impecuniosity. However in *Maes Finance Ltd v Sharp & Partners*[13] Judge Bowsher Q.C. held that in a case where there was no express instruction to report any doubts about the borrowers' ability to repay the loan, then no such duty would be implied, and the defendant solicitors were therefore not liable in failing to report such matters. He held that *Giffen Couch & Archer* and *Mortgage Express v Bowerman* could be distinguished from each other on the basis that one related to the value of the personal covenant, and the other to the value of the security property. The judge was influenced by the fact that the lender was primarily interested in the adequacy of the security, the solicitors had not been told what inquiries if any the lender had made about the borrowers' financial circumstances, and a court should be slow to impose a duty on a solicitor which may well lead to a conflict between his duties to lender and borrower clients.

11–215   **The purchase price, direct payments and fraud.** In one of the categories of cases considered by Chadwick J. *Bristol & West Building Society v Fancy & Jackson (a firm)*,[14] it was alleged that some of the defendants had failed to report direct payments of the deposit. The report on title in each case stated that the solicitor confirmed that the details of the transaction accorded with the offer of advance, which extended to the purchase price. A solicitor would therefore have to make the inquiries that a reasonably competent solicitor would make to satisfy himself that the stated purchase price was the true one. Where the purchase price passed through the hands of the solicitor, he was able to make such a confirmation. Where it did not, the solicitor should normally seek confirmation from the vendor's solicitor that all the moneys had been paid, although it would be sufficient if the vendor gave a receipt for the full purchase price, unless the solicitor should have realised that there may be a fraud. The judge considered that the Law Society's "Green Card" on mortgage fraud, published in March 1991, which referred to a deposit paid direct as a sign of fraud, could not be applied retrospectively to the transactions before him which happened at an earlier date. Thus in *Fancy & Jackson* itself the vendor was willing to give a full receipt, and there was no breach. In contrast, there was a breach in *Steggles Palmer* where the evidence before the solicitor suggested that the direct deposit had never been paid, and in *Baileys Shaw & Gillett* where the scanty evidence of payment of the deposit was contradicted by a number of factors.

11–216   In *Nationwide Building Society v Balmer Radmore (a firm)*,[15] Blackburne J. unsurprisingly held that it would ordinarily be an implied obligation of the solicitors to pass on information doubting the bona fides of the borrower.[16] The judge considered two main issues about price to which the issue of fraud may be

---

[13] (1999) 69 Con.L.R. 46.
[14] [1997] 4 All E.R. 582.
[15] [1999] P.N.L.R. 606.
[16] *ibid.* at 636C. This should not undermine the general principle in *Giffen Couch & Archer. cf. Shiokawa v Pacific Coast Savings Credit Union* (2005) 250 D.L.R. (4th) 656, where the British Columbia Court of Appeal held that the individual and cumulative effect of various unusual circumstances in some powers of attorney were not sufficient to oblige the lawyers acting for a lender to make further inquiries into them.

relevant. First,[17] there was an express obligation in the Nationwide's instructions for the solicitors to report discrepancies, which would include anything which in effect was a variation in price. This was in any event no more than a reflection of a general obligation connected with the possibility of fraud, and it was also implied in the report on title that the solicitor had made enquiries to satisfy himself that the stated purchase price was the true one. A vendor discharging the purchaser's costs and expenses would effectively be agreeing a reduction in purchase price, whereas the supply of a structural survey may not be. These principles were applied in *Nationwide Building Society v Vanderpump & Sykes*.[18] There were back-to-back sales at £120,000 and £138,000 when a valuation of £130,000 had been obtained by the lender. The solicitor was not in breach of duty by failing to report the first sale at £120,000. However, there were a number of other curious features about the transaction so that the solicitor was negligent in giving unqualified confirmation that the purchase price was £138,000. The second issue considered by Blackburne J. was direct payments.[19] The judge agreed with the approach in *Fancy & Jackson* towards direct payments by the purchaser to the vendor, with the gloss that it applied even in cases before the "Green Card" issued by the Law Society in March 1991 which warned that direct payments were a badge of mortgage fraud. In most cases the solicitor would seek an explanation from his client, and probably confirmation of the payment in a falling market. Thus the solicitor was liable in *Nationwide Building Society v J R Jones*[20] for failing to inform the lender of a direct payment of 31 per cent of the alleged purchase price.

Other matters. The two last categories of cases considered by Chadwick J. in **11–217** *Bristol & West Building Society v Fancy & Jackson (a firm)*[21] should be mentioned. First, it was alleged that some of the defendants failed to inform the claimant of the borrower's intention to act in breach of a special condition of the mortgage. As the solicitors' instructions required them to report any matter at variance with the offer of advance, the defendants were in breach if they failed to do so. In *Clearys* the solicitors failed to disclose the fact that the borrower intended to redeem the existing mortgage to his bank but to grant it a second charge. While there was not strictly a breach of the condition to redeem prior mortgages, the solicitors should have appreciated that the second charge may be material to its lending decision, and they were negligent.[22] Secondly, given the confirmation in the report on title that the solicitor had investigated the title to the

---

[17] (1999) 69 Con. L.R. at 646D–648F. For example, see *Nationwide Building Society v Goodwin Harte* [1999] Lloyd's Rep. P.N. 338, and *Nationwide Building Society v Richard Grosse & Co* [1999] Lloyd's Rep. P.N. 348 (where there was a large uplift in price and a direct deposit). In both cases there was also a breach of fiduciary duty, see para.11–024, above.

[18] [1999] Lloyd's Rep. P.N. 422.

[19] [1999] P.N.L.R. 606 at 648G–652D.

[20] [1999] Lloyd's Rep. P.N. 414.

[21] [1997] 4 All E.R. 582.

[22] *cf. Leeds & Holbeck Building Society v Alex Morison & Co (No.2)* [2001] P.N.L.R. 13, OH, where the defenders were not negligent in failing to report a prospective breach of mortgage condition in that the borrowers were seeking funds to use the property for business purposes.

security property and he considered it to be good and marketable,[23] it was beyond argument that a solicitor could not proceed to completion unless he had an official search certificate disclosing no adverse entries. Thus the solicitors were negligent in *Fancy & Jackson* for such a breach, although as the search was obtained shortly after completion only nominal damages were awarded. However, there would be no breach of the representation in the report on title if a solicitor accepted from the borrower's solicitor a mortgage deed that appeared on its face to be properly executed when it was not, and the defendants in *Cooke & Borsay* were not liable on that ground. Where a solicitor acted for the borrowers too, Chadwick J. held that he warranted that he acted with their authority.[24]

11–218   **Communicating with the client.** In *Nationwide Building Society v Balmer Radmore (a firm)*[25] Blackburne J. held that where a solicitor came across something he was obliged to report, he should do so in sufficiently clear and comprehensive terms to be understood by the receipient, and unless obvious he must explain what the reasons are for reporting the matter. Thus in *Nationwide Building Society v Littlestone & Cowan*[26] the judge held that on a remortgage with a valuation of £152,000 it was not sufficient to state in a report on title that the purchase price was £120,000. The solicitor also needed to give the date of the purchase, which was just three weeks earlier, and explain that the information might cast doubt on the valuation. In *UCB Bank Plc v Hepherd Winstanley Pugh*[27] the defendants sought consent from the claimant to a third charge over the property with a limit to the priority of the claimant's charge of £20,000. The claimant consented to the third charge, but not specifically to the priority. The Court of Appeal found the defendants liable for failing to have this specifically confirmed, and failing to obtain instructions directly from head office contrary to the claimant's standing instructions.

11–219   **Confidential information and fraud.**[28] The first decision to qualify the extent of the implied obligation to report relevant matters was *Bristol & West Building*

---

[23] In *Nationwide Building Society v Balmer Radmore (a firm)* [1999] P.N.L.R. 606 at 654B–655F, Blackburne J. held that to be satisfied with title the solicitor must have seen reasonably up to date office copy entries of the registered title showing that the vendor is the registered proprietor. For a case where there was a breach of this requirement see *Nationwide Building Society v ATM Abdullah* [1999] Lloyd's Rep. P.N. 616. A solicitor should verify the authority of the person who signed a sale agreement on behalf of a vendor company, see *National Commercial Bank Ltd v Albert Hwang, David Chung & Co* [2002] 2 HKLRD 409, Hong Kong High Court.

[24] This may not be quite correct, see para.11–075, above.

[25] [1999] P.N.L.R. 606 at 656B.

[26] [1999] Lloyd's Rep. P.N. 625.

[27] [1999] Lloyd's Rep. P.N. 963.

[28] See also, para.11–145. Compare the position in Scotland. In *Bank of East Asia v Shepherd & Wedderburn* [1995] S.L.T. 1074, the Inner House held that if a solicitor acting for a potential lender is already in possession of information which tends to show that the security is of significantly less value than he knows the potential lender thinks, then he must report the facts to the client. The duty would be no less incumbent on him if the solicitor was already acting for the potential borrower. However, there was no general duty to deal with the value of the property or financial status of the borrower. The *Bank of East Asia* case was followed in *Bristol & West Building Society v Aitken Nairn, W.S.* [2000] S.L.T. 762, Second Division. *cf.* also *Hilton v Parker Booth & Eastwood (a firm)* [2005] UKHL 8; [2005] 1 W.L.R. 567, noted at para.11–237.

Society v Baden Barnes Groves Co,[29] where Chadwick J. held that only information acquired in the course of the retainer by the claimant had to be reported, and any wider duty would be oppressive and unrealistic. In *Darlington Building Society v O'Rourke James Scourfield McCarthy*[30] the Court of Appeal similarly decided that if the solicitor is acting for the lender and borrower in a transaction, and the borrower in another transaction, information obtained in the other transaction is confidential, and should not be disclosed, unless there is reason to believe that the information shows a serious crime such as fraud by the borrower. The issue was discussed in more detail in *Nationwide Building Society v Balmer Radmore (a firm)*.[31] Blackburne J. held that by naming his own solicitor to the lender, the borrower must be taken to have authorised him to disclose whatever was necessary to comply with the lender's instructions. If the solicitor was in any doubt, he should seek the borrower's permission, and if consent was withheld, he should cease to act. If there was a conflict and the solicitor continued to act, conscious that he was benefiting the borrower at the expense of the lender, he would be in breach of fiduciary duty. The obligation to disclose information to the lender covered information acquired while doing the work that the lender had instructed him to do, but not, for instance, information that he obtained as a result of earlier transactions which he had carried out for the borrower.[32] The one exception to this limited disclosure obligation was that any information from any source which suggested that the borrower was intending to defraud the lender should be disclosed.

(iii) *Wills*[33]

General. In view of the decision in *White v Jones*[34] a solicitor who is negligent **11–220** in relation to a will may face an action by the disappointed beneficiary.[35] It should be noted that for there to be a breach of duty to the beneficiary, there must also be a breach to the testator: see *Punford v Gilberts Accountants (a firm)*,[36] and the scope of the duty owed to the beneficiary will not be wider than that owed to the testator, seesee *Cancer Research Campaign v Ernest Brown & Co*.[37] It has been decided in Canada that any contributory negligence of the testator is not to

---

[29] [2000] Lloyd's Rep. P.N. 788, decided in 1996.
[30] [1999] P.N.L.R. 365.
[31] [1999] P.N.L.R. 606 at 640G–646B.
[32] In an earlier case, *Omega Trust Company Ltd v Wright Son & Pepper (No.2)* [1998] P.N.L.R. 337, Douglas Brown J. had held, following previous decisions, that solicitors acting for a lender had no duty to disclose information about the borrower's poor financial state which they had acquired before the commencement of their retainer and which was confidential.
[33] See further, A. Borkowski, "Solicitor's negligence in the preparation of wills" (1986) 2 P.N. 151; C.N. von Benzon "Avoiding solicitors' negligence in probate and trust work" *Law Society Gazette*, January 29, 1986, p.263; A. Norris, "A sense of direction" (2001) New. L.J. 932.
[34] [1995] 2 A.C. 207; see para.11–048, above.
[35] However, it may be possible for the solicitor to avoid liability by procuring rectification of the will under s.20 of the Administration of Justice Act 1982.
[36] [1998] P.N.L.R. 763, CA. An accountant advised in relation to a transfer of the testator's home to his wife, and did not advise that if he predecease his wife, the bequest of the house to the claimant would be ineffective. There was no breach to the testator, as the matter was obvious to him, and thus there was no breach to the claimant. See also, *Trusted v Clifford Chance* (2000) 1 W.T.L.R. 1219, Jonathan Parker J., as authority for this proposition.
[37] [1998] P.N.L.R. 592, discussed at para.11–223, below.

be attributed to the beneficiary.[38] However, there is in some circumstances an obligation on the claimant to mitigate his loss by proceedings to rectify the will.[39]

11–221   **Taking instructions.** When a lay client seeks advice in imprecise and non-legal terms, the solicitor should clarify the extent and nature of the advice sought.[40] A solicitor is generally only required to consider and advise upon the issue of testamentary capacity when the circumstances are such as to raise doubts in the mind of a reasonably competent practitioner[41]; if there are such doubts, there is probably no duty not to execute the will, but a note should generally be made.[42] However, the position may be different if instructions are received from a third party, such as a will-writing company. If such instructions are received, the solicitor should obtain written instructions from the client that he or she wishes to act, and in any case of doubt the solicitor should see the client.[43] If instructions are given by an interested party, it may be the duty of the solicitor to satisfy himself thoroughly as to the testator's volition and capacity, and to make the necessary inquiries so that if called upon he can show that the testator fully appreciated the effect of what he was doing.[44] If there were any danger of lack of sufficient information, or doubt about capacity or undue influence, the solicitor

---

[38] *Earl v Wilhelm* [2001] W.T.L.R. 1275; (2000) 183 D.L.R. (4th) 45, Saskatchewan CA.

[39] See para.11–330, below.

[40] See *Gray v Buss Murton (a firm)* [1999] P.N.L.R. 882, Rougier J., where the solicitors failed to ask the intentions of the testator in a homemade will that erroneously gave a life interest to a beneficiary, rather than an absolute interest.

[41] See *Public Trustee v Till* [2001] 2 N.Z.L.R. 508, Randerson J.; there were no such circumstances in that case. In *Re Collicutt* 128 N.S.R. (2d) and 359 A.P.R. 81 the the Nova Scotia Probate Court suggested that with a very decrepit client, the solicitors should enquire about their mental competence and about the provisions of any former will. In. *Re Praught Estate* 2002 PESCTD 1; (2002) 208 Nfld. & P.E.I.R. 64 the Prince Edward Island Supreme Court held that a solicitor had to satisfy himself as to the testator's capacity, knowledge and approval, particularly if elderly or apparently suffering from delusions or lack of capacity. In *Hall v Estate of Bruce Bennett* [2003] W.T.L.R. 827; (2003) 227 D.L.R. (4th) 263, the Ontario Court of Appeal held that a solicitor has a duty to inquire into the client's testamentary capacity and be satisfied that it exists, particular care being required in suspicious circumstances such as the client being ill and elderly. The relevant question on liability in that case was not whether the client had capacity, but whether a reasonable and prudent solicitor could have concluded that he did not.

[42] The New Zealand Court of Appeal have held in *Knox v Till* [2000] P.N.L.R. 67 that there would be no duty to refuse to act if there were doubts about testamentary capacity, and in any event whether a testator has testamentary capacity is outside a solicitor's professional expertise. See also, *Ryan v Public Trustee* [2000] 1 N.Z.L.R. 700, where it was suggested that if there was doubt about capacity the will should be executed and the opinions on capacity recorded. The position in Canada is summarised in the decision of the Manitoba Court of Appeal in *Slobodianik v Podlasiewicz* (2003) 228 D.L.R. (4th) 610 that if there were suspicious circumstances as to testamentary capacity, the solicitor had to satisfy himself that capacity did exist, and if there were any possible doubt a note of the observations and conclusions should be made. If it were clear that the patient lacked capacity, the will should not be executed, see *Hall v Estate of Bruce Bennett* [2003] W.T.L.R. 827; (2003) 227 D.L.R. (4th) 263.

[43] See the Law Society's *Guide to the Professional Conduct of Solicitors* (8th edn, 1999) at para.12.05; for the updated *Guide* see the Law Society website. On the status of the *Guide* see paras 11–094 and 11–095, above.

[44] *Russel v Fraser* (1981) 118 D.L.R. (3d) 733 at 746, B.C.L.C., and cases referred to there. *Aylwin v Aylwin* [1902] P. 203 lends some indirect support to this proposition.

should see the client.[45] It is advisable for a solicitor to prepare an attendance note when taking instructions, and to record any advice given.[46]

Giving advice. A solicitor may fail to advise the testator properly. He should **11–222** take care to ensure that the client understands and agrees to the provisions of the will.[47] He may have to give advice on matters which he is not specifically asked to advise upon. Thus, if a solicitor knows that his client intends to marry in the near future, he should advise that the will is revoked on marriage unless expressly made in contemplation of marriage.[48] If a solicitor has given advice, and it is not accepted, he has no duty to persuade the testator to act differently. This is illustrated by the New Zealand case of *Sutherland v Public Trustee*.[49] The testator intended to leave his estate to his wife. The Public Trustee, who was in the same position as a solicitor, suggested to the testator that if his wife predeceased him, he could make a gift over to his step-children. The testator rejected this option. It was held, obiter, that there was no breach in failing to persuade the testator to change his mind.

The scope of the duty. The scope of the instructions and duty must be **11–223** examined. In *Cancer Research Campaign v Ernest Brown & Co*,[50] charities which were to benefit under the will of P claimed that the defendants were negligent in failing to advise P of the possibility of executing a deed of variation of the will of her brother N, under which she had inherited a substantial estate, and which deed would have substantially decreased the amount of inheritance tax payable. Harman J. held that the solicitors owed no duty to either the testator or the beneficiaries to advise on possible tax avoidance, the scope of their retainer being only to settle the will. In contrast, in *Earl v Wilhelm*[51] it was held that a solicitor should inquire into the client's circumstances, and in the special circumstances of that case enquiries should have been made with the testator's accountant. If this were done it would have been found that the land the testator intended to leave to the claimant beneficiaries belonged to his company. Similarly, in *MacKenzie v MacKenzie*[52] the Nova Scotia Court of Appeal found the defendant solicitor liable for failing to ask about the extent of the testator's estate, his earlier wills, and why six of his children were excluded from benefiting under his will. In *Carr-Glynn v Frearsons (a firm)*,[53] the solicitor pointed out to the 81-year-old

---

[45] See further the *Guide* at para.24.01.
[46] See C.N. von Benzon, "Avoiding solicitors' negligence in probate and trust work" *Law Society Gazette*, January 29, 1986 at 263, and para.11–175, above.
[47] " . . . it seems most unusual not to do one or other of two things, viz. either to read over the whole of the document which the party is about to sign or go through it passage by passage, and say there is a clause to this effect and a clause to that effect and so on," *per* Hannen P. in *Morrell v Morrell* (1882) 7 P.D. 68 at 72–73. See also, *Aylwin v Aylwin* [1902] P. 203, J. Turing, "The will making process" (1980) 124 S.J. 268 and *Russell v Fraser* (1981) 118 D.L.R. (3d) 733 at 746, British Columbia CA.
[48] *Hall v Meyrick* [1957] 2 All. E.R. 722, CA.
[49] [1980] 2 N.Z.L.R. 536, Jeffries J.
[50] [1998] P.N.L.R. 592.
[51] [2001] W.T.L.R. 1275 [1998] 2 W.W.R. 522, Saskatchewan QB, upheld on appeal at (2000) 183 D.L.R. (4th) 45.
[52] (1998) 162 D.L.R. (4th) 674.
[53] [1999] Ch. 326.

testatrix that it was not clear whether she was able to leave her share of a house to her niece, and it was agreed that the testatrix would obtain the deeds so that the position could be ascertained. The solicitor was negligent in failing to advise the testatrix to prepare a notice to sever what was in fact a joint tenancy, which could be done immediately, easily and unilaterally.[54]

11–224   **Knowledge of the law and attestation.** Although there may be exceptions for obscure points, in general "a lawyer who undertakes to attend a client and supervise the execution of a will can reasonably be expected to be familiar with all the comparatively simple provisions of the statute regulating the execution of wills and setting out the law in relation to gifts to witnesses and to the spouses of witnesses".[55] Several of the reported cases concern the signing of wills by the spouses of beneficiaries. For instance, in *Ross v Caunters*,[56] the defendant solicitors admitted negligence in failing to warn a testator that the will should not be witnessed by the spouse of a beneficiary, which then happened, with the result that the gift to the beneficiary was void.[57] In *Esterhuizen v Allied Dunbar Assurance Plc*[58] Longmore J. held that the defendant will-making company owed a duty to ensure proper attestation, and mere written instructions would not be sufficient; the client should be invited to the office to attest the will, or asked if he would like the solicitor to attend him at home to do so. Contrast *Gray v Richards Butler (a firm)*,[59] where Lloyd J. held that written instructions were sufficient, although there was a duty to check the attestation of a will where the solicitor did not personally supervise its execution. However, the minor irregularities apparent on the face of the will, in particular the misplaced signatures of witnesses who gave addresses in different parts of London, were not such as to put him on enquiry that the witnesses were not present at the time of the attestation.

11–225   **Time.** It may be important to act promptly in relation to wills. In *White v Jones*[60] the solicitors were negligent in failing to complete a new will within two months of being instructed and failing to keep two appointments made with the

---

[54] This conclusion of the Court of Appeal has been criticised by R. Kerridge and A. Brierley in "Negligence and conflicts of interest in will-making process" (1999) 115 L.Q.R. 201. They argue that although it was simple to serve a notice to sever, that could have soured relations between the testatrix and her nephew, who jointly owned the house. See also, *ibid.*, "Will making and the avoidance of negligence claims" [1999] Conv. 399.

[55] *Whittingham v Crease & Co* (1978) 88 D.L.R. (3d) 353 at 366, Aitkens J., British Columbia Supreme Court.

[56] [1980] 1 Ch. 297. The negligence was admitted, but Megarry V.C. approved the admission at 304D–F.

[57] See also: *Whittingham v Crease & Co* (1978) 88 D.L.R. (3d) 353: the solicitor was negligent in asking the wife of the beneficiary to witness the will; *Watts v Public Trustee for Western Australia* [1980] W.A.R. 97, Supreme Court Western Australia: the defendant was found to be negligent because he failed to enquire, on receipt of the signed will witnessed by "Margaret Watts, Housewife", whether she was married to the beneficiary Norval Watts.

[58] [1998] 2 F.L.R. 668.

[59] [2000] W.T.L.R. 143. In *Humblestone v Martin Tolhurst Partnership (a firm)* [2004] EWHC 151; [2004] P.N.L.R. 26, Mann J. also held that there was a duty to check the attestation of a will where the solicitor did not supervise the execution.

[60] [1995] 2 A.C. 207. For the facts see para.11–048.

testator. In *Smith v Claremont Haynes & Co*[61] a solicitor had the essence of an intended will made known to him by a testator. The testator had leukaemia, and the solicitor should have realised how ill she was. Despite prompting telephone calls, the solicitor failed to make an appointment to take full instructions for 33 days, by which stage the testator was too ill to give instructions. The solicitor was found to be "well short of the standards reasonably to be expected of a competent solicitor."[62] In *Hooper v Fynmores (a firm)*,[63] the solicitors were negligent in cancelling an appointment with an elderly client who was in hospital; this should not happen unless the client was content for the appointment to be missed. In contrast, Neuberger J. held that solicitors were not negligent in *X v Woollcombe Younge (a firm)*[64] when the solicitor took instructions from the testator in hospital, arranging to return next week, before which the client died. A reasonable solicitor could have formed the view that there was no real risk of the testator dying in the next few days, and it was not negligent not to recommend a holding codicil which might be disadvantageous. In *Atkins v Dunn & Baker (a firm)*[65] the Court of Appeal held that a solicitor who had sent a draft will to the testator had no duty to chase that client for a response, although there may be such a duty in some circumstances.

Other errors. It is likely that a solicitor will be held to be negligent for clerical **11–226** errors in the drafting of a will,[66] and it is advisable that the completed will should be checked by the solicitor who drafts it. Gifts to a solicitor must be treated with caution. As a matter of professional conduct, if the gift is of a significant amount, the solicitor must advise the client to be independently advised, and if the client declines to do this he must refuse to act.[67] The solicitor may have to prove that the testator knew and approved of the contents of the will if he wishes to keep the gift,[68] but he might also face an action from the estate for any wasted costs, or from a disappointed beneficiary.

---

[61] *The Times*, September 3, 1991, Judge Barnett Q.C. sitting as a deputy High Court judge. The report is very brief and does not record all the material facts, which are better explained in S. Baughen, "The will that never was: *Ross v Caunters* extended" (1992) 8 P.N. 99.

[62] Transcript, p.62. See also *Hawkins v Clayton* (1988) 78 A.L.R. 69, High Court of Australia: solicitors in possession of a will owed a duty of care to the executor in tort to take reasonable steps to locate the executor. There was a clear breach in failing to take any positive steps for six years. For the facts see para.11–044.

[63] [2002] Lloyd's Rep. P.N. 18, Pumfrey J.

[64] [2001] Lloyd's Rep. P.N. 274. For a commentary on this case see M. Jones, "Third party beneficiaries—disappointed again" (2001) 17 P.N. 113.

[65] [2004] EWCA Civ 263; [2004] W.T.L.R. 477.

[66] For an illustration in a case where the solicitor was not being sued, see *Re Morris* [1971] P. 62. A codicil removed parts of an earlier will to a greater extent than was intended by the testator, due to an error by a typist.

[67] See the Law Society's *Guide to the Professional Conduct of Solicitors*, (8th edn, 1999), p.318, para.15.05; for the current *Guide* see the Law Society website.

[68] See para.11–017, above.

3. DAMAGES

11–227 An award of damages or compensation is the principal remedy, and in most cases the only remedy,[69] which the court will grant for breach of duty by a solicitor.[70] Compensation may be awarded for breach of fiduciary duty, and damages for breach of contract or negligence. Where the solicitor's services are valueless to the client as a result of his breach of duty, the solicitor may also be debarred from recovering his costs or ordered to repay any costs which he has received from the client.[71]

(a) *Breach of Fiduciary Duty and Breach of Trust*

11–228 **Introduction.** In *Nocton v Ashburton*[72] the defendant solicitor advised the claimant in connection with a loan he sought. The borrowers were also clients of the defendant and he had a personal interest in the transaction. The security proved insufficient and the claimant suffered substantial losses. Neville J. at first instance found that the defendant had given bad advice and "fell far short of the duty which he was under as solicitor" but that he had not been fraudulent. Since the claim was pleaded in fraud, but not in negligence, the claimant's claim was dismissed. The House of Lords agreed with Neville J.'s findings, but by a majority held that the claimant was entitled to compensation for breach of fiduciary duty. Viscount Haldane L.C. explained that the solicitor's fiduciary duties were separate from his common law duties and that the remedies for breach were in the discretion of the court:

> "It did not matter that the client would have had a remedy in damages for breach of contract. Courts of Equity had jurisdiction to direct accounts to be taken, and in proper cases to order the solicitor to replace property improperly acquired from the client, or to make compensation if he had lost it by acting in breach of a duty which arose out of his confidential relationship to the man who had trusted him."[73]

Where the solicitor is in breach of fiduciary duty, the remedies are in the

---

[69] e.g. *British Mutual Investment Co v Cobbold* (1875) L.R. 19 Eq. 627: a solicitor acting for clients lending money upon a mortgage failed to spot a defect in the borrower's title to the mortgaged property. Upon the borrower's bankruptcy, the clients filed a bill in equity seeking a declaration that the solicitor was liable to make good the loss which they had sustained and take the property off their hands. Held that the claim was misconceived. The clients' remedy was to claim damages at common law.

[70] But see paras 11–126 *et seq.* for the wasted costs jurisdiction, an alternative remedy where a solicitor misconducts litigation. More diverse remedies are often available in equity, see para.11–228, below.

[71] This is discussed in para.11–318, as an instance of recovery by the client of "wasted expenditure". For further discussion of circumstances which may disentitle the solicitor to his fees, see Ch.3 paras 3–008—3–010.

[72] [1914] A.C. 932. For a helpful summary of what was decided by *Nocton v Ashburton*, see *Swindle v Harrison* [1997] 4 All E.R. 705 at 732, *per* Mummery L.J.

[73] *ibid.* at pp.956–957. See also the speech of Lord Dunedin at pp.964–965.

discretion of the court, and are not necessarily limited to compensation.[74] Where a solicitor trustee is in breach of duty he may be ordered to indemnify his co-trustees against any resulting liability.[75] Where a solicitor acts for a new client when there is a conflict of interest with an existing client, he may be ordered to disgorge profits.[76]

Claims in particular by lenders against their former solicitors have recently **11–229** been framed as breaches of trust in order to attempt to take advantage of the potentially superior remedies afforded by equity. The two main issues to be considered are whether the claimant has to prove that he would have acted differently but for the breach, and whether common law rules on remoteness and the like apply.

Brickenden. In the old case of *Brickenden v London Loan & Savings*[77] a **11–230** solicitor acted for the lender, the borrower, and had a personal interest in loan. He failed to disclose the existence of two other mortgages to the lender. The Privy Council held that:

> "When a party, holding a fiduciary relationship, commits a breach of his duty by non-disclosure of material facts, which his constituent is entitled to know in connection with the transaction, he cannot be heard to maintain that disclosure would not have altered the decision to proceed with the transaction, because the constituent's action would be solely determined by some other factors, such as the valuation by another party of the property proposed to be mortgaged. Once the Court has determined that the non-disclosed facts were material, speculation as to what course the constituent on disclosure, would have taken is not relevant".[78]

The case has been applied in a number of commonwealth cases where solicitors have failed to disclose material facts in breach of fiduciary duty.[79] The decision

---

[74] *Nocton v Ashburton* [1914] A.C. 932; *MacDonald v Lockhart* (1981) 118 D.L.R. (3d) 397, Nova Scotia CA. For examples of other remedies: where a solicitor has personal dealings with the client in breach of fiduciary duty, the transaction may be set aside, see, e.g. *Spector v Ageda* [1973] Ch. 30, Megarry J.; bribes or secret commissions can be recovered, e.g. *Islamic Republic of Iran v Denby* [1987] 1 Lloyd's Rep. 367, Leggatt J.

[75] *Re Linsley, Cattley & West* [1904] 2 Ch. 785, Warrington J.: a solicitor was ordered to indemnify a co-trustee against any liability for costs; *Re Partington, Partington v Allen* (1887) 57 L.T. 654, Stirling J.: a solicitor was primarily liable for the loss sustained by the beneficiaries. However, the solicitor is not liable to indemnify where the co-trustee actively participates in the breach of trust: *Head v Gould* [1898] 2 Ch. 250, Kekewich J.

[76] *3464920 Canada Inc v Strother* (2005) 256 D.L.R. (4th) 319 (British Columbia CA).

[77] [1934] 3 D.L.R. 465. For criticism of the case see Heydon (1994) 110 L.Q.R. 328 at 331–333.

[78] [1934] 3 D.L.R. 465 at 469.

[79] *Commerce Capital v Berk* (1989) 5 R.P.R. (2d) 177 and *Canada Trustco Mortgage Co v Bartlet & Richardes and Gates* (1996) 28 OR 768, both Ontario CA; *Roussel v Bertrand* (1996) 183 N.B.R. (2d) 81, New Brunswick CA (test interpreted as putting onus on solicitors); *Farrington v Rowe, McBride & Partners* [1985] 1 N.Z.L.R. 83, NZCA; *Commonwealth Bank of Australia v Smith* (1992) 102 A.L.R. 453, Federal Court of Australia, General Division, Full Court; *Stewart v Layton* (1992) 111 A.L.R. 687, Federal Court of Australia, General Division, Foster J.; *Unioil International Pty Ltd v Deloitte Touche Tohmatsu* [1997] 17 W.A.R. 98, High Court of Western Australia (*Brickenden* applied where there was a conflict between duty to client and the solicitor's own interest).

has been doubted in subsequent authority, discussed below. However, the question of its correctness does not arise when the remedy sought is one of recision.[80]

11–231   **The modern law.** In the leading English case of *Target Holdings Ltd v Redferns*[81] a different view was taken. The solicitors, Redferns, had acted for Target who were mortgagees lending £1,525,000 to a borrower. Redferns obtained the mortgage money, and paid it to the borrowers before the transfers of the property were executed rather than at execution. The money was held by Redferns on a bare trust, which was breached by the early payment. The House of Lords rejected the argument which had persuaded the Court of Appeal that immediately after the moneys were paid away in breach of trust there was an immediate loss and an immediate and continuing right to have the trust fund reconstituted. While common law rules of remoteness of damage and causation do not apply directly in equity, there needs to be a causal connection between the breach of trust and the loss of the estate, which will lead to the same result. Rules applicable to traditional trusts had no application to bare trusts in commercial situations, where the relations were governed by contract. *Target* has been applied in subsequent cases. In *Bristol & West Building Society v Daniels Co (a firm)*[82] it was held that the defendant solicitors were in breach of fiduciary duty in failing to inform the claimant lenders that they also acted for the vendors, but the claimant had to prove a causal link with the loss suffered. In contrast, in *Bristol & West Building Society v May May & Merrimans*,[83] solicitors had received funds in response to a request made on the basis of a report that the solicitor knew or must be taken to have known was misleading. Chadwick J. granted summary judgment, following *Brickenden*. However, that case was

---

[80] See *Maguire v Makaronis* (1997) 144 A.L.R. 729; [1955–1995] P.N.L.R. 35: the appellant solicitors loaned moneys to their client, and were in breach of fiduciary duty because they had not obtained fully informed consent to the transaction. The High Court of Australia set the transaction aside, but only on condition that the moneys were repaid. What the respondents would have done had they been informed of the need to obtain independent advice was not relevant, as the issue in the case was setting aside the transaction, and not equitable compensation. For a commentary on the decision, see S. Moriaty, "Fiduciaries and discretion" (1998) 114 L.Q.R. 9.

[81] [1996] 1 A.C. 421. For commentary, see R. Fletcher, "Mortgages, markets and the fiduciary principle" (1995) 11 P.N. 137. It should be noted that in some circumstances the trustee may be able to claim relief under s.61 of the Trustee Act 1925, which was not relied upon by the defendants in *Target*. The 1991 case of *Alliance & Leicester v Edgestop* [1999] Lloyd's Rep. P.N. 868, Hoffmann J., is probably consistent with the decision in *Target*, where the House of Lords approved but distinguished it. *cf. Jalmoon Pty Ltd v Bow* [1997] 2 Qd.R. 62, where the Queensland Court of Appeal found the defendant solicitor liable for breach of trust in paying over moneys received on behalf of the claimant company to its 49 per cent shareholder, on his instructions purportedly given on behalf of the claimant, and was liable for the amount of the payment made. In "Equity's place in the law of commerce" [1998] L.Q.R. 214 at 223–227, Lord Justice Millett argued that there are two disquieting features about the reasoning in *Target Holdings Limited v Redferns*. First, there is no sensible distinction to be drawn between traditional family trusts and bare trusts used commercially; trustees of a family settlement could have negligently parted with trust moneys before obtaining an executed mortgage in the same way as Redferns did. Secondly, there is no explanation of why the common law rules on causation apply, which the author explains by an analysis of how equity will take an account of a trustee's dealings with trust property. See also, S. Elliott, "Remoteness Criteria in Equity" (2002) 65 M.L.R. 588.

[82] [1997] P.N.L.R. 323, Ch. D.

[83] [1996] 2 All E.R. 802.

overruled by the Court of Appeal in *Bristol & West Building Society v Mothew*,[84] where Millett L.J. made it clear that the breach of fiduciary duty had to be deliberate.

Recent commonwealth authority. In *Canson Enterprises Ltd v Boughton*[85]   **11–232** the defendant solicitor acted for the claimant in the purchase of property. It was assumed for the purposes of a special case that the solicitor knew that the vendors were making an improper profit, but failed to inform the claimant, and that the claimant would not have entered the transaction if it had known of the secret profit. The Supreme Court of Canada held that the claimant could recover damages for breach of fiduciary duty. A majority held that damages were to be assessed according to common law principles,[86] and a minority held that foreseeability and similar common law limits on damages were not relevant. In *Beach Petroleum NL v Kennedy*[87] the New South Wales Court of Appeal held that causation had to be established, following *Target Holdings* and distinguishing *Brickenden*. In *Youyang Pty Ltd v Minter Ellison Morris Fletcher*[88] the High Court of Australia reached the same conclusion. In that case solicitors had instructions to release $500,000 to a third party to purchase a bearer deposit certificate. They released the monies in breach of trust in a number of respects, and as a result the monies were lost. Causation needed to be and was proved. If a trustee wished to assert that there was no loss because the beneficiary would have authorised the breach, there was an evidentiary onus on the trustee to prove that. In *Gilbert v Shanahan*[89] the New Zealand Court of Appeal made it clear that the claimant must show that he has suffered loss as a result of the defendant solicitor's breach of fiduciary duty.

Measure of compensation. In the other leading case on this subject, *Swindle*   **11–233** *v Harrison*,[90] the claimant solicitors loaned monies to their client, the defendant, in order for her to complete the purchase of a hotel. The business failed, and the claimants sought possession of the hotel. The defendant successfully claimed that the claimants were in breach of fiduciary duty as they had not disclosed the profit they were making from the loan. The Court of Appeal held that the defendant was not entitled to equitable compensation as she could not prove that she would not have accepted the loan if the claimants had made full disclosure to her. Evans L.J. also suggested that only if there were equitable fraud would the measure of loss be the same as for common law fraud, otherwise the ordinary common law principles would apply in assessing damages. However, it would appear that Hobhouse and Mummery LL.J. did not make any distinction between fraudulent and non-fraudulent breach of fiduciary duty. According to the interpretation of

---

[84] [1997] 1 Ch. 1, see further, para.11–023, above.
[85] (1992) 85 D.L.R. (4th) 129. For the later resolution of the case see *Canson Enterprises Ltd v Boughton* [1996] 1 W.W.R. 412.
[86] Thus the claimant has to prove causation, see *44246 BC Ltd v 0909 Management Inc* (2000) 80 B.C.L.R. (3d) 299, BCCA.
[87] (1999) 48 N.S.W.L.R. 1.
[88] [2003] H.C.A. 15; [2003] W.T.L.R. 751. See S. Elliott and J. Edelman, "*Target Holdings* considered in Australia" (2003) 119 L.Q.R. 545
[89] [1998] 3 N.Z.L.R. 528, not following *Brickenden*.
[90] [1997] 4 All E.R. 705. For a commentary, see Tjio and Yeo, "Limited liability for breach of fiduciary duty" (1998) 114 L.Q.R. 181.

the case by the Court of Appeal in *Collins v Brebner*,[91] the majority decided that the principles to be applied to all breaches of fiduciary duty were the same as for fraud at common law, requiring that the fraud induced the transaction and the loss flowed directly from that transaction, but not that the losses were reasonably foreseeable.

11-234   **Restitution.** Another attempt to obtain a superior remedy than that which existed in contract or tort was made in *Portman Building Society v Hamlyn Taylor Neck (a firm)*.[92] The defendant solicitors failed to inform the claimant lender that the security property was used as a guest house, although the loan was on the basis that the property was to be used as a private residence only. The claimant claimed in restitution for money had and received, arguing that it had paid monies over to the defendant solicitors in the mistaken belief that the property would be used as a private residence. The Court of Appeal struck the action out on the grounds that the defendant solicitors were not unjustly enriched by the payment, which it had applied to the purchase of the property, and the transaction was not ineffective.

(b) *Remoteness*

11-235   The assessment of damages at common law is subject, in every case, to the overriding principle that the damage in respect of which compensation is sought must not be too remote from the solicitor's breach of duty. Broadly speaking, this means that: (a) the breach of duty must have "caused" the damage[93] and (b) the damage in question was foreseeable.[94] The law has developed so that we should add a third requirement, which it is convenient to discuss under the heading of remoteness. This is (c) that the loss must be within the scope of the duty.[95]

(i) *Causation*

11-236   **"But for" causation.** Whether the claim is brought in contract or tort, it is first necessary to determine whether the solicitor's breach of duty was "the cause" of the alleged damage.[96] The burden of proof is on the claimant to prove causation.[97] Clearly, the breach of duty was not the cause if the damage would

---

[91] [2000] Lloyd's Rep. P.N. 587 at 589. See also *Nationwide Building Society v Balmer Radmore (a firm)* [1999] P.N.L.R. 606 at 660F–672C. Blackburne J. exhaustively analysed the authorities, including the Privy Council's decision in *Rama v Millar* [1996] 1 N.Z.L.R. 257 (where the Court required proof of causation) and concluded that unless the fiduciary had acted dishonestly or in bad faith, the court should assess the actual loss caused by the breach, and the claimant has to show in any event that but for the breach of duty he would not have acted in the way which caused his loss.

[92] [1998] 4 All E.R. 202.

[93] As to which see paras 11–236—11–243.

[94] As to which see paras 11–244—11–247.

[95] As to which see paras 11–248—11–253.

[96] For a statement of the general principles, see *McGregor* (17th edn), paras 6–005—6–074 (in relation to tort) and paras 6–126–6–143 (in relation to contract).

[97] See *Wilsher v East Essex Area HA* [1988] A.C. 1074, which was applied in a solicitor's negligence case by the British Columbia Court of Appeal in *Haag v Marshall* (1989) 1 C.C.L.T. (2d) 99, with the qualification that "in a situation where it is impossible, as a practical matter, to prove whether the breach of duty caused the loss, it is more in keeping with a common sense approach to causation as a tool of justice to let the liability fall on the defendant". See also, paras 11–268 and 11–287.

have occurred in any event.[98] In *Sykes v Midland Bank Executor & Trustee Co Ltd*,[99] for example, the Court of Appeal held that the claimants would have entered the underlease in question, even if they had been properly advised by their solicitors. Accordingly, nominal damages only were awarded.[1] It is necessary for the claimant to prove that if proper advice had been given he would have acted differently, and it is not enough merely to prove that he relied on the solicitors advice; however, where the solicitor negligently gave incorrect advice or information, it may be the case that the claimant needs only show that he would not have acted as he did if he had not been given such advice, and he does not have to show that he would not have acted as he did if he had been given the proper advice.[2] In *Vision Golf Ltd v Weightmans (a firm)*[3] the defendants

---

However, in *Etridge v Pritchard Englefield* [1999] P.N.L.R. 839, the solicitors were negligent in failing to give the claimant any advice about charges she was making on her property to raise money for her husband. The Court of Appeal held that there was no presumption that the client would have followed the advice which should have been given to her, and the burden remained on the claimant to prove on the balance of probabilities that she would have done so. Further, in *Boateng v Hughmans (a firm)* [2002] EWCA Civ 593; [2002] P.N.L.R. 40, the Court of Appeal emphasised that in all cases where failure to advise was alleged against a solicitor, the claimant had to plead and prove what he would have done if he had been properly advised. The claimant in that case failed to prove that he would have acted differently.

[98] Unless there are concurrent causes of the damage, as in *Baker v Willoughby* [1970] A.C. 495. The authors are not aware of any case in which this principle has been applied to a claim against solicitors. The principle was questioned by the House of Lords in *Jobling v Associated Dairies Ltd* [1982] A.C. 794. See further Hart and Honore, *Causation in the Law* (2nd edn), pp.247–248. For another case where the claimant failed to prove causation, see *Westbury v Sampson* [2001] EWCA Civ 407; [2002] 1 F.L.R. 166. The defendant solicitors acted for the claimant husband in ancillary relief proceedings, and failed to inform him that any lump sum settlement could be later varied by the court pursuant to s.31 of the Matrimonial Causes Act 1973, as in fact happened. The Court of Appeal held that the claimant could not establish causation as there was no way to protect him from the effect of s.31.

[99] [1971] 1 Q.B. 113. For the facts see para.11–262. This decision has been applied in a number of cases: *GP P Ltd v Bulcraig & Davies* (1986) 2 E.G.L.R. 148, although with the opposite result (see para.11–258); *Stratton Ltd v Weston, Financial Times*, April 11, 1990, Ch. D.: a solicitor negligently failed to register client's lease; there was no loss as the landlord would have sold free of the lease anyway under a prior equitable mortgage; *Polischuk v Hagarty* (1983) 149 D.L.R. (3d) 65: the solicitor for the purchaser accepted an undertaking from the vendor's solicitor without first consulting his client. At trial the claimant recovered nominal damages only, on the basis that (if consulted by the solicitor) he would probably have decided to accept the undertaking. This decision was reversed, however, by the Ontario Court of Appeal, who took a different view of the evidence: (1985) 14 D.L.R. (4th) 446; *Income Trust Co v Watson* (1984) 26 B.L.R. 228, Ontario High Court; *Hanflex Pty Ltd v NS Hope & Associates* [1990] 2 Qd.R. 218, Queensland Full Court.

[1] See, however, paras 11–261—11–268 on the differing approach taken in evaluating a chance.

[2] See *Bristol & West Building Society v Mothew* [1998] Ch. 1. In that case, misrepresentations were made, and by virtue of the easier test of causation just outlined, the claimant lender was able to obtain summary judgment. Millett L.J.'s view of the reliance required for negligent misstatements was based on his interpretation of the Court of Appeal's decision in *Downs v Chappell* [1997] 1 W.L.R. 426. Hobhouse L.J. subsequently suggested this interpretation is wrong in *Swindle v Harrison* [1997] 4 All E.R. 705 at 728. Millet L.J.'s interpretation is also criticised by J. O'Sullivan: in "Acts, omissions and negligence professionals: confusion over counterfactuals" (2001) 17 P.N. 272. However, in *White v Paul Davidson & Taylor (a firm)* [2004] EWCA Civ 1511; [2005] P.N.L.R. 15, the Court of Appeal were content to apply the *Mothew* distinction, despite scepticism about whether it was correct, observing that every case of giving incorrect advice necessarily involved a failure to give proper advice. The Court of Appeal also made clear that the special policy reasons in *Chester v Afshar* [2005] 1 A.C. 134, where the House of Lords afforded a remedy to a claimant who could not satisfy traditional causation principles, did not apply in professional negligence claims outside clinical negligence.

[3] [2005] EWHC 1675, Ch; *The Times*, September 1, 2005.

breached their duty in failing to apply to the court on behalf of their tenant clients for relief from forfeiture, which application would have succeeded. The defendants argued that this caused no loss because an application for relief by new solicitors would have succeeded. Lewison J. dismissed this argument. The loss would have been avoided if the defendants had acted as they should have. There was no claim that the subsequent solicitors had acted unreasonably, and thus it was irrelevant that a subsequent application may have succeeded, although the judge also held that it would have been a difficult one.

11–237   In *Hilton v Parker Booth & Eastwood (a firm)*[4] solicitors acted for the claimant purchaser and the vendor in the sale of development sites. The defendant solicitors were in breach of contract[5] in acting for both parties to the transaction, and also in breach for failing to disclose to the claimant that the defendant had just been released on licence from a sentence of imprisonment for fraudulent trading and other offences. While the solicitors had obtained that information while acting for the vendor in his criminal proceedings, it was not confidential, and it should have been disclosed. The defendants could not argue that no loss had caused as they should have insisted that the claimant instruct other solicitors, who would not have known of the vendor's criminal history. That first breach did not exonerate the solicitors from liability for the second and more serious breach.

11–238   **Proximity.** Assuming that the claimant overcomes this hurdle, he will still fail if the causal link between the solicitor's breach and the subsequent damage is too tenuous. Thus in *Braid v W L Highway & Sons*,[6] for example, the claimant was obliged to sell certain securities in order to meet liabilities which he had incurred to a third party, as a result of his solicitors' negligence. He recovered by way of damages all the sums which he had had to pay to the third party,[7] but he did not recover his stockbroker's fees for selling the securities. Roskill J. stated:

> " . . . it would seem contrary to all principle if this were allowed. What Mr. Braid had to pay was a sum of money. How he raised that money was a very long way from the defendants' breach."

In *Nash v Phillips*[8] the claimants recovered damages because they were unable to purchase the house of their choice, owing to their solicitors' negligence. One of the matters they complained of was that the house they did purchase ("Chynance") was less convenient that the house they had wished to buy. Foster J. refused to award the claimants damages under this head:

---

[4] [2005] UKHL 8; [2005] 1 W.L.R. 567. See J. Getzler "Inconsistent fiduciary duties and implied consent" (2006) 122 L.Q.R. 1.

[5] The claim was pleaded in contract, but the House of Lords made clear that the duties in question had their roots in the fiduciary duty of trust and confidence.

[6] (1964) 191 E.G. 433. See also, the New Zealand Court of Appeal case *Inder Lynch Devoy & Co v Surbritsky* [1979] 1 N.Z.L.R. 87: because of the delay in receiving the sale price of his former home, the building costs of the claimant's proposed new house increased. It was held that the claimant was not entitled to recover these additional building costs, because they were too remote.

[7] See para.11–312.

[8] (1974) 232 E.G. 1219.

" . . . in my judgment the inconvenience in this case did not result directly from the solicitor's negligence. The Nashes were not forced to purchase Chynance as a result of his negligence, and all the inconvenience stems from that purchase."

This principle was explored in the accountant's negligence case of *Galoo Ltd* **11–239** *v Bright Grahame Murray*,[9] which held that that a distinction must be drawn between a breach which gives the occasion for the loss and one which is the substantial cause of the loss. This rule may encompass the question of the intervening acts of the claimant or a third party which are discussed below. *Galoo* was applied in *Young v Purdy*.[10] Solicitors wrongfully terminated a retainer to act for the claimant in proceedings for ancillary relief. She continued to act for herself, and by remarrying she effectively lost the right to claim relief. The Court of Appeal concluded that the solicitor's negligence was the occasion and not the cause of the loss as the claimant acted negligently, and they also held that the loss was not foreseeable. However, in *Aneco Ltd v Johnson & Higgins Ltd*.[11] Evans L.J. suggested that the search for an effective cause has been replaced by an inquiry into the scope of the duty of care, following *Banque Bruxelles Lambert v Eagle Star Insurance*.[12]

Intervening act of the claimant. If the immediate cause of the damage in **11–240** question was some unwise action or inaction on the part of the claimant, then the court will more readily hold that the chain of causation has been broken. A number of cases illustrate this principle.[13] In *Simmons v Pennington*[14] the claimant, on the advice of his solicitors, decided not to re-sell his property, pending the outcome of certain litigation. During this period the property was damaged by fire and, since the insurance policy had lapsed, the claimant suffered loss. The Court of Appeal held that it was not necessary to determine whether the solicitor's advice was negligent, since the damages claimed were too remote. The claimant's loss was due to his own failure to insure.[15] In *Frank v Seifert Sedley & Co*[16] solicitors were acting for the purchaser of a lease. As a result of their negligence the vendor increased the asking price from £7,500 to £9,000. The client agreed to pay the increased price and contracts were exchanged on that basis. The client failed to complete and claimed damages of £1,500 against her

---

[9] [1994] 1 W.L.R. 1360, CA, on which see Ch.17, para.17–125, and see *Bernasconi v Nicholas Bennett* [2000] Lloyd's Rep. P.N. 285, discussed in Ch.12, para.12–043. See also, *MacMahon v James Doran & Co* [2002] P.N.L.R. 33 where the claimant ran up a sizeable overdraft as a result of the defendants solicitors delaying litigation on his behalf. Relying on *Galoo*, the Northern Ireland Court of Appeal held that the solicitors were not liable for the overdraft because the incurring of a capital obligation to repay was not a loss as it was balanced by the receipt of the sum advanced. The claimant could recover the interest payments.
[10] [1997] P.N.L.R. 130.
[11] [2000] P.N.L.R. 152 at 161C, an insurers brokers' case, on which see Ch.16, para.16–141.
[12] [1997] A.C. 191. For the law on scope of duty see paras 11–248 *et seq.*, below.
[13] See also, *Mallesons Stephen Jaques v Trenorth Ltd* [1999] 1 V.R. 727, Victoria CA. The defendant solicitors acted for the vendors of commercial premises. They were negligent in failing to include in their draft disclosure statement reference to a supplemental agreement with the tenant giving him a rent-free period. However, there was a break in the chain of causation by the vendor's fraudulent non-disclosure of that agreement to the purchaser.
[14] [1955] 1 W.L.R. 183.
[15] *per* Denning L.J. It was also held that the damage was not foreseeable.
[16] (1964) 108 S.J. 523.

solicitors. Melford Stevenson J. held that the claimant would have been able to raise the necessary money to pay the increased purchase price, and that her loss flowed from her own failure to complete. He awarded nominal damages. In *Clark v Kirby-Smith*[17] the claimants lost the opportunity to renew their lease of business premises as a result of their solicitors' negligence. On leaving the premises they were faced with a claim by their landlords for dilapidations, which they settled for £120. Plowman J. held that this loss was not caused by the solicitors' negligence, but by the claimants' own breach of covenant.

11–241   **Intervening act of a third party.**[18] The chain of causation may also be broken by the intervening negligence of some third party. However, not every mistake amounts to negligence.[19] In *Cook v Swinfen*,[20] for example, as a result of the solicitors' breach of duty the client did not defend divorce proceedings brought by her husband. About three months after the decree nisi the solicitors sought counsel's advice in conference on the matter. Counsel advised that they should not move to set aside the decree. Lawton J. held that counsel's advice was wrong, since a motion to set aside the decree nisi would probably have succeeded. However, he went on to hold that counsel's error was not negligent, and that it did not break the chain of causation. Therefore the solicitors were liable for the consequence, namely that there was a decree of divorce against the client. The case subsequently went to the Court of Appeal,[21] but this part of Lawton J.'s judgment was not challenged.[22]

11–242   A different principle was applied in *Connor v Ritzman*.[23] Solicitors who acted for the purchasers of leasehold property failed to note discrepancies in the leasehold conveyancing documents. The purchasers of the freehold wrongly refused to agree to rectification, but Robert Walker J. held that their intransigence was not a new intervening cause, as solicitors are paid to avoid trouble of this very kind, and the solicitors were liable for their clients' losses. Similarly, in *British Racing Drivers Club v Hextall Erskine Co (a firm)*[24] the defendant solicitors failed to advise the board of directors that a proposed investment which involved one of the directors needed the approval of a general meeting as a result of s.320 of the Companies Act 1985. It was argued that the subsequent loss was

---

[17] [1964] 1 Ch. 506.
[18] Some guidance as to whether the later negligence of solicitors will always break the chain of causation from the negligence of earlier solicitors may be derived from two Court of Appeal decisions in the context of clinical negligence cases: *Rahman v Arearose Ltd* [2001] Q.B. 351 at paras 26–33, and *Webb v Barclays Bank Plc* [2001] Lloyd's Med. L.R. 500 at paras 52–57.
[19] As discussed in the first two sections of this chapter.
[20] [1966] 1 W.L.R. 635.
[21] [1967] 1 W.L.R. 457.
[22] Another illustration of the same principle is to be found in *Hart & Hodge v Frame, Son & Co* (1839) 6 C. & F. 193: where an error by magistrates did not break the chain of causation. For the facts see para.11–312.
[23] (1995) 70 P.C.R. D41. See also, *Barnes v Hay* (1988) 12 N.S.W.L.R. 337, CA. The solicitors acted for a tenant of a shop, and negligently failed to warn him of the consequences of not taking a formal lease. The tenant was unwarrantably harassed by his lessor in an attempt to obtain vacant possession, which he was not in a position to be able to resist because of his precarious title. The lessor's conduct was not an intervening act which broke the chain of causation, for the solicitors had the duty to advise the tenant in part because he was apt to suffer the very kind of loss that he did, see Mahoney J.A. at 355E–F, and Hope and Priestley JJ.A. at 340F–341A.
[24] [1996] 4 All E.R. 667, Carnwarth J.

caused by the director's commercial misjudgment, so that the solicitor's negligence was the occasion for the loss rather than the substantial cause of the loss. The judge rejected this argument and held that the purpose of the statutory provision requiring approval of the general meeting was to protect a company against the directors' judgments being distorted by conflicts of interest and loyalties.

Intervening act of the defendant. In *Normans Bay Ltd v Coudert Brothers (a firm)* the Court of Appeal held that, as a matter of public policy, defendant solicitors cannot rely on their own intervening negligence to break the chain of causation.[25] The point will seldom arise as the claimant would normally amend to plead the alleged negligence. In that case, the claimant lost its investment in a Russian firm when a Russian court declared invalid its tender offering a five-year investment period, as the government had decreed a three-year maximum. The defendants could not rely on the allegation that no loss had been caused because they had failed to seek anti-monopoly permission.

11–243

(ii) *Foreseeability*

In order to succeed, the claimant must establish not only that the damage was caused by the solicitor's breach of duty, but also that it was foreseeable. If the claim is brought in contract, then at the time the contract was made the damage must have been "reasonably foreseeable as liable to result from the breach."[26] This has been interpreted narrowly in *The Heron II*[27]; the event must be "not unlikely", and "a type of damage which was plainly foreseeable as a real possibility but which would only occur in a small minority of cases cannot be regarded as arising in the usual course of events".[28] If the claim is brought in tort, then at the time the breach of duty was committed the damage (or at least the type of damage) must have been reasonably foreseeable as a consequence.[29] In many cases, of course, foreseeability poses no problem for the claimant, since the solicitor has special knowledge of his client's intentions.[30] In *McLoughlin v Jones*[31] the Court of Appeal held that the question of the foreseeability of

11–244

---

[25] *The Times*, March 24, 2004.

[26] *per* Asquith L.J. in *Victoria Laundry (Windsor) Ltd v Newman Industries Ltd* [1949] 2 K.B. 528. For a full discussion of the requirement of foreseeability in contract, see *McGregor* (17th edn), paras 6–144—6–184.

[27] [1969] 1 A.C. 350.

[28] *ibid.*, *per* Lord Reid at 385–386.

[29] For a full discussion of the requirement of foreseeability in tort, see *McGregor* (17th edn), paras 6–075—6–124. In *Cadoks Pty Ltd v Wallace Westley & Vigar Pty Ltd* [2000] VSC 167; (2000) 2 V.R. 569, Victoria Supreme Court., the loss was foreseeable in tort, but not contract. The defendant solicitors negligently failed to ensure their clients had finance in place for the purchase of a farm, causing a delay in purchase of 15 months. The solicitors knew that the claimant intended to resell, but the loss of the opportunity to sell at a favourable time was held to be too remote in contract although not in tort.

[30] e.g. *King v Hawkins & Co, The Times*, January 28, 1982, Mars-Jones J.: solicitors for the purchaser knew that their client intended to extend the property. It was foreseeable that he would incur substantial losses if he did not acquire good title to parts of the land.

[31] [2002] Q.B. 1312.

psychiatric injury, caused by the defendant solicitors' allegedly negligent handling of his criminal trial which resulted in his imprisonment, should be determined with the assistance of expert medical evidence.

11-245 **Illustrations.** In *Pilkington v Wood*[32] the claimant was not advised by his solicitor of the defect in title of a house which he bought in Hampshire. The defect only came to light when he needed to move to Lancashire because of a change in his employment. This meant that the claimant had difficulty in selling the property. He obtained temporary accommodation in Lancashire during the week and returned to the house in Hampshire, where his wife was still living, at weekends. The claimant recovered as damages the diminution in value of the property attributable to the defective title. He did not recover the costs of travel between Hampshire and Lancashire,[33] or the interest payable on his overdraft as a result of the delay in selling the property. Harman J. held that these items were not within the reasonable contemplation of the parties at the time when the solicitor was retained. The decision, at least with respect to the interest payments, must be in doubt given the conclusions in *Hayes v Dodd*,[34] discussed below.[35]

11-246 A similar argument was advanced by the defendant solicitors in *G & K Ladenbau Ltd v Crawley & De Reya*.[36] As a result of their negligence when acting on the purchase of certain property, rights of common which had been mistakenly registered against it did not come to light until the claimants sought to sell. As a result the sale was delayed and the claimants: (i) paid additional interest on their mortgage, and (ii) lost the interest which they could have earned by investment of the net proceeds of sale. Mocatta J. rejected the argument that these items were too remote, given that the defendants had been told by the claimants that they intended to develop part of the property and sell or let it:

> "the defendants should in my judgment have reasonably contemplated that if they failed to secure an unencumbered title for the claimants without warning them of the defect, the damages the claimants would suffer were "not unlikely" to be the loss of a handsome profit on resale."[37]

It should be noted that the defendants knew that the claimants intended to develop part of the land and let or sell the remainder. In the later Court of Appeal

---

[32] [1953] Ch. 770. For another example, see *Matlock Green Garage Ltd v Potter Brooke-Taylor & Wildgoose (a firm)* [2000] Lloyd's Rep. P.N. 935, where solicitors who failed to renew the claimant's business tenancy could not be expected to foresee the effect this might have on parts of the business carried on at other sites. For the facts see para.11–272. See also, *Parry v Edwards Geldard (a firm)* [2001] P.N.L.R. 44, where Jacob J. held that it was not foreseeable that, as a result of losing a right of pre-emption to purchase adjacent land, the claimant farmer would lose a milk quota which he would not have to pay for, as an earlier error by the valuer in failing to take account of the quota attached to the land was not foreseeable.

[33] For a similar decision on similar facts see *Douglas v Stuart Wyse Ogilvie Estates Ltd* [2001] S.L.T. 689, OH.

[34] [1990] 2 All E.R. 815, CA.

[35] At para.11–246. Another case where recovery was not allowed, perhaps surprisingly, is *Piper v Daybell, Court-Cooper & Co* (1969) 210 E.G. 1047. The defendant solicitors failed to notice a right of way. The claimants purchased the property, and sold it as a result of the inconvenience caused by the right of way. Nield J. held that this was not foreseeable, and did not allow recovery for professional fees for that transaction.

[36] [1978] 1 W.L.R. 266. For the facts see paras 11–093 and 11–199.

[37] *ibid.* at 289E–F.

case of *Hayes v Dodd*[38] the claimants acquired property principally for business purposes where there was no right of way over the only convenient access. It took the claimants five or six years to dispose of the property, and they recovered all the expenses they incurred during those years. There was a dispute over whether rates, insurance, redundancy payments, conveyancing costs and life insurance were too remote. The Court of Appeal decided they were not, although there was little discussion of the matter.[39]

Time to consider foreseeability. One of the problems concerning the con-   **11–247** tractual rules is that the point of time at which foreseeability must be considered is when the contract was made. This could work injustice to the claimant in solicitors' negligence cases, since much may happen between the date of the retainer and the date when the breach of duty occurs. In *Cook v Swinfen*,[40] for example, the claimant failed to recover damages for anxiety resulting in injury to her health, since this was not reasonably foreseeable when she first instructed the solicitor. In *Malyon v Lawrance, Messer & Co*,[41] however, Brabin J. awarded damages for neurosis resulting from the solicitors' negligence, even though this may not have been foreseeable at the time when they were initially retained. The judge refused to accept that the extent of the solicitor's liability was fixed by reference to the situation "which existed at the moment when the claimant, as it were, walked into the defendants' office."[42] It may be thought that the con-tractual rules as to remoteness were somewhat stretched in order to do justice in that case. However, it now seems that there is probably a parallel liability in tort, and the judge's conclusion can be justified on that basis. The problem referred to at the beginning of this paragraph can normally be avoided by applying the tortious rules as to remoteness of damage.

(iii) *The Scope of the Duty*[43]

The principle. In *Banque Bruxelles Lambert SA v Eagle Star Insurance Co*   **11–248** *Ltd*[44] the House of Lords held that someone under a duty to advise on what is the appropriate course of action will be liable for all the foreseeable consequences of the action taken in reliance, but a person under a duty to take reasonable care to provide information on which someone relies will generally be regarded as responsible for the consequences of the information being wrong, and not all the consequences of the reliance. As a result, negligent valuers sued by mortgage

---

[38] [1990] 2 All E.R. 815.

[39] *ibid.* at 818B, 824D–E, and 827B. It was unsuccessfully argued that the lessor's harassment was unforeseeable in *Barnes v Hay* (1988) 12 N.S.W.L.R. 337, CA. The court applied the tortious rules of foreseeability.

[40] [1967] 1 W.L.R. 457 at 462B, CA. See also, *Ekkebus v Lauinger* (1990) 73 O.R. (2d) 743 High Court. (defendant solicitors failed to ascertain whether hot tub on property being purchased by their clients complied with the appropriate byelaws; claimants liable to visiting child injured by falling into tub; defendants not liable to claimants as loss too remote).

[41] [1968] 2 Lloyd's Rep. 539.

[42] *ibid.* at 550–551.

[43] For a critical view see H. Evans, "The scope of the duty revisited" (2001) 17 P.N. 146; and H. Evans, *Lawyers' Liabilities* (2nd edn, 2002), Ch.9. The doctrine should be seen as one concerning the extent of liability, see L. Hoffmann "Causation" (2005) 121 L.Q.R. 593.

[44] [1997] A.C. 191, on which see Ch.10, paras 10–113—10–119. The case is often referred to under the name of *South Australia Asset Management Corp v York Montague Ltd*, or *SAAMCO*.

lenders were held to be liable only for the difference between their valuations and the correct valuations, and they were not liable for the further loss suffered by the lenders when the value of the security declined as a result of the fall in the property market. This principle is of significance in many solicitor's negligence cases, and most importantly in actions brought by lenders against solicitors who acted for them in the making of loans.[45] A number of cases involving solicitors apply the *BBL* principle, which will be discussed below.

10–249   **Information and advice.** It is submitted that solicitors advising in commercial transactions, like other professional advisers, are generally under a duty to provide specific information or advice and not to advise on the wisdom of transactions in general, and thus the loss for which they are responsible will be limited to the consequences of the specific information or advice being accurate. Of course the facts of any particular case may show that the solicitor is under a wider duty to advise on the wisdom of the transaction as a whole. In *Cottingham v Attey Bower & Jones (a firm)*[46] Rimer J. expressly agreed with this statement, and added that there were no fundamentally different considerations in a domestic conveyancing transaction. In that case solicitors acting for vendors of property failed to obtain a copy of building regulations consent for substantial renovations which had never in fact been granted. As the duty was only to provide information, the solicitors were liable for the overpayment due to defects which had not been noted in the survey report which the claimants had obtained and which assumed that building regulations had been complied with, but not for all the defects identified in the property.

11–250   Similarly, in *Green v Turner*[47] it was alleged that the defendant solicitors negligently advised the claimant property developer that the title of property which he was contemplating purchasing would be registered within four to six weeks, and that as a result he purchased the property and carried out a limited scheme of refurbishment, but the sale on was delayed by two months, so that he

---

[45] This issue is further explored at paras 11–304 and 11–305. Of particular importance is the *Steggles Palmer* case in *Bristol & West Building Society v Fancy & Jackson (a firm)* [1997] 4 All E.R. 582, an "information" case, where Chadwick J. held that the consequence of the solicitors' breach was that the claimant loaned money to a borrower whom they would not have wanted to lend to as the circumstances of the loan were suspicious, and the defendants were held liable for the full amount of the claimant's loss. It remains to be seen, particularly following the actuaries' negligence case of *Andrew v Barnett Waddingham (a firm)* [2006] P.N.L.R. 24, whether the distinction between information and advice, which may focus on the particular breach in question rather than the professional's role as a whole, is in fact different in principle or practice from an enquiry as to whether the negligent breach was central to the client's transaction.

[46] [2000] P.N.L.R. 557. *cf. Michael Gerson Investments Ltd v Haines Watts (a firm)* [2002] P.N.L.R. 34, where it was alleged that the defendant solicitors, by releasing documents in a tax saving scheme, impliedly advised that good title was available to the containers which underlay the scheme. The solicitors gave no tax advice but were only concerned with the question of good title. Rimer J. held that it was arguable that they gave advice rather than information, and were responsible for the wasted expenditure of the scheme which failed.

[47] [1999] P.N.L.R. 28, Ch. D. For another straightforward example see *Guild (Claims) Ltd v Eversheds (a firm)* [2000] Lloyd's Rep. P.N. 910, Jacobs J., where it was alleged that the solicitors were negligent in relation to the contents of a circular to the shareholders of Airbreak for the raising of capital to purchase Sunsail. Airbreak later went into liquidation. The purpose of the advice was to ensure that the circular was accurate for those who were going to rely on it, which did not include Airbreak. The solicitor's liability to that company was limited to claims against it brought by third parties based upon the misleading circular, of which there were none.

incurred a liability of £50,000 to a sub-purchaser. It was held that the alleged loss was caused by the investment decision, not the decision to purchase. Furthermore, the scope of the duty in any event did not include the alleged loss, as the duty covered the consequences of the information being wrong not the consequences of decisions made in reliance on that information.

An exception. In contrast, in *Carter v TG Baynes & Sons*[48] the defendant **11–251** solicitors failed to note that there were restrictive covenants preventing development of the site which the claimant intended to purchase, and advised him to go ahead with the transaction. The claimant recovered for all foreseeable losses, including those resulting from a fall in the market, as the advice had been to proceed with the works, and it was not limited to giving information.

Further cases.[49] The distinction between information and advice, and the **11–252** scope of the solicitor's duty, has been explored in cases where lenders have sued the solicitors they instructed, which are summarised below.[50] A number of cases in other areas have also addressed these issues. In *Pearson v Sanders Witherspoon*[51] the defendant solicitors were negligent in failing to prosecute their client's action timeously against Ferranti, which went into administration. The Court of Appeal held that the loss of opportunity to enforce the judgment obtained was not within the scope of the defendant's duty, which was to act with due expedition, unless expressly assumed by the solicitor, or he was given sufficient notice of the impecuniosity. In *Jenmain v Steed & Steed*[52] the defendant solicitors acted for the vendors in a contract race. It was held that they were also retained by the claimants, who were some of the proposed purchasers, in a limited capacity which required the solicitors to pass on the fact that they were also dealing with another proposed purchaser. The scope of the duty, based on rule 6A of the Solicitors' Practice Rules 1990, was to avoid wasted costs. The judge found they would have obtained the property if properly advised by the defendants. The Court of Appeal held that they could recover any wasted costs and also the difference between the price they would have paid and the value of the property. However, they could not recover the profits they would have made from the proposed development of the property. In contrast, in *Keydon Estates Ltd v Eversheds LLP*[53] the claimant purchased commercial property in order, as the defendants knew, to obtain an income stream. The defendants negligently advised that a sub-lease did not operate as an assignment, when in fact it did, and the subtenant went into liquidation and the income stream was lost. While an

---

[48] [1998] E.G.C.S. 109, Ch. D.
[49] For a further example in relation to the loss suffered as a result of a defective will, see *Corbett v Bond Pearce (a firm)* [2001] 3 All E.R. 769, CA, summarised at para.11–052, above. See also, *Trust Co of Australia v Perpetual Trustees* (1997) 42 N.S.W.L.R. 237, where McLelland C.J. in Equity applied *BBL* and held that a solicitor who failed to advise the trustee company that a conflict of duty would arise if it acquired property was not responsible for the losses it suffered from an improvident investment which had nothing to do with the solicitor's breaches.
[50] See paras 11–304 and 11–305.
[51] [2000] P.N.L.R. 110.
[52] [2000] P.N.L.R. 616.
[53] [2005] EWHC 972; [2005] P.N.L.R. 40.

"information" case, Evans-Lombe J. awarded the claimant the hypothetical rent it would have obtained on another notionally similar property in which it would have invested if properly advised, rather than the normal difference in value of the property at the date of purchase.

11–253   In *Petersen v Personal Representatives of Rivlin*,[54] the claimant purchased property which was subject to litigation with a neighbour, and in respect of which he gave an indemnity for 90 per cent of any liability and of the costs of the proceedings from the date of the contract. The defendant solicitor negligently failed to explain the indemnity provision properly, and the claimant would have withdrawn from the transaction if it had been explained. The failure to advise was a failure to provide information, and the claimant's claim for the vendors' legal fees in the proceedings with the neighbour were not within the scope of the duty, as he did understand and accept that the indemnity applied to costs liabilities incurred by the vendors after the exchange of contracts. In *McLoughlin v Jones*,[55] the claimant alleged that as a result of the defendant solicitors' negligent handling of his criminal trial he was imprisoned, which caused his psychiatric illness. The Court of Appeal held that it was arguable that the purpose of the defendants' engagement was to minimise the risks of wrongful conviction and of suffering psychiatric illness. They applied the tests of the scope of duty or purpose, and also the assumption of responsibility and the tripartite test of foreseeability, proximity and justice and reasonableness.

(c) *Measure of Damages*

11–254   Whether the claim is brought in contract or tort, the fundamental principle governing the measure of damages is that the claimant should be put, so far as money can do it, and subject to the rules as to remoteness which have just been discussed, in the position he would have occupied if the solicitor had discharged his duty.[56] Broadly speaking, this may be achieved in one of two ways, depending upon the particular facts of the case: (i) by paying to the claimant the monetary equivalent of any benefits of which he has been deprived; or (ii) by indemnifying the claimant against any expenses or liabilities which he has incurred. In practice, the assessment of damages is subject to a number of rules which are considered below.

---

[54] [2002] Lloyd's Rep. P.N. 386.
[55] [2002] Q.B. 1312.
[56] See: *Livingstone v Rawyards Coal Co* (1880) 5 App. Cas. 25 at 39 and *Dodds Properties v Canterbury CC* [1980] 1 W.L.R. 433 at 451, 454 and 456 (as to general principles); *Braid v WL Highway Sons* (1964) 191 E.G. 433, Roskill J.; *County Personnel (Employment Agency) Ltd v Alan R Pulver & Co* [1987] 1 W.L.R. 916, at 925C–E, CA, and *Hayes v Dodd* [1990] 2 All E.R. 815 at 817C and 818F, CA (all in relation to solicitors' negligence). See also, *Bartter v Gambril* (1932) 76 S.J. 868: the enrichment of a third party as a result of solicitor's alleged breach of duty was not relevant to assessment of damages. In *Welburn v Dibb Lupton Broomhead (a firm)* [2002] EWCA Civ 1601; [2003] P.N.L.R. 28 the claimant alleged that his solicitors had lost him the fruits of an arbitration by delay. The Court of Appeal held that he could claim no damages where the beneficial interest of the claim had been vested in the claimant's supervisor under an individual voluntary arrangement, although he retained the legal interest.

(i) *Date of Assessment*

The general rule. Damages are generally assessed as at the date of breach, **11–255**
unless justice requires that some other date should be taken.[57] This principle is
illustrated by a number of cases. In *Amerena v Barling*[58] the defendant solicitor's
negligently granted an option over shares in a company without the claimant's
authority, which would not have been forthcoming. The Court of Appeal summarised the law as follows: damages will normally fall to be assessed at the date
when the cause of action arose[59]; but this principle will not be applied mechanistically in circumstances where assessment at another date may more accurately
reflect the overriding compensatory principle.[60] The Court was not satisfied that
the taking of an assignment of the option two years later at a cost of £1.75m. was
reasonable. They considered that damages should be assessed at the date of
breach, when the benefits receivable under the option agreement were not less
than the value of the shares over which the claimant had granted an option. Only
nominal damages were therefore awarded. In *Ricci v Masons*[61] the diminution in
the value of the claimant's restaurant business caused by the fact that he had
obtained a new lease without statutory protection was assessed at the date of
breach, rather than at the date the new lease would have been obtained (where the
loss to the claimant would have been somewhat less) or at the date of trial. In
Mahoney v Purnell[62] the defendant solicitors were negligent in relation to the
sale by the claimant to his son-in-law of his interest in their jointly owned hotel.
May J. assessed damages at the date of sale in 1988, rather than the much higher
value of the shares when the hotel was about to be sold in 1989 or the value at
the date of trial which was zero.[63] In *Aylwen v Taylor Joynson Garrett*[64] the
claimant purchased a property from her estranged husband for £1.8 million
which was subject to a £1 million mortgage. She alleged that the defendant
solicitors had negligently failed to complete the purchase or inform her of
possession proceedings by the mortgagee, which sold the property for £1.2
million in June 1993. The Court of Appeal held that damages should be assessed
at the date of breach, and thus the action was struck out as there was no evidence
that the mortgagee sold the property at an undervalue. The claimant was not

---

[57] *Zakrzewski v Chas. Oldhams & Sons* (1981) 260 E.G. 1125, QBD. For general statements of
principle in cases which did not concern solicitors' negligence see *Banque Bruxelles Lambert v Eagle
Star* [1997] A.C. 191 at 220 (Lord Hoffmann) and *Smith New Court Securities Ltd v Scrimegeour
Vickers (Asset Management) Ltd* [1997] A.C. 254 at 266 (Lord Browne-Wilkinson). For a slightly
different view see *Reeves v Thrings & Long* [1996] 1 P.N.L.R. 265 at 278; the facts are summarised
at para.11–276.
[58] (1995) 69 P.C.R. 252.
[59] see *Miliangos v George Frank (Textiles) Ltd* [1976] A.C. 443, 468, *per* Lord Wilberforce.
[60] See *County Personnel Ltd v Alan R Pulver & Co* [1987] 1 W.L.R. 916 at 926, *per* Bingham L.J.
The exceptions to the difference in value rule set out at paras 11–275 *et seq.* provide many
illustrations also of exceptions to the principle that damages will normally be assessed at the date of
breach. Bingham L.J.'s dictum was also followed in *Roker House Investments Ltd v Saunders* [1997]
E.G.C.S. 137, Ch. D., where the date of assessment was held to be the date the negligence came to
light.
[61] [1993] 38 E.G. 154; see para.11–272 for the facts.
[62] [1996] 3 All E.R. 61.
[63] For a further example see *Wapshot v Davies Donovan & Co* [1996] 1 P.N.L.R. 361, summarised
at para.11–275, below. See also, *Griffiths v Last Cawthra Feather (a firm)* [2002] P.N.L.R. 27, T.C.C.,
following *Wapshot*.
[64] [2001] EWCA Civ 1171; [2002] P.N.L.R. 1.

entitled to claim for the loss of an opportunity to redevelop or enfranchise the property, which would entail valuing the case at a date of her choosing, and there was nothing to suggest that this property could not be replaced.[65]

11–256 **Exceptions.** In a number of cases a date of assessment some time after the breach has been chosen. In *McElroy Milne v Commercial Electronics Ltd*[66] the claimant was developing industrial property and found a tenant, Imagineering. It instructed the defendant solicitors to draft a lease guaranteed by Imagineering's principal shareholder, Studio. In late 1987, the defendant solicitors negligently failed to make Studio party to the lease. Imagineering, which was in financial difficulties, repudiated the lease. The New Zealand Court of Appeal agreed with the assessment by the trial judge: if the lease had been guaranteed, the claimant would have been able to sell the development fully let for NZ$5.25m. in January 1989. As a result of the fall in property prices, the claimant was instead left with an unsold development at the time of the trial in July 1990 which was worth about NZ$4m. Damages were assessed at NZ$1.25m, relying particularly on *Czarnikow v Koufos*,[67] subject to a deduction of 25 per cent for contingencies. The Court considered that assessing damages at the date of the breach, although the general rule, was artificial and unjust in this case, and that the fall in the property market was foreseeable.[68] More recently, in *Portman Building Society v Bevan Ashford (a firm)*[69] the defendant solicitors negligently failed to reveal information to the claimant building society which cast doubt on the reliability of the borrower and his covenant, and in particular that the balance of the purchase price was being raised by a loan secured by a second charge. Immediately after completion, the claimant knew of the second charge, and it was argued that the claimant could have extracted itself from the transaction at that stage with no loss. The Court of Appeal held that as the claimant reasonably did not know of the breach of duty of the defendants, it could recover the full loss it later sustained.

(ii) *Credit for Benefits*

11–257 **General principle.** The restitution principle[70] necessarily entails that the claimant should give credit for any incidental or compensating benefits which

---

[65] cf. *Cadoks Pty Ltd v Wallace Westley & Vigar Pty Ltd* [2000] VSC 167; (2000) 2 V.R. 569, summarised at para.11–334.
[66] [1993] 1 N.Z.L.R. 39. In *Snipper v Enever Freeman & Co* [1991] 2 E.G.L.R. 270 Sheen J. had to assess damages for the loss of enfranchisement rights caused by the defendant solicitor's negligence. If the loss of value at the date of breach in 1983 was taken along with the benefit of an extension to the lease which was obtained in a compromise of proceedings in 1987, that would be unfair to the claimant because of inflation between the two dates. The judge assessed the loss as at 1987. For a case similar to *McElroy* where damages were assessed at the date of an aborted sale in 1996 after a purchase by the claimant in 1994, see *Feerni Development Ltd v Daniel Wong & Partners* [2001] 2 HKLRD 13, Hong Kong High Court.
[67] [1969] 1 A.C. 350, HL.
[68] For an example see *Kennedy v KB Van Emden & Co* [1996] P.N.L.R. 409, summarised at para.11–282.
[69] [2000] P.N.L.R. 344.
[70] See para.11–254.

flow from the solicitor's breach of duty.[71] This factor is not uncommon in cases where, because of a solicitor's negligence, the client's business affairs have taken an altogether different course. For example, in *Port of Sheerness Ltd v Brachers*[72] the defendant solicitors failed to advise the claimants that dismissing dockers would lead to claims for unfair dismissal, and as a result the claimants settled claims at a cost of £2.5m. However, they had to give credit for the fact that the claimants did not have to reinstate or reengage the dockers, enabling them to move straight away to a cheaper system of contracting labour. In accordance with normal principles relating to insurance monies, lenders which sue solicitors for negligence in relation to mortgage transactions do not have to give credit for moneys obtained as a result of taking out a mortgage indemnity guarantee policy.[73]

Further illustrations. The evaluation of the benefit may not be straightforward. In *GP&P Ltd v Bulcraig & Davies*[74] the defendant solicitors were retained in relation to the purchase of new office accommodation for the claimant, an advertising agent. The solicitors failed to discover that the premises were in part subject to a conditional planning consent restricting the use of the ground floor premises to the printing trade. The claimant took the lease, which was at a very favourable rent, and expended large sums of money improving the premises. After a year and a half of occupation, the claimant went into liquidation, and the restrictive user clause was then discovered. The receiver was unable to dispose of the lease, and so surrendered it to the landlord. Damages were assessed on the basis of the expenditure wasted on effecting the improvements. In calculating the recoverable damages, credit was given for the sum received on the surrender of the lease to the landlords, and for the benefit enjoyed in occupying the premises for the period. The judge decided that the beneficial occupation had to be fixed on the basis of a rent taking into account the existence of the planning restriction, because the defendants would be taking advantage of their own wrongdoing in assessing the rent without such a restriction. That decision was not challenged on appeal. The judge also decided that the claimant should give credit for the beneficial occupation assessed as the difference between the rental value after the improvements of £118,000 and the rental value before the improvements of £88,000, rather than the difference between the £118,000 and the actual rent paid of £35,000. He did not consider that the claimant had to give credit for the favourable bargain it had reached with the landlord. The Court of Appeal came to the opposite conclusion on this issue: but for the defendants' error, there would have been no lease, and thus no favourable bargain with the landlord, and the claimant would have had to find premises elsewhere at an open market rent.

11–258

---

[71] e.g. *Nadreph v Willmett & Co* [1978] 1 W.L.R. 1537, Whitford J.: claimants had to pay compensation to their tenants, but got the benefit of vacant possession of the premises.

[72] (1997) I.R.L.R. 214.

[73] See *Bristol & West Building Society v May May & Merrimans (a firm) (No.2)* [1998] 1 W.L.R. 336, Chadwick J. (where the solicitors were given the opportunity to join the insurers before any payment was ordered to avoid any risk of double jeopardy), followed by the Court of Appeal in *Portman Building Society v Bevan Ashford (a firm)* [2000] P.N.L.R. 344, a solicitors' case, and *Arab Bank Plc v John D Wood Ltd* [2000] 1 W.L.R. 857, a surveyor's case. See further Ch.10, para.10–123.

[74] (1986) 2 E.G.L.R. 148, first instance; (1988) 1 E.G.L.R. 138, CA.

11–259   A curious problem on evaluating benefits was posed by *Teasdale v Williams &
Co*.[75] Owing to the negligence of his solicitors the tenant of business premises
did not acquire a new lease for five years at a rental of £20,000 per annum.
Instead he acquired a seven year lease at a rental of £19,000 for the first two years
and £26,500 for the last five years. Leonard J. awarded damages of £17,500,
representing the loss of £19,500 in years three to five less the gain of £2,000 in
years one and two. He declined to take into account the "gain" in years six and
seven (which would arise because there was no rent review at the end of year
five). The Court of Appeal upheld this decision. The "gain" in years six and
seven would be offset by the fact that a rent review at the end of year seven
would produce a higher figure than a rent review at the end of year five.
Forevermore the claimant's rent would be reviewed two years later than would
have been the case if the solicitors had not be negligent. This approach is surely
right. The court will not bring into the assessment of damages a gain which is
speculative or remote.

11–260   **Remote or incidental benefits.** Benefits may be too remote or incidental to be
taken into account. This is nicely illustrated by *Hayes v Dodd*.[76] The claimants
acquired property for business purposes where there was no right of way over the
only convenient access. It took them five or six years to dispose of it, during
which the value of the maisonette, which formed part of the property, increased
in value. The Court of Appeal decided that credit need not be given for that
increase, except to the extent of the interest charges over the maisonette during
that period to which the claimants were otherwise entitled.[77] It is submitted that
the distinction made is a sensible one, albeit difficult to justify logically. In *Royal
Bank of Canada v Clark*[78] the defendant solicitor negligently advanced the
bank's money without obtaining proper security. He was held to be liable to
repay the full amount of the advances, even though part of the advances were
used by the bank to reduce the borrower's overdraft.

(iii) *Evaluation of a Chance*[79]

11–261   In the course of assessing damages, it is frequently necessary to speculate what
would have happened if the solicitor had properly discharged his duty. Where the
matter is in doubt, an approach sometimes taken by the courts is (i) to assess

---

[75] (1984) 269 E.G. 1040.
[76] [1990] 2 All E.R. 815. See more generally *Hussey v Eels* [1990] 2 Q.B. 227, CA, and *Gardner v
Marsh & Parsons* [1996] P.N.L.R. 362. For an application see *Owen v Fielding* [1998] E.G.C.S. 110,
where Steel J. did not give the defendant credit for profits made on the sale of land when the claimant
had purchased it subject to rights of common due to the defendant solicitor's negligence.
[77] [1990] 2 All E.R. 815 at 818C, 822G, and 826F.
[78] (1978) 88 D.L.R. (3d) 76, aff'd by the Supreme Court of Canada 105 D.L.R. (3d) 85. See also
Lomond Assured Properties Ltd v McGregor Donald [2000] S.L.T. 797, OH, where it was held that
developers suing solicitors for obtaining securities which were postponed to other interests over
development land did not have to give credit for a settlement from a bank for issuing an unauthorised
cheque.
[79] See further: H. Evans *Lawyers' Liabilities* (2nd edn, 2002), Ch.12; *ibid*., "Damages for solicitors'
negligence: (3) damages for the loss of a chance" (1992) 8 P.N. 85; G. Reid, "The hypothetical
outcome in professional negligence claims" (2001) 17 P.N. 129; G. Reid: "The hypothetical outcome
in professional negligence claims: Part II" (2001) 17 P.N. 262, and J. Stapleton: "Cause-in-fact and
the scope of liability for consequences" (2003) 119 L.Q.R. 388 at 402–411.

damages on the basis of a particular hypothesis, and then (ii) to scale down the award according to the probability that the hypothesis is correct.[80] A distinction must, however, be drawn between what the claimant would have done and how a third party might have acted.

What the claimant would have done. If the question is what the claimant   **11–262**
himself would have done, he must prove on the balance of probabilities that he would have acted differently. In *Sykes v Midland Bank Executor & Trustee Co Ltd*[81] a solicitor going through an underlease with his clients failed to point out to them the effect of a somewhat onerous clause relating to change of user. The claimants were unable to say in evidence whether or not they would have taken the underlease, if they had been correctly advised. The Court of Appeal, reversing the decision of the trial judge, held that "on balance of probabilities" the claimants would have taken the underlease in any event and therefore they were only entitled to nominal damages.

What a third party would have done. If, however, the question is what some   **11–263**
third party would have done in the hypothetical scenario following competent advice from the defendant solicitor, then damages are assessed on the basis of the loss of a chance. This has been made clear by the Court of Appeal in *Allied Maples Group Ltd v Simmons & Simmons*.[82] The claimants wished to acquire some of the assets of Kingsbury Warehouse Limited, a part of the Gillow group of companies. While they had hoped to purchase only some properties, this was not possible because there were conditions against alienation and the like which were personal to Kingsbury. Therefore, the claimants decided to purchase Kingsbury itself and transfer unwanted properties from that company. The defendant solicitors failed to inform them that some properties which had previously been owned by Kingsbury had first tenant liabilities, which might involve claims against Kingsbury if the assignees of those properties defaulted. After the claimants bought Kingsbury, there were such claims. On a preliminary issue,

---

[80] The court may have to make a rough and ready assessment accounting for the fact that a range of outcomes are possible, as in *McMorran's Cordova Bay Ltd v Harman* (1979) 106 D.L.R. 495, British Columbia CA (loss of opportunity to sell property).
[81] [1971] 1 Q.B. 113. *cf. Otter v Church, Adams, Tatham & Co* [1953] Ch. 280, Upjohn J., where solicitors failed to advise that an airman on active service should execute a disentailing assurance promptly upon attaining 21. Had he done so, the value of his estate on death would have been increased by some £7,000. The court awarded £6,500 to reflect the possibility that the airman may, in any event, have decided not to disentail. The correctness of the case was doubted by Salmon L.J. in *Sykes v Midland Bank Executor & Trustee Co Ltd* [1971] 1 Q.B. 113 at 130B; *cf.* Karminski L.J. at 132A–C. In *Hall v Foong* (1995) 65 S.A.S.R. 281, the Full Court of South Australia followed *Sykes* and held that the claimant had not proved what she would have done if the defendant solicitor had not been negligent, and thus awarded her only nominal damages, as did the Supreme Court in *Smith v Moloney* [2005] S.A.S.C. 305; (2005) 223 A.L.R. 101.
[82] [1995] 1 W.L.R. 1602. *cf. Martin Boston & Co v Roberts* [1996] 1 P.N.L.R. 45; for facts see para.11–180, above. The defendant solicitors failed to obtain a charge over a house from a third party in support of her personal guarantee. A majority of the Court of Appeal held, following *Sykes*, that the question of whether the guarantee would have been obtained should be judged on the balance of probabilities. For an earlier example see *Nash v Phillips* (1974) 232 E.G. 1219, Foster J.: the claimants lost the opportunity to purchase a particular house as a result of their solicitor's negligence. Damages were reduced by 10% to reflect the possibility that they may not in any event have gone ahead with the purchase.

Turner J. found for the claimants, and held that as a result of their solicitors' negligence they had lost the opportunity of negotiating with the Gillow group to obtain protection against potential claims resulting from first tenant liabilities. The Court of Appeal held that provided the claimants could prove on the balance of probabilities that they would have negotiated with the Gillow Group, they could recover substantial damages if there was a significant chance that they might have succeeded in those negotiations. The claimants did not have to prove on the balance of probabilities that they would have succeeded in those negotiations, which would have depended on the hypothetical actions of a third party. Accordingly, the measure of damages was the value of the lost chance. On the facts, the Court held that the claimants had a realistic chance of renegotiating the deal.

11–264   **Illustrations.**[83] There are now a number of examples of the application of this principle.[84] In *Stovold v Barlows*[85] the defendant solicitors were negligent in sending deeds by DX when the purchaser's solicitors were not on the DX, and the claimant's sale then failed. The Court of Appeal considered that he had lost a chance of the sale going ahead, which they evaluated on the facts at 50 per cent on an assessment of how long the deeds might have taken to arrive by post and whether the purchaser might still have been tempted by an alternative property. In *Hartle v Laceys*[86] the Court of Appeal held that there was a 60 per cent chance of a deal going ahead with the proposed purchaser, but for the defendant solicitors' negligence. In *Inter-Leisure Ltd v Lamberts*[87] the judge had to evaluate the effect of the defendant solicitors negligently inserting an upwards/downwards rent review clause into a lease instead of an upward only one. He determined that there was a 75 per cent chance that the tenants would have accepted an upwards only rent review clause, and a one-third chance that the tenants would not have exercised a break clause at the end of a third year, so that 25 per cent of the full loss was awarded. In *Abraxas Computer Services Ltd v Rabin Leacock Lipkan (a firm)*[88] the defendant solicitors negligently failed to make applications to the court to extend leases under the Landlord and Tenant Act 1954. As a result, the claimant had three months to resolve its accommodation needs, instead of two and a half years. The judge held that the claimant lost the chance of obtaining a better deal on some other property equivalent to that which it did move into, which he assessed as 35 per cent of the difference between what the claimant paid and the offer from an alternative bidder. In *Lloyds Bank Plc v Parker Bullen (a firm)*[89] the defendant solicitors failed to inform the lender of a covenant against assignment. While the transaction would have gone ahead in any event, there was a prospect of obtaining a more favourable outcome to negotiations with

---

[83] See also the loss of a chance approach to lost litigation discussed at paras 11–284 *et seq.*
[84] See also: *Titanic Investments v McFarlanes* [1997] N.P.C. 105; *Rey v Graham & Oldham (a firm)* [2000] B.P.I.R. 354, McKinnon J. (failure to apply for adjournment of bankruptcy proceedings, 80% chance of avoiding bankruptcy, damages reduced by 20%); *Finley v Connell Associates (a firm)* [2002] Lloyd's Rep. P.N. 62 (if properly advised, development 60% likely to commence by May 1990, profits reduced by £30,000 if development started later, damages reduced by £12,000).
[85] [1996] 1 P.N.L.R. 91.
[86] [1999] Lloyd's Rep. P.N. 315, summarised at para.11–283, below.
[87] [1997] N.P.C. 49, QBD.
[88] [2000] E.G.C.S. 70; N.P.C. 63, QBD.
[89] [2000] Lloyd's Rep. P.N. 51.

the owner of the borrower. Longmore J. held that there was only a 15 per cent chance of the bank obtaining a more favourable deal, which would have avoided any loss. In *Motor Crown Petroleum Ltd v SJ Berwin & Co*[90] the Court of Appeal upheld a finding by the same judge that the claimants had a 40 per cent chance of obtaining planning permission if the solicitors had challenged in time the local council's designation of the land on which they wished to build a petrol station as open countryside. In contrast, in *Bacon v Howard Kennedy (a firm)*,[91] the testator's will, which would have left his estate to the claimant, was never concluded due to the defendants' negligence. The court rejected a submission that damages should be reduced because the testator might have made changes to his will, because such a possibility was merely speculative.

In *Channon v Lindley Johnstone*,[92] the defendant solicitors had failed to **11–265** prepare and present the claimant's case properly in an application for ancillary relief by his former wife. The Court of Appeal held that it should consider the best order that the claimant was reasonably likely to have obtained if his case was properly presented. On the basis of the revised figures which should have been presented to the District Judge, which showed that the claimant had a smaller income than had appeared originally, the financial split with the claimant's former wife would have been 50:50, and not 60:40 in her favour as had actually been ordered. Damages were reduced by 20 per cent to reflect the fact that the claimant was a bad witness who would not have inspired sympathy in the court, and that the court might have continued to award a split of 60:40. In *Maden v Clifford Coppock & Carter (a firm)*,[93] the defendants had given negligent advice in relation to a claim brought against the claimant, but for which he would have attempted to settle the claim by paying £20,000 plus costs. The Court of Appeal held that there was an 80 per cent likelihood of a settlement at that figure, given that the original claimant had offered to settle for £25,000 plus costs. In *Ball v Druces & Attlee (a firm)*[94] the defendant solicitors failed to protect the claimant's interest in the Eden Project, of which he was a co-founder, by suggesting an agreement with the trustees which would have cemented his right to a share in the profits. The claimant would have accepted that advice, and there was an appreciable chance that his co-founder, the trustees and the Millennium Commission, who were the principal funders of the project, would have agreed to such an arrangement. The claimant lost a 70 per cent chance of obtaining substantial benefits, being a 50 per cent chance of a £1 million buyout of his rights with a five year service agreement, and a 20 per cent chance of a buyout of such rights at £1.5 million with a five year service agreement.

---

[90] [2000] Lloyd's Rep. P.N. 438. The Court of Appeal rejected a submission that there was no loss, distinguishing *Hotson v East Berkshire Area HA* [1987] A.C. 750.

[91] [1999] P.N.L.R. 1, H.H. Judge Bromley Q.C., sitting as a Judge of the Chancery Division. In *Prosser v Castle Sanderson Solicitors (a firm)* [2003] Lloyd's Rep. P.N. 584, the defendant solicitors negligently failed to advise the claimant, during a hostile creditors' meeting in relation to his proposed individual voluntary arrangement, that he could seek and obtain an adjournment of the meeting. However, the Court of Appeal upheld the judge's conclusion that no loss was suffered, as there was no realistic chance of the decision of the creditors' meeting being any different if adjourned.

[92] [2002] EWCA Civ 353; [2002] P.N.L.R. 41.

[93] [2004] EWCA Civ 1037; [2005] 2 All E.R. 43.

[94] [2004] EWHC 1402; [2004] P.N.L.R. 39.

11–266   **The limits of the principle.** The courts are still working out all the circumstances in which losses should be considered on the basis of the loss of a chance rather than the balance of probabilities. Three particular instances should be noted. *Allied Maples* was applied in the context of the chances of a claimant being acquitted of criminal charges if further evidence had been forthcoming in *Acton v Graham Pearce & Co (a firm)*.[95] In contrast, in *Veasey v Millfeed Co Ltd*[96] the Court of Appeal assumed without deciding that the question of causation in wasted costs proceedings should be determined on the balance of probabilities, as full discovery and cross-examination did not take place in such an application. In *Cancer Research Campaign v Ernest Brown & Co*[97] Harman J. seemed to decide, obiter, and it is submitted correctly, that disappointed beneficiaries had to prove only that they lost the chance that they would have received benefits under a putative deed of variation of a will.

11–267   **The position in the Commonwealth.** The High Court of Australia came to an almost identical decision to *Allied Maples in Poseidon Ltd v Adelaide Petroleum NL*,[98] although in Canada different courts have adopted different views.[99] The New Zealand Court of Appeal upheld a 25 per cent discount to the damages awarded in *McElroy Milne v Commercial Electronics Ltd*[1] on the basis that even if there had been no breach, the claimants might have had some difficulties. In *Benton v Miller & Poulgrain (a firm)*,[2] the New Zealand Court of Appeal followed *Allied Maples* in deciding that what the claimant would have done had proper advice been given had to be decided on the balance of probabilities, but

---

[95] [1997] 3 All E.R. 908. For the facts of the case see para.11–183. *cf. Folland v Reardon* (2005) 249 D.L.R. (4th) 167 where the Ontario Court of Appeal held that a claimant who had been wrongly convicted and imprisoned allegedly as a result of his lawyers negligence would have to prove on the balance of probabilities that he would have avoided that result if his lawyers had acted competently.

[96] [1997] P.N.L.R. 100. See para.11–140 for the facts. In *Brown v Bennett (No.2)* [2002] 1 W.L.R. 713, Neuberger J. held that the applicant had to prove that the lawyers' conduct had caused the waste of costs on the balance of probabilities.

[97] [1998] P.N.L.R. 592 at 604. For a contrary view of what the judge found, see J. Murphy, "Probate solicitors, disappointed beneficiaries and the tortious duty to advise on tax avoidance" (1998) 14 P.N.L.R. 107.

[98] (1994) 68 A.L.J.R. 313 (a case which did not concern solicitors); *cf.* the earlier case of *Waribay Pty Ltd v Minter Ellison* [1991] 2 V.R. 391, Victoria App. Div.

[99] *Bossee v Clavette* (1984) 56 N.B.R. (2d) 375, New Brunswick CA: solicitors failed to secure release of client's obligations under mortgage; deduction as speculative whether release could have been obtained. *Fraser Park South Estates Ltd v Lang Michener Lawrence & Shaw* (2001) 3 C.C.L.T. (3d) 270, British Columbia CA: no loss of a substantial chance as a result of solicitor's negligence. *Graybriar Industries Ltd v Davis & Co* (1992) 46 B.C.L.R. (2d) 164, affd on damages 72 B.C.L.R. (2d) 190 by the British Columbia CA: claimant awarded $60,000 for the loss of the opportunity to continue negotiations which might have led to a more favourable agreement. *Papageorgiou v Seyl and Parkland Farm Power & Equipment Ltd* (1990) 45 B.C.L.R. (2d) 319, British Columbia CA: claimant awarded $15,000 for the loss of a chance to sell his restaurant. *cf. Clarke v Poje and Kenney* (1989) 38 B.C.L.R. (2d) 110, British Columbia CA: claimant could not prove that the defendant solicitor would probably have successfully negotiated a compromise with his bank reducing his liability.

[1] [1993] 1 N.Z.L.R. 39. For the facts see para.11–256, above. See also *Apatu v Peach Prescott & Jamieson* [1985] 1 N.Z.L.R. 50, at 69, Eichelbaum J.: loss of opportunity to purchase property, 10% deducted for contingencies.

[2] [2005] 1 N.Z.L.R. 66.

the reactions of third parties fell to be determined on the basis of the loss of a chance.

Burden of proof. As a matter of practice the courts tend to lean in favour of **11–268** the claimant when considering, hypothetically, what would have happened if the defendant solicitors had performed their duty.[3] A number of cases suggest that on some occasions the burden of proof shifts to the solicitors to show that the alleged benefit would not have materialised in that event,[4] but this must be wrong in the light of the House of Lords' decision in *Wilsher v East Essex Area Health Authority.*[5]

(d) *Heads of Damage*

The losses which may result from breaches of duty by solicitors cover a wide **11–269** variety of situations. However, certain types of loss are of common occurrence. It is hoped that the classification offered below will be of some assistance.

(i) *Loss of Opportunity to Acquire or Renew an Interest in Property*

Alternative methods of evaluation. Where, as a result of the solicitor's error, **11–270** the client is unable to proceed with an intended purchase or renewal, his loss is normally represented by (a) the value of the property he intended to buy less (b) the sum for which he would have bought it.[6] In *Stinchcombe & Cooper Ltd v Addison, Cooper, Jesson & Co,*[7] as a result of negligence by the purchasers' solicitors, the vendors were enabled to rescind a contract for the sale of building land. The contract price was £2,250. The value of the land at the time of rescission was £6,500. Damages were assessed at £4,250. An alternative method of quantifying damages was adopted in *Simpson v Grove Tompkins & Co.*[8] As a result of his solicitors' negligence the claimant was unable to purchase certain property in 1978. However, he was able to acquire the property (albeit at an overvalue) in 1979. The Court of Appeal held that the measure of damages was the difference between the market value in 1979, and the price which the claimant was originally asked to pay in 1978. By contrast, in *Endhill Pty Ltd v*

---

[3] e.g. *Kitchen v Royal Air Force Association* [1958] 1 W.L.R. 563, CA, and *Mount v Barker Austin (a firm)* [1998] P.N.L.R. 491, discussed at para.11–287, below.

[4] e.g. *Heywood v Wellers* [1976] Q.B. 446 at 459, (*per* Lord Denning M.R.). In *Ferris v Rusnack* (1984) 9 D.L.R. (4th) 183 the Alberta Court of Queen's Bench applied the same principle, following *Heywood v Wellers*.

[5] [1988] A.C. 1074.

[6] e.g. *Nash v Phillips* (1974) 232 E.G. 1219, Foster J.: loss of opportunity to purchase house. Value of house £5,250. Agreed purchase price, subject to contract, £4,750. Damages assessed at £500 less notional legal expenses and 10% discount to reflect the possibility that the purchase might not have proceeded. *Jarvis v T Richards & Co* (1980) 124 S.J. 793, Nourse J.: the claimant lost the opportunity to have the former matrimonial home conveyed to her. Held that damages should not only include the value of the property when the claimant lost it, but also should take account of inflation since that date. See also *Otter v Church Adams Tatham & Co* [1953] Ch. 280, Upjohn J. (discussed in para.11–262) in which the client lost the opportunity, at no cost, to make his interest in entailed property absolute.

[7] (1971) 115 S.J. 368, Brightman J.

[8] *The Times,* May 17, 1982.

Grasso Searles & Romano[9] the defendant solicitors negligently failed to settle a contract for the purchase of land in 1986, as a result of which the claimant was unable to obtain the property until 1989. The Queensland Court of Appeal held that the solicitors were not liable for the increased costs of acquiring and building on the land as they were proportionately no greater than inflation in the period of delay.

11–271   **Business tenancies.** Part 2 of the Landlord and Tenant Act 1954, which governs the renewal of business tenancies, gives rise to numerous claims against solicitors. If the tenant's solicitor fails to give notice or to issue proceedings within the specified time limits, the right to a renewal of the tenancy is forfeited. The measure of the tenant's loss in such circumstances is usually the value of the tenancy which would have been obtained (either by order of the court or by negotiation with the landlord).[10] In *Clark v Kirby-Smith*[11] Plowman J. held that the new tenancy would have been at market rent and that there was no evidence as to what its value would have been. He therefore awarded nominal damages only. In *Joliffe v Charles Coleman & Co.*[12] Browne J. was prepared to speculate in rather more detail. He considered that the county court judge would have been prepared to grant a 14-year lease at a rental of £900 per annum. He also considered that this was worth £200–£250 more than the lease which the landlords were prepared to offer after learning of the solicitors' mistake (and which the claimants, in order to mitigate their losses, ought to have accepted).[13]

11–272   A broadly similar approach was adopted by Leonard J. and the Court of Appeal in *Teasdale v Williams & Co*[14] where the tenant accepted a new lease but on less favourable terms. In *Hodge v Clifford Cowling & Co*[15] the claimant shopkeeper renewed his lease for five years instead of 14 years due to the

---

[9] [1993] 2 Qd.R. 136.

[10] If the claimant moves to alternative premises, he ought to recover the removal costs and incidental expenses as special damages, see para.11–279. For an example of the loss being the lost opportunity to obtain more favourable terms at another property, see *Abraxas Computer Services Ltd v Rabin Leacock Lipkan (a firm)* [2000] E.G.C.S. 70; N.P.C. 63, discussed at para.11–264, above.

[11] [1964] 1 Ch. 506.

[12] (1964) 219 E.G. 1608.

[13] The total damages awarded were £1,000 because the judge took into account the fact that during the course of the proceedings under the Landlord and Tenant Act 1954 the claimants would have continued to pay the old rent of £108 per annum.

[14] (1983) 269 E.G. 1040. See para.11–259, above.

[15] [1990] 2 E.G.L.R. 89, CA. A similar approach was adopted in *Aran Caterers Ltd v Stephen Lake Gilbert & Paling* [2002] 1 E.G.L.R. 697, Judge Howarth sitting as a High Court judge. The defendant solicitors negligently failed to make an application for a grant of a new tenancy under Pt II of the Landlord and Tenant Act 1954. The judge determined that if an application had been made, a four-year term would have been granted as the landlord intended to redevelop the building. Damages were calculated on the basis of the likely profits from the business, adjusted to £95,000, with a year's purchase multiplier of 2.75, and with a deduction of £30,000 for the value of the lease that the claimant had been forced to take from the landlord. Loss of disturbance compensation under the Act was added, discounted for accelerated receipt, and a total of £315,000 was awarded. Uncertainty of tenure forced the claimant to acquire a lease of alternative property, but no costs of relocation were awarded, in part because they would have been incurred in due course anyway.

defendant solicitors' negligence, although the rent was not affected. He recovered the difference in value of the business caused by the shorter lease. In *Ricci v Masons*[16] the defendant solicitors failed to serve a notice under s.25 of the Act. Their client, the claimant, was able to negotiate for a new lease. The judge determined that the claimant would have obtained a 10-year term with a six-month redevelopment break clause. The claimant was awarded the additional cost of the lease which he had to pay, his costs of abortive proceedings and disbursements, and the diminution in the value of his restaurant business caused by the fact that his lease now had no statutory protection. A different approach was adopted in *Matlock Green Garage Ltd v Potter Brooke-Taylor & Wildgoose (a firm)*[17] where the solicitors failed to renew a lease in 1992. But for the negligence, the claimant would have obtained leases for a further 10 years, and possibly for longer, rather than the two years which the landlord granted. The claimant ceased its garage business in 1994, and was awarded the stream of profits which would reasonably have been expected for the remaining period, capitalised on a conventional multipler/multiplicand basis. The judge did not account for the loss of profits on parts of the business on other sites, as those parts of the business were not bound to close, and the losses were not foreseeable as the defendants could not be assumed to have known about the interrelationship between parts of the business.

Agricultural tenancies. A more conventional result was reached in unusual circumstances in *Layzell v Smith Morton & Long*.[18] The claimant's father held an agricultural tenancy. When he died, the defendant solicitors negligently failed to claim a right of succession for the claimant pursuant to s.39 of the Agricultural Holdings Act 1986. Schiemann J. found that it was all but impossible to obtain a tenancy at the market equivalent to the one the claimant had lost as a result of the defendant's negligence. The claimant was awarded the cost of the freehold of an equivalent property, less what he could recover from selling the freehold and taking the leasehold on the terms of the one he had lost. The defendant argued that the claimant had only lost a source of cheap housing and a higher income than he would otherwise obtain, both of which could be compensated by applying an appropriate multiplier to the yearly loss. The court rejected this approach, which would have resulted in smaller damages; the claimant had expected to be a tenant farmer on his family farm, and the court would award damages to put him in the position he would have been but for the defendant's negligence. **11-273**

Difficulties in evaluation. It is not always possible to evaluate in precise monetary terms what the claimant has lost through being unable to remain in occupation of property. *Bryant v Goodrich*[19] illustrates how the court will treat **11-274**

---

[16] [1993] 38 E.G. 154, Mr L. Swift Q.C. sitting as a deputy judge of the Queen's Bench Division.
[17] [2000] Lloyd's Rep. P.N. 935.
[18] [1992] 1 E.G.L.R. 169.
[19] (1966) 110 S.J. 108.

such a difficulty. A wife gave up possession of the matrimonial home, after the breakdown of marriage, as a result of her solicitor's negligent advice. The court therefore had to assess how much worse off the wife was financially as a result of moving out. Lord Denning M.R. stated that this was "one of those cases, like the loss of a chance, which the court had to deal with as would a judge or jury." Damages were assessed at £600.

(ii) *Difference in Value of Property*

11–275   **The normal rule.** Where the purchaser's solicitor errs in his advice he gives or in the investigations which he makes on the client's behalf, the property purchased may prove to be less valuable than was assumed at the time of purchase. The normal measure of damages in such circumstances (as in the cases on surveyors' negligence)[20] is the amount by which the sum paid by the client exceeds the true value of the property at the date of purchase. For instance in *Wapshott v Davies Donovan & Co*[21] the Court of Appeal upheld an assessment of damages in relation to defective leases as the difference in value at purchase in 1986, and not when defects first became apparent in March 1988 when the claimants tried to sell the premises. In the majority of cases, the courts are ready to accept that the purchase price represents the value of the property in the condition described by the solicitor. Where, however, the purchase price corresponds with the value of the property in its actual condition, then the purchaser suffers no loss and will be entitled to no more than nominal damages.[22] In Scotland there is no such general rule, and

---

[20] As to which see Ch.10, paras 10–131 to 10–150. *cf.* the case where there is no valid transaction: see paras 11–309 and 316.

[21] [1996] 1 P.N.L.R. 361. The court held that here were no special circumstances requiring a later date of assessment. For further examples see *Lake v Bushby* [1949] 2 All E.R. 964, K.B.D.: property less valuable by reason of absence of planning permission for bungalow standing on it. Diminution assessed at £100; *Piper v Daybell Court-Cooper & Co* (1969) 210 E.G. 1047, Nield J.: property less valuable by reason of right of way running across it. Diminution assessed at £200; *Collard v Saunders* (1972) 221 E.G. 797, Mocatta J.: property less valuable by reason of defects. Diminution assessed at £250; *Trask v Clark & Sons* [1980] C.L.Y.B. 2588, Talbot J.: footpath ran across claimant's property, diminution assessed at £1,500; *Walker v Giffen Couch & Archer* [1988] E.G.C.S. 64, Peter Gibson J.: diminution in value from public footpath through property assessed at £8,000; *Twidale v Bradley* [1990] 2 Qd.R. 464, Queensland Supreme Court: grocery business less valuable without secure title of premises; *Owen v Fielding* [1998] E.G.C.S. 110, Steel J.: diminution in value assessed at 20% as part of land was subject to rights of common; *Greymalkin Ltd v Copleys (a firm)* [2004] EWHC 1155; [2004] P.N.L.R. 44 (Lawrence Collins J.); [2004] EWCA Civ 1754; [2005] P.N.L.R. 20 (upheld by the Court of Appeal): diminution of £45,000 awarded for three charges on title of hotel.

[22] *Ford v White* [1964] 1 W.L.R. 885: solicitors advised, incorrectly, that land was not subject to restriction against building. The price paid corresponded with the true value of the land, taking into account the building restriction. Pennycuick J. held that there was no loss. See further Ch.10, para.10–137. Similarly, the claimant was limited to the diminution in value, which was zero, in *Brown v Cuff Roberts* [1996] C.L.Y. 4499, CA, and the same result was reached in *422246 BC Ltd v 0909 Management Inc* (2000) 80 B.C.L.R. (3d) 299, British Columbia CA, where there was no evidenced of any difference in value.

each case falls to be considered on its own facts.[23] The difference in value rule applies in Ireland,[24] in Australia,[25] and in Canada.[26]

Exceptions to the rule, general statements. The principle is not an invariable one. In *County Personnel Ltd v Alan R Pulver*[27] Bingham L.J. stated: **11–276**

> "On the authorities as they stand the diminution in value rule appears almost always, if not always, to be appropriate where property is acquired following negligent advice by surveyors . . . That is not, however, an invariable approach, at least in claims against solicitors, and should not be mechanistically applied in circumstances where it may appear inappropriate."[28]

Two further Court of Appeal cases discuss the general approach to be adopted. In *Reeves v Thrings & Long*[29] the claimant purchased a hotel where access to the hotel car park was by licence only, and he spent some money rectifying this when the problem came to light four years later. The defendant solicitors were not found to be liable. Sir Thomas Bingham M.R., with whom Simon Brown L.J. agreed, considered, obiter, three approaches on damages, if it had been established that the claimant would not have entered into the transaction. First,

---

[23] This has been stated in: *Haberstich v McCormick and Nicholson* [1975] S.L.T. 181, IH (solicitor's negligence caused purchaser to obtain property without a wholly good and marketable title; damages assessed at difference in value at later sale of property after it had been improved); and *Di Ciacca v Archbald Sharp & Sons* [1994] S.L.T. 421, OH (purchaser entered property on payment of deposit, seller later proved to have no title, damages against negligent solicitor could include additional amount required to purchase other property on discovering the defect in title). However, in *Douglas v Stuart Wyse Ogilvie Estates Ltd* [2001] S.L.T. 689, OH, the diminution in value was said to be the preferred measure, with the cost of repairs as a potentially relevant cross-check.

[24] *Kelly v Finbarr J Crowley* [1985] I.R. 212, Murphy J.: diminution in value rule applied; *Doran v Delaney* [1999] 1 I.L.R.M. 225, Irish High Court: diminution in value as prima facie the measure of damages applied. cf. *Kehoe v Louth* [1992] I.L.R.M. 282, Supreme Court.: the damages awarded for negligently advising that premises were as good as freehold when the claimants purchased the property were the capital value of the annual increase in rates on the revaluation which would be needed under Irish law to enable such a conversion, and the cost of buying out the freeholder less what a reasonable person would think it would cost. The case could be justified as being based on a warranty. No cases were cited by the Court.

[25] *Kyriacou v Kogarah Municipal Council* (1995) 88 L.G.E.R.A. 110, Supreme Court N.S.W., in which *Ford v White* was cited with approval.

[26] *Messineo v Beale* (1978) 81 D.L.R. (3d) 713, in which *Ford v White* was cited with approval, *Toronto Industrial Leaseholds v Posesorski* (1995) 119 D.L.R. (4th) 193; and *789538 Ontario Ltd v Gambin Associates* (1999) 27 R.P.R. (3d) 210, *789538 Ontario Ltd v Gambin Associates* (2000) 27 R.P.R. (3d) 211, all Ontario CA; cf. *Poolton v Paci* (1999) 21 R.P.R. (3d) 212 where without referring to authority the Ontario Court of Appeal held that the cost of cure was the primary measure of loss rather than the diminution in value, although in that case there was no evidence that the claimant's imperfect title would ever be challenged and minimal damages were awarded.

[27] [1987] 1 W.L.R. 916.

[28] *ibid.* at 925F–G. This dictum was cited by many subsequent cases, e.g. Staughton L.J. in *Hayes v Dodd* [1990] 2 All E.R. 815, at 819B. A very similar approach is followed in Canada, see *Toronto Industrial Leaseholds v Posesorski* (1995) 119 D.L.R. (4th) 193 at 214, Ontario CA. It has been suggested that a claimant may be able to elect which method to adopt, see Hirst J. at first instance in *Hayes v Dodd* [1990] 2 All E.R. 815, at 820B. It is plainly implicit in later cases that it is for the court to determine the appropriate measure of damages, not the claimant, on the basis of the parties' pleaded cases and evidence.

[29] [1996] 1 P.N.L.R. 265 at 278.

damages might be the claimant's entire outlay on the purchase and refurbishment of the hotel, which the Judge considered would probably have overcompensated the claimant, because whatever he had invested in might have led to loss in the recession at that time. Secondly, it may have been preferable to apply the difference in value test at the date when the problem came to light rather than at the date of breach, although there might be additional claims too. Thirdly, the loss may have been calculated as the costs of rectifying the defect when the problem came to light. The Master of the Rolls concluded that it was undesirable to rule on the proper approach to damages in principle, because assessment of damages is ultimately a factual exercise. He stated that this "is an area in which legal rules may have to bow to the particular facts of the case."[30] In *Oates v Anthony Pitman & Co*[31] the Court of Appeal suggested that there were at least three possible approaches to the assessment of damages. First, there was the difference in value rule, which was applied by considering evidence of the value of comparable properties. Secondly, where the property was unusual, or was being purchased for a particular purpose to the knowledge of the solicitor, or there had been a substantial interval before the defect came to light, the estimated cost of correcting the defect might be the most reliable guide to the difference in value. There may be no satisfactory evidence to decide the market value. Thirdly, where the claimant has extracted himself from a transaction he would not have entered but for the negligence of the solicitor, damages should be assessed on the basis of the cost of extraction.

11–277   **Illustrations of exceptions.** A number of exceptions appear in the decided cases. Although they may be sensible decisions on their own facts, any general rules extracted from them may be somewhat artificial, and the following classification is tentative.[32]

11–278   **(1) Loss of use of property.** Where an encumbrance or defect in title interferes with the use to which the solicitors know the claimant intends to put the property, his loss may not be limited to the difference in value but may include the loss from such use of the property.[33] This is especially true if the claimant builds on the property before discovering that there is an easement upon which he has encroached.[34]

---

[30] Contrast the case of *Amerena v Barling*, para.11–255, above.
[31] [1998] P.N.L.R. 683.
[32] For a different view see H. Evans *Lawyers' Liabilities*, (2nd edn, 2002), Ch.10; and *ibid.*, "Damages for solicitors' negligence: (2) diminution in the value of property" (1992) 8 P.N. 29. See also *CEMP Properties (UK) Ltd v Dentsply Research & Development Corp* [1989] 2 E.G.L.R. 205, solicitors acting for a vendor who was sued by the purchaser for misrepresentation were ordered to indemnify their clients against the purchaser's claim for wasted expenditure, but not the overpayment the purchaser recovered.
[33] *King v Hawkins & Co, The Times*, January 28, 1982, Mars-Jones J.
[34] e.g. *Barclay-White v Guillaume* [1996] E.G.C.S. 123, QBD, where the claimant built on land which he did not in fact own due to the negligent of the solicitor in failing to ascertain the correct boundaries, and he recovered his wasted building costs; *Charette v Provenzano* (1978) 7 C.C.L.T. 23, Ontario High Court.

(2) Costs of extrication. Where the claimants would never have entered the **11–279**
transaction at all but for their solicitor's negligence, and have subsequently rid or
attempted to rid themselves of the property,[35] it may be appropriate to award as
damages the extrication costs.[36] Thus in *County Personnel (Employment Agency)
Ltd v Alan R Pulver & Co*[37] the claimant entered a lease which had no capital
value, and as a result of the negligence of its former solicitors exposed themselves to a longstanding liability. The damages were assessed as the cost actually
paid by the claimant to extricate itself from the lease. The Court of Appeal
considered that an assessment on the basis of the diminution in capital was
wholly artificial.[38] In *Hayes v Dodd* the claimants acquired property where there
was no right of way over the only convenient access.[39] It took the claimants five
or six years to dispose of the property, and they recovered all the expenses they
incurred during those years. Similarly, in *Connor v Ritzman*[40] the defendants
allowed the claimant to purchase a lease where there were discrepancies in the
conveyancing documents, and the purchasers of the freehold did not consent to
rectification. The claimant recovered the difference between the sums spent on
purchasing and improving the maisonette, the costs of the rectification action,
and the mortgage repayments after a failed resale, minus the value of the lease
at the date of judgment.

(3) Market value not reflect loss.[41] Although the claimants paid a market rate **11–280**
for the property acquired, in some cases the loss may not be nominal but clearly
of substance, so that the difference in value rule is inappropriate. Thus in *Murray*

---

[35] This category could be extended to include attempts by the claimants to rid themselves of the
encumbrance, as in *Toronto Industrial Leasholds Ltd v Posesorski* (1995) 119 D.L.R. (4th) 193 at 214,
Ontario CA where the costs of unsuccessful litigation to rid property of an option which the solicitor
had not noticed were awarded as well as the diminution in value.
[36] Such a measure of loss was not awarded in *Oates v Pitman* [1998] P.N.L.R. 683 because the
claimants did not base their claim on such a basis, and there was insufficient evidence to make the
calculations. Nor was it awarded in *Greymalkin Ltd v Copleys (a firm)* [2004] EWHC 1155; [2004]
P.N.L.R. 44 (Lawrence Collins J.); [2004] EWCA Civ 1754; [2005] P.N.L.R. 20 (upheld by the Court
of Appeal). In 1993 the claimants purchased a decrepit seaside hotel, and the defendant solicitors
failed to spot three charges on the title. The claimants were awarded the difference between the
purchase price and the true value at the time, which was £45,000. In fact the charges were removed
in 1996, and the claimants sold the hotel in 1999 as they were being pressed by their own bankers.
However, this was not an extrication case, as the property was not disposed of subject to the original
defect.
[37] [1987] 1 W.L.R. 916. See also *GP Ltd v Bulcraig & Davies* [1986] 2 E.G.L.R. 148 and [1988] 1
E.G.L.R. 138, where a planning restriction was only discovered after the claimant had gone into
receivership, and the lease was then surrendered. The claimant recovered all of its expenditure less
what it obtained on surrender.
[38] *ibid.* at 926B and 927H–928A. But see the explanation of Staughton L.J. in *Hayes v Dodd* [1990]
2 All E.R. 815, at 818–819, and Ralph Gibson L.J. in *Watts v Morrow* [1991] 1 W.L.R. 1421, cited
in Ch.10, para.10–148.
[39] [1990] 2 All E.R. 815 at 820A.
[40] (1995) 70 P.C.R. D41.
[41] See also *Powell v Whitman Breed Abbot & Morgan (a firm)* [2005] EWHC 1169; [2005] P.N.L.R.
1 the claimant bought the lease of property for investment in the name of a company rather than
personally. While the value was the same, there was a smaller class of potential buyers for company
leases so that it would take longer to sell, and Tugendhat J. therefore awarded damages at 6% of the
value of the lease at the date of purchase.

v Lloyd[42] the defendant solicitors negligently advised the claimant in 1981 to purchase a residential lease in the name of a company in order to save tax, rather than in her own name. Subsequently in 1986 the claimant was unable to have the lease assigned to her, and thus she was unable to obtain a statutory tenancy at the expiry of the lease in 1991. The claimant was awarded what it would cost her to acquire what she had lost, which was the cost of purchasing similar rights of occupation on similar terms in similar alternative accommodation. The evidence was that the freehold value of such a house was £460,000, and that a statutory tenancy depreciated the value by a quarter. As a result, the claimant was awarded £115,000. Similarly, the rule would not apply where the claimants obtained property which was more expensive than property that would suit their needs due to their solicitors' error. In *Computastaff Ltd v Ingledew Brown Bennison & Garrett*,[43] the defendant solicitors negligently advised the claimant that the rateable value of office premises it wished to lease was £3,305 rather than £8,305. The claimant would not have entered the lease for that sum. The defendants contended that the claimant suffered no loss because it obtained value for what it was paying. The Judge decided that, but for the defendants negligence, the claimant would have obtained other offices which were suitable to its needs for the price it wanted to pay.[44]

11–281   **(4) Loss of business profits.** Where premises are acquired for business use, the solicitor's error may affect the profitability of the client's business. In such a case difference in value may not be the measure of the client's loss.[45] In *Simple Simon Catering Ltd v Binstock Miller & Co*[46] the claimants took a lease of a restaurant. As a result of their solicitor's negligence, the lease contained a clause permitting the landlords and persons authorised by them to share the use of the kitchen. The trial judge awarded no damages under this head. The Court of Appeal reversed this decision on the grounds that the landlord's right to use the kitchen constituted a serious threat, and remitted the matter for rehearing and reassessment of damages. As to quantum, Lord Denning M.R. stated:

> "It seemed that loss was very much a matter of general assessment, one not to be measured necessarily by the difference in value of the reversion and so forth, but as a matter of general expectation of loss."

---

[42] [1989] 1 W.L.R. 1060, John Mummery sitting as a High Court judge. This case did not concern advice relating to the value of the property, which was perfectly sound in every way, but to the identity of the purchaser. The difference in value rule may have no application in such circumstances.

[43] (1983) 268 E.G. 906, McNeill J.

[44] See also *Carter v TG Baynes & Sons* [1998] E.G.C.S. 109, Ch. D. The defendant solicitors failed to note that there were restrictive covenants preventing development of the site which the claimant intended to purchase. The claimant recovered for his losses sustained as a result of being unable to sell the maisonettes he built, which he could have sold five years earlier but for the covenants, rather than the diminution in value.

[45] e.g. *Braid v WL Highway Sons* (1964) 191 E.G. 433, Roskill J. See also *Kienzle v Stringer* (1981) 35 O.R. (2d) 85: owing to the solicitor's negligence, the claimant acquired a defective title to a farm. The problem emerged when he sought to sell and the claimant incurred substantial costs resolving the situation, and the farm was less profitable. The Ontario Court of Appeal held that damages were not limited to the diminution in value.

[46] (1973) 228 E.G. 527.

However, *Oates v Anthony Pitman & Co*[47] suggests that loss of profits will normally not be recoverable. The defendant solicitors failed to advise that there was no grant of planning permission for the use of the property as holiday flats, which is what the claimant intended to use it for. The claimant did not recover any loss of profits for two reasons: it would appear that such losses would not be recoverable as they would not be attributable to the breach of duty[48]; and the claimant could not recover loss of profits from developing a property if he would not have purchased it but for the defendant solicitors' negligence.

(5) Radical change in circumstances. Changes in circumstances after the   **11–282**
purchase may make it inappropriate to award the difference in value at the date of purchase. In *Kennedy v KB Van Emden & Co*[49] the claimant purchased the underlease of property in 1983 at a premium. The defendant solicitors had failed to advise her that the premium was unlawful. The claimant claimed that as a result she would have been unable to assign the underlease at a premium, and she had therefore lost the premium she had paid. However, as a result of statutory changes in 1988 a premium was no longer unlawful. The Court of Appeal declined to award the difference in value at the date of purchase, as that would have given the claimant an undeserved windfall.[50] In *Gregory v Shepherds*[51] the claimant purchased a Spanish holiday flat in 1989, but was unable to sell it in 1991 due to a defect in title. The defect was eventually removed in June 1999, and the flat was sold in January 2000. The Court of Appeal held that it was inappropriate to award the difference in value, and the true measure of loss was the interest over eight years on the capital tied up, less 50 per cent for the personal use of the apartment over that time. The claimant was also awarded the costs of trying to procure the removal of the charge, and an enquiry was ordered into the capital losses sustained from inflation and the difference in exchange rates over the eight years. In *Dent v Davis Blank Furniss*[52] the defendant solicitors were negligent in 1991 in failing to carry out a search of the commons

---

[47] [1998] P.N.L.R. 683, CA. *cf. Keydon Estates Ltd v Eversheds LLP* [2005] EWHC 972; [2005] P.N.L.R. 40, where the claimant purchased commercial property in order, as the defendants knew, to obtain an income stream. The defendants negligently advised that a sub-lease did not operate as an assignment, when in fact it did, and the subtenant went into liquidation and the income stream was lost. Evans-Lombe J. awarded the claimant the hypothetical rent it would have obtained on another notionally similar property in which it would have invested if properly advised, and the difference in value rule was not applied.

[48] Relying on *Banque Bruxelles Lambert v Eagle Star* [1997] A.C. 191.

[49] [1996] P.N.L.R. 409. Contrast *Shaw v Fraser Southwell (a firm)* [1999] Lloyd's Rep P.N. 633. The defendants failed to inform purchasers of a lease that an assignment had to be to a limited company. One of the purchasers recovered his diminution in value of £11,500. He sold his share of the flat, which was now the whole of the flat rather than half of it due to his copurchaser's trustee in bankruptcy disclaiming his interest, back to the landlord eight years later. The Court of Appeal held that although the amount he received in excess of the true value of his interest in 1997 cancelled out the diminution in value of his interest in 1989, it was not a sufficiently unusual circumstance to displace the ordinary rule. *cf.* also *Gardner v Marsh & Parsons* [1997] P.N.L.R. 362, discussed at Ch.10, para.10–148, and which may not be easy to reconcile with *Kennedy v Van Emden*.

[50] Contrast the cases of *Amerena v Barling* (1995) 69 P.C.R. 252, see para.11–255, and *Wapshot v Davies Donovan & Co* [1996] 1 P.N.L.R. 361, see para.11–275.

[51] [2000] P.N.L.R. 769, CA, for the facts see para.11–202, above.

[52] [2001] Lloyd's Rep. P.N. 534. Followed obiter on similar facts in *Patel v Daybells (a firm)* [2001] P.N.L.R. 43, Gray J. This was not considered by the Court of Appeal, which overturned the finding of liability, see *Patel v Daybells (a firm)* [2001] EWCA Civ 1229; [2002] P.N.L.R. 6.

register in the purchase of a house and garden. The purchasers learned of the problem in 1994, but in 1996 they succeeded in having part of the land de-registered as common land, at a cost of £20,000. Blackburne J. assessed damages in 1996 as the difference between the open market value assuming it to be free from commons registration and the lesser of what the claimants had spent on the property (including acquisition and improvement costs) and its open market value as so improved.

11–283   **(6) Cost of cure.** There have been a few cases in which the claimant has been awarded the cost of cure.[53] Some of them share the feature that if the defect had been discovered before purchase, it would have been removed, and that subsequently it has been removed.[54] In *Creech v Mayorcas*[55] the solicitor for the purchaser of a lease failed to obtain the landlord's licence to assign or licence for change of user. It subsequently proved possible to obtain the licences at a cost of £120. The claimant recovered this sum by way of damages, together with the amount of rent which he had to pay before the licences were obtained (during which time he could not use the shop) and a small sum in respect of extra wages. In *Braid v WL Highway & Sons*[56] solicitors acting for the purchasers of a hotel business failed to give proper advice concerning the reversion expectant on the term of the lease. The claimants recovered, inter alia, the costs of buying out their landlord's interest. However, in *Fulham Leisure Holdings Ltd v Nicholson Graham & Jones*[57] the Claimant purchased a football club and the shareholders' agreement did not permit the dilution of the minority shareholder's interests when more than £60m had been invested. Mann J. did not award the cost of cure, which may otherwise have been legitimate,[58] because the purchase of the minority's shares put the Claimant in a better position than it otherwise would have been, and the £7.75m paid was not a reasonable sum to pay to cure the defect.

(iii) *Loss of Opportunity to Bring Proceedings*

11–284   **Claimant's claim statute-barred:** *Kitchen.* Where solicitors fail to issue proceedings within the limitation period, it is not always possible to discover

---

[53] See also *Kienzle v Stringer* (1981) 35 O.R. (2d) 85, Ontario CA.

[54] But see *Hartle v Laceys* [1999] Lloyd's Rep. P.N. 315. The claimant property developer purchased a plot of land subject to a restrictive covenant in favour of the covenantee which had not been registered and was thus void. The claimant purchased an adjoining plot, obtained planning permission to sell both plots, and agreed a sale to a third party. The defendant solicitor, who acted for the claimant and did not appreciate that the unregistered covenant was void, informed the covenantee of the proposed sale. The covenantee registered the covenant, and the sale to the third party did not go ahead. The Court of Appeal awarded the claimant the difference between the agreed sale price and the amount for which the plots were later sold, plus sums to release the covenants and solicitors' costs, with compound interest, reduced by 40 per cent for the chance of the sale not completing in any event.

[55] (1966) 198 E.G. 1091, Pennycuick J.

[56] (1964) 191 E.G. 433, Roskill J.

[57] [2006] EWHC 2017, Ch; [2006] All E.R. (D) 461.

[58] Following *Ruxley Electronics & Construction Ltd v Forsyth* [1996] A.C. 344.

what is the "loss" which the claimant has thereby suffered.[59] The court trying the professional negligence action can only speculate about the outcome of the original proceedings. The intended defendant to the original proceedings is not a party to the professional negligence action, although he may be, and quite commonly is, called as a witness in that action. The correct approach to such cases was considered by the Court of Appeal in *Kitchen v Royal Air Force Association*.[60] The Court rejected the argument that it should determine on balance of probabilities, whether the claimant would have succeeded in the original action. Lord Evershed M.R. (with whom Parker and Sellers L.JJ. agreed) continued:

> "If, in this kind of action, it is plain that an action could have been brought, and if it had been brought that it must have succeeded, of course the answer is easy. The damaged claimant then would recover the full amount of the damages lost by the failure to bring the action originally. On the other hand, if it be made clear that the claimant never had a cause of action, that there was no case which the claimant could reasonably ever have formulated, then it is equally plain that the answer is that she can get nothing save nominal damages for the solicitors' negligence. I would add, as was conceded by [counsel for the claimant], that in such a case it is not enough for the claimant to say: 'Though I had no claim in law, still, I had a nuisance value which I could have so utilized as to extract something from the other side and they would have had to pay something to me in order to persuade me to go away.'
>
> The present case, however, falls into neither one nor the other of the categories which I have mentioned. There may be cases where it would be quite impossible to try 'the action within the action' . . . In my judgment, assuming that the claimant has established negligence, what the court has to do in such a case as the present is to determine what the claimant has lost by that negligence. The question is: Has the claimant lost some right of value, some chose in action of reality and substance? In such a case it may be that its value is not easy to determine, but it is the duty of the court to determine that value as best it can."[61]

The general approach. The defendant solicitors do not step into the shoes of the original defendants. In the ordinary case, the court has to determine the value of the case at the date of a notional trial. This will involve making proper allowance for the probabilities of success and other contingencies. Interest will then be added from that notional trial date. The cases concerning loss of opportunity to sue decided before *Kitchen v Royal Air Force Association*[62] ought now to be treated with caution, at least in relation to quantum of damages.[63] The following paragraphs will illustrate and develop the principles set out in *Kitchen*

11–285

---

[59] If the claim was already statute-barred when the client consulted the solicitor, then he will have suffered no loss from any delay by the solicitor, as in *Coffin v MacBeath* (1990) 81 Nfld. & P.E.I.R. 333, Newfoundland CA.

[60] [1958] 1 W.L.R. 563.

[61] *Kitchen v Royal Air Force Association* [1958] 1 W.L.R. 563 at 574–575.

[62] [1958] 1 W.L.R. 563.

[63] e.g. *Clayton v Kearsey* (1935) 79 S.J. 180 failure to issue proceedings in respect of road traffic accident. Nominal damages only awarded; *Ashton v Philip Conway Thomas & Co* (1939) B.W.C.C. 246: failure to apply for review of an award under the Workmen's Compensation Act 1925. Damages of £133 were awarded, being the amount which would probably have been recovered on the review.

as they have developed in subsequent case law. *Kitchen* has been followed in Scotland,[64] Australia,[65] and by most Canadian courts.[66]

11–286   **Application of these principles in other circumstances.**[67] Loss of a chance principles will be applied in a variety of circumstances apart from the claimant's case being statute barred.[68] They will apply *mutatis mutandis* where the claimant loses the opportunity to bring proceedings to enforce a judgment.[69] In *Somatra Ltd v Sinclair Roche & Temperley*[70] the claimants lost confidence in their lawyers shortly before trial as a result of numerous breaches by them, and settled the claim for 66 per cent of its full worth. But for the negligence the case would have been settled for 75 per cent of its full worth, and they obtained damages based on the 11 per cent difference. In *Browning v Brachers (a firm)*[71] the claimants were unable to rely on evidence in the original action which had been served out of time because of the negligence of the defendants solicitors. The claim was compromised for £5,000, but was valued by the judge at £46,000.[72]

11–287   The same approach will be taken where the claimant's claim is dismissed for want of prosecution. In such cases, the claimant's solicitors are unlikely, in the majority of cases, to persuade the court that the claim had no value whatsoever. The fact that the defendant solicitors were bringing the action is evidence that they thought it had some prospect of success, so that if they wish to say that the case was hopeless they will need good evidence to rebut the initial factual

---

[64] *Yeoman v Ferries* [1967] S.C. 255, OH. The case was followed in *Kyle v P Stormonth Darling* [1994] S.L.T. 191, IH, and *Siraj-Eldin v Campbell Middleton Burness & Dickson* [1989] S.L.T. 122, IH.
[65] See, e.g. Johnson v Perez (1989) 82 A.L.R. 587 and *Nikolaou v Papasavas, Phillips & Co* (1989) 82 A.L.R. 617, both High Court of Australia.
[66] See, e.g. *Melanson v Cochrane Sargeant, Nicholson & Paterson* (1968) 68 N.B.R. (2d) 370, New Brunswick CA, and *Rose v Mitton* (1994) 111 D.L.R. 217, Nova Scotia CA. But see *Fisher v Knibbe* (1992) 3 Alta. L.R. (3d) 97.
[67] For an exploration of a problem of evaluating cases where an action is lost due to the failure to obtain sufficient evidence see H. Evans: "Lies, damn lies, and the loss of a chance" (2006) 22 P.N. 99.
[68] But see *Moffat v Burges Salmon (a firm)* [2002] EWCA Civ 1977; [2004] P.N.L.R. 13. The claimants did recover damages in the original action in relation to the operation of an unlawful milk quota scheme, but only for the six years before proceedings were commenced. They sued their solicitors for failing to issue proceedings earlier. The Court of Appeal held that they were entitled to rely on the findings of the original judge, including his determination that the losses which were more than six years old had been statute-barred, unless there was evidence that the judge had been capricious or irrational, because the issue was simply whether, if the claimants had brought proceedings earlier, they would in fact have recovered more.
[69] *Harrington v Binns* (1863) 3 F. & F. 942: measure of damages was the amount which the jury thought would have been realised if the attorney had issued execution; *Butler v Knight* (1867) L.R. 2 Ex. 109: judgment for 390 guineas. The claimant's attorney agreed to accept 100 guineas in full satisfaction. The claimant claimed the difference (i.e. 290 guineas), but there was some doubt as to what the judgment debtor would have been able to pay. 150 guineas damages awarded.
[70] [2003] EWCA Civ 1474; [2003] 2 Lloyd's Rep. 855, CA.
[71] [2004] EWHC 16; [2004] P.N.L.R. 28. Similarly, in *Feakins v Burstow* [2005] EWHC 1931, QB; [2006] P.N.L.R. 6, the defendant was negligent in failing to obtain proper documentary evidence in a claim which had failed before a judge. Jack J. held that there was a 60% chance of success in the original litigation, and the allegations were not an impermissible collateral attack on the original decision.
[72] A figure amended on appeal [2005] EWCA Civ 753.

presumption. In *Mount v Barker Austin (a firm)*[73] Simon Brown L.J. considered that the applicable principles were as follows:

(1) the legal burden lies on the claimant to prove that he has lost something of value, that is a case with real and substantial rather than merely a negligible prospects of success;

(2) the evidential burden lies on the defendants to show that despite acting for the claimant in the litigation it was in fact of no value to their client[74];

(3) if the court has greater difficulty in discerning the strength of the claimant's claim than it would have at the time of the original action, that counts against the defendant solicitors and not the claimant;

(4) one would expect the court to be generous to the claimant in assessing his prospects of success.

No trial within a trial. In *Sharif v Garrett & Co (a firm)*[75] the claimants' **11–288** warehouse was destroyed by fire causing a loss of £842,000, their insurers refused to pay, and their claim against their broker was struck out as a fair trial was impossible. In the solicitors' negligence action, the defendants called the broker who said that the risk was uninsurable in this country, although it might be placed abroad. The judge awarded only the insurance premium on the basis that the claimants had called no evidence to support their claim. The Court of Appeal held that the starting point was that no fair trial had been possible, and the judge should therefore not have attempted to try the issues himself, as he had done, although he may be assisted by evidence, including expert evidence, which would have been called in the first action. The judge should have attempted to make a realistic assessment of the claimants' prospects, and the Court of Appeal awarded £250,000 plus interest.[76]

It might be thought, consistent with Lord Evershed M.R.'s dictum in *Kitchen* **11–289** *v Royal Air Force Association*[77] and *Sharif v Garrett & Co (a firm)*[78] that where

---

[73] [1998] P.N.L.R. 493. This dictum has been cited and relied on in a large number subsequent lost litigation cases, for instance *Sharif v Garrett & Co (a firm)* [2001] EWCA Civ 1269; [2002] 1 W.L.R. 3118 and *Sharpe v Addison* [2003] EWCA Civ 1189; [2004] P.N.L.R. 23.

[74] For an illustration of the importance attached to the views of the lawyers instructed on the merits of the original action, see *Sharpe v Addison* [2003] EWCA Civ 1189; [2004] P.N.L.R. 23. There, two barristers had advised that the action had reasonable prospects of success, and the argument that the original action was of no value was dismissed in part because of the daily familiarity of barristers with valuing claims, and the fact that the allegation essentially meant that the two barristers had been negligent.

[75] [2001] EWCA Civ 1269; [2002] 1 W.L.R. 3118.

[76] It may be thought that, consistent with the loss of chance approach, the cause of action accrues against a solicitor who delays prosecuting an action when there is a substantial chance that the action may be struck out. However, three possibilities have been suggested in the cases: when the claim is bound to be struck out; when it is more likely than not that the claim will be struck out; and when there is a real risk of the claim being struck out. *Khan v Falvey* [2002] EWCA Civ 400; [2002] P.N.L.R. 8, CA may be interpreted as favouring the first or the last test, but Sir Anthony Evans in *Hatton v Chafes (a firm)* [2003] EWCA Civ 341; [2003] P.N.L.R. 24, CA and Davies J. in *Luke v Kingsley Smith & Co (a firm)* [2003] EWHC 1559; [2004] P.N.L.R. 12 appear to favour the first test.

[77] [1958] 1 W.L.R. 563.

[78] [2001] EWCA Civ 1269; [2002] 1 W.L.R. 3118.

a fair trial is possible, the original action should be tried in the normal way, and the loss of chance approach should not be followed. Two cases make it clear that this is not correct.[79] In *Hanif v Middleweeks*[80] The claimant's counterclaim against his insurers for an indemnity for the loss of his nightclub by fire was struck out. In the professional negligence action the Judge determined that the claimant had only a 25 per cent chance of proving that he had not set fire to the nightclub. The Court of Appeal held that the judge had and should have determined the chances of proving the claimant's dishonesty in the original action rather than whether the claimant had in fact set fire to his property.[81] The court stated that the fact of delay or absence of witnesses was only set of reasons why the court assesses prospects of success on a percentage basis, and only if the evidence or law showed that the prospects or overwhelming or negligible would a claim be assessed at 100 per cent or nothing; other reasons included the fact that other witnesses may have been called at a notional trial, the judge at the notional trial may have taken a different view of the matter, and that account should be taken of the prospects of settlement.[82] Following that analysis, Rix L.J. held in *Dixon v Clement Jones Solicitors (a firm)*[83] that:

> "there is no requirement in such a loss of a chance case to fight out a trial within a trial, indeed the authorities show as a whole that is what should be avoided. It is the prospects and not the hypothetical decision in the lost trial that have to be investigated."

That case concerned lost litigation against accountants, where the judge assessed the value of the lost claim at 30 per cent because he thought that the claimant would on balance pressed on with what turned out to be a disastrous business venture even if the accountants had given her the negative advice they should have done. The Court of Appeal upheld this conclusion.

11–290   **Early examples of the evaluation.** In *Kitchen v Royal Air Force Association.*[84] itself the claimant's husband was killed whilst using electrical equipment in the kitchen at home. The claimant alleged that the accident was due to a defect in the cooker, for which the electricity company who had connected it were liable. Her solicitors failed to issue proceedings within the time allowed by the

---

[79] *cf.* the approach in Alberta. In *Fisher v Knibbe* (1992) 3 Alta. L.R. (3d) 97 the Court of Appeal considered that the claimant would be awarded the value of the lost opportunity, rather than 100 per cent of the lost damages or nominal damages, only where a "trial within a trial" was impossible. In that case, the trial judge had decided that the original defendant was not negligent, and thus only nominal damages were awarded. The decision was applied in *Stealth Enterprises Ltd v Hoffman Dorchik* [2003] ABCA 58; [2003] 5 W.W.R. 205, Alberta CA. However, in *Henderson v Hagblom* 2003 SKCA 40; [2003] 7 W.W.R. 590, the Saskachewan Court of Appeal rejected that approach in favour of the English one.

[80] [2000] Lloyd's Rep. P.N. 920.

[81] Similarly, the claim should not be denied on public policy grounds as the judge had not found that the claimant had been the arsonist.

[82] [2000] Lloyd's Rep. P.N. 920 at paras 13–15, 21 56. *cf.* the remarks of Smith L.J. in *Dudarec v Andrews* [2006] EWCA Civ 256; [2006] 2 All E.R. 856 at para.60 that when the only issue is quantum and the evidence before the trial judge is substantially the same as would have been available at the notional trial, the judge should simply assess the damages on the basis of that evidence.

[83] [2004] EWCA Civ 1005; [2005] P.N.L.R. 6, para.27.

[84] [1958] 1 W.L.R. 563.

Fatal Accidents Acts 1846 to 1908. It was common ground that the maximum sum which would have been recovered in the original action was £3,000. In the professional negligence action the trial judge awarded £2,000 damages. The Court of Appeal upheld the decision, although observing that on the particular facts, the judge's assessment of the claimant's prospects was a generous one.[85] Where the original action raised serious issues both on liability and damages the evaluation of the chance which the claimant has lost becomes more difficult and more speculative. In *Yardley v Coombes*,[86] for example, the claimant, a lorry driver, sustained a fall when the grab handle came away from the cab of his lorry. Subsequently the tuberculosis which had been latent in the claimant's right shoulder became serious, and he required an arthrodesis of the joint. Edmund-Davies J. held that on liability the claimant had "a fair chance of success". On the question whether the accident had seriously aggravated the tuberculosis, the evidence was more difficult. The judge considered that the claimant "was not bound to fail in establishing that the fall was the cause of his tubercular shoulder." In the event of total victory in the original action the claimant would have recovered £3,000. Reviewing all the contingencies, Edmund-Davies J. awarded £1,000.

Further illustrations.[87] *Acton v Graham Pearce & Co (a firm)*[88] is unusual as   **11–291** it concerned the lost opportunity of avoiding a criminal conviction. The claimant was a solicitor who was convicted and imprisoned for obtaining money from the Law Society by deception by submitting false Green Forms to the Law Society. His appeal succeeded on the basis that memoranda implicating the claimant from a former employee were shown by a document examiner to have been typed on dates other than those they bore, and on evidence from the employee's former employer that she was dishonest. The claimant successfully sued his solicitors for failing to submit the memoranda to a document analyser or obtain statements from the former employers. Chadwick J. held that the claimant would still have had to explain at his criminal trial how he allowed clients to sign Green Forms which had not been completed, or how he thought he could claim costs for work above that allowed in the Green Form scheme. The Judge held that there was a

---

[85] See also *Gregory v Tarlo* (1964) S.J. 219, where McNair J. considered that the claimant could have made out a "quite a formidable case" and awarded 75 per cent of the full value of the claim. *Malyon v Lawrance, Messer Co* [1968] 2 Lloyd's Rep. 539 is a more complicated case. The claimant was injured in a road traffic accident in Germany, and the negligence of his English solicitors caused him to loss the opportunity to pursue his claim. After hearing evidence from German lawyers, Brabin J. decided that: (i) the claimant would have been held 50% to blame for the accident by a German court; (ii) the German courts would have valued his claim on full liability at £550 in respect of personal injuries and £3,500 in respect of loss of profits.

[86] (1963) 107 S.J. 575.

[87] See also *Gascoine v Ian Sheridan & Co* [1994] 5 Med L.R. 437, where Mitchell J. concluded that the claimant had lost a 60 per cent chance of successfully establishing negligence in a clinical negligence action alleging negligent irradiation treatment which had been struck out for want of prosecution.

[88] [1997] 3 All E.R. 909. *cf. Folland v Reardon* (2005) 249 D.L.R. (4th) 167 where the Ontario Court of Appeal held that a claimant who had been wrongly convicted and imprisoned allegedly as a result of his lawyers negligence would have to prove on the balance of probabilities that he would have avoided that result if his lawyers had acted competently.

50 per cent chance that he would not have been convicted, and directed an enquiry into the loss he had suffered as a result.

11–292   *Harrison v Bloom Camillin*[89] is one of the most detailed lost litigation cases to be tried, and it provides a very good illustration of the approach of the courts to evaluating such claims. The defendant solicitors admitted negligence in failing to serve a writ properly in November 1992 in a case where accountants were sued for negligence in relation to a new business venture which turned out disastrously. In relation to the assessment of damages, Neuberger J. held the matters of law should be resolved on the basis of the loss of a chance, as well as matters of fact, but that a court would be more ready to determine that the claimant would have succeeded or failed on a point of law. He also considered that the extent to which a court would be prepared to take a "broad brush" approach depended on the circumstances. In that case, he could form a detailed view on separate issues as there was very substantial evidence, and limited delay from the defendant's negligence. The judge found that there was a better than evens chance of establishing that the accountant's report was negligent, rather less than that in proving that they had made negligent verbal assurances, and there was a small discount in relation to reliance, so that the total discount so far was 35 per cent. There was no discount in relation to contributory negligence, as the judge was able to come to a firm conclusion that such an allegation would have failed. There was a further 20 per cent discount to reflect the fact that the business might have got into difficulties for reasons unconnected with the accountant's negligence. The total discount of 48 per cent[90] was applied to damages of £101,500 for each claimant for their lost investment, and £20,000 for the loss of earnings of the second claimant. The judge rejected the damages claims for the first claimant's loss of earnings as it was so weak in principle and in fact, and he also dismissed the claim for the increase in value of the claimants' homes because as a matter of law the prospect of its success was so slim. There was a deduction, without discount, for the accountants' fee claim.[91]

11–293   **The lower threshold.** In *Kitchen v Royal Air Force Association* it was stated that there had to be a claim in law, and not merely a nuisance claim.[92] The test has been expressed as the claimant having some prospect of success,[93] having anything above a certainty of failure,[94] and whether it would have been open to a reasonable tribunal to make the claimant an award.[95] A sum of $1,000, a little more than nominal damages, was awarded in *Appo v Barker*.[96] In a number of

---

[89] [2000] Lloyd's Rep. P.N. 89. See para.11–295 for the judge's views on the claimants's funding difficulties, para.11–296 in relation to settlement, para.11–298 on notional trial date, and para.11–300 on interest.

[90] See the further reasons at [2000] Lloyd's Rep. P.N. 404. The 52% chance of success is calculated as $(100 - 35) \times (100 - 20)$.

[91] See the further reasons at [2000] Lloyd's Rep. P.N. 404.

[92] [1958] 1 W.L.R. 563 at 574.

[93] *Buckley v National Union of General and Municipal Workers* [1967] 3 All E.R. 767, at 774F, Nield J., *Gouzenko v Harris* (1977) 72 D.L.R. (3d) 293, Ontario High Court.

[94] *Prior v McNabb* (1977) 78 D.L.R. (3d) 319, Ontario High Court.

[95] *Siraj-Eldin v Campbell Middleton Burness & Dickson* [1989] S.L.T. 122, IH.

[96] [1981] 50 F.L.R. 198, Supreme Court Northern Territory.

cases it has been held that the test was not satisfied and no[97] or only nominal damages[98] were awarded. For an illustration see *Green v Cunningham John & Co (a firm)*,[99] where the claimants were sued for defective construction. The defendant solicitors settled the case without authority and failed to advise their clients to pursue the local authority. The claimants recovered nothing as the settlement was a good one, and an action against the local authority was speculative, expensive and best avoided. In *Hatswell v Goldbergs*,[1] the Court of Appeal distinguished cases where there was loss of a right of value, and those which were bound to fail. In that case, the claimant and his witnesses had no possibility of establishing the correctness of their recollection that he was suffering night sweats and other symptoms which were reported to his doctor at the material time, which would rise to a claim for clinical negligence, as the doctors' notes had no such record. Sir Murray Stuart-Smith suggested that the court should consider a two-stage process: it should be satisfied that the claimant had lost something of value; and if that test was satisfied, the court should evaluate the lost claim in percentages.

The upper threshold: discount for risks of litigation. At the other extreme, **11–294** even the best case is not free from risk, and therefore it may be appropriate to make some discount for the hazards of litigation.[2] Thus in *Redman v Instant Nominees Pty Ltd*[3] the claimant lost his right of appeal due to his solicitor's negligence in a case where there was no fresh evidence. The Court of Appeal of Western Australia gave a 10 per cent discount on the basis that the appeal might not have succeed. However, each case must be considered on its own facts, and in some cases no discount may be appropriate.[4] Thus in *Charles v Hugh James Jones & Jenkins (a firm)*[5] the Court of Appeal held that there should be no

---

[97] In *Jemma Trust Co Ltd v Kippax Beaumont Lewis* [2005] EWCA Civ 248; [2004] W.T.L.R. 533 the deceased's landed estate was left to his nephew upon trust for life for his wife, who suffered from severe senile dementia, and then his nephew. The executors decided to mitigate liability to inheritance tax on the wife's death by advancing a sum to her on her releasing her life interest, and an application was made to the Court of Protection to enable this, which was opposed, but the opposition was withdrawn when the sum offerered increased to £750,000. The solicitors were negligent in failing to deal properly with the opponents, failing to obtain an actuarial report, and failing to make the application timeously. However it was pure speculation that, but for the negligence, the opposition to the application would have been withdrawn for any smaller price, and the claimant failed to obtain any damages.

[98] *Buckley v National Union of General and Municipal Workers* [1967] 3 All E.R. 767; *Gouzenko v Harris* (1977) 72 D.L.R. (3d) 293; *Siraj-Eldin v Campbell Middleton Burness & Dickson* [1989] S.L.T. 124; *Melanson v Cochrane Sargeant, Nicholson & Paterson* (1968) 68 N.B.R. (2d) 370, New Brunswick CA ($500 nominal damages awarded).

[99] (1995) 46 Con.L.R. 62, CA. See also *McFarlane v Wilkinson* [1997] P.N.L.R. 578, where an action brought against two barristers was struck out (inter alia) because the breach of statutory duty which it was alleged they should have pleaded would have been bound to fail on the facts.

[1] [2002] Lloyd's Rep. P.N. 359.

[2] e.g. *McNamara v Martin Mears & Co* (1983) S.J. 69, Peter Pain J; *Dolman v Penrose* (1983) 34 S.A.S.R. 481, South Australian Supreme Court *in banco*: a case "almost certain of success" was assessed at about 80% of the value on full liability.

[3] [1987] W.A.R. 277. In *Hunter v Earnshaw* [2001] P.N.L.R. 42 Garland J. made a similar discount of 10% for the small prospect of the original defendant establishing contributory negligence in the claimant's personal injury action.

[4] e.g. in *Johnson v Perez* (1989) 82 A.L.R. 587 and *Nikolaou v Papasavas, Phillips & Co* (1989) 82 A.L.R. 617.

[5] [2000] 1 W.L.R. 1278.

discount in a case where liability had been admitted and there was no evidence to suggest that the claimant might have recovered less in settlement or negotiation than the damages assessed by the judge in the professional negligence litigation. In *Dickinson v James Alexander & Co*[6] the defendant solicitors acted for the wife in divorce proceedings, and negligently failed to obtain full disclosure from the husband of his assets, with the result that she obtained a disadvantageous settlement. Douglas Brown J. assessed damages on the basis of what a court would have ordered the husband to pay or transfer to her. It was argued on behalf of the defendants that the matter might have been disposed of in negotiation for less than a court might award (presumably in response to a *Calderbank* letter). The judge considered that the husband was not a man who would have compromised the litigation, and therefore there should be no such discount.

11–295   **Funding difficulties and legal aid.** Defendants sometimes allege that the claimant would have been unable to fund the litigation, and thus should be awarded nothing for their lost opportunity. This issue can be particularly acute in legal aid or Community Legal Services funding cases, where funding would not be forthcoming for an action which had some prospects of success, although those prospects would have been less than fifty percent. In *Casey v Hugh James Jones & Jenkins*[7] the defendant solicitors failed to advise the clients about their rights of appeal after the withdrawal of legal aid. However, there was no real or substantial chance of the Legal Aid Board changing its mind if adequate representations had been made. The Court also held that there was no real chance of the claim succeeding at trial. The claimant recovered only nominal damages. In *Harrison v Bloom Camillin*[8] a different funding issue arose. It was alleged that legal aid was obtained dishonestly, as the claimants failed to disclose their financial circumstances to the Legal Aid Board. Neuberger J. held that, although funding with legal aid could not be taken into account if acquired dishonestly, the defendants had not proved that the claimants had been dishonest. Furthermore, the judge held that if the claimants had lost their legal aid funding after proceedings had been issued, which they would not have done as they would have refused to accept an income they received from their father. Further, they would have been able to and would have funded the action, and the judge was influenced by the fact that they had been able to fund privately the subsequent proceedings against their solicitors. It should be noted that the judge did not consider that these issues should be looked at as the loss of a chance, but on the basis of the balance of probabilities.

11–296   **Cost of the original action and settlement.** One factor which has received some attention in the reported decisions is the risk in costs which the claimant runs in any case where the outcome is uncertain.[9] In *McNamara v Martin Mears*

---

[6] (1990) 6 P.N. 205, at 207.
[7] [1999] Lloyd's Rep. P.N. 115, Thomas J.
[8] [2000] Lloyd's Rep. P.N. 89; see para.11–292 for the facts.
[9] See further H. Evans: *Lawyers' Liabilities*, (2nd edn, 2002), Ch.11, and *ibid.*, Damages for solicitors' negligence: (1) the loss of litigation (1991) 7 P.N. 201, where further dicta are cited. The point may develop a different significance in the context of conditional fee agreements.

& *Co*[10] Peter Pain J. gave a discount of a third from the award of £12,000 "for the costs and hazards of litigation, and for the acceleration of payment." and in the New Zealand case of *Thompson v Howley*[11] Somers J. held that the claimant would have won his case, and deducted a sum of $150 for irrecoverable costs, apparently on the agreement of counsel. In *Corfield v DS Bosher & Co*[12] the defendant solicitors failed to appeal an arbitrator's award in time. The judge held that the claimant had a one third chance of persuading a court to set the arbitration aside, and that in any further arbitration he would probably have obtained £23,380, of which he was awarded a third. The claimant recovered a third of the costs he had paid to the other side in a failed late appeal to the court. The judge held that in any arbitration the arbitrator would probably have required each party to bear their own costs and half of the arbitrator's fee, and so the claimant had to give credit for £6,500, based on agreed figures. In principle, the costs of the original action should be taken into account in appropriate circumstances. Similarly, account should be taken where appropriate of the chances of settlement.[13] In *MacKenzie v Middleton Ross & Arnot*[14] the Inner House of the Court of Session held that the pursuers' personal injury claim, which the defendant solicitors negligently failed to issue before the expiry of the limitation period, would have been compromised at approximately £25,000. In *Port of Sheerness Ltd v Brachers*[15] solicitors gave wrong advice in Industrial Tribunal proceedings which prevented settlement. The chance of settlement was assessed as a near certainty, and Buckley J. awarded the claimants 90 per cent of the costs they incurred. In *Harrison v Bloom Camillin*[16] Neuberger J. held that the court should take into account the possibility of the lost action settling, but he held that ordinarily the task of establishing the settlement value of a claim was likely to be similar to assessing the value of the lost opportunity of obtaining damages at trial. The issue was of some importance in that case, as the Judge made no deduction to reflect irrecoverable costs in the original action not least because it was likely to settle prior to trial in such a way as to cater for such costs. It is often the case that the claimant faces a potential liability to pay the costs of the other party against whom the original action failed. In such cases, it is common for the courts to award an indemnity to the claimant, sometimes subject to a percentage deduction where appropriate, as in *Browning v Brachers (a firm)*.[17]

Means of the original defendant. One qualification which should be added to the above discussion concerns the means of the original defendant. If he had no assets and no relevant insurance, then a judgment against him may have been **11–297**

---

[10] (1983) S.J. 69.

[11] [1977] 1 N.Z.L.R. 1 at 27.

[12] [1992] 1 E.G.L.R. 163, see esp. 168.

[13] "I think that the possibility of a reasonable compromise must not be forgotten in assessing the value of the lost right to bring an action", *per* Bollen J. in *Dolman v Penrose* (1983) 34 S.A.S.R. 481 at 492, South Australia CA.

[14] [1983] S.L.T. 286. Damages were also assessed on the basis of the likely settlement in *Smith v Lindsay & Kirk (No.2)* [2002] S.L.T. 335, OH.

[15] (1997) I.R.L.R. 214.

[16] [2000] Lloyd's Rep. P.N. 89; see para.11–292 for the facts.

[17] [2004] EWHC 16; [2004] P.N.L.R. 28, Jack J. The claimants successfully appealed on other matters, see [2005] P.N.L.R. 901. Garland J. awarded an indemnity in *Hunter v Earnshaw* [2001] P.N.L.R. 42.

valueless. In *Brinn v Russell Jones & Walker*[18] Gray J. held that the defendant had to plead the issue of the original defendant's impecuniosity, and had an evidential burden. As the defendants had satisfied this, the burden of proof rested on the claimant. The judge held that such impecuniosity would have had an effect on the likely settlement obtained.[19]

11–298   **The significance of the notional date of trial.** One matter which often has to be determined by the court in assessing damages is the date at which the original action should have come to trial or would have settled, if the defendant solicitors had carried forward the claimant's claim with due diligence. In *Johnson v Perez*[20] the High Court of Australia held that damages crystallised when the action was dismissed for want of prosecution, and in *Nikolaou v Papasavas, Phillips & Co*[21] the same court held that when no action was commenced, damages crystallised when the claim became statute-barred. In both cases the court held that a notional trial date should then be assessed. A court must assess the evidence that would have been available at that time, and the relevant principles of law then governing the assessment of damages.[22] Thus if the claimant's claim is in respect of personal injuries, the "tariff" prevailing at that date should be applied, rather than the "tariff" prevailing when the professional negligence action is heard. Furthermore, the claimant's prognosis at the time of the notional trial date must be assessed, and what actually happened later should generally be ignored.[23] The

---

[18] [2002] EWHC 2727; [2003] P.N.L.R. 16.
[19] The judge relied on *Redman v Instant Nominees Pty Ltd* [1987] W.A.R. 277, Western Australia CA. See similarly *Perri v Zaitman* [1984] V.R. 314, Supreme Court, where the pleadings point was not mentioned. A similar approach has been adopted in Canada, see *Alberta Workers' Compensation Board v Riggins* (1993) 95 D.L.R. (4th) 279, the defendant solicitors settled a personal injury claim at too low a level. After discussing conflicting Canadian decisions, the Alberta Court of Appeal considered that the burden lay on the claimant client to prove that he would have recovered the full amount which should have been awarded, but that the defendant solicitor had to place "collectability" in issue first. In that case the issue had not been pleaded and the limited evidence suggested that higher damages would have been collectable. See also the earlier cases of: *Page v A Solicitor* (1971) 20 D.L.R. 532, New Brunswick CA, aff'd 29 D.L.R. 386: following a road accident, a solicitor failed to sue the deceased driver; damages were assessed at the deceased's insurance cover in the absence of any evidence that he had any funds or property to satisfy any judgment; *Doiron v Caisse Populaire D'Inkerman Ltee.* (1985) 17 D.L.R. 660, New Brunswick CA; *Aikmac Holdings Ltd v Loewen* (1993) 86 Man. R. (2d) 56 Manitoba QB: claimant failed to discharge onus of proving that she would have recovered her damages; *Buerckert v Mattison* [1997] 1 W.W.R. 430, Saskatchewan QB: the Court determined that the original defendant would probably have gone bankrupt but would have had to pay half of the claimant's notional judgment debt on discharge, which was what the claimant was awarded; *Valness v MacLowich* (1998) 168 Sask.R. 45, Saskatchewan CA: there was sufficient evidence that the original claimant had the ability to satisfy the judgment.
[20] (1989) 82 A.L.R. 587.
[21] (1989) 82 A.L.R. 617. This was followed by Garland J. in *Hunter v Earnshaw* [2001] P.N.L.R. 42, who assessed damages in that case at the date the original action was struck out, and not at a later date when the action would otherwise have come to trial.
[22] See *Nikolaou v Papasavas, Phillips & Co* (1989) 82 A.L.R. 617 at 623 ll. 11–13.
[23] Evidence of what happened later may, in certain cases, assist in determining what a judge at the notional trial date would have done, and what evidence might have been brought then: see *Johnson v Perez* (1989) 82 A.L.R. 587, at 598–599. For instance, if there were no medical reports prepared at the notional trial date, later medical reports may assist in determining what reports would have said then. The longer the time has passed from the notional trial date, the less material the report will be.

same result has been reached in Canada.[24] The question of the date of the notional trial may be important in determining the applicable legal principles in an area of law where there has been significant development. For example, in *Harrison v Bloom Camillin*[25] the claimants argued that there would have been trial within two and three-quarter years, relying on the length of time the solicitors' negligence trial had taken to come to court, and the defendants suggested nearly six years, relying on statistical evidence. Neuberger J. held that there would have been a hearing in July 1996 and judgment in October 1996. Unusually, the issue was of some importance, as the House of Lords' decision in *Banque Bruxelles Lambert v Eagle Star*[26] would limit the damages recoverable if it was decided in time for the notional judgment, as the judge held it was.

The principles discussed above have been qualified by the Court of Appeal in **11-299** *Charles v Hugh James Jones & Jenkins (a firm)*.[27] The claimant suffered personal injuries in a road accident in 1990, and the defendant solicitors negligently allowed her subsequent action to be struck out. The judge held that the original action would have been tried in January 1996, but in assessing damages he took into account evidence in relation to the deterioration of the claimant's condition obtained after that date. The Court of Appeal held the court should consider evidence of the claimant's condition which would have been available at the notional trial date, even if the evidence in fact only emerged later. Furthermore, if a condition was of uncertain prognosis at the notional trial date, but became clearer afterwards, it was appropriate to admit later evidence of what in fact happened[28]; the court tentatively considered that evidence of some entirely new condition which manifested itself only after the notional trial date should not be admitted. The issue was revisited by the Court of Appeal in *Dudarec v Andrews*.[29] The claimant was injured in a road traffic action, but his solicitors negligently delayed the action so that it was struck out for want of prosecution in 1996. He issued proceedings against his solicitors in 2002, and a preliminary issue was ordered to decide whether the claimant failed to mitigate his damage by failing to have an operation to correct an aneurism which he said prevented him working. A scan showed that there was in fact no aneurism. The experts agreed that they would have wanted the 2004 scan performed in 1996 for the notional trial, and the Court of Appeal therefore held that it would not have been unreasonable in 1996 to refuse an operation for a problem that did not exist.

---

[24] *Rose v Mitton* (1994) 111 D.L.R. (4th) 217, Nova Scotia CA, expressly following the two Australian cases and para.4–189 in the 3rd edn of this book.

[25] [2000] Lloyd's Rep. P.N. 89. However at 116 col.2 the judge seemed to suggest that if a later authority laid down the law in a way which was not intended to be a departure from the past, that authority should be applied in any event. See para.11–292 for the facts of the case. For an apparent exception see *Cohen v Kingsley Napley (a firm)* [2005] EWHC 899, QB; [2005] P.N.L.R. 37, where Tugendhat J. held that the prospects of any action being struck out should be assessed by reference to subsequent law not the law as it then stood, although in fact there was no difference between the two.

[26] [1997] A.C. 191, discussed at para.11–248.

[27] [2000] 1 W.L.R. 1278.

[28] *ibid.* at 1290G, *cf.* 1295D–E, *per* Swinton Thomas L.J., with whom Robert Walker L.J. agreed, but Sir Richard Scott V.C. reserved his position. These comment were obiter see *Dudarec v Andrews* [2006] EWCA Civ 256; [2006] 2 All E.R. 856 para.33, *per* Waller L.J. It is submitted that they are difficult to reconcile with principle. They were doubted, obiter, by the Outer House in *Campbell v Imray* [2004] P.N.L.R. 1, where the potential problems with the reasoning were explained.

[29] [2006] EWCA Civ 256; [2006] 2 All E.R. 856, CA.

Smith L.J. went on to agree the comments made in *Charles*, and suggested that if the claimant died of unrelated causes between the notional and actual trial date, or won the lottery and gave up work, those matters should be taken into account.

11–300   **Interest after date of trial.** If the claimant would have recovered damages at a particular date which has been assessed, then those damages would have attracted judgment debt interest thereafter if they had not been paid. The Court of Appeal decided in *Pinnock v Wilkins & Sons*[30] that such interest is recoverable in an action against solicitors who have lost the claimants' right of action by their negligence. However, in *Harrison v Bloom Camillin*[31] Neuberger J. held that the appropriate rate of interest was a matter of discretion, and although many cases had awarded judgment rate interest, he considered it just to award the more flexibile short-term investment rate.

11–301   **Deduction of benefits.** One issue which frequently arises, but has not been the subject of any reported decision, is the effect of the deduction of statutory benefits from damages. In personal injury actions, the claimant will often recover significantly less than he is nominally awarded because the defendants are obliged to deduct most statutory benefits from the damages and send that deduction to the Compensation Recovery Unit.[32] The relevant legislation, in summary, only applies to compensation payments made in consequence of an accident by the person liable in respect of the accident.[33] Compensation payable by a solicitor to his client who has lost his personal injury action is therefore not subject to any such deduction. The consequence is that the negligent solicitor will have to pay less to the claimant than he would have been awarded at trial, due to the "CRU clawback" reducing the notional damages that would have been obtained, but the claimant will not lose out twice by having to pay any sum from the damages he recovers from the negligent solicitor to the Compensation Recovery Unit.

(iv) *Loss of Opportunity to Defend Proceedings*

11–302   Where a solicitor fails to put in a defence or to take some other procedural step, with the result that his client loses the opportunity to contest a claim against him, the court must consider the merits of the proposed defence. The damages should represent the value of the opportunity which has been lost, and many of the principles which have been discussed above will be applicable. In *Godefroy v*

---

[30] *The Times*, January 29, 1990. See further on the issue of interest Ch.3, paras 3–021 to 3–026.
[31] [2000] Lloyd's Rep. P.N. 404; see para.11–292 for the facts. Neuberger J.'s reasoning was followed, albeit not in the context of lost litigation, in *Griffiths v Last Cawthra Feather (a firm)* [2002] P.N.L.R. 27, TCC. In *Browning v Brachers (a firm)* [2004] EWHC 16; [2004] P.N.L.R. 28 Jack J. awarded interest at the ordinary commercial rate, broadly reflecting the cost of the claimants' borrowings.
[32] Where the claimant had an X% chance of success, the deduction should be X%, see *Green v Berry* [2001] 1 Qd.R. 605, Queensland CA.
[33] See s.1 of the Social Security (Recovery of Benefits) Act 1997, which is materially identical to earlier enactments.

Jay[34] it was held that the client had no defence and therefore nominal damages only were awarded. In *Cook v Swinfen*[35] the solicitor acting for a wife failed to defend divorce proceedings and allowed the husband to obtain a decree against her. It was held that, if the solicitors had performed their duty, it was probable that both parties would have obtained cross-decrees for adultery, but there was an outside chance that the wife alone would have obtained a decree. Lawton J. awarded (and the Court of Appeal approved) (i) damages of £200 for loss of the chance of obtaining a more favourable outcome of the divorce suit; and (ii) damages of £750 for loss of the chance of obtaining maintenance.[36]

(v) *Losses on Loans Secured by Mortgages*[37]

The basic calculation. The principles to be applied in lender's cases will generally be the same as those which have been extensively developed by the courts in the context of negligent surveys carried out for lenders.[38] In *Swingcastle Ltd v Alastair Gibson*,[39] a case concerning surveyor's negligence, the House of Lords held that the usual measure of loss recoverable by a lender is (i) the difference between the advance and any capital recovered, plus (ii) consequential expenses, plus (iii) interest to reflect the loss of use of the capital sum advanced, credit being given for any interest payments made. However, this will be subject to the type of breach in question which may restrict the damages recoverable.[40] The interest to be awarded will be at a simple rate only, unless there was evidence of foreseeability within the second limb of *Hadley v Baxendale*, see *Birmingham Midshires Mortgage Services Ltd v Phillips*.[41] The losses recoverable will include the cost of in-house lawyers, and estate agency commission where the work was undertaken by a separate legal entity, see *Portman Building Society v Bevan Ashford (a firm)*.[42] **11–303**

Scope of duty. The measures of loss discussed in the previous paragraph will be further subject to the principle in *Banque Bruxelles Lambert SA v Eagle Star* **11–304**

---

[34] (1831) 7 Bing. 413. It was also held that the burden of proof rested on the attorney to show that there was no defence to the original action.
[35] [1967] 1 W.L.R. 457.
[36] See also *Hill v Finney* (1865) 4 F. & F. 616 in which, as a result of his attorney's advice, the husband allowed his wife to obtain a decree of judicial separation undefended. In relation to quantum, Cockburn C.J. directed the jury to consider the merits of the proposed defence and to consider what damage the husband had suffered through not defending. The jury awarded one farthing.
[37] The duties of a solicitor acting for a client lending money are discussed in paras 11–208 to 11–219.
[38] See the discussion in Ch.10, paras 10–152 to 10–176. For earlier cases see: *Wilson v Rowswell* (1970) 11 D.L.R. (3d) 737, Supreme Court Canada; followed in *Collin Hotels Ltd v Surtees* [1988] 1 W.W.R. 272, Saskatchewan CA; *Wilson v Tucker* (1822) 3 Stark. 154; *Donaldson v Haldane* (1840) 7 C. & F. 762 and *Ronaldson v Drummond & Reid* (1991) 8 Rettie 767, Ct. Sess.; *Whiteman v Hawkins* (1878) 4 C.P.D. 13; *Campbell v Clason* (1838) 1 Dunlop 270 and (1840) 2 Dunlop 1113, Ct. Sess.; *Pretty v Fowke* (1887) 3 T.L.R. 845.
[39] [1991] 2 A.C. 223.
[40] See paras 11–248 *et seq.*, above.
[41] [1998] P.N.L.R. 468, QBD; *cf. The Mortgage Corp v Halifax (SW) Ltd* [1999] Lloyd's Rep. P.N. 159, a surveyor's claim.
[42] [2000] P.N.L.R. 344, CA.

Insurance Co Ltd.[43] Someone under a duty to advise on the appropriate course of action will be liable for all the foreseeable consequences of the action taken in reliance, but a person under a duty to take reasonable care to provide information on which someone relies will generally be regarded as responsible for the consequences of the information being wrong, and not all the consequences of the reliance. Thus surveyors sued by lenders were only responsible for the losses sustained up to the difference between the correct valuation and their negligent valuation. In *Bristol & West Building Society v Mothew*[44] the Court of Appeal applied this principle to a case where the defendant solicitors had misrepresented to the claimant lender that the borrower had no other indebtedness. While the claimant's loss from the loan was large, the loss within the scope of the broken duty appeared to be modest, as the small size of the borrower's liability may have a minimal or no effect on their ability to make mortgage repayments to the claimant. Determination of the size of the loss was left to the assessment of damages. While a solicitor's duty will be wider than that of a valuer, *Mothew* supports the view that there is no wide duty to advise on the appropriate course of action.[45]

11–305   **An exception: dishonest borrowers.** In *Bristol & West Building Society v Fancy & Jackson (a firm)*[46] Chadwick J. considered that the principles in *Banque Bruxelles Lambert* did apply to cases involving solicitors. However, in one of the cases he tried in that managed litigation, *Steggles Palmer*, the consequence of the solicitors' breach was that the claimant loaned money to a borrower whom they would not have wanted to lend to as the circumstances of the loan were suspicious. The defendants were held liable for the full amount of the claimant's loss (subject to mitigation and contributory negligence). In contrast, in *Colin Bishop*, the defendants had failed to report back to back sales, and the solicitors were liable only for the amount of the overvaluation of the property. Blackburne J. adopted the same approach in *Nationwide Building Society v Balmer Radmore (a firm).*[47] Thus, for instance, *Nationwide Building Society v ATM Abdullah*[48] was

---

[43] [1997] A.C. 191, see para.11–248, above. For a further explanation of how the principle works in the context of awarding interest, see *Nykredit Mortgage Bank Plc v Edward Erdman Group Ltd (No.2)* [1997] 1 W.L.R. 1627, considered in Ch.10, para.10–164. For the effect of contributory negligence on a claim which is subject to a limit from the scope of the duty owed, see *Platform Home Loans Ltd v Oyston Shipways Ltd* [2000] 2 A.C. 190, considered in Ch.10, paras 10–168 to 10–169.

[44] [1996] 4 All E.R. 698. See also *The Mortgage Corp v Tisdall Nelson Nari & Co* [1998] P.N.L.R. 81, QBD, which applied *Banque Bruxelles Lambert* to limit damages, and *Halifax Building Society v Richard Grosse & Co* [1997] E.G.C.S. 111.

[45] *cf.* the position in Scotland where it was held in *Bristol & West Building Society v Rollo Steven & Bond* [1998] S.L.T. 9, OH, that the solicitors effectively advised the building society to take a certain course of action and were responsible for the full loss. Similarly in *Leeds & Holbeck Building Society v Alex Morison & Co (No.2)* [2001] P.N.L.R. 13, OH, it was held that if the defenders had been negligent in failing to report that the borrowers intended in due course to use the property for business purposes, then they would have been liable for the full losses as the matter was relevant to the risk of default. See to similar effect *Newcastle Building Society v Paterson Robertson & Graham* [2001] P.N.L.R. 780 and [2002] S.L.T. 177, OH, where the alleged errors went to the heart of the trans-action.

[46] [1997] 4 All E.R. 582.

[47] [1999] P.N.L.R. 606.

[48] [1999] Lloyd's Rep. P.N. 616.

a *Colin Bishop*-type case, whereas in *Nationwide Building Society v JR Jones*[49] the lender recovered the full loss as a report on the back to back nature of the transaction and a direct payment would have meant that the lender would not have wanted to make any loan to that applicant. The approach of these two cases was approved by the Court of Appeal in *Portman Building Society v Bevan Ashford (a firm)*[50] where the solicitor failed to report matters relating to the borrower's financial condition. As a result, the claimant thought that there was no second charge and that the borrower was paying the balance of the purchase from his own resources, when in fact he had no personal equity and had fraudulently deceived the lender when signing the offer of advance. The claimant was entitled to recover its full loss. The Court of Appeal cast the relevant principle in very wide terms:

" . . . where a negligent solicitor fails to provide information which shows that the transaction is not viable or which tends to reveal an actual or potential fraud on the part of the borrowers, the lender is entitled to recover the whole of its loss."

This statement of principle has been followed by the Court of Appeal in *Lloyds Bank Plc v Crosse & Crosse*.[51] The defendant solicitors negligently failed to inform the claimant bank in 1989 that the plot of land over which security was taken was subject to restrictive covenants. The Court of Appeal applied *Portman* and limited the recoverable damages to the difference in value in 1989 between the plot without the restrictive covenants and the plot with those covenants.

(vi) *Loss of Some Other Financial Advantage*

Losses sustained on the sale of land. If, through the negligence of his **11–306** solicitor, the claimant is obliged to accept a forced sale or to sell his property at less than the full value, then the primary measure of his loss is the difference between the sum which he actually receives and the sum which he would have received in normal circumstances.[52] Alternatively, the solicitor's breach of duty might lead to a delay in the sale of land. In that event the measure of damages might comprise: (i) the amount of any mortgage interest paid during the period of delay, and (ii) the interest which could have been earned by investing the proceeds of sale throughout the period of delay.[53] In order to avoid double compensation, the "proceeds of sale" under the second head should be taken as the net proceeds after repayment of any mortgage.

Loss of earnings. Loss of earnings is not a usual consequence of negligence **11–307** by solicitors. It may arise, for example, where the solicitor advises a client to

---

[49] [1999] Lloyd's Rep. P.N. 414.

[50] [2000] P.N.L.R. 344.

[51] [2001] P.N.L.R. 34.

[52] *Rumsey v Owen White & Catlin* (1978) 245 E.G. 225, CA: as a result of the solicitors' negligence the claimant agreed to sell certain property with vacant possession, when in fact the tenants had security of tenure. The claimant recovered (i) the difference between what he actually received on the sale (£90,000) and what he would have received if he had sold without vacant possession (assessed at £112,000) and (ii) an indemnity against any future liability to the purchaser.

[53] *G & K Ladenbau Ltd v Crawley & De Reya* [1978] 1 W.L.R. 266, Mocatta J.; *Dorey Dorey v Romney* (1982) 51 N.S.R. (2d) and 102 A.P.R. 53, Nova Scotia Supreme Court.

pursue a course of conduct which results in the client being fairly dismissed. In *Malyon v Lawrance, Messer & Co*[54] (in which the claimant's claim for damages resulting from a road traffic accident became statute-barred) the claimant developed a neurosis which was not expected to clear up until after the conclusion of the litigation. Brabin J. awarded £2,000 compensation for loss of earnings caused thereby, in addition to damages in respect of the value of the original claim.[55]

11–308 **Loss of life policy.** In *McLellan v Fletcher*,[56] as a result in part of the defendant solicitor's negligence, the claimant failed to take out a life insurance policy. The claimant was killed shortly afterwards, and his personal representative argued that the deceased has lost the contingent interest in the envisaged life policy. Anthony Lincoln J., apparently giving no reasons for his decision, awarded the deceased the sum insured. This sum was reduced by 75 per cent for contributory negligence, minus the premium which would have been paid. The opposite conclusion was reached in *Lynne v Gordon Doctors & Walton*.[57] The defendant solicitors acted for a deceased mortgagee, and allegedly failed to ensure that his life was insured as part of the mortgage transaction. On a preliminary issue, Phillips J. decided that no loss was suffered by the deceased, assisted by an earlier Court of Appeal decision.[58] It is submitted that *Lynne v Gordon Doctors & Walton* should be followed.

11–309 **Loss of property.** In *Keep Point Development Ltd v Chan Chi Yim*[59] the claimant vendors assigned their units to a purchaser in return (inter alia) for options to purchase new units in the building to be constructed on the site. The option agreements provided that they would not be registered, with regard to which the solicitors were negligent. The purchaser got into financial difficulties and sold the land to a third party, and the claimants were left without remedy save against their solicitors. But for the defendants' negligence, the sales to the vendor would not have taken place. The Hong Kong Court of Final Appeal awarded the claimants: the capital value of their old units as would be assessed on the open market, taking account their development potential; the cost of removal to temporary accommodation and the rent for it; and the amount over and above the capital value of the old units required to acquire similar permanent premises when it became clear that the purchaser could not complete the construction of the new premises.

11–310 **Loss of company.** Solicitors may negligently fail to advise shareholders of the risk of relying on the credit of the purchasers of their company if payment for the company is deferred, as in *Matlaszek v Bloom Camillin (a firm)*.[60] Park J. valued

---

[54] [1968] 2 Lloyd's Rep. 539.

[55] As to which see para.11–247.

[56] (1987) 3 P.N. 202.

[57] *The Times*, June 17, 1991.

[58] *Griffiths v Fleming* [1909] 1 K.B. 805 at 820–821. See also in *Daniels v Thomson* [2004] P.N.L.R. 33, summarised at para.11–048, above. The Court of Appeal decided that where the solicitor's negligence caused the payment of inheritance tax, the testator could not suffer loss.

[59] [2003] 2 HKLRD 207. For further guidance by the Court of Final Appeals on quantum see [2005] 1 HKLRD 729.

[60] [2004] EWHC 2728; [2004] P.N.L.R. 17.

the loss of a small company with a limited trading history by establishing one year's maintainable earnings, and then multiplying that sum by the appropriate price/earnings ratio, which was obtained from publicly quoted companies in the most comparable business sector heavily discounted for a small business with a limited track record. Credit was then given for the small payments which had been made for the company.

Diminution in value of shareholding. Shareholders and directors sometimes   11–311
sue their company's solicitors for their own losses. In many cases contractual or tortious duties will be owed to them by the solicitors, and they may seek to recover the diminution in value of their shareholdings. The circumstances in which they may do so has reviewed by the House of Lords in *Johnson v Gore Wood & Co (a firm).*[61] While only a company may sue in respect of loss caused by a breach of duty to it, if the company suffers loss but has no cause of action, a shareholder who does have a cause of action may sue even thought the loss is the diminution in value of his shareholding. If the company suffers loss caused by a breach of duty to it, and the shareholder suffers a loss separate and distinct from that suffered by the company as a result of a breach of a duty independently owed to him, both can sue, but neither can recover loss caused to the other by breach of the duty owed to the other. In the latter case, if the shareholder's loss is merely reflective of the loss suffered by the company, the shareholder will have no right of action. Thus in *Johnson* the claimant could claim for sums he invested in the company, the cost of personal borrowings, the loss of some of his shareholdings, and his tax liability. As for an alleged diminution in value of his pension and shareholding in the company, the claimant could not claim for the enhancement of his pension by payments the company would have made, but he could for the enhancement of the value of the pension if the payments had been made. Thus, in summary, a shareholder cannot recover loss which is merely a reflection of the company's loss unless the company has no claim, see the Court of Appeal's decision in *Day v Cook.*[62] As a result, in that case, the claimant could not recover lost investments in property dealings made through his companies, given that the solicitor also owed duties to the companies.[63]

(vii) *Liability to Third Parties*

One consequence of the solicitor's mistake may be to expose the client to liability   11–312
to some third party: for example, the liability to pay mesne profits,[64] additional rates[65] or interest.[66] A more dramatic example is afforded by *Hart & Hodge v*

---

[61] [2002] 2 A.C. 1. For the analogous Canadian position, see *Martin v Goldfarb* (1999) 41 O.R. (3d) 161.

[62] [2001] EWCA Civ 592; [2001] P.N.L.R. 32.

[63] The Court of Appeal referred a number of the investments back to the judge for further determination.

[64] As in *Allen v Clark* (1863) 7 L.T. 781: solicitor acting for purchaser of leasehold property failed to discover that it was mortgaged. The claimant recovered, inter alia, the mesne profits which he was obliged to pay to the mortgagee.

[65] *Computastaff v Ingledew Brown Bennison & Garett* (1983) 268 E.G. 906, McNiell J.

[66] As in *Morris v Duke-Cohan & Co, The Times,* November 22, 1975, Caufield J.: interest was paid to vendor, because the claimants were unable to proceed with purchase.

Frame Son & Co.[67] The claimants instructed attorneys to take proceedings against their apprentices for misconduct. The attorneys brought proceedings under the wrong statute. The apprentices were convicted, but the convictions were quashed on appeal. The apprentices then sued the claimants for false imprisonment and recovered damages. The claimants recovered against their attorneys the full amount of their liability to the apprentices. In *Buckley v Lane Herdman & Co*[68] solicitors exchanged contracts for the sale of the claimants' house before the claimants had found a house to buy. The claimants were unable to move out on the completion date and therefore faced a claim for specific performance. The claimants ultimately had to pay the purchasers' costs in that action, amounting to £400. They recovered this sum, together with their own costs, from the solicitors. In *Braid v WL Highway & Sons*,[69] as a result of their solicitors' negligence, the claimants faced a claim by their landlord for breach of covenant. They settled this claim on terms amounting to a surrender, but recovered the amount of their liability from the solicitors.

11–313   **Solutions to uncertainty about claimant's liability.** Often the solicitor is joined as the third party in an action brought against his client. This may be important to avoid the risk of inconsistent findings. It is often convenient in such circumstances to try the third party proceedings immediately after the main action.[70] If, however, at the date of trial, the claimant's liability to some third party has yet to be determined, it may not be possible to assess damages against the solicitors. In *Rumsey v Owen White & Catlin*[71] the claimants were unable to give vacant possession of property which they had sold, as required by the contract. The purchasers' claim for damages had not yet been heard. The Court of Appeal therefore gave judgment for the amount of the claimants' loss so far, and ordered that the final assessment of damages should await the outcome of the other action. An alternative course, which was adopted in *Transportation Agency Ltd v Jenkins*,[72] is to grant a declaration that the solicitors are liable to indemnify the claimants against all sums which they may be held liable to pay to the party in question.

(viii) *Criminal Liability*

11–314   The client may find himself in breach of the criminal law, as a result of negligent advice or omissions by his solicitor. The fact of the solicitor's error may constitute excellent mitigation in the criminal proceedings, but will not constitute a defence if (for example) the offence is one of strict liability. The normal

---

[67] (1839) 6 C. & F. 193.
[68] [1977] C.L.Y.B. 3143, Judge Faye sitting as an Official Referee.
[69] (1964) 191 E.G. 433, Roskill J.
[70] e.g. *Cemp Properties (UK) Ltd v Dentsply Research & Development Corp, Estates Gazette*, August 31, 1991, CA, where, first, the liability of the defendant to the claimant was established, secondly the liability was quantified, thirdly the defendant's claim against their former solicitors was tried, and fourthly the solicitors appealed against the second order on quantum.
[71] (1978) 245 E.G. 225.
[72] (1972) 223 E.G. 1101, Kerr J.

measure of damages in such a case[73] is the amount of any fine or penalty imposed together with the costs of legal representation. In *Ashton v Wainwright*[74] as a result of their solicitors' negligence the claimants committed the offence of supplying drink at an unregistered club. They were convicted before the magistrates' court and fined. In the subsequent action against their solicitors the claimants recovered the amount of fines and costs which they were ordered to pay. Goddard J. dismissed as irrelevant the fact that the fines had been paid out of club funds: "If by the negligence of my solicitor I incur a fine, the fact that a charitable person helps me to pay it so as to enable me to escape imprisonment in default cannot afford him a defence."[75]

(ix) *Wasted Expenditure*

General rule: wasted expenditure. Where a solicitor fails to notice that a **11–315** transaction his client is entering is invalid, the normal measure of loss will be the client's wasted expenditure. Thus in *Clarke v Milford*[76] a solicitor acting for a purchaser of land failed to notice that the vendor was unable to convey any interest in the property. The client recovered money advanced on the purchase price and taxes he had paid on the property, and not the difference in value of the property.[77]

Wasted expenditure or anticipated gains. Where as a result of the solicitor's **11–316** breach of duty a transaction proves to be abortive, the client may recover by way of damages the whole of his expenditure in connection with that transaction. The client cannot at the same time claim the gains which he had anticipated receiving from the transaction, since that would give rise to double compensation. Claims for wasted expenditure and claims for anticipated gains are regarded as alternatives and the client must elect between the two.[78] If the client opts for the wasted expenditure basis, the authority of *Anglia Television v Reed*[79] allows for the recovery of expenses incurred before contract where the parties contemplate that the expenditure may be wasted upon breach. This may be the case where the solicitor's breach results in the loss of an expected benefit. However, in *GP & P v Bulcraig & Davis*[80] the defendant solicitors failed to discover that premises to be purchased by the claimant were in part subject to a restriction of user clause which rendered them unsuitable. The claimant was unable to recover wasted expenditure incurred before the breach, because they would have been incurred

---

[73] The client will only recover damages under this head in a case where there is no mens rea or culpable negligence on his part: *Osman v J Ralph Moss* [1970] 1 Lloyd's Rep. 313, CA. In other cases considerations of public policy preclude the recovery of any damages. For a general discussion of this topic, see *McGregor* (17th edn), paras 17–045 to 17–054.

[74] [1936] 1 All E.R. 805.

[75] *ibid.* at 812.

[76] (1987) 38 D.L.R. (4th) 139, Nova Scotia CA.

[77] For the difference in value approach see paras 11–275 to 11–283.

[78] For general principles, see *Cullinane v British "Rema" Manufacturing Co* [1954] 1 Q.B. 292; *Anglia Television v Reed* [1972] 1 Q.B. 60.

[79] [1972] 1 Q.B. 60, CA. See *McGregor* (17th edn), paras 2–018 to 2–025.

[80] (1986) 2 E.G.L.R. 148, 152. This point was not in issue on appeal in (1988) 1 E.G.L.R. 138. For the facts see para.11–258.

even if the defendants had discovered the restrictive user clause (in which case the claimant would not have entered the lease).

11–317　　**An illustration.** In *Transportation Agency Ltd v Jenkins*[81] the claimants purchased a restaurant business, including the lease of the premises where the business was carried on. Unfortunately, their solicitors failed to notice a number of provisions in the lease which put the venture in jeopardy, principally a covenant prohibiting cooking. By the time that the landlords sought to enforce this covenant the claimants had engaged a manager on terms which gave him a fairly free hand as to the running of the business. The claimants were in no position to stop him cooking. The claimants extricated themselves from the venture as best they could and ultimately the lease was forfeited for non-payment of rent. Kerr J. awarded by way of damages: (i) the total sum which the claimants had paid for the business, plus (ii) the three instalments of rent which they had paid, minus (iii) the total amount which they had received from the manager during the period of operation of the business.

11–318　　**Original solicitors' costs.** Where the solicitor's services are valueless as a result of his breach of duty, the client is entitled to recover any sum which he has paid to the solicitor by way of costs.[82] This may be regarded either as damages for wasted expenditure or as repayment of a sum for which the consideration has wholly failed.[83] Thus if the solicitor for a claimant sues in the wrong court[84] or commits some other error which renders the whole proceedings useless,[85] he will be debarred from recovering his costs and ordered to repay any costs which he has received. The same principle applies if the client brings a futile action as a result of negligent advice (or negligent lack of advice) by his solicitor.[86] Similarly, if the solicitor for a defendant allows proceedings to go by default, he forfeits his entitlement to remuneration.[87] Where part only of the solicitor's services are rendered valueless by his breach of duty, he may still be entitled to remuneration for the remainder of his services.[88]

---

[81] (1972) 223 E.G. 1101.

[82] See, e.g. *Heywood v Wellers* [1976] Q.B. 446 at 458, CA.

[83] One case which does not readily fit into this analysis is *Piper v Daybell Court-Cooper & Co* (1969) 210 E.G. 1047, Nield J.: solicitors acting for a purchaser failed to advise their client about a right of way. One item of damages (which was apparently conceded) was the amount of the solicitors' charges. However, it could hardly be said that there was a total failure of consideration or that the solicitors' services were valueless.

[84] *Gill v Lougher* (1830) 1 Cr. & J. 170; *Long v Orsi* (1856) 18 C.B. 610; *Cox v Leech* (1857) 1 C.B. (N.S.) 617.

[85] *Symes v Nipper* (1840) 12 Ad. & El. 377 n.; *Bracey v Carter* (1840) 12 Ad. & El. 373; *Saffery v Wray* (1846) 7 L.T. (O.S.) 183; *Lewis v Samuel* (1846) 8 Q.B. 685; *Stokes v Trumper* (1855) 2 K. & J. 232: this case concerned negligence by an attorney acting as advocate. See also *Clarke v Couchman* (1885) 20 L.J. 318: a solicitor entrusted the conduct of the case to another member of his firm, "through whose want of familiarity with the facts the claimant was non-suited." The claimant recovered, by way of damages for negligence, the costs which he had incurred. See also *Templer v McLachlan* (1806) 2 B. & P. (N.R.) 136.

[86] *Hill v Featherstonhaugh* (1831) 7 Bing. 570.

[87] *Ferguson v Lewis* (1879) 14 L.J. 700.

[88] e.g. *Cox v Leech* (1857) 1 C.B. (N.S.): Attorney sued in the wrong court, but was entitled to recover the costs of sending letters before action. "These letters are distinguishable. They might have produced the desired result." See also *Shaw v Arden* (1832) 9 Bing. 287.

Later solicitor's costs. A claimant may incur legal costs in litigation com-   **11–319**
menced to mitigate his loss. In *British Racing Drivers Club v Hextall Erskine Co
(a firm)*[89] it was held that the claimant could recover costs of proceedings
instituted against its former directors from the defendant solicitors on a standard
basis only, and not on an indemnity basis. The cost of pursuing the claim against
the defendant solicitors is recoverable as costs only and not as damages.

(x) *Incidental Expenses*

Clearly, any expenses which the claimant incurs as a result of the solicitor's   **11–320**
negligence will be recoverable,[90] in addition to the other heads of damage
discussed in this section. As illustrations, see *Bailey v Bullock*[91] or *Buckley v
Lane Herdman & Co.*[92]

(xi) *Physical Injury, Inconvenience and Distress*

Where as a result of the solicitor's breach of duty the claimant suffers non-   **11–321**
pecuniary loss, such as physical injury, inconvenience or (in some cases only)
distress, then (subject to the rules as to remoteness) he is entitled to general
damages.

Inconvenience. It has long been accepted that physical inconvenience and   **11–322**
discomfort resulting from a solicitor's breach of duty sound in damages. For
instance in *Wapshott v Davies Donovan & Co*[93] the Court of Appeal assessed

---

[89] [1996] 3 All E.R. 667, Carnwarth J. For the facts see para.11–242, above. For another example see *Savoie v Mailhot* 2004 NBCA 17; (2004) 268 N.B.R. (2d) 348, New Brunswick CA. The defendant solicitors' failure to describe the property properly in a deed of sale led to successful litigation by the claimant, who was unable to enforce his costs order and recovered those costs from the defendant solicitors. For a more detailed treatment of whether costs should be recovered on an indemnity or standard basis see *McGregor* (17th edn) paras 17–012 to 17–018, where it is argued that old authority permitting recovery on an indemnity basis should be preferred.

[90] Subject to the rules as to remoteness discussed in paras 11–238 to 11–253.

[91] [1950] 2 All E.R. 1167, KBD: owing to solicitors' negligence the claimants were unable to recover possession of their house from tenants for a period. They recovered inter alia the costs of storing furniture and garage expenses.

[92] [1977] C.L.Y.B. 3143, Judge Faye sitting as an Official Referee: the claimants recovered the incidental expenses of moving house, which was forced upon them by their solicitors' negligence. In *Lomond Assured Properties Ltd v McGregor Donald* [2000] S.L.T. 797, OH, the pursuers recovered for cost of the director's wasted time spent dealing with the problem caused by their solicitors, but not the time spent in the litigation.

[93] [1996] 1 P.N.L.R. 361. For further examples see: *Shilcock v Passman* (1836) 7 C. & P. 289: claimant was awarded £10 damages as compensation for two months which he spent in prison, as a result of the attorney's failure to secure his discharge. *Bailey v Bullock* [1950] 2 All E.R. 1167, Barry J.: claimant instructed the solicitors to recover possession of his house from the tenants. During two years' delay the claimant, his wife and child were forced to live with the wife's parents in cramped accommodation. Claimant awarded £300 damages for discomfort and inconvenience, but damages for annoyance and mental distress were irrecoverable. *Piper v Daybell Court-Cooper & Co* (1969) 210 E.G. 1047, Nield J.: claimants were awarded £50 for the inconvenience and loss of privacy resulting from a right of way running across their land. *Trask v Clark & Sons* [1980] C.L.Y. 1588, Talbot J.: claimant awarded £250 for the inconvenience, anxiety and loss of privacy caused by a public footpath running past his front door. *Buckley v Lane Herdman & Co* [1977] C.L.Y.B. 3143, Judge Faye sitting as an official referee: as a result of premature exchange of contracts by their solicitors, claimants were obliged to leave their home and to move to other unsuitable accommodation for two years at date of trial. They were awarded £750 damages each for inconvenience and distress.

damages in relation to inconvenience discomfort and distress of £3,000. The defendant solicitors were retained by two young couples each buying a single bedroom flat, and it was reasonably foreseeable that if the solicitors were negligent then their clients may have to remain in the flats in cramped conditions with young families. As the loss was not too remote, there was no rule of law preventing such damages being awarded.

11–323 **Distress affecting health.** Where the solicitor's breach of duty causes such distress as to affect the client's health, then this constitutes a separate head of damages. This is subject to the rules as to remoteness, which will often defeat a claim.[94] In *Malyon v Lawrance, Messer & Co*[95] the solicitors' negligence led to an extension of the period for which the claimant suffered neurosis, following a road traffic accident. £1,250 was awarded under this head.[96] A claim for distress affecting health means that the whole claim is subject to the three year limitation period appropriate for personal injuries.[97]

11–324 **Distress not affecting health.**[98] It used to be thought that mental distress not resulting in injury to health did not sound in damages.[99] However, decisions in other areas of law have established that, in principle, damages for disappointment or distress resulting from breach of contract can be awarded in some circumstances.[1] There are two Court of Appeal cases concerning solicitors which consider this matter, and one from the House of Lords.[2] In *Heywood v Wellers*[3] the Court of Appeal awarded damages to a claimant in respect of the anxiety,

---

[94] In *Cook v Swinfen* [1967] 1 W.L.R. 457 damages for injury to health were refused, on the grounds that such injury was not foreseeable (but see *Heywood v Wellers* [1976] Q.B. 446, at 459C, *per* Lord Denning M.R.). This was distinguished in *Dickinson v James Alexander & Co* (1990) P.N. 205 at 212.

[95] [1968] 2 Lloyd's Rep. 539, Brabin J. See also *Wales v Wales* (1967) 111 S.J. 946.

[96] Similarly, see *Curran v Docherty* [1995] S.L.T. 716 where the Outer House awarded the pursuer £3,000 with respect to the anxiety and distress caused by the defendant solicitor failing to obtain discharge of a mortgage over her house pursuant to a matrimonial settlement. It appears from the report that the distress did affect the pursuer's health.

[97] See: *Bennett v Greenland Houchen & Co* [1998] P.N.L.R. 458, CA; *Oates v Harte Reade & Co* [1999] P.N.L.R. 763, Singer J., (refusal to allow the personal injury part of the claim to be deleted); *Shade v The Compton Partnership (a firm)* [2000] P.N.L.R. 218, CA (allowing the personal injury part of the claim to be deleted). See further Ch.5, para.5–028.

[98] For a more detailed analysis see H. Evans, "Lawyers' Liabilities" (2nd edn, 2002), Ch.13. For a discussion of this topic see M. Jones and A. Morris: "The distressing effects of professional incompetence" [2004] 20 P.N. 118.

[99] e.g. *Groom v Crocker* [1939] 1 K.B. 194, CA: *Bailey v Bullock* [1950] 2 All E.R. 1167, KBD.

[1] *Jarvis v Swan's Tours* [1973] Q.B. 233; *Jackson v Horizon Holidays* [1975] 1 W.L.R. 1468 (both cases concerning an unsatisfactory holiday); *Bliss v South East Thames Regional HA* [1987] I.C.R. 700 (where nothing was awarded because the case did not come within the narrow circumstances where such an award is permitted).

[2] While the cases concern recovery in contract, the same rules will apply in tort, see *Verderame v Commercial Union* [1992] B.C.L.C. 793. Such damages were awarded in *Crossnan v Ward Bracewell & Co* (1989) 6 P.N. 103, at 107, Kennedy J., but without any discussion about the principles to be applied.

[3] [1976] Q.B. 446. While the outcome of the case is correct on the law as it has subsequently developed, the majority of the Court based its decision on foreseeability only, which can no longer be justified. That approach was followed in *Dickinson v James Alexander & Co* (1990) 7 P.N. 205 at 212–213, Douglas Brown J., and may be the explanation of the award for anxiety in *Buckley v Lane Herdman & Co* [1977] C.L.Y.B. 3143, and *Trask v Clark & Sons* [1980] C.L.Y. 1588.

vexation and distress caused by a man's continued molestation, when the defendant solicitors failed to bring proceedings to prevent such molestation. In *Hayes v Dodd*[4] the claimants decided to purchaser larger premises for their motor repair business. Their solicitors, the defendants, wrongly informed them that a right of way existed over the only proper access to the premises, which was at the rear. The claimants purchased the premises. The owner of adjacent property blocked the rear access, and as a result the business failed. The Court of Appeal did not allow the recovery of damages for anguish and vexation. The Court rejected the application of the foreseeability test alone and followed the classification provided by Dillon L.J. in *Bliss v South East Thames Regional Health Authority*[5]: that recovery of such damages would be limited to cases " . . . where the contract which has been broken was itself a contract to provide peace of mind or freedom from distress."[6] In *Johnson v Gore Wood & Co (a firm)*[7] the House of Lords struck out a claim by a claimant for damages for distress arising out of a commercial conveyancing contract. Their lordships adopted as an authoritative statement of the law the formulation of Bingham L.J. in *Watts v Morrow*,[8] a surveyor's case, that damages for distress should only be awarded where "the very object of a contract is to provide pleasure, relaxation, peace of mind or freedom from molestation", a test almost identical to *Hayes v Dodd*. However, in *Farley v Skinner*[9] a case concerning surveyors, the House of Lords have made it clear that it is sufficient if a major or important part of the contract was to secure pleasure, relaxation or peace of mind.

Application of the rule. *Hayes v Dodd* concerned the conveyance of commercial property,[10] as did *Johnson v Gore Wood & Co (a firm)*. The Court of Appeal did not allow damages for distress in *Watts & Watts v Morrow*,[11] a surveyor's negligence case concerning a domestic survey. It is submitted that, by analogy, damages for distress could not normally be recovered from solicitors for the conveyance of residential property.[12] In *McLeish v Amoo-Gottfried & Co*[13] Scott Baker J. concluded (without the contrary being argued) that the very essence of a retainer to act for a defendant in a criminal trial was to ensure his peace of mind. There, the solicitors' negligence caused the client to be convicted and fined £450 for assault and possessing an offensive weapon, before the Court of Appeal quashed the conviction over two years later. The client was awarded £6,000, **11–325**

---

[4] [1990] 2 All E.R. 815. The same result was reached in relation to commercial property by the Court of Appeal in *Hartle v Laceys* [1999] Lloyd's Rep. P.N. 315. In "Anguish, foreseeability and policy" (1989) L.Q.R. 43, K. Soh argues that anyone who approaches solicitors for conveyancing is asking for peace of mind.

[5] [1987] I.C.R. 700 at 718.

[6] [1990] 2 All E.R. 815 at 824A–B, *per* Staughton L.J. See also at 818D and 826H–827A.

[7] [2002] 2 A.C. 1. For the analogous Canadian position see *Martin v Goldfarb* (1999) 41 O.R. (3d) 161.

[8] [1991] 1 W.L.R. 1423.

[9] [2002] 2 A.C. 732.

[10] Some residential property was also conveyed, but the distress was entirely caused by problems with the commercial property.

[11] [1991] 1 W.L.R. 1421. See Ch.10, para.10–184.

[12] This was the conclusion of McDermott L.J. in *Smyth v Huey* [1993] N.I. 236, applying *Watts v Morrow*.

[13] [1994] 10 P.N. 102. See also *Boudreau v Benaiah* (2000) 182 D.L.R. (4th) 569, where the Ontario Court of Appeal awarded damages for mental anxiety relating to a forced guilty plea.

taking into account the distress he was caused by his loss of reputation. Following *McLeish*, in *Rey v Graham & Oldham (a firm)*[14] McKinnon J. awarded damages for the distress of being stigmatised as a bankrupt and for being unable to buy a house as a result of bankruptcy caused by the defendant solicitors' negligence. The judge considered that bankruptcy was somewhat akin to a criminal conviction. In *Channon v Lindley Johnstone*[15] the Court of Appeal held that damages for distress should not be awarded in a claim for ancillary relief. In *Hamilton-Jones v David & Snape (a firm)*[16] Neuberger J. awarded the claimant £20,000 damages for the distress occasioned by the loss of her children. She retained the defendant solicitors in a custody battle with her former husband, and they obtained orders prohibiting the removal of the children from the jurisdiction. However, they negligently failed to re-register the children with the passport agency, and the husband absconded with the children to Tunisia. A significant reason for the solicitors' retainer was to ensure that the claimant retained custody of her children for her own pleasure and peace of mind, and thus damages for mental distress were awarded.

(e) *Mitigation of Damage*

11–326   **Examples of Failure to Mitigate.** The claimant in a solicitors' negligence action, as in any other action, cannot recover damages in respect of any loss which he ought reasonably to have avoided. Thus in *Joliffe v Charles Coleman & Co*,[17] an action arising from the solicitors' failure to apply for a new tenancy under Pt 2 of the Landlord and Tenant Act 1954, it was held that the claimants acted unreasonably in refusing the new tenancy which was in fact offered by the landlords. The terms offered were not very much worse than the terms which could have been obtained upon an application under the Act. Damages were therefore assessed on the hypothetical assumption that the landlords' offer had been accepted.

11–327   **Generous treatment of the claimant.** The argument that the claimant has failed to mitigate his loss always suffers from the disadvantage that it is advanced by the guilty party. It is put forward as a criticism of the manner in which the innocent party has extricated himself from a situation of the defendant's making.

---

[14] [2000] B.P.I.R. 354. Applied in *Fraser v Gaskell* [2004] EWHC 894; [2004] P.N.L.R. 32, where H.H. Judge Rich Q.C. awarded £750 general damages for making the client vulnerable to bankruptcy.

[15] [2002] EWCA Civ 353; [2002] P.N.L.R. 41.

[16] [2003] EWHC 3147, Ch; [2004] 1 All E.R. 657, applying *Farley v Skinner* [2002] 2 A.C. 1.

[17] (1971) 219 E.G. 1608, Browne J. For the facts see para.11–271. For another example see *Matlock Green Garage Ltd v Potter Brooke-Taylor & Wildgoose (a firm)* [2000] Lloyd's Rep. P.N. 935, where solicitors failed to renew the claimant's business tenancy, but it was unreasonable of the claimants to close parts of the business carried on at other sites. For the facts see para.11–272. *cf. Baloch v Leonard & Kalin* [1996] E.G.C.S. 181, where the Court rejected an allegation of failure to mitigate as the claimant had no choice but to accept the landlord's terms. In *Dareway Properties Ltd v Glovers* [1998] C.L.Y. 4025, QBD, the defendant solicitors failed to ensure that the contract for the purchase of property included a condition that the Charity Commissioners' consent be obtained to develop part of the land. Consent was refused. The claimants refused to enter a similar agreement at no extra cost which would receive consent, as they hoped to unlock extra ransom value from the land. It was held that they had failed to mitigate their loss.

Thus, in the majority of cases,[18] the court tends to lean in favour of the claimant on this issue. In *Whiteman v Hawkins*,[19] for example, a case in which the security for a loan proved to be subject to an equitable charge, the court rejected the argument that the claimant should enforce other securities which were available, rather than sue his solicitor.[20] In *Transportation Agency Ltd v Jenkins*[21] the defendants argued that despite the covenant in the lease against cooking and the other difficulties referred to, the claimants ought not to have simply withdrawn from the transaction. They should have tried to iron out the difficulties with their landlords and to make the business viable. Kerr J. "had no hesitation" in rejecting this submission. In *Gregory v Shepherds*[22] where the claimants were unable to sell a Spanish holiday apartment for eight years, but they did not have to give credit for the rent he could have obtained during that period as they had not bought the property to let, and any such letting would impinge on the ability to conclude an early sale when they were encouraged to believe that the defect in title would be removed shortly.

Fresh litigation: the general rule.[23] An issue which frequently arises in **11–328** solicitors' negligence cases is whether the claimant ought to embark upon fresh litigation in order to mitigate his loss. In *Pilkington v Wood*,[24] it was argued that the claimant ought to have brought proceedings against the original vendor of his house in respect of the defect in title. This argument was rejected in view of the difficulties which that action would involve. Harman J. stated that the claimant's duty to mitigate "does not go so far as to oblige the injured party, even under an indemnity, to embark on a complicated and difficult piece of litigation against a third party."[25] The actual decision in that case is eminently reasonable. The

---

[18] See, e.g. *Dodds Properties v Canterbury CC* [1980] 1 W.L.R. 433 at 452C–D, *per* Megaw L.J. *King v Hawkins & Co, The Times,* January 28, 1982, Mars-Jones J.: the purchaser of property discovered a defect in title owing to his solicitors' negligence. He refused to abandon his plans for improving the property. Held that he was not in breach of his duty to mitigate. *Hayes v Dodd* [1990] 2 All E.R. 815, CA: the purchaser of two properties discovered that there was no right of way over the only convenient means of access; it was not unreasonable to attempt to sell both properties together, which had been done on advice, and caused a four year delay before they were sold. *Barnes v Hay* (1988) 12 N.S.W.L.R. 337, CA: it was not unreasonable for a tenant to refuse to go out of business when the solicitor's negligence enabled the lessor to harass him causing the business loss, because it was not unreasonable to expect that the position would improve when changes to the shopping complex were complete. For the facts see para.11–242, above.
[19] (1878) 4 C.P.D. 13.
[20] See also *Westlake v JP Cave* [1998] N.P.C.: no obligation to enhance value of land obtained in settlement by applying for planning permission.
[21] (1972) 223 E.G. 1101, Kerr J. For the facts see para.11–317.
[22] [2000] P.N.L.R. 769, CA. For the facts, see paras 11–202 and 11–282, above.
[23] See H. Evans, "Solicitors and mitigation of loss" (2001) 17 P.N. 93; *ibid., Lawyers' Liabilities* (2nd edn, 2002), Ch.14.
[24] [1953] Ch. 770. See also *Treloar v Henderson* [1968] N.Z.L.R. 1085, High Court (solicitor's negligence resulted in client being liable under a contract; it was reasonable for the claimant not to attempt to avoid the contract, because he would have been sued and probably lost). For a further example see *Williams v Glyn Owen & Co* [2003] EWCA Civ 367; [2004] P.N.L.R. 20. The vendor delayed the completion of the sale of a Welsh hill farm to the claimant, who as a result lost the profits he would have made if he had been able to purchase breeding ewes in time. His solicitors, the defendants, negligently failed to serve a completion notice. The Court of Appeal held that the claimant had no duty to mitigate his loss and sue the vendor for damages, particularly as the solicitor had not recommended such a course of action.
[25] *ibid.* at 777.

proposed litigation would have involved considerable delay and would have seriously interfered with the claimant's domestic arrangements.[26] Subsequent cases have explored how far the claimant must go in pursuing litigation against a third party.[27]

11–329   **Exceptions to the general rule.** In *Western Trust & Savings Ltd v Clive Travers & Co*[28] the Court of Appeal held that when a lender sues his solicitors for negligent advice in relation to a mortgage transaction, it should mitigate its loss by obtaining possession and selling the property. This was an ordinary feature of enforcing security, and would have been necessary whether or not there were defects in the security, as there in fact were. The fact that the defendants were not prepared to offer an indemnity was irrelevant. Delays in enforcing security were a failure to mitigate so that the lender was deprived of lost interest and outgoings for the period of delay in *Bristol & West Building Society v Fancy & Jackson (a firm)*.[29] In *Dickinson v James Alexander & Co*,[30] by reason of the defendant solicitors' negligence, the claimant received a very disadvantageous settlement on the divorce from her husband. She failed to apply to vary the original order, despite growing financial difficulties and her former husband's rising income which were evident in the year or two following the divorce settlement. When she did apply for the order to be varied, six years after the original order, she received a very large increase. Douglas Brown J. decided that the claimant had failed to mitigate her loss.

11–330   **Disappointed beneficiary cases.** Two Court of Appeal decisions concern cases brought by disappointed beneficiaries.[31] In *Walker v Medlicott*[32] the claimant claimed that the testatrix had informed him and others that she had left property to him, although no reference to such a devise appeared in the defendant solicitors' note of the testatrix's instructions. The Court of Appeal upheld the Judge's finding that negligence had not been proved. The Court also held that in such a case the evidence for a claim in negligence would be the same as that

---

[26] For the facts see para.11–245. The claimant was not entitled to recover the costs caused by the delay in selling his house.

[27] In *Halifax Plc v Gould & Swayne* [1999] P.N.L.R. 184 Auld L.J. suggested that *Pilkington v Wood* was not an exhaustive code of the criteria material to assessing whether the claimant should reasonably have litigated to mitigate its loss. Buxton L.J. appears to have cautiously agreed.

[28] [1997] P.N.L.R. 295. Contrast *Cottingham v Attey Bower & Jones (a firm)* [2000] P.N.L.R. 557, where claimants who had not been advised by solicitors that there was no building regulation consent for what were defective renovation works were not obliged to mitigate their loss by suing the surveyors who had also advised them.

[29] [1997] 4 All E.R. 582 at 623–62.

[30] (1990) 6 P.N. 205 at 211.

[31] For commentary see B. Rich, "Errors in will-drafting: the limits of a remedy in negligence" (1999) 15 P.N. 211.

[32] [1999] 1 W.L.R. 727. Note that Simon Brown L.J. specifically did not doubt the soundness of the basic rule and correctness of the decision in *Pilkington v Wood*, although the other two members of the Court of Appeal did not directly address that issue. In "Mistakes in wills: rectify and be damned." (2003) 62 C.L.J. 750 R. Kerridge and A. Brierley argue that *Walker v Medlicott* [1999] 1 W.L.R. 727 is wrongly decided as: a rectifiable misunderstanding by the draftsman is almost inevitably negligent; the alternative remedy of a rectification action may be fraught with difficulty as it may be almost impossible to work out whether the mistake falls within the limited ambit of s.20(1) of the Administration of Justice Act 1982 and so allows for rectification; and the facts cannot easily be distinguished from *Horsfall v Haywards* [1999] P.N.L.R. 583.

required in an action for rectification, and the claimant should have mitigated any loss he sustained by seeking the latter. Contrast *Horsfall v Haywards*[33] where the defendant solicitors negligently drafted the will leaving the testator's house to his widow rather than merely a life interest to her with a remainder to the claimants. The Court of Appeal held that the claimants had no obligation to sue the widow. The Court cited *Pilkington v Wood* with approval, and distinguished *Walker v Medlicott*. The solicitor, who had acted for the estate, had given no advice about rectifying the will or not sending the money to the widow in Canada, so it was reasonable for the claimants to have taken no action before the six months time limit for rectification expired.

Limits of the rule. It is submitted, if the claimant is simply asked to lend his **11–331** name to litigation, under a full indemnity as to costs, and the litigation involves no serious hardship for the claimant, it probably would be unreasonable for him to refuse. This situation often arises where solicitors allow a personal injuries claim to become statute-barred. The solicitors, or their insurers, may wish to make an application to the court, in the claimant's name, to override the time limit under s.33 of the Limitation Act 1980. If the application succeeds, the claimant will be restored to the position he would have occupied if the breach had not occurred (unless the delay has otherwise affected his prospects of success). It seems that, unless the proposed application is plainly hopeless, the claimant would be failing in his duty to mitigate if he did not allow it to proceed.

Change of solicitor. The client normally changes solicitors as soon as it **11–332** becomes apparent that he might have a claim for negligence against his original solicitors. If thereafter he acts in accordance with the advice of his new solicitors and counsel, he has strong grounds for arguing that he acted reasonably.[34]

4. SHARED RESPONSIBILITY

(a) *Contributory Negligence*[35]

The general rule. Contributory negligence is rarely in issue between an **11–333** unsophisticated lay client and his solicitor, and it will be unusual for there to be

---

[33] [1999] P.N.L.R. 583.
[34] See, e.g. *Attard v Samson* (1966) 110 S.J. 249; *Apatu v Peach Prescott & Jamieson* [1985] 1 N.Z.L.R. 50, at 72, Eichelbaum J. *cf. Dickinson v James Alexander & Co* (1990) 6 P.N. 205, Douglas Brown J. For discussion of an analogous problem in the construction context (first architect negligent, claimant instructs second architect and carries out remedial works in accordance with his advice) see Ch.9, para.9–304.
[35] The general principles of contributory negligence are referred to in Ch.5, paras 5–141 to 5–147. The issue can normally be raised at the stage of assessment of damages stage after summary judgment has been obtained, depending on what the judgment had decided, see *Maes Finance Ltd v AL Phillips, The Times*, March 25, 1997, Ch. D. For a helpful discussion and classification of contributory negligence, see J. Murdoch, "Client negligence: A lost cause?" (2004) 20 P.N. 97.

such a finding. For example, in *Manortarn Ltd v Rose & Bird*[36] the claimant, which was a property investment company mostly concerned with residential property, was not contributorily negligent in failing to read the commercial lease of property it was buying and thus failing to notice break clauses. The defendant solicitors were wholly liable for failing to bring them to the claimant's attention. Even where the client acts through legally qualified officers, there would ordinarily be no contributory negligence because those officers would be concerned with the business aspects of a transaction and would properly leave the legal aspects of it to the retained solicitors.[37] There are, however, exceptions. In *McLellan v Fletcher*[38] the defendant solicitor acted for the claimant in the purchase of some land. The claimant made his own arrangements about an endowment policy. The defendant solicitor was told by the claimant that he had arranged to pay premiums for the policy, but was held to be negligent in failing to confirm with the insurers or the building society whether the insurers were on risk. However, Anthony Lincoln J. found the claimant 75 per cent responsible. He had been informed by the insurance company that he had to pay the first premium if the cover was to commence, but believed without grounds that he had done so and informed his solicitor accordingly.

11–334   **Illustrations.** Commonwealth cases provide further illustrations of courts finding claimants contributorily negligent. In *Astley v Austrust Ltd*[39] the claimant trustee sought advice from the defendant solicitor in relation to its intention of becoming trustee of an existing trading trust. The solicitor negligently failed to advise the trustee about excluding his personal liability if the trust failed. At first instance, the claimant was held 50 per cent contributorily negligent in failing properly to assess the financial worth of the proposed venture. The High Court of Australia held that the claimant was guilty of contributory negligence even when the very purpose of the duty owed by the defendant was to protect the claimant against the loss that happened. However, on the construction of the relevant Australian legislation, contributory negligence did not give rise to an apportionment of the cause of action in contract, even where the contractual duty was concurrent with that in negligence. Contrast the English case of British *Racing Drivers' Club Ltd v Hextall Erskine Co,*[40] where Carnwath J. refused to

---

[36] [1995] E.G.C.S. 142, QBD. In dismissing a defence of contributory negligence in *Feakins v Burstow* [2005] EWHC 1931, QB; [2006] P.N.L.R. 6, Jack J. held that in a claim of negligence relating to the conduct of litigation it would be rare for the claimant to be held guilty of contributory negligence. For another example see *Hondon Development Ltd Powerise Investments Ltd* [2006] P.N.L.R. 1, [2005] 3 H.K.L.R. 605, HKCA, where the claimant, an experienced property developer was held not to be contributorily negligent in failing to spot the difference in two plans of property he was buying, which was the solicitor's error.

[37] *Central Trust Co v Rafuse* (1986) 31 D.L.R. (4th), Supreme Court of Canada. For the facts see para.11–085. Similarly, in *Alberta Workers' Compensation Board v Riggins* (1993) 95 D.L.R. (4th) 279, Alberta CA, the fact that the claimant had a staff of three lawyers was irrelevant once they sought the opinion of outside counsel, and they were not negligent in relying on the advice provided.

[38] (1987) 3 P.N. 202. The case is of limited authority because the principal finding of loss is dubious, see para.11–308.

[39] [1999] Lloyd's Rep. P.N. 758.

[40] [1996] 3 All E.R. 667.

impute to the company the negligence of its directors, when the negligence of the solicitors was a failure to advise the board that the transaction in question had to be approved by the members. The claimant has been found to be contributorily negligent in several Canadian cases,[41] and in New Zealand.[42] For another Australian example, see *Cadoks Pty Ltd v Wallace Westley & Vigar Pty Ltd*[43] where the defendant solicitors negligently failed to take steps to ensure that finance was available for the purchase of a farm, but there was a finding of 10 per cent

---

[41] *Bowles v Johnson* [1988] 4 W.W.R. 242, Manitoba QB: the lawyer acting for the vendors owed a duty of care to the unrepresented purchasers and was negligent in allowing the vendors to continue with a dubious sale at an inflated price; the purchasers were held 50% contributorily negligent in not making suitable enquiries, or determining the value of the land, or obtaining professional advice; *Doiron v Caisse Populaire D'Inkerman Ltee* (1985) 17 D.L.R. (4th) 660, New Brunswick CA: the defendant solicitors negligently failed to procure personal guarantees as security for a loan made by the claimant bank. The bank was 50% to blame in not giving clear instructions and not inspecting the documents to ascertain that the guarantees were missing; *Earl v Wilhelm* [2001] W.T.L.R. 1275, (2000) 183 D.L.R. (4th) 45, Saskatchewan CA, the defendant solicitor was negligent in failing to ensure that the claimant beneficiaries received the land intended by the testator under his will. At first instance there was a 25% deduction for the contributory negligence of the testator in failing to provide full and accurate instructions as to the ownership of the land, but on appeal it was held that the testator's contributory negligence was irrelevant; *Fasken Campbell Godfrey v Seven-Up Canada Inc* (1997) 142 D.L.R. (4th) 456, Ontario High Court, upheld (2000) 182 D.L.R. (4th) 315: solicitors should have advised a trustee that he required permission from the beneficiaries for a transaction which benefited himself, although no loss was caused thereby. The trustee was a former senior partner of the solicitors, and would have been 80% contributorily negligent; *Klingspon v Ramsay* [1985] 5 W.W.R. 411, British Columbia Supreme Court: a solicitor acting for a company negligently created the impression with an investor that her investment in the company was sound; the investor was held 75% responsible as she failed to pay proper attention to the material about the company which she had seen, or to obtain proper material or advice; *Lawrie v Gentry Developments Inc* (1990) 72 O.R. (2d) 512, Ontario High Court: solicitors failed to prepare mortgage documents on time; however the client was held to be 25% contributorily negligent for the delay in returning the documents to the solicitor; *Marbel Developments Ltd v Pirani* (1994) 18 C.C.L.T. (2d) 229, British Columbia Supreme Court: a solicitor was negligent in failing to warn the claimant company that a surveyor's certificate was about to expire, making approval for conversion more difficult. The claimant was found to be 50% contributorily negligent, having received some rudimentary education in property law and practice; *MacDonell v M & M Developments Ltd* (1998) 175 N.S.R. (2d) 89, Nova Scotia Supreme Court: the solicitor failed to review a dealership agreement the client was about to enter and thus failed to explain to him the requirement to notify the automobile manufacturer of an earlier share transfer; the client was equally responsible for the loss for ignoring the advice of his accountant to notify that manufacturer of the transfer; *Skirzyk v Crawford* (1990) 64 Man. R. (2d) 220, Manitoba QB, aff'd. Manitoba CA June 11, 1991: the solicitor was found negligent in failing to progress the claimant's personal injury litigation. The claimant was held 25% contributorily negligent in failing to pursue his claim with diligence.

[42] *Mouat v Clark Boyce* [1992] 2 N.Z.L.R. 559, NZCA: the claimant wished to assist her son by granting a mortgage over her home as security for loans to be made to him, and the defendant solicitors acted for both her and her son. Claimant found 50% to blame because she failed to act on the defendants' recommendation that she should take independent legal advice, and she told the defendants that she relied upon and trusted her son. On appeal, the Privy Council reversed the finding that the solicitors were liable, and thus it was not necessary to consider the cross-appeal against the finding of contributory negligence (see [1994] 1 A.C. 428 at 438D). In *Gilbert v Shanahan* [1998] 3 N.Z.L.R. 528, the defendant solicitor negligently failed to advise the claimant that he was not legally obliged to sign a guarantee for a lease taken by a company in which he had an interest. The New Zealand Court of Appeal held that the claimant was 10% contributorily negligent in failing to draw a preliminary agreement to the notice of the solicitor and enquire whether he was obliged to sign the guarantee as a result.

[43] [2000] V.S.C. 167; (2000) 2 V.R. 569, Victoria Supreme Court.

contributory negligence as a result of the claimant delaying applying for finance and failing to tell the solicitors of the situation concerning finance.

11–335 **Claims by lenders.** Contributory negligence is frequently an issue in actions brought by mortgage lenders against solicitors; and further guidance can be found in the analogous cases brought against surveyors.[44] Contributory negligence should be deducted only from the total loss, and save in exceptional circumstances not the "capped" loss which is within the scope of the duty.[45] A number of cases against solicitors consider the issue, and there has been a trend towards findings of a high degree of contributory negligence. In *Birmingham Midshires Mortgage Services Ltd v David Parry*[46] the solicitors were held not to have been negligent, but the claimant would have been contributorily negligent in making a non-status loan of 75 per cent of the valuation where the property was expensive, and in failing to apply its own lending criteria. In *Omega Trust Co Ltd v Wright Son & Pepper (No.2)*[47] Douglas Brown J. found the claimant lender 70 per cent to blame for its losses principally for seven instances of the lender's failure to follow its own criteria, such as failures to obtain relevant up-to-date valuations, to investigate the borrower's financial circumstances, to read the accounts and balance sheets property, to obtain references, or to obtain confirmation that judgment debts had been paid. In *Lloyds Bank Plc v Parker Bullen (a firm)*[48] solicitors failed to notify the lender of a covenant against alienation, and Longmore J. found the lender 50 per cent contributorily negligent for failing to obtain a valuation of its security leasehold interest. Very high findings of contributory negligence were made in some of the *Nationwide* cases.[49] In *UCB Bank Plc v Hepherd Winstanley Pugh*,[50] the defendants sought consent from the claimant to a third charge over the property with a limit to the

---

[44] See Ch.10, paras 10–168 to 10–174. See also H. Evans: "Contributory negligence by lenders" (1998) 14 P.N. 43; *ibid.*, *Lawyers' Liabilities*, (2nd edn, 2002), Ch.8., and T. Dugdale, "Contributory negligence: continuing controversy" (1999) 15 P.N.L.R. 164.

[45] *Platform Home Loans v Oyston Shipways* [2000] 2 A.C. 190.

[46] [1996] P.N.L.R. 495 upheld on appeal; [1997] N.P.L.C. 153 and [1997] E.G.C.S. 150.

[47] [1998] P.N.L.R. 337.

[48] [2000] Lloyd's Rep. P.N. 61.

[49] *Nationwide Building Society v Archdeacons* [1999] Lloyd's Rep. P.N. 549 (90% contributory negligence from borrower's known inconsistencies and uncertainties); *Nationwide Building Society v Balmer Radmore* [1999] Lloyd's Rep. P.N. 558 (75% contributory negligence, if defendants had been liable, for failing to investigate borrower's income, obtain a banker's reference, or heed previous arrears, and making a loan of 90% of the valuation); *Nationwide Building Society v Goodwin Harte* [1999] Lloyd's Rep. P.N. 338 (breach of fiduciary duty so no deduction, but otherwise 50% from instructing a valuer who was not independent of the applicant, and failing to examine the accounts or obtain proper references); *Nationwide Building Society v JR Jones* [1999] Lloyd's Rep. P.N. 414 (40% contributory negligence from failure to take up bank and credit references, obtain proper accounts, or to enquire why a single man wanted to buy a very large house); *Nationwide Building Society v Littlestone & Cowan* [1999] Lloyd's Rep. P.N. 625 (66% contributory negligence from in-house over valuation, failure to investigate borrower's ability to pay, and lending in excess of 75% of value); *Nationwide Building Society v Richard Grosse & Co* [1999] Lloyd's Rep. P.N. 348 (breach of fiduciary duty so no deduction, but otherwise would have been two-thirds from excessive valuation by employee and flawed assessment of borrower's creditworthiness); *Nationwide Building Society v Vanderpump & Sykes* [1999] Lloyd's Rep. P.N. 422 (50% reduction as lender made loan of 95% of valuation, had not investigated why there were so many credit searches against the borrower, and had failed to heed valuer's warning that the application might be suspect).

[50] [1999] Lloyd's Rep. P.N. 963.

priority of the claimant's charge of £20,000, and were negligent. The claimant consented to the third charge, but not specifically to the priority, of which the head office was justifiably ignorant. It was 25 per cent responsible for failing to appreciate that the only reason for the deed of priority was to limit their security.

Excess LTV. In *Bristol & West Building Society v Fancy & Jackson (a firm)*[51]   **11–336** Chadwick J. reduced the damages in two of the cases brought by the claimant building society against a number of solicitors because the claimant had loaned more than 75 per cent of the value of the security property, without any additional security. He held that the lender should bear all of the loss attributable to making the loan above that percentage. The claimant could not rely on the fact that it had prudently obtained a mortgage indemnity guarantee policy because insurance had to be ignored as *res inter alios acta*. Similarly, in *Nationwide Building Society v ATM Abdullah*[52] Blackburne J. held that the claimants should bear the losses caused by lending more than 75 per cent of the value of the security property.

Circumstances in which contributory negligence cannot be claimed. Any   **11–337** contributory negligence must have a contributory or causative effect on the loss caused by the defendants' negligence.[53] Contributory negligence cannot be raised as a defence against a claim in deceit, see *Alliance & Leicester Building Society v Edgestop Ltd*.[54] If a claimant can show breach of a contractual provision which does not depend on negligence, such as breach of an express instruction from a mortgagee, then the defendant may not be able to raise a plea of contributory negligence.[55] A solicitor who is in breach of fiduciary duty cannot claim that his client was contributorily negligent or its equitable equivalent, at least where the breach involved a deliberate act or omission, see Blackburne J.'s judgment in *Nationwide Building Society v Balmer Radmore (a firm)*.[56] The Judge held that no plea of contributory negligence could be raised against an allegation of breach of fiduciary duty, both on the construction of the Act, and in particular where the defendant's breach was a deliberate wrong. In contrast, the New Zealand Court of Appeal allowed a deduction on the grounds of contributory negligence in relation to a claim for breach of fiduciary duty in *Day v Mead*.[57] Contributory negligence is not a defence to a claim for breach of warranty of authority.[58]

---

[51] [1997] 4 All E.R. 582.

[52] [1999] Lloyd's Rep. P.N. 616.

[53] *UCB Corporate Services Ltd v Clyde & Co (a firm)* [2000] P.N.L.R. 841, CA, where a bank's decision to release a mortgage on the guarantor's house was held to have no causative effect on the loss caused by the solicitors negligence in failing to obtain an enforceable guarantee, which was the opportunity to recover from the guarantors. The bank was also not culpable as it thought it was sufficiently protected by the guarantee.

[54] [1993] 1 W.L.R. 1462, a case brought by a lender principally against a surveyor.

[55] As in *Bristol and West Building Society v Kramer, The Times,* February 6, 1995. But see para.11–008, above.

[56] [1999] P.N.L.R. 606 at 672D–677F. See the same judge's judgment in *Nationwide Building Society v Thimbleby* [1999] P.N.L.R. 733. For a commentary on the different views adopted on this issue in the Commonwealth, and the reasons for such positions, see R. Mulheron, "Contributory negligence in equity: Should fiduciaries accept all the blame?" (2003) 19 P.N. 422.

[57] [1987] 2 N.Z.L.R. 433, followed by the Supreme Court of Canada in *Canson Enterprises Ltd v Broughton & Co* (1992) 85 D.L.R. (4th) 129.

[58] See *Zwebner v The Mortgage Corp Ltd* [1997] P.N.L.R. 504, Lloyd J.

(b) *Apportionment of Liability*[59]

11–338 Recent developments in the law of tort have led to a growth in the number of claims which are made against more than one professional adviser. Thus the question of apportioning liability under the Civil Liability (Contribution) Act 1978 arises with increasing frequency. In the case of solicitors, three situations commonly give rise to problems of apportionment, usually in the context of settlement negotiations:

(a) Where the client has changed solicitors and both have been negligent.

(b) In a conveyancing-type transaction, where both solicitors and surveyors have been negligent.

(c) Where a financial scheme set up by solicitors and accountants, normally with the aim of reducing tax liability, has gone wrong.

Apportionment may arise in other circumstances.

11–339 **Successive solicitors.** Where different solicitors are sued, it used to be the case under the Solicitors' Indemnity Rules that the same insurers were involved, since both firms were covered by the same insurance policy. The position has now changed.[60] However, even where the same insurance company is involved, the apportionment of liability between solicitors is an important matter, since each firm has its own excess and the damages apportioned to each firm affect that firm's claims record and thus its premium level in future years. Where both firms proceed on the same mistaken basis, for instance that the proper defendant is X, whereas in fact the proper defendant is Y, each firm may be equally culpable; but the negligence of the second firm usually has a much closer causal link with the claimant's loss. In this example, the limitation period against Y may expire during the retainer of the second firm. If, of course, the limitation period had expired earlier, the first firm alone would be liable and no question of apportionment would arise. The result is similar where successive solicitors delay prosecuting an action with the result that it is dismissed for want of prosecution. Each firm may be equally culpable, but the negligence of the second firm usually has a much greater causative potency: if that firm had "got a move on" as soon as they were instructed the action would have been saved. If, of course, the action was by then so stale that it would have been struck out as soon as the next move was made, the first firm alone is liable and there is no question of apportionment. Thus where successive solicitors are liable for the same loss, in most cases the firm which acted later will have to pay the larger share of the damages.[61] These observations are, of course, made at a very general level and each case turns upon its own facts. The Australian case *Macpherson & Kelly v Kevin J Prunty*

---

[59] The general principles of apportionment are referred to in Ch.4.

[60] See para.11–003, above.

[61] In an extreme case the effect of the first solicitors' negligence may be spent, with the result that the second solicitors alone are liable. See paras 11–241 and 11–242, "Intervening act of a third party."

Associates[62] illustrates a situation in which the first solicitors were principally responsible for the fact that an action was not commenced within the three year limitation period. It is likely that the damage caused by the delays of successive solicitors, or the delay of one solicitor followed by the negligent undersettlement by another, will count as the "same damage" within the meaning of the Civil Liability (Contribution) Act 1978, see *Luke v Kingsley Smith & Co (a firm).*[63]

Apportionment of liability between solicitors and surveyors.[64] Solicitors   **11–340** and surveyors commonly have to liaise in conveyancing or related matters. For example, in the renewal of business tenancies under Pt 2 of the Landlord and Tenant Act 1954, the actual negotiations may take place between surveyors, whilst the respective solicitors take the appropriate procedural steps, such as service of notices and commencement of proceedings. If something goes wrong, possibly through lack of communication between the two firms, liability may well be shared. When considering the relative culpability of the two defendants, which is one factor in the apportionment, the surveyors must be taken to have a basic knowledge of the law relevant to their field of practice.[65] In the situation mentioned above, for example, the surveyors should be familiar with the procedural steps which are required under the Landlord and Tenant Act 1954 and the time limits within which those steps must be taken. Equally a solicitor who deals in property matters must have some idea of market values, the principles upon which rent is assessed and surveying practice.[66] An example of a failure by both professionals in relation to the same point is *Theodore Goddard v Fletcher & King Services Ltd.*[67] The claimant solicitors negligently failed to include rent review provisions in two leases which permitted only increases in the rent. They claimed a contribution from surveyors who had acted for the same client and were sent the leases for their approval, and the surveyors were found 20 per cent to blame.

The alternative situation in which liability is shared between solicitors and   **11–341** surveyors is where each firm makes a separate mistake, and both mistakes contribute to the same loss.[68] For example, the surveyor overvalues property and the solicitor fails to ascertain that there is an easement over it. In this situation it is even more difficult to formulate any general principles as to apportionment.

---

[62] [1983] V.R. 573, Supreme Court Victoria, Full Court. The first solicitors failed to institute proceedings for two years and nine months. There was a delay in forwarding their file to the second solicitors, who wrongly assumed that a writ had been issued. The apportionment was 80% to the first solicitors and 20% to the second solicitors.

[63] [2003] EWCA Civ 341; [2004] P.N.L.R. 12, Davis J.

[64] For an example of a solicitors' nominee company being a third contributorily negligent when suing a valuer, see *Kendall Wilson Securities Ltd v Barraclough* [1986] N.Z.L.R. 576, NZCA.

[65] See Ch.10, para.10–056.

[66] See also *Rieger v Croft & Finlay* (1992) 5 W.W.R. 700, British Columbia Supreme Court: selling realtor (estate agent) breached contractual duty in failing to advise about rent review provision, as did claimant's solicitor. Realtor 60% to blame and solicitors 40%.

[67] (1997) 32 E.G. 90.

[68] e.g. *Computastaff Ltd v Ingledew Brown Bennison & Garrett* (1983) 268 E.G. 906, McNeill J. For the facts of this case see para.11–280.

One factor which is sometimes of assistance is to consider the extent of each firm's involvement in the overall transaction. This is illustrated by *Anglia Hastings & Thanet Building Society v House & Son*[69]: the claimant building society claimed damages against both the valuers and the solicitors who had previously acted for the society when it took a mortgage over two properties. The borrowers defaulted and the two properties proved to be insufficient security. The valuers had produced a valuation which was "wildly wrong", but their overall involvement in the matter had been relatively brief. The solicitors had been involved over several months, and had failed to protect the building society's interests in a number of respects. Bingham J. apportioned liability 30 per cent to the valuers and 70 per cent to the solicitors.[70]

11–342   **Other cases concerning apportionment.** In taxation matters solicitors and accountants often work together closely. Where both solicitors and accountants are responsible for the failure of a "scheme" to reduce tax liability, it is certainly relevant to consider whether the mistake was essentially a "legal" one or a matter of accounting, and it is also necessary to consider who was the client's principal adviser.[71] Where both solicitors and counsel are found to be negligent, the issue of apportionment has arisen in a number of cases.[72] In *Burke v Lfot Pty Ltd*[73] the claimant had purchased a small shopping complex with a financially weak tenant. The vendors, who had misdescribed the tenant as high quality, sought a contribution from the claimant's solicitors for failing to advise his client to investigate the financial standing of the tenants. A majority of the High Court of Australia held that there should be no contribution on the grounds that the solicitor had gained nothing from his conduct and the vendor was merely repaying a sum which had been wrongly obtained. A similar result was reached in very unusual circumstances in *Dubai Aluminium Co Ltd v Salaam*.[74] The defendant solicitors had settled with the claimant in a case where dishonest assistance was alleged against

---

[69] (1981) 260 E.G. 1128; [1955–1995] P.N.L.R. 11. See para.11–209.
[70] For further examples see *Bristol & West Building Society v Christie* [1996] E.G. 53, where liability was apportioned equally, and *Cook v Power* (1992) 28 R.P.R. (2d) 207, Newfoundland Supreme Court (solicitors 80% liable for failing to discern potential discrepancies in title, and 25% liable for failing to ascertain the differences in boundaries). See also *Chelsea Building Society v Goddard & Smith* [1996] E.G.C.S. 157, where surveyors who overvalued a property for a building society were found equally liable with the solicitors who failed to report a back-to-back transaction.
[71] *Mathew v Maughold Life Assurance Co Ltd* (1985) 1 P.N. 142 concerned the apportionment between solicitors, accountants and counsel. The case is an illustration only, because on appeal the findings of liability against all parties except the claimants' solicitors were reversed: [1955–1995] P.N.L.R. 15. (See further Ch.12, para.12–034 on this case.)
[72] See Ch.12, para.12–045.
[73] (2002) 76 A.L.J.R. 749. In a similar Canadian case, *789538 Ontario Ltd v Gambin Associates* (1999) 27 R.P.R. (3d) 210, the court directed an assignment of the purchaser's cause of action against the vendors to the solicitors. In some cases no recovery would be allowed as the parties would not be responsible for the same damage, as in *Howkins & Harrison (a firm) v Tyler* [2001] P.N.L.R. 27, CA, where surveyors sued by a building society for a negligent valuation were not permitted to recover from the borrowers' directors for that reason, the test being whether payment by the third party would reduce the defendant's liability to the claimant.
[74] [2002] UKHL 48; [2003] 2 A.C. 366.

a former partner. Fraudsters who had stolen the money were ordered to contribute 100% to the innocent solicitors, who were nevertheless fixed with the assumed dishonest assistance by their partner, as the fraudsters retained considerable amounts of the stolen money.[75]

---

[75] For other examples see *Kyriacou v Kogarah Municipal Council* (1995) 88 L.G.E.R.A. 110, Supreme Court N.S.W.: council officer advised prospective purchasers that property could be used for wedding receptions, and claimant's solicitors failed to advise that this was not so; liability apportioned one third and two thirds respectively. In *Peake v Litwiniuk* (2001) 200 D.L.R. (4th) 534, the Alberta Court of Appeal held that lawyers who failed to bring proceedings for personal injury on behalf of their client could not claim in contribution from the driver who injured the client, as the parties were not liable for the same damage.

CHAPTER 12

BARRISTERS

1. GENERAL

(a) *The Function of a Barrister*

It is the function of barristers to appear as advocates before courts and tribunals, **12–001** to give advice and draft documents in connection with litigation, and to do such other advisory or drafting work as may properly be referred to them by solicitors.[1] Barristers no longer have the exclusive rights of audience before the House of Lords, the Court of Appeal, the High Court, and the Crown Court which they used to possess.[2] Barristers are subject to the discipline of the General Council of the Bar.[3] The Bar does now operate within some statutory framework[4]: barristers must be sole practitioners,[5] and it is a professional requirement that all practising barristers insure against claims for professional negligence.[6] In addition to the duties owed by a barrister to his client, which are discussed below, he will also owe duties to the court.[7]

Instructing barristers. Subject to certain recognised exceptions,[8] a barrister **12–002** can only act on the instructions of a solicitor, and is professionally obliged to

---

[1] This chapter is concerned with barristers in independent practice. There are also employed barristers who provide legal services to their employers in government, commerce and industry.

[2] Solicitors may now have full rights of audience, subject to satisfying the rules on experience and qualifications, pursuant to s.27 of the Courts and Legal Services Act 1980 and the Higher Courts Qualification Regulations 1992 made thereunder.

[3] The General Council of the Bar publishes the Code of Conduct of the Bar of England and Wales. The current edition is the sixth, published in 1998; for the current position see the Bar Council website. Under the draft Legal Services Act a new and independent Office for Legal Complaints will be established.

[4] The Courts and Legal Services Act 1990 has certain provisions that affect the practice of barristers.

[5] See the Code of Conduct of the Bar of England and Wales, 6th edn, para.207.

[6] *ibid.* para.302. Barristers must mutually insure with the Bar Mutual Indemnity Fund.

[7] For a helpful review of such duties, see D. Ipp, "Lawyers' duties to the court" (1998) 114 L.Q.R. 62.

[8] See the Code of Conduct of the Bar of England and Wales published by the General Council of the Bar, 6th edn 1998, at paras 102(a)(ii), 210, 306, 901 (for the definition of "professional client"), and Annex E (for the current code see the Bar Council's website).

accept instructions in a field in which he professes to practice.[9] The major exception is that a barrister may, in appropriate circumstances, accept a brief or instructions directly from clients who are members of a professional body that has been approved by the Bar Council. Direct professional access is not allowed for instructions to appear in court (other than a magistrates' court) or the Employment Appeals Tribunal.[10]

12–003   **Alternatives to litigation.** A disappointed client now has an alternative remedy to launching proceedings against a barrister. Clients can complain to the Bar Standards Board about inadequate professional service, and may be awarded up to £5,000 compensation, although compensation is limited to the loss which is recoverable at law. If the Board dismisses the complaint, then the client can complain to the Legal Services Ombudsman, who now has the power to award compensation.[11] Under the draft Legal Services Act a new and independent Office for Legal Complaints will be established.

(b) *Duties to Clients*

12–004   **No contractual duties.** In practice, a barrister does not enter a contract either with the solicitor who instructs him, or with the lay client on whose behalf he is instructed. This used to be a rule of law: see *Kennedy v Broun*[12] and *Rondel v Worsley.*[13] The rule of law preventing a barrister from entering into a contract for the provision of his services as a barrister was abolished by s.61(1) of the Courts and Legal Services Act 1990.[14] This statutory change does not affect the restrictions imposed by the Bar Council on who may instruct a barrister.[15] Furthermore, the Bar's terms of business include a provision that a barrister does not enter into any contractual relationship when he is instructed by a solicitor, unless the contrary is agreed in writing.[16]

12–005   **Tort and other duties.** A barrister will of course owe duties in tort to his lay client.[17] A barrister will also owe fiduciary duties, including duties of confidence, to the client.[18] For a salutary illustration see *China Light & Power Co Ltd v Michael Ford,*[19] where a barrister deliberately used confidential information

---

[9] The "cab rank" rule; *ibid.* para.209.
[10] *ibid.* Annex E, para.3.
[11] See Access to Justice Act 1999, s.49.
[12] (1863) 13 C.B. (N.S.) 677.
[13] [1969] 1 A.C. 191.
[14] The section came into force on January 1, 1991.
[15] See s.61(2) of the Act. For the restrictions imposed by the Bar Council, see para.12–002 above.
[16] See paras 25 and 26 of Annex B of the Code of Conduct of the Bar 1998, as amended.
[17] For confirmation of this obvious principle, see Lord Morris in *Rondel v Worsley* [1969] 1 A.C. 191 at 244A–B.
[18] *cf. McMullen v Clancy* [2005] IESC 10; [2005] 2 I.R. 445, where the Irish Supreme Court held that there was normally no fiduciary relationship between a barrister and client, although it could become one if the barrister derived valuable confidential information from the relationship.
[19] [1996] 1 H.K.L.R. 57, CA. See also *Stewart v Canadian Broadcasting Association* (1997) 150 D.L.R. (4th) 24, Ontario High Court, where a lawyer was held to be in breach of his continuing fiduciary duty by preferring his own financial interests, when he discussed his client's case on television and in part exaggerated his culpability. He was liable for damages for the emotional harm, and for the profits derived from his participation in the programme.

entrusted to him by his client, which was awarded damages. Barristers are self-employed, and there is no conflict of interest in appearing against or before members of the same chambers; furthermore, the organisation of barristers' chambers should normally prevent any danger of an accidental or improper dissemination of confidential information.[20] However, cohabiting counsel should avoid acting on opposite sides in criminal cases.[21] A barrister who is a witness in a case should generally not act.[22] It is improper for prosecuting counsel's speech to be xenophobic, inflammatory, or to make use of inadmissible and irrelevant material.[23]

(c) *Duties to Third Parties*[24]

Duties to clients' associates. There is limited authority specifically on the   **12–006**
duty of barristers to third parties. Duties of care may be owed in some circumstances to associates of the lay client. In *Mathew v Maughold Life Assurance Co Ltd* a barrister was instructed on behalf of an insurance company who marketed a tax avoidance scheme.[25] Leonard J. held that the barrister owed a duty to Mr and Mrs Mathew, the clients of the insurance company who were to benefit from the scheme. The point was not considered on appeal. In *Estill v Cowling*,[26] counsel and solicitors were instructed by E concerning the transfer of shares in her lifetime to her nephews and nieces. The advice was sought on behalf of the trustees of the proposed settlement of the shares. Arden J. held that a duty of care was owed to the trustees, although they had not been appointed yet.

No duty to other side. It is very unlikely that a duty of care is owed to the   **12–007**
other side in litigation.[27] In *Connolly-Martin v Davis*[28] the Court of Appeal struck out an action by the opposing party against a barrister where it was alleged that he had given an undertaking to the other side on his client's behalf without

---

[20] *Laker Airways Inc v FLS Aerospace Ltd and Burton* [1999] Lloyd's Rep. 45, Rix J. See also *Locabail (UK) Ltd v Bayfield Properties Ltd* [2000] Q.B. 451 for guidance on when a barrister should not act as a judge in a case.
[21] *R. v Blatt, The Times,* May 30, 1996. In *Geveran Trading Co Ltd v Skjevesland* [2002] EWCA Civ 1567; [2003] 1 W.L.R. 912, the Court of Appeal held that in exceptional circumstances the court could prevent an advocate from acting even where he did not possess confidential information if satisfied that there was a real risk that his continued participation would require the order made at trial to be set aside on appeal.
[22] *Beggs v Att-Gen* [2006] 2 N.Z.L.R. 129, High Court.
[23] *Benedetto v The Queen* [2003] 1 W.L.R. 1545.
[24] See also *O'Doherty v Birrell* [2001] VSCA 44 [2001] 3 V.R. 147, where the Victoria Court of Appeal held that a barrister owed no duty of care to another barrister retained in the same case to prevent financial loss to him.
[25] (1985) 1 P.N. 142, Leonard J.; [1955–1995] P.N.L.R. 51, CA.
[26] [2000] Lloyd's Rep. P.N. 378. In *Wakim v HIH Casualty & General Insurance Ltd* [2001] F.C.A. 103; [2001] 182 A.L.R. 353, the Federal Court of Australia held that a barrister instructed on behalf of a trustee in bankruptcy to advise on the prospects of legal proceedings owed a duty of care to the principal creditor, because he should have been aware that the applicant was the principal and sole indemnifying creditor, and there was a coincidence of interests between the trustee and the applicant. A similar duty was owed by the barrister's instructing solicitor.
[27] See the remarks of Sir John Donaldson M.R. in *Orchard v South Eastern Electricity Board* [1987] 1 Q.B. 565 at 571F–G, and Dillon L.J. at 581B–C.
[28] [1999] P.N.L.R. 827.

authority and then advised the client that the undertaking was not binding. The Court accepted that, in general, counsel owed no duties to those who were not his client, such as the lay client's adversary. While there would be a duty if there were a voluntary assumption of responsibility on which the other side could reasonably rely, there was no such assumption in that case.

(d) *The Standard of Skill and Care*

12–008 A barrister is subject to the same rules as other professional men, and the test as to whether there has been negligence is the standard of the ordinary skilled man exercising and professing to have that special skill.[29] In *Saif Ali v Sydney Mitchell & Co*[30] Lord Diplock stressed that not every error made by a barrister (or any other professional man) constitutes negligence, but only such an error "as no reasonably well-informed and competent member of that profession could have made."[31] In *Matrix Securities Ltd v Theodore Goddard*[32] Lloyd J. rejected allegations that tax counsel had any absolute duties to the client, and adopted the formulation of Lord Diplock in *Saif Ali*.[33] The tax silk's advice was to be judged by that of "the rather small and select group of silks specialising in tax matters." In *Estill v Cowling*,[34] Arden J. held that the standard of care to be applied to a Chancery barrister who gave advice on a settlement was that of a reasonably competent barrister in general Chancery practice, having experience in tax and trust matters, but not the standard of a barrister who specialised in tax. In *Hall v Simons*,[35] where the House of Lords abolished immunity, the standard of care for advocacy was expressed by Lord Hope[36] to be that of ordinary professional practice and ordinary skill, and by Lord Hobhouse[37] in identical terms to Lord Diplock in *Saif Ali v Sydney Mitchell & Co*.

(e) *Immunity*

12–009 In *Hall v Simons*[38] the House of Lords abolished the special immunity of advocates, unanimously in the case of civil actions, and by a majority of four to three in relation to criminal proceedings. Their Lordships considered and rejected

---

[29] *Mathew v Maughold Life Assurance Co Ltd* [1955–1995] P.N.L.R. 51, CA. *cf.* para.12–027.
[30] [1980] A.C. 198 at 218 and 229, For a qualification to Lord Diplock's views see *McManus Development Ltd v Barbridge Properties Ltd* [1996] P.N.L.R. 431 at 442, CA.
[31] A test adopted by the Court of Appeal in, e.g. *McFarlane v Wilkinson* [1997] P.N.L.R. 578, an action brought against two barristers, and in the wasted costs cases of *Ridehalgh v Horsefield* [1994] Ch. 205 and *Re a Barrister (Wasted Costs Order) (No.9 of 1999)* (2000) 16 P.N. 122.
[32] [1998] P.N.L.R. 290.
[33] As it was in *Green v Collyer-Bristow* [1999] Lloyd's Rep. P.N. 799 at 809, *per* Douglas Brown J.
[34] [2000] Lloyd's Rep. P.N. 378.
[35] [2002] 1 A.C. 615.
[36] *ibid.* at 726D–E.
[37] *ibid.* at 737G–H.
[38] [2002] 1 A.C. 615. For commentary see H. Evans, *Lawyers' Liabilities*, (2nd edn, 2002), Ch.5, and esp. 5–16 on the issue of whether the abolition of immunity is retrospective and to what extent, on which there is no decided authority. The subject of immunity is treated at some length in the 2nd edn of this work, and the 5th edn at paras 11–009 to 11–025, which includes a detailed analysis of *Hall v Simons*.

the reasons for immunity which were given in two House of Lords cases, *Rondel v Worsley*[39] and *Saif Ali v Sidney Mitchell & Co.*[40] Immunity still exists in Scotland in relation to criminal proceedings.[41] Elsewhere in the commonwealth, the position is more mixed. Immunity has recently been abolished in New Zealand.[42] In Australia, a bare majority of the High Court of Australia supported immunity in *Giannarelli v Wraith*,[43] on public policy grounds similar to those previously adopted by the House of Lords, and that decision has been recently confirmed by the High Court of Australia in *D'Orta-Ekenaike v Victoria Legal Aid*.[44] The extent of the immunity there is based on the *Rees v Sinclair* test.[45] Immunity does not exist in Canada.[46]

(f) *Abuse of Process*

If a barrister's client is convicted, the client may not be able to sue him on the **12–010** grounds of abuse of process, on the reasoning of the Court of Appeal in *Somasundaram v M Julius Melchior & Co.*[47] The Court of Appeal also considered that the objection could be taken when the original case under attack was a civil one.[48] In *Hall v Simons*[49] the House of Lords held that the abuse of process principle would ordinarily prevent a claimant suing for a wrongful criminal conviction, as it would be a collateral attack on the verdict of the criminal trial, but that in civil actions that principle will rarely have a place.[50]

(g) *Liability for Costs*

Unlike solicitors, a barrister used not be liable to pay the costs of his lay client **12–011** or of the opposing side which had been wasted by his defaults, either under the inherent jurisdiction or under the rules of court.[51] The jurisdiction to order the

---

[39] [1969] 1 A.C. 191.
[40] [1980] A.C. 198.
[41] *Wright v Paton Farrell* [2006] S.L.T. 59, IH.
[42] Immunity was established in *Rees v Sinclair* [1974] 1 N.Z.L.R. 180, CA. In *Lai v Chamberlains* [2006] NZSC 70 the Supreme Court of New Zealand abolished it.
[43] (1988) 91 A.L.R. 417.
[44] [2005] H.C.A. 12; (2005) 214 A.L.R. 92.
[45] *Giannarelli v Wraith* (1988) 91 A.L.R. 417, High Court of Australia; *Keefe v Marks* (1989) 16 N.S.W.L.R. 713, New South Wales CA: *Boland v Yates Property Corp Pty Ltd* (2000) 167 A.L.R. 575, High Court of Australia, *per* Gleeson C.J. and Callinan J., *cf.* Gaudron J. The *Rees v Sinclair* test is "that the protection exists only where the particular work is so intimately connected with the conduct of the cause in court that it can fairly be said to be a preliminary decision affecting the way that cause is to be conducted when it comes to a hearing".
[46] *Banks v Reid* (1977) 81 D.L.R. (3d) 730, Ontario CA (immunity doubted); *Demarco v Ungaro* (1979) 95 D.L.R. (3d) 385, Ontario High Court (no immunity for conduct of civil cases in court).
[47] [1988] 1 W.L.R. 1394. See further Ch.11, para.11–111.
[48] [1988] 1 W.L.R. 1394 at 1402E–1403B. The principle was applied in the context of civil litigation in *Palmer v Durnford Ford* [1992] 1 Q.B. 483 which has subsequently been doubted in *Walpole v Partridge & Wilson* [1994] Q.B. 106, CA.
[49] [2002] 1 A.C. 615.
[50] This difficult issue is discussed in Ch.11 paras 11–111 to 11–115.
[51] *Orchard v South Eastern Electricity Board* [1987] 1 Q.B. 565 at 571E–F and 581C, CA; *cf. Kelly v London Transport Executive* [1982] 1 W.L.R. 1055 at 1065, *per* Lord Denning M.R.; *Fozal v Gofur, The Times*, July 9, 1993, CA.

payment of wasted costs was amended by s.4 of the Courts and Legal Services Act 1990 to apply to any "legal or other representative", which is defined by subs.(13) to mean "any person exercising a right of audience or right to conduct litigation", which clearly includes barristers.[52] Since then, a large number of wasted costs applications have been made against counsel.

12–012   **Guidelines.** In *Re a Barrister (Wasted Costs Order) (No.1 of 1991)*[53] the Court of Appeal laid down guidelines for use in criminal cases. They can be summarised as follows:

(a) First, the wasted costs jurisdiction is draconian, and thus the court must formulate the complaint carefully and concisely.

(b) Secondly, where necessary, a transcript of the part of the proceedings under discussion should be available. A transcript of any wasted costs hearing should be made. (This is required by the 1991 Regulations.)

(c) Thirdly, a defendant should be present if it was in his interests, especially if the matter might affect the course of his trial. Other parties may make representations, and it might be appropriate for counsel for the Crown to be present.

(d) Fourthly, the court recommended a three-stage test:

> "(i) Had there been an improper, unreasonable or negligent act or omission? (ii) As a result had any costs been incurred by a party? (iii) If the answers to (i) and (ii) were yes; should the court exercise its discretion to disallow or order the representative to meet the whole or any part of the relevant costs, and if so what specific sum was involved?"

(e) Fifthly, it was inappropriate to propose any deal. The judge should state his complaint, invite comments, and make a ruling.

(f) Sixthly, the judge had to specify the sum to be ordered, or if that was impossible, substitute an alternative procedure.

In *Ridehalgh v Horsefield*[54] the Court of Appeal gave guidelines on wasted costs orders in civil litigation, which are summarised in Ch.10.[55] A number of decisions concerning barristers illustrate the procedure and application of the wasted costs jurisdiction.

12–013   **Scope of jurisdiction.** In *Brown v Bennett (No.2)*[56] defendants applied for wasted costs orders against the claimant's solicitors and barristers. Neuberger J.

---

[52] The section came into force on October 1, 1991. For the exercise of the jurisdiction, see Ch.11 paras 11–126 to 11–141.

[53] [1993] Q.B. 293. In *Re Mintz (Wasted Costs Order)*, *The Times*, July 16, 1999, the Court of Appeal held that before deciding to make a wasted costs order a judge should consider the relevant guidance given in the textbooks on the exercise of that power, such as *Archbold*. They also held that the complaint and grounds need to be carefully and concisely formulated; where necessary a transcript of the relevant part of the proceedings should be available; and the sum ordered must be specified.

[54] [1994] Ch. 205.

[55] Paras 11–130 to 11–136.

[56] [2002] 1 W.L.R. 713. The judge also held that causation had to be proved on the balance of probabilities.

held that on the true construction of s.51 of the Supreme Court Act 1981 a wasted costs order could be made in favour of one party against the legal representatives of another party to proceedings. Subsequently, in *Medcalf v Mardell*[57] the House of Lords rejected a submission that on the true construction of s.51 of the Supreme Court Act 1981 a wasted costs order could only be made in favour of the clients of the lawyers concerned. In *Brown v Bennett (No.2)*[58] the judge also held that the liability of a barrister was not limited to his conduct of the proceedings in court, but extended to his involvement in advising and drafting, which were included in the meaning of exercising a right to conduct litigation in s.51(13) of the Act. However, the judge dismissed at the show cause stage almost all of the application that the lawyers show cause why they should not pay the costs personally, which mostly related to allegedly improperly pleading dishonesty.[59]

Procedure.[60] In *Filmlab Systems International Ltd v Pennington*[61] Aldous J.   **12–014** held that it would rarely be right to apply for a wasted costs order until after the trial of the action. Contrast *B v B (Wasted Costs: Abuse of Process)*[62] where Wall J. held that it was appropriate to hear the application during the course of proceedings, because the lawyers concerned were no longer instructed in the litigation, and the issue was not going to be affected by the outcome of the case. In *Re Freudiana Holdings Ltd*[63] the Court of Appeal held that it was almost always appropriate for the trial judge to adjudicate on a wasted costs application. The court considered that unless the wasted costs hearing could take place in summary form soon after judgment it was unlikely to be appropriate. In that case, the court held that the judge had been correct to halt proceedings which he had instigated with an order to show cause when it became clear that there were numerous matters of fact in issue.[64] In *Royal Institution of Chartered Surveyors v Wiseman Marshall*[65] the Court of Appeal stated that it would rarely be appropriate to grant an adjournment to investigate whether the client was willing to waive privilege, as that would create complexity and delay. The barrister must

---

[57] [2002] UKHL 27; [2003] 1 A.C. 120.

[58] [2002] 1 W.L.R. 713.

[59] See also *Byrne v Sefton HA* [2001] EWCA Civ 1904; [2002] 1 W.L.R. 775, where the Court of Appeal held that no wasted costs order could be made against solicitors who had allegedly failed to issue proceedings within the limitation period, as they had not conducted litigation.

[60] See further the detailed guidance given in solicitor's negligence cases, summarised at Ch.11 paras 11–133 and 11–134.

[61] [1995] 1 W.L.R. 673.

[62] [2001] 1 F.L.R. 843. In that case there was no need to have a hearing to determine whether the lawyers should be given an opportunity to show cause, as the applicant's prima facie case had been established at the appeal hearing of which complaint was made. and the lawyers had had a reasonable opportunity to give reasons why the court should not make the order.

[63] *The Times,* December 4, 1995. To similar effect see *Re P (a Barrister) (Wasted Costs Order), The Times,* July 23, 2001, CA. In part because the judge who has conducted the trial will be aware of the conduct of the legal representatives, it will be very rare for the Court of Appeal to interfere with a judge's decision on a wasted costs order, particularly at the first stage, see *Persaud v Persaud* [2003] EWCA Civ 394; [2003] P.N.L.R. 26, CA.

[64] Similarly, one reason why Keen J. dismissed the application for wasted costs in *Chief Constable of North Yorkshire v Audsley* [2000] Lloyd's Rep. P.N. 675 was that the costs sought were £168,900, whereas the likely costs in the wasted costs application were £125–£135,000, and thus the costs in the application were unjustifiably disproportionate.

[65] [2000] P.N.L.R. 649.

be given the opportunity of considering his ground, taking advice, and obtaining representation: see *R. v Luton Family Proceedings Court Justices Ex p. R.*[66] This is illustrated by *S v M*,[67] where an application was made near the start of a hearing after a vital allegation of forgery had been withdrawn, without sufficient notice, due to lack of expert evidence. The order to show cause was made without a statement of what the barrister had done wrong, and without satisfying the requirement that a strong prima facie case had been made out before the respondent barrister was called upon. In fact there was no prima facie evidence that she had acted negligently or improperly. Pumfrey J. therefore granted the appeal against the Master's order to show cause.

12-015   **Privilege**. In *Medcalf v Mardell*,[68] leading and junior counsel signed a draft amended notice of appeal which made allegations of dishonesty against the claimant and his legal advisers. In relation to most of the allegations, no evidence was served supporting those allegations. The barristers submitted that there had been no waiver of privilege, that they were aware of their obligation imposed by the Bar's Code of Conduct not to draft any notice of appeal containing allegations of fraud without clear instructions to make them and reasonably credible material before them establishing a prima facie case of fraud, and that they would like to put material before the court full details of what material was before them but could not do so because of privilege. The House of Lords held that the court should not make a wasted costs order where privilege is not waived and the lawyers wished to put privileged material before the court unless a number of conditions were met: full allowance must be made for the inability of the lawyers to tell the story, and the lawyers are entitled to the benefit of any doubt, both of which will rarely be possible; where a lawyer is precluded from giving his account of the material before him, the court will be very slow to conclude that he had no sufficient material; and the court must be satisfied that it would be fair to make an order although the practitioner is precluded by privilege from advancing his full answer. As a result, the House of Lords reversed the wasted costs order made against the barristers by the Court of Appeal.

12-016   **Misjudgments as to the strength of a case.** It will be relatively rare that misjudgments on the strength of a case, an application, or an argument will lead to a wasted costs order. In the context of the inherent jurisdiction to make wasted costs orders, the Privy Council in *Harley v McDonald*[69] reversed a decision making a wasted costs order against a barrister for litigating a hopeless case. There were two important principles behind the decision. First, applications for wasted costs:

---

[66] [1998] C.L.Y. 496, CA.
[67] [1998] 3 F.C.R. 665.
[68] [2002] UKHL 27; [2003] 1 A.C. 120. In *Brown v Bennett (Wasted Costs) (No.2)* [2002] Lloyd's Rep. P.N. 242, Neuberger J. gave guidance as to what counsel could divulge as to what documents they had seen or known of if privilege was not waived.
[69] [2001] UKPC 18; [2001] 2 A.C. 678. For a case where it was alleged that the proceedings were hopeless, but no wasted costs order was made see *Daly v Martin Bernard Hubner* [2002] Lloyd's Rep. P.N. 461, summarised at Ch.11, para.11–137.

"should be confined strictly to questions which are apt for summary disposal by the court. Failures to appear, conduct which leads to an otherwise avoidable step in the proceedings or the prolongation of a hearing by gross repetition or extreme slowness in the presentation of evidence or argument are typical examples. The factual basis for the exercise of the jurisdiction in such circumstances is likely to be found in facts which are within judicial knowledge because the relevant events took place in court of are facts that can easily be verified."[70]

Secondly, fairness to the lawyers requires that notice should be given of allegations relating to issues about the nature or scope of the instructions which the client has given or the advice the lawyers may have tendered.[71] In that case the trial judge had taken account of matters relating to the conduct of the proceedings which took place before the events he observed at trial, and which were not fully tested in the evidence. It is rarely safe to assume that a hopeless case is being litigated on the advice of the lawyers, or that it demonstrates incompetence by the lawyers.

In *Persaud v Persaud*[72] the Court of Appeal made it clear that the legal **12–017** representative had to break a duty to the court itself. Thus, the failure of a barrister to follow the Bar Council's legal aid guidelines was not itself enough. In that case, the barrister was not unreasonable in concluding that two brothers who had convictions for dishonesty would be believed when they alleged that their father had promised them various benefits including a house if they worked for his company, and that if believed other legal hurdles would be overcome. The Court of Appeal appeared to hold that where the allegation was that the legal representative had pursued a hopeless case, mere negligence was not enough. However, the Court of Appeal in *Re Madden (a Barrister)*[73] thought that this gloss was unjustified and was not intended. A similar view was taken by the Court of Appeal in *Dempsey v Johnstone (Wasted Costs Order)*,[74] which considered that the observation in *Persaud* was wrong and inconsistent with *Medcalf v Mardell*,[75] although the court concluded that it was difficult to see how the question of negligence in the context of an allegation of pursuing a hopeless case could be answered affirmatively unless the legal representative had acted unreasonably, which was akin to an abuse of process.

Illustrations of no wasted costs order for misjudgments. In *Filmlab Sys-* **12–018** *tems International Ltd v Pennington*[76] Aldous J. found that counsel's erroneous advice in relation to a discovery application was not an error that no reasonably well-informed and competent member of the Bar could have made, and so he did not make a wasted costs order. Similarly, in *R. v Horsham DC Ex p. Wenman*[77] Brooke J. dismissed a wasted costs application against a barrister and solicitors in relation to judicial review proceedings because there was material on which the district council's decision could be challenged. The judge criticised a number

---

[70] [2001] UKPC 18; [2001] 2 A.C. 678, 703 para.50.
[71] *ibid.* at para.54.
[72] [2003] EWCA Civ 394; [2003] P.N.L.R. 26.
[73] [2004] EWCA Civ 754; [2004] P.N.L.R. 722.
[74] [2003] EWCA Civ 1134; [2004] P.N.L.R 25.
[75] [2002] UKHL 27; [2001] 1 A.C. 120.
[76] [1995] 1 W.L.R. 673.
[77] [1995] 1 W.L.R. 681, a case decided before *Ridehalgh*.

of departures from good practice which took place before the new wasted costs jurisdiction came into force. In *Sampson v John Boddy Timber Ltd*[78] the Court of Appeal set aside an order for wasted costs against a barrister who had referred to without-prejudice correspondence in open court. A majority considered that the questions of admissibility and privilege were not entirely clear. A legal representative should not be considered to be negligent if he took a point which was fairly arguable. In *Royal Institution of Chartered Surveyors v Wiseman Marshall*[79] a wasted costs order was sought, in proceedings brought against the RICS for expelling the claimant from that body, in relation to two allegations which had been pursued. On the first, that the decision to expel the claimant was unreasonable, the Court of Appeal held that counsel's advice that there were reasonable prospects of success was reasonable. In relation to the second, that the RICS had misdirected itself when expelling the claimant, the Court of Appeal refused to infer that counsel had advised that there was more than a 50 per cent chance of success, and they were also able to look at counsel's advice which concluded that there was no prospect of success on that issue. The court found that the client had instructed counsel to pursue that point, and he was not to be criticised for maintaining it until the end of the oral evidence. In *Chief Constable of North Yorkshire v Audsley*[80] an application was made for wasted costs against a barrister and solicitors in relation to civil litigation against the Chief Constable for malicious prosecution which had been dismissed at the outset of the trial. Keene J. held that this was not hopeless litigation, as there was evidence which could properly form the basis for an allegation that the prosecutor did not have an honest belief in the guilt of the accused, and in any event the court did not know what legal advice was given to the claimant and it was not improper for a lawyer to act for a party whose claim might seem doomed to fail.

12–019   **Exceptions.** Some wasted costs applications against barristers have succeeded on these grounds. In *R. v Secretary of State for the Home Office Ex p. Begum*[81] Harrison J. made a wasted costs order against a barrister where he had advised that documents, which the Treasury Solicitor wished to be put before the court on an *ex parte* application for judicial review, were irrelevant and did not need to be shown to the court. In *Dace v Redland Aggregates Ltd*[82] Blackburne J. ordered counsel and solicitors to pay the wasted costs of a vexatious application seeking a declaration that a lease had not been determined, which had no chance of success as it was *res judicata*, having being determined in an earlier action. In *B v B (Wasted Costs: Abuse of Process)*[83] Wall J. made a wasted costs order against solicitors and a barrister who had appealed an order vacating a trial date, as the directions which were given and which were not appealed made it inevitable that

---

[78] *Independent*, May 17, 1995.
[79] [2000] P.N.L.R. 649.
[80] [2000] Lloyd's Rep. P.N. 675.
[81] [1995] C.O.D. 176.
[82] [1997] E.G.C.S. 123.
[83] [20001] 1 F.L.R. 843. The judge was not impressed by the argument that privilege had not been waived, because, even assuming that the appeal was made on the client's instructions, the duty of the lawyers would have been to report to the Legal Services Commission that the client was making them act unreasonably. But see now *Persaud v Persaud* [2003] EWCA Civ 394; [2003] P.N.L.R. 26, noted at para.12–017, above.

the hearing would be postponed. In *Wasted Costs Order (No.5 of 1997)*[84] the Court of Appeal upheld wasted costs orders against two barristers who advised the issue of a witness summons for disclosure of social services files for the speculative purpose that useful material might come to light, when it was clearly established that a witness summons in such circumstances was not proper. In *Re Madden (a Barrister)*[85] the Court of Appeal upheld a wasted costs order against a barrister who called a witness despite indications that he would not be favourable to his client's case, which led to the jury being discharged.

Misjudgments on timing. In *Ridehalgh v Horsefield*[86] one of the appeals, **12–020** *Antonelli v Wade Gery Farr*, concerned a barrister whose conduct of a trial was impaired because she had accepted the brief at a very late stage. The Court of Appeal held that in accepting the brief, counsel was acting properly in accordance with the "cab rank" rule. The Court rejected each of the specific criticisms of counsel and set aside the wasted costs order made by the judge. In *Re a Barrister (Wasted Costs Order) (No.4 of 1993)*[87] the barrister had accepted a two-day trial at Derby followed immediately by another in Nottingham. The first trial overran. The Court of Appeal held that the barrister had been over-optimistic in failing to anticipate delays in the first trial, but his conduct was not unreasonable and no wasted costs order should have been made against him.

In contrast, in *Re a Barrister (Wasted Costs Order) (No.4 of 1992)*[88] a barrister **12–021** failed to appear at a trial because he had made no arrangements to ascertain the dates of cases in the relevant list. The Court of Appeal held that he should not have relied wholly on his instructing solicitors to notify him of the dates, but should have liaised with the listing officers, in accordance with normal practice. Similarly, in *R. v Secretary of State for the Home Department Ex p. Mahmood*[89] Richards J. made a wasted costs order against a barrister who accepted a case on a day when he had an existing commitment, without making contingency plans for the possibility of being unable to honour the new commitment. In *R. v Rodney*[90] a barrister did not attend an appeal because he had been erroneously told by his clerk that the appeal was not listed. The Court of Appeal made a wasted costs order against him, as a barrister is vicariously liable for the defaults of his clerk.

Other illustrations. In *Re G (Minors) (Care Proceedings: Wasted Costs)*[91] a **12–022** local authority applied for care orders in respect of three children, relying on

---

[84] *The Times*, September 7, 1999.
[85] [2004] EWCA Civ 754; [2004] P.N.L.R. 722.
[86] [1994] Ch. 205.
[87] *The Times*, April 21, 1995. In *R. v Duffy (Michael) (Wasted Costs)* [2004] EWCA Crim 330; [2004] P.N.L.R. 36 the Court of Appeal held that no wasted costs order should be made against a barrister who turned up late to court as a result of attending a hearing at another court. Both matters were originally listed at the same court, and the court was notified of the potential clash, but the court relisted the cases at different courts at 4 pm on the working day before the hearings. The problem was caused by the court, and it was uncertain that alternative counsel could be found at such short notice.
[88] *The Times*, March 15, 1994.
[89] [1999] C.O.D. 119.
[90] [1997] P.N.L.R. 489.
[91] [2000] Fam. 104.

expert medical opinion. The legal representatives failed to provide the first expert with the children's medical records, so that the witness was unable to complete her evidence on the arranged day and had to return another time. Despite assurances that no further problems would occur, a second expert had to be released to read documents. Wall J. held that a barrister instructed for the local authority in care proceedings was responsible for the presentation of the client's case, including ensuring that expert witnesses were aware of new developments and had digested new material. He held that counsel had acted unreasonably and negligently,[92] and a wasted costs order was made in relation to securing the first expert's reattendance, but not in relation to the second expert in respect of whom the judge was not confident that any costs were in fact wasted. In *Wall v Lefever*[93] the Court of Appeal held that a barrister was not negligent in misjudging that the principal issue in the case was whether a competent engineer could come to the conclusion that the property in question was stable, when in fact the issue was in failing to report the need for further investigation. In *Re a Barrister (Wasted Costs Order) (No.9 of 1999)*[94] a barrister acted for a defendant charged with sexual offences. He failed to obtain a record of his client's previous convictions before eliciting from the client in evidence that he had never had an allegation of a sexual nature made against him, which was in fact false. The Court of Appeal held that the barrister had made an error in not obtaining a copy of his client's record, but it was not an error which no reasonably informed and competent member of the Bar would have made. The barrister had asked for a copy of the record, which was not provided, his client had assured him that he had no previous conviction for sexual offences, and the prosecution counsel had said that he would not refer to previous convictions.

2. LIABILITY FOR BREACH OF DUTY

12-023   The respects in which barristers could be held negligent are almost as varied and numerous as those relating to solicitors.[95] In the case of contentious business, the following are among the more common areas of liability: failing to analyse or apply legal principles properly (for instance, failing to keep properly apprised of recent changes in the law); failing to determine the appropriate remedy or procedure; errors in pleading (such as the failure to claim an indemnity from a third party); failing to identify the appropriate parties to litigation; failing to attend to limitation defences; delays (as a result of which the client loses the chance to bring proceedings or has the proceedings struck out); and failures of advice, particularly on settlement. In the case of non-contentious business, claims have been made for failing to draft documents or advise correctly, leading to adverse tax consequences.

---

[92] He held that all counsel had acted unreasonably and negligently, but there was no practice direction or the like imposing an obligation on barristers in such non-adversarial litigation to ensure that other parties' experts were properly briefed. Thus a wasted costs order was only made against the local authority's barrister.

[93] [1998] 1 F.C.R. 605.

[94] (2000) 16 P.N. 122.

[95] As to which, see Ch.11, s.2.

Knowledge of the law. In *Copeland v Smith*[96] the Court of Appeal stated that   **12–024**
advocates owed a duty to the court to keep themselves up to date with the law.
Doubtless the same duty would be owed to a barrister's client. The court
indicated that an advocate should keep up to date with the general law reports,
which are the *Weekly Law Reports* and the *All England Law Reports*. The court
expressed no view about the need to keep up to date with specialist law reports,
but it is submitted that a barrister practising in a specialist field would be
negligent if he failed to do so. *Green v Collyer-Bristow*[97] is an illustration of a
mistake about the law being held to be negligent. Matrimonial counsel advised
the claimant that she should seek specific enforcement of an agreement with her
former husband to transfer real property to her. Counsel failed to notice s.2 of the
Law of Property (Miscellaneous Provisions) Act 1989, which imposed more
onerous requirements with respect to the need for such an agreement to be in
writing than the repealed s.40 of the Law of Property Act 1925, on which he had
advised. Although two of the three standard textbooks did not refer to the change
in the law, the barrister was held to be liable. In contrast, counsel's advice that
the claimant should seek to set aside an earlier court order of 1984 was not
negligent, although the "better opinion probably" was that such an application
would fail. Normally a barrister has no obligation to have a command of
unreported Court of Appeal decisions.[98]

Mistakes and mere errors of judgment. As in the case of solicitors,[99] there   **12–025**
are usually two stages[1] in determining whether the barrister is liable: (i) Was the
particular advice or other act or omission complained of "wrong" in the light of
the instructions and information placed before him?[2] (ii) If so, did the error
amount to negligence?

Is there an error? *Boland v Yates Property Corp Pty Ltd*[3] is an example of a   **12–026**
barrister's views being found to be correct. The claimant was entitled to receive
compensation for land which was taken by the Darling Harbour Authority, and

---

[96] [2000] 1 W.L.R. 371. see also *Yell Ltd v Garton, The Times,* February 26, 2004, CA.

[97] [1999] Lloyd's Rep. P.N. 798

[98] See *Moy v Pettman Smith (a firm)* [2002] EWCA Civ 875; [2002] P.N.L.R. 44, CA. This issue was not appealed to the House of Lords.

[99] Except where a breach of a specific duty arising under the retainer is alleged: see Ch.11 paras 11–008 to 11–010.

[1] In *Green v Hancocks* [2001] Lloyd's Rep. P.N. 212 at paras 60–61 Chadwick L.J. considered that where the advice was correct, it may well be irrelevant how the barrister arrived at it, but that each case must be judged on its own circumstances. In that case the allegations made included a failure to address the issues properly as well as the giving of wrong advice.

[2] The qualification (contained in the last 11 words) is added, because in the majority of work out of court the barrister is not an investigator of fact, but a processor of facts laid before him. If the barrister gives advice which is correct on the basis of his instructions, it cannot subsequently be said against the barrister that the advice is "wrong", simply because the instructions prove to be mistaken. However, the roles of barrister and solicitor cannot be too rigidly compartmentalised. If the barrister has a conference with the client or expert witness, he may well become an investigator of fact during the conference. Presumably a barrister's failure to elicit information could, in appropriate circumstances, constitute negligence. In addition a barrister may be under a duty to defer advising until further information has been obtained, see para.12–038.

[3] (2000) 167 A.L.R. 575. For an English example see *Naish v Thorp Wright & Puxon* [1998] C.L.Y. 4024. Counsel was held not to be negligent in advising that a restraint of trade clause was enforceable, as his advice was correct.

it was successfully argued on its behalf that the land had "special value" to it. The claimant later sued his lawyers, including counsel, alleging that they negligently failed to propound a theory of "special value" based on the argument that the claimant was in a position to develop the land more quickly than any hypothetical purchaser. The High Court of Australia held that there was an insufficient factual basis for such a theory. None of the lawyers were found to be negligent.

12–027　　　**Mistake or misjudgment?** In relation to the second of these questions, in the case of genuine mistakes, as opposed to misjudgments, there seems to be no reason why the barrister should be treated any more favourably than the solicitor. Indeed, since the barrister holds himself out as a specialist, presumably there are some mistakes which, if committed by a barrister, amount to negligence but, if committed by a solicitor, do not. There are a number of obiter dicta of the House of Lords on this subject. Lord Upjohn in *Rondel v Worsley*[4] expressed the view that counsel would only be guilty of actionable negligence[5] if he committed "some really elementary blunder". This view is difficult to reconcile with the standard of care expected of solicitors.[6] Lord Reid stated that the "the onus of proving professional negligence over and above error of judgment is a heavy one".[7] The point was discussed in *Saif Ali v Sidney Mitchell & Co*[8] by each of the three Law Lords who constituted the majority. Lord Wilberforce put the matter in this way[9]:

> "Much if not most of a barrister's work involves exercise of judgment—it is in the realm of art not science. Indeed the solicitor normally goes to counsel precisely at the point where, as between possible courses, a choice can only be made on the basis of judgment, which is fallible and may turn out to be wrong. Thus in the nature of things, an action against a barrister who acts honestly and carefully is very unlikely to succeed."

Lord Diplock stressed[10] that not every error made by a barrister (or any other professional man) constitutes negligence, but only such an error "as no reasonably well-informed and competent member of that profession could have made".[11] He pointed out[12] that the trial judge would be well qualified, without any need of expert evidence, to make allowance for the circumstances in which

---

[4] [1969] 1 A.C. 191 at 287 A–B.
[5] Which Lord Upjohn described as *"crassa negligentia"*, or "gross negligence".
[6] See Ch.11 paras 11–080, 11–081 and 11–087.
[7] [1969] 1 A.C. 191 at 230F.
[8] [1980] A.C. 198.
[9] *ibid.* at 214F–G.
[10] *ibid.* at 218D and 220D. For a qualification to Lord Diplock's views, see *McManus Development Ltd v Barbridge Properties Ltd* [1996] P.N.L.R. 431 at 442, CA. See further para.12–008, above.
[11] A test adopted in the wasted costs cases of *Ridehalgh v Horsefield* [1994] Ch. 205 and *Re a Barrister (Wasted Costs Order) (No.9 of 1999)* (2000) 16 P.N. 122. Applying this dictum, in *Bark v Hawley* [2004] EWHC 144; [2005] P.N.L.R. 3 Hughes J. struck out a claim against a barrister who advised that an application under s.33 of the Limitation Act 1980 in a claim for perinatal injuries would almost inevitably fail given the long delays since the claimant turned 21. Such an application might have succeeded on the basis that the delays of the claimant's lawyers would not be attributed to her, but that interpretation of the law was not established until after Counsel had advised.
[12] [1980] A.C. 198 at pp.220H–221A.

the allegedly negligent act or omission occurred. Similar observations were made by Lord Salmon[13] as to the nature of a barrister's work and the distinction between errors of judgment and negligence, and also by the House of Lords in *Hall v Simons*.[14]

llustrations. A number of cases now illustrate the distinction between errors **12–028** of judgment and negligence, and in most of them the barrister was found not to be negligent.[15] In *Cook v S*[16] the claimant consulted the defendant solicitor in connection with divorce proceedings brought against her by her husband. As a result of the defendant's negligence the proceedings were undefended and the husband obtained a decree nisi on the grounds of desertion. Had the proceedings been defended, the probabilities were that both parties would have obtained cross-decrees and the claimant's position in regard to maintenance would thereby have been improved. About a month after the decree nisi was pronounced, counsel advised that there was no evidence of adultery against the husband and he could see no point in defending. Lawton J. held that counsel's advice was wrong; that a motion to set aside the decree nisi would probably have succeeded and that this would have been to the claimant's advantage. Lawton J. went on to hold, however, that counsel was "not negligent, just mistaken as any lawyer and judge might be".[17] Accordingly, the chain of causation was not broken, and the defendant solicitor was liable for all the consequences of the fact that the husband had obtained an undefended decree.

In *Matrix Securities Ltd v Theodore Goddard*[18] the claimant promoted a tax **12–029** avoidance scheme. A tax silk was instructed to advise on a letter sent to the Inland Revenue which sought an assurance that certain capital allowances would be available, which assurance was given. The Inland Revenue later disowned the assurance, and the claimant's subsequent litigation with the Inland Revenue was pursued to the House of Lords, where it was held that the allowances were not available, and the Inland Revenue was not bound by the assurances as inadequate disclosure had been made in the letter. Most of the judges who considered the case thought that the letter was inaccurate or misleading, but, the judge trying the negligence action brought against the tax silk considered that counsel's advice on the contents of the letter was not negligent, and that the judgment he made was not one which no reasonably competent tax silk could make. In *Waters v*

---

[13] [1980] A.C. 198 at pp.220H–221A at 231C–D.

[14] [2002] 1 A.C. 615. See para.12–041, below for an exposition.

[15] See also *Nestle v Best* [1996] P.N.L.R. 444, where the Court of Appeal struck out an allegation made against solicitors and counsel of allowing an action to continue despite it being hopeless, as it had been supported by expert evidence which was rejected by the judge at trial.

[16] [1966] 1 W.L.R. 635.

[17] *ibid.* at 641E.

[18] [1998] P.N.L.R. 290. See also *Popat v Barnes* [2004] EWHC 741, QB; *The Times,* July 5, 2004. The claimant had been convicted of rape, and appealed unsuccessfully. On a second appeal the Court of Appeal quashed the conviction in part on the basis that an alibi direction was not given by the judge, and the claimant was acquitted at a retrial. Buckley J. held that the claimant's barrister was not negligent in failing to raise the issue before the trial judge or on the original appeal. She reasonably believed that an alibi direction was not required and may not have been to the claimant's advantage, and it was reasonable not to take the point on appeal when there had been a deliberate decision not to take the point at trial.

Maguire[19] Garland J. struck out a claim against a barrister who had exercised her judgment not to pursue a claim for direct discrimination based on acts of victimisation, but to pursue only a claim for vicarious liability for a sexual assault of a fellow employee which was in fact bound to fail.

12–030   **Settlement.** Many of the areas upon which a barrister is asked to advise are clearly matters of judgment. One question commonly referred to counsel is whether or not a payment into court or offer of settlement should be accepted.[20] Often there is no "right" or "wrong" answer to this question. Counsel must weigh up subjective matters such as his own assessment of the witnesses, his experience of the trial judge (when known) and the "merits" of the case, as well as purely legal considerations. In the Canadian case of *Karpenko v Paroian, Courey, Cohen & Houston*[21] Anderson J. expressed the view that only in exceptional cases would a lawyer's advice on such matters amount to negligence:

> "In my view, an important element of public policy is involved. It is in the interests of public policy to discourage suits and encourage settlements. The vast majority of suits are settled. It is the almost universal practice among responsible members of the legal profession to pursue settlement until some circumstance or combination of circumstances leads them to conclude that a particular dispute can only be resolved by a trial. I say nothing of the suits which are settled by reason of sloth, or inexperience, or lack of stomach for the fight. They have nothing to do with this case. What is relevant and material to the public interest is that an industrious and competent practitioner should not be unduly inhibited in making a decision to settle a case by the apprehension that some Judge, viewing the matter subsequently, with all the acuity of vision given by hindsight, and from the calm security of the Bench, may tell him he should have done otherwise. To the decision to settle a lawyer brings all his talents and experience both recollected and existing somewhere below the level of the conscious mind, all his knowledge of the law and its processes. Not least he brings to it his hard-earned knowledge that the trial of a lawsuit is costly, time-consuming and taxing for everyone involved and attended by a host of contingencies, foreseen and unforeseen. Upon all of this he must decide whether he should take what is available by way of settlement, or press on. I can think of few areas where the difficult question of what constitutes negligence, which gives rise to liability, and what constitutes at worst an error in judgment, which does not, is harder to answer. In my view it would be only in the case of some egregious error that negligence would be found."[22]

This dictum was cited with approval in *Chancellor, Masters and Scholars of Oxford University v John Stedman Design Group*,[23] and more importantly by the

---

[19] [1999] Lloyd's Rep. P.N. 855. The point is closely allied to the issue of pleading weak points, discussed at para.12–039, below. Garland J. also held that the barrister, who had no solicitor and was working for the Free Representation Unit, was not negligent in failing to take a more detailed proof or discovering further gender specific acts which could have been pleaded as direct discrimination, as she had a full note from the claimant who provided a different version of events.

[20] This topic has already been discussed in the context of solicitors: see Ch.11, para.11–192.

[21] (1981) 117 D.L.R. (3d) 383, Ontario High Court.

[22] *ibid.* at 397–398.

[23] (1991) 7 Const.L.J. 102 at 107, Judge Esyr Lewis Q.C. It was held that the defendants had acted reasonably in entering into a settlement on the advice of counsel, and thus were entitled to pursue contribution proceedings on the basis of that settlement.

House of Lords in *Moy v Pettman Smith (a firm)*.[24] In *Kelley v Corston*[25] Judge L.J. suggested, in the context of a consideration of immunity, that no case was bound to succeeed, and it is difficult to underestimate the value of certainty provided by settlement, factors which should "militate against successful proceedings based on criticism of advice leading to a settlement".

Illustrations. An extreme example of an allegation against counsel of advising **12–031**
an undersettlement can be found in *Hussain v Cuddy Woods & Cochrane (a firm)*,[26] where the Court of Appeal upheld an order striking the case out. There was no evidence that the claim was worth more than the £10,000 which the barrister had advised should be accepted in settlement on the third day of trial. Counsel was entitled to take into account the hazards of litigation, the enormous costs for the client if the claim were to fail, or if the payment in were not beaten. No inference could be drawn from the fact that counsel might have a financial interest in the case as his solicitors had not guaranteed payment of all his fees. A less extreme example is *McIlgorm v Bell Lamb & Joynson*.[27] The claimant was sued as a director of a small company, which had gone into liquidation, for negligently allowing an employee to be exposed to asbestosis. His barrister's advice to accept the settlement proposals of the other side was held by Gibbs J. to be within the range of reasonable views which a well informed barrister could have formed. The factors which he did and was entitled to take into account included: the evidence available as to whether the claimant personally directed or controlled the employees; the law, which included an unreported case on similar facts which had been drawn to his attention; and the fact that the offer to settle for about two-thirds of the value of the claim, with damages and costs being charged on the claimant's property and not to be enforced in his lifetime, meant that the claimant would keep his home. In *Luke v Wansboroughs (a firm)*[28] a barrister had advised in 2000 that a claim commenced in 1995 for malicious falsehood was very likely to be struck out, and the claimant should accept an offer of £10,000 plus costs. Davis J. held that the advice was reasonable, and the barrister was entitled to express her views strongly.

Exceptions. However, in *Griffin v Kingsmill*,[29] counsel and solicitors were **12–032**
found to be negligent in advising a claimant to accept £50,000 in a personal injury action which would have been worth about £500,000 on full liability. The claimant, who was 12 years old at the time, was a pedestrian hit by a car. There were only two witnesses. The claimant's grandfather said that the claimant was waiting on the side of the road, between the white line and the pavement, and the driver said that she ran alongside the road until she suddenly changed direction and ran into the road. The Court of Appeal held that this was essentially a simple case, and it would take cogent reasons to conclude that the grandfather's evidence was overwhelmingly likely to be rejected, which did not exist. The reasons given by counsel for rejecting the grandfather's evidence were untenable, and he

---

[24] [2005] UKHL 5; [2005] 1 W.L.R. 581 at para.59 (save for the first four lines quoted in the text).
[25] [1998] Q.B. 686 at 700E–F.
[26] [2001] Lloyd's Rep. P.N. 134.
[27] [2001] P.N.L.R. 28.
[28] [2003] EWHC 3151, QB; [2005] P.N.L.R. 1.
[29] [2001] Lloyd's Rep. P.N. 716.

did not properly assess the driver's evidence, which was inconsistent. In *Hickman v Blake Lapthorn*[30] a barrister attended court for a trial on liability in a personal injury action. A monetary settlement was proposed by the other side. The barrister was unfamiliar with most of the medical reports, but he advised on the proposed settlement. Jack J. held that he was negligent, as his advice was based on the assumption that the claimant would regain full time employment, which was wrong. A medical report in the trial bundle stated that a case manager was needed to combat the factors which could threaten the claimant's chances of satisfactory employment, and if the barrister had followed that up, he would have found that no progress had been made and there was a real issue as to whether the claimant would be able hold down a job.

12–033   **Failures of advice.** In *Estill v Cowling*[31] counsel was instructed in relation to the proposed transfer of shares in a company to the client's nephews and nieces. Arden J. held that the barrister was negligent in failing to advise that the proposed gift of shares to a settlement would be an immediately chargeable transfer for the purposes of inheritance tax, and failing to consider an interest in possession trust, which would have been a potentially exempt transfer.[32] In *Gosfield School Ltd v Birkett Long (a firm)*[33] a barrister advised an independent school on settling a claim for fees against the parents of two former children, and their counterclaim for losses allegedly from providing substandard eduction. Further proceedings were later brought by the children alleging a failure to provide an adequate education, which were also settled. The barrister, and his instructing solicitors, were not at fault in failing to warn about the risk of the further proceedings, as the risk was not sufficiently significant.

12–034   **Giving clear advice.** The question of how comprehensive a barrister's advice must be was considered in *Mathew v Maughold Life Assurance Co Ltd.*[34] In March 1974 Mr and Mrs Mathew entered into a scheme in order to minimise liability to estate duty on Mr Mathew's death. In order to achieve the desired result, it was necessary for Mrs Mathew to exercise an option by March 20, 1981, in the event that her husband survived until that date. Unfortunately she did not do so, and in consequence suffered loss. The family solicitor admitted liability, and unsuccessfully attempted to seek contribution from three other professional advisers, including a barrister. The case against the barrister related to advice which he had given orally in conference in 1974 and 1978 and to an opinion which he had written shortly after the 1978 conference. Leonard J. held that the barrister had given adequate advice in 1974, but that his advice in 1978 was inadequate in that he failed to make it clear that the option must be exercised by March 1981. The Court of Appeal reversed that finding and held that the barrister was not liable. At the conference in 1974 the barrister was instructed by the insurance company who had marketed the scheme, and not by Mr or Mrs Mathew. However, Leonard J. held that the barrister owed a duty to them to give

---

[30] [2005] EWHC 2714; [2006] P.N.L.R. 20, Jack J.
[31] [2000] Lloyd's Rep. P.N. 378.
[32] This was despite expert evidence from a silk that he was not aware of an interest in possession settlement, which was not mentioned in the predecent book.
[33] [2005] EWHC 2905; [2006] P.N.L.R. 19, Cook J.
[34] (1985) 1 P.N. 142, Leonard J.; [1955–1995] P.N.L.R. 51, CA.

an adequate explanation of the scheme to Mr Mathew's solicitor and accountant, who were present at the conference. In relation to the 1974 advice, Leonard J. considered that the barrister was entitled to assume that the solicitor and accountant were following what he said unless they indicated to the contrary and that Mr Mathew's professional advisers would familiarise themselves with the documents before Mr and Mrs Mathew were invited to sign them.[35] The Court of Appeal went further, and considered that even when the barrister was instructed on behalf of Mr Mathew in 1978, he owed no duty to ensure that the lay client fully understood the scheme given the presence of the other professional advisers. He was entitled to assume that his instructing solicitor was familiar with what had been arranged, and had explained it to the client.[36]

In *Moy v Pettman Smith (a firm)*[37] the claimant sued a health authority with   **12–035** respect to an injury to his leg, and judgment was entered with damages to be assessed. A barrister advised that a vital further medical report on causation should be obtained, but it was served only a month before trial, and an application to adduce it failed. The barrister then advised that the permission should be sought to rely on the report at trial. Her view was that there was a 50:50 chance of obtaining permission, but she did not communicate this to the claimant. At the door of the court she advised the client to proceed with the action rather than accept £150,000 offered by the health authority, which was an increase on their payment into court.[38] The House of Lords held that the barrister was not negligent in failing to tell the client of her views of the chances of obtaining permission to adduce the report. Particularly with advice on settlement at the door of the court, the advice could not be expected to precisely reasoned, and advocates were entitled to concentrate on giving clear and readily understood advice about the course of action that they recommended.

Predicting changes in the law. In *Heydon v NRMA Ltd*,[39] leading counsel and   **12–036** solicitors advised in relation to proposals to demutualise or convert NRMA companies limited by guarantee to companies limited by guarantee and shares, converting rights of members to shares. They advised that special resolutions were sufficient, and a scheme of arrangement was not required. Such advice was consistent with a recent Court of Appeal case called *Gambotto v WCP Ltd*, which was later reversed by the High Court of Australia. At first instance, the lawyers were held to be negligent in failing to advert to the grant of special leave by the High Court in *Gambotto*, failing to obtain a copy of transcript of the arguments on the application for leave, and failing to advise that if the appeal were upheld it might be on grounds which cast doubt on the validity of the proposed special resolutions. The New South Wales Court of Appeal unanimously allowed the

---

[35] (1985) 1 P.N. 142 at 145 col.3.
[36] (1987) 3 P.N. 98 at 104.
[37] [2005] UKHL 5; [2005] W.L.R. 581. The House of Lords overturned the decision of the Court of Appeal, [2002] EWCA Civ 875; [2002] P.N.L.R. 44, who has also held that a barrister was not negligent in miscalculating the prospects of admitting crucial late evidence of causation in a clinical negligence case at the start of a trial.
[38] The advice which should be given on a payment into court will generally be whether the claimant is likely to obtain more than that sum at court, and his liability in costs if he fails to obtain more from the judge, see Lord Hope at [2005] UKHL 5; [2005] W.L.R. 581 para.14.
[39] (2001) 51 N.S.W.L.R. 1.

appeal. There was nothing in the existing authorities which would have caused a competent lawyer to foresee or warn against the possibility of the High Court of Australia formulating a new principle, as in fact it did. A majority held that the suggested research was oppressive, and would effectively entail that a lawyer had a duty to identify all relevant applications for leave to appeal and examine copies of transcripts of the hearings, and pending changes in statute. Such detailed research would only be required in very exceptional cases.

12–037   **Advising where not instructed to do so.** One problem which sometimes arises is the extent to which barristers can be held liable for failing to advise on matters which are not specifically raised in their instructions. If the barrister is asked to advise on certain specific points only, it seem unlikely that he will be held liable for failing to advise on other matters. In the Canadian case of *Smith v McInnis*[40] a solicitor was instructed to pursue claims under insurance policies in respect of certain losses by fire. He engaged experienced insurance counsel to advise on the preparation of proofs of loss. The solicitor failed to bring proceedings within the limitation period. In the professional negligence action which followed, the solicitor claimed a contribution from the barrister. The claim failed. It was held by the Supreme Court of Canada that counsel specialising in insurance was not required to give advice about the limitation period. Presumably, however, if it is obvious from the instructions that instructing solicitors are under a misapprehension about some relevant matter on which the barrister's opinion is not specifically sought, or perhaps even that they have overlooked a point of critical importance, he would be held negligent for failing to correct that misapprehension.

12–038   **Obtaining full instructions.** A barrister may be negligent in some circumstance if he settles proceedings or advises on the basis of information or instructions which he ought to realise are inadequate.[41] Thus in medical negligence cases, it is necessary to see copies of the relevant medical notes as well as an expert's report before advising on the merits of a case.[42]

12–039   **Pleading weak points.** In *McFarlane v Wilkinson*[43] the claimant suffered psychiatric injury as a result of witnessing the catastrophic fire on the Piper Alpha oil-rig from a support vessel. His claim at common law succeeded at first instance, but failed on appeal. He sued his barristers for failing to plead breach of statutory duty. Reversing Rix J., the Court of Appeal held that such a claim

---

[40] (1979) 91 D.L.R. (3d) 190. For another example see *Heydon v NRWA* [2000] N.S.W.C.A. 374; (2001) 36 A.C.S.R. 462, N.S.W.CA.
[41] As Richard Fernyhough Q.C. points out at (1997) 13 Cons.L.J. 364, this may not apply in matters of urgency, and statements of case can be settled on the basis of limited information.
[42] See *Locke v Camberwell HA* (1990) 140 N.L.J. 205 at 206 col.1. On appeal, further facts came to light. The Court of Appeal stated that the barrister who was criticised by the judge did not, on the facts of the case, deserve censure, but the court did not consider the principle discussed: see [2002] Lloyd's Rep. P.N. 23.
[43] [1997] 2 Lloyd's Rep. 259. A similar result was reached by the British Columbia Court of Appeal in *Arbutus Bay Estates Ltd v Davis & Co* (2003) 8 B.C.L.R. (4th) 73, where a majority dismissed a claim against lawyers for failing to argue certain constitutional points in a dispute about a roadway, because they had no chance of success.

was bound to fail. Brooke L.J., with whom the other members of the court agreed, held that the relevant test was:

> "if a barrister omits to plead a cause of action in a situation where no other reasonably competent barrister, acting with ordinary care, would have failed to plead that cause of action, then he or she will be liable to compensate the client if loss flows foreseeable from that negligence. If on the other hand other reasonably competent barristers holding themselves out as competent to practise in the relevant field and acting with ordinary care might also have decided not to plead that cause of action, then there will be no question of professional negligence."

It was argued by the claimant that any properly arguable claim, such as breach of statutory duty in that case, should be pleaded, as it had some settlement value. Brooke L.J. suggested that a client would not thank counsel for taking properly arguable points which were likely to fail if as a consequence the litigation was longer and more expensive. In that case, counsel rightly judged that the plea of breach of statutory duty added nothing to the plea of negligence, and it was "quite absurd to consider that she could be liable in negligence for exercising her judgment in the way she did". The Court of Appeal struck out the claim.

McFarlane has been followed and applied in *Firstcity Insurance Group Ltd v*   **12–040**
Orchard.[44] The claimants were involved in litigation concerning their obligation to take certain premises subject to certain works being carried out and completed by December 24, 1995. The client advanced an argument that the agreement could be construed in such a way that the date of completion of the works was after the deadline. An experienced commercial Q.C. considered this argument and rejected it. He did not plead it, and did not change his view after seeing further information from the other side which appeared to follow the client's initial argument, but which he considered had been made by mistake. The case was lost at first instance, but on appeal the Court of Appeal raised the question of how the date of completion should be calculated, and eventually allowed the appeal on the basis of the client's initial argument. Forbes J. held that counsel was not negligent. The barrister reasonably took the view that the client's construction argument was not arguable, and he was not bound to plead or argue it for its settlement value. He had formed a considered view, and did not have to clutter up the case with other arguments. While a barrister must be prepared to review his advice, counsel could not be criticised in holding to his view when nothing of substance had occurred to cause him to change it.

Negligence in court. As a result of the abolition of immunity by the House of   **12–041**
Lords in *Hall v Simons*[45] barristers are vulnerable to being sued for mistakes they make in court. Three of their Lordships made observations about such actions in slightly different terms. In one of the two leadings judgments, Lord Steyn said[46]:

---

[44] [2003] P.N.L.R. 9.
[45] [2002] 1 A.C. 615.
[46] *ibid*. 681G–682C. Lord Steyn's speech was agreed with by Lord Browne-Wilkinson at 685E, and Lord Millett at 752B. Lord Steyn's observations were applied by the QBD in *Prettys v Carter* [2001] Lloyd's Rep. P.N. 832 at 836, where it was held that lack of robustness in cross-examination, especially in regard to credit, cannot normally hope to found an allegation of negligence.

"when such claims are made courts will take into account the difficult decisions faced daily by barristers working in demanding situations to tight timetables. In this context the observations of Sir Thomas Bingham M.R. in *Ridehalgh v Horsefield* [1994] Ch. 205 are instructive. Dealing with the circumstances in which a wasted costs order against a barrister might be appropriate he observed, at p.236:

'Any judge who is invited to make or contemplates making an order arising out of an advocate's conduct of court proceedings must make full allowance for the fact that an advocate in court, like a commander in battle, often has to make decisions quickly and under pressure, in the fog of war and ignorant of developments on the other side of the hill. Mistakes will inevitably be made, things done which the outcome shows to have been unwise. But advocacy is more an art than a science. It cannot be conducted according to formulae. Individuals differ in their style and approach. It is only when, with all allowances made, an advocate's conduct of court proceedings is quite plainly unjustifiable that it can be appropriate to make a wasted costs order against him.'

For broadly similar reasons it will not be easy to establish negligence against a barrister. The courts can be trusted to differentiate between errors of judgment and true negligence. In any event, a plaintiff who claims that poor advocacy resulted in an unfavourable outcome will face the very great obstacle of showing that a better standard of advocacy would have resulted in a more favourable outcome."

Lord Hope stated that an advocate's

"duty in the conduct of his professional duties is to do that which an advocate of ordinary skill would have done if he had been acting with ordinary care. . . . He must also exercise that judgment with the care which an advocate of ordinary skill would take in the circumstances. It cannot be stressed too strongly that a mere error of judgment on his part will not expose him to liability for negligence."[47]

Finally, Lord Hobhouse indicated that the standard of care to be applied was:

". . . the same as that applicable to any other skilled professional who has to work in an environment where decisions and exercises of judgment have to be made in often difficult and time constrained circumstances. It requires a plaintiff to show that the error was one which no reasonably competent member of the relevant profession would have made."[48]

3. DAMAGES

12–042 **Remoteness of damage.** Since there is normally no contract between the barrister and his client, the ordinary rules of remoteness in the law of tort[49] should be applied, in order to determine which losses flowing from the barrister's negligence sound in damages.

---

[47] [2002] 1 A.C. 615 at 726D–G.
[48] *ibid*. at 737G–H.
[49] For the general principles of remoteness in the law of tort, see *McGregor*, (17th edn), paras 6–075 to 6–124.

As in solicitors' negligence cases, the loss will have to be within the scope of **12–043** the defendant's duty, and be proximately caused by it. In *Green v Alexander Johnson (a firm)*[50] the defendant barrister negligently failed to advise the claimant freehold owners that their tenant did not have a long lease and were not entitled to a new lease pursuant to statute, as a result of which they entered a consent order agreeing the right to a new lease. Subsequent proceedings between landlord and tenant were compromised, with the landlord accepting £190,000 when the open market value was £278,000. However, it was insufficient to give credit for £190,000, as the compromise arose from the fact that counternotices may have been defective, which was extraneous to the original negligent advice. The credit to be given was the figure at which the Leasehold Valuation Tribunal would have valued the flats. In *Bernasconi v Nicholas Bennett*[51] the defendants, a barrister and a firm of solicitors, gave advice to directors on how their company could divest itself of four leases. The company's liquidator subsequently sued the directors for fraudulent preference. The directors' action against the lawyers, seeking an indemnity, was struck out. The lawyers were not the proximate cause of the loss. It was not alleged that the defendants acted dishonestly or encouraged the directors to act.

Measure of damages. The heads of damage will generally be similar to those **12–044** discussed in relation to solicitors.[52] Where the barrister's negligence has deprived the client of the chance of bringing or defending proceedings, the court must assess the value of the "chance" which has been lost, applying the principles formulated in *Kitchen v Royal Air Force Association*,[53] as was done in *Gascoine v Ian Sheridan & Co.*[54] A barrister was one of the defendants whose negligent delay caused the claimant's case to be struck out for want of prosecution. In *Griffin v Kingsmill*[55] counsel negligently advised that a case had no reasonable prospects of success, and as a result a settlement was accepted at about a tenth of the value of the claim on full liability. The Court of Appeal awarded 80 per cent of the full value of the claim, giving a discount for the uncertainties of litigation and the risk of a finding of contributory negligence. In assessing damages for wrongful imprisonment, a court will follow the guidance of *Thompson v Commissioner of Police of the Metropolis.*[56]

A more difficult question arises if counsel makes a mistake[57] as a result of **12–045** which the case is lost. Does the court have to determine on the balance of probabilities whether, but for that mistake, the case would have been won? And, if so, award the relief which should have been obtained in the earlier action? Alternatively, does the court have to assess the chances of a more favourable outcome, in the absence of the negligent mistake, and then scale down the award

---

[50] [2004] EWHC 1205; [2006] P.N.L.R. 40, Peter Smith J., appeal dismissed [2005] EWCA Civ 775; [2005] P.N.L.R. 45.
[51] [2000] Lloyd's Rep. P.N. 285.
[52] See Ch.11, s.3.
[53] [1958] 1 W.L.R. 563, CA.
[54] [1994] 5 Med. L.R. 437. For the facts see Ch.11, para.11–291.
[55] [2001] Lloyd's Rep. P.N. 716
[56] [1998] Q.B. 498. This was done in *Popat v Barnes* [2004] EWHC 741, QB; *The Times,* July 5, 2004, where Buckely J. awarded £50,000 for two years' imprisonment. The decision was obiter, as the case against the barrister failed on liability.
[57] e.g. advising wrongly on a period of limitation.

of damages accordingly? It would appear from the reasoning of Lord Diplock in *Saif Ali v Sidney Mitchell & Co,*[58] and from comments made by Lord Browne-Wilkinson in *Hall v Simons*[59] in the House of Lords, that the first course is to be preferred. If, therefore, the negligence of counsel transforms an action with a 40 per cent chance of success into an action with no prospect of success, the client would suffered no recoverable loss.[60] However, Lord Diplock's dictum should now be reconsidered in the light of the Court of Appeal's decision in *Allied Maples Group Ltd v Simmons & Simmons,*[61] and the law in relation to lost litigation.[62] It is submitted that his dictum is now unlikely to be followed.

4. SHARED RESPONSIBILITY

(a) *Apportionment of Liability*[63]

12–046 Apportionment between solicitors and barristers has arisen in a number of cases.[64] In two wasted costs applications, a division between the barrister and the solicitor was determined at 75/25,[65] but each case will depend on its own facts. There may be technical difficulties preventing contribution proceedings in wasted costs cases[66]; the wasted costs application is sometimes made against both solicitors and counsel, and the court will then normally determine that each will pay a proportion of the costs. In *Hickman v Blake Lapthorn,*[67] negligent advice was given on settlement at the start of a liability trial, which did not take into account the prospects of the claimant not working again. The barrister, who was a senior junior, had a leading role in valuing the claim and advising on settlement, but the solicitor had a greater knowledge of quantum. Responsibility was apportioned two thirds to one third.

---

[58] [1980] A.C. 198 at 222 D–E. The reasoning is similar to that of the Court of Appeal in *Sykes v Midland Bank Executor & Trustee Co* [1971] 1 Q.B. 113, CA.

[59] [2002] 1 A.C. 615 at 684G. cf. Lord Hoffman at 687E–F.

[60] Since damage is a necessary element in the tort of negligence, the claim would then fail altogether.

[61] [1995] 1 W.L.R. 1602, on which see Ch.11, para.11–263.

[62] See Ch.11 paras 11–284 *et seq.*

[63] The general principles of apportionment are referred to in Ch.4.

[64] See also *Moy v Pettman Smith (a firm)* [2002] EWCA Civ 875; [2002] P.N.L.R. 44. The Court of Appeal held that the solicitor, who failed to obtain a proper report on causation in a clinical negligence case, was 75% to blame. The barrister failed to inform her client of her assessment of the chances of the court permitting him to adduce late evidence on causation, as a result of which he turned down an offer of about half the value of the claim; she was found to be responsible for 25% of the loss. On appeal the House of Lords held that the barrister was not negligent, see [2005] UKHL 5; [2005] 1 W.L.R. 581.

[65] *R. v Secretarary of State of the Home Department Ex p. Begum* [1995] C.O.D. 176, Harrison J., where the solicitors wrongly relied on counsel's opinion in a judicial review application. See para.12–019 for the facts. *B v B (Wasted Costs: Abuse of Process)* [20001] 1 F.L.R. 843, Wall J. where an order vacating a trial date had been hopelessly appealed; the directions which were given and which were not appealed made it inevitable that the hearing would be postponed.

[66] See H. Evans, "The wasted costs jurisdiction" (2001) 64 M.L.R. 51 at 60–62.

[67] [2005] EWHC 2714; [2006] P.N.L.R. 20.

CHAPTER 13

MEDICAL PRACTITIONERS

1. GENERAL

In order to obtain registration, a medical practitioner must satisfy the require-   **13–001**
ments of the Medical Act 1983 (as amended by the Medical Qualifications
(Amendment) Act 1991) both as to qualifications and as to experience. Once
fully registered, a practitioner is eligible for appointment as a medical officer in

[895]

any hospital within or outside the National Health Service[1]; he is entitled to practise, and to hold himself out, as a registered medical practitioner[2]; he is also entitled to give medical certificates required by any enactment.[3] Medical practitioners are subject to the discipline of the General Medical Council, whose powers are now derived from the Medical Act 1983 and the Medical (Professional Performance) Act 1995.

Similarly, a registered dentist is a person who appears as such in the dentists' register maintained by the Registrar of the General Dental Council. In order to obtain registration, a dentist must satisfy the requirements of the Dentists Act 1984.[4] No one may practise dentistry who is not a registered dentist, a visiting EEC practitioner entered in the list of such practitioners or a registered medical practitioner.[5] Dentists are subject to the discipline of the General Dental Council, whose powers are derived from the Dentists Act 1984. Only a registered dentist is entitled to describe himself as "dentist", "dental surgeon" or "dental practitioner".[6]

Similar arrangements also exist in respect of other allied medically related professions.[7]

13–002   **Disciplinary proceedings.** Doctors, dentists and each of the allied medical professions referred to above are each subject to the disciplinary jurisdiction of statutory bodies established for that purpose.[8] Detailed consideration of the jurisdiction of those bodies is outside the scope of this work but it should be

---

[1] Medical Act 1983, s.47, amended by the Medical (Professional Performance) Act 1995, s.4.

[2] Unqualified persons are not prohibited from practising medicine or surgery. However, they are not permitted to sue for their charges: see Medical Act 1983, s.46. It is a criminal offence if such persons hold themselves out as being registered under the Medical Act 1983: see s.49.

[3] Medical Act 1983, s.48. For a fuller discussion of the privileges and duties of medical practitioners, see *Halsbury's Laws* (4th edn), vol.30, paras 13–18.

[4] See in particular s.15, as amended by the Dental Qualifications (Recognition) Regulations 1996 (SI 1996/1496).

[5] Dentists Act 1984, s.38. These provisions are more stringent than the equivalent provisions relating to general medical practice: see n.2 above.

[6] Dentists Act 1984, s.26.

[7] The registration of pharmacists is governed by the Pharmacy Act 1954: see ss.1–6 for the requirements that must be satisfied. The registration of nurses, midwives and health visitors is governed by the Nurses, Midwives and Health Visitors Act 1997, ss.7–9. The registration of opticians is governed by the Opticians Act 1989, ss.7–9. The registration of osteopaths is governed by the Osteopaths Act 1993, ss.2–4, 6. The registration of chiropodists, dieticians, medical laboratory technicians, occupational therapists, physiotherapists, radiographers, arts therapists, clinical scientists, speech and language therapists, orthoptists, prosthetists and orthotists, and paramedics is governed by the Professions Supplementary to Medicine Act 1960, ss.2–7. Acupuncturists may register with the British Medical Acupuncture Society, and the British Acupuncture Council; registration is voluntary.

[8] For example, doctors are subject to the disciplinary jurisdiction of the General Medical Council, dentists are subject to the disciplinary jurisdiction of the General Dental Council and nurses, midwives and health visitors are subject to the disciplinary jurisdiction of the Central Council for Nursing, Midwifery and Health Visiting. The activities of these regulatory bodies are now overseen by the Council for the Regulation of Health Care Professionals, and their decisions on disciplinary matters can be referred to the courts under s.29 of the National Health Service Reform and Health Care Professions Act 2002, if the Council considers the decision was unduly lenient, or should not have been made and that it would be desirable for the protection of members of the public for the Council to take action under this section. There have been a number of such references by the Council.

noted that in *McCandless v General Medical Council*[9] the Privy Council rejected an argument to the effect that the conduct of a general practitioner had to be "morally blameworthy" before he or she could be found guilty of "serious professional misconduct" and instead confirmed that "seriously negligent treatment" could support such a charge. In that case the care provided by the practitioner was found by the Council to have fallen "deplorably short of the standard which patients are entitled to expect from their general practitioners". The practitioner was struck off the Medical Register.

(a) *Duties to Patient*

(i) *Contractual Duties*

National Health Service patients. Most medical treatment is undertaken   **13–003** under the National Health Service scheme and there is almost certainly no contract between the patient and those by whom he is treated.[10]

Arguments have been sought to be put forward to the effect that a contract for services is concluded between a patient and his general practitioner at the time that the patient first enrolled (on the basis that by permitting his name to be added to that practitioner's list, he increases the remuneration to which the practitioner is entitled thereby providing consideration for the practitioner's services) or in respect of hospital treatment in the National Health Service's "internal market", where funding is intended to "follow the patient". Such arguments have been accepted at first instance in Canada[11] but rejected in England.[12]

---

[9] [1996] 1 W.L.R. 167. In *McCandless* the Privy Council followed its earlier decision in *Doughty v General Dental Council* [1988] A.C. 164.

[10] A similar conclusion is reached in Kennedy & Grubb's *Principles of Medical Law* (1998 edn) at sections 5.012–5.10. In addition, in its Report on Civil Liability and Compensation for Personal Injury, (1978, Cmnd. 7054) the Royal Commission, chaired by Lord Pearson, stated at para.1313: "Private patients may sue their doctors for a breach of contract . . . under the National Health Service, however there is no contract between patient and doctor and a plaintiff must rely on an action in tort. But the National Health Service patient is in no worse position than the private patient because the same considerations determine if there has been a breach of duty whether the case is brought in contract or tort". In *Hotson v East Berkshire AHA* [1987] 1 A.C. 750 at 760B Lord Donaldson M.R. was " . . . quite unable to detect any rational basis for a state of the law, if such it be, whereby in identical circumstances, Dr A who treats a patient under the National Health Service, and whose liability therefore falls to be determined in accordance with the law of tort, should be in a different position from Dr B who treats a patient outside the service, and whose liability therefore falls to be determined in accordance with the law of contract, assuming, of course, that the contract is in terms which impose upon him neither more nor less than the tortious duty"; see also *per* Croom-Johnson L.J. at 768F. The decision in *Hotson* concerned causation of loss and was reversed by the House of Lords without comment upon this point.

[11] See *Pittman Estate v Bain* (1994) 112 D.L.R. (4th) 257, Ontario High Court. Lang J. found a contract between a patient and the hospital where he was treated under a government funded healthcare scheme. The patient gave consideration by submitting himself for treatment, thereby enhancing the reputation of the hospital and increasing the level of government funding to which it became entitled.

[12] See *Reynolds v The Health First Medical Group* [2000] Lloyd's Rep. Med. 240 and [2000] Lloyd's Rep. Med. 244–245 for a commentary. The case concerned an allegedly negligent failure on the part of the defendant general practitioners practice to advise the claimant that she was pregnant. She subsequently gave birth to a healthy but unwanted child and sued for, inter alia, the cost of bringing up the child. Following the House of Lords' decision in *McFarlane v Tayside Health Board* [2000] 2 A.C. 59, she re-amended her claim to add a claim for breach of a contractual relationship with the defendant. The defendant succeeded in striking out the re-amended parts of the claim. His Honour

13–004   **Private patients.** Where a medical practitioner is privately engaged, he owes a contractual duty to attend and treat the patient and to exercise reasonable skill and care in so doing.[13] The fact that a surgeon agrees to perform an operation on a claimant on a private basis and to give the case his personal attention does not impose upon the defendant any greater responsibility than normal.[14]

It has been suggested by certain of the judiciary that there is also an (apparently separate) implied contractual duty "to act at all times in the best interests of the patient".[15] However, the implication of such a term is likely to give rise to obvious difficulties. In particular, if the patient's condition cannot be correctly diagnosed by the exercise of reasonable skill and care, the doctor will not know what action is in the best interests of the patient. If the suggested implied term is qualified to take account of such objections as this, the term would seem to add nothing to the implied contractual duty to exercise reasonable skill and care on the patient's behalf.[16]

Medicine is perhaps the classic example of a profession in which results are not guaranteed and are not expected to be guaranteed.[17] It is of course open to the medical practitioner in any given case to contract or warrant that the proposed

---

Judge Simmons declined to follow *Pittman Estate v Bain* (see n.11 above) and concluded that there was not "in this instance" a contractual relationship between the claimant and the defendant. Whilst the Judge properly restricted his conclusions to the particular facts of the case, it is likely that the same result will be reached in virtually every case where services have been provided to a patient under the National Health Services Act 1977.

[13] See *Shiells and Thorne v Blackburne* (1789) 1 H.Bl. 158; *Eyre v Measday* [1986] 1 All E.R. 488; *Thake v Maurice* [1986] Q.B. 644; Supply of Goods and Services Act 1982, s.13.

[14] See *Morris v Winsbury-White* [1937] 4 All E.R. 494 in which Tucker J. stated as follows at 500 A–D: "Mr Winsbury-White did say that he had pledged himself in terms to give this case his personal attention, although he agreed with me that in fact, in his view, that made very little difference as to the nature of his obligations. Of course, in any event his obligation was to perform the operation, and to give the necessary supervision thereafter until the discharge of the patient. I think it is, therefore, involved in that Mr Winsbury-White did expressly or impliedly intimate that the case would have his personal attention. Whether you call it a special contract or not is quite immaterial because, in my view, it merely emphasises, if necessary, or it merely contains, all the necessary ingredients of the ordinary case where a surgeon is retained to perform an operation of this kind. It is necessarily involved that he will perform the operation personally, and I think that it was necessarily involved in such a retainer that he would pay such subsequent visits as were necessary in the ordinary case."

[15] "The relationship between doctor and patient is contractual in origin, the doctor performing services in consideration for fees payable by the patient. The doctor, obedient to the high standards set by the medical profession impliedly contracts to act at all times in the best interests of the patient" *per* Lord Templeman in *Sidaway v Governors of Bethlem Royal Hospital* [1985] A.C. 871, 904B. The *ratio* of this decision (it is submitted) is contained in the speeches of Lord Diplock and Lord Bridge. The passage here quoted is obiter. See also *R. v Mid Glamorgan Family Health Services Authority Ex p. Martin* [1994] 5 Med. L.R. 383, 394–397 *per* Nourse L.J. (considering whether the common law confers a right of access to medical records).

[16] By contrast, it has been suggested that there is a positive duty to withdraw treatment where its continuance is not in the best interests of a patient who is incapable of making decisions about his treatment: see *Airedale N.H.S. Trust v Bland* [1993] A.C. 789, 819C *per* Butler-Sloss L.J., obiter. This suggestion was not adopted by the House of Lords: compare the dicta at 868H *per* Lord Goff, at 877A *per* Lord Lowry and at 884A *per* Lord Browne-Wilkinson. The decision is best understood as dealing with the lawfulness of treatment in the contexts of the law of trespass and the criminal law rather than as defining the scope of duties of care in contract or tort.

[17] See, e.g. *Eyre v Measday* [1986] 1 All E.R. 488: held that the defendant contracted to carry out a sterilisation operation; he did not contract to render the claimant absolutely sterile. Jones J. reached the same conclusion in *Grey v Webster* (1984) 14 D.L.R. (4th) 706 (New Brunswick).

treatment will be successful. In *Thake v Maurice*[18] it was held at first instance that the defendant surgeon had done precisely this, albeit unwittingly.[19] However, the Court of Appeal, by a majority, reversed this part of the decision.[20] It is clear that in the absence of extremely clear wording, a claim based on allegedly guaranteed results is likely to fail.[21]

(ii) *Statutory Duties*

Where a contract between a patient and a medical practitioner involves a transfer **13–005** of goods, there are statutory implied terms as to quality and fitness for purpose.[22] In *Samuels v Davis*[23] a dentist who agreed to make a denture for his patient was held in breach of an implied warranty as to fitness for purpose when the denture did not fit.

The question whether the statutory warranties are implied where treatment involves the supply of drugs, prosthetics or products of biological origin—such as blood products or donated semen used in artificial insemination procedures—has given rise to a number of cases.[24]

---

[18] [1986] Q.B. 644.

[19] "I am left in little doubt that the defendant did not intend to enter into a contract which absolutely guaranteed sterility; nor did he use any such word as 'guarantee'. But the test as to what the contract in fact was does not depend upon what the claimants or the defendant thought it meant, but upon what the court objectively determines that the words used meant . . . . I have been driven . . . to the conclusion that the contract was to make the male plaintiff irreversibly sterile": *ibid.* at 657D and 658C *per* Peter Pain J.

[20] [1986] Q.B. 644. The Court of Appeal applied broadly the same objective test as the trial judge, but on the evidence the majority came to the opposite conclusion. They attached considerable weight to "the common experience of mankind" that the results of medical treatment are uncertain. This reasoning is supported by A. Grubb in a case note: "Failed sterilisation: Is a Claim in Contract or Negligence a Guarantee of Success?" [1986] C.L.J. 196.

[21] In *Worster v City and Hackney HA The Times*, June 22, 1987 the claimant signed a consent form for a sterilisation operation which included the words "we understand that this means we can have no more children". Garland J. held that this was not a representation that the operation was bound to be successful.

[22] Supply of Goods and Services Act 1982, s.4, as amended by the Sale and Supply of Goods Act 1994.

[23] [1943] K.B. 526.

[24] Courts in Canada and Australia have considered whether a term of this nature can be implied at common law where medical treatment includes the supply of blood products and donated semen, so as to impose strict contractual liability when those substances are the conduit for infection by the HIV virus. In *ter Neuzen v Korn* (1995) 127 D.L.R. (4th) 577, Supreme Court of Canada, and *E v Australian Red Cross Society* (1991) 105 A.L.R. 53, Aus. Fed. CA; [1991] 2 Med.L.R. 303, the implication was rejected, on the basis that the supply of blood by transfusion was merely an incident of the provision of medical services. A separate contract for the supply of goods could not be identified. The same result was achieved in the Canadian case of *Pittman v Bain* (1994) 112 D.L.R. (4th) 257. Lang J. held that donated semen administered for the purposes of artificial insemination was not supplied subject to a warranty that it was free from disease. As a biological product (as opposed to manufactured equipment and supplies), the safety of donated semen was difficult to monitor. There are difficulties in applying this argument to blood products, many of which undergo some manufacturing process before use in treatment, and to drugs which are derived from biological sources (e.g. some hormones). The question in English law is a consideration of whether or not a warranty of fitness for purpose is to implied into the contract between the patient and the medical practitioner will be whether such products are "goods" within the meaning of the 1982 Act. However it is submitted that there is no good reason why "manufactured" or altered biological products should be treated any differently from other products of non-biological origin.

In the case of *Richardson v LRC Products Ltd*[25] the claimant became pregnant when a condom failed during sexual intercourse when the teat end became detached. She and her husband already had two children and considered their family to be complete, and she brought an action for damages in respect of the cost of the upbringing of the resulting third child. The claim was brought under the provisions of the Consumer Protection Act 1987 (which came into force on March 1, 1988) on the basis that (1) the failure of the condom had been caused by a weakening of the latex as a result of ozone damage before the condom left the factory, and (2) that the fact of the fracture of the condom indicated the existence of a defect for the purposes of the Act in any event. Ian Kennedy J. found that the claimant had not established that ozone damage to the condom had caused the failure, and that she had not established by the failure of the condom alone that there had been a defect in the condom for which the defendants were liable.

The case of *A v The National Blood Authority*[26] explored the defendants' liability for the supply of defective blood products under the Consumer Protection Act 1987 in detail. The claimants had been infected with Hepatitis C from March 1, 1988 to September 1, 1991 through transfusion of blood and blood products supplied by the defendants. Burton J. held that the infected blood was defective within the meaning of the Consumer Protection Act (and the Product Liability Directive 1985/374 by which the extent of the statutory obligation was defined), and that the defendants were liable to the claimants. After detailed analysis of the obligation on the defendants, Burton J. said:

> "I see no difficulty ... in an analysis which is akin to contract or warranty. Recital 6 [of the Product Liability Directive 1985/374] ('... the defectiveness of the product should be determined by reference not to its fitness for use but to the lack of safety which the public at large are entitled to expect') does not in my judgment counter-indicate an approach analogous to contract, but is concerned to emphasise that it is safety which is paramount".[27]

(iii) *Common Law Duty of Care*

13–006　It has long been accepted that a medical practitioner owes a duty to exercise reasonable skill and care in his treatment of a patient, even where no contract exists between them.[28] The medical practitioner assumes a duty of care to the

---

[25] [2000] Lloyd's Rep. Med. 280.

[26] [2001] Lloyd's Rep. Med. 187.

[27] *ibid.* at 218, para.66.

[28] For example in *Gladwell v Steggall* (1839) 5 Bing (N.C.) 733 the claimant, a 10-year-old girl, complained of a pain in her knee. Her father summoned the defendant, a clergyman who "also practised as a medical man". In this instance his treatment had disastrous consequences. Tindal C.J. ruled that the claimant was entitled to succeed despite the absence of any contract between them: "The declaration is not framed as in an action on a contract, but alleges a breach of duty arising out of the employment of the defendant by the plaintiff ... this is an action *ex delicto*." See also *Pippin v Sheppard* (1822) 11 Price 400; *Pimm v Roper* (1862) 2 F. & F. 783; *Edgar v Lamont*, 1914 S.C. 277. The duty of care arises out of the relationship of doctor and patient. The relationship and the duty are created when the doctor accepts the patient for treatment: see *Jones v Manchester Corp* [1952] 2 Q.B. 852, 867A *per* Denning J. In extremely limited circumstances, breach of the practitioner's duty might not be actionable. For example, in *Derry v Ministry of Defence* [1999] P.I.Q.R. P204 the Court of Appeal held that the M.O.D. was entitled to rely upon the statutory immunity from liability in tort conferred by s.10 of the Crown Proceedings Act 1947 to defeat a soldier's claim that a military doctor

patient, even when he renders his services gratuitously[29] or entirely voluntarily, for example by attending the victim of a road accident. The existence of a duty of care in such circumstances was confirmed obiter by the Court of Appeal in *Capital & Counties Plc v Hampshire County Council.*[30] However in giving the judgment of the Court, Stuart-Smith L.J. remarked that in such circumstances a doctor would be under no general obligation to provide assistance to such a victim and would only owe a duty of care to the victim should he choose to do so. Even then "if he volunteers his assistance his only duty as a matter of law is not to make the victim's condition worse". It is therefore important in a "rescue" case to analyse precisely what the medical practitioner has taken it upon himself to do. If he has continued to take some responsibility for an accident victim beyond initial first aid he may assume a duty of care which is no longer limited to not making matters worse.

An interesting extension of the scope of the doctor-patient relationship arises when the parents of children that have died give their consent to a post-mortem examination. Sufficient proximity and the fair, just and reasonableness test for imposing a duty of care was found to have been satisfied in *A & B v Leeds Teaching Hospital NHS Trust.*[31] The duty of care extended to giving the parents an explanation of the purpose of the post-mortem examination and what it entailed, including alerting the parents to the possibility of organs being retained. There had been a breach of this duty, but on only one of these three cases was the risk of psychiatric injury to the parents sufficiently probable to have been foreseen, resulting in a successful claim for damages for negligence.[32]

The duty of care in tort is additional to any contractual duties which may be **13–007** owed.[33] Where, therefore, a medical practitioner has been privately engaged by the claimant, it is normal to plead the claim both in contract and tort. Damage is a necessary element of the cause of action in tort. If a claimant shows that a doctor was negligent and in breach of contractual duties that were owed to him, but fails to prove that any loss or injury was caused thereby, then he will be entitled to recover nominal damages in respect of the breach of contract but nothing in respect of his claim in tort—in the latter case he will not be entitled to nominal damages and his claim will be dismissed.[34]

---

had negligently failed to diagnose and treat his carcinoma. The case is an oddity: following repeal by the Crown Proceedings (Armed Forces) Act 1987 the provisions of s.10 of the 1947 Act only remained in force in respect of acts or omissions committed before May 15, 1987.

[29] See, e.g. *Goode v Nash* (1979) 21 S.A.S.R. 419: defendant held liable for negligence, whilst giving his services gratuitously at a public screening for the detection of glaucoma.

[30] [1997] Q.B. 1004 at 1035D–E.

[31] [2004] EWHC 644, QB; [2005] Q.B. 506.

[32] The legislative control of use of human tissue is now contained within the Human Tissue Act 2004 which came into force on September 1, 2006. The Act and the regulations made thereunder provide for a new regime for the authorisation of taking, keeping and using human tissue to be licensed and supervised by the Human Tissue Authority. The Authority has already issued six Codes of Practice, approved by Parliament. Its website containing all the statutory and guidance material is at *www.hta.gov.uk.*

[33] The relationship between contractual and tortious duties has not generated the same amount of controversy in the case of doctors as it has in respect of other professions, no doubt because the damage caused is normally personal injury. The commencement of the relationship of doctor and private patient will depend upon the time and circumstances of formation of the contract.

[34] See, e.g. *Rich v Pierpont* (1862) 3 F. & F. 35; *Fish v Kapur* [1948] 2 All E.R. 176; *Barnett v Chelsea and Kensington Hospital Management Committee* [1969] 1 Q.B. 428; *Robinson v Post Office*

In light of the House of Lords' decision in *South Australia Asset Management Corp v York Montague Ltd*[35] it is important to avoid attempting to define the scope of a defendant's duty of care in a vacuum.[36] Problems as to the extent of a doctor's duty of care are more likely to arise in cases of advice than in treatment. But an example can be given: in an obstetric case the allegation was that the obstetrician should have diagnosed gestational diabetes in the mother, and that in consequence the baby should have been delivered not later than term. In fact the pregnancy was allowed to continue beyond term, and the baby was injured *in utero* at about 10 days after term by an unforeseen and unforeseeable ischaemic event which was unrelated to the gestational diabetes. The question is whether the doctor (on the assumption that he was negligent in failing to diagnose diabetes) should be liable for the injuries caused to the baby by the unrelated ischaemic event—which would have been avoided if the baby had been delivered at term. Such injuries should be outside the scope of the duty breached by the doctor, and he should not be liable.[37]

Thompson v Bradford[38] confirms that before a breach of duty will sound in damages it must be relevant to the risk that materialised and there must be a duty to prevent it. In that case, a two-month-old baby was taken to his general practitioner for polio immunisation. He was given the injection but contracted polio. It was found that this had occurred a boil on the child's buttock. At first instance the judge held that the defendant had not been negligent in advising that the vaccination should proceed. However he found that the general practitioner had been negligent in failing to inform the baby's parents that the abscess was unusual and that surgery might be needed, and that, if they had been informed of such matters, they would not have proceeded with the vaccine. The Court of Appeal allowed the appeal. They drew attention to the fact that the case against the defendant related to the child's contraction of polio and the only relevant breach of duty was one which would render the defendant liable for that state of affairs. However, it was common ground that the defendant could not have foreseen any increase in the risk of the baby contracting polio. Further, the failure to inform the child's parents that the abscess was unusual and might require surgery was also not a relevant breach of duty as no competent general practitioner would have contemplated any risk from that failure other than some further discomfort for the baby or an ineffective immunisation if there was a reaction to the vaccination. The case re-emphasises that it is not sufficient for a court to simply find that there is fault and then to move straight to the question of factual

---

[1974] 1 W.L.R. 1176. However, it would now be surprising to permit a claim to be litigated if nominal damages for breach of contract were all that were realistically being pursued. Unless a claimant could demonstrate that for some reason it was appropriate for such a case to be fought it is likely that it would be struck out under CPR 3.4 and/or the claimant would be likely to be heavily penalised on costs.

[35] [1997] A.C. 191.

[36] See page 213D for the example given by Lord Hoffmann in respect of a doctor. See also paragraphs 9–113 and 9–114 for an analysis of the decision.

[37] This decision was reached, obiter, in the unreported case of *O'Reilly v Whittington Hospital NHS Trust* by H.H.J. Mackay, sitting as a deputy judge of the QBD, on March 17, 2000. See also *Brown v Lewisham and North Southwark HA* [1999] 4 Lloyd's Rep. Med. 110 at 118.

[38] [2005] EWCA Civ 1439; (2006) Lloyd's Rep. Med. 95.

causation. The important question which also has to be asked and answered in the affirmative is whether there had been a relevant breach of duty and that depends on what the defendant can reasonably have foreseen as the consequence of any failure on his part.

The doctor as rescuer. Given that there is no obligation to rescue at common **13–008** law—only an obligation not to make the condition of a victim worse[39]—a doctor might be thought to be under no duty to attend and treat a person who has not hitherto been his patient, even in an emergency.[40] Despite the fact that such a duty has been held to arise in New South Wales,[41] it seems unlikely that in England there would be found to be any general duty to attend and treat a non-patient in an emergency.[42] Whether any duty arises, and the extent of such a duty, will depend upon detailed consideration of the particular factual circumstances of any case in which it is alleged and the application of ordinary "duty of care" principles.[43] In the context of a rescuing doctor the most important consideration will be the extent (if any) to which he has assumed responsibility for the victim, or is deemed to have done so.

The ambulance service. It has been held that the ambulance service owes a **13–009** duty to attend a member of the public within a reasonable time once four

---

[39] See para.13–006.

[40] In *Barnes v Crabtree*, *The Times*, November 1 and 2, 1955, it was conceded on behalf of the defendant general practitioner that his duty was to treat any person in an emergency. A general practitioner's contract with a health authority (formerly with a family health services authority, but now see the Health Authorities Act 1995, s.1) requires him on request to visit anyone in his practice area who is involved in an accident or an emergency: see the NHS (General Medical Services) Regulations 1992 (SI 1992/635).

[41] In *Lowns v Woods* (1996) Aust. Tort Reports 63,151 the Court of Appeal of New South Wales held that a doctor did owe a duty to attend a person in urgent need of medical care where a direct request had been made for him to do so and there was no reasonable impediment preventing him from attending. The claimant was an 11-year-old boy suffering a prolonged epileptic fit. His 14-year-old sister went on foot to a nearby surgery to summon a doctor. The defendant general practitioner refused to attend, allegedly advising that the child should be brought to his surgery. Applying the test of proximity outlined in *Sutherland Shire Council v Heyman* (1985) 157 C.L.R. 424, the majority in the Court of Appeal (Mahoney dissenting) found that there was sufficient proximity between the doctor and the claimant for a duty of care to arise. Relevant to the existence of such duty were (a) his physical proximity to the patient, (b) the "causal proximity" created by the information given to the doctor and his consequent understanding that this was a life-threatening emergency with dire likely consequences if he did not treat, and (c) the "circumstantial proximity". The last was created by the facts, inter alia, that the doctor was competent and equipped to treat, he was called upon at his surgery during surgery hours and no personal health or safety risk or existing disability prevented him from responding to the appeal for his professional services.

[42] In this regard see the obiter remarks of Stuart-Smith L.J. in *Capital & Counties Plc v Hampshire County Council* [1997] Q.B. 1004 at 1035D–E, at para.13–006 above. See also L. Haberfield, "*Lowns v Woods* and the duty to rescue" (1998) 6 Tort L.Rev 56 for a critical analysis of the majority judgments and their failure to reconcile the decisions reached with the established common law principle (and the exceptions to that principle) that there is no duty to rescue, R. Martin, "Further Thoughts on the Liability of Rescuers" (1998) 6 Tort L.Rev. 113 and the commentary on *Lowns v Woods* at (1998) 6 Med. L. Rev. 126.

[43] See Ch.2 at paras 2–013—2–053. See S. Smith, "Rights, Remedies and Normal Expectations in Tort and Contract" (1997) 113 L.Q.R. 426 for a further discussion on duties to assist.

qualifying conditions have been satisfied.[44] On the facts of that case, the London Ambulance Service was telephoned by the claimant's general practitioner and asked to send an ambulance to the claimant's home to take the claimant, who had suffered an asthma attack, to hospital "immediately". Despite two further telephone calls being made, and reassurances being given that an ambulance was on its way, no ambulance arrived for 40 minutes. Shortly before she arrived at hospital the claimant suffered a respiratory arrest leading to brain damage. The claim succeeded at first instance.[45]

The ambulance service appealed on the sole ground that it owed no duty of care to members of the public to provide an ambulance within a reasonable time in response to a 999 telephone call. The Court of Appeal dismissed the appeal, rejecting the defendant's argument that as a "rescuer" its only duty when responding to 999 telephone calls was not to add to damage already suffered by a claimant. In the only substantive judgment, Lord Woolf M.R. stated[46]:

> "Here what was being provided was a health service. In the case of health services under the Act of 1977 the conventional situation is that there is a duty of care. Why should the position of an ambulance staff be different from that of doctors or nurses? . . . The ambulance service is part of the health service. Its care function includes the transporting of patients to and from hospital when the use of an ambulance for this purpose is desirable. It is therefore appropriate to regard [the defendant] as providing services of the category provided by hospitals and not as providing services equivalent to those rendered by the police or fire service.[47]
>
> . . .
>
> The fact that it was a person who foreseeably would suffer further injuries by a delay in providing an ambulance, when there was no reason why it should not be provided, is important in establishing the necessary proximity and thus duty of care in this case. In other words, as there were no circumstances which made it unfair or unreasonable or unjust that liability should exist, there is no reason why there should not be liability if the arrival of the ambulance was delayed for no good reason."

13–010   **Communication of information.** A doctor will generally be found to owe a duty of care to his patient to avoid physical or psychological injury caused by his advice, treatment or diagnosis.[48] One area where there may still be some uncertainty concerns the communication of bad or distressing news to a claimant. In

---

[44] See *Kent v Griffiths* [2001] Q.B. 36. The four qualifying conditions were that (1) there had been an initiating call to the ambulance service, with sufficient information being provided to enable the ambulance service to understand the nature of the request for its services, (2) the ambulance service must have allocated an ambulance to meet the request, (3) the ambulance service must have been informed that time was of the essence, and (4) the ambulance must have failed to arrive at the casualty within a reasonable time: see at 453.

[45] [1999] Lloyd's Rep. Med. 424 *per* Turner J.

[46] [2001] Q.B. 36 at 52G–54B, paras 45 and 49.

[47] The Court of Appeal therefore distinguished its earlier decision in *Capital & Counties Plc v Hampshire County Council* [1997] Q.B. 1004; see para.13–006.

[48] See, e.g. *Kralj v McGrath and St Theresa's Hospital* [1986] 1 All E.R. 54 (damages for psychiatric illness caused by negligent treatment). In *M (a Minor) v Newham LBC*, reported *sub nom. X (Minors) v Bedfordshire County Council* [1995] 2 A.C. 633 a mother and child claimed damages for psychiatric illness occasioned by their separation as a result of the alleged negligence of a psychiatrist employed by the defendant authority. The claims were struck out on other grounds but in relation to recoverability for psychiatric injury Sir Thomas Bingham M.R. observed, "It would be little short of absurd if the child were held to be disentitled to claim damages for injury of the very type which the psychiatrist should have been exercising her skill to try and prevent", *ibid.* at 664C. The issue was

a number of cases defendant health authorities have conceded that they owed a duty to individuals to whom they were transmitting information to take reasonable care to ensure both that the information was correct and that it was communicated in a competent manner.[49] While no doubt justifiable on the peculiar facts of each case, these concessions have been the subject of academic criticism[50] and appear to have been inconsistent with the existing authorities. They should not be taken as necessarily implying that in all cases in which incorrect news is communicated to a patient or in which correct news is communicated to a patient in an improper manner, the communicating authority will be liable for psychological injury suffered by the receiving party. Each case will turn on its own facts and will no doubt depend upon the degree of proximity between the parties, the extent to which psychological harm is a reasonably foreseeable consequence of the authority's actions and whether it is fair, just and reasonable in the circumstances to impose a duty to care to prevent such harm.[51]

An example of a case in which a duty to avoid the risk of psychiatric harm was found to exist is *CJD Group B v The Medical Research Council*.[52] In that case each of the claimants had suffered from dwarfism as a child. For the purposes of a preliminary issue to determine the scope of the defendants' duty of care, it was assumed that each claimant had received injections of human growth hormone after July 1, 1977, despite the defendants being aware by that date that the injections carried a potentially lethal dose of the CJD agent. Each of the claimants had learned subsequently of the devastating and potentially fatal consequences of contracting CJD and, again for the purposes of the preliminary issue, it was assumed that each had a psychiatric injury derived from their awareness that "they may develop" CJD. In concluding that the defendants did

---

not mentioned by the House of Lords: *ibid*. In *Page v Smith* [1996] A.C. 155, a road traffic accident case, a majority in the House of Lords held that where personal injury to the claimant was foreseeable, liability would accrue for psychiatric injury even though physical injury did not occur.

[49] *AB v Tameside and Glossop HA* [1997] 8 Med. L.R. 91, *Allin v City & Hackney HA* [1996] 7 Med. L.R. 167. In *AB v Tameside and Glossop HA* a health worker employed by the defendant authority was diagnosed HIV positive. By letter the authority informed patients and former patients who had received obstetric treatment from the worker that there was a remote risk that they had been infected. Several of the individuals informed in this way claimed to have suffered psychological injury as a result of receiving the news in this way and alleged that the authority had acted negligently in failing to arrange for communication of the information via general practitioners or other health workers qualified to provide appropriate counselling. The authority conceded that it owed a duty to those to take care when communicating news of this nature. In *Allin* the claimant had been told that her newly born baby was dead when in fact it was still alive. She suffered psychiatric harm as a result of this inaccurate news. The defendant authority accepted that it was "under a duty of care in respect of statements of this sort made to the other".

[50] Dziobon and Tettenborn, "When the truth hurts: the incompetent transmission of distressing news" (1997) 13 P.N. 70; M. Jones, "Negligently inflicted psychiatric harm: is the word mightier than the deed?" (1997) 13 P.N. 111. For further comment see (1998) 6 Med. L. Rev. 338.

[51] See also *Bancroft v Harrogate HA* [1997] 8 Med. L.R. 398, a case in which the claimant sought to recover damages for psychiatric damage resulting, inter alia, from the manner in which a consultant had failed adequately to explain her condition to her, and failed adequately to explain to her a plan of treatment in which she could have confidence. The claim failed on the facts, but it seems to have been implicitly accepted that the claim made, if proved, would have justified an award of damages.

[52] [2000] Lloyd's Rep. Med. 161.

owe a duty to the claimants to avoid the risk of psychiatric injury from sub-sequent discovery of the risks that they faced, Morland J. found that:

"the defendants . . . could only have concluded that the risk of CJD becoming a reality could occur within a huge time span, that is within a year or two after injection or within many decades after injection . . .
. . . the evidence shows that the defendants not only should have reasonably foreseen the risk of psychiatric injury but did in fact do so."[53]

13–011   **Economic losses.** Whether a duty is owed to take care to avoid causing purely financial loss is also unclear. In one decision, such a claim failed on the grounds that the doctor's duty was limited to the sphere of medicine and that a doctor was not required to bear in mind possible third party liability to his patient save in special circumstances.[54] The decision might be understood as limiting the scope of a doctor's duty of care to exclude recovery for economic loss which is not consequent upon physical or psychological injury, save where the doctor knows or ought to know that reliance will be placed upon his negligent advice in a way which will directly affect the patient's economic fortunes.[55] In the latter circum-stances, it is difficult to see why liability for economic loss caused by negligent advice (or the performance of other medical services) should not now be founded upon the principle in *Hedley Byrne & Co Ltd v Heller & Partners Ltd*[56] at least

---

[53] [2000] Lloyd's Rep. Med. 161 at 166. See also *Farrell v Avon HA* [2001] Lloyd's Rep. Med. 458, in which an unemployed man with a history of drug and alcohol abuse was told on his arrival at hospital that his recently born and premature son had died an hour before. A dead baby was brought into the room and the claimant kissed it and cried over it. He was then told that a mistake had been made, and he was shown his baby son who was in fact still alive. It was held that he had suffered mild PTSD as a result of this, and that this was a foreseeable consequence of what had happened. He was awarded £10,000 in damages as a "primary victim". This is an example of a medical practitioner being held liable for the consequences of giving false information to someone who was not a patient. The reasoning appears to have been based on the fact that there was no other primary victim, the father was the only victim, and he was therefore a participant in the incident.

[54] See, e.g. *Stevens v Bermondsey & Southwark Group Hospital Management Committee* (1963) 107 S.J. 478 (*per* Paull J.): the claimant was involved in an accident caused by an employee of the borough council. He was treated at the defendant hospital and, on the strength of what he was told about the seriousness of his condition by the casualty officer, settled his claim against the council for a small sum. Subsequently learning that he had a serious congenital condition which had been activated by the accident, he alleged that, but for the casualty officer's negligence, he would have settled his claim for a larger sum. The action failed.

[55] See, e.g. *McGrath v Kiely & Powell* [1965] I.R. 497: the claimant recovered the difference between damages awarded to him in a third party action, and those which would have been awarded but for a negligent omission in a medical report prepared for the purposes of the litigation. See also *Kelly v Lundgard* (1996) 40 Alta. L.R (3d) 234 where Veit J. reached a similar result in the Alberta Queen's Bench Division. However, the author of a medical report prepared for disclosure in the third party action (rather than for the primary purpose of advising as to the merits of the action) will enjoy immunity from suit in respect of its contents: see *Landall v Dennis, Faulkner & Alsop* [1994] 5 Med. L.R. 268. Cited with approval by the Court of Appeal in *Stanton v Callaghan* [2000] Q.B. 75, which was followed in *Raiss v Paimano* [2001] P.N.L.R. 21. *cf.* the position of a doctor who provides a report in respect of his patient's injuries for use in negotiations before litigation has begun. Such a doctor will not enjoy immunity from suit as a witness since the report will not be preliminary to his giving evidence as an expert: *Hughes v Lloyd's Bank Plc* [1998] P.I.Q.R. P.98, CA.

[56] [1964] A.C. 465. *In Henderson v Merrett Syndicates* [1995] 2 A.C. 145, the House of Lords accepted that the principle applies to the performance of professional services generally and is not limited to the provision of advice or information.

where the claimant is the direct recipient of such advice or services and relies upon them.[57] However, such claims remain difficult ones to succeed in.[58]

The most recent consideration of the circumstances in which a duty to avoid causing financial loss might arise occurred in *Phelps v Hillingdon LBC*.[59] In that case educational psychologists employed by the defendant had assessed the claimants at school so as to advise the defendant as to the educational needs of each. The defendant had failed to diagnose that three of the claimants suffered from dyslexia. They had therefore received no special schooling. The claimants alleged that such failure had been negligent and had led to them suffering a lack of educational progress with inter alia a consequent reduction in their earning potential in later life. The first claimant succeeded in demonstrating that a duty of care was owed to her by the defendant to take reasonable care when carrying out an educational assessment of her needs, and that a reduction in her level of achievement and a loss of employment and wages was a reasonably foreseeable consequence of that duty being breached. The House of Lords expressly rejected the defendant's argument that any duty owed by its educational psychologists could be owed to them alone.[60]

---

[57] See *Goodwill v British Pregnancy Advisory Service* [1996] 2 All E.R. 161, discussed at para.13–018 below.

[58] In *Kapfunde v Abbey National Plc and another* [1999] Lloyd's Rep. Med. 48, CA the claimant had applied for employment with the first defendant and had completed a medical questionnaire in which she disclosed a history of sickle-cell anaemia. The defendant declined to employ the claimant after its part-time occupational health adviser, the second defendant, had assessed the claimant as being unsuitable for employment on the grounds that her medical history made her likely to have an above-average level of absences from work. The claimant alleged that the second defendant's conclusions were negligent and brought an action seeking damages for economic loss. The claim failed. While concluding that "financial loss is clearly foreseeable if a careless error in the doctor's assessment leads to the loss of an opportunity of employment" (p.56) Millett L.J. (with whom Hutchison L.J. agreed) confirmed that "this is not enough". Such duties that were owed by the defendant's adviser were owed to the defendant alone; the adviser had assumed no responsibility to the claimant to take care to ensure that his conclusions were accurate. In reaching this conclusion the Court of Appeal disapproved the decision of Robert Owen Q.C. in *Baker v Kaye* [1997] I.R.L.R. 219 which was to the effect that a doctor who had made a pre-employment assessment of a claimant, which included a physical examination and the taking of blood samples, owed him a duty of care. The claimant's claim for economic loss also failed in *R. v Croydon Health Authority* [1998] Lloyd's Rep. Med 44. In that case the claimant had undergone a pre-employment chest X-ray which ought to have alerted the radiologist to a significant abnormality from which a diagnosis of primary pulmonary hypertension (PPH) would have been made. It was common ground that pregnancy presents a threat to life in a PPH sufferer. The claimant's evidence was that, had she received such a diagnosis and been properly advised, she would at all costs have avoided becoming pregnant. Instead, the radiologist negligently passed the claimant as being fit for work. The claimant was then employed by the defendant Health Authority and subsequently became pregnant and gave birth to a healthy child, although excessive bleeding led to her undergoing a hysterectomy. She sought to recover damages for inter alia the costs of raising the child. The Court of Appeal concluded that the scope of the duty owed by the radiologist stopped short of "responsibility for the consequences of the decision, by the claimant and her husband, that she should become pregnant" (p.60). The cases of wrongful conception concerning the recoverability of the costs of bringing up an unwanted child have been decided on the basis that this aspect of the loss claimed is purely economic loss. See paragraph 13–158 and onwards below.

[59] [2000] 3 W.L.R. 776.

[60] Lord Slynn at 791C, Lord Nicholls at 803E-G, Lord Clyde at 811H. Applied by Buckley J. in *A&B v Essex County Council* [2002] EWHC 2707, reported at [2003] P.I.Q.R. P21, in finding that a duty was owed by the defendant authority to prospective adoptive parents for providing relevant information about the prospective adoptive child. The Court of Appeal has upheld this decision on appeal: reported at [2004] 1 W.L.R. 1881.

13–012   **Fiduciary duties.** The relationship of doctor and patient is capable of being characterised as a fiduciary relationship.[61] However, the case of *Bristol & West Plc v Mothew*[62] now makes clear that a claim for breach of a fiduciary duty will not arise merely because a defendant who stands in a fiduciary relationship to a claimant has breached a duty of care at common law that he owes to the claimant. Such a claim will only arise when the duty breached can truly be characterised as a fiduciary duty.[63]

A presumption of undue influence may unravel dispositions of property or finance in favour of a doctor who has abused the confidence of his patient.[64] It has been suggested that further development of the concept of fiduciary duties owed by doctors would be a useful complement to the law of negligence, particularly where questions arise as to the extent of the doctor's duty to disclose the risks and implications of proposed treatment, allowing the imposition of more extensive duties than would currently arise in contract or tort.[65] This analysis at one time gained limited support in Canada, where the Supreme Court has founded entitlement to access to medical records upon the fiduciary nature of the doctor-patient relationship[66] and has treated sexual exploitation of a patient by a doctor as breach of fiduciary duty[67] before being rejected in favour of a more traditional approach to fiduciary duty by McLachlin J. in *Smith v Arndt*.[68] However, the analysis has been rejected by the High Court of Australia in the context of a claim for access to medical records.[69]

The nature and extent of a doctor's fiduciary obligations in a range of factual situations has yet to be fully explored in the English courts. The analysis did not find favour in *Sidaway v Governors of Bethlem Royal Hospital*,[70] a decision concerning the extent of the duty to warn of the risks and implications of proposed treatment. In *R. v Mid Glamorgan Family Health Services Authority Ex*

---

[61] *Barclays Bank Plc v O'Brien* [1994] 1 A.C. 180, 189G *per* Lord Browne-Wilkinson.
[62] [1998] Ch. 1, CA.
[63] For the facts of *Bristol & West Plc v Mothew* and for further discussion see Ch.10, para.10–023 above.
[64] See *Sidaway v Governors of Bethlem Royal Hospital* [1984] Q.B. 498, 515D–G *per* Dunn L.J. and the authority there cited.
[65] See A. Grubb, "The Doctor as Fiduciary" (1994) C.L.P. 311. *cf.* "The Fiduciary Relationship— Doctors and Patients" in *Wrongs and Remedies in the Twenty-First Century* (P. Birks, edn, 1996) where Professor Kennedy argues that the fiduciary relationship in this context is a "false dawn". See also P. Bartlett, "Doctors as Fiduciaries: Equitable Regulation of the Doctor-Patient Relationship" (1997) 5 Med. L. Rev. 193.
[66] *McInerney v MacDonald* (1992) 93 D.L.R. (4th) 415 (and see commentary at (1993) 1 Med. L.Rev. 126). But a duty of disclosure of risks which is wider than that imposed in English law has been accepted in Canada without recourse to the fiduciary analysis: see *Reibl v Hughes* (1980) 114 D.L.R. (3d) 1. In *Arndt v Smith* [1996] 7 Med. L. R. 108, British Columbia CA, Lambert J.A. relied on a fiduciary analysis in deciding whether damage was caused by breach of a doctor's duty of disclosure.
[67] *Norberg v Wynrib* (1992) 92 D.L.R. (4th) 449; *Taylor v McGillivray* (1993) 110 D.L.R. (4th) 64, New Brunswick Court of Queen's Bench (and commentary at (1995) 3 Med. L. Rev. 108).
[68] (1997) 148 D.L.R. (4th) 48 at 63b–d.
[69] *Breen v Williams* (1996) 138 A.L.R. 259, declining to follow *McInerney v MacDonald* (above). Again, the wide duty to disclose which exists in Australian law rests on common law principles only: see *Rogers v Whitaker* [1993] 4 Med. L.R. 79, High Court of Australia.
[70] See [1984] Q.B. 493, CA, *per* Browne-Wilkinson L.J. at 518F–519E, Dunn L.J. at 515D–G and [1985] 1 A.C. 871, HL, *per* Lord Scarman at 884B.

p. Martin[71] the claimant asserted an entitlement at common law to access to his medical records, which were made before the Access to Health Records Act 1990 came into force.[72] The claimant argued that the health authority owed him a fiduciary duty to disclose to him all the information contained in his medical records. Ruling that there was no common law right to access, Popplewell J. specifically rejected the argument that the doctor-patient relationship was to be regarded as giving rise to equitable obligations for these purposes.[73]

(b) *Duties to Third Parties*

The general principles governing liability to third parties are stated above.[74]　**13–013** There is little authority concerning the application of those principles to medical practitioners and no unifying principle emerges therefrom.

Usually, a doctor's negligence will not cause personal injury to anyone other than his patient. However, in one Canadian case[75] the defendant removed the patient's only kidney during an operation, believing it to be an ovarian cyst. The patient's father gave one of his kidneys in an unsuccessful attempt to save her life. The defendant was held liable for the injury suffered by the father. It seems likely that an English court would adopt the same approach to this situation.

(i) *The "Nervous Shock" Cases*

In *McLoughlin v O'Brian*[76] the House of Lords recognised a right of action for　**13–014** psychiatric illness caused to a near relative who witnessed the suffering of family members injured in a violent road accident caused by the defendant's negligence, but did not witness the accident itself. This is the so-called "immediate aftermath" extension to the established principle of liability for foreseeable psychiatric illness suffered by a near relative who witnesses the negligent and traumatic infliction of injury or death.

The cases of *Alcock v Chief Constable of South Yorkshire Police*[77] and *Frost v Chief Constable of South Yorkshire Police*[78] both arose out of the Hillsborough football stadium disaster in 1989, when 95 people died and hundreds were injured as a result of overcrowding on a terrace.[79] In *Alcock* the claimants were relatives of those on the terrace, but none was a spouse or parent. Each of the

---

[71] [1994] 5 Med. L.R. 383. The decision was upheld on appeal, but without mention of the fiduciary analysis: [1995] 1 W.L.R. 110.

[72] On November 1, 1991. The Act applies only to records made after that date.

[73] [1994] 5 Med. L.R. 383, 391.

[74] See Ch.2, paras. 2–109–2–115, above. For a detailed discussion of this topic, including a review of the United States authorities, see K. C. de Haan, "My Patient's Keeper? The Liability of Medical Practitioners for Negligent Injury to Third Parties" (1986) 2 P.N. 86. See also paras 12–043 to 12–054 below.

[75] *Urbanski v Patel* (1978) 84 D.L.R. (3d) 650.

[76] [1983] 1 A.C. 410. For a full discussion of liability for nervous shock, see *Clerk & Lindsell on Torts* (19th edn), paras 7–62 to 7–83.

[77] [1992] 1 A.C. 310, HL.

[78] [1999] 2 A.C. 455, HL.

[79] For a summary of the categories of primary victims see Brooke L.J. in *Hunter v British Coal* [1999] Q.B. 140.

claimants had been present at the stadium, but remote from the terrace, or had witnessed the event live on television or in later news broadcasts. In *Frost* the claimants were police officers who had tended victims of the tragedy, either at the stadium itself or at a hospital to where bodies had subsequently been taken. Each of the claimants claimed damages against the police for nervous shock.

In *Alcock* the House of Lords held that each of the claimants was foreseeably injured, but each failed to satisfy the test of proximity in one or more of the three required respects, namely, (i) proximity of familial or analogous tie, and propinquity in (ii) time and (iii) space to the horrifying event or its immediate aftermath. In addition, the illness complained of had to be caused by "shock".[80]

13–015   In *Frost* once again, each of the claimants was a "secondary victim".[81] They were unable to demonstrate either that they had been at risk of physical injury or that they had reasonably perceived themselves to be at risk of physical injury. They did not satisfy the conditions necessary to found a claim for psychiatric injury and the claims therefore failed. *Alcock* and *Frost* were considered and applied in *W v Essex County Council*.[82] The claimants fostered children placed with them by the defendant. They had received an assurance that none of the children would be known sexual abusers. In fact one of the foster children was a known sexual abuser and, in the period during which he was placed with the claimants, he sexually abused the claimants' own children. The claimants alleged that they had suffered psychiatric illness upon learning that their own children had been abused. The House of Lords allowed the claimants' appeal and refused to strike out the claim, concluding that without a full investigation of the facts it would not be possible to determine (i) whether the claimants were primary or secondary victims, or (ii) the scope of the duty of care that was owed to them by the defendants.

A major difficulty in establishing liability for nervous shock in clinical negligence cases is the need to show that the claimant's psychiatric damage was caused by shock, that is, the sudden and direct appreciation of the horrifying event to which the breach of duty gives rise, as opposed to the stress, anxiety and grief which naturally attend the terminal illness or death of a loved one, or the

---

[80] In *Page v Smith* [1996] A.C. 155, 189 Lord Lloyd described these restrictions on a right to recover damages for psychiatric injury as "control mechanisms", intended to keep liability within what was regarded as acceptable bounds. The control mechanisms set out in *Alcock* were considered and approved by the New Zealand Court of Appeal in the context of a clinical negligence claim in *van Soest v Residual Health Management Unit* [2000] 1 N.Z.L.R. 179. The claimants were close relatives of individuals who had died during surgery carried out by the defendant. Each sued inter alia for mental suffering caused upon learning of their relatives' deaths. The defendant successfully struck out the claims since, even had the claimants been able to demonstrate that mental suffering had been a reasonably foreseeable consequence of the defendant's negligence towards their relatives, they still needed to demonstrate (i) a physical and temporal proximity to the accident, and (ii) that their mental suffering amounted to a recognisable psychiatric disorder or illness. They failed to show this.

[81] The claimants attempted to distinguish themselves from the bereaved relatives who had witnessed the tragedy at the stadium, and so argue that they were in fact primary victims, on the bases that (i) their attendance at the stadium had been pursuant to contracts of employment with the defendant, and/ or (ii) they ought to be classified as "rescuers" by virtue of their actions. Neither argument met with any success.

[82] [2000] 2 W.L.R. 601, HL.

gradual or even retrospective realisation of events.[83] Each case will turn very much on its own facts, although the suddenness with which the claimant learns of or perceives events, and the nature of the event will always be key factors.[84] Psychiatric illness on the part of a claimant resulting from a fear of what might have happened to another, or from what the claimant imagines might have happened to another, will not found a claim.[85]

---

[83] *Julia Ward v. Leeds Teaching Hospitals NHS Trust* [2004] EWHC 2106, QB, reported at [2004] Lloyd's Rep. Med. 530, is an example of a case where the judge held that the mother's illness was caused by the death of her daughter (itself caused by a vascular complication to surgery for wisdom teeth removal) and not any shocking or horrifying events at the hospital or mortuary. The decision turned on the lack of supportive expert psychiatric evidence. See also *Reilly v Merseyside HA* [1995] 6 Med. L.R. 246, CA, where claimants who suffered apprehension and fear while trapped in a lift by reason of the health authority's negligence could not recover under this principle. They had suffered "normal human emotions" and not a recognised psychiatric illness.

[84] In *Taylor v Somerset HA* [1993] 4 Med. L.R. 34 the defendants negligently failed to diagnose and treat the claimant's husband's heart condition, with the result that he suffered a fatal heart attack at work. Some 35 minutes after his death, the claimant viewed her husband's body in the hospital mortuary, partly because she refused to believe the doctor who told her that he was dead. Her action for damages for psychiatric injury was dismissed. Auld J. held that there was no traumatic event caused by the health authority's negligence which immediately caused injury to the claimant's husband. The heart attack was merely the final consequence of the gradual deterioration in his condition which the defendant had negligently failed to arrest. If there was no qualifying event, there could be no "immediate aftermath". Further, even were the heart attack to be treated as a qualifying event, the claimant did not see her husband's body soon enough after his death to convey to her the shock of the attack as well as its consequence. Similarly, the body bore no marks which would suggest to her the circumstances of death.

In *Sion v Hampstead HA* [1994] 5 Med. L.R. 170 the Court of Appeal struck out as disclosing no reasonable cause of action the claim of a father who suffered psychiatric damage as a result of witnessing over some two weeks the deterioration and consequent death (allegedly due to medical negligence) of his adult son, who had been injured in a road accident. The Court held that the claim described causation of illness by the claimant's gradual realisation of the seriousness of his son's condition over the two weeks before death and of the possibility of medical negligence after the inquest, as well as his natural attendant grief, rather than by any sudden and violent appreciation of events. It is noteworthy that, by contrast with the approach of Auld J. in *Taylor v Somerset HA*, Peter Gibson L.J. made clear that there need be no external traumatic event in such cases, the requirements of suddenness and violence attaching to the impact of the awareness of what has happened upon the claimant's mind, rather than to the relevant events themselves. By contrast in *Tredget v Bexley HA* [1994] 5 Med. L.R. 178 (Central London County Court) both parents of a child who died of the effects of asphyxiation two and a half days after its negligently mismanaged birth suffered a psychiatric grief reaction as a result of their experiences during the delivery, the child's death and its intervening illness. It was found that the delivery itself (at which both parents were present, although the mother's awareness was diminished) was a sufficiently traumatic event to have caused the psychiatric damage suffered by the parents. The judge further held that the course of events from the onset of labour to the child's death, a period of some 48 hours, could not realistically be treated as other than a single qualifying event. *Sion v Hampstead HA* was distinguished on the facts by the greater degree of involvement in and the immediacy of the parents to the birth of the child in *Tredget*.

In *Powell v Boladz* [1998] Lloyd's Rep. Med. 116 the defendant failed to diagnose a rare disease in the claimant's child, who later died as a result. It was alleged that one of the general practitioners then removed and falsified medical records pertaining to the death. The claimant alleged that this substitution of false documents had caused him to suffer psychiatric illness. The Court of Appeal struck out the claim. No duty of care was owed to the claimant in such circumstances. In any event, psychiatric injury was found not to be a foreseeable consequence of falsifying the records. For criticism of this decision see (1998) 6 Med. L. Rev. 112.

[85] *Palmer v Tees HA* [1999] Lloyd's Rep. Med. 350.

13–016   An example of a successful claim is *Walters v North Glamorgan NHS Trust*.[86] The claimant was the mother of a 10-month-old boy whose acute hepatic failure the defendants had failed to diagnose and treat. She was in his room when he suffered a major and dramatic epileptic seizure, leading to a coma and catastrophic brain damage. Some 36 hours later the baby was on a life support machine and the claimant was advised that her son's brain was so severely damaged that he would have no quality of life if he survived, and the life support machine was turned off, and he died in her arms. She was not a primary victim, but it was held that the period of 36 hours following the fit was a horrifying event, and the claimant recovered £20,000 as damages for her pathological grief reaction. The decision was upheld on appeal to the Court of Appeal.[87]

(ii) *Duty to Prevent Injury to Third Parties*

13–017   Where the practitioner is treating a patient with an infectious disease at his request, he owes a duty of care to persons whom he should foresee are likely to be infected.[88] Injury may foreseeably be caused to third parties unless the patient is warned to take suitable precautions, in which case a duty may be owed to the third party to advise the patient accordingly. In a Canadian case[89] the patient contracted the HIV virus through a blood transfusion. His general practitioner failed to inform him that he had been at risk of infection and did not advise him or his wife to take precautions against transmission of the virus to her through sexual contact. The doctor was held liable to the wife when she established that she had caught the virus from her husband and that, had he been warned, they would have taken precautions which would have protected her from infection.[90]

---

[86] [2002] Lloyd's Rep. Med. 227; [2003] P.I.Q.R. P2.

[87] [2002] EWCA Civ 1792 reported at [2003] P.I.Q.R. P16; [2003] Lloyd's Rep. Med. 49: where a series of events amounts to an inexorable progression from an accident, and the appreciation of the event or series of events is sudden, and the experience can be accurately described as horrifying, damages for nervous shock may be recovered. *Walters* was applied in *Atkinson v Seghal* [2003] EWCA Civ 697 reported at [2003] Lloyd's Rep. Med. 285, in which the claimant mother's visit to a mortuary two hours after a fatal road accident in which her daughter was killed was within the "immediate aftermath" of the accident. The claimant's extreme reaction to her daughter's death and her psychiatric condition was not solely due to being told of the accident, but also due to the mortuary visit when she saw and cradled her daughter's disfigured body.

[88] *Evans v Liverpool Corp* [1906] 1 K.B. 160 (where the defendants escaped liability not because they owed a duty to no one other than their patients, but because they were not vicariously responsible for the negligence of their visiting physician). See also *X and Y v Pal* (1991) 23 N.S.W.L.R. 26, [1992] 3 Med. L.R. 195, New South Wales Court of Appeal: negligent exposure of foetus to congenital syphilis in the womb. Held not causative of claimant's disfigurement and mental retardation.

[89] *Pittman Estate v Bain* (1994) 112 D.L.R. (4th) 257, Ontario High Court.

[90] The Court of Appeal of California found a duty of care to warn the patient so as to prevent infection of a third party in *Reisner v Regents of the University of California* 37 Cal. Rptr. 2d 518 (1995). The claimant was infected with the HIV virus following a sexual relationship with JL. JL had been negligently infected with the HIV virus following a blood transfusion carried out by the defendant several years earlier when she was 12 years old. The defendant knew that JL had been infected with the HIV virus but had elected not to divulge the information to her or her family. The California Court of Appeal found little difficulty in concluding that (i) the defendant owed a duty of care to warn JL and her family that JL was HIV positive (ii) JL and/or her family would in all probability have warned the claimant had they been aware that she was HIV positive; and (iii) the claimant was a foreseeable victim of the defendant's negligence even though not readily identifiable at the time of the defendant's negligence.

By analogy with the infection cases, it is suggested that a duty would be owed to both patient and third parties to warn a patient not to undertake an activity which would be hazardous to third parties by reason of debilitating effects of his condition or treatment. Suppose that the patient is an epileptic of whom it is known that his condition is not reliably controlled by medication and that his occupation involves driving heavy goods vehicles. It might reasonably be expected that his doctor would be found to owe a duty of care to other road users to warn the patient not to drive commercial vehicles.[91] The risk of personal injury or death to other road users in the event that the patient suffered a seizure while driving would be a clearly foreseeable result of failure to advise him in appropriate terms. Provided that the patient should have been regarded as likely to heed such a warning, it is arguable that a duty of care would arise on the principle of *Donoghue v Stevenson.*[92]

The limits of any such duty are likely to be extremely closely circumscribed. As illustrated by the Court of Appeal decision in *Goodwill v British Pregnancy Advisory Service.*[93] The defendants arranged a vasectomy operation for one M in November 1984 and advised him in April 1985 that since the operation had been successful, he need not use contraception in future. In 1988, M began a sexual relationship with the claimant and no contraception was used. The claimant became pregnant by M and gave birth to a daughter. She brought an action against the defendants for the costs associated with the delivery and upbringing of the child, which costs she alleged were caused by her reliance upon the defendant's negligent representations to M in 1985.[94] The Court of Appeal held that the defendant owed no duty of care to the claimant in advising M, for it was not and could not reasonably be alleged that the defendant knew or ought to have known that their advice to M was likely to be acted upon by the claimant. In 1985, she was one of an indeterminately large class of women who might be a future sexual partner of M. Accordingly, there was insufficient proximity between the parties to justify the imposition of a duty in favour of the claimant. Although the class of non-patients to whom a doctor advising in these circumstances would owe a duty did not arise for decision in this case, the suggestion was that this was limited to a current sexual partner of the patient of whom the doctor is aware and who is the direct recipient of his advice. However, it should be noted that the claim in *Goodwill* was, in substance and as pleaded, a claim

13–018

---

[91] A duty was found on similar facts to those here suggested in *Spillane v Wasserman* (1992) 13 C.C.L.T. 267, Ontario High Court: doctors treating an epileptic were held liable to a cyclist who was killed when the patient drove a heavy goods vehicle through a red traffic light during an epileptic fit. The doctors had failed to warn him not to drive and had failed to report his condition to the appropriate licensing authority.

[92] [1932] A.C. 562.

[93] [1996] 1 W.L.R. 1397.

[94] The claimant's claim was advanced as a justifiable increment to existing categories of negligence under the principle in *Hedley Byrne v Heller* [1965] A.C. 465 but was found wanting when analysed by reference to the criteria for proximity elaborated by Lord Oliver in *Caparo Industries Plc v Dickman* [1990] 2 A.C. 605 at 638. See Ch.2, para.2–031, above. In addition to the features mentioned in the text, the fact that the claimant had consulted her own doctor about the need for contraception was held to amount to foreseeable independent enquiry which rendered her reliance upon the defendant's advice to M unforeseeable: see at 169E–G *per* Peter Gibson L.J. and at 170E–G *per* Thorpe L.J. The claim was struck out.

wholly for financial loss.[95] The imposition of a duty of care to prevent pure economic loss is subject to far more stringent requirements than apply when a duty to guard against the infliction of personal injury is alleged.[96]

13–019   A related area is the potential liability of psychiatrists to persons foreseeably injured by patients under their care.[97] If a psychiatrist negligently permits the release of a dangerous patient detained under the Mental Health Act 1983 or pursuant to the order of the court, and the patient injures a third party, that third party should have a claim.[98] The position is more difficult where a psychiatrist is treating a voluntary patient, and has reason to believe that he might commit a crime.[99]

In *Palmer v Tees HA*[1] the claimant's daughter was abducted, abused and murdered by A. The claimant suffered psychiatric injury upon learning of her daughter's disappearance and subsequent violent death. A had previously been under the defendants' care as a psychiatric patient and (it was alleged) had confessed to having sexual feelings towards children and to an intention to murder a child upon his discharge. It was said by the claimant that the defendants ought to have diagnosed that there was a substantial risk that A would sexually abuse children and treated him accordingly. The claimant commenced proceedings on her own behalf and on behalf of her daughter's estate. The Court of Appeal struck out both claims. The claimant's daughter was not an identifiable victim and there was an insufficient degree of proximity between her and the defendants.[2]

However, despite the decision in *Palmer* there would be nothing to prevent a court finding that a duty of care exists in a case where sufficient proximity between defendant and victim existed (for example where the defendant's patient

---

[95] In *Walkin v South Manchester HA* [1995] 1 W.L.R. 1543, the Court of Appeal held that an unwanted conception is a species of personal injury within the meaning of s.11 of the Limitation Act 1980. It was not argued that the claim in *Goodwill* should be regarded in this light, however, and that case proceeded on the basis that the claim was for financial loss only.

[96] See Ch.2, paras 2–024—2–025, above.

[97] In the interesting case of *Broadmoor Special Hospital Authority v Robinson* [2000] Q.B. 775, CA the claimant hospital unsuccessfully sought injunctions to restrain publication of a book written by the defendant, who had been convicted of manslaughter and ordered to be detained in a special hospital. The claimant considered that if the book was published it would be likely to expose the defendant to risk of assault, undermine his mental state and cause distress to other patients and his victim's family. The Court of Appeal determined, by a majority, that it had jurisdiction to grant the injunctions sought but declined to do so as a matter of discretion. The Court held that the hospital authority could not bring proceedings to protect other patients' rights to privacy or confidence or to prevent distress to the victim's family unless the conduct complained of interfered with the performance of the authority's public responsibilities.

[98] *Holgate v Lancashire Mental Hospitals Board, Gill and Robertson* [1937] 4 All E.R. 19; *Dorset Yacht Co Ltd v Home Office* [1970] A.C. 1004. See also *Partington v Wandsworth LBC* [1989] C.L.Y. 2563. In *Reid v Secretary of State for Scotland* [1999] 2 A.C. 512 Lord Clyde referred at 532B–C to the interests of members of the public who may "reasonably require the assurance that there is no threat to the peaceful enjoyment of their own lives through the release of someone who has been suffering some form of mental disorder."

[99] The public policy objections to an action against the police by a victim of crime, discussed by the House of Lords in *Hill v Chief Constable of West Yorkshire* [1989] A.C. 53, would seem not to apply.

[1] [1999] Lloyd's Rep. Med. 351, CA.

[2] See Stuart-Smith L.J. at 359. For commentary on *Palmer* see [1999] Lloyd's Rep. Med. 364 and [1999] Med. L. Rev. 331.

had threatened to harm a particular victim or a victim from an identifiable class), essentially on the basis of *Dorset Yacht Co Ltd v Home Office*.[3] Some support for this proposition can be derived from the first instance judgment of Gage J. in *Palmer*, where the judge stated:

> " . . . in holding, as I do, that the defendants owed no duty of care to Rosie, I am not to be taken as holding that health authorities have any general immunity from suit. If the claimant's pleaded case had shown that there existed some distinctive feature or characteristic which demonstrated that Rosie was at some special risk from A other than the general risk to other young female members of the general public, I would have found that the requirement of proximity existed. Subject of course to arguments on fairness, justice and reasonableness in certain circumstances a court might then hold that a duty of care existed."[4]

(iii) *Unborn Children*

Where a medical practitioner is treating a pregnant woman, he owes a duty of **13–020** care to the unborn child. If, as a result of his negligent treatment, the child is born disabled, then, subject to the restrictions set out in s.1 of the Congenital Disabilities (Civil Liability) Act 1976, he may be liable to the child. If negligent treatment of either parent before conception causes a child to the born disabled, then, subject to s.1(4) of the Act, again the doctor may be liable to the child. Section 1A of the Congenital Disabilities (Civil Liability) Act 1976 was added by s.44 of the Human Fertilisation and Embryology Act 1990. This in effect extends the provisions of s.1 to children born as a result of artificial insemination. Subject to restrictions set out, such children can sue for disabilities caused by negligence prior to the artificial insemination. In respect of children born before the 1976 Act came into force, the position is governed by the common law.[5] The medical practitioner owes a "potential" or "contingent" duty of care to the unborn child, which vests at birth. If he negligently damages the embryo in his patient's womb, causing the baby to be born injured, the cause of action in negligence crystallises at birth.[6] In *X and Y v Pal*[7] the New South Wales Court of Appeal held that an

---

[3] [1970] A.C. 1004. In *Palmer* Stuart-Smith L.J. remarked obiter that the dicta from *Dorset Yacht Co v Home Office* were relevant to a consideration of whether it was just, fair and reasonable to impose a duty of care and not to the question of proximity.

[4] [1998] Lloyd's Rep. Med. 447 at 461. For further analysis of *Palmer* see M. Jones, "Liability for psychiatric patients: setting the boundaries" [2000] P.N. 3.

[5] At (1994) 10 P.N. 94, J. Murphy argues that the meaning of "disability" under the 1976 Act creates a residual role for common law claims for children born after 1976.

[6] At birth, the damage required to complete the cause of action accrues and the child acquires legal personality to sue: *Burton v Islington HA* [1993] Q.B. 204, CA. The principle has been accepted elsewhere: see *Hamilton v Fife Health Board* [1993] 4 Med. L.R. 201, Ct of Sess.; *Montreal Tramways v Leveille* [1933] 4 D.L.R. 337, Supreme Court of Canada. In *Cherry v Borsman* (1992) 94 D.L.R. (4th) 487, the British Columbia Court of Appeal held that if, in breach of duty to the mother, an abortion is negligently performed and the foetus preserved, the medical practitioner owes a duty of care to the foetus not to injure it. See also *Howarth v Adey* [1996] 2 V.R. 535, Court of Appeal of Victoria (duty to warn mother of need for Caesarean section in interests of unborn baby). See further A. Whitfield, "Common Law Duties to Unborn Children" (1993) 1 Med. L. Rev. 29.

[7] (1991) 23 N.S.W.L.R. 26, [1992] 3 Med. L.R. 195, (and see commentary at (1993) 1 Med. L. Rev. 119). This part of the claim failed because the injuries complained of were not caused by the syphilis. The difficulties of proving causation in a case where pre-conception injury is alleged are illustrated by *Reay v British Nuclear Fuels* [1994] 5 Med. L.R. 1, where the claimants failed to prove that paternal pre-conception irradiation was a material contributory cause of their cancers.

obstetrician and gynaecologist treating a woman owes a duty of care at common law to her future child, which need not have been conceived at the time of the treatment. Doctors consulted by X before and during her pregnancy negligently failed to test her for syphilis, with the result that Y was infected in *utero*.

(iv) *"Wrongful Life"*

13–021 A disabled child has no right of action either under the Act or at common law for "wrongful life": he cannot claim damages on the basis that, although his disabilities were unavoidable, the defendant was negligent in failing to ascertain his condition and recommend an abortion.[8]

(c) *The Standard of Skill and Care*

13–022 **The general principle.** Whether he is sued in contract or tort, the medical practitioner is not obliged to achieve success in every case that he treats.[9] His

---

[8] *McKay v Essex AHA* [1982] 1 Q.B. 1166. One of the claims advanced in that case was that if the defendants had not been negligent the mother (who had caught German measles while she was pregnant) would have had an abortion. The Court of Appeal held that this part of the child's claim should be struck out on grounds of public policy. This result was in line with a number of American decisions. The relevant American decisions are summarised by G. Robertson in an interesting case note on *McKay v Essex AHA*: see "Wrongful life" (1982) 45 M.L.R. 697. The decision also accords with the recommendations of the Royal Commission on Civil Liability and Compensation for Personal Injury, Cmnd. 7054 (1978), paras 1485–1486. Subsequent recent Australian case law has maintained this position, *Harriton v Stephens* [2006] HCA 15 and *Waller v James & Hoolahan* [2006] HCA 16, two appeals involving claims brought for damages for "wrongful life". Both were dismissed by a majority (Kirby J. dissenting in each) consisting of Gleeson CJ., Gummow J., Hayne J. Callinan J., Heydon J., and Crennan J. In 1997 the supreme administrative court in France (*Conseil d'Etat*), while compensating the parents, rejected a wrongful life claim by the child himself where a negligently performed amniocentesis deprived the mother of the choice of terminating her pregnancy, the English authority of *McKay* being cited with approval in the opinion of the *Commissaire du Gouvernement*. The position of the supreme civil court in France (*Cour de Cassation*) has been less clear. A decision in 1996 appeared to envisage such a claim (Civ 1ere, mars 26, 1996) and in 2000 judgment was given in the notorious *Perruche* case (*Assemblée Plénière*, novembre 17, 2000, Bull. No.9). In that case the mother contracted rubella while pregnant. Negligently she was not advised of the risk to her foetus of being born handicapped and therefore did not seek a termination. The child was born handicapped and the *Cour de Cassation* decided that he could recover damages in respect of his handicapped existence, in effect basing the recovery on the concept of "wrongful life". Inferior courts showed some reluctance in following this decision, which had provoked a storm of public interest, and in July 2001 three appeals in similar cases were heard by the *Cour de Cassation* (*Assemblée Plénière*). The *Avocat Général* (M. Sainte-Rose) in his opinion argued for a rejection of the principle that a "wrongful life" could be compensated. On July 13, 2001 the Court gave its judgment, which accepted the principle that a handicapped child could recover damages for his handicapped existence flowing from his mother being deprived of the choice of terminating the pregnancy, on condition that it was proved that the legal requirements justifying a therapeutic termination had existed in the cases in question. In all three cases the Court held that it had not been proved that those requirements had existed. It seems likely that the effect of these decisions of the *Cour de Cassation* will be overruled by statute to exclude claims for wrongful life.The child's claim for wrongful life was held properly to have been abandoned in *Arndt v Smith* (1994) 93 B.C.L.R. (2d) 220, British Columbia Supreme Court, following *McKay*. See further C. Stolker, "Wrongful Life and Limits of Liability" (1994) 43 I.C.L.Q. 521. Such claims have also recently been confirmed as not being permissible by the High Court of Australia: see *Harriton v Stephens* [2006] HCA 15 and *Waller v James; Waller v Hoolahan* [2006] HCA 16.

[9] Except in cases where the medical practitioner undertakes to achieve a specific result: see, for instance, *Thake v Maurice*, para.13–004 above.

duty, like that of other professional men, is to exercise reasonable skill and care as set out by McNair J. in *Bolam v Friern Hospital Management Committee*,[10] commonly known as "the *Bolam* test":

> "But where you get a situation which involves the use of some special skill or competence, then the test as to whether there has been negligence or not is not the test of the man on the top of a Clapham omnibus, because he has not got this special skill. The test is the standard of the ordinary skilled man exercising and professing to have that special skill. A man need not possess the highest expert skill; it is well established law that it is sufficient if he exercises the ordinary skill of an ordinary competent man exercising that particular art ... he is not guilty of negligence if he has acted in accordance with a practice accepted as proper by a responsible body of medical men skilled in that particular art ... Putting it another way round, a man is not negligent if he is acting in accordance with such a practice merely because there is a body of opinion who would take a contrary view."[11]

The *Bolam* test itself has been the subject of numerous judicial paraphrases and summaries. Lord Scarman in *Sidaway v Governors of Bethlem Royal Hospital*[12] has reformulated it thus:

> "a doctor is not negligent if he acts in accordance with a practice accepted at the time as proper by a responsible body of medical opinion even though other doctors adopt a different practice."

The *Bolam* test has withstood a series of attacks by determined claimants, sometimes armed with transatlantic authority. In *Whitehouse v Jordan*[13] the House of Lords held that the *Bolam* test was applicable to medical treatment. In *Maynard v West Midlands Regional HA*[14] the House of Lords held that the *Bolam* test was applicable to diagnosis. In *Sidaway v Governors of Bethlem Royal Hospital*[15] the House of Lords held by a majority[16] that the *Bolam* test was applicable to all aspects of a medical practitioner's work and in particular to the extent of the medical practitioner's obligation to inform a patient of the risks of a proposed course of treatment.[17] Lord Diplock stated:

---

[10] [1957] 1 W.L.R. 582, 586. This direction was approved by the Privy Council in *Chin Keow v Government of Malaysia* [1967] 1 W.L.R. 813, 816, and by Lord Edmund-Davies in *Whitehouse v Jordan* [1981] 1 W.L.R. 246.

[11] In *Bolitho v City of Hackney HA* [1998] A.C. 232, 239C Lord Browne-Wilkinson described this direction as the "*locus classicus*" of the test for the standard of care required of a doctor.

[12] [1985] A.C. 871, 881F.

[13] [1981] 1 W.L.R. 246.

[14] [1984] 1 W.L.R. 634.

[15] [1985] A.C. 871.

[16] Lord Diplock, Lord Bridge and Lord Keith (Lord Templeman and Lord Scarman agreed with the decision of the majority, but on different grounds).

[17] Canada and Australia took a different approach. Instead of considering what the doctors thought the patient should know, the Canadian approach was to consider what a reasonable patient would want to know. The doctor's duty is to give the patient sufficient information to make an informed decision as to their treatment. They must consider with the patient the nature of the illness and the proposed treatment, and they must explain the risks involved with the treatment, they must consider alternative treatments and the consequences of doing nothing. *Reibl v Hughes* (1980) 114 D.L.R. (3d) 1 Can. Sup. Ct; *Arndt v Smith* (1997) 148 D.L.R. (4th) 48, Can. Sup. Ct. In *Rogers v Whitaker* (1992) 109 A.L.R. 625, Aust. HC and [1993] Med. L.R. 79 the Australian High Court also rejected the approach in *Sidaway* and held that the extent of what a patient had to be told depended on a proper assessment of what the patient wanted to be told.

"The *Bolam* test is far from new, its value is that it brings up to date and re-expresses in the light of modern conditions in which the art of medicine is now practised an ancient rule of common law . . . [18]

In English jurisprudence the doctor's relationship with his patient which gives rise to the normal duty of care to exercise his skill and judgment to improve the patient's health in any particular respect in which the patient has sought his aid, has hitherto been treated as a single comprehensive duty covering all the ways in which a doctor is called upon to exercise his skill and judgment in the improvement of the physical or mental condition of the patient for which his services either as a general practitioner or specialist have been engaged. This general duty is not subject to dissection into a number of component parts to which different criteria of what satisfies the duty of care apply, such as diagnosis, treatment, advice . . . [19]

My Lords, no convincing reason has in my view been advanced before your Lordships that would justify treating the *Bolam* test as doing anything less than laying down a principle of English law that is comprehensive and applicable to every aspect of the duty of care owed by a doctor to his patient in the exercise of his healing functions as respects that patient."[20]

13–023　　In *Gold v Haringey HA*[21] the Court of Appeal held that the *Bolam* test applies even to non-therapeutic advice given by a medical practitioner. In *Re F (Mental Patient: Sterilisation)*[22] the House of Lords held that the *Bolam* test determined whether medical treatment carried out on a patient unable to consent was lawful. In *Airedale NHS Trust v Bland*[23] the House of Lords held that the *Bolam* test applies to the withdrawal of medical treatment from a patient who is incompetent to refuse treatment, even where this will lead to the death of the patient. Finally it seems implicit from the judgment of Kay J. in *Skelton v Lewisham and North Southwark HA*[24] that the *Bolam* test applies to an assessment of the standard of note-taking by a doctor.

Nor should the applicable standard of care vary with the circumstances in which medical treatment is rendered to a patient. In *Brooks v Home Office*[25] Garland J. held that, subject to the reasonable constraints of having to be transported and having her freedom restricted, a pregnant woman detained in prison was entitled to expect the same standard of obstetric care and observation as if she were at liberty.[26]

13–024　　In the past there had been controversy as to the status and significance of evidence from an expert to the effect that the management complained of by the

---

[18] [1985] A.C. 871, 881F at 892E.
[19] *ibid.* at 893D–E.
[20] *ibid.* at 893H–894A.
[21] [1988] Q.B. 481, 489F–H.
[22] [1990] 2 A.C. 1. See para.13–052, below.
[23] [1993] A.C. 789.
[24] [1998] Lloyd's Rep. Med. 324, 328.
[25] (1999) 48 B.M.L.R. 109.
[26] See *McGlinchey v The United Kingdom* (50390/99) reported at [2003] Lloyd's Rep. Med. 264 and (2003) 37 E.H.R.R. 41 for a case where the European Court of Human Rights found (in the absence of proceedings in negligence) there had been a violation of Art.3 and Art.13 of the European Convention on Human Rights when a detained prisoner with a history of heroin addiction died in custody, having lost 10kg of weight in five days with symptoms of vomiting, diarrhoea and abdominal pain. The European Court noted that the prison authorities had not monitored the weight loss or the prisoner's condition and had failed to treat her condition by hospital admission or seeking expert advice to control the symptoms.

claimant was approved by a responsible body of medical opinion. It had been thought that a claim of negligence against a doctor could be successfully defended by the defence calling an expert honestly to say that he would have acted in the same way as the defendant. However, this practice was held to be impermissible by the House of Lords in *Bolitho v City & Hackney HA*.[27] Patrick Bolitho, aged two, was admitted to hospital suffering from respiratory difficulties; he deteriorated and suffered a cardiac arrest which caused massive brain damage. At one stage a nurse was sufficiently concerned about Patrick's breathing difficulties that she summoned a doctor—but the doctor negligently failed to attend or send a deputy. It was accepted that if the doctor had attended and intubated Patrick, the respiratory failure which caused the cardiac arrest would not have occurred. The case was defended on the question of causation on the basis that even if the doctor had attended she would not have intubated the child, but the claimants made an assault in the House of Lords on the significance of the defendant's expert evidence.

Lord Browne-Wilkinson said in the only speech[28]:

> "[Counsel for the claimant] submitted that the judge had wrongly treated the Bolam test as requiring him to accept the views of one truthful body of expert professional advice even if he was unpersuaded of its logical force. He submitted that the judge was wrong in law in adopting that approach and that ultimately it was for the court, not for medical opinion, to decide what was the standard of care required of a professional in the circumstances of each particular case.
>
> My Lords, I agree with these submissions to the extent that, in my view, the court is not bound to hold that a defendant doctor escapes liability for negligent treatment or diagnosis just because he leads evidence from a number of medical experts who are genuinely of opinion that the defendant's treatment or diagnosis accorded with sound medical practice."

It now follows that any expert evidence supporting a defendant doctor's approach to treatment, diagnosis or the explanation of risk must be subjected to logical analysis, and (although such cases will obviously be rare) it need not be accepted by the court if the analysis is found wanting.[29]

**Standard of skill and care determined by reference to the current state of   13–025
knowledge.** Advances of medical science or medical knowledge between the date of the alleged negligence and the date of trial should be ignored when

---

[27] [1998] A.C. 232, HL.

[28] *ibid.* at 241.

[29] *Hucks v Cole* (1968) 112 S.J. 483; [1993] 4 Med. L.R. 393 is an example of this critical approach to expert evidence being applied in 1968; see also: *Pearce v United Bristol Healthcare NHS Trust* [1999] P.I.Q.R. 53, CA; and *Penney v East Kent HA* [2000] Lloyd's Rep. Med. 41, CA. See also the important lecture by Lord Woolf entitled "Are the courts excessively deferential to the Medical Profession?" (2001) 9 Med. L. Rev. 1. In *Reynolds v North Tyneside HA* [2002] Lloyd's Rep. Med. 459 Gross J. held that even if there had been a practice of not conducting a vaginal examination on admission (and there was no such practice at the material time, but the practice of conducting one was not uniform) it would not have been defensible. In *S R Burne v A* [2006] EWCA Civ 24 the Court of Appeal emphasised that a judge should not embark upon an examination of the Bolitho principle until expert witness had had a proper opportunity to explain why medical practice took the position that the use of open questions was a proper method to diagnose conditions.

determining whether the defendant exercised reasonable skill and care.[30] In *Roe v Minister of Health*[31] a spinal anaesthetic was kept in glass ampoules stored in phenol solution. The phenol penetrated the ampoules through invisible cracks. In October 1947 the anaesthetic, containing phenol, was injected into two patients, who thereby suffered severe injuries. The risk of such mishaps occurring was first drawn to the attention of the medical profession in 1951 when a book was published on lumbar puncture and spinal anaesthesia. The trial took place in 1953. McNair J. held that Dr G, who was responsible for the anaesthetic, was not negligent in failing to foresee and guard against[32] the risk of invisible cracks. The Court of Appeal affirmed that decision, emphasising that they were judging Dr G by the state of knowledge in 1947.[33] Denning L.J. observed that if the same mistake were made after 1951, it would amount to negligence.[34]

The ascertainment of the state of knowledge at the material time is sometimes a central issue at trial. This is determined in part by the recollection of expert witnesses, but largely by reference to the published literature. The question then arises at what point does published material become part of the current knowledge. In order that he not fall behind the development of accepted medical practice, the doctor has an obligation to keep himself informed. In practice, however, a professional person does not read every relevant publication, nor can he remember everything that he reads. Thus in *Crawford v Board of Governors of Charing Cross Hospital*[35] the Court of Appeal held that an anaesthetist was not negligent in failing to read a particular article in *The Lancet*.

Evidence of the current state of knowledge and standard practice in other countries may not be relevant to the standard of care applicable to doctors in this country. In *Whiteford v Hunter*[36] the defendant's mistaken diagnosis of prostate cancer was not negligent on account of his failure to use an instrument which was routinely used in such circumstances in the United States.

13–026   **Standard of skill and care determined by reference to the specialisation of the defendant.** In determining whether a medical practitioner has exercised due skill and care, regard must be had to his specialisation or lack of specialisation. Thus in *Hucks v Cole*[37] Lord Denning M.R. observed that the defendant "was to be judged as a general practitioner with a diploma in obstetrics". Conversely, as the House of Lords has pointed out on three occasions,[38] a practitioner who specialises in any particular area of medicine must be judged by the standard of

---

[30] See, e.g. *Chin Keow v Government of Malaysia* [1967] 1 W.L.R. 813, 817. In the case of claims for ante-natal injury, see s.1(5) of the Congenital Disabilities (Civil Liability) Act 1976.
[31] [1954] 2 Q.B. 66.
[32] The risk could have been guarded against quite easily by staining the phenol with a deep dye.
[33] See Somervell L.J., *ibid.* at 77, Denning L.J. at 86 and Morris L.J. at 92.
[34] *ibid.* at 86.
[35] *The Times*, December 8, 1953.
[36] [1950] W.N. 552, HL.
[37] (1968) 112 S.J. 483; [1993] 4 Med. L.R. 393.
[38] *Whitehouse v Jordan* [1981] 1 W.L.R. 246, 263B *per* Lord Fraser; *Maynard v West Midlands Regional HA* [1984] 1 W.L.R. 634, 638H, *per* Lord Scarman (with whom the other four law lords agreed); *Sidaway v Governors of Bethlem Royal Hospital* [1985] A.C. 871, 892G *per* Lord Diplock, 897C *per* Lord Bridge (with whom Lord Keith agreed).

skill and care of that speciality.[39] Lord Bridge (with whom Lord Keith agreed) said in *Sidaway v Governors of Bethlem Royal Hospital*[40]:

"The language of the *Bolam* test clearly requires a different degree of skill from a specialist in his own special field than from a general practitioner. In the field of neuro-surgery it would be necessary to substitute for Lord President Clyde's phrase, 'no doctor of ordinary skill', the phrase 'no neuro-surgeon of ordinary skill'."[41]

The specialist is required to meet the standards of the ordinarily competent member of his specialism, which need not be those of the most experienced or highly qualified members.[42]

Inexperience. Of necessity, treatment in hospitals is on occasions given by junior doctors of limited experience. The question arises, by what standard should they be judged? The standard of care to be expected of junior hospital doctors was the subject of detailed consideration by the Court of Appeal in *Wilsher v Essex AHA*.[43] The claimant was born prematurely and treated in a special care baby unit, staffed by two consultants, a senior registrar and several junior doctors. Mustill L.J. rejected the submission that a junior doctor should be judged by the standard "required of a person having his formal qualifications and practical experience". He considered that the duty of care related not to the individual but to the post which he occupied: **13–027**

"In a case such as the present, the standard is not just that of the averagely competent and well-informed junior houseman (or whatever the position of the doctor) but of such a person who fills a post in a unit offering a highly specialised service."[44]

Sir Nicolas Browne-Wilkinson V.C. favoured a lower standard:

"In my judgment, if the standard of care required of such a doctor is that he should have the skill required of the post he occupies, the young houseman or the doctor seeking to acquire specialist skill in a special unit would be held liable for shortcomings in the treatment without any personal fault on his part at all."[45]

On this issue Glidewell L.J. preferred the view of Mustill L.J.[46] The view of the majority in *Wilsher* was followed at first instance.[47]

---

[39] In *Poynter v Hillingdon HA* (1997) 37 B.M.L.R. 192 the authority's heart transplant team was "practising at the very highest level of expertise" and were thus required to meet a correspondingly high standard of care.

[40] [1985] A.C. 871, 897C.

[41] The relevant passage of Lord Clyde's judgment is set out in para.12–068, above.

[42] "A medical practitioner who holds himself out as being a specialist in a particular field is required to attain the ordinary level of skill amongst those who specialise in the same field. He is not required to attain the highest degree of skill and competence in that particular field" *O'Donovan v Cork County Council* [1967] I.R. 173, 190 *per* Walsh J., Supreme Court of Ireland.

[43] [1987] Q.B. 730. This aspect of the Court of Appeal's decision was not challenged on the appeal to the House of Lords: see [1988] A.C. 1074.

[44] [1987] Q.B. 730, 751B–C.

[45] *ibid.* at 777E-F.

[46] *ibid.* at 774D–E.

[47] *Djemal v Bexley HA* [1995] 6 Med. L.R. 269 and *Bova v Spring* [1994] 5 Med. L.R. 120. It should however be noted that failure properly to supervise inexperienced doctors may be a breach of a hospital authority's direct duty of care: see paras 13–060 to 13–062, below.

13–028   **Undertaking work beyond one's competence.** If a medical practitioner lacks the skill and experience to deal with a particular case, he should refer the matter to someone who is competent to deal with it.[48] In one case[49] the defendant's casualty officer incorrectly diagnosed the abdominal injuries of a man who had been kicked by a horse. Donovan J. held that the casualty officer was negligent in failing to have the man examined by a doctor of consultant rank.

13–029   **Undertaking work in an emergency.** The extent of the doctor's duty will depend on the facts of the situation, and what (if anything) the doctor took it upon himself to do. The standard of care to be provided by the doctor will be no more and no less than that which it is reasonable to expect of him in all the circumstances.

13–030   **Misadventure.** A great deal of medical treatment, even if administered with all due skill and care, involves some degree of risk. It is inevitable, therefore, that mishaps will occur for which the patient has no remedy.[50] By way of example, in one first instance case[51] during an operation on the claimant's right eye the surgeon accidentally cut the retina. Thompson J. acknowledged that the surgeon was operating within a very few millimetres, and held that he had exercised all reasonable skill, care and judgment. The claimant was a victim of mischance.

On occasions medical treatment involves making a choice between competing risks. This situation commonly arises where a doctor wishes to prescribe a drug which is known to have serious adverse effects. So long as he acts reasonably, he should not be held liable simply because the risks inherent in whichever course he takes materialise or simply because some other doctor (or the judge) feels that

---

[48] "It is, no doubt, conceivable that a qualified man may be held liable for recklessly undertaking a case which he knew, or should have known, to be beyond his powers." (*per* Lord Hewart C.J. in *R. v Bateman* (1925) 94 L.J.K.B. 791.) For Canadian cases in which a similar principle was applied, see *Fraser v Vancouver General Hospital* [1951] 3 W.W.R. (N.S.) 337, British Columbia Court of Appeal, affirmed [1952] 3 D.L.R. 785, Supreme Court of Canada (intern held to have been negligent in undertaking to interpret X-ray films, rather than referring them to an expert radiologist) and *Dillon v Le Roux* [1994] 6 W.W.R. 280, British Columbia Court of Appeal (family physician who was acting as a relief hospital emergency room doctor but had no emergency room training was negligent in failing promptly to call a hospital doctor to assist in diagnosis). See also *Miles v Judge* (1997) 37 C.C.L.T. 160, Ontario Court of Justice, General Division (surgeon adopted a form of laparoscopic surgery which was an acceptable method of treatment but which he had performed only twice before. Held that his inexperience had led him to perform the procedure negligently, causing damage to major blood vessels); *Brooks v Home Office*, *The Times*, February 18, 1999, Garland J. (a woman pregnant with twins who was detained in prison was entitled to expect the same careful standard of obstetric medical care and observation as if she were at liberty, that standard was not met because the prison medical service doctor had insufficient obstetrics experience to deal with one twin's lack of growth and failed to seek specialist obstetric advice for five days after the need for it arose, although the breach was not causative of the baby's death); *Marriott v West Midlands HA* [1999] Lloyd's Rep. Med. 23, CA (negligent failure to refer patient to hospital for full neurological testing where the general practitioner ought to have perceived a risk of intracranial lesion).
[49] *Payne v St Helier Group Hospital Management Committee* [1952] C.L.Y. 2442.
[50] *Fussell v Beddard* (1942) 2 B.M.J. 411, affords a striking example: as a result of a misunderstanding between the anaesthetist and the nurse, the claimant was given an excessive quantity of decicaine, from which he died. Lewis J. held that there was no negligence, but an "unfortunate mistake". See generally paras 1331–1332 of the Report of the Royal Commission on Civil Liability and Compensation for Personal Injury, (1978) Cmnd. 7054.
[51] *White v Board of Governors of Westminster Hospital*, *The Times*, October 26, 1961.

he would have taken the opposite course.[52] In *Whiteford v Hunter*[53] the defendant did not verify his diagnosis of cancer by means of a biopsy, because this would have involved serious risk of perforating the bladder wall and consequent ulceration. The House of Lords held (contrary to the trial judge) that the failure to do a biopsy did not amount to negligence.

In cases involving misadventure in the course of a patient's management, the true consideration of liability will usually depend upon whether the patient has been adequately warned if the misadventure was a known risk, and if inadequate warnings have been given, whether the patient would have decided upon a different course if properly warned.[54]

Failure to take precautions. Where a medical practitioner rejects precautions **13–031** for no good reason, then any resulting mishap is more likely to be treated as negligent.[55] The medical practitioner is, of course, only expected to take precaution against risks which he ought reasonably to anticipate.[56]

(d) *General and Approved Practice*

(i) *Acting in Accordance with General and Approved Practice: the Impact of Bolitho*

In *Bolitho v City & Hackney HA*[57-58] the claimant argued that ultimately it was **13–032** for the court, not for medical opinion, to decide the standard of care required of a practitioner in the circumstances of each case. The judge had said that, as a layman, he saw the force of the claimant's argument that it was unreasonable and illogical not to intubate. The claimant argued that the judge was wrong to treat the *Bolam* principle as requiring him to accept the views of one body of opinion

---

[52] An interesting example of this dilemma is the Australian case, *Battersby v Tottman* (1984) 35 S.A.S.R. 577: the first defendant prescribed a high dosage of melleril for the claimant (who was suffering from severe mental illness) in the knowledge that this posed a risk to the claimant's eyes. The risk materialised and the claimant suffered serious and permanent eye damage. It was held that the first defendant had acted reasonably in prescribing such a high dosage of melleril. The alternative risk, if the claimant had not been taking melleril, was that she would commit suicide: see *ibid*. at 584.

[53] [1950] W.N. 552. See also Wood J.'s description of the comparative risk assessment to be undertaken in deciding whether laparotomy or laparoscopy was the appropriate diagnostic technique to be used on a patient with a history of gynaecological problems: *Darley v Shale* [1993] 4 Med. L.R. 161 at 168, New South Wales Supreme Court.

[54] See paras 13–089 to 13–104.

[55] See, e.g. *Cardin v City of Montreal* (1961) 29 D.L.R. (2d) 492, Supreme Court of Canada: a doctor who continued to inject vaccine into the arm of a struggling child, with the result that the needle broke, was held to have been negligent. Given the serious consequences of a broken needle, immobilisation of the child's arm was an essential precaution. For a slightly different example of failure to take precautions, see *Stokes v Guest, Keen & Nettlefold* [1968] 1 W.L.R. 1776 (company medical officer failing to protect employees against scrotal cancer). See also *Le Page v Kingston and Richmond HA* [1997] 8 Med. L.R. 229 (failure to administer prophylactic blood transfusion at the start of a Caesarian section when it was known that the claimant was anaemic).

[56] In *Warren v Greig The Lancet*, February 9, 1935, p.330. a doctor allowed the extraction of all the patient's teeth in a single operation, without first carrying out a blood test to see whether the patient suffered from acute myeloid leukaemia. MacKinnon J. held that, having regard to the rarity of the disease, the doctor was not negligent in omitting this precaution.

[57-58] [1998] A.C. 232. For facts see para.13–024 above.

even though he was unpersuaded of its logical force. The appeal was dismissed. Lord Browne-Wilkinson (with whom Lords Slynn, Nolan, Hoffmann and Clyde agreed) said[59]:

"My Lords, I agree with these submissions to the extent that, in my view, the Court is not bound to hold that a defendant doctor escapes liability for negligent treatment or diagnosis just because he leads evidence from a number of medical experts who are genuinely of the opinion that the defendant's treatment or diagnosis accorded with sound medical practice. In the *Bolam* case itself, McNair J. stated ... that the defendant had to have acted in accordance with the practice accepted as proper by a 'responsible body of medical men'. Later ... he referred to 'a standard of practice recognised as proper by a competent reasonable body of opinion.' Again, in the passage which I have cited from Maynard's case, Lord Scarman refers to a 'respectable' body of professional opinion. The use of these adjectives—responsible, reasonable and respectable—all show that the court has to be satisfied that the exponents of the body of opinion relied upon can demonstrate that such opinion has a logical basis. In particular in cases involving, as they so often do, the weighing of risks against benefits, the judge before accepting a body of opinion as being responsible, reasonable or respectable, will need to be satisfied that, in forming their views, the experts have directed their minds to the question of comparative risks and benefits and have reached a defensible conclusion on the matter ... "

and at 243A–B:

"These decisions demonstrate that in cases of diagnosis and treatment there are cases where, despite a body of professional opinion sanctioning the defendant's conduct, the defendant can properly be held liable for negligence. (I am not here considering questions of disclosure of risk.) In my judgment that is because, in some cases, it cannot be demonstrated to the judge's satisfaction that the body of opinion relied upon is reasonable or responsible."

13-033   Lord Browne-Wilkinson expressly excluded from his remarks those cases where the negligence alleged is a failure to warn a patient of the risks of proposed treatment. It may be that the decision of the majority in *Sidaway v Governors of Royal Bethlem Hospital*[60] was regarded as of similar effect to that of the House of Lords in *Bolitho*. The majority in *Sidaway* held that, while the *Bolam* principle applied to such cases, it was open to the court to decide that a general practice of the profession in relation to warnings was inadequate to meet the needs of a particular claimant.

Lord Browne-Wilkinson emphasised that the court will rarely reject expert opinion as "indefensible", for two reasons. First, because in the vast majority of cases the fact that distinguished experts in the field are of a particular opinion would demonstrate the reasonableness of that opinion. Secondly, because the assessment of medical risks and benefits is a matter of clinical judgment which a judge would not normally be able to make without expert evidence. The Court found that *Bolitho* was not one of those exceptional cases where the judge ought to have rejected expert testimony. On the evidence, it could not be suggested that

---

[59] [1998] A.C. 232 (at 241G–242B).
[60] [1985] A.C. 871.

it was illogical for the defendant's expert, a most distinguished practitioner, to favour running what, in his view, was a small risk of total respiratory collapse rather than submitting the infant claimant to the invasive procedure of intubation.

(ii) *Departing from General and Approved Practice*

If a medical practitioner departs from the general and approved practice for no good cause, and damage results, he is likely to be held negligent.[61] *Clark v MacLennan*[62] offers an illustration of this principle. The claimant suffered stress incontinence after the birth of her first child. T, the consultant employed by the second defendants, decided that an anterior colporrhaphy should be performed four weeks after the birth. This was a departure from the normal practice, which was to defer such an operation until three months after the birth. Peter Pain J. held that there were no factors to justify this departure from normal practice and that the second defendants were therefore in breach of duty. Lord Clyde analysed the same principle in *Hunter v Hanley*[63] in these terms:

> "It follows from what I have said that in regard to allegations of deviation from ordinary professional practice ... such a deviation is not necessarily evidence of negligence. Indeed it would be disastrous if this were so, for all inducement to progress in medical science would then be destroyed. Even a substantial deviation from normal practice may be warranted by the particular circumstances. To establish liability by a doctor where deviation from normal practice is alleged, three facts require to be established. First of all it must be proved that there is a usual and normal practice; secondly it must be proved that the defender has not adopted that practice; and thirdly (and this is of crucial importance) it must be established that the course the doctor adopted is one which no professional man of ordinary skill would have taken if he had been acting with ordinary care."[64]

Novel treatment. More substantial departures from general and approved practice may occur when the medical practitioner applies a new technique or a new form of treatment. It is clearly in the public interest that new forms of treatment should be developed and any principle of law which stifles such development altogether is manifestly unsatisfactory. In *Sidaway v Governors of*

13–034

13–035

---

[61] See, e.g. *Chin Keow v Government of Malaysia* [1967] 1 W.L.R. 813 (doctor departed from normal practice in that he did not inquire into patient's medical history before prescribing penicillin); *Stokes v Guest, Keen and Nettlefold* [1968] 1 W.L.R. 1776 (company medical officer ignored warning leaflet issued by factory inspectorate); *Robinson v Post Office* [1974] 1 W.L.R. 1176 (doctor gave claimant a test dose of anti-tetanus serum, waited one minute and then gave the full dose. The normal practice was to wait half-an-hour after the test dose. The doctor only escaped liability because no damage was caused by his negligence); *Ritchie v Chichester HA* [1994] 5 Med. L.R. 187 (anaesthetic registrar failed to follow a procedure which was prescribed by his consultant and was safe); *Hepworth v Kerr* [1995] 6 Med. L.R. 139. In the case of claims for ante-natal injury, see s.1(5) of the Congenital Disabilities (Civil Liability) Act 1976.
[62] [1983] 1 All E.R. 416.
[63] 1955 S.C. 200.
[64] *ibid.* at 206.

Bethlem Royal Hospital[65] Lord Diplock stressed the importance of permitting the development of medical science:

"Those members of the public who seek medical or surgical aid would be badly served by the adoption of any legal principle that would confine the doctor to some long-established, well-tried method of treatment only, although its past record of success might be small, if he wanted to be confident that he would not run the risk of being held liable in negligence simply because he tried some more modern treatment, and by some unavoidable mischance it failed to heal but did some harm to the patient."[66]

Lord Diplock went on to state that the *Bolam* test itself provided adequate protection for a doctor who made use of some new form of treatment. This is likely once the new form of treatment has won the approval of a responsible body of medical opinion. However, there may be cases where a medical practitioner wishes to use some new form of treatment which has not even attained that degree of acceptance. It is submitted that in those circumstances the question whether the medical practitioner acted reasonably must be determined by reference to all the circumstances of the case, and the mere fact he departed from established practice should not lead automatically to a finding of negligence. Relevant factors would include the information available about the proposed new treatment, the likely effect of the other more established forms of treatment which were available, and the stated wishes of the patient after the relevant facts had been explained to him.[67]

13–036 **Clinical trials.** Yet further difficulties arise when it is desired to use some innovative treatment, not principally for the patient's benefit but for the purpose

---

[65] [1985] A.C. 871, 893A–B.

[66] In the unreported case of *Linque Pollard v Hugh Crockard and another*, January 22, 1997 Holland J. the defendant surgeon departed from usual practice in his approach to surgery, and adopted a relatively novel technique. The judge held that it was not negligent of him to have done so because he had established his expertise at the time in respect of this different approach and it was therefore for him an option consistent with accepted clinical practice. Neuro-surgeons without the necessary level of skill would not have been justified in adopting the approach.

[67] The question of explanations and warnings is dealt with in paras 13–089 to 13–104, below. Obviously this assumes greater importance where the proposed treatment is innovative. In *Zimmer v Ringrose* (1981) 16 C.C.L.T. 51 the Alberta Court of Appeal held that the defendant (who used an innovative technique to sterilise the claimant) was negligent in failing to tell the claimant that his technique had not been approved by the medical profession and in failing to give her a comparison between his method and other methods of sterilisation. See also *Coughlin v Kuntz* [1990] 2 W.W.R. 737, British Columbia Court of Appeal (negligent use of experimental technique for cervical spine discectomy). Two English cases illustrate the approach taken in this country. In *Waters v West Sussex HA* [1995] 6 Med. L.R. 362 a neurosurgeon carried out an operation comprising an unprecedented combination of procedures. There was no established practice either in support of or in opposition to his method. Buxton J. examined the decisions which the defendant had taken individually and in combination in the light of relevant medical literature and expert evidence. He held that the neurosurgeon was not negligent, for his actions were supported by expert witnesses who represented a competent body of professional opinion. The defendant anaesthetist in *Hepworth v Kerr* [1995] 6 Med. L.R. 139 deliberately reduced a patient's blood pressure to a dangerously low level in order to provide the surgeon with a blood-free operating field. Although he had used the technique in previous cases, it was both novel and essentially experimental, for it lacked any conventional scientific validation. Further, the surgeon did not in fact require so clean an operating field: thus the anaesthetist had subjected the patient to risks which were both scientifically unwarranted and unnecessary in the particular circumstances of the case. The patient suffered a spinal stroke and the defendant was held liable.

of gathering information. Clinical trials play an important part in the development of medical science and any principle of law which stifled them altogether would be undesirable.[68] Equally, however, there are sound reasons of policy why anyone who suffers injury as a result of participation in research or clinical trials should recover damages, irrespective of negligence by those who treated him.[69] The principles of law in this area have yet to be worked out.[70] In practice, however, it would seem likely that whether or not a patient who suffered injury as a result of receiving some experimental form of treatment would succeed on liability[71] would depend on the issues of informed consent and causation.[72] Often patients who are offered experimental treatment are faced with the likelihood of a poor outcome if nothing is done. They may agree to the treatment even if all of the uncertainties are properly explained; and it may be alleged that they would have agreed anyway if it can be established that not all of the uncertainties were, in fact, properly explained.

(e) *Expert Evidence*

In assisting the court on the question of liability, the expert witness has two **13-037** principal functions. First, he has an explanatory or didactic function, in that he explains the technical issues as fully as possible in language comprehensible to laymen. This generally involves explaining the nature of the patient's original condition, the nature of the treatment given, the consequences of the treatment and (where possible) how those consequences flowed from the treatment given. This aspect of the expert evidence may be largely or totally uncontroversial. For example, there may be no dispute that the claimant was suffering from a particular disease, that the defendant prescribed a new type of drug and that the claimant's present complaint is an adverse reaction to that drug. Clearly the court must understand (and resolve any conflicts between) this aspect of the expert reports before it can seriously consider the question of negligence. At this stage of the inquiry the court is largely in the hands of the expert witness. It cannot speculate upon medical matters or come to conclusions or diagnoses which are

---

[68] See H. A. F. Dudley, "Informed consent in surgical trials" (1984) 289 B.M.J. 937.
[69] See the Report of the Royal Commission on Civil Liability and Compensation for Personal Injury (1978) Cmnd. 7054, Ch.24.
[70] For the view that a distinctive regime of liability for harm suffered in the course of research and experimentation is unnecessary, see D. Giesen, "Civil Liability of Physicians for New Methods of Treatment and Experimentation: a comparative examination" (1995) 3 Med. L. Rev. 22.
[71] For discussion of international and national ethical codes applying to research on human subjects, see Kennedy & Grubb, *Principles of Medical Law* (1998 edn), Ch.14.
[72] In the case of *The Creutzfeldt-Jacob Disease Litigation Group B Claimants v The Medical Research Council* [2000] Lloyd's Rep. Med. 161, the claimants took part in clinical trials to treat their dwarfism. By July 1, 1977 the defendants were aware that the injections used in the experimental treatment included a potentially lethal dose of the CJD agent: Morland J. held that it was negligent to administer the experimental treatment after that date. See also *Simms v Simms* [2002] EWHC 2734, reported at [2003] Fam. 83; [2003] 2 W.L.R. 1465, for an instance where the lack of an alternative treatment (for two CJD victims) led their parents to seek declarations that their children should receive an experimental and untested treatment.

not supported by at least one of the experts.[73] On the other hand, where there is dispute upon an issue of medical fact, the court may prefer the evidence of one party's experts over that of the other's: the *Bolam* test does not apply to opinion evidence on matters of fact.[74]

The second function of the expert witness is to assist the court in deciding whether the acts or omissions of the defendant constituted negligence.[75] He will recount what was the current state of knowledge at the time the patient was treated,[76] what was the general and approved practice or what were the different schools of thought at that time relating to the patient's condition.[77] He will

---

[73] *In McLean v Weir* (1977) 3 C.C.L.T. 87, 101, British Columbia Supreme Court, Gould J. summarised the position in a manner which, it is submitted, is equally applicable in England. "It is true that the court may accept in whole or in part or reject in whole or in part the evidence of any witness on the respective grounds of credibility or plausibility, or a combination of both. But in technical matters, unlike in lay matters within the traditional intellectual competence of the court, it cannot substitute its own medical opinion for that of qualified experts. The court has no status whatsoever to come to a medical conclusion contrary to unanimous medical evidence before it even if it wanted to, which is not the situation in this case. If the medical evidence is equivocal, the court may elect which of the theories advanced it accepts. If only two medical theories are advanced, the court may elect between the two or reject them both; it cannot adopt a third theory of its own, no matter how plausible such might be to the court."

[74] See *Loveday v Renton* [1990] 1 Med. L.R. 117, 182 *per* Stuart-Smith L.J.; *Joyce v Merton, Sutton & Wandsworth HA* [1996] 7 Med. L.R. 1, 13 *per* Roch L.J. An example is *Corley v North West Herefordshire HA* [1997] 8 Med. L.R. 45. The claimant suffered cerebral palsy as a result of compression of the umbilical cord shortly before his birth. Cresswell J.'s finding that the health authority's obstetric staff had not been negligent in failing to effect a forceps delivery at an earlier stage largely followed from his findings as to the mechanism of cord compression, on which he preferred the evidence of the authority's expert and other witnesses. See, for a further example: *Scott v Wakefield AHA* [1997] 8 Med. L.R. 341 (allegation that ophthalmic surgeon should have referred claimant for micro-surgery failed on the judge's finding of fact that the cause of deterioration of the claimant's eyesight was one which was not amenable to cure by micro-surgery). In *Anderson v Heatherwood & Wrexham Park Hospitals NHS Trust*, June 16, 2005, Judge Eccles Q.C. carried out a detailed logical analysis of the expert evidence, and particularly the literature cited by those experts, before preferring one expert's view as to whether or not the claimant's wife was already past the point of no return when admitted, so that even had the defendant hospital not breached its duty of care, the fatal outcome would have been the same. In *Eastwood v Wright* [2005] EWCA Civ 564: (2005) 84 B.M.L.R. 51, the Court of Appeal upheld the judge's preference for the cautious approach of one expert. In *Roughton v Weston AHA* [2004] EWCA Civ 1509, a case concerning delay to treatment of cerebral vasculitis, the trial judge was criticised and the case remitted for re-trial because the judge had incorrectly concluded his view on causation before considering the state of general medical knowledge and literature. The judge had decided that the stabilisation of the claimant's condition following treatment had been spontaneous rather than caused by the treatment.

[75] In *Scott v Bloomsbury HA* [1990] 1 Med. L.R. 214, Brooke J. said that it was inappropriate for a complex medical negligence action to be brought, where the only supporting evidence was that given by a consultant who had long retired. Compare *Briffett v Gander & District Hospital Board* (1996) 29 C.C.L.T. (2d) 251, Newfoundland CA (cardiologists had qualified as general practitioners before specialising and so were qualified to testify as to the standard of care expected of the average general practitioner in a hospital emergency room). In this regard the expert witness plays a crucial role in the trial on liability.

[76] See para.13–026, above.

[77] See paras 13–032 to 13–036, above. In *Sharpe v Southend HA* [1997] 8 Med. L.R. 299, Cresswell J. stressed that an expert witness in a medical negligence case should make clear in his initial report (if it be the case) that while he would have adopted a practice or approach different from that which the defendant adopted, he accepts that the defendant's conduct was in accordance with an alternative approach or practice accepted as proper by a responsible body of practitioners in the relevant field. Had the claimant's expert done so in that case, the case against one of the defendants would not have begun. In the event, it was withdrawn following the expert's concessions in cross-examination.

thereby explain the gravity and foreseeability of the risks attaching to a particular course of treatment or medical procedure and identify any precautions which might have been taken to guard against such risks materialising. He may also state what is the experience and skill usually displayed by medical practitioners with the particular specialisation of the defendant, when they are called upon to diagnose or treat the injury or illness from which the claimant was suffering.[78] Ultimately, however, it is for the court to decide, on the totality of the evidence and applying the *Bolam* test, and the necessary logical analysis, whether the defendant exercised the requisite degree of skill and care. The question whether the defendant was "negligent" is a mixed question of fact and law. The court is not bound in every case by the opinion of the expert witnesses that there was or was not negligence, although in many cases the opinion of expert witnesses on matters within their province, if accepted as representative of a body of responsible professional opinion, leads inevitably to one or other of these conclusions.

On each of these questions, the court is entitled to, and should, assess the **13–038** weight of expert testimony using the normal principles of critical evaluation of evidence. The evidence of a particular expert witness may be rejected on grounds that the expert has become partial[79] or on grounds that his evidence lacks internal consistency or logic.[80] For example, in one case,[81] the evidence of an expert witness for the defence was rejected because the witness had lost his objectivity, his views were unsupported by the literature and his argument did not withstand analysis when tested by the views of other expert witnesses.[82]

Where the defendant's conduct cannot be defended by evidence that it conformed with a general approved practice, because no general practice or relevant school of thought exists, the decision whether reasonable care and skill were exercised will be informed but not constrained by expert evidence. The facts in *AB v Tameside and Glossop HA*[83] provide an extreme example. A health worker employed by the defendant authority was diagnosed HIV positive. By letter, the

---

[78] See paras 13–032 to 13–033, above.

[79] See, e.g. *Early v Newham HA* [1994] 5 Med. L.R. 214, 216; *Hepworth v Kerr* [1995] 6 Med. L.R. 139, 165.

[80] As in *McAllister v Lewisham and North Southwark HA* [1994] 5 Med. L.R. 343.

[81] *Murphy v Wirral HA* [1996] 7 Med. L.R. 99 (Kay J). See also *Robinson v Jacklin* [1996] 7 Med. L.R. 83 (the evidence of an expert witness called by the defendant was held not to support the existence of a body of competent professional opinion).

[82] See also Judge Eccles Q.C.'s analysis of the expert evidence in *Anderson v Heatherwood & Wrexham Park Hospitals NHS Trust*, June 16, 2005. For an example of a successful appeal on grounds of serious procedural or other irregularity under CPR 52.11(3)(b), see *Breeze (as personal representative of the Estate of Leonard Breeze, deceased) v Saeed Ahmad* [2005] EWCA Civ 223. The judge's decision was unjust based, in part at least, on the extent of literature that supported each expert's view. In so deciding against the claimant on causation the judge had taken "on trust" what one expert (the one whose evidence was ultimately preferred by the judge) had said about the contents of two epidemiological data research papers, without being shown the actual papers. The expert had unwittingly been wrong about those contents. The matter was remitted for re-trial. See *Rachael Brown (a patient by her litigation friend Angela Brown) v (1) Birmingham & Black Country Strategic HA (2) Patricia May Shukru (widow and personal representative of Umit Shukru, deceased) (3) Medical Defence Union* [2005] EWHC 1098, QBD, for an instance where the claimant's expert was criticised for loss of objectivity. The judge found this expert's evidence to be significantly influenced by hindsight knowledge of the claimant's true condition. The claimant failed to prove her case.

[83] [1997] 8 Med. L.R. 91.

health authority informed patients (and former patients) who had received obstetric treatment from the worker that there was a remote risk that they had been infected. A group of patients claimed to have suffered psychological injury as a result of receiving the news by those means, and alleged that the authority negligently failed to arrange communication via general practitioners or other health workers qualified to provide immediate counselling where necessary. The Court of Appeal reversed French J.'s finding that the authority was in breach of its (admitted) duty of care. Reasserting the established standard of care, the Court rejected the claimant's submission that the authority's duty was to employ the best method of communication. It accepted the authority's argument that the *Bolam* principle applied, in theory at least, but held that on the facts of that case the principle offered no practical assistance. The problem had not arisen in comparable circumstances before. Accordingly, there was no evidence of a generally approved practice—there was, in that sense, no adequate well of professional experience upon which the court could usefully draw. Once the authority had decided to provide the information, its duty was simply to take all such steps to implement that decision as were reasonable, having regard to the foreseeable risk that some patients might suffer psychological injury as a result of receiving the information. In deciding the scope of that duty, the Court was assisted by expert opinions offered on behalf of each party but was particularly impressed by the fact that, in guidelines published by the Department of Health's Expert Advisory Group on AIDS some two years after the authority's experience, the Group advised that the authority's approach be followed. The claimants' expert had been in the dissenting minority among the experts in the Group.[84]

(f) Res Ipsa Loquitur

13–039   Clinical negligence is the main area of professional negligence in which *res ipsa loquitur* assumes importance. The patient's position is such that he may very well not know, and not be able to establish, what treatment he received and how his injuries were caused. Where he is able to invoke the maxim *res ipsa loquitur*, the

---

[84] In *Penney v East Kent HA* [1999] Lloyd's Rep. Med. 123 a hospital's pathology laboratory failed to detect abnormal cells when testing the claimant's cervical smear sample. The initial screening process was carried out by biomedical scientists or by cytology screeners. Senior screeners and pathologists then examined any slide which was regarded by the first-stage screeners as showing possible abnormalities. It was common ground that the relevant standard of care was that of the reasonably competent cytoscreener exercising reasonable care. The unanimous expert evidence was that unless the cytoscreener was satisfied beyond reasonable doubt that a slide was negative, he should pass it up to the next stage for further consideration. H.H. Judge Pepitt Q.C. (sitting as a deputy High Court judge) held that the *Bolam* principle did not apply, for two reasons. First, since the medical expert witnesses agreed that a screener had been wrong not to classify the claimant's slide as borderline, and so requiring further checking, no question of acceptable practice arose. Second, the cytoscreeners' task was a mechanical one which did not involve diagnosis. The judge's decision was upheld on appeal by the Court of Appeal at [2000] Lloyd's Rep. Med 41: The judge was entitled to prefer the evidence of the claimants' experts as to what the slides showed. See also *MacPhail v Desrosiers* (1998) 170 N.S.R. (2d) 145, Nova Scotia CA: where expert evidence suggested that there was no generally adopted practice on the question whether a patient should be allowed to drive herself home after undergoing an abortion, the court was able to decide what the standard of reasonable skill and care required.

defendant cannot escape liability unless he calls evidence to rebut the inference of negligence which arises from the injury itself and its surrounding circumstances.

The classic exposition of the maxim is that of Erle C.J. in *Scott v London & St Katherine Docks*[85]:

> "There must be reasonable evidence of negligence. But where *the thing* is shown to be under the management of the defendant or his servants, and the accident is such as in the ordinary course of things does not happen if those who have the management use proper care, it affords reasonable evidence, in the absence of explanation by the defendants, that the accident arose from want of care."[86]

Application of the maxim to clinical negligence. If for the words "the thing" **13-040** (which have been italicised in the above quotation) are substituted the words "the treatment of the claimant", the application of the maxim to clinical negligence cases becomes apparent.[87] In *Ratcliffe v Plymouth and Torbay HA*,[88] the Court of Appeal conducted a review of the authorities in this area. Brooke L.J. summarised the relevant principles.[89] The court considered, in particular, whether a claimant is entitled to rely upon the maxim in the absence of expert evidence. It held that in simpler medical situations (for example, a surgeon cuts off the right foot instead of the left, or a swab is left in an operation site) expert evidence will not be necessary. But in most contested cases the claimant's evidence will normally be buttressed by expert evidence to the effect that the matter complained of would not ordinarily occur without negligence on the defendant's part.[90] Statistical evidence that the particular operation, although properly performed, fails in a small number of cases may also prevent the application of the maxim.[91] The maxim *res ipsa loquitur* will only apply where the injury suffered

---

[85] (1865) 3 H. & C. 596: three bags of sugar fell from an upper storey of a warehouse on to the claimant. This raised a presumption of negligence on the part of those in control of the sugar.

[86] *ibid.* at 601. The emphasis has been added.

[87] The argument that the maxim could not apply in clinical negligence cases was rejected in *Ritchie v Chichester HA* [1994] 5 Med. L.R. 187, 205.

[88] [1998] Lloyd's Rep. Med. 162.

[89] See pp.172–173.

[90] Other illustrations are afforded by *Saunders v Leeds Western HA* (1985) 129 S.J. 225; [1993] 4 Med. L.R. 355. and *Coyne v Wigan HA* [1991] 2 Med. L.R. 301. In the former case the claimant suffered a cardiac arrest during the course of an operation. The defendants were unable to rebut the inference of negligence and the claimant succeeded on *res ipsa loquitur*. In the latter case the claimant suffered hypoxia in the recovery ward after a routine operation. The defendants failed to rebut the inference of negligence and the claimant again succeeded on *res ipsa loquitur*. However, not every mishap in the course of treatment raises a presumption of negligence. Thus the maxim did not apply in *O'Malley-Williams v The Board of Governors of the National Hospital for Nervous Diseases* (1975) 1 B.M.J. 635 (neurological injury following an aortagram), *Hobson v Munkley* (1977) 74 D.L.R. (3d) 408 (damage to ureter in course of tubal ligation) or *Jacobs v Great Yarmouth and West Waveney HA* [1995] 6 Med. L.R. 192.

[91] See, e.g. *Considine v Camp Hill Hospital* (1982) 133 D.L.R. (3d) 11, Nova Scotia Supreme Court (the claimant was incontinent following an operation to remove tissue in the region of the prostate: since the evidence showed that 1–4% of such operations could cause incontinence, it was held that *res ipsa loquitur* did not apply); *Grey v Webster* (1984) 14 D.L.R. (4th) 706 (*res ipsa loquitur* held not to apply in a case of failure of sterilisation by means of tubal ligation).

by the claimant is not of a kind which might reasonably occur through misadventure in the course of treatment whether attributable to an inherent risk of the procedure even when carefully performed, or to the patient's particular susceptibility to injury.[92]

In *Mahon v Osborne*[93] (in which a swab was left in the patient's body after an operation) a majority[94] of the Court of Appeal considered that the maxim *res ipsa loquitur* applied. Goddard L.J. put the matter in this way:

"The surgeon is in command of the operation, it is for him to decide what instruments, swabs and the like are to be used, and it is he who uses them. The patient, or, if he dies, his representatives, can know nothing about this matter. There can be no possible question but that neither swabs nor instruments are ordinarily left in the patient's body, and no one would venture to say that it is proper, although in particular circumstances it may be excusable, so to leave them. If, therefore, a swab is left in the patient's body, it seems to me clear that the surgeon is called on for an explanation, that is, he is called on to show not necessarily why he missed it but that he exercised due care to prevent it being left there."[95]

Where the treatment of the patient is under the control of several persons, the maxim cannot apply unless the party sued is responsible for the acts of all those

---

[92] "I cannot for my part accept that medical science is such a precise science that there cannot in any particular field be any room for the wholly unexpected result occurring in the human body from the carrying out of a well-recognised procedure": *Delaney v Southmead HA* [1995] 6 Med. L.R. 355, 360 *per* Dillon L.J. See also the discussion of the application of *res ipsa loquitur* to medical negligence cases by the British Columbia Supreme Court in *Girard v Royal Columbian Hospital* (1976) 66 D.L.R. (3d) 676: the claimant was given a spinal anaesthetic in preparation for an operation. After the operation he was found to have permanent partial paralysis of both legs. Andrews J. held that the doctrine of *res ipsa loquitur* did not apply: "Although the treatment of the claimant was under the control of the defendant doctors it was not under their sole control in the sense that they could see, observe and react to the immediate effects of the external application of such treatment. It was hidden from their view and was subject to the unexplained mysteries of the claimant's own physiology . . . medical science has not yet reached the stage where the law ought to presume that a patient must come out of an operation as well or better than he went into it. From my interpretation of the medical evidence the kind of injury suffered by the claimant could have occurred without negligence on anyone's part. Since I cannot infer there was negligence on the part of the defendant doctors the maxim of *res ipsa loquitur* does not apply." In *Fallows v Randle* [1997] 8 Med. L.R. 160 in a failed sterilisation case the Court of Appeal held that *res ipsa loquitur* had no application where the fallope ring on a fallopian tube was found to be missing and pregnancy resulted. The judge had to decide the most probable explanation for its being missing on the basis of the possible explanations put forward by the two experts.
[93] [1939] 2 K.B. 14.
[94] Goddard and MacKinnon L.JJ.; Goddard L.J. dissented from the actual decision of the Court.
[95] *ibid.* at 50. Examples of other English cases in which the claimant has succeeded on the basis of *res ipsa loquitur* are *Clarke v Worboys, The Times*, March 18, 1952 (liability for severe burn after pad placed on claimant's left buttock for the purpose of electro-coagulation) and *Cooper v Nevill, The Times*, March 10, 1961 (abdominal pack left in claimant's body after operation). Canadian cases in which the claimant has succeeded on *res ipsa loquitur* include *Cox v Saskatoon* [1942] 1 D.L.R. 74 (injury to arm during an operation); *Cavan v Wilcox* (1973) 44 D.L.R. (3d) 42 (nurse injected bicillin into claimant's arm: some bicillin entered an artery and caused a blockage and gangrene developed); *Holmes v Board of Hospital Trustees of City of London* (1978) 81 D.L.R. (3d) 67 (tissue emphysema when oxygen injected at pressure could only occur if needle negligently displaced from trachea); *Feist v Gordon* [1991] 2 Med. L.R. 376 (eyeball pierced during periocular injection).

persons.[96] In *Cassidy v Ministry of Health*[97] the claimant was treated at Walton Hospital, Liverpool for Dupuytren's contraction of the third and fourth fingers of the left hand. Dr F performed the operation. After the operation (as was normal) the claimant's left hand and lower arm were kept rigid in a splint. When released from the splint the claimant's left hand was useless. The third and fourth fingers were bent and stiff. The two good fingers were also affected. The Court of Appeal, reversing the trial judge, held that the maxim *res ipsa loquitur* applied: "On the basis that the hospital was responsible for all those in whose charge the claimant was, the surgeon, the doctor and nurses, the result seems to me to raise a case of *res ipsa loquitur,*" *per* Somervell L.J.[98] The defendants did not, on the evidence, succeed in rebutting the inference that there had been some negligence by their staff and accordingly were held liable to the claimant.[99]

Inference of negligence rebutted. Defendants may displace the inference of   **13-041** negligence by adducing evidence to show either that due care was exercised, or that there is an alternative explanation for the claimant's injury which is consistent with the exercise of due care.[1] Cases where evidence of an alternative

---

[96] Thus in *Morris v Winsbury-White* [1937] 4 All E.R. 494 the doctrine was held not to apply. See also *McFadyen v Harvie* [1942] 4 D.L.R. 647. *cf. Thompson Estates v Byrne* (1993) 114 N.S.R. (2d) 395, Court of Appeal of Nova Scotia, where a patient under intensive care removed tubes from her body and suffered brain damage before she was retubated. She was not entitled to rely upon the maxim: since she was able to disturb her tubation, it was not under the sole management of the defendant hospital and her pre-existing condition was part of the cause of her injury, which could therefore have happened without negligence. See also *Elliott v Bickerstaff* (1999) 48 N.S.W.L.R. 214. New South Wales Court of Appeal, in which the case concerned an obstetric operation at a private hospital: the surgeon was sued (but the hospital was not) in respect of a surgical sponge left in the patient's abdominal cavity at the end of the operation. On the basis that the fault was that of the theatre nursing staff (for whom the surgeon was not responsible, but the hospital was) *res ipsa loquitur* did not apply.

[97] [1951] 2 K.B. 343.

[98] *ibid.* at 348. See also Singleton L.J. at 353 and Denning L.J. at 365–366.

[99] "They have busied themselves in saying that this or that member of their staff was not negligent. But they have not called a single person to say that the injuries were consistent with due care on the part of all the members of their staff. They called some of the people who actually treated the man . . . each of whom protested that he was careful in his part; but they did not call any expert at all, to say that this might happen despite all care. They have not therefore displaced the prima facie case against them . . . " *per* Denning L.J., *ibid.* at 366. See also *Bull v Devon AHA* [1993] 4 Med. L.R. 117 in which the majority in the Court of Appeal held that the maxim was properly applied in a case where breach of a health authority's primary duty to provide a safe system of care was alleged. Complications developed at the birth of a second twin in the hospital's maternity unit. As a result of difficulties and delay in tracing a suitably qualified medical practitioner to assist, the baby suffered hypoxia and consequent brain-damage. It was held that the most likely explanation for the delay was either inefficiency in the hospital's system for summoning doctors to obstetric emergencies or negligence by an individual or individuals in the operation of that system. Consequently, the maxim applied and the hospital had the evidential burden of justifying the delays. In *Hay v Grampian Health Board* [1995] 6 Med. L.R. 128 Ct of Sess. however, the maxim did not apply. The issue in that case was whether a patient's suicide while subject to the hospital's regime of close observation was caused by negligence. There was evidence of the explanation for the event, namely, that a nurse had allowed the patient to go to the bathroom unaccompanied. The question whether it was negligent for the health board's regime to provide such opportunity for self-harm was to be considered on ordinary principles.

[1] See *Delaney v Southmead HA* [1995] 6 Med. L.R. 355, 359 *per* Stuart-Smith L.J. Since the maxim describes only a prima facie inference of negligence, and the burden of proof remains on the claimant, the defendant need not show that an alternative explanation is more likely than not to be the correct

explanation has been accepted include *Roe v Minister of Health*,[2] *Brazier v Ministry of Defence*[3] and *Howard v Wessex Regional HA*.[4] In *Roe*, two patients suffered permanent paralysis from the waist down after being injected with a spinal anaesthetic at the defendant's hospital. The Court of Appeal held that the maxim *res ipsa loquitur* applied: the facts called for an explanation from the defendants.[5] However, the defendants had given an explanation of the disaster, which was consistent with due care on their part. The anaesthetic was kept in glass ampoules, stored in phenol solution. The phenol had penetrated the ampoules through invisible cracks, of which the defendants could not reasonably have been aware. Accordingly, the defendants escaped liability. In *Brazier*, a needle broke in the course of an injection. McNair J. held that *res ipsa loquitur* applied. However, the defendants had established on the balance of probabilities that the mishap was due to a latent defect in the needle. Accordingly, the claimant's claim failed.[6] In *Howard*, the claimant alleged that the tetraplegia which she suffered following maxillo-facial surgery must have been due to a traumatic injury negligently inflicted upon her cervical spine during surgery, relying on the maxim. She failed because the defendant health authority was able to show that there was another possible explanation. The explanation advanced was that the claimant's condition was caused by fibro-cartilaginous embolism (FCE). Notwithstanding that this was an extremely rare occurrence, the defendants were held not liable.[7] By contrast, the defendant's attempt to explain the claimant's condition as caused by extremely remote risks failed in *Glass v Cambridge HA*.[8] The claimant suffered cardiac arrest while under anaesthetic. The defendant's argument that this was caused by gas embolism resulting from the use of hydrogen peroxide to clean a wound was held to involve a highly unlikely combination of circumstances. As such, it failed to rebut the presumption that due care had not been exercised. In *Browne v Guys & Lewisham NHS Trust*[9] the defendant established that irritation (which resolved) following a second exploratory operation was not due to lack of care at the first operation, but due to keloid scarring which was removed by the further operation. In *Hopper v Young*[10] the Court of Appeal allowed an appeal by the defendant on the basis that there had been ample evidence that the kinking of a ureter following an operation could occur without negligence.

13–042   In the absence of an explanation for the claimant's condition which is consistent with the exercise of due care, the defendant may succeed if there is evidence that due care was in fact exercised. This is illustrated by cases where the

---

explanation. See also *Browne v Guys & Lewisham NHS Trust* [1997] 8 Med. L.R. 132; and *Hooper v Young* [1998] Lloyds' Rep. Med. 61.

[2] [1954] 2 Q.B. 66.

[3] [1965] 1 Lloyd's Rep. 26.

[4] [1994] 5 Med. L.R. 57.

[5] [1954] 2 Q.B. 66. at 80 (*per* Somervell L.J.), 81 (*per* Denning L.J.) and 88 (*per* Morris L.J.).

[6] *Hajgato v London Health Association* (1982) 36 O.R. (2d) 669, Ontario High Court is a Canadian decision to the same effect, affirmed: (1983) 44 O.R. (2d) 264.

[7] The judge concluded that there had not been negligent over-extension of the claimant's neck during surgery on the basis of evidence from the operating team that no one had noticed anything untoward.

[8] [1995] 6 Med. L.R. 91.

[9] 1997] 8 Med. L.R. 132.

[10] [1998] Lloyd's Rep. Med. 61.

negligence complained of took place during operative procedures carried out under general anaesthetic or on the part of anaesthetists themselves. The maxim is frequently called in aid in such cases, since the claimant's recollection of relevant events is unlikely to be sufficient to enable the precise conduct complained of to be identified. In *Jacobs v Great Yarmouth and Waveney HA*[11] and *Delaney v Southmead HA*[12] there are decisions to the same effect. In *Jacobs*, the claimant complained that she had experienced consciousness before and during an operation because of ineffective anaesthesia. The normal effect of muscle relaxant drugs administered as part of the pre-operative procedure was to paralyse the patient; she was thus unable to signal her awareness to theatre staff so as to obtain corroborative evidence of her complaint. The Court of Appeal upheld the judge's finding that, although the claimant had established a prima facie case of consciousness due to negligence before or during surgery, that case had been answered by the defendant's evidence that all proper steps were taken in administration of the anaesthetic.[13] In *Ratcliffe v Plymouth and Torbay HA*,[14] the claimant suffered a serious and unexpected neurological deficit from the waist down following an operation on his ankle which had involved a spinal anaesthetic. The anaesthetist's evidence as to the manner in which he had carried out the spinal injection was accepted and it was held that he had exercised due care. Since there was ample evidence to support the judge's findings, the claimant's appeal failed.[15]

A recent example of a case where the medical practitioner failed to rebut the inference is *Lillywhite v UCH*.[16] In this case a distinguished antenatal radiologist had failed to observe a serious abnormality of the brain. The claimant argued that

[11] [1995] 6 Med. L.R. 192.

[12] [1995] 6 Med. L.R. 355, CA.

[13] This decision highlights the difficulties of proof facing a claimant complaining of ineffective anaesthesia. The Court of Appeal upheld the judge's finding, on the evidence and as "a matter of common sense", that the claimant's memory was unreliable because of the fact that several drugs had been administered to her as part of the operative process. For further examples of non-application of the maxim see *Lindsay v Mid-Western Health Board* [1993] I.L.R.M. 550 (in which the Irish Supreme Court held that the claimant's failure to return to consciousness after a routine operation required explanation. The claimant was unable to point to any precise instance of negligence but was entitled to rely upon *res ipsa loquitur*. The health board escaped liability by showing that all reasonable care had been taken and was not required to prove an alternative cause of the claimant's condition) and *Delaney v Southmead HA* [1995] 6 Med. L.R. 355, CA (the claimant suffered an injury to the nerves serving his hand during an operation for removal of his gall bladder. He alleged that the only possible explanation was negligent over-rotation of his arm during administration of the general anaesthetic. The allegation failed, and the maxim did not apply, because on the evidence there was no such over-rotation and the defendants had exercised due care). The maxim also did not assist the claimant in *Vernon v Bloomsbury HA* [1995] 6 Med. L.R. 297. Injury following administration of gentamicin therapy at a dosage higher than that recommended by the manufacturers or by the pharmaceutical formularies raised an inference of negligence. However, the inference was displaced by evidence that the dosage conformed with the standard set by the responsible body of medical opinion which was represented by the defendant's experts.

[14] [1998] Lloyd's Rep. Med. 162.

[15] In *Jake Smith v Richard J Sheridan* [2005] EWHC 614, QBD, although Mr Justice McKinnon stated that he did not see the point of relying on the maxim and that he did not see it as a "*res ipsa loquitur*" case, because he found that the defendant must have used excessive force in delivering the claimant during an elective Caesarean section breech birth, the defendant did defend by offering a possible non-negligent explanation for the claimant's severe brain damage. The explanation was rejected as no more than a remote possibility which did not amount to a plausible explanation.

[16] [2005] EWCA Civ 1466; (2006) Lloyd's Rep. Med. 268.

he must have been negligent because the relevant structures required for normality were just not there to be seen. The defence pointed to the fact that two other specialists had come to the same conclusion at about the same time and that the evidence suggested that the consultant had set about his task with care. The judge at first instance rejected the claim on these grounds and because the possible explanations for the consultant "seeing" what was not there did not "point with clarity" to negligence. The majority of the Court of Appeal (Latham and Buxton L.JJ.) allowed the appeal on the ground that, after a detailed consideration of the evidence, no plausible explanation for the mistake had been produced. Therefore although it was accepted that the consultant had conducted the examination with great care he was found to have acted negligently. Buxton L.J. pointed out that a professional man is required to display not just care, but care and skill. *Ratcliffe* was distinguished because it involved a "mechanical process" where an acceptance that care had been used led to the conclusion that some unknown condition was the cause and that therefore the doctor was not responsible, whereas the present case involved one where skill and judgment were required in assessing what could be seen. In such circumstances, without reversing the burden of proof, the defendant must produce an explanation which at least raises a question mark over the original assumption of negligence.

(g) Consent to Treatment

13-043   A full discussion of consent to medical treatment is outside the scope of this book.[17] Shortly stated, however, medical treatment which is given without consent constitutes trespass to the person,[18-19] save in exceptional circumstances. A claim for assault and battery is sometimes pleaded in addition to (or in the alternative to) a claim for negligence, although such claims have greatly diminished following the decision of the House of Lords in *Sidaway v Governors of Bethlem Royal Hospital*.[20] Proof of consent is a defence to an allegation of trespass to the person.[21] In order to provide an answer to a claim in trespass, it must be shown that the consent given related to the treatment in question, that it

---

[17] For a general review of this subject, see Kennedy & Grubb, *Principles of Medical Law* (1988 edn), Chs 3 and 4; Powers & Harris, *Clinical Negligence* (1999), Ch.5.
[18-19] See, e.g. *Hamilton v Birmingham Regional Hospital Board* [1969] 2 B.M.J. 456 (sterilisation without consent); *Appleton v Garrett* [1996] 1 P.I.Q.R. 1 (unnecessary dental treatment without consent); *Schweizer v Central Hospital* (1974) 53 D.L.R. (3d) 494. "By going into hospital, he does not waive or give up his right of absolute security of the person; he cannot be treated in hospital as a mere specimen, or as an inanimate object which can be used for the purpose of vivisection; he remains a human being, and he retains his rights of control and disposal of his own body; he still has the right to say what operation he will submit to, and, unless his consent to an operation is expressly obtained, any operation performed upon him without his consent is an unlawful interference with his right of security and control of his own body and is a wrong entitling him to damages if he suffers any", *per* Watermeyer J. in *Stoffberg v Elliott* [1923] C.P.D. 148 (South Africa).
[20] [1985] A.C. 871.
[21] The burden of proof is on the defendant: see *Re F (Mental Patient: Sterilisation)* [1990] 2 A.C. 1, 27 *per* Neill L.J.; *Reibl v Hughes* (1980) 114 D.L.R. (3d) 1, 9, Supreme Court of Canada; *Secretary, Department of Health and Community Services v JWB* (1992) 106 A.L.R. 385, 453, High Court of Australia; *cf. Freeman v Home Office* [1984] Q.B. 524.

was given voluntarily, that the patient was appropriately informed before he consented and that he had capacity in law to consent.[22]

The exercise of reasonable care and skill in treating the patient or in advising beforehand as to the risks of proposed treatment is not a defence. This is one of the perceived advantages of framing a case in trespass: evidence as to general and approved practice in disclosure of risks is irrelevant. Another advantage lies in the test for causation. If it is not shown that the patient gave valid consent to the procedure administered, damages will follow for any injury suffered as a direct result of that procedure. Unlike a claim in negligence for failure to warn of the risks of treatment, the claimant need not prove that he would not have consented to the treatment had he been advised beforehand with due care. Further, he will recover damages for injury suffered when a risk inherent in the procedure materialises, notwithstanding that such injury was consistent with the exercise of due care in performance of the procedure. The English courts, however, have been unwilling to encourage actions brought in trespass.[23] The claimant in *Williamson v East London & City HA*[24] claimed damages on the grounds that she had consented to a less serious operation than the defendant's surgeon had performed, but argued that there had been a negligent failure to obtain consent, rather than a trespass. She recovered general damages for inter alia her shock upon discovering what had been done, the insult of a non-consensual operation and her loss of certainty that the operation had been necessary, which certainty she would have acquired had she been free to obtain further medical opinions.[25]

(i) *Limits to Consent*

Just as a practitioner will be liable if the treatment given exceeds the patient's consent, the patient may withdraw consent at any stage in the procedure. Difficulties arise when there are unexpected complications during the course of an operation. It is normally possible to obtain consent before carrying out the further treatment which is necessary, but it is highly inconvenient to take this course, not   **13-044**

---

[22] See paras 13–047 to 13–053, below.

[23] This reluctance is illustrated by *Davis v Barking, Havering and Brentwood HA* [1993] 4 Med. L.R. 85. Before undergoing a minor operation, the claimant signed a consent form which authorised the defendant health authority to perform the operation and to administer general, local and such other anaesthetics as were deemed necessary. The anaesthetist administered a general anaesthetic and, during the operation, a caudal block (a type of local epidural anaesthetic). The claimant alleged that she had not consented to the administration of the caudal block because no one had suggested to her before the operation that any anaesthetic other than general would be necessary and a caudal block was not in fact necessary. Dismissing the argument that separate consent was required for each type of anaesthesia used, McCullough J. observed that an approach which required consent for each aspect of treatment (a "sectional" approach) would encourage the bringing of actions in trespass rather than in negligence. *Ibid.* at 90. See also *Hills v Potter* [1984] 1 W.L.R. 641, 653 *per* Hirst J.; *Sidaway v Governors of Royal Bethlem Hospital* [1985] 1 A.C. 871, 883E *per* Lord Scarman.

[24] [1998] Lloyd's Rep. Med. 6.

[25] The case of *B v Leeds HA* 2001 EWCA Civ 51 was also a case brought in negligence, rather than trespass. The claimant's parents had successfully contended that the defendant had been negligent in the advice given about the infant claimant's treatment for acute lymphoblastic leukaemia. The defendant's appeal was allowed on the basis that in the circumstances, there had been no negligence.

least for the patient, who may be subjected to two operations where fuller consent would have made the second unnecessary.[26]

This problem is now less likely to arise, because the consent forms signed by patients before undergoing surgery usually refer to the specific operation proposed and then to "such further or alternative operative measures as may be found necessary during the course of such operation". The consent form should be construed in a reasonable manner[27] but the patient's signature is merely evidence of consent. Where the patient is incapable of understanding the form or has not been advised to the extent necessary to give him a broad understanding of the nature of the procedures contemplated, his signature on the form will not be conclusive.[28]

(ii) *Voluntary Consent*

13–045 Consent to medical treatment must be freely given. In other words, such consent must not be obtained by imposing unreasonable pressure on the patient. In many situations, of course, it will be reasonable for a doctor to put pressure on a patient to accept treatment which is plainly for his benefit. In prison, however, where the medical officer is also a prison officer, the doctor-patient relationship assumes a different character. In this context the question whether consent to medical

---

[26] Three Canadian cases shed light on this situation. In *Marshall v Curry* [1933] 3 D.L.R. 260 the defendant surgeon, in the course of a hernia operation, discovered a seriously diseased testicle, a condition which he could not reasonably have foreseen. He removed the testicle for the protection of the claimant's health and possibly his life. It was held that there was no assault. Similarly, in *Ciarlariello v Schacter* (1993) 100 D.L.R. (4th) 609 the patient insisted that an angiogram to which she had previously consented be stopped. The Supreme Court of Canada said that in such circumstances, the practitioner is entitled to continue a procedure only where failure to do so would be life-threatening or cause immediate and serious harm to the health of the patient. It was found on the facts that the claimant had in fact renewed her consent, so that the procedure was lawfully continued. In *Murray v McMurchy* [1949] 2 D.L.R. (4th) 609 however, it was held that a surgeon was not entitled to carry out an unauthorised procedure during the course of an operation merely because it was convenient or desirable to do so.

[27] See *Davis v Barking, Havering and Brentwood HA* [1994] 3 Med. L.R. 85, the facts of which are given at para.12–125 above; *Bruschett v Cowan* [1991] 2 Med. L.R. 271, Newfoundland CA (consent to muscle biopsy was sufficient to include consent to bone biopsy); *O'Bonswain v Paradis* [1994] 5 Med. L.R. 399, Ontario High Court (consent to "additional or alternative treatment or operative procedure as in the opinion of [the defendant] are immediately necessary" embraced consent to alternative means of access for dialysis); *cf. Pridham v Nash* (1986) 33 D.L.R. (4th) 304, where the Ontario High Court held that a consent form in similar terms signed before a laparoscopy (a minor investigative operation) entitled the surgeon to carry out any minor operation found necessary during the laparoscopy; but it would not entitle him to carry out major surgery.

[28] " . . . getting the patient to sign a pro forma expressing consent to undergo the operation 'the effect and nature of which have been explained to me' . . . would be no defence to an action based on trespass if no explanation had in fact been given. The consent would have been expressed in form only, not in reality": *Chatterton v Gerson* [1981] Q.B. 432, 443D–E *per* Bristow J. The same applies to signature of forms of refusal to consent: see *Re T (Adult: Refusal of Treatment)* [1993] Fam. 95, 114G–H *per* Lord Donaldson M.R. See, to similar effect, *Taylor v Shropshire HA* [1998] Lloyd's Rep. Med. 395. The claimant failed to prove that she had not been warned of the risk of failure of a sterilisation operation (although she recovered damages on the basis that the operation had been negligently performed). In so finding, however, Popplewell J. stated that he was not assisted by the defendant's specific consent form for sterilisations, which stated that the claimant had been warned of the risk of failure and was signed by her just before the operation. He regarded the form as "pure window dressing" on the facts of that case. NB: *Taylor* is per incuriam in so far as the decision awards damages for the cost of bringing up the child.

treatment was freely given may arise more often. This topic was considered in *Freeman v Home Office (No.2)*.[29] In that case McCowan J. rejected the contention that a prisoner could not give valid consent to treatment by the prison medical officer. However, he acknowledged that a prisoner may on occasions be overborne by the medical officer:

> "The right approach, in my judgment, is to say that where, in a prison setting, a doctor has the power to influence a prisoner's situation and prospects a court must be alive to the risk that what may appear, on the face of it, to be a real consent is not in fact so."[30]

The Court of Appeal, in affirming McCowan J.'s judgment, expressly approved this passage.[31]

Consent or refusal to consent may be vitiated by the undue influence of a third party. In *Re T (Adult: Refusal of Treatment)*,[32] T, a pregnant woman who had links with Jehovah's Witnesses, was injured in a road traffic accident and taken to hospital. T said that she did not want a blood transfusion. However, she said this at a time when she was under the influence of her mother (a Jehovah's Witness) and when a doctor had advised her that there were other procedures available. On the following day a Caesarean section was performed. The baby was stillborn, T's condition deteriorated and a blood transfusion became essential. The Court of Appeal upheld a declaration that it was not unlawful to administer a blood transfusion to T. The Court held that in the present case T's refusal was not effective, because at the time (a) she was under the undue influence of her mother and (b) she believed that alternative treatments would suffice.

(iii) *Informed Consent*

The doctrine of "informed consent", as developed in certain states in the United **13–046** States, holds that a patient's consent to medical treatment is vitiated if he is given inadequate information concerning the proposed treatment. Accordingly, he is entitled to claim damages for battery, despite the fact that he apparently consented to the treatment.[33]

---

[29] [1984] Q.B. 524.

[30] *ibid.* at 542H–543A.

[31] *ibid.* at 557B–C and 558.

[32] [1993] Fam. 95.

[33] *Salgo v Leland Stanford Jr University Board of Trustees* 154 Cal. App. 2d 560; 317 P. 2d 170 (1957); *Canterbury v Spence* 464 F. 2d 772 (D.C. Cir. 1972); Robertson, G., "Informed consent to Medical Treatment" (1981) 97 L.Q.R. 102. The Supreme Court of Canada, although imposing a higher duty of disclosure than the English courts, has declined to adopt this doctrine. In *Reibl v Hughes* (1980) 114 D.L.R. (3d) 1, 10–11 Laskin C.J., delivering the judgment of the court, stated:
"In my opinion, actions of battery in respect of surgical or other medical treatment should be confined to cases where surgery or treatment has been performed or given to which there has been no consent at all or where, emergency situations aside, surgery or treatment has been performed or given beyond that to which there was consent . . . . In situations where the allegation is that attendant risks which should have been disclosed were not communicated to the patient and yet the surgery or other medical treatment carried out was that to which the claimant consented . . . I do not understand how it can be said that the consent was vitiated by the failure of disclosure . . . [I]n my view, unless there has been a misrepresentation or fraud to secure consent to the treatment, a failure to disclose the attendant risks, however serious, should go to negligence rather than battery."

The American doctrine of informed consent was exhaustively reviewed by the Court of Appeal[34] and the House of Lords[35] in *Sidaway v Governors of Bethlem Royal Hospital*. The Court of Appeal held unanimously that failure to give a patient sufficient information would not vitiate his consent to an operation. In the House of Lords, although the law lords differed as to the extent of the duty of disclosure, they were unanimous in the view that inadequate disclosure of information did not vitiate the patient's consent to treatment. Even Lord Scarman, who favoured a more extensive duty of disclosure than his colleagues, agreed with Hirst J.'s comment in *Hills v Potter*[36] that it would be deplorable to base the law in medical cases of this kind on the torts of assault and battery.[37]

In *Appleton v Garrett*,[38] the defendant dentist administered excessive and unnecessary dental treatment to his patients on a massive scale. Dyson J. found that he deliberately withheld from his patients the information that their teeth were healthy and that the treatment was unnecessary, so as to secure their consent and his personal gain. The effect of his non-disclosure in bad faith was to vitiate the consents given and entitle the patients to sue in trespass.[39] But in the cases of *Halkyard v Mathew*[40] and *R. v Richardson*[41] in differing circumstances it was held that failures to disclose did not vitiate consent. In *Halkyard* the surgeon failed to disclose to his patient that he suffered from epilepsy: it was held that as long as his medical condition did not affect his capacity to perform the treatment he was under no obligation to disclose it; and in *Richardson* a dentist continued to carry out treatment on patients despite being suspended from practice. She was convicted of assault, but the convictions were overturned on appeal on the basis

---

[34] [1984] Q.B. 493.

[35] [1985] A.C. 871.

[36] [1984] 1 W.L.R. 641, 653D–E (Note).

[37] [1985] A.C. 871, 883E. See also *Davis v Barking, Havering and Brentwood HA* [1993] 4 Med. L.R. 85, 91 *per* McCullough J; and *Behrens v Smith* (1997) 153 Sask. R. 294 where Wimmer J. said: "The law imposes upon the medical practitioner a duty to provide sufficient information to enable the patient to reasonably balance the possible risks and benefits and make an informed decision about whether to undergo or forego a recommended treatment. The scope of the duty will vary according to the circumstances of the case and any special considerations affecting the particular patient. That which a patient should be made to understand are the nature, purpose, and likely benefits of the treatment; the recognised risks inherent in it; the availability of alternative treatments; and the possible consequences of leaving the condition untreated". The Canadian case of *Van Mol v Ashmore* (1999) 168 D.L.R. (4th) British Columbia CA considers the question of who has to consent. A 16-year-old girl underwent surgery to remedy narrowing of her aorta; in the course of difficulties in the operation she suffered paraplegia and damage to the laryngeal nerve. The judge held that the operation was not negligently carried out, and that proper consent had been obtained from the parents. The Court of Appeal held, by a majority, that the appeal should be allowed on the basis that the patient herself should have had the appropriate explanation about the risks and advantages of the operation, and that had this happened she would have probably have opted for a more conservative approach.

[38] [1997] 8 Med. L.R. 75. See para 13–157 below.

[39] At (1996) 4 Med. L.Rev. 311, the commentator argues that the law of trespass serves a useful purpose in such cases: the prospect of compensation for damage (injury to feelings) which does not sound in negligence should be an important deterrent against cynical conduct by health professionals.

[40] [1999] 67 Alta. L.R. (3d).

[41] [1999] Q.B. 444.

that fraud only vitiated the consent where the fraud was as to the identity of the person doing the act, or the nature of the act itself.[42-43]

(iv) *Capacity to Consent*

Legal capacity to consent depends upon the patient's ability to understand the **13–047** broad nature of the treatment which he is advised to undergo. The requirement for consent is a recognition of individual autonomy or a right to self-determination. A patient who has capacity in law to give his consent to treatment must also have the right to withhold consent. It follows that he is entitled to refuse consent for any reason whatever or for no reason at all.[44] Where a patient refuses treatment which is recommended for him and does so on grounds which appear to be irrational, there is a danger that he may be regarded as incompetent to give or refuse consent and that his wishes may be overridden. In *Re T (Adult: Refusal of Treatment)*[45] Lord Donaldson M.R. summarised the relevant principles:

"1. Prima facie every adult has the right and capacity to decide whether or not he will accept medical treatment, even if a refusal may risk permanent injury to his health or even lead to premature death. Furthermore, it matters not whether the reasons for the refusal were rational or irrational, unknown or even non-existent . . . . However the presumption of capacity to decide, which stems from the fact that the patient is an adult, is rebuttable.
2. An adult patient may be deprived of his capacity to decide by long-term mental incapacity . . . .
3. If an adult patient did not have the capacity to decide at the time of the purported refusal and still does not have that capacity, it is the duty of the doctors to treat him in whatever way they consider, in the exercise of clinical judgment, to be in his best interests.
4. Doctors faced with a refusal of consent have to give very careful and detailed consideration to what was the patient's capacity to decide at the time the decision was made. It may not be a case of capacity or no capacity. It may be a case of reduced capacity. What matters is whether at that time the patient's capacity was reduced below the level needed in the case of a refusal of that importance, for refusals can vary in importance. Some may involve a risk to life or of irreparable damage to health. Others may not."[46]

These principles were applied in *Re C (Adult: Refusal of Medical Treatment)*.[47] C was a chronic paranoid schizophrenic adult who refused to consent to the

---

[42-43] For a detailed criticism of the current position on informed consent under English law see the article "Informed Consent and Other Fairy Stories" by Professor Michael Jones (1999) 7 Med. L. Rev. 103.

[44] See *Sidaway v Governors of Royal Bethlem Hospital* [1985] A.C. 871, 904F *per* Lord Templeman.

[45] [1993] Fam. 95 at 115–116.

[46] In the case of *R. v Bournemouth Community and Mental Health NHS Trust Ex p. L.* [1999] 1 A.C. 458 the House of Lords confirmed the basic principle that if a person lacks capacity to take decisions about medical treatment, it is necessary for other appropriately qualified people to take the decisions for him. The principles of necessity may apply (125H–126B). In *Ms B v NHS Hospital Trust* [2002] EWHC 429 reported at [2002] 2 All E.R. 449, the President of the Family Division gave guidance for the treatment of future cases concerning adult refusal of treatment (at para.100).

[47] [1994] 1 W.L.R. 290.

amputation of his gangrenous foot. He was granted an injunction against the amputation of his foot without his express written consent. Thorpe J. had to consider whether or not C was competent to give or withhold consent at the time of his refusal. He analysed the process of deciding into three stages: comprehending and retaining treatment information, believing it, and weighing it in order to make an informed choice.[48] Applying that test, he found that C's general mental capacity was not so impaired by his schizophrenia that he was incapable of understanding the nature, purpose and effects of the treatment proposed, so that the presumption of competence (his right of self-determination) was not displaced and its expression governed all doctors with notice of it. The injunction merely added the sanction of contempt of court to what under the general law would be an assault. Thorpe J.'s approach to the question whether an adult patient has capacity to consent to or to refuse treatment in *Re C* was approved by the Court of Appeal in *Re MB*.[49]

13–048   Similarly, a competent adult who refuses treatment because of political or religious convictions is entitled to have that refusal honoured. *In Secretary of State for the Home Department v Robb*,[50] it was held that prison officials and medical staff could lawfully observe and abide by a prisoner's refusal to accept nutrition and hydration and could abstain from forcing them upon him, so long as he retained the mental capacity to refuse. By contrast in *R. v Collins and Ashworth Hospital Authority Ex p. Brady*[51] forcible feeding against the prisoner's will was sanctioned by the court on the basis that Brady had been incapacitated in all his decisions about refusing food by a mental disorder, and that the doctors were legally empowered to supply medical treatment in his best interests in accordance with their clinical judgment.

Medical treatment in the absence of consent may be given in an emergency.[52] This is a rule of common law, which is self-evidently necessary.[53] As to the ambit of the rule, it applies when a person is unable to consent (for example, because he is unconscious or mentally handicapped) and treatment is in his best interests.[54] The classic example of a case falling within this rule is the victim of a road accident lying unconscious, who requires a blood transfusion and possibly surgery to save his life. Even in this situation, however, doubt may arise if it is

---

[48] [1994] 1 W.L.R. 290 at 292E. The Court of Appeal has doubted whether a patient suffering anorexia nervosa has capacity to refuse food because of the effect of that disorder on the patient's understanding of the consequences of refusal: see *Re W (A Minor) (Medical Treatment)* [1993] Fam. 64; *B v Croydon HA* [1995] 1 All E.R. 683.

[49] [1997] 8 Med. L.R. 217.

[50] [1995] 2 W.L.R. 722. Feeding and hydration have also been regarded as treatment in the case of anorexics.

[51] [2000] Lloyd's Rep. Med. 355. See also Margaret Brazier's analysis of this and related cases in "Do No Harm—Do Patients Have Responsibilities Too?" [2006] C.L.J. 397

[52] See *Re F (Mental Patient: Sterilisation)* [1990] 2 A.C. 1, 55 (*per* Lord Brandon) and 712–78 (*per* Lord Goff).

[53] However, the juristic basis of the rule is uncertain. Lord Goff in *Re F (Mental Patient: Sterilisation)* [1990] 2 A.C. 1 expressed the view that it is founded on the principle of necessity. It is sometimes suggested that the rule is based upon implied consent, although this is somewhat artificial, since the patient has probably never directed his mind to the situation which has arisen.

[54] See *Re F (Mental Patient: Sterilisation)* [1990] 2 A.C. 1.

known that the victim is a Jehovah's Witness who would refuse the necessary treatment if he were in a position to do so. It has been suggested that in those circumstances a medical practitioner would not be held liable for taking whatever steps were necessary to save the patient's life.[55]

It follows from the above discussion that a patient of full age and capacity can   **13–049** effectively refuse medical treatment, even when it is necessary to save his life. Depending upon its terms, that refusal may include foreseeable future medical treatment even in the event that the patient later becomes incompetent to give or withhold consent.[56] It has been held that a refusal of consent to treatment may be overridden in circumstances where treatment is necessary to save the life of another. In *Re S (Adult: Refusal of Treatment)*[57] Sir Stephen Brown P. granted a declaration that a Caesarean section could be performed on a woman, despite her refusal on religious grounds, in order to save the life of the baby and avoid a serious risk of the mother's death. Urgent decisions in the course of the management of the last stages of pregnancy are the source of some difficult cases. The decision in *Re S*, which was given in circumstances of great urgency, was difficult to reconcile with the mother's right to refuse consent to treatment or with the principle that a foetus does not have legal personality until it is born alive.[58] In *Re MB*[59] following a comprehensive review of the authorities, Butler-Sloss L.J. said, obiter, that a woman who has the capacity to decide was entitled to refuse medical intervention, even though the consequence might be the death or serious handicap of the child she carries. It was held that the court did not have jurisdiction to take the interests of the unborn child into consideration in such cases. *Re S (Adult: Refusal of Treatment)*[60] was disapproved. The observations of

---

[55] See "Treatment without Consent: Emergency" (1985) 290 B.M.J. 1505. However, the Ontario Court of Appeal took a different view in *Malette v Shulman* [1991] 2 Med. L.R. 162 The claimant was seriously injured in a road traffic accident and admitted unconscious to hospital. A Jehovah's Witness card, found in her purse, requested that no blood be administered to her under any circumstances. The defendant doctor administered blood transfusions to her, which he considered necessary to preserve her life. It was held that the Jehovah's Witness card imposed a valid restriction on the emergency treatment which could be given to the claimant, and that the defendant was liable for battery.

[56] See *Re C (Adult: Refusal of Medical Treatment)* [1994] 1 W.L.R. 290. The effect of "advance directives" as to the patient's treatment wishes in the event that he later becomes incapable of making his own treatment decisions was recognised obiter in *Airedale NHS Trust v Bland* [1993] A.C. 789, 864F *per* Lord Goff. See *The NHS Trust v Ms T* [2004] EWHC 1279 (Fam) reported at [2005] 1 All E.R. 387, for an example of an "advance directive" by the patient that she no longer wanted to receive blood transfusions being overridden. The patient is a self-harmer, who believed that her own blood was evil. The court considered she had lacked capacity when signing the advance directive, and continued to lack capacity. The balance of competing factors came down in favour of giving the patient treatment to save her life.

[57] [1993] Fam. 123; see commentary at (1993) 2 Med. L.Rev. 92.

[58] The decision was criticised in Stern, K., "Court-Ordered Caesarian Sections: In Whose Interests?" (1993) 56 M.L.R. 238. The same outcome was achieved in the cases of *Norfolk and Norwich Healthcare NHS Trust v W* [1996] 2 F.L.R. 613 and *Rochdale Healthcare NHS Trust* [1997] 1 F.C.R. 274 (Johnson J. in both cases) in which neither woman was suffering from a mental disorder, but in one of which there was some doubt as to whether she was capable of understanding and retaining information about the proposed treatment.

[59] [1997] 8 Med. L.R. 217.

[60] [1993] Fam. 123.

Butler-Sloss L.J. in *Re MB* were adopted by the Court of Appeal in *St George's NHS Trust v S.*[61] S, who was 36 weeks pregnant, was diagnosed with pre-eclampsia and advised that she should be admitted to hospital for an induced delivery. She refused, since she wanted a natural birth. Against her will, she was admitted to a mental hospital for assessment under s.2 of the Mental Health Act 1983 and then transferred to another hospital, which obtained a declaration dispensing with her consent to treatment by Caesarean section. Her appeal, after the operation, was successful. The Court of Appeal held that an adult of sound mind was entitled to refuse treatment, even when his or her own life depended on receiving such treatment. That right was not diminished by reason of pregnancy merely because the decision to exercise it would result in the death of an unborn child and so might appear morally repugnant. The detention, treatment and transfer of S had been unlawful. The Court set out guidelines for use by medical practitioners, hospital authorities and health professionals generally when faced with a patient who refuses surgical or invasive treatment which is regarded as medically necessary.[62]

13-050   **Mentally disordered patients.** Consent is not required for lawful medical treatment of a patient who is detained under s.3 of the Mental Health Act 1983, provided that the treatment given is for the mental disorder.[63] Such treatment may be given notwithstanding a positive refusal to consent. In *Re KB (Adult) (Mental Patient: Medical Treatment)*,[64] the issue was whether an anorexic patient might lawfully be force-fed under these provisions despite her refusal to eat. It was argued that feeding was not treatment for her psychiatric disorder, but merely relief of the symptoms. Ewbank J. accepted the hospital's argument that relief of the symptoms of the patient's eating disorder was part of the treatment for that disorder, and was necessary in any event for treatment of the underlying disorder to be possible. It was held that forced-feeding of an anorexic patient amounted to "medical treatment given to [the patient] for a medical disorder" under s.63 of the 1983 Act, and so could be administered without consideration of her competence to refuse. That proposition was upheld and extended by the Court of Appeal in *B v Croydon HA.*[65] B was detained in hospital under s.3 of the 1983

---

[61] [1999] Fam. 26.
[62] See pages 702H–704J and for commentaries on this case, see (1998) 114 L.Q.R. 550 and [1998] C.L.J. 438. For a discussion of the decision in *Re MB*, see S. Michalowski, "Court-Authorised Caesarian Sections—The End of a Trend?" (1999) 62 M.L.R. 115.
[63] Mental Health Act 1983, s.63. See, generally, ss.512–564. In *R. (on the application of B) v (1) Dr A Haddock (2) Dr J Rigby (3) Dr Wood* [2005] EWHC 921, Admin, Collins J. held it was unnecessary to "classify" the detained claimant's disorder as mental illness or psychopathic disorder, provided it was convincingly shown that the proposed treatment was medically necessary to alleviate the claimant's condition.
[64] (1994) 19 B.M.L.R. 144; [1994] 2 F.C.R. 1051.
[65] [1995] Fam. 133 (and see commentary at (1995) 3 Med. L.Rev. 191). See also *Riverside Mental Health NHS Trust v Fox* [1995] 6 Med. L.R. 181, where a declaration that an anorexic woman could lawfully be forced-fed in order to keep her alive was quashed by the Court of Appeal on the grounds that the declaration granted purported to be an interim declaration, a form of relief which does not exist in English law. In "Feeding anorexics who refuse food" (1999) 7 Med. L.Rev. 21, P. Lewis examines the meaning of "best interests" in the context of the force-feeding of anorexic patients.

Act by reason of her borderline personality disorder. Although she was not anorexic, her disorder caused her to refuse food. B was refused an injunction against the hospital to prevent the staff feeding her by tube against her wish. Her appeal was dismissed. Treatment under s.63 had to be considered as a whole. Feeding, being designed to alleviate a symptom of her mental disorder, was ancillary to and a necessary prerequisite of the core treatment administered to deal with that disorder. Hoffmann L.J. said:

> "Nursing and care concurrent with the core treatment or as a necessary prerequisite to such treatment or to prevent the patient from causing harm to himself or to alleviate the consequences of the disorder are in my view all capable of being ancillary to a treatment calculated to alleviate or prevent a deterioration of the psychopathic disorder. It would seem to me strange if a hospital could, without the patient's consent, give him treatment directed to alleviating a psychopathic disorder showing itself in suicidal tendencies, but not without such consent be able to treat the consequences of a suicide attempt. In my judgment the term 'medical treatment . . . for the mental disorder' in section 63 includes such ancillary acts." [66]

On that basis, force-feeding of B was held to be treatment under s.63. The decision in *Re C (Adult: Refusal of Medical Treatment)* [67] was distinguished. Although C was a detainee under s.3 on account of his schizophrenia, that mental disorder was wholly unrelated to the gangrenous condition of his foot. [68]

In *R. (on the application of N) v Doctor M*, [69] the Court of Appeal applied the   **13–051**
standard of proof test from *Herczegfalvy v Austria (A/242B)*, [70] a decision of the European Court of Human Rights, that it had to be "convincingly" shown that the proposed treatment (and each part of that treatment) was a medical necessity. The Court stated that its duty was to consider whether or not the proposed treatment was in a detained patient's best interests; that this should be determined by reference to this high standard of proof ("the medical necessity test"), and that

---

[66] [1995] Fam. 133, *per* Hoffmann L.J. at 138H–139B. The Court of Appeal also doubted, without deciding, that B had capacity to refuse feeding when she did, by reason of the effect of anorexia nervosa on her understanding of the consequences of refusal. See also to this effect *Re W (A Minor) (Medical Treatment)* [1993] Fam. 64, CA.

[67] [1994] 1 W.L.R. 290, discussed at para.13–047, above.

[68] [1995] Fam. 133, 138H–139B *per* Hoffmann L.J., with whom Henry and Neill L.JJ. agreed. The approach adopted by the Court of Appeal in *B v Croydon HA* was applied by Wall J. in *Tameside and Glossop Acute Services NHS Trust v CH (a Patient)* [1996] 1 F.L.R. 762 CH was a 41-year-old schizophrenic, detained under the Mental Health Act 1983, who was found to be pregnant. Her obstetrician considered that there was a grave danger that her child would be still-born unless labour was induced and a Caesarian section performed. Her psychiatrist gave evidence that, in his opinion, the birth of a live baby was necessary for treatment of CH's schizophrenia to be effective. Accordingly, it was argued, induction and a Caesarean section were properly regarded as treatment ancillary to the core psychiatric treatment for the mental disorder. Wall J. accepted this reasoning. A declaration was granted that such procedures were lawful, notwithstanding CH's lack of consent to a Caesarean section, which had not even been discussed with her. Wall J. left open the question whether the court has power at common law to authorise the use of reasonable force as a necessary incident of treatment. The question was answered affirmatively by the Court of Appeal in *Re MB* [1997] 8 Med. L.R. 217.

[69] [2003] 1 W.L.R. 562.

[70] (1993) 15 E.H.R.R. 437. See also Chapter 7: Human Rights and Professionals.

the existence of a responsible body of opinion (the Bolam test) that the treatment was not in their best interests was not conclusive in favour of the patient.[71]

The exception annunciated by Butler-Sloss L.J. in *Re MB* namely where the detained patient is "unable to use the information and weigh it in the balance as part of the process of arriving at the decision" of whether to consent to the proposed treatment or not, was applied in *An NHS Trust v C*.[72] The case concerned an elderly patient, C, who was mentally ill, and had been detained under s.3 of the Mental Health Act 1983. A renal carcinoma was suspected but C was refusing to consent to a CT ultrasound scan. The court found that C lacked the capacity to consent; that her mental illness led to an inability to weigh the information and arrive at a decision and that it was in C's best interests for the CT scan to go ahead. The Court of Appeal confirmed that it was permissible for the court to make a judgment between two competing schools of expert evidence in this regard in *An NHS Trust v A*.[73] Such principles were again recently confirmed by the Court of Appeal in *R (on the application of B) v (1) SS (Responsible Medical Officer) (2) Second Opinion Appointed Doctor (3) Secretary of State for the Department of Health*[74] in which it was held that a patient detained under the Mental health Act 1983 who had the capacity to consent to medical treatment could be treated even though he refused consent where the proposed medical treatment was a medical or therapeutic necessity. It did not have to be shown that the treatment was necessary for the protection of the public or to prevent the patient suffering serious harm.

13–052   When is it lawful to treat an adult who is not detained under the Mental Health Act 1983, but whose mental disorder means that he or she is incompetent to make treatment decisions? This problem was considered by the House of Lords in *Re F (Mental Patient: Sterilisation)*,[75] where a declaration was upheld to the effect that a proposed sterilisation operation carried out on a 36-year-old mentally handicapped woman without her consent would not be unlawful. It was held that:

(i) the court had no *parens patriae* jurisdiction or jurisdiction under the Mental Health Act 1983 to approve the operation;

---

[71] See *R. (on the application of PS) v (1) Responsible Medical Officer; (2) Second Opinion Appointed Doctor* [2003] EWHC 2335, for a case confirming that forcible administration of treatment (anti-psychotic drugs) to a patient detained under the Mental Health Act 1983 was not "inhuman or degrading treatment" so as to engage the patient's rights under Art.3 of the European Convention on Human Rights 1950, or that those rights were not engaged due to the evident medical and therapeutic necessity of the treatment. See also *R. (on the application of B) v (1) Dr SS (Responsible MO), Broadmoor Hospital (2) Dr G (Second Opinion Appointed Doctor) (3) S of S for the Department of Health* [2005] EWHC 1936, Admin: if Art.3 was not engaged, the strict test of medical or therapeutic necessity (from *Herczegfalvy v Austria*) was not applicable; and this test did not apply to Art.8 rights.

[72] [2004] EWHC 1657 (Fam).

[73] [2005] EWHC Civ 1145; [2006] Lloyd's Med L.R. 29.

[74] [2006] EWCA Civ 28; (2006) 1 W.L.R. 810.

[75] [1990] 2 A.C. 1. Applied by the High Court of Hong Kong in *Hospital Authority v C* [2003] Lloyd's Rep. Med. 130 where the mother suffered irreversible brain damage when 12 weeks pregnant. By 32 weeks gestation her condition was deteriorating and the Hospital Authority wanted to deliver the foetus by Caesarean section and sought a declaration that the proposed surgery would be lawful. In opposition to the father's wishes, the declaration was granted as being in the mother's best interests.

(ii) where a person lacks the capacity to consent, medical treatment carried out in his best interests is not unlawful;

(iii) in determining whether particular treatment is, or was, in the best interests of such a person, the *Bolam* test applies[76];

(iv) the court has jurisdiction to make a declaration that a proposed operation is in a patient's best interests. It is good practice to apply for such a declaration before carrying out a sterilisation operation on an adult woman who is unable to consent because of mental incapacity.

In *R. v Bournewood Community and Mental Health NHS Trust*,[77] the House of Lords considered the lawfulness of treatment of an "informal patient". L was an autistic adult who was voluntarily admitted to hospital after becoming agitated at a day centre. Against the will of his carers, he remained in hospital and received treatment for his mental disorder. He lacked capacity to consent to treatment, but did not object to it. He was incapable of making a voluntary decision to leave hospital, but since he did not object, the procedures laid down by the Mental Health Act 1983 were not invoked to detain him or to justify his treatment. It was held that L was to be regarded as admitted under s.131(1) of the 1983 Act, which permits the admission to hospital of patients who lack capacity to consent but do not object. His treatment and care was justified by the common law principle of necessity. An examination of the legislative history of the 1983 Act revealed that its provisions did not exclude the application of the common law doctrine to the treatment of "informal patients" who are not detained under that Act. It was also held (Lords Nolan and Steyn dissenting) that L was not in fact detained, since he was in an open, unlocked ward, even although the hospital would have taken steps to detain him compulsorily under the 1983 Act had he tried to leave.

In *An NHS Trust v D*,[78] a case concerning an NHS Trust's application to court   **13–053** for a declaration prior to termination of a pregnancy of a mentally incapacitated person suffering severe schizophrenia, the Family Division of the High Court, Coleridge J., gave the following guidance as regards the making of an application to the court:

(i) An application to the court was not necessary where issue of capacity and best interests were beyond doubt.

---

[76] See Lord Bridge at 52D–E, Lord Brandon at 66G–68E and Lord Goff at 78B–C. This approach was followed by Hollis J. in *Re W (an Adult: Mental Patient: Sterilisation)* [1993] 1 F.L.R. 381, authorising the non-therapeutic sterilisation of a 20-year-old mentally disabled woman, notwithstanding that risk of her pregnancy was small. *cf. Department of Health & Community Services v JWB and SMB* (1992) 66 A.L.J.R. 300, where the High Court of Australia rejected the application of the *Bolam* test to the decision whether non-therapeutic sterilisation was in the best interests of a mentally disabled girl. For a comparative discussion of the law on sterilisation of mentally handicapped women in England and Australia, see N. Cica, (1993) 1 Med. L.Rev. 186. Cica argues that the *Bolam* principle in this context means that excessive regard will be paid to the opinion of medical practitioners on the social issues which bear upon the lawfulness of a proposed sterilisation. See also D. Giesen, "Comparative legal developments" in *Decision-Making and Problems of Incompetence* (A. Grubb, edn, 1994).

[77] [1999] 1 A.C. 458.

[78] [2003] EWHC 2793, reported at [2004] Lloyd's Rep. Med. 107.

(ii) An application should be made promptly where there was any doubt as to either issue.

(iii) Applications should ordinarily be made where:

     a. There was a realistic prospect of the patient regaining capacity during or shortly after pregnancy.

     b. There was disagreement between medical professionals as to the patient's best interests, or the patient, or her family, or the father expressed views inconsistent with termination.

     c. The procedures under s.1 of the Abortion Act 1967 had not been followed.

     d. There was some other exceptional circumstance, such as the pregnancy being the patient's last chance to bear a child.

(iv) A termination in accordance with the Abortion Act 1967 in the best interests of an incapacitated patient was a legitimate and proportionate interference with rights protected by Sch.1, Pt I, Arts 8(1) and 8(2).

13–054   **Withdrawal of Treatment from Insensate Patients.** In *Airedale NHS Trust v Bland*[79] the House of Lords applied the principles set out in *Re F*[80] in deciding whether medical treatment can lawfully be withdrawn from a patient who is permanently insensate. Anthony Bland was in a persistent vegetative state from which he would not recover. The hospital and physicians responsible for attending him sought and were granted declarations that they might lawfully discontinue medical treatment and care designed to keep him alive, including artificial ventilation, nutrition and hydration. It was held (1) that a medical practitioner is under no duty to provide medical treatment and care to a patient who is unable to benefit from it and (2) that the *Bolam* test applies to determine whether treatment and care is beneficial to, or in the best interests of, a patient who is unable to consent to their discontinuance.[81] Since there was a responsible medical opinion that neither life in a persistent vegetative state with no prospect of recovery nor the measures necessary to sustain life in that state were of benefit to Bland, those measures could lawfully be withdrawn. There was no question of balancing Bland's competing interests in continuance and cessation of treatment, respectively, for he had no interest in continuance. This would be so, notwithstanding the existence of a responsible body of medical opinion which supported the view that continuance of treatment was in the patient's interests.[82]

---

[79] [1993] A.C. 789.

[80] [1990] 2 A.C. 1.

[81] *ibid., per* Lord Keith at 362E, *per* Lord Goff at 373D–E, and *per* Lord Browne-Wilkinson at 385F–G. The application of the *Bolam* principle in this context is strongly criticised by J. Finnis in "Bland: Crossing the Rubicon?" (1993) 109 L.Q.R. 329; see also J. Keown, [1993] C.L.J. 209 and D. Robertson "The Withdrawal of Medical Treatment from Patients: Fundamental Legal Issues" (1996) 70 A.L.J. 723. *Airedale* was distinguished in the case of *SL (Adult Patient: Sterilisations: Patient's Best Interests)* [2000] Lloyd's Rep. Med. 339 where the Court of Appeal held in a case involving the possible sterilisation of a patient that the correct test was not the *Bolam* test, but whether or not the proposed treatment was in the best interests of the patient.

[82] Like reasoning has been applied in comparable cases in New Zealand (*Auckland AHA v Att-Gen* [1993] 1 N.Z.L.R. 235, High Court of New Zealand) and in South Africa (*Clarke v Hurst* (1992) 4 S.A. 630).

In *R. (on the application of Burke) v General Medical* Council,[83] it was held **13–055** at first instance that in cases concerning the proposed withdrawal of treatment seeking prior authorisation from the court was now a requirement in law where:

(i) There is any doubt or disagreement as to the capacity or competence of the patient.

(ii) There is a lack of unanimity amongst the medical professionals as to either the patient's condition, prognosis, best interests, the likely outcome of withdrawal or otherwise as to whether or not the treatment should be withdrawn.

(iii) There is evidence that the patient, when competent, would have wanted the treatment to continue in the relevant circumstances.

(iv) There is evidence that the patient (even if a child or incompetent) disputes or resists the proposed withdrawal of treatment.

(v) There are persons who, having a reasonable claim to have their views or evidence taken into account, such as parents, partners, close friends or long term carers, assert that withdrawal of treatment is contrary to the patient's wishes or not in the patient's best interests.

The Court of Appeal held that the declarations in fact given by Munby J. went **13–056** beyond the approach to competent patients in the claimant's position and set them all aside as unnecessary for the claimant's protection.[84] The claimant's concerns were already addressed by the law as it stood (i.e. the common law, but also Arts 2, 3 and 8 of the Convention). The claimant's competence and his expressed wish to be kept alive meant that any doctor who withdrew artificial nutrition and hydration from the claimant would be guilty of murder, not mere breach of duty. The Court of Appeal disapproved the judge's attempt to enunciate propositions of law "binding on the world" and counselled strongly against selective use of Munby J.'s judgment in future cases. The declaration of parts of the GMC Guidance as unlawful was disapproved as groundless in respect of the claimant's position, and the judge's postulation of a legal duty on the doctors to obtain court approval before treatment withdrawal was a misstatement of the law—it was good practice to do so when the legality of the proposed treatment was doubtful. The Court of Appeal, in a footnote to their judgment, stated that the GMC should be teaching understanding and promulgating implementation of the GMC Guidance at every level and in every hospital, to ensure patients like the claimant were confident of being treated properly and in accordance with good practice.[85]

---

[83] [2004] EWHC 1879, Admin, reported at [2005] Q.B. 424
[84] [2005] EWCA Civ 1003; (2005) 3 W.L.R. 1132.
[85] For a detailed commentary on the case see "Losing the Wood for the Trees: Burke and the Court of Appeal", Medical Law Review, 14, Summer 2006, pp.253–263.

13–057   **Children.** If a child has capacity to consent to medical treatment, the same principles apply as to an adult. There is a statutory presumption that a child has the same capacity to consent to treatment as an adult from the age of 16.[86] A child under 16 is capable of consenting to medical treatment, provided he or she has sufficient maturity to understand the implications of the proposed treatment[87] and the consequences of refusal of treatment.[88] However, where a child who is "*Gillick* competent" declines to consent to treatment, his parents or the court can do so on his behalf.[89] In the exercise of its wardship jurisdiction, the court may override a parent's wishes for treatment of a child. In *Re O (a Minor) (Medical Treatment)*,[90] the parents of an infant suffering respiratory distress syndrome refused to consent to the transfusion of blood to O on religious grounds. Johnson J. overrode their refusal, authorising a transfusion in the event that O's condition deteriorated to the point where, in the opinion of his doctors, a transfusion was necessary to avoid damage to his vital organs. By contrast, the Court of Appeal in *Re T (a Minor) Wardship: Medical Treatment*[91] upheld the parents' refusal to consent to a liver transplant operation upon their infant child. The unanimous opinion of the medical experts called was that the surgery was the accepted treatment and gave the child a good chance of an extended and reasonable quality of life, and that without the surgery the child would die at the age of two to two-and-a-half. In the very unusual facts of this case the Court held that in considering the future welfare of the child, it was entitled to take into account wider considerations than the prospects of success of the medical procedure proposed, including the effect on the baby's welfare of the mother's likely ability to cope

---

[86] Family Law Reform Act 1969, s.8(1). The presumption may be rebutted.

[87] See *Gillick v West Norfolk and Wisbech AHA* [1986] A.C. 112.

[88] See *Re E (a Minor) (Wardship: Medical Treatment)* [1993] 1 F.L.R. 386 (a 15-year-old Jehovah's Witness was not competent to refuse a blood transfusion because although he understood that he would die, he did not realise the full implications of the process of dying: transfusion lawful); on similar facts, *Re S (a Minor) (Consent to Medical Treatment)* [1994] 2 F.L.R. 1065 and *Re EE (a Minor) (Wardship: Medical Treatment)* [1994] 5 Med. L.R. 73. See also, on similar facts, the decision authorising transfusion in *Re L (Medical Treatment: Gillick Competency)* [1998] 2 F.L.R. 810. Commentaries on this decision appear at (1999) 62 M.L.R. 585 and at [1999] 7 Med. L.Rev. 58.

[89] See *Re W (a Minor) (Medical Treatment: The Court's Jurisdiction)* [1993] Fam. 64 (authorisation of removal to special hospital and treatment of 16-year-old anorexic), discussed by J. Eekelaar at (1993) 109 L.Q.R. 182 and by M. Mulholland at (1993) 9 P.N. 21. See also, on similar facts, *Re C (A Minor) (Detention: Medical Treatment)* [1997] 2 F.L.R. 180 commentary at (1999) 62 M.L.R. 595.

[90] [1993] 4 Med. L.R. 272. In *Re C (a Minor) (Medical Treatment)* [1998] Lloyd's Rep.Med. 1. The parents of a terminally ill infant refused consent to withdrawal of ventilation from her unless the hospital undertook to restore ventilation should she suffer respiratory arrest. The court granted leave to withdraw ventilation without such undertaking as in the infant's best interests. Neither the court nor parents can insist that treating doctors undertake a course of treatment which they do not consider medically justified. This decision is criticised at (1998) 6 Med. L.Rev. 99. See also *Re C (A Child) (HIV Testing)* [2000] Fam. 48: Wilson J. held that while there might be a rebuttable presumption of law that the united view of a baby's parents was correct in identifying where the welfare of the child lay, on the facts, the overwhelming advantages of testing for HIV a baby born to and breastfed by an HIV-positive woman overrode the wishes of the parents. If the test were to be conducted and was positive, advice could be given (and if necessary enforced by further orders of court) to which the afflicted baby would be entitled.

[91] [1997] 1 W.L.R. 242. For further discussion of *Re T (a Minor) (Wardship: Medical Treatment)*, see (1996) 4 Med. L.Rev. 315 and (1997) 60 M.L.R. 700.

with the care which the child would require during and after the operation. However, the court will not order that a particular medical procedure be administered where consent to treatment is not forthcoming from the child or from those with power to consent upon his behalf. The decision as to the appropriate treatment in the best interests of the patient is then for his attending doctors, and not for the court.[92]

(h) Allied Professions

This chapter is principally concerned with doctors and surgeons. The same   **13–058** principles apply, however, to nurses, midwives,[93] dentists and opticians. Any person who professes expertise in any aspect of medical treatment is required to exercise reasonable skill and care, judged by the standards of his own particular profession. Thus in *Lock v Scantlebury*[94] a dentist who dislocated the patient's jaw during treatment was held negligent for failing to notice what had occurred. He was not negligent, however, in causing the dislocation, since that could

---

[92] See *Re J (a Minor) (Child in Care: Medical Treatment)* [1993] Fam. 15 (refusal to order intensive resuscitation of profoundly mentally and physically handicapped child). This applies equally to the withdrawal of treatment: see *R. v Cambridge & District HA, Ex p. B* [1995] 1 W.L.R. 898, CA. See also *R. v Portsmouth Hospitals NHS Trust Ex p. Glass* [1999] Lloyd's Rep. Med. 367. Over the course of the Trust's treatment of a severely disabled child, disagreements arose between his mother and the Trust. His mother sought judicial review of the doctors' decisions. Scott Baker J. refused to grant a declaration as to the procedural steps which the doctors should take if disagreements arose in future between them and the child's mother as to the treatment to be given to or withheld from the child. There was an almost infinite number of considerations which might arise in the future. If the child's parents, having been fully consulted and fully understanding what doctors proposing to do, disagreed with what was proposed, the matter should be brought before the court for a decision as to what was required in the best interests of the child in the situation then pertaining. The Court of Appeal refused leave to appeal from this decision. See also *R. (on the application of Oliver Leslie Burke) v GMC & the Disability Rights Commission* [2005] EWCA Civ 1003 and *Portsmouth NHS Trust v (1) Derek Wyatt (2) Charlotte Wyatt (by her guardian CAFCASS) & Southampton NHS Trust (Intervenor)* [2004] EWHC 2247 (the treating hospital sought and obtained an order allowing it not to undertake ventilation of baby C, (despite parental disagreement) or any similar aggressive treatment, if baby C should catch a respiratory infection requiring ventilation, as such treatment was not in baby C's best interests. Baby C had never left hospital after a premature birth and suffered from chronic respiratory, kidney and neurological problems. The court held, applying *Re J (A Minor) (Wardship: Medical Treatment)* (1990) F.C.R. 370, that a valuable guide in the search for "best interests" in this kind of case was for the court to judge the quality of life the child would have if treated and whether such treatment would make life intolerable to that child. The Court of Appeal, (Laws L.J., Wall L.J. and Lloyd L.J.) [2005] EWCA Civ 1181 rejected the "intolerability" test, stating that the focus should be the "best interests" of the child. However the judge had approached the best interests question correctly and permission to appeal was refused. The matter was referred to the High Court of reconsideration based on an apparent change in C's respiratory condition which was an improvement. The Trust sought a declaration to the effect that the Trust would "have the final word" in the event of irreconcilable disagreement with C's parents. The court declined to give that declaration which would amount to a "treatment veto". The treating clinician had to act in the best interests of the child, not take orders from the parents, whilst accommodating their wishes so far as judgment and conscience permitted.
[93] See now the Nurses, Midwives and Health Visitors Act 1997, consolidating previous legislation.
[94] *The Times*, July 25, 1963.

happen despite the exercise of reasonable skill and care.[95] In *Parry v North West Surrey HA*[96] a midwife was held liable for failing properly to monitor the progress of the claimant's birth, so as to detect that there were difficulties, and for failing promptly to summon a doctor when the claimant's distress became apparent. Nurses occupy a somewhat different position. Traditionally, many of their duties are essentially ministerial. A finding of professional negligence will not be made against a nurse simply because a mishap occurs.[97] Where, however, a nurse makes an error within her area of expertise, she (and her employers) will be liable.[98]

The case of *Shakoor v Situ*[99] concerned a practitioner in traditional Chinese herbal medicine. He gave a course of traditional medicine, prepared with reference to a classic formula, to the claimant's husband for benign lipomata. After taking nine doses of the medicine the patient became seriously ill with liver failure and subsequently died. The experts agreed that the deceased had suffered an "idiosyncratic" reaction to the medicine, which was extremely rare and could not be predicted. The claim failed, but the interest is in the formulation of the duty of care on the practitioner of this alternative medicine. The claimant contended that he should be judged by the standards of a reasonably competent general medical practitioner concerned with skin disorders. The court held that it was not sufficient to judge the defendant simply by reference to other practitioners in Traditional Chinese Herbal Medicine, but he had also to take account of the fact that he was practising alongside orthodox medicine, and he had to take steps to satisfy himself that there were no adverse reports in orthodox journals which would affect his use of the remedy.

(i) *Hospitals and Health Authorities*

13–059   **Vicarious liability.** Broadly speaking, a person is liable for the negligence of his employees when acting in the course of their employment, but not (save in special circumstances) for the negligence of independent contractors.[1]

---

[95] See also *Fish v Kapur* [1948] 2 All E.R. 176; *Fletcher v Bench* (1973) 4 B.M.J. 117; *Gagnon v Stortini* [1974] 4 O.R. (2d) 270. Different considerations arise where a dentist agrees to make a set of dentures for a patient. Whether the contract is regarded as one for the sale of goods or as one for work and materials, it is an implied term that the dentures shall be reasonably fit for the purpose intended: *Samuels v Davis* [1943] K.B. 526.

[96] [1994] 5 Med. L.R. 259. See also *Gaughan v Bedfordshire HA* [1997] 8 Med. L.R. 182 (midwife negligently applied traction which was excessive in force and duration when it was apparent that the claimant's delivery was hindered by shoulder dystocia).

[97] For example, *Dryden v Surrey County Council* [1936] 2 All E.R. 535; *Thorne v Northern Group Hospital Management Committee* (1963) 108 S.J. 115. *cf. Strangeways-Lesmere v Clayton* [1936] 2 K.B. 11; *Selfe v Ilford and District Hospital Management Committee, The Times*, November 26, 1970.

[98] *Voller v Portsmouth Corp* (1947) 203 L.T.J. 264 (nurses allowed operating equipment to become infected); *Smith v Brighton and Lewes Hospital Management Committee, The Times*, May 2, 1958 (the doctor prescribed a course of 30 streptomycin injections for the claimant. The ward sister allowed 34 injections to be administered with the result that the patient lost her sense of balance).

[99] [2001] 1 W.L.R. 410.

[1] For a discussion of vicarious liability, which is beyond the scope of this book, see *Clerk & Lindsell on Torts* (19th edn), Ch.5.

The effect of the introduction of the NHS indemnity in January 1990 is that health authorities and NHS trusts do not now seek to argue that consultants (or agency staff) are not employees when engaged on NHS work, since the health authority or NHS trust is obliged to indemnify them against liability for medical negligence.[2]

General practitioners are not employees of health authorities. They will be liable for the negligence of nurses employed by them, but it is likely that locum doctors would be regarded as independent contractors.[3] The position may also be different for a private patient. A patient may engage a consultant directly and contract separately with an NHS hospital or a private clinic for nursing and ancillary care. The hospital or clinic will not be vicariously liable for the negligence of the consultant. It may be more difficult in such circumstances to succeed in a claim arising out of injury during an operation. The claimant may be unable to say whether the negligence was that of the surgeon or another member of the theatre staff.

Primary liability. Mishaps may occur not because of the negligence of   **13–060** individual doctors or nurses, but because of bad administration or an unsafe system of work. In those circumstances the hospital authority is primarily liable.

In *Robertson v Nottingham HA*[4] the Court of Appeal emphatically reaffirmed that a health authority or NHS trust has a non-delegable duty to provide to its patient a proper system of care. The infant claimant in that case had suffered catastrophic brain damage of a rare type. Her mother argued that it was caused by hypoxic insult to the foetus during and immediately before labour, which the staff of the defendant authority had failed to prevent by performing a caesarean section hours before they in fact did. The Court of Appeal upheld Otton J.'s finding that negligence had not caused the damage, which was the result of an unknown event which must have happened some days earlier. However, the Court overturned the judge's finding of negligence by the registrar. Instead, Brooke L.J. (for the Court) identified two significant types of breakdown in communications between hospital staff. First, there was no effective communication of information available from CTG traces operated by nurses and midwives to the doctors who were responsible for making the decisions on management of the birth. Secondly, there was a lack of effective communication of the doctors' instructions to the nurses and midwives who were responsible for monitoring the condition of the foetus before labour began. The defendant was in breach of its primary duty of care to the claimant in both respects.

Brooke L.J. stated the relevant principles to this effect:

(a) a hospital authority owes a non-delegable duty to establish a proper system of care, as it does to engage competent staff and provide proper and safe equipment and premises;

---

[2] See H.C. (89) 34, H.S.G. (96) 48.
[3] Where general practitioners practise in partnership, they will be jointly liable for the negligence of any one of them: see *Lindley & Banks on Partnership* 18th edn. (2002), paras 12–88 to 12–93.
[4] [1997] 8 Med. L.R. 1.

(b) if a hospital authority has put in place effective systems so as to ensure, so far as reasonably practicable, that communication breakdowns do not occur, the hospital is vicariously liable for negligent failure by a staff member to operate such systems effectively;

(c) if no such systems have been put in place, the hospital is directly liable to a patient who suffers injury as a result;

(d) if a patient is injured because of a negligent breakdown in the systems in place for communicating material information to the clinicians responsible for his care, he is not to be denied redress merely because no identifiable person is to blame for the deficiencies in setting up and monitoring the effectiveness of the relevant communication systems.[5]

13–061   Hospital authorities have been found to be in breach of a primary duty of care in several cases.[6] In *Robertson v Nottingham HA*[7] the Court of Appeal confirmed that the *Bolam* principle applies in deciding the standard of care applicable to the non-delegable duty. Brooke L.J. said (at 13):

"By reasonable regime of care we mean a regime of a standard that can reasonably be expected of a hospital of the size and type in question—in the present case a large teaching centre of excellence."

The Court of Appeal in *AB v Tameside and Glossop HA*[8-9] reached the same conclusion, but on the facts of this case, derived no assistance from the principle in deciding whether the authority was in breach of duty.

---

[5] There is a helpful commentary on *Robertson v Nottingham HA* at (1997) 5 Med. L.Rev. 342. In August 2001 the Secretary of State for Health announced that he was considering the possibility of permitting patients to be treated in other European Community countries where they had excess capacity, and when the patient would be subjected to a long waiting list if required to wait for treatment on the NHS in the United Kingdom. If NHS patients are treated in other European countries the concept of the non-delegable duty owed by a Trust or HA to its patients may become important if there has been negligence in the European hospital, and the patient wishes to sue the NHS hospital which made the referral abroad. If NHS patients are to be treated abroad new issues on liability may arise. In *A v The Ministry of Defence and Guy's and St Thomas' Hospital NHS Trust* [2003] Lloyd's Rep. Med. 339, the MoD had contracted the Trust to procure secondary elective healthcare for servicemen and their dependants in Germany, and admitted it owed a duty to exercise reasonable care and skill in selecting the secondary provider. The claimant (a child of a serviceman serving with the MoD in Germany) sought a declaration that the defendants owed a non-delegable duty to ensure that all reasonable skill and care was taken by the staff caring for servicemen at a designated hospital in Germany. Bell J. applying the general rule of no vicarious liability for acts or omissions of an independent contractor dismissed the claim. The MoD had discharged its obligations to the claimant by its contract with the Trust, the Trust had discharged its obligations by its exercise of reasonable care and skill in procuring the German services provider. The first instance trial judge was upheld on appeal. The Court of Appeal stated that the MoD did not owe the claimant a non-delegable duty of care; that the claimant was trying to extend the law of negligence and that the Court of Appeal found no policy grounds for so expanding the scope of tortious liability, [2004] EWCA Civ 641.

[6] See, e.g. *Bull v Devon AHA* [1993] 4 Med. L.R. 117 in which the health authority was found negligent in failing to operate an efficient and reliable system for securing the attendance of experienced doctors to deal with crises arising in the course of childbirth and *Lybert v Warrington HA* [1996] 7 Med. L.R. 71 in which the health authority was negligent in failing to adopt a proper and effective system for warning patients of the risk of failure of sterilisation operations.

[7] [1997] 8 Med. L.R. 1.

[8-9] [1997] 8 Med. L.R. 91.

The decisions in *Robertson* and *AB*, taken together with the House of Lords'   **13–062**
restatement of the *Bolam* principle in *Bolitho v City & Hackney HA*[10] appear to
allow the development of new arguments on liability in the area of "systems"
negligence. For example:

(a) It may no longer be sufficient in all cases to show that the systems in place
    in a defendant's hospital are in line with those adopted in some other
    hospitals. The defendant in *Early v Newham HA*[11] resisted liability
    because there was evidence that other hospitals directed their anaesthetists
    to follow a similar procedure whenever an attempt to intubate a patient
    failed. Therefore the procedure could not be said to be one which no
    reasonably competent authority could adopt. Today, the authority might be
    called upon specifically to justify that procedure, and it would be subjected
    to an objective and critical analysis.

(b) Systems failures are often failures to put in place, monitor or maintain
    systems of administration and non-clinical management, for example,
    those for effective communication between levels of staff in a department
    and between staff in different departments. Even where the system con-
    cerned is a system for clinical management, the relevant failure may be of
    an administrative nature, such as the keeping of drug records. In those
    cases, a judge who might be reluctant to find a logical flaw in a clinical
    decision might well feel able to find fault with the failures in administra-
    tion and management which led to the lack of a system, a badly designed
    system or the breakdown of a good system.

(c) In the light of *Robertson*, a hospital whose systems design is criticised by
    comparison with other hospitals will have to be prepared to identify its
    position in the spectrum which extends from "teaching centres of excel-
    lence" to cottage hospitals, and to justify its systems (or lack of them)
    from that point of view. This might prove a difficult and expensive
    exercise in evidential terms.

(d) The failure to provide appropriately qualified and experienced staff is a
    systems failure. It is clear law[12] that a treating doctor must meet the
    standard of care reasonably to be required of someone filling the post that
    he holds, for example, a senior house officer in an obstetric unit. His
    personal qualifications and experience are irrelevant. In *Wilsher v Essex
    AHA*[13] both Sir Nicholas Browne-Wilkinson V.C. and Glidewell L.J. said
    obiter that a hospital authority would be liable if it failed to provide
    doctors of sufficient skill and experience. A claimant might complain that,
    although the conduct of the senior house officer who treated her cannot be
    faulted on *Bolam* grounds, she ought to have been treated by a registrar.
    In the light of *Bolitho*, it may not be sufficient for the defendant to show

---

[10] [1998] A.C. 232. And see paras 13–032 to 13–033, above.
[11] [1994] 5 Med. L.R. 214.
[12] See paras 13–026 to 13–027, above.
[13] [1987] Q.B. 730.

that other, similar hospitals do not employ more senior staff to administer that sort of treatment.

The question whether and in what circumstances a health authority or a health service body (as defined in the National Health Service and Community Care Act 1990) could be liable in tort to an NHS patient for the manner in which it allocates limited resources as between competing demands has not yet been directly addressed by the courts. This raises some fundamental questions, which are beyond the scope of a book on professional negligence.

13–063   **Structure of National Health Service.** The Secretary of State is under a duty to provide throughout England and Wales, to such extent as he considers necessary to meet all reasonable requirements, hospital and similar accommodation; medical, dental, nursing and ambulance services; and other related facilities for the prevention and treatment of illness.[14] The local administration of these services is now entrusted to health authorities.[15] It is these authorities (rather than the Secretary of State himself) who should be sued in respect of negligence committed by staff at hospitals under their control.[16]

Under s.5 of the National Health Service and Community Care Act 1990 the Secretary of State is empowered to set up NHS trusts, to own and manage hospitals or other establishments or facilities formerly managed or provided by health authorities. Many NHS trusts have been set up. Under s.4 of the 1990 Act one health service body (e.g. a health authority or an NHS trust) may contract to provide goods or services to another health service body. If negligence occurs, the health service body actually providing the treatment will be liable to the patient. It is important to note, however, that liability for clinical negligence accruing before the institution of an NHS trust remains the responsibility of the health authority which the trust succeeds. NHS trusts do not inherit liabilities of this sort. Further, the acquiring authority may be liable if it places a contract which does not provide for an adequate standard of treatment.[17] However, the NHS contract itself does not give rise to any contractual rights or liabilities.[18]

---

[14] National Health Service Act 1977, s.3.
[15] Regional and district health authorities and family health services authorities were abolished, as from April 1, 1996, by the Health Authorities Act 1995. Health authorities are constituted under the National Health Service Act 1977, s.8, as amended by s.1 of the Health Services Act 1980, s.1 of the National Health Service and Community Care Act 1990 and s.1 of the Health Authorities Act 1995.
[16] See National Health Service Act 1977, Sch.5, para.15.
[17] See J. Jacob, "Lawyers go to Hospital" [1991] P.L. 255.
[18] s.4(3). For an analysis of the health care markets introduced into the National Health Service in 1991 and of the response of the medical profession, see F. Miller, "Competition Law and Anti-competitive Professional Behaviour Affecting Health Care" (1992) 55 M.L.R. 453. The possibility that the new structure of the health service will allow the formulation of new species of negligence claims is discussed by C. Newdick in "Rights to N.H.S. resources" (1993) 1 Med. L.Rev. 53. In "N.H.S. contracting: shadows of the law of tort" (1995) 3 Med. L.Rev. 161, K. Barker argues that the publication of standards for the purposes of NHS contracting may result in a higher individual standard of care or at least, an easing of the evidential burden on claimants seeking to allege negligence, by providing evidence of prevailing standards.

(j) *Apportionment of Liability*

Apportionment between hospital authorities and doctors. Prior to 1954 it **13–064**
was common for hospital authorities, when sued for negligence, to bring third
party proceedings against the member of their staff who was alleged to be at
fault. Thus in *Jones v Manchester Corp*[19] liability was apportioned, under s.6 of
the Law Reform (Married Women and Tortfeasors) Act 1935, 20 per cent to the
house surgeon and 80 per cent to the hospital board. After 1954, however, a
private arrangement existed between the hospital authorities and the bodies
representing medical practitioners, as a result of which liability was apportioned
by agreement in individual cases, and third party proceedings or contribution
proceedings were no longer brought.[20] With effect from January 1, 1990, a new
arrangement in respect of hospital doctors came into force.[21] Health authorities
are required to give them a full indemnity in respect of liability for negligence in
the course of their NHS employment.[22] However, any private work undertaken
by consultants in a NHS hospital falls outside the scheme,[23] so that questions of
apportionment can still arise in that context.[24]

Apportionment between medical practitioners and pharmacists. A phar- **13–065**
macist is a skilled professional man. He has a duty to satisfy himself about any
prescription which he makes up and, in case of doubt, to refer back to the
prescribing doctor.[25] In *Dwyer v Roderick*,[26] where a general practitioner made a
serious error in prescription, liability was apportioned 45 per cent to the prescribing doctor, 40 per cent to the pharmacist who failed to spot the error and 15 per
cent to a partner of the prescribing doctor who failed to spot the error. Where a
prescription is badly written, so that its meaning is unclear, the pharmacist should
refer back to the doctor. If the pharmacist goes ahead on his own interpretation
of the prescription and gets it wrong, he is likely to carry the greater share of
responsibility. In *Prendergast v Sam & Dee Ltd*[27] a general practitioner, intending
to prescribe Amoxil, wrote the prescription to a poor standard of legibility. The
pharmacist read this as Daonil, which for a number of reasons was an inappropriate reading of the prescription. The claimant suffered hypoglycaemia and
irreversible brain damage as a result of taking Daonil. The Court of Appeal
upheld an apportionment of 25 per cent to the doctor and 75 per cent to the
pharmacist.

---

[19] [1952] 2 Q.B. 852.
[20] For more details of the arrangement see C. R. A. Martin, *Law Relating to Medical Practice* (Pitman
Medical Publishing Co Ltd, 1979), pp.95–96.
[21] Set out in Department of Health Circular H.C. (89) 34 and Health Services Guidelines H.S.G. (96)
48.
[22] For discussion of the implications of this reform, see J. Jacob, "Lawyers go to Hospital" [1991]
P.L. 255, 264–265; M. Brazier, "N.H.S. Indemnity: The Implications for Medical Litigation" (1990)
6 P.N. 88.
[23] Department of Health Circular H.C. (89) 34, para.5. See further, H.S.G. (96) 48.
[24] As do general practitioners. However, H.C. (89) 34 asks the medical defence organisations and the
heath authorities to seek to reach agreement as to their respective liabilities and to co-operate in
presenting a defence.
[25] *Prendergast v Sam & Dee Ltd* [1989] 1 Med. L.R. 36, 37, col.2.
[26] (1982) 132 New L.J. 176.
[27] [1989] 1 Med. L.R. 36. A reproduction of the prescription form and the medicine label was before
the court and appears at p.39 of the report.

2. Liability for Breach of Duty

13–066   **General.** Breach of duty by a medical practitioner is likely to take one of two forms:

(i) Breach of the implied contractual duty to exercise reasonable skill and care.[28]

(ii) Breach of the duty of care owed by the medical practitioner to his patient, whether or not there is any contract between them.[29]

Both categories involve breaches of the same standard of skill and care and hereafter will be jointly described as "negligence". Where a medical practitioner is privately engaged by the patient, it is possible that he will find himself in breach of some specific contractual duty not involving negligence.[30] In the rare cases where a medical practitioner treats a patient without his consent, he may also be liable for assault.[31]

Instances in which medical practitioners are, or may be, liable for breach of duty are discussed below under seven headings. It is not suggested that this catalogue is exhaustive. The cases serve to illustrate how the principles stated above operate in practice and, in particular, what the courts consider to be the standard of skill and care which may reasonably be expected of medical practitioners.[32-33]

(a) *Failing to Prevent Illness*

13–067   **Prevention not cure.** The object of the medical profession is the promotion of good health and not simply the treatment of illness.[34] Failure to take reasonable steps to prevent illness may in appropriate circumstances amount to negligence. In one case[35] for example, it was held that the defendants' medical officer was negligent in failing to guard against scrotal cancer amongst employees in an engineering factory as he ought to have instituted six-monthly medical examinations and to have issued a notice about the risk, describing the symptoms and recommending reference to a doctor.

---

[28] See para.13–003, above.
[29] See paras 13–006 to 13–021, above.
[30] See para.13–003, above.
[31] See paras 13–043 to 13–048, above.
[32-33] For a general discussion of the standard of skill and care, see paras 13–022 to 13–036, above. As to the danger of treating particular cases as precedents, establishing what a medical practitioner ought or ought not to do, see *Mahon v Osborne* [1939] 2 K.B. 14 (surgeon not necessarily negligent for leaving swabs inside patient; negligence depends on the circumstances of each case).
[34] This is emphasised by ss.1, 3 of the National Health Service Act 1977 and the NHS (General Medical Services) Regulations 1992 (SI 1992/635), Sch.2, Terms of Service for Doctors in general NHS practice that requires general practitioners to have periodical consultations with their patients, directed to improving their health.
[35] *Stokes v Guest, Keen and Nettlefold* [1968] 1 W.L.R. 1776, Swanick J.

Infectious disease spread. The medical practitioner must take reasonable care   **13–068**
to prevent the spread of infectious diseases.[36] Thus in one case[37] the claimant was
admitted to a cottage hospital and put in the same ward as a "gravely suspicious
case", which turned out to be puerperal fever. The claimant contracted the
disease. Both the hospital authorities and the doctor in charge were found to be
negligent.[38]

In *Re HIV Haemophiliac Litigation*[39] haemophiliacs who had contracted the
HIV virus from contaminated imported blood products used in their treatment
alleged inter alia that the Department of Health had negligently failed to screen
donors, heat-treat the blood products so as to inactivate the virus, warn the
claimants and achieve NHS self-sufficiency in blood products. The action settled,
but the Court of Appeal accepted that the claimants had an arguable claim.[40]

(b) *Failing to Attend or Examine a Patient*

If a medical practitioner makes unwarranted assumptions about his patient's   **13–069**
condition without examining him, he is at risk of an action for negligence.

The hospital doctor. In *Wisniewski v Central Manchester HA*[41] the Court of   **13–070**
Appeal held that a senior house officer was negligent for failing to attend a
patient in a maternity ward and for relying on a midwife's assessment of a CTG
trace of a baby's heart rate as the mother went into labour.[42] Failure to attend and
examine in the later stages of treatment may also, of course, constitute negligence. In *Joyce v Merton, Sutton & Wandsworth HA*[43] the patient underwent
brachial cardiac catheterisation, a minor surgical procedure designed to assess
arterial disease and carried out on a day patient basis. In carrying out the

---

[36] In *Vancouver General Hospital v McDaniel* (1935) 152 L.T.R. 56, the claimant contracted
smallpox whilst being treated in the defendants' hospital. It was held that the defendants were not
negligent, since they had complied with the general and approved practice as to the containment of
smallpox patients. By contrast, it is likely to be difficult to establish liability for transmission of the
HIV virus from medical staff to a patient: see M. Mulholland, "AIDS, HIV and the Health Care
Worker" (1993) 9 P.N. 79.

[37] *Heafield v Crane The Times*, July 31, 1937, Simgleton J.

[38] *Marshall v Lindsey County Court* [1935] 1 K.B. 516 is to the same effect: claimant was admitted
to a maternity home in which there was a case of puerperal fever; the matron was held to be negligent.
Decision affirmed by the House of Lords at [1937] A.C. 97.

[39] [1996] P.N.L.R. 290.

[40] *ibid.* at 312–315. See also *Pittman Estate v Bain* (1995) 127 D.L.R. (4th) 577: the patient
contracted the HIV virus through a blood transfusion. He later died of an AIDS-related disease and
his wife discovered that she had contracted the virus. Her husband's general practitioner was
negligent in failing to inform her husband that he might be HIV-positive and in failing to advise him
or the claimant to take precautions against transmission of the virus to her through sexual contact.

[41] [1998] Lloyd's Rep. Med. 223.

[42] The trial judge found that the doctor had not been told of the baby's tachycardia, but since both
midwife and doctor were employed by the same defendant, no point was taken on the appeal. The trial
judge also considered whether the doctor had been properly prevented from attending by other events
that night at the hospital but found none had occurred. See *Cummings v Croydon HA*, unreported,
March 24, 1998, QBD for a case where the claimant failed to show that the defendant health authority
had not responded adequately to her complaints that she was in labour.

[43] [1996] 7 Med. L.R. 1, CA. The claimant failed on causation. See also *Cavanagh v Bristol & Weston
HA* [1992] 3 Med. L.R. 49 (failure to monitor patient's condition following eye operation).

procedure, the registrar sutured together the walls of the patient's brachial artery. This was a non-negligent mishap. However, the registrar and the nurse responsible for the patient's care on the day ward were negligent in discharging him home without impressing upon him that he should contact the hospital if he became concerned about any aspect of his recovery. Roch L.J. pointed out that a doctor must bear in mind that an oral warning may not be understood and remembered by a patient who has reacted badly to a procedure.[44] The result of the negligence was that the suturing error caused vascular complications which were not treated in time to avoid a catastrophic cerebral embolism.

13-071   **The general practitioner.** The general practitioner is entitled and bound to exercise some discretion in determining whether and when it is necessary to visit patients who cannot come to his surgery.[45] In a first instance case[46] it was held that it was not negligent of a general practitioner not personally to visit a baby reported to be unwell and having feeding problems. The doctor sent an experienced practice nurse instead. In another similar case,[47] a general practitioner who had given adequate instructions for the care of a sick infant to its mother was not under a duty to visit to ensure that his instructions were followed. The patient's past medical history and the complaint raised will obviously impact on whether the doctor acted reasonably in not attending or examining that patient.[48]

13-072   **Arranging follow-up.** Failure to arrange follow-up or to pursue results of tests may be negligent even where no treatment has been given. In *Major v Wilcox*[49] a general practitioner was negligent because he did not advise a patient to contact him if his condition did not improve over the weekend. The claimant had attended his GP twice, complaining of fever and sore throat. The GP diagnosed viraemia and properly concluded that treatment with antibiotics was unnecessary. The claimant was admitted to hospital on the Monday and died a few hours later

---

[44] [1996] 7 Med. L.R. 1, CA at 12.
[45] A general practitioner's contract with the health authority responsible for local family health services requires him to make a home visit if in his reasonable opinion it is inappropriate for the patient to attend normal surgery (or a night or emergency surgery where these are operated): see the NHS (General Medical Services) Amendment Regulations 1995 (SI 1995/80).
[46] *Stockdale v Nicholls* [1993] 4 Med. L.R. 191, Otton J. See also *Morrison v Forsyth* [1995] 6 Med. L.R. 6, Sc. Ct Sess. (on the basis of the information given to her, general practitioner not negligent in failing to visit patient or in failing to ask further questions which might have disclosed the true nature of the patient's condition). See also *D v Dr Ahmed*, unreported, March 26, 1998, QBD, David Steel, J.): a toddler developed a common reaction to the measles vaccine ("mini-measles"). On his father's telephoning the doctor's surgery, the doctor gave advice over the telephone but did not personally attend on the claimant. Over the next four days the claimant's condition deteriorated and he was hospitalised and diagnosed as suffering from haematemesis, hepatitis, pneumonia and possible viral encephalitis. The claimant alleged that the doctor should have attended him and that if he had done so he would have been treated with antibiotics, alternatively that he would have been admitted to hospital sooner. The claimant's case was dismissed, the doctor had quite properly given advice by telephone.
[47] *Durrant v Burke* [1993] 4 Med. L.R. 258.
[48] See *Sohal v Brar* [1999] 63 Alta. L.R. (3d) 280, Doctor held to be negligent for failing to immediately re-examine a diabetic patient whose minor foot injury had after three days become swollen and discoloured. Patient subsequently diagnosed with gangrene underwent amputation of part of foot. The claimant failed to show that the doctor's breach and delay had caused or materially contributed to the amputation.
[49] Unreported, February 4, 1999, CA, Kennedy, Chadwick and Laws L.JJ.

due to streptococcal septicaemia. The trial judge found no negligence in not treating with antibiotics, but held that the GP had breached his duty of care by not advising the claimant to contact him again if he did not improve, and that the claimant would have attended his GP again if he had been advised to do so. The Court of Appeal upheld the trial judge's findings on the evidence and on the expert opinion that giving such advice to a patient was good practice.[50] In *Judge v Huntingdon HA*[51] the patient was referred to a consultant surgeon for specialist opinion on a lump in her breast which she had found and her general practitioner had confirmed. The surgeon examined her but failed to find a lump. It was held that he negligently failed to arrange to see the patient again in a different phase of her menstrual cycle. When both the patient and her general practitioner were sure that a lump existed, the surgeon could not exclude the possibility that there was a lump, and it might be malignant.[52]

(c) *Wrong Diagnosis*

General. At the date of trial there is often no dispute as to what illness or injury the claimant was in fact suffering from at the time when he consulted the defendant. Thus there is no dispute as to whether the diagnosis made by the defendant was correct or incorrect. If the diagnosis was incorrect, often the sole question is whether the "mistake" was negligent. This issue is seldom resolved by reference to "general and approved practice" or "schools of thought". The question simply is whether, on the symptoms and material presented or available to the defendant, a reasonably careful and skilful medical practitioner might have made the same mistake.

13–073

If a medical practitioner fails to diagnose a relatively common or obvious illness or injury, then he is likely to be held negligent.[53] In one case[54] a casualty officer was held negligent in failing to discover a hole in the claimant's skull of one-quarter to one-half inch in diameter. The claimant was complaining of a

---

[50] The *Bolam* test appears to have been applied although there is no express reference to the case in the judgment.

[51] [1995] 6 Med.L.R. 223.

[52] For other examples see the following cases: *C v A Health Authority*, unreported, November 3, 1998, QBD, Ebsworth J: the defendant health authority had breached its duty by failing to offer the claimant an appointment for further tests for foetal defects (which the claimant contended would have resulted in her having a scan at 16 to 20 weeks of pregnancy); *Morea-Loftus v Wray Castle Ltd* [1999] Lloyd's Rep. Med. 159: failure by medical staff at a residential college to make an early morning check on the condition of a student in sickbay was a breach of duty, but the claimant was unable to establish that the breach was causative of his later-diagnosed meningitis.

[53] For example, *Edler v Greenwich and Deptford Hospital Management Committee*, *The Times*, March 7, 1953 (hospital casualty officer failed to diagnose appendicitis); *Saumarez v Medway and Gravesend Hospital Management Committee* (1953) 2 B.M.J. 1109 (failure to diagnose chip fracture of distal phalanx of left middle finger); *Riddett v D'Arcy* (1960) 2 B.M.J. 1607 (general practitioner examined a baby in the early stages of pneumonia but failed to diagnose the baby's condition, although symptoms of heart failure were present, Southampton County Court); *Gardiner v Mounfield* [1990] 1 Med. L.R. 205 (failure to diagnose pregnancy). See also *Lock v Scantlebury*, *The Times*, July 25, 1963 (dentist failed to notice that the claimant's jaw had become dislocated during extraction of teeth).

[54] *McCormack v Redpath Brown Co Ltd*, *The Times*, March 24, 1961.

blow on the head from a spanner. Paull J. considered that the fracture could not have been missed on any proper physical examination.[55]

In determining whether an incorrect diagnosis was negligent, the court must have regard to all the circumstances at the time the diagnosis was made. These include, obviously, the symptoms[56] exhibited by the patient, the information available to the doctor from other sources, the age of the patient and the rarity (or commonness) of the disease from which the patient was suffering. Thus in *Marriott v West Midlands Regional HA*[57] a general practitioner was negligent for failing to give sufficient weight to the patient's complaints and symptoms (of drowsiness and headaches) following a fall and head injury and relying too much on the results of neurological tests (no papilloedema, vomiting or other signs of raised intra-cranial pressure) leading to a missed diagnosis of skull fracture resulting in extradural haematoma and hemiplegia.[58] In the case of *Murphy v MOD*,[59] there was a failure correctly to diagnose a sub-arachnid haemorrhage (SAH). The judge emphasised that the claimant's presentation was far from being typical of SAH. He found that the claimant had a number of non-specific symptoms, none of which pointed to SAH, and he accordingly found that the defendants had not been negligent in not considering a diagnosis of SAH and in not acting on such a diagnosis. The case emphasises the importance of establishing exactly what the individual clinician would have been faced with, and how he should have acted on the patient's presentation.

13-074   Another relevant factor is the time spent and care taken in listening to the patient's history.[60] In *Djemal v Bexley HA*[61] an inexperienced casualty officer failed to elicit a full history from the patient or the patient's wife and failed to notice the patient's significant inability to swallow. Had he done so, he ought to have realised that advice from an ENT specialist was called for. In fact, the patient had epiglottitis, which, untreated, led to his deterioration to a persistent vegetative state. Sir Haydn Tudor Evans said:

> "I find that it is the duty of an examining doctor, and that includes a casualty officer, as an essential preliminary to making a diagnosis, to obtain a proper history and that it

---

[55] Other cases in which medical practitioners have been held negligent for failing to diagnose fractures after serious accidents are *Wood v Thurston*, *The Times*, May 25, 1951 and *Newton v Newton's Model Laundry Ltd*, *The Times*, November 3, 1959.

[56] See, e.g. *Serre v De Tilly* (1975) 8 O.R. (2d) 490, Ontario High Court (brain haemorrhage mistakenly diagnosed as hysteria. Held that the diagnosis was a reasonable one on the basis of the symptoms). *cf. Wipfli v Britten* (1982) 28 C.C.L.T. 104, British Columbia Supreme Court (1984) 13 D.L.R. (4th) 169 (failure to diagnose that claimant was carrying twins held negligent, because there were sufficient indicia of the existence of twins).

[57] [1999] Lloyd's Rep. Med. 23, CA.

[58] In *Rampling v Haringey HA*, unreported, July 30, 1996, Buxton J., the defendants negligently failed to revise their (mistaken) diagnosis of symphysis pubis because they paid too little attention to the patient's complaints of severe pain. As a result, her undisplaced stress fracture was allowed to become displaced during labour.

[59] [2002] EWHC 452.

[60] See, e.g. *Giurelli v Girgis* (1980) 24 S.A.S.R. 264, South Australia Supreme Court. White J. stated that listening to the patient's history was as much a part of diagnosis as clinical examination. The fact that the claimant was a difficult patient and tended to exaggerate his complaints of pain did not excuse the defendant's failure properly to listen to and investigate the claimant's complaints. See also *Meyer v Gordon* (1981) 17 C.C.L.T. 1 (nursing staff held negligent for failing to obtain claimant's obstetric history).

[61] [1995] 6 Med. L.R. 269.

is not correct medical practice simply to accept what is related by the patient or the person speaking for him."[62]

The amount of time spent by the doctor in examining the patient is also relevant.[63] *Parry v North West Surrey HA*[64] and *Wiszniewski v Central Manchester HA*[65] were cases in which a doctor was found to be negligent in failing to attend a patient in the early stages of labour. The result in each case was that the management of the labour was left to the midwife. In *Parry*, this meant that when a crisis developed and the doctor did attend, he lacked adequate first-hand knowledge of the patient to deal with it properly. In *Wiszniewski*, the doctor's neglect left the patient in the sole care of a midwife who was deemed not competent to recognise signs of increasing foetal distress.

On the other hand, the doctor risks a finding of negligence if he allows the patient's anxiety about a particular diagnostic test to overrule his own better judgment as to the need for it: in *Hutton v East Dyfed HA*,[66] a locum consultant physician did not call for a chest X-ray on a pregnant patient because of her anxiety about possible damage to her unborn child. Any such risk would have been reduced to a level acceptable to her by use of a lead apron, but the physician did not explain this to the patient. A chest X-ray would have revealed that the patient was at real risk of disastrous pulmonary embolism, which would have been prevented by administering heparin, but from which she later died.

13-075

Often, the correct diagnosis of a complaint is (at the material time) a matter of disagreement between practitioners. Where the defendant can call a reputable expert witness to say that on the material available he, too, would have made the same diagnosis, a finding of negligence will be difficult to sustain.[67] It was on this basis that the finding of negligence made by the trial judge in *Maynard v West Midlands Regional HA*[68] was reversed. The defendant will be in an even stronger

---

[62] [1995] 6 Med. L.R. 269 at 277. See also *Drake v Pontefract HA* [1998] Lloyd's Rep. Med. 425 (senior house officer negligently failed to diagnose (and accordingly failed to treat) the claimant's agitated depression, resulting in her depressive condition deteriorating until an attempt to commit suicide resulted in serious injury and disablement).

[63] In *Parkinson v West Cumberland Management Committee* (1955) 1 B.M.J. 977 a newly qualified hospital doctor spent an hour examining the patient but failed to diagnose coronary thrombosis. Ashworth J. held that the doctor's mistake did not amount to negligence. *cf. Seyfert v Burnaby Hospital Society* (1986) 27 D.L.R. (4th) 96 (claimant came to hospital casualty department with stab wound in left abdomen; the emergency physician negligently discharged claimant after an inadequate period of observation, and failed to discover that the stab wound had penetrated the transverse colon).

[64] [1994] 5 Med. L.R. 259.

[65] [1998] Lloyd's Rep. Med. 223. See also *Judge v Huntingdon HA* [1995] 6 Med.L.R. 223 (surgeon's failure to use diagnostic aids such as ultrasound scan or fine needle biopsy was not negligent, but their absence made it all the more important that he took proper care in carrying out his manual examination).

[66] [1998] Lloyd's Rep. Med. 335.

[67] For example, *Crivon v Barnet Group Hospital Management Committee, The Times*, November 19, 1958 (hospital pathologist wrongly diagnosed a specimen from the claimant's breast as cancer. At the trial Professor S, an acknowledged expert in the field, said that looking at the slide, he too would have diagnosed cancer. "In those circumstances could it be said to be negligence in a pathologist, when he came to a conclusion which a great expert might himself have come to?" (*per* Lord Denning)).

[68] [1984] 1 W.L.R. 634, HL.

position where a number of other doctors actually did make the same mistaken diagnosis as himself.[69]

13–076   **Failure to detect more serious condition.** In some cases negligence is established not on the basis that the defendant should have made a correct diagnosis, but on the basis that he should have been alerted to the risk of something serious,[70] or that he should have referred the claimant to hospital or to a specialist for assistance sooner.[71] In *Raji Abu Shkara v Hillingdon HA*[72] the claimant was admitted to the defendant's hospital with a tracheal wound and secondary infection. He suffered repeated episodes of respiratory distress, which were managed by use of oxygen and medication. Finally, he suffered respiratory arrest. He was resuscitated, but brain damage had been caused. The judge held that the nurse and senior house officer on duty the evening of the arrest had failed to suspect that he was suffering a developing hypoxia and had therefore failed to test his blood gases (which would have confirmed that suspicion) and summon appropriate assistance to prevent the arrest. The defendant's appeal succeeded, in part because the trial judge had not found that the claimant's hypoxia had manifested on that evening in a way that would suggest that it was more serious than on the previous occasions, when distress had not culminated in arrest. Moreover the evidence did not support such a finding.[73]

(d) *Error in the Course of Treatment*

13–077   **Mistakes and negligence.** Mistakes made in the course of treatment may be purely physical (as when the surgeon's hand slips or twitches during an

---

[69] As happened in *Pudney v Union Castle Mail Steamship Company Ltd* [1953] 1 Lloyd's Law Rep. 73 (claimant suffering from the early stages of osteo-arthritis. Ship's doctor diagnosed mild rheumatic condition. Subsequently other doctors who saw the claimant made the same mistake and diagnosed rheumatic fever. Devlin J. held that the ship's doctor was not negligent in his diagnosis).

[70] See, e.g. *R. v Croydon HA* [1998] Lloyd's Rep. Med. 44 for an example of admittedly negligent failure to recognise an abnormality that required investigation; *Dale v Munthali* (1978) 78 D.L.R. (3d) 588 (patient suffering from meningitis; defendant diagnosed flu. Held that the defendant was not negligent in failing to diagnose meningitis, because not all the symptoms were present. But he was negligent in failing to realise this was something more serious than flu. He should have arranged for the patient to be admitted to hospital immediately for further testing). See also *Sabapathi v Huntley* [1938] 1 W.W.R. 317; *Fraser v Vancouver General Hospital* [1951] 3 W.W.R.(N.S.) 337; *Bova v Spring* [1994] 5 Med. L.R. 120.

[71] See, e.g. *Sa'ad v Robinson* [1989] 1 Med. L.R. 40 (18-month-old child sucked hot tea from spout of teapot. General practitioners held negligent for failing promptly to refer the child to hospital and (subsequently) for making inadequate arrangements in respect of the child's admission to hospital).

[72] [1997] 8 Med. L.R. 114.

[73] Compare with *Fleury v Woolgar* [1996] 37 Alta. L.R. (3d) 346 (family practitioner who engaged in a significant obstetric practice was not negligent in not calling for assistance in delivering claimant of her baby. The obstetrician who was eventually summoned attempted the delivery by the same traction manoeuvre and this was the likely cause of the baby's fractured arm and brachial plexus injury. The defendant's delay did not contribute to the baby's injuries.)

operation), purely intellectual (as when the doctor prescribes the wrong drug) or they may fall somewhere between the two (for example, pulling too hard with a pair of forceps). Whichever form the mistake takes, there are two separate questions to consider, both of which may well be hotly contested: (i) whether the defendant made a "mistake" (judged by the circumstances in which he was acting); (ii) if so, whether the mistake was one which a reasonably careful and skilful medical practitioner would not have made. The claimant must, of course, succeed on both questions in order to establish negligence.[74]

The first question. In relation to the first question, the court must consider whether the defendant gave the "right" treatment, not whether the treatment "worked". Thus if a doctor summoned to an emergency gives the treatment which is obviously appropriate, but the patient dies, he cannot be said to have made a "mistake". This is so, even if the post mortem and the subsequent investigation of the patient's history reveal that a quite different course of action might have saved his life. Contrast this case with *Le Page v Kingston and Richmond HA*.[75] During delivery of her child by Caesarean section, the claimant haemorrhaged so seriously that a hysterectomy was required to arrest the bleeding. The authority's obstetric staff were held liable for failing to take precautions against deterioration of her condition to the point where the bleeding became uncontrollable and hysterectomy unavoidable. The judge distinguished between cases where the court was required to review a considered clinical decision and those where, as here, the conduct of medical and nursing staff could only be described as "a catalogue of errors".   **13–078**

The right procedure. The choice of one procedure in preference to another which in the event would have proved more beneficial (or less injurious) to the   **13–079**

---

[74] Examples include: *Gold v Essex County Council* [1942] 2 K.B. 293 (radiographer covered the claimant's face with a piece of lint only, before treating facial warts with Grenz rays); *Jones v Manchester Corp* [1952] 2 Q.B. 852 (house surgeon administered too much Pentothal too quickly); *Bayliss v Blagg* (1954) 1 B.M.J. 709 (matron of children's hospital failed to heed deterioration in condition of small girl with plaster cast on her leg. The leg, which was infected, remained in plaster and much of the calf muscle was destroyed); *Smith v Lewisham Group Hospital Management Committee, The Times*, June 21, 1955 and (1955) 2 B.M.J. 64 (claimant aged 86 and suffering from acute cholecystitis. Hospital staff left her on the trolley for a short time, during which she fell and fractured her thigh); *Munro v United Oxford Hospitals* (1958) 1 B.M.J. 167 (surgeon knocked out four of patient's front teeth during a tonsillectomy); *Hucks v Cole*, (1968) 112 S.J. 483; [1993] 4 Med. L.R. 393 (general practitioner treating claimant for fulminating septicaemia, failed to prescribe sufficient antibiotics); *Moffat v Witelson* (1980) 111 D.L.R. (3d) 712 (ophthalmologist failed to heed the serious danger that a penetrating wound of claimant's cornea was causing infection of the anterior chamber of the eye); *White v Turner* (1981) 120 D.L.R. (3d) 269 and (1983) 5 D.L.R. (4th) 282 (plastic surgeon removed insufficient tissue during mammoplasty); *Kay v Ayrshire and Arran Health Board* [1987] 2 All E.R. 417; (senior house officer gave greatly excessive dose of penicillin); *Gallant v Fialkov* (1989) 69 O.R. (2d) 297 (use of sutures to control bleeding after tonsillectomy as a matter of routine); *Bentley v Bristol and Weston HA (No. 2)* [1991] 3 Med. L.R. 1 (overstretching nerve during hip replacement operation); *Smith v Salford HA* [1994] 5 Med. L.R. 321 (use of inappropriate aneurism needle in spinal fusion).

[75] [1997] 8 Med. L.R. 229.

claimant is not negligent provided that all relevant factors and available evidence and risks bearing on the decision have been properly considered. Thus there are cases where it was not negligent to choose to deliver normally rather than by caesarean section[76] or to operate by laparoscopy and not laparotomy,[77] or to close and reverse a colostomy without undertaking a resection of the colon concerned.[78]

13-080   **The second question.** Sometimes the mistake made by the defendant is of such a kind that there is no room for serious argument on the second question. This is so, for example, where the defendant fails to observe a simple, routine procedure,[79] or where he makes a physical error of a kind which does not happen if the treatment is properly carried out.[80] Where the second question does arise, however, the defendant is likely to escape liability if he shows that he complied with a practice accepted as proper by a respectable part of the medical profession.[81] Alternatively, if there was no "practice" applicable to the particular circumstances in which the mistake occurred, he will escape liability if he shows that other reasonably careful and skilful medical practitioners might have made

---

[76] *Hinfey v Salford HA* [1993] 4 Med. L.R. 143. Compare with *Dowdie v Camberwell HA* [1997] 8 Med. L.R. 368 (the defendant's obstetric team were not negligent for using traction prior to intravaginal manipulation but were negligent for failing to proceed to delivery by caesarean section as soon as it was known (via the manipulation) that the baby was or was likely to be macrosomic).

[77] *Darley v Shale* [1993] 4 Med. L.R. 161, Supreme Court of New South Wales. See also *Early v Newham HA* [1994] 5 Med. L.R. 214 (abandonment of attempt to re-intubate patient for anaesthesia was in accordance with a procedure prescribed by the health authority after proper consideration of the risks).

[78] *McCafferty v Merton Sutton & Wandsworth HA* [1997] 8 Med. L.R. 387, QBD, in the absence of evidence of a diverticular problem affecting the colon, and considering the risks inherent in a resection operation.

[79] For example in *Goode v Nash* (1979) 21 S.A.S.R. 419, 423, Supreme Court of South Australia, the defendant medical practitioner gave his services gratuitously at a public screening for the detection of glaucoma. The tests were conducted by placing a tonometer on each patient's eye. After each test, the tonometer was sterilised in a flame. The defendant placed the tonometer on the claimant's eye before it had cooled sufficiently, and caused permanent injury. The court rejected the contention that this could be characterised as a mere error of judgment. "There was . . . no exercise of a decision-making process at all, nor the taking of a calculated risk. There was simply a failure, however unintentional and inadvertent, to observe the obvious but critical precaution of ensuring that the instrument was not too hot to place upon the patient's eye" (*ibid.* at 423).

[80] For example, *Gonda v Kerbel* (1982) 24 C.C.L.T. 222, Ontario Supreme Court: defendant caused a perforation of claimant's bowel, while carrying out a bowel examination using a sigmoidoscope. Compare with *Lavelle v Hammersmith and Queen Charlotte's Special HA*, unreported, January 16, 1998, CA (claimant alleged that a cardiovascular surgeon had mistakenly threaded a balloon catheter into his right middle lobe pulmonary vein during a balloon atrial septostomy operation. This had caused rupture of the vein leading to his severe brain damage. The Court of Appeal did not accept that the experienced doctor concerned had made such a careless mistake and concluded that the vein injury was more likely to have been caused as an attendant risk of the septostomy.

[81] See paras 13–032 to 13–036, above.

the same mistake.[82] If the defendant was dealing with an emergency, an error of judgment may be easier to justify.[83]

Mistakes and errors of judgment. The most important case in this area is   **13–081** *Whitehouse v Jordan*,[84] in which the House of Lords held that the *Bolam* test was applicable to actions for negligence in the course of medical treatment. In that case the claimant, who was born with severe brain damage, brought an action for negligence against inter alia the senior registrar who attended the birth and the health authority. Bush J. held that the registrar was negligent in that he "pulled too hard and too long" with forceps before delivering the claimant by Caesarean section. The Court of Appeal[85] by a majority held that the judge was wrong in this crucial finding of fact. Lord Denning M.R. and Lawton L.J. added that even if the defendant did make the mistake of pulling too hard and too long, that would not amount to negligence. The House of Lords upheld the Court of Appeal's decision, but solely on the basis that there was no evidence to support the judge's finding of fact (in other words, on the basis that no mistake was made).[86]

Adverse reaction to drugs or treatment. If the claimant suffers an adverse   **13–082** reaction to a drug prescribed or treatment administered by the defendant, this may be because the defendant was taking a calculated and reasonable risk (for example in vaccinating a normal child against whooping cough). If the defendant had failed to familiarise himself with the possible side effects of the drug or if the side effects were disproportionate to the benefit likely to be achieved,[87] an allegation of negligence will be more difficult to resist. Where the adverse reactions occur because the defendant is using a new drug or taking part in a clinical trial, different considerations arise.[88] In many cases of "adverse reaction", the decision to prescribe the drug cannot be impugned on the *Bolam*[89] test,

---

[82] See para.13–029, above. In *Pudney v Union Castle Mail Steamship Co Ltd* [1953] 1 Lloyd's Law Rep. 73 it was alleged that the ship's doctor was negligent in the treatment he prescribed, even on the basis of his own diagnosis. It was argued that, having diagnosed a mild rheumatic condition, the doctor was negligent in failing to take precautions against a more serious affliction; he should, for example, have advised immediate rest and prohibited walking. Devlin J. considered that the doctor had exercised reasonable skill and care in treatment and rejected this contention. See also *Spry v Calman and Camberwell HA*, unreported, April 6, 1998 (radiation treatment eradicated claimant's cancer but damaged small bowel. Claimant alleged that the doses had been excessive. No negligence as defendant was acting consistently with a leading cancer hospital's protocol (actually less radical doses were used), and the doses had to take account of different equipment. The defendant's practice was accepted as proper by a responsible body of clinicians.

[83] See, e.g. *Meyer v Gordon* (1981) 17 C.C.L.T. 1, British Columbia Supreme Court: doctor resuscitating a baby in an emergency situation used certain procedures which were unorthodox and an error of judgment. This did not amount to negligence in the circumstances.

[84] [1981] 1 W.L.R. 246.

[85] [1980] 1 All E.R. 650.

[86] See also *Knight v West Kent HA* [1998] Lloyd's Rep. Med. 18, CA (Court of Appeal overturned a finding that an excessive traction force had been used: on the evidence, the amount of force required was a matter of clinical judgment).

[87] *Graham v Persyko* (1986) 27 D.L.R. (4th) 699, Ontario Court of Appeal: negligent prescription of prednisone.

[88] See para.13–036, above.

[89] Examples include *Vernon v Bloomsbury HA* (1986) [1995] 6 Med. L.R. 297 (gentamicin therapy); *Battersby v Tottman* (1985) 37 S.A.S.R. 524, discussed at para.12–081, n.61, above; *Rowan v Steinberg* [1997] 8 Med L.R. 30, Sc. Ct Sess. (OH): general practitioner not negligent for failing to withdraw claimant from tranquilliser therapy to avoid her dependency on them because the risk of

and the patient's real complaint is that he was not warned of the side effects or properly consulted before the decision to treat him was made.[90] These cases are discussed below.[91]

13–083   **Injections.** Although the administration of an injection is a purely routine procedure, it does not follow that every mishap in the course of an injection constitutes negligence. This is illustrated by a number of reported cases. In *Williams v North Liverpool Hospital Management Committee*[92] a doctor injected Pentothal into the claimant's tissues instead of the vein. On the evidence the claimant's vein was not easy to find and the Court of Appeal reversed the trial judge's finding of negligence.[93] In three cases the needle broke during the administration of the injection without any negligence on the part of the practitioner involved.[94] However, negligence was established in a case[95] where nurses injected an excessive quantity[96] of paraldehyde, and where a ward sister allowed an excessive number of injections to be given.[97] Similarly, injection of the wrong drug may be negligent.[98]

---

such dependency had occurred in her case before the risk of dependency was generally known to the profession; *Robb v East London & City HA*, unreported, May 8, 1998 (Ebsworth J.): level of radiotherapy doses prescribed in 1980 was not negligent in the light of what was then perceived to be the risk of harm to the brachial tissues.

[90] In one case the claimant recovered general damages for distress and anxiety, even though, if properly informed at the outset, he would have accepted the drug and suffered the same adverse reaction: *Goorkani v Tayside Health Board*, 1991 S.L.T. 94 (Note).

[91] See para.13–097, below. In an unusual case a defendant anaesthetist was found liable for failing to diagnose or suspect that the claimant's incidence of bronchospasm during an anaesthetic given in 1995, might be due to an adverse drug reaction. The bronchospasm was effectively managed and the 1995 anaesthetic passed without further incident. A subsequent anaesthetic in 1997 passed without incident. In a subsequent anaesthetic in 1999 a repeat incident of bronchospasm left the claimant with permanent and constant breathing difficulty. The cause of the bronchospasm was identified in 1999 as an allergy to certain muscle relaxant drugs. The 1995 anaesthetist was liable for failing to suspect, report and investigate the possibility of an adverse drug reaction following the 1995 bronchospasm incident.

[92] *The Times*, January 17, 1959.

[93] See also *Prout v Crowley* (1956) 1 B.M.J. 580 (the defendant injected ferrivenin partly into the claimant's vein and partly into the surrounding tissue. Held by the Liverpool Court of Passage that there was no negligence); *Muzio v North West Hertfordshire HA* [1995] 6 Med. L.R. 184 (claimant suffered severe headaches when, as a result of penetration of a spinal membrane by a needle used to administer a spinal anaesthetic, leakage of cerebro-spinal fluid occurred. Her claim failed: the administering anaesthetist had exercised all reasonable care during insertion of the needle).

[94] *Gerber v Pines* (1935) 79 S.J. 13; *Brazier v Ministry of Defence* [1965] 1 Lloyd's Rep. 26; *Galloway v Hanley* (1956) 1 B.M.J. 580. In the first case it was held that the doctor was negligent in failing to inform the patient or her husband what had happened.

[95] *Strangeways-Lesmere v Clayton* [1936] 2 K.B. 11.

[96] The nurses misread their instructions and injected six ounces instead of six drachms.

[97] *Smith v Brighton and Lewes Hospital Management Committee*, *The Times*, May 2, 1958. The doctor prescribed a course of 30 streptomycin injections. As a result of the ward sister's failure to take proper precautions, 34 injections were administered.

[98] In *Collins v Hertfordshire County Council* [1947] 1 K.B. 598 a junior house surgeon prepared cocaine instead of procaine as a local anaesthetic, having misunderstood the surgeon's prescription. Hilbery J. held the surgeon liable on the grounds that he was responsible for checking that what he injected was the correct substance. The defendant health authority in *Ritchie v Chichester HA* [1994] 5 Med. L.R. 187 had a protocol for the administration of epidural anaesthetic, which required the midwife and the anaesthetist to check that the correct drug had been selected for injection. The trial judge found that the anaesthetist had injected a neurotoxin into the claimant, notwithstanding that this conclusion implied a series of errors on the part of the medical staff.

Operations. The courts have always recognised the dangers which are inher- **13–084**
ent in an operation.[99] Mistakes will occur on occasions, despite the exercise of
reasonable skill and care, and the patient may suffer grievous injuries in consequence. Even where a routine operation, which has been performed countless
times without mishap, fails, it does not necessarily follow that the surgeon was
negligent.[1] Where the operation is complex or unusual, any failure is easier to
justify.[2] However, where the claimant developed meningitis as a result of some
infection in the apparatus used during his operation, it was held that there must
have been some negligence by the hospital staff, for which the hospital authority
was responsible.[3] Where the operation is a race against time, the court will make
greater allowance for mistakes on the part of the surgeon or his assistants.[4] An
operation should be carefully planned.[5-6] The decision to operate, rather than to
treat conservatively, may be negligently hasty. Once negligence is established,
the claimant should be able to recover damages, even if the ill effects are purely
cosmetic.[7]

Failure to remove objects. Many claims arise from the surgeon's failure to **13–085**
remove objects from the patient's body at the end of an operation. In practice
such claims are usually settled. Even when they are contested, it is difficult for
the defendants to rebut the inference that someone involved in the operation must

---

[99] See, e.g. *Hajgato v London Health Association* (1982) 36 O.R. (2d) 669, 681 affirmed (1983) 44
O.R. (2d) 264, Ontario CA (risk of post-operative infection).
[1] *Ashcroft v Mersey Regional HA* [1983] 2 All E.R. 245 concerned a routine operation for the
removal of granulated tissue from the claimant's eardrum. The surgeon damaged the claimant's facial
nerve while removing the granulations with the use of forceps. With some hesitation Kilner-Brown
J. rejected the contention that the surgeon had used excessive force. Claimant's claim dismissed. This
decision was upheld on appeal: see [1985] 2 All E.R. 96 (Note).
[2] See *Lavelle v Hammersmith and Queen Charlotte Special HA*, para.12–189, fn.6 above for
facts.
[3] *Voller v Portsmouth Corp* (1947) 203 L.T.J. 264. The operation was performed in the ward rather
than the operating theatre, but Birkett J. did not consider that the doctors were negligent in adopting
this course.
[4] "A mistake which would amount to negligence in a 'cold' operation might be no more than
misadventure in a 'hot' operation." *Cooper v Nevill*, *The Times*, March 10, 1961.
[5-6] Failure to carry out further assessment by CT scan or myelogram before spinal surgery, so that
the surgery was planned on the basis of inadequate information, was held negligent in *Smith v Salford
HA* [1994] 5 Med. L.R. 321, but the claimant failed to show that the breach was causative of his post-
operative tetraplegia. See also *Tucker v Tees HA* [1995] 6 Med. L.R. 54: failure to perform an
ultrasound scan to exclude the possibility that the patient was pregnant before conducting a laparotomy to confirm a provisional diagnosis of ovarian cyst was negligent.
[7] *MacDonald v Ross* (1983) 24 C.C.L.T. 242, 247, Nova Scotia Supreme Court: following an
operation on claimant's breasts, one breast was appreciably larger than the other and the nipple was
misaligned. Surgeon held liable for negligent performance of the operation. "Cosmetic improvement
may not be in contemplation where surgery is performed for therapeutic reasons, but it must equally
be true that gross and entirely unnecessary, and I stress unnecessary, deformations are not acceptable
consequences within the appropriate standard of care in such cases." It is submitted that the English
courts would adopt the same approach.

have been negligent.[8] In *James v Dunlop*[9] a surgeon failed to remove all the swabs at the end of an operation. The Court of Appeal held that he was not exonerated simply because the nurse who was counting the swabs for him had made a mistake. A similar point arose in *Mahon v Osborne*.[10] At the end of an abdominal operation one of the swabs used to pack off adjacent organs was left in the patient's body, with the result that he died three months later. The system used for checking the removal of swabs was as follows: each swab had a tape attached with a Spencer-Wells forceps clipped to the tape, which would hang outside the patient's body as a signal. In addition, the theatre sister counted the swabs used. In the present case the surgeon made a visual search and concluded that all the swabs were removed. He asked the theatre sister if they were all removed and she said "yes". The surgeon did not make a further search by feel before sewing up. The jury found that the surgeon, but not the theatre sister, was negligent. On the surgeon's appeal the Court of Appeal, by a majority, ordered a re-trial on the grounds of the judge's misdirection to the jury. They observed that there was no general rule of law requiring a surgeon in an operation such as this one, after removing all the swabs of which he was aware, to make sure by a separate search by feel that no swabs were left in the patient's body.[11] The question whether the omission by the surgeon to remove a swab constituted failure to exercise reasonable skill and care was to be decided on the evidence given in the particular case. Where the surgeon discards a precaution which is available to ensure the removal of all swabs, he may be judged more harshly.[12]

---

[8] *Dryden v Surrey County Council* [1936] 2 All E.R. 535 (a wad of gauze was left in the claimant's body during a minor operation. It was held that the doctor who performed the operation was negligent, but the nurses were not); *Hocking v Bell* [1948] W.N. 21 (the defendant carried out a thyroidectomy on the claimant and temporarily placed a rubber drainage tube in the wound. He left part of the tube *in situ*, negligence established); *Cooper v Nevill*, *The Times*, March 10, 1961 (abdominal pack left in the claimant's body. Held that there must have been some negligence on the part of the surgeon or his assistant).

[9] (1931) 1 B.M.J. 730. See also the discussion of this case in *Mahon v Osborne* [1939] 2 K.B. 14. By contrast in *Elliott v Bickerstaff* (1999) 48 N.S.W.L.R. 214, the Court of Appeal of New South Wales held that even if leaving a sponge in the patient could be taken to indicate negligence by someone, this did not mean that the surgeon was negligent, as the theatre staff could have been negligent (wrongly informing the surgeon that the sponge count indicated all sponges were removed). The claimant was suing her surgeon personally and not the hospital or health authority responsible for employing both the theatre staff.

[10] [1939] 2 K.B. 14.

[11] In *Elliott v Bickerstaff*, see n.40 above, the Court of Appeal of New South Wales held (on the evidence in this case) that the surgeon's duty of care to his patient did require him to exercise reasonable skill and care in feeling for sponges in the abdominal cavity as well as asking theatre staff if the sponge count was satisfactory.

[12] See, e.g. *Urry v Bierer*, *The Times*, July 15, 1955. For a similar Canadian decision see *Chasney v Anderson* [1950] 4 D.L.R. 223: surgeon performed tonsil and adenoid operation on child using sponges. He did not use sponges with tapes attached which were available, nor did he have a nurse in attendance to count the sponges. It was held that his failure to remove one of the sponges was negligent. By contrast the surgeon's failure to wear his prescription glasses when performing the claimant's hysterectomy was not negligent in *Stefanyshyn v Rubin* (1996) 113 Man. R. (2d) 133 because his failure to wear glasses did not cause the suturing error that occurred (a ureter had been tied to the vagina, leading to a fistula and urine leakage), since the ureter was not visible during the surgery.

Post-operative care. The neglect of any reasonable post-operative precaution   **13–086**
may expose a surgeon to liability for a non-negligent mistake which occurred
during the course of the operation.[13] The requirement for post-operative aftercare
includes dealing with complications and investigating the patient's complaints,[14]
and pursuing the results of tests or undertaking further tests that are indicated or
ordered by another clinician.[15]

Overintervention. With the growing panoply of available medical treatments,   **13–087**
cases sometimes arise where medical practitioners attempt to treat the incurable
or embark on treatment which is worse than the original disability. Thus before
considering whether the method of treatment was negligent, it must sometimes
be asked whether medical intervention can be justified at all.[16] Whether or not the
intervention undertaken can be justified will be determined by the extent of
investigation, consideration of other less "invasive" regimes or management,
and on expert opinion of the appropriateness of the treatment used. The fact that

---

[13] See, e.g. *Lee v O'Farrell* (1988) 43 C.C.L.T. 269: fracture of femoral head occurred during surgery.
Defendant held negligent for failing to detect this by post-operative X-ray (the X-ray taken covered
too small a field). See also *Cherekwayo v Grafton* (1993) 84 Man. R. (2d) 81 (failure to provide
suitable post-operative care after breast implantation surgery led to corrective surgery being performed as an emergency); see also *Newbury v Bath District HA* [1998] 47 B.M.L.R. 138, QBD,
Ebsworth J. Defendant found liable for failure to test claimant for neurological deficit following
spinal surgery and consequent failure to re-operate to remove implants. Held that such removal within
24 hours of surgery would have given claimant more than 50% chance of recovery. This negligence
was a material cause of the claimant's damage (although selection of a technique using the offending
implants was not negligent).
[14] *Knight v Bradley*, unreported, May 5, 1998, defendant's negligent delay to dealing with the
claimant's post-operative complaints entitled the claimant to damages for the limited consequences
of the delay; *Tailleur v Grande Prairie General & Auxiliary Hospital* [2000] 74 Alta. L.R. (3d) 20,
Canadian Court of Appeal (claimant severed Achilles tendon and surgeon sutured tendon and wound
and then placed claimant's leg in cast, gas gangrene (rare, infectious disease caused by Clostridia
bacteria) developed leading to amputation of the leg. No evidence of negligence by surgeon since no
evidence that different type of cast or keeping claimant in hospital without a cast for observation
would have led to different result).
[15] See *Taylor v West Kent HA* [1997] 8 Med. L.R. 251, QBD (claimant's breast lump was aspirated,
and cytology report stated: "Blood and groups of mildly atypical epithelial cells possibly from a
fibroadenoma or fibrocystic disease. Consider biopsy to confirm." No biopsy undertaken, claimant
was reassured at two six-monthly reviews and her carcinoma was only diagnosed when the axillary
lymph nodes were involved. Held that no reasonable clinician ought to have taken the cytology report
as an exclusion of malignancy, or that no further investigation was necessary. At the very least, failure
to seek further clarification of the cytology was negligent. The result was that diagnosis and treatment
of the claimant's breast cancer was delayed by over one year. See also *Braun Estate v Vaughan* (1997)
124 Man. R. (2d) 1, where the doctor failed to follow up the cytology report of a routine PAP smear
taken from the claimant's cervix. The report showed evidence of abnormality that required further
investigation at the time, but for which there was a 100% probability of recovery with proper
treatment. The doctor was held negligent for having no independent system in place to ensure that
reports were returned to him, or to ensure that the hospital concerned had such a system in place. The
hospital had closed its gynaecological unit and the claimant's records held by the hospital were not
forwarded to her general practitioner. The claimant's cervical cancer was undetected for a year, in
which time it had become untreatable and the claimant subsequently died from the cancer. The claim
for damages succeeded.
[16] In *Atzori v Dr Chan King Pan* [1999] 3 HKLRD 77, the Court of First Instance found that an
orthopaedic surgeon: "had set his sights on surgery at a very early stage long before a proper trial of
conventional conservative treatment had been conducted and that this accounts in part for the absence
of careful neurological testing."

the patient or his parent has consented is not a defence in circumstances where no reasonably competent medical practitioner would have proceeded at all.[17] In *De Freitas v O'Brien and Connelly*[18] the claimant complained that she had been subjected to unnecessary spinal decompression surgery when there was no evidence that her back pain was caused by nerve root compression. The Court of Appeal upheld the conclusions of the trial judge that (a) spinal surgery was a specialism apart from other orthopaedic surgery and neurosurgery which, notwithstanding that it was practised by a very small number of surgeons, represented a respectable body of medical opinion, and (b) a spinal surgeon could reasonably and safely undertake exploratory surgery on the claimant because his expertise greatly reduced the risk of damage to nerve roots which were not directly involved in the procedure.[19]

(e) *Failure of Communication Between Hospitals or Medical Practitioners*

13–088 It is frequently necessary to transfer the treatment of a patient from one hospital, or one hospital department, to another or possibly from a hospital to the patient's own doctor. Plainly, there must be adequate communication between the parties as to the condition diagnosed, the treatment so far given and, possibly, the treatment required.

The question of communication arose in *Chapman v Rix*.[20] The patient, a butcher, stabbed himself in the abdomen while boning a rump of beef. The defendant examined him at the cottage hospital. He realised that the deep fascia had been cut but he concluded wrongly (though not negligently) that the wound had not penetrated the peritoneum. He ordered the wound to be stitched and dressed and then sent the patient home. The defendant told him that he thought it was a surface wound, but he gave emphatic instructions that he should see his own doctor that evening and tell him what had happened and what had been done. Symptoms of pain and nausea developed. The patient saw his own doctor (M) and told him that the hospital had said his wound was superficial. M diagnosed digestive disorder. Five days later the patient died as a result of the wound to his peritoneum. Barry J. held that the defendant was negligent in his failure to communicate directly with M. The Court of Appeal, by a majority, allowed the defendant's appeal. They observed that it might have been better if the defendant had sent a letter to M, but his omission to do so did not constitute professional negligence. The House of Lords, by a majority of three to two, upheld the Court of Appeal's decision. Lords Goddard, Morton and Hodson

---

[17] In *Doughty v North Staffordshire HA* [1992] 3 Med. L.R. 81 the claimant was born with a birthmark on her face. A plastic surgeon employed by the defendants carried out 11 to 13 operations during her childhood. As a result there was a considerable area of scarring on her face and the birthmark remained visible. The defendants were held liable on the basis that no body of reasonably competent medical opinion would have exposed the claimant to that course of plastic surgery.
[18] [1995] 6 Med. L.R. 109.
[19] Compare with the decision in *Atzori v Dr Chan King Pan* [1999] 3 HKLRD 77.
[20] [1994] 5 Med. L.R. 238.

considered that the steps taken by the defendant were sufficient to communicate to M that he did not think there was penetration of the peritoneum but there was a degree of risk and the patient needed watching.

In two Canadian cases,[21] the importance of proper consultation between different doctors treating a patient in the same hospital was emphasised. In *Bergen*, the trial judge condemned the practice of "kerbstone consultations", which occurred when the various doctors happened to meet in the hospital corridors. A hospital authority has a duty to devise and maintain an adequate system for summoning qualified or specialist assistance when required. In *Brown*, an injured child (the claimant) was admitted to the defendant hospital and the treating paediatricians failed to warn the mother of suspected child abuse (based on a CTG scan). The child was discharged and brought back having sustained severe and permanent brain damage. The radioneurologist noticed the suggestive CTG signs of brain haemorrhage due to violent shaking but did not communicate the significance of the finding to the treating paediatricians responsible for the claimant's discharge. The claimant's claim for damages succeeded. The trial judge stated:

> "While I do not conclude that [the radioneurologist] had any obligation to run to the child's side, read the entire history and in effect become the treating physician, it was his duty to advise at least [the paediatric resident] that these subdural bleeds were: (a) likely non-accidental in nature, and (b) because of their age, not consistent with recent trauma. That, in effect, is placing on [the radioneurologist] the obligation to tell [the paediatric resident] that child abuse is suspected."[22]

He continued:

> "Common sense, hospital policy and precise legislation mandate that the medical profession go beyond pure diagnosis and report to the proper authorities circumstances which suggest and especially those that scream child abuse is the likely cause of trauma to the child."[23]

In *Robertson v Nottingham HA*[24] the Court of Appeal identified two significant types of breakdown in communications between hospital staff. First, there was no effective communication of information available from CTG traces operated by nurses and midwives to the doctors who were responsible for making the decisions on management of the claimant's birth. Secondly, there was a lack of effective communication of the doctor's instructions to the nurses and midwives who were responsible for monitoring the condition of the foetus before labour

---

[21] *Bergen v Sturgeon General Hospital* (1984) 28 C.C.L.T. 155, 175, Alberta Court of Queen's Bench Division. See also *Brown v University of Alberta Hospital* [1997] 145 D.L.R. (4th) 63, Alberta Court of Queen's Bench. See also *Braun Estate v Vaughan* (1997) 124 Man. R. (2d) 1.

[22] *per* Marceau J. at p.114, para.197.

[23] *per* Marceau J. at p.114, para.200.

[24] [1997] 8 Med. L.R. 1.

began. The defendant was in breach of its primary duty of care to the claimant in both respects.[25]

(f) Failing to Explain Treatment or Warn of Risks

13-089   **General principle.** The fundamental principle that a patient should be informed of the treatment which is proposed and warned of any risks which are inherent in that treatment, has long been recognised. It was observed in 1767: "it is reasonable that a patient should be told what is about to be done to him, that he may take courage and put himself in such a situation as to enable him to undergo the operation."[26] The extent of the patient's right to information and of the medical practitioner's correlative duty to inform has been the subject of much judicial discussion in common law countries, leading to different approaches in Canada, England and Wales and Australia.[27-28]

13-090   **English law.** The most important case in this area is *Sidaway v Governors of Bethlem Royal Hospital*.[29] This case concerned a spinal operation performed on the claimant by the second defendant for the purpose of relieving pain in her neck, right shoulder and arms. Although the operation was performed with reasonable skill and care, the claimant suffered partial paralysis as a result. Skinner J. found that the second defendant had explained the nature of the operation to the claimant, had mentioned the possibility of disturbing a nerve root and its consequences, but had not mentioned the danger of damage to the spinal cord or the fact that this was an operation of choice rather than necessity. As to the operation, the judge found that the inherent dangers were damage to nerve roots and damage to the spinal cord. The risk of one or other occurring was between 1 and 2 per cent. Damage to the spinal cord was the less likely of the two risks but would lead to the worst consequences. Skinner J. found that the warning given by the second defendant was in accordance with accepted medical practice and, applying the *Bolam* test, dismissed the claim. The claimant

---

[25] See also *Taylor v West Kent HA*, para.12–184 above, for an example of a failure of adequate communication (by report) between clinicians within one hospital where the cytology report by the pathologist who carried out the needle aspiration suggested a benign diagnosis but was not entirely clear. The surgical registrar was negligent to interpret the report as excluding malignancy; at the very least the pathologist should have been asked for clarification.

[26] *Slater v Baker* (1767) 2 Wils.K.B. 359. See also the Canadian decision *Kenny v Lockwood* [1932] 1 D.L.R. 507, 525: "the duty cast upon the surgeon was to deal honestly with the patient as to the necessity, character and importance of the operation and its probable consequences and whether success might reasonably be expected to ameliorate or remove the trouble, but that such duty does not extend to warning the patient of the dangers incident to, or possible in, any operation, nor to details calculated to frighten or distress the patient."

[27-28] As to the American doctrine of informed consent, which has been rejected by the English courts, see paras 13–102 to 13–104, below.

[29] [1985] A.C. 871.

appealed unsuccessfully both to the Court of Appeal[30] and to the House of Lords.[31]

The Court of Appeal, in affirming Skinner J.'s decision, unanimously applied the *Bolam* test. In the House of Lords a bare majority, namely Lord Diplock,[32] Lord Bridge[33] and Lord Keith[34] considered that the *Bolam* test was applicable to claims against medical practitioners for inadequate advice.[35] Thus it has now been finally established (albeit by a bare majority) that in negligence actions based upon the omission or inadequacy of any advice, explanation or warning given by the defendant in relation to proposed medical treatment, the *Bolam* test is to be applied.

One merit of the *Bolam* test, as Lord Diplock observed,[36] is its flexibility. The **13–091** duty of disclosure changes as medical knowledge advances and medical practices change. Indeed the duty of disclosure ought to change as public knowledge of medical matters increases,[37] since one factor which a reasonably careful and skilful doctor would take into account is the patient's capacity to understand the information he is given.[38] In the foreseeable future it is most unlikely that the

---

[30] [1984] Q.B. 493. For discussion of the Court of Appeal's decision, see M. A. Jones, "Doctor Knows Best?" (1984) 100 L.Q.R. 355; I. Kennedy, "The Patient on the Clapham Omnibus" (1984) 47 M.L.R. 454; T. Hodgkinson, "Medical Treatment: Informing Patients of Material Risks" [1984] P.L. 414.

[31] [1985] A.C. 871. For discussion of the House of Lords' decision, see A. Grubb, "Medical law, 'Informed Consent' to Medical Treatment: Who Decides, the Patient or Doctor?" (1985) 44 C.L.J. 199; H. Teff, "Consent to Medical Procedures: Paternalism, Self-Determination or Therapeutic Alliance?" (1985) 101 L.Q.R. 432.

[32] [1985] A.C. 871, 893–895.

[33] *ibid.* at 900.

[34] *ibid.* at 895.

[35] Lord Templeman defined the duty of disclosure in different terms (at 904G), which may nevertheless lead to the same result as the *Bolam* test in many cases. Lord Scarman considered (at 885–890) that in actions for alleged inadequate warning by medical practitioners, the *Bolam* test should be discarded and that the principles enunciated by the United States Court of Appeals, District of Columbia Circuit in *Canterbury v Spence* should be applied.

[36] [1985] A.C. 871, 892–893.

[37] The merits of the *Sidaway* decision, as well as the dangers of relying too heavily on the medical standard, were discussed by *The Times* in a leading article on the day after the House of Lords' decision: "Even today, patients are very often far readier to learn about their illness than doctors are ready to recognise; and better able to understand, too. Medical education, as well as habit and pressure of time, all tend to obstruct the development of a relationship of mutual respect and trust. The *Sidaway* case had established that there is no place in English law for a rigid doctrine of informed consent. But it has underwritten a high level of information and consultation as an essential part of good clinical practice today."

[38] The main criticisms of the use of the *Bolam* test in this area of the law come from those who seek objective rules defining the extent of the information to which a patient is entitled. See, e.g.: M. A. Jones, "Doctor Knows Best?" (1984) 100 L.Q.R. 355. In "Consent to Medical Procedures: Paternalism, Self-Determination or Therapeutic Alliance?" (1985) 101 L.Q.R. 432, H. Teff argues that a greater measure of disclosure than that customarily made by doctors would assist in the formation of a "therapeutic alliance" between doctor and patient and would thus aid the treatment of the patient. For further academic criticism of Sidaway, see Giesen and Hayes, "The Patient's Right to Know—a Comparative View" (1992) An.-Am.L.R. 101; Professor Kennedy argues in "The Patient on the Clapham Omnibus" (1984) 47 M.L.R. 454 that there should be a duty (subject to certain defined exceptions) to disclose "any unusual and material risks inherent in the proposed treatment, and any feasible alternatives" and that the question of materiality should be decided by the court on the basis of the "prudent patient" test. Although academic debate on these questions continues, the direction of the law is probably now fixed (subject, of course, to legislation).

House of Lords will be persuaded to depart from the view of the majority in *Sidaway v Governors of Bethlem Royal Hospital.*[39]

The cases decided since *Sidaway* are helpful as illustrations of established principle.[40-41] Where the risks involved are relatively remote, the judgment of Bridge J. in *O'Malley-Williams v Board of Governors of the National Hospital for Nervous Diseases*[42] is still relevant. Bridge J. stated that there were obvious disadvantages in warning a patient of such risks: "On the one hand you alarm him unnecessarily, on the other hand, you may put him in a position where he feels that he should take the decision, albeit the doctor is obviously much better qualified to weigh up the advantages and the desirability of the proposed operation as against the risks". Where the proposed operation or treatment is purely elective, it is submitted that this consideration carries less weight. If the proposed operation or treatment is not necessary for the patient's welfare (e.g. because the patient is being asked to participate in an experiment), it is difficult to conceive of any justification for withholding information concerning the known risks. The decision of the Court of Appeal in *Pearce v United Bristol Healthcare NHS Trust*[43] is interesting in this context, as an example of the application of *Bolam*, subject to *Bolitho* scrutiny of the expert medical evidence (where the doctor had recommended non-intervention and conservative treatment). The claimant complained that she had not been advised of a risk of stillbirth in the event that her overdue baby was not induced or delivered by Caesarean section. Her doctor recommended that she waited for the delivery to commence naturally. The risk materialised and the baby was stillborn. It was held that the *Bolam* test applies to the giving of advice or failure to give advice as to the risks attaching to both interventionist and conservative treatment but that, in the ordinary event, the patient should be informed of any significant risk which would affect the judgment of a reasonable patient in deciding between treatment options. "Significant risk" is a matter for expert medical evidence (subject to the court's review on *Bolitho* principles). In this case, the risk was regarded by the defendant's medical experts and by the court as of such a low magnitude as to be insignificant. Notwithstanding that the court stated that it was applying *Sidaway* in formulating the requirement of the standard of care, the formula suggested is very close to the "prudent patient" test adopted by the High Court of Australia in *Rogers v Whittaker.*[44]

---

[39] [1985] A.C. 871.

[40-41] Examples include: *Moyes v Lothian Health Board* 1990 SLT 444, (applying the *Bolam* test, it was held that the claimant had been adequately warned as to the small risk of stroke); *Gold v Haringey HA* [1988] Q.B. 481, CA; *Blyth v Bloomsbury HA* [1993] 4 Med. L.R. 151, CA; *Smith v Salford HA* [1994] 5 Med. L.R. 321; *Poynter v Hillingdon HA* (1997) 37 B.M.L.R. 192 (the *Bolam* test was applied as modified by the remarks of Lord Bridge in *Sidaway*; *Newbury v Bath District HA* (1998) 47 B.M.L.R. 138, QBD (applying *Bolam* and *Bolitho*: on the facts and evidence, doctor under no duty to advise patient that his proposed surgical implant technique was unusual, and no duty to advise patient of alternative techniques available); *Williamson v East London & City HA* [1998] Lloyd's Rep. Med. 6 (damages were awarded for negligent failure to explain to the claimant that a more serious operation was required than that to which she had consented, even though she would have had the same operation in any event, albeit later).

[42] (1985) 1 B.M.J. 635.

[43] [1999] P.I.Q.R. P53.

[44] [1993] 4 Med. L.R. 79, 82–83, and see also paras 13–103 to 13–104, below. The court in *Rogers v Whittaker*, however, put forward this formulation as an express departure from *Bolam* and *Sidaway*, which it declined to follow. The decision in *Pearce* has attracted considerable academic attention: see

Specific considerations affecting what ought to be disclosed by a doctor advising upon treatment options are discussed below.

Explanation or warning curtailed because of the patient's condition or   **13–092**
state of mind. It is self-evident that any duty of disclosure or warning must be curtailed where the patient is unfit to receive such disclosure or warning (for example due to the effect of his physical condition on his ability to understand at the time when the information is given, or due to his emotional or mental condition).[45]

In *Smith v Salford HA*[46] the defendant failed to communicate to the patient the risks of surgery. Potter J. found that even if the defendant had made an attempt to warn of those risks, such warning was not given in terms which were adequate to register with the patient, bearing in mind his condition at the time. He had a headache and was suffering the general ill-effects of a recent myelogram. In an extreme case, where the patient is semi-conscious and in need of urgent treatment to save his life, the most laconic communication may be deemed sufficient. The position is more difficult where the doctor considers it contrary to the patient's best interests to give him an accurate explanation or warning, even though the patient would be capable of understanding it. The Supreme Court of Canada has recognised that the emotional condition of the patient and his fears relating to the operation may justify a surgeon in withholding or generalising information.[47]

Duty to answer patient's questions. Following Lord Woolf M.R.'s judgment   **13–093**
in *Pearce v United Bristol Healthcare NHS Trust*[48] the starting point is that if a patient asks his doctor about a risk, the doctor's duty is to give an honest answer. If the patient is not of sound mind there may be an acceptable reason for not giving an honest answer. In most of the cases relating to inadequate warning or explanation discussed above, the patient himself did not ask specific questions. Where, however, the patient does ask specific questions, generally speaking he is entitled to accurate answers, so far as the doctor is able to give them.[49]

Lord Woolf's statement of the law in *Pearce v United Bristol Healthcare NHS Trust*, was confirmed and approved by the Court of Appeal in *Wyatt v (1) Dr Anne Curtis; (2) Central Nottinghamshire HA.*[50] This case concerned Pt 20 proceedings brought by a GP against the health authority for a contribution

---

the commentary at [1999] 7 Med. L.Rev. 61 and Michael A. Jones, "Informed Consent and Other Fairy Stories" [1999] 7 Med. L.Rev. 103.
[45] See, e.g. *Male v Hopmans* (1967) 64 D.L.R. (2d) 105, Ontario CA.
[46] [1994] 5 Med. L.R. 321.
[47] See para.13–102, below, and *Reibl v Hughes* (1980) 114 D.L.R. (3d) 1, 13.
[48] [1999] P.I.Q.R. P53 at P54.
[49] See the passages in *Sidaway v Governors of Bethlem Royal Hospital* referred to at para.13–090 and n.29 above, and Lord Woolf M.R.'s judgment in *Pearce v United Bristol Healthcare NHS Trust* [1999] P.I.Q.R. P53, P54. Contrast with Sir Maurice Drake's obiter comments in *Poynter v Hillingdon HA* (1997) 37 B.M.L.R. 192.
[50] [2003] EWCA Civ 1779, October 30, 2003, unreported.

towards the GP's admitted liability to the claimant mother for her failure to warn the mother of the risk of severe harm to the baby due to the mother's contracting chicken pox during pregnancy. The GP had simply warned that the worst effect on the unborn baby would be chicken pox lesions. It was held that the subsequently treating house surgeon, who was not asked about the risk caused to the baby by chicken pox, but was aware of the mother's infection, was not under a duty to ascertain what advice the claimant had received from her GP and to correct the errors in that advice. As the Court of Appeal indicated the false impression of security arising from the GP's incorrect advice was still operating at the time of the second consultation and this caused the claimant not to ask questions of the second doctor concerning the chicken pox infection.[51]

13–094   The duty to advise in relation to the treatment of a minor patient was considered in *Thompson v Blake-James*.[52] The Court of Appeal there emphasised that the duty in such circumstances is to the child. Accordingly the doctor's obligation is to take reasonable care to see that the parents are in a position to make an informed decision as to treatment options which is in the patient's best interests. The doctor is not entitled to limit his advice because of the attitude of the parents to the treatment in question.[53]

However, a general enquiry by a patient about a drug does not impose on hospital staff an obligation to pass on all information available to the hospital about the drug.[54] In *Lee v South West Thames Regional HA*[55] the Court of Appeal expressed the view, obiter, that the duty to answer questions truthfully applied equally after treatment had been given. Thus, if some mishap had occurred, the patient was entitled to be given details.[56] A right to demand recorded information has been conferred by statute.[57] Under the Access to Health Records Act 1990, subject to certain limited exceptions, a person has a right of access to medical records relating to himself. The Act came into force on November 1, 1991. It does not apply to health records prepared before that date, save in so far as it is necessary to make subsequent health records intelligible.

---

[51] By contrast in *Deriche v Ealing Hospital NHS Trust* [2003] EWHC 3014, QB, Buckley J. found in very similar circumstances yet distinguishing *Wyatt*, that where a consultant had been the subsequent doctor he was not entitled to assume from the previous doctor's note that "full counselling" had been given, that the claimant had fully understood the nature of the risk involved.

[52] [1998] Lloyd's Rep. Med. 187.

[53] This decision was handed down in July 1997, three months after the decision of Sir Maurice Drake in *Poynter*. The Court of Appeal's guidance in *Pearce* and *Blake-James* suggests that the judge's obiter comments in *Poynter* were incorrect, and the approach to the withholding of information given to the parents should be limited to the facts of that case.

[54] *Blyth v Bloomsbury HA* [1989] 4 Med. L.R. 151.

[55] [1985] 1 W.L.R. 845, 850–851. Lord Donaldson M.R. reiterated these views in *Naylor v Preston AHA* [1987] 2 All E.R. 353, 360.

[56] Sometimes there is a duty to volunteer such information, whether requested or not. See, e.g. *Gerber v Pines* (1935) S.J. 13: needle broke in the course of an injection. Held that the doctor who administered the injection was negligent in failing to inform the claimant or her husband what had happened on the day of the accident. Damages only 5 guineas.

[57] There is no absolute right of access to medical records at common law: see *R. v Mid Glamorgan HA Ex p. Martin* [1994] 5 Med. L.R. 383, CA for the position in respect of medical records brought into being before November 1, 1991. The procedure for obtaining medical records under the clinical negligence protocol is contained in the CPR at C3–014 and C-3–019.

Warning required for patient's protection. Different considerations alto-   **13–095**
gether arise when a warning or explanation is necessary, not to satisfy the
patient's curiosity, but to protect him against the inherent risks of the treatment.[58]
When the patient is being admitted to a hospital or similar institution, failure to
inform him of a known risk of infection could also amount to negligence.[59-60] In
some circumstances, it may be negligent not to warn a patient to take precautions
for the protection of others.

Manner and scope of communication.[61] The manner in which the doctor   **13–096**
communicates a warning or explanation may itself be critical.[62] In *Lybert v
Warrington HA*[63] the claimant complained that she had not received an adequate
warning of the risk of failure of an operation to sterilise her. It was found that a
warning had been given but the claimant had not understood it. The Court of
Appeal upheld the conclusion of the trial judge that a doctor must take reasonable
care to give a warning which is adequate in scope, content and presentation and
to take steps to see that his warning is understood. These requirements apply not
only to information which the doctor has a duty to provide, but also to any
additional information which he volunteers. The warning given to the claimant
was given at an inappropriate time and under unsuitable conditions. It lacked
sufficient emphasis and clarity, and the doctor had obtained no assurance that it
was understood. Both the doctor and the health authority were liable, the latter on
the grounds that it failed to institute an effective system to ensure that proper
warnings were given in such cases. The case of *Smith v Tunbridge Wells HA*[64]
illustrates that the doctor must bear in mind that his duty to warn is owed to the
particular patient. He must take care to see that his explanation is sufficient in the
light of the characteristics of that individual, so far as he knows or ought to
appreciate them. The 24-year-old claimant was rendered impotent by an operation to repair a rectal prolapse. This was a recognised risk of the operation, but
the defendant was liable for failing effectively to communicate the risk to the
claimant. Morland J. said[65]:

---

[58] In *Clarke v Adams* (1950) 94 S.J. 599 for example, the defendant, a physiotherapist, was treating
the claimant for a fibrositic condition of the left heel. The instrument which he used was dangerous, because burns caused by it could lead to serious consequences. Before applying the treatment
the defendant gave the claimant an approved form of warning. Slade J. held that the warning was
not adequate to convey to a reasonable person "that his safety depended on his informing the
defendant the moment he felt more than a comfortable warmth". Accordingly the defendant was
liable for the claimant's injuries. For further examples, *Crichton v Hastings* (1973) 29 D.L.R. (3d)
692 (failure to inform claimant of possible side effect of anti-coagulant drug, in the event of
overdose or protracted use); contrast with *Webster v Chapman* (1997) 155 D.L.R. (4th) 82 (no
duty to advise patient of risk to foetus of anti-thrombotic drug, when patient told doctor she was
using birth control).
[59-60] See, e.g. *Marshall v Lindsey County Court* [1935] 1 K.B. 516, CA; [1937] A.C. 97, H.L.
[61] See also para.13–092, above: Explanation or warning curtailed because of the patient's condition
or state of mind.
[62] See *Bancroft v Harrogate HA* [1997] 8 Med. L.R. 398 (alleged psychiatric damage caused by the
manner in which a consultant explained the claimant's condition and his proposed treatment to her:
claim failed on the facts).
[63] [1996] 7 Med. L.R. 297.
[64] [1994] 5 Med. L.R. 334.
[65] [1994] 5 Med. L.R. 334 at 339. See also *McAllister v Lewisham and North Southwark HA* [1994]
5 Med. L.R. 343 (to leave the claimant with the impression that she had nothing to lose by undergoing
surgery was negligent).

"When recommending a particular type of surgery or treatment, the doctor, when warning of the risks, must take reasonable care to ensure that his explanation of the risks is intelligible to his particular patient. The doctor should use language, simple but not misleading, which the doctor perceives from what knowledge and acquaintanceship that he may have of the patient (which may be slight), will be understood by the patient so that the patient can make an informed decision as to whether or not to consent to the recommended surgery or treatment."[66]

The doctor will owe no duty to advise about treatment options if he cannot reasonably foresee that the patient will rely upon his advice. In *Thompson v Blake-James*[67] the defendant general practitioner was consulted by the claimant's parents on the question whether she should be vaccinated against measles. The normal age for vaccination was the second year of life. At the time of the consultation, the claimant was less than one year old. Further, the defendant was aware that the claimant's family were shortly to move to another country, so that another general practitioner would be involved in the ultimate decision whether the claimant should be vaccinated. The Court of Appeal held that, in those circumstances, it was not reasonably foreseeable by the defendant that his failure to inform the parents that an alternative method of vaccination might be suitable for the claimant would have any significant influence on their decision when the claimant reached the appropriate age.[68]

13–097   **Side effects of drugs.** Even where the benefits of a drug outweigh the harmful side effects, it is good medical practice to inform the patient of the side effects, so that he understands the treatment which he is accepting. In *Goorkani v Tayside Health Board*[69] the claimant, who had lost the sight of one eye, was given the

---

[66] The obligation on a clinician to take reasonable and appropriate steps to give a warning that was adequate in scope, content and presentation, and to satisfy themselves that the warning was understood was confirmed (applying *Lybert v Warrington HA*) in *Rana Al Hamwi v (1) Fiona Johnston (2) North West London Hospitals NHS Trust* [2005] EWHC 206, QBD; (2005) Lloyd's Rep. Med. 309. However the obligation did not extend to ensuring that the patient understood. In *Helen Cooper v Royal United Hospital Bath NHS Trust* [2004] EWHC 3381, QBD, (a trial of the question of breach only) the doctor, when advising the claimant on diagnostic options, had negligently given the claimant the impression that a repeat biopsy and a further mammogram were of equal diagnostic value. The repeat biopsy was in fact the preferred diagnostic test. Had the claimant been so advised, it was likely that she would have undergone a repeat biopsy, and her malignancy would have been detected.

[67] [1998] Lloyd's Rep. Med. 187.

[68] In *Thompson v Bradford* [2005] EWCA Civ 1439; (2006) Lloyd's Rep Med 95, a two month old baby was taken to his general practitioner for polio immunisation. He was given the injection but contracted polio. It was found that this had occurred via a boil on the baby's buttock. At first instance the judge held that the defendant had not been negligent in advising that the vaccination should proceed. However he found that the general practitioner had been negligent in failing to inform the baby's parents that the abscess was unusual and that surgery might be needed, and that, if they had been informed of such matters, they would not have proceeded with the vaccine. The Court of Appeal allowed the appeal. They drew attention to the fact that the case against the defendant related to the child's contraction of polio and the only relevant breach of duty was one which would render the defendant liable for that state of affairs. However, it was common ground that the defendant could not have foreseen any increase in the risk of the baby contracting polio. Further, the failure to inform the child's parents that the abscess was unusual and might require surgery was also not a relevant breach of duty as no competent general practitioner would have contemplated any risk from that failure other than some further discomfort for the baby if there was a reaction to the vaccination.

[69] 1991 S.L.T. 94 (Note).

drug chlorambucil to prevent deterioration in the other eye. He became infertile as a result of the drug. The Lord Ordinary held that the defendant was negligent in failing to warn the claimant of the risk of infertility, even though, properly advised, the claimant would have accepted the same treatment.[70] However, a concise statement of the risks and drawbacks is normally sufficient. The patient, especially one in pain or distress, will seldom welcome a medical lecture. In *Blyth v Bloomsbury HA*[71] the patient was a qualified nurse and made a general enquiry about Depo-Provera, a contraceptive with which she was to be injected. The Court of Appeal held that the hospital staff were not obliged to pass on to her all the information which was available to the hospital about the drug. Accordingly, the claimant's claim failed, even though she suffered from side-effects about which she had not been fully informed.[72] At the other end of the side effect spectrum, in *Shakoor v Kang Situ*,[73] a practitioner of traditional Chinese herbal medicine was sued for negligence in failing to warn his patient of the risk of injury from ingesting a decoction of herbs which he supplied.[74] The patient died of liver failure following what was described as an "idiosyncratic reaction" to the herbs. Quite apart from the impossibility of predicting such a unique reaction, the judge dismissed the allegation of failure to warn and said:

> "An adverse reaction of the type which occurred is such a rare event that I do not believe that a doctor would be obliged to give a warning and, if a warning were to be given, the risk could legitimately have been presented as being so small that I do not believe that an appropriate warning would have had the effect of dissuading anyone, let alone the deceased, from taking the treatment."[75]

Blood products. Blood products give rise to special problems. They are **13–098** known carriers of viral infection, but are highly necessary for certain groups of patients, notably haemophiliacs. The degree of risk varies, according to the type of blood product, whether it has been heat treated and so forth. It is good medical practice to inform the patient of the degree of risk involved. The extent of the warning required is, of course, governed by the state of medical knowledge at the material time; and medical knowledge in this area (especially in relation to AIDS) has changed considerably over the last 20 years. In the group hepatitis C action the claimants had all been infected with hepatitis C via blood transfusions. Although the risk of such infection was known, it was impossible to avoid either because the virus had not been discovered or because there was no way of testing

---

[70] General damages were awarded for the claimant's distress and anxiety arising from his subsequent discovery of the possibility that he was infertile.

[71] (1987) [1993] 4 Med. L.R. 151.

[72] Contrast with a Canadian case, *Lacroix v Dominique* (1999) 141 Man. R. (2nd) 1, where a doctor was negligent for not warning his patient of a 10% risk attached to anti-epileptic drugs of causing foetal abnormalities. The claim was dismissed on grounds of limitation.

[73] [2001] 1 W.L.R. 410, QBD, Bernard Livesey Q.C.

[74] Allegations of negligent failure to test liver function prior to treatment and failure to monitor liver function throughout treatment were not pursued at trial, however negligent prescription of the herb decoction was also alleged.

[75] *ibid.* 420F–G.

for its presence in the blood. The claimants' claims would have been defeated by this "knowledge of the time" defence (so far as they related to infections prior to the date on which detection and prevention of infection measures became available[76]) had they been brought in negligence. In *A v National Blood Authority*[77] the claimants succeeded on liability by bringing their claims under the Consumer Protection Act 1987 and a Directive[78] that imposed strict liability on the producer, subject to specific defences.[79] In Australia it has been held that the failure to warn a haemophiliac of the AIDS risk in September 1983 was negligent.[80]

13–099   **Risk of failure of sterilisation.** A sterilisation operation differs from most other operations in two important respects. First, it is not generally a therapeutic operation. So the justification for not mentioning remote risks given by Bridge J. in *O'Malley-Williams v Board of Governors of the National Hospital for Nervous Diseases*[81] would seem to have no application. Secondly, the patient needs to be warned of any risk of failure, not simply in order to decide whether to undergo the operation but also so that the patient and the patient's husband or wife may know how they stand thereafter. If the proposed form of sterilisation has a known risk of failure (whether 1 in 100 or 1 in 1,000), it is difficult to see any good reason why the patient should not be told. Thereafter it would be a matter for the patient and the patient's husband or wife to decide whether they wish to take any further precautions against so unlikely an eventuality. But these are arguments why medical practice might be expected to favour full disclosure. In the light of *Sidaway v Governors of Bethlem Royal Hospital*[82] these considerations would not lead the courts to override established medical practice—unless it was considered that it could not withstand logical scrutiny.

In *Gold v Haringey HA*[83] the claimant underwent a sterilisation operation at the defendant's hospital on the day after her third child was born. She subsequently conceived and bore a further child. Schiemann J. held that the operation had been carried out with reasonable care, but that the defendant had been negligent in failing to warn the claimant about the failure rate of such operations (2 per 1000, or 6 per 1000 if carried out immediately after childbirth). The expert witnesses all said that they personally would have warned about the risk of

---

[76] Either March 1, 1989 or March 1, 1990.
[77] [2001] 3 All E.R. 289, QBD.
[78] The Product Liability Directive (85/374/EEC), Art.6.
[79] The judge held that "avoidability" (of a defect) was not one of the circumstances to be taken into account under Art.6 since it fell outside the purpose of the Directive, which was intended to eliminate the requirement for proof of fault or negligence. The defence under Art.7(e) of the Directive did not apply because the existence of the defect was known or should have been known, and it was therefore immaterial that the defect was unavoidable in the product. The purpose of the Directive could not have been to permit a producer, in the face of a known risk, to continue to supply his products without accepting the responsibility for any injuries resulting (by insurance or otherwise) simply because he was unable to identify in which of his products the defect would occur.
[80] *H v Royal Alexandra Hospital* [1990] 1 Med. L.R. 297. The claimant failed on causation.
[81] (1975) 1 B.M.J. 635.
[82] [1985] A.C. 871.
[83] [1988] Q.B. 481.

failure, but that at the relevant time (1979) a substantial body of responsible doctors would not have given any such warning.[84] The judge held that the *Bolam* test only applied to therapeutic advice, and not to non-therapeutic (in this case contraceptive) advice. The judge applied his own judgment about what had been said, and concluded that the defendant ought to have warned the claimant about the failure rate. This decision was reversed on appeal. The Court of Appeal held that the *Bolam* test applies to both therapeutic and non-therapeutic advice.[85] On application of the *Bolam* test, it was held that the defendant was not liable. This decision has been criticised by legal writers,[86] but it would appear to be in line with the House of Lords' decision in *Sidaway v Governors of Bethlem Royal Hospital*.[87] In Canada, a medical practitioner was held negligent for failing to warn his patient of the risk of failure of a sterilisation operation.[88] However, a special feature of that case was that an alternative method of sterilisation existed, which was more likely to be permanent and which the claimant (if warned about the risks of failure) might have chosen.

Recently, however, claimants have succeeded in establishing liability under this head.[89] In *Lybert v Warrington HA*,[90-91] the Court of Appeal upheld a finding that although something had been said as to the risk of failure of a sterilisation, the doctor's warning had not been sufficiently clear and comprehensible to discharge his duty of care. In the unusual circumstances of that case, the fact that the claimant had behaved as if she had not been warned made it inherently likely that no proper warning had been given.[92]

Risk of disability of unborn baby. The development of techniques (such as **13–100** ultra-sound scans and amniocentesis) for detecting defects in unborn babies has given rise to a separate category of claim[93]: namely, that if the defendant had properly advised the claimant as to the condition of the foetus she was carrying,

---

[84] [1988] Q.B. 481 at 486B.

[85] *ibid*. at 489F–H.

[86] See S. Lee, "A Reversible Decision on Consent to Sterilisation" (1987) 103 L.Q.R. 515; A. Grubb, "Contraceptive advice and doctors—a law unto themselves" [1988] C.L.J. 12.

[87] [1985] A.C. 871.

[88] *Dendaas v Yackel* (1980) 109 D.L.R. (3d) 455, Supreme Court of British Columbia. But *cf. Grey v Webster* (1984) 14 D.L.R. (4th) 706.

[89] In *Newell and Newell v Goldenburg* [1995] 7 Med. L.R. 371 Mantell J. held that a vasectomist was negligent in 1985 in failing to warn of the risk of spontaneous recanalisation. It was the vasectomist's own normal practice to warn. He called experts who gave evidence that in 1985 there was a practice not to give such a warning. The defendant argued that, notwithstanding his own usual practice, he had complied with a practice approved by a responsible body of medical opinion. The judge rejected that contention, holding that such a practice was neither responsible nor reasonable.

[90-91] [1996] 7 Med. L.R. 71.

[92] [1996] 7 Med. L.R. 71, 74 *per* Otton L.J.

[93] See, e.g. *Gregory v Pembrokeshire HA* [1989] 1 Med. L.R. 81 (negligent failure to advise that amniocentesis had produced insufficient cultures to allow for testing for Down's syndrome. The claimant failed on causation, because she probably would not have had another amniocentesis anyway); *Rance v Mid-Downs HA* [1991] Q.B. 587 (claimant failed both on negligence and causation); *Arndt v Smith* [1996] 7 Med. L.R. 35 (first instance) and 108 (British Columbia CA) and [1997] 148 D.L.R. (4th) 48 (Supreme Court of Canada): negligent failure by general practitioner to warn of small but grave risks to foetus from mother's chickenpox held not causative because mother probably would not have had an abortion if warned.

then the claimant would have had an abortion. Thus the defendant's negligence has "caused" the claimant to have a handicapped baby.[94] The liability issues in these cases usually are (i) what tests were or should have been done, and (ii) what inferences should have been drawn from the results of such tests. It is normally accepted that full disclosure of any defects discovered in the foetus should be made, since the prime object of the tests is to obtain information for the parents. In practice, therefore, the *Bolam* test in this situation is primarily relevant to the gathering of information, rather than to the extent of disclosure.[95]

13–101   **The evidential problem: what did the doctor say?** A recurrent problem in this kind of case is to establish, as a matter of fact, what explanation, warning or advice the doctor gave. Typically, the doctor himself has no recollection of the conversation in question and the best he can do is tell the court what he usually says in the particular circumstances. The patient, on the other hand, generally does have a recollection of the conversation, because it was an important event in his life and something he often thought about afterwards. Although the opportunity for "reconstruction", even by the most honest of claimants, is present, one would expect that, in evidential terms, the claimant begins with an advantage. A striking feature, however, of the reported cases is that more often than not the court has accepted the defendant's evidence as to his usual practice in preference to the claimant's direct recollection of the particular conversation. In *Sidaway* Lord Scarman,[96] Lord Diplock,[97] Lord Bridge[98] and Lord Templeman[99] all expressed some surprise that the judge made such detailed findings as to what the second defendant said on the basis of evidence as to his usual practice. One case which went the other way is *Thake v Maurice*[1] which

---

[94] This category of claim is discussed and criticised by P. R. Glazebrook, in "Capable of Being, But No Right to Be, Born Alive?" [1991] C.L.J. 241. Glazebrook argues that a claim by parents that their handicapped child should have been killed before birth is so offensive that the action should be struck out.

[95] See *Carver v Hammersmith & Queen Charlotte's Special HA*, unreported, February 25, 2000, QBD: defendant negligently failed to explain to the claimant that Bart's test did not detect one in three Down's syndrome babies and, as such was not diagnostic of Down's syndrome (like amniocentesis). The claimant succeeded on causation that had she known this she would have sought amniocentesis (privately if necessary), and would have terminated the pregnancy (since on the balance of probabilities the amniocentesis would have diagnosed her baby's Down's syndrome); *Rand v East Dorset HA* [2000] Lloyd's Rep. Med. 181 on similar facts, where a routine pregnancy scan disclosed the likelihood of a Down's syndrome baby, but the parents were not told, thereby depriving them of the opportunity to terminate the pregnancy. Negligence and causation were admitted. Contrast with *Mickle v Salvation Army Grace Hospital* (1998) 166 D.L.R. (4th) 743, where the claimant parents failed on breach. The baby was born with asymmetrical limb development which was missed on ultrasound scan, but without negligence since no professional guidelines or customary practice required an examination of all of the limbs of a foetus. The claimants also failed on causation (the evidence did not support the parents' claim that they or a reasonable woman in their position would have terminated the pregnancy). *Carver v Hammersmith & Queen Charlotte's Special HA* [2000] WL 33201548.

[96] *ibid.* at 877G–H.

[97] *ibid.* at 891D.

[98] *ibid.* at 896C–E.

[99] *ibid.* at 901G–902A.

[1] [1986] Q.B. 644. See, to similar effect, *Lybert v Warrington HA* [1996] 7 Med. L.R 71, CA; and a Canadian case: *Joyal v Starreveld* [1996] 37 Alta. L.R. 19, where the claimant's recollection evidence (of receiving no warning of risks associated with reducing anti-epileptic treatment) was preferred over the defendant doctor's evidence of his standard practice of warning.

concerned an operation for sterilisation. Peter Pain J. accepted the claimants' evidence that they were given no warning (or at least no clear warning) of the risk that the first claimant might become fertile again. The defendant gave evidence that it was his normal practice to give such a warning and the judge was satisfied that all the witnesses were being honest. However, in this case the claimants' evidence was corroborated by their subsequent conduct. The Court of Appeal upheld the judge's finding of fact on this issue. By contrast with solicitors' negligence cases, the Courts are not prepared to infer any causative want of care on the basis of poor note keeping,[2] but in a case concerning brain damage resulting from hypotension during anaesthesia, where the paucity of note taking led the experts to conclude that the anaesthesia record was sub-standard for the time, the Court of Appeal held that the note taking was: "(not) negligent in the legal sense but that it is indicative of an unexplained carelessness, whether in breach of a duty of care or not."[3] In *Taylor v Shropshire HA*,[4] the claimant failed to prove that she had not been warned of the risk of failure of a sterilisation operation (although she recovered damages on the basis that the operation had been negligently performed). In so finding, however, Popplewell J. was not assisted by the defendant's specific consent form for sterilisations, which stated that the claimant had been warned of the risk of failure and was signed by her. He regarded the form as "pure window dressing" on the facts of the case.

Canadian law. Amongst Commonwealth countries, Canada has taken the lead **13-102** in developing this area of law. Although there are now important divergences between the law of Canada and English law, the Canadian decisions (especially those of the Supreme Court[5]) are frequently cited in English judgments and have certainly been taken into account by the English courts.[6] In *Hopp v Lepp*[7] the Supreme Court of Canada postulated an objective duty of disclosure (i.e. not one which was solely determined by the customs or practices of the medical profession[8]):

> "In summary, the decided cases appear to indicate that, in obtaining the consent of a patient for the performance upon him of a surgical operation, a surgeon, generally, should answer any specific questions posed by the patient as to the risks involved and should, without being questioned, disclose to him the nature of the proposed operation, its gravity, any material risks and any special or unusual risks attendant upon the performance of the operation. However, having said that, it should be added that the scope of the duty of disclosure and whether or not it has been breached are matters which must be decided in relation to the circumstances of each particular case."

---

[2] See *Faithfull v Wiltshire HA*, unreported, March 29, 2000, QBD, where the judge found that there was no substance to an allegation raised against a midwife of generally poor care based on her admitted poor note keeping.

[3] *Skelton v Lewisham & North Southwark HA* [1998] Lloyd's Rep. Med. 324, the claimant succeeded in his claim against the anaesthetists.

[4] [1998] Lloyd's Rep. Med. 395. NB: This decision was handed down the same day as judgment from the Committee of the House of Lords in *McFarlane*. *Taylor* is per incuriam in so far as the decision awards damages for the cost of bringing up the child.

[5] *Hopp v Lepp* (1980) 112 D.L.R. (3d) 67; *Reibl v Hughes* (1980) 114 D.L.R. (3d)1.

[6] For example in *Chatterton v Gerson* [1981] Q.B. 432.

[7] (1980) 112 D.L.R. (3d) 67, 81.

[8] Effectively the opposite of the *Bolam* test.

This statement was adopted by the Canadian Supreme Court in *Reibl v Hughes*,[9] where further elaboration was given as to the meaning of the crucial phrase "any material risks and any special or unusual risks attendant upon the performance of the operation". It includes any risks which the surgeon knows (or should know) that the patient deems relevant to the decision whether to undergo the operation. A risk which is a mere possibility is not "material", unless its occurrence may result in serious consequences such as paralysis or death.[10] The dangers inherent in any operation, such as the dangers of the anaesthetic or the risks of infection, do not have to be disclosed. The emotional condition of the patient and his fears relating to the operation may in certain cases justify the surgeon in withholding or generalising information. In *Reibl v Hughes*[11] itself the operation involved a significant risk of stroke. It was held that this was a material risk which ought to have been disclosed. In *Beherns v Smith*,[12] the trial judge further elucidated the extent of the duty to provide sufficient information to the patient:

> "In this regard, the law imposes upon the medical practitioner a duty to provide sufficient information to enable the patient to reasonably balance the possible risks and benefits and make an informed decision whether to undergo or forgo a recommended treatment. The scope of the duty will vary according to the circumstances of the case and any special considerations affecting the particular patient. That which a patient should be made to understand are the nature, purpose, and likely benefits of the treatment; the recognised risks inherent in it; the availability of alternative treatments; and the possible consequences of leaving the condition untreated."[13]

The Canadian cases since *Reibl* are, essentially, applications of these principles.

13–103   **Australian law.** The issue of informed consent came before the High Court of Australia in *Rogers v Whitaker*.[14] The claimant was almost blind in her right eye owing to an injury suffered in childhood. The defendant, an ophthalmic surgeon, offered an operation to remove scar tissue from the right eye. He said that the operation would improve the appearance of the right eye and also, probably, restore some of its vision. Despite the claimant's incessant questioning about possible complications of the operation, the defendant failed to warn the claimant of the very small risk of sympathetic ophthalmia (1 in 14,000—or slightly greater where, as here, there had been an earlier penetrating injury to the eye operated

---

[9] (1980) 114 D.L.R. (3d) 1.
[10] See also *White v Turner* (1981) 31 O.R.(2d) 773, HC at 789 for an explanation of "material" or "special or unusual risks": "In my view, material risks are significant risks that pose a real threat to the patient's life, health or comfort. In considering whether a risk is material or immaterial, one must balance the severity of the potential result and the likelihood of its occurring. Even if there is only a small chance of serious injury or death, the risk may be considered material. On the other hand, if there is a significant chance of slight injury this too may be held to be material. As always in negligence law, what is a material risk will have to depend on the specific facts of the case."
[11] *ibid*.
[12] (1997) 153 Sask.R. 294. The claimant underwent laparoscopic laser removal of abdominal adhesions, during which operation her small bowel was perforated. The court held that the claimant was aware of and understood the general risks of the surgery, and had been provided with sufficient information to make a reasoned decision. The claimant's claim was dismissed.
[13] *ibid*. at 297.
[14] (1992) 109 A.L.R. 625; [1993] 4 Med. L.R. 79.

upon) although the defendant was aware of that risk. If warned of the risk, the claimant would not have consented to the operation. The defendant carried out the operation with reasonable skill and care. Unfortunately, the operation did not achieve the intended improvement to the right eye, but did lead to sympathetic ophthalmia in the left eye, leaving the claimant almost totally blind.

The trial judge, the New South Wales Court of Appeal and the High Court of Australia all held that the defendant was liable for failing to warn the claimant of the risk of sympathetic ophthalmia. It was accepted that the failure to give such warning accorded with a practice accepted as proper by many reputable practitioners, but it was held that the *Bolam* test was inapplicable. In the single judgment given by five of the six judges in the High Court, the reasoning was as follows: **13–104**

 (i) There is a fundamental difference between (a) diagnosis and treatment and (b) provision of information and advice.

 (ii) In the case of diagnosis and treatment "A responsible professional opinion will have an influential, often a decisive role to play".

(iii) The question whether the patient was given all relevant information does not generally depend upon medical standards or practices.

(iv) A doctor has a duty (subject to the therapeutic privilege) to warn his patient of a material risk inherent in proposed treatment.

 (v) "A risk is material if, in the circumstances of the particular case, a reasonable person in the patient's position, if warned of the risk, would be likely to attach significance to it or if the medical practitioner is or should reasonably be aware that the particular patient, if warned of the risk, would be likely to attach significance to it."

(vi) In this case, the claimant had incessantly questioned the defendant as to, amongst other things, possible complications.

(vii) The risk of sympathetic ophthalmia was material because "a reasonable person in the patient's position would be likely to attach significance to the risk, and thus required a warning."[15]

In thus effectively adopting a "prudent patient" test for the standard of care in disclosure cases, the High Court of Australia specifically disapproved *Bolam v*

---

[15] See also *Hart v Chappell* [1994] 5 Med. L.R. 365, Supreme Court of New South Wales, upheld on appeal (on causation) by the defendant to the High Court of Australia [1999] Lloyd's Rep. Med. 223 (a doctor failed to warn his patient that an operation on her throat carried a risk to her voice, even though he was aware that she was a teacher, and she had expressly raised with him the question of possible damage to her voice. Applying the tests set out in *Rogers v Whitaker*, he was negligent.) *Rogers v Whitaker* has been adopted in South Africa in preference to the English approach: see *Castell v De Greef* (1994) (4) S.A. 408. For discussion of the decision in *Rogers v Whitaker*, see D. Chalmers, and R. Schwartz, "*Rogers v Whitaker* and Informed Consent in Australia: A Fair Dinkum Duty of Disclosure" (1993) 1 Med. L.Rev. 129; F. A. Trinidade, "Disclosure of Risks in Proposed Medical Treatment" (1993) 109 L.Q.R. 352. In "Malpractice—Medical Negligence in Australia" (1992) Aus.L.J. 67, D. Cassidy reviews the standing of the *Bolam* principle in Australia, and criticises *Rogers* as introducing an anomalous test for breach of a professional duty of care.

Friern Hospital Management Committee[16] and *Sidaway v Governors of Bethlem Royal Hospital.*[17] It is an important divergence from English law, but a case on the same facts might now be decided the same way in England on the basis that the view of a body of expert opinion that it was unnecessary for the patient to be told of this slight risk could not withstand logical analysis in the face of her specific and express desire to be told of just such a risk.

3. DAMAGES

13–105   **General.** An award of damages is the normal remedy sought for breach of duty by a medical practitioner whether the claim is brought in contract or tort. If the medical practitioner is privately retained by the patient and if, as a result of the breach of duty, his services are valueless, he would also be debarred from recovering his fees or ordered to repay any fees which he has received from the patient.

(a) *Scope of Duty*

13–106   It is well established law that a duty of care does not simply arise in the abstract, the same general principle applies to claims against clinicians.

> "It is always necessary to determine the scope of the duty by reference to the kind of damage from which A must take care to save B harmless."[18]

13–107   **Legal and factual causation.** In claims against clinicians, as with claims against all professionals, proof of legal causation is tantamount to proof of the scope of the duty of care, and the extent of protection that the law will afford. The interrelationship between the scope of duty and causation (which also involves consideration of remoteness and forseeability[19]) is sometimes described as "legal causation". In addressing this question a court will consider the scope of the duty as a rule affecting causation and the imposition of a liability.[20] The court's analysis will involve applying "rules" of causation (such as the "but for" test, material contribution, material increase of risk—these are sometimes described as "factual causation") as well as the limits on the scope of duty. For the purposes of this chapter these tests and rules will be addressed separately—in reality they will arise concurrently. As Lord Justice Laws stated in *Rahman v Arearose Ltd*[21]:

> "So in all these cases the real question is, what is the damage for which the defendant under consideration should be held responsible. The nature of his duty (here, the common law duty of care) is relevant; causation, certainly will be relevant—but it will

---

[16] [1957] 1 W.L.R. 582.
[17] [1985] A.C. 871.
[18] *Caparo Industries v Dickman* [1990] 2 A.C. 605 *per* Lord Bridge at 627.
[19] See also para.13–152.
[20] See Lord Hoffmann's extra-judicial discourse: "Causation" in (2005) 121 L.Q.R. 592.
[21] [2001] Q.B. 351 at 367–368, para.33, CA.

fall to be viewed, and in truth can only be understood, in light of the answer to the question: from what kind of harm was it the defendant's duty to guard the claimant? . . . . Novus actus interveniens, the eggshell skull, and (in the case of multiple torts) the concept of concurrent tortfeasors are all no more and no less than tools or mechanisms which the law has developed to articulate in practice the extent of any liable defendant's responsibility for the loss and damage which the claimant has suffered."

And as Lord Hoffmann stated in *Fairchild*[22]:   **13–108**

"In my opinion, the essential point is that the causal requirements are just as much part of the legal conditions for liability as the rules which prescribe the kind of conduct which attracts liability or the rules which limit the scope of that liability. If I may repeat what I have said on another occasion,[23] one is never simply liable, one is always liable for something—to make compensation for damage, the nature and extent of which is delimited by the law. The rules which delimit what one is liable for may consist of causal requirements or may be rules unrelated to causation, such as the forseeability requirements in the rule in *Hadley v Baxendale* (1854) 9 Exch 341. But in either case they are rules of law, part and parcel of the conditions of liability."

A claim against a clinician will not succeed unless the injury or loss caused falls within the scope of the duty owed. The claimant must show that the clinician was obliged to act or obliged to prevent the very type of injury or loss which is now complained or the claimant is entitled to compensation for the kind of loss claimed.[24]

For example, in *R. v Croydon HA*[25] the defendant health authority admitted negligent failure to warn the claimant to seek medical advice which would have revealed that she was suffering from a condition (PPH) that meant pregnancy would be life-threatening. Her diagnosis was not eventually made until the final stages of her pregnancy. She claimed damages for the cost of the care of the healthy child that was born, that she alleged would not have been conceived or born, and the pain and suffering of the pregnancy (including the complications caused by the PPH) and her reactive depression. The Court of Appeal held that, even were the claimant to be regarded as having suffered damage by the conception, birth and upbringing of a healthy and wanted child (which she was not applying *MacFarlane*), such damage was outside the scope of the defendant radiologist's duty. The claimant had only consulted the defendant's radiologist as part of her application for employment with the defendant (and the X-ray that disclosed the PPH was only taken for the purposes of the claimant's application for employment). The Court of Appeal held that her domestic life was outside the scope of duty owed by the defendant's radiologist.[26] Applying the principles of

---

[22] *Fairchild* at para.54.
[23] *Kuwait Airways Corp v Iraqi Airways Co (Nos 4 and 5)* [2002] UKHL 19 reported at [2002] 2 A.C. 1106, para.128.
[24] Applying the principle from *South Australia Asset Management Corp v York Montague Ltd*, ("SAAMCO") [1997] A.C. 191, HL.
[25] [1998] Lloyd's Rep. Med. 44.
[26] See also the unreported case of *O'Reilly v Whittington Hospital NHS Trust*, H.H.J. Mackay, sitting as a deputy judge of the QBD, March 17, 2000; and *Brown v Lewisham and North Southwark HA* [1999] Lloyd's Rep. Med. 110 at 118, referred to in para.13–007, above.

remoteness, her only recoverable loss was limited to the consequences of the late diagnosis of PPH, namely the complications in the pregnancy, her subsequent hysterectomy, the additional treatment of PPH that would otherwise have been avoided and exacerbation of her reactive depression.

13–109   **Economic loss.** For there to be liability for economic loss in addition to reasonable forseeability there must be sufficient proximity and it must be fair, just and reasonable to impose such a duty. These extra requirements make claims for such losses unlikely to succeed when the claims are pursued by employers[27] or against an employed doctor.[28] However, (applying *X v Bedfordshire County Council*[29] and *Phelps v Hillingdon Borough of London*[30]) a doctor can at least theoretically owe a duty of care in the absence of a patient-doctor relationship. Whether or not a duty actually exists depends on the facts of each case. In *West Bromich Albion Football Club Ltd v El-Safty*[31] the defendant surgeon negligently advised reconstructive surgery to treat the knee injury of a professional footballer signed to the claimant football club. The surgery was unnecessary and unsuccessful. The footballer retired from professional football. The club claimed for its resulting economic losses. Royce J. found there was no contractual relationship but held that a duty of care could exist in the absence of a patient—doctor relationship. The court applied the three-stage test from *Caparo v Dickman* as well as the headings applied by the Court of Appeal in the auditors' case of *James McNaughton v Hicks Anderson*.[32] On the facts of this case such a duty did not exist because there was insufficient proximity and it was not fair, just and equitable for there to be liability.

Where a medical practitioner is negligent in advising or reporting to or for his patient, the claimant may suffer economic loss as opposed to personal injuries. Although there are few reported cases of this kind,[33] the same principles would seem to apply as in the case of solicitors or accountants.[34]

---

[27] *West Bromwich Albion Football Club Ltd v El-Safty* [2005] EWHC 2866, reported at [2006] P.N.L.R. 18 and [2006] Lloyd's Rep. Med. 139. This decision was upheld on appeal to the Court of Appeal.

[28] *Kapfunde v Abbey National Plc* [1999] Lloyd's Rep. Med. 48, CA. See also para.13–011, fn.58 above for a summary of the facts of this case and other cases on economic loss.

[29] [1995] A.C. 633.

[30] [2000] 3 W.L.R. 776.

[31] *ibid.*

[32] [1991] 2 Q.B. 113. For these headings and discussion see paras 17–062; 17–048: Accountants and Auditors.

[33] In *Pimm v Roper* (1862) 2 F. & F. 783 the claimant failed on liability. In *Stevens v Bermondsey & Southwark Group Hospital Management Committee* (1963) 107 S.J. 478 the claimant failed on causation: see para.13–142, below. For an example of a case where the doctors were held to be liable for the losses caused by their negligent misrepresentations in a medico-legal report, see *Kelly v Lundegard* (1996) 40 Alta. L.R. (3d) 234. The doctors knew the intended purpose for the report and knew the claimant had sustained injuries that might result in infertility. Despite this they failed to raise this in their report, and thereby prevented the claimant from making a claim in respect of this additional effect of the injury.

[34] See, e.g. *McGrath v Kiely & Powell* [1965] I.R. 497: medical report prepared for litigation omitted material fact. Claimant recovered the difference between the damages actually awarded and the damages which should have been awarded in the original action.

Relevant breach. Another limit on the potential liability of a defendant **13–110** clinician is that the only relevant breach of duty is the one that would make the defendant clinician liable for the state of affairs in question.[35]

(b) *Remoteness*

Recovery of damages is subject, in every case, to the overriding principle that the **13–111** injury in respect of which compensation is sought must be sufficiently proximate to the medical practitioner's breach of duty, i.e. it must not be too remote. Broadly speaking, this means that:

(a) the breach of duty must have "caused" the injury[36] and

(b) the injury in question must have been foreseeable.[37]

(i) *Causation*

Normal rules of causation. Whether the claim is brought in contract or tort, **13–112** it is first necessary to determine whether the medical practitioner's breach of duty caused the injury complained of. The burden of proof of causation is as a matter of principle always on the claimant. Causation can be a simple matter of fact or a combined matter of fact and law. This leads to the need to consider different "tests" or rules for causation of the injury complained of, namely "but for" causation (also referred to as "orthodox" or "threshold" causation), material contribution, material increase in risk. The latter two tests might equally be considered to be modifications of the "but for" test, which are applied when certain circumstances arise. Those cases which might be described as exceptions to the usual need to prove causation (such as the House of Lords' decisions in *Fairchild v Glenhaven Funeral Services*[38] and *Chester v Afshar*[39]) are simply instances where a new rule on causation was applied or the orthodox rules were modified. These cases are not an indication of a general relaxation in the requirement on a claimant to prove causation. They are, and were always intended to be, of limited and exceptional application.[40] Subsequent decisions have confirmed that this is correct.[41] There may be many situations where it is

---

[35] *Thompson v Bradford* [2005] EWCA Civ 1439 reported at [2006] Lloyd's Rep. Med. 95.

[36] As to which, see paras 13–112 to 13–148, below.

[37] As to which see paras 13–149 to 13–154, below.

[38] [2002] UKHL 22 reported at [2003] 1 A.C. 32. See paras 13–119 to 13–124, below.

[39] [2004] UKHL 41 reported at [2005] 1 A.C. 134, HL. See paras 13–137 to 13–138, below.

[40] See *Fairchild:* Lord Bingham at para.9 and 34; Lord Nicholls at paras 37/38 and 43; Lord Hoffmann at para.47, 60 to 63, 67, 73, but compare with para.74; Lord Hutton at para.108 and 118; Lord Rodger at para.118/119 and 169/170.

[41] See *Barker v Corus (UK) Ltd,* [2006] UKHL 20 reported at [2006] 2 W.L.R. 1027; *Clough v First Choice Holidays & Flights Ltd* [2006] EWCA Civ 15 reported at [2006] P.I.Q.R. P22; *Thompson v Bradford* [2004] EWCA Civ 1439 reported at [2006] Lloyd's Rep. Med. 95; *Gregg v Scott* [2005] UKHL 2 reported at [2005] 2 A.C. 176, HL: the narrow limits of the application of *Fairchild*, the fact that it was an exception to the general principle that a claimant must prove the determinate cause, and the fact that the decision in *Fairchild* was a special rule imposing liability for conduct that only increased the chances of the claimant contracting the disease were again stated by their Lordships. NB: The claimant's alternative argument based on *Fairchild* was rejected, apparently—*per* Baroness Hale—without argument before the Committee. Lord Phillips described the decision as having: "*made a change in the law of negligence in the interests of justice.*", but cautioned in dramatic terms against making any such exception in Mr Gregg's case (at para.172):"My Lords it seems to me that

difficult to say which of a succession of factors in the negligent management of a patient might have caused an injury or condition, it would not be a common occurrence for those factors to constitute a single "agent" (or agents operating in the same way[42]) yet be the responsibility of different (or materially different) defendants.[43]

13–113   **"But for" or orthodox causation.** The "but for" test is often determinative of causation in clinical negligence cases but it does not invariably yield the right answer. For example, Lord Hoffmann's mountaineer's knee example in *SAAMCO*[44]:

> "A mountaineer about to undertake a difficult climb is concerned about the fitness of his knee. He goes to a doctor who negligently makes a superficial examination and pronounces the knee fit. The climber goes on the expedition, which he would not have undertaken if the doctor had told him the true state of his knee. He suffers an injury which is an entirely foreseeable consequence of mountaineering but has nothing to do with his knee."

One could claim that had the clinician not advised as he did, i.e. "but for" that advice (which advice may or may not have been negligent), the mountaineer would not have undertaken the very expedition on which he was injured. Lord Hoffmann's example shows how misleading this test can be as well as demonstrating the impact of the scope of duty owed.

13–114   **Would the damage have occurred in any event.** Another way of applying the "but for" test is to ask the question: would the damage have occurred in any event? If the damage would have occurred in any event,[45] it was not caused by

---

there is a danger, if special tests of causation are developed piecemeal to deal with perceived injustices in particular factual situations, that the coherence of our common law will be destroyed." See Professor Jane Stapleton's article on asbestos litigation in the USA, (2006) 122 L.Q.R. 189. Further cases outside the context of asbestos-related disease considering the impact of *Fairchild* are: *Phillips v Syndicate 992 Gunner* [2003] EWHC 1084 reported at [2004] Lloyd's Rep. I.R. 426; *Rupert St Loftus-Brigham v London Borough of Ealing* [2003] EWCA Civ 1490, reported at [2004] 20 Const. L.J. 82.

[42] See para.13–120, below.

[43] In his paper to the Professional Negligence Bar Association in September 2002, Adrian Whitfield Q.C. posed two possible examples: where a succession of healthcare professionals have negligently manhandled an accident victim with an unstable spine with the result that he is paralysed, but it is not possible to show which of them did the damage; and where a drug has been negligently over-prescribed by a series of doctors, but it cannot be shown which prescription made the critical difference. In a paper published in the Professional Negligence Law Review in August 2003, Issue 2, Martin Spencer Q.C. proposed similar factual examples involving transfers of patients from a private to an NHS hospital, or referral from a negligent GP to a negligent hospital. These might be examples where the principle in *Fairchild* would allow a claim to be brought against one or more of the negligent professionals where causation might not have been established before. See also Professor Jane Stapleton's article; "Occam's Razor Reveals an Orthodox Basis for Chester v Afshar" (2006) 122 L.Q.R. 426.

[44] *ibid.* at 213.

[45] See, e.g. *Kay v Ayrshire and Arran Health Board* [1987] 2 All E.R. 417, HL: the appellant being treated for meningitis at respondent's hospital was given a greatly excessive dose of penicillin and subsequently went deaf. The deafness was caused by the meningitis, not the excessive penicillin. See also *Marsden v Bateman* [1993] 4 Med. L.R. 181: brain damage in infant caused not by failure to diagnose and treat hypoglycaemia but by defective development at the foetal stage; *De Martell v Merton and Sutton HA (Liability) (No.2)* [1995] 6 Med. L.R. 234: cerebral palsy caused by abnormal

the medical practitioner's breach of duty—the claim fails on the "but for" test for causation.[46] In *Barnett v Chelsea & Kensington Hospital Management Committee*,[47] for example, it was held that a hospital casualty officer was negligent in failing to see and examine a patient who was complaining of vomiting. However, even if the patient had been examined by the casualty officer it appeared on the balance of probabilities that he would still have died (of arsenic poisoning). Therefore the defendants' negligence did not cause the patient's death and the claim was dismissed.[48]

Material contribution. The claimant does not have to show that the defendant's conduct is the *sole* or even the principal cause of his disease or injury— there can be other causes (e.g. self-caused or contributory negligence, other tortfeasors, other innocent parties, intervening causes). What the claimant must show is that the defendant's breach of duty was a "material" or "effective" cause of the disease or injury. Thus, there may be concurrent tortious and non-tortious causes, or intervening causes or intervening tortfeasors. The question is then whether the injury complained of was materially contributed to by the alleged cause.

13–115

This determination of material cause or contribution effectively means applying the balance of probabilities civil standard of proof to the evidence available. Thus where medical science cannot adequately inform as to the actual factual cause or where the actual trigger for the disease is elusive, (and there is an evidentiary gap) the courts will apply a test of material effect, be that material contribution or material increase in risk (of contracting the disease or injury). The courts' approach to these cases is as much one of policy as of application of any

---

foetal development and not by midwife's negligent delay in summoning a doctor to a difficult delivery; *Richardson v Kitching* [1995] 6 Med. L.R. 257: negligent failure to diagnose an ear tumour not causative because the prospects of success of an earlier operation would not have been significantly different; *Robertson v Nottingham HA* [1997] 8 Med. L.R. 1: claimant's brain damage was caused some time before mother's admission to hospital and culpable delay to delivery by Caesarean section did not contribute materially; *Oksuzoglu v Kay & Another* [1998] 2 All E.R. 361: amputation of leg for treatment of malignant tumour was not caused by doctor's negligent failure to refer to hospital, amputation was inevitable; Canadian cases: *Egedebo v Windermere District Hospital* (1993) 78 B.C.L.R. (2d) 63: paralysis already irreversible before its cause was negligently misdiagnosed and treated; *MacWilliam v Jeffrey* (1993) 127 N.B.R. (2d) 113: condition of claimant's mouth was unrelated to dental work performed by the defendant dentist; *Moore v Castlegar & District Hospital* (1996) 25 B.C.L.R. 188: RTA caused spinal injury, not care and management at defendant hospital; *Tailleur v Grande Prairie General and Auxiliary Hospital* (1999) 74 Atla. L. R. 20, CA: gangrene infection led to amputation of leg following severed Achilles tendon injury; no evidence that use of a different cast type would have resulted in earlier detection of gangrene, and insufficient evidence that hospitalisation without cast would have led to different result.
[46] See further, Hart and Honore, *Causation in the Law*, (2nd edn, Oxford at the Clarendon Press, 1985), pp.247–248.
[47] [1969] 1 Q.B. 42. See para.13–007, fn.34 above.
[48] See also *Fish v Kapur* [1948] 2 All E.R. 176: no loss due to failure to diagnose a broken jaw since there was no treatment that could have been given; *Robinson v Post Office* [1974] 1 W.L.R. 1176: a negligent failure to wait the required one-half hour following a test dose of a vaccine before administering the full dose did not cause the damage since the claimant's reaction would not have been apparent in that time anyway; *Peter Wardlaw v. Stephen Farrar* [2003] EWCA Civ 1719, reported at [2003] 4 All E.R. 1358, CA: death from pulmonary embolism was caused by failure of anti-coagulant therapy to prevent its formation, and not the seven days of delay to the claimant's hospital admission, which delay had been caused by the defendant's breach of duty.

causation rules: if the claimant's case will fail because the causative evidential link can never be proved, (an entirely different situation to one where the causative link is capable of being proved but has not been proved in that instant case) the courts will allow something less than clear proof of cause to suffice.

In *Bonnington Castings v Wardlaw*,[49] the claimant alleged breach of statutory duty against his employers. He had contracted pneumoconiosis from inhaling air containing silica dust. The dust came from two sources, only one of which was caused by a breach of that statutory duty (the swing grinders), and the evidence suggested the majority of the dust came from the other "innocent" source (the pneumatic hammers). The House of Lords concluded that the claimant had succeeded in showing causation so long as he was able to show (by the ordinary standard of proof in civil actions) that the "guilty" dust had materially contributed to the development of his disease/injury. It should be noted also that the disease was caused by the gradual accumulation of the dust in the lungs—there was no instant effect or threshold level. Lord Reid gave the main speech:

> "The medical evidence was that pneumoconiosis is caused by a gradual accumulation in the lungs of minute particles of silica inhaled over a period of years. That means, I think, that the disease is caused by the whole of the noxious material inhaled and, if that material comes from two sources, it cannot be wholly attributed to material from one source or the other. I am in agreement with much of the Lord President's opinion in this case, but I cannot agree that the question is: which was the most probable source of the respondent's disease, the dust from the pneumatic hammers or the dust from the swing grinders? It appears to me that the source of his disease was the dust from both sources, and the real question is whether the dust from the swing grinders materially contributed to the disease. A contribution which comes within the exception de minimis non curat lex is not material, but I think that any contribution which does not fall within that exception must be material. I do not see how there can be something too large to come within the de minimis principle but yet too small to be material."[50]

13–116   **Material increase in risk of developing disease.** In *McGhee v National Coal Board*,[51] the pursuer was employed to empty pipe kilns at a brickworks. One day he was sent to empty brick kilns where much hotter and dustier conditions prevailed causing irritation of his skin. Shortly afterwards he developed dermatitis—caused by repeated minute abrasion to the outer horny layer of skin followed by injury to the underlying cells by some unknown mechanism. The only actionable breach of duty against his employers was a failure to provide washing facilities/showers. This was admitted. It was also admitted that the dermatitis was attributable to the work in the brick kilns. Nevertheless the employers defended on causation: it could not be proved that the admitted breach of duty had caused the onset of the disease. The medical evidence (once again) fell short—it did not prove that provision of showers would have prevented the disease. However, the effect of the abrasion was cumulative—the longer the time that lapsed between the exposure and washing the worse the abrasion. The evidence did prove that washing would have materially reduced the risk of

---

[49] [1956] A.C. 613.
[50] *ibid.* at 621.
[51] [1973] 1 W.L.R. 1.

developing dermatitis. The pursuer's case would have failed because he could not prove something that was at that time scientifically impossible:

" . . . I think that in cases like this we must take a broader view of causation. The medical evidence is to the effect that the fact that the man had to cycle home caked with grime and sweat added materially to the risk that this disease might develop. It does not and could not explain why that is so. But experience shows that it is so. Plainly that must be because what happens while the man remains unwashed can have a causative effect, though just how that cause operates is uncertain."

Lord Reid, Lord Simon and Lord Salmon made no distinction between "materially increasing the risk" that a disease will occur and "making a material contribution" to its occurrence or dismissed it as "far too unreal to be recognised by the common law".[52] Lord Wilberforce and Lord Kilbrandon did distinguish between these two situations. The decision in the pursuer's favour was based on firm policy grounds—the evidential gap (the absence of proof that the presence of showers would have prevented the onset of dermatitis) should not deprive the pursuer of a remedy against an employer who should have but did not take precautions:

" . . . in the absence of proof that the culpable addition had, in the result, no effect, the employers should be liable for an injury, squarely within the risk which they had created and that they, not the pursuer, should suffer the consequence of the impossibility, forseeably inherent in the nature of his injury, of segregating the precise consequence of their default."[53]

Hotson v East Berkshire AHA[54] is an example of the House of Lords' applying **13–117** the normal causation requirement of a "material contribution" and concluding that it was missing. The claimant, a 13-year-old boy, fell from a tree and suffered a fracture of the left femoral epiphysis. He was taken to hospital on the same day but because of the defendants' negligence his injury was not diagnosed or treated for five days. The claimant developed avascular necrosis of the epiphysis. He alleged that the defendant's negligence had caused his disability. At first instance Simon Brown J.[55] treated the case as a "lost chance" claim and held that there was a 75 per cent chance that so many blood vessels had been ruptured by the fall that avascular necrosis was bound to result. He awarded £11,500 (being 25 per cent of the full damages for the injury) for loss of a 25 per cent chance of recovery. This decision was upheld by the Court of Appeal, but reversed by the House of Lords.[56] The House of Lords analysed the case in this manner: it follows from the judge's findings of fact that, on the balance of probabilities, the epiphysis was doomed before the defendants came under a duty to treat the claimant. There was a high probability (75 per cent) that, even with correct diagnosis and treatment, the claimant's disability would have occurred. Therefore the claimant had failed to establish causation (an element of liability) on the balance of probabilities and his claim must fail.

---

[52] [1973] 1 W.L.R. 1. Lord Reid at 5A; Lord Simon at 8C–F and Lord Salmon at 11G–12A and 12G–H.
[53] *ibid.* Lord Wilberforce at 7E–F.
[54] [1987] A.C. 750.
[55] *sub nom. Hotson v Fitzgerald* [1985] 1 W.L.R. 1036.
[56] [1987] A.C. 1250.

13–118   In *Wilsher v Essex HA*[57] the infant claimant had received excess oxygen following his premature birth. This was due to the defendant's negligent failure to monitor the oxygen levels. The claimant developed retrolental fibroplasias (RLF) rendering him almost blind. The RLF could have been caused by the excess oxygen, but equally there were a number of other factors present that could have caused the RLF. Nevertheless the Court of Appeal (by a majority, with Sir Nicholas Browne-Wilkinson, V.C. dissenting) gave judgment for the claimant, specifically by adopting the (then) presumed principle from *McGhee*: that if it is established that certain conduct by one party creates a risk of injury or increases an existing risk to another party to whom a duty is owed not to expose them to that harm, then the first party is taken to have caused the injury by his breach of duty. The House of Lords overturned the decision, and expressly approved the following passage from the Vice Chancellor's dissenting judgment.[58] In *Wilsher* there was more than one possible cause,[59] and the claimant could not show the excess oxygen had caused or materially contributed to his developing RLF:

> "To apply the principle in *McGhee v National Coal Board* [1973] 1 W.L.R. 1 to the present case would constitute an extension of that principle. In the *McGhee* case there was no doubt that the pursuer's dermatitis was physically caused by brick dust: the only question was whether the continued presence of such brick dust on the pursuer's skin after the time when he should have been provided with a shower caused or materially contributed to the dermatitis which he contracted. There was only one possible agent which could have caused the dermatitis, viz., brick dust, and there as no doubt that the dermatitis from which he suffered was caused by that brick dust. In the present case the question is different. There are a number of different agents which could have caused the RLF. Excess oxygen was one of them. The defendants failed to take reasonable precautions to prevent one of the possible causative agents . . . from causing RLF. But no one can tell in this case whether excess oxygen did or did not cause or contribute to the RLF suffered by the plaintiff."

13–119   **The *Fairchild* principle.** In *Fairchild v Glenhaven Funeral Services Ltd*[60] the claimants had developed mesothelioma following exposure to asbestos during the course of their employment. Before the Court of Appeal breach of duty was not in issue and it was accepted that the mechanism that triggered the condition of mesothelioma in any sufferer was unknown, but that it might be triggered by contact with a single asbestos fibre on a single occasion, and that once the condition had been caused, it would not be aggravated by further exposure to asbestos. Continued exposure to asbestos would not increase the severity of the condition, but it increased the likelihood of the condition being triggered. Since each claimant had been exposed by more than one employer, and while working in more than one environment, and the trigger might have been one single or very few fibres of asbestos, none of the claimants could prove their case on the

---

[57] [1988] A.C. 1074, HL.
[58] Lord Hoffmann did not accept this reasoning in *Fairchild*. See his judgment in *Barker v Corus (UK) Ltd*, *ibid.* at paras 18 to 24 under heading: *"Distinguishing Wilsher v Essex AHA [1988] A.C. 1074."*
[59] See para.13–120 below for discussion of the ratio of this decision.
[60] *ibid.*

balance of probabilities against any one employer applying the "but for" or orthodox principle of causation. The claimants thus failed on causation before the Court of Appeal. However the House of Lords reversed the Court of Appeal's decision and allowed the six claimants to recover their losses from their former employers. Their Lordships did so by reviewing the applicability of the orthodox test for causation and by choosing instead to apply a modified approach to proof of causation (namely that the breach of duty contributed substantially to the risk that the claimant would contract the disease) which was justified in certain specified circumstances or "conditions". According to Lord Bingham those conditions were:

(a) Where the claimant was employed at different times by different employers; and

(b) Where those employers were all subject to a duty to take reasonable care or all practicable measures to prevent the claimant inhaling asbestos dust due to the known risk that such inhalation might cause mesothelioma; and

(c) Those employers were in breach of that duty in relation to the claimant's employment; and

(d) The claimant suffered from mesothelioma; and

(e) Any cause of the claimant's mesothelioma apart from inhalation of asbestos dust at work could effectively be discounted; and

(f) The claimant cannot (due to the current limits on human science) prove on the balance of probabilities that his mesothelioma was the result of his inhaling asbestos dust during his employment.

When will proof of a material contribution/material increase in risk   **13–120**
suffice? It is not easy to reconcile the decisions and judgments in *McGhee*,[61] *Wilsher, Hotson, Wardlaw* and *Fairchild*. In *McGhee* the claimant won because it was apparently accepted that there was no substantial difference between materially increasing the risk of injury and making a material contribution to that injury. Lord Hoffmann in his opinion in *Barker v Corus (UK) Ltd*[62] preferred to restate their Lordships' opinions on this point in *McGhee*: " . . . when some members of the House . . . said that in the circumstances there was no distinction between materially increasing the risk of disease and materially contributing to the disease, what I think they meant was that, in the particular circumstances, a

---

[61] The House of Lords' decision is discussed by A. Grubb, in "Causation and Medical Negligence" [1988] C.L.J. 350. Grubb concludes that *McGhee* is consigned to the category of cases decided upon its own unique facts. A contrary view is expressed in A. Boon, "Causation and the Increase of Risk" (1988) 51 M.L.R. 508. See *Hossack v Ministry of Defence*, unreported, April 18, 2000, CA, [2000] WL 544153 CA: claimant's hypothesis for cause of his injury was only one of a number of possibilities, and the causative requirement had not been satisfied.
[62] [2006] 2 W.L.R. 1027, HL.

breach of duty which materially increased the risk should be treated *as if* it had materially contributed to the disease." (no emphasis added). It may be that *McGhee* is best recognised openly (as it was by Lord Nicholls in *Fairchild*[63]) as an instance where the court simply applied a different and less stringent test for causation.[64]

The rationale for the decision in *Wilsher* is particularly unclear. Following Lord Bingham's speech in *Fairchild* and Lord Hoffmann's speeches in both *Fairchild* and *Barker v Corus (UK)*, it is not clear if the claimant's failure was because the case involved different "noxious agents" or the fact that the different causes operated (or may have operated) in different ways:

Per Lord Bingham: "It is one thing to treat an increase of risk as equivalent to the making of a material contribution where a single noxious agent is involved, but quite another where any one of a number of noxious agents may equally probably have caused the damage."[65]

Per Lord Hoffmann: "If the distinction between Fairchild and Wilsher does not lie in the fact that in the latter case a number of very different causative

---

[63] [2006] 2 W.L.R. 1027, HL at 71B, para.45.
[64] In *Snell v Farrell* (1990) 4 C.C.L.T. 229 the Canadian Supreme Court approved and followed the House of Lords' approach to causation in *Wilsher*. The Ontario High Court came to a similar conclusion in *Gallant v Fialkov* (1989) 69 O.R. (2d) 297. However Sopinka J. observed that "[i]n many malpractice cases, the facts lie particularly within the knowledge of the defendant. In these circumstances, very little affirmative evidence on the part of the claimant will justify the drawing of an inference of causation in the absence of evidence to the contrary", *ibid.* at 300. See *Joyal v Starreveld* (1996) 37 Alta. L.R. 19 for an example of this approach to causation. The treating clinician failed to warn the claimant not to drive whilst under a reducing regime of anti-epileptic drug therapy. The court held that causation had been proved in the absence of any positive or scientific proof of causation adduced by the claimant and awarded damages because the court held that a seizure was the more likely cause of the claimant's car accident than the alternative causes suggested by the defendant and that if the claimant had received the appropriate warning then he would not have driven, or would not have agreed to the proposed reduction. Compare with *Meloche v Hotel Dieu Grace Hospital* (1999) 179 D.L.R. (4th) 77, Ontario, CA. The issue in that case was whether negligent delay in diagnosing the claimant's eye infection had caused his subsequent loss of sight. The court of first instance held, following *Snell v Farrell*, that in the absence of evidence to the contrary adduced by a defendant, an inference of causation may be drawn even though positive or scientific proof is lacking. However, the medical experts for both parties agreed that it would be speculative to associate delay in diagnosis with the claimant's blindness. The Ontario Court of Appeal held that in finding that there was a causal relationship, the judge at first instance had taken the "robust and pragmatic" approach from *Snell v Farrell* too far. He was not filling a lacuna in the evidence with common sense pragmatism, he was replacing two medical opinions with one of his own and was not entitled to do so. See *Pearce v United Bristol Healthcare NHS Trust* [1999] P.I.Q.R. P53, Lord Woolf, for an example of a rare and theoretical instance where the judge might replace medical opinion with his own (as to whether or not non-disclosure of a particular risk was a breach of the duty to adequately advise). By contrast in *Webster v Chapman* (1998) 155 D.L.R. 82, the Manitoba Court of Appeal applied the *McGhee* approach and saw no relevant distinction, on the facts of the case, between the statements that continued prescription of a drug materially increased the risk of damage to the claimant and that continued prescription had materially contributed to the damage which occurred. Since there was evidence to support the first statement, the claimant succeeded on causation. See *Meyers (Next friend of) v Stanley* (2005) 251 D.L.R. (4th) 345, Alberta Court of Appeal: The claimant was born with cerebral palsy probably due to maternal intrauterine infection. The risk created by failing to instruct the claimant's mother to monitor her temperature following discharge home after her premature rupture of membranes was that such an infection might go undetected. The creation of a risk of injury was a loss of a chance and this was not enough to create a liability.
[65] *Fairchild* at 57D–E.

agents were in play, I think it would be hard to tell from my *Fairchild* opinion what I thought the distinction was. In my opinion it is an essential condition for the operation of the exception that the impossibility of proving that the defendant caused the damage arises out of the existence of another potential causative agent which operated in the same way."[66]

In *Barker v Corus (UK) Ltd* it was proposed by Lord Hoffmann[67] that the **13–121** creation of the risk was the damage caused.[68] However in *Fairchild* their Lordships (including Lord Hoffmann) had not taken this step. The rationale adopted in *Fairchild* was either to make no distinction between materially increasing the risk and materially contributing to the disease, or to hold that a material increase in risk was sufficient to satisfy the causation requirements for liability, and Lord Hoffmann identified five factors[69] that ought to lead to be satisfied before such causation requirements were relaxed:

(1) The duty was specifically intended to protect the claimant from being unnecessarily exposed to the risk of a particular disease.

(2) The duty was intended to create a civil right to compensation for injury "relevantly connected" to the breach.

(3) It can be established that the risk of contracting the disease was increased by greater "exposure" to the agent (or breach of duty).

(4) Medical science cannot attribute the injury to any one exposure or breach of duty.

(5) The claimant has contracted the disease (i.e. he has suffered the very harm against which he would have been protected).

Thus, the five factors were present in *McGhee*, but absent in *Wilsher*. Indeed *McGhee* was described as an approved application of the Fairchild exception by Lord Hoffmann.[70]

In practice the "but for" test for causation is likely to be "modified" or **13–122** replaced with a material contribution test where:

(1) There is more than one defendant, each of whom has breached a duty of care to the claimant and exposed the claimant to the very harm against which he should have been rendered harmless, but where it is impossible to prove on the balance of probabilities that any one defendant's conduct is the one that is responsible for the harm actually suffered and where the mechanisms by which the harm was suffered in each case are identical: *Fairchild* and *Wilsher*.

---

[66] *Barker v Corus (UK) Ltd, ibid.* at para.24.
[67] Lord Scott agreed with his conclusions and reasons.
[68] At 1039H–1040A.
[69] *ibid.* at para.61.
[70] See Lord Hoffmann's speech in *Barker v Corus (UK) Ltd, ibid.* at 1034C.

(2) There is only one defendant, who is responsible for both culpable and non-culpable potential causes of the injury suffered, where it is impossible to prove on the balance of probabilities which of these causes was responsible for the actual injury/disease: *Wardlaw.*

(3) There is only one defendant, and where it is impossible to show on the balance of probabilities that the defendant's breach of duty caused the injury/disease, but the evidence shows that the breach of duty did significantly increase the risk of that injury/disease being suffered: *McGhee.*

13–123   **Extension of the *Fairchild* principle.** This relaxation of the requirement to show a material contribution to the injury only applies to cases that fall within the Fairchild exception, i.e. cases where the necessary "conditions" or five factors are present. Lord Bingham acknowledged that it was likely that the Fairchild principle would be the subject of incremental and analogical development, but he stated expressly that cases developing the principle had to be decided as they arose, and that he did not intend to decide more than was necessary for the disposals of the appeals in the case. *Chester v Afshar*[71] is an instance where this statement by Lord Bingham was relied on by Lord Steyn as justifying a departure from the normal rules of causation. However the case of *Chester v Afshar* should be regarded with caution since Lord Bingham and Lord Hoffmann, both of whom gave the judgment in *Fairchild*, dissented from the majority view in *Chester v Afshar.*[72]

13–124   **Limits on the application of the *Fairchild* principle.** In *Gregg v Scott*[73] and *Barker v Corus (UK) Ltd*[74] the House of Lords re-inforced the intended narrow nature of the exception made to the causation requirements by *Fairchild.*[75] In particular Lord Hoffmann made clear that where the precise cause of an injury could not be determined, the case did not sidestep causation by being expressed as a loss of a chance. The Fairchild principle is about a proven increased risk of injury or damage where there are potential other causative agents which operate to cause damage in the *same way* (that is by the same mechanism). Thus the purpose of the Fairchild exception is to assist[76] in cases where:

> "a defendant has materially increased the risk that the claimant will suffer damage and may have caused that damage but cannot be proved to have done so because it is

---

[71] *Barker v Corus (UK) Ltd* at para.24 at 1034C.
[72] See discussion of *Chester v Afshar* below at paras 13–137 to 13–138.
[73] [2005] UKHL 2 reported at [2005] 2 A.C. 176, HL.
[74] *ibid.*
[75] See para.13–112, above: Normal rules of causation. See *per* Lord Scott in *Barker v Corus (UK) Ltd* [2006] 2 W.L.R. 1027 at para.57.
[76] *per* Lord Scott in *Barker v Corus (UK) Ltd*: "Fairchild is explained as a pragmatic judicial response to what would otherwise have been an unjust and unsatisfactory denial of a remedy to a mesothelioma sufferer whose disease had been caused by one or other of a number of wrongdoers (in the sense of persons shown to have been in breach of duty) each of whose breach of duty may have caused the disease, and could not be shown not to have done so, but could not be shown to have done so."

impossible to show, on a balance of probability, that some other exposure to the same risk may have caused it instead".[77]

The decision in *McGhee v National Coal Board*[78] is an example of the *Fairchild* exception in operation—the defendant had failed to provide showers, thereby materially increasing the risk of dermatitis developing due to the abrasive effect of the brick dust on the skin. By contrast the case of *Wilsher v Essex AHA*[79] is not an example of the *Fairchild* exception because it involves not simply different causative agents, but agents which did not cause damage in the same way. However, in *Barker v Corus (UK) Ltd* Lord Hoffmann went further, the effect of *Fairchild*, is, he said, to treat the: "*creation of the risk as the damage caused by the Defendant*",[80] by measuring that defendant's liability according to his contribution to the risk, and apportioning the claimant's damages accordingly. Lord Hoffmann[81] reasoned that where causation was proved by ordinary tests, (such as "but for") there was no reason to reduce the defendant's liability simply because another party caused the same harm:

> "But when liability is exceptionally imposed because you may have caused harm, the same considerations do not apply and fairness suggests that if more than one person may have been responsible, liability should be divided according to the probability that one or other caused the harm."[82]

The introduction of "proportionate" damages is rationally defensible for *Fairchild* exception cases. The claimant is already benefiting from the protection of this new rule which by relaxing the normal rules of causation equates creation of a material risk of damage with actually causing damage, and thereby imposes liability. To add to this advantage the benefit of the separate rule that deems liability for an indivisible injury to be joint and several[83] is to tip the playing field too far and unfairly in the claimant's favour.[84] Because each defendant is already liable to the claimant according to his own contribution to the risk, there is no scope for contribution between defendants. Their Lordships left it to lower courts

---

[77] *Barker v Corus (UK) Ltd* at para.17.
[78] *ibid.*
[79] *ibid.*
[80] Lord Scott agreed with Lord Hoffmann's opinion. However this is a minority view since Lord Rodger (who had also given an opinion in *Fairchild*) disputed that this was the effect or the basis for the opinions given by their Lordships in that case, see paras 70/71, 80 to 84; Baroness Hale agreed with Lord Rodger and Lord Walker preferred to state that *Fairchild* was an explicit variation of the ordinary requirement for causation.
[81] Lord Scott and Lord Walker agreed with Lord Hoffmann on the question of apportionment. Lord Rodger dissented para.90/91: "The desirability of the courts, rather than Parliament, throwing this lifeline to wrongdoers and their insurers at the expense of claimants is not obvious to me . . . . In the meantime, however, I would adhere to the usual rule of liability in solidum which applies generally to defendants who are held to have made a material contribution to indivisible injuries such as mesothelioma."
[82] *ibid.* para.43.
[83] See para.13–125: Attributability of divisible injury.
[84] See *per* Lord Hoffmann *ibid.* at paras 27–43; Lord Scott at para.61, Lord Walker at para.109; Baroness Hale at para.127.

in the future to determine how relative contributions to the risk would be assessed.[85]

13–125   **Attributability of divisible injury.** Where the injury is indivisible liability will be joint and several between the potential defendants.[86] The mere fact that injuries may be concurrent will not mean that the injury may not be broken down into different parts, which can then be attributed to different causes or apportioned between tortfeasors. In such cases liability will not be joint and several and the claimant must pursue all the defendants who caused the total of his injuries. In *Rahman v Arearose Ltd*[87] the claimant was violently assaulted at work by two black youths, for which assault his employers, the first defendants, were found liable. He was admitted to the second defendant's hospital and underwent eye surgery. Through the second defendant's (admitted) negligence he lost the sight of this eye. The claimant developed post traumatic stress disorder, a severe depressive disorder of psychotic intensity, a specific phobia of Afro-Caribbean people and a personality change. The expert evidence enabled the Court to attribute the PTSD, the depressive disorder (and the personality change) largely to the loss of the eye and the specific phobia to the assault. Since each defendant's acts had caused distinct parts of the claimant's overall psychiatric condition, neither had caused all of it.[88] Whilst the second defendant had caused the claimant's blindness, the claimant's overall suffering had been caused by both defendants, and both should bear the damages claim, 75 per cent by the second defendant, 25 per cent by the first defendant, with some adjustments for specifically attributable heads of damage.

---

[85] See however the effect of the Compensation Act 2006 at para.13–170 Proportionate damages *in Fairchild exception cases.* The case of *Holtby v Brigham & Cowan (Hull) Ltd* [2000] 3 All E.R. 421 is an example of a proportionate approach to damages which pre-dated this decision. The case concerned a claimant who suffered asbestosis caused by tortious exposure to asbestos dust in the course of his working life. About half of his working life was spent with the defendants, and the balance with a number of other employers. On the basis that the exposure to the asbestos which was the responsibility of the defendants made a material contribution, but only a material contribution to the claimant's condition, he was awarded damages which reflected a 25% deduction to take account of the contribution to his condition that was made by the other employers who were not before the court. The Court of Appeal held that the court had to consider all of the evidence and apply common sense in deciding whether the claimant had proved that the defendant was responsible for the whole or a quantifiable part of his condition, and there was ample evidence to support the decision that the correct award was arrived at by making a 25% reduction to reflect the contribution to the claimant's condition that was the responsibility of the other employers who were not before the court.

[86] See *per* Devlin L.J. in *Dingle v Associated Newspapers Ltd* [1961] 2 Q.B. 162, 188–189:

"Where injury has been done to the claimant and the injury is indivisible, any tortfeasor whose act has been a proximate cause of the injury must compensate for the whole of it. As between the claimant and the defendant it is immaterial that there are others whose acts also have been a cause of injury and it does not matter whether those others have or have not a good defence. These factors would be relevant in a claim between tortfeasors for contribution, but the claimant is not concerned with that; he can obtain judgment for total compensation from anyone whose act has been a cause of his injury. If there are more than one of such persons, it is immaterial to the claimant whether they are joint tortfeasors or not . . . . It is essential for this purpose that the loss should be one and indivisible; whether it is so or not is a matter of fact and not a matter of law."

For a summary of the law on contribution see Ch.4: Contribution between Defendants.

[87] [2001] Q.B. 351.

[88] The defendant hospital's contention that both defendants had caused the "same damage" within the meaning of the Civil Liability (Contribution) Act 1978 was rejected.

(ii) *Loss of a Chance*

The position after *Gregg v Scott*.[89, 90] A claimant may claim that the   **13–126**
defendant's negligent failure to give him proper treatment has deprived him of an
improvement in his medical condition or has allowed him to deteriorate further.
In the majority of clinical negligence cases, the damage has occurred by the time
of trial—the case is not therefore really a "risk of damage" or "lost chance" case
since the chance in question has eventuated. The question then is whether the
doctor's conduct did or did not affect the claimant's present condition or prospects. However these cases include negligent failures to diagnose and treat
leading to a lost chance of gaining an improvement and also cases where the
failure to treat concerned a condition such as cancer leading to a greater risk of
spread/mortality and the possible loss of a chance of a cure. A problem arises:
should the law permit recovery for the lost chance or a reduction in the prospect
of a more favourable outcome in clinical negligence cases? To do so would
(arguably) mean replacing the normal requirement for probable causation, with
the lesser requirement of possible causation.[91] Following the House of Lords'
decision in *Gregg v Scott*,[92] the answer is in the negative and until a future case
arises on the point,[93] reduction in the prospect of a favourable outcome "a loss
of a chance" (where the chances were uncertain or less than 50 per cent) is not
a recoverable head of damage.[94] The present position is that in a case where
negligent medical treatment increased the risk of a particular injury occurring and
that very injury did occur, there is no short cut for the claimant. He must still
prove on balance of probabilities that it was the negligent treatment, rather than
some other factor, which caused the injury, unless he can bring himself within the
Fairchild rule/exception.

The causation requirement—balance of probabilities. If it is more likely   **13–127**
than not that the claimant's condition was amenable to treatment, then the
claimant will recover, and will recover in full. If on the balance of probabilities,
treatment would have made no difference, he will recover nothing. This "all or
nothing" policy derives from *Hotson* and *Wilsher*.

In *Hotson*,[95] the question of primary fact was whether or not a sufficient
number of blood vessels in the claimant's hip had survived his fall to make him

---

[89] [2005] 2 A.C. 176.
[90] For a summary of the applicable law prior to *Gregg v Scott*, see *Jackson & Powell on Professional
Negligence*, (5th edn), paras 12–251 to 261. Past cases where no discount was applied include:
Saumarez v Medway & Gravesend Hospital Management Committee (1953) 2 B.M.J. 1109; *Moffat
v Witelson* (1980) 111 D.L.R. (3d) 712; *Straddlers Groups A and C v Secretary of State for Health*
(2000) 54 B.M.L.R. 104; *Newbury v Bath District HA* (1998) 47 B.M.L.R. 138. For cases where a
discount was applied when the claimant, if properly treated, had a more than 50% chance of recovery
see: *Clark v MacLennan* [1983] 1 All E.R. 416; *Judge v Huntingdon HA* [1995] 6 Med. L.R. 223;
Barnett v Chelsea Kensington Hospital Management Committee [1969] 1 Q.B. 42.
[91] See per Lord Hoffmann's opinion in *Gregg v Scott*, *ibid.* at para.90.
[92] *ibid.*
[93] In the light of Lord Philips' reasoning (see para.13–130, below), the possibility of a future case
being an appropriate "vehicle" for an award of damages for the reduction of a prospect of a cure
cannot be ruled out.
[94] For a discussion and critique of their Lordships' opinions see "Loss of the Chance of Cure from
Cancer", by Professor Jane Stapleton, (2005) 68(6) M.L.R. 996.
[95] See para.13–117, above for a summary of the facts of this case.

one of the 75 out of every 100 patients who would respond to treatment. Since he could not show on the balance of probabilities that a sufficient number of his vessels had survived his original fall, he could not show that he would probably have responded to treatment, so as to establish causation.[96] In effect, he could not show that the damage had not already been done before the defendant's duty arose. His case was not therefore a loss of a chance case, although it was clearly treated as one at first instance and by the Court of Appeal.

13–128   In *Wilsher* the claimant received too much oxygen due to a negligent failure to properly place a catheter. The claimant suffered RLF which resulted in blindness. Excess oxygen was a possible cause of the development of RLF and had increased the chances of it developing. However the claimant also had various other conditions which were linked to the development of RLF by some unknown mechanism. His blind condition could thus have been caused by the excess oxygen, or the other conditions, or both. The claimant could not show the excess oxygen had in fact caused or materially contributed to his developing RLF. The Court of Appeal had awarded damages for the reduced chance of a favourable outcome. However the House of Lords overturned this decision. The claimant had to prove on the balance of probability that his injury (developing RLF) had been caused or materially contributed to by the excess oxygen. This he could not do.

Thus unless the claimant can show that proper treatment was more likely than not to have produced an improvement or arrested the deterioration, the claimant will be unable to show that the defendant's negligence caused his damage and he will recover nothing. In *Hardaker v Newcastle HA*,[97] Stanley Burnton J. considered the question of a "loss of a chance". The claimant was diving near Leith and, after the dive, he realised that he was suffering from decompression illness ("DCI"). He was taken to hospital at the RVI in Newcastle, but the decompression chamber nearby was closed. However, he was seen by the registrar in A&E who confirmed that he had DCI. He was then taken to Sunderland to the back-up decompression chamber, which was also closed and unattended when he arrived. Decompression began shortly afterwards, but there were no oxygen facilities, and the claimant suffered serious and disabling injuries. His claim against the HA was to the effect that there was culpable delay of about 30 minutes in treating his DCI, and that with earlier treatment there would have been a significantly better chance of a better outcome. The claimant failed to establish that the Health Authority had been negligent, but the judge also considered that since the expert evidence only showed an unquantified chance of a better but unidentified outcome, the claimant had failed to prove any loss since a chance of a better recovery below 50 per cent was not recoverable damage.

13–129   In the field of delay in diagnosis of cancer, the patient who has lost an estimated 40 per cent chance of successful treatment, but whose condition is now terminal, may justifiably feel aggrieved at the proposition that he or she has lost nothing of value. On the other hand defendants who are obliged to compensate a claimant as though a chance of a certain cure had been lost would be

---

[96] See *Richardson v Kitching* [1995] 6 Med. L.R. 257 for another case where the claimant failed to establish causation.
[97] [2001] Lloyd's Rep. Med. 512.

understandably aggrieved if the chance had in fact been rather less than certain.[98] In *Gregg v Scott* the claimant had developed non-Hodgkin's lymphoma, which was negligently misdiagnosed as benign. That misdiagnosis caused a delay to its treatment of nine months, which in turn led to the growth and spread of the lymphoma. At trial statistical evidence was presented and accepted by the trial judge to the effect that the claimant's chance of recovery (defined as surviving for a period of ten years) was only 42 per cent, even if it had been treated promptly. The trial judge found that the delay had reduced the chances of recovery to 25 per cent, but refused to award damages at 25 per cent of the full sum claimed because the chances of survival were in any event less than 50 per cent. The chances of a cure from the claimant's particular type of cancer were never as good as 50 per cent, (a fact which was not known at the outset of the proceedings) thus on the balance of probabilities the claimant could not show that the outcome would have been different had be been treated nine months earlier— he could not show that he would have recovered even without the negligent delay.

The decision of the House of Lords (upholding the Court of Appeal[99] and the trial judge) was a majority decision (3:2, Lord Nicholls and Lord Hope dissenting), but that majority did not present one uniform view.

Lord Hoffmann and Baroness Hale of Richmond applied the clear line of authority based on the "*Hotson*" and "*Wilsher*" requirement for a cause of the adverse consequence complained of to be identified and proved to be the result of the defendant's act or omission on the balance of probabilities, choosing against the apparent alternative of adopting a lower, mere possibility. Lord Phillips (also in the majority) adopted a different approach. Drawing on the fact that the claimant had by the time of their Lordships' judgment already survived post-diagnosis for nine years Lord Phillips noted that the claimant's pleaded and pursued case of delay affecting chances of survival appeared to fail on its facts, although the delay may have meant that "cure" involved more intrusive treatment. Lord Phillips viewed the essential basis of the claimant's claim for damages (his chance of long term survival for ten years fell from 42 per cent to 25 per cent as a result of the defendant's negligent misdiagnosis which resulted in a nine-month delay to treatment) to be fallacious and based on a misuse of

---

[98] Baroness Hale put this proposition the other way around at para.195: "If it is more likely than not that the defendant's carelessness caused me to lose a leg. I do not want my damages reduced to the extent that it is less than 100% certain that it did so. On the other hand, if it is more likely than not that the defendant's carelessness did not cause me to lose the leg, then the defendant does not want to have to pay damages for the 20% or 30% chance that it did. A 'more likely than not' approach to causation suits both sides."

[99] The Court of Appeal had dismissed the appeal by a majority, with Lathan L.J. distinguishing *Hotson*, but with Mance L.J. and Simon Brown L.J. feeling unable to do so. The Court of Appeal's decision provoked a reaction of "some disquiet" from Waller L.J. that the claimant should receive no damages for the chance that was lost (with whom Carnwath L.J. agreed) in *Coudert Brothers v. Normans Bay Ltd* [2003] EWCA Civ 215, a solicitor's negligence case where the solicitor defendant unsuccessfully challenged the claim and finding at first instance that this was a "loss of a chance" case. Laws L.J. added in *Coudert* (whilst noting that he understood and respected the decision of the majority on which *Hotson* had had influence): "If a man's chance of a cure from a potentially fatal cancer has been reduced by another's negligence from 42% to 25%, would not a reasonable jury say that he had been grievously hurt by the negligence?". As both Waller and Laws L.J.'s concluded, the correctness or otherwise of the decision in *Gregg v Scott* was a matter for the House of Lords. Their Lordships duly upheld the Court of Appeal.

statistics. Lord Phillips concluded that based on the instant case the law should not permit damages awards for the loss of a chance of a cure, when such claims and awards would be based on limited and difficult medical statistical evidence, even to redress the substantial injustice (identified by Lord Nicholls and Lord Hope) that no award would cause.

13–130 The outcome in *Gregg v Scott* seems to reflect a wish of the majority of the Committee to "rein in" the law of causation, which was proceeding down an incremental path of decisions made on the basis of specific facts and to address apparent injustices that arose from the mechanistic application of the normal rules of causation (namely *Fairchild* and *Chester v Afshar*). It is likely that this case is the end of claims for damages for clinical negligence where the chances of a cure fall, but were in any event less than 50 per cent. However Lord Phillips' decision is also a comprehensive critique of the evidence on which Mr Gregg's case was based and he expressly left open the possibility for an award of damages for the reduction of a prospect of a cure in some future case (at paragraph 190):

> "The complications of this case have persuaded me that it is not a suitable vehicle for introducing into the law of clinical negligence the right to recover damages for the loss of a chance of a cure. Awarding damages for the reduction of the prospect of a cure, when the long term result of treatment is still uncertain, is not a satisfactory exercise. Where medical treatment has resulted in an adverse outcome and negligence has increased the chance of that outcome, there may be a case for permitting a recovery of damages that is proportionate to the increase in the chance of the adverse outcome. That is not a case that has been made out on the present appeal."[1]

However it may be appropriate for the court to consider whether the culpable delay to diagnosis and treatment caused the treatment to be less likely to succeed.[2] Applying the usual "but for" test of causation produces an "all or nothing" result. Thus, if the chance that proper treatment would have secured the

---

[1] Perhaps, more prosaically, and ignoring the wider impact on loss of a chance cases, the decision in *Gregg v Scott* is simply not a case where their Lordships felt a departure from the standard criteria for causal requirements was justified. See the extrajudicial views of Lord Hoffmann, as expressed in a lecture given in Oxford in May 2005, the text of which is reported (2005) 121 L.Q.R. 592–603. Contrast the decision in *Gregg v Scott* with the "common sense" result of the New South Wales Court of Appeal in *Rufo v Kosking* [2004] N.S.W.C.A. 391. The claimant could not show on the balance of probabilities that she would not have suffered the spinal microfractures she sustained, which were not caused by the negligent treatment (there was a less than 50% chance of avoiding such fractures). Nevertheless Campbell AJA held, adopting a robust, pragmatic approach, that in the context of the claimant's pre-existing osteoporotic state and her skeletal vulnerability, it was more probable than not that the excessive corticosteroid administered by the defendant in treatment of her lupus condition caused the claimant's loss of chance that she would have suffered less spinal damage than she did. The court applied a similar test as applied in *Allied Maples*: did the claimant lose a valuable or material chance or a chance "of substance", not merely a speculative or remote chance? The claim was remitted to the trial judge for determination of damages for the loss of the chance. In *A v The National Blood Authority* [2001] 3 All E.R. 289, Burton J. in a defective product claim under s.3 of the Consumer Protection Act 1987, rejected the contention that the claimants' damages should be reduced to reflect a loss of a chance argument concerning the failure to introduce routine screening and surrogate testing earlier.

[2] *Dawn Demery v Cardiff & Value NHS Trust*, unreported, July 11, 2006, CA.

desired result was less than 50 per cent, the claimant cannot prove on the balance of probabilities that the damage would not have occurred in any event.

By maintaining the *Hotson* and *Wilsher* line of authority on causation, the **13-131** decision in *Gregg v Scott* means the alternative approach of awarding the claimant compensation for the loss of the chance of recovery, even if that chance is less than 50 per cent has been rejected. In that alternative approach the argument would be that, on the balance of probabilities, the claimant has been deprived of the opportunity to receive treatment. This much proof of causation would be necessary before proceeding to quantification of loss or the value of the damage suffered using "loss of a chance" discounting. The value of the opportunity which was lost would depend upon the chance that the treatment would have been successful but it is treated as a matter for the assessment of damages, not causation. This approach is commonly adopted in claims against solicitors for the lost chance of gaining some benefit, whether via litigation or not. Following *Gregg v Scott* the law as applied to loss of chance cases in clinical negligence is now fundamentally different to the law as applied in other areas of professional negligence, see for example *Allied Maples Group Ltd v Simmonds & Simmonds*[3] where the lost chance of renegotiating a contract (caused by a solicitor's negligence) was recoverable if the claimants could show, on the balance of probabilities that they would have so negotiated and that there was a "real or substantial" rather than "speculative" chance of succeeding in those negotiations. The claimants did not have to prove on the balance of probabilities that they would have succeeded—success being an uncertain future matter for a third party to decide, namely the vendor.

Canadian law. In *Lawson v Laferriere*[4] the Supreme Court of Canada **13-132** reviewed the issue both in the context of civil law and common law. In March 1971 the patient consulted the defendant, a cancer specialist, about a lump in her right breast. The defendant performed a biopsy, which revealed that the patient had cancer of the breast. The defendant negligently failed to inform the patient of her condition or to follow it up. In 1975 the patient's condition deteriorated and the doctors treating her confirmed the original diagnosis of cancer. The patient died in January 1978. The medical evidence indicated that, whatever treatment the patient had received since 1971, she would probably have died of cancer. The trial judge dismissed a claim by the patient's executor because causation was not established. The Quebec Court of Appeal, by a two to one majority, awarded the executor $50,000 for loss of the chance of a cure. The Supreme Court of Canada, by a majority of six to one, allowed the defendant's appeal in part. The court held that the patient's executor was not entitled to damages for loss of the chance of a cure; but she was entitled to damages for the distress and diminished quality of life which the patient suffered, as a result of the four-year delay in telling her of the diagnosis. Such damages were assessed at $17,500.

---

[3] [1995] 1 W.L.R. 1602 (discussed further at para.10–263).
[4] (1991) 78 D.L.R. (4th) 609, 654. Lord Hoffmann drew support for his opinion in *Gregg v Scott* from this decision, at para.81 of his speech.

The majority of the Supreme Court concurred with the judgment of Gonthier J. This judgment reviewed at length the civil law on damages for loss of a chance, surveying the judicial decisions and academic writings on the topic of France, Belgium and Quebec. Gonthier J. also reviewed more briefly the common law on this topic and noted the House of Lords' decision in *Hotson*. He concluded that the "lost chance" approach was inappropriate in all but the exceptional classical cases, such as loss of a lottery ticket. In such cases "the damage can only be understood in probabilistic or statistical terms and . . . it is impossible to evaluate sensibly whether or how the chance would have been realised in that particular case." He considered that such artificial analysis should not be extended to the medical context. Instead the courts should concentrate on what injury had been caused to the individual claimant, such as shorter life or greater pain.[5] *Lawson v Laferriere* was distinguished[6] (as a civil law case having no application to a common law case of a contract for medical services) by the Canadian Court of Appeal in *de la Giroday v Brough*[7] where the majority held that there was no basis for loss of a chance in an action based on tort, but that an action in contract for breach of an implied obligation to exercise reasonable care and skill could be decided using a loss of a chance approach.[8] By contrast, in *Brown v University of Alberta*,[9] the claimant's damages were reduced by 50 per cent to reflect the chances of the very same injury (violent shaking by father leading to brain damage) occurring (without negligence by any doctor) in the future life of the claimant, even if the missed diagnosis of child abuse had been made. The court accepted that contingencies for future events did not need to be proved on the balance of probabilities, thereby apparently accepting the principle of discounting damages for an uncertain future event derived from *Allied Maples, Davies v Taylor* and applied in *Judge*.

13–133   **Evidence of culpable delay.** For an example of a case where the lack of specific evidence (again) prevented the court making an award for a culpable delay in treatment see *Tahir v Haringey HA*.[10] The claimant sustained severe

---

[5] See *Sohal v Brar* (1999) 63 Alta. L.R. (3d) 280 where the applicability of the loss of chance doctrine was rejected. For an application of this approach in the UK see: *Sutton v Population Services Family Planning Programme Ltd*, *The Times*, November 7, 1981. A different view is expressed by Dr W. Scott in "Causation in Medico-Legal Practice: A Doctor's Approach to the 'Lost Opportunity' Cases" (1992) 55 M.L.R. 521. Scott argues that the "all or none" approach is unsatisfactory because of the practical difficulty in many borderline cases of saying on which side of the 50% line the probabilities fall. In view of the impossibility of precision, he suggests that the courts should deal in fixed bands: 10% chance, 25% chance, 33% chance and so forth. In cases which fall near the 50% borderline, justice to the parties would be much better served by adopting a proportionate approach. A proportionate approach would be workable. From a pragmatic viewpoint, this argument has considerable force. It merits serious consideration in any statutory scheme for compensation for medical accidents.

[6] Lord Hoffmann did not refer to this case. Mr Gregg had not privately retained the defendant general practitioner, and there was therefore no contractual nexus.

[7] (1997) 33 C.L.R. (3d) 171.

[8] See *per* Southin J.A. (with whom Newberg J.A. concurred) at para.42. However, these dicta are all obiter and for this reason Finch J.A. (who dissented on the question of breach of duty) declined to consider causation at all.

[9] (1997) 145 D.L.R. (4th) 63, Court of Queen's Bench.

[10] [1998] Lloyd's Rep. Med. 104.

neurological damage following surgery for a spinal abscess. He contended that the doctors' delay of 24 hours to diagnosis and treatment had caused a general increment in his injury. At trial, he was only able to establish two to three hours' of negligent delay. The trial judge awarded general damages of £4,000 to reflect the linear proportion of the general damages of £30,000 which would have been awarded had the claimant established 24 hours' negligent delay. The health authority's appeal was upheld. The claimant had failed to prove that some measurable damage was actually caused by the culpable two to three hours' of delay. The claimant's expert evidence was not directed towards proving breach of duty based on a culpable two to three hour delay, but only the main case of 24 hour delay. The court therefore had no evidential basis for determining what, if any deficit, was caused by the culpable delay and therefore had no real basis for assessing damages. The claimant's award for two to three hours' delay was overturned.[11]

(iii) *Warnings*

Normal rule. Where the claimant's case rests on the medical practitioner's **13–134** failure to give him proper warning of the risks entailed in treatment,[12] it is necessary to prove that (if properly advised) he would not have accepted the treatment (simple causation),[13] (or would not have accepted the treatment at that time—this arises from the House of Lords' decision in *Chester v Afshar*[14]). If the claimant fails to establish this hypothetical fact, then no loss flows from the defendant's breach of duty. Where, however, the claimant sues in trespass,[15] this is not a necessary element in his claim.[16]

Proving what the claimant would have done. In some cases, the nature of **13–135** the duty breached may increase the difficulty of proving causation. In *Smith v Salford HA*,[17] the defendant neurosurgeon negligently failed to give the claimant

---

[11] See also: *Robertson v Nottingham HA* [1997] 8 Med. L.R. 1. The Court of Appeal overturned the finding of negligence against the obstetric registrar, in part on the lack of proof that the culpable delay had contributed materially to the damage. By contrast the claimant in *Miles v Redbridge Waltham Forest HA* succeeded in his claim that the negligent delay in commencing ventilation after his premature delivery caused or materially contributed to his post-delivery brain haemorrhage and his consequent mental difficulties. The defendant doctors had negligently misdiagnosed foetal death during delivery, and given the mother a pethidine injection. The pethidine had depressed the claimant's respiration at birth and inadequate restorative measures were taken, leading to an excess of carbon dioxide in the claimant's blood (hypercarbia). The Court's decision is robust: the causative or contributing factors for the haemorrhage included prematurity itself, the birth process via the birth canal as well as the culpable injection of pethidine to the mother leading to hypercarbia. See also *Hardaker v Newcastle HA*, *ibid.* at para.13–128, above.
[12] See paras 13–089 to 13–104, above.
[13] *Bolam v Friern Hospital Management Committee* [1957] 1 W.L.R. 582, 590–591; *Chatterton v Gerson* [1981] Q.B. 432, 442G–H.
[14] *Chester v Afshar* [2004] UKHL 41 reported at [2005] 1 A.C. 134.
[15] On the grounds that the claimant was not told, even in broad terms, the nature of the treatment proposed. See paras 13–043 to 13–057: Consent to Treatment, above.
[16] *Chatterton v Gerson* [1981] Q.B. 432, 442H–443A.
[17] [1995] 6 Med. L.R. 321.

an adequate warning of the risks which attended the operation which he recommended. However, even had he given a proper warning, the likely benefits of the procedure for the claimant were such that the surgeon would have been entitled to emphasise that the risks of adverse effects were remote and to advise strongly that the surgery be undertaken. In those circumstances, Potter J. found that the claimant would probably have accepted the recommendation.[18] In *Poynter v Hillingdon HA*[19-20] the infant claimant failed to prove that doctors responsible for his heart transplant operation were negligent in not disclosing to his parents that the surgery carried a relatively small risk of permanent brain damage. Sir Maurice Drake was of the view, however, that even had such a warning been given, the parents would have consented to the operation. He attached greater weight to the circumstances in which they has actually consented, which involved them setting aside their own strong views against heart transplant so as to secure the claimant's survival, than to their testimony at trial that they would have refused even if told that the relevant risk was tiny in the extreme.

13–136   **Subjective approach.** In determining what the claimant would have done, if he or she had been properly advised, there are three possible approaches which could be adopted:

> (i) to consider what a reasonable person would have done in the claimant's position, if properly advised (the objective approach[21]);
>
> (ii) to consider what this particular claimant would have done, if properly advised, however reasonable or unreasonable that course of action may be (the subjective approach);

---

[18] See *Smith v Barking, Havering and Brentwood HA* [1994] 5 Med. L.R. 285: on the balance of probabilities the claimant would have gone ahead with the operation even if she had been properly advised of the risk of tetraplegia, so the failure to warn was not causative; *Smith v Salford HA* [1994] 5 Med. L.R. 321: there was a finding of no breach, but in addition the claimant had not satisfied the judge that the operation would have been refused if proper advice had been given; *Shakoor v Kang Situ* [2001] 1 W.L.R. 410, 420F–G: the claimant failed on breach and causation; *Pearce v United Bristol Healthcare NHS Trust* [1999] E.C.C. 167 for an example of the claimant failing to establish that had the proper warning been given by the clinician, the recommendation would not have been accepted by the patient. By contrast in *McAllister v Lewisham and North Southwark HA* [1994] 5 Med. L.R. 343 and *Smith v Tunbridge Wells HA* [1994] 5 Med. L.R. 334, the claimant succeeded because the judge was satisfied that if properly warned the claimant would not have consented to the operation in question. See also *Newbury v Bath District HA* [1998] 47 B.M.L.R. 138, QBD: the judge held that there was no negligence in obtaining consent and that in any event, the claimant would have gone ahead with the surgery if she had known of the 1–5% risk of neural damage.
[19-20] (1997) 37 B.M.L.R. 192.
[21] There are policy arguments in favour of the objective approach. Subject to the difficulties noted by the Court of Appeal of British Columbia in *Arndt v Smith* [1996] 7 Med. L.R. 108 it is easier to apply and it is less likely to lead to bizarre results. Its main drawback, however, is that if damages are awarded on this basis, they are less directly related to the loss actually suffered by the claimant as a result of the breach of duty. A claimant who was unable to show on the balance of probabilities that he would not have undergone the treatment offered, for example, could nevertheless succeed if a reasonable claimant (or, possibly, a significant number of reasonable claimants, *ibid. per* Lambert J.A. at 117) would.

(iii) to consider what a reasonable person having the characteristics or circumstances of the claimant would have done if properly advised (the modified
objective approach[22]).

It is implicit in McNair J.'s direction to the jury in *Bolam v Friern Hospital
Management Committee*[23] and in Bristow J.'s judgment in *Chatterton v Gerson*[24]
that in English law the subjective approach is correct.[25] The "missed abortion"

---

[22] The matter was considered in *Reibl v Hughes* (1980) 114 D.L.R. (3d) 1 by the Canadian Supreme
Court, which decided that the objective approach was correct. However, the court was at pains to
point out that this did not put the issue of causation completely in the hands of the medical
practitioner. "Merely because medical evidence establishes the reasonableness of a recommended
operation does not mean that a reasonable person in the patient's position would necessarily agree to
it." The patient's particular circumstances must also be taken into account (thereby modifying the
objective approach). In *Reibl v Hughes*, for example, the court attached importance to the fact that
the claimant needed to work another one and a half years in order to earn pension benefits. Naturally
he would not want to jeopardise those prospects. In that case it was held on balance of probabilities
that a reasonable person in the claimant's position, if properly advised, would not have submitted to
the treatment in question. As a result of the wide duty of disclosure in Canada coupled with the
objective approach to causation, in numerous cases since *Reibl v Hughes*, the modified objective test
has been applied. In *Arndt v Smith* [1996] 7 Med. L.R. 108, decision reversed by Supreme Court of
Canada, the claimant alleged that, had she been properly warned that the chickenpox which she
contracted during pregnancy created certain risks to her unborn child, she would have requested an
abortion. The trial judge held that she would not. The Court of Appeal of British Columbia allowed
her appeal on the grounds that the judge was not entitled, in applying the objective test, to take into
account the claimant's scepticism towards conventional medicine or that the pregnancy was carefully
planned and wanted. However, the court recognised that the objective test was inadequate in a case
where the hypothetical treatment decision would involve the balancing of overlapping personal,
ethical and medical considerations. It would be possible to conclude that some reasonable patients in
the position of the claimant would have undergone the treatment, but others, equally reasonable,
would not. The court suggested that it was time that the Supreme Court of Canada reconsidered the
question of causation in cases where negligence consists in a failure to warn. The majority in the
Supreme Court of Canada (1997) 148 D.L.R. (4th) 48, reversed the decision of the Court of Appeal
in British Columbia in *Arndt v Smith* upholding the finding of the trial judge that, even if warned that
her unborn child might be harmed by chicken pox during the pregnancy, the claimant would not have
had an abortion. In doing so the Supreme Court applied the modified objective test for causation (The
subjective approach appears to have been preferred by the three dissenting judges (MacLachlin,
Sopinka and Iacobucci JJ.)). The question to be asked is: "Would a reasonable patient in the
claimant's position have decided to have an abortion?", but in answering that question, the court may
take into account the claimant's "reasonable" beliefs, fears, desires and expectations. Thus the
claimant cannot rely on proof that she would have reacted unreasonably to the appropriate warning.
Under a subjective test she could. As an example of an unreasonable reaction, the majority judgment
suggested a patient who would have refused treatment if warned that it carried the risk of causing a
temporary rash because she believed that the rash would signal the presence of evil spirits in the body.
In "Causation and Disclosure of Medical Risks" L.Q.R. 1998 114 Jan. 52–55, Tony Honore argues
that, in cases concerning the duty to disclose the risks of treatment, resort to the modified test for
causation suggests that the duty to disclose has been too widely drawn. If the scope of the duty is
properly defined, the traditional subjective test for causation does not afford the claimant any undue
advantage. In "Causation and the emerging Canadian Doctrine of Informed Consent to Medical
Treatment" (1985) 33 C.C.L.T. 131, Philip Osborne advocates the subjective approach. See *Seney v
Crooks* [1998] 166 D.L.R (4th) 337, Alberta CA. The Court of Appeal upheld the trial judge's
decision and affirmed the use of the modified objective test of causation in cases concerning failure
to advise or warn.
[23] [1957] 1 W.L.R. 582, 590–591.
[24] [1981] Q.B. 432, 445B–D.
[25] The subjective approach is adopted in the case of solicitors: see *Sykes v Midland Bank Executor
and Trustee Co* [1971] 1 Q.B. 113, 124–125, 129 and 131–132. The objective approach is applied in
Canada: *Reibl v Hughes* (1980) 114 D.L.R. (3d). The subjective approach is adopted in Hong Kong.

cases (discussed below at paras 13–144 to 13–148) have also proceeded on this basis. In practice it appears that evidence of both will weigh with the court, the "modified objective approach". Thus in *Chester v Afshar* both the subjective and the objective approach to causation were applied, albeit that the objective approach was applied only to confirm that the same outcome was reached using either approach. In *Pearce v United Bristol Healthcare NHS Trust*,[26] the Court of Appeal adopted the subjective approach.[27] In *Smith v Barking, Havering and Brentwood HA*,[28] while accepting the subjective test as the correct one, Hutchison J. recognised the value of objective considerations in assessing the claimant's evidence on the point. The judge said:

> "Both counsel invited me to accept that in the end the matter must be one for decision on a subjective basis. This must plainly as a matter of principle be right, because the question must be: If this plaintiff had been given the advice that she should have been given, would she have decided to undergo the operation or not? However, there is a particular difficulty involved in this sort of case—not least for the plaintiff herself—in giving, after the adverse outcome of the operation is known, reliable answers as to what she would have decided before the operation had she been given proper advice as to the risks inherent in it. Accordingly, it would, in my judgment, be right in the ordinary case to give particular weight to the objective assessment. If everything points to the fact that a reasonable plaintiff, properly informed, would have assented to the operation, the assertion from the witness box, made after the adverse outcome is known, in a wholly artificial situation and in the knowledge that the outcome of the case depends upon that assertion being maintained, does not carry great weight unless there are extraneous or additional factors to substantiate it. By extraneous or additional factors I mean, and I am not doing more than giving examples, religious or some other firmly-held convictions; particular social or domestic considerations justifying a decision not in accordance with what, objectively, seems the right one; assertions in the immediate aftermath of the operation made in a context other than that of a possible claim for damages; in other words, some particular factor which suggests that the plaintiff had grounds for not doing what a reasonable person in her situation might be expected to have done. Of course, the less confidently the judge reaches the conclusion as to what objectively the reasonable patient might be expected to have decided, the more readily will he be persuaded by her subjective evidence."[29]

13–137   *Chester v Afshar.* In a case that was an exception to the normal rule, the claimant, Miss Chester, succeeded on causation though she could not prove that had she been warned as she alleged she should have been she would not have had the operation later, with the same attendant risk of sustaining the same injury she suffered. The Court of Appeal[30] held that, but for a negligent failure on the part of the clinician to give a proper warning of risks associated with treatment or an operative procedure, the patient would not have had that treatment or that operation then; that the claimant does not have to show that he or she would not

---

In America some states expressly adopt the subjective approach, others purport to adopt the objective approach but import so many subjective factors that the so-called objective test becomes indistinguishable from the subjective test.

[26] [1999] E.C.C. 167 (Lord Woolf, with whom L.JJ. Roche and Mummery agreed).

[27] As did Ebsworth J. in *Newbury v Bath District HA* (1999) 47 B.M.L.R. 138 at 150.

[28] [1994] 5 Med. L.R. 285.

[29] *ibid.* at 288–289. It was common ground in that case that the subjective test was correct.

[30] [2002] EWCA Civ 724 reported at [2003] Q.B. 356.

have had the treatment at a later stage, or that the risk which eventuated would have in any way been reduced if the procedure or operation had been undertaken at a later stage.

The House of Lords upheld this decision by a majority, (3:2 with Lord Bingham and Lord Hoffmann dissenting).[31] What might seem to be a major departure from the normal rules of causation should probably more simply be viewed as a decision based soundly on principles of legal public policy and caused by the majority of their Lordships' wish to "right wrongs". Although two of the majority view (Lord Steyn and Lord Walker) did partly base their decisions on a justified extension of the "principled" or "modified" approach to causation as enunciated in *Fairchild*, both of the dissenting opinions came from members of the Committee of the House of Lords that had actually given the judgment in *Fairchild*. In the light of this there must be doubt as to whether this more relaxed approach to causation can properly be said to be appropriate in this case, or to any other normal clinical negligence cases. As Lord Hoffmann put it, the case failed on causation, but should there be a special rule, to vindicate the affront to the claimant's right to choose for herself he proposed as a possible alternative a modest solatium.[32] The *Chester v Afshar* ratio is limited to cases where the injury complained of was the consequence of something about which the claimant should have been warned. In such cases the claimant only has to establish that he or she would not have accepted that treatment at that time in order to recover in full for the injury. By contrast the claimant who did not receive the same warning, but who would have accepted the treatment (or who fails to satisfy the judge that they would not have accepted) had the warning been given recovers nothing, yet each claimant has suffered the same breach of duty—a negligent failure to warn.

The outcome of the appeal to their Lordships in *Chester v Afshar* was   **13–138** influenced by the Australian case of *Chappel v Hart*,[33] where the claimant suffered from a progressive condition which sooner or later would require surgery. The defendant ENT surgeon failed to warn her that the operation carried a risk of perforation of the oesophagus, which in turn might lead to infection and partial loss of voice. It was found that had she been so warned, the claimant would have taken steps to have the surgery performed by "the most experienced [surgeon] with a record and reputation in the field". In fact the surgery was carried out by Dr Chappel, and, without negligence in the course of the operation, the claimant suffered infection and consequential voice loss. The claimant contended that the damage to her throat and voice was caused by the doctor's failure to warn her of the risk of infection. The doctor contended that there was no causal nexus between the failure to warn and the injury because she would have had to undergo the surgery in any event, and it could not be shown that there would have been a reduced risk of infection if the operation had been carried out by someone else. The evidence in the case showed that the claimant would have had the surgery in any event, and if she had had it on a later occasion, any reduction in

---

[31] [2005] 1 A.C. 134.
[32] Such a view accords with the majority view (4–3) in *Rees v Darlington Memorial Hospital NHS Trust* [2003] UKHL 52, reported at [2004] 1 A.C. 309, and Lord Millett's suggestion in *McFarlane* that a conventional award be made to mark the loss of the freedom to choose and in recognition of the wrong done, an approach that was rejected in *Rees* by Lord Steyn and Lord Hope.
[33] [1999] Lloyd's Rep. Med. 223.

the associated risk would have been very small and not in any way measurable. It may be thought surprising that she recovered damages on the basis of the full value of her injuries.[34] The defendant appealed on the issue of causation, arguing that the claimant's damage was not physical injury but the loss of the chance to have the operation performed by someone else and that therefore the damages should be discounted on the basis of a loss of a chance. The defendant further argued that the risk which materialised was a random event and was ever present, no matter who performed the operation. Therefore, it was said, the defendant's failure to warn had not caused the claimant to lose anything of value. The majority in the High Court of Australia rejected this argument. It was wrong to analyse the claimant's damage as the loss of a chance to have the operation performed by another surgeon. On the evidence, had she been properly warned, she would not have undergone the operation when she did. She would not have suffered loss of her voice when she did. The fact that she would have undergone the operation, bearing a risk of the same nature, at a later date did not prevent a finding that the defendant's failure to warn had caused her to suffer the injury of which she complained, namely the loss of her voice.[35]

(iv) *The Application of the* Bolam *Test in Causation*—Bolitho

13–139　The application of the *Bolam* test to the question of causation was considered by the House of Lords in *Bolitho v City & Hackney HA*.[36] It was held that in the generality of cases, the *Bolam* test has no part to play in deciding causation. However, in those cases where the breach of duty consisted of an omission to act, a two stage approach to causation was required. The court will ask first: what would have happened had the act been performed? On the facts of *Bolitho*, this question required an enquiry whether, as a matter of fact, the registrar would have intubated the claimant if she had attended him when called. If the answer is that such treatment would have been administered as would have avoided the injuries of which the claimant complains, the claimant has proved causation. Should the claimant fail to show that such treatment would have been administered, he will nonetheless succeed on causation if he can show that it would have been negligent not to administer such treatment—hence the role for the *Bolam* test. A defendant cannot escape liability by saying that the damage would have occurred in any event because he would have committed some further breach of duty after the initial failure. Lord Browne-Wilkinson (with whom the other four law lords agreed) approved the following passage from the judgment of Hobhouse L.J in the Court of Appeal:

> "... a plaintiff can discharge the burden of proof on causation by satisfying the court either that the relevant person would in fact have taken the relevant action (although she

---

[34] See the commentary at [1999] Lloyd's Rep. Med. 223 at 253 where Adrian Whitfield Q.C. argues that the decision of the majority is right, and in accordance with the whole basis of informed consent cases.

[35] The reasoning behind this decision (but not the outcome) has been criticised. See Marc Staunch: "Taking the Consequences for Failure to Warn of Medical Risks," [2000] 63 M.L.R. 261; Peter Cane: "A Warning about Causation" [1999] 115 L.Q.R. 21.

[36] [1998] A.C. 232, HL, for the Court of Appeal decision see [1993] 4 Med. L.R. 381. For the facts of this case see para.13–024, above.

would not have been at fault if she had not) or that the proper discharge of the relevant person's duty towards the plaintiff required that she take that action."[37]

On the facts, the claimant could not show that the registrar would in fact have intubated. Nor, on the evidence of medical experts, could the claimant show that there was no responsible body of medical opinion in support of the doctor's assertion that, had she attended, she would not have intubated. It was not the case, therefore, that no doctor of ordinary skill would have omitted to intubate the claimant, and accordingly, the claimant failed on causation.[38]

The majority view of the Court of Appeal in *Bolitho* was followed by the Court **13–140** of Appeal in *Joyce v Merton, Sutton & Wandsworth HA*.[39] The claimant underwent a cardiac catheterisation, in the course of which the walls of his brachial artery were (non-negligently) sutured together. He was negligently discharged home without instructions to contact the hospital if he became concerned about any aspect of his recovery. By the time that the suturing error was discovered, it was too late to prevent the claimant suffering cerebral infarct. There appeared to have been a period of 48 hours after the operation when this consequence might have been averted. To establish causation, the claimant had to show that, during that time, his condition in fact deteriorated sufficiently for it to have been brought back to the attention of the cardiologist, that the cardiologist would then have referred him to a vascular surgeon and that the vascular surgeon would have reopened the artery. According to Roch L.J., *Bolitho* established that:

> " . . . in such cases as these . . . the burden of proof that had the doctor not been negligent the child would have been intubated or the artery would have been explored, and that a failure to intubate or a failure to re-explore would have been negligent remains on the plaintiff."[40]

Roch L.J. thus appeared to take the view that it was insufficient for the claimant to show simply that the relevant doctors would have intervened to prevent his injury, it is necessary for him also to show that non-intervention would have been negligent.[41] Hobhouse L.J. took the view that *Bolitho* was authority for the proposition that, in such cases:

---

[37] See *Coudert Brothers v. Normans Bay Ltd* [2003] EWCA Civ 215 for a case where this passage of Lord Browne Wilkinson's judgment in *Bolitho* was approved as an example of the general rule of the common law that a party may not rely on his own wrong to secure a benefit.

[38] At the Court of Appeal Simon Brown L.J. dissented. He did not favour the introduction of the *Bolam* test on the issue of causation. He considered that the ordinary tests of factual causation were adequate to deal with the issue. The question was not whether it would have been unreasonable for an attending doctor to intubate the claimant, but whether on the balance of probabilities such a doctor would have intubated. The self-serving evidence of a doctor whose conduct in a hypothetical situation is in issue should be treated with caution, however, and an attending doctor probably would have done whatever she should have done in order to prevent harm to the claimant. Simon Brown L.J. considered that the existence of a responsible body of medical opinion against intubation in these circumstances did not prevent the court finding that, in all the circumstances, the particular claimant probably would have been intubated by an attending doctor. The House of Lords upheld the Court of Appeal.

[39] [1996] 7 Med. L.R. 1. See para.13–070, above.

[40] *ibid.* at 14.

[41] See *Hunt v National Health Service Litigation Authority* [2000] W.L. 1480071, QBD (failure to intervene in birth process and perform forceps delivery was negligent).

"a plaintiff can discharge the burden of proof on causation by satisfying the court either that the relevant person would in fact have taken the relevant action (although she would not have been at fault if she had not) or that the proper discharge of the relevant person's duty towards the plaintiff required that she take action ... Properly viewed, therefore, this rule is more favourable to a plaintiff because it gives him two routes by which he may prove his case—either proof that the exercise of proper care would have necessitated the relevant result, or proof that if proper care had been exercised it would in fact have led to the relevant result."[42]

13–141   Nourse L.J. agreed with both judgments. It appears, therefore, that a claimant who is unable to prove on the balance of probabilities that he would have secured the treatment he required, were it not for the defendant's negligence, will nevertheless succeed if he can show that the failure to provide such treatment would have been a further act of negligence. This approach was adopted by Thomas J. *in Wiszniewski v Central Manchester HA*,[43] and upheld on appeal by the Court of Appeal.[44]

The decision of the Court of Appeal in *Hallatt v North West Anglia HA*[45] demonstrates the need for care in seeking to apply the analysis in *Bolitho* to particular allegations of clinical negligence. In that case, the claimant's mother suffered gestational diabetes during her pregnancy. The chain of consequences was as follows: the claimant grew unusually large before birth, his delivery was complicated and delayed by shoulder dystocia, vaginal delivery was eventually abandoned in favour of Caesarean section but he had suffered oxygen deprivation which caused brain damage. It was argued on his behalf that a hospital doctor who saw his mother during the pregnancy negligently decided that a glucose tolerance test (GTT) was unnecessary because he had failed to appreciate that an earlier glucose test was not conclusive evidence of the absence of diabetes. Had he been aware of the limitations of the earlier test, it was alleged, he would have referred the claimant's mother to a consultant who ought to have ordered the test. The Court of Appeal held that there was no room for the application of the *Bolitho* analysis of causation in this case. The claimant's case was a straightforward allegation that the hospital staff failed to order a GTT because they negligently failed to appreciate the limitations of the earlier test. There was no

---

[42] 5 *ibid.* at 20.
[43] [1996] 7 Med. L.R. 248. See para.13–070, above.
[44] Reported at [1998] Lloyd's Rep. Med. 223. See also *Le Page v Kingston and Richmond HA* [1997] 8 Med. L.R. 229 (for a summary of the facts of this case see para.13–078, above), where John Samuels Q.C. (a deputy judge of the High Court) found that had the claimant's uterine haemorrhage been detected by the obstetric staff, as it ought to have been, the registrar would probably have induced a contraction to expel blood which had accumulated in the uterus and administered a drug to control the bleeding. "Would" here clearly meant "would and should", for the judge formulated the test for causation in *Bolam* terms: "Where there is a genuine disagreement as to the probable outcome among the expert witnesses, who have properly taken into account all the material facts relating to the claimant's treatment and condition at all times, the claimant will fail." See also *C v A Health Authority* unreported, November 3, 1998, QBD, Ebsworth J. See para.13–073, fn.52, above for the facts. See also *Brown v Lewisham & North Southwark HA*, the claimant established breach of duty on the part of one doctor in communicating his history to another, but failed to show that the treatment decision likely to have been taken by the second doctor if given the correct information would have prevented his injury.
[45] [1998] Lloyd's Rep. Med. 197.

question, as there had been in *Bolitho*, of a failure to follow correct procedures to procure the appropriate treatment.[46]

(v) *Intervening Events*

If some extraneous event intervenes between the negligence of the medical **13–142** practitioner and the loss or injury of which the patient complains, the causal connection may be broken.[47] In *Stevens v Bermondsey & Southwark Group Hospital Management Committee*[48] the claimant was injured in an accident caused by an employee of the borough council. The claimant was treated at the defendant's hospital. On the strength of the medical advice he received he settled his claim against the council for £125. He subsequently learnt that he had spondylolisthesis. The claimant claimed that because of the defendant's negligence, he had settled his claim against the council for less than its true value. Paull J. held that this loss was irrecoverable: "His claim against the council was either a *novus actus interveniens* or at least a severing of the direct line of causation stemming from the doctor's negligence."[49] In *Sabri-Tabrizi v Lothian Health Board*,[50] the claimant had undergone a sterilisation operation but due, she

---

[46] For examples of cases where the claimant failed on causation see: *D v Ahmed, ibid*. Claimant failed on both tests of causation. The defendant doctor had properly advised over the telephone, and if he had attended the claimant he would have given the same advice, which advice was not negligent; *Matthews v East Suffolk HA*, unreported, February 25, 2000, CA, [2000] W.L. 191250, CA: (failure to promptly administer antibiotics), the judge did not accept that the prompt administration would have avoided or quantifiably reduced the claimant's injuries; *Sherlock v North Birmingham HA* [1997] 40 B.M.L.R. 103, CA. Chadwick L.J. applied the *Bolitho* approach and found that the claimant failed on both tests of causation. The registrar (had he been informed) would not have transferred the claimant to the Intensive Therapy Unit; for a Canadian example see *Clinton v Regina District Health Board and Gellner* [1998] 171 Sask. R. 44. Only if the allegedly negligent omission (failure to detain a patient in hospital) would have resulted in the detection of the methanol that he had consumed such that his death from methanol poisoning could have been prevented, could causation be proved.
[47] See generally Ch.4: Contribution between Defendants; *Clerk & Lindsell*, (19th edn, Sweet & Maxwell, 2006), paras 2–078 to 2–106 and Hart and Honoré, *Causation in the Law*, (2nd edn, Oxford at the Clarendon Press, 1985), Ch.6. This is illustrated by *Thompson v Schmidt* (1891) 8 T.L.R. 120: the defendant gave a written opinion that the claimant was of unsound mind; on the basis of this the relieving officer in the exercise of his discretion under Lunacy Act 1890, s.20, temporarily detained the claimant. The Court of Appeal held, inter alia, that the defendant's certificate was not the cause of the detention. "Even though it might possibly be true that the act of the defendant was the *causa sine qua non*, it was not the *causa causans*. In other words, the confinement was not the direct result of the defendant's act, but it was the direct result and the sole result of the act of the relieving officer" (*per* Lord Esher M.R.). See also *Rahman v Arearose Ltd* [2001] Q.B. 351, the facts of which are discussed at para.13–125, above. *Joyal v Starreveld* [1996] 37 Alta. L.R. 19 for a case where failure to advise of the risk of epileptic seizures after reduction of anti-epileptic therapy was considered to be the continuing cause of the claimant's road traffic accident (presumed to have been caused by a seizure) and the injuries sustained.
[48] (1963) 107 S.J. 478. See para.13–011, fn.54, above.
[49] *cf*. A Canadian case: *Kelly v Lundgard* [1996] 40 Alta. L.R. (3d) 234. The claimant sustained internal injuries in a road traffic accident. In subsequent litigation the defendant (who had treated her by performing life saving surgery) provided a report on her condition including future prognosis. The report omitted to mention the risk of infertility resulting from abdominal adhesions. The claimant settled her claim without taking into account any risk of infertility materialising. Subsequently she discovered she was infertile due to the accident. She successfully claimed against her treating doctors, who should have identified the risk to her or her lawyers in the accident claim. The doctors knew the purpose for which the report was sought. The chain of causation was not broken.
[50] (1998) 43 B.M.L.R. 190.

alleged, to the defendant's negligence, she remained fertile. She became pregnant and underwent an abortion. She became pregnant a second time, which pregnancy ended in a stillbirth. The health board applied to strike out her claim for damages in relation to the second pregnancy, arguing that the claimant's decision to have sexual intercourse once she knew (because of the first pregnancy) that the sterilisation operation had failed, broke the chain of causation. The Scottish Court of Session (Outer House) accepted the argument and struck out that part of the claimant's claim.[51]

It is a common feature of medical treatment that the patient's care is shared between a number of different nurses, doctors and specialists. Where more than one person makes a mistake, it is largely a question of fact and degree whether the earlier error is an effective cause of the patient's injury. Although the citation of authority in this area is of limited value, *Prendergast v Sam & Dee Ltd*[52] and the Canadian case *Yepremian v Scarborough General Hospital*[53] do provide helpful illustrations. In *Prendergast* (the facts of which are set out above)[54] it was held that the pharmacist's negligence did not break the chain of causation flowing from the negligence of the prescribing doctor. In *Yepremian* a patient suffered cardiac arrest as the result of the negligence of an internist. It was held that the original failure of a physician and a general practitioner to diagnose the patient's condition (diabetes) was not the effective cause of his injury, and they escaped liability.[55] As to the question of apportionment, where more than one party is liable, see above: "Apportionment of Liability".[56] In *Thompson v Blake-James*,[57] advice on options for vaccination of the infant claimant was given successively

---

[51] *cf.* with *Emeh v Kensington & Chelsea & Westminster AHA* [1985] Q.B. 1012 (the claimant became pregnant following a negligently performed sterilisation operation by the defendant health authority. Her decision not to terminate the pregnancy was rejected by the Court of Appeal (thereby overturning the decision of the judge of first instance), as a *novus actus interveniens* between the health authority's original negligence and the claimant's claimed losses (the cost of bringing up the congenitally deformed child that was born). The Court of Appeal held that the negligent health authority could not expect a woman to terminate a subsequent pregnancy, and held the defendant liable for the claimed losses. See para.13–161, for the effect of *McFarlane* on *Emeh*.

[52] [1989] 1 Med. L.R. 36.

[53] (1980) 110 D.L.R. (3d) 513.

[54] See para.13–065, above.

[55] *cf. Powell v Guttman* (1979) 89 D.L.R. (3d) 180: After operating on P's hip, G negligently failed to advise the performance of an arthroplasty operation. This rendered P's femur more susceptible to fracture during any arthroplasty carried out later. Subsequently N carried out an arthoplasty, but in the process caused a fracture to the femur. The Manitoba Court of Appeal held that N's conduct did not amount to a novus actus interveniens. Therefore G was liable for the subsequent fracture. See also: *Law Estate v Simice* [1995] 4 W.W.R. 672, British Columbia CA (claimant's deferring of urgent surgery for brain aneurysm for four days so surgery could be performed in another town did not insulate the doctors who had failed to diagnose the condition thereby causing preceding delay to treatment from liability); *Seney v Crooks* [1998] 166 D.L.R. (4th) 337, Alberta CA (no contributory negligence by claimant for not telling her surgeon that she wanted a full recovery to her normal state after a fracture injury). See also *Kite v Malycha* [1998] 71 S.A.S.R. 325, Supreme Court (courts should not be quick to find contributory negligence on the part of a patient who has relied on a competent medical practitioner for advice and treatment—claimant was entitled to assume that if a cytology report was adverse, she would be told about it) and *Hughes v Cooper* [1998] 41 B.C.L.R. 109 (misdiagnosed as having Crohn's Disease for eight years, found to have colon cancer, onus on defendant doctor to show contributory negligence, patient is entitled to rely on physician's advice and was not contributorily negligent for not seeking additional medical advice).

[56] See also, paras 13–064 to 13–065; 13–156 and Ch.4: Contribution Between Defendants.

[57] [1998] Lloyd's Rep. Med. 187. See para.13–094, above.

by two general practitioners. It was foreseeable by the first that the second would advise on that point, and that such advice would be given closer to the time when the decision to vaccinate would normally be made. The second doctor advised in opposite terms to the first. Peter Gibson L.J. was of the view that the advice of the second doctor broke the chain of causation between the parents' decision not to vaccinate and the advice given by the first doctor.

(vi) *Contributory Negligence*

Successful medical treatment frequently depends upon co-operation by the patient, for example, in taking drugs as and when directed or in notifying his doctor if particular symptoms develop. Lack of co-operation by the patient could constitute contributory negligence or, in a more extreme case, break the chain of causation.[58] In *Pigeon v Doncaster HA*,[59] the claimant underwent extensive surgery for cervical cancer in 1997. In June 1988 a cervical smear that had been taken when the claimant was 22 was wrongly, and negligently, reported as negative. The smear was not repeated on the birth of the claimant's child in October 1988 because of the earlier (false) negative report. Between 1991 and 1997 the claimant was urged on many occasions both by her GP and by the FHSA to have further smear tests, but she refused to do so—because she had found the test that had been carried out in 1988 both painful and embarrassing. The judge held that this conduct by the claimant was not such as to break the chain of causation, but it did amount to substantial contributory negligence, and her damages were reduced by two-thirds accordingly.[60]

In *Crossman v Stewart*[61] the defendant prescribed a drug for the claimant without warning her that there were risks involved in prolonged use. The claimant continued to use the drug (which she obtained privately from a drug salesman) for a long time after the defendant had stopped prescribing it. The defendant was held negligent for failing to appreciate that the claimant was probably continuing to use the drug. But damages were reduced by two-thirds on account of the claimant's contributory negligence.[62]

13–143

---

[58] See *Richardson v LRC Products Ltd* [2000] Lloyd's Rep. Med. 280, QBD: claimant failed to mitigate her loss by not taking morning after pill, which would have been a reasonable step to take after a condom had failed during intercourse. Claim was dismissed.

[59] [2002] Lloyd's Rep. Med. 130.

[60] See also the case of *Hardaker v Newcastle HA* [2001] Lloyd's Rep. Med. 521: the judge dismissed the claim but would have found contributory fault against the claimant for aggravating his injuries before arriving at the hospital.

[61] (1977) 5 C.C.L.T. 45. See also *Brushett v Cowan* (1990) 69 D.L.R. (4th) 743, Newfoundland Supreme Court, Appeal Division (surgeon held negligent for failing to give claimant proper advice on the use of crutches which he had prescribed; 20% discount for contributory negligence by the claimant). *cf. Law Estate v Simice* [1996] W.W.R. 672, British Columbia CA (following a series of delays caused by negligent failures of communication by the defendant doctors, the claimant delayed further before undergoing an operation which, if taken earlier, would have prevented his death; held: claimant's delay was reasonable and did not insulate the doctors from the consequences of their negligence).

[62] See the discussion of novus actus interveniens in the case of *Emeh v Kensington and Chelsea and Westminster AHA* [1985] Q.B. 1012, bearing in mind that the decision has been overruled by *McFarlane* at least so far as the quantum of damages for a wrongful conception claim is concerned.

(vii) *Causation in Wrongful Birth and Wrongful Conception Claims*

13–144 **Failure to detect defects.** Where the complaint made is that the defendant failed to detect[63] and advise upon defects in an unborn baby, the issue which arises is what the mother would have done if properly advised. Would she have had any further tests necessary?[64] Once testing was complete, and competent advice given, would she have had an abortion? Has the opportunity to terminate the pregnancy been lost due to the defendant's negligence?

(a) In *Gregory v Pembrokeshire HA*[65] the defendants failed to inform the claimant that an amniocentesis had produced insufficient cultures. It was held that even if the claimant had been informed promptly, in view of the advanced stage of her pregnancy, she probably would not have had another amniocentesis. Her claim therefore failed on causation.

(b) By contrast in *Carver v Hammersmith & Queen Charlotte's Special HA*[66] the claimant was not told that Bart's test was not diagnostic of Down's syndrome, like amniocentesis, but was a screening test that only detected two-thirds of Down's syndrome foetuses. On the facts, the claimant succeeded in proving breach and causation. It was held that had she known the limitations of the test then she would have she would probably have insisted on amniocentesis and would have terminated the pregnancy.[67]

13–145 **Abortion Act 1967.** One further question to consider is whether the claimant could lawfully have had an abortion at the material time. For the claim to have a realistic prospect of success, it must be shown that the termination of the pregnancy would fall within the scope of s.1(1)(a) to (d) of the Abortion Act 1967 (as amended by s.37(1) to (3) of the Human Fertilisation and Embryology Act 1990). Termination of a pregnancy is now lawful:

" . . . if two registered medical practitioners are of the opinion, formed in good faith—

(a) that the pregnancy has not exceeded its twenty-fourth week and that the con- tinuance of the pregnancy would involve risk, greater than if the pregnancy were terminated, of injury to the physical or mental health of the pregnant woman or any existing children of her family; or

(b) that the termination is necessary to prevent grave permanent injury to the physical or mental health of the pregnant woman; or

(c) that the continuance of the pregnancy would involve risk to the life of the pregnant woman, greater than if the pregnancy were terminated; or

---

[63] See para.13–100, above.
[64] Assuming that the failure to detect, or the failure to advise was negligent and that the claimant would have sought such tests. See *C v A HA*, unreported, November 3, 1998, QBD, Ebsworth J. for an example of a case where the failure to advise the mother to attend an appointment for detection of defects was not negligent since attendance at the appointment would not have resulted in her having a scan capable of detecting her child's subsequent defect.
[65] [1989] 1 Med. L.R. 81.
[66] Unreported, February 25, 2000, QBD, Nelson J.
[67] See also *Rand v East Dorset HA* [2000] Lloyds Rep. Med. 181, QBD, Newman J. and para.13–153, below.

(d) that there is a substantial risk that if the child were born it would suffer from such physical or mental abnormalities as to be seriously handicapped."

Under this section (as amended) in certain circumstances an abortion can be carried out at any stage of the pregnancy. One such circumstance is "that there is a substantial risk that if the child were born it would suffer from such physical or mental abnormalities as to be seriously handicapped".[68]

Failure to warn adequately. Causation is also a problem for claimants where   **13–146**
the negligence complained of is failure to warn of the risk that a sterilisation operation has not been effective or may spontaneously reverse. In *Lybert v Warrington HA*,[69] the claimant was able to show that, had she been so warned, she would have continued to use contraception and so avoided pregnancy, but only because of her unusual history and circumstances. She had known that a further pregnancy would pose particular risks to her health and she had agreed to a hysterectomy before the sterilisation. The Court of Appeal accepted that, in normal circumstances, it would be intrinsically improbable that contraception would be used after a sterilisation, notwithstanding a proper warning.[70]

Choosing to proceed with unwanted pregnancy. An important question in   **13–147**
such cases is whether the conduct of the mother, in declining to have an abortion when she first discovers the unwanted pregnancy, breaks the chain of causation. This question received detailed consideration in *Emeh v Kensington and Chelsea and Westminster AHA*.[71] In that case Park J. held that the claimant's refusal to have an abortion was a novus actus interveniens, because it was so unreasonable as to eclipse the defendants' wrongdoing. Accordingly he held that she could not recover any damages in respect of the period after she had discovered that she was pregnant, save for the costs of a second sterilisation operation. This decision was reversed by the Court of Appeal. Waller L.J. based his decision on the particular circumstances of that case.[72] For example, he took into account the fact that the claimant decided not to have an abortion before she decided to sue the defendants. Slade L.J., however, dealt with the matter on a broader basis and concluded: "Save in the most exceptional circumstances, I cannot think it right that the court should ever declare it unreasonable for a woman to decline to have an abortion in a case where there is no evidence that there were any medical or

---

[68] By contrast in *Rance v Mid-Downs HA* [1991] Q.B. 587, it was held that at the material time the baby was "capable of being born alive" within the meaning of s.1 of the Infant Life (Preservation) Act 1929; therefore any abortion would have been unlawful under the law at that time. Accordingly the claim failed on causation (as well as breach). The basis of the claim in *Rance* is strongly criticised in P. R. Glazebrook, "Capable of Being, But No Right to Be, Born Alive?" [1991] C.L.J. 241.
[69] [1996] 7 Med. L.R. 71.
[70] *ibid.* at 75. A claimant may succeed in showing that, if properly warned of the risk that a vasectomy would spontaneously reverse, an alternative procedure with a lower failure rate would have been undertaken, such as a female sterilisation. That argument failed in *Newell & Newell v Goldenburg* [1995] 6 Med. L.R. 371 because sterilisation of the female claimant was contraindicated on medical grounds.
[71] [1985] Q.B. 1012.
[72] *ibid.* at 1019.

psychiatric grounds for terminating the particular pregnancy."[73] Purchas L.J. tended to agree with Slade L.J., although he indicated that if the claimant's sole motivation in refusing an abortion was to promote an action, it might break the chain of causation.[74]

13–148   It is clear from *Emeh*[75] that in the great majority of cases where the claimant refuses an abortion, such refusal will not break the chain of causation. Even if the prospect of recovering damages is one factor in her decision, she is likely to be influenced by other, more powerful, moral and emotional considerations. However, in the extreme case postulated by Purchas L.J. (where the claimant refuses an abortion purely in order to mount a claim for damages) the question remains open whether the claimant would succeed on causation. If one applies the general principle as formulated by Hart and Honoré: "The general principle of the traditional doctrine is that the free, deliberate and informed act or omission of an human being, intended to exploit the situation created by the defendant, negatives causal connection"[76] it would seem that the claimant should fail. However, in the situation under discussion this principle is in conflict with a higher principle, namely that it is the policy of the law to preserve life not to destroy it.[77] The mother is in certain circumstances entitled to have an abortion, but she can hardly be under a duty to do so in order to mitigate her loss or in order to reduce the liability of a negligent doctor. It is therefore submitted that of the various approaches adopted by the Court of Appeal in *Emeh v Kensington and Chelsea and Westminster AHA*[78] that of Slade L.J. is to be preferred.

Where the unwanted child results from a failed abortion, rather than a failed sterilisation, different considerations arise. The same objections of principle to the novus actus interveniens defence do not exist. To take an extreme example, if an attempted abortion is unsuccessful and the claimant declines to undergo an identical abortion procedure 24 hours later (with a high prospect of success) solely in order to mount a claim for substantial damages, it is submitted that the claimant's conduct would break the chain of causation from the doctor's initial negligence. In *Fredette v Wiebe*,[79] where a first attempted abortion failed, the British Columbia Supreme Court held that the claimant's refusal to undergo a second abortion was reasonable. But in that case the failure of the first abortion was not discovered until a late stage and the second abortion procedure would have been more drastic. Thus the decision turned upon the facts of the case, rather than upon any absolute principle. It is suggested that the same approach would be adopted in England.

---

[73] [1985] Q.B. 1012 at 1024.
[74] *ibid.* at 1027.
[75] Their Lordships appear to have overruled this decision in *McFarlane*, at least so far as the quantum of damages for a wrongful conception claim is concerned. See para.13–161, fn.40 below: Unwanted pregnancy leading to unwanted disabled child.
[76] *Causation in the Law* p.136.
[77] See, e.g. *McKay v Essex AHA* [1982] 1 Q.B. 1166, 1179–1180 and 1188. See also Art.2 of the European Convention for the Protection of Human Rights and Fundamental Freedoms. In *Paton v UK* (1980) 3 E.H.R.R. 408 it was left open whether Art.2 applies to an unborn but viable child.
[78] [1985] Q.B. 1012.
[79] (1986) 29 D.L.R. (4th) 534.

(c) *Foreseeability*

In order to succeed the claimant must establish not only that the injury was **13–149** caused by the medical practitioner's breach of duty but also that it was foresee-able. In the majority of medical negligence cases, the injury of which the claimant complains is either the continuance of some illness which ought to have been cured or prevented or else the infliction of some new injury in the course of treatment. In practice the injury is normally "foreseeable", whether the con-tractual or tortious test is applied. Since the defendant is a medical man, he is well placed to foresee the consequences of his own mistakes.

Forseeability in tort and contract. If the claim is brought in contract, this **13–150** means that, at the time the contract was made, the injury was "reasonably foreseeable as likely to result from the breach".[80] If the claim is brought in tort, it means that at the time the breach of duty was committed the injury (or at least the type of injury[81]) was reasonably foreseeable as a consequence.[82]

Egg shell skull rule.[83] There is a problem with accomodating the "egg shell **13–151** skull" rule with forseeability of injury because the characteristic of the egg shell skull claimant is that their vulnerability to injury is not apparent. That being the case how can the injury be "foreseeable"? This problem is usually overcome by the general statement that the extent of that damage need not be foreseeable, only the type of damage. In *Smith v Leech Brain and Co Ltd*[84] the claimant suffered a small burn on his lip when he was struck by a piece of molten metal. The court found that the burn was the promoting agency for the cancer which subsequently developed from its pre-malignant condition, and also found that but for the burn the cancer may not have developed. Accordingly although the claimant's ensuing death from cancer was not reasonably foreseeable as resulting from the burn, the defendant was held liable for the death. This permits the vulnerable claimant to recover in full for the unexpectedly devastating effect of a foreseeable type of injury.

Unforeseeable way of foreseeable injury occurring. An interesting decision **13–152** on the requirement of foreseeability was *Brown v Lewisham and North South-wark HA*.[85] Following heart surgery, the claimant was discharged from one hospital to another. At the time, he was suffering a chest infection and an

---

[80] *per* Asquith L.J. in *Victoria Laundry (Windsor) Ltd v Newman Industries Ltd* [1949] 2 K.B. 528. For a full discussion of the requirement of foreseeability in contract, see McGregor, (17th edn, Sweet & Maxwell, 2003), 6–125 *et seq.*

[81] See, e.g. *Graham v Persyko* (1984) 30 C.C.L.T. 84, 96, Ontario High Court: it was foreseeable that the claimant would suffer some side effect from the drug prescribed, although the side effect actually suffered was not reasonably foreseeable. Defendant held liable on the principle of *Hughes v Lord Advocate* [1963] A.C. 837. The decision was upheld by the Ontario Court of Appeal: (1986) 27 D.L.R. (4th) 699.

[82] For a full discussion of the requirement of foreseeability in tort, see McGregor, (17th edn, Sweet & Maxwell, 2003), 6.004 *et seq.*

[83] "If the wrong is established the wrongdoer must take his victim as he finds him." *per* Lord Wright in *Bourhill v Young* [1943] A.C. 92 at 109–110.

[84] [1962] 2 Q.B. 405.

[85] [1999] Lloyd's Rep. Med. 110.

undiagnosed deep vein thrombosis (DVT). The DVT was recognised at the second hospital, where the claimant developed a seriously adverse reaction to its treatment with heparin and ultimately lost his leg. The first hospital admitted that it was in breach of duty in discharging the claimant while he had a chest infection. It was held that this admission of breach was not sufficient to permit the claimant to recover against the first hospital in respect of the loss of his leg. The claimant argued that, once he had proved that personal injury of some kind was the foreseeable result of the defendant's breach, it was no defence that the injury in fact suffered came about in an unforeseeable way. The argument failed. Beldam L.J. (with whom Morritt and Mantell L.JJ. agreed) said:

"The public policy of limiting the liability of tortfeasors by the control mechanism of foreseeability seems to me as necessary in cases of medical as in any other type of negligence. I do not see on what policy ground it would be fair or just to hold a doctor to be in breach of duty who failed to diagnose an asymptomatic and undetectable illness merely because he was at fault in the management of a correctly diagnosed but unrelated condition. In short it must be shown that the injury suffered by the patient is within the risk from which it was the doctor's duty to protect him."[86]

In *Smith v Brighton & Lewes Hospital Management Committee*,[87] as a result of the ward sister's negligence, 34 streptomycin injections were administered to the claimant, rather than 30, as prescribed by the doctor. Following this treatment the claimant lost her sense of balance. Streatfeild J. held that it was the last injection which probably did the damage. The ward sister ought to have foreseen that some injury might result from giving more injections than the doctor prescribed.[88] It was not necessary that the quality and extent of the damage should be foreseen. Accordingly the claimant recovered damages for the injury she had in fact sustained. In *Hepworth v Kerr*,[89] the defendant was liable for the consequences of a spinal stroke which the claimant suffered because of his negligent treatment, even though the occurrence of a spinal stroke (as opposed to a cerebral stroke) was not specifically foreseeable in 1979. McKinnon J. held that a spinal stroke was within the general category of risk which was foreseeably caused by the negligence complained of, namely, thrombosis. In *Wiszniewski v Central Manchester HA*[90] the defendant's negligent mismanagement of the claimant's birth meant that he was deprived of oxygen and suffered from cerebral

---

[86] A slightly unusual point on foreseeability arose in *Kralj v McGrath and St Theresa's Hospital* [1986] 1 All E.R. 54. As a result of the defendants' negligence one of the claimant's twins died shortly after birth. The claimant already had one child and planned to have a family of three. Thus it was a consequence of the defendant's negligence that the claimant would have to undergo a further pregnancy in order to achieve her planned family. Woolf J. held that this head of damage was not too remote, even though the claimant had never specifically informed the defendants of her desire to have a family of three in any event. See also *R. v Croydon HA* [1998] Lloyd's Rep. Med. 75 (pregnancy in a married woman of the claimant's age was a foreseeable event, notwithstanding that she had not communicated her desire for a family to the defendant, but no recovery because the claimant's private life was outside the scope of the company doctor's duty).

[87] *The Times*, May 2, 1958.

[88] However, the probability of injury being caused appears to have been small. Streatfield J. considered that if a doctor had prescribed 34 injections rather than 30, that might well not have constituted negligence.

[89] [1995] 6 Med. L.R. 39. The facts are given at para.13–035, fn.67, above.

[90] [1996] 7 Med. L.R. 248, upheld in the Court of Appeal [1998] Lloyd's Rep. Med. 223.

palsy as a result. The umbilical cord had become knotted around his neck, restricting the foetal blood supply. The health authority argued that this was not a foreseeable consequence of their negligence in failing to notice and act upon signs of foetal distress. Thomas J. rejected this argument and the Court of Appeal endorsed his decision and reasoning.[91] The foreseeable result of the neglect was that the claimant would be born suffering the effects of pre-birth hypoxia. The precise mechanism by which the foetal blood supply was restricted was irrelevant. In *Thompson v Blake-James*[92] the defendant general medical practitioner was consulted by the claimant's parents on the question of whether she should be vaccinated against measles. He advised that she should not. She contracted measles and a rare complication left her severely brain damaged. The defendant resisted liability because, on the facts of the case, the Court of Appeal held that it was not reasonably foreseeable that his failure to inform her parents that an alternative method of vaccination might be suitable for the claimant would have had any significant influence upon their decision.

In *Rand v East Dorset HA*[93] the defendant health authority were found liable   **13–153** to the parents of a Down's syndrome child for failing to disclose the results of a routine pregnancy scan that showed the likelihood of a Down's syndrome foetus. The judge held that in the context of the Abortion Act 1967, the scan had been intended to offer a choice whether to terminate a pregnancy or not (where the likelihood was that the pregnancy involved a seriously disabled child). This had established the necessary proximity and foreseeability to make the defendant liable for the consequences of its omission.

In *Roe v Minister of Health*[94] nupercaine was kept in glass ampoules stored in phenol solution. The phenol penetrated the ampoules through invisible cracks and contaminated the nupercaine. The nupercaine was injected into two patients, who suffered permanent paralysis as a result. One of the allegations of negligence was that the nursing staff must have knocked the ampoules together in order to cause the cracking. Denning L.J.[95] held that this was the case. Somervell L.J.[96] and Morris L.J.[97] assumed that this was the case for the purpose of their judgments. The court unanimously held that the injuries in fact caused the patients by this mishap were not foreseeable. "The only consequence which could reasonably be anticipated was the loss of a quantity of nupercaine, but not the paralysis of a patient" (*per* Denning L.J.).[98] "In the case I am assuming, having knocked the ampoules the natural inference is that the nurse would look to see if they were cracked ... As the judge has found no visible crack and the nursing staff had no reason to foresee invisible cracks, the nurse would reasonably assume no harm had been done" (*per* Somervell L.J.).[99]

---

[91] [1996] 7 Med. L.R. 248, 243–245.
[92] [1998] Lloyd's Rep. Med. 187, CA. See para.13–096, above.
[93] *ibid.*, see para.13–144, above: Failure to detect defects.
[94] [1954] 2 Q.B. 66. See also paras 13–025 and 13–041, above.
[95] *ibid.* at 84.
[96] *ibid.* at 81.
[97] *ibid.* at 93.
[98] *ibid.* at 86.
[99] *ibid.* at 81.

13–154 **Psychiatric injury.** Of particular importance for medical practitioners is the decision of the House of Lords in *Page v Smith*.[1] It was held in that case that if physical injury to the claimant was a foreseeable result of the defendant's negligence, the defendant was liable for any psychiatric injury which occurred as a result of the negligence, even where the claimant did not in fact suffer physical injury and the psychiatric damage was not itself foreseeable. The effect of this decision is that psychiatric injury is to be treated as of the same type as physical injury. Thus where it is foreseeable that the negligence of a doctor will cause the patient to suffer physical injury, liability will follow for any psychiatric injury which results from apprehension of that physical harm, even although it does not materialise. The liability for this psychiatric injury is not limited in time to the period of the breach of duty. In *Creutzfeldt-Jakob Litigation Group B v Medical Research Council and Secretary of State for Health*[2] the defendants' duty to avoid foreseeable harm included a duty to avoid the risk of psychiatric injury caused to the patient as a consequence of receiving the news and information about the consequences and effects of CJD. Any patient who could prove a genuine psychiatric illness caused by the awareness of the risk of CJD was entitled to compensation.

(d) *Measure of Damages*

(i) *Damages for Personal Injury*

13–155 In the vast majority of medical negligence actions, the principal matter of complaint is that the defendant has caused, aggravated or failed to cure some form of personal injury. The claimant ordinarily claims general damages for pain, suffering and loss of amenity and special damages for financial losses suffered in consequence of the injury (such as loss of earnings or the cost of medical and nursing care). The same principles apply to the assessment of damages for personal injuries and death, whether resulting from medical negligence or from some other form of accident.[3]

(ii) *Reduced Damages Due to Successive Events*

13–156 In *Baker v Willoughby*[4] the effects of the first tort (a road traffic accident) which caused injury to the claimant's leg were obliterated by the second tort (an armed robbery resulting in the claimant being shot in the same leg) which resulted in amputation of the leg, but the House of Lords held that the damages flowing from the first tort should not be reduced. The court viewed the claimant's disability as having two concurrent causes. The second tortfeasor (applying the principle that a wrongdoer must take his victim as he finds him) would only have to pay for the

---

[1] [1996] A.C. 155. See the commentary on *Page v Smith* at [1997] C.L.J. 254. See para.13–010, above.

[2] [2000] Lloyd's Rep. Med. 161, QBD.

[3] Quantum of damages for personal injuries is too vast a topic for this book and is more than adequately dealt with elsewhere, for example Kemp & Kemp, *The Quantum of Damages* (Sweet & Maxwell).

[4] [1970] A.C. 67. This decision must now be regarded as confined to its facts since its ratio (the "concurrent causes") was comprehensively dismissed by their Lordships in *Jobling v Associated Dairies*.

additional loss caused, namely the fact that the leg was amputated rather than simply stiff. Lord Reid[5] stated the principle of "concurrent causes" thus:

> "If the later injury suffered before the date of the trial either reduces the disabilities from the injury for which the defendant is liable, or shortens the period during which they will be suffered by the plaintiff, then the defendant will have to pay less damages. But if the later injuries merely become a concurrent cause of the disabilities caused by the injury inflicted by the defendant, then in my view they cannot diminish the damages."

Lord Reid's principle was doubted by the House of Lords in *Jobling v Associated Dairies*.[6] The claimant suffered a back injury at work. Prior to trial he was diagnosed with an unconnected (previously present but dormant) disease which would have prevented his return to work in any event. The latter (non-tortious) event was taken into account (by the unanimous application of the "vicissitudes of life" principle) to reduce the damages he obtained for his back injury to ensure the claimant only received just and sufficient and not excessive compensation.

In *Heil v Rankin*[7] the Court of Appeal held that the principle that had developed whereby the occurrence of a second tort would be ignored when awarding damages against the first tortfeasor could not be justified on any juridical basis and that there was no general rule that supervening tortious (as compared with non-tortious) acts must be ignored in all circumstances when assessing damages. However, in some circumstances the second act may be ignored for purely pragmatic reasons to ensure just and full compensation is secured for the claimant, alternatively the court can award damages against each defendant that reflect the losses caused by that defendant alone, and apportion the liability for losses caused by both.[8] For example in *Webb v Barclays Bank*[9] a case concerning the apportionment of liability for the claimant's above-the-knee amputation between an employer and a hospital trust the claimant's employer was found to be 25 per cent liable (the first tort) and the negligent trust was found to be 75 per cent liable (the second tort).

(iii) *Aggravated Damages*

In *Kralj v McGrath and St Theresa's Hospital*[10] a claim for aggravated damages **13–157** was unsuccessfully advanced in a medical negligence action, on the basis of the allegedly outrageous conduct of the first defendant. This claim was rejected by Woolf J. as wholly inappropriate.[11] In *Appleton v Garrett*[12] the defendant dentist

---

[5] Lord Pearson also gave a speech, in which his main reason for rejecting the defendant's argument was that it would produce manifest injustice. Lord Guest, Lord Donovan and Viscount Dilhorne entirely agreed with the opinion of Lord Reid. The ratio of the case was thus the principle of concurrent causes.

[6] [1982] A.C. 794.

[7] [2001] Q.B. 272.

[8] See para.13–125: "Attributability of divisible injury" and also *Clerk & Lindsell on Torts*, (19th edn, Sweet & Maxwell, 2006), para.2–92: "Intervening medical treatment".

[9] [2001] Lloyd's Rep. Med. 500.

[10] [1986] 1 All E.R. 54.

[11] See para.13–010, fn.48. This decision was approved by the Court of Appeal in *AB v South West Water Services Ltd* [1993] 1 All E.R. 609.

[12] [1997] 8 Med. L.R. 75.

administered excessive dental treatment to his patients on a massive scale. Dyson J. held that the outrageous nature of the defendant's conduct also informed the appropriate remedy, awarding aggravated damages calculated as 15 per cent of each claimant's award for personal injury.[13] In New Zealand, the Court of Appeal indicated in *Ellison v L*,[14] that awards of exemplary damages should be reserved for cases of truly outrageous conduct (being conduct that was high-handed or in flagrant disregard for the patient's safety and going beyond mere negligence), which cannot be adequately punished in any other way (for example by an award of general damages). However in the case of *A v Bottrill*[15] the Privy Council considered the question of exemplary damages in New Zealand and concluded by a majority of 3:2, (reversing a decision of the Court of Appeal and restoring the order of the judge permitting a new trial in a claim against a pathologist who was for many years the only doctor examining cervical smears in the Gisborne area of New Zealand), that the power to award exemplary damages was not rigidly confined to cases where the defendant intended to cause the harm or was consciously reckless as to the risks involved. It is submitted that a similar approach should be adopted to awards of aggravated or exemplary damages in England and Wales.

(iv) *Damages in Wrongful Birth and Wrongful Conception Claims*

13-158   **An unwanted pregnancy is a personal injury.** Where the medical practitioner was negligent in the performance of a sterilisation or abortion, the principal "damage" suffered by the claimant is usually not personal injury, but the arrival of an unplanned baby. Pregnancy itself would not be regarded as personal injury if the claimant throughout wanted to become pregnant and to bear a child, even though she would not have done so if she had been warned that her general health made child-bearing dangerous.[16] Nevertheless, it has been held that an unwanted conception is a personal injury in the sense that it is an "impairment" of the

---

[13] In an Australian case, *Backwell v AAA* [1997] 1 V.R. 182, exemplary (punitive) damages were awarded to the claimant. The claimant was a participant in an artificial insemination programme run by the defendant, by whose negligence, she was artificially inseminated with semen from a donor of an incompatible blood type. She became pregnant and was advised by the defendant to have an abortion and that if she continued the pregnancy and subsequently miscarried, her identity might be revealed and adverse publicity might force the donor insemination programme to close. She was also told that if she did not agree to an abortion, it would be difficult for her to take part in that insemination programme or any other. The defendant admitted that those were false threats. The defendant's false threats had caused distress and placed the claimant in a false dilemma. They were designed to persuade her to act contrary to her religious and moral beliefs. Against her religious beliefs, the claimant underwent an abortion. It was held that it was open to the jury to award modest exemplary damages. The claimant was awarded A$125,000 in exemplary damages, reduced on appeal to A$60,000 (the same as the claimant's award for compensatory damages).

[14] [1998] 1 N.Z.L.R 416. See also *L v Robinson* [2000] 3 N.Z.L.R. 499, where the claimant had approached the defendant psychotherapist for treatment following sexual abuse. The defendant engaged in sexual misconduct whilst the claimant was his patient, thereby causing or risking causing further psychological or psychiatric harm to the claimant. The defendant was struck off the medical register, and the court also awarded compensatory and exemplary damages to reflect its condemnation of the defendant's outrageous conduct. Disciplinary action was held to be no bar to such an award.

[15] [2002] UKPC 44 reported at [2003] 1 A.C. 449.

[16] *R. v Croydon HA* [1998] Lloyd's Rep. Med. 44.

claimant's bodily condition: *Walkin v South Manchester HA*.[17] Similarly in *Das v Ganju*[18] also a case on limitation, it was held that the continuation of pregnancy in circumstances where it would have been terminated but for the alleged negligence, was "personal injury" for the purposes of s.11 of the Limitation Act 1980.

For claims resulting either from failed sterilisation or failed termination operations the trend in England and Wales[19] was to permit recovery under three main heads of damage[20]:

(1) General damages for the mother's pain and discomfort associated with pregnancy and the birth[21] (damage directly related to the pregnancy)

---

[17] [1995] 1 W.L.R. 1543, CA. This case concerned a failed female sterilisation operation that resulted in the birth of a healthy child. The claimant issued but did not serve her writ within the primary limitation period, and then issued and served a second writ seeking damages for economic loss arising out of the negligent advice and treatment that led to the unwanted birth. On a preliminary issue as to whether the shorter limitation period for personal injuries applied to the apparently economic loss claims in the second writ, the Court of Appeal held that the economic losses claimed were claims for "damages in respect of personal injuries" within the meaning of s.11(1) of the Limitation Act 1980, and that such claims for post-natal costs arose out of the same cause of action as the pre-natal pain and suffering, and that the unwanted pregnancy, whether caused by negligent advice or surgery, was a personal injury in the sense of an "impairment" within the meaning of s.38(1). Applied in *Saxby v Morgan* [1997] P.I.Q.R. P531, another case on limitation, where the Court of Appeal (Potter and Mummery L.JJ.) described the injury sustained by the claimant as being the continuation of an unwanted pregnancy. To the extent that the decision in *Walkin v South Manchester HA* is contrary to the judgments in *McFarlane v Tayside Health Board* [2000] 2 A.C. 59, HL, it has been disapproved by the Court of Appeal (Laws L.J.) in *Greenfield v Irwin* [2001] 1 W.L.R. 1279.
[18] [1999] Lloyd's Rep. Med. 198, QBD Garland J.
[19] In Scotland there was a general requirement of reasonableness in the particular circumstances of the case, see *Anderson v Forth Valley Health Board* (1997) 44 B.M.L.R. 108; *Allen v Greater Glasgow Health Board* (1998) S.L.T. 580. In Canada following *Kealey v Berezowski* [1996] 136 D.L.R. (4th) 708, the reasons for the sterilisation operation will be considered before the consequences of the failed sterilisation is accepted as a genuine injury or a "blessed event" and before the claim for healthy child-rearing costs is rejected. Thus, for example, if the birth of the unplanned child imposed unreasonable financial burdens on an impoverished family, a different outcome might result. In South Africa the Supreme Court of Appeal held in *Mukheiber v Raath* (2000) 52 B.M.L.R. 1065, in a judgment handed down on May 28, 1999 (Pre-*McFarlane*) that the liability of a doctor in a failed female sterilisation case in negligence and in negligent misrepresentation extended to covering the costs of the upbringing of the unplanned child, limited only to the parents' means and station in life and continuing until the child was reasonably able to support itself.
[20] Pre-*McFarlane* different considerations prevailed where the claimant did not want a child at all and, because of the defendant's negligence, had a handicapped child. In those circumstances the normal costs of upbringing, increased because of the handicap were recovered in: *Robinson v Salford HA* [1992] 3 Med. L.R. 270 (failed female sterilisation). In *Fish v Wilcox* [1994] 5 Med. L.R. 230 (failure to detect foetal abnormalities, loss of opportunity to terminate resulting in disabled child), the Court of Appeal held that a mother who gave up work to look after a handicapped child which would not have been born but for the defendant's negligence was not entitled to claim both the value of her nursing services and her loss of earnings.
[21] For cases where such an award was made see: *Scuriaga v Powell* (1979) 123 S.J. 406 (failed termination); *Udale v Bloomsbury AHA* [1983] 1 W.L.R. 1098 (failed female sterilisation); *Thake v Maurice* [1986] Q.B. 644, (failed male sterilisation), damages for expense of birth and loss of earnings, but no award for pain and distress of labour since the judge held that the joy of the birth offset the pain and distress of the labour; *Allen v Bloomsbury HA* [1993] 1 All E.R. 651 (failed termination).

> (2) Special damages for the financial expenditure or loss associated with or consequent upon the pregnancy and birth; and[22] (losses directly related to the pregnancy)

> (3) Economic loss caused after the birth of the unwanted child and incurred on the child's upbringing and care.[23]

13–159   **Unwanted pregnancy leading to unwanted but healthy child.** Following the decision in *McFarlane v Tayside Health Board*,[24] (a wrongful conception case where a healthy child was conceived and born as a result of a negligently performed and ineffective vasectomy) the loss claimed under the third head, namely the costs of bringing up the child is characterised as purely economic loss[25] and is not recoverable. Applying Lord Bridge's three stage test from *Caparo v Dickman*[26] for liability for economic loss to lie against a tortfeasor there must be a greater link between the negligent act and the damage than mere foreseeability. There must also be proximity and the imposition of the liability must be fair, just and reasonable. The majority held that this was the position for

---

[22] For cases where such an award was made see: *Udale v Bloomsbury AHA, ibid.; Allen v Bloomsbury HA; ibid.*

[23] For pre-*McFarlane* cases where such an award was made see: *Emeh v Kensington and Chelsea and Westminster AHA* [1985] Q.B. 1012, CA (failed female sterilisation), congenitally deformed child born; *Benarr v Kettering HA* (1988) 138 N.L.J. 179 (failed male sterilisation), where the damages included a sum for future private education as that was an expectation of this child in this particular family; *Thake v Maurice, ibid.* the defendant did not appeal against this part of the judgment, although he did appeal on liability. The claimant cross-appealed in relation to damages and recovered an additional £1,500 for pain and suffering during the unwanted pregnancy; *Gold v Haringey HA* [1988] Q.B. 481 (failed female sterilisation); *Allen v Bloomsbury HA, ibid.* It appears that no claim was made under this head in *Scuriaga v Powell* (presumably because a comparable claim for loss of earnings contingent upon the rearing of a child was conceded by the defendant, see *Greenfield v Irwin* [2001] 1 W.L.R. 1279, CA, *per* Buxton L.J. at 1288). This claim was rejected in *Udale v Bloomsbury AHA* on the grounds of public policy. *Cataford v Moreau* (1981) 114 D.L.R. (3d) 585 is a Canadian decision made at around the same time to the same effect. For a case where the claimant recovered only the additional costs of the handicap see *Salih v Enfield HA* [1991] 3 All E.R. 400 (incorrect diagnosis leading to unwanted handicapped child), the trial judge awarded the whole cost of upbringing of the handicapped child but the Court of Appeal allowed only the additional cost. However, in that case the birth of the handicapped child caused the parents to abandon their intention to have a second child, and this fact was crucial to the Court of Appeal's reasoning. The reasoning in *Salih v Enfield HA* is strongly criticised by P. R. Glazebrook in "Unseemliness Compounded by Injustice" (1992) 51 C.L.J. 226. It was argued that such litigation is morally unacceptable, and that such an action for financial loss is not maintainable in principle, following the House of Lords' decisions in *Governors of the Peabody Donation Fund v Sir Lindsay Parkinson* [1985] A.C. 210, *Caparo Industries v Dickman* [1990] 2 A.C. 605 and *Murphy v Brentwood DC* [1991] 1 A.C. 398.

[24] [2000] 2 A.C. 59

[25] The House was unanimous on the characterisation of the loss as purely economic: see Lord Slynn at 75F; Lord Steyn at 79E–G; Lord Hope at 89D; Lord Clyde at 101G, 105H; Lord Millett at 109A–C.

[26] [1990] 2 A.C. 605 at 617/618:

> "What emerges is that, in addition to the forseeability of damage, necessary ingredients in any situation giving rise to a duty of care are that there should exist between the party owing the duty and the party to whom it is owed a relationship characterised by the law as one of 'proximity' or 'neighbourhood' and that the situation should be one in which the court considers it fair, just and reasonable that the law should impose a duty of a given scope upon the one party for the benefit of the other."

a claim brought in tort against a clinician.[27] Lord Slynn, Lord Steyn and Lord Clyde envisaged that recovery of such costs would or might be permitted if an appropriate contract had been entered into, whereby the outcome was warranted.[28] Their Lordships therefore unanimously rejected the claim for the costs of upbringing of a healthy, unwanted child born as a result of a negligently performed sterilisation operation. The majority found that in cases concerning an unwanted pregnancy resulting in a healthy child, the scope of the duty of care owed by the doctors did not extend to being liable for the costs of bringing up that healthy child. Their Lordships appeared to reach this conclusion by the application of legal principle for recovery of economic rather than physical loss or loss consequent on physical damage. The mother's claim for general damages for the physical effects of the pregnancy and birth remains recoverable (head (a) above),[29] and the claim for special damages arising out of the pregnancy and birth is also recoverable.[30]

This application of the three-stage test for liability for economic loss essentially limits the scope of the defendant doctor's liability to what the court deemed was reasonable. The requirement for each head of damage claimed to pass a "reasonableness test" led the judge and then the Court of Appeal to reject the claim for the cost of a commercial surrogate pregnancy in *Briody v St Helen's & Knowsley HA*,[31] where the chances of success were very low. Applying the same test (and the "assumption of responsibility" test from *Hedley Byrne*) the genetic testing laboratory that prepared a tissue sample for pre-natal DNA analysis to screen for a hereditary blood disorder was sufficiently proximate to found a duty of care to the claimant mother who had given birth to a child with the disorder which was being screened for.[32]

Despite this clear majority approach in *McFarlane*, Lord Justice Buxton in **13–160** *Greenfield v Irwin*[33] considered the description of losses as physical or economic was not significant and that *McFarlane* had been decided by the application of a broad principle. He further considered that their Lordships' decision reached beyond the circumstances of unwanted pregnancy. There was no claim for loss of

---

[27] *per* Lord Slynn at 75F–76D; Lord Steyn at 83D–84B; Lord Hope at 94B, 95B–C, 96H–97E. Lord Clyde held at 101G–102D that the existence or otherwise of the liability was not the correct approach. He preferred a restitutionary approach with consideration of the extent of liability that the doctors thought they were undertaking and proportionality between the culpable breach and the loss caused.

[28] *per* Lord Slynn at 76C; Lord Steyn at 76H; Lord Clyde at 99E–G.

[29] *per* Lord Slynn at 74B–E (on the grounds that it is foreseeable and need not be characterised as "injury"); *per* Lord Steyn at 84C (who characterised the pregnancy as an injury); *per* Lord Hope at 87C–E and 89B–D (who considered that the physical effects of pregnancy and birth did not end with the birth and that losses sustained by the mother after the birth should be recoverable subject to remoteness); *per* Lord Clyde at 102B, 102F–H (who held that the pain, discomfort and inconvenience of the experience did qualify as a potential head of damages); Lord Millett dissenting at 114D–E held that the true loss suffered by the McFarlanes was the lost freedom to limit the size of their family. He valued this loss of personal autonomy in this case at not more than £5,000.

[30] *per* Lord Slynn at 74D; *per* Lord Steyn at 84D–E; *per* Lord Hope at 89B; Lord Clyde dissenting at 106D and Lord Millett dissenting at 114G–115A, but noting that such a claim may be possible.

[31] [2000] Lloyd's Rep. Med. 127, QBD, Ebsworth J., a case concerning the loss of a baby and subsequent emergency hysterectomy resulting in loss of fertility.

[32] *Hanan Basem Farraj & Basem M Farraj v King's Healthcare NHS Trust & Cytogenetic DNA Services Ltd* [2006] EWHC 1228, QB, reported at [2006] 2 F.C.R. 804; [2006] 90 B.M.L.R. 21.

[33] [2001] 1 W.L.R. 1279, CA.

earnings following the birth (rather than during the pregnancy) in the mother's claim for damages in *McFarlane*[34] but the issue arose in *Greenfield v Irwin*.[35] The defendant had failed to test for pregnancy before the claimant had received contraceptive injections. The claimant was pregnant and gave birth to a healthy child and claimed damages for the pain and suffering of the pregnancy and birth and loss of earnings caused by the claimant's decision to leave work and rear her child. The claim was rejected on a preliminary issue hearing and the decision upheld by the Court of Appeal. The question for decision was whether or not the general approach of *McFarlane* to remoteness of loss in negligence cases where pregnancies resulted from the negligence applied to the facts of the instant case. The loss of earnings in *McFarlane* was directly related to the pregnancy, and as such it fell within the limited recovery of damages arising out of the pregnancy. This claim was different and could not be distinguished from the rejected claim for the costs of maintenance of the child. Both were claims caused by the existence of the child, not the pregnancy, and were not recoverable at law.

13–161   **Unwanted pregnancy leading to unwanted disabled child.** Since the decision in *McFarlane v Tayside Health* Board, its most controversial effect has been its applicability (or otherwise) to cases where a disabled, unwanted child has been born as a result of either a failed sterilisation or a failure to detect a foetal defect.[36] Any reference in *McFarlane* to the recoverability of damages for the costs of bringing up a disabled child is strictly speaking obiter. The only express references were by Lord Clyde,[37] and Lord Steyn[38]:

> "If there is a distinction in cases of wrongful conception between those where the child is healthy and those where the child is unhealthy, or disabled or otherwise imperfect, it has to be noted that in the present case we are dealing with a normal birth and a healthy child." (*per* Lord Clyde.)
> "Secondly, counsel for the health board was inclined to concede that in the case of an unwanted child who was born seriously disabled the rule may have to be different. There may be force in this concession but it does not arise in the present appeal and it ought to await decision where the focus is on such cases." (*per* Lord Steyn.)

The scope of application of this decision was also limited by the fact that the claim for costs of upbringing in *McFarlane* did not include any claim for the cost of care and trouble of bringing up the child (as there almost invariably would be for a disabled child) and Lord Steyn's expressly limiting his speech to the issues that arose in the pleaded case.[39] However, the decision is reported as having overruled *Emeh v Kensington and Chelsea and Westminster HA*, which did

---

[34] Although Lord Steyn notes at 84 that the pleaded case also referred to the mother giving up work in the later stages of pregnancy.
[35] *ibid.*
[36] See Commentary following *Gail Taylor v Shropshire AHA* [2000] Lloyd's Rep. Med. 96, QBD at 107–108. NB: *Taylor* is per incuriam in so far as the decision awards damages for the cost of bringing up the child.
[37] At 99D–E.
[38] At 84A–B.
[39] *ibid.* at 77B–C.

concern a disabled child.[40] In the subsequent cases of *Parkinson v St James and Seacroft University Hospital NHS Trust*[41] and *Groom v Selby*[42] the Court of Appeal evidently considered the same economic loss test applied even where the claim concerned the wrongful birth of an unwanted, disabled child.[43]

In *Gail Taylor v Shropshire HA*[44] judgment was handed down at a quantum-only hearing on the same day as the judgment in *McFarlane*. His Honour Judge Nicholl (sitting as a High Court judge) noted that the argument in *McFarlane* had been heard, but wrongly thought that their Lordships had not yet delivered their opinions. Considering himself to be bound by the Court of Appeal authority of *Emeh v Kensington and Chelsea and Westminster HA* and the endorsement therein of the earlier case of *Scuriaga v Powell*[45] "unless or until the House of Lords repudiates them", the judge held that the reasonable costs of bringing up the unwanted and disabled child of a pregnancy that followed a failed sterilisation were recoverable, subject to offsetting the value of the child's aid and society for the period of the parent's life expectancy.[46] The mother recovered general damages of £15,000 for the physical and psychological effects of pregnancy, and an additional £25,000 for the additional burden and anxiety of bringing up a

---

[40] In the *All England Reports Emeh* is referred to as "considered". The reports also indicate that *Thake v Maurice* and *Allen v Bloomsbury HA* have been overruled. In *Rand v Dorset HA* [2000] Lloyd's Rep. Med. 181, Newman J. noted at 189 that it was unclear from the reports of the decision of the House of Lords in *McFarlane* whether the case of *Emeh* should be considered to be "overruled" as the *Weekly Law Reports* (and subsequently the *Law Reports* state), or "considered" as the All England Reports suggest. However, the judge noted that *Emeh* had proceeded on an erroneous analysis of "injury" and could not be a sound legal basis for the claims made in *Rand*. Henriques J. in *Hardman v Amin* [2001] P.N.L.R. 303, also noted at 325 that the criticism of *Emeh* was by the same two lords (Lord Steyn and Lord Clyde) who expressly reserved the application of their analysis to a case concerning a disabled child until such a case was brought before them. Accordingly, it appears to be the case that *Emeh* is only criticised in relation to the decision to award the total maintenance costs, rather than the additional cost of disability which did not arise as an alternative measure of damages for consideration in that case.

[41] [2001] EWCA Civ 560 reported at [2002] Q.B. 266, CA. The court awarded the extra costs of raising a disabled child.

[42] [2001] EWCA Civ 1522, reported at [2002] P.I.Q.R. P18; [2002] Lloyd's Rep. Med. 1.

[43] See para.13–163: Parkinson. In *Roberts v Bro Taf HA* [2001] W.L. 1422837, reported at [2002] Lloyd's Rep. Med. 182, Turner J. followed *Parkinson v St James and Seacroft University Hospital NHS Trust* in holding that a claim for the additional costs of looking after an unwanted disabled child should not be limited to what the family would have been able to afford. Following the House of Lords' decision in *Rees v Darlington Memorial Hospital NHS Trust* [2003] UKHL 52 and reported at [2004] 1 A.C. 309, the status of the Court of Appeal's decision in *Parkinson* is uncertain.

[44] *ibid.*, (a case where the mother had become pregnant following a negligent sterilisation operation and had given birth to a disabled child).

[45] *ibid.*

[46] The defendant had conceded that the claimant was entitled to damages for the pain and inconvenience of the pregnancy and further conceded that a claim for compensation for the extra "wear and tear" involved in bringing up a handicapped child where the burden of the additional anxiety and stress was not offset by the benefit and joy of the birth of a child, was recognised in law as a claim for a loss of the mother's amenity, see also *per* Lord MacFadyen in *McLelland v Greater Glasgow Health Board*, unreported, September 23, 1998. In respect of *McLelland v Greater Glasgow Health Board*, reported on appeal at (2001) S.L.T. 446: the damages representing the cost of looking after the child up to and including the age of 18 were limited to the additional costs consequent upon the child's disabilities. The rest of the damages award was upheld, including a sum in respect of the cost of care after the child reached the age of 40, modestly discounted to take account of the chance (but not certainty) that state benefits would be available.

disabled child, less £2,500, which was an arbitrary sum applied for the joy and comfort derived from the child. Past expenditure on the child was recovered and future expenditure was not to be limited to what the mother could afford. Services, past and present were valued on a scale that was a scaled-down version of the commercial costs of the services.[47] The decision in *Taylor* is clearly *per incuriam*.

13–162 **Unwanted healthy child born to a disabled mother.** *McFarlane* was affirmed by a seven-man committee of the House of Lords (Lord Bingham, Lord Nicholls, Lord Millett, Lord Scott, Lord Steyn, Lord Hope, Lord Hutton) in the case of *Rees v Darlington Memorial Hospital NHS Trust*.[48] The claimant suffered from retinitis pigmentosa. She was blind in one eye and had only limited vision in the other, with the effect that she was severely visually handicapped. She was sterilised in July 1995 because she felt that her eyesight would make it very difficult for her to look after a baby. The sterilisation was ineffective, and her healthy baby son was born in April 1997. Unfortunately the baby's father did not wish to be involved with him. The claimant sought the entire cost of bringing up this child, and the judge struck the claim out. On appeal the claim was limited to the additional costs of bringing up the child that were attributable to her own disability. Such costs were not identified in the Court of Appeal, and it is not clear what they might be. By a majority the Court of Appeal allowed the appeal with the effect that the claimant was entitled to claim such additional costs—if she could establish any. Hale L.J., in the majority, loyally (but perhaps reluctantly) followed the House of Lords decision in *McFarlane* categorising the principle in *McFarlane* as one of "deemed equilibrium" between the costs and benefits of bringing up a healthy child; Waller L.J. dissented, and both Waller L.J. and Robert Walker L.J. doubted the "deemed equilibrium" principle that Hale L.J. considered binding. On appeal the claimant had invited their Lordships to reconsider *McFarlane*, and a seven-man committee of the House of Lords: Lord Bingham, Lord Nicholls, Lord Millett, Lord Scott, Lord Steyn, Lord Hope, Lord Hutton declined to do so. All of their Lordships affirmed *McFarlane* and refused the claimant's appeal.

However, by a majority (four to three) a "gloss" was added to *McFarlane* in that this majority (which included Lord Millett, who had heard *McFarlane* before the Court of Appeal, and had then proposed an award of £5,000 to reflect the denial of personal autonomy and right to limit one's own family size) added a "conventional award" (in addition to the award for the pregnancy and the birth) to recognise the fact that the claimant had been a victim of a legal wrong. The

---

[47] This award has been considered in *Farrell v Merton Sutton & Wandsworth HA*, unreported, July 31, 2000, QBD, H.H.J. E. Steel Q.C., to be an adoption and extension of the proposed new head of claim for loss of the freedom to limit the size of one's own family suggested by Lord Millett in his dissenting opinion (and valued by him at not more than £5,000 in straightforward cases). Since the two judgments were handed down on the same day, this is doubtful.

[48] *ibid.* The respondent (claimant) effectively sought to overturn *McFarlane*. After the oral hearing and the High Court of Australia's decision in *Cattanach v Melchior* [2003] H.C.A. 38 (July 16, 2003), their Lordships sought written submissions from the parties dealing with that case, but evidently declined to follow it.

sum awarded was £15,000. Accordingly a fourth head of damages should now be added to the list in paragraph 13–158 above.[49]

Parkinson v St James and Seacroft University Hospital NHS Trust. The **13–163** status of the decision in *Parkinson* is uncertain following their Lordships' decision in *Rees v Darlington Memorial Hospital NHS Trust*:

- Lord Bingham described it as "arguably anomalous", and considered his conventional award for a legal wrong should be made irrespective of the presence of disability whether in parent or child, thereby implicitly over-ruling *Parkinson* (which had not been under appeal).

- Lord Nicholls made no direct mention of *Parkinson* but approved of Lord Bingham's reasons.

- In support of this view, Lord Millett described it as an "illegitimate gloss on *McFarlane*".

- Lord Scott expressly stated that it was inconsistent with *McFarlane*.

- However Lord Hope and Lord Hutton approved the decision and Lord Steyn approved *Parkinson*, as a "legitimate extension" of *McFarlane* (which had not involved considering a disabled child or parent).

The majority suggests that the decision was disapproved, but it is not clear that it has been overruled.[50]

Wanted pregnancy leading to unwanted disabled child. Where the claimant **13–164** wanted a child, but would have sought an abortion if she had been advised that the child she was carrying was handicapped, there are, again, two possible measures of damage to consider:

(i) the whole cost of bringing up the child; and

(ii) the additional cost of bringing up a handicapped child rather than a normal one.

In favour of the first measure it can be urged that, if she had received competent ante-natal advice, the whole cost of bringing up that child would have been avoided. On the other hand, the second measure reflects the difference between the cost which she had been led to expect (had the wanted pregnancy resulted in a healthy child) and the cost which she actually incurred (being the increased

---

[49] The House of Lords' approach in *McFarlane* was rejected by the High Court of Australia in *Cattanach v Melchior* which by a 4:3 majority held that claims for recovery of the cost of upkeep of the child born after a negligently performed sterilisation operation were allowed. As Kirby J. pointed out, since the majority approach in *McFarlane* was either implicitly or explicitly based on the three-stage test from *Caparo Industries Plc v Dickman* [1990] 2 A.C. 605, which test had been rejected by the courts of Australia (*Sullivan v Moody* (2001) C.L.R. 562), it is little surprise that the High Court of Australia declined to follow their Lordships' decision.

[50] It was presumed to "represent the law", by Mrs Justice Swift, sitting in the Court of Appeal in *Hanan Basem Farraj & Basem M Farraj v King's Healthcare NHS Trust & Cytogenetic DNA Services Ltd, ibid.*

costs of care of a disabled child). Furthermore if, after the hypothetical abortion, the claimant would have persisted in her attempt to have a normal child, the second measure may more truly reflect her actual loss. Decisions following *Mc Farlane* indicate that claims for the full cost of maintenance of a disabled child are not maintainable at law, but claims for the extra cost consequences of the child's disability will be recoverable, based on an extended principle of *Hedley Byrne v Heller*.[51]

13–165   In *Rand v East Dorset HA*[52] the defendant failed to inform the parents that a routine pregnancy scan had disclosed a likelihood of a Down's syndrome baby. It was undisputed that a termination of the pregnancy would have been chosen. Newman J. noted that following *McFarlane*, the case of *Emeh* was either overruled or erroneous. He considered that there was no distinction to be made between a healthy and a disabled child, and that the claim for costs of maintenance and care was still a claim for economic loss and as such must fail following *McFarlane* as not being maintainable in law. He also came to this conclusion on the grounds that any quantification of such a claim would involve "an invidious and morally offensive valuation" of the benefit to the claimants of their disabled child.[53] He drew a distinction between a "wrongful conception" case such as *McFarlane* and a "wrongful birth" case such as *Rand*, and noted that the breached duty in the latter case was not a duty to prevent conception. Nevertheless he held that the fact that a disabled child was born could not extend the duty wider than was permitted in *McFarlane*. However, the judge went on to note that the existence of the Abortion Act 1967 and its presumed purpose of permitting the lawful termination of pregnancies where the foetus was likely to be severely disabled meant that the defendant health authority was liable (based on the extended principle of *Hedley Byrne v Heller*[54]), for the financial consequences of its omission where that omission resulted in the loss of an opportunity to prevent the birth of a disabled child. He rejected the claims for the full cost of maintenance of the child, apparently on the grounds that this would extend the duty owed by the defendant to a wider extent than was permitted in *McFarlane*, the liability being limited to the consequences flowing from the child's disability only (i.e. the extra cost of care over and above the cost of care and maintenance of a healthy child, but limited to the parental means rather than the child's actual

---

[51] See *Rand v East Dorset HA* [2000] Lloyd's Rep. Med. 181; and *Parkinson v St James and Seacroft University Hospital NHS Trust* [2001] 3 All E.R. 97, CA. However, the status of the decision in *Parkinson* is uncertain following their Lordships' decision in *Rees v Darlington Memorial Hospital NHS Trust*. Lord Bingham described it as "arguably anomalous", and considered his conventional award for a legal wrong should be made irrespective of the presence of disability whether in parent or child, thereby implicitly overruling *Parkinson* (which had not been under appeal). Lord Nicholls made no direct mention of *Parkinson* but approved of Lord Bingham's reasons. In support of this view, Lord Millett described it as an "illegitimate gloss on *McFarlane*", and Lord Scott expressly stated that it was inconsistent with *McFarlane*. However Lord Hope and Lord Hutton approved the decision and Lord Steyn approved *Parkinson*, as a "legitimate extension" of *McFarlane* (which had not involved considering a disabled child or parent). The majority suggests that the decision was disapproved, but it is not clear that it has been overruled.
[52] [2000] Lloyd's Rep. Med. 181, QBD, Newman J. See also para.13–153, above.
[53] This valuation exercise was carried out by Judge Nicholl in *Taylor v Shropshire HA* [2000] Lloyd's Rep. Med. 96. NB: *Taylor* is per incuriam in so far as the decision awards damages for the cost of bringing up the child. See para.13–161, above.
[54] [2000] Lloyd's Rep. Med. at 193.

needs). The judge also awarded £30,000 to the claimants for the loss of amenity to their life of having to care for their disabled child.

Given the distinction made by the judge himself between wrongful conception and wrongful birth claims, there may be an argument that the strict application of the measure of damages from *McFarlane* to the latter class of case is not correct or is not required as a consequence of the *McFarlane* decision unless their Lordships should be taken to have meant their decision to apply to all wrongful birth claims and claims concerning disabled children.[55] In the light of the comments of Lord Clyde and Lord Steyn, (detailed above para.13–x) it is doubtful that this should be taken to be their intention. In *Nunnerly v Warrington HA*,[56] a disabled child was born following admittedly negligent advice. On a preliminary issue Morrison J. did not limit the claimants' award to 18 years because Morrison J. held applying the normal principles of compensation that they were entitled to be restored fully to the position they would have been in but for the negligent advice and it was likely, on the facts that they would continue to contribute to the cost of care of the child after its 18th birthday. The Court of Appeal refused the defendant permission to appeal.[57]

Loss of amenity award. In *Farrell v Merton Sutton & Wandsworth HA*[58] the judge held, relying on the new head of claim referred to by Lord Millett in his dissenting judgment as a claim for "loss of amenity", that the awards made to the parents in *Taylor* and *Rand* were not in respect of economic loss (and therefore presumably not within the ambit of *McFarlane*) but were awards to compensate for the loss of amenity to the lives of the parents of a disabled child, which imposed constraints beyond what would be expected to arise out of the birth of a healthy child. In *Rand* Newman J. expressly stated that the assessment of these general damages should not be calculated by reference to commercial costs or hourly rates for care since it was: "not an award for financial loss under the guise of general damages".[59] However, in *Taylor*, the use of discounted commercial care rates on the basis of the principle from *Housecroft v Burnett*[60] (commercial

13–166

---

[55] The principle that a claimant could not recover the costs of the upbringing of a healthy child was held by Ian Kennedy J. in *Richardson v LRC Products Ltd* [2000] Lloyd's Rep. Med. 280, to apply equally to claims brought for breach of statutory duty as to claims brought in negligence.

[56] [2003] Lloyd's Rep. Med. 365. In the period between the decision and the appeal, their Lordships' judgments in *McFarlane* was handed down. Permission to appeal was refused. The case was to be decided on the basis of pre-*McFarlane* law since the parties had entered into a compromise agreement.

[57] In *McLelland v Greater Glasgow Health Board* 1999 S.C. 305, Sc. Ct. Sess. (OH), the defendant's appeal was allowed (2001 S.L.T. 446) to the extent that the damages representing the cost of looking after the child up to and including the age of 18 were limited to the additional costs consequent upon the child's disabilities. The rest of the damages award was upheld. Both parents also recovered separately for mental distress (falling short of mental illness) suffered on discovery of the child's condition and during its upbringing. The court limited the award in that way because it took judicial notice of the fact that the state would provide benefits to keep a disabled adult. In the light of the more recent decisions concerning claims raised under the European Convention on Human Rights, it is submitted that this limiting approach may be incompatible with Art.8. See para.13–x below.

[58] (2001) 57 B.M.L.R. 158, a case concerning the birth of a disabled child following an emergency Caesarean section operation.

[59] [2000] Lloyd's Rep. Med. 181 at 201.

[60] [1986] 1 All E.R. 332, CA. NB: *Taylor* is per incuriam in so far as the decision awards damages for the cost of bringing up the child. See para.13–161, above.

costs of care scaled down by 25 per cent) had been expressly approved and was used in calculating the enhancement of the general damages award for the physical and psychological effects of pregnancy to take into account the additional burden and anxiety of bringing up a disabled child.

13–167　　　The current approach to each of the claims brought by the mother or parents of a disabled child in a wrongful birth claim was demonstrated by the judgment of Henriques J. in *Hardman v Amin*.[61] On the preliminary issue of the basis and extent of damages to be awarded and whether or not a claim for past and future care costs following a wrongful birth of a disabled child was barred after *McFarlane*, Henriques J. held that the claim was not precluded by their Lordships' decision and was not limited to the parents' means. The case concerned a child born disabled following the expectant mother's infection with rubella.[62] The defendant general practitioner admitted a failure to warn the claimant of the probable damage to her child. If she had been so warned the claimant would have terminated the pregnancy. Henriques J. held that the mother's claim for loss of earnings was a claim for loss consequential upon the personal injury claim of the suffering and inconvenience of the pregnancy.[63] The claim for past and future care given by the mother fell to be determined in accordance with *Housecroft v Burnett* and could alternatively be awarded as damages for the loss of amenity to private life caused by the anxiety and stress of the care of and obligations to a disabled child. As to the claim for maintenance and upkeep of the extra costs of a disabled child, this was a claim for pure economic loss, and that in circumstances where the claimant relied upon the defendant doctor not only to diagnose her rubella infection, but also to advise her of her lawful entitlement to a termination under the Abortion Act 1967, the extra requirements for establishing liability in addition to foreseeability of the loss (namely proximity and that imposition of such liability was fair just and reasonable) were present.[64] Recovery of the basic maintenance costs was not sought[65] and would, in any event not have been granted, applying both *McFarlane*, and, more particularly the factually similar case of *Salih v Enfield HA*, where the Court of Appeal took into account the claimants' decision to have no more children instead of continuing to increase their family. The decision has been followed in *Groom v Selby*,[66] where it was accepted, on behalf of the claimant that the causal proximity between the breach and the damage suffered in the cases of *Rand* and *Hardman* was stronger than in this case. In *Groom v Selby* the defendant failed to carry out a pregnancy test

---

[61] [2001] P.N.L.R. 303, QBD.

[62] Similar facts to *Salih v Enfield HA* [1991] 3 All E.R. 400.

[63] Citing Lord Clyde's speech in *McFarlane*. In this case the damages for the personal injury were agreed at a modest sum to reflect the fact that the claimant had wanted this pregnancy, and but for the negligence would have gone through a termination and become pregnant again on two further occasions, but had been subjected to a Caesarean section and the shock of realising that her child was born seriously disabled. The claim for loss of earnings was in principle allowed but in practice in this case was reduced to nil by virtue of a set-off of the loss and expense of a future pregnancy and childbirth.

[64] The judge also found that recovery was justified on the grounds of distributive justice and restitution for the wrong done.

[65] Counsel for the claimant reserved the right to raise the claim if the case went to the House of Lords, but recognised that the court of first instance was bound by *Salih*.

[66] [2001] Lloyd's Rep. Med. 39, QBD, Peter Clark J. Affirmed in the Court of Appeal at [2001] EWCA Civ 1522, reported at [2002] P.I.Q.R. P18; [2002] Lloyd's Rep. Med. 1.

before sterilising the claimant. The claimant was pregnant but discovered the pregnancy at a late stage when termination was rejected as an option. She gave birth prematurely to a disabled child. The necessary proximity was held to be present to make the defendant liable for the loss properly recoverable under the application of the fair, just and reasonable test from *Caparo* as approved in *McFarlane*. The maintenance costs (comparable to the costs of the upbringing of a healthy child) were again not claimed,[67] but the claim for the additional costs of the child's disability was allowed.[68]

The case of *AD v East Kent Community NHS Trust*[69] concerned a mental patient who had become pregnant as a result of (allegedly) negligent supervision in a mixed psychiatric ward where she was treated, having been sectioned under s.2 of the Mental Health Act 1983. The (healthy) child was looked after by the claimant's mother. Cooke J. held that the claimant could not claim in respect of the cost of looking after the child on the basis that she could not look after the child herself, and would incur no costs. But he did say[70] that he saw no distinction as a matter of principle between unwanted children born to mothers with physical disabilities and those born to mothers with mental disabilities. The decision was affirmed by the Court of Appeal.[71] The claimant petitioned the House of Lords for permission to appeal, but the intervening decision of their Lordships in *Rees v Darlington Memorial Hospital NHS Trust*[72] resulted in the petition being withdrawn.

(v) *Impact of the Human Rights Act 1998*

The more recent cases have included an additional claim under Art.8 of the European Convention for the Protection of Human Rights and Fundamental Freedoms. Article 8 entitles a person to "respect for his (her) private and family life and his home". It was noted in *Hardman v Amin*[73] by Henriques J. that although this entitlement had not been a determining factor in his decision, nevertheless his decision reached by the application of the common law was compatible with Art.8. The disabled child's family, was compensated for the additional costs of care, and the family was therefore able to make decisions concerning the child's care independently of the state. The compatibility of the award of damages limited to the additional costs of the disability with Art.8 (and Art.6) was affirmed in *Groom v Selby*,[74] and was held to be proportionate to the interests of both claimant and defendant,[75] and consistent with the principle of

13–168

---

[67] Counsel for the claimant reserved the right to raise the claim if the case went to the House of Lords.
[68] The claims for general and special damages arising out of or consequent upon the suffering and inconvenience of the pregnancy were conceded in principle by the defendant.
[69] [2003] P.I.Q.R. P3; [2002] Lloyd's Rep. Med. 424.
[70] At para.13 of his judgment.
[71] [2002] EWCA Civ 1872, reported at [2003] 3 All E.R. 1167.
[72] [2003] UKHL 52, reported at [2004] 1 A.C. 309.
[73] [2001] P.N.L.R. 303.
[74] [2001] Lloyd's Rep. Med. 39, Peter Clark J. Affirmed in the Court of Appeal at [2001] EWCA Civ 1522, reported at [2002] P.I.Q.R. P18; [2002] Lloyd's Rep. Med. 1. This point was not considered on appeal.
[75] Applying the principles of Lord Steyn's judgment in *Frost v Chief Constable of South Yorkshire Police* [1999] 2 A.C. 455.

distributive justice referred to by Lord Steyn in *McFarlane*.[76] In *Greenfield v Irwin*[77] Lord Justice Buxton reviewed the point more comprehensively and came to the conclusion that there was no reason to think that Art.8 imposed any requirements concerning regimes of damages in claims involving unwanted pregnancies or births.[78]

(vi) *Claims by Unwanted Disabled Child*[79]

13–169 A separate question which arises in such cases is whether the handicapped child can make his or her own claim to recover damages on the ground that he or she ought not to have been born at all. This was considered in *McKay v Essex AHA*.[80]

(vii) *Proportionate Damages in* Fairchild *Exception Cases*

13–170 Insofar as the House of Lords' decision in *Barker v Corus (UK) Ltd* (decision handed down on May 3, 2006) displaced the rule of joint and several liability for victims who have contracted mesothelioma as a result of exposure to asbestos it has been almost entirely overtaken by s.3 of the Compensation Act 2006 which received Royal Assent on July 25, 2006. This section provides for joint and several liability between responsible defendants. It has retrospective force except where a claim was settled (with or without issue of legal proceedings), or proceedings were determined before May 3, 2006. It would appear their Lordships' proposition of proportionate liability and damages where the *Fairchild* exception has been applied has now been displaced by act of Parliament.

---

[76] And by Lord Hoffmann in *Frost, ibid.*
[77] [2001] 1 W.L.R. 1279; [2001] EWCA Civ 113, paras 31–37, and para.48.
[78] See also Ch.7: Human Rights and Professionals.
[79] See also (iv) Wrongful life at para.13–021, above.
[80] [1982] 1 Q.B. 1166.

CHAPTER 14

REGULATION OF FINANCIAL SERVICES

1. General

14–001　　This chapter provides an overview of the regulatory regime under the Financial Services and Markets Act 2000 ("FSMA") to the extent relevant to this work. Aspects of the regime apply to a large number of practitioners. Accordingly, it is convenient to deal with them in a separate chapter. It is, however, beyond the scope of this chapter to provide a detailed review of the law relating to regulation of financial services in the United Kingdom. FSMA and related material, including other legislation, subsidiary legislation, rules, codes, European directives and published guidance, are extensive and complex. Reference should be made to specialist works.[1] It is also beyond the scope of this chapter to deal with the law relating to banking, insurance and pensions. The main focus is upon those activities of financial practitioners, principally those relating to investment, as are within the scope of the FSMA regulatory regime.

14–002　　The FSMA regulatory regime has now been in force since December 1, 2001. Preceding events are governed by predecessor regulatory regimes. The latter, especially the regime under the Financial Services Act 1986 Act ("the 1986 Act"), will remain of relevance for several years in the determination of claims, but are of diminishing significance. Predecessor regulatory regimes are not addressed in this book. For a summary description of the regime under the 1986 Act, reference should be made to the previous edition of this book.

14–003　　FSMA is much wider in scope than the 1986 Act, regulating not only investment businesses but also the banks and mortgage lenders, insurance companies and Lloyd's businesses as well "mutuals" (building societies and friendly societies). Despite its length, FSMA is distinctly and deliberately skeletal in some

---

[1] For the text of such material and detailed commentary, see Lomnicka and Powell, *Encyclopedia of Financial Services Law* (Sweet & Maxwell). This chapter draws considerably on some of that commentary.

areas. Extensive secondary legislative powers are given to the Treasury and the FSA. These powers have been exercised and there is an immense volume of instruments (including regulations, rules and guidance) made by the Treasury and the FSA which contain the body of the regulatory regime. Key terms to the scope of the regulatory regime are "regulated activities", "financial promotion" and "investment", the operative relevant definitions of which are contained in detailed orders made by the Treasury.[2] Rules and guidance made by the FSA are compiled in "The FSA Handbook".[3]

(a) The FSA

FSMA confers powers on a single statutory regulator, the FSA.[4] Nevertheless, **14–004** the Treasury retains overall responsibility for the regulatory regime as a whole and the Bank of England continues to be responsible for the stability of the financial sector. The regulatory capacity of the FSA is remarkably large in terms of scope, powers and discretion. It regulates the whole of the financial sector and concerns itself with both prudential and conduct of business aspects. It has very wide-ranging powers of rule-making,[5] authorisation of firms,[6] approval of key personnel,[7] monitoring, investigation, intervention and discipline.[8] It also undertakes the official listing function as the competent authority under EC Directives, styling itself as "UKLA" (the "UK Listing Authority").[9] The Act requires the FSA to discharge its "general functions" within a framework of four defined "regulatory objectives" and having regard to seven factors, although these operate at a very general level and are not expressed to be applicable to specific decisions.[10] The regulatory objectives are: market confidence, public awareness, the protection of consumers and the reduction of financial crime. The Act provides for a compensation scheme[11] and an ombudsman scheme (the Financial

---

[2] See further paras. 14–023 and 14–026, below as to the RAO and FPO.

[3] See further paras 14–034 *et seq.*, below.

[4] See its website: *www.fsa.gov.uk.*

[5] See especially FSMA, Pt X (ss.138–164, "Rules and Guidance"). The FSA has power to make rules under many other provisions in the Act.

[6] See *ibid.*, Pt IV (ss.40–55,"Permission to carry on Regulated Activities"). See further para.14-011, below.

[7] See *ibid.*, ss.59–70 (a new power). See further para.14–012, below.

[8] The broad nature of FSA's powers is apparent from the titles to the following Parts of the Act which confer various powers upon it: Pt V (ss.56–71,"Performance of Regulated Activities"); Pt VII (ss.104–117,"Control over Business Transfers"); Pt VIII (ss.118–131,"Penalties for Market Abuse"); Pt XI (ss.165–177, "Information Gathering and Investigations"); Pt XII (ss.178–192, "Control over Authorised Persons"); Pt XIII (ss.193–204,"Incoming Firms: Intervention by Authority"); Pt XIV (ss.205–211,"Disciplinary Measures"); Pt XVII (ss.235–284,"Collective Investment Schemes"); Pt XVIII, ss.285–301, "Recognised Investment Exchanges and Clearing Houses"); Pt XIX, ss.314–324, "Lloyd's"); Pt XX (ss.325–333,("Provision of Financial Services by Members of the Professions"); Pt XXI (ss.334–339, "Mutual Societies"); Pt XXII (ss.340–346) ("Auditors and Actuaries"); Pt XXIII (ss.347–354, "Public Record, Disclosure of Information and Co-operation"); Pt XXIV (ss.355–379, "Insolvency"); Pt XXV (ss.380–386, "Injunctions and Restitution"); Pt XXVI (ss.387–396, "Notices").

[9] FSMA, Pt XVI (ss.72–103). The FSA took over as the "competent authority" from The (London) Stock Exchange after it demutualised in May 2000.

[10] *ibid.*, s.2. For the "regulatory objectives" see s.2(2)) and ss.3–6. For the factors, see s.2(3). The factors are called "regulatory principles" by the FSA.

[11] *ibid.*, Pt XV (ss.212–224). See paras 14–125 to 14–139, below.

Services Ombudsman Scheme or "FOS").[12] A tribunal is established, the Financial Services and Markets Tribunal,[13] with powers of control over the FSA in the exercise of its decision-making powers over those persons it regulates. The FSA remains subject to judicial review in the exercise of its functions under FSMA, as under the 1986 Act.[14]

14–005   **Limited immunity.** FSMA[15] confers upon the FSA limited immunity from liability in damages (as did the 1986 Act),[16] including when acting as the UK Listing Authority.[17] Thus the FSA is generally not liable in damages for anything done, or omitted to be done, in the discharge or purported discharge of its functions. The same applies as regards any person who is, or acting as, a member, officer or member of the staff of the FSA. Such immunity is limited in two respects. First, the immunity is lost if the act or omission "is shown to have been in bad faith". Secondly, the immunity does not extend to awards of damages as a result of s.6(1) of the Human Rights Act 1998. Other bodies and persons are accorded like limited immunity.[18] In construing the meaning of "bad faith" it is relevant to have regard to the recent consideration of the concept by the House of Lords in the context of the tort of misfeasance in public office and the similar limited immunity provision in the Banking Act 1987.[19] The meaning of the term in the context of a like provision in 1986 Act[20] was considered by Lightman J. in *Melton Medes Ltd v Securities and Investments Board*[21] in striking out an action for damages against the SIB for disclosure of information in contravention of disclosure restrictions in the 1986 Act.[22] He considered that it connoted "either (a) malice in the sense of personal spite or a desire to injure for improper reasons; or (b) knowledge of absence of power to make the decision in question".[23]

---

[12] FSMA, Pt XVI (ss.225–234). See paras 14–103 to 14–125, below.

[13] *ibid.*, Pt IX (ss.132–137) and Sch.13. Its decisions are available from its website: *www.financeandtaxtribunals.gov.uk.*

[14] For examples of (unsuccessful) applications against the SIB (in the context of the pensions misselling review), see *R. v Securities and Investments Board Ex p. Independent Financial Advisers Association* [1995] 2 B.C.L.C. 76; *R. v Securities and Investments Board Ex p. Sun Life Assurance Society Plc* [1996] 2 B.C.L.C. 150. For a case on the judicial review of the FSA, see *R. v FSA Ex p. Davies* [2003] EWCA 1128.

[15] See FSMA, s.1(3) and Sch.1, para.19.

[16] 1986 Act, s.187.

[17] FSMA, s.102.

[18] i.e. the complaints investigator, not any person appointed to conduct an investigation on his behalf (see FSMA, Sch.1, paras 7, 8(8) and 19(2)): the FSA as the UK Listing Authority (s.102), the compensation scheme manager (s.222), recognised investment exchanges (RIEs) and recognised clearing houses (RCHs) (s.291) and ombudsmen (Sch.17, para.10). As to the position under the 1986 Act, s.187, the limited immunity did not extend to RIEs or RCHs.

[19] See Ch.15, para.15–031.

[20] 1986 Act, s.187.

[21] [1995] Ch. 137

[22] 1986 Act, s.179, a similar provision to FSMA, s.348.

[23] [1995] Ch. 137 at 147. He cited Wade, *Administrative Law* (6th edn, Oxford University Press, 1988) at p.782 which in turn relied on the discussion of "malice" in *Bourgoin SA v Ministry of Agriculture* [1986] Q.B. 716. See also *Three Rivers DC v Bank of England (No.3)* [2000] 1 W.L.R. 1220, HL.

(b) *The General Prohibition*

The regulatory regime under FSMA proceeds from the general prohibition[24] **14–006**
(specifically so called) against any person carrying on "a regulated activity"[25] in
the United Kingdom unless an authorised or exempt person. Contravention of the
general prohibition (the "authorisation offence")[26] attracts criminal liability[27]
and civil liability for which there are a range of remedies.[28]

Territorial scope. The general prohibition only relates to the carrying on of a **14–007**
regulated activity *in the United Kingdom*. The wording is apt to cover "inward"
activity which affects the United Kingdom market.[29] As regards "outward"
activity by persons in the United Kingdom targeting an overseas market, some
guidance is given in FSMA. Thus the natural meaning of "in the United
Kingdom" is extended by applying the so-called "home country control" principle of the single market directives whereby the "home state" has responsibility
for its firms no matter where within the EEA they operate.[30]

(c) *The Financial Promotion Restriction*

FSMA restricts "financial promotion"[31] by requiring that it is carried out only by **14–008**
or with the approval of an authorised person[32] (the "financial promotion restriction").[33] There are, however, a number of significant exceptions.[34] As in relation
to contravention of the general prohibition, contravention of the financial promotion restriction attracts criminal liability[35] and civil liability for which there are
a range of remedies.[36] Authorised persons cannot be in breach of the restriction,
but if they act in breach of the FSA's financial promotion rules applicable to
them,[37] the usual disciplinary consequences may follow and they may incur
statutory liability for damages under s.150 of FSMA.[38]

Territorial scope. Unlike the general prohibition, the financial promotion **14–009**
restriction is not expressed by reference to promotion "in the United Kingdom".
This is unsurprising given modern forms of communication. A distinction needs

---

[24] FSMA, s.19.
[25] As to the meaning of this term see paras 14–022 and 14–023, below.
[26] FSMA, ss.417(1), 23(2).
[27] *ibid.*, s.23.
[28] See paras. 14–071, 14–083 to 14–094 and 14–097, below.
[29] There are exclusions in the RAO (as to which see para.14–023, below) for investment business
activity by "overseas persons" (defined in RAO, art.3), e.g. RAO, art.72(1)(2).
[30] FSMA, s.418, as amended. As to the single market directives, see FSMA, Sch.3 and para.14–019,
below.
[31] For the meaning of financial promotion, see para.14–025, below.
[32] FSMA, s.21.
[33] So called not in FSMA but in the FPO (see para.14–026, below).
[34] Contained in the FPO: see para.14–026, below.
[35] FSMA, s.25.
[36] See paras 14–071, 14–083 to 14–094 and 14–097 below.
[37] Made under FSMA, s.145. For such rules, see para.14–029, below.
[38] See paras 14–077 to 14–079 and 14–102, below.

to be drawn between what may be termed "inward" and "outward" communications, i.e. communications originating from outside and inside the United Kingdom respectively. In the case of the former, the restriction only applies if it is "capable of having effect in the United "Kingdom".[39] This is hardly a significant limitation. Internet communications even from outside the United Kingdom would be caught by the restriction. As for "outward" communications originating from the United Kingdom, these are all prima facie caught, although the Treasury may by order provide otherwise in given circumstances.[40]

(d) *Authorised Persons*

14–010   There are a number of categories of authorised persons[41] (called "firms" in the FSA's Handbook) but there are two main categories. The first consists of domestic concerns authorised by virtue of having obtained a "Part IV permission"[42] from the FSA to carry on one or more regulated activities. The second consists of undertakings authorised in other EEA Member States and entitled to exercise their "single European passport" so as to establish branches or provide cross-border services in the United Kingdom. This second category of "incoming firms" is, in accordance with the United Kingdom's EC law obligations, granted automatic authorisation for the purposes of FSMA. The latter category comprises two types of such firms, "EEA firms"[43] and "Treaty firms".[44] They are subject to regulation as "authorised persons" by the FSA when they operate in the United Kingdom, but in a manner that is consistent with EC law which provides for a division of responsibility between "home" (i.e. another EEA Member State) and "host" (United Kingdom) regulators.[45]

14–011   **Part IV permission**. Part IV of FSMA[46] contains elaborate provisions relating to the grant of "Part IV permission" to domestic concerns to carry on regulated activities. The FSA is given a very wide discretion, especially as to the scope and terms of any permission it grants.[47] It may impose limitations[48] and requirements[49] as to how a person is, or is not, to act. The FSA must ensure that the person concerned will satisfy and will continue to satisfy the "threshold conditions" in Sch.6 in relation to a regulated activity.[50] Of central importance are the

---

[39] FSMA s.21(3). But note s.21(5).
[40] *ibid.*, s.21(5). See FPO, art.12. As to the FPO, see para.14–026 below.
[41] Listed in FSMA, s.31.
[42] See *ibid.*, s.40(4).
[43] Defined in FSMA, s.425(1)(a) and Sch.3 (essentially firms exercising their "passport" under single market financial services directives, i.e. the Banking Consolidation Directive, the Insurance Directives and the Investment Services Directive (soon to be the Markets in Financial Investments Directive) (see further FSMA, Sch.3).
[44] Defined in *ibid.*, s.425(2)(b) and Sch.4 (essentially firms exercising their rights under the EU Treaty).
[45] Similarly, UK authorised firms are also able to exercise their single European passport throughout the EEA and special provision is made for this in FSMA, s.37 and Sch.3, Pt III.
[46] ss.40–55.
[47] FSMA, s.42.
[48] *ibid.*, s.42(7).
[49] *ibid.*, s.43. This may include an "assets requirement" (s.48(4)) entailing the freezing of assets or their transfer to a trustee.
[50] *ibid.*, s.41 and Sch.6, as amended. See also the "COND" Module of the FSA Handbook.

requirements that the person concerned has adequate resources and is suitable (i.e. fit and proper). The FSA's procedures and policy as to the grant of permission is contained its Authorisation Manual ("AUTH") which forms part of the Regulatory Processes block in its Handbook.[51]

(e) *Approved Persons*

FSMA introduces an additional layer of regulation in the approved person regime.[52] Thus key persons within businesses that are authorised (either those with significant managerial control or those dealing with customers or their property) must be approved and regulated by the FSA.   **14–012**

(f) *Exempt Persons*

FSMA makes provision for certain "exempt persons".[53] Three categories of person are exempt: (1) "appointed representatives" of authorised persons[54]; (2) recognised investment exchanges and recognised clearing houses[55]; and (3) persons specified, or within a class specified, by Treasury order.[56] They do not contravene the general prohibition if they carry on a regulated activity in the United Kingdom as long as they are exempt persons in relation to that activity. Unlike authorised person status, exempt person status is generally conferred to a limited extent in relation to certain regulated activities. Thus if exempt persons stray outside such activities they lose exempt person status and breach the general prohibition (unless they become authorised in respect of that other activity). Although exempt persons are subject to the financial promotion restriction,[57] the relevant Treasury order exempts non-real time and solicited real-time communications made or directed by an exempt person for the purposes of his business in relation to which he is exempt.[58]   **14–013**

(g) *Appointed Representatives*

Persons authorised to carry on regulated activities under FSMA, including product provider firms and independent intermediaries, frequently do so through agents called "appointed representatives".[59] Specific provision is made for them under FSMA.[60] An appointed representative, rather than being required to become an authorised person, is accorded exempt person status,[61] but only so   **14–014**

---

[51] See paras 14–034 *et seq.*, below.
[52] See FSMA, ss.59–63.
[53] Defined in FSMA, s.417(1).
[54] FSMA, s.39. See further paras 14–014 to 14–016, below.
[55] *ibid.*, s.285.
[56] *ibid.*, s.38. See the FSMA (Exemption) Order 2002, SI 2001/1201, as amended.
[57] See para.14–008, above.
[58] The FPO, art.16. See para.14–026, below.
[59] FSMA, ss.417(1) and 39(2).
[60] FSMA, s.39.
[61] See para.14–013, above.

long as an authorised person, termed his "principal", takes responsibility, including regulatory responsibility, for him. Thus regulation of appointed representatives is, to some extent, sub-contracted to authorised persons.[62] A person cannot simultaneously be both an appointed representative in respect of some activities and an authorised person in relation to others. [63] The principal authorised person's Part IV permission must extend to all of his appointed representatives' activities.

(i) *Status Requirements*

14–015   To be exempt as an appointed representative, a person must fulfil two conditions.[64] First, he must be in a contractual relationship with an authorised person, "his principal", which complies with requirements prescribed by Treasury order and which requires or permits him to carry on business of a kind prescribed in the order. Business so prescribed[65] is generally that which comprises arranging deals in investment, safeguarding and administering investments, advising on investments and agreeing to carry on such activities as are defined in the RAO.[66] Secondly, the principal must accept responsibility in writing for the appointed representative's activities in carrying on that business. An appointed representative is only exempt in relation to those activities for which his principal has accepted responsibility and therefore he ceases to have that status and so potentially breaches the general prohibition[67] if he strays outside the scope of his principal's responsibility.

(ii) *Liability of Principal under FSMA*

14–016   Apart from ordinary common law principles[68] which will apply to render the principal liable for certain activities of his appointed representative, FSMA makes further provision clarifying the responsibility of the principal.[69] Nevertheless, these provisions only apply in relation to business for which the principal has accepted responsibility.[70] First, whatever the position at common law,[71] the principal is responsible for *anything* done or omitted to be done by the appointed representative in carrying out business for which his principal has accepted

---

[62] See esp. FSMA, s.39(3) and (4).

[63] See FSMA, s.39(1) (the words in parenthesis). Similarly a person cannot be both an exempt person by reason of his status as an appointed representative in relation to some activities and an exempt person other than by virtue of such status in relation to other activities: see FSMA, s.38(2).

[64] FSMA, s.39(1).

[65] See the Financial Services and Markets Act 2000 (Appointed Representatives) Regulations 2001 (SI 2001/1217), as amended.

[66] RAO, arts 25, 40, 53 and 64. As to the RAO, see para.14–023, below.

[67] In FSMA s.19. See paras 14–027 and 14–028, above.

[68] Especially in relation to agency (see Ch.15, para.15–024 below) and, as to criminal law, principles of vicarious liability.

[69] FSMA, s.39.

[70] Thus in *Emmanuel v DBS Management Plc* [1999] 2 Lloyd's Rep. P.N. 593 (a decision under the 1986 Act, s.44), the principal was not liable for activities which were held to be outside the scope of the business for which he had accepted responsibility and for activities undertaken before the agent became an appointed representative. See further as to this case, Ch.15, n.71 under para.15–038.

[71] Which to some extent limits the extent to which a principal is responsible for the activities of his agent.

responsibility "to the same extent as if he had expressly permitted it".[72] Thus the principal will be liable to third parties and accountable to the FSA as his regulator, for the activities of his appointed representative, in so far as this depends on such express permission. In particular, the principal will be liable to third parties on contracts made by his representative without the third party having to prove that the representative was actually (or ostensibly) authorised by the principal to act. And he may be liable as joint tortfeasor with the appointed representative on the basis that he is taken to have expressly permitted any tort the appointed representative engages in. Secondly, special provision is made in relation to determinations whether the principal has complied with a provision contained in or made under the Act (only). Here again anything done (or omitted) by the appointed representative in carrying on the business for which the principal has accepted responsibility is attributed to the principal.[73] Once more the wording of this subsection is apt to cover both civil and criminal (and disciplinary) liability but only under the Act. In particular, it enables the FSA to hold the principal responsible for all the activities of the appointed representative but only in deciding if the principal has complied with the regulatory regime. There is no direct attribution (for example, on analogy with the vicarious responsibility of an employer for the torts of his employee) of breaches by the appointed representative to the principal. There is only attribution of the representative's acts and omissions for the purposes of deciding if the principal himself has been in breach.

(h) *Members of Professions*

FSMA[74] replaced those provisions of the 1986 Act[75] which enabled some 15,000 **14–017** professionals, mainly solicitors and accountants, to become authorised persons by being "certified" by their "recognised professional body" ("RPB"). It replaces the concept of "recognised professional body" with "designated professional body" ("DPB"). All bodies which were RPBs immediately before FSMA was brought into force,[76] became DPBs.[77] The position under the 1986 Act was that professionals became authorised persons by virtue of their "certification" by their professional body. In contrast, FSMA exempts from the general prohibition the carrying on of certain incidental regulated activities by members of DPBs in certain circumstances.[78] Such incidental activities are termed

---

[72] FSMA, s.39(3).
[73] FSMA, s.39(4).
[74] Pt XX (ss.325–333).
[75] See 1986 Act, ss.15–21.
[76] Prior to the enactment of FSMA, there were nine RPBs: the three Law Societies (of England and Wales, Scotland and Northern Ireland), the three Institutes of Chartered Accountants (in England and Wales, Scotland and Northern Ireland), the Institute of Actuaries and the Association of Certified Accountants. The Insurance Brokers' Registration Council was an RPB, but ceased to be one in 2000.
[77] The Treasury (not the FSA) is empowered to "designate" professional bodies satisfying certain conditions: FSMA, s.326, and has done so: The Financial Services and Markets Act 2000 (Designated Professional Bodies) Order 2001, (SI 2001/1226), as amended by to add the Council for Licensed Conveyancers (see SI 2004/3352) and the Royal Institution of Chartered Surveyors (see SI 2006/58).
[78] See FSMA, s.327.

"exempt regulated activities".[79] The role of the FSA in relation to such professionals is limited.[80] The rulebook of a DPB, insofar as it covers "exempt regulated activities", is subject to the approval of the FSA,[81] but otherwise the FSA has very limited rule-making powers. Thus it can make "disclosure rules"[82] and it may issue directions generally limiting the scope of the exemption on investor protection grounds and thus requiring certain activities to be regulated directly by it.[83] As against any professional person, the FSA may issue a "disapplication order" disapplying the exemption from the general prohibition in relation to him if it deems him not "fit and proper".[84] The FSA has a more general power to make a prohibition order prohibiting any individual (including a professional) from performing a "specified function".[85]

14–018   Professional firms which carry on "mainstream" investment business need to be authorised by the FSA and are subject to all the provisions applicable to authorised persons. These are firms, for example, that give investment advice (such as arranging life assurance and personal pensions), manage investments on a discretionary basis or undertake major corporate finance advice. However, so that there is a "level playing field" for authorised and unauthorised members of the professions in relation to the carrying on of similar activities, the FSA disapplies or modifies parts of its Handbook in relation to authorised professional firms when they carry on "non-mainstream regulated activities" (as defined to mean, in essence, exempt regulated activities when carried on by authorised firms).[86]

(i) *European Aspects*

14–019 The financial services sector has long been the subject of European Community directives. These have been given effect in United Kingdom legislation. Leaving aside major directives relating to banking and insurance, significant directives relate to the prospectus requirements when securities are offered to the public or admitted to trading,[87] the disclosure obligations in relation to listed securities,[88]

---

[79] But members of a DPBs are not "exempt persons" (see para.14–013, above) for the purposes of FSMA.

[80] In order to enable it to exercise its residual regulatory control, it must keep itself informed as to DPBs (s.325(1)) and keep under review the desirability of exercising its Pt XX powers (s.325(3)).

[81] FSMA, s.332(5).

[82] *ibid.*, s.332(1)(2): for the purpose of ensuring that their clients are aware that the professionals concerned are not regulated by the FSA.

[83] *ibid.*, ss.328, 330. See the PROF Module of the FSA Handbook.

[84] *ibid.*, s.329. Note the usual procedural safeguards in s.331 of a "warning notice" (see s.387) followed by a "decision notice" (see s.388) and a right of reference to the Financial Services and Markets Tribunal (see Pt IX, ss.132–137).

[85] *ibid.*, s.56 (note s.56(8)(b)).

[86] See the PROF Module, Ch.5.

[87] See the Prospectus Directive, ("POD"), (Directive 2003/71 (replacing the Prospectus (Public Offers) Directive (Council Directive 89/298) as regards unlisted securities and amending the Consolidated Admissions and Reporting Directive (Council Directive 2001/34) as regards listed securites) This was given effect in the UK by Pt VI of FSMA.

[88] See the Transparency Obligations Directive, ("TOD"), (Council Directive 2004/109)—due for implementation on January 7, 2007, in part by amendment to Pt VI of FSMA.

collective investment schemes,[89] market abuse,[90] capital requirements,[91] investment services,[92] and investor compensation schemes.[93]

(j) *Human Rights Law*

The influence of the Human Rights Act 1998 ("the HRA")[94] can be clearly seen   **14–020**
in FSMA.[95] Nevertheless, it should not automatically be assumed that FSMA
safeguards all Convention rights and particular provisions should be examined
closely in light of the HRA. The FSA is clearly a public authority for the
purposes of the HRA, at least when it is carrying out functions of a public nature.
As such, it is prohibited from acting in a way that is incompatible with a
Convention right.[96] The limited immunity from liability in damages conferred
upon the FSA by FSMA, does not extend to an award of damages made against
it in relation to an act or omission which is unlawful as a result of s.6(1) of the
HRA.[97] Although the primary aim of the HRA is to protect the rights of
individuals, the European Court of Human Rights has long recognised that a
"company" may be a person for the purposes of the Convention and so have
rights capable of protection. In practice, such rights are likely to be far more
limited than the rights of an individual. However, rights such as those conferred
under Art.6,[98] Art.8,[99] Art.10[1] and Art.1 of Protocol No.1[2] will provide a degree
of protection to companies as well as individuals.

---

[89] See the UCITS Directive (Council Directive 85/611 [1985] O.J. L375/3), as amended. This has
been given effect in the UK formerly by Pt 1, Ch.VIII (ss.75–95) of the 1986 Act and now by Pt XVII
(ss.235–284) of FSMA and subsidiary rules thereunder.
[90] See the Market Abuse Directive, ("MAD"), (Council Directive 03/6), replacing in part, the Insider
Dealing Directive (Council Directive 89/592 [1989] O.J. L334/30).
[91] See the Capital Requirements Directive (Council Directives 2006/48 and 2006/49) which will
result in a "recast" Capital Adequacy Directive (Council Directive 93/6) and a "recast" Banking
Consolidation Directive (Council Directive 2000/12), in the light of "Basel 2".
[92] See the Markets in Financial Instruments Directive, ("MiFID"), (Council Directive 2004/39),
which will replace the Investment Services Directive (Council Directive 93/22) in October 2007.
[93] The Investor Compensation Directive (Council Directive 97/9 [1997] O.J. L84/22).
[94] For a detailed consideration of the impact of the Human Rights Act 1998 in the field of financial
services see L.-A. Mulcahy, *Human Rights and Civil Practice* (Sweet & Maxwell, 2001), Ch.14. See
also Ch.6 of this book.
[95] Especially in relation to the market abuse regime (FSMA, Pt VIII, ss.118–131), disciplinary powers
(FSMA, Pt XXVI, ss.387–396) and the Financial Services and Markets Tribunal (Pt IX, ss.132–137).
See the sourcebooks in the FSA Handbook (see paras 14–034 *et seq.*, below) relating to market
conduct, enforcement and decision making.
[96] Human Rights Act 1998, s.6(1).
[97] FSMA, s.1(3) and Sch.1, para.19 and (as competent authority—see para.14–004, above) s.102. See
further para.14–005, above. The extent of this immunity of the FSA can itself be challenged in the
event that it is shown to be disproportionate to the legitimate needs of society: see for example *Fayed
v United Kingdom* (1994) 18 E.H.R.R 393. FSMA confers like limited immunity from liability in
damages upon operators of the Financial Ombudsman Service and the Financial Services Compensation Scheme: see paras 14–124 and 14–139, below.
[98] The right to a fair trial.
[99] The right to privacy.
[1] The right to freedom of expression.
[2] The right to protection of property.

2. Application of the FSMA Regulatory Regime

14–021   The regulatory regime under FSMA, like that under the predecessor 1986 Act, contains a range of criteria for its application, graduated to the multifarious range of circumstances to which it relates. Ascertainment of the impact of the relevant regime consequently demands analysis of those criteria and their application to the circumstances of a case. In particular, the impact of the regulatory regime will depend on ascertaining: (i) whether or not the services provided involved carrying on a "regulated activity" in the United Kingdom; (ii) whether or not there was any "financial promotion"; (iii) whether or not an "investment" was involved and, if so, its type; (iv) the nature of the services provided; (v) the regulatory status of the provider; and (vi) the regulatory status of the recipient. Ascertaining each of these matters is at the forefront of analysis.

(a) *Regulated Activities*

14–022   The focus of the general prohibition is the carrying on of a "regulated activity" in the United Kingdom.[3] A regulated activity is an activity which is: (1) specified in an order made by the Treasury[4]; and (2) carried on "by way of business".[5] A regulated activity must fall within one of two categories. The first is a specified activity which relates to an "investment" also so specified. The second is a specified activity which relates to property of any kind, whether or not an investment.[6]

14–023   **The RAO**. The relevant order made by the Treasury is the Financial Services and Markets Act 2000 (Regulated Activities) Order 2001 ("the RAO").[7] Since it was originally made, it has frequently been amended as its scope has been fine-tuned and extended, in particular to implement EU directives. Amendments were made to give effect to the Insurance Mediation Directive.[8] Amendments will be made to give effect to MiFID which is due for implementation by October 1, 2007.[9] The RAO is divided into six Parts and four Schedules.

14–024   The scheme of Pt II of the RAO[10] is, broadly, to incorporate under "chapters" a series of articles relating to a "specified activity", the first article in the chapter defining the substantive activity and other articles defining specific exclusions or

---

[3] FSMA, s.19. See paras 14–006 and 14–007, above.
[4] The RAO: see para.14–023, below.
[5] See Lord Diplock's description of the word "business" as an "etymological chameleon" in *Town Investments Ltd v Department of the Environment* [1978] A.C. 359 at 383C. Note also as to the repetition element connoted, *Smith v Anderson* [1880] 15 Ch.D. 247 at 277–8. In the context of the meaning of the word in the 1986 Act, s.63 (predecessor to FSMA, s.412), see *Morgan Grenfell Co v Welwyn Hatfield DC* [1995] 1 All E.R. 1. The FSA has given guidance as to its interpretation of "by way of business" in the "PERG" Module of its Handbook.
[6] FSMA, s.22 and Sch.2.
[7] SI 2001/544 made under FSMA, s.22(5), as amended.
[8] Council Directive 2002/92. See Ch.16, para.16-008.
[9] Council Directive 2004/39.
[10] RAO, Pt II, arts 4–72F.

containing supplemental provisions. In addition, there are some general exclusions which apply to several specified kinds of activity.[11] Regulated activities which are specified activities relating to an "investment", also as specified in the RAO,[12] comprise the following: (1) accepting deposits[13]; (2) issuing electronic money[14]; (3) effecting and carrying out contracts of insurance[15]; (4) dealing in investments as principal[16]; (5) dealing in investments as agent[17]; (6) arranging deals in investments[18]; (7) managing investments[19]; (8) assisting in the administration and performance of a contract of insurance[20]; (9) safeguarding and administering investments[21]; (10) sending dematerialised instructions[22]; (11) establishing, etc. a collective investment scheme[23]; (12) establishing, etc. a pension scheme[24]; (13) providing basic advice on stakeholder products[25]; (14) advising on investments[26]; (15) advising, managing and arranging activities in relation to Lloyd's[27]; (16) entering as provider into a funeral plan contract[28]; (17) entering into a regulated mortgage contract or administering the same[29]; and (18) agreeing to carry on certain specified activities.[30] Each of such activities is defined in more detail and it is essential to have regard to the definitions including any applicable exclusions. Regulated activities which are specified activities relating to property of any kind, whether or not an investment, comprise the activities within (11) and (12).[31]

(b) *Financial Promotion*

The term "financial promotion" is not as such defined in FSMA, but it clearly   **14–025** covers not only advertising but all other forms of promoting certain investment activities. The financial promotion restriction prohibits a person, "in the course

---

[11] RAO, Pt II, arts 66–72F.

[12] RAO, Pt III, arts 73–89.

[13] RAO Pt II, Ch.II, art.5; it is subject to the exclusions in arts 5–9AA and 72A.

[14] *ibid.*, Ch.IIA, art.9B; it is subject to the exclusions in arts 9C–9G and 72A; see also supplemental provisions in arts 9H–9K.

[15] *ibid.*, Ch.III, art.10; it is subject to the exclusions in arts 11–12A and 72A; see also supplemental provision in art.13.

[16] *ibid.*, Ch.IV, art.14; it is subject to the exclusions in arts 15–20, 66, 68–72A.

[17] *ibid.*, Ch.V, art.21; it is subject to the exclusions in arts 22–24, 67–72B and 72D.

[18] *ibid.*, Ch.VI, arts 25 and 25A; it is subject to the exclusions in arts 26–36, 66 to 72D.

[19] *ibid.*, Ch.VII, art.37; it is subject to the exclusions in arts 38 and 39, 66, 68,69 72A and 72C.

[20] *ibid.*, Ch.VIIA, arts 39A and 39B; it is subject to the exclusions in arts 39C, 66 and 67, 72A–72D.

[21] *ibid.*, Ch.VIII, art.40; it is subject to the exclusions in arts 41–44, 66–69, 71, 72A and 72C.

[22] *ibid.*, Ch.IX, art.45; it is subject to the exclusions in arts 46–50, 66, 69 and 72A.

[23] *ibid.*, Ch.X, art.51; it is subject to the exclusion in arts 51A and 72A.

[24] *ibid.*, Ch.XI, art.52, as amended; it is subject to the exclusion in arts 52A and 72A.

[25] *ibid.*, Ch.XIA, art.52B.

[26] *ibid.*, Ch.XII, arts 53 and 53A; it is subject to the exclusion in arts 54 to 55, 66–70, 72, 72A, 72B and 72D.

[27] *ibid.*, Ch.XIII, arts 56–58; it is subject to the exclusion in arts 58A and 72A.

[28] *ibid.*, Ch.XIV, art.59; it is subject to the exclusions in arts 60, 60A and 72A.

[29] *ibid.*, Ch.XV, art.61; it is subject to the exclusions in arts 62–63A, 66, 72 and 72A.

[30] *ibid.*, Ch.XVI, art.64; it is subject to the exclusions in arts 65, 72 and 72A.

[31] *ibid.*, Ch.XI, art.4(2).

of business",[32] from communicating an invitation or an inducement to engage in investment activity, unless he is an authorised person or the content of the communication has been approved by an authorised person.[33] The term "engaging in investment activity" is defined by reference to other terms, "controlled activity" and "controlled investment".[34] The definition of these terms, along with the circumstances in which the prohibition is disapplied and other matters, are left to be detailed by Treasury order.

14–026   **The FPO.** The current order made is the Financial Services and Markets Act 2000 (Financial Promotion) Order 2005[35] ("the FPO"). It replaces the order made of the same name in 2001.[36] The provisions of the FPO are extensive. The definitions of "controlled activities" and "controlled investments" overlap, but do not coincide, with similar definitions of "regulated activities" and "specified investments" in the RAO[37] and hence the scope of the "general prohibition" and the "financial promotion restriction" are similar but not co-extensive. There are also definitions relating to different kinds of communications. "Real time communications" are distinguished from "non-real time communications", with "real time communications" being subdivided into "solicited" and "unsolicited" communications. There is a wide range of "exemptions" (some qualified) from the promotion prohibition, including by reference to the context of the promotion, the nature of the relevant investments and the categories of persons by whom and to whom the promotion is made.

(c) *Investment*

14–027   Investment is widely defined to include "any asset, right or interest" in the context of regulated activities[38] and financial promotion[39] respectively, but detailed definition of "specified investment" and "controlled investment" is left to subordinate legislation.[40] Relevant orders relating to each of those matters contain detailed definitions of the kind of investments to which they relate. In the context of regulated activities,[41] the RAO[42] contains detailed definitions of investments of a "specified kind". In the context of financial promotion,[43] the FPO[44] contains detailed definitions of "controlled investments". The definitions

---

[32] This phrase should be contrasted with the narrower term "by way of business" used in the "general prohibition" in s.19: see paras 14–006 and 14–007, above.
[33] FSMA, s.21. See further paras 14–008 and 14–009, above.
[34] *ibid.*, s.21(8).
[35] SI 2005/1529 made under FSMA s.21(15). Note it was amended by SI 2005/3392.
[36] SI 2001/1335 made under FSMA s.21(15). It was frequently amended.
[37] See para.14–023, above.
[38] FSMA, s.22(4).
[39] *ibid.*, s.21(14).
[40] *ibid.*, ss.22(5) and 21(15) and see the RAO and FPO.
[41] See *ibid.*, s.22 and Sch.2, Pt II.
[42] See para.14–023, above.
[43] See FSMA s.21, esp. subss.(9), (10) and (11), and Sch.2, Pt II.
[44] See para.14–026, above.

in the two orders generally correspond, but not precisely. The RAO and the FPO contain relevant definitions of the following kinds of investments: (1) deposits[45]; (2) electronic money[46]; (3) rights under a contract of insurance[47]; (4) shares[48]; (5) instruments creating or acknowledging indebtedness other than those of the next kind[49]; (6) government and public securities[50]; (7) warrants and other instruments entitling the holder to subscribe for any of the last three kinds[51]; (8) certificates representing certain securities[52]; (9) units in a collective investment scheme[53]; (10) rights under a pension scheme[54]; (11) options[55]; (12) futures[56]; (13) contracts for differences[57]; (14) Lloyd's syndicate capacity and syndicate membership[58]; (15) funeral plan contracts[59]; and (16) rights or interests in certain other investments.[60] Within the scope of the FPO, but not the RAO, are (17) agreements for "qualifying credit".[61] Within the scope of the RAO, but not the FPO, are (18) regulated mortgage contracts.[62]

The general prohibition and the financial promotion restriction in FSMA do **14–028** not only apply if an "investment" is involved. A regulated activity may relate not only to an investment but also to "property of any kind".[63] The financial promotion restriction is defined by reference to a "controlled activity" which, in turn, is defined in terms of not only an activity related to an investment but also an activity of a "specified kind" or a "specified class of activity".[64] A frequent source of confusion arises in the context of an alleged collective investment schemes. The fact that the underlying assets of such a scheme may not comprise investments may dupe the unwary into the misconception that no regulated investment is involved. The assets of a collective investment scheme may comprise "property of any description, including money"[65] and rights to participate in such a scheme are "investments". Indeed they are amongst the most heavily regulated kinds of investments. Problems may also arise as to the

---

[45] RAO, Pt III, art.74; FPO art.4(2) and Sch.1, para.12.
[46] *ibid.*, art.74A; no equivalent in FPO.
[47] *ibid.*, art.75; FPO art.4(2) and Sch.1, para.13.
[48] *ibid.*, art.76; FPO art.4(2) and Sch.1, para.14.
[49] *ibid.*, art.77; FPO art.4(2) and Sch.1, para.15.
[50] *ibid.*, art.78; FPO art.4(2) and Sch.1, para.16.
[51] *ibid.*, art.79; FPO art.4(2) and Sch.1, para.17.
[52] *ibid.*, art.80; FPO art.4(2) and Sch.1, para.18.
[53] *ibid.*, art.81; FPO art.4(2) and Sch.1, para.19.
[54] *ibid.*, art.82, as amended. FPO art.4(2) and Sch.1, para.20, as amended.
[55] *ibid.*, art.83; FPO art.4(2) and Sch.1, para.21.
[56] *ibid.*, art.84; FPO art.4(2) and Sch.1, para.22.
[57] *ibid.*, art.85; FPO art.4(2) and Sch.1, para.23.
[58] *ibid.*, art.86; FPO art.4(2) and Sch.1, para.24.
[59] *ibid.*, art.87; FPO art.4(2) and Sch.1, para.25.
[60] *ibid.*, art.89; FPO art.4(2) and Sch.1, para.27.
[61] FPO art.4(2) and Sch.1, para.26.
[62] RAO, Pt III, art.88.
[63] FSMA, s.22(1). See the RAO, arts 4(2), 51 and 52.
[64] FSMA, s.21, esp. s.21(9). See also the FPO, art.4(1) and Sch.1, paras 1–11.
[65] FSMA, s.235(1). See *Russell-Cooke Trust Company v Elliot* 2001 WL 753378, on the identically worded 1986 Act, s.75; applied by Lindsay J. in *Russell-Cooke Trust Company v Prentis* [2002] EWHC 2227 (Ch) (the "property" was mortgages); and *FSA v Fradley* 2004] EWHC 3008 (Ch) (the "property" was bets places on horse races).

appropriate classification of particular investments[66] which in turn will require consideration of relevant Treasury orders.

(d) *Nature of the Services*

14–029   The duties of a provider of financial services will vary according to the nature of the services provided. Generally, very little will be required where the services are limited to execution only. On the other hand, the duties will be far more extensive if the services are advisory or involve discretionary management of a portfolio of investments.

(e) *Status of Provider of Financial Services*

14–030   A person may contravene the general prohibition because he is neither an authorised person nor an exempt person. If he is authorised, he may contravene his permission requirement by carrying out a regulated activity not covered by his permission but this will not entail a breach of the general prohibition.[67] Similarly, an unauthorised person may contravene the financial promotion restriction by communicating an inducement to engage in investment activity without the approval of an authorised person. On the other hand, the particular circumstances in which financial services are provided may be such that their provider does not carry on any regulated or controlled activities by reason of a relevant exclusion in the RAO or FPO.

(f) *Status of Recipient of Financial Services*

14–031   This is relevant in a number of respects. In the FPO relevant exclusions are expressed by reference to the status of the recipient, e.g. an "investment professional",[68] a "certified high net worth individual",[69] "certified sophisticated investor"[70] and "self-certified sophisticated investor".[71] Again the nature and extent of the duties imposed under the Handbook upon a provider of financial services is graduated to the status of the recipient, e.g. "private customer" as defined.[72] The statutory right of action given for contravention of relevant rules by authorised persons is generally limited to a "private person" as defined.[73]

---

[66] e.g. as in *Larussa-Chigi v CS First Boston Ltd* [1998] C.L.C. 277.

[67] See paras 14–006 and 14–007, above. This can only be breached by someone who does not have the status of an authorised (or exempt) person. There may be disciplinary consequences for an authorised person acting outside his Pt IV permission.

[68] FPO, art.19. An investment professional includes an authorised person: *ibid.*, art.19(5)(a).

[69] FPO, art.48.

[70] FPO, art.50.

[71] FPO, art.50A.

[72] In the Glossary to the Handbook.

[73] See para.14–074, below.

3. Duties and Liabilities under FSMA

Integral to the regulatory regime under FSMA is an array of requirements **14–032** imposed not only directly by the Act itself but also by delegated powers given to the Treasury and the FSA. In particular, the FSA is accorded wide powers to make rules. The FSA is also empowered to give guidance and to issue statements of principle and codes of practice.[74] Contravention of some of statutory duties and rules may give rise to civil liability under relevant sections of the Act.[75]

4. Regulatory Rules and the FSA Handbook

(a) *General*

FSMA obliges the FSA to exercise its rule-making powers in writing and also to **14–033** publish all rule-making instruments in the way appearing to the FSA to be best calculated to bring it to the attention of the public.[76] The FSA has undertaken to publish all rule-making instruments in full on its website.[77]

(b) *FSA Handbook*

The rule-making instruments in force at any particular time are contained in the **14–034** FSA's Handbook. This is the title given to a continuously updated compendium of such instruments and other material, including published guidance. It is published on the FSA's website. In ascertaining the requirements under FSMA apposite to financial advisers and institutions it is vital to examine the relevant version of the Handbook at the relevant time(s).

(i) *Sourcebooks*

As explained in the introductory "Reader's Guide",[78] the Handbook is divided **14–035** into "sourcebooks" (providing sources of the FSA's requirements and guidance) and manuals (containing the processes to be followed). Each sourcebook in fact comprises the "rule-making instrument" by which the FSA is required to make rules.[79] The general form is a one page formal instrument and an Annex incorporating relevant rules as well as guidance. The contents page of the Handbook reflects its arrangement as of October 2, 2006 as follows:

---

[74] See para.14–043, below.
[75] See paras 14–069 to 14–082, below.
[76] FSMA, s.153.
[77] For the website, see n.4 under para.14–004, above. Para.4 of the Reader's Guide Instrument 2001 identifies this as "the definitive source for determining what the text was at any particular time for legal purposes". Note FSMA, s.154 as to verification of rules.
[78] It has the status of guidance issued under FSMA, s.157(1).
[79] FSMA, s.153(1), (2).

Block	Sourcebook or manual	Reference Code
Glossary	Glossary	Glossary
High Level Standards	Principles for Businesses	PRIN
	Senior Management Arrangements, Systems and Controls	SYSC
	Threshold Conditions	COND
	Statements of Principle and Code of Practice for Approved Persons	APER
	The Fit and Proper Test for Approved Persons	FIT
	General provisions	GEN
	Fees Manual	FEES
Prudential Standards	Integrated Prudential sourcebook	IPRU
	Integrated Prudential sourcebook for Banks	IPRU-BANK
	Integrated Prudential sourcebook for Building Societies	IPRU-BSOC
	Integrated Prudential sourcebook for Friendly Societies	IPRU-FSOC
	Integrated Prudential sourcebook for Insurers	IPRU-INS
	Integrated Prudential sourcebook for Investment Businesses	IPRU-INV
Business Standards	Conduct of Business	COB
	Insurance: Conduct of Business	ICOB
	Mortgages: Conduct of Business	MCOB
	Client Assets	CASS
	Market Conduct	MAR
	Training and Competence	TC
	Money Laundering (30/08/2006 is the last day this material was in force)	ML
Regulatory Processes	Authorisation	AUTH
	Supervision	SUP
	Enforcement	ENF
	Decision Making	DEC
Redress	Dispute Resolution: Complaints	DISP
	Compensation	COMP
	Complaints against the FSA	COAF

Block	Sourcebook or manual	Reference Code
Specialist sourcebooks	Collective Investment Schemes	CIS
	New Collective Investment Schemes	COLL
	Credit Unions	CRED
	Electronic Commerce Directive	ECO
	Electronic Money	ELM
	Lloyd's	LLD
	Professional Firms	PROF
	Recognised Investment Exchanges and Recognised Clearing Houses	REC
Listing, Prospectus and Disclosure	Listing Rules	LR
	Prospectus Rules	PR
	Disclosure Rules	DR
Handbook Guides	Energy Market Participants	EMPS
	Small Friendly Societies (12/06/2005 is the last day this material was in force)	FREN
	Oil Market Participants	OMPS
	Service Companies	SERV
	Using the FSA Handbook: an Overview for small IFA firms	SIFA
	Small Mortgage and Insurance Intermediaries: Part I–General Rules	MIGI
	Small Mortgage and Insurance Intermediaries: Part II–Mortgage Intermediaries (additional rules)	MOGI
	Small Mortgage and Insurance Intermediaries: Part III–Insurance Intermediaries (additional rules)	GIGI
Regulatory Guides	The Collective Investment Scheme Information Guide	COLLG
	The Perimeter Guidance Manual	PERG

Each sourcebook follows a similar structure. Each comprises: (1) a contents **14–036** page; (2) a schedule of transitional provisions (if any); (3) the main text, with any annexes or appendices; and (4) six schedules of requirements and supplementary information.[80] Of the schedules to each sourcebook, the fifth is useful in

---

[80] The schedules relate to: (1) any record-keeping requirements; (2) any notification requirements; (3) fees and other required payments; (4) powers exercised; (5) rights of action for damages; and (6) rules that can be waived.

identifying the extent to which the rules in the sourcebook attract the right of action granted under FSMA for contravention of certain rules.[81]

(ii) *Glossary*

14–037   This is a compendium of definitions of defined terms used in the various sourcebooks in the FSA Handbook. Defined terms are highlighted in the text. The definition of each defined term is readily accessible in the online version of the Handbook via a hypertext link to the Glossary. The definitions of defined terms are critical to understanding the rules and other provisions within the FSA Handbook. Many are complex and long, somewhat inevitably in order to ensure fine-tuning of the regulatory regime. It is beyond the scope of this chapter to deal with the definitions. The Glossary itself is a book.

14–038   Certain defined terms, albeit not their full definitions, bear mention. A "firm" is defined, generally, as an "authorised person".[82] A "client" is generally defined as any "person" with or for whom a "firm" conducts or intends to conduct "investment business" or any other "regulated activity". There are two types of "client": a "customer" and a "market counterparty". Sub-species of "customer" are a "private customer" and an "intermediate customer". These definitions enable graduation of the regulatory regime to the level of protection deemed appropriate to different categories of client.

(iii) *Rules*

14–039   The main text of each sourcebook or manual is sub-divided into chapters, sections and paragraphs. Each paragraph is accorded a regulatory status. "R" is used to denote a general or specialised rule made under FSMA[83] and other powers, other than an evidential rule. The legal effect of such a rule will vary according to the power under which it is made and on the language used in the rule. Contravention may render a firm liable to enforcement action[84] and/or an action for damages.[85] "D" is used to indicate a direction or requirement given under various powers conferred by FSMA.[86] Directions and requirements are binding on the persons or categories of persons to whom they are addressed. "P" is used to indicate a statement of principle for approved persons.[87] "C" is used to denote a paragraph of the Code of Market Conduct describing behaviour which, in the opinion of FSMA, does not amount to market abuse.[88] Such

---

[81] See FSMA, s.150, considered further in paras 14–077 to 14–079, below.

[82] But not a "professional firm" unless it is an "authorised professional firm".

[83] See as to general rules, FSMA, s.138 (general rule-making power) and s.139 (ancillary matters) and as to specialised rules, see in particular, s.140 (managers of authorised unit trust schemes), ss.141 and 142 (insurance business), s.143 (endorsement of take-over codes, to be repealed when the Takeover Directive is implemented), s.144 (price stabilisation), s.145 (financial promotion), s.146 (money laundering) and s.147 (control of information).

[84] See para.14–004, above.

[85] See paras 14–077 to 14–079, below.

[86] For example, under s.51(3) of FSMA about the form and content of applications for Pt IV permission.

[87] Made under FSMA s.64(1). See further para.14–043, below. As to approved persons, see para.14–012, above.

[88] Made under *ibid.*, s.119.

descriptions are conclusive for the purposes of FSMA.[89] "E" is used to identify an evidential provision.[90] Such a provision does not bind in its own right but instead relates to some other binding rule. Where provided for within the Handbook, compliance or non-compliance with an evidential provision may be relied upon as "tending to establish compliance" with or "tending to establish contravention" of the rule to which it relates. Evidential provisions thus create rebuttable presumptions of compliance with or contravention of the binding rules to which they refer. "E" is also used in relation to provisions of the Code of Practice for Approved Persons[91] and the Code of Market Conduct.[92]

(iv) *Guidance*

"G" is used to indicate guidance given by the FSA[93] and for certain other   **14–040** purposes. Guidance may be given for many purposes including to explain the implications of other provisions, to indicate possible means of compliance and to recommend a particular course or arrangement. Guidance is neither binding on those to whom FSMA or rules made under FSMA apply, nor does it have "evidential" effect. It need not be followed to achieve compliance with the relevant rule or other requirement. Nor does it attract disciplinary liability. Significantly (and in contrast to judicial statements in other contexts[94]) the Handbook expressly states that there is no presumption that departing from guidance is indicative of a breach of the relevant rule.[95]

(v) *Treatment*

Detailed treatment of the rules, guidance and evidential provisions contained   **14–041** within each sourcebook and manual in the Handbook is outside the scope of this chapter. However, of particular relevance to claims against financial services providers are the Principles for Business (referenced "PRIN") and the Conduct of Business sourcebook (referenced "COB") and the Insurance Conduct of Business sourcebook (referenced "ICOB").[96] Contravention of certain rules in COB may result in statutory liability in damages.[97] The Compensation sourcebook ("COMP") is discussed later in this chapter.[98]

---

[89] FSMA, s.122(1).
[90] Made under *ibid.*, s.149. Contravention of such rules do not give rise to the consequences set out in the Act for other rule breaches.
[91] Made under *ibid.*, s.64(2). See further para.14–043, below.
[92] Made under *ibid.*, s.119 (in relation to market abuse).
[93] Made under *ibid.*, s.157.
[94] See Ch.8, paras 8–156 to 8–159 and Ch.15, para.15–091.
[95] Reader's Guide, para.28.
[96] This is dealt with further in Ch.16
[97] Under FSMA s.150. See paras 14–077 to 14–078, below. Although providing guidance and evidential provisions, none of the High Level Standards sourcebooks (see para.14–035, above) provide for such statutory liability. Some of those sourcebooks contain no rules (e.g. the Fit and Proper Test for Approved Persons) while others (e.g. the Principles for Businesses) are specified under s.150(2) of FSMA as containing provisions giving rise to no such right of action.
[98] See paras 14–125 *et seq.*, below.

(c) *Principles for Businesses*

14–042   In general, the Principles for Business (referenced "PRIN") apply to authorised persons with respect to regulated activities. They are a general statement of the fundamental obligations of firms under the regulatory system. Although called "principles" they are not foreshadowed as such in FSMA, unlike the Statements of Principle for Approved Persons made under FSMA.[99] The regulatory status of the Principles for Businesses are in part rules made under rule-making powers in FSMA[1] and in part guidance.[2] They are made by a rule-making instrument which is incorporated as a sourcebook within the Handbook. Contravention of such a principle does not of itself attract the right of action under FSMA for contravention of certain rules, although it may make a firm liable to disciplinary sanctions. Nevertheless conduct which contravenes a principle may amount to a contravention of a rule which does attract that right of action. The 11 principles have some merit in the context of legal advice and forensic presentation as a first point of departure in order to explain the rationale which may be obscured in detailed and complex rules. Moreover, they are relied on extensively by the FSA when exercising its disciplinary powers against authorised persons. Hence their quotation in full:

1. **Integrity:** A firm must conduct its business with integrity.

2. **Skill, care and diligence:** A firm must conduct its business with due skill, care and diligence.

3. **Management and control:** A firm must take reasonable care to organise and control its affairs responsibly and effectively, with adequate risk management systems.

4. **Financial prudence:** A firm must maintain adequate financial resources.

5. **Market conduct:** A firm must observe proper standards of market conduct.

6. **Customers' interests:** A firm must pay due regard to the interests of its customers and treat them fairly.

7. **Communications with clients:** A firm must pay due regard to the information needs of its clients, and communicate information to them in a way which is clear, fair and not misleading.

8. **Conflicts of interest:** A firm must manage conflicts of interest fairly, both between itself and its customers and between a customer and another client.

9. **Customers: relationships of trust:** A firm must take reasonable care to ensure the suitability of its advice and discretionary decisions for any customer who is entitled to rely upon its judgment.

---

[99] FSMA, s.64. See further para.14–043, below.
[1] FSMA, ss.138, 145, 146, 150(2) and 156.
[2] Issued under FSMA, s.157.

10. **Clients' assets:** A firm must arrange adequate protection for clients' assets when it is responsible for them.

11. **Relations with regulators:** A firm must deal with its regulators in an open and cooperative way, and must disclose to the FSA appropriately anything relating to the firm of which the FSA would reasonably expect notice.[3]

(d) *Statements of Principle and Code of Practice for Approved Persons*

These,[4] presently seven in number, are similar in concept to the FSA's Principles   **14–043**
for Businesses applicable to authorised persons[5] but are tailored to meet the position of approved persons.[6] While the former focus on an authorised person's responsibilities when undertaking regulated activities, the Statements of Principle for Approved Persons focus on such persons' responsibilities when undertaking "controlled" functions[7] in the context of regulated activities. By issuing such Statements of Principle the FSA was required also to issue a code of practice to help determine compliance with them.[8] The code, divided into general and specific matters, has been issued and is incorporated together with the Statements of Principle as a sourcebook (referenced "APER") in the Handbook. Four Statements of Principle relate to every approved person. These statements require integrity, due skill and diligence and proper standards of market conduct in carrying out his controlled function and open and cooperative dealings with the FSA and other regulators and disclosure of information of which the FSA would reasonably expect notice. The other three Statements of Principle relate to those approved persons who perform a "significant influence position" in relation to his sphere of responsibility in his controlled function. They require the taking of reasonable steps to ensure proper organisation, regulatory compliance and the exercise of competence in management. Contravention of a Statement of Principle does not of itself give rise to any right of action or affect the validity of any transaction[9] but may attract disciplinary sanctions.[10]

(e) *"Conduct of Business" Sourcebook ("COB")*

COB, in common with other sourcebooks in the Handbook, contains rules,   **14–044**
evidential provisions and guidance.

(i) *Arrangement*

COB is divided into 14 chapters. A broad sense of the subject matter of each is   **14–045**
derived from their respective titles: 1. Application and general provisions;

---

[3] *cf.* the SIB's Statements of Principle issued under the FSA, s.47A on March 15, 1990, "the Ten Commandments". Contrasted with the original Ten Commandments, their quality was not divine and their reformulation into eleven under FSMA may have been intended to avoid that comparison.
[4] Issued under powers conferred under FSMA, s.64.
[5] See para.14–042, above.
[6] See further para.14–012, above.
[7] Not to be confused with "controlled activities" in relation to the financial promotion restriction, as to which see para.14–008, above.
[8] FSMA, s.64(2).
[9] *ibid.*, s.64(8).
[10] *ibid.*, s.66(2)(a).

2. Rules which apply to all firms[11] conducting designated investment business; 3. Financial promotion; 4. Accepting customers; 5. Advising and selling; 5A. Providing basic advice on stakeholder products; 6. Product disclosure and the customer's right to cancel or withdraw; 7. Dealing and managing; 8. Reporting to customers; 8A. Claims handling[12]; 9. Client assets; 10. Operators of collective investment schemes; 11. Trustee and depositary activities; and 12. Lloyd's. Each chapter is sub-divided into sections and each section follows a similar structure. At the beginning of each chapter, there are identified the firms and activities to which the various rules, guidance and evidential provisions are directed, as well as the Principles for Business which the provisions of the chapter are intended to amplify. The various rules, evidential provisions and guidance are then set out. Highlighted by italics in the text are terms which are defined in the Glossary to the Handbook. The definitions merit close scrutiny in order to evaluate the scope of the main text. A detailed consideration of COB (and thus of relevant rules and guidance) is beyond the scope of this book. Only some of more relevant matters are briefly dealt with.

(ii) Scope[13]

14–046 COB starts by describing to whom, for what activities and within what territorial limits it applies. Generally, but subject to exceptions,[14] the rules contained in COB apply to every "firm" with respect to the carrying on of all regulated activities[15] and, to the extent specified, non-regulated activities. Although not of direct application to a firm's appointed representatives,[16] a firm will always be responsible for the acts and omissions of its appointed representatives in carrying on business for which the firm has accepted responsibility.[17] Accordingly, anything done or omitted by a firm's appointed representative will be treated as having been done or omitted by the firm.[18]

(iii) Rules of General Application to all Firms conducting "Designated Investment Business"[19]

14–047 "Designated investment business "is defined to cover some but not all categories of regulated activities in the RAO,[20] which are carried on by way of business. Broadly, the categories covered by the term are (true) investment activities (such as were covered by the 1986 Act) as opposed to regulated activities such as accepting deposits and effecting contracts of insurance. A firm carrying on "designated investment business" is required to communicate information to a

---

[11] A "firm" is defined as an authorised person.
[12] This is limited to claims handling under "long-term care insurance contracts" as defined.
[13] See COB, Ch.1: General Application.
[14] One exception pertains to firms which engage in "insurance mediation activities" as defined for "non-investment insurance contracts", as defined. In their case, ICOB applies and COB does not apply: COB, 1.2.1A.
[15] The scope of the regulated activities (see paras 14–022 and 14–023, above) to which COB applies is determined by the description of the activity as set out in the RAO. A firm will therefore not generally be subject to COB in relation to any aspect of its business activities which fall within an exclusion found within the RAO.
[16] See paras 14–014 to 14–016, above.
[17] FSMA, s.39(3).
[18] *ibid.*, s.39(4).
[19] COB, Ch.2.
[20] See paras 14–023 and 14–024, above.

"customer"[21] in a way which is clear, fair and not misleading, except in circumstances in which the more detailed financial promotion requirements apply. The acceptance by such firm of inducements and soft commission is restricted. Rules are also made as to the extent to which such a firm may rely on information provided by others. It will be taken to be in compliance with any of the COB rules that require it to obtain information to the extent that it can show that it was reasonable for it to rely upon information provided to it in writing by another person. A firm will therefore be able to rely upon this provision when carrying out client classifications and obtaining sufficient information in order to satisfy the "know its customer" requirement.[22] Other rules of such general application pertain to Chinese walls and to restriction of liability.

Restriction of liability. Save in the case of an authorised unit trust scheme,[23]   **14–048**
there is no prohibition in FSMA itself on a financial practitioner seeking to exclude or limit its duties or its liabilities by means of a contractual term. However, every firm which communicates with a "customer"[24] while conducting "designated investment business"[25] is prohibited by COB from seeking in such communications to exclude or restrict or to rely on any exclusion or restriction of any duty or liability it may have to a customer under FSMA or the regulatory system.[26] Moreover, every such firm is also prohibited from seeking in communications to a "private customer"[27] to exclude or to restrict or to rely on any exclusion or restriction of any other duty or liability that it may have unless it is reasonable for it to do so.[28] Guidance is not given on the factors that might make any such restriction or exclusion reasonable. It is likely that matters similar to those set out in s.11 of and Sch.2 to the Unfair Contract Terms Act 1977 will be relevant. Limits in exclusion of liability are also imposed in relation to distance contracts to accept deposits.[29]

(iv) *Financial Promotion*[30]

A long chapter addresses "financial promotion"[31] and, with very limited excep-   **14–049**
tions, its provisions apply to every firm to which COB applies.[32] The purpose of

---

[21] Defined as a "client" who is a "private customer" or an "intermediate customer". The latter terms are also defined in the Glossary.
[22] See para.14–056, below.
[23] s.253 of FSMA provides that "Any provision of the trust deed of an authorised unit trust scheme is void in so far as it would have the effect of exempting the manager or trustee from liability for any failure to exercise due care and diligence in the discharge of his functions in respect of the scheme." This section reflects arts 9 and 16 of the UCITS Directive.
[24] See under para.14–047, above.
[25] See para.14–047 and n.219 thereunder.
[26] COB 2.5.1R and 2.5.3R. The "regulatory system" is defined as the arrangements for regulating a firm or other person in or under FSMA, including the threshold conditions, the Principles for Business and other rules, the Statements of Principle, codes and guidance.
[27] See paras 14–038 and 14–051, below.
[28] COB 2.5.1R and 2.5.4R.
[29] COB 2.5.1R and 2.5.4R.
[30] COB, Ch.3.
[31] Defined as in accordance with FSMA, s.21(1) as an invitation or inducement to engage in investment activity, see para.14–025, above.
[32] Those exceptions are limited to firms communicating or approving the content of a financial promotion solely for a deposit, a general insurance contract or a pure protection contract. In those cases only limited parts of the chapter apply.

the chapter is to provide promotion rules and guidance for firms (i.e. authorised persons) who wish to communicate and to approve a financial promotion. Restrictions on financial promotion by unauthorised persons are imposed by FSMA itself.[33] However, there are many exemptions to these restrictions as apparent from the FPO.[34] These exemptions have been integrated in the financial promotion rules together with other exemptions.[35] Recognising the extent to which e-mail and the internet are now used, COB expressly provides (albeit in the form of general guidance) that any material meeting the definition of a financial promotion, including any video or moving image material incorporated in any website containing a financial promotion, should comply with the financial promotion rules.[36] Other matters addressed in separate sections are territorial scope,[37] confirmation of compliance and approval,[38] records,[39] form and content of financial promotions,[40] "direct offer promotions",[41] "unsolicited real-time financial promotions",[42] unregulated collective investment schemes and qualified investor schemes[43] and financial promotions for an unauthorised person and overseas persons.[44]

14–050   Form and content requirements vary as between non-real-time promotions and real-time financial promotions.[45] In respect of the former, the firm must properly identify itself and be able to show that it has taken reasonable steps to ensure that the financial promotion was clear, fair and not misleading. Additional obligations are also imposed (as binding rules) where the financial promotion involves a comparison or contrast, or relates to a specific investment, or gives information about the past performance of an investment or fund or gives a projection. Real-time financial promotions must also be clear, fair and not misleading and further requirements are imposed as to manner of communication. The latter are more stringent if such promotions are unsolicited.[46]

(v) *Accepting Customers*[47]

14–051   Any firm intending to conduct, or conducting, designated investment business or ancillary activities relating to designated investment business is required to

---

[33] FSMA s.21. See para.14–008, above.
[34] See para.14–026, above.
[35] COB 3.5.
[36] COB 3.14.
[37] COB 3.3.
[38] COB 3.6.
[39] COB 3.7.
[40] COB 3.8.
[41] COB 3.9.
[42] COB 3.9: i.e. essentially cold calls.
[43] COB 3.10.
[44] COB 3.12 and 3.13.
[45] COB 3.8. A "real-time financial promotion" is one communicated in the course of a personal visit, telephone conversation or other interactive dialogue. A "non-real-time financial promotion" is a financial promotion that is not a real-time financial promotion and includes a financial promotion communicated by letter, e-mail or included in publications disseminated in paper format, in material displayed on a website or in sound or television broadcasts: see the Glossary to the Handbook. See PERG 8.10.2G. The distinction parallels that between "real time communications" and "non-real-time communications" in the FPO, art.7.
[46] COB 3.10.
[47] COB, Ch.4.

classify the persons with or for whom it intends to carry on that business or those activities.[48] The purpose of this requirement is to ensure that clients are correctly categorised so that regulatory protections are focused on those classes of client that need them most, while allowing an appropriately "light-touch" approach for inter-professional business. Firms are obliged to review their classifications of all clients other than private customers at least annually.[49] While the obligation to take reasonable steps to classify a customer is mandatory, it is possible for a firm to classify a client who would otherwise be a "private customer"[50] as an "intermediate customer", or intermediate customer as a "market counterparty", if certain conditions are met.[51] However, in each case the firm must advise the client of the regulatory protections that he will lose by being re-classified in this way.

Terms of business and customer agreements.[52] Subject to certain excep-   **14–052**
tions,[53] every firm conducting or intending to conduct "designated investment business" with or for a specific customer is required to provide "in good time" its "terms of business",[54] setting out the basis on which such business is to be conducted for the customer.[55] Moreover, such terms must be in "adequate detail".[56] Thus generally there must be provisions as to matters itemised in a table of general requirements and, if relevant, a table of requirements pertaining to managing investments on a discretionary basis.[57] A customer agreement is required of a firm intending to conduct any of the following designated investment business with or for a private customer: managing investments on a discretionary basis, a transaction in a "contingent liability investment",[58] stock lending activity or underwriting except in respect of a life policy.[59] Requirements are also imposed as to amendment of terms of business[60] and as to making a record of terms of business and times of retention of records.[61] Apart from requirements in the Conduct of Business sourcebook, additional requirements are imposed as to disclosure and client agreements in the Client Assets sourcebook (referenced "CASS").[62]

---

[48] COB 4.1. Note the rule in para.4.1.4: "Before conducting designated investment business with or for any client, a firm must take reasonable steps to establish whether that client is a private customer, intermediate customer or market counterparty".
[49] COB 4.1.15R.
[50] See para.14–038, above.
[51] COB 4.1.9R and 4.1.12R.
[52] COB 4.2. See further para.14–053, below.
[53] COB 4.2.5R and COB 4 Annex 1. The latter contains a table listing exceptions, including exceptions relating to "execution-only transactions" and "direct offer financial promotion".
[54] Defined as "a written statement, supplied to a client, of the terms on which a firm will conduct designated investment business with or for the client."
[55] COB 4.2.4G.
[56] COB 4.2.10R
[57] COB 4.2.11E and COB 4 Ann 2E and Ann 3E.
[58] As defined in the Glossary
[59] COB 4.2.7R. There is an exception relating to a private customer habitually resident outside the UK.
[60] COB 4.2.13R.
[61] COB 4.2.14R.
[62] CASS 2.3.

14–053   Terms of business or, as the case may be, a customer agreement will ordinarily form the starting point for analysis of the contractual relationship between the provider and recipient of financial services, including duties. While providers of financial services are free to design and negotiate their own terms of business, there are extensive evidential provisions relating to what should be included in order to provide adequate detail.[63] General requirements as to the content of terms of business[64] pertain to the following:

(1) A description of when and how the terms of business are to come into force.

(2) A statement as to the firm's statutory status.[65]

(3) A description of the customer's investment objectives.

(4) The identification of any restrictions on the type of designated investment in which the customer wishes to invest or the markets on which the customer wishes transactions to be executed.

(5) The identification of the services that the firm will provide.

(6) Details of any payment for services payable by the customer to the firm.

(7) Relevant details if the firm is to act as investment manager.

(8) A description of arrangements for accounting to the customer for any transaction executed on his behalf.

(9) A description of cancellation and withdrawal rights, options and consequences in respect of certain investments.

(10) Circumstances in which unsolicited real time financial promotion may be made to a private customer.

(11) Where a firm may act as principal in a transaction with the customer, a statement to that effect.

(12) A statement of the manner in which the firm will ensure fair treatment in the event of a material interest or conflict of interest.

(13) Where a firm acts as a broker fund adviser for a private customer, a statement of the firm's dual role as adviser to him and adviser to the life office or operator in question.

(14) The disclosure of any soft commission arrangements.

(15) The giving of relevant risk warnings.

(16) If advice or execution services are to be provided in relation to unregulated collective investment schemes, a statement to that effect.

---

[63] See the annexes to COB 4.
[64] COB 4.2.11E and COB 4 Annex 2E.
[65] See the General Provisions sourcebook: GEN 4 Annex 1.

(17) A statement as to as to any underwriting obligations to be entered on behalf of the customer.

(18) Details as to any stock lending activity which the firm may undertake with or for a private customer.

(19) The required information as to any contractual rights to realise a private customer's assets.[66]

(20) A description of how to make a complaint to the firm, and a statement, if relevant, that the customer may complain to the Financial Ombudsman Service ("FOS").[67]

(21) A statement as to the availability of compensation from the compensation scheme.[68]

(22) A description of the permissible methods of terminating the terms of business and the consequences of termination.

(23) A description of how transactions in progress may be dealt with on termination.

(24) The consequences of contracting out of best execution.

(25) In the case of an authorised professional firm conducting "non-main-stream regulated activity", an explanation of complaint procedures and any compensation arrangements.[69]

Other evidential requirements pertain to the contents of terms of business and client agreements for discretionary management of investments.[70] These pertain to the extent of discretion, periodic statements, valuation, borrowings and underwriting commitments.

(vi) *Advising and Selling*[71]

These matters are addressed in another long chapter under presently 9 sections entitled as follows: (1) Advising on packaged products; (2) Know your customer; (3) Suitability; (4) Customers' understanding of risk; (5) Information about the firm; (6) Excessive charges; (7) Disclosure of charges, remuneration and commission; (8) Customers introduced to clearing firms by introducing brokers and overseas introducing brokers; and (9) Corporate finance business issues.   **14–054**

(1) Advising on packaged products.[72] Specific requirements are imposed on a firm which (including through its appointed representatives[73]) gives advice on   **14–055**

---

[66] i.e. information required by COB 7.8.3R.
[67] As to FOS, see paras 14–103 to 14–124, below.
[68] As to the FSMA Compensation Scheme, see paras 14–125 to 14–139, below.
[69] As to "non-mainstream regulated activity", see the full definition in PROF 5.2.1R. Essentially it is a regulated activity of an "authorised professional firm" in respect of which certain conditions are satisfied.
[70] COB 4.2.11E and COB 4 Annex 3E.
[71] COB 5.
[72] COB 5.1.
[73] See paras 14–014 to 14–016, above.

investments to a private customer on packaged products,[74] other than when giving basic advice on a "stakeholder product". Their purpose is to ensure that private customers are adequately informed about the nature of the advice, in particular the scope and range of products and product providers on which the advice is based.[75]

14–056   **(2) Know your customer.**[76] Requirements of this nature are imposed upon firms in various circumstances.[77] For example, they include circumstances in which a firm, in relation to a private customer: (a) gives a personal recommendation concerning a designated investment or (b) acts as an investment manager.[78] In the latter circumstances the firm must take reasonable steps to ensure that it is in possession of sufficient personal and financial information about the customer relevant to the firm's services.[79] Record keeping requirements are imposed, including in relation to execution-only pension opt-outs and pension transfers.[80] In relation to a personal recommendation or the arranging of a life policy, requirements are imposed for the provision by a firm of a statement of the client's demands and needs.[81]

14–057   **(3) Suitability.**[82] Suitability requirements pertaining to certain advisory, management and promotional activities are a core element of the regulatory regime. There are a series of such requirements relating to a firm: (a) making a personal recommendation concerning a designated investment to a private customer; (b) acting as an investment manager for a private customer; (c) managing the assets of an OPS or a stakeholder pension scheme; (d) promoting a personal pension scheme by means of a direct offer financial promotion to a group or employees; or (e) if the firm is not an insurer, making a personal recommendation to an intermediate customer or a market counterparty to take out a life policy.[83] There is a general requirement in relation to a private customer that a firm, in the course of designated investment business, must take reasonable steps to ensure that it does not make a personal recommendation to buy or sell a designated investment, or effect a discretionary transaction for a private customer, unless the recommendation or transaction is suitable for the private customer, having regard to the facts disclosed by him and other relevant facts about him of which the firm is or

---

[74] A "packaged product" is defined in the Glossary as being: (a) a life policy, (b) a unit in a regulated collective investment scheme, (c) an interest in an investment trust savings scheme or (d) a stakeholder pension scheme. Products (a), (b) or (c) are packaged products whether or not they are held within a PEP or an ISA or a CTF and whether or not the packaged product is also a stakeholder product.

[75] COB 5.1.2G.

[76] COB 5.2.

[77] COB 5.2.1R. The requirements do not apply when a firm provides basic advice on a stakeholder product: see COB 5A.

[78] COB 5.2.1R.

[79] COB 5.2.5R.

[80] COB 5.2.9R and 5.2.10R.

[81] COB 5.2.12R.

[82] COB 5.3.

[83] COB 5.3. The requirements do not apply when a firm provides basic advice on a stakeholder product: see COB 5A. Nor do they apply to a firm in respect of a direct offer financial promotion, other than for the promotion of a personal pension scheme: COB 5.3.2G.

reasonably should be aware.[84] There is a like general requirement when the firm acts as an investment manager.[85] There are other specific suitability requirements, including in relation to packaged products,[86] life policies,[87] occupational and stakeholder pension schemes,[88] broker funds,[89] pensions transfers and optouts[90] and personal pension schemes.[91] Whether or not a recommendation or transaction is "suitable" will depend upon the facts of each case, although detailed guidance is given as to a range of matters.[92] In many circumstances an explanatory suitability letter is required[93] and guidance is given as to its contents.[94]

(4) Customers' understanding of risk.[95] In relation to a private customer, a   **14–058**
firm conducting designated investment business must not: (1) make a personal recommendation of a transaction; (2) act as a discretionary investment manager; (3) arrange a deal in a warrant or derivative; or (4) engage in stock lending activity, unless it has first taken reasonable steps to ensure that the customer understands the nature of the risks involved.[96] Once again, the steps that will need to be taken by a firm to satisfy this obligation will vary from customer to customer and from transaction to transaction. Evidential guidance of the types of risk warnings required for various transactions is provided.[97]

(vii) *Product Disclosure*[98]

Reflecting Principle for Business 7, which requires a firm to pay due regard to the   **14–059**
information needs of its clients, requirements are imposed to provide private customers with information about a product or proposed transaction in a prescribed "key features" or "simplified prospectus" format.[99] The design and content will vary according to the product and the transaction. Projections relating to life policies, "key features schemes", "simplified prospectus schemes" and stakeholder pension schemes are subject to separate requirements.[1] With certain defined exceptions, firms are prohibited from providing projections for life policies, schemes or stakeholder pension schemes unless the

---

[84] COB 5.3.5R.
[85] *ibid.* Note the qualification in respect of a pooled fund.
[86] COB 5.3.5R, 5.3.8A–R and 5.3.10A–R.
[87] COB 5.3.5R and 5.3.10B–R
[88] COB 5.3.12R.
[89] COB 5.3.13G and 5.3.20R.
[90] COB 5.3.13G, 5.3.21R to 5.3.27R.
[91] COB 5.3.13G and 5.3.28R.
[92] COB 5.3.13G and 5.3.29G (table).
[93] COB 5.3.14R, 5.3.14R to 5.3.18R and 5.3.19R; note the record keeping requirements in 5.3.19A.
[94] COB 5.3.30G (table).
[95] COB 5.4. The requirements do not apply when a firm provides basic advice on a stakeholder product: see COB 5A.
[96] COB 5.4.3R.
[97] COB 5.4.4E to 5.4.12E.
[98] COB 6.
[99] COB 6.1 to 6.5. Note also the information requirements in sections 8 and 9 (relating to insurance contracts and life policy guides) which are not confined to private customers.
[1] COB 6.6.

projection is calculated and presented in accordance with relevant rules.[2] In addition, any document containing a projection must include specified statements and warnings.[3] While the rules are numerous and detailed, of particular note are the specific rules that govern both the assumptions that may be made and the information that must be provided in pension projections[4] and the assumptions that are to be made in relation to rates of return for various types of contract.[5] Other sets of rules relate to life policies[6] and with-profit guides[7] and firms carrying on with-profit business.[8]

(viii) *The Customer's Right to Cancel and Withdraw*[9]

14–060 Rights to cancel and rights to withdraw from certain categories of agreements are given, principally to a "retail customer", in specified circumstances.

(ix) *Dealing and Managing*[10]

14–061 Rules and guidance relating to these matters reflect several Principles for Business, especially Principle 6 (fair treatment of customers) and common law duties relating to competence and fiduciaries. They are directed to guard against a range of potential abuses. Relevant provisions are arranged under 15 headings, some of which are dealt with in more detail below: (1) Conflict of interest and material interest; (2) Churning and switching; (3) Dealing ahead of investment research; (4) Customer order priority; (5) Best execution; (6) Timely execution; (7) Aggregation and allocation; (8) Realisation of a private customer's assets; (9) Lending to private customers; (10) Margin requirements; (11) Non-exchange traded securities; (12) Customer order and execution records; (13) Personal account dealing; (14) Programme trading; (15) Non-market-price transactions; (16) Investment research; (17) Investment research recommendations: required disclosures; and (18) Use of dealing commission.

14–062 **(1) Conflict of interest and material interest.**[11] Fair treatment is the critical criterion in this context. So, in specified circumstances, a firm conducting designated investment business with or for a customer is prohibited from knowingly advising or dealing in the exercise of its discretion unless its takes reasonable steps to ensure fair treatment of the customer. The circumstances are where, in relation to a transaction, the firm has a material interest or a relationship or interest of actual or potential conflict or other customers with conflicting interests.[12] While not intended to be a definitive list, a number of reasonable steps are instanced by way of guidance with a view to resolving conflicts. They might include disclosure of the interest to the customer, reliance upon a policy of

---

[2] COB 6.6.4R.
[3] COB 6.6.14R to 6.6.18R.
[4] COB 6.6.10R to 6.6.13R.
[5] COB 6.6.49R to 6.6.52R
[6] COB 6.8.
[7] COB 6.9.
[8] COB 6.10–6.13.
[9] COB 6.7. The provisions are complex.
[10] COB 7.
[11] COB 7.1.
[12] COB 7.1.3R.

independence, and/or the establishment and maintenance of Chinese walls.[13] In the event that a firm is unable to manage a conflict of interest using such methods, it should decline to act on behalf of the customer.[14] Further requirements are imposed upon a broker fund adviser, [15] product provider with a broker fund[16] and a UCITS management company which also manages investments.[17]

(2) Churning and switching.[18] Restrictions are imposed to guard against a   **14–063** firm entering into transactions for a customer with unnecessary frequency relative to his agreed investment strategy (churning). Thus a firm conducting designated investment business with or for a customer must not in engage in discretionary dealing or make personal recommendations in specified circumstances, unless it has reasonable grounds for believing it is in the customer's best interests, both when viewed in isolation and when viewed in the context of earlier transactions. Like restrictions are imposed to guard against switching within or between packaged products unnecessarily relative to what is suitable for a private customer.

(3) Dealing ahead.[19] Restrictions are imposed directed towards postponement   **14–064** of own account transactions by a firm or an associate when not in the interests of clients. The restrictions apply when a firm or its associate intends to publish "investment research" to its clients. The firm must not undertake an own account transaction in the relevant or any related designated investment and must take all reasonable steps to ensure that its associates do not do the same, until the clients for whom the publication was principally intended have had (or are likely to have had) a reasonable opportunity to act upon it. The restrictions are subject to exceptions.

(4) Best and timely execution. Duties are imposed to achieve best execution[20]   **14–065** and timely execution.[21] Every firm that executes a customer order in a designated investment must provide best execution. This has two facets. First, the firm must take reasonable care to ascertain the price which is the best available for the customer order in the relevant market at the time for transactions of the kind and size concerned. Secondly, it must execute the customer order at a price which is no less advantageous to the customer, unless it has taken reasonable steps to ensure that it would be in the customer's best interests not to do so.[22] There are exceptions.[23] As to timely execution, a firm, once it has agreed or decided in its

---

[13] COB 7.1.4G to 7.1.8G.
[14] COB 7.1.4G and 7.1.9G.
[15] COB 7.1.10R–7.1.12R.
[16] COB 7.1.13R.
[17] COB 7.1.14R.
[18] COB 7.2.
[19] COB 7.3.
[20] COB 7.5.
[21] COB 7.6.
[22] COB 7.5.1R, 7.5.3R and 7.5.5R. Note COB 7.5.6E containing evidential provisions as to what is required in order for a firm to take "reasonable care" and the guidance in COB 7.5.7G to 7.5.10G.
[23] COB 7.5.4R. These include exceptions relating to life policies, units in regulated collective investment schemes and circumstances where a firm relies on another person to provide best execution.

discretion to execute or arrange for the execution of a current customer order in a designated investment, it must do so as soon as reasonably practicable. However, it is not so obliged if it has taken reasonable steps to ensure that postponing execution is in the customer's best interests.[24] Guidance is given as to circumstances when particular care may be needed when assessing the timing of execution of all or part of a customer order and as to when there may be reasonable grounds for postponing execution.[25]

14–066   **(5) Aggregation and allocation.**[26] A series of duties relating to these practices are imposed on a firm conducting designated investment claims. A requirement is imposed as to aggregation and allocation only in accordance with standards and procedures which are recorded, consistent and compliant with COB requirements.[27] Further a firm must have reasonable grounds to believe that aggregation will work to the advantage of the customers concerned and disclose that aggregation may have the effect on some occasions of working to their disadvantage.[28] Other requirements pertain to timing, fairness and pricing of allocation, reallocation and record keeping.[29]

(x) *Reporting to Customers*[30]

14–067   Requirements are imposed as to written confirmation of transactions and, in appropriate cases, periodic statements. These reflect Principle for Business 7 relating to communications with clients.

(f) *The "Client Assets" Sourcebook ("CASS")*

14–068   This contains extensive requirements relating to safeguarding and administering investments ("custody rules"),[31] collateral (i.e. receipt or holding of assets to secure an obligation of a client)[32] and client money and mandates ("client money rules", "client money distribution rules" and "mandate rules").[33]

5. FSMA Imposed Regulatory Liabilities

14–069   FSMA imposes civil and sometimes criminal liability for a number of contraventions of the regulatory regime. The range of remedies available in relation to civil liabilities varies according to whether the claimant is a regulator or private

---

[24] COB 7.6.4R and 7.6.5R.
[25] COB 7.6.6G and 7.6.7G.
[26] COB 7.7.
[27] COB 7.7.3R.
[28] COB 7.7.4R.
[29] COB 7.7.5–7.7.18.
[30] COB 8.
[31] CASS 2.
[32] CASS 3.
[33] CASS 4 in relation to designated investment business and CASS 5 in relation to insurance mediation activities. Note CASS 4.2 and CASS 5.3 as to the statutory trust in relation to client money.

litigant.[34] For purposes of exposition, civil liabilities imposed by FSMA may be classified as follows: (i) liabilities related to lack of authorisation; (ii) liabilities related to authorised persons; (iii) liabilities related to EEA firms; and (iv) liabilities related to official listing of securities.

(a) *Liabilities Related to Lack of Authorisation*

These comprise: **14–070**

(a) liability for contravention of the general prohibition;

(b) liability for contravention of the financial promotion restriction.

(i) *Liability for Contravention of the General Prohibition*

Contravention entails civil (and criminal[35]) consequences under FSMA. Reg-   **14–071** ulators may seek a range of remedies.[36] Moreover, relevant agreements are potentially unenforceable and voidable.[37]

(ii) *Liability for Contravention of the Financial Promotion Restriction*

Contravention entails civil (and criminal[38]). Regulators may seek a range of   **14–072** remedies.[39] Moreover, relevant agreements are potentially unenforceable and voidable.[40]

(b) *Liabilities Related to Authorised Persons*

Authorised persons may incur civil liability under FSMA for: (a) acting outside   **14–073** permission; (b) employment of certain persons; and (c) contravention of FSA rules. The statutory right of action in respect of such a contravention is however, limited. In the case of (a), the contravention is actionable only in prescribed[41] cases. In the case of (b) and (c), the contravention is actionable only at the suit of a "private person"[42] and by other persons in prescribed cases.[43] Moreover, the right of action is available only to a person who suffers loss as a result of the

---

[34] See further paras 14–083 to 14–094 (regulator) and 14–096 to 14–101, (private litigant) below.
[35] FSMA, s.23.
[36] See paras 14–083 to 14–094, below.
[37] See paras 14–097 to 14–101, below.
[38] FSMA, s.25.
[39] See paras 14–083 to 14–094, below.
[40] See paras 14–097 to 14–101, below.
[41] i.e. in regulations made by the Treasury: FSMA s.417(1), see the FSMA (Rights of Action) Regulations 2001 (SI 2001/2256).
[42] See paras 14–073, 14–074 and 14–077 to 14–079, below. For a case under the predecessor provision (1986 Act, ss.62, 62A) where the claimant failed as he was not a "private customer", see *Diamantis Diamantides v JP Morgan Chase Bank* [2005] EWHC 263.
[43] *ibid.* and see the FSMA (Rights of Action) Regulations 2001 (SI 2001/2256).

contravention.[44] Further the right is subject to the defences[45] and other incidents[46] applying to actions for breach of statutory duty.

(i) *"Private Person"*

14-074 The definition covers two categories of individual. Within the first category[47] is any individual, unless he suffered the loss in question in the course of carrying on any regulated activity or any activity which would be a regulated activity apart from any exclusion made by articles in the RAO relating to overseas persons[48] and information society services.[49] However, an individual who suffers loss in the course of effecting or carrying out as principal contracts of insurance[50] written at Lloyd's,[51] is not to be taken to suffer loss in the course of carrying on a regulated activity.[52] Within the second category[53] is any person who is not an individual, unless he suffers the loss in question in the course of carrying on business of any kind, except a government, a local authority or an international organisation.

(ii) *Liability for Acting outside Permission*

14-075 In general, persons (unless they have the benefit of automatic authorisation) need to obtain Part IV permission in order to undertake any regulated activity.[54] If an authorised person carries on a regulated activity in the United Kingdom otherwise than in accordance with permission, the contravention is actionable in prescribed cases at the suit of a person who suffers consequent loss.[55] Under the relevant prescribing regulations,[56] the right of action is limited to a "private person" as therein defined[57] or a person acting in a fiduciary or representative capacity on behalf of a private person for the latter's benefit and also does not extend to a contravention of a Part IV financial resources requirement.

(iii) *Liability for Employment of Certain Persons*

14-076 Authorised persons are required to take reasonable care to ensure that functions in regard to regulated activities are not performed by a person who is the subject

---

[44] For a case under the predecessor provision (1986 Act, s.62) in which the claimant was found to have suffered no loss, see *ANZ Banking Group Ltd v Cattan* [2001] WL 825289 (unsuccessful claim: no loss), considered further in Ch.15, para.15–047.
[45] e.g. the defence of contributory negligence.
[46] e.g. limitation period. For a case under the predecessor provision (1986 Act, s.62) which was statute-barred, see *Martin v Britannia Life Ltd* [2000] Lloyd's Rep. P.N. 412, considered further in Ch.15, para.15-049.
[47] The FSMA (Rights of Action) Regulations 2001 (SI 2001/2256), reg.3(1)(a).
[48] RAO, art.72.
[49] RAO, art.72A.
[50] RAO, art.10.
[51] A Lloyd's Name.
[52] SI 2001/2256, reg.3(2).
[53] *ibid.*, reg.3(1)(b).
[54] As to the grant of permission, see paras 14–010 and 14–011, above.
[55] FSMA, s.20.
[56] The FSMA (Rights of Action) Regulations 2001 (SI 2001/2256), regs 4, 3.
[57] See para.14–074, above.

of a prohibition order made by the FSA.[58] Similarly they must take reasonable care to ensure that in relation to a "controlled function" they use only a person who has had the requisite FSA approval.[59] Contravention of either obligation is actionable at the suit of a "private person" and, in prescribed cases, by any other person who suffers consequent loss.[60] Under the relevant prescribing regulations,[61] the right of action is limited to a "private person" as therein defined[62] or a person acting in a fiduciary or representative capacity on behalf of a private person for the latter's benefit.

(iv) *Authorised Persons' Liability for Contravention of FSA Rules*

Section 150 of FSMA renders civilly actionable in certain circumstances, contravention by authorised persons of *rules* made by the FSA.[63] Such rules are deemed to impose statutory duties for the purposes of liability for their breach. In order to establish a contravention, the nature and extent of the duty need to be determined by interpreting the FSA rule. Moreover the claimant must be within the category of person which the rule, as a matter of interpretation, is intended to protect. Also, the right of action is subject to a number of qualifications.[64] It does not arise in the following circumstances. First, rules as to financial resources are excluded.[65] Secondly, the listing rules made by the FSA as "competent authority"[66] are excluded.[67] Thirdly, the FSA may specify that contravention of certain of its rules does not give rise to actionability.[68] Fourthly, the FSA has power to make evidential rules and to provide that contravention of such rules should not be actionable.[69] Moreover, although the FSA's "endorsing rules"[70] which endorse provisions in the Takeover Code[71] and SARs[72] are "rules", the endorsed provisions themselves are not "rules" and so breach of the endorsed provisions

14–077

---

[58] FSMA, s.56(6).

[59] *ibid.*, s.59(1), (2). See para.14–012, above.

[60] *ibid.*, s.71.

[61] The FSMA (Rights of Action) Regulations 2001 (SI 2001/2256), regs 5, 3.

[62] See para.14–074, above.

[63] FSMA, s.150. This follows a like provision in 1986 Act: s.62 as restricted by s.62A of the 1986 Act. For case law under s.62 see: *Morgan Stanley UK Group v Puglisi Consentino* [1998] C.L.C. 481, considered further in Ch.15, para.15–051; *Loosemoore v Financial Concepts* [2001] Lloyd's Rep P.N. 235, considered further in Ch.15, paras 15–020 and 15–050; *Gorham v British Telecommunications Plc* [2000] 1 W.L.R. 2129 (unsuccessful claim), considered further in Ch.15, para.15–035; *Martin v Britannia Life Ltd* [2000] Lloyd's Rep. P.N. 412 (statute-barred claim), considered further in Ch.15, para.15–049; *ANZ Banking Group Ltd v Cattan* [2001] WL 825289 (unsuccessful claim: no loss), considered further in Ch.15, para.15–047; *Diamantis Diamantides v JP Morgan Chase Bank* [2005] EWHC 263 (unsuccessful claim: claimant not "private customer"); *Seymour v Ockwell* [2005] EWHC 1137, considered further in Ch.15, para.15–052.

[64] See the definition of "rule" in FSMA, s.417(1).

[65] FSMA, s.150(4)(b). There is little point in giving a right of action for breach of these rules, as persons are only likely to suffer loss as a result of breaches if the authorised person becomes insolvent and a right of action would be worthless in such circumstances.

[66] Under FSMA Pt VI, s.74(4).

[67] *ibid.*, s.150(4)(a).

[68] *ibid.*, s.150(2) . It has done so in its *Handbook*. Reference should be made to the fifth schedule to each sourcebook. See para.14–036, above.

[69] *ibid.*, s.149.

[70] FSMA, s.143. This provision will be repealed when the Takeover Directive is implemented.

[71] i.e. the City Code on Takeovers and Mergers issued by the Panel on Takeovers and Mergers.

[72] i.e. the Rules Governing Substantial Acquisitions of Shares issued by the Panel.

in the Takeover Code or SARs are not actionable under the Act. Finally, the right of action for contravention of a rule is "subject to the defences and other incidents" described above.[73]

14–078 The s.150 right of action is limited to a "private person" as defined in regulations made by the Treasury,[74] and to other persons who have suffered loss as a result of a rule contravention in four cases prescribed in the same regulations.[75] The first is where the rule contravened prohibits an authorised person from seeking to make provision excluding or limiting liability.[76] The second case is where the rule contravened is directed against insider dealing.[77] The third case is where the action would be brought by a person acting in a fiduciary or representative capacity on behalf of a private person for the latter's benefit. The fourth case is where the contravened rule requires a "relevant authorised person"[78] to respond to a claim for compensation within a specified time limit or to pay interest in specified circumstances in respect of any such claim. The defendant to a s.150 right of action is the authorised person who is under the relevant obligation imposed by an FSA rule.[79]

14–079 As discussed below,[80] contravention of a FSA rule may well give rise to concurrent civil liability in tort or contract and so in practice s.150 liability may not add to the liability already existing at common law.[81] However, being able to point to an explicitly imposed duty, which has been broken with consequent liability under s.150, will often result in a more easily established liability. This is especially the case where the claimant wishes to make a claim under the compensation scheme established under Pt XV of FSMA.[82] Breach of a FSA rule does not give rise to any criminal liability.[83] Nor, in contrast to contravention of the general prohibition and the financial promotion restriction, does a breach of a rule as such provide a ground for vitiating any transaction.[84] Nevertheless,

---

[73] See para.14–073, above.

[74] See para.14–074, above. For a case under the predecessor provision (1986 Act, ss.62, 62A) where the claimant failed as he was not a "private customer", see *Diamantis Diamantides v JP Morgan Chase Bank* [2005] EWHC 263.

[75] *ibid.*, s.150(3); FSMA (Rights of Action) Regulations 2001 (SI 2001/2256), regs 6, 3.

[76] See para.14–048, above.

[77] i.e. a "rule directed at ensuring that transactions in any security or contractually based investment [within the meaning of the [RAO] are not effect with the benefit of unpublished information that, if made public, would be likely to affect the price of that security or investment."

[78] Defined in FSMA (Rights of Action) Regulations 2001 (SI 2001/2256), reg. (4)(a) as an authorised person with a Pt IV permission to effect or to carry out "relevant contracts of insurance" (essentially a motor accident contract of insurance) or to manage the underwriting capacity of a Lloyd's syndicate as managing agent, the members of which effect or carry out "relevant contracts of insurance" underwritten at Lloyd's.

[79] The power to make money laundering rules under FSMA, s.146 extends (exceptionally) beyond authorised persons (although the rules must be "in connection with the carrying on of regulated activities by authorised persons") but it is only the authorised persons to whom those rules apply that may be sued under s.150 for breach.

[80] See Ch.15, paras 15–019 to 15–021 and 15–032.

[81] See (under the predecessor provision, 1986 Act, s.62): *Loosemoore v Financial Concepts* [2001] Lloyd's Rep P.N. 235; considered further in Ch.15, paras 15–020 and 15–050; *Gorman v British Telecommunications Plc* [2000] 1 W.L.R. 2129, considered further in Ch.15, para.15–035; *Seymour v Ockwell* [2005] EWHC 1137, considered further in Ch.15, para.15–052.

[82] See paras 14–125 to 14–139, below.

[83] FSMA, s.151(1).

[84] *ibid.*, s.151(2).

conduct which is impugnable not only as a breach of a rule but also on other grounds, such as a misrepresentation, may presumably vitiate a transaction. A person is not to be regarded as having contravened a rule if the "rule-making instrument" had not been published sufficiently widely at the time.[85]

(c) Liabilities related to EEA Firms

The FSA as "host state" regulator is empowered to impose requirements on "incoming firms".[86] FSMA imposes liability for contravention of such requirements in prescribed cases, at the suit of any person suffering consequent loss.[87]   **14–080**

(d) Liabilities related to Listing Particulars and Prospectuses

FSMA, s.90 (as amended[88]) imposes a statutory liability in respect of misleading statements or omissions in: (i) listing particulars[89] (a document required to be produced when securities are admitted to the Official List[90] operated by the FSA as UKLA[91]) and (ii) prospectuses[92] (documents required to be produced when securities are offered to the public[93]).   **14–081**

FSMA, s.90. Section 90 imposes liability to pay compensation to a claimant meeting certain criteria if listing particulars[94] or a prospectus[95] have a defect consisting of an untrue or misleading statement or an omission from them of a matter required to be included.[96] This statutory liability is imposed upon persons "responsible for" the particulars or prospectus.[97] Such persons may escape liability if a relevant "exemption" is satisfied.[98] For further commentary on this   **14–082**

---

[85] FSMA, s.153(6), (4), (2). Note also s.154 as to verification of FSA rules in legal proceedings.

[86] See FSMA, Pt XIII (ss.193–204). As to incoming firms (comprising EEA firms and Treaty firms), see para.14–019, above.

[87] FSMA, s.202. See the Financial Services and Markets Act 2000 (Rights of Action) Regulations (SI 2000/2256), regs 7, 3.

[88] By the Prospectus Regulations 2005 (SI 2005/1433) which implemented the Prospectus Directive ("POD"), Directive 2003/71 and extended s.90 to cover prospectuses in relation to unlisted securities (previously covered by the Public Offers of Securities Regulations 1995 (SI 1995/1537).

[89] FSMA, s.90(1).

[90] FSMA, s.79.

[91] The FSA, styled as the UKLA, is now the "competent authority": see ss.74, 103(2) and para.14–004, above.

[92] FSMA, s.90(11).

[93] FSMA, s.85.

[94] FSMA, s.90(4). The same applies in relation to supplementary listing particulars, as to which see s.81.

[95] FSMA, s.90(11)(a). The same applies in relation to a supplementary prospectus (see s.87(8)), as to which see s.87G.

[96] As to which see, in relation to listing particulars and supplementary listing particulars, FSMA, s.90(1)(b), (3), (4) and in relation to prospectuses and supplementary prospectuses, ss.90(11)(a), 87A, 87G and 82.

[97] As defined in Treasury regulations made under s.79(3) in relation to listing particulars and in the Prospectus Rules (in the FSA Handbook) made under s.84.

[98] FSMA, s.90(2), (11) and Sch.10 (and see s.90(11)(b)).

statutory liability, reference should be made to specialist works.[99] However, it is relevant to note that liability is incurred to a claimant meeting certain cumulative criteria: (a) he must have acquired some of the securities to which the defective particulars or prospectus relate; (b) he must have suffered loss; (c) the loss must be in respect of the securities; and (d) the loss must be as a result of the relevant untrue or misleading statement or omission. Acquisition of securities is given an extended meaning to include circumstances in which the claimant contracted to acquire the securities or an interest in them.[1] Moreover, it is clear that acquisition of securities includes both subscribing for and purchase of securities. A claimant is thus not precluded from making a claim under s.90 by reason of being a purchaser in the market as distinct from a subscriber although he may be precluded from making a claim in tort for negligent misrepresentation on the same facts.[2] The statutory liability is in addition to any other liability which may be incurred in the same circumstances.[3]

6. FSMA REMEDIES

(a) Remedies Available to Regulators

14–083   FSMA confers a number of important enforcement powers, more extensive than those which existed under the 1986 Act,[4] which enable regulators to act on behalf of investors and obtain various remedies in the event of actual or potential breaches of the regulatory regime. The FSA or the Secretary of State may apply to the court for injunctions, "remedial orders" and "restitution orders" against persons contravening the regulatory regime as well as persons "knowingly concerned in the contravention".[5] The FSA may also so apply against persons engaging in market abuse.[6] Moreover the FSA is empowered to act extra-judicially and obtain "restitution" from authorised persons (only) contravening the regulatory regime[7] and any persons engaging in market abuse.[8]

---

[99] For a commentary on Pt VI of FSMA and Pt IV of the 1986 Act, see Lomnicka and Powell, *Encyclopedia of Financial Services Law*. For the development of 1986 Act provisions see Powell, *Issues and Offers of Company Securities: The New Regimes* (Sweet & Maxwell, 1988).

[1] FSMA, s.90(7); as to the 1986 Act, s.150(5).

[2] See *Al-Nakib Investments (Jersey) Ltd v Longcroft* [1990] 3 All E.R. 321.

[3] *ibid.*, s.90(6), but note s.90(8)–(9).

[4] 1986 Act, ss.6 and 61. In relation to s.6, see *Securities and Investments Board v Pantell SA* [1990] Ch.426 (*Mareva* injunction available) (noted Lomnicka [1989] J.B.L. 509); *Securities and Investments Board v Pantell SA (No.2)* [1993] Ch. 256 (noted Lomnicka [1993] J.B.L. 54); *Securities and Investments Board v Lloyd-Wright* [1993] 4 All E.R. 134 (no undertaking in damages for interlocutory relief); *Securities and Investments Board v Scandex Capital Management A/S* unreported but noted (1997) Co. Lawyer 217 and affirmed on appeal [1998] 1 W.L.R. 712. Similar powers were conferred on the Bank of England to apply to the court in respect of contraventions of the Banking Act 1987 in ss.48, 49 and 93 of that Act.

[5] FSMA, ss.380, 382.

[6] *ibid.*, ss.381, 383.

[7] *ibid.*, ss.384(1) and 386.

[8] *ibid.*, ss.384(2) and 386.

(i) *Grounds for Application to Court*

The FSA (only) may apply to the court for relevant orders in relation to a breach **14–084** of two types of "relevant requirements".[9] The first is a "requirement . . . imposed by or under this Act". In essence, this covers any breach of the regulatory regime, including breaches which are criminal offences.[10] The second is a "requirement . . . imposed by or under any *other* Act" (emphasis added) where the FSA has power under FSMA to prosecute for its breach.[11] Secondly, the Secretary of State may apply in relation to "a requirement . . . imposed by or under this Act" leading to a criminal offence where he has power to prosecute under FSMA.[12]

Requirements imposed by or under FSMA. Such requirements will include **14–085** requirements implied in the general prohibition[13] as well as the financial promotion restriction,[14] i.e. requirements not to contravene such prohibition or restriction. In relation to authorised persons, such requirements will include those pertaining to acting within the scope of their permission,[15] employment of certain persons[16] and compliance with FSA rules.[17]

Requirements imposed by or under any other Act. Such requirements **14–086** where the FSA has power under FSMA to prosecute for breach,[18] pertain to insider dealing[19] and money-laundering.[20]

(ii) *Persons against whom Orders Available*

Contravenors. Relevant orders may be obtained against any person contra- **14–087** vening (or, in the case of an injunction, likely to contravene) a "relevant requirement".[21] Thus the orders are available against authorised persons, exempt persons and any other persons—as long as they are subject to and have breached a "relevant requirement". Most of such requirements are imposed on authorised persons.

Persons knowingly concerned. Relevant orders may also be obtained against **14–088** "any other person who appears to have been knowingly concerned" in the contravention.[22] The phrase "knowingly concerned" has been transplanted from

---

[9] FSMA, ss.380(6)(a), 382(9). As to the meaning of "requirement" in FSMA, see Lomnicka [2001] J.B.L. 96.
[10] See *ibid.*, s.401(2)(a), for the FSA's prosecuting power, extending to any offence under FSMA or subordinate legislation thereunder: s.401(1).
[11] *ibid.*, s.402(1) See para.14–086, below.
[12] See *ibid.*, s.401(1), (2)(a): same prosecuting power as the FSA.
[13] See para.14–006, above.
[14] See para.14–008, above.
[15] See paras 14–011 and 14–075, above.
[16] See paras 14–012 and 14–076, above.
[17] See the requirements in the FSA Handbook (paras 14–034 *et seq.*, above).
[18] FSMA, s.402.
[19] Under Criminal Justice Act 1993, Pt V (insider dealing).
[20] Under "prescribed" (see FSMA, s.417(1)) regulations, i.e. the Money Laundering Regulations 2003 (SI 2003/3075).
[21] FSMA, ss.380(1), (2), (3), 382(1).
[22] *ibid.*, ss.380(2), (3), 382(1).

the 1986 Act,[23] but its precise meaning is unclear.[24] It has two components, one pertaining to the state of mind of the person and one pertaining to their involvement. The case law is sparse. A person who knowingly received the proceeds of another's wrongdoing was assumed to be "knowingly concerned" in the wrongdoing in the first of two decisions in the same case.[25] In the second decision[26] it was accepted that solicitors acting for the wrongdoer could also be knowingly concerned and "a person who was the moving light behind a company" was given as another example. In another case it was stated that a director could be someone "knowingly concerned" in the company's breach[27] and that a person could be so concerned "if he merely knew the facts giving rise to the breach, even if he erroneously thought a breach of the law was not occurring".[28] In relation to market abuse, a relevant order may be made against the person concerned, i.e. in actual or potential market abuse.[29]

(iii) Orders Available

14–089 These comprise a restraining injunction, a "remedial" order, an asset-freezing order and a restitution order.

14–090 **Injunction.** The court may grant an injunction (or in Scotland, an interdict) restraining contravention of a "relevant requirement".[30] It may do so if satisfied that there is a reasonable likelihood of a contravention or of continuance or repetition of a previous contravention.[31] It may also grant an injunction in relation to market abuse if similarly satisfied.[32]

14–091 **Remedial order.** The court may grant such an order requiring the taking of such steps as it may direct to remedy contravention of a "relevant requirement". The court may make an order if it is satisfied that there has been a contravention and there are steps which could remedy it.[33] It may also grant a remedial order in relation to market abuse if similarly satisfied.[34] The order need not actually require a complete remedy for the contravention but may merely require that the

---

[23] 1986 Act, ss.6(2), 61(1).
[24] See Lomnicka, "'Knowingly concerned?' Participatory liability to regulators" (2000) 21 Co. Lawyer 120.
[25] Securities and Investments Board v Pantell SA [1990] Ch. 426 (noted Lomnicka [1989] J.B.L. 509).
[26] Securities and Investments Board v Pantell SA (No.2) [1993] Ch. 256 (noted Lomnicka [1993] J.B.L. 54).
[27] Securities and Investments Board v Scandex Capital Management A/S unreported but noted (1997) 18 Co. Lawyer 217, per Carnworth J.
[28] Securities and Investments Board v Scandex Capital Management A/S [1998] 1 W.L.R. 712, CA; following Burton v Burton [1980] Ch. 240 at 246–247.
[29] FSMA, ss.381, 383.
[30] See further para.14–092, below.
[31] FSMA, s.380(1), (6).
[32] ibid., s.381(1).
[33] ibid., s.380(2).
[34] ibid., s.381(2).

effect of the breach be mitigated.[35] In a case[36] concerning the similarly worded provisions of the 1986 Act,[37] the relief available was described as in the nature of "statutory recission of unlawful transactions" in that it enabled the court to unravel transactions.[38] A contrast was drawn[39] with the position under separate restitutionary provisions enabling "disgorgement" and compensation orders to be made.[40] An analogy was drawn with common law rescission. Thus the counterparty to the transaction with the wrongdoer had to be willing to return anything received under the transaction,[41] although on appeal there was disagreement as to what was required of the counterparty in order to achieve this.[42] Moreover, the order had to be directed at specific, identifiable transactions.[43] So-called "class recovery" was only possible under the separate restitution provisions. The Court of Appeal took a narrow view of the restorative or remedial requirement in the case of contraventions (concerning misrepresentations and misleading advertisements) which did not involve the actual entry into transactions but merely steps preliminary to transactions. It doubted whether it could order the unravelling of the consequent transactions in that the contravention was not the actual making of the transactions but the preliminary steps and therefore the unravelling of the transaction would not remedy the contraventions.[44] Interim payment orders were held to be available under like provisions in the 1986 Act.[45]

Asset-freezing order. In relation to a contravention of a relevant requirement, the court may grant an asset-freezing order (similar to an old style *Mareva* injunction), restraining the disposal or dealing with assets in danger of dissipation.[46] It is enough if there "may have" been a contravention or knowing involvement in one. This contrasts with the freezing injunction jurisdiction, which requires proceedings to have been commenced or be imminent. As regards   **14–092**

---

[35] FSMA, s.380(5). The Explanatory Notes to FSMA at para.665 give the example of an order requiring a correction to be published of a previous misleading advertisement. In relation to market abuse, see s.381(6).

[36] *Securities and Investments Board v Pantell SA (No.2)* [1993] Ch. 256 (reporting both Sir Nicholas Browne-Wilkinson V.C.'s judgment at first instance and the judgments on appeal to the Court of Appeal—Neill, Scott and Steyn L.JJ.).

[37] 1986 Act, s.6(2): order for "restoring the parties to the position in which they were before the transaction [in contravention of s.3] was entered into"; s.61(1): order requiring the taking of steps "to remedy" the relevant contravention.

[38] *ibid.* at 264, 282, 277.

[39] *ibid.* at 265.

[40] 1986 Act, ss.6(3)(4) and 61(3)(4). Equivalent FSMA provisions are ss.382 and 383.

[41] *ibid.* at 277, Scott L.J.

[42] *ibid.* at 277–278, Scott L.J. and 283, Steyn L.J.

[43] *ibid.* at 278, 280, Scott L.J.; also at 265.

[44] *ibid.* at 279, 286. *Sed quaere.* See Lomnicka [1993] J.B.L. 53 where it is submitted that this was too cautious an interpretation in that the preliminary steps were undertaken in order to induce the transactions and it is difficult to see how the contraventions could be remedied other than by unravelling the transactions they induced. In any event, at common law, misrepresentations may render consequent transactions voidable. FSMA, s.380(2) (especially in the light of the new s.380(5)) should be given a broader interpretation.

[45] *Securities and Investments Board v Scandex Capital Management A/S* unreported but noted (1997) Co. Lawyer 217 and affirmed on appeal [1998] 1 W.L.R. 712; and *FSA v Lukka*, unreported, April 23, 1999, Ch. D.

[46] FSMA, s.380(3).

a person "knowingly concerned", just as the possibility of a breach by the main protagonist is enough, so it would seem that possible involvement in a possible breach is enough. Should proceedings be contemplated or have been commenced, ordinary freezing injunctions may be applied for instead of orders under FSMA.[47] It would seem that the latter, like freezing injunctions, operate *in personam* against any assets of the defendant and give no security interest in respect of the assets frozen.[48] This is in contrast to an injunction based on a proprietary (e.g. tracing claim).[49] Thus it would be advantageous for a person with a separate proprietary claim at common law, not to rely on the FSA acting under FSMA, but to apply for an injunction freezing specific assets in the hands of the defendant to which he can assert a proprietary claim. In this way he can claim priority over unsecured creditors of the defendant (including the FSA).

14–093   **Restitution orders.** This is the marginal note description of orders which the court may make for contravention of a relevant requirement and also in case of market abuse provided the court is satisfied that either profits have accrued to the defendant and/or loss or other adverse effect has been caused by the contravention or abuse.[50] Thus regulators may obtain financial redress—disgorgement of profits or compensation for loss—on behalf of investors who may not have the resources, inclination or stamina to pursue the wrongdoers. In effect it enables "class recovery" or collective enforcement of their rights.[51] In form it is an order that the persons concerned (whether the main contravenor or a person "knowingly concerned") initially make a payment to the FSA and that the FSA then distribute that award as directed by the court. Thus even if the Secretary of State brings an application as he may in relation to a contravention of certain relevant requirements, it is the FSA that is the initial recipient of the award with the obligation to distribute it. The amount of the award is at the discretion of the court, but the court must have regard to the profits appearing to have accrued and/or the extent of the loss caused. Thus it would appear that the amount awarded must bear some relation to the profits and/or loss and that the court may not award "punitive" or "exemplary" sums which are, for example, a multiple of the profits made. As an award may not be made against a person in respect of profits accruing unless they have accrued to him, it would seem that in calculating its amount, regard should be had to the same profits. If private proceedings have been or are being taken against the wrongdoer, then no doubt, the court in the exercise of its discretion under this provision, would take any amounts

---

[47] See *SIB v Pantell SA* [1990] Ch. 426: grant of *Mareva* injunction in support of 1986 Act, ss.6 and 61 claims. Noted Lomnicka [1989] J.B.L. 509.

[48] *Cretanor Maritime Co Ltd v Irish Maritime Management Ltd ("The Cretan Harmony")* [1978] 1 W.L.R. 966 (a *Mareva* case).

[49] For case law on this distinction in the case of *Mareva* injunctions, see *A v C* [1981] 2 W.L.R. 197 Goff J.; *A.J. Beckhor Co v Bilton* [1981] Q.B. 923, Ackner L.J.; *PCW v Dixon* [1989] 2 Lloyd's Rep. 197, Lloyd J.

[50] See FSMA, s.382 as regards contravention of a relevant requirement. Equivalent provisions under the 1986 Act, ss.6(3)(4) and 61(3)(4), only enabled a restitution order to be made against the main contravenor and not also (as under FSMA) a person knowingly concerned. See *Securities and Investments Board v Pantell SA (No.2)* [1993] Ch. 256 at 285 (no jurisdiction under s.6(3)(4) to make orders against third parties). See FSMA, s.383 as regards market abuse.

[51] As so described in relation to like provisions in the 1986 Act (ss.6(3)(4) and 61(3)(4)) in *Securities and Investments Board v Pantell SA (No.2)* [1993] Ch. 256 at 263, 278.

recoverable in those proceedings into account. The order would also direct the FSA as to how the award is to be distributed amongst qualifying persons. These are persons appearing to the court to be person to whom the profits are attributable or who have suffered the loss, as the case may be.

(iv) *The FSA's Extra-judicial Power to Require Restitution*

FSMA confers on the FSA a new power which did not exist under the 1986 Act.   **14–094**
It is a power, exercisable extra-judicially, to require authorised persons to make restitution if they make profits or cause loss as a result of breaching the regulatory regime.[52] A like power exists in relation to anyone committing market abuse.[53]

(v) *The FSA Enforcement Manual*

The FSA's policy in relation to the exercise of its various enforcement powers is   **14–095**
contained in this manual which forms part of the FSA Handbook.[54]

(b) *Remedies Available to Private Litigants*

FSMA confers an entitlement to certain remedies on private litigants (i.e. persons   **14–096**
other than regulators) in respect of certain contraventions of the regulatory regime.

(ii) *Recovery of Money or Property Paid under Agreements Made by or Through Unauthorised Person*

Contravention of the general prohibition (non-banking). What may be seen   **14–097**
as direct contravention and attributed contravention of the general prohibition[55] may render relevant agreements potentially unenforceable and voidable.[56] Thus an agreement made by a person conducting a regulated activity (other than banking)[57] in breach of the general prohibition (direct contravention) is rendered unenforceable against the other party (the customer) and voidable at the latter's instance.[58] Also rendered unenforceable against the customer and voidable at his instance is an agreement made in the course of a regulated activity (other than banking)[59] by an authorised person not in breach of the general prohibition but

---

[52] FSMA, s.384.
[53] *ibid.* As to market abuse, see FSMA, ss.417(1), 118.
[54] See paras 14–034 *et seq.*, above.
[55] See para.14–006, above.
[56] FSMA, ss.26, 27. As apparent from subs.(3) of each section, it is not retroactive, but note the equivalent provisions in the 1986 Act: ss.5 (relating to investment business) and 132 (relating to insurance contracts). In relation to EEA firms, see FSMA, Sch.3, paras 16(2) and 17(2): ss.26 and 27 do not apply in relation to agreements entered into by such firms which have not satisfied the conditions for authorisation under those Schedules. For a case under the 1986 Act's provisions, see *CR Sugar Trading Ltd v China National Sugar & Alcohol Group Corp* [2003] EWCA 79 (Comm).
[57] FSMA, s.26(4). As to banking, see para.14–100, below.
[58] *ibid.*, ss.26(1).
[59] *ibid.*, s.27(4). As to banking, see para.14–100, below.

in consequence of activity by a third party in breach of the general prohibition (attributed contravention).[60] An example would be an agreement with an author-ised person made by a customer on the basis of investment advice by an unauthorised financial adviser. An agreement is rendered unenforceable only if made after the relevant FSMA provision came into force and if its making or performance constituted or was part of the regulated activity.[61] Thus, agreements which are incidental to the regulated activity are not caught. The unenforceability is one-sided and there is nothing to stop the customer from holding the party in breach to the agreement. Moreover, the agreement is not illegal or void to any greater extent.[62]

14–098   **Court's discretion.** The court is given a discretion to uphold the agreement. The discretion arises if the court is satisfied that it is just and equitable to enforce the agreement or to allow retention of the money or property transferred.[63] In making that assessment the court is obliged to have regard to a certain factor (called "the issue") depending on whether the case is one of direct contravention or attributed contravention.[64] In the case of a direct contravention the issue is whether the person in breach of the general prohibition reasonably believed that he was not contravening the general prohibition.[65] The test is part subjective and part objective: the person must have both subjectively believed and reasonably believed that he was not in breach. Thus if he was negligent in not seeking authorisation, his agreements cannot be saved by the court. An honest but unreasonable belief is not enough, so ignorance of the provisions of the Act would not constitute reasonable belief. In contrast in the case of an attributed contravention the issue is whether the authorised person knew that the third party was in breach of the general prohibition.[66] The test here is clearly subjective. It is enough to show that the authorised person did not know that the third party was in breach of the general prohibition.

14–099   **Recovery.** In the event that the agreement remains unenforceable, the cus-tomer is entitled to recover both the money (and any other property) he trans-ferred and also "compensation for any loss" suffered as a result of the breach.[67] Although the statute states that the amount of compensation is that agreed between the parties, or in default of agreement, that determined by the court,[68] no guidance is given as to the calculation of the amount of the compensation. Nevertheless, on electing not to perform the agreement, the other party must also return what he obtained under the agreement by way of any money or property

---

[60] FSMA, ss.27(1).
[61] *ibid.*, ss.26(3), 27(3).
[62] *ibid.*, s.28(9). See *Lloyd v Popely* [2001] 1 C.L. 77.
[63] *ibid.*, s.28(3). The onus being on the person seeking to uphold the agreement with the customer.
[64] *ibid.*, s.28(4).
[65] *ibid.*, s.28(4), (5).
[66] *ibid.*, s.28(4), (6).
[67] *ibid.*, ss.26(2) and 27(2).
[68] *ibid.*, s.28(2).

or, if transferred to a third party, its value at the time of transfer.[69] Contravention of the general prohibition does not make an agreement illegal or invalid to any greater extent than provided under the relevant FSMA provisions.[70]

Contravention of the general prohibition (banking). Separate and narrower **14–100** provision is made for contravention of the general prohibition in relation to deposit-taking. Thus a depositor who has parted with deposits to a deposit-taker acting in breach of the general prohibition may apply to the court for an order for the return of his money if he is not otherwise entitled (as under a current account) to recover his money immediately on demand. The court is given a discretion whether or not to make the order.[71]

Contravention of the financial promotion restriction. FSMA provides for **14–101** similar civil consequences in relation to contravention of the financial promotion restriction[72] as in relation to a contravention of the general prohibition.[73] Thus it renders unenforceable against the customer and voidable at his instance, certain agreements made and certain obligations undertaken in consequence of a communication in relation to which there has been a contravention of the financial promotion restriction. Also the customer is entitled to recover both any money or other property transferred and also compensation for any loss suffered as a result of the transfer.[74] Nevertheless, the court is given a discretion to enforce the agreement or obligation in certain circumstances.[75]

(ii) *Damages or Compensation*

FSMA confers on persons other than regulators rights to recover damages or **14–102** compensation in respect of certain liabilities arising under the Act, as previously described.[76]

7. THE OMBUDSMAN SCHEME

(a) *Introduction*

Part XVI[77] and Sch.17 to FSMA provide for the establishment of a scheme under **14–103** which "certain disputes may be resolved quickly and with minimum formality by

---

[69] FSMA, s.28(7), (8).
[70] *ibid.*, s.28(9). Similarly under the 1986 Act, ss.5(6) and 132(6).
[71] *ibid.*, s.29. See Sch.3, para.16(4): disapplication in relation to EEA firms.
[72] *ibid.*, s.21. See para.14–008, above.
[73] *ibid.*, s.30.
[74] *ibid.*, s.30(2), (3).
[75] *ibid.*, s.30(4) (8).
[76] See paras 14–077 to 14–079, above.
[77] FSMA, ss.225–234.

an independent person".[78] Although called "the ombudsman scheme" in the Act itself, the scheme that was actually established is named the Financial Ombudsman Service ("the FOS").[79] The FOS is operationally independent of the FSA.[80] It is administered by a body corporate as the scheme operator, which must appoint and maintain a panel of suitably qualified persons to act as ombudsmen. One is appointed to act as Chief Ombudsman. However, the FSA retains a number of responsibilities in relation to the FOS. These include appointing the board of the scheme operator, determining the scope of the "compulsory jurisdiction",[81] approving the rules made in relation to the "consumer credit jurisdiction"[82] and the "voluntary jurisdiction",[83] and setting limits on the awards that can be made under the compulsory jurisdiction.[84]

14–104   The FOS replaces eight dispute resolution schemes that previously operated across the financial services sector.[85] These predecessor schemes were variously organised on a voluntary basis and as a result of statutory and regulatory requirements. Although a single scheme, the FOS creates three separate and non-overlapping jurisdictions: the compulsory jurisdiction, the consumer credit jurisdiction[86] and the voluntary jurisdiction. While the broad structure of those schemes is contained in FSMA itself, details of the operation and procedures of the schemes are to be set out in rules made by the FSA in respect of the compulsory jurisdiction,[87] and by the FOS and approved by the FSA in respect of the consumer credit and voluntary jurisdiction.[88] Complaint-handling rules are published under the title "Dispute Resolution: the Complaints Sourcebook" (DISP).[89]

---

[78] FSMA, s.225(1).

[79] Its website is *www.financial-ombudsman.org.uk*.

[80] There is however a close relationship between the two entities: see the *Memorandum of Understanding* that exists between them and that seeks to define their respective roles and responsibilities.

[81] FSMA, s.226. See para.14–105, below.

[82] *ibid.*, s.226A, added by the Consumer Credit Act 2006, s.59. See para.14–105, below. The jurisdiction is expected to come into in April 2007.

[83] *ibid.*, s.227. See para.14–107, below.

[84] See paras 14–121 to 14–123, below.

[85] i.e. the Office of the Banking Ombudsman ("OBO"), the Office of the Building Societies Ombudsman ("OBSO"), the Office of the Investment Ombudsman ("OIO"—for firms regulated by IMRO), the Insurance Ombudsman ("IOB"), the Personal Insurance Arbitration Service ("PIAS"), the PIA Ombudsman Bureau ("PIAOB"), the SFA Complaints Bureau and Arbitration Service ("SFA CB") and the (voluntary) FSA Direct Regulation Unit and Independent Investigator. The Consumer Credit Act 2006 extends the FOS's jurisdiction to disputes with those licensed under the Consumer Credit Act 1974.

[86] Expected to come in force in April 2007.

[87] FSMA, s.226(3)(a). Sch.17, para.14 provides that the scheme operator is to make rules ("scheme rules") setting out the procedure for reference of complaints and for their investigation, consideration and determination by an ombudsman.

[88] As to the consumer credit jurisdiction, see *ibid.*, s.226A(7), (8) and Sch.17, paras 16A–16G. As to the voluntary jursdiction, see ss.227(3)(a), (6) and Sch.17, paras 17–22. Sch.17, para.18 refers to the voluntary jurisdiction rules as "standard terms" for the determination of complaints.

[89] For a review of the Financial Services Ombudsman system, including the extent of its coverage, the accountability regime, its decision making policies, rules of complaint handling and related procedural issues, see Jones & Morris, "A brave new world in ombudsmanry?" [2002] P.L. 640–648.

(b) *Compulsory, Consumer Credit and Voluntary Jurisdiction*

(i) *The Compulsory Jurisdiction*

This is imposed upon all authorised firms[90] and extends to cover[91] all regulated **14–105**
activities,[92] lending money secured by a charge on land, lending money (other
than restricted credit), paying money by a plastic card (other than a store card),
and the provision of ancillary banking services. Such services include the
provision and operation of cash machines, safe deposit boxes, etc.

(ii) *The Consumer Credit Jurisdiction*[93]

The Consumer Credit Act 2006 extended the jurisdiction of FOS to disputes with **14–106**
holders of standard licences under the Consumer Credit Act 1974.[94]

(iii) *The Voluntary Jurisdiction*[95]

This is imposed upon "VJ participants". VJ participants are companies, firms, **14–107**
individuals or other businesses which have decided and agreed to participate in
the voluntary jurisdiction and to be bound by the standard terms fixed by the
scheme operator for VJ participants. The voluntary jurisdiction extends to
cover[96] complaints which fall outside the terms of the compulsory jurisdiction
but which relate to lending money secured by a charge over land and financial
services activities covered by predecessor schemes insofar as the VJ participant
was a member of that predecessor scheme in respect of that activity immediately
before N2.[97] In practice, the majority of complaints dealt with under the voluntary jurisdiction of the FOS relate to the activities of unauthorised persons.
However, the voluntary jurisdiction is potentially sufficiently broad to cover
activities of authorised firms which fall outside the scope of the activities covered
by the compulsory jurisdiction.

(c) *Complaint Handling Procedures for Firms*

As with its predecessor schemes, the FOS will not accept a complaint for **14–108**
investigation under either the compulsory or voluntary jurisdiction until that

---

[90] See FSMA, s.226(2).
[91] DISP 2.6.1. These activities include any ancillary activities, including advice, provided by the firm
in connection with those activities. Complaints about firms which are members of designated
professional bodies and which relate to any otherwise exempt regulated activity cannot be handled
under the Compulsory Jurisdiction of the FOS.
[92] FSMA, s.226(4) limits the activities which may be covered by the Compulsory Jurisdiction to
activities which are "regulated activities or which could be made regulated activities by an order
under section 22 [of FSMA]".
[93] See FSMA, s.226A, added by the Consumer Credit Act 2006, s.59. The jurisdiction is expected to
come into force in April 2007 and at the time of writing the relevant "consumer credit rules" have
not been finalised.
[94] And persons authorised to wind up a licensable business under the Consumer Credit Act 1974,
s.34A.
[95] See FSMA, s.227.
[96] DISP 2.6.8.
[97] December 1, 2001—when the FSMA regime came into force.

complaint has been referred to the firm or VJ participant concerned and investi-gated. For that reason, every firm and VJ participant is obliged[98] to have in place and operate appropriate and effective internal complaint handling procedures to deal with any expression of dissatisfaction, whether justified or not, from or on behalf of an "eligible complainant" about that firm's provision of or failure to provide a financial services activity.[99] In order to be an "eligible complainant" the complainant must satisfy the criteria set out in the rules.[1] Save in very limited circumstances,[2] there are strict time limits within which a firm or VJ participant must deal with any complaint received by it.[3] Within those limits the complaint must be investigated and the complainant provided with a "final response".[4] If the firm or VJ participant decides that redress is appropriate, the complainant should be provided with fair compensation for any acts or omissions for which the respondent was responsible, and the respondent should comply promptly with any offer of redress which the complainant accepts.[5]

(d) Jurisdiction of the FOS

14–109   If a complaint made to a firm is not satisfactorily resolved through the firm's internal complaints handling procedures[6] the complainant may be able to refer the complaint to the FOS. If so, it is the duty of the firm to co-operate fully with the FOS in the handling of the complaint.[7] Before the Ombudsman will deal with

---

[98] DISP Ch.1. There are exceptions for: (1) UCITS qualifiers and (2) firms which do not conduct business with "eligible complainants" and which have no reasonable likelihood of doing so, to the extent that the firm notifies the FSA of this fact: see DISP 1.1.1 and 1.1.5.

[99] DISP 1.2.1. The Guidance given in the remainder of DISP 1.2.4 provides that a firm's procedures should provide for: (1) receiving complaints, (2) responding to complaints, (3) the appropriate investigation of complaints, and (4) notifying complainants of their right to go to the FOS where relevant. The precise procedures required will depend upon the size and organisational structure of the firm, the type of business undertaken by the firm, the nature and likely complexity of any complaints it is likely to receive and the likely number of complaints it will receive and have to investigate.

[1] DISP 2.4. See para.14–109, below.

[2] Where the firm reasonably determines that: (1) the complaint has not been made by an eligible complainant, (2) the complaint does not relate to an activity of the firm which comes under the jurisdiction of the FOS, (3) the complaint does not involve an allegation that the complainant has suffered or may suffer financial loss, material distress or material inconvenience, or (4) the complaint has been resolved by close of business on the business day following its receipt: see DISP 1.3.1.

[3] The firm must: (1) acknowledge all complaints in writing within five days of receipt (DISP 1.4.1), (2) send a final or holding response within four weeks of receipt (DISP 1.4.4) and (3) (if a final response has not been sent within four weeks of receipt) send a final response or a response which inter alia informs the complainant that he may now refer the complaint to the FOS within eight weeks of receipt (DISP 1.4.5). Every final response provided by a firm must also inform the complainant that he may within six months refer the complaint to the FOS if he is dissatisfied with the final response.

[4] A "final response" is one in which the firm: (1) accepts the complaint and, where appropriate, offers redress, or (2) offers redress without accepting the complaint, or (3) rejects the complaint and gives reasons for doing so, and contains information about the right to refer the complaint to the FOS.

[5] DISP 1.2.14.

[6] For example, because no Final Response is forthcoming within eight weeks of the complaint being made or because the complainant refuses to accept the contents of the Final Response.

[7] DISP 1.6.1. Such co-operation includes, but is not limited to, producing requested documents, adhering to any specified directions, attending hearings when requested to do so and complying promptly with any settlements or awards.

any complaint, he will need to be satisfied that he has the necessary jurisdiction. In particular, he must be satisfied that[8] the complainant is an eligible complainant[9] and that the respondent to the complaint is subject to either the compulsory jurisdiction or the consumer credit jurisdiction or the voluntary jurisdiction.[10] Also he must be satisfied that the activity to which the complaint relates is subject to either the compulsory jurisdiction or the voluntary jurisdiction[11] and that the respondent to the complaint has failed to resolve the complaint to the satisfaction of the complainant within eight weeks of resolving it.[12]

The jurisdiction of the Ombudsman also depends in part upon both the timing **14–110** of the act or omission about which complaint is made and the timing of the complaint. Under the terms of FSMA the Ombudsman will not be able to deal with a complaint under the compulsory jurisdiction unless: (1) the respondent was an authorised person at the time of the relevant act or omission; and (2) the relevant act or omission occurred at a time when compulsory jurisdiction rules were in force in relation to the activity in question.[13]

Equally, under the terms of FSMA the Ombudsman will not be able to deal **14–111** with a complaint under the voluntary jurisdiction unless three conditions are met. First the respondent was a VJ participant at the time of the act or omission to which the complaint relates.[14] Secondly, the respondent was still a VJ participant at the time that the complaint was referred to the FOS.[15] Thirdly, the relevant act or omission occurred at a time when voluntary jurisdiction rules were in force in relation to the activity in question.[16] The scope of the voluntary jurisdiction has also been expanded by the scheme rules to permit the Ombudsman to consider a complaint even though the relevant act or omission occurred before the VJ participant was participating in the FOS and even though it may have occurred before N2 if: (1) the complaint could have been dealt with under a predecessor scheme; or (2) the VJ participant has agreed to such a course.[17]

The jurisdiction of the FOS has been widened to allow it to determine **14–112** "relevant existing complaints" and "relevant new complaints".[18] By definition,

---

[8] DISP 2.2.1.

[9] An exhaustive definition of precisely who is an "eligible complainant" is set out in DISP 2.4.3–2.4.12.

[10] i.e. the respondent must either be a firm or a consumer credit licensee or a VJ participant.

[11] See paras 14–105 and 14–107, above.

[12] This condition exists to maximise the prospects of a complaint being satisfactorily resolved through a firm's own internal complaints handling procedures.

[13] FSMA, s.226(2)(b) and (c).

[14] ibid., s.227(2)(b).

[15] ibid., s.227(2)(c).

[16] ibid., s.227(2)(d).

[17] DISP 2.2.1 and 2.6.10.

[18] A "relevant existing complaint" is defined in Art.2(1) of the Financial Services and Markets Act 2000 (Transitional Provisions) (Ombudsman Scheme and Complaints Scheme) Order 2001 as a complaint which: (a) was referred to a predecessor scheme (other than the PIAS) at any time before N2 by a person who was at that time entitled under the terms of the predecessor scheme to refer such a complaint, and (b) was not determined before N2. A "relevant new complaint" is defined in Art.3(1) of the Financial Services and Markets Act 2000 (Transitional Provisions) (Ombudsman Scheme and Complaints Scheme) Order 2001 as a complaint referred to the FOS which relates to an act or omission occurring *before* N2. The Compulsory Jurisdiction applies to a relevant new complaint only if: (1) the respondent was subject to a predecessor scheme prior to N2; (2) the activity about which complaint is made was an activity to which the predecessor scheme applied; and (3) the complainant is eligible and wishes to have the complaint dealt with by the FOS. The FOS is also

each of these types of complaint will relate to acts and omissions which occurred before the compulsory or voluntary jurisdiction rules were made. The procedure and scheme rules are modified in relation to relevant existing complaints and relevant new complaints.[19] In particular, the Ombudsman will determine relevant existing complaints by reference to such criteria as would have been applied to determine the complaint by the appropriate Ombudsman under the predecessor scheme.[20] Further, the Ombudsman will, when determining in relation to a relevant new complaint what is fair and reasonable in all the circumstances of the case and what constitutes fair compensation, take into account what determination the appropriate Ombudsman under the predecessor scheme might have been expected to reach.[21]

(e) Complaints Handling Procedures of the FOS

14-113   The procedures adopted by the Ombudsman under the compulsory and voluntary jurisdictions to consider and deal with complaints are very similar.[22] On receipt of a complaint the Ombudsman must consider four matters[23]: first, whether or not he has jurisdiction to deal with the complaint[24]; secondly, whether or not the complaint is within the relevant time limit[25]; thirdly, whether or not the complainant is an eligible complainant[26]; fourthly, whether or not the complaint is one which should be dismissed without consideration of its merits.[27]

---

granted jurisdiction in relation to a limited number of other categories of complaint under the Financial Services and Markets Act 2000 (Transitional Provisions) (Ombudsman Scheme and Complaints Scheme) Order 2001: see Arts 8 to 10.

[19] See Arts 4 and 5 of the Financial Services and Markets Act 2000 (Transitional Provisions) (Ombudsman Scheme and Complaints Scheme) Order 2001.

[20] Art.6 of the Financial Services and Markets Act 2000 (Transitional Provisions) (Ombudsman Scheme and Complaints Scheme) Order 2001. For a consideration of the principles applied under the various predecessor schemes, see Lomnicka and Powell, *Encyclopedia of Financial Services*.

[21] Art.7 of the Financial Services and Markets Act 2000 (Transitional Provisions) (Ombudsman Scheme and Complaints Scheme) Order 2001.

[22] DISP 4.2.6 provides that the rules and guidance contained in DISP 3 will apply to VJ participants for the purposes of the voluntary jurisdiction as if they were firms except where the application of DISP 3 to VJ participants is specifically excluded or necessarily inapplicable. That to be established under the consumer credit jurisdiction is also expected to be similar.

[23] DISP 3.2.1.

[24] In this regard see the observations of Auld L.J. in *R. v PIA and PIA Ombudsman Bureau Ex p. Burns Anderson Independent Network Plc* (10) A.L.R. 57 at 61–62.

[25] The Ombudsman will not entertain a complaint: (1) more than six months after the date on which the firm or VJ participant advised the complainant in its final response letter that he could refer his complaint to the FOS (DISP 2.3.1(b)); or (2) more than six years after the event complained of or (if later) more than three years from the date on which the complainant became aware or ought reasonably to have become aware that he had cause for complaint (DISP 2.3.1(c)). The Ombudsman does however have jurisdiction to consider complaints outside these time limits if, in his view, the failure to comply with the time limits has been the result of "exceptional circumstances" (DISP 2.3.2). Examples of exceptional circumstances include the incapacity of the complainant or a failure on the part of the firm or VJ participant to inform the complainant in its final response that any referral to the FOS should take place within six months.

[26] See para.14–109, above.

[27] DISP 3.3 identifies 17 instances in which the Ombudsman may dismiss a complaint without considering its merits, including: (1) if the complainant has suffered no financial loss, material distress or material inconvenience; (3) if the complaint has no reasonable prospect of success; (4) if the firm has already made a fair and reasonable offer of compensation which remains open for acceptance; (6) if the matter has already been considered by the FOS or a predecessor scheme; (8) if

(f) *The Investigation*

If the Ombudsman does not summarily dismiss the complaint, he will proceed to **14–114** carry out an investigation into the complaint. He has a considerable discretion as to the procedure to be adopted during the course of any investigation. The starting point for any investigation will generally be the complaint form which complainants are required to complete at the outset. That complaint form will usually be sent to the financial adviser and a response to the complaints invited. Directions can and frequently are given by the Ombudsman as to the issues that he wishes to be addressed, the evidence that he requires, how such evidence should be given and the like. Representations and submissions, either in writing or at a hearing, are frequently invited.[28] The Ombudsman is also empowered to require a party to provide specified information or documents to assist in his investigation if the information or documents in question are necessary for the determination of the complaint.[29] A failure to comply with a request for information or documents without reasonable excuse can be referred to the court, which may deal with the defaulter as if he were in contempt.[30] It will also be referred to the FSA. The Ombudsman has also on occasion published guidance as to the material he requires parties to particular types of complaints to provide.[31]

At an appropriate time during his investigation the Ombudsman will send to **14–115** the parties a provisional assessment, setting out the reasons for that assessment and inviting each party to respond within a specified period.[32] Thereafter the Ombudsman will proceed to determine the complaint. The complaint will be determined by reference to what, in the opinion of the Ombudsman, is fair and reasonable in all of the circumstances of the case. While many of the factors likely to bear upon the decision are those which would be relevant to a determination of legal liability by a court, the Ombudsman is not limited to taking a strictly "legal" approach. Thus matters such as delays in administration, delays in dealing with correspondence, poor quality of service and the manner in which the parties have behaved are all potentially relevant to an assessment of what is "fair and reasonable" in any particular case.[33]

While this "fair and reasonable jurisdiction" undoubtedly increases the scope **14–116** for uncertainty over what decision the Ombudsman may reach, guidance has

---

the complaint has been the subject of court proceedings in which there has been a decision on the merits; (9) if the complaint is at that time the subject of court proceedings, unless those proceedings have been stayed for the purpose of referring the complaint to the FOS; (13) the complaint is about investment performance; and (17) there is some other compelling reason why it is inappropriate for the FOS to deal with the complaint. If the Ombudsman is minded to dismiss a complaint on any such basis he must give the complainant an opportunity to submit representations as to why he should not do so.

[28] The Ombudsman is not fettered by the rules of evidence that would be applied by a court. He is permitted either to exclude evidence that would otherwise be admissible in a court or to include evidence that would not be admissible: DISP 3.5.2.

[29] FSMA, s.231(1).

[30] *ibid.*, s.232(2).

[31] Such guidance has for example been given in relation to complaints about endowment and zero dividend preference share mis-selling

[32] DISP 3.2.10.

[33] See s.228(2) of FSMA, DISP 3.8.1(1).

been given as to factors that he is obliged to take into account when reaching that decision. In particular, the Ombudsman must consider: (1) relevant law, regulations, regulators' rules, guidance and standards and Codes of Practice; and (2) where appropriate, good industry practice at the relevant time. He is not however obliged to make a decision in accordance with English law—if he considers that what is fair and reasonable differs from English law, or that the result that there would be under English law would not be fair and reasonable, he is free to make an award in accordance with that view provided that he has taken into account the matters identified in DISP 3.8. In *IFG Financial Services Ltd v Financial Ombudsman Services Ltd*[34] it was confirmed that FOS determinations may be made by reference to what the Ombudsman considers to be "fair and reasonable" and not necessarily in accordance with the law. Thus although the claimants obtained an opinion from a Q.C. to the effect that, on the facts, they were not liable for loss caused by the unforeseeable dishonesty loss of an investment manager, the court upheld the Ombudsman's determination that the claimant was liable on the basis that this result was "fair and reasonable".

14–117   Once the determination becomes final and binding,[35] there is no right of appeal. The only means open to a disgruntled respondent to challenge the determination is by way of judicial review on the basis that the determination was not in fact fair and reasonable.[36] As with predecessor schemes, it is likely that the only determinations potentially susceptible to judicial review will be those made under the compulsory jurisdiction and (as the scheme is compulsory for consumer credit licensees) the consumer credit jurisdiction. Determinations made under the voluntary jurisdiction will not be susceptible to judicial review.[37]

(g) The Award

14–118   If a complaint dealt with under the scheme is determined in favour of the complainant, the determination may include an award against the respondent of such amount as the ombudsman considers fair compensation for loss or damage[38] suffered by a complainant ("a money award").[39] Also, or alternatively, it may include a direction that the respondent take such steps in relation to the complainant as the Ombudsman considers just and appropriate.[40]

14–119   The scheme is effectively one-sided since if the complainant accepts the determination, the respondent will be bound by it. The respondent has no option

---

[34] [2005] EWHC 1153, Admin, Burnton J. esp. paras 12, 74–76.
[35] See para.14–119, below.
[36] For examples of (unsuccessful) challenges to decisions of the Ombudsman see *R. v FOS Ex p. (Norwich & Peterborough Building Society* [2002] EWHC 2379; [2003] 1 All E.R. (Comm) 65; *R. v FOS Ex p. Green Denham & Co* [2003] EWHC 338, Admin; *IFG Financial Services v FOS* [2005] EWHC 1153, Admin.
[37] See by way of example *R. v Personal Investment Authority Ombudsman Bureau Limited Ex p. Johannes Mooyer* [2001] EWHC Admin 247, unreported, April 5, 2001, Newman J.
[38] Defined in FSMA, s.229(3) as financial loss or any other loss or damage of a specified kind.
[39] *ibid.*, s.229(2)(a).
[40] *ibid.*, s.229(2)(b).

to reject the determination.[41] If the complainant rejects the determination, for whatever reason, he is free to pursue the respondent by other means. Enforcement of the award is available through the courts, both for money awards[42] and for directions to take steps.[43] There is no right of appeal against an accepted determination.

If a determination is rejected by a complainant who subsequently elects to **14-120** pursue a claim against the respondent through the courts, the question frequently arises as to what, if anything, can be done with the rejected determination. The short answer is that it will depend upon the facts of each particular case. Clearly the court will not be bound by the determination of the Ombudsman—indeed, the court may decline even to admit that determination in evidence since on one view it is nothing more than a statement of opinion of what is a "fair and reasonable" result in the particular case before the court. However, insofar as the determination or a statement of assertions made previously by the parties, the determination may become relevant to issues before the court and so become admissible, albeit for limited purposes.

Money awards. The Ombudsman is obliged to assess the amount which **14-121** would be fair compensation for the loss or damage suffered by the complainant. The approach taken to financial loss is, in general, that adopted by the courts. In addition, the Ombudsman is able to require that "fair compensation" be paid for other heads of loss or damage which would not generally be recoverable through the courts. These heads of loss are pain and suffering, damage to reputation and distress and inconvenience.[44]

The maximum money award that the Ombudsman may make is £100,000 **14-122** exclusive of the costs of the complaint.[45] The Ombudsman however can, in practice, make determinations the value of which exceed this monetary limit since the limit does not apply to directions to take steps[46] which may well have a monetary value. Interest may be added to the award.[47] Costs may be awarded to a successful complainant.[48] In addition, if the Ombudsman considers that the award necessary to compensate the complainant exceeds the £100,000 limit, he

---

[41] FSMA, s.228(5). DISP 3.9.13 obliges a firm to comply promptly with any money award or direction made by the Ombudsman. See *FSA v Matthews* [2004] EWHC 2966: refusal of authorised person to comply with the award of the PIA ombudsman (since replaced by FOS) held to be a "breach of a requirement" and hence amenable to a FSMA, s.382 order (see paras 14–081, 14–087 and 14–091, above).

[42] *ibid.*, s.229(8)(b) and Sch.17, para.16.

[43] For example, by injunction to compel required steps to be taken: s.229(9) of FSMA.

[44] DISP 3.9.2. Although s.229(4) permits the FSA to specify the maximum amount which may be regarded as fair compensation for pain and suffering, damage to reputation and distress and inconvenience, to date no ceiling has been specified.

[45] FSMA, s.229(4); DISP 3.9.4.

[46] Under FSMA, s.229(2)(b).

[47] FSMA, s.229(8)(a).

[48] See FSMA, s.230(1) and DISP 3.9.9. A complainant cannot be ordered to pay costs incurred by a respondent in dealing with a complaint: FSMA, s.230(3). S.230(4) provides for rules to be made permitting the FOS to make an award of costs against a complainant in its favour for the purpose of providing a contribution to resources deployed in dealing with the complaint if, in its opinion, the complainant's conduct was improper or unreasonable or the complainant was responsible for unreasonable delay. To date, there are no such rules, even in draft form.

can recommend that the respondent should pay the difference on a voluntary basis. However, that recommendation is not enforceable and the respondent is under no obligation to meet any higher money award.

14–123   **Non-money awards.** If the Ombudsman decides that it is just and appropriate to require something other than, or in addition to, a money award he may so require. It does not matter that a court would be unable to order the course of action required by the Ombudsman. Accordingly, the Ombudsman can and frequently does require respondents to reinstate inappropriately surrendered life policies, reissue and back-date units in a unit trust scheme and so forth. The one practical limit on the Ombudsman's power is that his direction will operate only as between the parties to the complaint. Accordingly, if the Ombudsman was to determine that a life policy had been surrendered as a result of inappropriate advice given not by the insurance company but by the complainant's adviser, the Ombudsman could not direct the insurance company to reinstate the policy. The options open to him would be to direct the adviser to seek, at his own expense, the reinstatement of the policy and, if the adviser was unable to achieve that result, to make a money award instead.

(h) *Limited Immunity*

14–124   The FOS has a limited immunity from action in damages while performing compulsory jurisdiction functions.[49] Similar immunity is provided under the scheme rules in relation to voluntary jurisdiction functions.[50] The scope of this immunity is similar to that of the FSA.[51] Hence, there is no immunity in respect of acts or omissions of the Ombudsman shown to have been in bad faith. Moreover, an award of damages can be made in respect of acts or omissions which were unlawful as a result of s.6(1) of the Human Rights Act 1998.[52]

8. Compensation Scheme

(a) *Introduction*

14–125   Part XV of FSMA provides for a compensation scheme. Two main obligations are imposed on the FSA. The first is to establish a scheme for compensating persons in cases where "relevant persons"[53] are unable or are likely to be unable to satisfy claims made against them.[54] This scheme is called the Financial

---

[49] FSMA, s.225(4) and Sch.17, para.10.
[50] *ibid.*, s.225(4) and Sch.17, para.18(5); DISP 4.2.7.
[51] Para.14–005, above.
[52] *ibid.*, s.1(3), Sch.17, para.10(2); DISP 4.2.7(2). See further para.13–025, above and Ch.7, paras 7–004 to 7–012, above for a consideration of the operation of s.6 of the Human Rights Act 1998.
[53] See para.14–131, below.
[54] FSMA, s.213(1).

Services Compensation Scheme ("the compensation scheme").[55] This single compensation scheme is designed to replace the numerous and varied compensation schemes which previously existed.[56] The second obligation is to establish a body corporate to act as "scheme manager" for the compensation scheme. This body corporate is the Financial Services Compensation Scheme Limited ("the FSCS").[57] While the Chairman and Board of the scheme manager are appointed by, and liable to removal from office, by the FSA, the actual operation of the compensation scheme by the FSCS is independent from the FSA.[58]

(b) *Purpose*

The purpose of the compensation scheme is broadly twofold. First, it is designed **14–126** to maintain consumer confidence and to provide a certain level of protection to consumers in the event of insolvency. Thus the scheme aims to ensure that the debts due to consumers will still be met to a greater or lesser extent, if the entity with which consumers have deposited money or taken out an insurance contract or to which they have provided funds with a view to investment, ceases trading or is declared insolvent. Secondly, it is designed to provide a degree of consistency and unity within the financial services sector.

(c) *Structure*

The broad structure of the compensation scheme is contained in FSMA itself. **14–127** The detail of how the compensation scheme operates is contained in rules set out in the Compensation Sourcebook (COMP) which came into force on December 1, 2001 and has been amended subsequently by a number of Instruments. The Compensation Sourcebook also contains Funding Rules in relation to the scheme.

(d) *Qualifying Conditions for Compensation*

Once an application for compensation has been received from a claimant, the **14–128** FSCS will proceed to investigate and then, if appropriate, will make an offer of compensation to the claimant. The FSCS is entitled, as part of its investigation, to require "relevant persons" to provide such information or documents as is necessary to enable the fair determination of the claim.[59] It is also entitled to inspect documents held by the liquidator of an insolvent relevant person[60] and by

---

[55] FSMA, s.213(2).
[56] These were the Investors Compensation Scheme, the Deposit Protection Scheme, the Building Societies Investor Protection Scheme, the Policyholders Protection Scheme, the Friendly Societies Protection Scheme, the compensation arrangements that each of the eight professional bodies recognised under the 1986 Act was required to have in place and the various "profession-specific" schemes that existed.
[57] This body took over the management of the Investors Compensation Scheme (under the 1986 Act) on February 1, 2001.
[58] FSMA, s.212(1)–(5).
[59] FSMA, s.219. If without reasonable excuse the relevant person fails to comply with such a request by the FSCS, the FSCS may refer the matter to the court and the court may deal with the defaulter as if he were in contempt: see s.221(2).
[60] *ibid.*, s.220.

the Official Receiver.[61] Once it has completed its investigation the FSCS may pay compensation[62] to an "eligible claimant" if from its investigations it is satisfied as to the relevant criteria. The first is that an eligible claimant has made an application for compensation.[63] Secondly, the claim must be in respect of a "protected claim" against a "relevant person" who is in default.[64] However, the FSCS has a discretion to reject an application for compensation if the application contains any material inaccuracy or omission, save where it considers that inaccuracy or omission to be wholly unintentional.[65] Moreover, it must reject the application for compensation if the liability of the relevant person to the claimant has been extinguished by operation of law or any civil claim against the relevant person would have been defeated by a defence of limitation at the earlier of two dates: (a) the date the relevant person is determined to be in default; or (b) the date the claimant first indicates in writing that he may have a claim against the relevant person.[66]

(i) Eligible Claimants

14–129   Every person is an "eligible claimant" for the purposes of the compensation scheme unless they fall within relevant categories of excluded persons.[67] Even

---

[61] FSMA, s.224. The purposes for which the FSCS may inspect documents held by the Official Receiver are limited to: (1) establishing the identity of persons to whom it might be liable to make a payment in accordance with the compensation scheme; and (2) establishing the amount of any payment which it might be liable to make.

[62] COMP 3.2.1. In respect of claims under protected contracts of insurance there is one additional qualifying condition, namely that it is not reasonably practicable or appropriate to take steps to secure continuity of insurance under COMP 3.3.1 and 3.3.4 or to take the measures specified in COMP 3.3.4(2) to provide assistance to an insurance undertaking in financial difficulties. See further para.14–138, below.

[63] Or, if an application is made by a person on behalf of another, the other on whose behalf the claim is made is an "eligible claimant" who would have been paid compensation by the FSCS had he been able to make the claim himself: COMP 3.2.2. Thus claims may be made under the compensation scheme by personal representatives on behalf of the deceased, by trustees on behalf of beneficiaries and so forth.

[64] COMP 3.2.1.

[65] COMP 8.2.1.

[66] COMP 8.2.3. The FSCS may however disregard a defence of limitation in respect of a claim made in connection with protected investment business if it considers that it would be reasonable to do so.

[67] See COMP 4.2.2. Persons excluded from the definition of "eligible claimants" are: (1) firms (other than a sole trader firm or a small business whose claim arises out of a regulated activity for which they do not have permission); (2) overseas firms; (3) collective investment schemes or operators or trustees of such a scheme; (4) pension or retirement funds or trustees of such a fund (other than a trustee of a small self-administered scheme or an occupational scheme of an employer which is not a large company or large partnership); (5) supranational institutions, governments and central administrative authorities; (6) provincial, regional, local and municipal authorities; (7) directors and managers of the relevant person in default (unless the relevant person in default is a mutual association which is not a large mutual association and the directors and managers do not receive a salary or other remuneration for services performed by them for the relevant person in default); (8) close relatives of persons excluded by (7); (9) bodies corporate in the same group as the relevant person in default; (10) persons holding 5% or more of the capital of the relevant person in default or of any body corporate in the same group; (11) the auditors of the relevant person in default or of any body corporate in the same group as the relevant person in default or the appointed actuary of a friendly society or insurance undertaking in default; (12) persons who in the opinion of the FSCS are responsible for or have contributed to the relevant person's default; (13) large companies; (14) large partnerships or mutual associations; (15) persons whose claim arises from transactions in connection

then, such a person can still be an "eligible claimant" if he is able to satisfy one of the several exemptions.[68]

(ii) *Protected Claims*

A protected claim[69] is: (1) a claim for a protected deposit; (2) a claim under a protected contract of insurance; or (3) a claim in connection with protected investment business[70] as each is defined.   **14–130**

(iii) *Relevant Persons*

A relevant person is a person who, at the time that the act or omission which gives rise to the complaint took place, was a participant firm or an appointed representative of a participant firm.[71]   **14–131**

(iv) *Default by Relevant Persons*

A relevant person is "in default" if the FSCS determines that the relevant person is unable, or is likely to be unable, to satisfy protected claims against it and is satisfied that a protected claim exists and there has been a relevant insolvency related event.[72]   **14–132**

(v) *Assignment of Rights*

As a pre-condition to a payment of compensation, the FSCS may require a claimant to assign the whole or any part of his rights against the relevant person or against any third party to the FSCS on such terms as it thinks fit.[73] Where this is done the FSCS is obliged to make "such recoveries as it reasonably can"   **14–133**

---

with which they have been convicted of an offence of money laundering; and (16) persons whose claim arises under the Third Parties (Rights against Insurers) Act 1930.

[68] In COMP 4.3. The exemptions vary according to whether the compensation is sought in respect of a protected deposit, a long-term insurance contract, a general insurance contract and a liability subject to compulsory insurance.

[69] "Claim" is defined for the purposes of COMP as "a valid claim made in respect of a civil liability owed by a relevant person to the claimant". This definition is sufficiently broad to include claims for the return of deposits from banks and building societies, claims for actionable breaches under FSMA and claims for actionable breaches of common law duties of care and skill.

[70] COMP 5.2.1, 5.3–5.5. Note also COMP 14.5.

[71] COMP 6.2.1. For appointed representatives, see para.14–014, above. A "participant firm" is any firm other than: (1) an incoming EEA firm which is a Banking Consolidation Directive (BCD) credit institution or Investment Services Directive (ISD) investment firm and whose permission is confined to cross border services; (2) an incoming EEA firm without top up cover which is (a) a BCD credit institution whose permission to carry on regulated activities from a UK branch is confined to accepting deposits, or (b) an ISD investment firm (including a credit institution which is an ISD investment firm) whose permission to carry on regulated activities from a UK branch is confined to passported activities; (3) a service company; (4) the Society of Lloyd's, in respect of activities included in its permission under section 315(2) of FSMA; (5) a member, in respect of effecting or carrying out Lloyd's policies; (6) an underwriting agent or member's adviser in respect of advising on syndicate participation at Lloyd's or managing the underwriting capacity of a Lloyd's syndicate as a managing agent at Lloyd's; (7) an authorised professional firm that is subject to the rules of the Law Society (England and Wales) or the Law Society of Scotland; (8) an ICVC (as defined to mean, in essence an open-ended investment company authorised by the FSA); and (9) a UCITS qualifier (as defined).

[72] See COMP 6.3.1–6.3.3. See also COMP 6.3.4.

[73] COMP 3.2.1(3), 7.2.1. Where such an assignment is required, there is no obligation on the part of the FSCS to provide the claimant with an indemnity against any liability for costs that might arise in

through the rights so assigned.[74] It is also obliged to pay any recoveries made through the pursuit of the assigned claim to the claimant, unless equivalent compensation has already been paid by the FSCS to him.[75]

(e) *Compensation*

(i) *Offers of Compensation*

14–134   The FSCS is obliged to ensure that a claimant does not suffer any disadvantage by promptly accepting any offer of compensation that might be made to him by the FSCS.[76] The amount of compensation payable to a claimant in respect of any type of protected claim is the amount of his "overall net claim" against the relevant person at the "quantification date".[77] A claimant's overall net claim is the sum of the protected claims of the same category that he has against a relevant person in default, less the amount of any liability which the relevant person may set off against any of those claims.[78] The FSCS will therefore offset against any award of compensation monies to which the relevant person could properly claim to be entitled from the claimant. It will also offset monies that the relevant person (or a third party) has already paid to the claimant, if such payment was connected with the relevant person's liability to the claimant.[79] The quantification date varies according to the type of protected claim in issue.[80]

---

any future proceedings pursued by the FSCS against the relevant body: *R. v Investors Compensation Scheme Ltd Ex p. Bowden* [1994] 1 W.L.R. 17; [1996] A.C. 261.

[74] COMP 7.2.3. An example of one of the compensation scheme's predecessor schemes taking such steps is to be found in *ICS Ltd v West Bromwich Building Society* [1999] Lloyd's L.Rep. P.N. 496.

[75] COMP 7.2.4. Where the claimant has already received equivalent compensation from the FSCS, any recoveries from the pursuit of the assigned rights will be payable to the FSCS rather than to the claimant: COMP 7.2.2.

[76] COMP 7.2.5. Suppose A and B each have a protected investment business claim of £60,000 against a relevant person in default. The FSCS offers each claimant £48,000 (the maximum available) as compensation. A accepts the offer of compensation and assigns his rights against the relevant person to the FSCS but B delays accepting the offer. The liquidator of the relevant person in default subsequently makes a payment of 50 pence in the pound to all creditors of the relevant person. A and B are therefore each prima facie entitled to £30,000. If the payment is made after A has accepted the FSCS's offer of compensation but before B does so: (1) B would receive £30,000 from the liquidator and could then claim the £30,000 balance of his £60,000 loss from the FSCS; but (2) A would already have assigned his rights against the relevant person in default to the FSCS, who would receive the £30,000 instead of A. In such circumstances, A's prompt acceptance of the FSCS's offer of compensation would have worked to his disadvantage when compared to B, who delayed accepting the offer. The FSCS would almost certainly in such circumstances pass on to A £12,000 of the £30,000 recovered by it from the liquidator.

[77] COMP 12.2.1. In addition, COMP 12.4–12.6 identifies a number of specific matters of which the FSCS must take account when assessing appropriate compensation under particular categories of protected claims.

[78] COMP 12.2.4.

[79] In *R. v Investors Compensation Scheme Ex p. Bowden* [1996] A.C. 261 investors challenged the decision of the ICS to make deductions from the compensation that was offered to them so that the amount offered fell below the investors' overall net claim. The House of Lords found that the ICS was entitled to exclude elements of a claim which it considered were not essential to provide fair compensation to investors and also to place a reasonable limit on the sums payable to investors in respect of their professional fees. It is doubtful whether the COMP rules would be interpreted so as to permit the FSCS to apply similar deductions or limitations.

[80] See COMP 12.3.1–12.3.6.

The FSCS may make reduced or interim offers of compensation if the amount   **14–135**
of compensation payable is uncertain or if the claimant has reasonable prospects
of recovering part of his loss from any other person.[81] Any offer of compensation
made by the FSCS must remain open for 90 days unless it appears during that
period that no offer should in fact have been made, or the offer is rejected in that
period. Upon the expiry of 90 days, the FSCS may withdraw the offer unless its
size has been disputed and consideration is being given to making a reduced or
interim offer.[82] No offer of compensation will exceed the limits payable by the
FSCS for protected claims.[83] For protected deposits, the limit is 100 per cent of
the first £2,000 of the claim, 90 per cent of the next £33,000 of the claim and a
maximum payment of £31,700. For a protected contract of insurance when the
contract is a relevant general insurance contract, the limit is 100 per cent of the
claim (to an unlimited maximum) where the claim is in respect of a liability
subject to compulsory insurance and 100 per cent of the first £2,000 of the claim
and 90 per cent of the remainder of the claim (to an unlimited maximum) in all
other cases. For a protected contract of insurance when the contract is a long term
insurance contract, the limit is at least 90 per cent of the value of the policy
(including future benefits declared before the date the relevant person is determined to be in default) to an unlimited maximum. For protected investment
business, the limit is 100 per cent of the first £30,000 of the claim and 90 per cent
of the next £20,000 of the claim, to a maximum payment of £48,000.[84]

These limits apply to the aggregate amount of claims in respect of each   **14–136**
category of protected claim that an eligible claimant has against a relevant
person. Consequently a claimant who, for example, has a claim against a relevant
person for two deposits each of £1,500, will not receive 100 per cent compensation on each deposit. He will only receive 100 per cent of £2,000 and 90 per cent
of the balance of £1,000, a total of £2,900.

(ii) *Acceptance of Offers of Compensation*

The FSCS is obliged[85] to pay a claim as soon as reasonably possible after it has   **14–137**
satisfied itself that the qualifying conditions for compensation have been met and
the amount of compensation due to the claimant has been calculated.[86] With
limited exceptions,[87] payment will be made to the claimant or to the order of the

---

[81] COMP 8.3.2 and COMP 11.2.4–11.2.5.

[82] COMP 8.3.1. The offer may also be withdrawn if it is rejected.

[83] See in COMP 10.2. Interest, which may be paid on the compensation sum under COMP 11.2.7, is
not to be taken into account when applying limits on the compensation sum payable.

[84] COMP 10.2.3.

[85] COMP 9.2.1.

[86] "As soon as reasonably possible" is not defined within the rules, although COMP 9.2.1 provides
that all payments must be made within three months unless the FSA has granted the FSCS an
extension of time. Even then, appropriate compensation must be paid within four months. COMP
9.2.2 does permit the FSCS in extremely limited circumstances to postpone paying compensation to
a claimant.

[87] COMP 11.2.2–11.2.3. These exceptions include: (1) claims made in connection with protected
investment claims covered by the pensions review (when the FSCS must pay any compensation to the
trustee of the occupational pension scheme or the personal pension scheme or other product
provider); and (2) claims under a protected contract of insurance against a relevant person that is in
provisional liquidation or liquidation (when the FSCS may inter alia make payments on behalf of the
claimant).

claimant unless arrangements have been or are to be made to secure continuity of insurance or the FSCS is taking measures to safeguard the claimant in respect of an insurance undertaking in financial difficulty.[88]

(iii) *Insurance*

14–138 Insurance, and in particular long-term insurance, can cause difficulty when the issue of compensation is considered. If, for example, a life policy is payable only upon the death of the policy holder or upon the policy holder reaching a certain age, and he is below that age at the material time, it is not immediately straightforward to see how best to compensate the policy holder. Particular provision is therefore made in FSMA for the FSCS to make arrangements *not* to make an immediate payment of monetary compensation to such persons. The FSCS may instead secure continuity of insurance for policy holders whose insurer is unable, or appears to be unable, to satisfy claims against it.[89] This may involve either securing or facilitating the transfer of all or part of the long-term insurance business of the relevant person in default to another firm or securing the issue of policies by another firm to eligible claimants in substitution for their existing policies.[90] The FSCS may also take measures to safeguard a policy holder whose insurer encounters financial difficulty.[91] This may involve securing or facilitating the transfer of all or part of the business of the relevant person which consists of carrying out contracts of insurance to another firm. Alternatively it may involve the provision of assistance to the relevant person to enable it to continue to effect or carry out contracts of insurance.[92]

(iv) *Challenging the FSCS*

14–139 The FSCS has a limited immunity from action in damages while performing functions as scheme manager of the compensation scheme.[93] Nevertheless, the decisions and actions of the FSCS are susceptible to judicial review.

---

[88] See COMP 3.3.3–3.3.6 and 11.2.1.
[89] FSMA, s.216. The rules governing the circumstances in which the FSCS is obliged to make arrangements to secure continuity of insurance are set out in COMP 3.3.1.
[90] COMP 3.3.2.
[91] FSMA, s.217. The rules governing the circumstances in which the FSCS is obliged to take measures to safeguard eligible claimants where the relevant person about whom complaint is made is an insurance undertaking in financial difficulty are set out in COMP 3.3.3–3.3.6.
[92] COMP 3.3.4.
[93] See FSMA, s.222(1). Note para.14–004, above in relation to the limited immunity of the FSA.

CHAPTER 15

FINANCIAL PRACTITIONERS

1. GENERAL

(a) *Scope*

This chapter concerns financial practitioners regulated by the Financial Services **15–001**
and Markets Act 2000 ("FSMA"), other than insurance brokers and underwriting
agents at Lloyd's, which are treated in other chapters.[1] They consist of a very

---

[1] See Ch.16 (Insurance Brokers) and Ch.19 (Members and Managing Agents at Lloyd's).

wide range of occupations. Many will fall outside the public perception of a professional. The term "financial practitioner" is used as a neutral generic description in this chapter.

15–002   An understanding of the FSMA regulatory regime is fundamental to any consideration of claims against regulated practitioners. The regime is complex and relevant to both financial and other practitioners; hence its treatment in a separate chapter, including statutory liabilities under FSMA.

15–003   Despite the impact of financial services legislation, the common law remains of fundamental relevance, particularly the common law relating to contract, tort, trust, fiduciaries, confidentiality, damages and restitution, as well as other statutes, e.g. the Misrepresentation Act 1967. Claims against financial practitioners cannot be corralled into a discrete pen which is the exclusive domain of what may be seen as somewhat recondite regulatory law. Statute-led regulatory law constitutes only another overlay to other areas of law and the task of the lawyer is to be acute to their interrelationship and the scope for development. Indeed, especially in relation to non-private customers, the common law may provide bases of claim in circumstances where regulatory duties do not.

(b) *The Financial Sector*

15–004   A generation ago the financial sector was much less developed and recognisable than now. The main players would have been identified as banks, including merchant banks, insurers, stockbrokers, and at the retail level "insurance" agents, (e.g. "the man from the Pru") and, to the more knowledgeable, some more recondite animals associated with specialist markets, such as discount houses in the gilt market. "The City" served as an embracing halo to identify an otherwise obfuscating cloud. As a generic description it was remarkable less for its precision than its mystique, inexplicable not only to the uninitiated but even to most of those initiated in financial affairs.

15–005   A series of events has shaped today's financial sector in the United Kingdom. They may be traced through the development of the euro dollar market, the abolition of exchange controls, "Big Bang", privatisation of state enterprises, the shift from occupational pension schemes to private provision for pensions, tax advantaged investment products, (e.g. PEPs and ISAs) and generally the encouragement of an investment culture. Internationally, currency and capital markets have burgeoned, with a broad trend towards floating exchange rates and free movement of capital. Securities markets have likewise grown, driven by increased mergers and acquisitions activity, privatisation and demutualisation issues and increasing demand from pensions, mutual funds and private sources, as well as by technological aids, principally computers and the internet.

15–006   These developments have spawned an increasing and constantly evolving range of occupations and specialities. Classification is difficult and various. The pantheon of financial activities includes analysis, research, reporting, advice, custody, management, dealing, regulation, compliance and administration. Similarly financial practitioners will include those identified generally as analysts, bankers, brokers, custodians, insurers, investment advisers, journalists, managers, traders, valuers, regulators and compliance officers, as well as more recognisable professions such as accountants, actuaries and lawyers. The difficulty of classification impacts significantly upon the ascertainment and setting of standards.

(c) *Regulation*

Developments in the financial sector were paralleled by increasing statutory **15–007** regulation of the financial sector, dating principally from the 1970s, and culminating in FSMA. Prior to FSMA, a series of statutes established specific regulatory regimes.[2] The main features of such regimes are now familiar. Generally, regulated institutions and firms needed to be authorised by an appropriate regulator as a condition of carrying on business in a relevant financial sector. Authorisation demanded compliance with a range of requirements relating to integrity, competence, avoidance of conflicts of interests, adequate financial resources, accounts and auditing, records and reporting etc. Regulators were given a panoply of powers including powers to take action to seek injunctions and restitution orders, intervention powers and powers to seek winding up and administration orders. These were backed by criminal, civil and disciplinary sanctions. Compensation from an established scheme was also usually available.

Regulation related to general investor protection was a relative latecomer. **15–008** Investment was formerly generally perceived as synonymous with speculation and the interest of a rich minority. Change the word from "investment" to "savings" or "pensions" and the perspective inevitably changes. This wider perspective resulted in the Financial Services Act 1986 ("the 1986 Act") directed mainly at regulating the conduct of investment business in the United Kingdom. While originally the system of regulation was at least portrayed as "statute backed self-regulation", gradually changes were effected so that eventually it could not be mistaken for anything other than a statutory regime of regulation. FSMA marks the inevitable shift to a fully statutory scheme.

(d) *Raising Standards*

The imposition and raising of standards are fundamental objectives of the **15–009** regulatory regimes. Doing so by what is effectively a statutory scheme takes the process of setting standards considerably further than that effected by self-regulation, but necessarily so. Given the past structure and utilisation of the retail investment sector in the United Kingdom, achieving those objectives requires a metamorphosis of culture, from that of salesman to professional adviser. That metamorphosis is far from complete. It is likely to remain incomplete so long as remuneration is contingent on an investment being made, however open (or less opaque) the commission disclosure requirements. Major scandals relating to mis-selling of home income plans, pensions and endowment policies illustrate how far the change in culture has to go. Indeed the Janus faces of representatives of product providers in the investment sector, one of salesman and the other of adviser, portends continuing misunderstanding, misconduct and litigation.

---

[2] e.g. Insurance Companies Acts 1974 and 1982; Banking Act 1979 and 1987; Building Societies Act 1986; Financial Services Act 1986; Pensions Act 1995.

2. DUTIES AND LIABILITIES

(a) *Sources*

15–010   The duties of financial advisers and institutions arise from a range of sources: statutes (especially regulatory statutes), the common law and codes of practice. Breach of these duties may (but not invariably) give rise to civil liability. Some liabilities are generally characterised by reference to a duty, (e.g. breach of contract) others may be characterised by reference to the relevant default, (e.g. misrepresentation). Whether and, if so, to what extent, liability may arise from one or more such sources will require close analysis of the circumstances and context of each case. Victims of unlawful acts of a public authority may bring proceedings against it.[3]

(b) *Relevant Approach*

15–011   In analysing claims from a financial context, the first main issue which needs to be addressed is one of regulatory application. Does any statute-based or other regulatory regime apply? If so, which? What is its impact, taking into account the regulatory classification of both claimant and defendant, the nature of the services provided and relevant contractual arrangements? Does it give rise to any duties and liabilities? To what extent, if at all, does it modify what would otherwise be the position? What is the significance, if any, of the regulatory regime for common law liabilities? The second main issue which needs to be addressed is the relevance of other potential causes of action. These may arise under other relevant statutes such as the Misrepresentation Act 1967. There may be common law causes of action such as breach of contract, tort (especially the torts of deceit and negligence) or breach of fiduciary and confidentiality duties.

(c) *The FSMA Regime*

15–012   The FSMA regime, including duties and statutory liabilities arising thereunder, is treated in Ch.14.

(d) *The Misrepresentation Act 1967*

(i) *Relevance*

15–013   The Misrepresentation Act 1967 is of general application. The Act, in particular s.2(1) (damages for "negligent" misrepresentation) and s.2(2) (damages in lieu of rescission), has particular relevance to claims against financial practitioners. This is because (especially as compared to other professionals and other service providers), there is generally a large element of promotion in their activities.

---

[3] Human Rights Act 1998, s.7(1) A "victim" is any person who is directly affected by the alleged breach of the EHR Convention. It is not necessary to show detriment: see, e.g. *De Jong, Baljet and Van den Brink v The Netherlands* (1984) 8 E.H.R.R. 20, paras 40–41.

There is frequent scope for invocation of alleged misrepresentations and related liabilities designed to undo consequent investment contracts or relieve their effect. Nevertheless, the 1967 Act is likely to be of significance only in relation claims by persons to whom the statutory right of action under the FSMA (as under the 1986 Act) for contravention of rules (including very prescriptive rules as to financial promotion and advice) is not available.[4] Detailed consideration of the provisions of the 1967 Act is a beyond the scope of this work,[5] but aspects of s.2(1) liability merit comment.

(ii) *Representations as to Suitability*

The traditional view that, to be actionable, a representation must be a statement **15–014** of fact rather than one of opinion has been considerably eroded in recent years.[6] It will provide no obstacle to an investor whose complaint is to the effect that an investment was misdescribed to him.[7] In contrast, it may be said that a representation as to "suitability" is more appropriately categorised as a representation of opinion rather than a representation of fact. Nevertheless, a representor will not escape liability under the 1967 Act merely because the representation is a statement of opinion or belief, if the statement carries with it the implication that there are reasonable grounds for holding that opinion or belief.[8] It is submitted that in almost every case where a financial practitioner recommends an investment as suitable for an investor, that recommendation carries with it implicit representations that (1) the nature of the investment has been carefully considered by the practitioner, (2) the investor's needs have been carefully assessed by the practitioner, and (3) viewed objectively, the investment meets those needs. If one or more of those implicit representations is false, the fact that the express representation might be one of opinion rather than of fact will be of no assistance to the maker of the representation.[9]

---

[4] See Ch.14, paras 14–074 and 14–078 as to whom the statutory right of action is available.

[5] See generally *Chitty on Contracts* (29th edn), Ch.6.

[6] See generally, *Chitty, op. cit.*, paras 6–004 to 6–019.

[7] In *Peekay Intermark Ltd v ANZ Banking Group Ltd* [2006] EWCA Civ 386 the claimant contended that he had been induced to invest in a particular product as a result of oral misrepresentations as to the nature of the product made by a representative of the defendant. In fact, a form subsequently initialled and signed by the claimant as part of the application process for making the particular investment had accurately described the investment and, had it been carefully read by the claimant, would have corrected any misapprehension in his mind that had occurred due to the earlier inaccurate oral misrepresentation. The claimant had however initialled and signed the application form without reading it. The claimant failed in his claim for damages. Although the product had been mis-described to him orally, the inducement for him signing the relevant documentation had not been that misrepresentation but rather had been "his own assumption that the investment product to which [the forms] related corresponded to the description he had previously been given". That assumption would and should have been shattered had he (as he ought to have done) read the forms.

[8] See *Brown v Raphael* [1958] Ch. 636.

[9] In *ICS Ltd v West Bromwich Building Society* [1999] Lloyd's L.Rep. P.N. 496 the defendant sought to argue that representations made to claimants who had subsequently entered into Home Income Plans ought to be viewed as nothing more than predictions as to the likely future performance of the Plans and not as actionable representations. In rejecting this argument Evans Lombe J. considered that, by making the predictions, the defendant had implicitly stated that it could justify them on reasonable grounds. Since the defendant could not in fact do so, the representations were prima facie actionable.

(iii) *False in a Material Respect*

15-015   No claim will lie under the 1967 Act unless the representation of which complaint is made is false. Difficulty can be encountered if a statement is literally true, but is nonetheless misleading in certain respects, or if a statement contains elements which are true and elements which are false. The test often applied has been to ask whether or not the representation was false in a "material respect".[10] The problem has also been addressed[11] by applying the test laid down in s.20(4) of the Marine Insurance Act 1906—a statement will be treated as being true if it is substantially correct and the difference would not have induced a reasonable person to enter the contract.

(iv) *Comparison with Common Law*

15-016   A claimant who has a cause of action under s.2(1) of the 1967 Act may also have a common law cause of action based on the tort of negligence. The former statutory cause of action has some relative advantages. First, there is no need to prove that a duty of care is owed by the maker of the representation to the recipient. Secondly, provided that the recipient is able to demonstrate that the representation is false, the burden will fall on the maker to demonstrate that, despite its falsity, he had reasonable grounds for believing that it was true. Thirdly, given that the liability in s.2(1) is expressed by reference to the position prevailing if the misrepresentation had been made fraudulently, it would seem that the damages recoverable fall to be assessed by reference to the more favourable measure applicable to the tort of deceit rather than that applicable to the tort of negligence.[12] Moreover, for the same reason, a defendant will be unable to contend for a reduction in any award on the grounds of the claimant's contributory negligence—unless there is a concurrent claim open to the claimant for negligent misstatement.[13]

(e) *Contractual Duties*

(i) *Relevant Contracts*

15-017   There will be usually be a contract between the provider and recipient of financial services. Indeed there may be several contracts. A recipient of financial services might well enter into a framework customer agreement at the outset of a

---

[10] i.e. is the respect in which the representation is false "capable of inducing the representee to enter the contract in question"?: see *Lonrho v Fayed* [1992] 1 W.L.R. 1.

[11] See *Avon Insurance v Swire* [2000] 1 All E.R. (Comm.) 573.

[12] See *Smith New Court Securities Ltd v Scrimgeour Vickers Ltd* [1997] A.C. 254 (wider measure of damages for the tort of deceit than for the tort of negligence); *Clef Aquitaine SARL v Laporte Materials (Barrow) Ltd* [2001] Q.B. 488.

[13] See *Chitty, op. cit.,* para.6–073. *Gran Gelato Ltd v Richcliff (Group) Ltd* [1992] Ch. 560. In the Canadian case of *Avco Financial Services Realty Ltd v Norman* unreported, April 16, 2003 the Ontario Court of Appeal concluded that while negligent misrepresentation and contributory negligence could co-exist at law, it would be necessary to consider in each case whether the conduct which amounted to reasonable and foreseeable reliance by a claimant on a defendant's representations was nonetheless open to sufficient criticism to justify a finding of contributory negligence on the part of that claimant. *Avco* was cited with approval by the Ontario Supreme Court in *C&B Corrugated Containers Inc v Quadrant Marketing Ltd* (2005) Can. L.I.I. 14005.

relationship and then enter into further separate contracts relating to individual or types of transactions from time to time thereafter. He might have a "services" contract with an independent intermediary and a "product" contract with a product provider. Especially where the facts involve discretionary portfolio management or a contingent liability investment there will usually be several agreements dealing with different aspects of the relationship between the provider and the recipient of the services. Confirmations of transactions and periodic statements will be evidentially relevant in ascertaining the contractual position.[14] Proper analysis of the inter-relationship between the parties will usually require careful consideration of the whole contractual matrix. General principles for analysis, in particular as to interrelationship and effect of relevant documentation and as to incorporation[15] and implication of terms, are no different in investment contexts than in other contractual contexts. However, the regulatory dimension needs to be taken into account.

(ii) *Regulatory Requirements as to Terms of Business and Customer Agreements*

Extensive requirements are imposed under the FSMA regulatory regime in relation to terms of business and customer agreements.[16]   **15–018**

(iii) *Incorporation of Regulatory Duties in Contract*

Regulatory duties such as those imposed by the FSA Handbook or market codes   **15–019** of practice or other codes may also be incorporated as contractual duties, whether expressly or by implication. Contravention may then be actionable at common law as a breach of contract as well as, in some cases, being actionable by reason of a regulatory statute. What terms fall to be implied in a contract is a question of law[17] to be determined in accordance with usual principles for implication of terms.[18] These principles were considered in a financial services context in *Clarion Ltd v National Provident Institution.*[19] It was alleged that the defendant mutual life office had agreed to grant the claimant investment advisers a special block switching arrangement for their clients' investments. The defendant contended that the SIB Principles were implicitly incorporated as a term of that agreement.[20] Rimer J. rejected the contention. He reasoned, first, since both claimant and defendant were already subject to the SIB Principles at the time that the agreement was made, there was no point in incorporating those principles into the contract. Secondly, a number of the SIB Principles were either irrelevant to or inapplicable to the relationship between claimant and defendant. Thirdly, there was no basis for classifying the agreement between the parties as a generic

---

[14] See Ch.14, para.14–067 as to regulatory reporting requirements.
[15] e.g. by reference, as in *Brandeis (Brokers) Ltd v Herbert Black* [2001] 2 Lloyd's Rep. 359 Toulson J. (SFA rules incorporated in contract between LME broker and clients).
[16] See Ch.14, paras 14–052 and 14–053.
[17] *Mosvolds Rederi A/S v Food Corp of India* [1986] 2 Lloyd's L.Rep. 68 at 70.
[18] See generally *Chitty on Contracts* (29th edn, 2004) Chs 13–01 to 13–10.
[19] [2000] 1 W.L.R. 1888.
[20] The defendant contended both that it was a matter of obvious inference that the SIB Principles were incorporated and that the agreement with the claimant was of a particular generic type which required the implication of the SIB Principles.

type which required the implication of the SIB Principles. A contrasting conclusion was reached obiter in *Larussa-Chigi v CS First Boston Ltd.*[21] Thomas J. held that relevant agreements between the parties expressly incorporated the London Code of Conduct.[22] He went on to opine that had this not been the case, the code would have been incorporated as an implied term since it was not intended that the foreign exchange transactions in question be unregulated. The implied term to exercise reasonable care and skill[23] may provide another, indirect, route to the incorporation of regulatory rules or code of practice. Thus such rules or code will usually be relevant in ascertaining what is required in order to meet the standard in question.[24]

(iv) *Duty of Care and Skill*

15–020   **The duty and the standard.** In common with other providers of relevant services acting in the course of business, a provider of financial services will be under an implied if not express contractual duty to exercise reasonable care and skill in carrying out the services required of him.[25] The standard of care and skill will be that to be expected of a like provider engaged to provide the relevant services. Evaluating that standard will generally involve consideration of applicable regulatory requirements. It may also involve considering expert evidence from like practitioners to the defendant as to relevant practices, procedures and safeguards, perhaps in relation to highly specialised investments or markets. The evidence of such practitioners is not determinative. Ultimately the standard is for the court to determine and it may reject even general practice as failing to meet the required standard, as did the Privy Council in 1983 in relation to a conveyancing practice of Hong Kong solicitors.[26] For the court to impose its own higher standard is rare and is more likely in cases where the court is relatively familiar with the practices of the occupation concerned, as in relation to solicitors. Yet as courts become more familiar with claims against financial practitioners, the greater the scrutiny of their practices and the greater the likelihood of a court occasionally imposing its own view of the required standard, as in a recent pension misselling case, *Loosemore v Financial Concepts.*[27] The finding of breach of duty was made even though the court appears to have accepted that a reasonable body of financial practitioners would have provided advice of a standard similar to (or even worse than) the advice provided by the defendant:

" . . . in comparison with what many financial advisers and companies were doing at this time—which was to encourage people to opt out and transfer, [the defendant] did well. For he did give some warning. It was not however enough. The Financial Services

---

[21] [1998] C.L.C. 277.
[22] i.e. promulgated by the Bank of England and applicable to the defendant as a listed institution under the 1986 Act, s.43. The full title of the code is "A Guide to Accepted Best Practice in the Wholesale Markets in Sterling, Foreign Exchange and Bullion".
[23] See para.15–020, below.
[24] See *Brandeis (Brokers) Ltd v Herbert Black* [2001] 2 Lloyd's Rep. 359, *per* Toulson J. at para.20.
[25] See Supply of Goods and Services Act 1982, s.13.
[26] *Edward Wong Finance Co Ltd v Johnson, Stokes & Master* [1984] A.C. 296. See Ch.10, para.10–085.
[27] [2001] Lloyd's L.Rep. P.N. 235, Judge Raymond Jack Q.C. For facts, see para.15–050, below.

Act 1986 and the rules made under it by the supervisory agencies brought in radically new standards."[28]

Utility. In many cases the statutory cause of action for breach of a relevant **15–021** regulatory rule may provide a more straightforward basis of claim to a private investor.[29] Reliance also on breach of the contractual duty to exercise reasonable care and skill may then be superfluous. Usually a breach of such rule will also amount to a breach of that contractual duty. On the other hand, the statutory cause of action may not be available to the claimant.[30] The duty of care and skill will then be an important basis of claim, including as an indirect means of invoking breaches of regulatory rules.[31] Moreover, it may not be possible to point to breach of a specific rule. Further, regulatory rules may have limited application or relevance to a claimant, as for example in relation to corporate investors in respect of sophisticated investments such as options, futures and contracts for differences or portfolio management. In such circumstances it will be necessary to fall back on the common law, especially the duty of care and skill.

"Bracket" claims. This is an intriguing subject for consideration. In the **15–022** context of valuers, liability for negligent valuation of a property is usually deduced by reference to whether the impugned valuation fell within a "bracket" of "competent valuations" ascertained from expert valuation evidence and often derived from sales of comparable properties. It remains to be seen whether this "bracket" approach will commend itself to the courts in the context of claims against fund managers who have consistently performed well below average. The plethora of performance league tables as well as rating agencies have established a vast information base which can be drawn in aid of a "bracket" negligence claims against bad performers. A "bracket" claim is likely to face considerable scepticism in an investment context. Less important than mere demonstration that the impugned investment performance fell outside the alleged bracket of competence will be the reasons why it did so. In the event of a severe market fall it may be possible to show that, in the case of a large fund, relevant protections through put options and other devices, which kept other funds within the bracket, were not in place. Relevant analogies may be drawn from negligence claims by Names against Lloyd's underwriters who failed to take out adequate reinsurance or stop loss insurance.[32]

(v) *Agency*

Appointed representatives. Persons authorised under the FSMA regulatory **15–023** regime may carry on regulated activities through "appointed representatives". They are essentially agents of their authorised principals. The position of an

---

[28] [2001] Lloyd's Rep. P.N. 235 at 242.
[29] See Ch.14, paras 14–077 to 14–079.
[30] See Ch.14, paras 14–078 and 14–074 as to whom the statutory right of action is available.
[31] See para.15–019, above.
[32] See Ch.19, paras 19–052 to 19–064, 19–067 to 19–068, 19–075 and 19–076.

appointed representative and the liability of authorised persons for the defaults of such representatives are treated in Ch.14.

15–024   **Common law agency principles.** An agent has implied authority to do whatever is necessary for, or ordinarily incidental to, the effective execution of his express authority in the usual way.[33] Thus, while the terms of an appointed representative's express authority might be limited to providing investment advice to customers in relation to particular products of his principal, conduct that is incidental to the provision of that advice (such as soliciting the customers, identifying the financial and personal circumstances of the particular customer, assisting in any application that the customer might choose to make) will still fall within the actual authority of that representative.[34] Secondly, irrespective of whether or not the agent has actual authority to act on the principal's behalf in the relevant way, a principal will be bound by such acts of an agent if the agent has ostensible or apparent authority to act in that way.[35] Thus if a firm has knowingly or even unwittingly led a customer to believe that an authorised representative is authorised to conduct business on its behalf of a type that he is not in fact authorised to conduct, the firm will be bound by the acts and omissions of the representative and will be liable for his defaults.[36]

(f) Tort-based Duties

(i) Deceit or Fraudulent Misrepresentation

15–025   **General.** The tort of deceit or fraudulent misrepresentation[37] is committed if: (1) the defendant makes a statement of fact; (2) the statement of fact is false; (3) the defendant makes such a statement knowing it to be untrue, or not believing it to be true, or being reckless as to whether or not it is true; (4) the defendant intends that the recipient of the statement should act upon it; and (5) the recipient is in fact influenced to act upon the statement to his detriment.

15–026   There are advantages to a claimant who is able to pursue a claim of fraud against a defendant. First, the damages recoverable in such a claim are likely to

---

[33] See *Bowstead & Reynolds on Agency* (17th edn, 2001) at paras 3–018 *et seq.*

[34] See in the context of the 1986 Act, s.44, *Martin v Britannia Life Ltd* [2000] Lloyd's L.Rep. P.N. 412 at 426–428, *per* Jonathan Parker J. In *Martin* the issue was whether the Defendant was liable for advice given by one of its authorised company representatives in relation to a remortgage as well as other "investments". The representative was authorised only to give advice in relation to "investments" issued by the defendant. A mortgage of real property was not an "investment" for the purposes of the 1986 Act. Nonetheless, it was held that the representative had had actual authority to give such advice since the advice was inherently bound up with and incidental to the advice given by the representative in relation to the other investments.

[35] See generally as to ostensible authority, *Freeman & Lockyer v Buckhurst Park Properties (Mangal) Ltd* [1964] 2 Q.B. 480 at 503, *per* Diplock L.J. and *Bowstead & Reynolds, op. cit.*

[36] In *Martin* (above) the representative gave a business card (with which he had been supplied by the defendant) to the customer which bore the defendant's name and logo, the representative's name and the words "Financial Adviser". Jonathan Parker J. held that this was sufficient on the facts of the case to provide the representative with ostensible authority to advise in a far wider capacity than that in which the defendant had expressly authorised him to advise. The defendant was therefore liable for the representative's conduct.

[37] See generally *Clerk & Lindsell on Torts* (19th edn, 2006), paras 18–04 to 18–035.

be more favourable than in a claim of negligent misstatement.[38] Secondly, a defendant is unable to pursue a plea of contributory negligence against a claimant who has been the victim of fraud.[39] Thirdly, time will not begin to run for limitation purposes against the victim of a fraud until the fraud has been discovered or could with reasonable diligence have been discovered.[40] Fourthly, a victim of fraud need not show the same "special relationship" as is necessary to demonstrate a duty of care at common law.

However, such advantages must be weighed against the increased onus that a plea of fraud places upon a claimant. Any such plea is a "very serious matter" and should only be advanced when there is "reasonably credible material" available which appears to justify such an allegation.[41]   **15–027**

In a retail financial contest, two particular types of fraud are frequently encountered. First, the employee or representative of the provider deliberately or recklessly misrepresents the nature of the proposed investment or some key element in that investment. This type of fraud is often motivated by a desire on the part of the fraudster to maximise the benefit to himself through commission or the like. Secondly, the employee or representative deliberately or recklessly suggests an investment to the investor which he in fact has no authority to suggest. Such investments are frequently ones with which the employee or representative himself has an association or an interest and are often motivated by a simple desire to part the investor from his own money, which is then misappropriated.   **15–028**

In either case, the issue likely to be of primary importance to the victim of the fraud will be whether or not he can recover his losses from the principal of the employee or representative, i.e. whether or not the principal is vicariously liable for the fraud.[42] A principal cannot per se avoid responsibility for the conduct of his agent merely because that conduct was fraudulent and, unless the conduct fell outside the scope of the actual or ostensible authority of the representative,[43] the principal will find himself bound by the fraudulent conduct of the representative.[44] Thus a principal may find himself liable for the actions of a representative who knowingly and deliberately either mis-sells a product to a client which,   **15–029**

---

[38] This is particularly so if the scope of the duty of care owed by the defendant at common law is too narrow to enable the entirety of the claimant's loss to be recovered in a claim for negligent misstatement: see *South Australia Asset Management Corp v York Montague* [1997] A.C. 191 at 215G–H; *Smith New Court Securities Ltd v Scrimgeour Vickers Ltd* [1997] A.C. 254; *Clef Aquitaine SARL v Laporte Materials (Barrow) Ltd* [2001] Q.B. 488.

[39] *Alliance & Leicester BS v Edgestop Ltd* [1993] 1 W.L.R. 1462; *Nationwide BS v Thimbleby* [1999] Lloyd's L.Rep. P.N. 359. In *Standard Chartered Bank v Pakistan National Shipping Corp (Nos 2 and 4)* [2002] UKHL 43; [2003] 1 A.C. 959 the House of Lords concluded that, since there was no common law defence of contributory negligence in the case of fraudulent misrepresentation, there was no possibility of an apportionment of liability in such a case between claimant and defendant under the Law Reform (Contributory Negligence) Act 1945. Note however that Lord Rodger preferred to leave open the question of whether or not a defence of contributory negligence might be open to a defendant in other cases of intentional harm to a claimant.

[40] s.32(1) of the Limitation Act 1980. See further Ch.5, paras 5–099 *et seq.*, above.

[41] *Medcalf v Mardell* [2002] UKHL 27; [2003] 1 A.C. 120 at para.22.

[42] The circumstances in which a principal may himself owe a duty of care at common law to such victims to supervise its employees and representatives and/or to prevent them committing such frauds are rare: see para.15–038, below.

[43] See para.15–024, above.

[44] See, e.g. *Hambro v Burnand* [1904] 2 K.B. 10.

while unsuitable, is nonetheless of a type which the representative is actually authorised by the principal to sell, or mis-sells a product to a client which he is not authorised by his principal to sell but which the victim nonetheless believes that the representative has authority to sell.

15–030   In this latter scenario, the liability of the principal will depend to a very great extent on the basis for the victim's belief. Only if the victim's erroneous belief as to the authority of the representative has been induced by the words or conduct of the principal will the principal be vicariously liable for the representative's actions. If his belief is based solely on the words or conduct of the fraudulent representative, the principal will not be bound by the representative's actions.[45] Equally, if the victim's belief as to the authority of the representative is unreasonable, (i.e. the victim ought to have appreciated that the representative had no authority to act as he did) then the principal will escape liability for the actions of the representative.[46]

(ii) *Misfeasance in Public Office*

15–031   A regulator may be liable to an individual claimant or class of claimants who have lost money as the result of the collapse of an institution for which the regulator had regulatory responsibility if the claimant is able to demonstrate that the regulator was guilty of the tort of misfeasance in public office.[47] In *Three Rivers DC v Governor and Company of the Bank of England*,[48] 6,000 former depositors in the United Kingdom Branch of BCCI commenced proceedings against the Bank of England on the basis that the Bank of England's decisions (1) to grant BCCI a licence, and (2) not to revoke that licence when it knew or suspected that BCCI would probably collapse, amounted to misfeasance in public office. The House of Lords concluded that, as a matter of law, the claim as pleaded was not bound to fail.[49] In particular, it held that "bad faith" meant that a public officer exercised his power by acting illegally (or possibly even by omitting to act) either: (1) with specific intention to injure the claimant or a class of persons of which the claimant was a member, or (2) with knowledge of, or with reckless indifference to, the probability of causing injury to the claimant or a class of persons of which the claimant was a member.

(iii) *Negligence*

15–032   **Clients.** A financial practitioner will generally owe a duty of care in tort to his client quite apart from any contract that exists between them. As with most professions, that duty will usually be not only concurrent with,[50] but also

---

[45] See generally *Armagas Ltd v Mundogas Ltd* [1986] A.C. 717. For an example in the field of financial services see *Emmanuel v DBS Management Plc* [1999] Lloyd's L.Rep. P.N. 593.
[46] *Houghton & Co v Nothard Lowe & Wills Ltd* [1927] 1 K.B. 246 at 260, *per* Bankes L.J. The decision of the Court of Appeal was affirmed by the House of Lords at [1928] A.C. 1.
[47] As to the FSA's limited statutory immunity from damages liability, see Ch.14, para.14–005.
[48] [2000] 2 W.L.R. 1220.
[49] Although ultimately the trial of the the claim collapsed.
[50] See, e.g. *Midland Bank Trust Co Ltd v Hett, Stubbs & Kemp (a firm)* [1979] Ch. 384 and more generally Ch.10, paras 10–013 to 10–015.

consistent with,[51] the contractual duty to exercise reasonable care and skill.[52] Consequently, if the parties to a contract have expressly or implicitly agreed a limitation on the scope of the practitioner's duties under the contract, his tortious duty of care will almost certainly be similarly limited. For example, in an execution-only transaction there will be no contractual (nor regulatory) duty to advise on the merits of the transaction. The practitioner's tortious duty of care will be similarly limited, except in very exceptional circumstances.

Third parties. A financial practitioner may owe a tortious duty of care to third 15–033 parties, i.e. a person between whom and the practitioner there is no contractual relationship. Whether such duty arises in particular circumstances falls to be decided in accordance with general tests for the determination of its existence.[53] Nevertheless, in the present, as in other contexts, critical factors will be any statutory context or contractual matrix, the purpose for which any information, advice or other services was provided and the availability of other causes of action or means of redress.

In *Seymour v Caroline Ockwell & Co and Zurich IFA Ltd*[54] the first defendant IFA recommended investment in "the Alpha Fund" to the claimants. Those recommendations were made by the first defendant in light of information previously given to her about the Alpha Fund by the second defendant, who was marketing a bond wrapper within which the Alpha fund could be held. There had at no time been any direct contact between the claimants and the second defendant. After reviewing many of the recent authorities considering the principles governing the existence of duties of care, His Honour Judge Havelock-Allan Q.C. concluded that no duty of care had been owed by the second defendant to the claimants when providing information about the Alpha Fund to the first defendant: "the contractual chain and the framework of statutory duties tell against the imposition of a direct duty of care on [the second defendant]". The Judge concluded that to find such a duty on the facts of the case would "by-pass the regulatory regime and side-step the contractual remedy". The claimants' direct claim against the second defendant therefore failed.

In contrast, in *Riyadh Bank & RBE London Ltd v Ahli United Bank*[55] the defendant bank, which had provided advice to a corporate investment vehicle established by the claimant but not directly to the claimant itself, was found to have owed a duty of care both to the investment vehicle and to the claimant. The claimant was thus able to recover from the defendant losses that it had sustained itself.

Prospectus cases. Statutory causes of action provide in most circumstances 15–034 easier bases of claim in respect of misleading statements in prospectuses, as well as listing particulars.[56] Nevertheless, the tortious duty of care may be invoked also, as well as in circumstances where the statutory provisions may not apply.

---

[51] See *Henderson v Merrett Syndicates Ltd* [1995] 2 A.C. 145 at 193A–D.
[52] See by way of example *Investors Compensation Scheme Ltd v West Bromwich Building Society* [1999] Lloyd's L.Rep. P.N. 496 at 504.
[53] See Ch.2, paras 2–013 to 2–080.
[54] [2005] EWHC 1137; [2005] P.N.L.R. 39.
[55] [2006] EWCA Civ 780.
[56] See Ch.14, paras 14–081 and 14–082.

There are two relevant English cases. In *Al-Nakib Investments (Jersey) Ltd v Longcroft*,[57] CT Plc decided to float M Ltd, a subsidiary, on the Unlisted Securities Market and issued a prospectus inviting CT shareholders to subscribe for shares in M and CT under a rights issue. The claimant CT shareholder acquired 400,000 shares by subscription under the rights issue and later acquired further CT and M shares through purchases made through the stock exchange. The claimant alleged that the prospectus contained misrepresentations and that since all of its acquisitions had been made in reliance upon the prospectus, it was entitled to recover the losses sustained from CT and its directors based on breaches of duties of care owed by them. Mervyn Davies J. struck out the claim in respect of the purchase transactions. He held that the prospectus had been addressed to the claimant for a particular purpose, (i.e. subscription under the rights issue) and not for the purpose of purchasing shares in the market. Accordingly neither CT nor its directors owed any duty of care to the claimant in respect of the purchase transactions. The opposite conclusion was reached in *Possfund Custodian Trustee Ltd v Diamond*.[58] The defendant had issued a prospectus in connection with the flotation of its shares on the unlisted securities market. The prospectus specifically stated that, as part of the same exercise as allotment, the facility would be available for shares to be dealt with subsequently on the unlisted securities market. Two classes of claimant, the first of which had purchased shares at the time of their original placing and the second of which had subsequently bought shares in the unlisted securities market, sought damages from the defendant in deceit and negligence in relation to alleged material representations contained in the prospectus as to the financial position of the defendant which, it was said, had induced them to purchase shares. Lightman J. refused to strike out any part of the claims. An after-market purchaser could sustain a claim in negligence against the issuer of a prospectus if he could establish that he was intended by the issuer to rely upon the prospectus for that purpose, that he had in fact relied upon it for that purpose, and if he could demonstrate the necessary connection between himself and the issuer of the prospectus to render the imposition of a duty of care just, fair and reasonable. On the facts of the case, it was arguable that the prospectus had been worded in such a way as to inform and encourage after-market purchasers in addition to those who had relied on the prospectus when deciding whether to subscribe to the original placing of the shares, and so to give rise to a duty of care to such persons.

15–035   **Pension beneficiaries.** Cases involving these often raise the issue whether, expressed generically, a duty of care may be owed by an adviser to a claimant who did not directly rely on his advice or expertise, but who has suffered loss as result of advice provided to another. In *Gorham v British Telecommunications Plc*[59] G had, prior to 1991, been an employee of Cable & Wireless and thereafter, until his death, of BT. In early 1992, shortly after joining BT and following advice by a representative of Standard Life Assurance Company, G opted to take

---

[57] [1990] 3 All E.R. 321.
[58] [1996] 2 All E.R. 774.
[59] [2000] 1 W.L.R. 2129, C.A. *Gorham* was cited with approval in *Dean v Allin & Watts* [2001] Lloyd's L. Rep. (PN) 249 at 261, a solicitor's negligence claim. For the facts of *Dean* see Ch.10, paras 10–005 and 10–060.

out a personal pension scheme with that company and to transfer thereto the transferable value of benefits accumulated under the Cable & Wireless scheme. He was eligible to join BT's occupational pension scheme but did not do so, although by October 1992 he believed that he had done so (contrary to his previous belief).[60] BT treated G as having opted out.[61] In November 1992 he ceased paying premiums to Standard Life and there was evidence that he had rung the company's helpline and been advised that the BT scheme was better. The claimant dependants of G (his wife and two children) succeeded in their claim for damages against Standard Life, which was based on breach of an alleged duty of care in tort owed by the company to them in advising G. The recoverable damages related to the capital value of the greater pension rights under the BT occupational pension scheme relative to the personal pension scheme. The claimants failed to recover claimed damages for loss of a lump sum death benefit because there had been a break in the chain of causation consisting of G's failure to act upon the helpline advice.[62]

As to duty, Standard Life accepted that it owed a duty of care in advising G and   **15–036** that it was in breach on the basis that its representative had failed to advise G about the differences between an occupational pension scheme and a personal pension scheme. Consequently, he should have refused to sell the latter to G unless satisfied that G had made an informed choice between the two schemes. Reflecting polarisation requirements current at the time,[63] Standard Life was not entitled to advise G as to the merits of the BT scheme. Standard Life disputed that it owed the dependants any duty of care. Nevertheless the Court of Appeal held that it did owe such a duty. It rejected the company's contention that since the dependants did not fall within the category of claimant to which statutory right of action under the 1986 Act[64] extended, there should be no wider duty of care owed at common law.[65] The Court held that a duty of care was owed to the defendants for like reasons to those given by the House of Lords in *White v Jones*[66]:

> "[G] intended to create a benefit for his wife and children in the event of his predeceasing them . . . It is fundamental to the giving and receiving of advice upon a scheme for pension provision and life insurance that the interests of the customer's dependents will arise for consideration. In my judgment, practical justice requires that the disappointed beneficiaries should have a remedy against an insurance company in circumstances such as the present . . . Advice was expected and was directed not only to the interests of [G] but to the interests of his dependents should he predecease them.

---

[60] G had been told by BT that, unless he positively chose to opt out of its occupational scheme, he would be automatically joined to the scheme and appropriate deductions made from his salary. He did nothing to lead BT to conclude that he had elected to opt out.

[61] Claims against BT and the trustees of the BT pension scheme were dismissed at first instance.

[62] Sir Murray Stuart-Smith dissented on this point, holding that the causation chain was not broken.

[63] The polarisation principle required a firm giving advice to a private customer upon packaged products to be within one, but not the other, of two categories: a provider firm or an independent intermediary: see Ch.13, para.13–055 of the 5th edition of this book. The term "polarisation" is not referred to as such in the judgments, though its effect is described.

[64] See 1986 Act, ss.62 and 62A. These are the predecessor provisions to FSMA, s.150: see Ch.14, paras 14–077 to 14–079 and 14–074.

[65] [2000] 1 W.L.R. 2129 at 2141.

[66] [1995] 2 A.C. 207.

The advice was given on the assumption that their interests were involved. Moreover, the provision for them was not merely a windfall in the sense that a legacy may be a windfall; it was central to purpose of the venture into insurance."[67]

In the context of the case the scope of the duty was expressed as "not to give advice to the customer which adversely affects [his dependants'] interest."

15–037   Although the situation did not arise in *Gorham*, Stuart-Smith L.J. doubted whether a duty of care would be owed to beneficiaries such as the claimants in the event that their interests conflicted with the interests of the original recipient of the financial advice.[68] However Pill L.J., with whom Schiemann L.J. agreed, concluded that on a proper analysis of the scope of the duty that was owed by defendants such as Standard Life, no difficulty would in fact arise.[69] The duty owed by Standard Life to the dependants was not one to take care to ensure that they were properly provided for, but rather was a duty not to give negligent advice to the customer which would adversely affect their interests as he intended them to be. In the circumstances (given polarisation requirements) the duty, put at its simplest, was not to sell a Standard Life policy to G.

15–038   **Principal or employer.** Claimants have on a number of occasions attempted to fashion a duty of care on the part of financial services providers to take care to protect them against misconduct on the part of appointed representatives or employees of the provider in circumstances where no other remedy is open to them.[70] In the absence of an express or implied assumption of responsibility for such conduct of the representative or employee, such a duty will be rare.[71] In *Lloyds TSB General Insurance Holdings Ltd v Lloyds Bank Group Insurance Co Ltd* the claimants had been sued by individuals to whom they had sold personal

---

[67] [2000] 1 W.L.R. 2129 at 2140, 2141–2142.
[68] *ibid.*, at 2147. The example that Schiemann L.J. gave was an investor who wished to enhance his own pension at the expense of his wife's pension.
[69] In carrying out such analysis, Pill L.J. followed the well-known passage from the speech of Lord Bridge in *Caparo* that: "It is never sufficient to ask simply whether A owes B a duty of care. It is always necessary to determine the scope of the duty by reference to the kind of damage from which A must take care to save B harmless" and the similar views expressed by Lord Hoffman in *SAAMCO v York Montague Ltd* [1997] A.C. 191 at 211.
[70] For example, if the representative or employee was acting fraudulently, outside the course of his employment and/or actual and ostensible authority.
[71] In *Hornsby v Clark Kenneth Leventhal* [1998] P.N.L.R. 635 the claimant was defrauded by an employee of the defendant firm of accountants who had persuaded him to invest in an "International Fund". The claimant was unable to demonstrate any vicarious liability on the part of the defendant and so contended that the defendant had owed him a duty to supervise and investigate its employees to prevent such frauds being perpetrated. The Court of Appeal held that the defendant owed no such duty to the claimant. Such a duty would arise only if the defendant had actually known of the fraud or been reckless as to its existence. Similarly, in *Emmanuel v DBS Management Plc* [1999] Lloyd's L.Rep. P.N. 593 the defendant had appointed ITIP to act as its appointed representative under the 1986 Act. ITIP persuaded the claimants to enter into two separate investment transactions neither of which fell within the scope of that for which the defendant had accepted responsibility under the terms of ITIP's appointment. Consequently the claimants were unable to rely upon the provisions of 1986 Act, s.44. They attempted to circumvent this difficulty by arguing that the defendant owed them a duty of care at common law to take care to protect them against losses of the type that they suffered at the hands of ITIC. The Judge (Jonathan Sumption Q.C.) struck out the claim. There was no basis for holding that the defendant owed a duty of care to the claimant (as a member of the class of persons with whom ITIC had dealt) simply by virtue of having appointed ITIP as its appointed representative in respect of other unrelated transactions.

pension plans. Each individual had alleged that the claimants' representatives had failed to give best advice at the time that the policies were entered into. The claimants sought indemnities against the claims from the defendant underwriters. An issue arose as to whether the individual claims were properly to be treated for insurance purposes as a series of individual claims resulting from poor advice or a single claim resulting from the claimants' failure to provide training to their representatives that was adequate to enable them to give proper advice to the individuals. The Court of Appeal[72] concluded (albeit obiter) that, in order to for a claim to result from a circumstance, the circumstance had to be the "proximate cause of" or "immediately causative of" the claim in question. Accordingly although a lack of training might have created the antecedent state of affairs which led to the bad advice and/or been the underlying reason for the bad advice, the claims themselves resulted from the bad advice and not the lack of training provided to the claimants' representatives. The House of Lords[73] approved this aspect of the Court of Appeal's decision—the absence of adequate training and monitoring on the part of the claimant was irrelevant to the civil liability in issue since any such absence was not an "act or omission" from which a liability on the part of the claimants had resulted—the relevant "act or omission" had in each case been the failure of the claimants' representatives to provide best advice. However, (reversing the Court of Appeal) the House of Lords concluded that each case arose from a separate contravention of the relevant statutory framework and so should be treated as a separate claim for the purpose of the policy. The fact that each case might be of similar nature and/or arise from the same underlying cause was not sufficient to bring them within the aggregation clause.

Employee. There may be occasions in which it is necessary to consider the extent to which an employee of a provider of financial services owes a duty of care to the recipient of those services independently to any duty owed by the provider itself.[74] In *Hale v Guildarch Ltd*[75] the claimants entered into transactions in reliance upon financial advice given to them by the defendants, P and T, both of whom were employees of ADC Group Ltd. By the time the transactions had gone disastrously wrong, ADC was insolvent and uninsured. The judge rejected the claimants' contention that P and T owed them a duty of care.[76] It is submitted that an employee does not owe a duty of care in respect of a task unless at least (1) he clearly and voluntarily intimates that he is undertaking responsibility in a personal capacity and (2) the recipient of the advice is able to demonstrate that he reasonably relied upon that personal acceptance of responsibility for the task.   **15–039**

Regulators. Irrespective of the limited statutory immunity from liability in damages granted to regulators and others,[77] regulators do not generally owe a duty of care to investors in the performance of their functions. Considerations   **15–040**

---

[72] [2001] EWCA Civ 1643; [2002] Lloyd's L.Rep. (P.N.) 211.

[73] [2003] UKHL 48 [2003]; 4 All E.R. 43.

[74] e.g. if the provider is in liquidation and/or uninsured.

[75] [1999] P.N.L.R. 44, Judge Raymond Jack Q.C.

[76] *cf. Merrett v Babb* [2001] 3 W.L.R. 1, CA: see Ch.9, paras 9–014, 9–035 and 9–047.

[77] See Ch.14, paras 14–005 (the FSA), 14–124 (FOS) and 14–139 (FSCS).

decisive to negate a duty of care alleged to have been owed to a third party by statutory, ministerial, administrative, regulatory and complaints-handling bodies[78] have been the availability of alternative bases of redress and regulatory overkill,[79] even though such redress may be of little value to the third party concerned.

(g) *Fiduciary Duties*

15–041   **General.** The law relating to fiduciary duties[80] in its application to the financial sector and to the interrelationship of such duties and regulatory duties is still in a relatively immature state of development. Its undeveloped state motivated the involvement of the Law Commission. Following an earlier Consultation Paper,[81] it published its final report "Fiduciary Duties and Regulatory Rules"[82] in December 1995. In both reports it addressed the law and its application in the financial services sector. A classic statement as to when a person is a fiduciary is that of Professor Finn: "A person will be a fiduciary in his relationships with another when and insofar as that other is entitled to expect that he will act in that other's interest or (as in a partnership) in their joint interest, to the exclusion of their several interests." This statement has the advantage of recognising the feature, important in a financial services context, that a person may be a fiduciary in some but not all aspects of his relationship with another. While fiduciary duties may be variously classified, the Law Commission in both reports formulated four basic rules: the "no conflict" rule,[83] the "no profit" rule,[84] the undivided loyalty rule (which embraces a disclosure requirement)[85] and the duty of confidentiality.[86]

---

[78] As to a regulatory context see *Yeun Kun Yeu v Att-Gen of Hong Kong* [1988] A.C. 175, PC; *Minories Finance Ltd v Arthur Young* [1989] 2 All E.R. 105 and *Davis v Radcliffe* [1990] 1 W.L.R. 821, PC, but *cf. Lonrho v Tebbit* [1992] 4 All E.R. 280, CA; for a ministerial context see *Rowling v Takaro Properties Ltd* [1988] 1 A.C. 473, PC; and an administrative context, see *Jones v Department of Employment* [1989] Q.B. 1 CA. See further Ch.2, para.2–088.

[79] See *Rowling v Takaro Properties Ltd* [1988] 1 A.C. 475, PC at 502.

[80] For a general consideration of fiduciary obligations in the context of professional liability claims see Ch.2, paras 2–128 to 2–144. Also see generally Finn, "Fiduciary obligations" (1979) and "Commercial Aspects of Trust and Fiduciary Obligations" (McKendrick, edn, 1992). Significant recent English cases are *Kelly v Cooper* [1993] A.C. 205; *Henderson v Merrett Syndicates Ltd* [1995] 2 A.C. 145; *Bristol and West BS v Mothew* [1996] 4 All E.R. 698. Fiduciary duties have been subject to close scrutiny in Canada: see especially *Lac Minerals Ltd v International Corona Resources Ltd* [1990] F.S.R. 441. But Canadian cases must be read subject to the caution that they may be too broadly expressed for entire consumption by an English court.

[81] Law Commission Consultation Paper No.124 (1992).

[82] Law Commission Paper No.236.

[83] i.e. a fiduciary must not place himself in a position where his own interest conflicts with that of his customer, the beneficiary; there must be "real possibility of conflict".

[84] i.e. a fiduciary must not profit from his position at the expense of his customer, the beneficiary.

[85] i.e. a fiduciary owes undivided loyalty to his customer, the beneficiary, not to place himself in a position where his duty towards one customer conflicts with a duty that he owes to another customer; a consequence of this duty is that a fiduciary must make available to a customer all the information that is relevant to the customer's affairs.

[86] A fiduciary must only use information obtained in confidence from his customer, the beneficiary, for the benefit of the customer and must not use it for his own advantage, or for the benefit of any other person.

The range of services provided by financial conglomerates, the composition of **15–042** their customer base and the different capacities in which they conduct business are significant factors in generating potential conflicts of interest and duty. Instances include dealing off one's book or buying on one's own account, matching orders (agency cross), buying from a customer and selling immediately to another customer (riskless principal transactions), dealing in property in which the customer has an interest, preferential or discriminatory treatment in the allocation of investment opportunities and failure to use all the information which the attribution acknowledgment rule deems to be available to a firm. However, the normal incidents of a fiduciary relationship may be modified by any underlying contractual relationship between the parties.[87] The source of fiduciary duties in a financial services context (as in any other context) is not the retainer itself but rather all the circumstances (including the retainer) which create a relationship of trust and confidence and from which flow obligations of loyalty and transparency. As long as that confidential relationship exists, the financial practitioner must not place himself in a position where his duty to act in the interests of the confiding party and his personal interest in acting for his own benefit may conflict. The termination of a retainer will not automatically terminate all fiduciary duties.[88]

The normal incidents of a fiduciary relationship may be modified by regulatory requirements, including as to Chinese walls.[89]

Illustrations. The application of the above principles was considered in the **15–043** context of the rules and practices of the London Metal Exchange by Toulson J. in *Brandeis (Brokers) Ltd v Herbert Black*.[90] He dismissed a challenge by LME brokers to an arbitral award made against them in favour of their former clients. He endorsed the arbitrators' conclusions that certain rules of the Securities and Futures Authority, the self-regultory organisation (the "SRO") of which the brokers were members, were incorporated in contracts made between the brokers and their clients and also that the brokers owed fiduciary duties to their clients. He concluded that the relationship between the parties was such that the brokers were acting as principal and not as agent for an undisclosed principal, but in all other respects the substance of the relationship was much more closely akin to that of agency than of buyer and seller. Agency was by its nature a form of fiduciary relationship. This impacted on allocation of orders (brokers were required to process the orders of different clients in due turn). Moreover, "front-running" (the placing by a broker of a prior order in advance of placing a client's order anticipated to move the market) and misuse of confidential information

---

[87] In *Ratiu v Conway* [2005] EWCA Civ 1302 the claimant alleged that fiduciary duties were owed to him by an individual who had stood behind a company with whom the claimant had contracted. Giving the principal judgment of the Court, Auld L.J. concluded that "there is . . . a powerful argument of principle in this intensely personal context of considerations of trust, confidence and loyalty for lifting the corporate veil where the facts require it to include those in or behind the company who are in reality the persons whose trust in reliance upon the fiduciary may be confounded" (at para.78),

[88] *Longstaff v Birtles* [2001] EWCA Civ 1219; [2002] 1 W.L.R. 470 at 471F–G.

[89] See Ch.14, para.14–062, above.

[90] [2001] 2 Lloyd's Rep. 359. See further para.15–055, below.

would involve a breach of fiduciary duties. Similarly in another case[91] it was held that the defendant bank owed a "fiduciary obligation" based on "classic principles" to the claimant investor when it performed discretionary management functions for him, but not when performing other functions including execution-only functions.

3. BREACH OF DUTY

(a) *General*

15–044   The object of this section is to provide some case illustrations of breaches of duties in various financial contexts. The section is arranged under various categories, some reflecting titles in the FSA Handbook,[92] but the categories are far from covering the multifarious circumstances in which relevant breaches may arise. In other chapters of this work the main relevant duty for consideration is the practitioner's duty of care, whether arising in contract and/or tort, and the focus of case law is the types of conduct amounting to its breach. The equivalent section in those chapters is arranged around categories reflecting the broad nature of the offending conduct. In contrast, in a financial context the duty of care subsists along with other very specific duties imposed by or under regulatory legislation. Many of those duties are expressed by reference to specific kinds of conduct, whether in terms of prescribing good conduct or prohibiting bad conduct. Hence the focus in a financial context on ascertaining the nature and scope of relevant duties which, once properly ascertained, frequently result in an inevitable conclusion on breach.

(b) *Misleading Promotion*

(i) *Old Prospectus Cases*

15–045   There is a large volume of reported cases on misleading statements in a prospectus. Most were decided in the half century or so preceding the First World War—the legal flotsam of victims of the heady entrepreneurial optimism of late Empire. These cases must now be approached with some caution and with due regard to the state of the law and to methods and practices for the issue of securities current at the time.[93] However, much of the reasoning remains of enduring relevance. Thus a half truth represented as a whole truth may be tantamount to a false statement.[94] The following observation by Lord Halsbury L.C. merits invocation in many financial promotion contexts:

> "I do not care by what means it is conveyed—by what trick or device of ambiguous language: all those are expedients by which fraudulent people seem to think they can

---

[91] *Ata v American Express Bank Ltd* C.A., unreported, June 17, 1998 upholding Rix J., unreported, October 7, 1996. See further, paras 15–061, 15–070 and 15–071, below.

[92] Ch.14, paras 14–034 *et seq.*

[93] For an account see Powell, *Issues and Offers of Company Securities: The New Regimes* (1988).

[94] See *Aaron's Reefs v Twiss* [1896] A.C. 273.

escape from the real substance of the transaction. If by a number of statements you intentionally give a false impression and induce a person to act upon it, it is not the less false if one takes each statement by itself there may be difficulty in shewing that any specific statement is untrue."[95]

(ii) *Financial Promotion Documents*

Prospectus requirements formerly contained in companies legislation relating to   **15–046** a prospectus have now, almost entirely, been superseded by provisions made in or under FSMA.[96] FSMA imposes liability in respect of any "untrue or misleading statement" as well as certain omissions.[97] Other rules relating to financial promotion in the FSMA may give rise to s.150 liability in respect of both misleading statements and omissions.[98] Civil liability may also be incurred under the Misrepresentation Act 1967 and at common law for untrue or misleading statements in promotional and reporting documents. Examples of misleading promotion may be found in recent caselaw but apart from being illustrative they are fact specific and do not give rise to any new principle.[99] Section 397 of FSMA, provides for criminal liability in respect of misleading etc. statements and practices, as did the equivalent s.47 of the 1986 Act. Neither of these provisions gives rise to a civil claim for damages.[1]

(iii) *Customer Classification*

Under the FSMA regime, as under previous regulatory regimes, the nature and   **15–047** scope of a financial practitioner's duties are dependant upon his properly classifying his customers.[2] Failure to do so may result in a consequential failure to perform duties appropriate to the correct classification. Classification was the central issue in *ANZ Banking Group Ltd v Cattan*.[3] The defendant resisted a claim for debts arising from trading losses in the Emerging Market Debt ("EMD") sector on the basis that the claimant had wrongly classified him as a "non-private customer" under IMRO rules. He maintained that but for that classification the claimant would not have permitted him to make relevant trades and he would not have suffered the losses. Morison J. concluded that the defendant had been correctly classified. The judgment made about him by the

---

[95] *Aaron's Reefs v Twiss* [1896] A.C. 273 at 281. Note also the observations of Lord Watson at 287.
[96] See Ch.14, paras 14–081 and 14–082.
[97] Ch.14, para.14–082.
[98] See Ch.14, paras 14–049 and 14–050, and 14–077 to 14–079.
[99] See, e.g. *Ball v Banner* [2000] Lloyd's L.Rep. P.N. 569 (misleading statements in a prospectus for an EZPUT); *Re Market Wizard Systems (UK) Ltd* [1988] 2 B.C.L.C. 282 (misleading statements used by the Secretary of State as the basis for an application to wind up the respondent on public interest grounds); *Securities and Investment Board v Vandersteen Associates NV* [1991] B.C.L.C. 206 (breaches of s.57 of the 1986 Act resulting from cold-calling by telephone and post); *Secretary of State for Trade and Industry v Grant,* unreported, September 15, 2000, Neuberger J. (distribution of misleading material relating to collective investment schemes).
[1] See in relation to the 1986 Act, s.47: *Norwich Union Society v Qureshi* [1998] C.L.C. 1605; *Aldrich v Norwich Union Life Insurance Co Ltd* [1999] 2 All E.R. (Comm) 707.
[2] See Ch.14, para.14–051.
[3] Unreported, August 21, 2001, Morison J.

claimant's representative was both reasonable and right: he had sufficient under-standing and experience to waive the protection provided for private customers. Morison J.'s judgment contains a useful analysis of the factors taken into account under the following headings: (1) the source of the defendant's introduction, (2) the knowledge displayed by him, (3) the discussions that took place between the claimant and the defendant which suggested a degree of familiarity with the EMD market "beyond the normal", (4) his background and experience, (5) his familiarity with another EMD trader, and (6) the way he presented himself: "a man who knew his way around the international financial circuit".

(iv) *Advising and Selling*

15–048 There are many and varied requirements in the FSA Handbook[4] relating to advising and selling. Like requirements imposed under the predecessor 1986 Act regime have generated several cases, especially requirements relating to "know your customer", customer understanding of risk and suitability.

15–049 *Martin v Britannia Life Ltd*[5] provides numerous examples of these types of failures. In 1991 the claimants contacted the predecessors of the defendant ("LAS") for advice. They met one of LAS's authorised representatives who purported to obtain an overview of the claimants' financial position. LAS subsequently advised the claimants to surrender five life policies, to replace them with a life policy offered by LAS, to remortgage their house and charge the new life policy as collateral security for the mortgage and to set up a new pension policy with LAS. Although the judge found that the claims brought by the claimants in tort and pursuant to s.62 of the 1986 Act[6] were statute barred, he was extremely critical of LAS.[7] In particular, he found that (1) no adequate steps had been taken to assess the personal and financial circumstances of the claimants— LAS had not "got to know" its customer, (2) the investments that LAS had advised were wholly unsuitable for the claimants,[8] (3) LAS had failed to provide any adequate warning of the risks posed by entering into the investments that were proposed,[9] (4) no adequate advice had been given of the advantages and

---

[4] See Ch.14, paras 14–054 to 14–058.

[5] [2000] Lloyd's L.Rep. P.N. 412, Jonathan Parker J. For a further example see *Primavera v Allied Dunbar Plc*, unreported, December 14, 2003, H.H.J. Hawkesworth Q.C. sitting as a High Court Judge. Although the Court of Appeal subsequently varied the Judge's Order on the issue of the measure of loss (see [2002] EWCA Civ 1327; [2003] Lloyd's L. Rep. (PN) 14 and para.15–077, below) the Judge's findings on liability were undisturbed.

[6] The equivalent provsion in FSMA is s.150, as to which see Ch.14, paras 14–077 to 14–179.

[7] [2000] Lloyd's L.Rep. P.N. 412, esp. at 429 to 431.

[8] *ibid.* at 429: "I have no doubt that in giving his advice [LAS] was under no illusions that in entering into the package [the claimants] would be extending their commitments well beyond the limits of what they could reasonably afford; but that did not deter [LAS] from his endeavours to procure them to take out policies with LAS".

[9] *ibid.* at 429: "it was plainly [LAS's] duty to advise [the claimants] in the strongest terms that if they entered into the package they would be undertaking very substantial ongoing commitments which they might well find hard to meet . . . The adviser's duty is to make sure, so far as he can, that the client's decision is an informed one. In my judgment, [LAS] clearly failed in that duty in this case".

disadvantages of entering into the package,[10] (5) the advice given to the claimants that it was appropriate to fund a personal pension by means of a remortgage was simply wrong, and (6) the endowment policy advised by LAS was unnecessary and unsuitable since the claimants could have used monies payable under the pension plan as security for the remortgage.

The extent to which advice should comply with the letter, as well as the spirit, **15–050** of the 1986 Act and FIMBRA rules were considered in *Loosemore v Financial Concepts*.[11] The claimant was an NHS employed nurse who in 1988 was considering starting a personal pension plan in order to be independent of the NHS. She was already a member of the NHS occupational pension scheme. She consulted the defendant IFA, who advised that the claimant was "better off" in the NHS scheme while she could remain a member. The claimant ignored the advice, opted out of the NHS scheme and took out a personal pension plan. She subsequently sued the defendant, alleging that the advice that she had received had been negligent and that the defendant had breached s.62 of the 1986 Act. Although the judge found that the defendant's advice in 1988 had been correct, nonetheless he concluded that the advice was deficient in several respects. First, the defendant had failed to establish precisely what benefits the claimant was entitled to under the NHS scheme or to present those benefits to her in order to enable her to consider them. Secondly, he had not compared the amounts that the claimant might expect to receive under the NHS scheme and the personal pension plan. Thirdly, he had failed to take all reasonable steps to ensure that the claimant understood the risk that opting out of the NHS scheme and starting up a personal pension plan might entail. The defendant had therefore breached FIMBRA rules[12] and had been negligent and, despite advising correctly, had deprived the claimant of the opportunity to make an informed decision whether to remain in or opt out of the NHS scheme.[13]

One of the more striking examples of a financial practitioner's failure to assess **15–051** suitability is to be found in the decision of Longmore J. in *Morgan Stanley UK Group v Puglisi Cosentino*.[14] The defendant resisted a claim for substantial losses sustained in a principal exchange rate linked security ("PERLS") investment with the claimant bank. The bank had provided 90 per cent of the funding for the investment by way of a loan to the defendant. In dismissing the bank's claim the judge concluded that the bank had been guilty of a "serious under-appreciation of the Financial Services Act".[15] The bank was authorised to carry on investment business under the 1986 Act by virtue of its membership of the Securities Association ("TSA"), then an SRO, and so was bound by its rules. First the transaction was one which necessitated a risk warning being given under the TSA's rules, but no such warning had in fact been given. Secondly, although the

---

[10] In particular, LAS did not warn that: (1) substantial penalties would be incurred upon early surrender of their existing endowment policies, (2) the premiums under the new policies would increase substantially over time, or (3) the new policies, unlike the old ones, would not qualify for life assurance premium relief.

[11] [2001] Lloyd's L.Rep. P.N. 235, Judge Raymond Jack Q.C.

[12] FIMBRA, rr. 4.1, 4.2 and 4.3. FIMBRA was one of the self-regulating organisations under the 1986 Act regime. See para.13–010 of the 5th edition of this book.

[13] See further para.15–020, above.

[14] [1998] C.L.C. 481, Longmore J.

[15] At 498C.

bank had ascertained that the defendant had experience of high-value foreign exchange dealings, it had taken no steps to determine the defendant's wealth or the amount that he was prepared or could afford to lose. Thirdly, the transaction had been structured in such a way that although the borrowing arrangement agreed with the defendant entitled the bank to cease financing the investment at the end of every three- or six-month period (and thus to require the defendant to find money from his own resources to replace the bank's funding at short notice) the investment itself was relatively illiquid and could not be readily realised. Fourthly, the investment was not suitable for the defendant and the bank had no reasonable grounds for believing that it was suitable, contrary to the suitability requirement in TSA's rules. But for the relevant breaches of the rules, the defendant would not have invested in the PERLS transaction. Consequently, the bank was unable to enforce the debt that had been incurred by the defendant on the PERLS investment.

15–052   Examples of failures by financial practitioners to ensure an adequate understanding on the part of the customer of the risks associated with a proposed investment can be found in *Australia & New Zealand Banking Group Ltd v Cattan*,[16] *Investors Compensation Scheme Ltd v West Bromwich Building Society*[17] and *Seymour v Caroline Ockwell & Co and Zurich IFA Ltd*.[18] The bank in *Cattan* failed to take the defendant through a warning letter, but this occasioned no loss. In contrast, in *ICS v West Bromwich* the financial practitioner was guilty not only of a wholesale failure to warn investors that the home income plan in which they were proposing to invest created a significant risk of substantial loss but also of positively providing misleading advice to the effect that the home income plan would provide a safe and secure investment for the remainder of the investors' lives. In reality nothing could have been further from the truth. The plan was vulnerable not only to a falling property market but also to one which was static or "only" rising slowly. In normal market conditions it could be expected to last no more than 10 years. It was therefore totally unsuitable for any investor who might have 25 years or more to live. In *Seymour* the first defendant IFA recommended investment in "the Alpha Fund" to the claimants. To the first defendant's knowledge the claimants required an investment that was short term, low risk and income producing. The Alpha Fund satisfied none of these criteria. The claim was nonetheless defended by the first defendant on two bases: (1) that as an "average high-street IFA" the first defendant was not to be criticised for failing to appreciate the unsuitability of the Alpha Fund as an investment for the claimant and (2) that the defendant was in any event entitled to rely upon information and recommendations (negligently) provided to her about the Alpha Fund by the second defendant. Neither defence succeeded. In relation to the first His Honour Judge Havelock-Allan Q.C. concluded that any competent high-street IFA ought to have realised the unsuitability of the Alpha Fund as an investment for the claimants. In relation to the second, the fact that the first defendant may have innocently received and relied upon information provided by the second defendant could not excuse her from liability to the claimant in

---

[16] Unreported, August 2, 2001, Morison J. For the full facts of *Cattan* see para.15–047, above.
[17] [1999] Lloyd's L.Rep. P.N. 496, Evans Lombe J.
[18] [2005] EWHC 279; [2005] P.N.L.R. 39.

circumstances where her duty to advise the claimants was non-delegable. The Judge concluded:

"It is not a defence for her to say that she relied upon the advice or opinion of others as to the suitability of the Alpha Fund if that advice or opinion was itself negligent ... It was for [the first defendant] to form her own opinion in the light of information available to her. She needed to exercise an independent judgment. No amount of reassurance or comfort from [the second defendant] absolved her from examining the product particulars with a critical eye or entitled her to abandon the healthy scepticism she would otherwise have had for a product such as the Alpha fund."

The first defendant did however succeed in making out a Pt 20 claim against the second defendant. The second defendant was ordered to make a 66 per cent contribution towards the first defendant's liability to the claimants.

(v) *Dealing and Managing*

Chapter 7 of the COB sourcebook[19] now sets out the regulatory framework governing these areas.[20] Cases decided under the regime of the 1986 Act may provide assistance for the interpretation of the rules and guidance contained therein.　**15–053**

Many of the cases decided under the 1986 Act regime concerned perceived conflicts of interest on the part of the financial practitioner. Such conflicts can take many forms. In *Australia & New Zealand Banking Group Ltd v Cattan*[21] one of the allegations unsuccessfully advanced by the defendant was that the claimant bank had advised him to buy EMD at the same time as it had itself been reducing its own proprietary positions. In rejecting the allegation Morison J. found that the bank had successfully kept its proprietary book entirely separate from its trading desk where its salesmen bought and sold on customers' behalf and that there was no evidence to suggest that its own decision to sell EMD from its proprietary book influenced the advice that it gave to its customers. He concluded:　**15–054**

"There is nothing wrong or disreputable for a bank to take a different view of the market in relation to its own holdings from the view properly advised to their customers. The reason is obvious: the bank may decide to off-load assets in a particular field for a whole variety of reasons which have nothing to do with an appreciation of how the market is going to respond in the future."[22]

The bank was able to demonstrate that an adequate Chinese wall was in place to prevent any inference being drawn that one department had in any way influenced the other.

One case in which a financial practitioner was found to have acted in a manner that conflicted with the interests of its clients is *Brandeis (Brokers) Limited v Black.*[23] The claimant was an LME broker who commenced arbitration proceedings against various of its clients seeking to recover US$12.5m in relation to　**15–055**

---

[19] See Ch.14, para.14–035 as to sourcebooks in the FSA Handbook.
[20] See Ch.14, paras 14–061 to 14–066.
[21] See also para.15–047, above.
[22] At para.40.
[23] [2001] 2 Lloyd's Rep. 359, Toulson J. See further para.15–043, above.

dealings in copper futures. The respondents countered the claim by alleging mispricing,[24] front-running[25] and misuse of confidential information[26] by the claimant. The arbitrators found that the claimant had indeed been guilty of the majority of the transgressions of which it was accused. The claimant's appeal was dismissed by Toulson J.[27]

15–056   The nature of criticisms made of financial practitioners within the sphere of dealing and managing investments on behalf of a client will frequently depend on the degree of discretion given to the practitioner to deal on the client's behalf. A practitioner who accepts an instruction to act on behalf of a discretionary client will breach the duties of care and skill that he owes to his client if he fails to deal with or manage the client's investment in a way in which a reasonably competent practitioner would have done in the circumstances of the particular transaction. However, no practitioner should to be judged with the benefit of hindsight. It will therefore be necessary in each case to consider whether, on the basis of the information which was available or ought to have been available to the practitioner at the material time, the practitioner has fallen below that standard.[28] The exercise of discretion will, however, entail the financial practitioner owing fiduciary duties to his client, as recognised in *Ata v American Express Bank Ltd*[29] in a discretionary management context. As observed in the same case "a discretion to trade is precisely that: a discretion and not an obligation" and "it was not obliged to trade had it in its discretion felt it inappropriate to do so, let alone to

---

[24] Defined and explained by the arbitrators as follows: "When the broker executing an order in the market on behalf of a client does not give the correct execution to the client, that is to say . . . the broker has executed a transaction at one price but, leaving aside commission, has given a different price."

[25] Defined and explained by the arbitrators as follows: "Front running occurs where, after a broker has taken an order from a client, the broker goes into the market on its own account (or for the benefit of a discretionary or closely associated client) and carries out a transaction for itself or such other client ahead of the client who has given the order. The broker does this because it believes that the client's order will move the market. The broker wants to deal ahead of the client so as to benefit from the market movement or confer a benefit on others or to avoid a loss on its existing position as a result of the market movement. The client may well suffer loss or damage because the broker's transaction and others which may be triggered by it could move the market against the client."

[26] Which the arbitrators explained as occurring when "a broker discloses to outside parties or uses for its own purposes confidential information in its possession about a client's positions, transactions or intended transactions. Such information would include information about the client's present own future positions and financial position. Information would not come within this definition if it is in the public domain or merely consists of general gossip or speculation." Front running is a particular form of misuse of confidential information.

[27] The claimant's appeal was on grounds of serious irregularities during the arbitration and errors of law on the part of the arbitrators. The findings of fact made by the arbitrators did not therefore fall to be considered by Toulson J.

[28] In *Stafford and Comstock Ltd v Conti Commodity Services Ltd* [1981] 1 Lloyd's Rep. 466 the claimant alleged that the claimant commodities broker had negligently failed to "handle" its investments. In rejecting that claim Mocatta J. concluded (at 474–475): "a broker cannot always be right in the advice that he gives in relation to so wayward and rapidly changing market as the commodities futures market. An error of judgment, if there be an error of judgment, is not necessarily negligent . . . Similarly, losses made on the commodity market do not of themselves, in my judgment, provide evidence of negligence on the part of a broker even if he advised both parts of the particular transaction which produced the loss . . . I am satisfied that with the best advice in the world in such an unpredictable market as this it would require exceedingly strong evidence from expert brokers in relation to individual transactions to establish negligence on the part of the defendants."

[29] CA unreported, June 17, 1998, upholding Rix J. unreported, October 7, 1996.

trade in any particular way". Nevertheless, the defendant bank's fiduciary duty entailed recognising the existence of its discretion and thus a positive obligation to consider the investor's open positions from time to time so as to decide whether or not to trade. While on the facts it was in breach of that duty, the investor failed to establish any consequent loss.

Where a client is an execution-only client, the primary duty on the financial **15–057** practitioner will be to comply with instructions given by the client.[30] The practitioner will have no duty to provide advice about the transaction which the client wishes to undertake and will not be open to criticism should the transaction prove to be disadvantageous to the client.[31] He will however be obliged to comply with instructions within a reasonable time of receipt—if he does not, he will be in breach of his duty of care and skill.[32]

4. DEFENCES AND RELIEF

(a) *General*

Statutory rights of action granted under the FSMA are expressly subject to "the **15–058** defences and other incidents applying to actions for breach of statutory duty." Such defences would include, in particular, contributory negligence. Common law causes of action will be subject to defences specific to each particular cause of action.

(b) *Limited Immunity of the FSA from Liability in Damages*

This is addressed in Ch.14.[33] **15–059**

(c) *Restriction of Liability by Contract*

FSMA regulatory regime. Limitations are imposed under this regime upon **15–060** restriction of liability.[34]

Unfair Contract Terms Act 1977. Generally, UCTA has limited relevance. **15–061** First, ss.2 to 4 of UCTA do not apply to any contract of insurance or any contract so far as it relates to the creation or transfer of securities or of any right or interest

---

[30] See, e.g. *Bank fur Handel und Effekten v Davidson* (1975) 55 D.L.R. (3d) 303.
[31] See, e.g. *Valse Holdings SA v Merrill Lynch International Bank Ltd* [2005] EWHC 2471, Comm. In that case the claimant criticised the defendant bank in relation to a number of loss-making trades that it had made on his behalf. Morison J rejected the criticisms, holding that the defendant had traded investments in accordance with the instructions of the claimant who he described as a "knowing and informed trader" who had been "master of the account". Although advice undoubtedly had been given by the defendant to the claimant, no criticism was to be made of that advice. See also *Laskin v Bache & Co Ltd* (1972) 23 D.L.R. (3d) 385.
[32] See, e.g. *Pankhurst v Gairdner Co* (1960) 25 D.L.R. (2d) 515.
[33] See Ch.14, para.14–005.
[34] For a detailed consideration of this topic in a professional liability context, see Ch.5.

in securities.[35] This was one of the reasons why it was held that UCTA was not applicable to contracts governing the relationship between a bank regulated by IMRO[36] and an investor whereby the bank agreed to effect trading transactions on his behalf relating to emerging market debt.[37] Secondly, it does not apply to any contractual provision authorised or required by the express terms or necessary implication of an enactment.[38] It is submitted that it would not apply to contractual provisions authorised or required in the FSA's Handbook.[39] Thirdly, a contract term is to be taken for the purposes of UCTA as satisfying the requirement of reasonableness if it is incorporated or approved by, or incorporated into a contract pursuant to, a decision or ruling of a "competent authority" acting in the exercise of any statutory jurisdiction or function and is not a term of a contract to which the competent authority is itself a party.[40] It is submitted that the FSA is a "competent authority" as defined *qua* a "public authority". Consequently any term incorporated into a contract entered into by a financial practitioner with an investor by reason of a requirement of the FSA will be deemed to be reasonable. This will include requirements contained within the Handbook.[41] In the emerging market debt case IMRO was taken to be a "competent authority" and since the bank's terms of business reflected IMRO requirements, they were to be taken as reasonable.[42]

(d) *Statutory Relief*

15–062 A director of a company may seek relief from liability under s.727 of the Companies Act 1985, although it would seem that such relief is available only in respect of a claim against him by or on behalf of or for the benefit of the company.[43] Relief is neither a defence nor a right, but a discretionary power given to the court in proceedings against the director for negligence, default, breach of duty or breach of trust, to relieve him wholly or partly from his liability on such terms as the court thinks fit, if certain criteria are satisfied. These are, if in the opinion of the court, the director has acted honestly and reasonably and that, having regard to all the circumstances of the case, including those of his

---

[35] See UCTA, s.1(2) and Sch. para.1(1)(a) and(e) of UCTA. "Securities" is not defined. In *Micklefield v SAC Technology* [1990] 1 W.L.R. 1002 it was accepted that the word covered shares and that the disapplication provision covered an employment contract which incorporated a share option.

[36] The Investment Managers Regulatory Organisation, one of the self-regulating organisations under the 1986 Act regime.

[37] *Australia & New Zealand Banking Group Ltd v Louis Cattan*, unreported, August 2, 2001, Morison J.

[38] UCTA, s.29(1)(a).

[39] See Ch.14.

[40] UCTA, s.29(2),(3).

[41] In *Australia & New Zealand Banking Group Ltd v Cattan*, unreported, August 2, 2001, Morison J.

[42] *ibid.* Note also *Ata v American Express Bank Ltd*, CA, unreported, June 17, 1998, upholding the decision of Rix J., unreported, October 7, 1996: it was assumed that UCTA applied in a discretionary management context but the investor's contention that terms relied upon by the bank did not satisfy the requirement of reasonableness was rejected. For facts, see para.15–070, below.

[43] *Customs and Excise Commissioners v Hedon Alpha Ltd* [1981] 2 All E.R. 697, CA.

appointment, he ought fairly to be excused.[44] In the context of claims arising from a regulatory context, there is nothing in principle to prevent the grant of such relief but the circumstances in which it is granted are likely to be exceptionally rare given the regulatory responsibilities of directors.[45]

5. REMEDIES INCLUDING DAMAGES

(a) General

The title to this section of the chapter is different from the usual title to the **15-063** equivalent section in other chapters, which is limited to damages. The explanation is that in relation to financial practitioners the range of remedies frequently sought is wider than damages. There are several reasons for this. First, in the case of other professions the contract of engagement will generally precede the services provided and be the prime basis of claim. Damages for breach of that contract and a concurrent tortious remedy will usually be the only appropriate remedy. In the case of financial practitioners, however, promotion (whether in a prospectus or other advertisement) or investment advice may often precede a contract (e.g. to purchase an investment). The relevant complaint may then be misrepresentation and the remedies sought would be the rescission of that contract and restitution or damages in lieu. Secondly, the impact of regulatory regimes entails that there are statutory causes of action in addition to those at common law. Thirdly, regulatory regimes enable regulators to bring proceedings for the benefit of investors and to seek a wider range of remedies than those available to private litigants.

(b) Remedies Available to Regulators

Under FSMA, the FSA or the Secretary of State are empowered to seek certain **15-064** remedies. The topic is addressed in Ch.14.[46]

(c) Remedies Available to Private Litigants

There are a range of remedies available to private litigants (persons other than **15-065** regulators) in respect of claims arising from a financial context.

(i) Rescission of Contract Induced by Misrepresentation

It will be open to a claimant to seek an order for rescission of a contract which **15-066** he was induced to enter into by a misrepresentation (e.g. in an investment

---

[44] This section reflects similar protection given to trustees; see Trustee Act 1925, s.61. In *Re Duomatic* [1969] 2 Ch. 365, the Companies Act 1948, s.448, the predecessor provision to the Companies Act 1985, s.727, was considered in relation to a director. In *Re D'Jan of London Ltd* [1994] 1 B.C.L.C. 561, Hoffmann L.J. granted relief under s.727 to a director.

[45] Note in the FSA Handbook the sourcebook, "Senior Management Arrangements, Systems and Controls". As to the Handbook, see Ch.14, paras 14–034 *et seq.*

[46] See Ch.14, paras 14–083 to 14–095.

advertisement). Usual common law principles for the grant of rescission will apply. The court has power under s.2(2) of the Misrepresentation Act 1967 to award damages in lieu of rescission.

(ii) *Recovery of Money Paid or Property Transferred Under Agreements Made by or Through Unauthorised Persons*

15–067 Counterparties to agreements made by unauthorised persons in breach of the general prohibition or the financial promotion restriction may be entitled to recover money paid or property transferred pursuant to such agreements. This topic is addressed in Ch.14.[47]

(iii) *Damages or Compensation*

15–068 Damages may be claimed on one or more of several bases: statutory liability for damages under FSMA,[48] breach of contract, tort or damages in lieu of rescission under the Misrepresentation Act 1967. Compensation also may be claimed for defects in listing particulars and a prospectus.[49] Where damages or compensation are claimed, usual general principles for quantification apply.

15–069 **Remoteness.** Although a breach of duty may be established, no loss and damage will be recoverable if too remote. The claimant must establish that, broadly, the loss and damage (a) were caused by the relevant breach of duty and (b) were foreseeable. Moreover, whether or not the starting point for damages assessment is ascertaining the scope of the duty undertaken or imposed,[50] that issue is an important factor in addressing remoteness.

15–070 **Causation illustrations.** That the burden is upon the claimant to prove that the defendant's's default caused loss is apparent from two cases. In *Australia & New Zealand Banking Group Ltd v Cattan*[51] the clamant was held to have committed "at best technical" breaches of IMRO requirements as to completion of certain formalities before the defendant could be classified as a non-private customer and as such allowed to make certain trades. Nevertheless it was held that such breaches had not caused any loss. Even if he had not been able to enter the relevant trades before the required formalities had been completed, upon their completion he would still have entered the same trades. There was no evidence to indicate that then there would have been any difference in price in the defendant's favour. The effect of there being no loss was fatal to the statutory right of action relied upon, loss being an ingredient of that right of action. Similarly, in *Ata v American Express Bank Ltd*[52] the claimant failed to establish that the defendant bank's breach of fiduciary duty caused him any loss. The judge found as a matter of fact that even if the bank had traded the claimant's open

---

[47] See Ch.14, paras 14–097 to 14–101.
[48] See Ch.14, paras 14–102, 14–073 to 14–080.
[49] FSMA, s.90. Equivalent to 1986 Act, s.150. See Ch.14, paras 14–073 to 14–079, above.
[50] See *South Australia Asset Mgmt Corp v York Montague* [1997] A.C. 191.
[51] Unreported, August 2, 2001, Morison J. For other aspects of the case, see paras 15–047 and 15–052, above.
[52] CA, unreported, June 17, 1998 upholding Rix J., unreported, October 7, 1996. As to other aspects of the case, see paras 15–047 and 15–054, above.

positions, further losses were as likely as any profits. The Court of Appeal rejected the contention that in assessing what the claimant's financial position would have been but for the defendant's default, every presumption should be made against the defendant. It overruled a previous first instance decision to the effect that in assessing damages against a stockbroker who had prematurely sold an investor's shares in breach of contract, the measure of damages was the highest price at which the shares could have been later sold by the investor.[53] The "chain of causation" from the defendant's relevant failure may be broken by the act or omission of the claimant or some third person. This happened in *Gorham v British Telecommunications Plc* (summarised above)[54] where the deceased's failure to act on helpline advice indicative of the superiority of the BT occupational scheme precluded his dependants recovering a element of loss consisting of lump sum death benefit.

In *Beary v Pall Mall Investments*[55] the defendant financial adviser had recommended to the claimant that his pension fund be transferred into a Scottish Equitable managed fund ("the PMI fund"), that a tax-free lump sum be withdrawn, that part of that tax-free lump sum be invested in an offshore bond and that the claimant should draw down from his investments the maximum sum available to him each year. The claimant had done what the defendant had recommended and the funds had soon dwindled. The claimant criticised the advice that he had been given. The defendant admitted that he had negligently failed to advise the claimant of alternative methods of dealing with the pension fund—in particular, that he had failed to advise the claimant on the possibility of buying an immediate annuity. However, the judge found as a fact that even had the defendant advised the claimant of the possibility of purchasing an annuity in place of the other investments, the claimant would not have done so. Causation was therefore not established and the claimant recovered nothing on that element of his claim. On appeal the claimant sought to overcome that hurdle by two imaginative means. Firstly he argued that on a proper application of the *Bolitho*[56] principle the Court ought to have considered what the defendant *would* have done had he not been negligent, ought to have concluded that the defendant would have advised the purchase of an immediate annuity and ought to have concluded that, as with every other recommendation made by the defendant, the claimant would have followed that advice. The Court of Appeal rejected that argument— the proper question for the court to have asked (and the question that the judge had in fact asked) was what *should* the defendant have done. The answer to that question was simply "advise on the possibility of buying an immediate annuity". Secondly the Claimant argued that he was entitled to rely upon the reasoning in *Chester v Afshar*[57] to recover damages even if he could not demonstrate that, but for the negligence of the defendant, he would on a balance of probabilities have chosen to purchase an immediate annuity. The Court of Appeal rejected this argument also. On the facts of the case there was no reason to depart from the conventional approach to causation adopted by the judge. In any event, the

---

[53] *Michael v Hart* [1901] 2 K.B. 161, Wills J.
[54] [2001] P.N.L.R. 21. For facts see paras 15–035 to 15–037, above.
[55] [2005] EWCA Civ 415.
[56] See Ch.13.
[57] [2005] UKHL 41; [2005] 1 A.C. 134. See Ch.13, para.13–137.

departure in *Chester v Afshar* from established principles of causation was exceptional, justified only by the particular policy considerations in that case.

15–071   **Evaluation of chance.** In other contexts[58] damages are sometimes calculated by reference to the value of the chance of which the defendant's default deprived the claimant. However, for this approach to be adopted the claimant must first prove as matter of causation that he had a real or substantial chance as opposed to a speculative one.[59] This would appear to present claimants with an insuperable obstacle to recovery of damages on a lost chance basis in an investment context. It was so held in a commodity trading context in *Bailey v Balholm Securities*.[60] Kerr J. distinguished cases in which damages had been assessed on a lost chance basis:

> "But those were all cases in which the plaintiff might or might not have obtained some pecuniary advantage or benefit and lost the chance of doing so as the result of the defendant's wrongful act. He therefore lost the chance of being better off than he was, but he was not exposed to the risk of being worse off. In cases like the present, on the other hand, a person who is prevented from speculating in cocoa or sugar futures may have lost the chance of making money or may have been saved from losing money. A cynical view would be that there is an equal chance either way. No doubt experience and skill play a large part, and to this extent there may be said to be a better chance of winning rather than losing. But in my view this is not the kind of situation which the law should recognize as giving a right to damage for the loss of a chance. Even though in law trading in commodity futures does not amount to gambling, the loss of the general opportunity to trade—as opposed to the loss of the particular bargain—is in my view much too speculative to be capable of having any monetary value placed upon it. A wrongful refusal to trade with a person in futures would therefore in my judgment normally only give rise to the recovery if nominal damages."[61]

This reasoning was followed in rejecting a claim for damages based on lost chance in a investment management context in *Ata v American Express Bank Ltd*.[62]

15–072   **Measure of damages.** The fundamental principle governing the measure of damages is that the claimant must be put so far as money can do it in the position he would have occupied if the financial practitioner had properly discharged his duty.[63] Broadly speaking, this can be achieved in one of two ways, depending upon the particular facts of the case (i) by paying to the claimant the monetary equivalent of any benefits of which he has been deprived, or (ii) by indemnifying the claimant against any expenses or liabilities which he has incurred.

---

[58] See e.g. Ch.10, paras 10–256 to 10–262.
[59] See *Allied Maple Group v Simmons & Simmons* [1995] 1 W.L.R. 1602 at 1614.
[60] [1973] 2 Lloyd's Rep. 404, Kerr J.
[61] *ibid.* at 415–6.
[62] CA unreported, June 17, 1998, upholding Rix J., unreported, October 7, 1996. For further aspects of the case, see paras 15–043, 15–061 and 15–070.
[63] See *Livingstone v Rawyards Coal Co* (1880) 5 App.Cas. 25, 39 and *Dodd Properties (Kent) Ltd v Canterbury CC* [1980] 1 W.L.R. 433, 451, 454 and 456 (as to general principles).

In *Keydon Estates Ltd v Eversheds*[64] the claimant purchased an investment property in the belief that its tenant represented a long-term, blue-chip covenant. That belief was the result of negligent advice received from its solicitors. The claimant's case was that had those solicitors not advised negligently, it would not have bought the subject property but would instead have sought out and purchased an alternative investment property offering a return comparable to that which it believed it was to receive from the subject property. Evidence was adduced as to the availability of such comparable alternative properties. The Court accepted that the claimant would have done as it contended and awarded damages to reflect (i) the losses that the claimant had in fact suffered as a result of purchasing the subject property when it would not have done so, and (ii) the sums that it would have received by way of income from the hypothetical comparable alternative property that it would have bought instead. The judge used the level of income that the claimant had been led to believe would be generated from the subject property as an indicator of the likely income that it would have received from a comparable alternative property, although discounted those figures by 5 per cent to reflect the possibility that the hypothetical comparable alternative property might not have proved to be so lucrative an investment as the subject property had appeared to be.

Although that case was one of solicitors negligence, there is no reason why similar principles would not be applied when assessing the damages to be awarded to a claimant who, in reliance on negligent financial advice, invested in product X when, had he been properly advised, he would have invested in product Y. Subject to adducing the necessary evidence and discharging the necessary burdens of proof, such a claimant should be able to recover both the profits that he would have made from investing in product Y as well as the losses that he in fact made from investing in product X.

Benefits received. Some difficult issues have arisen in the context of the mass **15–073** of claims arising from misselling of home income plans, pension policies and endowment policies as to treatment of certain benefits received in assessing compensation or damages.[65] In *R. v Investors Compensation Scheme Ltd Ex p. Bowden* the issue was whether in compensating investors for inadequate advice by financial advisers in consequence of which they had taken out home income plans (whereby they raised money on mortgage in order to provide an income), ICS was entitled not to provide compensation for sums received and expended. The context of the proceedings was a judicial review application. Hence the critical question was not whether such sums were compensatable in damages as a matter of common law. Rather the question was whether it was open to ICS as a reasonable public authority to exclude such sums from compensation pursuant to the compensation scheme which it administered. The House of Lords[66] answered that question affirmatively in favour of ICS and declined to resolve the question whether such sums would have been recoverable in a damages claim as a matter of common law. In so doing the House of Lords overruled the Court of

---

[64] [2005] EWHC 972, Ch; [2005] P.N.L.R. 40.
[65] See *McGregor on Damages* (17th edn, 2003), esp. 7–089 to 7–150.
[66] [1996] A.C. 261. See further Ch.14, para.14–135.

Appeal[67] which had ruled against ICS. The Court of Appeal did address the common law position, concluding as follows:

> "Whether dissipated benefit is a recoverable loss must depend on the circumstances. But here the very purpose of the transaction advised by the financial advisers was the achievement of an increase in income. To establish that it is unnecessary to look further than the newspaper advertisement placed by the advisers to which the investor responded. That being so expenditure of money, once it had been paid to the investors, was plainly foreseeable and if that expenditure was on ephemera so that no lasting benefit accrued there was a loss in terms of increased mortgage debt which sounds in undiminished damages against the financial advisers."[68]

15–074   The problem arises again in the context of the misselling of endowment policies. Many house owners who were induced to invest in an endowment policy intended to produce a capital sum sufficient to repay a related mortgage debt, are faced with a funding shortfall and are bringing claims against financial advisers for negligently advising the endowment route as opposed to the route of a repayment mortgage. In assessing damages by reference to the capital difference between the value of the endowment policy and the amount which would have been repaid under a repayment route, should credit be given for any lesser outgoings under the endowment route relative to the repayment route, even though such outgoings may have been dissipated on everyday expenditure? The solution apposite to a person on low income who "stretched" to buy and relied on the financial adviser in order to make an informed decision not only as to mortgage type but also as to consequent budgeting, may not be apposite to a person with substantial free assets or high income. Considerations of fair allocation of risk may merit a credit in case of the latter, not least since he can finance a shortfall from future income.[69]

15–075   The formulation of a distinguishing principle poses difficulty. Might it be that credit or some credit should be given unless the claimant can establish on a balance of probabilities that it is unreasonable to require him to give such credit in his or particular circumstances, having regard to his existing and foreseeable other commitments? Might the credit be rationalised in terms of mitigation? Mitigation rules will not require the impecunious to provide the credit. It may be argued that mitigation does not extend to the expenditure of money. But is not the position different where the expenditure in the form of higher future outgoings reflects the benefit of lower outgoings in the past as a consequence of the claimed default?

15–076   In *Needler Financial Services v Taber*[70] the issue was whether in assessing compensation for negligent pension misselling based on the difference between the greater benefits under an occupational pension scheme and a personal pension plan, a credit should be given for benefits received by the investor upon demutualisation of the plan provider. It was held that no credit should be given. Following a review of relevant authorities, the critical question was formulated

---

[67] [1995] Q.B. 107.
[68] *ibid.* at 120G–H.
[69] See further Powell [2001] P.N. 206.
[70] [2002] 3 All E.R. 501. For a critical analysis of *Needler*, see *Swinton* S.L.G. 2002 70(2), 48–49 and Turner *"Heads I win, Tails you lose"* Corp Brief 2001 15(9) 6–8.

as "whether the negligence which caused the loss also caused the profit in the sense that the latter was part of a continuous transaction of which the former was the inception." This was a question of fact and was answered in the negative.[71]

In *Primavera v Allied Dunbar Assurance Plc*[72] the claimant had been advised **15–077** by the defendant in 1987 to invest in an executive retirement plan ("ERP") with the aim by 1995 of being able to draw down a tax-free sum of £500,000 from the fund to repay a loan and to purchase an annuity with the balance of the fund. However, the defendant neglected to advise the claimant that in order for the ERP to produce the necessary tax free sum to enable the loan to be repaid, the claimant would have to receive schedule E earnings of a particular level for at least three consecutive years during the seven year life of the ERP. He could have arranged to receive such earnings, but due to his ignorance of any need to do so, did not in fact receive such remuneration. As a result, although by 1995 the fund value of the ERP was £792,896, the tax free lump sum available to the claimant from the ERP was only £125,875. Had he received higher schedule E earnings, that tax free lump sum would have been approximately £101,000 greater. Between 1997 and 2000 the claimant did in fact arrange his affairs so as to receive the necessary Schedule E salary payments and by 2000 a sufficient tax free lump sum to repay the loan had become available under the ERP. In addition, by that date the value of the fund had risen to such an extent that the Claimant was able to purchase a substantially larger annuity than he would have been able to purchase in 1995 had he received the necessary schedule E earnings prior to 1995. The claimant was found to be entitled to recover the additional tax free lump sum that would have been available to him in 1995 had he received the necessary Schedule E salary payments. However, an issue arose as to whether the claimant should have to give credit against that sum for increases in the value of the fund after 1995 from which he would not in fact have benefited had the ERP been used to pay off the loan in 1995. The Court of Appeal concluded that he did not. That benefit was not a consequence of the defendant's misconduct and it was wrong to characterise the claimant's conduct after 1995 as action taken in order to mitigate loss suffered by him as a result of the defendant's failings. Instead that conduct was properly to be described as the claimant's own "*speculation*", in relation to the consequences of which the defendant could have no risk or benefit.

Account of profits. This is a well established remedy for breach of fiduciary **15–078** duty as well as for breach of confidence.[73]

---

[71] *Sed quaere*. The decision seems out of accord with the sentiment expressed by Lord Hoffman in *Dimond v Lovell* [2000] 2 W.L.R. 1121 at 1133A–C. The effect of the compensation payable in such circumstances not being reduced by a credit for demutualisation benefits is to burden the whole community with a cost referable to higher pension contributions.

[72] [2002] EWCA Civ 1327; [2003] P.N.L.R. 12. For an examination of this decision, see Gibbons' "Breaking chains of causation in the avoidance of loss" N.L.J. Vol.152 1714. *Primavera* was distinguished by the Court of Appeal in *JP Morgan Chase Bank v Springwell Navigation Corp* [2006] EWCA Civ 161.

[73] See *Peter Pan Manufacturing Corp v Corsets Silhouette Ltd* [1964] 1 W.L.R. 96; *Att-Gen v Guardian Newspapers Ltd (No.2)* [1990] 1 A.C. 109. As recognised in a financial services context in *Brandeis (Brokers) Ltd v Herbert Black* [2001] 2 Lloyd's Rep. 359, Toulson J.

6. Shared Responsibility

(a) *Contributory Negligence*[74]

15–079   In principle, this defence is available to financial practitioners in respect of claims made against them to the same extent as it is available to other defendants.[75] In particular, it is available in respect of a claim based on the statutory liability under the FSMA for contravention of regulatory rules,[76] as indeed recognised in relation to like statutory liability under the 1986 Act.[77] Nevertheless, the circumstances in which the defence is successfully invoked in relation to claims by claimants in a retail investment context are likely to be relatively rare.

(b) *Contribution*

15–080   Contribution[78] is not a defence but a right conferred by statute[79] upon a defendant, D1, to recover a proportion of the damages for which he is liable to C, from other persons, D2, D3 etc., each of whom is also liable to C in respect of the same damage, based on that other person's share in the responsibility for the damage. While each of D1, D2 and D3 is liable to C, as between themselves the damages are shared as appropriate, e.g. a third each.[80] Financial practitioners who advise a claimant successively may make contribution claims as between themselves, as they may where they advise a claimant contemporaneously, whether on the same or different aspects of the transaction complained of.

7. The Process of Resolving Claims

15–081   As in other contexts, many cases are not susceptible to resolution other than by litigation but there are other processes for the resolution of disputes. These include arbitration as well as conciliation and mediation procedures. Specific to

---

[74] For a detailed consideration of this topic in the context of professional liability claims, see Ch.5, paras 5–141 to 5–148.

[75] But the defence is not available to a claim based on the tort of deceit (see para.15–026, above) and may be limited in respect of a claim based on the Misrepresentation Act 1967, s.2(1) (see para.15–016, above).

[76] FSMA, s.150. See Ch.14, paras 14–074 to 14–079.

[77] 1986 Act, ss.62, 62A. See *Morgan Stanley UK Group v Puglisi Cosentino* [1998] C.L.C. 481; *Gorham v British Telecommunications Plc* [2001] P.N.L.R. 21.

[78] For a detailed consideration of this topic in the context of professional liability claims, see Ch.4, paras 4–001 to 4–017.

[79] The Civil Liability (Contribution) Act 1978.

[80] In *Seymour v Caroline Ockwell & Co and Zurich IFA Ltd* [2005] EWHC 1137; [2005] P.N.L.R. 39 the defendant IFA recovered a 66% contribution from the Pt 20 defendant product provider towards her own liability to the claimants. However, she did so *not* on the basis that each had breached a duty owed to the claimant (since the judge had found that the Pt 20 defendant in fact owed no such duties to the claimant directly) but on the basis that the Pt 20 defendant had breached contractual and tortuous duties of care owed directly to her, thereby causing her to suffer in the form of a liability to the claimants.

the financial services context is a (now) unified Ombudsman scheme ("FOS").[81] Moreover, in relation to pension mis-selling, regulators utilised their disciplinary powers to compel authorised firms to carry out a review of relevant previous business. Judicial review applications directed to resist such exceptional use of disciplinary powers were unsuccessful.[82] There is also a compensation scheme.[83]

8. PARALLEL PROCEEDINGS

Consideration of claims arising from a financial regulatory context would be incomplete without mention of problems arising from parallel proceedings, though detailed consideration is beyond the scope of this book. A scandal from a regulatory context frequently spawns a range of different proceedings and often in different jurisdictions. The problems reflect the different aims of the different proceedings which may be brought. Investigatory (e.g. by liquidators, regulatory and professional bodies), criminal, civil and regulatory proceedings all have different aims. There is no obvious hierarchy which may be invoked to prescribe a priority sequence of general application. Different events will merit different sequences. Moreover, much will depend on the will of the various potential initiators of different proceedings. Applications are often made to stay disciplinary proceedings pending the outcome of civil proceedings. The general principle seems now to be clear: **15–082**

> "the court has power to intervene to prevent injustice where the continuation of one set of proceedings may prejudice the fairness of the trial of other proceedings. But it is a power which has to be exercised with great care and only where there is real risk of serious prejudice which may lead to injustice."[84]

Disclosure problems. Regulatory and investigatory proceedings generate documents which attract disclosure applications in civil proceedings. These applications are frequently met with claims to various kinds of privilege, e.g. public interest immunity, legal professional privilege[85] and privilege against self-incrimination, and invocation of human rights legislation. As to information obtained by regulators pursuant to statutory powers to obtain such information, restrictions are imposed on disclosure *by them* of such information subject to a range of exceptions including in favour of other regulators.[86]   **15–083**

---

[81] See Ch.14, paras 14–103 to 14–124.
[82] *R. v Securities and Investments Board Ex p. Independent Financial Advisers Association* [1995] 2 B.C.L.C. 76; *R. v Securities and Investments Board Ex p. Sun Life Assurance Society Plc* [1996] 2 B.C.L.C. 150.
[83] See Ch.14, paras 14–125 to 14–139.
[84] *R. v Panel on Takeovers and Mergers Ex p. Fayed* [1992] B.C.C. 524, CA, *per* Neill L.J. at 531. Compare the (frequently criticised) decision of the Court of Appeal in *R. v Institute of Chartered Accountants in England and Wales Ex p. Brindle* [1994] B.C.C. 297 in which disciplinary proceedings were stayed with the more orthodox later decision of the Divisional Court in *R. v Chance Ex p. Smith* [1995] B.C.C. 1095.
[85] See in the context of the 1986 Act, *Kaufmann v Credit Lyonnais* [1995] C.L.C. 300.
[86] See FSMA Pt XXIII, ss. 347 to 354.

CHAPTER 16

INSURANCE BROKERS

1. GENERAL

Some insurance contracts are arranged directly between an insurer and an insured. However, the majority of insurance contracts are arranged through intermediaries, most of which fall within one of two categories: insurance agents and insurance brokers. The term "insurance agent" is used to describe persons who normally act as agents of the insurers for the purpose of effecting insurance policies. Insurance agents are commonly employed by particular insurance companies or groups of companies and they do not profess to give disinterested advice about the services which are offered by their competitors.[1]

16–001

---

[1] Where the usual requirements for the imposition of a duty of care are satisfied (as to which, see Ch.2, paras 2–017 *et seq.*) insurance agents will be held to owe duties of care to those seeking insurance. See, e.g. *Gorham v British Telecommunications Plc* [2000] 1 W.L.R. 2129 in which the defendant insurance company conceded that it owed a duty of care to the purchaser of one of its personal pensions. In such cases the same principles relating to breach, causation and loss and damage as set out in this chapter will apply. Similarly, in appropriate circumstances other parties may

16–002   The term "insurance broker", by contrast, is used to describe persons who normally act as agents of the insured (or reinsured) for the purpose of effecting insurance (or reinsurance) policies. Insurance brokers hold themselves out as experts in insurance generally, or in certain fields of insurance, and offer their services to persons who are seeking the benefit of insurance. Insurance brokers effect policies of insurance or reinsurance on behalf of their clients, give advice in connection with such policies, and, on occasions, assist their clients in making claims against the insurers or reinsurers as the case may be. Although insurance brokers usually draw their remuneration from the insurers (in the form of commission), they are expected to act in the best interests of the insured. An intermediary should inform his client whether he is acting as an insurance agent or an insurance broker.[2] This chapter is concerned with claims against insurance brokers

16–003   As stated above, the insurance broker generally acts as the agent of the insured and not of the insurer.[3] This applies both when he is effecting insurance[4] and when he is handling claims which arise under the policy.[5] There are, however, exceptions to this general rule.[6] The broker may be authorised by particular insurers to effect insurance on their behalf, and when so doing he acts as the agent of those insurers.[7] In non-marine insurance the broker often has implied authority to grant interim insurance (which is normally evidenced by cover notes) and, again, when so doing he acts as agent of the insurers rather than the insured.[8]

---

be found to have assumed the responsibility of an insurance broker. Such an allegation against a bank succeeded at first instance in *Frost v James Finlay Bank* [2001] Lloyd's Rep. P.N., but the judge's finding was over-turned on appeal: [2002] EWCA Civ 667; [2002] Lloyd's Rep. P.N. 473.

[2] Para.3.1 of the General Insurance Standards Council Code for Private Customers (2000) states: "We will explain the service we can offer and our relationship with you, including: whether we act for an Insurer or act independently for you as an intermediary; whether we act as an agent of another intermediary or agent; the choice of products and services we can offer you." R.4.2 of the ICOB sourcebook sets out the information that an insurance intermediary must provide to its customer, including information regarding the intermediary's status.

[3] In *Searle v Hales Co* [1996] Q.B. 68, Adrian Whitfield Q.C. (sitting as a deputy High Court judge) held, allowing the insurer's application to strike out the client's claim, that "prima facie, insurance agents and brokers are agents of the insured and not the insurer . . . This relationship is not altered by the fact that a broker's commission may be deducted from the premium": *ibid.* at 71.

[4] *Rozanes v Bowen* (1928) 32 Ll. L. Rep. 98; *McNealy v The Pennine Insurance Co Ltd* [1978] 2 Lloyd's Rep. 18, CA; *Velos v Harbour Insurance* [1997] 2 Lloyd's Rep. 461 (H.H.J. Hallgarten Q.C.). In New Zealand a broker who receives commission from the insurer is deemed to be the insurer's "representative", so that the insurer is fixed with the broker's knowledge of all matters material to the insurance contract: s.10 of the Insurance Law Reform Act 1977 as applied in *Helicopter Equipment Ltd v Marine Insurance Co Ltd* [1986] 1 N.Z.L.R. 448; and *Gold Star Insurance Co Ltd v Gaunt* [1998] 3 N.Z.L.R. 80, NZCA. He is not thereby deemed to be the insurer's agent, however. In Australia the Insurance (Agents and Brokers) Act 1984 modifies the role of the broker: see *Manufacturers' Mutual Insurance Ltd v John H Boardman Insurance Brokers Pty Ltd* (1994) 68 A.L.J.R. 385.

[5] *Anglo-African Merchants Ltd v Bayley* [1970] 1 Q.B. 311; *North and South Trust Co v Berkeley* [1971] 1 W.L.R. 470; *Callaghan and Hedges v Thompson* [2000] Lloyd's Rep. I.R. 125, Steel J.

[6] That a broker is agent of the insured is essentially a presumption which can be rebutted: *Winter v Irish Life Assurance Plc* [1995] 2 Lloyd's Rep. 274 at 282, *per* Sir Peter Webster.

[7] As in *Woolcott v Excess Insurance Co Ltd (No.2)* [1979] 2 Lloyd's Rep. 210; *Excess Life Assurance Co Ltd v Firemen's Insurance Co of Newark, New Jersey* [1982] 2 Lloyd's Rep. 599, 621.

[8] *Stockton v Mason* [1978] 2 Lloyd's Rep. 430.

Even where the broker is acting as agent for the insurers, however, he still owes a duty of care to the insured.[9]

An insurance broker may be an individual, a partnership or a company. If the   **16–004** broker is a company, then the claim will usually be against the company. However, in appropriate circumstances it may be possible to maintain an action against an employee of the company. This will be particularly relevant where the company is insolvent and uninsured. In *Punjab National Bank v de Boinville*[10] the Court of Appeal held that the first two defendants, who were principals of their respective insurance broking companies, were personally liable. More recently, in *European International Reinsurance Co Ltd v Curzon*[11] the Court of Appeal held that it was arguable that a broker's employees had voluntarily assumed the duties of a broker and were therefore personally liable.[12]

Regulation of brokers prior to January 2005. Until April 2001 the business   **16–005** of insurance brokers was regulated by the Insurance Brokers (Registration) Act 1977 and the rules and orders made thereunder. The governing body of the profession was the Insurance Brokers Registration Council, established under s.1 of the 1977 Act. Sections 2 and 4 of the Act required the Council to establish and maintain a register of insurance brokers and a list of bodies corporate carrying on business as insurance brokers.[13] It was an offence for individuals who were not registered or for companies which were not enrolled in the list to describe themselves as "insurance brokers"[14]: such parties typically described themselves as "insurance consultants" or "insurance intermediaries".[15] A Code of Conduct for the guidance of insurance brokers was drawn up by the Council, pursuant to s.10 of the Act, and was contained in the Insurance Brokers Registration Council (Code of Conduct) Approval Order 1994.[16]

The Insurance Brokers (Registration) Act 1977 was repealed by the Financial   **16–006** Services and Markets Act 2000 ("FSMA"),[17] and the Insurance Brokers Registration Council was abolished. The General Insurance Standards Council (GISC), an independent and non-statutory body, was established to take its place. The

---

[9] *London Borough of Bromley v Ellis* [1971] 1 Lloyd's Rep. 97, 99.

[10] [1992] 1 W.L.R. 1138 (the facts of which are set out at para.16–028, below).

[11] [2003] EWCA Civ 1074; [2003] Lloyd's Rep. I.R. 793.

[12] The court stated that the decision of the Court of Appeal in *Punjab* was not necessarily inconsistent with the decision of the House of Lords in *Williams v Natural Life* [1998] 1 W.L.R. 830.

[13] The qualifications for registration were set out in s.3 of the Insurance Brokers (Registration) Act 1977. The construction of s.3 is discussed in *Pickles v Insurance Brokers Registration Council* [1984] 1 W.L.R. 745. The statutory scheme is briefly discussed in *Macmillan v AW Knott Becker Scott Ltd* [1990] 1 Lloyd's Rep. 98.

[14] Insurance Brokers Registration Act 1977, s.22. In *Harvest Trucking Co Ltd v Davis* [1991] 2 Lloyd's Rep. 638 the defendant was not registered as an insurance broker and described himself as an "insurance intermediary". H.H.J. Diamond Q.C., sitting in the High Court, stated that although Mr Davis's business was indistinguishable from that of a small insurance broker, "no possible criticism can be made of the fact that Mr Davis carried on business in the way he did".

[15] Many insurance intermediaries who were not members of the Insurance Brokers Registration Council were instead members of the Association of British Insurers. The ABI produced its own Code of Practice to regulate the activities of its members.

[16] SI 1994/2569. Before November 21, 1994 the Code of Conduct was contained in the Insurance Brokers Registration Council (Code of Conduct) Approval Order 1978 (SI 1978/1394).

[17] The Insurance Brokers (Registration) Act 1977 was repealed on April 30, 2001 when the relevant provisions of FSMA were brought into force by the Financial Services and Markets Act 2000 (Commencement No.2) Order (SI 2001/1282).

GISC was to be the sole body for the regulation of the general insurance industry, including insurers and independent intermediaries. However, membership of the GISC was voluntary. The GISC produced two Codes of Conduct, one relating to private investors and one for commercial customers.[18]

16–007   **Regulation of brokers after January 2005.** Since January 15, 2005, the usual activities of an insurance broker have amounted to a "regulated activity" within the meaning of FSMA.[19] An insurance broker or other intermediary may not carry on a "regulated activity" unless he is either an authorised person or an exempt person.[20] An agreement made in breach of this general prohibition is unenforceable by the broker against the innocent party, who may be entitled to recover any money paid under the agreement together with compensation.[21]

16–008   The expansion of the regulation of insurance intermediaries was necessary so that the UK complied with its obligations under the Insurance Mediation Directive.[22] The Directive has been implemented through amendments to FSMA and certain regulations made under that Act. The Directive sets minimum standards covering matters such as fitness and propriety, training and competence, and complaints handling. It also requires that certain minimum pre-sale information is given to customers.

16–009   The consequence of the amendments to the Act and regulations and rules thereunder is that since January 2005 the Financial Services Authority ("FSA") has been responsible for regulating insurance brokers, who are required to be authorised by the FSA. Further, all insurance brokers are required to comply with the applicable rules in the Insurance: Conduct of Business sourcebook ("ICOB") which forms part of the FSA's handbook.[23] In the context of claims against insurance brokers, the most important rules are contained in Chs 4 and 5 of the sourcebook. Chapter 4 sets out minimum standards for advising and selling (in particular the requirements of "suitability"), and Ch.5 contains rules regarding product disclosure. Pursuant to s.150 of the Act, a breach of the rules by an

---

[18] The two codes are the General Insurance Standards Council Code for Private Customers (2000) and the General Insurance Standards Council Commercial Code. For the full text of these codes, and commentary on them, see R. W. Hodgin, *Insurance Intermediaries, Law and Regulation*, Ch.4.

[19] Before 2001 insurance brokers were subject to the regime of the Financial Services Act 1986 in so far as they carried on "investment business" as defined. From December 2001 insurance brokers were subject to the regime of FSMA insofar as they carried on a "regulated activity" within the meaning of the FSMA. However, prior to January 15, 2005 the definition of a "regulated activity" was restricted and did not include advising on contracts of general insurance. See paras 14–007 and 14–008 of the 5th edition of this work.

[20] See the general prohibition set out in s.19 of the FSMA. See Ch.14, paras 14–006 *et seq.*, above. A breach of the general prohibition is a criminal offence (ss.23–25). Detailed guidance on whether or not a person needs authorisation is contained within the Perimeter Guidance Manual (PERG) which is contained within the FSA's Handbook.

[21] See ss.26–28 of FSMA. See Ch.14, above. The same remedies were set out in s.5 of the Financial Services Act 1986.

[22] (2002/92). The Directive was approved in September 2002 and had to be implemented by all Member States by January 15, 2005.

[23] The full text of the handbook can be found on the FSA's website: www.fsa.gov.uk. In addition, the online version of the handbook includes a useful facility by which it is possible to ascertain what rules were in force at any given date in the past.

authorised broker may be actionable at the suit of a private person[24] who suffers loss as a result of that breach, subject to the defences and other incidents applying to actions for breach of statutory duty.[25]

Lloyd's brokers. Lloyd's consists of a number of syndicates, each made up of **16–010** a number of "names", who undertake unlimited liability for their proportion of any given risk. Each syndicate has an active underwriter who enters into contracts on its behalf in "the room" at Lloyd's. With limited exceptions,[26] only Lloyd's brokers (i.e. those accredited by the Society of Lloyd's) are allowed to effect contracts of insurance with underwriters in the room.[27] For this privilege Lloyd's brokers are subject to Lloyd's regulations and disciplinary procedures.[28] Previously all Lloyd's brokers were required to become members of the General Insurance Standards Council and to comply with the Council's Commercial Code. They are now required to be authorised by the FSA because they carry on a regulated activity within the meaning of FSMA.[29] Lloyd's brokers are obliged to enter into Terms of Business Agreements with all managing agents with whom they place business.[30]

(a) *Duties to Client*

(i) *Contractual Duties*

In most cases a contract is made, either expressly or by implication, between the **16–011** insurance broker and his client. Although the client does not normally pay a fee,

---

[24] The definition of a "private person" for the purposes of s.150 is set out in reg.3 of the Financial Services and Markets Act 2000 (Rights of Action) Regulations 2001 (SI 2001/2256). The definition includes (a) any individual, unless he suffers the loss in question in the course of carrying on any regulated activity and (b) any person who is not an individual, unless he suffers the loss in question in the course of carrying on business of any kind. Further, governments, local authorities and international organisations are specifically excluded. See Ch.14, para.14–074, above.

[25] See further Ch.14, para.14–073, above.

[26] Paras 27–29 of the Lloyd's Underwriting Byelaw (No.2 of 2003) (as amended) sets out the limited circumstances in which business may be accepted from or through a person who is not a Lloyd's broker.

[27] But see *Johns v Kelly* [1986] 1 Lloyd's Rep. 468, which concerned an "umbrella" agreement whereby a non-Lloyd's broker gained access to the room under the name of a Lloyd's broker. The same arrangement was used in *Velos v Harbour Insurance* [1997] 2 Lloyd's Rep. 461; and *Callaghan and Hedges v Thompson* [2000] Lloyd's Rep. I.R. 125. Lloyd's syndicates give binding authorities to brokers and others so that it is possible to effect insurance with Lloyd's outside the room: see para.16–023, below.

[28] Lloyd's brokers are required to comply with the Lloyd's Brokers Byelaw (No.7 of 2004), the text of which can be found on the Lloyd's website (*www.lloyds.com*). Prior to the coming into force of that byelaw on December 1, 2004 Lloyd's brokers were required to comply with the Lloyd's Brokers Byelaw (No.17 of 2000).

[29] See FSMA, s.22 and the Financial Services and Markets Act 2000 (Regulated Activities) Order (SI 2001/544). See further Ch.14, paras 14–022 *et seq.*, above.

[30] The requirement for Lloyd's brokers to enter into Terms of Business Agreements with managing agents was introduced by the Lloyd's Broker Byelaw (No.17 of 2000). The requirement is now contained within the Lloyd's Brokers Byelaw (No.7 of 2004).

by placing his insurance through the broker he enables the broker to draw a commission, and this constitutes sufficient consideration. The contract may relate to the insuring of a single risk or class of risks. Alternatively, the brokers may handle all the client's insurance affairs. In any contract between an insurance broker and his client, there is implied by law[31] a term that the broker will exercise reasonable skill and care.[32]

16–012	In addition to the implied duty to exercise reasonable skill and care, other specific duties are commonly imposed on the broker by his contract with the client.[33] The broker may, for example, agree that he will obtain a particular form of insurance for the client, not merely that he will use reasonable skill and care to do so.[34] Much of the work done by insurance brokers is of a purely routine nature and such that there is no excuse for a failure to carry out the client's instructions.[35] In such cases the client's instructions (once accepted) may be regarded as imposing specific contractual obligations, for breach of which the broker would be held liable, without any consideration of the question of negligence.[36]

16–013	It is not normally the function of an insurance broker to decide what kinds of insurance the client should have.[37] However, the broker may by contract assume such a task and then it becomes his duty to investigate the client's activities, in order to identify the risks to be insured. In the Canadian case of *Fine's Flowers*

---

[31] Unless successfully excluded. See Ch.5, paras 5–001 *et seq.*

[32] The nature of the contract between insurance broker and client was considered at some length by the Australian Supreme Court in *Ogden & Co Pty Ltd v Reliance Fire Sprinkler Co Pty Ltd* [1975] 1 Lloyd's Rep. 52. As in the case of any other contract for professional services, the obligation to exercise reasonable skill and care is implied in order to give business efficacy: see p.68, col.1. This common law principle is now embodied in s.13 of the Supply of Goods and Services Act 1982.

[33] The broker's general duty to exercise reasonable skill and care may be broken down into the performance of specific tasks, but unless there is a clear agreement to the contrary the broker will not be under an absolute obligation to perform those tasks, merely to bring to their performance reasonable skill and care: see *Youell v Bland Welch & Co Ltd (No.2)* [1990] 2 Lloyd's Rep. 431, 458 (the "Superhulls Cover" case) (for the facts of this case see para.16–022, below.

[34] See para.16–047, below. Thus in *Texas Homecare Ltd v Royal Bank of Canada Trust Co (Jersey) Ltd* [1996] C.L.C. 776 (for the facts, see para.16–031, below) brokers had contracted to place insurance with an insurers of "at least AA status (or equivalent)".

[35] For example, if there is an issue as to whether the broker has obtained insurance which meets his client's instructions or requirements, the issue is not so much whether the broker was negligent as whether the insurers are liable on the policy: if they are not, the broker will have been negligent: see, e.g., *Seavision Investment SA v Evennett, The Tiburon* [1990] 2 Lloyd's Rep. 418, discussed at para.16–043, below; and *Flying Colours Film Co Ltd v Assicurazioni Generali SpA* [1993] 2 Lloyd's Rep. 184 where the argument was solely between the insurers and the brokers, the client standing on the touchline.

[36] See, e.g., the reasoning of Atkin J. in *Dickson & Co v Devitt* (1916) 86 L.J.K.B. 315, discussed at para.16–047, below. By omitting the words "and/or steamers" from one of the insurance slips, the defendant's clerk failed to carry out the claimant's instructions. This constituted a specific breach of contract, which was separate from (and additional to) the failure to exercise reasonable skill and care.

[37] For example in *O'Brien v Hughes-Gibb & Co Ltd* [1995] L.R.L.R. 90 the owners of a racehorse asked the brokers to arrange cover for "mortality only". Rattee J. held that the brokers had not been in breach of duty for failing to advise the owners to obtain cover against theft or to obtain it for them. Nor is a broker under a duty to advise on the financial wisdom of a transaction: *Moore v Zerfahs* [1999] Lloyd's Rep. P.N. 144, CA.

Ltd v General Accident Assurance Co of Canada[38] it was held that the brokers
had assumed such a duty:

> "But there are other cases, and in my view this is one of them, in which the client gives
> no such specific instructions but rather relies upon his agent to see that he is protected
> and, if the agent agrees to do business with him on those terms, then he cannot
> afterwards, when an insured loss arises, shrug off the responsibility he has assumed. If
> this requires him to inform himself about his client's business in order to assess the
> foreseeable risks and insure his client against them, then this he must do. It goes without
> saying that an agent who does not have the requisite skills to understand the nature of
> his client's business and assess the risks that should be insured against should not be
> offering this kind of service."[39]

(ii) *Duties Independent of Contract*

The question of concurrent liability in contract and tort, which has been so much **16–014**
discussed in the context of other professions, has provoked little controversy in
the case of insurance brokers. The English courts have accepted for some time
that the insurance broker owes a duty of care to his client, and may be liable to
him in negligence, whether or not there is a contract between the parties.[40]

---

[38] (1977) 81 D.L.R. (3d) 139: claimant relied on defendant to obtain adequate insurance cover for his
horticultural business. Defendant obtained insurance under a policy which did not cover damage to
plants by freezing caused by the failure of a water pump (a foreseeable risk). Held that the defendant
was liable for breach of contract and negligence. Followed in *McCann v Western Farmers Mutual
Insurance Co* (1978) 87 D.L.R. (3d) 135; and *Kadaja v CAA* (1995) 23 O.R. (3d) 275, Ontario Court,
General Division. In Canada this decision has been treated as establishing one of the normal
incidents of a broker or insurance agent: see, e.g. *Fletcher v Manitoba Public Insurance Co*
(1990) 74 D.L.R. (4th) 636 (for the facts, see para.16–093, n.8, below); and *Miller v Guardian
Insurance Co of Canada* (1995) 127 D.L.R. (4th) 717 (for the facts see para.16–060, n.79,
below). This is not the case in England and Wales: *O'Brien v Hughes-Gibb & Co Ltd* [1995]
L.R.L.R. 90 (see the preceding footnote). *Fletcher v Manitoba Public Insurance Co* (1990) 74
D.L.R. (4th) 636 continues to be followed in Canada (see, e.g. *Payer v Peerless Plating Rack Co*
(1998) 37 O.R. (3d) 781, Ontario Court of Appeal), but evidence that the client relied upon the
broker to give such advice is an essential ingredient of a claim on that basis: see *Kalkinis v
Allstate Insurance Co of Canada* (1998) 41 O.R. (3d) 528, Ontario Court of Appeal. Further, the
broker's duty to inform and to advise is contingent upon and limited by the insured's description
of the nature of his business, see *St Isidore Asphalte Ltee v Luminex Signs Ltd* (1996) 176
N.B.R.(2d) 135 (for facts see para.16–059, n.78, below).
[39] *ibid.* at 149, *per* Wilson J.A. (with whom Blair J.A. agreed).
[40] See, e.g. *British Citizens Assurance Co v L Woolland & Co* (1921) 8 Ll. Rep. 89; *Strong & Pearl
v S Allison & Co Ltd* (1926) 25 Ll. Rep. 504 (brokers held liable to their clients both in contract and
tort); *Coolee Ltd v Wing, Heath & Co* (1930) 47 T.L.R. 78; *Sarginson Bros v Keith Moulton & Co*
(1942) 73 Ll. Rep. 104; *Osman v J Ralph Moss Ltd* [1970] 1 Lloyd's Rep. 313; *London Borough of
Bromley v Ellis* [1971] 1 Lloyd's Rep. 97; *Cherry Ltd v Allied Insurance Brokers Ltd* [1978] 1
Lloyd's Rep. 274; *Mint Security Ltd v Blair* [1982] 1 Lloyd's Rep. 188; *Dunbar v A & B Painters
Ltd* [1985] 2 Lloyd's Rep. 616; *Forsikringsaktieselskapet Vesta v Butcher* [1989] A.C. 852, CA,
particularly at 860 and 879; *Macmillan v AW Knott Becker Scott Ltd* [1990] 1 Lloyd's Rep. 98; *Youell
v Bland Welch & Co Ltd (No.2)* [1990] 2 Lloyd's Rep. 431 (the *"Superhulls Cover"* case); *Punjab
National Bank v de Boinville* [1992] 1 W.L.R. 1138.

The same view is accepted in Canada,[41] but has been questioned in Australia.[42]

16–015   Where the appointment of an insurance broker is terminated, the client will normally wish to retain his cover whilst making alternative arrangements for insurance. Even after the termination of their appointment, the brokers owe a duty of care to their former client in any transitional arrangements which they make or in any advice which they give as to the continuation of cover. In *Cherry Ltd v Allied Insurance Brokers Ltd*[43] the defendant brokers, shortly after the termination of their appointment, led the claimants to believe that their original insurance policy against consequential loss would remain in force for another four months and that the sensible thing to do was to cancel the new policy. Two days later the original policy was cancelled but the defendants did not advise the claimants of this fact. As a result the claimants were uninsured against consequential loss when a fire occurred shortly afterwards. Cantley J., applying the principles stated in *Hedley Byrne & Co Ltd v Heller & Partners Ltd*,[44] held that the defendants owed a duty of care to the claimants in the advice which they gave and were liable for the breach of that duty.

16–016   **Fiduciary duties.** Since an insurance broker is the agent of the insured, he is the insured's fiduciary and owes fiduciary duties to the insured.[45] As a result, he may not put himself in a position in which there is a conflict between his own interests and his duty to the insured; he must act honestly, faithfully and loyally in the best interests of the insured; and he may not make a secret profit.[46]

(b) *Duties to Third Parties*

16–017   Today an insurance broker often performs functions beyond the straightforward effecting of policies of insurance for his client and he may assume responsibilities to others involved in the transaction. The broker's client may not be the only

---

[41] See, e.g. *Myers v Thompson & London Life Insurance Co* (1967) 63 D.L.R. (2d) 476 (life insurance agent liable in tort to the insured's estate); *Fine's Flowers Ltd v General Accident Assurance Co of Canada* (1978) 81 D.L.R. (3d) 139 (para.16–013, above); *Wilcox v Norberg & Wiggins Insurance Agencies Ltd* [1979] 1 W.L.R. 414; *Firestone Canada Inc v American Home Assurance Co* (1989) 67 O.R. (2d) 471.

[42] In *Ogden & Co Pty Ltd v Reliance Fire Sprinkler Co Pty Ltd* [1975] 1 Lloyd's Rep. 52, 73–74, MacFarlan J. tentatively expressed the view that the existence of a contract between the parties precluded any liability in negligence. But see *Mitor Investments Pty Ltd v General Accident Fire and Life Assurance Corp Ltd* [1984] W.A.R. 365.

[43] [1978] 1 Lloyd's Rep. 274.

[44] [1964] A.C. 465.

[45] See generally Ch.2, paras 2–128 *et seq.*

[46] Para.1.1 of the General Insurance Standards Council Code for Private Customers (2000) states: "As Members of the GISC, we promise that we will: avoid conflicts of interest or, if we cannot avoid this, explain the position fully to you." The Core Principles of the General Insurance Standards Council Commercial Code state: "In the course of their General Insurance Activities Members should: seek to avoid conflicts of interest, but where a conflict is unavoidable or does arise, manage it in such a way as to avoid prejudice to any party. Members will not unfairly put their own interests above their duty to any Commercial Customer for whom they act."

person interested in the policy of insurance or claim which he is handling for his client. Claimants other than the insured have claimed that insurance brokers owed them duties and the courts have upheld some of those claims. The cases can usefully be divided between those where the person asserting the duty was an insurer and those concerning other third parties.

(i) *Duties to Insurers*

Contractual duties. In a straightforward contract of insurance or reinsurance   **16–018**
a broker will be in a contractual relationship with, and be the agent of, the insured or reinsured. Generally the broker will not be in a contractual relationship with the insurer or reinsurer, so that no contractual duty to exercise skill and care arises.[47] Although the broker is typically paid commission by the insurer, this does not mean that the broker is undertaking to perform any obligation in favour of the insurer.[48] However, Lloyd's brokers are obliged to enter into Terms of Business Agreements with managing agents with whom they place business.[49]

Duty to disclose. When seeking to procure insurance for a client the broker   **16–019**
owes an obligation to insurers to disclose all material facts. That obligation is imposed by s.19 of the Marine Insurance Act 1906, and is owed by the broker personally and not just as the agent of his client.[50] The broker is obliged to disclose (a) every material circumstance which is known to himself; and (b) every material circumstance which the assured is bound to disclose, unless it comes to his knowledge too late to communicate it to the broker.[51] The duty imposed by s.19 is only owed by the placing broker, i.e. the broker who actually arranges the insurance with the insurer.[52] The duty to disclose on the broker is neither contractual nor tortious, and a breach of it does not sound in damages between the broker and the insurer: the only remedy is avoidance of the insurance

---

[47] *Pryke v Gibbs Hartley Cooper* [1991] 1 Lloyd's Rep. 602, 615 (Waller J.), following *Empress Assurance v Bowring* (1906) 11 Com. Cas. 107 and *Glasgow Assurance Co v Symondson* (1911) 16 Com. Cas. 109. However, a contract may arise if the broker makes a specific promise to the insurer: *General Accident Fire and Life Assurance Corp v Tanter, The "Zephyr"* [1985] 2 Lloyd's Rep. 529, 537, CA.

[48] See the reasoning of Waller J. in *Pryke v Gibbs Hartley Cooper Ltd* [1991] 1 Lloyd's Rep. 602, 614–615.

[49] The requirement for Lloyd's brokers to enter into Terms of Business Agreements with managing agents was introduced by the Lloyd's Broker Byelaw 17/2000. The provisions of the model Terms of Business Agreement were considered by the Court of Appeal in *Goshaw Dedicated Ltd v Tyser & Co Ltd* [2006] EWCA Civ 54; [2006] 1 Lloyd's Rep. 566. In that case the Court held that even before Terms of Business Agreements were concluded between Lloyd's brokers and managing agents there was an implied contract between the brokers and underwriters, since business necessity required such a contract. As a result, the brokers were obliged to make available to the underwriters documents necessary for the effective performance of the insurance contracts.

[50] The position is the same for non-marine insurance: *Pryke v Gibbs Hartley Cooper Ltd* [1991] 1 Lloyd's Rep. 602.

[51] Marine Insurance Act 1906 subss.19(a) and (b).

[52] See *PCW Syndicates v PCW Reinsurers* [1996] 1 Lloyd's Rep. 241, *per* Saville L.J. at 259 and, *per* Rose L.J. at 257; which was applied in *ERC Frankona Reinsurance v American National Insurance* [2005] EWHC 1381 (Andrew Smith J.).

contract.[53] However, if a broker dishonestly or recklessly withholds information from the insurer which he knows to be material, then this may amount to a fraudulent misrepresentation which would entitle the insurer to avoid the policy and then bring a claim against the broker for damages.[54]

16–020   **Tortious duties.** In the ordinary course of events a broker will not owe a tortious duty of care to the insurer without more.[55] However, in certain circumstances (including those set out immediately below) a duty of care in tort may arise, particularly if the broker makes a statement to an insurer. There are few reported examples, not least because any default by a broker while acting as the agent of the insured, whether negligent or not in the case of non-disclosure, usually enables the insurer to avoid liability under the policy of insurance so that he suffers no loss.[56]

16–021   **Broker giving a signing indication.** There are, however, circumstances in which an insurer may rely on what a broker tells him when entering a contract of insurance but will be unable to avoid that contract by reason of the inaccuracy of what he was told. One such situation is where a broker gives a "signing indication" to the underwriters who write lines on his slip. A "signing indication" is a statement by the broker of the extent to which he intends that the slip will be oversubscribed. If, for example, the slip is oversubscribed by 100 per

---

[53] *Banque Keyser Ullmann SA v Skandia (UK) Insurance Co Ltd* [1990] 1 Q.B. 665, CA (the decision of the House of Lords [1991] 2 A.C. 249 did not involve this point, although Lord Templeman indicated that he agreed with the Court of Appeal on it); *Bank of Nova Scotia v Hellenic Mutual War Risks Association (Bermuda) Ltd, The "Good Luck"* [1990] 1 Q.B. 818, CA (overturned on other grounds on appeal [1992] 1 A.C. 233); *PCW Syndicates v PCW Reinsurers* [1996] 1 Lloyd's Rep. 241 at 255 ("[s.19] does not, as it seems to me, impose an obligation or duty owed by the agent to the insurer, which could be enforced by an order for specific performance or give rise to a remedy in damages for breach": *per* Staughton L.J.); *HIH Casualty v Chase* [2001] 1 Lloyd's Rep. 30 (Aikens J.) at paras 100–105 (this part of the decision was not appealed); *HIH Casualty v Chase* [2003] UKHL 6; [2003] 1 Lloyd's Rep. 230 ("non-disclosure (whether dishonest or otherwise) does not as such give rise to a claim in damages", *per* Lord Hoffmann at para.75).

[54] *HIH Casualty v Chase* [2003] UKHL 6; [2003] 1 Lloyd's Rep. 230, (*per* Lord Bingham at [21]).

[55] See *Tai Hing Cotton Mill Ltd v Liu Chong Hing Bank Ltd* [1986] A.C. 80; *HIH Casualty v Chase* [2001] 1 Lloyd's Rep. 30 (Aikens J.). The decisions in *Empress Assurance v Bowring* (1906) 11 Com. Cas. 107; and *Glasgow Assurance Co v Symondson* (1911) 16 Com. Cas. 109 to the effect that no duty of care was owed in tort followed *Le Lievre v Gould* [1893] 1 Q.B. 491 which was overruled by *Hedley Byrne & Co Ltd v Heller & Partners Ltd* [1964] A.C. 465. They are therefore no longer sound: see *General Accident Fire and Life Assurance Corp v Tanter, The "Zephyr"* [1984] 1 Lloyd's Rep. 58, 84; and *Pryke v Gibbs Hartley Cooper Ltd* [1991] 1 Lloyd's Rep. 602, 618. In *HIH Casualty v Chase* [2001] 1 Lloyd's Rep. 30 Aikens J. held (at paras 106–115) that, absent a specific assumption of responsibility, a broker owes no common law duty to the insurer to disclose material facts the breach of which is actionable in damages. The broker did not owe a common law duty to the insurer "to speak up." This part of his decision was not appealed.

[56] In *Adams-Eden Furniture Ltd v Kansa General International Insurance Co* (1996) 113 Man.R.(2d) 142, (Manitoba Court of Appeal), the insurer settled insured's claim, but then sought an indemnity against the broker on the ground the broker had not disclosed all material facts. The insurer's claim for an indemnity was rejected on the basis that the broker owed no duty of care to the insurer. The claim by insurers against their agent failed for a different reason in *Hunt v Brandie* (1998) 38 O.R. (3d) 154, (Court of Appeal for Ontario): the agent had not followed the correct procedures, but had he done so, insurers would have been obliged to accept the relevant business. They had therefore suffered no loss.

cent, each underwriter only carries half the risk which is shown on the line that he has signed. In this example the slip is "signed down" by 50 per cent. If the broker gives a signing indication of, say, 50 per cent or 30 per cent which is not fulfilled, the underwriters may have legitimate cause for complaint against the broker but they have no conceivable grounds for avoiding the contract of insurance. Each underwriter may then carry a risk which is substantially greater than he expected or intended when writing his line on the slip. In *General Accident Fire and Life Assurance Corp v Tanter, The "Zephyr"*[57] the question arose whether a broker who gave a signing indication to an underwriter owed a duty in tort to that underwriter to take reasonable steps to see that the signing down indication was achieved. Hobhouse J. held that the broker did owe such a duty. Although this issue was not directly raised on appeal, the Court of Appeal expressed considerable misgivings as to this part of the decision. Mustill L.J.[58] said that a signing indication may in some circumstances give rise to a collateral contract between the broker and the underwriter. But in the absence of such a contract, Mustill L.J. did not see how the broker could owe a tortious duty to achieve the signing down which he had indicated: that entailed a positive obligation to act which would usually only arise in contract.[59] However, he added that, had the signing indication been a negligent misrepresentation of existing fact, liability in tort could not have been denied, thus recognising that liability on the basis of *Hedley Byrne & Co Ltd v Heller and Partners Ltd*[60] could arise between broker and insurer. The signing indication given was a representation of existing fact, namely that the broker honestly believed it to be accurate on reasonable grounds. In that sense it was accurate so that there was no negligent misstatement. The insurers' complaint was that it had not been acted on subsequently.

Misstatement regarding reinsurance. Another situation in which an insurer **16–022** may rely upon a statement by a broker when deciding to enter a contract of insurance is where the broker has provisionally arranged reinsurance and makes a representation to the insurer as to the existence or terms of that reinsurance. If it transpires that the reinsurance cover is not as represented the insurer will not be entitled to avoid liability under the policy of insurance. In *Youell v Bland Welch & Co Ltd (No.2)*[61] (the *"Superhulls Cover"* case), cover was sought against builders' risks during the construction of three LNG ships with a value of US$100m each. Cover of that size necessarily involved reinsurance. The brokers therefore arranged reinsurance cover before approaching potential insurers. The

---

[57] [1984] 1 Lloyd's Rep. 58 (Hobhouse J.); [1985] 2 Lloyd's Rep. 529, CA.
[58] With whom Stephen Brown and Oliver L.JJ. agreed.
[59] It is not clear, however, whether this aspect of Mustill L.J.'s reasoning can survive the recognition by the House of Lords of liability for economic loss caused by negligent omissions: see *Henderson v Merrett Syndicates Ltd* [1995] 2 A.C. 145 at 180F–G and 181E–F; and *White v Jones* [1995] 2 A.C. 207 at 268H–269A. It is possible that a broker might now be under a tortious duty to exercise reasonable skill, care and diligence in seeking to obtain subscriptions in accordance with the signing indication he has given. He would not, however, warrant that he would actually obtain subscriptions.
[60] [1964] A.C. 465.
[61] [1990] 2 Lloyd's Rep. 431, Phillips J.

reinsurance arranged included a clause under which cover of any particular vessel terminated 48 months after the commencement of its construction. There was no such clause in the contract of insurance. When seeking to persuade the insurers to subscribe to the insurance contract the brokers informed them that there was reinsurance available, without mentioning the 48-month clause, so that the reasonable inference was that the reinsurance cover was on the same terms as the insurance policy. The insurers were thereby induced to write larger lines on the insurance policy than they would otherwise have done. Phillips J. found the brokers negligent on various grounds,[62] including a negligent failure to describe the reinsurance properly. That breach occurred before insurers had instructed the brokers to obtain reinsurance for them (and so before any contractual relationship arose), but Phillips J. held that a broker who seeks to persuade an insurer to write a line of original insurance by informing him that specific reinsurance cover is available is in a relationship which gives rise to a duty of care in tort, independent of any contractual relationship.[63]

16–023   **Coverholders.** Contracts of insurance are not always effected between the insurer in person and a broker acting for the insured. Insurers give authority to insurance brokers and others to issue insurance policies on their behalf under binding authorities. These will give the holder of the binding authority (often called the coverholder) the authority to make contracts of insurance on the insurer's behalf, subject to restrictions as to class of risk, size of risk and, in some cases, the rate of premium to be paid. For present purposes binding authorities can be divided into two classes: those where the broker is the coverholder and those where the broker acts as an intermediary between the coverholder and the insurer.

16–024   Where the broker is the coverholder there is no doubt that he owes a duty to the insurer to exercise reasonable skill and care. He is in a direct contractual relationship with the insurer and will also owe a concurrent duty of care.[64] Thus in *Woolcott v Excess Insurance Co Ltd*[65] brokers effected household insurance for the claimant with the defendant insurers under a binding authority granted to them by the insurers. The brokers knew that the claimant had a serious criminal record, but failed to pass this information on to the insurers. The claimant's house was subsequently destroyed by fire. The insurers denied liability, on the grounds of non-disclosure of the claimant's criminal record. This defence failed because the insurers were fixed with the brokers' knowledge. In third-party proceedings, however, the insurers recovered an indemnity against the brokers on the grounds

---

[62] See paras 16–055, 16–087 and 16–090, below.
[63] When seeking to obtain reinsurance of a risk which he is trying to insure for his immediate client, a broker acts as agent of the potential insurers and not of his immediate client, so that any knowledge he acquires in seeking reinsurance is that of the potential insurers and not of his immediate client: *Société Anonyme d'Intermediaries Luxembourgeois v Farex* [1995] L.R.L.R. 116. It would appear to follow that the broker owed a duty of care in tort to the potential insurers when seeking reinsurance, but not to his immediate client, the intended insured.
[64] See para.16–014, above.
[65] [1978] 1 Lloyd's Rep. 633, Caulfield J.; [1979] 1 Lloyd's Rep. 231, CA; [1979] 2 Lloyd's Rep. 210, Cantley J. on retrial.

of the brokers' failure to pass on the information.[66] Given that the broker is in a contractual relationship with the insurer, it is open to the insurer to bring an action against the broker pursuant to the Misrepresentation Act 1967 if the insurer enters into the coverholder arrangement with the broker after a misrepresentation has been made to it by the broker.[67]

Where the broker is not himself the coverholder, but acts as an intermediary, **16–025** he is in a contractual relationship with his coverholder who is his client. There is no contract between the broker and the insurer, and therefore the broker owes the insurer no contractual duty to exercise skill and care when acting as intermediary.[68] Nor does a broker owe the insurer a duty of care in tort, without more.[69] However, a broker may come to owe a duty of care to an insurer when acting as an intermediary. In *Pryke v Gibbs Hartley Cooper Ltd*[70] a coverholder in the United States had been authorised to write fire insurance by a London insurance company and a group of Lloyd's syndicates, the defendant brokers acting as intermediaries. The insurance company and the leading underwriter at Lloyd's learnt that the coverholder might have issued a financial guarantee policy. This would not only have been beyond the coverholder's own authority but was a type of insurance which the Lloyd's underwriters were forbidden to write and which the company did not write as a matter of policy. Upon being contacted by the insurance company and by the leading underwriter the brokers raised the matter with the coverholder and passed his explanation on to the company and leading underwriter. The brokers were about to visit the coverholder and said that they would look into the matter when in the United States. They were held to owe a duty of care in tort to the company, the leading underwriter and to the other syndicates (who knew nothing of the matter at the time) when investigating the matter and reporting back. The duty of care arose because the brokers chose to

---

[66] Other cases where insurers brought claims against coverholders for breach of a duty to exercise reasonable skill and care are: *Gore Mutual Insurance Co v Barton* (1979) 12 B.C.L.R. 261: failure to advise insurer of material change in risk insured, which would have caused the insurer to refuse to continue insurance. Agent liable; *Canadian General Insurance Co v Lacey, Stoyles Insurance Services Ltd* (1985) 56 Nfld. & P.E.I.R. 125, Newfoundland District Court: coverholder negligently exceeded its authority by accepting premium under a policy which had been cancelled and negligently reported a subsequent loss without informing the insurer of the cancellation; *Gibraltar General Insurance Co v LE Yingst Co Ltd* (1990) 89 Sask. R. 93; Saskatchewan Court of Queen's Bench: coverholder failed to include a clause incorporating a statutory one-year limitation period for claims under a policy; *Bos v Brauer* (1992) 3 Alta.L.R. (3d) 318, where a broker coverholder was found to be in breach of duty in failing to provide accurate information to insurers. However, since there was no evidence that insurers would have acted differently had they received accurate information, they recovered only nominal damages.

[67] Such a claim was brought against a broker in *Avon Insurance Plc v Swire Fraser Ltd* [2000] Lloyd's Rep. I.R. 535 (Rix J.), but the claim failed on the facts.

[68] *Pryke v Gibbs Hartley Cooper Ltd* [1991] 1 Lloyd's Rep. 602, 615; following *Empress Assurance Corp Ltd v CT Bowring & Co Ltd* (1905) 11 Com. Cas. 107; and *Glasgow Assurance Corp Ltd v William Symondson & Co* (1911) 104 L.T. 254.

[69] *ibid*. The *Empress* and *Glasgow* decisions to the effect that no duty of care was owed in tort followed *Le Lievre v Gould* [1893] 1 Q.B. 491 which was overruled by *Hedley Byrne & Co Ltd v Heller & Partners Ltd* [1964] A.C. 465. They are therefore no longer sound: see *General Accident Fire and Life Assurance Corp v Tanter, The "Zephyr"* [1984] 1 Lloyd's Rep. 58 and *Pryke v Gibbs Hartley Cooper Ltd* [1991] 1 Lloyd's Rep. 602, 618. See also *Adams-Eden Furniture Ltd v Kansa General International Insurance Co* (1996) 113 Man.R.(2d) 142, Manitoba Court of Appeal.

[70] [1991] 1 Lloyd's Rep. 602, Waller J.

do more than act as the coverholder's messenger and undertook personal responsibility towards the insurers.

(ii) *Duties to Other Third Parties*

16–026 The broker's client may not be the only person interested in the policy of insurance which the broker is instructed to effect. There may be other persons who are to directly benefit from the insurance (either by being insured themselves or otherwise) and there may be third parties whose claims against the broker's client will be covered by the proposed insurance. A duty may exist in the former case, but is less likely to do so in the latter. In each case the issue of whether or not the broker owed the third party a duty of care will be resolved in accordance with the usual principles used to determine when a party owes another a duty of care in respect of economic loss.[71]

16–027   **Potential beneficiaries.** One of simplest examples of third parties deriving benefit from another's insurance is the beneficiaries of pension and life insurance policies. In *Gorham v British Telecommunications*[72] the Court of Appeal considered whether an insurance company which owed a duty of care to one its customers when giving advice in relation to his pension and life insurance cover also owed a duty of care to potential beneficiaries other than himself. The court held that in such a case the position of the customer was analogous to that of a client who seeks his solicitor's advice regarding a will. Applying *White v Jones*[73] the Court held that a duty was owed to the potential beneficiaries. Pill L.J. described the duty in the following way: "The duty is not one to ensure that the dependants are properly provided for. It is, in the present context, a duty to the dependants not to give negligent advice to the customer which adversely affects their interests as he intends them to be."

16–028   **Third parties with a known financial interest.** A duty of care may also be owed to a third party if, to the broker's knowledge, that third party has a direct financial interest in the insurance being arranged and is actively involved in the arranging of the insurance. In *Punjab National Bank v De Boinville*[74] the third party was a bank which was providing finance to one of its customers. The bank required its customer to effect insurance to protect the bank's position. The policies were taken out in the name of the customer, which assigned its interest in the policies to the bank soon after they were effected. The Court of Appeal upheld the judge's finding that at times when the bank was not in a contractual relationship with the brokers, it was owed a tortious duty of care by the brokers. Following the approach of Brennan J. in *Sutherland Shire Council v Heyman*[75] Staughton L.J.[76] held that it was a justifiable increment to hold that an insurance broker owed a duty of care to the specific person who he knew was to become

---

[71] See generally Ch.2 para.2–024, above.
[72] [2000] 1 W.L.R. 2129.
[73] [1995] 2 A.C. 207. See Ch.2, para.2–047, and Ch.11, paras 11–048 *et seq.*
[74] [1992] 1 W.L.R. 1138.
[75] (1985) 60 A.L.R. 1, 43–44: see Ch.2, para.2–038.
[76] With whom Mann and Dillon L.JJ. agreed.

an assignee of the policy, at all events if, to the broker's knowledge, that person actively participated in giving instructions for the insurance, as was the case.

It is not enough that the third party has a financial interest in the transaction **16–029** which is the subject of the insurance policy, or is a major creditor of the insured.[77] *In Punjab National Bank v De Boinville*[78] Staughton L.J. doubted whether the fact that the broker knew that the bank had some financial interest in the underlying transaction and a right of recourse against the insured, who was the broker's client, would give rise to a duty of care. A more direct interest in the insurance policy is needed. This is illustrated by the decision of Evans J. in *Macmillan v AW Knott Becker Scott Ltd.*[79] There, the third parties were former clients of an insolvent professional (a Lloyd's broker). They brought proceedings against the brokers who had negligently failed to ensure that the professional's errors and omissions insurance was effective, with the result that the professional was not insured in relation to their claims against him. The preliminary issue before Evans J. was whether the brokers effecting the errors and omissions insurance owed a duty of care to their professional client's clients and others to whom that professional might be liable for negligence. Evans J. held that loss was foreseeable and that there was sufficient proximity, but that it would not be just and reasonable to impose a duty which would leapfrog the contractual chain. Following the speech of Lord Griffiths in *Smith v Eric S Bush*[80] he concluded that brokers could not be deemed to have assumed responsibility towards the claimants.

The need for the third party to have a direct interest (whether present or future) **16–030** in the contract of insurance is also shown by the decision of the Court of Appeal in *Verderame v Commercial Union Assurance Co Ltd.*[81] There the sole directors and shareholders of a limited company were in effect carrying on business through the medium of the company in quasi-partnership. They brought a claim in tort against the company's insurance brokers on the basis that the company had suffered an uninsured loss by reason of the brokers' negligence and that the company had been unable to continue trading as a result, causing loss to them as individuals. The claim was struck out on several grounds, one of them being that the directors were seeking to go behind the corporate status of the company, the brokers' actual client.[82] Their interest was not in the insurance policy, but in the intended insured.

Even if the third party does have a direct interest in the contract of insurance, **16–031** which is immediate and known by the broker, this will not necessarily outweigh

---

[77] In *South Pacific Manufacturing Co Ltd v New Zealand Security Consultants & Investigations Ltd* [1992] 2 N.Z.L.R. 282 the New Zealand Court of Appeal considered a claim by the creditors of an insured against a private investigator employed by the insurer to inquire and report on the cause of a fire on the insured's property. The claim was struck out on the basis that even if the investigator owed a duty of care to the insured, such a duty would not extend to persons financially interested in the insured.
[78] [1992] 1 W.L.R. 1138. (for the facts see para.16–028, above).
[79] [1990] 1 Lloyd's Rep. 98.
[80] [1990] 1 A.C. 831, 862D–E; Ch.2, paras 2–030 *et seq.*
[81] [1992] B.C.L.C. 793.
[82] Other grounds were that the loss claimed was irrecoverable in law (as to which see para.16–143, below), that it would allow directors and shareholders to circumvent the rules governing the winding up of companies, exposing brokers to the risk of having to make double restitution and that the claim advanced was novel and would not be a "justifiable increment" to any existing category.

other factors so as to give rise to a duty of care. Thus in *Texas Homecare Ltd v Royal Bank of Canada Trust Co (Jersey) Ltd*[83] the third party was a retailer which contracted with Y that Y would obtain insurance for a "cash-back scheme" with insurers who were "at least AA status or equivalent". The third party was to be the insured. Y then retained the brokers to effect that insurance. They failed to do so and the insurers with whom they placed the risk became insolvent. The third party claimed in tort directly against the brokers. That claim failed,[84] essentially because it would have cut across the contractual chain by which the parties had chosen to regulate their relationships and which was the origin of the obligation to obtain insurance with an insurer of the required class.[85]

16–032   **Misstatements to third parties.** If a broker choses to give advice or information to a third party, without any effective disclaimer of responsibility, in circumstances in which a reasonable person would know that he was being trusted or that his skill or judgment was being relied upon, then he may be found to owe a duty of care to that third person.[86] If the broker fails to exercise reasonable skill and care then he will be found to have breached his duty.[87] For example, in *Baron v Hartford Fire Insurance Co*[88] the son of the deceased insured contacted the deceased's broker to ascertain whether his father had any life insurance. The broker incorrectly led the son to believe that no cover was in place and in so doing was found to have owed a duty of care to the son, which he breached in failing to give an accurate answer.

(c) *Sub-brokers*

16–033   It is not unusual for the broker directly instructed by a client to engage sub-brokers to place the insurance.[89] For example, a non-Lloyd's broker will need to use a Lloyd's broker if a risk is to be brokered in Lloyd's. In the ordinary course, if there is a breach of duty by either the broker or the sub-broker, then the client will sue his broker, either on the basis of the broker's own breach of duty (which

---

[83] [1996] C.L.C. 776.

[84] The third party's claim against Y in contract succeeded, as did Y's claim against the brokers.

[85] See generally Ch.2, paras 2–096 *et seq.*

[86] *Hedley Byrne & Co Ltd v Heller & Partners Ltd* [1964] A.C. 465. For a discussion of the general principles see Ch.2, para.2–024.

[87] *Cherry Ltd v Allied Insurance Brokers Ltd* [1978] 1 Lloyd's Rep. 274 (for the facts, see para.16–015, above). See also *London Borough of Bromley v Ellis* [1971] 1 Lloyd's Rep. 97 (brokers acting as agents for the insurer owed insured a duty of care when they had undertaken to arrange the transfer of insurance to him).

[88] [1998] 1 HKLRD 411, Court of First Instance, Seagroatt J. The son's claim ultimately failed because there had been a material misrepresentation to the insurers which entitled them to avoid the policy and the court was not satisfied that the deceased had not colluded in the making of that misrepresentation.

[89] The broker engaged by the client is known as the "producing broker" (because he has produced the business) while the sub-broker is known as the "placing broker" (because he places the risk). Importantly only the placing broker is subject to the duty of disclosure imposed by s.19 of the Marine Insurance Act 1906 (see para.16–019, above).

may include the negligent selection or instruction of the sub-broker), or on the basis that the broker is liable for the acts and omissions of his agent, (i.e. the sub-broker).[90] If it is the sub-broker who was at fault, then the broker may seek to pass his liability on up the contractual chain to the sub-broker.[91] However, there may be reasons why the client wishes to sue the sub-broker, for example if the broker is insolvent and uninsured. In that event the issues of whether or not the client can bring any contractual or tortious claim against the sub-broker will arise.

Contractual claim. In order to bring a contractual claim against the sub-broker, the client must show that there was in fact a contract between him and the sub-broker. In *Prentis Donegan & Partners Ltd v Leeds & Leeds Co Inc*[92] Rix J. held that usually no direct contract will be made. Only if the client, the broker and the sub-broker all intend that a direct contractual relationship should arise will it do so. Rix J. held that cases where a direct contractual relationship was found (such as *De Bussche v Alt*[93]) were exceptional. In *Pangood Ltd v Barclay Brown & Co Ltd*[94] the Court of Appeal held that whether the Lloyd's broker was to be taken as having contracted directly with the insured depended upon the terms upon which he was instructed. The instructions from the broker to obtain a quotation and then to effect insurance in accordance with its terms did not form an adequate basis for holding that the Lloyd's broker had assumed direct contractual responsibility to the insured. The effect of these two decisions is that it is only in exceptional circumstances that a contract will be found to exist between a client and a sub-broker.[95]   **16–034**

Tortious claim. The question of whether a claim in negligence against a sub-broker will succeed will depend upon the nature of the instructions given to the   **16–035**

---

[90] For an analysis of the circumstances in which a principal is liable for the torts committed by his agent, see *Bowstead & Reynolds on Agency* (17th edn) at 8–177. In *Thomas Cheshire v Vaughan Brothers* [1920] 3 K.B. 240 (the facts of which are set out in para.16–127, n.45, below) Atkin L.J. stated that he could imagine circumstances in which a country agent might not be responsible for the negligence of a London sub-agent if the agent had used reasonable care in the selection of the sub-agent. In *Youell v Bland Welch (Superhulls No.2)* [1990] 2 Lloyd's Rep. Phillips J. held that in accordance with "well established principles of English law of agency" one broker was liable for the acts and omissions of another broker who it had employed to perform part of the first broker's duties to its principal. A distinction may be drawn between those cases where the broker employs a sub-broker to perform duties which it (the broker) could have performed, and those cases where the broker employs a sub-broker to perform duties which it could not have performed, (e.g. where a non-Lloyd's broker employs a Lloyd's broker to place a risk in the Lloyd's market).
[91] There will typically be a contract between the broker and the sub-broker, and the sub-broker will owe the broker a duty to carry out his instructions with reasonable skill and care.
[92] [1998] 2 Lloyd's Rep. 326.
[93] (1878) 8 Ch.D. 286.
[94] [1999] Lloyd's Rep. I.R. 405.
[95] In some cases it may be possible for the client to bring a contractual claim against the sub-broker pursuant to the Contracts (Rights of Third Parties) Act 1999, i.e. if the contract between the broker and sub-broker expressly provides that the client may enforce it, or if the contract purports to confer a benefit on the client and (on a proper construction of the contract) the broker and sub-broker intended the contract to be enforceable by the client.

sub-broker and the nature of the duty alleged to have been breached.[96] For example, it is likely that a sub-broker will be found to owe a duty to the client not to make any misrepresentation to the insurer, but less likely that the sub-broker will be found to owe a duty to the client to advise upon the terms and conditions of the policy obtained.[97] In *Pangood Ltd v Barclay Brown & Co Ltd*[98] the Court of Appeal held that the Lloyd's broker did not owe any general duty of care in tort to the insured: any assumption of responsibility to the insured was confined to obtaining a quotation and communicating it accurately to the other brokers. It did not extend to a duty to draw the attention of the other brokers to a warranty which formed part of the quotation obtained and which was usually included in the sort of policy which was being broked. The Lloyd's brokers were entitled to treat their client, the other brokers, as knowledgeable brokers. More recently, in *European International Reinsurance Co Ltd v Curzon Insurance Ltd*,[99] where it was alleged that a Lloyd's sub-broker had failed to make disclosure to a reinsurer, the Court of Appeal held that it was arguable that a Lloyd's sub-broker owed a tortious duty of care to the client. The Court held that it was at least arguable that someone who held himself out as "A Lloyd's Broker" assumed a personal liability to the insured even if he was acting as the agent of another broker. Indeed, the Court expressed surprise that the Lloyd's broker would wish to argue that in presenting a reinsurance slip it did not accept any responsibility to the reinsured under that slip. In *BP Plc v AON Ltd (No.2)*.[1] Colman J. held that sub-brokers who had taken on the responsibility of making declarations to insurers under an open-cover agreement owed a tortious duty of care to the companies intended to be insured under that agreement.

(d) *The Standard of Skill and Care*

16–036   Whether he is sued in contract or tort, the insurance broker is required to exercise reasonable skill and care[2]: in other words that degree of skill and care which is

---

[96] In a number of cases it has been conceded that the Lloyd's brokers who had been instructed by the producing broker did owe a duty of care to the insured: *Mint Security Ltd v Blair* [1982] 1 Lloyd's Rep. 188 (Staughton J.) (the basis of the concession appears to have been that the Lloyd's broker was in a direct contractual relationship with the assured); *O'Brien v Hughes-Gibb & Co Ltd* [1995] Lloyd's Rep. I.R. 90 (it is doubtful whether the concession was made that a duty was owed in tort only rather than a duty in both contract and tort); *Tudor Jones II v Crawley Colosso Ltd* [1996] 2 Lloyd's Rep. 619 (it was conceded that the Lloyd's brokers owed a duty to the producing broker and/ or the assured). The basis of the concessions in each of these cases was considered by Colman J. in *BP Plc v AON Ltd (No.2)* [2006] EWHC 424 (at paras 90–92).

[97] In *Coolee Ltd v Wing Heath & Co* (1930) 47 T.L.R. 78 (the facts of which are set out at para.16–073, below) the insured's claim succeeded against both its broker and the Lloyd's sub-broker on the basis that they both breached duties they owed to the insured. However, it is not clear from the report whether the liability of the Lloyd's sub-broker was based upon there being in privity of contract with the claimant or upon their owing a duty of care. In *BP Plc v AON Ltd (No.2)* [2006] EWHC 424; [2006] 1 All E.R. (Comm) 789 Colman J. suggested (at [89]) that it was more likely that liability was based upon there being privity of contract.

[98] [1999] 2 Lloyd's Rep. I.R. 405.

[99] *European International Reinsurance Co Ltd v Curzon Insurance Ltd* [2003] EWCA Civ 1074; [2003] Lloyd's Rep. I.R. 793.

[1] [2006] EWHC 424; [2006] 1 All E.R. (Comm) 789.

[2] e.g. *Hurrell v Bullard* (1863) 3 F. & F. 445.

exercised by reasonably competent insurance brokers.[3] In *Chapman v Walton*,[4] Lord Tindal C.J. described the broker's duty in these terms:

> "For the defendant did not contract that he would bring to the performance of his duty, on this occasion, an extraordinary degree of skill, but only a reasonable and ordinary proportion of it; and it appears to us, that it is not only an unobjectionable mode, but the most satisfactory mode of determining this question, to show by evidence whether a majority of skilful and experienced brokers would have come to the same conclusion as the defendant. If nine brokers of experience out of ten would have done the same as the defendant under the same circumstances, or even if as many out of a given number would have been of his opinion as against it, he who only stipulates to bring a reasonable degree of skill to the performance of his duty, would be entitled to a verdict in his favour."[5]

Specialist markets. Where a broker undertakes work in a specialist market, he **16–037** will be required to exercise reasonable skill and care in the context of that market. In *Sharp and Roarer Investments Ltd v Sphere Drake Insurance Plc, The Moonacre*[6] the judge[7] had to consider the standard of skill required of an insurance broker who undertook to obtain insurance for a yacht when considering whether a broker had been negligent in relation to a particular clause of a marine insurance policy. He referred to *Duchess of Argyll v Beuselinck*[8] and said:

> "In deciding whether their standard of skill was sufficiently high, it is appropriate . . . to require that a non-specialist marine broker should bear no greater skill than that which would be expected from a reasonably skilled non-specialist broker. This is not the same thing as saying that the standard is that of a marine broker substantially inexperienced in the insurance of large yachts. It is rather the standard of a broker who has such general knowledge of the yacht insurance market and the cover available in it as to be able to advise his client on all matters on which a lay client would in the ordinary course of events predictably need advice, in particular in the course of the selection of cover and the completion of the proposal."[9]

Expert evidence. Evidence as to the general practice of insurance brokers **16–038** carries great weight in the determination whether, in any given case, the defendant brokers owed a particular duty[10] or exercised reasonable skill and care.[11]

---

[3] In *Harvest Trucking Co Ltd v Davis* [1991] 2 Lloyd's Rep. 638 Judge Diamond Q.C. (sitting as a High Court judge) said: "The liability of an insurance agent to his employer for negligence is comparable to that of any agent. He is bound to exercise reasonable care in the duties which he has undertaken. In no case does the law require an extraordinary degree of skill on the part of the agent but only such a reasonable and ordinary degree as a person of average capacity and ordinary ability in his situation and profession might fairly be expected to exert": *ibid.* at 643.

[4] (1833) 10 Bing. 57. For the facts, see para.16–066, below.

[5] *ibid.* at 63–64. See also *O'Connor v BDB Kirby & Co* [1972] 1 Q.B. 90, 101C, quoted at para.16–083, below.

[6] [1992] 2 Lloyd's Rep. 501; for the facts see para.16–058, below.

[7] A.D. Colman Q.C., sitting as a deputy judge of the High Court.

[8] [1972] 2 Lloyd's Rep. 172.

[9] [1992] 2 Lloyd's Rep. 501 at 523, col.2.

[10] In *Great North Eastern Railway Ltd v JLT Corporate Risks Ltd* [2006] EWHC 1478 Cresswell J. stated that the court was likely to be informed and assisted by expert evidence as to the relevant practice of brokers when deciding whether or not a broker owed the insured a continuing duty after the placement of a risk.

[11] See, e.g. *Fanhaven Pty Ltd v Bain Dawes Northern Pty Ltd* [1982] 2 N.S.W.L.R. 57, 63.

However, as has been already pointed out,[12] the court cannot abdicate to expert witnesses the responsibility for deciding what does and what does not amount to reasonable skill and care. In exceptional cases the court may consider that the ordinary practice of insurance brokers (as described by expert witnesses) is unduly lax and that the "reasonably competent broker" should do better.[13] Conversely, the ordinary practice of insurance brokers might on occasions be regarded as going beyond their strict legal duty.[14] This was the view taken by McNair J. in *United Mills Agencies Ltd v RE Harvey Bray & Co.*[15]

16–039   **Legal knowledge.** Since the insurance broker's work revolves around the formation of a special kind of legal relationship, some legal knowledge is essential. Familiarity with the general principles of insurance law and agency forms part of the "reasonable skill" which the broker is required to possess.[16] If a legal problem arises which is beyond the broker's competence, he should advise the client to consult a solicitor.[17] If the broker chooses to give legal advice himself, then he does so at his peril.[18]

---

[12] See Ch.6, paras 6–008 *et seq.*, above.

[13] In *Lewis v Tressider Andrews Associates Pty Ltd* [1987] 2 Qd.R. 533 a broker had received financial details of a new insurance company. There was evidence that the average broker would not have been able to interpret the material and would not have taken any steps to satisfy himself of the solvency and responsibility of the insurer. Connolly J. held that a broker was under a duty to exercise greater skill and care.

[14] Or that the ordinary practice of insurance brokers may not be evidence of or give rise to a duty: *Pryke v Gibbs Hartley Cooper Ltd* [1991] 1 Lloyd's Rep. 602 (for the facts of which, see para.16–025, above) where evidence of practice in the Lloyd's market was held not to establish any legal duty.

[15] [1951] 2 Lloyd's Rep. 631; for the facts see para.16–089, n.58, below. When considering whether the defendant brokers were negligent in failing to send the claimants promptly a copy of the cover note, McNair J. disposed of the claimants' contentions in these terms: "It is said that there was, accordingly, failure on the part of the defendants to cause the claimants to be notified promptly of the terms of the cover. On that point evidence was called from an independent broker—and I think, substantially agreed to by Mr Davey—that it is the practice of, at any rate, these two offices of insurance brokers (and I have no doubt the practice of brokers as a whole) that when cover has been placed the clients are notified as soon as possible. That seems to me to be good business and prudent office management, but on the evidence I am completely unable to hold that it is part of the duty owed by the broker to the client so to notify him, in the sense that a failure so to notify him would involve him in legal liability. No case was spoken to in which any broker had ever been held liable or had ever paid any client money in respect of such a failure. It seems to me to put quite an intolerable and unreasonable burden on a broker to say that as a matter of law, apart from prudent practice, he is bound to forward the cover note as soon as possible. It is no doubt prudent to do so, both to allay the client's anxiety and possibly to enable the client to check the terms of insurance. That is a very different thing from saying it is part of his duty." *ibid.* at 643.

[16] See, e.g. *Park v Hammond* (1816) 6 Taunt. 495 (insurance broker held negligent for ignorance of an established rule of law (that an insurance to commence from the loading of goods at a certain point would not attach on goods previously laden)); *Fanhaven Pty Ltd v Bain Dawes Northern Pty Ltd* [1982] 2 N.S.W.L.R. 57, 65. Patent agents are in a similar position: *Lee v Walker* (1872) L.R. 7 C.P. 121, where the defendant was held negligent as a result of his ignorance of a recent Chancery decision affecting the procedure for obtaining letters patent.

[17] In *Lewis v Tressider Andrews Associates Pty Ltd* [1987] 2 Qd.R. 533 a broker had received financial details of a new insurance company. Connolly J. held that, if the broker could not himself interpret the documents, he should have gone to his accountant or auditor for advice.

[18] *Sarginson Bros v Keith Moulton & Co* (1942) 73 Ll. Rep. 104. See paras 16–095 to 16–096, below. See also *Bates v Barrow Ltd* [1995] 1 Lloyd's Rep. 680 at 690 (for the facts, see para.16–067, n.92, below).

2. LIABILITY FOR BREACH OF DUTY

Broadly speaking, breach of duty by an insurance broker to his client may take **16–040** one of four forms[19]: (i) breach of a specific contractual duty[20]; (ii) breach of the implied contractual duty to exercise reasonable skill and care[21]; (iii) breach of the duty of care owed by the insurance broker to his client independently of his contractual duties[22]; or (iv) breach of certain requirements under FSMA or applicable rules and regulations made thereunder.[23] Negligence is not an essential element of liability under the first head,[24] nor under the fourth. The second and third heads involve breaches of the same standard of skill and care, and are jointly referred to in this chapter as "negligence".

Instances in which it has been held that insurance brokers are, or may be, liable **16–041** for breach of duty are discussed below under different headings. This catalogue is not, of course, exhaustive.[25] The cases serve to illustrate how the principles stated above operate in practice and, in particular, what the courts consider to be the standard of skill and care which may reasonably be expected of insurance brokers.

(a) *Failing to Effect Insurance*

A total failure to effect insurance is the clearest form of breach of duty which the **16–042** broker could commit.[26] It would only be justified if the broker had done all that was reasonably possible but the required insurance was unobtainable.[27] See, for

---

[19] In Canada, negligence by insurance brokers and agents is often held to constitute a breach of fiduciary duty as well (see, e.g. *Fine's Flowers Ltd v General Accident Assurance Co* (1977) 81 D.L.R. (3d) 139). This does not appear to add anything to the claim and cannot survive the analyses of Lord Browne-Wilkinson in *Henderson v Merrett Syndicates Ltd* [1995] 2 A.C. 145, 204–206; and of Millett L.J. in *Bristol & West Building Society v Mothew* [1998] Ch. 1.

[20] See para.16–011, above.

[21] See para.16–011, above.

[22] See para.16–014, above.

[23] See para.16–009, above. See also Ch.13.

[24] Although breach of a specific contractual duty is commonly accompanied by, or due to, negligence, as in *Dickson & Co v Devitt* (1916) 86 L.J.K.B. 315.

[25] Indeed there are other areas in which insurance brokers might incur liability; e.g. fraud in the presentation of claims to underwriters (see *The Litsion Pride* [1985] 1 Lloyd's Rep. 437, in which the broker's duty was discussed in the context of litigation between insured and insurer). There are other cases where brokers have been found negligent which are less obvious. For example, *Johns v Kelly* [1986] 1 Lloyd's Rep. 468 concerned the negligent supervision by a Lloyd's broker of a non-Lloyd's broker with whom it had an "umbrella arrangement" whereby the non-Lloyd's broker gained access to Lloyd's under the Lloyd's broker's name.

[26] e.g. *Transport & Trading Co Ltd v Olivier & Co Ltd* (1925) 21 Ll. Rep. 379. *Cosyns v Smith* (1983) 146 D.L.R. (3d) 622, Ontario CA: insurance agents instructed by claimant to obtain insurance against wind damage to his greenhouses, but failed to do so.

[27] *Avonale Blouse Co Ltd v Williamson & Geo. Town* (1948) 81 Ll. Rep. 492, where the broker was held to have discharged his duty (for the facts, see para.16–046, below). In *Markal Investments Ltd v Morley Shafron Agencies Ltd* (1990) 67 D.L.R. (4th) 422, British Columbia CA the broker was asked to obtain cover against the collapse under the weight of snow of a tent in which the client operated a flea market. The broker approached the insurer among those with whom he regularly dealt who was most likely to accept the risk. The insurer declined and the broker made no further enquiries. He was held liable at first instance (44 D.L.R. (4th) 745), but on appeal the action was dismissed because there was no evidence that any other insurer would have accepted the risk.

example, *Smith v Cologan*[28]: "if a person to whom such orders are sent do what is usual to get the insurance made, that is sufficient, because he is no insurer, and is not obliged to get insurance at all events". Even in those circumstances the broker will still be liable unless he promptly reports the position to his client.[29] Otherwise "he deprives the other of any opportunity of applying elsewhere to procure the insurance".[30] In *Eagle Star Insurance Co Ltd v National Westminster Finance Australia Ltd*[31] the Privy Council defined the duty of the defendant insurance brokers in these terms:

> "Their duty was to use all reasonable care and skill in seeking to obtain the cover in London which had been sought by their principals, and if for any reason, notwithstanding that they had used that reasonable care and skill, their efforts failed, it was then their further duty to report their failure and, if necessary, to seek further instructions. But they did not undertake that cover would be procured."

16–043   Where a broker purports to effect insurance on behalf of a client, but the insurers successfully deny that they were effectively bound, the broker will almost invariably be found to have been negligent. Thus in *Seavision Investment SA v Evennett, The Tiburon*[32] brokers had purported to obtain war risks cover for a ship owned by a Panamanian company by declaring it under an open cover for ships in German ownership. A loss was suffered and one underwriter denied liability on the basis that the owner was not German so that the risk did not fall within the terms of the open cover. The owner brought proceedings against both the underwriter and the brokers. The brokers conceded at trial that if the underwriter was not liable, they were, a concession which Steyn J. said "anticipated what would have been an inevitable conclusion". He went on to find that the underwriter was not liable and gave judgment against the brokers.[33] The brokers in *Mander v Commercial Union Assurance Co Plc*[34] were held liable on similar grounds: they had purported to reinsure their client's liabilities by making a declaration under an open cover. However, at trial Rix J. held that the declarations were not effective to create a binding contract. In the circumstances the brokers could not and did not dispute that they were in breach of duty.

16–044   In exceptional circumstances the broker may bind himself to effect or renew insurance in any event. In those circumstances any non-performance by the broker will render him liable for breach of contract,[35] although not necessarily for

---

[28] (1788) 2 T.R. 188n.

[29] *Smith v Lascelles* (1788) 2 T.R. 187; *Callander v Oelrichs* (1838) 5 Bing.N.C. 58. See para.16–087, below.

[30] *Smith v Lascelles* (1788) 2 T.R. 187.

[31] (1985) 58 A.L.R. 165, 174 (appeal from Supreme Court of Western Australia).

[32] [1990] 2 Lloyd's Rep. 418.

[33] See also *Block Brothers Industries Ltd v Westland Insurance Centre Ltd* (1993) 84 B.C.L.R.(2d) 319, where brokers had purported to issue a policy on behalf of an insurer who had not agreed to provide cover on that basis. The brokers were held liable when the insurer successfully resisted a claim by the client on the purported policy.

[34] [1998] Lloyd's Rep. I.R. 93.

[35] *Turpin v Bilton* (1843) 5 Man. & G. 455; *Hood v West End Motor Car Packing Co* [1917] 2 K.B. 38 (in particular at 47); *United Marketing Co v Hasham Kara* [1963] 1 Lloyd's Rep. 331. See also the judgment of Hobhouse J. in *General Accident Fire and Life Assurance Corp v Tanter, The "Zephyr"* [1984] 1 Lloyd's Rep. 58, at 80, col.2 to 81, col.1 (for the facts of the case see para.16–021, above).

negligence. It is, however, unusual for a broker to undertake an absolute obligation to procure insurance, since he is generally in no position to compel insurers
to accept the risk.[36]

If an insurance broker is retained to effect insurance but does not in fact do so, **16–045**
he may nevertheless in the course of his enquiries gain information material to
the risk. In these circumstances the broker, possibly, owes no duty to disclose that
information to the client for onward transmission to new brokers or insurers.[37]

Amendment or renewal of existing cover. The same principles as those **16–046**
stated in the preceding paragraphs apply where the broker is instructed to effect
an enlargement, variation or renewal of existing insurance. Thus in *Avonale
Blouse Co Ltd v Williamson & Geo. Town*[38] brokers were instructed to transfer
cover from one property to another. They had transferred cover against fire, but
not against burglary, when a loss occurred. They were held not to have been
negligent, because it was not possible to transfer cover against burglary until a
survey of the new premises had been carried out.[39]

(b) *Effecting Insurance, but not on the Terms Specified by the Client*

Where the client defines the risk against which he wishes to be insured, the **16–047**
broker is expected to carry out these instructions (if it is possible to do so)
precisely.[40] In *Dickson & Co v Devitt*[41] the claimants instructed the defendant
broker to arrange for the insurance of certain machinery to be shipped on the
"*Suwa Maru* and/or steamers" against marine and war risks. As a result of an
error by the defendant's clerk the words "and/or steamers" were omitted from
the slip relating to war risks. The machinery was shipped on a steamer other than
the *Suwa Maru* and lost as a result of enemy action. Atkin J. held that the

---

[36] Thus in *TL Creda Ltd v Hay Fielding Ltd*, unreported, October 30, 1984, UB 1568, CA, there was
a written agreement between the claimants and the defendant brokers under cl.1 of which the
defendants agreed "to obtain a policy document with Lloyd's in accordance with the attached draft
policy". The Court of Appeal held that on its true construction this agreement did not impose an
absolute obligation on the brokers, but merely an obligation to exercise due diligence and skill in
obtaining such a policy, if it was possible.

[37] *Blackburn Low & Co v Vigors* (1887) 12 App.Cas. 531, 537, in which it was held that the client
was not fixed with knowledge of information gained by his previous brokers.

[38] (1948) 81 Ll. Rep. 492.

[39] See also *MacDonald v Charlie Cook Insurance Inc* (1985) 55 Nfld. & P.E.I.R. 248; (1985) 162
A.P.R. 248, Prince Edward Island Supreme Court (brokers who undertook to find an alternative
insurer when the existing insurer declined to renew held liable when they failed to do so); and
Galambos v Kindrachuk Enterprises Ltd (1988) 63 Sask.R. 229, Saskatchewan Court of Queen's
Bench (broker who failed to procure an extension of cover for two new granaries was held to have
been negligent).

[40] See, e.g. *Barron v Fitzgerald* (1840) 6 Bing.N.C. 201: a broker who effected life insurance, but not
exactly on the terms specified, was held to be in breach of duty and not entitled to recover the
premiums which he had paid. See also *Zulu Airwear Inc v Khanna Holdings Ltd* (1998) 55 B.C.L.R.
(3d) 136, British Columbia Supreme Court, in which the broker was found liable in both contract and
tort for failing to carry out his landlord client's instructions to obtain comprehensive general liability
("CGL") coverage. Instead the broker obtained owners', landlords' and tenants' coverage, which
contained an exclusion not found in the CGL policy; and see *Newsome v Bennie S Cohen & Son (Qld)
Pty Ltd* [1941] Q.S.R. 270.

[41] (1916) 86 L.J.K.B. 315.

defendant was liable on two grounds: first, failure to carry out the claimants' specific instructions and secondly, (through his clerk) failure to exercise reasonable skill and care. Similarly, it is a breach of duty if a broker, who is instructed to insure goods for their replacement value, only obtains insurance on the basis of actual value.[42] A broker, who is instructed by various companies in the same group to arrange insurance for their respective properties will be in breach of duty to the company which owns a particular property if, despite being informed that that company owns the property, he obtains insurance for that property in the name of a different company.[43] In the context of reinsurance, the broker must usually[44] ensure that the risk reinsured is defined in identical terms to the risk covered by the primary policy of insurance. Any failure to do so is a breach of his express instructions and, almost inevitably, negligent.[45] If a broker fails to effect insurance on the terms specified by the client, then it is arguable that he comes under a continuing duty after the placement of the risk either to obtain the cover on the terms specified or to warn the insured that such cover has not been obtained.[46]

16–048   **Ambiguous instructions.** Where the client's instructions are ambiguous, the broker will not be liable if he interprets them in a reasonable manner[47] or in accordance with the usual practice of insurance brokers.[48] In *Vale v Van Oppen and Co Ltd*[49] the claimants instructed the defendants (shipping agents) to insure their consignment of goods against "all risks". Contrary to the claimants'

---

[42] *Coyle v Ray F Fredericks Insurance Ltd* (1984) 64 N.S.R. (2d); and (1984) 143 A.P.R. 93, Nova Scotia Supreme Court. See also *McNicol v Insurance Unlimited (Calgary) Ltd* (1992) 5 Alta.L.R. (3d) 158: a broker instructed to obtain insurance against ice hazards negligently obtained a policy which excluded cover for damage caused by floods. In *National Insurance and Guarantee Corp v Imperio Reinsurance Co (UK) Ltd* [1999] Lloyd's Rep. I.R. 249, Colman J., the brokers were asked to seek confirmation that a policy already obtained included cover for losses represented by self-funding interest. They obtained an endorsement which did not provide the requisite confirmation and were held to have been negligent for having mistakenly formed the view that it did.

[43] *Austcan Investments Pty Ltd v Sun Alliance Insurance Ltd* (1992) 57 S.A.S.R. 343 at first instance (on appeal, *ibid.*, it was held that the correct company had been insured, but that the broker had been negligent in another respect: see para.16–090, n.59, below).

[44] An insurer may choose not to obtain reinsurance which exactly mirrors the underlying risk: see *Deeny v Gooda Walker Ltd* [1996] L.R.L.R. 183 at 200–1.

[45] *British Citizens Assurance Co v L Woolland & Co* (1921) 8 Ll. Rep. 89 (brokers, arranging reinsurance of a ship, failed to describe it as a sailing vessel). See also *Youell v Bland Welch & Co Ltd (No.2)* [1990] 2 Lloyd's Rep. 431 (the *"Superhulls Cover"* case) (for the facts, see para.16–022, above).

[46] *Great North Eastern Railway Ltd v JLT Corporate Risks Ltd* [2006] EWHC 1478 (Cresswell J.). The insured issued proceedings more than six years after the policy had been effected and the broker applied for summary judgment on the basis that the claim was statute barred. The insured maintained that the broker was under a continuing duty after the policy had been effected. The judge held that the issue of whether or not the broker was under such a continuing duty was a matter on which expert evidence as to relevant broking practice was required and it was not suitable for summary determination.

[47] *Dixon v Hovill* (1828) 4 Bing. 665; *Veljkovic v Vrybergen* [1985] V.R. 419: V, a subcontractor on a building project instructed an insurance agent to obtain insurance. The agent obtained insurance against employers' liability but not against injury to V himself. The Supreme Court of Victoria held that the insurance agent had not been negligent to interpret his instructions in this manner. See also *Ireland v Livingston* (1872) L.R. 5 H.L. 395.

[48] *Enlayde Ltd v Roberts* [1917] 1 Ch. 109, 120–121, (obiter dictum of Sargant J.).

[49] (1921) 37 T.L.R. 367.

intentions, the defendants took the phrase "all risks" to mean "all risks covered by an ordinary marine policy", and effected insurance accordingly. Roche J. held that they had discharged their obligations to the claimants.[50] It is suggested, however, that where an ambiguity is patent, the broker is under a duty to seek clarification from the client before carrying out the instructions.

Specified insurance unavailable. Except in the unusual circumstances mentioned above,[51] the broker has a good defence if he can show that insurance on the particular terms specified was not available, but he effected insurance on the best terms that he reasonably could.[52] In *Waterkeyn v Eagle Star & British Dominions Insurance Co Ltd*[53] the claimant claimed damages from the defendant brokers for failing properly to insure his deposit accounts in various Russian banks after the Bolshevik revolution. Greer J. heard evidence "at length" as to the negotiations carried on by the defendants' representative and concluded that he had discharged his duty: " . . . he is not responsible for the fact that this insurance was not as wide as was desired . . . it is all that could have been got from the Underwriters in the circumstances".   **16–049**

(c) *Effecting Insurance which does not meet the Client's Requirements*

An insurance broker is under a duty to ensure, so far as he reasonably can,[54] that he effects insurance which meets the client's requirements.[55] Rule 4.3.1 of the ICOB sourcebook provides that: "An insurance intermediary must take reasonable steps to ensure that, if in the course of insurance mediation activities it makes any personal recommendation to a customer to buy or sell a non-investment insurance contract, the personal recommendation is suitable for the customer's demands and needs at the time the personal recommendation is made."[56]   **16–050**

A broker should ensure that the risk against which the client wishes to be insured is correctly described in the policy and that the client will be entitled to   **16–051**

---

[50] The position is otherwise, however, where someone who is not an insurance broker agrees to effect insurance against all risks: *Yuill & Co v Robson* [1908] 1 K.B. 270: *Enlayde Ltd v Roberts* [1917] 1 Ch. 109.

[51] See para.16–044, above.

[52] See, e.g. *McIntyre & Co v FJ Krutwig* (1922) 10 Ll.L.R. 430; *King (or Fiehl) v Chambers & Newman (Insurance Brokers) Ltd* [1963] 2 Lloyd's Rep. 130. As to the duty to notify the client in these circumstances, see para.16–085, below.

[53] (1920) 4 Ll. Rep. 178; (1920) 5 Ll. Rep. 42.

[54] This obligation is particularly onerous in cases where the broker accepts instructions to arrange insurance for the client against all foreseeable risks. See para.16–013, above.

[55] Para.3.2 of the General Insurance Standards Council Code for Private Customers (2000) states: "We will make sure, as far as possible, that the products and services we offer you will match your requirements: We will offer you products and services to meet your needs, and match any requirements you have. If we cannot match your requirements, we will explain the differences in the product or service that we can offer you. If it is not practical to match all your requirements, we will give you enough information so that you can make an informed decision about your insurance." Similarly, para.11 of the General Insurance Standards Council Commercial Code states: "If members are unable to match Commercial Customer's requirements they will explain the differences in the insurance proposed."

[56] Breach of this rule gives rise to a cause of action at the suit of a "private person" (see para.16–009, above).

claim if the need should arise.[57] Thus in an Australian case, brokers who were instructed to obtain insurance against damage by storm, tempest and flood were held negligent for obtaining a policy which excluded "damage caused directly or indirectly by the sea". Having regard to the location of the property, the brokers ought to have appreciated that the only flooding which could occur would be from the sea.[58] Similarly, in *Niagara Frontier Caterers Ltd v Continental Insurance Co of Canada,*[59] brokers were held negligent for obtaining an insurance policy subject to a "co-insurance clause" which had the effect of reducing cover under the policy to thirty-five ninetieths of any loss. In *Cee Bee Marine Ltd v Lombard Insurance Co Ltd,*[60] cover was arranged in the name of one of two clients. Stock belonging to the other was lost in a fire. The client named on the insurance policy had no insurable interest in the lost stock and so it could not claim under the policy. The other client was not an insured. The broker was held liable. Where the client has specific requirements as to the identity or status of any insurer, the broker should either obtain insurance from an appropriate insurer or advise his client accordingly.[61]

16–052　　　The defendant brokers in *Strong & Pearl v S Allison & Co Ltd*[62] were also held liable for failure to obtain a policy on terms appropriate for their client's needs. The claimants instructed the brokers to arrange insurance for their motor yacht while it was laid up for repair. The defendants knew that the claimants proposed to live on board during this period. Nevertheless, they effected a "lying-up policy" in the standard form, which did not cover the yacht while the owners were on board and contained a "no petrol warranty". Subsequently an

---

[57] e.g. *Peter Unruh Construction Co Ltd v Kelly-Lucy & Cameron Adjusters Ltd* [1976] 4 W.W.R. 419, Alberta Supreme Court, where the agent obtained a policy which excluded cover for loss caused by excavation, although he knew that the insured carried out such work. Held liable for failing to notice this exclusion upon receipt of the policy. See also *McCann v Western Farmers Mutual Insurance Co* (1978) 87 D.L.R. (3d) 135 where the defendant arranged insurance of claimant's premises, on part of which (as he knew) the claimants carried on business. Held liable for effecting a policy which excluded business use. In *Kadaja v CAA* (1995) 23 O.R. (3d) 275, Ontario Court General Division, the insured asked his insurer to transfer his car insurance from an old vehicle to a new one and asked for "full coverage". The insurer was found to owe the insured the same duty to advise as that owed by a broker, and was found negligent in failing to advise him of a gap in his cover, namely that the policy which was transferred did not cover him for collision/comprehensive damage. In *All Lift Consultants Ltd v Adam Crane Service (1980) Ltd* (1988) 88 A.R. 208, Alberta Court of Queen's Bench, the broker obtained and renewed cover which did not extend to a part of the insured's activities of which the broker knew. The broker was held liable. See also *Mitzner v Miller & Beazley Ltd* (1993) 11 Alta.L.R. (3d) 108: broker held liable for not properly investigating his client's requirements with the result that the policy procured did not cover loss and damage to tools.

[58] *Mitor Investment Pty Ltd v General Accident Fire & Life Assurance Corp Ltd* [1984] W.A.R. 365, Supreme Court of Western Australia. In contrast, in *New Forty-Four Mines Ltd v St Paul Fire & Marine Insurance Co* (1987) 78 A.R. 364 the Alberta Court of Appeal held that a broker who offered a warranty to insurers that the insured premises would be watched 24 hours a day was not liable when insurers successfully denied liability for breach of that warranty. The broker had reasonable grounds for believing that the warranty would be complied with.

[59] (1990) 74 O.R. (2d) 191, Ontario High Court. In *GKN Keller Canada Ltd v Hartford Fire Insurance Co* (1983) 27 C.C.L.T. 61, Ontario High Court, brokers were held to have been negligent in obtaining an insurance policy with an exemption clause which rendered the cover inadequate for the claimants' needs.

[60] [1990] 2 N.Z.L.R. 1.

[61] *Texas Homecare Ltd v Royal Bank of Canada Trust Co Ltd* [1996] C.L.C. 776: for the facts, see para.16–031, above.

[62] (1926) 25 Ll. Rep. 504.

explosion occurred and the insurers denied liability. Greer J. held that the defendants were negligent and in breach of the implied terms of their employment in failing to obtain insurance which covered the actual circumstances under which the yacht was being laid up.[63]

A further illustration is provided by *Paul Tudor Jones II and Marsh &* **16–053** *McLennan Inc v Crowley Colosso Ltd*[64] in which the defendants were English brokers engaged by American brokers to obtain contractor's all risk insurance for a development in the Bahamas. They obtained insurance on terms that cover would ot be provided for any part of the works which had been taken over by the employer or for which a certificate of completion had been issued. The development was carried out in phases and the client required and believed that he had obtained cover which would protect his interest in the development until all phases had been completed. The marina had been completed when it suffered substantial damage during a hurricane. The insurers declined to pay. At the time the risk was broked the American brokers, but not the English brokers, had known that there would be certificates of completion for phases of the works. The English brokers had sent the proposed wording to the American brokers for approval. Mance J. held that the English brokers were at fault in failing to draw the attention of the American brokers to the term and the American brokers were at fault in failing to notice it.

Client becoming involved in legal dispute. If the insurance obtained by the **16–054** broker is such that his client becomes involved in a legal dispute with the insurer then, unless the position taken by the insurer is absurd,[65] the broker will be found to be in breach of duty. In *FNCB Ltd v Barnet Devanney (Harrow) Ltd*[66] the defendant brokers were held liable for failure to obtain a policy on terms appropriate for their client's needs. The brokers were acting for both mortgagor and mortgagee in relation to a composite policy insuring their respective interests in the mortgaged property. They failed to have included a mortgagee protection clause, which insurers would have agreed to at no additional cost. The mortgaged property was damaged by fire and insurers purported to avoid cover because of non-disclosure and misrepresentation by the mortgagor. The mortgagee compromised its claim against insurers and sued the brokers. The Court of Appeal held that the brokers were in breach of duty. The law as to the separate rights of two insured under a composite policy was not clear at the time the risk was broked[67]:

> "it is not the function of an insurance broker to take a view on undetermined points of law. The protection to be afforded to the client should, if reasonably possible, be such

---

[63] The second ground of liability was the defendants' failure to give proper advice to the claimants, as to which see para.16–093, below.

[64] [1996] 2 Lloyd's Rep. 619.

[65] In a Canadian case, *Messagemate Aust Pty Ltd v National Credit Insurance (Brokers) Pty Ltd* [2002] S.A.S.C. 327 the insurer refused to provide the insured with an indemnity, and the insured sued both the insurer and its broker. The claim against the insurer succeeded. Williams J. stated (at para.93) that he did not consider that the broker's duty of care "required it to anticipate and warn against the absurd construction which [the insurer] now seeks to give the policy."

[66] [1999] Lloyd's Rep. I.R. 459.

[67] It has subsequently been clarified: *New Hampshire Insurance Co v MGN Ltd* [1997] L.R.L.R. 24; following *Dixey & Sons v Parsons* (1964) 192 E.G. 197.

that the client does not become involved in legal disputes at all. As in the case of a solicitor the insurance broker should protect his client from unnecessary risks including the risk of litigation".

That conclusion was also supported by the absence of evidence that the brokers had acted in accordance with responsible market practice.[68] More recently in *Talbot Underwriting Ltd v Nausch Hogan & Murray Inc*[69] Cooke J. stated that: "the duty of the broker is, so far as possible, to obtain insurance coverage which clearly and indisputably meets its clients' requirements." He held that if the broker breached that duty with the result that a dispute arose between the insured and the insurer, then the broker would be liable for the resulting costs, expenses and losses.

16–055   **Defects in policy wording.** The broker may also be responsible for defects in the wording of the policy of insurance which render it unsatisfactory from his client's point of view. Thus in *Youell v Bland Welch & Co Ltd (No.2)* (the *"Superhulls Cover"* case),[70] one ground upon which Phillips J. held the brokers liable was their failure to draft the contract of reinsurance with reasonable clarity, obscuring the difference between the cover under the original insurance and that under the reinsurance.[71] In *Firestone Canada Inc v American Home Assurance Co*[72] the brokers arranged a policy to insure against the manufacturers of snow tyres being called upon to honour a weather warranty. As a result of a difference between the clause describing cover and the formula for calculating the premium due, the insured had to pay premium on sales which were not subject to the

---

[68] The decisions set out in this section should be contrasted with *Fomin v Oswell* in which the defendant brokers were instructed to effect insurance on a vessel bound for Petersburgh. The captain had stated in conversation that he intended to carry simulated papers, although there was no reference to this in the written instructions to insure. The defendants duly effected insurance, but without any clause permitting the vessel to carry simulated papers. It was held that they had discharged their duty. "Notwithstanding the prior conversation, the captain might have resolved not to carry any [simulated papers]", *per* Lord Ellenborough. This decision is a surprising one. It might be thought that the brokers should at least have investigated the matter, before effecting a policy which assumed that no simulated papers would be carried. A possible explanation of the decision is that the claimant in this case (unlike the claimants in *Strong & Pearl v S Allison & Co Ltd* and *Sharp and Roarer Investments Ltd v Sphere Drake Insurance Plc, The Moonacre*) was well versed in marine insurance and could be presumed to have given accurate and complete instructions. Alternatively, it may be that a lower standard of skill and care was expected of insurance brokers in the early 19th century and that, had the case arisen more recently, it would have been decided differently.
[69] [2005] EWHC 2359; [2005] 2 C.L.C. 868. The broker had failed to ensure that an intended insured was named on the policy placed by the broker with the insurer. As a result of that failure, the insurer denied that the intended insured was an insured under the policy. Cooke J. tried a number of preliminary issues, including whether the claim in damages against the broker had a real prospect of success. He held that it did. This part of his decision was not challenged in the subsequent appeal [2006] EWCA Civ 889; [2006] 2 Lloyd's Rep. 195.
[70] [1990] 2 Lloyd's Rep. 431 (for the facts see para.16–022, above).
[71] Similarly, in *GE Reinsurance Corp v New Hampshire Insurance Co* [2003] EWHC 402; [2004] Lloyd's Rep. I.R. 404, a film finance case, the brokers admitted that they owed the insurer a duty to obtain reinsurance which was co-extensive with the insurer's liabilities under the insurance contract. In rejecting the broker's submission that the insurer was contributorily negligent, Langley J. stated (at para.73) that "in a transaction of this novel type, the onus [was on the broker] to 'get it right' and to alert insurers to any risks."
[72] (1989) 67 O.R. (2d) 471, Ontario High Court.

warranty or to the cover provided. The brokers were found to have been negligent.

Broker's duty to enquire. The broker is expected to have a basic knowledge **16–056** of insurance law[73] and, on occasions, to question the client himself so as to elicit relevant information which may not otherwise be volunteered.[74] Rule 4.3.2 of the ICOB sourcebook states that in assessing his customer's demands and needs an insurance intermediary "must seek such information about the customer's circumstances and objectives as might reasonably be expected to be relevant in enabling the insurance intermediary to identify the customer's requirements."

McNealy v The Pennine Insurance Co Ltd[75] the claimant, a property repairer **16–057** and part-time musician, instructed the defendant brokers to effect motor insurance on his behalf. The defendants effected insurance with the Pennine Insurance Company, which offered low rates. Unfortunately a number of categories of persons were excluded from benefiting under the policy, one of which was "whole or part-time musicians". On the occurrence of an accident the claimant was unable to claim on the policy. Evidence was given that the brokers had filled in the proposal form on the basis of information given by the claimant. When asked what his occupation was, the claimant replied "property repairer" and the brokers recorded this answer without further enquiry. The Court of Appeal held that the brokers had failed in their duty. They possessed a leaflet setting out all the categories of excluded persons. They should have gone through the leaflet with the claimant, so as to make sure that he did not fall into any of the excluded categories.

A further example is provided by the decision in *Sharp and Roarer Invest-* **16–058** *ments Ltd v Sphere Drake Insurance Plc, The Moonacre.*[76] In that case brokers were held to have been negligent in arranging insurance for a yacht on terms which included an exclusion of cover for any period when the yacht was used as a houseboat. The insured's crew lived on his yacht when it was laid up over winter and this allowed insurers to rely upon the exclusion when a loss occurred. When preparing the proposal form the broker had asked whether the insured or his family would live on the yacht over winter, but failed to ask whether anyone else would. He was therefore held to have been negligent.

There are, however, limits to the scope of a broker's duty to make enquiries. **16–059** A broker will not be found to have acted negligently if he fails to raise questions about the risk to be covered which he had no reason to ask. For example, in

---

[73] See *Park v Hammond* (1816) 6 Taunt. 495, where the defendant through ignorance of an established rule of law, failed properly to define in the terms of cover the risk against which the client was seeking insurance.

[74] Para.3.2 of the General Insurance Standards Council Code for Private Customers (2000) states: "We will make sure, as far as possible, that the products and services we offer you will match your requirements: If it is practical, we will identify your needs by getting relevant information from you." Para. 7 of the General Insurance Standards Council Commercial Code states: "Members will seek from Commercial Customers such information about their circumstances and objectives as might reasonably be expected to be relevant in enabling them to identify the Commercial Customer's requirements and fulfil their responsibilities to their Commercial Customers."

[75] [1978] 2 Lloyd's Rep. 18, CA.

[76] [1992] 2 Lloyd's Rep. 501, A.D. Colman Q.C., sitting as a deputy judge of the High Court.

Dallinga v Sun Alliance Insurance Co[77] the owner of goods stored at his son's property arranged contents cover for his son through the defendant broker but did not tell the broker that the goods were his. They were stolen. The son had no insurable interest and the father was not named on the policy, so neither could claim for the loss. The broker had no reason to believe that the goods belonged to the father and the claim against him was dismissed. Obviously if the broker does ask the appropriate questions and the insured withholds essential information from the broker then the broker will not be held responsible for any resulting gap in the insured's cover.[78]

16–060   **Client giving clear instructions.** A broker who receives clear instructions from his client as to the insurance to be effected is not under an obligation to suggest that the client obtain more extensive cover unless he has undertaken to give such advice.[79] Thus in *The Town of Rosetown v Wilson Agencies Ltd*[80] a town decided to place its insurance business out to tender, specifying the cover it wanted. It failed to seek or obtain excess automobile liability insurance and, on finding itself facing a claim in respect of which it was underinsured, sued both its broker before it went out to tender and the broker whose tender it had accepted. The claim was dismissed. A fortiori a client who is adequately informed of possible coverage but decides not to obtain it cannot complain if he then suffers a loss which would have been covered.[81]

16–061   **Appropriate level of cover.** A broker should obtain cover not only against the relevant risks but also at a suitable level to protect his client. This is usually done not by the broker valuing the insured property or interest himself, but by the

---

[77] (1993) 10 Alta.L.R. (3d) 59. See also *National Insurance and Guarantee Corp v Imperio Reinsurance Co (UK) Ltd* [1999] Lloyd's Rep. I.R. 249, Colman J.: brokers not in breach of duty for failing to realise that the insured wanted excess of loss cover to include loss of interest on the insured's own funds applied as part of the insured scheme.

[78] *St Isidore Asphalte Ltee v Luminex Signs Ltd* (1996) 176 N.B.R. (2d) 135, New Brunswick Court of Queen's Bench: insured ran a sign-painting business. A vehicle was stolen from his premises, but his insurance did not extend coverage to vehicles. Broker found not liable because the insured withheld essential information from the broker and thereby failed to adequately describe the nature of the business.

[79] In Canada such a duty is readily found: see para.16–013, n.38, above. For example in *Miller v Guardian Insurance Co Ltd* (1995) 127 D.L.R. (4th) 717 the client wanted "full coverage" and the agent was held liable for failing to advise him to obtain the uninsured motorist endorsement. An appeal in *Miller v Guardian Insurance Co of Canada* was unsuccessful: (1997) 149 D.L.R. (4th) 375. However, a client who brings such a claim must prove that he relied upon the broker to give such advice and that the broker knew or ought to have known that he would do so: *Kalkinis v Allstate Insurance Co of Canada* (1998) 41 O.R. (3d) 528, Ontario CA.

[80] (1989) 77 Sask.R. 42, Saskatchewan Court of Queen's Bench. See also *O'Brien v Hughes-Gibb & Co Ltd* [1995] L.R.L.R. 90: owners of racehorse requested cover for "mortality only"; brokers held not liable for failing to advise of or obtain cover against theft.

[81] *Davca Building Supplies Ltd v Wedgewood Insurance Ltd and Clarke* (1992) 99 Nfld. & P.E.I.R. 203. The client was informed of possible cover in respect of liability for damage to trailers towed by his truck but chose not to obtain it. His action against the broker failed. See also *Conway v Home Securities Ltd* (1996) 108 Man.R. (2d) 58 (client informed of optional sewer back-up coverage, decided not to pay the small additional premium, and then claimed unsuccessfully against broker when he suffered an uninsured loss); and *Madole v State Farm Mutual Automobile Insurance Co* (1995) 32 Alta.L.R. (3d) 265 (client informed of possibility of comprehensive cover for existing car, chose not to have it, purchased new car and insured it on same terms as before; his claim against the insurance agent for failing to advise him to obtain comprehensive cover for the new car failed).

broker drawing his client's attention to the consequences of underinsurance (which may need checking on each renewal, particularly if the policy covers damage to property on the basis of the cost of reinstatement).

In *JW Bollom & Co Ltd v Byas Mosley & Co Ltd*[82] the insured was under-   **16–062** insured. Moore-Bick J. emphasised that insurance brokers are not valuers and so could not be expected to advise as to the value of a particular piece of property. However, he found that the brokers had acted negligently in failing to advise the insured of the need to obtain cover for the full cost of reinstatement of the property insured and to obtain cover accordingly. Where, however, the broker takes it upon himself to value the property to be insured and negligently underestimates the level of cover needed, he will be in breach of duty. Thus in *Evans v State Farm Fire and Casualty Co*[83] brokers who used a computer software program to calculate the reinstatement cost of their client's house, rather than ask questions about the house, were found to have been in breach of duty when their client was underinsured as a result.

By contrast, in *William Jackson & Sons Ltd v Oughtred & Harrison (Insurance*   **16–063** *Ltd)*[84] the claimant suffered a loss at a time when its premises were greatly under-insured. The premises had been valued by an independent firm of surveyors, but their valuation was negligently low. Thereafter the premises were developed and the level of insurance was varied as the development progressed based on the cost of the building works. Morison J. rejected the claimant's allegation that the brokers were negligent in failing to advise the claimant to have a further valuation carried out at some stage during the development works.

Client with changing requirements. If a broker is aware that his client's   **16–064** insurance requirements will change then he may come under a duty to monitor his client's requirements and ensure that those requirements are met. In a Canadian case, *Etter and Hart v Commercial Union Assurance Co*,[85] the client purchased a property which included a derelict barn. He advised his broker that he intended to conduct renovations and instructed his broker to arrange the appropriate insurance. The broker arranged insurance, but when the barn was destroyed in a storm the insurer refused liability on the basis that the original barn covered by the policy had been torn down and a new one constructed in its place. The broker was held to have been under a duty to keep himself appraised of his client's renovation plans and activities and to ensure that the client was either insured with the existing coverage or, if not, to advise that other cover was required. The broker had failed to do so and the finding of negligence against him was upheld on appeal.

Cost of cover. One of the main functions that a broker carries out on behalf of   **16–065** his client is obtaining quotes from different insurers to ensure that the client pays no more for his insurance than is necessary. Typically the broker will test the

---

[82] [1999] Lloyd's Rep. P.N. 598, Moore-Bick J. See also *Kennedy (BJ) Agency (1984) Ltd v Kilgour Bell Ins* (1999) 139 Man.R.(2d) 276, Manitoba Court of Queen's Bench, in which the broker was negligent in failing to advise his client of the availability of "replacement cost coverage" and the limitations of "actual value" coverage.

[83] (1993) 15 O.R. (3d) 86.

[84] [2002] Lloyd's Rep. I.R. 230 (Morison J.).

[85] (1998) 166 N.S.R. (2d) 299, Nova Scotia CA.

market prior to renewal to ensure that the premium payable to the existing insurer is competitive. If a broker fails to test the market in this way, with the result that the insured pays over the odds for his cover, then the insured may have a claim against the broker for the difference between the amount of premium paid and the amount which would have been payable had the broker acted with due skill and care.[86]

(d) *Failing to Exercise Discretion Reasonably*

16–066 If the client leaves the choice of insurer[87] or the terms of insurance[88] to the judgment or discretion of his broker, the latter will not be liable if he acts reasonably and in accordance with the usual practice of insurance brokers. In *Chapman v Walton*[89] the defendant broker was instructed to effect five policies of insurance on goods being shipped from London to St Thomas, with leave to call at Madeira and Tenerife. Subsequently the client received a letter indicating that the voyage was altered. He took it to the defendant and told the defendant "to do the needful with it". The meaning of the letter was not as clear as it might have been, but the defendant effected such alterations to the policies as he considered appropriate. In the event the ship sank off the Grand Canary Island and, as this was not covered by any of the alterations to the policy, the underwriters refused to pay. At the trial the defendant called "several policy brokers" as witnesses, each of whom expressed the opinion that an insurance broker would have done ample justice to the instructions contained in the letter by procuring the alterations which were in fact made. The jury found for the defendant and a subsequent application to set aside their verdict was dismissed. Lord Tindal C.J. stressed that the issue was not whether the defendant's decision was ultimately proved correct, but whether he exercised reasonable skill, care and judgment.[90]

16–067 On the other hand, a broker who chooses an insurer for his client will be liable if he fails to exercise sufficient skill and care in making his choice. In *Lewis v Tressider Andrews Associates Pty Ltd*,[91] the broker chose to place a risk with a new insurer, having received financial details of that insurer. Properly understood, they gave rise to grounds for believing that the insurer was not reliable or sound. The broker was held liable when the policy proved worthless.[92] A broker

---

[86] In a Scottish case, *McCrindle Group Ltd v Willis Corroon Scotland Ltd* 2002 S.L.T. 209, the Outer House of the Court of Session refused to summarily dismiss such a claim.

[87] *Moore v Mourgue* (1776) 2 Cowp. 479; *Comber v Anderson* (1808) 1 Camp. 523; *Dixon v Hovill* (1828) 4 Bing. 665 (it is part of the broker's duty to "take reasonable care that the policy [is] underwritten by responsible and solvent persons"); *Hurrell v Bullard* (1863) 3 F. & F. 445, (*per* Cockburn C.J. at 453).

[88] *Vale v Van Oppen & Co Ltd* (1921) 37 T.L.R. 367.

[89] (1833) 10 Bing. 57.

[90] See para.16–036, above.

[91] [1987] 2 Qd.R. 533.

[92] Similarly in *Bates v Barrow Ltd* [1995] 1 Lloyd's Rep. 680 Gatehouse J. would have found brokers who placed stop loss insurance with unauthorised insurance companies liable if he had not held that the policies were enforceable by reason of s.132 of the Financial Services Act 1986.

who fails to insert in the policy a clause which is normally inserted,[93] will be liable for any loss thereby caused to the client.[94]

(e) *Failing to Act with Reasonable Speed*

Any professional person owes a duty to his client to act with reasonable speed.   **16–068**
If an insurance broker is guilty of unreasonable delay in effecting or renewing insurance cover and in consequence the client suffers loss for which he is uninsured, then the broker will be liable.[95] What constitutes unreasonable delay is a question of fact.[96] The nature of an insurance broker's business is such that a large part of his work is attended by some degree of urgency. Relevant factors to consider in each case are the nature of the risk to be covered, whether the client is uninsured in the meantime and the availability of the particular insurance required. In *Cock, Russell & Co v Bray, Gibb & Co Ltd*[97] the defendants, marine insurance brokers, were instructed by the claimants on a Friday afternoon to cover the claimants for all risks in a Spanish steamer which was expected shortly. The defendants did nothing that day. On the Saturday they approached various underwriters but without success. On Monday the steamer arrived before the start of business and it transpired that a large part of the cargo was lost. Bailhache J. considered that, having regard to the nature of the risk, the defendants were not guilty of unreasonable delay. On the other hand in *Fraser Valley Mushroom Growers' Co-operative Association v MacNaughton & Ward Ltd*,[98] brokers were held liable for failure to act with reasonable speed. They were requested to place coverage on goods but had not done so two hours later when the goods were destroyed by fire.[99] A fortiori, if a broker receives a request from a client and fails to act on it at all he will be in breach of duty. In *Forsikringsaktieselskapet Vesta v Butcher*[1] the broker's reinsured client told the broker that the insured under the original insurance could not comply with a warranty that the insured property be

---

[93] As to which the evidence of other insurance brokers is admissible: *Mallough v Barber* (1815) 4 Camp. 150.

[94] See also *Gibraltar General Insurance Co v LE Yingst Co Ltd* (1990) 89 Sask.R. 93, discussed in para.16–024, n.66, above.

[95] *Turpin v Bilton* (1843) 5 Man. & G. 455; *London Borough of Bromley v Ellis* [1971] 1 Lloyd's Rep. 97, 99; *Irish Nationwide BS v Malone* (1999) I.L.T. 243 (Irish Supreme Court stated that the normal duties of a broker required close attention to the progress of a matter until it had been completed or abandoned).

[96] In *Icarom Plc (formerly Insurance Corp of Ireland Plc) v Peek Puckle (International) Ltd* [1992] 2 Lloyd's Rep. 600 the claimant alleged that the defendant broker, having been instructed on January 19, had been negligent in failing to obtain facultative reinsurance cover until January 22, by when a total loss had occurred on the underlying policy. Webster J. held that the brokers had only been instructed on the 22nd, so that the claim failed on its facts. It appears to have been considered to be at least arguable that the brokers would have been negligent had they taken four days to obtain reinsurance cover.

[97] (1920) 3 Ll. Rep. 71.

[98] (1982) 37 B.C.L.R. 20, British Columbia Supreme Court.

[99] See also *Labreche Estate v Harasymiw* (1992) 89 D.L.R. (4th) 95 where an employee of a credit union who assisted a mortgagor in applying for life insurance was held to be in breach of a tortious duty of care in taking three months to complete an application form and generally failing to progress the application.

[1] [1986] 2 All E.R. 488, Hobhouse J. (the brokers did not seek to challenge this finding on appeal: [1989] A.C. 852, CA and HL).

watched 24 hours a day and asked for confirmation that this was acceptable to reinsurers. The broker failed to act at all and was held by Hobhouse J. to have been in breach of duty.

(f) *Liability Arising out of Material Non-disclosure*

16–069   Insurance contracts are contracts of the utmost good faith. The insured is obliged to disclose all material facts which he either knows or is deemed to know, both before the contract is made and on the negotiation of any renewal of that contract.[2] The insured's broker owes a separate personal duty of disclosure.[3] In the event that the broker breaches his personal duty of disclosure, then the insurer will have a right to avoid the policy even if the insured was entirely unaware that such non-disclosure had occurred.[4] If the broker fails to disclose material facts, with the result that the insurers subsequently repudiate,[5] he will be liable for the loss sustained.[6] There is a substantial body of case law on what constitutes a "material" fact, but a discussion of these authorities is outside the scope of this work.[7] In brief, however, a fact is material if it was one which would have an effect (not necessarily decisive) on the mind of a prudent underwriter in deciding whether to accept the risk or the premium to be asked.

16–070   In order to avoid the policy for non-disclosure the insurer must also show that he had been induced to enter the contract of insurance on the terms he did by the non-disclosure.[8] In *Container Transport International Inc v Oceanus Mutual Underwriting Association (Bermuda) Ltd*[9] (a case in which marine insurers

---

[2] See *MacGillivray on Insurance Law* (10th edn) at Ch.17.

[3] See para.16–019, above. The evidence of other insurance brokers as to whether they would have considered the facts material is not admissible: *Campbell v Rickards* (1833) 5 B. Ad. 840.

[4] For example, in *Hazel v Whitlam* [2004] EWCA Civ 1600; [2005] 1 Lloyd's Rep. I.R. 168, CA motor insurers were found to be entitled to avoid the policy where the broker had given incomplete and misleading answers in a proposal form regarding the nature of the insured's occupation.

[5] There may be a failure to disclose a material fact without negligence: see *Banque Keyser Ullmann SA v Skandia (UK) Insurance Co Ltd* [1990] 1 Q.B. 665, 781; *Bank of Nova Scotia v Hellenic Mutual War Risks Association (Bermuda) Ltd, The "Good Luck"* [1990] 1 Q.B. 818. However, a broker will find it difficult to establish that any non-disclosure of information known to him was not negligent: see para.16–072, below.

[6] e.g. *Maydew v Forrester* (1814) 5 Taunt. 615. In *WE Acres Crabmeal Ltd v Brien's Insurance Agency Ltd* (1988) 90 N.B.R. (2d) 77 and 228 A.P.R. 77, New Brunswick Court of Queen's Bench, brokers failed to disclose the insured's claims history, entitling insurers to avoid the policy and rendering themselves liable. In *Akedian Co Ltd v Royal Insurance Australia Ltd* (1999) 1 V.R. 80, Supreme Court of Victoria, the brokers were found to have breached their duty to the client in failing to disclose to insurers the purchase price of machinery to be insured. In New Zealand, insurers would not be able to repudiate, if, as is customary, the broker receives commission from them, being fixed with the broker's knowledge of all matters material to the contract of insurance by s.10 of the Insurance Law Reform Act 1977: *Helicopter Equipment Ltd v Marine Insurance Co Ltd* [1986] 1 N.Z.L.R. 448; and *Gold Star Insurance Co Ltd v Gaunt* [1998] 3 N.Z.L.R. 80, NZCA. In *Roberts v Plaisted* [1989] 2 Lloyd's Rep. 341, 345, col.1, Purchas L.J. expressed dissatisfaction that in English law an insured who has made full disclosure to a broker could nevertheless find himself uninsured because his broker failed to make full disclosure to insurers.

[7] See *MacGillvray on Insurance Law* (10th edn), Ch.17.

[8] *Pan Atlantic Insurance Co Ltd v Pine Top Insurance Co Ltd* [1995] 1 A.C. 501

[9] [1984] 1 Lloyd's Rep. 476, 496–497 (now partly overruled by *Pan Atlantic Insurance Co Ltd v Pine Top Insurance Co Ltd* [1995] 1 A.C. 501).

avoided a contract of insurance under s.18(1) of the Marine Insurance Act 1906)
Kerr L.J. summarised the broker's duty in these terms:

" . . . one way of formulating the test as to the duty of disclosure and representation to
cases such as the present . . . is simply to ask oneself: 'Having regard to all the
circumstances known or deemed to be known to the insured and to his broker, and
ignoring those which are expressly excepted from the duty of disclosure, was the
presentation of the risk in summary form to the underwriter a fair and substantially
accurate presentation of the risk proposed for insurance, so that a prudent insurer could
form a proper judgment—either on the presentation alone or by asking questions if he
was sufficiently put on enquiry and wanted to know further details—whether or not to
accept the proposal, and, if so, on what terms?' This is not an onerous duty for brokers
to discharge in practice".

In *Pan Atlantic Insurance Co Ltd v Pine Top Insurance Co Ltd*[10] it was held **16–071**
by the trial judge and the Court of Appeal that there was no non-disclosure of a
disastrous claims record by a broker who had the statistics with him when
broking the risk, but conducted himself so as to reduce the likelihood of the
underwriter asking to see them. In the House of Lords Lord Mustill indicated that
there might well have been non-disclosure, but that, if there had, the underwriter
would have waived it. However a broker who approaches underwriters on that
basis acts at his peril. Thus in *Newbury International Ltd v Reliance National
Insurance Co (UK) Ltd*[11] Hobhouse J. rejected a submission that underwriters
had had the opportunity to ask further questions, holding that they could only be
expected to make such enquiries after a fair presentation of the risk. He held that
underwriters were entitled to avoid the policy and, in the circumstances, the
brokers conceded that they were in breach of duty.[12]

Failing to make disclosure. Where the broker fails to disclose a material fact **16–072**
which is or should be within his own knowledge, he will almost inevitably be
negligent. Thus the fact that the broker has forged his client's signature on the
proposal form is a material fact even if the client would have readily signed the
form as completed himself. In *Sharp and Roarer Investments Ltd v Sphere Drake
Insurance Plc, The Moonacre*,[13] a broker who did so without authority was held
liable when insurers avoided cover for non-disclosure.

---

[10] [1995] 1 A.C. 501.
[11] [1994] 1 Lloyd's Rep. 83
[12] Potter J. expressed similar views in *Aiken v Stewart Wrightson Members Agency Ltd* [1995] 1
W.L.R. 1281 at 1315–1316: see Ch.19, para.19–028. In *Aneco Reinsurance Underwriting (in
liquidation) v Johnson and Higgins Ltd* [1998] 1 Lloyd's Rep. 565, Cresswell J. stated that it was
highly desirable that means be found to record in a form which precluded later dispute what was said
between brokers and underwriters when the risk was broked. When documents are presented to
underwriters it is good practice to obtain their initial (or "scratch") on them to confirm that they have
been seen. In *Mander v Commercial Union Assurance Co Plc* [1998] Lloyd's Rep. I.R. 93 (for the
facts see para.16–043, above) Rix J. indicated that a broker who failed to record adequately his
presentation of a risk might be in breach of duty, but that there could be no relevant breach of such
a duty unless it were shown that the presentation were faulty.
[13] [1992] 2 Lloyd's Rep. 501: for other grounds upon which the broker was held liable, see paras
16–058, 16–093 and 16–097, above.

16–073   In *Coolee Ltd v Wing Heath & Co*[14] the claimants were engaged in quarrying sand from pits. They instructed the first defendants, who were insurance brokers but not Lloyd's brokers, to arrange employers' liability insurance for them. The first defendants employed the second defendants, who were Lloyd's brokers, to effect the insurance. The claimants did not originally use explosives in their work and they so stated on the proposal form. When the policy came up for renewal the claimants sent a letter to the first defendants in which they mentioned that they had started using explosives. The first defendants did not appreciate the significance of this point. However, they forwarded a copy of the letter to the second defendants. The second defendants, too, did not notice the point, with the result that the underwriters were never informed. Two workmen were subsequently injured in an explosion, and the underwriters denied liability. Rowlatt J. held that the first defendants were negligent in failing to spot the point and draw it to the attention of the second defendants. On receiving the letter "they ought to have turned up their record of insurance and had the matter adjusted with underwriters". The second defendants were also negligent in failing to notice the point for themselves. Rowlatt J. held that both defendants were liable for the whole of the claimants' loss.

16–074   **Duty to advise the client.** The insurance broker should advise his client of the duty to disclose all circumstances material to the insurance, and the consequences of failing to do so.[15] Rule 4.3.2 of the ICOB sourcebook imposes an obligation on a broker to "explain to the customer his duty to disclose all circumstances material to the insurance and the consequences of any failure to make such disclosure, both before the non-investment contract commences and throughout the duration of the contract."

16–075   The client may not appreciate which facts are "material". It is part of the insurance broker's expertise to recognise matters which ought to be disclosed and he should make sure that they are disclosed to the insurers.[16] In *Akedian Co Ltd v Royal Insurance Australia Ltd*,[17] Byrne J. described the broker's duty as follows:

> "The duty of a broker is to disclose material facts known to it and to have a knowledge and understanding of the requirements of the law relating to the duty to disclose and,

---

[14] (1930) 47 T.L.R. 78.

[15] Para.3.7 of the General Insurance Standards Council Code for Private Customers (2000) states: "We will explain your duty to give Insurers information before cover begins and during the policy, and what may happen if you do not." Para. 18 of the General Insurance Standards Council Commercial Code states: "Members will explain to Commercial Customers their duty to disclose all circumstances material to the insurance and the consequences of any failure to make such disclosure, both before the insurance commences and during the policy."

[16] For example, in *O & R Jewellers Ltd v Terry* [1999] Lloyd's Rep. I.R. 436 (Sir Godfrey le Quesne Q.C., sitting as a deputy High Court judge) the brokers conceded that they were under a duty to advise the claimant jewellers to disclose that the managing director of its parent company had convictions for burglary, if they were aware of that fact. The brokers were also found to be in breach of duty in failing to pass on to insurers information as to where the keys to the insured's safes were kept overnight, a failure which also led to avoidance of the policy.

[17] (1999) 1 V.R. 80, Supreme Court of Victoria. The brokers were found negligent in failing to disclose to insurers the purchase price of machinery which was to be insured, as required by s.24(1) of the Marine Insurance Act 1909.

in particular, as to the materiality of the given fact . . . It is part of the function of a broker to advise its client as to what must be disclosed in this technical area [of Marine Insurance] as well as to communicate the fact or circumstance in question to the insurer so that the policy issued to the insured is not at risk."[18]

If the broker is in doubt as to whether or not a fact is material, the proper and prudent course is to advise the client that it should be disclosed. If in reality the fact is not material, then its disclosure is most unlikely to prejudice the client in obtaining insurance. If in reality the fact is material but it is not disclosed, then it is no defence for the brokers to say that the question was a borderline one or one on which the most eminent lawyers might differ in their conclusion[19]: in *Aiken v Stewart Wrightson Members Agency Ltd*,[20] Potter J., considering the care to be exercised by a reasonably competent Lloyd's managing agent when effecting aggregate excess loss reinsurance for his syndicate, held that the duty "extended to disclosure of facts which were arguably material so as to avoid unnecessary risk of avoidance".[21]

16–076

Duty to make enquiries. The broker's duty in this regard is not limited to spotting material facts contained in the information given by his client. There may be other matters that ought to be disclosed, which the client has not thought it necessary to mention. The broker should take reasonable care to elicit such information for himself.[22] Thus in the Australian case *Ogden & Co Pty Ltd v Reliance Fire Sprinkler Co Pty Ltd*,[23] MacFarlan J. held that it was the duty of the brokers "to collect such information regarding the nature of the company's business and its claims history as the underwriters could properly require, and . . . to pass on that information to the underwriters".[24] This duty is particularly important where the client is a private individual with limited experience of insurance matters. In *McNealy v The Pennine Insurance Co Ltd*[25] it was a material fact that the claimant was a part-time musician. The claimant did not appreciate the significance of the fact and did not communicate it to the brokers.

16–077

---

[18] (1999) 1 V.R. 80 at 86–87.

[19] In *Chariot Inns Ltd v Assicurazioni Generali Spa* [1981] I.R. 199 the broker took the view that certain facts did not have to be disclosed and Keane J., taking broadly the same view, held that the insurers were not entitled to repudiate. The Irish Supreme Court took a different view (viz. that the facts were material and ought to have been disclosed) and accordingly held the brokers liable in negligence.

[20] [1995] 1 W.L.R. 1281: see Ch.19, para.19–028.

[21] *ibid*. at 1313H. In *Akedian Co Ltd v Royal Insurance Australia Ltd* (1999) 1 V.R. 80, Supreme Court of Victoria. Byrne J. suggested that "the test of materiality as it affects the broker's duty to advise the client insured to make a disclosure may be more extensive than the same test as it affects the insurer's right to avoid the policy": *ibid*. at 87.

[22] Rule 4.3 of the ICOB sourcebook provides that an insurance intermediary must take reasonable steps to ensure that any personal recommendation of a policy is suitable for the customer's needs (r.4.3.1). A policy will not be suitable if it is voidable for material non-disclosure. Consequently, the reasonable steps that the intermediary must take will include taking reasonable care to elicit information about any material facts which ought to be disclosed.

[23] [1975] 1 Lloyd's Rep. 52. See para.16–085, below.

[24] *ibid*. at 69.

[25] [1978] 2 Lloyd's Rep. 18, CA. For the facts see para.16–057, above.

The Court of Appeal held that by the exercise of reasonable care the brokers could and should have elicited the matter for themselves.[26]

16–078   There is, however, a limit to the information which a reasonably competent and careful broker can be expected to elicit from the client. To take an extreme example, if an apparently reputable company instructs brokers to arrange insurance of its premises, it can hardly be said that the brokers are negligent if they fail to enquire whether the company's directors have criminal records.[27] In *Lyons v JW Bentley Ltd*[28] brokers effected a householder's comprehensive insurance policy for the claimant. The claimant did not disclose his or his wife's claims history to the brokers, and consequently this was not passed on to the insurers. The insurers later repudiated for non-disclosure. The claimant's claim for negligence against the brokers was dismissed.[29]

16–079   **Reinsurance.** Where a broker is placing a reinsurance treaty he should be careful to describe fully the nature of the underlying risk which he is seeking to reinsure. Failure to do so will expose his client to a risk that the reinsurance will be avoided for non-disclosure and the broker to a claim for damages. In *Aneco Reinsurance Underwriting (in liquidation) v Johnson and Higgins Ltd*[30] brokers failed to advise potential reinsurers under a reinsurance treaty that the underlying reinsurance business in respect of which their client wished to obtain cover was limited to a single facultative/obligatory treaty with a number of Lloyd's syndicates, rather than a quota share treaty.[31] The reinsurers had successfully avoided the treaty in arbitration for non-disclosure and in subsequent court proceedings, Cresswell J. held that the brokers were in breach of duty on the same basis. He also held that the brokers were in breach of duty because they had misrepresented

---

[26] See also *Bolton v New Zealand Insurance Co Ltd* [1995] 1 N.Z.L.R. 224, where the broker negligently failed to ask his client whether there would be any changes to the crew of the yacht to be insured, although the broker should have realised that the identity of the crew was a material fact.

[27] *Fanhaven Pty Ltd v Bain Dawes Northern Pty Ltd* [1982] 2 N.S.W.L.R. 57: the New South Wales Court of Appeal held that brokers were not negligent in these circumstances. The court also held that the brokers were not under a duty to advise the claimants generally as to their duty of disclosure. However, if the broker had notice of some questionable matter the position may be different: *Quinby Enterprises Ltd (in liquidation) v General Accident Fire and Life Assurance Corp Public Ltd Co* [1995] 1 N.Z.L.R. 726, *per* Barker J.

[28] (1944) 77 Ll.L.R. 335.

[29] The claim against the brokers also failed in *Gunns v Par Insurance Brokers* [1997] 1 Lloyd's Rep. 173, Sir Michael Ogden, sitting as a deputy High Court judge. The claimant was dyslexic, but this had not prevented him from becoming a successful businessman, and the suggestion that brokers should have done more than they did because of their client's dyslexia was rejected. The Judge stated: "Stupid, illiterate, senile people, and other such persons in similar categories may well call for a broker to take unusual precautions when proposal forms are filled in. In my view in this case there was no call for [the brokers] to do more than they did."

[30] [1998] 1 Lloyd's Rep. 565. The finding of breach of duty was not challenged on appeal.

[31] Under a facultative/obligatory treaty the reinsured is able to choose which risks are ceded to the reinsurer, who has no choice but to accept them. Under a quota share treaty all risks within the defined parameters must be ceded by the reinsured. Facultative/obligatory treaties are less attractive to reinsurers because they allow the reinsured to select the risks which are reinsured. There is therefore a risk that the reinsured's selection will be unbalanced, producing a concentration of risk (whereas his whole account or defined area of account should be balanced) or that the reinsured will simply choose to reinsure his worst business.

the nature of the proposed reinsurance to the lead underwriter and had failed to disclose this to the following market.

(g) *Making a Misrepresentation to the Insurers*

If the insurance broker makes a representation to the insurers which he knows,   **16–080**
or should know, may be false, he will be liable for any loss thereby caused to the client.[32] For example, in *Warren v Henry Sutton & Co*[33] the claimant instructed the defendants to arrange an extension of his motor insurance policy, so that a friend, Mr Wright, with whom he was proposing to go on holiday, would be permitted to drive his car. The defendants enquired about Mr Wright's driving record and the claimant may have given some such answer as "no convictions so far as I know". The defendants then informed the insurers (incorrectly) that Mr Wright had no accidents, claims or disabilities. Subsequently an accident occurred and the insurers denied liability on the grounds of misrepresentation. The Court of Appeal by a majority[34] held that the defendants were liable on the grounds that nothing said by the claimant justified the positive representation which they made to the insurers. The obligation on a broker not to make a misrepresentation to the insurer exists both before the policy incepts and during the currency of the policy.[35]

Approval by the client. If the client expressly approves or confirms a commu-   **16–081**
nication from the brokers to his insurers containing misrepresentations, he cannot thereafter hold the brokers liable for the consequences.[36] In *Bell v Tinmouth*[37] the client wanted to insure his paintings while on display at M's house. The client referred his broker to M for information about the house and M inaccurately stated that the house was permanently occupied. The paintings were stolen in M's absence and insurers successfully denied cover. The client's claim against

---

[32] e.g. *Everett v Hogg Robinson & Gardner Mountain (Insurance) Ltd* [1973] 2 Lloyd's Rep. 217 (broker wrongly stated that no plastics were used by the insured); *Sharp and Roarer Investments Ltd v Sphere Drake Insurance Plc, The Moonacre* [1992] 2 Lloyd's Rep. 501 (broker who forged his client's signature on the proposal form without his client's authority thereby made a misrepresentation to insurers and so was in breach of duty to his client); and *Akedian Co Ltd v Royal Insurance Ltd* (1999) 1 V.R. 80, Supreme Court of Victoria (broker knowingly misrepresented the age of machinery which was to be insured).
[33] [1976] 2 Lloyd's Rep. 276.
[34] Lord Denning M.R. dissented on the grounds that the claimant was well aware of Mr Wright's bad driving record and the cause of the loss was his own failure to disclose it to the brokers.
[35] *Gaughan v Tony McDonagh & Co Ltd* [2005] EWHC 739; [2005] P.N.L.R. 36. The claimant's broker sent a fax to the insurer during the policy period. Subsequently the insurer avoided the policy and alleged that the information contained in the broker's fax was incorrect. The claim form was issued within six years of the fax being sent, but more than six years after the policy period had commenced. The defendant applied for summary judgment on the basis (among others) that the claim was statute barred. Gloster J. dismissed the application, stating: "Clearly, on [the day the fax was sent] the defendant was under an obligation to report accurately what it had been told by the claimant. It cannot be said that, as broker, the defendant was in any sense *functus officio* or was discharged from any continuing obligation at that stage."
[36] See *Commonwealth Insurance Co of Vancouver v Groupe Spinks SA* [1983] 1 Lloyd's Rep. 67, 82, *per* Lloyd J.
[37] (1988) 53 D.L.R. (4th) 731, British Columbia Court of Appeal.

the broker failed, the broker reasonably having relied upon the information he received from M and having transmitted it reasonably accurately to insurers.[38]

16–082   The factual basis for a finding that brokers were in breach of duty for making a misrepresentation to insurers will often also support a finding of breach for failing to disclose material facts. Thus, in *Aneco Reinsurance Underwriting (in liquidation) v Johnson and Higgins Ltd*,[39] Cresswell J. held that the brokers were also in breach of duty for misrepresenting the nature of the underlying business to reinsurers.

16–083   **Completion of the proposal form.** Where new insurance is being arranged for the client, it is quite common for the broker to fill in the proposal form, reading out the questions to the client and recording his answers.[40] The broker's duty in such circumstances was described by Megaw L.J. in *O'Connor v BDB Kirby & Co*[41] in these terms:

> "When the broker took it on himself to fill in the proposal form, the duty upon him was to use such care as was reasonable in all the circumstances towards ensuring that the answers recorded to the questions in the proposal form accurately represented the answers given to the broker by the insured. But the duty was not a duty to ensure that every answer was correct."[42]

---

[38] In *Rivard v Mutual Life Insurance Co of Canada* (1992) 9 O.R. (3d) 545, Ontario Court (General Division) an insurance agent was held to have been in breach of duty to an intended beneficiary of a policy of life insurance for allowing the person whose life was to be insured to represent falsely that he had never smoked. The misrepresentation was unequivocal and the basis upon which the agent (who had some reason to question what was said) was held negligent is not clear. Yates J. appears to have applied a particularly rigorous standard of care.

[39] [1998] 1 Lloyd's Rep. 565 (discussed in para.16–079, above). Cresswell J.'s finding of breach of duty was not challenged on appeal. A similar duplication of findings was made in *Sharp and Roarer Investments Ltd v Sphere Drake Insurance Plc, The Moonacre* [1992] 2 Lloyd's Rep. 501 (discussed in paras 16–058, 16–072, 16–093 and 16–097), above.

[40] Para.19 of the General Insurance Standards Council Commercial Code states: "Members will make it clear to Commercial Customers that all answers or statements given on a proposal form, claim form, or any other material document, are the Commercial Customer's own responsibility. Commercial Customers should always be asked to check the accuracy of information provided." Para.20 provides: "If Members believe that any disclosure of material facts by their Commercial Customers is not true, fair or complete, they will request their Commercial Customers to make the necessary true, fair or complete disclosure, and if this is not forthcoming must consider declining to continue acting on their Commercial Customer's behalf."

[41] [1972] 1 Q.B. 90, 101C. See also *Hudson Turner Furs Ltd v American Insurance Co* (1964) 43 D.L.R. (2d) 323 (Ontario High Court) where the broker read out and explained the questions on the proposal form to the insured and wrote down the answers. He did not show the completed form to the insured. He was held not to be liable when the insurers avoided liability for breach of a warranty made by answers to those questions. The client's appeal was dismissed (1965) 48 D.L.R. (2d) 508.

[42] See also *Moore v Zerfahs* [1999] Lloyd's Rep. P.N. 144 in which Stuart-Smith L.J. stated: "It was not the responsibility of the [broker] to advise [the claimant] as to the financial wisdom of the loan, merely to complete the application form honestly and carefully." The broker may be absolved from the consequences of negligence in this regard, if the client checks the proposal form and fails to correct the errors: see para.16–109, below. See also example (20) of the Insurance Brokers Registration Council Code of Conduct (SI 1994/2569): "In the completion of the proposal form . . . insurance brokers shall make it clear that all answers are the client's own responsibility. The client should always be asked to check the details and told that the inclusion of incorrect information may result, inter alia, in a claim being repudiated. On request, a client shall be supplied with a copy of the proposal form . . . at the time of completion."

Different considerations arise where the questions in the proposal form are directed to matters of which the brokers have greater knowledge than their clients, such as details of previous claims which the brokers handled or details of previous insurance which the brokers arranged. The brokers are then under a duty to answer such questions correctly and cannot rely upon their clients.[43]

The broker cannot avoid his responsibility by putting evasive answers in the proposal form. This is illustrated by the Australian case of *Ogden & Co Pty Ltd v Reliance Fire Sprinkler Co Pty Ltd*.[44] In that case brokers completed and signed a proposal form for public and products liability insurance on behalf of the F Group of Companies. Questions 1 and 2 of the proposal form, relating to prior claims and cancellations of policies, were bracketed together and answered "not known to brokers". In fact the Group had a record of claims which ought to have been disclosed. MacFarlan J. held that the answer to questions 1 and 2 amounted to misrepresentation. The insurers were entitled to repudiate both for misrepresentation and for non-disclosure of material facts. He held that in giving the answer "not known to brokers", the brokers were in breach of their implied contractual duty to exercise reasonable skill and care.[45]

16–084

(h) *Failing to Keep the Client Properly Informed as to the Existence or Terms of Cover*

Existence of cover. An insurance broker should keep the client properly informed as to the presence or absence of cover. If the insurance broker is unable to effect insurance at all[46] or, alternatively, is unable to effect insurance on the specific terms required,[47] he is under a duty to notify the client promptly. Where a broker receives information casting doubt on the reliability or solvency of an insurer of one of his clients, he should pass that information to his client even if

16–085

---

[43] *Dunbar v A & B Painters Ltd* [1985] 2 Lloyd's Rep. 616: proposal form contained misstatement on matters within the brokers' knowledge. Brokers held liable. This case went to the Court of Appeal, but not on the issue of liability: [1986] 2 Lloyd's Rep. 38. See further para.16–127, below. See also *Porter v Prudential of America General Insur. Co* (1995) 146 N.S.R.(2d) 81, Nova Scotia Supreme Court: proposal form completed by broker. Form silent on client's previous loss of which the broker was aware. Broker held negligent in completing the proposal incorrectly and not in accordance with the information he had been provided with, and in not asking the client all the relevant questions.

[44] [1975] 1 Lloyd's Rep. 52.

[45] *ibid.* at 71: "The answer divorced from the anterior circumstances to which I have already referred was, of course, untrue. Secondly, in its character as an untrue statement it exposed the client, Reliance, and the validity of the policy thereafter to be issued to the risk, as should have been well known to an experienced broker, that the policy would be avoided."

[46] *Smith v Lascelles* (1788) 2 T.R. 187; *Reardon v Kings Mutual Insurance Co* (1981) 120 D.L.R. (3d) 196 and see generally paras 16–042 to 16–046, above.

[47] *Callander v Oelrichs* (1838) 5 Bing.N.C. 58 and see paras 16–050 to 16–053, above. Similarly, if the broker is instructed to obtain insurance cover generally for the client's business, he is under a duty to notify the client if there is any foreseeable risk which is not covered by the policy he effects: *Fine's Flowers Ltd v General Accident Assurance Co of Canada* (1977) 81 D.L.R. (3d) 139; *Mitor Investments Pty Ltd v General Accident Fire and Life Assurance Corp Ltd* [1984] W.A.R. 365. Thus *Dueck v Manitoba Mennonite Mutual Insurance Co* (1993) 83 Man.R.(2d) 291: agent negligently failed to advise clients that new policy was for specific perils rather than for all risks.

he is personally satisfied with the insurer.[48] Where, however, the insurance broker receives instructions from a trade union or association of which the insured is a member, his duties to keep the insured informed are necessarily more restricted.[49]

16–086   A claimant who suffers a loss while uninsured may put his case on the basis that, had he known he was uninsured, then he would have taken greater care to avoid the loss which he suffered. However, in *Sharif v Garrett & Co*[50] the Court of Appeal indicated that such a claim is unlikely to succeed. For an insured is required to act in the same way as a prudent uninsured. Accordingly, an insurance broker cannot be expected to foresee that someone who thinks he is insured would take different precautions if he knew he was uninsured.

16–087   **Where client becomes uninsured.** If the client becomes uninsured for any reason, the broker should notify him as a matter of urgency. In *London Borough of Bromley v Ellis*[51] the brokers were held liable for failing to inform the defendant that his motor insurance policy had been cancelled by the insurers. In *Osman v J Ralph Moss Ltd*[52] the defendants arranged motor insurance for the claimant with a company which subsequently became insolvent. The defendants then sent a letter to the claimant, which was ambiguous in its terms and did not indicate the seriousness of his position. The defendants were held liable for (inter alia) failing to warn the claimant in clear terms that he was uninsured. In *Youell v Bland Welch & Co Ltd (No.2)* (the "*Superhulls Cover*" case)[53] a further ground upon which the brokers were held to have been negligent was breach of a duty to ensure that the insurers were warned that reinsurance cover was about to expire because of the 48-month cut-off clause and to exercise reasonable skill and care to make available to the insurers reasonable extensions of cover under the reinsurance contract.[54]

---

[48] *Lewis v Tressider Andrews Associates Pty Ltd* [1987] 2 Qd.R. 533 (for the earlier facts, see para.16–067, above). After effecting the insurance the broker received further communications which tended to show that the insurer was not reliable or sound, but failed to pass the information on to his client. He was held to have been negligent.

[49] In *Norwest Refrigeration Services Pty Ltd v Bain Dawes (W.A.) Pty Ltd* (1984) 55 A.L.R. 509, High Court of Australia, brokers received instructions from a fishermen's co-operative to arrange insurance of the claimants' fishing vessel. The vessel was duly added to the fleet policy which the brokers had previously arranged. Under the policy liability was excluded in the case of a vessel which did not have a current certificate of survey. The claimants were not told of this exclusion and the vessel was lost at a time when it did not have a current certificate of survey. The co-operative were held liable in negligence, but the brokers were held not liable: "we think it was reasonable for Bain Dawes to proceed on the basis that the Co-operative, in the performance of its role of caring for its members, would have made any specific enquiry that was considered necessary in a particular case and that it was sufficient for it simply to act as an intermediary between the Co-operative and the insurer consistently with any specific instructions received from the former". *ibid.* at 517.

[50] [2001] EWCA 1269; [2002] Lloyd's Rep. I.R. 11 (for the facts see para.16–134, below).

[51] [1971] 1 Lloyd's Rep. 97.

[52] [1970] 1 Lloyd's Rep. 313.

[53] [1990] 2 Lloyd's Rep. 431 (for the facts, see para.16–022, above).

[54] See also *Grainary Restaurant Ltd v American Home Insurance Co* (1987) 81 N.B.R. (2d) 151 and 205 A.P.R. 151, New Brunswick CA: brokers were held liable for failing to inform their client that insurers would not grant further endorsements suspending a condition excluding cover if the premises were unoccupied for more than 30 days and that the existing endorsements had expired.

There are, however, limits to a broker's duties when his client is in danger of becoming uninsured. In *Pacific and General Insurance Co Ltd*[55] the reinsured went into liquidation without putting the broker in funds to pay the premium for its reinsurance. The provisional liquidator made it clear to the brokers that funds would not be forthcoming, but gave them no instructions to cancel the policies. The brokers' accounts at Lloyd's were automatically debited with the premiums, although it was held by Moore-Bick J. that they were not personally liable to the underwriters for the premiums and had had no authority from the reinsured to make the payments. The reinsurers cancelled the policies *ab initio*, on the suggestion of the brokers. The reinsured claimed against the brokers on the ground that they should have advised the provisional liquidator before doing so. Moore-Bick J. dismissed the claim, observing that once the provisional liquidator had decided not to provide funds to pay the premium the brokers were entitled to protect their own interests and that, if the premiums were not paid, there was little if anything the brokers could do to prevent the reinsurers from cancelling them.

16–088

Provision of policy documents. Chapter 5 of the ICOB sourcebook contains rules which impose obligations on insurance intermediaries to provide information about policies to their clients.[56] Rule 5.3 requires that an intermediary provides a policy summary[57] to a retail customer before the conclusion of the contract, and a policy document immediately after conclusion of the contract. Where the client is a commercial customer, Rule 5.4 requires that before the contract is concluded an intermediary must provide its client with "sufficient information to enable the commercial customer to make an informed decision about the contract being proposed." On conclusion of the contract an intermediary must provide his commercial customer with a policy document "promptly."[58]

16–089

---

[55] [1997] L.R.L.R. 65

[56] The General Insurance Standards Council Codes also imposed obligations regarding the provision of policy documents. Para.4.3 of the General Insurance Standards Council Code for Private Customers (2000) states: "We will send you full policy documentation promptly." Similarly, para.27 of the General Insurance Standards Council Commercial Code states: "Members will forward full policy documentation without avoidable delay where this is not included with the confirmation of cover".

[57] The policy summary must contain certain specified information, including: "significant or unusual exclusions or limitations" (ICOB 5.5.5).

[58] Before obligations were imposed on brokers by the General Insurance Standards Council's Codes and by the ICOB rules, it seem that, whilst it was prudent practice to send the client a copy of the cover note or policy immediately, the broker was not generally under a legal duty to do so: *United Mills Agencies Ltd v RE Harvey Bray Co* [1951] 2 Lloyd's Rep. 631. In that case the claimants instructed the defendants to effect export cover on their goods, which were at the time in the hands of packers. The claimants omitted to tell the defendants that there was no existing insurance to cover the goods whilst they were at the packers. The defendants duly effected export insurance, but did not insert any clause relating to attachment of risk while the goods were at the packers. Cover was effected on the Monday morning. On the Wednesday the defendants sent a copy of the cover note to the claimants, which was received the following day. On the night of Wednesday/Thursday a fire occurred at the premises of the packers, in which the claimants' goods were destroyed. McNair J. held: (i) the defendants, who were instructed to effect export insurance, were not negligent in failing to tell the claimants that such insurance did not cover the goods while at the packers. The defendants were entitled to assume that the claimants had conducted their business prudently and had arranged the appropriate form of insurance while the goods were at the packers; (ii) the defendants were not

16–090   **Advice on terms of cover.** If any onerous term or restriction is included in the policy, this should be drawn to the attention of the client[59] and a failure to do so will amount to a breach of duty.[60] If necessary the broker should explain to his client the nature and effect of any significant or unusual restrictions or exclusions in the policy.[61]

16–091   **Renewal.** It is the normal practice of insurance brokers to notify their client shortly before a policy falls due for renewal.[62] Chapter 5 of the ICOB sourcebook contains rules imposing obligations on insurance intermediaries in relation to

---

negligent in delaying for two days before sending a copy of the cover note to the claimants. McNair J. accepted that it was the general practice of insurance brokers to notify clients of the cover as soon as possible, but held that failure to comply with this practice was not negligent. See para.16–038, above.

[59] Para.3.3 of the General Insurance Standards Council Code for Private Customers (2000) states: "We will explain all the main features of the products and services we offer, including: any significant or unusual restrictions or exclusions; any significant conditions or obligations which you must meet." Para.10 of the General Insurance Standards Council Commercial Code states: "Members will advise Commercial Customers of the key features of the insurance proposed, including the essential cover and benefits, any significant or unusual restrictions, exclusions, conditions or obligations, and the period of cover. In so doing, Members will take into consideration the knowledge held by their Commercial Customers when deciding to what extent it is appropriate for Commercial Customers to have the terms and conditions of a particular insurance explained to them." In the Australian case of *Austcan Investments Pty Ltd v Sun Alliance Insurance Ltd* (1992) 57 S.A.S.R. 343 brokers were held to have assumed a duty to advise their client of a clause whereby the policy was avoided if there was a change of use of the insured premises during the policy period unless agreed by insurers.

[60] See *King (or Fiehl) v Chambers & Newman (Insurance Brokers) Ltd* [1963] 2 Lloyd's Rep. 130 (client adequately informed; brokers held not liable); *Theriault v Assurance Levesque et autres* (1995) 162 N.B.R.(2d) 365, New Brunswick Court of Queen's Bench (broker negligent in failing to advise his client that his property was not covered for damages caused by freezing because the property was vacant). In *Youell v Bland Welch & Co Ltd (No.2)* [1990] 2 Lloyd's Rep. 431 (the *"Superhulls Cover"* case) (for the facts see para.16–022, above) Phillips J. held that the brokers were in breach of duty in failing to inform insurers of the 48-month cut-off of cover under the reinsurance after that reinsurance had been obtained for them (this was a separate breach from the failure to advise insurers of the clause when inviting them to enter the insurance contracts). In *JW Bollom & Co Ltd v Byas Mosley & Co Ltd* [1999] Lloyd's Rep. P.N. 598 the brokers accepted that their duty extended to taking reasonable steps to ensure that the client is aware of the nature and terms of insurance and, in particular, drawing to his attention and if necessary explaining any terms the breach of which might result in his being uninsured. In *George Barkes (London) Ltd v LFC (1988) Ltd* [2000] 1 P.N.L.R. 21, H.H.J. Hallgarten Q.C. the claimant instructed brokers to renew its contents and property insurance. The brokers procured insurance from a new insurer which provided a lower quotation that the original insurer. Subsequently a theft occurred in circumstances which were excluded under the terms of the new policy (but which would have been covered by the original policy), and the insurers declined to provide any indemnity. The brokers were found to have acted negligently in failing to advise the claimant of the restrictions in the new policy.

[61] In *Harvest Trucking Co Ltd v Davis* [1991] 2 Lloyd's Rep. 638 Judge Diamond Q.C. (sitting as a High Court judge) said: "If the only insurance which the intermediary is able to obtain contains unusual, limiting or exempting provisions which, if they are not brought to the notice of the assured, may result in the policy not conforming to the client's reasonable and known requirements, the duty falling on the agent, namely, to exercise reasonable care in the duties which he has undertaken, may in those circumstances entail that the intermediary should bring the existence of the limiting or exempting provisions to the express notice of the client, discuss the nature of the problem with him and take reasonable steps either to obtain alternative insurance, if any is available, or alternatively to advise the client as to the best way of acting so that his business procedures conform to any requirements laid down by the policy." *ibid.* at 643.

[62] Para.5.3 of the General Insurance Standards Council Code for Private Customers (2000) states: "We will tell you when you need to renew you policy or, when it will end, in time to allow you to

renewal.[63] Rule 5.3.18[64] provides that, if the insurer is willing to renew a policy for a retail client, then at least 21 days prior to renewal the intermediary should take reasonable steps to provide its retail customer with certain specified information, including any changes to the terms of the policy.[65] If the insurer is not willing to invite renewal then the intermediary must take reasonable steps to notify the customer of that fact. Rule 5.4.11 contains similar provisions in relation to commercial customers. A broker's duty on renewal does not oblige him to renew a policy automatically without his client's instructions.[66]

If, on renewal of the policy, there is any significant variation in the terms, the   **16–092** broker should bring this to the specific attention of his client, who might not otherwise notice the change, even if sent a copy of the policy.[67] Where the terms of insurance are varied on renewal, but there is delay in issuing the new policy, the broker clearly ought to inform his client of the material changes in the terms. Thus in *Mint Security Ltd v Blair*[68] Lloyd's brokers were held liable for failing to inform the client's principal insurance brokers that upon renewal of a cash in transit policy, the terms of a proposal form completed two-and-a-half years earlier were incorporated. In the intervening two-and-a-half years the clients had varied their procedures from those described in the original proposal form. The

---

consider and arrange any continuing cover you may need." Similarly para.32 of the General Insurance Standards Council Commercial Code states: "Members will notify Commercial Customers of the renewal or expiry of their policy in time to allow them to consider and arrange any continuing cover they may need."

[63] A broker's duties in relation to renewal have been considered in 2 Canadian cases. In *Morash v Lockhart Ritchie Ltd* (1978) 95 D.L.R. (3d) 647 the defendant brokers, who failed to send the claimant a renewal form for his fire insurance or to inform him that the policy was expiring, were held liable in negligence. However, in the later Canadian case of *Bijeau v Pelletier and the Co-operators General Insurance Co* (1996) 176 N.B.R.(2d) 241, New Brunswick CA (claim against insurer's agent dismissed because agent had not given the claimant an undertaking to renew the policy) it was held that there is no duty to renew an insurance policy, or to notify an insured that a policy is about to expire, unless the broker has expressly or (as in *Morash*) impliedly undertaken to effect renewal. See also *King v Sullivan Insurance Inc* (1993) 109 Nfld. & P.E.I.R. 227, where the broker not only failed to inform his clients that their policy had not been renewed, but led them to believe that it had been.

[64] Rule 5.3.18 does not apply where the intermediary has reason to believe the retail customer does not wish to renew the policy, or the intermediary has notified the customer that it does not wish to act for him at renewal, or the customer has already been advised that the insurer will not invite renewal (see r.5.3.22).

[65] The information is set out in ICOB rule 5.3.21 and includes "a statement of any changes to the terms of the policy" and "an explanation of those changes, where necessary."

[66] In *Roy v Edmond Vienneau Assurance Ltee* (1986) 67 N.B.R. (2d) 16 and 172 A.P.R. 16, New Brunswick CA the insured received a renewal notice but failed to act on it. He sued his broker after suffering a loss when uninsured, alleging that the broker owed a duty to renew automatically as a result of a conversation some years before. Even if there had been such a conversation, the brokers had continued to renew only upon receipt of instructions and the claim failed.

[67] *Harvest Trucking Co Ltd v Davis* [1991] 2 Lloyd's Rep. 638 (H.H.J. Diamond Q.C. sitting as a High Court judge): intermediary held liable for failing to draw client's attention to new clause excluding cover for theft from vehicles which were not individually attended, a new and onerous provision. In *Michaels v Valentine* (1923) 16 Ll. Rep. 244, Mayor's and City of London Ct, where the broker sent a copy of the new policy to the client without commenting on one important variation in the terms, it was held that the broker was not in breach of duty. However, this case is only briefly reported and it is doubtful whether it could now be relied upon even as persuasive authority.

[68] [1982] 1 Lloyd's Rep. 188.

insurers escaped liability on this ground, and the claimants recovered against the Lloyd's brokers.[69]

(i) *Failing to Give Proper Advice*[70]

16–093   Anyone who gives advice on insurance matters in the course of his business owes a duty to exercise reasonable skill and care.[71] In the case of insurance brokers, the giving of advice is one of their most important functions.[72] Insurance brokers are expected to have a basic knowledge of insurance law,[73] to understand the insurance policies which they effect and to be reasonably familiar with the insurance market, or at least that part of it in which they practise. In *Osman v J Ralph Moss Ltd*[74] the Court of Appeal considered that one respect in which the defendants were negligent[75] was in their initial advice to the claimant to insure with a company which was generally known to be in financial difficulties.[76] In *Strong & Pearl v S Allison & Co Ltd*[77] the defendants failed to appreciate that unless and until the insurers agreed to vary the terms, the policy which they had effected would only cover the vessel if it were laid up in one particular boatyard. Accordingly the second ground upon which the defendants were held liable[78] was that they had incorrectly advised the claimants that the vessel would be covered if it were moved to a different boatyard. A similar conclusion was reached in *Sharp and Roarer Investments Ltd v Sphere Drake Insurance Plc, The Moonacre*.[79] In *Engel v Janzen*[80] the insured were going abroad for two months and asked their broker whether they should cancel their motor insurance policies. The broker advised that they should without pointing out that if they did cancel they would lose insurance cover against personal injury by uninsured or under-insured motorists. The insured acted on the advice and suffered serious injuries

---

[69] [1982] 1 Lloyd's Rep. 188 at 199–200.

[70] Insurance brokers who are subject to the regulatory regime of FSMA (as to which see para.16–007, above) may incur civil liability to their clients under s.150 of the Act for failure to give proper advice. For example they may be in breach of the "Suitability" rules.

[71] *M'Neill v Millen & Co Ltd* [1907] 2 I.R. 328 (garage owners held liable for wrongly advising claimant that his car was insured); *Gomer v Pitt & Scott* (1922) 12 Ll. Rep. 115; *Random Ford Mercury Sales Ltd v Noseworthy* (1992) 95 D.L.R. (4th) 168 (agent negligently advising unpaid vendor of boat that his interest was covered under insurance arranged for the purchaser; vendor allowed purchaser to take boat which was lost).

[72] The IBRC Code of Conduct provides that brokers shall "provide advice objectively and independently". Code of Conduct, example (1). See also example (11): "Insurance brokers shall explain to the client the differences in, and the relative costs of, the principal types of insurance . . . which in the opinion of the insurance broker, would suit the client's needs . . . "

[73] See para.16–039, above.

[74] [1979] 1 Lloyd's Rep. 313. For the facts see para.16–087, above.

[75] In addition to the ground discussed at para.16–087, above.

[76] See also *Lewis v Tressider Andrews Associates Pty Ltd* [1987] 2 Qd.R. 533, discussed at para.16–067, above.

[77] (1926) 25 Ll. Rep. 504. For the facts see para.16–052, above.

[78] In addition to the ground discussed above at para.16–052, above.

[79] [1992] 2 Lloyd's Rep. 501 (for the facts see para.16–058, above).

[80] (1990) 65 D.L.R. (4th) 760, British Columbia CA.

at the hands of an impecunious and uninsured motorist. The broker was held liable.[81]

16–094 There are, of course, limitations on a broker's duty to advise. The duty to advise is contingent upon and limited by the insured's description of the nature of his business.[82] A broker will not necessarily be under a duty to advise as to coverage beyond that specifically sought by his client. Nor will a broker be held liable for failing to advise a client that his policy does not provide a certain type of cover if the client is already aware of that and has made his own, informed decision not to obtain the additional cover.[83] The scope and nature of a broker's duty to advise will also be affected by the nature of his client and other surrounding circumstances. For example, a broker acting for a large organisation with an experienced property department will not be expected to give the same level of advice as one acting for an individual or small company.[84]

16–095 **Advice on the law.** In *Sarginson Bros v Keith Moulton & Co*[85] the claimants (timber merchants and manufacturers) asked the defendants (insurance brokers) whether it was possible to insure their stock of timber against war risks under the Commodity Insurance Scheme. This scheme was contained in the War Risks Insurance Act 1939 and rious statutory instruments. The defendants replied, incorrectly, that the timber could not be insured under the scheme. Before giving that advice the only step taken by the defendants was to consult one insurance company. The insurance company told the defendants that a builder's stock of timber did not come within the scheme and showed them certain entries in the list of Board of Trade replies to questions concerning the scheme (which were not directly on point). Hallett J. considered that the defendants had not taken "the steps which a reasonably prudent person would clearly have deemed necessary before that answer could be given with reasonable safety" and accordingly held that the defendants were liable in negligence.

---

[81] See also *Fletcher v Manitoba Public Insurance Co* (1990) 74 D.L.R. (4th) 636: public insurance corporation held to be in breach of tortious duty of care in failing to advise insured of availability and importance of underinsured motorist coverage. This decision was followed in *Payer v Peerless Plating Rack Co Ltd* (1994) 37 O.R.(3d) 781. In the latter case, brokers were held liable for failing to advise their client of a life insurance policy taken out by his employer, the benefit of which he could have retained when his employment ended. These Canadian decisions followed *Fine's Flowers Ltd v General Accident Assurance Co of Canada* (1977) 81 D.L.R. 135 (as to which see para.16–013, above).

[82] *St Isidore Asphalte Ltee v Luminex Signs Ltd* (1996) 176 N.B.R. (2d) 135, New Brunswick Court of Queen's Bench (for facts see para.16–059 n.78, above).

[83] *Diamond v Ranger Unicity Insurance Brokers Ltd* (1997) 119 Man.R. (2d) 99 (clients found to be sophisticated and intelligent people who took a keen interest in their insurance cover; their claim against brokers for failing to advise them to obtain sewer back-up cover failed on the facts). See also *Kalkinis v Allstate Insurance Co of Canada* (1998) 41 O.R. (3d) 528 where the Court of Appeal for Ontario, when allowing an appeal by an insurance agent (who was treated as having similar duties to an insurance broker), stressed the need for a claimant to show that he had relied upon the broker to advise as alleged and that the broker knew or ought to have known that he was being relied upon to give such advice.

[84] See *William Jackson & Sons Ltd v Oughtred & Harrison (Insurance) Ltd* [2002] Lloyd's Rep. I.R. 230 (Morison J.) (for the facts of which see para.16–063, above).

[85] (1942) 73 Ll. Rep. 104.

16–096   This case raised the question, what standard of skill and competence is expected of the insurance broker when called upon to advise on a matter of law. Hallett J. approached the question, as one of general principle, in this way:

> "In my view, if people occupying a professional position take it upon themselves to give advice upon a matter directly connected with their own profession, then they are responsible for seeing that they are equipped with a reasonable degree of skill and a reasonable stock of information so as to render it reasonably safe for them to give that particular piece of advice. One has a great deal of sympathy, I suppose, with every professional man nowadays, at the way in which his operations are affected by a mass of emergency legislation, emergency regulations and emergency rules and orders. They pour out in unceasing flow, and I can well understand that it is most difficult for those concerned to keep up to date with them. I can well understand that there is always a danger of their being caught out by something. I do not for one moment say they are bound to be acquainted with everything. I think it is open to them always to say: 'Well, this is a difficult matter; I shall have to look this up; I shall have to make enquiries.' They can say, if they like: 'This is a matter for a solicitor, not for me'; and if they went to a solicitor he very likely would say: 'You had better consult Counsel.' No-one is under obligation to give advice on those difficult matters. If they are going to give advice, they can always qualify their advice and make it plain that it is a matter which is doubtful or upon which further investigation is desirable; but if they do take it upon themselves to express a definite and final opinion, knowing, as they must have known in this case, that their clients would act upon that, then I do think they are responsible if they give that information without having taken reasonable care to furnish themselves with such information, of whatever kind it may be, as will render it reasonably safe, in the view of a reasonably prudent man, to express that opinion."[86]

Similar views were expressed by Hutley J.A. in the New South Wales Court of Appeal.[87]

16–097   **Seeking the insurer's advice.** If the client inquires whether his insurance policy covers a particular risk, and there is any doubt about the matter, the broker commonly refers the question to the insurers. Indeed he would be well advised to do so.[88] In these circumstances the broker's "advisory" function involves little more than acting as a messenger.[89] It is, however, vital that he should accurately transmit the client's queries and the insurers' advice. Any failure in this regard

---

[86] (1942) 73 Ll. Rep. 104 at 107.

[87] *Fanhaven Pty Ltd v Bain Dawes Northern Pty Ltd* [1982] 2 N.S.W.L.R. 57, 65: "Because law provides the framework of commerce, sometimes a confining and obstructive framework, professional advisers in the field of commerce cannot avoid giving advice on legal topics. Thus, a broker in advising what policies are required by a business is an adviser on legal matters, namely, the types of risk for which the operation of the business may attract liability and the appropriate policies, and if he takes upon himself to so advise and does not do so competently as a broker, he would be liable for loss occasioned by his failure and he could not avoid it by pointing to the fact that his advice involved legal issues."

[88] In *Dodson v Dodson Insurance Services* [2001] 1 W.L.R. 1012 the Court of Appeal suggested (at para.21) that, if there was some uncertainty about the scope of cover afforded by a policy, then the broker should not give advice in unqualified terms or without first confirming the scope of cover with insurer.

[89] e.g. *Coles v Sir Frederick Young (Insurances) Ltd* (1929) 33 Ll. Rep. 83.

would normally amount to negligence, if the client suffers loss in consequence.[90] If a broker chooses to answer the query without recourse to the insurer, he does so at his peril.[91] Thus in *Sharp and Roarer Investments Ltd v Sphere Drake Insurance Plc, The Moonacre*[92] when finding the broker negligent in relation to the houseboat exclusion clause, the Judge[93] said: "If there was any doubt in [the broker's] mind as to the matter it was the duty of the broker to ask the insurers what meaning they attached to the question and the houseboat exclusion."[94]

(j) *Failings after the Risk has been Placed*

A number of cases have raised the question of the extent to which a broker owes   **16–098** a continuing duty to his client after he has placed the risk. This issue may be of particular importance in relation to limitation if proceedings are commenced more than six years after the inception of the risk. It will also be of importance when the acts and omissions complained of occurred after the broker had placed the risk. Given that brokers owe their clients certain duties in relation to renewal, it is clear that the duties owed by a broker do not cease when a risk is placed.[95] The nature and extent of the continuing duty will depend on all the circumstances.

In *Youell v Bland Welch & Co (No.2)*[96] Phillips J. held that the broker owed the   **16–099** reassured a duty to warn him that reinsurance cover was about to expire because of a 48-month cut-off clause which did not apply to the underlying insurance. He also held that the duty extended to taking steps to procure extensions to reinsurance. The post-placement duty arose out of the earlier breach by the broker of his duty in placing the reinsurance which was intended to be on the same terms as the insurance.[97] There had also been a breach of duty by the broker when placing

---

[90] In *Melik & Co Ltd v Norwich Union Fire Insurance Society Ltd* [1980] 1 Lloyd's Rep. 523 the claimants asked their broker, K, whether the insurance of their warehouse premises was still effective, despite a breakdown of the telephones at the premises. After making inadequate inquiries of the insurers, K advised the claimants that they were covered. In the event, Woolf J. held that that advice was correct. If it had not been, however, K would have been liable to the claimants: "it was K's duty to raise the matter much more clearly than he did with the insurers and to get the clear and positive answer [the claimants] required. Instead, he relied upon his own judgment, his own view, that the claimants were insured, and if they were not insured, in my view, he would have been in default in that respect and that would have been sufficient to find liability assuming that there was a loss in respect of that default" (at 534, col.1.).
[91] In *T O'Donoghue Ltd v Harding* [1988] 2 Lloyd's Rep. 281 the brokers answered a query about the extent of cover themselves. Otton J. held that their interpretation of the cover was correct and held the insurers liable. However he went on to say of the broker: "Whether he was wise to give such unequivocal advice to the insured without referring to underwriters is a matter I do not have to decide. Suffice it to say that if I had found the facts marginally different, then Mr Ellis [of the brokers] . . . might well have been shown to be not merely imprudent but even negligent" (at 291, col.1).
[92] [1992] 2 Lloyd's Rep. 501 (for the relevant facts, see para.16–058, above).
[93] A.D. Colman Q.C., sitting as a deputy judge of the High Court.
[94] *ibid.* at 525, col.2.
[95] See para.16–091, above.
[96] [1990] 2 Lloyd's Rep. 431 (Phillips J.) (the facts of which are set out at para.16–022, above).
[97] See *HIH Casualty & General Insurance Ltd v JLT Risk Solutions Ltd* [2006] EWHC 485; [2006] Lloyd's Rep. I.R. 493 (Langley J.) at para.130.

the risk in *Great North Eastern Railway Ltd v JLT Corporate Risks Ltd*.[98] The breach related to the inclusion of a particular exclusion clause in the policy which was contrary to the claimant's instructions. Subsequently a loss occurred in circumstances which fell within the exclusion clause. The insured commenced proceedings against the broker more than six years after the policy had incepted, but less than six years after the loss. The broker applied for summary judgment on the basis that the claim was time barred. Cresswell J. dismissed the application on the basis that it was arguable that the broker owed a continuing duty to the broker up until the loss occurred to obtain the cover requested or to advise that such cover had not been obtained.

16–100 In *HIH Casualty & General Insurance Ltd v JLT Risk Solutions Ltd*,[99] a film finance case, a broker placed reinsurance on behalf of the claimant. Subsequently the broker was sent risk management reports which indicated that there was or might be a breach of a warranty in the claimant's reinsurance policies. Langley J. rejected the broker's submission that it was under no duty to act unless instructed to do so. Instead he held that the broker should have read the reports carefully, and if any of the information contained in them was or ought to have been thought to be a matter of at least potential concern on coverage issues then the broker should have alerted the claimant to it.

16–101 If after the risk has been placed the broker does act on behalf of the insured, then the broker owes the insured a duty to act with reasonable skill and care. For example, in *Gaughan v Tony McDonagh & Co Ltd*[1] the claimant's broker sent a fax to the insurer during the policy period. Subsequently the insurer avoided the policy and alleged that the information contained in the broker's fax was incorrect. In dismissing an application by the broker for summary judgment Gloster J. stated: "Clearly, on [the day the fax was sent] the defendant was under an obligation to report accurately what it had been told by the claimant. It cannot be said that, as broker, the defendant was in any sense *functus officio* or was discharged from any continuing obligation at that stage." In *BP Plc v AON Ltd (No.2)*.[2] the broker owed a duty to make declarations to insurers under an open-cover policy, and was found to have acted negligently in failing to make timely declarations as required.

(k) *Failings relating to Claims against the Insurer*

16–102 Typically when an insured suffers a loss he will inform his broker of the fact, and will rely on the broker to notify his insurer as required. The broker may give the insured further assistance in relation to the making of the claim. When doing so,

---

[98] [2006] EWHC 1478 (Cresswell J.).
[99] [2006] EWHC 485; [2006] Lloyd's Rep. I.R. 493 (Langley J.). See in particular para.133.
[1] [2005] EWHC 739; [2005] P.N.L.R. 36. The claimant's broker sent a fax to the insurer during the policy period. Subsequently the insurer avoided the policy and alleged that the information contained in the broker's fax was incorrect. The claim form was issued within six years of the fax being sent, but more than six years after the policy period had commenced. The defendant applied for summary judgment on the basis (among others) that the claim was statute barred.
[2] [2006] EWHC 424; [2006] 1 All E.R. (Comm) 789 (Colman J.).

the broker must act with due skill, care and diligence.[3] The broker must take care to ensure that he notifies the correct insurer, complies with any time-limits for notifications (so far as still possible) and complies with (or advises the insured to comply with) any notification requirements.

The brokers duty includes an obligation to assess the information provided to **16–103** it and consider what notifications (if any) should be made to the insurer. In *Alexander Forbes Europe Ltd v SBJ Ltd*[4] it was alleged that the brokers had been negligent in failing to notify "circumstances likely to give rise to a claim." The brokers maintained they had only been instructed to notify a specific claim. The brokers were found to have acted negligently in failing to notify circumstances to the insurer based on information received from the insured. David Mackie Q.C. described the duties of a broker who has received information from an insured as follows:

> "Brokers owe duties going beyond those of a post box. It was for the brokers to get a grip on the proposed notification, to appraise it and to ensure that the information was relayed to the right place in the correct form . . . it was the duty of [the brokers] to have a strategy in place . . . that ensured that when such information was received from clients, the broker was alive to making such notifications accurately and promptly."

The insured will be unable to bring a claim against the insurer if neither he nor **16–104** his broker knows or has a record of the identity of the relevant insurer. Such a situation gave rise to a claim against Lloyd's brokers in *Johnston v Leslie Goodwin Financial Services Ltd* [1995] L.R.L.R. 472. The Lloyd's brokers had failed to maintain records of reinsurance obtained for a Lloyd's syndicate so as to enable it to make claims (it is an established custom in the Lloyd's market for brokers to retain such information for underwriters). Clarke J. held that the brokers owed a general duty to exercise reasonable skill and care to collect claims on the reinsured's behalf. As part of that duty they were obliged to retain the original slip "for so long as a reasonable broker would regard a claim as possible" so that the reinsurers could be identified.

3. DAMAGES

An award of damages is the principal remedy which the court will grant for **16–105** breach of duty by an insurance broker. Since an insurance broker is not normally remunerated by his client, no question of forfeiture or repayment of fees generally arises.[5]

---

[3] *Bousfield v Creswell* (1810) 2 Camp. 545; Rule 7.4.3 of the ICOB sourcebook states: "An insurance intermediary, when acting for a customer in relation to a claim, must act with due care, skill and diligence." See also the GISC Codes for Commercial (paras 35–38) and Private Codes (para.6).
[4] [2003] Lloyd's Rep. I.R. 432 (David Mackie Q.C. sitting as a deputy High Court judge).
[5] Where the client is charged a fee, presumably the same principles would apply to insurance brokers as to other professions. See Ch.3, paras 3–008 *et seq.*

(a) *Remoteness*

16–106 The assessment of damages is subject, in every case, to the overriding principle that the damage in respect of which compensation is sought must be sufficiently proximate to the insurance broker's breach of duty. Broadly speaking, this means that (a) the breach of duty must have "caused" the damage,[6] and (b) the damage in question was foreseeable.[7]

(b) *Causation*

16–107 Whether the claim is brought in contract or tort, it is first necessary to determine whether the insurance broker's breach of duty was "the cause" of the damage of which complaint is made.[8] Arguments as to causation normally take one of three forms: (1) sometimes it is contended that a particular error or omission on the claimant's part was the sole reason why he was uninsured; (2) sometimes it is argued that even if the broker had fully discharged his duty, the claimant would not have been insured against the loss which actually occurred; or (3) sometimes it is argued that if the full facts had been known, the required insurance would not have been obtained. These three topics will be discussed separately.

(i) *Intervening Error or Omission of the Claimant*

16–108 **Failure to check the documents.** In the ordinary way, after the insurance broker has effected insurance he sends a copy of the cover note or the policy to the client. Where the insurance has been effected on the wrong terms, it is sometimes suggested that the client alone is responsible for the loss, since he ought to have checked the documents himself. This is not usually an attractive argument. In *Dickson & Co v Devitt*[9] Atkin J., rejecting the point, said:

> "It appears to me, however, that the question is whether or not the loss which the claimants have sustained is a reasonable and natural consequence of the defendant's breach of contract. In my opinion, when a broker is employed to effect an insurance, especially when the broker employed is a person of repute and experience, the client is entitled to rely upon the broker carrying out his instructions, and is not bound to examine the documents drawn up in performance of those instructions and see whether his instructions have, in fact, been carried out by the broker. In many cases the principal would not understand the matter, and would not know whether the document did in fact carry out his instructions. Business could not be carried on if, when a person has been employed to use skill and care with regard to a matter, the employer is bound to use his

---

[6] As to which see paras 16–107 to 16–132, below.

[7] As to which see para.16–133, below.

[8] For a statement of the general principles, see *McGregor on Damages* (16th edn), paras 139–191 (in relation to tort) and paras 232–246 (in relation to contract). The damage suffered must be loss in respect of which the broker owed a duty: *Banque Bruxelles Lambert SA v Eagle Star Insurance Co Ltd* [1997] A.C. 191. The application of this decision to insurance brokers is discussed further in para.16–140, below.

[9] (1916) 86 L.J.K.B. 315. For the facts see para.16–047, above. Followed in *British Citizens Assurance Co v L Woolland & Co* (1921) 8 Ll. Rep. 89.

own care and skill to see whether the person employed had done what he was employed to do."[10]

Approval of the proposal form. Where the broker's breach of duty consists of negligence in completing the proposal form, then the subsequent negligence (or dishonesty) of the client in checking the form may exonerate the broker from liability. In *O'Connor v BDB Kirby & Co*[11] the claimant instructed the defendant broker to arrange motor insurance on his behalf. The defendant filled in the proposal form on the basis of information given to him by the claimant. In answer to one question, however, as a result of a slip or misunderstanding, the broker wrongly stated that the claimant's car was kept in a garage. After completing the proposal form the defendant handed it to the claimant. The claimant glanced at the form, did not notice the mistake and signed it. Some time later, as a result of the misstatement in the proposal form, the insurers repudiated liability. The claimant then brought an action against the broker, but his claim was dismissed. The Court of Appeal held that the claimant's failure properly to check the proposal form was the sole effective cause of his loss.[12] Davies L.J. conceded that the position would be different if the claimant was unable to read or in some degree illiterate.[13] The position is also different where the erroneous answer relates to a matter peculiarly within the broker's knowledge[14] or where (as sometimes unfortunately happens) the client at the broker's invitation signs an uncompleted or partly completed proposal form and leaves it to the broker to answer the remaining questions. In the latter situation the broker deprives the client of the opportunity to check his answers and any error subsequently made by the broker is the immediate cause of the client's loss.[15]

16–109

---

[10] (1916) 86 L.J.K.B. 315 at 317, 318. In *Youell v Bland Welch & Co Ltd (No.2)* [1990] 2 Lloyd's Rep. 431 (the *"Superhulls Cover"* case) Phillips J. rejected an argument by counsel for the insurers that *Dickson v Devitt* and *General Accident Fire & Life Assurance Corp Ltd v JH Minet & Co Ltd* (discussed at para.16–113, below) demonstrated that insurers were entitled not to check a policy of reinsurance effected for them: see para.16–149, below. There is a Canadian line of authority which suggests that an insured is not required to examine or read his policy: see *Miller v Guardian Insurance Co of Canada* (1995) 127 D.L.R. (4th) 717, at 729 (for the facts, see para.16–060, n.79, above). It is suggested that in an appropriate case an insured will be contributorily negligent for failing to do so. An appeal in *Miller v Guardian Insurance Co of Canada* was unsuccessful: (1997) 149 D.L.R. 375. The Alberta Court of Appeal held that the insured had no duty to inquire as to the omission of a particular type of cover from his policy in the absence of any knowledge of the availability, importance and effect of the relevant provision.

[11] [1972] 1 Q.B. 90.

[12] *per* Davies and Karminski L.JJ. The other ground of the decision was that negligence was not established, *per* Davies and Megaw L.JJ.

[13] See also *Gunns v Par Insurance Brokers* [1977] 1 Lloyd's Rep. 173 (Sir Michael Ogden, sitting as a deputy High Court judge), at para.16–078, n.29. In *Porter v Prudential of America General Insur. Co* (1995) 146 N.S.R.(2d) 81, Nova Scotia Supreme Court, the broker completed the proposal, knew that the client did not read the proposal before signing it, and it was obvious to him that the client was relying on him to complete the proposal accurately. The broker was held negligent in failing to note on the proposal a previous loss of which he was aware.

[14] *Dunbar v A & B Painters Ltd* [1985] 2 Lloyd's Rep. 616, 620. (The case went to the Court of Appeal, but not in relation to this point: [1986] 2 Lloyd's Rep. 38.)

[15] The broker would also be in breach of the IBRC Code of Conduct, see example (20) of the Insurance Brokers Registration Council Code of Conduct (SI 1994/2569): "In the completion of the proposal form . . . insurance brokers shall make it clear that all answers are the client's own responsibility. The client should always be asked to check the details and told that the inclusion of incorrect information may result, inter alia, in a claim being repudiated . . . "

16–110　　　*O'Connor v BDB Kirby & Co* was applied by the Court of Appeal in *Ramesh Kumar Kapur v J. W. Francis & Co.*[16] In that case an earlier claim was not disclosed on the proposal form and as a result the insurers subsequently avoided the policy for non-disclosure. The Court of Appeal found that the claimant had noticed the omission of the claim from the proposal and held that this was the sole effective cause of the claimant's loss. Therefore, notwithstanding the broker's negligence, the claim failed.[17]

16–111　　　**Failing to notice a deficiency in the terms of cover.** Failure by a client to notice an error on the face of the policy is most unlikely to be held to have been the sole effective cause of the loss. A finding of contributory negligence is the more probable outcome.[18] Thus in *Youell v Bland Welch & Co Ltd (No.2)* (the *"Superhulls Cover"* case)[19] the brokers sought to argue that the insurers' negligent failure to appreciate that the reinsurance contract contained an exclusion not present in the contract of insurance broke the chain of causation. Phillips J. rejected this argument, but reduced the award of damages by 20 per cent to take account of insurers' negligence. In *Forsikringsaktieselskapet Vesta v Butcher*[20] the brokers were held liable for failure to act on a request by their client, the reassured, to contact the reinsurers. The reinsured failed to chase up the brokers for several months. Hobhouse J., whose judgment was upheld by the Court of Appeal's,[21] held that the reassured's negligence did not prevent the broker's negligence from being a cause of the loss, although he attributed three-quarters of the blame to the reassured. In *Paul Tudor Jones II and Marsh & McLennan Inc v Crowley Colosso Ltd*[22] the English brokers sought to argue that the failure of the American brokers to notice the term as to partial completion broke the chain of causation between their breach and the loss and damage. Mance J. rejected that argument and apportioned the loss equally between the two firms of brokers.

16–112　　　**Approval of the policy.** Where the client does examine the cover note or policy, notices the error or omission and approves what has been done, then the brokers may not be liable for any loss subsequently sustained.[23] In *General Accident Fire & Life Assurance Corp Ltd v JH Minet & Co Ltd*[24] the defendants

---

[16] [1999] Lloyd's Rep. P.N. 834; [2000] Lloyd's Rep. I.R. 361.
[17] In *Stowers v GA Bonus Plc* [2003] Lloyd's Rep. P.N. 402 (H.H.J. Knight Q.C.) the insurer successfully avoided the claimant's policy for material non-disclosure on the basis that the proposal form was incomplete. The claimant alleged that his brokers should have noticed that the proposal form was incomplete and queried this with him. His claim against the brokers failed on the ground (among others) that even if they had queried the incompleteness of the proposal form with the claimant, he would not have made any further disclosure, with the result that the insurer would have been entitled to avoid the policy in any event.
[18] See paras 16–148 to 16–152, below.
[19] [1990] 2 Lloyd's Rep. 431 (for the facts see para.16–022, above).
[20] [1986] 2 All E.R. 488.
[21] [1989] A.C. 852.
[22] [1996] 2 Lloyd's Rep. 619 (for the facts, see para.16–053, above).
[23] This was one of the grounds upon which the defendants succeeded in *Smith v Cologan* (1788) 2 T.R. 188n.
[24] (1942) 74 Ll. Rep. 1.

failed to arrange reinsurance for the claimants in accordance with their instructions. The defendants argued, however, that they had delivered a cover note to the claimants, which clearly showed the terms of reinsurance effected and which the claimants had accepted without question. In rejecting this argument the Court of Appeal set out what a broker must show to succeed in such a defence:

> "To succeed on this point the defendants must show that there was a ratification of their action, a ratification, that is, of their having effected a reinsurance different from that which their instructions required. The evidence entirely fails to prove this. Apart from the question whether the claimants were under any duty to read the cover note, I am satisfied that the defendants have not proved that the claimants understood that it did not represent the protection they desired and always desired. Mr. Bunton [of the claimants], who was a marine underwriter, never, I think, understood the position under the original policy, and I am sure never intended anything less than he had instructed Mr. McRobert to obtain."[25]

In *Youell v Bland Welch & Co Ltd (No.2)* (the "*Superhulls Cover*" case)[26] the **16–113** brokers argued that the insurers were estopped from asserting that the reinsurance was defective, alleging that the failure of the insurers to comment on the terms of the reinsurance contract when they saw it amounted to a representation that those terms were acceptable to them. The argument failed. Phillips J. held that the insurers had not made an unequivocal representation that they were aware that the reinsurance cover differed from the insurance contract. The brokers, being themselves ignorant of the difference by reason of their own negligence, had not altered their position in reliance on any representation. Phillips J. also held that mere silence by insurers could not be a representation unless the insurers owed the brokers a duty to speak, and following *Dickson v Devitt*[27] and *General Accident Fire & Life Assurance Corp Ltd v JH Minet & Co Ltd*[28] held that the insurers owed no such duty.[29]

Similar arguments on behalf of negligent brokers were rejected by Colman J. **16–114** in the more recent case of *National Insurance and Guarantee Corp v Imperio Reinsurance Co (UK) Ltd*.[30] In that case the client had received the defective endorsement and had stated to the broker that it seemed to do what the client wanted. The brokers sought to raise defences of waiver, estoppel and ratification. All three failed, the first two for essentially the same reasons as those given by Phillips J., the third because an agent whose principal has indicated that he is prepared to treat a contract made by the agent as binding as between the principal and the other contracting party is not necessarily entitled to assume that the principal is thereby releasing him from all claims and, on the facts, the brokers were not so entitled.

---

[25] (1942) 74 Ll. Rep. 1 at 9, col.2.
[26] [1990] 2 Lloyd's Rep. 431 (for the facts, see para.16–022, above).
[27] (1916) 86 L.J.K.B. 315.
[28] (1942) 74 Ll. Rep. 1.
[29] Phillips J. also held that *Dickson v Devitt* and *General Accident Fire & Life Assurance Corp Ltd v JH Minet & Co Ltd* did not establish that insurers could not be contributorily negligent in failing to check the reinsurance policy. He held that on the facts before him insurers were 20% to blame, but that was because they had failed to have proper regard for their own interests as opposed to being in breach of a duty owed to the brokers: see para.16–149, below.
[30] [1999] Lloyd's Rep. I.R. 249 (for the relevant facts see para.16–047, above).

16–115   In practice, therefore, it seems that where as a result of the broker's breach of duty insurance is not effected on the terms required by the client, it will be difficult to establish that the client's subsequent conduct was the sole cause of his loss unless the client actually noticed that the insurance was not as he had required but failed to do anything about it.

16–116   **Failure to obtain a replacement policy.** In some cases a claimant will discover before he suffers a loss that, as a result of his brokers, he does not have the benefit of the insurance which he should have had. In such a case, the claimant should take steps to obtain a new policy to replace the non-existent or inadequate cover. If he fails to do so, and then suffers a loss while he is either uninsured or inadequately insured, then any claim against the broker is likely to fail.[31]

(ii) *Where the Claimant would not have been Insured in any Event*

16–117   Typically a claimant in a broker's negligence action will have suffered a loss for which he is not properly insured. His allegation against his broker will be that, but for the broker's negligence, he would have been properly insured and would have received a payment from his insurer. In such cases the broker may be able to establish that, even if he had acted properly, the claimant would not have been insured for the particular loss which he has suffered. This may be for one (or more) of several reasons.

16–118   **Claimant would have chosen not to obtain the required insurance.** If a claimant alleges that owing to his broker's negligence he was not properly insured, it will be a good defence for the broker to show that the claimant would not have purchased the required insurance even if he had been properly advised. For example,[32] in *Kennedy (BJ) Agency (1984) Ltd v Kilgour Bell Ins*[33] the claimant's business was destroyed by fire. However, his insurance covered only a portion of his loss because cover was for "actual value" rather than "replacement cost" coverage. The broker was found to have been negligent in failing to advise the claimant of the availability of "replacement cost" coverage. However, the claim failed on causation. The court found that even if the broker had given the proper advice, the claimant would not have purchased the "replacement cost" coverage because it was more expensive than the "actual value" cover.

16–119   **Claimant would not have complied with a policy condition.** If a claimant establishes that a broker negligently failed to advise him of a particular condition or warranty in a policy, then his claim will fail unless he can also establish that, had the broker acted with reasonable skill and care, then he would have complied

---

[31] *BP Plc v AON Ltd (No.2)* [2006] EWHC; [2006] 1 All E.R. (Comm) 789 (Colman J.) at paras 317–318.

[32] See also *George Barkes (London) Ltd v LFC (1988) Ltd* [2000] 1 P.N.L.R. 21 in which the terms of the insured's cover excluded certain types of theft. A theft occurred in circumstances which were excluded. The brokers were found to have acted negligently in failing to advise the claimant of the restrictions in the policy. However, H.H.J. Hallgarten Q.C. found that even if the claimant had been properly advised it would still have accepted the policy. Therefore the claimants were entitled to no more than nominal damages.

[33] (1999) 139 Man.R.(2d) 276, Manitoba Court of Queen's Bench.

with the condition or warranty. The claim in *Bhopal v Sphere Drake Insurance Plc*[34] failed on that basis. In that case the insurers denied liability on basis that the claimant was in breach of a heating warranty. The insured brought a claim against his broker alleging that they failed to give him any explanation as to the significance and effect of the warranty. The claim was summarily dismissed on the basis that, on the evidence, the inexorable conclusion was that no advice on the part of the brokers about the effect of the warranty would have led the claimant to act differently. In *JW Bollom & Co Ltd v Byas Mosley & Co Ltd*[35] the brokers also argued that their failure to draw a condition to the attention of the insured was not causative of any loss because, even if the condition had been drawn to the insured's attention, the insured would not have complied with it. Moore-Bick J. accepted that the burden of proof was on the claimant to show that, if properly advised, it would have satisfied the condition and was satisfied that this would have been the case. Accordingly, the defence failed.

Claimant with no insurable interest. In *Newbury International Ltd v Reli-*   **16–120**
ance National Insurance Co (UK) Ltd[36] insurers had avoided a policy for non-disclosure by the brokers. The policy was a device for raising money to finance a season of Formula 3 motor racing. Hobhouse J. held that the claimants had no insurable interest in the policy and so would not have been entitled to recover under had it not been avoided. He therefore declined to award substantial damages against the brokers.[37]

Insurer entitled to reject the claim for a reason for which the broker is not   **16–121**
responsible. In many cases there may be more than one basis upon which an insurer is entitled to reject a claim. For example, there may have been a material non-disclosure when the policy was effected, and also a breach of condition when the loss occurred. The insurer may reject the claim on the basis of the non-disclosure or the breach of condition, or both. It is also often the case that the broker is responsible for one, but not both, of the grounds upon which the insurer is entitled to reject the insured's claim. This may provide the broker with a good defence on causation.

Where the insurer rejects liability on the ground for which the broker is not   **16–122**
responsible before the other ground is detected then the matter is relatively straightforward. The broker will be able to show (for example) that the material non-disclosure for which he is responsible did not cause the claimant any loss because the insurer had already repudiated liability owing to the claimant's

---

[34] [2002] Lloyd's Rep. I.R. 413, CA.

[35] [1999] Lloyd's Rep. P.N. 598.

[36] [1994] 1 Lloyd's Rep. 83.

[37] See also *Fomin v Oswell* (1813) 3 Camp. 357, 359: "For omitting to include the premiums, the defendants would certainly be liable if the claimant had thereby sustained any damage: but the court has decided that he was not entitled to recover upon the policy; and he would not have been in a better situation if the premiums had been included. As to the first complaint (see para.16–054, n.68, above), there is a loss without an injury; as to the second, there is an injury without a loss. I am therefore of the opinion that on neither ground can the action be maintained", (*per* Lord Ellenborough). Where the broker in breach of a duty owed to the insurer fails to include a customary limitation clause in a policy he issues on the insurer's behalf, there will be no loss if the insurer would have been liable on the policy in any event: *Gibraltar General Insurance Co v LE Yingst Co* (1990) 89 Sask.R. 93, Saskatchewan Court of Queen's Bench.

breach of condition in any event. However, the position is more difficult where (as more typically happens) the insurer rejects liability on the ground for which the broker is responsible. For example, if the insurer repudiates liability on the ground of non-disclosure, for which the broker is responsible, the broker will wish to argue that the insurer could and would have exercised its right to reject the claim on the basis of the breach of condition, for which the broker was not responsible. The difficulty arises when it is unclear whether or not the insurer would indeed have rejected the claim on the basis of the breach of condition.

16–123   In such a case the brokers must satisfy the court that the insurers would in fact have exercised their rights and declined to meet the claim.[38] Only if this is established can it properly be said that no loss flows from the broker's breach of duty. Such a defence was successful in *Gunns v Par Insurance Brokers*.[39] There the brokers successfully argued that the claimant would not have recovered under the policy (which had been avoided for non-disclosure) because the insured was in breach of a condition that he should take all reasonable steps to avoid loss and damage and to safeguard the property insured from loss and damage.

16–124   The defence was unsuccessful in *Fraser v BN Furman (Productions) Ltd*,[40] in which an employer instructed its brokers to arrange employers' liability insurance on its behalf. The brokers failed to do so and consequently the employer was uninsured when an employee brought a claim for damages for negligence and breach of statutory duty. It was common ground that if insurance had been effected it would have been with the Eagle Star. The brokers argued that since the employer was in breach of one of the standard conditions of the Eagle Star's employers' liability policies, the insurers would have been entitled to repudiate in any event and therefore no loss flowed from the brokers' breach of duty. The Court of Appeal rejected this argument on two grounds: first, the insurers would not have been entitled to repudiate on the grounds alleged. Secondly (and in the alternative) it was considered "highly improbable" that the Eagle Star would have wished to take the point. In dealing with the second issue Diplock L.J. stated that the court must consider "the chances that an insurance company of the highest standing and reputation, such as Eagle Star, notwithstanding their strict legal rights, would, as a matter of business have paid up under the policy".[41]

16–125   *Fraser v BN Furman (Productions) Ltd* was followed by the New Zealand Court of Appeal in *Cee Bee Marine Ltd v Lombard Insurance Co Ltd*.[42] In that case stock was lost as a result of the client's negligence. The broker was held to have been negligent in failing to effect insurance covering the stock. He argued that, had insurance been arranged, the insurers would have avoided liability

---

[38] In *Everett v Hogg Robinson and Gardner Mountain (Insurance) Ltd* [1973] 1 Lloyd's Rep. 217 it was held that the burden of proof was on the broker to show that the reinsurers would have repudiated liability in any event (for the facts, see para.16–128, below).

[39] [1997] 1 Lloyd's Rep. 173, Sir Michael Ogden, sitting as a deputy High Court judge. Such arguments may not always result in a reduction of damages, however: see the decision of Moore-Bick J. in *JW Bollom & Co Ltd v Byas Mosley & Co Ltd* [1999] Lloyd's Rep. P.N. 598, discussed in para.16–062, above.

[40] [1967] 1 W.L.R. 898.

[41] *ibid.* at 904E–F.

[42] [1990] 2 N.Z.L.R. 1 (for the facts, see para.16–051, above).

under a clause requiring the insured to take reasonable precautions. The New Zealand Court of Appeal held that when considering whether a clause would have excluded liability the policy should be construed so as to have regard to its commercial objectives. On that basis there was no breach of the term and the broker was liable for the loss. *Fraser v BN Furman (Productions) Ltd* was also followed by the British Columbia Supreme Court in *LB Martin Construction Ltd v Gaglardi.*[43] In that case the brokers admitted liability for having incorrectly informed their client that they had obtained insurance. The insurance which they should have obtained would have contained a relevant exclusion clause, but Taylor J. held that the insurers would have been prepared to compromise a claim under the policy and awarded the clients half their loss.

Where this line of defence is put forward, evidence from the proposed insurers **16-126** (or, if their identity is not known, from any representative insurers) is admissible to show whether or not they would have repudiated on the grounds suggested. In *Fraser v BN Furman (Productions) Ltd* Diplock L.J. indicated that the absence of such evidence was one of the weaknesses of the third party's case.[44]

It may be that, having heard the evidence, the court is uncertain whether the **16-127** insurers would have availed themselves of the opportunity to repudiate. Alternatively, the court may consider that the insurers would have attempted to repudiate, although the outcome of any subsequent litigation is uncertain. In these circumstances the client has suffered some loss as a result of the broker's breach of duty—namely the loss of the chance of recovering a full or partial indemnity from the insurers. The measure of damages is the value of the chance which the client has lost. The correctness of this approach was reaffirmed by the Court of Appeal in *Dunbar v A & B Painters Ltd*[45] although the court went on

---

[43] (1978) 91 D.L.R. (3d) 393.

[44] [1967] 1 W.L.R. 898, 909. Diplock L.J. held that the burden was on the brokers to show that the policy would not have covered their client's loss. In *Cee Bee Marine Ltd v Lombard Insurance Co Ltd* [1990] 2 N.Z.L.R. 1 the New Zealand Court of Appeal took the same view; but in *Toikan International Insurance Broking Pty Ltd v Plasteel Windows Australia Pty Ltd* (1988) 15 N.S.W.L.R. 641 the New South Wales Court of Appeal held that the onus was on the client.

[45] [1986] 2 Lloyd's Rep. 38. May L.J., with whom the other members of the court agreed, said at 42, col.2: "the proper approach for the learned Judge to have adopted in the present case was to have assessed the chances that the insurers would have taken the height point and, having so assessed the chances, tailored his award of damages accordingly". One case which does not at first sight appear to fit into the scheme of the more recent cases is *Thomas Cheshire & Co v Vaughan Bros & Co* [1920] 3 K.B. 240. In that case the claimants instructed the defendants to effect a PPI policy on a cargo of nitrate which was due to arrive shortly at Liverpool. PPI policies were in common use at the time, and were strictly speaking gaming policies within s.4(2)(b) of the Marine Insurance Act 1906, and therefore null and void. Nevertheless, it was not the practice of marine insurers to take this point, and evidence was given that they would not have done so in the present case. As a result of the defendants' breach of duty the insurers were entitled to, and did, deny liability because of non-disclosure of a material fact. The Court of Appeal held that since the policy would have been null and void in any event, the claimants were not entitled to recover damages. The Court of Appeal declined to take into account the fact that the insurers would not have relied upon s.4 of the Marine Insurance Act. It is now thought that this case was decided on grounds of public policy and it has no application to cases where the insurance (or the proposed insurance) is not rendered void or illegal by statute or common law, (e.g. *Webster v De Tastet* (1797) 7 T.R. 157 (failure to insure slaves)). It was on this basis that the Court of Appeal in *Fraser v BN Furman (Productions) Ltd* succeeded in distinguishing the decision. (See the judgment of Diplock L.J. at 908H–909B.)

to hold (on the facts of that case) that it was certain that the insurers would not have taken advantage of a particular term to avoid liability.

16–128 In *Everett v Hogg Robinson & Gardner Mountain (Insurance) Ltd*[46] the defendants effected reinsurance for the claimants, but wrongly (and negligently) told the reinsurers that plastic was not used in the products of the insured. The reinsurers subsequently repudiated. The defendants contended that no loss had been caused, since the reinsurers could and would have repudiated in any event, owing to the claimants' failure to disclose their adverse claims record. Kerr J. found that the reinsurers would, initially, have attempted to repudiate. However, Kerr J. continued, considering the friendly relations between the claimants and the reinsurers and "the relative minor importance of this difference in terms of money against the background of their business relations as a whole . . . I am convinced that the result would . . . have been . . . a compromise".[47] What the compromise would have been was a matter of guesswork. However, as "a fair and reasonable assessment of the chances in all the circumstances" the claimants were awarded two-thirds of the full value of their claim.[48]

(iii) *Where the Required Insurance would not have been Granted if the Full Facts had been Known*

16–129 Where the insurer repudiates for non-disclosure or misrepresentation on the part of the broker, any claim by the insured against the broker is based upon the premise that if the true facts had been declared valid insurance would have been obtained. However, the true facts may be so alarming that the client was effectively uninsurable. In these circumstances it may be that no loss was caused by the broker's negligence.[49] Alternatively, it may be that, if the truth had been declared, only limited cover could have been obtained. In this situation the loss caused by the broker's negligence is correspondingly reduced but not eliminated.

---

[46] [1973] 2 Lloyd's Rep. 217.
[47] *ibid.* at 224. See also *Beattie v Furness-Houlder Insurance (Northern) Ltd* 1976 S.L.T. (Notes) 60.
[48] In *Pryke v Gibbs Hartley Cooper Ltd* [1991] 1 Lloyd's Rep. 602 (for the facts of which see para.16–025, above) one element of the insurer's claim against the brokers was the loss of the chance to sue their American coverholder while it had solvent errors and omissions insurers. The brokers argued that the coverholder's errors and omissions insurers would have relied upon two exclusions in the policy. Waller J. accepted that they would have relied upon both, although they only had a real chance of establishing one, and even that was not certain. He held that given the possibility that neither exclusion would avail them and their exposure to costs and a possible claim for punitive damages in the United States for "bad faith denial of coverage" the errors and omissions insurers would have been prepared to contribute 50% of the sum needed to meet insurers' exposure in the United States as a result of their coverholder's excess of authority, proceeding on the basis of loss of a chance.
[49] A similar argument was accepted in *Gooderham v Bank of Novia Scotia* [2000] 47 O.R. 3d 554, Canadian Supreme Court of Justice, in which the defendant bank was found to have acted negligently in failing to forward the claimant's application forms to the insurer. On the facts it was found that the bank acted as the agent of the insurer so that a valid contract of insurance existed. However, the court went on to hold that if no such contract had existed, the claimant would only have been entitled to nominal damages because he was uninsurable as at the date the insurance application was made.

Arguments of this nature necessarily depend on speculation and are not likely **16–130** generally to appeal to the court.[50] In *Mint Security Ltd v Blair*[51] Staughton J. held that if there had been no failure of communication, "some accommodation would have been reached between the claimants and their insurers. Either the procedures would have been improved so far as they could be or a small extra premium would have been charged with the procedures as varied. In the last resort, of course, the claimants need not have carried the cash at all, and then there would have been no loss."[52]

In *Cee Bee Marine Ltd v Lombard Insurance Co Ltd*[53] the risk which was **16–131** uninsured by reason of the broker's negligence was a fibreglass boat repair business carried on in a wooden building. This was not a risk likely to appeal to insurers. The New Zealand Court of Appeal held that the measure of damages was the loss of the chance to obtain insurance elsewhere. The award of damages should reflect the value of that chance. The court was satisfied that the client would not knowingly have carried on its business without insurance, so that the four most obvious possible outcomes were:

  (i) the client would have obtained insurance with a higher premium;

  (ii) the client would have obtained insurance conditional upon a change in the structure of the building;

  (iii) the insured would have moved its business elsewhere and obtained insurance;

  (iv) it would have ceased to carry on its business so preserving the value of its stock.

The court discounted the award of damages slightly to take account of these possibilities, including something for the sums which might have had to be expended on the premium and expenses in order to obtain cover. This approach was followed in *O & R Jewllers Ltd v Terry.*[54] The evidence in that case was that so long as the convicted burglar remained managing director of the claimant's parent company, the claimant was uninsurable. Even had it been obtained, there

---

[50] Such arguments were rejected by the Privy Council in *Eagle Star Insurance Co Ltd v National Westminster Finance Australia Ltd* (1985) 58 A.L.R. 165. *In Youell v Bland Welch & Co Ltd (No.2)* [1990] 2 Lloyd's Rep. 431 (the "*Superhulls Cover*" case) (for the facts of which, see para.16–022, above) the insurers admitted on their pleadings the brokers' contention that reinsurance could not have been obtained without the 48-month cut-off clause. As Phillips J. remarked, this may have been a shrewd tactical move on the part of the insurers, rather than a recognition that the broker's contention was correct, because it allowed the insurers to argue that they would not have entered the insurance contracts but for the brokers' negligence, since it was clear that they would not have done so had there been no reinsurance on offer. As explained in para.16–140, below, the decision of Phillips J. on this point and similar arguments now need to be considered in the light of *Aneco Reinsurance Underwriting (in liquidation) v Johnson and Higgins Ltd* [2001] UKHL 51; [2002] 1 Lloyd's Rep. 157 (for the facts, see para.16–079, above) and *Banque Bruxelles Lambert SA v Eagle Star Insurance Co Ltd* [1997] A.C. 191.

[51] [1982] 1 Lloyd's Rep. 188; for the facts of this case see para.16–092, above.

[52] *ibid*. at 201.

[53] [1990] 2 N.Z.L.R. 1. For the facts see para.16–051, above.

[54] [1999] Lloyd's Rep. I.R. 436, Sir Godfrey le Quesne, sitting as a deputy High Court judge (for the facts see para.16–075, n.16, above).

were further defences which underwriters could and would have raised, although they might not have succeeded. The judge followed *Cee Bee Marine* and awarded damages on the basis that the claimant would have tried to have the dishonest director removed and that, while underwriters would have raised other defences, they might have compromised a claim or lost at trial and, taking the matter broadly, awarded damages representing 30 per cent of full recovery.

16–132   The court in *Cee Bee Marine Ltd v Lombard Insurance Co Ltd*[55] followed the dictum of Lord Diplock in *Mallett v McMonagle*[56] which allows a court when deciding what the chance was that something would have happened (as opposed to deciding what did happen) to decide that the chance was more or less than 50 per cent and award damages accordingly. In *Markal Investments Ltd v Morley Shafron Agencies Ltd*[57] the British Columbia Court of Appeal took a different view and held that a client whose broker had failed to obtain insurance had to show on the balance of probabilities that insurance would have been obtained. It is submitted that in the context of claims against brokers for failure to obtain cover, the approach taken in *Cee Bee Marine Ltd v Lombard Insurance Co Ltd*[58] is to be preferred. Where the availability of insurance is in doubt, the damage should be characterised as a loss of opportunity.[59]

(c) *Foreseeability*

16–133   Whether the claim is brought in contract or tort, the claimant must establish not only that his loss was caused by the defendant's breach of duty, but also that it was foreseeable. In practice, questions of foreseeability do not generally arise in actions against insurance brokers, because the kinds of loss suffered fall within such a narrow compass.[60] However, where a claimant seeks to recover damages

---

[55] [1999] Lloyd's Rep. I.R. 436.

[56] [1970] A.C. 166, 176: "The role of the court in making an assessment of damages which depends upon its view as to what will be and what would have been is to be contrasted with its ordinary function in civil actions of determining what was. In determining what did happen in the past a court decides on the balance of probabilities. Anything that is more probable than not it treats as certain. But in assessing damages which depend upon its view as to what will happen in the future or would have happened in the future if something had not happened in the past, the court must make an estimate as to what are the chances that a particular thing will or would have happened and reflect those chances, whether they are more or less than even, in the amount of damages which it awards."

[57] (1990) 67 D.L.R. (4th) 422 (for the facts see para.16–042, n.27, above). The court followed *Hotson v East Berkshire Area HA* [1987] A.C. 750; and *Wilsher v Essex Area HA* [1988] A.C. 1074. In those cases the House of Lords was concerned with the level of proof needed to establish the cause of an event which had actually occurred. Thus in *Hotson* the claim failed because, on the balance of probabilities, too many blood vessels had been ruptured at the time of the negligent diagnosis.

[58] [1990] 2 N.Z.L.R. 1.

[59] In *Allied Maples Group Ltd v Simmons & Simmons* [1995] 1 W.L.R. 1602 (a solicitors' case) the Court of Appeal, holding that the claimants' claim was for loss of a chance, proceeded on the basis that the same principles applied to claims against solicitors as insurance brokers and relied upon *Dunbar v A & B Painters Ltd* [1986] 2 Lloyd's Rep. 38 (see para.16–127, above).

[60] See paras 16–135 to 16–147, below. The claim against the brokers in *Bates v Barrow Ltd* [1995] 1 Lloyd's Rep. 680 (for the facts see para.16–067, n.92, above) would have failed because it was not reasonably foreseeable that an insurer would plead its own breach of the Insurance Companies Acts as a defence to a claim under an illegal policy. However, if it was negligent for the broker to expose his client to that risk, as Gatehouse J. found, it is hard to see how it was not foreseeable that the risk might turn out to be real.

for losses other than the sum which he would have recovered under an insurance policy, the defendant broker may successfully argue that such losses were not reasonably foreseeable. That argument was successful in *Bolton v New Zealand Insurance Co Ltd*.[61] The client claimed damages for losses allegedly caused by the need to sell a farm in order to finance repairs of his uninsured yacht, but this head of loss was rejected as being unforeseeable.

The issue of foreseeability will arise where an uninsured claimant puts his case **16–134** on the basis that, if he had been aware he was uninsured, then he would have taken greater care to avoid the loss which he suffered. In *Sharif v Garrett & Co*,[62] a claim against solicitors, the Court of Appeal had to consider the claimant's prospects of success in an earlier claim against his brokers which had been struck out. The court found that the claimant had negligible prospects of success in his claim against the brokers which was to have been put on the basis that, if he had known he was uninsured, he would have taken further precautions to avoid the loss. An insured is required to act in the same way as a prudent uninsured. For that reason an insurance broker cannot be expected to foresee that someone who thinks he is insured would take different precautions if he knew he was uninsured.

(i) *Measure of Damages*

The fundamental principle governing the measure of damages is that the claimant **16–135** should be put, so far as money can do so, in the position he would have been in had the defendant discharged his duty.[63] In claims against insurance brokers, the claimant typically alleges that he was uninsured when, but for his broker's negligence, he would have been insured. Therefore the main (and often the only) item of damages claimed is the amount which would have been payable by the insurers (or reinsurers) but for the broker's breach of duty. If there is no doubt that the insurers (or reinsurers) would have satisfied the client's claim, then this loss is plainly recoverable.[64]

The measure of damages is the difference between the sum the claimant should **16–136** have received had his broker acted properly and that which (if anything) he actually received.[65] Therefore if the insurance policy which should have been effected contained a term limiting liability to a sum lower than the claimant's loss, the damages recoverable against the broker will be limited to the same extent.[66] Similarly, where the broker arranges valid but inadequate insurance, the measure of damages will be the difference between the sum recoverable under

---

[61] [1995] 1 N.Z.L.R. 224; for the facts see para.16–077, n.26, above.
[62] [2001] EWCA 1269; [2002] Lloyd's Rep. I.R. 11.
[63] *Livingstone v The Rawyards Coal Co* (1880) 5 App. Cas. 25, 39; *Dodd Properties (Kent) Ltd v Canterbury CC* [1980] 1 W.L.R. 433, 451, 454 and 456.
[64] See, e.g. *Smith v Price* (1862) 2 F. & F. 748; *British Citizens Assurance Co v L Woolland & Co* (1921) 8 Ll. Rep. 89; *General Accident Fire & Life Assurance Corp Ltd v JH Minet & Co Ltd* (1942) 74 Ll. Rep. 1; *London Borough of Bromley v Ellis* [1971] 1 Lloyd's Rep. 97; *Ramwade Ltd v WJ Emson & Co Ltd* [1987] R.T.R. 72.
[65] In *Alexander Forbes Europe Ltd v SBJ Ltd* [2002] EWHC 3121; [2003] Lloyd's Rep. I.R. 432, David Mackie Q.C. (sitting as a deputy High Court judge) commented on the proper approach to the assessment of damages as follows (at 443): "I am not strictly concerned with what as a matter of law a claimant was entitled to under a policy but with what, on the balance of probabilities, would have occurred had there been no breach of duty."
[66] *Mint Security Ltd v Blair* [1982] 1 Lloyd's Rep. 188.

the policy and the sum which ought to have been recoverable.[67] Where insurers make an *ex gratia* payment, credit should be given for it.[68] In one case, where the insurers paid up under the policy in error but the insured voluntarily reimbursed them, the amount which the insured voluntarily repaid was also recovered in damages.[69]

16–137   In some cases it will be open to the defendant broker to argue that, even if he had fulfilled his duty, the insurers would not have satisfied the client's claim. This may be for a number of reasons, but typically it is alleged that the insurers would have been entitled to repudiate liability in any event. As discussed above, in such cases damages are assessed on a loss of a chance basis, i.e. the court will value the chance the claimant had of recovering a full or partial indemnity from the insurers.[70]

16–138   **Settlement with insurers.** As a result of his broker's breach of duty, an insured may find himself with doubtful or uncertain rights against insurers when he should have had a clear, unequivocal right to indemnity for a loss. If the client enters a reasonable compromise of his claim against the insurers, the measure of loss against the broker is the difference between what he actually recovered from insurers and what he would have recovered had the broker not been negligent.[71] This is illustrated by the decision of the High Court of Australia in *Unity Insurance Brokers Pty Ltd v Rocco Pezzano Pty Ltd.*[72] There the brokers had failed to disclose their client's extensive previous claims record. Section 28 of the Australian Insurance Contracts Act 1984 provides that, save in the case of fraud, insurers are not entitled to avoid for non-disclosure or misrepresentation. They are, however, entitled to reduce the amount payable under the contract to that which would have been payable had there been proper disclosure or the misrepresentation had not been made. The client compromised its claim against the insurers for just over half the full value of the claim. The High Court of Australia held that the brokers were liable for the full shortfall.[73]

---

[67] See, e.g. *Coyle v Ray F Fredericks Insurance Ltd* (1984) 64 N.S.R. (2d); and (1984) 143 A.P.R. 93, Nova Scotia Supreme Court: insurance agents insured boat for actual value, not replacement value as instructed.

[68] *Harvest Trucking Co Ltd v Davis* [1991] 2 Lloyd's Rep. 638.

[69] *Maydew v Forrester* (1814) 5 Taunt. 615.

[70] See paras 16–127 to 16–128, above.

[71] See, e.g. *Akedian Co Ltd v Royal Insurance Australia Ltd* (1999) 1 V.R. 80 (Supreme Court of Victoria) (insurer avoided the claimant's policy for non-disclosure and misrepresentation. Claimant brought proceedings against the insurer under the policy and against the brokers for negligence. Claimant settled its action against the insurer and recovered from the brokers the amount recoverable under the policy less the amount received in the settlement with the insurers); *Bollom v Byas Mosley* [2000] Lloyd's Rep. I.R. 136.

[72] (1998) 154 A.L.R. 361.

[73] See also *FNCB Ltd v Barnet Devanney (Harrow) Ltd* [1999] Lloyd's Rep. I.R. 459 (for the facts see para.16–054, above). The mortgagee insured had compromised its claim against the insurer, who had relied upon non-disclosure, misrepresentation and breach of condition by the mortgagee, who was also an insured under the composite policy. A subsequent decision of the Court of Appeal (*New Hampshire Insurance Co v MGN Ltd* [1997] L.R.L.R. 24) held that the non-disclosure, misrepresentation and breach of condition of one insured, the mortgagor, under a composite policy did not affect the claim of another, the mortgagee, but that was too late for the mortgagee. The result of the brokers' negligence was that there was no mortgagee protection clause. The Court of Appeal held that, had there been, the insurers would have settled the mortgagee's claim in full within a reasonable time and that the brokers' breach of duty had caused the lower recovery on settlement. Damages were awarded

Where a client has compromised his claim against the insurers, it is open to the **16–139** brokers to claim that the settlement was unreasonably low. The correct approach in such a case was discussed by Rix J. in *Mander v Commercial Union Assurance Co Plc*.[74] Rix J. expressed the view that it was not appropriate to re-litigate the dispute between insured and insurers, but rather to assess the chances of the insured's claim succeeding and then to consider whether the settlement was reasonable or unreasonable in the light of that assessment.[75] In *BP Plc v AON Ltd (No.2)* Colman J.[76] stated that the fact that the terms of the settlement were entered into upon legal advice establishes that they were prima facie reasonable, and that it was then for the defendant to displace that inference by evidence to the contrary be establishing, for example, that some vital matter was overlooked. He then stated the test as follows[77]:

> The test is therefore whether the settlement arrived at was, in all the circumstances which the settling party knew or ought reasonably to have known at the time of the settlement, within the range of settlements which reasonable commercial men might have made. To the extent that such settlement was excessive, the settling party cannot recover.

Other heads of loss. The insured may try to claim further losses on the basis **16–140** that had he realised that his insurance policy was not or might not be effective, he would have acted differently and so not have incurred those further losses. The starting point when considering whether the insured is entitled to recover damages for his additional losses is to establish the extent of the broker's duty in accordance with the principles set out by Lord Hoffmann in *Banque Bruxelles Lambert SA v Eagle Star Insurance Co Ltd*.[78] In a straightforward case where the broker negligently fails to disclose a material fact to insurers, the broker's duty (and so the measure of any damages for breach of that duty) will be confined to the policy of insurance which is later avoided. The insured will not be able to recover other losses even if they resulted from his having entered a transaction in reliance on the insurance being in place. However, brokers can undertake a wider role so that the scope of their duty (and so their potential exposure in damages) to their client will be greater. If the brokers undertake to advise their client whether or not a course of action should be taken, then they may be held responsible for all the foreseeable loss which was a consequence of that course of action having been taken.

Broker obtaining insurance and reinsurance. One example is where a **16–141** broker approaches an insurer with a substantial risk which he knows the insurer is only likely to accept if reinsurance is available and the broker offers to obtain that reinsurance. The broker is then acting both for the insured (in seeking to

---

for the difference between the full claim and the sums recovered on settlement and sale of the mortgaged property.
[74] [1998] Lloyd's Rep. I.R. 93, at 148–9.
[75] For a discussion of the appropriate measure of damages in cases where it is alleged that the insurer would have repudiated liability even if the broker had acted properly, see paras 16–127 to 16–128, above.
[76] [2006] EWHC 424; [2006] 1 All E.R. (Comm) 789.
[77] *ibid* at para.283.
[78] [1997] A.C. 191. See also Ch.3, paras 3–002 *et seq.*, and Ch.10, paras 10–113 *et seq.*

place the insurance contract) and for the insurer/reinsured (in seeking to obtain reinsurance cover). On one view the broker's duty to the insurer/reinsured is limited to the reinsurance contract and does not extend to the underlying contract of insurance. On that basis unreinsured losses suffered on the insurance contract are not within the scope of the broker's duty to the insurer/reinsured and so not recoverable as damages for breach of that duty. However, if the broker has taken an active part in setting up the insurance and reinsurance and has negligently failed to disclose material facts to reinsurers so that they accepted the risk, whereas had the broker made proper disclosure he would have discovered that it was not possible to obtain reinsurance on commercially acceptable terms and would have been under a duty to report accordingly to the insurer/reinsured, then the scope of the broker's duty may be wider. That was the conclusion of the majority of the House of Lords in *Aneco Reinsurance Underwriting (in liquidation) v Johnson and Higgins Ltd.*[79] The claimant in that case had only recovered damages at the first instance to the extent that it would have recovered under the reinsurance treaties which had been avoided. However, the Court of Appeal reversed that finding and held that the client was entitled to recover damages for the whole of the loss which it suffered as a result of having accepted the underlying reinsurance business. The House of Lords upheld the Court of Appeal's decision. In his speech Lord Lloyd stated that "brokers (and others) are liable in contract for the foreseeable consequences of their negligence, including the adverse consequences of entering into a transaction with a third party, provided such a consequence can fairly be held to fall within the scope of the defendant's duty of care." He went on to state that *Banque Bruxelles Lambert SA v Eagle Star Insurance Co Ltd*[80] was an example of a special class of case where the scope of the defendant's duty is confined to the giving of specific information. If the brokers duty had been confined to the obtaining of reinsurance, then damages would have been limited to the value of the reinsurance which the brokers failed to obtain. However, the scope of the duty owed by the brokers was not so limited since they had undertaken to advise the client as to what course of action to take. Accordingly, the brokers were liable for all the foreseeable consequences of their negligence, namely the full amount of the loss suffered by the client as a result of having entered into the transaction. In reaching this conclusion the House of Lords approved the decision of Phillips J. in *Youell v Bland Welch & Co Ltd (No.2)* (the *"Superhulls Cover"* case).[81] Lord Millett dissented on the basis that the proper measure of damages should reflect the fact that the brokers were not liable for all the foreseeable consequences of the client having entered into the transaction, but only for the consequences of it having done so on a false basis, namely that it had effective reinsurance cover.[82]

---

[79] [2001] UKHL 51 (October 18, 2001) (Lord Millett dissenting), upholding the judgment of the Court of Appeal, [2000] Lloyd's Rep. P.N. 1 (Evans and Ward L.JJ., Aldous L.J. dissenting). The Court of Appeal had reversed the decision of Cresswell J. on the point; (for the facts see para.16–079, above).

[80] [1997] A.C. 191.

[81] [1990] 2 Lloyd's Rep. 431 (see paras 16–022 and 16–130, n.50, above).

[82] Lord Millett considered that the concession made by counsel in *Youell v Bland Welch & Co Ltd (No.2)* (the *"Superhulls Cover"* case) regarding the appropriate measure of loss had been wrongly made.

The central issue in *Aneco* was the scope of the duty of care owed by the **16–142**
brokers, i.e. whether it was limited to the giving of specific information, or
extended to advising the client whether or not to enter into the transaction. The
brokers advised on the availability of reinsurance. However, and this was the
determinative point, the availability of reinsurance was indicative of the market's
assessment of the risk and thus the merits of the transaction. Accordingly, the
duty to advise on the availability of reinsurance encompassed a duty to advise on
the merits of the transaction. If the brokers had correctly advised the client that
the reinsurance was not available, then the transaction would not have proceeded
at all. Therefore, the brokers were liable for all the losses suffered by the client
as a result of entering into the transaction.

Damages caused by failure to receive insurance moneys. The client may **16–143**
also seek to claim further damages caused by failure to receive payment under
the insurance policy. Thus in *Ramwade Ltd v WJ Emson & Co Ltd*[83] the client's
lorry was damaged beyond repair. Owing to the broker's negligence the client
was uninsured and so received no payment from the insurers. The client lacked
sufficient funds to buy a replacement vehicle and therefore hired a replacement.
The client then sought to recover from the brokers the replacement value of the
vehicle and the hire charges, on the basis that if the broker's had acted properly
it would have received a prompt payment from the insurers and would never have
had to incur any hire charges. The Court of Appeal allowed the claim for the
replacement value of the lorry but rejected the claim for the hire charges, because
the reason why hire charges were incurred was either: (i) the client's impecuniosity, in which case damages could not be recovered[84]; or (ii) the failure of the
brokers to satisfy their client's claim for damages promptly (i.e. the client was
seeking to recover damages for non-payment of damages, and the law does not
recognise such a claim). The first reason is no longer good law.[85] The second
reason, however, is currently good law.[86] *Ramwade Ltd v WJ Emson & Co Ltd*
was followed by the Court of Appeal in *Verderame v Commercial Union Assurance Co Plc*[87] when striking out the claim for consequential losses allegedly
caused by failure to recover under the insurance policy. A similar claim was
rejected by the High Court of New Zealand in *Bolton v New Zealand Insurance*

---

[83] [1987] R.T.R. 72.
[84] Applying *Owners of Liesbosch Dredger v Owners of Steamship Edison* [1933] A.C. 449.
[85] In *Lagden v O'Connor* [2003] UKHL 64; [2004] 1 A.C. 1067 the House of Lords decided that the
rule in the *Liesboch* should no longer be followed and stated that its application in *Ramwade* was "an
isolated instance . . . The trend of the authorities has been almost always in the contrary direction."
(at para.53).
[86] The principle that the law does not recognise a claim for damages for the late payment of damages
was confirmed by the Court of Appeal in *Sprung v Royal Insurance (UK) Ltd* [1999] Lloyd's Rep.
I.R. 111. In that case the insured was seeking to recover from his insurer damages for the
consequential losses he had suffered as a result of the insurer's failure to pay a valid claim. His claim
for such damages failed on the basis that he was seeking to recover damages for the non-payment of
damages (because the insurer's liability to pay the sum due under the policy was itself a liability to
pay damages since the primary obligation under a contract of indemnity is to hold the insured
harmless against the insured event). The principle has been subject to considerable criticism (see
Clarke, *Law of Insurance Contracts*; Browne [1998] I.J.I.L. 250 at 256; and Hemsworth [1998]
L.M.C.L.Q. 154.
[87] [1992] B.C.L.C. 793 (for the facts see para.16–030, above).

Co Ltd[88] on the grounds both of lack of a sufficient causal link and lack of foreseeability.

16–144   **Litigation costs.** Where as a result of the broker's negligence the client finds himself uninsured, he may engage in litigation in an attempt to avoid the loss or to obtain reimbursement from some third party. The client may sue the insurer and then the broker in separate actions, or may sue them together. If the client reasonably sues the insurer and then (having lost in whole or in part against the insurer) sues the broker, then the costs of the first action will be a head of loss in the claim against the broker. If the client reasonably sues the insurer and the broker in the same action and succeeds only against one of them, then in the ordinary course the court will make an order requiring the losing defendant to pay the client's costs. The "costs" in both scenarios are (a) the costs payable to the successful defendant; and (b) the client's own costs, both to be assessed on the standard basis.[89] Where the client acts unreasonably in bringing or defending such proceedings, he will not be able to recover the costs against the broker.[90]

16–145   **Claimant prosecuted.** If as a result of the broker's negligence the client is prosecuted and convicted of driving whilst uninsured, the amount of the fine and the costs of his own defence are also recoverable as damages against the broker.[91] In the unlikely event that the client is also disqualified (for example under the penalty points system) it is submitted that, subject to questions of causation and foreseeability, he may be entitled to general damages for the actual inconvenience caused by such disqualification. However, where as a result of the broker's negligence the client suffers distress or anxiety, as opposed to inconvenience, he should not usually recover general damages for that distress or anxiety.[92] Such awards should be very rare, because damages for distress are only recoverable if the subject-matter of the contract or tortious duty of care is to provide peace of

---

[88] [1995] 1 N.Z.L.R. 224; for the facts see para.16–077, n.26, above.

[89] *Strong & Pearl v S Allison & Co Ltd* (1926) 25 Ll. Rep. 504, 508. In *Seavision Investment SA v Evennett, The Tiburon* (for the facts of the underlying trial see para.16–043, above) Steyn J., when considering the basis upon which the brokers should pay the claimant's costs of suing the underwriter, said that he derived little assistance from the older cases and awarded costs taxed on the standard basis, rather than on a solicitor and own client or indemnity basis. His judgment on this point is not reported at first instance, but the claimant sought to appeal and the relevant part is set out in the judgments of the Court of Appeal: *Seavision Investment SA v Evennett, The Tiburon* [1992] 2 Lloyd's Rep. 26. The Court of Appeal held that pursuant to s.18(1)(f) of the Supreme Court Act 1981, it had no jurisdiction to entertain an appeal on the question of costs alone because Steyn J. had refused leave to appeal. Having initially expressed "considerable doubt" as to Steyn J.'s decision (29, col.1), after hearing further argument Parker L.J. indicated that he had decided that his initial doubts were misplaced (34, col.2). Scott L.J. agreed that the claimant could only recover the assessed costs incurred in unsuccessfully suing one defendant, and that such assessment should be on the standard basis (35, col.2).

[90] *Osman v J. Ralph Moss Ltd* [1970] 1 Lloyd's Rep. 313.

[91] *ibid.* at 316, 318 and 320. But where there is a degree of *mens rea* or culpable negligence on the part of the client, he cannot recover the fine by way of damages. For a general discussion of this topic, see *McGregor*, paras 748–757.

[92] In *Gaunt v Gold Star Insurance Co Ltd* [1991] 2 N.Z.L.R. 341, Gallen J. awarded general damages against a broker for the disruption caused to the claimant's life by the insurer's refusal to accept liability. This judgment was confirmed on appeal, although the judgment against the insurer was overruled on other grounds: *Gold Star Insurance Co Ltd v Gaunt* [1998] 3 N.Z.L.R. 80.

mind or freedom from distress,[93] whereas insurance brokers are usually retained to obtain monetary protection against contingencies. Thus in *Verderame v Commercial Assurance Co Plc*[94] the directors claimed damages for anxiety, depression and inconvenience. The Court of Appeal held that such damages would not be recoverable against a broker in contract and therefore should not be recoverable in tort.[95]

Credit for saved premium. Where as a result of the broker's breach of duty   **16–146**
a cheaper policy or no policy is effected or, alternatively, the policy is avoided *ab initio*, the client makes a small "gain", namely the amount of the premium saved or refunded. The client should give credit against his claim for the amount of this gain,[96] although it is usually relatively modest. In *Bollom v Byas Mosley*[97] Moore-Bick J. held that the client had to give credit for the additional premium which would have been payable in the year in which the client's loss occurred, but not for premiums payable in earlier years.[98] However, in *Eagle Star Insurance Co Ltd v National Westminster Finance Australia Ltd*[99] (where the policy was avoided as a result of the brokers' negligence) the Privy Council rejected the brokers' contention that the claimants should give credit for the amount of premium refunded.[1] In *Sharif v Garrett & Co*,[2] a claim against solicitors, the Court of Appeal had to consider the value of the claimant's earlier claim which had been struck out. The earlier claim was a claim against brokers who had failed to obtain cover. In assessing the value of that lost claim, the Court held that the

---

[93] See *Hayes v Dodd* [1990] 2 All E.R. 818; and *Watts v Morrow* [1991] 1 W.L.R. 1421.

[94] [1992] B.C.L.C. 793 (for the facts see para.16–030, above).

[95] But damages for "the disruption worry and stress occasioned by the failure to pay out" under the insurance policy were awarded by the New Zealand High Court against the negligent broker in *Bolton v New Zealand Insurance Co Ltd* [1995] 1 N.Z.L.R. 224: the English authorities were not referred to in the judgment and it is hard to reconcile this decision with them.

[96] In *Charles v Altin* (1854) 15 C.B. 46, 63 Jervis C.J. recognised that credit should usually be given for the amount of premium saved. Allowance was made for the saving of premium in *Lewis v Tressider Andrews Associates Pty Ltd* [1987] 2 Qd.R. 533; and *Cee Bee Marine Ltd v Lombard Insurance Co Ltd* [1990] 2 N.Z.L.R. 1. In *Sharp and Roarer Investments Ltd v Sphere Drake Insurance Plc, The Moonacre* [1992] 2 Lloyd's Rep. 501, A.D., Colman Q.C., sitting as a deputy judge of the High Court, appeared to consider it appropriate for credit to be given for returned premium, although he left the point open for further argument.

[97] [2000] Lloyd's Rep. I.R. 136 (for the facts see para.16–119, above).

[98] Moore-Bick J. rejected the broker's argument that the client had to give credit for the additional amounts which would have been payable by way of increased premiums throughout the period in which the client would, but for the broker's negligence, have paid higher premiums: "The fallacy in the argument lies in the assumption that [the client's] claim is based on a single continuous breach of duty or on a series of breaches of duty over the years up to and including 1996. It is not. The claim is based on a failure to give proper advice in relation to the renewal of the policy for the 1996/97 year." *ibid.* at 151.

[99] (1985) 58 A.L.R. 165 (Appeal from Supreme Court of Western Australia).

[1] "Their Lordships . . . do not accept that A.I.B. are entitled to credit for the premiums which the Goldbergs will recover from underwriters. The measure of damages is for the loss which the Goldbergs suffered by not recovering $1,000,000 under the policies. That is $1,000,000." *ibid.* at 175. In *George Barkes (London) Ltd v LFC (1988) Ltd* [2000] 1 P.N.L.R. 21 (for the facts see para.16–090, n.60, above) H.H.J. Hallgarten Q.C. declined to follow *Eagle Star Insurance Co Ltd v National West Finance Australia Ltd*. He held that if the claimant was entitled to substantial damages, then the defendants would be entitled to deduct from those the amount of premium the claimant had saved as a result of acting on the broker's advice.

[2] [2001] EWCA 1269; [2002] Lloyd's Rep. I.R. 11.

factor which would have affected the quantum of the claim against the brokers included the facts that the insured would almost certainly have had to pay a large premium to obtain cover, and that they would probably have had to pay for expensive security measures and take a share of any risk as a condition of obtaining cover. Similarly in *BP Plc v AON Ltd (No.2)*[3] Colman J. stated that the normal measure of damages for breach of a broker's duty to procure insurance was "the amount which the insurance would have paid . . . less the cost of the premium."[4]

16–147   Where the broker has negligently failed to obtain effective "primary" cover but the client has effective "secondary" cover, the client need not give credit for the latter if any recovery against the brokers diminishes the amount of the claim under the secondary cover, thus precluding the possibility of double recovery.[5]

(ii) *Contributory Negligence*

16–148   While the courts are slow to find that the client's own negligence broke the chain of causation between the broker's breach of duty and the client's loss,[6] they are prepared to reduce an award of damages to reflect want of care on the client's part.[7] Unless the claim is for breach of an absolute contractual obligation,[8] the courts may do this whether the claim is brought in tort or contract or both.[9]

16–149   Whether a claimant has been contributorily negligent will depend upon the facts of each case rather than upon any fixed rules of law. So in *Youell v Bland Welch & Co Ltd (No.2)* (the *"Superhulls Cover"* case),[10] the insurers had received a copy of the contract of reinsurance (which did not match the terms of the insurance they had granted) on three occasions. The insurers failed to notice that the reinsurance was not on the same terms as the insurance. The brokers claimed that the insurers were at fault. The insurers cited *Dickson v Devitt*[11] and *General Accident Fire & Life Assurance Corp Ltd v JH Minet & Co Ltd*[12] as authorities for the proposition that they were entitled to rely upon the brokers and were not negligent in failing to compare the wording of the insurance and reinsurance policies and spot the difference between them. Phillips J. rejected

---

[3] [2006] EWHC 424; [2006] 1 All E.R. (Comm) 789.

[4] *ibid.* at para.317.

[5] *FNCB Ltd v Barnet Devanney (Harrow) Ltd* [1999] Lloyd's Rep. I.R. 459 (for the facts see para.16–054, above).

[6] See paras 16–108 to 16–116, above.

[7] In *Cosyns v Smith* (1983) 146 D.L.R. (3d) 622, however, the Ontario Court of Appeal held that where an insurance agent failed to arrange insurance as instructed, the claimant's failure "to check up on the agent" could not in law amount to contributory negligence. The court followed *Becker v Medd* (1897) 13 T.L.R. 313, CA, a case decided before the passing of the Law Reform (Contributory Negligence) Act 1945. *Cosyns v Smith* was distinguished in *Firestone Canada Inc v American Home Insurance Co* (1989) 67 O.R. (2d) 471 on the ground that each case turned on its own facts.

[8] See para.16–011, above.

[9] *Forsikringsaktieselskapet Vesta v Butcher* [1986] 2 All E.R. 488, Hobhouse J.; [1989] A.C. 852, CA; *Youell v Bland Welch & Co Ltd (No.2)* [1990] 2 Lloyd's Rep. 431 (the *"Superhulls Cover"* case), Phillips J.

[10] [1990] 2 Lloyd's Rep. 431 (for the facts, see para.16–022, above).

[11] (1916) 86 L.J.K.B. 315 (see para.16–113, above).

[12] (1942) 74 Ll. Rep. 1 (see para.16–113, above).

that argument and held the insurers 20 per cent to blame.[13] The low percentage may well have owed much to the fact that the brokers had so drafted the reinsurance contract as to make the relevant term difficult to understand[14]: where the wording is straightforward and the person reading it is another broker, a higher percentage may well be justified. Thus in *Paul Tudor Jones II and Marsh & McLennan Inc v Crowley Colosso Ltd*[15] Mance J. reduced the damages payable by the English brokers by a third to reflect the negligence of the American brokers in failing to appreciate the effect of the relevant term, which was easy to understand. For similar reasons a reduction of 30 per cent was made by Colman J. in *National Insurance and Guarantee Corp v Imperio Reinsurance Co (UK) Ltd.*[16] In reaching his decision Colman J. mentioned the desirability of a broadly consistent approach to the application of contributory negligence to claims against brokers.

Insurers. Whilst contributory negligence is not readily found in cases of professional negligence,[17] courts are not slow to hold that insurers, being as knowledgeable about insurance matters as insurance brokers, were contributorily negligent. So in *Forsikringsaktieselskapet Vesta v Butcher*[18] Hobhouse J. held the insurers 75 per cent to blame for failing to chase up the brokers, who had negligently failed to act on a request to contact the reinsurers about an exclusion clause. This award was upheld on appeal, although it would appear that the Court of Appeal thought that the percentage fixed by Hobhouse J. was at the higher end of the acceptable range.[19] However each case will depend on its facts, and a finding that an insurer was contributorily negligent is not at all inevitable. Thus in *Pryke v Gibbs Hartley Cooper Ltd*[20] the brokers alleged that the leading underwriter at Lloyd's had been contributorily negligent. He had been given the coverholder's initial explanation, which suggested that the policy issued was not a financial guarantee, and was led to believe by the brokers that their investigations in the United States generally supported that explanation, which suggested that the coverholder had breached the spirit, but not the letter, of his contract. The underwriter had not been shown the copy of the offending policy which the

16–150

---

[13] "*Dickson v Devitt* and *General Accident v Minet* were cases decided on their own facts and do not lay down some inflexible rule of law as to what a broker's client can properly be expected to do in the exercise of reasonable care to protect his own interests. In the present case those clients were Lloyd's agents. The personnel involved were marine underwriters of great experience. They admitted that they should have read carefully the terms of the cover on the three separate occasions when they received it." [1990] 2 Lloyd's Rep. 431, 460, col.2. It must be borne in mind that both *Dickson v Devitt* and *General Accident Fire & Life Assurance Corp Ltd v JH Minet & Co Ltd* were decided before the Law Reform (Contributory Negligence) Act 1945.

[14] See para.16–055, above and *Youell v Bland Welch & Co Ltd (No.2)* [1990] 2 Lloyd's Rep. 423 (the "*Superhulls Cover*" case) where Phillips J. had to decide what the effect of the clause in the reinsurance policy was (his decision was upheld by the Court of Appeal: [1992] 2 Lloyd's Rep. 127).

[15] [1996] 2 Lloyd's Rep. 619 (for the facts see para.16–053, above).

[16] [1999] Lloyd's Rep. I.R. 249 (for the relevant facts see para.16–047, n.42, and para.16–114, above).

[17] See generally Ch.5, paras 5–141 *et seq.*

[18] [1986] 2 All E.R. 388 (see para.16–068, above).

[19] [1989] A.C. 852. No member of the court endorsed the apportionment wholeheartedly and Sir Roger Ormrod said he was somewhat surprised (at 879).

[20] [1991] 1 Lloyd's Rep. 602 (see para.16–025, above).

brokers had, nor was he shown a telex from the coverholder which showed that the brokers had a copy of the policy. He did not pursue the matter further. Waller J. held that the underwriter had not been negligent, but indicated that had he seen the documents the position would have been different.[21] Similarly, in *GE Reinsurance Corp v New Hampshire Insurance*,[22] a film finance case, Langley J. rejected the broker's submission that the insurer was contributorily negligent in failing to notice differences between the terms of insurance and re-insurance, principally because the insurer had not received notice of their terms until it was too late. The Judge stated: "In my judgment in a transaction of this novel type the onus on [the broker] 'to get it right' and to alert the insurers to any risks was such that it would not be fair to attribute fault to [the insurer] in failing to spot the problem."

16–151   **Others.** Where the claimant is not an insurer or a person with relevant expertise, the courts are likely to be slower to find contributory negligence. However, they will not be deterred from apportioning a significant part of the blame to the failure of the lay client to have due regard for his own interests if the facts warrant it. Thus in *Morash v Lockhart & Ritchie Ltd*[23] a client who failed to take any action for 18 months after his existing policy expired was held 75 per cent to blame. In *Firestone Canada Inc v American Home Insurance Co*[24] the client, acting by its advertising manager, was held 50 per cent to blame. The advertising manager had read the clause which was either incomplete or contrary to his understanding of what had been agreed, but did nothing about it. In *Labreche Estate v Harasymiw*[25] the mortgagor was held to have been 50 per cent negligent for failing to respond in a timely manner to requests from the potential insurers for further information which he should have known they would require before granting cover.

16–152   The courts are unlikely to find that a client without any expertise is contributorily negligent in failing to realise that his broker has not appreciated the purpose or effect of a particular clause. Thus in *Sharp and Roarer Investments Ltd v Sphere Drake Insurance Plc, The Moonacre*[26] the argument that the client should have appreciated the effect of the houseboat exclusion clause was rejected as "entirely misconceived".[27] Similarly in *JW Bollom & Co Ltd v Byas Mosley & Co Ltd*[28] the brokers contended that the insured was negligent in failing to appreciate the need to set the alarm and in not obtaining an adequate level of cover. Moore-Bick J., following a passage from the judgment of Beldam L.J. in

---

[21] [1991] 1 Lloyd's Rep. 602 at 624, col.2. The claim by the brokers that their client, an underwriter himself, should have realised that the risk to be reinsured was inaccurately described in a material way failed in *Aneco Reinsurance Underwriting (in liquidation) v Johnson and Higgins Ltd* [1998] 1 Lloyd's Rep. 565 (for the facts see para.16–079, above). The client did not have sufficient experience of the relevant market to appreciate this (whereas the brokers claimed special expertise) and had no knowledge of what oral presentation of the risk would be made by the brokers.

[22] [2003] EWHC 402; [2004] Lloyd's Rep. I.R. 404.

[23] (1978) D.L.R. (3d) 647 (see para.16–091, n.63, above).

[24] (1989) 67 O.R. (2d) 471 (see para.16–055, above).

[25] (1992) 89 D.L.R. (4th) 95 (for the facts see para.16–068, n.99, above).

[26] [1992] 2 Lloyd's Rep. 501 (for the relevant facts see para.16–058, above).

[27] A similar conclusion was reached in *Peter Unruh Construction Co Ltd v Kelly-Lucy & Cameron Adjusters Ltd* [1976] 4 W.W.R. 419 (for the facts, see para.16–051, n.57, above).

[28] [1999] Lloyd's Rep. P.N. 598.

Barclays Bank Plc v Fairclough Building Ltd[29] rejected those contentions: the insured was entitled to expect the brokers to act with reasonable skill and care so that it was not negligent in failing to guard against the possibility that the broker had failed to do so.

Negligence relating to the insured event. Where the negligence of the client **16–153** causes an accident in respect of which the client would have been insured but for his broker's negligence, it might be thought that no account should be taken of the client's negligence. However, in *Bolton v New Zealand Insurance Co Ltd*[30] a finding of 50 per cent contributory negligence was made on the grounds of the client's negligence in causing damage to the uninsured yacht. It is suggested that this is wrong in principle: the purpose of the insurance was to provide indemnity against loss of the yacht, even if the client had been negligent. It was for loss of that indemnity rather than loss of the yacht that the broker was liable and the client did not contribute to that loss.

(iii) *Mitigation of Loss*

A claimant cannot recover damages in respect of any loss which he ought **16–154** reasonably to have avoided. In an insurance brokers' negligence action an issue which a claimant will often have to consider is whether or not he is obliged to commence proceedings against an insurer who has rejected his claim in an attempt to mitigate his loss. For example, if the insurer has avoided the policy as a result of non-disclosure for which the broker is responsible, should the insured commence proceedings to challenge the insurer's entitlement to avoid? In *Alexander Forbes Europe Ltd v SBJ Ltd*[31] the Judge rejected the broker's argument that the insured had failed to mitigate its loss by failing to sue its insurer. He commented that: "While there is no invariable rule that a claimant does not have to embark on litigation as part of mitigating damage this is in practice generally the case."

4. CLAIMS FOR CONTRIBUTION

Claims against insurance brokers do not often give rise to claims for an indem- **16–155** nity or contribution under the Civil Liability (Contribution) Act 1978. However, were a broker and sub-broker both found liable to the insured then a claim for contribution would arise.

Claims are brought against insurance brokers because a claimant has suffered **16–156** a loss. Frequently that loss has been caused by the negligence or breach of contract by some third party. Can the insurance broker bring a contribution claim against that third party on the basis that he is liable to the claimant for the same damage as the broker? Such a claim was allowed by the Court of Appeal in

---

[29] [1995] Q.B. 241 at 226G.
[30] [1995] 1 N.Z.L.R. 224 (for the facts see para.16–077, n.26, above).
[31] [2002] EWHC 3121; [2003] Lloyd's Rep. I.R. 432 (David Mackie Q.C., sitting as a deputy High Court judge). The judge also approved the section headed "Generous treatment of claimant" at para.10–317 in the 5th edition of this work.

Hurstwood Developments Ltd v Motor & General,[32] where the third party's negligence had resulted in the claimant's factory being damaged, and the broker had failed to obtain appropriate insurance. However, the decision was promptly over-ruled by the House of Lords in *Royal Brompton NHS Trust v Hammond*.[33] The House of Lords held that the third party and the brokers were not liable for the "same damage" because the former were liable for damage to the claimant's building while the latter were liable for the loss of insurance cover for such damage.[34]

---

[32] [2001] EWCA Civ 1785; [2002] Lloyd's Rep. I.R. 185.

[33] [2002] UKHL 14; [2002] 1 W.L.R. 1397 (at para.33).

[34] In *Great North Eastern Railway Ltd v JLT Corporate Risks Ltd* [2006] EWHC 1478 Cresswell J. held that the third party whose negligence had caused the claimant to suffer a loss and the broker were not liable in respect of the same damage. He also held that it was not an abuse of process for the claimant to bring proceedings against the third party, recover damages, and then bring separate proceedings against the broker to recover the amount by which the damages already recovered from the third party were less than the amount of the indemnity that would have been received from the insurer under the claimant's policy of insurance had the broker acted with reasonable skill and care.

CHAPTER 17

ACCOUNTANTS AND AUDITORS

1. INTRODUCTION

The expanding domain. From its origins as a profession concerned primarily   **17–001**
with book-keeping and the preparation and investigation of accounts, accountancy has embraced a wide range of functions. Apart from those original functions, including auditing, the range covers extensive advisory, reporting,
investigatory, regulatory and administrative services. Advice includes most notably taxation matters but also business problems such as organisational structures,
managerial efficiency and take-overs and mergers. Administration includes
administering trusts, receiverships and liquidations, and usually involves a considerable advisory and reporting element. This proliferation of functions has
necessarily resulted in specialisation. While an individual practitioner may be

competent to deal with a wide range of functions commonly performed by accountants, very rarely will he be sufficiently competent to deal with them all. Indeed the same applies to the smaller-sized firms of accountants. The larger firms will usually be able to offer the whole range of accountancy services through partners or employees. It will be apparent that professional negligence on the part of accountants may arise within very broad contexts. This chapter will be mainly concerned with liability in the context of the preparation and investigation of accounts and reporting thereon, particularly auditing, and on the part of accountants in private practice. Owing to the substantial amount of specific statutory provisions relevant to the discharge of their duties, consideration of professional liability on the part of receivers and liquidators belongs more properly to specialist works on receivership and liquidation than to a book on professional liability covering a number of different professions. Accordingly, professional liability on the part of receivers and liquidators is not discussed. The domain of auditors and accountants continues to expand. Their roles are likely to become more extensive and intrusive. Three major propellants of this trend merit specific mention: corporate governance, regulation of the financial sector and privatisation of governmental functions.

17–002   **Corporate governance.** A basically Victorian structure is reflected in current company legislation. A company's constitution is embodied in its memorandum and articles of association. Ownership by the shareholders is separated from management and day-to-day control by the directors. The latter are accountable for the conduct of the company's affairs to the shareholders who may exercise their collective powers to reward, appoint or remove the directors. To that end, shareholders are entitled to an annual report from the directors as to their conduct of the company's affairs. Shareholders are also entitled to a report from independent auditors in order to ensure, so far as possible, that financial information as to the company's affairs prepared by the directors accurately reflects the company's position. Around that basic structure, patchy encrustations of duties have developed through legislation, the common law and regulation in certain sectors—the accumulated product of pragmatic development reflecting the vicissitudes of the moment.

Over the last three decades, corporate governance has become a major legal and political issue in the United Kingdom, as elsewhere. The problems attendant upon separation of management from ownership may be encountered in even the most basic company structure. They magnify and proliferate in the case of groups of companies, and especially so in the case of multinationals with a range of subsidiaries incorporated in various jurisdictions, shareholders, directors and managers of different nationalities and sometimes with share listings on more than one investment exchange. Diversity of management and ownership brings diversity of cultures, expectations and standards.

Reform initiatives have already resulted in the Companies (Audit, Investigation & Community Enterprise) Act 2004.[1] More significant changes, presaged by

---

[1] See paras 17–010 *et seq.*, below.

the Department of Trade and Industry's Company Law Review[2] and the White Paper on Company Law Reform published in March 2005,[3] are reflected in the Companies Bill which is expected to be enacted soon. Provisions of the Bill of particular relevance to this chapter pertain to Company Directors (Pt 10), Accounts and Reports (Pt 15) and Audit (Pt 16). Auditors are enabled to limit their liability by liability limitation agreements.[4] The new Companies Act, when enacted, will be a major statute modifying as well as consolidating existing companies law. As provisions of the new Act are brought into force, they will replace those contained in existing legislation. Presently, however, this chapter reflects companies legislation existing as at September 30, 2006. Future supplements will update the chapter to take account of the new Companies Act.

Regulation in the financial sector. A feature of the last three decades or so   **17–003** has been increasing statutory regulation of the financial sector. Prior to the Financial Services and Markets Act 2000 ("FSMA 2000") and the regime and sub-regimes established thereunder, various statutes[5] established separate regulatory regimes for insurance, banking, building societies and financial services. As in predecessor regimes, in the FSMA 2000 regime contained in the statute itself and in regulations and rules made thereunder, there are detailed provisions relating to accounts and monitoring and reporting by accountants and auditors. These provisions are designed to achieve regulatory objectives and go considerably further than requirements in company legislation.[6] Part XXII of FSMA 2000 (ss.340 to 346) pertains to auditors and actuaries.

Privatisation of governmental functions. Another feature initiated in the   **17–004** 1980s has been an extensive programme of privatisation of state-owned enterprises and (previously perceived) government functions. Privatisation has nevertheless been accompanied by the establishment of varying degrees of regulation, designed to ensure achievement of prescribed objectives, as apparent from implementing legislation. Monitoring and reporting by accountants, auditors and others are generally required. In many cases the implementing legislation provides for a formal regulator.

The structure of the profession. Anybody may call himself an accountant.   **17–005** There are currently six main professional bodies for accountants in the United Kingdom: the Institutes of Chartered Accountants in England and Wales, of Scotland and in Ireland, the Association of Chartered Certified Accountants, the Chartered Institute of Management Accountants, and the Chartered Institute of Public Finance and Accountancy. These bodies together comprise the Consultative Committee of Accounting Bodies ("CCAB"). Each body prescribes its own membership requirements, being primarily a combination of examinations

---

[2] See the DTI's website and, in particular *http://www.dti.gov.uk/cld/review.htm*, for a succinct account of the Company Law Review and White Papers, with excellent hyperlinks to relevant papers.
[3] Cmnd. 6456.
[4] See Pt 16 of the Bill. For the present law as to limitation of liability, see para.17–053, below.
[5] The major statutes preceding Financial Services and Markets Act 2000 were: Insurance Companies Acts 1974 and 1982, Banking Acts 1979 and 1987, Building Societies Act 1986 and the Financial Services Act 1986.
[6] See further Ch.14.

and practical training, and regulates its members. The first four are designated professional bodies under FSMA 2000.[7] The CCAB is involved in the organisations responsible for setting accounting[8] and auditing[9] standards.

2. DUTIES

17–006   **Overview.** The primary source of an accountant's duties is the contract of engagement between the accountant (or usually his firm) and his client. In addition, the accountant usually assumes a tortious duty of care to his client which typically, but not necessarily, coincides with his contractual duty. He may, in special circumstances, assume a tortious duty of care to third parties. The relationship of accountant and client usually gives rise also to fiduciary duties. Because accountants are often engaged to perform statutory functions such as audit, it is necessary to look at the statutory and regulatory framework; this provides the context in which contractual, tortious and fiduciary duties arise.

(a) *The Statutory Context*

17–007   A large number of functions performed by accountants are prescribed and regulated by statute. The prime example is the company audit. Accordingly, in assessing most professional liability claims against accountants, the starting point is the relevant statutory context. Detailed treatment of the various statutory contexts is beyond the scope of this book. However, certain provisions in the Companies Acts and in FSMA 2000 merit specific mention.

(i) *Companies Legislation: the Company Audit*

17–008   Relevant provisions are presently[10] contained in the Companies Acts of 1985 to 2004. These will be superseded by provisions in the present Companies Bill, when enacted and brought into force. Detailed consideration of these provisions is outside the scope of a book on professional liability and for such consideration reference should be made to the standard textbooks on company law.[11] A brief outline is given below. It should be noted that the obligation to file audited accounts does not apply to many small and medium-sized companies.[12]

17–009   **Rationale for the company audit.** The approach adopted by the courts[13] is that the management of a company is entrusted to the board of directors which is answerable to the shareholders in general meeting. The auditor's function is to ensure that the financial information prepared by the board is accurate, first to protect the company itself from undetected errors or wrongdoing (e.g. declaring

---

[7] See further Ch.14, para.14–017.
[8] See paras 17–012 *et seq.* and 17–058, below.
[9] See para.17–051, below.
[10] September 30, 2006
[11] See *Palmer's Company Law*, Pt 9.
[12] See para.17–012, below.
[13] *Caparo Industries Plc v Dickman* [1990] 2 A.C. 605, 630, *per* Lord Oliver. See also Bingham L.J.'s judgment in the Court of Appeal in the same case: [1989] Q.B. 653, 676. For the facts see para.17–029, below.

dividends out of capital) and secondly to provide shareholders[14] with reliable information for the purpose of enabling them to scrutinise the conduct of the company's affairs and to exercise their collective powers to reward, control or remove the directors. The Companies Acts do not reflect the wider commercial purpose of enabling those to whom the accounts were addressed or circulated to make informed investment decisions, for example to sell or buy shares.[15] This perception has been the foundation for the rejection of claims in tort by shareholders and parties, other than the company itself, against auditors based on allegedly negligent audit reports.[16]

Appointment of auditors. Part II (comprising ss.24 to 54) of the Companies Act 1989 is designed to ensure "that only persons who are properly supervised and appropriately qualified are appointed as company auditors, and that audits by persons so appointed are carried out properly and with integrity and with a proper degree of independence".[17] A person may be appointed as a company auditor only if he is a member of a recognised supervisory body ("RSB") and is eligible for the appointment under its rules.[18] An RSB must maintain and enforce rules as to eligibility for appointment as company auditors and as to the conduct of company audit work.[19] Generally every company must appoint an auditor or auditors.[20] It must do so at the general meeting at which accounts are laid[21] and the appointment then continues from the conclusion of that meeting until the conclusion of the next meeting at which accounts are laid.[22]   **17–010**

Remuneration. The remuneration of auditors appointed by the company in general meeting is fixed by the meeting and is required to be stated in the accounts.[23] These rules are designed to ensure that the auditor's independence is safeguarded by proper disclosure.   **17–011**

---

[14] See para.17–039, below.

[15] [1990] 2 A.C. 605 at 631. In *Berg Son & Co Ltd v Mervyn Hampton Adams* [1993] B.C.L.C. 1045, 1064 Hobhouse J. stressed that the statutory purpose was limited to providing information but not advice. He said that the statutory purpose was simply to furnish the shareholders with accurate information; what the shareholders did with that information fell outside the scope of the purpose.

[16] However, this does not preclude a claim in tort where there are special circumstances: see paras 17–026 *et seq.*, below.

[17] Companies Act 1989, s.24(1). Part II implements the European Council's Eighth Council Directive on company law harmonisation (No. 84/253). See also ss.1–6 of the Companies (Audit, Investigation & Community Enterprise) Act 2004.

[18] *ibid.*, s.25. See paras 17–005, above and 17–051, below.

[19] *ibid.*, s.30.

[20] Companies Act 1985 (as modified by the Companies Act 1989 s.119) s.384(1). There are exceptions in favour of dormant companies and certain categories of small companies: s.388A.

[21] *ibid.*, s.384(2). There is a modified procedure in the case of a private company which has dispensed with the laying of accounts: see ss.384(2), 385A and 386.

[22] *ibid.*, s.385(2). In default of appointment by the company, the Secretary of State may appoint an auditor: *ibid.*, s.387.

[23] *ibid.*, s.390A. This requirement extends to expenses and benefits in kind. There are also regulations requiring disclosure in the accounts of remuneration for non-audit work: *ibid.*, s.390B and see the Companies Act 1985 (Disclosure of Remuneration for Non-Audit Work) Regulations 1991 SI 1991/2128. Section 390B is replaced with effect from October 1, 2005 by s.7 of the Companies (Audit, Investigation & Community Enterprise) Act 2004 (see the Commencement Order: SI 2004/3322).

17–012   **The preparation of accounts.** The directors of a company are under a duty[24] to prepare accounts for each financial year, comprising a balance sheet and a profit and loss account.[25] There are specific requirements as to the form and content of accounts and as to additional information to be provided by way of notes to the accounts.[26]

Important changes in accounting standards have been introduced for financial years beginning on or after January 1, 2005.[27] Henceforth, listed companies are required to prepare their accounts in accordance with international financial reporting standards ("IFRSs").[28] Most other companies may prepare accounts in compliance either with IFRSs or with generally accepted accounting practice in the United Kingdom ("UK GAAP").[29] IFRS 1 on First Time Adoption of International Financial Reporting Standards contains important provisions for companies which are moving from the old regime to the new.[30] However, given that claims against auditors usually relate to historic accounts, it is likely that the impact of the new rules will not be felt in the field of professional liability for some time. Accordingly, we have continued to refer to UK GAAP where relevant, but readers should bear in mind the progressive impact of the new regime over time.

The cornerstone of prudent accounting is the requirement that accounts must give a "true and fair view".[31] This concept is the subject of a number of accounting standards[32] and it is given statutory effect in the Companies Act.[33] Standards are promulgated by the Accounting Standards Board ("ASB"), which is set up under the aegis of the Financial Reporting Council ("FRC"). The FRC

---

[24] Directors have a statutory responsibility for the accounts and will not be allowed to hide behind the auditor's certificate: *Re Queen's Moat Houses Plc* [2005] 1 B.C.L.C. 136; [2004] EWHC 1730, Ch, Sir D. Rattee.

[25] Companies Act 1985, s.226. In the case of a group, the directors of the parent company are under a duty to prepare group accounts also: *ibid.*, s.227. See further para.17–041, below.

[26] *ibid.*, s.226(3) and Sch.4.

[27] These changes are made by Companies Act 1985 (International Accounting Standards and Other Accounting Amendments) Regulations 2004 SI 2004/2947, which gives effect to EC Regulation 2002/1606. The impact of these Regulations is discussed in DTI Guidance for British Companies on Changes to the Accounting and Reporting Provisions of the Companies Act 1985 (see *http://www.dti.gov.uk/files/file21617.doc*). There is also a fuller discussion in *Palmer's Company Law* paras 9.201 *et seq.*

[28] IFRSs are developed by the International Accounting Standards Board and include International Accounting Standards (IASs) which were issued by the predecessor to the IASB.

[29] Section 235(1A) of the Companies Act 1985 (introduced by the 2004 Regulations) will require the audit report to specify whether the accounts have been prepared in accordance with IFRS or UK GAAP.

[30] See also APB Bulletin 2005/3 giving guidance to auditors on first-time application of IFRSs.

[31] It should be noted that the IFRS requirement is for the accounts to "present fairly". Freshfields advised the Financial Reporting Review Panel on June 22, 2005 that references in any statute to "true and fair view" should be construed in relation to accounts prepared under IFRS GAAP as referring to the requirement to "present fairly", and that IFRS GAAP seeks to maintain the principle that the accounts show a true and fair view. The advice may be found at *http://www.frc.org.uk/images/uploaded/documents/220605%20-%20True%20and%20Fair%20Opinion.pdf.*

[32] Although the accounting standards are not limited to accounts of companies registered under the Companies Acts, this is the context in which their application most frequently arises. They are therefore discussed at this point in the chapter, but the reader should be aware that accounting standards are also relevant in other contexts.

[33] s.226(2).

comprises the CCAB[34] as well as representatives from Government and industry. Standards issued by the predecessor to the ASB but which have been adopted by the ASB are known as Statements of Standard Accounting Practice ("SSAPs"); standards issued by the ASB are known as Financial Reporting Standards ("FRSs").[35] Although these standards do not directly have the force of law, it was held in 1987 that they are very strong evidence of the proper standard to be applied by the courts.[36] Since then, they have been given added status in two respects.[37] The first is that they are now promulgated by the FRC which represents interests wider than just the accountancy profession. Secondly, SSAPs and FRSs have now been given statutory recognition in the Companies Acts.[38] The purpose behind the SSAPs and FRSs is to provide a consistent approach to accounting. It is beyond the scope of this book to examine these standards in detail.[39] Their single most important objective is to put flesh on the bare bones of the overriding requirement that the accounts show a true and fair view. Anyone who is concerned with a claim against an accountant should ensure that he looks at the accounting standards which were in force at the date of the alleged breach of duty.

In almost every case, an accountant who follows accounting standards will be above criticism whilst one who departs from them may expose himself to criticism. Nevertheless, these standards should not be applied slavishly. Prudent accounting should always involve an exercise of judgment. Accounting standards make good servants but bad masters. They represent standards agreed within the profession as being generally appropriate for measuring the financial state of business entities, but the overriding objective is to convey a true and fair view.[40] Standards are constantly being reviewed by the ASB to reflect changes in commerce, but there may be rare cases in which either the standards are out of date or they need modification in order for the accounts to give a true and fair view.[41]

---

[34] See para.17–005, above.

[35] The accounting standards and related documents referred to in this section of the chapter will be found in the volume entitled *Accounting Standards* produced annually by the ICAEW.

[36] *Lloyd Cheyham v Littlejohn* [1987] B.C.L.C. 303, 313, *per* Woolf J.

[37] See the Opinion of Mary Arden Q.C. (now Arden L.J.) dated April 1993 which is set out as an Appendix to the APB's Forward to Accounting Standards (reproduced in *Palmer's Company Law*, s.F.

[38] This is achieved as follows: the Companies Act 1985, s.256 (added by the 1989 Act) makes provision for statements of standard accounting practice to be made by prescribed bodies; the Accounting Standards Board Ltd has been prescribed as a standard setting body (SI 1990/1667); the 1985 Act, s.226(3) requires accounts to comply with Sch.4; Sch.4 para.36A requires the accounts to state whether they have been prepared in accordance with applicable accounting standards and to give particulars of any material departure from those standards and the reason for such departure.

[39] The objectives of the ASB in issuing accounting standards are set out in the Statement of Principles for Financial Reporting, a document which does not itself have the status of an accounting standard but which provides an overview of the subject. However, the reader should exercise caution in relation to Chapter One of that Statement, which says that the objective of financial statements is to provide information that is useful to a wide variety of users for assessing the stewardship of the entity's management and for making economic decisions. This is considerably wider than the scope of the duty recognised in law as being owed to third parties: see paras 17–026 *et seq.*, below. Some of the FRSs and SSAPs are considered at paras 17–054 *et seq.*, below.

[40] Save as modified in the case of small and medium-sized companies: see para.17–012, below.

[41] *Kripps v Touche Ross & Co* (1997) 33 B.C.L.R. (3d) 254, 275, British Columbia CA.

The Companies Act requires that the balance sheet and the profit and loss account should each give a true and fair view.[42] This is not defined in the Act, which indirectly refers to FRSs and SSAPs.[43] Compliance with this requirement may require additional information to be given[44] and, in special circumstances, may justify departure from prescribed specific requirements.[45] However, many small and medium-sized companies are permitted to deliver abbreviated accounts to the Registrar of Companies[46]; it is recognised that these abbreviated accounts will not give a true and fair view,[47] although there is still a requirement that they be prepared properly in accordance with the relevant provisions.[48]

17–013   **The auditing of accounts.** In theory, the directors prepare the accounts first and the auditors audit them afterwards. In practice, however, the directors usually involve the auditors at an early stage and discuss the draft accounts with them. This may have important ramifications in cases where a reasonably competent auditor would have given appropriate advice at the stage when he was initially consulted or before he gave his audit certificate.[49] Where immediate steps need to be taken by the company (e.g. in order to prevent further fraud), auditors have a duty to inform the management as soon as possible after becoming aware of the situation, and not to wait until the audit is completed.[50]

Once appointed, the role of the company's auditors is to make a report to the company's members on all annual accounts of the company of which copies are laid before the company in general meeting during their tenure of office.[51] In the report the auditors must state whether in their opinion the annual accounts have been prepared in accordance with the Companies Act 1985 and in particular must state whether "a true and fair view" is given of certain matters. They are:

"(a) in the case of an individual balance sheet, of the state of affairs of the company as at the end of the financial year,
(b) in the case of an individual profit and loss account, of the profit or loss of the company for the financial year,

---

[42] Companies Act 1985, s.226(2).
[43] See para.17–012, above.
[44] Companies Act 1985, s.226(4).
[45] *ibid.*, s.226(5).
[46] *ibid.*, ss.246–9. The limits for small companies have been raised with effect from March 30, 2004 to £5.6 million in respect of turnover and £2.8 million in respect of balance sheet total: the Companies Act 1985 (Accounts of Small and Medium-sized Enterprises and Audit Exemption) (Amendment) Regulations 2004 (SI 2004/16).
[47] See APB Bulletin 1997/1 (The Special Auditors' Report on Abbreviated Accounts in Great Britain) para.13 (printed in *Auditing and Reporting* published annually by the ICAEW).
[48] Companies Act 1985, s.247B(2)(b).
[49] *Coulthard v Neville Russell* [1998] P.N.L.R. 276, CA: for the facts see para.17–042, below. See also *Pacific Acceptance Corp Ltd v Forsyth* [1970] 92 W.N. (N.S.W.) 29, 50 and 59 (for the facts see para.17–052, below). A different view was taken in *Nelson Guarantee Corp Ltd v Nelson* [1958] N.Z.L.R. 609, but we suggest that *Pacific* is to be preferred.
[50] *Sasea Finance Ltd v KPMG* [2000] 1 All E.R. 676 at 681, CA.
[51] Companies Act 1985, s.235(1). The duty is discharged by sending the report to the Company secretary: *Re Allen Craig & Co (London) Ltd* [1934] Ch. 483. If the secretary fails to pass it on to the members, it may be difficult for them to show reliance on it. See also *John (Elton) v Price Waterhouse* [2001] EWHC Ch. 438, Ferris J.

(c) in the case of group accounts, of the state of affairs as at the end of the financial year, and the profit and loss for the financial year, of the undertakings included in the consolidation as a whole, so far as concerns the members of the company."[52]

The auditors must also consider whether the information contained in the directors' report for the financial year for which the annual accounts are prepared is consistent with the accounts. If they consider that is not the case, they must state the fact in their report.[53] The auditors' report must contain the name of the auditors and be signed by them.[54]

In preparing their report the auditors must carry out such investigations as will enable them to form an opinion as to:

"(a) whether proper accounting records have been kept by the company and proper returns adequate for their audit have been received from branches not visited by them; and

(b) whether the company's individual accounts are in agreement with the accounting records and returns."[55]

The auditors must specify in their report if their opinion as to (a) or (b) is adverse and if they fail to obtain all the information and explanations which to the best of their knowledge and belief are needed for the purposes of their audit. Further, if the requirements of Sch.6, which concerns disclosure of emoluments and other benefits of directors and others, are not complied with in the annual accounts, the auditors must give the relevant particulars in their report, so far as they are able to do so.[56]

Rights of auditors. For the purpose of performing their role, auditors are **17–014** given certain rights. They have a right of access at all times to the company's books, accounts and vouchers and they may require from the company's officers such information and explanations as they think necessary for the performance of their duties as auditors.[57] An officer who provides misleading information

---

[52] Companies Act 1985, s.235(2).

[53] *ibid.*, s.235(3).

[54] *ibid.*, s.236(1). The same applies to the copy sent to the registrar of companies and to every copy laid before the company in general meeting or which is otherwise circulated, published or issued. Contravention of these requirements exposes the company and every officer to a criminal penalty under s.236(4).

[55] *ibid.*, s.237(1). For a discussion as to auditing standards, see paras 17–051 *et seq.*, below.

[56] *ibid.*, s.237. If the auditors consider that the directors were not entitled to take advantage of the exemption from the need to prepare group accounts conferred by s.248, they must state that fact in their report: *ibid.*, s.237(4A).

[57] *ibid.*, s.389A(1). Requirements are also imposed relating to subsidiary undertakings in order to secure the provision of information to the auditors of any parent company: see s.389A(3) and (4). Section 389A is replaced with effect from April 6, 2005 by s.8 of the Companies (Audit, Investigation & Community Enterprise) Act 2004 (see the Commencement Order: SI 2004/3322). In *Cuff v London and County Land and Building Co Ltd* [1912] 1 Ch. 440, company auditors, threatened with proceedings for negligence against them by the company, were refused a mandatory injunction giving them access to the company's books.

exposes himself to criminal penalties.[58] Auditors also have a right to receive notices and other communications relating to any general meeting, to attend that meeting and to be heard on any part of the business which concerns them as auditors.[59]

17–015 **Removal of auditors.** An auditor may be removed from office at any time by a company by ordinary resolution, notwithstanding anything in any agreement between them.[60] Special notice is required for a resolution at a general meeting of a company for the removal of an auditor before the expiration of his term of office or for the appointment as auditor of a person other than a retiring auditor.[61] The auditor proposed to be removed or the retiring auditor may make representations and provision is made for them to be circulated to members or to be read out at the general meeting, unless the court otherwise directs.[62] Also he must deposit a notice under s.394.[63]

17–016 **Resignation of auditors.** An auditor may resign his office by depositing a written resignation notice at the company's registered office; he must simultaneously deposit a statement under s.394, otherwise his resignation notice is not effective.[64] A s.394 notice is required where an auditor ceases to hold office for any reason. The notice must state either any circumstances connected with the auditor's ceasing to hold office which he considers ought to be brought to the attention of the company's members or creditors or, if he considers that there are no such circumstances, it must state that there are none.[65] In the former case, the company must circulate copies of the statement to every person entitled to be sent copies of the accounts, unless, on the company's application, the court otherwise directs.[66] Moreover, in the same case an auditor proposing to resign may deposit with his resignation notice a signed requisition notice calling on the company's directors forthwith to convene an extraordinary general meeting in order to receive and consider an explanation of the circumstances connected with his resignation, which he wishes to place before the meeting.[67] The auditor may request the company to circulate its members with a statement of the relevant circumstances and, unless the request is received too late, the company must comply, unless the court otherwise directs.[68]

---

[58] *ibid.*, s.389A(2). The requirements relating to subsidiary undertakings (see previous note) are also backed by criminal sanctions: see. s.389A(3), (4) and (5).

[59] *ibid.*, s.390.

[60] *ibid.*, s.391. Notice of the passing of such a resolution must be given to the registrar of companies: *ibid.* s.391(2).

[61] *ibid.*, s.391A(1).

[62] *ibid.*, s.391A(3) to (6).

[63] See the next paragraph.

[64] *ibid.*, s.392.

[65] *ibid.*, s.394.

[66] *ibid.*, s.394(3) to (7). An auditor may incur criminal liability under s.394A for contravention of s.394. The time limit for objecting to an auditor's resignation statement under s.394 is mandatory: *P & P Design Plc v PriceWaterhouse Coopers*, Ferris J. [2002] 2 B.C.L.C. 648; [2002] EWHC 446, Ch.

[67] *ibid.*, s.392(2). If the directors do not comply, they may incur criminal liability under s.392A(5). The resigning auditor is entitled to attend and be heard at the meeting convened: s.392A(8).

[68] *ibid.*, s.392A(3) to (7).

Alternative summary procedure. The usual remedy for breach of duty by an   **17–017**
accountant is an award of damages in a claim brought by way of action for breach
of contract or negligence or for equitable compensation for breach of fiduciary
duty. However, s.212 of the Insolvency Act 1986 provides an alternative summary procedure, formerly known as a misfeasance summons. The section
replaces similar provisions under predecessor legislation. Several claims against
company auditors discussed in this chapter originated by way of misfeasance
summons. A number of points arise in respect of the section[69]:

(1)   An auditor is not described as such in this section and he will come within
      it only if he is an "officer of the company". An auditor is not necessarily
      an officer of a company.[70] He is an officer, and thus can be proceeded
      against under the section, if he is duly appointed to the office of auditor by
      the company.[71] But an auditor appointed ad hoc for a limited purpose is
      not an officer.[72]

(2)   This section is procedural only. It does not create any new right or liability
      but merely provides a summary procedure for enforcing in the liquidation
      of a company existing rights which might otherwise have been enforced
      by ordinary action.[73]

(3)   There was authority in relation to the predecessor to s.212 that it did not
      cover claims based exclusively on common-law negligence.[74] However,
      the better view was that the summary procedure did extend to negligence
      claims, at least against auditors.[75] The current drafting has laid to rest any
      doubts by referring to "breach of fiduciary or other duty" instead of the
      narrower wording formerly used ("breach of trust").[76]

---

[69] Only the main points, and only so far as they concern auditors, are here mentioned. For detailed
consideration of the section see *Palmer's Company Law*, paras 15.466 *et seq.* 8.544 *et seq.* (in relation
to directors), 9.607 and (in relation to auditors).

[70] *Re Western Counties Steam Bakeries & Milling Co* [1897] 1 Ch. 617 at 627, *per* Lindley L.J.

[71] See *Re London and General Bank* [1895] 2 Ch. 166; *Re Kingston Cotton Mill Co Ltd (No.2)* [1896]
2 Ch. 279. *cf. Lipschitz v Wolpert & Abrahams* [1977] 2 S.A.L.R. 732.

[72] *R. v Shacter* [1960] 2 Q.B. 252, 256; also *Re Western Counties Steam Bakeries & Milling Co*
[1897] 1 Ch. 617 (accountants employed by one of directors of a company to audit its accounts and
to prepare a balance sheet but not appointed by the shareholders in general meeting held not to be
"officers" of the company for the purposes of Companies (Winding-Up) Act 1890, s.10; proceedings
consequently stayed); and *Mutual Reinsurance Co Ltd v Peat Marwick Mitchell & Co* [1997]
B.C.L.C. 1, CA (accountant appointed to carry out a specific audit function without being appointed
the company's auditor).

[73] *Re Canadian Land Reclaiming and Colonizing Co, Coventry and Dixon's Case* (1880) 14 Ch.D.
660 at 670; *Re City Equitable Fire Insurance Co Ltd* [1925] 1 Ch. 407 at 507 and 527; *Re B Johnson
& Co (Builders) Ltd* [1955] Ch. 634 at 648.

[74] *Re B Johnson & Co (Builders) Ltd, ibid.* at 648; see also *Re Kingston Cotton Mill Co Ltd (No.2)*
[1986] 2 Ch. 279 at 283 and 288.

[75] *per* Kay L.J. in *Re Kingston Cotton Mill Co Ltd (No.2), ibid.* at 291.

[76] In making this change Parliament broadly accepted the recommendation of the Jenkins Committee
(Cmnd. 1796, para.503(d)). In *Re D'Jan of London Ltd* [1994] 1 B.C.L.C. 561 Hoffmann J. accepted
sub silentio that s.212 applied to a claim for common-law negligence against a director. See also
Cohen v Selby [2001] 1 B.C.L.C. 176 at 183B–G.

(4) Only loss to the company consequent upon the auditor's breach of duty is recoverable under the section.[77] A frequent head of recoverable loss is the amount of dividend paid out of capital as opposed to profits in consequence of audited financial statements incorrectly showing profits instead of losses.[78]

(5) Under the section a discretion is given to the court both as to whether or not to order payment of compensation and as to the amount of compensation ordered.[79]

(ii) *Regulatory Statutes relating to the Financial Sector*

17–018 Since the 1970s, the financial sector in the United Kingdom has been the subject of several statutes imposing regulatory regimes, primarily in relation to insurance, banking, building societies, financial services and pensions. An important feature of the regimes has been extensive provisions relating to accounts and audit. The main regulatory statute is now FSMA 2000.[80] Part XXII (ss.340–346) relates to auditors and actuaries.

In considering claims arising from a regulatory context[81] it is important to have regard to specific provisions in the relevant statute, subordinate legislation and rules,[82] as well as non-statutory rules and guidance issued by regulatory organisations and professional bodies. Regulatory regimes are subject to continuing modification and amendment, frequently effected by delegated legislation.

A New Zealand case illustrates[83] how the extent of the duty is moulded by the terms of the relevant legislation. The Securities Regulations in New Zealand required a deposit-taking company to appoint a trustee who would receive periodic reports from the directors and the auditor. Section 50(2) the Securities Act 1978 imposed an express duty on the auditor to send a written report to the company and the trustee upon becoming aware of any matter which in his opinion was relevant to the exercise of the trustee's powers or duties.[84] In March 1986 the auditor became concerned about loans due from associated companies but he failed to submit any report. The company went into liquidation in August 1986. On a claim by the trustee against the auditor, the Privy Council held that s.50(2) created the necessary relationship of proximity between the auditor and

---

[77] Thus in *Re Liverpool and Wigan Supply Association Ltd* [1907] Acct. L.R. 4 where creditors sustained loss consequent upon continuing to trade with a company in reliance upon incorrect and misleading balance sheets certified by the company auditor, the liquidator failed to recover such loss upon proceeding by way of a misfeasance summons.

[78] See para.17–073, below.

[79] The giving of this discretion is somewhat inconsistent with statements that the section is procedural in nature. This discretion is additional to the court's power to grant relief to an auditor under s.727 of the Companies Act 1985: see para.17–044, below.

[80] See Ch.14 above.

[81] See paras 17–018 *et seq.*, above.

[82] Note also the Accountant's Report Rules made under the Solicitors Act 1974 (*Law Society v KPMG* [2000] 1 W.L.R. 1921: see para.17–044, below).

[83] *Deloitte Haskins & Sells v National Mutual Life Nominees Ltd* [1993] A.C. 774, PC.

[84] Contrast the English legislation, which imposes a wider duty on the auditor: *ibid.* at 787D. The current English legislation is considered at para.17–013, above.

the trustee, but the auditor's only duty was to send the report once he had actually formed an opinion. There was no statutory duty, and no basis for superimposing a tortious duty, to form an opinion. There was therefore no breach of duty before March 1986. There was a breach of duty between March and August 1986, but no loss was caused, since the money would have been lost, even if the breach had been reported in March.

In a more recent New Zealand case[85] an investor claimed against an auditor who was required by the Securities Regulations to produce a report. The court held that the Regulations contemplated that the report would be relied on by potential investors and that this created a duty of care to investors. The Regulations required a report which gave a true and fair view but they did not require the auditor to make any recommendation as to whether or not to invest. Accordingly, in order to succeed, it was not enough for an investor to show that he relied on the fact of there being a report; he had to go further and show that he read the accounts and relied on the certificate which said that the accounts gave a true and fair view.

(iii) *Whistle-blowing*

An important feature of regulatory statutes is provision for "whistle-blowing", **17–019** i.e. communication by an auditor to the relevant regulatory authority, particularly in relation to suspected fraud.[86] FSMA 2000 provides that no duty (e.g. of confidence) to which the auditor may be subject is contravened by disclosure to the FSA of information on a matter acquired *qua* auditor of an authorised person or his opinion on such matter. This is contingent upon the auditor acting in good faith and upon the information or opinion being relevant to any of the FSA's functions.[87] Moreover, an auditor is obliged to communicate certain matters to the FSA in circumstances prescribed by regulations.[88] Whistle-blowing duties may have causation ramifications in the context of claims against auditors and accountants.[89]

(b) *Duties to Client*

(i) *Contractual Duties*

The duties of an accountant primarily depend upon the contract between him and **17–020** his client. This regulates the nature and extent of his task and the standard of its

---

[85] *Boyd Knight v Purdue* [1999] N.Z.L.R. 278.
[86] See FSMA 2000, ss.342, 343. See also Pt VII of the Proceeds of Crime Act 2002 in respect of money-laundering. Guidance for auditors is provided by ISA 250 Section B (for ISAs, see para.17–094, below) and APB Practice Note 12 on Money-Laundering.
[87] FSMA 2000, s.343 creates a further exception where the auditor is auditor both of an authorised person and of another person having "close links" with the authorised person.
[88] Financial Services and Markets Act 2000 (Communications by Auditors) Regulations 2001 SI 2001/2587.
[89] See paras 17–063 *et seq.*, below.

performance.[90] It is prudent for an accountant to record his precise instructions in writing to his client. It is particularly important to establish the nature of the task, for example whether it is an audit or some more limited accountancy function.[91] The extent of investigations required is much greater in the case of the former than in the case of the latter.[92] Conversely, analysis of the contract in the context of its factual matrix may show in a particular case that the accountant has assumed a greater duty than that of an auditor.[93] An accountant who prepares a report for use in connection with an investment circular may be required to assume a responsibility which differs from that of an auditor in the following respects: (i) he may be responsible for the presentation (not merely the auditing) of the information in his report; (ii) he may need to make adjustments to information previously reported so that it gives a true and fair view for the purposes of the investment circular; and (iii) he may be required to comment on financial information which has previously been the subject of an audit.[94] It may be prudent for an accountant to have separate engagement letters where he is

---

[90] See, e.g. *International Laboratories Ltd v Dewar* (1933) 3 D.L.R. 665, Manitoba CA, *per* Robson J.A. at p.698:

> "It cannot be doubted that the measure of the responsibility of auditors depends on the terms of the employment in the particular case. That the relation did exist here is a fact though regard must be had to its exact terms. The defendants were appointed auditors at the shareholders' meeting only on one occasion . . . when the terms of appointment were general. There was discussion during the argument as to whether the audit was to be merely the statutory audit under [the relevant company statute]. I think the Court will have to ascertain the duty and obligation of the defendants from the correspondence by which their work was defined and that the limit of the statutory requirement will not prevail against that understanding."

This passage was cited with approval in *Jamieson, Austin Mitchell Ltd v Battrum* [1934] 1 W.W.R. 324. See also *Nelson Guarantee Corp Ltd v Hodgson* [1958] N.Z.L.R. 609, 610.

[91] Contrast *The Trustee of the Property of Apfel (a bankrupt) v Annan Dexter Co* (1926) 70 Acct. L.R. 57 with *Smith v Sheard* (1906) 34 Acct. L.R. 65. See also *Fox v Morrish, Grant & Co* [1918] T.L.R. 126; *Armitage v Brewer & Knott* (1932) 77 Acct. L.R. 28 (in that case the terms of the auditor's instructions required him to undertake comprehensive checking and vouching and not merely testing); and *Haig v Bamford* (1976) 72 D.L.R. (3d) 66, 71, S. Ct of Canada. In *Dairy Containers Ltd v NZI Bank Ltd* [1995] 2 N.Z.L.R. 30, given the terms of his letter to the claimant outlining his responsibilities, the Auditor-General was held to have undertaken voluntarily more extensive duties than would ordinarily arise in the case of an audit under the Companies Act. See also *Bloor Italian Gifts Ltd v Dixon* (2000) 48 O.R. (3d) 760, Ontario CA (see para.17–053, below).

[92] *McBride's Ltd v Rooke and Thomas* [1941] 4 D.L.R. 45, 48 (more required by way of examination in the case of a special investigation, as, for example, into the defalcations of a particular employee, than in the case of an audit).

[93] In *Nederlandse Reassurantie Groep Holding BV v Bacon & Woodrow* [1997] L.R.L.R. 678, a firm of accountants was retained to carry out a "due diligence" exercise on the take-over of a reinsurance company. Colman J. held (at 745), having regard to the factual matrix and to the purpose for which the advice was sought, that the standard of care required was "somewhat higher than that to be expected from accountants whose function was to advise a company in respect of its annual accounts or its annual setting of loss reserves". *Fawkes-Underwood v Hamiltons* (unreported, March 24, 1997, Goudie Q.C.) is an example of a contract which imposed a higher duty on an accountant than that usually imposed on an auditor. In this case the accountant was advising on investment in a Lloyd's syndicate. In *Stanilite Pacific Ltd v Seaton* (2005) 55 ASCR 460, the S Ct of NSW, CA, held that prima facie a higher duty of care applies to an opinion in an audit certificate than applies to his opinion given in a prospectus; however, it is theoretically possible that an accountant may assume a higher degree of responsibility in relation to a prospectus if it is clear that he is warranting facts, and not merely giving an opinion.

[94] APB Statements of Investment Circular Reporting Standards, e.g. SIR 2000 para.18 (published in *Auditing & Reporting*).

providing both auditing and accountancy services, since the responsibilities undertaken in each case are different.[95]

Audit: scope of the contract. Even where the nature of an engagement is **17–021** agreed to be an audit, questions may arise as to the scope of the audit contract. As previously noted, a large part of the necessary framework is provided by legislation. In the case of an audit of a company's accounts, the scope of the contract may also be affected by the company's articles of association.[96] An auditor auditing the accounts of a group has a duty to be satisfied with the accounts of the subsidiary companies in so far as they are relevant to the group.[97] The standard expected of an auditor is to a large extent regulated by International Standards on Auditing ("ISAs").[98]

ISA 210 says that an auditor should agree his terms of engagement in an engagement letter.[99] The letter should record acceptance of the audit appointment and summarise responsibilities of the directors and the auditors, the scope of the engagement and the form of any reports.[1] There are procedural requirements imposed as to regular review and changes in the nature of the engagement.[2]

As is apparent from the wording of s.235 of the Companies Act 1985,[3] each audit engagement is a separate contract. This may be important if a limitation issue arises. The fact that auditors have negligently performed their duties by failing to report a particular matter in one year does not by itself establish that the absence of a report about the same matter in the next year is negligent. Where what is complained of is an omission to note a particular point the circumstances giving rise to that omission in the year in question need to be examined.[4]

It has been held in Canada in relation to the audit of company's accounts required under companies legislation, that although shareholders are entitled by resolution to appoint and remove auditors, that does not give rise to a contract

---

[95] ISA 210 para.3 (SAS 140.5). Also, liability may be limited in relation to accountancy, but not audit, functions: see para.17–053, below.
[96] *Re City Equitable Fire Insurance Co Ltd* [1925] 1 Ch. 407, 520–521, *per* Warrington L.J.:
"I think that that article . . . does in such a case as the present form part of the contract between the company and the auditors, and for the reason that auditors are engaged without any special terms of engagement. When that is the case, then if the articles contain provisions relating to the performance by them of their duties and to the obligations imposed upon them by the acceptance of their office, I think it is quite plain that the articles must be taken to express the terms upon which the auditors accept their position. Of course, if the terms of their employment are expressed as a separate document, then that document must be taken to define the conditions of their engagement, and it would not be proper to assume any implied terms either from the provisions of the articles or elsewhere. But in the present case I think it is quite plain that the terms of Art.150 do, according to their proper construction, whatever that may be, effect a modification in what would prima facie be, but for that article, the obligation and liability of the auditors."
[97] *ADT v Binder Hamlyn* [1996] B.C.C. 808 at 836.
[98] See paras 17–051 *et seq.*, below for a discussion of ISAs and SASs.
[99] ISA 210 (Terms of Audit Engagements) (the SAS equivalent is SAS 140).
[1] ISA 210 para.5.1 (SAS 140.4).
[2] ISA 210 paras 10 to 19 (SAS 140.2 and 140.3).
[3] See para.17–013, above.
[4] *John (Elton) v Price Waterhouse* [2001] E.W.H.C. Ch. 438 para.268, Ferris J. See also *Midland Bank v Hett Stubbs & Kemp* [1979] Ch. 384, 403C.

between them (as distinct from the company) and the auditors.[5] We suggest that the same applies in relation to an audit required under companies legislation in the United Kingdom.[6]

17–022   **Implied duties.** Apart from duties, usually express, defining the nature of a particular engagement, an accountant will invariably be under an implied[7] if not express contractual duty to exercise reasonable care and skill. In addition, he will generally be under an implied if not express duty to take reasonable care to keep his client's affairs secret.[8] The implication of particular duties in a contract with an accountant will be governed by rules applicable to implication of terms in contracts generally.[9]

(ii) Duty in Tort

17–023   In common with other professional persons, an accountant generally owes a tortious duty of care to his client quite apart from any contract between them.[10] Although the tortious duty of care is usually co-extensive with the contractual duty, there are cases in which it assumes some practical importance, e.g. because the limitation period is different.[11]

(iii) Fiduciary Duties

17–024   **Fiduciary duties.**[12] An accountant will generally owe fiduciary duties to his client. An accountant's duty has been held to be a duty *uberrimae fidei* and of

---

[5] See *Roman Corp Ltd v Peat Marwick Thorne (No.1)* (1992) 8 B.L.R. 43, Ontario Court of Justice, Farley J. See also *Roman Corp Ltd v Peat Marwick Thorne (No.2)* (1993) 12 B.L.R. (2d) 10, Ontario Court of Justice, in which Farley J. struck out an allegation that the company contracted with the auditors as agent for the claimants who constituted a "control block" of shareholders.

[6] However, this does not preclude the court from finding a duty of care in tort: see para.17–039, below.

[7] See Supply of Goods and Services Act 1982, s.13. See further Ch.2, above.

[8] *Weld-Blundell v Stephens* [1919] 1 K.B. 520, CA; [1920] A.C. 959, HL. In that case an accountant was asked to investigate the affairs of a company. He was given information about two officials which proved to be libellous and he accidentally left the letter at the company's offices. It was held that he was in breach of an implied term to use reasonable care to keep the contents of the letter secret. See also *Fogg v Gaulter* (1960) 110 L.J. 718 and see para.17–038, below.

[9] *Investors Compensation Scheme v West Bromwich Building Society* [1998] 1 W.L.R. 896, 912–913, *per* Lord Hoffmann. For an illustration in relation to auditors see *Simonius Vischer & Co v Holt & Thompson* [1979] 2 N.S.W.L.R. 322, in which the auditors sought to imply terms: (a) that the client company would inform them of all and any breaches of authority by its employees of which the auditors were not aware; (b) that the company would take all reasonable steps to avoid suffering loss due to the acts or omissions of its employees; and (c) that the company would inform the auditors of any matters which indicated breaches by its staff of directions which would have a financially disadvantageous effect upon its business. The CA of NSW refused to imply these terms on the ground that they were not required to give business efficacy to the audit contract and were too vague.

[10] See Ch.2, paras 2–103 *et seq.* A concurrent duty in tort was expressly accepted by Lord Bridge in *Caparo Industries Plc v Dickman* [1990] 2 A.C. 605, 619C.

[11] Thus in *Pech v Tilgals* (1994) 28 A.T.R. 197 proceedings were commenced more than six years after the date of the audit certificate but within six years of the loss.

[12] See generally, Ch.2, paras 2–128 *et seq.*

complete and full disclosure of all facts properly coming within the ambit of the inquiry he was conducting.[13] However, we suggest that to describe an accountant, or indeed any other person, as a fiduciary without more would be meaningless:

"To say that a man is a fiduciary only begins analysis; it gives direction to further inquiry. To whom is he a fiduciary? What obligations does he owe as a fiduciary? In what respect has he failed to discharge those obligations? And what are the consequences of his deviation from duty?"[14]

There are three particular duties or disabilities which are usually labelled "fiduciary",[15] namely: (i) the duty of loyalty, which subsists during the accountant's or auditor's retainer, (ii) the principle of undue influence and (iii) the duty of confidentiality. Cases on breaches of the duty of loyalty, typically involving actual or potential conflicts of interest or secret profits, tend to involve solicitors[16] rather than accountants or auditors. This is no doubt because the relationship of solicitor and client is traditionally seen as a fiduciary relationship in a way that the relationship of accountant or auditor and client is not. Nevertheless there may be cases in which an accountant does assume a duty to act loyally in the best interests of the client.[17] Similarly in relation to undue influence: the relationship of accountant and client does not necessarily have the required features of ascendancy on the one side and dependency on the other, but it may be possible to establish a relationship of influence on the facts of a particular case. One important reason why claimants may seek to allege a breach of fiduciary duty is that contributory negligence is no defence.[18]

In a Canadian case[19] a client retained the defendant accountant for tax-planning and investment advice. The accountant had a financial relationship with the developer of a housing investment, from whom he received fees. The accountant recommended this investment to the client without disclosing the relationship. The client had no previous experience of this type of investment and was heavily reliant on the accountant. The majority of the court held that the defendant was in a fiduciary position towards the claimant. La Forest J. distinguished between relationships which were generally regarded as giving rise to a duty of loyalty and those where the relationship was created ad hoc. In the latter case it was necessary to look at all the circumstances in order to see whether the relationship was fiduciary. The circumstances included: (i) the scope for the defendant to exercise some discretion or power; (ii) the scope for the defendant

---

[13] *Morton v Arbuckle (No.2)* [1919] V.L.R. 487, 491, *per* Irvine C.J.

[14] Quoted by Lord Mustill in *Re Goldcorp Exchange Ltd* [1995] A.C. 74, 98.

[15] This is the classification adopted by Sir Peter Millett in *Equity's Place in the Law of Commerce* [1998] 114 L.Q.R. 214, 219.

[16] e.g. *Bristol & West Building Society v Mothew* [1998] Ch.1, 16–22, CA: see Ch.11, paras 11–023 *et seq.*

[17] As is shown by *Hodgkinson v Simms* (see below).

[18] For a recent discussion of this point, see the article by Mulheron: "Contributory Negligence in Equity: should fiduciaries accept all the blame?", 2003 P.N. 421.

[19] *Hodgkinson v Simms* (1994) 97 B.C.L.R. (2d) 1, S. Ct. of Canada.

to exert undue influence over the claimant; (iii) the opportunity for the defendant to exercise his power or discretion unilaterally so as to affect the claimant's legal or practical interests; and (iv) the claimant's peculiar vulnerability to such exercise of discretion or power. What was required was something more than a simple assumption of responsibility to provide information and execute orders; the extra ingredient was a mutual understanding that the defendant had relinquished his own self-interest and had assumed a duty of loyalty, i.e. a duty to act in the best interests of the claimant.[20] The court looked at the professional rules in force in British Columbia, which required full disclosure, and said that equity would not hold him to a lower standard.[21] The majority went on to hold that the accountant in that case was in breach of fiduciary duty as well being in breach of contract, and that the claimant was entitled to compensation on a restitutionary basis.

In an Australian case,[22] an issue arose as to whether an accountant owed a fiduciary obligation and was in breach of it. KO was a public company which was proposing to take over another public company, WU. KO's directors were required by Listing Rules to obtain for the benefit of KO's shareholders an accountant's report on the proposed take-over. The defendant accountant reported that the proposed price was fair and reasonable. In reliance on this, the shareholders of KO voted in favour of the take-over, which proved to be a disaster. KO was wound up and its liquidator sued the accountant, alleging (among other things) that he had owed a fiduciary obligation to KO not to report unless he was able to do so without a conflict of interests, and that he had been in breach of duty by making a report despite his close personal and business connections with WU and with KO's directors The High Court of Australia held (by majority) that no relevant fiduciary obligation had been owed by the accountant. Fiduciary duties are usually proscriptive rather than prescriptive; there are specific prohibitions (such as not acting for two clients with conflicting interests) rather than a positive requirement to act in the best interests of a client. Although an accountant required by Listing Rules to make a report had to be independent, the majority said that neither lack of independence nor evidence of a previous close association between the KO directors and the defendant was sufficient to establish a conflict of interests. It is submitted that there is force in the dissenting judgment of Kirby J., who held that the accountant's duty to report for the purpose of Listing Rules was fiduciary (in the sense of imposing a duty of loyalty) and that on the facts he could only discharge that duty by declining to act.

17–025   **Confidentiality.** As in the case of other professionals, an accountant owes to his client a duty of confidence. This duty continues in equity even after the termination of an accountant's contract of engagement. Aspects and consequences of this duty are addressed in Ch.2, including the leading case of *Prince*

---

[20] (1994) 97 B.C.L.R. (2d) 1, S. Ct. of Canada at 21–22.
[21] *ibid.* at 33–34, *per* La Forest J.
[22] *Pilmer v Duke Group Ltd* [2001] 2 B.C.L.C. 773, H Ct Aus. The case is discussed by Nolan and Prentice, (2002) 118 L.Q.R. 180.

Jefri Bolkiah v KPMG.[23] One consequence of the duty is that the accountant may not disclose information confidential to a client to any third party without the client (or former client)'s consent.[24] This is a strict duty, not merely a duty to use reasonable endeavours to keep the information confidential.[25] Nevertheless, the duty of confidence may be overridden by the statutory "whistle-blowing" duty.[26]

The second consequence of the duty of confidence is that the former client may be entitled to an injunction to restrain the accountant from acting for another client with an adverse interest. The burden of proof is on the first client to show (i) that the accountant is in possession of information which is confidential to him and to the disclosure of which he has not consented and (ii) that the information is or may be relevant to the new matter in which the interest of the other client is or may be adverse to his own.[27]

(c) *Duties to Third Parties*

(i) *Overview*

The basic rule. Accountants, like other professionals, owe duties of care to   **17–026** their own clients but do not owe them to third parties in the absence of some special factor. The courts recognise that negligent advice or information is capable of causing loss to many more claimants than a negligent product. In order to keep the tort within reasonable bounds, the courts require some extra ingredient beyond mere foreseeability of loss.[28] If there were no extra ingredient, then there would be a risk of imposing "a liability in an indeterminate amount for an indeterminate time to an indeterminate class".[29] This is particularly important in the case of accountants, since the range and number of persons who may suffer

---

[23] [1999] 2 A.C. 222, HL.

[24] In some cases consent may be implied, e.g. a report to shareholders in a company audit or disclosure of assets to the Revenue in a tax return completed by an accountant for a client. In *Nam Tai Electronics Inc v Pricewaterhouse Coopers* (2005) 2 H.K.L.R.D. 461 (Hong Kong), NTE appointed PwC to conduct due diligence into Albatronics, a company which it was proposing to acquire. The acquisition went ahead. Albatronics then went into liquidation and there was a proposal to appoint a partner in PwC as liquidator. NTE objected, alleging a conflict of interests. PwC submitted a liquidation proposal to creditors summarising why there was no conflict. NTE then sued PwC for breach of confidence. Waung J. dismissed the claim on various grounds. One ground was that NTE was to be taken as having waived the confidence (*cf. Lillicrap v Nalder*, discussed in Ch.11 (Solicitors) para.11–145). The judge reasoned that, by alleging conflict of interests, NTE had brought the previous retainer into the public domain and the absolute right to confidentiality was relative and not absolute (*Bolkiah* not followed).

[25] *Prince Jefri Bolkiah v KPMG* [1999] 2 A.C. 222, 235G, HL.

[26] See para.17–030, above. It has been suggested that a similar "whistle-blowing" duty arises at common law where an auditor suspects fraud on the part of the company's management and it may be necessary for him to report directly to a third party without the knowledge of management: *Sasea Finance Ltd v KPMG* [2000] 1 All E.R 676 at 681. Such a duty to report to a third party is explicable as an aspect of the auditor's contractual and tortious duty of care owed to the company.

[27] *Bolkiah, ibid.* at 235C-F.

[28] *Murphy v Brentwood DC* [1991] 1 A.C. 398, 468G, *per* Lord Oliver.

[29] *per* Cardozo C.J. in *Ultramares Corp v Touche* (1931) 174 N.E. 441, 444, Court of Appeals of New York.

loss consequent upon negligent performance of certain engagements by them, especially an audit report, are very large.[30]

The current state of the law, which is considered in more detail below, may be summarised as follows:

(1) The scope of the duty will depend upon the purpose to be discerned from an analysis of the relevant statute or regulatory context. In the case of an audit under the Companies Act, the statutory purpose is to provide shareholders with information about the company's financial position so that they are fully informed at the general meeting; it is not to provide the shareholders or anyone else with information so that they may make investment decisions.

(2) Nevertheless, there may be cases where the accountant has undertaken a specific responsibility to a third party or class of third parties. In order to establish this, the claimant must prove:

(3) that the accountant was aware of the nature of the transaction which the claimant had in mind;

(4) that the accountant knew or ought to have known that his statement would be communicated to the claimant, either directly or as a member of a class;

(5) that the accountant knew or ought to have known that the claimant was likely to rely on the statement in deciding whether or not to proceed with the transaction; and

(6) that the claimant did rely on the statement.

Some auditors have now started to add the following words to their audit reports so to reflect the basic rule as set out in this paragraph:

"This report is made solely to the Company's members, as a body, in accordance with Section 235 of the Companies Act 1985. Our audit work has been undertaken so that we might state to the company's members those matters we are required to state to them in an Auditor's report and for no other purpose. To the fullest extent permitted by law, we do not accept or assume responsibility to anyone other than the company and the company's members as a body, for our audit work, for this report, or for the opinions we have formed."[31]

17–027   **The different tests.** Over the years, various tests or approaches have been formulated in order to determine whether on particular facts the defendant owed to the claimant a duty of care in tort.[32] These have included (i) the three-fold test based on (a) foreseeability of loss, (b) proximity of relationship and (c) whether

---

[30] *Caparo Industries Plc v Dickman* [1990] 2 A.C. 605, 632. Various categories of claimant are considered in paras 17–038 *et seq.*, below.

[31] This was apparently done in response to the original decision in *Royal Bank of Scotland Plc v Bannerman Johnston Maclay* (discussed at para.17–066, below).

[32] See generally, Ch.2 para.2–022 *et seq.*

it would be just and reasonable to impose a duty,[33] (ii) the assumption of responsibility test[34] and (iii) the incremental approach.[35] Each of these were reviewed by Sir Brian Neill in an audit negligence context in *Bank of Credit Commerce International (Overseas) Ltd v Price Waterhouse (No.2)*.[36] He concluded that, at least for the purpose of an application to strike out a claim, the court should look at all three tests. He said that it was likely that they all would all lead to the same result, if the facts were properly analysed.[37] The three tests or approaches were recently reviewed by the House of Lords in a banking context in *Customs & Excise Commissioners v Barclays Bank Plc*[38] and their relevant potency (including in an audit context) must now be assessed in light of the judgments in that case.

In the light of these authorities the following approach is suggested:

(1) If there is a sufficiently compelling analogy with a previous decided case, the incremental approach will be a useful starting point.

(2) In cases which are equivalent to contract, the most useful test is likely to be that of assumption of responsibility. This is especially so where the case involves an acceptance of responsibility for particular information provided by a particular defendant to a particular claimant for a particular purpose. In such a case the enquiry will focus upon what can reasonably be inferred from the parties' conduct against the background of the factual matrix.[39]

(3) The more notional the assumption of responsibility becomes, the less useful the test. In such a case one should instead look at the three-fold test, but bearing in mind the inherent vagueness of the test which limits its usefulness. It is vital not to lose sight of the critical issues which are likely to be: purpose, knowledge and reliance, i.e. (i) the purpose for

---

[33] This test was adopted in *Caparo* although it was observed in that case that proximity is "no more than a label which embraces not a definable concept but merely a description of circumstances from which, pragmatically, the courts conclude that a duty of care exists": [1990] 2 A.C. 605 at 633D, *per* Lord Oliver; see also *ibid.* at 617B, *per* Lord Bridge. However in *BCCI (No.2)* the court said that the test was useful in focussing attention on the three essential questions of foreseeability, proximity and fairness. This test was also adopted in *Law Society v KPMG* [2000] 1 W.L.R. 1921. The courts in Canada have used element (iii) in a different fashion: they have continued to follow the wider pre-*Caparo* test set out in *Anns v Merton LBC* [1978] A.C. 728, 751–752 but they have refused on policy grounds to allow claims where these would result in indeterminate liability: *Hercules Managements Ltd v Ernst & Young* [1997] 146 D.L.R. 577, 586 and 597.

[34] *Henderson v Merrett Syndicates Ltd* [1995] 2 A.C. 145, 180–181 and 192–193, *per* Lord Goff; *White v Jones* [1995] 2 A.C. 207, 268H and 273G, *per* Lords Goff and Browne-Wilkinson. However, in *Caparo* [1990] 2 A.C. 605, 628 and 637, Lords Roskill and Oliver said that it was a convenient label but that it did not tell one anything about the circumstances from which such attribution arose. The assumption of responsibility was found by Moore-Bick L.J. to be a helpful test in *Man Nutzfahrzeuge AG v Freightliner Ltd* [2005] EWHC 2347 (Comm), para.340.

[35] *Sutherland Shire Council v Heyman* (1984) 147 C.L.R. 424, H. Ct. of Aus., quoted with approval in *Caparo, ibid.* at 618 and 633 by Lords Bridge and Oliver.

[36] [1998] P.N.L.R. 564, 583, CA. For the facts, see para.17–030, below.

[37] *BCCI (No. 2), ibid.* at 586F.

[38] [2006] 3 W.L.R. 1. See Ch.2 para.2–053.

[39] Lord Hoffmann in *Customs & Excise Commissions v Barclays Bank Plc, ibid.* at para.35.

which the statement was made and communicated, (ii) the knowledge of the maker of the statement and (iii) reliance by its recipient.[40]

(4) Whichever general test is applied, it is important to focus on the particular context in which the alleged duty arises. In evaluating a claim against accountants arising from a statutory or regulatory context, it is critical to assess the relevant statute or regulatory scheme. Considerations decisive in such a context to negate a duty of care alleged to have been owed to a third party by statutory, ministerial, administrative, regulatory and complaints-handling bodies have been the availability of alternative bases of redress[41] and regulatory overkill,[42] even though such redress may be of little value to the third party concerned. Like considerations apply in evaluating claims against accountants. Moreover, it is vital not to lose sight of the critical issues which are likely to be: purpose, knowledge and reliance, i.e. (i) the purpose for which the statement was made and communicated, (ii) the knowledge of the maker of the statement and (iii) reliance by its recipient.[43]

Most of the reported decisions against accountants since *Caparo* have arisen out of applications to strike out the claim on the ground that no duty of care was owed to the claimant. In general, the courts have taken the view that duties owed to third parties by accountants and auditors is a developing area of law and, provided that something is alleged which might arguably be sufficient to constitute a special factor, the claim should be allowed to proceed to trial.[44] The moral is that, unless it is clear that the claimant's claim must fail, it may be better for the defendant to proceed to trial instead of attempting to strike out. However, it remains to be seen whether the current move towards active judicial case-management will bring about a change of climate.

---

[40] Note in particular the speeches in *Caparo Industries Plc v Dickman, ibid.* of Lord Bridge at 620–621, Lord Oliver at 638 and Lord Jauncey at 659–660 (esp. at 630E "the fundamental question of purpose"). Note also the emphasis on purpose in *James McNaughton Paper Group Ltd v Hicks Anderson & Co* [1991] 2 Q.B. 113, 125–127.

[41] As to a statutory context see *Caparo, ibid.*, and *Murphy v Brentwood* [1991] 1 A.C. 398. As to a regulatory context, see *Yuen Kun Yeu v Att-Gen of Hong Kong* [1988] A.C. 175, PC and *Davies v Radcliffe* [1990] 1 W.L.R. 821, PC. As to a ministerial context, see *Rowling v Takaro Properties Ltd* [1988] 1 A.C. 475, PC. As to an administrative context see *Jones v Department of Employment* [1989] Q.B. 1, CA. For like reasoning in the context of copyright, see *CBS Songs Ltd v Amstrad Consumer Electronics Plc* [1988] A.C. 1013, 1059–1060, HL, and receivership, see *Downsview Ltd v First City Corp Ltd* [1993] A.C. 295, 316, PC.

[42] See *Rowling v Takaro Properties Ltd* [1988] 1 A.C. 475, 502, PC.

[43] Note in particular the speeches in *Caparo Industries Plc v Dickman, ibid.* of Lord Bridge at 620–621, Lord Oliver at 638 and Lord Jauncey at 659–660 (esp. at 630E "the fundamental question of purpose"). Note also the emphasis on purpose in *James McNaughton Paper Group Ltd v Hicks Anderson & Co* [1991] 2 Q.B. 113, 125–127.

[44] *Equitable Life Assurance Society v Ernst & Young* [2004] P.N.L.R. 16; [2003] EWCA Civ 1114, CA, para.128. See also *Coulthard v Neville Russell* [1998] P.N.L.R. 276, 288–289 (for the facts see para.17–042, below); *Andrew v Kounnis Freeman* [2000] Lloyd's Rep. P.N. 263, 272, CA (for the facts see para.17–044, below); *Siddell v Smith Cooper* [1999] P.N.L.R. 511, 520–522 (for the facts see para.17–033, below).

After considering the basic principles enunciated in *Caparo* we seek to analyse the case law both by reference to factors identified in the cases and by reference to categories of typical advisee. The analysis should be taken as no more than indicative as to a court's approach on similar facts. A claimant will have made considerable headway in getting his claim off the ground if he can show that his facts are similar to those of a previous decision in which a duty of care was held to exist, at least if the courts adopt the incremental approach. However, where a novel set of facts comes before the court, the fact that they do not fit into any established category is not necessarily a reason for holding that there is no duty of care. It is usually necessary to go back to first principles.

(ii) *Caparo*

The law prior to *Caparo*.[45] It used to be thought that there was no liability for   **17–028** a negligent misrepresentation made by one person to another who had acted upon it to his detriment, in the absence of any contractual or fiduciary relationship between the parties or of fraud. It was on this basis that the majority of the Court of Appeal in *Candler v Crane Christmas & Co*[46] dismissed the claim of the claimant who had invested money in a company in reliance upon accounts negligently prepared by the defendant accountants and who had lost his investment upon the company's liquidation. Denning L.J., however, in his classic dissenting judgment, took the view that the claimant was owed a duty of care by the accountants and was entitled to recover. The majority's decision was overruled and Denning L.J.'s judgment was approved by the House of Lords in *Hedley Byrne & Co Ltd v Heller & Partners Ltd.*[47] His judgment was also expressly approved in *Caparo*[48] and there can be little doubt that in the same circumstances as those in *Candler* today, the claimant would succeed.

Denning L.J.'s judgment[49] laid the foundations for the modern law in relation to claims by third parties against accountants. He considered the types of statements in respect of which professional accountants owe a general duty of care and the persons and transactions to which that duty extends.

(1) Types of statement: he considered that accountants were not liable for (a) casual remarks made in the course of conversation; nor for (b) statements made outside their work; nor for (c) statements not made in their capacity as accountants. But they were "in proper cases", apart from any contract in the matter, under a duty to use reasonable care in the preparation of their accounts and in the making of their reports.

(2) Persons to whom accountants owe a duty of care: he said that the test of proximity in these cases was: Did the accountants know that the accounts were required for submission to the claimant and use by him?

---

[45] For a more detailed discussion of the law before *Caparo* see the fourth edition of this work, paras 8–34 to 8–46.
[46] [1951] 2 K.B. 164.
[47] [1964] A.C. 465.
[48] [1990] 2 A.C. 605, 623.
[49] [1951] 2 K.B. 164, 174–185.

(3) Nature of the transactions: he confined liability to transactions for which the accountants knew their accounts were required.[50]

The next milestone was *Hedley Byrne & Co Ltd v Heller & Partners Ltd*.[51] Although not a claim against accountants, it proved of crucial relevance in the development of the law relating to accountants' negligence. All their Lordships agreed that in certain circumstances liability could be incurred for a negligent misrepresentation by one person to another even in the absence of any contractual or fiduciary relationship between them or of fraud. They were nevertheless concerned to limit the parameters of such liability. The case is generally regarded as requiring a special relationship to exist for one person to owe another a duty of care in the giving of advice or information. None of their Lordships gave precise criteria for this relationship, all relying upon broad formulations of general principle. Not all these formulations are identical in substance and they differ in emphasis. Nevertheless the following passage from a speech of Lord Morris, which Lord Hodson endorsed, broadly reflects the current view of what *Hedley Byrne* established:

> "if in a sphere in which a person is so placed, that others could reasonably rely upon his judgment or his skill or upon his ability to make careful inquiry, a person takes it upon himself to give information or advice to, or allows his information or advice to be passed on to, another person who, as he knows or should know, will place reliance upon it, then a duty of care will arise."[52]

17–029   **The facts of *Caparo Industries Plc v Dickman*.**[53] The claim arose out of the takeover in 1984 of Fidelity Plc by Caparo Industries Plc, both listed companies, and was brought against two of Fidelity's directors and the auditors of its accounts for the year ended March 31, 1984. In early March 1984 a press release was issued forecasting a significant profits shortfall. Over that month Fidelity's share price fell sharply. In May 1984 the auditors reported upon the accounts giving a clean certificate to the effect that they were properly prepared and gave a true and fair view of relevant matters. The next day Fidelity's directors announced profits well down on predictions. On June 8, Caparo began to buy Fidelity shares. The accounts were sent to the shareholders on June 12, 1984, but Caparo was not registered as a shareholder until later. Nor did it attend Fidelity's annual general meeting on July 4, 1984 when the auditors' report was read and the accounts adopted. Two days later Caparo had acquired 29.9 per cent of Fidelity's issued shares. In September it made a bid for the remaining shares and subsequently acquired them, some compulsorily.

Caparo maintained that the accounts were inaccurate and misleading, in particular in overvaluing stock and undervaluing after-sales credits, with the

---

[50] In this respect the law has developed: the accountant would also be liable today if he *ought* to have known: *Hedley Byrne, ibid.* at 486. On the particular facts in *Candler*, the defendants did actually know of the claimant's reliance and it was therefore unnecessary to consider the question whether they ought to have known of it. Note also Denning L.J.'s observation (*ibid.* at 184) that a lawyer is never called upon to express his personal belief in the truth of his client's case, whereas an auditor is always called on to express his opinion that the accounts give a true and fair view.

[51] [1964] A.C. 465.

[52] *ibid.* at 503, 514.

[53] [1990] 2 A.C. 605.

result that there was in fact a loss of £400,000 instead of reported profits of £1.3m. It alleged that its share purchases subsequent to the sending of the accounts to shareholders were made in reliance on those accounts and that, if it had known the true position, it would not have bid for them at the price paid or at all. It commenced proceedings against the two directors alleging deceit and against the auditors alleging negligence. It contended that the auditors in carrying out their functions in April and May 1984 owed a duty of care to investors (in the sense of existing shareholders) and potential investors, including Caparo. In support it maintained that the auditors: (1) knew or ought to have known of (a) the press release in early March, (b) the slide in the share price from 143p on March 1 to 75p on April 2, and (c) Fidelity's need for financial assistance; and (2) ought to have foreseen that Fidelity was vulnerable to a takeover bid and that bidders such as Caparo might well rely on the accounts in assessing a bid and suffer loss if the accounts were inaccurate.

An order was made for the trial of a preliminary issue: whether on the alleged facts the auditors owed a duty of care to Caparo (a) as potential investors in Fidelity or (b) as shareholders in Fidelity as from June 8 and/or 12, 1984, in respect of the audit of the relevant accounts. The judge at first instance, Sir Neil Lawson, held that the auditors owed no duty of care to Caparo in either capacity. On Caparo's appeal, the Court of Appeal by a majority (Bingham and Taylor L.JJ., O'Connor L.J. dissenting in part) allowed the appeal.[54] The court was unanimously of the view that the requisite relationship of proximity was not established between potential investors in a company and its auditor. Bingham and Taylor L.JJ. concluded that it was established between existing shareholders and the auditor. Thus if an individual shareholder sustained loss by acting in reliance on negligently prepared accounts, whether by selling or retaining his shares or by purchasing additional shares, he was entitled to recover in tort. O'Connor L.J. disagreed and rejected a duty of care in that case also.

The House of Lords took the same view as O'Connor L.J. and the judge at first instance and restored the latter's decision, holding that there was no duty of care owed to Caparo either as an existing shareholder or as a potential investor. The main speeches were delivered by Lords Bridge and Oliver.[55]

Lord Bridge propounded the three-fold test of foreseeability, proximity and fairness, although he warned that these were imprecise terms and he saw the wisdom of following the incremental approach.[56] He distinguished *Smith v Eric S Bush*[57] by saying that in that case the defendant knew (i) the nature of the transaction which the claimant had in contemplation, (ii) that the information or advice would be communicated to the claimant and (iii) that the claimant was very likely to rely on it. The defendant could therefore be expected specifically to anticipate (a) that the claimant would rely on the advice or information for the very purpose for which he did rely on it and (b) that the claimant would

---

[54] [1989] Q.B. 653.
[55] Lord Roskill gave a short speech agreeing with Lords Bridge and Oliver (*ibid.* at 627F), Lord Ackner (at 629E) agreed with all the speeches, and Lord Jauncey gave a speech which concurred with the main speeches (at 654–663).
[56] See para.17–027, above.
[57] [1990] 1 A.C. 831. In that case it was held that a surveyor who valued a modestly priced house for a mortgagee but whose fee was paid by the borrower might owe the latter a duty of care.

reasonably suppose that he was entitled to rely on it. This is to be contrasted with a statement, such as an audit certificate, which is put into general circulation.[58] He concluded:

"It is never sufficient to ask simply whether A owes B a duty of care. It is always necessary to determine the scope of the duty by reference to the kind of damage from which A must take care to save B harmless."[59]

Lord Oliver took as his starting point the statutory context.[60] He said that it should not be assumed that the purpose of the auditor's certificate was anything other than the fulfilment of the statutory duty of carrying out the annual audit. The statutory purpose of the audit was simply to furnish the shareholders with information.[61] Although it was foreseeable that shareholders and other investors would make investment decisions based on that information, this was not its statutory purpose.[62] He considered the three different tests summarised above[63] and found the greatest assistance in the incremental approach.[64] He then went on to consider the law of negligence and the need for something more than mere foreseeability as a way of controlling the floodgates of liability. A defective bottle of ginger-beer may damage one consumer, but a defective statement may be repeated endlessly and relied on in different ways by different people. He regarded *Smith v Eric S Bush* as the high-water mark and distinguished it on the ground that the loss in the present case was strictly unrelated to the intended recipient or to the purpose for which the advice was required. Importantly, he saw no policy reason to extend the law.[65] He said in relation to proximity that:

"it is not a duty to take care in the abstract but a duty to avoid causing to the particular claimant damage of the particular kind which he has in fact sustained"[66]

---

[58] [1990] 1 A.C. 831 at 620.

[59] *ibid.* at 627D. The importance of analysing the scope of the duty was emphasised by Lord Hoffmann in *South Australia Asset Management Co Ltd v York Montague Ltd* [1997] A.C. 191 (see para.17–064, below).

[60] This is a reference to the Companies Act: see paras 17–009 *et seq.*, above. Lord Jauncey took the same approach: *ibid.* at 658G. Surprisingly, it would appear that no consideration was given to the listing requirements made by the Council of the Stock Exchange and contained in its publication Admission of Securities to Listing ("The Yellow Book") which are now statutory requirements by virtue of Pt VI of FSMA 2000, although they were not at the time of the facts giving rise to the claim in *Caparo*. These include specific requirements relating to publication of financial information, including on a continuing basis. The Stock Exchange is an investment market and potential investors are clearly in contemplation.

[61] See para.17–009, above.

[62] *ibid.* at 631. See also Lord Jauncey *ibid.* at 661G–662B.

[63] See para.17–027, above.

[64] *ibid.* at 632–638.

[65] *ibid.* at 642F–H. In *Morgan Crucible Co Plc v Hill Samuel & Co Ltd* [1991] Ch. 295 Hoffmann J. at first instance justified the distinction between *Smith v Bush* and *Caparo* in policy terms (i.e. differences between the economic relationships of (i) corporate investor and auditor and (ii) house purchaser and valuer respectively and differences between the markets in which the different professionals operated) but the Court of Appeal in that case downgraded the importance of this policy factor (for the facts of this case, see para.17–040, below.)

[66] *ibid.* at 651F.

He concluded that:

> "The purpose for which the auditors' certificate is made and published is that of providing those entitled to receive the report with information to enable them to exercise in conjunction those powers which their respective proprietary interests confer upon them, and not for the purposes of individual speculation with a view to profit. The same considerations as limit the existence of a duty of care also, in my judgment, limit the scope of the duty."[67]

The House of Lords in *Caparo* held that the duty was owed to the shareholders as a body and not to individual shareholders.[68] In practice their collective interests are indistinguishable from the interests of the company itself and therefore any loss suffered by the shareholders as a body will be recouped by a claim brought by the company.[69]

(iii) *Factors which may be Relevant*

In evaluating claims based upon the assertion of a duty of care in care owed to third party by an accountants, in particular the issue of proximity, the six factors adopted in three cases by Sir Brian Neill (as Neill L.J. in the first) in the Court of Appeal provide a useful framework for analysis. As he cautioned, some of the factors overlapped and the did not intend the list of factors to be comprehensive. The facts of the three cases merit summary before enumeration and consideration of the factors. As Sir Brian Neill in *Bank of Credit Commerce International (Overseas) Ltd v Price Waterhouse (No.2)*[70] and *Peach Publishing Ltd v Slater & Co*[71] he evaluated the claims by reference to the same factors. **17–030**

The claim in *James McNaughton Paper Group Ltd v Hicks Anderson*[72] arose out of the agreed takeover if a company, MK, by the claimant company. In the course of takeover negotiations, draft financial statements were provided by the defendants who were MK's auditors. These showed a net loss for the year. Also at a meeting between the chairman of the claimant company and a representative of the defendants, the latter confirmed that MK was breaking even or doing marginally worse. The take-over went ahead and the claimant later discovered errors in the accounts. The Court of Appeal held that there was insufficient proximity and hence no duty was owed to the claimant.

The claim in *Bank of Credit Commerce International (Overseas) Ltd v Price Waterhouse (No.2)*,[73] ("*BCCI (No.2)*") arose out of a massive fraud. Liquidators acting on behalf of a holding company and two subsidiary companies, S1 and S2, in the same banking group brought claims on various bases against two firms of

---

[67] [1990] 1 A.C. 831 at 654.

[68] It is suggested that a preferable formulation is that the duty was owed to the company as represented by all its shareholders, and not to individual shareholders.

[69] *ibid.* at 626C–E (Lord Bridge). See para.17–039, below.

[70] [1998] P.N.L.R. 564, 583, CA.

[71] [1998] P.N.L.R. 364, CA. *cf. ADT v Binder Hamlyn* [1996] B.C.C. 808, where the accountant was aware that the confirmation which the purchaser sought from him was "the final hurdle" to be surmounted before the purchaser agreed to purchase.

[72] [1991] 2 Q.B. 113.

[73] [1998] P.N.L.R. 564, 583, CA.

auditors. All three companies were operated as a single economic unit to the knowledge of both firms of auditors. One of head of claim was by S1 against the auditors of S2, based on alleged breach of a duty of care in tort owed by the S2 auditors to S1 in failing to communicate information about S2 to S1 and its auditors, which was relevant to the S1 audit. The S2 auditors sought to strike out the claim on the basis that they did not owe a duty of care to S1. The Court of Appeal held that, although auditors did not usually owe a duty to a non-client, it was arguable on the facts that the S2 auditors did owe such a duty.

In *Peach Publishing Ltd v Slater & Co*[74] the claimant was proposing to buy the share capital of ASA. The claimant's representative said that the purchase would not proceed unless the seller gave a warranty as to the accuracy of certain management accounts of ASA. The seller would not give the warranty without approval from the defendant, who was both his personal accountant and ASA's auditor. At a meeting the claimant's representative pressed the defendant to give his approval, which he did. After the purchase, it emerged that the accounts were inaccurate and the buyer sued the accountant. The Court of Appeal held that, although the accountant's assurance had been given both voluntarily and direct to the claimant's representative, the purpose of the assurance had been solely to advise the seller that he could give the warranty and the defendant had not assumed a duty to the claimant.

17–031　　　**Factor (1): The purpose for which the statement was made.** Where a statement is made for the express purpose of communicating it to the advisee, this is a factor in favour of finding the necessary proximity. Where it is not express, it might in a suitable case be implied from the circumstances.[75] By contrast, where the document is an auditor's certificate in relation to a company audit and there is no indication as to the purpose for which it was made, the court will conclude that it was made merely for the statutory purpose of giving information to the shareholders as a body.[76] In one case[77] it was held that the purpose of the defendant's audit work was limited to the statutory purpose, but that representations made by the auditor at a meeting were made for the purpose of providing the takeover bidder with information upon which he could rely without further enquiry.

17–032　　　**Factor (2): The purpose for which the statement was communicated.** It is necessary to ask whether it was communicated for information only or with a view to some action being taken. Further, if a statement was made for one purpose, it may be unreasonable to impose liability in relation to a different

---

[74] [1998] P.N.L.R. 364. *cf. ADT v Binder Hamlyn* [1996] B.C.C. 808, where the accountant was aware that the confirmation which the purchaser sought from him was "the final hurdle" to be surmounted before the purchaser agreed to purchase.

[75] *Customs & Excise Commissioners v Barclays Bank Plc* [2006] 3 W.L.R. 1; [2006] UKHL 28, para.35 (Lord Hoffmann).

[76] See para.17–009, above.

[77] *ADT v Binder Hamlyn* [1996] B.C.C. 808, May J.; see also *Barings v Coopers & Lybrand* [2002] P.N.L.R. 16, Evans-Lombe J.

purpose.[78] In one case[79] an accountant was held liable to a third party notwithstanding that he did not intend to proffer information as a means of persuasion; it was sufficient that he knew (or ought to have known) that the information would be relied upon.

Factor (3): The relationship between the advisee and any relevant third   **17-033**
party. Where the information or advice was initially prepared for someone other than the advisee, it is necessary to consider whether the advisee was likely to look to the third party, and through him to the defendant, for advice or information. Where the statement is communicated through a third party, it is necessary to ask whether such communication was intended or envisaged[80] by the defendant. In *BCCI (No.2)*[81] the Court of Appeal found the necessary proximity in the close relationship between three companies which were operated as a single economic unit and the two firms of auditors who between them audited the accounts of the companies. The court noted that each auditor relied on information supplied by the other and that the correspondence referred to the interdependence of the companies and the auditors and to the need for close liaison between them.

In another case[82] the claimants were shareholders in a private company which borrowed money from a bank on the security of guarantees from the claimants. The defendants were the company auditors and were also its accountants. The company went into receivership as a result of financial irregularities which the defendants had failed to notice. The claimants' guarantee was called upon and the claimants then sought to recover from the defendant. The Court of Appeal refused to strike out the claimants' claim, saying that it was not plain and obvious that the claim would fail. In the first place the defendants were not simply auditors but also accountants providing advice to the company as well as quarterly management accounts. Secondly, the company was a small quasi-

---

[78] e.g. the facts of *Caparo* itself: see paras 17–029 *et seq.*, above.

[79] *ADT v Binder Hamlyn* [1996] B.C.C. 808, May J.; see also *Andrew v Kounnis Freeman* [2000] Lloyd's Rep. P.N. 263, CA: for the facts see para.17–044, below. In *Royal Bank of Scotland Plc v Bannerman Johnstone Maclay* [2005] P.N.L.R. 43 at para.49, the Court of Session (Inner House) held, (under the Scottish equivalent of an application to strike out), that in order to show a duty of care owed by the auditor to the company's bankers, it was not necessary to prove that the auditor expressly intended that the accounts be relied on by the bank. It was sufficient that the audited accounts were provided to the company in the knowledge that (i) the accounts would be passed to the bank for the purpose satisfying itself that the company was able to continue as a going concern and (ii) that the bank would be likely to place reliance on the accounts for that purpose. The court placed reliance on the fact that the auditor had not disclaimed responsibility to the bank (*ibid.* para.63).

[80] *Kripps v Touche Ross & Co* (1997) 33 B.C.L.R. (3d) 254, British Columbia CA: in that case a company which sold certain debentures was required by the local law to file an annual prospectus containing financial statements for the previous year and an unqualified auditors' report. The claimant claimed to have purchased debentures in reliance on the defendant auditors' report and sued for negligent misrepresentation. It was held on appeal that, although the auditors did not expressly consent to the inclusion of their report in the prospectus, they knew when they provided their report that its purpose was to facilitate the sale of debentures to the public and they must be taken to have given implicit consent to its inclusion in the prospectus.

[81] [1998] P.N.L.R. 564, 583, CA: for the facts see para.17–030, above.

[82] *Siddell v Smith Cooper* 1999] P.N.L.R. 511, CA.

partnership, which made it more likely that the company's shareholders would rely on advice from its accountants. The fact that the defendant had a contractual relationship with the company does not necessarily preclude a duty in tort from being owed to the claimant.

17–034   **Factor (4): The size of any class to which the advisee belongs.** The larger the class, the harder to establish proximity. The court should look not only at the number of advisees but also at the nature of the class to which they belong.[83]

17–035   **Factor (5): The state of knowledge of the adviser.** The court will ask whether he knew or should reasonably have known: (i) the purpose for which the statement was made or required in the first place, (ii) the purpose for which it was communicated to the advisee,[84] and (iii) that the advisee would rely on the statement without obtaining independent advice.[85] Despite dicta to the contrary, the better view is that liability depends, not on whether the defendant consciously assumed a duty of care, but on whether in all the circumstances it would be reasonable to regard him as having assumed such a duty: "the touchstone of liability is not the state of mind of the defendant".[86] However, reasonableness depends on more than just foreseeability: hence the need to consider all the factors which are put into the melting pot in order to decide whether there is sufficient proximity.[87]

17–036   **Factor (6): Reliance by the advisee.** The court asks: (i) was it reasonable to rely on the statement? and (ii) did the advisee actually rely on it?[88] The cases show that the following have been treated as factors which point towards it being unreasonable to rely on the accountant's statement[89]: that the accounts are labelled "draft" accounts[90]; that if the accounts themselves show that the company is in a poor financial state, this might make it unreasonable to rely on a statement which paints a rosier picture[91]; that the claimant is an experienced businessman who might be expected to seek his own advice[92]; that the defendant's answer was a very general one upon which it was not reasonable for the

---

[83] *Siddell v Smith Cooper, ibid.* at 524.
[84] *Al Saudi Banque v Clarke Pixley* [1990] Ch. 313 and *Esanda Finance Corp Ltd v Peat Marwick Hungerfords* (1997) 71 A.L.J.R. 448 (for the facts of both cases see paras 17–043 *et seq.*, below).
[85] See also *Siddell v Smith Cooper, ibid.* at 525.
[86] *Electra Private Equity Partners Ltd v KPMG Peat Marwick* [1999] Lloyd's Rep. P.N. 670, 682; *Customs & Excise Commissioners v Barclays Bank Plc* [2006] 3 W.L.R. 1; [2006] UKHL 28.
[87] In *JEB Fasteners Ltd v Marks Bloom & Co* [1981] 3 All E.R. 289 at 296J Woolf J. held an auditor liable to an investor on the ground that it was foreseeable that the investor would rely on the valuation of stock in the accounts. In *Caparo* [1990] 2 A.C. 605, 625 Lord Bridge said that the reasoning in *JEB* was wrong but the decision might be right on its facts, since the auditors did have actual knowledge of the specific purpose for which the accounts were to be relied upon.
[88] For actual reliance, see para.17–065, below.
[89] In *BCCI (No.2)* [1998] P.N.L.R. 564 the factors making it unreasonable to rely on the statement were held to outweigh the fact that the advice had been given expressly to the claimant.
[90] *McNaughton* [1991] 2 Q.B. 113, 127H and 129E.
[91] *ibid.* at 128B.
[92] *ibid.* at 128C.

claimant to rely without further enquiry[93]; and that it is unreasonable to rely on audited accounts beyond a limited period (i.e. an audit certificate impliedly has a "sell-by" date).[94]

There is no need to show that the adviser actually intended the advisee to rely, as long as it would be reasonable for the advisee to rely in the circumstances.[95] But it is necessary for the advisee to show that he was aware of the statement[96] and actually relied on it.[97]

Other factors. Other important factors which are not listed in *McNaughton* are: the relationship between the adviser and the advisee (was it a general relationship or an ad hoc one?)[98]; whether the adviser had the opportunity to issue a disclaimer[99]; and the terms of the defendant firm's internal manual.[1]   **17–037**

(iv) *Categories of Advisee*

The categories of claimant who most frequently claim to be owed duties of care by accountants are as follows: **17–038**

(1) Existing shareholders.

(2) Potential investors.

(3) Other companies in the group.

(4) Directors.

(5) Banks and other creditors.

The list is not exhaustive. We shall now consider these and other miscellaneous categories in more detail.

Existing shareholders. The paradigm case is *Caparo*,[2] which established that, unless there are special factors to the contrary, the duty is limited to a duty to the shareholders as a body. In most cases this is identical to the duty owed to the company itself: it is not easy to see what loss the shareholders as a body might   **17–039**

---

[93] [1991] 2 Q.B. 113, 127H and 129E at 128D.
[94] *Berg Son & Co v Mervyn Hampton Adams* [1993] B.C.L.C. 1045 at 1055; *Barings Plc v Coopers & Lybrand* [2003] Lloyd's Rep. I.R. 566; [2003] EWHC 1319, Ch, Evans-Lombe J., paras 839 *et seq.*
[95] *BCCI (No.2) ibid.* at 588; see also *Yue Xiu Finance Co Ltd v Dermot Agnew (formerly trading as Deloitte Haskins & Sells)* [1996] 1 H.K.L.R. 137: for the facts see para.17–040, below).
[96] *Abbott v Strong* [1998] 2 B.C.L.C. 420, Ferris J.: an accountant, who advised directors on what to include in the prospectus for a rights issue, owed no duty of care to shareholders who were unaware that he was advising.
[97] See para.17–065, below.
[98] *BCCI (No.2), ibid.* at 587.
[99] *ibid.* at 587.
[1] *ADT Ltd v Binder Hamlyn* [1996] B.C.C. 808, 837E.
[2] See paras 17–029 *et seq.*, above.

suffer independently of the company itself.[3] We suggest that it is wrong to permit the shareholders as a class to sue independently of the company, both because it conflicts with the general rule that duties are owed only to the client company and because it gives rise to the problems of duplication of remedies.[4] Although the company as a going concern is often identified with its shareholders,[5] this is no longer the case when the company becomes insolvent; at that point the interests of creditors become paramount.[6] In such a case we suggest that there are strong policy grounds why the claim of the liquidator (effectively acting for the creditors) should prevail over the claim of the shareholders.[7]

Despite the general rule, there may be a duty to shareholders individually where there is sufficient proximity as discussed above. This would be relevant if a shareholder sells his shares at an undervalue in reliance on the audit certificate.[8] Thus, where the company's articles of association gave a right of pre-emption to the surviving shareholders to buy back shares at a valuation following death of a shareholder, it was held to be arguable that the accountant owed those shareholders a duty to exercise care in giving a valuation to the company, since he knew or ought to have known that his valuation would affect them.[9]

17–040   **Potential investors.** *Caparo*[10] established that there is no duty of care to investors unless there is sufficient proximity. However, there is usually little difficulty in establishing a duty of care to recipients of takeover circulars or promotional documents, by an accountant who has consented to the inclusion of information provided by him. Such documents are known to be directed to

---

[3] *Berg Son & Co v Mervyn Hampton Adams* [1993] B.C.L.C. 1045, 1064, Hobhouse J. In *Man Nutzfahrzeuge AG v Freightliner Ltd* [2005] EWHC 2347, Comm, paras 324–7, Moore-Bick L.J. (sitting at first instance) held that an auditor's duty was to protect the shareholders' interest in the proper management of the company; this is the same as the duty to the company and hence a separate claim may not be brought by the shareholders unless there was a separate assumption of responsibility towards them. We suggest that this is preferable to the conclusion reached by Cooke J. in an application to strike out in the same proceedings ([2004] P.N.L.R. 19; [2003] EWHC 2245, Comm). Cooke J. held that, where there is only one shareholder, in practice he may be able to control the administration of the company (e.g. by dismissing employees), and hence the auditor's negligence might arguably be the cause of the shareholder's failure to take the steps which he would have taken, had he been alerted to the employee's defalcations.

[4] See para.17–079, below as to reflective loss.

[5] Hence the principle that the shareholders are entitled to ratify irregular decisions of the board which are not ultra vires: *Re Duomatic Ltd* [1969] 2 Ch.365.

[6] *Winkworth v Baron* [1986] 1 W.L.R. 1512, 1516E-F, HL (duty owed by directors to the company and its creditors to see that affairs of the company are properly administered and not dissipated); *West Mercia Safetywear Ltd v Dodd* [1988] B.C.L.C. 250, CA (where company is insolvent, duty to creditors overrides duty to members); *Kinsella v Russell Kinsella Pty Ltd* [1986] 5 A.C.L.C. 215, CA of Aus. (where company is insolvent, the interests of creditors intrude and they become prospectively entitled, through the mechanism of liquidation, to displace the power of shareholders and directors and to deal with the assets.).

[7] *Duke Group Ltd v Pilmer* (1999) 31 A.C.S.R. 213, 259 (reversed in part, but not on this point: [2001] 2 B.C.L.C. 773); see also *Carr-Glynn v Frearsons* [1999] Ch. 326, 337–338.

[8] *Morgan Crucible Co Plc v Hill Samuel & Co Ltd* [1991] Ch. 295, 305A, *per* Hoffmann J. (obiter) at first instance.

[9] *Killick v PriceWaterhouseCoopers* [2001] P.N.L.R. 1, Neuberger J. There was no such assumption of responsibility in *Man Nutzfahrzeuge AG v Freightliner Ltd* [2005] EWHC 2347, Comm, para.349 *et seq.*, Moore-Bick L.J.

[10] See paras 17–029 *et seq.*, above.

particular recipients or classes of recipient, who may rely on them for investments purposes.[11] In *Morgan Crucible Co Plc v Hill Samuel & Co Ltd*[12] a circular was issued in the course of a contested takeover of a public company. The circular referred to financial statements relating to the target company and made by its auditors; the circular also included a letter from the auditors saying that the forecast had been properly compiled. The claimant company increased its offer for the target company and its bid was successful. It then sued various defendants, including the auditors, alleging that it had increased its bid in reliance on their statements. The Court of Appeal considered it arguable that the necessary relationship of proximity could be found on the assumptions that the defendants knew: (i) that the claimant would rely on them for the purpose of making an increased bid, (ii) that the defendant intended the claimant so to rely, and (iii) that the claimant did so rely. On these assumed facts, the representations were made to the claimant and not merely to the company.

In *Possfund Custodian Trustee Ltd v Diamond*[13] a prospectus was issued in connection with a flotation of shares in a company. The claimants subscribed for shares and subsequently bought more shares in the aftermarket. The claimants then sued various defendants including the auditors, claiming they had made both purchases in reliance on the prospectus and that the prospectus was inaccurate. The defendants sought to strike out the claim in relation to the aftermarket.[14] Lightman J. held that it was arguable that the duty of care continued in relation to the aftermarket, provided that the representor's intention that the representee should rely could be objectively established. This required the claimant to show either (i) that the representor communicated this intention to the representee or (ii) that the representee reasonably assumed that the representor intended him to rely. Proof of such objective intention would arguably be sufficient to establish proximity.[15]

By contrast, it has been held in New Zealand[16] that it is not sufficient to show that it was foreseeable in a general sort of way that the accounts might be relied on in the course of a takeover; the claimant must show that the auditor knew or

---

[11] In addition, an accountant may incur stautory liability under Pt VI of FSMA as a "person responsible" for listing particulars or a prospectus: see Ch.14, para.14–081, above.

[12] [1991] Ch. 295, CA held that it was arguable on the facts that the accountant knew that the investor would rely on his financial statements and forecast for the purpose of making an increased bid.

[13] [1996] 1 W.L.R. 1351, Lightman J.

[14] The defendants sought to rely on *Peek v Gurney* (1873) L.R. 6 H.L. 377, in which the House of Lords had held that a prospectus could reasonably be relied on only for the purpose for which it was intended, i.e. the subscription of shares in the course of the flotation and not the purchase of shares in the aftermarket.

[15] For other examples of cases where there was (or was arguably) sufficient proximity see: *ADT v Binder Hamlyn* [1996] B.C.C. 808 (for the facts see para.17–031, above); *Yorkshire Enterprises Ltd v Robson Rhodes*, unreported, June 17, 1998, Bell J.; *Haig v Bamford* (1976) D.L.R. (3d) 68, S. Ct of Can.: (discussed by Bingham L.J. in the CA in *Caparo* [1989] Q.B. 653, 693–694); and *Yue Xiu Finance Co Ltd v Dermot Agnew* [1996] 1 H.K.L.R. 137 (accountant instructed to certify valuation of company in circumstances where he knew or ought to have known that vendor would rely on valuation in deciding whether to exercise put option to sell shares in the company. The relationship was as close as it was possible to have, short of contract).

[16] *Scott Group Ltd v McFarlane* [1978] 1 N.Z.L.R. 553, *per* Richmond P. Although he formed part of the majority which dismissed the appeal of the takeover bidder in that case, the other judge did so on different grounds. Nevertheless, it was this statement by Richmond P. which was approved in *Caparo* [1990] 2 A.C. 605, 624 and 644–645.

ought to have known that his report would be relied on by a particular person or class of persons for a specific purpose.[17]

In addition to liability for information in take-over circulars and offer documents, an accountant might also owe a duty of care in tort in respect of statements made in negotiations on behalf of a client. Whether such a duty arises depends very much on the particular circumstances and the proper analysis of the purpose of the relevant statement and to whom it was directed. For example, in negotiations for the sale of a company an accountant or auditor may be asked to give the prospective purchaser some assurance as to the accuracy of relevant financial statements, including draft statements. He should tread carefully, as the giving of such assurance may result in liability in tort, which may appear hugely disproportionate to the degree of culpability. Relevant case law in this area demonstrates some fine distinctions and differences of analyses.[18]

17–041   **Other companies in the group.** Although an auditor who is instructed to audit the accounts of one company in a group usually owes no duty to other companies in the group,[19] there may be a duty if the facts indicate a sufficiently close relationship. One example is is *BCCI (No.2)*,[20] where it was held arguable that the auditor of subsidiary A owed a duty of care to subsidiary B in circumstances creating a sufficiently close interdependence. However, even if Company B is able to establish that a duty of care was owed to it, it may fall at the next hurdle, if the loss proves to be merely reflective of the loss suffered by Company A.[21]

---

[17] For other examples of cases where there was insufficient proximity see: *Al-Nakib Investments (Jersey) Ltd v Longcroft* [1990] 1 W.L.R. 1390 (doubted in *Possfund*); *James McNaughton Paper Group Ltd v Hicks Anderson* [1991] 2 Q.B. 113 (for the facts see para.17–030, above); *Peach Publishing Ltd v Slater & Co* [1998] P.N.L.R. 364 (for the facts see para.17–030, above); *Dimond Manufacturing Co Ltd v Hamilton* [1969] N.Z.L.R. 609, NZCA; and *Boyd Knight v Purdue* [1999] N.Z.L.R. 278 (for the facts see para.17–018, above).

[18] *James McNaughton Papers Group Ltd v Hicks Anderson & Co* [1991] 2 Q.B. 113, CA (first instance judge held duty owed, but reversed on appeal: very general statement in respect of draft accounts); *ADT Ltd v BDO Binder Hamlyn* [1996] B.C.C. 808, May J. (duty owed: £65 million damages award settled before appeal); *Downs v Chappell* [1997] 1 W.L.R. 426, CA (duty owed); *Electra Private Equity Partners v KPMG Peat Marwick* [1999] Lloyd's Rep. P.N. 670, CA (refusal to strike out claim by purchaser of controlling interest in company against its auditors arising from allegedly incorrect information supplied during acquisition negotiations: reversing Carnwath J. at first instance reported at [1998] P.N.L.R. 135); *Peach Publishing Ltd v Slater & Co* [1998] P.N.L.R. 364, CA (held liable by Rimer J. on basis that a duty was owed to the claimant third party, but reversed on appeal); *Yorkshire Enterprise Ltd v Robson Rhodes*, unreported, June 17, 1998, Bell J. (duty owed); *HIT Finance Ltd v Cohen Arnold* [2000] Lloyd's Rep. P.N. 125, CA (accountants of a guarantor of a company's indebtedness did owe a limited duty of care in respect of financial information provided about the guarantor, but held not in breach; on its true construction the relevant letter merely passed on information provided by the guarantor and did not amount to verification of guarantor's net worth as held by Mantell J. at first instance: [1998] 1 E.G.L.R. 140); *Man Nutzfahrzeuge AG v Freightliner Ltd* [2005] EWHC 2347, Comm at para.478, Moore-Bick L.J. (drawing a distinction between cases where it is foreseeable that an identifiable third party may rely on the accounts when deciding on a course of action and cases where the auditor has stepped outside his statutory functions by entering into a closer relationship with the third party).

[19] In *Barings v Coopers & Lybrand* [2002] P.N.L.R. 16, Evans-Lombe J.

[20] [1998] P.N.L.R. 564: for the facts see para.17–030, above. The claim failed for other reasons: see para.17–036, above.

[21] See para.17–079, below.

Directors. In *Coulthard v Neville Russell*[22] a company carrying on business as   **17–042**
a Lloyd's managing agent was taken over by another company, which used
money from the managing agent to fund the takeover in breach of s.151 of the
Companies Act 1985. The directors were subsequently disqualified from acting
as directors and they sued the auditor who had failed to warn of the breach. The
Court of Appeal, on an application to strike out, held that it was arguable that the
auditor owed a duty of care to the directors. The court said that Companies Act
1985[23] read in isolation might suggest that the auditors are not instructed until the
directors have submitted completed accounts to them. But in practice the directors usually discuss the draft accounts with the auditors before they are approved
by the directors. Although it is no part of the auditor's statutory duty to protect
the directors personally from the consequences of their mistakes, he may assume
such a duty in the course of those discussions. In this case it was arguable that
he should have warned the directors that the proposed loan might lead to a
qualified auditor's report.

Creditors. There is not usually sufficient proximity between creditors of a   **17–043**
company and the auditors but there may be exceptional cases. These tend to
involve either guarantors[24] or else banks or other major investors.[25] In *Al Saudi
Banque v Clarke Pixley*[26] a claim was brought by banks which lent money to a
company or failed to call in their loan in reliance on unqualified audit certificates.
The judge dismissed the claim on a preliminary point. In the case of the banks
which lent money after the date of the balance sheet, they were in the same
position as the potential investors in a company, to whom no duty of care was
usually owed. As for the banks which were already creditors at the date of the
balance sheet and which allowed their loans to remain outstanding, there was less
proximity in their case than there was in the case of existing shareholders of the
company. The banks had played no part in appointing the auditors; the auditors
had no statutory obligation to report to the banks; the auditors did not supply a
copy of their report to the banks, nor did they supply them to the company with
the intention or in the knowledge that they would be supplied to the banks. The
fact that the banks in question were a small and limited class was insufficient to
create the necessary proximity. Further, it was not just and reasonable to impose
a duty of care, since this might result in liability in an indeterminate amount if
the bank subsequently lent further sums without the auditor's knowledge.

In an Australian case[27] a financier who made loans to a company in reliance
on audited accounts sought to recover damages for negligence from the auditor.

---

[22] [1998] P.N.L.R. 276, CA.
[23] See para.17–079, below.
[24] *Siddell v Smith Cooper* [1999] P.N.L.R. 511, CA: for the facts see para.17–033, above; for other
examples see *Huxford v Stoy Hayward & Co* (1989) 5 B.C.C. 421, Popplewell J. and *AGC (Advances)
Ltd v R Lowe Lippman Figdor & Franck* (1990) 4 A.C.S.R. 337, S. Ct of Vict.; *Craig v Troy* (1997)
16 W.A.R. 96, S. Ct. of W. Aus. For an example of a case where no duty was owed see *Ikumene
Singapore Pte Ltd v Leon Chee Leng* [1993] 3 S.L.R. 24, CA of Sing.
[25] e.g. *Electra Private Equity Partners v KPMG Peat Marwick* [1999] Lloyd's P.N. 670.
[26] [1990] Ch. 313, Millett J. This judgment was approved by the House of Lords in *Caparo* [1990]
2 A.C. 605, 623 and 640.
[27] *Esanda Finance Corp Ltd v Peat Marwick Hungerfords* (1997) 71 A.L.J.R. 448, H. Ct. of Aus. See
also *Temseel Holdings Ltd v Beaumonts Chartered Accountants* [2003] P.N.L.R. 27; [2002] EWHC
2642, Comm, Tomlinson J.

Reference was made to the Australian Accounting Standard AAS5, which provided that the test for materiality in financial statements depended on the likely prime users of the statement. The High Court of Australia struck out the claim on the ground that that it was necessary for the claimant to prove that the auditor knew or ought to have known that his certificate would be relied on by the claimant, either individually or as a member of a class. It was not sufficient for the claimant to cite AAS5, as he had done.[28]

17–044   **Bodies which are liable to compensate third parties.** *Andrew v Kounnis Freeman*[29] concerned the Air Travel Trust, a reserve fund which compensated stranded travellers. In that case an auditor negligently audited the accounts of a travel company which was insolvent. The Civil Aviation Authority ("CAA") had initially refused to renew the company's licence but had agreed following a meeting with the auditor at which the auditor had promised to provide some financial information. The company then continued trading until it collapsed, leaving passengers stranded abroad. The CAA and the Trust, which had to compensate the passengers, made a claim against the auditor. The Court of Appeal refused to strike out the claim. The mere fact that an auditor repeated his statutory report to a third party was not sufficient by itself to amount to an assumption of responsibility to that third party, but it was capable of doing so in the circumstances of this case. Beldam L.J. found the necessary assumption of responsibility in the fact that a reasonable auditor would have realised that the claimants were relying on the certificate and would not be obtaining independent advice and that the defendant did nothing to qualify his liability.[30] Buxton L.J. based his decision on the fact that the auditor, by providing accounts to the claimants in the unusual circumstances of this case, was impliedly giving advice to them and not merely information.[31] The third judge agreed with both judgments.[32]

Law Society v KPMG[33] concerned the Accountant's Report Rules made under s.34 of the Solicitor's Act 1974. These rules require every solicitor to produce a report from an accountant as a pre-condition to the renewal by the Law Society of his practising certificate. In this case the accountant negligently failed to notice and report on defalcations by partners in a firm of solicitors, as a result of which claims were made by clients of the firm against the Compensation Fund (a fund

---

[28] The six judges gave five reasoned judgments, each containing different reasons. Brennan C.J. endorsed Lord Oliver's test in *Caparo*, whilst McHugh J. considered a number of policy factors which constituted socio-economic reasons for restricting auditor's liability. The other judgments adopted intermediate positions.

[29] [2000] Lloyd's Rep. P.N. 263, CA.

[30] *ibid.* at 270.

[31] *ibid.* at 271.

[32] In *Independents' Advantage Insurance Co Ltd v Cook* [2004] P.N.L.R. 3, CA, the defendant audited accounts for a travel agency in the knowledge that the accounts would be submitted to ABTA and IATA and that the requisite travel bond might be provided by an insurer such as IAIC. Although there was no allegation that the defendant had the particular insurer in mind, the law was still in a transitional state and therefore it would be wrong to strike out without knowing all the facts.

[33] [2000] 1 W.L.R. 1921, CA: leave to appeal was refused: [2001] 1 W.L.R. 1122. In New Zealand it has been held that an auditor appointed under the Solicitors Audit Regulations owes duties both to clients whose money was put into the firm's trust account (*Price Waterhouse v Kwan* [2000] 3 N.Z.L.R. 39, CA) and to innocent partners who are required to make good any loss suffered by clients (*Stringer v Peat Marwick Mitchell & Co* [2000] 1 N.Z.L.R. 450, Chisholm J.).

set up by the Law Society to make payments to victims of fraud by solicitors). The Court of Appeal held that, where a body such as the Law Society has different functions, it was not sufficient to ask whether a duty of care was owed to that body generally; one had to focus on the specific capacity in which the body sued.[34] However, in that case there was a duty of care for the following reasons: the body which granted practising certificates was the same legal entity as the body which set up the Fund; it was obvious to a reasonable accountant that his negligence in giving his report might cause the Law Society to make future payments out of the Fund[35]; there was no reason why the accountant should not owe a private law duty to take reasonable care to safeguard the Law Society from exposure to a public law liability to compensate third parties; and there was sufficient proximity and it was fair, just and reasonable to impose a duty of care.[36]

Others. It has been held that there is insufficient proximity arising from the mere fact that the claimant is a beneficiary under a trust of which the company is trustee[37] or an employee whose salary was equal to 99 per cent of the profit of the company set up to exploit his talents as a pop star.[38] There may be cases in which an accountant is retained to provide a report for shareholders, but may owe a duty of care to the company itself, which in this situation is not the client.[39] **17–045**

(v) *Policy Considerations: Duplication of Remedies*

We suggest that the courts, when considering whether it is just and reasonable to impose a duty of care in favour of a third party, should have regard to the following policy issues which arise where the claim overlaps with a claim in contract by the client: **17–046**

---

[34] [2000] 1 W.L.R. 1921 at 1928 paras 19–20.

[35] The unique nature of the Fund proved to be critical in *Law Society v Sephton* [2006] 2 W.L.R. 1091; [2006] UKHL 22, HL, where an issue arose as to the limitation period for a claim by the Law Society against a reporting accountant who had negligently failed to uncover fraud by a firm of solicitors. The Law Society has a duty to maintain the Compensation Fund, but grants out of the Fund are wholly discretionary and will not be made where the misappropriation has been made good by some other means. In *Sephton* the House of Lords held that, at least until a claim on the Fund was actually made in proper form, there was no actual loss and hence no cause of action had accrued. (see Lord Hoffmann *ibid.* at paras 30–1 and Lord Mance at para.80).

[36] *ibid.* at 1928–1930. The court suggested obiter (at 1930B) that a duty might not be owed to the Solicitors' Indemnity Fund, since this Fund is the solicitor's insurer and since the accountant's report is not prepared for its benefit. For criticism of this decision, see Powell [2001] P.N. 206.

[37] *Anthony v Wright* [1995] 1 B.C.L.C. 236, 241. In *Richards v Hughes* [2004] EWCA Civ 266; [2004] P.N.L.R. 35, the Court of Appeal held that it was strongly arguable that an accountant instructed by parents as trustees of a trust to advise on investments owed a duty to the trustees and not the beneficiaries, but court was not prepared to strike out claim on the particular facts. (The case is discussed by O'Sullivan, 2005 P.N. 144). The opposite result has been reached in Australia: *Edwards Karawacki Smith & Co Pty Ltd v Jacka Nominees Pty Ltd* (1994) 15 A.C.S.R. 503. See also *Price Waterhouse v Kwan* [2000] 3 N.Z.L.R. 39, noted at para.17–044, above.) However, the trustee may be the proper claimant: see *Deloitte Haskins & Sells v National Mutual Life Nominees Ltd* [1993] A.C. 774, PC: for the facts see para.17–018, above.

[38] *John (Elton) v Price Waterhouse* [2001] EWHC Ch. 438 para.219, Ferris J.

[39] *Duke Group Ltd v Pilmer* (1999) 31 A.C.S.R. 213, 258 (reversed in part, but not on this point: [2001] 2 B.C.L.C. 773).

(1) The risk of different defences being available: in some cases there might be a defence of causation or contributory negligence if the client knew or ought to have known of the breaches of duty or did not rely on the accountant.[40] The English courts have not yet considered the question whether it is just and reasonable to permit this defence to be circumvented by bringing the proceedings in the name of a third party.[41]

(2) The problem of double recovery: see para.17–079, below.

(3) The "loss of a chance" problem: in cases where the claimant is the alter ego of the client (e.g. a director or majority shareholder where the company is the client), we suggest that the client should not be regarded as a third party for the purpose of the "loss of a chance" doctrine.[42]

(vi) *The Contracts (Rights against Third Parties) Act 1999*

17–047 The Contracts (Rights against Third Parties) Act 1999 came into force on November 11, 1999 in relation to contracts made after May 1, 2000. Section 1 permits a contract to be enforced by a third party in two cases: the first is where it expressly so provides; the second is where it purports to create a benefit on him, unless it appears on the true construction of the contract that he was not to benefit.[43]

(vii) *The Human Rights Act 1998*

17–048 It has been held that the restrictions on the duty of care embodied in *Caparo* do not breach the claimant's right to a fair hearing under Art.6 of the European Convention on Human Rights (the right to a fair trial).[44]

(d) *The Standard of Skill and Care*

(i) *General*

17–049 In common with other professionals, the standard required of an accountant in carrying out an engagement is that of the reasonable skill and care of an ordinary

---

[40] See paras 17–063 *et seq.* and 17–080 *et seq.*

[41] e.g. the facts of *Law Society v KPMG* [2001] 1 W.L.R. 1921 (see para.17–044, above).

[42] *Allied Maples Group Ltd v Simmons & Simmons* [1995] 1 W.L.R. 1602, 1612C. For a discussion of the "loss of a chance" principle, see para.17–069, below.

[43] As to whether a third party who relies on audited accounts is able to take the benefit of the 1999 Act, see articles by Burbidge, [2002] P.N. 40 at 59, and Arnull, *ibid.* 146 at 153.

[44] *Hands v Coopers & Lybrand* [2001] Lloyds Rep. P.N. 732. See also *Z v United Kingdom* (2001) 34 E.H.R.R. 97 (where the European Court of Human Rights said that the "just and reasonable" criterion was a substantive part of the tort and not merely a ground for immunity, so that a claimant who failed to persuade the court that it was just and reasonable to impose liability had no grounds for complaint under Art.6 if his claim was struck out) and *Matthews v Ministry of Defence* [2003] 1 A.C. 1163; [2003] UKHL 4 (where the House of Lords likewise held that immunity from suit (in that case, Crown immunity) was a substantive, not a procedural, bar). See article by P. Burbidge, "Liability of statutory auditors to third parties—is the European writing on the wall for *Caparo v Dickman*?" (2002) P.N. 40. The Convention is now enshrined in the Human Rights Act 1998 and has been directly enforceable in the English courts since October 2000. See Ch.7 above.

skilled person carrying out the same engagement.[45] The standard will not be lower for an accountant with limited experience or if a low fee is charged, although the amount of the fee may be some indication of the nature of the engagement.[46] The standard generally remains constant irrespective of the nature of the particular engagement, although what steps will be required to fulfil the standard will vary according to the engagement.[47] The court should guard against hindsight and only take account of knowledge reasonably available at the time of the alleged breach.[48]

Sources of evidence. In a New Zealand case, *Dairy Containers Ltd v NZI Bank Ltd*[49] the court listed the following sources of evidence: **17–050**

(1) The standard required as a matter of contract and under the relevant statutes or regulations.[50]

(2) Expert evidence: the court is usually unwilling to find a professional person negligent in the absence of evidence from a professional in the same field.[51] In professional negligence claims it is usually necessary to adduce such evidence, especially if it is alleged that a particular default was the consequence of departure from general practice.[52] But it is not within the province of expert witnesses on the subject of general practice to determine what was the duty of an accountant in a particular case or

---

[45] *Re Kingston Cotton Mill Co Ltd (No.2)* [1896] 2 Ch. 279, 288, CA. See also *Calne Gas Co v Curtis* (1918) 59 Acct. L.R. 17, 20; and *International Laboratories Ltd v Dewar* (1933) 3 D.L.R. 665, 692. In *Whiteoak v Walker* (1988) 4 B.C.C. 122 the judge rejected the claimant's argument that the standard was that of a accountant who professed "specialist skills in valuing unquoted shares"; instead he held that the required standard was that of "a reasonably competent chartered accountant in general practice acting as an auditor who has agreed to a request to undertake the valuation task".

[46] Note *Henry Squire, Cash Chemist Ltd v Ball Baker & Co (also Mead v Ball Baker & Co)* (1912) 106 L.T. 197, 199–200. In discussing the nature of the defendant accountants' duty, Lord Alverstone C.J. attached no importance to their scale of remuneration.

[47] *e.g. ibid.* at 199–200, *per* Lord Alverstone C.J.: "I do not agree that their duty as auditors would be less than their duty in advising a purchaser when he was buying the business." See also *HIT Finance Ltd v Cohen Arnold* [2000] Lloyd's Rep. P.N. 125 (CA held on the facts of the case that a letter to a lender stating the borrower's net worth was not a warranty but was a statement that the accountant had taken reasonable care in writing the letter based on information from the borrower).

[48] *Re City Equitable Fire Insurance Co Ltd* [1925] 1 Ch. 407, 505. In *Stanilite Pacific Ltd v Seaton* (2005) 55 ASCR 460, the S Ct of NSW, CA. held that an accountant had misconstrued the relevant accounting standard (AASB 109) but that this was not negligent, given the ambiguous wording of the standard (note that the trial judge had also misconstrued it). Nevertheless, even adopting the accountant's wrong construction of the standard, he was negligent on the facts in giving an unqualified audit certificate.

[49] [1995] 2 N.Z.L.R. 30.

[50] See paras 17–006 and 17–022, above.

[51] *Sansom v Metcalfe Hambleton* [1998] P.N.L.R. 542. See also *Pacific Acceptance Corp Ltd v Forsyth* (1970) 92 W.N. (N.S.W.) 29, 74–75. In *Sceptre Resources Ltd v Deloitte Haskins & Sells* (1991) 83 Alta. L.R. (2d) 157 the Supreme Court of Alberta said: "The law allows differing opinions among accountants as it does within the medical and legal professions. Acting in concert with an opinion or practice held by a significant fraction of the profession, is almost always a defence to a suit for malpractice . . . The only exception arises where the practice of the profession is totally unreasonable."

[52] *Henry Squire, Cash Chemist Ltd v Ball Baker & Co* (1912) 106 L.T. 197, 202.

whether he was in breach of it. That is for the court to determine.[53] In some cases the nature of the negligence may be such as not to require expert evidence to be adduced.[54]

(3) Auditing and accounting standards[55]: in practice these are usually the most important source of evidence. Professional standards, whilst not conclusive, are very strong evidence as to what is a proper standard; third parties reading the accounts are entitled to assume that they have been drawn up in accordance with approved practice unless the accounts state otherwise.[56] However, more recently a Canadian court has emphasised that professional standards do not supplant the degree of care called for by the law: the court had in mind the risk that the profession might set a standard lower than the courts thought reasonable.[57]

(4) The defendant's internal office manuals.[58]

Older caselaw should be treated with caution since, although the test has always been that of the reasonably competent accountant, the standard to be expected of a reasonably competent practitioner is substantially higher today than it was in the nineteenth century.[59]

(ii) *Auditing*

17–051   **Auditing standards.** The Auditing Practices Board ("APB") of the Financial Reporting Council, established by the CCAB,[60] issues auditing standards. The APB has adopted the International Standard on Quality Control 1 (ISQC 1) and the International Standards on Auditing (ISAs) issued by the International Auditing and Standards Board with effect from December 15, 2004. Where necessary, the APB has added additional standards and guidance to the ISQCs in order to maintain the requirements and clarity of previous UK and Irish auditing standards. We shall refer to both sets of standards in this text, but it is obviously crucial in any case to determine which set of standards applies and to ensure that one looks at the standards for the relevant year.[61]

---

[53] *Pacific Acceptance Corp Ltd v Forsyth* (1970) 92 W.N. (N.S.W.) 29, 75; *Nelson Guarantee Corp Ltd v Hodgson* [1958] N.Z.L.R. 609, 613.

[54] *Murray Bourne Dyck v FMA Farm Management Associates Ltd* (1996) 3 W.W.R. 509, 512, *per* Wedge J. "If it is found as fact that a filing deadline is missed through the negligence of an accounting professional, then I am satisfied that no expert evidence is required to establish such a common sense standard of competence."

[55] For accounting standards, see paras 17–012, above and 17–058, below. For auditing standards, see paras 17–051, *et seq.*

[56] *Lloyds Cheyham v Littlejohn* [1987] B.C.L.C. 303, Woolf J.

[57] *Kripps v Touche Ross & Co* (1997) 33 B.C.L.R. (3d) 254, British Columbia CA: for the facts see para.17–033, above.

[58] *ADT Ltd v Binder Hamlyn* [1996] B.C.C. 808, 837E.

[59] *Re Thomas Gerrard & Son Ltd* [1968] Ch. 455, 475; *Pacific Acceptance Corp Ltd v Forsyth* (1970) 92 W.N. (NSW) 29, 73–74.

[60] See para.17–005, above.

[61] ISAs and other documents referred to in this section are printed in *Auditing & Reporting* published annually by the ICAEW. The previous standards, known as Statements of Auditing Standards (SASs), will be found in older editions of that publication. We have referred primarily to the ISAs, but we have referred to the old SASs in brackets.

Although auditing standards do not directly have the force of law, compliance with them is powerful evidence that the auditor has acted reasonably, whilst failure to comply without adequate explanation is powerful evidence to the contrary.[62] There are two reasons why this is so. The first is that the APB is constituted under the aegis of the CCAB[63] and the standards accordingly represent the agreed view of all the major professional bodies of accountants as to what constitutes good practice. The second is that the standards are given additional status by the Companies Act, in that every auditor of the accounts of a company registered under the Companies Acts is required to belong to a RSB,[64] every RSB is required to have auditing standards and all the professional bodies which make up the CCAB have undertaken to adopt all the standards.[65] In practice, the standard of skill and care in any claim against an auditor is more likely to be found in the standards than in any caselaw.

The following basic principles emerge from the auditing standards and the cases:

(1) The responsibility for managing the business[66] and for preparing financial statements belongs to the directors of the entity. The auditor is responsible for giving an opinion on those statements.[67] It is no part of his duty to give advice as to the prudence or imprudence of the company's business. His duty is to see that the shareholders receive independent and reliable information respecting the true financial position of the company at the time of the audit, so that they can exercise their own judgment.[68]

(2) An audit is not a warranty: in ISA 200,[69] the objective of an audit of financial statements is described as:

(3) "to enable the auditor to express an opinion whether the financial statements are prepared, in all material respects, in accordance with an applicable financial reporting framework. The phrases used to express the auditor's opinion are 'give a true and fair view' or 'present fairly, in all material respects', which are equivalent terms."

---

[62] In *Barings v Coopers & Lybrand* [2002] 2 B.C.L.C. 410; [2002] EWHC 461, Ch, Evans-Lombe J. considered the extent to which the auditors had complied with Singapore auditing standards.

[63] See para.17–005, above.

[64] See para.17–009, above.

[65] Paras 17–013 of The Scope and Authority of APB Pronouncements (formerly SAS 010 para.10) and see para.17–012, above.

[66] See para.17–081(4), below.

[67] ISA 200 para.24 (the SAS equivalent is SAS 100 para.(6); and see para.17–009, above.

[68] *Re London and General Bank (No.2)* [1895] 2 Ch. 673, 682–683, *per* Lindley L.J.: in that case an auditor presented a confidential report to directors pointing out the insufficiency and difficulty of realisation of securities on which loans by the company were advanced. But in his report to the shareholders he merely made the vacuous comment that the value of the assets was dependent on realisation. He was held liable upon a misfeasance summons by the liquidator of the company. He had not reported the true financial position of the company and the shareholders had consequently been deceived into voting for a dividend which in the event was proved to have been paid from capital and not from income. This dividend the auditor was required to make good to the liquidator.

[69] ISA 200 para.2 (Objective and general principles governing an audit of financial statements) (SAS 100 is in similar terms, but without reference to "present fairly"). See further para.17–057, below.

(4) A degree of imprecision is inevitable because of inherent uncertainties and the need to use judgment in making accounting estimates[70] and selecting appropriate accounting policies. The auditor's duty is to provide reasonable assurance.[71]

(5) The auditor should recognise the possibility that fraud or error may materially affect the financial statements.[72]

(6) The auditor's responsibility is a personal one: It is his opinion which must be expressed in his report and not for example that of an in-house accountant employed by the company.[73] It is nevertheless recognised that many engagements including a company audit, are beyond the capacity of a single person to perform and that he may employ others to assist him.[74] But an accountant cannot by delegating abdicate his responsibility, and he will continue to be under a duty to exercise reasonable skill and care although many tasks required by a particular engagement are performed by assistants.[75] The accountant should properly supervise his assistants and be careful not to give them tasks beyond their capacity and experience.[76]

(7) In general it is no answer for an auditor to say that he was working under time constraints. If he needs more time, he should ask the directors to adjourn the general meeting; if they refuse, he should attend and explain the position.[77]

17–052   **The detection of fraud.** One especially important issue in relation to audit work is the question of whether the auditor ought to have detected fraud or

---

[70] ISA 540 para.3 (Audit of Accounting Estimates) provides that "accounting estimate" means an approximation of the amount of an item in the absence of a precise measurement, e.g. allowances to reduce stock and debtors to their estimated realisable value, depreciation, accrued revenue, profits or losses on construction contracts in progress and provision for deferred taxation, for losses from litigation, and for warranty claims. It is inherent in such estimates that they will be less conclusive than other evidence and that more judgment is required in order to decide whether the evidence is sufficient and appropriate (The SAS equivalent is SAS 420 para.4).

[71] In one old case it was said that "when it is shewn that audited balance-sheets do not shew the true financial condition of the company and that damage has resulted, the onus is on the auditors to shew that this is not the result of any breach of duty on their part": *Re Republic of Bolivia Exploration Syndicated Ltd* [1914] 1 Ch. 139 at 171, *per* Astbury J. However we suggest that a modern court would not be prepared to reverse the burden of proof in this way but would wish to decide for itself whether the claimant had established breach of duty.

[72] See para.17–052, below.

[73] *Dominion Freeholders Ltd v Aird* (1966) 67 S.R. (N.S.W.) 150 at 156–157, *per* Wallace P. and see para.17–055, below.

[74] e.g. *The Irish Woollen Co Ltd v Tyson* (1900) 27 Acct. L.R. 13, Irish CA at 14. This issue is discussed in ISA 220 (Quality Control for Audit Work) (the SAS equivalent is SAS 240).

[75] See *Henry Squire, Cash Chemist Ltd v Ball Baker & Co* (1912) 106 L.T. 197, 201: "with some slight exceptions, where judgment and discretion come in, the skill of the head clerk must be the same as the skill of the principal. That is to say the principal cannot excuse himself of his clerk's negligence by saying that he [employed a] clerk", *per* Lord Alverstone C.J. (Bracketed words taken from report in 44 Acct. L.R. 25); *Armitage v Brewer and Knott* (1932) 77 Acct. L.R. 25 (auditors could not get rid of their responsibility by delegating it to junior clerks: *per* Talbot J.).

[76] See *Pacific Acceptance Corp Ltd v Forsyth* (1970) 92 W.N. (N.S.W.) 29, 79 and 117–118.

[77] *Re Thomas Gerrard & Son Ltd* [1968] Ch. 455, 477; *Pacific Acceptance, ibid.* at 107.

defalcations. The classic statements are in *Re London and General Bank (No.2)*[78] and *Re Kingston Cotton Mill Co (No.2)*.[79] In the former case Lindley L.J. stressed that an auditor is not an insurer and does not guarantee the accuracy of the company's books in general or the balance sheet in particular.[80] In the latter case Lopes L.J. said that an auditor is "not bound to be a detective" and that he is "a watchdog but not a bloodhound".[81] The traditional approach was to draw a firm distinction between cases where suspicion was excited, in which case the auditor's duty was to probe to the bottom, and cases where there was nothing to excite suspicion, in which case very little inquiry would usually suffice.[82]

The modern approach is set out in ISA 200: "The auditor should plan and perform an audit with an attitude of professional scepticism recognising that circumstances may exist that cause financial statements to be materially misstated."[83] Further guidance is provided in ISA 240: "The auditor should maintain an attitude of professional scepticism throughout the audit, recognising that possibility that a material misstatement due to fraud could exist, notwithstanding the auditor's past experience with the entity about the honesty and integrity of management and those charged with governance."[84] The auditor's responsibility is not to prevent fraud or error but to exercise reasonable care in detecting it. Accordingly, failure by an auditor to detect fraud or negligence is not of itself proof of negligence by him; the likelihood of detecting error is greater than that of detecting fraud, since fraud is usually deliberately concealed.[85] When planning the audit he should assess the risk of fraud or error and should design audit procedures which take account of that risk.[86] He should examine "critically and with professional scepticism" the information and explanations provided by the management.[87] If he becomes aware of information indicating that fraud or error may exist, he should obtain an understanding of the circumstances; if he believes that the possible fraud or error might have a material effect on the financial

---

[78] [1895] 2 Ch. 673, 683, CA: for facts see para.17–051, above.

[79] [1896] 2 Ch. 279, CA: for the facts see para.17–057(3), below.

[80] See also *Calne Gas Co v Curtis* (1918) 59 Acct. L.R. 17, 20. In *Re City Equitable Fire Insurance Co* [1925] 1 Ch. 407, 480, Romer J. said that if in the course of his "long and arduous audit" the auditor concerned had in even one instance fallen short of "the strict duty of an auditor" he could not be excused merely because in general he displayed the highest degree of care and skill. The statement requires qualification. To the extent that it implies that an auditor is strictly liable for any error, it is incorrect, being inconsistent with the standard of reasonable skill and care which allows some degree of error.

[81] By contrast, the detection of fraud was described as one of the main objects of an audit and of primary importance, in the Australian case of *Frankston and Hastings Corp v Cohen* (1960) 102 C.L.R. 607, 617; see also *Pacific, ibid.* at 52. *cf.* Davison and Khan, "Contractual liability of an auditor" [1980] A.B.L.R. 300, 303–304: arguing that the detection of fraud had not been a primary aim of the audit for some considerable time from the profession's viewpoint and to that extent its viewpoint was at variance with the legal interpretation of an audit.

[82] In *Pacific, ibid.* at 62 Moffitt J. cautioned against the traditional approach.

[83] ISA 200 para.6 (SAS 110.1)

[84] ISA 240 para.24 (SAS 110.1). In *Dairy Containers Ltd v NZI Bank Ltd* [1995] 2 N.Z.L.R. 30, 54, Thomas J. said that metaphors about dogs and detectives tended to obscure the basic duty to plan and carry out the audit cognisant of the possibility of fraud.

[85] ISA 240 paras 17–22 (SAS 110 paras 18–22); *Pacific, ibid.* at 65. See also *Re Kingston Cotton Mill Co Ltd (No.2)* [1896] 2 Ch. 279, 290; *International Laboratories Ltd v Dewar* (1933) 3 D.L.R. 665, 682 and 693.

[86] ISA 240, 315 and 330 (SAS 110.2 and 110.3).

[87] ISA 240 paras 23–6 (SAS 100 para.11).

statements, he should perform appropriate procedures; he should document his findings and discuss them with the appropriate level of management; and he should consider the implication of his findings on other aspects of the audit.[88] The auditor "is not confined to the mechanics of checking vouchers and making arithmetical computations"; he is required to approach his task "with an inquiring mind—not suspicious of dishonesty . . . but suspecting that someone may have made a mistake somewhere and that a check must be made to ensure that there has been none".[89] His role is "verification, not detection".[90]

In the Australian case of *Pacific Acceptance Corp Ltd v Forsyth*[91] Moffitt J. in a detailed judgment analysed the function and duties of an auditor having regard to modern audit practice and procedures, particularly auditors' increasing reliance upon a company's internal system of accounting control. The facts were that the auditors of a finance company (Pacific) failed to discover frauds in relation to loans made to T and to entities with which T was connected and gave an unqualified audit report. The loans were intended to be secured. Thereafter Pacific's business relationship with T deepened in several ways. First, it entered into a joint venture with T's company through a company named Pavic and it advanced money to Pavic which was lost. Secondly, it took over various interests of T. Thirdly, Pavic became a wholly owned subsidiary of Pacific and T became a principal shareholder and director of Pacific. Within the framework of the joint venture and takeover T committed further frauds and misappropriation. Fourthly, there was a further takeover whereby Pacific acquired almost all T's assets at a time when T's companies were in grave financial difficulties. The court held that Pavic's auditors had qualified their report on Pavic but that the defendant had ignored this qualification.

Moffitt J. concluded that the contracts being open had imported into them promises to perform the duties prescribed by the relevant Companies Act and also the articles of association of the company.[92] The relevant statute,[93] however, merely required the auditors to report to the shareholders and to give their

---

[88] ISA 240 paras 83–9 and 93–101 (SAS 110.4, 110.5 and 110.6). If the auditor comes across irregular or unusual matters, he should not separate them into watertight compartments *Pacific, ibid.* at 62. See also para.17–019, above ("whistle-blowing" duties).

[89] *Fomento (Sterling Area) Ltd v Selsdon Fountain Pen Co Ltd* [1958] 1 W.L.R. 45, 61: see para.17–057(4), below.

[90] *Re City Equitable Fire Insurance Co Ltd* [1925] Ch. 407, 509.

[91] (1970) 92 W.N. (N.S.W.) 29. The case raises issues relevant to a number of subject headings in this chapter and particular issues will be more fully discussed in their appropriate context. For further statements, see *International Laboratories Ltd v Dewar* [1933] 3 D.L.R. 665, 670; *McBride's Ltd v Rooke & Thomas* [1941] 4 D.L.R. 55; *Dimond Manufacturing Co Ltd v Hamilton* [1969] N.Z.L.R. 609, 637; and *Scott Group Ltd v McFarlane* [1978] 1 N.Z.L.R. 553, 580.

[92] See also *Re City Equitable Fire Insurance Co Ltd* [1925] 1 Ch. 407, 520–521 (para.17–021 above.)

[93] The Australian Companies Act 1936, s.115. Of the similar Companies (Consolidation) Act 1908, s.113, Warrington L.J. in *Re City Equitable Fire Insurance Co Ltd* [1925] 1 Ch. 407, 525 observed:

"It says nothing as to what [the auditors] are to do in order to form that opinion, or to ascertain the truth of the facts to which they are to certify. That is left to be determined by the general rules which, in point of law, are held to govern the duties of the auditors, whether those rules are to be derived from the ordinary law, or from the terms under which the auditors are to be employed."

cf. now the UK Companies Act 1985, s.237(1) (duty to carry out certain investigations: see para.17–013, above).

opinion on certain matters. It did not state what the auditors had to do in order to form their opinions. It was contended for the Pacific auditors that they were required to do no more than report to the shareholders using due care and skill. This contention was rejected:

> "In the absence of express terms the scope of the audit will depend on what is directly or indirectly required or indicated by the particular provisions of the Companies Act and of the articles and any relevant surrounding circumstances. However, whatever the precise content of his audit duty, the auditor promises, first, to conduct an audit of some description and, second, to provide a report of his opinion based on his audit work, which report has to comply with the Companies Act and the articles, and also impliedly agrees to exercise reasonable skill and care in the conduct of the audit and in the making of the report."[94]

The duty to audit carried with it an incidental duty to warn the appropriate level of management or the directors, during the course of the audit, of fraud or suspicion of fraud uncovered.[95] Thus, if in the course of vouching work, the Pacific auditors had uncovered matters which reasonably required them to take further steps which they did not take and which would have uncovered or led them to the uncovering of T's fraudulent and irregular dealings, a breach would have occurred at that time.[96] As for the scope of a statutory audit, Moffitt J. took the view that in planning and carrying out his work an auditor must pay due regard to the possibility of error and fraud.[97] A modern audit of a large company will inevitably rely on the company's own internal systems where possible.[98]

(e) *Limitation of Liability*

Under existing companies legislation,[99] it is not open to an auditor of a company to seek to exclude or limit his liability in relation to the company for negligence **17–053**

---

[94] (1970) 92 W.N. (N.S.W.) 29, 51. See also at 50:
"[A duty to report on the accounts, records required to be kept by statute and the articles and on the balance sheet] would not admit logically of a duty to report to management a discovery of fraud or misappropriation by an employee during the course of the audit year, and it would not admit a right to recover damages arising from a negligent failure to uncover fraud in the course of the audit, as distinct from damage flowing from the falsity in the balance sheet and an opinion negligently given of the shareholders in respect thereof."
The issues as to what were the relevant duties and when breaches thereof occurred had particular relevance in the case owing to the defence of limitation raised by many of the partners of the Pacific auditors. Moffitt J. derived support for the existence of a duty to audit from the cases of *Frankston and Hastings Corp v Cohen* (1960) 102 C.L.R. 607 and *Re Thomas Gerrard & Son Ltd* [1968] 1 Ch. 455, 475 ("basically [the auditor's] duty has always been to audit the company's accounts with reasonable care and skill").
[95] *ibid.* at 45, 50–54. Note also at 54, *per* Moffitt J.:
"Even if I am wrong and there is no separate duty to audit with an incidental duty to warn, I would not accept, despite the lack of logic that would then appear to exist, that the duty to report in terms of the statute would not include at least at the time of the report a duty to warn somebody at that date; if not the directors, then the shareholders of fraud uncovered."
See also *Sasea Finance Ltd v KPMG* [2000] 1 All E.R. 676 (discussed at para.17–064, below).
[96] *ibid.* at 50–54.
[97] *ibid.* at 63.
[98] *ibid* at 55. See para.17–056, below for discussion about internal control systems.
[99] See para.17–004, above as to provision in the Companies Bill for liability limitation agreements.

or other breach of duty[1]. This is the effect of s.310 of the Companies Act 1985 which declares as void any provision which seeks to do so, whether contained in the articles or a contract with the company or otherwise.[2] The same applies in relation to a provision for an indemnity against such a liability. The company may, however, purchase and maintain insurance against such liability. It may also indemnify the auditor against any liability incurred in defending proceedings against him in which judgment is given in his favour or he is acquitted, or in connection with an application under s.727 of the Companies Act 1985 in which he is granted relief by the court.[3] Section 310 applies only in the context of a company audit.[4]

Engagement letters by accountants relating to engagements other than audits are nowadays replete with provisions directed to control or limit liability. They take many forms. It is prudent to describe the nature and parameters of the task to be undertaken and in as precise and unambiguous terms as the circumstances allow. Inherent constraints or limitations are frequently pointed out. Requirements of the client merit mention. There is usually an express statement that the services to be provided are for the benefit of the client only and not any third party. Express disclaimers of responsibility to third parties are common.[5] There may also be provisions seeking to limit liability to clients. These may be variously expressed and by reference to various formulae, e.g. a fee multiple. A well drawn limitation of liability clauses should in general survive attack by reference to the Unfair Contract Terms Act 1977[6] or the Unfair Terms in Consumer Contracts Regulations,[7] though much depends on the circumstances of each particular case. Statute apart, a limitation of liability provisions may be challenged on the ground that as a matter of construction it is not effective to exclude or restrict liability[8] or that it has not been incorporated into the relevant

---

[1] In March 2005 the DTI published a White Paper on Company Law Reform, including the proposed repeal of s.310. If enacted, this will enable auditors to limit their liability, subject to disclosure and shareholder approval (see *http://www.dti.gov.uk/files/file13958.pdf?pubpdfdload=05%2F928*). One recent development which will have a practical impact on the extent of auditor's liability is the change in the law which allows accountants and auditors to form limited liability partnerships.

[2] In *Re City Equitable Fire Insurance Co Ltd* [1925] 1 Ch. 407 auditors, although held in breach of their duty to the company, were also held not liable on the basis of an article which protected the auditors and other officers from liability for losses not due to their "wilful neglect or default". Such an article would now be void by reason of s.310.

[3] As to s.727, see para.17–083, below.

[4] See para.17–002, above for the proposed repeal of s.310.

[5] See para.17–026, above.

[6] In *Killick v PriceWaterhouseCoopers* [2001] P.N.L.R. 1, 8, Neuberger J., in refusing to grant summary judgment on the efficacy of an exclusion clause, listed a number of factors to be taken into account in deciding whether it was reasonable. These included: the way in which the term came into being and was used generally; the strength and bargaining position of the parties relative to each other; whether the client had an opportunity of entering into a similar contract with other persons without having to accept a similar term; how far it would have been practical and convenient to go elsewhere; the reality of the client's consent to the term; the size of the limit compared with other limits and widely used standard terms; the availability of insurance to the accountant; and the possibility of allowing for an option to contract without the limitation clause but with a price increase in lieu.

[7] SI 1999/2083, giving effect to Directive 93/13/EEC.

[8] e.g. in *Dairy Containers Ltd v NZI Bank Ltd* [1995] 2 N.Z.L.R. 30, 53, Thomas J., the issue concerned the following provision in the Auditor-General's contract: "The audit examination should not be relied upon to disclose defalcations or other irregularities, but their disclosure, if they exist,

contract. The courts have not yet resolved the question whether such a provision is effective against a third party to the contract.[9]

3. LIABILITY FOR BREACH OF DUTY

(a) *Auditing*

As we have seen,[10] the most relevant material in measuring the standard of skill   **17–054**
and care expected of an auditor is to be found in the auditing standards. The overriding principle is that the auditor is required only to provide reasonable assurance.[11]

(i) *Planning, Control and Recording*

An auditor should plan his work so as to perform the audit effectively. In order   **17–055**
to do so, he should develop and document an overall audit plan. He should develop and document the nature, timing and extent of planned audit procedures required to implement the overall audit plan and should keep these procedures under review.[12] An important part of his preparatory work is to obtain a knowledge of the business sufficient to enable him to identify and understand the matters which might materially affect the financial statements.[13] An auditor who has audited the company's financial statements in previous years will obviously have more knowledge of the company's affairs than a new auditor; on the one hand he is not expected to remember all the details of previous audits; on the other hand he is not working in a vacuum.[14] Another aspect to be considered at the planning stage is materiality. An error in the financial statements is relevant

---

may result from the audit tests undertaken." Thomas J. held that the provision did no more than confirm the position relating to detection of such fraud and irregularities, prescribed in relevant professional auditing standards, and was not effective to restrict his liability. See also *Bloor Italian Gifts Ltd v Dixon* (2000) 48 O.R. (3d) 760, Ontario CA: a clause saying that responsibility for the prevention of defalcations rested with the claimant was insufficient to protect an accountant from liability for negligence in failing to notice that the company had (innocently) underpaid tax. *University of Keele v Price Waterhouse* [2004] P.N.L.R. Case 43; [2004] EWCA Civ 583, CA, is a recent example of an exemption clause which failed to exclude liability on the plain meaning of the clause.

[9] The question was expressly left open by Neuberger J. in *Killick v PriceWaterhouseCoopers, ibid.* at 9–14 and by Moore-Bick L.J. in *Man Nutzfahrzeuge AG v Freightliner Ltd* [2005] EWHC 2347, Comm at para.411. In the latter case Moore-Bick L.J. expressed. the provisional view that the terms of an exclusion clause between company and auditor were part of the factual matrix as between the auditor and the third party and that it was relevant to ask whether the third party knew of the terms of the engagement letter or, if not, whether he should have realised that the auditor was assuming responsibility only on limited terms. See also *Royal Bank of Scotland Plc v Bannerman Johnston Maclay* [2005] P.N.L.R. 43 (see para.17–032, above).

[10] See para.17–051, above for an explanation of auditing standards.

[11] See para.17–051(2), above.

[12] ISA 300 (Planning) (SAS 200).

[13] SAS 210 (Knowledge of Business) (ISA 315). See also *Bloor Italian Gifts Ltd v Dixon* (2000) 48 O.R. (3d) 760, Ontario CA: accountant engaged to prepare financial statements (less than a full audit) was negligent in failing to make intelligent enquiries of management which would have alerted him to the fact that the company paid insufficient retail sales tax.

[14] *Pacific, ibid.* at 62.

only if it is "material"; the question whether it is likely to be material is case-sensitive and calls for a exercise of judgment.[15]

Failure to comply with auditing standards at the planning stage is likely to be neither necessary nor sufficient to give rise to liability for breach of duty. The issue is more likely to turn on the failure to detect or report on material misstatement in the financial statements. Nevertheless, the source of many failures can be found in the absence of proper planning. The absence of proper planning is likely to be a relevant consideration if the auditor seeks to assert that he could not reasonably have been expected to detect the fraud or error in question.

In *Pacific Acceptance Corp Ltd v Forsyth*[16] Moffitt J. recognised that it was the usual practice in all but the simplest cases for auditors to lay out a written programme of work which served many purposes. First, it acted as a direction to clerks as to the checks they were required to make. Secondly, it acted as a document against which the reviewing audit manager or partner should check and review the work of those under him. Thirdly, it facilitated, with minimum risk of error, changes in the audit staff during the course of the audit. The preparation or approval of a programme called for the skill and care of a person of sufficient seniority and experience, especially where reliance was placed on the company's internal system of control, since selection of appropriate sampling procedures involved some degree of sophistication. He recognised that there was (in that case) no statutory or contractual obligation to provide or work to a written programme and considered that omissions from the programme in themselves would not be sufficient to make the claimant's case. But if there were omissions from the programme and if undiscovered error or fraud occurred in the same area, then failure by the auditors to amend the programme would tend to indicate that the shortcomings were due to negligence. The business of the claimant company in that case consisted of lending money on security. On the facts, Moffitt J. concluded that the omission from the audit programme of procedures to vouch mortgage loan securities was the key to the omissions and deficiencies in the work of the defendant auditors' clerks. In failing to amend the programme to provide for such procedures, the auditors were held negligent. He took a similar view in respect of the employment of inexperienced staff to do work beyond their capacity. If the work was properly done by them, there was no breach of duty by the auditors employing them. But if work was left to audit clerks who were inexperienced and insufficiently supervised and their work was not properly reviewed, then these circumstances would tend to indicate that any shortcomings in the work were due to negligence. He concluded on the facts that the defendant auditors had employed inexperienced staff and failed properly to supervise them.

(ii) *Accounting and Internal Control Systems*

17–056 The company or other entity being audited will have its own accounting and internal control systems. The auditor needs to understand these in order to be able

---

[15] ISA 320 (Materiality and the Audit) (SAS 220).
[16] (1970) 92 W.N. (N.S.W.) 29, 76–79 and 102 (for the facts see para.17–052, above). See also *Dairy Containers Ltd v NZI Bank Ltd* [1995] 2 N.Z.L.R. 30, 59–62, in which the Auditor-General was held negligent in various respects, including lack of planning.

to form the necessary professional judgment as to the audit risk[17] and to design audit procedures which will reduce that risk to an acceptably low level.[18] Audit risk of material financial misstatement is divided into three categories.[19] The first is inherent risk, including the risk that the management might be fraudulent or negligent or that the accounts might contain errors of judgment (e.g. in valuing assets or liabilities). The second is control risk, i.e. the risk of a failure in the entity's own accounting and internal control systems.[20] The third is detection risk, i.e. the risk that the auditor's substantive procedures[21] fail to detect material misstatement. Given the fact that the audit is not expected to involve an examination of every item or class of transactions, that any internal system of accounting and control will be imperfect and that most audit evidence is persuasive rather than conclusive,[22] the auditor is not required to eliminate audit risk but to reduce it to an acceptable level. There are cases in which the auditor may properly decide that the cost of substantive procedures will be disproportionate to their benefit.[23] In other words, before the auditor carries out any substantive procedures,[24] he should make a preliminary assessment of the risks and benefits of these procedures.

In *Pacific Acceptance Corp Ltd v Forsyth*[25] Moffitt J. said:

"First, there must be a proper inquiry to ascertain the company's system. This would include ascertaining such features as indicate the strength and weaknesses of the system and hence its reliability. Second, there must be appraisal of it in that a person of sufficient auditing competence should make a decision as to the extent, if any, that the auditors can properly rely upon it. He should decide what procedures should be adopted to check that it is operating as intended and what other conditions should be met before reliance can be placed upon it. Third, there must be testing of its operation. All these essentials may call for revision in the course of the audit. For example, because of the result of testing it might be necessary to make a decision in the course of the testing to extend the testing or even not to rely on the system."

---

[17] ISA 315 paras 41–99 (Accounting and Internal Control Systems and Audit Risk Assessments) contains a detailed analysis of audit risk which is summarised in this paragraph. (SAS 300; see also SAS 400.2).

[18] ISA 315 and 330 (SAS 300.1).

[19] ISA 200 paras 20–3.

[20] The auditor should beware of relying on an internal system where it is operated by or is within the control of one person: *Irish Woollen Co Ltd v Tyson* (1900) 27 Acct. L.R. 13, Irish CA. In general the smaller the company, the fewer the internal controls, or at least the fewer the internal controls upon which an auditor may reasonably rely: SAS 300 para.26 (ISA paras 45, 48, 66 and 79) and see *Guardian Insurance Co v Sharp* [1941] 2 D.L.R. 417, 433.

[21] ISA 610 (Considering the Work of Internal Audit): The external auditor has sole responsibility for his audit but it may be reasonable for him to rely to some extent on the work of internal auditors (SAS 500).

[22] ISA 200 para 9 (SAS 100.10).

[23] ISA 330 para.70 (SAS 300.25).

[24] Substantive procedures are considered in para.17–057, below.

[25] (1970) 92 W.N. (N.S.W.) 29, 87–8 and 125 (for the facts see para.17–052, above). See also *Daniels v Anderson* (1995) 16 A.C.S.R. 607, 623–628, 642–644 and 651–652 (and the same case in the lower court: (1992) 7 A.C.S.R. 759, 796–802 and at 834–835). For further illustrations, see *Re SP Catterson & Sons Ltd* (1937) 81 Acct. L.R. 62; *International Laboratories Ltd v Dewar* [1933] 3 D.L.R. 665, Manitoba CA; *McBride's Ltd v Rooke & Thomas* [1941] D.L.R. 45, 49 and 53; *Guardian Insurance Co v Sharp* [1941] 2 D.L.R. 417; and *Dairy Containers Ltd v NZI Bank Ltd* [1995] 2 N.Z.L.R. 30, 61.

On the facts he held that the defendant auditors had failed in respect of each prerequisite and had not properly addressed themselves to questions of internal control in relation to mortgage loan vouching. He further stressed the importance of independence in the audit approach. The claimant's system was unjustifiably absolutely relied upon without any real independent consideration. He further rejected the contention for the auditors that they were justified in not checking documents in that they relied upon the employment of the solicitor seen as part of the company's system of internal control.[26]

(iii) *Evidence*

17–057   **Sufficient appropriate evidence.** ISA 500 states that "the auditor should obtain *sufficient appropriate* audit evidence to be able to draw *reasonable conclusions* on which to base the audit opinion".[27] Audit evidence is usually persuasive rather than conclusive; auditors therefore need to obtain evidence from a variety of sources. Sufficiency refers to quantity of evidence, appropriateness to quality. As regards quality, although the reliability of audit evidence will vary from case to case, as a general rule it may be said that: external evidence is more reliable than evidence from the entity's own records; evidence from the entity's own records is more reliable where the internal control systems operate effectively; evidence obtained directly by the auditor is more reliable than that obtained by or from the entity; written evidence is more reliable than oral; and original documents are more reliable than copies.[28]

ISA 500 (Audit Evidence) is of critical importance and is likely to form the core of most allegations of breach of duty against auditors. The key is the interrelationship between "sufficient appropriate" evidence and "reasonable conclusions". As we have seen,[29] the auditor seeks to provide reasonable, not absolute assurance. There is inevitably an element of risk, e.g. in the fact that he relies on sampling[30] and does not examine every transaction. In considering whether he was negligent in running a risk, one looks at matters such as an assessment of the nature and degree of risk of misstatement, the nature of the accounting and internal control systems, the materiality of the item being examined, the auditor's knowledge of the business including experience gained during previous audits, the findings from audit procedures and the source and reliability of information available.[31]

The steps which need to be taken include:

(1) Inspection: reviewing or examining records, documents or tangible assets. An auditor's duty to examine the books in order to satisfy himself

---

[26] Note also *Dairy Containers Ltd v NZI Bank Ltd* [1995] 2 N.Z.L.R. 30, 62–65, in which the Auditor-General was held negligent in various respects, including failure to obtain adequate evidence especially in regard to investments and security documents.

[27] ISA 500 para.2 (Audit Evidence) (SAS 400.1).

[28] ISA 500 para.9 (SAS 400.16).

[29] See para.17–051(2), above.

[30] ISA 530 (Audit Sampling) (SAS 430). Care should be taken over the design and selection of the sample, having regard to the specific audit objectives, the nature of the population which the auditor wishes to sample and the sampling and selecting methods. The sample items should be selected so as to be representative. See *Dairy Containers Ltd v NZI Bank Ltd* [1995] N.Z.L.R. 30, 69.

[31] ISA 500 para.7 (SAS 400 paras 5–6).

that they show the true financial position of the company was given early recognition.[32] If a document under the control of the entity is material to the audit, the auditor should look at it for himself unless there are special circumstances why it is reasonable to make do with something less.[33]

(2) Observation: looking at an operation or procedure being performed by others with a view to determining its manner of performance, e.g. stock counting.

(3) Enquiry and confirmation from knowledgeable persons inside the entity.[34] As regards those inside the entity, enquiry should be directed to management or staff at the appropriate level; in deciding that level the interest of the person concerned is a relevant matter. Thus in a matter calling for an explanation concerning the authority of an employee or otherwise reflecting on the performance of his duty, prima facie he is not the person from whom an explanation should be sought or if sought, from whom it should be accepted without verification.[35] It may be important to consider who should make the enquiry: where it relates to a matter of

---

[32] *Leeds Estate, Building and Investment Co v Shepherd* (1887) 36 Ch.D. 787, 802 (for facts, see para.17–057(3), below); and *Re London and General Bank (No.2)* [1895] 2 Ch. 673, 682–683 (for facts see para.17–051(1), above). Note the Canadian case of *Revelstoke Credit Union v Miller* (1984) 28 C.C.L.T. 17, 31, *per* McEachern C.J.S.C.:

"A court must be careful about drawing inferences from the mere recording of facts in voluminous books of record or computer printouts. This is because it is a reality of commercial life that the diffusion of clerical and accounting functions between several members of a department often deprives an organisation such as a credit union of real notice of what is happening, and although a meticulous scrutiny of printouts may tell the whole story, it is useful to remember Mr (Sherlock) Holmes' admonition (to observe what is seen). The crucial question is not whether the facts are recorded and seen but whether they should have been recognised and observed, and, if observed, they should have led to a sceptical or critical train of inquiry in the face of assurances given by trusted persons in authority."

[33] *Pacific Acceptance Corp Ltd v Forsyth* (1970) 92 W.N. (N.S.W.) 29, 67–68. It may be argued that Moffitt J. over-emphasises the importance of personal inspection of documents. His view seems over-influenced by the nature of the particular documents not properly inspected on the facts in *Pacific Acceptance*, namely original mortgage and title deeds. It is evident, however, that the courts continue to attach considerable importance to actual inspection of material documents by auditors and their staff. But see *Cork Mutual Benefit Terminable Society v Atkins Chirnside & Co* (1905) 45 Acct. L.R. 13 (no duty to examine the pass books of each member of a building society).

[34] *Leeds Estate, Building and Investment Co v Shepherd* (1887) 36 Ch.D. 787, 802, Stirling J. In that case an auditor did not acquaint himself with the articles of association of a company and did not carry out appropriate inquiries as required by them. He relied on inaccurate balance sheets prepared by the secretary and manager of the company and relied without further inquiry upon the same person's statement that securities upon which monies were lent were worth more than those monies. He nevertheless certified the accounts in terms indicating that he had carried out proper examination and inquiries. He was held to have been in breach of his duty to the company.

[35] *Pacific, ibid.* at 71: *ADT v Binder Hamlyn* [1996] BCC 808 at 836–7. The point is graphically illustrated by the *Barings* debacle in which the auditors relied on representations made by Nick Leeson (discussed at 017–81 above). Note also *WA Chip & Pulp Co Pty Ltd v Arthur Young & Co* (1987) 12 A.C.L.R. 25 Pidgeon J., and on appeal, *sub nom. Arthur Young & Co v WA Chip & Pulp Co Pty Ltd* (1988) 13 A.C.L.R. 283. *cf. Short & Compton v Brackett* (1904) Acct. L.R. 8 (no negligence in failing to notice that clerk had made out wages bills for more than was due) and *Cameron Publications Ltd v Piers, Conrod & Allen* (1986) 35 B.L.R. 32, Nova Scotia Supreme Court, Appeal Division.

substance and where the enquiry is to be made of a senior executive, it might require the attention of a person of experience and seniority.[36] Management representations should be recorded in writing. If the representations relate to matters material to the financial statement, the auditor should seek corroborative evidence; if he fails to obtain it, he should consider whether his report needs to be qualified.[37] However, in some circumstances he might reasonably conclude that the cumulative weight of the management representations and the corroborative evidence is sufficient, even though neither would have sufficed without the other.[38]

(4) Enquiry and confirmation from knowledgeable persons outside the entity: One important source of confirmation is from the entity's bankers. There is now a standard form for requests for information from banks,[39] but the auditor should always consider whether the standard form is appropriate in the circumstances. In appropriate cases the auditor should make enquiries of other persons outside the entity,[40] such as creditors or debtors of the entity, the auditors of a wholly owned subsidiary company[41] or appropriate experts.[42]

(5) Computation: checking arithmetical accuracy or performing independent calculations.

(6) Analytical procedures[43]: analysing the relationships between different items of data or between comparable financial information deriving from different period or different entities, in order to identify consistencies and predicted patterns or significant fluctuations and unexpected relationships.[44]

---

[36] *Pacific* at 72. Moffitt J.'s remarks concerning enquiry were particularly directed towards a branch office audit which in his view was a potential danger point.

[37] ISA 580 (Management Representations) (SAS 440). It was formerly held that the auditor was entitled to believe tried servants in whom the entity had placed confidence: *Re Kingston Cotton Mill Co Ltd (No.2)* [1896] 2 Ch. 279, 288 (for the facts see para.17–058(3), below), but we suggest that a modern auditor would be expected to show more professional scepticism: *Re City Equitable Fire Insurance Co Ltd* [1925] 1 Ch. 407, 531; and *Re Thomas Gerrard & Son Ltd* [1968] Ch. 455. In *ADT v Binder Hamlyn* [1996] B.C.C. 808, 836B, May J. said that an auditor does not discharge his obligation to express an independent opinion simply by accepting what the directors say; hence management representations are a low grade of audit evidence.

[38] *ADT v Binder Hamlyn, ibid.* at 838.

[39] APB Practice Note 16 (Bank Reports for Audit Purposes).

[40] *Fomento (Sterling Area) Ltd v Selsdon Fountain Pen Co Ltd* [1958] 1 W.L.R. 45, 61, HL, *per* Lord Denning: The issue in that case was whether auditors engaged by patent licensors to ascertain the amount of royalties due from licensees were entitled to require production by the licensees of specimens or specifications of particular products in order to establish whether they were patented articles or not.

[41] *Pacific, ibid.* at 107–114. See also ISA 600 (Relationship between Principal Auditors and Other Auditors) (SAS 510).

[42] ISA 620 (Using the Work of an Expert) (SAS 520); *AWA Ltd v Daniels t/a Deloitte Haskins & Sells* (1992) 7 A.C.S.R. 759, 775. (The case went to appeal *sub nom. Daniels v Anderson* (1995) 16 A.C.S.R. 607.)

[43] ISA 520 (Analytical Procedures) (SAS 410).

[44] ISA 500 para.38 and ISA 520 (SAS 400 para.19–25).

At the conclusion of the process of gathering evidence the auditor should carry out a review of the financial statements in conjunction with the evidence obtained and should consider whether the information in the financial statements accords with statutory requirements and whether accounting policies accord with accounting standards properly disclosed, consistently applied and appropriate to the entity.[45]

Particular items in the accounts.   17–058

(1) Fixed and intangible assets: the auditor should consider whether the asset has been valued in accordance with appropriate accounting standards, including depreciation.[46]

(2) Securities and investments: an auditor must take reasonable steps to satisfy himself that the securities exist, are in safe and proper custody and are sufficient. This is particularly important in the case of a finance company the business of which consists of lending money on security. It has been suggested that a company's stockbrokers however respectable or responsible are not proper persons to have the custody of its securities except for short periods of necessity.[47] It has also be said[48] that an auditor is never justified in omitting to make a personal inspection of securities in improper custody whenever such personal inspections are practicable. Failure to inspect supposed securities, mainly first mortgages on freehold property, for loans made by the claimant finance company, was the prime default by the defendant auditors in *Pacific Acceptance Corp Ltd*

---

[45] ISA 700 (SAS 470).

[46] e.g. SSAP 12 (Accounting for Depreciation), SSAP 19 (Accounting for Investment Properties); SSAP 21 (Accounting for Leases and Hire Purchase Contracts); FRS 7 (Fair Value in Acquisition Accounting); FRS 10 (Goodwill and Intangible Assets); and FRS 11 (Impairment of Fixed Assets and Goodwill). (For a general discussion about SSAPs, FRSs and IFRSs, see para.17–021, above.)

[47] *Re City Equitable Fire Insurance Co Ltd* [1925] 1 Ch. 407, 498, *per* Romer J. at first instance. On appeal Pollock M.R. seemed to concede that during such short periods it might be permissible to accept from stockbrokers a certificate of possession of securities but generally he considered that it was an auditor's duty to take such a certificate only from a person who was not only "respectable" or "trustworthy" but also was within a class of persons who in the ordinary course of their business kept securities for their customers (*ibid.* at 512–513. Sargant L.J. at 530 instanced bankers or safe deposit companies as persons accustomed to keep securities.) In that case there was a large deficiency upon the winding-up of an insurance company, in large part attributable to the managing director's fraud. He was also the senior partner of a firm of stockbrokers through which the company placed investments. It was alleged that the auditors were liable for damage occasioned by the stockbrokers pledging to their customers and losing various securities belonging to the company but in the possession of the stockbrokers. Romer J. at first instance (*ibid.* at 498) and the CA (*ibid., per* Pollock M.R. at 515 and seemingly reluctantly, *per* Warrington L.J. at 527; *cf., per* Sargant L.J. at 531) held that the auditors were negligent (i) in accepting a certificate from the stockbrokers that they held large blocks of the company's securities and (ii) in neither insisting upon those securities being put in proper custody nor reporting the matter to the shareholders. However the auditor escaped liability by reason of an exemption clause (see para.17–053, above).

[48] *ibid., per* Romer J. at 497–498. Note *Re London and General Bank (No.2)* [1875] 2 Ch. 673, 684 where Lindley L.J. seems to have considered it to be the auditor's duty to see that the bills and securities entered in the books were held by the bank (for facts see para.17–051, above).

v Forsyth.[49] The fact that the person whom the duty of attending to the execution and registration of mortgages is a professional man does not place him outside the audit field.[50] It is also the auditor's duty to satisfy himself of the sufficiency of the securities.[51]

(3) Stock-in-trade[52]: it has been held that it is not an auditor's duty to take stock.[53] Nevertheless the exercise of reasonable care may still require reasonable steps to be taken to verify figures concerning stock-in-trade.[54] If the auditor discovers irregularities in documents relating to stock, he may need to go further than an explanation from an employee or director.[55]

---

[49] (1970) 92 W.N. (N.S.W.) 29, 81: for the facts see para.17–052, above. In that case the preparation of security documents was entrusted by the company to a solicitor who also acted for the borrowers. It was the practice of the relevant branch office of the company to allow solicitors to hold the security documents. The auditors did not inspect the documents. Had they done so they would have discovered that the company had been duped into making loans, sometimes to fictitious companies, which were unsecured. Moffitt J. considered that at the very least auditors of a finance company should satisfy themselves by some proper means that the securities for each of the material loans during the audit year, or outstanding at the balance date, had as promised been executed and registered. He held that the defendant auditors in neither inspecting the security documents for themselves nor obtaining appropriate certificates from the supposed custodian were negligent.

[50] *Pacific, ibid.* at 86.

[51] *Leeds Estate, Building and Investment Co v Shepherd* (1887) 36 Ch.D. 787: for the facts see para.17–112(1) and 17–112(3), above. In that case the auditor of a finance company was held to be negligent in accepting a manager's statement that the securities on which the moneys were lent were not only equal to but worth more than the amount placed against them, without making any proper investigation of the company's accounts. We suggest, however, that the extent of the inquiry into the sufficiency of securities expected of an auditor is in the absence of special circumstances limited, since this is essentially for the management or the directors of the company and not for its auditors to decide: *Re London and General Bank (No.2)* [1895] 2 Ch. 673, 682.

[52] See SSAP 9 (Stocks and Long Term Contracts) and AG (Auditing Guideline) 405 (Attendance at Stocktaking).

[53] *Re Kingston Cotton Mill Co Ltd (No.2)* [1896] 1 Ch. 331 (first instance); [1896] 2 Ch. 275, CA. In that case auditors relied upon certificates as to stock value given by a director of the company which were deliberately overstated. Dividends paid on the basis that the balance sheets were correct were found after discovery of the fraud to have been paid out of capital rather than income. If the auditors had added to the stock-in-trade at the beginning of any of the relevant audit years the purchases of raw material in the same year, and had deducted therefrom their sales, they would have seen that the statement of stock-in-trade at the end of the year was so remarkable as to call for explanation. Lindley and Lopes L.JJ. held that it was not an auditor's duty to take stock and that he was entitled to rely on other people for details of stock-in-trade in the absence of suspicion being aroused. However we suggest that a higher standard might be imposed today. AG 405 para.5 says that an auditor should attend at stocktaking where the stocks are material in the financial statements and the auditor is relying on the management's stocktake.

[54] *Henry Squire, Cash Chemist Ltd v Ball Baker & Co* (1912) 106 L.T. 197, 201 and 203: it is the duty of an auditor to make a reasonable and proper investigation of stock sheets and if he concludes something was wrong to report the matter. See also *Re Liverpool and Wigan Supply Association Ltd* [1907] Acct. L.R. 4 and *Colmer v Merrett, Son & Street* (1914) 50 Acct. L.R. 21.

[55] *Re Thomas Gerrard & Son Ltd* [1968] 1 Ch. 455, 476. In that case a company's managing director caused the value of its stock-in-trade to be falsified and overstated. When questioned about altered invoices he gave an explanation which the auditor accepted. Pennycuick J. considered that the auditors should not have contented themselves with the managing director's explanation for the altered invoices but should have examined suppliers' statements and where necessary have communicated with suppliers. Having ascertained the true facts they should then have informed the board. In the circumstances their suspicions ought emphatically to have been aroused. (For discussion of this case see Pennington, 78 *Accountancy*, 694; Baxt [1970] 33 M.L.R. 413.)

(4) Work in progress: it has been held to be the auditor's duty to satisfy himself that nothing is included in the work in progress or the balance sheet which was done after that date and that all expenses or liabilities incurred by the company in connection with the work so valued have been brought into account.[56] If a large proportion of work in progress is subject to reservation of title clauses in favour of suppliers, an auditor should make express reference to this in his report.[57] Moreover in certain circumstances it may be prudent for an auditor to seek legal advice upon the effect of a particular reservation of title clause.

(5) Debtors: the overriding concept is that of prudence.[58] An auditor must take care that he does not bring into his balance sheet at face value a debt that is not a good one.[59] He must make reasonable inquiries as to the provision made for bad debts. If circumstances call for inquiry, the auditor must make proper inquiry.[60] It is nevertheless recognised that in the writing off and the making of provision for bad debts an auditor is dependent upon those who run the audited enterprises since their knowledge of the debtors is generally far greater than his.[61] It is now established practice in the United Kingdom to verify a sample of debtor balances by direct communication with the debtors concerned.[62] On the other hand, auditors are not expected to be so astute as to discover whether debts are bad because there is some technical legal defence to their recoverability.[63]

(6) Cash: reasonable steps must be taken to inspect cash records.[64] If an enterprise is large and has many branches it will be impracticable for auditors to check all cash records. Moreover, internal control systems are usually designed to prevent abstraction of money and fabrication of records to conceal the consequent loss. If an auditor has properly relied upon and tested an internal control system[65] it may be difficult to prove him negligent in failing to carry out an inspection of particular documents which would have revealed fraud.[66] On the other hand, where the

---

[56] *Re Westminster Road Construction & Engineering Co Ltd* (1932) Acct. L.R. 38 (also referred to as *Smith v Offer*).

[57] ICAEW Recommendation (Accounting for Goods Sold Subject to Reservation of Title).

[58] *ADT Ltd v Binder Hamlyn* [1996] B.C.C. 808, 848F.

[59] *Re City Equitable Fire Insurance Co Ltd* [1925] 1 Ch. 407, 483.

[60] *Arthur E Green & Co v The Central Advance and Discount Corp Ltd* (1920) 63 Acct. L.R. 1.

[61] See *Scarborough Harbour Commission v Robinson, Coulson Kirby & Co* (1934) 78 Acct. L.R. 65, 69; see also *Irish Woollen Co Ltd v Tyson* (1900) 27 Acct. L.R. 13, 14 and *Jamieson, Austin & Mitchell Ltd v Battrum* [1934] 1 W.W.R. 324, 330.

[62] See para.17–057, above as to audit sampling.

[63] *Frank M Wright (Construction) Ltd v Frodoor Ltd* [1967] 1 W.L.R. 506, 523: accountants asked to value shares on the basis of excess of assets over liabilities were not bound when valuing those liabilities to consider whether or not the Moneylenders Acts would apply.

[64] *London Oil Storage Co Ltd v Seear, Hasluck & Co* (1904) 31 Acct. L.R. 1; *Fox v Morrish, Grant & Co* [1918] T.L.R. 126. see also *Re Kingston Cotton Mill & Co Ltd (No.2)* [1896] 2 Ch. 279, 287.

[65] See para.17–056, above.

[66] Compare *Guardian Insurance Co v Sharp* [1941] 2 D.L.R. 417 and *McBride's Ltd v Rooke and Thomas* [1941] 4 D.L.R. 45 in regard to inspection of bank slips when internal control system relied upon.

enterprise is small or where there is no internal control system the taking of reasonable steps may require detailed inspection of original cash records such as receipts and bank slips and of cash in hand. Also when there is cause for suspicion,[67] detailed inspection will be required. One cause for suspicion may be dishonoured cheques.[68]

(7) Creditors: accounting standards[69] set out the principles of accounting for provisions, contingent liabilities and contingent assets. The objective is to ensure that appropriate recognition criteria and measurement bases are applied and that sufficient information is disclosed in the notes to enable the user to understand their nature, timing and amount. A frequent device resorted to for giving an over-favourable picture of the state of affairs of an enterprise is the suppression of liabilities, frequently by carrying them over from the accounting period subject of an audit to the next. An auditor must take reasonable steps to ascertain liabilities including contingent liabilities, but even the taking of such steps may not lead to discovery of suppressed liabilities.[70] In certain circumstances, such as upon the discovery of the alteration of invoice dates, an auditor should call for statements from creditors and may be held negligent in failing to do so.[71] Specific inquiries concerning liabilities will also be required of an auditor where creditors commonly delay sending invoices and in consequence liabilities incurred cannot be ascertained from invoices received owing to insufficient lapse of time for receipt of all relevant invoices.[72]

(8) Unauthorised transactions: an auditor who comes upon a payment which is *ultra vires* or improper is to inquire into it and, if need be, to disallow it.[73] On the other hand, an auditor of a company is rarely equipped with the knowledge of a lawyer. While he may be liable for failure to discover that a particular transaction is unauthorised owing to the absence of a prerequisite resolution of the directors or shareholders, he will not be liable for failure to ascertain as unauthorised a transaction which only a lawyer would have been likely to recognise as such.[74] But if he ought to realise that there might be a problem, he should make the necessary

---

[67] e.g. *Hardy Employees' Credit Union Ltd v Moll Chadwick & Co* [1980] Qd.R. 362 (failure properly to investigate suspiciously large payments).

[68] *Pacific Acceptance Corp Ltd v Forsyth* (1970) 92 W.N. (N.S.W.) 29, 98–99 and 102.

[69] FRS (Financial Reporting Standard) 12 (Provisions, Contingent Liabilities and Contingent Assets).

[70] In *Henry Squire, Cash Chemist Ltd v Ball Baker & Co* [1912] L.T. 197, 204 auditors were absolved of negligence in not discovering suppressed liabilities since there was no entry in the books of the audited company which would have revealed them

[71] *Re Thomas Gerrard & Son Ltd* [1968] 1 Ch. 455. See also *Irish Woollen Co Ltd v Tyson* (1900) 27 Acct. L.R. 13.

[72] See *Re Westminster Road Construction & Engineering Co Ltd* (1932) Acct. L.R. 38.

[73] *Fomento (Sterling Area) Ltd v Selsdon Fountain Pen Co Ltd* [1958] 1 W.L.R. 45, 61, HL: see para.17–057(4), above. See also ISA 250 Section A (Consideration of Law and Regulations) (SAS 120).

[74] Note *Trustee of the Property of Blue Band Navigation Co Ltd v Price Waterhouse & Co (No.2)* [1934] 3 D.L.R. 404, 433, British Columbia CA.

inquiries[75] and, if appropriate, take expert advice.[76] It has long been recognised as part of the function of an auditor of a local authority to take reasonable steps to check that there are no unauthorised, illegal or improper payments and to report to the authority if any are discovered.[77]

(9) Related party transactions: the audit should be planned and performed with the objective of obtaining sufficient audit evidence regarding the adequacy of disclosure of related party transactions.[78]

(10) Post-balance sheet events: the auditor should consider the effect of subsequent events on the financial statements.[79] He should perform procedures devised to obtain sufficient appropriate evidence that all material subsequent events have been identified and properly reflected in the financial statements. Where events happen or are discovered after the date of the auditor's report but before the financial statements are issued, he should consider whether the financial statements need amendment. If the events which happen are discovered after the statements have been issued but before they have been laid before the members, he should consider whether the statements need revision. The important point is that the auditor's duty is not discharged where the audit certificate, although reasonable in the light of facts known at the time, proves to be incorrect before it is relied upon.

(iv) *Reporting*

The product of an audit is a report by the auditor upon the entity's financial   **17–059**
statements. Errors in conducting the audit will usually be reflected in the report. For example, in consequence of inadequate inspection of material documents an unqualified report might be given when, if a proper inspection had been made, the report would need to have been qualified. Various statutes contain provisions making specific requirements concerning the contents of an auditor's report.[80] The Companies Act 1985 requires the report to state that the company's financial statements have not only been properly prepared in accordance with the Act but also give a "true and fair view."[81] Indeed, until recently statutory obligations concerning the audit of an enterprise related exclusively to the audit report rather

---

[75] See *AWA Ltd v Daniels t/a Deloitte Haskins & Sells* (1992) 7 A.C.S.R. 759, 787. On appeal, see *Daniels v Anderson* (1995) 16 A.C.S.R. 607.
[76] See para.17–057(3), above.
[77] *Thomas v Devonport Corp* [1900] 1 Q.B. 16, 21, approved in *Roberts v Hopwood* [1925] A.C. 578, 605 and *Re Risdel, Risdel v Rawlinson* [1947] 2 All E.R. 312, 315–316; also *Frankston and Hastings Corp v Cohen* (1960) 102 C.L.R. 607, 619. Ultra vires has always been a particular concern in relation to public authorities; accordingly care needs to be taken in applying these cases to other entities.
[78] ISA 550 (Related Parties) (SAS 460); see also FRS 8 (Related Party Disclosures).
[79] ISA 560 (Subsequent Events) (SAS 150).
[80] See paras 17–007 *et seq.*, above.
[81] s.235: see para.17–012, above.

than both to the audit itself and the consequent report. A prior audit was contemplated, but an auditor's duties incidental and preparatory to making a report were left for the courts to decide. The current Companies Act expressly takes into account the audit itself, by requiring an auditor to carry out such investigations as will enable him to form an opinion on various matters.[82] Nevertheless, the nature of appropriate investigating steps is not defined in the Act but remains within the province of the courts to decide, having regard to the facts of particular cases and the practice of the profession. Indeed somewhat inversely to the statutory approach, the courts' approach to deciding professional negligence cases against auditors is to consider primarily errors in the course of an audit as opposed to errors in the audit report. Moreover, comparative to the number of judicial comments concerned with what should be done in the course of an audit, there are few concerned with the contents or form of the report itself. The point is usually of no great significance, however, since if an auditor has failed to discover a matter in the course of an audit, it goes without saying that he will also have failed to deal with it in his report. Nevertheless, the manner of stating the results of an audit is often crucial.

An ISA contains specific requirements as to the contents of auditors' reports on financial statements.[83] The primary requirement is that such statements should "contain a clear expression of opinion, based on review and assessment of the conclusions drawn from evidence in the course of the audit". Since the auditor's role is to provide reasonable, not absolute, assurance, it is important that the report indicates the context in which it is given. The ISA states the form which the report should take.[84] The report should contain a clear expression of opinion on the financial statements.[85] Before the auditor can properly express an unqualified opinion, he must be satisfied that the financial statements give a true and fair view and have been prepared in accordance with appropriate accounting policies consistently applied. If there is a limitation on the scope of his examination or if he disagrees with the treatment or disclosure of a matter, he should give a qualified report. If his disagreement is so material or pervasive that he considers the financial statements to be seriously misleading, he should give an adverse opinion. Where the possible effect of a limitation on scope is so material or pervasive that he has been unable to obtain sufficient evidence, he should issue a disclaimer of opinion.[86] Further, he should consider whether the view expressed in the financial statements could be affected by inherent uncertainties which are fundamental; if this is so but the uncertainty is adequately disclosed in the

---

[82] s.237(1): see para.17–013, above.

[83] ISA 700 (SAS 600). See also APB Practice Note 8 (Reports by auditors under company legislation in the United Kingdom); APB Bulletin 1997/1 (The Special Auditors' Report on Abbreviated Accounts in Great Britain); APB Bulletin 1999/6 (The Auditors' Report on the Summary Financial Statement); and APB Bulletin 2001/2 (Revisions to the Wording of Auditors' Reports on Financial Statements and the Interim Review Report).

[84] In *Re John Fulton & Co Ltd* [1932] N.I. 35 an auditor who signed balance sheets "Audited Henry Jenkinson" but who had failed to audit and report on the balance sheets was held to have been in breach of his duty.

[85] *Re London and General Bank (No.2)* [1895] 2 Ch. 783, CA (for facts see para.17–051(1), above). Also note *Shorrock Ltd v Meggitt Plc, The Times*, June 4, 1991, CA.

[86] ISA 700 para.38 (SAS 600 paras 32–37).

financial statement, he should add an explanatory paragraph to his report but without qualifying his opinion.[87]

In some cases the disclosure of sensitive information might be damaging to the company. We suggest that the correct approach is to look at the scope of the auditor's duty and to consider whether he has discharged his duty to the person or class of persons to whom the duty is owed.[88] A less extensive reporting duty has been recognised in the case of an audit of a company the shareholders of which are also directors than in the case of a company with a large body of shareholders, where an auditor has already communicated material matters to the directors.[89] However, the fact that the shareholders are also directors should not excuse an auditor from performing his statutory duties in making his report.

In addition to his report to the general meeting, the auditor should consider whether to make a separate report to directors or management on matters coming to his attention during the audit, including material weakness in accounting and internal control systems.[90] This is in addition to, not instead of, a report to the general meeting.[91] We suggest that, where an auditor discovers wrongdoing within a company and considers that all or some of the management is unaware of the wrongdoing, he may come under a duty to the company to alert the management.[92] If the management is party to the fraud, the auditor may come under "whistle-blowing" duties.[93]

(b) Other Breaches of Duty

Valuation. Accountants are sometimes asked to act as valuers.[94] The articles of association of a private company often have rights of pre-emption requiring a shareholder who wishes to dispose of his shares to offer them to the other **17–060**

---

[87] ISA 700 paras 31–2 (SAS 600.6).
[88] *Pacific Acceptance Corp Ltd v Forsyth* (1970) 92 W.N. (N.S.W.) 29, 58. In *Re London and General Bank (No.2)* [1895] 2 Ch. 783 (for the facts see para.17–051(1), above) Lindley L.J. recognised that the disclosure of certain information in the shape of a printed document circulated among a large body of shareholders might by its consequent publicity be damaging to their interests. In such circumstances he was unwilling to hold an auditor in breach of his duty if instead of publishing his report in such a way as to ensure publicity, he made a confidential report to the shareholders, invited their attention to it and told them where they could see it.
[89] *Pendlebury's Ltd v Ellis Green & Co* (1936) 80 Acct. L.R. 39; also *International Laboratories Ltd v Dewar* (1933) 3 D.L.R. 665, 697.
[90] ISA 260 (SAS 610); *Sasea Finance Ltd v KPMG* [2000] 1 All E.R. 676. In *Canadian Woodmen of the World v Hooper* [1933] 1 D.L.R. 168 auditors of a fraternal order discovered that the order's stockbroker had purchased bonds different from those required by the directors of the order and that this had been concealed from the directors by the order's head clerk. In reliance upon the clerk's and the stockbroker's promises to rectify the matter, the auditors did not report it to the directors until three years later when the promises remained unfulfilled. In failing to report the matter upon original discovery to the directors, the auditors were held negligent.
[91] *Re London and General Bank (No.2)* [1895] 2 Ch. 783, CA (see para.17–051(1), above).
[92] See para.17–013, above.
[93] See para.17–030, above.
[94] In *Goldstein v Levy Gee* [2003] P.N.L.R. 35, Lewison J. held that negligence in the process of valuation is irrelevant, as long as the end result is within the range of reasonable values. He applied *Arab Bank v John D Wood* (see Ch.10 (Surveyors) para.10–097, above). (*Goldstein* is discussed in an article by Dugdale, [2004] P.N. 21.)

shareholders at a price to be determined by the auditor. If the auditor is acting as expert, not arbitrator, he will owe a duty of care to the parties.[95]

17–061   **Preparation of tax returns.** An accountant may be liable if, as a result of his acts or omissions, there is undue delay in submitting a tax return or the tax return is inaccurate.[96] Needless to say, it will be particularly important in this context to consider whether the client has caused or contributed to the loss and whether he would have acted differently, if properly advised.[97]

17–062   **Advice.** Accountants frequently give advice on tax, insolvency[98] or business matters. The principles to be applied are broadly the same as those which apply in the case of solicitors.[99] If the accountant assumes a responsibility for advising the client as to what investment policy he should adopt, he may find that he has crossed the line between "information" and "advice".[1]

An auditor's working papers belong to the auditor.[2] The same goes for an accountant's working papers. However, the Professional Negligence Pre-Action Protocol[3] imposes duties on both sides to co-operate in an early exchange of information. If the auditor or accountant refuses to give early disclosure of working papers and the claimant can demonstrate a need for such disclosure in order to be able to plead his case, he may make an application for pre-action disclosure under CPR r.31.16. The Court of Appeal has so far refused to lay down guidelines for early disclosure but has said that it may be appropriate in a vast range of cases.[4]

---

[95] *Arenson v Casson Beckman, Rutley & Co* [1977] A.C. 405. As to challenges to the valuation on the ground of mistake, see *Jones v Sherwood Computer Services Plc* [1992] 1 W.L.R. 277. As to the standard of care, see *Whiteoak v Walker* (1988) B.C.C. 122 (para.17–91).

[96] *United Project Consultants Pte Ltd v Leong Kwok Onn* [2005] 4 S.L.R. 214: in that case a company sued its auditor and tax agent to recover the penalty imposed by the Inland Revenue Authority of Singapore for under-reporting directors' fees in its tax return. The Singapore Court of Appeal held that the defendant had actual knowledge of the amount of the fees, since it also acted as tax agent for one of the directors. Although the defendant was entitled to rely on management representations to some extent, it had a duty to satisfy itself and was more than a mere form filler. It was therefore liable for negligence. The decision was based on actual knowledge, but it seems that having the means of knowledge might suffice: *Pech v Tilgals* (1994) 28 A.T.R. 197.

[97] See paras 17–063 *et seq.*, 17–065 *et seq.* and 17–080 *et seq.*, below.

[98] *Wade v Poppleton & Appleby* [2004] 1 B.C.L.C. 674, is an example of the duty of care owed by an insolvency practitioner to the company and its shareholders.

[99] See Ch.11 (Solicitors) para.11–153.

[1] *South Australia Asset Management Co Ltd v York Montague Ltd* [1997] A.C. 191 (see para.17–064, below). For an example, see *Craig v Troy* (1997) 16 W.A.R. 96, Supreme Court of Western Australia, where an accountant was held liable for negligent advice as to the feasibility of a hotel development. In *Aneco Reinsurance Underwriting Ltd v Johnson & Higgins Ltd,* [2002] P.N.L.R. 8, the House of Lords held by a majority that an insurance broker who wrongly advised an insurer that reinsurance was available was giving advice and not merely information. Although the House of Lords categorised this as an appeal which realised no point of principle, it might be seen as a retreat from *SAAMCO.*

[2] *Chantrey Martin v Martin* [1953] 2 Q.B. 286.

[3] Para.B4.3 and Guidance Note C5.1: White Book Vol.1 sections C7–005 and 017.

[4] *Bermuda International Securities Ltd v KPMG* [2001] Lloyd's Rep. P.N. 392. See also *Medisys Plc v Arthur Andersen* [2002] P.N.L.R. 22; *Black v Sumitomo* [2002] 1 W.L.R. 1562 and *Three Rivers DC v Bank of England (No.4)* [2003] 1 W.L.R. 210.

4. Damages

(a) *Remoteness*

(i) *Causation*

General. An accountant is only liable for such loss as has been caused by his **17–063**
breach of duty.[5] In accordance with the usual rule, the burden is on the claimant
to establish causation. It is always necessary to consider whether the loss falls
within the scope of the accountant's duty.[6] Once it is established that an accountant's negligence was causative of the relevant loss, he remains liable notwithstanding that there may have been other causes of equal efficacy.[7]

Effective cause. In cases involving accountants as in other cases, causation **17–064**
gives rise to difficulties, primarily in the application of principle to the huge
variety of circumstances which arise. The perennial problem is to establish
whether one or more putative causes provide the required link in law between the
duty breached and the loss claimed. The "but for" test is necessary but not
sufficient.[8] It is an exclusionary test serving only to filter out non-causal occa-

---

[5] The question of effective cause is considered in paras 17–064, *et seq.*, below. For specific
illustrations in cases involving accountants see the following: *London Oil Storage Co Ltd v Seear,
Hasluck & Co* (1904) 31 Acct. L.R. 93 (Lord Alverstone C.J. directed the jury:
"You must not put upon him the loss by reason of theft occurring afterwards or before, but you
must put upon him such damages as you consider in your opinion were really caused by his not
having fulfilled his duty as Auditor of the company.");
Re City Equitable Fire Insurance Co [1925] 1 Ch. 407, 482–483 and 511 (the claim against the
auditors for misdescription of certain debts in a balance sheet failed since no one would have been
misled by it. Note Romer J. at 482: if proper description of the debts had induced any director or
shareholder to make some inquiry as to their nature, the matter would have been different); *JEB
Fasteners Ltd v Marks Bloom & Co* [1981] 3 All E.R. 289, CA (it was held that the claimant would
have acted no differently even if it had known the true position as to the accounts); *Canadian
Woodmen of the World v Hooper* [1933] 1 D.L.R. 168, 171, *per* Middleton J.A. (see para.17–059,
above); *Guardian Insurance Co v Sharp* [1941] 2 D.L.R. 417 and 426; *West Coast Finance Ltd v
Gunderson, Stokes, Walton & Co* (1974) 44 D.L.R. (3d) 232 (first instance); (1974) 56 D.L.R. (3d)
468, British Columbia CA; *Toromont Industrial Holdings Ltd v Thorne, Gunn, Helliwell & Christenson* (1975) 62 D.L.R. (3d) 225 (first instance); (1976) 73 D.L.R. (3d) 122, Ontario CA; *Cambridge
Credit Corp Ltd v Hutcheson (No.1)* (1983) 8 A.C.L.R. 123; *(No.2)* (1983) 8 A.C.L.R. 513; *(No.3)*
(1983) 8 A.C.L.R. 526; *Northumberland Insurance Ltd v Alexander* (1984) 8 A.C.L.R. 882; (1988)
13 A.C.L.R. 170; *Cambridge Credit Corp Ltd v Hutcheson* (1985) 9 A.C.L.R. 545; 9 A.C.L.R. 669
and *Alexander v Cambridge Credit Corp Ltd* (1985) 10 A.C.L.R. 42; (1987) 12 A.C.L.R. 202.
[6] See para.17–064, below.
[7] *WA Chip & Pulp Co Pty Ltd v Arthur & Young Co* (1987) 12 A.C.L.R. 25, 42–43; on appeal, *sub
nom. Arthur & Young Co v WA Chip & Pulp Co Pty Ltd* (1988) 13 A.C.L.R. 283, Supreme Court of
Western Australia. However, these other causes may give rise to a claim for contributory negligence
or contribution (see paras 17–080 *et seq.*, below). Where the other effective cause was reckless
conduct (as distinct from negligence), the recklessness will ordinarily be treated as the sole cause:
Barings Plc v Coopers & Lybrand [2003] Lloyd's Rep. I.R. 566; [2003] EWHC 1319, Ch, Evans-
Lombe J., at paras 835–6.
[8] *Kuwait Airways Corp v Iraqi Airways Co (Nos 4 and 5)* [2002] 2 A.C. 883 at 1090–2 (paras
69–75), *per* Lord Nicholls; applied in the context of auditor's negligence in *Barings, ibid.* at paras
718–6.

sions for the loss. Putative causes may survive that test but may still not qualify as "effective causes".[9]

In seeking the elusive ingredient which is additional to the "but for" test, the Courts have speaking travelled broadly speaking along two routes. The first is to leave it to judicial "common sense" or to speak of "effective cause" without attempting to analyse what makes a cause effective. This was the approach adopted by the Court of Appeal in *Galoo v Bright Grahame Murray*.[10] In that case a parent company made loans to its subsidiaries and claimed to have done so in reliance on the negligence of the subsidiary's auditor in failing to uncover the subsidiary's insolvency. Glidewell L.J. said that it was necessary to establish whether the negligence was the "effective" or "dominant" cause of the loss and that this was done "by the application of the Court's common sense". The Court held that the negligent audit certificate merely created the opportunity for the subsidiaries to incur and continue to incur trading losses, the effective cause of the losses being the unsuccessful trading. In *Smith New Court Securities Ltd v Scrimgeour Vickers (Asset Management) Ltd*[11] Lord Steyn said that there was no single satisfactory theory of causation capable of solving the infinite variety of practical problems confronted by the courts. Judges sometimes applied a pragmatic test of asking whether the condition in question was a substantial factor in producing a result and others asserted "common sense" as the guiding criterion. There was no material difference.

Galoo has been trenchantly criticised in New Zealand.[12] It was said that common sense can never provide a test as such, but should simply reflect the

---

[9] In *Downs v Chappell* [1997] 1 W.L.R. 426, 443D–F, CA, Hobhouse L.J. applied a "but for" test in relation both to a claim for fraudulent misrepresentation against a director and to a claim for negligent misstatement against an accountant. We suggest that this approach, whilst unexceptionable in relation to fraud, is not the correct test in relation to negligence (the point was expressly left open by Lord Hoffmann in *SAAMCO, ibid.* at 214H). Hobhouse L.J. also applied a cross-check by comparing the contract price with the value which the business would have had, if the representation had been true, but this was disapproved in *Smith New Court Securities Ltd v Scrimgeour Vickers (Asset Management) Ltd* [1997] A.C. 254, 283. On one reading of Hobhouse L.J.'s judgment, he appeared to apply a different causation test in relation to negligent acts from that which he applied in relation to negligent omissions. That, at least, is how Millett L.J. understood the judgment in *Bristol & West Building Society v Mothew* [1998] Ch. 1, 11. However Hobhouse L.J. has since made it clear that he was not intending to lay down any such general principle: *Swindle v Harrison* [1997] 4 All E.R. 705, 727. We suggest that there is no basis for such a distinction: the duty arises out of an obligation to provide accurate information or advice; it should be immaterial whether the breach of duty occurs because the wrong information was provided or because the right information was not provided (see *White v Jones* [1995] 2 A.C. 207, 268H, *per* Lord Goff).

[10] [1994] 1 W.L.R. 1360, 1374–1375, following the reasoning in *Alexander v Cambridge Credit Corp Ltd* (1987) 9 N.S.W.L.R. 310, 333–335. In *Equitable Life v Ernst & Young* [2004] P.N.L.R. 16; [2003] EWCA Civ 1114 at para.133, CA said obiter: "Although *Galoo* was a case of summary disposal, the facts of the case were idiosyncratic. Since, ex hypothesi, the company was insolvent, the losses suffered by continuing to trade were really suffered by the creditors (or by the company's parent), and so, although the case was not argued in that way, the real question may well have been whether the auditors owed any duty to the creditors" (see Lord Hoffmann's lecture to the Chancery Bar Association, June 15, 1999, Common Sense and Causing Loss).

[11] [1997] A.C. 254, 284–285 (the case was concerned with the measure of damages for fraudulent misrepresentation).

[12] *Sew Hoy & Sons Ltd v Coopers & Lybrand* [1996] 1 N.Z.L.R. 392, CA of NZ; see especially Thomas J. at 408–411.

approach which any judge will take to a "jury" question. The distinction between the effective cause and the opportunity for the loss was criticised as unhelpful. Instead it was said that the right approach was to treat causation as an issue of fact and to break it down into subsidiary questions. Thus, instead of simply asking whether the negligent audit caused the loss, one should ask: (i) Did the negligent audit lead the company to believe that it was trading profitably? and (ii) Did the company continue trading at a loss in reliance on that belief? If the answer to both questions was "yes", then the auditor was prima facie liable for such loss as was a necessary consequence of continued trading.[13]

Other judges, notably Lord Hoffmann, have analysed in terms of "scope of duty" the extra ingredient which goes to make up causation. The starting point is the principle affirmed in *Caparo* that it is always necessary to consider whether the loss falls within the scope of the accountant's duty, and that the scope of the duty is determined by reference to the kind of damage from which the accountant must take care to save the claimant harmless.[14] As stated above,[15] Lord Oliver in *Caparo* held that the statutory purposes of a company auditor's function were limited to (i) protecting the company from the consequences of undetected errors or wrongdoing and (ii) providing its shareholders with reliable information so as to enable them to scrutinise the conduct of the company's affairs and to exercise their collective powers to reward, control or remove the directors. The analysis was taken a step further in *South Australia Asset Management Corp v York Montague Ltd*[16] ("*SAAMCO*"), where Lord Hoffmann said that a claimant has to prove both that he has suffered loss and that the loss falls within the scope of the duty of care. Lord Hoffmann's thesis is perhaps most clearly expressed in *Environment Agency v Empress Car Co (Abertillery) Ltd*,[17] where he said that common-sense answers to questions of causation will differ according to the purpose for which the question is asked. This in turn depends upon the purpose and scope of the rule by which responsibility is being attributed.

---

[13] The Court in *Sew Hoy* treated *Galoo* as a decision on its facts but said that, if *Galoo* laid down a principle of law that losses caused by continued trading could never be recovered, then it was wrongly decided. As regards the measure of damages, it was said in *Sew Hoy* that this was prima facie the difference between (i) the losses attributable to continued trading (but excluding losses arising from any imprudent trading decisions) and (ii) the losses which would have resulted if the company had ceased to trade. *Sew Hoy* was itself criticised at first instance in Hong Kong in *Guang Xin Enterprises Ltd v Kwan Wong Tan* [2002] 2 HKLRD 319, but on appeal ([2003] 3 HKLRD 527) the judgment in the latter case was upheld without discussing this criticism. However *Sew Hoy* has been cited with approval in *Temseel Holdings Ltd v Beaumonts Chartered Accountants* [2003] P.N.L.R. 27; [2002] EWHC 2642, Comm, (Tomlinson J. held at para.52 that the complaint in *Temseel* was not simply that the company was allowed to carry on trading, but that it continued trading in a particular manner as a result of the auditor's breach, and that the way in which it traded was responsible for the losses.)

[14] *Caparo Industries Plc v Dickman* [1990] 2 A.C. 605: see paras 17–029 *et seq.*, above.

[15] See para.17–009, above.

[16] [1997] A.C. 191, 218B. Although Lord Hoffmann, *ibid.* at 211A, described the issue in terms of the scope of the duty of care, he has since accepted extra-judicially that it should be described in terms of causation: [2005] 121 L.Q.R. 592.

[17] [1999] 2 A.C. 22, 29–31, HL; see also and *Reeves v Commissioner of Police of the Metropolis* [2000] 1 A.C. 360, HL. These two cases were applied to auditor's negligence in *Barings, ibid.* at para.739 (discussed at para.17–081, below).

SAAMCO has been applied in a number of recent cases involving accountants, most notably *Sasea Finance Ltd v KPMG*,[18] where the Court of Appeal held that it was the auditor's duty was to report to the company's management the fraud of a senior employee as soon as the auditor discovered it or should reasonably have discovered it. *Galoo* was distinguished on the ground that, where the auditor's duty was to draw attention to a fraud, he was responsible for the company continuing to trade fraudulently. The subsequent frauds were "the kind of transactions against the risk of which the auditor had a duty to warn". Although this is helpful as far as it goes, the position remains that it is a fact-sensitive enquiry which might be masked by taking an unduly wide or unduly narrow approach to the categorisation of transactions as being of the same "kind". Another potential difficulty arising from *SAAMCO* is the distinction between "information" and "advice"; however the cases to date have accepted that the product of an auditor's work usually falls on the "information" side of the line.[19]

In *Barings Plc v Coopers & Lybrand*[20] Evans-Lombe J. said *SAAMCO* was a one-transaction case (i.e. a case where one loan had been made in reliance on the over-valuation), and that he found it difficult to apply the *SAAMCO* test in a case where the auditor's failure to alert the company was one of the causes of its continuing with its course of unauthorised trading. This unauthorised trading was foreseeable at the date of the audit, albeit that it was funded from an unforesee-able source. The judge noted that there was a distinction between a case where an investor spent a sum of money acquiring an asset and a case (such as *Barings*) where an insolvent company continued to incur losses. In the former case the accountant would expect the amount for which he was assuming responsibility to be limited to the amount of the investment. In the latter case, he would not be able to foresee the amount of the losses, which might bear no relation to the

---

[18] [2000] 1 All E.R. 676, CA. See also *Yorkshire Enterprises Ltd v Robson Rhodes*, unreported, June 17, 1998, Bell J.; *BCCI v Price Waterhouse* [1999] B.C.C. 351 (Laddie J. struck out a claim in respect of trading losses allegedly incurred in reliance on a negligent audit certificate on the ground that it was outside the scope of the duty of care; it appears that he would have taken a different view, had the continued trading been a continuation of the fraudulent type of business which the auditor should have discovered); *HIT Finance v Cohen Arnold* [2000] Lloyd's Rep. P.N. 125 at 129, 141 and 142, CA; *Johnson v Gore Wood (No.2)* [2003] EWCA Civ 1728, CA (a solicitor's negligence case where Arden L.J. said obiter at para.98 that the scope of an auditor's duty "must in principle encompass anything which the company in general meeting could, having regard to the statutory scheme for annual accounts and audit, be expected to do on the strength of those unqualified accounts"); and *Man Nutzfahrzeuge AG v Freightliner Ltd* [2005] EWHC 2347, Comm, Moore-Bick L.J., paras 328–31 (where the kind of loss caused by the fraud was held to be different from the kind of loss for which the claimant was suing) and para.352 (loss falling within the scope of the duty will usually be limited to difference between the true asset value and that shown in the accounts; it will not include losses caused by the fraud of someone for whom the company is vicariously responsible).

[19] *Boyd Knight v Purdue* [1999] N.Z.L.R. 278, 292, (NZ CA held that an auditor's report required by the Securities Commission gave information not advice, in that it contained no recommendation to potential investors as to whether or not to invest in the company); *Berg Son & Co v Mervyn Hampton Adams* [1993] B.C.L.C. 1045, 1064, Hobhouse J. (para.17–009, above); and *Temseel Holdings Ltd v Beaumonts Chartered Accountants* [2003] P.N.L.R. 27; [2002] EWHC 2642, Comm, Tomlinson J., paras 38 and 60. However, in *Equitable Life Assurance Society v Ernst & Young* [2004] P.N.L.R. 16; [2003] EWCA Civ 1114, para.128, CA cautioned against deciding on which side of the *SAAMCO* line the case fell until all the facts were known. See also para.17–062, above.

[20] [2003] Lloyd's Rep. I.R. 566; [2003] EWHC 1319, Ch, Evans-Lombe J., paras 816–825.

negligence.[21] Nevertheless, the judge held that to exclude these losses from the scope of the auditor's duty would be to narrow the *SAAMCO* test.[22]

Reliance. Where a claim is brought for negligent misstatement, reliance is **17–065** usually a necessary ingredient of the claim. In such a case the claimant must prove that he relied[23] on the information or advice given by the accountant's certificate.[24] It is necessary for a claimant company to point to at least one natural person within the company who relied on, and was misled by, the accountant's negligence.[25] The effects of this case in the context of whistle-blowing duties[26] have yet to be tested. Thus a fraudulently misled company may (e.g. by its liquidator) be able to point to a regulator who would not have been misled by the fraud and who would have intervened to prevent further loss, if its auditor or other accountant reporting upon it had "whistle-blown".[27] The fact that all the shareholders and directors of the company may have been fraudulent and were not misled may not then be fatal to the success of the claim. Hence a claimant will be denied recovery of loss which is the product of his own unlawful act even though the accountant was negligent in failing to discover that loss. It is not sufficient for an investor to show merely that he relied on the fact that the accountant had written a report; the claimant has to go further and show that he read the accounts and relied on the report which certified that they gave a true and fair view.[28]

It is always necessary to go back to first principles in order to see whether reliance (and, if so, what degree of reliance) is necessary. Where the claim is based on negligent misstatement, it is likely that the causative mechanism will be reliance. Where the negligence consists of a negligent act or omission, it has been suggested that there may be cases in which the necessary causative link may be established without reliance.[29] However we suggest that, save in exceptional cases, mere foreseeability will not have the necessary causative potency and that

---

[21] The judge referred to *Al-Saudi Banque v Pixley* [1990] 1 Ch. 313 at 337; Millett J. and *Esanda Finance Corp Ltd v Peat Marwick Hungerfords* (1997) 71 A.L.J.R. 448 (see para.17–043, above).

[22] This conclusion has been criticised in an article by Butcher, [2004] P.N. 248. However, the judge limited the damages by imposing a cut-off date (see 17–081, below).

[23] The claimant must also show that it was reasonable to rely on the information or advice: see para.17–036, above.

[24] *Boyd Knight v Purdue, ibid.* at 292; *Howael Ventures (1984) Inc v Arthur Anderson & Co* [1996] 7 W.W.R. 383.

[25] *Berg Son & Co v Mervyn Hampton Adams* [1993] B.C.L.C. 1045, 1065. In *Edwards Karawacki & Smith Co Pty Ltd v Jacka Nominees Pty Ltd* (1994) 15 A.C.S.R. 503, the Supreme Court of Western Australia inclined to the view (i) that the fraud of the director was to be treated as the fraud of the company, but (ii) that this did not relieve the auditor from liability for negligence. We suggest that this approach has much to commend it, provided of course that there is an innocent victim of the auditor's breach of duty. However it still leaves open the issue of contributory negligence (see para.17–081(2), below).

[26] See para.17–019, above.

[27] This is analogous to the position in *Law Society v KPMG* [2000] 1 W.L.R. 1921 (see para.17–044, above).

[28] *Luscombe v Roberts and Pascho* (1962) 106 S.J. 373.

[29] *White v Jones* [1995] 2 A.C. 207, 272D–G, *per* Lord Browne-Wilkinson (a solicitor's case: see Ch.11, para.11–043.). However care needs to be taken in applying this principle. *White v Jones* was an exceptional case in which the House of Lords fashioned a remedy in order to avoid injustice (*ibid.* at 260G and 267H–268E, *per* Lord Goff). It does not follow that mere foreseeability of loss will usually suffice.

a claimant will need to demonstrate reliance, even if it is only general reliance on the defendant's skill and care.[30]

Where a negligent misstatement or omission is likely to induce the claimant to act (or refrain from acting) in a particular way and he does in fact act (or refrain from acting) in that way, we suggest that the court may presume reliance although no direct evidence is called; however this is no more than an inference of fact, not a presumption of law.[31]

17–066   **Intervening act of claimant or third party.** The chain of causation may be broken by the act or omission of the claimant or some third person.[32] In order to ascertain whether the chain of causation will be broken, it is necessary to go back to Lord Hoffmann's formulation[33]: where the defendant's duty is to guard against the risk of fraud or mistake by a third party, then any such fraud or mistake on the part of the third party will not constitute an intervening act which breaks the chain of causation.[34] An auditor may be liable for loss which continues after he has retired and a new auditor has been appointed; the question is whether it is the old or the new auditor who is the effective cause of the loss.[35]

(ii) *Foreseeability*

17–067   In order to succeed the claimant must establish not only that the loss was caused by the breach of duty of the defendant accountant, but also that it was foresee-

---

[30] In *Duke Group Ltd v Pilmer* (1999) 31 A.C.S.R. 213, 284, Supreme Court of Southern Australia (reversed in part, but not on this point: [2001] 2 B.C.L.C. 773) the Court held that the accountant's breach of duty to the company had caused loss notwithstanding that the directors of the company knew that the statement was inaccurate. The necessary causative link was to be found in the fact that the directors would have been unable to call the necessary shareholders' meeting without a favourable accountant's report and that, if a meeting had been called following an unfavourable report, the shareholders would have been unlikely to vote in favour of the transaction in question.

[31] We suggest that this represents the law in relation to misrepresentation generally: *Smith v Chadwick* (1884) 9 App. Cas. 187, 196; however, the weight to be given to this presumption is not settled: see *Chitty*, para.6–034 n.67. In South Australia this presumption was applied in *Duke Group Ltd v Pilmer*, *ibid*. at 282–4; however, in Western Australia a claim was dismissed in the absence of positive evidence of reliance: *Strategic Minerals Corp NL v Basham* (1997) 25 A.C.S.R. 470, Full Court of Supreme Court.

[32] See paras 17–080 *et seq.* for contributory negligence and contribution.

[33] See para.17–064, above.

[34] *Re London and General Bank (No.2)* [1895] 2 Ch. 673. 688 and 696–697 (for facts see para.17–051(1), above); *Re Thomas Gerrard & Son Ltd* [1968] Ch. 455, 477–8 (for facts see 17–058(3), above); *Craig v Troy* (1997) 16 W.A.R. 96, Supreme Court of Western Australia (the negligence of the first firm of accountants remained causatively potent notwithstanding the negligence of the second firm); and *Duke Group Ltd v Pilmer* (1999) 31 A.C.S.R. 213, 287–289 (reversed in part, but not on this point: [2001] 2 B.C.L.C. 773) (stock market crash did not break chain of causation because it was foreseeable that the accountant's report would be relied on after the crash). In contrast, in *Weld-Blundell v Stephens* [1920] A.C. 956 an accountant who was in breach of his duty to take reasonable care to keep secret a libellous document was not liable to indemnify the claimant for damages for libel, since the document had been brought to the attention of the person libelled by the intervening act of the person who had shown it to him. In *Sayers v Clarke Walker* [2002] 2 B.C.L.C. 16, an accountant gave advice within his general field of competence but suggested that the client seek a second opinion from a specialist; CA held that the client did not break the chain of causation by ignoring this suggestion.

[35] *Sasea Finance Ltd v KPMG* [2000] 1 All E.R. 676; *Barings Plc v Coopers & Lybrand* [2003] Lloyd's Rep. I.R. 566; [2003] EWHC 1319, Ch, Evans-Lombe J., para.789.

able.[36] If the claim is brought in contract, this means that, at the time the contract was made, the loss was reasonably foreseeable as likely to result from the breach.[37] If the claim is brought in tort, it means that at the time the breach of duty was committed the damage (or at least the type of damage) was reasonably foreseeable as a consequence. What is foreseeable will depend upon the facts of each case.[38] In practice this issue rarely arises for separate consideration since any loss which falls within the scope of the duty is likely to be foreseeable.[39]

(b) *Measure of Damages*

Whether the claim is brought in contract or tort or by way of misfeasance summons the fundamental principle governing the measure of damages is that the claimant must be put so far as money can do it in the position he would have occupied if the accountant had properly discharged his duty.[40] Broadly speaking, this can be achieved in one of two ways, depending upon the particular facts of the case: either (i) by paying to the claimant the monetary equivalent of any benefits of which he has been deprived, or (ii) by indemnifying him against any expenses or liabilities which he has incurred. **17–068**

Loss of a chance. In some cases the complaint is that the accountant's breach of duty has prevented the claimant from doing (or not doing) something which might have produced a gain or avoided a loss. He cannot prove that he would actually have done (or refrained from doing) the thing in question, because it is hypothetical. His loss is the loss of the chance of doing (or refraining from doing) it. The Court of Appeal in *Allied Maples Group Ltd v Simmons & Simmons*[41] has **17–069**

---

[36] For a full discussion of the requirement of foreseeability in contract and tort, see *McGregor on Damages* (17th edn), Ch.6.

[37] *per* Asquith L.J. in *Victoria Laundry (Windsor) Ltd v Newman Industries Ltd* [1949] 2 K.B. 528.

[38] e.g. *Re Kingston Cotton Mill Co Ltd (No.2)* [1896] 1 Ch. 331 (for the facts see paras 17–057(3), 17–058(2), 17–058(3), above: at first instance Vaughan Williams L.J. held the auditors liable for preference dividends wrongly passed on the basis of the inaccurate balance sheet signed by the auditors, but CA, [1896] 2 Ch. 279 reversed the decision on liability); *Re Thomas & Son Ltd* [1968] Ch. 455, 476–477 (for facts see para.17–058(3), above: although the defendant was held liable under only one of the three heads of breach alleged, the judge held that it was rightly conceded that the compensation was the same as if breach had been found under all heads, since once put on their guard under any one head the auditors ought to have taken steps which would have led to the detection of the frauds under the other heads); *McBride's Ltd v Rooke & Thomas* [1941] 4 D.L.R. 45, 55 (it was held that, if in the course of an audit defalcations of an employee are not discovered, it was foreseeable that they would be continued by him); and *Duke Group Ltd v Pilmer* (1999) 31 A.C.S.R. 213, 288 (reversed in part, but not on this point: [2001] 2 B.C.L.C. 773) (stock market crash held to be foreseeable).

[39] Although there is an overlap between the two concepts, foreseeability is concerned with the kind of loss, whilst scope of duty looks at quantification: *Platform Home Loans Ltd v Oyston Shipways Ltd* [2000] 2 A.C. 190, 209G, *per* Lord Hobhouse. In *Law Society v KPMG* [2000] 1 W.L.R. 1921, 1930, CA left open the possibility of an argument based on foreseeability.

[40] See *Livingstone v Rawyards Coal Co.* (1880) 5 App. Cas. 25, 39 and *Dodd Properties (Kent) Ltd v Canterbury CC* [1980] 1 W.L.R. 433, 451, 454 and 456 (as to general principles). Also see the cases mentioned at para.17–063, above.

[41] [1995] 1 W.L.R. 1602 (see Ch.3, para.3–007 and Ch.11, para.11–263). Although this was a case involving solicitors, the same principles should apply in relation to accountants. *Allied Maples* has been followed in relation to accountants in *First Interstate Bank of California v Cohen Arnold* [1996] P.N.L.R. 17, CA, and in *Eqiutable Life Assurance Society v Ernst & Young* [2004] P.N.L.R. 16; [2003] EWCA Civ 1114, CA, para.94.

drawn a distinction between the hypothetical acts or omissions of the claimant and those of a third party. In the former case, the issue has to be decided on the balance of probabilities. But where the issue turns on what a third party[42] might hypothetically have done or not done, then the courts assess damages by reference to the value of the chance that the third party would have acted (or refrained from acting) as alleged. This is an exception to the usual principle that issues of fact in a civil case are decided on the balance of probabilities.[43] The "loss of a chance" principle may be categorised under either causation or quantum.[44]

The following principles have emerged in relation to quantifying damages:

(1) If the chance of the hypothesis being fulfilled is negligible, it will be treated as nil; conversely, if it is a near certainty, it will be treated as certain.[45]

(2) The legal burden of proof is on the claimant, but in some cases the defendant may have the evidential burden of showing that the chance was no more than negligible.[46]

(3) There is a difference of judicial opinion as to how far the court should delve into the hypothetical question of fact.[47]

(4) Where the outcome depends on two or more hypothetical facts, the courts need to consider their interrelationship. If each is independent of the other, then the right approach is usually to multiply the percentages in order to ascertain the overall chance.[48] But where the hypothetical facts are interdependent, it may be appropriate to take make one single discount.[49]

(5) The measure of damages is the amount recoverable if the hypothesis had been fulfilled multiplied by the percentage chance of it being fulfilled.

---

[42] Where the third party is very closely identified with the claimant, the court might treat them as one and the same (i.e. apply the balance of probabilities test): *Allied Maples, ibid.* at 1612C, *per* Stuart-Smith L.J. (commenting on *Otter v Church Adams Tatham* [1953] Ch. 280), but see also Millett L.J. in *Allied Maples, ibid.* at 1623H. An example of such a situation would be a claim by a director or shareholder who had control of the company whose accounts were audited by the defendant.

[43] We suggest that the distinction is wrong in principle and has little support in previous authorities, but that by now it is probably too well established to be overturned by any court below the House of Lords.

[44] In most cases it will not matter whether it is categorised under causation or quantum, as long as the parties know when it is to be argued if there is a split trial: see the cautionary tale of *Allied Maples, ibid.* at 1609, 1618–1619.

[45] *Allied Maples, ibid.* at 1614C said that the chance had to be "substantial", not "speculative", but in *Mount Barker v Austin* [1998] P.N.L.R. 493, CA preferred the term "negligible" to "speculative". We suggest that this is intended to be nothing more than a rough-and-ready way of saving the courts from becoming embroiled in fine-tuning the damages. The courts might take a different view if the alleged loss was (say) a 1% chance of £1 billion.

[46] *Mount Barker v Austin, ibid.*

[47] Contrast the view of Stuart-Smith L.J. in *Allied Maples, ibid.* at 1614F with that of Millett L.J., *ibid.* at 1623D. A close examination of the evidence on the hypothetical question proved to be decisive in *Pearson v Sanders Witherspoon* [2000] P.N.L.R. 110, CA (a solicitor's case).

[48] *Harrison v Bloom Camillin (No.1) and (No.2)* [2000] Lloyd's Rep. P.N. 89 and 404, Neuberger J. (a claim against a solicitor for failing to prosecute a claim against accountants for a negligent report which persuaded the claimant to invest in a company).

[49] *Hanif v Middleweeks* [2000] Lloyd's Rep. P.N. 920, CA (a solicitor's case).

Thus if a claimant has lost a 75 per cent chance of making a gain, or avoiding a loss, of £1 million, the damages would prima facie be £750,0000. If the claimant has lost the chance of being in position X instead of position Y, the measure of damages is prima facie (X–Y) multiplied by the chance (or multiple chances).[50]

(c) Heads of Damage

The losses which may result from breach of duty by accountants cover a wide   **17–070** variety. Certain types of losses are of frequent occurrence and are considered below. The discussion is far from definitive of the types of loss for which liability may be incurred and ultimately the appropriate measure of loss and the types of loss depend upon the facts of each case. In particular much will depend upon the nature of the relationship of the claimant to the defendant. In broad terms a distinction may be drawn between losses caused by negligent auditing and losses caused by other negligence of accountants.

(i) Lost Investment or Advance

Upon the insolvency of an enterprise, a person may fail to recover an investment   **17–071** made originally in reliance upon overstatement of the enterprise's financial position in an offer document or a report upon financial statements, for which an accountant is responsible. Provided entitlement to recovery against the account-ant can be demonstrated, the normal measure of damages is the amount of the lost investment.[51] A like position prevails where a loan, as distinct from an equity investment, is made.[52] Credit must be given for any amount recovered upon distribution of any available assets of the enterprise among creditors.[53]

(ii) Overpayment

In consequence of negligent advice by an accountant, an investor may pay more   **17–072** for acquiring shares in a company than he would have done if proper advice or information had been given. In the latter event the usual measure of the damages recoverable against the accountant is the amount of the overpayment. The overpayment is to be calculated by comparing what would have been paid for the

---

[50] In *First Interstate Bank of California v Cohen Arnold* [1996] P.N.L.R. 17, CA, the claimant bank was held to have lost a two in three chance of being able to sell a property for £3 million; it actually sold the property for £1.4 million. CA assessed damages at £600,000, i.e. (£3 million × 66%) less £1.4 million. We suggest that the amount of damages should have been £1.066 million, i.e. (£3 million − £1.4 million) × 66%. The £1.4 million was a certainty: the lost chance related only to the excess of £1.6 million.

[51] *Candler v Crane Christmas & Co* [1951] 2 K.B. 164, *per* Denning L.J. (discussed at para.17–028, above); and *Haig v Bamford* (1972) D.L.R. 68.

[52] See *AGC (Advances) Ltd v R Lowe Lippman Figdor & Franck* (1990) 4 A.C.S.R. 337, Supreme Court of Victoria. Vincent J. awarded damages representing increased loans made following date of negligent certification of the relevant accounts by the defendant auditors; a claim in respect of loans made earlier, consisting of alleged recoveries that would have been effected by an earlier receivership of liquidation of the audited company, failed. Note also *Al Saudi Banque v Clark Pixley* [1990] 1 Ch. 313, 338.

[53] Note *Colmer v Merrett, Son and Street* (1914) 50 Acct. L.R. 21.

shares if proper advice or information had been given, with what was actually paid. Unless it can be shown that in the latter events the value of the shares would have been calculated by simple deduction of the company's liabilities from its assets, that method of calculation is usually not appropriate for assessing the overpayment. A number of contingencies may need to be taken into account, e.g. the investor may have been prepared to pay more for the shares than their net asset backing.[54] In *Pilmer v Duke Group Ltd*[55] a company ("KO") took over another company ("Western") by acquiring the shares in Western in exchange for shares in KO plus cash. KO sued Western's auditor for negligent misstatement in relation to Western's value. The High Court of Australia held that the measure of damages was limited to the loss suffered by the claimant, KO, rather than by its shareholders. Since KO was not permitted to trade in its own shares which it had allotted to Western's shareholders, its loss extended to the cash which it had paid (less the value received) but did not extend to the value of the shares allotted.

(iii) *Moneys Wrongly Paid Out*

17–073   Where in consequence of the negligence of the auditors of a company its shareholders are induced to vote for dividends which would not have been voted if the auditors had properly discharged their duty, since it would have entailed payment of dividend from capital, the normal measure of damages recoverable by the company from the auditors is the amount of the dividend wrongly paid out.[56] Similarly bonuses to directors, wrongly paid out in consequence of negligently audited accounts falsely showing profits to have been made, have been held to be recoverable from auditors.[57] However, as we have seen,[58] continued trading losses are usually excluded either on causation grounds or on the ground that they fall outside the scope of the duty of care; but they may be recoverable where they are a continuation of the very wrongdoing which the auditor ought to have discovered and reported.

---

[54] e.g. see *Dimond Manufacturing Co Ltd v Hamilton* [1969] N.Z.L.R. 609, 645; *Scott Group Ltd v McFarlane* [1978] 1 N.Z.L.R. 553, 576–580 and 582–589. (If these facts were to arise today within England and Wales, it is likely that the courts would apply the "loss of a chance" principle: see para.17–069 above.)

[55] [2001] 2 B.C.L.C. 773, High Court of Australia (on appeal from Supreme Court of Southern Australia).

[56] See *Leeds Estate Building and Investment Co v Shepherd* (1887) 36 Ch.D. 787; *Re London and General Bank (No.2)* [1985] 2 Ch. 673; *Re Westminster Road Construction and Engineering Co Ltd* (1932) Acct. L.R. 38; *Re Thomas Gerrard & Son Ltd* [1968] Ch. 455 (in this case the auditors were also held liable for the costs of recovering excessive tax paid but not recovered in respect of the non-existent profits); *Sasea Finance Ltd v KPMG* [2000] 1 All E.R. 676; *Barings* (see para.17–081, below). See also *Segenhoe Ltd v Akins* [2002] Lloyd's Rep. P.N. 434, Supreme Court of NSW, Giles J., where the above text in a previous edition of this book was referred to (*ibid.* at 701). Note *Galoo Ltd v Bright Grahame Murray* [1994] 1 W.L.R. 136: the claim for the amount of £500,000 dividend (*ibid.* at 1368) appears to have been overlooked and, we suggest, wrongly struck out. (This sentence was approved by Collins J. in *Sasea Finance Ltd v KPMG*, *The Times*, August 25, 1998; the judgment was reversed but not on this point: [2000] 1 All E.R. 676.)

[57] See *Leeds Estate, Building and Investment Co v Shepherd* (1887) 36 Ch.D. 787; *Re Westminster Road Construction and Engineering Co Ltd* (1932) Acct. L.R. 38

[58] See paras 17–063 *et seq.*, above.

(iv) *Defalcations by Director or Employee*

Where owing to an accountant (or auditor's) negligence the defalcations of a   **17–074**
director or employee remain undiscovered for longer than should have been the
case, the normal measure of damages recoverable against the accountant is so
much of the loss as would have been avoided (whether by prevention of further
defalcations or by recovery from the director or employee) given competence on
the part of the accountant.[59]

(v) *Costs of Fresh Audit and Investigations*

When consequent upon an auditor's negligence, a fresh audit or an investigation   **17–075**
is necessary, the costs thereof together with any incidental but necessary legal
expenses may be recovered in damages against the auditor.[60]

(vi) *Tax Advice and Returns*

Negligent tax advice by an accountant may result in a client paying more in tax   **17–076**
than would have been paid given competent advice. In that event the normal
measure of damages is the excess tax paid together with interest thereon.[61] On the
other hand, negligence by an accountant may result in tax being paid later than
due and the client incurring penalties for late payment. In that event the amount
of the penalties are recoverable from the accountant, but credit must be given for
the benefit of the use of the amount of the tax due between the time when it was
properly payable and when it was in fact paid.[62]

(vii) *Late Notices and Returns*

A frequent basis of claim against accountants is late filing of notices, elections[63]   **17–077**
or returns in consequence of which losses are caused to their clients consisting of
lost benefits[64] or higher incidence of tax.

---

[59] See *Fox v Morrish, Grant & Co* (1918) T.L.R. 126; *Armitage v Brewer and Knott* (1932) 77 Acct.
L.R. 25; *McBride's Ltd v Rooke and Thomas* [1941] 4 D.L.R. 45; *Revelstoke Credit Union v Miller*
(1984) 28 C.C.L.T. 17.
[60] See *Toromont Industries Holdings Ltd v Thorne, Gunn, Helliwell & Christenson* (1976) 73 D.L.R.
(3d) 122.
[61] e.g. *Walker v Hungerfords* (1987) 19 A.T.R. 745, Supreme Court of Southern Australia, Full Court;
Slattery v Moore Stephens [2004] P.N.L.R. 14; [2003] EWHC 1869, Ch (failure to advise claimant
of the tax benefits of receiving payment off-shore). In *Grimm v Newman* [2002] S.T.C. 1388, CA held
that, although a tax scheme upon which the accountants advised would not have worked, the claimant
had failed to establish that any other scheme would have worked and had therefore suffered no loss.
Note also the Australian case of *Jindi (Nominees) Ltd v Dutney* (1993) 26 A.T.R. 206. Owing to the
negligence of the defendant accountants in regard to the manner that they acquired shares in
company, the claimants were compelled to delay acceptance of a take-over offer for the shares and
consequent receipt of the proceeds in order to avoid a liability to tax on the profits from sale of the
shares within 12 months of acquisition. Damages were assessed on the basis of interest referable to
lost use of the proceeds during the period of delayed receipt, net of tax on the interest.
[62] e.g. the Australian case of *Pech v Tilgals* (1994) 28 A.T.R. 197, esp. at 206–208. See also *Bloor
Italian Gifts Ltd v Dixon* (2000) 48 O.R. (3d) 760, Ontario CA.
[63] e.g. a partnership continuation election under s.113(2), Income and Corp Taxes Act 1988.
[64] e.g. in the Canadian case of *Murray Bourne Dyck v FMA Farm Management Associates Ltd* (1996)
3 W.W.R. 509.

(viii) *Negligent Advice*

17–078   Accountants sometimes give legal or general business advice. Where such advice is negligent and the negligence causes loss, damages are quantified in a similar way to claims against solicitors.[65]

(ix) *Avoidance of Double Recovery*

17–079   The law has been comprehensively reviewed by the House of Lords in *Johnson v Gore Wood*,[66] from which the following principles emerge[67]:

(1) In many cases the cause of action (if any) will be vested in the company alone and not in its shareholders.[68] There may be other cases in which the cause of action (if any) is vested in the shareholders and not the company[69]: in those cases the shareholders may sue for their own loss, measured by the diminution in value of their shareholding. In neither of these two categories is there any problem of double recovery.

(2) However, there are cases in which duties are owed both to the company and to its shareholders, and in which both suffer loss. In such cases the shareholders are not usually permitted to sue for diminution in the value of their shares or for loss of dividends, since this merely reflects the loss suffered by the company. Protection of the interests of creditors requires that the company is allowed to recover to the exclusion of the shareholders.[70] However, an exception may be made where the wrongdoer has ensured that the company will not be able to sue.[71]

(3) Nevertheless, a shareholder is permitted to sue for any loss which is suffered by him personally if this is additional to any loss suffered by the company, since in such a case there is no problem of double recovery.

(4) Where a claim is brought by a third party which duplicates a claim by the

---

[65] See generally Ch.11 para.11–153. A recent example is *Punsford v Gilberts* [1998] P.N.L.R. 763, CA, where an accountant advised a testator on the drafting of a will. It was held that he owed no duty to a beneficiary to advise the testator against making a subsequent gift which caused the bequest to that beneficiary to adeem.

[66] [2002] 2 A.C. 1; [2000] UKHL 65. In this case a solicitor was negligent in acting for a company on exercise of an option; the company sued but compromised its claim, leaving open the possibility of claim by its director, who then sued the solicitor. HL held that the second action was not an abuse of process in the particular circumstances and that in principle the director could sue for any loss which was not merely a reflection of the company's loss. (For a fuller account of this case, see Ch.11 (Solicitors) para.11–117.) These principles were applied in the context of auditor's negligence in *Barings Plc v Coopers & Lybrand* [2002] P.N.L.R. 16, Evans-Lombe J. Note that the earlier decision in *Barings Plc v Coopers Lybrand* [1997] P.N.L.R. 179, CA, was disapproved in *Johnson, ibid.* at 36A and 65C.

[67] For a critique of this area of the law, see Mitchell on Shareholders' Claims for Reflective Loss (2004) 120 L.Q.R. 457.

[68] *Caparo Industries Plc v Dickman* [1990] 2 A.C. 605; this principle was applied in *Man Nutzfahrzeuge AG v Freightliner Ltd* [2005] EWHC 2347, Comm, paras 324–7, Moore-Bick L.J (see para.17–039, above).

[69] e.g. where the accountant has assumed a responsibility directly towards an investor.

[70] See para.17–039, above.

[71] *Giles v Rhind* [2003] Ch. 618 para.35, CA.

company, it has been suggested[72] that both claims should be brought in one set of proceedings, so as to avoid the risk of double recovery.[73]

(5) The rule against reflective loss also applies to a claim for breach of fiduciary duty, on the ground that the purpose of the rule is to bar double recovery of certain types of loss, irrespective of the nature of the cause of action; the rule is not limited to claims brought qua shareholder but extends claims brought by a shareholder qua creditor.[74]

It was held in *Johnson v Gore Wood* that the following heads of loss were arguably recoverable by the shareholder: sums invested in the company and lost; the cost of personal borrowings (in principle recoverable, provided that this was not a disguised claim for loss of dividend); loss of shares which were transferred to a lender as security for the personal borrowing; and additional tax liability of the shareholder. However a claim to diminution in the value of his pension was struck out, in so far as it related to payments which the company would have made into a pension fund for the shareholder, on the ground that this was merely a reflection of the company's loss.[75]

(d) *Contributory Negligence and Contribution Proceedings*

General. Contributory negligence is a defence provided by statute[76] which **17-080** enables the court to reduce the damages otherwise due from the defendant, based on the share of the claimant in the responsibility for the damage. The precise reduction will depend on the facts of the particular case. The defence is frequently advanced on behalf of accountants in claims against them.[77] It has been

---

[72] *Barings Plc v Coopers & Lybrand* [1997] P.N.L.R. 179, 186–187, CA: for the facts see para.17–041, above.

[73] An analogous issue which has been considered in Australia is the effect of the negligence of the claimant's own employee, which gives rise to a problem as to the interrelationship between contribution and contributory negligence: see para.17–081(3), below.

[74] *Gardner v Parker* [2004] 2 B.C.L.C. 554; [2004] EWCA Civ. 781, CA.

[75] The House of Lords, by a majority, also struck out a claim for damages for mental distress on the ground that such damages were irrecoverable under a commercial contract. This is likely to apply a fortiori to a claim against an accountant.

[76] Law Reform (Contributory Negligence) Act 1945.

[77] e.g. *De Meza v Apple* [1975] 1 Lloyd's Rep. 498 (damages reduced by 30%); *Slattery v Moore Stephens* [2004] P.N.L.R. 14; [2003] EWHC 1869, Ch (damages reduced by 50% for claimant's negligence in failing to query a tax refund which would have revealed his mistake in assuming that he was being received money off-shore).
    In the Australian case of *Pech v Tilgals* (1994) 28 A.T.R. 197, the claim against the defendant accountants for negligent failure to prepare and complete accurate income tax returns was reduced by 20% for contributory negligence on account of the claimant's failure to read tax returns before signing them and to check their accuracy.
    In the Australian case of *Daniels v Anderson* (1995) 16 A.C.S.R. 607, 720–733, the CA of NSW held that the management of the company was negligent in disregarding advice it was given, in failing to set up or implement proper management and control structures and in failing to keep proper records, that the chief executive was negligent in failing to heed warnings about weaknesses in the system and that the board was negligent in failing to set policy to set up or implement a proper system of reporting to the board; nevertheless the auditor's negligence was of a higher order, in that he knew that there were no internal controls in existence, that the records were a shambles, and that no steps

held that the defence is available, not merely where the contributory negligence prevented or hindered an auditor from carrying out his own duties, but also where the claimant failed generally to look after its own interests.[78] As in any professional negligence claim, the standard expected of the claimant will depend upon the factual matrix, in particular the claimant's level of experience and understanding, the accountant's reasonable perception of the same and the scope of the accountant's retainer.[79]

Contribution is not a defence but a right conferred by statute[80] upon a defendant, D1, to recover a proportion of the damages for which he is liable to C, from other persons, D2, D3 etc., each of whom is also liable to C in respect of the same damage,[81] based on that other person's share in the responsibility for the damage; while each of D1, D2 and D3 is liable to the C, as between themselves the damages are shared as appropriate, e.g. a third each. Thus an auditor sued by a company may claim contribution from its directors based on

---

had been taken to rectify these defects; the court reduced the damages by one third for contributory negligence, but would have made a bigger reduction, but for the later breaches compounding the auditor's original negligence.

In the New Zealand case of *Dairy Containers v NZI Ltd* [1995] 2 N.Z.L.R. 30, Thomas J. held that the directors had failed in their primary duty to monitor the business and management of the company and had thereby created an environment in which fraud could thrive; damages were reduced by 40% for contributory negligence.

In the Australian case of *Duke Group Ltd v Pilmer* (1999) 31 A.C.S.R. 213, 326–336, S. Ct. of S. Aus., Full Court, the company, through its directors, was at fault, first in knowingly providing unreliable information to the accountant for the purpose of the valuation, even though it was the accountant's duty to check that information, and secondly in accepting a valuation when the directors, being sophisticated businessmen, must have known that it was wrong; damages were reduced by 35% for contributory negligence. (Reversed in part, but not on this point: [2001] 2 B.C.L.C. 773.)

See also *Mirage Entertainment Corp Ltd v Arthur Young* (1992) 6 N.Z.C.L.C. 68, 213 (negligence by auditors in valuing assets; wrong accounting methodology; reduction of 40%). See also the following Canadian cases: *West Coast Finance Ltd v Gunderson, Stokes, Walton & Co* (1974) 44 D.L.R. (3d) 233 (50% reduction, but finding of liability reversed on appeal: (1975) 56 D.L.R. 461); *HE Kane Agencies Ltd v Coopers & Lybrand* (1983) 23 C.C.L.T. 233; (1985) 17 D.L.R. (4th) 695 (50% reduction); *Revelstoke Credit Union v Miller* (1984) 28 C.C.L.T. 17; (1984) 2 W.W.R. 297 (15% reduction); and *Bloor Italian Gifts Ltd v Dixon* (2000) 48 O.R. (3d) 760 (50% reduction).

[78] In other words, the contributory negligence does not need to be causally connected to the defendant's negligence; it is sufficient that it is a cause of the same damage: *Dairy Containers Ltd v NZI Bank Ltd* [1995] 2 N.Z.L.R. 30, 74; see also *Platform Home Loans Ltd v Oyston Shipways Ltd* [2000] 2 A.C. 195, 215, *per* Lord Millett (a valuer's case).

[79] Contrast *De Meza v Apple* [1975] 1 Lloyd's Rep. 498 (court reduced damages by 30% because client should have noticed an obvious arithmetical error) with *Walker v Hungerfords* (1987) 44 S.A.S.R. 532, 553–554, Bollen J., upheld on appeal: 19 A.T.R. 745, 747, Supreme Court of Southern Australia, Full Court (no reduction for arithmetical error made by clerk employed by company, since it was reasonable for him to assume that any errors would be checked by the accountant.) See also *Craig v Troy* (1997) 16 W.A.R. 96, Supreme Court of Western Australia (no contributory negligence where accountant informed client of relevant facts but failed to explain their significance).

[80] Civil Liability (Contribution) Act 1978. See further, Ch.4. Where the purchaser of a company has claims against the vendor for deceit and against the auditors for negligence, these are to be regarded as the "same damage" to the extent that the loss falls within the scope of the auditor's duty of care: *Man Nutzfahrzeuge AG v Freightliner Ltd* [2005] EWHC 2347, Comm, para.485, Moore-Bick L.J. See also *Dominion Freeholders Ltd v Aird* (1966) 67 S.R. (N.S.W.) 150.

[81] In *Eastgate Group Ltd v Lindsey Morden Group Inc* [2002] 1 W.L.R. 642; [2001] EWCA Civ 1446, CA, it was held that a claim against the vendor of shares for breach of warranty was a claim for the "same damage" as a claim against accountants for negligent advice.

breach of duties owed by the directors to the company and/or, in an appropriate case, on breach of duties owed direct to the auditor.[82]

Claims against auditors. In *Barings Plc v Coopers & Lybrand*[83] a Singapore   **17–081**
subsidiary of the bank sued its auditor Deloitte & Touche for losses arising from
the failure to warn of frauds committed by the company's employee Nick
Leeson. The auditor counterclaimed for deceit on the basis that (i) Leeson had
been fraudulent in making management representations to the auditor, (ii) the
company was vicariously liable for these representations, which were made by
Leeson in the course of his employment, (iii) the company's vicarious liability
for deceit "trumped" the auditor's liability for negligence, since it is no defence
to a claim for fraud that the victim (in this case, the auditor) was negligent.[84]
Evans-Lombe J. held that, in the context of a contract, the question of vicarious
liability depends upon whether the employee has acted within the scope of his
authority, whilst in the context of a tort claim, it depends upon whether the
employee has acted within the scope of his employment. There needs to be some
connection between the wrongful act and the employment but this was satisfied
in this case, since Leeson's duties as manager extended to the provision of
information to the auditors. The judge went on to hold that prima facie the
company was vicariously liable for Leeson's frauds, notwithstanding that it was
the company which was the primary victim of those frauds,[85] and that no such
special rule of attribution should be fashioned in order to avoid this result.[86]
However, the judge went on to hold that the auditor's duty to the company in this
case included a duty to investigate the bona fides of the management representa-

---

[82] In an Australian case, *Employers Corporate Investments Pty Ltd v Cameron* (1977) 3 A.C.L.R. 120
in which auditors were sued by a company for negligence in failing to discover a fraud by the
company's employee, the court refused to strike out cross-claims by the auditors against its directors
based on (a) alleged breach of duties by the directors to the claimant company, i.e. a statutory
contribution claim and (b) alleged breach of a duty of care owed by the directors to them as auditors.
In a Canadian case, *Harvey Credit Union Ltd v GH Ward & Partners* (1981) 15 B.L.R. 307, the court
also refused to strike out a statutory contribution claim against the claimant company's directors
based on alleged breach of duties by the directors to the company.
[83] [2003] Lloyd's Rep. I.R. 566; [2003] EWHC 1319, Ch, Evans-Lombe J.
[84] *Alliance & Leicester Building Society v Edgestop* [1993] 1 W.L.R. 1462, Mummery J.
[85] The judge (at paras 692–717) refused to follow *Dairy Containers v NZI Bank* [1995] 2 N.Z.L.R.
30, NZ, where Thomas J. had held that the company was not vicariously liable for the actions of
employees in concealing the frauds of other employees, since this was "dramatically and deliberately
hostile to the employer's interest". We suggest that Evans-Lombe J. was right to reject this view: see
Lester v Hesley Hall Ltd [2002] 1 A.C. 215.
[86] It was argued on behalf of the company that a special rule of attribution should be fashioned on the
ground that the auditors were "insiders", so that the Leeson's fraudulent representations were not
attributed to the company. The judge rejected this argument both on the trial of a preliminary issue
([2002] P.N.L.R. 39; [2002] EWHC 461, Ch, paras 155–9) and at the full hearing (paras 718–9). We
suggest that the principle of vicarious liability operates counter-intuitively in a case such as *Barings*
and that this may justify fashioning a special rule of attribution having regard to the purpose of the
rule which requires it, e.g. where there are innocent shareholders who would otherwise suffer for the
fraud of the directors, or where the directors and shareholders are all fraudulent but the company is
insolvent and there are innocent creditors whose only recourse is through a claim by the liquidator.
A recent example is *Bank of India v Morris* [2005] 2 B.C.L.C. 328; [2005] EWCA Civ 693, where
CA fashioned a special rule of attribution in a case of fraudulent trading.

tions and that the auditor had been negligent in failing to uncover the fraud.[87] The judge then considered the question of contributory negligence. Given that the directors were responsible for managing the company's business, the failure of the board, or of any employees to whom it had delegated specific tasks, was to be attributed to the company.[88] He held on the facts that contributory negligence should result in reductions ranging from 50 per cent to 80 per cent.

In the light of *Barings*, we suggest that the following principles apply when considering how to apportion fault between the auditor and the company:

(1) Where the loss results from the fraud of the company's employee and the auditor could not be expected to have discovered the fraud, this will be a complete defence.[89]

(2) Where the auditor is under a duty to discover the employee's fraud, he may be be liable, but this does not preclude the court from holding that the company is also partly to blame.[90]

(3) Where the company's employee has been reckless or has been so negligent as to break the chain of causation from the auditor's negligence, the auditor will have a complete defence.[91]

(4) When considering the responsibility of the company's directors (including responsibility for supervising employees), it should be borne in mind that it is the directors who are primarily responsible for managing the business. Evans-Lombe J. held that there was a "level playing-field" between the directors and the auditor. He said: "There is nothing special about auditors which requires of them a special standard of skill and judgment in their investigation of an audit client's affairs, over other professional men and, in particular, over the directors and officers of the commercial companies they audit".[92]

(5) If it is proper to take account of the fraud of the company's officers, should this be done by way of contributory negligence or by way of contribution proceedings or both? There is an obvious need to avoid double-counting. In some cases the same acts or omissions of the officer

---

[87] The judge (at paras 727–749) relied on *Environment Agency v Empress Engineering* [1999] 2 A.C. 22, 29–31, HL, and *Reeves v Commissioner of Police of the Metropolis* [2000] 1 A.C. 360, HL, (see para.17–064, above). This is an application of the principle that answers to questions of causation will differ according to the purpose for which the question is asked; this in turn depends on the purpose and scope of the rule by which responsibility is being attributed. If the auditor was himself under a duty to investigate the *bona fides* of the dishonest answers being given by the company's employee, then the company *is* allowed to say that the auditor's negligence was also a cause of the loss.

[88] *ibid.* paras 908–9.

[89] So held by Evans-Lombe J. on the preliminary issue in *Barings* ([2002] P.N.L.R. 39; [2002] EWHC 461, Ch.

[90] [2003] Lloyd's Rep. I.R. 566, paras 698–720 and 961–3.

[91] *ibid.* paras 837–8 and 878. The judge held that the auditor's negligence ceased to be the effective cause after the point in time at which it should have been obvious to the company that there had been unauthorised trading, or at least that there was a need for an investigation which would have revealed the unauthorised trading. In view of this conclusion, the company did not have to give credit for gains accruing after the cut-off date (para.886). However, the defendant was entitled to choose the cut-off date, as long as it was not before the date when the negligence ceased to be operative (para.889).

[92] *ibid.* para.1059.

in question might be relied on by the defendant, either to found a defence of contributory negligence against the company or to claim contribution from that officer. In order to prevent double-counting, the courts have refused to allow contribution proceedings on the ground that it would not be just and equitable to do so.[93] It has also been held that a defendant is not permitted to elect between the two courses of action. Contributory negligence should logically be considered before contribution proceedings.[94]

(e) *Failure to Mitigate*

The usual principles of mitigation apply to claims against accountants.[95] In **17–082** particular: the claimant is under a duty to take reasonable steps to mitigate his loss; the burden of proving failure to mitigate lies on the defendant; but the court will not impose a high standard of reasonableness on the claimant. These principles have been applied in relation to auditors in an Australian case[96] in which the company paid out a dividend in reliance on a negligent audit certificate. The court held that the company's duty to mitigate did not require it to bring uncertain litigation against the shareholders for the recovery of the dividend.

(f) *Statutory Relief*

An auditor may seek relief from liability under s.727 of the Companies Act 1985 **17–083** although it would seem that such relief is available only in respect of a claim against him by or on behalf of or for the benefit of the company.[97] Relief is neither a defence nor a right, but a discretionary power given to the court in proceedings against the auditor of a company (whether or not also an officer of the company) for negligence, default, breach of duty or breach of trust, to relieve him wholly or partly from his liability on such terms as the court thinks fit, if certain criteria are satisfied. These are that, if in the opinion of the court, the auditor has acted honestly and reasonably and that, having regard to all the circumstances of the case, including those of his appointment, he ought fairly to be excused.[98] The test of reasonableness has (unsurprisingly) been held to be an

---

[93] *Daniels v Anderson* (1995) 16 A.C.S.R. 607, 734–735, approving Glanville Williams' *Joint Torts and Contributory Negligence* at 446. See also *Barings, ibid.* at para.1073.

[94] *Dairy Containers Ltd v NZI Bank Ltd* [1995] 2 N.Z.L.R. 30, 86. This was based on *Fitzgerald v Lane* [1989] A.C. 328, 338–9 and 345D–E, HL. See also *Daniels v Anderson, ibid.* at 735.

[95] See *McGregor on Damages* (17th edn), Ch.7.

[96] *Segenhoe Ltd v Akins* (1990) 1 A.C.S.R. 691, S. Ct of N.S.W. Giles J. considered it to be a matter of doubt whether a company could recover dividends paid out of capital which were innocently received by the shareholders. He therefore applied the principle in *Pilkington v Wood* [1953] Ch. 770, Harman J., that the duty to mitigate did not require the claimant to embark on a complicated and difficult piece of litigation against a third party, even under an indemnity. (We suggest that that the dictum that the claimant is not required to sue even under an indemnity is too widely stated.)

[97] *Customs and Excise Commissioners v Hedon Alpha Ltd* [1981] 2 All E.R. 697, CA. See also *Dimond Manufacturing Co Ltd v Hamilton* [1969] N.Z.L.R. 609, 645, CA of NZ, and *Jagwar Holdings Ltd v Julian* (1992) 6 N.Z.C.L.C. 68,041 at 68,070.

[98] This section reflects similar protection given to trustees; see Trustee Act 1925, s.61. In *Re Duomatic* [1969] 2 Ch. 365, the Companies Act 1948, s.448, the predecessor provision to the Companies Act 1985, s.727, was considered in relation to a director. In *Re D'Jan of London Ltd* [1994] 1 B.C.L.C. 561, Hoffmann L.J. granted relief under s.727 to a director.

objective one.[99] It might be thought that this would make it unlikely that the defence would be available in many cases of professional negligence.[1] However, in *Barings Plc v Coopers & Lybrand*[2] Evans-Lombe J. held that it is possible for an auditor to have acted reasonably even though he had been negligent, e.g. if the negligence was minor or technical. In the light of his finding that the proven breaches were lapses in an otherwise proper audit, he held that the threshold under s.727 had been satisfied and that he had a discretion to grant relief. The factor which persuaded him to grant relief was the profits made by other Barings companies out of the Leeson tradings. Although the judge had held that these profits should not be brought into account when quantifying Barings' loss (given that the other companies were separate legal personalities), they should be taken into account when exercising the broad discretion under s.727.

It has been held in Australia that the word "reasonably" is not limited in its area of operation to circumstances connected with the discharge of the auditor's duty, but that the court may take into account his conduct after the breach of duty including his conduct in defending the claim against them.[3] There is a difference of opinion in Australia as to whether the negligence of the directors is a relevant factor in relieving the auditor from liability.[4] We suggest that the question whether the auditor acted honestly and reasonably should be considered by focussing solely on his own acts and omissions, against the background of all the circumstances of the case[5]; however, if the auditor surmounts this hurdle, the court is given a wide discretion in considering whether he ought fairly to be excused. The court is required to consider all the circumstances, which ought surely to include the conduct of the directors.

---

[99] *Re MDA Investment Management Ltd* [2004] 1 B.C.L.C. 217, Park J.

[1] *Dimond Manufacturing Co Ltd v Hamilton* [1969] N.Z.L.R. 609, NZCA. The Court, while recognising that the section could be invoked even in the case of negligence, considered that there would not be many cases where a negligent auditor could be said to have acted reasonably.

[2] [2003] Lloyd's Rep. I.R. 566; [2003] EWHC 1319, Ch, Evans-Lombe J., paras 1133, 1137 and 1142–3.

[3] *Pacific Acceptance Corp Ltd v Forsyth* (1970) 92 N.S.W. (W.N.) 29, Moffitt J.: for the facts see para.17–052 above. We suggest that the better approach is to bring subsequent conduct into account, not in relation to reasonableness, but in considering whether the auditor ought fairly to be excused.

[4] In *Pacific Acceptance*, *ibid.*, Moffitt J. said that it was irrelevant; however in *AWA Ltd v Daniels* (1992) 7 A.C.S.R. 759, 854–856 Rogers J. said that the section was an appropriate provision for allocation of fault. He added that, if he were wrong in his view that the defence of contributory negligence was available to the defendant auditors the same facts would enliven the operation of the provisions of the section. (On appeal the CA of NZ quoted Rogers J.'s view but found it unnecessary to decide the question: *Daniels v Anderson* (1995) 16 A.C.S.R. 607, 685–686.)

[5] This may include the fact that fraud on the part of the directors is frequently more difficult to detect than negligence: see para.17–052 above.

CHAPTER 18

ACTUARIES

1. INTRODUCTION

The role of an actuary. The core skill of an actuary is to apply financial and   **18–001**
statistical theories to analyse and predict future events, especially in the areas of
life and general insurance, pensions and investment. The theory of probability
which lies at the heart of actuarial science may be traced back to Edmund Halley,
who produced the first life table in 1693, and then went on to work out how much
someone of a given age should pay to buy an annuity. It is impracticable in a
general work on professional liability to describe the entire range of functions
performed by actuaries but the focus of this chapter will be on the main issues
which are likely to arise in claims against actuaries.[1]

The professional bodies. There are two professional bodies which regulate   **18–002**
the conduct of actuaries in the United Kingdom. These are the Institute of
Actuaries (in England) and the Faculty of Actuaries (in Scotland). These two
bodies issue Professional Conduct Standards and formerly issued Actuarial
Professional Standards. However, in March 2005 the Morris Review,[2] commissioned by the Government following Lord Penrose's enquiry into Equitable Life,
recommended that the Financial Reporting Council ("FRC") should become
responsible for overseeing the UK Actuarial Profession and for setting actuarial
technical standards. The Board of Actuarial Standards ("BAS"), created under
the auspices of the FRC, is responsible for setting standards with effect from May
18, 2006, but it has adopted, as BAS standards, most of the technical Guidance

---

[1] For a general introduction to the work of actuaries, see the profession's own website at
www.actuaries.org.uk.
[2] The Final Report of Sir Derek Morris's Review of the Actuarial Profession may be found at
www.hm-treasury.gov.uk/media/A62/3D/Morris_final_150305.pdf.

Notes previously forming part of the Manual of Actuarial Practice.[3] It is suggested that failure to comply with Guidance Notes will not in itself be conclusive proof of negligence but it will be relevant evidence.[4]

18–003   **The paucity of authority.** At the time of writing, there are few reported cases in which actuaries have been sued to judgment for professional liability. Nevertheless, the subject of actuarial negligence is likely to be an important one over the next few years. There are several reasons for this, including the high value of the financial products with which actuaries are concerned, the greater willingness of the courts to entertain claims against professionals in general and actuaries in particular, the increasing regulation of the industry and the collapse of high-profile insurers such as Independent. Because of the paucity of reported cases involving actuaries, it is necessary to go back to first principles and to look for analogies involving other professions. However, there is an obvious danger in using an analogy blindly without considering whether it is a good analogy. One should always bear in mind the words of Lord Bridge in *Caparo Industries Plc v Dickman*[5]:

> "It is never sufficient to ask simply whether A owes B a duty of care. It is always necessary to determine the scope of the duty by reference to the kind of damage from which A must take care to save B harmless."

One needs to look at the entire context of the relationship between the claimant and the actuary in order to see whether the actuary's function, in respect of which the claimant wishes to allege a breach of duty, is analogous to that of an auditor, a solicitor, a valuer or some other professional. For example, where an actuary is advising one party on an acquisition, his role may be analogous to that of a solicitor. If he is producing a valuation to be published with pension accounts, his role is more like that of an auditor, but within a different statutory context from that of an auditor. If he is advising a pension scheme on an issue arising between the scheme as a whole and one member (e.g. transfer value), he may be in a position similar to the surveyor in *Smith v Eric S Bush*.[6] In other cases he may be acting as an expert determining an issue between two or more parties.

2. DUTIES

18–004   The primary source of an actuary's duties is contractual, but usually he will also owe a duty of care in tort to his client. In special circumstances he may assume a duty of care in tort to a third party. In addition, he will typically be in a fiduciary relationship, which may be particularly important because of the potential for

---

[3] Guidance Notes ("GN") produced or adopted by the BAS may be found on the FRC's website: *www.frc.org.uk/bas/actuarial/index.cfm*. Guidance Notes constituting Actuarial Professional Standards may be found on the profession's website (see above). The Guidance Notes are regularly updated; it is therefore important to ensure that reference is made to the version which was current at the date of the alleged breach of duty.

[4] *cf. Johnson v Bingley* [1997] P.N.L.R. 392 (a solicitor's case).

[5] [1990] 2 A.C. 605 at 627D, HL (an accountant's case).

[6] [1990] 1 A.C. 831, HL.

conflicts of interest. Some of the functions of actuaries, especially in relation to pension schemes, are very heavily regulated. It is therefore necessary to begin with the statutory and regulatory framework since this may provide the context in which the actuary's duties arise.

(a) *The Statutory Context*

(i) *Pensions*

Occupational pension schemes. Occupational pension schemes[7] are usually   **18–005**
either "money-purchase" schemes (under which a fund is created for each member out of his contributions) or "defined benefit" schemes (under which each member is entitled to a fixed benefit) or some hybrid of the two:

(1) Defined benefit schemes: The advantage to the member of a defined benefit scheme is that he is assured of a fixed pension, provided that the scheme remains solvent. Defined benefit schemes often depend upon the employee contributing a fixed percentage of his income every year, with the employer making up any shortfall.

(2) Money-purchase schemes: The simplest money-purchase schemes are those in which the member is entitled to such benefits as can be purchased with his notional fund. In such cases the actuary will need to project forward the size of fund on retirement and the amount of benefits which can be purchased. In more complex schemes the benefits are calculated by reference to a notional rate of return. If the actual return proves to be better than the notional return, a non-refundable bonus will be declared.

In each of these cases the actuary plays a crucial role in carrying out the necessary projections and calculations, which include determining the solvency of the scheme, the level of contributions and the level of benefits. The potential for conflict between the trustee (who is frequently also the employer or closely linked to him), the employer and the members is obvious and needs to be carefully managed.[8]

Contracted-out schemes. Many occupational pension schemes are contracted   **18–006**
out of SERPS (the second State pension). In order to be contracted out, the scheme has to comply with certain procedures, which include the provision to NICO (the National Insurance Contributions Office) of an actuarial certificate confirming that the scheme offers benefits which are at least equivalent to those offered by SERPS.[9]

---

[7] For a detailed consideration of occupational pension schemes, the reader is referred to *Ellison on Pensions Law & Practice* (Sweet & Maxwell).

[8] See paras 18–019 *et seq.* below.

[9] Pension Schemes Act 1993, ss.12A to 12D and Occupational Pension Schemes (Contracting-out) Regulations 1996 (SI 1996/1172) (as amended).

18–007   **Exempt approved schemes.** Section 592 of the Income and Corporation Taxes Act 1988 provides for schemes to be "exempt approved" and to benefit from a more favourable income-tax regime. The scheme actuary would usually provide a report or advice in support of the application for Inland Revenue approval. One particular concern of the Revenue has been to prevent schemes from being used as tax havens for sheltering profits. Accordingly, Sch.22 to the 1988 Act enabled the Revenue to make regulations to deter schemes from being "over-funded". In order to avoid being taxed on the notional overfunding, it was necessary either to increase benefits or to give the employer or the employees a contributions "holiday". Once again, the potential for conflict between the interests of the employer and the members is obvious. The Revenue's sole concern was to prevent schemes from being used as tax havens, but the consequence of the legislation was to deplete a purely notional surplus and leave schemes with insufficient cushion when the stock market fell in 2000. The provisions as to exempt approved schemes have been repealed and replaced with effect from April 6, 2006 by Pt 4 of the Finance Act 2004, which provides instead for a system of registration of pension schemes.

18–008   **The Pensions Act 1995.** Following the Maxwell scandal, Parliament formalised the role of actuaries in the funding of pension schemes. Section 47(1)(b) of the Pensions Act 1995 requires most occupational pension schemes to have a scheme actuary[10] appointed by the trustees or managers. Section 47(9) provides that regulations may be made imposing duties on the actuary to disclose information to the trustees or managers and vice versa. Section 48 imposes whistle-blowing duties[11]; it is unlikely to be held that these give rise to any civil remedy.[12] Regulations made under the 1995 Act provide that any actuarial valuation required under certain provisions of the Act is to be made available on request to members, beneficiaries and trade unions.[13] The valuation will comprise two elements, viz. a statement of certain prescribed aspects of the method of valuation and a certification of the adequacy of the rates of contribution for the purpose of meeting statutory minimum funding requirements. These Regulations are likely to play a critical role in any claim brought by members of beneficiaries against the actuary. In the first place, they may enable any member or beneficiary to argue that he is within the class of persons intended by Statute to be entitled to rely on the valuation. Secondly, it may be important to see whether the claimant relied on the valuation for its intended statutory purpose. Whereas the purpose of audited accounts is to present a record of the scheme's performance over a previous period, the purpose of the valuation is to confirm that, based on certain actuarial techniques and assumptions, the actuary is satisfied that the scheme ought in the future to meet minimum funding requirements. It may therefore follow that the actuary's report shows a different picture from the accounts, and may also show a different picture from an actuary's report prepared for a different purpose. The actuary is also given an important role in the

---

[10] s.47(1)(b) requires the appointment to be of an individual actuary, not a firm.

[11] See also s.33A of the Pension Schemes Act 1993, added by the 1995 Act.

[12] *cf.* FSMA 2000, s.150, which expressly confers a civil remedy for contravention of FSA rules.

[13] Occupational Pension Schemes (Disclosure of Information) Regulations 1995 (SI 1995/1655).

modification of schemes. Section 67(4)(a) requires an actuary to certify that the power of modification is not exercised so as to affect adversely any member of the scheme without his consent.[14]

The Pensions Act 2004. The trustees or managers of a defined benefit scheme   **18–009** were formerly required to obtain an actuarial valuation every three years stating whether the contributions payable were adequate for the purpose of meeting statutory minimum funding requirements.[15] However, the rules as to minimum funding requirements have been replaced by Pt 3 of the Pensions Act 2004. The basic scheme of Pt 3 is to impose primary duties on the trustees or managers of the scheme, who will discharge those duties with the assistance of the scheme actuary. Section 222 of the 2004 Act requires every scheme to have sufficient and appropriate assets to cover its "technical provisions", i.e. the amount required, on an actuarial calculation, to make provision for the scheme's liabilities. Section 223 requires the trustees or managers to prepare a statement of funding principles (including a statement of policy for securing that the statutory funding objective is met). Section 224 requires the trustees or managers to obtain actuarial valuations and reports; however, provided that the actuary produces a report annually, he need only make a full valuation every three years. Section 225 requires the actuary to certify the method of calculating the technical provisions. Section 226 requires the trustees or managers to prepare or revise a recovery plan where it appears that the statutory funding objective is not met. Section 227 requires the trustees or managers to prepare, review and revise a schedule of contributions (i.e. a statement showing the contributions to be made by the employer and the members). Section 230 requires the trustees or managers to obtain the advice of the actuary before making any decision as to the methods or assumptions to be used in calculating the technical provisions, preparing or revising the statement of funding principles, the recovery plan or the schedule of contributions, or modifying the scheme as regards future accrual of benefits. These provisions are supplemented by Regulations[16] which apply in respect of valuations dates after September 22, 2005. It can thus be seen that the scheme actuary has a key role in relation to defined benefit schemes under the 2004 Act.

(ii) *Life Insurance*

Subject to a few exceptions, every long term insurer and many friendly socie-   **18–010** ties[17] are required to have an actuary,[18] who was formerly known as "the

---

[14] This may give rise to particular problems for actuaries, since it is likely to involve issues of law as much as valuation.

[15] Pensions Act 1995, s.57 and Occupational Pension Schemes (Minimum Funding Requirement and Actuarial Valuations) Regulations 1996 (SI 1996/1536 (as amended)).

[16] Occupational Pension Schemes (Scheme Funding) Regulations 2005 (SI 2005/3377). See also GN9 (Funding defined benefits—Presentation of actuarial advice) and GN49 (Occupational pension schemes—Scheme funding matters on which advice of actuary must be obtained).

[17] A friendly society is a society registered under the Friendly Societies Acts 1974 and 1992 which carries on certain activities, including life and general insurance (s.7(1)(a) and Sch.2 to the 1974 Act).

[18] FSMA, s.340 provides that rules may require an authorised person to appoint an actuary. The relevant rules are in SUP4, (i.e. Ch.4 of the Supervision Manual forming part of the FSA Handbook; this is available on the FSA website at *http://fsahandbook.info/FSA/html/handbook/*).

appointed actuary" and is now called "the approved person". His role comprises "the actuarial function" and "the with-profits function". The actuarial function[19] is, in summary, to provide actuarial advice to the firm's[20] senior management on methods and assumptions for the actuarial investigation and on the risks being run by the insurer.[21] The approved person's particular focus is on the risks the firm runs insofar as they may have a material impact on the firm's ability to meet liabilities to policyholders in respect of long-term insurance contracts as they fall due. The with-profits function[22] may be summarised as the provision of ongoing advice to a with-profits insurer's senior management on its use of discretion and providing assurance to the regulators and to policyholders on its compliance with Principles and Practices of Financial Management. Each function involves giving advice to the firm's management at the level of seniority which is appropriate to the advice in question.[23] The appointed actuary had a statutory right of access to the books and records of the firm.[24] There were also whistle-blowing provisions.[25]

18–011   The FSA further provides for another function known as that of the "reviewing actuary".[26] The FSA rules require the firm's auditor to take advice from an independent actuary as to the calculation of the firm's policyholder liabilities. The reviewing actuary need not necessarily be the same person as the approved person. His advice is given on a different purpose and he may therefore reach a different conclusion from that of the approved actuary.

18–012   In addition, FSA rules require most friendly societies to have a valuation carried out by the appropriate actuary[27] every three years.[28] There are a number of further ways in which actuaries are given a statutory role in friendly societies. For example, a friendly society may amend its rules to provide for it to carry on re-insurance to the extent approved by an actuary.[29] A friendly society has a duty to annex to its balance sheet details of the appointed actuary, including certain information showing whether or not the actuary has any personal interest conflicting with his duties as actuary.[30] If there is any investigation on behalf of the FSA into the affairs of a friendly society, the actuary has a statutory duty to cooperate with the FSA and to produce documents to any inspector appointed by

---

[19] Described in SUP 4.3.13 and GN40.

[20] The term "firm" is used in SUP to describe a long-term insurer or friendly society.

[21] See GN1 (The prudential supervision in the UK of long-term insurance business).

[22] Described in SUP 4.3.16 and GN41.

[23] SUP 4.3.13.

[24] FSMA, s.341 and see SUP 4.3.17.

[25] FSMA, s. 342 says that the actuary will not contravene any duty to his client if he gives information to the FSA in good faith and in the reasonable belief that this information is relevant to the FSA's functions. However, FSMA 2000 (Communications by Actuaries) Regulations 2003 (SI 2003/1294) goes further and imposes a positive duty of whistle-blowing in certain circumstances; see also GN37.

[26] IPRU(INS) 9.35(1A) (i.e. paras 9.4 and 9.35(1A) of the Interim Prudential Sourcebook: Insurers); see also GN42.

[27] The appropriate actuary is the appointed actuary, if any. In the case of a friendly society which is not required to have an appointed actuary, the appropriate actuary is appointed ad hoc in order to carry out the triennial valuation.

[28] Interim Prudential Sourcebook: Friendly Societies (see *www.fsa.gov.uk/pubs/hb-releases/rel30/rel30iprufsoc.pdf*), SUP 4.4; see also GN43.

[29] 1974 Act, ss.23 and 23A.

[30] 1992 Act, s.77.

the FSA.[31] Where a friendly society proposes to transfer any part of its engagements to another friendly society, the transferee must furnish the FSA with a
report by the actuary showing that the transferee will have the necessary margin
of solvency.[32]

(b) *Duties to Client*

(i) *Contractual Duties*

An actuary should always agree the terms of his engagement in writing. This is   **18–013**
good practice for any professional, but it is particularly important in the case of
actuaries. In the first place, it may be vital in determining the identity of the client
and the capacity in which the client is instructing the actuary, given that the
actuary's report or valuation is likely to be read by a number of different parties
and that each party may be wearing more than one hat. Secondly it should
identify the nature of the valuation or report which the actuary is required to
produce and the purpose for which it is being produced.

As we have seen, the Pensions Act 1995 created the office of scheme actuary.[33]   **18–014**
The provisions of s.47 of the Act are likely to be impliedly incorporated into the
contract which is created by an appointment as scheme actuary.[34] Guidance Note
29[35] sets out various provisions which the scheme actuary ought to require to be
included in his appointment. For example, para.2.3 provides for a letter of
appointment to be sent to the scheme actuary, and paras 2.5 to 2.8 provide that
he should obtain the written agreement of the trustees or managers to advise him
of certain material facts and to allow him access to certain information.[36]
Trustees and managers continue to engage actuaries to perform tasks additional
to those performed by the scheme actuary as such. If these tasks are to be
performed by a different actuary, there should be a written division of responsibilities.[36a] If the additional tasks are performed by the scheme actuary, it is
important to have written a letter of engagement distinguishing between the two
roles and making it clear to whom the additional duties are owed and for what
purpose. The actuary should also consider carefully whether the role of adviser
to one party is compatible with that of scheme actuary.

An actuary will be under an implied, if not an express, duty to exercise   **18–015**
reasonable skill and care.[37] He will also be under a duty to take reasonable care
to keep the affairs of his client confidential, subject to any "whistle-blowing"
duties.[38]

---

[31] 1992 Act, ss.62 to 67. See also FSMA 2000, ss.175 and 342.
[32] 1992 Act, s.87.
[33] See para.18–008, above.
[34] *cf. Brandeis Brokers Ltd v Black* [2001] 2 Lloyd's Rep. 359, where Toulson J. held that, on the facts
of that case, the relevant parts of the SFA rules were incorporated into a contract made by a London
Metal Exchange broker.
[35] See para.18–002, above for Guidance Notes.
[36] GN29: "Occupational Pension Schemes—Advisers to the Trustees or a Participating
Employer".
[36a] GN29 para.5.
[37] Supply of Goods and Services Act 1982, s.13.
[38] This follows from the fiduciary obligations of an actuary: see below. For whistle-blowing duties,
see paras 18–008 and 18–010, above.

18–016   In theory it is possible that third parties may be identified in the actuary's contract and hence fall within the Contracts (Rights Against Third Parties) Act 1999. In practice, as with other areas of professional negligence, the Act has so far been of little practical significance.

(ii) *Duty in Tort*

18–017   In common with other professionals, an actuary ought in principle to owe a duty to his client in tort which is co-extensive with his duty in contract. In practice this is likely to matter only where on the particular facts of the case it may give the claimant the benefit of a longer limitation period.

(iii) *Fiduciary Obligations*

18–018   In common with other professionals, an actuary is usually in a fiduciary relationship with his client.[39] The principal fiduciary obligations (or, more accurately, disabilities) are (i) the duty of loyalty, (ii) the principle of undue influence and (iii) the duty of confidentiality. The first and last of these are likely to be particularly relevant to actuaries.

18–019   **Loyalty.** The different facets of the duty of loyalty were described by Millett L.J. in *Bristol & West Building Society v Mothew*.[40] The duty usually ends on the termination of the retainer. In practice the most important facet of the duty is likely to be the duty to avoid conflicts of interest. As we have seen, actuaries are frequently required to produce certificates or valuations which are likely to be relied on by parties with conflicting interests. In addition, trustees are likely to seek actuarial advice before making decisions which have an impact on individual members or classes of members, e.g. decisions in relation to disposal of any surplus in a scheme. The statutory background will be relevant in helping the courts to decide what duties are owed and to whom, as are the terms of any letter of engagement.

18–020   The Morris Review[41] concluded that there is an obvious potential for conflict between the trustees, whose interest it is to maximise the assets of the scheme, and the scheme sponsor (who is usually the employer), who is required to fund it. At present the same actuary may act for both. This reflects the reality that the trustee is often the same person as the employer (or is a related company). The Review recommended that the trustees, the scheme sponsor and the scheme actuary should explicitly agree that there are no material conflicts of interest before the scheme actuary advises both the trustees and the scheme sponsor. If at any point any of these parties considers that a conflict has arisen, the trustees should have the option of retaining the scheme actuary and the scheme sponsor should seek separate actuarial advice.

18–021   If the court concludes that an actuary has undertaken irreconcilable duties to parties with conflicting interests, it is no answer to say that the duty to Client A

---

[39] See Ch.2 paras 2–128 *et seq.* See also para.2.5 (confidentiality) and para.5 (conflict of interest) of the Professional Conduct Standards. In addition, there are references to confidentiality and conflict in many of the Guidance Notes.

[40] [1998] Ch. 1 at 16–22, CA (a solicitor's case).

[41] Para.16 of the Final Report: see para.18–002, above.

prevents the actuary from discharging his duty to Client B. He must either discharge both duties to the fullest extent, or else pay compensation to the client whose duty he is unable to discharge.[42]

Confidentiality. Unlike the duty of loyalty, a professional's duty of confidenti- **18–022**
ality survives the termination of the retainer. An actuary is therefore under a duty, both to current and to former clients, to maintain confidentiality. This is particularly relevant in relation to advisory work, where it is likely to prevent an actuary from advising a rival party if privy to relevant confidential information. This will obviously apply to the actuary himself, but may also extend to his firm, unless a suitable Chinese wall can be erected.[43] The whistle-blowing duties are an important statutory restriction on confidentiality.[44] The Morris Review noted that there was only a small number of firms capable of advising the largest pension schemes.[45] This may result in the Court taking a more pragmatic approach towards the erection of ad hoc Chinese walls.[46]

(c) *Duties to Third Parties*

An important issue in relation to all professionals is whether they owe duties to **18–023**
third parties. This is particularly important in the case of actuaries, since their advice, reports and valuations are frequently relied on by third parties. *Precis (521) Plc v William M Mercer Ltd*[47] is the first reported case to consider the extent of duties owed to third parties. Before considering this case, it is worth looking at the general approach which the courts are likely to adopt, having regard to analogies with other professions.

In considering whether to extend duties of care to third parties, the courts have **18–024**
tended to adopt three different but overlapping approaches, viz. (i) the three-fold approach, (ii) the assumption of responsibility and (iii) the incremental approach. These three approaches were reviewed by the House of Lords in *Customs & Excise Commissioners v Barclays Bank Plc.*[48]

As noted above,[49] analogies are dangerous unless applied with care. It is **18–025**
important to look at the function which the actuary is performing in order to find an appropriate analogy. A useful starting-point is to compare and contrast the House of Lords' decisions in *Smith v Eric S Bush*[50] and *Caparo Plc v Dickman*.[51] In *Smith*, it was held that a surveyor who surveyed a house on behalf of a proposed mortgagee also owed a duty of care to the mortgagor, if he was aware

---

[42] *Hilton v Barker Booth & Eastwood* [2005] 1 W.L.R. 567, HL (a solicitor's case).
[43] *Prince Jefri Bolkiah v KPMG* [1999] 2 A.C. 222, HL (an accountant's case).
[44] See paras 18–008 and 18–010, above.
[45] Para.4 of the Final Report (details of the Final Report are at para.8–002, above).
[46] For a more pragmatic approach than was taken in *Bolkiah, ibid.* at 239D, see *Young v Robson Rhodes* [1999] 3 All E.R. 524, Laddie J. and see the discussion on Chinese walls in Ch.2 para.2–176 and Ch.11 para.11–029, above.
[47] [2005] P.N.L.R. 28; [2005] EWCA Civ 114, CA.
[48] [2006] 3 W.L.R. 1; [2006] UKHL 28. For a discussion of the three approaches see Ch.2 paras 2–022 *et seq.*
[49] See para.18–003, above.
[50] [1990] 1 A.C. 831, HL.
[51] [1990] 2 A.C. 605 at 631, HL.

that the mortgagor was likely to rely on his survey and was paying for it. However, it was made clear that the decision might not necessarily extend to industrial property, large blocks of flats or very expensive houses, where it may be reasonable to expect the mortgagor to obtain his own report.[52] By contrast, in *Caparo* it was held that prima facie an auditor's duty of care was limited to a duty to the company and to the shareholders as a body. It did not extend to future investors, nor to individual shareholders who might be considering the purchase of further shares. The House of Lords distinguished *Smith* on the ground that the auditor's case involved a statement which was put into more or less general circulation and may foreseeably be relied on by strangers to the makers of the statement for any one of a variety of purposes which the maker of the statement had no specific reason to anticipate.[53]

18–026   The arguments in favour of extending the duty of care to individual members or beneficiaries include the following:

(1) Just as Lord Oliver in *Caparo* took as his starting-point the provisions of the Companies Act, which showed that statutory purpose of the audit was simply to furnish the shareholders as a body with information, so one might expect the courts to look at the statutory provisions in relation to the scheme actuary. However, it does not necessarily follow that the application of this approach will lead to the same result in the case of actuaries as it does in the case of auditors. As we have seen, the scheme actuary may be required to make his report available on request to members and beneficiaries.[54]

(2) Although the amounts of money involved and the class of persons who might suffer are potentially large, both are likely to be finite and also foreseeable at the date of the actuary's report. Hence there is unlikely to be a risk of liability in an indeterminate amount for an indeterminate time to an indeterminate class.

(3) The individual members or beneficiaries might well be persons of relatively modest means. In many cases it might be unreasonable to expect them to seek their own independent actuarial advice. The actuary might argue that the member or beneficiary does not pay directly for the scheme actuary's report or valuation, unlike the mortgagor in *Smith*, but the claimant might retort that the members do pay indirectly, because the actuary's fees are an expense of the scheme.

18–027   However, where the loss is suffered by all the members, it is likely to be suffered by the scheme as a whole. For example, where a scheme is underfunded as a result of the actuary's negligent valuation, the loss may be suffered by the employer (if he is required to pay more) or by the members (if the employer becomes insolvent and there are insufficient funds to pay pensions). But if the trustee or manager sues the actuary and recovers damages, this may restore the scheme to solvency, which will thereby indirectly benefit the employer and the

---

[52] [1990] 1 A.C. 831 at 859G.
[53] *Caparo* at 621B.
[54] See para.18–008, above.

members. The actuary might argue that, if he had valued the liabilities with reasonable care, the employer would have had to pay more into the scheme. The employer (if solvent) should therefore make good the shortfall, and the only loss is the loss suffered by the employer to the extent that it is more expensive to make good the shortfall later rather than sooner. Where the trustee is the proper claimant, the court is likely to disallow claims by members or beneficiaries, unless the trustee wrongfully refuses to sue and the members seek to bring a derivative claim on behalf of the whole scheme.[55] The argument in favour of allowing members to sue is stronger where the loss has been suffered by an individual member rather than by all members collectively, especially if the individual member suffers a loss but the trustee does not.[56] An example would be a valuation which affected the transfer value for a particular member.

Different issues arise where the advice, valuation or report is relied on by third   **18–028**
parties other than the employer, the members or the beneficiaries acting as such. Where the role of the actuary is to advise one party or negotiate on its behalf, there is a more obvious divergence or conflict between the interests of his client and those of a third party. In such a case, there may be a closer analogy with the position of a solicitor, who does not usually owe duties of care to the party with whom his client is negotiating.[57] However, an argument to the contrary may be based on GN9 (8th edition). This says that that the client may wish to make a piece of advice available to third parties and that any limitations to which third parties can rely must be set out in the advice. Guidance Note 9 seems to be suggesting that the actuary may assume a responsibility by default towards third parties, but it remains to be seen how far this will be taken to represent the general law.[58]

In *Precis (521) Plc v William M Mercer Ltd*[59] Precis made a take-over bid for   **18–029**
Stoves Group Plc. Mercer had prepared an actuarial report for Stoves which negligently underestimated its liabilities. Stoves agreed to supply information to Precis but on the basis of excluding liability for the negligence of any of its agents. Precis's solicitors contacted Mercer, who answered some questions and sent a copy of the report to Precis's solicitors. Precis's solicitors advised that Precis should obtain its own report but it did not do so. The Court of Appeal approached the matter by asking whether there had been an assumption of

---

[55] *Hayim v Citibank* [1987] A.C. 730 at 748F, PC; *Anthony v Wright* [1995] B.C.L.C. 236, Lightman J. For an example of a derivative claim where the Court made a pre-emptive order for costs in favour of the members of an occupational pension scheme, see *MacDonald v Horn* [1995] 1 All E.R. 961, CA. For a general discussion of the analogous principle of "reflective loss", see Ch.17 (Accountants and Auditors) para.17–148.

[56] In such a case there may be an analogy with *White v Jones* [1995] 2 A.C. 207 at 260G and 267H–268E, where Lord Goff fashioned a remedy in order to fill a lacuna and hence prevent injustice.

[57] *Gran Gelato Ltd v Richcliff (Group) Ltd* [1992] Ch. 560.

[58] See also GN30 (Compensation for Professional Shortcomings) para.1.2, which says that "A duty of care includes working to appropriate professional standards at all times (whether the work is full or part-time), considering how advice may be interpreted by third parties who can reasonably be expected to rely on that advice and communicating any significant uncertainty or risk." This is written in the context of disciplinary proceedings; it is suggested that it does not purport to lay down the general law and in any event would not displace the court's function to decide for itself whether a duty of care had been assumed to a third party, albeit that it may be relevant as part of the factual matrix. See the reference to *Johnson v Bingley* in para.18–002, above.

[59] [2005] P.N.L.R. 28; [2005] EWCA Civ 114, CA.

responsibility by Mercer towards Precis. This meant, not simply a voluntary assumption of responsibility, but a matrix of fact from which the court could reasonably infer an assumption of responsibility.[60] The facts upon which the court relied were:

(1) The original report had been intended, not for the purpose of a take-over bid but for the purpose of reviewing the company contribution rate.

(2) There was no pre-existing relationship between Mercer and Precis.

(3) Mercer expected Precis to have its own advisers (which it did).

(4) Precis had no direct communication with Mercer.

(5) Mercer impliedly agreed that Precis could have the report but they knew only that some kind of corporate transaction was involved. They did not know that it was a take-over bid and did not agree to the report being used for that purpose.

(6) The information provided was historic (i.e. it gave a snapshot at a past date).

(7) The information could just as easily have been sent by Stoves. Mercer's role was effectively simply helping Stoves to put together the information.

The Court of Appeal concluded that in the circumstances there had been no assumption of responsibility for the purpose for which the report was used.

(d) The Standard of Skill and Care

18–030   There was a time when the function of an actuary was regarded by the courts as being a mystery into which the courts were reluctant to delve. In *Re George Newnes Group Pension Fund*,[61] Buckley J. said that:

"The function of an actuary in advising how a pension scheme of this kind should be dealt with on the determination of the scheme is to achieve the greatest practicable degree of fairness between the various persons interested under the scheme consistent with the rules governing that scheme. . . . In performing this function an actuary must employ an expertise of great refinement which involves assessing the weight to be given to many and various contingencies and near imponderables. Some of these, such as mortality tables, may depend on statistical data and may be susceptible of more or less demonstrable validation. Others must necessarily be largely a matter of personal judgment. There is considerable scope for justifiable differences of approach and opinion among actuaries, and as the actuary's function is essentially one of estimation, one actuary may very possibly reach a conclusion in a particular case which varies, perhaps widely, from the conclusion of another actuary on the same facts. The court should be very slow to criticise or seek to control the exercise of any discretion or

---

[60] For a general analysis of the validity of assumption of responsibility as a tool of analysis, see the *Barclays Bank* case mentioned in para.18–024, above.
[61] July 25, 1969 (reported in (1972) JIA 251; the judgment can also be found at *www.actuaries.org.uk/ files/pdf/library/JIA-098/0251–0262.pdf*). This decision was followed by Walton J. in *Re Imperial Foods Ltd Pension Scheme* [1986] 1 W.L.R. 717.

judgment reposed in or required of an expert of this kind in the exercise of a function of this character. . . .

Where a discretion of this kind is reposed in an expert, the burden rests on any party who criticizes the decision of the expert to show that the expert has acted fraudulently or with some improper motive or that he has been guilty of a mistake of a substantial character or has materially misdirected himself."

Before considering the extent to which the court's former deferential approach **18–031** to actuaries may have changed, it should be noted that no issue arose in *Newnes* as to whether the actuary had been negligent. The issue was whether the court should interfere in the exercise of a discretion conferred on the actuary by the scheme rules upon the dissolution of the scheme. The court applied the principle that, where the parties agree in advance that an expert's a valuation or report should be conclusive, it may not be challenged unless it can be shown that the expert has departed from his instructions to a material extent, so that it can be said that he has no done what he was appointed to do. The application of this principle raises different issues from those which arise in a negligence claim.[62]

Nederlandse Reassurantie Groep Holding NV v Bacon & Woodrow[63] **18–032** ("NRG") is the first case in which a claim for negligence against an actuary was pursued to judgment. Insofar as it is possible to summarise briefly the facts of an 87-day trial, NRG retained the actuary B to advise on its proposed acquisition of Victory Reinsurance. B advised on the valuation of Victory Re's non-life reserves and on the adequacy of retrocessional cover for a non-life portfolio. The acquisition went ahead but was disastrous, in that the liabilities proved to be very much greater than had been predicted. NRG sued B for negligence. Colman J. held that:

"The standard of care to be expected is measured by reference to the quality of work reasonably to be expected from a professional firm or organisation possessed of the skills which by undertaking the work in question that firm or organisation has warranted that it has.

If the skill that is warranted is a specialist skill, the client is entitled to the standard of work reasonably to be expected of a specialist professional possessed of that skill."[64]

Colman J. held that the standard of care depended on the purpose of the advice. **18–033** Where the purpose was to provide information to assist the client in deciding

---

[62] In *Campbell v Edwards* [1976] 1 W.L.R. 403 at 409, CA, Geoffrey Lane L.J. considered that no claim for negligence should lie. In the first place it would lead to anomalies if the disappointed party could sue the other party and the valuer in the same action, thereby obtaining disclosure against the valuer which could be used to assist in setting aside the valuation. Secondly, if the valuation was set aside for manifest error, this would mean that the valuer's negligence would have caused no loss. In *Baber v Kenwood Manufacturing Co Ltd* [1978] 1 Lloyd's Rep. 175 at 181, CA, Lawton L.J. said that an expert determination test would not necessarily be set aside on the ground of negligence: "Now experts can be wrong; they can be muddle-headed; and unfortunately on occasions they can give their opinions negligently. Anyone who agrees to accept the opinion of an expert accepts the risk of these sorts of misfortunes happening. What is not acceptable is the risk of the expert being dishonest or corrupt". See also *Jones v Sherwood Computer Services Plc* [1992] 1 W.L.R. 277 at 286G, CA.
[63] [1997] 1 L.R.L.R. 678, Colman J.
[64] *ibid.* at 744 paras 385–6.

whether or not to buy a reinsurer, the standard was higher than advising the reinsurer in relation to its annual accounts. This was because the decision to purchase was irrevocable and therefore had irreversible consequences. By contrast, a company which was negligently advised as to its assets or loss reserves could put right the negligence as soon as it was discovered.[65]

18–034   One argument advanced by NRG was that B had used a novel method of evaluation and should have warned NRG that this method had not been tried and tested. Colman J. rejected this argument, on the basis this was a "non-prototype situation" in which the new technique could be fully evaluated without testing. There was no need to warn the client that a new and untried technique was being used, if the client was entitled to assume that the actuary had exercised reasonable care both in concluding that old techniques were inadequate and in devising the new technique.[66]

18–035   In considering whether B was negligent, Colman J. explained that the problem was one which had not been appreciated within the profession when B gave its advice in 1990. The issue concerned the "third tier" of the London Excess of Loss Market ("LMX"), in which Victory Re participated. The third tier of the LMX market had a number of unusual features.[67] In the first place, any participant business was far removed from the original insurance business and was therefore likely to know much less about the original risk. Secondly, it might take a considerable time for claims under the primary policy to be notified to the third-tier insurer. These feature made it very difficult to judge whether a particular large loss was likely to fall within its own third tier. Thirdly, this was exacerbated by the practice of marine insurers of re-insuring non-marine losses; it would not always be obvious that the reinsurance of the whole account of a marine insurer might involve non-marine losses. Fourthly, there were few participants in the market at this level. The combination of these unusual features resulted in the so-called LMX spiral, i.e. the tendency of losses from large catastrophes, such as hurricanes, to be re-circulated within a small number of insurers as a result of higher-tier retrocession. Colman J. accepted that actuaries in 1990 had an imperfect understanding of the potential impact of the LMX spiral on loss development patterns. Hence, although B's prediction was seriously over-optimistic, this was held not to have been negligent when judged by the standards of a reasonable actuary at the time[68] (save in one small respect). The reasoning in NRG suggests that negligence claims against actuaries are governed by the same principles as those which apply to claims against other professionals, but there is room for argument as to whether those principles were applied with unusual leniency or whether this was simply a highly unusual case from which no general conclusions can be drawn.

18–036   A modern court is likely to approach the issue of an actuary's professional liability in the same way as it would in relation to that of any other professional.[69] In other words, it will ask whether the alleged acts or omissions fell below the

---

[65] [1997] 1 L.R.L.R. 678 at 745 paras 387–9.
[66] *ibid.* at 750–1 paras 423–6.
[67] *ibid.* at 691–5 paras 18–25.
[68] *ibid.* at 756–7 and 760, paras 460–2 and 475–6.
[69] This was implicit in the judgments in *Precis* (para.18–029, above) and in the judgment of Cox J. in *Andrews v Barnett Waddingham LLP* [2006] P.N.L.R. 2 (reversed in relation to causation: see para.18–039, below).

standard reasonably to be expected of any competent actuary. This is likely to involve hearing expert evidence from another actuary as to the standard to be expected of a competent actuary.[70] The fact that there may be different legitimate approaches to a particular issue (as was held to be the case in *Newnes*) would, of course, be a good defence to a claim for negligence, but the court would be particularly astute in such a case to ensure that an actuary who is exercising his discretion does so untainted by any conflict of interests.[71]

(e) *Limitation of Liability*

A friendly society is not permitted by its constitution to exempt the actuary from **18–037** any liability, but the actuary is permitted to raise a defence in the same terms as s.727 of the Companies Act 1985.[72] Letters of engagement often exclude liability to third parties.[73] The Morris Review recommended that consideration be given to proportionate liability clauses in letters of engagement.[74]

3. LIABILITY FOR BREACH OF DUTY

In order to see whether the actuary has been negligent, it is necessary to consider **18–038** the function performed by him which is the subject of the complaint. The following analysis may assist:

(1) Was he acting as expert or as adviser? If he was acting as expert determining an issue between two or more parties, he will owe duties to each of them which will include a duty of fairness. It may be impossible for the actuary to discharge that duty if he is closely connected with one of the parties who has a personal interest in the outcome (i.e. not merely a trustee owing duties to all other interested parties).[75]

(2) Was the valuation made on the (or, at least, an) appropriate basis? Unlike the valuation of a house, which is often concerned merely to establish the current market value, pensions valuations are usually undertaken for a much more precise and limited purpose. As we have seen,[76] one of the principal purposes is to value liabilities so that a proper comparison can be made of assets and liabilities. This is done in accordance with particular formulae. One therefore has to see whether the actuary has deviated from the formulae. By contrast, an employer may also need a

---

[70] *cf. Sansom v Metcalfe Hambleton* [1998] P.N.L.R. 542.
[71] In *Re Belfield Furnishing Ltd*, unreported, January 27, 2006, the deputy judge held that a valuation of shares under a pre-emption agreement was not conclusive where the valuer was not in a position to exercise independent judgment. See also paras 18–013 and 18–019, above.
[72] 1992 Act, s.106. For a discussion as to s.727, see Ch.17 para.17–154, above.
[73] There was an exclusion of liability to third parties in *Precis 521 Plc v William M Mercer Ltd* (see para.18–029, below), but the terms of this exclusion clause were held to be irrelevant, since they were unknown to the claimant.
[74] para.2.16 of the Morris Review (see para.18–002, above).
[75] See para.18–036, above.
[76] See paras 18–005 to 18–009, above.

valuation for the purposes of its own accounts; clearly this valuation may be made on a different basis and for a different purpose.

(3) Was the basis of valuation applied in a reasonable manner? For example, did the actuary assemble the relevant factual material and apply his methodology in a reasonable manner, without arithmetical error? It may be arguable that negligence in the reasoning is not relevant, provided that the result is a reasonable one. This was the approach taken by the Canadian court in *Re Simon Fraser University Administrative/Union Pension Plan*.[77] Tysoe J. accepted that the chosen assumptions were reasonable. Errors had been made in applying those assumptions but the errors were self-cancelling and the final result was within the range of conclusions which a reasonable actuary might reach.

4. DAMAGES

18–039 In accordance with the usual principles, an actuary is liable only for loss caused by his negligence and falling within the scope of his duty of care. In *Andrews v Barnett Waddingham LLP*,[78] A had engaged W to advise him on the best way to achieve maximum long-term security from his pension provision and had specifically sought advice about the protection afforded by the Policyholders Protection Act 1975. In reliance on W's advice A had purchased a with-profits annuity with Equitable Life. Five years later the House of Lords gave its well-publicised ruling,[79] as a result of which the with-profits annuity became substantially less valuable than A had originally envisaged. A sued W for negligence in failing to explain how the 1975 Act would impact on an annuity of this type. The trial judge held that W had been negligent in failing to advise A that, if Equitable Life became insolvent, the Act did not provide protection for non-guaranteed bonuses, and that A would not have purchased the annuity if correctly advised about the Act. W appealed against the finding that his negligence had caused loss, relying on the principle in *South Australia Asset Management Corp v York Montague Ltd*[80] (*"SAAMCO"*) that a claimant has to prove both that he has suffered loss and that the loss falls within the scope of the duty of care. The Court of Appeal held that the fact that A would not have entered into the loss-making transaction, but for the negligent advice, was a necessary but not a sufficient condition of liability. A had never alleged that it was negligent to recommend to him the purchase of a with-profits Equitable Life annuity. The only breach of duty relied upon was the failure to explain how the 1975 Act would operate in connection with an annuity of that type, and since the operation of the 1975 Act was an

---

[77] 1997 Can.L.I.I. 1314, S. Ct. of British Columbia. This conclusion is similar to that reached in *Goldstein v Levy Gee* [2003] P.N.L.R. 35, where Lewison J. held that negligence in the process of valuation is irrelevant, as long as the end result is within the range of reasonable values (see Ch.17 para.17–119, above). The contrary approach was taken by Lord Hoffmann in *Lion Nathan Ltd v C-C Bottlers Ltd* [1996] 1 W.L.R. 1438 at 1445, PC. It may be that the distinction turns on whether the recipient is likely to rely solely on the resulting figure or on the reasoning as well.
[78] [2006] P.L.R. 101; [2006] EWCA Civ 93.
[79] *Equitable Life Assurance v Hyman* [2002] 1 A.C. 408, HL.
[80] [1997] A.C. 191 at 218B.

irrelevance in the events that have happened, Mr Andrews had suffered no loss as a result of that breach of duty.

Care needs to be taken to ensure that the loss claimed has been suffered by the claimant.[81] In some cases the negligence may be curable without loss, if the decision made in reliance on the negligent valuation can be set aside, e.g. where trustees have exercised their discretion in reliance on a flawed valuation[82] or where the valuer acting as expert has materially departed from his instructions.[83] In such cases it may be argued that the claimant is under a duty to mitigate his loss by applying to set it aside.[84]   **18–040**

The usual principles of contributory negligence and contribution apply.[85] In practice issues of contribution are most likely to arise between the actuary and the auditor or solicitor or between the scheme actuary and another actuary retained to give advice to a pension scheme.[86] There may also be an issue as to whether the actuary can reduce or extinguish a claim by relying on the negligence of the client's management. It is suggested that the Court is likely to follow the approach of Evans-Lombe J. in *Barings Plc v Coopers & Lybrand.*[87]   **18–041**

---

[81] See para.18–027, above.
[82] *Sieff v Fox* [2005] 1 W.L.R. 3811 para.119, Lloyd L.J.
[83] See para.18–031, above.
[84] *cf. Walker v Geo H Medlicott* [1999] 1 W.L.R. 727, CA (a solicitor's case).
[85] See Ch.4.
[86] See para.18–013, above.
[87] [2003] Lloyd's Rep. I.R. 566; [2003] EWHC 1319, Ch, Evans-Lombe J. (see Ch.17 paras 17–151 *et seq.* above).

MEMBERS' AND MANAGING AGENTS AT LLOYD'S

1. GENERAL

(a) *Lloyd's of London*

The Society of Lloyd's is the cornerstone of the London insurance market. It is **19–001**
established and regulated by the Lloyd's Act 1982 and byelaws made under that
Act from time to time.[1] It also falls within the general regulatory regime
established by the Financial Services and Markets Act 2000 ("FSMA"),[2] but
with modifications to reflect the unique position of Lloyd's and its members. The
Financial Services Authority ("the FSA") is given considerable discretion as to

---

[1] The byelaws can be found on the Lloyd's website (*www.lloyds.com*).
[2] See further para.19–005, below, and see generally Lomnicka and Powell, *Encyclopaedia of Financial Services Law* (Sweet & Maxwell).

how it discharges its general duty and powers in relation to Lloyd's, given the regulatory role of Lloyd's governing body, the Council of Lloyd's.[3]

19–002   Lloyd's is not itself an insurer: the insurers in Lloyd's are a multitude of members, each member writing insurance for himself but not for the others (so that liability is several and not joint).[4] The membership of Lloyd's includes a number of different types of member or "capital provider" including: (a) individual members or "Names" who are high net worth individuals and whose exposure to the insurance risks they underwrite is unlimited, and (b) corporate members which are limited liability companies formed exclusively to underwrite insurance business at Lloyd's. For convenience, in this chapter all types of member are referred to as "Names".

19–003   Names belong to one or more syndicates, which are groupings of members.[5] Individual Names tend to belong to a number of syndicates, whereas some corporate members only underwrite through a single syndicate. Names join syndicates for particular years of account, covering all business written in a particular year. After three years, a year of account will be closed, if appropriate,[6] usually by reinsuring the liabilities of that year into the next year of account of the same syndicate. Each syndicate is required to have an active underwriter, who is the individual with principal authority to accept risks on behalf of the members of the syndicate.[7]

19–004   It would be impossible for each member to enter each insurance contract and deal with each claim on his own behalf. Save to the extent that they are themselves actively involved in underwriting at Lloyd's, members act through agents known as underwriting agents. It is with the duties and liabilities of the two types of underwriting agents that this chapter is concerned, namely:

(a) Members' agents: Each member is obliged to appoint a members' agent to act on his behalf.[8] Members agents are companies specifically established to provide services and perform duties for members. These services and duties include advising members on which syndicates they should participate in and their level of participation within such syndicates, and liaising with the members' managing agents. A members' agent provides the link between individual members of Lloyd's and their syndicates.

---

[3] See Ch.14, para.14–004.

[4] For a summary of the operation of the Lloyd's market and the structure of Lloyd's, see *Society of Lloyd's v Clemston* [1997] L.R.L.R. 175 at 188–189, Cresswell J. Lloyd's does not owe syndicate members a contractual or statutory or common law duty to regulate the market with reasonable skill and care, see *Price and Price v Society of Lloyd's* [2000] Lloyd's Rep.I.R. 453, Colman J.

[5] A syndicate's core functions are to enter contracts of insurance (including reinsurance), whether directly or through agents, decide upon and implement a reinsurance programme, deal with claims, invest premiums and to consider whether and on what terms the year of account can be reinsured to close. The managing agent is also responsible for maintaining the syndicate's records and preparing its annual audited accounts. See *Society of Lloyd's v Clemston* [1997] L.R.L.R. 175 at 188–189, Cresswell J.

[6] This is discussed in detail in paras 19–075 and 19–076, below.

[7] Underwriting Byelaw (No.2 of 2003) para.41.

[8] By s.8(2) of the Lloyd's Act 1982 each member is required to appoint a members' agent to conduct his affairs at Lloyd's, unless the Name is himself an underwriting agent. If a member has more than one members' agent acting for him then he must appoint one of them as his co-ordinating agent.

(b) Managing agents: Managing agents are companies specifically established to manage the underwriting of one or more syndicates. A managing agent's principal functions are underwriting contracts of insurance, reinsuring such contracts, and paying claims on such contracts.

The activities of both types of underwriting agents are regulated activities under FSMA.[9] Accordingly, such an agent needs to become an authorised person by obtaining a Pt IV permission.[10]

(b) *The Regulatory Regime*

The Society of Lloyd's is a corporate body incorporated under the Lloyd's Act 1871. Special provision for Lloyd's is made in Pt XIX of FSMA.[11] The Society itself is an "authorised person"[12] and is subject to regulation by the FSA. Requirements specific to Lloyd's and Lloyd's members are contained in the Lloyd's sourcebook, which is one of the specialist sourcebooks that form part of the FSA's Handbook.[13] The Lloyd's sourcebook contains rules which require the Society to make appropriate byelaws regarding a number of issues.[14]   **19–005**

The Lloyd's Act 1982 established the Council of Lloyd's and defined the functions and powers of the Council. In particular, the Council was given the power to make byelaws for various purposes.[15] At the time of writing, 56 such byelaws are in force. The byelaws are supplemented by (a) a set of Core Principles, (b) a number of Codes of Conduct which set out in detail how underwriting agents can best meet their responsibilities, and (c) various business guidance documents. Copies of all of these are contained in the Codes Handbook.[16] The Core Principles and the Codes of Conduct supplement the byelaws. FSMA provides that the FSA may exercise its powers by giving directions to either the Society or the Council.[17]   **19–006**

The typical activities of members' and managing agents are regulated activities for the purposes of FSMA.[18] Accordingly, they need to be authorised by the FSA to carry on a regulated activity and must comply with the regulatory regime established under the Act. In particular, they must comply with the requirements   **19–007**

---

[9] As to regulated activities, see Ch.14, para.14–022.

[10] See Ch.14, paras 14–010 and 14–011.

[11] FSMA, ss.314–324.

[12] FSMA, s.315. It is given permission to carry on the regulated activities of the kinds set out in s.315(2).

[13] The FSA's handbook can be found on the FSA's website at *www.fsa.gov.uk*.

[14] For example, r.8.2.1 requires the Society to maintain byelaws establishing appropriate arrangements to compensate members if underwriting agents are unable to satisfy claims made against them by those members. Breach of the rules contained within the Lloyd's sourcebook does not give rise to a right of action for damages: see Sch.5 to the Lloyd's sourcebook.

[15] Lloyd's Act 1982, s.6(2).

[16] The full text of the Codes Handbook can be found on the Lloyd's website: *www.Lloyds.com*.

[17] FSMA, s.318.

[18] See generally Ch.14, paras 14–022 *et seq.* as to regulated activities and the "RAO" (SI 2001/544). The RAO provides that the following activities are specified activities for the purposes of s.22 of the Act and thus regulated activities: advice on syndicate participation at Lloyd's (art.56); managing the underwriting capacity of a Lloyd's syndicate (art.57); arranging deals in contracts of insurance written at Lloyd's (art.58, note the exclusion in art.58A relating to information society services).

in the sourcebook (within the FSA's Handbook) entitled "Insurance: Conduct of Business" ("ICOB").

19–008   Consequently, managing agents and members' agents are required to comply with the following rules and regulations:

(a) The applicable ICOB rules, which can be found on the FSA's website (*www.fsa.gov.uk*).

(b) The byelaws made by the Council of Lloyd's. The text of the byelaws can be found on the Lloyd's website (*www.lloyds.com*).

(c) The Lloyd's Core Principles, the Codes of Practice, and the business guidance documents, all of which are contained within the Codes Handbook. The text of the Handbook can be found on the Lloyd's website (*www.lloyds.com*).

19–009   **Prescribed agreements.** A member at Lloyd's is required to enter into an agreement with both his members' agent and directly with the managing agent of each syndicate of which he is a member. His members' agent enters a separate agreement with each managing agent. The terms of those agreements is prescribed by the Agency Agreement Byelaw.[19] The members' agent is not contractually responsible for the underwriting conducted by the managing agent.[20]

19–010   **The core principles.** The introduction to the Core Principles for underwriting agents states that: "The high standard demanded of Lloyd's agents ensures we remain the world's leading insurance market." The Core Principles are as follows:

Integrity. An agent should observe high standards of integrity and deal openly and fairly.

Skill, care and diligence. An agent should act with due skill, care and diligence.

Market conduct. An agent should observe high standards of conduct and should take all reasonable steps to avoid causing harm to the standing or reputation of Lloyd's.

Conduct towards members. An agent should conduct the affairs of each of the members for whom it acts in a manner which does not unfairly prejudice the interests of any such member.

Information. An agent should seek from members its advises any information about their circumstances and objectives which might reasonably be expected to

---

[19] Byelaw No.8 of 1988. The byelaw has been amended on numerous occasions since it commenced on December 7, 1988, but its name remains unchanged. The standard forms of the agency agreements are set out in schedules to the Byelaw.

[20] *The Lloyd's Litigation* [1994] 2 Lloyd's Rep. 193 at 201–202, *per* Saville J. and *Deeny v Gooda Walker Ltd* [1996] L.R.L.R. 183, at 186, *per* Phillips J. Both judges were speaking obiter.

be relevant in enabling it to fulfil its responsibilities to them. An agent should also take all reasonable steps to give members it advises or for whom it exercises discretion, in a comprehensive and timely way, any information needed to enable them to make balanced and informed decisions. An agent should also be ready to provide members with a full and fair account of the fulfilment of its responsibilities to them.

Conflicts of interest. An agent should seek to avoid any conflict of interest arising, but where a conflict does arise, should make comprehensible and timely disclosure of that conflict and of the steps to be taken to ensure the fair treatment of any members affected. An agent should not unfairly put its own interests above its duty to any members for whom it acts.

Assets. An agent should deal with assets and rights received or held on behalf of a member prudently and in accordance with the terms of any applicable trust deed or agreement with the member.

Financial resources. An agent should maintain adequate financial resources to meet its commitments and to withstand the normal risks to which it is subject.

Internal organisation. An agent should organise and control its affairs in a responsible manner, maintaining proper records and systems for the conduct of its business and the management of risk. It should have adequate arrangements to ensure that staff and others whom it employs are suitable, adequately trained and properly supervised and that it has well-defined compliance procedures.

Relations with Lloyd's. An agent should deal with Lloyd's in an open and co-operative manner and keep Lloyd's promptly informed of anything concerning the agent which Lloyd's might reasonably expect to be disclosed to it.

19–011 A breach by a managing or members' agent of one of the Core Principles does not of itself give rise to a cause of action against that agent. However, a reasonably competent managing or members' agent will comply with the Core Principles. Therefore a failure to comply with any of the Core Principles will amount to a failure to act with reasonable skill and care.

19–012 **The codes of conduct.** At the time of writing there are 11 Codes and 12 business guidance documents contained in the Codes Handbook. The Codes and the guidance cover a range of subject matters. The Code which is most relevant to the liability of a members' agent is the Code for Members' Agents: Responsibilities to Members. The Codes which are most likely to be relevant to the liability of a managing agent are those on Managing Underwriting Risk, Management of Investment Risk, and Management of Reserving Risk. The Foreword to the Codes Handbook states that the codes "seek to promote best practice, but should not be taken as exhaustive." It continues: "Compliance with a code provides strong evidence of the adequacy of an underwriting agent's procedures. Underwriting agents should not assume however that in all circumstances compliance with a code will discharge all their responsibilities, nor that the regulatory division would not accept some other, equally effective, procedure." An underwriting agent's compliance with, or failure to comply with, the requirements of a Code will be cogent evidence in assessing whether the agent acted with reasonable skill and care, but is unlikely to be determinative of that question.

19–013 **The old regime.** In the early 1990s there was a spate of litigation involving Lloyd's underwriting agents which largely related to events in the 1980s. Since then there have been significant changes to the way in which business is conducted at Lloyd's. However, an understanding of how business used to be conducted at Lloyd's is necessary to put some of the authorities from the 1990s into context.

19–014 Historically all Names were individuals who undertook unlimited personal liability. Upon joining Lloyd's, Names who were not themselves underwriting agents had to appoint a members' agent to act for them, either in person or through sub-agents. The relationship between a Name and a members' agent was contractual. Before January 1, 1987 there was no prescribed form of contract, but in practice standard forms of agreement were used.[21] Thereafter agreements had to conform with the Agency Agreements Byelaw (No.1 of 1985).[22] Members' agents would place Names on one or more syndicates for each year of account.

19–015 Each syndicate had one or more active underwriters, who did the actual underwriting. The active underwriters were employed by an agency which managed the syndicate's affairs.[23] These agencies either concerned themselves solely with the management of underwriting, in which case they were known as managing agents, or acted as members' agents as well, in which case they are known as combined agents. The agreements between Names and members' agents gave the members' agents the power to conduct underwriting on their behalf. This power was either exercised by the members' agents themselves, if they were combined agents, or delegated to managing agents.[24] Where the members' agent was also the managing agent names were known as "direct Names". Where the members' agent entered into a sub-agency agreement with a managing agent they were known as "indirect Names".[25]

19–016 **LMX business.** The litigation in the early 1990s concerning Lloyd's largely, if not exclusively, concerned losses suffered as a result of London Market excess of loss ("LMX") business having been written in the late 1980s. By excess of loss reinsurance ("XL") insurers seek to limit their exposure to a particularly large risk or to an aggregation of risks which are all exposed to the same event.

---

[21] *Henderson v Merrett Syndicates Ltd* [1995] 2 A.C. 145 at 171A–C. Some of the provisions are set out in the speech of Lord Goff at 175B–H. The full terms are set out in the appendices to the judgment of Saville J. in *Henderson v Merrett* at first instance (reported as *The Lloyd's Litigation* [1994] 2 Lloyd's Rep. 193; the agreement appears at 202–210).

[22] Set out at [1994] 2 Lloyd's Rep. 211–226.

[23] A syndicate's core functions are to enter contracts of insurance (including reinsurance), whether directly or through agents, decide upon and implement a reinsurance programme, deal with claims, invest premiums and to consider whether and on what terms the year of account can be reinsured to close. The managing agent is also responsible for maintaining the syndicate's records and preparing its annual audited accounts. See *Society of Lloyd's v Clemston* [1997] L.R.L.R. 175 at 188–189, Cresswell J.

[24] A sample sub-agency agreement is appended to the judgment of Saville J. in *The Lloyd's Litigation* [1994] 2 Lloyd's Rep. 193 at 208–210.

[25] See *Henderson v Merrett Syndicates Ltd* [1995] 2 A.C. 145 at 170–171, *per* Lord Goff.

At the highest levels of such reinsurance cover the insurer is seeking protection from catastrophes. In the London insurance market of the 1980s relatively few insurers wrote XL business. They were therefore highly exposed in the event of any catastrophic event or series of events. This exposure was compounded by "the spiral", which Phillips J. described in these terms in *Deeny v Gooda Walker Ltd*[26]:

> "Many syndicates which wrote XL cover took out XL cover themselves. Those who reinsured them were thus writing XL on XL. They, in their turn, frequently took out their own XL cover. There thus developed among the syndicates and companies which wrote LMX business a smaller group that was largely responsible for creating a complex intertwining network of mutual reinsurance, which has been described as the spiral. When a catastrophe led to claims being made by primary insurers on their excess of loss covers, this started a process whereby syndicates passed on their liabilities, in excess of their own retentions, under their own excess of loss covers from one to the next, rather like a multiple game of pass the parcel. Those left holding the liability parcels were those who first exhausted their layers of excess of loss reinsurance protection . . .
>
> There were at least two significant ways in which spiral business was written:
>
> *XL on XL*: This described the grant of excess of loss cover in respect of an excess of loss account.
>
> *Whole account*: An underwriter who took out, without exclusion, excess of loss cover in respect of his whole account would thereby obtain excess of loss cover in respect of that part of his whole account which itself comprised excess of loss business."[27]

(c) *Duties to Client*

(i) *Contractual Duties*

Members' agents. The contractual duties of a members' agent are set out in (a) the written contract between the member and the members' agent, and (b) the written contract between the members' agent and the managing agent. The Standard Members' Agent's Agreement[28] prescribes the services to be provided by the members' agent for a Name, including the provision of advice in respect of syndicate selection, the performance of syndicates on which a member participates, reserve requirements and a member's compliance with all relevant

19–017

---

[26] [1996] L.R.L.R. 183 at 190.

[27] See also Robert Kiln, *Reinsurance in Practice*, (3rd edn, 1991), Witherby & Co. pp.286–287:
"In general the underwriting of LMX business requires very special skills, knowledge and nerve. The London market place is one market and all its constituent members tend to write shares in the same business and on the same exposures, for example, oil rigs. Therefore, the accumulation hazard on a book of LMX business can be very large indeed. All such covers tend to be directly additional to each other and the risk of a large proportion of them being involved in the same disaster is very high indeed.
This is not to say that such a book of business, properly selected, will not be profitable, but it will have a high profitability in loss free years and a high risk of a large accumulating loss when the bad years occur."
For a further description of the "spiral", see *Society of Lloyd's v Clemston* [1997] L.R.L.R. 175 at 207–209, Cresswell J.

[28] Contained within Sch.1 of the Agency Agreements Byelaw (No.8 of 1988) (as amended).

regulatory requirements. In addition the Agreement prescribes the duties of the agent, including acting in what it believes to be the best interests of the member, forwarding promptly to the member reports, etc. received from the managing agent, disclosing certain information to the member and maintaining proper records relating to all transactions effected by the agent concerning the member's Lloyd's business.

19–018   The role of a members' agent was set out in these terms by Gatehouse J. in *Brown v KMR Services Ltd*[29]:

> "(a) to advise the name which syndicates to join and in what amounts, (b) to keep him informed at all times of material factors which may affect his underwriting, (c) to provide him with a balanced portfolio and appropriate spread of risk; a balanced spread of business on syndicates throughout the main markets at Lloyd's, (d) to monitor the syndicates on which it places the name, and to make recommendations whether the name should increase his share on a syndicate, join a new syndicate, reduce his share, or withdraw, (e) to keep regularly in touch with the syndicates to which the name belongs, and (f) to advise and discuss with the name the prospects and past results on which he could be placed."[30]

19–019   Members' agents also advise members of, and if appropriate about, personal stop loss insurance[31] and estate protection policies.[32] It is a term of the contract that the members' agent will bring reasonable skill and care to the performance of those functions.[33] If a members' agent gives an assurance that he will perform his agency in a particular way, he will be liable for breach of contract if performs his agency in a different way.[34]

19–020   **Managing agents.** The contractual duties of managing agents are set out in (a) the written agreement between the member and the managing agent, and (b) the written agreement between the members' agent and the managing agent. Those duties include an express contractual duty to the Names to exercise reasonable skill and care.[35] The Standard Managing Agent's agreement prescribes the services to be provided by a managing agent for a Name including determining the underwriting policy of the syndicate, appointing and supervising the active underwriter and other staff of the syndicate, accepting risks on behalf of the

---

[29] [1994] 4 All E.R. 385 at 390f–h. The facts are set out in para.19–040, below. For a summary of the relationship between Names and agents see also *Society of Lloyd's v Clemston* [1997] L.R.L.R. 175 at 199, Cresswell J.

[30] See also *Henderson v Merrett Syndicates Ltd* [1995] 2 A.C. 145 at 170E, *per* Lord Goff.

[31] This is discussed further in para.19–042, below.

[32] These are policies insuring against liability of Names' estates for years of account left open after a Name's death.

[33] cl.6.2 (a) of the standard Members' Agent's Agreement (Sch.1 to the Agency Agreements Byelaw) provides expressly that the members' agent will "use such skill, care and diligence as could reasonably be expected of a members' agent carrying on business at Lloyd's and as is necessary for the proper provision of services, performance of duties and exercise of powers by it under this Agreement."

[34] *Brown v KMR Services Ltd* [1994] 4 All E.R. 385 at 400b–f.

[35] cl.4.2 (a) of the standard Managing Agent's Agreement (Sch.3 to the Agency Agreements Byelaw, No.8 of 1988) provides that the managing agent will "use such skill, care and diligence as could reasonably be expected of a managing agent carrying on business at Lloyd's and as is necessary for the proper provision of services, performance of duties and exercise of powers by it under this Agreement."

syndicate, determining the reinsurance policy of the syndicate, effecting and managing any reinsurance programme, settling and paying claims, and effecting the reinsurance to close for the syndicate in respect of each year of account if it is appropriate to close the year.

(ii) *Tortious Duties*

Members' agents. Members' agents owe a concurrent tortious duty to their **19–021** Names.[36] That tortious duty is co-extensive with their contractual duty of care. The duties of members' agents in relation to underwriting (which is carried out by the managing agent) has been described as follows:

> "the common law duty of care is no more than expected and required of a competent members' agent (*qua* members' agent) and therefore that, in respect of the detailed conduct of the underwriting function and the day-to-day management of the Syndicate's affairs in connection with it, the common law duty to be imposed is no more than one of reasonable care in the selection of and liaison with the managing agent coupled with general oversight of the members' interests, it being no part of the members' agent's function (unless put on inquiry as to the competence of the managing agent) to supervise or interfere in managing or controlling the syndicate's affairs. It is the managing agents who are employed for that purpose pursuant to the practice and requirements of the Lloyd's market."[37]

In the absence of an assumption of personal responsibility, a director or **19–022** employee of a members' agent will not owe a duty of care to a Name. In *Noel v Poland*[38] the claimant Name alleged that she had been misled into becoming and remaining a Name by the defendants, who were the directors of a members' agent. Her claim was summarily dismissed on the basis that any arguable case which she might have had lay against the company not against the defendants personally.

Managing agents. Managing agents owe Names a tortious duty concurrent **19–023** with their contractual duty. The active underwriter employed by the managing agent owes a tortious duty of care to the Names on whose behalf he acts.[39]

(iii) *Fiduciary Duties*

Both members' and managing agents are subject to the fiduciary obligation not **19–024** to allow their duty to act in the interests of their Names to conflict with their own interests.[40] This is now expressly acknowledged in the prescribed forms of

---

[36] *Henderson v Merrett Syndicates Ltd* [1995] 2 A.C. 145: the actual decision concerned the tortious liability of managing agents to direct and indirect names, but it must follow that members' agents owe a duty of care in tort to their names.
[37] *ibid.*, at 1300B–C. See P. Cane, "Contract, tort and the Lloyd's debacle" in *Consensus ad Idem* (F. D. Rose edn, Sweet & Maxwell, 1996) at 100–103.
[38] [2002] Lloyd's Rep. I.R. 30 (Toulson J.).
[39] *Wynniatt-Husey v RJ Bromley (Underwriting Agencies) Plc* [1996] L.R.L.R. 310, Langley J.; *Henderson v Merrett Syndicates Ltd* [1997] L.R.L.R. 265, Cresswell J.
[40] See generally, Ch.2, paras 2–128 *et seq*. Additionally, there is a fiduciary relationship between the Names in a syndicate and the active underwriter of that syndicate: *Sphere Drake Insurance Ltd v Euro International Underwriting Ltd* [2003] EWHC 1636, (*The Times*, August 11, 2003) (Thomas J.).

agreement.[41] The question of whether members' or managing agents owed Names any separate fiduciary duty to exercise skill and care was raised in the appeal in *Henderson v Merrett Syndicates Ltd.*[42] Both Saville J. and the Court of Appeal had not addressed the question, having found that sufficient contractual and tortious duties were owed. In the House of Lords only Lord Browne-Wilkinson considered the point and rejected it as misconceived: while a fiduciary may owe a duty of care, that is "not a separate head of liability but the paradigm of the general duty to act with care imposed by law on those who take it upon themselves to act for or advise others".[43] Moreover, the extent of the fiduciary duties owed, including any duty to exercise skill and care, falls to be determined by reference to the terms of any underlying contract.[44]

(iv) *Duties Imposed by the FSA*

19–025 As previously noted, members' and managing agents are required to be authorised by the FSA and are required to comply with the regulatory regime established under the Act. In particular they must comply with the applicable rules set out in the ICOB sourcebook.[45] Breach of rules within ICOB is actionable at the suit of a private person[46] who suffers loss as a result of that breach, subject to the defences and other incidents applying to actions for breach of statutory duty.[47]

(d) *Duties to Third Parties*

19–026 Apart from the question of duties owed by managing agents to indirect Names which arose in relation to the old regime, the question of the duties owed by members' or managing agents to persons other than the Names with whom a members' or managing agent has contracted has rarely arisen in practice.

19–027 **Reinsurance to close.** Reinsurance to close is a contract whereby one year of account of a syndicate is reinsured into another, usually the following year of account of the same syndicate number.[48] The effect is to release Names on the reinsured syndicate from further liability for that year's account (unless and to the extent that they are also Names on the reinsuring syndicate) and to allow them to take any profit. In return for a substantial premium the Names on the

---

[41] See cl.6.2(b), (c) and (d) of the Members' Agent's Agreement (Sch.1 to the Agency Agreements Byelaw, No.8 of 1988) and cl.4.2(b), (c) and (d) of the Managing Agent's Agreement (Sch.3 to the Agency Agreements Byelaw, No.8 of 1988).

[42] [1995] 2 A.C. 145. See P. Cane, "Contract, Tort and the Lloyd's Debacle" in *Consensus ad Idem* (F. D. Rose edn, Sweet & Maxwell, 1996) at 118–119.

[43] *ibid.*, at 205F.

[44] See also *Kelly v Cooper* [1993] A.C. 205. For an alternative view see J. D. Heydon Q.C., (1995) 111 L.Q.R. 1.

[45] See para.19–007, above.

[46] The definition of a "private person" for the purposes of s.150 is set out in reg.3 of the Financial Services and Markets Act (Rights of Action) Regulations 2001 (SI 2001/2256). The definition includes (a) any individual, unless he suffers the loss in question in the course of carrying on any regulated activity, and (b) any person who is not an individual, unless he suffers the loss in question in the course of carrying on business of any kind.

[47] FSMA, s.150. See further Ch.14, paras 14–077 *et seq.*

[48] The Names on the syndicate will vary from year to year as will their individual lines.

reinsuring syndicate will take over the business of the year being closed, which will include the business of all earlier years of account reinsured into that year. They will also enjoy the benefit of all reinsurance obtained for the old years of account (and of any recoveries made) and it is they, rather than the Names on the old years, who will suffer losses should that reinsurance prove to be ineffective because they will have reinsured the liability of the old Names. Where the managing agent is negligent in effecting reinsurance so that the reinsurer avoids the policy several years later, the loss will fall not on the Names at the time the reinsurance was originally effected but in the earliest year of account still open at the date of avoidance.

In *Aiken v Stewart Wrightson Members Agency Ltd*[49] the managing agent had **19–028** arranged aggregate excess of loss reinsurance for all liabilities which the syndicate might incur on its 1975 and earlier years of account. This was for the immediate benefit of the 1979 Names but had obvious possible consequences for Names on future years who would reinsure to close on the basis that the risk of losses above a certain sum on pre-1976 business had been effectively reinsured by others. In 1989 the reinsurer avoided the aggregate excess of loss policy for non-disclosure of material facts. On a trial of preliminary issues Potter J. had to decide whether the managing agent owed a duty of care in tort to Names on following years. He held that it did, not only to the Names on the two years immediately following 1979 (where the identity and interests of the Names were known at the time the reinsurance was made) but also for later years, including 1985 (being the earliest open year when the aggregate excess of loss policy was avoided), even though their identities and interests were not known at the time the policy had been effected. Potter J. had no difficulty in finding that a duty was owed to the 1980 and 1981 Names on the basis of the evidence of the managing agents as to their intention in effecting the aggregate excess of loss policy at the time.[50] As for later years, he adopted the three-stage test[51] and the incremental approach advocated in *Caparo Industries Ltd v Dickman*[52] and applied in *Punjab National Bank v de Boinville*.[53] He held that, in effect, a syndicate at Lloyd's continues from year to year and that, "managing agents are *in reality* concerned to deal on behalf of the Syndicate, protecting its interests without regard to the identity of its Names."[54] While at the time the aggregate excess of loss policy was obtained the managing agents did not know the identities of the Names for future years beyond 1981, they were an identifiable class at any given time and the total liability of the managing agents would not be increased as a result of any changes in the membership of the syndicate.[55]

Change of managing agent. In *Wynniatt-Husey v RJ Bromley (Underwriting* **19–029**
Agencies) Plc[56] the Names claimed not only against the managing agent at the

---

[49] [1995] 1 W.L.R. 1281.
[50] *ibid.*, at 1305H–1306H.
[51] See Ch.2, para.2–030.
[52] [1990] 2 A.C. 605: see Ch.17, paras 17–029 *et seq.*
[53] [1992] 1 W.L.R. 1138; see Ch.16, para.16–029.
[54] *ibid.*, at 1312G–H; the emphasis is that of Potter J.
[55] However, the brokers employed to effect the reinsurance would not owe a duty of care to later Names: *Deeny v Walker* [1996] L.R.L.R. 276, Gatehouse J.
[56] [1996] L.R.L.R. 310.

relevant time, but also against its predecessor. The claim was founded upon an undertaking given to Lloyd's by the predecessor when the management of the syndicate was transferred to the new managing agent. By the undertaking the predecessor promised to provide such support as the successor considered necessary. The claim failed because the Names had not been aware of the undertaking and the undertaking itself did not require the predecessor to supervise its successor, but merely to provide support on request. The successor had not in fact requested any support.

2. The Standard of Care

19–030 Where the members' or managing agent owes a duty to exercise reasonable skill and care, he (or those for whom he is liable) will only be in breach of that duty if he falls below the standards of a reasonably competent members' or managing agent at the relevant time and with the knowledge which such a members' or managing agent had or should have had.[57] In the context of Lloyd's, the standards are those of the Lloyd's market[58] or, if appropriate, the relevant section of the Lloyd's market. However, while expert evidence is of importance in determining the question, it is ultimately for the court to decide what constitutes reasonable competence. The court is not bound to accept that compliance with a widely followed practice or standard is sufficient and it may be that the approach of a specialised section of the Lloyd's market over a period will not amount to sufficient evidence of what constitutes the exercise of reasonable care. Thus in *Deeny v Gooda Walker Ltd*[59] Phillips J. addressed the question of the standard of care to be expected of those underwriting excess of loss business in the LMX spiral[60] in these terms:

" . . . this action is concerned with one area of underwriting, excess of loss reinsurance. At the heart of the action lies one aspect of excess of loss underwriting, the writing of spiral business. That was a business which developed rapidly in the period of the eight years or so that led up to the events with which this action is concerned. Only a relatively small proportion of Lloyd's underwriters specialised in writing spiral business. The London market no longer writes spiral business—at least on the scale and in the manner which developed in the last decade. In these circumstances I do not consider that one can automatically regard the practices of those who wrote spiral business as constituting strong evidence of what constituted the exercise of reasonable skill and care. It is necessary to approach this case with the possibility in mind that, for many

---

[57] See, for example, *The Lloyd's Litigation* [1994] 2 Lloyd's Rep. 468 at 474, col.1, *per* Bingham M.R.: " . . . any successful claim against the agent in negligence would, as in any other case, have to show a failure to show the standard of skill and care reasonably to be expected of such an agent at the time and with the knowledge that he had or should have had. His judgment could not be impugned simply because events showed it to be wrong." See also *Brown v KMR Services Ltd* [1994] 4 All E.R. 385 at 397d–j, *per* Gatehouse J. (members' agent) and *Henderson v Merrett Syndicates Ltd (No.2)* [1996] 1 P.N.L.R. 32, Cresswell J. (managing agent).

[58] In the case of underwriting, the standards are those of a reasonably competent underwriter, whether at Lloyd's or elsewhere.

[59] [1996] L.R.L.R. 183.

[60] See para.19–016, above.

involved, a significant involvement in spiral business may not have been compatible with competent underwriting."[61]

Moreover, where Names are being exposed to very great potential liabilities, an appropriate level of skill is to be expected of those who are so exposing them.[62]

In considering whether a members' or managing agent's conduct fell below the standards of a reasonably competent members' or managing agent, the court will be heavily influenced by whether or not the agent complied with the Core Principles, the Codes, and any applicable provisions of the ICOB sourcebook. **19–031**

[THE NEXT PARAGRAPH IS 19–033]

3. LIABILITY FOR BREACH OF DUTY

Broadly speaking breach of duty by a members' or managing agent may take one of four forms: **19–033**

(i) Breach of a specific contractual duty.

(ii) Breach of an express or implied duty to exercise reasonable skill and care.

(iii) Breach of a tortious duty of care.

(iv) Breach of one or more of the FSA's Conduct of Business rules.[63]

Proof of negligence will not be necessary to establish liability under the first or fourth head, but in order to establish liability under the second and third heads a failure to exercise the same standard of skill and care must be shown. Such a failure is referred to as "negligence" in this chapter.

The principal respects in which members' and managing agents might be held to have been negligent are discussed below under seven heads, being those which have featured most prominently in the decided cases. However, the catalogue of errors is not closed and this chapter does not attempt to speculate as to other circumstances in which a members' or managing agent might be negligent. **19–034**

---

[61] [1996] L.R.L.R. 183 at 207. See also at 205: "As a broad proposition, any professional who engages in a particular speciality can be expected to demonstrate the level of skill and care appropriate to that speciality."

[62] *ibid.*, at 207–208. But see *Wynniatt-Husey v RJ Bromley (Underwriting Agencies) Plc* [1996] L.R.L.R. 310 at 313, *per* Langley J.:

"As to the standard of care, that is the standard of a professional underwriter holding himself out as possessing the skill and experience reasonably required to underwrite a marine account which on any view of the evidence, contained a significant proportion of excess of loss ('XL') business. There is no dispute that such business is of a high risk nature. That does not mean in my judgment that some special and stricter standard of care applies in the sense that the standard differs from that of a reasonable underwriter but only that his conduct is to be considered in the context of underwriting an account which included such business."

[63] This may give rise to liability pursuant to FSMA, s.150. (see para.19–007, above).

(a) Members' Agent—Failure to Advise Adequately as to Syndicate Participation

19–035 **"Knowledge your principal".** Before giving any advice on which (if any) syndicates a member or prospective member should participate in, the members' agent should seek from the Name any information which might reasonably be expected to be relevant in enabling it to fulfil its responsibilities to him. Such an obligation is expressly imposed on a members' agent by Core Principles,[64] the Code for Members' Agents: Responsibilities to Members[65] and by r.4.3.2 of ICOB. The Code states that the information which should be obtained by the members' agent includes details of his personal circumstances, financial circumstances including available means, and financial objectives including whether participation should be on a limited or unlimited basis. The Code states that such information should be updated at least annually.

19–036 **Suitability for membership.** The first obligation on a members' agent is to advise a prospective member on his suitability for membership of Lloyd's, and on the type of underwriting participation. The Code for Members' Agents: Responsibilities to Members[66] states that a members' agent should advise a prospective member of any information which it considers to be material to that prospective member in deciding whether to become a member. This must include a recommendation from the members' agent whether, in its opinion, membership of Lloyd's is suitable for the prospective member. Similarly, advice should be provided to an existing member on whether underwriting at Lloyd's remains a suitable activity for him. Such advice should be updated regularly. Rule 4.3.1 of ICOB requires a members' agent to take reasonable steps to ensure that, if it makes any personal recommendation to buy or sell a non-investment insurance contract, the recommendation is suitable for the customer's demands and needs at the time the personal recommendation is made.

19–037 If the members' agent is of the view that membership of Lloyd's is suitable for the prospective member, then the members' agent should advise the prospective member on the type of underwriting participation that is suitable for him, i.e. whether as an individual Name or via some type of corporate membership.[67] Once a member has joined Lloyd's, then the members' agent should advise on whether an alternate type of membership is appropriate in the event of, for example, a change in the member's personal circumstances or changes in the structure of the Lloyd's market. This will include advice on conversion from unlimited to corporate membership.

19–038 **Choice of syndicates.** Once a member has joined Lloyd's then the members' agent must give him advice as to the choice of syndicates to join. This is the most important task carried out by a members' agent. The Members' Agent's Agreement imposes an express obligation on the members' agent to:

---

[64] See para.19–010, above.
[65] Code for Members' Agents: Responsibilities to Members, para.4.1.
[66] Code for Members' Agents: Responsibilities to Members, paras 5.1 and 5.2.
[67] Code for Members' Agents: Responsibilities to Members, paras 5.3 & 5.4.

"advise the Name as to the syndicates in which he should participate, as to the amounts of his overall premium limit which should from time to time be allocated to each such syndicate and as to the exercise of any rights of the Name, or the response to any offer made to the Name, with respect to the Name's right of participation in any such syndicate" and "keep under review and report to the Name as and when appropriate on the performance of the Contracted Syndicates."[68]

The Code for Members' Agents: Responsibilities to Members also imposes **19–039** obligations on members' agents regarding the giving of advice on syndicate selection.[69] The extent to which Names will seek or accept such advice will vary: at one extreme they will rely entirely upon their members' agent, while, at the other extreme, "working Names" will be directly involved in Lloyd's and might be as well as or better informed than a competent members' agent. A members' agent is not under a duty to warn of a risk which he knows his Name is aware of,[70] and a working Name who makes his own choice of syndicate without reference to his members' agent may thereby absolve his members' agent from any duty to advise.[71] However, save in those unusual circumstances the duties of a members' agent have been authoritatively summarised in these terms by Hobhouse L.J.:

"The relevant duties of the members' agent are stated in the express or implicit provisions of the contract between the member and the agent. They are to the same effect: 'to advise the Name which syndicates to join and in what amounts.' This is a duty which has to be performed each year when the decisions have to be made for the following underwriting year. The advice must therefore cover both the selection of the syndicates and the amount of premium to be allocated to each. In selecting the syndicates regard must be had to the classes of business in which the member wishes to become involved, to the quality of the individual syndicates, what business they write and to the sectors of the market to be covered. The agent must make recommendations which are of the appropriate quality, both having regard to the individual syndicates and the composition of the portfolio as a whole. Linked with this must be advice as to the amount of the allocation that the member should make to each syndicate. This must have regard to the same considerations—the character and quality of the syndicate and the need to obtain an appropriate spread and maintain a proper balance.

Such considerations must apply to every member whom the agent is advising. Certain members may need additional advice because of their special need to avoid risk . . . Regard may be had to other information which has been given by the member to the agent about the member's requirements or circumstances . . .

Further, the agent must give the member such information as is necessary for the member to make a reasonably informed decision about the recommendations which the agent is making. The more that the member is himself getting involved in the actual decisions (as opposed to leaving it to the agent), the more it is necessary that the advice given to the member should include the appropriate information . . . The agent need not

---

[68] See cll.4(a) & 4(c) of the Members' Agent's Agreement.
[69] Code for Members' Agents: Responsibilities to Members, paras 6.1 *et seq.*
[70] *Brown v KMR Services Ltd* [1995] 4 All E.R. 598 at 617b, *per* Stuart-Smith L.J.
[71] *Berriman (Sir David) v Rose Thomson Young (Underwriting) Ltd* [1996] L.R.L.R. 426, *per* Morrison J. at 486. Where the members' agent had warranted that the underwriting on those syndicates chosen by the Name would be carried out with reasonable skill and care, he would be liable for breach of contract even if it was the Name and not he who had chosen the syndicates (*ibid.*).

in the ordinary course repeat the warnings that have already been given. But where a particular syndicate involves some additional risk it is incumbent upon the agent . . . to give an appropriate additional warning coupled with appropriate information."[72]

19–040   The duties owed to Names with very different requirements and attitudes were considered in *Brown v KMR Services Ltd.*[73] One claimant Name, Mr Sword-Daniels, was of relatively modest means, so that he would find losses particularly hard to fund, and wished to adopt a conservative, cautious approach to underwriting. His members' agent placed him on a high proportion of syndicates which were high risk without informing him of the potential liabilities to which he was exposed as a result. Gatehouse J. found the members' agent to have been negligent. The same conclusion was reached in the case of the other claimant Name, Mr Brown. Mr Brown was experienced and knowledgeable both as to business and investment matters generally and, by the relevant period, as to the Lloyd's market. He took an active interest in his choice of syndicates (based largely upon their profitability in preceding years) and was aware that some of them involved a higher degree of risk than others. He was nevertheless prepared to participate to a large extent on syndicates which wrote catastrophe excess of loss business. Gatehouse J. held that he was still entitled to receive advice as to the particular risks to which his proposed underwriting would expose him. The Court of Appeal held that the members' agent was under a duty to do more than just warn of the risk. In order to discharge his duty properly in such circumstances the members' agent should have told Mr Brown which of his proposed syndicates were high risk, the nature of the risk, the degree to which the risks on the proposed syndicates overlapped, the proportion of his total allocation which it was prudent to allocate to such syndicates and the appropriate allocation to make to each of the high risk syndicates.[74]

19–041   **Knowledge of syndicates.** In assessing the advice which a members' agent should give as to particular syndicates or types of business, he is to be judged by the knowledge which he had or ought to have had. As well as a reasonable understanding of the various classes of business underwritten at Lloyd's, a members' agent should know and understand the underwriting philosophy and the nature of the business underwritten by those syndicates he advises his Names to join. That will include some knowledge of the reinsurance protection which the underwriter proposes to obtain. However, a members' agent is "not required so to question the underwriter of any particular syndicate as to endeavour to second guess the way the risks were written".[75] In *Brown v KMR Services Ltd*[76] Gatehouse J. held that a combined agency[77] whose underwriters were aware of the inherent risks of writing excess of loss reinsurance was under a duty to communicate that knowledge to those of its employees who advised Names in

---

[72] *Brown v KMR Services Ltd* [1995] 4 All E.R. 598 at 633f–634c.
[73] [1994] 4 All E.R. 385 (*Sword-Daniels and Brown*), Gatehouse J.; [1995] 4 All E.R. 598 (*Brown*), CA.
[74] [1995] 4 All E.R. 598, at 634e–g, *per* Hobhouse L.J., with whom the other members of the Court of Appeal agreed on this point.
[75] *Berriman (Sir David) v Rose Thomson Young (Underwriting) Ltd* [1996] L.R.L.R. 426 at 482 (Morrison J.).
[76] [1994] 4 All E.R. 385.
[77] i.e. an agency which acted both as a member's agent and managed one or more syndicates.

the capacity of members' agent. On the facts of that case the knowledge in question was such as might be expected to be held by a reasonably competent members' agent in any event. However, in general it would be wrong to require a higher degree of knowledge of a combined agent when acting as a members' agent by reason of the knowledge of its active underwriters: the contractual and tortious expectation of the Name should not depend upon whether his members' agent is also a managing agent.

Stop loss insurance. A members' agent may advise a Name to take out **19–042** personal stop loss insurance as part of his underwriting strategy. Personal stop loss insurance insures Names against losses on their underwriting at Lloyd's in a given year, subject both to a deductible and a limit, the Name retaining the risk of losses falling within the former and above the latter. Although this will provide an element of protection to the Name, a members' agent who has otherwise exposed a Name to risks of which the Name was not but should have been informed will still be in breach of duty.[78]

(b) *Managing Agent—Failure to Plan Properly*

Like all insurers, Names risk making losses. Every time an underwriter makes an **19–043** insurance contract on their behalf he exposes them to the risk of a claim or claims under that policy. Claims can be met from premiums received or by reinsurance. If both are exhausted, then the Names will make a loss. By the exercise of skill and judgment the underwriter should reduce the risk of loss. An underwriter therefore should seek to write a range of business both in terms of class of business and geographical area. This should allow claims on one class of risk written in a particular area (for example property damage caused by a hurricane) to be met by premiums on policies not affected by the underlying event. An underwriter will also wish to reinsure against large claims or aggregations of claims. A proper plan is a vital tool for the underwriter in that regard. The Underwriting Byelaw imposes an obligation on a managing agent each year to prepare a business plan relating to each syndicate it manages.[79] The Code for Managing Agents: Managing Underwriting Risk states that the plan should state the business intentions of the active underwriter and should state how it is intended the portfolio of the syndicate will be protected by outward reinsurance. The plan should reflect the levels of risk to be retained and the potential for the accumulation of risk, taking into consideration the realistic disaster scenarios and the need for the reinsurance programme to be consistent with the underwriting plan. The plan must be submitted to the Franchise Board of Lloyd's.[80]

Establishing the PML. In order to formulate such a plan the underwriter **19–044** needs to establish the probable maximum loss ("PML") to which the syndicate will be exposed by a single event. The PML is not the same as the aggregate of all the sums payable under the policies to be underwritten, although, if a

---

[78] *Brown v KMR Services Ltd* [1994] 4 All E.R. 385 at 394. Gatehouse J. also held that Names need not give credit for sums recovered under personal stop loss policies: see para.19–091, below.
[79] Underwriting Byelaw (No.2 of 2003) at para.14. This obligation was previously contained in para.57A of the Underwriting Agents Byelaw, No.4 of 1984 as amended.
[80] Underwriting Byelway (No.2 of 2003) para.14.

syndicate writes excess of loss business, its underwriter will need to know the aggregates.[81] Having calculated his aggregates the underwriter should then identify an appropriate event as the source of the PML. The catastrophe chosen should be remote, but nevertheless a practical possibility.[82] If the underwriter chooses one such event rather than another without having any good reason for believing that the PML which might result from the former would be lower than that which might result from the latter, the underwriter will be in breach of duty.[83]

19–045   Having identified an appropriate event, the underwriter should proceed to calculate its potential impact. That involves a difficult exercise of judgment by the underwriter. In *Deeny v Gooda Walker Ltd*.[84] Phillips J. described the task of the underwriter as follows:

> "To calculate his exposure to a single event he needs to know how many of the covers that he has written are exposed to the risk of a claim should that event occur. He thus has to divide into different categories the covers that can aggregate. In practice this is normally done by a system of coding the different aggregates. The more carefully the business is recorded under appropriately chosen codes the more confident the underwriter will be able to be as to the limit of his exposure to a single event. As I have already said there will be some categories where it is unlikely, or indeed inconceivable, that a single event will result in a claim on every cover. In respect of those categories the true exposure will be, not the aggregate, but the PML. The estimation of PML has to be made by the application of judgment to the data available."

An underwriter should therefore maintain sufficient data to enable him to make a reasonable estimate of his syndicate's PML. If he fails to do so, he will be in breach of duty.[85]

19–046   If an underwriter has sufficient data, he must bring reasonable skill and care to the task of assessing it.[86] Thus in *Deeny v Gooda Walker Ltd*[87] one underwriter

---

[81] *Deeny v Gooda Walker Ltd* [1996] L.R.L.R. 183 at 198; *Wynniatt-Husey v RJ Bromley (Underwriting Agencies) Plc* [1996] L.R.L.R. 310 at 320.

[82] "An underwriter is not to be criticised for preferring to take one sensible event as opposed to another, or for excluding some events (which might be described as cataclysmic) as being so massive and so destructive as to destroy the world wide insurance market" (Morrison J. in *Berriman (Sir David) v Rose Thomson Young (Underwriting) Ltd* [1996] L.R.L.R. 426 at 442).

[83] *Arbuthnott v Feltrim Underwriting Agencies Ltd* [1995] C.L.C. 437 at 476: underwriter decided not to use an earthquake as the relevant catastrophe, because he lacked adequate data to put a realistic figure on the PML which an earthquake might cause. However, his alternative choice of a windstorm was unsatisfactory, because an earthquake was a practical possibility and there was no basis for concluding that its consequences would be less than those of a windstorm. Generally, however, the choice of an appropriate catastrophe should be relatively straightforward: *Wynniatt-Husey v RJ Bromley (Underwriting Agencies) Plc* [1996] L.R.L.R. 310 at 320.

[84] [1996] L.R.L.R. 182 at 198.

[85] *Deeny v Gooda Walker Ltd* [1996] L.R.L.R. 183 at 218: business coded to assess profitability, not to allow aggregates or PML to be calculated: held to have been negligent. See also *Wynniatt-Husey v RJ Bromley (Underwriting Agencies) Plc* [1996] L.R.L.R. 310 (where the coding system adopted by the underwriter was defective) and *Berriman (Sir David) v Rose Thomson Young (Underwriting) Ltd* [1996] L.R.L.R. 426.

[86] "The calculation of the PML amount will involve judgment. And an underwriter is not to be criticised for making a calculation of the PML amount merely because others would or might have made a different calculation." (*per* Morrison J. in *Berriman (Sir David) v Rose Thomson Young (Underwriting) Ltd* [1996] L.R.L.R. 426 at 442–443).

[87] [1996] L.R.L.R. 182.

claimed to have applied a PML of 15 per cent to whole account reinsurance.[88] Phillips J. held that he had not made any attempt to calculate his syndicate's PML in that way, but that, if he had, he would have been negligent in applying such a low percentage to risks which included a substantial amount of spiral business.[89] Detailed critiques of the assessments of other underwriters have been made in other cases.[90] An underwriter who fails altogether to estimate his syndicate's PML is negligent[91] as is an underwriter who discounts the PML on the basis that it is unlikely to occur.[92]

Level of reinsurance and exposure. Having established his syndicate's PML   **19–047** an underwriter can plan how much reinsurance cover he should seek to obtain[93] and what unreinsured risk should remain with the Names. At least in the context of excess of loss underwriting it is not necessarily negligent for an underwriter to plan on the basis that the Names will suffer a substantial loss on some years of account, but make a profit over a number of years. However, an underwriter who adopts such an approach should inform the Names of his decision to do so and of the scale of losses which they will be exposed from time to time.[94] There are also limits to the extent to which a reasonably competent managing agent could decide to expose the Names on its syndicates. To a certain extent that will depend upon the nature of the syndicate, but it has been held that the managing agent of a syndicate which is avowedly high risk could not reasonably decide to leave Names exposed to a loss greater than 100 per cent of stamp capacity.[95] The level of risk to which the Names could reasonably be exposed on any given syndicate is the level of exposure which those Names, properly advised by their members' agents, should have realised they were accepting by participating in that syndicate.[96]

---

[88] i.e. excess of loss cover in respect of a whole account. The account so reinsured might include excess of loss business liable to a claim by reason of an event which impacted upon the excess of loss business written directly by the syndicate. A far higher percentage was therefore appropriate.

[89] See para.19–016, above.

[90] *Arbuthnott v Feltrim Underwriting Agencies Ltd* [1995] C.L.C. 437 at 476–481, Phillips J. (two out of five allegations of negligence accepted) and 482 (assessment negligent on two grounds); *Berriman (Sir David) v Rose Thomson Young (Underwriting) Ltd* [1996] L.R.L.R. 426 (failure to include relevant aggregates was negligent; failure to include aggregation for exposure on personal stop loss policies not negligent). See also *Wynniatt-Husey v RJ Bromley (Underwriting Agencies) Plc* [1996] L.R.L.R. 310, where Langley J. had to decide what factors a reasonably competent underwriter would have applied to the various classes of business, the actual underwriter having failed to do so at all. He held that the underwriter had been negligent for failing to carry out a calculation in accordance with his findings.

[91] e.g. *Deeny v Gooda Walker Ltd* [1996] L.R.L.R. 183; *Arbuthnott v Feltrim Underwriting Agencies Ltd* [1995] C.L.C. 437; *Wynniatt-Husey v RJ Bromley (Underwriting Agencies) Plc* [1996] L.R.L.R. 310.

[92] *Berriman (Sir David) v Rose Thomson Young (Underwriting) Ltd* [1996] L.R.L.R. 426.

[93] As to which see paras 19–053 to 19–059, below.

[94] *Deeny v Gooda Walker Ltd* [1996] L.R.L.R. 183 at 197; *Arbuthnott v Feltrim Underwriting Agencies Ltd* [1995] C.L.C. 437 at 484.

[95] *Arbuthnott v Feltrim Underwriting Agencies Ltd* [1995] C.L.C. 437 at 484–489. Stamp capacity is the amount of net premium which a syndicate is allowed to receive in a year of account.

[96] *Wynniatt-Husey v RJ Bromley (Underwriting Agencies) Plc* [1996] L.R.L.R. 310, at 332. The syndicate in that case was presented as a medium risk/medium reward syndicate and Langley J. concluded that the greatest level of exposure to which the Names should have been exposed was 50% (*ibid.*, at 336). See also *Berriman (Sir David) v Rose Thomson Young (Underwriting) Ltd* [1996] L.R.L.R. 426 (40%).

19–048   If an underwriter does warn of the risk of losses in certain circumstances, he will still be in breach of duty if his approach to underwriting in fact exposes his Names to greater risks, either in terms of their financial exposure to a single event or by reference to the type of event or scale of loss which would exhaust the syndicate's reinsurance programme. Thus in *Deeny v Gooda Walker Ltd*[97] the active underwriter of one syndicate stated in a report to his Names that a loss of 200 per cent of the amount allocated to the syndicate might be suffered. He believed that only the most severe catastrophe would lead to such a loss. That belief was unsound and had he carried out a proper calculation of aggregates and PML he would have known better. Phillips J. held that he had been negligent.

19–049   Assessment of PML, reinsurance cover and exposure to be retained within the syndicate is only part of the plan which a reasonably competent underwriter should make. He should also project the premium which he will receive and the premium he intends to pay for reinsurance.

19–050   **LMX market.** The need for and adequacy of a managing agent's plans has been considered in the context of excess of loss underwriting and, in particular, the LMX market.[98] An underwriter who is writing XL business should formulate and follow a plan as to the extent to which Names are to be exposed to the risk of unreinsured loss.[99] If he does not do so at all, he will be negligent.

(c) *Managing Agent—Unjustified Departure from Plan*

19–051   The Underwriting Byelaw provides that a managing agent shall only underwrite in accordance with its business plan.[1] However, a managing agent may at any time submit a request to the Franchise Board to amend the business plan.[2] An underwriter should have regard to his plan throughout the year of account and, if circumstances change, consider what changes, if any, should be made to his policy to take account of those changes. For example, if it appears that the target aggregate exposure in a particular area will be exceeded if further business is written, then either the underwriter should cease to accept new business or he should obtain an appropriate increase in reinsurance protection.[3] In *Arbuthnott v Feltrim Underwriting Agencies Ltd*[4] one underwriter departed materially from

---

[97] [1996] L.R.L.R. 183.
[98] See para.19–016, above. The decisions discussed in the following paragraphs all concerned XL business.
[99] *Deeny v Gooda Walker Ltd* [1996] L.R.L.R. 183 at 198; *Arbuthnott v Feltrim Underwriting Agencies Ltd* [1995] C.L.C. 437, at 444–445; *Wynniatt-Husey v RJ Bromley (Underwriting Agencies) Plc* [1996] L.R.L.R. 310, at 320–321.
[1] Underwriting Byelaw (No.2 of 2003) para.25.
[2] Underwriting Byelaw (No.2 of 2003) para.15.
[3] *Arbuthnott v Feltrim Underwriting Agencies Ltd* [1995] C.L.C. 436 at 462, *per* Phillips J. See also *Wynniatt-Husey v RJ Bromley (Underwriting Agencies) Plc* [1996] L.R.L.R. 310 at 332, *per* Langley J.: "I am quite satisfied on the evidence that a prudent underwriter should have kept under regular review the aggregates he was writing or being asked to write relative to the level of protection he had acquired. By regular review I mean that he should have had in mind *at all times* what his protections and aggregates were and ensured that there was sufficient level of cover to match his PML less only the risk of loss to which it was appropriate to expose his Names."
[4] *ibid.*

his planned aggregate exposure. He advanced several possible commercial reasons to justify this departure. Phillips J. rejected them: the effect of the underwriter's decision had been to increase the exposure of the names by some US$28 million, when they were already overexposed.[5]

(d) *Managing Agent—Failure to Obtain Adequate Reinsurance*

An adequate programme of reinsurance is an important means of minimising the **19-052** Names' exposure to loss. The Code for Managing Agents: Managing Underwriting Risk provides that each syndicate should maintain written guidelines for the purchase and monitoring of reinsurance, and states that any reinsurance programme should be monitored on a regular basis to ensure that it continues to provide an appropriate level of protection. Underwriters must exercise reasonable skill and care when deciding what reinsurance to seek and in trying to obtain it. This involves the following:

 (i) determining what reinsurance cover to seek to obtain;

 (ii) nominating the reinsurers from whom that reinsurance is to be sought or approving the choice of reinsurers made by brokers for them;

 (iii) ensuring that the rate at which reinsurance is obtained is commercial, so that the syndicate has a reasonable prospect of making a profit;

 (iv) trying to ensure that the reinsurance is valid and not liable to be avoided for non-disclosure or misrepresentation.

Each of those tasks will be considered in turn.

(i) *Deciding What Reinsurance Cover to Seek*

The underwriter must decide what amount of "vertical" and "horizontal" cover **19-053** should be acquired. The amount of "vertical" protection is the amount of cover for a single loss or aggregation of losses. The amount of "horizontal" protection is the number of losses at a particular level which will be covered, usually the number of times a policy is reinstated after an initial loss.

Vertical cover. In order to make a reasonable decision as to what vertical **19-054** cover to seek an underwriter needs to know what his aggregates and PML are.[6] In the absence of that information he will be relying upon luck rather than proper professional judgment. If it transpires that he has thereby exposed his Names to a greater loss than that which he had informed them they would be exposed he will be negligent and liable for any resulting loss.[7]

---

[5] [1995] C.L.C. 436 at 480–481.

[6] As to which see paras 19–044 to 19–046, above and *Arbuthnott v Feltrim Underwriting Agencies Ltd* [1995] C.L.C. 437 at 446 and *Berriman (Sir David) v Rose Thomson Young (Underwriting) Ltd* [1996] L.R.L.R. 426.

[7] *Deeny v Gooda Walker Ltd* [1996] L.R.L.R. 183; *Arbuthnott v Feltrim Underwriting Agencies Ltd* [1995] C.L.C. 437; *Wynniatt-Husey v RJ Bromley (Underwriting Agencies) Plc* [1996] L.R.L.R. 310 at 321; *Berriman (Sir David) v Rose Thomson Young (Underwriting) Ltd* [1996] L.R.L.R. 426 at 451.

19–055   An underwriter who makes a reasonable assessment of his syndicate's PML is not required to obtain reinsurance for the entire amount so assessed. He is entitled to decide to retain a degree of net exposure.[8] This may be either above or below the reinsurance he seeks to procure, although in practice he will usually have to accept a level of retention below the reinsurance obtained. However, if he is to proceed on this basis, the underwriter should ensure that the Names are informed of his policy and of the extent of the potential exposure which they face as a result.[9]

19–056   Moreover, an underwriter's decision as to what exposure the Names on his syndicate should risk must be a reasonable one. In *Arbuthnott v Feltrim Underwriting Agencies Ltd*[10] one underwriter approached the question of exposure not on the basis of the maximum that the syndicate could afford to run, but rather by reference to the amount of reinsurance protection which it could afford to buy. Phillips J. held that his failure to address the matter from the former point of view was negligent.[11] In the same case Phillips J. also had to consider the maximum exposure to which it was reasonable to decide to expose the Names. He held that in view of the need to aim to balance losses with profits over a period of years, the highest level of exposure which a competent managing agent could decide was 100 per cent of the syndicate's stamp capacity.[12]

19–057   **Horizontal cover.** The same principles apply to an underwriter's decision as to the amount of horizontal cover to seek. Again the underwriter needs to make a reasonably informed decision and again he is not necessarily obliged to seek to obtain reinsurance which will reinstate as many times as the insurance cover he writes on behalf of his syndicate. For smaller, more frequent claims it would make little sense to try to match reinsurance cover to the underlying business written for the syndicate. However, in the context of catastrophe excess of loss business, where the potential claims are far greater in amount but far less frequent, any failure to match reinstatements must be for some good reason and, in the absence of such a reason an underwriter will be held to have been negligent.[13] A good reason for these purposes might be that an underwriter had to offer a greater number of reinstatements on the business he was writing than he could obtain at a commercial rate on the reinsurance available to him.[14] If an underwriter chooses not to match reinstatements, he will be exposing his Names to risk and should bear this in mind when considering the extent to which the Names are exposed vertically.[15]

---

[8] *Arbuthnott v Feltrim Underwriting Agencies Ltd* [1995] C.L.C. 437 at 446.
[9] *Deeny v Gooda Walker Ltd* [1996] L.R.L.R. 183 at 197–199; *Arbuthnott v Feltrim Underwriting Agencies Ltd* [1995] C.L.C. 437 at 446.
[10] [1995] C.L.C. 437.
[11] *ibid.*, at 481–482. See also *Wynniatt-Husey v RJ Bromley (Underwriting Agencies) Plc* [1996] L.R.L.R. 310 and para.19–065, below.
[12] *ibid.*, at 486–489. See also *Wynniatt-Husey v RJ Bromley (Underwriting Agencies) Plc* [1996] L.R.L.R. 310, where the syndicate should have been perceived as medium risk/medium reward and Langley J. held that the maximum exposure should have been 50% of stamp capacity.
[13] *Deeny v Gooda Walker Ltd* [1996] L.R.L.R. 183 at 191–201 and 217–218.
[14] *Berriman (Sir David) v Rose Thomson Young (Underwriting) Ltd* [1996] L.R.L.R. 426 at 469; but see paras 19–065 & 19–066, below.
[15] *ibid.*

Joint reinsurance. Where joint reinsurance protection is obtained for more **19–058**
than one syndicate, the underwriter should consider carefully the implications of
such reinsurance and the adequacy of the joint cover obtained. In *Arbuthnott v
Feltrim Underwriting Agencies Ltd*[16] one underwriter obtained a single whole
account reinsurance cover for two syndicates, one non-marine and the other
marine. If, as was perfectly possible, a single catastrophe produced claims
against both syndicates so as to exhaust both syndicates' specific reinsurance
programmes, then both would seek to rely upon the same whole-account reinsurance. The underwriter failed to consider and provide properly for this possibility,
even though the marine syndicate had written a considerable amount of non-
marine business. Phillips J. held that the underwriter should have been aware of
this risk and provided against it. He held him to have been negligent for failing
to do so.[17]

Reinsurance terms. The underwriter should also seek reinsurance on appro- **19–059**
priate terms. In *Arbuthnott v Feltrim Underwriting Agencies Ltd*[18] the Names
alleged that an underwriter had been negligent for accepting a reinsurance policy
which overvalued the US dollar against the pound sterling. Phillips J. rejected
this claim, because the underwriter reasonably acted on the basis that the
syndicate's dollar exposure was more significant than its exposure in sterling. In
the circumstances he was entitled to agree to rates which resulted in a lower
sterling excess point and a lower sterling limit of cover.[19]

(ii) *Choosing the Reinsurer*

It is not enough to identify the amount of reinsurance which is needed to afford **19–060**
reasonable protection to the Names. Unless the reinsurers who agree to provide
such reinsurance are solvent when claims come to be made the reinsurance
obtained will be worthless. Therefore, it is essential that steps are taken to assess
and monitor the solvency of reinsurers. The Code for Managing Agents: Managing Underwriting Risk states that the security of reinsurers should be monitored
as part of managing the reinsurance programme.

Reinsurance will typically be purchased through brokers instructed by the **19–061**
underwriter. Those brokers will themselves owe a duty to exercise skill and care
in the choice of reinsurer.[20] They should themselves be reasonably satisfied that
the reinsurance security they put before the underwriter is appropriate for the
type of risk being reinsured, for example if it is includes a substantial amount of
long tail business.[21] However, the brokers will have a less detailed knowledge of
the risk to be reinsured than the underwriter. In *Berriman (Sir David) v Rose
Thomson Young (Underwriting) Ltd*[22] Morrison J. described the different roles of
broker and underwriter as follows:

---

[16] [1995] C.L.C. 437.
[17] *ibid.*, at 470–474.
[18] [1995] C.L.C. 437.
[19] *ibid.*, at 475.
[20] See Ch.16, para.16–067, above.
[21] i.e. business on which claims can be expected to take a considerable time to be advised or settled.
[22] [1996] L.R.L.R. 426 at 455–466, Morrison J.

"The list of approved companies prepared by the broker was compiled for general use, although some would be more appropriate than others in some instances. But all the companies on the list would have been approved as sound, in principle. It would be quite inappropriate for a broker to maintain within that list different tiers or levels of soundness. The underwriter, on the other hand, knows better than the broker the nature of the risks which he is writing and the length of tail, if any. He will know how much risk he intends to cede, and he will have been able to evaluate the nature of those risks and the likely impact on them of foreseeable events. The roles of broker and underwriter neatly complement one another: in normal circumstances, an underwriter would be entitled to assume that the broker would only have presented him with a prospective reinsurer which the broker considered to be generally sound, and the broker can assume that a competent underwriter will make a judgment as to the appropriateness of that security having regard to his particular needs . . . The names on the brokers' list are 'off the peg', whereas the underwriter must tailor the material to meet his own special needs."

19–062   An underwriter should therefore obtain sufficient information about a proposed reinsurer to enable him to judge whether it is suitable security for the risk to be reinsured. Thus an underwriter who has no real information about a reinsurer and decides to accept it because the individual underwriter he meets seems to be "very nice" will be in breach of duty.[23] An underwriter needs to understand properly the information he obtains. It is no good being told a rating if he misinterprets it. In *Berriman (Sir David) v Rose Thomson Young (Underwriting) Ltd*[24] the brokers made it clear that they took no responsibility for the suitability of one proposed reinsurer and the underwriter misunderstood the rating of that reinsurer. Morrison J. held that he was negligent in accepting that reinsurer as security for 30 per cent of the risk being reinsured. However the underwriter was not negligent for accepting a North Korean company, which depended upon the willingness of the North Korean government to provide funds in bad years. The evidence was that the brokers regarded the company as reasonable security and, in that instance, the underwriter would have been entitled to rely upon their judgment.[25]

19–063   **Inter-syndicate reinsurance.** Because Names are members of more than one syndicate, they may find themselves, as members of one syndicate, reinsuring their own liabilities as members of another. In the final analysis they derive no benefit from such reinsurance.[26] To a certain extent that is an inevitable consequence of the structure of Lloyd's, which will depend upon the extent of the overlap between memberships of the reinsured and the reinsuring syndicates. Thus, where both syndicates are managed by the same combined agent who, in his capacity as members' agent, regularly advises Names to join both of the agency's syndicates, there will be a large overlap in membership and any inter-syndicate reinsurance will be of little benefit to the Names. In *Deeny v Gooda Walker Ltd*[27] the Names alleged that it was negligent for one of the four Gooda

---

[23] [1996] L.R.L.R. 426 at 456–460.
[24] [1996] L.R.L.R. 426.
[25] *ibid.*, at 466.
[26] Unless their line on the reinsuring syndicate is lower than that on the reinsured syndicate or the reinsured syndicate in turn reinsures part of the risk reinsured.
[27] [1996] L.R.L.R. 183.

Walker syndicates to obtain reinsurance for another, given that the majority of Names on one of the four syndicates were members of at least two of the other three. Phillips J. rejected the allegation that in those circumstances it was negligent without more to obtain inter-syndicate reinsurance, because it depended upon the consequences for the reinsured Names. Given the nature of the spiral,[28] those consequences were very hard to assess. However, he did observe that where there was a high degree of common membership it would usually make sense to avoid inter-syndicate reinsurance and that, in the context of the spiral, the fact that some reinsurance was being provided by the same Names should have reduced the comfort which the underwriter derived from his reinsurance programme.[29]

A further problem which can arise with the choice of reinsurer is where the   **19–064**
reinsurer in turn obtains cover against his liability under the reinsurance which is, either directly or through reinsurance, provided by the reinsured. The under-writers in *Deeny v Gooda Walker Ltd*[30] were alleged to have been negligent for obtaining and providing reinsurance to the same syndicates or companies. Phil-lips J. refused to hold that such reciprocal reinsurance was negligent in itself.[31]

(iii) *Maintaining Commercial Viability*

The cost of reinsurance is met by the syndicate from the premium received in   **19–065**
relation to the underlying business. A reasonably competent underwriter should therefore ensure that the relationship between the premiums received by the syndicate for accepting the risks and the premiums paid for reinsuring against claims on those risks is such that there is a reasonable prospect of making a profit. If the cost of reinsurance is so high that a profit is unlikely to be made, then he should consider whether the rates at which he is accepting business are appropriate[32] and whether he should be continuing to write business of the relevant class.[33] Thus in *Deeny v Gooda Walker Ltd*[34] one active underwriter sought to increase his syndicate's reinsurance cover following the Piper Alpha disaster. The cost was such that the excess of loss business he continued to write at low rates was "doomed to be loss making" and Phillips J. held that the losses so suffered were the result of the underwriters' incompetence.[35]

An underwriter whose reinsurance programme is based essentially upon the   **19–066**
cost of obtaining reinsurance rather than upon a proper assessment of the vertical and horizontal cover needed to obtain appropriate protection will be in breach of

---

[28] As to which see para.19–016, above.
[29] [1996] L.R.L.R. 183 at 208.
[30] [1996] L.R.L.R. 183.
[31] *ibid.*, at 208–209. See also *Berriman (Sir David) v Rose Thomson Young (Underwriting) Ltd* [1996] L.R.L.R. 426 at 457, where Morrison J. criticised the underwriter for his mistaken view that by obtaining reinsurance with a company outside the London market he would reduce the effects of the spiral: the underwriter should have realised that the reinsurer would in turn obtain cover in the London market.
[32] See paras 19–069 to 19–073, below.
[33] *Wynniatt-Husey v RJ Bromley (Underwriting Agencies) Plc* [1996] L.R.L.R. 310 at 321.
[34] [1996] L.R.L.R. 183.
[35] *ibid.*, at 217.

duty. Thus in *Arbuthnott v Feltrim Underwriting Agencies Ltd*[36] one under-writer's reinsurance programme involved obtaining as much cover as possible by spending approximately half the syndicate's gross premium income. This approach was condemned by Phillips J. as unacceptable.[37]

(iv) *Obtaining Valid Reinsurance*

19–067 As stated above,[38] the underwriter will know more about the risk to be reinsured than the broker instructed to obtain the reinsurance. Underwriters should also be aware of the duty of an insured or reinsured to make full disclosure of all material facts and not to make any misrepresentation to the reinsurer.[39] They should therefore take care that the broker is informed of all material facts and that the information they provide to the broker for presentation to the proposed reinsurers is full and accurate. In *Aiken v Stewart Wrightson Members Agency Ltd*[40] the managing agent made an unintentional but material misrepresentation to the reinsurers. They also failed to disclose their own reserves for asbestosis and diethylstilboestrol ("DES") claims, both of which were material. Potter J. held that they had thereby been negligent. He described the duty of the managing agent, Pulbrook, in these terms:

> " . . . it was the duty of Pulbrook as prudent managing agents seeking unlimited protection in respect of the whole of the account for the years up to 1979 to consider with care what required to be disclosed to a prospective reinsurer. This duty applied especially to the matters which were giving Pulbrook concern and were arguably, if not obviously, material to the prudent reinsurer, in particular the mounting claims for asbestosis and DES which were the reason why the reinsurance was being sought in the first place. Further, that duty extended to disclosure of facts which were arguably material, *so as to avoid unnecessary risk of avoidance.*"[41]

19–068 If there are "grey areas" which might require disclosure the managing agent should apply his mind to them or, if he wishes to rely upon the broker for advice, he should provide the broker with the information to enable the broker to resolve the question.[42]

(e) *Managing Agent—Negligent Underwriting of Individual Risks*

19–069 Insurance allows the risk of loss to be shared: a number of insureds pay premiums to insurers to reflect the risk of loss and the insurers use the premiums

---

[36] [1995] C.L.C. 437.

[37] *ibid.*, at 468F–H: "I do not find it negligent per se that Mr Fagan budgeted to spend not more than 50 per cent of his premium income on reinsurance. On the contrary, any competent underwriter would need to decide the maximum that he could afford to spend if the account were to remain viable. What is not satisfactory is Mr Fagan's statement that his programme was based on buying as much cover as he could for the money that he could afford to spend. The correct approach should have been to work out, on the basis of PML calculations, how much reinsurance he needed and then to calculate whether he could afford to buy it. If he could not, he should have concluded that his programme was not viable and attempted to redesign it accordingly." See also para.19–044, above.

[38] In para.19–052.

[39] See Ch.16, paras 16–069 and 16–080.

[40] [1995] 1 W.L.R. 1281; for the facts see para.19–027, above.

[41] *ibid.*, at 1313G–H; the emphasis is Potter J's. See also Ch.16, para.16–076, above.

[42] *ibid.*, at 1314A–E.

of all to meet the losses of few. The insurers should be left with sufficient to meet their expenses and to make a profit. That should be the case if the premiums required by insurers are properly rated. The decision whether to accept a risk and at what premium is a matter of professional judgment for the underwriter. In order to exercise that judgment with reasonable competence he needs:

(i) to form a reasonably informed view of the nature of the risk which he is being asked to accept on behalf of his syndicate, and

(ii) to determine and require a premium which adequately reflects that risk.

Run-off contracts. Particular difficulties arise when the proposed risk is a   **19–070**
"run-off" contract. Run-off contracts involve the reinsurance of another syndicate's or insurer's portfolio of business, so that, subject to the solvency of the reinsurer and any deductible, the reinsured is relieved of any further liability on that portfolio. The premium paid is almost invariably very substantial. However, where the underlying business contains a significant amount of long tail business,[43] particular care is needed because "no one knows the length of the tail, and tails have a habit of wagging for a very long time and wagging very vigorously".[44] The dangers inherent in underwriting such risks were the subject of the decision of Cresswell J. in *Henderson v Merrett Syndicates Ltd*.[45] That case concerned the writing of 11 run-off contracts in the late 1970s and early 1980s, a time of increasing perception of the losses which were arising and which might arise from claims relating to asbestos (both personal injury and property damage) and pollution. In respect of nine of the 11 contracts the underwriter was held to have been negligent, mainly because each "contract exposed the claimants to potentially huge liabilities, unlimited in time or amount, which were not capable of reasonable quantification on the material before [the underwriter]. There was insufficient placing or other information available at the time the risk was considered to enable a reliable assessment to be made with a reasonable degree of confidence of [the syndicate's] ultimate net retained potential liability under the contract."[46] If such contracts were to be written at all, then full details of the IBNR[47] loss reserves for both asbestos and non-asbestos related claims and of the methodology used to calculate those reserves should have been required. Underwriting involves an acceptance of risk, but the underwriter should have a reasonable perception of what that risk is, particularly where the potential liability is unlimited in time or amount.

The premium. Having obtained a reasonable understanding of the risk which   **19–071**
is being broked to him, the underwriter's next task is to consider the adequacy of the premium offered. In *Deeny v Gooda Walker Ltd*[48] Phillips J. summarised the correct approach to rating in these terms:

---

[43] i.e. business on which claims can be expected to take a considerable time to be advised or settled.
[44] Robert Kiln, *Reinsurance in Practice* (3rd edn, Witherby & Co), p.384.
[45] [1997] L.R.L.R. 265.
[46] *ibid.*, at 324.
[47] "Incurred but not reported", i.e. losses which have been suffered but not advised to the insurer.
[48] [1996] L.R.L.R. 183.

" . . . it is a fundamental principle applying to all insurance business that the underwriter must satisfy himself that the premium received is commensurate with the risk assumed. If not so satisfied he should not write the risk. This basic principle is subject to pragmatic exceptions. Sometimes it will be politic to accept an unattractive risk as a loss leader to a broker who has more attractive business in his gift. The majority of business written tends to be renewal business. Such business, once rejected will find another home and not return. This again may justify the short term expedient of accepting a risk at an unattractive rate."[49]

19–072   Four elements make up an adequate premium: the basic risk premium, a loading for random fluctuations, a loading for administrative expenses and brokerage and a loading for profit. Generally an underwriter can and should rely upon past experience of the market in general and of his own syndicate in particular.[50]

19–073   That task is more difficult when the risk being insured is catastrophe excess of loss business. It is in the nature of such cover that losses will usually be infrequent and irregular. Moreover, the degree of risk will depend upon the nature of the insured's exposure to loss from a single event or aggregation of events. Historic experience is therefore not a useful guide. The correct approach is for the underwriter to consider the type and level of event which would result in a claim on such cover and the likelihood of such an event. That would involve a high degree of judgment rather than mathematical precision, but if not attempted at all the underwriter would have no proper basis at all for agreeing a premium and so be negligent.[51] The information which the underwriter needs is essentially the same as that required for a proper calculation of PML.[52] An underwriter who underwrites high layers of excess of loss business at low rates on the basis that no claims will be made will be negligent: he should derive no comfort from the claims history of such business and ignores the fact that protection is being sought by those he is reinsuring.[53] Nor should a reasonably competent underwriter accept such business at whatever rate was offered simply on the basis of recent claims history.[54]

(f) Managing Agent—Inadequate Supervision of Active Underwriter

19–074   While the acts and omissions of the active underwriter are inevitably the primary source of findings of liability against managing agents, it is the managing agents and not the underwriters who contract to carry out the underwriting. The active underwriters are their employees, but they are not just entitled to leave them to run their syndicates on their own. While an allegation of lack of supervision of the active underwriter will generally cause no loss unless the underwriter himself

---

[49] [1996] L.R.L.R. 183 at 201. See also *Arbuthnott v Feltrim Underwriting Agencies Ltd* [1995] C.L.C. 437 at 444B–E, *per* Phillips J. for a discussion of the particular problems of rating excess of loss business at Lloyd's.

[50] *ibid.*, at 201.

[51] *Deeny v Gooda Walker Ltd* [1996] L.R.L.R. 183 at 202.

[52] See paras 19–044 to 19–046, above.

[53] *Deeny v Gooda Walker Ltd* [1996] L.R.L.R. 183 at 212.

[54] *ibid.*, at 215–216. However, it is extremely hard to show that an underwriter should have decided to cease to write business at all: *ibid.*, at 216.

has also been negligent,[55] the board of a managing agency has a separate duty to consider and approve the active underwriter's underwriting policy and to monitor its implementation.[56] The Code for Managing Agents: Managing Underwriting Risk provides that the performance of the active underwriter should be reviewed. The review should consider whether the business written is in line with the business plan, whether the realistic disaster scenarios remain appropriate, whether the level of reinsurance cover and reserving levels will remain adequate, and whether the syndicates cashflows will be sufficient to meet ongoing liabilities. It is not sufficient for the board of the managing agent to rely upon the underwriter's assurance that all is well.[57] The board should therefore possess sufficient expertise to analyse and question the approach of the active underwriter.[58]

(g) *Managing Agent—Negligence in Relation to Reinsurance to Close*

The decision as to whether to effect reinsurance to close[59] and on what terms, is one of the most important functions of a managing agent. Once effected it is final and there is no means of adjusting the rights between the parties.[60] If the managing agent also manages the reinsuring syndicate he must act equitably between the Names on the syndicate which is to be closed and the Names on that which is to reinsure them. The managing agent should therefore only effect reinsurance to close between succeeding years of the same syndicate if he is in a position to form a reasonable judgment as to the liabilities which are to be reinsured. That involves considering the likely level of claims, because that is a critical ingredient of the premium. For these purposes there are two classes of claim: those known to be outstanding and those incurred[61] but not reported. Assessment of the latter can never be certain and requires the exercise of judgment by the underwriter. A reasonable projection can usually be made on the basis of past experience and the knowledge of the underlying business to be reinsured. However, if the underwriter is unable to arrive at a reasonably accurate assessment of the appropriate premium, he should leave the year open.

In *Henderson v Merrett Syndicates Ltd*[62] the portfolios of the relevant syndicates contained not only a large account of business which was likely to give rise to asbestos and pollution-related claims but also 11 run-off contracts which also

19–075

19–076

---

[55] *Deeny v Gooda Walker Ltd* [1996] L.R.L.R. 183 at 186–190; *Wynniatt-Husey v RJ Bromley (Underwriting Agencies) Plc* [1996] L.R.L.R. 310 at 319.
[56] *Arbuthnott v Feltrim Underwriting Agencies Ltd* [1995] C.L.C. 437 at 483; *Berriman (Sir David) v Rose Thomson Young (Underwriting) Ltd* [1996] L.R.L.R. 426 at 454–455.
[57] *ibid.*, at 483–484.
[58] *Wynniatt-Husey v RJ Bromley (Underwriting Agencies) Plc* [1996] L.R.L.R. 310 at 319. The Code for Managing Agents: Managing Underwriting Risk sets out the key characteristics required of whoever is to review the active underwriter's conduct, including independence from the day to day operations of the syndicate, relevant experience and skills, and the status, authority and independence to challenge the active underwriter and, where necessary, the tenacity to follow up any concerns to a satisfactory conclusion.
[59] See para.19–027, above.
[60] *Henderson v Merrett Syndicates Ltd (No.2)* [1997] L.R.L.R. 265, Cresswell J.
[61] i.e. claims to be made on policies already written.
[62] [1997] L.R.L.R. 265, Cresswell J.

included significant amounts of such business.[63] The underwriter effected rein-surance to close over a period of years when it was increasingly known that the level of such claims was likely to be substantial, but when it was not clear how high it might be. He was sued on the basis that he should not have effected such reinsurance at all.[64] Cresswell J. rejected that allegation in respect of the first three years in question. However in later years there were significant areas of uncertainty, as more of the 11 run-off contracts formed part of the underlying portfolio and as the potential scale of asbestos and pollution claims became clearer. By the fourth year there were fundamental uncertainties as to the future development of asbestos claims (both personal injury and property damage) and pollution claims. Those uncertainties were compounded by the run-off contracts. The underwriter failed to make sufficient enquiries as to the likely exposure, either on the syndicate's own direct business or under the run-off contracts. He was therefore held to have been negligent.

4. Damages

19–077 An award of damages is the usual ultimate remedy against members' and managing agents. However, because of the uncertain and continuing extent of the liabilities to which Names may become exposed as a result of breaches of duty by their members' and managing agents, declarations that the Names are entitled to be indemnified against certain types of loss in the future may also be obtained in appropriate cases.[65] The scope of any such indemnity should, however, be the same as that of any award of damages made after the true extent of the relevant liabilities had become known. The question of abatement of the members' or managing agents' fees to reflect their defective discharge of their duties[66] has not been the subject of significant judicial decision.

(a) Remoteness

19–078 It is not enough for a Name to show that his members' or managing agent was negligent and that he suffered losses in the relevant year of account of the syndicate in question. He must show that the losses of which he complains were sufficiently related to the breach of duty which he has proved. To do so he must show that (a) the losses were "caused" by that breach of duty,[67] and (b) the loss and damage was reasonably foreseeable.[68]

(b) Causation

19–079 In order to recover damages for a particular loss, a Name must show that there was a sufficient causal link between that loss and the breach of duty (whether

---

[63] As to which see para.19–070, above.
[64] An allegation that the premium should have been higher would have been of little use to the claimants, given the enormous scale of the losses eventually suffered.
[65] The courts have also awarded damages on an interim basis.
[66] See Ch.3, paras 3–008 et seq.
[67] As to which see paras 19–079 to 19–087, below.
[68] As to which see para.19–088, below.

contractual or tortious) which he has established. This has proved to be a fruitful area for arguments both by Names and on behalf of members' and managing agents. In response the courts have adopted a pragmatic approach rather than embarking upon any overly technical and precise exercise, which would have increased costs but not produced a materially different result.

(i) *Members' Agents—Consequences of Failure to Advise Adequately as to Syndicate Participation*

As a result of the shortcomings of his members' agent, a Name may receive inadequate advice as to which syndicates he should join and as to the extent to which he should participate in them. Those syndicates may then suffer losses in the relevant years and the Name may seek damages to the extent that they do. The following arguments have arisen in that context:

19–080

   (i) The Name would have joined the same syndicates even if properly advised.

  (ii) The Name would have joined other syndicates which would have made losses.

 (iii) There was an insufficient causal link between the losses which the Name suffered on the syndicate and the inadequate advice given by the members' agent.

It is for the Name to show that he would have acted differently, but for the members' agent to show that he would have joined other, loss-making syndicates or that the losses were caused by some intervening event.

The Name must show that he would have acted differently had he received correct advice and that, had he so acted, he would have avoided or reduced his losses. The question as to what difference proper advice would have been made is to be approached on the basis that the Name should have received all that advice which a reasonably competent members' agent would have given. Thus if a Name appreciates that certain types of syndicate are higher risk than others and shows a predilection for membership of such syndicates, he is nevertheless entitled to advice as to the proper balance of his portfolio. If he does not receive such advice and is able to satisfy the court that he would have acted upon it, at least to a certain extent, then he will be entitled to damages accordingly.[69]

19–081

On the other hand, a Name who should not have been placed on a high risk syndicate should not give credit for the average loss suffered by Lloyd's syndicates in the relevant year of account. That average would include high risk syndicates and it would be hard to show that the Name would have suffered a loss, albeit smaller, because he would have joined some other, unspecified syndicate had he been correctly advised.[70] It might be different if a specific alternative syndicate had been considered at the time the Name was being advised.

19–082

---

[69] *Brown v KMR Services Ltd* [1995] 4 All E.R. 598, CA; varying [1994] 4 All E.R. 385 (*Brown's Case*).

[70] *Brown v KMR Services Ltd* [1994] 4 All E.R. 385 at 399g–400a, *per* Gatehouse J. (*Sword-Daniels' Case*, which was not the subject of appeal).

19–083   In *Brown v KMR Services Ltd*[71] the members' agent sought to argue that the breach of duty which resulted in Mr Sword-Daniels being on certain syndicates was the occasion for the loss rather than the effective cause of the loss.[72] This argument was rejected on the facts: Mr Sword-Daniels had been placed on high risk syndicates, i.e. syndicates with a high risk of high losses. The members' agent had not argued that the managing agents of those syndicates had conducted the underwriting negligently and that that negligence broke the chain of causation. Such a plea would not have been of avail, because the members' agent was contractually liable for any want of care by the managing agent.[73]

(ii) *Losses Caused by Negligent Underwriting*

19–084   Where underwriting has been carried out negligently, it does not follow that the Names are entitled to recover all losses suffered as members of the syndicate for the relevant year of account. They are entitled only to recover damages for the losses which were actually caused by the negligent acts or omissions of the underwriter. If, for example, the underwriter was at fault as to the amount of "vertical" reinsurance he obtained,[74] the Names could not recover all their losses, some of which would relate to business underwritten in earlier years or arise from lack of "horizontal" reinsurance cover.[75] Moreover, proof of negligent underwriting in one respect will not lead to the drawing of the inference that the underwriter was negligent in other respects so as to circumvent the need to show a sufficient causal link.[76] Nor is it possible simply to compare the losses suffered by the syndicate in question with the results of a hypothetical syndicate writing similar business in a competent manner: that would be an "artificial and unrealistic exercise".[77]

19–085   The fact that the consequences of negligent underwriting of catastrophe business have been exacerbated by a concatenation of catastrophes does not give rise to a defence of causation. There is nothing in the occurrence of catastrophes to break the chain of causation, because they are by their nature random events.[78] However, if they are such as to have caused losses to syndicates whose underwriters had not been negligent, then an appropriate reduction in damages should be made.[79]

19–086   Different considerations apply where an underwriter has negligently obtained reinsurance with reinsurers who are unlikely to be good security for the risk reinsured and, on the strength of that reinsurance, has underwritten business upon which losses have subsequently been suffered. In those circumstances there is no sufficient link between the total losses on the loss-making business underwritten

---

[71] [1994] 4 All E.R. 385 (*Sword-Daniel's Case*, which was not subject to appeal); for the facts see para.19–040, above.

[72] The argument relied upon, inter alia, *Galoo Ltd v Bright Grahame Murray (a firm)* [1994] 1 W.L.R. 1360, as to which see Ch.17, paras 17–064 *et seq.*

[73] [1994] 4 All E.R. 385 at 398a–g and [1995] 4 All E.R. 598 at 643g. Under the present regime the members' agent may well be in a better position: see para.19–009.

[74] See para.19–054, above.

[75] *Deeny v Gooda Walker Ltd* [1996] L.R.L.R. 183 at 224–225.

[76] *ibid.*, at 227–228.

[77] *ibid.*, at 228.

[78] *Wynniatt-Husey v RJ Bromley (Underwriting Agencies) Plc* [1996] L.R.L.R. 310 at 314.

[79] *Deeny v Gooda Walker Ltd* [1996] L.R.L.R. 183 at 225–227.

and the inadequate reinsurance. The Names are entitled to damages only for that part of their total losses which was ineffectively reinsured with inappropriate reinsurers.[80]

Where the negligence consists of failure to make full disclosure to reinsurers   **19–087** or in making a misrepresentation to reinsurers,[81] it might be argued that, had the potential reinsurers been given full and accurate information no reinsurance could have been obtained. Similar issues have arisen in the context of claims against insurance brokers.[82] Save in extreme cases the courts are unlikely to adopt an "all or nothing" approach. Rather, they are likely to approach the question on the basis of loss of a chance or, if there is sufficiently clear evidence, to hold that reinsurance would have been obtained, either at the same or a higher premium.[83]

(c) *Foreseeability*

In cases against members' agents for negligent advice and against both members'   **19–088** agents and managing agents for negligent underwriting defendants have sought to argue that losses caused by one or more catastrophes were not reasonably foreseeable. In the context of catastrophe XL business[84] such a plea is unsustainable: the risk being underwritten is loss caused by one or more catastrophes and if negligent advice or underwriting exposes a Name unduly to the risk of such losses, those who so exposed him cannot be heard to say that the losses were not reasonably foreseeable.[85] As against members' agents who negligently place their Names on syndicates writing catastrophe XL business, loss caused by catastrophes should have been foreseeable, even if its extent was not.[86]

(d) *Measure of Damages*

In both contract and tort, damages are awarded to compensate the injured party   **19–089** for the wrong he has suffered. The award of damages is calculated so far as possible to put him in the position in which he would have been had his legal right not been invaded.[87] The principle is easily stated. Its strict application would present serious practical difficulties in claims against members' and managing agents and has led the courts to adopt a pragmatic approach to the calculation of some losses.

---

[80] *Berriman (Sir David) v Rose Thomson Young (Underwriting) Ltd* [1996] L.R.L.R. 426 at 485.
[81] See para.19–067, above.
[82] See Ch.16, at para.16–129.
[83] *Aiken v Stewart Wrightson Members Agency Ltd* [1995] 1 W.L.R. 1281, reported in summary only on this point.
[84] See para.19–016, above.
[85] *Arbuthnott v Feltrim Underwriting Agencies Ltd* [1995] C.L.C. 437 at 491H–492B.
[86] *Brown v KMR Services Ltd* [1994] 4 All E.R. 385 at 398j–299a, Gatehouse J.; [1995] 4 All E.R. 598 at 630f–621j; Stuart-Smith L.J. and 641j–643h, Hobhouse L.J.
[87] *The Albazero* [1977] A.C. 744 at 841, *per* Lord Diplock, cited in *Deeny v Gooda Walker Ltd* [1996] L.R.L.R. 183 by Phillips J. at 229.

(i) *Members' Agents—Consequences of Failure to Advise Adequately as to Syndicate Participation*

19–090   Subject to questions of causation[88] a Name who suffers losses on a syndicate which he would not have joined had he been properly advised, is entitled to damages equivalent to his losses on that syndicate.[89]

19–091   The Name may have been advised by his members' agent to take out stop-loss insurance as part of his overall underwriting philosophy. If he did so and thereby mitigated his losses it might be thought that, as against the members' agent who advised him to obtain that insurance, the Name should give credit for sums so recovered. However, in *Brown v KMR Services Ltd*[90] that argument was rejected. Gatehouse J. followed a well-established line of authority that a contract of insurance was to be regarded as *res inter alios acta* and so disregarded for the purposes of assessing damages.[91] Although a Name is bound to account to his stop loss insurers if he recovers damages for losses caused by negligent underwriting for which he has already been compensated by those insurers,[92] so that credit should not be given where the breach of duty relates to negligent underwriting,[93] it is hard to see why a members' agent sued for negligent advice as to a Name's underwriting philosophy should not be entitled to a credit for recoveries which were made as a result of that same advice.

19–092   A Name may participate in a syndicate for a number of years as a result of negligent advice from his members' agent. He may make a profit on some years followed by a loss on others. However, the Name need not give credit for those earlier profits when claiming damages for the later losses: he was entitled to proper advice in respect of each year and had a separate cause of action for each year.[94]

19–093   A Name who makes an underwriting loss will be able to claim tax relief for that loss. However, no credit should be given by reason of such relief. This is because the damages recovered by the Name will themselves be subject to tax.[95]

(ii) *Losses Caused by Negligent Underwriting*

19–094   Where the underwriter negligently fails to obtain adequate "vertical" reinsurance[96] and his Names suffer serious losses as a result of one or more catastrophes, the correct measure of loss may be difficult to establish in practice. Difficult questions as to the effect of catastrophic and other less serious losses on the complicated reinsurance programmes which Lloyd's syndicates have and as to the problems in practice which the underwriter would have had in obtaining sufficient reinsurance cover might arise. It is not practicable to seek to unravel or

---

[88] See para.19–079, above.
[89] *Brown v KMR Services Ltd* [1994] 4 All E.R. 385, Gatehouse J.; [1995] 4 All E.R. 598, CA. For the facts see para.19–040, above.
[90] [1994] 4 All E.R. 385 (not subject to appeal on this point).
[91] *Bradburn v Great Western Railway Co* (1874) L.R. 10 Exch. 1; *Parry v Cleaver* [1970] A.C. 1.
[92] *Napier and Ettrick (Lord) v Hunter* [1993] A.C. 713.
[93] See para.19–098, below.
[94] *Brown v KMR Services Ltd* [1995] 4 All E.R. 585 at 640c–641j, *per* Hobhouse L.J., with whom Peter Gibson L.J. agreed.
[95] *Deeny v Gooda Walker Ltd (No.2)* [1996] 1 W.L.R. 426, HL.
[96] See para.19–054, above.

to rewrite an entire year's business. The courts have adopted a pragmatic, but broadly just, approach.

The starting point is to establish the PML.[97] The next stage is to establish the **19–095** extent to which a reasonably competent underwriter could have decided to expose his Names to the risk of loss in the event of the PML. That will depend upon the information as to the syndicate's approach to underwriting which the Names should have known, either directly or through their members' agent.[98] The next stage is to compare the vertical reinsurance cover actually obtained with that which should have been obtained (on the assumption that it could have been obtained). That reinsurance should have left the Names' exposed to the permitted extent only when it was exhausted and not at any lower level. Then the cost of such reinsurance should be estimated and credit given for it.[99] Finally the unreinsured losses which would have been reinsured need to be established.[1] Those losses, subject to credit for the notional reinsurance premiums, represent the basic measure of loss.[2]

That general approach has been refined in a number of respects, some of them **19–096** extremely technical.[3] To the extent that Names fail to establish that it was incompetent deliberately to choose to retain exposure at low layers, losses resulting from that decision are not recoverable.[4] Where the underwriter instructed brokers to seek reinsurance but they were unable to obtain it, then the Names cannot complain of the underwriter's acts or recover damages for the lack of such reinsurance from those liable for his acts.[5] Where no allegation of negligence leading to any lack of "horizontal" reinsurance cover is established, damages should be reduced to allow for the reduction of the reinsurance cover which should have been obtained by a series of minor losses.[6] On the other hand, the allowance for deliberate exposure should be treated as being above the reinsurance cover which should have been obtained, not below it or in the middle of it.[7] Unless and to the extent that it is shown that the reinsurance strategy of the underwriter was negligent, the additional notional cover should be on the same

---

[97] See para.19–044, above.

[98] See para.19–047, above.

[99] This may be an essentially theoretical exercise, if such reinsurance would have been hard or impossible to obtain. However, the alternative approach (on the basis that the underwriter should have ceased to accept risks in the absence of adequate reinsurance) involves a complex and impracticable exercise which should lead to the same result: see the comments of Phillips J. in *Deeny v Gooda Walker Ltd* [1996] L.R.L.R. 183 at 230.

[1] Thus damages will not be recoverable for losses which exceed a competently calculated PML.

[2] See *Deeny v Deeny Walker* [1996] L.R.L.R. 183; *Arbuthnott v Feltrim Underwriting Agencies Ltd* [1995] C.L.C. 437, *Arbuthnott v Feltrim Underwriting Agencies Ltd (No.2)* [1995] C.L.C. 1550; *Arbuthnott v Feltrim Underwriting Agencies Ltd (No.3)* [1996] C.L.C. 714; *Berriman (Sir David) v Rose Thomson Young (Underwriting) Ltd* [1996] L.R.L.R. 426.

[3] See, for example, *Arbuthnott v Feltrim Underwriting Agencies Ltd (No.3)* [1996] C.L.C. 714, where Longmore J. had to decide a sequence of detailed issues as to the assessment of damages.

[4] *Deeny v Gooda Walker Ltd* [1996] L.R.L.R. 183 at 230.

[5] *ibid.* Unless they could show that the underwriter was negligent to continue to accept business given the unavailability of the reinsurance he had sought to obtain.

[6] *ibid.*

[7] *Arbuthnott v Feltrim Underwriting Agencies Ltd (No.2)* [1995] C.L.C. 1550, at 1551–1552, *per* Phillips J.

basis as that actually obtained, both as to type of cover and as to any co-insurance[8] reasonably made by the underwriter. Credit should be given for the the losses which would have been retained as a consequence of that strategy.[9] Where, as a result of the underwriter's reasonable decision to obtain reinsurance cover which undervalued one currency[10] as opposed to another, the Names are entitled to recover damages in the undervalued currency on the basis of the reinsurance obtained and not at some other rate.[11]

19–097   Where reinsurance cover is successfully avoided or fails to respond to claims as a result of the underwriter's negligence then the basic measure of loss is the sum which would have been recovered from such reinsurance.[12] If the court concludes that reinsurers would have required a higher premium had they been fully informed, then credit should be given for the additional premium.[13]

19–098   As in claims against members' agents for failure to give proper advice, credit need not be given for recoveries made by Names on stop loss insurance,[14] for profits on earlier years,[15] or for tax relief on losses.[16]

19–099   Apart from the basic measures of loss set out above, Names may also be able to recover consequential losses. For example, where a syndicate goes into run-off[17] as a result of losses caused by the underwriter's negligence, each Name on that syndicate will incur a share of the costs of that run-off which otherwise would have been borne by the syndicate into which the open year was reinsured to close. Such costs are recoverable.[18] If a Name's personal expenses at Lloyd's are increased as a result, damages may be recovered for the increase.[19] The same is true of losses caused by the effect of movements of exchange rates on losses caused by the underwriter's negligence.[20]

---

[8] i.e. a retention of a percentage of the risk reinsured.

[9] *Arbuthnott v Feltrim Underwriting Agencies Ltd (No.2)* [1995] C.L.C. 1550 at 1552–1553, *per* Phillips J.

[10] See para.19–059, above.

[11] *Arbuthnott v Feltrim Underwriting Agencies Ltd (No.3)* [1996] C.L.C. 714, 717, *per* Longmore J.

[12] Unless the court proceeds on the basis of "loss of a chance", as to which see para.19–087, above.

[13] *Aiken v Stewart Wrightson Members Agency Ltd* [1995] 1 W.L.R. 1281.

[14] See para.19–091, above and *Deeny v Gooda Walker Ltd* [1996] L.R.L.R. 183 at 231; *Arbuthnott v Feltrim Underwriting Agencies Ltd* [1995] C.L.C. 437 at 492. It follows that Names who failed to take out stop loss insurance are not precluded from recovering damages for losses which would have been recovered from such insurance.

[15] See para.19–092, above and *Arbuthnott v Feltrim Underwriting Agencies Ltd* [1995] C.L.C. 437 at 492.

[16] See para.19–093, above.

[17] i.e. where there is no reinsurance to close so that the syndicate is left open.

[18] *Deeny v Gooda Walker Ltd* [1996] L.R.L.R. 183 at 231.

[19] *ibid.*

[20] *ibid.*

CHAPTER 20

INFORMATION TECHNOLOGY PROFESSIONALS

1. GENERAL

This chapter considers the professional liability of providers of information technology services.[1] The principal services considered are the supply, develop-   **20–001**

---

[1] Much of the chapter concerns the supply of software, which may be the subject of copyright and/or duties of confidentiality. Liability arising from breaches of copyright and/or confidence are, however,

ment and maintenance of computer systems and software. No professional body has yet been established in respect of consultants and others who provide services in these fields.[2] As yet, therefore, there is no code of conduct, regulatory framework or any other guidelines which govern the appointment or work of such consultants. However, this makes information technology professionals no less suitable for inclusion in this book than (for example) architects or engineers. The development of the legal principles governing the liability of the latter professionals is rarely influenced (at least expressly) by the fact or nature of such self-regulation. In any event, as will be seen below, in practice the absence (to date) of a recognised professional body and/or self-regulation has not deterred or hindered the courts in their adaptation of the common law to provide principles governing the duties owed by information technology professionals to their clients.

(a) Standard Software

20–002   Only brief mention is made here of the supply of standard ("off the shelf") software, since it is unlikely ever to be categorised as a supply of services,[3] and therefore falls outside the scope of this chapter.[4] When a standard software package is sold this is invariably on a medium such as a compact disc,[5] in which case the agreement to supply the "CD" is a contract for the sale (or, depending on its terms, the hire) of goods. Whether the goods can be regarded as also including the software on the CD, so that the statutory implied warranties of satisfactory quality and fitness for purpose apply not only to the CD itself but also to the software, is a separate (and difficult) question. However, in England and Wales the answer to this question is probably yes.[6] As yet the question has only arisen directly in Scotland, where the Scottish Court of Session determined that such a contract should be treated as *sui generis*: *Beta Computers (Europe) Ltd v Adobe Systems (Europe) Ltd*.[7]

---

beyond the scope of this book, and the reader is referred to Toulson and Phipps, *Confidentiality*, and *Copinger and James on Copyright*.

[2] A kitemark offering accreditation and training was, however, launched by the British Government in 1999.

[3] Many of the reasons for this are discussed in paras 20–004 onwards, and apply here a fortiori.

[4] For a discussion of the legal issues arising from the supply of standard software, see D. Rowland and E. Macdonald, *Information Technology Law*, esp. pp.106–116.

[5] It may, however, be electronically transmitted by downloading or email, for example. If so, the question of whether the transfer can amount to a sale of goods is a still more difficult one, raising similar issues to those considered below at paras 20–005 to 20–007.

[6] This is the view expressed (obiter) by the Court of Appeal in *St Albans City and DC v International Computers Ltd*: see paras 20–014 to 20–018, below. It also accords with common sense. "Most consumers would be surprised, and rightly so, at the suggestion that the retailer from whom their software was bought guaranteed only the floppy disc and the system documentation (the handbook)— not the performance and quality of the programs recorded on it": Napier, "The future of information technology law" [1992] C.L.J. 46 at 56.

[7] [1996] F.S.R. 387. The case concerned the supply of a "shrink-wrapped" software package, i.e. software packaged so as to indicate that the software (the copyright of which belonged to a third party, I) was subject to a strict end-user licence. The pursuers sought to recover payment for the supply of the software. The defenders contended that there was an absolute right to reject the package until it was opened. Lord Penrose reasoned (at 375) that what the defenders sought to have supplied was access to I's intellectual property in a medium which they could use and from which they could copy the software onto their own hardware, in order to use it for business purposes. The subject of

Standard software of this kind is usually sold on the basis that the purchaser **20–003** is granted a conditional licence to use the software by the copyright owner, usually a "shrink wrap" licence, in which the customer agrees to licence conditions by opening the packaging to the software. However, since the owner of the copyright is invariably a third party to the contract of sale, and the packaging is generally only opened after that contract (i.e. the purchase) has been concluded, it is doubtful that in such circumstances the licence conditions are validly incorporated into the contract of sale.[8]

(b) *Bespoke and Modified Standard Software*

This chapter is instead concerned with the position where information technology **20–004** professionals contract to supply either tailor-made ("bespoke") software (i.e. software which is written for the client from scratch), or *modified* standard software. In such cases two difficult and interrelated questions arise:

(i) does such software (i.e. the program itself) represent "goods", so that a contract for its supply is capable of being treated as a traditional nominate contract for the sale of goods[9]; and

(ii) even if software is goods, is the contract for the supply of the software in fact one for the supply of goods, or instead a contract for the supply of services.

These questions are potentially important because, ordinarily, the law applies a different regime of warranties depending on whether a particular contract is for the supply of services, or for the supply of goods; namely, fault-based warranties of reasonable skill and care if the contract is for the supply of services, or strict liability warranties (of satisfactory quality and fitness for purpose) if the contract is for the supply of goods.

(c) *The Nature of Software*

The difficulties in answering these questions stem partly from the nature of **20–005** software itself. The term software is probably synonymous (at least for the purposes of this chapter) with "computer program", a convenient definition for which appears in the United States Copyright Act, at s.101: "a set of statements or instructions to be used directly or indirectly in a computer in order to bring about a particular result". On this basis, programs and software are a form of information. However, it is well established that, in general, information is not

---

the contract was thus a complex product, comprising the medium (i.e. the disk) and the manifestation on it of particular intellectual property. Lord Penrose considered that there were no true analogies to this type of product, and that the only acceptable view is that the supply of proprietary software for a price is a contract "*sui generis*".

[8] Arguably, by opening the packaging the user enters into a separate contract with the copyright owner.

[9] This first question arises equally in the case of standard software: see para.20–002, above.

property at all.[10] For this reason it has been said[11] that software, of itself, does not fall within the conventional legal definition of goods, namely the definition contained in s.61 of the Sale of Goods Act 1979, which defines goods as "including all personal chattels other than things in action and money".[12]

20–006   The difficulty is compounded by the fact that, in the case of a contract for the supply of bespoke (or modified standard) software, the subject-matter of the contract, i.e. the software itself, does not exist (at least not in the form in which it is required) at the time the contract is made.

(d) *Software as Services or Goods*

20–007   The question whether software constitutes goods has not arisen directly for decision in the English courts.[13] The Court of Appeal has, however, expressed the view, obiter, that software per se is not goods: *St Albans City and DC v International Computers Ltd.*[14] Similarly the provision of software alone is treated as the provision of services, and not goods, for the purposes of VAT[15], unless it is transmitted by a tangible medium, such as a CD, in which case it is generally treated as goods.[16] The US courts have, however, been prepared to treat software as falling within the definition of goods contained in the Uniform Commercial Code,[17] which is comparable to the definition contained in s.61 of the Sale of Goods Act 1979, even where it is transmitted independently of any tangible medium such as a CD.[18] In reaching this conclusion, the US courts appear to have been much influenced by commercial and policy considerations, including the importance of software in the commercial world, and the desirability of its supply being subject to regulation specifically devised for commercial transactions (namely, in the United States, the Uniform Commercial Code).[19] These considerations appear to apply equally in this country. Accordingly, and given that even information other than software has now become an established form of merchandise,[20] the time may well have come to recognise software as at

---

[10] *Boardman v Phipps* [1967] 2 A.C. 46, *per* Lord Upjohn at 127F.

[11] *St Albans City and DC v International Computers Ltd* [1996] 4 All E.R. 481; [1997] 1 F.S.R. 251.

[12] For a more detailed analysis of whether software represents goods, see A. Scott, "Software as goods: nullum simile est idem" [1987] Comp. Law & Practice 133.

[13] See further para.20–008, below. Nevertheless warranties corresponding to those imposed by statute will generally be imposed by the common law: see para.20–009, below.

[14] [1996] 4 All E.R. 481; [1997] 1 F.S.R. 251.

[15] "For VAT and duty purposes, all supplies of digitised products are treated as services": para 3.9.2 of VAT Notice 741 (March 2002). Para 3.9.1 of the same provision defines digitised products as "software—'off the shelf' or customised".

[16] Export of Goods, Transfer of Technology and Provision of Technical Assistance (Control) Order 2003: "goods means tangible goods, both used and unused and includes any goods on which 'software' or 'technology' is recorded".

[17] Art.2–105 of the Uniform Commercial Code defines goods as "all things (including specifically manufactured goods) which are movable at the time of identification to the contract for sale other than the money in which the price is to be paid, investment securities and things in action."

[18] *Schroders Incorporated v Hogan Systems Inc* 522 NYS 2d 404; *Communications Groups Inc v Warner Communications* Misc. 2d 80.

[19] *Advent Systems Ltd v Unisys Corp* 925 F 2d 670, US Court of Appeal, Weis J.

[20] Customer databases are frequently sold for mail-shot purposes, for example.

least being capable of representing goods and therefore subject to the whole of the Sale of Goods Act 1979.

Traditionally, the legal categorisation of a contract as one for the supply of **20-008** services or for the supply of goods is performed by applying the "substance of the contract" test: is the substance of the contract the skill and expertise to be exercised by the contractor, or its end product?[21] If this test is applied, the answer to the two questions posed at para.20-004 above will of course depend on the particular facts of each case. However, if, as the Court of Appeal has indicated,[22] the end product (i.e. the software) is no more than information, and therefore not capable of amounting to goods in the legally recognised sense, then it appears that a contract for the provision of software alone must be one for the supply of services. This reasoning and conclusion becomes unattractive, however, once it is recognised that software is very often supplied to the client on CD, in which case (as appears now to be relatively uncontroversial[23]) the CD and software together do represent goods. If A agrees to write bespoke software for B and to supply it to him on CD, then, at least in circumstances where the substance of the contract is the provision of the software itself rather than the service of writing it, the contract is one for the supply of goods. However, as matters presently stand, if A agrees to provide software by email, the contract can only be one for services, and not goods, even if the essence of the agreement is the supply of the end product: i.e. the software itself. This appears to be an unsatisfactory and artificial distinction, given that the particular mode of supply of the software may well be a matter of complete indifference to the parties themselves, and would appear to be entirely irrelevant to the appropriate categorisation of the contract as one either for the supply of goods or the supply of services. Ultimately, however, it may make little difference for the purposes of determining the potential professional liability of the software supplier, since the implied terms governing the agreement are likely to be the same in each case, as is discussed in the next section.

(e) *Implied Warranties at Common Law*

These considerations appear to have been recognised in *St Albans City and DC* **20-009** *v International Computers Ltd*,[24] in which obiter dicta of the Court of Appeal suggest that the supply of bespoke software by electronic transmission rather than on CD, although not a sale of goods within the scope of the 1979 Act, will be subject to implied terms of quality and fitness for purpose imposed by the common law.[25] However, and perhaps importantly, any apparent harshness in imposing strict liability on computer consultants in this way has been mitigated by the courts in granting latitude to computer consultants in determining what is

---

[21] See, e.g. *Robinson v Graves* [1935] 1 K.B. 584.
[22] *St Albans City and DC v International Computers Ltd* (1996) 4 All E.R. 481; [1997] 1 F.S.R. 251.
[23] See para.20-002, above, and the VAT provisions referred to in para.20-007, above.
[24] [1996] 4 All E.R. 481; [1997] 1 F.S.R. 251.
[25] See further paras 20-014 to 20-018, below.

reasonably fit for the client's purpose,[26] in allowing consultants opportunity to rectify errors emerging in their software,[27] and by requiring co-operation on the part of the client.[28]

2. Duties

(a) *Duties to Client*

(i) *Bespoke Software: Warranties of Satisfactory Quality and Fitness for Purpose*

20–010 Where a software contractor (or "software house" as they are also known) contracts for the supply not only of software but also of the hardware on which it is to be used, the contract will generally be regarded as one for the provision of an entire computer system, and thus for the sale of goods.[29] Warranties of satisfactory quality and reasonable fitness for purpose will therefore apply to the whole system, i.e. to the operation of both the hardware and software.[30]

20–011   This situation arose in the Australian case of *Toby Construction Products Ltd v Computer Bar Sales Pty Ltd*.[31] The defendant agreed to supply the claimant, by way of purchase, "the following computer hardware and software collectively referred to as 'the Equipment' ". The claimant alleged that the Equipment was deficient and brought a claim for lost profits, relying on implied conditions and warranties said to arise in the contract of purchase pursuant to statute.[32] The statutes only applied if the Equipment was "goods" within the meaning of the statutes.[33] Rogers J. determined the preliminary issue of whether the statute applied to the contract by applying the "substance of the contract" test.[34] He concluded that the substance of the contract was the sale of a total computer system, i.e. hardware and software, which, "whilst representing the fruits of much research and work, was in current jargon off the shelf, in a sense mass produced. There can be no comparison with a one off painting. Rather is the comparison with a mass produced print of a painting."[35]

---

[26] See paras 20–024 to 20–025, below.

[27] See paras 20–032 to 20–035, below.

[28] See paras 20–036 to 20–041, below.

[29] See *Toby Construction Products Ltd v Computer Bar Sales Pty Ltd*, discussed at paras 20–011 and 20–012, below; and, for an example of the same approach being taken in Canada, *Lalese Enterprises Inc v Arete Technologies Inc* (1994) 59 C.P.R. 3d 438, British Columbia Supreme Court. However, this will not necessarily be so in every case. See further *Gretton & Starkey (trading as Open Systems Design) v British Millerain Co Ltd*, unreported, July 29, 1998, H.H.J. Thornton Q.C., discussed at paras 20–023 to 20–024, below. The judge's reasoning might, in appropriate cases, apply as much to a contract for the supply of hardware and bespoke software as to hardware and standard software.

[30] Pursuant to ss.14(2) and 14(3) of the Sale of Goods Act 1979.

[31] [1983] 2 N.S.W.L.R. 48.

[32] The Sale of Goods Act 1923 and/or the Trade Practices Act 1974.

[33] The statutes each defined "goods" as "including" various specific items not relevant to the facts of the case.

[34] See *Robinson v Graves* [1935] 1 K.B. 579; para.20–008, above.

[35] At 51G.

In *Toby Construction Products Ltd v Computer Bar Sales Pty Ltd*[36] Rogers J. **20–012** specifically left open the question whether software by itself represents "goods". This issue arose in the English case of *Eurodynamic Systems v General Automation Ltd.*[37] ED specialised in the design and development of bespoke business/ technical and accounting software. GA was a computer manufacturer. In 1980 ED entered into negotiations with GA to become one of its franchisees, with a view to marketing complete computer systems. ED used a programming language known as Cobol. GA primarily used Fortran, but indicated that their systems could also be used in Cobol. In 1981 ED agreed to purchase a "Boss 2" computer system from GA and entered into a franchise agreement with it. Under the franchise agreement GA was obliged to provide, maintain and update the Boss 2 system software, such support being free for 12 months. During the first year of use of the computer system ED complained that the system software, and the technical support offered by GA, were inadequate, principally because of the limited availability of facilities in Cobol language. ED alleged that these failures represented breaches by GA of implied terms of the franchise agreement that the Boss 2 computer system would be fit for purpose and of merchantable quality. GA denied that the franchise agreement was subject to these implied terms, since (1) there was no sale of the system software, only a licence to use it and to transfer it to customers, and (2) software does not constitute goods.

Steyn J. rejected the first of these contentions, since the licence provision in the **20–013** franchise agreement could not on its own take the transaction outside the scope of the Sale of Goods Act: "Although the ideas and concepts in the software remained GA's intellectual property, the reality of the transaction is that there has been a transfer of a product."[38] However, he found the second contention to be "far more formidable".[39] Steyn J. considered that the materials placed before him[40] indicated that the problem was far more complex than realised during oral argument, and was not prepared to decide such "important issues of legal principle" without further argument. He was, however, prepared to proceed on the assumption that the implied terms were established.[41] He went on to find that although there had been no breach of any such implied terms, GA had repudiated the contract by unequivocally refusing to deal with ED's complaints regarding the system, which repudiation had been validly accepted by ED.[42] Judgment was therefore given for ED.

The issue of whether the supply of bespoke software alone is a supply of goods **20–014** or of services came before the Court of Appeal in *St Albans City and DC v International Computers Ltd.*[43] The claimant local authority engaged the defendant (ICL) to supply a computer system to be used in administering its

---

[36] [1983] 2 N.S.W.L.R. 48.
[37] Unreported, September 6, 1988, QBD, Steyn J.
[38] At 20 of the transcript. Steyn J.'s reasoning is supported in an article by Mr Graham Smith in *Reed: Computer Law* (2nd edn) at 44.
[39] At 20.
[40] He appears to have been particularly influenced by Mr Andrew Scott's article "Software as goods: nullum simile est idem" (1987) Computer Law and Practice 133.
[41] Steyn J. went on to hold (at p.22) that even if the implied terms existed ED had not established breaches of them. However, he was satisfied that GA had repudiated the contract by an unequivocal refusal to deal with the complaints raised by ED regarding the operating software.
[42] At 22–23 of the transcript.
[43] (1996) 4 All E.R. 481; [1997] F.S.R. 251.

collection of the community charge. The claimant used the system to determine the population in its area. An error in the software resulted in the figure being overstated by some 3,000. The claimant set its community charge based on that figure, and suffered significant losses as a result, which it sought to recover from ICL in an action for breach of express, alternatively implied, terms of the contract. The Court of Appeal held that ICL was in breach of an express term that it would supply software which enabled the authority accurately to determine the population in its area.[44] It was further held that, even in the absence of an express term, a contract of the kind in this case (i.e. "a contract for the transfer into a computer of a program intended by both parties to instruct or enable the computer to achieve specified functions")[45] would in any event be subject to implied terms of quality and fitness for purpose arising at common law[46] which were to the same effect.

20–015   The reasoning of the Court of Appeal, which is contained in the judgment of Sir Iain Glidewell,[47] began with consideration of the commonly arising situation in which a computer program is transferred to the client on disk. In such a case, in Sir Iain Glidewell's view, the disk is within the statutory definition of goods, but the program itself is not. However, if the program is defective, then the seller or hirer of the disk is in breach of the statutory implied terms of quality and/or fitness for purpose. This followed, according to the Sir Iain Glidewell, from an analogy with the position of the seller of a vehicle instruction manual, and the following reasoning. Such a manual, including the instructions, would be goods. If the manual contains erroneous instructions likely to cause users to damage their vehicles the defect in the instructions would constitute a breach of the statutory implied terms. There is no logical reason why this should not also be correct in relation to a computer disk/CD containing a defective program or instruction.

20–016   The second part of the court's reasoning[48] recognised that on the particular facts of the case the relevant programs were not supplied on disk, but were transferred directly onto the authority's computer by ICL employees. According to the Court of Appeal, the transfer of a program in this way does not constitute a transfer of goods. There is therefore no statutory implication of terms as to quality/fitness for purpose. Nevertheless, in "a contract for the transfer into a computer of a program intended by both parties to instruct or enable the computer to achieve specified functions", a term requiring fitness for purpose can and should be implied as a matter of common law, since the parties must have

---

[44] At 487h. One of the central issues in the case was as to the measure of loss suffered by the authority, which had recouped its loss by increasing subsequent community charges. On this issue the Court of Appeal reduced the level of damages awarded by Scott Baker J. at first instance.

[45] At 494c.

[46] Applying the *dictum* of Lord Pearson in *Trollope & Colls Ltd v North West Metropolitan Regional Hospital Board* [1973] 1 W.L.R. 601 at 609: "An unexpected term can be implied if and only if the courts find that the parties must have intended that term to form part of their contract; it is not enough for the court to find that such a term would have been adopted by the parties as reasonable men if it had been suggested to them; it must have been a term that went without saying, a term which, though tacit, formed part of the contract which the parties made for themselves".

[47] At 492, Nourse and Hirst L.JJ. agreed (at 487h and 492c).

[48] At 493h onwards.

intended such a term to form part of the contract, and such a term "went without saying".[49]

Since the contract in this case was found to contain corresponding express terms, the whole of the reasoning was obiter. The first part of the reasoning (at para.20–015, above) is doubly so, since (as the court recognised at the second stage) the software in question was not in fact supplied on disk. This part of the reasoning, and the analogy on which it is based (a vehicle instruction manual), are not without difficulty, however. There are significant differences between a computer program and an instruction manual, including their purpose and mode of use. Printed material is used directly and independently by reading for enjoyment or interest, whereas software generally has to be copied for use, and can only be used by interaction with hardware.[50] Moreover, on established principles it may well be that the writing of an instruction manual should give rise to an obligation only to exercise reasonable skill and care, not a warranty of fitness for purpose. If, for example, an accountant gives general tax advice to his clients orally, only a warranty of reasonable skill and care is provided. If he reproduces his advice in a publication which he sells to interested clients, it would be surprising if the contents of the publication were subject to a warranty of fitness for purpose. The same may well be true, at least in some cases, with an instruction manual. On the other hand, it has been suggested[51] that the conclusion is supported by the approach which has been taken in criminal law to the problem of computer hacking, in which the physical form which a program takes on the CD is emphasised.[52]

In any event, the second part of the Court of Appeal's reasoning (at **20–018** para.20–016, above) seems to the current editors to be clearly sound.[53] Moreover that reasoning would appear to apply to most contracts for the supply of bespoke software, irrespective of how it is to be supplied, provided that both parties intend

20–017

---

[49] Applying the above mentioned (n.47) dictum of Lord Pearson in *Trollope & Colls Ltd v North West Metropolitan Regional Hospital Board* at 609.

[50] In an interesting case comment on the *St Albans City and DC v International Computers Ltd* decision ((1995) 58 M.L.R. 585), Elizabeth Macdonald points out that "software is not simply a set of instructions, like some sort of manual, telling an individual what to do. In contrast with the manual, the software interacts directly with the hardware. If there is a defect in it, there may well not be any point at which an individual has an opportunity to assess what is occurring and intervene to prevent some unexpected and unwanted result. Software may be information but it is not pure information." Since, however, the manual's instructions are normally beyond the reader's knowledge and expertise, this opportunity (and the ground of distinction) may be little more than theoretical. In the Scottish case of *Beta Computers (Europe) Ltd v Adobe Systems (Europe) Ltd* [1996] F.S.R. 366, Lord Penrose rejected the analogy with printed material (at 376) and identified a number of further potential grounds of distinction between printed material and software on disk.

[51] D. Rowland and E. Macdonald, *Information Technology Law*, p.106; and Elizabeth Macdonald 58 M.L.R. 585 at 590.

[52] In *R. v Whiteley* (1991) 93 Cr.App.Rep. 25 the Court of Appeal (Criminal Division) had to determine whether the alteration or deletion of files on computer disks represented criminal damage within s.1(1) of the Criminal Damage Act 1971. In answering this question in the affirmative, Lord Lane C.J. stated: "There can be no doubt that the magnetic particles upon the metal disc were part of the discs and if the appellant was proved to have intentionally and without lawful excuse altered the particles in such a way as to cause an impairment of the value or usefulness of the disc to the owner, there would be damage within the meaning of s.1. The fact that the alteration could only be perceived by operating the computer did not make the alteration any less real . . . ".

[53] See further para.20–008, above.

the program "to instruct or enable the computer to achieve specified functions",[54] which, it is to be expected, will generally be the case. Accordingly, even if the reasoning in the first part of the passage is susceptible to criticism, the latter reasoning appears to justify the imposition of strict liability implied terms (i.e. of satisfactory quality and fitness for purpose) in all, or virtually all, cases of software supply.

(ii) *Modified Standard Software*

20–019   Where a software house is appointed not to write software from scratch but to supply and modify, or "tailor", an existing software package (whether produced by that software house or a third party), the contract might be categorised as either:

(a) the supply of goods (i.e. the standard software) together with associated services (the tailoring); or

(b) a single transaction, for the supply of the tailored software.[55]

In any particular case the modification process envisaged by the parties might be only very limited, so that the finished product remains in substantially the same form as the original standard product, or so extensive as to render the finished product more in the nature of bespoke software, and the original software simply part of the fabric of construction. The former case would appear to be more likely to fall into category (a) and the latter into category (b). The distinction is potentially important because in category (a) the contract may well be subject to implied terms as to fitness for purpose and satisfactory quality only in relation to the standard software, and (depending on the circumstances) only terms requiring reasonable skill and care for the tailoring process. By contrast, in category (b), applying the *St Albans* case, the tailored software is likely to be subject to the stricter warranty of fitness for purpose and satisfactory quality, regardless of how it is transmitted.

20–020   An illustration of a case which clearly falls into category (a) is provided by the decision of the Technology and Construction Court in *Jonathon Wren & Co Ltd v Microdec Plc*.[56] W was a recruitment company and M a producer of specialist

---

[54] The need for consistency of approach irrespective of the mode of transfer has been emphasised both in court and in published articles: see, e.g. Lord Penrose in *Beta v Adobe* [1996] F.S.R. 366 at 376.

[55] The difficulty in categorisation is analogous to the classification of supply for the purposes of determining the application of VAT. In *Levob Verzekeringen BV v Staatssecretaris van Financien* [2006] S.T.C. 766, a US company F supplied software to a Dutch insurer L for a specified price and in CD form for L to take back to the Netherlands. L paid a second sum for F to customise the software for the Dutch market, and a third charge to install it and train L's staff. The European Court was asked whether this constituted a multiple supply, of first goods (the software on CD) and then the services of customisation then installation and training. In the opinion of the Attorney General (a) standard software supplied by CD is a supply of goods under Art.5.1 of the EC 6th VAT Directive; (b) however, customised software should be considered the supply of services under Art.6.1 of the same Directive; (c) the present case was to be treated as a single supply of services, since the agreement of separate prices is not determinative of the classification of supply, and here the services aspect of the supply dominated.

[56] [1999] 65 Con. L.R. 157.

software for use by staff recruitment agencies. Between 1983 and 1996 M developed a number of different versions of the software, known as Profile versions 3 to 7. In April 1996 M offered W a demonstration of Profile version 7, also known as "Profile 2000", which was then a new product. W was impressed with the demonstration and in May 1996 entered a contract with M (which made reference to M's standard terms and conditions) for the purchase of Profile 2000,[57] together with the following associated services, namely installation, maintenance and a specified number of days of staff training. W alleged that the package was defective and that as a result its business failed and it ceased trading.

In a trial of preliminary issues as to the terms of this agreement, H.H.J.   **20–021** Bowsher Q.C. held that M's standard terms and conditions had not been validly incorporated into the contract. However, the agreement was subject to implied terms that (i) the application software and services would fulfil W's objective of fully computerising its recruitment process; (ii) the application software, Profile 2000, would be of reasonably satisfactory quality and reasonably fit for the purposes of W; (iii) the associated services to be provided by M, including the installation of the software on W's existing computer system, would be performed by M with reasonable skill and care; and (iv) those services (including in particular the installation of the software) would be performed within a reasonable time.[58] There was no discussion of the basis on which these terms were implied.

In *Jonathon Wren v Microdec* any tailoring process was limited indeed;   **20–022** effectively it comprised no more than implementation of the standard software on the client's own computer system. However, it provides a useful illustration of the implied terms which might well arise in contracts for the supply of standard software with relatively limited tailoring services. Another decision of the Technology and Construction Court which is closer to the border between categories (a) and (b) referred to in para.20–019, above, but ultimately found to lie within category (a), is *Gretton & Starkey (trading as Open Systems Design) v British Millerain Co Ltd*.[59]

In *Gretton & Starkey,* BM was a fabric dyeing and coating company. OSD was   **20–023** a small software house which worked predominantly with clients in the textile industry. Its principal asset was a software package called TEXpro, which provided accounting, stock control and management facilities. TEXpro could be tailored to the individual requirements of each customer. BM entered into negotiations directly with OSD in which, as the Judge found, OSD described the functions and attributes of the systems it offered and BM decided whether these met their general requirements. OSD did not provide a detailed list of its requirements, indeed BM was not even clear as to what it wanted. The intention was that the software would be tailored to meet BM's reasonable requirements when those were communicated to OSD, though this was to be only after the contract was entered into. The contract ultimately executed was for the supply of specified hardware and software, together with associated services including

---

[57] It is not clear from the judgment whether the software package was delivered on disk or installed onto W's computer network by M's employees, but the latter seems more likely.
[58] At 171, 172.
[59] Unreported, July 29, 1998, H.H.J. Thornton Q.C.

software support, staff training, on-site implementation and consultancy. The software comprised a number of modules of the TEXpro package, which were to be delivered in phases, together with a Global 2000 accounting package. The services were to include an unusually "high degree of post-contract tailoring", not least because BM's requirements were largely to be identified as the contract was being performed.[60]

20–024   In determining what terms were to be implied into the contract as to merchantability,[61] fitness for purpose and the exercise of reasonable skill and care the judge referred to the reasoning of Sir Iain Glidewell in the *St Albans* case[62] as offering the clearest statement of principle.[63] He considered that in the case before him, however, the contract in question was in truth three contracts in one: (i) a contract for the supply of hardware and disks or other software media; (ii) a contract for the supply of software modules; and (iii) a contract for the provision of specialised services, namely the tailoring of the modules to achieve the functions appropriate to BM's needs.[64] The hardware and disks were not the subject of criticism in the case. As to (ii) and (iii), the judge asked himself what implied terms arose at common law by applying the dictum of Lord Pearson in *Trollope & Colls Ltd v North West Metropolitan Regional Hospital Board*.[65] He concluded that (a) the modules, in their untailored forms, were required to be fit for their purpose for use in textile manufacturing stock control and monitoring systems and suitable to be tailored for a use reasonably associated with such a purpose; (b) the tailoring, training, help facilities, report writing and after-sales services to be provided by OSD had to be provided with the exercise of reasonable skill and care.[66]

20–025   The judge's reasoning was that it went without saying that *some* quality standard was to be imported into the contract, and that the appropriate standard was that which mirrored similar terms as to quality in similar contracts. Accordingly, since the contract in this case comprised three "sub-agreements", the appropriate implied term in sub-agreement (ii) was the term at (a) above, since sub-agreement (ii) was analogous to the transfer of computer programs in the *St Albans* case itself. In the case of (iii), the appropriate term was (b) on the basis that "[a]ny contract which consists entirely of the supply of professional services has implied into it a term as to the exercise of reasonable skill and care".[67]

20–026   Although it is not entirely clear from the judgment, it does not appear to have been argued in *Gretton & Starkey* that the contract was subject to an implied term that the *tailored* software would be of merchantable quality and/or fit for its purpose.[68] Applying the judge's own reasoning, i.e. that "the appropriate standard was that which mirrored similar terms as to quality in similar contracts", if

---

[60] Para.24 of judgment.
[61] The contract was entered into prior to the Sale of Goods Act 1994, which replaced this term with "satisfactory quality".
[62] Paras 20–015 to 20–018, above.
[63] Para.45 of judgment.
[64] Para.46 of judgment.
[65] See para.20–014, n.46 above.
[66] The judge went on to find that BM had failed to establish that any of its 411 complaints against OSD represented breaches of these contractual terms.
[67] At 12 of the judgment.
[68] This may well be because, as already indicated above, BM had not identified its precise requirements at the time of the contract. See, however, the decision in *Saphena* below.

the contract had been described not as three sub-agreements but as a single one for the provision of tailored software, then by analogy with the provision of bespoke software in the *St Albans* case the appropriate warranty would have been that the *tailored* software would be of merchantable quality and/or fit for its purpose. However, this conclusion was effectively ruled out by the particular (and somewhat unusual) facts of the case. Had OSD specified its requirements at the outset, and BM agreed to provide TEXpro software duly tailored to meet those needs, the case might well have fallen within category (b).

(iii) *Communication of Client's Purpose*

The implied obligation on the software supplier to provide software which is "fit for purpose" does not extend to all of the client's purposes, whatever they may be, even if not communicated to the supplier. Only those purposes which are within the supplier's (objective) knowledge are included in the scope of the warranty. This point arose in *Saphena Computing Ltd v Allied Collection Agencies Ltd.*[69] The claimant, SCL, was a software supplier and the defendant, ACA, a debt-collecting agency. In January 1985 SCL agreed to supply batch software to ACA. This was supplied in February 1985, and a number of initial defects were rectified by SCL. Later, in about May 1985, ACA instructed SCL to supply online software. This also suffered numerous defects, and caused fresh defects in the batch software. SCL was in the process of rectifying the various defects when, in February 1986, the parties agreed to terminate their relationship. ACA alleged (by counterclaim) that SCL had breached implied terms that the software would be fit for its purpose. Mr Recorder Havery Q.C. (as he then was) held that both supply contracts were subject to the following implied term of fitness for purpose:

> "In my judgment it was an implied term of each contract for the supply of software that the software would be reasonably fit for any purpose which had been communicated to the claimants before the contract was made and for any further purpose subsequently communicated, provided in the latter case that the claimants accepted the defendants' instructions to make the relevant modification. The making of the modification constitutes or implies acceptance of the instructions".[70]

The counterclaim for breach of this implied term in each of the software contracts failed since, by entering into the termination agreement in February 1986, ACA agreed to accept the software in its then condition, and deprived SCL of further opportunity to rectify the defects.

The latter part of the passage extracted above from the judgment of Mr Recorder Havery Q.C. appears simply to confirm that the parties are free to vary the terms of the contract by mutual consent at any time after it is executed. If the client does give instructions to make modifications, however, the circumstances (and in particular the terms of the original contract) will have to be considered carefully to determine whether an acceptance by the supplier (in making the

20-027

20-028

---

[69] [1995] F.S.R. 616. An appeal to the Court of Appeal (at [1995] F.S.R. 646), which was dismissed, did not disturb any of the Recorder's findings. The decision of the Court of Appeal is discussed further below at paras 20–032 to 20–033.
[70] At 644.

modifications) is unconditional or in consideration of (reasonable) payment by the client. The continuing duties of the supplier are considered further below,[71] and if the making of the modifications fall within their scope then no further payment will be due. This was the position in *Gretton & Starkey*,[72] where the original contract contemplated that the supplier would carry out significant modifications to the software after installation in order to meet the needs of the client as identified post-contract. Otherwise, the circumstances will usually be such that the supplier will be entitled to reasonable remuneration for the work involved in carrying out the modification.

20–029   Since the supplier's obligation to provide software fit for its purpose is potentially the client's principal safeguard in ensuring proper performance by the supplier, it is obviously of critical importance that the client takes care to identify, and communicate, all of its objectives and requirements to the supplier. For this reason it is now common practice for clients to appoint computer consultants specifically for this purpose, whose task is to prepare and develop, in consultation with the client, a detailed functional specification for the proposed computer software or system.

20–030   The importance to the client of clearly communicating its requirements to the supplier is illustrated by *Micron Computer Systems Ltd v Wang (UK) Ltd*.[73] In that case Micron claimed that a computer system comprising hardware and software supplied to it by Wang suffered from a number of faults, including (principally) an inability to perform "transaction logging". The express terms of the contract of supply included a warranty by Wang that the software would conform substantially with Micron's functional specification for a period of 90 days. In addition Micron relied on implied terms that the system would be fit for the purpose for which it was sold and of merchantable quality. In dismissing Micron's claim for alleged breaches of contract by Wang in this (and all other) respects, Steyn J. said[74]:

> "The acknowledged absence of a transaction logging facility is not in reality a fault in the system which was sold. Micron can only complain about its absence if Micron can establish a contractual term, express or implied, or an actionable representation, to the effect that the system included such a facility. In order to make good its case on transaction logging, Micron must therefore establish that they made known to Wang that they required such a facility."

The judge found that Micron did not in fact communicate to Wang that it required transaction logging. Its functional specification did not refer to transaction logging, and at best Micron only referred to transaction logging in vague phrases ("simultaneous background back-up") which were insufficient to alert Wang to what they intended to convey.[75] Accordingly there was no "fault" in the system in this (or any other) respect, and Wang were not in breach of the express or implied terms of the contract.

20–031   It is clearly not the case, however, that only purposes which are specifically and expressly communicated by the client to the supplier will become the subject

---

[71] At paras 20–042 *et seq.*
[72] Unreported, July 29, 1998, H.H.J. Thornton Q.C.; paras 20–023 to 20–026, above.
[73] Unreported, May 9, 1990, QBD, Steyn J.
[74] At 9 of the transcript.
[75] At 10 of the transcript.

of the implied (or any express) term requiring fitness for purpose. It might be implicit from the client's instructions, from earlier dealings between the parties or from normal trade practice that the client has a particular purpose for the software (or system) ordered from the supplier. *Jonathon Wren v Microdec*,[76] the facts of which are set out above in para.20–020, provides an example. In that case it was held that a contract for the supply of software was subject to implied terms requiring the software to be of reasonably satisfactory quality and reasonably fit for the purposes of the client (W). The judge went on to identify what those purposes were.[77] The first was the overall objective of the client (which was communicated to the supplier, M) to fully computerise its recruitment process. In addition, however, the judge found that the purposes for which the software was to be fit included six specific requirements identified in the client's statement of case.[78] Four of these functions (such as a rapid search facility) had not been communicated to M, but had simply been extracted from M's sales literature as to the software's alleged capabilities.[79] The requirements were nonetheless included by the judge in the list of warranted purposes, apparently on the basis that the supplier "would have understood [them] as the common aim"[80] of W and/or because they were promised in the sales literature[81] which was provided to the client before it ordered the software. In other words, these requirements were implicit in the client's instructions, and the circumstances of the transaction.

(iv) *Implementation and Testing*

In a contract for the provision of bespoke or modified standard software there will invariably be an express provision dealing with the implementation and testing to be carried out by the supplier. This will include the process of debugging. In the absence of express provision, a corresponding obligation will normally arise by necessary implication at common law. Unless specified otherwise, the supplier will ordinarily be obliged to complete these processes within a reasonable time. These propositions follow from the decision of the Court of Appeal in *Saphena Computing Ltd v Allied Collection Agencies Ltd*,[82] the facts of which are set out above in para.20–027.[83] The judgment of Staughton L.J. contains the following important passage[84]:   **20–032**

---

[76] [1999] 65 Con. L.R. 157.

[77] At 172, para.58.

[78] Namely those at para.8 of the statement of case, which is extracted both at pp.163 and 172 of the judgment.

[79] At 163, 172.

[80] At 163.

[81] At 172.

[82] [1995] F.S.R. 616, Mr Recorder Havery Q.C.; *ibid.*, 646, CA.

[83] See further the decision in *Eurodynamic Systems Plc v General Automation Ltd* discussed in para.20–012, above. At 17 of the judgment Steyn J. stated that, according to the expert evidence in the case, it is acceptable and normal practice to supply software which contains bugs and errors. He added that the basis of that practice was that "pursuant to the supplier's support obligation (free or chargeable as the case may be) the supplier will correct errors or bugs that prevent the product from being properly used." Hence on the particular facts in that case the supplier was not in breach of any obligation to supply software which was fit for purpose and of merchantable quality (the existence of which Steyn J. was prepared to assume) even though there were minor errors requiring correction.

[84] At 652.

"It was, we are told, common ground that the law governing these contracts was precisely the same whether they were contracts for the sale of goods or for the supply of services.[85] It is therefore unnecessary to consider into which category they might come. But it is important to remember that software is not necessarily a commodity which is handed over or delivered once and for all at one time. It may well have to be tested and modified as necessary. It would not be a breach of contract at all to deliver software in the first instance with a defect in it . . .

[Delivery of the software] will necessarily be accompanied by a degree of testing and modification. Naturally it could be expected that the supplier will carry out those tasks. He should have both the right and the duty to do so . . . No doubt there was a time limit for that purpose—a reasonable time is that which the law would ordinarily supply."[86]

20–033   In *Saphena Computing Ltd v Allied Collection Agencies Ltd* this process of testing and modification was still continuing on February 11, 1986, more than six months after even the second contract had been entered into. Nevertheless a reasonable time was not found to have elapsed by then. On that date the parties terminated their relationship. Accordingly SCL were not obliged, or entitled, to do any more work on the software, and therefore were not liable for any defects which had not been remedied as at that date.

20–034   What constitutes a "reasonable time" within which to complete implementation was considered by Seymour Q.C. in *Astea (UK) Ltd v Timegroup Ltd.*[87] The claimant was a supplier of software packages for use in call centres, which could be used independently or linked to other software systems. The defendant ran a call centre and wished to replace its existing computer system with a number of software packages including a package supplied by the claimant. The claimant and defendant entered into a licence and support agreement whereby the claimant granted the defendant a licence to use the software and agreed to provide implementation services, including configuring the software and integrating it with the other software packages. At trial it was agreed that the claimant's obligation was to complete that implementation within a reasonable time. After some months of implementation the defendant declined to pay the claimant's invoices and alleged that the claimant's delay in completing implementation constituted a repudiatory breach of contract. The claimant sued for its outstanding fees and the defendant counterclaimed for damages for repudiatory breach. Judge Seymour held that it was necessary to take a broad consideration of what in all the circumstances was a reasonable time for performance, and that the following factors should be taken into account:

(1) any estimate given by the performing party of how long it would take it to perform;

---

[85] The "common ground" referred to in passing by the learned Lord Justice has been described by the editors of the *Encyclopaedia of Information Technology Law* as a "remarkable statement". Since different statutory regimes apply depending on whether the supply was of goods or services the statement certainly seems to be doubtful. It may be that the parties agreed no more than that even if the contract was one for the supply of services it was nonetheless subject to an implied term of fitness for purpose by operation of the common law, so that the law governing the contract was "precisely the same" for the purposes of that case.

[86] These views were based on a passage contained in one of the expert reports in the case, but appear to be of general application.

[87] [2005] EWHC 725.

(2) whether any estimate had been exceeded, and if so in what circumstances;

(3) whether the party for whose benefit the relevant obligation was to be performed needed to participate in the performance or not at all;

(4) whether it was necessary for third parties to collaborate with the performing party in order to enable it to perform;

(5) what exactly was the cause, or what were the causes, of the delay to performance.

On the particular facts in *Astea (UK) Ltd v Timegroup Ltd* Judge Seymour held that at the time when the defendant purported to accept the claimant's repudiation a reasonable time for performance had not passed. He was particularly influenced by the fact that the defendant itself was late in preparing to receive the software, and that the claimant had been willing and helpful throughout the testing period. Judge Seymour went on to conclude (obiter) that even if a reasonable time for performance had passed, the delay did not deprive the defendant of substantially the whole benefit of the contract, and, since the claimant intended to complete the implementation, and was applying appropriate resources, it would not have represented a repudiatory breach of contract.

The approach adopted by Judge Seymour in *Astea (UK) Ltd v Timegroup Ltd*   **20–035**
as to what constitutes a reasonable time for performance was cited with approval by the Court of Appeal in *Peregrine Systems Ltd v Steria Ltd*.[88] In the latter case the Court of Appeal upheld another of Judge Seymour's decisions regarding (amongst others) the obligation of a supplier (S) of software and associated implementation services to perform such services within a reasonable time. In that case the central issue was the scope of implementation services which S was required to provide. The Court of Appeal agreed with Judge Seymour's conclusion that S had not been required to complete implementation by a particular date, and was only obliged to provide implementation services up to a particular value. It followed that the contract could contain no implied term to complete implementation within a reasonable time, though it was common ground that whatever S *was* required to do, it was obliged to do it within a reasonable time. The Court of Appeal also emphasised that the obligation to complete within a reasonable time was distinct from the concept of time being "of the essence", and that a breach of the former obligation was not necessarily repudiatory.

(v) *The Importance of Co-operation between the Parties*

In any contract for the supply of software, or an entire computer system, success   **20–036**
is usually heavily dependent on a high level of co-operation between the parties at all stages of the contract, but particularly at the stage of implementation and testing. The law therefore generally implies mutual contractual obligations of co-operation accordingly. The relevant principles were recently considered in the Technology and Construction Court in relation to a contract for the supply of a "standard" computer system in *Anglo Group Plc v Winther Brown & Co*.[89] WB

---

[88] [2005] EWCA Civ 239.
[89] Unreported, March 1, 2000, QBD, TCC, H.H.J. Toulmin C.M.G. Q.C.

(a distributor of decorative mouldings) purchased a computer system from BML comprising both hardware and a standard software package ("Charisma"). The principal agreement was entered into on December 21, 1995, on BML's standard form. Delivery was to take place in February/March 1996 and the system was to go live by July 1996. The system did go live on July 1, 1996, but WB raised a number of complaints regarding its performance. BML sought to deal with these, but by April 1997 WB was so dissatisfied with the system that it purported to repudiate the agreement and claimed damages from BML for (inter alia) breaches of the agreement. In an important section of the judgment[90] entitled "The contract: Parties' Duty of Co-operation", Judge Toulmin stated:

> "126. It is important to understand the nature of the contracts between WB and BML. It is well understood that the design and installation of a computer system requires the active co-operation of both parties. Frequently a client employs a consultant to assist it in the process . . . WB did not do that in relation to Charisma. Instead it invited proposals from selected hardware and software suppliers and developed its requirements in discussions with potential suppliers.[91] It is clear that WB was always interested only in a package system and was not prepared to spend money on bespoke software which could adapt the computer system to WB's particular working practices. It was almost inevitable in these circumstances that while Charisma (or any other standard system) could be expected to provide an 80% fit or better with WB's existing procedures, it was unlikely to provide a 100% fit. This meant that it was inevitable that there would be some procedures of WB which WB would have to adapt to Charisma . . .
>
> 127. The duty of co-operation in my view extends to the customer accepting where possible reasonable solutions to problems that have arisen. In the case of unimportant or relatively unimportant items that have been promised and cannot be supplied each party must act reasonably, consistent, of course, with its rights.
>
> 128. In relation to a contract for the supply of a standard computer system it is an implied term that:
>
> (a) the purchaser communicates clearly any special needs to the supplier;
> (b) the purchaser takes reasonable steps to ensure that the supplier understands those needs;
> (c) the supplier communicates to the purchaser whether or not those precise needs can be met and if so how they can be met. If they cannot be met precisely the appropriate options should be set out by the supplier;
> (d) the supplier takes reasonable steps to ensure that the purchaser is trained in how to use the system;
> (e) the purchaser devotes reasonable time and patience to understanding how to operate the system;
> (f) the purchaser and supplier work together to resolve the problems which will almost certainly occur. This requires active co-operation from both parties. If such co-operation is not present it is likely that the purchaser will not achieve the desired results from the system."

20–037   Judge Toulmin then considered whether, in the light of these obligations, the numerous alleged defects constituted breaches of the agreement, and if so

---

[90] Paras 125 to 129.
[91] Judge Toulim considered that where, as in this case, the client of a computer company has limited computer knowledge and nevertheless chose not to employ its own computer consultant, the need for active co-operation between the parties *throughout the project* was "of crucial importance" (para.126 of judgment).

whether there was such a fundamental breach as to entitle WB to repudiate the agreement. The judge rejected virtually all of WB's complaints, largely on the basis that BML had put forward reasonable solutions to the various problems, and/or WB had unreasonably refused to adopt those solutions. Judge Toulmin rejected the claim for repudiation, therefore, stating that, while a failure by a computer company to deliver individual requirements (and particularly those which constitute expected enhancements in a replacement computer system) can, in principle, amount to a fundamental breach leading to a repudiation, this had not happened in the present case. Most of WB's complaints had been rejected. Those few complaints which were not rejected either had been or could, given reasonable co-operation by WB, have been remedied before April 1997. Taken as a whole they did not amount to a fundamental breach of contract giving rise to a right of repudiation by WB.[92] As to the minority of complaints which did represent breaches of the agreement by BML, such as delay in resolving various bugs, Judge Toulmin found that WB had failed to prove any associated loss.

In *Anglo Group Plc v Winther Brown & Co* the implied terms requiring   **20–038**
co-operation on the part of the customer were said to be based on the fact that (i) standard not bespoke software was ordered, rendering it "inevitable" that post-installation adaptation would be required; and (ii) the client (WB) lacked computer knowledge and chose not to employ a computer consultant. However, as has already been seen,[93] in all or virtually all instances of the supply of computer software or systems it is implicit that some level of testing and modification will be required. In *Saphena Computing Ltd v Allied Collection Agencies Ltd*, which concerned bespoke software, the Court of Appeal stated that the supplier is not only under a duty to carry out the processes of testing and modification but that he should have the "right" to do so. It is clearly inherent in such a right that the supplier should be given reasonable opportunity to carry out testing and modification, and therefore that he should be given appropriate level of co-operation in order to achieve this.

Anglo Group Plc v Winther Brown & Co illustrates that the extent of the   **20–039**
obligation of co-operation probably differs in every case depending on precisely what was (or ought to have been) envisaged by the parties at the outset as to the level of "fit" of the software or system at the time of delivery. Where (as in *Anglo Group*) (i) the customer has chosen not to have software specifically written for him; and (ii) has not spelt out his requirements in detail in advance, there is a heavy onus on that customer to assist the supplier in the process of adaptation following delivery.[94] If, on the other hand, the contract is to supply bespoke software, and a clear and comprehensive specification has been provided by the customer at the outset, it will usually be incumbent on the supplier, at the time of delivery, to supply software which has already been written with those particular requirements in mind. Ordinarily, therefore, it would not be open to the

---

[92] Para.232 of judgment.

[93] Para.20–032 and *Saphena Computing Ltd v Allied Collection Agencies Ltd*, above.

[94] *Gretton & Starkey*, discussed in para.20–023, above, is another example of a case in which the points at (i) and (ii) were present. As in *Anglo Group*, the customer had onerous post-delivery obligations, all the more so in Gretton & Starkey, since not only was there a limited specification of requirements in advance (i.e. point (ii)), but it was specifically envisaged that there would be a high level of input by the customer as the contract was being performed, i.e. in actually bringing the software into operation: see para.24 of judgment.

supplier at that stage to require the customer to co-operate in a modification process necessitated by a requirement which could and should have already been taken into account (though not necessarily met)[95] by that stage.[96]

20–040 Following delivery of the software or system the process of implementation will often lead to reappraisal of the specification by the customer. If the customer reasonably revises his requirements during the process, the duty of co-operation will oblige the supplier to respond accordingly. In particular, if the contract is for modified standard software and the revision is simply the result of the "inevitable" inability of the software in its original standard form to meet all of the customer's requirements, and is a reasonable step towards achieving the overall objective, the supplier will be obliged to meet the revised specification without further payment.[97] If, on the other hand, the revision is independent of the implementation process the supplier will usually be entitled to reasonable remuneration for the further work involved. Where no detailed list of the customer's requirements is prepared in advance of the contract, it will often be difficult to draw this distinction in practice.

20–041 The duty of co-operation in a contract for the supply of software was also recognised by the Court of Appeal in *Systems Team Plusmark Ltd v Kingswood Fluid Power Group Plc*.[98] This was a claim by a computer and software supplier (STP) for damages for breach of a contract with KFP for the supply of computer equipment and tailored software. STP relied on implied terms of the contract that KFP would (i) co-operate with STP so as to enable STP to perform the contract; (ii) ensure that the representative of KFP appointed to supervise the project would perform his duties in a proper manner; and (iii) ensure that instructions, information and details required by STP were given or made available in reasonable time so as not to impede STP in performance of the contract. The case came before the Court of Appeal on an appeal by KFP as to whether judgment entered against it in default of its service of a defence ought to be set aside. KFP had to establish an arguable defence with a real prospect of success. In the course of argument the existence of the implied terms was neither challenged by KFP nor doubted by the court. Interestingly, Hutchison L.J. noted that the particular contract in this case was "in many ways similar to a standard building contract",[99] particularly in that the whole of the work was subject to supervision by KFP's project manager. There was also a 16-week contract programme, in relation to which the parties had proceeded as if party to a building contract: STP had requested an extension of time arising from (inter alia) late information and alleged repudiation by KFP for its refusal to provide these. In its reasoning the court did not need to draw upon principles applicable to construction law

---

[95] It is unlikely that a supplier could ever reasonably be expected to have met a particular requirement of software at the very time of delivery: see paras 20–090 to 20–091, below.

[96] This proposition also derives support from a passage in the judgment of Nourse L.J. in *St Albans City and DC v ICL* [1996] 4 All E.R. 481: "Parties who respectively agree to supply and acquire a system recognising that it is still in the course of development cannot be taken, merely by virtue of that recognition, to intend that the supplier shall be at liberty to supply software which cannot perform the function expected of it at the stage of development at which it is supplied."

[97] This follows from the sixth of the implied terms listed in the *Anglo Group* case.

[98] Unreported, April 30, 1996, CA.

[99] At 1 of the judgment.

contracts in order to determine that KFP did indeed have a meritorious defence, but the case appears to leave open such a course in any future similar case.

(vi) *Duties of Support*

When implementation and "acceptance testing" have been successfully effected **20-042** in respect of all of the components of the software or system supplied, the customer's right to reject the system is lost. However, even at this stage it is perfectly normal, and acceptable, for bugs to appear in the software or system from time to time. The process of testing will rarely result in a program being totally bug free. Rather, the expression "bug free" has to be seen as meaning "acceptably free from bugs". As Ian J. Lloyd points out[1]: "It is impossible to test even the simplest program in an exhaustive fashion. This is because of the myriad possibilities for interaction (whether desired or not) between the various elements of the program." For this reason contracts for the supply of software or a computer system invariably require the supplier to provide support facilities following implementation. Often this is free during the first year or other specified period ("the warranty period") and then at an agreed cost thereafter. In the absence of express provision an implied term will usually arise for the provision of such a warranty period requiring correction of bugs. The duration of that period will be a reasonable length of time having regard to the expectation of the parties and the circumstances of the contract. In the absence of express agreement, however, it will usually be difficult to imply a further obligation of continuing (paid) support facilities.

Problems can arise post implementation where the client's contractual entitle- **20-043** ment, and in particular the precise deliverables under the contract, are not precisely defined. An example arose in *Psychometric Services Ltd v Merant International Ltd*,[1a] in which the dispute concerned whether the claimant was entitled to access to a software source code. The claimant provided psychometric testing services for companies interested in assessing job applicants. The defendant agreed to develop websites for the claimant which would enable it to offer companies the opportunity to test candidates on their own home computers via the internet. The claimant secured a number of lucrative clients for the service, but the defendant was unable to overcome defects in the software. The claimant wished to approach a third party to remedy the defects, but needed access to the source code to do so, which the defendant declined to provide. The claimant therefore sought an interim injunction requiring delivery up of the source code, relying on a number of provisions of the software agreement including (a) its entitlement to the "software deliverables" and (b) the provisions in relation to ownership of the source code. Granting the injunction, Laddie J. held that the claimant had an arguable claim to access to the source code under (b) but not under (a), since, in a normal software development context, the term "software deliverables" would include the object code, but not the source code.

(vii) *Staff Training*

The supplier's obligation to provide a computer system or software which is fit **20-044** for the customer's purpose will carry with it an obligation to ensure that it is fit

---

[1] *Information Technology Law* (2nd edn, Butterworths), p.409.
[1a] [2002] F.S.R. 147.

for use by the customer's own staff. If the staff are already computer literate and versed in the use of the kind of system or software which is to be provided then no problem will arise, provided of course that use of the system/software is indeed within their capabilities. If, on the other hand, complete retraining of the staff is required, which was not agreed with or envisaged by the customer at the outset, this may constitute a breach of the implied obligation of fitness for purpose, giving rise to a liability in damages for the associated disruption to the customer. Between these two extremes lies the usual case, in which the parties envision (and the contract therefore impliedly provides) that use of the software or system will be within the reasonable capabilities of the customer's staff following appropriate training by the supplier, which the supplier is therefore usually duty bound to provide.[2]

(viii) *User's Operation Manual*

20–045 Usually a computer or software supply contract will also be subject to an implied term that both a system specification (detailing the technical specification and capabilities of the system, and demonstrating how it meets the functional requirements) and a user manual will be supplied to the customer. Moreover the user manual should be in a form which the intended users will understand. British Standard BS 7649 "Guide to design and preparation of documentation for users of application software" contains recommendations for the preparation and content of user manuals and provides helpful guidance as to the likely extent of this obligation.

(ix) *Implied Terms of Reasonable Skill and Care*

20–046 We have already seen that a contract for the supply of software is likely to be subject to an implied (and often an express) term requiring the software to be of satisfactory quality and (reasonably) fit for its purpose. In most circumstances the latter obligation is likely to be more onerous than an obligation to exercise reasonable skill and care. However, there may nevertheless be circumstances in which the client of a software house will wish to assert and rely on an obligation that the supplier will exercise reasonable skill and care in performing the services it is required to provide under the contract. This might be, for example, (i) where the installation of the software has not (yet) been completed (so that a requirement of fitness for purpose is of limited assistance)[3] and the client is dissatisfied with the supplier's performance to date; or (ii) where installation of bespoke or modified standard software has been completed, and the software is (or might be) technically fit for its purpose, but the performance of the software is not such as is reasonably to be expected from a software house exercising the appropriate

---

[2] An example of a supplier being criticised for breach of its duty to train the purchaser's employees in the use of the software is *SAM Business Systems Ltd v Hedley & Co* (TCC, H.H.J. Bowsher Q.C., December 19, 2002 unreported, at para.83 of the judgment). The case also offers an example of a representation made by the supplier during the pre-contractual phase that the system was going to be operable by people who were not technically qualified (para.21 of the judgment). Both of these factors were invoked to defeat the supplier's contention that the system was not working properly because of the purchaser's defective operation of the system.

[3] But see below at para.20–089 for the continuing and evolving nature of the fitness for purpose obligation.

level of skill and care in and about writing or modifying the particular software.

An example of the first situation arose in *Salvage Association v CAP Financial*   **20–047**
Services Ltd.[4] SA was a marine surveying company which required computer accounting software. CAP was a computer software house. CAP entered into two contracts with SA: in March 1987, to carry out an analysis of SA's requirements and to specify how these were to be achieved, and in September 1987 to develop the appropriate software for SA. Pursuant to the first contract, in July 1987 a "System Specification" and "User Requirement Specification" were produced by CAP and approved by SA. Pursuant to the second contract, system software was developed and delivered by CAP to SA in September 1988. However, the software suffered from numerous faults. These were still not resolved by July 1989. As a result SA terminated the second contract and claimed damages from CAP for breach.

SA did not allege that the second contract was subject to an implied term of   **20–048**
fitness for purpose, only that, pursuant to s.13 of the Sale of Goods and Services Act 1982, it was subject to an implied term as to reasonable care and skill.[5] The judge accepted that the contract was one for the supply of a service to which this part of the Act applied, and that the term was not negatived by any of the express provisions of the second contract. He held that SA had been entitled to terminate the contract since CAP were in repudiatory breach, in that they had delivered a system which, after two-and-a-half years, was still unusable because of significant deficiencies in CAP's performance.[6] Moreover SA were entitled to terminate the contract, i.e. accept CAP's repudiation, since there was no prospect of CAP completing the system within a reasonable time.[7] CAP's liability for damages is considered further below.[8]

In *Salvage Association v CAP* the court had no difficulty in finding an implied   **20–049**
term to exercise reasonable skill and care in a contract which was subject to an express term requiring fitness for purpose. The question arises as to whether a contractual obligation to exercise reasonable skill and care can and should be implied in a contract which is not subject to an express term requiring fitness for purpose but only an implied one. If the contract is one for the supply of software on disk or CD then, according to the *St Albans* case, an implied term requiring fitness for purpose will be imposed by statute.[9] In such a case there seems to be no reason in logic or principle why an implied term requiring the supplier to

---

[4] [1995] F.S.R. 654, H.H.J. Thayne Forbes Q.C.: judgment delivered October 21, 1992.
[5] It should be noted, however, that the second contract contained an express term that CAP would provide the System to SA as described in the User Requirement Specification, by July 1988: [1995] F.S.R. 654 at 660.
[6] The judge considered that the fundamental problems with the system were "the inevitable result of a significant lack of knowledge, experience and expertise . . . on the part of those assigned to the project by CAP. In addition . . . the project had throughout been mismanaged by CAP at all levels": [1995] F.S.R. 654 at 679.
[7] The judge found that "SA were fully justified in coming to the conclusion that CAP had failed to deliver a useable system and that there was no prospect that it either would or could do so by January 1, 1990 or within a reasonable timescale thereafter. In all the circumstances of this case, I have every sympathy with SA's loss of confidence both in the sysem itself and in CAP's ability to complete it satisfactorily." [1995] F.S.R. 654 at 680.
[8] See para.20–106, below.
[9] [1996] 4 All E.R. 481 at 493h.

exercise reasonable skill and care in and about carrying out the services required of it (writing or modifying the software, or implementing it, for example) should not also apply, whether pursuant to s.13 of the Sale of Goods and Services Act 1982 or at common law. Moreover, there is again no reason to treat a contract for the provision of bespoke or modified standard software other than on disk/CD (which, according to the *St Albans* case, will ordinarily be subject to a common law implied term requiring fitness for purpose) any differently. It follows that all contracts for the supply of bespoke or modified standard software are probably subject not only to implied terms requiring that the software be fit for its purpose, but also implied terms requiring the supplier to exercise reasonable skill and care in and about performing the services it is contractually obliged to provide.

(x) *Common Law Duty of Care*

20–050 In any event, the supplier of bespoke software will usually owe a common law duty of care to its client to exercise reasonable skill and care in and about performing the services of writing the relevant software, on the basis that, in the ordinary case, there will almost certainly have been an assumption of responsibility towards the client.[10] Moreover; (i) economic loss[11] would almost certainly be a foreseeable consequence of any negligence on the part of the supplier; (ii) the relationship would usually be one of sufficient proximity (given the supplier's special knowledge and the client's likely reliance) and it would appear to be fair, just and reasonable to impose such a duty.[12] The duty will extend not only to the writing and/or modification of the software, but also to the associated services of implementation, testing and staff training, for example. *DSL Group Ltd v Unisys International Services Ltd*[13] (which is discussed further below at para.20–054) provides an example of a case in which a software house was found to owe a *Hedley Byrne v Heller* type duty of care not only in respect of pre-contract statements but also in relation to advice given after the contract was entered into as to the design of the software database.[14]

(xi) *Supply of Standard/Modified Standard Software: Consultant or Supplier?*

20–051 A more difficult question is whether a particular supplier of either standard or modified standard software, or of a computer system including such software, assumed the position of a professional consultant, or was merely acting as a supplier. Only in the former case will the supplier owe a duty of care to the client

---

[10] *Henderson v Merrett Syndicates Ltd* [1995] 2 A.C. 145.

[11] Needless to say, if the software is intended for "safety-critical" application, such as in a medical or emergency service computer system, the case for a duty of care would be even stronger, and probably irresistible.

[12] Applying the test for the existence of a *Hedley Byrne v Heller* type duty stipulated by the House of Lords in *Caparo v Dickman* [1990] 2 A.C. 605. The fact that the tortious duty may be wider than any corresponding one does not appear to be a ground of objection: *Holt v Payne Skillington* [1996] P.N.L.R. 179, CA.

[13] October 19, 1994, reported at [1995] Masons C.L.R. 5, discussed in para.20–039, above.

[14] The availability of a remedy in negligence not only in tort but also in contract is not merely of academic interest. The client may prefer to bring his claim in tort rather than in contract in order to take advantage of a more favourable limitation period, for example. (The cause of action in tort only accrues, and the limitation period commences, on proof of loss, which may be later than the date of breach, which triggers accrual of the contractual claim.)

to advise on the suitability of what is being supplied. The distinction is often very difficult to draw. In *Jonas & Erickson Software v Fitz-Wright Co Ltd*,[15] for example, FW contracted with JE (a software house) for the supply of a computer system to integrate its production and accounting. The system was to include software in standard form (known as "TABS") but which could be customised to meet FW's needs, together with ongoing support services. In a claim by FW for (inter alia) negligent misstatement, JE contended that it was no more than a supplier selling software and hardware. However, the judge found that FW were "essentially computer illiterate", had no separate consultant assisting them and were relying on JE to act as consultants on their behalf. Moreover JE were aware of all of the foregoing, and, the judge found, had held themselves as consultants for FW. For all of these reasons JE owed FW a duty of care to ensure that the product they sold FW was adequate for their needs and capable of fulfilling them.[16]

By contrast, the supplier of hardware, software and associated services was **20–052** held not to owe a duty of care in *Comyn Ching Ltd v Linkirk Hardware Ltd*.[17] In that case SWEL were architectural ironmongery wholesalers who, in about 1988, wished to computerise their operations. ABT supplied computers and software to three of SWEL's sites. There was no formal written contract. In 1994 SWEL brought proceedings against ABT for negligent misstatement, misrepresentation and breach of contract and collateral contract, claiming damages in excess of £3 million. The duty of care alleged against ABT was not a general duty to take reasonable skill and care but a specific one, either to take proper steps to ascertain the user's requirements or to warn SWEL that they had not taken such steps. It was significant, however, that at the outset SWEL had deliberately decided not to employ a consultant, even though they had limited knowledge of computers. ABT had offered to investigate their requirements but that offer was rejected. For this reason, H.H.J. Bowsher Q.C. held, the case was distinguishable from *Jonas & Erickson Software v Fitz-Wright Co Ltd*, and ABT owed no duty of care to SWEL.

This last decision illustrates that, in order for a duty of care to arise, there must **20–053** be not only (foreseeable) reliance by the client on the supplier as a consultant, but that reliance must be reasonable. Where the client has, without good reason, declined either to appoint his own consultant or to accept an offer by the supplier himself to provide consultancy, there can be little difficulty in concluding that he has acted unreasonably in this regard and/or that it would not be fair, just and reasonable to impose a duty of care on the supplier to provide appropriate consultancy *gratis*.

(xii) *Negligent Misstatements*

It is clear that statements made by any computer supplier or software house **20–054** (whether acting as a consultant or otherwise) during the course of pre-contractual negotiations can give rise to a *Hedley Byrne v Heller*-type duty of care and a liability for negligent misstatement. In *DSL Group Ltd v Unisys International*

---

[15] Unreported, October 5, 1990, Supreme Court of British Columbia, Selbie J.
[16] At 2 of the judgment.
[17] Unreported, April 1997, QBD, Official Referees, H.H.J. Bowsher Q.C.

Services Ltd,[18] for example, DSL, a software house, obtained a computer and operating software from another computer/software supplier, U. These were for onward supply to one of DSL's clients, TR. Disenchanted with the software's capabilities, TR terminated its contract with DSL and sued DSL for damages. That action was settled. DSL in turn sued U, claiming inter alia that U was guilty of negligent misstatement (and deceit) in relation to the software's capabilities. H.H.J. Hicks Q.C. considered that U owed DSL a duty of care in relation to these pre-contract statements because inter alia: (i) the purpose of the statements had been to induce DSL (and its client) to contract with U; (ii) DSL relied on U for guidance in relation to the subject matter of the statements; and (iii) U were aware of DSL's reliance. In addition, U owed a duty of care and were guilty of negligent misstatement (and deceit) in relation to one of the statements made by them to DSL after the contract was entered into, which was to the effect that DSL's approach to the design of the system was adequate.

(xiii) *Collateral Contract*

20–055   It should also be noted that pre-contract statements can, as in any commercial context, be such as to give rise to a collateral warranty on the principles in *Esso Petroleum Co Ltd v Mardon*.[19] In *Mackenzie Patten & Co v British Olivetti Ltd*, for example, pre-contractual representations made by a computer supplier to a firm of solicitors regarding the capabilities of the computer were found to give rise to a collateral contract.[20]

(xiv) *Advice on Computer Systems*

20–056   The liability of computer consultants employed to advise in connection with the acquisition of a computer system was considered in *Stephenson Blake (Holdings) Ltd v Streets Heaver Ltd*.[21] SBH employed SH to advise it on a new computerised accounting system. On SH's recommendation, SBH placed a purchase order with a company, O, for such a system, but was dissatisfied with it. SBH alleged that SH was negligent in recommending O's system. In an action for damages brought before the (then) Official Referees of the Queen's Bench Division, Hicks J. held that the contract was subject to the following implied terms:

(1) where the client has put forward a specification, the consultant is under a duty of reasonable care and skill to ensure that the recommended system conformed to the description;

(2) the consultant must warn the client in plain terms when budgetary constraints or other difficulties mean that the requirements of the client cannot be met;

(3) if the consultant has any concerns about the ability of the client's staff to cope with the changes acquired by the new system it must communicate those concerns to the client;

---

[18] October 19, 1994, reported at [1995] Masons C.L.R. 5.
[19] [1976] Q.B. 801.
[20] Unreported, January 11, 1984, QBD.
[21] [1994] Masons C.L.R. 17; [1998] Masons C.L.R. Rep. 25.

(4) the consultant is under an independent duty to ensure that the hardware and software are compatible with the specification—it cannot rely on the assurances of the supplier who has a vested interest;

(5) the consultant has a duty to ensure that the suppliers recommended had the requisite skilled staff to provide maintenance and support;

(6) if the requirements of the client changed then the consultant has a duty to warn of any incompatibility between the system and any changes.

Further the consultant must air any concerns he has at an early stage during the **20–057** currency of the project. The court found that most of the elements of the system recommended by SH were either incomplete or "not well proven" in commercial use, that the system was unaccpetably deficient in its capacity to carry out the functions required of it and that it contained an excessive number of faults. The hardware was also seriously inadequate. In relation to some of the software defects the court was not satisfied that SBH had shown that SH should have carried out more exhaustive testing to discover them. However, as to the hardware it was clear that SH had advised calamitously without any independent testing or calculation of their own, on the recommendation of a supplier who had an obvious incentive to under-supply. Accordingly SH were in breach of the above implied terms and liable for damages which were to be assessed.

(xv) *Grant of Quiet Possession: "Time Bombs"*

Licensors of standard software sometimes include in the software supplied to **20–058** their customers a device commonly known as a "time bomb" which enables the licensor to deactivate the software if, for example, the licensor discovers that the licensee is in breach of the licence provisions. The legality of such devices was considered by the Court of Appeal in the recent case of *Rubicon Computer Systems Ltd v United Paints Ltd.*[22] R sold a computer system to UP to replace its ageing system. UP withheld about 15 per cent of the purchase price as a result of a dispute over whether R was obliged to transfer data from the old system to the new one. R still had access to the system and put a time lock device in it which, if activated, prevented the system working. R then activated the device, which rendered the system useless. The Court of Appeal held that s.12(2)(b) of the Sale of Goods Act 1979 applied to the contract and introduced into it an implied term that the buyer "will enjoy quiet possession of the goods except so far as it may be disturbed by the owner or other person entitled to the benefit of any charge or encumbrance so disclosed or known." On ordinary principles, wrongful interference with the goods (the hardware and software system) by the seller after property in the goods had passed constituted a breach of that implied term. Moreover, the breach was repudiatory in nature, notwithstanding that the device was easily removed.

Applying the reasoning of the Court of Appeal in the *St Albans*[23] case, it would **20–059** appear that such a term ought to be implied at common law even where the Act does not itself apply, for example where software alone is supplied other than on

---

[22] [2000] Masons C.L.R. 3, CA.
[23] [1996] 4 All E.R. 481.

CD. It has been suggested, however,[24] that the decision in *Rubicon* extends the meaning of "quiet possession" to an unacceptable degree since, ordinarily, the statutory implied term is only invoked where the buyer is deprived of physical possession by someone claiming title or a right to possession of the goods. However, any such extension would appear to be justified given the need for an effective remedy in these circumstances, and is certainly consistent with the interpretation placed on "quiet possession" in landlord and tenant cases.

(b) *Duties other than to Client*

(i) *Common Law Liability to Third Parties*

20–060   As in the case of all professionals, the question of whether a software house or computer supplier owes a common law duty of care to a person other than its client depends upon the type of loss suffered by that third party.[25]

20–061   **Personal injury/damage to other property.** It is now commonplace for software or computer systems to be supplied in circumstances in which the foreseeable consequence of negligence on the part of the supplier, leading to an error or defect in the software or system, is personal injury or damage to other property. Examples include software or computer systems for safety critical applications such as in aircraft and hospital equipment, or for the operation of industrial machinery.

20–062   In the case of the supply of an entire system for such applications, such as the control unit for an industrial laser, it is clear that such a system represents goods,[26] and therefore a product, to which the principles established in *Donoghue v Stephenson*[27] apply. Accordingly, provided that personal injury or property damage is indeed a foreseeable consequence of negligence on the part of the supplier, the necessary proximity for a duty of care to arise will almost inevitably be established,[28] so that a duty of care will exist in favour of all persons who suffer such injury or damage. This would appear to be so even if the product is one which provides factual information for the user, such as an aircraft altimeter.[29]

20–063   If the supply is of software alone, and the software is supplied on CD or some other medium, then (as already seen in the last section) the law treats this as the supply of goods.[30] There seems to be no reason why, in the present context, such a supply should not also be treated as the supply of a product and therefore one in relation to which a duty of care is owed by the supplier to eventual users (or

---

[24] Case Commentary of Mr Richard Stephens, [2000] Masons C.L.R. 3 at 4.

[25] See *South Australia Asset Management Corp v York Montague Ltd* [1996] 3 W.L.R. 87.

[26] *Toby Construction Products Ltd v Computer Bar Sales Pty Ltd* [1983] 2 N.S.W.L.R. 48.

[27] [1932] A.C. 562, HL.

[28] The position has now been reached where foreseeability of phyiscal damage will in itself give rise to a sufficient relationship of proximity for a duty of care to arise in respect of such damage: see Ch.2. Such a duty would therefore only be displaced if, for public policy reasons, it would not be fair, just and reasonable for such a duty to be imposed. It is difficult to imagine a situation in which this would be the case, at least where the relevant loss is personal injury.

[29] A different view is, however, expressed in the *Encyclopaedia of Information Technnology Law* at para.7.34.

[30] *St Albans City and DC v International Computers Ltd* [1996] 4 All E.R. 481.

persons affected) who ultimately suffer foreseeable personal injury or property damage. The same is true where software is provided other than on CD, by downloading or by telephone line, for example (which is becoming far more usual with the modern prevalence of high-speed broadband lines able to handle the transfer of large amounts of data almost instantaneously). It would clearly be illogical to apply different legal principles to such forms of supply.

However, in some circumstances the supply of a computer system or software 20–064 depends upon input from professionals who are required to exercise judgment and express opinions which become incorporated into the software itself. Often the very essence of such a system or software is that it provides recommendations or advice to the user. Examples include the supply of medical equipment (or associated software) which provides diagnoses of medical conditions, or software which provides management or accounting guidance. In such cases, although a particular recommendation is supplied to the user through a computer program or equipment, there seems to be no reason why the liability of the person responsible for the recommendation or opinion ought to be determined any differently from how it would be had the recommendation been provided in writing or orally. Such liability would be determined in accordance with the principles stated by the House of Lords in *Caparo v Dickman*.[31] Again, where physical damage has been suffered, the requirements for establishing a duty of care will almost inevitably be made out on the basis of physical damage alone.

If the particular professional who is the author of the recommendation is 20–065 someone other than the actual supplier of the software or computer, then it would appear that no liability in common law negligence attaches to the supplier, provided that the professional was chosen with due care.[32] However, liability would arise on the part of the professional who made the recommendation, provided that the three-stage test established in *Caparo v Dickman* is satisfied.

"Other property". The criteria considered above apply to negligence claims 20–066 in respect of personal injury or damage to property other than the computer system or software which is itself being supplied. Where the complaint is that the very system or software supplied is defective, the claim is one for economic loss. The principles relevant to such a claim are discussed further below. If software alone has been supplied and, when it is loaded onto hardware, it causes damage to that hardware, then such damage is clearly physical damage recoverable under *Donoghue v Stephenson* principles. A more difficult question arises where the software destroys or damages particular files or other software on that hardware. Should this be categorised as damage to "other property"? Although there is no direct authority on the point, the decision of the Court of Appeal (Criminal Division) in *R. v Whiteley*,[33] which has already been considered above,[34] suggests that the answer is yes. If files or software other than that supplied are erased or corrupted (for example), this represents an impairment of the usefulness of the CD on which the files or software are stored (i.e. the hardware, or conceivably

---

[31] [1990] 2 A.C. 605.
[32] *Taylor v Rover Co Ltd* [1966] 1 W.L.R. 1491.
[33] [1993] F.S.R. 168, CA.
[34] At para.20–017, n.52, above.

a CD), which constitutes physical damage for the purpose of the Criminal Damage Act 1971. Arguably precisely the same approach should apply in determining whether the owner of the hardware (or CDs) on which the damaged files or software are stored has a civil right to compensation under the tort of negligence.[35]

20–067   However, if the same reasoning is applied to the case of the supply of a complete computer system, the corruption or erasure of files stored on that system would represent damage to the system itself, and therefore, on the face of it, irrecoverable economic loss. On the other hand it would be recoverable property damage if the erasure or corruption was to files stored on a CD or other medium separate from the original system supplied. The distinction appears to be arbitrary and irrelevant to the question of whether damages ought to be recoverable in respect of the loss of or damage to the particular file.

20–068   Two alternative approaches are: (i) to treat damage to computer files as no more than economic loss; or (ii) to treat damage to files stored in the system itself as property damage, i.e. damage to property other than the system as originally supplied. The first proposition is unattractive since it would lead to the conclusion that where an item of package software on CD is rendered useless by a defective computer system even this would not give rise to an action for damages under *Donoghue v Stephenson* principles. This would be a surprising and unsatisfactory position. Some support for the proposition at (ii) might be drawn from some of the obiter dicta in the decision of the House of Lords in *D & F Estates Ltd v Church Commissioners*.[36] In that case Lord Bridge considered that it may well be arguable that in the case of complex structures or chattels one element of the structure or chattel should be regarded as distinct from another for the purpose of determining whether damage is to "other property". If so, then if any one component of the structure or chattel malfunctions and causes damage to another of the components the supplier of the defective component, if he was negligent, ought to be liable for that damage provided that the two components are sufficiently distinct for the second component to be properly regarded as "other property". This proviso might be satisfied, for example, if the defect in the system is in a physical component which is distinct from the hard disk on which the corrupted or erased file was stored. If, on the other hand, the defect in the system is in fact a defect in software which is stored on the same hard disk as the affected files then the complex structure argument still leads to the conclusion that the loss is purely economic. It may well be that, arbitrary as this distinction appears to be, it is the inevitable conclusion of the application of the established common law principles.

20–069   **Economic loss.** If the loss of which a third party complains is based upon (i) a defect or error in the very system or software supplied or recommended; or (ii) the financial consequences of such a defect or error, then the loss is properly categorised as economic loss. Since economic detriment of this kind is clearly the most likely form of loss to be occasioned to third parties by the negligence of IT professionals, this area could form the backdrop to a renewed challenge of the

---

[35] This is the view expressed by the authors of the *Encyclopaedia of Information Technology Law*, at para.7.79.
[36] (1988) 41 B.L.R. 1.

restrictive rules of recovery in respect of economic losses in English law. As the law currently stands, third parties can only recover damages for pure economic loss where the loss is the result of a negligent misstatement by the tortfeasor upon which they reasonably relied, or where the tortfeasor has assumed responsibility for the task from which the loss flows.[37] In relation to information technology, it is more likely that consultants will fall within the former category,[38] whilst suppliers could only usually be potentially liable within the latter.

In the context of information technology, in which the level of expertise and   **20–070**
understanding of IT products and systems of those outside the industry is often limited, it will often be difficult for an IT supplier or consultant to argue either that their client did not rely on them, or that they did not assume responsibility for the task in question. However, with more sophisticated clients such defences might conceivably be available.[39]

(ii) *The Consumer Protection Act 1987*

Given the proliferation of computer technology in purely private, non-commer-   **20–071**
cial applications, the potential liability of producers and importers of computer products under the Consumer Protection Act 1987 should not be ignored. Under this Act, the producer (or, in certain circumstances, importer) of a product is liable for any personal injury or damage to (non-commercial) property resulting from a defect in that product, providing that the product was produced during the course of a business.

Liability under the Act is strict,[40] but attaches only to "products". It is clear   **20–072**
that any defect in hardware comes within the terms of the Act, but it remains open to doubt whether software could properly be classified as a "product" under the statute. Section 1(2) provides that "product" means any goods or electricity and . . . includes a product which is comprised in another product, whether by virtue of being a component part or raw material or otherwise." The inter-pretations of "goods" and "substances" in the interpretation section of the Act (s.45) do not assist: the former being a non-exhaustive list of examples of things that can be goods, the latter an unhelpful definition of elemental substances.

Software as a "product". It seems clear (for the reasons given above in the   **20–073**
discussion as to whether software constitutes "goods" or "services") that soft-ware provided by physical medium (e.g. by CD) would fall within the definition of "product" in the Act. However, real doubt remains as to whether software which is downloaded directly, or provided in some other non-tangible way, would constitute a "product" for the purposes of the Act.

The courts have not yet addressed this matter. However, it would be a   **20–074**
surprising, and arbitrary, state of affairs if the manner in which the software is downloaded were to be determinative of the liability of its producer for defects within it. The definition of product within the Act is, it is submitted, drafted

---

[37] See Ch.2, above.
[38] Provided the requirements laid down by the House of Lords in *Caparo Industries v Dickman* are met—see Ch.2, above.
[39] The level of expertise of the client also has ramifications for any allegations of contributory negligence: see below at paras 20–130 *et seq.*
[40] Subject to the limited defences discussed below at paras 20–075 to 20–076, below.

sufficiently widely to allow a court to find that software in itself constitutes a product, and therefore to avoid such a state of affairs. It should be noted, however, that the preponderance of academic opinion is that software transmitted in an "intangible" form would *not* be a "product" for the purposes of the Act.[41]

20–075   **Defences.** By s.3(1) of the Act, a product is defective if it is not as safe as those using it are entitled to expect. Thus the producer may have a defence in relation to the use to which the product was being put at the time of the alleged malfunction, for example that the use was not one which was reasonably envisaged or provided for by the producer.[42]

20–076   There is also the possibility that a producer could utilise a "state of the art" defence in accordance with s.4(1)(e). Under this section it is a defence to show "that the state of scientific and technical knowledge at the relevant time was not such that a producer of products of the same description as the product in question might be expected to have discovered the defect if it had existed in his products while they were under his control." This kind of defence is discussed further at para.20–094, below.

(iii) *"Safety-Critical" Information*

20–077 It is not difficult to imagine the courts imposing a relatively strict duty upon the suppliers of and consultants for computer equipment and software which generate information critical to the physical safety of others. Items falling within this category include the hardware and software in systems regulating the passage of trains on a rail network, or air traffic control, for example. Provided that the proximity aspect of the duty of care test is present, there is no reason why the providers of equipment and systems which generate such information ought not to be liable for foreseeable personal injury which results from their negligence. It is anticipated that the standard of care to be attained by people voluntarily dealing in such critical equipment would be a stringent one.

3. STANDARD OF CARE AND BREACH

(a) *Standard of Care*

(i) *Contracts for Services*

20–078 As already discussed, in many cases involving the recommendation and/or provision of software and hardware, there is likely to be a term implied into the relevant contract of retainer that the equipment or software will be of satisfactory quality and reasonably fit for its purpose. This standard is explored further below. However, there will remain cases in which the contract is clearly for the provision of services alone, or is construed by the court as comprising both a goods *and* a services aspect, and in those circumstances the usual professional duty of care attaches to the services part of the performance, i.e. a duty to act with

---

[41] See, e.g. Lloyd, *Information Technology Law* (2nd edn), p.446; and Reed, *Computer Law* (3rd edn), p.89.
[42] See s.3(2).

all the skill, diligence and care to be expected of a reasonably competent member of the profession.

Since there is, as yet, no professional body regulating the IT industry,[43] there is no obvious point of reference for determining an industry-wide level of acceptable practice in areas of IT consultancy practice. However, there are a number of project management and development methodologies which are widely used, and which give some guidance as to good practice in the provision of consultancy services.[44] Nevertheless a failure to adopt such methodologies will not necessarily be evidence of negligence. Whether there has been a breach of duty will be a matter of fact in each case, and close regard must of course be had to express terms of the retainer and communicated requirements of the client.   **20–079**

As set out in paras 20–085 to 20–089, below, it is accepted as an idiosyncrasy of the IT industry that no software or system can be expected to be entirely free of bugs and errors. Thus it is clear that any professional who has recommended or provided a modified system which does not operate perfectly is not necessarily negligent or in breach of contract. It is a matter of fact and degree on the particular facts of each case as to what constitutes an unacceptable operating standard for the software or system recommended or provided. The further question then arises as to whether the consultant or modifier was in breach of contract/duty in recommending or providing such a system. As discussed below (at para.20–094), it is anticipated that a "state of the art" or "frontiers of knowledge" defence will rarely be available: IT consultants and software modifiers are expected to be circumspect in their assessments of what can be achieved, and to make such assessments and recommendations to clients in the light of the current state of knowledge within the industry.   **20–080**

(ii) *Contracts for Sale/Supply of Goods*

What is satisfactory quality/reasonably fit for purpose? Where the contract between the parties is for the provision of goods (hardware or bespoke software), there is implied by statute (or by common law, where the software is provided by a non-physical medium: the *St Albans* case, above) there is normally a requirement that the goods will be of "satisfactory quality" and "fit for their purpose". Section 14 of the Sale of Goods Act 1979 provides, materially, as follows: **20–081**

> "**14—2**) . . . Where the seller sells goods in the course of a business, there is an implied term that the goods supplied under the contract are of satisfactory quality.
>
> (2A) For the purposes of this Act, goods are of satisfactory quality if they meet the standard that a reasonable person would regard as satisfactory, taking account of any description of the goods, the price (if relevant) and all the other relevant circumstances.
>
> (2B) For the purposes of this Act, the quality of goods includes their state and condition and the following (among others) are in appropriate cases aspects of the quality of goods—

---

[43] See further para.20–001, above.
[44] Included in this category are PRINCE ("Projects in Controlled Environments"), DSDM ("Dynamic Systems Development Method"), and SSADM ("Structural Systems Analysis and Design Method").

(a) fitness for all the purposes for which goods of the kind in question are commonly supplied,
(b) appearance and finish,
(c) freedom from minor defects,
(d) safety, and
(e) durability.

(2C) The term implied by subsection (2) above does not extend to any matter making the quality of the goods unsatisfactory—

(a) which is specifically drawn to the buyer's attention before the contract is made,
(b) where the buyer examines the goods before the contract is made, which that examination ought to reveal . . .

(3) Where the seller sells goods in the course of a business and the buyer, expressly or by implication, makes known . . . any particular purpose for which the goods are being bought, there is an implied term that the goods supplied under the contract are reasonably fit for that purpose . . . except where the circumstances show that the buyer does not rely, or that it is unreasonable for him to rely, on the skill or judgment of the seller . . . "

20–082   The Supply of Goods and Services Act 1982 applies to "contracts for the transfer of goods", defined by s.1 of that Act as "a contract under which one person transfers or agrees to transfer to another the property in goods . . . " The relevant parts of s.4 of the Act are identical to subss.14(2) and (3) of the Sale of Goods Act 1979 (above), and imply terms of satisfactory quality and fitness for purpose.

20–083   In cases in which there is no physical medium transferred between the parties, and to which the judgment of the Court of Appeal in *St Albans City and DC v International Computers Ltd* applies, the term requiring fitness for purpose and satisfactory quality to be implied by the common law is probably to be given the same meaning as has been given to those terms when construed by the courts in a statutory context.[45]

20–084   The issue, however, of whether software is fit for its purpose is potentially far from straightforward, as in many cases the software is to some extent unique to the recipient in question and the precise "purpose" for which the software is to be used is often very loosely defined in the contracts for the supply of the software. A recent case[46] (albeit not in the context of computer software) suggests that the courts will be willing to take a purposive approach to the interpretation of a specification, and be prepared to fill in any gaps in the favour of the recipient in holding that where both parties know the commercial purpose to which a product is intended to be put, it should be fit for that purpose. Providers of software should accordingly be astute to define closely and carefully the purpose for which the software will be fit upon installation.

---

[45] The judgment of Sir Iain Glidewell does not elaborate upon the content of the term to be implied. In relation to contracts for the transfer of software alone, he states that "such a contract is subject to an implied term that the program will be reasonably fit for, i.e. reasonably capable of achieving, the intended purpose." [1996] 4 All E.R. 481 at 494d. Immediately preceding this passage the learned judge discusses the relevant terms implied elsewhere by the Sale of Goods Act 1979 and the Supply of Goods and Services Act 1982, and he can only have had a term identical to those in mind.
[46] *Filobake Ltd v Rondo Ltd* [2005] EWCA Civ 563.

(b) *"Bugs" and "Bedding In"—Inevitable Defects and Software*

As can be seen from the above definitions, there is an objective element to the   **20–085**
test of both fitness and satisfactory quality. However, the objectively reasonable
view to be taken of fitness and quality must relate to the *specific* goods in
question. Hence the determination of what constitutes "satisfactory quality" or a
product "reasonably fit for its purpose" is subject to the idiosyncracies of the IT
industry. For example, in *Eurodynamic Systems v General Automation Ltd*,[47] a
case in which the High Court was concerned with a dispute as to the quality of
an operating system for a computer, Steyn J. observed that:

> "The expert evidence convincingly showed that it is regarded as acceptable practice to
> supply computer programmes [*sic*] (including system software) that contains errors and
> bugs. The basis of the practice is that, pursuant to his support obligation (free or
> chargeable as the case may be), the supplier will correct errors and bugs that prevent the
> product from being properly used. Not every bug or error in a computer programme can
> therefore be categorised as a breach of contract."

Note should also be taken of the (obiter) observation of Staughton L.J. in   **20–086**
Saphena that (emphasis added): *"Just as no software developer can reasonably
expect a buyer to tell him what is required without a process of feedback and
reassessment,* so no buyer should expect a supplier to get his programs right first
time".[48]

In *Micron Computer Systems Ltd v Wang*[49] the claimant purchased a computer   **20–087**
system consisting of both hardware and software from the defendant. Discussing
the problems experienced by the claimant with the running of the software, Steyn
J. noted that: "Some of the problems were plainly only the teething problems
which are commonplace in the installation of any such computer system",[50] and
that "It was simply teething problems in the installation process which is
perfectly normal in the computer industry".[51]

It is apparent from these passages that the expectation in the IT industry is that   **20–088**
software will not be free from error upon delivery or activation, but that some
period of "bedding in" or "debugging" is to be expected.[52] It is a matter of
degree in each case as to how many faults or errors are acceptable, and the
timescale within which the provider ought to have the system running acceptably
bug free.[53] This has ramifications for the compliance of the buyer with its duty

---

[47] Unreported, September 6, 1988, QBD.
[48] See also the observations of Staughton L.J. in the same case, in the passage reproduced at
para.20–032, above.
[49] Unreported, May 9, 1990, QBD. See further para.20–030, above.
[50] At 7 of the transcript.
[51] At 12 of transcript.
[52] It is doubtful that the courts would be so lenient in relation to faults in hardware. It is also doubtful
whether standard (i.e. non-bespoke) software would be accorded the same degree of indulgence.
Again it is a matter of fact and degree in each case.
[53] As the IT industry matures, however, it may well be that customers' and the court's acceptance of
the inevitably of bugs will gradually erode.

of co-operation[54] (i.e. in relation to the period over which this duty is in operation), with the implied term that the seller or provider has a right to test and modify the system and with the need for the buyer to mitigate any losses it suffers.[55]

20–089   Particular problems arise in relation to the meaning of fitness for purpose where the purpose in question is communicated to the supplier late, or in gradual stages. In some computer contracts, the buyer collaborates with the seller/supplier in the design process for bespoke software by working out its requirements during the currency and progression of the contract. In such cases the buyer is under a duty to sufficiently and timeously communicate its requirements.[56] However, assuming that this duty is complied with, the fact that the obligation was an evolving one will not absolve the supplier from liability if the final product does not comply with the specification as ultimately agreed. As Nourse L.J. said in *St Albans City and DC v ICL*[57]:

> "Parties who respectively agree to supply and acquire a system recognising that it is still in the course of development cannot be taken, merely by virtue of that recognition, to intend that the supplier shall be at liberty to supply software which cannot perform the function expected of it at the stage of development at which it is supplied."

(c) *The Time when the Obligation of Fitness for Purposes Arises*

20–090   In sale of goods law the obligation to provide goods which are of satisfactory quality and fit for their purpose arises, in the absence of anything to the contrary in the relevant contract, at the time the property in the goods passes. On the basis of the authorities referred to above,[58] it would appear that in cases involving bespoke (or in some circumstances modified) computer software the relevant obligation only arises at a later stage, at a point when reasonable testing, refinement and adjustment have allowed the system to run in an acceptably bug-free manner, and to perform the functions for which it was acquired.

20–091   Although the issue has not been put directly in this way in the reported cases, it would appear that this conclusion is based on the existence of an implied term to this effect. This is consistent with the passages cited above, and any departure from the usual point in time at which the obligation arises (i.e. as laid down by

---

[54] See above, para.20–036. The attitude of the courts in relation to standard software has recently been demonstrated in the decision of H.H.J. Bowsher Q.C. in *SAM Business Systems Ltd v Hedley & Co* ([2002] EWHC 2733). In that case the software in question was called InterSet and was described by the judge as:

> "not as simple as going into a shop and buying a shrink wrapped package, but it is not a bespoke system. The customer can make choices between certain modules and certain services, but it is sold as a developed system." (para.8 of judgment).

In relation to the acceptability of bugs within the software the judge said this:

> " . . . InterSet was sold as a developed system allegedly already working well in other places. This is a much stronger case than St Albans against toleration of bugs. I am in no doubt that if a software system is sold as a tried and tested system it should not have any bugs in it and if there are any bugs they should be regarded as defects. Of course, if the defects are speedily remedied without charge, it may be that there will be no consequential damage." (para.20 of judgment).

[55] See discussion below, paras 20–128 to 20–129.

[56] See discussion above, paras 20–027 to 20–031.

[57] [1996] 4 All E.R. 481.

[58] See paras 20–085 to 20–087, above.

the relevant statutes) offers the advantage that it is equally applicable to cases in which software is downloaded or transferred without any physical medium, to which the statutory provisions do not strictly relate by virtue of the absence of a transfer of property.

(d) *The Time when the Obligation Ceases*

Whilst, in general, the supplier's obligation to test and modify the system or software ends when the system becomes of satisfactory quality or fit for its purpose, the parties can of course vary the contract and thereby end the obligation sooner. In *Saphena v Allied Collection Agencies*[59] the parties (the supplier and purchaser of online software) agreed to end their relationship *before* the bugs had been satisfactorily worked out of the system. Mr Recorder Havery Q.C. held[60] that this was a consensual variation of the contract such that the supplier would not be liable to the purchaser for the system's failure to be fit for its purpose as the contract work had not been completed. **20–092**

Another way in which the obligation to test and modify can be brought to an end is by the purchaser accepting the goods. Whilst the nature of software again makes the precise application of the Sale of Goods Act provisions problematic,[61] in relation to acceptance it is submitted that the buyer can clearly indicate acceptance of the goods at any time. The clearest indication of such acceptance might be by means of systems acceptance tests, especially so if such tests are specified in the contract.[62] **20–093**

(e) *"State of the Art" Defence*

Given the rapidly evolving nature of information technology, it may be that defendants will attempt to argue that the system or software they contracted to provide could not in fact have been provided by any party, and that, as a result, and given the state of knowledge in the industry at the time, it cannot be said that they were negligent in contracting to provide it. In support of this, it might be argued that to condemn as negligent those who attempt to push back the boundaries of technology would be unduly restrictive and would hinder progress in the industry. Such an argument was advanced on behalf of the defendants in the building case of *IBA v EMI and BICC*.[63] In that case the House of Lords found that negligence could properly be found even where the defendant's work could be said to be at the "cutting edge", if the party in question had not approached the project with sufficient circumspection. A similar approach can **20–094**

---

[59] [1995] F.S.R. 616. See further para.20–027, above.

[60] *ibid.*, at 640.

[61] s.35(1) of that Act deems the buyer to have accepted goods "when he intimates to the seller that he has accepted them; or when the goods have been delivered to him and he does any act in relation to them inconsistent with the ownership of the seller." The latter of these is problematic in relation to software, but the former ought to present no difficulties provided the acceptance is clearly and unequivocally communicated.

[62] See further Rowland and MacDonald, *Information Technology Law*, p.87.

[63] (1980) 14 B.L.R. 1.

probably be expected by the courts in the area of Information Technology.[64] It is not thought that an argument as bold, and unattractive, as this is ever likely to succeed, at least in the absence of a specific warning from the software provider.

4. Causation

20–095   The related facts that no IT system can be bug- or error-free, and that there appears to be an implied term in IT contracts that the consultant/supplier is entitled to a reasonable period of time to correct errors and ensure that the system is running in an acceptable manner, may present difficulties for claimants in establishing causation of loss. In borderline cases in which, for example, a system is found to have only marginally more bugs than is acceptable; or in which the problems are reduced to an acceptable level but outside the timescale in which this result would have been reasonably expected, it may be difficult for a claimant to establish which part or parts of its loss are causally attributable to the default of the defendant, and which parts are attributable to the "acceptable" initial errors in the system.

20–096   Questions of causation may also arise in situations in which software is subsequently modified by a different party, and then becomes inoperative. There may be difficult causation issues as to whether the more recent modification was the operative cause of the defect, or whether the original program was defectively designed. Such cases would turn upon the expressed requirements of the client in the original contract (i.e. in relation to future modification), and in all probability upon expert evidence.

20–097   There are also difficulties in IT cases in proving exactly what losses have flowed from the defects in hardware or software of which complaint is made. These problems result largely from the fact that contracts for the provision of software and computer systems are aspirational in nature: they are entered into as a means of improving the efficiency and profitability of businesses, and measuring the expected results is often problematic.[65] These difficulties are discussed further in the context of remedies, below.

An additional causation question and one related to the implied duty of co-operation upon the purchaser (see paras 20–036 to 20–041, above) is whether or not the purchaser would in any event have been ready to implement the new system at the contractually agreed date. In the *CWS* case (see para.20–126, below), the judge found (at paras 239 and 266 of the judgment) that the purchaser

---

[64] See the observations of Nourse L.J. in *St Albans DC v International Computers Ltd* [1996] 4 All E.R. 481 at 487c and of Hirst L.J. in *Professional Reprographic Services v DPS Typecraft*, unreported, February 15, 1993, CA, approving the comments of the trial judge on this issue.

[65] However, these problems were given short shrift by H.H.J. Bowsher Q.C. in the case of *Horace Holman Group Ltd v Sherwood International Group Ltd* (unreported, November 7, 2001, TCC), in which damages were awarded for various "aspirational" heads of loss. See discussion of this case in para.20–104, below. The same judge adopted a similar approach in *SAM Business Systems Ltd v Hedley & Co* (discussed further at para.20–126, below).

would have been unable to implement the new system in time owing to deficiencies in its own understanding of and preparation for the new system.

5. REMEDIES

The remedies available in respect of a breach of contract and/or duty by an IT   **20–098**
professional are no different from those available under the general law of
contract and tort. The issue of quantification of damages for pecuniary loss, and
the related question of election between "reliance" and "expectation" loss,
presently represent the main area of interest in IT contract disputes. This area is
examined at paras 20–106 to 20–111, below.

(a) *Contract*

The provision of hardware, and of software conveyed by physical medium,   **20–099**
constitutes a sale of goods in accordance with the Sale of Goods Act 1979. The
terms implied by that Act as to satisfactory quality and fitness for purpose are, by
virtue of s.14(6), deemed to be conditions of the contract. Accordingly breach of
these conditions gives the buyer a right to repudiate the contract.

(b) *Repudiation: When Possible?*

As has already been discussed (at para.20–090), there appears to be an implied   **20–100**
term in contracts for the provision of software that the time for compliance with
these conditions is *not* the point at which property in the goods passes (as in
general sale of goods law), but is some later point in time at which it is
reasonably to be expected that the system will be operating in an acceptably bug-
free manner.[66] In these circumstances it is not always clear exactly when the
buyer is entitled to repudiate the contract. Advising on this point may therefore
prove to be a very delicate exercise. Buyers must be careful that a severance of
their relationship with the supplier is not construed as a variation of contract as
opposed to a repudiation.[67]

(c) *Acceptance: When Deemed?*

Where there is a continuing relationship between supplier and buyer after   **20–101**
delivery it is often difficult to establish when the buyer can be deemed to have
"accepted" the goods[68] and thereby lost his right of repudiation. In the absence
of a contractual provision for defined acceptance tests, it may be difficult to

---

[66] As mentioned above, there appears to be no such concession in relation to defects in hardware.
[67] See in this respect the *Saphena* case (para.20–033, above), in which an agreement between supplier
and buyer to sever relations before the bugs had been satisfactorily removed from a system was held
to be a consensual variation of contract which terminated the supplier's obligation to make right the
defect.
[68] See s.35 of the Sale of Goods Act 1979 and the discussion of this point at para.20–093, above.

advise upon when "acceptance" has taken place, and a careful review of all the circumstances will be required.

(d) *Time of the Essence?*

20–102   Of course the parties may oust or modify the implied term as to continued relationship after supply of software by including a contractual term as to the date upon which the system must be operating satisfactorily. It will be a matter of construction in each case as to whether a provision as to the time for completion has been made a condition or "of the essence" of the contract.[69]

20–103   Where the defendant is not the supplier of the goods (or non-physically delivered software) but the consultant who recommended the items or system in question, the claimant will not generally be able to sue upon a condition of quality or fitness for purpose, and the contractual measure of damages will reflect what would have happened had the consultant's advice been to the standard required (i.e. non-negligent). In most circumstances the quantum of loss will be the same in relation to claims against consultants as those against suppliers, i.e. the amount required to put the claimant in the position he would have been in had the advice been correct and had the system delivered the required functionality.

20–104   **Damages.** The normal measure of contractual damages applies, namely the amount to put the claimant in the position he would have been in had the contract been properly performed. In contracts for the supply of computer equipment and software (and contracts for advice on which equipment or software to obtain) this is often very difficult to calculate. The reason why people and businesses usually install and upgrade computer equipment is to improve the efficiency of, and often to expand, their business. As H.H.J. Hicks Q.C. stated in *Stephenson Blake (Holdings) Ltd v Streets Heaver Ltd,*[70] the assessment of what would have happened had the hardware or system worked properly is "necessarily hypothetical".[71] These hypothetical losses will often include a claim for lost profits, for which cogent evidence is required. It seems, however, that the difficulties in proving such losses are far from insuperable. In *Horace Holman Group Ltd v Sherwood International Group Ltd*[72] H.H.J. Bowsher Q.C. awarded the claimant more than £2.6 million in damages, under heads of loss such as "predicted in-house savings", "audit savings not made", and "staff not made redundant earlier". Under this last head of damage the claimant was awarded over £1.7 million in relation to staff costs they would have saved had the system in question worked as it was supposed to. The claimants also recovered a significant amount under the head of loss "Time wasted by Directors and Staff". The judge considered the leading case of *Tate & Lyle v GLC*[73] (which held that a court

---

[69] Examples of time being "of the essence" in IT contracts can be found in the *South West Water* case, and in *Salvage Association v CAP.*

[70] Unreported, March 2, 1994, ORB; case note at [1994] Masons C.L.R. 17.

[71] Para.158 of judgment.

[72] TCC, November 7, 2001, unreported.

[73] [1982] 1 W.L.R. 149.

could not award damages under this head in the absence of good evidence on the point), but distinguished the case thus:

> "the case before me differs from the case before Forbes J in that while he had no evidence of the amount of time spent, there is before me evidence in the form of a reconstruction from memory of events from the past. I cannot and do not say, in the absence of records there is to be no recovery." (para.73)

The arguments of the parties were rehearsed in paras 74 to 77 of the judgment, before the judge concluded that:

> "I do not accept the distinction that [D's expert] seeks to make between short and long periods of wasted time nor his distinction between senior and less senior posts. In all cases, the claimants were paying for time which was to be a benefit to them and they lost the benefit of that time . . . it is unrealistic to try to distinguish between profit makers and non-profit makers as the defendants have sought to do." (para.78 of judgment—Damages of £135,567.95 awarded under this head).

Accordingly it would seem that the courts are evincing a willingness to recognise the "aspirational" nature of software contracts and to award aspirational or expectation damages more readily in this area of law. The application of the defendant for permission to appeal *Holman* was rejected by Dyson L.J. on February 7, 2002.[74] H.H.J. Bowsher Q.C. reiterated his commitment to the approach in *Holman* when assessing (obiter) damages in the *SAM v Hedley* case (para.20–126, below).

Given, however, the remaining uncertainties in the calculation of what is **20–105** generally described as "expectation loss", a claimant in an IT case will often seek to include in its claim a measure of the "reliance loss" suffered, for example the costs incurred in preparing to implement the systems and equipment contracted for, which have subsequently been wasted.[75] Whether this is a sustainable head of loss depends of course on the facts of the case, but in situations where there is at least a prima facie case for recovery under this head, the issue arises as to whether the claimant must make an election between reliance and expectation loss, or whether elements of both are recoverable.

(e) *"Reliance Loss" and "Expectation Loss": Election Necessary?*

Since Lord Denning's pronouncement in *Anglia TV v Reed*[76] the traditional **20–106** position has been that such an election must be made, so that the claimant does not obtain double recovery by being awarded both the costs of setting up a business opportunity *and* the lost profits that such an opportunity or venture would have generated. This was the position adopted by H.H.J. Thayne Forbes in *Salvage Association v CAP Financial Services*,[77] in which Lord Denning's dictum in *Anglia TV* was applied.

---

[74] [2002] EWCA Civ 170.
[75] In certain circumstances this can include even pre-contractual expenditure—see *Anglia TV v Reed* [1972] Q.B. 60.
[76] [1972] Q.B. 60 at 64.
[77] [1995] F.S.R. 654.

20-107   However, this position was recently examined in the IT case of *Kwik Fit Insurance Services Ltd v Bull Information Systems Ltd*.[78] In that case, KFIS had retained Bull as prime contractor to design, develop, deliver, install and implement an enterprise-wide computer system. Various breaches of contract were alleged against Bull and it was contended that the result of these breaches was that the system was never operational. KFIS claimed losses under heads including: restitution of the moneys paid to Bull under the agreement; costs and expenses directly incurred by KFIS in contemplation of and pursuant to the agreement between the parties, to the extent that such costs and expenses would be wasted if an alternative solution was implemented by another supplier; and "indirect" or consequential losses (i.e. "expectation losses") consisting mainly of projected losses of revenue.

20-108   The case came before Mr Colin Reese Q.C., sitting as a deputy in the Technology and Construction Court, for the hearing of certain preliminary issues and applications. One of the applications made by Bull was that KFIS should be compelled to make an election at an early stage before trial as to whether they were going to pursue "reliance losses" (which came to around £1.4 million) or "expectation losses" (which came to over £25 million and would take much time, effort and expense to investigate). It was submitted on behalf of KFIS that the terms "expectation loss" and "reliance loss" were not terms of art, and indeed were not used in the *Anglia TV* case itself. All that was established was that a claimant could not "have his cake and eat it" by claiming the cost of setting up a business venture and the gross profits that would have been generated from it. The set-up costs and the generated profits were not alternative measures of loss but different ways of approaching the same loss, and whilst the claimant might choose at some stage to limit his claim to the costs incurred, this was not a true "election". There was no necessary inconsistency between a claim for expenses incurred in reliance on the contract and a claim for loss of profit, provided there was no double-counting.

20-109   In support of this proposition KFIS cited para.27–063 of *Chitty on Contract* (28th edn):

> "Claiming for wasted expenditure in addition to net loss of expected profit. In principle the claimant should be entitled to claim damages both for his wasted expenditure incurred up to the date of his terminating the contract and also for the net loss of profit which he would have made but for the breach. There can be no valid objection to this, provided the calculations show that there is no overlapping in the claimant's recovery, *viz.* his net loss of profits is calculated by deducting from his expected gross return both the cost of his performance and reliance expenditure to the date of termination and the cost of the further expenditure which he would have incurred after that date if he had completed his performance. However the Court of Appeal (in *Cullinane v British 'Rema' Manufacturing Co Ltd*[79]) has ruled that the claimant must choose between claiming for his wasted reliance expenditure and claiming for his loss of expected profits, holding that he is not entitled to recover both. This position is correct if it is interpreted to mean that the claimant should not recover both his gross return or profits expected under the contract (or from the activity in question) and also the (now wasted expenditure) incurred in reliance on the contract which he had intended to meet from

---

[78] Unreported, June 23, 2000, TCC.
[79] [1954] 1 Q.B. 292.

that gross return. But it is submitted that the ruling against a 'split' claim cannot be justified if the claimant can show that there is no overlapping between the two claims."

Similar passages in *Treitel on Contract* (10th edn) were also cited. The deputy judge accepted these propositions and ruled that KFIS did not have to make any such "election".[80]   **20–110**

The approach outlined above and endorsed in *Kwik Fit Insurance Services Ltd v Bull Information Systems Ltd* appears to the present authors to be sound in principle, and should be carefully considered by claimants when calculating and pleading losses for breach of IT contracts.[81]   **20–111**

(f) *Quantum: Difficulties in Calculation*

There are numerous additional difficulties to calculating the quantum of a claim in this area. One example of this is where a defective system corrupts or destroys data already held by the claimant. The best view appears to the present authors to be that, by analogy to the approach taken in the criminal case of *R. v Whiteley*,[82] this would represent (recoverable) damage to property. However, the quantification of such a loss is often difficult. Such cases can only be dealt with on their individual facts, and it is anticipated that cogent (possibly expert) evidence will be required to establish the value to a claimant of raw data.[83]   **20–112**

Restitution. Restitution of the moneys paid to the defendant under an IT contract has been sought in a number of cases where the systems provided ultimately transpired to be useless, on the basis of a total failure of consideration. In both *Stephenson Blake (Holdings) Ltd v Streets Heaver Ltd*[84] and the *Salvage Association* case[85] such claims failed, in the latter case H.H.J. Thayne Forbes commenting that it is "well nigh impossible to prove a total failure of consideration unless no part of the service contracted is provided for".[86]   **20–113**

This is in line with the general approach in the law of restitution. However, a different view was taken by H.H.J. Toulmin Q.C. in *South West Water Services*   **20–114**

---

[80] See para.80 of judgment.
[81] The normal contractual rules of remoteness of course apply to IT contracts, and lost profits can accordingly only be recovered in accordance with the rule in *Hadley v Baxendale*.
[82] [1993] F.S.R. 168, see discussion at para.20–066, above.
[83] See for example the case of *Logical Computer Ltd v Euro Carparks Ltd* (unreported, June 19, 2001, QB), in which two grossly incompetent repair operatives damaged the defendant's hard disk and erased data from the payroll, the nominal ledger, the suppliers database and the sales ledger. The claimant sued for its fees for this and other work. The defendant's counterclaim included a claim for the value of lost data. The Court found that the lost data would never in fact be re-inputted, and for this reason a claim for the cost of so doing was disproportionate to the benefit to be obtained and therefore, in accordance with *Ruxley Electronics v Forsyth* [1996] 1 A.C. 344, should not be allowed. Mr R. Fernyhough Q.C., sitting as a deputy judge in the Technology and Construction Court, held that the correct way of dealing with this particular claim was as a diminution in value of the system as a whole, relying on *Chaplin v Hicks* [1911] 1 K.B. 786 as the justification of such an award of general damages. The judge assessed the diminution in value of the system without the lost data at £15,000. The claim for the cost of re-inputting the data had been just over £45,000.
[84] Unreported, March 2, 1994.
[85] [1995] F.S.R. 654.
[86] [1995] F.S.R. 654 at 682.

Ltd v International Computers Ltd[87] in which the claimant did obtain restitution of the contract price. The contracted for computer system was never received, the judge holding that "SWW did not contract in a vacuum to receive management know-how. They contracted to receive management services to enable the computer system to be delivered and not as an end in itself . . . The buyer did not get any part of that for which they paid the purchase money."

20–115   It is suggested that this case is likely to be confined to its specific facts as the general position in the law of restitution is that the contract price is not recovered unless no part of the service contracted for is provided.[88] It will be rare that restitution of the contract price is ordered in situations in which the defendant has clearly gone some way towards performing its obligations under the contract.

(g) *Tort*

20–116   It will be relatively rare for claimants to have to rely upon a claim in tort, as there is almost invariably a contractual relationship between the party seeking to acquire or upgrade IT equipment or software and those who supply or advise upon such products. The situations in which a tortious claim might arise have already been discussed above,[89] for example where the ultimate user of software has no direct relationship with supplier or manufacturer. In situations in which a duty can be established, the measure of loss is the usual tortious one, i.e. the amount to put the claimant into the situation he would have been in had the tort not occurred. This can include pure economic loss,[90] and where the relevant relationship is established, the tortfeasor will be liable for losses in relation to which he had a duty to keep the claimant harmless.[91]

20–117   A potentially interesting problem in relation to recovery in tort presents itself when the loss claimed is for damage to software not "attached" to any physical medium. It is well established that for liability in tort to attach the victim must have property in the damaged item at the time damage occurs—*Leigh & Sillivan Ltd v Aliakmon Shipping Co Ltd*[92]—which would technically mean that damage to software alone would not be susceptible to a claim in tort, unless a court was willing to find that software could represent "property" for this purpose.

6. EXCLUSION AND LIMITATION OF LIABILITY

20–118   There are no special rules applicable to the IT industry in relation to exclusion and limitation clauses. However, such clauses are invariably used in IT contracts.

---

[87] Unreported, June 29, 1999, TCC; case note at [1999] Masons C.L.R. 400.
[88] See *Chitty on Contracts,* paras 30–048 *et seq.*
[89] Paras 20–060 to 20–070, above.
[90] See above, para.20–069.
[91] See *South Australia Asset Management Corp v York Montague Ltd* [1997] A.C. 191, and discussion thereof in Ch.10, above. As far as a claim in tort ever needs to be relied upon against an IT consultant, it is worth noting that such consultants will very rarely be retained to provide bare information. They almost always give positive advice on a course of action, and under *SAAMCO* principles they would accordingly be liable for all the consequences of that advice being wrong.
[92] [1986] A.C. 785.

This is understandable given the potentially substantial liability that can arise as a result of a defect in modern IT systems. Accordingly the construction and/or application of exclusion clauses arises as an issue in many of the reported IT cases. As set out at para.20–125, below, the Court of Appeal in *Watford Electronics Ltd v Sanderson CFL Ltd*,[93] in a case involving the defective supply of software and the specific issues thrown up by such contracts, has given general guidance as to when the exclusion of liability, limitation of liability, and entire agreement clauses are reasonable as between commercial parties operating at arm's length. The decision seeks to place as few restrictions as possible on commercial parties' freedom of contract. Accordingly the parties to an IT contract should when negotiating the contract give very careful thought indeed to the terms of any limitation or exclusion of liability clauses contained therein.

It should also be noted that a new Unfair Contract Terms Act (which will **20–119** repeal in their entirety the Unfair Contract Terms Act 1977 and the Unfair Terms in Consumer Contracts Regulations 1999) is shortly to be promulgated. Assuming no late revisions to the Bill which has been produced, the new Act will provide a new and special protection for "small businesses", i.e. those businesses with nine or fewer staff. Such businesses will be entitled to challenge *any* standard term that has not been altered through negotiation and is not the main subject-matter of the contract or the price. If the small business can show that the term is unfair (and the onus is on the small business to establish unfairness), it will not be enforceable. Exemptions to the special "small businesses" protection are: (i) where the business is part of a group which overall has more than nine employees; (ii) where the value of the contract in issue is greater than £500,000 (or if there is a series of transactions whose aggregated value is greater than £500,000); or (iii) terms relating to intellectual property are exempt. The "fair and reasonable" test under the new act is to take into account (a) the extent to which the term is transparent; and (b) the substance and effect of the term, and all the circumstances existing at the time it was agreed. There is a list of considerations which the court must take into account in considering the substance and effect and all the circumstances of the contract, which is in similar (but not identical) terms to Sch.2 to the present Act. It is thought therefore that the authorities dealing with the question of reasonableness under the old Act will be a useful aid to the courts when considering the question under the new Act. The new Act will be prospective only in effect. The foregoing is by necessity only a very brief summary of some of the facets of the new Act, and practitioners should of course familiarise themselves with the entirety of the Act itself upon promulgation.

Contracting on the other party's standard terms. In *Salvage Association v* **20–120** *CAP Financial Services*[94] it was held that, although the parties had negotiated some important points in their first contract, there had been no negotiation or alteration of the general terms or conditions, and accordingly the parties had contracted on the defendant's standard terms. The exclusion clauses in the contract therefore had to pass the test of reasonableness laid down in s.11 of the Unfair Contract Terms Act 1977 (UCTA). In relation to the second contract

---

[93] [2001] 1 All E.R. (Comm) 696.
[94] [1995] F.S.R. 654.

between them, the claimant had considered and received advice on each term of the contract, and where it had sought changes these had generally been agreed. Accordingly the parties had been of equal bargaining power and the UCTA requirement of reasonableness did not apply to the exclusion clauses contained in this contract.[95]

20–121 Many of the cases to date deal with the issue of whether one of the party's standard terms were incorporated into the contract, which is usually decided on (and specific to) the facts of the individual case. In *St Albans DC v ICL*[96] the Court of Appeal discussed the decision of Thayne Forbes Q.C. in *Salvage Association v CAP*, and held that dealing on standard terms was not dependent upon the absence of negotiations. Even if there had been negotiations over the terms in question the learned judge would still have found that the parties had contracted on the defendant's standard terms.

20–122 **Reasonableness of term.** In the *St Albans* case, the Court of Appeal upheld the trial judge's decision that the term in question, which purported to limit ICL's liability for breach of contract to the price of the equipment or service in question or £100,000, whichever was the lesser, and to exclude liability entirely for "any direct or consequential loss or loss of business profits sustained by the customer", was unreasonable.[97]

20–123 In the *Salvage Association* case, the court held that a clause which purported to limit the defendant's liability for any failure of their warranty to repair defects in the system provided within a reasonable period of time to the lesser of the price of the repair or £25,000, was unreasonable. In reaching this decision the judge emphasised the fact that the claimant was unable to insure effectively against the risk of non-performance by the defendant, whereas the defendant had considerable insurance cover and, in recent similar contracts, had adopted the policy of raising the limitation to £1,000,000.

20–124 In *South West Water v ICL*,[98] clauses which purported to exclude the defendant's liability for fraudulent misrepresentation prior to the contract, and to limit its liability to £250,000 if the system did not make it to the stage of acceptance testing, were both found to be manifestly unreasonable.

20–125 The Court of Appeal decision in *Watford Electronics Ltd v Sanderson CFL Ltd*[99] has now set out authoritative guidance on the approach to be taken in considering whether exclusion and entire agreement clauses are reasonable as between commercial entities. The relevant guidance given by Chadwick L.J. was as follows:

"[31] In order to decide whether the relevant contract term was a fair and reasonable one to be included having regard to the circumstances which were, or ought reasonably to have been, known to or in the contemplation of the parties when the contract was

---

[95] It should be noted, however, that both contracts imposed duties on the defendant, breach of which would have constituted negligence. Accordingly the exclusion clauses attempted to exclude liability for negligence and thereby fell foul of s.2 of UCTA, meaning that they in fact had to comply with the requirements of reasonableness in s.11. It is submitted that this will often be the case, and practitioners should be alert to the operation of UCTA in this manner.
[96] [1996] 4 All E.R. 481 at 491.
[97] [1996] 4 All E.R. 481 at 492b.
[98] [1999] Masons C.L.R. 400.
[99] [2001] 1 All E.R. (Comm) 696.

made it is necessary, as it seems to me, to determine, first, the scope and effect of that term as a matter of construction. In particular, it is necessary to identify the nature of the liability which the term is seeking to exclude or restrict. Whether or not a contract term satisfies the 'requirement of reasonableness' within the meaning of s 11 of the 1977 Act does not fall to be determined in isolation. It falls to be determined where a person is seeking to rely upon the term in order to exclude or restrict his liability in some context to which the earlier provisions of the 1977 Act (or the provisions of s 3 of the 1967 Act) apply.

[54] It seems to me that the starting point in an enquiry whether, in the present case, the term excluding indirect loss was a fair and reasonable one to include in the contract which these parties made is to recognise (i) that there is a significant risk that a non-standard software product, 'customised' to meet the particular marketing, accounting or record-keeping needs of a substantial and relatively complex business (such as that carried on by Watford), may not perform to the customer's satisfaction, (ii) that, if it does not do so, there is a significant risk that the customer may not make the profits or savings which it had hoped to make (and may incur consequential losses arising from the product's failure to perform), (iii) that those risks were, or ought reasonably to have been, known to or in the contemplation of both Sanderson and Watford at the time when the contract was made, (iv) that Sanderson was in the better position to assess the risk that the product would fail to perform but (v) that Watford was in the better position to assess the amount of the potential loss if the product failed to perform, (vi) that the risk of loss was likely to be capable of being covered by insurance, but at a cost, and (vii) that both Sanderson and Watford would have known, or ought reasonably to have known, at the time when the contract was made, that the identity of the party who was to bear the risk of loss (or to bear the cost of insurance) was a factor which would be taken into account in determining the price at which the supplier was willing to supply the product and the price at which the customer was willing to purchase. With those considerations in mind, it is reasonable to expect that the contract will make provision for the risk of indirect or consequential loss to fall on one party or the other. In circumstances in which parties of equal bargaining power negotiate a price for the supply of product under an agreement which provides for the person on whom the risk of loss will fall, it seems to me that the court should be very cautious before reaching the conclusion that the agreement which they have reached is not a fair and reasonable one.

[55] Where experienced businessmen representing substantial companies of equal bargaining power negotiate an agreement, they may be taken to have had regard to the matters known to them. They should, in my view, be taken to be the best judge of the commercial fairness of the agreement which they have made; including the fairness of each of the terms in that agreement. They should be taken to be the best judge on the question whether the terms of the agreement are reasonable. The court should not assume that either is likely to commit his company to an agreement which he thinks is unfair, or which he thinks includes unreasonable terms. Unless satisfied that one party has, in effect, taken unfair advantage of the other—or that a term is so unreasonable that it cannot properly have been understood or considered—the court should not inter-fere."

In *SAM Business Systems Ltd v Hedley & Co*[1] the freedom of contract **20–126** approach espoused by the court in *Watford Electronics* was adopted by H.H.J. Bowsher Q.C., the learned judge finding that the customer in question was "well able to look after itself" and that it had made no attempt to alter the terms of the

---

[1] TCC, H.H.J. Bowsher Q.C., December 19, 2002.

clause in question. The judge also made clear that the question of the reasonableness of any term could only properly be determined by looking at other relevant terms in the contract dealing with the attribution of risk between the parties:

> "As was made plain by Chadwick LJ in *Watford* at page 16 paragraph 50, the reasonableness of each term to which the 1977 Act applies must be considered separately even to the extent of looking to see whether each clause contains one term or more than one, although, of course, in considering whether that requirement is satisfied in relation to each term, the existence of the other term in the contract is relevant . . . As I understand it, the effect of [Watford] is that, by way of example, I might find that the virtually total exclusion of liability for breach of warranties is unreasonable but at the same time find that the limitation of the amount of liability to getting one's money back is reasonable." (para.62).

In the event the judge found that:

> "If SAM had not offered [the] 'standard money back guarantee on licence', I would have regarded the exclusion of liability and entire agreement clauses as quite unreasonable though I would have regarded the limitation of liability to the amount of money paid under the licence agreement as reasonable. But on the evidence before me . . . I find that all of the terms to which objection is taken in the contract were reasonable." (para.72).

On the issue of whether SAM could recover their service charges under the maintenance agreement for putting right defects in relation to which they had successfully excluded their liability, the judge was forthright in his view:

> " . . . I cannot see that it is right that SAM should be paid for putting right a defect in respect of which they have excluded liability to pay damages . . . no customer would or should accept liability to pay for rectification of defects existing in goods on delivery even if there was no contractual liability on the part of the supplier to pay damages arising out of those defects . . . Exclusion clauses exclude liability for breach of contract: they do not amount to an agreement that performance has been given by providing equipment that is fit to be maintained: nor do they amount to an agreement that the purchaser should pay for any efforts made by the supplier to put right the defects." (para.78).

20–127   Accordingly it is clear that exclusion and limitation of liability clauses will often be effective in IT contracts between commercial parties operating at arm's length, but that the court's will subject the clauses in question (and any other relevant risk allocation clauses) to careful scrutiny to ensure that the allocation of risk has been considered between the parties and that at least a justifiable (i.e. not obviously unjust) balance has been struck.

7. MITIGATION

20–128   The principles of mitigation are the same in contract and tort, namely that the claimant should take all reasonable steps to mitigate its losses and is not entitled to recover damages in respect of losses which could and should reasonably have been avoided.[2] This can present problems in IT disputes where there is an express

---

[2] See, e.g., *McGregor on Damages* (16th edn), paras 282 *et seq.*

or implied term that the supplier is to be allowed a reasonable amount of time to ensure that the system or software runs satisfactorily and free from bugs. Where this is the case, it is difficult for a claimant to know the point at which he ought to start taking steps of his own to remedy the situation. If he starts too soon, he will be in breach of his obligation to allow the supplier reasonable time and any expense he incurs may not be deemed reasonable; if he waits too long he may well face the argument that he failed to reasonably mitigate his losses.

Other arguments which may succeed in the IT sphere include the contention   20–129
that the claimant ought not to have replaced the defective system with an entirely new one. There are occasions where the claimant can be shown to have replaced hardware as well as software unnecessarily, since different software could have fulfilled the claimant's purposes whilst using the same hardware.[3]

8. CONTRIBUTORY NEGLIGENCE

A defence of contributory negligence is not of course available in relation to   20–130
breaches of contract, save where the contractual term imposes no more than a duty to take reasonable care alongside an attendant obligation in tort.[4] Consequently no defence of contributory negligence will be available for a defendant who is in breach of the contractual terms of satisfactory quality and/or fit for their purpose.

Accordingly contributory negligence will usually only be available as a   20–131
defence to consultants who do not supply the goods themselves. As indicated earlier, in a specialist field such as IT, where lay knowledge is generally very limited, a defendant will have significant difficulties in establishing contributory negligence on the part of the claimant. The defendant in *Stephenson Blake v Streets Heaver*[5] argued that its client, the claimant, had negligently contributed to its own loss in a number of ways (including a failure to carry out adequate systems testing, and going "live" with the system too early). All of the allegations failed, primarily on the basis that the defendant had been kept informed of the intended actions of the claimant and yet said nothing to prevent the actions being taken. The claimant did not know enough about computer systems to realise that what it was doing was likely to cause or contribute towards their loss. It is to be expected that this will normally be the correct analysis.[6]

However, there will be cases in which the alleged contributory negligence   20–132
relates to a matter so basic and obvious that even a claimant with no specific technical knowledge will be held to have been negligent. Such a situation arose

---

[3] An argument along these lines was partially successful for the defendant in *Stephenson Blake (Holdings) Ltd v Streets Heaver Ltd*, unreported, March 2, 1994, QB.
[4] *Forsikringsaktieselskapet Vesta v Butcher* [1989] A.C. 852.
[5] [1994] Masons C.L.R. 17; [1998] Masons C.L.R. Rep. 25.
[6] It should not be forgotten that the client is under an obligation to co-operate with his IT supplier—see *Anglo Group Plc v Winther Brown*, unreported, March 1, 2000—and where such co-operation is not forthcoming and the breach in question is not related to a term for satisfactory quality or fitness for purpose, it is submitted that this would be likely to be construed as either a failure to mitigate or contributory negligence on the client's part, depending upon exactly how they had failed to co-operate.

in *Logical Computer Ltd v Euro Carparks Ltd*.[7] In that case the negligence of the claimant's operatives had caused the defendant's system to crash, destroying a quantity of crucial data on the defendant's hard disk. The claimant sued for its fees and the defendant counterclaimed for its losses attendant upon the disruption to its business. In relation to the counterclaim, the claimant contended that the defendant had been negligent in failing to ensure that their system was regularly backed up.

20–133   The judge held that the claimant had indeed been negligent, in three respects: ordering the wrong backup tapes and failing to check that they were the correct type; failing to check at any time that the backup system was working satisfactorily; and in failing to detect the error message that had been shown on the server. The judge observed that:

> "In my judgment, in this day and age, these were serious shortcomings. The Defendant's business was heavily dependant upon the proper functioning of its computer systems and this was well understood. They also knew that the backup system was a vital defence against computer malfunction which is, unfortunately, far from rare. It is therefore vital that this line of defence is regularly checked to see that it is functioning properly for, if not, the consequences can be disastrous. It should be common practice in every business which uses computers for the backup system to be regularly checked for malfunction. I do not consider this a matter of special expertise or knowledge possessed only by the qualified few. To my mind it is a matter of business common sense and risk management. If the Defendant did not have sufficiently qualified or experienced personnel to understand and take steps to avoid this risk, then they could have employed outside assistance and advice for this purpose. But to place this line of defence in the hands of an employee who did not understand how it worked or, more importantly, how to verify that it was working satisfactorily was, in my judgment, a major error."

20–134   The learned judge reduced the damages on the counterclaim by 50 per cent for contributory negligence. Accordingly practitioners should always be astute as to whether the claimant can justifiably be criticised for not doing enough to guard against computer failure.

9. Limitation

20–135   There are no special rules of limitation in this area. However, the reasonable period which suppliers and advisers appear to have to put right defects in installed software and systems[8] may present difficulties in pinning down the precise date upon which the contract was breached, and accordingly in determining the date upon which the contractual limitation period began to run.

20–136   The limitation period in tort will in most cases only be relevant where the damage accrues some considerable time after the installation of the relevant

---

[7] Unreported, June 19, 2001, QB.
[8] See above, paras 20–090 to 20–091.

hardware/system, and there is a problem with contractual limitation. For example, a defective system that destroys crucial data and files some years after its installation. Where the loss suffered is pure economic loss, questions will arise as to when the limitation period starts running, i.e. date of "damage" or date of discoverability, an area less than clear in English law.[9]

---

[9] See Ch.5, above.

CHAPTER 21

PATENT AGENTS AND TRADE MARK ATTORNEYS

1. GENERAL

There are very few reported cases against patent agents or trade mark attorneys.[1] **21–001**
Reference should therefore be made to the general principles to be applied to
professionals, set out in the first part of this work, and, given the analogous
nature of much of their work, to the chapters on solicitors and barristers.[2] The
main professional body in the United Kingdom is the Chartered Institute of
Patent Attorneys which was incorporated in 1882 and received a Royal Charter
in 1891.[3]

(a) *The Function of a Patent Agent*[4]

Patent agents deal with matters related to patents. Their functions can broadly be **21–002**
divided into two: applying for and obtaining patents on their client's behalf,[5] and
advising on intellectual property rights, including questions of validity and
infringement. A patent agent's work includes clerical tasks such as filing forms
at the Patent Office and paying renewal fees, but also matters requiring technical
and legal skill such as drafting patent specifications and advising on validity and
infringement. Considerable care will usually be required in order to try and
protect a client's interest by, for example, drafting a patent specification which
provides appropriately wide protection but which is nevertheless valid. There
will usually be a trade-off between certainty or relative certainty in obtaining a

---

[1] In part this is due to the small size of the profession. There are about 1,600 registered patent agents
and 900 registered trade mark attorneys, with about 600 of these being dually qualified.

[2] See Chs 11 and 12.

[3] The CIPA website, *www.CIPA.ork.uk* contains useful reference material including the Charter and
byelaws of the Institute.

[4] For a general exposition of the law relating to patents, see *Terrell on the Law of Patents* (15th edn,
2000). For the statutory framework relating to patent agents, see *Halsbury's Laws of England* (4th
edn, reissue), Vol.35, paras 692 to 713.

[5] A patent agent in the UK will normally himself deal with patents in the UK and with European
patents. Given the necessity for international protection, a patent agent will often also apply for
patents in other jurisdictions, normally through a foreign agent.

valid patent which will resist challenge (which may involve making relatively narrow claims) and protecting a client's commercial interests (which will usually involve seeking to obtain a patent which grants the maximum possible monopoly).

21–003   **Court proceedings.** Patent agents may conduct proceedings relating to patents before the Comptroller.[6] They can do anything in connection with proceedings before the patents county court which a solicitor may do,[7] which will include appearing as an advocate. They may also appear on behalf of any party to an appeal from the Comptroller to the Patents Court.[8] The Chartered Institute of Patent Agents is an appropriate body under the Courts and Legal Services Act,[9] and thus Patent Agents have a right to conduct litigation and appear as an advocate in relation to a wider range of proceedings,[10] subject to certain restrictions.[11] European patent agents may appear before the European Patent Office. Patent agents may instruct counsel directly.[12]

21–004   **Regulation.** While anyone may practice before the Patent Office, only registered patent agents may call themselves patent agents or patent attorneys,[13] and in practice almost all practitioners are registered. The register of patent agents is maintained by the Chartered Institute of Patent Agents,[14] which for most practical purposes is the professional regulatory body.[15] Registered patent agents must pass qualifying examinations and complete a period of practice under the supervision of a patent agent or suitably qualified lawyer for two years.[16] Only someone on the European list may call himself a European patent agent or attorney.[17]

21–005   **Alternatives to litigation.** A disappointed client now has an alternative remedy to launching proceedings. The Chartered Institute of Patent Agents can issue a reprimand or exclude or suspend a member for breach of the Rules of

---

[6] Copyright, Designs and Patents Act 1988, s.274(1). The Comptroller General of Patents, Designs and Trade Marks controls the Patents Office, see Patents and Designs Act 1907, s.62. Any person may appear in person or as a representative before the Comptroller, see the Patents Act 1977, s.102A.
[7] Save for preparing a deed. See Copyright, Designs and Patents Act 1988, s.292.
[8] Patents Act 1977, s.102A.
[9] ss.27 and 28. See the Chartered Institute of Patents Order (SI 1999/3137).
[10] Essentially conducting litigation in respect of intellectual property in the county court, the Chancery Division and appeals therefrom.
[11] The patent agent must hold a certificate permitting him to conduct litigation issued by the Chartered Institute, which has (inter alia) training and experience requirements—see further *www.cipa. org.uk.*
[12] In Pt IV, para.401(a) of the Code of Conduct of the Bar of England and Wales, a barrister in independent practice may only supply services to a professional client, a BarDIRECT client or if appointed by the court. In the definitions of Pt X, para.1001, "professional client" includes a patent agent and trade mark agent.
[13] Copyright, Designs and Patents Act 1988, s.276.
[14] Pursuant to the Register of Patent Agents Rules 1990 (SI 1990/1457), which are made under the Copyright, Designs and Patents Act 1988, s.275.
[15] However, only the Secretary of State for Trade and Industry can remove someone from the register for misconduct.
[16] In theory it is possible to qualify by passing the examinations and carrying out unsupervised practice for four years, although it would not appear that this route is ever followed.
[17] Copyright, Designs and Patents Act 1988, s.277.

Professional Conduct, but it also has the power to require a member to pay compensation to a client, forgo fees, or pay a fine, where the client has not received the service expected of a patent agent.

(b) *The Function of a Trade Mark Attorney*[18]

It is the function of a trade mark attorney to advise on trade mark law, including **21-006** protection and infringement of trade marks, and to act for clients to obtain registration of a trade mark. His work includes clerical tasks such as filing forms at the Trade Mark Registry and paying renewal fees, but also matters requiring technical and legal skill such as selecting new marks and advice on infringement. Trade mark attorneys have no rights of audience in the High Court or county court, but along with any other agent, they may appear before the registrar or on appeal before the appointed person.[19] They may instruct counsel directly.[20]

Regulation. While any person may carry out any procedure relating to a trade **21-007** mark,[21] only a registered trade mark agent can describe himself as such.[22] Registration is undertaken by the Institute of Trade Mark Attorneys, which determines the necessary examination qualification.

(c) *Duties to Clients*

In accordance with normal principles, a patent agent or trade mark attorney will **21-008** owe contractual duties to the client, and also concurrent duties in tort.[23] Equitable duties will be owed, in particular not to breach the confidence of the client.[24]

(d) *Duties to Third Parties*

In appropriate circumstances, duties may be owed to third parties, although there **21-009** are no reported cases of such third parties suing patent agents or trade mark attorneys. As with solicitors, it will in general be very rare that duties of care will be owed to third parties who are in conflict with the client, particularly if there are proceedings between the third party and the client.[25]

---

[18] For the law relating to trademarks, see *Kerly's Law of Trade Marks and Tradenames* (14th edn, 2005).
[19] See the Trade Marks Act 1994, s.82. Appeals to the appointed person are pursuant to s.76 of the Act.
[20] See para.21-003, n.21, above.
[21] Trade Marks Act 1994, s.82.
[22] *ibid.*, s.84.
[23] See *Henderson v Merrett Syndicates Ltd* [1995] 2 A.C. 145; and Ch.2, paras 2-108 *et seq.*
[24] This is particularly important as an invention can only be patented, if it is new, see Patents Act 1977, ss.1 and 2. See also the Chartered Institute of Patents Agents' Rules of Professional Conduct, r.4 dealing with conflicts of interest, and the corresponding guidance in the Guidelines Concerning the Observance of the Rules of Professional Conduct
[25] See Ch.11 para.11-064.

(e) *The Standard of Skill*

21–010 **General.** Patent agents and trade mark attorneys are required to exercise reasonable care and skill.[26] The test of what is required is an objective one. In *Andrew Master Hones Ltd v Cruikshank and Fairweather*[27] Graham J. held:

> "The degree of knowledge and care to be expected is thus seen to be that degree possessed by a notional duly qualified person practising that profession. The test is, therefore . . . an objective test referable to the notional member of the profession, and not a subjective test referable to the particular professional man employed."

21–011 **Codes of conduct.** Both the Chartered Institute of Patents Agents and the Institute of Trade Mark Attorneys have produced codes of practice.[28] Such codes of conduct do not determine the law, but in practice the courts are very ready to follow them as establishing the duties and common practice of a profession.[29] The Code of Practice of the Institute of Trade Mark Attorneys is likely to be of limited assistance in any professional negligence litigation, being largely concerned with publicity, relations between trade mark attorneys and change of agents. The Chartered Institute of Patents Agents' Rules of Professional Conduct, and Guidelines Concerning the Observance of the Rules of Professional Conduct, may be of more assistance.[30]

(f) *Immunity*

21–012 Although there was no direct judicial authority for the proposition, it appeared clear that a patent agent or trade mark attorney acting as an advocate had the same immunity as a barrister,[31] but such immunity has now been abolished.[32]

(g) *Liability for Costs*

21–013 When undertaking litigation, patent agents may be made liable for wasted costs in the same way as a solicitor or barrister may be,[33] in relation to proceedings before the Court of Appeal, High Court and county court.[34] It would appear that

---

[26] s.13 of the Supply of Goods and Services Act 1982. This provision simply restates the common law.

[27] [1980] R.P.C. 16 at 18. This was not an issue on appeal. For the facts of the case see para.18–017, below.

[28] The Chartered Institute of Patents Agents has promulgated both Rules of Professional Conduct, and Guidelines Concerning the Observance of the Rules of Professional Conduct.

[29] See Ch.11, para.11–094, above.

[30] See in particular the Rules of Professional Conduct for Patent Agents Holding and Acting within the Scope of Litigation Right Certificates. See generally *www.cipa.org.uk*

[31] See in particular the Supply of Services (Exclusion of Implied Terms) Order 1982 (SI 1982/1771), which provided that s.13 of the 1982 Supply of Goods and Services Act does not apply to "the services of an advocate in court or before any tribunal, inquiry or arbitrator and in carrying out preliminary work directly affecting the conduct of the hearing."

[32] *Hall v Simons* [2002] 1 A.C. 615. See generally Ch.12, para.12–009.

[33] On which see Ch.11, paras 11–126 to 11–141 and Ch.12, paras 12–011 to 12–022.

[34] The Supreme Court Act 1981, s.51(6) permits a court to make a wasted costs order against a "legal or other representative." The Civil Procedure Rules Pt 48.7 refers to "legal representative", which is defined in r.2.3 as including "other authorised litigator (as defined in the Courts and Legal Services Act 1990)", on which see para.21–003, above.

a wasted costs order may be made by the Trade Mark Registry against a trade mark attorney.[35]

(h) *Privilege*

Communications between a patent agent or European patent attorney and his client relating to intellectual property are privileged in the same way as those between a solicitor and his client.[36] There is a similar privilege with respect to communications beween a trade mark agent and his client.[37] It should follow that a former client suing a patent agent or trade mark attorney will waive privilege, within certain limits, in the same way as if he sued his solicitor.[38] **21–014**

2. LIABILITY FOR BREACH OF DUTY

General. Given the paucity of reported cases, there are few illustrations of the type of circumstances in which patent agents or trade mark attorneys may be found to be negligent. One particular area in which patent agents and trade mark attorneys are obviously vulnerable is in relation to missing deadlines for the registration of documents. An illustration is afforded by *Finecard International Ltd v Urquhart Dyke & Lord*[39] where the defendant patent agents failed to register an exclusive licence timeously in accordance with their client's express instructions. The defendants failed to comply with their instructions for some 15 months and admitted that they were in breach of duty in so doing. In the context of a dispute as to the consequences of this failure,[40] Smith J. pointed out that s.68 of the Patents Act 1977 provided severe consequences for a failure to register a transaction within six months in that an assignee would not be entitled to damages or an account of profits for the period prior to registration. This was justified on the basis that the section was designed to encourage openness in, as the Judge put it, an "Admiral Byng" sense. **21–015**

Ignorance of the law. A patent agent or trade mark attorney must have adequate knowledge of the law and practice of intellectual property. This is illustrated by the old case of *Lee v Walker*.[41] The claimants retained the defendant patent-agent to obtain a patent for a "new automaton vase or depot for holding coals", and he filed a provisional specification on April 30, 1870. In accordance with ordinary practice, he intended to wait until the expiration of four months before giving notice of intention to proceed with the patent, and then to wait two **21–016**

---

[35] See *Sun Microsystems Inc's Trade Mark Application* [2001] R.P.C. 461, where such an application failed.
[36] Copyright, Designs and Patents Act 1988, s.280. By the Patents Act 1977, s.103, legal professional privilege will extend to communications between a solicitor and his client relating to pending or contemplated proceedings before the Comptroller or courts under certain conventions. Thus this privilege will extend to communications between a patent agent and his client.
[37] Trade Marks Act 1994, s.87.
[38] See further Ch.11.
[39] [2005] EWHC 2481.
[40] See further para.21–021, below.
[41] (1872) L.R. 7 C.P. 121.

more months before filing the complete specification and obtaining the patent. In the meantime, on June 15, 1870 one Perman filed for a provisional specification for "improvements in coal vases", which turned out to be substantially the same as the claimants' invention, and on September 10, 1870 he obtained a grant of patent for it. The Attorney-General rejected the claimants' application on the authority of a case decided in May 1869, *Ex p. Bates*,[42] which decided that the second application for provisional protection was entitled to have his letters-patent sealed, in the absence of fraud. Brett and Grove JJ. affirmed the decision of Lush J. that the patent agent was negligent. Grove J. hesitated to impute negligence on the basis of delay in giving notice of intention to proceed with the patent until the end of the prescribed notice, or on the basis of the defendant's ignorance of the fact that Perman's invention, of which the defendant had notice, was in substance the same. However, the judges agreed that the defendant was negligent in failing to know of *Ex p. Bates*. According to Brett J.:

" . . . an agent of this kind is not bound to be accurately acquainted with the whole law of patents: but I think he is bound to know the law as to the practice of obtaining patents; and, as this was a most important decision with respect to the sealing of patents, the very practice the conduct of which he undertook for reward, I think he was bound to know it. Since that decision, patent-agents are not entitled to carry on their business as they had done before."[43]

The case is, of course, of some antiquity. The relevant law has changed greatly, and the knowledge of the law and practice of intellectual property required of patent agents and trade mark attorneys will probably have increased since then.[44]

21–017   **Taking proper instructions.**[45] It is essential that a patent agent takes full and proper instructions from the client about his invention if there is a question of an earlier similar patent or "prior art".[46] This is illustrated by *Andrew Master Hones Ltd v Cruikshank and Fairweather*.[47] The claimant had developed a device for

---

[42] (1869) L.R. 4. Ch. 577.

[43] (1872) L.R. 7 C.P. 121 at 126, and see the similar comments of Grove J.

[44] For another example, in the context of trade mark attorneys, see *Halifax Building Society v Urquart-Dykes and Lord* [1997] R.P.C. 55 at 77, ll.20–25, where the defendant was held to be negligent in an "elementary failure" to understand the procedure adopted by the registrar on separate applications by different persons of marks that are identical or nearly resemble each other pursuant to s.12(3) of the Trade Marks (Amendment) Act 1984, which was set out in the registrar's Work Manual. For the facts of the case see para.21–018, below.

[45] For another example, in the context of trade mark attorneys, see *Halifax Building Society v Urquart-Dykes and Lord* [1997] R.P.C. 55 at 67, ll.22 to 25, where Jacob J. stated that the duty "extends to informing his client of any matter in relation to which he needs instructions on the facts to give proper advice . . . the client may not have the expertise to know what facts matter and what do not. The client is entitled to expect his agent to ask for the information necessary to give proper advice", and at 76, ll.9–10: "A trade mark agent's job in making or pursuing an application normally involves finding out just what his clients do."

[46] Similarly, it will be important to obtain detailed instructions in drafting an application so it is properly defined.

[47] [1980] R.P.C. 16. The issue of negligence was not canvassed on appeal on the defendants' concession, on the assumption that the claimant's specification was sufficiently different from the two earlier patents, that they were negligent in failing to bring to the claimant's attention that the application would become void unless it was put in order by April 7, 1970, and that if it had been put in order it would have been accepted by the Patent Office, see [1981] R.P.C. 389 at 396.

reconditioning *in situ* marine crankshafts, which were large and could not realistically be removed from ships. The machine was an inverted lathe consisting of rings, encircling the crankshaft, connected by bars, one of which held a cutting tool, with the whole cage driven by a pair of belts so that it rotated around the shaft. The claimant instructed the defendant patent agents, who filed a provisional[48] specification, but an objection was raised by the examiner, based on two earlier patents. The defendants informed the claimant that as a result it would be unable to obtain a valid patent, and on receiving no further instructions they took no further steps. The defendants were found to be negligent as they failed to ascertain from the claimant what were the features of the invention which distinguished it from the prior art and which resulted in success in practice. They were also liable in three other respects: they took a superficial and incorrect view of one of the earlier patents; they failed to explain that the client might still obtain a valid patent despite their views[49]; and they should not have assumed that the client had decided to take their advice and abandon the application.

Giving proper advice, including commercial advice.[50] While a patent agent   **21–018** or trade mark attorney will generally owe no duty to give commercial advice, giving sufficient legal advice may entail suggesting that the client considers the commercial consequences. In *Halifax Building Society v Urquart-Dykes and Lord*[51] Jacob J. explained what was required:

> "I think that where a trade mark agent undertakes to pursue a trade mark application for a client then his duties to that client extends to advising in relation to all legal pitfalls reasonably connected with the application. The trade mark agent is not under a duty to give commercial advice as such, but he is under a duty to keep his client informed of the legal problems which may arise and his duty extends to warning his client to consider any commercial problems which may arise as a result of the legal problems which he, as trade mark agent, should reasonably discern."

In that case, the claimant instructed the defendant trade mark agents to make a series of applications involving the word "Halifax", which it did on September 30, 1986. The next day, Provident Financial Group Plc applied to register the same name for motor insurance services, which they had carried out through a subsidiary, Halifax Insurance Company Limited, from 1966. The registry cited Provident's application, and sent the defendants Provident's evidence of prior use. The claimant was dilatory in providing evidence of its prior use, and in a letter dated February 5, 1990 the defendants correctly informed their client that the registry had indicated that it would allow Provident's application to proceed to registration unless the claimant could provide evidence in respect of motor insurance before 1966. However, the defendants were negligent in failing to explain in detail how the system of applications would work and what the claimant should do, in particular that if it failed to provide evidence to rebut the

---

[48] Abolished by the Patents Act 1977, s.15.
[49] But compare the position of solicitors, where the law is uncertain as to whether a solicitor has to explain that his view of the law may not be correct, see Ch.11, para.11–154.
[50] See also Ch.11, paras 11–170 to 11–173 in relation to giving commercial advice.
[51] [1997] R.P.C. 55 at 67, ll.11–20.

priority claim, its application would be suspended. Most importantly, the defendants failed to inform their client that it was open to them to resolve the conflict with Provident by agreement to the satisfaction of the registrar, and that a failure to reach agreement would be likely to lead to cross-oppositions.[52]

21–019   **Instruction of foreign agents.** In *Arbiter Group Plc v Gill Jennings and Every (a firm)*[53] the claimants sought advice from the defendant patent agents as to whether their new kind of jukebox might infringe an existing US patent, as they had been warned at a fair where they had exhibited the jukebox that it infringed two US patents. The patent agents instructed US patent searchers to carry out a search to check this, who reported erroneously that the patent was still in force, when it had in fact lapsed through non-payment of annual renewal fees, which the defendants passed on to the claimant. The claimant alleged that by the time they discovered that the advice was erroneous, three years later, it was too late to sell the jukebox successfully in the United States, and they sued the defendant patent attorneys.[54] Swinton Thomas L.J. held:

> "A professional man in appropriate circumstances is entitled to delegate tasks. Whether he is entitled to delegate a particular task will depend on the nature of the task. He is entitled to delegate some tasks to others but is not entitled to delegate others. It all depends on the nature of the task involved. If he does delegate he must delegate to a suitably qualified and experienced person."[55]

The court recognised that there was a risk that the person to whom the task is delegated may make a mistake, and the question to be considered was the degree of risk and whether it was appropriate that the delegator should take it. In that case, the defendants were entitled to delegate the search to US patent searchers, and they were entitled to rely on the results and not carry out further inquiries themselves.[56]

3. Damages

21–020   **Causation and loss of a chance.** Consonant with the general law,[57] a claimant will have to prove on the balance of probabilities that he would have acted differently if properly advised, for instance in prosecuting a patent application. This is a question of causation, but quantification of damages only has to satisfy an easier test: the claimant will recover substantial damages if there was a

---

[52] [1997] R.P.C. 55 at 71, l.33 to 72, l.13 and 81, ll.1–3. The defendants were also negligent in other respects, see para.21–016, n.44 and para.21–017, n.45, and in failing later, when told that the claimant intended to offer motor insurance in addition to their other services to advise that this required serious and in depth consideration as Provident would obtain registration, see [1997] R.P.C. 55 at 78, ll.18–25. In fact, no loss was caused by the negligence, see paras 21–021 and 21–022, below.

[53] [2000] P.N.L.R. 680.

[54] The American patent agent searchers were second defendants, but they had gone out of business.

[55] *ibid.* at 686.

[56] The claimant further relied on *Edward Wong Finance Co Ltd v Johnson Stokes & Master* [1984] A.C. 296, which was distinguished, see Ch.11, para.11–088, above.

[57] See *Allied Maples v Simmons & Simmons* [1995] 1 W.L.R. 1602, CA.

significant chance (for instance) that it might have obtained a valuable patent. This may involve considering whether the patent would have been granted, whether revocation proceedings might have been brought[58] and what the results of those proceedings would have been, and whether a competitor could easily have avoided infringing such claims.[59]

The scope of protection. Because it is part of the function of a patent agent **21–021** to provide protection to a client against possible problems and disputes, a negligent patent agent will be responsible for the consequences of having exposed a client to an unnecessary dispute. Thus in *Finecard International Ltd v Urquhart Dyke & Lord*,[60] the defendant patent agents negligently failed to register an exclusive licence dated September 9, 1999 in accordance with the express instructions of their client. A judge held that the consequences of the failure to register within six months was to disentitle the clients to damages or an accounting of profits until it was eventually registered in accordance with the provisions of s.68 of the Patents Act 1977. When proceedings were brought against the patent agents, they sought to argue that the judge had been wrong and that reliance could have been placed on an earlier exclusive licence. Smith J. rejected this argument on its facts but also pointed out that the defendants had exposed the claimant to the risk that it might not make recovery with the result that the claimant was entitled to protection even if it was arguable that the original Judge had been wrong. As a consequence he struck out those parts of the defence which sought to impugn the original decision.

Halifax Building Society v Urquart-Dykes and Lord[61] is a salutary example of **21–022** a claimant failing to produce sufficient evidence to prove its case. The trade mark attorneys essentially failed in 1990 to advise their client to negotiate with Provident, which was attempting to register the name "Halifax" for motor insurance services. Eventually, proceedings were commenced by Provident, and in 1993 Halifax negotiated an assignment of all Provident's registrations and applications, with Provident ceasing to use the name, for £2 million. The claimant failed to produce as witnesses any of their commercial men to prove that it would have negotiated with Provident earlier if properly advised, and the claim failed on causation. Jacobs J. also held that it was entirely speculative that the claimants missed a valuable chance of obtaining a better deal from Provident if it had negotiated in 1990 rather than 1993, and the £2 million. price was a good one at either time.

Remoteness and scope of duty. In the normal way, a claimant will have to **21–023** establish that his loss is not too remote, and that it was within the scope of the

---

[58] Pursuant to the Patents Act 1977, s.72. Compare *Alexander Turnbull & Co Ltd v Cruickshank and Fairweather* (1905) 22 R.P.C. 521, where the Inner House of the Court of Session struck out a plea in a patent agent's negligence case that the patent was invalid for want of novelty, a decision which would probably not be followed now.

[59] Some indication of the factors that may have to be taken into account are given by Buckley L.J. in *Andrew Master Hones Ltd v Cruikshank and Fairweather* [1981] R.P.C. 389 at 403, ll.29–38.

[60] [2005] EWHC 2481—see further para.21–015, above.

[61] [1997] R.P.C. 55 at 83 to 87. See para.21–018, above for the facts. While Jacobs J. did not cite the case of *Allied Maples v Simmons & Simmons* [1995] 1 W.L.R. 1602, he correctly applied the law which it lays down.

duty the defendant owed. Jacobs J. addressed both of these issues in *Halifax Building Society v Urquart-Dykes and Lord*.[62] He considered that the loss within the scope of the duty was the foreseeable loss, which was the chance of the claimant acting in accordance with the advice which should have been given.[63] The claimant claimed, inter alia, for the litigation and administrative costs of the proceedings brought by Provident. Jacobs J. rejected this claim. The defendants had advised the claimant not to proceed with motor insurance, which advice it ignored, and they were not responsible for the claimant when it "wilfully sailed into the eye of the storm".[64]

21–024   **Valuation of lost patent.** In *Andrew Master Hones Ltd v Cruikshank and Fairweather*[65] the defendants had failed to advise the claimant fully on a patent application, which was not pursued. The Court of Appeal held that the claimant company lost whatever benefits might have accrued to the company if the application had been accepted by the Patent Office.[66] The Court held that the logical method of assessing damages may be to quantify the price at which the claimant could have disposed its right to pursue is application on the open market on the assumption that it had been accepted by the Patent Office,[67] which would involve a potential purchaser forming a view on matters such as the potential success of revocation proceedings, and the potential profitability of any patent which might be obtained. In that case, an enquiry was directed as to damages.

---

[62] [1997] R.P.C. 55 at 83 to 87. See paras 21–018 and 21–021, above for the facts.
[63] Applying *Banque Bruxelles Lambert v Eagle Star Insurance* [1997] A.C. 191, on which see Ch.3, paras 3–02 to 3–04, and Ch.10, paras 10–113 to 10–119. Essentially it would appear that this principle would not prevent recovery of the claimed loss of profits on motor insurance during the period of the injunction, the legal costs of defending the action, the internal costs, and the loss of a chance of obtaining a better settlement with Provident. The claim failed on other grounds.
[64] [1997] R.P.C. 55 at 87; applying *Galoo Ltd v Bright Grahame Murray* [1994] 1 W.L.R. 1360, on which see Ch.17, para.17–064, above.
[65] [1981] R.P.C. 389, esp. at 403. For the facts see para.21–017, above.
[66] Presumably discounted by the chances of the Patent Office not accepting the patent, which was plainly very large on the facts, see *ibid.*, at 403, 1.35.
[67] In principle, if this assumption is made, then the resulting valuation should be reduced to account for the contingency of the patent not being accepted, see the previous paragraph.

INDEX